THE
VIDEO
TAPE & DISC GUIDE TO
HOME
ENTERTAINMENT

THE VIDEO TAPE & DISC GUIDE TO HOME ENTERTAINMENT®
Seventh Edition
is an original publication of
The National Video Clearinghouse, Inc.
100 Lafayette Drive
Syosset, NY 11791 (516)364-3686

Printed in Canada
ISBN: 0-935478-31-0
Library of Congress: 83-62240

Cover design: Costas Mendonis

Bookstore Distribution: International Specialized Book Services, Inc., Portland, OR

A MONUMENTAL BREAKTHROUGH

★ ★ ★ ★ ★

FIVE STAR COLLECTION II

GREAT ENTERTAINMENT AT A GREAT PRICE, $29.98*

CLASSICS
The Adventures Of
    Robin Hood
The African Queen
Angels With Dirty Faces
Arsenic And Old Lace
Casablanca
Yankee Doodle Dandy

ACTION/ADVENTURE
Live And Let Die
Moonraker
Octopussy
Patton
Raise The Titanic
The Spy Who Loved Me

DRAMA
Rocky
Rocky II
Rocky III

WESTERN
The Alamo
A Fistful Of Dollars
The Legend Of
    The Lone Ranger

MUSICALS
All That Jazz
Cabaret
Doctor Dolittle
Guys And Dolls
Hello, Dolly!
Man Of LaMancha
My Fair Lady
New York, New York
Oklahoma!
The Sound Of Music
South Pacific
West Side Story

COMEDY
Revenge Of
    The Pink Panther
Some Like It Hot

HORROR
Alien
Carrie
The Omen

FAMILY
The Muppets Take
    Manhattan

ADD TO YOUR COLLECTION TODAY!

Presenting three dozen reasons why CBS/FOX VIDEO is a leader in home
video entertainment. It's our new Five Star Collection II. 36 of the world's most
popular films on videocassette for just $29.98 each. That's quite a deal.

Because the CBS/FOX VIDEO Five Star Collection II is the very best of our best.
From Bogart and Bergman in CASABLANCA to Cagney as Cohan in YANKEE
DOODLE DANDY. We've got westerns with Wayne and Eastwood. Laughs galore
with Sellers and Lemmon. Stallone slugs it out in ROCKY I, II & III and Bond is back,
of course. There are musicals, too! From OKLAHOMA to MY FAIR LADY.

It's a collection of the classics, the dramas, the westerns, the musicals, the
comedies, the horror, family and action/adventure films known and loved the
world over. The Five Star Collection II. Only from CBS/FOX VIDEO.

Available in Stores Everywhere.

Preface

The Video Tape & Disc Guide to Home Entertainment®, 7th Edition, is designed to provide home viewers with detailed information on more than 10,000 video programs available to them. Most of the titles included herein are easily available from your local video retailer; if he doesn't have them in stock, he may be able to special order them. Other tapes described in this Guide are generally available directly by mail order from the program sources listed.

Special features included in this edition are the 8mm Index, and a listing of all the Video Subject Categories. The 8mm Index is a complete listing of all videocassettes available in this new format.

The Subject Categories listing enables the reader to see at a cursory glance the types of tapes contained in this guide: Drama, Comedy, Western, Cartoons, etc.

This publication has been compiled from catalogs, supplementary lists and additional information provided by the video program sources. The wholesalers or distributors do not pay to have their programs listed, nor does the publisher pay them for information about their titles. The publisher is not responsible for any program changes, withdrawals, or additions, or for the listing of any unauthorized distribution of any title.

Our editorial staff has sought to provide you, the home video viewer, with the most comprehensive, up-to-date, useful guide to home video available.

FREE

CATALOG

Table of Contents

Acknowledgements

This guide is an original work compiled by the staff of the National Video Clearinghouse, Inc. Those who have contributed to its creation include: George Hatch, Chairman of the Board; Harvey Seslowsky, President; Robert M. Reed, Vice President; Liz Doris, Editor; David J. Weiner, Director of Information and Data Services; Robin Ames, Gregory P. Fagan, Valerie Tantillo; Editorial Coordinators; Michael Atkinson, Editorial Assistant; Arnold Menis, Director of Marketing; Barbara Levine, Assistant Sales Manager; Christine D. Schmidt, Sales Coordinator; Costas Mendonis, Graphic Designer; Christine Mercieca, Editorial Secretary.

Use Guide

*The Video Tape and Disc Guide to Home Entertainment®,
Seventh Edition,* is divided into seven major sections:
(1) Program Listings; (2) Subject Category Index; (3) Videodisc
Index; (4) 8 Millimeter (8mm) Index; (5) Closed Captioned
Index; (6) Cast Index; and (7) Video Program Sources
Index. A description of each section is given below.

(1) PROGRAM LISTINGS

The main body of this book consists of more than 10,000 program
listings. Each entry may contain up to 19 different pieces of
information, most of which is supplied by the distributor, or "video
program source." Standard film and video reference materials are
utilized to obtain pertinent information when not supplied by the
distributor. Full explanations of the information included are given
below; consult the Key for illustrated examples.

ALPHABETIZATION
Each program is listed alphabetically. "A", "an" and "the" and their
foreign counterparts are not considered in alphabetization.

RELEASE DATE
"Release date" is defined as the year in which the film or program
was initially made available for public viewing.

SUBJECT CATEGORY
Each title has been assigned a specific subject heading, i.e.,
"Comedy," "Music Video," etc. This descriptive category will identify
the contents of the program . In some entries, a second category
has also been assigned.

ACCESSION NUMBER
Each title is assigned an accession number. The number is simply
an identifying code for the publisher and has no other meaning.

RUNNING TIMES
The running time of a program is listed as "88 mins." When edited
or different versions of a program are available, they are listed
separately with the appropriate running times.

COLOR AND BLACK AND WHITE
Each title listing indicates whether the program is available in color
(C) or black and white (B/W).

X

FORMAT AVAILABILITY

Each entry includes the video formats available for that particular program. The most common home video formats are Beta and VHS, although others are listed, when available. Laser optical videodisc (LV) and capacitance electronic disc (CED) availabilities are also included.

TELEVISION STANDARDS

All programs listed in the *Guide* are available on the U.S. television standard (NTSC).

PROGRAMS FOR THE HEARING IMPAIRED

When a program has been captioned or signed for the hearing impaired, the entry includes the notation "Open Captioned," "Closed Captioned" or "Signed" below the accession number.

CAST/STARS/HOSTS/GUESTS

The major stars or other members of the cast of dramatic television programs or movies are listed. In some instances, the director is listed as well. For instructional, talk show and documentary programs, the host, narrator or instructor is given, when known.

SERIES: NUMBER OF PROGRAMS

The number of programs in a generic series is listed as "11 pgms." The individual titles of each program within the series are listed in the sequence in which they are given by the distributor. When the distributor will make programs available either as a series or individually, the individual programs may also be listed in the main text.

PROGRAM DESCRIPTION

The narrative program descriptions are designed to briefly identify the major plot, subject, or theme of the program.

AWARDS

The major awards and the year of the award are listed in each entry. Unless there is an obvious abbreviation for well-known awards, the awards are spelled out. Nominations are normally not listed.

ANCILLARY MATERIALS

Brochures, study guides, and other printed and audio materials are occasionally available from the distributor to aid in the use of the program. This is noted by the phrase "AM Available."

AUDIENCE RATING

For theatrical films, the standard Motion Picture Association of America ratings are listed according to the MPAA Classification and Rating Program.

VCR USERS USE HOME VIEWER

Video is the hottest TV network of the '80s. Home Viewer is your indispensable guide to everything that's new, exciting, and available to play on your video machine. Over 300 new releases every issue. With the most informative and entertaining descriptions you'll find anywhere, for every title listed! From Jane Fonda exercise tapes to 'Cotton Club' and every other movie Francis Ford Coppola ever made, we cover the glamorous world of video like nobody else can. In fact, here's our incomparable guarantee: "Any new release you find at your favorite video outlet will be listed and described in the pages of Home Viewer." That's why we say, "If It's on Home Video, It's in Home Viewer." There's nothing else like it.

THE LEADING PUBLISHER OF PERIODICALS FOR PEOPLE WHO BUY, SELL AND WATCH HOME VIDEO PROGRAMS.

HOME VIEWER PUBLICATIONS. 11 NORTH 2ND STREET. PHILADELPHIA. PENNSYLVANIA 19106. (215) 629-1588

FOREIGN LANGUAGE

Virtually all titles found in this publication are available in English. Some foreign films have retained their original foreign language soundtrack; other English-language films have been dubbed into foreign languages. The availability of a foreign language version is indicated according to the following codes:

EL	English	JA	Japanese
AF	Afrikaans	LA	Latin
AB	Arabic	LI	Lithuanian
BE	Belgian	NE	Nepalese
CH	Chinese	NO	Norwegian
CZ	Czech	PO	Polish
DA	Danish	PR	Portuguese
DU	Dutch	RU	Russian
EG	Egyptian	SE	Serbo-Croatian
FI	Finnish	SP	Spanish
FL	Flemish	SA	Swahili
FR	French	SW	Swedish
GE	German	TH	Thai
GR	Greek	TU	Turkish
HE	Hebrew	WE	Welsh
IT	Italian		

When EL is not given along with a foreign language code, the program is not available in English.

SILENT/DUBBED/SUBTITLES

Silent films or those with dubbing or different language soundtracks are noted in the program descriptions. Similarly, a program with subtitles is so indicated at the end of the program description.

ORIGINAL PRODUCER

The original producer (studio, company, and/or individual person) is listed in each entry. When the actual producer cannot be determined, but the country of origin (other than the U.S.) is known, that information wll be listed.

VIDEO PROGRAM SOURCES

The video program source, also known as the wholesaler or distributor, appears to the right of the original producer in the listing. More than one source will be listed when the program is legitimately available from more than one wholesaler. This normally occurs when the program is in the public domain, or when it is available from one source on cassette and from another on disc. When multiple sources are listed, the format and acquisition availabilities apply to the first source. Most of the alternate sources will make the program available in Beta and VHS formats; special notations for those companies offering videodisc formats will be found in the Video Program Sources Index at the back of this book.

ACQUISITION AVAILABILITY

Video programs may be acquired in several ways. Full explanations of the information included are given; consult the Key for illustrated examples.

(2) VIDEO SUBJECT CATEGORIES/ SUBJECT CATEGORY INDEX

Each title in this Guide has been assigned a subject category. A complete listing of all subjects found herein appears after the main body and is followed by the Subject Category Index. When a program has been assigned two different subjects, that title is indexed under both. This index is intended to help the reader quickly locate programs in any of over 200 specific areas of interest.

(3) VIDEODISC INDEX

The Videodisc Index is a compilation of all programs available on CED and LV disc formats at the time of publication. For complete information on any title, refer to the Program Listings. NOTE: as of June 1986, RCA has officially discontinued production of CED discs. We continue to list this format as a viewer guide to those titles which may still be acquired through some dealers.

(4) 8 MILLIMETER (8mm) INDEX

All titles currently available in the new 8mm videocassette format are indexed in this section.

(5) CLOSED CAPTIONED INDEX

The Closed Captioned Index is a listing of cassettes and discs which are closed captioned for the hearing impaired. Full information on each title may be found in the Program Listings.

(6) CAST INDEX

Complete videographies for over 320 actors, actresses and directors have been compiled in this section. Readers can easily check which films of a favorite performer are currently on video by consulting the Index.

(7) VIDEO PROGRAM SOURCES INDEX

The full corporate name, address, and telephone number(s) for each video program source whose entries appear in *The Guide* are listed alphabetically in the Video Program Sources Index at the back of this book. Contact the individual program sources for further information about their titles.

KEY

This sample entry will assist the reader in interpreting the individual Program Listings. For a complete explanation of each code, please refer to the USE GUIDE.

COLOR DESIGNATION
C = Color   B/W = Black & White

LENGTH ⌐ FORMAT (see below)

TITLE	New Wave:
	The Real Auteurs, The
SUB-CATEGORIES	Film-History/Filmmaking
ACCESSION NO.	11548 60 mins ──── C B,V,8mm,LV P
CAPTIONED/SIGNED	Closed Captioned
CAST/HOST/STARS	Narrated by John Badham, Kevin Kline, Tina Weymouth, John Percival, William Hurt, directed by Gerald Cuesta
NO. OF PROGRAMS IN SERIES	5 pgms
PROGRAM DESCRIPTION	A documentary series which outlines the careers and dubious achievements of several unfairly maligned directors, who are now considered to be examples of inverted genius. Subtitled; in HiFi Stereo.
IND. PROGRAM TITLES	1. Edward D. Wood Jr.: The Brighter Side of Deviation 2. Phil Tucker: Schizophrenic Ineptitude 3. Mario Bava: The Spastic Zoom Lens 4. Stuart Margolin: Undiscovered Genius 5. J. Lee Thompson: Auteur Without Shame
AWARDS	Largo Film Festival '86: Biere d'Or Award.

RELEASE DATE
1986 ACQUISITION
(see below)

ANCILLARY
MATERIALS
PRODUCER

MPAA RATING ⌐   FOREIGN
A   MPAA: R ┘   EL,CZ,NE,WE ── LANGUAGE
TDC Productions–101 Video ─────── DISTRIBUTOR

FORMAT			¾U	=	¾" U-Matic	**ACQUISITION**		
			1C	=	1" Broadcast type			
CV	=	¼" compact			"C"	R	=	Rent/lease
		videocassette	Q	=	2" Quad	L	=	Loan
B	=	Beta	LV	=	Laser optical	P	=	Purchase
V	=	VHS			videodisc	D	=	Duplication
8mm	=	8 millimeter	CED	=	Capacitance	S	=	Subscription
		videocassette			electronic disc	T	=	Trade-In
EJ	=	½" reel	FO	=	Other than listed	FL	=	Free Loan
						FD	=	Free Duplication
						DL	=	Duplication License
						OR	=	Off-Air Record

A

A, B & C   1968
Drama
79896   52 mins   C   B, V   P
Patrick McGoohan, Katherine Kath, Colin Gordon
Number two attempts to find out why the Prisoner resigned from his previous profession by drugging The Prisoner to enter his dreams.
Patrick McGoohan — *MPI Home Video*

A Mi Las Mujeres N, Fu, N, Fa   1980
Comedy
64499   90 mins   C   B, V   P
This musical comedy features the well-known Spanish and Latin American singer Peret.
English title: "I Don't Care for Women."
SP
Jose Antonio Cascales Guijarro — *Media Home Entertainment*

A Nos Amours   1984
Drama
80787   99 mins   C   B, V   P
Sandrine Bonnaire, Maurice Pialat, Evelyne Ker, Maurice Pialat
A young girl is having casual affairs while searching for the love and attention she was denied at home. With English subtitles.
MPAA:R
Triumph Films — *RCA/Columbia Pictures Home Video*

A Nous La Liberte   1931
Satire
06212   87 mins   B/W   B, V   P
Raymond Cordy, Henri Marchand, directed by Rene Clair
A tramp becomes a wealthy and powerful leader in this satire that provided the inspiration for Chaplin's "Modern Times." French dialogue with English subtitles.
FR
France — *Hollywood Home Theater; Discount Video Tapes; Western Film & Video Inc*

Aaron Loves Angela   1975
Drama
81432   99 mins   C   B, V   P
Irene Cara, Moses Gunn, Kevin Hooks, Robert Hooks, Jose Feliciano, directed by Gordon Parks, Jr.
A Puerto Rican girl falls in love with a black boy amidst the harsh realities of the Harlem ghetto. Available in VHS and Beta Hi-Fi.
MPAA:R
Columbia Pictures — *RCA/Columbia Pictures Home Video*

Abba   1980
Music-Performance
48539   60 mins   C   B, V   P
Abba
Popular Swedish rock band gives a visual concert performance which includes their hits "Waterloo" and "Dancin' Queen."
Unknown — *MCA Home Video*

Abba   1983
Music-Performance
66008   60 mins   C   B, V   P
The internationally-famous group performs "Knowing Me, Knowing You," "Take a Chance on Me," "The Name of the Game," "Dancing Queen" and other hits.
Polar Music International — *Monterey Home Video*

Abba, Again   1983
Music-Performance
76797   30 mins   C   B, V   P
The popular rock group performs such hits as "Supertrooper" and "When All Is Said And Done" in this taped concert.
Polar Music International — *Monterey Home Video*

Abba in Concert   1979
Music-Performance
64832   ? mins   C   LV   P
This concert combines sequences from an American tour and London's Wembley Arena in 1979. Features songs such as "I Have a Dream," "Gimme! Gimme! Gimme!," "Summer Night," and "Dancing Queen." In stereo.
Curt Edman — *Pioneer Video Imports*

Abbott and Costello Cartoon Festival   1966
Cartoons
59932   60 mins   C   B, V   P
Animated 3 pgms
Animated Abbott and Costello involved in a series of comic mishaps. Cartoons include: "Cherokee Choo Choo," "Pinocchio's Double Trouble," "Son of Kong," "Teenie Weenie Genie," "Indestructible Space Suit," "Bouncing Rubber Man," "Germ Squirm," "Marauding Mummy," and "Wizardland."
Hanna Barbera — *United Home Video*

Abbott and Costello in Hollywood   1945
Comedy
58292   83 mins   B/W   B, V   P
Bud Abbott, Lou Costello, Frances Rafferty, Warner Anderson, Lucille Ball
Bud and Lou appear as a barber and porter of a high class tonsorial parlor in Hollywood.
MGM — *MGM/UA Home Video*

Abbott and Costello Meet Captain Kidd — 1952
Comedy
00384   70 mins   C   B, V   P
Abbott and Costello, Charles Laughton
With Captain Kidd on their trail, Abbott and
Costello follow up on a treasure map.
Warner Brothers — *United Home Video*

Abbott and Costello Meet Dr. Jekyll and Mr. Hyde — 1952
Comedy/Horror
65204   77 mins   B/W   B, V   P
Bud Abbott, Lou Costello, Boris Karloff, Helen Westcott
Abbott and Costello take on evil Dr. Jekyll, who
has transformed himself into Mr. Hyde, and is
terrorizing London.
Universal — *MCA Home Video*

Abbott and Costello Meet Frankenstein — 1948
Comedy
47680   83 mins   B/W   B, V, LV   P
Bud Abbott, Lou Costello, Lon Chaney Jr., Bela Lugosi
Chick and Wilbur, two unsuspecting baggage
clerks, deliver a crate containing the last
remains of Dracula and Frankstein's monster.
Universal — *MCA Home Video*

ABC—Mantrap — 1983
Music-Performance
65461   ? mins   C   B, V   P
A music video that follows "Mantrap" on a path
that leads from obscurity to international
stardom. Includes many of their top hits: "Look
of Love," "All of My Heart," and "Poison
Arrow." In stereo VHS and Beta Hi-Fi.
Michael Hamlyn — *RCA/Columbia Pictures Home Video; RCA VideoDiscs*

Abduction — 1975
Drama
65373   100 mins   C   B, V   P
Leif Erickson, Dorothy Malone, Judith-Marie Berigan
"Abduction" is the explicit and straight-forward
account of Patricia Prescott's transformation
from distraught captive to knowing participant.
Based on the novel by Harrison James.
MPAA:R
Kent E Carroll — *Media Home Entertainment*

Abduction from the Seraglio, The — 1980
Opera
84660   129 mins   C   B, V   P
Carolyn Smith-Meyer, Barbara Sternberger, the Dresden State Opera conducted by Harry Kupfer
A Dresden-based version of this Mozart opera.
Recorded in Hi-Fi.
GE
Harry Kupfer — *V.I.E.W. Video*

Abductors, The — 1971
Adventure
63084   90 mins   C   B, V   P
Ginger
Sexy Ginger infiltrates a ring of kidnappers by
offering her body as bait.
Abductors Productions — *Monterey Home Video*

Abdulla the Great — 1956
Adventure
57344   89 mins   C   B, V, FO   P
Gregory Ratoff, Kay Kendall, Sydney Chaplin
A dissolute Middle-East monarch falls for a
model, who spurns him for an army officer
critical of the King.
Gregory Ratoff — *Video Yesteryear*

Abe Lincoln: Freedom Fighter — 1978
Drama/Biographical
65723   54 mins   C   B, V   P
Allen Williams, Andrew Prine, Brock Peters
A turning point in the young life of Abe Lincoln,
the 16th President of the United States, is re-
created in this moving historical drama.
James L Conway — *VidAmerica; Lucerne Films*

Abe Lincoln in Illinois — 1939
Drama
00260   110 mins   B/W   B, V, 3/4U   P
Raymond Massey, Gene Lockhart, Ruth Gordon
Massey portrays a very human backwoods
lawyer involved with his two loves—Ann
Rutledge and Mary Todd.
RKO; Max Gordon — *Nostalgia Merchant*

Abilene Town — 1946
Western
08601   90 mins   B/W   B, V, 3/4U   P
Randolph Scott, Ann Dvorak, Lloyd Bridges, Rhonda Fleming, Edgar Buchanan
Kansas town becomes the scene of conflict
between cattlemen and homesteaders,
following the Civil War.
United Artists; Jack Broder — *Movie Buff Video; Prism; Cable Films; Video Connection; Hollywood Home Theater; Discount Video Tapes; Kartes Video Communications*

Abominable Dr. Phibes, The — 1971
Horror
64897   90 mins   C   B, V   P
Vincent Price
An evil genius decides that the surgical team
that let his wife die shall each perish by a
different biblical plague.

American International Pictures — *Vestron Video*

Abraham Lincoln   1930
Drama
11218   93 mins   B/W   B, V   P, T
Walter Huston, Una Merkel, Henry B. Walthall, directed by D. W. Griffith
D.W. Griffith's first talking movie takes Lincoln from his birth through his assassination. This restored version includes the original slavery sequences which were thought lost. Musical score included.
United Artists — *Movie Buff Video; Blackhawk Films; Hal Roach Studios; Video Yesteryear; Cable Films; Hollywood Home Theater; Discount Video Tapes; Kartes Video Communications*

Abraham's Sacrifice   1979
Drama/Bible
55016   58 mins   C   B, V   P
Gene Barry, Andrew Duggan, Beverly Garland, Ross Martin, Lainie Kazan, Ed Ames, narrated by Victor Jory
The story of Abraham and his son Isaac. Part of the "Greatest Heroes of the Bible" series.
Sunn Classics — *Magnum Entertainment; Vanguard Video; Lucerne Films*

Absence of Malice   1981
Drama
59602   116 mins   C   B, V, LV   P
Paul Newman, Sally Field, Melinda Dillon, Bob Balaban, directed by Sydney Pollack
A private citizen suddenly reads that he is the subject of a criminal investigation when an investigative reporter writes a story that was purposely leaked. A drama about the responsibility of the press.
MPAA:PG
Columbia — *RCA/Columbia Pictures Home Video; RCA VideoDiscs*

Absent-Minded Professor, The   1961
Comedy
55567   97 mins   C   B, V, LV   P
Fred MacMurray, Keenan Wynn, Tommy Kirk, Ed Wynn, Leon Ames, Nancy Olson, directed by Robert Stevenson
A professor accidentally invents an anti-gravity substance called flubber, causing inanimate objects and people to become airborne. Crazy complications arise in this newly-colored version of the Disney classic.
MPAA:G
Walt Disney — *Walt Disney Home Video; RCA VideoDiscs*

AC/DC: Let There Be Rock   1982
Music-Performance
81788   98 mins   C   B, V   P
Australian hard rockers AC/DC perform such headbangers as "Live Wire" and "Highway to Hell" in this 1980 concert filmed in Paris.
MPAA:PG
Warner Bros; High Speed Productions — *Warner Home Video*

Academy Award Winners Animated Short Films   1984
Film/Cartoons
77179   60 mins   C   B, V, CED   P
Animated
This is a collection of six short films that includes Jimmy Picker's "Sunday in New York," "The Hole," "Munro" and "Closed Mondays." Academy Award '84: Best Short Subject (Picker).
Videoline Inc — *Vestron Video*

Accident   1967
Drama
63340   100 mins   C   B, V   P
Dirk Bogarde, Michael York, Stanley Baker, Jacqueline Sassard
A tangled web of guilt, remorse, humor and thwarted sexuality is unravelled against the background of the English countryside in this story of an Oxford love triangle.
Royal Avenue Chelsea Productions Ltd — *THORN EMI/HBO Video*

Ace Drummond   1936
Drama/Serials
01773   250 mins   B/W   B, V   P
John King, Jean Rogers, Noah Beery
Complete 13-chapter serial about a murdering organization trying to stop several countries from forming a world wide clipper ship air service. Thirteen untitled episodes.
Unknown — *Hollywood Home Theater; Video Connection; Discount Video Tapes; Video Yesteryear; Captain Bijou*

Acqua e Sapone   1983
Comedy
87757   100 mins   C   B, V   P
Natasha Hovey, Carlo Verdone, directed by Carlo Verdone
A young innocent model goes to Rome under the watchful eyes of an appointed priest-chaperone, but finds love, fun and other sinful things.
MPAA:PG
Mario and Vittorio Cecchi Gori — *RCA/Columbia Pictures Home Video*

Across the Great Divide   1976
Adventure
63382   102 mins   C   B, V   P

Robert Logan, George "Buck" Flower, Heather Rattray
Two orphans must cross the rugged snow-covered Rocky Mountains in 1876 in order to claim their inheritance—a 400-acre plot of land in Salem, Oregon.
MPAA:G
Pacific International Enterprises — *Media Home Entertainment*

Act, The 1982
Comedy
73033   90 mins   C   B, V   P
Jill St. John, Eddie Albert
This is a satire about political double dealing.
MPAA:R
Film Ventures — *Vestron Video*

Act of Aggression 1973
Drama
80118   100 mins   C   B, V   P
Jean Louis Trintignant, Catherine Deneuve, Claude Brasseur
When a Parisian man finds his wife and daughter murdered at a summer resort, he takes the law into his own hands.
MPAA:R
Joseph Green Pictures — *King of Video*

Act of Passion (The Lost Honor of Kathryn Beck) 1983
Drama
86170   100 mins   C   B, V   P
Marlo Thomas, Kris Kristofferson, George Dzunda, John De Vries
Based loosely on a novel by Heinrich Boll, the film deals with an innocent woman who, after messing with a terrorism suspect, is beleaguered by police and the press.
Open Road/ComWorld — *Vidmark Entertainment*

Act of Vengeance 1984
Drama
70949   90 mins   C   B, V   P
Brutalized victims of a rapist unite in an organized and deadly hunt for their criminally degenerated attacker.
MPAA:R
Buzz Feitshans — *THORN EMI/HBO Video*

Action 1985
Filmmaking
82309   60 mins   C   B, V   P
This is a behind-the-scenes look at how special effects for "The Terminator," "Life Force" and "Missing in Action" were done by the Hollywood masters of the art.
Drew Cummings — *Karl/Lorimar Home Video*

Action in Arabia 1944
War-Drama/Adventure
82183   75 mins   B/W   B, V   P
George Sanders, Virginia Bruce, Gene Lockhart, Robert Armstrong
A newsman uncovers a Nazi plot to turn the Arabs against the Allies while investigating a colleague's murder in Damascus.
RKO — *RKO HomeVideo*

Adam 1983
Drama
Closed Captioned
81255   100 mins   C   B, V   P
Daniel J. Travanti, Jobeth Williams, Martha Scott, Richard Masur, directed by Michael Tuchner
This is the true story of John and Reve Walsh's search for their six-year-old son Adam who was kidnapped from a large department store.
Alan Landsburg Productions — *U.S.A. Home Video*

Adam Had Four Sons 1941
Drama
76023   81 mins   B/W   B, V   P
Ingrid Bergman, Warner Baxter, Susan Hayward, Fay Wray, and Robert Shaw
An intense drama of love, jealousy, and hatred; a governess to a man's four sons sees them growing up.
Robert Sherwood — *RCA/Columbia Pictures Home Video*

Adam's Rib 1949
Comedy
44647   101 mins   B/W   B, V   P
Katherine Hepburn, Spencer Tracy, Tom Ewell, Judy Holliday, directed by George Cukor
A husband and wife lawyer team clash when the wife defends a woman on trial for shooting her spouse. The other half of the team (the husband) is the prosecutor.
MGM — *MGM/UA Home Video*

Adios, Hombre 1975
Western
84895   90 mins   C   B, V   P
Craig Hill, Giulia Rubini
An innocent man who was imprisoned for murder escapes from prison and seeks revenge.
Italian — *Unicorn Video*

Adrian Belew: Electronic Guitar 1985
Music
87920   60 mins   C   B, V   P
The great journeyman guitarist instructs in tuning, fretless guitars, electronic effects and two-handed fingerboards. Musical illustrations include selections from his solo albums and work with King Crimson.

DCI Music Video — *DCI Music Video*

Adriana Lecouvreur   1985
Opera
88134   135 mins   C   B, V   P
Dame Joan Sutherland, conducted by Richard Bonynge
The Elizabethan Sydney Opera performs the classic Francesco Cilea opera, in French with English subtitles.
FR
The Australian Opera — *Sony Video Software*

Adventure 1: Trailers on   1984
Tape
Movie and TV trailers/Adventure
66480   61 mins   C   B, V   P
Nearly 40 trailers for adventure movies are compiled on this tape, including "Rebel Without a Cause," "Lost Horizon," "Torn Curtain," "From Russia With Love," "Wild in the Street," "The Wild One" and "Sunset Boulevard." Some black and white segments.
Universal et al — *San Francisco Rush Video*

Adventure Called   1982
Menudo, An
Musical
69540   90 mins   C   B, V   P
Xavier, Miguel, Johnny, Ricky and Charlie (the members of Menudo) sing 14 songs in this story of their misadventures, which begin with a flight in a balloon. In Spanish.
SP
Embassy Communications — *Embassy Home Entertainment*

Adventurer, The   1917
Comedy
58970   20 mins   B/W   B, V, 3/4U   P
Charlie Chaplin
As an escaped convict, Charlie is invited as a house guest by two women who believe he is a gallant sportsman. Silent with music track.
Mutual — *Cable Films; Festival Films*

Adventurers, The   1952
Adventure
82231   82 mins   B/W   B, V   P
Dennis Price, Jack Hawkins, Siobhan McKenna, Peter Hammond, Bernard Lee
In 1902, two Boers and an English officer set out to recover stolen diamonds hidden in the jungles of South Africa.
J. Arthur Rank — *Monterey Home Video*

Adventures in Paradise   1982
Documentary/Sports-Water
77452   79 mins   C   B, V   P
Champion surfers Mike Ho, Chris Lassen, and Bobby Owens go on a worldwide search for the perfect wave. Available in Beta Hi Fi and VHS Stereo.
Scott Dittrich Films — *Monterey Home Video*

Adventures of Black   1972
Beauty, The
Adventure/Cartoons
75891   50 mins   C   B, V   P
Animated   6 pgms
The endearing childrens story is told once again in this six volume series. Programs are available individually.
LWI Productions; Tablot Television — *Sony Video Software*

Adventures of Buckaroo   1984
Banzai, The
Science fiction/Fantasy
80047   100 mins   C   B, V, LV,   P
                                CED
Peter Weller, Ellen Barkin, Jeff Goldblum, Christopher Lloyd, John Lithgow, directed by W.D. Richter
Neurosurgeon/physicist Buckaroo Banzai travels through the eighth dimension to battle with Dr. Emilie Lizardo and his lectoids for control of the overthruster.
MPAA:PG
Twentieth Century Fox — *Vestron Video*

Adventures of Buster the   1978
Bear, The
Cartoons
53142   52 mins   C   B, V   P
Animated
Joe the Otter doesn't want to share the fish in the stream with Buster, until Grandfather Bullfrog shows him that sharing makes life fun.
EL, SP
Ziv Intl — *Family Home Entertainment*

Adventures of Captain   1980
Future Volume 1, The
Science fiction/Cartoons
53159   54 mins   C   B, V   P
Animated
Captain Future and his crew use a time machine to go back a million years into the past to save a planet. They encounter strange prehistoric creatures.
EL, SP
Ziv Intl — *Family Home Entertainment*

Adventures of Captain   1980
Future Volume 2, The
Science fiction/Cartoons
53160   54 mins   C   B, V   P
Animated
Captain Future and his crew save an entire planet from destruction by solving the problem of finding a safe energy source.
EL, SP

Ziv Intl — *Family Home Entertainment*

Adventures of Captain Fabian
1951
Adventure
80030   100 mins   B/W   B, V   P
Errol Flynn, Vincent Price, Agnes Moorehead, Micheline Prelle.
When the captain of the "China Sea" learns that a beautiful woman has been falsely imprisoned, he comes to her rescue.
Republic Pictures — *Republic Pictures Home Video*

Adventures of Captain Marvel
1941
Adventure/Serials
07334   240 mins   B/W   B, V, 3/4U   P
Tom Tyler, Frank Coghlan Jr., Louise Currie
A serial about the adventures of Captain Marvel in his fight against crime. In twelve episodes.
Republic — *Video Connection; Republic Pictures Home Video*

Adventures of Curley and His Gang, The
1947
Comedy
66112   54 mins   C   B, V   P
Larry Olsen
The children's favorite teacher is replaced.
Hal Roach — *Unicorn Video*

Adventures of Don Juan
1949
Adventure/Romance
71142   111 mins   C   B, V   P
Errol Flynn, Viveca Lindfors, Robert Douglas, Romney Brent, Alan Hale, Raymond Burr, Aubrey Mather, Ann Rutherford, directed by Vincent Sherman
Don Juan de Marana saves Queen Margaret from her evil first minister; and swashbuckles his way across Spain and England in order to win her heart. Flynn's last spectacular costume epic.
Academy Awards '49 Best Costume Design.
Warner Bros — *MGM/UA Home Video*

Adventures of Droopy, The
1955
Cartoons
81052   53 mins   C   B, V   P
Animated, directed by Tex Avery
This is a collection of seven classic cartoons featuring that sad-eyed bloodhound Droopy including: "Domb-Hounded," "Wags to Riches," "Champ Champ" and "Deputy Droopy."
MGM — *MGM/UA Home Video*

Adventures of Eliza Fraser, The
1976
Comedy
80820   114 mins   C   B, V, LV   P
Susannah York, Trevor Howard, Leon Lissek, Abigail, Noel Ferrier, Carole Skinner
A young shipwrecked couple move from bawdy pleasures to cannibalism after their tropical island's aborigines capture them.
Hexagon Productions — *New World Video*

Adventures of Ellery Queen, The
1951
Mystery/Crime-Drama
47487   25 mins   B/W   B, V, FO   P
Richard Hart, Sono Osato, Kurt Katch
The first television portrayal of Ellery Queen featured Richard Hart as the famed detective. In this episode, Ellery solves the murder of a carnival acrobat.
Dumont — *Video Yesteryear*

Adventures of Felix the Cat, The
1960
Cartoons
65482   56 mins   C   B, V   P
Animated
In this episode of light-hearted episodes, Felix is joined by a whole array of amazing characters—the devious and evil Professor, the absent-minded Poindexter, and the Strongman Rock Bottom.
Joseph Oriolo — *Media Home Entertainment*

Adventures of Frontier Fremont, The
1975
Adventure
35366   95 mins   C   B, V   P
Dan Haggerty, Denver Pyle
A rough and tumble story of a man who makes the wilderness his home and the animals his friends.
Sunn Classic — *United Home Video; Lucerne Films*

Adventures of Grizzly Adams at Beaver Dam, The
198?
Adventure
65759   60 mins   C   B, V   P
Dan Haggerty
Fearing that a dam will flood his valley, Grizzly tries desperately to convince a misplaced family of beavers to build their dam elsewhere.
Charles E Sellier Jr — *United Home Video*

Adventures of Huckleberry Finn, The
1939
Adventure
52744   89 mins   B/W   B, V   P
Mickey Rooney, Lynne Carver, Rex Ingram, William Frawley

Mark Twain's immortal classic about a boy who runs away down the Mississippi on a raft, accompanied by a runaway slave, is the basis of this film.
MGM — *MGM/UA Home Video; VidAmerica*

Adventures of Huckleberry Finn, The   1978
Adventure
75616   97 mins   C   B, V   P
Forrest Tucker, Larry Storch
The classic adventure by Mark Twain of a Missouri boy and a runaway slave.
Sunn Classic Productions — *VidAmerica; Children's Video Library*

Adventures of Huckleberry Finn, The   1984
Cartoons
80395   48 mins   C   B, V   P
Animated
An animated version of the Mark Twain classic novel about the friendship between a young boy and a runaway slave.
Unknown — *Embassy Home Entertainment*

Adventures of Huckleberry Finn, The   1984
Adventure
82079   121 mins   C   B, V   P
Sada Thompson, Lillian Gish, Richard Kiley, Jim Dale, Barnard Hughes, Patrick Day
This is an adaptation of the Mark Twain story about the adventures Huckleberry Finn and a runaway slave encounter when they travel down the Mississippi River. Available in VHS and Beta Hi-Fi Mono.
The Great Amwell Company — *MCA Home Video*

Adventures of Little Lulu and Tubby Volume 1, The   1978
Cartoons
53135   50 mins   C   B, V   P
Animated
In "Good Luck Guard," Lulu tries to join Tubby's club for boys. In "The Endurance Test," Lulu gets back at Tubby when they go on an all-day hike, without any food for Tubby.
EL, SP
Ziv Intl — *Family Home Entertainment*

Adventures of Little Lulu and Tubby Volume 2, The   1978
Cartoons
53136   50 mins   C   B, V   P
Animated
In "Save the Prisoners," Lulu helps Tubby escape from the dreaded Westside gang. In "Little Fireman," Lulu fools all the boys and becomes the first one on the block to ride in a real fire truck.

EL, SP
Ziv Intl — *Family Home Entertainment*

Adventures of Mighty Mouse-Volumes IV & V, The   194?
Cartoons
29125   60 mins   C   B, V   P
Animated
Paul Terry's Mighty Mouse character is featured in two cartoon collections, both available individually. Volume IV runs 90 minutes.
EL, SP
Viacom International — *CBS/Fox Video*

Adventures of Ozzie and Harriet, The   1966
Comedy
38994   57 mins   C   B, V, FO   P
Ozzie, Harriet, David and Ricky Nelson
2 pgms
Two episodes from the long-running television series: "Wally the Author" and "The Sheik of Araby." Commercials are included; they are in black and white.
ABC — *Video Yesteryear*

Adventures of Ozzie and Harriet, The   1964
Comedy/Television
57346   55 mins   C   B, V, FO   P
Ozzie, Harriet, David and Ricky Nelson
Two complete episodes of the long-running situation comedy: "Ricky's Horse," where Ricky finds himself the proud owner of a horse after a financial "discussion" between Ozzie and Harriet, and "Ozzie the Babysitter," where Ozzie's in big trouble after damaging a slot car set belonging to the nine-year-old he's babysitting. Black and white commercials included.
ABC — *Video Yesteryear; Discount Video Tapes*

Adventures of Ozzie and Harriet I thru VIII, The   195?
Comedy
45022   120 mins   B/W   B, V, 3/4U   P
Ozzie, Harriet, David and Ricky Nelson
Each tape in this series includes four shows with the original commercials left in. Some later editions of the program were aired in color.
ABC — *Shokus Video*

Adventures of Reddy the Fox, The   1978
Cartoons
53143   52 mins   C   B, V   P
Animated
While Granny Fox is away, Reddy the Fox gets into all kinds of trouble, until, much to his relief, Granny returns to set everything right.

EL, SP
Ziv Intl — *Family Home Entertainment*

Adventures of Robin Hood, The   1938
Adventure
58832   102 mins   C   B, V, LV   P
Errol Flynn, Basil Rathbone, Claude Rains, Olivia de Havilland, Alan Hale
Errol Flynn stars as the rebel outlaw who outwits Sir Guy of Gisbourne and Prince John and saves the throne for the absent King Richard. Academy Awards '38: Interior Decoration; Film Editing; Original Score (Erich Wolfgang Korngold). EL, SP
United Artists — *CBS/Fox Video; RCA VideoDiscs*

Adventure of Sherlock Holmes, The   1985
Mystery
84522   58 mins   C   B, V   P
Jeremy Brett, David Burke   6   pgms
Sir Arthur Conan Doyle's immortal detective returns in this series of new adventures, originally televised on PBS's "Mystery" series.
1.A Scandal in Bohemia 2.The Speckled Band 3.The Blue Corbuncle 4.The Dancing Men 5.The Naval Treaty 6.The Solitary Cyclist
Granada TV; PBS — *Simon and Schuster Video*

Adventures of Sherlock Holmes' Smarter Brother, The   1978
Comedy
29126   91 mins   C   B, V   P
Gene Wilder, Madeline Kahn, Marty Feldman, Dom DeLuise
The unknown brother of the famous Sherlock Holmes takes on some of his brother's more disposable excess cases and makes some hilarious moves.
MPAA:PG
20th Century Fox — *CBS/Fox Video*

Adventures of Sinbad, The   1979
Fantasy
84713   47 mins   C   B, V   P
The adventures of the Arabian mythic hero in an animated film version.
API Television Prod — *MGM/UA Home Video*

Adventures of Sinbad the Sailor, The   1973
Cartoons/Adventure
53138   88 mins   C   B, V   P
Animated
Sinbad receives a map to a treasure island where fabulous stores of jewels are hidden, and,

in his search, falls in love with the King's daughter.
International Film Exchange — *Lightning Video; Family Home Entertainment*

Adventures of Sinbad the Sailor, The   1985
Fantasy
86549   47 mins   C   B, V   P
Narrated by Telly Savalas
An animated version of the classic Sinbad stories.
Cori & Orient — *Children's Video Library*

Adventures of Superman, The   194?
Cartoons
53799   55 mins   C   B, V, FO   P
Animated
Seven cartoons from 1942 and 1943 are included in this package: "Underground World," "Terror on the Midway," "Volcano," "Destruction Inc.," "Secret Agent," "Billion Dollar Limited," and "Showdown." Some black and white.
Paramount; Max Fleischer — *Video Yesteryear*

Adventures of Tartu, The   1943
Adventure
29753   103 mins   C   B, V   P
Robert Donat, Valerie Hobson, Glynis Johns
A British secret agent, sent to blow up Nazi poison gas factory in Czechoslavakia, poses as a Romanian.
MGM — *Hollywood Home Theater; Video Connection*

Adventures of Tarzan, The   1921
Adventure/Serials
11390   153 mins   B/W   B, V, FO   P
Elmo Lincoln
The screen's first Tarzan in an exciting jungle thriller. Silent.
Artclass — *Video Yesteryear*

Adventures of the Flying Cadets   1944
War-Drama
54163   169 mins   B/W   B, V   P
Johnny Downs, Regis Toomey
An early war adventure serial in thirteen complete chapters.
Universal — *Video Connection; Video Yesteryear*

Adventures of the Lone Ranger: Count the Clues, The   1957
Western
87368   72 mins   C   B, V   P
Clayton Moore, Jay Silverheels

Three episodes from the classic TV series, involving the masked man's investigation and apprehension of a corrupt cattle baron.
Wrather Corp. — *MGM/UA Home Video*

Adventures of the Masked Phantom, The   1938
Adventure
78092   56 mins   B/W   B, V, FO   P
Monte Rawlins, Betty Burgess, Larry Mason, Sonny Lamont
This film presents the exciting adventures of the Masked Phantom.
Monogram — *Video Yesteryear*

Adventures of the Scrabble People in a Pumpkin Full of Nonsense   1986
Fantasy/Language arts
87210   30 mins   C   B, V   P
This animated film for kids teaches spelling in a fun way, through the exploits of some wordy adventurers.
Children's Video Library — *Children's Video Library*

Adventures of the Wilderness Family, The   1976
Adventure
47749   100 mins   C   B, V, LV   P
Robert F. Logan, Susan Damente Shaw
The story of a modern-day pioneer family who becomes bored with the troubles of city life and head for life in the wilderness.
MPAA:G
Arthur R Dubs — *Media Home Entertainment*

Adventures of Tom Sawyer, The   1973
Adventure
81441   76 mins   C   B, V   P
Jane Wyatt, Buddy Ebsen, Vic Morrow, John McGiver, Josh Albee, Jeff Tyler
Tom Sawyer is a mischievous Missouri boy who gets into all kinds of trouble in this adaptation of the Mark Twain book. Available in VHS and Beta Hi-Fi.
Universal TV — *MCA Home Video*

Adventures of Tom Sawyer, The   1938
Adventure
52736   77 mins   C   B, V, CED   P
Tommy Kelly, Jackie Moran, Ann Gillis, Walter Brennan, May Robson, Victor Jory
Mark Twain's classic about a Missouri boy whose adventures range from tricking the neighborhood into whitewashing the fence for him to running away on a raft to become a pirate.

United Artists; David O. Selznick — *CBS/Fox Video*

Adventures of Topper, The   1953
Comedy
78360   120 mins   B/W   B, V   P
Leo G. Carroll, Anne Jeffreys, Bob Sterling, Lee Patrick
When a bank president purchases a house, he inherits the three ghosts who lived there before him. Four episodes from the long-running TV series.
Loveton Schubert Productions — *U.S.A. Home Video*

Adventures of Ultraman, The   1981
Cartoons/Adventure
58541   90 mins   C   B, V   P
Animated
The adventures of Ultraman, a futuristic hero from a distant plant.
EL, SP
Tsuburaya Productions — *Family Home Entertainment*

Adventures—Past, Present and Future Featurettes   1985
Movie and TV trailers/Adventure
81890   58 mins   C   B, V   P
This is a rousing collection of trailers from such films as "Doc Savage," "Alien," "Futureworld" and "Airport 77."
20th Century Fox et al — *San Francisco Rush Video*

Aerobic Dancing   1982
Physical fitness
63167   56 mins   C   B, V   P
Jacki Sorensen
Aerobic dancing, a blend of dancing and jogging, is demonstrated on this workout tape by its creator, Jacki Sorensen. She performs a complete exercise session at three activity levels: walking, jogging and running. VHS is in stereo, with music on one track and instructions on the other.
Feeling Fine Productions; Jacki Sorensen's Aerobic Dancing Inc — *MCA Home Video*

Aerobic Dancing—Encore   1983
Physical fitness/Dance
65205   57 mins   C   B, V   P
Jacki Sorensen
A blending of dancing and jogging into a complete workout. The program is choreographed to strengthen the heart and lungs while firming up the entire body.

Priscilla Ulene — *MCA Home Video*

Aerobic Self-Defense 1984
Physical fitness/Martial arts
72890   60 mins   C   B, V   P
A "How to" program that combines aerobics
and the martial arts.
NTA — *Republic Pictures Home Video*

Aerobicise: The Beautiful 1981
Workout
Physical fitness
58875   113 mins   C   B, V, LV   P
Aerobic dancing to original music, produced by
Ron Harris, fashion photographer. An erotic
exercise program.
Ron Harris — *Paramount Home Video; RCA
VideoDiscs*

Aerobicise: The 1982
Beginning Workout
Physical fitness
63427   96 mins   C   B, V, LV   P
This is a basic, simple exercise regimen for the
uninitiated aerobiciser.
Ron Harris — *Paramount Home Video; RCA
VideoDiscs*

Aerobicise: The Ultimate 1983
Workout
Physical fitness
66032   100 mins   C   B, V, LV   P
The last installment of Paramount's Aerobicise
trilogy is the most advanced, designed for those
in excellent shape. In stereo.
Ron Harris — *Paramount Home Video*

Aesop and His Friends 1982
Fairy tales/Cartoons
58577   50 mins   C   B, V   P
A collection of Aesop's most beloved fables:
"The Fox and the Crow," "The Lion and the
Mouse," "The Grasshopper and the Ant," "The
City Mouse and the Country Mouse," plus "The
Snowman's Dilemma" and "The Owl and the
Pussycat" as told by Cyril Ritchard. Others
included as well.
McGraw Hill — *Mastervision*

Aesop's Fables 1985
Fairy tales/Cartoons
81790   60 mins   C   B, V   P
Animated
The young shepherd Aesop discovers what
happens when you yell "wolf"once too often
and picks up some pointers for an industrious
ant along the way. Available in VHS and Beta
Hi-Fi.
Turner Program Services — *RCA/Columbia
Pictures Home Video*

Aesop's Fables 1986
Fantasy
84952   30 mins   C   B, V   P
Bill Cosby
Combining live action and computer animation,
this film portrays Aesop's fable-telling and his
fables.
Lou Scheimer; Norm Prescott — *Blackhawk
Films*

Affair of the Pink Pearl, 1984
The
Mystery
80447   60 mins   C   B, V   P
James Warwick, Francesca Annis
The husband and wife private investigation
team of Tommy and Tuppence must find the
culprit who stole a valuable pink pearl within
twenty four hours. Based on the Agatha Christie
story.
London Weekend Television — *Pacific Arts
Video*

Affairs of Annabel 1938
Comedy
29491   68 mins   B/W   B, V   P, T
Lucille Ball, Jack Oakie, Ruth Donnelly
The first of the popular series of Annabel
pictures Lucy made in the late 30's. This
appealing adolescent is zoomed to movie
stardom by her press agent's stunts. A behind-
the-scenes satire on Hollywood, stars, and
agents.
RKO, Lou Lusty Republic — *Blackhawk Films;
RKO HomeVideo*

Africa Screams 1949
Comedy
00386   79 mins   B/W   B, V   P
Abbott and Costello
Abbott and Costello go on an African safari in
possession of a secret map. Then the trouble
begins.
United Artists — *Prism; American Video Tape;
Hollywood Home Theater; Media Home
Entertainment; VCII; Video Connection; Video
Yesteryear; Discount Video Tapes; Nostalgia
Merchant; Vestron Video (disc only); Kartes
Video Communications; Hal Roach Studios*

Africa Texas Style 1967
Adventure
80031   109 mins   C   B, V   P
*Hugh O'Brien, John Mills, Nigel Green, Tom
Nardini*
An East African rancher hires an American
cowboy and his Navajo sidekick to help run his
wild game ranch.
Paramount; Ivan Tors — *Republic Pictures
Home Video*

African Queen, The 1951
Adventure
08471   105 mins   C   B, V, LV   P
Humphrey Bogart, Katharine Hepburn, Robert Morley, Theodore Bikel, directed by John Huston
In the Congo during World War I, a spinster persuades a dissolute captain to try to destroy a German gunboat.
Academy Awards '51: Best Actor (Bogart). EL, SP
United Artists; Horizon Romulus
· Prod — *CBS/Fox Video; RCA VideoDiscs*

After Hours 1985
Comedy
Closed Captioned
88038   97 mins   C   B, V, LV   P
Griffin Dunne, Rosanna Arquette, John Heard, Teri Garr, Catherine O'Hara, Verna Bloom, Cheech & Chong, Linda Fiorentino, directed by Martin Scorcese
A surreal, absurd comedy about an uptown New York yuppie who innocently meets a girl downtown, and finds himself thereafter drawn by chance into a series of wild, malevolent and paranoid adventures, unable to get back home.
Cannes Film Festival '86: Best Director (Scorcese). MPAA:R
Geffen Co.; Warner Bros. — *Warner Home Video*

After Mein Kampf 1942
World War II/Propaganda
52321   40 mins   B/W   B, V   P
British propaganda film which blends German cartoons and contemporary footage to illustrate the rise of Hitler and the Third Reich.
British — *Prism; International Historic Films*

After Mein Kampf (The Story of Adolf Hitler) 1940
Documentary/World War II
69575   43 mins   B/W   B, V, FO   P
This combination of newsreel footage and recreations presents the life story of Hitler, made by the British as a propaganda move during the early months of World War II.
British Lion — *Video Yesteryear; Discount Video Tapes*

After the Fall of New York 1985
Science fiction
80928   95 mins   C   B, V   P
Michael Sopkiw, Valentine Monnier, Roman Geer, George Eastman
The sole survivors of a nuclear war to New York City seeking the final fertile femme fatale on Earth.
MPAA:R
Almi Pictures — *Vestron Video*

After the Fox 1966
Comedy
72894   103 mins   C   B, V   P
Peter Sellers, Victor Mature
A con artist disguises himself as a film director in order to steal gold from Rome.
Delegate Productions — *CBS/Fox Video*

After the Rehearsal 1984
Drama
77377   72 mins   C   B, V   P
Erland Josephson, Ingrid Thulin, Lena Olin, directed by Ingmar Bergman·
Three actors reveal their hearts and souls on an empty stage after the rehearsal of a Strindberg play. Swedish with English subtitles.
MPAA:R SW
Triumph Films — *RCA/Columbia Pictures Home Video*

After the Thin Man 1936
Mystery/Comedy
71156   113 mins   B/W   B, V   P
William Powell, Myrna Loy, James Stewart, Elissa Landi, Joseph Calleia; Jessie Ralph, Alan Marshall, directed by W.S. Van Dyke III
The Charles', Nick, Nora and Asta seek out a murderer among Nora's own blue-blooded relatives.
MGM — *MGM/UA Home Video*

Aftermath 1985
Science fiction
80323   96 mins   C   B, V   P
Steve Barkett, Larry Latham
Three astronauts who return to Earth are shocked to discover that the planet has been ravaged by a nuclear war.
Independent — *Prism*

Against A Crooked Sky 1975
Drama
79315   89 mins   C   B, V   P
Richard Boone, Stewart Peterson, Clint Richie, directed by Earl Bellamy
A young boy and an elderly trapper set out to find his sister who was captured by the Indians.
MPAA:G
Cinema Shares — *Vestron Video*

Against All Odds 1984
Drama
Closed Captioned
70185   122 mins   C   B, V, CED   P
Jeff Bridges, Rachel Ward, James Woods, Alex Karras, directed by Taylor Hackford
An ex-football player travels to Mexico in search of his friend's girl. When he finds her, things become complicated as they fall passionately in love. In Beta Hi-Fi Stereo and VHS Hi-Fi Dolby Stereo.

Columbia Pictures — *RCA/Columbia Pictures Home Video*

Against All Odds 1969
Adventure
76830   93 mins   C   B, V   P
Christopher Lee, Richard Greene, Shirley Eaton
Fu Manchu plans to murder several world leaders by using beautiful slave girls saturated with poisonous venom that will instantly kill any man who kisses them.
Commonwealth — *Republic Pictures Home Video*

Against the Drunken Cat Paws 1975
Martial arts
82278   94 mins   C   B, V   P
Chia Ling, Ou-Yang Ksiek
A blind young martial arts student seeks to regain her sight and avenge the death of her father.
Foreign — *Unicorn Video*

Agatha 1979
Mystery
47391   98 mins   C   B, V   P
Dustin Hoffman, Vanessa Redgrave, Timothy Dalton, Helen Morse, Tony Britton, Timothy West, Celia Gregory
Agatha Christie mysteriously disappears when faced with a failing marriage. Numerous people turn out to search the British countryside for some sign of her.
MPAA:PG
Warner Bros — *Warner Home Video*

Age to Age—Amy Grant 1985
Music-Performance
82330   90 mins   C   B, V   P
Amy Grant performs such contemporary gospel favorites as "El Shadai" and "Sing Your Praise to the Lord" in this concert which is available in VHS Dolby Hi-Fi Stereo and Beta Hi-Fi Stereo.
A&M Video — *A & M Video; RCA/Columbia Pictures Home Video*

Agency 1981
Drama
62778   94 mins   C   B, V, CED   P
Robert Mitchum, Lee Majors, Valerie Perrine
An advertising agency attempts to manipulate public behavior and opinion through the use of subliminal advertising.
MPAA:R
Jensen Farley Pictures — *Vestron Video*

Ages of Humankind, The 1986
Film-History/Cartoons
70942   30 mins   C   B, V   P
Animation by Faith and John Hubley

This tape compiles several jazzy short subjects from the famed independent filmmakers, Faith and John Hubley. These productions look at people and relationships. Included are: "The Tender Game," "Dig," "WOW," "People, People, People" and "Cockaboody."
Walt Disney Productions — *Walt Disney Home Video*

Agnes of God 1985
Drama
Closed Captioned
85278   99 mins   C   B, V   P
Jane Fonda, Anne Bancroft, Meg Tilly
A young, naively innocent nun gives birth and kills the baby. The subsequent investigation into her religious fervor is spearheaded by a neurotic psychiatrist and worldly mother-superior.
MPAA:PG-13
Patrick Palmer; Norman Jewison — *RCA/Columbia Pictures Home Video*

Aida 1981
Opera
59878   210 mins   C   LV   P
Verdi's tragic opera performed live at the Arena Di Verona. In stereo.
Covent Garden Video — *Pioneer Artists*

Aida 1984
Opera
80055   150 mins   C   B, V   P
Maria Chiara, Nicola Martinucci
A performance of Giuseppe Verdi's opera taped at the Arena di Verona in Italy.
Radiotelevision Italiana — *THORN EMI/HBO Video*

AIDS: Profile of an Epidemic—Update 1986
Diseases
86844   68 mins   C   B, V   P
Narrated by Edward Asner
A documentary on AIDS' effect on families, with a current update covering recent advances in the public knowledge of the disease.
WNET New York — *MPI Home Video*

A.I.P. Collection: Trailers on Tape, The 1979
Movie and TV trailers
81883   59 mins   C   B, V   P
This is a collection of coming attractions from the studios of American International Pictures including such favorites as "Beach Blanket Bingo," "The Raven" and "I Was a Teenage Werewolf." Some segments in black and white.
American International Pictures — *San Francisco Rush Video*

Air Force 1943
War-Drama
65064   124 mins   B/W   CED   P
John Garfield, Gig Young, Arthur Kennedy, directed by Howard Hawks
This film about the early days of World War II follows the exploits of the crew of a Flying Fortress bomber as they see action at Pearl Harbor, Manila and the Coral Sea.
Warner Bros — *RCA VideoDiscs*

Air Supply Live in Hawaii 1982
Music-Performance
76024   60 mins   C   B, V   P
This concert features Air Supply's biggest hits, including "Lost in Love," "The One That You Love" and "Event the Nights Are Better."
Danny O'Donovan — *RCA/Columbia Pictures Home Video*

Airplane! 1980
Comedy
54667   88 mins   C   B, V, 8mm, LV   P
Kareem Abdul-Jabbar, Lloyd Bridges, Peter Graves, Ethel Merman, Robert Hays, Jimmie Walker, directed by Jim Abrahams
A comical twist to disaster films. First the passengers on a flight to Chicago are poisoned by their fish dinners. Then the plane must be landed by a shell-shocked veteran who has a drinking problem.
MPAA:PG
Paramount, Howard W Koch — *Paramount Home Video; RCA VideoDiscs*

Airplane II: The Sequel 1982
Comedy
64505   84 mins   C   B, V, LV   P
Robert Hays, Julie Hagerty, Lloyd Bridges, Raymond Burr, Peter Graves, William Shatner
There's a mad bomber aboard the first lunar shuttle in this loony sequel to "Airplane," which spoofs the familiar cliches of disaster movies.
MPAA:PG
Paramount — *Paramount Home Video; RCA VideoDiscs*

Airport 1970
Drama
53395   137 mins   C   B, V   P
Dean Martin, Burt Lancaster, Jean Seberg, Jacqueline Bisset, George Kennedy, Helen Hayes, Van Heflin, Maureen Stapleton
The first of the "Airport" movies is based on Arthur Hailey's novel about a snow storm, a mired plane, and an aircraft in dire distress after a bomb explodes on it.
Academy Award '70: Best Supporting Actress (Hayes). MPAA:G
Universal; Ross Hunter — *MCA Home Video; RCA VideoDiscs*

Airport 1975 1975
Adventure
84630   107 mins   C   B, V   P
Charlton Heston, Karen Black, George Kennedy, Gloria Swanson, Helen Reddy, Sid Caesar, Efrem Zimbalist, Jr, Susan Clark, Dana Andrews, Linda Blair, Myrna Loy, Susan Clark, directed by Jack Smight
A standard disaster formula, with a jetliner left pilotless and wrecked in flight. Arthur Hailey's novel "Airport" inspired this and its predecessor, "Airport" ('70).
MPAA:PG
William Frye; Universal — *MCA Home Video*

Airport '77 1977
Adventure
84631   114 mins   C   B, V   P
Jack Lemmon, James Stewart, Lee Grant, Brenda Vaccaro, Joseph Cotton, Olivia de Havilland, Darren McGavin, Christopher Lee, George Kennedy, directed by Jack Smight.
A jet-liner plunges into the ocean and stays there, distressing the passengers and hijackers while endangering the priceless art collection on board.
MPAA:PG
William Frye; Universal — *MCA Home Video*

Al Capone 1959
Crime-Drama
70990   104 mins   C   B, V   P
Rod Steiger, Fay Spain, Murvyn Vye, Nehemiah Persoff, Martin Balsam, James Gregory, Joe de Santis, directed by Richard Wilson
Using documentary style, this film traces the life of one of the roaring 20's most colorful gangsters.
Lorimar; Allied Artists — *Key Video*

Al Capone: Chicago's Scarface 198?
Documentary/Crime and criminals
87342   110 mins   C   B, V   P
Narrated by Geraldo Rivera
A documentary using vintage footage about the mob king of the 1920's and his eventual demise.
Unknown — *MPI Home Video*

Al Ponerse el Sol 197?
Romance
49746   90 mins   C   B, V   P
Serena Hercan
The plot revolves around the relationships between women auditioning for a Madrid stage show, and the men who will choose them.
SP
Independent — *Media Home Entertainment*

Alabama—Greatest Video Hits 1986
Music video
84610   37 mins   C   B, V   P

The famed country group performs nine of their hits.
RCA Video — *RCA/Columbia Pictures Home Video*

Alabama's Ghost   1974
Horror
70871   96 mins   C   B, V   P
Christopher Brooks, E. Kerrigan Prescott, directed by Fredric Hobbs
A musician steals a dead master magician's secrets, incurring the wrath of the paranormal populace.'
MPAA:PG
Vistar Int'l Prods. — *Thriller Video*

Aladdin and His Magic Lamp   1976
Fairy tales
81682   90 mins   C   B, V   P
This is the story of Aladdin, a young boy who owns a magic lamp and the merchant who will stop at nothing to gain control of the lamp.
Majestic International Pictures — *United Home Video*

Aladdin and His Magic Lamp   1985
Fantasy
84103   70 mins   C   B, V   P
Animated directed by Jean Image
An animated feature, version of the classic children's story of the young Arabian boy, the powerful genie and the evil magician vying for ownership of the world.
Target Intl-Jean Image — *Lightning Video*

Aladdin and His Wonderful Lamp   1984
Fairy tales
Closed Captioned
82094   60 mins   C   B, V   P
Valerie Bertinelli, Robert Carradine, Leonard Nimoy, James Earl Jones
This is the story of Aladdin, a young man who finds a magical oil lamp when he is trapped in a tiny cave. From the "Faerie Tale Theatre" series. Available in VHS and Beta Hi-Fi Stereo.
Platypus Productions; Lion's Gate Films — *CBS/Fox Video*

Aladdin and the Wonderful Lamp   1982
Cartoons/Adventure
59668   65 mins   C   B, V   P
Animated
Aladdin must use his magical lamp to defeat the wicked wizard and own the most valuable treasures in the land.
Toei Company — *Media Home Entertainment*

Alamo, The   1960
Western
31660   161 mins   C   B, V, CED   P
John Wayne, Richard Widmark, Laurence Harvey, Frankie Avalon, directed by John Ford
An historical account of the men who came to the aid of Texas in its fight for freedom against the Mexican army.
Academy Awards '60: Best Sound Recording.
EL, SP
United Artists — *CBS/Fox Video*

Alamo Bay   1985
Drama
Closed Captioned
71107   99 mins   C   B, V   P
Ed Harris, Ho Nguyen, Amy Madigan, directed by Louis Malle
This tale of contemporary racism pits an angry Vietnam veteran against a Vietnamese refugee who, he feels, threatens his livelihood as a fisherman. A Hi Fi recording.
Tri-Star — *RCA/Columbia Pictures Home Video*

Alarm: Spirit of '86, The   1986
Music-Performance
87180   90 mins   C   B, V   P
A performance by the Welsh rock band at UCLA, featuring "Strength," "68 Guns," "Absolute Reality" and "Spirit of '76."
Jay Boberg; Ian Wilson; International Record Syndicate Inc. — *MCA Home Video*

Alaska   1981
Travel
70861   30 mins   C   B, V   P
This program introduces viewers to the wonders of Alaska, and offers travel tips to prospective tourists.
Dennis Burkhart — *Encounter Productions*

Alaska: Once in a Lifetime   1985
Fishing
82509   72 mins   C   B, V, 3/4U,   P
                              1C
Two fishermen go after silver salmon, arctic char, and rainbow trout amidst grizzly bears and other furry beasts.
Grunko Films — *Grunko Films*

Alaskan King   1985
Fishing
82510   51 mins   C   B, V, 3/4U,   P
                              1C
Seven fishermen go on a quest for the elusive 30-pound King salmon.
Grunko Films — *Grunko Films*

Alaskan Safari   1987
States-US/Wildlife
88166   92 mins   C   B, V   P

A scenic tour of the 49th state, concentrating on its vast array of unspoiled wildlife.
United Home Video — *United Home Video*

Alberta Hunter   1982
Music-Performance
88123   58 mins   C   B, V, 8mm   P
The famed jazz vocalist gets righteous at the Smithsonian with "Rough and Ready Man," "Remember My Name," "Handyman," and other hits.
Adler Ent.; Sony — *Sony Video Software*

Albino   197?
Mystery/Drama
53943   85 mins   C   B, V   P
Christopher Lee, Trevor Howard, Sibyle Danning, Horst Frank
An albino, played by Horst Frank, stalks the street in search of his female victim.
MPAA:R
Jurgen Goslar — *Media Home Entertainment*

Alcatraz   197?
Prisons/Crime and criminals
87343   54 mins   C   B, V   P
Narrated by William Conrad
A documentary outlining the history, security and denizens of the famed prison.
Tom Thayer — *MPI Home Video*

Alchemy—Live Dire   1984
Straits
Music-Performance
79266   95 mins   C   B, V   P
The exciting progressive rock sounds of Dire Straits are captured live in concert.
Polygram Music Video — *Music Media*

Aldrich Family, The   1950
Comedy
42973   27 mins   B/W   B, V, FO   P
Jackie Kelk, House Jameson, Lois Wilson, Robert Casey
Upset because he hasn't received an invitation to a costume party, Henry decides to go as the rear end of a horse.
NBC — *Video Yesteryear*

Alexander Nevsky   1938
Drama
08701   107 mins   B/W   B, V   P
Nikolai Cherkasov, N.P. Okholopkov, Al Abrikossov, directed by Sergei Eisenstein
A story of the invasion of Russia in 1241 by the Teutonic Knights, "Alexander Nevsky" emerges as more than a film spectacle. Dubbed in English.
Russian — *International Historic Films; Discount Video Tapes; Video Yesteryear; Hollywood Home Theater; Western Film &*

Video Inc; International Home Video; Kartes Video Communications

Alexander the Great   1955
Biographical
80626   135 mins   C   B, V   P
Richard Burton, Fredric March, Claire Bloom, Harry Andrews, Peter Cushing, directed by Robert Rossen
This is the life story of Alexander the Great who conquered the world before the age of thirty three.
Rossen Films; United Artists — *MGM/UA Home Video*

Alfa Romeo   1986
Automobiles
88398   60 mins   C   B, V, 3/4U   P
How to tune-up, basically maintain and perform minor repairs on the entitled vehicle.
Peter Allen Prod. — *Peter Allen Video Productions*

Alfie   1966
Drama/Comedy
71135   114 mins   C   B, V   P
Michael Caine, Shelley Winters, Millicent Martin, Julia Foster, Jane Asher, directed by Lewis Gilbert
This tale of a mid-60's British mod with more than an eye for the ladies brought Caine to international acclaim.
Paramount — *Paramount Home Video*

Algiers   1938
Drama
01786   96 mins   B/W   B, V   P
Charles Boyer, Hedy Lamarr, Sigrid Gurie, Gene Lockhart, directed by John Cromwell
Spoiled rich girl falls under romantic spell of Pepe Le Moko, the Casbah's most notorious citizen.
U A; Walter Wanger — *Hollywood Home Theater; Movie Buff Video; Cable Films; VCII; Video Connection; Video Yesteryear; Western Film & Video Inc; Discount Video Tapes; Kartes Video Communications*

Ali: Skill, Brains and Guts   1975
Boxing
07874   90 mins   C   B, V   P
Muhammad Ali
From teenage Golden Glove to Heavyweight champion, Ali tells his own story with highlights of over twenty-five fights.
Big Fights Inc — *VidAmerica*

Alibaba's Revenge   1984
Cartoons
70582   53 mins   C   B, V   P
Animated, voice of Jim Backus, directed by H. Shidar

The efforts of Al Huck, his rodent side-kick, and a goofy genie combine to overthrow the tyrannical king of Alibaba. The Alibaban peasants (all cats) revolt behind Huck's leadership in response to unfair food and luxury taxes.
ATA Trading Corporation — *MPI Home Video*

Alice Adams 1935
Drama
45103 99 mins B/W   B, V   P, T
Katharine Hepburn, Fred MacMurray
Girl from small, midwestern town falls in love with a man from the upper level of society and tries to fit in.
Pandro S Berman — *Blackhawk Films; Nostalgia Merchant*

Alice Cooper and Friends 1978
Music-Performance
12044 50 mins C   B, V   P
Alice Cooper, The Tubes, Nazareth, Sha-Na-Na
A rock extravaganza, taped at the Anaheim Stadium in California in the summer of 1978, featuring the exotic stylings of Alice Cooper.
Drew Cummings — *Media Home Entertainment*

Alice Cooper: Welcome to My Nightmare 1975
Music
65134 66 mins C   B, V   P
Alice Cooper, Vincent Price
An elaborate video version of the "Welcome to My Nightmare" record album, featuring such ghoulish tunes as "Department of Youth," "Ballad of Dwight Frye" and "Cold Ethyl."
Alive Enterprises — *Warner Home Video*

Alice Doesn't Live Here Anymore 1975
Drama/Comedy
52706 113 mins C   B, V   P
Ellen Burstyn, Kris Kristofferson, Diane Ladd, Jodi Foster, Harvey Keitel, directed by Martin Scorcese
A young woman's husband dies suddenly, leaving her to care for their eleven-year-old son. She heads toward Monterey, California, where she was once a singer, but gets delayed in Phoenix where she falls for a rancher.
MPAA:PG
Warner Bros; David Suskind; Audrey Maas — *Warner Home Video; RCA VideoDiscs*

Alice Goodbody 1976
Comedy
66288 83 mins C   B, V   P
Sharon Kelly, Daniel Kauffman, Keith McConnell
A sex spoof of a lonely girl's misadventures in Hollywood.
MPAA:R

Tom Scheuer — *Media Home Entertainment*

Alice in Wonderland 1951
Fantasy/Cartoons
53794 75 mins C   CED   P
Animated
Disney's version of Lewis Carroll's fable about a girl who falls into a hole and ends up in Wonderland with the Mad Hatter, the Cheshire Cat, and the Queen of Hearts.
Walt Disney — *RCA VideoDiscs*

Alice in Wonderland 1977
Satire
55212 76 mins C   B, V   P
Kristine DeBell
Adult version of the classic tale starring Playboy cover girl Kristine DeBell.
MPAA:R EL, SP
General National Enterprises — *Media Home Entertainment*

Alice in Wonderland 1982
Musical/Fantasy
63841 81 mins C   B, V   P
Annie Enneking, Solvieg Olsen, Wendy Lehr, Jason McLean, Gary Briggle, Elizabeth Fink
All of Lewis Carroll's beloved characters come alive in this musical adaptation of his classic tale, performed by the Children's Theatre Company and School. VHS in stereo.
Television Theater Company — *MCA Home Video*

Alice in Wonderland 1951
Fantasy
82227 83 mins C   B, V   P
Carol Marsh, Stephen Murray, Pamela Brown, Felix Aylmer, Ernest Milton
This is the other version of the Lewis Carrol classic which combines the usage of puppets and live action to tell the story.
Souvaine Selective Pictures — *Monterey Home Video*

Alice in Wonderland 1951
Fantasy
85530 75 mins C   B, V   P
Voices of Kathryn Beaumont, Ed Wynn, Sterling Holloway, Jerry Colonna
The classic Disney animated version of Lewis Carroll's famous children's story about a girl who falls down a rabbit hole into a magical world populated by strange creatures.
MPAA:G
Walt Disney Studios — *Walt Disney Home Video*

Alice Sweet Alice 1976
Suspense
29498 112 mins C   B, V   P
Brooke Shields, Linda Miller, Paula Sheppard

A spine-chilling story of macabre murders: who and why is this masked person butchering their victims?
Allied Artists — *Movie Buff Video; Spotlite Video; Sound Video Unlimited; Hollywood Home Theater; World Video Pictures; Discount Video Tapes*

Alice Through the Looking Glass 1966
Adventure
70679   72 mins   C   B, V   P
Judi Rolin, Ricardo Montalban, Nanette Fabray, Robert Coote, Agnes Moorehead, Jack Palance, Jimmy Durante, The Smothers Brothers, Roy Castle, Richard Denning, directed by Alan Handley
Based on Lewis Carroll's classic adventure, this show follows the further adventures of young Alice. After a chess piece comes to life, it convinces Alice that excitement and adventure lie through the looking glass.
NBC; Alan Handley; Bob Wynn — *Embassy Home Entertainment*

Alice's Adventures in Wonderland 1973
Fantasy
69614   97 mins   C   B, V   P
Peter Sellers, Sir Ralph Richardson, Dudley Moore, Michael Horndern, Spike Mulligan
This adaptation of Lewis Carroll's classic tale features an all-star cast.
Josef Shaftel — *United Home Video; Vestron Video; Children's Video Library*

Alice's Restaurant 1969
Comedy/Drama
65333   111 mins   C   B, V, CED   P
Arlo Guthrie
A young folk singer has difficulties with the police, the draft board and a Massachusetts community of flower children.
MPAA:R
United Artists — *CBS/Fox Video*

Alien 1979
Science fiction
44930   116 mins   C   B, V, LV, P
CED
Tom Skerritt, Sigourney Weaver, Veronica Cartwright
Seven astronauts on a routine mission encounter an awesome galactic horror.
MPAA:R
20th Century Fox — *CBS/Fox Video*

Alien Factor, The 1978
Science fiction
69803   82 mins   C   B, V   P
John Leifert, Tom Griffiths, Mary Mertens
A spaceship crashes in the countryside, and a small town is jolted out of its sleepy state by

havoc wreaked by a host of grotesque extraterrestrial monsters.
MPAA:PG
Don Dohler — *United Home Video*

Alien Warrior 1985
Science fiction
88024   100 mins   C   B, V   P
Brett Clark, Pamela Saunders, directed by Edward Hunt
An extraterrestrial fights a street pimp to save a crime-ridden Earth neighborhood.
MPAA:R
Shapiro Ent. — *Vestron Video*

Aliens from Spaceship Earth 1977
Science fiction
33805   107 mins   C   B, V   R, P
Donovan, Lynda Day George
Are strange, celestial forces invading our universe? If they are, is man prepared to defend his planet against threatening aliens of unknown strength?
International TF Productions — *Video Gems*

Alison's Birthday 1983
Horror
70048   99 mins   C   B, V   P
A teenage girl learns that some of her family and friends are Satan worshipers at a terrifying birthday party.
David Hannay — *VidAmerica*

All About Eve 1950
Drama
29127   138 mins   B/W   B, V   P
Bette Davis, Anne Baxter, Gary Merrill, Celeste Holme, George Sanders, Marilyn Monroe, directed by Joseph L. Mankiewicz
An aspiring young actress ingratiates herself with a prominent group of theatre people, but passion to perform and jealousy consume her as she viciously betrays her colleagues in her struggle for success.
Academy Awards '50: Best Picture; Best Supporting Actor (Sanders); Best Direction (Mankiewicz); Best Screenplay (Mankiewicz).
20th Century Fox — *CBS/Fox Video*

All in a Night's Work 1961
Mystery
16136   94 mins   C   B, V   P
Dean Martin, Shirley MacLaine, Cliff Robertson
The founder of a one-man publishing empire is found dead with a smile on his face.
EL, SP
Paramount; Hal Wallis Prod — *CBS/Fox Video*

All Mine to Give 1956
Drama
10400   102 mins   C   B, V   P

Glynis Johns, Cameron Mitchell
Saga of a family of eight who braved frontier
hardships, epidemics, and death in the
Wisconsin wilderness a century ago.
RKO — *United Home Video*

All Night Long   1981
Comedy
59682   100 mins   C   B, V   P
*Gene Hackman, Barbra Streisand, Dianne Ladd,
Dennis Quaid*
A man who is passed over for a promotion
begins his comic liberation and joins the drifters,
weirdos and thieves of the night at his new job.
MPAA:R
Universal — *MCA Home Video*

All Night Long/Smile   1924
Please
Comedy
85142   66 mins   B/W   B, V   P
*Harry Langdon, Natalie Kingston, Jack Cooper,
Alberta Vaughn*
Two classic comedies by the most overlooked
of the great silent clowns, both produced by
slapstick progenitor Mack Sennett.
Mack Sennett — *Video Yesteryear*

All of Me   1984
Comedy
80329   93 mins   C   B, V   P
*Steve Martin, Lily Tomlin, Victoria Tennant,
Selma Diamond, Richard Libertine, directed by
Carl Reiner*
A lawyer inherits the soul of a dead woman by
accident and it winds up taking over the right
side of his body.
MPAA:PG
Universal — *THORN EMI/HBO Video*

All Over Town   1937
Comedy
81735   52 mins   B/W   B, V   P
Ole Olsen, Chic Johnson, Mary Howard
Two vaudevillians with a trained seal find
themselves involved in a murder when they are
kidnapped by a gang of thugs.
Republic Pictures — *Kartes Video
Communications*

All Quiet on the Western   1979
Front
Drama
55528   150 mins   C   B, V   P
*Richard Thomas, Ernest Borgnine, Donald
Pleasance, Patricia Neal*
A sensitive German youth plunges excitedly into
World War I and discovers its terror and
degradation. Based on the novel by Erich Maria
Remarque.
Norman Rosemont Prods; Marble Arch
Prods — *CBS/Fox Video*

All Quiet on the Western   1930
Front
Drama
55556   103 mins   B/W   B, V   P
Lew Ayres, Louis Wolheim, John Wray
A dramatization of Erich Maria Remarque's
novel about a young German soldier facing the
horrors of World War I.
Universal — *MCA Home Video*

All Screwed Up   1974
Film-Avant-garde
37406   104 mins   C   B, V   P
*Luigi Diberti, Lina Polito, directed by Lina
Wertmuller*
The story of a group of young immigrants in
Milan—where everything is in its place—but
nothing is in order.
New Line Cinema — *CBS/Fox Video*

All-Star Batting Tips   1975
Baseball
33844   28 mins   C   B, V   P
*Tony Kubek, Mickey Mantle, Stan Musial, Pete
Rose, Willie Mays, Harmon Killebrew*
Tony Kubek moderates an All-Star panel as
they discuss their philosophies on hitting and
teach the six essential steps necessary to
become a better hitter.
Major League Baseball — *Major League
Baseball Productions*

All Star Cartoon Parade   19??
Cartoons
66470   54 mins   C   B, V   P
Animated
A collection of popular vintage cartoons,
starring such favorites as Little Lulu, Casper the
Friendly Ghost, Betty Boop and Raggedy Ann
and Andy.
Famous Studios — *Republic Pictures Home
Video*

All-Star Catching and   1975
Base Stealing Tips
Baseball
35533   28 mins   C   B, V   P
*Johnny Bench, Thurman Munson, Carlton Fisk,
Steve Yeager, Del Crandall*
The fine points of catching and the art of
stealing bases are the featured topics on this
program. Game-action footage of today's stars
is presented in an easy-to-understand manner.
Major League Baseball — *Major League
Baseball Productions*

All-Star Game, 1967   1967
Baseball
49550   30 mins   C   B, V   P
Tony Perez' 15th inning home run off Catfish
Hunter gives the National League a 2-1 victory
in the longest All-Star game ever played. Young

Mets' pitcher Tom Seaver gets credit for the victory.
Winik Films — *Major League Baseball Productions*

All-Star Game, 1970: What Makes an All-Star
1970

Baseball
45030   30 mins   C   B, V   P
The National League wins its eighth straight midsummer classic, 5-4, in 12 innings. Pete Rose barrels into American League catcher Ray Fosse at home plate to score the winning run on Jim Hickman's single.
W and W Prods — *Major League Baseball Productions*

All-Star Game, 1971: Home Run Heroes
1971

Baseball
33843   26 mins   C   B, V   P
Some or the great home run sluggers of the past are paid tribute, including Babe Ruth, Hank Greenberg, Mel Ott, and Mickey Mantle. The game itself produces six home runs, one of them a mammoth blast by Oakland's Reggie Jackson, and the American League goes on to a 6-4 victory.
W and W Productions — *Major League Baseball Productions*

All-Star Game, 1972: Years of Tradition, Night of Pride
1972

Baseball
33841   26 mins   C   B, V   P
Highlights from the first All-Star Game in 1933 to the present ones are shown prior to the National League's 10-inning, 4-3 victory at Atlanta Stadium. Hank Aaron thrills the home-team crowd with a dramatic home run.
W and W Prods — *Major League Baseball Productions*

All-Star Game, 1973: A New Generation of Stars
1973

Baseball
33840   26 mins   C   B, V   P
The great Willie Mays plays in his last All-Star Game, while the up-and-coming stars such as Bobby Bonds and Johnny Bench lead the National League to victory.
W and W Productions — *Major League Baseball Productions*

All-Star Game, 1974: Mid-Summer Magic
1974

Baseball
33839   26 mins   C   B, V   P
Write-in candidate Steve Garvey leads the National League to its third straight victory at

Pittsburgh's Three Rivers Stadium. A sequence of ironic dream game performances by All-Stars throughout the years is included.
W and W Productions — *Major League Baseball Productions*

All-Star Game, 1975: All-Star Fever
1975

Baseball
33838   28 mins   C   B, V   P
National League home runs by Steve Garvey and Jimmy Wynn give them an early lead. Carl Yastrzemski's homer ties the game for the American leaguers. The Nationals score three times in the ninth inning with Bill Madlock's single the key hit in a 6-3 victory at County Stadium in Milwaukee.
Major League Baseball — *Major League Baseball Productions*

All-Star Game, 1976: Champions of Pride
1976

Baseball
33837   28 mins   C   B, V   P
The National League celebrates its 100th anniversary with another victory over the American League. Unusual viewpoints are featured, including Randy Jones' sinkerball, the many motions of Luis Tiant, the aggressive play of Pete Rose and Mickey Rivers, and the zany antics of Tigers' pitcher, "The Bird," Mark Fidrych.
Major League Baseball — *Major League Baseball Productions*

All-Star Game, 1977: The Man Behind the Mask
1977

Baseball
33836   29 mins   C   B, V   P
This program highlights the game and the individual stars of the National League's 7-5 victory over the American League, while featuring the work of home plate umpire Bill Kunkel, from his pre-game preparation to the final out.
Major League Baseball — *Major League Baseball Productions*

All-Star Game, 1978: What Makes an All-Star
1978

Baseball
33835   26 mins   C   B, V   P
Los Angeles Dodger first baseman Steve Garvey collects two hits, two RBI's, and the game's MVP award as the National League defeats the American League 7-3 in San Diego. "Mr. Cub," Ernie Banks, comments from the stands along with the youngsters who won the "Pitch, Hit, and Run" competition.
Major League Baseball — *Major League Baseball Productions*

All-Star Game, 1979: Inches and Jinxes
1979
Baseball
45029   30 mins   C   B, V   P
The National League is victorious again. A 7-6 win in Seattle's Kingdome is highlighted by Lee Mazzili's home run and Dave Parker's throw to home plate to nail Brian Downing, a potentially important run for the American League. Ron Guidry walks Mazzili to force in the winning run.
Major League Baseball — *Major League Baseball Productions*

All-Star Game, 1980: Heroes to Remember
1980
Baseball
49549   30 mins   C   B, V   P
Cubs' relief pitcher Bruce Sutter wins the game's MVP award, as he nails down yet another victory for the National League in the Midsummer's Classic.
Major League Baseball — *Major League Baseball Productions*

All-Star Game, 1981
1981
Baseball
59376   30 mins   C   B, V   P
In the first baseball game played since the great strike, Gary Carter of the Expos captures the MVP award by crashing two home runs in leading the National League to still another victory over the American League, at Cleveland's Municipal Stadium.
Major League Baseball Prods — *Major League Baseball Productions*

All-Star Game, 1982
1982
Baseball
64658   30 mins   C   B, V   P
American and National League All-Star Players
The National League wins again. Cincinnati Reds' shortstop Dave Concepcion homers and is named MVP of this All-Star Game at Montreal. Montreal's own Steve Rogers is the winning pitcher, and Boston's Dennis Eckersley takes the 4-1 loss for manager Billy Martin's American League squad. Detroit catcher Lance Parrish stars in defeat, throwing out three NL runners attempting to steal bases.
Major League Baseball — *Major League Baseball Productions*

All-Star Game, '84: Something Special
1984
Baseball
81130   25 mins   C   B, V   P
Here are highlights from the 1984 mid summer classic where the National League triumphad over the American League once again.
Major League Baseball — *Major League Baseball Productions*

All-Star Pitching Tips
1975
Baseball
33845   28 mins   C   B, V   P
Whitey Ford, Tom Seaver, Claude Osteen, Bert Blyleven, Catfish Hunter, Mike Marshall, Nolan Ryan
The basics of pitching are explained by host and Hall of Famer Whitey Ford, along with helpful hints from many major league pitching stars.
Major League Baseball — *Major League Baseball Productions*

All-Star Swing Festival
1972
Music-Performance
87214   52 mins   C   B, V   P
Dizzy Gillespie, Duke Ellington, Earl Hines, Count Basie, Joe Williams, Arvell Shaw, The Benny Goodman Quartet, Ella Fitzgerald, Bobby Hackett
Doc Severinsen hosts this once-in-a-lifetime teaming of jazz greats, taped at Lincoln Center's Phiharmonic Hall. A highlight of the concert was the reunion of the original Benny Goodman Quartet: Benny, Lionel Hampton, Teddy Wilson and Gene Krupa.
Lincoln Center; Vestron Musicvideo — *Vestron Video*

All-Star Game, 1983: Golden Memories
1983
Baseball
81129   25 mins   C   B, V   P
The American League wins the All-Star Game for the first time in twelve years by a score of 13 to 3. Fred Lynn hits the first grand slam home run in the fifty-year history of the game.
Major League Baseball — *Major League Baseball Productions*

All That Jazz
1979
Musical-Drama
48515   120 mins   C   B, V, LV, CED   P
Roy Scheider, Jessica Lange, Ann Reinking, Ben Vereen, John Lithgow, directed by Bob Fosse
A show business personality is so obsessed by his career that it takes a heart attack to bring him down to earth. Along the way, the tensions, sweat, and tears that go into the making of a Broadway show are exposed.
Academy Awards '79: Best Film Editing, Best Art Direction, Best Costume Design, Best Song Adaptation Score MPAA:R
Twentieth Century Fox — *CBS/Fox Video*

All the Best from Russia
1977
Dance/Variety
58564   58 mins   C   B, V   P
An inside look at the Russian Winter Arts Festival which includes performances by the Bolshoi Ballet, the Don Cossack dancers and the American Folk Ensemble.

Canadian — *Mastervision*

All the King's Men   1949
Drama
85281   109 mins   B/W   B, V   P
Broderick Crawford, Mercedes McCambridge,
John Ireland, Joanne Dru, John Derek, Anne
Seymour, directed by Robert Rossen
This classic film, based upon the Robert Penn
Warren book, follows the rise and fall of a Huey
Long-style politician.
Academy Awards '49: Best Actor(Crawford);
Best Supporting Actress (McCambridge); Best
Picture.
Robert Rossen — *RCA/Columbia Pictures*
Home Video

All the Marbles   1981
Comedy
59365   113 mins   C   B, V, CED   R
Peter Falk, Burt Young
A manager of two beautiful lady wrestlers has
dreams of going to the top.
MPAA:R
MGM — *MGM/UA Home Video*

All the President's Men   1976
Drama
38939   135 mins   C   B, V   P
Robert Redford, Dustin Hoffman, Jason
Robards, directed by Alan J. Pakula
The investigation into the Watergate break-in by
Washington Post reporters Bob Woodward and
Carl Bernstein is dramatized in this powerful
film.
Academy Awards '76: Best Supporting Actor
(Robards); Best Adapted Screenplay (William
Goldman) MPAA:PG
Warner Bros — *Warner Home Video; RCA*
VideoDiscs

All the Right Moves   1983
Drama
Closed Captioned
65752   90 mins   C   B, V, CED   P
Tom Cruise, Lea Thompson, Craig T. Nelson
A young man attempts to move up in the world
and out of the dying mill town where he grew up.
MPAA:R
20th Century Fox — *CBS/Fox Video*

All the Way Boys   1973
Adventure/Comedy
80042   105 mins   C   B, V   P
Bud Spencer, Terence Hill
Two adventurers crash-land a plane in the
Amazon jungles to find riches and danger.
MPAA:PG
Joseph E. Levine; Italo Zingarelli — *Embassy*
Home Entertainment

All This and Heaven Too   1940
Drama
71143   141 mins   B/W   B, V   P
Charles Boyer, Bette Davis, Barbara O'Neil,
Virginia Weidler, Jeffrey Lynn, Helen Westley,
Henry Daniell, Harry Davenport, directed by
Anatole Litvak
When a governess arrives at a Parisian
aristocrat's home in the 1840's, she causes
jealous tension between the husband and his
wife. The wife is soon found murdered. Based
on Rachel Field's best-seller.
Warner Bros — *MGM/UA Home Video*

All You Need Is Cash   1978
Comedy/Music
65335   70 mins   C   B, V   P
Eric Idle, Neil Innes, Rikki Fataar, Dan Ayleroyd,
Gilda Radner, John Belushi, George Harrison,
directed by Eric Idle
"The Rutles" star in this parody of The Beatles'
legend, from the early days of the "Pre-Fab
Four" in Liverpool to their worldwide success.
Lorne Michaels — *Pacific Arts Video*

Allegheny Uprising   1939
Western
10074   81 mins   B/W   B, V   P
John Wayne, Claire Trevor, George Sanders,
Brian Donlevy, Chill Wills
Set in 1759, man clashes with military
commander in order to stop sale of firearms to
Indians.
RKO — *Blackhawk Films; RKO HomeVideo*

Alley Cat   1984
Martial arts
73042   82 mins   C   B, V   P
Karin Mani
A woman fights back against a street gang that
attacked her.
MPAA:R
Film Ventures — *Vestron Video*

Alligator   1980
Horror/Satire
84889   92 mins   C   B, V   P
Robert Foster, Michael Gazzo, Jack Carter,
Henry Silva
A giant alligator runs amok through a
midwestern city in this John Sayles farce.
MPAA:R
Group I — *Lightning Video*

Allman Brothers Band: 1985
Brothers of the Road,
The
Music-Performance
85234   85 mins   C   B, V   P
A performance concert by the legendary band,
featuring "Pony Boy," "Jessica," and "Ramblin'
Man."

RCA Video Prods. — *RCA/Columbia Pictures Home Video*

Almost Angels 1962
Musical-Drama
84806   85 mins   C   B, V   P
Vincent Winter
Two boys romp in Austria as members of the Vienna Boys Choir.
Walt Disney Prod — *Walt Disney Home Video*

Almost Perfect Affair, An 1979
Comedy/Romance
81117   92 mins   C   B, V   P
Keith Carradine, Monica Vitti, Raf Vallone, Christian deSica, directed by Michael Ritchie
An American Filmmaker falls in love with the wife of an Italian producer during the Cannes Film Festival.
MPAA:PG
Paramount; Terry Carr — *Paramount Home Video*

Almost You 1985
Romance
Closed Captioned
70994   91 mins   C   B, V   P
Brooke Adams, Griffin Dunne, Karen Young, Joe Silver, Josh Mostel, Marty Watt, directed by Adam Brooks
Normal marital conflicts and uncertainties grow exponentially when a wealthy New York City couple hires a lovely young nurse to help care for the wife's dislocated hip.
MPAA:R
20th Century Fox — *Key Video*

Aloha, Bobby and Rose 1974
Drama
77521   90 mins   C   B, V   P
Paul LeMat, Dianne Hull, Robert Carradine, Tim McIntire, directed by Floyd Mutrux
A mechanic and his girlfriend become accidentally involved in an attempted robbery and murder.
MPAA:PG
Columbia Pictures — *Media Home Entertainment*

Alone in the Dark 1982
Horror
65063   92 mins   C   CED   P
Jack Palance, Donald Pleasance, Martin Landau
The inmates of an insane asylum escape during a power blackout and terrorize an isolated family.
MPAA:R
New Line Cinema — *RCA VideoDiscs*

Alone in the Dark 1982
Horror
68262   92 mins   C   B, V   P
Jack Palance, Donald Pleasance, Martin Landau
Three patients from a mental hospital decide that they must kill their doctor. They get this chance when there is a city-wide blackout.
MPAA:R
Robert Shaye; New Line Cinema — *RCA/Columbia Pictures Home Video*

Along Came Jones 1945
Western/Comedy
73974   93 mins   B/W   B, V   P
Gary Cooper, Loretta Young, Dan Duryea, William Demarest
A cowboy is the victim of mistaken identity as the good guys and the bad guys pursue him.
United Artists — *Key Video*

Alpha Incident, The 1977
Drama/Science fiction
65366   86 mins   C   B, V   P
Ralph Meeker, Stafford Morgan, John Goff, Carol Irene Newell
A frightening doomsday drama about an alien organism with the potential to destroy all living things.
MPAA:PG
Bill Rebane — *Media Home Entertainment*

Alphabet City 1984
Drama
73659   85 mins   C   B, V   R, P
Vincent Spano, Michael Winslow, Kate Vernon, directed by Amos Poe
A drug king pin who runs New York's Lower East Side must burn down his mother's apartment building for the insurance money. The music is composed and performed by Nile Rodgers of Chic.
MPAA:R
Andrew Braunsberg — *CBS/Fox Video*

Alpine Ski School 1984
Sports-Winter
73704   76 mins   C   B, V   P
This program shows you everything you'll need to know about skiing before hitting the slope. When you buy the videocassette, you get a tote bag as a bonus.
AM Available
Special Projects International Inc — *Embassy Home Entertainment*

Altered States 1980
Science fiction/Drama
58215   103 mins   C   B, V, LV   P
William Hurt, Blair Brown, directed by Ken Russell

A research scientist experimenting with altered states of consciousness discovers horrors in the secret landscapes of the mind. Based on the novel by Paddy Chayefsky.
MPAA:R
Warner Bros — *Warner Home Video; RCA VideoDiscs*

Alternative, The   1976
Drama
80130   90 mins   C   B, V   P
Wendy Hughes, Peter Adams, Mary Mackie
An unmarried pregnant magazine editor is caught in a tug of war between the baby's father and her lover.
Grundy Organization — *King of Video*

Alvarez Kelly   1966
Western
44786   116 mins   C   B, V   P
William Holden, Richard Widmark, Janice Rule
Holden and Widmark employ some two-fisted action amidst the Civil War setting.
Sol C Siegel — *RCA/Columbia Pictures Home Video*

Alvin Purple   1973
Comedy
81253   97 mins   C   B, V, LV   P
Graeme Blundell, George Whaley, Elli Maclure, Jacki Weaver
This film chronicles the adventures of Alvin Purple, a man who is constantly being pursued by throngs of sexually insatiable women.
MPAA:R
Hexagon Productions — *New World Video*

Alvin Rides Again   1974
Comedy
80662   89 mins   C   B, V   P
Graeme Blundell, Alan Finney, Brionny Behets, Frank Thring, Jeff Ashby
The sexually insatiable Alvin Purple is asked to impersonate an American gangster who was accidentally killed.
Hexagon Productions — *New World Video*

Always   1985
Comedy-Drama
88023   105 mins   C   B, V   P
Henry Jaglom, Patrice Townsend, directed by Henry Jaglom
Jaglom fictionally documents his divorce in this film that stars his ex-wife and friends, and is set in their real-life house.
MPAA:R
Samuel Goldwyn Company — *Vestron Video*

Always Ready   1985
Documentary/History-US
70685   45 mins   C   B, V   P

Narrated by Ken Howard, directed by Fred Warshofsky
Part of the "In Defense of Freedom" series, this program traces the history of the U.S. Coast Guard.
A.B. Marian — *MPI Home Video*

Am I Normal?   1979
Adolescence/Sexuality
63878   24 mins   C   B, V   P
Focusing on three fictional characters, this program presents the facts about male sexual development, while raising important questions about masculinity, identity and peer pressure.
Copperfield Films — *MGM/UA Home Video; New Day Films*

Amadeus   1984
Drama
81827   158 mins   C   B, V   P
F. Murray Abraham, Tom Hulce, Jeffrey Jones, Elizabeth Berridge, directed by Milos Foreman
This is an adaptation of the Peter Shaffer play about the intense rivalry between 18th century composer Antonio Salreri and Wolfgang Amadeus Mozart. Available in VHS and Beta Hi-Fi Stereo.
Academy Awards '84: Best Picture; Best Director (Foreman); Best Actor (Abraham); Best Adapted Screenplay (Shaffer). MPAA:PG
Saul Zaentz — *THORN EMI/HBO Video*

Amante Para Dos   1981
Drama
47858   95 mins   C   B, V   P
Alberto Olmedo, Tato Bores, Maria Casan
Mauricio is a serious man and loves his wife, but his weakness is Monica, his lover. Alberto, another married man, is also Monica's lover, until both men decide that she is dangerous. In Spanish.
SP
Nicolas Carreras; Luis Repetto — *Media Home Entertainment*

Amarcord   1974
Comedy
54798   124 mins   C   B, V   P
Magall Noel, Bruno Zanin, Pupella Maggio, Armando Brancia, directed by Federico Fellini
The life of a small Italian coastal town in the 1930's is recalled by a director with a superstar's access to the resources of the Italian film industry.
Academy Awards '74: Best Foreign Film.
MPAA:R
Warner Bros, New World Pictures — *Warner Home Video*

Amateur, The   1982
Adventure
62776   112 mins   C   B, V, CED   P

John Savage, Christopher Plummer, Marthe Keller, Arthur Hill
A computer technologist dives into a plot of international intrigue when he investigates the death of his girlfriend, murdered by terrorists.
MPAA:R
20th Century Fox — *CBS/Fox Video*

Amazing Adventure, The 1937
Comedy
81736   63 mins   C   B, V   P
Cary Grant, Mary Brian
A millionaire wins a bet when he rises from a chauffeur's position to the executive boardroom without using his wealth.
Grand National — *Kartes Video Communications*

Amazing Adventures of Joe 90, The 1968
Cartoons
71344   90 mins   C   B, V   P
Supermarionation
Joe is the supermarionette with an insatiable appetite for adventure. These tapes include three such outings.
Gerry & Sylvia Anderson — *Family Home Entertainment*

Amazing Apes, The 1977
Animals/Documentary
29128   93 mins   C   B, V   P
This feature reveals never-before-known facts about these fascinating primates through absorbing highlights such as monkey worship, life-style of snow monkeys in Japan, and studies of gorillas and chimps in the wild.
Bill Burrud Productions — *Walt Disney Home Video*

Amazing Dobermans, The 1976
Adventure
47818   96 mins   C   B, V, 3/4U   P
Fred Astaire, Barbara Eden, James Franciscus
The owner of five trained dogs assists an undercover agent in foiling a small-time criminal's gambling and extortion racket.
MPAA:G
Golden Films — *Media Home Entertainment; Nostalgia Merchant*

Amazing Howard Hughes, The 1977
Biographical/Drama
63341   119 mins   C   B, V   P
Tommy Lee Jones, Ed Flanders, James Hampton, Tovah Feldshuh, Lee Purcell
This film reveals the full story of the legendary millionaire's life and career, from daring test pilot to inventor to Hollywood film producer to death as a paranoiac in isolation.

Roger Gimbel Productions; EMI Television Programmes — *THORN EMI/HBO Video*

Amazing Masters of the Martial Arts 1985
Martial arts
70858   60 mins   C   B, V   P
Sonny Chiba, Bruce Lei, Carter Wong, directed by Domonic Paris
This showcase compiles clips from some of Kung Fu filmdom's brightest stars.
Paris Productions — *Lightning Video*

Amazing Mr. Blunden, The 1972
Suspense
82480   100 mins   C   B, V   P
Laurence Naismith, Lynne Frederick, Garry Miller, Marc Granger, Rosalyn London, Diana Dors
Two youngsters travel back in time to change history: to try to save the lives of two murdered children.
MPAA:G
Media — *Media Home Entertainment*

Amazing Spider-Man, The 1982
Cartoons/Adventure
59038   100 mins   C   B, V   P
A collection of Spider-Man's most exciting adventures.
Marvel Comics Group — *MCA Home Video*

Amazing Spider-Man, The 1977
Adventure
Closed Captioned
59334   94 mins   C   B, V   P
Nicholas Hammond, David White, Lisa Eilbacher
Spider-Man's unique powers are put to the test when he comes to the rescue of the government by preventing an evil scientist from blackmailing the government.
Edward S Montagne — *Playhouse Video*

Amazing Things 198?
Cartoons
87341   60 mins   C   B, V   P
2   pgms
A cartoon Dr. Misterio entertains children for parties and rainy afternoons.
Maljack Prod. — *MPI Home Video*

Amazing World of Psychic Phenomena, The 1977
Occult sciences
45039   91 mins   C   B, V   P
Hosted and narrated by Raymond Burr
A look at the mysteries of parapsychology.
Sunn Classic — *VidAmerica; Lucerne Films*

Ambassador, The   1984
War-Drama
88215   97 mins   C   B, V   P
Robert Mitchum, Rock Hudson, Ellen Burstyn, directed by J. Lee Thompson
An American ambassador to the Mid-East, in trying to solve the area's political problem, becomes the target for terrorism from every side, including the President himself. Hudson's last feature film.
Cannon Prod. — *MGM/UA Home Video*

Ambassador's Boots, The   1985
Mystery/Drama
70661   60 mins   C   B, V   P
James Warwick, Francesca Annis
In this chapter of the "Partners in Crime" series, the Beresfords aid the American Ambassador to England in answering some curious queries regarding the handling of his luggage.
Unknown — *Pacific Arts Video*

Ambrose Bierce: The Man   1978
and the Snake/The
Return
Literature-American/Mystery
58733   60 mins   C   B, V   P
A pair of stories by American author Ambrose Bierce.
Independent — *Mastervision*

Ambush Murders, The   1982
Drama
81809   93 mins   C   B, V   P
James Brolin, Dorian Harewood, Alfre Woodard, Antonio Fargas, directed by Steven Hilliard Stern
This is the true story of how a lawyer cleared an innocent black man, framed for the murders of two policemen. Available in VHS Stereo and Beta Hi-Fi.
David Goldsmith — *U.S.A. Home Video*

America at the Movies   1976
Film-History/Documentary
44776   116 mins   C   B, V   P
John Wayne, Orson Welles, Peter Sellers, James Dean, Gene Hackman, Burt Lancaster, Julie Harris, Deborah Kerr, Al Pacino, Robert De Niro
Scenes from over eighty of the finest American motion pictures tell the story of American movies and give a portrait of America as it has been seen on screen for half a century. Scenes from "The Birth of a Nation," "Citizen Kane," "Dr. Strangelove," "East of Eden," "The French Connection," and "From Here to Eternity," are among the many included. Some black and white scenes.
American Film Institute — *RCA/Columbia Pictures Home Video*

America Between the   1978
Great Wars
History-US/Documentary
10153   60 mins   B/W   B, V   P, T
Covers celebrations and tragedies from the roaring twenties. Includes the century of Progress Exposition in Chicago, the Prohibition era, Hindenburg disaster, and off-screen activities of Charlie Chaplin.
Blackhawk — *Blackhawk Films*

America Live in Central   1981
Park
Music-Performance
59876   53 mins   C   LV   P
Conceptual sequences combine with stirring performances as the folk-rock group America offers this concert of hits including "Tin Man," "Ventura Highway," "Horse with No Name." In stereo.
Peter Clifton — *Pioneer Artists*

America/The Fall of   1924
Babylon
Drama
84950   68 mins   B/W   B, V   P
Constance Talmadge, Neil Hamilton, Lionel Barrymore
Two condensed dramas from the silent days, the latter being the Babylon sequence from Griffith's "Intolerance."
Biograph — *Blackhawk Films*

America/The Fall of   1924
Babylon
Film-History
50636   56 mins   B/W   B, V   P, T
Neil Hamilton, Lionel Barrymore, Constance Tallmadge, Elmer Clifton, Alfred Paget
A double feature containing abridged versions of these two motion pictures. In "America", a Boston patriot and the daughter of an aristocratic Virginia Tory fall in love during the Revolutionary War. "The Fall of Babylon" is one of the stories in D.W. Griffith's "Intolerance." Silent.
D W Griffith — *Blackhawk Films*

American Alcoholic,   1981
The/Reading, Writing and
Reefer
Drug abuse/Alcoholism
52609   102 mins   C   CED   P
Two important contemporary issues—alcoholism and marijuana abuse—are explored in two enlightening documentaries.
NBC — *RCA VideoDiscs*

American Ballet Theatre   1985
at the Met
Dance
85027   97 mins   C   B, V   P

Mikhail Baryshnikov leads the ABT in a performance of three separate ballets and a pas de deux.
ABT — *THORN EMI/HBO Video*

American Caesar 1985
Biographical/World War II
81450   300 mins   C   B, V   P
Hosted by John Huston
This documentary examines the life and military career of General Douglas MacArthur.
John McGreevey; Ian McLeod — *Embassy Home Entertainment*

American Commandos 1984
War-Drama
87631   96 mins   C   B, V   P
Christopher Mitchum, John Phillip Law, Franco Guerrero
An ex-Green Beret slaughters the junkies who killed his son and raped his wife, and then joins his old buddies for a secret, Ramboesque mission in Vietnam.
MPAA:R
Panorama Films — *Lightning Video*

American Documents, 1976
The
History-US
57782   55 mins   C   B, V   P
Narrated by Lowell Thomas; Theodore Bikel, Gloria Swanson, Ossie Davis, Jean Stapleton, William Shatner   13   pgms
This patriotic series documents America's history through rare newsreels, archive photographs and excerpts from Hollywood films. Each program is available individually.
1.The Age of Ballyhoo 2.Black Shadows on a Silver Screen 3.The Building of the Capitol 4.The Empty Frame 5. How We Got the Vote 6.Inaugural Souvenir 7.Just Around the Corner 8.We All Came to America 9.A Moment in Time 10.Patent Pending 11.The Legendary West 12.Working for the Lord 13.America's Romance with Space
Post Newsweek Stations — *Republic Pictures Home Video; Lucerne Films*

American Dream 1981
Drama
80422   90 mins   C   B, V   P
Stephen Macht, Karen Carlson, John Karlen, Andrea Smith, John McIntire
A mid western family leaves the suburbs and move into a Chicago inner city neighborhood.
Mace Neufield Productions — *Unicorn Video*

American Dreamer 1984
Comedy/Adventure
Closed Captioned
81171   105 mins   C   B, V   P
Jobeth Williams, Tom Conti, Giancarlo Giannini, Coral Browne, directed by Rick Rosenthal

A housewife wins a trip to Paris as a prize from entering a mystery writing contest. Silly from a blow on the head, she begins living the fictional life of her favorite literary adventures. Hi-Fi Stereo for both formats.
MPAA:PG
CBS Theatrical Films — *CBS/Fox Video*

American Empire 1942
Western
10921   82 mins   B/W   B, V   P
Preston Foster, Richard Dix, Frances Gifford, Leo Carrillo, directed by William McGann
Two Civil War heroes struggling to build a cattle empire in Texas are hampered by Mexican rustlers.
United Artists; Harry Sherman Prods — *Movie Buff Video; Discount Video Tapes; Video Yesteryear; Cable Films; Independent United Distributors; Kartes Video Communications*

American Flyers 1985
Drama
Closed Captioned
84536   113 mins   C   B, V, LV   P
Kevin Costner, David Grant, Rae Dawn Chong, Alexandra Paul, directed by John Badham.
Written by Steve Tesich, this is about yet another bicycle race upon which rests the dreams and happiness of two brothers. Lively performances, lots of bikes.
MPAA:PG-13
Gareth Wigan; Paula Weinstein — *Warner Home Video*

American Friend 1982
Drama
72178   127 mins   C   B, V   P
Dennis Hopper, Bruce Ganz
Reverence is paid to Hitchcock and Fuller in this gripping thriller.
Wim Wenders — *Pacific Arts Video*

American Gigolo 1979
Drama
48507   117 mins   C   B, V, LV   P
Richard Gere, Lauren Hutton
A professional lover becomes involved with the wife of a California state senator, then is framed for murder.
MPAA:R
Jerry Bruckheimer — *Paramount Home Video; RCA VideoDiscs*

American Graffiti 1973
Comedy
11565   112 mins   C   B, V, LV   P
Richard Dreyfuss, Ronny Howard, Cindy Williams, Mackenzie Phillips, Wolfman Jack, directed by George Lucas
A look at one hectic night in the life of a group of high school friends just before they go off to college, jobs, or the army.

MPAA:PG
Universal; Francis Ford Coppola — *MCA
Home Video; RCA VideoDiscs*

American Haute—Skiing The High Country Huts   1984
Sports-Winter
84277   15 mins   C   B, V   P
Skiing cross-country through the Aspen-to-Vail trail.
Video Travel Inc — *Video Travel*

American Health   1986
Health education
87730   60 mins   C   B, V   P
2 pgms
An expanding series of programs, based on the popular magazine, dealing with subjects such as stress, fitness and nutrition.
Geoffrey Drummond; American Health — *Karl/Lorimar Home Video*

American History: America Grows Up (1850-1900's)   1982
History-US
58572   50 mins   C   B, V   P
America's growth from a nation of farms and villages to one of the leading industrial nations of the world from 1850 to 1900 is discussed.
McGraw Hill — *Mastervision*

American History: Americans Courageous (1600-Today)   1982
History-US
58566   50 mins   C   B, V   P
Two films featuring tales of courage: "The Gloucesterman," a filmed celebration of the townsfolk of the historic Massachusetts village who go down to the sea in ships, and "Not for Ourselves Alone," a 200 year history of America's Armed Forces.
WGBH Boston — *Mastervision*

American History: Colonial America (1500's-1600's)   1982
History-US
58567   50 mins   C   B, V   P
A look at the days when France, Spain, and England were fighting for the riches of the New World.
McGraw Hill — *Mastervision*

American History: Gathering Strength (1840-1914)   1982
History-US
58571   50 mins   C   B, V   P

The differences between the old immigrants from northern Europe and the new wave of settlers from the counties of eastern and southern Europe are discussed.
McGraw Hill — *Mastervision*

American History: Opening the West (1860-1900)   1982
History-US
58570   50 mins   C   B, V   P
Lincoln's efforts to reunite the nation after the bloody fratricide of the Civil War and begin the epic westward expansion are discussed.
McGraw Hill — *Mastervision*

American History: Roots of Democracy (1700's)   1982
History-US
58568   50 mins   C   B, V   P
This program portrays the relationship between foreign trade and domestic activity which led to the rebellion against English restraints and the American Revolution.
McGraw Hill — *Mastervision*

American History: The Game of Monopoly (1870-1914)   1982
History-US
58573   50 mins   C   B, V   P
This program examines the rise to wealth and power of the industrial titans under the leadership of such men as Morgan, Carnegie, Rockefeller, and Vanderbilt.
McGraw Hill — *Mastervision*

American History: Two Great Crusades (1930-1945)   1982
History-US/World War II
58575   50 mins   C   B, V   P
The New Deal and the Second World War are the focus of this look at the U.S.'s two modern crises.
McGraw Hill — *Mastervision*

American History: War Between the States (1800's)   1982
History-US
58569   50 mins   C   B, V   P
This program analyzes the institution of slavery and shows how it came to divide our country.
McGraw Hill — *Mastervision*

American History: Warring and Roaring (1914-1929)   1982
History-US/World War I
58574   50 mins   C   B, V   P

This program examines the U.S. involvement in
World War I and the spirited 1920's, which
ended with the stock market crash of '29.
McGraw Hill — *Mastervision*

American Hot Wax   1978
Comedy
64781   91 mins   C   CED   P
*Chuck Berry, Jerry Lee Lewis, Tim McIntire,
Laraine Newman*
1950's rock 'n' roll is revived in this tribute to
pioneering disk jockey Alan Freed.
MPAA:R
Paramount — *RCA VideoDiscs*

American in Paris, An   1951
Musical
39092   113 mins   C   B, V, LV,   P
CED
*Gene Kelly, Leslie Caron, Oscar Levant,
directed by Vincente Minnelli*
Gene Kelly plays an ex-G.I. artist living in Paris,
who is torn between his love for a dancer, Leslie
Caron, and his artistic mentor, Nina Foch.
George Gershwin score includes a 15-minute
ballet based on "An American in Paris." Winner
of seven Academy Awards, including Best
Picture.
Academy Awards '51: Best Picture; Best Story
and Screenplay; Best Musical Scoring.
MGM — *MGM/UA Home Video*

American Nightmare   1983
Drama
64231   85 mins   C   B, V   P
Lawrence Day, Lora Stanley, Lenore Zann
A young man searches for his missing sister
against a background of pornography, drug
peddling and prostitution in the slums of a city.
Independent — *Media Home Entertainment*

American Ninja   1985
Martial arts
82349   90 mins   C   B, V   P
*Michael Dudikoff, Steve James, Guich Koock,
Judie Aronson*
An American soldier uses his martial arts skills
to stop a Ninja army from selling stolen
weapons to the South American black market.
MPAA:R
Cannon Productions — *MGM/UA Home Video*

American Werewolf in   1981
London, An
Horror
58629   95 mins   C   B, V, LV   P
*David Naughton, Griffin Dunne, Jenny Agutter,
Frank Oz, Brian Glover, directed by John Landis*
Special effects highlight this telling of the
werewolf story, as two young Americans
backpacking in northern England are attacked
by a werewolf.
MPAA:R

Universal; George Folsey Jr — *Vestron Video;
RCA VideoDiscs*

Americana   1983
Drama
65603   90 mins   C   B, V   P
David Carradine, Barbara Hershey
The gripping drama captures the pain and
determination of a Vietnam veteran struggling to
rebuild his life.
MPAA:PG
David Carradine — *Vestron Video*

Americano, The   1955
Adventure
80032   85 mins   C   B, V   P
*Glenn Ford, Frank Lovejoy, Abbe Lane, Cesar
Romero, directed by William Castle*
A cowboy travelling to Brazil with a shipment of
Brahma bulls discovers the rancher he's
delivering them to has been murdered.
RKO; Robert Stillman Productions — *Republic
Pictures Home Video*

Americano, The/Variety   192?
Adventure
10119   54 mins   B/W   B, V   P, T
Douglas Fairbanks, directed by John Emerson
"The Americano" (1917) features Douglas
Fairbanks, Sr. saving a revolt-ridden Caribbean
country. "Variety" portrays the Flying Artinellis,
a trapeze act hampered by jealous love. Both
films are abridged.
Fine Arts Triangle; Unknown — *Blackhawk
Films*

America's Best-Loved   1985
Cartoons
Cartoons
88223   60 mins   C   B, V   P
2 pgms
A compilation of vintage Casper, Bugs Bunny
and Daffy Duck cartoons.
Warner Bros. et al. — *Master Arts Video*

America's Music   1983
Music-Performance/Documentary
84783   57 mins   C   B, V   P
6 pgms
A series of programs on various types of
American music.
*1.Gospel 2.Blues 3.Soul 4.Jazz 5.Rhythm and
Blues 6.Folk*
Skylark Prods — *Video Associates*

America's National Parks   1985
Travel
70863   60 mins   C   B, V   P
This travelogue captures the beauty of
seventeen National Parks in breathtaking
videography.

Dennis Burkhart — *Encounter Productions*

America's Team: The Dallas Cowboys 1975-79 — 1982
Football
63164   120 mins   C   B, V, FO   P
Dallas Cowboys
A compilation of individual Dallas Cowboys team highlight films from the second half of the 1970's.
NFL Films — *NFL Films Video*

Americathon — 1979
Comedy
80888   85 mins   C   B, V   P
John Ritter, Nancy Morgan, Harvey Korman, Peter Riegart, Fred Willard, Meat Loaf, directed by Neal Isreal
It is the year 1998 and the United States is almost bankrupt, so the President decides to stage a telethon to keep the country from going broke. The soundtrack features music by The Beach Boys and Elvis Costello.
MPAA:PG
Lorimar Productions — *Karl/Lorimar Home Video*

Amin: The Rise and Fall — 1982
Drama/Biographical
69677   101 mins   C   B, V   P
This is a dramatization of Idi Amin's 8-year reign of terror in Uganda, which resulted in the deaths of a half million people and the near ruin of a nation.
Sharad Patel — *THORN EMI/HBO Video*

Amityville Horror, The — 1979
Horror
53505   117 mins   C   B, V   P
James Brolin, Margot Kidder, Rod Steiger, Don Stroud, Murray Hamilton
The tale of the Lutz family and their supernatural experiences in their Long Island home, once the scene of a mass murder.
MPAA:R
American International Pictures — *Warner Home Video; RCA VideoDiscs; Vestron Video (disc only)*

Amityville 3D — 1983
Horror
65473   98 mins   C   B, V, CED   P
Tony Roberts, Tess Harper
The infamous Amityville house is once again the centerpiece of terror.
MPAA:R
Stephen F Kesten — *Vestron Video*

Amityville II: The Possession — 1982
Horror
60438   110 mins   C   B, V, LV, CED   P
Burt Young, Andrew Prine, Moses Gunn, Rutanya Alda
This prequel to "The Amityville Horror" tells the story of how the house became possessed by demonic forces.
MPAA:R
Dino DeLaurentiis — *Embassy Home Entertainment*

Among the Cinders — 1983
Drama
81252   103 mins   C   B, V, LV   P
Paul O'Shea, Derek Hardwick, Rebecca Gibney, Yvonne Lawley, Amanda Jones
A sixteen-year-old New Zealand boy runs away to his grandfather's farm to forget about his friend's accidental death. At the farm, he meets an older woman and compromises his virtue.
Pacific Films — *New World Video*

Amor Perdoname — 197?
Drama
86188   100 mins   C   B, V   P
Julio Aleman, Kitty De Hoyos
A mismatched man and woman marry, but are able to work it out.
SP
Spanish — *Unicorn Video*

Amsterdam Connection — 197?
Martial arts/Adventure
47705   90 mins   C   B, V   P
Chen Shing, Jason Pai Piu, Kid Sherrif
A film company acts as a cover for prostitution and drug smuggling, with the girls acting as international couriers.
KK Wong — *Master Arts Video*

Amsterdam Kill, The — 1978
Adventure
64574   93 mins   C   B, V   P
Robert Mitchum, Richard Egan, Keye Luke, Leslie Nielsen, Bradford Dillman
An ex-agent of the U.S. Drug Enforcement Agency is hired to hunt down the kingpin of a narcotics syndicate.
MPAA:R

Columbia — *RCA/Columbia Pictures Home Video*

Amy 1981
Drama
53795   100 mins   C   B, V   P
Jenny Agutter, Barry Newman, Kathleen Nolan, Margaret O'Brien, Nanette Fabray, Chris Robinson, Lou Fant, directed by Vincent McEveety
Set in the early 1900's, the story follows the experiences of a woman after she leaves her well-to-do husband to teach at a school for the deaf and blind.
MPAA:G
Walt Disney Productions — *Walt Disney Home Video*

Anarchy, U.S.A. 1966
Propaganda
69574   78 mins   B/W   B, V, FO   P
A blatantly propagandistic film which offers the premise that the Civil Rights Movement in America is part of a worldwide scheme organized by Soviet Communists to enslave mankind.
Independent — *Video Yesteryear*

Anchors Aweigh 1985
Documentary/History-US
70682   45 mins   C   B, V   P
Narrated by Ken Howard, directed by Fred Warshofsky
Part of the "In Defense of Freedom" series, this program looks at the history of the United States Navy.
A.B. Marian — *MPI Home Video*

And Baby Makes Six 1979
Drama
71297   97 mins   C   B, V   P
Colleen Dewhurst, Warren Oates, Maggie Cooper, Al Corley, Tim Hutton, Allyn Ann McLerie, Mildred Dunnock, Maria Melendez, directed by Waris Hussein
A middle-aged couple with three grown children experience shock and dismay when the wife discovers that she is pregnant.
Alan Landsburg Productions — *U.S.A. Home Video*

And God Created Woman 1957
Drama
58894   93 mins   C   B, V   P
Brigitte Bardot, Curt Jurgens, Jean-Louis Trintignant, Christian Marquand
An eighteen-year-old is given a home by a local family with three handsome young sons.
MPAA:PG
Raoul J Levy — *Vestron Video; Time Life Video*

And God Said to Cain 196?
Western
85541   95 mins   C   B, V   P
Klaus Kinski
Another Biblically-titled western from the prolific Kinski, about a put-upon gunman who must fight for his life.
Foreign — *Unicorn Video*

And Hope to Die 1972
Drama
81833   95 mins   C   B, V   P
Robert Ryan, Jean-Louis Trintignant, Aldo Ray, Tisa Farrow, directed by Rene Clement
A gang of hardened criminals go ahead with their plans to kidnap a retarded girl even though she is already dead. Available in VHS and Beta Hi-Fi.
20th Century Fox — *Monterey Home Video*

...And Justice for All 1979
Drama
52750   120 mins   C   B, V   P
Al Pacino, Jack Warden, John Forsythe, Lee Strasberg, directed by Norman Jewison
A young lawyer battles not only one-on-one injustice in the courts, but the whole system as well.
MPAA:R
Norman Jewison; Patrick Palmer — *RCA/Columbia Pictures Home Video; RCA VideoDiscs*

And Nothing But the Truth 1984
Drama
80213   90 mins   C   B, V   P
Glenda Jackson, Jon Finch, Kenneth Colley, James Donnelly
A multinational corporation is out to ruin the investigative TV report team trying to do a story on the company.
Castle Hill Productions — *Monterey Home Video*

And Now for Something Completely Different 1972
Comedy
47782   89 mins   C   B, V   P
John Cleese, Michael Palin, Eric Idle, Graham Chapman, Terry Gilliam, Terry Jones
A compilation of skits from BBC-TV's "Monty Python's Flying Circus" featuring Monty Python's own weird, hilarious brand of humor.
Patricia Casey — *RCA/Columbia Pictures Home Video*

And Now My Love 1974
Drama/Romance
82255   121 mins   C   B, V   P
Marthe Keller, Andre Dussollier, Carla Gravina, directed by Claude Lelouch

This is the romantic tale of two people who meet and fall in love instantly. This film is dubbed into English.
MPAA:PG
Joseph E Levine — *Embassy Home Entertainment*

And Now the Screaming Starts   1973
Horror
54913   87 mins   C   B, V, 3/4U   P
Peter Cushing, Herbert Lom, Patrick Magee, Ian Ogilvy, Stephanie Beacham, Geoffrey Whitehead, Guy Rolfe, directed by Roy Ward Baker
The young bride-to-be of the lord of a British manor house is greeted by bloody faces at the window, a severed hand, and five corpses.
MPAA:R
Cinerama Releasing — *Nostalgia Merchant*

And Soon the Darkness   1980
Suspense
85899   94 mins   C   B, V   P
Pamela Franklin, Sandor Eles, Han-Marie Pravda, directed by Robert Fuest
One of two vacationing young girls disappears where a teenager was once murdered and the search is on.
MPAA:PG
Levitt-Pickman Film Corp. — *THORN EMI/HBO Video*

And the Ship Sails On   1984
Drama
80371   130 mins   C   B, V   P
Freddie Jones, Barbara Jefford, Janet Suzman, Peter Cellier, directed by Federico Fellini
A group of devoted opera lovers take a luxury cruise to pay their respects to a recently deceased opera diva. With English subtitles and Available in Beta Hi-Fi.
MPAA:PG IT
Triumph Films — *RCA/Columbia Pictures Home Video*

And Then There Were None   1945
Mystery
11602   97 mins   B/W   B, V   P
Louis Hayward, Barry Fitzgerald, Walter Huston
Based on Agatha Christie's play about ten people invited to an island who are murdered one by one.
20th Century Fox — *United Home Video*

Anderson Tapes, The   1971
Suspense
21279   98 mins   C   B, V   P
Sean Connery, Dyan Cannon, Martin Balsam, directed by Sidney Lumet

The story of an epic million-dollar robbery of a luxury apartment house. Based on the novel by Lawrence Sanders.
MPAA:PG
Columbia — *RCA/Columbia Pictures Home Video*

Android   1982
Science fiction
76019   80 mins   C   B, V   P
Klaus Kinski, Don Opper, Brie Howard
A classic saga of men versus machines combining science fiction, suspense and cloned romance.
MPAA:PG
Mary Ann Fisher — *Media Home Entertainment*

Andromeda Strain, The   1971
Science fiction
58213   131 mins   C   B, V   P
Arthur Hill, David Wayne, James Olson, Kate Reid, Paula Kelly, directed by Robert Wise
A satellite falls back to earth carrying a deadly bacteria which must be identified in time to save the population from extermination.
MPAA:G
Universal; Robert Wise — *MCA Home Video*

Andy Warhol's Dracula   1975
Horror
56928   106 mins   C   B, V   R, P
Joe Dallesandro, Udo Kler, Arno Juergling, directed by Paul Morrissey
Sex and camp humor, as well as a large dose of blood, highlight this tale of the gardener who beds the young ladies and finally does Dracula in.
MPAA:R
Bryanston Pictures — *Video Gems*

Andy Warhol's Frankenstein   1975
Horror
56929   95 mins   C   B, V   R, P
Joe Dallesandro, Monique Van Vooren, Udo Kler, directed by Paul Morrissey
One of the most outrageous versions of Frankenstein, featuring plenty of gore and sex.
MPAA:R
Bryanston Pictures — *Video Gems*

Angel   1975
Cartoons/Adventure
56747   48 mins   C   B, V   P
Animated
An animated adventure laced with fantasy, magic, and music which tells the story of an independent girl and her travel companions, a lovable dog and a talking cat. Available in English and Spanish versions.
EL, SP

ZIV International — *Media Home Entertainment*

Yesteryear; Kartes Video Communications; United Home Video

Angel   1984
Drama
65744   94 mins   C   B, V   P
Donna Wilkes, Cliff Gorman, Susan Tyrell, Dick Shawn
A 15-year old honor student attends an expensive Los Angeles private school during the daytime and by night becomes Angel, a streetwise prostitute making a living amid the slime and sleaze of Hollywood Boulevard.
MPAA:R
Roy Watts; Donald P Borchers — *THORN EMI/HBO Video*

Angel and the Badman   1947
Western
00282   100 mins   B/W   B, V   P
John Wayne, Gail Russell, Irene Rich
Notorious badman is humanized by the love of a young Quaker girl.
Republic — *Movie Buff Video; Prism; Nostalgia Merchant; Discount Video Tapes; Video Dimensions; Cable Films; VCII; Republic Pictures Home Video; Video Connection; Video Yesteryear; Hollywood Home Theater; Cinema Concepts; Western Film & Video Inc; Media Home Entertainment; Hal Roach Studios; Spotlite Video; Kartes Video Communications*

Angel and the Badman   1947
Western
71027   100 mins   C   B, V   P
John Wayne, Gail Russell, Irene Rich
Hal Roach Studios used the Colorization process to enhance this copy of the Wayne western classic.
Republic — *Hal Roach Studios*

Angel of H.E.A.T.   1982
Adventure
62862   90 mins   · C   B, V, LV,   P
                                 CED
Marilyn Chambers
A female super-agent is on a mission to save the world from total destruction.
MPAA:R
Myrl A. Schreibman; Hal Kant — *Vestron Video*

Angel on My Shoulder   1946
Fantasy
08862   101 mins   B/W   B, V, 3/4U   P
Paul Muni, Claude Rains, Anne Baxter, Onslow Stevens
A murdered convict returns to earth as a respected judge.
United Artists — *Hollywood Home Theater; Cable Films; VCII; Video Connection; Discount Video Tapes; Hal Roach Studios; Video*

Angel on My Shoulder   1980
Fantasy
64982   96 mins   C   B, V, CED   · P
Peter Strauss, Richard Kiley, Barbara Hershey, Janis Paige
In this remake of the 1946 classic, a small-time hood wrongfully executed for murder comes back as an incorruptible district attorney, with a little help from the devil.
Mace Neufeld Productions — *Embassy Home Entertainment*

Angela   1977
Drama
65430   91 mins   C   B, V   P
Sophia Loren, Steve Railsback, John Huston
An extraordinary love story which transpires between a mother and son who after a twenty-three year separation meet again, unaware that they are related.
20th Century Fox — *Embassy Home Entertainment*

Angelo My Love   1983
Drama
66350   91 mins   C   B, V   P
Robert Duvall wrote this compassionate tale of New York's gypsy community, following the adventures of 12-year-old Angelo Evans, the streetwise son of a fortune teller.
MPAA:R
Cinecom International — *RCA/Columbia Pictures Home Video*

Angels Die Hard   1974
Drama
35364   86 mins   C   B, V   P
William Smith
Trouble follows an outlaw's entrance into a small town. Motorcycle gang action, extremely violent.
Charles Beach Dickerson — *Hollywood Home Theater*

Angels Die Hard   1984
Adventure
80462   86 mins   C   B, V, LV   P
William Smith
A marauding gang of bikers confronts a mob of angry townspeople in a series of brutal attacks, beatings and other incidents.
MPAA:R
New World Pictures — *New World Video*

Angels with Dirty Faces   1938
Drama
66076   97 mins   B/W   B, V, CED   P
James Cagney, Pat O'Brien, Humphrey Bogart, Ann Sheridan, George Bancroft, Dead End Kids

A classic in which two young hoodlums grow up-one to the priesthood and one to prison. The priest then tries to keep a group of young toughs from idolizing the famed gangster and following in his footsteps.
Warner Bros — *CBS/Fox Video*

AngKor: Cambodia Express   1984
Drama
81165   96 mins   C   B, V   P
Robert Walker, Christopher George
An American journalist travels back to Vietnam — to search for his long lost love.
Monarex Hollywood Corp. — *Vestron Video*

Animal Alphabet, The   1985
Language arts/Children
71056   30 mins   C   B, V   P
Geoffrey the Giraffe, animation by Bill Davis
13   pgms
The cassettes in this series feature live action and animated sequences designed to help youngsters learn the alphabet. Broadway composer Elizabeth Swados wrote a special song for each letter and animal footage adds a mnemonic device.
Geoffrey Drummond — *Karl/Lorimar Home Video*

Animal Crackers   1930
Comedy
14018   98 mins   B/W   B, V, LV   P
Marx Brothers, Lillian Roth, Margaret Dumont, directed by Victor Neerman
One of the funniest Marx Brothers films, "Animal Crackers" is a screen classic. Complete with the Harry Ruby music score—including Groucho's "Hooray for Captain Spaulding."
Paramount — *MCA Home Video; RCA VideoDiscs*

Animal Farm   1955
Satire
53287   73 mins   C   B, V, FO   P
Animated, directed by John Halas and Joy Batchelor
An animated version of George Orwell's classic political satire about a barnyard full of animals who parallel the growth of totalitarian dictatorships.
Louis de Rochemont; Halas and Batchelor — *Video Yesteryear; Movie Buff Video; Video Connection; Vestron Video; Hollywood Home Theater; Cable Films; Western Film & Video Inc; Discount Video Tapes; Phoenix Films & Video; Texture Films*

Animal House   1978
Comedy
11567   109 mins   C   B, V   P

John Belushi, Tim Matheson, John Verna, Donald Sutherland, Thomas Hulce, directed by John Landis
Every college tradition from fraternity rush week to the homecoming pageant, is irreverently and relentlessly mocked in this wild comedy.
MPAA:R
Universal; Matty Simmons; Ivan Reitman — *MCA Home Video; RCA VideoDiscs*

Animal Quiz #1   1984
Animals
65638   60 mins   C   B, V   P
This series is an invitation to children and their parents to test their animal expertise. This volume features "Looney Gooney," a look at the comical aerodynamics of the Gooney bird of Midway Island; the dragon-like lizards of Indonesia in "Komodo Dragons"; and the San Diego Zoo's collection of animal infants in "Zoo Babies."
Walt Disney — *Walt Disney Home Video*

Animal Quiz #2   1984
Animals
65639   60 mins   C   B, V   P
This volume takes viewers to the arid state of Chihuahua, Mexico, for a glimpse of the "Mexican Grizzly", an oasis-like watering hole in Africa for "Kenya's Spring of Life"; and the frigid, desolate realm of the Emperor penguin in "Adventure Antarctica."
Walt Disney — *Walt Disney Home Video*

Animal Quiz #3   1984
Animals
65640   60 mins   C   B, V   P
The third volume provides insights to "The Strange Creatures of the Galapagos," and traces the training and breeding of racehorses in "Thoroughbred" and the monkeyshines performed by "The Apes of Gibraltar."
Walt Disney — *Walt Disney Home Video*

Animal Quiz #4   1984
Animals
72799   84 mins   C   B, V   P
Viewers are shown the creatures of the Sonoran desert, visit the famed Masai warriors of Africa and participate in a Pacific shark watch.
Walt Disney Productions — *Walt Disney Home Video*

Animal Quiz #5   1984
Animals
72800   84 mins   C   B, V   P
Viewers witness unique structures built by animals, visit the Mexican desert where jaguars roam and observe the crocodile population of the Nile.

Walt Disney Productions — *Walt Disney Home Video*

Animal Quiz #6   1984
Animals
72801   84 mins   C   B, V   P
The big cats of South Africa are filmed in their habitat, as are Japan's snow monkeys.
Walt Disney Productions — *Walt Disney Home Video*

Animal Quiz #7   1985
Animals
80357   83 mins   C   B, V   P
Here's a chance to test your knowledge about the jungle jaguar, the brown bears of Alaska, and New Zealand sheep dogs.
Walt Disney Productions — *Walt Disney Home Video*

Animal Quiz #8   1985
Animals
80358   83 mins   C   B, V   P
This volume visits the Yagua Indian tribe and looks at the various animals who inhabit a Kenyan game reserve.
Walt Disney Productions — *Walt Disney Home Video*

Animal Quiz #9   1985
Animals
80359   83 mins   C   B, V   P
In this volume, find out about the elephants of Thailand, Kenya's pink flamingos, and a colony of fur seals on the Pribilof Islands.
Walt Disney Productions — *Walt Disney Home Video*

Animal Talk   1980
Literature/Children
70983   45 mins   C   B, V   P
Anthony Newley, Keith Mitchell, Lance Kerwin, Spencer Mulligan, John Quade
Hosted by Newley as Dr. Doolittle, this program adapts three classic stories about animals for children. The stories are: Jack London's "Call of the Wild," Sterling North's "Rascal," and an excerpt Mel Ellis' "The Flight of the White Wolf."
Asselin Productions — *Video Gems*

Animal Talk   1984
Literature
73649   50 mins   C   B, V   P
Anthony Newley
Dr. Dolittle introduces stories where humans and animals communicate, including "Call of the Wild," "Rascal" and "Flight of the White Wolf."
Bosustow Entertainment; Asselin Productions — *Kartes Video Communications*

Animals Are Beautiful People   1974
Wildlife/Documentary
58216   92 mins   C   B, V   P
Narrated by Paddy O'Byrne, directed by Jamie Uys
A profile of the African wilderness that captures the unique mood of the animal community.
MPAA:G
Mimosa Films — *Warner Home Video*

Animalympics   1980
Cartoons
47378   78 mins   C   B, V   P
Voices of Gilda Radner, Billy Crystal, Harry Shearer, Michael Fremer
In this animated feature, animals from all over the world gather for the first Animal Olympics—and the fur really flies.
Lisberger Studios Film — *Warner Home Video*

Animation in the 1930's   193?
Cartoons
11288   57 mins   B/W   B, V, FO   P
Animated
A collection of nine cartoons from the studios of Warner Brothers and Max Fleischer, including "Crosby, Columbo and Vallee," "Three's a Crowd," "Hollywood Capers," "Songs You Like to Sing—Margie," "Grampy's Indoor Outing," "Betty in Blunderland," "Let's Sing with Popeye," "Happy You and Me," and "Sinkin' in the Bathtub."
Warner Bros; Max Fleischer — *Video Yesteryear*

Animation Wonderland   1975
Cartoons
58587   75 mins   C   B, V   R, P
Animated
A collection of delightful animated shorts for children.
Peabody Award: Best Children's Entertainment.
MPAA:G
John Wilson — *Video Gems*

Anita de Montemar   196?
Drama
86187   127 mins   C   B, V   P
Amparo Rivelles, Fernando Solar
A man is torn between his wife and his child-bearing girlfriend.
SP
Spanish — *Unicorn Video*

Ann Vickers   1933
Drama
76842   76 mins   B/W   B, V   P
Irene Dunne, Walter Huston, Bruce Cabot, Conrad Nagel
A dashing young army captain wins over the heart of a dedicated social worker.

RKO; Pandro S. Berman — *RKO HomeVideo*

Anna Christie   1930
Drama
80210 90 mins B/W   B, V   P
Greta Garbo, Marie Dressler, Charles Bickford,
George F. Marion, directed by Clarance Brown
An adaptation of the classic Eugene O'Neill play
about a prostitute who fights her past for the
man she loves.
MGM — *MGM/UA Home Video*

Anna Russell: The (First)   1984
Farewell Concert
Music-Performance/Satire
81945   85 mins   C   B, V   P
Anna Russell performs her unique version of
Wagners "Ring Cycle" and "Wind Instruments I
Have Known" in this concert recorded at
Baltimore's Museum of Art.
Phillip Byrd; Maryland Public TV — *Video Arts*
International

Anna to the Infinite   1984
Power
Drama
65466   ? mins   C   B, V   P
Dina Merrill, Martha Byrne, Mark Patton
Based on the book of the same name, this
powerful drama follows a young girl who
desperately seeks to unravel the mystery of her
life. In Beta Hi-Fi.
Bruce Graham; Blue Marble Company
Films — *RCA/Columbia Pictures Home Video*

Annabel Takes a   1938
Tour/Maids Night Out
Comedy
76844 131 mins B/W   B, V   P
Lucille Ball, Jack Oakie, Ruth Donnelly, Joan
Fontaine, Allan Lane, Hedda Hopper
A delightful comedy double feature: In "Annabel
Takes a Tour" a fading movie star falls in love
with a writer while on a tour to boost her career,
and in "Maids Night Out" a heiress and a
millionare fall in love.
RKO — *RKO HomeVideo*

Anne of Green Gables   1934
Drama
76843 79 mins B/W   B, V   P
Anne Shirley, Tom Brown, O.P. Heggie
A lonely couple have their hands full when they
adopt a little girl whose background causes
them problems.
RKO; Kenneth McGowan — *RKO HomeVideo*

Anne of the Thousand   1969
Days
Biographical/Drama
77211 145 mins C   B, V   P

Richard Burton, Genevieve Bujold, Irene
Pappas, Anthony Quayle, directed by Charles
Jarrott
England's Henry VIII separates from Queen
Katherine to pursue a romance with feisty Anne
Boleyn.
MPAA:R
Hal B. Wallis; Universal Pictures — *MCA Home*
Video

Annie   1982
Musical
63437 130 mins C   B, V, LV   P
Aileen Quinn, Carol Burnett, Albert Finney,
Bernadette Peters, Ann Reinking, Tim Curry,
directed by John Huston
Based on the hit Broadway musical, this is the
story of America's favorite orphan, a plucky,
red-haired girl who dreams of a life outside her
dingy orphanage.
MPAA:PG
Columbia; Ray Stark — *RCA/Columbia*
Pictures Home Video; RCA VideoDiscs

Annie Hall   1977
Comedy
13322   94 mins   C   B, V, LV   P
Woody Allen, Diane Keaton, Paul Simon, Carol
Kane, directed by Woody Allen
Autobiographical love story with incisive
Allenisms on romance, relationships, fame, and
other topics.
Academy Awards '77: Best Picture; Best
Actress (Keaton); Best Direction (Allen); Best
Screenplay (Allen, Brickman). MPAA:PG
United Artists; Jack Rollins; Charles H
Joffe — *CBS/Fox Video; RCA VideoDiscs*

Annie Oakley   1935
Drama
66335 90 mins B/W   B, V   P
Barbara Stanwyck, Preston Foster, Melvyn
Douglas, directed by George Stevens
A biographical drama based on the life and
legend of sharpshooter Annie Oakley and her
on-off relationship with Wild Bill Hickok.
RKO — *RKO HomeVideo; Nostalgia Merchant*

Annie Oakley   1985
Western
Closed Captioned
86374   30 mins   C   B, V   P
Jamie Lee Curtis, Cliff DeYoung, Brian Dennehy
This biography of the acclaimed shooting star
covers her career from age 15 to retirement,
including some actual silent footage of Miss
Oakley filmed by Thomas Edison in 1923.
Platypus & Gaylord Prods.; Shelley
Duvall — *Playhouse Video*

Annihilators, The   1985
Adventure
85079   87 mins   C   B, V   P

Christopher Stone, Andy Wood, LAwrence Hilton-Jacobs
A band of mercenaries attempt to save a Southern town from a gang of urban terrorists.
MPAA:R
Unknown — *New World Video*

Another Country   1984
Drama
79698   90 mins   C   B, V   P
Rupert Everett, Colin Firth, Michael Jenn, Robert Addie, Rupert Wainwright
Two English boarding school friends wind up as spies for the Soviet Union.
Goldcrest Films — *Embassy Home Entertainment*

Another Time, Another   1983
Place
War-Drama
80760   101 mins   C   B, V   P
Phyllis Logan, Giovanni Mauriello, Gian Luca Favilla, Paul Young, Tom Watson, directed by Michael Radford
A bored young Scottish housewife falls in love with an Italian prisoner-of-war who works on her farm during World War II.
MPAA:R
Samuel Goldwyn Co. — *Embassy Home Entertainment*

Another Time, Another   1958
Place
Drama
85241   98 mins   B/W   B, V   P
Lana Turner, Barry Sullivan, Glynis Johns, Sean Connery, Terrence Langdon
An American woman suffers a nervous breakdown when her British lover is killed in World War II.
Paramount — *Kartes Video Communications*

Antarctica   1984
Adventure
Closed Captioned
76930   112 mins   C   B, V   P
Ken Jakakura, Masako Natsume, Keiko Oginome
A group of scientists leave a pack of fifteen huskies chained to posts on a frozen glacier in the Antarctic.
TLC Films — *CBS/Fox Video*

Anthony Adverse   1936
Drama
82394   137 mins   B/W   B, V   P
Frederic March, Olivia de Haviland, Anita Louise, directed by Mervyn LeRoy
Set in the Napoleonic era, this story traces the struggles of two lowborn lovers who eventually achieve fame, fortune, and independence.
Academy Awards '36: Best Supporting Actress (Gale Sondergaard)

Warner Bros Pictures — *MGM/UA Home Video*

Antony and Cleopatra   1973
Drama
81443   150 mins   C   B, V   P
Charlton Heston, Hildegarde Neff, Fernando Rey, Eric Porter, directed by Charlton Heston
This is an adaptation of the Shakespeare play that centers on the torrid romance between Mark Antony and Cleopatra.
MPAA:PG
Peter Snell — *Embassy Home Entertainment*

Anti-Smoking Card... All   1984
Choked Up!, The
Video
73635   5 mins   C   B, V   P
On this reusable two hour videocassette is the perfect message for those who do not appreciate cigarette smoke.
Kartes Productions — *Kartes Video Communications*

Ants   1977
Suspense
77208   88 mins   C   B, V   P
Lynda Day George, Myrna Loy, Robert Foxworth, Suzanne Sommers
An army of killer ants are terrorizing the guests of a posh summer resort.
Alan Landsburg Productions — *U.S.A. Home Video*

Any Which Way You Can   1980
Comedy
58217   116 mins   C   B, V, LV   P
Clint Eastwood, Sondra Locke, Ruth Gordon
This sequel to "Every Which Way But Loose" finds brawler Philo Beddoe and Clyde the orangutan facing a big bout with big bucks at stake.
MPAA:PG
Warner Bros — *Warner Home Video; RCA VideoDiscs*

Anyuta   197?
Dance
87353   68 mins   C   B, V   P
Ekaterina Maximova, choreographed by Vladimir Vasiliev
The Bolshoi, Kirov and Maly ballet companies get together for a performance of this classic piece.
Russian — *Kultur*

Apache   1954
Western
55583   91 mins   C   CED   P
Burt Lancaster, John Mc Intire, Jean Peters

The chronicle of a bitter battle between the Indians and the U.S. cavalry in the struggle for the west.
EL, SP
United Artists — *CBS/Fox Video*

Apache Rose   1947
Western
44149   75 mins   B/W   B, V   P
Roy Rogers, Dale Evans, Olin Howlin, George Meeker
A gambling boat owner plots to gain control of oil found on Vegas Ranch. This is the original, unedited version of the film.
Republic — *Captain Bijou; Video Connection; Discount Video Tapes*

Apando, El   198?
Drama
77351   85 mins   C   B, V   P
Salvador Sanchez, Manuel Ojeda
A group of prisoners are sentenced to the world's worst prison.
SP
Foreign — *Unicorn Video*

Apartment, The   1960
Comedy-Drama
58948   125 mins   B/W   CED   P
Jack Lemmon, Shirley MacLaine, Fred MacMurray, Ray Walston, Edie Adams, directed by Billy Wilder
A lonely, ambitious clerk rents out his apartment to philandering executives and finds that one of them is after his own girl.
Academy Awards '60: Best Picture; Best Director; Best Screenplay (Wilder, I.A.L. Diamond).
United Artists — *RCA VideoDiscs*

Ape, The   1940
Horror
81741   62 mins   B/W   B, V   P
Boris Karloff, Maris Wrixon, Henry Hall, Gertrude Hoffman
A mad scientist disguises himself as an ape in order to kill humans to use their blood for an experimental serum.
Monogram Pictures — *Kartes Video Communications*

A*P*E*   1976
Horror
82172   87 mins   C   B, V   P
Rod Arrants, Joanna DeVarona, Alex Nicol
A*P*E* is thirty-six feet and ten tons of animal fury who destroys anything that comes between him and the actress he loves. Available in VHS and Beta Hi-Fi Stereo.
MPAA:PG
Worldwide Entertainment — *New World Video*

Ape Man, The   1943
Horror
10372   70 mins   B/W   B, V, 3/4U   R, P
Wallace Ford, Bela Lugosi
A scientist turns himself into a murderous ape.
Prime TV — *Cable Films; Video Connection; Discount Video Tapes; Kartes Video Communications*

Aphrodite   1983
Drama
65360   89 mins   C   B, V   P
Valerie Kaprisky
A steamy drama based on Pierre Louy's masterpiece of erotic literature.
Adolphe Viezzi — *Vestron Video*

Apocalypse Now   1979
Drama
58493   139 mins   C   B, V, LV   P
Marlon Brando, Martin Sheen, Robert Duvall, Fredric Forrest, Sam Bottoms, Dennis Hopper, directed by Francis Ford Coppola
Coppola's epic set during the Vietnam War, concerning one officer's trip through the jungle to locate and eliminate a megalomaniac officer whose methods have become "unsound."
Academy Awards '79: Best Cinematography; Best Sound. MPAA:R
United Artists; Francis Ford Coppola — *Paramount Home Video; RCA VideoDiscs*

Apple Dumpling Gang, The   1975
Comedy
44299   100 mins   C   B, V   P
Bill Bixby, Susan Clark, Don Knotts, Tim Conway, David Wayne, Slim Pickens, Harry Morgan
Three frisky kids strike it rich and trigger the wildest bank robbery in the gold-mad West.
MPAA:G
Walt Disney — *Walt Disney Home Video; RCA VideoDiscs*

Apple Dumpling Gang, The   1975
Comedy/Western
70672   100 mins   C   B, V   P
Bill Bixby, Susan Clark, Don Knotts, Tim Conway
Slapstick shenanigans abound in cops and robbers comedy set in California's gold rush. Everyone gets beaten at their own game on their way to an explosive climax.
MPAA:G
Walt Disney Productions — *Walt Disney Home Video*

Apple Dumpling Gang Rides Again, The — 1979
Western/Comedy
81657　89 mins　C　　B, V　　　P
Tim Conway, Don Knotts, Tim Matheson, Jack Elam, Ruth Buzzi, Harry Morgan
The two charter members of the gang who are trying to go straight find themselves in trouble again when they are accused of robbing a bank.
Walt Disney Productions — *Walt Disney Home Video*

Apple Dumpling Gang Rides Again, The — 1979
Comedy/Western
55570　88 mins　C　　B, V　　　P
Tim Conway, Don Knotts, Tim Matheson, Kenneth Mars, Harry Morgan, Jack Elam, directed by Vincent McEveety
Two lovable hombres terrorize the West in their bungling attempt to go straight.
Walt Disney — *Walt Disney Home Video*

Appointment, The — 1984
Horror
88139　90 mins　C　　B, V　　　P
Edward Woodward, Jane Merrow
A cheap suspenser about a mysterious supernatural force that enters the minds and bodies of a family and makes them do crazy things.
Unknown — *Sony Video Software*

Appointment in Honduras — 1953
Adventure
80804　79 mins　C　　B, V　　　P
Glenn Ford, Ann Sheridan, Zachary Scott, directed by Jacques Tourneur
An adventurer goes on a dangerous trek through the Central American jungles to deliver funds to the Honduran President.
RKO — *Buena Vista Home Video*

Apprenticeship of Duddy Kravitz, The — 1974
Comedy-Drama
59859　121 mins　C　　B, V　　　P
Richard Dreyfuss, Randy Quaid, Denholm Elliot, Jack Warden, Micheline Lanctot, Joe Silver, directed by Ted Kotcheff
A young Jewish man in Montreal circa 1948 is driven by an insatiable need to be a "somebody."
MPAA:PG
Paramount — *Paramount Home Video*

April Fools, The — 1969
Comedy-Drama
82240　95 mins　C　　B, V　　　P
Jack Lemmon, Catherine Deneuve, Sally Kellerman, Peter Lawford, Charles Boyer, Myrna Loy, Harvey Korman, directed by Stuart Rosenberg
A bored stockbroker falls in love with a beautiful woman who turns out to be married to his boss. Marvin Hamlisch's score resounds in VHS and Beta Hi-Fi.
MPAA:PG
National General - Cinema Center — *Key Video*

April Wine — 1981
Music-Performance
58467　67 mins　C　　B, V　　　P
The hard-rock group, April Wine, performs hits from their Capitol LP's.
EMI Music — *THORN EMI/HBO Video; Pioneer Artists*

April Wine — 1980
Music video
88088　15 mins　C　　B, V　　　P
A video compilation of the rock group's favorite songs, including "Just Between You and Me" and "Sign of the Gypsy Queen."
Sony Video — *Sony Video Software*

Aquaman — 1967
Cartoons/Fantasy
81087　60 mins　C　　B, V　　　P
Animated
Here is a collection of eight animated adventures featuring that mighty superhero, Aquaman.
Filmation — *Warner Home Video*

Arabella — 1984
Opera
87741　154 mins　C　　B, V　　　P
Ashley Putnam, Gianna Rolandi, Regina Sarfaty, directed by John Cox
A recording of Richard Strauss' opera at the Glyndebourne Festival Opera, conducted by Bernard Haitink.
Glyndebourne Festival; Thorn EMI — *THORN EMI/HBO Video*

Arabesque — 1966
Mystery
87627　105 mins　C　　B, V　　　P
Gregory Peck, Sophia Loren, directed by Stanley Donen
A college professor is drawn into international espionage by a beautiful woman and a plot to assassinate an Arab prince. Available in HiFi Mono. Music by Henry Mancini.
Stanley Donen; Universal — *MCA Home Video*

Arch of Triumph — 1948
Drama
64537　120 mins　B/W　　B, V　　　P
Ingrid Bergman, Charles Boyer, Charles Laughton, directed by Lewis Milestone
An Austrian refugee searches for the Gestapo agent who tortured him and killed his friends.

United Artists; Enterprise — *Spotlite Video*

Archery Tactics for Deer   1984
Hunting
86870   30 mins   C   B, V   P
Chuck Adams
Tips and instruction on bow hunting deer.
AM Available
Warburton Prod. — *Warburton Productions*

Archie   1978
Cartoons
69624   60 mins   C   B, V   P
Animated
Three separate cartoons feature the escapades
of Archie, Jughead, Veronica, Betty, Reggie, Mr.
Weatherbee and the rest of the gang from
Riverdale High.
Filmation — *THORN EMI/HBO Video*

Archie   1964
Comedy
85143   43 mins   B/W   B, V   P
John Simpson, Roland Winters
A television pilot for a live-action version of the
comic strip that never made it, which predated
the cartoon version. Included are program
pitches for sponsors.
CBS — *Video Yesteryear*

Archie, Volume II   1978
Cartoons
65745   23 mins   C   B, V   P
Animated
Archie and the "Gang" carry on with their
hilarious pranks, while Mr. Weatherbee loses his
glasses and thinks Hot Dog is the Commodore
of a ship.
Filmation — *THORN EMI/HBO Video*

Archie, Volume 3   1984
Cartoons
78392   60 mins   C   B, V   P
Animated
Here's the third installment of the animated
escapades of Archie Andrews and all of his
friends at Riverdale High.
Filmation Studios — *THORN EMI/HBO Video*

Archie, Cassette #4   1968
Cartoons
81183   60 mins   C   B, V   P
Animated
Archie and the rest of the Riverdale High gang
are back to cause more comic commotion in this
collection of three episodes from the series.
Filmation — *THORN EMI/HBO Video*

Are You in the House Alone?   1978
Suspense
65664   100 mins   C   B, V   P
*Blythe Danner, Kathleen Beller, Tony Bill, Scott
Colomby*
A high school coed becomes the target of a
terror campaign.
Charles Fries — *Worldvision Home Video*

Arf!   1984
Pets
73636   60 mins   C   B, V   P
This program is designed for dogs to help them
relate to their peers and give them role models
to emulate.
Kartes Productions — *Kartes Video
Communications*

Arf!   1985
Pets/Variety
81721   30 mins   C   B, V   P
Here's proof that video is going to the dogs.
This tape features such canine favorites as
"Fitness With Fifi," "Boners" and "Bark Along
With Mitch."
Kartes Video Communications — *Kartes Video
Communications*

Far Frontier, The   1948
Western
70572   60 mins   B/W   B, V   P
Roy Rogers, Andy Divine
Roy saves the day by thwarting a band of no-
good niks who are smugglingthemselves across
the border in soy bean-oil cans.
Republic — *Captain Bijou*

Argentinisima I   1972
Music
47860   115 mins   C   B, V   P
Inspired by the verses of famed singers like
Mercedes Sosa and Atahualpa Yupanqui,
various singers and groups relate the tales of
the different regions and music from past and
present Argentina. In Spanish.
SP
Luis Repetto — *Media Home Entertainment*

Arizona Days   1937
Western
08791   56 mins   B/W   B, V   P
Tex Ritter, Eleanor Stewart
Cowboys join a minstrel group and rescue the
show when a group of toughs try to break it up.
Grand National — *United Home Video; Video
Connection; Video Yesteryear; Discount Video
Tapes*

Arizona Raiders   1965
Western
11603   88 mins   C   B, V   P

Audie Murphy, Buster Crabbe
Arizona rangers hunt down killers who have
been terrorizing the territory.
Columbia; Grant Whytock — *Movie Buff Video;
United Home Video; Video Connection*

Arizona Stagecoach   1942
Western
87670   58 mins   B/W   B, V   P
*Ray Corrigan, Max Terhune, Kermit Maynard,
Charles King, John King*
The Range Busters set out to bust a notorious,
guiltless, devil-may-care outlaw gang.
Monogram — *Captain Bijou*

Armed Forces Workout   1984
Physical fitness
72536   75 mins   C   B, V, CED   P
A U.S. Marine Corps drill instructor instructs a
program of daily exercises designed to
strengthen one's body and attitude toward
working-out.
K Tel International Inc — *Vestron Video*

A.R.M.S. Concert, The   1983
Music-Performance
76642   60 mins   C   B, V   P
Jeff Beck, Eric Clapton, Bill Wyman
An ensemble of rock-n-roll stars from Eric
Clapton to Bill Wyman perform in this live
benefit concert.
Glyn Johns — *Music Media*

A.R.M.S. Concert Part II,   1984
The
Music-Performance
70916   59 mins   C   B, V   P
*Ronnie Lane, Eric Clapton, Steve Winwood,
Jimmy Page, Jeff Beck, Bill Wyman, Kenny
Jones, Ray Cooper*
This further compilation of British rock from
these four consecutive benefit concerts
includes staples like "Stairway to Heaven,"
"Layla," and "Who's to Blame" in Dolby Hi-Fi
Stereo sound.
Glyn Johns — *Music Media*

Army Brats   1984
Comedy
85659   103 mins   C   B, V   P
*Akkemay, Frank Schaafsma, Peter Faber,
directed by Ruud van Hemert*
A military family goes bloodily and comically to
war with itself.
Chris Brouwer; Haig Balian — *Warner Home
Video*

Arnold   1973
Comedy
70693   96 mins   C   B, V   P
*Stella Stevens, Roddy McDowell, Elsa
Lanchester, Victor Buono, Bernard Fox, Farley*

*Granger, Shani Wells, directed by Georg
Fenady*
A dead man's brother plots to have his girl friend
marry the cadaver in order to claim the
deceased man's estate. The wedding is most
unusual.
MPAA:PG
Bing Crosby Productions — *Lightning Video*

Arnold Schwarzenegger: 1982
Mr. Olympia (The
Comeback)
Sports-Minor/Physical fitness
59566   50 mins   C   B, V   P
Hosted by Arnold Schwarzenegger
A filmed record of the seventh annual body-
building contest for the World Title, comprised
of former Mr. Universe winners.
Aspac Prods — *Mastervision*

Around the World in 80   1956
Days
Adventure
65322   178 mins   C   B, V   P
*David Niven, Shirley MacLaine, Frank Sinatra,
Marlene Dietrich, Robert Newton, Cantinflas*
An unflappable Victorian Era Englishman
wagers that he can circumnavigate the earth in
four-score days, which sends him on a
spectacular journey. In VHS stereo and Beta Hi-
fi.
MPAA:G
Michael Todd — *Warner Home Video*

Around the World in 80   1972
Days
Cartoons
78904   60 mins   C   B, V   P
Animated
An animated adaptation of the Jules Verne
novel about a man who bets 20,000 pounds that
he can go around the globe in eighty days via
balloon, elephant, ship and railroad.
Air Programs International — *Prism*

Around the World Under   1965
the Sea
Adventure
79209   111 mins   C   B, V   P
*David McCallum, Shirley Eaton, Gary Merill,
Keenan Wynn, Brian Kelly*
A group of scientists race against time to plant
earthquake detectors along the ocean floor.
Ivan Tors — *MGM/UA Home Video*

Around the World With   1981
Willy Fog
Cartoons
82383   30 mins   C   B, V   P
Animated
This animated series, inspired by the Jules
Verne story "Around the World in 80 Days,"

chronicles the adventures of Willy Fog and his friends, Rigodon and Tico.
Sony Corporation of America — *Sony Video Software*

Arrangement, The   1969
Drama
81491   126 mins   C   B, V   P
Kirk Douglas, Faye Dunaway, Deborah Kerr, Richard Boone, directed by Elia Kazan
A veteran advertising executive sets out to search for the meaning of life as he attempts to patch up his "arrangements" with his wife, his mistress and his father.
MPAA:R
Warner Bros; Elia Kazan — *Warner Home Video*

Arrival, The   1968
Drama
79894   52 mins   C   B, V   P
Patrick McGoohan, Virginia Maskell, Guy Doleman
This pilot episode of "The Prisoner" series explains how Number 6 wound up in The Village.
Patrick McGoohan — *MPI Home Video*

Arrowsmith   1931
Drama
84869   95 mins   B/W   B, V   P
Ronald Colman, Helen Hayes, directed by John Ford
A small-town doctor travels to the West Indies to confront his life and career goals. Based on the classic Sinclair Lewis novel.
Samuel Goldwyn — *Embassy Home Entertainment*

Arsenic and Old Lace   1944
Comedy/Mystery
64459   158 mins   B/W   B, V   P
Cary Grant, Josephine Hull, Jean Adair, Raymond Massey, Jack Carson, John Ridgely, James Gleason, Peter Lorre, directed by Frank Capra
Grant plays Mortimer Brester, an easygoing drama critic, who discovers that his gentle maiden aunts derive pleasure from poisoning gentlemencallers and burying them in the cellar.
Warner Bros — *CBS/Fox Video; RCA VideoDiscs*

Art and Science of Making Movies, The   1957
Filmmaking/Film-History
80750   58 mins   B/W   B, V   P
Here are three fascinating documentaries on films and filmmaking: "Origins of the Motion Picture" (1956) traces the evolution of moving pictures; "Film Editing—Interpretation and Values" shows the editing of a "Gunsmoke"

sequence; while "The Soundman" (1949) examines the evolution of sound in the movies.
U.S. Navy; et al — *Video Yesteryear*

Art Blakey   1982
Music-Performance
88120   58 mins   C   B, V, 8mm   P
The legendary jazz drummer and his Great Messengers perform and converse about their history at a Smithsonian jazz festival.
Adler Ent. — *Sony Video Software*

Art Farmer   1980
Music-Performance
88122   58 mins   C   B, V, 8mm   P
A look at the concert work and life of the famed jazz flugelhorn player.
Adler Ent.; Sony — *Sony Video Software*

Arte Johnson's Kid Stuff   1986
Toys
86909   19 mins   C   B, V   P
Arte Johnson
Johnson instructs kids in ingenious and inexpensive methods of having fun with just about anything at hand, including all sorts of common household junk.
Mort Kasman — *Embassy Home Entertainment*

Arthur   1981
Comedy
58218   97 mins   C   B, V, LV   P
Dudley Moore, Liza Minnelli, John Gielgud, Geraldine Fitzgerald, directed by Steve Gordon
A billionaire stands to lose everything unless he gives up the woman he loves. Music by Burt Bacharach. Also available with Spanish subtitles.
MPAA:PG
Orion Pictures — *Warner Home Video; RCA VideoDiscs*

Arthur's Hallowed Ground   1984
Drama
88214   75 mins   C   B, V   P
Jimmy Jewel, Jean Bolt, Michael Elphick, directed by Freddie Young
A cricket field caretaker battles the board of directors over the fate of his favorite plot of sod.
Techno Sunley Leisure Ltd.; David Puttnam — *MGM/UA Home Video*

Artur Rubinstein   1981
Music-Performance
57252   78 mins   B/W   B, V   P
Artur Rubinstein, Gregor Piatigorsky, Jascha Heifetz
Rare footage never before seen showcases this great violinist in his home and in the recording studio. Rubinstein is featured in two solo spots

---

and in a trio with cellist Gregor Piatigorsky and violinist Jascha Heifetz.
Kultur — *Kultur*

As You Like It   1936
Comedy
11393   96 mins   B/W   B, V, FO   P
Elisabeth Bergner, Laurence Olivier, Henry Ainley
A Duke's banished daughter poses as a man in this Shakespearian comedy.
Inter Allied — *Video Yesteryear; Blackhawk Films; Prism; Cable Films; Video Connection; Hollywood Home Theater; Western Film & Video Inc; Discount Video Tapes*

Asesinos, Los   1968
Western
80492   95 mins   C   B, V   P
Nick Adams, Regina Torne, Pedro Armendariz, Elsa Cardenas
Two rival bandits arrive in a lawless town and fight for control. Dialogue in Spanish.
SP
Spanish — *Unicorn Video*

Ashes and Diamonds   1959
Drama/World War II
71254   105 mins   B/W   B, V   P
Zbigniew Cybulski, Eva Krzyzewska, Adam Pawlikowski, directed by Andrzej Wajda
In the closing days of World War II, a Polish resistance fighter assassinates the wrong man. Available in Polish with English subtitles or dubbed into English.
Venice Film Festival '59: International Film Critics Award; British Film Critics Guild: Best Foreign Film EL, PO
Film Unit KADR — *Embassy Home Entertainment*

Ashford and Simpson   1982
Music-Performance
63351   75 mins   C   B, V   P
Nick Ashford, Valerie Simpson
This well-known duo perform their greatest hits live in concert, including "Ain't No Mountain High Enough," "Ain't Nothing Like the Real Thing" and "Let's Get Stoned."
EMI Music — *THORN EMI/HBO Video; Pioneer Artists; RCA VideoDiscs*

Ashford and Simpson   1984
Music-Performance
75912   21 mins   C   B, V   P
This program presents the popular 60's group Ashford and Simpson performing their best songs.
Capital Records Inc — *Sony Video Software*

Asi No Hay Cama Que   1980
Aguante
Comedy
47856   95 mins   C   B, V   P
Chico Novarro, Patricia Dal
Horacio and Claudio pretend to have money to win the friendship of Marcela and Silvana, who appear to be wealthy. In Spanish.
SP
Nicolas Carreras; Luis Repetto — *Media Home Entertainment*

Asia in Asia   1983
Music-Performance
72217   60 mins   C   B, V   P
Fusion rock group Asia plays a concert at Budokan, Japan.
Independent — *Vestron Video*

Asphalt Jungle, The   1950
Drama
71145   112 mins   B/W   B, V, LV   P
Sterling Hayden, Sam Jaffe, Louis Calhern, Jean Hagen, Marilyn Monroe, James Whitmore, John McIntire, Marc Lawrence, directed by John Huston
An aging criminal emerges from his forced retirement (prison) and assembles the old gang for one final heist.
Loews Inc; MGM — *MGM/UA Home Video*

Asphyx, The   1972
Horror
84831   98 mins   C   B, V   P
Robert Stephens, Robert Powell, Jane Lapotaire
An obscure supernatural power is meddled with by irresponsible men to acquire eternal life. Naturally, it doesn't work out.
MPAA:PG
Unknown — *United Home Video; Magnum Entertainment*

Assassin, The   1979
Martial arts
64906   86 mins   C   B, V   P
Sonny Chiba
An athletic karate fighter poses as an underworld figure and infiltrates the largest gang in Japan where he is hired as a hit man.
Toei Company — *CBS/Fox Video; Unicorn Video*

Assault   1970
Drama
59827   89 mins   C   B, V   P
Suzy Kendall, Lesley-Anne Down, Frank Finlay
Violent sex murders in a girl's school have the police baffled. The school's pretty art teacher offers to act as bait in order to catch the murderer.

* George H Brown — *Embassy Home Entertainment*

Assault on Agathon   197?
Adventure
59349   95 mins   C   B, V   R, P
Nina Van Pallandt, Marianne Faithful
An "executed" W.W. II guerilla leader returns to
lead a revolution.
MPAA:PG
Heritage Enterprises — *Video Gems; Prism*

Assault on Precinct 13   1979
Horror
42910   91 mins   C   B, V
This movie from the producers of "Halloween"
takes a frightening look at the destruction of law
and order.
EL, SP
Irwin Yablans — *Media Home Entertainment*

Assault with a Deadly   1982
Weapon
Adventure/Drama
71331   86 mins   C   B, V   P
*Richard Holliday, Sandra Foley, Lamont
Jackson, Rinaldo Rincon, Arthur Kennedy,
directed by Walter Gaines*
A city's government can no longer afford
adequate police protection, and crime spreads
unchecked. Several eager young cops dash the
rulebook aside and mount a counter-offensive.
MPAA:R
Terry Levene — *U.S.A. Home Video*

Assignment, The   1978
Drama
82412   92 mins   C   B, V   P
*Christopher Plummer, Thomas Hellberg,
Carolyn Seymour, Fernando Rey*
The assassination of a high-ranking officer in an
uneasy Latin American nation spurs violence
and political instability. A Swedish diplomat is
assigned the tremedous task of restoring peace
and stability between the political factions.
New World Video — *New World Video*

Assisi Underground, The   1984
War-Drama
82246   115 mins   C   B, V   P
*James Mason, Ben Cross, Maximilian Schell,
directed by Alexander Ramati*
This is the true story of how the Catholic Church
helped to save several hundred Italian Jews
from being executed by the Nazis during the
1943 German occupation of Italy.
Cannon Productions — *MGM/UA Home Video*

Asterix and Cleopatra   1985
Cartoons
81650   72 mins   C   B, V   P
Animated
The gallant warrior Asterix, and his friends,
battle Queen Cleopatra in ancient Egypt.
Productions Dargaud Films — *Walt Disney
Home Video*

Asterix the Gaul   1985
Cartoons
76816   67 mins   C   B, V   P
Animated
Asterix the Gaul and his sidekick Obelix take on
an inept legion of Roman warriors when they try
to take over Asterix's Gallic territory.
Productions Dargaud Films — *Walt Disney
Home Video*

Astro Zombies, The   1970
Horror
05526   83 mins   C   B, V   P
John Carradine, Wendell Corey
Human transplants go berserk and threaten the
safety of a city.
MPAA:PG
Ram Ltd — *Wizard Video*

Asylum   1972
Horror
54912   100 mins   C   B, V, 3/4U   P
*Peter Cushing, Herbert Lom, Britt Ekland,
Barbara Parkins, Patrick Magee, Barry Morse,
directed by Roy Ward Baker*
A search of an eerie insane asylum for its former
director, now a raving maniac, leads a young
psychiatrist on a tour of terror. His interviews
with inmates reveal their case histories in
flashback—all weird, horrible, or murderous.
MPAA:PG
Cinerama Releasing — *Nostalgia Merchant*

Asylum of Satan   1972
Horror
81684   87 mins   C   B, V   P
Charles Kissinger, Carla Borelli
A beautiful concert pianist is savagely tortured
by a madman in the Asylum of Satan.
Majestic International Pictures — *United Home
Video*

At Gunpoint   1955
Drama
65687   81 mins   C   B, V   P
Fred MacMurray, Dorothy Malone
A store owner becomes the town hero when, by
accident, he shoots and kills a bank robber.
Allied Artists — *Republic Pictures Home Video*

At Sword's Point   1952
Adventure
00295   81 mins   C   B, V, 3/4U   P
Cornel Wilde, Maureen O'Hara
Adventure tale based on "The Three
Musketeers."

RKO — *Nostalgia Merchant*

At the Circus　1939
Comedy
59360　87 mins　B/W　B, V　　　　P
*The Marx Brothers, Margaret Dumont, Kenny
Baker, Florence Rice, Eve Arden, Nat
Pendleton, Fritz Feld*
The Marx Brothers, as circus performers, cause
their usual comic insanity. Groucho sings,
"Lydia the Tattooed Lady."
MGM — *MGM/UA Home Video*

At the Earth's Core　1976
Science fiction
65135　90 mins　C　B, V　　　　P
Doug McClure, Peter Cushing, Caroline Munro
A Victorian scientist invents a giant burrowing
machine, which he and his crew use to dig
deeply into the Earth. To their surprise, they
discover a lost world of subhuman creatures
and prehistoric monsters.
MPAA:PG
American International — *Warner Home Video*

At War with the Army　1950
Comedy
39009　93 mins　B/W　B, V　　　　P
Dean Martin, Jerry Lewis, Polly Bergen
Martin and Lewis' first starring appearance, as
soldiers getting mixed up in all kinds of wild
situations at their army base.
Paramount — *American Video Tape; Cable
Films; Video Connection; Video Yesteryear;
Discount Video Tapes*

Atalante, L'　1934
Film-Avant-garde
06225　82 mins　B/W　B, V　　　　P
*Dita Parlo, Jean Daste, Michel Simon, directed
by Jean Vigo*
A bride on her honeymoon becomes bored and
starts flirting with other men. French with
English subtitles.
FR
J L Nounez; Gaumont — *Hollywood Home
Theater; Video Yesteryear; Western Film &
Video Inc; Discount Video Tapes*

Atlanta Braves: Team　1984
Highlights
Baseball
81132　30 mins　C　B, V　　　　P
*Hank Aaron, Dale Murphy, Bob Horner, Chris
Chambliss　4　pgms*
This series highlights the many shining
moments from the Atlanta Braves' past
seasons.
*1.1966: Here Come The Braves 2.1982: Coming
To America 3.1983: The A Team 4.1984: Ready
To Rebound*

Major League Baseball — *Major League
Baseball Productions*

Atlantic City　1981
Drama
53930　104 mins　C　B, V, LV　　　P
*Burt Lancaster, Susan Sarandon, Kate Reid,
Michel Piccoli, Hollis Mc Laren, directed by
Louis Malle*
A smalltime, aging mafia hood falls in love with a
clam bar waitress, and they share the spoils of a
big score against the backdrop of a changing
Atlantic City.
MPAA:R
Dennis Heroux; Cine Neighbor; Selta
Films — *Paramount Home Video; RCA
VideoDiscs*

Atlantic Starr: As the　1985
Band Turns... The Video
Music-Performance/Music video
85669　15 mins　C　B, V　　　　P
A concert taping by the popular dance-music
group.
A&M Video — *A & M Video*

Atoll K　1951
Comedy
05436　82 mins　B/W　B, V　　　　P
*Stan Laurel, Oliver Hardy, Suzy Delair, directed
by John Berry*
Laurel and Hardy inherit an island and turn it into
a Utopia, but their peace is disturbed when
uranium is discovered. This film is also known
as "Utopia" and "Robinson Crusoeland."
Sirius Films;Franco-London Films — *Hal
Roach Studios; Video Yesteryear; Discount
Video Tapes*

Atom Age Vampire　1961
Horror
65198　71 mins　B/W　B, V　　　　P
Alberto Lupo, Susanne Loret, Sergio Fantoni
A mad scientist falls in love with a woman who
has been disfigured in an auto crash. To remove
her scars, he treats her with a formula derived
from the glands of freshly killed women. English
dubbed.
Lion Film; Topaz Film Corp — *Video
Yesteryear*

Atom Ant　196?
Cartoons
47686　53 mins　C　B, V　　　　P
Animated
Eight episodes in which the ant with atomic
strength battles Ferocious Flea and Karate Ant.
Hanna Barbera — *Worldvision Home Video*

Atom Ant, Volume II　1965
Cartoons
82320　40 mins　C　B, V　　　　P

The mightiest little hero in the universe, Atom Ant, is back to fight crime in this collection of six episodes from the series.
Hanna-Barbera — *Worldvision Home Video*

Atomic Cafe, The   1982
Documentary/Satire
64210   92 mins   C   B, V   P
A chillingly humorous compilation of newsreels and government films of the 1940's and 1950's that show America's preoccupation with the A-Bomb. Some sequences are in black and white.
Archives Project Inc — *THORN EMI/HBO Video*

Atomic Submarine   1959
Science fiction
70816   80 mins   C   B, V   P
Arthur Franz, Dick Foran, Bob Steele, Brett Halsey, Joi Lansing
Alien invaders wage war against an atomic-powered submarine far below the arctic ice.
Alex Gordon — *Monterey Home Video*

Ator the Fighting Eagle   1983
Adventure/Fantasy
69392   98 mins   C   B, V   P
Miles O'Keeffe
According to legend, Ator, son of Thorn, must put an end to the tragic Dynasty of the Spiders.
MPAA:PG
Comworld Pictures — *THORN EMI/HBO Video*

Attack and Reprisal   1946
World War II
78972   55 mins   C   B, V   P
Two short films about the Japanese attack on Pearl Harbor and the bombing of Hiroshima.
Maljack Productions — *MPI Home Video*

Attack Force Z   1984
Adventure
74107   84 mins   C   B, V   P
Mel Gibson, John Philip Law, John Waters
An elite volunteer corps, Force Z, is given the dangerous mission of finding a defected Japanese government official who was lost in a plane crash somewhere in the South Pacific.
Lee Robinson — *VCL Home Video*

Attack from Outer Space   1980
Documentary/Speculation
84854   90 mins   C   B, V   P
This speculative movie explores the possibility of extraterrestrial life.
Unknown — *United Home Video*

Attack of the Killer   1977
Tomatoes
Comedy
42912   87 mins   C   B, V   P
In this low-budget spoof, tomatoes suddenly turn savage and begin attacking people. Many familiar cliches of the science fiction genre are parodied and a few musical numbers are included.
MPAA:PG   EL, SP
Four Square Productions — *Media Home Entertainment*

Attack of the Robots   1966
Comedy
66133   88 mins   B/W   B, V, FO   P
Eddie Constantine, Fernando Rey
A spy spoof about individuals being turned into robots.
American Intl Pictures — *Video Yesteryear*

Attack of the Swamp   1975
Creature
Horror
81744   96 mins   C   B, V   P
Frank Crowell, David Robertson
A deranged scientist transforms himself into a swamp creature and terrorizes a small town.
Aquarius Video — *Thriller Video*

Attack!—The Battle of   1944
New Britain
World War II
53654   45 mins   B/W   B, V, 3/4U   P
Frank Capra supervised production on this film, which provides a record of the attacks on Arawa and Cape Gouster on New Britain.
Unknown — *International Historic Films; Spotlite Video*

Attic, The   1980
Drama
79335   92 mins   C   B, V   P
Carrie Snodgrass, Ray Milland
A young woman isolates herself from the world by hiding away in her parent's attic.
MPAA:R
Raymond M. Dryden; Phillip Randall — *Key Video; Monterey Home Video*

Audi 5000   1986
Automobiles
88399   60 mins   C   B, V, 3/4U   P
How to tune-up, repair and maintain the Audi.
Peter Allen Prod. — *Peter Allen Video Productions*

Auditions   1973
Comedy
60436   82 mins   C   B, V   P
Real, bizarre, erotic and outrageously funny auditions for X-rated stardom.

MPAA:R
Charles Band Productions — *Wizard Video*

Audrey Rose   1977
Horror
72464   113 mins   C   B, V   P
Marsha Mason, Anthony Hopkins, John Beck
The parents of a young girl are traumatized
when a man tells them his dead daughter lives
on inside her.
MPAA:PG
United Artists — *MGM/UA Home Video*

Audubon Society's   1986
Videoguide to the Birds
of North America
Birds
85270   96 mins   C   B, V   P
4   pgms
A series of lushly photographed studies of North
American bird life.
Audubon Society — *Mastervision*

Auntie Mame   1958
Comedy
47620   161 mins   C   B, V   P
*Rosalind Russell, Patrick Knowles, Roger
Smith, Peggy Cass*
A young boy is brought up by his only surviving
relative—flamboyant and eccentric Auntie
Mame. Part of the "A Night at the Movies"
series, this tape simulates a 1958 movie
evening, with a Road Runner cartoon, "Hook,
Line and Stinker," a newsreel and coming
attractions for "No Time for Sergeants" and
"Chase a Crooked Shadow."
Warner Bros — *Warner Home Video*

Aurora Encounter   1985
Science fiction
87622   90 mins   C   B, V   P
*Jack Elam, Peter Brown, Carol Bagdasarian,
Dottie West*
Aliens surreptitously infiltrate a small town in
1897, and spread benevolence everywhere.
MPAA:PG
New World — *New World Video*

Australia Now   1984
Music-Performance/Documentary
81192   60 mins   C   B, V   P
*Little River Band, Inxs, Men at Work, Midnight
Oil, Split Enz, Moving Pictures*
This documentary takes a look at the people
and the music from the lands down under,
Australia and New Zealand.
Pom Oliver; Peter Clifton — *Music Media*

Author! Author!   1982
Comedy
63391   100 mins   C   B, V, CED   P

*Al Pacino, Tuesday Weld, Dyan Cannon, Alan
King, directed by Arthur Hill*
Al Pacino portrays a struggling playwright whose
wife leaves him with their son and four children
from her previous marriage. Pacino becomes
involved with the leading lady of his new
Broadway play, but she is more concerned with
the social scene than with his children.
MPAA:PG
20th Century Fox — *CBS/Fox Video*

Auto Video   1986
Automobiles
86190   60 mins   C   B, V   P
A general survey of personal car care, from
maintainance to the early warning signs of a
breakdown.
Larry Denauger — *Total Productions*

Autobiography of Miss   1974
Jane Pittman, The
Drama
52333   110 mins   C   V   P
Cicely Tyson, Odetta, Joseph Tremice
This program, based on the novel by Ernest J.
Gaines, tells the story of a courageous black
woman whose life spans from the Civil War to
the Civil Rights movement in the 1960's.
Tomorrow Entertainment — *Prism; RCA
VideoDiscs; Learning Corp of America*

Autumn Born   1979
Drama
60411   76 mins   C   B, V   P
Dorothy Stratten
A young heiress is abducted by her guardian
and imprisoned while she's taught to obey his
will.
MPAA:R
North American Pictures Ltd — *Monterey
Home Video*

Autumn Leaves   1956
Drama
71110   108 mins   B/W   B, V   P
*Cliff Robertson, Joan Crawford, Vera Miles,
Lorne Green, directed by Robert Aldrich*
Suspicion leads to terror for a woman when her
husband becomes more secretive and his
explanations seem inconsistent.
Columbia — *RCA/Columbia Pictures Home
Video*

Autumn Portrait   1985
Music video
82064   60 mins   C   B, V   P
The music of the Windham Hill family of artists is
featured in this impressionistic portrait of
autumn. Available in VHS and Beta Hi-Fi Stereo.
Dann Moss; Windham Hill
Productions — *Paramount Home Video;
Pioneer Artists*

Avalanche 1978
Suspense
65072   91 mins   C   B, V, CED   P
Rock Hudson, Mia Farrow, Robert Forster, Rick Moses
Vacationers at a new winter ski resort are at the mercy of a monster avalanche which leaves a path of terror and destruction in its wake.
New World Pictures, — *Embassy Home Entertainment*

Avant Garde and 193?
Experimental Film
Program No. 1
Film-Avant-garde
11290   55 mins   B/W   B, V, FO   P
A collection of five avant-garde films: "Un Chien Andulou," by Luis Bunuel and Salvador Dali; "Rain," by Joris Ivens and Mannus Franken; "Umberfall," by Erno Marzner; "Hearts of Age," directed by and starring Orson Welles; and "Ballet Mecanique," by Fernand Leger.
Unknown — *Video Yesteryear*

Avant-Garde #2 192?
Film-Avant-garde
58266   42 mins   B/W   B, V, FO   P
Three avant-garde films: "Symphonie Diagonale" (1921, Germany), by Viking Eggeling, a Dada-ist; "L'Etoile de Mer" (1928, France), directed by Man Ray, an early surrealist; and, "Entr'acte" (1924, France), directed by Rene Clair, pure cinematic imagery.
Germany; France — *Video Yesteryear*

Avengers 198?
Music-Performance/Music video
84051   30 mins   C   B, V   P
Avengers
Three live performances of Avengers, a reknowned and politically idealistic punk group of the late '70's.
Target Video — *Target Video*

Avengers, The 196?
Adventure
54135   50 mins   B/W   B, V   P
Diana Rigg, Patrick Macnee
This program contains an episode entitled "Dial a Deadly Number" from this classic TV series.
Associated British Corp — *Video Dimensions; Video Yesteryear*

Avenging Angel 1985
Drama
80818   94 mins   C   B, V, LV   P
Betsy Russell, Rory Calhoun, Susan Tyrell, Ossie Davis, Barry Pearl, Ross Hagen
Law student Molly "Angel" Stewart is back out on the streets again to retaliate against the men who killed the policeman who saved her from a life of prostitution.
MPAA:R

New World Pictures — *New World Video*

Avenging Conscience, 1914
The
Film-History
11388   78 mins   B/W   B, V, FO   P
Henry B. Walthall, Blanche Sweet, directed by D.W. Griffith
An early eerie horror film, based on tales of Edgar Allen Poe. D.W. Griffith's first large-scale feature. Silent.
Biograph — *Video Yesteryear*

Aventura Llamada 1982
Menudo, Una
Adventure/Music video
86914   90 mins   C   B, V   P
A video movie with the Latin group running into danger and many young girls amid 14 of their songs.
EL, SP
Embassy — *Embassy Home Entertainment*

Average White Band 1984
Shine
Music-Performance
79893   30 mins   C   B, V   P
The popular soul band plays their greatest hits in this taped concert from their European tour.
Independent — *VCL Home Video*

Aviation Volume I 19??
Aeronautics
10151   60 mins   B/W   B, V   P, T
Newsreels highlight aviation history from Wright Brothers through evolution of the helicopter. Includes de Pinedo's death, the Graf Zeppelin, Lindberg's trans-Atlantic flight, and Pan American Clippers.
Unknown — *Blackhawk Films*

Aviator, The 1985
Adventure/Drama
81773   98 mins   C   B, V   P
Christopher Reeve, Rosanna Arquette, Jack Warden, Tyne Daly, Marcia Strassman, directed by George Miller
A pilot haunted by the memory of a fatal crash is hired to transport a young woman to Washington. The two fall in love after their biplane crashes in the mountains. Available in VHS and Beta Hi-Fi.
MPAA:PG
United Artists — *MGM/UA Home Video*

Awakening of Candra, 1981
The
Drama
85779   96 mins   C   B, V   P
Blanche Baker, Cliff De Young, Richard Jaeckel
A young couple is assaulted in the mountains by a lunatic, who rapes the girl, kills the husband,

and then brainwashes her into thinking it was all an accident.
Telefeature — *Video Gems*

B

Awakening of Cassie, The   1985
Romance
87692   90 mins   C   V   P
A romance novel brought to video life, as a beautiful artist discovers the pains and pleasures of love.
Prism Video — *Prism*

Awakening, The   1980
Horror
52717   102 mins   C   B, V   P
Charlton Heston, Susannah York, Stephanie Zimbalist
An archeologist discovers the tomb of a murderous queen, but upon opening the coffin, the mummy's spirit is transferred to his baby daughter, born at that instant.
MPAA:R
Orion Pictures — *Warner Home Video*

Away All Boats   1956
War-Drama
87175   114 mins   C   B, V   P
Jeff Chandler, George Nader, Richard Boone, Julie Adams, Lex Barker
The true story of Captain Hawks, who led a crew of misfits to victory in World War II aboard the U.S.S. Belinda.
Universal; Howard Christie — *MCA Home Video*

Awful Truth, The   1937
Comedy
87268   92 mins   B/W   B, V   P
Irene Dunne, Cary Grant, Ralph Bellamy, Alexander D'Arcy, Cecil Cunningham, directed by Leo McCarey
A married couple get divorced and then spend their time sabotaging each other's romantic liasons. One of the greatest screwball comedies of the 1930s.
Academy Awards '37: Best Director (McCarey).
Columbia — *RCA/Columbia Pictures Home Video*

Ay Jalisco No Te Rajes!   197?
Drama
52792   90 mins   C   B, V   P
Rodolfo De Anda, Angel Garasa, Sonia Infante
General Carvajal forbids Salvador Perez Gomez to woo his daughter. Salvador kills him and must flee from the general's sons. One year later he finds the daughter in a convent, and she professes her love for him. In Spanish.
SP
Gonzalo Elvira — *Media Home Entertainment*

B.C. Rock   1984
Fantasy/Cartoons
80923   82 mins   C   B, V   P
Animated
A cave man learns how to defend himself and has some prehistoric fun with a tribe of female amazons.
MPAA:R
Almi Pictures — *Vestron Video*

Babar the Elephant Comes to America   1985
Fantasy
85902   23 mins   C   B, V   P
Animated, narrated by Peter Ustinov
Based on Jean de Brunhoff's famous character, this animated film depicts Babar's adventures in Hollywood.
Children's Video Library — *Children's Video Library*

Babes in Arms   1939
Musical
80858   91 mins   B/W   B, V   P
Judy Garland, Mickey Rooney, Charles Winninger, Guy Kibbee, June Preisser, directed by Busby Berkeley
The children of several vaudeville performers team up to put on a show to raise money for their financially impoverished parents. The Rodgers and Hart score features "Where or When" and "I Cried For You."
MGM; Arthur Freed — *MGM/UA Home Video*

Babes in Toyland   1961
Musical
63124   119 mins   C   B, V   P
Annette Funicello, Ray Bolger, Tommy Sands, Ed Wynn, Tommy Kirk
A lavish production of Victor Herbert's timeless operetta, with Toyland being menaced by the evil Barnaby and his Bogeymen.
Walt Disney Productions — *Walt Disney Home Video*

Babine Steelhead   1985
Fishing
82508   50 mins   C   B, V, 3/4U,   P
1C
Two men attempt to catch a twenty-pound steelhead trout with a fly rod in the wilds of British Columbia.
Grunko Films — *Grunko Films*

Baby, The   1972
Suspense
01648   85 mins   C   B, V   P, T
Anjanette Comer, Ruth Roman, Marianna Hill, directed by Ted Post

Bizarre story of a social worker attempting to free a retarded man-child from over-protection of his mother and sisters. Murder follows.
Scotia Intl Films — *King of Video; World Video Pictures*

Baby Comes Home   1986
Infants
86161   60 mins   C   B, V   P
A program outlining initial infant care, from bonding to breast feeding to educational games. Part of "Parents Video Magazine."
Arnold Shapiro; Karl-Lorimar; Jean O'Neill — *Karl/Lorimar Home Video*

Baby Doll   1956
Drama
81492   115 mins   B/W   B, V   P
Eli Wallach, Carroll Baker, Karl Malden, Mildred Dunnock, directed by Elia Kazan
When a slow-witted Mississippian is frustrated by his nubile child bride, he becomes an arsonist and burns down his competitor's cotton gin. However, the competitor has a surprise in store for the couple.
Warner Bros; Newtown Prods — *Warner Home Video*

Baby Dynamics   1985
Childbirth/Physical fitness
81456   36 mins   C   B, V   P
2   pgms
Linda Westin, the co-founder of the Baby Dynamics program demonstrates an exercise regiment that aids in developing young children's motor skills and coordination.
Sheri Singer — *Embassy Home Entertainment*

Baby Huey the Baby Giant   1962
Cartoons
86366   60 mins   C   B, V   P
A compilation of the Baby Huey cartoons.
Harvey Films Inc. — *Worldvision Home Video*

Baby Love   1983
Comedy
81774   80 mins   C   B, V   P
Nerds get revenge against the freshmen who run the local frat house.
Noah Films — *MGM/UA Home Video*

Baby—Safe Home, The   1985
Safety education
81621   60 mins   C   B, V, 8mm   P
Consumer advocate David Horowitz and his wife Suzanne show the areas of the home that could be dangerous to infants and what can be done to prevent accidents.
Eagle/Horowitz Productions — *Embassy Home Entertainment*

Baby...Secret of the Lost Legend   1985
Fantasy/Adventure
81979   92 mins   C   B, V   P
William Katt, Sean Young, Patrick McGoohan, Julian Fellowes, directed by BWL Norton
A sportswriter and his paleontologist wife risk their lives to reunite a hatching brontosaurus dinosaur with its mother in the African jungle.
MPAA:PG
Buena Vista; Touchstone Films — *Touchstone Home Video*

Baby, the Rain Must Fall   1964
Drama
66351   100 mins   B/W   B, V   P
Steve McQueen, Lee Remick, Don Murray, directed by Robert Mulligan
A rootless drifter, paroled from prison, returns home to his wife and daughter, but his outbursts of violence make the reunion difficult.
Columbia; Alan Pakula — *RCA/Columbia Pictures Home Video*

Babylon Story from "Intolerance," The   1916
Drama
58645   25 mins   C   B, V, FO   P
Constance Talmadge, Alfred Paget, directed by D. W. Griffith
A condensation of the Babylon sequence from Griffith's epic, "Intolerance." The story concerns the simple mountain girl befriended by Belshazzar, King of Babylonia, who tries to warn the city of its impending doom. Silent with music score, tinted color.
D W Griffith — *Video Yesteryear*

Babysitter, The   1980
Mystery/Drama
82024   96 mins   C   B, V   P
William Shatner, Patty Duke-Astin, Quinn Cummings, Stephanie Zimbalist, John Houseman
A mysterious woman manipulates and exploits the three members of a family, driving them to the edge of destruction.
Moonlight Productions; Filmways — *THORN EMI/HBO Video*

Bachelor and the Bobby Soxer, The   1947
Comedy
44814   95 mins   B/W   B, V   P, T
Cary Grant, Myrna Loy, Shirley Temple, Rudy Vallee
A playboy is brought before Judge Myrna for disturbing the peace and sentenced to court her teenage sister.
Academy Awards 1947: Best Original Screenplay (Sidney Sheldon).

Dore Schary — *Blackhawk Films; Nostalgia Merchant*

Bachelor Bait   1934
Comedy
44985   75 mins   B/W   B, V   P, T
Stuart Erwin, Rochelle Hudson, Pert Kelton, Skeets Gallagher
A marriage license clerk who's tired of just handing out licenses opens a matrimonial service for men.
Pandro S Berman — *Blackhawk Films*

Bachelor Mother   1939
Comedy
10037   82 mins   B/W   B, V   P, T
Ginger Rogers, David Niven, Charles Coburn
Single salesgirl causes scandal when she finds abandoned baby.
RKO; B G DeSylva — *Blackhawk Films; Nostalgia Merchant*

Bachelor Party   1984
Comedy
Closed Captioned
76928   105 mins   C   B, V   P
Tom Hanks, Tawny Kitaen, George Grizzard, Adrian Zmed, directed by Neal Israel
When a young couple plans to marry, her parents and his friends do all that they can to prevent it.
20th Century Fox — *CBS/Fox Video*

Back Among the   1984
Best/NFL '83
Football
72940   46 mins   C   B, V, FO   P
San Francisco 49'ers
Highlights from the San Francisco 49'ers 1983 season and "NFL 83."
NFL Films — *NFL Films Video*

Back from Eternity   1956
Drama
11608   97 mins   B/W   B, V   P
Robert Ryan, Rod Steiger
Eleven survivors of a plane crash are stranded in a headhunter region of South America's jungle.
Universal; John Farrow — *United Home Video*

Back (Rehabilitation and   1978
Injury)
Physical fitness
52760   30 mins   C   B, V   P
Hosted by Ann Dugan
Back strengthening exercises to help overcome weaknesses, relieve pain, and condition muscles and tissue to prevent further stress.
Part of the "Rehabilitation and Injury" series.

Health 'N Action — *RCA/Columbia Pictures Home Video*

Back Roads   1981
Comedy-Drama
53939   94 mins   C   B, V, CED   P
Sally Field, Tommy Lee Jones, David Keith, directed by Martin Ritt
A Southern hooker meets a down-on-his-luck boxer and both head out for the better life in California.
MPAA:R
Ronald Sheldo — *CBS/Fox Video*

Back Street   1961
Drama
70555   107 mins   C   B, V   P
Susan Hayward, John Gavin, Vera Miles, directed by David Miller
The forbidden affair between a married man and a beautiful fashion designer carrys on through many anxious years to a tragic end. This lavish third film version of the Fanny Hurst novel features Hi-Fi Mono sound in all formats.
Universal — *MCA Home Video*

Back to Bataan   1945
War-Drama
10073   95 mins   B/W   B, V   P
John Wayne, Anthony Quinn
Colonel forms guerrilla army to raid Japanese and to help Americans landing on Leyte.
RKO; Robert Fellows — *Blackhawk Films; RKO HomeVideo*

Back to the Future   1985
Fantasy/Comedy
Closed Captioned
84849   116 mins   C   B, V, LV   P
Michael J Fox, Christopher Lloyd, Lea Thompson, Crispin Glover, directed by Robert Zemeckis
The neighborhood tinkerer constructs a time machine, and his youthful companion accidentally transports himself to 1955. There, he uses contemporary savvy to bring his parents together, elude the local bully, and get back...to the future. The Hi-Fi soundtrack features Huey Lewis and the News, and Lewis makes a cameo appearance early in the film.
MPAA:PG
MCA;Universal — *MCA Home Video*

Backaid   1985
Back disorders/Physical fitness
84691   90 mins   C   B, V   P
Charisse Layne
Created by Doctors, an exercise and stretching program for back maintenance of all ages.
Medical Prods; Four Point Ent — *Four Point Entertainment*

Backcountry   1984
**Skiing—Telemarking in
the 80's**
Sports-Winter
84278   15 mins   C   B, V   P
Another colorful skiing film, this time
interspersed with introductions to telemarking.
Video Travel Inc — *Video Travel*

Backstage at the Kirov   198?
Dance
72179   80 mins   C   B, V   P
A unique look at the Russian Kirov ballet
company mixed with a profile of Leningrad.
Dr Armand Hammer — *Pacific Arts Video*

Bad   1977
Comedy
80763   105 mins   C   B, V   P
*Carroll Baker, Perry King, Susan Tyrell, Stefania
Cassini, Mary Boylon*
A suburban housewife runs a side business of
providing hit women to perform other people's
dirty deeds.
MPAA:X
New World Films — *Embassy Home
Entertainment*

Bad Boys   1983
Drama
69039   123 mins   C   B, V, CED   P
Sean Penn
Two young hoodlums who hate each other are
sent to a Juvenile Hall together and end up in
the same dorm. Backed into a corner by their
mutual hatred and the escalating peer pressure,
the two are pushed over the brink into a final
and shattering fight-to-the-death.
Robert Solo — *THORN EMI/HBO Video*

Bad Bunch, The   197?
Crime-Drama
86553   82 mins   C   B, V   P
*Greydon Clark, Tom Johnigam, Jacqulin Cole,
Aldo Ray, Jock Mahoney*
A white liberal living in Watts tries to befriend a
ruthless black street gang, but is unsuccessful.
MPAA:R
Greydon Clark — *United Home Video*

B.A.D. Cats   1980
Suspense/Drama
81125   74 mins   C   B, V   P
*Asher Brauner, Michelle Pfeiffer, Vic Morrow,
Jimmie Walker, Steve Hanks, La Wanda Page*
Two members of a police burglary auto detail
chase after a group of car thieves who are
planning a million-dollar gold heist.
Aaron Spelling and Douglas S.
Cramer — *Karl/Lorimar Home Video*

Bad Company   1972
Western
88421   93 mins   C   B, V   P
*Jeff Bridges, Barry Brown, Jim Davis, John
Savage, directed by Robert Benton*
Two Civil War draft dodgers roam the Western
frontier and eventually turn to a fruitless life of
crime.
MPAA:PG
Paramount — *Paramount Home Video*

Bad Georgia Road   1977
Crime-Drama
84830   85 mins   C   B, V   P
Gary Lockwood, Carol Lynley
A New Yorker inherits a moonshine operation
from her uncle, and fights off the syndicate for
its profits.
Demension Pictures — *United Home Video*

Bad Manners   1984
Comedy
79709   85 mins   C   B, V   P
Martin Mull, Karen Black
A group of orphans attempt to rescue a young
boy adopted by a wealthy family.
MPAA:R
New World Pictures — *THORN EMI/HBO
Video*

Bad Medicine   1985
Comedy
Closed Captioned
85372   97 mins   C   B, V   P
*Steve Guttenberg, Alan Arkin, Julie Hagerty, Bill
Macy, Curtis Armstrong*
A youth who doesn't want to be a doctor is
accepted by a highly questionable Latin
American school of medicine.
MPAA:PG-13
Alex Winitsky; Arlene Sellers — *Playhouse
Video*

Bad News Bears, The   1976
Comedy
38606   102 mins   C   B, V, 8mm,   P
                                 LV
*Walter Matthau, Tatum O'Neal, Vic Morrow,
Joyce Van Patten, Jackie Earle Haley*
Family comedy about a misfit Little League team
which gets whipped into shape by a cranky
sloppy beer-drinking coach.
MPAA:PG
Paramount — *Paramount Home Video; RCA
VideoDiscs*

Bad News Bears in   1977
Breaking Training, The
Comedy
10984   97 mins   C   B, V   P
William Devane, Clifton James
With a chance to play the Houston Toros for a
shot at the Japanese champs, the Bears devise

---

a way to get to Texas to play at the famed Astrodome.
MPAA:PG
Paramount; Leonard Goldberg — *Paramount Home Video; RCA VideoDiscs*

Badge 373   1973
Crime-Drama
88423   116 mins   C   B, V   P
Robert Duvall, Verna Bloom, Eddie Egan, directed by Howard W. Koch
A follow-up to "The French Connection," in which a Doyle/Egan-esque New York cop is suspended and decides to battle crime his own way.
MPAA:R
Paramount — *Paramount Home Video*

Badlands   1974
Drama
51988   95 mins   C   B, V, LV   P
Martin Sheen, Sissy Spacek, Warren Oates
A garbage man from South Dakota falls in love with a 15-year-old girl. He doesn't hesitate to kill anyone who tries to interfere with their romance.
MPAA:PG
Warner Bros — *Warner Home Video*

Badman's Territory   1946
Western
81029   97 mins   B/W   B, V   P
Randolph Scott, Gabby Hayes, Steve Brodie
A straight-shooting marshal has to deal with such notorious outlaws as the James and Dalton boys in a territory outside of government control.
RKO — *RKO HomeVideo*

Baer vs. Louis/Louis vs.   193?
Schmeling
Boxing
60056   54 mins   B/W   B, V   P, T
Max Baer, Joe Louis
Joe Louis meets ex-champ Max Baer at Yankee Stadium on September 24, 1935. On June 19, 1936 Joe Louis fights with Max Schmeling at Yankee Stadium.
Unknown — *Blackhawk Films*

Baffled   1972
Suspense/Drama
59341   96 mins   C   CED   P
Leonard Nimoy, Susan Hampshire, Vera Miles
A story of the supernatural, blending drama and suspense with comic undertones.
ATV — *CBS/Fox Video*

Bakery, The/The Grocery   1921
Clerk
Comedy
63994   55 mins   B/W   B, V   P, T

Larry Semon, Oliver Hardy, Lucille Carlisle, directed by Larry Semon
A package of shorts featuring crazy comedian Larry Semon, getting tangled up in mayhem and molasses. Silent with piano score.
Vitagraph — *Blackhawk Films*

Bal, Le   1984
Musical
74207   112 mins   C   B, V   P
This movie captures a 50-year span of contemporary history through the music and dance of periods from the 1930s through 1983. French Academy Awards '83: Best Picture; Best Director (Scola); Best Music Score.
Giorgio Silvagni — *Warner Home Video*

Balance, La   1982
Drama
Closed Captioned
70763   103 mins   C   B, V   P
Philippe Leotard, Nathalie Baye, Richard Berry, directed by Reymond LePlont
"La Balance" is the underworld stool-pigeon recruited by the Parisian police to blow the whistle on a murderous mob. Hi-Fi stereo sound available in all formats.
MPAA:R
Les Films Ariane — *CBS/Fox Video*

Balanced Fitness   1986
Workout Program
Physical fitness
85655   30 mins   C   B, V   P
Art Ulene
A light-impact aerobic program designed chiefly for flexibility and optimum muscle tone.
ACOG — *Warner Home Video*

Balboa   1982
Drama
84093   92 mins   C   B, V   P
Tony Curtis, Carol Lynley, Chuck Connors, directed by James Polakof
Set on sun-baked Balboa Island, this is a tale of high-class power, jealousy and intrigue. Special guest appearances by Sonny Bono and Cassanora Peterson, also known as horror hostess Elvira.
Simcom — *Vestron Video*

Balkan Express   1985
Adventure
86088   102 mins   C   B, V   P
A crew of unlikely slobs become heroes in war-ravaged Europe.
Unknown — *New World Video*

Ball of Fire   1942
Comedy
81477   111 mins   B/W   B, V, LV   P

Gary Cooper, Barbara Stanwyck, Dana Andrews, Gene Krupa, directed by Howard Hawks
A professor of semantics gets more than he can handle when he consults a stripper for his study of slang in the English language.
Sameul Goldwyn — Embassy Home Entertainment

Ballad in Blue   1966
Drama
79326   88 mins   B/W   B, V   P
Ray Charles, Tom Bell, Mary Peach, Dawn Addams, directed by Paul Henried
The pianist befriends a blind British boy and his mother and guides them through the trials and tribulations of everyday life. In Beta Hi-Fi and VHS Stereo.
Alexander Salkind — U.S.A. Home Video

Ballad of a Gunfighter   1964
Western
81709   84 mins   C   B, V   P
Marty Robbins, Bob Barron, Joyce Redd
A feud between two outlaws reaches the boiling point when they both fall in love with the same woman.
Bill Ward — Prism

Ballad of a Soldier   1959
Drama
29755   88 mins   B/W   B, V   P
Vladimir Ivashov, Shanna Prokhorenko, directed by Grigori Chukrai
As a reward for demolishing two German tanks, a nineteen-year old Russian soldier receives a six day pass so he can see his mother. After much effort, he manages to see her briefly...for the last time.
Russian — International Home Video; Hollywood Home Theater; International Historic Films; Western Film & Video Inc; Discount Video Tapes; Video Dimensions; Movie Buff Video

Ballad of Cable Hogue, The   1970
Western
82340   122 mins   C   B, V   P
Jason Robards, Stella Stevens, David Warner, L Q Jones, Strother Martin, Slim Pickens, directed by Sam Peckinpah
A prospector, who had been left to die in the desert by his double-crossing partners finds a waterhole. A surprise awaits his former friends when they visit the remote well.
MPAA:R
Warner Bros — Warner Home Video

Ballad of Gregorio Cortez, The   1983
Drama
64990   99 mins   C   B, V   P
Edward James Olmos
Based on one of the most famous manhunts in Texas history, this is the story of a Mexican cowhand who killed a Texas sheriff in self-defense and tried to elude the law, all because of a misunderstanding of the Spanish language.
EL, JA
Moctesuma Esparza Productions — Embassy Home Entertainment

Ballerina: Karen Kain   1980
Dance
58562   58 mins   C   B, V   P
A profile of the dancer about whom Nureyev has said "in her the star quality is unmistakable." Includes scenes from "Carmen," "Romeo and Juliet," and "Cappelia."
MasterVision — Mastervision

Ballerina: Lynn Seymour   1980
Dance
58563   58 mins   C   B, V   P
Rudolph Nureyev
Prima ballerina Lynn Seymour is seen dancing with some of the world's leading male stars. Scenes from "Romeo and Juliet" and "The Two Pigeons" are included.
MasterVision — Mastervision

Ballet Class for Beginners, A   1982
Dance
47366   60 mins   C   B, V   P
Basic ballet movements are taught by renowned dancer Dave Howard.
American Home Video Library — Kultur

Ballet Class for Intermediate—Advanced   1983
Dance
79302   45 mins   C   B, V   P
Former Royal Ballet soloist David Howard teaches the intermediate and advanced levels of dance movement.
New Age Video — New Age Video Inc; Kultur

Ballo in Maschera, Un   1980
Opera
82536   150 mins   C   B, V, LV   P
Katia Ricciarelli, Louis Quilico, Judith Blegen, Bianca Berini, Luciano Pavarotti conducted by Giuseppe Patone
This production of Verdi's opera is set in 18th century Boston, on the eve of the American revolution. It was taped at N.Y.'s Metropolitan Opera House and is subtitled in English.
IT
Elija Moshinsky — Paramount Home Video; Pioneer Artists

Balloonatic, The/One Week   192?

Comedy
60051   48 mins   B/W   B, V   P, T
Buster Keaton, Phyllis Haver, Sybil Seely
"The Balloonatic" (1923) features Keaton in
several misadventures. In "One Week" (1920)
Buster and his new bride, Sybil, receive a new
home as a wedding gift—the kind you have to
assemble yourself. Silent.
Buster Keaton Prods; Metro — *Blackhawk
Films*

Baltimore Bullet, The   1980

Adventure
55533   97 mins   C   B, V   P
*James Coburn, Omar Sharif, Bruce Boxleitner,
Ronee Blakely, Jack O'Halloran*
Two men make their living traveling through the
country as pool hustlers, bilking would-be pool
sharks. Features ten of the greatest pool
players in the world.
MPAA:PG
Avco Embassy; John Brascia — *Charter
Entertainment*

Baltimore Orioles: Team Highlights   1984

Baseball
81134   30 mins   C   B, V   P
*Jim Palmer, Earl Weaver, Rick Dempsey, Eddie
Murray, Ken Singleton, Benny Ayala*   4   pgms
Here are highlights from the Baltimore Orioles
four successful early eighties seasons.
*1.1981: Oriole Magic 2.1982: Something Magic
Happened 3.1983: O's What A Feeling 4.1984:
A Winning Tradition*
Major League Baseball — *Major League
Baseball Productions*

Bamboo Saucer   1967

Science fiction
80181   103 mins   C   B, V   P
Dab Duryea, John Ericson
Two groups of Russian and American scientists
race to find a U.F.O. in Red China
NTA — *Republic Pictures Home Video*

Banana Monster   1972

Comedy/Horror
84105   80 mins   C   B, V   P
John Landis, Saul Kahan, Eliza Garrett
From the director of "Animal House" and
"Spies Like Us," comes this, his first feature
film, about an ape-man who proceeds through a
town committing Banana Murders. Previously
entitled "Schlock," it features Landis in the lead
role, and make-up by Rick Baker.
MPAA:PG
Empire — *Lightning Video*

Banana Splits & Friends, The   197?

Cartoons
66279   60 mins   C   B, V   P
Four large furry creatures, the Banana Splits,
perform their slapstick antics and present
cartoons.
Hanna Barbera — *Worldvision Home Video*

Bananarama: And That's Not All...   1984

Music-Performance/Music video
84490   35 mins   C   B, V   P
The harmonious female new wave trio's
conglomeration of videos and performances.
Polygram Music Video Ltd — *Sony Video
Software*

Bananas   1971

Comedy
58484   82 mins   C   B, V   P
*Woody Allen, Louise Lasser, Carlos Montalban,
Howard Cosell, Sylvester Stallone, directed by
Woody Allen*
A frustrated product tester from New York runs
off to South America, where he volunteers his
support to the revolutionary force of a shaky
Latin-American dictatorship and winds up the
leader.
MPAA:PG
United Artists; Rollins Jaffe; Jack
Grossberg — *CBS/Fox Video; RCA
VideoDiscs*

Band Reunion, The   1984

Music-Performance
78369   87 mins   C   B, V   P
The Band is together again performing their
greatest hits at a concert taped in Vancouver,
Canada.
Jack McAndrew — *Music Media*

Bandits, The   1973

Western
47667   83 mins   C   B, V   P
*Robert Conrad, Jan Michael Vincent, Roy
Jenson*
Three cowboys team up with a band of Mexican
outlaws to fight a Mexican traitor.
Lone Star Pictures — *Unicorn Video*

Bandolero!   1968

Adventure
Closed Captioned
65412   106 mins   C   B, V   P
*James Stewart, Raquel Welch, Dean Martin,
George Kennedy, Will Geer, Andrew Prine*
In Texas, two fugitive brothers run into trouble
with their Mexican counterparts.
MPAA:PG
20th Century Fox — *Playhouse Video*

Band Wagon, The   1953
Musical
59136   112 mins   C   B, V   P
Fred Astaire, Cyd Charisse, Oscar Levant,
Nanette Fabray, Jack Buchanan, directed by
Vincente Minnelli
A Hollywood song-and-dance man finds trouble
when he is persuaded to star in a Broadway
musical. Songs by Howard Dietz and Arthur
Schwartz include "That's Entertainment," and
"Dancing in the Dark."
MGM;Arthur Freed — *MGM/UA Home Video*

Bang the Drum Slowly   1973
Drama
59390   97 mins   C   B, V, LV   P
Robert DeNiro, Michael Moriarty, Vincent
Gardenia, Phil Foster, Ann Wedgeworth,
Heather MacRae, Selma Diamond
The story of a major league catcher who suffers
from a fatal illness, and his friendship with a
quiet, senstive teammate.
NY Film Critics Awards '73: Best Supporting
Actor (DeNiro). MPAA:PG
Paramount — *Paramount Home Video*

Banjo the Woodpile Cat   1985
Fantasy
85903   27 mins   C   B, V   P
Animated
This children's film features a country cat who
visits the big city, encountering mishaps every
step of the way.
Children's Video Library — *Children's Video*
Library

Bank Dick, The   1940
Adventure/Comedy
69030   73 mins   B/W   B, V, LV   P
W.C. Fields, Cora Witherspoon, Una Richard
Purcell, Jack Norton
W.C. Fields wrote the screenplay and stars in
this comedy about a man who accidentally trips
a bank robber and winds up as a guard. Side
two of the laserdisc is in CAV format, which
allows single frame access to the frenetic cops
and robbers chase sequence.
Universal — *MCA Home Video*

Bank on the Stars   1954
Game show
42980   30 mins   B/W   B, V, FO   P
Bill Cullen
Contestants watch an action scene from a
newly released movie and then answer
questions based on what they've seen. Scenes
on this show are from "Apache," "Johnny
Dark," "Mr. Hulot's Holiday," and "The Caine
Mutiny."
NBC — *Video Yesteryear*

Barabbas   1961
Drama
64239   144 mins   C   B, V   P
Anthony Quinn, Silvana Mangano, Arthur
Kennedy, Jack Palance
Barabbas, a thief and murderer, is freed by
Pontius Pilate in place of Jesus, but he is
haunted by this event for the rest of his life.
Columbia; Dino de
Laurentiis — *RCA/Columbia Pictures Home*
Video

Barbra Streisand Putting   1986
it Together—The Making
of the Broadway Album
Music video/Documentary
84757   40 mins   C   B, V   P
Barbra Streisand
A behind-the-scenes look at the recording
sessions for Streisand's popular "Broadway
Album," showing her at work in the studio. The
tape also includes music videos of several
tracks from the album.
CBS/Fox — *CBS/Fox Video*

Barbara Woodhouse   1985
Goes to Beverly Hills
Pets
81701   52 mins   C   B, V   P
Barbara Woodhouse, Britt Ekland, David Soul,
William Shatner, Lorne Greene
The world-famous animal expert discovers why
Hollywood is going to the dogs as she visits top
celebrities and their canine pals.
Nigel Turner — *Pacific Arts Video*

Barbarella   1968
Fantasy
38615   98 mins   C   B, V, LV   P
Jane Fonda, John Phillip Law, David Hemmings,
directed by Roger Vadim
Based on the popular French sci-fi comic strip
drawn by Jean-Claude Forest, this popular film
stars Jane Fonda as a sexually emancipated
space woman who vanquishes evil robots and
monsters and rewards the many men she meets
in her travels.
MPAA:PG
Paramount — *Paramount Home Video; RCA*
VideoDiscs

Barbarian Queen   1985
Adventure
84087   71 mins   C   B, V, LV   P
Lana Clarkson, Frank Zagarino, Katt Shea,
directed by Hector Olivera
Female warriors seek revenge for the capturing
of their tribe's men in this sword and sorcery
epic available as well in an unrated version.
MPAA:R
New Horizons — *Worldvision Home Video*

Barbarosa   1982
Western
63398   90 mins   C   B, V, CED   P
Willie Nelson, Gilbert Roland, Gary Busey
Nelson stars as an aging, legendary outlaw
whose Mexican in-laws never succeed in killing.
He takes in a naive farmboy and teaches him his
survival skills to continue the legend.
MPAA:PG
ITC Entertainment — *CBS/Fox Video*

Barbary Coast   1935
Adventure
81625   90 mins   B/W   B, V, LV   P
Edward G. Robinson, Walter Brennan, Brian
Donleavy, Joel McCrea, Miriam Hopkins,
directed by Howard Hawks
A ruthless club owner tries to win the love of a
young girl by building her into a star attraction
during San Francisco's gold rush days.
Samuel Goldwyn — *Embassy Home
Entertainment*

Barber Shop, The   1933
Comedy
59401   21 mins   B/W   B, V   P, T
W.C. Fields, Elise Cavanna, Harry Watson,
Dagmar Oakland, Frank Yaconelli
Fields portrays the bumbling, carefree barber
Cornelius O'Hare, purveyor of village gossip and
solver of problems. Havoc begins when a
gangster enters the shop and demands that
Cornelius change his appearance.
Paramount — *Blackhawk Films*

Barcelona Kill, The   197?
Suspense
73147   86 mins   C   B, V   P
Linda Hayden, John Austin, Simon Andrew,
Maximo Valverde
When a journalist and her boyfriend get in too
deep with the Barcelona mob, their troubles
begin.
Michael Klinger Production — *VCL Home
Video*

Barefoot Contessa, The   1954
Drama
55584   128 mins   C   CED   P
Ava Gardner, Humphrey Bogart, Edmond
O'Brien
The story, told in flashback, of a girl's rise to
stardom and the loneliness she finds at the top.
Academy Awards '54: Best Supporting Actor
(O'Brien).
United Artists — *CBS/Fox Video*

Barefoot Executive, The   1971
Comedy
82029   92 mins   C   B, V   P
Kurt Russell, John Ritter, Harry Morgan, Wally
Cox, Heather North, directed by Robert Butler
A mailroom boy who works for a national
television network finds a chimpanzee that can
pick hit shows.
Walt Disney Productions — *Walt Disney Home
Video*

Barefoot in the Park   1967
Comedy
54675   105 mins   C   B, V, LV   P
Robert Redford, Jane Fonda, Charles Boyer,
Mildred Natwick, directed by Gene Saks
A newly wedded bride tries to get her husband
to loosen up and be as free spirited as she is.
Paramount, Hal Wallis — *Paramount Home
Video; RCA VideoDiscs*

Barn Burning   1980
Drama
82103   40 mins   C   B, V   P
Tommy Lee Jones, Diane Kagan, Shawn
Whittington, hosted by Henry Fonda
A tenant farmer's son is torn between
attempting to win his father's acceptance and
his aversion to the man's violent nature.
Available in VHS Stereo and Beta Hi-Fi.
Cal Skaggs — *Monterey Home Video*

Barney Bear Cartoon Festival   1948
Cartoons
88217   32 mins   C   B, V   P
Four Barney Bear adventures: "The Bear That
Couldn't Sleep," "The Bear and the Bean,"
"The Bear and the Hare" and "A Rainy Day."
MGM; Loew's Inc. — *MGM/UA Home Video*

Barney Oldfield's Race for a Life/Super-Hooper-Dyne Lizzies   19??
Comedy-Drama
60057   42 mins   B/W   B, V   P, T
Barney Oldfield, Mack Sennett, Mabel
Normand, Ford Sterling, Billy Bevan, Andy Clyde
In the first of two shorts on this tape from 1913,
Barney chases a villain who has abducted a
lovely girl. In the second film from 1925, radio-
controlled Model-T Fords co-star with comic
Billy Bevan.
Mack Sennett; Pathe — *Blackhawk Films*

Baron and the Kid, The   1984
Drama
Closed Captioned
81556   100 mins   C   B, V   P
Johnny Cash, Darren McGavin, June Carter
Cash, Richard Roundtree, directed by Gary
Nelson
A pool shark finds out that his opponent at a
charity exhibition game is his long-lost son.
Based upon Johnny Cash's song. Available in
VHS and Beta Hi-Fi.
Telecom Entertainment — *Playhouse Video*

Barry Gibb: Now Voyager   1984
Music-Performance/Music video
70558   79 mins   C   B, V   P
Barry Gibb, Michael Hordern
The prominent Mr. Gibb dives headlong into the conceptual video world with this unified production of nine songs. His exotic and musical travels with singers and dancers feature stereo sound on all formats.
Polygram Musicvideo — *MCA Home Video*

Barry Lyndon   1975
Drama
68232   184 mins   C   B, V   P
Ryan O'Neal, Marisa Berenson
Ryan O'Neal stars as an Irish scoundrel and gentleman in this film.
MPAA:PG
Warner Brothers — *Warner Home Video*

Barry Manilow Live at the Greek   1982
Music-Performance
72445   75 mins   C   LV   P
Pop star Barry Manilow thrills his audience in this live performance at the Greek Theater.
Marty Pasetta; Barry Manilow — *Pioneer Video Imports*

Barry McKenzie Holds His Own   1975
Comedy
77013   93 mins   C   B, V   P
Barry Humphries, Barry Crocker, Donald Pleasence, directed by Bruce Beresford
When a young man's aunt is mistaken for the Queen of England, two emissaries of Count Plasma of Transylvania kidnap her to use as a Plasma tourist attraction.
Satori Entertainment — *VidAmerica*

Baseball: Fun and Games   1980
Baseball
29231   60 mins   C   B, V   P
Features great baseball trivia quizzes and gives you another chance to see the close plays and make the calls.
Major League Baseball
Productions — *VidAmerica; RCA VideoDiscs*

Baseball: The Now Career   1975
Baseball
33830   26 mins   C   B, V   P
Chuck Connors, Nolan Ryan, Johnny Bench, Tug McGraw
Television star Chuck Connors, a former ballplayer, helps tell the story of the road to the major leagues, along with several of the game's stars.
Major League Baseball — *Major League Baseball Productions*

Baseball the Pete Rose Way   1986
Baseball
Closed Captioned
85621   60 mins   C   B, V, 8mm   P
Rose demonstrates the art of playing baseball, using a group of youngsters to demonstrate his lessons.
Embassy — *Embassy Home Entertainment*

Baseball the Yankee Way   1965
Baseball
88174   45 mins   C   B, V   P
Roger Maris, Mickey Mantle, Whitey Ford, Elston Howard, Al Downing
Footage of the '65 Yankees in training, as they each demonstrate their own batting, pitching or attitudinal finesse.
NY Yankees — *Rhino Video*

Baseball's Hall of Fame   1981
Baseball
51658   60 mins   C   B, V, CED   P
Hosted by Donald Sutherland
The most glorious moments in baseball history are relived through speeches and footage of some of baseball's greatest players, such as oldtimers Babe Ruth, Mel Ott, Ted Williams, and Bob Feller, and newer inductees such as Al Kaline, Mickey Mantle, Duke Snider, and Warren Spahn.
Major League Baseball — *VidAmerica*

Basic Art By Video I: Painting   1984
Painting
76968   120 mins   C   B, V   P
Instructor Charles Haddock teaches the basic techniques of painting.
Charles Haddock — *Mastervision*

Basic Art By Video II: Drawing & Design   1984
Drawing
76969   120 mins   C   B, V   P
Instructor Charles Haddock teaches the basic skills needed for drawing.
Charles Haddock — *Mastervision*

Basic Art By Video III: Color   1984
Painting
76970   120 mins   C   B, V   P
Instructor Charles Haddock demonstrates the color techniques used by painters from the Renaissance through modern times.
Charles Haddock — *Mastervision*

Basic Chords for Guitar   1985
Music/Education
70777   85 mins   C   B, V   P

Johnny Kay
This course provides the viewer with an
introduction to the seven basic chords in major,
minor and 7th keys.
K-Video — *K Video*

Basic English for   1985
Hispanics by Video
Languages-Instruction
76965   90 mins   C   B, V   P
An introductory course for Hispanics that
teaches the basics of the English language.
L Productions; Mastervision — *Mastervision*

Basic English Grammar   1983
by Video
Languages-Instruction
74489   90 mins   C   B, V   P
This tape is designed to teach the basic
fundamentals of English grammar.
Mastervision — *Mastervision*

Basic French by Video   1983
Languages-Instruction
74488   90 mins   C   B, V   P
This tape is designed to teach basic
conversational French.
Mastervision Inc — *Mastervision*

Basic Italian by Video   1983
Languages-Instruction
66205   90 mins   C   B, V   P
A basic, working vocabulary of Italian is taught
in this program.
Mastervision — *Mastervision*

Basic Spanish by Video   1983
Languages-Instruction
66204   90 mins   C   B, V   P
This program is designed to provide the viewer
with a working vocabulary of Spanish.
Mastervision — *Mastervision*

Basic Training   1986
Comedy
87215   85 mins   C   B, V   P
*Ann Dusenberry, Rhonda Shear, Angela
Aames, directed by Andrew Sugarman*
Three sexy ladies wiggle into the Pentagon in
their efforts to clean up the government.
The Movie Store — *Vestron Video*

Basket Case   1982
Horror
63891   89 mins   C   B, V   P
*Kevin Van Hentenryck, Terri Susan Smith,
Beverly Bonner*
A pair of Siamese twins, one deformed and one
normal, set out to avenge their surgical
separation.

Edgar Ievins — *Media Home Entertainment*

Basketball with Gail   1982
Goodrich
Basketball
60439   30 mins   C   B, V   P
Gail Goodrich
Two pros take the viewer through basic
shooting, free throws, jump shots, jumps from
the dribble and shots close to the basket. For
novice and advanced player alike.
MPAA:G
Unknown — *Embassy Home Entertainment*

Bass Tactics that Work   1984
Fishing
86867   30 mins   C   B, V   P
Larry Nixon
An instructional tape on bass fishing, including
tips on casting, water reading and bait use.
AM Available
Warburton Prod. — *Warburton Productions*

Bataan   1943
War-Drama
88211   115 mins   B/W   B, V   P
*Robert Taylor, George Murphy, Thomas
Mitchell, Desi Arnaz, Lloyd Nolan, Robert
Walker, directed by Tay Garnett*
A rugged war-time combat drama following a
small platoon in the Phillipines endeavoring to
blow up a pivotal Japanese bridge.
MGM; Loew's Inc. — *MGM/UA Home Video*

Batman   1967
Cartoons/Fantasy
81088   60 mins   C   B, V   P
Animated
The caped crusader and his faithful sidekick
Robin battle crime in Gotham City in this
collection of eight animated adventures.
Filmation — *Warner Home Video*

Batman   1966
Adventure
Closed Captioned
82334   104 mins   C   B, V   P
*Burt Ward, Adam West, Burgess Meredith,
Cesar Romero, Frank Gorshin, Lee Meriwether*
The caped crusaders battle The Penguin, The
Joker, The Riddler and The Catwoman who
threaten to take over the world with a secret
invention. Available in VHS and Beta Hi-Fi.
20th Century Fox — *Playhouse Video*

Battered   1979
Drama
82293   95 mins   C   B, V   P
*Karen Grassle, Mike Farrell, Le Var Burton, Chip
Fields, Joan Blondell, Howard Duff*
This is the tragic story of three couples whose
marriages are scarred by wife beating.

Henry Jaffe Enterprises — *Prism*

Battle Beneath the Earth   1968
Science fiction
75540   112 mins   C   B, V   P
Kerwin Mathews, Peter Arne
American scientists discover a Chinese plot to
invade the U.S. via a series of underground
tunnels.
MGM — *MGM/UA Home Video*

Battle Beyond the Stars   1980
Science fiction
66100   103 mins   C   B, V, CED   P
*Richard Thomas, Robert Vaughn, George
Peppard*
A variety of extraordinary aliens set out on an
intergalactic mission.
MPAA:PG
Orion Pictures — *Vestron Video*

Battle Cry   1955
War-Drama
47617   170 mins   C   B, V   P
*Van Heflin, Aldo Ray, Mona Freeman, Tab
Hunter, Dorothy Malone, Anne Francis*
A group of U.S. Marines train, romance, and
enter battle in World War II. Part of the "A Night
at the Movies" series, this tape simulates a
1955 movie evening, with a cartoon, "Speedy
Gonzales," a newsreel and coming attractions
for "Mr. Roberts" and "East of Eden."
Warner Bros — *Warner Home Video*

Battle for Cassino   1985
Documentary/World War II
82555   50 mins   C   B, V, 3/4U   P
*Narrated by Bernard Archard, directed by Peter
Batty*
This film deals with the controversy surrounding
the bombing by the Allies of the historic
Benedictine monastery atop Monte Cassino
Peter Batty — *Evergreen International*

Battle for Dien Bien Phu   1985
Documentary/Korean War
82554   50 mins   C   B, V, 3/4U   P
*Narrated by Bernard Archard, directed by Peter
Batty*
This war documentary traces the story of the
1954 siege at Dien Bien Phu by the Vietminh,
from France's colonization of Indo-China to the
end of the siege.
Peter Batty — *Evergreen International*

Battle for the Bulge   1985
Documentary/World War II
82553   50 mins   C   B, V, 3/4U   P
Directed by Peter Batty
This highly acclaimed war documentary
chronicles the last major German offensive of

World War II. It includes previously unreleased
footage from Germany.
Peter Batty — *Evergreen International*

Battle for the Falklands   1984
Great Britain/Documentary
75925   110 mins   C   B, V   P
This program documents the complete account
of the dramatic battle for the Falklands.
Thorn — *THORN EMI/HBO Video*

Battle for the Planet of   1973
the Apes
Science fiction
Closed Captioned
81544   96 mins   C   B, V   P
*Roddy McDowall, Lew Ayres, John Huston, Paul
Williams, directed by J. Lee Thompson*
A tribe of human atomic bomb mutations are out
to make life miserable for the peaceful ape tribe
in the year 2670 A.D.
MPAA:G
20th Century Fox — *Playhouse Video*

Battle for Warsaw   1985
Documentary/World War II
82556   50 mins   C   B, V, 3/4U   P
*Narrated by Bernard Archerd, directed by Peter
Batty*
This new documentary chronicles the 2-month
Warsaw uprising of 1944 and includes rare
archive material and interviews with the
survivors.
Peter Batty — *Evergreen International*

Battle Hell   1956
War-Drama
80938   112 mins   B/W   B, V   P
Richard Todd, Akim Tamiroff, Keye Luke
This film tells the true story of how a British ship
was attacked by the Chinese Peoples Liberation
Army on the Yangtze River in 1949.
Distributors Corp. of America — *VidAmerica*

Battle of Austerlitz   1960
Drama
79192   180 mins   C   B, V   P
*Orson Welles, Rossaro Brazzi, Jack Palance,
Claudia Cardinale, Vittorio de Sica*
An account of how Napoleon became Emperor
after winning a series of battles is presented in
this dramatization.
MPAA:PG
Michael Salkind; Alexander Salkind — *U.S.A.
Home Video*

Battle of Britain, The   1943
World War II/Documentary
50615   55 mins   B/W   B, V   P
Directed by Frank Capra

Britain stands alone in her "finest hour,"
through a tremendous Nazi air onslaught. Part
of the "Why We Fight" series.
US War Department — *MPI Home Video;
Hollywood Home Theater; Western Film &
Video Inc; Discount Video Tapes*

Battle of China, The 1944
Documentary/World War II
44993 67 mins B/W B, V P
Directed by Frank Capra
A look at the people, culture, and industry of
China, and Japan's total commitment to
conquer the country during World War II,
through authentic newsreel footage.
US War Department — *MPI Home Video;
Hollywood Home Theater; Western Film &
Video Inc; Discount Video Tapes*

Battle of Neretva 1970
Drama
65459 112 mins C B, V P
Yul Brynner, Curt Jurgens, Orson Welles
Yugoslav partisans are facing German and
Italian troops and local Chetniks as they battle
for freedom.
American International — *Republic Pictures
Home Video*

Battle of Russia, The 1944
Documentary/World War II
44994 83 mins B/W B, V P
Directed by Frank Capra
Hitler's forces are victorious in Moscow and
Leningrad but are thoroughly defeated at the
battle of Stalingrad. Authentic newsreel footage.
US War Department — *Hollywood Home
Theater; Blackhawk Films; Western Film &
Video Inc; MPI Home Video; Discount Video
Tapes*

Battle of the Bombs 1985
Movie and TV trailers/Exploitation
84353 60 mins C B, V P
A collection of excerpts from the worst films of
all time.
Impulse Ent — *Rhino Video*

Battle of the Bulge, The 1965
War-Drama
73012 141 mins C B, V P
*Henry Fonda, Robert Shaw, Robert Ryan, Dana
Andrews, Pier Angeli*
A recreation of the famous offensive by Nazi
Panzer troops on the Belgian front during 1944-
45, an assault that could have changed the
course of World War Two.
Sidney Harmon; Warner Bros — *Warner Home
Video*

Battle of the Commandos 1971
War-Drama
81420 94 mins C B, V P
*Jack Palance, Curt Jurgens, Thomas Hunter,
Robert Hunter*
A tough Army colonel leads a group of convicts
on a dangerous mission to destroy a German
built cannon before it's used against the Allied
Forces.
Commonwealth United — *Republic Pictures
Home Video*

Battle of the Last Panzer, 1980
The
War-Drama
77393 90 mins C B, V P
Guy Madison, Stan Cooper
A beautiful French girl and a German
commander swap excess passion while trapped
behind Allied lines during World War II.
MPAA:R
Prodimex; Hispaner Film — *Wizard Video*

Battle of Valiant 1963
Adventure
70786 90 mins C B, V P
*Gordon Mitchell, Ursula Davis, Max Serato,
directed by John Gentil*
Thundering hordes of invading barbarians
trample the splendor of ancient Rome beneath
their grimy sandals.
Empire — *Force Video*

Battle Shock 1956
Mystery/Drama
76831 88 mins C B, V P
Ralph Meeker, Janice Rule, Paul Henried
A painter on a honeymoon with his wife in
Mexico is accused of murdering a cantina
waitress.
Republic Pictures — *Republic Pictures Home
Video*

Battlestar Galactica 1978
Science fiction
14066 125 mins C B, V, LV P
*Lorne Greene, Richard Hatch, Dirk Benedict,
Ray Milland, directed by Richard A Colla*
A spaceship tries a desperate attempt to reach
the ancient planet called Earth. Spectacular
special effects. A movie made for television.
MPAA:PG
Glen Larson — *MCA Home Video*

Battlestar Galactica 1979
Science fiction
82364 47 mins C B, V P
*Lorne Greene, Richard Hatch, Dirk Benedict,
Maren Jensen, Noah Hathaway* 8 pgms
Join the crew of the Battlestar Galactica as they
battle the Cylons in their quest to find Earth.
Each episode is available individually.

1.The Long Patrol 2.The Young Lords 3.The Lost Warrior 4.The Magnificent Warriors 5.The Man With Nine Lives 6.Fire in Space 7.Murder on Rising Star 8.Baltar's Escape
Universal Television — MCA Home Video

Battling Bunyan   1924
Drama
85495   71 mins   B/W   B, V   P
Chester Conklin, Wesley Barry, Molly Malone, Jackie Fields
A wily youngster becomes a comedy boxer for profit, and eventually gets fed up and battles the champ. Silent.
Arthur S. Kane — Video Yesteryear

Batty World of Baseball, The   1982
Baseball
59381   ? mins   C   B, V   P
A humorous look at the personalities who make the game interesting: managers like John McGraw, Leo Durocher, Casey Stengel, and Billy Martin, and a rarely-seen side of Babe Ruth.
Major League Baseball Prods — RCA/Columbia Pictures Home Video

---

Bauhaus: Live at the University of London   198?
Music-Performance
84052   60 mins   C   B, V   P
Bauhaus, Chrome
A tape of live performance by the English punk band Bauhaus, and the San Francisco punk group Chrome.
Target Video — Target Video

Bayadere, La   197?
Dance
87351   126 mins   C   B, V   P
Gabriella Komleva, Tatiana Terekhova, Rejen Abdeyev
A performance of the famous 'temple dance' by the Kirov Ballet, taped at the Kirov Theatre.
Kirov Theatre — Kultur

Bayou Romance   1986
Romance/Drama
71239   90 mins   C   V   P
Introduced by Louis Jourdan
A painter inherits a Louisiana plantation, moves in, and falls in love with a young gypsy.
Commworld; Romance Theater — Prism

B.B. King Live At Nick's   1983
Music-Performance
84487   60 mins   C   B, V   P
The great blues artist performs his greatest hits at Nick's in Dallas, Texas.
Uptown/Ten Prods — Sony Video Software

B.C. The First Thanksgiving   1984
Cartoons/Holidays
78349   25 mins   C   B, V   P
Animated
The caveman B.C. and his friends are trying to find a turkey to flavor their rock soup in this animated featurette.
King Features — Embassy Home Entertainment

Be My Valentine, Charlie Brown/Is This Goodbye, Charlie Brown   1983
Cartoons
76847   50 mins   C   B, V   P
Animated
Here are two Peanuts specials: In "Be My Valentine, Charlie Brown," Charlie waits by his mailbox hoping for a valentine and in "Is This Goodbye, Charlie Brown," Linus and Lucy are moving because of their father's job transfer to another city.
Lee Mendelson; Bill Melendez — Snoopy's Home Video Library

Beach Blanket Bingo   1965
Comedy/Musical
81828   96 mins   C   B, V   P
Frankie Avalon, Annette Funicello, Linda Evans, Don Rickles, Buster Keaton, Paul Lynde, Harvey Lembeck, directed by William Asher
A gang of teenagers who are fascinated by skydiving become involved in a kidnapping plot.
MPAA:G
American International Pictures — THORN EMI/HBO Video

Beach Boys: An American Band, The   1985
Documentary/Music-Performance
80684   103 mins   C   B, V, LV   P
Brian Wilson, Carl Wilson, Dennis Wilson, Mike Love, Al Jardine, Bruce Johnson, directed by Malcolm Leo
This film takes an in-depth look at the lives and music of the Beach Boys with a soundtrack that features over forty of their songs.
MPAA:PG-13
High Ridge Productions — Vestron Video

Beach Girls, The   1982
Comedy
64030   91 mins   C   B, V, LV   P
Debra Blee, Val Kline, Jeana Tomasina
Three voluptuous coeds intend to re-educate a bookish young man and the owner of a beach house.
MPAA:R
Crown International Pictures — Paramount Home Video; RCA VideoDiscs

---

(For explanation of codes, see Use Guide and Key)

Beach House   1982
Comedy
66187   89 mins   C   B, V   P
Adolescents frolic on the beach, get inebriated
and listen to rock 'n' roll.
Unknown — *THORN EMI/HBO Video*

Beach Party   1963
Comedy/Musical
64892   101 mins   C   CED   P
*Frankie Avalon, Annette Funicello, Bob
Cummings*
A scientist studying the mating habits of
teenagers intrudes on a group of surfers, beach
bums and motorcyclists.
American International Pictures — *Warner
Home Video; Vestron Video (disc only)*

Beachcomber, The   1939
Drama
12401   88 mins   B/W   B, V   P
*Charles Laughton, Elsa Lanchester, Robert
Newton, Tyrone Guthrie*
Beachcomber falls in love with missionary's
prim sister when plague breaks out. Story by W.
Somerset Maugham.
Mayfair — *Discount Video Tapes; Kartes Video
Communications*

Beany and Cecil   196?
Cartoons
Closed Captioned
72922   60 mins   C   B, V   P
Animated
The lovable little boy Beany joins his pal Cecil
the Seasick Sea-Serpent in this series of
adventures. Each tape includes six or seven
programs.
Bob Clampett — *RCA/Columbia Pictures
Home Video*

Beany & Cecil, Volume VII   196?
Cartoons
Closed Captioned
77372   60 mins   C   B, V   P
Animated
Join Beany, Cecil and Captain Huffenpuff as
they board the Leakin' Lena for seven animated
adventures.
Bob Clampett — *RCA/Columbia Pictures
Home Video*

Bear Island   1980
Adventure
77358   102 mins   C   B, V   P
*Donald Sutherland, Richard Widmark, Barbara
Parkins, Vanessa Redgrave, Christopher Lee,
Lloyd Bridges*
A group of secret agents disguising themselves
as U.N. weather researchers, converge upon
Bear Island in search of a Nazi U-Boat.

MPAA:PG
Taft International Pictures — *Media Home
Entertainment*

Bear Who Slept Through   1983
Christmas, The
Christmas
65161   60 mins   C   B, V   P
*Animated, voices of Tommy Smothers, Arte
Johnson, Barbara Feldon, Kelly Lange*
As Christmas approaches, all the bears are
getting ready to go to sleep for the winter,
except Ted E. Bear, who wants to see just what
Christmas is.
Dimenmark International — *Family Home
Entertainment*

Bears and I, The   1975
Adventure
56874   88 mins   C   CED   P
*Patrick Wayne, Chief Dan George, Andrew
Duggan, Michael Ansara*
A young war veteran in search of himself heads
for the wilderness, befriends a trio of orphaned
bears, and helps an Indian tribe in their struggle
to retain their rights.
MPAA:G
Walt Disney — *RCA VideoDiscs*

Beast, The   1975
Horror
58555   82 mins   C   B, V   P
Edward Connell, Barbara Hewitt
Two teenagers are menaced by a gigantic
mutant ape after discovering a devil-
worshipping cult.
MPAA:PG
Tonlyn; Jack Harris — *Wizard Video*

Beast Must Die, The   1975
Horror
55563   93 mins   C   B, V, 3/4U   P
Peter Cushing, Calvin Lockhart
A millionaire sportsman invites a group of men
and women connected with bizarre deaths or
the eating of human flesh to spend the cycle of
a full moon at his isolated lodge.
MPAA:PG
Cinerama Releasing; Max
Rosenberg — *Nostalgia Merchant; Prism*

Beast of I.R.S. Volume I,   1984
The
Music video
72864   40 mins   C   B, V   P
Some of I.R.S. artists' best video clips are
featured. The Alarm and the Go-Go's are
included.
International Record Syndicate Video — *IRS
Records*

Beast of the Yellow Night ·   1972
Horror
84815   87 mins   C   B, V   P
John Ashley, Mary Wilcox
A pervert makes a deal with the devil and kills
many people horribly.
MPAA:R
Eddie Romero — *United Home Video*

Beast Within, The   1982
Horror
64568   98 mins   C   B, V, CED   P
*Ronny Cox, Bibi Besch, Paul Clemens, Don
Gordon*
A young woman is raped by an unseen creature
in a Mississippi swamp. Seventeen years later,
her son begins to act strangely, forcing a return
to the rape scene. In stereo.
MPAA:R
MGM/UA — *MGM/UA Home Video*

Beastmaster, The   1982
Adventure
68239   119 mins   C   B, V, CED   P
Marc Singer, Tanya Roberts, and Rip Torn
This adventure film is set in a wild and primitive
world. The Beastmaster is involved in a life and
death struggle with overwhelming forces of evil.
In stereo.
MPAA:PG
MGM/UA — *MGM/UA Home Video*

Beasts   1983
Adventure/Drama
80892   92 mins   C   B, V   P
Tom Babson, Kathy Christopher, Vern Potter
A young couple's plans for a romantic weekend
in the Rockies are slightly changed when the
pair are savagely attacked by wild beasts.
American National Enterprises — *Prism*

Beat Goes On, The   1981
Football
51168   23 mins   C   B, V, FO   R, P
Houston Oilers
Coach Bum Phillips predicted 1980 would be
the year that his team 'broke down the door' to
the Super Bowl. Instead, at season's end, he
was shown the door. However, when Oiler stars
such as Ken Stabler and Earl Campbell were
good, there were few better.
NFL Films — *NFL Films Video*

Beat of the Live Drum, The   1985
Music video/Music-Performance
80881   75 mins   C   B, V   P
Rick Springfield
Guitarist/singer/songwriter Rick Springfield
performs such hits as "Jessie's Girl", "Affair of
the Heart" and "Love Somebody" in this
concert taped in Tuscon, Arizona. This tape also
features three conceptual music videos from his
"Tao" LP.
Z Street Films; Famous Dog
Productions — *RCA/Columbia Pictures Home
Video*

Beat Street   1984
Musical
70151   106 mins   C   B, V   P
This quasi-documentary about break dancing
features the music of Ruben Blades, Afrika
Bambaata and the Soul Sonic Force, and Grand
Master Melle Mel and the Furious Five.
MPAA:PG
Harry Belafonte; David Picker;
Orion — *Vestron Video*

Beat the Devil   1953
Drama/Comedy
Closed Captioned
71117   89 mins   C   B, V   P
*Humphrey Bogart, Gina Lollabrigida, Peter
Lorre, Robert Morley, Jennifer Jones, directed
by John Huston*
Each person on a slow boat to Africa has a
scheme to beat the other passengers to the
uranium-rich land that they all hope to claim. An
unusual black comedy.
Columbia — *RCA/Columbia Pictures Home
Video*

Beat the Odds   1969
Game show
85144   22 mins   B/W   B, V   P
Warren Hull
A typical word game show complete with a bad-
luck 'Mr. Whammie'and standard prizes. Taped
in Los Angeles.
KTLA — *Video Yesteryear*

Beatlemania—The Movie   1983
Music-Performance
65445   60 mins   C   B, V   P
This program pictorially and musically reflects
the tumultuous events of the 60's, featuring 30
of the greatest songs of John Lennon and Paul
McCartney. In stereo VHS and Beta Hi-Fi. Not
the Beatles, but an incredible simulation.
Edie and Ely Landau — *U.S.A. Home Video*

Beatles—Comedy Featurettes   1984
Movie and TV trailers/Comedy
66484   57 mins   C   B, V   P
Behind the scenes glimpses of the making of
seven comedy films are combined in this
package: "The Owl and the Pussycat," "Cold
Turkey," "Return of the Pink Panther," "A Hard
Day's Night," "Yellow Submarine" and "A
Funny Thing Happened..."
Walter Shenson et al — *San Francisco Rush
Video*

Beatles Live, The   1985
Music-Performance
82009   20 mins   B/W   B, V   P
*John Lennon, Paul McCartney, Ringo Starr,
George Harrison*
The Fab Four perform "Twist and Shout" "Roll
Over Beethoven" and nine other songs in this
compilation of clips from the "Ready Steady
Go" series. Available in VHS and Beta Hi-Fi
Stereo.
Dave Clark Limited; EMI Records — *Sony
Video Software*

Beau Mariage, Le   1982
Romance/Comedy
85597   100 mins   C   B, V   P
*Beatrice Romand, Arielle Dombasle, Andre
Dussollier, directed by Eric Rohmer*
An award-winning comedy from the great
French director about a girl trying to find a
husband. In French with English subtitles.
Venice Film Festival '82: Best Actress
(Romand). MPAA:R FR
French — *Media Home Entertainment*

Beau Pere   198?
Comedy
82490   125 mins   C   B, V   P
*Patrick Dewaere, Nathalie Baye, directed by
Bertrand Bier*
A film about the romance between a thirty-year
old man and his precocious 14-year old
stepdaughter. French dialogue.
FR
Foreign — *Media Home Entertainment*

Beautifull The Total Look   1985
Nutrition/Physical fitness
70767   60 mins   C   B, V   P
Beverly Sassoon
This video reference guide for feminine beauty
offers seven chapters of information: color
analysis, make-up, fashion, hair, skin, nutrition
and exercise.
Moving Targets, Inc. — *Video Associates*

Beauty and the Beast   1984
Fairy tales
Closed Captioned
73851   60 mins   C   B, V, LV,   P
                                        CED
*Susan Sarandon, Klaus Kinski, directed by
Roger Vadim*
From "Faerie Tale Theatre" comes the story of
a Beauty who befriends a Beast and learns a
lesson about physical ugliness.
Gaylord Productions; Platypus
Productions — *CBS/Fox Video*

Beauty and the Beast   1946
Drama/Romance
82570   90 mins   B/W   B, V, LV   P
*Jean Marais, Josette Day, directed by Jean
Cocteau*
This ethereal romantic drama brings to life the
classic fable of the ugly but gentle Beast and
the Beauty who is forced to live with him.
Jean Cocteau — *Embassy Home
Entertainment*

Because of the Cats   1975
Horror
70600   90 mins   C   B, V   P
*Bryan Marshall, Alexandra Stewart, Sylvia
Kristel, Sebastian Graham Jones, directed by
Fons Rademakers*
A police inspector uncovers an evil cult within
his seaside village while investigating a bizarre
rape/burglary.
American Transcontinental Pictures — *Prism*

Becket   1964
Drama
51574   148 mins   C   B, V   P
Richard Burton, Peter O'Toole, John Gielgud
A drama dealing with 12th century friendship
between Becket and the King of England,
Becket's appointment as Archbishop of
Canterbury, and the furor which arises when he
takes his position too seriously.
Academy Awards '64: Best Screenplay (Edward
Anhalt).
Paramount; Hal Wallis — *MPI Home Video;
United Home Video*

Becky Sharp   1935
Drama
81726   83 mins   C   B, V   P
*Miriam Hopkins, Frances Dee, Sir Cedric
Hardwicke, Billie Burke, Pat Nixon, directed by
Rouben Mamoulian*
This premiere Technicolor film tells the story of
Becky Sharp, a wicked woman who finally
performs one good deed.
RKO — *Kartes Video Communications; Movie
Buff Video; Discount Video Tapes*

Bedazzled   1968
Comedy
58951   107 mins   C   B, V   P
*Dudley Moore, Peter Cook, Eleanor Bron,
Michael Bates, Raquel Welch, directed by
Stanley Donen*
A short-order cook is saved from suicide by a
man who offers him seven wishes in exchange
for his soul.
EL, SP
20th Century Fox — *CBS/Fox Video*

Bedford Incident, The   1965
Adventure
44787   102 mins   B/W   B, V   P
*Richard Widmark, Sidney Poitier, James
MacArthur, Martin Balsam, Wally Cox*

The U.S.S. Bedford discovers an unidentified submarine in North Atlantic waters. The Bedford's commander drives his crew to the point of nerve-taut exhaustion when they find themselves the center of a fateful controversy. James B Harris, Richard Widmark, Columbia — *RCA/Columbia Pictures Home Video*

Bedknobs and Broomsticks   1971
Fantasy
44298   117 mins   C   B, V   P
Angela Lansbury, David Tomlinson, Sam Jaffe, Roddy McDowall
In 1940, three abandoned children and a kindly witch ride a magic bedstead and repel the invasion of England.
MPAA:G
Walt Disney — *Walt Disney Home Video*

Bedknobs and Broomsticks   1971
Fantasy/Musical
81672   112 mins   C   B, V   P
Angela Lansbury, Roddy McDowell, David Tomlinson, Bruce Forsyth, directed by Robert Stevenson
A novice witch and three cockney waifs join forces to stop the Nazis from invading England during World War II.
Academy Awards '71: Best Visual Effects.
MPAA:G
Walt Disney Productions — *Walt Disney Home Video*

Bedlam   1945
Horror
00317   79 mins   B/W   B, V, 3/4U   P
Boris Karloff, Anna Lee, Richard Fraser
Horror melodrama of a seventeenth century insane asylum and a sane female reformer.
RKO — *Nostalgia Merchant*

Bedtime for Bonzo   1951
Comedy
56872   83 mins   B/W   B, V   P
Ronald Reagan, Diana Lynn, Walter Slezak, Jesse White, Bonzo the Chimp, directed by Fred deCordova
A professor adopts a chimp to prove that environment determines a child's future, disproving the Dean's theory that his children-to-be might inherit criminal tendencies because his father was a crook.
Universal — *MCA Home Video*

Beer   1985
Comedy
88160   83 mins   C   B, V   P
Loretta Swit, Rip Torn, Dick Shawn, David Alan Grier, Kenneth Mars

A female advertising executive devises a dangerous sexist campaign for a cheap beer, and both the beer and its nickname become nationwide obsessions.
MPAA:R
Orion Pictures — *THORN EMI/HBO Video*

Bees, The   1978
Drama
53506   93 mins   C   B, V   P
John Saxon, John Carradine, Angel Tompkins
A strain of bees have ransacked South America and are threatening the rest of the world.
MPAA:PG
New World; Bee One Panorama Films — *Warner Home Video*

Beethoven/Schumann/Brahms   1985
Music-Performance
88128   55 mins   C   B, V   P
An orchestral concert featuring short works by the three composers.
Sony Video — *Sony Video Software*

Before I Hang   1940
Horror/Mystery
78965   60 mins   B/W   B, V   P
Boris Karloff, Evelyn Keyes, Bruce Bennett, Edward Van Sloan
When a doctor invents a youth serum from the blood of a murderer, he'll stop at nothing to keep his secret. In Beta Hi-Fi.
Columbia Pictures — *RCA/Columbia Pictures Home Video*

Beginner's Luck   1984
Comedy
86608   85 mins   C   B, V   P
Sam Rush, Riley Steiner, Charles Homet, Kate Talbot
A young man convinces his neighbors to engage in swinging activities, leading to predictable and raunchy situations.
MPAA:R
Frank & Caroline Mouris — *New World Video*

Beginning Four Harness Weaving   1985
Handicraft
85652   86 mins   C   B, V   P
Deborah Chandler
For ultimate beginners, the essentials of four-harness loom weaving are demonstrated.
Victorian Video Prod. — *Victorian Video Productions*

Beguiled, The   1970
War-Drama
64797   109 mins   C   B, V   P
Clint Eastwood, Geraldine Page, Elizabeth Hartman, directed by Donald Siegel

A wounded Union soldier is taken in by the women at a girl's school in the South. He manages to seduce both a student and a teacher, and jealousy and revenge ensue.
MPAA:R
Universal — *MCA Home Video*

Behave Yourself!   1952
Comedy
84812   81 mins   B/W   B, V   P
Shelley Winters, Farley Granger, William Demarest, Lon Chaney Jr., directed by George Beck
A married couple adopts a dog who may be the key for a million-dollar hijacking set up by a gang of hoodlums.
RKO; Jerry Wald; Norman Krasna — *United Home Video*

Behind the Rising Sun   1943
War-Drama
82181   88 mins   B/W   B, V   P
Tom Neal, J. Carrol Naish, Robert Ryan, Mike Mazurki, directed by Edward Dmytryk
A Japanese father is in for a big surprise when his son returns home after graduating from an American college during the 1930's.
RKO — *RKO HomeVideo*

Behind the Screen   1916
Comedy
10644   20 mins   B/W   B, V, 3/4U   R, P, DL
Charlie Chaplin
Chaplin starts out as a property man on a movie set and winds up in a pie-throwing sequence.
(Silent; musical soundtrack added.)
RKO — *Cable Films; Festival Films*

Behind Your Radio Dial   1948
Mass media/Documentary
12844   45 mins   B/W   B, V, FO   P
An early TV show which gives the viewer an entertaining glimpse of NBC radio and many of its stars.
NBC — *Video Yesteryear*

Behold a Pale Horse   1964
Drama
66015   118 mins   B/W   B, V   P
Gregory Peck, Anthony Quinn, Omar Sharif, Mildred Dunnock, directed by Fred Zinneman
A post-Spanish Civil War tale concerning an ideological battle between a guerilla leader and a cruel police captain.
Columbia — *RCA/Columbia Pictures Home Video*

Behold the Man!   1950
Religion
85145   66 mins   B/W   B, V   P

The Gospels are narrated over a performance of the final days of Jesus, with all the high points.
Unknown — *Video Yesteryear*

Being, The   1983
Horror
73022   82 mins   C   B, V   P
Ruth Buzzi, Martin Landau, Jose Ferrer
People in Idaho are terrorized by a freak who became abnormal after radiation was disposed in the local dump.
William Osco — *THORN EMI/HBO Video*

Being Different   1985
Documentary
82471   102 mins   C   B, V   P
Narrated by Christopher Plummer, directed by Harry Rasky
A docu-drama of deformed men and women who have learned to live their lives to the fullest.
Independent — *Vestron Video*

Being There   1979
Comedy
54838   126 mins   C   B, V, CED   P
Peter Sellers, Shirley MacLaine, Melvyn Douglas, directed by Hal Ashby
A feeble-minded gardener whose entire knowledge of life comes from watching television is sent out into the real world when his employer dies. Equipped with his prize possession, his remote control unit, the gardener encounters a series of hilarious events.
Academy Awards '79: Best Supporting Actor (Douglas). MPAA:PG
Lorimar Prods, Andrew Braunsberg
Prod — *CBS/Fox Video*

Belafonte Presents   1975
Fincho
Africa/Documentary
58580   79 mins   C   B, V   P
Hosted by Harry Belafonte, directed by Sarn Zebba
A docudrama shot in Nigeria concerning the problems a jungle village faces when suddenly brought into the 20th Century.
Rohauer Films — *Mastervision*

Belfast Assassin, The   1984
Drama
80326   130 mins   C   B, V   P
Derek Thompson, Ray Lonnen
A British anti-terrorist agent goes undercover to find an IRA assassin who shot a British cabinet minister.
Independent — *Prism*

Bell, Book and Candle   1959
Comedy
35378   103 mins   C   B, V   P
James Stewart, Kim Novak, Jack Lemmon, Elsa
Lanchester, Ernie Kovacs, Hermione Gingold
A young witch makes up her mind to refrain from
using her powers. When an interesting man
moves into her building, she forgets her decision
and enchants him with a love spell.
Columbia — RCA/Columbia Pictures Home
Video

Bell from Hell, A   1974
Mystery
84070   80 mins   C   B, V   P
Viveca Lindfors, Renaud Verley, Alfredo Mayo,
directed by Claudio Guerin Hill
A tale of insanity and revenge, wherein a young
man, institutionalized since his mother's death,
plots to kill his aunt and three cousins.
EL, SP
Santiago Moncada Productions — Unicorn
Video

Bell Jar, The   1979
Drama
65474   113 mins   C   B, V   P
Marilyn Hasset, Julie Harris, Barbara Barrie,
Anne Bancroft
Based on poet Sylvia Plath's acclaimed semi-
autobiographical novel, this is the story of a
young woman who becomes the victim of
mental illness.
MPAA:R
Avco Embassy — Vestron Video

Bellboy, The   1960
Comedy
81811   72 mins   B/W   B, V   P
Jerry Lewis, Alex Corry, Bob Clayton, Milton
Berle, directed by Jerry Lewis
A bumbling bellboy turns a plush Miami hotel
upside down as he misplaces room keys and
fouls up calls. Available in VHS Stereo and Beta
Hi-Fi.
Paramount Pictures; Jerry Lewis — U.S.A.
Home Video

Belles of St. Trinian's,   1953
The
Comedy
66020   86 mins   B/W   B, V   P
Alastair Sim
Alastair Sim is superb in a dual role as the prim
headmistress of a private girls school and her
slick bookmaker brother.
Lauder Gillist Productions — THORN
EMI/HBO Video

Bellhop/The Noon   1922
Whistle, The
Comedy
84933   46 mins   B/W   B, V
Stan Laurel, Oliver Hardy
Two comedic shorts back to back featuring the
famous comics separately.
Hal Roach — Blackhawk Films

Bells, The   1926
Drama
69563   92 mins   B/W   B, V, FO   P
Lionel Barrymore, Boris Karloff
The Burgomeister of an Alsatian village kills a
wealthy merchant and steals his money. The
murderer experiences pangs of guilt which are
accentuated when a traveling mesmerist comes
to town who claims to be able to discern a
person's darkest secrets. Silent with music
score.
Independent — Video Yesteryear

Bells Are Ringing   1960
Musical/Comedy
58294   126 mins   C   B, V   P
Judy Holliday, Dean Martin, Fred Clark, Eddie
Foy Jr., Jean Stapleton, directed by Vincente
Minnelli
A girl who works for a telephone answering
service can't help but take an interest in the
lives of the clients, especially a playwright with
an inferiority complex. Based on Adolph Green
and Betty Comden's Broadway musical.
MGM — MGM/UA Home Video

Bells of Rosarita   1945
Western
07055   54 mins   B/W   B, V   P
Roy Rogers, Dale Evans, Gabby Hayes
Roy helps to foil a play by crooks to swindle a
girl out of the ranch her father left her.
Republic — Video Connection; Discount Video
Tapes; Cable Films

Bells of St. Mary's, The   1945
Drama
47989   126 mins   B/W   B, V   P
Bing Crosby, Ingrid Bergman, Henry Travers,
directed by Leo McCarey
An easy-going priest finds himself in a subtle
battle of wits with the Sister Superior over how
the children of St. Mary's school should be
raised. Songs include the title tune and "Aren't
You Glad You're You?"
Academy Awards '45: Best Sound. NY Film
Critics Award '45: Best Female Performance
(Bergman).
RKO — Republic Pictures Home Video

Belly Dance for Fitness   1984
and Fun
Physical fitness
65696   28 mins   C   B, V, 3/4U   P
3   pgms
Narrated by Alicia Dhanifu, this program will
teach proper posture and hip movements,
snake arm-arched bends, Egyptian head slides

and costuming, the basic repertoire of the belly dancer.
AM Available
A. Dhanifu Productions — *A M Productions Home Video*

Below the Belt   1980
Drama
63330   92 mins   C   B, V   P
Regina Baff, Mildred Burke, John C. Becher
A street-smart woman from New York City becomes part of the blue-collar "circus" of lady wrestling.
MPAA:R
Aberdeen/RLF/Tom-Mi
Productions — *THORN EMI/HBO Video*

Belstone Fox, The   1973
Adventure
59828   103 mins   C   B, V   P
Eric Porter, Rachel Roberts, Jeremy Kemp
An orphaned fox goes into hiding, and is hunted by the hound he has befriended and his former owner.
Julian Wintle — *Embassy Home Entertainment*

Ben   1972
Horror
71203   95 mins   C   B, V   P
Joseph Campanella, Lee Harcourt Montgomery, Arthur O'Connell, Rosemary Murphy, Meredith Baxter, directed by Phil Karlson
This sequel to "Willard" find police Detective Kirtland on the hunt for a killer rat pack led by Ben, king of the rodents. The title song was a number 1 pop hit by Michael Jackson.
MPAA:PG
Cinerama; BCP Productions — *Prism*

Ben Hur   1959
Drama
44648   217 mins   C   B, V, CED   P
Charlton Heston, Jack Hawkins, Stephen Boyd, Hugh Griffith, Sam Jaffe, directed by William Wyler
Jewish nobleman Ben Hur struggles against Roman tyranny in first-century Palestine. Winner of ten Academy Awards.
Academy Awards '59: Best Picture; Best Actor (Heston); Best Supporting Actor (Griffith); Best Director (Wyler).
MGM — *MGM/UA Home Video*

Ben Turpin Rides Again   1923
Comedy
42948   45 mins   B/W   B, V, FO   P
Ben Turpin   3   pgms
Ben Turpin, the cross-eyed wonder, stars in three shorts by Mack Sennett.
1. The Daredevil 2. Yukon Jake 3. The Eyes Have It
Mack Sennett — *Video Yesteryear*

Bend of the River   1952
Western
84020   91 mins   C   B, V   P
James Stewart, Arthur Kennedy, Rock Hudson
A haunted, hardened guide leads a wagon train through Oregon territory, pitting himself against Indians, the wilderness and a former comrade-turned-hijacker.
Aaron Rosenberg — *MCA Home Video*

Beneath the Planet of the Apes   1970
Science fiction
Closed Captioned
81541   95 mins   C   B, V   P
Charlton Heston, James Franciscus, Kim Hunter, Maurice Evans, Victor Buono, directed by Ted Post
An astronaut discovers an underground society of mutated aliens when he is sent to New York to find a fellow astronaut believed to be lost in the rubble of an atomic blast.
MPAA:G
Apjac Productions, 20th Century Fox — *Playhouse Video*

Beneath the 12-Mile Reef   1953
Adventure
80058   102 mins   C   B, V   P
Robert Wagner, Terry Moore, Gilbert Roland, Richard Boone, Peter Graves, J. Carrol Naish
Two rival groups of divers are competing for sponge beds off the Florida coast.
20th Century Fox — *World Video Pictures; Video Gems; Discount Video Tapes; Hal Roach Studios*

Benji   1973
Comedy-Drama
49626   87 mins   C   B, V   P
Benji, Peter Brek, Christopher Connelly, Patsy Garrett, Deborah Walley, Cynthia Smith, directed by Joe Camp
In the loveable pooch's first feature-length movie, he falls in love with a female named Tiffany, and saves Paul and Cindy from the danger of sinister intruders.
MPAA:G
Mulberry Square Prods; Joe Camp — *Vestron Video; CBS/Fox Video (disc only)*

Benji Takes a Dive at Marineland/Benji at Work   1982
Animals
72230   60 mins   C   B, V   P
Television's Adam Rich goes to Marineland with Wonder-dog Benji, and chronicles the canine's busy work schedule.
Carolyn Camp — *Children's Video Library*

Benji's Very Own Christmas Story   1983
Fantasy/Christmas
69532   60 mins   C   B, V   P
Benji and his friends go on a magic trip and
meet Kris Kringle and learn how Christmas is
celebrated around the world. Also included:
"The Phenomenon of Benji," a documentary
about Benji's odyssey from the animal shelter to
international stardom.
Mulberry Square Productions — *Children's
Video Library*

Benny Carter   1982
Music-Performance
88121   57 mins   C   B, V, 8mm   P
The archetypal jazz saxophonist, mentor to
Miles Davis and Charlie Parker, performs "A
Train," "Honeysuckle Rose" and "Autumn
Leaves."
Adler Ent.; Clark Santee; Delia Gravel
Santee — *Sony Video Software*

Berenstain Bears' Comic Valentine, The   1982
Cartoons
65418   25 mins   C   B, V   P
Animated
The whole Berenstain Bear family gets in on the
fun when Brother Bear receives a mysterious
Valentine from Miss Honey Bear, a secret
admirer; but can he keep his mind on the
upcoming Valentine's Day Championship
Hockey Game against the Beartown Bullies?
Buzz Potamkin — *Embassy Home
Entertainment*

Berenstain Bears' Easter Surprise, The   1981
Cartoons
65437   25 mins   C   B, V   P
Animated
Boss Bunny, who usually controls the seasons,
has quit, Poppa Bear's vainglorious effort to
construct his own Easter egg machine is a
failure; and Brother Bear anxiously awaits his
"Extra Special" Easter Surprise.
Buzz Potamkin — *Embassy Home
Entertainment*

Berenstain Bears Meet Big Paw, The   1980
Cartoons
78352   25 mins   C   B, V   P
Animated
Brother and Sister Bear meet up with the
monster Big Paw and find out he is not a beast
at all.
Buzz Potamkin — *Embassy Home
Entertainment*

Berenstain Bears Play Ball, The   1983
Cartoons
74081   25 mins   C   B, V   P
Animated
In this animated feature, Papa Bear learns a
valuable lesson about winning and losing.
Buzz Potamkin — *Embassy Home
Entertainment*

Bergonzi Hand, The   1970
Drama
78096   62 mins   C   B, V, FO   P
Keith Mitchell, Gordon Jackson, Martin Miller
A drama about two scoundrels of the world of
art who are astonished when an immigrant
admits to painting a forged "Bergonzi."
ABC — *Video Yesteryear*

Berkshires and Hudsons of the Boston & Albany/Railroading in the Northeast   195?
Trains
62870   30 mins   B/W   B, V   P, T
Railroad buffs will enjoy these scenes of classic
steam locomotives from the New Haven, New
York Central, Central Vermont, Delaware &
Hudson and B & A lines.
J W Deely; E R Blanchard — *Blackhawk Films*

Berlin   1983
Music video
88089   21 mins   C   B, V   P
The best video clips from the innovative new
wave group, including "The Metro" and "No
More Words."
Sony Video — *Sony Video Software*

Berlin Alexanderplatz   1980
Drama
66463   920 mins   C   B, V   P
*Gunter Lamprecht, Hanna Schygulla, Barbara
Sukowa, directed by Rainer Werner Fassbinder*
Fassbinder's 15 1/2-hour epic, originally
produced for German television, follows the life,
death and resurrection of Franz Biberkof, a
former transit worker who has just finished a
lengthy prison term. With the Berlin of the
1920's as a backdrop, Fassbinder has contrived
a melodramatic parable with Biblical overtones.
Teleculture Films; Peter
Martheshmeimer — *MGM/UA Home Video*

Berlin Express   1948
War-Drama
00306   86 mins   B/W   B, V, 3/4U   P
Robert Ryan, Merle Oberon, Paul Lukas
Battle of wits between the Allies and Nazi
fanatics seeking to keep Germans disunited.
RKO — *Nostalgia Merchant*

Berlin Tunnel 21 1981
Adventure
85024   141 mins   C   B, V   P
Richard Thomas, Jose Ferrer, Horst Bucholz
Five American soldiers attempt a daring rescue
under the Berlin wall for a beautiful German girl.
Filmways Prod — *THORN EMI/HBO Video*

Bermuda Triangle, The 1979
Documentary/Speculation
29227   94 mins   C   B, V   P
Brad Campbell
One of the world's great mysteries, still
unsolved in our time. The facts are that in the
last 300 years more than 700 boats and planes
and thousands of people have vanished without
a trace in the area we call "The Bermuda
Triangle."
MPAA:G
Sunn Classic Pictures — *VidAmerica; Lucerne
Films*

Bernadette Peters in 1981
Concert
Music-Performance
55561   47 mins   C   B, V   P
Bernadette Peters, directed by John Blanchard
This two-sided stereo disc presents Bernadette
Peters' live performance, recorded at the 3,000
seat Jubilee Auditorium in Edmonton, Canada.
Doug Holtby; Nicholas Wry — *MCA Home
Video*

Bernice Bobs Her Hair 1977
Comedy
84032   49 mins   C   B, V   P
*Shelly Duvall, Bud Cort, Veronica Cartwright,
directed by Joan Micklin Silver, introduced by
Henry Fonda*
An ugly and shy girl's cousin revamps her into a
seductress. From the director of "Chilly Scenes
of Winter," part of the American Short Story
Collection.
Paul R Gurian — *Monterey Home Video*

Berry Gordy's The Last 1985
Dragon
Martial arts
Closed Captioned
70762   108 mins   C   B, V   P
*Vanity, Christopher Murney, Julius J. Cary III,
Taimak, directed by Michael Schultz*
It's time for a Kung Fu showdown on the streets
of Harlem, for there is scarcely enough room for
even one dragon. Available in VHS and Beta Hi-
Fi.
MPAA:PG-13
Berry Gordy; Tri-Star — *CBS/Fox Video*

Best Defense 1984
Comedy
80397   94 mins   C   B, V, LV,   P
                            CED

*Dudley Moore, Eddie Murphy, Kate Capshaw,
Helen Shaver, directed by Willard Huyck*
A U.S. Army tank operator is sent to Kuwait to
test a new state-of-the- art tank in a combat
situation.
MPAA:R
Gloria Katz; Paramount Pictures — *Paramount
Home Video*

Best Foot Forward 1943
Musical
88205   95 mins   C   B, V   P
*Lucille Ball, June Allyson, Tommy Dix, Nancy
Walker, Virginia Weidler, Gloria DeHaven,
William Gaxton, Harry James and His Orchestra*
A vintage musical about a movie star who
agrees to accompany a young cadet to a military
ball. Based on the popular Broadway show;
songs include "Buckle Down, Winsocki," "The
Three B's (Barrelhouse, Boogie Woogie and the
Blues), "Alive and Kicking" and Harry James'
"Two O'Clock Jump." The film debuts of
Walker, Allyson and DeHaven.
MGM; Loew's Inc. — *MGM/UA Home Video*

Best Friends 1982
Comedy
66121   108 mins   C   B, V, LV,   P
                            CED
*Goldie Hawn, Burt Reynolds, Jessica Tandy,
Barnard Hughes, Audra Lindley, Keenan Wynn,
Ron Silver, directed by Norman Jewison*
A team of screenwriters decide to marry after
years of living and working together.
MPAA:PG
Warner Bros — *Warner Home Video*

Best Legs in the 8th 1984
Grade
Comedy/Romance
70853   60 mins   C   B, V   P
*Tim Matheson, Jim Belushi, Annette O'Toole,
Kathryn Harrold, directed by Tom Patchett*
A handsome attorney bumps into the gorgeous
homeroom angel who had ignored his nebbishly
dull countenance in grade school.
Telecom — *Lightning Video*

Best Little Whorehouse 1982
in Texas, The
Musical/Comedy
63168   111 mins   C   B, V, LV   P
*Dolly Parton, Burt Reynolds, Dom De Luise,
Charles Durning, Jim Nabors, Lois Nettleton,
directed by Colin Higgins*
Dolly Parton is the buxom owner of The Chicken
Ranch, a house of ill-repute that may be closed
down unless Sheriff Burt Reynolds can think of
a way out. Based on the long-running Broadway
musical.
MPAA:R
Universal — *MCA Home Video*

Best of Alfred Hitchcock Presents, The   1958
Mystery
84635   78 mins   B/W   B, V   — P
Barbara Bel Geddes, Tom Ewell, John Williams, etc.
Each tape in this series features three original episodes, uncut, from the long-running TV series.
Alfred Hitchcock Exec — *MCA Home Video*

Best of Amos 'n Andy Vol. 1, The   195?
Comedy
44851   100 mins   B/W   B, V, 3/4U   P
Alvin Childress, Spencer Williams
Four classic television shows are contained in this volume. They include "Young Girls," "The Rare Coin," "The Turkey Dinner," and "The Secretary."
CBS — *Nostalgia Merchant*

Best of Benny Hill, The   1981
Comedy
58457   104 mins   C   B, V   P
Benny Hill
Humorous sketches featuring the off-beat comedy of this British funnyman.
Thames Video — *THORN EMI/HBO Video*

Best of the Benny Hill Show, Vol. 5, The   1985
Comedy
80814   97 mins   C   B, V   P
Here is another volume of madcap comedy from British funnyman Benny Hill. Available in VHS and Beta Hi Fi.
Thames Video — *THORN EMI/HBO Video*

Best of Betty Boop, The   1935
Cartoons
85146   56 mins   B/W   B, V   P
Directed by Dave Fleischer
A collection of nine Boop classics, including the immortal "Betty Boop's Ker-choo."
Max Fleischer — *Video Yesteryear*

Best of Betty Boop, Volume I, The   193?
Cartoons
64836   90 mins   C   B, V   P
Animated, voice of Mae Questal
Sweet Betty Boop sashays through eleven of her classic cartoon adventures in this collection of original shorts. Mastered from the original negatives.
Max Fleischer; Paramount — *Republic Pictures Home Video*

Best of Betty Boop Volume II   19??
Cartoons
66471   85 mins   C   B, V   P
Animated
Another collection of original cartoons starring the "Boop-Oop-a-Doop" girl, assisted by Bimbo and Koko the Clown. These black-and-white cartoons have been recolored for this release.
Max Fleischer — *Republic Pictures Home Video*

Best of Blondie, The   1981
Music-Performance
58880   60 mins   C   B, V   P
Deborah Harry, Jimmy Destri, Chris Stein, Nigel Harrison, Frank Infante, Clem Burke
Original footage from the group's early days combines with promotional videos to present fifteen Blondie hits linked with film shot in New York locations. Songs include: "Rapture," "The Tide is High," "Heart of Glass," "Call Me" and others.
Chrysalis Records — *Pacific Arts Video*

Best of Broadway, "The Philadelphia Story," The   1958
Drama
12847   55 mins   B/W   B, V, FO   P
Dorothy McGuire, John Payne, Richard Carlson, Herbert Marshall, Mary Astor, Charles Winninger, Dick Moran
A superb dramatization of the Philip Barry play.
CBS — *Video Yesteryear*

Best of Bugs Bunny and Friends, The   1940
Cartoons/Comedy
82405   53 mins   C   B, V   P
Animated
This collection includes classics from great cartoon stars Bugs Bunny, Daffy Duck, Tweety Pie and Porky Pig. Includes "Duck Soup to Nuts," "A Feud There Was" and "Tweetie Pie." Academy Awards '47: Cartoon ("Tweetie Pie").
The Vitaphone Corporation — *MGM/UA Home Video*

Best of Candid Camera, The   1985
Comedy
82470   56 mins   C   B, V   P
Alan Fund, Woody Allen, Angie Dickinson, Loni Anderson, Buster Keaton, Robby Benson
This tape compiles some of the best "Candid Camera" episodes.
Alan Funt Productions — *Vestron Video*

Best of Candid Camera, Vol. II   1986
Outtakes and bloopers/Comedy
84793   57 mins   C   B, V   P

Allen Funt
Various segments of unbelievable hilarity from the TV show.
Allen Funt — *Vestron Video*

Best of Comic Relief, The   1986
Comedy-Performance
87307   120 mins   C   B, V   P
Whoopi Goldberg, Robin Williams, Billy Crystal, Carl Reiner, Harold Ramis, Martin Short, Jerry Lewis, Howie Mandel, Eugene Levy, Steve Allen, Doc Severinsen, Sid Caesar, John Candy, George Carlin
This all-star comedic array of stand-up acts was taped "live" in concert, to raise money for America's homeless.
Comic Relief; Karl-Lorimar Home Video — *Karl/Lorimar Home Video*

Best of Elvis Costello and   1985
the Attractions, The
Music video
82274   65 mins   C   B, V   P
This is a compilation of twenty-two conceptual music videos that brought Elvis Costello critical acclaim. Here "Watching the Detectives" and "Pump It Up" in VHS and Beta Hi-Fi Stereo.
CBS Records — *CBS/Fox Video*

Best of Heckle and   19??
Jeckle and Friends, The
Cartoons
69609   60 mins   C   B, V   P
Animated
This cartoon collection features such memorable characters as Heckle and Jeckle, Deputy Dawg, Sad Cat, Possible Possum and Sidney, the baby elephant.
Terrytoons — *Children's Video Library*

Best of Heckle and   194?
Jeckle—Volumes IV & V,
The
Cartoons
29130   90 mins   C   B, V   P
Animated
Terrytoons' characters Heckle and Jeckle are featured in two programs, both available individually.
EL, SP
Viacom International — *CBS/Fox Video*

Best of John Belushi, The   1985
Comedy
82222   60 mins   C   B, V   P
John Belushi, Dan Aykroyd, Chevy Chase, Jane Curtain, Rob Reiner, Buck Henry, Robert Klein
This is a compilation of sixteen of John Belushi's funniest "Saturday Night Live" routines including "Samurai Deli," "Godfather Therapy" and "Star Trek" in VHS and Beta Dolby Hi-Fi Stereo.

Broadway Video — *Warner Home Video*

Best of Judy Garland,   1985
The
Music-Performance
82203   85 mins   B/W   B, V   P
Judy Garland
Judy Garland shines brightly in this TV concert that features such standards as "The Man That Got Away", "Over The Rainbow" and "Swanee" in VHS and Beta Hi-Fi Stereo.
RCA Video Productions — *RCA/Columbia Pictures Home Video*

Best of Kids   1984
Incorporated, The
Children
88474   60 mins   C   B, V   P
Cuts from the popular kid's show, with songs, dancing and comedy are featured.
Hal Roach Studios — *Hal Roach Studios*

Best of Little Lulu   19??
Cartoons
65688   60 mins   C   B, V   P
Animated
Mischief-prone Little Lulu returns in this special collection of cartoon adventures.
Paramount — *Republic Pictures Home Video*

Best of Little Rascals,   193?
The
Comedy
79878   103 mins   B/W   B, V   P
A collection of six classic "Our Gang" two reelers featuring everyone's favorite rascals Spanky, Alfalfa, Stymie and Buckwheat.
Hal Roach — *Republic Pictures Home Video*

Best of Marvel Comics,   1982
The
Fantasy/Cartoons
62878   112 mins   C   B, V   P
Animated
Five episodes featuring Marvel Comics favorites: Spiderman, Mr. Fantastic, Invisible Girl, Spiderwoman and The Thing. Titles are "The Great Magini," "The Mole Men," "The Menace Magneto," "Calamity on Campus" and "Diamond Dust."
Marvel Comics — *MCA Home Video*

Best of Mary Hartman,   1976
Mary Hartman, Volume II,
The
Comedy
76908   70 mins   C   B, V, LV   P
Louise Lasser, Greg Mullavey, Mary Kay Place, Dody Goodman, Debralee Scott
The town of Fernwood, Ohio is jumping with excitement as everyone's trying to guess the identity of the Fernwood Flasher.

Jerry Adler; Lou Gallo — *Embassy Home Entertainment*

The Best of New Wave Theatre 1985
Music-Performance/Exploitation
84351   60 mins   C   B, V   P
The Blasters, Black Flag, Circle Jerks, Dead Kennedys
Here are the grooviest highlights from various soft- and hard-core punk bands as shown on the New Wave Theatre television program.
Impulse Entertainment — *Rhino Video*

Best of Popeye, The 1983
Cartoons
65109   56 mins   C   B, V, CED   P
Animated
Eight classic Popeye cartoons are included in this compilation.
MGM/UA Home Entertainment Group; Max Fleischer — *MGM/UA Home Video*

Best of Sex and Violence, The 1981
Movie and TV trailers
47756   78 mins   C   B, V   P
Narrated by John Carradine, directed by Ken Dixon
A collection of trailers, or coming attractions, from films which feature blood, sexploitation, soft porn, bizarre comedy, bike flicks, blacksploitation, Kung fu, etc.
S and V Prods; Charles Band — *Wizard Video*

Best of 60 Minutes, The 1984
History-Modern/Television
Closed Captioned
65754   60 mins   C   B, V, CED   P
Mike Wallace, Morley Safer, Harry Reasoner, Ed Bradley, Andy Rooney
Included in this program are 4 of the most gripping segments ever shown on this long running news series.
Don Hewitt; CBS News — *CBS/Fox Video*

Best of 60 Minutes Volume 2, The 1985
History-Modern/Television
Closed Captioned
77466   60 mins   C   B, V   P
Mike Wallace, Morley Safer, Harry Reasoner, Ed Bradley, Andy Rooney, Dan Rather
A collection of five hard hitting stories from those intrepid investigative reporters of television's longest running news magazine.
Don Hewitt; CBS News — *CBS/Fox Video*

Best of Terrytoons, The 1983
Cartoons
69530   60 mins   C   B, V, CED   P
Animated

This is a compilation of cartoons featuring Mighty Mouse, Heckle and Jeckle, Deputy Dawg, Gandy Goose, Dinky Duck, Terry Bears and Little Roquefort.
Terrytoons — *Children's Video Library*

Best of the Benny Hill Show, Vol. II, The 1981
Comedy
63346   115 mins   C   B, V   P
Benny Hill
Another compilation of humorous sketches from "The Benny Hill Show."
Thames Video — *THORN EMI/HBO Video*

Best of the Benny Hill Show, Vol. III, The 1983
Comedy
65092   110 mins   C   B, V   P
Benny Hill
British funnyman Benny Hill mugs and jokes his way through a new collection of comedy sketches from his popular television series.
Thames Video — *THORN EMI/HBO Video*

Best of the Benny Hill Show Volume 6, The 1985
Comedy-Performance
82025   120 mins   C   B, V   P
British funnyman Benny Hill's unique brand of humor comes through in this collection of sketches from his TV series.
Thames Television — *THORN EMI/HBO Video*

Best of the Benny Hill Show, Volume 4, The 1984
Comedy
78391   95 mins   C   B, V   P
Here's another collection of zany sketches from British funnyman Benny Hill.
Thames Television — *THORN EMI/HBO Video*

Best of the Big Laff-Off, The 1983
Comedy-Performance
65546   60 mins   C   B, V   P
Featuring top comics delivering their most hilarious routines, emphasis is from waistlines to punchlines. It's the best, funniest and fastest-moving segments of "The Big Laff-Off".
Premiers Eddie Murphy and Robin Williams.
Chuck Braverman — *Karl/Lorimar Home Video*

Best of the Football Follies, The 1985
Football
Closed Captioned
82289   44 mins   C   B, V   P

This is a compilation of the humorous events that often occur on the football field.
NFL Films — *NFL Films Video*

Best of the Kenny Everett Video Show, The   1981
Comedy
59705   104 mins   C   B, V   P
Kenny Everett
Great scenes from the popular British late-night TV show combining new wave rock music, outrageous dancing and innovative video special effects.
David Mallett — *THORN EMI/HBO Video*

Best of the New York Erotic Film Festival Parts I & II   197?
Film
64841   210 mins   C   B, V   P
Two cassette collections of prize-winning and specially selected films presented at the annual New York Erotic Film Festival.
Various — *HarmonyVision*

Best of Times, The   1986
Comedy
Closed Captioned
87191   105 mins   C   B, V, LV   P
Robin Williams, Kurt Russell, M. Emmet Walsh, Pamela Reed, Holly Palance, Margaret Whitton, directed by Roger Spottiswoode
Two grown men attempt to redress the failures of the past by reenacting a football game they lost in high school due to a single flubbed pass.
MPAA:PG
Gordon Carroll; Universal — *Embassy Home Entertainment*

Best of Upstairs Downstairs, The   1971
Drama
79711   50 mins   C   B, V   P
Jean Marsh, Lesley Anne Down, David Longton, Simon Williams, Angela Baddeley
The foibles of London's Bellamy Family and their servants at the turn of the century are chronicled in these fourteen untitled programs.
London Weekend Television — *THORN EMI/HBO Video*

Best of Wally's Workshop, The   1979
Home improvement
81729   90 mins   C   B, V   P
6   pgms
This series of six programs consists of edited highlights from the television series.
1.Floors 2.Decorating 3.Ceilings and Fireplaces 4.Bath and Kitchen 5.Walls 6.Security and Weatherproofing
Wally Bruner — *Kartes Video Communications*

Best of W.C. Fields, The   193?
Comedy
80464   58 mins   B/W   B, V   P
W.C. Fields, Elsie Cavenna
Three of W.C. Field's Mack Sennett shorts are presented in their complete, uncut form.
Mack Sennett — *Spotlite Video*

Best Revenge   1983
Crime-Drama
87908   92 mins   C   B, V   P
John Heard, Levon Helm, Alberta Watson, John Rhys Davies, Moses Znaimer, directed by John Trent
Two aging hippies engage in a Moroccan drug deal in order to free a kidnapped friend from a sleazy gangster, but they get caught by the police, and escape, searching for the engineers of the frame-up.
Michael Lebowitz — *Karl/Lorimar Home Video*

Best Years of Our Lives, The   1946
Drama
80946   170 mins   B/W   B, V, LV   P
Frederic March, Harold Russell, Myrna Loy, Dana Andrews, Virginia Mayo, Hoagy Carmichael, directed by William Wyler
Three World War II veterans return to the homefront attempting to pick up the threads of their lives.
Academy Awards '46: Best Picture. Best Director (Wyler). Best Actor (March). Best Supporting Actor (Russell).
Samuel Goldwyn — *Embassy Home Entertainment*

Bete Humaine, La   1938
Film-Avant-garde
06223   90 mins   B/W   B, V   P
Jean Gabin, Simone Simon, directed by Jean Renoir
Son of drunkard finds his own abstinence from drink is no escape from self-hate and sadness.
French; English subtitles.
FR
France — *Hollywood Home Theater; Cable Films; Video Yesteryear; Discount Video Tapes*

Betrayal   1983
Drama
65490   95 mins   C   B, V, CED   P
Ben Kingsley, Patricia Hodge, Jeremy Irons
An unusual drama, beginning at the end of a seven-year adulterous affair and finally ending at the start of the betrayal of a husband by his wife and his best friend.
MPAA:R
20th Century Fox International Classics — *CBS/Fox Video*

Betrayal 1978
Drama
70909   95 mins   G   B, V   P
Lesley Ann Warren, Rip Torn, Ron Silver,
Richard Masur, Steven Elliot, John Hillerman,
Peggy Ann Garner, directed by Paul Wendkos
Producers based this telefilm on the book by
Lucy Freeman and Julie Roy about a historic
malpractice case involving a psychiatrist and
one of his female patients. The doctor
convinced the woman that sex with him would
solve her problems.
EMI Television Programs — VCL Home Video

Betsy, The 1978
Drama
65753 / 125 mins   C   B, V, CED   P
Laurence Olivier, Kathleen Beller, Robert
Duvall, Lesley-Anne Down, Tommy Lee Jones,
Katherine Ross, Jane Alexander
A story of romance, money, power and mystery
centering around the wealthy Hardeman family
and their automobile manufacturing business.
MPAA:R
Harold Robbins International
Productions — CBS/Fox Video

Bette Midler: Art or Bust 1984
Music-Performance/Comedy
77410   82 mins   C   B, V, CED   P
Bette Midler
The outrageous Bette Midler performs in the
concert taped at the University of Minnesota in
Minneapolis.
HBO — Vestron Video

Bette Midler Show, The 1976
Music-Performance
65419   84 mins   C   B, V, LV,   P
                              CED
Bette Midler, accompanied by the Harlettes,
jokes, dances and belts out a medley of songs
ranging from the Andrew Sisters' "Boogie
Woogie Bugle Boy" to "Friends."
Home Box Office — Embassy Home
Entertainment

Better Off Dead 1985
Comedy
Closed Captioned
84128   97 mins   C   B, V   P
John Cusak, Curtis Armstrong, Diane Franklin,
directed by Savage Steve Holland
A compulsive teenager's girlfriend leaves him
and he decides to end it all. After several
abortive attempts, he decides instead to out-ski
his ex-girlfriend's obnoxious new boyfriend.
MPAA:PG
Warner Bros — Key Video

Better Team, A 1980
Football
50080   24 mins   C   B, V, FO   R, P

Seattle Seahawks
Highlights of the 1979 Seattle Seahawks'
football season.
NFL Films — NFL Films Video

Betty Boop Special 193?
Collector's Edition II
Cartoons
81874   90 mins   B/W   B, V   P
Animated
That boop-a-doop girl is back in this collection
of classic cartoons that features Cab Calloway
and his orchestra.
Paramount; Max Fleischer — Republic
Pictures Home Video

Betty Boop Cartoon 193?
Festival
Cartoons
55339   55 mins   B/W   B, V   P
Animated
Max Fleischer produced and directed these
campy, racy cartoons of the 1930's including
such titles as "Baby Be Good," "Betty Boop
with Grampy," "Betty Boop with Henry,"
"Candid Candidate," "Ding Dong Doggie," and
"Ker-choo."
Paramount; Max Fleischer — Hollywood Home
Theater; Discount Video Tapes

Betty Boop Classics 19??
Cartoons
65689   60 mins   C   B, V   P
Animated
A compilation of Betty Boop and her cartoon
pals most fun-filled escapades.
Paramount — Republic Pictures Home Video

Betty Boop Special 193?
Collectors Edition
Cartoons
65740   60 mins   B/W   B, V   P
Animated, directed by Max Fleischer
Betty Boop returns in this collection of vintage
cartoons, presented in their original black-and-
white form, with appearances by jazz stars Louis
Armstrong, Cab Calloway and Don Redman.
Paramount; Max Fleischer — Republic
Pictures Home Video

Between Friends 1983
Drama
72225   105 mins   C   B, V   P
Elizabeth Taylor, Carol Burnett
Two women help each other through the
traumatic period following their respective
divorces.
Robert Cooper Films — Vestron Video

Between the Lines 1977
Comedy
59871   101 mins   C   B, V, CED   P

John Heard, Lindsay Crouse, Jeff Goldblum, Jill
Eikenberry, Stephen Collins, Lewis J. Stadlen,
Michael J. Pollard, Marilu Henner, directed by
Joan Micklin Silver
A comic exploration of the rapidly changing
world of a group of friends working together on
a small alternative newspaper.
MPAA:R
Raphael D Silver; Midwest Film
Productions — Vestron Video

Between Wars   1974
Drama
77015   97 mins   C   B, V   P
Corin Redgrave
A young doctor in Australia's Medical Corps
encounters conflict when he tries to introduce
Freud's principles into his work.
Satori Entertainment — VidAmerica

Beulah Show, The   1952
Comedy
82284   115 mins   B/W   B, V, 3/4U   P
Louise Beavers, Hattie McDaniel, Ernest
Whitman, Butterfly McQueen, Ruby Dandridge
Here are three episodes from the series
chronicling the adventures of a black
housekeeper and the family she takes care of.
Also featured on this tape are five racist
cartoons including "Jasper's in a Jam" and
"Jungle Jitters."
ABC — Shokus Video

Beulah Show, The   1952
Comedy
39001   51 mins   B/W   B, V, FO   P
Louise Beavers, Ruby Dandridge, Ernest
Whitman, Arthur Q. Bryan 2 pgms
Lovable housemaid Beulah outwits her
employers as usual in these episodes from the
early 1950's TV series: "Marriage on the
Rocks" and "Imagination."
ABC — Video Yesteryear

Beverly Hills Cop   1984
Comedy
Closed Captioned
82523   105 mins   C   B, V, 8mm,   P
                          LV
Eddie Murphy, Judge Reinhold, John Ashton,
Lisa Eilbacher, directed by Martin Brest
A brash, smooth-talking Detroit policeman
traces a murderer to the posh streets of Beverly
Hills in this hard-edged comedy.
MPAA:PG-13
Paramount — Paramount Home Video

Beyond and Back   1978
Documentary/Speculation
48265   93 mins   C   B, V   P
Narrated by Brad Crandall
The supposed reincarnation experiences of a
dozen people are explored in this documentary.

Sunn Classic — United Home Video; Lucerne
Films

Beyond Atlantis   1973
Fantasy
84817   91 mins   C   B, V   P
John Ashley, Patrick Wayne, George Nader,
directed by Eddie Romero
An ancient underwater tribe is discovered as it
kidnaps land-lubbin' women with which to mate.
MPAA:PG
John Ashely; Eddie Romero — United Home
Video

Beyond Belief   1976
Documentary/Occult sciences
84852   94 mins   C   B, V   P
Uri Geller
Footage of such phenomena as ESP, automatic
writing, telekinesis, etc., featuring Geller
bending flatware (without touching it.)
American Int'l Entprs. — United Home Video

Beyond Death's Door   1979
Death/Speculation
60350   106 mins   C   B, V   P
Tom Hallick, Howard Platt, Jo Ann Harris,
Melinda Naud
A documentary look at people who have seen
death but lived to tell about it.
MPAA:PG
Stan Siegel; Sunn Pictures — United Home
Video; Lucerne Films

Beyond Evil   1980
Horror
65111   98 mins   C   B, V   P
John Saxon, Lynda Day George, Michael Dante,
Mario Milano
A newlywed couple moves into an old mansion
despite rumors that the house is haunted. The
wife becomes possessed by the vengeful spirit
of a woman murdered 200 years earlier, and a
reign of terror begins.
MPAA:R
David Baughn; Herb Freed — Media Home
Entertainment

Beyond Fear   1975
Drama
15720   92 mins   C   B, V   P
Michael Boquet
Explores moral implications of a man forced to
aid a gang in robbery while they hold his wife
and son captive.
France — Prism; Cinema Concepts

Beyond Reason   1982
Drama
81190   88 mins   C   B, V   P
Telly Savalas, Laura Johnson, Diana Muldaur,
Marvin Laird, directed by Telly Savalas

A psychologist uses unorthodox methods, treating the criminally insane with dignity and respect.
Howard W. Koch — *Media Home Entertainment*

Beyond Reasonable Doubt   1984
Drama/Mystery
65396   117 mins   C   B, V   P
David Hemmings, John Hargreaves
A chilling true life murder mystery which shatters the peaceful quiet of a small New Zealand town and eventually divides a country.
Satori Entertainment Corporation — *VidAmerica*

Beyond the Door   1975
Horror
47853   97 mins   C   B, V   P
Juliet Mills, Richard Johnson
A San Francisco woman finds herself pregnant with a demonic child.
MPAA:R
Avido Assonnitis — *Media Home Entertainment*

Beyond the Door II   1979
Horror
69303   90 mins   C   B, V   P
John Steiner, Daria Nicolodi, David Colin Jr., Ivan Rassimov
A family is tormented by supernatural revenge.
MPAA:R
Film Ventures — *Media Home Entertainment*

Beyond the Limit   1983
Drama
65398   103 mins   C   B, V   P
Michael Caine, Richard Gere
The story of an intense and darkly ominous love triangle which takes place in the South American coastal city of Corrientes. Based on Graham Greene's novel "The Honorary Consul."
MPAA:R
Norma Heyman — *Paramount Home Video*

Beyond the Living Dead   1974
Horror
82091   91 mins   C   B, V   P
Stanley Cooper, Vickie Nesbitt
A Spanish police inspector is sent to investigate the strange deaths that have occurred at the reading of a landowner's will.
Bernard Woolner — *Unicorn Video*

Beyond the Poseidon Adventure   1979
Adventure
87678   115 mins   C   B, V   P

Michael Caine, Sally Field, Telly Savalas, Peter Boyle, Jack Warden, Slim Pickens, Shirley Knight, Shirley Jones, Karl Malden, Mark Harmon
A sequel to the 1972 film in which salvage teams and ruthless looting vandals compete for access to the sinking ocean liner.
MPAA:PG
Irwin Allen — *Warner Home Video*

Beyond the Valley of the Dolls   1970
Drama
56458   109 mins   C   B, V   P
Edy Williams, Dolly Reed, directed by Russ Meyer
Russ Meyer's story of an all-girl rock combo and their search for Hollywood stardom.
MPAA:X
Twentieth Century Fox — *CBS/Fox Video*

Beyond the Walls   1985
Drama
82499   107 mins   C   B, V   P
Arnan Zadok, Muhamad Bakri, directed by Uri Barbash
The opposing factions of a hellish Israeli prison unite to beat the system. Available in both subtitled and dubbed versions.
1984 Venice Film Festival: (Best Film).
MPAA:R   HE
April Films — *Warner Home Video*

Beyond Tomorrow   1940
Comedy
12402   84 mins   B/W   B, V   P
Richard Carlson, C. Aubrey Smith, Jean Parker, Charles Winninger
Young romance is guided from the spirit world during the Christmas season, as two "ghosts" come back to help young lovers.
RKO — *Hollywood Home Theater; Discount Video Tapes*

Bible, The   1966
Drama
34287   155 mins   C   B, V   P
Richard Harris, Stephen Boyd, George C. Scott, directed by John Huston
The book of Genesis is dramatized, including the stories of Adam and Eve, Cain and Abel, and Noah and the Flood.
EL, SP
Twentieth Century Fox, Dino DeLaurentiis — *CBS/Fox Video*

Bible Stories—Tales From the Old Testament   1985
Bible/Cartoons
82040   60 mins   C   B, V   P
Animated
This is an animated collection of Biblical stories from the Old Testament.

Video Japonica — *Children's Video Library*

Bicycle Racing U.S.A.   1985
Bicycling
84275   30 mins   C   B, V   P
A marathon viewing experience for those who
love speed bike racing.
Video Travel Inc — *Video Travel*

Bicycling America,   1985
Volume 1
Physical fitness/Bicycling
70779   60 mins   C   B, V   P
This program permits stationary exercising
bicyclists to experience the beauty of Yosemite
National Park.
AM Available
Videocassette Marketing
Corp. — *Videocassette Marketing*

Big Bad Mama   1974
Drama
54805   83 mins   C   B, V   P
*Angie Dickinson, William Shatner, Tom Skerritt,
Susan Sennett, Robie Lee, Noble Willingham,
directed by Steve Carver*
A tough, intelligent, pistol-packing mother
moves her two teenage daughters out of
poverty-stricken Texas in 1932. They become
bank robbers.
MPAA:R
New World Pictures; Roger Corman — *Warner
Home Video; RCA VideoDiscs*

Big Bands, The   1985
Music
80521   50 mins   B/W   B, V   P
11 pgms
A series of eleven videotapes which offer
original film shorts by the great swing bands of
the 1930's and 40's.
*1.Duke Ellington; Count Basie; Lionel Hampton
2.Harry James; Ray McKinley; Si Zentner; Ralph
Marterie; 3.Tex Beneke; Ralph Flanagan; Les &
Larry Elgart; Vaughn Monroe 4.Tex Beneke;
Gene Krupa; Jerry Wald; Stan Kenton 5.Larry
Clinton; Jimmy Dorsey; Red Nichols; Bunny
Berigan; Ina Ray Hutton 6.Lawrence Welk; Russ
Morgan; Hal Kemp; Jan Garber 7.Guy
Lombardo 8.Count Basie; Lionel Hampton;
Duke Ellington 9.Hal Kemp; Johnny Long;
Frankie Carle; Jan Garber; Art Mooney 10.Ray
McKinley; Dick Stabile; Sam Donahue; Stan
Kenton 11.Count Basie; Duke Ellington; Harry
James*
Vitaphone; Universal, et al — *Kartes Video
Communications*

Big Bands at Disneyland   1984
Music-Performance
77536   60 mins   C   B, V   P
*Peter Marshall, Lionel Hampton, Woody
Herman, Cab Calloway* 3 pgms

The swinging big band sounds of Lionel
Hampton, Woody Herman, and Cab Calloway
are captured in these three concerts taped at
Disneyland. Available in VHS Stereo and Beta
Hi-Fi.
Walt Disney Productions — *Walt Disney Home
Video*

Big Bird Cage   1972
Drama
54801   88 mins   C   B, V   P
*Pam Grier, Sid Haig, Anitra Ford, Candice
Roman, Teda Bracci, Carol Speed, Karen
McKevic, directed by Jack Hill.*
Several females living out prison terms in a rural
jail decide to defy their homosexual guards and
plan an escape. They are aided by
revolutionaries led by a Brooklynese expatriate
and his lover. Two of the girls survive the
escape massacre.
MPAA:R
New World Pictures — *Warner Home Video*

Big Blue Marble   1981
Adventure
59304   105 mins   C   CED   P
Two segments from the award-winning
children's series of the same name: "My
Seventeenth Summer" (1978), an adventure
story that crackles with intrigue and suspense
while imparting a lesson in understanding
people of different origins; and "Flying for Fun,"
which examines everything from a frisbee
championship to the flight of a sailplane (1981).
EL, JA
Blue Marble Co — *RCA VideoDiscs*

Big Brawl, The   1980
Martial arts
78622   95 mins   C   B, V   P
Jackie Chan, Jose Ferrer, Mako, Rosalind Chao
A Chicago gangster recruits a martial arts expert
to fight in a free-for-all match in Texas.
MPAA:R
Warner Bros; Golden Harvest — *Warner Home
Video*

Big   193?
Breakdowns—Hollywood
Bloopers of the 1930's,
The
Outtakes and bloopers
47468   27 mins   B/W   B, V, FO   P
*Joan Blondell, Humphrey Bogart, James
Cagney, Bette Davis, Errol Flynn, John Garfield,
Leslie Howard, Boris Karloff, Dick Powell,
Edward G. Robinson*
Leftover shots, gag scenes, flubs and goofs
from Warner Brothers films of the late 30's,
featuring nearly every contract player on the lot.
Warner Bros — *Video Yesteryear*

Big Bus, The — 1976
Comedy/Adventure
60217   88 mins   C   B, V   P
Joseph Bologna, Stockard Channing, Ned Beatty, Ruth Gordon, Larry Hagman
The wild adventures of the world's first nuclear-powered bus as it makes its maiden voyage from New York to Denver.
MPAA:PG
Fred Freeman; Lawrence J. Cohen — *Paramount Home Video*

Big Bust Out, The — 1973
Exploitation
88349   75 mins   C   B, V   P
Vonetta McGee, Monica Taylor, Linda Fox, Karen Carter
Seven beautiful convicts escape from prison, get sold into white slavery and face additional tortures every step of the way.
MPAA:R
Richard Jackson — *Embassy Home Entertainment*

Big Cat, The — 1949
Western
08611   75 mins   C   B, V, 3/4U   P
Lon McCallister, Peggy Ann Garner, Preston Foster, Forrest Tucker
Mountain valley in Utah is ravaged by a cougar; tense excitement is heightened by hatred between two men over a woman who is dead.
Eagle Lion — *Discount Video Tapes; Kartes Video Communications*

Big Chill, The — 1983
Comedy-Drama
72930   108 mins   C   B, V, CED   P
Tom Berenger, Glenn Close, Jeff Goldblum, William Hurt, Kevin Kline, Mary Kay Place, Meg Tilly, Jobeth Williams, directed by Lawrence Kasdan
A group of college graduates from the 1960's reunite at the funeral of a friend.
MPAA:R
Michael Shambers — *RCA/Columbia Pictures Home Video*

Big City Comedy — 1985
Comedy
88029   56 mins   C   B, V   P
John Candy, Billy Crystal, Tim Kazurinsky, Martin Mull, Fred Willard
These famous comics return to stand-up work before a live audience; a highlight is Mull's "Noses Run in My Family."
Vestron Video — *Vestron Video*

Big Combo, The — 1955
Crime-Drama
80501   87 mins   B/W   B, V   P
Cornel Wilde, Richard Conte, Jean Wallace, Lee Van Cleef, Brian Donlevy, Earl Holliman

A gangster's ex-girlfriend helps a cop to smash a crime syndicate.
Allied Artists — *Prism; World Video Pictures; King of Video*

Big Country, The — 1958
Western
86781   168 mins   C   B, V   P
Gregory Peck, Charlton Heston, Burl Ives, Jean Simmons, Carroll Baker, Chuck Connors, directed by William Wyler
A sprawling western epic dealing with a frontier family war and the Easterner who tries to settle it peacefully.
Academy Awards '58:Best Supporting Actor (Ives).
Anthony Worldwide Prod.; UA — *MGM/UA Home Video*

Big Country Live — 1984
Music-Performance
72889   75 mins   C   B, V   P
Big Country
This is a concert taped in Scotland on New Year's Eve 1984. Big Country performs "Wonderland" "Fields of Fire" and "In a Big Country."
Aubrey Powell — *Music Media*

Big Doll House — 197?
Adventure/Crime-Drama
82586   93 mins   C   B, V   P
Judy Brown, Pam Grier, Roberta Collins, Pat Woodell
A group of tormented female convicts decide to break out of jail.
MPAA:R
Jane Schaffer — *Embassy Home Entertainment*

Big Fights, Vol. 1—Muhammad Ali's Greatest Fights, The — 1980
Boxing
56878   90 mins   C   CED   P
Thrilling moments from the career of Muhammad Ali, including bouts with Sonny Liston, Archie Moore, Floyd Patterson, Ken Norton, Joe Frazier, and Leon Spinks.
ABC — *RCA VideoDiscs*

Big Fights, Vol. 2—Heavyweight Champions' Greatest Fights, The — 1981
Boxing
59017   89 mins   C   CED   P
Muhammad Ali, Jack Johnson, Jack Dempsey, Gene Tunney, Joe Louis, Rocky Marciano, Floyd Patterson
All of the heavyweight greats are seen in this collection of boxing's greatest heavyweight

matches. Contains rare early footage. Some black and white footage.
ABC — *RCA VideoDiscs*

Big Fights, Vol. 3—Sugar Ray Robinson's Greatest Fights, The   1982
Boxing
60377   90 mins   C   CED   P
The career of boxer Sugar Ray Robinson is examined in this program, which highlights his greatest title matches.
ABC — *RCA VideoDiscs*

Big Fix, The   1978
Mystery/Crime-Drama
70867   108 mins   C   B, V   P
Richard Dreyfuss, Susan Anspach, Bonnie Bedelia, John Lithgow, F. Murray Abraham, Fritz Weaver, directed by Jeremy Paul Kagan
Private investigator Moses Wine finds himself in an ironic situation: searching for a fugitive alongside whom he'd protested in the 60's.
MPAA:PG
Universal — *MCA Home Video*

Big Game America   1968
Football
50086   51 mins   C   B, V, FO   R, P
Pro football's fascinating first fifty years. Don Meredith wired for sound in his last game as a Cowboy is also included.
NFL Films — *NFL Films Video*

Big Heat, The   1963
Drama
13227   90 mins   B/W   B, V   P
Glenn Ford, Lee Marvin, Gloria Grahame, Jocelyn Brando, Alexander Scourby, directed by Fritz Lang
A detective's wife is killed in an explosion meant for him, as he pursues his quest to trap a nest of criminals.
Columbia; Robert Arthur — *RCA/Columbia Pictures Home Video*

Big Mo   1973
Biographical/Drama
76770   110 mins   C   B, V   P
Bernie Casey, Bo Svenson, Stephanie Edwards, Janet MacLahlan
This is the true story of the friendship that developed between Cincinnati Royals basketball stars Maurice Stokes and Jack Twyman after a strange paralysis hits Stokes.
MPAA:G
National General — *Vestron Video*

Big Push, The   1977
Adventure
70986   98 mins   C   B, V   P

Joseph Cotton, Claude Akins, Cesar Romero, Tab Hunter, Rosey Grier, Leon Ames, Stubby Kaye, Patricia Medina, directed by Tay Garnett
Originally entitled "Timber Tramps," a motley but O.K. bunch of Alaskan lumberjacks get together to save a poor widow's logging camp from a pair of greedy mill owners.
MPAA:PG
Chuck D Kean — *Video Gems*

Big Red   1962
Drama
65637   89 mins   C   B, V   P
Walter Pidgeon, Gilles Payant
Set amid the spectacular beauty of Canada's Quebec Province, an orphan boy protects a dog which later saves him from a mountain lion.
Buena Vista — *Walt Disney Home Video*

Big Red One, The   1980
War-Drama
52742   113 mins   C   B, V, CED   P
Lee Marvin, Robert Carradine, directed by Sam Fuller
Fuller's semi-autobiographical account of the U.S. Army's famous First Infantry Division in World War II, the "Big Red One." A rifle squad composed of four very young men cut a fiery path of conquest from the landing in North Africa to the liberation of the concentration camp at Falkenau, Czechoslovakia.
MPAA:PG
Lorimar Prods — *CBS/Fox Video*

Big Score, The   1983
Drama
79309   88 mins   C   B, V   P
Fred Williamson, John Saxon, Richard Roundtree, Nancy Wilson, EdLauter, Ron Dean
When a policeman is dismissed from the Chicago Police Department he goes after the men who stole money from a drug bust.
MPAA:R
Almi Pictures — *Vestron Video*

Big Show   1937
Western
07971   54 mins   B/W   B, V   P
Gene Autry, Smiley Burnette
A western adventure featuring Gene Autry.
Republic; Gene Autry — *Video Connection; Movie Buff Video; Captain Bijou*

Big Showdown, The   197?
Martial arts
82086   90 mins   C   B, V   P
Shiang Hwa Chyang, Jin Fu War
A young man uses his martial arts skills against the man who murdered his sister and father.
Foreign — *Unicorn Video*

Big Sky, The   1952
Western
81028   122 mins   B/W   B, V   P
Kirk Douglas, Dewey Martin, Arthur Hunnicutt,
directed by Howard Hawks
It's 1830, and a rowdy band of furtrappers
embark upon a back breaking expedition up the
uncharted Missouri River.
RKO — RKO HomeVideo

Big Sleep, The   1946
Suspense
59303   114 mins   B/W   B, V   P
Humphrey Bogart, Lauren Bacall, Martha
Vickers, Elisha Cook Jr, Dorothy Malone,
directed by Howard Hawks
Bogie protrays private eye Philip Marlowe, hired
to protect a young woman from her own
indiscretions, and falls in love with her older
sister.
Warner Bros — CBS/Fox Video; RCA
VideoDiscs

Big Steal, The   1949
Adventure
33901   72 mins   B/W   B, V   P
Robert Mitchum, William Bendix, Jane Greer,
Ramon Novarro
An Army officer recovers a missing payroll and
captures the thieves after a tumultuous chase
through Mexico.
RKO — Nostalgia Merchant

Big Surprise, The   1956
Game show
42979   30 mins   B/W   B, V, FO   P
Mike Wallace, Errol Flynn
This $100,000 prize quiz extravaganza was
NBC's answer to the "$64,000 Question." Mike
Wallace hosts as Errol Flynn wins $30,000
answering questions on ships and the sea.
NBC — Video Yesteryear

Big Switch, The   1970
Mystery
84036   68 mins   C   B, V   P
Sebastial Breaks, Virginia Wetherell, Erlka
Raffael, directed by Pete Walker
A gambler is framed for murder and becomes
embrolled in the plot to reinstitute an old
gangster kingpin.
MPAA:R
Pete Walker — Monterey Home Video

Big Trees, The   1952
Drama
66509   89 mins   C   B, V   P
Kirk Douglas, Patrice Wymore, Eve Miller, Alan
Hale Jr., Edgar Buchanan
A ruthless lumberman attempts a takeover of
the California Redwood Timberlands that are
owned by a group of peaceful homesteaders.

Warner Bros — Hal Roach Studios; Discount
Video Tapes; World Video Pictures; Video Gems

Big Trouble   1986
Comedy
87266   93 mins   C   B, V   P
Alan Arkin, Peter Falk, Beverly D'Angelo,
directed by John Cassavetes
An insurance broker endeavors to send his
three sons to Yale by conspiring in a fraud
scheme with a crazy couple that goes awry in
every possible manner.
MPAA:R
Columbia; John Cassavetes — RCA/Columbia
Pictures Home Video

Big Wednesday   1978
Drama
81085   120 mins   C   B, V   P
Jan Michael-Vincent, Gary Busey, William Katt,
Lee Purcell, Patti D'Arbanville, directed by John
Millius
Three California surfers from the early sixties
get back together after the Vietnam war to
reminisce about the good old days. Available in
VHS and Beta Hi-Fi Stereo.
MPAA:PG
Warner Bros. — Warner Home Video

Big Wheel   1942
Adventure
84846   92 mins   B/W   B, V   P
Mickey Rooney, Michael O'Shea, Thomas
Mitchell, Spring Byington, Mary Hatcher, Allen
Jenkins, directed by Edward Ludwig
A boy wants to follow in his dead father's
footsteps as a car racer.
UA — United Home Video

Big Foot and Wild Boy   1978
Adventure
76909   48 mins   C   B, V   P
Ray Young, Joseph Butcher
A collection of two episodes from the series: In
"The Secret Invasion" the Lorcan monsters
vow to get revenge on Big Foot and in "Space
Prisoner" Bigfoot and wildboy must save a
friend from an evil space criminal.
Sid and Marty Krofft — Embassy Home
Entertainment

Bigfoot and Wildboy   1987
Adventure
82580   72 mins   C   B, V   P
An adventurous threesome battles for justice in
this action-packed feature.
Sid and Marty Krofft — Embassy Home
Entertainment

Bikini Beach   1964
Musical
65068   100 mins   C   B, V   P

Annette Funicello, Frankie Avalon, Martha Hyer, Harvey Lembeck, Don Rickles, Stevie Wonder
The surfing teenagers at Bikini Beach and a visitor, British recording star The Potato Bug, join forces to keep their beach from being turned into a retirement community. Songs include "Bikini Drag," "Love's a Secret Weapon" and "Because You're You."
Alta Vista Productions; American International — *Embassy Home Entertainment*

Bilitis   1977
Drama
50729   95 mins   C   B, V   P
Patti D'Arbanville, Bernard Giraudeau, Mona Kristensen, directed by David Hamilton
A young girl from a private girls' school is initiated into the pleasures of sex and the unexpected demands of love.
MPAA:R
Topar; Sylvio Tabet; Jacques Nahum — *Media Home Entertainment*

Bill   1981
Drama
73532   97 mins   C   B, V   R, P
Mickey Rooney, Dennis Quaid
The true story of Bill Sackler, a mentally retarded adult who was released from a mental institution after 44 years. Available in Beta Hi-Fi and VHS stereo.
Emmy Awards '82: Best Actor (Mickey Rooney); Best Story.
Alan Landsburg — *U.S.A. Home Video*

Bill and Coo   1947
Fantasy
45023   61 mins   C   B, V   P
An unusual love story with a villian and hero using an all bird cast.
Academy Award '47; Special Award.
Republic, Ken Murray — *Hollywood Home Theater; Discount Video Tapes; Video Connection*

**Bill Bruford: Bruford and
the Beat**   1985
Music
87932   30 mins   C   B, V   P
Bruford, former drummer for King Crimson and Yes, discusses drumming and music, with an analysis of his work on King Crimson's "Discipline" recording. Guest appearances by Steve Howe and Robert Fripp.
Axis Video — *DCI Music Video*

Bill Cosby, Himself   1981
Comedy-Performance
Closed Captioned
70349   104 mins   C   B, V   P
Bill Cosby
This film features Bill Cosby recorded at Toronto's Hamilton Place Performing Arts

Center sharing his hilarious observations of marriage, drugs, alcohol, dentists, child-bearing and child-rearing. This film is available in Beta Hi-Fi and VHS-Stereo formats.
MPAA:PG
20th Century Fox — *CBS/Fox Video*

**Bill Cosby's
Picturepages—Volume I**   1985
Language arts
76817   55 mins   C   B, V   P
Bill Cosby teaches lessons that describe and demonstrate shapes, senses, and sizes for toddlers.
Walt Disney Productions — *Walt Disney Home Video*

**Bill Cosby's
Picturepages—Volume 2**   1985
Language arts
76821   55 mins   C   B, V   P
Bill Cosby combines humor with solid instructional material to teach basic concepts to pre-schoolers.
Walt Disney Productions — *Walt Disney Home Video*

**Bill Cosby's
Picturepages—Volume 4**   1985
Language arts/Children
81652   56 mins   C   B, V   P
Bill Cosby teaches pre-schoolers reading readiness in this collection of twelve lessons.
AM Available
Walt Disney Productions — *Walt Disney Home Video*

Bill Watrous   1983
Music-Performance
76672   24 mins   C   B, V   P
This program presents the jazz trombonist Bill Watrous performing with his Refuge West Band.
Dig it Recordings — *Sony Video Software*

Bill Wyman   1983
Music-Performance
64930   11 mins   C   B, V   P
Bill Wyman of the Rolling Stones performs three songs solo on this Video 45: "Si Si (Je Suis Un Rock Star)," "A New Fashion" and "Come Back Suzanne."
Ripple Records — *Sony Video Software*

Billion Dollar Hobo, The   1978
Comedy
58707   96 mins   C   B, V, CED   P
Tim Conway, Will Geer, Eric Weston, Sydney Lassick
Tim Conway stars as a poor, unsuspecting heir of a multimillion dollar fortune, who must duplicate his benefactor's experience as a hobo

during the Depression in order to collect his inheritance.
MPAA:G
Samuel Goldwyn Home Entertainment — *CBS/Fox Video*

Billy Crystal: A Comic's Line   1983
Comedy-Performance
80519   59 mins   C   B, V, LV   P
Billy Crystal
Comedian Billy Crystal performs a one-man show, highlighting spoofs, of rock videos and other stand-up comics. In stereo.
Crystal/R.J.M.B. Productions — *Paramount Home Video*

Billy Jack   1971
Drama
52705   112 mins   C   B, V   P
Tom Laughlin, Delores Taylor, Clark Howat
A half-breed ex-Green Beret stands between a redneck town and a Freedom School for runaways located on an Arizona Indian Reservation.
MPAA:PG
Warner Bros; National Student Film Corp — *Warner Home Video; RCA VideoDiscs*

Billy Joel: Live from Long Island   1983
Music-Performance
65413   80 mins   C   B, V, LV, CED   P
A recording of Billy Joel's dynamic New Year's Eve performance at Nassau Coliseum. Classic tunes showcased include "Piano Man," "Allentown," "You May Be Right," and "Still Rock and Roll to Me." In VHS stereo and Beta Hi-Fi.
CBS Fox — *CBS/Fox Video*

Billy Liar   1963
Comedy-Drama
66188   94 mins   B/W   B, V   P
Tom Courtenay, Julie Christie
A young Englishman dreams of escaping from his working class family and dead-end job.
Continental — *THORN EMI/HBO Video*

Billy Martin's Big League Baseball   1982
Baseball
65133   26 mins   C   B, V   P
Hosted by Billy Martin 11 pgms
Eleven programs make up this "how-to" series on baseball, conducted by major league all-stars. Programs are available individually; each tape concentrates on the area or position identified in the title.
1.Ron Guidry on Pitching 2.Gary Carter on Catching 3.Steve Garvey at First Base 4.Frank

---

White at Second Base 5.Larry Bowa at Shortstop 6.Graig Nettles at Third Base 7.Dwayne Murphy in the Outfield 8.Rickey Henderson on Baserunning 9.Rod Carew on Bunting 10.George Brett on Hitting 11.Billy Martin Special Show
Hal Larson — *Action Distributors*

Billy: Portrait of a Street Kid   1977
Drama
77153   96 mins   C   B, V   P
Le Var Burton, Tina Andrews, Ossie Davis, Michael Constantine
A ghetto youngster tries to better himself through education but complications arise when his girlfriend becomes pregnant.
Mark Carliner Productions — *Worldvision Home Video*

Billy Squier   1982
Music-Performance
63350   60 mins   C   B, V   P
Billy Squier
Billy Squier performs some of his best songs live in concert, including "In the Dark," "Rich Kids" and "My Kinda Lover."
EMI Music — *THORN EMI/HBO Video; Pioneer Artists*

Billy the Kid Returns   1938
Western
07187   60 mins   B/W   B, V   P
Roy Rogers
Roy is mistaken for the legendary outlaw, Billy the Kid.
Republic — *Hollywood Home Theater; Video Connection; Video Dimensions; Cable Films; Discount Video Tapes; Kartes Video Communications*

Billy the Kid Versus Dracula   1966
Horror/Western
69568   73 mins   C   B, V, FO   P
John Carradine, Chuck Courtney
Dracula travels to the Old West, anxious to "put the bite" on a pretty lady ranchowner. Her fiance, the legendary outlaw Billy the Kid, steps in to save his girl from becoming a vampire herself.
Avco Embassy — *Video Yesteryear*

Bimini Code   1984
Adventure
80896   95 mins   C   B, V   P
Vickie Benson, Krista Richardson
Two female adventurers accept a dangerous mission where they wind up on Bimini Island in a showdown with the mysterious Madame X.
American National Enterprises — *Prism*

Bing Crosby Festival 193?
Musical
01604 60 mins B/W B, V P
Bing Crosby
Features three of Bing's musical short subjects.
Includes "Billboard Girl," "Blue of the Night," "I
Surrender Dear."
Mack Sennett — *Hollywood Home Theater;*
Discount Video Tapes; See Hear Industries

Bingo Long Traveling All-
Stars & Motor Kings, The 1976
Comedy
64796 111 mins C B, V P
Billy Dee Williams, James Earl Jones, Richard
Pryor, directed by John Badham
Set during the Depression of 1939, this film
follows the comedic adventures of a lively group
of black ball players who have defected from
the old Negro National League. The All-Stars
travel the country challenging local white teams.
MPAA:PG
Universal — *MCA Home Video*

Bionic Woman, The 1975.
Drama/Fantasy
71165 96 mins C B, V P
Lindsay Wagner, Lee Majors, Richard
Anderson, Alan Oppenheimer, directed by
Richard Moder
A sky-diving accident leaves tennis pro Jaimie
Somers crippled and near death. Her bionic
buddy, Steve Austin, gets his friends to rebuild
her and make her better than she was before.
The pilot for the TV series.
Universal — *MCA Home Video*

Bird of Paradise 1932
Romance
51611 80 mins B/W B, V P
Joel McCrea, Dolores Del Rio, Lon Chaney Jr.
An exotic South Seas romance in which an
adventurer falls in love with a native girl.
RKO — *Hollywood Home Theater; Cable*
Films; Video Connection; Discount Video Tapes;
Kartes Video Communications; Movie Buff
Video

Bird with the Crystal 1970
Plumage, The
Mystery
51575 98 mins C B, V P
Tony Musante, Susy Kendall, Eva Renzi
An alleged murderer is cleared when the woman
believed to be his next victim is revealed to be a
psychopathic murderer.
MPAA:PG
UMC; Salvatore Argento — *United Home*
Video

Birdman & Galaxy Trio 197?
Cartoons
66280 60 mins C B, V P

Animated
Birdman, a former secret agent, is bestowed
with powerful wings.
Hanna Barbera — *Worldvision Home Video*

Birdman of Alcatraz, The 1961
Drama
59342 148 mins B/W CED P
Burt Lancaster, Karl Malden, Thelma Ritter,
Edmond O'Brien, Neville Brand, Telly Savalas,
directed by John Frankenheimer
An imprisoned murderer makes a name for
himself as an ornithologist.
United Artists — *RCA VideoDiscs*

Birds, The 1963
Horror
45001 120 mins C B, V, LV P
Rod Taylor, Tippi Hedren, Jessica Tandy,
directed by Alfred Hitchcock
A small shore town north of San Francisco is
attacked by thousands of birds of varying
shapes, sizes, and colors.
Universal — *MCA Home Video; RCA*
VideoDiscs

Birds and the Bees, The 1956
Comedy
85242 94 mins C B, V P
Mitzi Gaynor, David Niven, George Gobel,
Reginald Gardner, Hans Conreid
A millionaire falls in love with an alluring card
shark, and then calls it all off when he learns of
her profession, only to fall in love with her again
when she disguises herself. A remake of
Preston Sturges' 1941 classic, "The Lady Eve."
Paramount — *Kartes Video Communications*

Birds of Paradise 1984
Drama
80119 90 mins C B, V P
Three attractive women who inherit a yacht
travel to the Florida Keys to find romance.
MPAA:R
Playboy Video — *King of Video*

Birds of Prey 1972
Drama
70603 81 mins C B, V P
David Janssen, Ralph Meeker, Elayne Heilveil
This action film pits a WWII army pilot against a
group of kidnapping thieves in an airborne
chopper chase.
Tomorrow Entertainment — *Prism*

Birdy 1984
Drama
Closed Captioned
80879 120 mins C B, V P
Matthew Modine, Nicholas Cage, John Harkins,
Sandy Baron, Karen Young, directed by Alan
Parker

This film chronicles the friendship of two young men from their youth in Philadelphia, to their participation in the Vietnam War. One of the characters enters a psychological bird land upon their return, straining their relationship. Peter Gabriel's soundtrack enjoys Beta and VHS Stereo Hi-Fi reproduction.
MPAA:R
Tri Star Pictures — *RCA/Columbia Pictures Home Video*

Birth of a Legend, The   1984
Theater
76011   25 mins   B/W   B, V   P, T
Mary Pickford, Douglas Fairbanks Sr.
A documentary showing the on and off antics of Miss Pickford and Mr. Fairbanks when they reigned as the King and Queen of the movies in 1926.
Matty Kemp; Mary Pickford Company — *Blackhawk Films*

Birth of a Nation, The   1915
Film-History/War-Drama
47465   175 mins   B/W   B, V, FO   P
Lillian Gish, Henry B. Walthall, Mae Marsh, directed by D. W. Griffith
The Civil War-era classic by D. W. Griffith, presented here from the most complete print of the film known to exist.
Epoch — *Video Yesteryear*

Birth of a Nation   1915
Film-History
57204   158 mins   B/W   B, V   P, T
Lillian Gish, Henry B. Walthall, Mae Marsh, Wallace Reid, directed by D.W. Griffith
A special tinted and musically scored print of D.W. Griffith's milestone classic recalling the Civil War and Reconstruction.
Epoch — *Blackhawk Films; Glenn Video Vistas; Discount Video Tapes; Cinema Concepts; Kartes Video Communications*

Birth of a Nation, The   1915
Film-History
08635   124 mins   C   B, V, 3/4U   P
Lillian Gish, Henry B. Walthall, Mae Marsh, Miriam Cooper, Wallace Reid, directed by D.W. Griffith
D. W. Griffith's dramatization of the events leading up to the Civil War. Based on "The Clansman," by Thomas Dixon.
Epoch — *VCII; International Historic Films; Cable Films; Video Connection; Hollywood Home Theater; Western Film & Video Inc*

Birth of the Bomb   1985
Documentary/Nuclear warfare
82558   50 mins   C   B, V, 3/4U   P
Narrated by Bernard Archard, directed by Peter Batty

The story of the A-Bomb is traced from early atomic experimentation to its actual implementation.
Peter Batty — *Evergreen International*

Bishop's Wife, The   1948
Fantasy
78642   109 mins   B/W   B, V, LV   P
Cary Grant, Loretta Young, David Niven, Monty Wooley, Elsa Lanchester
An angel comes down to earth to help a young bishop, his wife and his parishioners.
RKO; Samuel Goldwyn Productions — *Embassy Home Entertainment*

Bitch, The   1978
Drama
63337   90 mins   C   B, V   P
Joan Collins
This continuation of "The Stud" tells of the erotic adventures of a beautiful divorcee playing sex games for high stakes on the international playgrounds of high society.
MPAA:R
Brent Walker Film Productions — *THORN EMI/HBO Video*

Bite the Bullet   1975
Western
76025   131 mins   C   B, V   P
Gene Hackman, James Coburn, Candice Bergen, Jan-Michael Vincent
This exciting action-adventure featuring an all-star cast tells of a grueling 700-mile horse race in the rugged west of the early 1900's.
MPAA:PG
Richard Brooks — *RCA/Columbia Pictures Home Video*

Bitter Harvest   1981
Drama
71314   98 mins   C   B, V   P
Ron Howard, Art Carney, Torah Nutter, Richard Dysart, Jim Haynie, David Kneel, directed by Roger Young
Calves die at birth, cows develop lesions, and production drops dramatically on a young dairy farmer's ranch. When the disease spreads to his infant daughter, he suspects radioactivity, and alerts the media.
Charles Fries Productions — *U.S.A. Home Video*

Bizarre Bizarre   1939
Comedy
07249   90 mins   B/W   B, V   P
Louis Jouvet, Michel Simon, Francoise Rosay
A revue of comedy-farce sketches that include slapstick, burlesque, black humor and comedy of the absurd. French dialogue with English subtitles.
FR

French — *Movie Buff Video; Hollywood Home Theater; Festival Films; Discount Video Tapes*

Bizarre Music Television 1985
Music video
84362   60 mins   C   B, V   P
Barnes and Barnes, The Weirdos
A motley collection of strange and pointless videos, with wrestlers, kazoos, fish heads and more.
Impulse Ent — *Rhino Video*

Black and Tan/St. Louis Blues 1929
Musical
60048   36 mins   B/W   B, V   P, T
Duke Ellington and his Cotton Club Orchestra, Fredi Washington, Bessie Smith, the Hall Johnson Choir
Two early jazz two-reelers are combined on this tape: "Black and Tan" is the first film appearance of Duke Ellington's Orchestra, featuring Cootie Williams and Johnny Hodges. "St. Louis Blues" is the only surviving film made by legendary blues singer Bessie Smith. She is backed by the Hall Johnson Choir, members of the Fletcher Henderson band directed by James P. Johnson and dancer Jimmy Mordecai.
RKO; Dudley Murphy — *Blackhawk Films*

Black Arrow 1984
Adventure
77537   93 mins   C   B, V   P
Oliver Reed, Benedict Taylor, Georgia Slowe, Stephan Chase
An exiled bowman returns to England to avenge the injustices of a villainous nobleman.
Walt Disney Productions — *Walt Disney Home Video*

Black Beauty 1978
Cartoons
47687   49 mins   C   B, V   P
Animated
The tale of a sweet-tempered horse sold into the slavery of a harsh master.
Hanna Barbera — *Worldvision Home Video*

Black Beauty 1946
Adventure
70809   74 mins   B/W   B, V   P
Mona Freeman, Richard Denning, Evelyn Ankers
In this adaptation of Anna Sewell's familiar novel, a young girl develops a kindred relationship with an extraordinary horse.
20th Century Fox — *Nostalgia Merchant*

Black Beauty 1971
Drama
82549   105 mins   C   B, V   P
Mark Lester, Walter Slezak

The classic horse story by Anna Sewell is dramatized in this film. The story is an argument for the humane treatment of animals.
MPAA:G
Tigon British Film Production — *Paramount Home Video*

Black Beauty/Courage of Black Beauty 19??
Adventure
59151   145 mins   C   B, V, 3/4U   P
Mona Freeman, Johnny Crawford
Two feature-length films based on Anna Sewell's novel about the love of a child for a black stallion comprise this cassette. "Black Beauty" was first released in 1946; "Courage of Black Beauty" in 1957.
20th Century Fox — *Nostalgia Merchant*

Black Belt 1973
Martial arts
63862   92 mins   C   B, V   P
Two masters of Kung Fu clash when both attempt to steal a shipment of gold bullion.
MPAA:R
United International Pictures — *Hollywood Home Theater*

Black Belt Jones 1974
Martial arts
78623   87 mins   C   B, V   P
Jim Kelly, Gloria Hendry, Scatman Crothers
A martial arts expert fights the mob to save a school of self defense in Los Angeles' Watts district.
MPAA:R
Warner Bros; Golden Harvest — *Warner Home Video*

Black Belt Karate I 1982
Martial arts
59571   60 mins   C   B, V   P
Hosted by Jay T. Will
An introduction to the basic philosophy and moves of this Oriental self-defense system.
Professional Karate Assn — *Mastervision*

Black Belt Karate II 1982
Martial arts
59572   60 mins   C   B, V   P
Hosted by Jay T. Will
Jay T. Will takes the aficionado up the ladder and sets the athletic stage for the student's next upward move to karate expertise.
Professional Karate Assn — *Mastervision*

Black Belt Karate III 1981
Martial arts
59573   60 mins   C   B, V   P
Hosted by Jay T. Will
This program takes the practitioner into the rarefied atmosphere of the highest karate plane.

Professional Karate Assn — *Mastervision*

Black Bird, The 1975
Comedy
62814   98 mins   C   B, V   P
George Segal, Stephane Audran, Lionel Stander, Lee Patrick
In this satiric "sequel" to "The Maltese Falcon," detective Sam Spade, Jr. searches for the mysterious black falcon statuette that caused his father such trouble.
MPAA:PG
Columbia — *RCA/Columbia Pictures Home Video*

Black Cat, The/The Raven 193?
Horror
63842   126 mins   B/W   B, V   P
Boris Karloff, Bela Lugosi, Jacqueline Wells, John Carradine, Irene Ware, Lester Matthews
Both parts of this double feature star Boris Karloff and Bela Lugosi in leading roles. "The Black Cat" (1934, 65 minutes) features an architect who preserves the corpses of young girls and a doctor who plays chess in an attempt to keep a new bride from becoming a sacrifice to Satan. In "The Raven" (1935, 61 minutes), an insane plastic surgeon who is obsessed by the works of Edgar Allan Poe creates an elaborate torture chamber.
Universal — *MCA Home Video*

Black Devil Doll from Hell 1984
Horror/Exploitation
84543   70 mins   C   B, V   P
Shirley T Jones, Rickey Roach, Marie Sainvilvs
This shot-on-video movie deals with a nasty little doll with cornrow hair that likes to kill its owners.
Chester T Turner — *Hollywood Home Theater*

Black Dragons 1949
War-Drama
08758   62 mins   B/W   B, V   P
Bela Lugosi, Joan Barclay, George Pembroke, Clayton Moore
A war drama involving sabotage by the Japanese.
Monogram — *Movie Buff Video; Video Connection; Cable Films; Capital Home Video; Discount Video Tapes; Video Yesteryear*

Black Emanuelle 1976
Drama
60584   121 mins   C   B, V   P
Karin Schubert, Angelo Infanti, Don Powell
Emanuelle travels to Africa on an assignment, but work turns to play as she becomes a willing partner.
Independent — *CBS/Fox Video*

Black Flag TV Party 198?
Music-Performance
84053   60 mins   C   B, V   P
Black Flag
Live performances by Black Flag, America's most infamous slam-dancing punk group.
Target Video — *Target Video*

Black Fury 1935
Drama
73975   95 mins   B/W   B, V   P
Paul Muni, Barton MacLane, Henry O'Neill, directed by Michael Curtiz
A coal miner tries to shed light on the poor working conditions that exist in the mines.
Warner Bros — *Key Video*

Black Godfather, The 1974
Crime-Drama/Exploitation
84513   90 mins   C   B, V   P
Rod Perry, Damu King, Don Chastain, Jimmy Witherspoon
The grueling all-black story of a hood clawing his way to the top of a drug-selling mob.
MPAA:R
Cinemation Ind — *Magnum Entertainment*

Black Hand, The 1976
Drama
77256   90 mins   C   B, V   P
Lionel Stander, Mike Placido
An unemployed Italian immigrant becomes drawn into a web of murder and betrayal after he is attacked by an Irish gang.
Stiletto Productions — *Magnum Entertainment*

Black Hole, The 1979
Science fiction
44297   97 mins   C   B, V, LV   P
Maximilian Schell, Anthony Perkins, Ernest Borgnine, Yvette Mimieux
This is your basic mad scientist movie, with Maximilian Schell as a man determined to acquire the secrets of the universe by plunging into a black hole. In preparation for his journey he has manufactured an army of robots to assist him such as his body guard robot, Maximilian.
MPAA:G
Walt Disney — *Walt Disney Home Video; RCA VideoDiscs*

Black Jack 1950
Drama
66363   112 mins   B/W   B, V   P
George Sanders, Agnes Moorhead, Herbert Marshall, Patricia Roc, directed by Julien Duvivier
A Riviera socialite pretends to be an undercover agent, but she is actually a dope smuggler. Also known as "Captain Black Jack."
United Artists; Walter Gould — *Movie Buff Video; U.S.A. Home Video*

Black Jazz and Blues   **1938**
Musical
85147   44 mins   B/W   B, V   P
Bessie Smith, Duke Ellington, Louis Jordan,
Billie Holiday
Three classic jazz/blues shorts,"St. Louis
Blues,""Symphony in Black,"and "Caldonia."
RKO et al. — *Video Yesteryear*

Black Like Me   **1964**
Drama
45049   110 mins   B/W   B, V   P
Roscoe Lee Browne, James Whitmore, Clifton
James, Dan Priest
This movie is based on the true story of a white
writer who chemically changes the color of his
skin and travels through the South experiencing
the humiliation and terror of the black man.
Continental, Alan Enterprises — *United Home*
Video; Continental Video

Black Magic   **1949**
Adventure
45148   105 mins   B/W   B, V, 3/4U   P
Orson Welles, Akim Tamiroff, Nancy Guild
Cogliostro the magician becomes involved in a
plot to supply a double for Marie Antoinette.
Edward Small; United Artists — *Nostalgia*
Merchant

Black Magic Terror   **1979**
Horror/Suspense
70571   85 mins   C   B, V   P
Suzanna, W.D. Mochtar, Alan Nuary, directed by
L. Sudjio
That old queen of black magic has got
everybody under her spell. Troublestarts when
she turns her back on one of her subjects.
World Northal — *Twilight Video*

Black Marble, The   **1979**
Crime-Drama
56454   110 mins   C   B, V   P
Paula Prentiss, Harry Dean Stanton, Robert
Foxworth
A beautiful policewoman is paired with a
policeman who drinks too much, is divorced,
and is ready to retire. Surrounded by urban
craziness and corruptness, they eventually fall
in love. Based on the Joseph Wambaugh novel.
MPAA:PG
Avco Embassy, Frank Capra Jr — *Embassy*
Home Entertainment

Black Moon Rising   **1986**
Adventure
Closed Captioned
86085   100 mins   C   B, V   P
Tommy Lee Jones, Linda Hamilton, Richard
Jaeckel, Robert Vaughn
Based on an idea by John Carpenter, this film
deals with a new fast car and the people who
are fighting brutally over it.

MPAA:R
New World — *New World Video*

Black Narcissus   **1947**
Drama
50914   101 mins   C   B, V   P
Deborah Kerr, Jean Simmons, Flora Robson,
Sabu, David Farrar
A group of Anglican nuns attempting to found a
hospital and school in the Himalayas confront
native distrust and their own human frailties.
Universal — *VidAmerica; Learning Corp of*
America

Black Oak Conspiracy   **1977**
Adventure
84528   92 mins   C   B, V   P
Jesse Vint
Based on a true story, this film deals with a
mining company conspiracy discovered by an
inquisitive stuntman.
MPAA:R
Jesse Vint; Tom Clark — *Charter*
Entertainment

Black Orchid, The   **1959**
Drama
85243   96 mins   B/W   B, V   P
Sophia Loren, Anthony Quinn, Ina Ballin, Mark
Richmond, Jimmie Baird
A businessman and a crook's widow fall in love
and try to persuade their children it can work
out.
Paramount — *Kartes Video Communications*

Black Orpheus   **1959**
Drama
52741   98 mins   C   B, V, CED   P
Breno Mello, Marpessa Dawn, Lourdes De
Oliveira, directed by Marcel Camus
The legend of Orpheus and Eurydice unfolds
against the colorful background of the carnival
in Rio de Janeiro. In the black section of the city,
Orpheus is a street-car conductor and Eurydice
a country girl fleeing from a man sworn to kill
her. Dubbed in English.
Cannes Film Festival '59: Grand Prize Winner;
Academy Awards '59: Best Foreign Language
Film.
France; Brazil; Lopert Pictures — *CBS/Fox*
Video

Black Panther, The   **1977**
Suspense
87212   90 mins   C   B, V   P
Donald Sumpter, Debbie Farrington, directed by
Ian Merrick
The true story of psychokiller Donald Neilson,
who murdered heiress Lesley Whittle in England
in the 1970's.
Alpha Films — *Vestron Video*

Black Pirate, The   1926
Adventure
47460   122 mins   B/W   B, V, FO   P
Douglas Fairbanks, Donald Crisp, Billie Dove
A shipwrecked mariner vows revenge on the
pirates who destroyed his father's ship.
Quintessential Fairbanks, this film features
astounding athletic feats and exciting
swordplay. Originally filmed in Technicolor, this
print is in black and white. Silent film with music
score.
Elton Corp; Douglas Fairbanks — *Video
Yesteryear; Discount Video Tapes*

Black Planet, The   1983
Cartoons
65707   78 mins   C   B, V   P
Animated
The distant planet of Terre Verte is rapidly
running out of energy. To keep the remaining
fuel, warhawks Senator Calhoun and General
McNab think their part of the Planet should blow
up the other part. Will the whole planet be
destroyed?
Paul Williams — *Embassy Home
Entertainment*

Black Room, The   1982
Horror
76774   90 mins   C   B, V   P
Couples are lured to a mysterious mansion
where a brother and his sister promise to satisfy
their sexual desires.
MPAA:R
Butler/Cronin Productions — *Vestron Video*

Black Room, The   1935
Horror/Mystery
78964   70 mins   B/W   B, V   P
*Boris Karloff, Marian Marsh, Robert Allen,
Katherine De Mille, directed by Roy William Neill*
As an evil count lures victims into his castle of
terror, the count's twin brother returns to fulfill
an ancient prophecy. In Beta Hi-Fi.
Columbia Pictures — *RCA/Columbia Pictures
Home Video*

Black Sabbath   1964
Horror
84420   99 mins   C   B, V   P
Boris Karloff, Mark Damon
An omnibus horror film with three parts,
climaxing with Boris Karloff as a Wurdalak, a
vampire who must kill those he loves.
American Intl — *THORN EMI/HBO Video*

Black Sabbath Live   1984
Music-Performance
76645   60 mins   C   B, V   P
Heavy metal superstar, Ozzy Osbourne, as a
member of Black Sabbath, performs such hits
as "War Pigs," "Never Say Die" and
"Paranoid."

VCL — *VCL Home Video*

Black Shampoo   197?
Exploitation
86554   90 mins   C   B, V   P
*John Daniels, Tanya Boyd, Joe Ortiz, directed
by Greydon Clark*
A black hairdresser on the Sunset Strip fights
the mob with a chainsaw.
Alvin L. Fast — *United Home Video*

Black Six, The   1974
Drama
79324   91 mins   C   B, V   P
*Gene Washington, Carl Eller, Lem Barney,
Mercury Morris, Joe Greene, directed by Matt
Cimber*
Six black Vietnam veterans are out to avenge
the white gang who killed one of the black
men's brother.
MPAA:R
Cinemation Industries — *Unicorn Video*

Black Stallion Returns, The   1983
Adventure/Drama
69375   103 mins   C   B, V, LV   P
                              CED
Kelly Reno, Teri Garr
This sequel to "The Black Stallion" follows the
adventures of young Alec as he travels to North
Africa to search for his beautiful horse, which
was stolen by an Arab chieftain.
MPAA:PG
Zoetrope — *CBS/Fox Video; RCA VideoDiscs*

Black Stallion, The   1979
Adventure
47058   120 mins   C   B, V, LV   P
*Kelly Reno, Mickey Rooney, Teri Garr, Clarence
Muse, directed by Carroll Ballard*
A young boy and a wild Arabian Stallion are the
only survivors of a shipwreck, and they develop
a deep affection for each other. Music by
Carmine Coppola.
MPAA:PG
United Artists, Francis Coppola — *CBS/Fox
Video; RCA VideoDiscs*

Black Sunday   1977
Drama
64451   143 mins   C   B, V   P
*Robert Shaw, Bruce Dern, Marthe Keller, Fritz
Weaver, Steven Keats*
An Arab terrorist group plots to kidnap the
Goodyear blimp and load it with explosives with
the intent for it to explode over a Miami Super
Bowl game to assassinate the U.S. president
and to kill all the fans.
MPAA:R
Paramount — *Paramount Home Video; RCA
VideoDiscs*

Black Sunday: Highlights of Super Bowl XVII   1984
Football
72934   46 mins   C   B, V, FO   P
Highlights from SuperBowl XVIII include playoffs for each of the nine teams that qualified; also included in the program is "NFL 83" a summary of the NFL 1983 Season.
NFL Films — *NFL Films Video*

Black Tights   1960
Musical/Dance
81944   120 mins   C   B, V   P
Cyd Charisse, Zizi Jeanmarie, Moira Shearer, Maurice Chevalier, Roland Petit
Maurice Chevalier introduces four stories told in dance by Roland Petit's Ballet de Paris company: "The Diamond Crusher," "Cyrano de Bergerac," "A Merry Mourning" and "Carmen."
Talam Films — *Video Arts International; Movie Buff Video*

Black Tower, The   1950
Mystery
78110   54 mins   B/W   B, V, FO   P
Peter Cookson, Warren Williams, Anne Gwynn, Charles Calvert
An interesting murder mystery telling the story of an impoverished medical student who needs money desperately.
PRC — *Video Yesteryear*

Blackbeard's Ghost   1967
Comedy
59810   107 mins   C   B, V   P
Peter Ustinov, Dean Jones, Suzanne Pleshette, Elsa Lanchester, Richard Deacon
The famed 18th-century pirate's spirit returns to play havoc in a modern-day college town.
Walt Disney Productions — *Walt Disney Home Video*

Blackenstein   1974
Horror
03562   87 mins   C   B, V   P
A doctor restores a man's arms and legs, but a jealous assistant causes the man to turn into a monster who starts attacking people.
MPAA:R
Prestige Pictures Releasing Corp — *Media Home Entertainment*

Blackmail   1929
Mystery
01742   86 mins   B/W   B, V   P
Anny Ondra, John Longdon, Sara Allgood, Charles Paton, directed by Alfred Hitchcock
Britain's first sound film and an early visualization of some typical Hitchcockian themes. The story follows the police investigation of a murder, and a detective's attempts to keep his girlfriend from being involved.

British Intl; Wardour — *Hollywood Home Theater; Cable Films; Western Film & Video Inc; Discount Video Tapes; Movie Buff Video; Kartes Video Communications*

Blackout   1978
Suspense/Crime-Drama
84526   86 mins   C   B, V   P
Jim Mitchum, Robert Carradine, Ray Milland, June Allyson
Four Killers terrorize an office building during an electrical blackout. Soon, the police enter, confront them, and the fun starts.
MPAA:R
Nicole M. Boisvert, Eddy Matalon, John Dunning — *Charter Entertainment*

Blacksmith, The/Cops   1922
Comedy
60052   38 mins   B/W   B, V   P, T
Buster Keaton, Virginia Fox
"The Blacksmith" is a burlesque of Longfellow's famous poem "The Village Blacksmith." In "Cops" Buster tries a new business venture to win his girl's hand. Chaos ensues. Silent.
Comique Film Company — *Blackhawk Films*

Blacksmith, The/The Balloonatic   192?
Comedy
56909   57 mins   B/W   B, V, FO   P
Buster Keaton, Virginia Fox, Phyllis Haver
Two Buster Keaton shorts: "The Blacksmith (1922) features Buster as the local blacksmith's apprentice who suddenly finds himself in charge. "The Balloonatic" (1923) presents Buster trapped in a runaway hot air balloon. Both films include music score.
First National — *Video Yesteryear*

Blackstar   1981
Cartoons/Adventure
66006   60 mins   C   B, V   P
Animated
Blackstar fights the forces of evil in three animated adventures.
Filmation — *Family Home Entertainment*

Blackstar Volume III   1981
Cartoons
73368   60 mins   C   B, V   P
Animated
John Blackstar and his friends take on the evil overlord in three adventures: "The Mermaid of Serpent Sea," "Lightning City of the Clouds" and "The Airwhales of Anchar."
Filmation Associates — *Family Home Entertainment*

Blackstar, Volume 2   1981
Cartoons/Adventure
69805   60 mins   C   B, V   P

Animated
John Blackstar and his friends on the planet
Sagar continue their never-ending battle against
the cruel and ruthless Overlord in three
animated adventures.
Filmation — *Family Home Entertainment*

Blackstone on Tour   1984
Magic
78659   60 mins   C   B, V   P
Here are highlights from magician Harry
Blackstone's cross country tour.
RKO — *RKO HomeVideo*

Blacula   1972
Horror
81481   92 mins   C   B, V   P
*William Marshall, Thalmus Rasulala, Denise
Nicholas, Vonetta Mcgee*
The African Prince Mamuwalde is stalking the
streets of Los Angeles trying to satisfy his
insatiable desire for blood.
MPAA:PG
American International Pictures — *THORN
EMI/HBO Video*

Blade   1972
Crime-Drama
59351   79 mins   C   B, V   R, P
*Steve Landesburg, John Schuck, Kathryn
Walker*
An honest cop challenges a dirty cover-up in
killer-stalked New York.
MPAA:PG
Heritage Enterprises — *Video Gems*

Blade Master   1984
Adventure
78342   92 mins   C   B, V   P
Miles O'Keefe, Lisa Foster
Ator, The Blade Master leads a small band of
men to the castle of knowledge to obtain the
ultimate weapon.
MPAA:PG
Chris Trainor — *Media Home Entertainment*

Blade Runner   1982
Science fiction
60437   122 mins   C   B, V, 8mm,   P
                                   LV
*Harrison Ford, Rutger Hauer, Sean Young,
Darryl Hannah, M. Emmet Walsh, Joanna
Cassidy, directed by Ridley Scott*
A hard-boiled ex-cop (known as Blade Runner)
is forced out of retirement for an extremely
dangerous mission. He must track down and kill
a group of genetically manufactured beings
impersonating humans.
MPAA:R
Ladd Co; Sir Run Run Shaw; Warner
Bros — *Embassy Home Entertainment*

Blake of Scotland Yard   1936
Drama/Serials
10931   70 mins   B/W   B, V   P
*Ralph Byrd, Lloyd Hughes, directed by Robert
Hill*
Feature film version of this exciting serial, with
Blake up again a villain who has constructed a
murderous death ray.
Victory — *Movie Buff Video; Discount Video
Tapes; Video Connection; Video Yesteryear*

Blame It on Rio   1984
Comedy
72908   90 mins   C   B, V   P
*Michael Caine, Joseph Bologna, Demi Moore,
Michelle Johnson*
A middle-aged man has a fling with his best
friend's daughter while on a vacation in Rio de
Janeiro.
MPAA:R
Sherwood Productions — *Vestron Video*

Blame It on the Night   1984
Musical-Drama
81930   85 mins   C   B, V   P
*Nick Mancuso, Byron Thames, Leslie
Ackerman, Billy Preston, Merry Clayton*
A rock star gets to take care of the son he never
knew after his mother suddenly dies. Available
in VHS and Beta Hi-Fi.
MPAA:PG-13
Tri-Star Pictures — *Key Video*

Blancmange   1984
Music video
88090   16 mins   C   B, V   P
A small slew of music videos by the strange new
wave group.
Sony Video — *Sony Video Software*

Blasphemer, The   1921
Drama/Religion
78116   89 mins   B/W   B, V, FO   P
A well-crafted, engrossing drama about
misfortune that befalls someone who disobeys
one of the sacred Commandments. Silent music
score.
Religious Film Association — *Video Yesteryear*

Blastfighter   1985
Crime-Drama
82433   93 mins   C   B, V   P
*Michael Sopkiw, Valerie Blake, George
Eastman*
After local hoodlums kill his daughter, an ex-con
cop goes on a spree of violence and revenge.
MPAA:R
Unknown — *Vestron Video*

Blazing Saddles   1974
Comedy
38945   90 mins   C   B, V, LV   P

Cleavon Little, Harvey Korman, Madeleine
Kahn, Gene Wilder, Mel Brooks, directed by Mel
Brooks
A wild, wacky spoof by Mel Brooks of every
cliche in the western film genre, telling the story
of a black sheriff who is sent to clean up a
frontier town, with unpredictable results.
MPAA:R
Warner Bros — Warner Home Video; RCA
VideoDiscs

Bless the Beasts & Children
1971

Drama
81210   109 mins   C   B, V   P
Bill Mumy, Barry Robins, Miles Chapin, Darel
Glaser, Bob Kramer, directed by Stanley Kramer
A group of six teenaged boys at a summer camp
attempt to save a herd of buffalo from slaughter
at a national preserve.
MPAA:R
Columbia, Stanley Kramer — RCA/Columbia
Pictures Home Video

Blessercize
1982

Physical fitness
75701   60 mins   C   B, V   P
Marie Chapian
Minister-psychotherapist-author Marie Chapian
combines aerobics and Bible teachings in this
program designed to fortify viewers' physical
and mental health. Available as a 60-minute
tape or two 30-minute tapes. This program is
also known as "Fun to Be Fit."
Marie Chapian — Video Associates; Video
Bible Library

Blind Date
1984

Mystery
77218   100 mins   C   B, V   P
Joseph Bottoms, Kirstie Alley
A blind man agrees to have a visual computer
implanted in his brain in order to help the police
track down a psychopathic killer.
MPAA:R
Wescom Productions — Lightning Video

Blind Fist of Bruce
197?

Martial arts/Adventure
47696   92 mins   C   B, V   P
Bruce Li
A rich, idle young man learns the techniques of
Kung Fu from a former warrior.
Luk Suie Yee — Master Arts Video

Blind Husbands
1919

Drama
11391   98 mins   B/W   B, V, FO   P
Erich von Stroheim, directed by Erich von
Stroheim
An Austrian officer is attracted to the pretty wife
of a dull surgeon. This film was considered
shocking at the time of its release.

Universal — Video Yesteryear

Blind Rage
1983

Martial arts
73363   81 mins   C   B, V   P
Fred Williamson
When the United States Government transports
fifteen million dollars to Manilla, five blind Kung
fu masters want a piece of the action.
MPAA:R
MGM; Cannon Films — MGM/UA Home Video

Bliss
1986

Comedy/Fantasy
88187   112 mins   C   B, V   P
Barry Otto, Lynette Curran, Helen Jones,
directed by Ray Lawrence
A savage, surreal Australian comedy about an
advertising executive who dies suddenly for a
few minutes, and upon his awakening he finds
the world maniacally, bizarrely changed.
Australian Academy Awards '86: Best Picture.
MPAA:R
Jay Lawrence; Australian — New World Video

Blob, The
1958

Science fiction
52611   83 mins   C   B, V   R, P
Steve McQueen, Aneta Corseaut, Olin Howlin,
Earl Rowe
McQueen's first starring role in this science
fiction thriller about a small town's fight against
a slimy invader from space.
Paramount; Jack Harris — Video Gems

Blockheads
1938

Comedy
33909   55 mins   B/W   B, V, 3/4U   P
Stan Laurel, Oliver Hardy, Billie Gilbert, Patricia
Ellis, James Finlayson
Stan is a famous WWI soldier who stays on the
battleground for eighteen years after the war
had ended, since nobody told him it was over.
Old friend Ollie finds him later at an old soldiers'
home, and brings him to his house to live.
Hal Roach, MGM — Nostalgia Merchant;
Blackhawk Films

Blockheads
1938

Comedy
63984   75 mins   B/W   B, V   P, T
Stan Laurel, Oliver Hardy, Billy Gilbert, Patricia
Ellis, Jimmy Finlayson
Twenty years after the end of World War I,
soldier Stan is found, still in his foxhole, and
brought back to America, where he moves in
with old pal Ollie. This tape also includes a 1934
Charley Chase short, "I'll Take Vanilla."
Hal Roach; MGM — Blackhawk Films

(For explanation of codes, see Use Guide and Key)

Blondie—Eat to the Beat 1980

Music-Performance
54690 60 mins C B, V P
Blondie
This program features the multi-million seller platinum album, "Eat to the Beat," taped on location and in a studio. The program contains twelve songs, including the hit singles "Dreaming" and "The Hardest Part."
Warner Bros — *Warner Home Video; RCA VideoDiscs*

Blondie Live 1983

Music video
75015 55 mins C B, V P
This tape features the group Blondie's last concert. Among the tunes performed are "Heart of Glass," "Call Me" and "Rapture."
MCA Home Video — *MCA Home Video*

Blood and Black Lace 1965

Horror
79224 90 mins C B, V P
Cameron Mitchell, Eva Bartok, Mary Arden
A police inspector must solve a series of grisly murders at a fashion salon.
Allied Artists — *Media Home Entertainment*

Blood and Sand 1922

Drama/Romance
58613 80 mins B/W B, V, 3/4U R, P
Rudolph Valentino, Nita Naldi, Lila Lee, Walter Long
Classic film based on Vincente Blasco Ibanez's novel about the tragic rise and fall of a matador, and the women in his life. (Silent).
Paramount — *Cable Films; Video Connection; Blackhawk Films; Western Film & Video Inc*

Blood and Sand/Son of the Sheik 1926

Film-History
50637 56 mins B/W B, V P, T
Rudolph Valentino, Lila Lee, Vilma Banky
A double feature containing two abridged versions of these motion pictures. In "Blood and Sand," an idolized matador meets another woman just before his wedding. In "Son of the Sheik," a man believes he has been betrayed by a dancing girl, and he abucts her to seek revenge. Silent.
Famous Players Lasky Corp; United Artists — *Blackhawk Films*

Blood Beach 1981

Horror
59047 92 mins C B, V P
David Huffman, Marianna Hill, John Saxon, Burt Young
A group of teenagers is devoured by menacing sand which keeps people from getting to the water.
MPAA:R

Shaw Beckerman Productions — *Media Home Entertainment*

Blood Beast Terror, The 1969

Horror
84037 81 mins C B, V P
Peter Cushing, Robert Flemyng, Wanda Ventham, directed by Vernon Sewell
An entomologist transforms his own daughter into a Deathshead Moth and she proceeds to terrorize and drink innocent victims' blood.
MPAA:G
Arnold L Miller — *Monterey Home Video*

Blood Couple 1973

Horror
80798 83 mins C B, V R, P
Duanne Jones, Marlene Clark
A newlywed vampire couple pursue their favorite nocturnal pastime-blood sucking.
MPAA:R
Karl Munson — *Video Gems*

Blood Cult 1985

Horror
81681 92 mins C B, V P
Chuck Ellis, Julie Andelman, Jim Vance, Joe Hardt
A bizarre series of murder-mutilations take place on a small midwestern campus. Contains graphic violence that is not for the squeamish. This film was created especially for the home video market.
Linda and Christopher Lewis — *United Home Video*

Blood Feud 1979

Drama
65004 112 mins C B, V P
Sophia Loren, Marcello Mastroianni, Giancarlo Giannini, directed by Lina Wertmuller
Set in Italy preceding Europe's entry into WWII, a young widow is in mourning over the brutal murder of her husband by the Sicilian Mafia. A rivalry between two men in her life ensues.
ITC Entertainment — *CBS/Fox Video*

Blood for a Silver Dollar 1966

Western
78118 98 mins C B, V, FO P
Montgomery Wood, Evelyn Stewart
An action-filled western, telling an ambitious tale of murder, revenge and romance.
Italio-France Co-productions — *Video Yesteryear*

Blood Legacy 1973

Horror
58549 77 mins C B, V R, P
John Carradine, John Russel, Faith Domergue
Four heirs must survive a night in a lonely country estate. Also titled "Legacy of Blood."

MPAA:R
ASW Films Inc — *Video Gems*

Blood Lust 1987
Horror
80127   90 mins   C   B, V   P
Dr. Jekyll returns to London to wreak havoc upon the human race.
Independent — *King of Video*

Blood Mania 1970
Horror
79758   90 mins   C   B, V   P
Peter Carpenter, Maria de Arogon
A retired surgeon's daughter decides to murder her father to collect her inheritance prematurely.
MPAA:R
Crown International — *United Home Video*

Blood of a Poet 1930
Film-Avant-garde
08688   55 mins   B/W   B, V   P
Jean Cocteau, directed by Jean Cocteau
A realistic documentary composed of unreal happenings. Built around the central character of a poet who "lives what he creates". French with English subtitles.
FR
France — *Movie Buff Video; Hollywood Home Theater; Video Yesteryear; Discount Video Tapes*

Blood of Dracula's Castle 1969
Horror
60347   84 mins   C   B, V   P
John Carradine, Paula Raymond, Alex D'Arcy
Young lovers move into an inherited castle, only to find it occupied by immovable vampires.
Al Adamson — *United Home Video*

Blood on the Moon 1948
Western
00288   88 mins   B/W   B, V, 3/4U   P
Robert Mitchum, Robert Preston, Walter Brennan
Well-acted film about a cowboy's involvement in a friend's underhanded schemes who mends his ways to aid a girl.
United Artists — *Nostalgia Merchant*

Blood on the Sun 19??
Suspense
01794   98 mins   B/W   B, V   P
James Cagney, Sylvia Sydney, Robert Armstrong, directed by Frank Lloyd
Politics, violence, and intrigue are combined in this story of Japan's plans for Pearl Harbor and world conquest.
United Artists — *Hollywood Home Theater; Prism; Video Yesteryear; Discount Video Tapes; Video Dimensions; Kartes Video Communications; Movie Buff Video*

Blood on the Sun 1975
Martial arts/Adventure
59070   81 mins   C   B, V   R, P
Martial arts action highlights this tale of adventure.
Dandrea Releasing Corp — *Video Gems*

Blood Simple 1985
Suspense/Mystery
81198   96 mins   C   B, V, LV   P
John Getz, M. Emmet Walsh, Dan Hedaya, Frances McDormand, directed by Joel Coen
A jealous husband hires a sleazy private eye to murder his adulterous wife and her lover. Plot twists around, though, and everybody gets into trouble. Available in VHS and Beta Hi-Fi.
MPAA:R
River Road Productions — *MCA Home Video*

Blood Voyage 1977
Horror
81398   80 mins   C   B, V   P
Jonathon Lippe, Laurie Rose, Midori, Mara Modair
A crewman aboard a pleasure yacht must find out who is killing off his passengers one by one. Available in VHS Stereo and Beta Hi-Fi.
MPAA:R
Gene Levy — *Monterey Home Video*

Blood Wedding (Bodas de Sangre) 1981
Dance
88305   71 mins   C   B, V   P
Antonio Gades, Christina Hoyos, Marisol, Carmen Villena
A dance film choreographed by Saura and Antonio Gades, based on an original story by famed author Federico Garcia Lorca. Subtitled.
SP
Carlos Saura; Spanish — *Media Home Entertainment*

Bloodbath at the House of Death 1985
Satire/Horror
82494   92 mins   C   B, V   P
Kenny Everett, Pamela Stephenson, Vincent Price
Vincent Price and his compatriots fight a team of mad scientists in this satirical spoof of popular horror films.
Ray Cameron — *Media Home Entertainment*

Bloodbrothers 1978
Drama
52702   116 mins   C   B, V   P
Richard Gere, Paul Sorvino, Tony LoBianco, Marilu Henner, directed by Richard Mulligan
An Italian New York family battle with each other in this story of emotional problems, and a son who wants to break out of his family existence.

MPAA:R
Warner Bros; Stephen Friedman — *Warner Home Video*

Bloodstalkers   1978
Horror
86168   91 mins   C   B, V   P
Kenny Miller, Celea Ann Cole, Jerry Albert, directed by Robert W. Morgan
Two vacationers in Florida meet up with a band of slaughtering, swamp-based lunatics.
Ben Morse — *Vidmark Entertainment*

Bloodsuckers   1985
Horror
70249   90 mins   C   B, V   P
Patrick Macnee, Peter Cushing, Patrick Mower
Three friends search for a professor who has been abducted by a blood drinking cult. They rescue him from the lips of the coven's leader.
VCL Communications — *VCL Home Video*

Bloodsuckers from Outer   1983
Space
Horror
85913   80 mins   C   B, V   P
Directed by Glenn Coburn
Texas is mysteriously overrun by ordinary citizens who have become vampire-like maniacs.
Gary Boyd Latham — *Karl/Lorimar Home Video*

Bloodsucking Freaks   1975
Horror/Comedy
65380   89 mins   C   B, V   P
This outrageous comedic bloodbath has developed a tremendous cult following, second only to the "Rocky Horror Picture Show."
MPAA:R
Joel Reed — *Vestron Video*

Bloody Birthday   1986
Horror
87682   92 mins   C   B, V   P
Susan Strasberg, Jose Ferrer, Lori Lethin, Melinda Cordell, Julie Brown
Three youngsters, coming up on their 10th birthdays, all plan to kill everyone around them that ever gave them problems.
MPAA:R
Gerald T. Olson — *Prism*

Bloody Fight, The   197?
Martial arts/Adventure
47704   89 mins   C   B, V   P
Alan Tang, Yu In Yin, Tan Chin
Two young people learn the cost of courage and the high price of justice when they avenge a murderer.
Chiang Chung Pin — *Master Arts Video*

Bloody Fist   197?
Martial arts/Adventure
47700   90 mins   C   B, V   P
An exciting story set in China with outstanding martial arts scenes.
Independent — *Master Arts Video*

Bloody Mama   1970
Drama
64896   90 mins   C   B, V, CED   P
Shelley Winters, Robert DeNiro, Don Stroud, Pat Hingle, Bruce Dern, Diane Varsi
The story of the infamous Barker Gang, led by the bloodthirsty and sex-crazed Ma Barker.
MPAA:R
American International Pictures — *Vestron Video*

Bloopers from Star Trek   1966
and Laugh-In
Outtakes and bloopers
43022   26 mins   C   B, V, FO   P
William Shatner, Leonard Nimoy, Bill Cosby, Milton Berle, Jonathan Winters, Orson Welles, Dick Martin, Dan Rowan
Some well-known faces are seen and heard cracking up in this compilation of hilarious goofs, flubbed lines, and kidding around in the NBC studios.
NBC — *Video Yesteryear*

Blotto   1983
Music video
88091   12 mins   C   B, V   P
A collection of the tongue-in-cheek San Fransisco-based group's favorite tunes, including "I Want to Be a Lifeguard."
Sony Video — *Sony Video Software*

Blow Out   1981
Suspense
51992   107 mins   C   B, V   P
John Travolta, Nancy Allen, John Lithgow, Dennis Franz, directed by Brian De Palma
When a prominent senator is killed in a car crash, a sound effects engineer becomes involved in political intrigue when he tries to expose a conspiracy with the evidence he has gathered.
MPAA:R
Filmways Pictures — *Warner Home Video; RCA VideoDiscs; Vestron Video (disc only)*

Blow-Up   1966
Drama
54101   110 mins   C   B, V   P
David Hemmings, Vanessa Redgrave, Sarah Miles, directed by Michelangelo Antonioni
A young London photographer takes some pictures of a couple in the park. After blowing the pictures up he discovers what looks like a murder involving the couple.

Carlo Ponti — *MGM/UA Home Video*

South Australian Film Corporation/Hal McElroy — *Embassy Home Entertainment*

Blue Angel, The   1930
Film-Avant-garde
08676   93 mins   B/W   B, V, 3/4U   P
Marlene Dietrich, Emil Jannings, directed by Josef von Sternberg
A film classic about how a cheap chanteuse morally destroys a professor who loves her. German with English subtitles.
GE
Paramount, Korda; German — Kartes Video Communications; VCII; Video Connection; Discount Video Tapes; Video Dimensions; Cable Films; Hollywood Home Theater; Western Film & Video Inc; International Home Video; Video Yesteryear

Blue Canadian Rockies   1952
Western
60050   58 mins   B/W   B, V   P, T
Gene Autry, Pat Buttram
Gene's employer sends him to Canada to discourage his daughter from marrying a fortune hunter. The daughter has turned the place into a dude ranch and wild game preserve. When Gene arrives, he encounters some mysterious killings.
BLA — *Blackhawk Films*

Blue Collar   1978
Drama
47412   114 mins   C   B, V   P
Richard Pryor, Harvey Keitel, Yaphet Kotto, directed by Paul Schrader
An auto assembly line worker, tired of the poverty of his life, hatches a plan to rob his own union.
MPAA:R
Universal — *MCA Home Video*

Blue Country   1978
Comedy
76026   104 mins   C   B, V   P
Brigitte Fossey, Jacques Serres
A joyful romantic comedy about a pair of free souls who leave their stagnant lives behind to seek out a more idyllic existence. This movie is subtitled in English.
MPAA:PG FR
Alain Poire — *RCA/Columbia Pictures Home Video*

Blue Fin   1978
Adventure
70681   93 mins   C   B, V   P
Hardy Kruger, Greg Rowe, directed by Carl Schultz
When their tuna boat is shipwrecked, and the crew disabled, a young boy and his father learn lessons of love and courage as the son tries to save the ship.

Blue Fire Lady   1978
Drama
65289   96 mins   C   B, V   P
Cathryn Harrison, Mark Holden, Peter Cummins
This is the heartwarming story of a young girl and her obsession for horses.
Antony I Ginnane — *Media Home Entertainment*

Blue Hawaii   1962
Musical
08385   101 mins   C   B, V, LV   P
Elvis Presley, Angela Lansbury, Joan Blackman, Roland Winters
Soldier, returning to Hawaiian home, takes job with tourist agency against parents' wishes.
EL, SP
Paramount; Hal Wallis — *CBS/Fox Video; RCA VideoDiscs*

Blue Heaven   1984
Drama
84798   100 mins   C   B, V   P
Leslie Denniston, James Eckhouse
A marriage harbors a dark, horrible secret.
Five Point — *Vestron Video*

Blue Knight, The   1975
Drama
81810   72 mins   C   B, V   P
George Kennedy, Alex Rocco, Glynn Turman, Verna Bloom, directed by J. Lee Thompson
Los Angeles policeman Bumper Morgan is The Blue Knight, a streetwise cop who sets out to bust a drug addict and an informer. Based upon Joseph Wambaugh's novel. Available in VHS Stereo and Beta Hi-Fi.
Lorimar Productions — *U.S.A. Home Video*

Blue Lagoon, The   1980
Drama
58434   105 mins   C   B, V   P
Brooke Shields, Christopher Atkins, Leo McKern, William Daniels, directed by Randal Kleiser
Two beautiful teenagers marooned on a desert isle discover love without the restraints of society.
MPAA:R
Columbia; Randal Kleiser — *RCA/Columbia Pictures Home Video; RCA VideoDiscs*

Blue Max, The   1966
Drama
29133   155 mins   C   B, V   P
George Peppard, James Mason, Ursula Andress
During World War II a young German, fresh out of aviation training school, competes for the

coveted "Blue Max" flying award with other members of a squadron of seasoned flyers of the aristocratic set. Based on a novel by Jack D. Hunter.
EL, SP
20th Century Fox — *CBS/Fox Video*

Blue Money   1984
Comedy
85056   82 mins   C   B, V   P
Tim Curry
A wild, comedic caper film about a nightclub impressionist who absconds with a briefcase packed with cash and is pursued by everyone, even the I.R.A.
London Weekend TV — *Sony Video Software*

Blue Note I, II   1983
Music-Performance
88114   115 mins   C   B, V, 8mm   P
On two volumes, a great variety of blues and jazz performers are captured in concert.
Sony Video — *Sony Video Software*

Blue Ribbon Bluesman   1986
Music
88295   30 mins   C   B, V   R, P
A portrait of the late Mississippi Delta bluesman Robert B.J. Johnson.
Hank Madden; Nancy Madden; Video Moviemakers — *Video Moviemakers*

Blue Skies Again   1983
Comedy
69312   91 mins   C   B, V   P
Robyn Barto, Harry Hamlin, Mimi Rogers, Kenneth McMillan, Dana Elcar
A spunky young woman determined to play major league baseball locks horns with the chauvinistic owner and the gruff manager of her favorite team. In Beta Hi-Fi and stereo VHS.
MPAA:PG
Lantana Productions — *Warner Home Video*

Blue Steel   1934
Western
08827   55 mins   B/W   B, V, 3/4U   P
John Wayne
Typical John Wayne excitement as he rides into danger and violence.
Monogram — *Video Connection; Video Dimensions; Discount Video Tapes; Cable Films; Nostalgia Merchant; Spotlite Video; Sony Video Software*

Blue Sunshine   1977
Horror
72909   94 mins   C   B, V   P
A certain brand of L.S.D. called Blue Sunshine starts to make its victims go insane.
MPAA:R

Excel Video — *Vestron Video*

Blue Thunder   1983
Adventure
65314   110 mins   C   B, V   P
Roy Scheider, Daniel Stern, Malcolm McDowell, Candy Clark, Warren Oates
Roy Scheider is the police helicopter pilot who is chosen to test an experimental high-tech chopper that can see through walls, record a whisper and level a city block. In VHS stereo and Beta Hi-Fi.
MPAA:R
Gordon Carroll — *RCA/Columbia Pictures Home Video; RCA VideoDiscs*

Blue Yonder, The   1986
Drama
70941   90 mins   C   B, V   P
Art Carney, Peter Coyote, Huckleberry Fox
In this made-for-video feature, a young boy travels back in time to meet the grandfather he never knew, risking historical integrity.
Walt Disney Productions — *Walt Disney Home Video*

Bluebeard   1944
Drama
01651   73 mins   B/W   B, V   P
John Carradine, Jean Parker, Nils Asther, directed by Edgar G. Ulmer
Tormented painter with apsychopathic urge to strangle his models is seen in this film.
PRC — *Hollywood Home Theater; Cable Films; Discount Video Tapes; Kartes Video Communications; Movie Buff Video*

Bluebeard   1972
Drama
65446   128 mins   C   B, V   P
Raquel Welch, Richard Burton, Joey Heatherton, Virna Lisi, Sybil Danning
An American dancer, married to an Australian aristocrat, discovers the frozen bodies of seven women in his refrigerated vault, and fights for her survival.
MPAA:R
Alexander Salkind — *U.S.A. Home Video*

Blues Alive   1983
Music-Performance
64780   91 mins   C   B, V   P
Albert King, Junior Wells and Buddy Guy join John Mayall in a concert celebration of their blues roots. Also appearing are ex-Rolling Stone Mick Taylor and Fleetwood Mac's John McVie.
Monarch Entertainment — *RCA/Columbia Pictures Home Video; RCA VideoDiscs*

Blues Brothers, The   1980
Musical/Comedy
48608   133 mins   C   B, V   P

John Belushi, Dan Aykroyd, James Brown, Cab Calloway, Ray Charles, Aretha Franklin, Carrie Fisher, directed by John Landis
As an excuse to run rampant on the city of Chicago, Jake and Elwood Blues attempt to raise $5,000 for their childhood parish by putting their old band back together.
MPAA:R
Universal, Robert K Weiss — *MCA Home Video; RCA VideoDiscs*

Blues 1   1983
Music-Performance
65224   58 mins   C   B, V   P
Linda Hopkins, B.B.King, Leatta Galloway, Ernie Andrews, Eddie "Cleanhead" Vinson, Vi Reed, "Pee Wee" Crayton
Brock Peters is the host of this historic journey to "the roots" of the Blues. In Beta Hi-Fi and VHS stereo.
Skylark Savoy Productions Ltd — *Video Gems*

Blume in Love   1973
Comedy/Drama
58219   115 mins   C   B, V   P
George Segal, Susan Anspach, Kris Kristofferson, Shelley Winters, Marsha Mason, directed by Paul Mazursky
An ironic comedy/drama about a man now hopelessly in love with his ex-wife who divorced him for cheating on her while they were married.
MPAA:R
Warner Bros — *Warner Home Video*

BMW 6 Cylinder   1986
Automobiles
88401   60 mins   C   B, V, 3/4U   P
How to tune-up, maintain and pamper the entitled BMW engines.
Peter Allen Prod. — *Peter Allen Video Productions*

BMW 320, 381   1986
Automobiles
88400   60 mins   C   B, V, 3/4U   P
How to tune-up, maintain and repair these BMW models.
Peter Allen Prod. — *Peter Allen Video Productions*

Boarding School   1983
Comedy
72222   100 mins   C   B, V   P
Nastassia Kinski
A group of restless young women hatch a plan to turn their spare time into money.
MPAA:R
Atlantic Releasing — *Vestron Video*

Boat, The   1982
War-Drama
63432   150 mins   C   B, V   P

Jurgen Prochnow, Herbert Gronemeyer
"The Boat" (original title: "Das Boot") is a World War II drama about a German submarine and its crew on patrol in the North Atlantic and their fight for survival. Stereo soundtrack, dubbed in English.
MPAA:PG
Gunter Rohrback; Bavaria Atelier — *RCA/Columbia Pictures Home Video; RCA VideoDiscs*

Boat Is Full, The   1962
Drama
81623   104 mins   C   B, V   P
Tina Engel, Curt Bais, directed by Markus Imhoof
A group of refugees pose as a family in order to escape from Nazi Germany as they seek asylum in Switzerland. Available in German with English subtitles or dubbed into English.
GE
George Reinhart — *Embassy Home Entertainment*

Boating: Cold Water   1983
Survivial
Boating/Safety education
70177   60 mins   C   B, V   P
This program explains what all boaters should know about hypothermia and cold water survival techniques.
Video Travel — *Video Travel; RMI Media Productions*

Boatniks, The   1970
Comedy
65635   99 mins   C   B, V   P
Robert Morse, Stefanie Powers, Phil Silvers, Norman Fell, Wally Cox, Don Ameche
An accident-prone Coast Guard ensign finds himself in charge of the "Times Square" of waterways: Newport Harbor. Adding to his already "titanic" problems is a gang of ocean-going jewel thieves who won't give up the ship!
Ron Miller — *Walt Disney Home Video*

Bob & Carol & Ted &   1969
Alice
Comedy
47435   104 mins   C   B, V   P
Natalie Wood, Robert Culp, Dyan Cannon, Elliot Gould, directed by Paul Mazursky
Two California couples, influenced by a group sensitivity session, decide to loosen their sexual inhibitions and try wife-swapping.
MPAA:R
Columbia — *RCA/Columbia Pictures Home Video*

Bob & Ray, Jane, Laraine   1983
& Gilda
Comedy
66284   75 mins   C   B, V   P

Bob & Ray, Jane Curtin, Laraine Newman, Gilda Radner, Willie Nelson, Leon Russell
The whimsical world of Bob & Ray is transferred to video.
Jean Doumanian; Lorne Michaels — *Pacific Arts Video*

Bob Hope Chevy Show I, The   1957
Comedy/Variety
64827   120 mins   B/W   B, V, 3/4U   P
Bob Hope, Joan Davis, Julie London, Perry Como, Rosemary Clooney, Lana Turner, Wally Cox
Two complete programs that were originally telecast on November 11, 1956 and March 10, 1957. Bob and his guest do spoofs of "Playhouse 90" and the Elvis Presley craze; Julie London, Perry Como and Rosemary Clooney sing their current hits. All original commercials are included.
NBC — *Shokus Video*

Bob Hope Chevy Show II, The   1957
Comedy/Variety
64828   120 mins   B/W   B, V, 3/4U   P
Bob Hope, Eddie Fisher, Betty Grable, Harry James, Rowen and Martin, Frank Sinatra, Natalie Wood, Janis Paige
Bob Hope and a stellar array of guest stars present songs and comedy routines in these two complete programs, originally telecast on January 25, 1957 and April 5, 1957. All original commercials are included.
NBC — *Shokus Video*

Bob Hope Chevy Show III, The   1956
Comedy/Television
84696   120 mins   B/W   B, V, 3/4U   P
Bob Hope, Vic Damone, Leo Durocher, Desi Arnaz
Complete with those amazing car commercials of yesteryear, two classic Hope shows fill this tape.
NBC — *Shokus Video*

Bob Le Flambeur   1955
Drama
65464   106 mins   B/W   B, V   P
Roger Duchesne, Isabel Corey, Daniel Cauchy
The story of a compulsive gambler who decides to take a final fling by robbing the casino at Deauville. Subtitled in English. In stereo VHS and Beta Hi-Fi.
FR
Jean Pierre Melville — *RCA/Columbia Pictures Home Video; Video Dimensions*

Bob Marley and the Wailers Live from the Santa Barbara Bowl   1980
Music-Performance
59880   59 mins   C   LV   P
Reggae king Bob Marley, accompanied by a 12-piece band performs his hits in this stereo presentation filmed during his last complete U.S. tour in the Fall of 1979. Songs include "I Shot the Sheriff," "Jamming," and "Africa Unite." Also includes a personal interview.
Avalon Attractions — *Pioneer Artists*

Bob Marley & the Wailers—Live at the Rainbow   1977
Music-Performance
85832   40 mins   C   B, V   P
Marley and his group are seen in a performance taped at the height of their popularity. Songs include "Exodus" and "Get Up Stand Up."
Taped at London's Rainbow Theatre.
Island Records Inc. — *RCA/Columbia Pictures Home Video*

Bob Marley—Legend   1984
Music-Performance
81791   55 mins   C   B, V   P
This rockumentary looks at the life and music of Bob Marley and features thirteen of his songs. Available in VHS Dolby, Hi-Fi Stereo and Beta Hi-Fi Stereo.
Don Letts — *RCA/Columbia Pictures Home Video*

Bob Rosburg's Golf Tips   1980
Golf
44336   58 mins   C   B, V   P
This program covers twelve different golf tips for shots on and around the green, including chipping, putting, and bunker play, which can take four or five strokes from the average golfer's scores.
Video Sports Prods — *Video Sports Productions*

Bob the Quail   1978
Cartoons
71343   60 mins   C   B, V   P
Animated
Taken from the "Fables of the Green Forest," this tale follows Bob's hunt for a good tree that will safely house his family.
Gene Wilkin Enterprises — *Family Home Entertainment*

Bob Welch and Friends   1982
Music-Performance
47805   81 mins   C   CED   P
This stereo concert features the one-time member of Fleetwood Mac, joined by members of Fleetwood Mac, drummer Carmine Appice,

and Ann Wilson of Heart. Songs include "Gold Dust Woman," "Rattlesnake Shake," and "Sentimental Lady."
RCA — *RCA VideoDiscs*

Bob Wilber   1984
Music-Performance
88126   59 mins   C   B, V   P
Wilber, in dedication to his mentor Sidney Bechet, plays sax at the Smithsonian: "Down in Honky Tonk," "Coal Cart Blues," "Kansas City Man Blues," and others.
Sony Video — *Sony Video Software*

Bobby Deerfield   1977
Drama
58220   123 mins   C   B, V   P
Al Pacino, Marthe Keller, Anny Duperey, Romolo Valli, directed by Sydney Pollack
A cold-blooded Grand Prix driver comes face to face with death each time he races, but finally learns the meaning of life when he falls in love with a critically ill woman.
MPAA:PG
Columbia Pictures; Warner Bros — *Warner Home Video*

Bobby Jo and the Outlaw   1976
Drama/Adventure
64895   89 mins   C   B, V, CED   P
Lynda Carter, Marjoe Gortner
A woman who wants to be a country singer and a man who emulates Billy the Kid are fugitives from the law.
MPAA:R
American International Pictures; Mark L. Lester — *Vestron Video*

Bobby Raccoon   1985
Cartoons/Adventure
70360   60 mins   C   B, V   P
Animated
Bobby learns to trust and respect his friendly neighborhood forest critters in this program. The masked mammal's adventures can be enjoyed in stereo on all formats.
Filmation — *Family Home Entertainment*

Bobby Short and Friends   1986
Music-Performance
86372   60 mins   C   B, V   P
Bobby Short
Suave vocal stylist Bobby Short performs his favorite show tunes in this program taped live at New York's Cafe Carlyle. There are also guest appearances by Jack Lemmon, Lucie Arnaz and Tony Bennett.
MGM/UA — *MGM/UA Home Video*

Bobby Short at the Cafe Carlyle   1981
Music-Performance
84649   65 mins   C   B, V   P
New York's most popular saloon singer performs in the heart of the city. Recorded in Hi-Fi Stereo.
Lou Tyrell — *V.I.E.W. Video*

Bobby Vinton   1984
Music-Performance
75285   60 mins   C   B, V   P
This tape features singer Bobby Vinton performing some greatest hits at the Sands Hotel in Las Vegas. In Beta Hi-Fi stereo and VHS Dolby stereo.
RKO Home Video — *RKO HomeVideo*

Bobo, The   1967
Comedy
58221   105 mins   C   B, V   P
Peter Sellers, Britt Ekland, Rossano Brazzi, Adolfo Celi
A third-rate matador has three days to woo and win a legendary beauty.
Gina Productions; Warner Bros — *Warner Home Video*

Bocuse A La Carte   1985
Cookery
81724   30 mins   C   B, V   P
13 pgms
This series provides step-by-step instructions on such French dishes as Pumpkin Soup, Beef Burgundy and Strawberry Pie.
Kartes Video Communications — *Kartes Video Communications*

Body and Soul   1947
Drama
47991   104 mins   B/W   B, V   P
John Garfield, Lilli Palmer, Hazel Brooks, Anne Revere, William Conrad, Canada Lee, directed by Robert Rossen
A young boxer fights his way unscrupulously to the top.
United Artists — *Republic Pictures Home Video*

Body and Soul   1981
Drama
68240   109 mins   C   B, V, CED   P
Leon Isaac Kennedy, Jayne Kennedy, Peter Lawford, Muhammad Ali
A hard hitting film about a boxer who loses his perspective in the world of fame, fast cars and women.
MPAA:R
Cannon Films — *MGM/UA Home Video*

Body by Jake   1984
Physical fitness
78893   55 mins   C   B, V   P
Jake Steinfield
The man who keeps Hollywood celebrities
looking good with his "Smokin' Workout" brings
his secrets to home video.
Marie Cantin — *MCA Home Video*

Body Double   1984
Drama/Suspense
Closed Captioned
70560   114 mins   C   B, V   P
*Craig Wasson, Melanie Griffith, directed by
Brian De Palma*
A voyeuristic unemployed actor peeps on a
neighbor's nightly disrobing and sees more than
he wants to. A grisly murder leads him into an
obsessive guest through the world of
pornographic film-making. In Hi-Fi Stereo on all
formats.
MPAA:R
Columbia Pictures — *RCA/Columbia Pictures
Home Video*

Body Heat   1981
Suspense/Drama
51993 __ 113 mins   C   B, V, LV   P
*William Hurt, Kathleen Turner, Richard Crenna,
Ted Danson*
Two people involved in a steamy love affair plot
to kill the woman's husband in this atmospheric
melodrama.
MPAA:R
Ladd Company — *Warner Home Video; RCA
VideoDiscs*

Body Music   1984
Music video
88092   30 mins   C   B, V   P
A compilation of breakdance/dance/disco
videos.
Sony Video — *Sony Video Software*

Body Rock   1984
Musical-Drama
77164   93 mins   C   B, V   P
*Lorenzo Lamas, Vicki Frederick, Ray Sharkey,
Carole Ita White*
A Brooklyn breakdancer deserts his buddies to
work at a chic Manhattan nightclub.
MPAA:PG-13
New World Pictures — *THORN EMI/HBO
Video*

Body Sculpture System,   1985
The
Physical fitness
85609   90 mins   C   B, V   P
Beth Johnson, Tina Plakinger
Designed for women, this exercise program
"sculpts" one's physique without promoting

excessive muscularity. With music by Alien
Nation.
C.W. Cressler — *Key Video*

Body Snatcher, The   1945
Horror
00315   77 mins   B/W   B, V, 3/4U'   P
Boris Karloff, Bela Lugosi
Based on R.L. Stevenson's novel about a grave
robber who supplies corpses to research
scientists.
RKO — *Nostalgia Merchant; RKO HomeVideo*

Bodyguard, The   197?
Adventure/Martial arts
59045   89 mins   C   B, V   P
Sonny Chiba, Aaron Banks, Bill Louie, Judy Lee
The "yellow mafia" and New York's big crime
families face off in this martial arts
extravaganza.
MPAA:R
Terry Levene — *Media Home Entertainment*

Bog   1984
Science fiction
71220   90 mins   C   B, V   P
*Gloria De Haven, Marshall Thompson, Leo
Gordon, Aldo Ray*
A boggy beast from the Arctic north awakens to
eat people. Scientists mount an anti-monster
offensive.
MPAA:PG
Independent — *Prism*

Bogie: The Last Hero   1980
Biographical/Drama
79327   99 mins   C   B, V   P
*Kevin O'Connor, Kathryn Harrold, Ann
Wedgeworth, Drew Barrymore, directed by
Vincent Sherman*
How Bogie coped with trying to balance out his
image as a tough guy on the screen and his
gentle off screen image is the subject of this
biopic. In Beta Hi-Fi and VHS Stereo.
Charles Fries Productions — *U.S.A. Home
Video*

Boheme, La   1982
Opera
60575   116 mins   C   B, V   P
*The Royal Opera, Ileana Cortrubas, Neil Shicoff,
Marilyn Zschau, Thomas Allen, Gwynne Howell*
Puccini's opera about the lives and loves of four
19th century Parisian Bohemians performed at
the Covent Garden Opera House on February
16, 1982. Includes libretto. In stereo.
Covent Garden — *THORN EMI/HBO Video;
Pioneer Artists*

Boheme, La   1982
Opera
82537   231 mins   C   B, V, LV   P

Teresa Stratas, Renata Scotto, Jose Carreras,
Richard Stilwell, Alan Monk, conducted by
James Levine
This critically acclaimed performance of the
popular Verdi opera was performed at N.Y.'s
Metropolitan in the original Italian with English
subtitles.
IT
Franco Zeffirelli — *Paramount Home Video;
Pioneer Artists*

Bohemian Girl, The   1936
Musical/Comedy
47139   74 mins   B/W   B, V, 3/4U   P
*Stan Laurel, Oliver Hardy, Mae Busch, Darla
Hood, Jacqueline Wells, Thelma Todd, Jimmy
Finlayson*
The last of Laurel and Hardy's comic operettas
finds them as guardians of a young orphan,
whom no one realizes is actually a kidnapped
princess.
Hal Roach; MGM — *Nostalgia Merchant;
Blackhawk Films*

Boiling Point   1932
Western
14206   67 mins   B/W   B, V   P
Hoot Gibson
Lawman proves once again that justice always
triumphs.
Allied Artists — *United Home Video; Discount
Video Tapes; Video Connection*

Bold Caballero, The   1936
Adventure
56599   69 mins   B/W   B, V   P
Robert Livingston, Heather Angel
Rebel chieftain Zorro overthrows oppressive
Spanish rule in the days of early California.
Republic — *Video Dimensions; Video
Connection; Nostalgia Merchant; Discount
Video Tapes*

Bolero   1982
Drama
63970   173 mins   C   B, V, CED   P
*James Caan, Geraldine Chaplin, Robert
Hossein, Nicole Garcia, Jacques Villeret,
directed by Claude Lelouch*
Beginning in 1936, this international epic traces
the lives of four families across three continents
and five decades, highlighting the music and
dance that is central to their lives.
Films 13; TF1 Films — *Vestron Video*

Bolero   1984
Romance/Drama
79186   106 mins   C   B, V   P
*Bo Derek, George Kennedy, Andrew Occhipinti,
Ana Obregon, directed by John Derek*
A young college graduate sets off on a
worldwide quest to lose her virginity.
MPAA:X

Bo Derek; The Cannon Group — *U.S.A. Home
Video*

Bolo   197?
Martial arts/Adventure
47698   90 mins   C   B, V   P
Yang Sze
The authorities pardon two tough prison
inmates, setting the scene for revenge.
Star Film Company — *Master Arts Video*

Bolshoi Ballet   1967
Dance
57255   90 mins   C   B, V   P
*Raissa Struhkova, Maya Samokhvalova,
Vladimir Vasiliev, Ekaterina Maximova, Natalie
Bessmertnova, The Bolshoi Ballet and Bolshoi
Symphony*
The world-famous dancers of the Bolshoi Ballet
are featured in excerpts from eight works,
including Ravel's "Bolers" and "La Valse,"
Prokofiev's "Stone Flower," music by Paganini
and Rachmaninoff and"Bolshoi Ballet '67."
Kultur — *Movie Buff Video; Kultur*

Bolshoi Ballet: Les   1984
Sylphides, The
Dance/Music-Performance
84663   34 mins   C   B, V   P
*Natalia Bessmertnova, Alexandre Beofatyriov,
Galina Kozlova, choreographed by Mikhail
Fokine*
A live Bolshoi performance of this famed Chopin
ballet. Recorded in Hi-Fi.
Russian TV — *V.I.E.W. Video*

Bomb at 10:10   1967
War-Drama
81878   87 mins   C   B, V   P
*George Montgomery, Rada Popovic, Peter
Banicevic*
An American pilot escapes from a German POW
camp and plots to assassinate a camp
commandant.
Ika Povic — *Video Gems*

Bombardier   1943
War-Drama
82179   99 mins   B/W   B, V   P
*Pat O'Brien, Randolph Scott, Robert Ryan,
Eddie Albert, Anne Shirley*
A group of cadet bombardiers discover the
realities of war on raids over Japan during World
War II.
RKO; Robert Fellows — *RKO HomeVideo*

Bombs Away!   1986
Comedy
88148   90 mins   C   B, V   P
*Michael Huddleston, Pat McCormick, directed
by Bruce Wilson*

An atomic bomb is mistakenly shipped to a
seedy war surplus store in Seattle, and causes
much chicanery.
Bruce Wilson; Bill Fay — *Charter
Entertainment*

Bon Jovi: Breakout   1984
Music-Performance/Music video
84497   23 mins   C   B, V   P
The currently popular band performs its greatest
hits in videos and concerts.
Polygram Records Inc — *Sony Video Software*

**Bon Voyage, Charlie
Brown**   1980
Comedy/Cartoons
48508   76 mins   C   B, V, LV   P
Animated
The comic strip group from "Peanuts" become
exchange students in Europe, led by Charlie
Brown, Linus, Peppermint Patty, Marcie, and the
irrepressible beagle, Snoopy.
MPAA:G
Lee Mendelson, Bill Melendez — *Paramount
Home Video*

Bongo Man   1980
Musical-Drama
70716   89 mins   C   B, V   P
Jimmy Cliff
A reggae star brings some hope of peace, love
and unity to his troubled homeland, Jamaica.
New World Pictures — *VCL Home Video*

Bongo Man   1980
Musical
70905   89 mins   C   B, V   P
Jimmy Cliff, directed by Stefan Paul
This reggae concert, filmed at the festival of
Somerton in Jamaica's Montego Bay, features
performances of many Cliff favorites including
"The Harder They Come" and "Stand Up-Fight
Back."
Sunpower Productions — *VCL Home Video*

Bonnie and Clyde   1967
Drama
44588   105 mins   C   B, V, LV   P
*Warren Beatty, Faye Dunaway, Michael J.
Pollard, Gene Hackman, Estelle Parsons,
directed by Arthur Penn*
The story of the two infamous bank robbers,
Clyde Barrow and Bonnie Parker, who spent
their days adrift in the Southwest during the
depression era.
Academy Awards '67: Best Supporting Actress
(Parsons).
Warner Bros — *Warner Home Video; RCA
VideoDiscs*

Bonnie's Kids   1975
Drama
76658   107 mins   C   B, V   P
*Tiffany Bolling, Robin Mattson, Scott Brady,
Alex Rocco*
A story about two sisters who become involved
in murder, sex and stolen money.
MPAA:R
General Film Corp — *Monterey Home Video*

Boob Tube, The   1975
Comedy
81616   74 mins   C   B, V   P
John Alderman, Sharon Kelly, Lois Lane
Television station KSEX is out to change their
audience's viewing habits with their unusual
programming.
MPAA:R
Christopher Odin — *Video Gems*

Boogey Man, The   1980
Horror
52864   86 mins   C   B, V   P
John Carradine, Suzanna Love, Ron James
A horrifying story of a brother and sister and the
power of a broken mirror. The sister views the
reflection of her brother murdering their
mother's lover in a hallway mirror. The memory
haunts the sister twenty years later.
MPAA:R EL, SP
Jerry Gross Organization — *Wizard Video;
Vestron Video (disc only)*

**Booker T. Washington:
The Life and the Legacy**   1986
Biographical/Civil rights
85706   30 mins   C   B, V   P
Maurice Woods
A dramatized biography of the negro humanist
and leader.
William Greaves — *Your World Video*

Boom in the Moon   1945
Comedy
81258   83 mins   B/W   B, V   P
Buster Keaton, Angel Grassa, Virginia Serret
An American GI is set adrift in the Atlantic
Ocean at the end of World War II. When the ship
runs aground, the soldier thinks that he's landed
in Japan but it is actually Mexico. Available in
VHS Stereo and Beta Hi-Fi.
Alexander Salkind — *U.S.A. Home Video*

Boomerang   1976
Adventure
86182   101 mins   C   B, V   P
*Alain Delon, Carla Gravina, Dora Doll, directed
Jose Giovanni*
A father rescues his wrongly-convicted son from
prison. Dubbed.
Alain Delon — *Unicorn Video*

Boots and Saddles 1937
Western
11383 54 mins B/W B, V, FO P
Gene Autry, Judith Allen, Smiley Burnette
A young English lord wants to sell the ranch he has inherited but Gene Autry is determined to make him a real Westerner.
Republic — *Video Yesteryear; Blackhawk Films; Video Connection; Hollywood Home Theater; Discount Video Tapes; Nostalgia Merchant*

Border, The 1982
Drama
59681 107 mins C B, V,.LV P
Jack Nicholson, Harvey Keitel, Valerie Perrine, Warren Oates, directed by Tony Richardson
A border guard faces corruption and violence within his department and tests his own sense of decency when the infant of a poor Mexican girl is kidnapped.
MPAA:R
Universal — *MCA Home Video*

Border Romance 1930
Western
38982 58 mins B/W B, V, FO P
Don Terry, Armide, Marjorie Kane
Three Americans have their horses stolen by bandits while riding through Mexico. Trouble with the Rurales follows in this early sound western.
Tiffany — *Video Yesteryear*

Borderline 1980
Drama
65005 106 mins C B, V P
Charles Bronson, A. Wilford Brimley, Bruno Kirby, Benito Morales, Ed Harris
This contemporary human action drama depicts the plight of illegal Mexican aliens.
MPAA:PG
ITC Entertainment — *CBS/Fox Video*

Boris Godunov 1954
Opera
78960 108 mins B/W B, V P
Alexander Pirogov
A filmed version of the Mussorgsky opera about the rise and fall of Russian czar Boris Godunov.
Corinth Films — *Video Arts International*

Born Again 1978
Biographical/Drama
78643 110 mins C B, V P
Dean Jones, Anne Francis, Dana Andrews, directed by Irving Rapper
This is the filmed adaptation of Charles Colson's biography of why he became a born again Christian.
Avco Embassy — *Embassy Home Entertainment*

Born Free 1966
Adventure
21280 95 mins C B, V P
Virginia McKenna, Bill Travers
A game warden in Kenya and his wife raise three orphan lion cubs. When the last cub is old enough they try to return her to the wild.
Academy Awards '66: Best Song.
Columbia — *RCA/Columbia Pictures Home Video; RCA VideoDiscs*

Born Invincible 1976
Martial arts
87186 90 mins C B, V P
Lo Lieh, Carter Wong, Nancy Yan, directed by Joseph Kuo
A Kung Fu master avenges the kick-death of a student by kick-killing any number of possible suspects.
Foreign — *Video Gems*

Born Losers 1967
Drama
66098 103 mins C B, V, CED P
Tom Laughlin
The original "Billy Jack" film in which the Indian martial arts expert takes on a group of incorrigible bikers.
American International Pictures — *Vestron Video*

Born to Kill 1947
Mystery
57127 92 mins B/W B, V P
Lawrence Tierney, Claire Trevor, Walter Slezak
A ruthless killer marries a girl for her money.
RKO — *King of Video*

Born Yesterday 1950
Comedy
21281 103 mins B/W B, V P
Judy Holliday, Broderick Crawford, William Holden, directed by George Cukor
A wealthy racketeer hires a writer to instruct his girl friend in etiquette. Based on the Broadway play.
Academy Awards '51: Best Actress (Holliday).
Columbia — *RCA/Columbia Pictures Home Video*

Borneo 1937
Documentary/Africa
65197 76 mins B/W B, V P
Martin Johnson, Osa Johnson, narrated by Lowell Thomas and Lew Lehr
Explorer and naturalist Martin Johnson investigates the many unusual sights and inhabitants of Borneo in this pioneering documentary.
Osa Johnson; 20th Century Fox — *Video Yesteryear*

Boss Foreman 1939
Comedy
85496   58 mins   B/W   B, V   P
Henry Armetta
A langorous, entwining comedy of errors about
a construction foreman and his misadventures
with the mob.
Unknown — *Video Yesteryear*

Boss' Son, The 1979
Drama
72223   97 mins   C   B, V   P
Rita Moreno, James Darren
A coming of age tale, as a young man tries to
implement his dreams in the real world.
Boss Son Productions — *Vestron Video*

Boston and Maine—Its Fitchburg Division and Hoosac Tunnel in Steam Days 195?
Trains
64825   11 mins   B/W   B, V   P, T
This vintage film shows steam locomotive
activity on many parts of the B&M Fitchburg
Division, which stretches west from Boston to
Troy and Mechanicsville, N.Y.
J W Dealey; E R Blanchard — *Blackhawk Films*

Boston Strangler, The 1968
Suspense
08437   116 mins   C   B, V   P
*Tony Curtis, Henry Fonda, George Kennedy,
Murray Hamilton, Sally Kellerman, directed by
Richard Fleisher*
Based on Gerold Frank's factual book about the
killer who terrorized Boston for about a year and
a half.
SP
20th Century Fox — *CBS/Fox Video*

Bostonians, The 1984
Drama
77181   120 mins   C   B, V, LV   P
*Christopher Reeve, Vanessa Redgrave, Linda
Hunt, directed by James Ivory*
A faith healer's daughter is forced to choose
between the affections of a militant suffragette
and a young lawyer in 19th Century Boston.
MPAA:PG
Almi Pictures — *Vestron Video*

Botany Bay 1953
Adventure
85244   99 mins   C   B, V   P
*Alan Ladd, James Mason, Patricia Medina, Sir
Cedric Hardwicke*
A rousing costumer about a convict ship in the
1700's that, after a trying voyage, lands in
Australia, wherein a framed doctor conquers the
local plague.

Paramount — *Kartes Video Communications*

Bottoms Up '81 1981
Variety
55547   75 mins   C   B, V   P
A screen recreation of this long-running comedy
revue, combining slapstick, satire, beautiful
showgirls, and lavish musical numbers. Taped
on location at Harrah's Lake Tahoe.
Breck Wall Prods — *Paramount Home Video*

Boum, La 1983
Comedy
65699   90 mins   C   B, V   P
*Sophie Marceau, Claude Brasseur, Brigitte
Fossey*
A teenager adjusting to the changes brought
about by a move to a new home is compounded
by her parents, who are having marital
problems.
Alain Poire — *RCA/Columbia Pictures Home
Video*

Bound for Glory 1976
Drama/Biographical
87376   149 mins   C   B, V   P
*David Carradine, Ronny Cox, Melinda Dillon,
directed by Hal Ashby*
The award-winning biography of American folk
singer Woody Guthrie, set against the backdrop
of the Depression and featuring many of his
songs. In VHS and Beta Hi-Fi.
MPAA:PG
United Artists — *MGM/UA Home Video*

Bounty, The 1984
Drama/Adventure
82427   130 mins   C   B, V   P
*Mel Gibson, Anthony Hopkins, Lord Laurence
Olivier, George Donaldson*
A new version of "Mutiny on the Bounty," with
emphasis on a more realistic relationship
between Fletcher Christian and Captain Bligh.
The sensuality of Christian's relationship with a
Tahitian beauty also receives greater
importance here.
Orion — *Vestron Video*

Bourgeois Gentilhomme, Le 1958
Comedy
59371   97 mins   C   B, V, FO   P
Translated "The Would-Be Gentleman." A
comedy-ballet in five acts in prose, performed
by the Comedie Francais. Subtitled in English.
FR
France — *Video Yesteryear*

Boxcar Bertha 1972
Drama
66096   89 mins   C   B, V, CED   P

Barbara Hershey, David Carradine, directed by Martin Scorcese
Scorcese's vivid portrayal of the South during the 1930's Depression.
MPAA:R
American International Pictures — *Vestron Video*

Boxing's Greatest Champions
1980
Boxing
29230   59 mins   B/W   B, V   P
Hosted by Curt Gowdy, Barney Ross, Rocky Marciano, Archie Moore, Sugar Ray Robinson, Joe Louis
Presented are "the greatest" in each division, as selected by the Boxing Writers Association. Match your boxing knowledge against the Boxing Writers.
Big Fights Inc — *VidAmerica*

Boy and His Dog, A
1976
Science fiction
42909   87 mins   C   B, V   P
Don Johnson, Susanne Benton, Jason Robards
This is a movie adaptation of Harlan Ellison's novella about a misogynistic society in the post World War IV civilizaton of 2024.
EL, SP
Alvy Moore — *Media Home Entertainment*

Boy, Did I Get a Wrong Number!
1966
Comedy
81550   100 mins   C   B, V   P
Bob Hope, Phyllis Diller, Marjorie Lord, Elke Sommer, directed by George Marshall
A real estate agent gets more than he bargained for when he accidentally dials a wrong number.
Available in VHS and Beta Hi-Fi.
United Artists — *Playhouse Video*

Boy in the Plastic Bubble, The
1976
Drama
80296   100 mins   C   B, V   P
John Travolta, Robert Reed, Glynnis O'Connor, Diana Hyland, Ralph Bellamy
A young man born with immunity deficiencies grows up in a specially controlled plastic environment.
Aaron Spelling; Leonard Goldberg — *Prism*

Boy Named Charlie Brown, A
1969
Cartoons
Closed Captioned
78885   80 mins   C   B, V   P
Animated, music by Vince Guaraldi and Rod McKuen
Charlie Brown enters the National Spelling Bee in New York and makes the final rounds with one other contestant.

Cinema Center Films — *Playhouse Video*

Boy of Two Worlds
1970
Adventure
59358   103 mins   C   B, V   R, P
Jimmy Sternman
Because he is of a lineage foreign to his late father's town, a boy is exiled to the life of a junior Robinson Crusoe.
MPAA:G
GG Communications — *Video Gems*

Boy Takes Girl
1983
Drama
82355   93 mins   C   B, V   P
Gabi Eldor, Hillel Neeman, Dina Limon
A little girl finds it hard adjusting to life on a farming cooperative during a summer recess.
Guy Film Productions Ltd — *MGM/UA Home Video*

Boy Who Left Home to Find Out About the Shivers, The
1981
Fairy tales
73145   60 mins   C   B, V, CED   P
Peter MacNicol, Christopher Lee, Vincent Price, directed by Graeme Clifford
From "Faerie Tale Theatre" comes the story of a young man, played by Peter MacNicol, who had no fear.
Shelley Duvall — *CBS/Fox Video*

Boy with the Green Hair, The
1948
Drama
59061   82 mins   C   B, V   P
Pat O'Brien, Robert Ryan, Barbara Hale, Dean Stockwell, directed by Joseph Losey
When he hears that his parents were killed in an air raid, a boy's hair turns green.
RKO — *King of Video*

Boys from Brazil, The
1978
Drama
44935   123 mins   C   B, V, LV   P
Gregory Peck, James Mason, Sir Laurence Olivier
Incredible plot of human cloning when children formed from Hitler's likeness are used to implement a neo-Nazi takeover.
MPAA:R
20th Century Fox — *CBS/Fox Video; RCA VideoDiscs*

Boys from Brooklyn, The
1952
Comedy
53432   60 mins   B/W   B, V, FO   P
Bela Lugosi, Duke Mitchell, Sammy Petrillo
Two comedians that bear a striking resemblance to Dean Martin and Jerry Lewis

get mixed up with a mad scientist and crazed gorillas in Africa.
Jack Broder — *Video Yesteryear; Discount Video Tapes; See Hear Industries*

Boys in Company C, The   1977
War-Drama
47786   125 mins   C   B, V   •   P
Stan Shaw, Andrew Stevens, James Canning, Michael Lembeck, Craig Wasson
A frank, hard-hitting drama about five young men involved in the Vietnam War.
MPAA:R
Andre Morgan — *RCA/Columbia Pictures Home Video*

Boys in the Band, The   1970
Drama
54102   120 mins   C   B, V, CED   P
Frederick Combs, Cliff Gorman, Lawrence Luckinbill, Kenneth Nelson, Leonard Frey, directed by William Friedkin
Mart Crawley adapts his own award-winning play concerning the lives of a group of homosexuals. While playing a parlor game where each is to call out the one he loves, they learn a lot about themselves and their way of life.
MPAA:R
National General, Cinema Center Films — *CBS/Fox Video*

Boys Next Door, The   1985
Drama
85081   90 mins   C   B, V   P
Maxwell Caulfield, Charlie Sheen, directed by Penelope Spheeris
Two California lads, due to causeless-rebel-type rage, kill and go nuts during a weekend in Los Angeles.
MPAA:R
New World Pictures — *New World Video*

Boys of Summer, The   1983
Baseball
66002   90 mins   C   B, V, LV,   P
                                    CED
Duke Snider, Roy Campanella, Carl Erskine, Preacher Roe
Based on Roger Kahn's best-selling book, this program tells the story of the 1947-57 Brooklyn Dodgers.
Video Corporation of America; Thorn EMI Video Programming — *VidAmerica*

Bozo the Clown Volumes 1-4   196?
Cartoons
47659   59 mins   C   B, V   P
Animated
Bozo the Clown and his pals are featured in these collections of cartoon adventures.

EL, SP
Larry Harmon — *Unicorn Video*

Brady's Escape   1984
War-Drama
75670   90 mins   C   B, V, LV,   P
                                    CED
An American World War II pilot is shot down in the Hungarian countryside and befriended by Hungarian Csikos (cowboys).
Satori Entertainment Corp — *VidAmerica*

Brain, The   1965
Horror
81402   83 mins   B/W   B, V   P
Anne Heywood, Peter Van Eyck, Bernard Lee
A scientist finds himself being manipulated by the dead man's brain he's trying to keep alive.
Available in VHS Stereo and Beta Hi-Fi.
Raymond Stross Prods. — *Monterey Home Video*

Brain From Planet Arous, The   1957
Science fiction
73546   70 mins   B/W   B, V   P
Robert Fuller, John Agar
An evil brain from the Planet Arous possesses a scientist's body intending to conquer the world.
Howco Films — *Monterey Home Video; Admit One Video*

Brain of Blood   1971
Horror
86491   107 mins   C   B, V   P
Grant Williams, Kent Taylor, Reed Hadley
Also known as "The Creature's Revenge," this film deals with a scientist who transplants the brain of a politician into the body of a deformed idiot. The change is minimal.
Hemisphere Prod. — *Magnum Entertainment*

Brain 17   1982
Science fiction
71345   72 mins   C   B, V   P
A ten-year-old lad named Stevie helps the giant robot, "Brain 17," battle an evil scientist who is bent on word domination.
MFTV Inc — *Family Home Entertainment*

Brain That Wouldn't Die, The   1963
Science fiction/Horror
65136   70 mins   B/W   B, V   P
Herb Evers, Virginia Leith, Adele Lamont
A brilliant surgeon keeps the decapitated head of his fiancee alive after an auto accident while he searches for a suitable body to transplant the head onto.
American International — *Warner Home Video*

Brainwaves   1982
Science fiction
66042   83 mins   C   B, V   P
Suzanna Love, Tony Curtis, Kier Dullea
A young woman is treated by a noted
neuroscientist with a mysterious form of
treatment, "the Clavins Process."
MPAA:R
Ulli Lommel — *Embassy Home Entertainment*

Braingames   1985
Games
81829   60 mins   C   B, V   P
Test your knowledge of history, art and music
with this collection of games designed to
challenge the mind.
Sheila Nevins — *THORN EMI/HBO Video*

Braingames, Cassette # 2   1985
Games
82026   60 mins   C   B, V   P
Here is another collection of games designed to
test your knowledge of history, art, music and
sports.
Sheila Nevins — *THORN EMI/HBO Video*

Braingames, Cassette #3   1985
Games
82264   60 mins   C   B, V   P
This is a new collection of computerized trivia
games that the whole family can play.
Sheila Nevins — *THORN EMI/HBO Video*

Brainstorm   1983
Science fiction
66456   106 mins   C   B, V, CED   P
*Natalie Wood, Christopher Walken, Cliff
Robertson, Louise Fletcher, directed by
Douglas Trumbull*
A scientist invents a device that can record
dreams and allow other people to experience
them. Stereo VHS and CED.
MPAA:PG
MGM UA Entertainment Co — *MGM/UA
Home Video*

Brainwash   1984
Drama
76020   98 mins   C   B, V   P
*Yvette Mimieux, Christopher Allport, John
Considine*
Yvette Mimieux stars in a shocking and dramatic
commentary on the capitalist system, and the
lengths to which people will go to acquire wealth
and power.
MPAA:R
Gary L Mehlman — *Media Home
Entertainment*

Branded Men   1931
Western
84832   70 mins   B/W   B, V   P

Ken Maynard, June Clyde
Standard early talkie 'B' western, with outlaws,
horses, gunfights and a rescuing, flawless hero.
Tiffany — *United Home Video*

Brandy Sheriff   1978
Western
51105   90 mins   C   B, V   P
Alex Nicol, Maria Contrera, Antonio Casas
A former outlaw tries to make up for the time he
lost in prison. In Spanish.
SP
Spanish — *Hollywood Home Theater*

Braniac, The   1961
Horror
51101   75 mins   B/W   B, V   P
*Abel Salazar, Ariadne Welter, Mauricio Garces,
Rosa Maria Gallardo*
A sorcerer sentenced for black magic returns to
strike dark deeds upon the descendants of
those who judged him. He turns himself into a
hideous monster, feeding on his victims' brains
and blood.
Mexican — *Hollywood Home Theater*

Brannigan   1975
Suspense/Crime-Drama
58829   111 mins   C   CED   P
*John Wayne, John Vernon, Mel Ferrer, Daniel
Pilon, James Booth, Richard Attenborough*
The Duke travels across the Atlantic to arrest a
racketeer who has fled the States rather than
face a grand jury indictment.
MPAA:PG
United Artists — *CBS/Fox Video*

Brave Bunch, The   1970
War-Drama
87327   110 mins   C   B, V   P
*Jhon Miller, Peter Funk, Maria Xenia, introduced
by Sybil Danning*
A Greek soldier during World War II attempts to
save his friends and country with his heroic
exploits.
Carar Films — *U.S.A. Home Video*

Brave One, The   1956
Drama
84031   100 mins   C   B, V   P
*Michael Ray, Rodolfo Moyos, Joi Lansing,
directed by Irving Rapper.*
A love story between a Spanish boy and bull
who saves his life and is later carted off to the
bull rings. Award-winning Screenplay by the
then-blacklisted Dalton Trumbo, as "Robert
Rich."
Academy Awards '56: Best Screenplay
Maurice King; Frank King — *United Home
Video*

Brazil   1985
Fantasy
Closed Captioned
87172   131 mins   C   B, V, LV   P
Jonathon Pryce, Robert DeNiro, Michael Palin,
Katherine Helmond, Kim Greist, Bob Hoskins,
Ian Holm, Peter Vaughn, directed by Terry
Gilliam
The acclaimed nightmare comedy by Gilliam
about an Everyman trying to survive in a surreal
paper-choked bureaucratic society. There are
copious references to "1984" and "The Trial,"
fantastic mergings of glorious fantasy and stark
reality, and astounding visual design.
L.A. Film Critics Assoc. Awards '85: Best
Picture; Best Director. MPAA:R
Universal; Arnon Milchan — *MCA Home Video*

Breaker, Breaker!   1977
Drama/Martial arts
63371   86 mins   C   B, V   P
Chuck Norris, George Murdock
A convoy of angry truck drivers launch an
assault on the corrupt and sadistic locals of a
small Texas town.
MPAA:R
American International — *Embassy Home*
Entertainment

Breaker Morant   1980
Drama
58496   107 mins   C   B, V   P
Edward Woodward, Jack Thompson, John
Waters, Bryan Brown, directed by Bruce
Beresford
In 1901 South Africa, three Australian soldiers
are put on trial for avenging the murder of a
comrade.
MPAA:PG
Matt Carroll; South Australian Film
Corp — *RCA/Columbia Pictures Home Video;*
Embassy Home Entertainment (disc only)

Breakfast at Tiffany's   1961
Comedy
38587   114 mins   C   B, V, LV   P
Audrey Hepburn, George Peppard, Patricia
Neal, directed by Blake Edwards
Truman Capote's story of an eccentric New
York City playgirl and her shaky romance with a
young writer. Music by Henry Mancini.
Academy Awards '61: Best Song ("Moon
River").
Paramount — *Paramount Home Video; RCA*
VideoDiscs

Breakfast Club, The   1985
Comedy-Drama
Closed Captioned
81436   92 mins   C   B, V, LV   P
Ally Sheedy, Molly Ringwald, Judd Nelson,
Emilio Estevez, Anthony Michael Hall, directed
by John Hughes

Five students at a Chicago suburban high
school bare their souls to each other and wind
up becoming friends while spending a Saturday
detention together.
MPAA:R
Universal; A&M Films — *MCA Home Video*

Breakfast in Hollywood   1946
Comedy
11224   93 mins   B/W   B, V, FO   P
Tom Breneman, Bonita Granville, Eddie Ryan,
Beulah Bondi, Billie Burke, Zasu Pitts, Hedda
Hopper, Spike Jones and His Slickers
A movie about the popular morning radio show
of the 1940's hosted by Tom Breneman—a
coast-to-coast coffee klatch.
United Artists — *Video Yesteryear; Movie Buff*
Video

Breakfast in Paris   1981
Drama
86609   85 mins   C   B, V   P
Rod Mullinar, Barbara Parkins
Two American professionals in Paris, both
crushed from past failures in the love
department, find each other.
John D. Lamond — *New World Video*

Breakheart Pass   1976
Western
64936   92 mins   C   CED   P
Charles Bronson, Ben Johnson, Richard
Crenna, Jill Ireland, Charles Durning, Archie
Moore
A governor, his female companion, a band of
cavalrymen and a mysterious man travel on a
train through the mountains of Idaho in 1870.
The mystery man turns out to be a murderer.
MPAA:PG
United Artists — *CBS/Fox Video*

Breakin'   1984
Film/Dance
78045   87 mins   C   B, V, CED   P
This program presents the movie about the
dance phenomenon break dancing along with
the hit songs that accompany the film.
Allen DeBevoise; David Zito — *MGM/UA*
Home Video

Breakin' Metal   1985
Music-Performance
71016   70 mins   C   B, V   P
Hanoi Rocks, Lords of the New Church, Thin
Lizzy
This compilation offers a look and listen to some
of England's top new hard rock acts.
Polygram — *Passport Music Video*

Breakin' Metal   1985
Music-Performance
82391   59 mins   C   B, V   P

Rock Goddess, Wrathchild, Sledgehammer and others
A compilation of budding metal group performances; recorded at the Camden Palace Theater and the Marquee Club in London. Features tunes such as "Let the Blood Run Red," and "Road Rat."
Trilion PLC — *Sony Video Software*

Breakin' Through   1984
Musical
81663   73 mins   C   B, V   P
Ben Vereen, Donna McKechine, Reid Shelton, directed by Peter Medak
The choreographer of a troubled Broadway-bound musical decides to energize his shows with a troupe of street dancers.
Walt Disney Productions — *Walt Disney Home Video*

Breaking Away   1979
Comedy
37410   100 mins   C   B, V, CED   P
Dennis Christopher, Dennis Quaid, Daniel Stern, Jackie Earle Haley
A comedy about a high school graduate's addiction to bicycle racing whose dreams are tested against the realities of a crucial race. Shot on location at Indiana University. Academy Awards '79: Best Original Screenplay.
MPAA:PG
20th Century Fox — *CBS/Fox Video*

Breaking Glass   1980
Musical
54674   104 mins   C   B, V   P
Hazel O'Connor, Phil Daniels, Jon Fich, Jonathan Pryce, directed by Brian Gibson
A "New Wave" musical that gives an insight into the punk record business and at the same time tells of the rags-to-riches life of a punk rock star.
Paramount — *Paramount Home Video*

Breaking the Ice   1938
Musical
42954   79 mins   B/W   B, V, FO   P
Bobby Breen, Charles Ruggles, Dolores Costello, Billy Gilbert
An improbable mixture of Mennonites and a big city ice skating show. Musical numbers abound with backing by Victor Young and his Orchestra.
RKO; Sol Lesser — *Movie Buff Video; Video Yesteryear; Discount Video Tapes*

Breaking with the Mighty   1984
Poppalots
Dance
70150   60 mins   C   B, V   P
The break dance group The Mighty Poppalots teach all aspects of break dancing from moon walks to windmills in this instructional program.
Adler Enterprises — *Vestron Video*

Breakout   1975
Drama
21282   96 mins   C   B, V   P
Charles Bronson, Jill Ireland, Robert Duvall, John Huston
The wife of a man imprisoned in Mexico hires a Texas bush pilot to help her husband escape.
MPAA:PG
Columbia — *RCA/Columbia Pictures Home Video; RCA VideoDiscs*

Breakthrough   1979
War-Drama
65666   96 mins   C   B, V   P
Richard Burton, Robert Mitchum, Rod Steiger, Michael Parks, Curt Jurgens
German and American officers join forces to assassinate Hitler.
Wolf C Hartwig; Hubert Lukowski — *Worldvision Home Video*

Breath of Scandal, A   1960
Comedy
85245   98 mins   C   B, V   P
Sophia Loren, John Gavin, Maurice Chevalier, Angela Lansbury
An American diplomat in Vienna rescues a princess when she is thrown off a horse, and falls like a ton o' bricks. Viennese politics complicate things.
Paramount — *Kartes Video Communications*

Breathless   1983
Drama
65340   105 mins   C   B, V, LV   P
Richard Gere, Valerie Kaprisky
Richard Gere is a car thief turned cop killer, who has a torrid love affair with a French student studying in Los Angeles as the police slowly close in. This is a remake of Jean-Luc Godard's 1960 classic.
MPAA:R
Jean Luc Godard — *Vestron Video; RCA VideoDiscs*

Breeders' Cup 1985   1985
Horse racing
85405   60 mins   C   B, V   P
Narrated by Dick Enberg
Seven exciting horse races are included, as the contenders vie for the title cup.
NBC Sports — *U.S.A. Home Video*

Brewster McCloud   1970
Comedy
79211   101 mins   C   B, V   P
Bud Cort, Sally Kellerman, Shelley Duvall, Michael Murphy, directed by Robert Altman
A killer is on the loose in Houston and the likely suspect is a young man who lives in the Astrodome where he is building giant wings.
MPAA:R

MGM — *MGM/UA Home Video*

Brewster's Millions   1945
Comedy
70741   79 mins   B/W   B, V   P
Dennis O'Keefe, June Havoc, Eddie Anderson,
Helen Walker, directed by Allan Dwan
If Brewster, an ex-GI, can spend a million dollars
in one year, he will inherit a substantially greater
fortune.
United Artists — *Nostalgia Merchant*

Brewster's Millions   1985
Comedy
Closed Captioned
82074   101 mins   C   B, V, LV   P
Richard Pryor, John Candy, Lonette McKee,
Stephen Collins, Pat Hingle, Hume Cronyn,
directed by Walter Hill
An aging minor league baseball player must
spend 30 million dollars in order to collect an
inheritance of 300 million dollars. In HiFi Stereo.
MPAA:PG
Universal Studios — *MCA Home Video*

Brian's Song   1971
Drama
Closed Captioned
44788   73 mins   C   B, V   P
James Caan, Billy Dee Williams, Jack Warden,
Shelley Fabares, Judy Pace
The story of the unique relationship between
Gale Sayers, the Chicago Bears' star running
back, and his teammate Brian Piccolo. The
friendship between the Bears' first interracial
roommates ended suddenly when Brian Piccolo
lost his life to cancer.
MPAA:G
Paul Junger Witt, CPT — *RCA/Columbia*
Pictures Home Video; RCA VideoDiscs;
Learning Corp of America

Bride, The   1985
Horror/Drama
Closed Captioned
84603   118 mins   C   B, V   P
Sting, Jennifer Beals, David Rappaport,
Geraldine Page, directed by Franc Roddam
A twist on the Frankenstein tale, with the female
monster gaining independence and social
acceptance.
MPAA:PG-13
Victor Drai — *RCA/Columbia Pictures Home*
Video

Bride of Frankenstein   1935
Horror
70156   75 mins   B/W   B, V, LV   P
Boris Karloff, Elsa Lanchester, Ernest Thesiger
O.P. Heggie, directed by James Whale
When an evil doctor meets a lonely
Frankenstein, he decides to build him a mate in
this horror classic. Side two of the laserdisc

---

version is CAV formatted to allow single frame
access to your favorite scenes.
Universal Pictures — *MCA Home Video*

Bride of the Monster   1956
Horror
57347   70 mins   B/W   B, V, FO   P
Bela Lugosi, Tor Johnson, Loretta King, Tony
McCoy
Lugosi stars as a mad doctor trying to create a
race of giants.
Banner Prods; Edward Wood Jr — *Video*
Yesteryear; Hollywood Home Theater

Bride Walks Out, The   1936
Comedy
80238   81 mins   B/W   B, V   P
Barbara Stanwyck, Gene Raymond, Robert
Young, Ned Sparts, Willie Best
A rich woman learns how to adjust to living on
her husband's poor salary.
RKO — *RKO HomeVideo*

Bridge of Love   1984
Video
73634   5 mins   C   B, V   P
On this reusable two hour videocassette is a
brief expression to the one you share your love
with.
Kartes Productions — *Kartes Video*
Communications

Bridge of San Luis Rey,   1944
The
Drama
81221   89 mins   B/W   B, V, LV   P
Lynn Bari, Francis Lederer, Louis Calhern
A priest investigates the famous bridge collapse
in Lima Peru that left five people dead. Based
upon the novel by Thorton Wilder.
United Artists — *New World Video*

Bridge on the River Kwai,   1957
The
Drama
13232   161 mins   C   B, V, LV   P
William Holden, Alec Guinness, Sessue
Hayakawa, James Donald, directed by David
Lean
A British Colonel is forced to labor in building a
bridge for the enemy during World War II, and
Holden is assigned to destroy it.
Academy Awards '57: Best Picture; Best Actor
(Guinness); Best Director (Lean).
Columbia; Sam Spiegel — *RCA/Columbia*
Pictures Home Video; RCA VideoDiscs

Bridge Too Far, A   1977
War-Drama
47144   175 mins   C   B, V, CED   P
James Caan, Michael Caine, Sean Connery,
Elliot Gould, Gene Hackman, Laurence Olivier,

Ryan O'Neal, Robert Redford, Liv Ullmann, Dirk
Bogarde, directed by Richard Attenborough
A meticulous recreation of one of the most
disastrous battles of World War II, the Allied
defeat at Arnhem in 1944. Misinformation,
adverse conditions, and overconfidence
combined to prevent the Allies from capturing
six bridges that connected Holland to the
German border.
MPAA:PG
United Artists; Joseph E. Levine — *CBS/Fox
Video*

Brig, The 1964
Theater
86477   65 mins   B/W   B, V   P
A film by Jonas Mekas documenting the Living
Theatre's infamous performance of Kenneth H.
Brown's experimental play. Designed by Julian
Beck.
Venice Film Festival '64: Best Documentary
Feature.
Jonas Mekas; The Living Theatre — *Mystic
Fire Video*

Brigadoon 1954
Musical
53349   108 mins   C   B, V, LV,   P
                            CED
*Gene Kelly, Van Johnson, Cyd Charisse,
directed by Vincente Minnelli*
The story of a magical, 18th century Scottish
village which awakens once every 100 years,
highlighted by Lerner and Loewe's score. Songs
include: "Heather on the Hill," "Almost Like
Being in Love," "I'll Go Home with Bonnie
Jean," "Wedding Dance."
MGM; Arthur Freed — *MGM/UA Home Video*

Brighton Strangler, The 1945
Mystery
73696   67 mins   B/W   B, V
John Loder, June Duprez
An actor who plays a murderer takes his part
too seriously.
RKO — *RKO HomeVideo*

Brighton Strangler, 1945
The/Before Dawn
Mystery
80427   128 mins   B/W   B, V   P
*John Loder, June Duprez, Miles Mander, Stuart
Oland, Dorothy Wilson*
A mystery double feature: In "The Brighton
Strangler," an actor takes his part too seriously
as he murders Londoners at night and in
"Before Dawn" a brilliant scientist turns to a life
of murderous crime.
RKO — *RKO HomeVideo*

Brimstone and Treacle 1982
Drama
68243   85 mins   C   B, V, CED   P

Sting, Denholm Elliot, Joan Plowright, Suzanna
Hamilton, directed by Richard Loncraine
A mysterious man charms his way into the lives
of a middle-aged couple whose pretty daughter
has been paralyzed since a car accident. In
stereo.
MPAA:R
Namara Films — *MGM/UA Home Video*

Brink of Life 1957
Drama
65201   82 mins   B/W   B, V   P
*Eva Dahlbeck, Ingrid Thulin, Bibi Andersson,
Max Von Sydow, directed by Ingmar Bergman*
Three pregnant women in a hospital maternity
ward await their respective births with mixed
feelings. Swedish dialogue with English subtitles
SW
Svenskfilmindustri — *Video Yesteryear*

Brink's Job, The 1978
Comedy/Adventure
70866   103 mins   C   B, V   P
*Peter Falk, Peter Boyle, Warren Oates, Gena
Rowlands, Paul Sorvino, Sheldon Leonard,
Allen Goorwitz, directed by William Friedkin*
This film recreates the "crime of the century,"
Tony Pino's heist of 2.7 million dollars from a
Brink's truck. The action picks up five days
before the statute of limitations is about to run
out. In Hi-Fi Mono.
MPAA:PG
Universal — *MCA Home Video*

Britannia Hospital 1982
Comedy
69625   111 mins   C   B, V   P
*Malcolm McDowell, Leonard Rossiter, Graham
Crowden, Jean Plowright*
This is a portrait of a hospital at its most chaotic:
the staff threatens to strike, demonstrators
surround the hospital, a nosey BBC reporter
pursues an anxious professor, and the eagerly-
anticipated royal visit degenerates into a total
shambles.
MPAA:R
Independent — *THORN EMI/HBO Video*

British Rock—The First 1985
Wave
Documentary/Music-Performance
81938   60 mins   C   B, V   P
*Narrated by Michael York, directed by Patrick
Montgomery*
The British musical invasion of the 1960's is
fondly remembered in this documentary that
features footage of the Beatles and the Rolling
Stones performing. Available in VHS Dolby Hi-Fi
Stereo and Beta Hi-Fi Stereo. Also seen are
Gerry and the Pacemakers, Eric Burdon and the
Animals, Herman's Hermits, The Kinks, The
Yardbirds and The Who.

Patrick Montgomery — *RCA/Columbia Pictures Home Video*

Broadway Danny Rose   1984
Comedy
72224   85 mins   B/W   B, V, LV,   P
                                CED
Woody Allen, Mia Farrow
Second rate booking agent Woody Allen has a
paternal relationship with his third-rate acts in
this funny-poignant film.
MPAA:PG
Orion — *Vestron Video*

Broadway Highlights   1936
Nightclub
56911   40 mins   B/W   B, V, FO   P
*Narrated by Ted Husing, Milton Berle, George
Jessel, Babe Ruth, Jack Dempsey, Ed Wynn,
Fannie Brice, Burns and Allen, Jimmy Durante,
Ed Sullivan*
Four different tours through the nightlife of New
York City in the 1930's, with visits to restaurants,
nightclubs, and theaters.
Unknown — *Video Yesteryear; Discount Video
Tapes*

Broken Blossoms   1919
Drama/Film-History
55813   102 mins   B/W   B, V   P
*Lillian Gish, Richard Barthelmess, Donald Crisp,
directed by D. W. Griffith*
One of Griffith's most widely acclaimed films,
photographed by Billy Bitzer, about a young
Chinaman in London's squalid Limehouse
district hoping to spread the peaceful philosphy
of his Eastern religion. He befriends a pitiful
street waif who is mistreated by her brutal
father, resulting in tragedy. Silent.
United Artists; D W Griffith — *Hollywood Home
Theater; Festival Films; Western Film & Video
Inc; Movie Buff Video*

Broken Strings   1940
Drama
11225   50 mins   B/W   B, V, FO   P
*Clarence Muse, Sybil Lewis, William
Washington, Stymie Beard*
An all-black feature in which a concert violinist
must come to terms with himself after an auto
accident limits the use of his left hand.
International Roadshows — *Video Yesteryear;
Video Connection; Discount Video Tapes;
Glenn Video Vistas*

Bronco Billy   1980
Comedy
58222   118 mins   C   B, V   P
*Clint Eastwood, Sondra Locke, directed by Clint
Eastwood*
A Wild West Show entrepreneur leads his
ragged troupe from one improbable adventure
to the next.

MPAA:PG
Warner Bros — *Warner Home Video; RCA
VideoDiscs*

Bronson Lee, Champion   1978
Adventure/Martial arts
66127   81 mins   C   B, V   P
Kung-fu and karate highlight this action
adventure.
MPAA:PG
Unknown — *Warner Home Video*

Bronze Buckaroo/Harlem   1939
Rides the Range
Western
51946   120 mins   B/W   B, V   P
*Herb Jeffries, Lucious Brooks, Artie Young,
Spencer Williams*
This double feature presents two examples of
the black film industry of the 1930's. All the
western elements, along with some comedy are
represented.
Independent — *Hollywood Home Theater*

Brood, The   1979
Drama/Horror
65420   92 mins   C   B, V   P
*Samantha Eggar, Oliver Reed, directed by
David Cronenberg*
A man, whose wife is in a mental hospital
seemingly unable to get better, finds himself
somehow involved in a series of murders, but
neither the doctors nor the police will help him.
MPAA:R
New World — *Embassy Home Entertainment*

Brother, Can You Spare a   1975
Dime?
History-US/Documentary
35381   103 mins   C   B, V   P
A compilation of documentary film footage from
the 1930's—Hollywood in its heyday, Dillinger
vs. the G-men, bread liners, and other
memorabilia.
Sandy Lieberson, David Puttnam — *United
Home Video*

Brother from Another   1984
Planet, The
Science fiction/Adventure
Closed Captioned
80728   109 mins   C   B, V   P
*Joe Morton, Dee Dee Bridgewater, Ren Woods,
Steve James, Maggie Renzi, directed by John
Sayles*
An alien slave escapes captivity from his native
planet and winds up in Harlem where he's
pursued by two alien bounty hunters. Available
in VHS and Beta Hi-Fi stereo.
A-Train Films — *Key Video*

Brother Sun, Sister Moon 1973
Drama
60329   122 mins   C   B, V   P
*Graham Faulkner, Judi Bowker, Alec Guinness,
Leigh Lawson, Kenneth Cranham, Lee
Montague, Valentina Cortese*
The life of Francis of Assisi. Musical score by
Donovan.
MPAA:PG
Paramount — *Paramount Home Video*

Brother Where You 1985
Bound—Supertramp
Music video
82328   30 mins   C   B, V   P
Supertramp performs "Cannonball," "Better
Days" and "Brother Where You Bound" in VHS
Dolby Hi-Fi Stereo and Beta Hi-Fi Stereo.
A&M Video — *A & M Video; RCA/Columbia
Pictures Home Video*

Brotherhood of Death 1976
Drama
77237   85 mins   C   B, V   P
Roy Jefferson, Larry Jones, Mike Bass
Three black Vietnam veterans return to their
southern hometown to get even with the
Klansmen who slaughtered all of the
townspeople.
MPAA:R
Cinema Shares International — *MPI Home
Video*

Brothers Lionheart, The 1985
Adventure
77300   120 mins   C   B, V   P
The Lion brothers fight for life, love and liberty
during the Middle Ages.
Olle Nordemar — *Pacific Arts Video*

Brothers O'Toole, The 1973
Comedy/Western
80660   94 mins   C   B, V   P
*John Astin, Steve Carlson, Pat Carroll, Hans
Conried, Lee Meriwether*
This film depicts the misadventures of a pair of
slick drifters who, by chance, ride into a broken-
down mining town in the 1890's.
Gold Key Entertainment — *United Home Video*

Brubaker 1980
Drama
56900   131 mins   C   B, V, CED   P
Robert Redford, Jane Alexander
Drama about a reform warden who risks his life
to replace brutality and corruption with humanity
and integrity in a state prison farm.
MPAA:R
Twentieth Century Fox, Ron
Silverman — *CBS/Fox Video*

Bruce Lee Fights Back 1976
from the Grave
Martial arts
63892   97 mins   C   B, V   P
Bruce Lee, Deborah Chaplin, Anthony Bronson
Bruce Lee returns from the grave to fight the
Black Angel of Death and to wreak vengeance
on the evil ones who brought about his untimely
demise.
MPAA:R
Bert Lenzi — *Media Home Entertainment*

Bruce Lee, the Legend 1984
Martial arts/Biographical
Closed Captioned
70764   88 mins   C   B, V   P
*Bruce Lee, Steve McQueen, James Coburn,
narrated by James B. Nicholson*
This video tribute to the king of karate films
features rare footage and interviews with many
of the star's closest friends. Hi-Fi sound in both
formats.
Galaxy; Leonard Ho — *CBS/Fox Video*

Bruce Lee The Man/The 1984
Myth
Biographical/Martial arts
77221   90 mins   C   B, V   P
A dramatization of the life and times of martial
arts master Bruce Lee.
Cinema Shares International — *Lightning
Video*

Bruce Le's Greatest 1980
Revenge
Adventure/Martial arts
56922   94 mins   C   B, V   R, P
Kung-fu action and martial arts fighting highlight
this film, in which a martial arts student gets
involved in a clash between Chinese and a
discriminatory European Club.
MPAA:R
Fourseas Film Company — *Video Gems*

Bruce Li in New Guinea 1980
Adventure/Martial arts
56924   98 mins   C   B, V   R, P
Bruce Li
The tribe of a remote island worships the
legendary Snake Pearl. Two masters of Kung-fu
visit the isle and discover they must defend the
daughter of the murdered chief against a cruel
wizard.
MPAA:PG
Fourseas Film Company — *Video Gems*

Bruce's Deadly Fingers 198?
Martial arts
70985   90 mins   C   B, V   P
*Bruce Lee, Lo Lien, Chan Wai Man, Nora Miao,
Rose, Yuen Man Chi, Chang Leih, Young Zee,
Wuk Ma No Hans*

Bruce Lee kept a boook of deadly finger techniques for Kung Fu killing. When a vicious gangster kidnaps the Master's ex-girlfriend, one of his followers must rescue her and maintain the book's integrity.
MPAA:R
Independent — *Video Gems*

Bruce's Fists of Vengeance
1984
Martial arts
86702   87 mins   C   B, V   P
Bruce Le, Jack Lee, Ken Watanabe, Romano Kristoff, Don Gordon
Le and Lee guard master Bruce Lee's kicking secrets from an evil adversary.
Foreign — *Video Gems*

Brute Man, The
1946
Drama
73539   62 mins   B/W   B, V   P
Rondo Hattan, Tom Neal, Jane Adams
After a young man is disfigured by his school mates, he goes out on a trail of revenge later in life.
PRC — *Sony Video Software; Admit One Video*

Bryan Adams, Reckless
1984
Music video
77247   30 mins   C   B, V   P
Directed by Steve Barron
A conceptual music video EP featuring guitarist/vocalist Bryan Adams playing five songs from his "Reckless" album.
Simon Fields; Limelight — *A & M Video; RCA/Columbia Pictures Home Video*

Buccaneer, The
1959
Adventure
85246   121 mins   C   B, V   P
Yul Brynner, Charlton Heston, Claire Bloom, Inger Stevens, Charles Boyer, Henry Hull, E.G. Marshall, directed by Anthony Quinn
A swashbuckling version of the adventures of pirate Jean LaFitte and his association with president Andrew Jackson.
Paramount — *Kartes Video Communications*

Buck and the Preacher
1972
Comedy-Drama/Western
64576   102 mins   C   B, V   P
Sidney Poitier, Harry Belafonte, Ruby Dee, Cameron Mitchell, Denny Miller, directed by Sidney Poitier
A trail guide and a conman join forces to help a wagon train of former slaves who are seeking to homestead out West.
MPAA:PG
Columbia — *RCA/Columbia Pictures Home Video*

Buck Privates
1941
Comedy
69031   84 mins   B/W   B, V, LV   P
Bud Abbott, Lou Costello, Lee Norman, Alan Curtis, The Andrews Sisters
Abbott and Costello star as two dim-witted tie salesmen, running from the law, who become buck privates during World War II.
Universal — *MCA Home Video*

Buck Rogers Conquers the Universe
1939
Science fiction
29134   91 mins   B/W   B, V   P
Buster Crabbe, Constance Moore, Jackie Moran
The story of Buck Rogers, written by Phil Nolan in 1928, was the first science fiction story done in the modern super-hero space idiom. Many of the "inventions" seen in this movie have actually come into existence—spaceships, ray guns (lasers), anti-gravity belts—as a testament to Nolan's almost psychic farsightedness.
Viacom International — *CBS/Fox Video*

Buck Rogers in the 25th Century
1981
Science fiction
82365   47 mins   C   B, V   P
Gil Gerard, Erin Gray, Mel Blanc, Tim O'Connor, Gary Coleman, Jerry Orbach 8 pgms
Blast off with Buck Rogers as he travels through the galaxy in search of adventure. Each episode is available individually.
1.Vegas in Space 2.Return of the Fighting 69th 3.Unchained Woman 4.Happy Birthday Buck 5.A Blast for Buck 6.Space Vampire 7.Space Rockers 8.The Guardian
Universal Television — *MCA Home Video*

Buck Rogers in the 25th Century
1979
Science fiction
48628   90 mins   C   B, V   P
Gil Gerard, Pamela Hensley, Erin Gray, Henry Silva
An American astronaut, preserved in space for 500 years, is brought back to life by a passing Draconian flagship. Outer space adventures begin when he is accused of being a spy from Earth. Based on the classic movie serial.
MPAA:PG
Universal — *MCA Home Video*

Buck Rogers: Planet Outlaws
1938
Science fiction
08630   70 mins   B/W   B, V, 3/4U   P
Buster Crabbe, Constance Moore, Jackie Moran
Drama of the world as it might exist in the 25th century. Compiled from the "Buck Rogers" serial.
Universal — *Video Yesteryear*

Buddy Barnes 1982
Music-Performance
88113   30 mins   C   B, V, 8mm   P
The renowned jazz pianist and composer
performs with Sylvia Sims, including "My Ship,"
"Don't Fight It, It's Chemistry" and "I've Been to
Town."
Studio B; Sony Video — *Sony Video Software*

Buddy Buddy 1981
Comedy
59845   96 mins   C   B, V, CED   P
*Jack Lemmon, Walter Matthau, directed by Billy
Wilder*
A professional hitman's well-ordered
arrangement to knock off a state's witness
keeps being interrupted by the suicide attempts
of a man in the next hotel room.
MPAA:R
MGM — *MGM/UA Home Video*

Buddy Hackett: Live and 1984
Uncensored
Comedy-Performance
66610   72 mins   C   B, V   P
Buddy Hackett
Comedian Buddy Hackett lets loose in a no-
holds-barred recording of his nightclub show.
USA — *U.S.A. Home Video*

Buddy Rich 1985
Music-Performance
82012   55 mins   C   B, V   P
Buddy Rich and his band play such standards
as "Sophisticated Lady" and "One O'Clock
Jump" along with "No Exit" and "Norwegian
Wood" in this concert taped at King Street.
Available in VHS and Beta Hi-Fi Stereo.
Bogue-Reber Productions — *Sony Video
Software*

Buddy System, The 1983
Drama
Closed Captioned
76042   110 mins   C   B, V   P
*Richard Dreyfuss, Susan Sarandon, Jean
Stapleton*
A tale of contemporary love and the modern
myths that outline the boundaries between
lovers and friends.
MPAA:PG
Alain Chammas — *Key Video*

Budo 1981
Martial arts/Documentary
70607   75 mins   C   B, V   P
This program explores the Eastern techniques
of Kendo, karate, akido, and judo while it
discusses the history of Oriental philosophical
and theological thought.
Prism Entertainment — *Prism*

Buffalo Bill and the 1976
Indians
Western
76044   135 mins   C   B, V   P
*Paul Newman, Geraldine Chaplin, Joel Grey,
Will Sampson*
A story about the rough-and-tumble days of Wild
Bill Hickok's traveling Wild West Show.
MPAA:PG
David Susskind — *Key Video*

Bug 1975
Horror/Science fiction
60215   100 mins   C   B, V   P
Bradford Dillman, Joanna Miles
The city of Riverside is threatened with
destruction after a massive earth tremor
unleashes a super-race of mega-cockroaches.
MPAA:PG
William Castle — *Paramount Home Video*

Bugs Bunny and Elmer 1944
Fudd Cartoon Festival
Cartoons
85545   54 mins   C   B, V   P
*Bugs Bunny, Elmer Fudd, Daffy Duck, voices by
Mel Blanc*
Seven classic Bugs & Elmer shorts, including
"Wabbitt Twouble," "Stage Door Cartoon" and
"The Big Snooze."
Warner Bros. — *MGM/UA Home Video*

Bugs Bunny Cartoon 1944
Festival
Cartoons
84715   34 mins   C   B, V   P
The animated antics of the nefarious rabbit in
four early cartoons.
Vitaphone Corp. — *MGM/UA Home Video*

Bugs Bunny/Road 1979
Runner Movie, The
Comedy/Cartoons
38948   90 mins   C   B, V   P
Animated
A compilation of classic Warner Brothers
cartoons, starring Bugs Bunny, Daffy Duck,
Elmer Fudd, the Road Runner, Wile E. Coyote,
Porky Pig, and Pepe Le Pew, including some all-
new animated sequences.
MPAA:G
Warner Bros — *Warner Home Video; RCA
VideoDiscs*

Bugs Bunny's 3rd Movie: 1982
1,001 Rabbit Tales
Cartoons
60560   74 mins   C   B, V   P
Animated, voices by Mel Blanc
A compilation of old and new classic cartoons
featuring Bugs, Daffy, Sylvester, Porky, Elmer,
Tweety, Speedy Gonzalez and Yosemite Sam.

MPAA:G
Warner Bros — *Warner Home Video*

Bugs Bunny's Wacky Adventures   1957
Cartoons
81571   59 mins   C   B, V   P
Animated, voice of Mel Blanc
Here is a collection of that rascally rabbit's classic cartoons featuring "Ali Baba Bunny", "Hare Do" and "Duck! Rabbit! Duck!".
Warner Bros. — *Warner Home Video*

Bugsy Malone   1976
Musical
58709   94 mins   C   B, V, LV   P
Jodie Foster, Scott Baio, directed by Alan Parker
An all-children's cast highlights this spoof of '30's gangster movies. Songs by Paul Williams.
MPAA:G
Paramount; Alan Marshall — *Paramount Home Video*

Building Blocks of Life, The   1982
Biology/Science
59561   61 mins   C   B, V   P
A no-nonsense look at the basic unit of life, the cell, of which 60 trillion are required to constitute the human body.
McGraw Hill — *Mastervision*

Bulldog Courage   1935
Western
08818   66 mins   B/W   B, V   P, T
Tim McCoy, Lois January
Young man is out to avenge his father's murder.
Puritan — *Video Connection; Discount Video Tapes; United Home Video*

Bulldog Drummond   1929
Adventure
84868   85 mins   B/W   B, V   P
Ronald Colman, directed by F Richard Jones
A World War I vet, bored with civilian life, is enlisted by a beautiful woman to help her father in various adventures.
Samuel Goldwyn — *Embassy Home Entertainment*

Bulldog Drummond Comes Back   1937
Mystery
10936   67 mins   B/W   B, V   P
John Howard, John Barrymore, Louise Campbell, Reginald Denny, Sir Guy Standing
Drummond, aided by Colonel Nielson, rescues his fiancee from the hands of desperate kidnappers.

Paramount — *Movie Buff Video; Discount Video Tapes; Cable Films*

Bulldog Drummond Double Feature   193?
Mystery
57759   119 mins   B/W   B, V   P
John Howard
Two Bulldog Drummond films: "Bulldog Drummond's Bride" (1939), wherein Drummond decides to marry, but not until after bomb explosions, a bank robbery, and a rooftop chase; and "Bulldog Drummond Comes Back" (1937), in which Drummond is on the trail of a clever criminal who is looking to get at him by kidnapping his fiancee.
Paramount — *Hollywood Home Theater*

Bulldog Drummond Escapes   1937
Mystery
08764   67 mins   B/W   B, V, 3/4U   P
Ray Milland, Heather Angel, Reginald Denny, Sir Guy Standing
Drummond, aided by his side-kick and valet, rescues a beautiful girl from spies. He then falls in love with her.
Paramount — *Video Yesteryear*

Bulldog Drummond's Bride   1939
Mystery
80736   69 mins   B/W   B, V   P
John Howard, Heather Angel, H. B. Warner, E. E. Clive, Reginald Denny
Ace detective Bulldog Drummond has to interrupt his honeymoon in order to pursue a gang of bank robbers across France and England.
Paramount — *Hal Roach Studios; Discount Video Tapes*

Bulldog Drummond's Peril   1938
Mystery
05514   77 mins   B/W   B, V, 3/4U   R, P
John Barrymore, John Howard, Louise Campbell, Reginald Denny
Murder and robbery drag Drummond away from his wedding; he pursues the villains until they are behind bars.
Paramount — *Cable Films*

Bulldog Drummond's Secret Police   1939
Mystery
85150   54 mins   B/W   B, V   P
John Howard, Heather Angel, H.B. Warner, Reginald Denny, E.E. Clive
The 15th Drummond film, featuring a million-pound treasure stashed in the Drummond

---

manor and the murderous endeavors to retrieve
it.
Paramount — *Video Yesteryear*

Bullfighter and the Lady · 1950
Drama
76825   87 mins   B/W   B, V   P
Robert Stack, Gilbert Roland, Katy Jurado
An American comes to Mexico to learn the fine
art of bullfighting from a matador to impress a
beautiful woman.
Republic Pictures — *Republic Pictures Home
Video*

Bullfighters, The · 1945
Comedy
81549   61 mins   B/W   B, V   P
*Stan Laurel, Oliver Hardy, Margo Wood, Richard
Lane, directed by Mal St. Clair*
Stan and Ollie are in hot pursuit of a dangerous
criminal which leads them to Mexico where Stan
winds up in a bull ring. Available in VHS and
Beta Hi-Fi.
20th Century Fox — *Playhouse Video*

Bullitt · 1968
Drama
44589   105 mins   C   B, V   P
*Steve McQueen, Robert Vaughn, Jacqueline
Bisset, Don Gordon, Robert Duvall, directed by
Peter Yates*
A detective lieutenant has an assignment to
keep a star witness out of danger for 48 hours.
He senses that something is fishy about the
setup and before the night is out has a murder
on his hands. Based on the novel "Mute
Witness" by Robert L. Pike.
MPAA:PG
Warner Bros — *Warner Home Video; RCA
VideoDiscs*

Bullpen · 1974
Baseball
33834   22 mins   C   B, V   P
*Joe Page, Jim Konstanty, Roy Face, Hoyt
Wilhelm, Ron Perranoski, Tug McGraw*
This program about baseball's relief pitchers
goes behind the scenes into the relievers' home
away from home, the bullpen. Some of the best
"firemen" of the past and present are seen in
action. Some black and white sequences.
W and W Productions — *Major League
Baseball Productions*

Bullshot · 1983
Comedy
70960   84 mins   C   B, V   P
*Alan Shearman, Diz White, Ron House, Frances
Tomelty, Michael Aldridge, Ron Pember,
Christopher Good, directed by Dick Clement*
This zany English satire sends up the legendary
Bulldog Drummond. In the face of mad
professors, hapless heroines, devilish Huns and

deadly enemies our intrepid hero
remains...British.
MPAA:PG
Island Alive — *THORN EMI/HBO Video*

Bullshot Crummond · 1984
Satire
78664   90 mins   C   B, V   P
The Low Moan Spectacular comedy troupe
performs this satire that trashes oldtime
adventure serials.
RKO — *RKO HomeVideo*

Bullwhip · 1958
Western
80843   80 mins   C   B, V   P
*Guy Madison, Rhonda Fleming, James Griffith,
Peter Adams*
A man falsely accused of murder saves himself
from the hangman's noose by agreeing to a
shotgun wedding.
Allied Artists — *Republic Pictures Home Video*

Bullwinkle & Rocky and · 1960
Friends, Volume I
Cartoons
64709   95 mins   C   CED   P
Animated
A collection of cartoon segments featuring all
the "Rocky and His Friends" characters,
including Rocket J. Squirrel, Bullwinkle Moose,
Boris Badenov, Natasha, Dudley Doright, Mr.
Peabody and Sherman.
Filmtel; Jay Ward — *RCA VideoDiscs*

Bummer · 1973
Adventure
51748   90 mins   C   B, V   P
Kipp Whitman, Dennis Burkley, Carol Speed
A rock band's wild party turns into tragedy when
the bass player goes too far with two groupies.
MPAA:R
Entertainment Ventures Inc — *Magnum
Entertainment*

Bunco · 1983
Drama
80887   60 mins   C   B, V   P
*Tom Selleck, Robert Urien, Donna Mills, Will
Geer, Arte Johnson, Alan Feinstein*
Two policemen working for the Los Angeles
Police Department's Bunco Squad discover a
college for con artists complete with tape-
recorded lessons and on the job training.
Lorimar Productions — *Karl/Lorimar Home
Video*

Bundle of Joy · 1956
Comedy
11643   98 mins   C   B, V   P
Debbie Reynolds, Eddie Fisher

Salesgirl, who saves an infant from falling off the steps of a foundling home, is mistaken for the child's mother.
Universal; Edmund Grainger — *United Home Video*

Bunnicula—The Vampire Rabbit   1982
Cartoons
80641   23 mins   C   B, V   P
Animated
Strange things happen to a family after they adopt an abandoned bunny so their dog and cat team up to prove that their furry friend is a vampire in disguise.
Ruby-Spears Prods. — *Worldvision Home Video*

Burial Ground   1985
Horror
84092   85 mins   C   B, V   P
Karen Well, Peter Bark, directed by Andrea Bianchi
A classically grisly splatter film in which the hungry dead rise and proceed to kill the weekend denizens of an isolated aristocratic mansion.
Film Concept Group — *Vestron Video*

Burn!   1970
Drama
76045   113 mins   C   B, V   P
Marlon Brando, Evarist Marquez, Renato Salvatori
An Italian-made saga about the rise of a people from slavery to freedom.
United Artists — *Key Video*

Burning, The   1982
Horror
59694   90 mins   C   B, V   P
Brian Matthews, Leah Ayres
A story of macabre revenge set in the dark woods of a seemingly innocent summer camp.
MPAA:R
Harvey Weinstein — *THORN EMI/HBO Video*

Burning Bed, The   1985
Drama
Closed Captioned
84883   95 mins   C   B, V   P
Farrah Fawcett, Paul LeMat, Penelope Milford, Richard Masur
A made-for-TV dramatic expose about wife-beating.
Carol Schreder — *CBS/Fox Video*

Burnt Offerings   1976
Horror
78632   116 mins   C   B, V   P
Oliver Reed, Karen Black, Bette Davis, Burgess Meredith, directed by Don Curtis

A family rents a house for the summer and they become affected by evil forces that possess the house.
MPAA:PG
United Artists — *MGM/UA Home Video*

Bury Me an Angel   1971
Drama
80663   85 mins   C   B, V, LV   P
Dixie Peabody, Terry Mace, Clyde Ventura, Dan Haggerty
A female biker sets out to seek revenge against the men who killed her brother.
New World Pictures — *New World Video; Hollywood Home Theater*

Bus Stop   1956
Comedy
08460   96 mins   C   B, V, CED   P
Marilyn Monroe, Arthur O'Connell, Hope Lange, Don Murray, Hans Conried, directed by Joshua Logan
A motley collection of travelers arrive at some truths about themselves while snowbound at an Arizona bus stop. Based on William Inge's play.
20th Century Fox — *CBS/Fox Video*

Bushido Blade, The   1980
Adventure/Suspense
59697   92 mins   C   B, V   P
Richard Boone, James Earl Jones, Frank Converse
An action-packed samurai thriller of adventure and betrayal set in medieval Japan.
Arthur Rankin Jr — *THORN EMI/HBO Video*

Buster and Billie   1974
Drama
81431   100 mins   C   B, V   P
Jan-Michael Vincent, Joan Goodfellow, Clifton James, Pamela Sue Martin, directed by Daniel Petrie
Tragedy ensues when a popular high school student falls in love with the class tramp in rural Georgia in 1948. Available in VHS and Beta Hi-Fi.
MPAA:R
Columbia Pictures — *RCA/Columbia Pictures Home Video*

Buster Keaton Rides   1965
Again/The Railrodder
Comedy/Documentary
65229   81 mins   C   B, V, FO   P
Buster Keaton
"The Railrodder" is a silent comedy short that returns Buster Keaton to the type of slapstick he made famous in his legendary 20's films. "Buster Keaton Rides Again" (in black-and-white) is a documentary-style look at Keaton filmed during the making of "The Railrodder." Besides scenes of Keaton at work, there is also a capsule rundown of his career.

National Film Board of Canada — *Video Yesteryear*

Buster Keaton: The Great Stone Face   1968
Documentary/Comedy
17236   60 mins   B/W   B, V   P
Narrated by Henry Morgan
This program from the Rohauer Collection contains footage of Buster Keaton in "Fatty at Coney Island," "Cops," "Ballonatics," "Day Dreams," and "The General."
Funnyman Inc — *Mastervision*

Bustin' Loose   1981
Comedy
58211   94 mins   C   B, V, LV   P
Richard Pryor, Cicely Tyson, Robert Christian, George Coe, Bill Quinn, directed by Oz Scott
A fast-talking con man reluctantly shepherds a busload of misplaced kids and their keeper cross-country.
MPAA:R
Universal; Richard Pryor; Michael Glick — *MCA Home Video*

Bustling Narrow Gauge/White Pass and Yukon/Rio Grande Southern/Trestles of Ophir   1951
Trains
77362   56 mins   B/W   B, V   P, T
This collection of four short films fondly recalls classic trains such as the San Juan and the White Pass.
Woodrow Gorman — *Blackhawk Films*

Butch and Sundance: The Early Days   1979
Western
82495   111 mins   C   B, V   P
Tom Berenger, William Katt
This film traces the origins of the famous outlaw duo. It contains the requisite shoot-outs, hold-ups and escapes. A "prequel" to "Butch Cassidy and the Sundance Kid."
MPAA:PG
20th Century Fox — *Playhouse Video*

Butch Cassidy and the Sundance Kid   1969
Adventure
09093   110 mins   C   B, V, LV   P
Paul Newman, Robert Redford, Katharine Ross
A couple of legendary outlaws at the turn of the century take it on the lam with a beautiful, willing ex-school teacher.
Academy Awards '69: Best Song (Raindrops Keep Falling on My Head). MPAA:PG   EL, SP
20th Century Fox — *CBS/Fox Video*

Butler's Dilemma, The   1943
Comedy
63620   75 mins   B/W   B, V, FO   P
Richard Hearne, Francis Sullivan, Hermione Gingold, Ian Fleming
A jewel thief and a playboy both claim the identity of a butler who never existed, with humorous results.
British National — *Movie Buff Video; Video Yesteryear*

Butterflies Are Free   1972
Comedy-Drama
13234   109 mins   C   B, V   P
Goldie Hawn, Edward Albert, Eileen Heckart, Michael Glaser, directed by Milton Katselas
An actress helps a blind man gain independence from his over protective mother.
Academy Awards '72: Best Supporting Actress (Heckart). MPAA:PG
Columbia; MJ Frankovich — *RCA/Columbia Pictures Home Video*

Butterfly   1982
Drama
59658   105 mins   C   B, V   P
Pia Zadora, Stacy Keach, Orson Welles, Edward Albert, James Franciscus, Lois Nettleton, Stuart Whitman
James M. Cain's novel about an amoral young woman who uses her beauty and sensual appetite to manipulate the men in her life, including her father. Set in Nevada of the 1930's, father and daughter are drawn into a daring and forbidden love affair by their lust and desperation.
Golden Globe Awards '82: Newcomer of the Year (Zadora). MPAA:R
Analysis Films — *Vestron Video*

Butterfly Ball, The   1976
Musical/Fantasy
80269   85 mins   C   B, V   P
Twiggy, Ian Gillian, David Coverdale, narrated by Vincent Price.
This retelling of the 19th century classic combines the music of Roger Glover, live action and animation by Halas and Batchelor for a unique film experience.
Tony Klinger — *VCL Home Video*

Buzzy the Funny Crow   1962
Cartoons
86369   60 mins   C   B, V   P
A compilation of the popular Buzzy cartoons.
Harvey Films Inc. — *Worldvision Home Video*

By Design   1982
Comedy
63329   90 mins   C   B, V   P
Patty Duke Astin, Sara Botsford

Two women who live together want to have a
baby, so they embark on a search for the
perfect stud.
MPAA:R
Atlantic Releasing Corp; Beryl Fox and Werner
Aellen — *THORN EMI/HBO Video*

Bye, Bye, Birdie   1963
Musical
21283   112 mins   C   B, V   P
*Dick Van Dyke, Janet Leigh, Ann-Margret, Paul
Lynde, Bobby Rydell, Trudi Ames, directed by
George Sidney*
The film version of the Broadway musical in
which a rock and roll idol is drafted. Songs
include "Put on a Happy Face."
Columbia — *RCA/Columbia Pictures Home
Video*

Bye Bye Brazil   1979
Drama
53507   100 mins   C   B, V   P
*Jose Wilker, Betty Faria, Fabio Junior, directed
by Carlos Diegues*
A changing Brazil is seen through the eyes of
four wandering minstrels, gypsy actors exploring
the exotic and picturesque north.
Lucy Barreto; Brazil — *Warner Home Video*

C

Cabaret   1972
Musical-Drama
55207   119 mins   C   B, V, CED   P
*Liza Minnelli, Joel Grey, Michael York, directed
by Bob Fosse*
In early 1930's Berlin, singer Sally Bowles
shares her English lover with a homosexual
German baron. Songs include "Money, Money,
Money," "Wilkommen," and "Mein Herr."
Academy Awards '72: Best Actress (Minnelli);
Best Supporting Actor (Grey); Best Director
(Fosse); Best Cinematography; Best Editing.
MPAA:PG
ABC Pictures; Allied Artists — *CBS/Fox Video*

Cabin in the Sky   1943
Musical/Fantasy
82114   99 mins   C   B, V   P
*Ethel Waters, Eddie "Rochester" Anderson,
Lena Horne, Rex Ingram, Louis Armstrong,
Duke Ellington, directed by Vincente Minnelli*
A poor woman fights to keep her husband's soul
out of the devil's clutches. The Harold Arlen-
E.Y. Harburg score features "Happiness Is Just
a Thing Called Joe" and "Taking a Chance On
Love."
MGM — *MGM/UA Home Video*

Cabinet of Dr. Caligari   1919
Film-Avant-garde
06215   52 mins   B/W   B, V   P
*Conrad Veidt, Werner Krauss, directed by
Robert Wiene*
Silent classic in surrealistic style about a
somnambulist under spell of mad doctor. New
sound track and music.
Decla Bioscop — *Movie Buff Video; Hollywood
Home Theater; International Historic Films;
Discount Video Tapes; Video Yesteryear;
Western Film & Video Inc; Kartes Video
Communications*

Cabo Blanco   1981
Drama
66599   87 mins   C   B, V   P
*Charles Bronson, Jason Robards, Dominque
Sanda*
A remake of "Casablanca," set in a South
American village in the years just after World
War II.
MPAA:R
Paul Joseph; Lance Hool — *Media Home
Entertainment*

Cactus Flower   1969
Comedy
59604   103 mins   C   B, V   P
*Walter Matthau, Goldie Hawn, Ingrid Bergman,
directed by Gene Saks*
A middle-aged bachelor dentist gets involved
with a kookie mistress and his prim and proper
receptionist.
Academy Awards '69: Best Supporting Actress
(Hawn). MPAA:PG
Columbia — *RCA/Columbia Pictures Home
Video*

Caddie   1981
Drama
63338   107 mins   C   B, V   P
Helen Morse, Jack Thompson
This is the story of a woman who leaves her
unfaithful husband to face hardship and
romance on her own in 1930's Australia.
Anthony Buckley Productions — *THORN
EMI/HBO Video*

Caddyshack   1980
Comedy
54808   99 mins   C   B, V, LV   P
*Chevy Chase, Rodney Dangerfield, Ted Knight,
Michael O'Keefe, Bill Murray, directed by Harold
Ramis*
This comic spoof takes place at Bushwood
Country Club, where a young caddy is bucking
to win the club's college scholarship. Within this
context we meet an obnoxious club president, a
playboy who is too laid back to keep his score, a
vulgar, loud, extremely rich, but hated man, and
a gopher-hunting groundskeeper.
MPAA:R

Warner Bros — *Warner Home Video; RCA VideoDiscs*

Caesar and Cleopatra   1945
Comedy
79106   135 mins   C   B, V   P
Claude Rains, Vivien Leigh, Stewart Granger, Flora Robson
A filmed adaptation of the classic George Bernard Shaw play.
Rank/Gabriel Pascal — *VidAmerica*

Caesar's Hour   1956
Comedy/Variety
52460   52 mins   B/W   B, V, FO   P
Sid Caesar, Carl Reiner, Howard Morris, Nanette Fabray
This episode of Sid Caesar's famous series is the last show of the 1956 season. Nanette Fabray plays Sid Caesar's long-suffering wife in one of several featured sketches.
NBC — *Video Yesteryear*

Caesar's Hour   1954
Television/Comedy
63624   59 mins   B/W   B, V, FO   P
Sid Caesar, Howard Morris, Carl Reiner
First telecast on October 25, 1954, this is the fourth show of the comedy-variety series. Slapstick sketches, dance, and a circus act are featured, and original commercials for Speidel, Glenn Miller Records, and others are included.
NBC — *Video Yesteryear*

Caesar's Hour   1957
Comedy/Variety
78098   45 mins   B/W   B, V, FO   P
Sid Caesar, Carl Reiner, Howard Morris, Janet Blair, Shirl Conway, Pat Carroll, Hugh Downs
A comedy show from Sid Caesar's variety series that was the replacement for "Your Show of Shows."
NBC — *Video Yesteryear*

Cage Aux Folles III: The   1986
Wedding, La
Comedy
87752   88 mins   C   B, V   P
Michel Serrault, Ugo Tognazzi, directed by Georges Lautner
The kooky gay duo must feign normalcy by marrying and fathering a child in order to collect a weighty inheritance.
MPAA:PG-13
Tri-Star Pictures; Marcello Danon — *RCA/Columbia Pictures Home Video*

Cage aux Folles, La   1979
Comedy
55585   91 mins   C   B, V, LV   P
Ugo Tognazzi, Michel Serrault

A situation comedy about a club in St. Tropez notorious for putting on a drag show featuring men dressed as women, focusing on the manager of the club and the club's headliner who share an apartment.
MPAA:R
United Artists — *CBS/Fox Video; RCA VideoDiscs*

Cage Aux Folles II, La   1980
Comedy
58844   100 mins   C   B, V, CED   P
Ugo Tognazzi, Michel Serrault, Marcel Bozzuffi, Michel Galabru, directed by Edouard Molinaro
The sequel to the highly successful "La Cage aux Folles." Albin sets out to prove to his companion that he still has sex appeal.
United Artists; Da Ma Produzione — *CBS/Fox Video*

Caged Fury   1980
Drama/Adventure
79389   90 mins   C   B, V   P
Bernie William, Taafee O'Connell, Jeniffer Lane
American P.O.W's being held captive in Southeast Asia are brainwashed into becoming walking time bombs.
MPAA:R
Emily Blas — *World Premiere*

Caged Terror   1972
Exploitation
88184   76 mins   C   B, V   P
Percy Harkness, Elizabeth Suzuki, Leon Morenzie
Two urbanites hit the countryside for a weekend, and meet a band of crazy rapists who ravage the wife and set the husband raging with bloodthirsty revenge.
Unknown — *New World Video*

Caged Women   1984
Drama
73038   97 mins   C   B, V   P
An undercover journalist enters a women's prison.
MPAA:R
Motion Picture Marketing — *Vestron Video*

Cahill: United States   1973
Marshal
Western
74208   103 mins   C   B, V   P
John Wayne, Gary Grimes, George Kennedy
The "Duke" stars as a marshal who comes to the aid of his sons who are mixed up with a gang of outlaws.
MPAA:PG
Michael Wayne; Batjac Productions — *Warner Home Video*

Caine Mutiny, The   1954
Drama
Closed Captioned
77240   125 mins   C   B, V   P
*Humphrey Bogart, Jose Ferrer, Van Johnson,
Fred Mac Murray, directed by Edward Dmytryk*
A group of naval officers revolt against a
Captain they consider mentally unfit.
Columbia; Stanley Kramer — *RCA/Columbia
Pictures Home Video*

Cain's Cutthroats   1971
Western
80827   87 mins   C   B, V   R, P
Scott Brady, John Carradine, Robert Dix
A former Confederate army captain and a
bounty hunting preacher team up to settle the
score with the soldiers who gang raped his wife
and murdered his son.
MPAA:R
Fanfare Productions — *Video Gems*

Cal   1984
Drama
77266   104 mins   C   B, V   P
*Helen Mirren, John Lynch, Donal McCann, Kitty
Gibson, directed by Pat O'Connor*
A 19-year-old IRA activist falls in love with a
widowed Protestant librarian. The music is by
Dire Straits guitarist Mark Knopfler.
Cannes Film Festival '84: Best Actress (Mirren).
MPAA:R
Warner Bros.; Goldcrest — *Warner Home
Video*

Caledonian Dreams   1982
Photography/Music
60577   46 mins   C   LV   P
Directed by Shoji Otake
This sequel to "Oriental Dreams" follows the
intimate escapades of three beautiful women as
they explore the exotic lifestyle of the South
Seas. Music by Norio Maeda and Windbreakers.
Stereo.
Japanese — *Pioneer Video Imports*

California Angels: Team   1982
Highlights
Baseball
81135   30 mins   C   B, V   P
*Bob Boone, Reggie Jackson, Fred Lynn, Bobby
Grich 3 pgms*
This series chronicles the first twenty-one years
of the California Angels.
*1.1961-1971: The First Ten Years 2.1981: In
The Groove For '82 3.1982: Something To
Prove*
Major League Baseball — *Major League
Baseball Productions*

California Dreaming   1979
Drama
80701   93 mins   C   B, V   P
*Dennis Christopher, Tanya Roberts, Glynnis
O'Connor, John Calvin, Seymour Cassel*
A young man heads west to California where he
meets up with a beach groupie and a surfer who
teach him something about life and love.
MPAA:R
American International Pictures — *Vestron
Video*

California Girls   1984
Comedy
70225   83 mins   C   B, V   P
*Al Music, Mary McKinley, Alicia Allen, Lantz
Douglas, Barbara Parks*
A radio station stages an outrageous contest,
and three sexy ladies prove to be tough
competition. Soundtrack features music by The
Police, Kool & the Gang, Blondie, Queen and
10cc.
William Webb; Monica Webb — *VCL Home
Video*

California Gold Rush   1981
Adventure
65760   100 mins   C   B, V   P
Robert Hays, John Dehner, Ken Curtis
In 1849, a young aspiring writer in search of
adventure arrives in Sutter's Fort and takes on a
job at the local sawmill. When gold is found,
Sutter's Fort is soon overrun with fortune
hunters whose greed, violence and corruption
threaten to tear apart the peaceful community.
James L Conway — *Magnum Entertainment*

California Reich, The   1975
Documentary
84533   55 mins   C   B, V   P
Directed by Walter F Parkes, Keith Critchlow
A searing chronicle of the actions and
ideologies of a growing sect of California-based
Neo-Nazis. A frightening record of perversely
motivated American-fringe life.
City Life Films Inc — *Paramount Home Video*

California Suite   1978
Comedy
47023   103 mins   C   B, V, LV   P
*Alan Alda, Michael Caine, Bill Cosby, Jane
Fonda, Walter Matthau, Richard Pryor, Maggie
Smith*
This Neil Simon comedy has four different story
lines, all set in the Beverly Hills Hotel.
Academy Award '78: Best Supporting Actress
(Smith). MPAA:PG
Columbia; Ray Stark — *RCA/Columbia
Pictures Home Video; RCA VideoDiscs*

Caligula   1980
Drama
65475   143 mins   C   B, V   P
*Malcolm McDowell, Sir John Gielgud, Peter
O'Toole*

Impeccably faithful to the historical events of Caligula's Rome, this program also captures in detail the decadence and debauchery that marked his reign. Explicit sex and violence.
Bob Guccione; Franco Rossellini — *Vestron Video*

Caligula 1980
Drama
65476   105 mins   C   B, V, LV,   P
                                    CED
Malcolm McDowell, Sir John Gielgud, Peter O'Toole
A slightly edited version, with some of the sexually explicit scenes toned down.
MPAA:R
Bob Guccione; Franco Rossellini — *Vestron Video*

Call Him Mr. Shatter 1974
Crime-Drama
85368   90 mins   C   B, V   P
Stuart Whitman, Peter Cushing, Anton Diffring
A hired killer stalks a tottering Third World president and becomes embroiled in international political intrigue.
MPAA:R
Michael Carreras; Vee King Shaw — *Charter Entertainment*

Call of the Canyon 1942
Western
44987   71 mins   B/W   B, V   P, T
Gene Autry, Smiley Burnette
A crooked agent for a local meat packer won't pay a fair price, so Gene goes off to talk to the head man to set him straight.
Republic — *Blackhawk Films; Video Connection*

Call of the Wild 1972
Adventure
47389   105 mins   C   B, V   P
Charlton Heston, Michele Mercier, George Eastman
Jack London's famous story about a man whose survival depends upon his knowledge of the Alaskan wilderness comes to life in this film version.
MPAA:PG
Intercontinental Releasing Corp — *Warner Home Video*

Call of the Wild 1983
Adventure/Cartoons
81169   68 mins   C   B, V   P
Animated
This is an adaptation of the Jack London story about a dog's trek across the Alaskan tundra.
Northstar Productions — *Vestron Video*

Call Out the Marines 1942
Comedy/Adventure
73692   67 mins   B/W   B, V   P
Victor McLaglen, Binnie Barnes, Paul Kelly, Edmund Lowe
A group of army buddies re-enlist to break up a spy ring.
RKO — *RKO HomeVideo*

Call to Glory 1984
Drama
81106   120 mins   C   B, V   P
Craig T. Nelson, Cindy Pickett, Gabriel Damon, Keenan Wynn, Elisabeth Shue, G.D. Spradlin
This is the premier episode of the series about the turbulent times faced by an Air Force pilot and his family during the Cuban Missile Crisis.
Tisch/Avnet Productions; Paramount TV — *Paramount Home Video*

Callao, El (The Silent One) 197?
Crime-Drama
86540   90 mins   C   B, V   P
Jose Albar, Olga Agostini
A Puerto Rican gang in New York City is gunning for their former leader; when they mistake a look-alike priest for him, trouble begins.
SP
Spanish — *Master Arts Video*

Callie & Son 1981
Drama
88143   97 mins   C   B, V   P
Lindsay Wagner, Dabney Coleman, Jameson Parker, Michele Pfeiffer
A made-for-TV film detailing the sordid, murderous and episodic intertwining lives of a socialite woman and her rebellious, illegitimate son.
Rosilyn Heller Prod.; Hemdale Pres.; City Films & Motown Pictures — *Sony Video Software*

Came a Hot Friday 1985
Comedy
Closed Captioned
84524   101 mins   C   B, V   P
Peter Bland, Phillip Gordon, directed by Ian Mune
Two cheap conmen arrive in a southern town and their tables turn.
MPAA:PG
Larry Parr — *Charter Entertainment*

Camel Boy, The 1984
Adventure
76779   78 mins   C   B, V   P
Animated
This is the true story of a young Arabian boy who befriends a camel and their treacherous trek across the desert.

Yorum Gross Films — *Vestron Video*

Camelot 1967
Musical
58223   150 mins   C   B, V, LV   P
Richard Harris, Vanessa Redgrave, Daivd Hemmings, directed by Joshua Logan
The long-running Broadway musical about King Arthur, Guinevere, and Lancelot. Score by Lerner and Loewe includes "If Ever I Would Leave You," "How to Handle a Woman" and "Camelot."
Warner Bros — *Warner Home Video*

Cameo 1984
Music video
88094   27 mins   C   B, V   P
A compilation of videos from the little-known, emerging rock band.
Sony Video — *Sony Video Software*

Camila 1984
Drama
81913   105 mins   C   B, V   P
Susu Pecoraro, Imanol Arias, Hector Alterio, Elena Tasisto, directed by Maria-Luisa Bemberg
This is the true story of the tragic romance between an Argentinian socialite and a Jesuit priest in 1847. Available in Spanish with English subtitles or dubbed into English.
SP
European Classics — *Embassy Home Entertainment*

Camouflage 194?
World War II
11227   20 mins   C   B, V, FO   P
Animated
A training film by the Walt Disney studios for the Armed Forces, in which Yehudi the Chameleon teaches camouflage to young Air Corps fliers. Contains some condemning attitudes towards Japan.
Walt Disney Productions — *Video Yesteryear*

Campus Corpse, The 1977
Horror
76767   92 mins   C   B, V   P
Charles Martin Smith
A young man discovers evil doings when he pledges to a college fraternity.
The Miraleste Company — *Vestron Video*

Can I Do It...Till I Need Glasses? 1980
Comedy
56740   72 mins   C   B, V   P
Robin Williams, Roger Behr, Debra Klose, Moose Carlson, Walter Olkewicz
This suggestive comedy features outrageous, risque humor, and stars TV's "Mork," Robin Williams.

Mike Callie — *Media Home Entertainment*

Can She Bake a Cherry Pie? 1983
Comedy-Drama
72448   118 mins   C   B, V   P
Karen Black, Michael Emil, Michael Margotta, Frances Fisher, Martin Frydberg
This critically acclaimed film concerns the doubts involved when two people contemplate getting married. The official U.S. selection at the 1983 Cannes Festival.
International Rainbow Pictures; Jagfilm Productions — *Monterey Home Video*

Canadian Capers... Cartoons Volume I 19??
Cartoons/Christmas
65231   61 mins   C   B, V, FO   P
Animated
A collection of innovative animated shorts produced by the National Film Board of Canada. Titles include: "The Great Toy Robbery," "The Animal Movie," "The Story of Christmas," "The Energy Carol," "The Bear's Christmas," "Carrousel" and "TV Sale."
National Film Board of Canada — *Video Yesteryear*

Canadian Capers... Cartoons Volume II 19??
Cartoons
65232   58 mins   C   B, V, FO   P
Animated
A second collection of thought-provoking cartoons from the National Film Board of Canada, including "Spinnolio," "Doodle Film," "Hot Stuff," "The Cruise," "The Specialists" and "No Apple for Johnny."
National Film Board of Canada — *Video Yesteryear*

Cancion en el Alma (Song from the Heart) 197?
Drama
86537   70 mins   C   B, V   P
Luis Fernando Ramirez, Claudia Osuna
A talented boy singer is stuck in a greedy custody battle over his potential revenues in the wide world of Puerto Rican entertainment.
SP
Spanish — *Master Arts Video*

Candid Candid Camera 1985
Comedy
66106   55 mins   C   B, V   P
Allen Funt 4 pgms
Each volume in this series is a compilation of funny hidden camera clips which were deemed too risque for general television audiences.
Allen Funt — *Vestron Video*

Candidate, The 1972
Satire
44590   105 mins   C   B, V   P
Robert Redford, Peter Boyle, Don Porter, Allen Garfield, Karen Carlson, Melvyn Douglas, directed by Michael Ritchie
A true to life look at politics and political campaigning. A young, idealistic lawyer is talked into trying for the Senate seat and learns the truth about running for office.
Academy Awards '72: Best Story and Screenplay (Larner).   MPAA:PG
Warner Bros — *Warner Home Video; RCA VideoDiscs*

Candles at Nine 1944
Mystery
85151   84 mins   B/W   B, V   P
Jessie Matthews
An innocent showgirl must spend a month in her late uncle's mansion in order to inherit it, much to the malevolent chagrin of the rest of the family.
English — *Video Yesteryear*

Candleshoe 1978
Comedy/Adventure
77530   101 mins   C   B, V   P
Helen Hayes, David Niven, Jodie Foster
A Los Angeles street kid poses an an English matron's long lost granddaughter in order to steal a fortune hidden in her country estate, Candleshoe.
MPAA:G
Walt Disney Productions — *Walt Disney Home Video*

Candy-Candy 1981
Cartoons
53157   60 mins   C   B, V   P
Animated
This animated program for children is designed in soap opera fashion.
Ziv Intl — *Family Home Entertainment*

Candy Tangerine Man, The 197?
Drama
80423   88 mins   C   B, V   P
John Daniels, Tom Hankerson, Eli Haines, Marva Farmer
A respectable businessman leads a double life as a loving father and as Los Angeles most powerful pimp.
Matt Cimber — *Unicorn Video*

Canned Heat Boogie Assault 1983
Music-Performance
65212   60 mins   C   B, V   P
America's premier boogie band comes to life in their very first rock video. In Beta Hi-Fi and stereo VHS.

Full Circle Productions — *Monterey Home Video*

Cannery Row 1982
Comedy-Drama
59846   120 mins   C   B, V, CED   P
Nick Nolte, Debra Winger, directed by David S. Ward
Steinbeck's tale of down-and-outers who struggle to survive in a seedy part of town is brought to life in this screen adaptation.
MPAA:PG
MGM — *MGM/UA Home Video*

Cannon Ball, The/The Eyes Have It 192?
Comedy
58599   41 mins   B/W   B, V   P, T
Chester Conklin, Keystone Cops, Ben Turpin, Georgia O'Dell, Helen Gilmore, Jack Lipson
Chester Conklin stars in "The Cannon Ball" (1915), as an explosives expert in the Boom Powder Factory. "The Eyes Have It" (1928), stars Ben Turpin involved in another misunderstanding with wifey and mother-in-law. Silent.
Mack Sennett — *Blackhawk Films*

Cannonball 1976
Adventure
51989   93 mins   C   B, V   P
David Carradine, Bill McKinney, Veronica Hamel, Gerrit Graham, Robert Carradine
A variety of ruthless and determined people compete for the $100,000 grand prize in an illicit cross-country auto race.
MPAA:PG
New World Pictures — *Warner Home Video*

Cannonball/Dizzy Heights & Daring Hearts, The 1916
Comedy
85152   71 mins   B/W   B, V   P
Chester Conklin
Two classic comedies featuring Conklin, the Keystone Kops and wacky aeroplanes from the irrepressible Mack Sennett.
Mack Sennett; Tri-Stone Pictures — *Video Yesteryear*

Cannonball Run, The 1981
Comedy
58895   95 mins   C   B, V, LV, CED   P
Burt Reynolds, Farrah Fawcett, Roger Moore, Dom DeLuise, Dean Martin, Sammy Davis Jr, Jack Elam, Adrienne Barbeau, Peter Fonda
Reynolds and sidekick Dom DeLuise disguise themselves as paramedics in order to foil the cops while they compete in the cross-country Cannonball race.
MPAA:PG

20th Century Fox — *Vestron Video*

Cannonball Run II   1984
Comedy
78621   109 mins   C   B, V, LV   P
Burt Reynolds, Dom DeLuise, Jamie Farr, Marilu Henner, Shirley MacLaine, direct by Hal Needham
A group of race car drivers are after a one million dollar prize in a no holds barred cross country car race.
MPAA:PG
Warner Bros; Golden Harvest — *Warner Home Video*

Can't Stop the Music   1980
Musical
58456   120 mins   C   B, V   P
Valerie Perrine, Bruce Jenner, Steve Guttenberg, Paul Sand, The Village People, directed by Nancy Walker
A retired model invites friends from Greenwich Village to a party to help the career of her roommate, an aspiring disco composer.
MPAA:PG
Allan Carr; Associated Film Distributors — *THORN EMI/HBO Video*

Cantinflas   1984
Cartoons
74077   60 mins   C   B, V   , P
Animated
The delightful cartoon character Cantinflas takes you on a trip through history to meet King Tut, Daniel Boone, Madame Curie and many other famous people.
Diamexsa — *Family Home Entertainment*

Cantinflas, Volume II: 1984
Galaxies and Gomes
Cartoons
78373   60 mins   C   B, V   P
Animated
Cantinflas takes a tour of the galaxy in an alien's space scooter and learns all about sports in his return visit to Earth.
Family Entertainment — *Family Home Entertainment*

Cantonen Iron Kung Fu   197?
Martial arts/Adventure
47706   90 mins   C   B, V   P
Liang Jia Ren
The ten tigers of Quon Tung perfect martial arts skills known as Cantonen Iron Kung Fu.
Jing Kno Jung — *Master Arts Video; World Video Enterprises*

Capricorn One   1978
Science fiction
45059   123 mins   C   B, V, LV,   P
                          CED

Elliot Gould, James Brolin, Brenda Vaccaro
The whole world is watching America's first manned space flight to Mars. But before the countdown ends, three astronauts are plunged into a battle for survival in an incredible cover-up conspiracy.
MPAA:R
Warner Brothers — *CBS/Fox Video*

Captain Apache   1972
Western
12028   95 mins   C   B, V   P
Lee Van Cleef, Carroll Baker, Stuart Whitman
An Apache is assigned by Union intelligence to investigate an Indian commissioner's murder.
Philip Yordan; Official Films — *King of Video; Prism*

Captain Blood   1935
Adventure
60427   99 mins   B/W   B, V, CED   P
Errol Flynn, Olivia DeHavilland, Basil Rathbone, J. Carrol Naish, Guy Kibbee, Lionel Atwill
An exciting adaptation of the Sabatini adventure story of a pirate and his swashbuckling exploits.
Warner Bros — *CBS/Fox Video; RCA VideoDiscs*

Captain Caution   1940
Adventure
64373   84 mins   B/W   B, V, 3/4U   P
Victor Mature, Louise Platt, Bruce Cabot, Alan Ladd
During the War of 1812, a young girl takes over her late father's ship and does battle with the British.
Hal Roach — *Nostalgia Merchant*

Captain Future in Space   197?
Cartoons/Science fiction
56748   54 mins   C   B, V   P
Animated
The outer-space adventures of Captain Future and his crew aboard the spaceship Comet, fighting evil and making the universe safe for mankind. Available in English and Spanish versions.
EL, SP
ZIV International — *Media Home Entertainment*

Captain Harlock   1980
Science fiction/Cartoons
53158   60 mins   C   B, V   P
Animated
Captain Harlock, the space pirate, is left alone to protect Earth from invasion by an evil alien planet.
Ziv Intl — *Family Home Entertainment*

(For explanation of codes, see Use Guide and Key)

Captain Harlock 1981
Cartoons/Adventure
69811   60 mins   C   B, V   P
Animated
The stardate is 2977, and Earth is in grave
danger of being attacked by a mysterious alien
force. Only one man—the famous freedom
fighter, Captain Harlock—can save the planet
from total destruction.
Ziv International — *Family Home
Entertainment*

Captain Kangaroo and 1985
His Friends
Children
70593   60 mins   C   B, V   P
*Bob Keeshan, Phil Donahue, Joan Rivers, Dolly
Parton*
Composed of short clips from the Captain's
library of shows, this program introduces the
young viewer to many of the Kangaroo guy's
buddies.
Encyclopedia Britannica Educational
Corporation — *MPI Home Video*

Captain Kangaroo and 1985
the Right Thing to Do
Children
70594   60 mins   C   B, V   P
Bob Keeshan
Composed of short clips from the Captain's
library of shows, this program offers advice for
life to youngsters.
Encyclopedia Britannica Educational
Corporation — *MPI Home Video*

Captain Kangaroo and 1985
the Right Thing to Do
Ethics
81849   58 mins   C   B, V   P
Captain Kangaroo narrates this collection of
short stories that teaches children the
importance of making the right choice.
Jim Hirschfeld — *MPI Home Video*

Captain Kangaroo's Baby 1985
Animal Album
Children
70591   60 mins   C   B, V   P
Bob Keeshan
Composed of short clips from the Captain's
library of shows, this program features
segments designed to inform young humans
about baby critters.
Encyclopedia Britannica Educational
Corporation — *MPI Home Video*

Captain Kangaroo's Fairy 1985
Tales and Funny Stories
Variety/Fairy tales
71069   60 mins   C   B, V   P
Bob Keeshan

The Captain recites "Sleeping Beauty,"
"Rapunzel" and "Little Red Riding Hood" with
his characteristic warmth.
Jim Hirschfeld — *MPI Home Video*

Captain Kangaroo's 1985
Favorite Stories
Fairy tales
76924   58 mins   C   B, V   P
Bob Keeshan, Lumpy Brannum, Gus Allegretti
Captain Kangaroo reads from his favorite
children's stories.
Jim Hirschfeld — *MPI Home Video*

Captain Kangaroo's 1985
Merry Christmas Stories
Variety/Christmas
71062   58 mins   C   B, V   P
Bob Keeshan
The Captain narrates a selection of animated
and live-action tales to lift the Christmas spirits
including: "The Gift of the Little Juggler," "The
Fir Tree," and Clement Moore's "A Christmas
Carol."
Jim Hirschfeld — *MPI Home Video*

Captain Kangaroo's Tales 1985
of Magic and Mystery
Mystery
84625   50 mins   C   B, V   P
Bob Keeshan
A series of mysterious short stories aimed at the
very young.
Encyclopedia Britannica Educational
Corporation — *MPI Home Video*

Captain Kidd 1945
Adventure
01795   83 mins   B/W   B, V   P
*Charles Laughton, John Carradine, Randolph
Scott, directed by Lew Landers*
Adventures of Captain Kidd and his treasure
search on high seas.
UA; Sol Lesser — *Movie Buff Video; Hollywood
Home Theater; Discount Video Tapes; Cable
Films; Video Yesteryear; Kartes Video
Communications*

Captain Kronos: Vampire 1974
Hunter
Horror/Science fiction
60216   91 mins   C   B, V   P
Horst Janson, John Carson, Caroline Munro
Captain Kronos sets out to capture a vampire
before more beautiful young girls fall prey to his
curse.
MPAA:R
Albert Fennell — *Paramount Home Video*

Captain Pugwash 1975
Cartoons/Adventure
87315   80 mins   C   B, V   P

An animated collection of high seas adventures for children, made in England.
British — *Family Home Entertainment*

Captain Scarlet Vs. The Mysterons ## 1980
Science fiction
77422   90 mins   C   B, V   P
Animated
When Captain Scarlet's expeditionary team mistakenly fires upon an extraterrestrial military complex, the humorless aliens retaliate by setting out to destroy the world.
ITC Entertainment — *Family Home Entertainment*

Captain Scarlett ## 1953
Adventure
80033   75 mins   C   B, V   P
Richard Greene, Leonora Amar, Isobel del Puerto, Nedrick Young
A nobleman and his friend take on French Royalists who demand loyalty payments from poor French citizens.
United Artists; Howard Dimsdale — *Republic Pictures Home Video; World Video Pictures; Video Gems; Hal Roach Studios; Discount Video Tapes*

Captains Courageous ## 1937
Drama
53407   116 mins   B/W   B, V   P
Spencer Tracy, Lionel Barrymore, Freddie Bartholemew, Mickey Rooney, Melvyn Douglas, Charley Grapewin, John Carradine
A spoiled rich boy falls off a cruise liner and lives for a while among fisher folk who teach him about life. Based on the Rudyard Kipling novel. Academy Award '37: Best Actor (Tracy).
MGM; Louis D Lighton — *MGM/UA Home Video*

Captain's Paradise, The ## 1954
Comedy
66019   89 mins   B/W   B, V   P
Alec Guinness, Yvonne de Carlo
The amiable Captain of the Golden Fleece marries two women.
London Films — *THORN EMI/HBO Video*

Captive Planet ## 1978
Science fiction
84374   95 mins   C   B, V   P
Sharon Baker, Chris Auran, Anthony Newcastle, directed by Al Bradly
Earth is at instellar war. You thought it couldn't happen here.
Nais Film — *Mogul Communications*

Car Wash ## 1976
Comedy
53392   97 mins   C   B, V   P
Franklyn Ajaye, Sully Boyar, Richard Brestoff, George Carlin, Richard Pryor, Ivan Dixon, Antonio Fargas
A day in the lives of the people involved in a car wash operation including the pot-smoking owner's son and a cab driver looking for a missing passenger.
MPAA:PG
Universal; Art Linson and Gary Stromberg — *MCA Home Video*

Carbon Copy ## 1981
Comedy
59333   92 mins   C   B, V, LV,   P
                                CED
George Segal, Susan St. James, Jack Warden, Paul Winfield, Dick Martin, Vicky Dawson, Tom Poston, directed by Michael Schultz
A business executive faces the arrival of his heretofore unknown son who happens to be black.
MPAA:PG
Carter De Haven; Stanley Shapiro — *Embassy Home Entertainment*

Card Weaving ## 1985
Handicraft
85651   97 mins   C   B, V   P
Candace Crockett
A course in the variables of card weaving which explains how to measure a warp and thread and stitch bands together.
Victorian Video Prod. — *Victorian Video Productions*

Care Bears ## 1985
Cartoons
71052   33 mins   C   B, V   P

Animated
The tapes in this series include three episodes of the TV and toy stars' adventures.
LBS Communications; DIC Enterprises — *Karl/Lorimar Home Video*

Care Bears Battle the Freeze Machine, The ## 1984
Fantasy
Closed Captioned
66615   60 mins   C   B, V   P
Animated
The Care Bears' adventure with the Freeze Machine leads off this tape wich also includes two read-a-long Care Bears stories, "The Witch Down the Street" and "Sweet Dreams for Sally."
CPG Products Corp — *Family Home Entertainment*

Care Bears in the Land Without Feeling, The ## 1983
Cartoons
69809   60 mins   C   B, V   P

Animated
The Care Bears attempt to save a little boy
named Kevin from the icy spell of Professor
Coldheart and turn the Land Without Feeling
into a land of friendship and love.
CPG Products Corp — *Family Home
Entertainment*

Care Bears Movie, The　　　1985
Cartoons
80692　90 mins　C　　B, V　　　P
*Animated, voices of Mickey Rooney and
Georgia Engel*
The Care Bears leave their cloud home in care-
a-lot to try and teach earthlings how to share
their feelings of love and caring for each other.
MPAA:G
Samuel Goldwyn — *Vestron Video*

Career Strategies 1　　　1985
Personal finance/Business
71003　60 mins　C　　B, V　　　P
Robert J. Waterman, Jr, Dick Cavett
Top executives offer tips for moving ahead
within a corporation.
Esquire — *Esquire Video*

Career Strategies 2　　　1985
Personal finance/Business
71004　60 mins　C　　B, V　　　P
Kurt Einstein, Putney Westerfield, Dick Cavett
This program discusses career moves,
headhunting and the principle of leveraging.
Esquire — *Esquire Video*

Carefree　　　1938
Musical
00272　83 mins　B/W　　B, V　　　P
Fred Astaire, Ginger Rogers
Dizzy radio singer falls for her psychiatrist in this
classic musical with an Irving Berlin score.
RKO; Pandro S Berman — *RKO HomeVideo;
Nostalgia Merchant*

**Careful He Might Hear
You**　　　1984
Drama
Closed Captioned
70350　113 mins　C　　B, V　　　P
*Wendy Hughes, Robyn Nevin, John
Hargreaves, directed by Carl Schultz*
This Australian film follows the story of a six-
year-old boy who becomes the object of a bitter
custody battle between his rich aunt, his poor
aunt, and his father—a grieving drunken
widower with an eye for adventure. The program
comes in Beta Hi-Fi and VHS Stereo.
MPAA:PG
20th Century Fox — *CBS/Fox Video*

Caring for Your Newborn　　　1985
Infants
81535　55 mins　C　　B, V　　　P
Dr. Avner Kauffman and Frank Beaman answer
the most often asked questions concerning
newborn children.
Maljack Productions — *MPI Home Video*

**Caring for Your Newborn
with Dr. Benjamin Spock**　　　1980
Infants
44953　111 mins　C　　B, V　　　P
In this program Dr. Benjamin Spock gives
advice and guidance on baby care. He
demonstrates with clear visual presentations
everything from bathing the baby to treating
early disorders and discomforts.
Gregory Jackson — *VidAmerica; RCA
VideoDiscs*

Carlin at Carnegie　　　1983
Comedy-Performance
65216　60 mins　C　　B, V, CED　　P
It's George Carlin at his funniest, with his classic
routine of the "Seven Words You Can Never
Say on Television."
Brenda Carlin — *Vestron Video*

Carlin on Campus　　　1984
Comedy-Performance
80115　59 mins　C　　B, V, LV,　　P
　　　　　　　　　　　CED
George Carlin performs his classic routines and
new material in this concert filmed at UCLA's
Wadsworth Theater.
Carlin Productions — *Vestron Video*

Carlton Browne of the　　　1959
F.O.
Comedy
86893　88 mins　C　　B, V　　　P
Peter Sellers, Terry-Thomas, Luciana Paluzzi
A bumbling British diplomat visits a tiny Pacific
island, after its king has died, to insure a
tenuous international agreement.
British — *THORN EMI/HBO Video*

Carmen　　　1973
Dance
69836　73 mins　C　　B, V　　　P
Maya Plisetskaya, Nikol Fadeyechev
A compilation of Maya Plisetskaya's most
famous roles. The centerpiece is of Carmen and
also included are scenes from Raymonda,
Prelude, and Dying Swan.
Sovexportfilm USSR — *Video Arts
International*

Carmen　　　1983
Drama
79223　99 mins　C　　B, V　　　P

Antonio Gades, Laura Del Sol, Paco De Lucia, Cristina Hoyos, directed by Carlos Saurá
A choreographer casting a dance production of "Carmen" falls in love with his leading lady and winds up acting out the Bizet opera in real life. In Spanish with English Subtitles.
MPAA:R SP
Orion Classics — *Media Home Entertainment*

Carmen 1984
Music-Performance/Opera
81792   151 mins   C   B, V   P
Julia Migenes-Johnson, Placido Domingo, Faith Esham, directed by Francesco Rosi
This is the Bizet opera about a gypsy tobacco worker who has torrid affairs with a lieutenant and a toreador. Available in VHS Dolby Hi-Fi Stereo and Beta Hi-Fi Stereo with English subtitles.
MPAA:PG FR
Triumph Films — *RCA/Columbia Pictures Home Video*

Carnage 1984
Horror
84671   91 mins   C   B, V   P
Leslie Den Dooven, Michael Chiodo, Deeann Veeder, directed by Andy Milligan
A haunted house consumes its inhabitants in a variety of gory ways, as the title will attest.
Shapiro Ent — *Media Home Entertainment*

Carnal Knowledge 1971
Drama
08369   96 mins   C   B, V, LV,   P
                       CED
Jack Nicholson, Candice Bergen, Art Garfunkel, Ann-Margret, Rita Moreno, directed by Mike Nichols
This adult satire takes a look at two young men from their college days in the 1940's and follows them into the seventies, exploring the way they treat their women.
MPAA:R EL, JA
Avco Embassy; Mike Nichols
Production — *Embassy Home Entertainment; RCA VideoDiscs*

Carnival of Blood 1987
Horror
88221   80 mins   C   B, V   P
Someone is killing the customers at an unlucky carnival. Not for the squeamish.
Unknown — *Master Arts Video*

Carnival of the Animals 1985
Puppets
84776   28 mins   C   B, V   P
A puppet performance of the Saint-Saens music and story.
F Prod/Vistar Int'l — *Video Associates*

Carnival Story 1954
Drama
75933   94 mins   C   B, V   R, P
Anne Baxter, Steve Cochran, Lye Bettger, George Nader
The story of a German girl who joins an American-owned carnival in Germany.
RKO — *Video Gems; Discount Video Tapes*

Carnivores, The 1983
Documentary/Animals
63668   90 mins   C   B, V   P
The flesh-eaters of the animal kingdom—bears, lions, tigers, and others—and their survival instincts are the focus of this nature documentary.
Bill Burrud Productions — *Walt Disney Home Video*

Carny 1980
Drama
56755   102 mins   C   B, V, CED   P
Gary Busey, Robbie Robertson, Jodie Foster, directed by Robert Kaylor
A carnival "bozo" and the carnival "patchman" both fall in love with a young runaway in this drama set in a traveling carnival.
MPAA:R
Robbie Robertson, Lorimar, Jonathan Taplin — *CBS/Fox Video*

Carol Burnett Show: Bloopers and Outtakes, The 1977
Comedy/Outtakes and bloopers
47489   92 mins   B/W   B, V, FO   P
Carol Burnett, Dick Van Dyke, Tim Conway, Steve Lawrence, Eydie Gorme, Harvey Korman, Don Crichton
A collection of flubs, missed lines, malfunctioning props and other goofs from "The Carol Burnett Show," featuring the whole cast cracking up over their mistakes.
CBS — *Video Yesteryear*

Carols for Christmas 1985
Music-Performance/Christmas
82020   60 mins   C   B, V   P
The Christmas story is told through masterpieces from the collections of the Metropolitan Museum of Art and traditional carols sung by the Royal College of Music Chamber Choir.
Office of Film and TV Metropolitan Museum of Art — *THORN EMI/HBO Video*

Carpathian Eagle, The 1981
Horror/Mystery
77441   60 mins   C   B, V   P
Suzzane Danielle, Sian Phillips, Pierce Brosnan, Anthony Valentine, directed by Francis Megahy

The police are baffled by a bizzare series of murders where the victims' hearts are ripped out.
Hammer House of Horror — *Thriller Video*

Carpenters, Yesterday   1985
Once More, The
Music video
77248   60 mins   C   B, V   P
Richard Carpenter, Karen Carpenter
This is a retrospective look at the musical career of The Carpenters.
A & M Video — *A & M Video; RCA/Columbia Pictures Home Video*

Carpetbaggers, The   1964
Drama
82069   150 mins   C   B, V   P
George Peppard, Carroll Baker, Alan Ladd, Elizabeth Ashley, Lew Ayres, Robert Cummings, directed by Edward Dmytryk
This is an adaptation of the Harold Robbins novel about a wealthy industrialist and the women in his life. Joan Collins introduces the film which is available in VHS and Beta Hi-Fi.
Paramount Pictures — *Paramount Home Video*

Carrie   1976
Horror
55590   98 mins   C   B, V, LV,   P
                                CED
Sissy Spacek, Piper Laurie, John Travolta, William Katt, Amy Irving, directed by Brian de Palma
A withdrawn teenager lives in a ramshackle house with her religious fanatic mother. On the night of the senior prom, Carrie gets revenge on all who have hurt her, through her special powers. Based on the novel by Stephen King. MPAA:R
United Artists — *CBS/Fox Video; RCA VideoDiscs*

Carrington, V.C.   1955
Drama
82232   100 mins   B/W   B, V   P
David Niven, Margaret Leighton, Noelle Middleton, Laurence Naismith, directed by Anthony Asquith
A British army major is brought up for a court-martial trial on the charges that he embezzled funds.
Kingsley International — *Monterey Home Video*

Carrott Gets Rowdie   1984
Comedy-Performance
66358   60 mins   C   B, V   P
Popular English comedian Jasper Carrott comments upon the differences between British and American people in this concert taped in Tampa Bay, Florida.

Pacific Arts — *Pacific Arts Video*

Carry On Behind   1975
Comedy
59829   95 mins   C   B, V   P
Kenneth Williams, Elke Sommer, Joan Sims
The "Carry On" crew head for an archeological dig and find themselves sharing the site with a holiday caravan.
Peter Rogers — *Embassy Home Entertainment*

Carry On Cleo   1965
Satire/Comedy
66026   91 mins   C   B, V   P
Sidney James, Amanda Barrie, Kenneth Williams, Kenneth Connor, Jim Dale, Charles Hawtrey, Joan Sims
A saucy spoof of Shakespeare's "Antony and Cleopatra" in the inimitable "Carry On" style.
Governor Films — *THORN EMI/HBO Video*

Carry On Cowboy   1966
Comedy
86264   91 mins   C   B, V   P
Sidney James, Kenneth Williams, Jim Dale
A raucous western parody of "High Noon," in the Carry On tradition, also known as "Rumpo Kid."
Anglo-Amalgamated — *THORN EMI/HBO Video*

Carry On Cruising   1962
Comedy
87740   89 mins   C   B, V   P
Sidney James, Kenneth Williams, Liz Fraser
The Carry On gang attack the sailing world with customary low humor and inoffensive raunchiness.
Governor Films — *THORN EMI/HBO Video*

Carry On Nurse   1958
Comedy
43012   86 mins   B/W   B, V, FO   P
Shirley Eaton, Kenneth Connor, Hattie Jacques, Wilfred Hyde-White
The men's ward in a British hospital declares war on their nurses and the rest of the hospital. English slapstick. The first of the "Carry On" series.
Governor Films; British — *Video Yesteryear; Movie Buff Video; THORN EMI/HBO Video*

Cars—How to Buy a New   1986
or Used Car & Keep It
Running Almost Forever
Consumer education/Automobiles
86160   50 mins   C   B, V   P
An instructional tape designed to make clear the best ways to buy cars and maintain them for maximum performance.
AM Available

Consumer Reports TV; Major H. Prod.; George
Paige Assoc. — *Karl/Lorimar Home Video*

Cars: 1984-1985—Live, The

1985

Music-Performance
81160   60 mins   C   B, V, LV,   P
CED
*Ric Ocasek, Elliot Easton, Greg Hawkes, David
Robinson, Ben Orr*
The Cars perform such hits as "You Might
Think," "Drive" and "Hello Again" in this
concert video. Hi-Fi stereo sound in both
formats.
FF Productions — *Vestron Video*

Carson City Kid

1940

Western
14375   54 mins   B/W   B, V   P
Roy Rogers, Dale Evans
Roy sings and fights his way to justice and love.
Republic — *Video Connection; Nostalgia
Merchant; Discount Video Tapes*

Cartoon Carnival #1

193?

Cartoons
53805   51 mins   C   B, V   P
Animated
This package includes "Song of the Birds" (Max
Fleischer), "Jerky Turkey" (MGM), "The Talking
Magpies" (Terrytoons), "Jasper in the Haunted
House" (George Pal), "It's a Hap Hap Happy
Day" (Max Fleischer), "Boy Meets Dog" (Walter
Lantz), and "The Friendly Ghost" (Harvey
Cartoons).
Max Fleischer et al — *Hollywood Home
Theater*

Cartoon Carnival #2

193?

Cartoons
63852   55 mins   C   B, V   P
Animated
A compilation of 8 classic cartoons: "Pincushion
Man," "Mary's Little Lamb" and "Jack Frost,"
all by Ub Iwerks; Max Fleisher's "Cobweb
Hotel"; "Farm Frolics," a Merrie Melodies
cartoon; Porky Pig in "Timid Toreador"; "Pantry
Panic," starring Woody Woodpecker; and a
Looney Tunes cartoon, "Hollywood Capers."
Ub Iwerks et al — *Hollywood Home Theater*

Cartoon Carnival Volume I

194?

Cartoons
64837   90 mins   C   B, V   P
Animated
A collection of ten original Max Fleischer
cartoons, featuring Little Lulu and others, plus
two "Bouncing Ball" sing-alongs. Mastered from
the original negatives.
Max Fleischer; Paramount — *Republic
Pictures Home Video*

Cartoon Carnival Volume II

194?

Cartoons
64838   90 mins   C   B, V   P
Animated
Another package of ten Max Fleischer cartoons,
featuring Casper and several "Bouncing Ball"
sing-alongs. Mastered from the original
negatives.
Max Fleischer; Paramount — *Republic
Pictures Home Video*

Cartoon Cavalcade

1935

Cartoons
77365   23 mins   C   B, V   P, T
Animated
Here are three classic cartoons from Burt
Gillette and UB Iwerkes: "Molly Moo Cow and
the Indians," "The Three Bears," and "Molly
Moo Cow and Rip Van Winkle."
RKO Radio Pictures — *Blackhawk Films*

Cartoon Classics, Volumes 1 thru XIV

194?

Cartoons
66055   45 mins   C   B, V, LV   P
Animated 14 pgms
These compilations provide a videocassetted
history of Disney animation. Each tape includes
six cartoons linked either thematically or by a
common star. Many of these won Academy
Awards for Best Cartoon Short Subject.
*1.Chip 'n' Dale Featuring Donald Duck 2.Pluto
3.Disney's Scary Tales 4.Sport Goofy
5.Disney's Best of 1931-1948 6.More Sport
Goofy 7.More of Disney's Best of 1932-1946
8.Sport Goofy's Vacation 9.Donald Ducks First
Fifty Years 10.Mickey's Crazy Careers
11.Continuing Adventures of Chip 'n' Dale
Featuring Donald Duck 12.Disney's Tall Tales
13.Silly Symphonies Fanciful Fables 14.Silly
Symphonies Animal Tales.*
Walt Disney Productions — *Walt Disney Home
Video*

Cartoon Classics #3

1921

Cartoons
85153   52 mins   B/W   B, V   P
Directed by O'Brien, Iwerks, Terry et al.
A compilation of 6 silent cartoons, including
pioneering efforts in stop-motion animation by
Willis O'Brien, creator of "King Kong."
Disney; Bray; Edison — *Video Yesteryear*

Cartoon Classics #4

1936

Cartoons
85154   55 mins   B/W   B, V   P
Directed by Freleng, Clampett, Terry
A collection of 8 classic cartoons, including a
few of Porky Pig's first appearances.
Warner Bros.; Freleng; Fleischer et al. — *Video
Yesteryear*

Cartoon Classics #5   1934
Cartoons
85155   60 mins   B/W   B, V   P
Directed by Lantz, Iwerks, Messmer
Another collection of rare, classic cartoons,
featuring Bosko and Felix the Cat.
Van Beuren; Lantz; Disney et al. — *Video
Yesteryear*

Cartoon Classics in Color   1934
#1
Cartoons
78088   60 mins   C   B, V, FO   P
Animated
Eight cartoon classics filled with color,
movement and lots of fun comprise this tape:
"Little Black Sambo," "Jack Frost," "Sinbad the
Sailor," "Simple Simon," "Ali Baba," Molly Moo
Cow and the Butterflies," "The Toonerville
Trolley," and "Somewhere in Dreamland."
RKO; Van Beuren — *Video Yesteryear*

Cartoon Classics in Color   194?
#2
Cartoons
78119   60 mins   C   B, V, FO   P
Animated
Eight fun and exciting, animated cartoons
featuring some of cartoon favorites: Daffy Duck
in "Yankee Doodle Duffy," Porky Pig in "Ali
Baba Bound" and Bugs Bunny in "Falling
Hare."
Warner Bros; Max Fleischer — *Video
Yesteryear*

Cartoon Classics of the   193?
1930's
Cartoons
03591   58 mins   C   B, V   P
Animated
Eight cartoon classics of the 1930's including
"Felix the Cat," "Daffy and the Dinosaur," and
"Bold King Cole."
Ub Iwerks; Warner Bros; Fleischer — *Media
Home Entertainment*

Cartoon Collection I   194?
Cartoons
33686   115 mins   C   B, V, 3/4U   P
*Bugs Bunny, Daffy Duck, Betty Boop, Popeye,
Donald Duck, Casper the Friendly Ghost*
A collection of sixteen classic cartoons from the
thirties, forties and fifties. Included are Bugs
Bunny in, "All This and Rabbit Stew," Daffy
Duck in, "Scrap Happy Daffy," Popeye in
"Eugene the Jeep," and "Poop Deck Pappy,"
and Betty Boop in "Minnie the Moocher." Some
in black and white.
Warner Bros; Max Fleischer; Walt
Disney — *Shokus Video*

Cartoon Collection II: 194?
Warner Brothers
Cartoons
Cartoons
33687   115 mins   C   B, V, 3/4U   P
Animated
A collection of sixteen favorite Warner Brothers
cartoons from the forties and fifties including
Bugs Bunny in "Fresh Hare," and "Falling
Hare," Daffy Duck in "The Daffy Commando,"
and Daffy's Southern Exposure," and Porky Pig
in "Notes to You," and "Porky's Midnight
Matinee."
Warner Bros — *Shokus Video*

Cartoon Collection III: 194?
Vintage Warner Bros.
Cartoons
Cartoons
66458   115 mins   B/W   B, V, 3/4U   P
Animated
Another package of 16 Warner Bros. cartoons
from the 1930's and 40's, featuring Bugs Bunny,
Daffy Duck and Porky Pig. Titles include "Coal
Black and de Sebben Dwarfs," "Calling Dr.
Porky," "Tom Turkey and Daffy" and "Daffy
Doc."
Warner Bros — *Shokus Video*

Cartoon Collection IV: 193?
Early Animation
Cartoons
76012   110 mins   B/W   B, V, 3/4U   P
Animated
Sixteen golden classics from the depression
era, all in their original fully-animated form in
glorious black and white.
Max Fleischer et al — *Shokus Video*

Cartoon Collection V: 194?
Saturday at the Movies
Cartoons
82283   120 mins   C   B, V, 3/4U   P
Animated
Here is a compilation of classic cartoons from
the 30's and 40's including "Bugs Bunny Bond
Rally," "Little Black Sambo," "Congo Jazz" and
"The Japoteurs."
Warner Bros; et al — *Shokus Video*

Cartoon Fun   1958
Cartoons
85926   40 mins   C   B, V   P
A compilation of cartoons featuring Casper the
Ghost, Betty Boop, Little Lulu and other
notables.
Hanna-Barbera; Fleischer; et al. — *Spotlite
Video*

Cartoon Magic   1985
Cartoons
65223   45 mins   C   B, V   P

Animated
Each tape in this series contains four or five classic MGM cartoons from the 1930's and 1940's, and feature characters such as Barney Bear, Doctor D and Screwball Squirrel.
MGM — *MGM/UA Home Video*

Cartoon Parade No. 1   194?
Cartoons
07345   120 mins   C   B, V, 3/4U   P
Animated
A collection of cartoons starring Bugs Bunny, Daffy Duck, Porky Pig, Popeye, Superman, and more.
Warner Bros — *Nostalgia Merchant*

Cartoon Parade No. 2   194?
Cartoons
44857   117 mins   C   B, V, 3/4U   P
Animated
Laugh with some of your favorite cartoon characters. Included are Bugs Bunny in "Wabbit Who Came to Supper," Popeye in "Popeye Meets Ali Baba," Superman in "Terror on the Midway," Little Lulu in "Bored of Education," and many more.
Warner Bros — *Nostalgia Merchant*

Cartoon Parade No. 3   194?
Cartoons
44858   110 mins   C   B, V, 3/4U   P
Animated
A collection of cartoon classics including "Falling Hare" with Bugs Bunny, "Cheese Burglar" staring Herman and Katnip, "Somewhere in Dreamland," "Robin Hood Makes Good," and others.
Warner Bros — *Nostalgia Merchant*

Cartoon Parade No. 4   194?
Cartoons
47141   120 mins   C   B, V, 3/4U   P
Another collection of popular cartoons from the 30's and 40's, featuring Max Fleischer's Bouncing Ball, Little Lulu, Superman, Bugs Bunny, and Porky Pig. Some cartoons are in black and white.
Warner Bros et al — *Nostalgia Merchant*

Cartoonal Knowledge: Farmer Gray and the Mice   1929
Cartoons
85497   55 mins   B/W   B, V   P
Seven vintage silent cartoons featuring the irascible Farmer Gray and his adventures with barnyard beasts. Directed by Paul Terry. Silent.
Paul Terry — *Video Yesteryear*

Cartoonal Knowledge: Farmer Gray Looks At Life   1926
Cartoons
85522   55 mins   B/W   B, V   P
Directed by Paul Terry, this compilation features seven Gray silent shorts, with a musical score.
Paul Terry — *Video Yesteryear*

Cartoonies   193?
Cartoons
79876   50 mins   C   B, V   P
Animated
A collection of Max Fleischer's best loved cartoons including Betty Boop, Gabby, Casper, and Little Lulu.
Fleischer Studios; Paramount — *Republic Pictures Home Video*

Cartoons Go to War, The   1943
Cartoons
87663   58 mins   C   B, V   P
A compilation of cartoons made during World War II, which hilariously propound caricatured propagandistic messages.
Warner Bros. et al. — *Victory Video*

Cas du Dr. Laurent, Le   1957
Drama
69562   88 mins   B/W   B, V, FO   P
Jean Gabin
A country doctor in a small French town tries to introduce methods of natural childbirth to the native women, but meets opposition from the superstitious townspeople.
France — *Video Yesteryear*

Casa Flora   197?
Comedy
52795   106 mins   C   B, V   P
Maximo Valverde, Antonio Garisa, Rafael Alonso
When the funeral of an important bullfighter is held in a small Andalusian town, the president of the Bullfighting Club decides to use every lodging possible, including those in a hotel of questionable reputation. In Spanish.
SP
Moviola Films — *Media Home Entertainment*

Casablanca   1943
Drama
13316   102 mins   B/W   B, V, LV   P
Humphrey Bogart, Ingrid Bergman, directed by Michael Curtiz
Classic story of an American expatriot who involves himself in romance and espionage in North Africa during World War II.
Academy Awards '43: Best Picture; Best Screenplay; Best Direction (Curtiz). EL, SP
Warner Bros; Hal Wallis — *CBS/Fox Video; RCA VideoDiscs*

Case of Libel, A 1983
Drama
73531   90 mins   C   B, V   P
Daniel J. Travanti, Edward Asner
This movie documents the true story of lawyer
Louis Nizer's account of the libel suit Quentin
Reynolds brought against Westbrook Pegler.
Available in Beta hi-fi and VHS stereo.
Showtime — *U.S.A. Home Video*

Case of the Missing Lady, 1983
The
Mystery/Suspense
81706   51 mins   C   B, V   P
Francesca Annis, James Warwick
A famous Arctic explorer asks Tommy and
Tuppence to find his missing fiancee. Based
upon the Agatha Christie story.
London Weekend Television — *Pacific Arts
Video*

Casey at the Bat 1985
Baseball
88081   30 mins   C   B, V   P
An installment of Shelley Duvall's Fairie Tale
Theatre, in which the immortal poem is brought
to life.
Platypus Prod.; Gaylord Prod. — *Playhouse
Video*

Casey's Shadow 1978
Comedy-Drama
63443   116 mins   C   B, V   P
*Walter Matthau, Alexis Smith, Robert Webber,
Murray Hamilton*
The eight-year-old son of an impoverished
horse trainer raises a quarter horse and enters it
in the world's richest horse race.
MPAA:PG
Columbia; Ray Stark — *RCA/Columbia
Pictures Home Video*

Cash 1934
Comedy
81388   71 mins   B/W   B, V   P
Robert Donat, Wendy Barrie, Edmund Gwenn
A bankrupt financier uses counterfeit money to
promote a new company.
British — *Kartes Video Communications;
Discount Video Tapes*

Casino Royale 1967
Comedy
86384   130 mins   C   B, V   P
*David Niven, Woody Allen, Peter Sellers, Ursula
Andress, Orson Welles, Charles Boyer, Joanna
Pettet, John Huston, William Holden, George
Raft*
The product of five directors, three writers and a
mismatched cast of dozens, this virtually
plotless spoof of James Bond films stands as
one of the low-water marks for 1960's comedy.

Charles K. Feldman; Jerry
Bresler — *RCA/Columbia Pictures Home
Video*

Casper and the Angels 1979
Cartoons
47688   55 mins   C   B, V   P
Animated
Five episodes in which the world's friendliest
ghost teams up with the Angels—Mini and
Maxi—the first policewomen in outer space.
Hanna Barbera — *Worldvision Home Video*

Casper and the Angels II 1979
Cartoons
69292   55 mins   C   B, V   P
Animated
Five more exciting adventures of Casper the
friendly ghost, Mini, and Maxi.
Hanna-Barbera — *Worldvision Home Video*

Casper and the Angels 1979
Vol III
Cartoons
77158   55 mins   C   B, V   P
Animated
Casper along with two space patrol women
Minnie and Maxie blast off for another series of
intergalactic adventures.
Hanna-Barbera — *Worldvision Home Video*

Casper the Friendly 1953
Ghost
Cartoons
86365   60 mins   C   B, V   P
A compilation of Casper cartoons.
Harvey Films Inc. — *Worldvision Home Video*

Cass 1978
Drama
77006   76 mins   C   B, V   P
A disenchanted filmmaker returns home to
Australia to experiment with alternative
lifestyles.
Don Harley — *VidAmerica*

Cast a Giant Shadow 1966
War-Drama
86046   138 mins   C   B, V   P
*Kirk Douglas, Senta Berger, Angie Dickinson,
John Wayne, James Donald, Frank Sinatra, Yul
Brynner, directed by Melville Shavelson*
This film follows the career of Col. David
Marcus, who became Israel's first general in
2000 years.
U.A. — *Key Video*

Castaway Cowboy, The 1974
Adventure
72792   91 mins   C   B, V   P
James Garner, Robert Culp

A shanghaied cowboy becomes partners with a widow when she turns her Hawaiian potato farm into a cattle ranch.
Walt Disney Productions — *Walt Disney Home Video*

Castle of Evil   1966
Horror
70202   81 mins   C   B, V   P
Scott Brady, Virginia Mayo, Hugh Marlowe
A group of heirs gather on a deserted isle to hear the reading of a will. One by one, they fall victim to mysterious "accidents."
World Entertainment — *Republic Pictures Home Video*

Cat and Mouse   1978
Mystery
39015   107 mins   C   B, V   P
Michele Morgan, Serge Reggiani, Jean-Pierre Aumont, directed by Claude Lelouch
A very unorthodox police inspector is assigned to investigate a millionaire's mysterious death. Who done it? French dialogue with English subtitles.
MPAA:PG FR
Quartet Films — *RCA/Columbia Pictures Home Video*

Cat and the Canary, The   1978
Mystery
58959   96 mins   C   B, V   P
Carol Lynley, Olivia Hussey, Daniel Masey, Honor Blackman, Wilfred Hyde White
A stormy night, a gloomy mansion, and a mysterious will combine to create an atmosphere for murder.
Grenadier Films Ltd — *RCA/Columbia Pictures Home Video*

Cat and the Canary, The   1927
Mystery
57348   99 mins   B/W   B, V, FO   P
Laura La Plante, Creighton Hale, Tully Marshall, Gertrude Astor
One of the great silent ghost stories, about the ghost of a madman that wanders nightly through the corridors of an old house.
Universal — *Video Yesteryear; Hollywood Home Theater*

Cat Ballou   1965
Western
13237   96 mins   C   B, V   P
Jane Fonda, Lee Marvin, Michael Callan, Dwayne Hickman, Nat King Cole, Stubby Kaye
School teacher and cattle rustler stage a train robbery.
Academy Awards '65: Best Actor (Marvin).
Columbia; Harold Hecht — *RCA/Columbia Pictures Home Video; RCA VideoDiscs*

Cat from Outer Space, The   1978
Comedy
69317   103 mins   C   B, V   P
Ken Berry, Sandy Duncan, Harry Morgan, Roddy McDowall, McLean Stevenson
An extraterrestrial cat named Jake crashlands his spaceship on Earth and leads a group of people on endless escapades.
MPAA:G
Buena Vista; Walt Disney Prods — *Walt Disney Home Video*

Cat Hunting in Tanzania   1984
Hunting
87646   45 mins   C   B, V   P
Ken Wilson, Dave Harshbarger, Luke Samaras
Filmed in Selous, the great white hunters go stalking the native Tanzanian feline in the wild brush.
Sportsmen On Film — *Sportsmen on Film*

Cat on a Hot Tin Roof   1958
Drama
53409   108 mins   C   B, V, LV,   P
                              CED
Paul Newman, Burl Ives, Elizabeth Taylor, Jack Carson, directed by Richard Brooks
Tennessee Williams' play about deception destroying a patriarchal Southern family.
MGM; Lawrence Weingarten — *MGM/UA Home Video*

Cat on a Hot Tin Roof   1984
Drama
80683   148 mins   C   B, V, LV,   P
                              CED
Jessica Lange, Tommy Lee Jones, Rip Torn, directed by Jack Hofsiss
An adaptation of the Tennessee Williams play wherein a young couple face difficulties over the husband's uncertain sexuality.
International TV Group — *Vestron Video*

Cat People   1942
Horror
00311   73 mins   B/W   B, V, 3/4U   P
Simone Simon, Kent Smith, Tom Conway
Young bride believes she's the victim of a curse that can change her into a deadly panther.
RKO — *Nostalgia Merchant; King of Video; RKO HomeVideo*

Cat People   1982
Horror
47679   118 mins   C   B, V, LV   P
Nastassia Kinski, Malcolm McDowell, John Heard, Annette O'Toole, directed by Paul Schrader
A beautiful young woman learns that she has inherited a feline characteristic, making a relationship with a man impossible.
MPAA:R

Universal — *MCA Home Video*

Cat Women of the Moon — 1953
Science fiction
33479   65 mins   B/W   B, V   P
Sonny Tufts, Marie Windsor, Victor Jory
Scientists land on the moon and encounter an
Amazon-like force of female chauvinists.
Astor Pictures — *Mossman Williams
Productions; Nostalgia Merchant*

Catamount Killing, The — 197?
Suspense
70391   82 mins   C   B, V   P
Horst Bucholz, Ann Wedgeworth
The story of a small town bank manager and his
lover. They decide to rob the bank and run for
greener pastures only to find their escape
befuddled at every turn.
MPAA:PG
Manfred Durnick — *VidAmerica*

Catch a Rising Star's 10th — 1983
Anniversary
Variety
80380   66 mins   C   B, V   P
*Pat Benatar, Billy Crystal, Gabe Kaplan, Joe
Piscopo, Robin Williams*
Some of the biggest names in comedy and
music got together to celebrate the tenth
anniversary of this New York night club.
Rising Star Video Pictures
Ltd — *RCA/Columbia Pictures Home Video*

Catch Me a Spy — 1971
Suspense/Drama
80298   94 mins   C   B, V   P
*Kirk Douglas, Tom Courtenay, Trevor Howard,
Marlene Jobert*
A foreign agent attempts to lure an innocent
man into becomming part of a swap for an
imprisoned Russian spy.
Ludgate Films; Capitole Films — *Prism*

Catch-22 — 1970
Satire
38930   121 mins   C   B, V, LV   P
*Alan Arkin, Martin Balsam, Art Garfunkel, Jon
Voight, directed by Mike Nichols*
An adaptation of Joseph Heller's black comedy
about a group of fliers in the Mediterranean
during World War II; biting anti-war satire.
MPAA:R
Paramount — *Paramount Home Video; RCA
VideoDiscs*

Catherine and Co. — 1976
Comedy
55259   91 mins   C   B, V   P
A lonely, penniless girl arrives in Paris and
"opens shop" on the streets of Paris. As

business booms, she takes a cue from the big
corporations and sells stock in herself.
MPAA:R
Warner Bros — *VidAmerica*

Catherine the Great — 1934
Drama
81457   93 mins   B/W   B, V, LV   P
Douglas Fairbanks Jr., Elizabeth Bergner
This is the story of how the Russian czarina's
life was ruined through a rigidly planned
marriage.
Alexander Korda — *Embassy Home
Entertainment; Movie Buff Video; VCII; Cable
Films; Video Yesteryear; Hollywood Home
Theater; Discount Video Tapes; Kartes Video
Communications*

Catherine Wheel, The — 1984
Dance
73652   180 mins   C   B, V   P
Twyla Tharp and her troupe perform "The
Catherine Wheel" with original music composed
and performed by David Byrne from Talking
Heads.
BBC-TV — *Kartes Video Communications*

Catherine Wheel, The — 1984
Dance/Music-Performance
70961   90 mins   C   B, V   P
Two leading contemporary artists,
choreographer Twyla Tharp and composer
David Byrne, collaborated on this work originally
performed at the Brooklyn Academy of Music.
BBC-TV — *THORN EMI/HBO Video*

Catholic Hour, The — 1960
Drama/Biographical
80756   30 mins   B/W   B, V   P
Edward Cullen, Arthur Gary
A dramatized version of the life story of Thomas
Frederick Price who co-founded the Maryknoll
Missionaries in the early 1900's.
The National Council of Catholic Men — *Video
Yesteryear*

Catholics — 1973
Drama
65438   86 mins   C   B, V   P
Martin Sheen, Trevor Howard
A sensitive exploration of contemporary mores
and changing attitudes within the Roman
Catholic church. Based on Brian Moore's short
novel.
Glazier Productions — *U.S.A. Home Video;
Carousel Film & Video*

Cat's Eye — 1985
Suspense
Closed Captioned
81964   94 mins   C   B, V   P

Drew Barrymore, James Woods, Alan King,
Robert Hays, Candy Clark, directed by Lewis
Teague
This is an anthology of three Stephen King short
stories connected by a stray cat who wanders
through each tale. Available in VHS and Beta Hi-
Fi.
MPAA:PG-13
MGM/UA; Dino De Laurentis — Key Video

Cattle Queen of Montana   1954
Western
52578   88 mins   C   B, V   P
Ronald Reagan, Barbara Stanwyck, directed by
Allan Dwan
Reagan stars as an undercover federal agent
investigating livestock rustlings and Indian
uprisings.
RKO — Weiss Global Enterprises; Buena Vista
Home Video

Caught   1949
Drama
77478   90 mins   B/W   B, V   P
James Mason, Barbara Bel Geddes, Robert
Ryan, directed by Max Ophuls
An unhappily married woman falls in love with
the struggling physician she works for.
MGM — Republic Pictures Home Video

Cauldron of Blood   1968
Horror
70201   101 mins   C   B, V   P
Boris Karloff, Viveca Lindfors, Jean Pierre
Aumont
A blind sculptor uses human skeletons as the
framework for his popular art pieces.
Robert D. Weinbach Prods — Republic
Pictures Home Video

Cavalcade of Stars   1951
Variety
11270   55 mins   B/W   B, V, FO   P
Jackie Gleason, Art Carney, Georgia Gibbs, The
June Taylor Dancers, Arthur Lee Simpson
"The Great One" clowns and sings with support
from Carney in comedy sketches. Simpson
sings, "Back in Donegal," and Gibbs performs
"I Can't Give You Anything But Love," in this
comedy-variety hour.
DuMont — Video Yesteryear

Cavaleur, Le (Practice   198?
Makes Perfect)
Comedy
76036   90 mins   C   B, V   P
jean Rochfort
A light hearted comedy about a philandering
concert pianist features Jean Rochfort with
Nicole Aarcia, Annie Girardot, Lila Kedrova and
Catherine Leprince as some of the women in his
life.

EL, FR
Georges Dancigers; Alexandre
Mnouchkine — RCA/Columbia Pictures Home
Video

Cavalier, The   198?
Martial arts
73959   90 mins   C   B, V   P
Tang Wei, Loon Fei, Yeh Yuen, Tseng Tsao
A Chinese cavalier faces love, danger and
intrigue in this martial arts film.
Independent — Unicorn Video

Cavegirl   1985
Comedy/Adventure
70874   85 mins   C   B, V   P
Daniel Roebuck, Cindy Ann Thompson, directed
by David Oliver
After falling through a time-warp, a social pariah
makes a hit with a pre-historic honey.
MPAA:R
Crown International — RCA/Columbia Pictures
Home Video

Caveman   1981
Comedy
58823   92 mins   C   B, V, CED   P
Ringo Starr, Barbara Bach, John Matuszak,
Dennis Quaid, Jack Gilford, Shelley Long
A group of cavemen banished from different
tribes band together to form a tribe called "The
Misfits."
MPAA:PG
United Artists; Lawrence Turman; David
Foster — CBS/Fox Video

CBS/Fox Guide to   1983
Complete Dog Care, The
Pets
65411   60 mins   C   B, V, CED   P
A guide to home pet care from feeding to
grooming.
CBS Fox — CBS/Fox Video

CBS/FOX Guide to Home   1983
Videography, The
Video
65007   45 mins   C   B, V   P
This original home video production follows the
adventures of a fictitious character who owns a
new video camera. Five easy to follow
segments include camera movement, framing
and composition, lighting and sound planning
and production and advanced techniques.
CBS/FOX Video — CBS/Fox Video

C.C. and Company   1970
Drama
76906   91 mins   C   B, V   P
Joe Namath, Ann-Margret, William Smith,
Jennifer Billingsley

A young man who joins a rowdy motorcycle gang becomes the enemy in the camp because he does not adhere to their rules.
MPAA:PG
Rogallan Productions; Avco Embassy — *Embassy Home Entertainment*

Cease Fire   1985
War-Drama
85768   97 mins   C   B, V   P
Don Johnson, Robert F. Lyons, Lisa Blount
The sordid story of a troubled Vietnam vet who finds solace in a veterans' therapy group.
MPAA:R
Independent — *THORN EMI/HBO Video*

Celanese Theatre, The   1951
Drama
85156   60 mins   B/W   B, V   P
Eduardo Cianelli, Ludwig Donath, Ralph Morgan, Royal Dano
A live-television performance of Sherwood Anderson's classic play "Winterset."
ABC — *Video Yesteryear*

Celanese Theatre, The   1952
Drama
85157   60 mins   B/W   B, V   P
MacDonald Carey, Walter Abel, Richard Kiley, Jack Klugman
A live-television performance of Sidney Howard's play "Yellowjack."
ABC — *Video Yesteryear*

Celanese Theatre   1952
Drama
85507   60 mins   B/W   B, V   P
Ralph Morgan, Billy Chapin, Melville Cooper, Mildred Dunnock
A live television performance of "On Borrowed Time."
ABC — *Video Yesteryear*

Celebration, A   1981
Music-Performance
65213   60 mins   C   B, V   P
Glen Campbell, Kris Kristofferson, Tanya Tucker, Roger Miller
A star-studded tribute in memory of a musical legend—Dorsey Burnett. Available in Beta Hi-fi and stereo VHS.
DID Productions — *Monterey Home Video*

Celestial Navigation   1984
Simplified
Boating
78963   40 mins   C   B, V   P
Narrated by William F. Buckley
A step by step demonstration of the art of celestial navigation is presented in this program.

Avant Communications — *Avant Communications; Force Video*

Cenerentola, La   1984
Opera
73656   180 mins   C   B, V   P
Kathleen Kuhlmann, Marta Taddei, Laura Zannini
Rossini interprets "Cinderella" in his grand operatic fashion with Donato Renzetti conducting The London Philarmonic from Glyndebourne.
BBC TV — *Kartes Video Communications; THORN EMI/HBO Video*

Cenerentola (Cinderella)   1948
Opera
84652   94 mins   B/W   B, V   P
Fedora Barbieri
A film version of the classic Rossini opera.
IT
Italian — *V.I.E.W. Video*

Centennial Gala   1983
Opera
82538   231 mins   C   B, V, LV   P
Roberta Peters, Joan Sutherland, Kiri Te Kanawa, Marilyn Horne, Placido Domingo, Luciano Pavarotti
Almost one hundred of the world's leading singers, seven conductors, and the Met Orchestra, Opera, and Ballet perform some of the most acclaimed operas and arias in the Met's history. With English subtitles.
Metropolitan Opera — *Paramount Home Video; Pioneer Artists*

Centerfold   1980
Photography
57453   60 mins   C   B, V   P
The side of the centerfold model we never see—in the dressing room preparing for a shooting session. Model Martha Thomsen talks candidly about her conflicts with men, how she felt posing nude for the first time, and her years growing up "plain."
At Home Video — *VidAmerica*

Centerfold Girls, The   197?
Suspense
59043   93 mins   C   B, V   P
Andrew Prine, Tiffany Bolling
A deranged man is determined to kill the voluptuous young women who have posed nude for a centerfold.
MPAA:R
Charles Stroud — *Media Home Entertainment*

Century of Progress 1937
Exposition, The/New
York World's Fair 1939-40
Documentary
60055 19 mins B/W B, V P, T
Fox Movietone newsreels of Chicago's Century
of Progress Exposition of 1933-34 and the most
impressive exhibits of the New York World's Fair
of 1939-1940 are combined on this tape.
Blackhawk Movietone
Compilation — *Blackhawk Films*

Certain Fury 1985
Adventure/Drama
81766 88 mins C B, V, LV P
Tatum O'Neal, Irene Cara, Peter Fonda
Two sheepish women go on the lam when they
are mistaken for escaped prostitutes who shot
up a courthouse. Available in VHS and Beta Hi-
Fi.
MPAA:R
New World Pictures — *New World Video*

Certain Sacrifice, A 1979
Horror/Exploitation
70904 60 mins C B, V P
*Madonna Ciccone, Jeremy Pattnosh, Charles
Kurtz*
This unusual film of love, passion and
contemporary human sacrifice features the
platinum-selling singer's first filmed effort.
Jon Lewicki — *Virgin Video*

Cesar 1933
Comedy
06231 117 mins B/W B, V P
*Raimu, Pierre Fresnay, directed by Marcel
Pagnol*
Third part in Pagnol's trilogy depicting lives,
loves, joys, and sorrows of the people of
Provence, France. French film, English subtitles.
FR
France — *Hollywood Home Theater*

Chain Gang Killings, The 1985
Adventure
77401 99 mins C B, V P
Ian Yule, Ken Gampu
A pair of shackled prisoners, one black the other
white, escape from a truck transporting them to
prison.
Clive Harding — *VCL Home Video*

Chain Reaction, The 1980
Suspense
78353 87 mins C B, V P
Steve Bisley, Ross Thompson
When a nuclear scientist is exposed to radiation
after an accident at an atomic power plant, he
must escape to warn the public of the danger.
David Elfick — *Embassy Home Entertainment*

Chained Heat 1983
Drama
65341 97 mins C B, V P
Linda Blair, Stella Stevens, Sybil Danning
A startling and explicit saga exposing the vicious
reality of life for women behind bars.
MPAA:R
Billy Fine — *Vestron Video*

Challenge, The 1938
Drama/Adventure
57349 77 mins B/W B, V, FO P
Luis Trenker, Robert Douglas
This classic mountaineering film features
incredible avalanche scenes, as it follow the
courageous party of explorers who conquered
the Matterhorn.
England — *Video Yesteryear; Movie Buff
Video*

Challenge, The 1982
Adventure
60425 108 mins C B, V, CED P
Scott Glenn, Toshiro Mifune
A contemporary action spectacle which
combines modern swordplay with the mysticism
and fantasy of ancient Samurai legends.
MPAA:R
CBS Theatrical Production — *CBS/Fox Video*

Challenge of the Gobots: 1985
Volumes I thru V
Cartoons
71019 48 mins C B, V P
Animated 5 pgms
Go Bots convert themselves from walking
robots into sports cars, jets and other high-
speed vehicles. Each program in the series
depicts the evil Renegades battling the good
Guardians for the control of Earth.
Hanna-Barbera — *Children's Video Library*

Challenge of the Gobots: 1986
The Gobotron Saga
Cartoons
85628 101 mins C B, V P
A children's made-for-video fantasy saga.
Hanna-Barbera — *Vestron Video*

Challenge to Be Free 1974
Adventure
63379 90 mins C B, V P
Mike Mazurki, Jimmy Kane
This is the legend of a man named Trapper, who
struggles across 1,000 miles of frozen
wilderness while being pursued by 12 men and
100 dogs.
MPAA:G
Pacific International Enterprises — *Media
Home Entertainment*

THE VIDEO TAPE & DISC GUIDE

Chamber of Fear 197?
Horror
79325 88 mins C B, V P
Boris Karloff, Isela Vega, Julissa and Carlos East
A madman inhabits a castle where he practices mental torture on innocent victims.
Luis Enrique Vergara — *Unicorn Video*

Chamber of Horrors 1940
Horror
72949 80 mins B/W B, V P
Leslie Banks, Lilli Palmer
A family is brought together at an English castle to claim a fortune left by an aristocrat. But there's one catch—there are seven keys that could open the vault with the fortune.
Monogram — *United Home Video*

Champ, The 1979
Drama
44650 121 mins C B, V, LV, CED P
Jon Voight, Faye Dunaway, Ricky Schroder, Jack Warden, directed by Franco Zeffirelli
An ex-fighter with a weakness for gambling and drinking is forced to return to the ring in an attempt to keep the custody of his son. A remake of the 1931 classic.
MPAA:PG
MGM — *MGM/UA Home Video*

Champagne for Caesar 1950
Comedy
65156 90 mins B/W B, V P
Ronald Colman, Celeste Holm, Vincent Price, Art Linkletter, directed by Richard Whorf
A self-proclaimed genius on every subject goes on a TV quiz show and proceeds to win everything in sight. The program's sponsor, in desperation, hires a femme fatale to distract the contestant before the final program.
Universal — *United Home Video*

Champion 1949
Drama
64542 99 mins B/W B, V P
Kirk Douglas, Arthur Kennedy, Marilyn Maxwell, Ruth Roman
An ambitious prizefighter alienates the people who helped him on the way to the top.
United Artists — *Republic Pictures Home Video*

Champions, The 1983
Drama
Closed Captioned
64987 90 mins C B, V P
John Hurt, Ben Johnson, Edward Woodward
This is the story of two championsa courageous, cancer-stricken British jockey and the horse he rode to victory in the Grand National, who came back from a severe, near-fatal injury.

Unknown — *Embassy Home Entertainment*

Champions 1984
Drama
72877 113 mins C B, V, LV P
John Hurt
The true story of Bob Champion, who overcame cancer to win England's Grand National, a top horse racing event.
Peter Shaw — *Embassy Home Entertainment*

Champions of the AFC East 1982
Football
47711 23 mins C B, V, FO P
Team highlights of the 1981 Miami Dolphins, who won the AFC Eastern Division with a strong defense.
NFL Films — *NFL Films Video*

Chandu on the Magic Island 1940
Mystery/Adventure
53357 67 mins B/W B, V, FO P
Bela Lugosi, Maria Alba, Clark Kimball Young
Chandu the Magician takes his powers of the occult to the mysterious lost island of Lemuri to battle the evil cult of Ubasti.
United Artists; Sol Lesser — *Movie Buff Video; Video Yesteryear*

Chanel Solitaire 1981
Drama
72906 124 mins C B, V P
Karen Black, Marie-France Pisier, Rutger Hauer
The biography of Gabrielle "Coco" Chanel, as portrayed by Marie-France Pisier, follows her career as a fabulous dress designer.
MPAA:R
George Kaczender — *Media Home Entertainment*

Change of Habit 1969
Drama/Comedy
55555 93 mins C B, V P
Elvis Presley, Mary Tyler Moore, Barbara McNair
Three novitiates undertake to learn about the world before becoming full-fledged nuns. While working at a ghetto clinic a young doctor forms a strong, affectionate relationship with one of them.
MPAA:G
Universal; Joe Connelly — *MCA Home Video*

Change of Mind 1968
Adventure/Fantasy
70581 52 mins C B, V P
Patrick McGoohan, Angela Brown, John Sharpe, directed by Joseph Serf

In this thirteenth episode of "The Prisoner" TV series, Number 2 uses drugs and ultra-sonic waves to break the Prisoner's resolve.
Associated TV Corp. — *MPI Home Video*

Change of Seasons, A   1980
Romance/Comedy
55456   102 mins   C   B, V, CED   P
Shirley MacLaine, Bo Derek, Anthony Hopkins, Michael Brandon, Mary Beth Hurt
A sophisticated comedy that looks at contemporary relationships and values. The wife of a college professor learns of her husband's affair with a seductive student and decides to have a fling with a younger man. The situation reaches absurdity when the couples decide to vacation together.
MPAA:R
Twentieth Century Fox — *CBS/Fox Video*

Change Your Job to   1986
Change Your Life
Occupations
84955   60 mins   C   B, V   P
Hosted by Walt Slaughter
This tape outlines strategies, tips and tactics in job hunting, including interviewing, resume writing and career planning.
Idea Marketing Inc — *Karl/Lorimar Home Video*

Changeling, The   1980
Horror
44918   114 mins   C   B, V, LV,   P
                        CED
George C. Scott, Trish Van Devere, John Russell
A music teacher moves into an old house and discovers that a young boy's ghostly spirit is her housemate.
MPAA:R
Associated Film Distribution — *Vestron Video*

Chaplin: A Character Is   197?
Born/Keaton: The Great
Stone Face
Comedy/Film-History
64842   90 mins   C   B, V   P
Narrated by Keenan Wynn and Red Buttons
Wynn narrates "A Character Is Born," with scenes from "Little Champ," "The Pawnshop," "The Rink" and "The Immigrant." Buttons presents "The Great Stone Face" featuring scenes from "Cops," "The Playhouse" "The Boat" and "The General."
SL Film Productions — *HarmonyVision*

Chaplin Essanay Book 1,   1915
The
Comedy
84948   51 mins   B/W   B, V   P
Charles Chaplin, Edna Purviance, Ben Turpin

Two of Chaplin's early shorts are featured on this tape: "The Tramp" and "The Champion."
Essanay — *Blackhawk Films*

Chaplin Revue, The   1958
Comedy
08395   121 mins   B/W   B, V   P
Charlie Chaplin
The "Revue," put together by Chaplin in 1958, consists of three of his best shorts: "A Dog's Life" (1918), "Shoulder Arms" (1918), and "The Pilgrim" (1922).
rbc Films — *Playhouse Video*

Chapter Two   1979
Romance
Closed Captioned
44789   120 mins   C   B, V, LV   P
James Caan, Marsha Mason, Valerie Harper, Joseph Bologna
A shy mystery writer and widower wins the heart of a young divorcee. The memory of his deceased wife nearly ruins their new marriage.
MPAA:PG
Ray Stark — *RCA/Columbia Pictures Home Video*

Charade   1963
Mystery/Comedy
58212   113 mins   C   B, V   P
Cary Grant, Audrey Hepburn, Walter Matthau, James Coburn, George Kennedy, directed by Stanley Donen
After her husband is murdered, a young wife finds herself on the run from crooks and double agents who want 250,000 dollars her husband stole during World War II. Filmed on location in Paris. Music by Henry Mancini.
Film Daily Poll 10 Best Pictures of the Year '63.
Universal; Stanley Donen — *MCA Home Video*

Charge of the Light   1936
Brigade, The
Drama
64783   115 mins   B/W   B, V, CED   P
Olivia De Havilland, Errol Flynn, David Niven, Nigel Bruce, directed by Michael Curtiz
An army officer deliberately starts the Balaclava charge to even an old score with Surat Khan, who's on the other side.
Warner; Hal B. Wallis; Sam Bischoff — *CBS/Fox Video; RCA VideoDiscs*

Charge of the Model T's   1979
Comedy
69553   94 mins   C   B, V   P
Louis Nye, John David Carson, Herb Edelman, Carol Bagdasarian, Arte Johnson
Set during World War I, this comedy is about a German spy who tries to infiltrate the U.S. army.
MPAA:G

Jim McCullough — *Embassy Home Entertainment*

Chariots of Fire   1981
Drama
47788   123 mins   C   B, V, LV   P
Ben Cross, Ian Charleson, Nigel Havers, Nick Farrell, John Gielgud, Alice Krige, Nigel Davenport, Ian Holm, Patrick Magee, Cheryl Campbell, Lindsay Anderson
Motivation and the will to win are poignantly and dramatically portrayed in this story of two British track athletes striving to win major events at the 1924 Paris Olympics.
Academy Awards '81: Best Picture. MPAA:PG
Enigma Productions; David Puttnam — *Warner Home Video; RCA VideoDiscs*

Chariots of the Gods   1973
Documentary/Speculation
14643   98 mins   C   B, V   P
Directed by Dr. Harold Reinl
The possibility of extraterrestrial visitors inhabiting Earth many years ago is examined.
MPAA:G
Sun International Productions — *United Home Video*

Charley Varrick   1973
Drama
68257   111 mins   C   B, V   P
Walter Matthau, Joe Don Baker, Felicia Farr
A crop dusting pilot robs a bank only to find that the bank belongs to the Mafia.
MPAA:PG
Universal — *MCA Home Video*

Charlie and the Great   1982
Balloon Chase
Comedy-Drama/Adventure
60176   98 mins   C   B, V   P
Jack Albertson, Adrienne Barbeau
Jack Albertson stars as a grandfather who takes his grandson on a cross-country balloon trip hotly pursued by the boy's mother, her stuffy fiance (who wants the boy in military school), the FBI, a reporter, and the Mafia. They make it to Virginia and are cheered as heroes.
Daniel Wilson — *Lightning Video; Time Life Video*

Charlie Boy   1981
Horror
82099   60 mins   C   B, V   P
Leigh Lawson, Angela Bruce, Marius Goring, directed by Robert Young.
The new owner of an ancient African idol enters the world of the supernatural when he casts a death spell on six people. Available in VHS Stereo and Beta Hi-Fi.
Hammer Films — *Thriller Video*

Charlie Bravo   198?
War-Drama
87759   83 mins   C   B, V   P
Bruno Pradal, Karen Veriler, Jean-Francois Poron
A commando group are commanded to rescue a captured nurse in Vietnam. Dubbed.
MPAA:R
French — *Video Gems*

Charlie Brown Christmas,   1965
A
Cartoons
79264   25 mins   C   B, V   P
Animated
Disillusioned by the commercialization of the holiday season, Charlie Brown sets out to find the true meaning of Christmas.
Lee Mendelson—Bill Melendez Productions — *Snoopy's Home Video Library*

Charlie Brown Festival, A   1981
Cartoons
56889   120 mins   C   CED   P
Animated
Four complete stores featuring Charlie Brown, trying to cope with Peppermint Patty, a losing baseball team, the Junior Olympics, and his love for the little red-haired girl.
United Features Syndicate — *RCA VideoDiscs*

Charlie Brown Festival   1981
Vol. II, A
Cartoons
59019   102 mins   C   CED   P
Four animated adventures featuring the Peanuts gang: "Be My Valentine, Charlie Brown," "It's the Easter Beagle, Charlie Brown," "He's Your Dog, Charlie Brown," and, "Life is a Circus, Charlie Brown."
United Features Syndicate — *RCA VideoDiscs*

Charlie Brown Festival   1982
Vol. III, A
Cartoons
47803   102 mins   C   CED   P
Animated
The Peanuts Gang are featured in this compilation containing "It Was a Short Summer Charlie Brown" (1969); "It's the Great Pumpkin Charlie Brown" (1966); "You're Not Elected Charlie Brown" (1972); and "A Charlie Brown Thanksgiving" (1973).
United Features Syndicate — *RCA VideoDiscs*

Charlie Brown Festival   1983
Vol. IV, A
Cartoons
64327   102 mins   C   CED   P
Animated
Snoopy is a super detective, Lucy is after Schroeder and Charlie Brown is facing a player walk-out in this collection of Peanuts favorites.

United Features Syndicate — *RCA VideoDiscs*

Mutual — *Republic Pictures Home Video*

Charlie Chan and the Curse of the Dragon Queen
1981

Satire/Comedy
66060   97 mins   C   B, V   P
Peter Ustinov, Lee Grant, Angie Dickinson, Richard Hatch, Brian Kieth, Roddy McDowall.
The famed Oriental sleuth confronts his old enemy the Dragon Queen, and reveals the true identity of a killer.
MPAA:PG
American Cinema — *Media Home Entertainment*

Charlie Chaplin Carnival
1916

Comedy
08711   80 mins   B/W   B, V, 3/4U   P
This features: "The Vagabond," "The Fireman," "The Count," and "Behind the Screen." Sound effects and music added. Silent.
Mutual — *Hollywood Home Theater*

Charlie Chaplin Cavalcade
1916

Comedy
08712   81 mins   B/W   B, V, 3/4U   P
Features Chaplin's: "One A.M.," "Pawnshop," "Floorwalker," and "The Rink."
Mutual — *Hollywood Home Theater*

Charlie Chaplin Festival
1917

Comedy
82163   80 mins   B/W   B, V   P
Charlie Chaplin
Here is a collection of four Charlie Chaplin short subjects: "The Cure," "The Adventurer," "The Immigrant" and "Easy Street."
Mutual — *Prism*

Charlie Chaplin Festival, The
1917

Comedy
08674   115 mins   B, V, 3/4U   P
Charlie Chaplin, Edna Purviance, Henry Bergmna, Eric Campbell, directed by Charlie Chaplin
Features four Chaplin shorts: "The Immigrant," "The Adventurer," "The Cure," and "Easy Street."
Mutual — *Hollywood Home Theater*

Charlie Chaplin—The Early Years, Volume I
1917

Comedy
10076   62 mins   B/W   B, V   P
Charlie Chaplin, Edna Purviance, John Rand, Eric Campbell, James T. Kelley
Package includes Chaplin's "The Immigrant," "The Count," and Easy Street." Silent.

Charlie Chaplin—The Early Years, Volume II
1917

Comedy
10080   61 mins   B/W   B, V   P
Charlie Chaplin, Edna Purviance, Eric Campbell, Albert Austin, Henry Bergman, John Rand
Package includes Chaplins "The Pawnshop" (1916), "The Adventurer" (1917), and "One A.M." (1916).
Mutual — *Republic Pictures Home Video*

Charlie Chaplin—The Early Years, Volume III
1916

Comedy
10084   64 mins   B/W   B, V   P
Charlie Chaplin, Edna Purviance, Eric Campbell, Albert Austin
Package includes Chaplin's "The Cure" (1916), "The Floorwalker" (1916), and "The Vagabond."
Mutual — *Republic Pictures Home Video*

Charlie Chaplin—The Early Years, Volume IV
1916

Comedy
10088   63 mins   B/W   B, V   P
Charlie Chaplin, Edna Purviance, Eric Campbell, Lloyd Bacon, Albert Austin, James T. Kelly
Package includes Chaplin's, "Behind the Screen," "The Fireman" (1916), and "The Rink" (1916).
Mutual — *Republic Pictures Home Video*

Charlie Chaplin: The Funniest Man in the World
1981

Documentary/Comedy
58561   93 mins   B/W   B, V   P
Charlie Chaplin, Fatty Arbuckle, Mabel Normand, Ben Turpin, Stan Laurel, narrated by Douglas Fairbanks Jr.
A profile of Chaplin, from his youth in England through his vaudeville days in America to his triumph in Hollywood.
Vernon Becker; Mel May — *Mastervision*

Charlie Chaplin's Keystone Comedies
1914

Comedy
58655   59 mins   B/W   B, V, FO   P
Charlie Chaplin, Mabel Normand, Mack Swain
Six one-reelers which Chaplin filmed in 1914, his first movie-making year: "Making a Living," Chaplin's first, in which he plays a villain; "Kid Auto Races," in which Charlie now sports baggy pants, bowler hat and cane; "A Busy Day," featuring Charlie in drag; "Mabel's Married Life;" "Laughing Gas;" and "The New Janitor." Silent with musical score.

Sennett; Keystone — *Video Yesteryear*

Charlie Chaplin's Keystone Comedies #2   1914
Comedy
88064   60 mins   B/W   B, V   P
Charlie Chaplin, Mabel Normand, Mack Swain, Mack Sennett
Three hilarious early Chaplin shorts, "His Trysting Place(s)," "Getting Acquainted" and "The Fatal Mallet." Silent withmusic score.
Mack Sennett — *Video Yesteryear*

Charlie Chaplin's Keystone Comedies #3   1914
Comedy
85505   59 mins   B/W   B, V   P
Charlie Chaplin, Mack Swain, Mabel Normand, Chester Conklin
Three more vintage early Chaplin shorts: "Caught in a Cabaret," "The Masquerader" and "Between Showers."
Mack Sennett; Keystone — *Video Yesteryear*

Charlie Chase and Ben Turpin   1921
Comedy
85158   67 mins   B/W   B, V   P
Ben Turpin, Charlie Chase, Wallace Beery, Juanita Hansen
Three silent comedy classics, "All Wet," "Publicity Pays," and "A Clever Dummy."
Hal Roach; Mack Sennett — *Video Yesteryear*

Charlie Daniels Band: The Saratoga Concert, The   1982
Music-Performance
59133   75 mins   C   B, V, LV,   P
                          CED
The Charlie Daniels Band performs live in concert at Saratoga Springs, New York, September 4, 1981. The program also includes two "conceptualized" songs filmed in North Carolina and narrated by Charlie Daniels. Songs include: "In America," "The Devil Went Down to Georgia," "South's Gonna Do It Again."
Richard Namm — *CBS/Fox Video*

Charlie Grant's War   1980
War-Drama/World War II
71044   130 mins   C   B, V   P
Jan Rubes, R.H. Thompson
Tales of Nazi brutality push Canadian businessman Charlie Grant into action. This film follows the true story of Grant's efforts to save European Jews from persecution.
British Independent — *Hal Roach Studios*

Charlie, the Lonesome Cougar   1967
Drama
82296   100 mins   C   B, V   P
Ron Brown, Brian Russell, Clifford Peterson
Life for a rugged logger will never be the same after he adopts an orphaned cougar.
MPAA:G
Walt Disney Productions — *Walt Disney Home Video*

Charlotte's Web   1972
Musical/Cartoons
38607   94 mins   C   B, V, LV   P
Animated, voices of Debbie Reynolds, Agnes Moorehead, Paul Lynde, Henry Gibson
E.B. White's famous story of Wilbur the pig and his friendship with Charlotte the spider, transformed into a cartoon musical for the whole family.
MPAA:G
Paramount — *Paramount Home Video; RCA VideoDiscs*

Charmkins, The   1983
Cartoons
80973   60 mins   C   B, V   P
Animated, voices of Ben Vereen, Sally Struthers, Aileen Quinn
Here are the animated adventures of Lady Slipper and her friends in Charm World where they battle the evil Dragonweed.
Sunbow Prods; Marvel Prods. — *Family Home Entertainment*

Chartbusters from Kids Incorporated   1985
Music video
87764   30 mins   C   B, V   P
Ten songs performed by kids are taken from the popular children's show, including "Walking on Sunshine," "Material Girl" and "Freeway of Love."
Hal Roach Studios — *Hal Roach Studios*

Chase, The   1966
Suspense
86385   135 mins   C   B, V   P
Marlon Brando, Robert Redford, Angie Dickinson, E.G. Marshall, Jane Fonda
An idealistic sheriff tracks down an escaped convict, who is innocent, despite the antagonism of the entire town. Written by Lillian Hellman from the play by Horton Foote.
Sam Spiegel — *RCA/Columbia Pictures Home Video*

Chaste and Pure   1977
Drama
81633   90 mins   C   B, V   P
Laura Antonelli
A young woman is torn between her blooming sexuality and her vows of chastity.
Italian — *Magnum Entertainment*

Chattanooga Choo Choo   1984
Comedy
80649   102 mins   C   B, V   P
Barbara Eden, Joe Namath, George Kennedy, Melissa Sue Anderson, directed by Bruce Bilson
A football team owner must restore the Chattanooga Choo Choo and make a twenty-four hour run from Chattanooga to New York in order to collect one-million dollars left to him in a will.
MPAA:PG
April Fools Prods. — *THORN EMI/HBO Video*

Chatterbox   1976
Comedy
66099   73 mins   C   B, V, CED   P
Candice Rialson
A young starlet has a very conversant anatomy.
Bruce Cohn Curtis — *Vestron Video*

Chatterer the Squirrel   1983
Cartoons
65655   60 mins   C   B, V   P
Animated
Chatterer the Squirrel learns a much-needed lesson in humility in "The Big Boast," and in "Captive Chatterer," the farmer's son tries to make a house pet out of Chatterer, but a new home and plenty of food are no substitute for freedom!
Ziv International — *Family Home Entertainment*

Cheaper to Keep Her   1980
Comedy-Drama
68222   92 mins   C   B, V   P
Mac Davis, Tovah Feldshuh, Jack Gilford, Rose Marie
Upon leaving his wife, Bill Dekker (Mac Davis) begins a new job working for a feminist attorney who has him investigating husbands of clients, who happen to be in the same predicament that he is in.
MPAA:R
American Cinema — *Media Home Entertainment*

Cheaters   1984
Theater/Drama
78660   103 mins   C   B, V   P
Peggy Cass, Jack Kruschen
Two middle class couples are having affairs with each other's spouses and complications arise when their respective children decide to marry each other.
Showtime — *RKO HomeVideo*

Check and Double Check   1930
Comedy
11226   75 mins   B/W   B, V, FO   P
Freeman Gosden and Charles Correll (Amos 'n' Andy), Duke Ellington and His Orchestra
Radio's original Amos 'n' Andy help solve a lover's triangle in this film version of the popular radio series. Duke Ellington's band plays "Old Man Blues" and "Three Little Words."
RKO — *Video Yesteryear; Discount Video Tapes; Video Connection; Hollywood Home Theater; Western Film & Video Inc; Kartes Video Communications; See Hear Industries*

Checkmate   1968
Suspense/Fantasy
77417   52 mins   C   B, V   P
Patrick McGoohan, Ronald Radd, Peter Wyngarde, directed by Don Chaffey
The Prisoner participates in an unusual chess game in the Village. An episode from "The Prisoner" series.
ITC Productions — *MPI Home Video*

Cheech and Chong: Get   1985
Out of My Room
Comedy/Music video
82073   53 mins   C   B, V   P
Cheech and Chong perform four comedic conceptual music videos from their album "Get Out of My Room" in VHS and Beta Hi-Fi Stereo.
Koo Koo Banana Inc. — *MCA Home Video*

Cheech and Chong's   1980
Next Movie
Comedy
48629   99 mins   C   B, V, LV   P
Cheech Marin, Tommy Chong, Evelyn Guerrero
A pair of messed-up bumblers adventure into a welfare office, massage parlor, nightclub, and flying saucer, while always living in fear of the cops.
MPAA:R
Universal — *MCA Home Video*

Cheech & Chong's Nice   1981
Dreams
Comedy
60344   97 mins   C   B, V, LV   P
Richard "Cheech" Marin, Tommy Chong, Evelyn Guerrero, Stacy Keach
The spaced-out duo are selling their own "specially mixed" ice cream to make cash and realize their dreams.
MPAA:R
Columbia — *RCA/Columbia Pictures Home Video; RCA VideoDiscs*

Cheerleaders, The   1973
Comedy
59081   84 mins   C   B, V   P
The locker room hi-jinks of rival football teams and a squad of uninhibited cheerleaders mix and match in this racy comedy.
MPAA:R
Paul Glickler; Richard Lerner — *HarmonyVision*

Cheerleaders' Wild Weekend
1985

Comedy
77413   87 mins   C   B, V   P
Jason Williams, Kristine DeBell
A group of cheerleaders plot to escape from their kidnapper, a disgruntled former football star.
MPAA:R
Fountain Productions — *Vestron Video*

Cheers for Miss Bishop
1941

Drama
63622   95 mins   B/W   B, V, FO   P
Martha Scott, William Gargan, Edmund Gwenn, Sterling Holloway, Rosemary DeCamp
This is the story of a young girl who graduates from a new college and stays on to teach English for over 50 years.
United Artists — *Movie Buff Video; Video Yesteryear; Kartes Video Communications*

Cherry Hill High
1976

Comedy
62783   86 mins   C   B, V   P
Carrie Olsen, Nina Carson, Lynn Hastings, Gloria Upson, Stephanie Lawlor
Five high school coeds decide to have a contest to see which of them can lose her virginity first.
MPAA:R
Cannon Films — *MCA Home Video*

Cheryl Ladd—Fascinated
1982

Music-Performance
66018   50 mins   C   B, V   P
The ex-Angel performs "Just Like Old Times," "I Love How You Love Me," "Cold as Ice" and more.
EMI Music — *THORN EMI/HBO Video*

Chess Moves
1986

Music video
88360   25 mins   C   B, V   P
Five video songs from the acclaimed Tim Rice musical "Chess," including "One Night in Bangkok" and "I Know Him So Well."
RCA Video — *RCA/Columbia Pictures Home Video*

Chesty Anderson U.S. Navy
1976

Comedy
47672   90 mins   C   B, V   P
Shari Eubank, Dorri Thompson, Rosanne Katon, Marcie Barkin, Scotman Crothers, Frank Campanella, Fred Willard
The comic adventures of a W.A.V.E.S. unit populated by well-endowed ladies.
Unknown — *Unicorn Video; World Video Pictures*

Cheyenne Autumn
1964

Western
82339   158 mins   C   B, V   P
James Stewart, Edward G Robinson, Sal Mineo, Richard Widmark, Carrol Baker, Karl Malden, Ricardo Montalban, directed by John Ford
This is the newly-restored version of the western classic about three hundred Cheyenne Indians who migrate from Oklahoma to Wyoming in 1878. Available in VHS and Beta Hi-Fi Stereo.
Warner Bros — *Warner Home Video*

Cheyenne Rides Again
1938

Western
11261   60 mins   B/W   B, V, FO   P
Tom Tyler, Lucille Browne, Jimmy Fox
Cheyenne poses as an outlaw to hunt a gang of rustlers.
Victory — *Video Yesteryear; Video Connection*

Chicago Bears 1984 Team Highlights
1985

Football
70544   70 mins   C   B, V, FO   P
Like their '84 Cubby cousins, the Chicagoans awoke from hibernation to win their division in a "Fight to the Finish." The tape features 47-minutes of highlights from the entire NFL's '84 season as well.
NFL Films — *NFL Films Video*

Chicago Cubs: Team Highlights
1984

Baseball
81136   30 mins   C   B, V   P
Dave Kingman, Mel Hall, Ryne Sandberg, Ron Cey, Leon Durnham, Jody Davis 6 pgms
The Chicago Cubs' meteoric rise from the National League baseball to division champions is chronicled in this series.
1.1978: We Love The Cubs 2.1979: Summer of '79 3.1980: Summer of '80 4.1981: Summer of '81 5.1982: Summer of '82 6.1984: Cubs Win
Major League Baseball — *Major League Baseball Productions*

Chicago White Sox: Team Highlights
1984

Baseball
81137   30 mins   C   B, V   P
Carlton Fisk, Steve Trout, Greg Luzinski, Tom Seaver, Harold Baines 4 pgms
This series describes how the Chicago White Sox clinched the American League western division title by "winning ugly" in 1983.
1.1981: On The Beginning 2.1982: One Step Closer 3.1983: Winning Ugly 4.1984; Chicago White Sox '84
Major League Baseball — *Major League Baseball Productions*

Chick Corea 1980
Music-Performance
88115   60 mins   C   B, V, 8mm   P
Corea reunites with his influential band Return to Forever, performing the blues classics "500 Miles High," "Guernica" and "L's BOP."
Sony Video — Sony Video Software

Chick Corea & Gary 1985
Burton Live in Tokyo
Music-Performance
70663   60 mins   C   B, V   P
Chick Corea, Gary Burton
The talents of this Grammy award-winning duo thrill the audience at Yuhbin Chokin Hall in Tokyo. This tape of their performance includes favorites like "La Fiesta," "Senor Mouse," and "Children's Songs" all in Hi-Fi sound.
Pacific Arts Music Video — Pacific Arts Video

Chick Corea/Gary Burton 1981
Live in Tokyo
Music-Performance
64829   58 mins   C   LV   P
The music of pianist/composer Corea and vibraphonist Burton is captured in a live performance. Features Corea compositions such as "La Fiesta," "Senior Mouse" and "Children's Songs." In stereo.
Chick Corea; Gary Burton — Pioneer Artists

Chicken Chronicles, The 1977
Comedy
80775   94 mins   C   B, V   P
Phil Silvers, Ed Lauter, Steve Guttenberg, Lisa Reeves, Meridith Baer
The rich high school students of Beverly Hills bring the sixties and their teen years to a close by experimenting with sex and drugs.
MPAA:PG
AVCO Embassy — Embassy Home Entertainment

Chicken Ranch 1983
Documentary
65381   84 mins   C   B, V   P
This documentary focuses on the women who work at and the men who frequent "The Chicken Ranch," the country's best-known legal brothel.
MPAA:R
Nick Broomfield — Vestron Video

Chico Hamilton 1982
Music-Performance
88117   53 mins   C   B, V, 8mm   P
The boss jazz drummer performs at NYC's Village Vanguard, doing "Encore," "Sweet Dreams Too Soon," "Frist Light" and "Erika."
Sony Video — Sony Video Software

Chiefs 1983
Crime-Drama
85077   200 mins   C   B, V   P
Charlton Heston, Paul Sorvino, Keith Carradine, Brad davis, directed by Jerry London
A made-for-TV movie about a police chief in a Southern town who investigates old murders previously covered up over the years by the town's most powerful men.
New World — New World Video

Chien Andalou, Un 1928
Film-Avant-garde
06242   20 mins   B/W   B, V   P
Pierre Batcheff, Simone Marevil, Jaime Miravilles, directed by Luis Bunuel
Succession of surreal images. Silent.
Foreign — Hollywood Home Theater; Texture Films

Child Bride of Short 1981
Creek
Drama
80299   100 mins   C   B, V   P
Diane Lane, Conrad Bain, Christopher Atkins, Kiel Martin, Helen Hunt
Two young people are trapped in a town where the government is out to stop the community's practice of polygamy.
Lawrence Schriller Productions — Prism

Childbirth Preparation 1985
Program
Parents/Childbirth
82125   56 mins   C   B, V   P
Narrated by Dr. Art Ulene
Dr. Ulene demonstrates techniques that pregnant women in labor can use to promote relaxation and relieve discomfort.
Feeling Fine Programs Inc — Feeling Fine Programs; Warner Home Video

Children, The 1980
Mystery/Suspense
65609   93 mins   C   B, V   P
A New England town is unprepared after a school bus passes through a mysterious yellow cloud and the children are transformed to terrifying, powerful menaces.
MPAA:R
World Northal — Vestron Video

Children of An Lac, The 1980
Drama
71298   98 mins   C   B, V   P
Shirley Jones, Ina Balin, Beulah Quo, Alan Fudge, Ben Piazza, directed by John Llewellyn Moxey
As the American Army prepares to leave Saigon, two courageous women work to evacuate a school-load of orphans.

Charles Fries Productions — *U.S.A. Home Video*

Children of Divorce   1980
Drama
87325   96 mins   C   B, V   P
Lance Kerwin, Barbara Feldon, Stacey Nelkin, Billy Dee Williams
Bratty, affluent kids, awash in understanding and kindness, suffer as their parents get divorced. A made-for-TV movie.
Charles B. Fitzsimons — *U.S.A. Home Video*

Children of Sanchez   1979
Drama
76659   103 mins   C   B, V   P
Anthony Quinn, Dolores Del Rio, Katy Jurado, Lupita Ferrer
A story of one man's attempts to provide for his family with very little except faith and love.
MPAA:R
Paul Bartlett Films — *Monterey Home Video*

Children of the Corn   1984
Horror
74089   93 mins   C   B, V, LV,   P
                                    CED
This is another spine-tingling horror epic from that master of horror, Stephen King. This one is set in a small town in Nebraska where the local children worship the corn by making adult sacrifices.
MPAA:R
Donald P. Borchers; Terrence Kirby — *Embassy Home Entertainment*

Children of the Full Moon   1984
Horror
80478   60 mins   C   B, V   P
Christopher Cazenove, Celia Gregory, Diana Dors, Jacof Witken, Robert Urquhart
A young couple find themselves lost in a forest that is the home of a family of werewolves. In Beta Hi-Fi and VHS stereo.
Hammer Films — *Thriller Video*

Children of Theatre Street, The   1977
Documentary/Dance
81568   100 mins   C   B, V   P
Narrated by Princess Grace of Monaco
This is a behind-the-scenes look at the students who attend the Kirov Ballet School in Leningrad, Russia.
Earle Mack Films — *Kultur*

Children's Carol, The   1980
Drama/Christmas
Closed Captioned
71047   94 mins   C   B, V   P
Judy Norton-Taylor, Jon Walmsley, Mary McDonough, Eric Scott, Kami Cotler, Joe
Conely, Ronnie Clare, Leslie Winston, Peggy Rea, directed by Lawrence Dobkin
The winter solstice brings no special joy to Walton's mountain; World War II has taken many men with short wave reports of the Nazi terror spreading across Europe. But huddled in the glow of Walton's barn, the children rediscover the true meaning of Christmas.
Lorimar — *Karl/Lorimar Home Video*

Children's Island   1984
Adventure
84495   200 mins   C   B, V   P
A two-volume saga, sold in one package, about children who, after being shipwrecked on an island during World War II, begin a democratic mini-society.
Creative Film GmbH — *Sony Video Software*

Children's Songs and   1985
Stories with the Muppets
Variety
Closed Captioned
80746   56 mins   C   B, V   P
Kermit the Frog, Scooter, Twiggy, Julie Andrews, Charles Aznavour, Brooke Shields, Judy Collins
The Muppets and their special guests perform unique renditions of well loved childrens songs.
Henson Associates — *Playhouse Video*

Children's Video   197?
Playground
Cartoons/Fairy tales
71230   30 mins   C   V   P
Animated 10 pgms
These features bring the beloved family tales from Mark Twain, Lewis Carroll and many others to the screen.
1.Alice in Wonderland 2.Arabian Nights 3.Cinderella 4.Tom Sawyer 5.Snow White 6.Sleeping Beauty 7.Hiawatha 8.Robinson Crusoe 9.Swiss Family Robinson 10.Robin Hood
Rankin-Bass — *Prism*

Chilly Scenes of Winter   1979
Comedy
82401   96 mins   C   B, V   P
John Heard, Mary Beth Hurt, Peter Riegert, directed by Joan Micklin Silver
In this quirky romantic comedy a woman is torn between an indifferent husband and an eager lover. The lover, in turn, is surrounded by unhappy women, whose lives embody some of the more questionable aspects of modernity.
MPAA:PG
United Artists — *MGM/UA Home Video*

Chimes of Big Ben, The   1968
Drama
79895   52 mins   C   B, V   P
Patrick McGoohan, Nadia Gray, Leo McKern

The Prisoner and a new arrival to the Village attempt an escape.
Patrick McGoohan — *MPI Home Video*

China Seas 1935
Drama/Adventure
71159   89 mins   B/W   B, V   P
Clark Gable, Jean Harlow, Wallace Beery, Rosalind Russell, Lewis Stone, C. Aubrey Smith, Dudley Digges, Robert Benchley, directed by Tay Garnett
The captain of a commercial steamship on the China route has to fight off murderous Malay pirates and a raging typhoon to reach port safely.
MGM — *MGM/UA Home Video*

China Syndrome, The 1979
Drama
Closed Captioned
44784   122 mins   C   B, V, LV   P
Jack Lemmon, Michael Douglas, Jane Fonda
A television news reporter and cameraman try to make public a dangerous incident which they stumbled upon at a nuclear power plant. The integrity of a nuclear engineer makes him a murder target.
MPAA:PG
Michael Douglas — *RCA/Columbia Pictures Home Video; RCA VideoDiscs*

Chinatown 1974
Mystery
38592   131 mins   C   B, V, LV   P
Jack Nicholson, Faye Dunaway, John Huston, Diane Ladd, directed by Roman Polanski
A complex tangled mystery involving Jack Nicholson as a private detective working on a seemingly routine case that mushrooms into more than he bargained for.
Academy Awards '74: Best Original Screenplay (Robert Towne).   MPAA:R
Paramount — *Paramount Home Video; RCA VideoDiscs*

Chinese Boxes 1984
Suspense/Adventure
82444   87 mins   C   B, V   P
Will Patton, Adelheid Arndt, Robbie Coltrane, directed by Christopher Petit
An American man is framed in a murder and becomes caught in an international web of crime and intrigue.
Palace Productions — *Vestron Video*

Chinese Connection, The 1973
Adventure/Martial arts
55831   107 mins   C   B, V   P
Bruce Lee, James Tien, Robert Baker
Revenge is the motive as Lee sets out to catch the men who murdered the revered teacher of his martial arts school.
MPAA:R

National General Pictures — *CBS/Fox Video; Video City Productions; Master Arts Video; Spotlite Video*

Chinese Gods 1980
Folklore/China
44341   90 mins   C   B, V   R, P
Animated
This program is an animated story of Chinese mythology. It explains the battles and rivalries occurring circa 1000 B.C. in the period of the Shang Dynasty. Cruel King Cheo's troops defeated the troops of the Marquis Hsi-pa in a huge war. After an evil flying serpent tries but fails to kill him, the Marquis, Chiang, wins a series of battles, and his rival, Cheo, eventually burns himself to death.
MPAA:G
Four Seas Films — *Video Gems*

Chinese Web, The 1978
Adventure
Closed Captioned
66069   95 mins   C   B, V   P
Nicholas Hammond, Robert F Simon, Rosalind Chao
A Spider-man adventure in which Spidey becomes entwined in international intrigue.
Lionel E Siegel — *Playhouse Video*

Chino 1975
Western
47384   97 mins   C   B, V   P
Charles Bronson, Jill Ireland, directed by John Sturges
A half-breed horse trainer with an independent streak "adopts" a runaway fifteen-year-old boy.
MPAA:PG
Intercontinental Releasing Corp — *Warner Home Video*

Chisholms, The 1979
Adventure/Drama
71325   300 mins   C   B, V   P
Robert Preston, Brian Keith, Ben Murphy, Charles Frank, Rosemary Harris, Glynnis O'Conner, directed by Mel Stuart
Set on the American frontier of the 1840's, this two-cassette package portrays the trials of the closely-knit Chisholm family as they made their way from Virginia to California.
Alan Landsburg Productions — *U.S.A. Home Video*

Chisum 1970
Western
51962   111 mins   C   B, V   P
John Wayne, Forrest Tucker, Geoffrey Deuel
A cattle baron meets Billy the Kid and together they fight the corrupt town government.
MPAA:G
Warner Bros — *Warner Home Video*

Chitty Chitty Bang Bang   1968
Musical/Fantasy
58483   142 mins   C   B, V, CED   P
*Dick Van Dyke, Sally Ann Howes, Lionel
Jeffries, directed by Ken Hughes*
An eccentric inventor spruces up an old car and,
in fantasy, takes his children to a land where the
evil rulers have forbidden children.
MPAA:G   EL, SP
United Artists; Albert R Broccoli — *CBS/Fox
Video*

C.H.O.M.P.S.   1979
Comedy
88177   90 mins   C   B, V   P
*Valerie Bertinelli, Wesley Eure, Conrad Bain,
Chuck McCann, Red Buttons*
A young inventor devises a robotic guard-dog
which becomes both a national phenomenon
and hazard.
MPAA:PG
Orion Pictures; American Int'l — *Warner Home
Video*

Choose Me   1984
Drama/Romance
77357   106 mins   C   B, V   P
*Genevieve Bujold, Keith Carradine, Lesley Ann
Warren, Rae Dawn Chong, directed by Alan
Rudolph*
A neurotic radio psychologist becomes involved
in a menage a trois with a drifter and a nightclub
owner. Teddy Pendergrass sings the title song.
MPAA:R
Island Alive — *Media Home Entertainment*

Chorus Line, A   1985
Musical/Drama
85021   118 mins   C   B, V, 8mm,   P
LV, CED
*Michael Douglas, Audrey Landers, Gregg Burge,
Alyson Reed, Janet Jones, Michael Blevins,
directed by Richard Attenborough*
This adaptation of the Pulitzer Prize-winning
Broadway musical follows the lives of a group of
chorus dancers who are auditioning for a new
show. Music by Marvin Hamlisch. In HiFi Stereo.
MPAA:PG-13
Polygram Pictures — *Embassy Home
Entertainment*

Chosen, The   1981
Drama
65404   107 mins   C   B, V   P
Rod Steiger, Robby Benson, Barry Miller
This is the story of two young Jewish men
whose friendship survives the deep conflicts
arising from having been raised in two different
worlds. Based on Chaim Potok's acclaimed
novel.
MPAA:PG
Edie and Ely Landau — *CBS/Fox Video*

Christ Stopped at Eboli   1979
War-Drama
85283   118 mins   C   B, V   P
*Gian Maria Volonte, Irene Papas, Paolo
Bonacelli, Francois Simon, directed by
Francesco Rosi*
In the classic Levi story, a political activist visits
a tiny town and witnesses the peasants'
strength during war.
Moscow Film Festival '79: Grand Prize.
Franco Cristaldi; Nicola
Carraro — *RCA/Columbia Pictures Home
Video*

Christian the Lion   1976
Documentary
82275   87 mins   C   B, V   P
Virginia McKenna, Bill Travers
This is the true story of Christian, a lion cub
raised in a London zoo, who is transported to
Africa to learn to live with other lions.
MPAA:G
Scotia American — *Unicorn Video*

Christiane F   1982
Drama
78343   120 mins   C   B, V   P
Natja Brunkhorst, Thomas Haustein
A true story about a fourteen year old girl who
becomes a junkie and a prostitute in Berlin's
Zoo Station. David Bowie makes a guest
appearance in the film and sings "Heroes".
MPAA:R
Bernd Eichinger; Hans Weth — *Media Home
Entertainment*

Christina   1974
Suspense/Drama
70583   95 mins   C   B, V   P
*Barbara Parkins, Peter Haskell, directed by Paul
Krasny*
An unemployed and lonely man meets a
beautiful woman who offers him $25,000 to
marry him. She then vanishes. Obsessed and in
love, he searches for clues that lead him
through haunted mansions and other evil
locations.
MPAA:PG
New World Pictures — *MPI Home Video*

Christine   1984
Suspense
76034   110 mins   C   B, V   P
*Keith Gordon, John Stockwell, Alexandra Paul,
Robert Prosley, Harry Dean Stanton, directed by
John Carpenter*
Christine is a sleek red and white 1958
Plymouth Fury that seduces a teenage boy and
demands his complete and unquestioned
devotion. Anyone who gets in her way becomes
a victim of Christine's wrath. Based on the
Stephen King novel.
MPAA:R

Richard Kobritz — *RCA/Columbia Pictures Home Video*

Christine McVie Concert, The   1984
Music-Performance
72535   60 mins   C   B, V, CED   P
Concert footage is intermixed with state-of-the-art videos of Fleetwood Mac's Christine McVie, who is enjoying a successful solo venture.
Time Life Multimedia — *Vestron Video*

Christmas Carol, A   1985
Dance/Christmas
82378   90 mins   C   B, V   P
Richard Hilger, J Patrick Martin, Jonathan Fuller, Peter Thoemke, and Stephen D'Ambrose
A visually stimulating dance interpretation of the classic Dickens holiday tale.
Guthrie Theater of Minneapolis — *Apollo Video*

Christmas Carol, A   1984
Fantasy
86319   72 mins   C   B, V   P
Animated
An animated version of the Dickens story.
Burbank Films — *Children's Video Library*

Christmas Carol, A   1951
Drama
11659   86 mins   B/W   B, V   P
Alastair Sim, Kathleen Harrison
Dickens' classic story of how a miserly old man is brought to change on Christmas Eve.
United Artists; Renown Pictures — *United Home Video*

Christmas in July   1940
Comedy
82358   67 mins   C   B, V   P
Dick Powell, Ellen Drew, Raymond Walburn, directed by Preston Sturges
A young man goes on a spending binge when he thinks that he has won a contest. Things take a turn for the worse when he finds out that it was all a practical joke.
Paramount — *MCA Home Video*

Christmas Lilies of the Field   1979
Drama
78969   98 mins   C   B, V   P
Billy Dee Williams, Maria Schell, Fay Hauser, Judith Piquet, directed by Ralph Nelson
An ex-soldier volunteers his skills as a carpenter to help a church build an orphanage for nine children.
Rainbow Productions; Osmond Television — *MPI Home Video*

Christmas on Grandfather's Farm   1959
Christmas
00831   14 mins   C   B, V   P, T
An old-fashioned Christmas celebration at Grandma and Grandpa's big farmhouse reveals what the holiday celebration was like in the 1890's.
Coronet Films — *Blackhawk Films; Coronet Films*

Christmas Raccoons, The   1984
Cartoons/Christmas
73706   30 mins   C   B, V   P
Animated, narrated by Rich Little
The Raccoons have their very own special animated Christmas story to tell, and with a purchase of this videocassette a wand is included.
AM Available
Kevin Gillis — *Embassy Home Entertainment*

Christmas Story, A   1983
Comedy
79206   95 mins   C   B, V   P
Peter Billingsley, Darren McGavin, Melinda Dillon, directed by Bob Clark
An adaptation of the Jean Shepherd story about a little boy's efforts to own a Red Ryder air rifle.
MPAA:PG
MGM/UA Entertainment — *MGM/UA Home Video*

Christmas to Remember, A   1978
Drama/Christmas
70852   96 mins   C   B, V   P
Jason Robards, Eva Marie Saint, Joanne Woodward, directed by George Englund
This film shows the sadly ironic side of the holiday season as a father mourns the early death of his beloved son.
Time/Life Films — *Lightning Video*

Christmas Tree, A/Puss-In-Boots   198?
Cartoons
78900   60 mins   C   B, V   P
Animated
An animated double feature: In "A Christmas Tree," two young children return a stolen Christmas tree from an evil giant, and in "Puss-In-Boots," a magical cat helps his master woo a princess.
Rankin-Bass Productions — *Prism*

Christmas Tree, The   1969
Drama
45054   110 mins   C   B, V   P
William Holden, Virna Lisi, Andre Bourvil, Brook Fuller

When the son of an extremely wealthy businessman contracts radiation poisoning and is given only a few months to live, his father devotes his entire life to the boy's happiness.
MPAA:G
Alan Enterprises — *United Home Video*

Christopher Strong 1933
Drama
76841 77 mins B/W B, V P
Katherine Hepburn, Billie Burke, Colin Clive, Helen Chandler, directed by Dorothy Arzner
A daredevil aviatrix falls in love with a married British statesman who also has a family.
RKO; David O. Selznick — *RKO HomeVideo*

Chu Chu and the Philly Flash 1981
Comedy
58824 102 mins C B, V, CED P
Alan Arkin, Carol Burnett, Jack Warden, Danny Aiello, Ruth Buzzi, Lou Jacobi
A has-been baseball player and a lame dance teacher meet while hustling the same corner; he sells hot watches, she's a one-man band. A briefcase full of government secrets soon involves them with the feds, the mob, and a motley collection of back-alley bums.
MPAA:PG
United Artists; Lawrence Turman; David Foster — *CBS/Fox Video*

C.H.U.D. 1984
Science fiction
76648 90 mins C B, V P
John Heard, Daniel Stern, Christopher Curry, Kim Griest
This program is based on a true New York Times story about life in the tunnels and caverns under the city and the exposure of a possible U.S. government plan to store wastes in these underground passages.
Andrew Bonime — *Media Home Entertainment*

Chump at Oxford, A 1940
Comedy
47140 63 mins B/W B, V, 3/4U P
Stan Laurel, Oliver Hardy, James Finlayson, Wilfrid Lucas, Peter Cushing, Charlie Hall
Street cleaners Laurel and Hardy foil a bank robbery and receive an all-expenses-paid education at Oxford as their reward.
Hal Roach — *Nostalgia Merchant; Blackhawk Films*

Chump at Oxford, A 1940
Comedy
63986 83 mins B/W B, V P, T
Stan Laurel, Oliver Hardy, Jimmy Finlayson, Wilfred Lucas, Peter Cushing
As a reward for foiling a bank robbery, Stan and Ollie receive a free education at Oxford

University. This tape also includes a Charley Chase short, "The Tabasco Kid," made in 1932.
Hal Roach; MGM — *Blackhawk Films*

Churchill and the Generals 1981
Biographical/World War II
81080 180 mins C B, V P
Timothy West, Joseph Cotten, Arthur Hill, Eric Porter, Richard Dysart, narrated by Eric Sevareid
This is the true story of how Winston Churchill led England away from the bleak Dunkirk battle and rallied the Allied generals to a D-Day victory. Based upon Churchill's memoirs.
BBC — *Prism*

Ciao Federico! 1970
Filmmaking/Documentary
88035 45 mins C B, V P
A document of Federico Fellini's filming of Petronius' "Satyricon," portraying the Italian filmmaker's larger-than-life directorial approach and relation with his actors.
Gideon Bachmann — *Mystic Fire Video*

Cincinnati Kid, The 1965
Drama
60591 104 mins C B, V, CED P
Steve McQueen, Edward G. Robinson, Ann-Margret, Tuesday Weld, Karl Malden, Joan Blondell
A young New Orleans gambler is determined to take the expert crown away from an old dapper man known as the King of Stud Poker.
MGM — *MGM/UA Home Video*

Cincinnati Reds: Team Highlights 1984
Baseball
81138 30 mins C B, V P
Pete Rose, Dave Concepcion, Johnny Bench, Dan Driessen, George Foster, Dave Parker
6 pgms
The sagas of "The Big Red Machine" and Pete Rose's return to the Reds as player/manager are chronicled in this series.
1.1979: 25 Men 2.1980: A Good Year 3.1981: Baseball's Real Winners 4.1982: Building For '83 5.1983: A New Beginning 6.1984: The Hustle's Back
Major League Baseball — *Major League Baseball Productions*

Cinderella 1984
Fairy tales
Closed Captioned
73575 60 mins C B, V, CED P
Jennifer Beals, Jean Stapleton, Matthew Broderick, Eve Arden
From the "Faerie Tale Theatre" comes the story of a girl who gets even with her three

stepsisters and ends up going to the ball to
meet the man of her dreams.
Gaylord Productions; Platypus
Productions — *CBS/Fox Video*

Cinderella Ballet   1977
Opera/Dance
84662   75 mins   C   B, V   P
Choreographed by Tom Schilling
The Berlin Comic Opera performs Prokofiev's
fantastical dance-piece. Recorded in Hi-Fi.
Peter Schilling — *V.I.E.W. Video*

Cinderella   1984
Seahawks/NFL '83, The
Football
72941   46 mins   C   B, V, FO   P
Seattle Seahawks
Highlights from the 1983 season of the Seattle
Seahawks and "NFL 1983."
NFL Films — *NFL Films Video*

Cinderfella   1960
Comedy
81812   91 mins   C   B, V   P
*Jerry Lewis, Ed Wynn, Anna Maria Alberghetti,
Judith Anderson, Henry Silva, directed by Frank
Tashlin*
This is a comedic takeoff on the fairy tale where
an orphaned man is forced to cook and clean
for his evil stepmother and her two stepsons.
Available in VHS Stereo and Beta Hi-Fi.
Paramount Pictures — *U.S.A. Home Video*

Cinemagic   1985
Horror/Science fiction
81845   60 mins   C   B, V   P
This is a compilation of four short horror and
science fiction films including "Nightfright," "Dr.
Dobermind," "Illegal Alien" and "The Thing in
the Basement."
Damon Santostefano; Linda Laias — *MPI
Home Video*

Circle of Iron   1978
Adventure
37419   102 mins   C   B, V   P
*Jeff Cooper, David Carradine, Roddy McDowall,
Eli Wallach, Christopher Lee*
Plenty of action and martial arts combat abound
in this story of one man's eternal quest for truth.
MPAA:R
New World — *Embassy Home Entertainment*

Circus Angel   1965
Fantasy
87916   80 mins   B/W   B, V   P
*Philippe Avron, Mirielle Negre, directed by
Albert Lamorisse*
The renowned director of "The Red Balloon"
creates a fantasy about a klutzy burglar
transformed by a found nightgown into an angel.

He begins to serve the dreams and actions of a
odd lot of characters. Subtitled in English.
Cannes Film Festival '65: Best Visual Effects.
FR
French — *Embassy Home Entertainment*

Circus, The/Day's   1928
Pleasure, A
Comedy
81552   105 mins   B/W   B, V   P
*Charlie Chaplin, Merna Kennedy, Allan Garcia,
Harry Crocher, directed by Charlie Chaplin*
A comedy double feature: In "The Circus"
Chaplin falls in love with a circus owner's
equestrian stepdaughter and nothing seems to
go right for a man and his family when they seek
"A Day's Pleasure."
Academy Awards '27/'28: Special Achievement
Award: (Chaplin).
RBC Films — *Playhouse Video*

Circus of Horrors   1960
Horror
70950   87 mins   C   B, V   P
*Anton Diffring, Erika Remberg, Yvonne Monlaur,
Jane Hylton, Kenneth Griffith*
After some permanently disfiguring malpractice,
a plastic surgeon and his assistant run away and
join the circus, where their past haunts them.
AI; Julian Wintle Parkwyn Prod — *THORN
EMI/HBO Video*

Circus World   1964
Drama
16808   137 mins   C   B, V   P
John Wayne, Rita Hayworth
American circus owner in Europe searches for
aerialist he loved 15 years before and whose
daughter he has reared.
Paramount; Samuel Bronston — *United Home
Video; Lightning Video*

Cities at War   1968
World War II/Cities and towns
86629   60 mins   B/W   B, V   P
3 pgms
A series that uses interviews and rare footage to
outline three European cities' experiences
during the war.
*1.The First City-London 2.The Hero City-
Leningrad 3.The Doomed City-Berlin*
Granada TV Prod. — *Simon and Schuster
Video*

Citizen Kane   1941
Drama
00255   120 mins   B/W   B, V   P
*Orson Welles, Joseph Cotton, Agnes
Moorehead*
Citizen Kane is the story of a powerful
newspaper publisher, told by those who thought
they knew him best.

Academy Awards '41: Best Original Screenplay;
N.Y. Film Critics Award '41: Best Motion Picture
RKO — *RKO HomeVideo; King of Video;
VidAmerica; RCA VideoDiscs*

Citizen Kane 1941
Drama
70787 120 mins B/W LV P
Orson Wells, Joseph Cotten, Agnes Moorehead
This special three-disc set, reproduced from a
superior negative, features extensive liner notes
and running commentary by film historian
Robert J. Carringer.
Academy Awards '41: Best Original Screenplay;
N.Y. Film CriticsAward '41: Best Motion Picture
RKO — *The Criterion Collection*

Citizen Soldiers 1985
Documentary/History-US
70686 45 mins C B, V P
*Narrated by Ken Howard, directed by Fred
Warshofsky*
Part of the "In Defense of Freedom" series, this
program traces the history of the United States
Army.
A.B. Marian — *MPI Home Video*

City Heat 1984
Comedy
Closed Captioned
80955 98 mins C B, V, LV P
*Clint Eastwood, Burt Reynolds, Jane Alexander,
Irene Cara, Madeline Kahn, Richard Roundtree,
directed by Richard Benjamin*
A tough cop and a wisecracking private eye
team up to find out who murdered the
detective's partner in Kansas City during the
1930's. Available in VHS and Beta Hi-Fi.
MPAA:PG
Malapso Company; Deliverance
Prods — *Warner Home Video*

City Lights 1931
Comedy
08420 86 mins B/W B, V P
*Charlie Chaplin, Virginia Cherrill, Harry Myers,
Henry Bergman, Jean Harlow, directed by
Charlie Chaplin.*
The story is of a tramp (Chaplin) who, by a
series of lucky accidents, is able to restore the
sight of a blind flowergirl.
United Artists — *Playhouse Video; RCA
VideoDiscs*

City Limits 1985
Science fiction
84795 85 mins C B, V, LV P
*John Stockwell, Kim Cahrall, Darrell Larson,
Rae Dawn Chong, Robby Benson, James Earl
Jones, directed by Aaron Lipstadt*
In a post-apocalyptic city, young people clash as
predictably as government-owned Volvos into
brick walls.

MPAA:PG-13
SHO Films/Videoform Pictures — *Vestron
Video*

City of Gold/Drylanders 19??
Documentary/Canada
65233 92 mins B/W B, V, FO P
This tape combines two riveting Canadian
documentaries: "City of Gold" (1957), which is
about the Klondike Gold Rush of the 1890's,
and "Drylanders" (1962), the story of a city
family's attempt to live on a lonely Sakatchewan
farm.
National Film Board of Canada — *Video
Yesteryear*

City on Fire 1978
Suspense
85365 101 mins C B, V P
*Barry Newman, Susan Clark, Shelley Winters,
Leslie Nielsen*
An arsonist starts a fire that could engulf an
entire city.
MPAA:R
Claude Heroux — *Charter Entertainment*

City's Edge, The 1983
Drama
81507 86 mins C B, V P
A young man becomes involved with the
mysterious residents of a boarding house on the
edge of the ocean.
Australia Film Office — *MGM/UA Home Video*

Clan of the Cave Bear, The 1986
Fantasy/Drama
Closed Captioned
80036 100 mins C B, V P
*Daryl Hannah, James Remar, Pamela Reed,
John Doolittle, directed by Michael Chapman.*
This is the story of a beautiful, blonde-haired
Cro-Magnon woman who was orphaned as a
child and raised by a group of Neanderthals.

MPAA:R
Gerald I Isenberg — *CBS/Fox Video*

Clarence Darrow 1974
Drama/Biographical
56888 90 mins C CED P
Henry Fonda
Henry Fonda's tour-de-force, one-man show
portraying the controversial trial lawyer who
defended over one hundred accused
murderers, including Leopold and Loeb, and
made history in the Scopes Monkey Trial.
Dome Prods — *RCA VideoDiscs*

Clash by Night   1952
Drama
11661   105 mins   B/W   B, V   P
*Barbara Stanwyck, Paul Douglas, Marilyn
Monroe*
Lonely woman marries fishing boat captain and
falls in love with his best friend.
RKO; Jerry Wald; Norman Krasna; Harriet
Parsons — *United Home Video*

Clash of the Titans   1981
Adventure
58702   118 mins   C   B, V, LV,   P
                               CED
*Laurence Olivier, Maggie Smith, Claire Bloom,
Ursula Andress, Burgess Meredith*
Special effects highlight this telling of ancient
Greek mythology and Nordic legends.
MPAA:PG
MGM — *MGM/UA Home Video*

Clash—This Is Video   1985
Clash, The
Music video
84759   31 mins   C   B, V   P
The famed English punk band's best video hits
are seen in this compilation.
CBS/Fox — *CBS/Fox Video*

Class   1983
Comedy
65361   98 mins   C   B, V, LV   P
*Jacqueline Bisset, Rob Lowe, Andrew
McCarthy, Cliff Robertson*
A rich and funny farce, this is the outrageous
story of a young prep school student whose
torrid new love turns out to be his roommate's
mother.
MPAA:R
Martin Ransohoff — *Vestron Video*

Class of '44   1973
Comedy
88039   92 mins   C   B, V   P
*Gary Grimes, Jerry Houser, Oliver Conant,
Deborah Winters*
The sequel to "Summer of '42" wherein three
teenage guys enter college and the military after
high school.
MPAA:PG
Warner Bros. — *Warner Home Video*

Class of 1984   1982
Drama
66092   93 mins   C   B, V, LV,   P
                               CED
*Perry King, Roddy McDowall, Timothy Van
Patten*
An explosive portrait of a school gang on the
loose. A confrontation between the humanity of
the past and a darkly violent future.
MPAA:R

United Film — *Vestron Video*

Class of '63   1973
Drama
81719   74 mins   C   B, V   P
*James Brolin, Joan Hackett, Cliff Gorman,
directed by John Korty*
An unfulfilled woman finally secures the lover
she lost nearly ten years ago at her college
reunion.
MPC/Stonehenge Productions — *Karl/Lorimar
Home Video*

Classic Comedy Video   1949
Sampler
Comedy
76918   78 mins   B/W   B, V   P
Bud Abbott, Lou Costello, Moe Howard
This is a collection of classic comedy shorts
featuring Amos and Andy, The Three Stooges,
and Abbott and Costello.
Max Fleischer, et al — *United Home Video*

Classic Cooking   1985
Cookery
85140   60 mins   C   B, V   P
A video cookbook sampler featuring nine
recipes from start to finish, including Spinach
Lasagna.
AM Available
Barrons Educational Series — *Barron's
Educational Series*

Classic Creatures: Return   1983
of the Jedi
Filmmaking
Closed Captioned
82333   49 mins   C   B, V   P
Hosted by Carrie Fisher and Billy Dee Williams
This is a behind-the-scenes look at how
Hollywood's special effects wizards gave life to
the creatures of the "Star Wars" galaxy.
Available in VHS and Beta Hi-Fi.
Lucasfilm Ltd — *Playhouse Video*

Classic Performances   1984
Music-Performance
79712   150 mins   C   B, V   P
Maria Chiara, Kirite Kanawa 3   pgms
Three of the greatest operas and ballets are
now available in one package.
1. Messiah 2.Aida 3.Die Fledermaus
Metropolitan Opera et al — *THORN EMI/HBO
Video*

Claude Bolling: Concerto   1982
for Classic Guitar and
Jazz Piano
Music-Performance
47810   ? mins   C   LV   P
Pianist George Shearing appears with guitarist
Angel Romero, drummer Shelly Manne, and

bassist Brian Torff in this definitive performance of Bolling's piece. In stereo.
Unknown — *Pioneer Artists*

Claws — 1977
Adventure
80789   100 mins   C   B, V   R, P
Leon Ames, Jason Evers, Anthony Caruso, Glenn Sipes, Carla Layton
A woodsman, a game commissioner and an Indian band together to stop a grizzly bear who is killing residents of a small Alaskan town.
MPAA:PG
Alaska Pictures — *Video Gems*

Clay Pigeon, The — 1949
Drama
73693   63 mins   B/W   B, V   P
Bill Williams, Barbara Hale, Richard Loo, directed by Richard Fleischer
A veteran wrongly accused of treason goes after the man who set him up.
RKO — *RKO Home Video*

Clean Slate (Coup de Torchon) — 1981
Comedy-Drama
81442   128 mins   C   B, V   P
Philippe Noiret, Isabelle Huppert, Jean-Pierre Marielle, Stephane Audran, directed by Bertrand Tavernier
An easy-going police officer has a sudden change of heart when he starts killing off residents of a small French West African village in 1938. Available in French with English subtitles or dubbed into English.
FR
Adolphe Viezzi — *Embassy Home Entertainment*

Clearing the Range — 1931
Western
11660   60 mins   B/W   B, V   P
Hoot Gibson
A cringing coward by day becomes a fearless champion by night in this western.
M H Hoffman — *Video Connection; Discount Video Tapes; United Home Video*

Cleopatra — 1963
Drama
08431   246 mins   C   B, V, CED   P
Elizabeth Taylor, Richard Burton, Rex Harrison, Pamela Brown, directed by Joseph L. Mankiewicz
After the death of Julius Caesar, Cleopatra, Queen of Egypt, becomes infatuated with Mark Antony. In stereo.
Academy Awards '63: Best Cinematography.
20th Century Fox; Walter Wanger — *CBS/Fox Video*

Cleopatra Jones — 1973
Crime-Drama
85657   89 mins   C   B, V   P
Tamara Dobson, Shelley Winters, Bernie Casey, directed by Jack Starrett
A kung-fu woman cop butts heads with a fat crime queenpin.
William Tennant — *Warner Home Video*

Clergyman's Daughter, The — 1984
Mystery
80450   60 mins   C   B, V   P
James Warwick, Francesca Annis
A clergyman's daughter calls upon detectives Tommy and Tuppence to investigate some murders at the family's country house. Based on the Agatha Christie story.
London Weekend Television — *Pacific Arts Video*

Cleveland Browns 1985 Team Highlights — 1985
Football
86797   23 mins   C   B, V   P
Glimpses of the Browns' '85 season are herewith preserved, including the playoff battle they lost to Miami.
NFL Films — *NFL Films Video*

Cleveland Indians: Team Highlights — 1984
Baseball
81139   30 mins   C   B, V   P
Julio Franco, Bert Blyleven, Andre Thornton, Pat Tabler 5 pgms
This series highlights the Cleveland Indians' best moments from their past seasons.
1.1978: Good Vibrations 2.1981:A Baseball Tradition 3.1982: 50 Years at Municipal Stadium 4.1983: Building An Indian Uprising 5.1984: It's A Whole New Ballgame
Major League Baseball — *Major League Baseball Productions*

Cliffhangers — 194?
Movie and TV trailers
87669   57 mins   C   B, V   P
2   pgms
Two volumes of collected movie serial coming attractions from the heyday of Saturday matinees, including "Blackhawk," "Gangbusters," "Captain America," "Mysterious Dr. Satan" and "Tim Tyler's Luck."
Captain Bijou; Various producers — *Captain Bijou*

Cliffhangers, Comebacks, and Character — 1982
Football
47714   23 mins   C   B, V, FO   P

Team highlights of the 1981 San Diego Chargers, who had the most prolific offense in NFL history.
NFL Films — *NFL Films Video*

Climax Blues Band—Live from London   1985
Music-Performance
85833   60 mins   C   B, V   P
The British blues band performs at London's Marquee Club, featuring "Gotta Have More Love," and "Couldn't Get it Right."
RCA Video Prod. — *RCA/Columbia Pictures Home Video*

Clinic, The   1983
Comedy
77016   95 mins   C   B, V   P
Chris Haywood, Simon Burke, Gerda Nicolson
A humorous look at an average day in a VD clinic.
Film House; Generation Films — *VidAmerica*

Cloak and Dagger   1984
Suspense/Adventure
Closed Captioned
80074   101 mins   C   B, V, LV   P
Dabney Coleman, Henry Thomas, Michael Murphy, directed by Richard Franklin
A young boy depends upon his imaginary friend to help him out when some agents are after his video game. Available in Beta Hi-Fi Stereo and VHS Dolby B Stereo.
MPAA:PG
Allan Carr; Universal — *MCA Home Video*

Clockwork Orange, A   1971
Science fiction
54118   137 mins   C   B, V, LV   P
Malcolm McDowell, Patrick Magee, Adrienne Corri, directed by Stanley Kubrick
The head of a gang of punks is imprisoned for rape. When he is released he finds the world to be even more violent, especially when he is brutally beaten by his old adversaries. Based on the novel by Anthony Burgess.
MPAA:R
Warner Bros, Stanley Kubrick — *Warner Home Video; RCA VideoDiscs*

Clodhopper, The   1917
Drama
84936   47 mins   B/W   B, V   P
Charles Ray, Margery Wilson
A drama of a young man traveling to New York to find fame and fortune. Music by R. Cameron Menzies.
Charles Ray Films — *Blackhawk Films*

Clones, The   1973
Science fiction
84100   90 mins   C   B, V   P

Michael Greene, Gregory Sierra, directed by Paul Hunt and Lamar Card
A doctor discovers a government experiment engineered to murder him with a perfect clone.
MPAA:PG
Film Makers Intl — *Lightning Video*

Clones of Bruce Lee, The   1980
Adventure/Martial arts
50731   87 mins   C   B, V   P
Dragon Lee, Bruce Le, Bruce Lai, Bruce Thai, directed by Joseph Kong
A Kung-Fu fan's delight, as gallant warriors from the Far East battle to reign supreme over the land of exotic self-defense.
MPAA:R
Newport Releasing — *Media Home Entertainment*

Clonus Horror, The   1979
Science fiction
85921   90 mins   C   B, V   P
Timothy Donnelly, Keenan Wynn, Peter Graves, Dick Sargent, Paulette Breen
In the tradition of "Coma," this film is about a project that freezes bodies alive to use their parts in surgery. A scientist finds out and tries to tell the world.
Group 1 — *Lightning Video*

Close Encounters of the Third Kind (The Special Edition)   1980
Science fiction
Closed Captioned
54107   152 mins   C   B, V, LV   P
Richard Dreyfuss, Teri Garr, Melinda Dillon, Francois Truffaut, directed by Steven Spielberg
A middle class American couple, who have had encounters of the first and second kinds, sighting UFO's and finding physical evidence of them, are determined to have the third encounter—actual contact with the occupants. In this special edition, which contains about 15 extra minutes, the man does go inside the UFO and makes contact.
MPAA:PG
Columbia Pictures — *RCA/Columbia Pictures Home Video; RCA VideoDiscs*

Closely Watched Trains   1966
Drama
72927   89 mins   C   B, V   P
A young man who works in a train station during World War Two is going through his rites of passage. This film is subtitled.
CZ
Filmove Studio Barrandov — *RCA/Columbia Pictures Home Video*

Cloud Dancer   1980
Drama
66630   108 mins   C   B, V   P

David Carradine, Jennifer O'Neill, Joseph
Bottoms, directed by Barry Brown
A champion acrobatic trapeze flier selfishly
pursues his career to the exclusion of those who
care about him.
MPAA:PG
Blossom Pictures; Melvin Simon
Productions — Prism

Clouds Over Europe   1939
Mystery
81458   82 mins   B/W   B, V, LV   P
Laurence Olivier, Valerie Hobson, Ralph
Richardson, directed by Tim Whelan
A test pilot and a man from Scotland Yard team
up to find out why new bomber planes are
disappearing.
Alexander Korda — Embassy Home
Entertainment

Clown, The   1952
Comedy-Drama
58870   91 mins   B/W   B, V   P
Red Skelton, Jane Greer, Tim Considine, Steve
Forrest
A derelict ex-comedian, after several attempts
at a comeback, faces his last chance in a make-
or-break situation.
MGM — MGM/UA Home Video

Clown Princes of   1958
Hollywood, The
Comedy
84941   25 mins   B/W   B, V   P
Charles Chaplin, Buster Keaton, Harold Lloyd,
Oliver Hardy
A compilation of clips from the silent screen's
funniest men.
Pathe; Schenck, Sennett et al. — Blackhawk
Films

Clowns, The   1971
Drama
03560   90 mins   C   B, V   P
Directed by Federico Fellini
Directed by Federico Fellini, this movie
recreates some of the most famous clown acts
in circus history, presents the two major types of
clowns, and suggests that the world is peopled
with clowns.
Universal — Media Home Entertainment;
Discount Video Tapes

Clue   1985
Comedy/Mystery
Closed Captioned
88294   96 mins   C   B, V, LV   P
Leslie Ann Warren, Tim Curry, Martin Mull,
Madeleine Kahn, Michael McKean, Christopher
Lloyd, Eileen Brennan, directed by Jonathan
Lynn
A comedy/mystery filmization of the popular
board game, with three alternate endings, all of
which are fortunately included in the video
version.
MPAA:PG
Paramount; Jon Peters; John Landis; Peter
Guber; George Folsey Jr. — Paramount Home
Video

Coach   1978
Comedy
63893   100 mins   C   B, V   P
Cathy Lee Crosby, Michael Biehn, Keenan
Wynn, Sidney Wicks
A female coach is hired to make a losing high
school boys' basketball team into a
championship one.
MPAA:G
Mark Tenser — Media Home Entertainment

Coal Miner's Daughter   1980
Drama
45104   125 mins   C   B, V   P
Sissy Spacek, Tommy Lee Jones
The rags-to-riches story of how Loretta Lynn
became "the queen of country music."
Academy Awards '80: Best Actress (Spacek).
MPAA:PG
Universal, Bernard Schwartz — MCA Home
Video; RCA VideoDiscs

Coast to Coast   1980
Comedy-Drama
54673   95 mins   C   B, V, LV   P
Dyan Cannon, Robert Blake, Quinn Redeker,
Michael Lerner, Maxine Stuart, Bill Lucking,
directed by Joseph Sargent
A woman whose playboy husband is trying to
have her judged insane rather than grant her the
divorce she wants escapes from an East Coast
hospital and hitches a ride with a trucker. The
action centers on their cross-country trip, during
which they are pursued by a detective (hired by
the husband) and a finance company thug who
is trying to repossess the trucker's vehicle.
MPAA:PG
Paramount — Paramount Home Video

Coaster Adventure of the   1981
John F. Leavitt
Boating/Documentary
73567   91 mins   C   B, V   P
This movie tells the story of a young man who
built a 97-foot wooden schooner and became a
modern day merchant adventurer.
Jon Craig Cloutier; Atlantic Film
Group — Atlantic Film Group I

Cobham Meets Bellson   1983
Music-Performance
84645   36 mins   C   B, V   P
Billy Cobham, Louis Bellson with the Louis
Bellson Big Band

A thrilling performance by the two leading big band drummers highlights this concert taped in Switzerland. Recorded in Hi-Fi Stereo.
Stanley Dorfman — *V.I.E.W. Video*

Coca-Cola Kid, The   1985
Comedy
Closed Captioned
82428   94 mins   C   B, V, LV,   P
                                      CED
Eric Roberts, Greta Scacchi, George Kerr, directed by Dusan Makavejev
A market researcher is sent to Australia to boost sales of Coca-Cola. He is hampered by an amorous secretary, his resemblance to a C.I.A. agent, and a homegrown soda entrepreneur.
MPAA:R
Film Gallery — *Vestron Video*

Cocaine Cowboys   1979
Drama
42913   90 mins   C   B, V   P
Jack Palance, Andy Warhol, Tom Sullivan, Suzanna Love
This modern day thriller tells the story of a rock and roll band smuggling cocaine to help their expenses and, in doing so, run afoul of the mob.
MPAA:R
International Harmony Films — *Media Home Entertainment; Video Gems*

Cocaine Fiends   1937
Drama/Exploitation
03854   74 mins   B/W   B, V   P
Lois January, Noel Madison, directed by W.A. Conner
A camp classic from the 1930's warning of the evils of cocaine. A brother and sister are led to the depths of degradation upon trying cocaine; heroin addiction, prostitution, and suicide are the inevitable results.
New Line Cinema — *Media Home Entertainment; Hollywood Home Theater; Video Dimensions; Discount Video Tapes*

Cocaine: One Man's   1983
Seduction
Drama/Drugs
71335   97 mins   C   B, V   P
Dennis Weaver, Karen Grassle, Pamela Bellwood, David Aykroyd, directed by Paul Wendkos
This docudrama shows how the elite sellers of cocaine often use subtle inducements in order to bring new clients into their expensive world.
Charles Fries Productions — *U.S.A. Home Video*

Cockeyed Cavaliers   1934
Comedy
44809   70 mins   B/W   B, V   P, T
Wheeler and Woolsey, Dorothy Lee, Thelma Todd

Wheeler and Woolsey are stockaded for stealing the Duke's horses and carriage. To escape jail they swap clothes with some drunken royalty.
RKO — *Blackhawk Films*

Cockfighter   1974
Drama
74082   84 mins   C   B, V   P
Warren Oates
This is the story of a man so obsessed with cockfighting he loses his money, possessions and lover because of it.
MPAA:R
Roger Corman — *Embassy Home Entertainment*

Cocoon   1985
Science fiction/Fantasy
Closed Captioned
84882   117 mins   C   B, V, LV   P
Wilford Brimley, Brian Dennehy, Steve Guttenberg, Don Ameche, Tahnee Welch, Hume Cronyn, Jessica Tandy, Gwen Verdon, Maureen Stapleton, Tyrone Power Jr, directed by Ron Howard
A group of oldsters stumble upon the hidden secret headquarters of four aliens who have come to Earth on an important mission. In Hi-Fi Stereo.
MPAA:PG-13
Richard D. Zanuck, David Brown, Lili Fini Zanuck — *CBS/Fox Video*

C.O.D.   1983
Comedy
80688   96 mins   C   B, V   P
Corinne Alphen, Carol Davis
Two comedy advertising executives must create an exciting ad campaign for the Beaver Bra Company.
MPAA:PG
Lone Star Pictures International — *Vestron Video*

Code Name: Emerald   1985
War-Drama
Closed Captioned
84421   95 mins   C   B, V   P
Ed Harris, Max Von Sydow, Eric Stoltz, Horst Buckholz
A tale of espionage surrounding D-Day and a captured lieutenant who knows the Allies' plans.
MPAA:PG
Martin Starger — *Playhouse Video*

Code of Silence   1985
Crime-Drama
82260   100 mins   C   B, V   P
Chuck Norris, Henry Silva, Bert Remsen, Molly Hagan, Nathan Davis, directed by Andy Davis
A police sergeant has a tough decision to make—should he inform on a fellow cop who

shot an innocent Hispanic youth during a drug
bust or keep it to himself?
MPAA:R
Orion Pictures — *THORN EMI/HBO Video*

Cold Feet   1984
Comedy-Drama
80136   96 mins   C   B, V   P
Griffin Dunne, Blanche Baker, Mark Cronogue
A television director tired of his wife leaves her
for a lab researcher.
MPAA:PG
Cinecom International Films — *CBS/Fox
Video*

Cold River   1981
Drama
65406   94 mins   C   B, V, CED   P
An experienced Adirondacks guide takes his
two children on an extended trip through the
Adirondacks. For the children, it's a fantasy
vacation until their father succumbs to a heart
attack in the chilly mountains. "Cold River" is a
journey of survival, and an exploration of human
relationships.
MPAA:PG
Fred G Sullivan — *CBS/Fox Video*

Cold Room, The   1984
Mystery/Suspense
76862   95 mins   C   B, V   P
*George Segal, Renee Soutenjijk, Amanda Pays,
Warran Clarke, Anthony Higgins*
A teenaged girl on vacation with her father in
East Berlin discovers the horrors hidden in an
antiquated hotel room.
Mark Forstater; Bob Weis — *Media Home
Entertainment*

Cold Steel for Tortuga   1965
Adventure
86858   95 mins   C   B, V   P
*Guy Madison, Rick Battaglia, Inge Schoener,
directed by Luigi Capuano*
An Italian epic about a mercenary rescuing his
woman and his gold from an evil governor.
Dubbed.
Liber Films — *Lightning Video*

Cold Sweat   1974
Crime-Drama
85780   94 mins   C   B, V   P
*Charles Bronson, Jill Ireland, Liv Ullman, James
Mason*
A gang of hoods hold a woman hostage as her
brutal-minded husband quietly kills them off one
by one.
MPAA:PG
Foreign — *Video Gems*

Colditz Story, The   1955
War-Drama
63343   93 mins   B/W   B, V   P
*John Mills, Eric Portman, Lionel Jeffries, Bryan
Forbes, Ian Carmichael*
Prisoners of war from the Allied countries join
together in an attempt to escape from Colditz, a
castle-prison deep within the Third Reich,
reputed to be escape-proof.
British Lion; Ivan Foxwell — *THORN EMI/HBO
Video*

Coleman's Guide to   1986
Camping
Camps and camping
87746   60 mins   C   B, V   P
Bruce Jenner
Coleman Camping Products presents this
instructional tape of camping tips for the
neophyte.
Twin Tower; Video Publishing — *Twin Tower
Enterprises*

Colgate Comedy Hour,   195?
The
Variety
63853   55 mins   B/W   B, V   P
*Eddie Cantor, Brian Donlevy, Eddie Fisher,
Frank Sinatra, Harold Arlen*
Eddie Cantor does a "Maxie the Taxi" sketch,
then joins Brian Donlevy for a Western sketch.
Eddie Fisher and Frank Sinatra sing, and Harold
Arlen plays a medley of his classic songs.
NBC — *Hollywood Home Theater*

Colgate Comedy Hour,   1953
The
Comedy
75637   60 mins   C   B, V   P
Bud Abbott, Lou Costello
This comedy is based around President
Eisenhower's inauguration. Abbott and Costello
end up destroying the ball with their skits.
NBC — *Great Comedy Shows*

Colgate Comedy Hour I,   1951
The
Variety
79238   60 mins   B/W   B, V, 3/4U   P
*Bud Abbott, Lou Costello, Vera Zorina, Joe Kirk,
Bobby Barber*
A series of comic complications arise as Abbott
and Costello take a cruise to Paris.
NBC — *Shokus Video*

Colgate Comedy Hour,   1952
The
Variety
79239   60 mins   C   B, V, 3/4U   P
*Keefe Braselle, Sonja Henie, Bud Abbott, Lou
Costello*

Abbott and Costello take a tour of a movie studio's prop department and meet up with the Creature From The Black Lagoon, plus Sonja Henie ice skates in this vintage 1952 kinescope.
NBC — *Shokus Video*

Colgate Comedy Hour, III, The   1951
Comedy
77188   60 mins   B/W   B, V   P
Bud Abbott, Lou Costello, Lon Chaney Jr
Abbott and Costello wander into Lon Chaney Jr's haunted mansion and perform a comic opera "Don Juan Costello" in this Kinescope that includes the original commercials.
NBC — *Shokus Video*

Colgate Comedy Hour, IV, The   1951
Comedy
77189   60 mins   B/W   B, V   P
Bud Abbott, Lou Costello, Charles Laughton
Bud and Lou head off to New York to make an appearance at the premiere of their latest movie.
NBC — *Shokus Video*

Colgate Comedy Hour (The Eddie Cantor Show)   1952
Variety
42964   60 mins   B/W   B, V, FO   P
Eddie Cantor, Kirk Douglas, Robert Clary
Aired January 20, 1952, this program stars Eddie Cantor singing and in comedy routines such as "Cantor Goes to College" and "The Detective Story," with Eddie playing the lead.
NBC — *Video Yesteryear*

Collector, The   1965
Drama
13245   119 mins   C   B, V   P
Terence Stamp, Samantha Eggar, Maurice Dallimore, directed by William Wyler
Lonely clerk kidnaps a girl and locks her in the cellar hoping she will fall in love with him.
Filmdoms Famous Five '65: Best Actress (Eggar); Outstanding Director (Wyler).
Columbia — *RCA/Columbia Pictures Home Video; RCA VideoDiscs*

Collectors Item: The Left Fist of David   1960
Mystery
38999   27 mins   B/W   B, V, FO   P
Vincent Price, Peter Lorre
The pilot program for a TV series that was never produced, featuring Price and Lorre as a pair of art dealers who become embroiled in mysterious doings.
CBS — *Video Yesteryear*

College   1927
Comedy
10093   60 mins   B/W   B, V   P, T
Buster Keaton, A. Cornwall, directed by James W. Horne
Keaton graduates valedictorian from high school, tries out for every sport in college, and works as a soda jerk. Musical score by John Muri.
United Artists — *Blackhawk Films; Video Dimensions; Video Yesteryear*

Colonel Effingham's Raid   1945
Comedy
81737   70 mins   B/W   B, V   P
Joan Bennett, Charles Coburn, William Eythe
A retired army colonel uses military tactics to keep an old historical courthouse open and defeat some crooked politicians in the process.
20th Century Fox — *Kartes Video Communications*

Color Adventures of Superman, The   194?
Cartoons
57350   52 mins   C   B, V, FO   P
Animated
Seven cartoon adventures of the Man of Steel, as animated by the Fleischer Studio; produced between 1941 and 1943. Titles include "Superman," "The Mechanical Monsters," "The Magnetic Telescope," "The Japoteurs," "The Bulleteers," "Jungle Drums," and "The Mummy Strikes."
Max Fleischer — *Video Yesteryear*

Color Me Beautiful   1984
Cosmetology
76932   60 mins   C   B, V   S
Author Carole Jackson and Image Consultant Cindy Howard demonstrate the "Color Me Beautiful" make up process for women. A book also comes with a purchase of the videocassette.
AM Available
C.B. Wismar — *Kartes Video Communications*

Color Them Tough   1981
Football
51169   23 mins   C   B, V, FO   R, P
New York Jets
1980 never materialized for the Jets the way they, their fans, and the experts had expected. Key injuries, offensive problems, and defensive inconsistency provided the problems. Still, they did manage to score upsets over strong clubs like Houston, Miami, and Atlanta.
NFL Films — *NFL Films Video*

Colorado   1940
Western
64390   54 mins   B/W   B, V, 3/4U   P
Roy Rogers, Gabby Hayes

Roy and Gabby bring law and order to the untamed Colorado Territory.
Republic — *Nostalgia Merchant; Discount Video Tapes*

Colt Is My Law (Mi   197?
Revolver es la Ley), The
Western
88315   95 mins   C   B, V   P
Anthony Clark, Lucy Gilly, Michael Martin
Bandits steal a railroad-funding gold shipment, and are pursued relentlessly by mysterious masked men.
SP
Pegaso Film — *JCI Video*

Columbia Pictures   1980
Cartoons Volume I: Mr.
Magoo
Comedy/Cartoons
44848   40 mins   C   B, V   P
Animated
The famous near-sighted old codger is seen in five of his adventures: "Barefoot Flatfoot," "Bungled Bungalow," "Bwana Magoo," "Destination Magoo," and "Madcap Magoo."
UPA — *RCA/Columbia Pictures Home Video*

Columbia Pictures   1980
Cartoons Volume II: Mr.
Magoo
Comedy/Cartoons
44849   40 mins   C   B, V   P
Animated
Mr. Magoo, through the voice of Jim Backus, entertains in his near-sighted fashion in: "Magoo Beats the Heat," "Magoo Breaks Par," "Magoo Goes Overboard," "Magoo Goes West," and "Magoo Saves the Bank."
UPA — *RCA/Columbia Pictures Home Video*

Columbia Pictures   1980
Cartoons Volume III:
Gerald McBoing-Boing
Cartoons
44850   30 mins   C   B, V   P
Animated
This is a compilation of four Gerald McBoing-Boing cartoons: "Gerald McBoing-Boing," "Gerald McBoing-Boing on the Planet Moon," "Gerald McBoing-Boing's Symphony," and "How Now Boing-Boing."
UPA — *RCA/Columbia Pictures Home Video*

Columbia Pictures   1980
Cartoons Volume IV: UPA
Classics
Cartoons
44839   40 mins   C   B, V   P
Animated
A collection of five favorite cartoons from UPA: "Christopher Crumpet's Playmate," "The

---

Emperor's New Clothes," "The Jay Walker," "The Man on the Flying Trapeze," and "The Tell Tale Heart."
UPA — *RCA/Columbia Pictures Home Video*

Columbia Pictures   1983
Cartoons Volume V: Mr.
Magoo
Comedy/Cartoons
63444   60 mins   C   B, V   P
Animated
Eight more misadventures with the near-sighted Mr. Magoo: "Stage Door Magoo," "Magoo's Glorious July 4th," "Sloppy Jalopy," "Magoo's Homecoming," "Trouble Indemnity," "Fuddy Duddy Buddy," "Magoo's Masquerade" and "Magoo Saves the Bank."
UPA — *RCA/Columbia Pictures Home Video*

Columbia Pictures   19??
Cartoons, Volume VI
Cartoons
66013   60 mins   C   B, V   P
Animated
Eight classic cartoons: "Pete Hothead," "Unicorn in the Garden," "Family Circus," "Ballet-Oop," "Christopher Crumpet," "Popcorn Story," "The Rise of Duton Lang," and "Four Wheels, No Breaks."
Columbia — *RCA/Columbia Pictures Home Video*

Columbia Pictures   196?
Cartoons, Volume VII
Comedy
68265   60 mins   C   B, V   P
Animated, voice of Jim Backus
Eight more amusing adventures of Mr. Magoo.
UPA — *RCA/Columbia Pictures Home Video*

Columbia Pictures   1954
Cartoons, Volume VIII
Cartoons
87758   60 mins   C   B, V   P
Eight Mr. Magoo cartoons, including "Rockhound Magoo," "Gumshoe Magoo" and "When Magoo Flew."
Academy Awards '54: Best Cartoon Short Subject ("When Magoo Flew").
Columbia Pictures — *RCA/Columbia Pictures Home Video*

Coma   1978
Suspense
44641   113 mins   C   B, V, LV,   P
                            CED
Genevieve Bujold, Michael Douglas, Elizabeth Ashley, Rip Torn, Richard Widmark, Lois Chiles, Harry Rhodes, directed by Michael Crichton
A young doctor at Boston hospital finds that patients, one of which is her best friend, suffer irreparable brain damage when supposed minor operations are performed. All these operations

---

take place in the same operating room. Based on the novel by Robin Cook.
MPAA:PG
MGM — *MGM/UA Home Video*

Comancheros, The   1961
Western
64903   108 mins   C   B, V, CED   P
John Wayne, Stuart Whitman, Nehemiah Persoff
Wayne, a Texas Ranger, penetrates the ranks of the Comancheros, an outlaw gang supplying guns and liquor to the dreaded Comanches.
20th Century Fox — *CBS/Fox Video*

Combat America   1944
Aeronautics
84911   61 mins   C   B, V   P
American B-17's, in vintage footage, stomp the German front in World War II.
Interurban Films — *Interurban Films; Victory Video*

Combat Diary—Volume 1   1942
World War II/Documentary
81606   56 mins   B/W   B, V   P
This volume covers the combat history of 24th and 32nd Infantry Divisions during World War II.
U.S. Office of War Information — *Victory Video*

Come Back   1984
Champions/NFL '83
Football
72936   46 mins   C   B, V, FO   P
Detroit Lions
Highlights from the Detroit Lions' 1983 season and "NFL 83."
NFL Films — *NFL Films Video*

Come Back Little Reba   1986
Drama
Closed Captioned
87605   60 mins   C   V   P
A semi-educational film about a young black boy and his lovable aging dog.
AM Available EL, FR
J. Fuccello — *Club Reba Video*

Come Back to the 5 and   1982
Dime Jimmy Dean, Jimmy
Dean
Drama
60559   109 mins   C   B, V, CED   P
Sandy Dennis, Cher, Karen Black, Sudie Bond, directed by Robert Altman
In 1975, the workers and customers of a small town 5 and Dime are celebrating the 20th anniversary of the death of James Dean. A complex look into the past begins when a woman announces that her son is the product of a one-night stand with the late actor twenty years ago.

Cinecom Intl — *Embassy Home Entertainment*

Come Dancing with the   1986
Kinks
Music video
86792   35 mins   C   B, V   P
Ray Davies leads the sturdy English band in their biggest hits, including concert footage of "Lola" and "You Really Got Me."
RCA Video — *RCA/Columbia Pictures Home Video*

Come On, Cowboys   1937
Western
64419   54 mins   B/W   B, V, 3/4U   P
Bob Livingston, Ray Corrigan
The Three Mesquiteers rescue an old circus friend from certain death.
Republic — *Nostalgia Merchant; Discount Video Tapes*

Comeback   1983
Drama/Music
65659   105 mins   C   B, V   P
Eric Burdon
This is the story of a disillusioned rock star who gives up his life in the fast lane and tries to go back to his roots... and to himself.
TeleCulture Inc — *MGM/UA Home Video*

Comeback Kid, The   1980
Comedy
87614   97 mins   C   B, V   P
John Ritter, Susan Dey, directed by Peter Levin
An ex-big league basball player is connived into coaching an urban team of smarmy street youths, and falls for their playground supervisor.
Louis Randolph — *Charter Entertainment*

Comedian, The   1957
Drama
86033   90 mins   B/W   B, V   P
Mickey Rooney, written by Rod Serling
An uncorrigible comedian makes life miserable for his family in this made-for-TV live play.
Rod Serling — *MGM/UA Home Video*

Comedies, Cartoons and   1985
Bloopers I
Cartoons/Outtakes and bloopers
81891   58 mins   C   B, V   P
Animated
Here is a collection of classic cartoons including "One Froggy Evening," "The Dove," "You Oughta Be in Pictures" and the legendary "Coal Black and the Sebben Dwarfs". Some cartoons are in black and white.
Warner Bros. — *San Francisco Rush Video*

Comedies, Cartoons and Bloopers II   196?
Cartoons/Outtakes and bloopers
81892   52 mins   C   B, V   P
Animated
Here is a collection of such comedic oddities as
"Dumb Dicks," "Shivering Shakespeare" and
"Bambi Meets Godzilla," with some segments
in black and white.
Hal Roach — *San Francisco Rush Video*

Comedy 1: Trailers on Tape   1984
Movie and TV trailers/Comedy
66479   60 mins   C   B, V   P
Over thirty theatrical trailers for comedy films
are compiled on this tape, including "Paper
Moon," "Born Yesterday," "Airplane," "Monty
Python and the Holy Grail," "The Producers,"
"Some Like It Hot," "The Errand Boy" and "The
Seven Year Itch." Some black-and-white
segments.
20th Century Fox et al — *San Francisco Rush
Video*

Comedy and Kid Stuff I   1952
Comedy
33688   120 mins   C   B, V, 3/4U   P
A collection of four light-hearted shows from the
50's including single episodes from "The Burns
and Allen Show," and "I Married Joan," "Winky
Dink," with host Jack Barry, and "Carson's
Cellar," starring a twenty-five year old Johnny
Carson and the late Jack Bailey.
CBS et al — *Shokus Video*

Comedy and Kid Stuff II   195?
Comedy
33689   120 mins   C   B, V, 3/4U   P
Four episodes from popular TV shows of the
1950's; "The Burns and Allen 1951 Christmas
Show," "The Abbott and Costello Show,"
featuring the "Who's on First" routine and the
retired actor's home, "Howdy Doody," and "The
Lucy Show." Some black and white.
CBS et al — *Shokus Video*

Comedy and Kid Stuff III   1959
Comedy
77193   120 mins   B/W   B, V   P
*Jack Benny, Art Linkletter, Andy Devine, Bob
Hope, Senor Wences*
A collection of three comedies from the 50's:
Jack Benny clowns around with Bob Hope on
"The Jack Benny Hour", Art Linkletter talks to
kids on "House Party" and Andy Devine hosts a
childrens show, "Andy's Gang."
CBS et al — *Shokus Video*

Comedy and Kid Stuff, IV   1955
Comedy/Variety
87204   115 mins   B/W   B, V, 3/4U   P

*Jack Carter, Don Ameche, Buffalo Bob, Phineas
T. Bluster*
Four episodes of various '50's TV shows: "The
Goldbergs," "The Farmer Alfalfa Show,"
"Howdy Doody" and "Saturday Night Revue."
CBS et al. — *Shokus Video*

Comedy II: Trailers on Tape   1985
Movie and TV trailers/Comedy
81888   59 mins   B/W   B, V   P
The laughs abound in this collection of trailers
from such comedy classics as "My Little
Chickadee," "The Road to Morocco," "The
Fortune Cookie" and "The Thrill of It All;" with
color segments.
Universal et al — *San Francisco Rush Video*

Comedy Classics of Mack Sennett and Hal Roach, The   1915
Comedy
78103   51 mins   B/W   B, V, FO   P
This program presents three comedy silent
films: "Love, Loot and Crash"; "Looking for
Trouble"; and "A Desperate Scoundrel."
Mack Sennett; Hal Roach — *Video Yesterycar*

Comedy Festival #1   193?
Comedy
00430   60 mins   B/W   B, V   P
Collection of three comic films: "Speed in the
Gay Nineties," with Andy Clyde; "Disorder in the
Court," with Three Stooges; "Hail Brother," with
Billy Gilbert.
Columbia et al — *Hollywood Home Theater*

Comedy Festival #2   193?
Comedy
00434   60 mins   B/W   B, V   P
Collection of Comedy films: "Bashful Romeo,"
with Gil Lamb; "Super Snooper," with Andy
Clyde; "Super Stupid," with Billy Gilbert.
RKO et al — *Hollywood Home Theater*

Comedy Festival #3   193?
Comedy
00438   60 mins   B/W   B, V   P
Collection of comic films: "Big Flash," with
Harry Langdon; "Half A Hero;" "Pardon My
Papa," with Shirley Temple.
Educational et al — *Hollywood Home Theater*

Comedy Festival #4   193?
Comedy
00442   60 mins   B/W   B, V   P
A collection of comic films: "His Weak
Moment," "Fainting Lover," "Shopping with the
Wife."
Mack Sennett et al — *Hollywood Home
Theater*

Comedy in Music 1956
Comedy/Variety
85160 60 mins B/W B, V P
Victor Borge
An entire hour of the Danish comic's musical hilarity.
CBS — *Video Yesteryear*

Comedy Music Videos 1986
Music video/Comedy
82454 60 mins C B, V, LV P
Mel Brooks, John Candy, Eugene Levy, Dan Aykroyd, John Belushi, Martin Mull, Eric Idle
Thirteen vignettes by well-known comics combine music with humor. Included are: "Rapmaster Ronnie," the Rutles' "Piggy in the Middle" and a parody of the Rod Stewart hit "Do You Think I'm Sexy?"
Vestron Video — *Vestron Video*

Comedy Tonight 1977
Comedy-Performance
59307 76 mins C B, V, CED P
Hosted by David Steinberg, Andy Kaufman, Robin Williams, Gallagher, Ed Bluestone, Richard Libertini, McIntyre Dixon
Los Angeles' "Improv" club is the scene for this night of stand-up comedy. Andy Kaufman performs his infamous Tony Clifton routine. Robin Williams reveals his X-rated side, and Gallagher offers his "Sledge-O-Matic" routine.
Home Box Office — *Vestron Video*

Comes a Horseman 1978
Western
58954 119 mins C B, V P
James Caan, Jane Fonda, Jason Robards, Richard Farnsworth, Jim Davis, Mark Harmon, directed by Alan J. Pakula
A cattle baron, attempting to gobble up all the land in his territory, must contend with a woman who has the courage to stand up to him.
MPAA:PG
United Artists — *CBS/Fox Video*

Comet Halley 1985
Documentary
84486 60 mins C B, V P
A fun look back and ahead on the clockwork phenomenon of Halley's Comet.
Greater Washington Telecom — *Sony Video Software*

Comfort and Joy 1984
Comedy
77213 93 mins C B, V P
Bill Paterson, Eleanor David, C.P. Grogan, directed by Bill Forsyth
A Scottish disc jockey is forced to reevaluate his life when his kleptomaniac girlfriend walks out on him. The music is by Dire Straits guitarist Mark Knopfler.
MPAA:PG

Davina Belling; Clive Parsons — *MCA Home Video*

Comic, The 1969
Drama
85286 96 mins C B, V P
Dick Van Dyke, Mickey Rooney, Michele Lee, Cornel Wilde
Written by Carl Reiner, this film deals with the rising career of a silent screen comedian and his sudden failure after talkies arrive.
Carl Reiner; Aaron Ruben — *RCA/Columbia Pictures Home Video*

Comic Book Kids, The 1982
Musical/Fantasy
64950 90 mins C B, V R, P
Joseph Campanella, Mike Darnell, Robyn Finn, Jim Engelhardt, Fay De Witt
Two youngsters enjoy visiting their friend's comic strip studio, since they have the power to project themselves into the cartoon stories.
MPAA:G
Century Video — *Video Gems*

Coming Attractions # 1—The Super Stars 1975
Movie and TV trailers
42953 31 mins C B, V, FO P
This program in partial color is a collection of movie trailers from 12 all-time hits, starring some of Hollywood's biggest stars. Titles include "Presenting Lily Mars" with Judy Garland, "The Singing Kid" with Al Jolson, "Funny Lady" with Barbra Strisand, and others dating back to 1930.
MGM et al — *Video Yesteryear*

Coming Home 1978
Drama
16051 127 mins C B, V, LV P
Jane Fonda, Jon Voight, Bruce Dern, directed by Hal Ashby.
Fonda falls in love with paraplegic Voight while her husband is overseas. A look at the effect of the Vietnam War on people.
Academy Awards '78: Best Actor (Voight), Best Actress (Fonda). MPAA:R
Jerome Hellman — *CBS/Fox Video; RCA VideoDiscs*

Coming of Age: The Story of the Dallas Cowboys 1970-74 1982
Football
63163 120 mins C B, V, FO P
Dallas Cowboys
A compilation of individual Dallas Cowboys team highlight films from the first half of the 1970's.
NFL Films — *NFL Films Video*

Coming Soon 1983
Movie and TV trailers
69029   55 mins   C   B, V   P
Narrated by Jamie Lee Curtis
This program features over 50 excerpts from the "previews of coming attractions" of the most famous and infamous of the horror films.
Universal — *MCA Home Video*

Commando 1985
Adventure
Closed Captioned
84127   90 mins   C   B, V, LV   P
Arnold Schwarzenegger, Rae Dawn Chong, James Olson, directed by Mark Lester
An ex-commando leader's daughter is kidnapped in a blackmail scheme to make him depose a South American president. He doesn't, and proceeds to rescue his daughter amid a torrential flow of falling bodies.
MPAA:R
Joel Silver — *CBS/Fox Video*

Commando Attack 1967
War-Drama
84068   90 mins   C   B, V   P
Michael Rennie, Monica Randall, Bob Sullivan, directed by Herman Mankiewicz
A tough sergeant leads a group of misfit soldiers to blow up a German radio transmitter the day before D-day.
Foreign — *Unicorn Video*

Commandos 1973
War-Drama
59355   100 mins   C   B, V   R, P
Lee Van Cleef, Jack Kelly
A 48-hour odyssey of courage lays the groundwork for Rommel's eventual defeat in Africa.
MPAA:PG
Heritage Enterprises — *Video Gems; Prism*

Commies Are Coming, 1957
The Commies Are
Coming, The
Documentary/Politics and government-US
70676   60 mins   B/W   B, V   P
Jack Webb, Andrew Duggan, Robert Conrad
This film, a cult classic, will leave viewers red from laughing in disbelief. Jack Webb's famed delivery captures the paranoia of the times through tales of terrible totalitarian tyranny.
Jack Webb/US Government — *Rhino Video*

Commitment to 1983
Excellence/NFL '82
Football
66223   45 mins   C   B, V, FO   P
Highlights of the L.A. Raiders' 1982-83 season plus an overview of the whole NFL season.
NFL Films — *NFL Films Video*

Committee, The 1968
Satire/Comedy
66028   88 mins   C   B, V   P
Howard Hesseman, Barbara Bosson, Peter Bonerz, Gary Goodrow, Carl Gottlieb
A comedy film of the seminal comedy troupe "The Committee," specialists in short, punchy satire.
Allen Myerson; Del Jack — *Pacific Arts Video*

Company of Wolves, The 1985
Horror/Fantasy
Closed Captioned
81162   95 mins   C   B, V, LV   P
Angela Lansbury, David Warner, Tusse Silberg, Sarah Patterson, Brian Glover, directed by Neil Jordan
A young girl on the threshold of womanhood dreams of a medieval fantasy world inhabited by wolves and werewolves.
MPAA:R
ITC Entertainment; Palace Productions — *Vestron Video*

Les Comperes 1984
Comedy
82475   92 mins   C   B, V   P
Gerard Depordieu, Pierre Richard, Anny Duperey, directed by Francis Veber
A mother enlists two former lovers to find her runaway son, convincing each that he is the real father. Wild chases, mishaps and general hilarity ensues.
FR
Fideline Films; Efve Films; D.D. Prods — *Media Home Entertainment*

Competition, The 1980
Drama
58480   125 mins   C   B, V   P
Richard Dreyfuss, Amy Irving, Lee Remick, directed by Joel Oliansky
Two virtuoso pianists meet at an international competition and fall in love—something their careers have taught them to avoid.
MPAA:PG
Columbia — *RCA/Columbia Pictures Home Video*

Compleat Al, The 1985
Music video/Satire
81758   97 mins   C   B, V   P
This is the story of the life and music of "Weird" Al Yankovic. Features his "Like a Surgeon" and "Eat It" music videos.
CBS/Fox Video Music — *CBS/Fox Video*

Compleat Beatles, The 1982
Music
47738   120 mins   C   B, V, LV, P
CED

The Beatles, George Martin, Brian Epstein, Billy
Preston, Milt Oken, Bruce Johnston, Roger
McGuinn, Mike McCartney, Mick Jagger
Music interviews, film clips, animation and live
performances make up this "rockumentary" on
the Beatles. New interviews are featured, as
well as vintage film clips and studio footage. The
first U.S press conference, legendary Hamburg
footage, and an in-depth interview with George
Martin are highlights.
Delilah Films — *MGM/UA Home Video*

Compromising Positions   1985
Comedy/Mystery
Closed Captioned
84530   99 mins   C   B, V, LV   P
*Susan Sarandon, Raul Julia, Edward Herrmann,
Judith Ivey, Mary Beth Hurt, Josh Mostel, Anne
De Salvo, directed by Frank Perry*
A philandering dentist is killed on Long Island,
and a bored housewife begins to investigate,
uncovering scandal after scandal.
MPAA:R
Frank Perry — *Paramount Home Video*

Computability   1984
Computers
74075   60 mins   C   B, V   P
This program, hosted by Steve Allen and Jayne
Meadows, is the complete guide to computer
software. It was developed to help viewers
understand how their needs might best be
served by current computer software.
Karl Home Video — *Karl/Lorimar Home Video*

Computer Wizard   1977
Comedy
70222   91 mins   C   B, V   P
*Henry Darrow, Kate Woodville, Guy Madison,
Marc Gilpin*
An 8-year-old boy with a genius I.Q. builds a
powerful electronic device. His intentions are
good, but the invention disrupts the entire town
and lands him in big trouble.
MPAA:G
William H White; Torga Brown — *VCL Home
Video*

Computer Wore Tennis   1969
Shoes, The
Comedy
82027   87 mins   C   B, V   P
*Kurt Russell, Cesar Romero, Joe Flynn, William
Schallert, Allan Hewitt, directed by Robert Butler*
A slow-witted college student turns into a genius
after a "shocking" encounter with the campus
computer.
Walt Disney Productions — *Walt Disney Home
Video*

Compututor   1984
Computers
78644   90 mins   C   B, V   P

This series of twelve untitled programs instructs
in the usage of micro computer operation and
technology.
Embassy Home Entertainment — *Embassy
Home Entertainment*

Con Artists, The   1980
Crime-Drama
69585   86 mins   C   B, V   P
Anthony Quinn, Adriano Celentano
A con man recently sprung from prison and his
protege set up a sting operation in Italy.
Unknown — *VidAmerica*

Conan the Barbarian   1982
Adventure
47848   115 mins   C   B, V, LV   P
*Arnold Schwarzenegger, James Earl Jones,
Max von Sydow, directed by John Milius*
Conan sets out to avenge the murder of his
parents and retrieve the sword bequeathed him
by his father.
MPAA:R
Universal — *MCA Home Video*

Conan the Destroyer   1984
Adventure/Fantasy
Closed Captioned
78891   101 mins   C   B, V, LV   P
*Arnold Schwarzenegger, Grace Jones, Wilt
Chamberlain, Sarah Douglas, directed by
Richard Fleischer*
Conan is manipulated by Queen Tamaris into
searching for a treasure in return for bringing
Conan's love Valeria back to life.
MPAA:PG
Raffaella De Laurentis; Universal
Pictures — *MCA Home Video*

Concert For Bangladesh,   1972
The
Music-Performance
75926   90 mins   C   B, V   P
*George Harrison, Bob Dylan, Ringo Starr, Billy
Preston, Eric Clapton, Ravi Shankar, Kalus
Voorman*
This program presents the concert held in 1971
for the benefit of the needy.
Thorn — *THORN EMI/HBO Video*

Concorde—Airport '79,   1979
The
Adventure
84632   113 mins   C   B, V   P
*Alain Delon, Susan Blakely, Robert Wagner,
Sylvia Kristel, John Davidson, Charo, Sybil
Danning, Jimmie Walker, Eddie Albert, Bibi
Andersson, Monica Lewis, Andrea Marcovicci,
Martha Raye, Cicely Tyson*
A supersonic film in the "Airport" tradition has
the Concorde chased by missiles and fighter
aircraft before it crashes in the Alps. David

Lowell Rich directed and Mercedes
McCambridge also appears.
MPAA:PG
Jennings Lang; Universal — *MCA Home Video*

Concrete Beat   1984
Crime-Drama
87685   74 mins   C   B, V   P
*Kenneth MacMillan, John Getz, Darlanne
Fleugel, Rhoda Gemignani*
A newspaper reporter simultaneously searches
for a murderer, tries to win his ex-wife back, and
writes headline-worthy stories for his editor and
ex-father-in-law.
Jay Daniel; Viacom — *Prism*

Concrete Jungle, The   1982
Drama
64242   106 mins   C   B, V   P
Tracy Bregman, Jill St. John, Barbara Luna
After being set up by her boyfriend, a woman is
sent to a correctional facility for drug smuggling.
MPAA:R
Columbia; Billy Fine — *RCA/Columbia Pictures
Home Video*

Condorman   1981
Comedy
58623   90 mins   C   B, V   P
*Michael Crawford, Oliver Reed, Barbara
Carrera, James Hampton, Jean-Pierre Kalfon,
directed by Charles Jarrott*
Woody Wilkins, an inventive comic book writer,
adopts the identity of his own character,
Condorman, in order to help a beautiful Russian
spy defect.
MPAA:PG
Walt Disney Productions — *Walt Disney Home
Video*

Coney Hatch   1985
Music-Performance
82386   17 mins   C   B, V   P
Coney Hatch
This Canadian band electrifies head-banging
hordes with their Ozzy Osborne-influenced
tunes including "Shake It" and "Devils Deck."
Polygram/Records Inc — *Sony Video
Software*

Confessional, The   1980
Suspense/Horror
80287   108 mins   C   B, V   P
*Anthony Sharp, Susan Pehaligon, Stephanie
Beacham, Norman Eshley*
A mad priest unleashes a monster from his
confessional to wreak havoc upon the world.
MPAA:R
Lone Star Pictures — *Prism*

Confessions of a Police   1972
Captain
Drama
80389   104 mins   C   B, V   P
Martin Balsam, Franco Nero, Marilu Tolo
A police captain is trying to wipe out the
corruption that is infecting his city.
MPAA:PG
Bruno Turchetto; Mario Montanari — *Embassy
Home Entertainment*

Confessions of a Young   1978
American Housewife
Drama
59675   85 mins   C   B, V   P
Jennifer Wells, Rebecca Brooke, Chris Jordan
A recent divorcee moves in with two younger
couples and experiences sexual liberation.
MPAA:R
Joe Sarno — *Media Home Entertainment*

Confessions of Tom   1972
Harris
Drama
70815   90 mins   C   B, V   P
*Don Murray, Linda Evans, David Brian, directed
by John Derek*
Somewhere between all the prizefighting,
legbreaking for the mob, and jail terms, Tom
Harris finds time for a life-changing encounter
with love.
MPAA:PG
Don Murray — *Monterey Home Video*

Confidentially Yours   1983
Suspense
87336   110 mins   B/W   B, V   P
*Fanny Ardant, Jean-Louis Trintignant, directed
by Francois Truffaut*
Truffaut's homage to Hitchcock, based on
Charles Williams' "The Long Saturday Night,"
deals with a small-town real estate agent who is
framed for a rash of murders, while his secretary
tries to clear his name. One of the great
director's last films.
MPAA:PG
Roissy — *Key Video*

Conformist, The   1971
Drama
60330   115 mins   C   B, V   P
*Jean-Louis Trintignant, Stefania Sandrelli,
Dominique Sanda, Pierre Clementi, directed by
Bernardo Bertolucci*
Repressing his homosexual drives, Marcello
Clerici strives for an "acceptable" life as a
member of the Italian Fascist Secret Service,
and middle-class would-be wife-chaser, until an
odd series of events make him a willing
murderer.
MPAA:R
Paramount — *Paramount Home Video*

Connection, The   1961
Theater
86478   105 mins   B/W   . B, V   P
*Warren Finnerty, Carl Lee, the Freddie Redd
Quartet*
An acclaimed film by Shirley Clarke showing the
Living Theatre's ground-breaking performance
of Jack Gelber's play.
Cannes Film Festival '61: Critic's Prize.
Shirley Clarke; The Living Theatre — *Mystic
Fire Video*

Conqueror, The   1956
Adventure
65120   111 mins   C   B, V   P
*John Wayne, Susan Hayward, William Conrad,
Agnes Moorehead, directed by Dick Powell*
John Wayne stars as Genghis Khan in this tale
of the warlord's early life and involvement with
the kidnapped daughter of a powerful enemy.
Universal; Howard Hughes; RKO — *MCA
Home Video*

Conqueror and the   1964
Empress, The
Adventure
88323   89 mins   C   B, V   P
*Guy Madison, Ray Danton, Mario Petri, Albert
Farnes*
English explorers roust an island prince from his
throne, motivating him to engage in inspired
blood-letting.
Liber Films — *Force Video*

Conquest   1983
Fantasy/Adventure
77361   92 mins   C   B, V   P
George Rivero, Andrea Occhipinti, Violeta Cela
Two valiant warriors team up to destroy an evil
sorceress who controls a planet's life-giving
sun.
MPAA:R
Giovanni Di Clemente — *Media Home
Entertainment*

Conquest   1986
Space exploration
84623   180 mins   C   B, V   P
A taped history of space travel from the Von
Braun rockets to the 80's shuttle flights.
MPI Home Video — *MPI Home Video*

Conquest of the Planet of   1972
the Apes
Science fiction
Closed Captioned
81543   87 mins   C   B, V   P
*Roddy McDowell, Don Murray, Ricardo
Montalban, Hari Rhodes, directed by J. Lee
Thompson*
The apes turn the tables on the human Earth
population when they lead a revolt against their
cruel masters.

MPAA:PG
Apjac Productions; 20th Century
Fox — *Playhouse Video*

Conrack   1974
Biographical/Drama
Closed Captioned
81555   111 mins   C   B, V   P
*Jon Voight, Paul Winfield, Madge Sinclair, Hume
Cronyn, directed by Martin Ritt*
This is the true story of how Pat Conroy tried to
teach a group of ignorant black children in a
dilapidated schoolhouse in South Carolina.
Available in VHS and Beta Hi-Fi.
MPAA:PG
20th Century Fox — *Playhouse Video*

Constructing Stud Walls   1984
Home improvement
Closed Captioned
77259   30 mins   C   B, V   P
Carpenter George Giangrante demonstrates the
proper procedures for constructing a stud wall.
You Can Do It Videos — *You Can Do It Videos*

Contempt   1964
Drama
65428   102 mins   C   B, V   P
Brigitte Bardot, Jack Palance, Fritz Lang
A struggling playwright accepts a writing offer
from a crude, manipulative American producer
to please his wife. When the producer is
attracted to the wife, she thinks her husband is
trying to push her into an affair.
Avco Embassy — *Embassy Home
Entertainment*

Contes D'Hoffman, Les   1984
Music-Performance
80816   135 mins   C   B, V   P
*Placido Domingo, Ileana Cotrubas, Agnes
Baltsa*
A performance of the Offenbach opera where in
a poet tells of his rivals thwarting of his last
three romantic encounters. Available in VHS
and Beta Hi Fi.
John Schlesinger — *THORN EMI/HBO Video*

Continental Divide   1981
Comedy/Romance
59036   103 mins   C   B, V, LV   P
*John Belushi, Blair Brown, Allen Goorwitz,
directed by Michael Apted*
A hard-nosed political columnist takes off for the
Colorado Rockies on an "easy
assignment"—interviewing a reclusive
arnithologist he eventually falls in love with.
MPAA:PG
Universal — *MCA Home Video*

Conversation, The   1974
Drama
58494   113 mins   C   B, V, LV   P
Gene Hackman, John Cazale, Frederick
Forrest, Cindy Williams, Robert Duvall, directed
by Francis Ford Coppola
A professional eavesdropper's conscience
interferes with his job when he fears that he
might be acting as an accomplice to murder.
MPAA:PG
Paramount; Francis Ford
Coppola — Paramount Home Video

Conversation Piece   1975
Drama
82261   112 mins   C   B, V   P
Burt Lancaster, Silvana Mangano, Helmut
Berger, directed by Luchino Visconti
An aging art historian's life is turned upside
down when a Countess and her daughter rent
out the penthouse in his estate.
New Line Cinema — THORN EMI/HBO Video

Convoy   1978
Adventure
73018   106 mins   C   B, V   P
Kris Kristofferson, Ali McGraw, Ernest Borgnine
A trucker is out to form an indestructible truck
convoy to Mexico. The film was inspired by the
song "Convoy" by C. W. Mc Call.
MPAA:R
Robert M Sherman — THORN EMI/HBO
Video

Coogan's Bluff   1968
Drama
47413   100 mins   C   B, V   P
Clint Eastwood, Lee J. Cobb, Tisha Sterling,
Don Stroud, Betty Field
An Arizona deputy sheriff travels to New York in
order to extradite an escaped murderer.
MPAA:PG
Universal — MCA Home Video

Cooking for Compliments   1984
Cookery
70570   72 mins   C   B, V   P
Lee Gerovitz, Steve Cassarino
Two professional chefs show viewers a lively
approach to meal preparation on this tape. They
offer recipes for ten dinners, four breakfasts,
side dishes, and even make table setting
suggestions. Bound recipe cards are included.
AM Available
Television Communications Network — Clever
Cleaver Productions

Cool Cats: 25 Years of   1983
Rock 'n' Roll Style
Music/Documentary
66457   90 mins   C   B, V   P
The effect of rock music on contemporary style
and mores is the subject of this "rockumentary"

which features performance clips and interviews
by thirty-four rock trendsetters, including Elvis,
The Beatles, Culture Club, David Bowie and
many others.
Delilah Films; Stephanie Bennett — MGM/UA
Home Video

Cool Hand Luke   1967
Drama
58224   126 mins   C   B, V, LV   P
Paul Newman, George Kennedy, J. D. Cannon,
Strother Martin, Jo Van Fleet, directed by Stuart
Rosenberg
A man sentenced to sweat out a term on a
prison farm refuses to compromise with
authority.
Warner Bros; Jalem Productions — Warner
Home Video

Cool it Carol   1968
Exploitation
86585   101 mins   C   B, V   P
Robin Askwith, Janet Lynn, Jess Conrad,
Stubby Kaye
A sluttish young girl leaves with her current
boyfriend for the city life where she gyrates her
way to success.
Pete Walker — Monterey Home Video

Cool World, The   1963
Documentary/Drama
63628   107 mins   B/W   B, V, FO   P
This docudrama, set on the streets of Harlem,
focuses on a 15-year-old black youth whose
one ambition in life is to own a gun and lead his
gang.
Frederick Wiseman — Video Yesteryear

Copacabana   1947
Musical/Comedy
64543   91 mins   B/W   B, V   P
Groucho Marx, Carmen Miranda, Steve
Cochran, Gloria Jean, Andy Russell
A quick-thinking theatrical agent books a
nightclub singer into two shows at the same
time, which leads to the expected
complications.
United Artists — Republic Pictures Home
Video

Coppelia with Fernando   1982
Bujones
Dance
47406   110 mins   C   B, V   P
Fernando Bujones
Mr. Bujones, the featured dancer of
Barishnikov's American Ballet Theater, plays
Franz, the young lover. Recorded with the
Ballets de San Juan.
Kultur — Kultur

Copperhead 1984
Horror
79759   90 mins   C   B, V   P
Jack Renner, Gretta Ratliff, David Fritts, Cheryl Nickerson
A group of copperhead snakes attack a family who possess a stolen Incangold necklace.
MPAA:R
Independent — *United Home Video*

Cord and Discords/A Naughty Nurse 1928
Comedy
85512   50 mins   B/W   B, V   P
Fred Parker, Jack Cooper, Ella MacKenzie, Spencer Williams
Two vintage silent shorts featuring some lesser known slapstick clowns cavorting in blackface.
Bray Prods. — *Video Yesteryear*

Cornbread, Earl and Me 1975
Drama
86894   89 mins   C   B, V   P
Moses Gunn, Rosalind Cash, Bernie Casey, Tierre Turner, Antonio Fargas
A high school basketball star from the ghetto is mistaken for a murderer by cops and shot, causing a subsequent furor of corruption, protest and racial hatred.
American Int'l.; Joe Manduke — *THORN EMI/HBO Video*

Cornered 1945
Suspense
81024   102 mins   B/W   B, V   P
Dick Powell, Walter Slezak, Micheline Cheirel, Luther Adler, directed by Edward Dmytryk
When a Canadian airman is released from a German prison camp he pursues a Nazi war criminal to Buenos Aires to avenge the death of his wife and child.
RKO — *RKO HomeVideo*

Corpse Vanishes, The 1942
Mystery
16158   64 mins   B/W   B, V   P
Bela Lugosi
Scientist experiments with various potions and turns himself into an ape.
Prime TV — *VidAmerica; Kartes Video Communications*

Corrupt 1984
Crime-Drama
72183   99 mins   C   B, V   P
Harvey Keitel
A policeman becomes involved in illegal activities in order to catch a murderer.
MPAA:PG
Elda Ferri — *THORN EMI/HBO Video*

Corrupt Ones, The 1967
Adventure
76905   87 mins   C   B, V   P
Robert Stack, Elke Sommer, Nancy Kwan, Christian Marguand
Everyone's after a photographer who has a medallion that will lead to buried treasure in Red China.
Warner Bros. — *Embassy Home Entertainment*

Corsair 1931
Drama
84150   73 mins   B/W   B, V   P
Chester Morris, Thelma Todd, Frank McHugh, Ned Sparks, Mayo Methot
A gorgeous debutante and a handsome gangster become inexplicably involved with sea-bound bootlegging pirates.
UA — *Movie Buff Video; Kartes Video Communications*

Corsican Brothers, The 1984
Comedy/Adventure
77217   91 mins   C   B, V   P
Richard "Cheech" Marin, Tommy Chong
The Corsican Brothers join forces to battle against an evil French Baron.
MPAA:PG
Orion Pictures — *Lightning Video*

Corsican Brothers, The 1942
Adventure
55352   111 mins   B/W   B, V, 3/4U   P
Douglas Fairbanks Jr, Akim Tamiroff, Ruth Warrick, J. Carrol Naish
Alexandre Dumas' classic about siamese twins who, although separated, remain spiritually tied through various adventures.
Edward Small; United Artists — *Nostalgia Merchant*

Cosh Boy 1961
Drama
82237   90 mins   B/W   B, V   P
Joan Collins, James Kennedy
Vicious male youths stalk women on the streets of London.
British — *Monterey Home Video*

Cosi Fan Tutte 1985
Opera
85028   139 mins   C   B, V   P
Ann Christine Biel, Maria Hoglino, Lars Tibell
A performance of the Mozart Lyric Opera at Sweden's 18th-century Drohningham Court Theatre.
Thomas Olofsson — *THORN EMI/HBO Video*

Cosmic Eye, The 1971
Film-Avant-garde
82301   71 mins   C   B, V   P

Animated, voices of Dizzy Gillespie, Maureen Stapleton, directed by Faith Hubley
This is the story of three musicians from outer space who come to earth to spread the message of worldwide peace and harmony.
Faith Hubley — *Walt Disney Home Video*

Cosmic Monsters   1958
Science fiction
49902   75 mins   B/W   B, V   P
Forrest Tucker, Gaby Andre, Alec Mango, Hugh Latimer
Alien beings in flying saucers terrorize a countryside with giant insects and other strange things from outer space.
DCA — *United Home Video; Mossman Williams Productions*

Cosmos: The   1981
Championship Years
1977-1980
Soccer
51086   115 mins   C   B, V   P
New York Cosmos
Highlights of the past four seasons of New York Cosmos soccer, featuring Pele, Giorgio Chinaglia, Franz Beckenbauer, and championship moments, are included in this program.
Cosmos Soccer Club — *Warner Home Video*

Cotter   1972
Drama/Western
84820   94 mins   C   B, V   P
Don Murray, Carol Lynley, Rip Torn, Sherry Jackson
A drunk rodeo clown is responsible for a cowboy's death. Fleeing to his native lands, he finds himself accused of causing yet another death.
Gold Key Ent — *United Home Video*

Cotton Club, The   1984
Musical-Drama
80426   121 mins   C   B, V, 8mm   P
Diane Lane, Richard Gere, Gregory Hines, Lonette McKee, directed by Francis Ford Coppola
A musician playing at The Cotton Club falls in love with gangster Dutch Schultz's girlfriend. Songs featured include "Crazy Rhythm," "Am I Blue," "Cotton Club Stomp," "Jitter Bug" and "I'll Wind."
MPAA:R EL, FR, SP
Robert Evans; Orion Pictures — *Embassy Home Entertainment*

Cougar Country   1986
Wildlife
86029   91 mins   C   B, V   P
The life and maturation of a wild cougar is caught on film.
MPAA:G

Unknown — *United Home Video*

Could It Happen Here?   198?
War-Drama
87344   90 mins   C   B, V   P
Luc Merenda, Marc Michelangeli, directed by Massimo Pirri
A lurid Italian spectacle about a metropolis thrown into a state of chaotic martial law by terrorism. Dubbed.
Italian — *Mogul Communications*

Count, The   1916
Comedy
10643   20 mins   B/W   B, V, 3/4U   R, P, DL
Charlie Chaplin
Chaplin pretends to be the secretary of his boss, who in turn is posing as a count. (Silent; musical soundtrack added.)
RKO — *Cable Films; Festival Films*

Count Basie Live at the   1984
Hollywood Palladium
Music-Performance
79874   60 mins   C   B, V   P
One of the Count's last concerts taped at the Hollywood Palladium. Songs performed include "Shiny Stockings," "Splanky" and "Big Stuff."
VCL Home Video — *VCL Home Video*

Count Dracula   1971
Horror
70199   90 mins   C   B, V   P
Christopher Lee, Herbert Lom, Klans Kinski
A "new" version of the Dracula legend, based closely on the original novel by Bram Stoker.
Independent — *Republic Pictures Home Video*

Count of Monte Cristo,   1934
The
Adventure
55349   114 mins   B/W   B, V, 3/4U   P
Robert Donat, Elissa Landi, Louis Calhern, directed by Rowland V. Lee
Alexandre Dumas' classic about Edmon Dantes who, after years in prison, escapes and avenges himself on those who framed him.
Edward Small; Reliance; United Artists — *Nostalgia Merchant; Blackhawk Films*

Count of Monte Cristo,   1974
The
Drama/Adventure
56892   104 mins   C   B, V   P
Richard Chamberlain, Kate Nelligan, Donald Pleasence, Alessio Orano, Tony Curtis, Louis Jourdan, Trevor Howard
The Alexandre Dumas classic with the swashbuckling Edmond Dantes and the villainous Mondego.

Norman Rosemont Productions,
ITC — *Playhouse Video; RCA VideoDiscs*

Count of Monte Cristo, The
1980

Cartoons
66578   52 mins   C   B, V   P
Animated
An animated version of the classic Alexander
Dumas story of a swordsman who seeks
revenge on the men who wrongly imprisoned
him.
Hanna-Barbera Productions — *Worldvision
Home Video*

Count of Monte Cristo, The
1912

Film-History
48697   90 mins   B/W   B, V   P
James O'Neill
One of the first full length features made starring
popular stage stars of the day. The first truly
American feature. Silent.
Adolph Zukor, Famous Players
Company — *Video Yesteryear*

Count, The/The Adventurer
1917

Comedy
58657   52 mins   B/W   B, V, FO   P
*Charlie Chaplin, Eric Campbell, Edna Purviance,
Frank Coleman, directed by Charlie Chaplin*
Two Chaplin two-reelers: "The Count (The
Phoney Nobleman)" (1916), in which Charlie
impersonates a count at the home of Miss
Moneybags, and "The Adventurer" (1917),
Chaplin's final film for Mutual, in which he plays
an escaped convict with the law relentlessly on
his trail. Silent with musical score.
Mutual — *Video Yesteryear*

Count Yorga, Vampire
1970

Horror
81180   90 mins   C   B, V   P
*Robert Quarry, Roger Perry, Michael Murphy,
Michael MacBrady*
The vampire Count Yorga conducts a seance to
conjure up the spirit of a young girl's recently
deceased mother. Things get weird at his
mansion. Available in VHS Stereo and Beta Hi-
Fi.
MPAA:PG
American International Pictures — *THORN
EMI/HBO Video*

Countdown
1968

Science fiction
65356   102 mins   C   B, V   P
*James Caan, Robert Duvall, Michael Murphy,
Ted Knight, Joanna Moore, Barbara Baxley,
Charles Aidman*

Robert Altman directed this thrilling adventure
about the first moon mission and its toll on the
astronauts and their families.
Warner Brothers — *Warner Home Video*

Countdown to World War II
194?

World War II
10154   59 mins   B/W   B, V   P, T
Newsreels cover rise of Hitler and Mussolini.
Unknown — *Blackhawk Films*

Country
1984

Drama
76851   109 mins   C   B, V   P
*Jessica Lange, Sam Shepard, Wilford Brimley,
Matt Clark, directed by Richard Pearce*
A farm family's life starts to unravel when the
government attempts to foreclose on their land.
MPAA:PG
Far West Productions; Pangaea Corporation
Productions — *Touchstone Home Video*

Country Comes Alive
1986

Music video
88362   30 mins   C   B, V   P
Various country singers appear in their most
popular videos, including Ronnie Milsap doing
"Lost in the 50's Tonight," Alabama does
"There's No Way" and The Judds wing "Love Is
Alive."
RCA Video — *RCA/Columbia Pictures Home
Video*

Country Gentlemen
1936

Comedy
46347   54 mins   B/W   B, V, FO   P
*Ole Olsen, Chic Johnson, Joyce Compton, Lila
Lee*
Olsen and Johnson play fast-talking conmen
who sell shares in a worthless oil field to a
bunch of World War I veterans.
Republic — *Video Yesteryear; Discount Video
Tapes; See Hear Industries*

Country Girl, The
1982

Drama
63344   137 mins   C   B, V   P
Dick Van Dyke, Faye Dunaway, Ken Howard
An aging, alcoholic actor, desperate for a
comeback, blames his fiercely loving wife for his
downfall.
Group W Productions — *THORN EMI/HBO
Video*

Country Girl, The
1954

Drama
64506   104 mins   B/W   B, V   P
*Bing Crosby, Grace Kelly, William Holden, Gene
Reynolds, directed by George Seaton*

The wife of an alcoholic actor is unfairly blamed for his sodden condition. Based on the play by Clifford Odets
Academy Awards '54: Best Actress (Kelly); Best Screenplay (George Seaton).
Paramount — *Paramount Home Video; RCA VideoDiscs*

Country Lovers, City Lovers   1972
Drama
78635   121 mins   C   B, V   P
Here are two adaptations of short stories by South African novelist Nadine Gordimer about interracial love.
Profile Productions — *MGM/UA Home Video*

Country Music with the Muppets   1985
Variety/Music-Performance
Closed Captioned
81547   55 mins   C   B, V   P
Rowlf, Kermit the Frog, Fozzie Bear, Johnny Cash, Roy Clark, Crystal Gayle, Roger Miller
Join Rowlf as he plays some of his favorite country music videos in this collection of highlights from "The Muppet Show".
Henson Associates — *Playhouse Video*

Country-Western All-Stars   1956
Music-Performance/Variety
47479   52 mins   B/W   B, V, FO   P
Carl Smith, Jim Reeves, Faron Young, Hank Snow, Minnie Pearl, Tex Ritter, The Sons of the Pioneers
A live country-western variety show broadcast from the Ryman Auditorium in Nashville.
WSM Nashville — *Video Yesteryear*

Countryman   1983
Drama/Adventure
65371   103 mins   C   B, V   P
Countryman, Hiram Keller, Kristine St. Clair
Countryman is no ordinary man. He is a man of the sea, a man of knowledgde, in effortless harmony with everything that lives and breathes.
MPAA:R
Chris Blackwell — *Media Home Entertainment*

Courage of Rin Tin Tin, The   1983
Adventure
79336   90 mins   C   B, V   P
James Brown, Lee Aaker
Rusty and his faithful dog Rin Tin Tin help the cavalry soldiers of Fort Apache keep law and order in a small Arizona town.
Screen Gems — *Monterey Home Video*

Courageous Dr. Christian, The   1940
Drama
47458   66 mins   B/W   B, V, FO   P
Jean Hersholt, Dorothy Lovett, Tom Neal
Dr. Christian is faced with an epidemic of meningitis among the inhabitants of a shanty town.
RKO — *Video Yesteryear; Discount Video Tapes*

Courageous Mr. Penn, The   1944
Biographical/Drama
84152   78 mins   B/W   B, V   P
Clifford Evans, Deborah Kerr
This is a British film outlining the achievements of William Penn, founder of Pennsylvania.
Alternate title: "Penn of Pennsylvania."
JH Hoffberg — *Movie Buff Video; Video Yesteryear*

Courier of Death   1984
Crime-Drama
88229   77 mins   C   B, V   P
Joey Johnson, Barbara Garrison, directed by Tom Shaw
A courier is embroiled in a mob war/struggle over a locked briefcase with mysterious contents.
Tom Shaw Prod. — *Lightning Video*

Court Jester, The   1956
Comedy
79182   101 mins   C   B, V   P
Danny Kaye, Glynis Johns, Basil Rathbone, Angela Lansbury, directed by Norman Panama and Melvin Frank
A former circus clown teams up with a band of outlaws who attempt to get rid of a tyrant king and replace him with the real king.
Paramount — *Paramount Home Video*

Cousin, Cousine   1976
Drama/Comedy
52745   95 mins   C   B, V, CED   P
Marie-Christine Barrault, Marie-France Pisier, Victor Lanoux, Guy Marchand, directed by Jean-Charles Tacchella
Distant cousins who meet at a round of family parties, funerals, and weddings fall in love with each other, but their relationship soon becomes more than platonic.
France; Libra Films — *CBS/Fox Video*

Cousteau—Diving for Roman Plunder   1978
Oceanography
47392   59 mins   C   B, V   P
Jacques Cousteau and the crew of the Calypso embark upon an underwater search for ancient Roman artifacts.

Cousteau Society — *Warner Home Video*

Cousteau—The Nile   1979
Travel/Documentary
47388   116 mins   C   B, V   P
Jacques Cousteau
A double-length episode of the "Cousteau
Odyssey" series, taking the viewer on a
spectacular journey down the Earth's longest
river to reveal the fabled past and challenging
present of the Nile River.
Cousteau Society — *Warner Home Video*

Covergirl   1983
Drama
65746   98 mins   C   B, V   P
Jeff Conaway, Irena Ferris, Cathie Shirriff
Covergirl tells the story of one girl's meteoric
rise to become a superstar model. The
heartaches and struggles involved in the climb
to success are also depicted.
MPAA:R
Claude Heroux — *THORN EMI/HBO Video*

Cow Town   1950
Western
66307   70 mins   B/W   B, V   P, T
Gene Autry, Gail Davis, Jock Mahoney
A range war results when ranchers begin
fencing in their land to prevent cattle rustling.
Columbia — *Blackhawk Films*

Coward of the County   1981
Drama
85910   115 mins   C   B, V   P
Kenny Rogers, directed by Dick Lowry
A devout pacifist is put to the test when his
girlfriend is raped.
Ken Kragen; John Marias — *Karl/Lorimar
Home Video*

Cowboy Counselor   1933
Western
84840   60 mins   B/W   B, V   P
Hoot Gibson
A cowboy-lawyer outwits a gang-mob of rustler-
outlaws, and wins the innocent-chaste girl-
maiden.
Universal — *United Home Video*

Cowboy Previews # 1   194?
Movie and TV trailers/Western
64416   60 mins   B/W   B, V, 3/4U   P
A collection of theatrical trailers from over thirty-
five "B" westerns. Titles include "Riders in the
Sky," "King of the Bullwhip," "Utah Wagon
Train," "Trail of Robin Hood," "Sioux City Sue"
and many others.
Republic et al — *Nostalgia Merchant*

Cowboys, The   1972
Western
74209   128 mins   C   B, V   P
John Wayne, Roscoe Lee Browne, Bruce Dern
Wayne stars as a cattle rancher who is forced to
hire eleven schoolboys to help him drive his
cattle 400 miles to market.
MPAA:PG
Mark Rydell — *Warner Home Video*

Cowboys from Texas   1939
Western
64402   54 mins   B/W   B, V, 3/4U   P
*Bob Livingston, Raymond Hatton, Duncan
Renaldo, Carole Landis*
The Three Mesquiteers bring about a peaceful
settlement to a fight between cattlemen and
homesteaders.
Republic — *Nostalgia Merchant*

Cowboys of the Saturday   1984
Matinee
Western/Movie and TV trailers
84402   75 mins   B/W   B, V   P
*Gene Autry, Tex Ritter, Roy Rogers, hosted by
James Coburn*
The history of B-movie westerns is traced from
the beginning of the sound era.
Karl-Lorimar Video — *Karl/Lorimar Home
Video*

Crack Shadow Boxers   197?
Martial arts/Adventure
47699   91 mins   C   B, V   P
Ku Feng, Chou Li Lung
Through a series of misadventures, Wu Lung
and Chu San battle to protect the inhabitants of
a small village from the onslaught of relentless
bandits.
United Enterprises Ltd — *Master Arts Video*

Cracker Factory, The   1979
Drama
81805   90 mins   C   B, V   P
*Natalie Wood, Perry King, Shelley Long, Vivian
Blaine, Juliet Mills, directed by Burt Brickerhoff*
A young woman who is committed to a mental
institution attempts to charm her way out of
treatment.
Roger Gimbel Prods; EMI Television — *VCL
Home Video*

Crackers   1984
Comedy
74090   92 mins   C   B, V, LV   P
Donald Sutherland, Jock Warden, Sean Penn
This is the off beat story of two bumbling thieves
who round up a gang of equally inept neighbors
and go on the wildest crime spree you have ever
seen.
MPAA:PG
Universal — *MCA Home Video*

Cracking Up   1983
Comedy
66323   90 mins   C   B, V   P
*Jerry Lewis, Herb Edelman, Foster Brooks,
Milton Berle, Sammy Davis Jr., directed by Jerry
Lewis*
Jerry Lewis stars as an accident-prone misfit
whose mishaps on the road to recovery create
chaos for everyone he meets.
MPAA:PG
Warner Bros — *Warner Home Video*

Crackler, The   1984
Mystery
80446   60 mins   C   B, V   P
James Warwick, Francesca Annis
During the 20's, a husband and wife private
investigation team set out to find a gang of
forgers operating in high society circles. Based
on a story by Agatha Christie.
London Weekend Television — *Pacific Arts
Video*

Cradle Will Fall, The   1983
Mystery
88190   103 mins   C   B, V   P
*Lauren Hutton, Ben Murphy, James Farentino,
Charita Bauer, Peter Simon*
A made-for-TV adaptation of the pulpy
bestselling mystery by Mary Higgins Clark about
a woman who cannot convince anyone she
witnessed a murder. The cast of "The Guiding
Light" appear in this film.
Cates Films; Proctor &
Gamble — *Karl/Lorimar Home Video*

Craig Claiborne's New   1985
York Times Video
Cookbook
Cookery
81488   120 mins   C   B, V   P
"The New York Times" food editor Craig
Claiborne prepares twenty of his most
requested recipes and gives expert cooking
advice in this program.
NYT Productions — *Warner Home Video*

Craig's Wife   1936
Drama
87754   75 mins   B/W   B, V   P
*Rosalind Russell, John Boles, Alma Kruger,
Jane Darwell, Billie Burke, directed by Dorothy
Arzner*
A classic soap opera about a woman driven to
total ruin by her desire for social acceptance
and material wealth. Based on a George Kelly
play.
Columbia — *RCA/Columbia Pictures Home
Video*

Cramps: A Free Concert   1981
at the Napa State
Hospital
Music-Performance
84054   60 mins   C   B, V   P
Cramps, Zev
Live performances by two notorious punk
forces, Cramps, and Zev.
Target Video — *Target Video*

Crash of Flight 401, The   1982
Drama
75459   101 mins   C   B, V   P
*William Shatner, Adrienne Barbeau, Lloyd
Bridges*
This jetliner story is based on an incident that
occurred during a landing at Miami's airport.
King Features — *U.S.A. Home Video*

Crater Lake Monster, The   1977
Horror
59655   85 mins   C   B, V   P
*Richard Cardella, Glenn Roberts, Mark Siegel,
Bob Hyman*
A meteor crashes into a mountain lake causing
it to warm up. The dormant egg of a prehistoric
creature lying at the bottom is incubated, and
the newborn creature heads for land.
MPAA:PG
William R Stromberg — *United Home Video*

Crawling Eye, The   1958
Science fiction/Horror
44349   87 mins   B/W   B, V, 3/4U   P
*Forrest Tucker, Laurence Payne, Janet Munro,
Jennifer Jayne*
Hidden in a radioactive fog, the crawling eye
decapitates its victims and returns these
humans to Earth to threaten mankind. Includes
previews of coming attractions from classic
science fiction films.
VCC Films — *Nostalgia Merchant*

Crawling Hand, The   1963
Horror/Science fiction
59348   89 mins   B/W   B, V   R, P
Alan Hale, Rod Lauren
An astronaut's hand takes off without him, on an
unearthly spree of stranglings.
Medallion — *Video Gems*

Crazy Mama   1975
Drama
65074   81 mins   C   B, V, CED   P
*Cloris Leachman, Stuart Whitman, Ann
Southern, Jim Backus*
A band of female outlaws turn to crime on the
way to Arkansas to repossess the family farm
that was sold during the Depression.
MPAA:PG
New World Pictures — *Embassy Home
Entertainment*

Creation of the Humanoids
1962

Science fiction
81834   84 mins   C   B, V   P
Don Megowan, Frances McCann, Erica Elliot
There's a war going on between the human race and purplish green robots after a nuclear holocaust. Available in VHS Stereo and Beta Hi-Fi.
Emerson Film Enterprises — *Monterey Home Video*

Creative Camera, The
1982

Photography
63424   60 mins   C   LV
This interactive videodisc is a primer of single lens reflex photography offering a practical and detailed introduction to SLR photographic techniques.
Valley Isle Productions; Jac Holzman — *Pioneer Video Imports*

Creative Parenting: The First Twelve Months
1985

Parents/Children
71121   60 mins   C   B, V   P
Narrated by Beau Bridges
This tape is designed to help new families over some of the hurdles they'll face in their baby's first year.
Sherry Goldsher Marsh; A&M Video — *RCA/Columbia Pictures Home Video*

Creator
1985

Fantasy/Comedy
70956   108 mins   C   B, V   P
Peter O'Toole, Mariel Hemingway, Vincent Spano, Virginia Madsen, David Ogden Stiers, John Dehner, Karen Kopins, directed by Ivan Passer
A Frankenstein-like scientist plans to construct a being based on his wife, who died thirty years ago. As his experiments begin to show positive results, his romantic attention turns towards his beautiful lab assistant.
MPAA:R
Universal — *THORN EMI/HBO Video*

Creature
1985

Horror/Science fiction
Closed Captioned
81897   100 mins   C   B, V   P
Klaus Kinski, Stan Ivar, Wendy Schaal, Lyman Ward
A two thousand-year-old alien life form is killing off astronauts exploring a wasteland planet. Available in VHS and Beta Hi-Fi.
Cardinal Entertainment — *Media Home Entertainment*

Creature from Black Lake
1976

Horror
80666   95 mins   C   B, V   P
Jack Elan, Dub Taylor, Dennis Fimple, John David
Two anthropology students from Chicago travel to the Louisiana swamps searching for the creature from Black Lake.
MPAA:PG
Jim McCullough Prods. — *Lightning Video*

Creature from the Haunted Sea
1960

Satire
56914   76 mins   B/W   B, V, FO   P
Antony Carbone, Betsy Jones-Moreland
A monster movie satire set in Cuba shortly after the revolution and centering around an elaborate plan to loot the Treasury and put the blame on a strange sea monster.
Roger Corman — *Movie Buff Video; Video Yesteryear*

Creepers
1985

Horror/Science fiction
71181   82 mins   C   B, V   P
Jennifer Connelly, Donald Pleasance, directed by Dario Argento
Jennifer is a normal young girl; except for the fact that she can talk to bugs and get them to follow instructions. She sics a cadre of her creepy crawling comrades on a psychopathic killer.
MPAA:R
Dacfilm-Rome — *Media Home Entertainment*

Creeping Flesh, The
1972

Horror
62808   89 mins   C   B, V   P
Peter Cushing, Christopher Lee, Lorna Heilbron
A scientist decides he can cure evil by injecting his patients with a serum extracted from the blood of evil humans. The plan backfires.
MPAA:PG
Columbia — *RCA/Columbia Pictures Home Video*

Creeping Terror
1964

Horror
59653   81 mins   B/W   B, V   P
Vic Savage, Shannon O'Neal, William Thourlby
A spaceship discovered in the Rocky Mountains contains a creeping monster that devours its human victims while computing their metabolism and sending the information to the mother craft somewhere in space.
A J Nelson — *United Home Video*

Creepshow
1982

Horror
60561   120 mins   C   B, V, CED   P
Hal Holbrook, Adrienne Barbeau, Viveca Lindfors, E.G. Marshall, Stephen King, Leslie Nielsen, Carrie Nye, Fritz Weaver, Ted Danson, directed by George A. Romero

Stephen King's tribute to E.C. Comics, those pulp horror comic books that delight in the grizzly, the grotesque and morbid humor.
MPAA:R
Warner Bros — *Warner Home Video*

Cria (The Secret of Anna) ·   1977
Drama
86534   115 mins   C   B, V   P
Geraldine Chaplin, Ana Torrent, Conchita Perez, directed by Carlos Saura
The award-winning story of a 9-year-old girl's struggle to mature and to deal with the adult world.
MPAA:PG   SP
Jason Allen; Larry Gordon Pres. — *Master Arts Video*

Cricket, The   1983
Drama
80037   90 mins   C   B, V   P
Clio Goldsmith, Virna Lisi, Anthony Franciosa, Renato Saluatori
The sparks fly when a woman and her seventeen year old daughter become rivals for the affections of the same man.
IT
Ibrahim Moussa; Samuel Goldwyn — *Embassy Home Entertainment*

Cricket in Times Square, A   1973
Cartoons
71360   30 mins   C   B, V   P
Animated, voices of Mel Blanc, Les Tremayne, June Foray, Kerry MacLane
This bug produces dulcet violin-like tones by rubbing his fore wings together. He becomes artist-in-residence at a downtown Manhattan newsstand.
Chuck Jones — *Family Home Entertainment*

Cricket on the Hearth, The   1923
Drama/Christmas
66353   68 mins   B/W   B, V   P
Paul Gerson, Virginia Brown Faire, Paul Moore, Joan Standing
An adaptation of Charles Dickens' short story about the life of a mail carrier and his bride, who find the symbol of good luck, a cricket on the hearth, when they enter their new home. Silent with organ score.
Paul Gerson Pictures; Selznick Releasing — *Blackhawk Films*

Cries and Whispers   1972
Drama
54802   94 mins   C   B, V   P
Harriet Andersson, Ingrid Thulin, Liv Ullman, Kary Sylway, Erland Josephson, directed by Ingmar Bergman

A Bergman production that dramatizes states of mind. It is the story of the lives of three sisters, all in their thirties. The middle sister is dying of cancer and the other two, along with a peasant woman, take care of her.
MPAA:R
New World Pictures — *Warner Home Video*

Crime and Passion   1975
Comedy/Crime-Drama
84791   92 mins   C   B, V   P
Omar Sharif, Karen Black, Joseph Bottoms, directed by Ivan Passer
Two rich lovers plan to get even richer by the woman's marrying a multimillionaire and suing for a quick divorce.
MPAA:R
American Intl — *Vestron Video*

Crimes of Passion   1984
Drama
Closed Captioned
80459   101 mins   C   B, V, LV   P
Kathleen Turner, Anthony Perkins, directed by Ken Russell
A prostitute becomes the object of a disturbed priest's erotic fantasies. Music score by Rick Wakeman.
New World Pictures — *New World Video*

Criminal Code, The   1931
Drama
78879   98 mins   B/W   B, V   P
Walter Huston, Boris Karloff, Constance Cummings, directed by Howard Hawks
A young man is jailed for killing a man in self defense and his life worsens at the hands of a sadistic prison warden. In Beta Hi-Fi.
Harry Cohn; Columbia
Pictures — *RCA/Columbia Pictures Home Video*

Crimson   1985
Horror
81035   90 mins   C   B, V   P
Paul Nash, Sylvia Solar
A criminal goes on a bloody rampage when he receives a brain transplant.
MPAA:R
Empire Entertainment — *Wizard Video*

Crisis at Central High   1980
Drama
80673   120 mins   C   B, V   P
Joanne Woodward, Charles Durning, William Ross, Henderson Forsythe, directed by Lamont Johnson
This is a dramatic recreation of the events that lead up to the integration of Central High in Little Rock, Arkansas in 1957.
Time Life TV — *Lightning Video*

Crocodile 1981
Horror
65510   95 mins   C   B, V   P
Nat Puvanai, Tany Tim, directed by Herman Cohen
Nature strikes with unbelievable fury, creating the largest and most savage crocodile on earth. No experts can kill this monster animal that is too huge and powerful to trap. Soon the giant crocodile attacks a beach town, killing and devouring dozens of people.
MPAA:R
Dick Randall; Robert Chan — *THORN EMI/HBO Video*

Crosby, Stills & Nash: 1983
Daylight Again
Music-Performance
64792   108 mins   C   B, V, LV,   P
                                CED
Directed by Tom Trbovich
This video concert taped in November 1982 at the New Universal Amphitheater in Los Angeles represents the group's first tour since 1977. Includes such songs as "Just a Song Before I Go," "Chicago," "Suite: Judy Blue Eyes," and from the recent "Daylight Again" album, "Wasted on the Way." In stereo.
Universal Pay TV; Neal Marshall — *MCA Home Video*

Cross Country 1983
Crime-Drama/Suspense
65421   95 mins   C   B, V   P
Richard Beymer, Nina Axelrod, Michael Ironside
Action revolves around the brutal murder of a call girl with initial suspicion falling on a TV advertising director involved with the woman. The story twists and turns from the suspect to the investigating detective.
MPAA:R
Pieter Kroonenburg — *Embassy Home Entertainment*

Cross Creek 1983
Adventure/Biographical
69678   120 mins   C   B, V, CED   P
Mary Steenburgen, Rip Torn
This film is based on the life of Marjorie Kinnan Rawlings who, after 10 years as a frustrated reporter/writer, moved to the remote and untamed Everglades, where she received the inspiration to write numerous bestsellers.
Universal — *THORN EMI/HBO Video*

Cross of Iron 1976
War-Drama
47815   120 mins   C   B, V, 3/4U   P
James Coburn, Maximilian Schell, James Mason, David Warner, Senta Berger, directed by Sam Peckinpah
During World War II, two antagonistic German officers clash over personal ideals as well as

strategy in combatting the relentless Russian attack.
MPAA:R
ITC Entertainment — *Nostalgia Merchant; Media Home Entertainment*

Crossfire 1947
Drama
64368   86 mins   B/W   B, V, 3/4U   P
Robert Young, Robert Mitchum, Robert Ryan, Gloria Grahame, Paul Kelly, directed by Edward Dmytryk
A Jewish hotel guest is murdered and three soldiers are suspected of the crime, one of whom is violently anti-Semitic. The first Hollywood film that explored racial bigotry.
RKO — *Nostalgia Merchant*

Crossover 1982
Drama
84112   96 mins   C   B, V   P
James Coburn, Kate Nelligan, directed by John Guillermin
A devoted male nurse works the graveyard shift in the psychiatric ward and neglects his personal life.
MPAA:R
Simcom — *Lightning Video*

Crucible of Terror 1972
Horror
58548   95 mins   C   B, V   R, P
Mike Raven, Mary Maude, James Bolam
A mad sculptor covers beautiful models with hot wax, then imprisons them in a mold of bronze.
Scotia Barber — *Prism; Video Gems; World Video Pictures*

Crucifix and M.D.C.: 198?
Compilation
Music-Performance
84055   60 mins   C   B, V   P
Crucifix, M.D.C. (Millions of Dead Cops)
Live performances by both San Francisco-based punk groups, including the hits 'No Limbs," 'John Wayne was a Nazi" and 'Dead Cops."
Target Video — *Target Video*

Cruel Sea, The 1953
War-Drama
58459   121 mins   B/W   B, V   P
Jack Hawkins, Stanley Baker, Denholm Elliott
The story of a Royal Navy corvette on convoy duty in the Atlantic.
Ealing Studios — *THORN EMI/HBO Video; Learning Corp of America*

Cruise Into Terror 1978
Suspense/Drama
80300   100 mins   C   B, V   P

Ray Milland, Hugh O'Brian, John Forsythe, Christopher George, Stella Stevens
A sarcophagus brought aboard a pleasure cruise ship unleashes an evil force which starts to slowly kill off the ship's passengers.
Aaron Spelling Productions — *Prism*

Cruise Missile   1978
Suspense
60415   100 mins   C   B, V   P
Peter Graves, Curt Jurgens, Michael Dante
A unique task force is on a mission to keep the world from nuclear holocaust.
Noble Production — *Monterey Home Video*

Cruising   1980
Drama
56753   102 mins   C   B, V, CED   P
Al Pacino, Paul Sorvino, Karen Allen, directed by William Friedkin
A bizarre murder-mystery set in the homosexual nightlife scene of New York's West Village.
Music by Jack Nitzsche.
MPAA:R
Jerry Weintraub, Lorimar — *CBS/Fox Video*

Crusaders Live!, The   1984
Music-Performance
80851   52 mins   C   B, V   P
Joe Sample, Wilton Felder, Stix Hooper
The infectious jazz-fusion sounds of the Crusaders are captured in this taped concert.
Available in VHS and Beta Hi Fi.
MCA Home Video — *MCA Home Video*

Cry For Love, A   1981
Drama
80633   98 mins   C   B, V   P
Susan Blakely, Powers Boothe, Gene Barry, Lainie Kazan, Charles Siebert, Herb Edelman
A divorced woman hiding her amphetamine addiction begins a near tragic romance with an alcoholic. Adapted from Jill Robinson's "Bed/Time/Story". Available in Beta Hi-Fi and VHS Stereo.
Charles Fries Prods.; Alan Sacks
Prods. — *U.S.A. Home Video*

Cry of a Prostitute: Love   1972
Kills
Drama
71244   86 mins   C   V   P
Henry Silva, Barbara Bouchet, directed by Andrew Bianchi
A former prostitute joins with a professional assassin in an effort to pacify rival gangsters in Italy.
MPAA:R
Joseph Brenner — *Prism*

Cry of Battle   1963
War-Drama
71191   99 mins   B/W   B, V   P
Van Heflin, Rita Moreno, James MacArthur
Anxious for the challenges of manhood, a well-heeled young man chooses to join a guerrilla militia in the Philippines.
Allied Artists — *Prism; King of Video*

Cry of the Innocent   1980
Adventure
74108   93 mins   C   B, V   P
Rod Taylor, Joanna Pettet, Nigel Davenport
An action-packed thriller about a Vietnam veteran who is out to find a group of Irish terrorists that killed his family.
Michael O'Herlihy — *VCL Home Video*

Cry of the Wild   1972
Wildlife
86027   87 mins   C   B, V   P
A documentary about wolves in their natural habitat, their raising of young, and methods of survival.
MPAA:G
Bill Mason; Pat Crawley — *United Home Video*

Cry Panic   1974
Mystery/Drama
80301   74 mins   C   B, V   P
John Forsythe, Anne Francis, Earl Holliman, Ralph Meeker
A man is thrown into a strange series of events after accidentally running down a man on a highway.
Spelling/Goldberg Productions — *Prism*

Cry Uncle   1971
Comedy
86861   85 mins   C   B, V   P
Allen Garfield, Paul Sorvino, directed by John G. Avildsen
A private eye investigates a blackmailing case involving film of orgies in which he has participated.
Troma — *Prism*

Crystal Gayle Live   1984
Music-Performance
66495   60 mins   C   V   P
Crystal Gayle
Country music's long-haired lovely sings the songs which won her Favorite Female Singer honors at the American music awards. Titles include "Talkin' in Your Sleep," "Half the Way" and the Grammy-winning "Don't It Make My Brown Eyes Blue."
Prism — *Prism*

Cuando Tu No Estas   197?
Drama
49743   90 mins   C   B, V   P

Maria Jose Alfonso, Ricardo Lucia, Margaret Peters, Jose Martin
A young man leaves his provincial town, looking for success in the city. He becomes familiar with the works of a female journalist, and she does likewise with his. Finally they meet, and love runs its course. In Spanish.
SP
Independent — *Media Home Entertainment*

Cucaracha, La   1934
Musical-Drama
12832   21 mins   C   B, V, FO   P
Steffi Duna
A lavish production filled with Mexican songs and dances. The first three-strip, live-action Technicolor film ever made.
Academy Awards '34: Best Comedy Short Subject.
RKO — *Video Yesteryear*

Cuchillo ("Knife")   1984
Adventure
72960   90 mins   C   B, V   P
Cuchillo is the weapon of the Apaches which they use to fight the white man in this violent tale of revenge and murder.
SP
Foreign — *Unicorn Video*

Cuckoo Clock That   1958
Wouldn't Cuckoo, The
Fairy tales/Cartoons
00666   12 mins   C   B, V   P, T
Animated
An animated fable of a clockmaker who tries to get the cuckoo in the royal cuckoo clock to break his silence.
Coronet Films — *Blackhawk Films; Coronet Films*

Cuisines and Folklores   1984
Around the World
Travel/Cookery
84282   40 mins   C   B, V   P
4   pgms
International travel highlights are spiced up by some of the best chefs in the world cooking their most famous dishes.
Video Travel Inc — *Video Travel*

Cujo   1983
Horror
66324   94 mins   C   B, V, LV,   P
                                        CED
Dee Wallace, Daniel Hugh-Kelly, Danny Pintauro, Ed Lauter, Christopher Stone
A rabid dog goes berserk and attacks a mother and her child who are trapped inside a broken-down car. Based on the Stephen King bestseller.

MPAA:R
Warner Bros — *Warner Home Video*

Culture Club: Kiss Across   1984
the Ocean
Music-Performance
72188   60 mins   C   B, V   P
America's favorite drag queen, Boy George, leads his pop group Culture Club through a string of hits performed live at the Hammersmith Odeon in London.
Tessa Watts and Richard Branston — *CBS/Fox Video*

Cure, The   1917
Comedy
58969   20 mins   B/W   B, V, 3/4U   P
Charlie Chaplin
Charlie arrives at a spa to take a rest cure, accompanied by a trunk full of liquor that somehow gets dumped into the water at the resort. Silent with music track.
Mutual — *Cable Films; Festival Films*

Curious George   1982
Cartoons
75892   30 mins   C   B, V   P
3   pgms
This program is a three-volume animated series of adventures of the monkey Curious George.
LWI Productions; Tablot Television — *Sony Video Software*

Curious George   1980
Cartoons
88137   83 mins   C   B, V   P
A full-length animated story featuring H.A. Rey's troublesome monkey.
Sony Video — *Sony Video Software*

Curley   1947
Comedy
29758   53 mins   C   B, V   P
Larry Olsen, Frances Rafferty, Eilene Janssen, Walter Abel
A part of the Hal Roach Comedy Carnival in which youngsters play pranks on their schoolteacher.
United Artists — *Hollywood Home Theater*

Curley and His Gang in   1947
the Haunted Mansion
Comedy/Mystery
66111   54 mins   C   B, V   P
Larry Olsen
An eccentric scientist gets involved in a haunted mansion mystery.
Hal Roach — *Unicorn Video*

Currier & Ives Christmas, A
1983

Christmas
66309   90 mins   C   B, V   P
A video music Christmas album that sets the
classic American art of Currier & Ives and other
early lithographers to a continuous background
of favorite Christmas music.
NTA — *Republic Pictures Home Video*

Curse of Frankenstein, The
1957

Horror
81901   83 mins   C   B, V   P
*Peter Cushing, Christopher Lee, Hazel Court,
Robert Urquhart*
Young Victor Frankenstein reenacts his father's
experiments with creating life from the dead
resulting in a terrifying, hideous creature.
Hammer Films — *Warner Home Video*

Curse of King Tut's Tomb, The
1980

Drama/Suspense
70565   98 mins   C   B, V   P
*Robin Ellis, Harry Andrews, Eva Marie Saint,
Raymond Burr, Wendy Heller, directed by Philip
Leacock*
It's 1922 and archeologists have opened
Tutankhamens tomb. The curse of the Boy King
seems unleashed as tragic events bring the
adventurers uncommon gloom.
Stromberg-Kerby Prods. in assoc. with CPT and
H.T.V. West — *RCA/Columbia Pictures Home
Video*

Curse of the Alpha Stone
1985

Horror
84816   90 mins   C   B, V   P
A professor experiments with an ancient
formula on a student, creating a babbling
maniac who slaughters freshman girls.
Unknown — *United Home Video*

Curse of the Cat People
1944

Fantasy
44802   70 mins   B/W   B, V, 3/4U   P
*Simone Simon, Kent Smith, Jane Randolph,
directed by Robert Wise*
A young sensitive girl is guided by the vision of
her dead mother.
RKO — *Nostalgia Merchant; RKO HomeVideo*

Curse of the Crying Woman, The
1961

Horror
51098   74 mins   B/W   B, V   P
*Rosita Arenas, Abel Salazar, Rita Macedo,
Carlos Lopez Moctezuma*
An unknowing descendant of a witch is lured to
her aunt's home to perform the act that will
revive the monstrous crying woman and renew
a reign of evil.

Mexican — *Hollywood Home Theater*

Curse of the Mummy, The/The Robot vs. the Aztec Mummy
195?

Horror
51953   130 mins   B/W   B, V   P
*Ramon Gay, Rosita Arenas, Crox Alvarado, Luis
Aceves Cantaneda, directed by Rafael Portillo*
A vengeful mummy of an Aztec warrior stalks
those who attempt to steal a fabulous treasure.
A mad, criminal scientist wants the treasure and
uses gangsters and a human robot to get what
he wants.
Azteca — *Hollywood Home Theater*

Curse of the Pink Panther, The
1983

Comedy
72465   110 mins   C   B, V   P
*Ted Wass, David Niven, Robert Wagner,
Herbert Lom, Capucine, Harvey Korman,
directed by Blake Edwards*
Ted Wass stars as Clifton Sleigh, an inept New
York City detective, assigned to find the missing
Inspector Clouseau. The plot is complicated by
an assortment of gangsters and aristocrats who
cross paths with the detective.
MPAA:PG
Tital Productions & United Artists
Corporation — *MGM/UA Home Video*

Curse of the Screaming Dead
1984

Horror
85376   90 mins   C   B, V   P
An unpredictable zombie yarn.
Unknown — *Mogul Communications*

Curse of the Yellow Snake, The
1963

Adventure
85162   98 mins   C   B, V   P
Joachim Berger, Werner Peters
Written by Edgar Wallace, this voluminous yarn
features a running battle over an ancient
Chinese artifact, with crazed Chinese cultists
running through foggy London streets.
German — *Video Yesteryear*

Curtain Call—USA
1978

Music-Performance
84855   90 mins   C   B, V   P
*Helen O'Connell, Johnny Desmond, Benny
Goodman*
A trip down memory lane with stars from the big
band era recreating the hits of the 40's.
Unknown — *United Home Video*

Curtains
1983

Horror
65351   90 mins   C   B, V   P

John Vernon, Samantha Eggar
A director has a clash of wills with a film star that spells "Curtains" for a group of aspiring actresses.
MPAA:R
Peter and Richard Simpson — *Vestron Video*

Custodio de Senoras   1979
Suspense
47857   100 mins   C   B, V   P
Augusto Larreta, Carlos Rotundo
Monica is threatened by death by a grudging boyfriend. George, the detective, becomes Monica's protector. In Spanish.
SP
Nicolas Carreras; Luis Repetto — *Media Home Entertainment*

Cut Above, A   1980
Football
45130   24 mins   C   B, V, FO   R, P
Pittsburgh Steelers
Highlights of the 1979 Pittsburgh Steelers World Championship season
NFL Films — *NFL Films Video*

Cut Above/NFL '83, A   1984
Football
72942   46 mins   C   B, V, FO   P
Washington Redskins
Highlights from the Washington Redskins' 1983 season and "NFL 83."
NFL Films — *NFL Films Video*

Cut-Pile Rug Weaving   1985
Handicraft
85653   101 mins   C   B, V   P
Orlo Duker
A beginners course in weaving cut-pile oriental rugs.
Victorian Video Prod. — *Victorian Video Productions*

Cutter's Way   1981
Mystery/Drama
63109   105 mins   C   B, V, CED   P
Jeff Bridges, John Heard, Lisa Eichhorn, directed by Ivan Passer
Two friends, one an embittered Vietnam veteran, become involved in a puzzling murder. Originally titled "Cutter and Bone."
MPAA:R
United Artists — *MGM/UA Home Video*

Cycling Through China   1983
Variety/Documentary
71103   52 mins   C   B, V   P
Ben Vereen, Kate Jackson, Joe Cunningham, Lorne Greene, directed by John Ripper
This travelogue features nine popular American entertainers who sing, dance, mime, dribble basketballs and cycle their way across the Asian continent.
Walt Disney Productions — *Walt Disney Home Video*

Cyclops   1956
Horror
82100   72 mins   B/W   B, V   P
Tom Drake, Gloria Talbot, Lon Chaney, Jr., James Craig
When an expedition party searches throughout Mexico for a woman's long lost brother, they are shocked when they find out he has turned into a one-eyed monster. Available in VHS Stereo and Beta Hi-Fi.
Allied Artists — *Thriller Video*

Cyrano   1974
Cartoons
79241   48 mins   C   B, V   P
Animated, voice of Jose Ferrer
An animated version of the classic story of a physically unattractive man who uses an attractive man to express his feelings to the woman he loves.
Hanna-Barbera Productions — *Worldvision Home Video*

Cyrano de Bergerac   1946
Drama
39008   112 mins   B/W   B, V   P
Jose Ferrer, Mala Powers, William Prince, Elena Verdugo, Morris Carnovsky, directed by Michael Gordon
The classic film version of the story of Cyrano, the tragic wit renowned for his nose, but longing of the love of a beautiful lady, Roxanne. Based on Edmond Rostand's play of 17th century Paris.
Academy Awards '50: Best Actor (Ferrer)
United Artists, Stanley Kramer — *Prism; Republic Pictures Home Video; American Video Tape; Video Yesteryear; Nostalgia Merchant; Cable Films; Video Connection; Hollywood Home Theater; Select-a-Tape; Western Film & Video Inc; Discount Video Tapes*

D

D-Day Plus 40 Years   1984
World War II/Documentary
86291   52 mins   C   B, V   P
Narrated by Tom Brokaw
The 40th anniversary of D-Day is celebrated through speeches by President Reagan, Queen Elizabeth and Pierre Trudeau. Also included are interviews with veterans of the famous battle.
NBC News — *Embassy Home Entertainment*

Daddy Long Legs
1982

Fantasy
72231 60 mins C B, V P
Animated
Jean Webster's story about an orphaned girl who is sent to school by an anonymous benefactor is animated for the first time.
Bunker Jenkins — *Children's Video Library*

Daffy Duck Cartoon Festival
194?

Cartoons
71150 35 mins C B, V P
Animated Daffy Duck, Porky Pig
There's wacky down-filled humor galore in this compilation tape. The cartoons include: "Ain't That Ducky," "Daffy Duck Slept Here," "Hollywood Daffy," "Conrad the Sailor" and "The Wise Cracking Duck," all from 1942-47.
The Vitaphone Corp — *MGM/UA Home Video*

Daffy Duck: The Nuttiness Continues...
1956

Cartoons
81572 59 mins C B, V P
Animated, voice of Mel Blanc
Daffy Duck runs amuck in this collection of cartoon classics that include "Beanstalk Bunny", "Deduce You Say", "Dripalong Daffy" and "The Scarlet Pumpernickel".
Warner Bros. — *Warner Home Video*

Daffy Duck's Movie: Fantastic Island
1983

Comedy/Cartoons
65323 78 mins C B, V, LV, P
CED
Animated
A compilation of classic Warner Brothers cartoons, starring Daffy Duck, Speedy Gonzales, Bugs Bunny, Porky Pig, Sylvester, Tweety, Pepe Le Pew, Pirate Sam, Granny, Foghorn Leghorn and the Tasmanian Devil.
MPAA:G
Warner Brothers — *Warner Home Video*

Dagora, the Space Monster
1965

Science fiction/Horror
69570 80 mins C B, V, FO P
Yosuke Natsuki, Yoko Fujiyama
A giant, slimy, pulsating mass from space lands on Earth and begins eating everything in sight. Scientists join together in a massive effort to destroy the creature.
Toho — *Video Yesteryear*

Dain Curse, The
1978

Mystery/Suspense
64972 118 mins C B, V P
James Coburn, Jason Miller, Jean Simmons, Beatrice Straight

In 1928, private eye Hamilton Nash must recover stolen diamonds, solve a millionaire's suicide, avoid being murdered, and end an insane family curse. Based on the novel by Dashiell Hammett.
Martin-Poll Productions — *Embassy Home Entertainment*

Daisy Miller
1974

Drama
86158 93 mins C B, V P
Cybill Shepherd, Eileen Brennan, Cloris Leachman
An adaptation of Henry James' novella about an emancipated woman who scandalizes Victorian society.
MPAA:G
Paramount — *Paramount Home Video*

Dakota
1945

Western
00284 82 mins B/W B, V P
John Wayne, Vera Ralston, Walter Brennan
Brawling saga with Wayne battling land grabbers in Dakota.
Republic — *Republic Pictures Home Video*

Dakota Incident
1956

Western
74484 88 mins C B, V P
Dale Robertson, Ward Bond
This is the story of a group of people brought together by a stagecoach ride across the dangerous Cheyenne territory.
Republic — *Republic Pictures Home Video*

Dallas Cowboys 1984 Team Highlights
1985

Football
70545 70 mins C B, V, FO P
The Cowboys proved that you don't need to make the playoffs to have a "Silver Season" in '84. This tape features 47-minutes of highlights from the entire NFL's '84 season as well.
NFL Films — *NFL Films Video*

Dallas Cowboys 1985 Team Highlights
1985

Football
86798 23 mins C B, V P
A program of highlights from the Cowboys' '85 season and their capture of the Eastern division title.
NFL Films — *NFL Films Video*

Dam Busters, The
1955

War-Drama
63353 119 mins B/W B, V P
Michael Redgrave, Richard Todd
In 1942 London, a scientist develops a plan to destroy the great Moehne and Eder dams in Germany.

ABPC; Richard Clark — *THORN EMI/HBO Video*

Dames 1934
Musical
73981   95 mins   B/W   B, V   P
Dick Powell, Joan Blondell, Ruby Keeler, ZaSu Pitts, Guy Kibbee, directed by Ray Enright
A fanatical puritanistic millionaire tries to stop the opening of a Broadway show. Songs from this movie include "I Only Have Eyes for You" and choreography by Busby Berkeley.
Warner Bros — *Key Video*

Damien—Omen II 1978
Horror
45106   110 mins   C ' B, V, CED   P
William Holden, Lee Grant, Lew Ayres, Robert Foxworth, Sylvia Sidney, directed by Don Taylor
This sequel to "The Omen" is about a young boy, possessed with mysterious demonic powers, who kills those people he comes in contact with.
MPAA:R EL, SP
20th Century Fox, Harvey Bernard — *CBS/Fox Video*

Damien: The Leper Priest 1980
Biographical/Drama
81261   96 mins   C   B, V   P
Ken Howard, Mike Farrell, Wilfred Hyde-White, William Daniels, David Ogden Stiers
This is the true story of Father Damien, a Roman Catholic priest who devoted his life to helping Hawaiian lepers on Molokai island. Available in VHS stereo and Beta Hi-Fi.
Tomorrow Entertainment — *U.S.A. Home Video*

Damn Yankees 1958
Musical
74202   110 mins   C ' B, V   P
Gwen Verdon, Ray Walston, Tab Hunter
This musical feature is adapted from the Broadway hit about a baseball fan who makes a pact with the devil.
George Abbott; Stanley Donen — *Warner Home Video*

Damnation Alley 1977
Science fiction/Drama
70698   87 mins   C   B, V   P
George Peppard, Jan-Michael Vincent, Paul Winfield, Dominique Sanda, Jackie Earle Haley, directed by Jack Smigth
A warrior, an artist and a biker set off in search of civilization after armageddon. Hi-Fi stereo sound in both formats.
MPAA:PG
20th Century Fox — *Key Video*

Damned, The 1969
Drama
58225   150 mins   C   , B, V   P
Dirk Bogarde, Ingrid Thulin, Helmut Griem, Charlotte Rampling, directed by Luchino Visconti
Visconti's study of a family's disintegration in greed, lust, and the madness of pre-war Germany. English language version.
MPAA:R
Warner Bros — *Warner Home Video*

Damsel in Distress, A 1937
Musical
63992   101 mins   B/W   B, V   P
Fred Astaire, Joan Fontaine, George Burns, Gracie Allen, Ray Noble, directed by George Stevens
Fred falls for an upper-class British girl, whose family wants her to have nothing to do with him. George and Ira Gershwin's memorable songs include "A Foggy Day," "Nice Work If You Can Get It," "Stiff Upper Lip" and "Put Me to the Test."
RKO — *RKO HomeVideo; Blackhawk Films; Nostalgia Merchant*

Dan Candy's Law 1973
Western
87684   90 mins   C   B, V   P
Donald Sutherland, Gordon Tootoosis, Chief Dan George, Kevin McCarthy
A Canadian mountie becomes a driven hunter, and then a desperate prey, when he tries to track down the Indian who killed his partner.
Cinerama — *Prism*

Dance Hall 1941
Adventure
88062   73 mins   B/W   B, V   P
Cesar Romero, Carole Landis
A Pennsylvania dance hall owner is propelled into libidinal confusion with the advent of a sultry blond dancer into his club.
20th Century Fox — *Kartes Video Communications*

Dance of the Dead 1968
Adventure/Fantasy
76921   50 mins   C   B, V   P
Patrick McGoohan
The members of the village use a succession of women in an attempt to break The Prisoner's will. An episode from "The Prisoner" TV series.
ITC — *MPI Home Video*

Dance with a Stranger 1985
Drama
Closed Captioned
86356   101 mins   C   B, V, LV   P
Miranda Richardson

A biography of Ruth Ellis, who ended her obsessive life with the notoriety of being the last woman hanged in Britain.
Cannes Film Festival '85: Best Picture   MPAA:R
The Samuel Goldwyn Company — *Vestron Video*

Dancing Princesses, The   1984
Fairy tales
Closed Captioned
81764   60 mins   C   B, V   P
Lesley Ann Warren, Peter Weller, Sachi Parker, Roy Dotrice, directed by Peter Medak
A handsome prince becomes invisible to follow five princesses into a magical fantasy world.
From the "Faerie Tale Theatre" series.
Lion's Gate Films; Platypus Productions — *CBS/Fox Video*

Danger   1952
Suspense
85508   77 mins   B/W   B, V   P
Don Hammer, Olive Deering, Joey Walsh, Eli Wallach, Kim Stanley
Three live "TV noir" thrillers directed by Sidney Lumet: "The Lady on the Rock," "Death Among the Relics" and "The System."
CBS — *Video Yesteryear*

Danger Lights   1930
Drama
44992   73 mins   B/W   B, V   P, T
Jean Arthur, Loius Wohleim
This movie depicts the railroads and the railroad men's dedication to the tenet of giving the best possible care to each other and their trains.
RKO — *Blackhawk Films; Interurban Films; Video Yesteryear; Kartes Video Communications*

Dangerous Holiday   1937
Adventure
12811   54 mins   B/W   B, V, FO   P
Hedda Hopper, Franklin Pangborn, Guinn Williams, Jack La Rue
A young violin prodigy would rather be just "one of the boys." He runs away from his greedy relatives but begins to hang out with a gang of kidnappers.
Republic — *Video Yesteryear*

Dangerous Mission   1954
Mystery
33900   75 mins   B/W   B, V   P
Victor Mature, Piper Laurie, Vincent Price, William Bendix
A New York girl witnesses a gangland murder and flees to the Midwest, pursued by killers and the police.
RKO;Irwin Allen — *Nostalgia Merchant*

Dangerous Moves   1984
Drama
87196   96 mins   C   B, V   P
Liv Ullman, Michel Piccoli, Leslie Caron, Alexandre Arbatt, directed by Richard Dembo
A drama built around the World Chess championship competition between a renowned Russian master and a young, rebellious dissident. The chess game serves as both metaphor and background for the social and political tensions it produces. With English subtitles.
Academy Awards '84: Best Foreign Film.   FR
Arthur Cohn — *Karl/Lorimar Home Video*

Dangerous Summer, A   1982
Suspense
73148   100 mins   C   B, V   P
James Mason, Tom Skeritt
James Mason is sent to Australia to investigate a murderous insurance fraud.
McElroy & McElroy Prods — *VCL Home Video*

Dangerous When Wet   1953
Musical
85635   96 mins   C   B, V   P
Esther Williams, Fernando Lamas, Charlotte Greenwood, William Demarest, Jack Carson, directed by Charles Walters, music by Arthur Schwartz & Johnny Mercer
A typical Williams water-musical, dealing with a farmgirl who decides to swim the English Channel. One famous number pairs Esther with cartoon characters Tom & Jerry in an underwater frolic.
MGM — *MGM/UA Home Video*

Danguard Ace   1982
Cartoons/Science fiction
63119   100 mins   C   B, V   P
Animated
A heroic young fighter pilot seeks the aid of Danguard Ace, mighty robot, to combat the evil forces of Komisar Krel.
Toei Animation; MK Company; Jim Terry Production Services — *Family Home Entertainment*

Daniel   1983
Drama
66410   130 mins   C   B, V   P
Timothy Hutton, Amanda Plummer, Mandy Patinkin, Lindsay Crouse
The children of a couple who were executed for espionage suffer many agonizing trials as they grow to maturity with the constant reminder of their parents' treasonous activities. Based on E.L. Doctorow's "The Book of Daniel."
MPAA:R
Paramount — *Paramount Home Video*

Daniel and Nebuchadnezzar   1979
Drama/Bible
55020   51 mins   C   B, V   P
Donny Most, Hans Conreid, David Hendison,
Jerry Houser, Linwood Boomer, Vic Morrow,
narrated by Victor Jory
The story of the young Hebrew Daniel, who is
imprisoned but set free once he interprets a
dream of the King's. Part of the "Greatest
Heroes of the Bible" series.
Sunn Classics — Magnum Entertainment;
Vanguard Video; Lucerne Films

Daniel Boone   1936
Western
65228   77 mins   B/W   B, V   P
George O'Brien, Heather Angel, John Carradine
Daniel Boone guides a party of settlers from
North Carolina to the fertile valleys of Kentucky,
facing Indians, food shortages and bad weather
along the way.
RKO — Movie Buff Video; Hal Roach Studios;
Video Connection; Hollywood Home Theater;
Discount Video Tapes; Kartes Video
Communications

Daniel in the Lion's Den   1979
Drama/Bible
55019   39 mins   C   B, V   P
Robert Vaughn, David Birney, Sherry Jackson,
Nehemiah Persoff, Dean Stockwell
The story of the Hebrew Daniel, caught in a
sinister plot and condemned to the lion's den.
Part of the "Greatest Heroes of the Bible"
series.
Sunn Classics — Magnum Entertainment;
Vanguard Video; Lucerne Films

Danny   1979
Drama
76800   90 mins   C   B, V   P
Rebecca Page, Janet Zarish, Gloria Maddox,
George Luce
A young girl begins to mature when a
mysterious benefactor gives her a pony.
MPAA:G
Wombat Prods — Monterey Home Video

Danny Boy   1946
Comedy-Drama
12864   67 mins   B/W   B, V, FO   P
A returning war dog has difficulty adjusting to
normal life. Things get worse for him and his
young master when Danny Boy is assumed to
be dangerous.
PRC — Video Yesteryear

Danny Boy   1984
Drama
77243   92 mins   C   B, V   P

Stephen Rea, Honor Heffernan
A young saxophone player who witnesses a
murder embarks on a path to find the killer.
MPAA:R
Triumph Films — RCA/Columbia Pictures
Home Video

Danspak   1983
Music video
88095   20 mins   C   B, V   P
A collection of performance clips from some of
New York/Greenwich Village's stranger new
wave club bands.
Sony Video — Sony Video Software

Danspak II   1984
Music-Performance
76667   30 mins   C   B, V   P
Six different New York groups combining night-
life scenes, dance routines, humor and much
more. The groups include: The Jim Carroll Band,
The Lenny Kaye Connection, Strange Party,
Michael Musto and the Must, Go Ohgami, Jason
Harvey.
Co Directions Inc — Sony Video Software

Danton   1982
Biographical
72921   136 mins C   B, V   P
Gerard Depardieu
An historical period film about the leader of the
French Revolution, Georges Danton. This film is
in French with subtitles.
MPAA:PG   FR
Les Films Du Losange Maragret
Menegoz — RCA/Columbia Pictures Home
Video

Darby O'Gill and the Little People   1959
Fantasy
53796   93 mins   C   B, V   P
Albert Sharpe, Janet Munro, Sean Connery,
Estelle Winwood, directed by Robert Stevenson
Set in Ireland, a roguish old story teller tumbles
into a well and visits the land of leprechauns,
who give him three wishes in order to rearrange
his life.
Walt Disney — Walt Disney Home Video

Daredevil Flyers   1986
Aeronautics/Documentary
71225   30 mins   C   V   P
General Chuck Yeager, Rob Kells, Jimmy
Franklin
The wide world of flight, from breaking the
sound barrier to hang gliding and hot-air
balloons, fills this made-for-video presentation.
Prism Video Collection — Prism

Daring Dobermans, The   1973
Crime-Drama
Closed Captioned
70992   88 mins   C   B, V   P
Charles Robinson, Tim Considine, David Moses, Claudio Martinez, JoanCaulfield, directed by Byron Ross Chudnow
In this sequel to "The Doberman Gang," the barking bank-robbers wind up with a new set of crime-planning masters. A young Indian boy who loves the dogs may thwart their perfect crime.
MPAA:G
Morin; Rosamond Prods Inc — *Key Video*

Daring Game   1968
Adventure
80034   100 mins   C   B, V   P
Lloyd Bridges, Brock Peters, Michael Ansara, Joan Blackman, directed by Laslo Benedek
A group of scuba divers attempt to rescue a woman's husband and daughter from an island dictatorship.
Paramount; Ivan Tors — *Republic Pictures Home Video*

Dark, The   1979
Horror
47317   92 mins   C   B, V   P
William Devane, Cathy Lee Crosby, Richard Jaeckel, Keenan Wynn, Vivian Blaine
A supernatural beast commits a string of gruesome murders.
MPAA:R
Dick Clark; Film Ventures International — *Media Home Entertainment*

Dark August   1976
Horror
88233   87 mins   C   B, V   P
J.J. Barry, Carole Shelyne, Kim Hunter, directed by Martin Goldman
A New Yorker drops out and transplants to rural Vermont, where he accidentally kills a young girl, and then suffers numerous horrors as a result of a curse put on him by the girl's grandfather.
MPAA:PG
Raffia Prod. — *Lightning Video*

Dark Command   1940
Western
66310   95 mins   B/W   B, V   P
John Wayne, Walter Pidgeon, Claire Trevor, Roy Rogers, Marjorie Main
The story of Quantrell's Raiders, who patrolled Kansas territory during the Civil War, in search of wrongdoers.
Republic — *Republic Pictures Home Video*

Dark Crystal, The   1982
Fantasy/Adventure
69390   93 mins   C   B, V, CED   P
Directed by Jim Henson
Jen and Kira, two of the last surviving Gelflings, attempt to return a crystal shard (discovered with the help of a sorceress) to the castle where the Dark Crystal lies, guarded by the cruel and evil Skeksis.
MPAA:PG
ITC Entertainment; Jim Henson and Gary Kurtz — *THORN EMI/HBO Video*

Dark Forces   1983
Mystery/Suspense
81092   96 mins   C   B, V   P
Robert Powell, David Hemmings, Broderick Crawford
Things get weird for a Senator when an enigmatic stranger comes to visit him.
MPAA:PG
Antony I. Ginnane — *Media Home Entertainment*

Dark Journey   1937
Drama
47773   82 mins   B/W   B, V, 3/4U   R, P
Vivien Leigh, Conrad Veidt, Joan Gardner, Anthony Bushell
A world War I tale of espionage and romance between a British spy and the head of the German Secret Service.
United Artists — *Cable Films; Discount Video Tapes; Kartes Video Communications; See Hear Industries*

Dark Mirror, The   1946
Mystery
76832   85 mins   B/W   B, V   P
Olivia de Havilland, Lew Ayres, Thomas Mitchell, Garry Owen
A psychologist and a detective must determine which twin sister murdered a prominent physician.
Nunnally Johnson — *Republic Pictures Home Video*

Dark of the Night   1985
Suspense
88225   88 mins   C   B, V   P
Heather Bolton, David Letch, directed by Gaylene Preston
In a story very much like Stephen King's "Christine," a car becomes possessed and goes on a killing rampage.
Castle Hill Prod. — *Lightning Video*

Dark Passage   1947
Drama/Mystery
73967   107 mins   B/W   B, V   P
Humphrey Bogart, Lauren Bacall, Agnes Moorehead, Bruce Bennett, Tom D'Andrea
A convict escapes from San Quentin to prove he was framed for the murder of his wife, aided by a women who believes his story.

Warner Bros — *Key Video*

Dark Places
1973

Horror
65426   91 mins   C   B, V   P
Joan Collins, Christopher Lee, Robert Hardy
Masquerading as a hospital administrator, a
former mental patient inherits the ruined
mansion of a man who had killed his wife and
children and died insane. As he lives in the
house, the spirit of its former owner seems to
overcome him, and the bizarre crime is
repeated.
MPAA:PG
Cinerama — *Embassy Home Entertainment*

Dark Ride, The
198?

Horror
82487   83 mins   C   B, V   P
James Luisi, Susan Sullivan, Martin Speer
A thriller based on the actions of serial murderer
Ted Bundy.
Media — *Media Home Entertainment*

Dark Room, The
1984

Suspense/Drama
80491   90 mins   C   B, V   P
A disturbed young man becomes obsessed with
his father's voluptuous mistress and longs to
possess her.
VCL Communications — *VCL Home Video*

Dark Side of Love
1979

Exploitation
86603   94 mins   C   B, V   P
*James Stacy, Glynnis O'Connor, Jan Sterling,
Mickey Rooney*
A young girl enters the underbelly of New
Orleans, gets pregnant and experiences utter
degradation.
EMI Television Prod. — *Video Gems*

Dark Star
1974

Science fiction
01657   95 mins   C   B, V   P
*Dan O'Bannon, Brian Narelle, directed by John
Carpenter*
Scientists try to destroy unstable planets and
are forced into a fight with aliens whose
technology may dominate the human race.
MPAA:G
Bryanston; John Carpenter — *Hollywood
Home Theater; Video Dimensions*

Dark Star—The Special Edition
1974

Science fiction
66029   91 mins   C   B, V   P
*Dan O'Brian, Brian Narelle, directed by John
Carpenter*
A scoutship is entrusted with clearing a path in
space for a Colony's ships.

MPAA:G
John Carpenter; Bryanston Pictures — *United
Home Video*

Dark Victory
1939

Drama
64707   106 mins   B/W   CED   P
*Bette Davis, George Brent, Geraldine
Fitzgerald, Humphrey Bogart, Ronald Reagan*
Bette Davis portrays a young heiress who
discovers she is dying from a brain condition.
She attempts to pack a lifetime into a few
months.
Warner Bros — *Key Video; RCA VideoDiscs*

Dark Waters
1944

Drama
81222   93 mins   B/W   B, V, LV   P
*Merle Oberon, Franchot Tone, Thomas Mitchell,
directed by Andre de Toth*
A woman is convinced that someone is trying to
drive her insane when she returns to her
mansion after a sailing disaster.
United Artists — *New World Video*

Darling
1965

Drama
64991   122 mins   B/W   B, V   P
Julie Christie, Laurence Harvey, Dirk Bogarde
A young model, searching for love in the world
of the jet set, leaves her husband and manages
to reach the top of European society by
marrying a prince. She learns that life at the top
can be very empty.
Academy Awards '65: Best Actress (Christie).
Avco-Embassy — *Embassy Home
Entertainment*

D.A.R.Y.L.
1985

Science fiction
Closed Captioned
82551   100 mins   C   B, V, LV   P
Mary Beth Hurt, Michael McKeon, Barret Oliver
The American military has a top-secret interest
in an extraordinarily gifted child that threatens
his very existence.
MPAA:PG
World Film Services — *Paramount Home
Video*

Daryl Hall & John Oates—The Liberty Concert
1986

Music-Performance
86791   30 mins   C   B, V   P
Hall & Oates' are captured at their concert for
the restoration of the Statue of Liberty,
performing their numerous hits.
RCA Video — *RCA/Columbia Pictures Home
Video*

Daryl Hall & John Oates   1985
Live at the Apollo
Music-Performance
70878   30 mins   C   B, V   P
Daryl Hall, John Oates, David Ruffin, Eddie Kendrick, Boy George, Andy Warhol, Kool & the Gang
Ruffin and Kendrick, former Temptations, join Hall and Oates on stage at the Apollo's grand re-opening for a rousing performance of some of their pop hits. In Hi-Fi Stereo.
RCA Video Prods. — *RCA/Columbia Pictures Home Video*

Daryl Hall & John   1983
Oates—Rock 'n Soul Live
Music-Performance
66349   50 mins   C   B, V   P
Taped during their 1983 "H2O" tour, Daryl Hall and John Oates perform a program of hits including "She's Gone," "Family Man" and "Maneater." Stereo VHS and Beta Hi-Fi.
RCA — *RCA/Columbia Pictures Home Video*

Daryl Hall and John Oates   1984
Video Collection: 7 Big
Ones
Music video
80367   30 mins   C   B, V   P
A collection of conceptual music videos from those masters of blue eyed soul, Daryl Hall and John Oates. Available in VHS Hi-Fi Dolby Stereo and Beta Hi-Fi Stereo.
RCA Video Productions — *RCA/Columbia Pictures Home Video*

Dastardly & Muttley   196?
Cartoons
66274   53 mins   C   B, V   P
Animated
The villainous commanders of the Vulture Squadron will stop at nothing in their diabolical, do-anything flying machines.
Hanna Barbera — *Worldvision Home Video*

Dastardly and Muttley's   1970
High Flying Fun
Cartoons
84080   50 mins   C   B, V   P
The cartoon flying aces in their jaunty jalopies endlessly pursue the paragon of wartime mail efficiency, Yankee Doodle Pigeon.
Hanna Barbera — *Worldvision Home Video*

Datsun, Nissan 210 & 240,   1986
260, 280Z
Automobiles
88402   60 mins   C   B, V, 3/4U   P
2   pgms
How to repair, maintain and tune-up the various Datsun engines.

Peter Allen Prod. — *Peter Allen Video Productions*

Datsun "Z" Tune-Up, The   1984
Automobiles
78377   36 mins   C   B, V, 3/4U   P
How to tune up the Datsun "Z" series of cars is demonstrated in this instructional videocassette.
Videovision Productions Inc — *Peter Allen Video Productions*

Dave Mason in Concert   1984
Music-Performance
77231   60 mins   C   B, V   P
The guitarist performs such hits as "We Just Disagree" and "Feeling' Alright" in this taped concert.
Neal Marshall — *Monterey Home Video*

Dave Mason Live at   1982
Perkins Palace
Music-Performance
47811   ? mins   C   LV   P
The veteran rock singer/guitarist performs "We Just Disagree," "Every Woman," "Let It Go," "Feelin' Alright," "Take It to the Limit" and other hits. In stereo.
Unknown — *Pioneer Artists*

David and Goliath   1979
Drama/Bible
55013   37 mins   C   B, V   P
Ted Cassidy, Jeff Corey, John Dehner, Roger Kern, Hugh O'Brian
The story of the battle between the young Israelite David and the Philistine giant Goliath. Part of the "Greatest Heroes of the Bible" series.
Sunn Classics — *Magnum Entertainment; Vanguard Video; Lucerne Films*

David Bowie   1983
Music-Performance
75902   14 mins   C   B, V   P
This program presents David Bowie at his best performing "Let's Dance," "China Girl" and "Modern Love."
EMI America Records — *Sony Video Software*

David Bowie: Ricochet   1984
Music-Performance/Documentary
71013   60 mins   C   B, V   P
David Bowie, directed by Gerry Troyna
Filmed during the Far Eastern leg of Bowie's "Serious Moonlight" tour in '83, this film includes some unusual interviews with Oriental Bowie fans.
Maya Vision — *Passport Music Video*

David Bowie—Serious   **1984**
Moonlight
Music-Performance
65683   90 mins   C   B, V   P
Drawing from all phases of his career, Bowie
performs 19 songs that have made him rock's
most enigmatic and commanding performer.
Included are "Space Oddity," "Young
Americans," "Let's Dance," and "China Girl."
Anthony Eaton — *Music Media*

David Copperfield   **1983**
Cartoons
77177   72 mins   C   B, V, CED   P
Animated
An animated adaptation of the Dickens classic
about a young boy growing up in 19th century
England.
Burbank Films — *Children's Video Library*

David Copperfield   **1935**
Drama
81499   132 mins   B/W   B, V   P
*Lionel Barrymore, W.C. Fields, Freddie
Bartholomew, Maureen O'Sullivan, Basil
Rathbone, Lewis Stone, directed by George
Cukor*
This is an adaptation of the Charles Dickens
novel about David Copperfield who undergoes a
great deal of struggles and hardship in Victorian
England.
MGM — *MGM/UA Home Video*

David Oistrakh: **1985**
Remembering a Musician
Music-Performance
87346   60 mins   C   B, V   P
A collection of rare performances by Oistrakh,
featuring rare footage from Soviet archives,
including Lalo's Symphonie Espagnole,
excerpts from Shostakovich's F minor Sonata
and more.
Unknown — *Kultur*

David Steinberg in   **1984**
Concert
Comedy-Performance
78661   60 mins   C   B, V   P
Comedian David Steinberg performs some of
his best routines in this concert taped in
Toronto.
Nordic Productions; Global Television
Network — *RKO HomeVideo*

Davy Crockett and the   **1956**
River Pirates
Western
81654   81 mins   C   B, V, LV   P
Fess Parker, Buddy Ebsen, Jeff York
Davy Crockett becomes involved in a keelboat
race down the Ohio River.
MPAA:G

Walt Disney Productions — *Walt Disney Home
Video*

Davy Crockett and the   **1956**
River Pirates
Adventure
55566   81 mins   C   B, V, LV   P
Fess Parker, Buddy Ebsen, Jeff York
The King of the Wild Frontier meets up with
Mike Fink, the King of the Ohio River, and the
two engage in a furious keelboat race, and then
unite to track down a group of thieves
masquerading as Indians and threatening the
peace.
MPAA:G
Walt Disney — *Walt Disney Home Video*

Davy Crockett, King of   **1955**
the Wild Frontier
Western/Adventure
77528   89 mins   C   B, V   P
*Fess Parker, Buddy Ebsen, Hans Conried, Ray
Whiteside, Pat Hogan*
This film chronicles the life and adventures of
Davy Crockett from his days as an Indian fighter,
to his gallant death in defense of the Alamo.
Walt Disney Productions — *Walt Disney Home
Video*

Davy Crockett on the   **1973**
Mississippi
Cartoons
66582   47 mins   C   B, V   P
Animated
The animated adventures of the American folk
hero during his days as a frontiersman along the
Mississippi River.
Hanna-Barbera — *Worldvision Home Video*

Dawn!   **1983**
Biographical/Drama
77012   114 mins   C   B, V   P
Bronwyn Mac Kay-Payne, Tom Richards
This is the true story of Dawn Fraser, the
Olympic champion swimmer who really was an
unfulfilled woman who fought for her happiness.
Satori Entertainment — *VidAmerica*

Dawn of the Dead   **1978**
Horror
69627   126 mins   C   B, V   P
Directed by George Romero
Flesh-eating zombies run amok in a shopping
mall.
MPAA:R
Richard P Rubinstein — *THORN EMI/HBO
Video*

Dawn of the Mummy   **1982**
Horror
64213   93 mins   C   B, V   P

From the depths of a pharaoh's tomb, a mummy awakes to kill the tomb's desecrators—four beautiful American models.
Frank Agarna; Harmony Gold Productions — *THORN EMI/HBO Video*

Dawn of the Pirates (La Secta de los Tughs), The   197?
Adventure
88312   95 mins   C   B, V   P
An adventurer stumbles upon a murderous tribe of Tughs and the beautiful white woman they captured.
SP
Spanish — *JCI Video*

Dawn on the Great Divide   1942
Western
11671   57 mins   B/W   B, V   P
Buck Jones, Tim McCoy, Ray Hatton
Western adventure with the Three Mesquiteers as the heroes.
Monogram — *Video Connection; Cable Films; Discount Video Tapes; Kartes Video Communications*

Dawn Patrol, The   1938
Drama/World War I
70696   103 mins   B/W   B, V   P
Errol Flynn, David Niven, Basil Rathbone, directed by Edmund Goulding
The brave fighters of WW I's air war face their deaths each time they fly. This film focuses on the effects of that pressure on three British airmen. Hi-Fi sound on both formats.
United Artists; Warner Bros. — *Key Video*

Dawn Rider   1935
Western
51635   60 mins   B/W   B, V   P
John Wayne, Marion Burns, Yakima Canutt
Love and gunfights in the action-filled old American West.
Monogram — *Sony Video Software; Spotlite Video; Discount Video Tapes*

Dawn Rider/Frontier Horizon   1938
Western
81018   114 mins   B/W   B, V   P
John Wayne, Jennifer Jones, Marion Burns
This is a double feature of two of John Wayne's earliest western films.
Republic Pictures — *Spotlite Video*

Day After, The   1983
Drama/Nuclear warfare
65387   126 mins   C   B, V, LV,   P
                                        CED
A powerful drama which graphically depicts the nuclear bombing of a midwestern city and its aftereffects on the survivors.

ABC Circle Films — *Embassy Home Entertainment*

Day and the Hour, The   1963
War-Drama
81835   110 mins   B/W   B, V   P
Simone Signoret, Stuart Whitman, Genevieve Page, directed by Rene Clement
A young woman becomes accidentally involved in the resistance movement during the Nazi occupation of France in World War II. Available in VHS and Beta Hi-Fi.
MGM — *Monterey Home Video*

Day at Disneyland, A   1982
Travel
47411   39 mins   C   B, V   P
A colorful souvenir of the attractions at Disneyland. Highlights include a ride down Main Street, a visit to Sleeping Beauty's castle and trips through Adventureland, Frontierland, Fantasyland and Tomorrowland.
Walt Disney Prods — *Walt Disney Home Video*

Day at the Races, A   1937
Comedy
53938   109 mins   B/W   B, V, LV,   P
                                        CED
Marx Brothers, Allan Jones, Maureen O'Sullivan
The Marx Brothers help a girl who owns a sanitorium and a race horse.
MGM — *MGM/UA Home Video*

Day for Night   1973
Drama
58226   116 mins   C   B, V   P
Jacqueline Bisset, Jean-Pierre Aumont, directed by Francois Truffaut
An affectionate look at the profession of moviemaking—its craft, its character, and the personalities that interact against the performances commanded by the camera. English language version.
Academy Awards '73: Best Foreign Language Film. MPAA:PG
Les Films Du Carrosse — *Warner Home Video*

Day of Freedom-Our Fighting Forces   1935
Propaganda
85163   17 mins   B/W   B, V   P
Directed by Leni Reifenstahl
A recently discovered film by the world-class filmmaker, showing the Reich's military power which der Fuehrer thought was missing from "Triumph of the Will."
The Third Reich — *Video Yesteryear*

Day of Frustration—Season of Triumph
1984

Football
72938   46 mins   C   B, V, FO   P
Miami Dolphins
Highlights from the Miami Dolphins' 1983 season and "NFL 83."
NFL Films — *NFL Films Video*

Day of Judgement
1981

Horror
80332   101 mins   C   B, V   P
A mysterious stranger arrives in a town to slaughter those people who violate the Ten Commandments.
E.O. Corporation — *THORN EMI/HBO Video*

Day of the Animals
1977

Horror
47316   97 mins   C   B, V   P
Christopher George, Leslie Nielsen, Lynda Day George, Richard Jaeckel, Michael Ansara, Ruth Roman
Animals begin attacking human beings when the earth's ozone layer is depleted to a critical level.
MPAA:PG
Edward Montoro; Film Ventures International — *Media Home Entertainment*

Day of the Cobra, The
1984

Adventure
80271   95 mins   C   B, V   P
Franco Nero, Sybil Danning, Mario Maranzana, Licinia Lentini
A corrupt narcotics bureau official hires an ex-cop to find a heroin kingpin on the back streets of Genoa, Italy.
Turi Vasile — *Media Home Entertainment*

Day of the Dead
1985

Horror
85595   91 mins   C   B, V   P
Lori Cardillo, Terry Alexander, directed by George Romero
This is the third in Romero's trilogy of films about flesh-eating zombies taking over the world. For adult audiences.
George A. Romero — *Media Home Entertainment*

Day of the Dolphin, The
1973

Adventure
08370   104 mins   C   B, V   P
George C. Scott, Trish Van Devere, Paul Sorvino, Fritz Weaver, directed by Mike Nichols
Research scientist, after successfully working out a means of teaching dolphins to talk, finds his animals kidnapped.
MPAA:PG
Avco Embassy — *Embassy Home Entertainment*

Day of the Dolphins/NFL '82
1983

Football
66220   45 mins   C   B, V, FO   P
Highlights of the 1982-83 season for the Miami Dolphins combined with an overview of the whole NFL season.
NFL Films — *NFL Films Video*

Day of the Jackal, The
1973

Suspense
60590   142 mins   C   B, V   P
Edward Fox, Alan Badel, Tony Britton, Derek Jacobi, Cyril Cusack, Olga Georges-Picot, directed by Fred Zinnemann
Frederick Forsyth's best-selling novel of political intrigue concerning a suave British assassin hired to kill DeGaulle is the basis of this film.
MPAA:PG
Universal — *MCA Home Video*

Day of the Locust
1975

Drama
66035   140 mins   C   B, V   P
Donald Sutherland, Karen Black, Burgess Meredith, William Atherton, Geraldine Page, directed by John Schlesinger
Nathaniel West's novel concerning the dark side of 1930's Hollywood is brought to life in this film.
MPAA:R
Paramount; Jerome Hellman — *Paramount Home Video*

Day of the Triffids
1963

Science fiction
01658   94 mins   C   B, V   P
Howard Keel, Janet Scott, Nicole Maurey, directed by Steve Sekely
Giant pea-pods drop to earth and become man-eating plants. A professor finally discovers a way to destroy them.
Allied Artists — *Media Home Entertainment; Prism; King of Video; Hollywood Home Theater; World Video Pictures*

Day of Wrath
1943

Horror
07365   110 mins   B/W   B, V   P
Directed by Carl Theodor Dreyer
A psychological horror story based on records of witch trials of the early 1600's.
Danish — *Western Film & Video Inc; Cable Films*

Day the Bookies Wept, The
1939

Comedy
29470   50 mins   B/W   B, V   P, T
Betty Grable, Joe Penner, Tom Kennedy, Richard Lane

A cab driver who loves pigeons is tricked into buying an old nag who loves alcohol and entering him in the big race.
RKO, Robert Sisk — *Blackhawk Films*

Day the Earth Caught Fire, The 1962
Science fiction
58461   100 mins   B/W   B, V   P
Janet Munro, Edward Judd, Leo McKern
World powers unite to save the earth after faulty nuclear tests.
Val Guest — *THORN EMI/HBO Video*

Day the Earth Stood Still, The 1951
Science fiction
08433   92 mins   B/W   B, V   P
Michael Rennie, Patricia Neal, Hugh Marlowe, Bobby Gray
An emissary from another planet lands on Earth on a mission of peace and is brutally shot down by Washington, D.C. policemen.
EL, SP
20th Century Fox — *CBS/Fox Video*

Day the Loving Stopped, The 1982
Romance
75458   96 mins   C   B, V   P
Dennis Weaver, Valerie Harper
A couple goes through a difficult break-up.
King Features — *U.S.A. Home Video*

Day They Gave Diamonds Away, The 1964
Adventure/Comedy
82189   52 mins   B/W   B, V   P
David Niven, Gig Young, Charles Boyer, Robert Coote, Gladys Cooper, James Gregory
The Flemings are up to their old tricks as they threaten the international diamond market with a machine that makes perfect gemstones. An episode from "The Rogues" series.
Four Star Television — *RKO HomeVideo*

Day Time Ended, The 197?
Science fiction
42916   80 mins   C   B, V   P
Chris Mitchum, Jim Davis, Dorothy Malone
A pair of glowing UFO's streaking across the sky and an alien mechanical device with long menacing appendages are only two of the bizarre phenomena in a house that is slipping into different dimensions.
Wayne Schmidt; Steve Neil; Paul Gentry — *Media Home Entertainment*

Daydreamer, The 1966
Fantasy/Fairy tales
64974   98 mins   C   B, V   P

Paul O'Keefe, Ray Bolger, Jack Gilford, Margaret Hamilton, voices of Tallulah Bankhead, Boris Karloff, Burl Ives, Terry Thomas
Young Hans Christian Andersen falls asleep and dreams some of his most famous fairy tales"The Little Mermaid," "The Emperor's New Clothes," and "Thumbelina." Live action is combined with animation and highlighted with songs.
Avco-Embassy — *Embassy Home Entertainment*

Days of Heaven 1978
Drama
38593   95 mins   C   B, V, LV   P
Richard Gere, Brooke Adams, Sam Shepard, directed by Terence Malick
Critically acclaimed story of a drifter (Gere) who becomes involved in the lives of a Texas sharecropper family. Story and screenplay by Terence Malick.
MPAA:PG
Paramount — *Paramount Home Video; RCA VideoDiscs*

Days of Wine and Roses 1962
Drama
63451   134 mins   B/W   B, V   P
Jack Lemmon, Lee Remick, Charles Bickford, Jack Klugman, directed by Blake Edwards
A harrowing tale of an alcoholic advertising man who gradually drags his wife down with him into a life of booze. Part of the 'A Night at the Movies" series, this tape simulates a 1962 movie evening, with a Bugs Bunny cartoon, "Martian Through Georgia," a newsreel and coming attractions for "Gypsy" and "Rome Adventure."
Academy Awards '62: Best Song ("Days of Wine and Roses").
Warner Bros — *Warner Home Video*

Days of Wine and Roses, The 1958
Drama
65014   89 mins   B/W   B, V   P
Cliff Robertson, Piper Laurie, directed by John Frankenheimer
The original "Playhouse 90" television version of J.P. Miller's story about a young couple whose social drinking becomes total dependence.
CBS — *MGM/UA Home Video*

Dazzledancin 1984
Dance
65611   60 mins   C   B, V   P
The dance spectacle of the 80's gives an inside look at the raw, acrobatic finesse of the most energetic breakdancers, spinners, and poplockers.
Four Star International — *U.S.A. Home Video*

D.C. Cab 1984
Comedy
Closed Captioned
65516 100 mins C B, V, LV P
Mr. T., Adam Baldwin, Charlie Barnett, Irene Cara, Anne De Salvo, Max Gail, Gloria Gifford, Gary Busey
A rag-tag Washington D.C. cab company is the setting for a young man who brings pride and esteem to a group of society's outcasts. Closed captioned in VHS and Beta only. In stereo VHS and Beta Hi-Fi.
MPAA:R
Universal — *MCA Home Video*

Dead and Buried 1981
Horror
64875 95 mins C B, V, CED P
James Farentino
A sheriff is bewildered and bewitched by the perpetrator of a series of strange murders in his town.
MPAA:R
Ronald Shusett; Robert Bentruss — *Vestron Video*

Dead Don't Die, The 1975
Adventure
79248 74 mins C B, V P
George Hamilton, Ray Milland, Linda Cristal, Ralph Meeker, directed by Curtis Harrington
When a young man tries to prove his brother was wrongly executed for murder, he encounters a man who wants to rule the world with an army of zombies.
Douglas S. Cramer Company — *Worldvision Home Video*

Dead Easy 1984
Mystery/Suspense
76662 92 mins C B, V P
Scott Burgess
A cop and two street characters team-up to run a scam and, in the process, cross a hoodlum who turns every one of his allies on them.
Unknown — *VCL Home Video*

Dead End 1937
Drama
82576 92 mins B/W B, V, LV P
Sylvia Sidney, Joel McCrea, Humphrey Bogart, Wendy Barrie, Claire Trevor, Allen Jenkins, directed by William Wyler
This film version of the Sidney Kingsley play traces the lives of various inhabitants of New York's Lower East Side.
Samuel Goldwyn — *Embassy Home Entertainment*

Dead for a Dollar 197?
Western
82090 92 mins C B, V P
John Ireland, George Hilton, Piero Vida, Sandra Milo
A Colonel, a con man, and a mysterious woman team up to search for the two hundred thousand dollars they robbed from a local bank.
Foreign — *Unicorn Video*

Dead Men Don't Wear Plaid 1982
Comedy
62779 91 mins B/W B, V, LV P
Steve Martin, Rachel Ward, Reni Santoni, Carl Reiner, directed by Carl Reiner
A private detective encounters a bizarre assortment of suspects while trying to find out the truth about a scientist's death. This black-and-white film is ingeniously interspliced with clips from old Warner Brothers films, featuring Humphrey Bogart, Bette Davis, Alan Ladd, Burt Lancaster, Ava Gardner, Barbara Stanwyck, Ray Milland and others.
MPAA:PG
Universal — *MCA Home Video*

Dead of Night 1945
Suspense
47302 102 mins B/W B, V P
Sir Michael Redgrave, Sally Ann Howes, Basil Radford, Naunton Wayne, Mervyn Johns, Roland Culver
This suspense classic, set in a remote country house, follows a small group of people as they find their worst nightmares becoming reality.
Universal International — *THORN EMI/HBO Video*

Dead of Night 1977
Horror
81745 60 mins C B, V P
Joan Hackett, Ed Begley, Jr., Patrick Macnee, Anjanette Comer, directed by Dan Curtis
This trilogy features Richard Matheson tales of the Supernatural: "Second Chance", "Bobby" and "No Such Thing As a Vampire."
Dan Curtis Prods; NBC — *Thriller Video*

Dead Wrong 1983
Adventure
76863 93 mins C B, V P
Britt Ekland, Winston Rekert, Jackson Davies
An undercover agent falls in love with the drug smuggler she's supposed to bring to justice.
Len Kowalewich — *Media Home Entertainment*

Dead Zone, The 1983
Suspense
Closed Captioned
65615 103 mins C B, V, LV, P
CED
Christopher Walken, Brooke Adams, Tom Skerritt, Martin Sheen

A man gains extraordinary psychic powers following a near-fatal accident. He is forced to decide between seeking absolute seclusion in order to escape his frightening visions, or using his "gift" to save mankind from impending evil.
MPAA:R
Debra Hill — *Paramount Home Video*

Deadline   1981
Suspense
79170   94 mins   C   B, V   P
Barry Newman, Trisha Noble, Bill Kerr
A journalist must find out the truth behind a minor earthquake in Australia.
Hanna-Barbera/PTY Limited — *Worldvision Home Video*

Deadly and the Beautiful, The   1974
Adventure
59673   82 mins   C   B, V   P
Nancy Kwan, Ross Hagen
Dr. Tsu sends her "deadly but beautiful" task force to kidnap the world's prime male athletes for use in her private business enterprise.
MPAA:PG
Ross Hagen — *Media Home Entertainment*

Deadly Blessing   1981
Horror
60440   104 mins   C   B, V, CED   P
Ernest Borgnine, Maren Jensen, Jeff East, Lisa Hartman, Lois Nettleton
Imminent danger and relentless psychological terror highlight this frightening story of a young woman who marries a member of a bizarre religious sect.
MPAA:R
Polygram — *Embassy Home Entertainment*

Deadly Chase (La Persecucion Mortal)   197?
Crime-Drama
88317   95 mins   C   B, V   P
Police investigate a series of violent acts by an elusive baron in a presumably antiquarian European country.
SP
Spanish — *JCI Video*

Deadly Dust, The   1985
Fantasy
Closed Captioned
88079   93 mins   C   B, V   P
Nicholas Hammond, Robert F. Simon, Chip Fields, directed by Ron Satlof
A live-action episode of Spider-Man, as he attempts to prevent a city-destroying plutonium accident.
Robert Janes; Ron Satlof — *Playhouse Video*

Deadly Encounter   1982
Adventure
81415   90 mins   C   B, V   P
Larry Hagman, Susan Anspach
A helicopter pilot is surprised when his ex-girlfriend comes to visit him in Mexico. She asks him to help her find a black book that her deceased husband kept information that could put many people behind bars.
Paul Cameron, Robert Boris — *VCL Home Video*

Deadly Eyes   1983
Horror
69311   87 mins   C   B, V   P
Sam Groom, Sara Botsford, Scatman Crothers
A genetically altered urban colony of super-rats seeks a new source of food—man.
MPAA:R
Golden Harvest — *Warner Home Video*

Deadly Force   1983
Suspense
64970   95 mins   C   B, V, CED   P
Wings Hauser
An ex-cop turned private detective stalks a killer in Los Angeles who has left an "X" carved in the forehead of each of his 17 victims.
MPAA:R
Sandy Howard/Hemdale — *Embassy Home Entertainment*

Deadly Game, The   1982
Drama/Suspense
60441   108 mins   C   B, V   P
George Segal, Robert Morley
A reunion at a remote hotel leads to an ordeal of psychological terror and murderous intrigue.
Ely and Edie Landau; Hillard Elkins — *Embassy Home Entertainment*

Deadly Games   1980
Horror
63082   94 mins   C   B, V   P
Sam Groom, JoAnn Harris, Steve Railsback, Dick Butkus, June Lockhart
A mysterious strangler terrorizes young women, seemingly at random.
Great Plains Entertainment Corp — *Monterey Home Video*

Deadly Harvest   1976
Science fiction/Drama
84119   86 mins   C   B, V   P
Clint Walker, Nehemiah Persoff, Kim Cattrall
A tale set in the near future where food is scarce and civilisation has turned savage as a result. A farmer is beset by hordes of hungry city dwellers, who slaughter his family, spurring him to action.
New World Pictures — *New World Video*

Deadly Hero　　1975
Crime-Drama
84861　102 mins　C　　B, V　　　　P
Don Murray, James Earl Jones, Diahn Williams
A thriller about a psychotic who senselessly kills
a thief, and is hailed as a hero.
MPAA:R
Thomas J. McGrath — *Embassy Home
Entertainment*

Deadly Impact　　1984
Suspense
82467　90 mins　C　　B, V　　　　P
Bo Svenson, Fred Williamson, Marica Cungon
A thriller about an illegal gambling operation that
turns into a most deadly game.
European International Films — *Vestron Video*

Deadly Intrigue　　1974
Suspense
82004　93 mins　C　　B, V　　　　P
Alex Rocco, Keenan Wynn, Andy Robinson
A newlywed woman seduces her husband's son
in order to get closer to his fortune. However, a
surprise awaits the couple when their plans to
murder her husband goes awry.
Arthur Productions — *Arena Video*

Deadly Intruder, The　　1984
Horror
77167　86 mins　C　　B, V　　　　P
A quiet vacation spot is being terrorized by an
escapee from a mental institution.
Independent — *THORN EMI/HBO Video*

Deadly Mission　　1967
War-Drama
87633　99 mins　C　　B, V　　　　P
Bo Svenson, Peter Hooten, Fred Williamson
Five soldiers in World War II France are
convicted of crimes against the Army, escape
and become focal points in a decisive battle.
MPAA:R
Neve Int'l Films — *Lightning Video*

Deadly Passion　　1985
Mystery
84098　100 mins　C　　B, V　　　　P
*Brent Huff, Harrison Coburn, Lynn Maree,
directed by Larry Larson*
A James Cain-like thriller about a private eye
getting carnally involved with a beautiful and
treacherous woman who is manipulating her
late husband's estate through murder and
double-crossing.
MPAA:R
Video Vision — *Lightning Video*

Deadly Sanctuary　　196?
Drama
70813　95 mins　C　　B, V　　　　P

*Jack Palance, Klaus Kinski, Akim Tamiroff,
Mercedes McCambridge, Sylva Koscina,
Romina Power*
Censors stopped production of this film several
times. Violence and intrigue abound in this
political adventure thriller
Italian/Spanish — *Monterey Home Video*

Deadly Sunday　　1982
Drama
70850　85 mins　C　　B, V　　　　P
*Dennis Ely, Henry Sanders, Gylian Roland,
Douglas Alexander, directed by Donald M.
Jones*
Jewel thieves detour a family's Sunday drive
into a terrifying hostage situation.
Media Gallery — *Lightning Video*

Deadly Thief　　1984
Drama
73559　90 mins　C　　B, V　　　　P
Rex Harrison, John Saxon, Sylvia Miles
A retired jewel thief comes out of retirement to
challenge his protege to steal the world's most
precious gem as the prize.
Unknown — *Prism*

Dead Men Walk　　1943
Horror
76917　65 mins　B/W　　B, V　　　　P
A deadman returns from the netherworld to
haunt the man who murdered him.
Sigmund Newfeld — *United Home Video*

Deal of the Century　　1983
Comedy
69799　99 mins　C　　B, V, LV,　　P
　　　　　　　　　　　　　　　CED
*Chevy Chase, Sigourney Weaver, Gregory
Hines, directed by William Friedkin*
A first-rate hustler and his cohorts sell second-
rate weapons to third-world nations, but their
latest deal threatens to blow up in their
faces—literally. In stereo on all formats.
MPAA:PG
Warner Bros. — *Warner Home Video*

Dealers in Death　　1984
Documentary
77235　60 mins　B/W　　B, V　　　　P
Narrated by Broderick Crawford
This documentary looks at the gangsters who
have left their impact on American history such
as Al Capone and John Dillinger.
John McNaughton — *MPI Home Video*

**Dean Martin and Jerry
Lewis Television Party
for Muscular Dystrophy**　　1951
Variety
45099　105 mins　B/W　　B, V　　　　P
Dean Martin, Jerry Lewis

An early television rarity of wild off-the-cuff clowning and fun entertainment, featuring Phil Silvers, Jane Wyman, and Eddie Cantor.
Unknown — *Hollywood Home Theater*

Dear Detective 1979
Crime-Drama
64998   92 mins   C   B, V   P
Brenda Vaccaro
A woman head of police homicide takes on the most challenging case of her career.
Viacom Enterprises — *U.S.A. Home Video*

Dear Diary 1981
Adolescence/Sexuality
63877   25 mins   C   B, V   P
Focusing on three fictional characters, this program presents facts about female sexuality and physical development, and addresses the issues of self-image, peer pressure, and pressure to date.
Copperfield Films — *MGM/UA Home Video; New Day Films*

Dear Wife 1949
Comedy
85247   88 mins   B/W   B, V   P
William Holden, Joan Caulfield, Edward Arnold, Billy DeWolfe
A young man and his father-in-law run for the same small-town Senate seat, at the instigation of a bratty young girl.
Paramount — *Kartes Video Communications*

Death at Love House 1975
Mystery
80302   74 mins   C   B, V   P
Robert Wagner, Kate Jackson, Sylvia Sydney, Joan Blondell, John Carradine
A screen writer and his wife are hired to write the life story of a silent movie queen.
Spelling/Goldberg Productions — *Prism*

Death Challenge 1980
Martial arts
84897   94 mins   C   B, V   P
Steve Leving, Susan Wong
Gangs battle without weapons, motive or discretion in this kung fu extravaganza.
Foreign — *Unicorn Video*

Death Driver 1978
Drama
78388   93 mins   C   B, V   P
Earl Owensby, Mike Allen
In order for a stuntman to make a comeback, he attempts to do a stunt that had ended his career ten years before.
Independent — *THORN EMI/HBO Video*

Death Duel of Mantis 1984
Martial arts
72958   90 mins   C   B, V   P
A martial arts film featuring Chin Yin Fei.
Foreign — *Unicorn Video*

Death Force 198?
Drama
80126   90 mins   C   B, V   P
Jayne Kennedy, Leon Issac Kennedy
When a Vietnam veteran comes to New York City, he becomes a hitman for the Mafia.
MPAA:R
Independent — *King of Video*

Death Game 1976
Drama
80188   91 mins   C   B, V   P
Sondra Lucke, Colleen Camp, Seymour Cassel
When a man lets two girls into his house to make a phone call the pair lead the man through 48 hours of sheer terror.
MPAA:R
First American Films — *United Home Video*

Death Games 1982
Suspense
72532   78 mins   C   B, V   P
Two young men shooting a documentary about an influential music promoter ask too many wrong questions, causing the powers-that-be to want them out of the picture for good.
Williams and Gardiner — *VidAmerica*

Death Hunt 1981
Adventure
58851   98 mins   C   B, V, LV,   P
CED
Charles Bronson, Lee Marvin, Ed Lauter, Andrew Stevens, Carl Weathers, Angie Dickinson
A man unjustly accused of murder pits his knowledge of the wilderness against the superior numbers of his pursuers.
MPAA:R
20th Century Fox — *CBS/Fox Video*

Death in Venice 1971
Drama
58227   127 mins   C   B, V   P
Dirk Bogarde, Mark Burns, Bjorn Andresen, directed by Luchino Visconti
Thomas Mann's novel about a man obsessed by ideal beauty is brought to life in this film.
Cannes Film Festival '71: Grand Prize Winner.
MPAA:PG
Alta Cinematografica — *Warner Home Video*

Death Journey 1976
Adventure
47669   mins   C   B, V   P
Fred Williamson, D'Urville Martin

Fred Williamson portrays Jesse Crowder, a man-for-hire hired by the New York D.A. to escort a key witness cross-country.
MPAA:R
Po Boy Productions — *Unicorn Video*

Death Kiss 1977
Drama
80281   90 mins   C   B, V   P
Larry Daniels, Dorothy Moore
When a man hires a psychopath to murder his wife, a strange series of events starts to happen that foils his plot.
MPAA:R
Joseph Brenner Associates — *Prism*

Death Kiss, The 1933
Mystery
08757   75 mins   B/W   B, V   P
Bela Lugosi, David Manners, Adrienne Ames
Eerie doings at a major Hollywood film studio where a sinister killer does away with his victims while a cast-of-thousands movie spectacular is under production.
World Wide; KBS Prod — *Movie Buff Video; Cable Films; Discount Video Tapes; Kartes Video Communications*

Death Machines 1976
Suspense/Martial arts
51117   93 mins   C   B, V   P
Ron Marchini, Michael Chong, Joshua Johnson
A young karate student must face the "Death Machines," a team of deadly assassins who are trained to kill on command.
MPAA:R
Crown International — *VidAmerica*

Death of a Centerfold 1981
Drama
75535   96 mins   C   B, V   P
Jamie Lee Curtis, Bruce Weitz, Robert Reed, Mitch Ryan, Bibi Besch
A drama based on the life of Dorothy Stratten.
Larry Wilcox Productions — *MGM/UA Home Video*

Death of a Hooker 1971
Crime-Drama
84670   90 mins   C   B, V   P
Red Buttons, Sam Waterston, Sylvia Miles, Conrad Baw, directed by Ernie Pintoff.
Also known as "Who Killed Mary What's'ername?," it features a few has-beens who, spurred by indifference to a hooker's murder, seek the killer.
MPAA:PG
George Manassee — *Video Gems*

Death of a Scoundrel 1956
Mystery
84810   119 mins   B/W   B, V   P

George Sanders, Zsa Zsa Gabor, Yvonne DeCarlo, Victor Jory, directed by Charles Martin
A womanizing entrepeneur is murdered, and the culprit could be any one of his betrodden romantic conquests. Also known as "Loves of a Scoundrel."
U-1 — *United Home Video*

Death of Adolf Hitler, The 1984
Biographical
88189   107 mins   C   B, V   P
Frank Finlay, Caroline Mortimer, directed by Rex Firlin
An English made-for-TV film depicting Hitler's last, drug-addled, suicidal, Eva Braun-haunted hours of life.
Rex Firlin; London Weekend
TV — *Karl/Lorimar Home Video*

Death on the Nile 1978
Mystery
58455   135 mins   C   B, V, CED   P
Peter Ustinov, Jane Birkin, Lois Chiles, Bette Davis, Mia Farrow, David Niven, Olivia Hussey, Angela Lansbury, Jack Warden, Maggie Smith
Agatha Christie's fictional detective, Hercule Poiret, is called upon to discover who killed an heiress aboard a steamer cruising down the Nile.
MPAA:PG
EMI; Paramount — *THORN EMI/HBO Video*

Death Race 2000 1975
Drama
54800   80 mins   C   B, V   P
David Carradine, Simone Griffeth, Sylvester Stallone, directed by Paul Bartel
Five racing car contenders challenge the national champion of a cross country race in which drivers score points by killing pedestrians. Based on the 1956 story by Ib Melchior.
MPAA:R
New World Pictures; Roger Corman — *Warner Home Video*

Death Rage 1977
Suspense
44913   92 mins   C   B, V   P
Yul Brynner, Martin Balsam
A hitman comes out of retirement to handle the toughest assignment he has ever faced: search for and kill the man who murdered his brother. But he is trapped by a Mafia doublecross, with himself as the real target.
MPAA:R
S. J. International — *VidAmerica*

Death Riders 1976
Motorcycles/Automobiles-Racing
81921   83 mins   C   B, V   P
This documentary chronicles the daring exploits of the "Death Riders," a group of daredevils who perform motorcycle and automobile stunts.

Four Star International — *VidAmerica*

Death Rides the Plains   1944
Western
11269   53 mins   B/W   B, V, FO   P
Bob Livingston, Fuzzy St. John, Nica Doret, Ray Bennet
A man lures prospective buyers to his ranch, kills them, and steals their money.
PRC — *Video Yesteryear*

Death Rides the Range   1940
Western
15483   57 mins   B/W   B, V, 3/4U   P
Ken Maynard
Action western with a mystery angle.
NTA — *Discount Video Tapes; Video Connection; United Home Video*

Death Screams   1983
Horror
86604   88 mins   C   B, V   P
Susan Kiger, Jennifer Chase, Jody Kay, William T. Hicks
A slew of comely co-eds have a party and get hacked to pieces for their troubles by a machete-wielding maniac.
MPAA:R
David Nelson — *Video Gems*

Death Sentence   1974
Suspense/Drama
80303   74 mins   C   B, V   P
Cloris Leachman, Laurence Luckinbill, Nick Nolte, William Schallert
When a woman juror on a murder case finds out that the wrong man is on trial, she is stalked by the real killer.
Spelling/Goldberg Productions — *Prism*

Death Sport   1978
Adventure
52703   83 mins   C   B, V   P
David Carradine, Claudia Jennings, Richard Lynch
A popular game of the future involves gladiators willing to lose their lives against lethal motorcyclists.
MPAA:R
New World; Roger Corman — *Warner Home Video*

Death Squad   1973
Drama
80304   74 mins   C   B, V   P
Robert Forster, Melvyn Douglas, Michelle Phillips, Claude Akins
A police commissioner hires an ex-cop to find a group of vigilante cops who are behind a series of gangland style executions.
Spelling/Goldberg Productions — *Prism*

Death Stalk   1974
Adventure
59353   90 mins   C   B, V   R, P
Vince Edwards, Vic Morrow, Anjanette Comer, Robert Webber, Carol Lynley
Two couples' dream holiday turns into a hostage nightmare.
Heritage Enterprises — *Video Gems; World Video Pictures*

Death Target   1983
Drama
81822   72 mins   C   B, V   P
Jorge Montesi
Three former mercenaries team up to capture oil-rich land on a Canadian Indian reservation.
Cintel Film Productions Ltd. — *Prism*

Death Valley   1981
Drama
59678   90 mins   C   B, V   P
Paul LeMat, Catherine Hicks, Peter Billingsley
A trio sets out to drive through Death Valley, a trip which soon becomes a nightmare of danger and insanity.
MPAA:R
Universal — *MCA Home Video*

Death Valley Days   1965
Western
78358   60 mins   B/W   B, V   P
Clint Eastwood, hosted by Ronald Reagan and Robert Taylor
Two episodes from the long-running Western anthology television series are contained on this tape.
Madison Productions — *U.S.A. Home Video*

Death Valley Days,   196?
Volume II
Western
79328   75 mins   C   B, V   P
Jim Davis, Forrest Tucker, Tom Skerritt, Robert Blake, James Caan
A second volume of two episodes from the series that features stories about the old west.
In Beta Hi-Fi and VHS Stereo.
Madison Productions — *U.S.A. Home Video*

Death Warmed Up   1985
Horror
84088   83 mins   C   B, V   P
Michael Hurst, Margaret Umbers, David Letch, directed by David Blyth
A crazed brain surgeon turns ordinary people into bloodthirsty mutants and a small group of young people travel to his secluded island to stop him.
Skouras — *Vestron Video*

Death Watch 1979
Drama
72881 117 mins C B, V, LV P
Harvey Keitel, Romy Schneider, Max Von Sydow
A television director implants a video camera in a man's brain to film a documentary on a dying woman without her knowledge.
MPAA:R
Planfilms; Selta Films — *Embassy Home Entertainment*

Death Weekend 1976
Suspense
82460 89 mins C B, V P
Brenda Vaccaro, Don Stroud, Chuck Shamata, Richard Ayres, Kyle Edwards
A woman is stalked by a trio of murderous, drunken hoodlums who seek to spoil her weekend.
Quadrant Films — *Vestron Video*

Death Wish 1974
Drama
38594 93 mins C B, V, LV P
Charles Bronson, Vincent Gardenia, William Redfield, Hope Lange, directed by Michael Winner
Charles Bronson turns vigilante after his wife and daughter are violently attacked and raped by a gang of hoodlums. He stalks the streets of New York seeking revenge on other muggers, pimps, and crooks. Music by Herbie Hancock.
MPAA:R
Paramount — *Paramount Home Video; RCA VideoDiscs*

Death Wish II 1982
Adventure
60337 89 mins C B, V P
Charles Bronson, Jill Ireland, Vincent Gardenia, Anthony Franciosa, directed by Michael Winner
Bronson recreates the role of Paul Kersey, an architect who takes the law into his own hands when his family is victimized once again.
MPAA:R
City Films — *Warner Home Video; Vestron Video (disc only)*

Death Wish III 1985
Adventure
85542 100 mins C B, V P
Charles Bronson, Martin Balsam, Deborah Raffin, directed by Michael Winner
Once again, Charles Bronson blows away the lowlifes who have killed those who were dear to him and were spared in the first two films.
MPAA:R
Cannon Films — *MGM/UA Home Video*

Deathcheaters 1976
Adventure
77004 96 mins C B, V P
The Australian Secret Service offers two stuntmen a top secret mission in the Phillipines.
MPAA:G
Brian Trenchard Smith — *VidAmerica*

Deathmask 1969
Drama/Mystery
71242 102 mins C V P
Farley Granger, Ruth Warrick, Danny Aiello, directed by Richard S Friedman
A 4-year-old boy's corpse is found buried in a cardboard box. Detective Douglas Andrews begins an obsessive investigation into the murder.
Gloria and Louis K Sher — *Prism*

Deathmoon 1978
Horror
82217 90 mins C B, V P
Robert Foxworth, Joe Penny, Debralee Scott, Dolph Sweet, Charles Haid
A businessman plagued by recurring werewolf nightmares goes on a Hawaiian vacation to try and forget his troubles.
Roger Gimbel Prods; EMI-TV — *VCL Home Video*

DeathStalker 1984
Fantasy
80048 80 mins C B, V, CED P
Richard Hill, Barbi Benton, Richard Brooker, Vicrot Bo, Lana Clarkson
Deathstalker sets his sights on seizing the evil wizard Munkar's magic amulet so he can take over Munkan's castle.
MPAA:R
Palo Alto Productions — *Vestron Video*

Deathtrap 1982
Suspense
60336 116 mins C B, V P
Michael Caine, Christopher Reeve, Dyan Cannon, directed by Sidney Lumet
Ira Levin's Broadway smash concerning a creatively blocked playwright of mysteries, his ailing rich wife and a former student who has written a surefire hit worth killing for.
MPAA:PG
Warner Bros — *Warner Home Video*

Debbie Does Las Vegas 1985
Variety/Nightclub
81962 55 mins C B, V P
Debbie Reynolds
Debbie Reynolds performs her knockout Las Vegas show that features impressions of Dolly Parton and Mae West and such show-stoppers as "Tammy" and "Broadway Melody."
Jackie Barnett — *Lightning Video*

Decade of the Waltons, A 1985
Drama
80890   120 mins   C   B, V   P
Richard Thomas, Ellen Corby, Will Geer, Michael Learned, Ralph Waite, narrated by Earl Hamner
"The Waltons" creator Earl Hamner narrates this retrospective program which features poignant highlights from the series.
Lorimar Productions — *Karl/Lorimar Home Video*

Decameron Nights 1953
Drama
75932   87 mins   C   B, V   P
Louis Jourdan, Joan Fontaine, Binnie Barnes, Joan Collins
A trio of tales about a beautiful young wife of an older man who is pursued by a tempestuous lover.
RKO — *Hal Roach Studios; Video Gems; Discount Video Tapes; World Video Pictures*

Decline of Western Civilization, The 1981
Documentary/Music-Performance
81193   100 mins   C   B, V   P
X, Circle Jerks, Black Flag, Fear, Germs, Catholic Discipline, directed by Penelope Spheeris
This documentary examines the L.A. hard core punk scene.
Penelope Spheeris — *Music Media*

Decoys and Duck Calls—Two Secrets for Success 1986
Hunting
86875   30 mins   C   B, V   P
Bob Brister
How to kill ducks via decoys, duck calls and other surprise strategies.
AM Available
Warburton Prod. — *Warburton Productions*

Deep, The 1977
Suspense
21284   123 mins   C   B, V   P
Nick Nolte, Jacqueline Bisset, Robert Shaw
An underwater search for a shipwreck. Based on the novel by Peter Benchley.
Columbia — *RCA/Columbia Pictures Home Video; RCA VideoDiscs*

Deep in My Heart 1954
Biographical/Musical
85636   132 mins   C   B, V   P
Jose Ferrer, Merle Oberon, Paul Henreid, Walter Pidgeon, Helen Traubel, Rosemary Clooney, Jane Powell, Howard Keel, Cyd Charisse, Gene Kelly, Ann Miller, directed by Stanley Donen
A musical biography of the life and times of composer Sigmund Romberg, with guest appearances by many MGM stars.
MGM — *MGM/UA Home Video*

Deep in the Heart 1984
Drama
73023   99 mins   C   B, V   P
Karen Young, Clayton Day
When a young woman gets raped at gunpoint on a second date she takes the law into her own hands. This film is based upon a true story.
MPAA:R
Tony Garrett and David Streit — *THORN EMI/HBO Video*

Deep Red: Hatchet Murders 1982
Horror/Suspense
63358   100 mins   C   B, V   P
David Hemmings, Daria Nicolodi
A composer reads a book on the occult that relates to the brutal murder of his neighbor. He goes to visit the book's author and discovers that she has been horribly murdered as well.
Rizzoli Films — *THORN EMI/HBO Video*

Deep Six, The 1958
War-Drama
29800   110 mins   C   B, V   P
Alan Ladd, William Bendix, James Whitmore, Keenan Wynn, Efrem Zimbalist Jr., Joey Bishop
A World War II drama that examines the conflict between pacifism and loyalty to country in wartime. A staunch Quaker is called to active duty as a lieutenant in the U.S. Navy. His pacifism puts him into disfavor with shipmates.
Warner Bros — *United Home Video*

Deer Hunter, The 1978
Drama
31585   183 mins   C   B, V, LV   P
Robert DeNiro, Christopher Walken, John Savage, Meryl Streep, directed by Michael Cimino
Three buddies from a Pennsylvania steel town go to Viet Nam and learn that war is a human roulette game. The town, their loves, and their lives will never be the same.
Academy Awards '78: Best Picture; Best Director (Cimino). MPAA:R
Universal — *MCA Home Video; RCA VideoDiscs*

Deerslayer, The 1978
Drama
45052   98 mins   C   B, V   P
Steve Forrest, Ned Romero, John Anderson, Joan Prather
Based on the classic novel by James Fenimore Cooper, this movie about the intrepid frontiersman Hawkeye and his Indian companion Chingachgook who set out to rescue

a beautiful Indian maiden and must fight bands of hostile Indians and Frenchmen along the way.
Schick Sunn Classic — *United Home Video; Magnum Entertainment*

Defiance   1979
Drama
64362   101 mins   C   B, V, CED   P
Jan-Michael Vincent, Art Carney, Theresa Saldona
A former merchant seaman moves into a tenement in a bad area of New York City. When a local street gang begins terrorizing the neighborhood, he decides to take a stand.
MPAA:PG
American International — *Vestron Video*

Defiant, The   1970
Crime-Drama
85917   93 mins   C   B, V   P
Kent Lane, John Rubenstein, Tisha Sterling, directed by Hall Bartlett
Two rival street gangs clash when one admits an young orphan girl.
Arista — *Lightning Video*

Defiant Ones, The   1958
Drama
65006   97 mins   B/W   B, V, CED   P
Tony Curtis, Sidney Poitier, Theodore Bikel, Cara Williams, directed by Stanley Kramer
This symbolic story about racism revolves around two prisoners in a chain gang in the rural south who escape. Their societal conditioning to distrust and dislike each other dissolves as they face each constant peril together.
United Artists; Stanley Kramer — *CBS/Fox Video*

Degas, Erte and Chagall   1977
Arts/Painting
58565   60 mins   C   B, V   P
"Degas in New Orleans" is a dramatization of the pictures painted when he visited this city. "Erte" is a profile of French designer Romain de Tirtoff. The last film features Marc Chagall giving viewers an inside look at his paint-on-glass technique.
Gary L. Goldman; Chuck Olin — *Mastervision*

Deja View   1986
Music video
86906   50 mins   C   B, V   P
Teri Garr, Harry Dean Stanton, Graham Nash, Brian Wilson, Michael Pare
A retrospective of hits of the 1960's in video productions starring personalities from the 1980's, including one original song by John Sebastian, "You and Me Way Go Back."
Joel Gallen — *Karl/Lorimar Home Video*

Deja Vu   1984
Drama
82398   95 mins   C   B, V   P
Jaclyn Smith, Nigel Terry, Claire Bloom
A romantic thriller about the tragic deaths of two lovers and their supposed reincarnation 50 years later.
MPAA:R
Dixon Films — *MGM/UA Home Video*

Delinquent Daughters   1944
Drama
47637   71 mins   B/W   B, V, FO   P
June Carlson, Fifi Dorsay, Teala Loring
After a high school girl commits suicide, a cop and a reporter try to find out why so many kids are getting into trouble.
PRC Pictures; American Prods Inc — *Video Yesteryear*

Delinquent Schoolgirls   1984
Drama/Exploitation
81166   89 mins   C   B, V   P
Michael Pataki, Bob Minos, Stephen Stucker
Three escapees from an asylum get more than they bargained for when they visit a Female Correctional Institute to fulfill their sexual fantasies.
MPAA:R
Rainbow Distributors — *Vestron Video*

Deliverance   1972
Drama
38943   105 mins   C   B, V, LV   P
Jon Voight, Burt Reynolds, Ned Beatty, John Boorman
A superb action film about four men who go riding down a wild river for a weekend that turns into a disaster. Based on James Dickey's novel.
MPAA:R
Warner Bros — *Warner Home Video; RCA VideoDiscs*

Delivery Boys   1984
Comedy
70894   94 mins   C   B, V   P
Joss Marcano, Tom Sierchio, Jim Soriero
The "Delivery Boys," three breakdancers aiming to win the $10,000 New York City Break-Off, find unusual perils that may keep them from competing.
MPAA:R
New World — *New World Video*

Delta Force, The   1985
Adventure
Closed Captioned
87188   125 mins   C   B, V   P
Lee Marvin, Chuck Norris, Shelley Winters, Martin Balsam, George Kennedy, Hanna Schygulla, Susan Strasberg, Bo Svenson, Joey Bishop, Lainie Kazan

Two Arab terrorists hijack an airliner full of motley characters, and the Delta Force rubs them out.
Cannon Films — *Media Home Entertainment*

Delusion   1984
Drama
72878   93 mins   C   B, V   P
Joseph Cotten
A young woman comes to a house to nurse an elderly man only to have a fling with his sixteen year old grandson.
MPAA:R
Unknown — *Embassy Home Entertainment*

Demented   1980
Horror
59662   92 mins   C   B, V   P
Sally Elyse, Bruce Gilchrist
A beautiful and talented woman is brutally gang-raped by four men but her revenge is sweet and deadly as she entices each to bed and murders them.
MPAA:R
Arthur Jeffreys; Mike Smith — *Media Home Entertainment*

Dementia 13   1963
Horror
11315   75 mins   B/W   B, V, FO   P
William Campbell, Luana Anders, Bart Patton, written and directed by Francis Ford Coppola
A woman drives her husband to a heart attack as her family clings strangely to the memory of a sister who drowned years ago.
American Intl; Roger Corman — *Video Yesteryear; Hollywood Home Theater; Video Dimensions; Cable Films; Movie Buff Video; Discount Video Tapes; World Video Pictures*

Demon, The   1981
Horror
51120   94 mins   C   B, V   P
Cameron Mitchell, Jennifer Holmes
A small town may be doomed to extinction, courtesy of a monster's thirst for the blood of its inhabitants.
MPAA:R
Hollard Productions — *THORN EMI/HBO Video; United Home Video; VidAmerica*

Demon Barber of Fleet   1936
Street, The
Horror
84354   68 mins   B/W   B, V   P
Tod Slaughter, Eve Lister
Released in the United States in 1945, this film about a psychotic, greedy barber inspired the 1978 smash play.
Select Films; George King — *Rhino Video*

Demon Lover, The   1975
Horror
47665   87 mins   C   B, V   P
A young girl is the victim of psychic attack from a demonologist.
MPAA:R
Donald G Jackson; Jerry Younkins — *Unicorn Video*

Demon Rage   1982
Horror
64843   98 mins   C   B, V   P
Britt Ekland, Lana Wood, John Carradine
A neglected housewife drifts under the spell of a phantom lover.
MPAA:R
MPM — *HarmonyVision*

Demon Seed   1977
Science fiction/Horror
73362   97 mins   C   B, V   P
Julie Christie, Fritz Weaver
When a scientist and his wife separate so he can work on his computer, the computer takes over the house and impregnates the wife.
MPAA:R
MGM — *MGM/UA Home Video*

Demoniac   1979
Horror
77396   87 mins   C   B, V   P
A depraved religious fanatic subjects a group of demon worshipers to gruesome rites of exorcism.
MPAA:R
Foreign — *Wizard Video*

Demonoid   1981
Horror
63386   85 mins   C   B, V   P
Samantha Eggar, Stuart Whitman, Roy Cameron Jenson
The discovery of an ancient temple of Satan worship drastically changes the lives of a young couple when the husband become possessed by the Demonoid.
MPAA:R
Zach Motion Pictures; Panorama Films — *Media Home Entertainment*

Demons, The   198?
Horror
73957   90 mins   C   B, V   P
Anne Libert, Britt Nichols, Doris Thomas, Karen Field
A woman accused of being a witch vows a curse of death upon her accusers.
Independent — *Unicorn Video*

Demons of the Mind   1971
Horror
85770   85 mins   C   B, V   P

Michael Hordern, Patrick Magee, Yvonne Mitchell, Paul Jones
A sordid psychological horror film about a hypnotist who travels to a 19th-century castle and unlocks mental horrors galore.
MPAA:R
Hammer Films — *THORN EMI/HBO Video*

Dennis De Young—Three Piece Suite   1986
Music video
87273   15 mins   C   B, V   P
A three-song concept video by the singing leader of the pop group Styx, featuring "Desert Moon," "Don't Wait for Heroes" and "Call Me."
Picture Music International; One Heart Prod. — *A & M Video*

Dennis the Menace in Mayday for Mother   1980
Cartoons/Comedy
84636   24 mins   C   B, V   P
Animated
An animated film of Hank Ketcham's comic strip, centering on Dennis' efforts to celebrate Mother's's Day.
David H DePatie; Friz Freleng — *MCA Home Video*

Dentist, The   1932
Comedy
59402   22 mins   B/W   B, V   P, T
W.C. Fields, Elise Cavanna, Babe Kane, Bud Jamison, Zedna Farley
Fields treats several oddball patients in his office.
Paramount — *Blackhawk Films; Festival Films*

Denver Broncos First Tastes of Glory: 1977, 1978, 1979, 1984   1985
Football
88076   93 mins   C   B, V   P
Footage of the Broncos' most outstanding seasons is collected on this tape.
NFL Films — *NFL Films Video*

Denver Broncos 1984 Team Highlights   1985
Football
70546   70 mins   C   B, V, FO   P
The Broncos crisp no-bucking-around style of play led them to a 13-3 record as they went about "The Winning of the West," the NFL's toughest division. This tape features 47-minutes of highlights from the entire NFL's '84 season as well.
NFL Films — *NFL Films Video*

Departamento Compartido   1985
Comedy
81643   100 mins   C   B, V   P
Alberto Olmedo, Tato Bores, Graciela Alfano, Camila Perisse
A notorious ladies man and his shy friend become unlikely roommates after their wives kick them out of their homes.
SP
Nicolas Carreras; Luis Repetto — *Media Home Entertainment*

Derby   1970
Drama/Sports
85086   91 mins   C   B, V   P
Charlie O'Connell, Lydia Gray, Janet Earp, Ann Colvello, Mike Snell
The story of the rise to fame of a roller-derby star.
MPAA:R
William Richert — *Prism*

Derek and Clive Get the Horn   1978
Comedy
59931   90 mins   C   B, V   P
Peter Cook, Dudley Moore
England's favorite comedy team in a four-letter funfest.
Peter Cook — *Pacific Arts Video*

Dernier Combat, Le (The Last Battle)   1984
Drama
70564   93 mins   B/W   B, V   P
Pierre Jolivet, Fritz Wepper, Jean Reno, Jean Bouise, Christiane Kruger, directed Luc Besson
This dialogueless, stark film about life after a devastating war marks the directorial debut of Besson. The characters wander through the rubble, staking claims to turf and forming new relationships with other survivors. In stereo on all formats.
MPAA:R
Triumph Films — *RCA/Columbia Pictures Home Video*

Desde el Abismo   19??
Drama
66415   115 mins   C   B, V   P
Thelma Biral, Alberto Argibay, Olga Zubarry
After the birth of her son, a young mother takes to drink while in the throes of post-partum depression.
SP
Spanish — *Media Home Entertainment*

Desert Fox, The   1951
War-Drama
08436   87 mins   B/W   B, V   P

James Mason, Sir Cedric Hardwicke, Jessica
Tandy, directed by Henry Hathaway
Personal and political sides of Field Marshal
Rommel are featured.
EL, SP
20th Century Fox; Nunnaly
Johnson — *CBS/Fox Video*

Desert of the Tartars, The   1982
Adventure
74083   140 mins   C   B, V, CED   P
This is the story of a young soldier who dreams
of war and discovers that the real battle for him
is with time.
MPAA:PG
Buz Potamkin; Hal Hoffer — *Embassy Home
Entertainment*

Desert Tigers (Los Tigres   197?
del Desierto), The
War-Drama
88313   95 mins   C   B, V   P
Allied soldiers escape from a German POW
camp and battle for survival across the African
deserts.
SpanishSfISP — *JCI Video*

Desert Trail   1935
Western
08828   57 mins   B/W   B, V, 3/4U   P
John Wayne
John Wayne stars as a rough-and-tough
cowboy in this action-packed Western
adventure.
Monogram — *Discount Video Tapes; Video
Dimensions; Cable Films; Video Connection;
Nostalgia Merchant; Spotlite Video; Sony Video
Software; Kartes Video Communications*

Deserters, The   198?
Drama
70898   110 mins   C   B, V   P
*Alan Scarfe, Dermot Hennelly, Jon Bryden,
Barbara March*
Sergeant Hawley, a Vietnam era hawk, hunts
deserters and draft-dodgers in Canada. There,
he confronts issues of war and peace head-on.
Independent — *Magnum Entertainment*

Desire Under the Elms   1958
Drama
85248   114 mins   B/W   B, V   P
Sophia Loren, Anthony Perkins, Burl Ives
A father and son clash over a woman in 19th
century New England. Loren's first American
appearance. Based on the play by Eugene O'
Neill.
Paramount — *Kartes Video Communications*

Despair   1979
Drama
66128   120 mins   C   B, V   P

Dirk Bogarde, Andrea Ferreal, directed by
Rainer Werner Fassbinder
A chilling and comic study of a victimized factory
owner's descent into madness, set against the
backdrop of Nazi Germany.
New Line Cinema — *Warner Home Video*

Desparate Lives   1982
Drama
85402   96 mins   C   B, V   P
*Diana Scarwid, Helen Hunt, William Windom,
Doug McKeon, Sam Bottoms*
A new high school counselor is faced with a
heinous drug abuse situation among her
students. Made for TV.
Lew Hunter; Lorimar — *U.S.A. Home Video*

Desperate   1922
Scoundrel/The Pride of
Pikeville, The
Comedy
84932   44 mins   B/W   B, V   P
Ford Sterling, Ben Turpin, The Keystone Cops
Two classic comedy films back to back featuring
the best of the early silent comics.
Pathe Exchange Inc — *Blackhawk Films*

Desperate Teenage   1984
Lovedolls
Exploitation
84542   60 mins   C   B, V   P
*Jennifer Schwartz, Hilary Rubens, Steve
McDonald, Tracy Lea, directed by David Markey*
A trashy view of the formation of a tacky all-girl
punk group.
We Got Power Prods — *Hollywood Home
Theater*

Desperate Women   1978
Western/Comedy
81260   98 mins   C   B, V   P
*Dan Haggerty, Susan Saint-James, Ronee
Blakley, Ann Dusenberry, directed by Earl
Bellamy*
A hired gun rescues three female convicts from
a stranded prison wagon in the desert.
Problems arise when they are chased across
the desert by an outlaw gang.
Lorimar Prods. — *U.S.A. Home Video*

Desperately Seeking   1985
Susan
Comedy/Adventure
81479   104 mins   C   B, V, LV   P
*Rosanna Arquette, Madonna, Aidan Quinn,
Robert Joy, Steven Wright, directed by Susan
Seidelman*
A bored New Jersey housewife's life starts to
get exciting when a case of mistaken identity
ensues after she answers a personal ad placed
by a mysterious woman's boyfriend.
MPAA:PG-13

Orion Pictures — *THORN EMI/HBO Video*

Destination Moon   1950
Science fiction
49899   91 mins   C   B, V, 3/4U   P
*Warner Anderson, Tom Powers, Dick Wesson,
Erin O'Brien Moore*
This story of man's first lunar voyage contains
Chesley Bonstell's astronomical artwork and a
famous Woody Woodpecker cartoon. Includes
previews of coming attractions from classic
science fiction films.
Academy Award '50: Special Effects.
George Pal — *Nostalgia Merchant*

Destination Moonbase   1975
Alpha
Science fiction
64904   93 mins   C   B, V   P
Martin Landau, Barbara Bain
In the 21st century, an explosion has destroyed
half the moon, causing it to break away from the
earth's orbit. The moon is cast far away, but the
311 people manning Alpha, a research station
on the moon, must continue their search for
other life forms in outer space.
ITC Entertainment — *CBS/Fox Video*

Destination Nicaragua   1985
Documentary
88179   60 mins   C   B, V   P
Hosted by Tyne Daly
A politically explosive documentary that follows
Americans into the war-torn Central American
country to see the Sandinistas and Contras
argue their respective cases. Taped on video.
Rhino Video — *Rhino Video*

Destination Saturn   1939
Science fiction
07368   90 mins   B/W   B, V, 3/4U   R, P
Buster Crabbe, Constance Moore
Buck Rogers awakens from suspended
animation in the twenty-fifth century.
Universal — *Cable Films*

Detective, The   1968
Mystery
34286   114 mins   C   B, V   P
Frank Sinatra, Lee Remick
A beautiful woman requests the services of a
detective in order to discover her husband's
killer.
SP
Twentieth Century Fox — *CBS/Fox Video*

Detour   1946
Crime-Drama
11672   69 mins   B/W   B, V   P
Tom Neal, Ann Savage

New York piano player hitchhikes west to be
with singer in California. He encounters murder
along the way.
Producers Releasing Corp — *Movie Buff
Video; Video Yesteryear; Western Film & Video
Inc; Festival Films; Kartes.Video
Communications*

Detroit 9000   1973
Drama
81830   106 mins   C   B, V   P
*Alex Rocco, Scatman Crothers, Hari Rhodes,
Vonetta McGee, Herbert Jefferson Jr.*
A pair of Detroit policemen investigate a robbery
that occurred at a black congressman's
fundraising banquet.
MPAA:R
General Film Corporation — *THORN
EMI/HBO Video*

Deutsche Wochen-Schau,   194?
Die (Nazi Newsreel)
World War II/Propaganda
52466   50 mins   B/W   B, V, FO   P
This wartime propaganda film shows the power
of the Nazi war machine, and the way that
people on the home front helped to produce
planes, tanks, and troops that conquered all
obstacles in their path. Original German
narration, no subtitles.
GE
Germany — *Video Yesteryear*

Devil and Daniel Mouse,   1978
The
Fantasy
54692   30 mins   C   B, V   P
Animated
A young songstress, Jan Mouse, sells her soul
to the Devil in exchange for fame, fortune, and
old records. Features John Sebastian's original
songs.
Nelvana Prods Ltd — *Warner Home Video*

Devil and Daniel Webster,   1941
The
Drama/Fantasy
81910   109 mins   B/W   B, V   P
*James Craig, Edward Arnold, Walter Huston,
Simone Simon, Gene Lockhart*
A young farmer who sells his soul to the devil is
saved from a trip down below when Daniel
Webster steps in to defend him.
Academy Awards '41: Best Dramatic Score
(Bernard Herrmann).
RKO — *Embassy Home Entertainment*

Devil and Leroy Basset,   1973
The
Drama/Western
71214   85 mins   C   B, V   P

Cody Bearpaw, John F Goff, George "Buck"
Flower, directed by Robert E Pearso
Keema Gregwolf kills a deputy, breaks from jail
with the Basset brothers, hijacks a church bus,
kidnaps a family and much more in his posse-
eluding cross-country adventure.
MPAA:PG
American National Enterprises — Prism

Devil and Max Devlin, The   1981
Comedy/Fantasy
58624   95 mins   C   B, V   P
Elliott Gould, Bill Cosby, Susan Anspach, Adam
Rich, Julie Budd, directed by Steven Hilliard
Stern
The recently deceased Max Devlin strikes a
bargain with the devil—he will be restored to life
if he can convince three mortals to sell their
souls. Music by Marvin Hamlisch.
MPAA:PG
Walt Disney Productions — Walt Disney Home
Video

Devil and Miss Jones, The   1941
Comedy
65738   90 mins   B/W   B, V   P
Jean Arthur, Robert Cummings
A rich department store owner poses as an
employee in order to learn about impending
labor trouble.
RKO — Republic Pictures Home Video

Devil at 4 O'Clock, The   1961
Drama
65189   126 mins   B/W   B, V   P
Spencer Tracy, Frank Sinatra, Kerwin Mathews,
Jean-Pierre Aumont, directed by Mervyn LeRoy
An alcoholic missionary and three convicts work
to save a colony of leper children from a South
Seas volcano.
Columbia — RCA/Columbia Pictures Home
Video

Devil Bat, The   1941
Horror
66370   70 mins   B/W   B, V   P
Bela Lugosi, Dave O'Brien, Suzanne Kaaren
A crazed madman trains a swarm of monstrous
blood-sucking bats to attack whenever they
smell perfume.
Producers Releasing Corp — Movie Buff
Video; Prism; Discount Video Tapes; Hal Roach
Studios

Devil Bat's Daughter   1946
Science fiction/Mystery
82019   66 mins   B/W   B, V   P
Rosemary La Planche, Michael Hale, John
James, Molly Lamont
A young woman consults a psychiatrist when
she starts to have violent nightmares.
PRC — Sony Video Software

Devil Dog: The Hound of   1978
Hell
Horror
80668   95 mins   C   B, V   P
Richard Crenna, Yvette Mimieux, Kim Richards,
Victor Jory, directed by Curtis Harrington
A family has trouble with man's best friend when
they adopt a dog who is the son of the "Hound
of Hell".
Zeitman-Landers-Roberts Prods. — Lightning
Video

Devil Girl from Mars   1955
Science fiction
49898   76 mins   B/W   B, V, 3/4U   P
Patricia Laffan, Hazel Court, Hugh McDermott,
Adrienne Corri
A female creature from Mars and her very large
robot terrorize the English countryside where
they land. The robot is capable of causing mass
incineration.
Danzigers — Nostalgia Merchant; Mossman
Williams Productions; Hal Roach Studios

Devil Thumbs a Ride, The   1947
Drama
73697   63 mins   B/W   B, V   P
Ted North, Lawrence Tierney, Nan Leslie
A traveller picks up a hitchhiker not knowing
he's wanted for murder.
RKO — RKO HomeVideo

Devil Thumbs a   1947
Ride/Having Wonderful
Crime
Mystery
79320   132 mins   B/W   B, V   P
Lawrence Tierney, Pat O'Brien, George Murphy,
Carole Landis
A mystery double feature: in ""Devil," a ruthless
killer hitches a ride from a travelling salesman
and in ""Having..." a criminal lawyer
investigates the disappearance of a magician.
RKO — RKO HomeVideo

Devil Times Five   1982
Horror
47751   87 mins   C   B, V   P
Gene Evans, Sorrel Booke, Shelly Morrison
To take revenge for being incarcerated in a
mental hospital, five children methodically
murder the adults who befriend them.
MPAA:R
Dylan Jones; Michael Blowitz — Media Home
Entertainment

Devil's Gift, The   1984
Horror
82462   112 mins   C   B, V   P
Bob Mendlesohn, Vicki Saputo, Steven
Robertson
A young boy's toy is possessed by a demon and
havoc ensues.

Zenith International Pictures — *Vestron Video*

Devils, The 1971
Drama
53508   108 mins   C   B, V   P
Vanessa Redgrave, Oliver Reed, directed by Ken Russell
In 1631 France, a young priest is accused of commerce with the devil and of sexually abusing a convent. Based on Aldous Huxley's "The Devils of Loudun."
MPAA:X
Warner Bros; Robert H. Solo; Ken Russell — *Warner Home Video*

Devil's Daughter, The 1939
Horror
11229   60 mins   B/W   B, V, FO   P
Nina Mae McKinney, Jack Carter, Ida James, Hamtree Harrington
A sister's hatred and voodoo ceremonies play an important part in this all-black drama.
Unknown — *Video Yesteryear*

Devil's Eye 1960
Comedy-Drama
65627   90 mins   B/W   B, V   P
Bibi Anderson, Jarl Kulle, directed by Ingmar Bergman
The devil dispatches Don Juan to tempt and seduce a young virgin bride-to-be.
Janus Films — *Embassy Home Entertainment*

Devil's Nightmare 1972
Horror
86584   90 mins   C   B, V   P
Jean Servais, Erika Blanc, Daniel Emilfork, Lucien Raimbourg
In World War II Berlin, a Nazi stabs his infant daughter to death, and is visited years later by the devil in retribution.
Cetelci S.A. Bruxelles — *Monterey Home Video*

Devil's Party, The 1938
Drama
71035   65 mins   B/W   B, V   P
Victor McLaglen, Paul Kelly, William Gargan
Some of the "old-boys" from the tenements reunite, and find themselves in a deadly trap.
U-I — *Hal Roach Studios*

Devil's Playground, The 1946
Western
81609   59 mins   B/W   B, V   P
William Boyd, Andy Clyde, Rand Brooks
A beautiful young woman enlists the aid of Hopalong Cassidy and his friends to make sure that a gold fortune falls into the right hands.
United Artists — *Buena Vista Home Video*

Devil's Rain 1975
Horror
35368   85 mins   C   B, V   P
Ernest Borgnine, Ida Lupino, William Shatner, Eddie Albert, Keenan Wynn
This gruesomely horrifying film relates the rituals and practices of devil worship, possession, and satanism.
MPAA:PG
Sandy Howard — *United Home Video*

Devils Triangle, The 1978
Documentary
81058   59 mins   C   B, V   P
Narrated by Vincent Price
This documentary examines the unexplained incidents which have occurred in the Bermuda Triangle.
Richard Winer Productions — *MGM/UA Home Video*

Devil's Undead, The 1975
Suspense
65451   90 mins   C   B, V   P
Christopher Lee, Peter Cushing
When a Scottish orphanage is besieged by a rash of cold blooded murders, the police are summoned to investigate. Their relentless search to determine the truth leads to a climax as shocking as it is terrifying.
MPAA:PG
Charlemagne Inc — *Monterey Home Video*

Devil's Wanton, The 1949
Drama
81358   80 mins   B/W   B, V   P
Doris Svedlund, Eva Henning, Hasse Ekman, directed by Ingmar Bergman
A group of filmmakers discuss some rather unpleasant projects but put them aside as unsatisfactory. With English subtitles.
SW
Terrafilm — *Discount Video Tapes; Video Yesteryear*

Devil's Wedding Night, The 1973
Horror
79761   85 mins   C   B, V   P
Mark Damon, Sara Bay
An archaeologist and his twin brother fight over a ring that lures Virgins into Count Dracula's Transylvanian castle.
MPAA:R
Dimension Pictures — *United Home Video*

Devo 1983
Music-Performance
75919   54 mins   C   B, V   P
This program presents a combination of videos from the group Devo.
Devovision — *Sony Video Software*

Devo: The Men Who Make the Music   1979
Music-Performance
42905   55 mins   C   B, V   P
New Wave rock group Devo perform robot-like interpretations from their first album, "Q—Are We Not Men? A—We Are Devo." Electronic music tinged thematically with de-evolution processes.
Chuck Statler — *Warner Home Video*

Devonsville Terror, The   1983
Horror
64985   97 mins   C   B, V   P
Suzanna Love, Robert Walker, Donald Pleasance
Strange things begin to happen when a new school teacher arrives in Devonsville, a town which has a history of torture, murder and witchcraft. The hysterical townspeople begin a 20th century witch hunt.
Unknown — *Embassy Home Entertainment*

Diabolique   1955
Mystery
06216   107 mins   B/W   B, V   P
Simone Signoret, Vera Clouzot, Paul Meurisse, Charles Vanet, directed by Henri-Georges Clouzot
Mistress of a school master and his wife plot elaborate murder scheme. French film with English subtitles.
FR
Henri Georges Clouzot — *Movie Buff Video; Hollywood Home Theater; VCII; Video Dimensions; Cable Films; Video Connection; Western Film & Video Inc; Cinema Concepts; Video Yesteryear; International Home Video*

Dial "M" for Murder   1954
Suspense
47616   123 mins   C   B, V   P
Ray Milland, Grace Kelly, Robert Cummings, John Williams, directed by Alfred Hitchcock
An unfaithful husband plots to murder his wife for her money. Part of the "A Night at the Movies" series, this tape simulates a 1954 movie evening, with a Daffy Duck cartoon, "My Little Duckaroo," a newsreel and coming attractions for "Them" and "A Star Is Born."
Warner Bros — *Warner Home Video; RCA VideoDiscs*

Dialogues of the Carmelites   1985
Opera
88136   155 mins   C   B, V   P
Dame Joan Sutherland, conducted by Richard Bonynge
The Elizabethan Sydney Opera performs the classic Poulenc opera in French with English subtitles.
FR
The Australian Opera — *Sony Video Software*

Diamanda Galas: The Litanies of Satan   1985
Music-Performance
84057   30 mins   C   B, V   P
Diamanda Galas
A line performance by Galas, of Avant-Garde, Quasi-Punk music based on Baudelaire, taped at San Francisco's I-Beam.
Target Video — *Target Video*

Diamonds   1972
Crime-Drama/Suspense
84525   108 mins   C   B, V   P
Robert Shaw, Richard Roundtree, Barbara Seagull, Shelley Winters
A tense big-caper film wherein the Israel Diamond Exchange is looted by a motley array of criminal heisters.
MPAA:PG
Menahem Golan — *Charter Entertainment*

Diamonds Are Forever   1971
Adventure
59302   120 mins   C   B, V, LV,   P
CED
Sean Connery, Jill St. John, Charles Gray
Connery's last outing as James Bond finds him taking a lighter approach to the spy business, highlighted by spectacular stunt work and special effects.
United Artists — *CBS/Fox Video; RCA VideoDiscs*

Diana Ross in Concert   1982
Music-Performance
63439   90 mins   C   B, V   P
Diana Ross
Diana Ross performs her greatest hits live at Caesar's Palace, including "Baby Love," "Ain't No Mountain High Enough," "Love Hangover," and "Reach Out and Touch."
Diana Ross Enterprises — *RCA/Columbia Pictures Home Video; RCA VideoDiscs*

Diary of a Mad Housewife   1970
Comedy-Drama
47414   94 mins   C   B, V   P
Carrie Snodgress, Richard Benjamin, Frank Langella
Despairing of her miserable family life, a housewife has an affair with a writer, only to find him to be more selfish and egotistical than her husband.
MPAA:R
Universal — *MCA Home Video*

Diary of a Teenage Hitchhiker   1982
Drama
60183   96 mins   C   B, V   R, P

THE VIDEO TAPE & DISC GUIDE

Charlene Tilton, Dick Van Patten
A 17-year-old girl ignores family restrictions and
police warnings about a homicidal rapist stalking
the area and continues to thumb rides to her job
at a beach resort until one night she is picked up
for a one-way ride to terror.
Stan Shpetner — *Lightning Video; Time Life
Video*

Diary of Anne Frank, The   1959
Drama
29140   150 mins   C   B, V, CED   P
*Millie Perkins, Joseph Schildkraut, Shelley
Winters, Richard Beymer, Gusti Huber, Ed Wynn*
In June 1945, a liberated Jewish refugee returns
to the hidden third floor of an Amsterdam
factory where he finds the diary kept by his
younger daughter during their years in hiding
from the Nazis.
National Board of Review '59: Best Picture;
Academy Awards '59: Best Supporting Actress
(Winters).
20th Century Fox — *CBS/Fox Video*

Diary of a Young Comic   1979
Drama
70664   74 mins   C   B, V   P
*Stacey Keach, Dom DeLouise, Richard Lewis,
Bill Macy, George Jessel, Gary Muledeer, Nina
Van Pollandt.*
The story of a New York comedian in search of
the meaning of lunacy. He finds it in Los
Angeles.
Late Nite Prods — *Pacific Arts Video*

Dias de Ilusion   1980
Suspense
47861   94 mins   C   B, V   P
Andrea Del Boca, Luisina Brando
The fantasy world in which Lucia and her sister
live was created for only one reason, and only
Lucia's diary has the secret. In Spanish.
SP
Hector Olivera; Luis Repetto — *Media Home
Entertainment*

Dick Cavett's Hocus   1979
Pocus, It's Magic
Magic
39079   101 mins   C   B, V, CED   P
*Mark Wilson, Harry Blackstone Jr., Slydini,
hosted by Dick Cavett*
Amateur magician Dick Cavett hosts this tribute
to the great magicians, with many of today's
master wizards performing their most
spectacular tricks and illusions.
MPAA:G
Unknown — *Vestron Video; VERVE Films Inc*

Dick Clark's Best of   1985
Bandstand
Music-Performance
86548   60 mins   C   B, V, LV   P

*The Big Bopper, the Everly Brothers, Sam
Cooke, Chubby Checker*
Dick Clark hosts this made-for-video collection
of vintage American Bandstand performances,
also featuring Dion and the Belmonts, Fabian,
Mark Dinning and Paul Anka.
Vestron MusicVideo — *Vestron Video*

Dick Deadeye   1976
Adventure
59326   80 mins   C   B, V   P
Animated
From the operas of Gilbert and Sullivan, based
on drawings by Ronald Searle, comes the
unlikeliest of heroes, Dick Deadeye. Sporting an
I.Q. of zero, Dick is hired to wipe out pirates,
thieves, and a sorcerer.
Sandy Cobe; David Baugh — *Family Home
Entertainment*

Dick Tracy   1937
Crime-Drama
11689   100 mins   B/W   B, V   P
Ralph Byrd, Smiley Burnett
Dick Tracy faces the fiend, "Spider," and his
demented hunchback.
Republic — *United Home Video*

Dick Tracy   1937
Crime-Drama/Serials
14618   310 mins   B/W   B, V   P
Ralph Byrd, Smiley Burnett
Serial, based on the comic strip character, in
fifteen chapters. The first chapter is thirty
minutes and each additional chapter is twenty
minutes.
Republic — *United Home Video; Video
Connection; Video Yesteryear; Discount Video
Tapes*

Dick Tracy   1945
Crime-Drama
58658   62 mins   B/W   B, V, FO   P
*Morgan Conway, Anne Jeffreys, Mike Mazurki,
Jane Greer, Lyle Latell*
The first Dick Tracy feature film, in which
Splitface is on the loose, a schoolteacher is
murdered, the Mayor is threatened, and a nutty
professor uses a crystal ball to give Tracy the
clue needed to connect the crimes.
RKO — *Movie Buff Video; Video Yesteryear;
Nostalgia Merchant; Hal Roach Studios*

Dick Tracy Detective   1945
Crime-Drama
84818   62 mins   B/W   B, V   P
Morgan Conway, Mike Mazurki, Jane Greer
The comic-strip character brought to hard-
boiled life, battling a scar-faced villian.
RKO — *United Home Video*

(For explanation of codes, see Use Guide and Key)   **213**

Dick Tracy Double Feature #1   194?
Crime-Drama
45053   122 mins   B/W   B, V   P
Ralph Byrd, Lyle Latelle, Morgan Conway, Anne Jeffreys
This video double feature presents two Dick Tracy adventures: "Dick Tracy Detective," "Dick Tracy's Dilemma", a mystery-adventure package starring Chester Gould's popular comic strip hero.
RKO, Gold Key — *United Home Video*

Dick Tracy Double Feature #2   194?
Mystery/Adventure
45005   127 mins   B/W   B, V   P
Boris Karloff, Ralph Byrd, Morgan Conway, Anne Jeffreys
Chester Gould's famous comic strip character is personified in: "Dick Tracy Meets Gruesome," "Dick Tracy vs. Cueball;" a double feature videocassette featuring Dick Tracy battling two of his arch enemies.
RKO, Gold Key — *United Home Video*

Dick Tracy Meets Gruesome   1947
Crime-Drama
58642   66 mins   B/W   B, V, FO   P
Boris Karloff, Ralph Byrd, Lyle Latell
Gruesome and his partner in crime, Melody, stage a bank robbery using the secret formula of Dr. A. Tomic. Tracy has to solve the robbery before word gets out and people rush to withdraw their savings, destroying civilization as we know it.
RKO — *Video Yesteryear; United Home Video; Video Connection; Hal Roach Studios; Western Film & Video Inc; Nostalgia Merchant; Admit One Video*

Dick Tracy Returns   1938
Crime-Drama
11694   100 mins   B/W   B, V   P
Ralph Byrd, Charles Middleton
Public Enemy Paw Stark and his gang set out on a wave of crime that brings them face to face with Dick Tracy.
Republic — *United Home Video*

Dick Tracy Returns   1938
Crime-Drama/Serials
14619   310 mins   B/W   B, V   P
Ralph Byrd, Charles Middleton
Serial, based on the comic strip character, in fifteen chapters. The first chapter is thirty minutes and each additional chapter is twenty minutes.
Republic — *United Home Video; Video Connection*

Dick Tracy vs. Crime Inc.   1941
Crime-Drama/Serials
14620   310 mins   B/W   B, V   P
Ralph Byrd, Ralph Morgan
Serial, based on the comic strip character, in fifteen chapters. The first chapter is thirty minutes and each additional chapter is twenty minutes.
Republic — *United Home Video; Video Connection*

Dick Tracy vs. Crime Inc.   1941
Crime-Drama
07220   100 mins   B/W   B, V   P
Ralph Byrd, Ralph Morgan
Dick Tracy encounters many difficulties when he tries to track down a criminal who can make himself invisible.
Republic — *United Home Video*

Dick Tracy vs. Cueball   1946
Mystery
80738   62 mins   B/W   B, V   P
Morgan Conway, Anne Jeffreys
Dick Tracy has his work cut out for him when the evil gangster Cueball appears on the scene. Based upon Chester Gould's comic strip.
RKO — *Hal Roach Studios; United Home Video; Video Yesteryear*

Dick Tracy's Dilemma   1947
Mystery
80737   60 mins   B/W   B, V   P
Ralph Byrd, Lyle Latelle
The renowned police detective Dick Tracy becomes involved in a nearly unsolvable case. Based upon the Chester Gould comic strip.
RKO — *Hal Roach Studios; United Home Video; Video Yesteryear*

Dick Tracy's G-Men   1939
Crime-Drama
11692   100 mins   B/W   B, V   P
Ralph Byrd, Jennifer Jones
Tracy and his G-Men must stop international spy, Aarnoff, from stealing America's top secrets.
Republic — *United Home Video*

Dick Tracy's G-Men   1939
Crime-Drama/Serials
14621   310 mins   B/W   B, V   P
Ralph Byrd, Irving Pichel
Serial, based on the comic strip character, in fifteen chapters. The first chapter is thirty minutes and each additional chapter is twenty minutes.
Republic — *United Home Video; Video Connection*

Didn't You Hear? 1983
Fantasy/Drama
82213   94 mins   C   B, V   P
Dennis Christopher, Gary Busey, Cheryl Waters, John Kauffman
An alienated college student discovers that dreams have a life of their own when he becomes immersed in his own fantasy world.
MPAA:PG
American National Enterprises — *Prism*

Die Laughing 1980
Comedy
52716   108 mins   C   B, V   P
Robby Benson, Charles Durning, Bud Cort, Elsa Lanchester
A cab driver unwittingly becomes involved in murder, intrigue, and the kidnapping of a monkey that has memorized a scientific formula that can destroy the world.
MPAA:PG
Orion Pictures — *Warner Home Video*

Die Sister, Die! 1974
Horror/Suspense
70578   88 mins   C   B, V   P
Jack Ging, Edith Atwater, Kent Smith, directed by Randall Hood
This gothic-mansion-with-a-secret-in-the-basement thriller features a battle between a senile, reclusive sister and her disturbed, tormenting brother.
Randall Hood — *MPI Home Video*

Different Story, A 1978
Comedy/Romance
76903   107 mins   C   B, V   P
Perry King, Meg Foster, Valerie Curtain, Peter Donat, Richard Bull
Romance develops when a lesbian real estate agent offers a homosexual chauffeur a job with her firm.
MPAA:PG
Alan Belkin; Avco Embassy — *Embassy Home Entertainment*

Digby, the Biggest Dog in the World 1973
Fantasy
71209   88 mins   C   B, V   P
Jim Dale, Angela Douglas, Spike Milligan, Dinsdale Landen, directed by Joseph McGrath
Digby wanders around a scientific laboratory, drinks an experimental fluid and grows a lot.
MPAA:G
Cinerama — *Prism*

Digital Dreams 1983
Music video
77526   70 mins   C   B, V   P
Animated, Bill Wyman, Astrid Wyman, James Coburn
This film presents a surrealistic journey into the life of Rolling Stones bassist Bill Wyman from his electronic childhood to his adult obsession with computers.
Bill and Astrid Wyman — *Music Media*

Dillinger 1973
Crime-Drama
64894   106 mins   C   B, V, CED   P
Warren Oates, Michelle Phillips, Richard Dreyfuss, Cloris Leachman
The most colorful period of criminality in America is brought to life in this story of John Dillinger, "Baby Face" Nelson and the notorious "Lady in Red."
MPAA:R
American International Pictures — *Vestron Video*

Dillinger 1945
Crime-Drama
70989   70 mins   C   B, V   P
Lawrence Tierney, Edmund Lowe, Anne Jeffreys, Elisha Cook, directed by Max Nosseck
John Dillinger's notorious career, from street punk to public enemy number one, receives a thrilling fast-paced treatment in this film.
Lorimar; Monogram — *Key Video*

Diner 1982
Comedy-Drama
47777   110 mins   C   B, V, CED   P
Steve Guttenberg, Daniel Stern, Mickey Rourke, Kevin Bacon, directed by Barry Levinson
The bittersweet experiences of a group of Baltimore teenagers growing up, circa 1959.
MPAA:R
MGM — *MGM/UA Home Video*

Dingaka 1965
Drama
87612   96 mins   C   B, V   P
Stanley Baker, Juliet Prowse, Ken Gampu, directed by Jamie Uys
A controversial drama from the writer and director of "The Gods Must Be Crazy" about a South African tribesman who avenges his daughter's murder by tribal laws, and is then tried by white man's laws. A crusading white attorney struggles to acquit him.
Jamie Uys — *Charter Entertainment*

Dinner at Eight 1933
Comedy-Drama
77378   110 mins   C   B, V, LV   P
John Barrymore, Lionel Barrymore, Wallace Beery, Madge Evans, Jean Harlow, Billie Burke, Marie Dressler, Phillips Holmes, Jean Hersholt, directed by George Cukor
A social climbing woman and her husband throw a dinner party where each of the guests reveal something about themselves.

MGM; David O. Selznick — *MGM/UA Home Video*

Dinner at the Ritz   1937
Drama
11392   78 mins   B/W   B, V, FO   P
David Niven, Annabella, Paul Lucas
Daughter of a murdered Parisian banker vows to find his killer with help from her fiance.
20th Century Fox — *Video Yesteryear; Cinema Concepts; Cable Films; Hollywood Home Theater; Western Film & Video Inc; Kartes Video Communications*

Dino   1957
Drama
77479   96 mins   B/W   B, V   P
Sal Mineo, Brian Keith, Susan Kohner, directed by Thomas Carr
A social worker joins a young woman in helping a seventeen-year-old delinquent to re-enter society.
Allied Artists — *Republic Pictures Home Video*

Dinosaurs and Monsters   1986
Fairy tales
Closed Captioned
88077   64 mins   C   B, V   P
Segments of Fred Rogers' PBS program featuring dinosaurs, mythical beasts and fairy tales are compiled on this tape.
Public Broadcasting System — *Playhouse Video*

Dinosaurus   1960
Science fiction
82410   85 mins   C   B, V   P
Ward Ramsey, Kristina Hanson, Paul Lukather, directed by Irvin S Yeaworth, Jr
Large sadistic dinosaurs appear in the modern world. They eat, burn, and pillage their way through this film. Also includes a romance between a Neanderthal and a modern-age woman.
New World Video — *New World Video*

Dionne Quintuplets   1978
Biographical/History-Modern
46693   87 mins   C   B, V, FO   P
The true story of five identical girls born in 1934 who were taken from their parents by a court order. This program presents the tragic story of exploitation and publicity that surrounded this family and the hardships they endured as a result.
National Film Board of Canada — *Video Yesteryear; National Film Board of Canada*

Dionne Warwick Live   1983
Music-Performance
75492   120 mins   C   V   P
Dionne Warwick

Dionne Warwick's Chicago 1983 concert includes great hits such as "Alfie," "Walk On By," "Do You Know the Way to San Jose" and "Deja Vu."
MusicAmerica Live — *Prism*

Diplomaniacs   1933
Comedy
65227   62 mins   B/W   B, V   P
Bert Wheeler, Robert Woolsey, Marjorie White, Hugh Herbert
Wheeler and Woolsey, official barbers on an Indian reservation, are sent to the Geneva peace conference to represent the tribe.
RKO — *Blackhawk Films*

Dire Straits   1981
Music-Performance
52709   21 mins   C   B, V   P
Dire Straits
The English rock group performs songs from the album "Making Movies" including "Romeo and Juliet," "Tunnel of Love," and "Skateaway."
Mervyn Lloyd — *Warner Home Video*

Directions '66   1966
Drama
85165   29 mins   B/W   B, V   P
Nancy Marchand, Lawrence Keith
A live one-set television drama about a pious couple who take the troubles of local youngsters upon their own shoulders.
ABC — *Video Yesteryear*

Dirt Band Tonight, The   1982
Music-Performance
64830   58 mins   C   B, V   P
Filmed at Denver's Rainbow Music Hall, The Dirt Band performs such classics as "Mr. Bojangles," "Rocky Top," "Will the Circle Be Unbroken" and "Make a Little Magic." In stereo.
EMI Music Video — *THORN EMI/HBO Video; Pioneer Artists*

Dirt Bike Kid, The   1986
Comedy
Closed Captioned
88155   91 mins   C   B, V, LV   P
Peter Billingsley, Anne Bloom, Stuart Pankin, Patrick Collins
A precocious brat is stuck with a used motorbike that has a mind of its own. Shenanigans follow.
MPAA:PG
Julie Corman — *Charter Entertainment*

Dirt Bike Stars   1986
Motorcycles/Documentary
71227   30 mins   C   V   P
This made-for-video highlight tape shows top motocrossers in action like Brock Glover, David Baily, Johnny O'Mara and Jeff Ward.
Prism Video Collection — *Prism*

Dirt Gang, The   1971
Drama
81532   89 mins   C   B, V   P
Paul Carr, Michael Pataki, Michael Forest
A motorcycle gang terrorize the members of a
film crew on location in the desert.
MPAA:R
Shermart Distributing Co. — MPI Home Video

Dirty, Dirty Jokes   1984
Comedy-Performance
79306   60 mins   C   B, V   P
Redd Foxx hosts this program that features up
and coming stand-up comics.
Vestron Video — Vestron Video

Dirty Dozen, The   1967
War-Drama
39090   149 mins   C   B, V, CED   P
Lee Marvin, Ernest Borgnine, Charles Bronson,
Jim Brown, George Kennedy
A tough Army major is assigned to train and
command twelve hardened convicts on the
suicidal mission into Nazi Germany in 1944.
Academy Awards '67: Best Sound Effects.
MGM — MGM/UA Home Video

Dirty Gertie From Harlem   1946
U.S.A.
Drama
08889   60 mins   B/W   B, V, 3/4U   P
Gertie LaRue
An all-black cast does a variation on Somerset
Maugham's "Rain." Gertie goes to Trinidad to
hide out from her jilted boyfriend.
Unknown — Video Yesteryear; Discount Video
Tapes

Dirty Harry   1971
Drama
38947   103 mins   C   B, V, LV   P
Clint Eastwood, directed by Don Siegel
Clint Eastwood is detective Harry Callahan, who
is attempting to track down a psychopathic
rooftop killer before a kidnapped girl dies.
MPAA:R
Warner Bros — Warner Home Video; RCA
VideoDiscs

Dirty Mind of Young Sally,   1972
The
Comedy
53147   84 mins   C   B, V   P
Sharon Kelly
Sally's erotic radio program broadcasts from a
mobile studio, which must stay one step ahead
of the police.
MPAA:R
Valiant Intl Pictures — Monterey Home Video

Dirty Tricks   1981
Comedy
65070   91 mins   C   B, V   P
Elliot Gould, Kate Jackson, Arthur Hill, Rich
Little, directed by Arthur Hill
A history professor searches for an incriminating
letter that was written by George Washington.
MPAA:PG
Filmplan International — Embassy Home
Entertainment

Disappearance, The   1981
Suspense
65607   80 mins   C   B, V   P
Donald Sutherland, David Hemmings, John
Hurt, Christopher Plummer
A hired assassin discovers an ironic link
between his new target and his missing wife.
MPAA:R
World Northal — Vestron Video

Disappearance of Aimee,   1976
The
Drama
81813   96 mins   C   B, V   P
Faye Dunaway, Bette Davis, James Woods,
directed by Anthony Harvey
This is the true story of evangelist Aimee
Semple McPherson's disappearance in 1926
and her subsequent return one month later.
Available in VHS Stereo and Beta Hi-Fi.
Tomorrow Entertainment — U.S.A. Home
Video

Disaster—Adventure   1984
Featurettes
Movie and TV trailers/Adventure
66483   61 mins   C   B, V   P
This group of movie promotion featurettes show
behind the scenes activities during the making
of "The Towering Inferno," "The Poseidon
Adventure," "The Cassandra Crossing," "The
Ten Commandments," "The Train" and "The
Golden Voyage of Sinbad." Also included is an
additional featurette, "Oscar: The First 50
Years."
Paramount et al — San Francisco Rush Video

Discreet Charm of the   1972
Bourgeoisie, The
Satire
81893   100 mins   C   B, V   P
Fernando Rey, Delphine Seyrig, Jean-Pierre
Cassel Bulle Ogier, Stephane Audran, directed
by Luis Bunuel
Six socialites find themselves being constantly
distracted during a posh dinner. In French with
English subtitles.
MPAA:R
20th Century Fox — Media Home
Entertainment

Dishonored Lady 1947
Suspense
66371 85 mins B/W B, V P
Hedy Lamarr, Dennis O'Keefe, William Lundigan, John Loder
A lady art director is accused of murdering her ex-boyfriend and refuses to testify in her own defense.
Mars Films — *Movie Buff Video; Kartes Video Communications*

Disney Cartoon Parade, Vol. 1 1981
Cartoons
56877 120 mins C CED P
Animated
Mickey Mouse, Goofy, Minnie, Pluto, Donald, Chip 'n Dale, and Peg-leg Pete star in "On Vacation with Mickey Mouse and Friends," and "The Adventures of Chip 'n Dale."
Walt Disney Productions — *RCA VideoDiscs*

Disney Cartoon Parade, Vol. 2 1982
Cartoons
59020 88 mins C CED P
Animated
This Disney compilation includes "At Home with Donald Duck" (1956), a festival of classic cartoons featuring Donald , Mickey, Pluto, and Goofy, and "The Coyote's Lament" (1961), featuring Pluto out West.
Walt Disney Productions — *RCA VideoDiscs*

Disney Cartoon Parade, Vol. 3 1982
Cartoons
59641 100 mins C CED P
Animated
Some of Disney's most memorable cartoons: "Kids Is Kids" features the zany antics of Donald Duck and his nephews, as Prof. Ludwig von Drake tries to answer why kids are hard to handle; "Goofy's Salute to Father" follows Goofy's hilarious misadventures from bachelorhood to the altar to bottles and diapers.
Walt Disney Productions — *RCA VideoDiscs*

Disney Cartoon Parade, Vol. 4 1982
Cartoons
60389 85 mins C CED P
Animated
This volume contains "Thru the Mirror," "The Sleepwalker," "Donald's Golf Game," "Pluto and Gopher," "Dragon Around, " "The Whalers," "Society Dog Show," "Pluto's Sweater," "Donald Applecore," "The Little Whirlwind," "Donald's Diary" and "Pluto's Blue Note."
Walt Disney Productions — *RCA VideoDiscs*

Disney Cartoon Parade, Vol. 5 1983
Cartoons
64328 90 mins C CED P
Animated
This collection includes such Disney favorites as "Goofy Over Sports," "Boat Builders," and "Pluto's Quintuplets," plus many others.
Walt Disney Productions — *RCA VideoDiscs*

Disney Christmas Gift, A 1984
Cartoons
79178 46 mins C B, V P
Animated
A collection of Christmas scenes from such Disney classics as ""Peter Pan," ""The Sword In The Stone," and ""Cinderella."
Walt Disney Productions — *Walt Disney Home Video*

Disney Classics, The 1985
Children/Literature
70938 30 mins C B, V P
Animated
From the Disney Video-A-Long series, this program offers a read-along lesson that teaches children three favorite stories: "Pinocchio," "Robin Hood" and "101 Dalmations."
Walt Disney Productions — *Walt Disney Home Video*

Disney's American Heroes 1982
Cartoons/Folklore
63190 39 mins C B, V P
Animated, the voices of Roy Rogers and the Sons of the Pioneers
Two Disney tall tales of American folk heroes: "Pecos Bill" and "Paul Bunyan."
Walt Disney Productions) — *Walt Disney Home Video*

Disney's Greatest Lullabies 1986
Children/Music
70940 25 mins C B, V P
Each tape in this series compiles 5 or so bedtime ballads, culled from classic Disney films, designed to bring somnolent bliss to the kiddies.
Walt Disney·Productions — *Walt Disney Home Video*

Disney's Halloween Treat 1984
Cartoons/Holidays
73792 47 mins C B, V P
Animated
Scenes from Disney classics, such as "Snow White and the Seven Dwarfs," "Fantasia", "Peter Pan" and "The Sword and the Stone" are tied together with a Halloween theme.
Walt Disney — *Walt Disney Home Video*

Disney's Storybook Classics — 1982
Cartoons
63127   121 mins   C   B, V   P
Animated, the voice of Sterling Holloway and the Andrews Sisters
A collection of classic children's fables, featuring "Little Toot" (1948-excerpted from "Melody Time"), The story of a little harbor tugboat; "Chicken Little" (1943); "The Grasshopper and the Ants" (1934—a Silly Symphony) and "Peter and the Wolf" (1946—excerpted from "Make Mine Music"), a Disneyized version of Prokofiev's famous concert piece.
Walt Disney Productions — *Walt Disney Home Video*

Displaced Person, The — 1977
Drama
87318   58 mins   C   B, V   P
Irene Worth, John Houseman, introduced by Henry Fonda
In this adaptation of Flannery O'Connor's story, the inhabitants of a 1940's Georgia farm find their lives disrupted by a Polish refugee.
Matthew Herman; Robert Geller — *Monterey Home Video*

Diva — 1982
Suspense/Romance
60394   123 mins   C   B, V, CED   P
Frederic Andrei, Roland Bertin, Richard Bohringer, Gerard Darmon, Jacques Fabbri, Wilhelmenia Wiggins Fernandez, Dominique Pinon
A young mail courier with a passion for opera manages to tape his idol who has avoided the recording studio. At the same time, a prostitute hides a tape recording in his delivery bag which fingers a local drug kingpin. Bizarre chases and plot twists follow.
Galaxie Films; Greenwich Films — *MGM/UA Home Video*

Divide and Conquer — 1943
World War II/Documentary
50614   60 mins   B/W   B, V, 3/4U   P
Directed by Frank Capra
Hitler's Nazis invade Belgium, Holland, Denmark, and Norway. They take France, and drive the British into the sea of Dunkirk. Part of the "Why We Fight" series.
US War Department — *Western Film & Video Inc; MPI Home Video; National AudioVisual Center*

Divine Madness — 1980
Music-Performance
47374   87 mins   C   B, V   P
Bette Midler
Bette Midler is captured at her best in a live concert at Pasadena Civic Auditorium.
MPAA:R

The Ladd Company — *Warner Home Video; RCA VideoDiscs*

Divorce Hearing — 1958
Documentary
85166   27 mins   B/W   B, V   P
Presented by Dr. Paul Popenoe
A real-life divorce case is taped and shown, as a couple lay into each other about their troubled 38 year marriage. Intended as a diatribe against divorce.
Syndicate — *Video Yesteryear*

Divorce His, Divorce Hers — 1972
Drama
70713   144 mins   C   B, V   P
Richard Burton, Elizabeth Taylor
The first half of this drama shows the crumbling of a marriage through the husband's eyes. The second half offers the wife's perspective.
John Heyman — *VCL Home Video*

Divorce of Lady X — 1938
Drama
07120   92 mins   C   B, V   P
Merle Oberon, Laurence Olivier, directed by Tom Whelan
British debutante, in guise of "Lady X", makes a woman-hating divorce lawyer eat his words through romance and marriage.
United Artists; Alexander Korda;
British — *Embassy Home Entertainment; Unicorn Video; Hal Roach Studios*

Dixie: Changing Habits — 1983
Drama
80899   96 mins   C   B, V   P
Suzanne Pleshette, Cloris Leachman, Kenneth McMillan, John Considine, Geraldine Fitzgerald
The flamboyant madam of a New Orleans bordello is sent to a convent for ninety days of rehabilitation. Available in VHS Stereo and Beta Hi-Fi.
George Englund Productions — *U.S.A. Home Video*

Dixie Dynamite — 1976
Drama
80950   88 mins   C   B, V   P
Warren Oates, Christopher George, Jane Anne Johnstone, Kathy McHaley, R.G. Armstrong
The two daughters of a Georgia moonshiner set out to avenge the murder of their father. The music is performed by Duane Eddy and Dorsey Burnette.
MPAA:PG
Dimension Pictures — *United Home Video; Continental Video*

Dixie Jamboree — 1944
Comedy/Musical
57351   69 mins   B/W   B, V, FO   P

Guy Kibbee, Frances Langford, Louise Beavers, Charles Butterworth
A gangster "on the lam" uses an unusual method of escape from St. Louis—the last Mississippi Showboat.
Producers Releasing Corp — *Video Yesteryear; Discount Video Tapes; See Hear Industries*

Dizzy Gillespie   1981
Music-Performance
75895   19 mins   C   B, V   P
This program presents a jazz concert by Dizzy Gillespie featuring his compositions "Be Bop" and "Birks' Works."
Jazz America Ltd — *Sony Video Software*

Dizzy Gillespie's Dream   1981
Band
Music-Performance
75896   16 mins   C   B, V   P
This program presents a concert by Dizzy Gillespie featuring his songs "Groovin' High" and "Hothouse," played by an all star band of Gillespie alumni.
Jazz American Ltd — *Sony Video Software*

Django   1968
Western
81516   90 mins   C   B, V   P
Franco Nero, Loredana Nusciak, Angel Alvarez
Django is a stranger who arrives in a Mexican border town to settle a dispute between a small band of Americans and Mexicans.
MPAA:PG
Sergio Corbucci Prods — *Magnum Entertainment*

Django Shoots First   1974
Western
78117   96 mins   C   B, V, FO   P
Glenn Saxon, Evelyn Stewart, Alberto Lupo
A colorful western with plenty of action and plot twists.
Italy — *Video Yesteryear*

Do It Debbie's Way   1984
Physical fitness
66496   85 mins   C   B, V   P
Debbie Reynolds, Teri Garr, Florence Henderson, Rose Marie, Virginia Mayo, Terry Moore, Dionne Warwick
Debbie Reynolds leads her friends through a workout routine that is designed for people of all shapes and sizes who are new to exercise. The tape features a musical track of big band favorites in VHS stereo and Beta Hi-Fi stereo.
Judy Franklin; Paul Brownstein; Rick Melchior — *Video Associates*

Do Not Forsake Me Oh   1968
My Darling
Adventure/Fantasy
76922   50 mins   C   B, V   P
Patrick McGoohan
The Prisoner's mind is needed to find a professor who's developed a process which can transmit the mind and personality of one man into the body of another. An episode from "The Prisoner" TV series.
ITC — *MPI Home Video*

Do They Know It's   1984
Christmas?
Music video/Documentary
80364   30 mins   C   B, V   P
Bob Geldof, Sting, Phil Collins, Paul Young, Bono Vox, Simon Le Bon, Boy George
A documentary about how over forty of rock's biggest stars got together to record "Do They Know It's Christmas" plus a music video of the song. Available in VHS and Beta Hi-Fi.
Vestron Music Video — *Vestron Video*

D.O.A.   1949
Suspense
33495   83 mins   B/W   B, V, FO   P
Edmond O'Brien, Pamela Britton, directed by Rudolph Mate
A man is accidentally given a lethal, slow-acting poison. As his time runs out, he frantically seeks to learn who is responsible and why he was poisoned.
United Artists — *Video Yesteryear; Cable Films; Western Film & Video Inc; United Home Video; Kartes Video Communications; Hal Roach Studios*

Doberman Gang, The   1972
Crime-Drama
Closed Captioned
70991   85 mins   C   B, V   P
Byron Mabe, Hal Reed, Julie Parrish, Simmy Bow, JoJo D'Amore, directed by Byron Ross Chudnow
Clever thieves train a gang of Doberman Pinschers in the fine art of bank robbing.
MPAA:G
Morin; Rosamond Prods, Inc — *Key Video*

Doc Savage   1975
Adventure/Fantasy
82500   100 mins   C   B, V   P
Ron Ely, directed by Michael Anderson
Doc and The Amazing Five fight a murderous villain who plans to take over the world. Based on the novels of Kenneth Robeson.
MPAA:G
George Pal — *Warner Home Video*

Doctor at Large   1957
Comedy
73793   98 mins   C   B, V   P

Dirk Bogarde, Donald Sinden, Anne Heywood
A doctor blunders his way to his dream of being
a surgeon.
J Arthur Rank — *VidAmerica*

Doctor at Sea   1956
Comedy-Drama
73794   93 mins   C   B, V   P
Dirk Bogarde, Brigitte Bardot
To escape his marriage, a doctor signs on a
cargo boat as a ship's doctor and becomes
involved with a French girl.
J Arthur Rank — *VidAmerica*

Dr. Black, Mr. Hyde   1976
Horror
35383   88 mins   C   B, V   P
Rosalind Cash, Stu Gilliam
Horrifying tale of a black man who can't control
himself when drinking the special potion.
MPAA:R
Charles Walker, Manfred Bernhard — *United
Home Video*

Dr. Bud Muehleisen on   1980
Racquetball
Sports-Minor
50095   25 mins   C   B, V, 3/4U   P
Dr. Bud Muehleisen
In this seven segment program, the "father of
raquetball" demonstrates tips and drills of the
world's fastest growing sport. A teaching aid for
clubs and schools.
VideoSports — *VideoSports*

Doctor Butcher M.D.   1980
Horror
60403   81 mins   C   B, V   P
*Ian McCulloch, Alexandra Cole, Peter O'Neal,
Donald O'Brian*
A mad doctor's deranged dream of creating
"perfect people" by taking parts of one person
and interchanging them with another backfires
as his creations develop strange side effects.
MPAA:R
Terry Levene; Aquarius Releasing — *Paragon
Video Productions; American Video Tape;
Thriller Video*

Dr. Death   1973
Horror/Science fiction
71205   93 mins   C   B, V   P
*John Considine, Barry Coe, Cheryl Miller,
Stewart Moss, Leon Askin, directed by Eddie
Saeta*
The evil doctor discovered a process for
transmigrating his soul into the bodies of people
he murdered 1000 years ago. Now, someone
wants to stop him.
MPAA:R
Pictures International — *Prism*

Dr. Detroit   1983
Comedy
65117   91 mins   C   B, V, LV   P
Dan Aykroyd, Howard Hesseman, Donna Dixon
A meek college professor becomes involved
with four beautiful hookers and creates another
identity as their flamboyant pimp, Dr. Detroit.
MPAA:R
Universal — *MCA Home Video*

Doctor Doolittle   1967
Musical
08456   144 mins   C   B, V, CED   P
*Rex Harrison, Samantha Eggar, Anthony
Newley, Richard Attenborough*
An adventure about a 19th century English
doctor who embarks on linguistic lessons for his
animals. Based on Hugh Lofting's stories.
Academy Awards '67: Best Song ("Talk to the
Animals"). EL, SP
20th Century Fox; APJAC — *CBS/Fox Video*

Doctor Doom Conquers   1985
the World
Adventure/Cartoons
81711   90 mins   C   B, V   P
Animated
Spider Man battles the evil Doctor Doom who
uses his scientific skills to conquer the world.
Marvel Productions — *Prism*

Dr. Frankenstein's Castle   1974
of Freaks
Horror
86494   87 mins   C   B, V   P
Rossano Brazzi, Michael Dunn
Frankenstein and his midget assistant
reanimate a few Neanderthals that are
terrorizing a nearby Rumanian village.
Foreign — *Magnum Entertainment*

Doctor Gore   1975
Horror/Exploitation
84814   90 mins   C   B, V   P
J G Patterson, Jenny Driggers, Roy Mehaffey
A demented pediatrician tries to assemble a
facsimile of his dead wife with pieces of other
women. He doesn't make it.
Pat Patterson — *United Home Video*

Dr. I. Q.   1953
Game show
42971   30 mins   B/W   B, V, FO   P
*George Ansbro, Art Fleming, Bob Shepherd,
Jimmy McLain*
Early television quiz fun abounds as the good
doctor, Jimmy McLain, gives away silver dollars
for the correct answers to questions like "Who
wrote the quote, "To err is human, to forgive
divine?"
ABC — *Video Yesteryear*

Doctor in Distress 1963
Comedy
73795   102 mins   C   B, V   P
Dirk Bogarde, Leo McKern, Samantha Eggar
An aging chief surgeon falls in love with a
physiotherapist and tries to recapture his youth.
J Arthur Rank — *VidAmerica*

Dr. Jekyll and Mr. Hyde 1941
Horror
82112   113 mins   B/W   B, V, LV   P
*Spencer Tracy, Ingrid Bergman, Lana Turner,
Donald Crisp, directed by Victor Fleming*
This is an adaptation of the Robert Louis
Stevenson story about a doctor's experiment on
himself to separate good and evil.
MGM — *MGM/UA Home Video*

Dr. Jekyll and Mr. Hyde 1920
Horror
48293   65 mins   B/W   B, V   P, T
John Barrymore, Nita Naldi, Brandon Hurst
The first American film version of Robert Louis
Stevenson's horror tale about a schizophrenic
physician. Silent.
Famous Players Lasky Corp — *Blackhawk
Films; Festival Films; Western Film & Video Inc;
Discount Video Tapes*

Dr. Kildare's Strange 1940
Case
Drama
05478   76 mins   B/W   B, V   P
Lew Ayres, Lionel Barrymore, Loraine Day
Dr. Kildare administers daring treatment to a
man suffering from a mental disorder of a
dangerous nature.
MGM — *Hollywood Home Theater; Discount
Video Tapes*

Dr. Mabuse vs. Scotland 1936
Yard
Mystery
85168   90 mins   B/W   B, V   P
Sabine Bethmann, Peter Van Eyck
A sequel to the Fritz Lang classics, this film
features the archcriminal attempting to take
over the world with a mind-controlling camera.
German — *Video Yesteryear*

Dr. Misterio's "Patented" 1985
Video Almanac of Fun
Variety
71061   56 mins   C   B, V   P
Written and directed by Tom Shutter
Designed to entertain the kiddies on rainy days,
this tape includes several "how-to" projects,
games and neat tricks.
Tom Shutter — *MPI Home Video*

Dr. No 1963
Adventure
58822   111 mins   C   B, V, LV,   P
                                 CED
*Sean Connery, Ursula Andress, Joseph
Wiseman, Jack Lord*
James Bond, investigating murders in Jamaica,
discovers a nuclear base established to divert
the course of rockets projected from Cape
Canaveral.
United Artists; Eon Prods — *CBS/Fox Video;
RCA VideoDiscs*

Doctor of Doom 1962
Horror
51947   77 mins   B/W   B, V   P
*Lorene Velazquez, Armando Silvestre, Elizabeth
Campbell, Roberto Canedo, directed by Rene
Cardona*
A mad surgeon conducts an insane series of
brain transplants, defying law and order. Two
lady wrestlers try to stop him.
Unknown — *Hollywood Home Theater*

Doctor Phibes Rises 1972
Again
Horror
82469   89 mins   C   B, V   P
Vincent Price, Robert Quarry, Peter Cushing
The diabolical Doctor Phibes tries to bring his
wife's corpse back to life.
MPAA:PG
Orion Pictures — *Vestron Video*

Doctor Snuggles 1984
Cartoons
80040   60 mins   C   B, V   P
Animated
Doctor Snuggles pursues the evil Professor
Emerald after a strange series of events occurs.
Jim Terry — *Embassy Home Entertainment*

Dr. Strangelove 1964
Comedy
63962   93 mins   B/W   B, V   P
*Peter Sellers, George C. Scott, Sterling Hayden,
Keenan Wynn, Slim Pickens, directed by
Stanley Kubrick*
Peter Sellers plays a triple role in Stanley
Kubrick's classic black comedy about a group of
war-eager military men and the psychotic genius
who is behind a scheme to attack Russia.
Columbia — *RCA/Columbia Pictures Home
Video; RCA VideoDiscs*

Dr. Syn 1937
Drama
08765   90 mins   B/W   B, V, 3/4U   P
*George Arliss, Margaret Lockwood, John Loder,
directed by Roy Neil*
The story tells of a seemingly respectible vicar
of Dymchurch who is really a former pirate.

Gaumount; British; London Film
Production — *Cable Films; Discount Video
Tapes; Kartes Video Communications*

Dr. Terror's House of Horrors
1965

Horror
70200   92 mins   C   B, V   P
Christopher Lee, Peter Cushing
Six traveling companions have their fortunes
told by a mysterious doctor through the use of
Tarot cards.
Hammer — *Republic Pictures Home Video*

Dr. Who and the Daleks
1965

Science fiction
81181   78 mins   C   B, V   P
*Peter Cushing, Roy Castle, directed by Gordon
Fleming*
The time-lord Dr. Who and his three
grandchildren accidentally transport themselves
to a futuristic planet inhabited by the Daleks,
who capture the travelers and hold them
captive. Available in VHS and Beta Hi-Fi.
Joe Vegoda — *THORN EMI/HBO Video*

Doctor Zhivago
1965

Drama
44642   197 mins   C   B, V, LV,   P
                              CED
*Omar Sharif, Julie Christie, Geraldine Chaplin,
Rod Steiger, Alec Guinness, Tom Courtenay,
directed by David Lean*
An historical account of the lives of the people
who lived through the dark days of the Russian
Revolution. Based on the Nobel Prize winning
novel by Boris Pasternak.
Academy Awards '65: Best Screenplay From
Another Medium (Bolt); Best Costume Design,
Color (Dalton); Best Cinematography (Young);
Best Art Direction, Color (Box and Marsh).
MGM — *MGM/UA Home Video*

Doctors and Nurses
1982

Comedy
85877   90 mins   C   B, V   P
A children's satire of soap operas wherein the
adults play the children and vice-versa.
Unknown — *VidAmerica*

Dodes 'ka-den
1970

Drama
86096   140 mins   C   B, V   P
*Yoshitaka Zushi, Junzaburo Ban, Kiyoko Tange,
directed by Akira Kurosawa*
In this departure from his samurai genre films,
Kurosawa depicts a throng of fringe-dwelling
Tokyo slum inhabitants in a semi-surreal
manner. Nominated for the Best Foreign Film
Academy Award in 1971.
Toho Prod. — *Embassy Home Entertainment*

Dodge City
1939

Western
68229   104 mins   C   B, V   P
Errol Flynn, Olivia De Havilland
Errol Flynn stars as Wade Hutton, the roving
cattleman who becomes the sheriff of Dodge
City. His job is to run the ruthless outlaw and his
gang out of town.
Warner Bros — *CBS/Fox Video*

Dodsworth
1936

Drama
81467   101 mins   B/W   B, V, LV   P
*Walter Huston, David Niven, Paul Lukas, John
Payne, Mary Astor, directed by William Wyler*
The lives of an American businessman and his
wife are drastically changed when they take a
tour of Europe. Based upon the Sinclair Lewis
novel.
Samuel Goldwyn — *Embassy Home
Entertainment*

Dog Day
1983

Suspense
81959   101 mins   C   B, V   P
Lee Marvin, Miou Miou, Victor Lanoux
An American traitor who is on the lam from the
government and his cronies takes refuge on a
small farm. A surprise awaits him when the
farmers come up with an unusual plan to
bargain for his life.
Norbert Saada — *Lightning Video*

Dog Day Afternoon
1975

Comedy-Drama
44591   120 mins   C   B, V   P
*Al Pacino, John Cazale, Charles Durning, James
Broderick, Chris Sarandon, Carol Kane, directed
by Sidney Lumet*
The true story of a bank robbery that occured on
August 22, 1972 in the early morning of a
scorching New York summer day. The gunmen
turned the robbery into a bizarre event—from
the way they handled their hostages, to their
demands, to their order for take-out pizza.
Academy Awards '75: Best Original Screenplay
(Pierson). MPAA:R
Warner Bros — *Warner Home Video; RCA
VideoDiscs*

Dog of Flanders, A
1959

Drama
81100   96 mins   C   B, V   P
David Ladd, Donald Crisp, Theodore Bikel
A young Dutch boy and his grandfather find a
badly beaten dog and restore it to health.
20th Century Fox; Robert
Radnitz — *Paramount Home Video*

Dogpound Shuffle
1974

Adventure/Comedy
Closed Captioned
70903   98 mins   C   B, V   P

Ron Moody, David Soul, written and directed by
Jeffrey Bloom
Two drifters form a new song and dance act in
order to raise the funds necessary to win their
dog's freedom from the pound.
MPAA:PG
Bulldog Productions; Inc — Playhouse Video

Dogs of Hell   1983
Horror
81093   90 mins   C   B, V   P
Earl Owensby, Bill Gribble, Jerry Rushing
The sheriff of an idyllic resort community must
stop a pack of killer dogs from terrorizing the
residents.
MPAA:R
Earl Owensby — Media Home Entertainment

Dogs of War, The   1981
Adventure/Drama
47147   102 mins   C   B, V, CED   P
Christopher Walken, Tom Berenger, Colin
Blakely
A group of professional mercenaries are hired to
overthrow the dictator of a new West African
nation. Based on the novel by Frederick
Forsythe.
MPAA:R
United Artists — CBS/Fox Video

Dogtanian and the Three   1981
Musketeers
Cartoons/Adventure
84496   25 mins   C   B, V.   P
Based on Dumas' classic, a dog musketeer
romps through animated France.
BRB Int'l — Sony Video Software

Doin' Time   1985
Comedy
71169   80 mins   C   B, V   P
Richard Mulligan, Jimmie Walker, John Vernon,
Colleen Camp, Pat McCormick, Mike Mazurki,
Jeff Altman, Dey Young, directed by George
Mendeluk
At John Dillinger Penitentiary, the inmates have
taken over the asylum. Under the supervision of
warden "Mongo," silliness prevails along the
order of chain-gang kick lines,
MPAA:R
Ladd Company — Warner Home Video

Doin What the Crowd   1973
Does
Horror
66108   89 mins   C   B, V   P
Robert Walker Jr, Cesar Romero
The tale of the death of Poe's lover Lenore.
MPAA:PG EL, SP
William Herbert — Unicorn Video

Dolce Vita, La   1960
Drama
47990   174 mins   B/W   B, V   P
Morcello Mastroianni, Anita Ekberg, Anouk
Aimee, directed by Federico Fellini
A journalist mixes in modern Roman high
society and is alternately bewitched and
sickened by what he sees.
Riama; Pathe Consortium — Republic Pictures
Home Video

Doll Face   1946
Musical
41075   80 mins   B/W   B, V   P
Vivian Blaine, Dennis O'Keefe, Perry Como,
Carmen Miranda, Martha Stewart, Reed Madley
This entertaining film includes songs such as
"Somebody's Walking in My Dream," "Hubba
Hubba," "Here Comes Heaven Again," and
"Chico Chico."
20th Century Fox — Hollywood Home Theater;
Discount Video Tapes; Video Yesteryear; See
Hear Industries

Dollars   1971
Suspense/Comedy
80784   119 mins   C   B, V   P
Warren Beatty, Goldie Hawn, Gert Frobe, Scott
Brady, Robert Webber, directed by Richard
Brooks
A bank employee and his dizzy assistant plan to
steal its assets while installing a new security
system in the bank. Music by Quincy Jones.
Available in Beta Hi-Fi.
MPAA:R
Columbia Pictures; M.J.
Frankovich — RCA/Columbia Pictures Home
Video

Dolls, The   1983
Drama
87216   96 mins   C   B, V   P
Tetchie Agbayani, Max Thayer, Carina Schally,
Richard Seward
A tropically-located fashion photographer
recruits a native beauty into the fashion world
with his winning smile and macho charm, only to
have native traditions forbid her to follow him.
Platinum Pictures — Vestron Video

Doll's House, A   1959
Drama
66455   89 mins   B/W   B, V   P
Julie Harris, Christopher Plummer, Jason
Robards, Hume Cronyn, Eileen Heckart,
Richard Thomas
An all-star cast is featured in this original
television production of Henrik Ibsen's classic
play about an independent woman's quest for
freedom in ninettenth-century Norway.
Sonny Fox Productions — MGM/UA Home
Video

THE VIDEO TAPE & DISC GUIDE

Doll's House, A — 1973
Drama
66492   98 mins   C   V   P
Jane Fonda, Edward Fox, Trevor Howard, David Warner
Jane Fonda plays Nora, a subjugated housewife who breaks free to establish herself as an individual. Based on Henrik Ibsen's classic play.
MPAA:G
World Film Services; Tomorrow Entertainment — Prism; RCA VideoDiscs

Dolly in London — 1983
Music-Performance
69623   50 mins   C   B, V   P
Dolly Parton
Dolly Parton is featured in a video concert from London's Dominion Theatre singing such hits as "9 to 5," "Jolene" and "Here You Come Again," among others. In stereo VHS and Beta Hi-Fi.
Stan Harris; Speckled Bird Inc — RCA/Columbia Pictures Home Video; RCA VideoDiscs

Dominique Is Dead — 1979
Drama
66493   95 mins   C   B, V   P
Cliff Robertson, Jean Simmons, Jenny Agutter, Simon Ward, Ron Moody
A woman is driven to suicide by her greedy husband—now someone is trying to drive him mad.
Sword and Sorcery Productions — Prism

Domino Principle, The — 1977
Drama/Prisons
46151   97 mins   C   CED   P
Gene Hackman, Candice Bergen, Richard Widmark, Mickey Rooney, Edward Albert, Eli Wallach, directed by Stanley Kramer
Gene Hackman plays a convict plotting to escape from San Quentin prison.
MPAA:G
Stanley Kramer, Avco Embassy — CBS/Fox Video

Don Amigo/Stage to Chino — 194?
Western
80429   122 mins   B/W   B, V   P
Duncan Renaldo, Leo Carrillo, George O'Brien
A western double feature: The Cisco Kid and Pancho ride together again in "Don Amigo" and in "Stage to Chino" a postal inspector investigates a gang who robs rival stage lines.
RKO — RKO HomeVideo

Don Carlo — 1983
Opera
82535   214 mins   C   B, V, LV   P
Placido Domingo, Nicolai Ghiaurov, Mirella Freni, Grace Bumbry, Louis Quilico, conducted by James Levine
The spectacular Verdi opera, based on a play by Schiller, is performed at N.Y.'s Metropolitan Opera House in Italian with English subtitles.
IT
John Dexter — Paramount Home Video; Pioneer Artists

Don Daredevil Rides Again — 1951
Serials
64426   180 mins   B/W   B, V, 3/4U   P
Ken Curtis
Don Daredevil flies into danger in this twelve-episode serial.
Republic — Nostalgia Merchant

Don Giovanni — 1977
Music-Performance
77457   173 mins   C   B, V   P
Benjamin Luxon, directed by Peter Hall
A production of the Mozart opera taped at the Glyndebourne Festival in Great Britain. With English subtitles.
IT
Southern Television — Video Arts International

Don Kirshner's Rock Concert, Vol. 1 — 1981
Music-Performance
52606   77 mins   C   CED   P
Don Kirshner presents seventeen magnetic performances by Motown superstars Billy Preston, The Commodores, Smokey Robinson, and Bonnie Pointer.
Don Kirshner Prods — RCA VideoDiscs

Don Q., Son of Zorro — 1925
Adventure
47791   111 mins   B/W   B, V, 3/4U   P
Douglas Fairbanks Sr, Mary Astor
Zorro's son takes up his father's fight against evil and injustice.
United Artists — Western Film & Video Inc; Blackhawk Films; Discount Video Tapes; Video Yesteryear

Don Quixote — 1984
Dance
80815   135 mins   C   B, V   P
Mikhail Baryshnikov, Cynthia Harvey
This tape offers a production of the Richard Strauss work, choreographed by Baryshnikov, and performed at the Metropolitan Opera House in New York. Available in VHS and Beta Hi Fi.
Mikhail Baryshnikov — THORN EMI/HBO Video

Don Rickles—Buy this Tape, You Hockey Puck   1985
Comedy-Performance
81320   51 mins   C   B, V   P
Don Rickles, Don Adams, Jack Klugman, Michele Lee
Don Rickles performs some of his best stand up and put down routines in this comedy video.
Paul Brownstein — *Lightning Video*

Don Winslow of the Navy   1943
Adventure/Serials
08876   234 mins   B/W   B, V, 3/4U   P
Don Terry, Walter Sands, Ann Nagel
Thirteen episodes centered around the evil Scorpion, who plots to attack the Pacific Coast.
Universal — *Video Connection; Video Yesteryear; Discount Video Tapes; Nostalgia Merchant*

Dona Flor and Her Two Husbands   1978
Comedy
53509   106 mins   C   B, V   P
Sonia Braga, Jose Wilker, Mauro Mendonca, directed by Bruno Baretto
A woman becomes a widow when her philandering husband finally expires from drink, gambling, and women. She remarries, but her new husband is so boringly proper, she begins fantasizing husband number one's return.
New Yorker Films; Brazil — *Warner Home Video*

Donner Pass—The Road to Survival   1984
Drama
69802   98 mins   C   B, V   P
Robert Fuller, Diane McBain, Andrew Prine, John Anderson, Michael Callan
Stranded in a mountain pass during an unexpected snowstorm in 1846, a group of settlers trying to reach California is faced with two choices: starvation or cannibalism. Based on a true episode in American history.
James Simmons — *United Home Video; Magnum Entertainment*

Donnie Iris and the Cruisers   1983
Music video
88097   46 mins   C   B, V   P
The quasi-punk video adventures of Iris and the guys, including their only 'hit', "Love You Like a Rock."
Sony Video — *Sony Video Software*

Donovan's Reef   1963
Comedy/Romance
64023   109 mins   C   B, V, LV   P
John Wayne, Lee Marvin, Elizabeth Allen, Dorothy Lamour
Two ex-Navy buddies are enjoying life on a South Pacific island, where they spend most of their time in the local saloon—until the arrival of a straight-laced Boston woman in search of her father.
Paramount — *Paramount Home Video*

Don's Party   1982
Comedy
65730   91 mins   C   B, V   P
John Hargreaves
This off-beat comedy focuses on a party that is not what anyone expected.
Phillip Adams — *VidAmerica*

Don't Answer the Phone   1980
Horror
47854   94 mins   C   B, V   P
James Westmoreland, Flo Gerrish, Ben Frank
A deeply troubled photographer stalks and attacks the patients of a beautiful psychologist talk show hostess.
MPAA:R
Robert Hammer — *Media Home Entertainment*

Don't Be Afraid of the Dark   1973
Suspense
77207   74 mins   C   B, V   P
Kim Darby, Jim Hutton, Barbara Anderson, William Demarest
Mysterious gnomes terrorize a young couple who have inherited an old house.
Lorimar Productions — *U.S.A. Home Video*

Don't Change My World   1983
Drama
69536   89 mins   C   B, V   P
Roy Tatum, Ben Jones
To preserve the natural beauty of the north woods, a wildlife photographer must fight a villainous land developer and a reckless poacher.
MPAA:G
George P Macrenaris — *Children's Video Library*

Don't Cry, It's Only Thunder   1981
Drama
69622   108 mins   C   B, V   P
Dennis Christopher, Susan Saint James
A young army medic who works in a mortuary in Saigon becomes involved with a group of Vietnamese orphans and a dedicated army doctor.
MPAA:PG
Sanrio Communications — *RCA/Columbia Pictures Home Video*

Don't Drink the Water   1969
Comedy
71247   100 mins   C   B, V   P
Jackie Gleason, Estelle Parsons, Joan Delaney,
Ted Bessell, directed by Howard Morris
Based on Woody Allen's hit play, this film places
an average Newark, NJ family behind the Iron
Curtain, where their vacation photo-taking gets
them accused of spying.
MPAA:G
AVCO Embassy Corp — *Embassy Home*
Entertainment

Don't Go in the House   1980
Horror
59666   90 mins   C   B, V   P
Dan Grimaldi, Robert Osth, Ruth Dardick
A long dormant psychosis is brought to life by
the death of a young man's mother.
MPAA:R
Ellen Hammill — *Media Home Entertainment*

Don't Go in the Woods   1981
Suspense/Horror
65217   88 mins   C   B, V   P
Four young campers are being stalked by a
crazed killer.
MPAA:R
James Bryan — *Vestron Video*

Don't Look Back   1967
Documentary/Music
87566   95 mins   B/W   B, V   P
Bob Dylan, Joan Baez, Donovan, directed by
D.A. Pennebaker
A famous documentary about Bob Dylan at the
beginning of his career--on the road, in
performance and during private moments. From
the director of "Monterey Pop."
D.A. Pennebaker — *Paramount Home Video*

Don't Look Now   1974
Drama
57280   110 mins   C   B, V, LV   P
Donald Sutherland, Julie Christie, Hilary Mason,
directed by Nicholas Roeg
Psychic terror in a Gothic setting provides the
chilling backdrop in this tale of a couple's
search for the ghost of their dead child.
MPAA:R
Paramount — *Paramount Home Video; RCA*
VideoDiscs

Don't Open the Door!   1980
Horror
81615   90 mins   C   B, V   P
Susan Bracken, Gene Ross, Jim Harrell
A young woman is terrorized by a killer located
inside her house.
MPAA:PG
Cinema Shares International — *Video Gems*

Don't Open Till Christmas   1984
Horror
82434   86 mins   C   B, V   P
Edmund Purdom, Caroline Munro, Belinda
Mayne
A weirdo with little sense of the festive murders
various Santa Clauses in assorted gory ways.
MPAA:R
Unknown — *Vestron Video*

Don't Raise the Bridge,   1968
Lower the River
Comedy
21285   99 mins   C   B, V   P
Jerry Lewis, Terry-Thomas
After his wife leaves him, an American with
crazy, get-rich-quick schemes turns her
ancestral English home into a Chinese
discotheque.
Columbia — *RCA/Columbia Pictures Home*
Video

Don't Shove/Two Gun   1919
Gussie
Comedy
64823   27 mins   B/W   B, V   P, T
Harold Lloyd, Bebe Daniels, Noah Young, Snub
Pollard
Two early Harold Lloyd shorts feature the
comedian's embryonic comic style as a young
fellow impressing his date at a skating rink
("Don't Shove") and a city slicker out West
("Two Gun Gussie"). Silent with piano scores.
Rolin Film; Pathe — *Blackhawk Films*

Don't Watch That, Watch   1985
This!
Music video
84493   48 mins   C   B, V   P
2   pgms
This two-volume compilation tape contains the
finest in new wave video music, from Big
Country to Bananarama to Band Aid.
Polygram Music — *Sony Video Software*

Doobie Brothers Live,   1981
The
Music-Performance
60381   65 mins   C   CED   P
The seminal rock group performs in Santa
Barbara, California, for over 20,000 fans. Songs
include "Minute by Minute," "Takin It to the
Streets," "What a Fool Believes," "Listen to the
Music."
Doobro Corp — *RCA VideoDiscs*

Doomed to Die   1940
Mystery
08755   67 mins   B/W   B, V   P
Boris Karloff, Marjorie Reynolds, Grant Withers

Cargo of stolen bonds leads to a tong war and the murder of a shipping millionaire. Part of Mr. Wong series.
Monogram — *Kartes Video Communications; Cable Films; Discount Video Tapes*

Doomsday Flight, The   1966
Adventure
84633   100 mins   C   B, V   P
Jack Lord, Edmund O'Brien, Van Johnson, John Saxon, Katherine Crawford, written by Rod Serling
A Psychopath plans to blow up a Jet-liner in mid-flight, and the race is on.
Frank Price — *MCA Home Video*

Doomwatch   1972
Horror
86089   89 mins   C   B, V   P
Ian Bannen, Judy Geeson, John Paul, Simon Oates, George Sanders
A scientist discovers a chemical company is dumping poison into local waters, deforming the inhabitants of an isolated island.
Avco Embassy — *Embassy Home Entertainment*

Doonesbury Special, A   1978
Cartoons/Satire
69022   30 mins   C   B, V   P
Animated
This animated program features Doonesbury, Zonker, Joanie Caucus, Mike, B.D, Marcus and Jimmy.
Cannes Film Festival: Special Jury Award.
Barry Trudeau; John and Faith Hubley — *Pacific Arts Video*

Doors: A Tribute to Jim   1981
Morrison, The
Music-Performance
47387   60 mins   C   B, V   P
Jim Morrison, Ray Manzarek, Bobby Krieger, John Densmore
Interviews and live performance footage capture the power of this famous rock group and its quixotic leader, Jim Morrison. Songs performed include "Light My Fire" and "The End."
Independent — *Warner Home Video*

Doors, Dance on Fire,   1985
The
Music video/Documentary
77212   65 mins   C   B, V   P
Jim Morrison, John Densmore, Robby Krieger, Ray Manzarek
This is a musical documentary that chronicles the music and wild times of Jim Morrison and The Doors with a new conceptual music video for "L.A. Woman." Available in VHS and Beta Hi Fi Stereo.

MCA Home Video — *MCA Home Video*

Doozer Music   1983
Music-Performance
65641   16 mins   C   B, V   R, P
An exclusive collection of tuneful highlights from Jim Henson's "Fraggle Rock" series. In stereo VHS and Beta Hi-Fi.
Jim Henson — *MuppetMusic Home Video*

Dorian Gray   1971
Horror
66311   91 mins   C   B, V   P
Richard Todd, Helmut Berger, Herbert Lom
A modern-day version of the famous tale by Oscar Wilde about an ageless young man whose portrait reflects the ravages of time.
MPAA:R
Towers of London Productions — *Republic Pictures Home Video*

Dorm That Dripped   1982
Blood, The
Horror
65374   84 mins   C   B, V   P
Laura Lopinski, Stephen Sachs, Pamela Holland
Five college students volunteer to close the dorm during their Christmas vacation. In a series of grisly and barbaric incidents, the students begin to disappear. As the terror mounts, the remaining students realize that they are up against a terrifyingly real psychopathic killer.
MPAA:R
Jeffrey Obrow — *Media Home Entertainment*

Dorothy in the Land of Oz   1981
Cartoons/Fantasy
66180   60 mins   C   B, V   P
Animated, narrated by Sid Ceasar
The further adventures of L. Frank Baum's characters from the "Wizard of Oz."
Muller Rosen Productions — *Family Home Entertainment*

Dorothy Stratten: The   1985
Untold Story
Documentary/Biographical
71049   85 mins   C   B, V   P
Dorothy Stratten
This telling of the Stratten story includes a wealth of footage from Playboy's film and photo vaults, as well as some interviews with the 1980 Playmate of the Year's comtemporaries.
Playboy Video; Marshall Flaum — *Karl/Lorimar Home Video*

Dos Chicas de Revista   197?
Drama
49747   90 mins   C   B, V   P
A former film actor now recovering from a mental breakdown and drug addiction comes across a book written about him when he was

big-time. He meets the girl who wrote the book and they enjoy a happy relationship. In Spanish. SP
Independent — *Media Home Entertainment*

Dot and Santa Claus 1979
Fantasy
65326   73 mins   C   B, V, CED   P
Animated
Dot has lost her kangaroo and through fate, meets Santa Claus who helps her find him in Central Park's zoo.
Yoram Gross — *Playhouse Video*

Dot and the Bunny 1982
Cartoons
Closed Captioned
65506   79 mins   C   B, V, CED   P
Animated
The adventures of a spunky young red-haired heroine on her quest for a missing baby kangaroo named Joey are followed.
Satori — *Playhouse Video*

Dot and the Kangaroo 1981
Fantasy
58834   75 mins   C   B, V, CED   P
Animated
Dot, the small daughter of a settler, wanders into the forest and gets lost. She meets a friendly kangaroo who takes her on a fabulous journey.
Satori Prods — *Playhouse Video*

Double Agents 1959
War-Drama/Suspense
69567   81 mins   B/W   B, V, FO   P
Marina Vlady, Robert Hossein
Two double agents are sent on a rendezvous to exchange vital government secrets. Dubbed in English.
French Italo Productions — *Video Yesteryear*

Double Deal 1984
Drama/Suspense
79891   90 mins   C   B, V   P
Louis Jourdan, Angela Punch-McGregor
An unfaithful woman and her lover plot to steal her husband's priceless opal.
Brian Kavanagh; Lynn Baker — *VCL Home Video*

Double Exposure 1982
Suspense
64876   95 mins   C   B, V, CED   P
Michael Callan, James Stacy, Joanna Pettet
A young photographer has violent nightmares which seem to become the next day's headlines.
Michael Callan; Von Deming; William Byron Hillman — *Vestron Video*

Double Face 1970
Drama/Mystery
84069   84 mins   C   B, V   P
Klaus Kinski
A wealthy industrialist kills his lesbian wife with a car bomb, but she seems to haunt him through pornographic films.
ZIV Pictures — *Unicorn Video*

Double Life, A 1947
Drama
64536   103 mins   B/W   B, V   P
Ronald Colman, Shelley Winters, Signe Hasso, Edmond O'Brien, directed by George Cukor
A Shakespearean actor becomes obsessed by the role of Othello and begins to duplicate the character's actions.
Academy Awards '47: Best Actor (Colman).
Universal; Garson Kanin — *Republic Pictures Home Video*

Double McGuffin, The 1979
Comedy
49625   100 mins   C   B, V   P
Ernest Borgnine, George Kennedy, Elke Sommer, Ed "Too Tall" Jones, Lisa Whelchel, directed by Joe Camp
A plot of international intrigue is uncovered when a prime minister and her security guard pay a visit to a small Virginia community.
MPAA:PG
Mulberry Square Prods; Joe Camp — *Vestron Video*

Double Trouble 1967
Musical
80153   92 mins   C   B, V   P
Elvis Presley, Annette Day, John Williams Yvonne Romain
When a rock star falls in love with an English heiress, he winds up involved in an attempted murder.
Metro Goldwyn Mayer — *MGM/UA Home Video*

Doughnuts and Society 1936
Comedy
69558   70 mins   B/W   B, V, FO   P
Louise Fazenda, Maude Eburne, Eddie Nugent, Ann Rutherford, Hedda Hopper, Franklin Pangborn
Two elderly ladies who run a coffee shop suddenly strike it rich and find that life among the bluebloods is not all it's cracked up to be.
Mascot — *Video Yesteryear*

Down Among the Z Men 1952
Comedy
79113   71 mins   B/W   B, V   P
Peter Sellers, Spike Milligan, Harry Secombe, Carole Carr
An enlisted man helps a girl save an atomic formula from spies.

E.J. Fancey Productions — *Pacific Arts Video*

Richard Gregson — *Paramount Home Video*

Down and Out in Beverly Hills 1986
Comedy
88337   120 mins   C   B, V   P
Nick Nolte, Bette Midler, Richard Dreyfuss, Little Richard, Mike the Dog, directed by Paul Mazursky
A modern retelling of Jean Renoir's classic "Boudu Sauve Des Eaux" wherein a spoiled wealthy couple reform a suicidal bum; now, chiefly satirizing trendy Beverly Hills affluence. In Hi-Fi Stereo.
MPAA:R
Touchstone Films — *Touchstone Home Video*

Down Mexico Way 1941
Western
77363   78 mins   B/W   B, V   P, T
Gene Autry, Smiley Burnette, Fay McKenzie, Duncan Renaldo, Champion
Two cowboys come to the aid of a Mexican town whose residents have been hoodwinked by a phony movie company.
Republic Pictures — *Blackhawk Films*

Down On the Farm with Captain Kangaroo and Mr. Green Jeans 1985
Children
70592   60 mins   C   B, V   P
Bob Keeshan
Composed of short clips from the Captains' library of shows, this program features segments that look at farm living, where land stretches out so far and wide.
Encyclopedia Britannica Educational Corporation — *MPI Home Video*

Down to the Sea in Ships 1922
Adventure
66338   83 mins   B/W   B, V   P
Marguerite Courtot, Raymond McKee, Clara Bow
Clara Bow made her movie debut in this drama about the whalers of the 19th-century Massachusetts. Exciting action scenes of an actual whale hunt are the film's highlight. Silent with music score and original tinted footage.
Whaling Film Corp; Hodkinson Corp — *Blackhawk Films; Darryl L. Sink & Associates; Classic Video Cinema Collector's Club*

Downhill Racer 1969
Drama
48510   102 mins   C   B, V, LV   P
Robert Redford, Camilla Sparv, Gene Hackman
An undisciplined American skier conflicts with his coach and new-found love on his way to becoming an Olympic superstar.
MPAA:PG

Doyle Against the House 1961
Drama
82185   52 mins   B/W   B, V   P
Milton Berle, Jan Sterling, Gavin Macleod, directed by Ralph Nelson
A professional card dealer decides to scam the house in order to raise funds for his daughter's operation. An episode from "The Dick Powell Theatre" series.
Four Star Television — *RKO HomeVideo*

Dr. Jekyll's Dungeon of Death 1979
Horror
81749   90 mins   C   B, V   P
James Mathers, Dawn Carver Kelly, Jake Pearson
Dr. Jekyll and his lobotomized sister, Hilda, scour the streets of San Francisco looking for human blood to recreate his great-grandfather's secret serum.
Rochelle Film Distributors — *Magnum Entertainment*

Dr. Seuss: The Cat in the Hat/Dr. Seuss on the Loose 1971
Cartoons
Closed Captioned
81510   51 mins   C   B, V   P
Animated
A Dr. Seuss double feature: "The Cat in the Hat" helps two young children fight boredom on a rainy day and "Dr. Seuss on the Loose" features stories about "The Sneetches," "The Zax" and "Green Eggs and Ham." Available in VHS and Beta Hi-Fi Stereo.
DePatie-Freleng Productions — *Playhouse Video*

Dr. Tarr's Torture Dungeon 1975
Horror
81750   90 mins   C   B, V   P
Claude Brook, Ellen Sherman, Robert Dumont
A mysterious man is sent to the forest to investigate the bizarre behavior of Dr. Tarr who runs a torture asylum.
MPAA:R
Electra Entertainment — *Magnum Entertainment*

Dr. Seuss: The Lorax/Hoober Bloob Highway 1975
Cartoons
Closed Captioned
81511   51 mins   C   B, V   P
Animated

Here are two animated adaptations of Dr. Seuss' stories: "The Lorax" is a creature who is trying to stop the greedy Once-ler from destroying the forest, and Mr. Hoober-Bloob is the proprietor of "The Hoober-Bloob Highway" a floating island that sends babies to Earth. Available in VHS and Beta Hi-Fi Stereo.
DePatie-Freleng Productions — *Playhouse Video*

Dracula   **1931**
Horror
14023   75 mins   B/W   B, V   P
Bela Lugosi, David Manners, directed by Tod Browning
A vampire terrorizes the countryside in its search for human blood. From Bram Stoker's novel, "Horror of Dracula".
Universal — *MCA Home Video; RCA VideoDiscs*

Dracula   **1979**
Horror
45046   109 mins   C   B, V, LV   P
Frank Langella, Sir Laurence Olivier
Remake of the classic story of the count who is among the undead and needs human blood for nourishment.
MPAA:R
Universal — *MCA Home Video*

Dracula   **1984**
Cartoons/Horror
70092   90 mins   C   B, V   P
Animated
The prince of darkness returns looking for blood in this animated adaptation of Bram Stoker's classic novel.
Northstar Productions — *Vestron Video*

Dracula   **1974**
Horror
82101   105 mins   C   B, V   P
Jack Palance, Simon Ward, Fiona Lewis, Nigel Davenport, directed by Dan Curtis
The Transylvanian count scours the countryside to quench his thirst for blood in this adaptation of the Bram Stoker novel. Available in VHS Stereo and Beta Hi-Fi.
Dan Curtis Productions — *Thriller Video*

Dracula and Son   **1976**
Horror/Satire
62809   88 mins   C   B, V   R, P
Christopher Lee, Bernard Menez, Marie Breillat
A Dracula spoof, in which the Count fathers a son who prefers girls and football to blood.
MPAA:PG
Quartet Films — *RCA/Columbia Pictures Home Video*

Dracula Sucks   **1979**
Satire
55217   91 mins   C   B, V   P
Jamie Gillis, Annette Haven, John Holmes
The erotic undertones of the vampire legend are made quite explicit in this version of the Dracula tale.
MPAA:R
MR Productions — *Media Home Entertainment*

Dracula/The Garden of Eden   **1928**
Film-History
50638   52 mins   B/W   B, V   P, T
Max Schreck, Alexander Granach, Corrine Griffith, Charles Ray, Louise Dressler
The abridged version of the chilling "Nosferatu" is coupled with "The Garden of Eden," in which Tini Le Brun meets her Prince Charming while vacationing with her Baroness friend.
Janus Films; Lewis Milestone — *Blackhawk Films*

Dracula—Up in Harlem   **1983**
Horror/Satire
69630   90 mins   C   B, V   P
When the Prince of Darkness gets together with the people of the night, the Pentagon rolls out the heavy metal.
Mike Rodgers — *Strike Force Films*

Dracula's Dog   **1978**
Horror
48474   90 mins   C   B, V   P
Michael Pataki, Reggie Nalder, Jose Ferrer
An explosion unearths the tomb of one of Dracula's servants and his dog. The dog puts other dogs under his spell to help the two vampires search for their new master.
MPAA:R
Crown International — *United Home Video*

Dracula's Great Love   **1972**
Horror
81071   96 mins   C   B, V   P
Paul Naschy, Charo Soriano
The insatiable count is looking for a woman to join his world of darkness.
MPAA:R
International Amusement Corp. — *MPI Home Video*

Dragnet   **1954**
Adventure
68256   71 mins   C   B, V   P
Jack Webb, Ben Alexander, Richard Boone, Ann Robinson
The Dragnet team tries to solve a mob slaying but has a rough time. Sgt. Joe Friday and Officer Frank Smith figure it out just in time.
Universal — *MCA Home Video*

Dragon from Shaolin, The 197?
Martial arts
70817   90 mins   C   B, V   P
Bruce Lee
The Shaolin monks match wits, chops and kicks
with the brutal Ching government.
Foreign — *Master Arts Video*

Dragon Lee Vs. the Five 1981
Brothers
Martial arts
70702   89 mins   C   B, V   P
Dragon Lee
Mr. Lee thwarts an attempted overthrow of the
Ching Government with his furiously brutal
fighting talents.
master Arts — *Master Arts Video*

Dragon Lives Again, The 198?
Martial arts
64962   90 mins   C   B, V   P
Bruce Leong, Alexander Grand, Jenny
A martial arts adventure that is dedicated to the
memory of Bruce Lee.
Dragon Lady Productions — *Unicorn Video*

Dragon Seed 1944
Drama
81500   148 mins   B/W   B, V   P
*Katherine Hepburn, Walter Huston, Agnes
Moorehead, Akim Tamiroff*
The lives of the residents of a small Chinese
village are turned upside down when the
Japanese invade it.
MGM — *MGM/UA Home Video*

Dragon Strikes Back, The 1975
Martial arts
63864   92 mins   C   B, V   P
A Chinese immigrant, a master of Kung Fu,
stands up to a gang of white toughs who are
brutally terrorizing and killing poor Mexican
farmers.
MPAA:R
United International Pictures — *Hollywood
Home Theater*

Dragon's Claws 198?
Martial arts
87760   90 mins   C   B, V   P
*Jimmy Liu, Hwang Cheng Li, directed by Joseph
Kuo*
A young man's parents are murdered, and he
trains in shaolin skills in order to exact revenge.
Foreign — *Video Gems*

Dragonslayer 1981
Fantasy/Adventure
59423   108 mins   C   B, V, LV   P
*Peter MacNicol, Caitlin Clarke, Ralph
Richardson, John Hallam, Albert Salmi*

A sorcerer's apprentice suddenly finds himself
the only person who can save the kingdom from
a horrible, firebreathing dragon.
Academy Awards '81: Best Special Effects.
MPAA:PG
Walt Disney Productions; Paramount; Barwood
Robbins Productions — *Paramount Home
Video; RCA VideoDiscs*

Drama—Romance: 1984
Trailers on Tape
Movie and TV trailers/Drama
66481   60 mins   C   B, V   P
Forty theatrical trailers for dramatic movies are
included on this tape, with such titles as "The
Godfather," "Lifeguard," "Shampoo," "Pride of
the Yankees," "Boys in the Band," "One Flew
Over the Cuckoo's Nest" and "Fortune and
Men's Eyes." Some black-and-white segments.
Columbia et al — *San Francisco Rush Video*

Draw! 1981
Western
82485   98 mins   C   B, V   P
*Kirk Douglas, James Coburn, directed by David
Hillard Stern*
Two has-been outlaws warm up their pistols
again in this old-fashioned Western.
Independent — *Media Home Entertainment*

Draw & Color a Cartoony 1986
Party with Uncle Fred
Arts
Closed Captioned
86376   61 mins   C   B, V   P
Fred Lasswell
The creator of Barney Google & Snuffy Smith
inspires artistic fun for children eight and under.
Fred Lasswell — *Playhouse Video*

Draw and Color Your 1984
Very Own Cartoonys
Right Along With Uncle
Fred
Arts/Hobbies
Closed Captioned
81868   60 mins   C   B, V   P
"Barney Google and Snuffy Smith" creator Fred
Laswell demonstrates how anyone can draw
"cartoons". Available in VHS and Beta Hi-Fi.
Fred Lasswell — *Playhouse Video*

Dream Called Walt Disney 1981
World, A
Documentary
58628   25 mins   C   B, V   P
This souvenir of Orlando, Florida's Walt Disney
World discusses the creation of the magnificent
theme park.
Walt Disney Productions — *Walt Disney Home
Video*

Dream Chasers, The 1984
Comedy-Drama
Closed Captioned
81873 97 mins C B, V P
Harold Gould, Justin Dana
A bankrupt old codger and a 11-year-old boy
stricken with cancer run away together during
the Great Depression.
MPAA:PG
A.R. Dubs Prod. — *Playhouse Video*

Dream Continues, The 1985
Documentary
87601 60 mins C B, V, 3/4U P
A look at Elvis' fans almost ten years after his
death, and how they feel about their idol today.
Monticello Prod. — *Monticello Productions*

Dream for Christmas, A 1973
Christmas/Drama
71299 98 mins C B, V P
*Hari Rhodes, Beah Richards, Lynn Hamilton,
Juanita Moore, Zara Cully, George Spell, Robert
Do Qui, directed by Ralph Senensky*
After moving his family from a small Arkansas
town to an inner-city Los Angeles parish, a
minister discovers that his new pastorate is
soon to be razed for a shopping center.
Lorimar Productions — *U.S.A. Home Video*

Dream Street 1921
Drama
58646 138 mins B/W B, V, FO P
*Carol Dempster, Ralph Graves, Charles Mack,
Tyrone Power Sr., directed by D. W. Griffith*
A morality tale of London's lower depths. Two
brothers, both in love with the same dancing girl,
woo her in their own way. Silent with music
score.
D W Griffith — *Video Yesteryear*

Dreamchild 1985
Drama
85897 90 mins C B, V P
Carol Browne, Ian Holm, Peter Gallagher
A poignant story of the autumn years of Alice
Hargreaves, the model for Lewis Carroll's "Alice
in Wonderland." The film follows her on a visit to
New York in the I930's, with fantasy sequences
invoking the obsessive Reverend Dodgson.
MPAA:PG
Universal — *THORN EMI/HBO Video*

Dreaming Lips 1937
Drama
13646 70 mins B/W B, V P, T
Raymond Massey, Elizabeth Bergner
Orchestra conductor's wife falls in love with her
husband's friend. Tragedy befalls the couple.
United Artists; Max Schach; British — *Movie
Buff Video; Blackhawk Films*

Dreams 1955
Drama
82577 86 mins B/W B, V P
*Harriet Andersson, Gunnar Bjornstrand, Eva
Dahlbeck, directed by Ingmar Bergman*
A probing film about the lives and loves of two
successful women.
SW
Rune Walderkranz — *Embassy Home
Entertainment*

Dreams of Gold 1983
Sports
72180 60 mins C B, V P
Members of the U.S. Olympic team were filmed
during a qualifying competition. A dramatic
musical score accompanies and enhances the
film.
Bruce Goronsky — *Pacific Arts Video*

Dreams of Gold 1984
Sports
79110 55 mins C B, V P
A unique visualization of the American Olympic
hopefuls competing in events to qualify for the
Summer Olympic Games, set to the music of
Ken Nordine.
Pacific Arts Video Records — *Pacific Arts
Video*

Dreamscape 1984
Science fiction/Fantasy
79706 99 mins C B, V P
*Dennis Quaid, Max Von Sydow, Christopher
Plummer, Eddie Albert, Kate Capshaw*
When a doctor teaches a young psychic how to
enter into other people's dreams, somebody
else wants to use this psychic for evil purposes.
MPAA:PG-13
Zupnick Curtis Enterprises — *THORN
EMI/HBO Video*

Dressed to Kill 1946
Mystery
01753 72 mins B/W B, V, 3/4U P
*Basil Rathbone, Nigel Bruce, Patricia Morison,
directed by Roy William Neill*
Sherlock Holmes finds a music box holds the
key to plates stolen from the Bank of England.
Universal; Howard Benedict — *Hal Roach
Studios; Prism; Cable Films; Western Film &
Video Inc; Discount Video Tapes; Hollywood
Home Theater; VCII; Kartes Video
Communications; Movie Buff Video; Nostalgia
Merchant; Video Yesteryear*

Dressed to Kill 1980
Suspense
53510 105 mins C B, V P
*Angie Dickinson, Michael Caine, Nancy Allen,
Keith Gordon, Dennis Franz, directed by Brian
De Palma*

A woman is brutally slashed to death and her son teams up with a prostitute who saw the killer in order to reveal the identity of the attacker.
MPAA:R
George Litto; Samuel Z Arkoff — *Warner Home Video; RCA VideoDiscs; Vestron Video (disc only)*

Dresser, The   1983
Drama
Closed Captioned
73858   119 mins   C   B, V, CED   P
Albert Finney, Tom Courtenay, Edward Fox, directed by Peter Yates
The film adaptation of the Broadway play about an English actor/manager, his dresser and their theatre company that tours war-torn England during World War II. In Beta Hi-Fi.
MPAA:PG
Peter Yates; Columbia Pictures — *RCA/Columbia Pictures Home Video*

Driller Killer   1974
Horror
77253   78 mins   C   B, V   P
Jimmy Laine, Carolyn Marz, Bob De Frank, directed by Abel Ferrara
A frustrated artist goes insane and begins to kill off Manhattan residents with a carpenter's drill.
MPAA:R
Mavaron Films — *Magnum Entertainment*

Drive-In Massacre   1974
Horror
77255   78 mins   C   B, V   P
Jake Barnes, Adam Lawrence
Two police detectives investigate a bizarre series of double murders at the local drive-in.
MPAA:R
Independent — *Magnum Entertainment*

Driver, The   1978
Adventure
Closed Captioned
80656   131 mins   C   B, V   P
Ryan O'Neal, Bruce Dern, Isabelle Adjani, Ronee Blakely, directed by Walter Hill
A police detective will stop at nothing to catch "The Driver," a man who has the reputation of driving the fastest getaway car around.
Available in VHS and Beta Hi-Fi.
MPAA:PG
20th Century Fox — *CBS/Fox Video*

Driver's Seat, The   1975
Suspense
64971   101 mins   C   B, V   P
Elizabeth Taylor, Ian Bannon, Mona Washbourne
A deranged woman looks for a man to whom she can give herself completely, but when she finds him she demands much more than love.

MPAA:R
Avco Embassy — *Embassy Home Entertainment*

Driving for Distance   1985
Golf
88069   25 mins   C   B, V   P
John Elliot demonstrates ways of improving tee shots.
NFL Films; Golf Digest — *NFL Films Video*

Dropzone: Normandy   1943
World War II
87664   71 mins   B/W   B, V   P
A dramatized version of D-Day from the American point of view.
Unknown — *Victory Video*

Drowning Pool, The   1975
Mystery
72917   109 mins   C   B, V   P
Paul Newman, Joanne Woodward, Tony Franciosa
Paul Newman returns as detective Lew Harper to solve another case—the murder of a New Orleans businessman.
MPAA:PG
Warner Bros — *Warner Home Video*

Drug Free Kids: A   1986
Parent's Guide
Drug abuse
88082   70 mins   C   B, V   P
Jane Alexander, Ned Beatty, Bonnie Franklin, Elliott Gould, Adam Rich
A program for parents that teaches children about the dangers of substance abuse.
AM Available
Video Associates; SCP Prod.; Scott Newman Foundation — *Video Associates*

Drum   1976
Drama
85634   101 mins   C   B, V   P
Ken Norton, Warren Oates, Pam Grier, Yaphet Kotto, Fiona Lewis
This steamy sequel to "Mandingo" eals with the sordid interracial sexual shenanigans at a Southern plantation.
MPAA:R
Dino De Laurentiis — *Vestron Video*

Drum Beat   1954
Western
11701   111 mins   C   B, V   P
Alan Ladd, Charles Bronson, Marisa Pavan
Unarmed Indian fighter sets out to negotiate peace treaty with renegade Indian leader.
Warner Bros — *United Home Video*

Drum Taps 1933
Western
58723 55 mins B/W   B, V   P
Ken Maynard, Dorothy Dix, Junior Coughlin
Ken saves the day for a young girl who is being
pushed off her land by a group of speculators.
Worldwide — *Video Dimensions; Video
Yesteryear; Video Connection; United Home
Video*

Drums 1938
Adventure
81459 96 mins B/W   B, V, LV   P
*Sabu, Raymond Massey, Valerie Hobson,
directed by Zoltan Korda*
A native prince helps to save the British army in
India from being anihilated by a tyrant.
Alexander Korda — *Embassy Home
Entertainment*

Drums in the Deep South 1951
War-Drama
80800   87 mins C   B, V   R, P
*James Craig, Guy Madison, Craig Stevens,
Barbara Dayton, Barton Maclare*
A rivalry turns ugly as two former West Point
roommates wind up on opposite sides when the
Civil War breaks out.
RKO — *Videograf; United Home Video; Video
Gems*

Drumset: A Musical 1985
Approach, The
Music
87930   120 mins C   B, V   P
Narrated by Ed Soph
This program gives detailed instruction about
the handling, positioning and tuning of a
professional drumset.
AM Available
Yamaha — *DCI Music Video*

Drying Up the Streets 1976
Drama
80697   90 mins C   B, V   P
Len Cariou, Don Francks
The members of a police drug squad are out to
terminate the pattern wherein young women are
turned to a life of prostitution and drugs.
Movie Store Prods. — *Vestron Video*

DTV—Golden Oldies 1984
Cartoons/Music video
79175   46 mins   C   B, V   P
Animated
Animator-director Chuck Brauerman took some
of the best Disney animation and recut them to
the music of Annette Funicello and others for
this collection of music videos.
Walt Disney Productions — *Walt Disney Home
Video*

DTV—Love Songs 1985
Music video/Cartoons
77532   45 mins   C   B, V   P
Animated, Directed by Chuck Braxerman
All your favorite Disney characters swoon and
sway to the music in this collection of love song
music videos.
Walt Disney Productions — *Walt Disney Home
Video*

DTV—Pop and Rock 1984
Cartoons/Music video
79176   46 mins   C   B, V   P
Animated
Classic Disney animation has been recut to the
music of the fifties and sixties for this collection
of music videos.
Walt Disney Productions — *Walt Disney Home
Video*

DTV—Rock, Rhythm and 1984
Blues
Cartoons/Music video
79177   46 mins   C   B, V   P
Some of Walt Disneys' best animation has been
re-edited to the music of Hall and Oates and
The Doobie Brothers for this collection of music
videos.
Walt Disney Productions — *Walt Disney Home
Video*

Duchess and the 1976
Dirtwater Fox, The
Comedy/Western
09095   105 mins C   B, V   P
George Segal, Goldie Hawn
A music-hall girl meets a man on the make.
MPAA:PG EL, SP
20th Century Fox — *CBS/Fox Video*

Duck Soup 1933
Comedy
44810   72 mins   B/W   B, V   P
The Marx Brothers
Groucho becomes a dictator in a mythical land
while Chico and Harpo run a peanut stand.
Paramount — *MCA Home Video; RCA
VideoDiscs*

Ducks Unlimited's 1986
Videoguide to Waterfowl
and Game Birds
Birds
85271   75 mins   C   B, V   P
A beautifully photographed guide to the various
North American waterfowl.
Ducks Unlimited — *Mastervision*

Dude Bandit, The 1932
Western
11702   68 mins   B/W   B, V   P

THE VIDEO TAPE & DISC GUIDE

Hoot Gibson, Gloria Shea
Unscrupulous money-lender tries to gain control of ranch.
Allied Artists — *Video Connection; United Home Video*

Duel　1971
Suspense
14069　90 mins　C　B, V　　　P
Dennis Weaver, Lucille Benson, Eddie Firestone, Cary Loftin, directed by Steven Spielberg
The story of a man's desperate attempt to stay alive. What begins as an ordinary business trip becomes a life and death battle for a man who is followed by a menacing psychopath.
Universal — *MCA Home Video*

Duel of Champions　1961
Adventure
70782　90 mins　C　B, V　　　P
Alan Ladd, Francesca Bett, directed by Frederick Baldi
It's ancient Rome, and the prodigal gladiator has come home. Now the family must have a duel to decide who will rule the globe.
Empire; Medallion — *Force Video*

Duel of the Iron Fist　1972
Martial arts
63863　98 mins　C　B, V　　　P
David Chiang, Ti Lung, Wang Ping, Yu Hui
A master of the martial arts must do battle with a brutal gang to save his own group from extinction.
MPAA:R
United International Pictures — *Hollywood Home Theater; United Home Video*

Duellists, The　1978
Drama
33714　101 mins　C　B, V　　　P
Keith Carradine, Harvey Keitel, Albert Finney, Edward Fox, Christina Raines, Diana Quick, directed by Ridley Scott
A beautifully photographed picture about the long running feud between two French officers during the Napoleonic wars.
MPAA:PG
Paramount — *Paramount Home Video*

Dumbo　1941
Cartoons
Closed Captioned
55564　64 mins　C　B, V, LV,　　P
　　　　　　　　　　　CED
Animated
The story of an elephant who is ridiculed for his large ears, until he discovers he can fly.
EL, SP
Walt Disney — *Walt Disney Home Video; RCA VideoDiscs*

Dunderklumpen　197?
Fantasy
40730　85 mins　C　B, V　　　R, P
Animated
Dunderklumpen is a little creature from the forest who is only two feet tall and sneaks into Carmilla's room and steals her dolls. From then on magical things keep happening.
MPAA:G　EL, SP
21st Century — *Video Gems; Vestron Video (disc only)*

Dune　1984
Science fiction/Fantasy
77451　137 mins　C　B, V, LV　　P
Kyle MacLachlan, Francesca Annis, Jose Ferrer, Sting, Max Von Sydow, Sean Young, directed by David Lynch
Controlling the spice of Arrakis permits control of the universe. Paul, the heir of the Atreides family leads the Freemen in a revolt against the evil Harkhonens who have violently seized control of Arrakis, also known as Dune, the desert planet. Adapted from Frank Herbert's popular novel. Music by Brian Eno and Toto. Available in VHS and Beta HiFi stereo.
MPAA:PG13
Universal; Raffaella De Laurentiis — *MCA Home Video*

Dungeonmaster, The　1985
Fantasy
81153　80 mins　C　B, V　　　P
Jeffrey Byron, Richard Moll, Leslie Wing
A warlord forces a computer operator to participation in a bizarre "Dungeons and Dragons" styled game.
MPAA:PG-13
Empire Pictures; Charles Band — *Lightning Video*

Dunwich Horror, The　1970
Horror
64984　90 mins　C　B, V　　　P
Sandra Dee, Dean Stockwell, Lloyd Bochner, Ed Begley
The town of Dunwich has a history of weird and evil happenings. When a young man acquires a rare and banned book on the occult, the horror begins again.
American International Pictures — *Embassy Home Entertainment*

Duran Duran　1982
Music-Performance
66027　55 mins　C　B, V　　　P
The hot new-music group performs "Planet Earth," "Rio," "Hungry Like the Wolf," and others.
EMI Music Video — *THORN EMI/HBO Video; RCA VideoDiscs*

Duran Duran 1983
Music-Performance
75918   10 mins   C   B, V   P
This program presents the popular British band singing their hits "Girls on Film" and "Hungry Like the Wolf."
Tritec Music Limited — Sony Video Software

Duran Duran: Arena 1985
Music-Performance
70945   58 mins   C   B, V   P
In a ten-number songfest, the members of Duran Duran reveal the source of their name. Hi-Fi Stereo recording enhances this mix of sci-fi, music, fantasy and reality.
EMI Music Video — THORN EMI/HBO Video

Duran Duran: Girls on Film/Hungry Like the Wolf 1982
Music/Video
66160   11 mins   C   B, V   P
A hot, sexy music video clip featuring the smash new group from England. In stereo.
Capitol; EMI MusicVideo — Sony Video Software

Dusty 1985
Drama
82481   89 mins   C   B, V   P
Bill Kerr, Noel Trevarthen, Carol Burns, Nicholas Holland, John Stanton
An Australian farmhand befriends a doomed sheepdog.
Foreign — Media Home Entertainment

Dvorak's Slavic Dance 1981
Music-Performance
60578   72 mins   C   LV   P
Recorded at Dvorak Hall in Prague, Czechoslovakia, this program presents Dvorak's sixteen colorful and rhythmical Slavonian dances. In stereo.
Koichi Takemoto — Pioneer Video Imports

D.W. Griffith: An American Genius 1975
Film-History/Documentary
29495   56 mins   C   B, V   P, T
Narrated by Richard Schickel
A penetrating documentary of a legendary filmmaker, narrated by the renowned film critic Richard Schickel. Excerpted works include early Biographs, "Birth of a Nation," "Way Down East," and "Intolerance."
Unknown — Blackhawk Films

D.W. Griffith Triple Feature 1913
Drama
81725   50 mins   B/W   B, V   P
Mae Marsh, Lillian Gish, Mary Pickford, Blanche Sweet, Charles West, directed by D.W. Griffith
Here is a collection of three short D.W. Griffith films including "The Battle of Elderbush Gulch" "Iola's Promise" and "The Goddess of Sagebrush Gulch."
Biograph — Kartes Video Communications

Dying Room Only 1973
Drama/Suspense
71322   74 mins   C   B, V   P
Cloris Leachman, Dabney Coleman, Ross Martin, Ned Beatty, Louise Latham, directed by Phillip Leacock
A stop at a roadside hotel turns into mysterious kidnapping case for a couple returning from vacation.
Lorimar Productions — U.S.A. Home Video

Dynamite Chicken 1970
Musical
15786   75 mins   C   B, V   P
Joan Baez, Richard Pryor, Lenny Bruce, Jimi Hendrix, Sha-Na-Na
Focuses on the attitudes of American youth in the 70's. Includes performances by Joan Baez, Lenny Bruce, B. B. King, and others.
MPAA:R
EYR — Monterey Home Video

Dynamite Pass 1950
Western
64405   61 mins   B/W   B, V, 3/4U   P
Tim Holt, Richard Martin
Disgruntled ranchers attempt to stop the construction of a new road.
RKO — Nostalgia Merchant

Dynamite Ranch 1932
Western
84833   60 mins   B/W   B, V   P
Ken Maynard
Ranchers fight tooth and nail to keep their rights and property.
Tiffany; Ken Maynard — United Home Video

Dynamo 1980
Martial arts
81472   81 mins   C   B, V   P
A glamorous advertising executive pursues a kung fu expert to sign a contract with her agency for a kick boxing contest.
MPAA:R
World Northal Corporation — Embassy Home Entertainment

E

E. Nick: A Lengend in His Own Mind   1986
Comedy
86580   75 mins   C   B, V   P
Don Calfa, Cleavon Little, Pat McCormick, Andra Akers, Carol Wayne
An " adult" parody of soft and hard core video shows.
Paul Hertzberg — *U.S.A. Home Video*

Eagle, The   1925
Drama
08851   72 mins   B/W   B, V, 3/4U   P
Rudolph Valentino, Vilma Banky, Louise Dresser
Romantic adventure story of a Russian Robin Hood.
United Artists — *Video Yesteryear; Cable Films; Video Connection; Discount Video Tapes; Western Film & Video Inc*

Eagle Has Landed, The   1977
War-Drama
45062   123 mins   C   B, V   P
Michael Caine, Donald Sutherland, Robert Duvall
German paratroopers stage a dramatic attempt to kidnap Winston Churchill.
MPAA:PG
Columbia — *CBS/Fox Video*

Eagles Attack at Dawn   1974
War-Drama
80937   96 mins   C   B, V   P
Rick Jason, Peter Brown, Joseph Shiloal
After escaping from an Arab prison, an Israeli soldier vows to return with a small commando force and kill the sadistic commander of the prison.
MPAA:PG
Yoram Globus — *VidAmerica*

Early Days   1981
Comedy/Drama
60585   67 mins   C   B, V   P
Sir Ralph Richardson
A cantankerous, salty, once-powerful politician now awaits death wandering around the garden rambling on about his life.
Independent — *CBS/Fox Video*

Early Elvis   1956
Music-Performance
58653   56 mins   B/W   B, V, FO   P
Ed Sullivan, Charles Laughton, Elvis Presley
Elvis appears on "Stage Show" with the Tommy and Jimmy Dorsey Orchestra, on the "Steve Allen Show" where he also participates in a comedy sketch, and the "Ed Sullivan Show." Ten songs in all.
CBS et al — *Video Yesteryear*

Early Frost   1984
Mystery
76647   95 mins   C   B, V   P
Diana McLean, Jon Blake, Janet Kingsbury, David Franklin
A suspenseful whodunit, centering around a simple divorce investigation that leads to the discovery of a corpse.
David Hannay; Geoff Brown — *VCL Home Video*

Earth   1930
Drama/Film-History
52343   56 mins   B/W   B, V, 3/4U   P
Semyon Svashenko, Stephan Shkurat, directed by Alexander Dovzhenko
Classic Russian silent film with English subtitles. Problems begin in a Ukranian village when a landowner resists handing over his land for a collective farm.
USSR — *International Historic Films; Blackhawk Films*

Earth, Wind & Fire in Concert   1982
Music-Performance
66094   60 mins   C   B, V, CED   P
The funky R&B band performs "Sing a Song," "Fantasy," and "Shining Star." (Stereo).
Mike Schultz; Gloria Schultz; Maurice White — *Vestron Video*

Earth, Wind and Fire   1983
Music-Performance
72218   60 mins   C   B, V   P
Using spectacular special effects, Earth, Wind and Fire puts on one of their typically engaging shows.
Independent — *Vestron Video*

Earthling, The   1981
Drama
0C003   98 mins   C   B, V, CED   P
William Holden, Ricky Schroder
A tale of two people alone in the Australian wilderness, learning survival and caring.
MPAA:PG
Filmways — *Vestron Video*

Earthquake   1974
Drama
53397   129 mins   C   B, V   P
Charlton Heston, Ava Gardner, George Kennedy, Lorne Greene, Genevieve Bujold, Richard Roundtree, Marjoe Gortner, Barry Sullivan
The effects of a major earthquake in Los Angeles on the lives of an engineer and his spoiled wife, his mistress, his father-in-law and a suspended policeman make up the central theme of this drama.
Academy Award '74: Special Achievement for Visual Effects. MPAA:PG

Universal — *MCA Home Video*

East End Hustle 1976
Drama
76773   86 mins   C   B, V   P
A high-priced call girl rebels against her pimp
and sets out to free other prostitutes as well.
Also available in an 88-minute unrated version.
MPAA:R
Troma Films — *Vestron Video*

East of Borneo 1931
Drama/Romance
53449   75 mins   B/W   B, V   P
Charles Bickford, Rose Hobart
An idyllic tropical romance.
Universal — *Movie Buff Video; Kartes Video
Communications; Discount Video Tapes*

East of Eden 1954
Drama
38940   105 mins   C   B, V   P
*James Dean, Julie Harris, Richard Davalos,
Raymond Massey, Jo Van Fleet, directed by Elia
Kazan*
John Steinbeck's sprawling novel provides the
basis for this World War I-era retelling of the
Biblical tale of Cain and Abel. James Dean's
first starring role.
Warner Bros — *Warner Home Video; RCA
VideoDiscs*

East of Eden 1980
Drama
65439   240 mins   C   B, V   P
*Jane Seymour, Bruce Boxleitner, Timothy
Bottoms, Lloyd Bridges*
John Steinbeck's sprawling novel of family
passions is wholly captured in this adaptation
from the popular television mini-series. The
1955 movie version only used a third of the
original story.
Viacom International — *U.S.A. Home Video*

East of Elephants Rock 1981
Drama
72879   93 mins   C   B, V   P
John Hurt, Jeremy Kemp, Judi Bowker
In 1948, a young first secretary of the British
Embassy returns from leave in England to a
tense atmosphere in a Colony in Southeast
Asia.
Great Britian — *Embassy Home Entertainment*

Easter Bunny Is Coming to Town, The 1978
Holidays
75618   60 mins   C   B, V   P
Narrated by Fred Astaire
This animated tale is about the Easter Bunny
and Easter traditions.

Rankin Bass Productions — *Children's Video
Library*

Easter Parade 1948
Musical
39089   103 mins   C   B, V   P
*Fred Astaire, Judy Garland, Peter Lawford, Ann
Miller, directed by Charles Walters*
A big musical star splits with his partner,
claiming that he could mold any girl to replace
her in his act, and he tries, with much difficulty.
Astaire and Garland in peak form, aided by a
classic Irving Berlin score.
Academy Awards '48: Best Musical Scoring
MGM — *MGM/UA Home Video*

Easy Come, Easy Go 1967
Musical
29768   95 mins   C   B, V   P
*Elvis Presley, Dodie Marshall, Pat Priest, Pat
Harrington*
A Navy frogman accidentally locates what he
believes to be a vast sunken treasure, only to
find it filled with copper coins of little value.
Paramount, Hal Wallis — *Paramount Home
Video*

Easy Money 1983
Comedy
Closed Captioned
65385   95 mins   C   B, V   P
Rodney Dangerfield
A basic slob has the chance to inherit millions...
if he can give up smoking, drinking and
gambling! It's an effort that nearly kills him!
MPAA:R
John Nicolella — *Vestron Video; RCA
VideoDiscs*

Easy Rider 1969
Drama
52752   88 mins   C   B, V, LV   P
Peter Fonda, Dennis Hopper, Jack Nicholson
Two young men undertake a motorcycle trip to
New Orleans, meeting hippies, rednecks,
prostitutes, and drugs along the way.
MPAA:R
Columbia; Pando Co; Raybert
Prods — *RCA/Columbia Pictures Home Video;
RCA VideoDiscs*

Easy Street 1916
Comedy
10641   20 mins   B/W   B, V, 3/4U   R, P, DL
Charlie Chaplin
Chaplin portrays a derelict who reforms the
residents of Easy Street. (Silent with musical
soundtrack added.)
RKO — *Cable Films; Festival Films*

Eat My Dust   1976
Drama
65388   89 mins   C   B, V   P
Ron Howard, Christopher Norris, Warren Kemmerling
The teenage son of a California sheriff steals the best of stock cars from a race track to take the town's heart throb for a joy ride and leads the town on the wildest car chase ever filmed.
MPAA:PG
New World Pictures; Roger Corman Production — *Embassy Home Entertainment*

Eat or Be Eaten   1985
Comedy/Satire
71112   30 mins   C   B, V   P
Phil Proctor, Peter Bergman, Phil Austin
The "Firesign Theatre" lampoons TV and anything else lying around in this made-for-video presentation. Supposedly, a killer vine threatens the village—and demands a virgin sacrifice.
RCA Video Productions — *RCA/Columbia Pictures Home Video*

Eat to Win   1985
Physical fitness
77228   60 mins   C   B, V   P
Judy Landers, Audrey Landers
A video adaptation of the Robert Haas bestseller that details a fourteen day diet plan and a daily aerobic workout.
Bob Giraldi — *Karl/Lorimar Home Video*

Eaten Alive   1976
Horror
73558   90 mins   C   B, V   P
Neville Brand, Mell Ferrer, Stuart Whitman, directed by Tobe Hooper
A resident of the Southern swamps takes an unsuspecting group of tourists into a crocodile death trap.
Unknown — *Prism*

Eating Raoul   1982
Comedy
69377   87 mins   C   B, V   P
Mary Woronov, Paul Bartel
This is the story of a happily married couple who share many interests: good food and wine, entrepreneurial dreams and an aversion to sex.
MPAA:R
Quartet Films — *CBS/Fox Video*

Echo Murders, The   1945
Crime-Drama
85494   75 mins   B/W   B, V   P
David Farrar, Dennis Price
A Sexton Blake mystery wherein he investigates a mine owner's murder opening up a veritable can of murdering, power-hungry worms.
English — *Video Yesteryear*

Echoes   1983
Suspense/Drama
80940   90 mins   C   B, V   P
Gale Sondergaard, Mercedes McCambridge, Richard Alferi, Nathalie Nell
A young painter's life slowly comes apart as he is tormented by a past incarnation.
MPAA:R
Herbeval Productions — *VidAmerica*

Ecstasy   1933
Drama
08887   70 mins   B/W   B, V   P
Hedy Lamarr, Jaromir Rogoz, directed by Gustav Machaty
A romantic, erotic story about a young woman married to an older man. This film brought world fame and notoriety to Hedy Lamarr. Original title: Extase.
Universal Elektra Film — *Movie Buff Video; Kartes Video Communications*

Ed Thigpen: On Jazz Drumming   1985
Music
87925   60 mins   C   B, V   P
Various musical techniques for use by jazz drummers are demonstrated by the renowned artist.
DCI Music Video — *DCI Music Video*

Ed Wynn Show, The   1949
Comedy/Variety
63782   110 mins   B/W   B, V, 3/4U   P
Ed Wynn, guests Mel Torme, Dinah Shore, Virginia O'Brien, Buster Keaton, the Lud Gluskin Orchestra
Three complete kinescopes of Ed Wynn's early variety series, originally telecast October-December 1949. Original Speidel commercials included. Also on this tape is a 20-minute documentary produced by NBC and RCA in color which reviews the history of television and promotes the latest innovation—color TV.
CBS — *Shokus Video*

Ed Wynn Show, The   1949
Variety/Comedy
11274   24 mins   B/W   B, V, FO   P
Ed Wynn, Diana Lynn
A rare piece of entertainment featuring one of television's great clowns in an early example of TV comedy/variety.
CBS — *Video Yesteryear*

Eddie and the Cruisers   1983
Drama
64989   90 mins   C   B, V, LV, CED   P
Tom Berenger, Michael Pare
In the early 1960's, Eddie and the Cruisers had one hit album; years later, a former band

member begins a search for the missing tapes of the Cruisers' unreleased second album.
MPAA:PG
Embassy Pictures — *Embassy Home Entertainment*

Eddie Macon's Run   1983
Drama
68252   95 mins   C   B, V, LV   P
Kirk Douglas, John Schneider, Lee Purcell, Leah Ayers
Based on a true story, Eddie Macon has been unjustly jailed in Texas and plans an escape to run to Mexico. He is followed by a tough cop who is determined to catch Eddie so his dignity will not be hurt.
MPAA:PG
Universal — *MCA Home Video*

Eddie Murphy "Delirious"   1983
Comedy-Performance
82504   69 mins   C   B, V   P
Eddie Murphy, Richard Tienken, Robert Wachs
Eddie Murphy raps about life, sex, childhood etc. in this scathing, scatological stand-up performance.
Paramount — *Paramount Home Video*

Edgar Kennedy Slow   19??
Burn Festival, The
Comedy
65196   59 mins   B/W   B, V   P
Edgar Kennedy, Florence Lake, Dot Farley, Jack Rice, Vivien Oakland, Tiny Sandford
Popular 30's comedian Edgar Kennedy stars in three shorts from his long-running "Average Man" series: "Poisoned Ivory" (1934), "Edgar Hamlet" (1935) and "A Clean Sweep" (1938).
RKO — *Video Yesteryear*

Edge of Fury   198?
Martial arts
80128   90 mins   C   B, V   P
Bruce Li, Andrew Sage, Michael Danna, Tommy Lee
When a businessman is unjustly arrested on a drug charge, it is up to his chauffer to clear the man's name.
German Valder — *King of Video*

Edie in Ciao! Manhattan   1972
Drama
65469   90 mins   C   B, V   P
Edie Sedgwick, Baby Jane Holzer, Roger Vadim, Paul America, Viva
The real-life story of Edie Sedgwick, Warhol superstar and international fashion model, whose life in the fast lane led to ruin.
MPAA:R
David Weisman — *Pacific Arts Video*

Edison Twins, The   1985
Adventure
84881   45 mins   C   B, V   P
Andrew Sabiston, Marnie McPhail
Two youngsters get into a series of predicaments, and use instructive scientific concepts to get themselves out. A series produced for the Disney channel.
DIC Enterprises; Canadian Film Board — *RCA/Columbia Pictures Home Video*

Edith and Marcel   1983
Romance
82476   180 mins   C   B, V   P
Evelyne Bouix, Marcel Cerdan, Jr, Charles Aznavour, Jacques Villeret, directed by Claude Lelouch
A fictionalization of the love affair between chanteuse Edith Piaf and boxer Marcel Cerdan.
FR
Parafrance Productions — *Media Home Entertainment*

Educating Rita   1983
Comedy-Drama
Closed Captioned
72803   110 mins   C   B, V
Michael Caine, Julie Walters, Michael Williams, Maureen Lipman, directed by Lewis Gilbert
A young hairdresser decides to take some college courses in an effort to improve herself.
Columbia — *RCA/Columbia Pictures Home Video*

Edward and Mrs.   1980
Simpson
Drama
59700   260 mins   C   B, V   P
Edward Fox, Cynthia Harris
The dramatic reconstruction of the years leading to the abdication of King Edward VII, who gave up the British throne in 1936 so that he could marry American divorcee Wallis Simpson.
Emmy Awards '80: Best Drama.
Andrew Brown; Thames Television — *THORN EMI/HBO Video*

Eegah!   1962
Horror/Exploitation
84356   93 mins   C   B, V   P
Richard Kiel, Arch Hall Jr
Another Arch Hall epic wherein an anachronistic Neanderthal falls in love in '60's California. Reputed to be one of the worst films of all time.
Fairway Prods — *Rhino Video*

EEOC Story   1978
Minorities
88387   38 mins   C   B, V, 3/4U   R, P
A look at how the Equal Employment Opportunity Commission works, why and by whom.

EEOC — *Your World Video*

Eiger Sanction, The   1975
Suspense
59067   125 mins   C   B, V   P
Clint Eastwood, George Kennedy, Vonetta McGee, Jack Cassidy, directed by Clint Eastwood
An art teacher returns to the CIA as an exterminator, and finds himself in a party climbing the Eiger.
MPAA:R
Universal — *MCA Home Video*

---

8 1/2   1963
Drama
66102   135 mins   B/W   B, V   P
Marcello Mastroianni, directed by Federico Fellini
Fellini's surreal self-portrait, a cinematic classic. Academy Awards '63: Best Foreign Film.
Embassy — *Vestron Video*

---

8 Minute Makeovers   1984
Cosmetology
76931   60 mins   C   B, V   P
Makeup artist and author Clare Miller demonstrate how women can create beautiful faces in only eight minutes. A book also comes with a purchase of the videocassette.
AM Available
C.B. Wismar — *Kartes Video Communications*

Eisenstein   1958
Film-History/Documentary
12805   48 mins   B/W   B, V, FO   P
A well-done biography of Sergei Eisenstein, the famous Russian director. Footage of his early life, first works and masterpieces such as "Potemkin" and "Ivan the Terrible."
Unknown — *Video Yesteryear*

El Cid   1961
Adventure
16809   187 mins   C   B, V, CED   P
Charlton Heston, sophia Loren, raf Vallone, Hurd Hatfield, Genevieve Page, directed by Anthony Mann
This is the story of El Cid, the legendary eleventh century Christian hero who freed Spain from the Moorish invaders. The music is by Miklos Roza.
Allied Artists; Samuel Bronston — *Lightning Video; United Home Video; Vestron Video (disc only)*

El Dorado   1967
Western
64509   126 mins   C   B, V   P
John Wayne, Robert Mitchum, James Caan, Charlene Holt, Ed Asner, directed by Howard Hawks

A gunfighter rides into the frontier town of El Dorado in order to bring peace between a cattle baron and farmers who are fighting over land rights.
Paramount — *Paramount Home Video; RCA VideoDiscs*

Electric Boogaloo,   1984
Breakin' 2
Musical
80853   94 mins   C   B, V, LV   P
Lucinda Dickey, Adolfo "Shabba Doo" Quinones, Michael "Boogaloo Shrimp" Chambers
Break-dancers Kelly, Ozone and Turbo stage a fundraising dance to prevent a greedy real-estate developer from tearing down their community center. Available in VHS and Beta Hi-Fi Dolby Stereo.
MPAA:PG
Cannon Films — *MGM/UA Home Video*

Electric Dreams   1984
Drama
80360   96 mins   C   B, V, LV   P
Bud Cort, Lenny Von Dohlen, Virginia Madsen, directed by Steve Barron
When a young man buys a computer, it winds up taking over his life. Available in VHS and Beta Hi-Fi.
MPAA:PG
MGM — *MGM/UA Home Video*

Electric Horseman, The   1979
Drama
29734   120 mins   C   B, V, LV   P
Robert Redford, Jane Fonda, John Saxon
A newspaper woman seeking a story discovers the reason behind a rodeo star's kidnapping of a prized horse. In the process she falls in love with the rodeo star.
MPAA:PG
Columbia, Ray Stark — *MCA Home Video; RCA VideoDiscs*

Electric Light Orchestra   1978
Live at Wembly
Music-Performance
44936   58 mins   C   B, V, CED   P
The ELO perform some of their greatest hits, including "Roll Over Beethoven," "Do Ya," "Living Thing" and "Evil Woman," live from the arena in Wembley, England.
MGM — *CBS/Fox Video*

Electric Light Voyage   1980
Film-Avant-garde/Video
56741   60 mins   C   B, V   P
Animated
This electronic fantasy featuring computer animation can control and change your moods of elation and tranquility. The animated visuals are in sync with a mesmerizing soundtrack.

Astralvision Productions — *Media Home Entertainment*

Elephant Boy 1937
Adventure
81460   81 mins   B/W   B, V, LV   P
Sabu, Walter Hudd, W.E. Holloway
An Indian boy helps government conservationists locate a herd of elephants in the jungle.
Alexander Korda — *Embassy Home Entertainment*

Elephant Hunting in Tanzania 1984
Hunting
87648   41 mins   C   B, V   P
Ken Wilson, Dave Harshbarger
Ken and Dave set out to hunt and shoot the fearsome Tanzanian elephant.
Sportsmen On Film — *Sportsmen on Film*

Elephant Man, The 1980
Drama
55537   123 mins   B/W   B, V, LV   P
Anthony Hopkins, John Hurt, Anne Bancroft, directed by David Lynch
The tragic, true-life story of John Merrick, a hideously deformed man who went from freak show to the attraction of London society.
MPAA:PG
Paramount; Jonathan Sanger — *Paramount Home Video; RCA VideoDiscs*

Elephant Parts 1981
Music/Comedy
51226   60 mins   C   B, V, CED   P
A video album by Michael Nesmith, which contains several amusing comedy sketches and original music by Nesmith.
Grammy Awards '81: Video of the Year Award.
Michael Nesmith; Kathryn Nesmith — *Pacific Arts Video; Pioneer Artists*

---

11 Harrow house 1974
Crime-Drama/Comedy
Closed Captioned
70902   95 mins   C   B, V   P
Charles Grodin, Candice Bergen, James Mason, Trevor Howard, John Gielgud, directed by Aram Avakian
The Consolidated Selling System at 11 Harrow house, London controls much of the world's diamond trade. Four adventurous thieves plot a daring heist relying on a very clever cockroach.
MPAA:PG
Twentieth Century Fox — *Playhouse Video*

Elfego Baca: Six Gun Law 1962
Western
84801   77 mins   C   B, V   P
Robert Loggia, James Dunn, Lynn Bari, Annette Funicello
An Arizonian DA tackles a seemingly clear-cut murder case.
Walt Disney Prod — *Walt Disney Home Video*

Eliminators 1986
Science fiction
87171   95 mins   C   B, V   P
Roy Dotrice, Patrick Reynolds, Denise Crosby, Andrew Prine, Conan Lee
A cyborgian creature endeavors to avenge himself on his scientist creator with help from a Kung Fu expert and a Mexican.
MPAA:PG
Altar Prod.; Charles Bond — *Playhouse Video*

Elixir of Love 1946
Opera
84655   90 mins   B/W   B, V   P
Tito Gobbi, Nelly Corradi, Italo Tajo
A feature film version of the Donizetti opera offers another great Gobbi rendition.
IT
Italian — *V.I.E.W. Video*

Ellie 1983
Comedy
81163   90 mins   C   B, V   P
Shelley Winters, Sheila Kennedy, Pat Paulsen, George Gobel, Edward Albert
A murderous widow's stepdaughter tries to save her father from being added to the woman's extensive list of dearly departed husbands.
MPAA:R
Rudine-Wittman Productions — *Vestron Video*

Elmer 1976
Drama/Adventure
70694   82 mins   C   B, V   P
Elmer Swanson, Phillip Swanson, directed by Christopher Cain
This film follows the exploits of a temporarily blind youth and a lovable hounddog who meet in the wilderness and together set off in search of civilization.
Film Advisory Board '76: Award of Excellence
MPAA:G
Cinema Shares — *Lightning Video*

Elmer Fudd Cartoon Festival 194?
Cartoons
71151   33 mins   C   B, V   P
Animated Elmer Fudd, Sylvester, Bugs Bunny
Fussy Elmer Fudd gets little respect, and more than his share of torment from "wascals." This tape includes: "An Itch in Time," "Hardship of Miles Standish," "Elmer's Pet Rabbit" and "Back-Alley Oproar," all from 1940-47.
Vitaphone Corp — *MGM/UA Home Video*

Elmer Gantry 1960
Drama
68225   146 mins   C   B, V, CED   P
Burt Lancaster, Jean Simmons, Shirley Jones
Burt Lancaster stars as Elmer Gantry, the
charismatic preacher who promises eternal
salvation, but in return pursues wealth and
power.
United Artists — *CBS/Fox Video*

Elton John 1982
Music-Performance
76670   14 mins   C   B, V   P
This program presents this rock-n-roll Superstar
performing his greatest hits.
Sunport Productions Intl Inc — *Sony Video
Software*

Elton John Live in Central Park 1984
Music-Performance
74109   59 mins   C   B, V   P
The largest concert audience in the U.S. since
Woodstock was the setting for a fabulous free
concert in New York's Central Park. Among the
songs performed are "Your Song," "Goodbye
Yellow Brick Road" and "Benny and the Jets."
Danny O'Donovan — *VCL Home Video*

Elton John—Night and Day: The Nighttime Concert 1975
Music-Performance
80691   53 mins   C   B, V   P
*Elton John, Davey Johstone, Dee Murray, Fred
Mandel, Nigel Olsson*
The outlandish rock superstar performs such
hits as "Your Song," "Crocodile Rock" and "I
Guess That's Why They Call It the Blues" in this
concert taped at London's Wembley Stadium.
John Reid, Mike Mansfield — *Vestron Video*

Elton John: Visions 1982
Music-Performance
47847   45 mins   C   B, V, LV,   P
CED
Elton John performs "Breaking Down Barriers,"
"Just Like Belgium," "Nobody Wins," "Elton's
Song," and other classics.
Al Schoenberger — *Embassy Home
Entertainment*

Elusive Corporal, The 1962
Drama
47648   109 mins   B/W   B, V, FO   P
*Jean-Pierre Cassel, Claude Brasseur, O. E.
Hasse, directed by Jean Renoir*
Set in a P.O.W. camp on the day France
surrendered to Germany, the story of the
French and Germans, and memories of a
France that is no more is told.
France — *Video Yesteryear*

Elvira Madigan 1967
Romance
63339   90 mins   C   B, V   P
Pia Degermark, Thommy Berggren
This film, based on a true incident, chronicles
the 19th-century romance between a young
officer and a beautiful circus dancer.
MPAA:PG
Atlantic Releasing; Europa Films — *THORN
EMI/HBO Video*

Elvis...Aloha from Hawaii 1973
Music-Performance
38118   60 mins   C   B, V   P
Elvis Presley
Elvis' 1973 Hawaiian concert appearance.
RCA Record Tours — *Media Home
Entertainment; RCA VideoDiscs*

Elvis—1968 Comeback Special 1968
Music-Performance
64453   76 mins   C   B, V   P
Elvis Presley, the Jordanaires
Elvis is showcased in this famous TV special,
which sparked his return to live performances.
Featured are a medley of Elvis' 50's hits, plus
newer tunes including "Guitar Man," "If I Can
Dream" and "Let Yourself Go."
NBC — *Media Home Entertainment; RCA
VideoDiscs*

Elvis on Tour 1972
Music-Performance/Documentary
63110   93 mins   C   B, V, CED   P
Elvis Presley
A revealing glimpse of Elvis Presley, on stage
and off, during a whirlwind concert tour.
MGM — *MGM/UA Home Video*

Elvis—One Night with You 1968
Music-Performance
82482   53 mins   C   B, V   P
Elvis Presley
The celebrated crooner performs such
memorables as "Heartbreak Hotel," "Blue
Suede Shoes" and "Are You Lonesome
Tonight" in this unedited performance from his
1968 Christmas Special.
Joe Rascoff — *Media Home Entertainment*

Elvis Presley's Graceland 1984
Documentary
88034   60 mins   C   B, V   P
Hosted by Priscilla Presley
Elvis' ex-wife takes the viewer on a tour of the
famous Memphis mansion, which was the rock
star's home from 1957 until his death in 1977.
Congress Video — *Congress Video*

Emanuelle Around the World   1980
Drama
72954   92 mins   C   B, V   P
Laura Gemser
The further erotic adventures of that insatiable
lady Emanuelle.
Jerry Gross — *Wizard Video*

Emmanuelle 4   1984
Exploitation
84719   81 mins   C   B, V   P
*Sylvia Kristel, Mia Nygren, Patrick Bauchau,
directed by Francis Giacobetti*
Emmanuelle undergoes plastic surgery to
become a young model.
MPAA:R
Sara Films/AS Prods — *MGM/UA Home
Video*

Emanuelle in America   1976
Drama
58737   95 mins   C   B, V, CED   P
Laura Gemser
Provocative reporter Emanuelle sets out to
expose the inner secrets of the Jet Set at play.
MPAA:R
Monarch — *VidAmerica*

Emanuelle in Bangkok   1978
Drama
55258   94 mins   C   B, V, CED   P
Emanuelle's exotic, erotic experiences in the
Far East include the royal masseuse, suspense,
and the Asian arts of love.
MPAA:R
Monarch Releasing Corp — *VidAmerica*

Emanuelle the Queen   1975
Drama
63419   90 mins   C   B, V   P
Laura Gemser
Seeking revenge, Emanuelle plots the murder of
her sadistic husband. The lecherous assassin
she hires in turn tries to blackmail her, and she
challenges him at his own game of deadly
seduction.
Othello Films; Andromeda Films — *VidAmerica*

Embryo   1982
Science fiction
75460   103 mins   C   B, V   P
Rock Hudson, Roddy McDowell, Diane Ladd
A scientist develops a growth hormone that
allows embryos to become adults in 4 1/2
MPAA:PG
King Features — *U.S.A. Home Video*

Emerald Forest, The   1985
Adventure/Drama
81905   113 mins   C   B, V, 8mm,   P
                          LV

*Powers Boothe, Meg Foster, Charley Boorman,
Dira Pass, Rui Polonah, directed by John
Boorman*
A father ventures into the Brazilian jungle to
look for his son who was kidnapped ten years
earlier. Based upon a true story.
MPAA:R
Embassy Pictures — *Embassy Home
Entertainment*

Emilienne   1978
Drama
55257   94 mins   C   B, V   P
An artistic young couple toys with the sexual
possibilities that exist outside of, and within, a
marriage.
MPAA:X
Gades Films International — *VidAmerica*

Emily   1977
Drama
63120   87 mins   C   B, V, CED   P
Koo Stark
Returning from her exclusive Swiss finishing
school, young Emily is ready for erotic
encounters at the hands of her willing
"instructors."
Christopher Neame — *MGM/UA Home Video*

Emma and Grandpa   1985
Drama/Seasons
84781   120 mins   C   B, V   P
4 pgms
Available as either one program or four 30-
minute shows, this story of a young girl's year on
her grandfather's farm, is told through rhyming
narration.
1.Summer 2.Fall 3.Winter 4.Spring
Joy Whitby — *VidAmerica; New World Video*

Emmanuelle   1974
Drama
55261   92 mins   C   B, V   P
Sylvia Kristel, Alain Cuny, Marika Green
Filmed in Bangkok, a young, beautiful, and
restless woman is introduced to an uninhibited
world of sensuality where she experiences her
wildest dreams.
MPAA:X
Columbia; Yves Rousset
Rouard — *RCA/Columbia Pictures Home
Video*

Emmanuelle Black and White   1978
Drama
77394   95 mins   C   B, V   P
Anthony Gizmond, Mary Longo
The jilted fiance of a plantation owner in the old
south begins a depraved quest for revenge
against her former lover.
S.E.F.I. — *Wizard Video*

Emmanuelle in the Country 1978
Drama
77257   90 mins   C   B, V   P
Laura Gemser
Emmanuelle becomes a nurse in an attempt to
bring comfort to those in need.
Monarch Releasing Corp. — *Magnum Entertainment*

Emmanuelle, the Joys of a Woman 1976
Drama
55512   92 mins   C   B, V, LV   P
Sylvia Kristel, Umberto Orsini, Frederic Lagache
The amorous exploits of a sensuous, liberated
couple take them and their erotic companions to
exotic Hong Kong, Bangkok, and Bali.
MPAA:X
Paramount — *Paramount Home Video*

Emmet Otter's Jug-Band Christmas 1977
Comedy
47349   50 mins   C   B, V   R, P
Emmet Otter and his Ma enter the Frog Town
Hollow talent contest and try to beat out a rock
group called the Riverbottom Nightmares for the
prize money, which will enable them to have a
merry Christmas.
Henson Associates — *Muppet Home Video*

Emotions of Life, The 1982
Psychology/Alcoholism
59564   63 mins   C   B, V   P
This program examines three of the most
interesting and critical manifestations of the
human psyche: aggression, depression, and
addiction.
McGraw Hill — *Mastervision*

Emperor Jones, The 1933
Drama
12296   72 mins   B/W   B, V   P
Paul Robeson, Dudley Diggs, Frank Wilson
Based on Eugene O'Neill's classic story, this
program portrays the rise and fall of a Pullman
porter to a king of Haiti.
United Artists — *Hollywood Home Theater;
Western Film & Video Inc; Phoenix Films &
Video; Cable Films*

Emperor's New Clothes, The 1984
Fairy tales
Closed Captioned
73572   60 mins   C   B, V, CED   P
Art Carney, Alan Arkin, Dick Shawn
From "Faerie Tale Theatre" comes the story of
an emperor and the unusual outfit he gets from
his tailor.

Gaylord Productions; Platypus
Productions — *CBS/Fox Video*

Empire of the Ants 1977
Science fiction
80765   89 mins   C   B, V   P
*Joan Collins, Robert Lansing, John David
Carson, Albert Salmi, Jacqueline Scott*
A group of enormous, unfriendly ants stalk a real
estate dealer and his prospective buyers when
they look at some undeveloped ocean front
property.
MPAA:PG
American International Pictures — *Embassy
Home Entertainment*

Empire of the Dragon 198?
Martial arts
64964   90 mins   C   B, V   P
Chen Tien Tse, Chia Kai, Chang Shan
A rip-roaring martial arts adventure.
Dragon Lady Productions — *Unicorn Video*

Empire Strikes Back, The 1980
Science fiction/Adventure
78890   124 mins   C   B, V   P
*Mark Hamill, Carrie Fisher, Harrison Ford, Billy
Dee Williams, David Prowse, Kenny Baker,
Frank Oz, directed by Irvin Kershner*
While the Rebel Alliance hides from Darth Vader
on the frozen planet Hoth, Luke Skywalker
learns how to be a Jedi knight from Jedi master
Yoda. In Beta and VHS Hi-Fi.
MPAA:PG
Gary Kurtz; 20th Century Fox; Lucas
Film — *CBS/Fox Video*

Enchanted Forest 1945
Adventure
81223   77 mins   C   B, V, LV   P
*Harry Davenport, Edmund Lowe, Brenda Joyce,
directed by Lew Landers*
An elderly man teaches a boy about life and the
beauty of nature when he gets lost in a forest.
PRC — *New World Video*

Enchanted Island 1958
Drama
72943   94 mins   C   B, V   P
Jane Powell, Dana Andrews
Based upon Herman Melville's "Typee", Dana
Andrews is a whaler who stops on an island to
find provisions and ends up falling in love with a
cannibal princess.
RKO Radio Pictures — *United Home Video*

**Enchanted Studio,
The/More from the
Enchanted Studio** 1907
Film-History
63982   57 mins   B/W   B, V   P, T

A collection of short films produced by Pathe Freres studios during the early years of this century. Titles include: "Policeman's Little Run," "The Dog and His Various Merits," "A Diabolical Itching," "The Red Spectre," "The Yawner," "Poor Coat," "Wiffles Wins a Beauty Prize," "I Fetch the Bread" and "Down in the Deep." Silent with music score. Some color-tinted sequences.
Pathe Freres — *Blackhawk Films*

Encounter with Disaster — 1979
Disasters
59330   93 mins   C   B, V   P
Using authentic footage from some of the worst and most frightening events of the century, this film explores how tragic events unfold—and how man has prevailed.
MPAA:PG
Charles E Sellier Jr; James Conway — *United Home Video; Lucerne Films*

Encounter with the Unknown — 1975
Adventure
11704   90 mins   C   B, V   P
Narrated by Rod Serling
Relates three fully documented supernatural events including a death prophesy and a ghost.
Gold Key — *United Home Video*

End, The — 1978
Comedy
44941   100 mins   C   B, V, CED   P
Burt Reynolds, Sally Field, Dom DeLuise, Carl Reiner, Joanne Woodward
Burt Reynolds plays a young man who finds out that he is dying from a rare disease. Deciding not to prolong his suffering, he tries various tried-and-true methods for committing suicide, with little success.
MPAA:R
United Artists — *CBS/Fox Video*

End of the Road — 1970
Drama
Closed Captioned
82243   110 mins   C   B, V   P
James Earl Jones, Stacy Keach, James Coco, Harris Yullin, Dorothy Tristan, directed by Aram Avakian
A troubled college professor undergoes bizarre treatments from his psychologist which produce tragic results. Available in VHS and Beta Hi-Fi.
MPAA:X
Allied Artists — *Key Video*

End of the World — 1977
Science fiction
33889   88 mins   C   B, V   P
Christopher Lee, Sue Lyon, Lew Ayres, MacDonald Carey

A coffee machine explodes, sending a man flying and screaming through a window and into a neon sign, where he is electrocuted. A haunted priest witnesses this and retreats to a convent where he meets his double and heads for more trouble.
MPAA:PG
Irwin Yablans Company — *Media Home Entertainment*

Endangered Species — 1982
Drama
64570   97 mins   C   B, V, CED   P
Robert Urich, Jobeth Williams, Paul Dooley, Hoyt Axton
A New York cop on vacation in Wyoming becomes involved in a mysterious series of cattle killings.
MPAA:R
MGM/UA — *MGM/UA Home Video*

Endgame — 1985
Science fiction/Fantasy
77360   96 mins   C   B, V   P
Al Oliver, Moira Chen, Jack Davis
Grotesquely deformed survivors of World War III fight their way out of radioactive New York City to seek a better life.
Independent — *Media Home Entertainment*

Endless Love — 1981
Drama
58495   115 mins   C   B, V   P
Brooke Shields, Martin Hewitt, Don Murray, Shirley Knight, Beatrice Straight, Richard Kiley
Scott Spencer's novel concerning two teenagers' doomed romance and sexual obsession.
MPAA:R
Universal; Dyson Lovell — *Vestron Video; RCA VideoDiscs*

Endless Night — 1972
Mystery
63356   95 mins   C   B, V   P
Hayley Mills, Hywel Bennett
This screen adaptation of an Agatha Christie tale focuses on a young chauffeur who wants to build a dream house, and his chance meeting with an heiress.
British Lion — *THORN EMI/HBO Video*

Endless Summer, The — 1966
Documentary/Sports-Water
59928   90 mins   C   B, V, LV, CED   P

Directed by Bruce Brown
Director Bruce Brown follows two young surfers around the world in their search for the perfect wave.
Bruce Brown — *Pacific Arts Video*

Enemy Mine   1985
Science fiction
87642   108 mins   C   B, V.   P
Dennis Quaid, Lou Gossett Jr., directed by
Wolfgang Peterson
A space fantasy in which two pilots from warring
planets, one an Earthling, the other an asexual
reptilian Drac, crash land on a barren planet and
are forced to work together to survive.
MPAA:PG-13
Stephen Friedman — *CBS/Fox Video*

Enforcer, The   1976
Crime-Drama
58228   97 mins   C   B, V   P
Clint Eastwood, Tyne Daly, Harry Guardino,
Brad Dillman
Dirty Harry takes on a vicious terrorist group
threatening the city of San Francisco.
MPAA:R
Warner Bros — *Warner Home Video; RCA*
VideoDiscs

Engelbert Humperdinck   1986
in Concert
Music-Performance
85622   60 mins   C   B, V   P
Humperdinck performs at London's Royal Albert
Hall, singing "After the Lovin'," "I'll Walk Alone"
and "Help Me Make It Through the Night" and
many of his other hits.
Vestron Musicvideo — *Vestron Video*

Enigma   1983
Drama/Adventure
66043   101 mins   C   B, V, LV,   P
                     CED
Martin Sheen, directed by Jeannot Szwarc
Five assassins from the Soviet's KGB are sent
to the West to eliminate five Soviet dissidents.
MPAA:PG
Ben Arbeid; Peter Shaw — *Embassy Home*
Entertainment

Enigma   1983
Suspense
69545   101 mins   C   B, V   P
Martin Sheen, Brigitte Fossey, Sam Neill
Trapped behind the Iron Curtain, a double agent
tries to find the key to five pending murders by
locating a Russian coded microprocessor
holding information that would unravel the
assassination scheme.
MPAA:PG
Filmcrest International Corp — *Embassy Home*
Entertainment

Enjoying Wine   1982
Alcoholic beverages
64925   120 mins   C   B, V   P
Paul Gillette

The author of "Playboy's Book of Wine"
demonstrates how to judge wine with seven
complete tastings.
Celluloid — *Video Associates*

Enola Gay   1980
War-Drama
70743   150 mins   C   B, V   P
Patrick Duffy, Billy Crystal, Kim Darby, Gary
Frank, Gregory Harrison, Ed Nelson, Robert
Walden, directed by D.L. Rich
Based on the best-selling book by Gordon
Thomas and Max Gordon Witts, this film tells
the story of the airmen aboard the B-29 that
dropped the first atomic bomb on Hiroshima.
Viacom in assoc. with The Production
Co. — *Prism*

Ensign Pulver   1964
Comedy
73013   104 mins   C   B, V   P
Robert Walker, Walter Matthau, Burl Ives,
directed by Joshua Logan
A continuation of the further adventures of the
crew of the U.S.S. Reluctant from "Mister
Roberts," which was adapted from the
Broadway play.
Joshua Logan; Warner Bros — *Warner Home*
Video

Enter Laughing   1967
Comedy
87271   112 mins   C   B, V   P
Rene Santoni, Jose Ferrer, Elaine May, Shelley
Winters, Jack Gilford, Don Rickles, Michael J.
Pollard, Janet Margolin, directed by Carl Reiner
Based on Reiner's semi-autobiographical novel
and play, this film depicts the botched efforts of
a Bronx-born shlump to become an actor.
Carl Reiner; Joseph Stein — *RCA/Columbia*
Pictures Home Video

Enter the Dragon   1973
Adventure/Martial arts
38946   90 mins   C   B, V, LV   P
Bruce Lee, John Saxon, Jim Kelly
Martial arts film starring Bruce Lee, with
spectacular fighting sequences featuring karate,
judo, tai kwan do, tai chi chuan, and hapkido
techniques.
MPAA:R   EL, SP
Warner Bros — *Warner Home Video; RCA*
VideoDiscs

Enter the Ninja   1981
Martial arts/Adventure
60593   101 mins   C   B, V, CED   P
Franco Nero, Susan George
The story of the Ninja warrior's lethal, little-
known Art of Invisibility.
MPAA:R

Cannon Films Release — *MGM/UA Home Video*

David Lynch — *RCA/Columbia Pictures Home Video*

Enter the Panther · 1979
Martial arts
85018 91 mins C B, V P
Bruce Li, Tsao Chen, Tse Lan
Amidst, and regardless of, a double-crossing plot featuring a treacherous family and a sought-after gold mine, a young man kicks and punches his way to fame.
Foreign — *Video Gems*

Entertaining Mr. Sloane · 1970
Drama
58886 90 mins C B, V P
Beryl Reid, Harry Andrews, Peter McEnery, Alan Webb
Playwright Joe Orton's masterpiece of black comedy concerning a handsome criminal who becomes the guest and love interest of a widow and her brother.
Pathe; Canterbury — *THORN EMI/HBO Video*

Entity, The · 1982
Horror
69376 119 mins C B, V, CED P
Barbara Hershey
An unseen entity repeatedly torments a woman both physically and mentally.
MPAA:R
20th Century Fox — *CBS/Fox Video*

Entre Nous (Between Us) · 1983
Drama
80497 110 mins C B, V P
Isabelle Huppert, Miou-Miou
Two attractive young French mothers find in each other the fulfillment their husbands cannot provide. French dialogue with English subtitles.
MPAA:PG FR
Alexandre Films — *MGM/UA Home Video*

Equus · 1977
Drama/Mystery
81770 138 mins C B, V P
Richard Burton, Peter Firth, Jenny Agutter, Joan Plowright, directed by Sidney Lumet
A psychiatrist undertakes the most challenging case in his career when he tries to figure out why a boy blinded horses with a metal stick. Based upon the play by Peter Shaffer.
MPAA:R
United Artists — *MGM/UA Home Video*

Eraserhead · 1977
Film-Avant-garde/Satire
47783 90 mins C B, V P
John Nance, Charlotte Stewart
A cult classic, with special effects that create an eerie, dreamlike world, about a very strange couple and their deformed child.

Erendira · 1983
Drama
81895 103 mins C B, V P
Irene Papas, Claudia Ohana, Michael Lonsdale, Rufus, Jorge Fegan, directed by Ruy Guerra
A teenaged girl and her lover plot to kill the grandmother who turned her into a sexual slave. With English subtitles.
SP
Miramax Films — *Media Home Entertainment*

Eric Clapton—Live '85 · 1986
Music-Performance
82426 56 mins C B, V P
Eric Clapton
Filmed at the Hartford Civic Center, this performance includes such Clapton classics as "Cocaine," "Lay Down Sally" and "Tulsa Time."
Vestron Music Video — *Vestron Video*

Erick Friedman Plays Fritz Kreisler · 1982
Music-Performance
59393 60 mins C B, V P
A recital of music composed by famed violinist Fritz Kreisler and performed by American violinist Erick Friedman and pianist Pavel Ostrosky. Selections include: "Tambourin Chinois," "Caprice Viennois," "The Old Refrain," "Song without Words" and "Schon Rosmarin."
Kultur — *Kultur*

Erik, The Viking · 1972
Adventure
84894 95 mins C B, V P
Givliano Gemma, Gordon Mitchell
The Norse Warrior discovers the New World and traitorous subordinates among his crew, calling for drastic measures.
Italian — *Unicorn Video*

Ernani · 1984
Music-Performance
77172 135 mins C B, V P
Placido Domingo, Mirella Freni, Renato Bruson
A performance of the Verdi opera taped at the Teatro Alla Scala in Italy.
National Video Corporation Limited — *THORN EMI/HBO Video*

Ernani · 1983
Opera
86880 142 mins C B, V P
Luciano Pavarotti, Leona Mitchell, Ruggero Raimondi

Conducted by James Levine, the Metropolitan Opera performs Verdi's classic opera, with English subtitles.
AM Available IT
Metropolitan Opera; Paramount — *Paramount Home Video*

Ernie Kovacs: Television's Original Genius 198?
Television/Comedy
66603   86 mins   C   B, V, LV   P
Ernie Kovacs, Edie Adams, Steve Allen, Jack Lemmon, Chevy Chase, hosted by John Barbour
A comedic tribute to one of television's pioneers, humorist Ernie Kovacs. His career is chronicled through clips from his numerous series and specials. Some black-and-white segments.
Simcom — *Vestron Video*

Eroticise 1983
Physical fitness
64336   60 mins   C   B, V, CED   P
Kitten Natividad
Kitten and her entourage guide the viewer into a sensual exercise workout, designed for adults. In stereo.
Pisanti Productions — *Vestron Video*

Errand Boy, The 1961
Comedy
80241   95 mins   B/W   B, V   P
Jerry Lewis, Brian Donlevy, Fritz Feld, directed by Jerry Lewis
A Hollywood studio head hires an errand boy to spy on his employees.
Paramount — *U.S.A. Home Video*

Eruption: St. Helens Explodes 1980
Volcanoes/Documentary
54108   25 mins   C   B, V   P, T
A look at the eruption of Mount St. Helens on May 18, 1980. Station KOIN-TV in Portland, Oregon shot the blast, showing the volcanic peak being torn away. They almost lost a $70,000 remote broadcast truck while shooting.
KOIN Portland — *Blackhawk Films*

Escapade in Florence 1962
Mystery
84433   81 mins   C   B, V   P
Tommy Kirk, Annette Funicello, directed by Steve Previn
As two students in Florence paint their way to immortality, an elaborate art-forging ring preys upon their talents.
Walt Disney Prods — *Walt Disney Home Video*

Escapade in Japan 1957
Adventure/Drama
79767   93 mins   C   B, V   P
Cameron Mitchell, Teresa Wright, Jon Provost, Roger Nakagawa
A Japanese and an American boy frantically search the city of Tokyo for their parents.
RKO — *United Home Video*

Escape 1978
Adventure
77390   100 mins   C   B, V   P
Anthony Steffen, Ajita Wilson
Two women escape from a sadistic penal colony and are pursued by a man who wants them to become his personal sex slaves.
Mark Alabiso — *Wizard Video*

Escape Artist, The 1980
Drama
85624   94 mins   C   B, V, LV   P
Griffin O'Neal, Raul Julia, Teri Garr, Joan Hackett, Desi Arnaz, directed by Caleb Deschanel
Award-winning cinematographer Deschanel's first directorial effort is this quirky film about a teenage escape artist.
Orion Pictures — *Vestron Video*

Escape from Alcatraz 1979
Drama
44752   112 mins   C   B, V, LV   P
Clint Eastwood, Patrick McGoohan, directed by Don Siegel
A fascinating account of the one and only successful escape from the maximum security prison at Alcatraz by three men who were never heard from again.
MPAA:PG
Paramount, Don Siegel — *Paramount Home Video; RCA VideoDiscs*

Escape from Cell Block Three 1978
Adventure
81710   82 mins   C   B, V   P
Carolyn Judd, Teri Gusman, Bonita Kalem
Five escaped female convicts take it on the lam for Mexico and freedom.
Independent — *Prism*

Escape from New York 1981
Science fiction/Adventure
65193   99 mins   C   B, V, LV   P
Kurt Russell, Lee Van Cleef, Isaac Hayes, Adrienne Barbeau, Season Hubley, directed by John Carpenter
In 1997, the island of Manhattan has been turned into a maximum security prison inhabited by millions of felons. When the President's plane crashes there, a convicted criminal is sent in to save him.
MPAA:R EL, JA

Avco Embassy — *Embassy Home
Entertainment; RCA VideoDiscs*

Escape from the Bronx   1985
Adventure/Science fiction
81188   82 mins   C   B, V   P
*Mark Gregory, Henry Silva, Valeria D'Obici,
Timothy Brant, Thomas Moore, Andrea Coppola*
Invading death squads seek to level the Bronx.
Local street gangs cry foul and ally to defeat the
uncultured barbarians.
*Fabrizio De Angelis — Media Home
Entertainment*

Escape from the Planet   1971
of the Apes
Science fiction
Closed Captioned
81542   97 mins   C   B, V   P
*Roddy McDowell, Kim Hunter, Sal Mineo,
Ricardo Montalban, William Windom, directed
by Don Taylor*
Two intelligent apes from the future travel back
in time and find themselves in present-day
America where they are the targets of a
relentless search.
MPAA:G
*Apjac Productions; 20th Century
Fox — Playhouse Video*

Escape of the One-Ton   1978
Pet, The
Cartoons
71362   73 mins   C   B, V   P
*Animated, voices of Stacy Swor, James
Callahan, Michael Morgan, Richard Yniguez,
directed by Richard Bennett*
When her pet calf grows into a full-grown steer,
a young girl's father asks her to find a new pet.
*Jean Anne Moore — Family Home
Entertainment*

Escape to Athena   1979
Adventure
57460   102 mins   C   CED   P
Roger Moore, Telly Savalas, David Niven
A group of losers are in a German POW camp
on a Greek island digging up Greek art
treasures. When they manage to escape, the
rumors abound.
MPAA:PG
*Associated Film Distributors — CBS/Fox
Video*

Escape to Burma   1955
Adventure
81610   86 mins   C   B, V   P
*Barbara Stanwyck, Robert Ryan, Reginald
Denny, directed by Allan Dwan*
A man on the run for a murder he did not commit
finds refuge and romance in an isolated jungle
home.

RKO — *Buena Vista Home Video*

Escape to Love   1986
Romance/Drama
71237   90 mins   C   V   P
Introduced by Louis Jourdan
A beautiful lady journalist helps a famous
dissident escape Poland, only to lose him to
another heroic venture.
Commworld; Romance Theater — Prism

Escape to the Sun   1972
Adventure/Suspense
66633   94 mins   C   B, V   P
*Laurence Harvey, Josephine Chaplin, John
Ireland, Jack Hawkins*
A pair of Russian university students plan to flee
their homeland so they can be allowed to live
and love free from oppression.
MPAA:PG
*Transamerican Productions — Monterey
Home Video*

Escape to Witch   1975
Mountain
Fantasy
29745   97 mins   C   B, V, LV   P
*Kim Richards, Ike Eisenmann, Eddie Albert, Ray
Milland*
Two young orphans with supernatural powers
find themselves on the run from a greedy
millionaire who wants to exploit their amazing
powers for his own gains.
MPAA:G
*Walt Disney, Jerome Coutland — Walt Disney
Home Video; RCA VideoDiscs*

Escape 2000   1983
Science fiction
69541   80 mins   C   B, V   P
Steve Railsback, Olivia Hussey, Michael Craig
In a future society where individuality is
considered a crime, those who refuse to
conform are punished by being hunted down in
a jungle.
MPAA:R
Unknown — Embassy Home Entertainment

Escapes   1986
Fantasy
86392   72 mins   C   B, V   P
*Vincent Price, Jerry Grisham, Lee Canfield,
John Mitchum, Gil Reade*
In the tradition of "The Twilight Zone," Vincent
Price introduces five short thrillers featuring time
travel, aliens and telepathy. Produced with
computer assistance for sharper, more
contrasty images.
*Visual Perceptions Prod.; David Steensland;
Angela Sanders — Prism*

(For explanation of codes, see Use Guide and Key)

Escapist, The   1984

Suspense
82461   87 mins   C   B, V   P
Bill Shirk
A professional escape artist becomes involved
in a perverted corporate plot and must escape
to save his life and livelihood.
Mid America Promotions — *Vestron Video*

Escort Girls   1974

Drama
80797   77 mins   C   B, V   R, P
*David Dixon, Maria O'Brien, Marika Mann, Gil
Barber, Helen Christie*
The escort girls are a group of actresses,
models and secretaries who really know how to
show their clients a good time.
Donovan Winter — *Video Gems*

Esposa y Amante   197?

Drama
49744   95 mins   C   B, V   P
*Ramiro Oliveros, Ricardo Merino, Victoria Abril,
Frika Wallner*
While her daughter contemplates suicide, a
mother remembers the happy early years of her
marriage, followed by the wrongdoings of her
husband which caused her to seek comfort in
the arms of an old lawyer friend. Her daughter is
now suffering for the problems of her marriage.
In Spanish.
SP
Independent — *Media Home Entertainment*

Esquire Great Body   1986
Series

Physical fitness
85377   30 mins   C   B, V   P
Deborah Crocker 6 pgms
A series of exercise programs sponsored by
Esquire magazine.
*1.Upper Body Beautiful 2.Dynamite Legs
3.Super Stomach 4.Low-Impact Aerobics
5.Total Body Tone-Up 6.Stretching for Energy*
Esquire Associates; Kartes Video
Corp. — *Kartes Video Communications*

Estate of Insanity   1970

Horror
81806   90 mins   C   B, V   P
An English lord and his second wife become
involved in a web of death when a maniac stalks
their ancient estate.
British — *VCL Home Video*

Eternally Yours   1939

Comedy
00395   95 mins   B/W   B, V   P
*David Niven, Loretta Young, Hugh Herbert,
Broderick Crawford*
Witty magician's career threatens to break up
his marriage.

United Artists; Tay Garnett — *Hollywood Home
Theater; Cable Films; Movie Buff Video; Kartes
Video Communications*

Eubie!   1982

Musical
59387   100 mins   C   CED   P
*Gregory Hines, Maurice Hines, Leslie Dockery,
Alaina Reed, Lynnie Godfrey, Mel Johnson Jr.,
Jeffrey V. Thompson*
The popular Broadway musical revue based on
the life and songs of Eubie Blake is presented in
a video transfer. Some of Eubie's best known
songs, performed here by members of the
original cast, include "I'm Just Wild About
Harry," "Memories of You," "In Honeysuckle
Time" and "The Charleston Rag." In stereo.
American Video Productions — *Warner Home
Video; Video Tape Network; RCA VideoDiscs*

Eureka!   1983

Drama
82352   130 mins   C   B, V   P
*Gene Hackman, Theresa Russell, Joe Pesci,
Rutger Hauer, Micky Rourke, Jane Lapotaire,
directed by Nicholas Roeg*
A bored, wealthy gold prospector has his death
wish satisfied when a Mafia hit man
assassinates him on his Canadian Island.
MPAA:R
Sunley Productions Ltd — *MGM/UA Home
Video*

Europeans, The   1979

Drama
56935   90 mins   C   B, V   P
*Lee Remick, Lisa Eichorn, directed by James
Ivory*
Henry James' satirical novel about two fortune-
seeking expatriates and their sober American
relations.
MPAA:G
Ismail Merchant — *Vestron Video*

Eurythmics—Sweet   1983
Dreams (The Video
Album)

Music-Performance
66347   50 mins   C   B, V   P
Directed by Derek Burbidge
Eurythmics' David Stewart and Annie Lennox
perform their hits "Sweet Dreams (Are Made of
This)" and "Love Is a Stranger" plus twelve
other songs in a combination of live concert
performances and music videos. In stereo VHS
and Beta Hi-Fi.
Jon Roseman — *RCA/Columbia Pictures
Home Video; RCA VideoDiscs; Pioneer Artists*

Eve, The   1980

Music-Performance
59872   60 mins   C   LV   P

The Inner Galaxy Orchestra, a contemporary ensemble led by Bingo Miki of the Japanese jazz scene, performs "The Eve," an incredible trip through his audiovisual fantasies. In stereo.
Yutaka Shigenobu — *Pioneer Video Imports*

Evel Knievel 1971
Drama/Biographical
75694   90 mins   C   B, V   P
George Hamilton, Bert Freed, Rod Cameron
The life of stuntman Evel Knievel is depicted in this movie, as portrayed by George Hamilton.
MPAA:PG
Fanfare — *MPI Home Video*

Evening with Liza Minnelli, An 1981
Music-Performance
59626   50 mins   C   B, V   P
Liza Minnelli
Liza is seen performing everything from blues to ballads at this concert recorded at the New Orleans Theater of the Performing Arts. Songs include "Cabaret" and "New York, New York."
Artel Home Video — *CBS/Fox Video*

Evening with Paul Anka, An 1986
Music-Performance
71320   87 mins   C   B, V   P
Paul Anka, directed by Joshua White
These ninety melodic minutes of Anka's finest, recorded at New Haven, Connecticut's Palace Theater, include the hits "Hold Me 'Til the Mornin' Comes" and "Diana" among many others.
Don Spielvogel — *U.S.A. Home Video*

Evening with Quentin Crisp, An 1981
Biographical/Theater
58582   90 mins   C   B, V   P
Introduction by John Hurt
Taped during performances of Crisp's one-man show during his first theatrical tour of the U.S., this program presents the "gospel according to Crisp," and features Crisp fielding questions from the audience.
Hillard Elkins — *Family Home Entertainment*

Evening with Ray Charles, An 1981
Music-Performance
58807   40 mins   C   B, V   P
Ray Charles
The living legend, Ray Charles, performs live at the Jubilee Auditorium in Edmunton, Canada, showcasing his many musical moods. Songs include: "Riding Thumb," "Busted," "Georgia on My Mind," "Oh What a Beautiful Morning," "Some Enchanted Evening," "Hit the Road Jack," "I Can't Stop loving You," "Take These

Chains from My Heart," "I Can See Clearly Now," "What'd I Say," and "America the Beautiful."
Allarco Prods Ltd; Optical Programming Associates — *MCA Home Video; Optical Programming Associates*

Evening with Robin Williams, An 1983
Comedy-Performance
64501   92 mins   C   B, V   P
Robin Williams
Robin Williams explodes all over the screen in this live nightclub performance taped at the Great American Music Hall in San Francisco.
Don Mischer — *Paramount Home Video; RCA VideoDiscs*

Evening with Sir William Martin, An 1981
Comedy
49676   30 mins   C   B, V   P
Bill Martin, Michael Nesmith
A "Mr. Toad" encounters his senile father, who is later transported to another planet. Then a moose hands him a cigarette which instantly transports him to Antarctica. This program probably has to be seen to be believed.
Pacific Arts Video Records — *Pacific Arts Video*

Evening with the Royal Ballet, An 1963
Dance
81203   87 mins   C   B, V   P
Rudolph Nureyev, Margot Fonteyn
Rudolph Nureyev and Margot Fonteyn join with the Royal Ballet to perform excerpts from such favorites as "The Sleeping Beauty" and "Les Sylphides."
British Home Entertainment Ltd. — *MCA Home Video*

Evening with the Royal Ballet, An 197?
Dance
56886   100 mins   C   CED   P
Rudolf Nureyev, Margot Fonteyn
Performances of "La Valse," "Les Sylphides," "Le Corsaire," "Aurora's Wedding," and the last act of "The Sleeping Beauty."
RCA — *RCA VideoDiscs*

Evening with Utopia, An 1983
Music-Performance
60587   85 mins   C   B, V   P
Directed by Joshua White
Utopia, the popular rock group and brainchild of Todd Rundgren, in concert. The 21 songs include "Feet Don't Fail Me Now" and others from the LP "Utopia." Stereo.

Neo Utopian Laboratories Ltd — *MCA Home Video*

Evergreen   1934
Musical
33506   90 mins   B/W   B, V, FO   P
Jessie Matthews, Sonnie Hale, Betty Balfour, Barry Mackey
The daughter of a retired British music hall star is mistaken for her mother and it is thought that she has discovered the secret of eternal youth.
Gaumont British — *Video Yesteryear; Cable Films; Western Film & Video Inc; Video Dimensions*

Everly Brothers Album: 1984
Flash, The
Music-Performance
84488   26 mins   C   B, V   P
The Everly Brothers demonstrate their timeless contribution to modern music in this video album.
Delilah Films Inc — *Sony Video Software*

Everly Brothers Reunion   1983
Concert
Music-Performance
65658   60 mins   C   B, V   P
After years of bitter separation and crises, the undisputed NO. 1 duo of the golden age of rock 'n' roll join together at London's Royal Albert Hall and perform such megahits as "Bye Bye Love," "Wake Up Little Susie," "All I Have To Do Is Dream," and "Cathy's Clown."
Delilah Films Inc; The Everly Brothers — *MGM/UA Home Video*

Every Girl Should Be   1948
Married
Comedy
73686   84 mins   B/W   B, V   P
Cary Grant, Betsy Drake, Diana Lynn
A shopgirl uses her wiles to land herself a bachelor doctor.
RKO — *RKO HomeVideo*

Every Girl Should Have   1978
One
Comedy
87185   90 mins   C   B, V   P
Zsa Zsa Gabor, Robert Alda, Alice Faye, Sandra Vacey, John Lazar
A rambunctious comedy about a chase following a million dollar diamond theft.
Robert Hyatt — *Video Gems*

Every Man for Himself   1975
and God Against All
Drama
69621   110 mins   C   B, V   P
Bruno S., directed by Werner Herzog

This film tells the story of Kaspar Hauser, a young man who mysteriously appears in a small German town, hardly able to speak, write or even function in the world of 1828. In German with English subtitles.
Cannes Film Festival: Grand Special Jury Prize.
Werner Herzog; Almi — *RCA/Columbia Pictures Home Video*

Every Which Way But   1978
Loose
Comedy/Adventure
54119   119 mins   C   B, V   P
Clint Eastwood, Sondra Locke, Geoffrey Lewis, Beverly D'Angelo, Ruth Gordon, directed by James Fargo
A beer guzzling, country music-loving truck driver earns a living as a barroom brawler. He and his orangutan travel to Colorado in pursuit of a woman he loves. Behind him are a motorcycle gang and an L.A. cop. All have been victims of his fists.
MPAA:R
Warner Bros — *Warner Home Video; RCA VideoDiscs*

Everybody Rides the   1975
Carousel
Psychology/Identity
81702   72 mins   C   B, V   P
Animated, directed by John and Faith Hubley
This film looks at the eight stages of Psychologist Erick Erikson's theory of personality development.
John and Faith Hubley — *Pacific Arts Video*

Everyday with Richard   1983
Simmons: Family Fitness
Physical fitness
60558   90 mins   C   B, V   P
This exercise regimen includes a 15-minute warm-up, an hour long exercise session, and emphasis on toning the face, stomach, legs, and thighs.
Karl Video Corp — *Karl/Lorimar Home Video*

Everything You Always   1972
Wanted to Know About
Sex But (Were Afraid to
Ask)
Comedy
44942   88 mins   C   B, V   P
Woody Allen, John Carradine, Lou Jacobi, Louise Lasser, Anthony Quayle, Lynn Redgrave, Tony Randall, Burt Reynolds, Gene Wilder, directed by Woody Allen
A series of comical sketches involving sex, such as a timid sperm cell, an oversexed court jester, and a giant disembodied breast.
MPAA:R
United Artists — *CBS/Fox Video; RCA VideoDiscs*

Everything You Always   **1984**
Wanted to Know About
Computers But Were
Afraid to Ask
Computers
79208   88 mins   C   B, V   P
John Wood presents in a clear cut fashion
everything you need to know to operate a
computer.
MGM UA Home Entertainment
Group — *MGM/UA Home Video*

Evictors, The   **1979**
Horror
65218   92 mins   C   B, V   P
Vic Morrow, Michael Parks, Jessica Harper
Three innocent victims are caught up in the
horror surrounding an abandoned farmhouse in
a small Louisiana town.
MPAA:PG
Charles B Pierce — *Vestron Video*

Evil, The   **1978**
Horror
81906   90 mins   C   B, V   P
Richard Crenna, Joanna Pettet, Andrew Prine,
Victor Buono
A psychologist must destroy an evil force that is
killing off the members of his research team
residing at an old mansion.
MPAA:R
New World Pictures — *Embassy Home*
Entertainment

Evil Dead, The   **1979**
Horror
69674   126 mins   C   B, V   P
Five vacationing college students unwittingly
resurrect demons which transform the students
into monsters.
New Line Cinema — *THORN EMI/HBO Video*

Evil Mind, The   **1935**
Drama
08760   68 mins   B/W   B, V   P
Claude Rains, Fay Wray, Jane Baxter
Fraudulent mindreader predicts many disasters
that start coming true.
British — *Kartes Video Communications; VCII;*
Video Yesteryear; Cable Films; Video
Connection

Evil That Men Do, The   **1984**
Drama
Closed Captioned
80375   90 mins   C   B, V   P
Charles Bronson, Rene Enriquez, Jose Ferrer,
Theresa Saladana
A hitman comes out of retirement to break up a
Central American government's political torture
ring. Available in VHS and Beta Hi-Fi.
MPAA:R

Tri-Star Pictures — *RCA/Columbia Pictures*
Home Video

Evil Under the Sun   **1981**
Mystery
63332   102 mins   C   B, V, CED   P
Peter Ustinov, Jane Birkin, Maggie Smith, Colin
Blakely, Roddy McDowall, Diana Rigg, Sylvia
Miles, James Mason
An opulent beach resort is the setting as
Hercules Poirot attempts to unravel a murder
mystery. Based on the Agatha Christie novel.
MPAA:PG
Universal — *THORN EMI/HBO Video*

Evils of the Night   **1984**
Horror
85915   85 mins   C   B, V   P
John Carradine, Julie Newmar, Tina Louise,
Neville Brand, Aldo Ray
Teenage campers are abducted by sex-crazed
aliens.
Mars Prod. — *Lightning Video*

Evilspeak   **1982**
Horror
59629   89 mins   C   B, V, CED   P
Clint Howard, Don Stark, Lou Gravance, Lauren
Lester
A bumbling misfit enrolled at a military school is
mistreated by the other cadets. He retaliates
with satanic power.
MPAA:R
Leisure Investments — *CBS/Fox Video*

Evolutionary Spiral   **1983**
Music-Performance/Video
76668   45 mins   C   B, V   P
A combination of visual imagery and a musical
soundtrack by the group Weather Report.
Earth Sky and Open Sky Productions — *Sony*
Video Software

Ex-Mrs. Bradford, The   **1936**
Mystery/Comedy
44854   80 mins   B/W   B, V, 3/4U   P
William Powell, Jean Arthur, James Gleason,
Eric Blore, Robert Armstrong, directed by
Stephen Roberts
Amateur sleuth Dr. Bradford teams up with his
ex-wife Jean Arthur to solve the race track
murders. Sophisticated comedy-mystery.
RKO — *Nostalgia Merchant*

Excalibur   **1981**
Fantasy
58229   140 mins   C   B, V   P
Nicol Williamson, Nigel Terry, Helen Mirren,
directed by John Boorman
An elegant version of the King Arthur legend
focusing on the rise of Christian civilization out

of the magic, murder, and chaos of the Dark Ages.
MPAA:R
Orion Pictures — *Warner Home Video; RCA VideoDiscs*

Executioner's Song, The 1982
Biographical/Drama
77386 157 mins C B, V P
Tommy Lee Jones, Rosanna Arquette, Eli Wallach, Christine Lahti, directed by Lawrence Schiller
An adaptation of the Norman Mailer book about the last nine months of convicted murderer Gary Gilmore's life. Available in Beta Hi Fi and VHS Stereo.
Lawrence Schiller — *U.S.A. Home Video*

Executioner, The 197?
Drama
70984 84 mins C B, V P
A brutal feud rocks the Mafia and a crime kingpin's passionate son seeks revenge on his father's slayers.
MPAA:R
Independent — *Video Gems*

Executioner, The 1970
Mystery
85282 107 mins C B, V P
George Peppard, Joan Collins, Keith Mitchell, directed by Sam Wanamaker
A spy thriller involving switched identities, backstabbing, betrayal and sabotage.
MPAA:PG
Charles H. Schneer — *RCA/Columbia Pictures Home Video*

Executioner of Venice, The 1963
Adventure
70785 90 mins C B, V P
Guy Madison, Lex Barker, Sandra Panaro, directed by Louis Capauno
Marauding pirates swarm in from the Adriatic Sea and attempt to rob the Venetians blind. The Doge and his godson come to the rescue.
Empire — *Force Video*

Executive Action 1973
Drama
44753 90 mins C B, V P
Burt Lancaster, Robert Ryan, Will Geer, Gilbert Green, John Anderson, directed by David Miller
A recreation of the events that led up to the assassination of JFK. A millionaire pays a professional spy to organize a secret conspiracy; their mission—kill President Kennedy.
MPAA:PG
National General — *Warner Home Video*

Exercise 1983
Physical fitness
60412 60 mins C B, V P
An adults-only erotic exercise program.
Appaloosa Productions — *Monterey Home Video*

Exercise Now! 1981
Physical fitness
52766 50 mins C B, V P
An intensive, two-part aerobic exercise program set to popular music and led by professional exercise instructors, complete with a poster detailing each exercise.
AM Available
Karl Video — *Karl/Lorimar Home Video*

Exit the Dragon, Enter the Tiger 1976
Adventure/Martial arts
37361 84 mins C B, V P
"Exit the Dragon, Enter the Tiger" is a motion picture about the death of karate specialist Bruce Lee.
Dimension — *United Home Video; Trans World Entertainment*

Exodus 1960
Drama
37523 207 mins C B, V P
Paul Newman, Eva Marie Saint, Lee J. Cobb, Sal Mineo, Ralph Richardson, Peter Lawford, Jill Haworth, John Derek, directed by Otto Preminger
Based on the novel by Leon Uris and filmed in Cyprus and Israel, this is the story of an Israeli underground leader who leads a group of Jewish refugees into Israel, and an American nurse who becomes involved with the movement.
Academy Award '60: Best Music Score.
United Artists, Otto Preminger — *CBS/Fox Video*

Exorcist, The 1973
Suspense
38944 120 mins C B, V, LV P
Ellen Burstyn, Linda Blair, Jason Miller, Max Von Sydow, directed by William Friedkin
A harrowing film based on William Peter Blatty's novel of a young girl who is possessed by a demon, raising havoc with her family and the priests who attempt to exorcise her.
MPAA:R EL, SP
Warner Bros — *Warner Home Video; RCA VideoDiscs*

Exorcist II: The Heretic 1977
Horror
44804 118 mins C B, V P
Richard Burton, Linda Blair, Louise Fletcher, Kitty Winn, James Earl Jones, Ned Beatty

---

A sequel to the 1973 hit "The Exorcist." After four years Blair is still under psychiatric care, suffering from the effects of being possessed by the devil.
MPAA:R
Warner Bros — *Warner Home Video*

Expansion of Life, The   1982
Biology/Science
59560   58 mins   C   B, V   P
This program deals with the fundamentals of cell division, invertebrates and fish life in the early seas, amphibians and reptiles, and the emergence of man.
McGraw Hill — *Mastervision*

Experience Preferred...   1982
But Not Essential
Comedy
75539   77 mins   C   B, V   P
Produced by David Puttnam
An English schoolgirl gets her first job at a resort where she learns about life.
MPAA:PG
Samuel Montagu & Co Ltd — *MGM/UA Home Video*

Experiment in Terror   1962
Suspense
86389   123 mins   B/W   B, V   P
Lee Remick, Glenn Ford, Stephanie Powers, Ross Martin, directed by Blake Edwards
A psychopath kidnaps a girl in order to blackmail her sister, a bank teller, into embezzling $100,000.
Blake Edwards — *RCA/Columbia Pictures Home Video*

Expertos en Pinchazos   1979
Comedy
47855   100 mins   C   B, V   P
Porcel and Olmedo
Albert and George, experts at giving injections to women, inject a patient with venom by mistake. Now they must find her within 48 hours. In Spanish.
SP
Luis Osvaldo Repetto; Nicolas Carreras — *Media Home Entertainment*

Explorers   1985
Fantasy
Closed Captioned
82550   109 mins   C   B, V, LV   P
Ethan Hawke, River Phoenix, Jassan Presson
Three young boys use a contraption from their makeshift laboratory to travel to outer space.
MPAA:PG
Paramount Pictures — *Paramount Home Video*

Exposed   1983
Suspense
66450   100 mins   C   B, V, CED   P
Nastassia Kinski, Rudolph Nureyev, Harvey Keitel, directed by James Toback
A high fashion model falls in with a terrorist gang, while at the same time, a group of anti-terrorists want to use her for their purposes.
MPAA:R
United Artists — *MGM/UA Home Video*

Express to Terror   1979
Drama
82294   120 mins   C   B, V   P
Steve Lawrence, George Hamilton, Vic Morrow, Broderick Crawford, Robert Alda, Don Stroud, Fred Williamson, directed by Dan Curtis
Passengers aboard an atomic-powered train en route to Los Angeles attempt to kill a sleazy theatrical agent. Pilot for the "Supertrain" series.
Dan Curtis Productions; NBC-TV — *Prism*

Exterminator, The   1980
Suspense
63369   101 mins   C   B, V, CED   P
Christopher George, Samantha Eggar
A man seeks vengeance and becomes the target of the police, the CIA and the underworld in this tale of murder and intrigue.
MPAA:R
Avco Embassy; Interstar Productions — *Embassy Home Entertainment*

Exterminator II   1984
Adventure
80499   88 mins   C   B, V   P
Robert Ginty
The Exterminator battles the denizens of New York's underworld after his girlfriend is crippled by the ruthless Mr. X.
MPAA:R
Cannon Films — *MGM/UA Home Video*

Exterminators of the Year   1983
3000
Adventure
80330   101 mins   C   B, V   P
Alan Collins, Fred Harris
The Exterminator and his mercenary girlfriend battle with nuclear mutants over the last remaining tanks of purified water on Earth.
MPAA:R
Samuel Goldwyn — *THORN EMI/HBO Video*

Eye for an Eye, An   1981
Adventure
60346   106 mins   C   B, V, CED   P
Chuck Norris, Christopher Lee, Richard Roundtree, Matt Clark
A story of pursuit and revenge with Chuck Norris as an undercover cop pitted against San Francisco's underworld and high society.

MPAA:R EL, JA
Avco Embassy — *Embassy Home
Entertainment*

Eye Hears, the Ear Sees, The　1970
Filmmaking
36349　59 mins　C　B, V, FO　P
Norman McLaren
This introduction to Norman McLaren and his
work shows how he has created many
innovative films which have become classic
examples of film art. McLaren discusses and
demonstrates some of his techniques, and
excerpts from his films are shown.
BBC — *Video Yesteryear; National Film Board
of Canada*

Eye of the Needle　1981
Suspense
58848　118 mins　C　B, V　P
*Donald Sutherland, Kate Nelligan, directed by
Richard Marquand*
Ken Follett's novel about a German spy posing
as a shipwrecked sailor on a deserted English
island during World War II.
MPAA:R
United Artists — *CBS/Fox Video*

Eyeball　1978
Horror
80288　91 mins　C　B, V　P
John Richardson, Martine Brochard
An intrepid policeman must keep an eye out for
the madman who is removing eyeballs from his
victims.
MPAA:R
Joseph Brenner Associates — *Prism*

Eyes of a Stranger　1980
Horror
58230　82 mins　C　B, V　P
*Lauren Tewes, John Disanti, Jennifer Jason
Leigh, directed by Ken Wiederhorn*
A terrifying maniac stalks his female prey by
watching their every move.
MPAA:R
Georgetown Productions — *Warner Home
Video*

Eyes of Laura Mars　1978
Mystery
Closed Captioned
35377　104 mins　C　B, V　P
Faye Dunaway, Tommy Lee Jones
A photographer (Dunaway) exhibits strange
powers—she can foresee a murder before it
happens. Title song performed by Barbra
Streisand.
MPAA:R
Columbia — *RCA/Columbia Pictures Home
Video; RCA VideoDiscs*

Eyes of Texas　1948
Western
14374　54 mins　B/W　B, V　P
Roy Rogers, Lynne Roberts, Andy Devine
Westerner turns his ranch into a camp for war-
orphaned boys.
Republic — *Video Connection; Captain Bijou*

Eyes of the Amaryllis, The　1982
Horror
80926　94 mins　C　B, V　P
Ruth Ford, Marsha Byrne, Guy Boyd
A young girl becomes involved in a mysterious
game when she arrives in Nantucket to care for
her invalid grandmother.
MPAA:R
Amaryllis Company — *Vestron Video*

Eyes Right　1926
Comedy-Drama
11387　65 mins　B/W　B, V, FO　P
Francis X. Bushman
An interesting portrayal of life in a military prep
school. (Silent.)
Goodwill — *Video Yesteryear*

Eyes, The Mouth, The　1983
Drama
70194　100 mins　C　B, V　P
*Lou Castel, Angela Molina, directed by Marco
Bellochio*
A young man has an affair with his dead twin
brother's fiancee. Happiness eludes them as
they are haunted by the dead man's memory. In
Beta Hi-Fi.
MPAA:R
Triumph Films — *RCA/Columbia Pictures
Home Video*

Eyewitness　1981
Suspense
47154　102 mins　C　B, V, CED　P
*William Hurt, Sigourney Weaver, Christopher
Plummer, James Woods, Steven Hill, directed
by Peter Yates*
The janitor of an office building tells a TV
reporter that he knows something about a
murder that took place in his building.
MPAA:R
20th Century Fox; Peter Yates — *CBS/Fox
Video*

F

Fables of the Green Forest　19??
Cartoons/Adventure
56750　55 mins　C　B, V　P

Animated
Johnny Chuck, Peter Cottontail, Chatter the Squirrel and other memorable Thorton W. Burgess characters come to life in "Whose Footprint Is That?" and "Johnny's Hibernation." Available in English and Spanish versions.
EL, SP
ZIV International — *Media Home Entertainment*

Fabulous Adventures of   1979
Baron Munchausen, The
Adventure/Cartoons
80689   77 mins   C   B, V   P
Animated
The legendary Baron Munchausen tells the story of his trek to the strange and beautiful land of Trukesban.
Jean Image Productions — *Vestron Video*

Fabulous Dorseys, The   1947
Musical/Drama
01609   91 mins   B/W   B, V   P
Tommy and Jimmy Dorsey and Orchestras, Janet Blair, Paul Whiteman, Directed by Alfred E. Green
The musical lives of Tommy and Jimmy Dorsey are portrayed in this biographical film. Guest stars include Art Tatum, Charlie Barnet, Ziggy Elman, Bob Eberly and Helen O'Connell.
UA; Charles R Rogers — *Movie Buff Video; Hal Roach Studios; Hollywood Home Theater; Video Connection; Video Yesteryear; Discount Video Tapes; Nostalgia Merchant; Republic Pictures Home Video; Kartes Video Communications*

Fabulous Fifties, The   19??
History-US/Documentary
10150   mins   B/W   B, V   P, T
Film covers MacArthur's "Old Soldier's Speech," Eisenhower and Nixon, Korea, Stalin's death, hydrogen bomb testing, Suez Canal crisis, the Cold War, and Castro.
Unknown — *Blackhawk Films*

Fabulous Fleischer Folio,   193?
The
Cartoons
76813   50 mins   C   B, V   P
Animated 4 pgms
This series features classic cartoons from the early days of color at Max Fleischer's Studios.
Max Fleischer Studios — *Walt Disney Home Video*

Fabulous Funnies   1978
Cartoons
75493   60 mins   C   B, V   P
The cartoons in this video include Alley Oop, Broomhilda, Nancy and Sluggo and Tumbleweeds.

Unknown — *Prism*

Fabulous Funnies Volume   1984
2
Cartoons
70613   60 mins   C   B, V   P
Animated
Many familiar comic strip characters appear in this volume including Nancy and Sluggo, Alley Oop, Broomhilda, and the Captain and the Kids.
Videocraft International Ltd. — *Prism*

Fabulous Joe, The   1974
Comedy
66113   54 mins   C   B, V   P
Walter Abel
A dog named Joe gets involved in a necklace caper.
Hal Roach — *Unicorn Video*

Face in the Crowd, A   1957
Drama
81493   126 mins   B/W   B, V   P
Andy Griffith, Patricia Neal, Lee Remick, Walter Matthau, Anthony Franciosa, directed by Elia Kazan
A hillbilly entertainer becomes a major success thanks to his television program. Things take a turn for the worse when he starts to believe his own publicity.
Warner Bros; Newtown Prods. — *Warner Home Video*

Faces of Death   1974
Death/Documentary
65154   88 mins   C   B, V   P
Narrated by Dr. Frances B. Gross
This gruesome documentary looks at death experiences around the world, uncensored film footage offers graphic coverage of autopsies, suicides, executions, and animal slaughter. Not for the squeamish.
Rosilyn T Scott — *MPI Home Video; Gorgon Video*

Faces of Death Part II   1985
Death/Documentary
70580   84 mins   C   B, V   P
This sequel to "Faces of Death" further explores violent termination of man by man and by nature in a graphic-grisly gala. Not for the squeamish.
Rosilyn T. Scott — *MPI Home Video*

Fade to Black   1980
Horror/Suspense
63894   100 mins   C   B, V   P
Dennis Christopher, Tim Thomerson, Linda Kerridge
A young man obsessed with movies loses his grip on reality and adopts the personalities of

---

cinematic characters to seek revenge on people
who have wronged him.
MPAA:R EL, SP
Irwin Yablans; Sylvio Tabet — *Media Home
Entertainment*

Faerie Tale Theatre   1983
Fairy tales
Closed Captioned
69320   60 mins   C   B, V, LV,   P
                                 CED
*Shelley Duvall, Robin Williams, Elliot Gould, Jeff
Bridges, Christopher Reeve, Tatum O'Neal et al
17 pgms*
"Faerie Tale Theatre," conceived and produced
by Shelley Duvall, is a series of hour-long
enactments of classic fairy tales featuring many
well-known actors and actresses. All programs
are available individually.
*1.The Tale of the Frog Prince 2.Jack and the
Beanstalk 3.Rapuznel 4.Sleeping Beauty
5.Goldilocks and the Three Bears 6.Little Red
Riding Hood 7.Hansel and Gretal 8.
Rumpelstiltskin 9.Boy Who Left Home to Find
Out About the Shivers 10. Pinocchio 11.The
Snow Queen 12. The Three Little Pigs 13.The
Emperor's New Clothes 14.The Pied Piper of
Hamlin 15.Puss 'N Boots 16.Cinderella 17.The
Little Mermaid 18.The Dancing Princesses
19.The Princess Who Had Never Laughed.*
Shelley Duvall — *CBS/Fox Video*

Faeries   1981
Cartoons
71359   30 mins   C   B, V   P
*Animated, voices of Morgan Brittany, Hans
Conreid, June Foray*
The mystical inhabitants of "Faerie" dabble in
magic and illusion. Based on Brian Froud and
Alan Lee's best-selling book.
Tomorrow Entertainment — *Family Home
Entertainment*

Fahrenheit 451   1966
Science fiction
81817   112 mins   C   B, V   P
*Julie Christie, Oskar Werner, Cyril Cusack,
Anton Peffring, directed by Francois Truffaut*
This is a chilling adaptation of the Ray Bradbury
novel about a society that uses firemen to burn
books forbidden by the government. Available in
VHS and Beta Hi-Fi.
Universal Pictures; Vineyard Films Ltd — *MCA
Home Video*

Fail Safe   1964
Drama
Closed Captioned
63440   111 mins   B/W   B, V   P
*Henry Fonda, Dan O'Herlihy, Walter Matthau,
directed by Sidney Lumet*
A computer malfunction sets off events that
may possibly result in a nuclear war.

Columbia; Max E.
Youngstein — *RCA/Columbia Pictures Home
Video*

Fairy Tale Classics: 1983
Volumes I thru III
Fairy tales
69533   50 mins   C   B, V, CED   P
Animated 3 pgms
Each tape in this series compiles five or more
popular fairy tales from "Ali Baba and the Forty
Thieves" to Aesop's "The Tiger King."
MPAA:G
Toei Animation Productions — *Children's
Video Library*

Fairy Tale Classics: 19??
Volume II
Fairy tales
69612   60 mins   C   B, V   P
Animated
This collection of animated fairy tales includes
"The Owl and the Pussycat," "The Three
Bears," Aesop's fable of "The Tiger King,"
"Beanstalk Jack," and more.
Viacom International — *Children's Video
Library*

Fairy Tale of Tsar Saltan,   1978
The
Opera
84657   98 mins   C   B, V   P
*Lidija Rushizkaja, Rolf Wollard, Barbara Hoene,
the Dresden State Opera conducted by Harry
Kupfer*
A highly original and partly animated version of
the opera by Rimsky-Korsakov. Recorded in Hi-
Fi
RU
German — *V.I.E.W. Video*

Fairy Tales, Volume Two   1977
Fairy tales/Cartoons
73664   55 mins   C   B, V   P
Animated
Five animated versions of fairy tale classics are
available in one program: "Snow White," "The
Emperor's New Clothes," "The Twelve
Months," "The Happy Prince" and "The Three
Wishes."
Unknown — *Embassy Home Entertainment*

Fairy Tales, Volume I   1977
Cartoons
72868   55 mins   C   B, V   P
Some of the world's best fairy tales come to life,
including "Cinderella" and "Beauty and the
Beast."
Unkown — *Embassy Home Entertainment*

Fairytales 1979
Satire
55218   83 mins   C   B, V   P
Don Sparks, Prof. Irwin Corey, Brenda Fogarty
An enchanting musical fantasy for adults. In
order to save the kingdom, the prince must
produce an heir. The problem is that only the girl
in the painting of "Princess Beauty" can
"interest" the prince—and she must be found.
MPAA:R
Fairytales Distributing Company — *Media
Home Entertainment*

Fake Out 1982
Suspense/Drama
78389   89 mins   C   B, V   P
Pia Zadora, Telly Savalas, Desi Arnaz, Jr
A nightclub singer is caught between the mob
and the police who want her to testify against
her gangland lover.
Matt Cimber — *THORN EMI/HBO Video*

Falco: Rock Me Falco 1985
Music video
85668   20 mins   C   B, V   P
Four songs are performed by the German
dance-music artist.
A&M Video — *A & M Video*

Falcon and the Snowman, 1985
The
Suspense
Closed Captioned
77185   110 mins   C   B, V, CED   P
*Sean Penn, Timothy Hutton, Lori Singer, Pat
Hingle, directed by John Schlesinger*
This is the true story of two childhood friends
who become spies and sell American
intelligence secrets to the KGB. Pat Metheny
and Lyle Mays perform the musical score.
MPAA:R
Orion Pictures — *Vestron Video*

Falcon in Mexico, The 1944
Mystery
64381   70 mins   B/W   B, V, 3/4U   P
Tom Conway, Mona Maris, Nestor Paiva
The manhunt for a dangerous killer leads the
Falcon to Mexico.
RKO — *Nostalgia Merchant*

Falcon Takes Over, 1949
The/Strange Bargain
Mystery
76839   131 mins   B/W   B, V   P
*George Sanders, Ward Bond, Allen Jenkins,
Martha Scott, Henry Morgan, Hans Conried*
An exciting mystery double feature: In "The
Falcon Takes Over," The Falcon becomes
involved in a bogus fortunetelling scheme and in
"Strange Bargain" an underpaid bookkeeper
gets in on an insurance swindle.

RKO — *RKO HomeVideo*

Falcon's Adventure, 1950
The/Armored Car
Robbery
Mystery
81026   122 mins   B/W   B, V   P
*Tom Conway, Madge Meredith, William Talman,
Charles McGraw, Adele Jergens*
A mystery double feature: The Falcon uncovers
a vicious plot to steal a formula for synthetic
diamonds in "The Falcon's Adventure," and
four participants in an armored car robbery flee
after slaying a policeman in "Armored Car
Robbery."
RKO — *RKO HomeVideo*

Falcon's Brother, The 1942
Mystery
11299   64 mins   B/W   B, V, FO   P
*Tom Conway, George Sanders, Keye Luke,
Jane Randolph*
Enemy agents intent on killing a South
American diplomat are the targets of the
Falcon's brother.
RKO — *Nostalgia Merchant*

Fall of the House of 1960
Usher, The
Horror
53511   85 mins   C   B, V   P
*Vincent Price, Myrna Fahey, Mark Damon,
directed by Roger Corman*
The last of the Usher line is buried alive by her
brother and returns to wreak vengeance. Also
titled "House of Usher." Based on the story by
Edgar Allen Poe.
American Intl; Roger Corman — *Warner Home
Video*

Fall of the House of 1979
Usher, The
Drama
37362   101 mins   C   B, V   P
*Martin Landau, Robert Hays, Charlene Tilton,
Ray Walston*
Another version of Edgar Allan Poe's classic
tale of a family doomed to destruction through
insanity.
MPAA:PG
Sunn Classic — *United Home Video; Lucerne
Films*

Fall of the Roman Empire, 1964
The
Drama
16810   153 mins   C   B, V   P
Sophia Loren, Alec Guiness
The licentious son of Marcus Aurelius arranges
for his father's murder and takes over as
emperor.

Paramount; Samuel Bronston — *United Home Video; Lightning Video*

Fallen Idol   1949
Drama
03858   92 mins   B/W   B, V   P
Sir Ralph Richardson, Bobby Henrey, Michele Morgan, directed by Carol Reed
A young boy wrongly believes that a man he idolizes is guilty of murder, so the child tries to influence the police investigation of the crime. Screenplay by Graham Greene from his short story, "The Basement Room."
Selznick; British — *Prism; Hollywood Home Theater; Cable Films; Western Film & Video Inc; Movie Buff Video; Kartes Video Communications*

Falling for the Stars   1985
Documentary/Filmmaking
70667   58 mins   C   B, V   P
Richard Farnsworth, Harvey Perry, Polly Burson, Buddy Ebsen, Robert Duvall, Robert Conrad, Betty Thomas
This film shows both stars and their stunt-doubles talking about the perils involved in movie stunts. Using spectacular clips and insightful commentary, the program steps back from the camera to show familiar camaraderie of the stunt trade.
Walt Disney Productions — *Walt Disney Home Video*

Falling In Love   1984
Drama
Closed Captioned
70760   106 mins   C   B, V, LV   P
Robert De Niro, Meryl Streep, Harvey Keitel, Dianne Wiest, George Martin, directed by Ulu Grosbard
Two married New Yorkers unexpectedly fall in love after a coincidental meeting at the Rizzoli Book Store.
MPAA:PG-13
Paramount; Marvin Worth — *Paramount Home Video*

Falling in Love Again   1980
Comedy/Romance
64966   103 mins   C   B, V, CED   P
Elliot Gould, Susannah York
A middle-aged dreamer and his realistic wife travel from Los Angeles to their hometown of New York, where the man is filled with nostalgia for his youth.
MPAA:PG
Steven Paul — *Embassy Home Entertainment*

Fallout   1968
Fantasy/Adventure
70688   52 mins   C   B, V   P
Patrick McGoohan, Leo McKern, Alexis Kanner, Kenneth Griffith, directed by Patrick McGoohan

The final suspenseful episode of "The Prisoner" shows Number 6 in his final showdown with Numbers 1 and 2.
Associated TV Corp. — *MPI Home Video*

False Colors   1943
Western
80751   54 mins   B/W   B, V   P
William Boyd, Robert Mitchum, Andy Clyde, Jimmy Rogers
Hopalong Cassidy unmasks a crook posing as a murdered ranch heir. A rare print with Portugese subtitles.
United Artists — *Video Yesteryear*

False Faces   1932
Crime-Drama
85171   80 mins   B/W   B, V   P
Lowell Sherman, Peggy Shannon, Lila Lee, Joyce Compton, directed by Lowell Sherman
A ruthless, money-hungry quack is hounded by the law and the victims of his unscrupulous plastic surgery.
Samuel Goldwyn — *Video Yesteryear*

Falstaff   1983
Opera
72446   140 mins   C   LV   P
Shakespeare's Falstaff is brought to life in this operatic version of the rogue's exploits.
BBC Television; Covert Garden Video Productions Ltd — *THORN EMI/HBO Video; Pioneer Artists*

Falstaff   1976
Music-Performance
81584   123 mins   C   B, V   P
Donald Gramm, Bernard Dickerson, Ugo Trama, Reni Penkova, Kay Griffel.
This is a production of the Verdi opera performed by the Glyndebourne Festival Opera. With English subtitles.
IT
Dave Heather — *Video Arts International*

Fame   1980
Musical-Drama
56751   133 mins   C   B, V, LV,   P
                                CED
Irene Cara, Barry Miller, Paul McCrane, Anne Meara, Joanna Merlin, directed by Alan Parker
Eight talented teenagers from New York's High School of Performing Arts struggle to perfect their skills while aspiring to stardom.
Academy Awards '80: Best Song ("Fame"); Best Original Score (Michael Gore). MPAA:R
MGM — *MGM/UA Home Video*

Family, The   1973
Crime-Drama
72059   94 mins   C   B, V   P

Charles Bronson, Jill Ireland, Telly Savalas,
directed by Sergio Sollima
As a hit-man who resists joining the mob,
Charles Bronson initiates an all-out war on the
syndicate and its boss, played by Telly Savalas.
International Corp; Unidis and Fono
Roma — *MPI Home Video*

Family Circus Christmas, A
1979

Cartoons/Christmas
75468   30 mins   C   B, V   P
Animated
Cartoonist Bil Keane animates the Family Circus
at Christmas time.
Cullen Kasden Productions Ltd — *Family
Home Entertainment*

Family Circus Easter, A
1980

Cartoons/Holidays
75470   30 mins   C   B, V   P
Animated
Cartoonist Bil Keane animates an Easter with
the Family Circus.
Cullen Kasden Productions Ltd — *Family
Home Entertainment*

Family Circus Valentine
1978

Cartoons
76971   25 mins   C   B, V   P
Animated
The Family Circus Kids learn a lesson in humility
after making fun of baby PJ's Valentine's Day
card for his parents.
Cullen-Kasdan Productions — *Family Home
Entertainment*

Family Enforcer
1977

Drama
81685   82 mins   C   B, V   P
Joseph Cortese, Joe Pesci, Anne Johns
A small-time hoodlum is bent on becoming the
best enforcer in an underworld society.
MPAA:R
First American Films — *United Home Video*

Family Entertainment Playhouse, Vol. 2
1979

Literature
59644   106 mins   C   CED   P
A compilation of stories for children: "The
Ransom of Red Chief," based on O. Henry's
famed short story about a banker's son who is
kidnapped by bumbling conmen; "Mr. Gimme,"
about a boy who wants everything; "Shoeshine
Girl," where a young girl finds that a first job is
more than hard work; "Best Horse," about a
strong-willed teenager determined to win a
horse race.
Robert McDonald — *RCA VideoDiscs*

Family Game, The
1967

Game show
80749   29 mins   C   B, V   P
Hosted by Bob Barker
In "The Newlywed Game" fashion, mom and
dad return from the isolation booth to guess
what their children said about them in their
absence.
Chuck Barris — *Video Yesteryear*

Family Life
1972

Drama
59382   108 mins   C   B, V   P
*Sandy Ratcliff, Bill Dean, Grace Cave, directed
by Ken Loach*
A portrait of a 19-year-old girl in the midst of an
identity crisis (Also titled, "Wednesday's Child).
Cinema Five — *RCA/Columbia Pictures Home
Video*

Family Plot
1976

Suspense
11579   120 mins   C   B, V   P
*Karen Black, Bruce Dern, Barbara Harris,
William Devane, directed by Alfred Hitchcock*
Alfred Hitchcock's last film; the search for a
missing heir is undertaken by a phony psychic
and her private eye boyfriend. Their search ends
when they discover that the heir is dead—or is
he?
MPAA:PG
Universal — *MCA Home Video*

Family Upside Down, A
1978

Drama
85240   100 mins   C   B, V   P
*Helen Hayes, Fred Astaire, Efrem Zimbalist Jr.,
Patty Duke Astin*
An aging couple fight eventual separation after
the husband has a heart attack and is put into a
nursing home. Made for TV.
Ross Hunter; Jacque Mapes — *RCA/Columbia
Pictures Home Video*

Famous Generals
1964

Biographical
78970   60 mins   C   B, V   P
These two short films about the life and military
career of George S. Patton are narrated by
Ronald Reagan and President Dwight D.
Eisenhower.
Maljack Productions — *MPI Home Video*

Famous T and A
1982

Variety
59765   70 mins   C   B, V   P
*Ursula Andress, Brigitte Bardot, Jacqueline
Bisset, Sybil Danning, Claudia Jennings,
Nastassia Kinski, Joan Prather, Laurie Walters,
Edy Williams*
An all-star collection of recognizable
personalities who have displayed their celebrity
skins for the camera.

Ken Dixon — *Wizard Video*

Fan, The 1981
Suspense
53931   95 mins   C   B, V, LV   P
Lauren Bacall, Maureen Stapleton, James Garner, Hector Elizondo, directed by Edward Bianchi
A Broadway star is threatened by a lovestruck fan who feels he has been rejected by his idol.
MPAA:R
Robert Stigwood — *Paramount Home Video*

Fanciulla Del West, La 1983
Music-Performance/Opera
81487   135 mins   C   B, V   P
Placido Domingo, Carol Neblett, Silvano Carroli
This is a production of the Puccini opera about the California gold rush performed at London's Royal Opera House in Covent Garden.
National Video Corporation Ltd. — *THORN EMI/HBO Video*

Fandango 1985
Comedy
81084   91 mins   C   B, V   P
Judd Nelson, Kevin Costner, Sam Robards, Chuck Bush, Brian Cesak, directed by Kevin Reynolds
Five college roommates take a wild weekend drive across the Texas Badlands for one last fling before graduation. Available in VHS and Beta Hi-Fi Stereo.
MPAA:PG
Warner Bros., Amblin Entertainment — *Warner Home Video*

Fangface 1983
Cartoons
66573   60 mins   C   B, V   P
Animated
The adventures of Fangface, the teenage werewolf, and his crime-fighting friends Biff, Kim and Puggsy are featured on this tape.
Ruby Spears — *Worldvision Home Video*

Fangs 197?
Horror/Suspense
70980   90 mins   C   B, V   P
Les Tremayne, Janet Wood, Bebe Kelly, Marvin Kaplan, Alice Nunn
Unfriendly reptile-stomping villagers take the life of Mr. Snakey's favorite serpent. He sends his slithering pets on a vengeful and poisonous spree.
MPAA:R
Worldwide Films — *Video Gems*

Fanny 1932
Comedy
06320   128 mins   B/W   B, V   P
Raimu, Pierre Fresnay, Directed by Marcel Pagnol
Second part of Pagnol's trilogy depicting the lives, loves, joys, and sorrows of the people of Provence, France. French film, English subtitles.
FR
France — *Hollywood Home Theater; Discount Video Tapes*

Fanny 1961
Drama
63450   150 mins   C   B, V   P
Leslie Caron, Maurice Chevalier, Charles Boyer, Horst Buchholz
A young girl is left with child by an adventuresome sailor in the picturesque port of Marseilles. Part of the "Night at the Movies" series, this tape simulates a 1961 movie evening, with a Tweety Pie cartoon, "The Last Hungry Cat," a newsreel and coming attractions for "Splendor in the Grass" and "The Roman Spring of Mrs. Stone."
Warner Bros — *Warner Home Video*

Fanny and Alexander 1983
Drama
64992   197 mins   C   B, V, LV   P
Ewa Froling, Erland Josephson, directed by Ingmar Bergman
Set in a rural Swedish town in 1907, this film tells the story of one year in the lives of the Ekdahl family, focusing on the young children, Fanny and Alexander. In Swedish with English subtitles.
Academy Awards '83: Best Foreign Language Film Best Cinematography, Best Art Direction, Best Costume Design MPAA:R EL, SW
Cinematograph AB — *Embassy Home Entertainment*

Fantasies 1973
Drama
80134   81 mins   C   B, V   P
Bo Derek, Peter Hooten, directed by John Derek
Two unrelated children raised as brother and sister find that their childhood affection changes to passionate love as they grow older.
John Derek — *CBS/Fox Video*

Fantastic Adventures of Unico, The 1984
Cartoons
Closed Captioned
73860   89 mins   C   B, V   P
Animated
This is the animated story of a magical unicorn who can make everyone around him happy. With a purchase of the video cassette comes a Unico School Fun Kit. This program is available in Beta Hi-Fi.
AM Available
Shintaro Tsuji — *RCA/Columbia Pictures Home Video*

Fantastic All-Electric Music Movie, The — 1985
Music video/Video
70982   73 mins   C   B, V   P
Animated with music by Sonny and Cher, the Kinks, Melanie, Stan Kenton, Joni Mitchell, Jim Croce
This program combines some award-winning short cartoons with popular music soundtracks.
John Wilson — *Video Gems*

Fantastic Animation Festival — 1977
Fantasy/Cartoons
05415   91 mins   C   B, V   P
Animated
Fourteen award-winning animated shorts are combined into one feature-length program. Included are 'Closed Mondays," "The Last Cartoon Man," "French Windows," "Moonshadow," and "Cosmic Cartoon."
MPAA:PG
Crest Film Distributors — *Media Home Entertainment*

Fantastic Balloon Voyage, The — 198?
Adventure
64949   100 mins   C   B, V   R, P
Hugo Stiglitz, Jeff Cooper
Three men embark on a journey across the equator in a balloon, encountering countless adventures along the way.
MPAA:G
Unknown — *Video Gems*

Fantastic Planet — 1973
Science fiction
57352   68 mins   C   B, V, FO   P
Animated, directed by Rene Laloux
Mind-boggling imagery, vivid colors, and music tell the story of the "Revolt of the Oms"—survivors of Earth who are kept as pets.
Cannes Film Festival: Grand Prix.
New World Pictures — *Movie Buff Video; Embassy Home Entertainment; Video Yesteryear*

Fantastic Voyage — 1966
Science fiction
08425   100 mins   C   B, V   P
Stephen Boyd, Edmond O'Brien, Raquel Welch, Arthur Kennedy, Donald Pleasence, Arthur O'Connell
A famous scientist, rescued from behind the Iron Curtain, is so severely wounded by enemy agents that surgery is impossible.
Academy Awards '66: Best Art Direction.
20th Century Fox; Saul David — *CBS/Fox Video*

Fantasy in Blue — 197?
Drama
59547   81 mins   C   B, V   P
The search for the solution to a sexual stalemate results in a couple's strange experimentation.
Frederick Fox — *Media Home Entertainment*

Fantasy Island — 1976
Drama
80305   100 mins   C   B, V   P
Ricardo Montalban, Bill Bixby, Sandra Dee, Peter Lawford, Carol Lynley
Three people fly out to an island paradise and get to live out their fantasies.
Spelling/Goldberg Productions — *Prism*

Far Country, The — 1955
Western
85249   97 mins   C   B, V   P
James Stewart, Ruth Roman, Walter Brennan, Harry Morgan, Corinne Calvert, directed by Anthony Mann
Cattlemen must battle the Alaskan tundra and frontier lawlessness in this classic in the Mann canon.
U-1 — *Kartes Video Communications*

Far East — 1985
Drama
85911   105 mins   C   B, V   P
Bryan Brown, Helen Morse, directed by John Duigan
Two ex-lovers meet in Southeast Asia and join forces to find the woman's missing husband, a reporter.
Richard Mason — *Karl/Lorimar Home Video*

Far Out Space Nuts, Vol. I — 1975
Comedy
80768   48 mins   C   B, V   P
Bob Denver, Chuck McCann
Two NASA ground crewmen accidentally launch a spacecraft propelling themselves into the vastness of outer space.
Sid and Marty Krofft — *Embassy Home Entertainment*

Far Pavilions, The — 1984
Romance/Adventure
80331   108 mins   C   B, V   P
Ben Cross, Amy Irving, Omar Sharif, Christopher Lee
A British Officer falls in love with an Indian princess during the second Afghan War.
HBO; Goldcrest — *THORN EMI/HBO Video*

Farewell, My Lovely — 1975
Mystery
56456   95 mins   C   B, V   P
Robert Mitchum, Charlotte Rampling, Sylvia Miles, John Ireland

A remake of the 1944 Raymond Chandler mystery, "Murder, My Sweet," featuring private eye Phillip Marlowe hunting for an ex-convict's lost sweetheart.
MPAA:R
Avco Embassy — *Embassy Home Entertainment; RCA VideoDiscs*

Farewell to Arms, A   1932
Drama
11215   85 mins   B/W   B, V, FO   P
Helen Hayes, Gary Cooper
The original film version of Ernest Hemingway's novel about a tragic love affair between an ambulance driver and a nurse during World War I.
Academy Awards '33: Best Cinematography; Best Sound Recording.
Paramount — *Prism; Hal Roach Studios; Kartes Video Communications; Cable Films; Video Connection; Discount Video Tapes; Western Film & Video Inc; Cinema Concepts; Hollywood Home Theater; Video Yesteryear*

Fargo Express   1932
Western
11714   60 mins   B/W   B, V   P
Ken Maynard
Stagecoach hold-up in the Old West.
World Wide — *Video Connection; Discount Video Tapes; United Home Video*

Farmer's Daughter, The   1947
Comedy
64902   97 mins   B/W   B, V   P
Loretta Young, Joseph Cotten, Ethel Barrymore, Charles Bickford, Rhys Williams, Rose Hobart
Young portrays Katrin Holmstrom, a Swedish farm girl who runs for Congress and captures the heart of a congressman along the way.
Academy Awards '47: Best Actress (Young).
RKO; David O. Selznick — *CBS/Fox Video*

Farouk: Last of the Pharaohs   1985
Documentary
82561   50 mins   C   B, V, 3/4U   P
Narrated by Bernard Archard, directed by Peter Batty
This film chronicles the history of Egypt's last king, the infamous Farouk. The film also encompasses the growth of Egyptian nationalism and the beginnings of the Arab-Israeli conflict.
Peter Batty — *Evergreen International*

Fast Break   1979
Comedy
64238   107 mins   C   B, V   P
Gabe Kaplan, Harold Sylvester, Randee Heller
A deli clerk who is a compulsive basketball fan talks his way into a college coaching job.
MPAA:PG

Columbia — *RCA/Columbia Pictures Home Video*

Fast Fists, The   1987
Martial arts
64959   90 mins   C   B, V   P
Jimmy Wang Tu
A martial arts adventure.
Dragon Lady Productions — *Unicorn Video*

Fast Forward   1985
Musical
Closed Captioned
81428   110 mins   C   B, V   P
John Scott Clough, Don Franklin, Tracy Silver, Cindy McGee, directed by Sidney Poitier
A group of eight teenagers learn how to deal with success and failure when they enter a national dance contest in New York City.
Available in VHS Dolby Hi-Fi Stereo and Beta Hi-Fi Stereo.
MPAA:PG
Columbia; John Patrick Veitch — *RCA/Columbia Pictures Home Video*

Fast Lane Fever   1982
Drama
80854   94 mins   C   B, V   P
A drag racer challenges a factory worker to a no-holds-barred race. Available in Dolby Hi Fi Stereo for both formats.
MPAA:R
Cannon Films — *MGM/UA Home Video*

Fast Money   1983
Comedy/Adventure
71332   92 mins   C   B, V   P
Sammy Allred, Sonny Carl Davis, Marshall Ford, Doris Hargrave, Lou Perry, directed by Doug Holloway
Three Tex-Mex pot smugglers find that they've been double-crossed, and take to the air to avoid federal marshals.
MPAA:R
Doug Holloway — *U.S.A. Home Video*

Fast Talking   1986
Comedy
87910   93 mins   C   B, V   P
Rod Zuanic
The story of a quick-talking, charismatic, fifteen-year-old Australian boy's humorous though tragic criminal schemes.
Australian Critics Circle '86: Best Picture.
Australian — *Embassy Home Entertainment*

Fast Times at Ridgemont High   1982
Comedy
63359   92 mins   C   B, V, LV   P
Sean Penn, Jennifer Jason Leigh, Judge Reinhold, Phoebe Cates, Ray Walston

Based on the bestselling book by Cameron Crowe, this is the story of teenagers' struggles with independence, success, sexuality, money, maturity and school.
MPAA:R
Universal — *MCA Home Video*

Fast Walking   1981
Drama
81068   116 mins   C   B, V   P
James Woods, Kay Lenz, M. Emmet Walsh, Robert Hooks, Tim McIntire
A bigoted prison guard is offered fifty-thousand dollars to help a militant black leader escape from jail. Available in VHS and Beta Hi-Fi.
MPAA:R
Pickman Films; Lorimar Productions — *Key Video*

Fat Albert and the Cosby   1978
Kids
Cartoons
69626   60 mins   C   B, V   P
Animated, voice of Bill Cosby
In three separate cartoon episodes, Fat Albert and the Cosby Kids learn something important about life, growing up, and the people around them.
Filmation Studios — *THORN EMI/HBO Video*

Fat Albert and the Cosby   1982
Kids Cassette #2
Cartoons
65747   23 mins   C   B, V   P
Animated
This tape consists of two episodes, with Fat Albert teaching the viewer something important about life, the people around them and growing up.
Filmation — *THORN EMI/HBO Video*

Fat Albert and the Cosby   1984
Kids Cassette #3
Cartoons
78393   60 mins   C   B, V   P
Animated, voice of Bill Cosby
Fat Albert and the Cosby Kids are back with more cartoon fun and lessons about growing up.
Filmation Studios — *THORN EMI/HBO Video*

Fat Albert and the Cosby   1978
Kids, Cassette #4
Cartoons
81182   60 mins   C   B, V   P
Animated, voice of Bill Cosby
Fat Albert and the Cosby Kids are back to have some fun and teach everyone some important values in this collection of three episodes from the series. Available in Beta and VHS Hi-Fi.
Filmation — *THORN EMI/HBO Video*

Fat Boys on Video: Brr,   1986
Watch 'Em!
Music video
87630   30 mins   C   B, V   P
Darren Robinson, Mark Morales, Damon Wimbley
The three bovine doyens of aural percussion do their 'thing' in a series of videos.
Kris P.; Julie Pantelich; Lynda West — *MCA Home Video*

Fatal Attraction   1980
Drama
71128   90 mins   C   B, V   P
Sally Kellerman, Stephen Lack, John Huston, Lawrence Dane, directed by Michael Grant
Two lovers enjoy playing dangerous games with each other; but as the plots grow more involved, the stakes also rise.
Parasol Group — *Vestron Video*

Fatal Games   1984
Suspense
72904   88 mins   C   B, V   P
Young female athletes are mysteriously disappearing at the Falcon Academy of Athletics and a crazed killer is responsible.
Christopher Mankeiwicz — *Media Home Entertainment*

Fatal Glass of Beer, The   1933
Comedy
59403   18 mins   B/W   B, V   P, T
W.C. Fields, Rosemary Theby, George Chandler, Richard Cramer
Field's son returns to his home in the North Woods after serving a jail term.
Paramount — *Blackhawk Films; Festival Films*

Fatal Glass of Beer/The   1932
Pool Shark, The
Comedy
84949   29 mins   B/W   B, V   P
W.C. Fields
These two comedy shorts feature Fields at his slapstick best.
Sennett — *Blackhawk Films*

Father   1967
Drama
47459   89 mins   B/W   B, V, FO   P
After World War II, a Hungarian youth becomes obsessed with the facts surrounding his father's death at the hands of the enemy. Hungarian dialogue with English subtitles.
Hungarofilm — *Video Yesteryear*

Father Figure   1980
Drama
81155   94 mins   C   B, V   P
Hal Linden, Timothy Hutton, Cassie Yates, Martha Scott, Jeremy Licht

---

When a divorced man attends his ex-wife's funeral, he discovers that he must take care of his estranged sons.
Finnegan Associates; Time-Life Films — *Lightning Video*

Father Goose 1964
Comedy
64538   116 mins   C   B, V   P
Cary Grant, Leslie Caron, Trevor Howard
During World War II, a plane-spotter stationed on a remote Pacific isle finds himself stuck with a group of French refugee schoolgirls and their teacher.
Universal — *Republic Pictures Home Video*

Father Guido Sarducci Goes to College 1985
Comedy-Performance
70383   60 mins   C   B, V   P
Don Novello
The satirical character of the title is shown performing at a campus concert. The tape also includes footage from the padre's campus tours, and a glimpse into Sarducci's secret Vatican film archives.
Steve Binder — *Vestron Video*

Father Sergius 1917
Film-History
52344   84 mins   B/W   B, V, 3/4U   P
Directed by Yakov Protazanov
Classic Russian silent film, subtitled in English.
USSR — *International Historic Films; Video Yesteryear*

Father's Little Dividend 1951
Comedy
80739   82 mins   B/W   B, V   P
Spencer Tracy, Joan Bennett, Elizabeth Taylor, Don Taylor, directed by Vincette Minnelli
A father fears that his peace and quiet is about to be interrupted when he finds that he'll soon be a grandfather.
MGM — *Hal Roach Studios; Prism; Discount Video Tapes; Kartes Video Communications; Video Yesteryear*

Fats Domino Live! 1985
Music-Performance
87182   19 mins   C   B, V   P
The Fats performs in Los Angeles, featuring "Blueborry Hill," "Blue Monday," "Ain't That a Shame" and "I'm Ready."
Silver Eagle Records; MCA Home Video — *MCA Home Video*

Fatty and Mabel Adrift/Mabel, Fatty and the Law 1916
Comedy
64824   40 mins   C   B, V   P, T

Fatty Arbuckle, Mabel Normand, Al St. John, Minta Durfee, Teddy the Dog
Fatty and Mabel have problems enjoying their wedded bliss in these two silent shorts, which have a newly recorded orchestral score on the soundtrack.
Triangle Film; Keystone Film — *Blackhawk Films*

Fatty Finn 1984
Comedy
85881   91 mins   C   B, V   P
A children's gagfest about young kids and bullies during the Depression, based on Syd Nicholls' comic strip.
Unknown — *VidAmerica*

Fatty's Tin-Type Tangle/Our Congressman 192?
Comedy
59410   44 mins   B/W   B, V   P, T
Roscoe "Fatty" Arbuckle, Louise Fazenda, Edgar Kennedy, Frank Hayes, The Keystone Cops, Will Rogers, Jimmy Finlayson
In "Fatty's Tin-Type Tangle" (1915), Fatty and Louise are snapped by a traveling tintyper. In "Our congressman" (1924), Will Rogers offers an "expose" of political life.
Mack Sennett; Hal Roach — *Blackhawk Films*

Favorita, La 1952
Music-Performance
12823   80 mins   B/W   B, V, FO   P
Sophia Loren, voices of Palmira Vitali Marini, Gino Sinimberghi, Paolo Silveri, Alfredo Colella
The great Italian opera with Sophia Loren in a supporting role. Narrated in English.
Unknown — *Video Yesteryear*

Faye Emerson Show, The 1950
Variety
85172   29 mins   B/W   B, V   P
Faye Emerson, Nancy Talbot, Russell Patterson
Two complete Emerson shows, featuring the celebrity interviewing various cultural icons of the time.
NBC; CBS; ABC — *Video Yesteryear*

Fear 1981
Horror
77397   87 mins   C   B, V   P
A movie company arrives at an isolated island to make a film and winds up involved in murder, witchcraft, and deadly passion.
Independent — *Wizard Video*

Fear City 1985
Suspense
81480   93 mins   C   B, V   P

Billy Dee Williams, Tom Berenger, Jack Scalia, Melanie Griffith, Rae Dawn Chong, Joe Santos, Rossano Brazzi, directed by Abel Ferrara
Two partners who own a talent agency are after the psychopath who is killing off their prized strippers.
MPAA:R
Zupnick Curties Enterprises — THORN EMI/HBO Video

Fear in the Night   1972
Horror/Suspense
63342   82 mins   C   B, V   P
Judy Gesson, Joan Collins, Ralph Bates, Peter Cushing
The young bride of a school master in a boys' prep school becomes convinced that her husband intends to kill her while the school is closed for the holidays.
Hammer Films — THORN EMI/HBO Video

Fear No Evil   1980
Horror
64986   90 mins   C   B, V, CED   P
Stefan Arngrim, Kathleen Rowe McAllen, Elizabeth Hoffman
A teenager who is the human embodiment of the demon Lucifer commits acts of demonic murder and destruction. His powers are challenged by an 18-year-old girl, who is the embodiment of the archangel Gabriel.
MPAA:R
Avco Embassy — Embassy Home Entertainment

Fearless   1978
Drama/Mystery
84120   89 mins   C   B, V   P
Joan Collins, Maurizio Merli
An Italian detective has found a Viennese banker's daughter, but continues to pursue the unanswered questions of the case and embroils himself in a web of intrigue and plotting.
New World Pictures — New World Video

Fearless Young Boxer,   1973
The
Martial arts
84076   94 mins   C   B, V   P
A young man trains in martial arts in order to exact revenge for his father's murder.
Jimmy Shaw — Unicorn Video

Feel My Pulse   1928
Comedy
85486   86 mins   B/W   B, V   P
Bebe Daniels, Richard Arlen, William Powell, directed by Gregory La Cava
A rich fanatic leaves everything in his will to his young niece on the stipulation that she lead a germ-free life; when she reaches 21, she moves into the sanitarium she's inherited, not knowing

it has become a base for prohibition-era rumrunners.
Paramount — Video Yesteryear

Feel the Motion   1986
Musical
87606   98 mins   C   B, V   P
Sissy Kelling, Frank Meyer-Brockman, Ingold Locke, Falco, Meat Loaf
A young girl strives to rise to the top of the music business, amid established rock stars plying their wares.
Peter Zenk — Vidmark Entertainment

Feelin' Up   1976
Drama
80117   84 mins   C   B, V   P
A young man sells all his possessions to come to New York in search of erotic adventures.
MPAA:R
Troma Productions — Vestron Video

Fela in Concert   1981
Music-Performance
84647   57 mins   C   B, V   P
Fela Anikulapo Kuti and the Africa 70
A Paris concert by Fela Anikulapo Kuti, the Nigerian musician. This Afro-Pop festival is punctuated by exotic tribal dances and rituals. Recorded in Hi-Fi Stereo.
French — V.I.E.W. Video

Felix in Outer Space   1985
Cartoons
76861   55 mins   C   B, V   P
Animated
Felix and Poindexter travel through the galaxy to do battle with the evil duo of the Professor and Rock Bottom.
Felix the Cat Productions; Joseph Oriolo — Media Home Entertainment

Felix's Magic Bag of   1984
Tricks
Cartoons
72900   60 mins   C   B, V   P
Animated
The professor is after Felix's Magic Bag of Tricks once again in this collection of cartoon favorites.
Felix the Cat Productions; Joe Oriolo — Media Home Entertainment

Female Impersonator   1985
Pageant, The
Variety
80821   74 mins   C   B, V, LV   P
Hosted by Ruth Buzzi and Lyle Waggoner
Thirty of America's top female impersonators compete for the coveted title of Female Impersonator of the Year.

New World Video — *New World Video*

Fer-De-Lance   1974
Suspense
80488   120 mins   C   B, V   P
David Janssen, Hope Lange, Ivan Dixon, Jason Evers
A stricken submarine is trapped at the bottom of the sea, with a nest of deadly snakes crawling through the ship.
Leslie Stevens Productions — *Worldvision Home Video*

Ferry to Hong Kong   1959
Adventure
59831   103 mins   C   B, V   P
Curt Jurgens, Orson Welles, Sylvia Sims
A world-weary traveler comes aboard the "Fat Annie," a ship skippered by the pompous Captain Hart. The two men clash, until an act of heroism brings them together.
George Maynard — *Embassy Home Entertainment*

Festival of Funnies, A   1980
Football
50089   48 mins   C   B, V, FO   R, P
The lighter side of pro football. Wacky plays and zany players provide fun and entertainment in a new collection of NFL comedy action. Contains "Sym Funny," "The Jar 'Em and Daze 'Em Circus," "Believe It or Else," and other shorts.
NFL Films — *NFL Films Video; Champions on Film and Video*

Feud of the West   1935
Western
14656   60 mins   B/W   B, V   P
Hoot Gibson
Old West disagreements settled with guns.
Grand National — *United Home Video; Video Connection; Discount Video Tapes*

Ffolkes   1980
Adventure
81201   99 mins   C   B, V   P
Roger Moore, James Mason, Anthony Perkins, David Hedison, Michael Parks, directed by Andrew V. McLaglen
Rufus Excalibur ffolkes is in eccentric underwater expert who is called upon to stop a madman from blowing up an oil rig in the North Sea.
MPAA:PG
Universal; Elliott Kastner — *MCA Home Video*

Fiction Makers, The   1967
Adventure/Suspense
68230   102 mins   C   B, V   P
Roger Moore, Sylvia Sims
Roger Moore stars as Templer, a sophisticated detective who is hired to help Amos Klein. Amos

Klein is just an alias for a beautiful novelist who is being threatened by the underworld crime ring.
ATV/ITC — *CBS/Fox Video*

Fiddler on the Roof   1971
Musical
37524   184 mins   C   B, V, LV   P
Topol, Norma Crane, Leonard Frey, Molly Picon, directed by Norman Jewison
This movie, based on the long-running Broadway musical, is the story of a poor Jewish farmer at the turn of the century in a small Ukranian village, his five dowry-less daughters, his lame horse, his wife, and his companionable relationship with God.
Academy Awards '71: Best Cinematography; Best Adaptation and Original Song Score; Best Sound. MPAA:G
United Artists — *CBS/Fox Video; RCA VideoDiscs*

Fidelio   1979
Music-Performance
77458   130 mins   C   B, V   P
A production of the Beethoven opera taped at the Glyndebourne Festival in Great Britain. With English subtitles.
GE
Southern Television — *Video Arts International*

Field Dressing and   1985
Trophy Care for the
Wilderness Hunter
Hunting
87653   102 mins   C   B, V   P
Hughie Lyons, Mike O'Haver
These two taxidermists demonstrate how to harvest deer and antelope corpses, with special attention paid to eyes, lips and salting.
Sportsmen On Film — *Sportsmen on Film*

Fiend   1983
Drama/Horror
70597   93 mins   C   B, V   P
Don Liefert, Richard Nelson, Elaine White, George Stover
Longfellow, the small-town music teacher, feeds parasitically on his students to satisfy his supernatural hunger. His neighbor suspects some discord.
Unknown — *Prism*

Fiend, The   1973
Horror
85374   87 mins   C   B, V   P
Ann Todd, Patrick Magee, Tony Beckley, Madeline Hinde
A religious cultist, already unbalanced, grabs a knife and starts hacking away Jack-the-Ripper style.
MPAA:R

Robert Hartford-Davis — *Monterey Home Video*

Fiend Without a Face   19'5
Science fiction
59404   77 mins   B/W   B, V   P, T
Marshall Thompson, Terence Kilburn
A scientist materializes primal human impulses into blood-thirsty flying brains with tails that besiege a house of isolated victims. A ridiculous, surreal closed-cage of a film, with a great gory, paranoid climax.
Producers Associates — *Blackhawk Films; Republic Pictures Home Video*

Fiendish Plot of Dr. Fu   1980
Manchu, The
Comedy
52718   108 mins   C   B, V   P
Peter Sellers, David Tomlinson, Sid Caesar
Peter Sellers' last film concerns Dr. Fu's desperate quest for the necessary ingredients for his secret life-preserving formula.
MPAA:PG
Orion Pictures — *Warner Home Video*

Fiesta   1941
Musical/Comedy
56908   44 mins   C   B, V, FO   P
Anne Ayars, George Negrete, Armida
A girl comes from Mexico City to her father's hacienda where her old boyfriend awaits her return with a proposal of marriage. Full of authentic Mexican dances and music.
Hal Roach — *Video Yesteryear; Discount Video Tapes; Hal Roach Studios*

Fifth Avenue Girl   1939
Comedy
79683   83 mins   B/W   B, V   P
Ginger Rogers, Walter Connolly, Tim Holt, James Ellison, directed by Gregory La Cava
An unhappy millionaire takes a poor homeless girl into his care to brighten his life.
RKO — *RKO HomeVideo*

Fifth Day of Peace, The   1972
Drama/World War II
71190   95 mins   C   B, V   P
Richard Johnson, Franco Nero, Larry Aubrey, Helmut Schneider
Set in the War's closing days, this story finds 2 German P.O.W.s on trial for desertion. The Canadian commandant of the camp faces a great moral crisis when the ranking Nazi prisoners demand the right to execute their traitors.
MPAA:PG
Scotia Int'l; Silvio Clementelli — *Prism*

Fifth Floor, The   1980
Mystery/Suspense
69304   90 mins   C   B, V   P
Bo Hopkins, Dianne Hull, Patti D'Arbanville, Mel Ferrer
An alleged suicide victim struggles to prove her innocence and maintain her sanity within the walls of an asylum. The only way out is to escape.
MPAA:R
Howard Avedis — *Media Home Entertainment*

55 Days at Peking   1963
Drama
16811   150 mins   C   B, V   P
Charlton Heston, Ava Gardner
The Chinese people's resentment against the infiltration of Western ideas erupts into violence against missionaries and foreigners.
Samuel Bronston — *Lightning Video; United Home Video*

$50,000 Reward   1925
Western
65226   49 mins   B/W   B, V   P
Ken Maynard, Esther Ralston, Tarzan the Horse
Ken Maynard's first Western finds him being victimized by an unscrupulous banker who wants Ken's land deeds for property on which a new dam is being built.
Davis Distributing — *Blackhawk Films*

50 Years of Baseball   1980
Memories
Baseball
33829   30 mins   B/W   B, V   P
Babe Ruth, Lou Gehrig, Tris Speaker, Ty Cobb, Mel Ott, Joe DiMaggio, Warren Spahn, Mickey Mantle
A thrilling and nostalgic look at some of the most outstanding players in baseball history. Scenes of baseball's most memorable moments, dating back to the teens and twenties, are included.
Lou Fonseca — *Major League Baseball Productions*

Fight for Survival   1977
Martial arts
65327   101 mins   C   B, V   P
Shang Kuan Ling-Feng
A young female aspirant of kung fu must recover sacred books that were stolen by disguised kung fu masters.
MPAA:R
Fann Jiann Gong; Lee Lin Lin — *CBS/Fox Video*

Fight for Your Life   1979
Drama
79332   89 mins   C   B, V   P
William Sanderson, Robert Judd, Lela Small

Three criminals who narrowly escape from an accident take a hostage and head for the Canadian border.
Canada — *Monterey Home Video*

Fighter, The   1983
Drama
75454   96 mins   C   B, V   P
Gregory Harrison, Glynnis O'Connor
An out of work millworker decides to become an amateur boxer against his wife's wishes.
King Features — *U.S.A. Home Video*

Fightin' Ranch   1930
Western
84834   60 mins   B/W   B, V   P
Ken Maynard
A famous lawman saves his reputation, previously tainted. A Maynard classic.
Tiffany; Ken Maynard — *United Home Video*

Fighting Back   1982
Crime-Drama
82539   99 mins   C   B, V   P
Tom Skerritt, Patti LuPone, Michael Sarrazin, Yaphet Kotto, directed by Lewis Teague
An angry resident in a crime-ridden neighborhood organizes a patrol of armed civilian vigilantes.
MPAA:PG-13
Dino De Laurentiis — *Paramount Home Video*

Fighting Black Kings   1976
Martial arts/Adventure
66129   90 mins   C   B, V   P
Martial arts and karate masters appear in this tale of action.
MPAA:PG
Unknown — *Warner Home Video*

Fighting Caravans   1932
Western
11373   80 mins   B/W   B, V, FO   P
Gary Cooper
Great outdoor adventure based on a story by Zane Grey.
Paramount — *Video Yesteryear*

Fighting Kentuckian, The   1949
Western
00283   100 mins   B/W   B, V, 3/4U   P
John Wayne, Oliver Hardy, Vera Ralston
Two-fisted story of romance and adventure set on the 1814 frontier.
Republic — *Nostalgia Merchant; Republic Pictures Home Video*

Fighting Life   1980
Martial arts/Adventure
60513   90 mins   C   B, V   P
The tale of two brothers who overcome immense physical and emotional handicaps and become vital members of society. The two stars of the film are both physically handicapped.
Unknown — *Master Arts Video*

Fighting Marines, The   1936
War-Drama
57353   69 mins   B/W   B, V, FO   P
Jason Robards, Grant Withers, Ann Rutherford, Pat O'Malley
The U.S. Marines are trying to establish an airbase on Halfway Island in the Pacific, but are thwarted by the "Tiger Shark," a modern-day pirate. First appeared as a serial.
Mascot — *Video Yesteryear*

Fighting Parson   1935
Western
84843   65 mins   B/W   B, V   P
Hoot Gibson
In order to infiltrate a lawless town, Hoot dresses as a revivalist preacher.
Universal — *United Home Video*

Fighting Prince of   1966
Donegal, The
Adventure
88343   110 mins   C   B, V   P
Peter McEnery, Susan Hampshire, Tom Adams, Gordon Jackson, Andrew Keir
An Irish prince swashbuckles and battles the invading British in 16th Century Ireland.
Walt Disney Prod. — *Walt Disney Home Video*

Fighting Seabees, The   1944
War-Drama
59092   100 mins   B/W   B, V   P
John Wayne, Susan Hayward, Dennis O'Keefe
A salute to the Navy's construction corps, with the Duke as a tough foreman fighting the Japanese and Navy regulations.
Republic — *Republic Pictures Home Video*

Fille Mal Gardee, La   1981
Dance
59873   110 mins   C   B, V   P
Two young lovers must overcome a disapproving mother as well as divergent social standing in this performance by the Royal Ballet.
Covent Garden Video — *THORN EMI/HBO Video; Pioneer Artists*

Film Firsts   1960
Film-History
10155   51 mins   B/W   B, V   P, T
Documentary-style look at early film segments from the "History of the Motion Picture" series. Includes the first attempt at science fiction with Georges Melies' "Trip to the Moon" (1902); and the first cartoon and western.
Killiam — *Blackhawk Films*

Film House Fever 1986
Exploitation
88031   58 mins   C   B, V   P
Jamie Lee Curtis, James Keach, Lon Chaney
Jr., Harvey Korman
A compilation of clips from sleazy, cult-esque
movies, including "Blood Feast" and "Hot
Night at the Go Go Lounge."
Vestron Video — Vestron Video

Filming the Big 193?
Thrills/Filming the
Fantastic
Documentary/Disasters
60054   20 mins   B/W   B, V   P, T
"Big Thrills" includes scenes of the 1920's
Florida hurricane, 1930's floods of the
Mississippi and Ohio rivers, the tragedy of the
Hindenburg, and more. "Fantastic" shows giant
boys and midget girls, a library of books inside a
walnut, a young man wearing a drape of
honeybees and more.
20th Century Fox — Blackhawk Films

Final Assignment 1982
Suspense/Drama
80045   97 mins   C   B, V, CED   P
Genevieve Bujold, Michael York, Burgess
Meredith, Colleen Dewhurst.
A Canadian television reproter agrees to
smuggle a dissident Soviet scientist's ill
granddaughter out of Russia for treatment.
Persephone Productions — Vestron Video

Final Comedown, The 1972
Exploitation
86596   84 mins   C   B, V   P
Billy Dee Williams, directed by Oscar Williams
A black revolutionary attempts to get white
radicals behind his war against racism. He fails
and starts a racial bloodbath.
MPAA:R
Oscar Williams — Charter Entertainment

Final Conflict, The 1981
Horror
58846   108 mins   C   B, V, CED   P
Sam Neill, Lisa Harrow, Barnaby Holm, Rossano
Brazzi
The third installment in the "Omen" series,
concerning Damien, now 32, who has become
the head of an international conglomerate.
MPAA:R
20th Century Fox — CBS/Fox Video

Final Countdown, The 1980
Drama
64893   92 mins   C   B, V, CED   P
Kirk Douglas, Martin Sheen, Katherine Ross,
James Farentino, Charles Durning
A nuclear warship is transported back in time to
Pearl Harbor just hours before the fateful
bombing that started World War II.

MPAA:PG
Bryna Company; Peter Vincent
Douglas — Vestron Video

Final Exam 1981
Horror
66050   90 mins   C   B, V, CED   P
Cecile Bagdadi, Joel Rice
A psychotic killer stalks college students during
exam week.
MPAA:R
John Chambliss — Embassy Home
Entertainment

Final Executioner, The 1983
Fantasy/Adventure
82354   95 mins   C   B, V   P
William Mang, Marina Costo, Harrison Muller,
Woody Strode
A valiant man finds a way to stop the slaughter
of innocent people in a post-nuclear world.
L'Immagine — MGM/UA Home Video

Final Justice 1984
Crime-Drama
82449   90 mins   C   B, V   P
Joe Don Baker, Rossono Brazzi, Patrizia
Pellegrino
A small-town Texan sheriff wages a war against
crime and corruption that carries him to Italy and
the haunts of Mafia hitmen.
MPAA:R
Arista Films — Vestron Video

Final Mission 1984
Crime-Drama
70957   101 mins   C   B, V   P
Richard Young, John Dresden, Kaz Garaz,
Christine Tudor
A vengeful one-man army follows the
professional hit man who slaughtered his family
from L.A. to Laos. His pursuit leads to a jungle
showdown.
Independent — THORN EMI/HBO Video

Final Programme, The 1981
Science fiction/Fantasy
63328   85 mins   C   B, V   P
Jon Finch, Jenny Runacre, Sterling Hayden,
Patrick Magee
In this futuristic story, a man must rescue his
sister and the world from their brother who
holds a microfilmed plan for global domination,
and himself from a bisexual computer
programmer who wants to make him father to a
new, all-purpose human being.
EMI Films Ltd — THORN EMI/HBO Video

Final Terror, The 1984
Horror
76776   90 mins   C   B, V, CED,   P
                                   LV

Daryl Hannah, Rachel Ward, Adrian Zmed
A group of campers are stalked by a mad killer stalking the forest looking for innocent victims.
MPAA:R
Samuel Arkoff — *Vestron Video*

Find A Way—Amy Grant   1985
Music video
82329   30 mins   C   B, V   P
Amy Grant delivers her own brand of gospel rock in this collection of three music videos from her "Unguarded" album. In VHS Dolby Hi-Fi Stereo and Beta Hi-Fi Stereo.
A&M Video — *A & M Video; RCA/Columbia Pictures Home Video*

Finders Keepers   1984
Comedy
81838   96 mins   C   B, V   P
Michael O'Keefe, Beverly D'Angelo, Ed Lauter, Louis Gossett Jr., Pamela Stephenson, Jim Carrey, David Wayne, directed by Richard Lester
A wild assortment of characters on board a train en route from California to Nebraska search for five million dollars hidden in the baggage car. Available in VHS and Beta Hi-Fi.
MPAA:R
CBS Theatrical Films — *Key Video*

Finding Your Own   1985
Fundamentals
Golf
88068   25 mins   C   B, V   P
Jim Flick demonstrates pre-swing golf essentials.
NFL Films; Golf Digest — *NFL Films Video*

Fine Madness, A   1966
Comedy
88180   104 mins   C   B, V   P
Sean Connery, Joanne Woodward, Jean Seberg, Patrick O'Neal, Colleen Dewhurst, Clive Revill, John Fiedler, directed by Irvin Kershner
A near-classic comedy about a lusty, rebellious poet thrashing against the pressures of the modern world, and fending off a bevy of lobotomy-happy psychiatrists.
Jerome Hellman — *Warner Home Video*

Finessing the King   1984
Mystery
80449   60 mins   C   B, V   P
James Warwick, Francesca Annis
Private eyes Tommy and Tuppence follow a mysterious newspaper notice to a masked ball where a murder is about to occur. Based on the Agatha Christie Story.
London Weekend Television — *Pacific Arts Video*

Finest Hours, The   1964
World War II/Documentary
71189   116 mins   C   B, V   P
Directed by Peter Baylis, narrated by Orson Welles
Sir Winston Churchill, removed as Lord of the Admiralty after World War I's Dardanelles campaign, later went on to lead Great Britain as Prime Minister through the Second World War. This film studies that period in his life.
Peter Baylis — *Prism*

Fingers   1978
Crime-Drama
84131   89 mins   C   B, V   P
Harvey Keitel, Tisa Farrow, directed and written by Jambe Toback
A hard-line debt collector approaches the brink of reason because of his fading dreams to be a concert pianist and his obsession with an uninterested prostitute.
MPAA:R
Georg Barrie — *Media Home Entertainment*

Finian's Rainbow   1968
Musical
74204   141 mins   C   B, V, LV   P
Fred Astaire, Petula Clark
This is the story of a leprechaun who is out to resteal a pot of gold taken by an Irishman and his daughter.
MPAA:G
Joseph Landon — *Warner Home Video*

Fiona   1978
Drama
66199   82 mins   C   B, V   P
Fiona Richmond, Victor Spinetti
A ravishing blonde exposes her legendary sexual appetite.
Assay Films Ltd — *U.S.A. Home Video*

Fire   1977
Adventure
87679   98 mins   C   B, V   P
Ernest Borgnine, Vera Miles, Patty Duke Astin, Alex Cord, Donna Mills
A fire raging through Oregon timberland is the focal dramatic point in this made-for-TV Irwin Allen disaster drama.
Irwin Allen — *Warner Home Video*

Fire and Ice   1983
Adventure/Fantasy
65463   81 mins   C   B, V   P
Animated, directed by Ralph Bakshi
An animated adventure film that culminates in a tense battle between good and evil, surrounded by the mystical elements of the ancient past. In stereo VHS and Beta Hi-Fi.
MPAA:PG

Ralph Bakshi; Frank Frazetta; Producers Sales Organization — *RCA/Columbia Pictures Home Video*

Fire Down Below   1957
Adventure
87753   116 mins   C   B, V   P
Robert Mitchum, Jack Lemmon, Rita Hayworth, directed by Robert Parrish
Two buddies smuggle a lovely, mysterious woman onto a Caribbean island, and succumb to her charms and their own conflicting desires.
Columbia; Warwick Film Prod. — *RCA/Columbia Pictures Home Video*

Fire in the Night   1985
Martial arts
88185   89 mins   C   B, V   P
Graciela Casillas, John Martin
In a small Southern town, a beautiful and sharp-footed woman battles the illimitable resources of the town's predominant dynastic family.
Unknown — *New World Video*

Fire Over England   1937
Drama
11232   81 mins   B/W   B, V, FO   P
Flora Robson, Raymond Massey, Laurence Olivier, Vivien Leigh
Spain and Great Britain engage in war while Queen Elizabeth is torn between duty and personal desire.
United Artists, British — *Movie Buff Video; Video Yesteryear; Hollywood Home Theater; Cable Films; Discount Video Tapes; Western Film & Video Inc; Kartes Video Communications; Prism*

Firebird 2015 A.D.   1981
Science fiction
65717   97 mins   C   B, V   P
Darren McGavin, Doug McClure
A tongue-in-cheek adventure involving a 21st century society where automobile use is banned because of extreme oil shortage.
MPAA:PG
Glen Ludlow — *Embassy Home Entertainment*

Firecracker   1971
Martial arts/Adventure
63086   83 mins   C   B, V   P
Jillian Kessner, Darby Hinton
A female Martial arts expert retaliates against the crooks who murdered her sister.
New World Pictures — *Monterey Home Video*

Firefox   1982
Adventure
62886   136 mins   C   B, V, LV,   P
                                        CED
Clint Eastwood, directed by Clint Eastwood

A special agent sneaks into the Soviet Union to steel a top-secret Russian warplane and fly it out of the country. VHS in stereo.
MPAA:PG
Warner Bros — *Warner Home Video*

Fireman, The   1916
Comedy
10648   20 mins   B/W   B, V, 3/4U   R, P, DL
Charlie Chaplin
Chaplin portrays a fireman who becomes a hero. (Silent; musical soundtrack added.)
RKO — *Cable Films; Festival Films*

Firemen's Ball   1968
Comedy
66014   73 mins   C   B, V   P
Josef Svet, directed by Milos Forman
A comedy about an honorary ball held for a retiring fire chief. Czech dialogue, subtitled in English.
CZ
Barrandov Film Studios — *RCA/Columbia Pictures Home Video*

Firepower   1979
Drama/Suspense
69381   104 mins   C   B, V   P
Sophia Loren, James Coburn, O.J. Simpson, Christoper F. Bean
A U.S. government agent is sent to the Caribbean to capture an American multimillionaire engaged in illegal activities and bring him to justice.
MPAA:R
Associated Film Distributors — *CBS/Fox Video*

Fires on the Plain   1959
Drama
51948   105 mins   B/W   B, V   P
Eiji Funakoshi, Osamu Takizawa, Mickey Custis, Asao Suno, directed by Kon Ichikawa
A group of men from the Japanese Army struggle to survive the perils of war in this disturbing drama. One soldier maintains his humanity while those around him resort to any crime. Japanese dialogue, English subtitles.
JA
Japanese — *Hollywood Home Theater; Festival Films; Video Action; Discount Video Tapes*

Fireside Theatre: 195?
Sergeant Sullivan
Speaking
Comedy-Drama
66120   24 mins   B/W   B, V   P, T
William Bendix, Joan Blondell, William Fawcett, Sarah Selby

From the TV series "Return Engagement," a romance blossoms over the telephone between a youthful widow and a police sergeant.
Procter and Gamble — *Blackhawk Films*

Firesign Theatre Presents Nick Danger in The Case of the Missing Yolk, The   1983
Comedy
63389   60 mins   C   B, V, CED   P
The Firesign Theatre (Phil Proctor, Phil Austin, Peter Bergman)
Firesign characters Nick Danger and Rocky Rococo are featured in this story of a truly interactive family who live through their television set.
VHD Programs; Pacific Arts Corporation — *Pacific Arts Video*

Firestarter   1984
Horror
70157   115 mins   C   B, V, LV   P
Drew Barrymore, George C. Scott, Heather Locklear, David Keith, directed by Mark Lester
A C.I.A. like organization is after a little girl who has the ability to set anything on fire in this filmed adaptation of Stephen King's bestseller.
MPAA:R
Universal; Dino De Laurentis — *MCA Home Video*

First Aid: The Video Kit   1984
First aid
Closed Captioned
65755   95 mins   C   B, V   P
This program provides the viewer with "eyes-on" experience of basic first aid principles that could make the difference in those crucial seconds when a crisis strikes.
CBS Fox Video — *CBS/Fox Video*

First Aid Video Book, The   1981
First aid
52768   40 mins   C   B, V   P
Several emergencies, such as choking, poisoning, and shock are covered, with instructions on how to handle each emergency quickly.
Karl Video — *Karl/Lorimar Home Video*

First and Ten   1985
Comedy
82439   88 mins   C   B, V   P
Delta Borke, Geoff Scott, Reid Shelton, Ruta Lee, Fran Tarkenton
A failing football team emphasizes sexual, rather than athletic conquests, under the guidance of their female owner.
P and D Partners — *Vestron Video*

First Blood   1982
Drama
64335   96 mins   C   B, V, LV   P
Sylvester Stallone, Richard Crenna, Brian Dennehy, Jack Starrett
Stallone portrays a former Green Beret survivor of Vietnam whose nightmares of wartime horrors are triggered by a wrongful arrest.
MPAA:R
Orion Picture — *THORN EMI/HBO Video; RCA VideoDiscs*

First Born   1984
Drama
77446   100 mins   C   B, V, LV   P
Terri Garr, Peter Weller, Christopher Collet, directed by Michael Apted
A divorced woman's son tries to save her from her evil cocaine dealing boyfriend.
MPAA:PG-13
Paramount Pictures — *Paramount Home Video*

First Deadly Sin, The   1980
Drama
72918   112 mins   C   B, V   P
Frank Sinatra, Faye Dunaway, David Dukes, Brenda Vaccaro
A police lieutenant tracks down a homicidal killer in spite of family troubles which intrude on his work.
MPAA:R
Filmways; Artanis; Cinema Seven — *Warner Home Video*

First Family   1980
Comedy
58231   100 mins   C   B, V   P
Bob Newhart, Madeline Kahn, Gilda Radner, Richard Benjamin, directed by Buck Henry
A biting satire of life in the White House for one President and his family.
MPAA:R
Warner Bros — *Warner Home Video*

First Howie Mandel Special, The   1986
Comedy-Performance
87643   53 mins   C   B, V   P
The offbeat stand-up comic performs his favorite bits on stage at the Variety Dinner Theater in Toronto.
CBS/Fox — *CBS/Fox Video*

First Legion, The   1951
Drama
88235   77 mins   B/W   B, V   P
Charles Boyer, Barbara Rush, William Demarest, Leo G. Carroll, directed by Douglas Sirk
A rare, minor piece of Sirkian cinema about priests who are confronted with a supposed miracle.

United Artists — *Lightning Video*

First Love 1977
Romance
29765 92 mins C B, V P
William Katt, Susan Dey, John Heard, Beverly D'Angelo
A story of an idealistic college student who takes love, and especially making love, more seriously than the rest of his peers, including his girlfriend.
MPAA:R
Paramount — *Paramount Home Video*

First Love 1970
Drama
65158 90 mins C B, V P
John Moulder-Brown, Dominique Sanda, Maximilian Schell, Valentina Cortese, directed by Maximilian Schell
In the days before the 1917 Revolution, a young Russian boy meets and becomes infatuated with an impoverished princess. Years later, after war and strife have swept the country, he seeks her out again.
MPAA:R
Franz Seitz Filmproduktion; UMC Pictures — *United Home Video*

First Man Into Space 1959
Science fiction/Adventure
70810 78 mins B/W B, V P
Marshall Thompson, Marla Landi, Robert Ayres, Carl Jaffe, Bill Edwards, directed by Robert Day
A daring young space cadet leaves behind the sweetheart he loves to make the grade in outer space.
MGM; John Croydon; Charles F. Vetter, Jr. — *Monterey Home Video*

First Monday in October 1981
Comedy
58710 99 mins C B, V, LV P
Walter Matthau, Jill Clayburgh, Barnard Hughes, James Stephens, directed by Ronald Neame
A comedy concerning the first woman appointed to the Supreme Court and her colleague, a crusty but benign liberal judge.
MPAA:R
Paramount — *Paramount Home Video*

First Nudie Musical, The 1975
Comedy
12700 93 mins C B, V P
Cindy Williams, Stephan Nathan, Diana Canova, Bruce Kimmel
Producer attempts success by staging a nudie musical in 1930's style.
MPAA:R
Jack Reeves — *Media Home Entertainment; Hollywood Home Theater*

First Spaceship on Venus, The 1964
Science fiction
11717 78 mins C B, V P
Yoko Tani
Eight scientists set out for Venus and find the remains of a civilization far in advance of Earth's.
Crown International — *United Home Video*

First Time, The 1982
Comedy
66023 96 mins C B, V P
A comedy about a college student who can't quite succeed with women.
Sam Irvin — *THORN EMI/HBO Video*

First Turn On, The 1983
Adolescence/Exploitation
70691 84 mins C B, V P
Sheila Kennedy, Michael Sanville, Googy Gress, Jenny Johnson, Heide Basset, directed by Michael Hertz and S. Weil
Not to be confused with "The Thomas Edison Story," this film follows the adventures of five young campers who decide to die happy when an avalanche leaves them un-rescueably trapped in a cave. A longer unrated version is available.
MPAA:R
Troma — *Lightning Video*

First Yank Into Tokyo 1945
War-Drama/Adventure
82182 83 mins B/W B, V P
Tom Neal, Richard Loo, Barbara Hale, Marc Cramer, directed by Gordon Douglas
An American army pilot undergoes plastic surgery, in order to infiltrate Japanese lines and rescue an American scientist.
RKO — *RKO Home Video*

Fish Hawk 1979
Adventure
72903 95 mins C B, V P
Will Sampson
When an alcoholic Indian, Fish Hawk, meets a young boy in the forest, and they strike up a friendship.
MPAA:G
Edgar J. Scherick; Stanley Chase — *Media Home Entertainment*

Fish that Saved Pittsburgh, The 1979
Comedy
80889 104 mins C B, V P
Jonathan Winters, Stockard Channing, Flip Wilson, Julius Erving, Meadowlark Lemon
A floundering basketball team hires an astrologer to try and change their luck.
MPAA:PG

Lorima Productions — *Karl/Lorimar Home Video*

Fishing U.S.A.   1969
Fishing
59072   105 mins   C   B, V   R, P
R. Vernon "Gadabout" Gaddis
Outdoor scenes from Maine to California,
including bass fighting on the line, are featured
in this program about fishing in America.
GG Communications — *Video Gems*

Fishing with Jimmy   1986
Houston Vol. 1
Fishing
86024   63 mins   C   B, V   P
The expert fisherman catches his biggest fish,
and in between gives tips on baiting, PH
breakline and crankbaits.
United Ent. — *United Home Video*

Fishing with Jimmy   1986
Houston Vol. 2
Fishing
86025   60 mins   C   B, V   P
Houston catches more huge fish and gives
advice on milking spinnerbaits,topwater baits
and fishing clear water.
United Ent. — *United Home Video*

F.I.S.T.   1978
Drama
53451   145 mins   C   B, V, CED   P
*Sylvester Stallone, Rod Steiger, Peter Boyle,
Melinda Dillon, Tony Lo Bianco, Kevin Conway,
Cassie Yates, directed by Norman Jewison*
The story of an idealistic labor union organizer
who works his way to the top of the union by
accepting mob favors which cost him his
integrity.
MPAA:R
United Artists; Norman Jewison — *CBS/Fox Video*

Fist   1979
Adventure/Martial arts
59085   84 mins   C   B, V   P
Richard Lawson, Annazette Chase, Dabney Coleman
A street fighter battles his way through the
urban jungle seeking personal freedom and
revenge.
MPAA:R
Larrabure Kaye — *HarmonyVision*

Fist of Fear—Touch of   1980
Death
Adventure
52858   90 mins   C   B, V   P
Bruce Lee, Fred Williamson, Lee Van Cleef

The three greatest martial arts masters star in
this kung-fu action adventure film. A compilation
of clips from Bruce Lee's films.
MPAA:R
Aquarius Releasing — *Wizard Video*

Fist of Vengeance   197?
Martial arts/Adventure
47703   90 mins   C   B, V   P
Shoji Karada, Lu Pi Chen
The East Asia Society hires a Samurai to kill a
young Chinese officer.
Sung Kuang Lung — *Master Arts Video*

Fistful of Dollars, A   1967
Western
58825   96 mins   C   B, V   P
*Clint Eastwood, Gian Maria Volonte, Marianne
Koch, directed by Sergio Leone*
An avenging stranger gets involved in a feud
between two powerful families.
United Artists; Harry Colombo; George
Papi — *CBS/Fox Video; RCA VideoDiscs*

Fists of Fury   1973
Adventure/Martial arts
55833   102 mins   C   B, V   P
Bruce Lee, Maria Yi
Bruce Lee stars in this violent Kung Fu action
adventure in which Lee must defend his honor
and break a solemn vow to avoid fighting.
MPAA:R
National General Pictures — *CBS/Fox Video;
Video City Productions; Master Arts Video;
Discount Video Tapes; Spotlite Video*

Fists of Fury II   1980
Adventure/Martial arts
44340   90 mins   C   B, V   R, P
Bruce Li, Ho Chung Do, Shum Shim Po
This story centers around character Chen Shan
(Bruce Li) and his efforts to survive the
Organizations' onslaughts to kill him. He
escapes their perilous plots only to return to
battle against them after they had killed his
mother for her inability to disclose Chen's hiding
place. Finally Chen defeats the evil Organization
himself.
MPAA:R
Four Seas Films — *Video Gems*

Fitzcarraldo   1982
Drama
66124   150 mins   C   B, V   P
*Klaus Kinski, Claudia Cardinale, directed by
Werner Herzog*
The epic story of a charismatic Irishman's
impossible quest to build an opera house in the
middle of the Amazon jungles.
Cannes Film Festival '82: Best Director.
MPAA:PG
New World Pictures — *Warner Home Video*

Five Came Back — 1939
Adventure
76837   93 mins   B/W   B, V   P
Lucille Ball, Chester Morris, John Carradine,
Wendy Barrie, Kent Taylor, directed by John
Farrow
When a plane with twelve passengers crashes
in the South American jungle, extenuating
circumstances cuts the number of survivors
down to five.
RKO — RKO HomeVideo

Five Days One Summer — 1982
Romance
66123   108 mins   C   B, V   P
Sean Connery, Betsy Brantley, Lambert Wilson,
directed by Fred Zinnemann
The story of a haunting and obsessive love
affair between a married Scottish doctor and a
younger woman.
MPAA:PG
Ladd Company — Warner Home Video

Five Golden Dragons — 1967
Crime-Drama
88173   92 mins   C   B, V   P
Robert Cummings, Christopher Lee, Brian
Donlevy, Klaus Kinski, George Raft, Dan
Duryea, Margeret Lee, directed by Jeremy
Summers
A typical actioneer about ruthless gold
trafficking in Hong Kong.
Harry Alan Towers — Republic Pictures Home
Video

Five Mile Creek — 1985
Adventure
70668   96 mins   C   B, V   P
Jack Taylor, Con Madigan, Jay Kerr, Liz Burch,
Gus Mercurio, Rod Mullinar, Louise Caire Clark,
Michael Caton, Priscilla Weems 13   pgms
Each tape in this series features two episodes
of this Australian frontier drama. Set against the
backdrop of the outback, settlers attempt to
establish footholds and fortunes while
preserving traditional values.
1. "Making Tracks" and "Horses for Courses"
2. "Love Before a Fall" and "A Few Surprises"
3. "The Scrub Bulls" and "Mothers and Fathers"
4. "Gold Fever" and "Annie" 5. "Home and
Away" and "The Awakening" 6. "The Prize" and
"Tricks of the Trade" 7. "Thanksgiving" and
"The Hangman's Noose" 8. "The Challenge"
and "Blood, Sweat and Faith" 9. "Mail Order
Brides" and "Maggie" 10. "Elaborate Practical
Joke" and "Desparate Bid to Save Him"
11. "Across the Great Divide" and "Missing,
Presumed Lost"
Walt Disney Productions — Walt Disney Home
Video

Five Weeks in a Balloon — 1962
Adventure
81512   101 mins   C   B, V   P

Fabian, Peter Lorre, Red Buttons, Sir Cedric
Hardwicke, Barbara Eden, directed by Irwin
Allen
This is an adaptation of the Jules Verne novel
about a British expedition that encounters many
adventures on their balloon trek to Africa.
Available in VHS and Beta Hi-Fi.
20th Century Fox — Playhouse Video

Fixx: Live in the USA, The — 1984
Music-Performance
81202   58 mins   C   B, V   P
New wave rockers The Fixx, perform such hits
as "Saved by Zero," "Deeper and Deeper" and
"One Thing Leads to Another" in this concert
video. Available in Hi-Fi stereo for both formats.
Loading Dock Film and Video — MCA Home
Video

Flame of the Barbary Coast — 1945
Western
00285   91 mins   B/W   B, V, 3/4U   P
John Wayne, Ann Dvorak
Cowboy vies with a gambling czar for a beautiful
dance hall queen and control of the Barbary
Coast.
Republic — Nostalgia Merchant; Republic
Pictures Home Video

Flame of the Islands — 1955
Adventure
88172   92 mins   C   B, V   P
Yvonne De Carlo, Howard Duff, Zachary Scott,
James Arness
Yvonne plays a sultry, passionate woman who
struggles with gangsters for possession of a
Bahamian casino.
Republic — Republic Pictures Home Video

Flaming Frontiers — 1938
Western/Serials
08872   300 mins   B/W   B, V, 3/4U   P
Johnny Mack Brown, Eleanor Hanson, Ralph
Bowman
A frontier scout matches wits against gold mine
thieves. In fifteen episodes.
Universal — Video Connection; Video
Yesteryear; Hollywood Home Theater; Discount
Video Tapes

Flaming Star — 1960
Drama
64931   92 mins   C   B, V   P
Elvis Presley, Dolores del Rio, Barbara Eden,
Steve Forrest, John McIntire
Set in 1870's Texas, a mixed Indian and white
family is caught in the midst of an Indian
uprising. A half-Indian youth must choose which
side he is on.
20th Century Fox — Key Video; CBS/Fox
Video (disc only)

Flamingo Kid, The   1984
Comedy
Closed Captioned
76764   100 mins   C   B, V, CED   P
Matt Dillon, Richard Crenna, Hector Elizondo, Jessica Walter, directed by Garry Marshall
A Brooklyn teenager finds out about life and love when he gets a summer job at a fancy beach club on Long Island.
MPAA:PG-13
Michael Phillips, Twentieth Century Fox — *Vestron Video*

Flamingo Lead   1939
Western
84835   57 mins   B/W   B, V   P
Ken Maynard
Maynard aids a female calvary horse-raiser amid various western adversities.
Ken Maynard — *United Home Video*

Flash Gordon   1980
Science fiction
56870   111 mins   C   B, V, LV   P
Sam J. Jones, Melody Anderson, Topol, Max von Sydow
Dino DeLaurentiis-produced version of the adventures of Flash Gordon in outer space. This time, Flash and Dale Arden are forced by Dr. Zarkov to accompany him on a mission to far-off Mongo, where Ming the Merciless is threatening the destruction of Earth. Music by Queen.
MPAA:PG
Universal, Dino DeLaurentiis — *MCA Home Video*

Flash Gordon Battles the   1979
Galactic Forces of Evil
Science fiction/Cartoons
81187   59 mins   C   B, V   P
Animated
Flash Gordon returns to battle with Ming The Merciless in this collection of adventures.
Don Christensen — *Media Home Entertainment*

Flash Gordon Conquers   1940
the Universe
Science fiction/Serials
08629   240 mins   B/W   B, V   P
Buster Crabbe, Carol Hughes, Charles Middleton, Frank Shannon
Ravaging plague strikes the earth and Flash Gordon undertakes to stop it. A serial in twelve chapters.
Universal — *Video Connection; Cable Films; Video Yesteryear; Discount Video Tapes*

Flash Gordon: Mars   1938
Attacks the World
Science fiction
08634   87 mins   B/W   B, V   P
Buster Crabbe, Jean Rogers, Charles Middleton

The earth is plagued by the evil Ming, but Flash Gordon steps in.
Universal — *Cable Films; Movie Buff Video*

Flash Gordon: 1936
Rocketship
Science fiction
13694   75 mins   B/W   B, V, FO   P
Buster Crabbe, Charles Middleton
Flash Gordon saves Earth from a planet that almost collides with it.
Universal — *Prism; Video Yesteryear; Cable Films; Cinema Concepts; Movie Buff Video*

Flash Gordon—Space   1979
Adventurer
Science fiction/Cartoons
81186   58 mins   C   B, V   P
Animated
Join Flash Gordon, Dale Arden and Dr. Zarkov as they encounter all kinds of adventures while traveling through outer space.
Don Christensen — *Media Home Entertainment*

Flash of Green, A   1985
Drama
71178   122 mins   C   B, V   P
Blair Brown, Richard Jordon, Ed Harris, George Coe, written and directed by Victor Nunez
A crooked politician is helping a construction firm exploit valuable waterfront property. He enlists the influence of an irresolute local journalist, who then falls for the woman leading the homeowner's conservation drive against the development plan.
Richard Jordan — *Media Home Entertainment*

Flashdance   1983
Musical-Drama
Closed Captioned
65096   96 mins   C   B, V, 8mm,   P
LV, CED
Jennifer Beals, Michael Nouri, Belinda Bauer, Lilia Skala
A young female welder dreams of becoming a professional ballet dancer, trying out her original dance routines every night at a local bar. Title song sung by Irene Cara. In stereo.
MPAA:R
Paramount — *Paramount Home Video*

Flashpoint   1984
Suspense
77163   95 mins   C   B, V   P
Treat Williams, Kris Kristofferson, Tess Harper, directed by William Tannen
A pair of Texas border patrolmen discover an abandoned jeep that contains evidence of a conspiracy.
MPAA:R
Tri-Star Pictures — *THORN EMI/HBO Video*

Flashpoint Africa 1984
Adventure
79890   99 mins   C   B, V   P
*Trevor Howard, Gayle Hunnicutt, James
Faulkner*
When a news team follows a terrorist group's
activities it winds up being a power struggle with
terrifying consequences.
Barrie Saint Clair — *VCL Home Video*

Flask of Fields, A 193?
Comedy
58654   61 mins   B/W   B, V, FO   P
*W.C. Fields, Babe Kane, Elsie Cavanna, Bud
Jamison, Rosemary Theby*
Three classic Fields shorts: "The Golf
Specialist" (1930), in which J. Effington
Bellweather finds himself teaching a lovely
young lady how to play the game; "The Fatal
Glass of Beer" (1933); and "The Dentist"
(1932), in which Fields tackles a room filled with
patients.
RKO; Paramount — *Video Yesteryear*

Flat Top 1952
War-Drama
81421   85 mins   C   B, V   P
*Sterling Hayden, Richard Carlson, Keith Larsen,
John Bromfield*
This is the story of how the Navy fighter pilots
were trained aboard "Flat Top" during World
War II.
Monogram — *Republic Pictures Home Video*

Flavors of China 1979
Cookery
38956   119 mins   C   B, V   P
Master chef Titus Chan guides the viewer
through classic Chinese recipes that can be
prepared at home. Chinese cooking utensils are
explained, and basic techniques of cooking
such as stir frying, steaming, poaching, and
deep frying are presented. Contains instructions
on such dishes as lemon chicken, beef with
oyster sauce, chicken with cashews, sweet and
sour pork, and many others.
AM Available
Valley Isle Productions — *Warner Home Video*

Fledermaus, Die 1985
Opera
88135   142 mins   C   B, V   P
*Dame Joan Sutherland, conducted by Richard
Bonynge*
The Elizabethan Sydney Opera performs the
classic Strauss opera in German with English
subtitles.
GE
The Australian Opera — *Sony Video Software*

Fledermaus, Volume I, Die 1984
Opera
80052   90 mins   C   B, V   P
*Kirite Kanawa, Hermann Prey, Charles
Aznavour, Benjamin Luxon*
Placido Domingo conducts this production of
Johann Strauss' opera taped at the Royal
Opera House in Covent Garden.
BBC Television; Arts International — *THORN
EMI/HBO Video*

Fledermaus Volume II, Die 1984
Opera
80053   90 mins   C   B, V   P
*Kirite Kanawa, Hermann Prey, Charles
Aznaibur, Benjamin Luxon*
Placido Domingo makes his British conducting
debut in this production of Johann Strauss'
opera taped at the Royal Opera House in
Covent Garden.
BBC Television; Arts International — *THORN
EMI/HBO Video*

Fleetwood Mac, Documentary and Live Concert 1980
Music-Performance
54687   60 mins   C   B, V   P
Fleetwood Mac
Both interviews with members of Fleetwood
Mac and footage from their recent tour are
featured in this program. Musical selections
include "Sarah," "Sisters of the Moon," "Go
Your Own Way," "Angel," and "Tusk."
Warner Bros — *Warner Home Video; RCA
VideoDiscs; MCA Home Video (disc only)*

Fleetwood Mac in Concert—Mirage Tour 1982 1982
Music-Performance
64240   80 mins   C   B, V   P
Filmed during Fleetwood Mac's 1982 tour, this
concert tape features such songs as
"Rhiannon," "Gypsy," "Go Your Own Way,"
and "Songbird." In Dolby stereo.
Marty Callner — *RCA/Columbia Pictures
Home Video; RCA VideoDiscs*

Flesh and Blood 1985
Adventure
84091   126 mins   C   B, V, LV   P
*Rutger Hauer, Jennifer Jason Leigh, Tom
Burlinson, directed by Paul Verhoeven*
A lavish romantic medieval spectacle with
clashing armies, kidnapped maidens and evil
kings. By the same director of Hauer's first
internationally known film, "Soldier of Orange."
MPAA:R
Orion Pictures — *Vestron Video*

Flesh and Blood Show, The　1973

Horror
70811　93 mins　C　B, V　P
Robin Askwith, Candace Glendenning, Tristan Rogers, Ray Brooks, Jenny Hanley, Luan Peters, Patrick Barr, directed by Peter Walker
Rehearsal turns into an execution ritual for a group of actors at a mysterious London theatre-pier.
MPAA:R
British; Peter Walker — *Monterey Home Video*

Flesh Gordon　1974

Satire
55213　70 mins　C　B, V　P
Jason Willaims, Suzanne Fields
An adult super-spoof of science fiction films. The Earth is thrown into carnal chaos by a mysterious sex ray, and Flesh travels to the planet Porno to save the earth from an evil emperor.
MPAA:X　EL, SP
Graffitti Productions Corp — *Media Home Entertainment*

Fleshburn　1984

Adventure
80273　91 mins　C　B, V　P
An Indian Vietnam War veteran escapes from a mental institution to get revenge on the four psychiatrists who committed him.
MPAA:R
Beth Gage — *Media Home Entertainment*

Fletch　1985

Comedy/Suspense
Closed Captioned
82356　98 mins　C　B, V, LV　P
Chevy Chase, Tim Matheson, Joe Don Baker, Dana Wheeler-Nicholson, Geena Davis, Richard Libertini, directed by Michael Ritchie
Fletcher, a journalist, stumbles onto a great story when a dying, wealthy businessman asks that he kill him to alleviate his pain. Available in Hi-Fi Stereo Surround Sound for all formats.
MPAA:PG
Universal Studios — *MCA Home Video*

Flight from Vienna　1958

Drama
69566　54 mins　B/W　B, V, FO　P
Theodore Bikel, John Bentley, Donald Gray
A high-ranking Hungarian security officer, disenchanted with communism, stages a daring escape from his country. In Vienna, he asks the British for political asylum, but is sent back to Hungary to help a scientist escape.
E J Fancey — *Video Yesteryear*

Flight of Dragons　1982

Fantasy
69613　98 mins　C　B, V　P
Animated, voices of John Ritter, Victor Buono, James Earl Jones
This animated tale takes place between the Age of Magic and the Age of Science, in a century when dragons ruled the skies.
Rankin Bass — *Children's Video Library*

Flight of the Grey Wolf, The　1976

Drama/Wildlife
84805　82 mins　C　B, V　P
Bill Williams, Barbara Hale, Jeff East
A tame, innocent wolf is mistaken for a killer and must run for his life with the help of his boy-owner.
Walt Disney Prod — *Walt Disney Home Video*

Flight of the Phoenix, The　1966

Adventure
Closed Captioned
82097　147 mins　C　B, V, LV　P
James Stewart, Richard Attenborough, Peter Finch, Hardy Kruger, Ernest Borgnine, Ian Bannen, directed by Robert Aldrich
A group of men stranded on a desert island after a plane crash attempt to rebuild their plane in order to escape from the island. Available in VHS and Beta Hi-Fi.
20th Century Fox — *CBS/Fox Video*

Flight to Mars　1952

Science fiction
44355　72 mins　C　B, V, 3/4U　P
Cameron Mitchell, Marguerite Chapman, Arthur Franz
An expedition crash lands on the red planet and discovers an advanced underground society. Includes previews of coming attractions from classic science fiction films.
Monogram, Walter Mirisch — *Nostalgia Merchant*

Flights and Flyers　193?

Documentary/Biographical
50635　30 mins　B/W　B, V　P, T
Three Fox-Movietone newsreels covering stories about famous flyers such as Will Rogers, Amelia Earhart, Howard Hughes, Eddie Rickenbacker, and Wrong Way Corrigan, to name a few.
Blackhawk; Movietone — *Blackhawk Films*

Flights and Flyers: Amelia Earhart　19??

Documentary/Biographical
50632　11 mins　B/W　B, V　P, T
The flying exploits and heroics of Amelia Earhart are chronicled in this program. The determination of a woman who made both cross-country and trans-Atlantic flights, and vowed to follow her failures with successes, is emphasized.

Blackhawk; Movietone — *Blackhawk Films*

Flights of Fancy   1986
Film-History/Cartoons
70943   30 mins   C   B, V.   P
animation by Faith and John Hubley
The renowned animators, Faith and John
Hubley, produced several whimsical short
subjects through the '50's and '60's. This tape
includes several, including: "The Adventure of
an *," "Moonbird," "Windy Day" and
"Zuckerkandl."
Academy Award '59: Best Cartoon Short
Subject ("Moonbird")
Walt Disney Productions — *Walt Disney Home
Video*

Flim-Flam Man, The   1967
Comedy
Closed Captioned
81514   104 mins   C   B, V   P
*George C. Scott, Michael Sarrazin, Slim
Pickens, Sue Lyon, Jack Albertson, Harry
Morgan, directed by Irvin Kershner*
A con man teams up with an army deserter to
teach him the fine art of flim-flamming as they
travel through small southern towns.
20th Century Fox — *Playhouse Video*

Flintstones, The   1960
Cartoons
77156   50 mins   C   B, V   P
*Animated, voices of Alan Reed, Mel Blanc, Jean
Vander Pyl, Bea Benaderet*
The foibles of two Stone Age families The
Flintstones and the Rubbles are chronicled in
these two episodes of this classic series.
Hanna-Barbera — *Worldvision Home Video*

Flintstones Comedy   1985
Show, The
Cartoons
81970   60 mins   C   B, V   P
Animated
Fred and Barney find themselves knee-deep in
trouble in this collection of episodes from the
popular TV series.
Hanna-Barbera — *Worldvision Home Video*

Flintstones Comedy   1985
Show 2, The: Curtain Call
Cartoons
84077   60 mins   C   B, V   P
Animated
The Flintstone gang romp through an animated
adventure intended to educate as well as
entertain.
Hanna-Barbera — *Worldvision Home Video*

Flintstones Meet Rockula   1980
and Frankenstone, The
Cartoons
77154   52 mins   C   B, V   P
Animated
Fred, Wilma, Barney and Betty win a trip to
Rocksylvania and meet up with Count Rockula
and his monster, Frankenstone.
Hanna-Barbera — *Worldvision Home Video*

Flock of Seagulls, A   1983
Music-Performance
76669   13 mins   C   B, V   P
This program presents the British band
performing "Wishing (If I Had a Photograph of
You)," "Nightmares" and "I Ran."
Zomba Productions Inc — *Sony Video
Software*

Flood!   1976
Adventure
87680   98 mins   C   B, V   P
*Robert Culp, Martin Milner, Barbara Hershey,
Richard Basehart, Carol Lynley, Roddy
McDowell, Cameron Mitchell, Teresa Wright,
Francine York*
Another Irwin Allen made-for-TV disaster film,
involving a dam which threatens to bust and
flood lots of homes.
Irwin Allen — *Warner Home Video*

Flood of Fury   1952
Adventure
10034   25 mins   B/W   B, V   P, T
Kirby Grant
Town is flooded by ravaging rain, escaped
prisoners rob bank, and Penny and Clipper are
kidnapped. Sky King attempts to help. From the
TV series "Sky King."
CBS — *Blackhawk Films*

Floorwalker, The   1917
Comedy
10647   20 mins   B/W   B, V, 3/4U   R, P,
                                          DL
Charlie Chaplin
Chaplin becomes involved with a dishonest
floorwalker in a department store. (Silent;
musical soundtrack added.)
RKO — *Cable Films; Festival Films*

Florida Connection, The   1974
Adventure
47673   90 mins   C   B, V   P
An action thriller set in the Florida Swamps with
a collection of villains.
Samuel Hyman — *Unicorn Video*

Flower Angel, The   1980
Cartoons
53664   46 mins   C   B, V   P
Animated

The Flower Angel and her friends, a white kitty and a lovable brown dog, are searching for the Flower of Seven Colors. In their travels they help a lonely old man and his beautiful daughter find the love they have for each other.
EL, SP
Ziv Intl — Family Home Entertainment

Flower Drum Song   1961
Musical
87628   133 mins   C   B, V
Nancy Kwan, Jack Soo, James Shigeta, Miyoshi Umeki, Juanita Hall
Rodgers and Hammerstein wrote the score of this Broadway adaptation about family life in San Francisco's Chinatown. Songs include "I Enjoy Being a Girl," "Sunday," "A Hundred Million Miracles" and "Love, Look Away." In HiFi Stereo.
Ross Hunter — MCA Home Video

Flower Out of Place, A   1974
Music
05413   50 mins   C   B, V   P
Concert performances by Johnny Cash, Roy Clark, Linda Ronstadt, and Foster Brooks.
Independent — Media Home Entertainment

Fly, The   1958
Science fiction
80732   94 mins   C   B, V   P
Vincent Price, David Hedison, Herbert Marshall, Patricia Owens, directed by Kurt Neumann
During an experiment with atomic energy, a scientist accidentally transforms his atomic structure onto a common housefly. Available in VHS and Beta Hi-Fi Stereo.
20th Century Fox — Key Video

Fly Casting—Game   1981
Fishing
Fishing
84268   65 mins   C   B, V   P
Arthur Oglesby, Hugh Falkus
The two top European fly fishers demonstrate their fishing styles in various exotic locations, chasing salmon. The two programs are 30 and 35 minutes in length, respectively.
Video Travel Inc — Video Travel

Fly Fishing   1983
Fishing
70176   49 mins   C   B, V   P
Through an on-stream casting lesson, this program provides an introduction to tackle, rods, reels, fly tying, fly selection, line selection and clothing.
Video Travel — Video Travel

Fly in the Pink, A   1966
Cartoons/Comedy
82406   57 mins   C   B, V   P

Animated
These classic cartoons from the debonair Pink Panther include "Pink Flea," "A Fly in the Pink," "Keep our Forest Pink" and "Pink in the Clink."
Mirisch-Geoffrey-DF — MGM/UA Home Video

Flying—A Man, a Plane   1983
and a Dream/Flight of the
Bluebird II
Aeronautics
70173   50 mins   C   B, V   P
"A Man, a Plane and a Dream" is the story of Elgin Long, who flew his light plane around the world solo. "Flight of the Bluebird II" covers the 30-day flight of two twin Comanches down and back the length of South America.
Video Travel — Video Travel

Flying Deuces, The   1939
Comedy
08577   70 mins   B/W   B, V   P
Stan Laurel, Oliver Hardy, Jean Parker, Reginald Gardner
Laurel and Hardy join the Foreign Legion.
RKO — Prism; Hal Roach Studios; Kartes Video Communications; Republic Pictures Home Video; Media Home Entertainment; Nostalgia Merchant; United Home Video; VCII; Hollywood Home Theater; Cable Films; Video Yesteryear; Discount Video Tapes; Video Connection; Vestron Video; Vestron Video (disc only)

Flying Down To Rio   1933
Musical
00268   89 mins   B/W   B, V, 3/4U   P
Fred Astaire, Ginger Rogers
First Astaire-Rogers musical, featuring Vincent Youmans' score, including "The Carioca."
RKO; Merian C Cooper — Nostalgia Merchant

Flying Leathernecks   1951
War-Drama
29343   102 mins   C   B, V   P
John Wayne, Robert Ryan, Janis Carter
A tough squadron leader wins the admiration and devotion of his fliers. This memorable World War II film deals with war in human terms.
RKO — RKO HomeVideo; VidAmerica

Flying Saucer, The   1950
Science fiction
44348   120 mins   B/W   B, V   P
Mikel Conrad, Pat Garrison, Hanz Von Teuffen
U.S. and Russian scientists search for a huge flying saucer that is hidden under a glacier. This was the first movie to deal with flying saucers. The cassette includes animated opening and closing sequences plus previews of coming attractions.
Film Classics — Mossman Williams Productions; United Home Video

Flying Tigers 1942
War-Drama
81425 101 mins B/W B, V P
John Wayne, Paul Kelly, John Carroll, Anna Lee
A squadron leader and his pal are both vying for
the affections of a pretty nurse while fighting the
Japanese during World War II.
Republic Pictures — *Republic Pictures Home
Video*

Fog, The 1978
Horror
56460 91 mins C B, V, LV, P
CED
*Hal Holbrook, Adrienne Barbeau, Jamie Lee
Curtis, Janet Leigh, John Houseman, directed
by John Carpenter*
John Carpenter's contemporary tale of
supernatural horror concerns a ghostly fog that
reappears to fulfill a curse.
MPAA:R
Avco Embassy, Debra Hill — *Embassy Home
Entertainment; RCA VideoDiscs*

Follow Me, Boys! 1966
Comedy
65636 120 mins C B, V P
*Fred MacMurray, Vera Miles, Lillian Gish,
Charles Ruggles, Elliott Reid, Kurt Russell,
Luana Patten, Ken Murray*
After one year too many on the road with a
ramshackle jazz band, a simple man decides to
put down roots and enjoy the quiet life—a life
that is suddenly just a memory when he
volunteers to head a troop of high-spirited
youngsters.
Buena Vista — *Walt Disney Home Video*

Follow that Car 1980
Adventure
85366 96 mins C B, V P
Dirk Benedict, Tanya Tucker, Teri Nunn
Three southern kids become FBI agents and
begin a thigh-slappin', rip-snortin' down-home
escapade.
MPAA:PG
James Sbardellati; Thomas M.
Hammel — *Charter Entertainment*

Follow the Fleet 1936
Musical
01611 110 mins B/W B, V P
*Fred Astaire, Ginger Rogers, Randolph Scott,
directed by Mark Sandrich*
Set to Irving Berlin's score, song and dance
man joins Navy with pal and meets two sisters in
need of help. Look for Betty Grable, Lucille Ball,
and Tony Martin in minor roles.
RKO — *RKO HomeVideo; Nostalgia Merchant*

Food of the Gods, The 1976
Horror
80696 88 mins C B, V P
*Marjoe Gortner, Pamela Franklin, Ralph
Meeker, Ida Lupino, Jon Cypher*
A farmer on a secluded island creates a race of
giant rats who crave for human flesh, blood,
bones, organs and other assorted body parts.
MPAA:PG
American International — *Vestron Video*

Foolin' Around 1980
Comedy/Romance
64978 101 mins C B, V, CED P
*Gary Busey, Annette O'Toole, Eddie Albert,
Tony Randall, Cloris Leachman*
An innocent Oklahoma farm boy arrives at
college and falls in love with a beautiful heiress.
He will stop at nothing to win her overincluding
crashing her lavish wedding ceremony.
MPAA:PG
Columbia — *Embassy Home Entertainment*

Foolish Wives 1922
Drama
12428 75 mins B/W B, V P
*Erich von Stroheim, Maude George, Mae Busch,
directed by Erich von Stroheim*
Monte Carlo: Posing as a Russian Count with
two accomplices, a fiendish man takes
advantage of women. Silent with music track.
Universal — *Hollywood Home Theater*

Foolish Wives 1922
Drama
47821 107 mins B/W B, V P, T
*Erich Von Stroheim, Mae Busch, Maud George,
Cesare Gravina, directed by Erich Von Stroheim*
A reconstruction of Von Stroheim's classic
depicting the confused milieu of post-war
Europe traced through the actions of a bogus
count and his seductive, corrupt ways. This
version is as close as possible to the original
film.
Universal; Carl Laemmle — *Blackhawk Films*

Fools 1970
Drama/Romance
71193 93 mins C B, V P
*Jason Robards, Katherine Ross, Scott Hylands,
directed by Tom Gries*
Two lonely people-he an aging horror film actor
and she a young woman estranged from her
husband—start a warm romance when they
meet in San Francisco.
MPAA:PG
Cinerama; Translor Productions — *Prism*

Fools: World Dance Party, The 1985
Music-Performance/Comedy
71011 30 mins C B, V P
The Fools
This band, best known as Van Halen's opening
act, aim for the funny bone as well as the ear in
this 4-cut tape.

Warner Bros — *Passport Music Video*

Paramount — *Paramount Home Video*

Football Follies   1969
Football
45125   22 mins   C   B, V, FO   R, P
The original chaos and comedy collection of
wild and wacky events that sometimes happen
on the one-hundred yard stage.
NFL Films — *NFL Films Video; Champions on
Film and Video*

Football   1980
Follies/Highlights of
Super Bowl V
Football
56790   46 mins   C   B, V   P
A collection of hilarious snafus by the great pro
football players, plus highlights of the Cowboys
and Colts "Blooper Bowl."
NFL Films — *VidAmerica*

Football   1981
Follies/Sensational 60's
Football
51698   47 mins   C   LV   P
Two of the NFL's most popular programs,
"Football Follies," a collection of slips, trip,
fumbles and falls, and "Sensational 60's,"
featuring highlights from football's golden
decade narrated by John Facenda, comprise
this disc offering.
NFL Films — *NFL Films Video*

Footlight Frenzy   1984
Satire
78665   110 mins   C   B, V   P
The Law Moan Spectacular comedy troupe are
at it again as they perform a benefit play where
everything goes wrong.
RKO — *RKO HomeVideo*

Footlight Parade   1933
Musical
73983   104 mins   B/W   B, V   P
*Ruby Keeler, James Cagney, Dick Powell, Joan
Blondell, directed by Lloyd Bacon*
Despite great difficulty a producer manages to
get the show on in the Busby Berkeley
choreographed musical that features a 20,000
gallon aquacade and the song "By A Waterfall."
Warner Bros — *Key Video*

Footloose   1984
Musical-Drama
75808   106 mins   C   B, V, 8mm,   P
                          LV, CED
*Kevin Bacon, Lori Singer, music by Kenny
Loggins*
A teenage boy tries to bring rock music to a
small, religious town.
MPAA:PG

For a Few Dollars More   1967
Western
64705   125 mins   C   CED   P
Clint Eastwood, Lee Van Cleef
A band of cutthroats has a sadistic leader who is
pursued by two bounty hunters. When the two
offer to help the outlaws crack a stolen safe, the
vicious leader is shot. Sequel to "A Fistful of
Dollars."
MPAA:PG
United Artists — *CBS/Fox Video; RCA
VideoDiscs*

For Ladies Only   1981
Drama
65312   94 mins   C   B, V   P
Gregory Harrison, Lee Grant
Gregory Harrison is a struggling, unemployed
actor by day and an exotic male stripper by
night.
Viacom International — *U.S.A. Home Video*

For Love of Ivy   1968
Comedy/Drama
47148   102 mins   C   B, V   P
*Sidney Poitier, Abbey Lincoln, Beau Bridges,
Carroll O'Connor, directed by Daniel Mann*
When the black maid of a wealthy family
decides to quit, the family tries to find a
boyfriend for her so she will stay on. Based on a
story by Sidney Poitier.
MPAA:PG
Cinerama Releasing; Palomar — *CBS/Fox
Video*

For Pete's Sake   1974
Comedy
44833   90 mins   C   B, V   P
*Barbra Streisand, Michael Sarrazin, Estelle
Parsons, William Redfield, Molly Picon*
Topsy-turvy comedy about a woman who goes
to great lengths for her husband.
MPAA:PG
Martin Erlichman, Columbia — *RCA/Columbia
Pictures Home Video*

For the Love of Angela   1986
Romance/Drama
71236   90 mins   C   V   P
Introduced by Louis Jourdan
A pretty young shop clerk involves herself with
both the shopkeeper and his son.
Commworld; Romance Theater — *Prism*

For the Love of Benji   1977
Comedy-Drama
49627   85 mins   C   B, V, CED   P
*Benji, Patsy Garrett, Cynthia Smith, Allen Finzat,
Ed Nelson, directed by Joe Camp*

Benji and his companion Tiffany join their human friends for a Greek vacation. But Benji is kidnapped to be used as a messenger for a secret code. He escapes, and the case is on.
MPAA:G
Mulberry Square Prods; Joe Camp — *Vestron Video*

For the Love of Benji   1983
Animals
75614   85 mins   C   B, V   P
Benji battles an international spy ring.
Mulberry Square Productions — *Children's Video Library*

For the Love of It   1980
Comedy
66616   98 mins   C   B, V   P
Deborah Raffin, Jeff Conaway, Don Rickles, Tom Bosley, Henry Gibson, William Christopher
A young couple steal some top-secret Soviet documents and become the target of bumbling FBI agents.
Charles Fries Productions — *U.S.A. Home Video*

For Your Eyes Only   1981
Adventure
58845   127 mins   C   B, V, LV,   P
                                 CED
Roger Moore, Carole Bouquet, Lynn-Holly Johnson
Another James Bond epic, in which 007 is called upon to keep the Soviets from getting hold of the valuable instrument aboard a sunken British spy ship.
MPAA:PG
United Artists — *CBS/Fox Video; MGM/UA Home Video (disc only)*

Forbidden   1985
Drama/World War II
71309   114 mins   C   B, V   P
Jacqueline Bisset, Jurgen Prochnow, Irene Worth, Osman Ragheb, directed by Anthony Page
A German countess oversees an underground railroad smuggling Jews from Nazi territory. Her developing romance with a heroic Hebrew who refuses to leave his people complicates matters. Adapted from "The Last Jews in Berlin," by Leonard Gross.
Mark Forstater; Gerald Isenberg — *U.S.A. Home Video*

Forbidden City, The   1973
China
02937   60 mins   C   B, V   P
The splendor of the great Kung Ku is portrayed in this film. The Peking palace housed Chinese emperors from 1421 to 1911 and remains today as an unmatched museum of Chinese history and culture.

San Francisco Film Festival
Lucy Jarvis — *Monterey Home Video; Films Inc*

Forbidden Planet   1956
Science fiction
55210   98 mins   C   B, V, LV,   P
                                 CED
Walter Pidgeon, Anne Francis, Leslie Nielsen, directed by Fred McLeod Wilcox
In 2200 A.D., a space cruiser visits the planet Altair Four to uncover the fate of a previous mission of space colonists, and discovers a former civilization.
MGM; Nicholas Nayfack — *MGM/UA Home Video*

Forbidden Trail   1933
Western
15436   60 mins   B/W   B, V   P
Buck Jones, Tim McCoy, Raymond Hatton
This adventure set in the old West features the "Roughriders."
Columbia — *Video Connection; Discount Video Tapes; United Home Video*

Forbidden World   1982
Science fiction/Horror
65715   82 mins   C   B, V   P
Jesse Vint, Dawn Dunlap
The lives of a genetic research team become threatened by the very life form they helped to create: a man-eating organism capable of changing its genetic structure as it grows and matures.
MPAA:R
Roger Corman — *Embassy Home Entertainment*

Forbidden Zone   1980
Film-Avant-garde/Science fiction
66600   75 mins   B/W   B, V   P
Herve Villechaize, Susan Tyrrell, The Kipper Kids, Viva
Frenchy Hercules is flung headlong into the sixth dimension. This kingdom is ruled by the midget, King Fausto and inhabited by dancing frogs, bikini-clad tootsies, robot boxers and degraded beings of all kinds. Original music by Oingo Boingo.
MPAA:R
Richard Elfman — *Media Home Entertainment*

Force Beyond, The   197?
Speculation/Occult sciences
47314   85 mins   C   B, V   P
Don Elkins, Peter Byrne, Renee Dahinden
This program provides a look at inexplicable phenomena, including psychic investigation, alien encounters, Bigfoot, and the Bermuda Triangle.
Donn Davidson — *Media Home Entertainment*

Force: Five 1981
Adventure
68223 95 mins C B, V P
Joe Lewis, Pam Huntington, Master Bong Soo Han
The daughter of a very powerful man has been taken to Rhee's Island, a retreat for people involved in the cult. The mission is to get her back and ruin Rhee's Island. Only a force of five agents can do this job.
MPAA:R
American Cinema — *Media Home Entertainment*

Force of Evil 1949
Drama
76826 80 mins B/W B, V P
John Garfield, Thomas Gomez, Marie Windsor, directed by Abraham Polonsky
An attorney who works for a mobster tries to break out of the numbers racket.
MGM — *Republic Pictures Home Video*

Force of One, A 1979
Martial arts/Adventure
66062 91 mins C B, V P
Chuck Norris, Bill Wallace, Jennifer O'Neill
A team of undercover narcotics agents is being eliminated mysteriously.
MPAA:PG
Alan Belkin — *Media Home Entertainment*

Force 10 from Navarone 1978
War-Drama
64301 118 mins C B, V P
Robert Shaw, Harrison Ford, Barbara Bach, Edward Fox
During World War II, five desperate Allied soldiers and one beautiful woman plot to blow up a dam and destroy an impregnable bridge.
MPAA:PG
Orion Pictures — *Warner Home Video; Vestron Video (disc only)*

Forced Entry 1980
Suspense
59082 92 mins C B, V P
Tanya Roberts, Ron Max, Nancy Allen
A psychopathic killer rapist becomes obsessed with a beautiful woman.
MPAA:R
Jim Sotos — *HarmonyVision*

Forced Vengeance 1982
Adventure/Martial arts
60568 103 mins C B, V, CED P
Chuck Norris, Mary Louise Weller
The story of a Vietnam vet pitted against the Underworld of the Far East.
MPAA:R
MGM; SLM Entertainment — *MGM/UA Home Video*

Forces of Life, The 1982
Chemistry/Physics
59562 56 mins C B, V P
This program examines the essential properties which make up our physical universe.
McGraw Hill — *Mastervision*

Ford Startime 1960
Drama
69577 50 mins B/W B, V, FO P
Audie Murphy, Thelma Ritter
An original television drama, "The Man" is a psychological study of an unbalanced veteran who visits the mother of an old army buddy and proves impossible to get rid of.
NBC — *Video Yesteryear*

Foreign Correspondent 1940
Suspense
81152 120 mins B/W B, V P
Joel McCrea, Laraine Day, Herbert Marshall, George Sanders, Robert Benchley, directed by Alfred Hitchcock
A reporter is sent to Europe during World War II to cover a pacifist conference in London, where he becomes romantically involved with the daughter of the group's founder and he friends an elderly diplomat. When the diplomat is kidnapped, the reporter uncovers a Nazi spy-ring headed by his future father-in-law.
United Artists; Walter Wanger — *Lightning Video*

Foreplay 1975
Comedy
64879 100 mins C B, V, CED P
Pat Paulsen, Jerry Orbach, Estelle Parsons, Zero Mostel
A trilogy of hilarious comedy segments. Also known as "The President's Women."
Cinema National Corp — *Vestron Video*

Forest, The 1983
Horror
71216 90 mins C B, V P
Spooks and a cannibalistic killer terrrorize a group of campers.
Independent — *Prism*

Forest Duel 1985
Martial arts
84506 83 mins C B, V P
Revenge is sweet in this rural Kung Fu epic.
Telefilm Co Inc — *Sony Video Software*

Forever Emmanuelle 1982
Drama
69282 89 mins C B, V P
Annie-Belle, Emmanuelle Arsan, Al Cliver
A sensual young woman finds love and the ultimate erotic experience in the wilds of the South Pacific.

MPAA:R
A-Erre Cinematografica — *Vestron Video*

Forever Fairytales   1985
Children/Fantasy
85106   72 mins   C   B, V   P
4 pgms
Available separately or together, these
animated programs relate stories told by four
great scribes.
*1.Brothers Grimm 2.Hans Christian Andersen
3.Rudyard Kipling 4.Charles Perrault*
Vidamerica — *VidAmerica*

Forever Young   1983
Drama
86777   85 mins   C   B, V   P
*James Aubrey, Nicholas Gecks, Alec McCowen,
directed by David Drury*
A young boy immerses himself into the world of
rock and roll, until a friend from the past
appears, stirring bad memories.
David Puttnam; Enigma Prods — *MGM/UA
Home Video*

Formula, The   1980
Drama
55206   117 mins   C   B, V, CED   P
*Marlon Brando, George C. Scott, directed by
John G. Avildsen*
Steve Shagan's novel about a hard-nosed Los
Angeles policeman who, despite numerous
attempts on his life, continues to search for the
formula that could end America's dependence
on foreign oil forever.
MPAA:R
Steve Shagan — *MGM/UA Home Video*

Fort Apache   1948
Western
00277   125 mins   B/W   B, V   P
John Wayne, Henry Fonda, Shirley Temple
Indian attacks and conflict between men on the
Western frontier arise in this film.
RKO; John Ford — *RKO HomeVideo;
VidAmerica*

Fort Apache, The Bronx   1981
Drama
58896   123 mins   C   B, V, LV,   P
                              CED
*Paul Newman, Ed Asner, Ken Wahl, Danny
Aiello, Rachel Ticotin, Pam Grier, Kathleen
Beller, directed by Daniel Petrie*
A police drama set in the beleaguered South
Bronx of New York City, based on the real-life
experiences of two former New York cops who
served there.
MPAA:R
Time-Life Films — *Vestron Video; Time Life
Video*

Fortress   1985
Suspense
86896   90 mins   C   B, V   P
Rachel Ward, Sean Garlick, Rebecca Rigg
A teacher and her class are kidnapped from
their one-room Australian schoolhouse into the
Outback, having only their ingenuity and wits on
which to depend to save their lives.
Australian — *THORN EMI/HBO Video*

Fortune's Fool   1921
Comedy
11231   60 mins   B/W   B, V, FO   P
*Emil Jannings, Daguey Servaes, Reinhold
Schunzel, directed by Reinhold Schunzel*
A beef king and profiteer marries a younger
woman and soon discovers the problems that
ambition can cause.
UFA — *Video Yesteryear; Discount Video
Tapes*

Forty Carats   1973
Comedy
63964   110 mins   C   B, V   P
*Liv Ullman, Edward Albert, Gene Kelly, Binnie
Barnes, Deborah Raffin*
A middle-aged, divorced woman falls in love
with a young man half her age; in turn, her
young daughter marries a widower who is in his
forties.
MPAA:PG
Columbia Pictures — *RCA/Columbia Pictures
Home Video*

---

48 Hrs.   1982
Comedy
66034   100 mins   C   B, V, LV   P
Nick Nolte, Eddie Murphy
A convict and a detective make an unlikely team
trying to solve a crime in San Francisco.
MPAA:R
Paramount — *Paramount Home Video; RCA
VideoDiscs*

---

48 Hours to Live   1960
Crime-Drama
88140   86 mins   B/W   B, V   P
*Anthony Steel, Ingemar Johannson, Marlies
Behrens*
A reporter travels to a nuclear scientist's
secluded island only to find the scientist held
hostage by nuclear weapon-seeking terrorists.
Foreign — *Sony Video Software*

45/85: America and the   1985
World Since WWII
History-US
87220   60 mins   C   B, V   P
Hosted by Peter Jennings and Ted Koppel
4 pgms
This series examines the major news events in
American history from 1945 to 1985.
1.1945-52 2.1953-60 3.1961-75 4.1976-85

ABC — *Vestron Video*

Paramount — *Paramount Home Video; RCA VideoDiscs*

Forty Ninth Parallel, The   1941
World War II
75673   90 mins   B/W   B, V   P
Laurence Olivier, Leslie Howard, Eric Portman, Raymond Massey, Glynis Johns
Six Nazi servicemen, seeking to reach neutral American land, are trapped and their U-boat is sunk by Royal Canadian Air Force bombers.
Rank Film Distributors — *VidAmerica*

42nd Street   1933
Musical
55582   89 mins   B/W   B, V   P
Warner Baxter, Ruby Keeler, Bebe Daniels, Dick Powell, Guy Kibbee, Ginger Rogers, Una Merkel, directed by Lloyd Bacon
A Broadway musical producer has troubles during rehearsal but reaches a successful opening night. Choreography by Busby Berkeley. Songs by Harry Warren and Al Dubin include the title song, "You're Getting to Be a Habit with Me," "Young and Healthy," and "Shuffle Off to Buffalo."
Warner Bros — *CBS/Fox Video; RCA VideoDiscs*

Forty Thousand   1941
Horsemen
War-Drama
85173   84 mins   B/W   B, V   P
Chips Rafferty, Grant Taylor, Betty Bryant, Pat Twohill
The story of the ANZACS of Australia, created to fight Germany in the Middle East during World War I, full of cavalry charges, brave young lads, and "Waltzing Matilda."
Australian — *Video Yesteryear*

Fotografo de Senoras   1985
Comedy
81644   110 mins   C   B, V   P
Jorge Porcel, Graciela Alfano, Tristan
A novice photographer finds himself being mistaken for a rapist when naked women keep popping up in front of his camera.
SP
Nicolas Carreras; Luis Repetto — *Media Home Entertainment*

Foul Play   1978
Comedy
38931   118 mins   C   B, V, 8mm,   P
                              LV
Goldie Hawn, Chevy Chase, Dudley Moore, directed by Colin Higgins
Chevy Chase is a San Francisco detective who becomes involved with Goldie Hawn and a plot to kidnap the Pope in this lighthearted comedy thriller.
MPAA:PG

Fountainhead, The   1949
Drama
73973   113 mins   C   B, V   P
Gary Cooper, Patricia Neal, Raymond Massey, directed by King Vidor
An idealistic architect clashes with big business over his designs for a housing project. Adapted from Ayn Rand's novel.
Warner Bros — *Key Video*

4-D Man, The   1959
Science fiction
82169   84 mins   C   B, V   P
Robert Lansing, Lee Meriwether, Patty Duke, James Congdon
A physicist makes two fateful discoveries while working on a special project that sets off a deadly chain of events. Available in VHS and Beta Hi-Fi Stereo.
Jack H. Harris — *New World Video*

Four Deuces, The   1975
Drama
77168   87 mins   C   B, V   P
Jack Palance, Carol Lynley
A gang war is underway between the Chico Hamilton mob and Vic Morano and the Four Deuces during the depression.
Cinema Shares International — *THORN EMI/HBO Video*

Four Faces West   1948
Western
81859   90 mins   B/W   B, V   P
Joel McCrea, Frances Dee, Charles Bickford
A stranger robs a small town bank in order to save his father's ranch from being foreclosed.
United Artists — *Spotlite Video*

Four Feathers, The   1978
Adventure
47796   95 mins   C   B, V   P
Beau Bridges, Jane Seymour, Simon Ward, Harry Andrews
Determined to return the symbols of cowardice-four feathers-to his friends and fiancee, a man courageously saves his friends' lives and regains the love of his lady.
Trident Films Ltd; Norman Rosemont Productions — *THORN EMI/HBO Video*

Four Feathers, The   1939
Adventure
81461   130 mins   C   B, V, LV   P
John Clements, Ralph Richardson, C. Aubrey Smith, June Duprez, directed by Zoltan Korda
A coward redeems himself when he goes underground to rescue a friend during the Sudan campaign of the late nineteenth century.

Alexander Korda — *Embassy Home Entertainment*

Four for Thrills   1982
Cartoons/Literature-American
58578   50 mins   C   B, V   P
Narrated by Herschel Bernardi and Harry Belafonte
A quartet of colorful animated, shorts containing Edgar Allen Poe's classic "Masque of the Red Death," Harry Belafonte's presentation of the Hand," the immortal, "Casey at the Bat," and Herschel Bernardi's presentation of "The Hangman."
McGraw Hill — *Mastervision*

Four Friends   1981
Comedy-Drama
60338   116 mins   C   B, V   P
Craig Wasson, Jodi Thelen, Michael Huddleston, Jim Metzler, Reed Birney, directed by Arthur Penn
Set against the turbulence of the 1960's, a young immigrant comes of age, learning of life and love from his friends.
MPAA:R
Filmways Pictures — *Warner Home Video; Vestron Video (disc only)*

Four Horsemen of the   1962
Apocalypse, The
Drama
81498   153 mins   C   B, V   P
Glen Ford, Charles Boyer, Lee J. Cobb, Paul Henried, Yvette Mimieux, directed by Vincente Minnelli
The members of a German family find themselves fighting on opposite sides during World War II.
MGM — *MGM/UA Home Video*

---

400 Blows, The   1959
Drama
87331   97 mins   B/W   B, V   P
Jean-Pierre Leaud, Claire Maurier, Albert Remy, Guy Decomble, Georges Fiamant, Patrick Auffay, directed by Francois Truffaut
The classic, ground-breaking semi-autobiography that initiated Truffaut's career and catapulted him to international acclaim, about the trials and rebellions of a 12-year-old French schoolboy. One of the greatest, and most influential of films, and the first of Truffaut's career-long Antoine Doinel series. With English subtitles.
Cannes Film Festival '59: Best Director (Truffaut); Time Magazine Ten Best List '59; The New York Times Ten Best List '59. FR
Roissy — *Key Video*

Four in a Jeep   1951
War-Drama
84499   83 mins   B/W   B, V   P

Ralph Meeker, Viveca Lindfors, Joseph Yadin, directed by Leopold Lindtberg
In Vienna in 1945, soldiers from different countries clash as a result of political demands and their love for the same woman.
Lazar Weshsler — *Sony Video Software*

Four Infernos to Cross   197?
Drama
82085   90 mins   C   B, V   P
Musung Kwak, Kyehee Kim
This is the story of the struggle the Korean people encountered while under Japanese rule before World War II.
Foreign — *Unicorn Video*

Four Musketeers, The   1973
Comedy/Adventure
60374   107 mins   C   CED   P
Raquel Welch, Richard Chamberlain, Faye Dunaway, Michael York
A bawdy continuation of the "Three Musketeers" based on the classic Dumas novel.
MPAA:R
Ilya Salkind — *RCA VideoDiscs*

Four Musketeers, The   1974
Adventure
66617   103 mins   C   B, V   P
Michael York, Oliver Reed, Raquel Welch, Faye Dunaway, Charlton Heston, directed by Richard Lester
This continuation of "The Three Musketeers" finds Athos, Porthos, Aramis and D'Artagnan continuing their adventures against the evil forces of Cardinal Richelieu.
MPAA:PG
20th Century Fox; Film Trust SA — *U.S.A. Home Video*

Four Rode Out   1969
Western
65209   99 mins   C   B, V   P
Pernell Roberts, Leslie Nielsen
The story of a woman in love with a suspected killer. To save his life, she rides out with his would be captors.
MPAA:R
Sagittarius Productions — *U.S.A. Home Video*

Four Seasons, The   1981
Comedy
58433   107 mins   C   B, V, LV   P
Alan Alda, Carol Burnett, Sandy Dennis, Len Cariou, Jack Weston, Rita Moreno, Bess Armstrong
Three upper-middle-class New York couples share their vacations together, as well as their friendship, their frustrations and their jealousies.
MPAA:PG
Universal; Martin Bregman — *MCA Home Video; RCA VideoDiscs*

Four Seasons, The 1984
Music
66597   45 mins   C   B, V   P
Orchestre National de France, conducted by Lorin Maazel
Vivaldi's famous concert piece is performed with a visual background of travelog scenes of Paris, New York, Moscow and Venice. In stereo.
Curiator Spiritus Company Ltd; Promedifilm; MGM UA — *MGM/UA Home Video*

4th Man, The 1984
Mystery/Suspense
76858   104 mins   C   B, V   P
Jeroen Krabbe, Renee Soutendijk, Thom Hoffman, directed by Paul Verhoeven
A Dutch writer en route to an out of town speaking engagement has a grisly series of visions that foretell his future. With English subtitles.
DU
Bob Houwer — *Media Home Entertainment*

Fourth Wish, The 1975
Drama
80767   107 mins   C   B, V   - P
John Meillon, Robert Bettles
When a single father learns that his son is dying, he vows to make his son's last months as fulfilling as possible.
Matt Carroll — *Embassy Home Entertainment*

Foxes 1980
Drama
86044   106 mins   C   B, V   P
Jodie Foster, Cherie Currie, Marilyn Kagan, Scott Baio, Sally Kellerman, Randy Quaid, directed by Adrian Lyne
Four trampy San Fernando Valley girls try to cope with maturation, their parents and life in the fast lane.
MPAA:R
David Puttnam; Gerald Ayres — *Key Video*

Foxfire Light 1984
Drama
86860   102 mins   C   B, V   P
Tippi Hedren, Laura Parker, Leslie Nielsen, Barry Van Dyke
A young girl is torn between her desire for a cowboy and her mother's social aspirations.
Bill Dailey — *Prism*

Foxtrot 1976
Drama
84041   91 mins   C   B, V   P
Peter O'Toole, Charlotte Rampling, Max Von Sydow, directed by Arturo Ripstein
A wealthy count isolates himself on an island but cannot escape his past or the horrors of World War II.
MPAA:R

Gerald Green — *Charter Entertainment*

Fozzie's Muppet Scrapbook 1985
Variety
Closed Captioned
81866   56 mins   C   B, V   P
Fozzie Bear, Kermit the Frog, Milton Berle, Beverly Sills, Raquel Welch
Fozzie Bear looks into his scrapbook and discovers why he is the first bear of comedy.
Available in VHS and Beta Hi-Fi.
Henson Associates — *Playhouse Video*

Fraggle Songs, Volume One 1983
Fantasy/Music
65306   52 mins   C   B, V, LV,   R, P
                              CED
The Fraggles, furry little creatures who come in every color of the rainbow, sing and dance their way into your heart. This program is in stereo on all formats.
Henson Associates — *Muppet Home Video*

Fraidy Cat 1974
Cartoons
75498   45 mins   C   B, V   P
This program includes four animated fantasies for children.
Filmation — *Prism*

Framed 1975
Crime-Drama
88425   106 mins   C   B, V   P
Joe Don Baker, Gabriel Dell, Brock Peters, Conny Van Dyke, John Marley
A nightclub owner is framed for murder, which understandably irks him. He determines to get paroled and then seek revenge.
MPAA:R
Paramount — *Paramount Home Video*

Frances 1982
Drama
66021   134 mins   C   B, V, CED   P
Jessica Lange, Kim Stanley, Sam Shepherd
The tragic story of Frances Farmer, the beautiful and talented screen actress driven to a mental breakdown by a neurotic, domineering mother.
Universal — *THORN EMI/HBO Video*

Francis Gary Powers: The True Story of the U-2 Spy Incident 1976
Drama
80485   120 mins   C   B, V   P
Lee Majors, Noah Beery Jr, Nehemiah Persoff, Brooke Bundy, directed by Delbert Mann
A dramatization of the true experiences of Gary Powers, a CIA spy pilot whose plane was shot down over the Soviet Union in 1960. His

capture, trial and conviction are all portrayed in graphic detail, taken from Power's own reminiscences.
Worldvision Enterprises — *Worldvision Home Video*

Frank Shorter's Run   1984
Running
65690   57 mins   C   B, V   P
America's foremost authority on running, world-class marathoner Frank Shorter gives information and instruction on warm-up racing and tempo running, injury prevention and treatment.
Paul Rost; Bruce Miller — *Media Home Entertainment*

Frank Sinatra: Portrait of   1985
an Album
Documentary/Music
82397   65 mins   C   B, V, LV   P
Frank Sinatra, Quincy Jones and His Orchestra
A documentary of the making of the album "L.A. Is My Lady," this film includes live recordings of hits such as "Stormy Weather," "Mack the Knife" and "How Do You Keep the Music Playing."
Quincy Jones Productions — *MGM/UA Home Video*

Frank Zappa's Does   1986
Humor Belong in Music?
Music-Performance
84624   57 mins   C   B, V   P
Frank Zappa
This lively and irreverent concert tape by Frnk Zappa is deliberately unrated. Songs include "Dancin' Fool," "Dinah-Moe Humm" and "Zoot Allures."
Barking Pumpkin Prod — *MPI Home Video*

Franken and Davis at   1984
Stockton State
Comedy-Performance
79109   55 mins   C   B, V   P
Former "Saturday Night Live" writers-stars Al Franken and Tom Davis perform stand-up comedy in this concert taped at Stockton College in New Jersey.
Broadway Video — *Pacific Arts Video*

Franken and Davis   1984
Special, The
Comedy-Performance
66359   60 mins   C   B, V   P
Writer-performers Al Franken and Tom Davis, once featured on "Saturday Night Live," star in this live comedy concert taped in New Jersey
Pacific Arts — *Pacific Arts Video*

Frankenstein   1931
Horror
14025   71 mins   B/W   B, V   P
Boris Karloff, Mae Clark, Colin Clive, John Boles
An adaptation of the Mary Shelley novel about Dr. Henry Frankenstein, the scientist who creates a terrifying yet strangely sympathetic monster.
Universal — *MCA Home Video; RCA VideoDiscs*

Frankenstein   1984
Cartoons/Horror
70091   90 mins   C   B, V   P
Animated
This is an animated version of the classic Mary Shelley novel about Dr. Frankenstein and his new creation.
Northstar Productions — *Vestron Video*

Frankenstein   1973
Horror
77442   130 mins   C   B, V   P
Robert Foxworth, Bo Svenson, Willie Aames, Susan Strasberg
A brilliant scientist unleashes an adaptation of the classic Mary Shelley novel from the remains of the dead.
Dan Curtis Productions — *Thriller Video*

Frankenstein   1984
Horror
84109   81 mins   C   B, V   P
Robert Powell, Carrie Fisher, David Warner, Sir John Gielgud, directed by James Ormerod
A remake of the horror classic, closely following the original story, wherein the creature speaks (and waxes philosophical), the doctor sees him as his dark subconscious, and the two die in an arctic confrontation.
Western World TV — *Lightning Video*

Frankenstein Island   198?
Mystery
75583   97 mins   C   B, V   P
John Carradine, Andrew Duggan, Cameron Mitchell
Four balloonists get pulled down in a storm and end up on Frankenstein island.
MPAA:PG
Unknown — *Monterey Home Video*

Frankie and Johnnie   1936
Musical-Drama
59407   68 mins   B/W   B, V   P, T
Helen Morgan, Chester Morris
Based on the song of the same name, Helen Morgan portrays a nightclub floozie who shoots her unfaithful lover.
Republic — *Blackhawk Films*

Frankies Goes to Hollywood—From A Wasteland to an Artificial Paradise   1985
Music video
81939   28 mins   C   B, V   P
This is a compilation of the four controversial music videos that brought notoriety to British new wavers Frankie Goes to Hollywood. In VHS Dolby Hi-Fi Stereo and Beta Hi-Fi Stereo.
Trevor Horn — *RCA/Columbia Pictures Home Video*

Frankie Laine Show with Connie Haines   1955
Variety
12843   50 mins   B/W   B, V, FO   P
Frankie Laine, Connie Haines, the Harry Zimmerman Orchestra
Two TV shows featuring plenty of songs, variety acts, knife throwers, and girl bagpipers.
CBS — *Video Yesteryear*

Frankie Valli—Hits from the 60's   1983
Music-Performance
75497   100 mins   C   V   P
Frankie Valli
Frankie Valli's Chicago 1982 concert includes great hits such as "Grease," "My Eyes Adored You," "Sherry," "Walk Like a Man" and "Rag Doll."
MusicAmerica Live — *Prism*

Franklin D. Roosevelt, Declaration of War   1941
Presidency-US/World War II
59651   9 mins   B/W   B, V   P, T
Franklin D. Roosevelt
This Fox Movietone newsreel captures FDR's declaration of war following the December 7th bombing of Pearl Harbor.
William Fox — *Blackhawk Films*

Frantic   1958
Drama
12803   92 mins   B/W   B, V, FO   P
Maurice Ronet, Jeanne Moreau
A former commando commits murder of an employer's wife, making it look like suicide. A teenage prank then frames him for murders he did not commit.
Times Films; Irenee Leriche — *Movie Buff Video; Video Yesteryear; Hollywood Home Theater; Discount Video Tapes*

Fraternity Vacation   1985
Comedy
Closed Captioned
81767   95 mins   C   B, V, LV   P
Stephen Geoffreys, Britt Eckland, Cameron Dye, Tim Robbins, John Vernon
Two college fraternity men show a nerd the greatest time of his life while he's on vacation in Palm Springs.
MPAA:R
New World Pictures — *New World Video*

Fraulein Devil   1981
Drama/World War II
70931   90 mins   C   B, V   P
Malisa Longo, Olivier Mathot, directed by Mark Stern
In this wartime nazi adventure, we meet the leather-booted leader of the Fuhrer's elite pleasure corps. She uses her womanly wiles to weed out dissidents within the party's upper echelon.
Eurocine; Brux International Films — *Wizard Video*

Freaky Friday   1977
Comedy/Fantasy
47409   95 mins   C   B, V   P
Barbara Harris, Jodie Foster, Patsy Kelly, Dick Van Patten, Ruth Buzzi
A housewife and her teenage daughter inadvertently switch bodies and each then tries to carry on the other's normal routine.
MPAA:G
Walt Disney — *Walt Disney Home Video*

Fred Astaire: Change Partners and Dance   1980
Musical/Documentary
70184   60 mins   C   B, V   P
Fred Astaire, Leslie Caron, Cyd Charisse, Barrie Chase, narrated by Joanne Woodward
Fred Astaire's post-Ginger Rogers career is the subject of this documentary that features scenes from Fred's films of the '40s and '50s, plus segments from his '60s TV specials. Some sequences are in black and white.
PBS — *RKO HomeVideo*

Fred Astaire: Puttin' on His Top Hat   1980
Musical/Documentary
70183   60 mins   C   B, V   P
Fred Astaire, Ginger Rogers, Adele Astaire, narrated by Joanne Woodward
Fred Astaire's career in Hollywood from 1933-1939 is the focus of this documentary, with scenes from his RKO films with Ginger Rogers. Some segments are in black and white.
PBS — *RKO HomeVideo*

Freddie Hubbard   1981
Music-Performance
76663   59 mins   C   B, V   P
A top rate jazz performance by one of the greatest trumpet players of our time, Freddie Hubbard.
Audio Visual Images — *Sony Video Software*

Frederick Douglass: An American Life — 1986
Biographical/Civil rights
85707   30 mins   C   B, V   P
Hugh Morgan
A dramatized biography of the negro leader and abolitionist.
William Greaves — *Your World Video*

Free for All — 1968
Adventure/Fantasy
80417   50 mins   C   B, V   P
Patrick McGoohan, Angelo Muscat, Colin Gordon, Alexis Kanner, Leo McKern, directed by Patrick McGoohan
The Prisoner runs for the position of Number Two in the Village hoping to meet Number One. An episode from the popular TV series.
Associated TV Corp. — *MPI Home Video*

Free to Be... You and Me — 1983
Identity/Children
69534   45 mins   C   B, V   P
Marlo Thomas, Alan Alda, Harry Belafonte, Mel Brooks, Diana Ross, Rosey Grier
This is a joyful celebration of childhood through song, story and poetry—created to let children feel "free to be who they are and who they want to be."
Marlo Thomas; Carole Hart — *Children's Video Library*

Freebie and the Bean — 1974
Comedy
79553   114 mins   C   B, V   P
Alan Arkin, James Caan, Loretta Swit, Valerie Harper, directed by Richard Rush
Two San Francisco cops nearly ruin the city in their pursuit of a mobster.
MPAA:R
Richard Rush; Warner Bros. — *Warner Home Video*

Freedanse — 1985
Physical fitness/Dance
85092   60 mins   C   B, V   P
Marine Jahan
With choreography by Jackie Sleight, the stand-in dancer from "Flashdance" dances and outlines an exercise program.
AM Available
MTI Prods — *MTI Home Video*

Freedom — 1981
Drama
80936   102 mins   C   B, V   P
Jon Blake, Candy Raymond, Jad Capelja, Reg Lye, John Clayton
A young man finds the price of freedom when he tries to escape from Australian society in a silver Porsche.
Matt Carroll — *VidAmerica*

Freedom Force, The — 1984
Adventure/Cartoons
66494   60 mins   C   B, V   P
Animated
The Freedom Force takes on the powers of evil and triumphs over the forces of darkness.
Prism — *Prism*

Freedom Road — 1979
Drama
84082   186 mins   C   B, V   P
Kris Kristofferson, Muhammad Ali
A made-for-TV drama about a Reconstruction Era ex-slave who is elected to the Senate and subsequently killed while trying to obtain total freedom for his race. In 2 volumes.
Zev Braun Television — *Worldvision Home Video*

French Connection, The — 1971
Crime-Drama
08432   102 mins   C   B, V, LV   P
Gene Hackman, Fernando Rey, Roy Scheider, Tony LoBianco, Marcel Bozzuffi
Two N.Y. hard-nosed narcotics detectives stumble onto what turns out to be the biggest narcotics haul to that time.
Academy Awards '71: Best Picture; Best Actor (Hackman); Best Director (William Friedkin).
MPAA:R   EL, SP
20th Century Fox; Philip D'Antoni — *CBS/Fox Video*

French Connection II — 1975
Drama
Closed Captioned
80653   118 mins   C   B, V   P
Gene Hackman, Fernando Rey, Bernard Fresson, directed by John Frankenheimer
New York policeman "Popeye" Doyle goes to Marseilles to crack a heroin ring headed by his arch nemesis, Frog One, who he failed to stop in the United States. Available in Beta and VHS Hi-Fi.
MPAA:R
20th Century Fox — *CBS/Fox Video*

French Detective, The — 1975
Suspense
63960   90 mins   C   B, V   P
Lino Ventura, Patrick Dewaere, Victor Lanoux
A cunning detective and an ambitious young politician clash in this story of murder and intrigue. Dubbed in English.
Les Films Ariane; Quartet Films — *RCA/Columbia Pictures Home Video*

French Lesson — 1986
Romance
87339   90 mins   C   B, V   P
Alexandre Sterling, Jane Snowdon, directed by Bruce Gilbert

A romantic British farce from a screenplay by cartoonist Posy S. Simmonds, dealing with an English girl going to school in Paris and finding love.
MPAA:PG
Enigma Prod.; Goldcrest — *Warner Home Video*

French Lieutenant's Woman, The 1981
Drama
59392   124 mins   C   B, V, LV   P
Meryl Streep, Jeremy Irons, directed by Karel Reisz
John Fowles' best seller which intertwines two love stories, one between two present-day actors and one between the historical characters they portray.
MPAA:R
United Artists — *CBS/Fox Video; MGM/UA Home Video (disc only)*

French Line 1954
Comedy
10030   102 mins   C   B, V   P, T
Jane Russell, Gilbert Roland, Craig Stevens
Millionairess beauty travels incognito while trying to sort out which men are after her money, and which ones aren't.
RKO; Edmund Graiger — *Blackhawk Films*

French Postcards 1980
Drama/Romance
81119   91 mins   C   B, V   P
Miles Chapin, Blanche Baker, Valerie Quennessen, Debra Winger, Mandy Patinkin, Marie-France Pisier, directed by Willard Huyck
Three American students study all aspects of French culture when they spend their junior year of college at the Institute of French Studies in Paris.
MPAA:PG
Paramount; Gloria Katz — *Paramount Home Video*

French Quarter 1978
Drama
47404   101 mins   C   B, V   P
Bruce Davison, Virginia Mayo, Lindsay Bloom, Alisha Fontaine, Lance Legault, Ann Michelle
A young girl travels to the French Quarter in New Orleans. Desperate for work, she falls victim to an old woman who practices witchcraft and voodoo. The woman's voodoo causes the young girl to "slip" away. She awakens in the year 1900, under the care of prostitutes.
MPAA:R
Crown Intl Pictures; Dennis Kane — *United Home Video*

French Quarter Undercover 1985
Crime-Drama
88226   84 mins   C   B, V   P
Michael Parks, Bill Holiday, directed by Joe Catalanotto
Two undercover cops in New Orleans thwart a terrorist plot aimed at the World's Fair.
MPAA:R
Shapiro Ent. — *Lightning Video*

French Woman, The 1979
Drama
55595   97 mins   C   B, V   P
Francois Fabian, Klaus Kinski
A sensuous story of blackmail, murder, and sex involving French cabinet ministers mixing passion and politics.
MPAA:R
Monarch Pictures; Claire Duval — *VidAmerica*

Frenzy 1972
Suspense
11582   116 mins   C   B, V   P
Jon Finch, Barry Foster, Barbara Leigh-Hunt, Anna Massey, Directed by Alfred Hitchcock
A sex criminal known as The Necktie Murderer is terrorizing London, and Alfred Hitchcock has everyone guessing who the culprit is—including Scotland Yard.
MPAA:R
Universal; Alfred Hitchcock — *MCA Home Video*

FRESHSTART: 21 Days to Stop Smoking 1985
Smoking
70885   60 mins   C   B, V   P
Robert Klein
This American Cancer Society-approved program takes smokers from the day-one jitters to off-the-hook status in three weeks.
Simon and Schuster — *Simon and Schuster Video*

Friday the 13th 1980
Horror
54669   95 mins   C   B, V, LV   P
Betsy Palmer, Adrienne King, Harry Crosby, Laurie Bartrarr, Mark Nelsor, directed by Sean S. Cunningham
A New Jersey camp that's been closed for 20 years after a history of "accidental" deaths reopens and the horror begins again. Six would-be counselors arrive to get the place ready. Each are progressively murdered—knifed, speared, and axed.
MPAA:R
Paramount — *Paramount Home Video; RCA VideoDiscs*

Friday the 13th, Part 2   1981
Horror
53932   87 mins   C   B, V, LV   P
Amy Steel, John Furey, Adrienne King, Betsy Palmer, directed by Steve Miner
A group of teen camp counselors are gruesomely executed by yet another unknown assailant.
MPAA:R
Steve Miner — *Paramount Home Video; RCA VideoDiscs*

Friday the 13th, Part 3   1982
Horror
64021   96 mins   C   B, V, LV   P
Dana Kimmell, Paul Krata, Richard Brooker
Yet another group of naive counselors at Camp Crystal Lake fall victim to the maniacal Jason.
MPAA:R
Jason Productions — *Paramount Home Video*

Friday the 13th, The Final   1984
Chapter
Horror
79183   90 mins   C   B, V   P
Kimberly Beck, Ted White, Peter Barton
Jason escapes from the morgue to once again slaughter and annihilate teenagers at a lakeside cottage.
MPAA:R
Paramount — *Paramount Home Video*

Friday the 13th, Part V—A   1985
New Beginning
Horror
Closed Captioned
81509   92 mins   C   B, V   P
John Shepherd, Shavar Ross, Richard Young
Jason rises from the dead to slice up the residents of a secluded halfway house.
MPAA:R
PARAMOUNT — *Paramount Home Video*

Friendly Persuasion   1956
Drama
Closed Captioned
80140   140 mins   C   B, V   P
Gary Cooper, Dorothy McGuire, Anthony Perkins, Marjorie Main, directed by William Wyler
The outbreak of the Civil War disrupts the lives of a Quaker family in southern Indiana.
William Wyler — *CBS/Fox Video*

Fright Night   1985
Horror
Closed Captioned
84602   106 mins   C   B, V   P
William Ragsdale, Chris Sarandon, Amanda Bearse, Roddy McDowell, Stephen Geoffreys, directed by Tom Holland
It's Dracula versus the teens time, and when Charley suspects that his new neighbor

descends from the Count Vlad's line, he calls in Peter Vincent to help de-ghoul the neighborhood. Mr. Vincent hosts a late-evening horror film series on local TV entitled "Fright Night."
MPAA:R
Herb Jaffe — *RCA/Columbia Pictures Home Video*

Frightmare   1983
Horror
64874   84 mins   C   B, V   P
A great horror star dies, but he refuses to give up his need for adoration and revenge.
MPAA:R
Patrick and Tallie Wright — *Vestron Video*

Frightmare   1976
Horror
80289   86 mins   C   B, V   P
Deborah Fairfax, Kim Butcher, Rupert Davies, Sheila Keith
There's a strange coincidence when a pair of sisters are involved in a gruesome series of murders similar to ones their parents committed years earlier.
MPAA:R
Joseph Brenner Associates — *Prism*

Frightmare II   1976
Horror
71217   86 mins   C   B, V   P
A young woman makes some startling discoveries. Firstly, her parents were locked away for committing several gruesome murders. Secondly, her sister is a delinquent. Third, police report a new series of mutilations. Finally, she's invited to a family reunion.
Independent — *Prism*

Frisco Kid, The   1979
Comedy
58232   119 mins   C   B, V   P
Gene Wilder, Harrison Ford, directed by Robert Aldrich
An orthodox rabbi from Poland sets out for the wild west.
MPAA:PG
Warner Bros — *Warner Home Video*

Fritz the Cat   1972
Comedy
59850   77 mins   C   B, V   P
Animated
Ralph Bakshi's animated tale for adults about a cat's adventures as he gets into group sex, college radicalism and other hazards of life in the 60's.
MPAA:X
Steve Krantz — *Warner Home Video*

Frog Prince, The 1971
Fairy tales
47346   50 mins   C   B, V, LV   R, P
The Muppets
Kermit the Frog narrates the Muppet version of
this classic fairy tale. A handsome prince has
been turned into a frog by an evil witch's spell,
and only the kiss of a beautiful princess can
change him back.
RLP Canada/Henson Associates — *Muppet
Home Video*

Frogs 1972
Horror
64839   91 mins   C   B, V   P
*Ray Milland, Sam Elliott, Joan Van Ark, Adam
Roarke, Judy Pace, directed by George
McCowan*
Amphibians and reptiles on a tropical island
take revenge against the family of a wildlife-
hating recluse.
MPAA:PG
American International Pictures — *Warner
Home Video; Vestron Video (disc only)*

Frolics on Ice 1940
Comedy
38976   65 mins   B/W   B, V, FO   P
*Roscoe Karns, Lynne Roberts, Irene Dare,
Edgar Kennedy*
Pleasant comedy-musical about a family man
saving to buy the barber shop he works at. Irene
Dare is featured in several ice skating
production numbers.
Hal Roach — *Video Yesteryear*

From Broadway to 193?
Hollywood
Film-History
10157   48 mins   B/W   B, V   P, T
Ed Sullivan, Eddie Cantor, Shirley Temple
Includes highlights from the 30's such as Shirley
Temple's "Biggest Little Star of the Thirties"
and Lew Lehr's "Cwazy Monkies." Also
features Ed Sullivan, Eddie Cantor, Jack
Dempsey, and Little Rascals.
Educational et al — *Blackhawk Films*

From China with Death 1973
Martial arts
63859   90 mins   C   B, V   P
After a vicious War Lord wipes out his family, a
young man trains under a martial arts master to
prepare himself for revenge.
MPAA:R
United International Pictures — *Hollywood
Home Theater*

From D-Day to Victory in 1985
Europe
History-US/World War II
70752   112 mins   C   B, V   P
Written and narrated by Max Hastings

Based on Mr. Hastings best selling novel, this
program combines original battlefield fontage
with computer graphics for a thorough
description of the War's turning point.
Bob Hunter — *MPI Home Video*

From Hell to Victory 1979
War-Drama
79222   100 mins   C   B, V   P
*George Peppard, George Hamilton, Horst
Bucholz, Anny Duprey, Sam Wanamaker,
Capucine*
A group of friends who meet in Paris before
World War II vow to return there again to
reminisce about old times.
MPAA:PG
New Film Productions — *Media Home
Entertainment*

From Russia with Love 1963
Suspense
53787   118 mins   C   B, V, LV,   P
                         CED
*Sean Connery, Robert Shaw, Daniela Bianchi,
Lotte Lenya*
A Russian spy joins an international crime
organization and develops a plan to kill James
Bond and steal a coding machine. The second
Bond feature.
United Artists; Eon; Harry Saltzman; Albert
Broccoli — *CBS/Fox Video; RCA VideoDiscs*

From "Star Wars" to 1983
"Jedi": The Making of a
Saga
Science fiction/Filmmaking
Closed Captioned
84422   65 mins   C   B, V   P
Narrated by Mark Hamill
Using copious amounts of actual footage from
the films, this movie follows the production of all
three "Star Wars" sagas, concentrating on the
special effects involved.
Richard Schickel — *Playhouse Video*

From the Czar to Stalin 1982
Documentary/USSR
75702   93 mins   C   B, V   P
Leon Trotsky, Joseph Stalin, Nikolai Lenin
The powers who changed the world in rare
footage of Russian history makers.
Unknown — *Video Associates*

From the Earth to the 1958
Moon
Science fiction
11723   100 mins   C   B, V   P
George Sanders, Joseph Cotton
Jules Verne's thriller in which three men and a
woman rocket to the moon.
Warner Bros — *United Home Video*

From the Life of the Marionettes   1980
Drama
81262   103 mins   C   B, V   P
Robert Atzorn, Christine Bucheggar, Martin Benrath, Rita Russek, directed by Ingmar Bergman
This film follows a rich businessman's descent into madness as he murders and sexually assaults a prostitute that resembles his nagging wife. With English subtitles. Available in VHS Stereo and Beta Hi-Fi.
MPAA:R SW
ITC; Martin Starger — U.S.A. Home Video

From the New World   1982
Music-Performance
47807   ? mins   C   LV   P
Dvorak's "Symphony No. 9 in E minor, Op.95—From the New World" is performed by the Czech Philharmonic Orchestra (stereo).
Unknown — Pioneer Video Imports

From These Roots   1984
Performing arts
88378   28 mins   B/W   B, V, 3/4U   P
Narrated by Brock Peters, this view of the 1920's 'Harlem Renaissance' features the work of Cab Calloway, Paul Robeson, Ethel Waters, Duke Ellington, Langston Hughes and Claude MacKay. Music by Eubie Blake.
Your World Video — Your World Video

From Worst to First   1980
Football
45131   24 mins   C   B, V, FO   R, P
Tampa Bay Buccaneers
Highlights of the 1979 Tampa Bay Buccaneers football season.
NFL Films — NFL Films Video

Front, The   1976
Drama
58961   95 mins   C   B, V   P
Woody Allen, Zero Mostel, Herschel Bernardi, Michael Murphy, Diana Marcovicci, directed by Martin Ritt
A bookmaker becomes a "front" for blacklisted writers during the communist witch hunts of the 1950's.
MPAA:PG
Columbia — RCA/Columbia Pictures Home Video

Front Page, The   1931
Comedy
57760   101 mins   B/W   B, V   P
Adolph Menjou, Pat O'Brien, Edward Everett Horton, directed by Lewis Milestone
The original version of the Hecht-MacArthur play about a battling newspaper reporter and his editor in Chicago.

United Artists — Hollywood Home Theater; Discount Video Tapes; Cable Films; Video Connection; Video Yesteryear; Western Film & Video Inc; Kartes Video Communications

Frontier Horizon   1948
Western
56601   55 mins   B/W   B, V, 3/4U   R, P
John Wayne, Phyllis Isley (Jennifer Jones), Ray Carrigan
A promoter is swindling ranchers out of land in order to build a dam to flood the land for a reservoir.
Republic — Spotlite Video; Cable Films

Frontier Pony Express   1939
Western
64389   54 mins   B/W   B, V, 3/4U   P
Roy Rogers
Roy and Trigger do their best to help the Pony Express riders who are being attacked by marauding gangs.
Republic — Nostalgia Merchant; Discount Video Tapes

Frontier Vengeance   1940
Western
64420   54 mins   B/W   B, V, 3/4U   P
Don "Red" Barry
A stagecoach driver helps a young girl who is being terrorized by crooks.
Republic — Nostalgia Merchant

Frosty's Winter Wonderland/The Leprechaun's Gold   197?
Christmas/Cartoons
70849   50 mins   C   B, V   P
Animated, voices by Andy Griffith, Shelley Winters, Art Carney, Peggy Cass, directed by Arthur Rankin Jr and Jules Bass
This tape features two holiday programs. In Frosty, Jack Frost threatens the Snowman and his wife, while in the second story a young boy discovers a magical island of leprechauns at Christmas.
Telepicture — Lightning Video

Fuerte Perdido (Fort Lost)   1978
Western
51102   90 mins   C   B, V   P
Esther Rojo, German Cobos, Mario Vidal
Settlers battle for their lives against hostile Indians led by Geronimo. In Spanish.
SP
Spanish — Hollywood Home Theater

Fugitive Samurai   1984
Martial arts
81862   92 mins   C   B, V   P
Kinnosuke Yorozuya, Katzutaka Nishikawa

A Shogun High Executioner sets out on a trail of revenge against the people who have betrayed him.
Nippon Television Network — *Sony Video Software*

Fugitive: The Final Episode, The   1967
Drama
53788   103 mins   C   B, V   P
David Janssen, Barry Morse, Bill Raisch, Diane Baker, Joseph Campanella, Michael Constantine
The final episode of the acclaimed series, aired on August 29, 1967, in which Dr. Richard Kimble meets up with the one-armed man who murdered his wife. This episode was the highest rated program up to that time.
Quinn Martin Prods — *Worldvision Home Video; RCA VideoDiscs*

Fugitive, The (The Taking of Luke McVane)   1915
Western
66134   28 mins   B/W   B, V, FO   P
William S. Hart, Enid Markey
An early silent western in which Hart upholds the cowboy code of honor.
Thomas Ince — *Video Yesteryear*

FUHRER! Rise of a Madman   1985
Documentary/World War II
71064   108 mins   B/W   B, V   P
This film documents the life of Adolph Hitler, one of history's most notorious villians.
Independent — *MPI Home Video*

Full Hearts and Empty Pockets   1963
Drama
63623   88 mins   B/W   B, V, FO   P
Linda Christian, Gino Cervi, Senta Berger
This film follows the happy-go-lucky adventures of a young, handsome, impoverished gentleman on the loose in Rome. Dubbed in English.
Screen Gems — *Video Yesteryear*

Full Moon in Paris   1984
Romance
85607   101 mins   C   B, V   P
Pascale Ogier, Tcheky Karyo, Fabrice Luchini, directed by Eric Rohmer
A young woman in Paris moves out on her lover in order to experience freedom and finds it brings only misery. With English subtitles.
Venice Film Festival'84: Best Actress (Ogier).
MPAA:R   FR
French — *Media Home Entertainment*

Fuller Brush Man, The   1948
Comedy
80786   93 mins   B/W   B, V   P
Red Skelton, Janet Blair, Don McGuire, Adele Jergens, directed by Frank Tashlin
A newly hired Fuller Brush man becomes involved in murder and romance as he tries to win the heart of his girlfriend.
Columbia Pictures — *RCA/Columbia Pictures Home Video*

Fun and Fancy Free   1947
Musical/Comedy
63126   96 mins   C   B, V   P
Edgar Bergen, Charlie McCarthy, Jiminy Cricket, Mickey Mouse, Donald Duck, Goofy, the voice of Dinah Shore
This part-animated, part-live-action feature is split into two segments: "Bongo," with Dinah Shore narrating the story of a happy-go-lucky circus bear; and "Mickey and the Beanstalk," a "new" version of an old fairy tale.
Walt Disney Productions — *Walt Disney Home Video*

Fun Factory/Clown Princes of Hollywood   196?
Comedy
10110   56 mins   B/W   B, V   P, T
Mack Sennett, Charlie Chaplin, Buster Keaton, Charley Chase, Ben Turpin, Stan Laurel
Collection of various slapstick situations including Keystone Cops segments. From the "History of Motion Pictures" series.
Mack Sennett et al — *Blackhawk Films*

Fun in Acapulco   1963
Musical
08382   97 mins   C   B, V   P
Elvis Presley, Ursula Andress, Elsa Cardenas, Paul Lukas
Elvis romances two beauties and acts as a part-time lifeguard and night club entertainer.
EL, SP
Paramount; Hal Wallis — *CBS/Fox Video; RCA VideoDiscs*

Fun with Dick and Jane   1977
Comedy
21286   104 mins   C   B, V   P
George Segal, Jane Fonda, Ed McMahon
An upper-middle class couple turn to armed robbery to support themselves when the husband is fired from his job.
MPAA:PG
Columbia — *RCA/Columbia Pictures Home Video*

Funeral for an Assassin   1977
Adventure
52610   92 mins   C   B, V   R, P
Vic Morrow, Peter Van Dissel

A professional assassin seeks revenge for his imprisonment by the government of South Africa, a former client. Planning to kill all of the country's leading politicians, he masquerades as a black man, a cover which is designed to fool the apartheid establishment.
MPAA:PG
Walter Brough; Ivan Hall — *Video Gems*

Funeral in Berlin   1966
Mystery
88427   102 mins   C   B, V   P
Michael Caine, Eva Renzi, Oscar Homolka, directed by Guy Hamilton
The second of the Caine-Harry Palmer espionage films, in which the deadpan British secret serviceman arranges the questionable defection of a Russian colonel.
Paramount — *Paramount Home Video*

Funhouse, The   1981
Horror
47415   96 mins   C   B, V   P
Elizabeth Berridge, Shawn Carson, Cooper Huckabee, Largo Woodruff, Sylvia Miles, directed by Tobe Hooper
Four teenagers spend the night at a carnival funhouse and are brutally hacked and maimed by a crazed father and son.
MPAA:R
Universal — *MCA Home Video*

Funny Face   1957
Musical
77447   103 mins   C   B, V, LV   P
Fred Astaire, Audrey Hepburn, Kay Thompson, Suzy Parker, directed by Stanley Donen
A fashion photographer turns a girl working in a bookstore into a high fashion model. The musical score features such Gershwin songs as "Bonjour Paris" and "Funny Face".
Paramount Pictures — *Paramount Home Video*

Funny Farm, The   1982
Comedy
69675   90 mins   C   B, V   P
Miles Chapin, Eileen Brennan, Peter Ackroyd
A group of ambitious young comics strive to make it in the crazy world of comedy at Los Angeles' famous club, The Funny Farm.
Independent — *THORN EMI/HBO Video*

Funny Girl   1968
Musical-Drama
64237   151 mins   C   B, V   P
Barbra Streisand, Omar Sharif, Walter Pidgeon, Kay Medford, Anne Francis, directed by William Wyler
This films follows the early career of Fanny Brice, her rise to stardom with the Ziegfeld Follies and her stormy romance with Nick Arnstein. The classic songs "People" and

"Don't Rain on My Parade" are featured. In stereo.
Academy Awards '68: Best Actress (Streisand).
MPAA:G
Columbia; Ray Stark — *RCA/Columbia Pictures Home Video; RCA VideoDiscs*

Funny Guys and Gals of   193?
the Talkies
Comedy
11285   60 mins   B/W   B, V, FO   P
W.C. Fields, Shirley Temple, Charlotte Greenwood, Groucho Marx, Marlene Dietrich
Four short pictures featuring the comedy stars of the early talking pictures: "The Golf Specialist," "Pardon My Pups," "Girls Will Be Boys," and "Band Rally Radio Show."
Mack Sennett et al — *Video Yesteryear*

Funny Money   1982
Comedy/Adventure
84892   92 mins   C   B, V   P
Gregg Henry, Elizabeth Daily, Gareth Hunt
The mob comically chases a pair of credit card thieves.
Norfolk Int'l Pictures — *Lightning Video*

Funny Thing Happened   1966
on the Way to the Forum,
A
Comedy
47794   99 mins   C   B, V, LV,   P
                                    CED
Zero Mostel, Phil Silvers, Jack Gilford, Buster Keaton, directed by Richard Lester
A bawdy Broadway farce set in ancient Rome where a conniving, eager-to-be-free slave sees his way to freedom.
United Artists — *CBS/Fox Video; RCA VideoDiscs*

Funstuff   193?
Comedy
10042   59 mins   B/W   B, V   P, T
Shirley Temple, Harold Lloyd
Shirley Temple and friends struggle for stardom. Harold Lloyd plays "Non-Stop Kid" and Snub Pollard strives to be an artist.
Educational et al — *Blackhawk Films*

Furious Avenger, The   1976
Martial arts
87604   84 mins   C   B, V   P
Hsiung Fei, Fan Ling, Chen Pai Ling, Tien Yeh, Wang Mo Chou
A released convict, on his way to avenging his family's murder, stops a rape and takes on nemesis after nemesis in a rousing kickfest. Dubbed.
King Kai — *Unicorn Video*

Fury, The 1978
Horror
56903   117 mins   C   B, V   P
Kirk Douglas, John Cassavetes, Carrie
Snodgress, Andrew Stevens, Amy Irving,
Charles Durning, directed by Brian dePalma
The head of a government institute for psychic
research finds that his own son is wanted by
terrorists who wish to use his lethal powers.
MPAA:R
Twentieth Century Fox, Frank
Yablans — CBS/Fox Video

Fury of the Wolfman, The 1974
Horror
84074   84 mins   C   B, V   P
A murdering werewolf is captured by a female
scientist who tries to cure his lycanthropy with
drugs and brain implants.
EL, SP
Spanish-Embassy — Unicorn Video

Future Kill 1985
Horror/Adventure
71122   83 mins   C   B, V, LV   P
Edwin Neal, Marilyn Burns, Doug Davis, directed
by Ronald W. Moore
Anti-nuclear activists battle fraternity brothers in
this grim futuristic world. Shakey political
alliances form between revenge-seeking
factions on both sides.
MPAA:R
International Film Marketing — Vestron Video

Futureworld 1976
Science fiction
53512   107 mins   C   B, V   P
Peter Fonda, Blythe Danner, Arthur Hill, Yul
Brenner, Stu Margolin
In the sequel to "Westworld," two reporters
junket to the new "Futureworld," where they
support a scheme to clone and control world
leaders.
MPAA:PG
American Intl Pictures — Warner Home Video;
Vestron Video (disc only)

Fuzz 1972
Adventure/Comedy-Drama
69383   92 mins   C   B, V, CED   P
Burt Reynolds, Tom Skerritt, Yul Brynner,
Raquel Welch
Combining fast action and sharp-edged humor,
this film portrays the life of a band of police
officers trying to keep the streets of Boston
safe.
MPAA:PG
United Artists — CBS/Fox Video

Fyre 1978
Drama
55215   90 mins   C   B, V   P

The story of a young beautiful girl who moves
from the midwest to Los Angeles unfolds as she
becomes a prostitute and encounters many new
experiences.
MPAA:R
Fyre Productions — Media Home
Entertainment

G

Gas-s-s-s 1970
Comedy
81318   79 mins   C   B, V   P
Cindy Williams, Ben Vereen, Talia Shire, Bud
Cort, Elaine Giftes, directed by Roger Corman
When a defense plant in Alaska springs a gas
main, everyone over twenty five dies. Those still
alive take over the world with humorous results.
MPAA:PG
Roger Corman — Lightning Video

Gabi und Frank 1986
Languages-Instruction
87198   60 mins   C   B, V   P
A twelve-lesson video course that teaches
conversational German.
AM Available
Gessler Ed. Software — Gessler Educational
Software

Gabriela 1984
Comedy
80632   105 mins   C   B, V   P
Marcello Mastroianni, Sonia Braga, Nelson
Xavier, Antonio Cantafora, directed by Bruno
Barreto
A hot and sultry romance develops between a
Brazilian tavern keeper and the new cook that
he's just hired. Music by Antonio Carlos Jobim.
With English subtitles.
MPAA:R
United Artists — MGM/UA Home Video

Gaiety 1943
Musical
08737   40 mins   B/W   B, V, 3/4U   P
Antonio Moreno, Armida, Anne Ayers
Explores the lighter side of lion hunting.
Hal Roach — Hal Roach Studios

Gaiking 1982
Cartoons
64199   100 mins   C   B, V   P
Animated
The mighty flying rubork, Gaiking, becomes
earth's strongest and most heroic defense
against the cunning Davius.
EL, SP

Toei Animation; Jim Terry Production — *Family Home Entertainment*

Galactica III: Conquest of the Earth · 1980
Science fiction
59684   99 mins   C   B, V   P
Lorne Greene, Kent McCord, Barry Van Dyke, Robin Douglas, Robert Reed
In an encounter with Earth, Commander Adama sends Lt. Troy and Lt. Dillon to the U.S. in order to bring the earthlings up to their level of technology.
MPAA:R
Universal — *MCA Home Video*

Galaxina · 1981
Science fiction/Comedy
55550   96 mins   C   B, V, LV   P
Dorothy Stratten, Avery Schreiber, Stephen Macht
In the 31st century, a beautiful robot woman capable of human feelings is created. A parody of superspace fantasies.
MPAA:R
Crown International; Marilyn Tenser — *MCA Home Video*

Galaxy Express · 1980
Fantasy/Cartoons
65709   94 mins   C   B, V   P
Animated, voices by Booker Bradshaw, Corey Burton
A young boy sets out to find immortality by traveling on The Galaxy Express, an ultra-modern 35th century Ospace train that carries its passengers in search of their dreams.
MPAA:PG
Toei — *Embassy Home Entertainment*

Galaxy Invader, The · 1985
Science fiction
77199   90 mins   C   B, V   P
Richard Ruxton, Faye Tilles, Don Liefert
Chaos erupts when an alien explorer crashlands his spacecraft in a backwoods area of the United States.
MPAA:PG
Moviecraft Entertainment — *United Home Video*

Galaxy of Terror · 1981
Science fiction/Horror
65719   85 mins   C   B, V   P
Erin Moran, Edward Albert, Ray Walston
The mind's innermost fears become reality when a spaceship rescue mission lands on a dark and barren planet.
MPAA:R
Roger Corman; Marc Siegler — *Embassy Home Entertainment*

Gallagher—Over Your Head · 1986
Comedy-Performance
71381   58 mins   C   B, V   P
Gallagher
The popular comedian expounds on politicians, ancient history, childbearing and other topical subjects.
Wizard of Odd — *Paramount Home Video*

Gallagher—Stuck in the 60's · 1984
Comedy-Performance
80400   60 mins   C   B, V, LV, CED   P
Comic Gallagher describes what his life was like in the 1960's in this concert performance.
Showtime — *Paramount Home Video*

Gallagher--The Bookkeeper · 1985
Comedy-Performance
87567   58 mins   C   B, V   P
The notorious comic takes a stand-up aim at bureaucracy and the trials of modern life.
Paramount — *Paramount Home Video*

Gallagher—The Maddest · 1984
Comedy-Performance
80399   60 mins   C   B, V, LV, CED   P
The madcap comedy of Gallagher is captured in this concert.
Showtime — *Paramount Home Video*

Gallipoli · 1981
Drama
59203   111 mins   C   B, V, LV   P
Mel Gibson, Mark Lee, directed by Peter Weir
History blends with the destiny of two friends as they become part of a legendary World War I confrontation between Australia and the German Allied Turks.
MPAA:PG
Paramount; Robert Stigwood — *Paramount Home Video*

Galyon · 1977
Adventure
77234   92 mins   C   B, V   P
Stan Brock, Lloyd Nolan, Ina Balin
A soldier of fortune is recruited by an oil tycoon to find his daughter and son-in-law in South America.
MPAA:PG
Ivan Tors — *Monterey Home Video*

Gamble on Love · 1986
Romance/Drama
71241   90 mins   C   V   P
Introduced by Louis Jourdan

A woman returns to her father's Las Vegas casino, and falls for the man who manages the gaming room.
Commworld; Romance Theater — *Prism*

Gambler, The   1974
Drama
59425   111 mins   C   B, V, LV   P
James Caan, Lauren Hutton, Paul Sorvino, Burt Young, directed by Karl Reisz
The story of a college professor who is also a compulsive gambler who falls into debt and trouble with the mob.
MPAA:R
Paramount — *Paramount Home Video*

Game of Death   1979
Martial arts/Adventure
59624   100 mins   C   B, V, CED   P
Bruce Lee, Dean Jagger, Colleen Camp
Bruce Lee's final kung fu thriller about a young martial arts movie star who gets involved with the syndicate.
MPAA:R
Galaxy Films — *CBS/Fox Video*

Game of Seduction   1976
Drama
70907   90 mins   C   B, V   P
Sylvia Kristel, Nathalie Delon, Jon Finch, directed by Roger Vadim
Countesses, killers, knaves and oversexed, conniving schemers compete in Parisian society's favorite participatory sport.
Roger Vadim — *VCL Home Video*

Game Show Program   195?
Game show
33692   120 mins   B/W   B, V, 3/4U   P
Exciting quiz shows of the 1950s are seen in their entirety: "Do You Trust Your Wife," with Edgar Bergen and Charlie McCarthy, "You Bet Your Life," with Groucho Marx, "The Price Is Right," with Bill Cullen, and "Play Your Hunch," with Merv Griffin.
CBS et al — *Shokus Video*

Game Show Program II   196?
Game show
33693   120 mins   B/W   B, V, 3/4U   P
A collection of four game show programs including: "People Are Funny," with Art Linkletter, "Take a Good Look," with Ernie Kovacs, "Concentration," with Hugh Downs, and "I've Got a Secret," starring Steve Allen and a celebrity panel.
CBS et al — *Shokus Video*

Game Show Program III   196?
Game show
33695   120 mins   C   B, V, 3/4U   P

Four favorite game shows of the past twenty years are seen in their entirety: "The Price Is Right," "Truth or Consequences," "The Face Is Familiar," and "PDQ." Some black and white.
NBC et al — *Shokus Video*

Game Show Program, IV   1956
Game show
87206   120 mins   B/W   B, V, 3/4U   P
Bud Collyer, Ernie Kovacs, Groucho Marx, George Fenneman, Cesar Romero
Four episodes of vintage game shows: "You Bet Your Life," "Take a Good Look," "Bride and Groom" and "Beat the Clock."
CBS et al. — *Shokus Video*

Games Girls Play   1975
Comedy
81399   90 mins   C   B, V   P
Christina Hart, Jane Anthony, Jill Damas, Drina Pavlovic, directed by Jack Arnold
The daughter of an American diplomat organizes a contest at a British boarding school to see which of her classmates can seduce important dignitaries. Available in VHS Stereo and Beta Hi-Fi.
Peter J. Oppenheimer — *Monterey Home Video*

Gandhi   1982
Drama
65186   188 mins   C   B, V   P
Ben Kingsley, Candice Bergen, Edward Fox, John Gielgud, John Mills, Martin Sheen, directed by Sir Richard Attenborough
A sprawling biography of Mahatma Gandhi, India's man of peace, which follows his life from his simple beginnings as a lawyer in South Africa through his struggle to free India from colonial rule.
Academy Awards '82: Best Picture; Best Actor (Kingsley); Best Director.   MPAA:PG
Columbia — *RCA/Columbia Pictures Home Video; RCA VideoDiscs*

Gangbusters   1938
Mystery/Serials
07381   253 mins   B/W   B, V, 3/4U   R, P
Kent Taylor, Irene Hervey, Robert Armstrong
Men battle crime in the city. A serial based on the popular radio series of the same name. In thirteen episodes.
Universal — *Cable Films; Video Connection; Video Dimensions; Video Yesteryear; Discount Video Tapes*

Gangs, Inc.   1941
Crime-Drama
58515   72 mins   B/W   B, V, 3/4U   P
Alan Ladd, Joan Woodbury, Jack LaRue, Linda Ware, John Archer, Vince Barnett

The story of how a woman with an unhappy past turned to a life of crime. Also known as "Paper Bullets."
Producers Releasing Corp — *Discount Video Tapes; Kartes Video Communications*

Gangster Wars, The   1981
Crime-Drama
47416   121 mins   C   B, V   P
Michael Nouri, Joe Penny
A specially edited-for-video version of the television mini-series, "The Gangster Chronicles." Based on fact, it deals with the growth of organized crime in America from the early days of this century, concentrating on three ghetto kids who grow up to become powerful mobsters.
Universal — *MCA Home Video*

Gap Band Video Train   1985
Music video
84491   23 mins   C   B, V   P
The Gap band performs their best funk/pop hits on video.
Polygram Records Inc — *Sony Video Software*

Garbo Talks   1984
Comedy
Closed Captioned
70658   104 mins   C   B, V   P
Anne Bancroft, Ron Silver, Carrie Fisher, Catherine Hicks, Steven Hill, Howard DaSilva, Dorothy Loudon, directed by Sidney Lumet
A dying eccentric's last request is to meet the reclusive screenlegend Greta Garbo. Her son goes to extreme and amusing lengths in order to fulfill this wish. Available in Hi-Fi stereo.
MPAA:PG13
MGM/UA — *CBS/Fox Video*

Garden of the Finzi-   1971
Continis, The
Drama
37519   90 mins   C   B, V   R, P
Dominique Sanda, Helmut Berger, Lino Capolicchio, Fabio Testi, directed by Vittorio De Sica
The story of an aristocratic Jewish family living under increasing Fascist opporession in pre-World War II Italy.
MPAA:R
Cinema 5 — *RCA/Columbia Pictures Home Video*

Gardening in the City: I   1982
Gardening/Plants
59574   60 mins   C   B, V   P
Members of the world-famous New York Botanical Gardens' staff offer an illuminating introduction to plant life.
New York Botanical Gardens — *Mastervision*

Gardening in the City: II   1982
Gardening/Plants
59575   60 mins   C   B, V   P
The scientists of the New York Botanical Gardens give examples of proper soil and planting conditions and offer lessons in the use of fertilizers and correct pruning methods.
New York Botanical Gardens — *Mastervision*

Garry Shandling Show,   1985
25th Anniversary Special,
The
Comedy-Performance
87568   57 mins   C   B, V   P
A comedy special in which stand-up comic Shandling salutes his fictional long-running talk show.
Showtime — *Paramount Home Video*

Gary Numan—The   1980
Touring Principal '79
Music-Performance
54689   60 mins   C   B, V   P
Gary Numan
This program features Gary Numan, the British singer/composer, on his 1979 world tour. Material includes selections from his second album "The Pleasure Principle" including the hit single. "Cars."
Warner Bros — *Warner Home Video*

Gary Player on Golf   1985
Golf
85093   90 mins   C   B, V, 8mm   P
Player instructs the viewer on the basics and nuances of the game.
Master Source Video Inc — *North American Video*

Gary Yanker's Walking   1985
Workouts
Physical fitness
84634   56 mins   C   B, V   P
Directed by Ron Brody
A work-out concentrating on walking aerobically.
Bruce Cohn — *MCA Home Video*

Gas   1981
Comedy
58711   94 mins   C   B, V   P
Donald Sutherland, Susan Anspach, Sterling Hayden, Peter Aykroyd, Helen Shaver
A gas shortage hits an average American town.
MPAA:R
Paramount; Claude Heroux — *Paramount Home Video*

Gas Pump Girls   1982
Comedy
59657   102 mins   C   B, V   R, P

THE VIDEO TAPE & DISC GUIDE

Five lovely ladies manage a gas station and use their feminine wiles to win the battle against a shady oil sheik.
MPAA:R
David A Davies — *Vestron Video*

Gaslight   **1944**
Mystery/Drama
80208 114 mins B/W B, V, LV P
Charles Boyer, Ingrid Bergman, Joseph Cotten, Angela Lansbury, Terry Moore, directed by George Cukor
An evil man tries to conjure up ways to drive his wife insane.
Academy Awards '44: Best Actress (Bergman); Best Art Direction, Black and White.
MGM — *MGM/UA Home Video*

Gathering, The   **198?**
Drama
78069 94 mins C B, V P
Ed Asner, Maureen Stapleton
A dying man seeks out the wife and family he has alienated for a final Christmas gathering.
Harry R Sherman — *Worldvision Home Video*

Gathering Storm   **1974**
Drama/Biographical
71223 72 mins C V P
Richard Burton, Virginia McKenna, Ian Bannen
Based on the first book of memoirs from Sir Winston Churchill, this drama examines the pre-World War II years.
BBC; Clarion Productions; LeVien International — *Prism*

Gator   **1976**
Adventure
63401 116 mins C B, V P
Burt Reynolds, Jerry Reed, Lauren Hutton, directed by Burt Reynolds
This sequel to "White Lightning" follows the adventures of Gator (Reynolds), who is recruited to gather evidence to convict a corrupt political boss.
MPAA:PG
United Artists — *CBS/Fox Video*

Gauntlet, The   **1977**
Crime-Drama/Adventure
58233 111 mins C B, V P
Clint Eastwood, Sondra Locke, directed by Clint Eastwood
A cop is ordered to Las Vegas to bring back a key witness for an important trial—but the witness turns out to be a beautiful prostitute being hunted by killers.
MPAA:R
Warner Bros — *Warner Home Video; RCA VideoDiscs*

Gay Divorcee, The   **1934**
Musical
00269 107 mins B/W B, V, 3/4U P
Fred Astaire, Ginger Rogers, Edward Everett Horton, Alice Brady, Erik Rhodes, Betty Grable
Fred pursues Ginger to an English seaside resort, where she mistakes him for her hired co-respondent. Songs include "Night and Day," "Don't Let It Bother You" and "Needle in a Haystack."
Academy Awards '34: Best Song (The Continental; Con Conrad and Herb Magidson).
RKO; Pandro S Berman — *Nostalgia Merchant*

Gay Ranchero, The   **1942**
Western
10700 55 mins B/W B, V P
Roy Rogers, Andy Devine
A sheriff hunts for a commercial airways plane that has disappeared.
Republic — *Video Connection; Cable Films*

Gemini Affair   **198?**
Romance
73956 88 mins C B, V P
Marta Kristen, Kathy Kersh, Anne Seymour
Two women go to Hollywood to become rich and famous but end up being very disappointed.
Independent — *Unicorn Video*

Gene Autry Matinee   **1953**
Double Feature #2
Western
82177 117 mins B/W B, V P
Gene Autry, Champion, Smiley Burnette, Al Bridges
An exciting western double feature: A cowboy goes after the man who stole his rodeo winnings in "Melody Trail" and a territorial ranger investigates a series of Indian raids in "Winning of the West."
Republic Pictures — *Republic Pictures Home Video*

Gene Autry Matinee   **1953**
Double Feature #3
Western
82178 113 mins B/W B, V P
Gene Autry, Champion, Smiley Burnette
An exciting Roy Rogers double feature: In "Susanna Pass," he discovers a conspiracy to acquire the deed to a lake rich in oil deposits. In "Sons of the Pioneers" (black and white), Roy investigates a series of livestock murders in Rogers City.
Republic Pictures — *Republic Pictures Home Video*

General, The   **1968**
Adventure/Fantasy
80419 50 mins C B, V P
Patrick McGoohan, Angelo Muscat, Colin Gordon, Alexis Kanner, Leo McKern

---

The General, a mysterious, unseen figure is introducing a new technique of speed learning to the Villagers.
Associated TV Corp. — *MPI Home Video*

General, The   1927
Comedy
12429   78 mins   B/W   B, V   P
Buster Keaton, Marion Mack, directed by Buster Keaton, Clyde Bruckman
A Civil War espionage spoof. A Confederate soldier almost wins the war single handedly when he goes behind Northern lines to recover his beloved locomotive. (Silent).
United Artists — *Hollywood Home Theater; Video Yesteryear; Prism; Video Dimensions; Cable Films; Western Film & Video Inc; Discount Video Tapes; Kartes Video Communications; Blackhawk Films*

General Della Rovere   1960
Adventure
76638   139 mins   B/W   B, V   P
Vittorio De Sica, Hannes Messemer, Sandra Milo
A petty con man fleeces his victims by posing as a Colonel.
Zebra; Gaumont — *Hollywood Home Theater*

General Electric Theatre, The   1955
Variety
85175   89 mins   B/W   B, V   P
Ralph Bellamy, George Montgomery, Fred Waring, Joe Louis, Jesse White
A trio of television drama-sketches, from melodrama to musical tour: "Outpost at Home," "American Tour," and "The Return of Gentleman Jim."
CBS — *Video Yesteryear*

General Motors 8 Cylinder   1986
Automobiles
88415   60 mins   C   B, V, 3/4U   P
A program demonstrating basic maintenance and tune-up procedures for the entitled American engine.
Peter Allen Prod. — *Peter Allen Video Productions*

General, The/Slapstick   1926
Film-History
50639   56 mins   B/W   B, V   P, T
Buster Keaton, Marion Mack, Charlie Murray, Mabel Normand, Fatty Arbuckle, Edgar Kennedy
A double feature composed of abridged versions of the Buster Keaton spoof on Civil War espionage, and a Mack Sennett anthology of slapstick comedy.
United Artists — *Blackhawk Films*

General/Slapstick, The   1926
Comedy
84951   40 mins   B/W   B, V   P
Buster Keaton, Mabel Normand, Fatty Arbuckle
The two-part program consists of a condensation of the Keaton Classic, and a compilation of silent slapstick bits.
Pathe et al. — *Blackhawk Films*

Generation   1969
Drama
86090   109 mins   C   B, V   P
David Janssen, Kim Darby, Carl Reiner, Peter Duel, Andrew Prine
A very pregnant bride informs everyone she'll give birth at home without doctors, and creates a panic.
Avco Embassy — *Embassy Home Entertainment*

Genesis/Three Sides Live   1982
Music-Performance
63352   90 mins   C   B, V   P
Rock supergroup Genesis performs some of their greatest hits live in concert, including "No Reply at All," "Misunderstanding" and "Behind the Lines."
Rooster Video — *THORN EMI/HBO Video*

Genevieve   1953
Comedy
59904   86 mins   C   B, V   P
Dianah Sheridan, John Gregson, Kay Kendall, Kenneth More, directed by Henry Cornelius
Two friendly rivals engage in a race on the way back from the Brighton veteran car rally.
Rank — *Embassy Home Entertainment*

Gentle Giant   1967
Adventure
79877   93 mins   C   B, V   P
Dennis Weaver, Vera Miles, Ralph Meeker, Clint Howard
An orphaned bear is taken in by a boy and his family and grows to be a 750 pound giant.
Ivan Tors Productions — *Republic Pictures Home Video*

Gentleman Jim   1942
Drama
53671   104 mins   B/W   CED   P
Errol Flynn, Alan Hale, Alexis Smith, Jack Carson, Ward Bond, William Frawley, directed by Raoul Walsh
The rise to fame of boxer Jim Corbett, during the 1880's when boxing was outlawed.
Warner Bros; Robert Buckner — *RCA VideoDiscs*

Gentlemen Prefer Blondes 1953
Comedy
08441　91 mins　C　　B, V　　　　P
Marilyn Monroe, Jane Russell, Charles Coburn, Elliot Reid, directed by Howard Hawks
Two showgirls land in police court while seeking rich husbands or diamonds.
20th Century Fox — *CBS/Fox Video*

George 1970
Comedy-Drama
80951　87 mins　C　　B, V　　　　P
Marshall Thompson, Jack Mullaney, Inge Schoner
A carefree bachelor takes his girlfriend and his 250 pound St. Bernard on a trip to the Swiss Alps where he proves that a dog is not always man's best friend.
MPAA:G
Marshall Thompson — *United Home Video*

George Burns and Gracie Allen Show, The 1952
Comedy
77191　115 mins　B/W　　B, V　　　P
George Burns, Gracie Allen, Bea Benaderet, Fred Clark, Harry Von Zell, Ronnie Burns
This is a collection of four live episodes of the show including the first television appearance of Burns and Allen from 1950.
CBS — *Shokus Video*

George Burns and Gracie Allen Show, The 1951
Comedy
38991　30 mins　B/W　　B, V, FO　　P
George Burns, Gracie Allen, Harry Von Zell, Bea Benaderet, Fred Clark
A live Christmas show from the first year of the popular series. Gracie gives her unique version of "A Christmas Carol." Originally telecast December 23, 1951.
CBS — *Video Yesteryear*

George Burns and Gracie Allen Show, The 1952
Comedy
Closed Captioned
71109　60 mins　B/W　　B, V　　　P
George Burns, Gracie Allen, Jack Benny, Harry Von Zell, Bea Benadaret, Fred Clark
This series includes two episodes from the Burns' timeless TV comedies of the fifties. The original commercials are left in.
Jesse Goldstein — *RCA/Columbia Pictures Home Video*

George Burns in Concert 1982
Comedy-Performance
80239　60 mins　C　　B, V　　　　P
George Burns

The ageless comedian reminisces about his long show business career in this concert taped in Ontario.
GBF Productions — *U.S.A. Home Video*

George Burns Show, The 1959
Comedy
58638　30 mins　B/W　　B, V, FO　　P
George Burns, Harry Von Zell, Larry Keating, Ronnie Burns, Bea Benaderet, Judi Meredith, Lisa Davis, Carol Channing
Carol Channing sues George in this episode, "The Hollywood Television Courtroom." George sings "Please Don't Take Me Home," and Harry steals the show as an announcer forced to drink his sponsors' products. Sponsored by Colgate, Fab and Ajax, with original commercials included.
NBC — *Video Yesteryear*

George Melies, Cinema Magician 1978
Science fiction/Film-History
59405　17 mins　C　　B, V　　　P, T
A look at film pioneer George Melies who originated the use of special effects in cinema. (Some black and white).
Patrick Montgomery — *Blackhawk Films*

George White's Scandals 1945
Musical
13644　95 mins　B/W　　B, V　　　P, T
Joan Davis, Jack Haley, Jane Greer
Musical comedy look at show biz world. Jazz numbers by Gene Krupa and his band.
RKO; George White — *Blackhawk Films*

Geppetto's Music Shop 1982
Fairy tales
64953　90 mins　C　　B, V　　　R, P
Kindly toymaker Geppetto gathers the children of the village in his house to tell them stories, seen in animation, all drawn from the greats of children's literature.
MPAA:G
Century Video — *Video Gems*

Germicide 1974
Science fiction/Drama
71243　90 mins　C　　V　　　　P
Rod Taylor, Bibi Andersson
A scientist tries to warn the world of the threat posed by a horrifying bacterial weapon. Terrorists and his mistress hatch plots against him.
Independent — *Prism*

Gerry Mulligan 1981
Music-Performance
75897　18 mins　C　　B, V　　　　P

This program presents the jazz music of Gerry Mulligan featuring his compositions "K4 Pacific" and "North Atlantic Run."
Jazz America Ltd — *Sony Video Software*

Get Crazy   1983
Comedy/Musical
64981   90 mins   C   B, V, LV,   P
                                CED
Malcolm McDowell, Allen Goorwitz, Daniel Stern, Gail Edwards
The owner of the Saturn Theatre is attempting to stage the biggest rock-and-roll concert of all time on New Year's Eve 1983, and everything is going wrong.
Unknown — *Embassy Home Entertainment*

Get Fit, Stay Fit   1978
Physical fitness
42778   60 mins   C   B, V   P
Ann Dugan
This series of three 20-minute programs is intended for all ages interested in total body conditioning.
Health N Action — *RCA/Columbia Pictures Home Video*

Get Happy   193?
Comedy
10043   59 mins   B/W   B, V   P, T
Shirley Temple, Weber and Fields, Bessie Smith
Includes Shirley Temple in "Glad Rags to Riches," Weber and Fields in "Beer is Here," and Bessie Smith in "St. Louis Blues." Also a Flip the Frog Cartoon.
Educational et al — *Blackhawk Films*

Get Out Your Handkerchiefs   1978
Comedy
47372   109 mins   C   B, V   P
Gerard Depardieu, Patrick Dewaere, Carole Laure, directed by Betrand Blier
Two men try to make one woman happy, then lose her to a precocious, 13-year-old boy.
Academy Awards '78: Best Foreign Language Film. MPAA:R
Springmill Productions — *Warner Home Video*

Get Started   1985
Physical fitness
82306   60 mins   C   B, V   P
Richard Simmons introduces his unique exercise and dietary program for those people who have never before embarked on a fitness program.
Visual Eyes Productions — *Karl/Lorimar Home Video*

Getaway, The   1972
Adventure
68233   122 mins   C   B, V   P

Steve McQueen, Ali MacGraw
Steve McQueen and Ali MacGraw star as husband and wife bank robbers traveling across Texas to get away from a corrupt politician and the state police.
MPAA:PG
Warner Brothers — *Warner Home Video*

Getting It On   1983
Comedy
72226   100 mins   C   B, V   P
A high school student uses his new-found video equipment for voyeuristic activity.
MPAA:R
Cromworld — *Vestron Video*

Getting of Wisdom, The   1980
Drama
52743   100 mins   C   CED   P
Susannah Fowle, directed by Bruce Beresford
An adaptation of the classic Australian novel, about the trials of an extraordinary teenage girl at an exclusive finishing school in turn of the century Melbourne, the heroine—Laura Rambotham—a gifted pianist who struggles to assert her individuality in the stuffy climate of Victorian conformity.
Australia; Southern Cross Films — *CBS/Fox Video*

Getting Straight   1970
Comedy/Satire
70191   124 mins   C   B, V   P
Elliott Gould, Candice Bergen
A former student activist returns to his alma mater as a teacher and tries unsuccessfully to avoid involvement in the student radical movement.
MPAA:R
Columbia Pictures — *RCA/Columbia Pictures Home Video*

Getting Wasted   1980
Comedy
59331   98 mins   C   B, V   P
Brian Kerwin, Stephen Furst, Cooper Huckabee
Set in 1969 at a military academy for troublesome young men, chaos ensues when the cadets meet the hippies.
MPAA:PG
David Buanno — *United Home Video*

Ghastly Ones, The   1965
Horror
79347   81 mins   C   B, V   P
Three couples are invited to a strange island to participate in the reading of a will.
Andy Milligan — *Video Home Library*

Ghidrah the Three Headed Monster   1965
Science fiction
01668   85 mins   C   B, V   P
Yosuke Natsuki, Yuriko Hoshi, Rodan and Mothra, Directed by Inoshiro Honda
When three-headed monster from outer-space threatens world, humans appeal to the friendly Mothra, Rodan, and Godzilla.
Toho Productions — *Hollywood Home Theater; Movie Buff Video; Video Connection; VCII; Discount Video Tapes; Video Yesteryear; Admit One Video*

Ghost Goes West, The   1936
Comedy
81911   82 mins   B/W   B, V   P
Robert Donat, Jean Parker, Eugene Pallette, directed by Rene Clair
The ghost of a Scottish rogue returns to the United States to help out a young member of his family.
Alexander Korda — *Embassy Home Entertainment*

Ghost in the Noonday Sun   1974
Comedy
70718   95 mins   C   B, V   P
Peter Sellers, Anthony Franciosa, Spike Milligan, Peter Boyle, Clive Revell, James Villiers, Directed by Peter Medak
A group of silly pirates search for buried treasure under the direction of their zang chief who turns everything into a mess.
Gareth Wigan — *VCL Home Video*

Ghost in the Noonday Sun   1974
Comedy
70906   90 mins   C   B, V   P
Peter Sellers, Spike Milligan, Anthony Franciosa, Clive Revill, Rosemary Leach, Peter Boyle, directed by Peter Medak
The wacky international crew of a treasure-seeking pirate ship sets sail for high sea silliness in this slapstick adventure film.
British Independent; Gareth Wigan — *VCL Home Video*

Ghost Patrol   1936
Western
11728   57 mins   B/W   B, V   P
Tim Mc Coy
G-Men of the West ride hard in this action western.
Puritan — *Video Connection; United Home Video*

Ghost Ship   1953
Mystery
77202   69 mins   B/W   B, V   P

Dermot Walsh, Hazel Court
A young couple is tortured by ghostly apparitions when they move into an old yacht with a dubious past.
Lippert Productions — *United Home Video*

Ghost Story   1981
Suspense
47417   110 mins   C   B, V, LV   P
Fred Astaire, Melvyn Douglas, Douglas Fairbanks Jr., John Houseman, Patricia Neal
Four elderly men, members of an informal social club called the Chowder Society, share a terrible secret buried deep in their pasts. Based on the best-selling novel by Peter Straub.
MPAA:R
Universal — *MCA Home Video*

Ghost Town Law   1942
Western
15412   62 mins   B/W   B, V   P
Buck Jones, Tim McCoy, Raymond Hatton
A sheriff's badge brings trouble. The Three Mesquiteers step into save the day.
Monogram — *Video Connection; Cable Films; Discount Video Tapes*

Ghostbusters   1984
Comedy/Science fiction
Closed Captioned
82198   103 mins   C   B, V   P
Bill Murray, Dan Aykroyd, Harold Ramis, Rick Moranis, Sigourney Weaver, directed by Ivan Reitman
The "Ghostbusters" are a team of parapsychologists who travel throughout New York City eliminating troublesome apparitions. Ray Parker Jr. performs the title song; in VHS and Beta Hi-Fi Stereo.
MPAA:PG
Columbia Pictures — *RCA/Columbia Pictures Home Video*

Ghosts of Berkeley Square, The   1947
Comedy
63621   61 mins   B/W   B, V, FO   P
Robert Morley, Felix Aylmer
The ghosts of two retired soldiers of the early 18th century are doomed to haunt their former home, and only a visit from a reigning monarch can free them.
NTA Pictures — *Video Yesteryear*

Ghosts on the Loose   1943
Mystery
08759   67 mins   B/W   B, V, 3/4U   P
Bela Lugosi, East Side Kids, Ava Gardner
Leo Gorcy and Huntz Hall tackle naughty Nazis and Ava Gardner in a haunted house. Spooky and zany.

Monogram — *Hollywood Home Theater; Discount Video Tapes; Cable Films; Video Connection; Kartes Video Communications*

Ghosts That Still Walk   1977
Horror/Documentary
70891   92 mins   C   B, V   P
Ann Nelson, Matt Boston
Spooky phenomena occur. The demons possessing a young lad's soul may be responsible.
Jim Flocker Productions — *United Home Video*

Ghoul, The   1975
Horror
58282   88 mins   C   B, V   P
Peter Cushing, John Hurt
A group of stranded travellers is reduced in number when they take shelter in the house of a former clergyman.
MPAA:R
J Arthur Rank; Tyburn Studios — *Media Home Entertainment; American Video Tape; VCL Home Video*

Ghoulies   1985
Horror
80694   81 mins   C   B, V   P
Lisa Pelikan, Jack Nance, Scott Thompson, Tamara DeTreaux
A young boy gets more than he bargained for when he inherits his father's house inhabited by evil little creatures, the ghoulies.
MPAA:PG13
Empire Pictures — *Vestron Video*

G. I. Blues   1960
Musical
08386   104 mins   C   B, V   P
Elvis Presley, Juliet Prowse, Robert Ivers, James Douglas
Three G. I.'s form a musical combo while stationed in Germany.
EL, SP
Paramount; Hal Wallis — *CBS/Fox Video; RCA VideoDiscs*

G.I. Executioner, The   1984
Adventure
82456   86 mins   C   B, V   P
Tom Kenna, Vicki Racimo, Angelique Petty John
An adventure set in Singapore, this film features a Vietnam veteran turned executioner.
MPAA:R
Troma Inc — *Vestron Video*

G.I. Joe   1985
Cartoons
71347   30 mins   C   B, V   P
Animated

These single-episode tapes pit G.I. Joe against the forces of COBRA deploying a variety of armaments in defense of national honor.
Sunbow Productions — *Family Home Entertainment*

G.I. Joe: A Real American   1983
Hero
Cartoons
79204   94 mins   C   B, V   P
Animated
G.I. Joe and his army must fight off Cobra to control a device that reduces people and objects to a molecular level.
Sunbow Productions — *Family Home Entertainment*

G.I. Joe: A Real American   1984
Hero, The Revenge of
Cobra Vol. 2
Cartoons
76973   99 mins   C   B, V   P
Animated
G.I. Joe's army must destroy COBRA's weather dominator which is pointed at the nation's capitol.
Sunbow Productions — *Family Home Entertainment*

Giant   1956
Drama
Closed Captioned
81490   201 mins   C   B, V, LV   P
Elizabeth Taylor, Rock Hudson, James Dean, Carroll Baker, Chill Wills, Jane Withers, Sal Mineo, Mercedes McCambridge, directed by George Stevens
This is the epic saga of a wealthy Texan who marries a strong willed Maryland woman and the problems they have adjusting to life on a ranch. Available in Stereo Hi-Fi for all formats.
Academy Awards '56: Best Director (Stevens).
Warner Bros — *Warner Home Video*

Giant Step, A   1982
Football
47712   23 mins   C   B, V, FO   P
Team highlights of the 1981 New York Giants who posted their first appearance in NFL post-season play in almost 20 years.
NFL Films — *NFL Films Video*

Gideon's Trumpet   1980
Drama
66277   104 mins   C   B, V   P
Henry Fonda, Jose Ferrer, John Houseman, Dean Jagger, Sam Jaffe, Fay Wray
A true story of how one man's fight for justice changed the course of U.S. legal history.
John Houseman — *Worldvision Home Video*

Gidget 1959
Comedy-Drama
81209 95 mins C B, V P
*Sandra Dee, James Darren, Cliff Robertson,
Mary Laroche, Arthur O'Connell*
A plucky teenaged girl discovers romance and
wisdom when she becomes a mascot for a
group of college boys as they spend the
summer surfing at Malibu.
Columbia — *RCA/Columbia Pictures Home
Video*

Gidget Goes Hawaiian 1961
Comedy
81430 102 mins C B, V P
*Deborah Walley, James Darren, Carl Reiner,
Peggy Cass, Michael Callan, Eddie Foy, Jr.*
There's trouble in paradise for Gidget when
someone starts a nasty rumor about her while
she's on vacation in Hawaii. Available in VHS
and Beta Hi Fi.
Columbia Pictures — *RCA/Columbia Pictures
Home Video*

Gielgud's Chekhov 1 1981
Literature
58557 52 mins C B, V P
Hosted by John Gielgud
Three tales of escape, literal and figurative:
"The Fugitive," "Desire for Sleep," and
"Rothschild's Violin."
MasterVision — *Mastervision*

Gielgud's Chekhov 2 1981
Literature
58558 52 mins C B, V P
A pair of tales dealing with illicit love: "Volodya"
and "The Boarding House."
MasterVision — *Mastervision*

Gielgud's Chekhov 3 1981
Literature
58559 51 mins C B, V P
A pair of works which investigate the inner world
of hopes and dreams: "Revenge" and "The
Wallet."
MasterVision — *Mastervision*

Gift for Heidi, A 1962
Drama
11731 71 mins C B, V P
Sandy Descher, Van Dyke Parks
An allegorical tale of Heidi and the lessons she
learns upon receiving three carved figures on
her birthday. They represent Faith, Hope and
Charity and bring her three adventures to teach
their meaning.
RKO — *United Home Video*

Gift Horse, The 1952
War-Drama
82230 99 mins B/W B, V P

*Trevor Howard, Richard Attenborough, Sonny
Tufts, Bernard Lee*
A British officer reluctantly takes over an old US
destroyer donated to Great Britain in 1940.
George Pitcher — *Monterey Home Video*

Gift, The (Le Cadeau) 1982
Drama
69040 105 mins C B, V P
The story of 55-year-old Gregoire Dufour, who
chooses early retirement with the hope of
somehow changing his dull and boring life.
Unknown to Gregoire, his co-workers have
arranged the ultimate retirement gifta woman.
Michel Zemer — *THORN EMI/HBO Video*

Gift of Winter, The 1974
Cartoons
71361 30 mins C B, V P
Animated
Mr. Winter takes heat from some small town
residents who feel that he welched on a promise
for snow.
John Leach & Jean Rankin — *Family Home
Entertainment*

Gigglesnort Hotel 1976
Puppets/Children
80885 45 mins C B, V P
The puppets inhabiting the Gigglesnort Hotel
teach kids to cope with the foibles of growing
up.
BILL JACKSON — *Karl/Lorimar Home Video*

Gigi 1958
Musical
47056 119 mins C B, V P
*Leslie Caron, Louis Jourdan, Maurice Chevalier,
Hermoine Gingold, directed by Vincente Minnelli*
A young Parisian girl is trained by her worldly-
wise grandmother to become a courtesan, but
Gigi decides that she prefers marriage. Based
on the novel and play by Colette. The musical
score by Lerner and Loewe includes "Thank
Heaven for Little Girls," "I Remember It Well"
and "The Night They Invented Champagne."
Winner of nine Academy Awards.
Academy Awards '58: Best Picture; Best
Director (Minnelli); Best Song ("Gigi"); Best
Screenplay; Best Color Cinematography; Film
Daily Poll 10 Best Pictures of the Year.
MGM — *MGM/UA Home Video*

**Gil Evans and His
Orchestra** 1983
Music-Performance
84643 57 mins C B, V P
The reknowned composer and pianist performs
in Switzerland with his jazz concert orchestra.
Works by Gershwin, Charlie Mingus, Thelonius
Monk and Jimi Hendrix are among those
performed in Hi-Fi stereo.

(For explanation of codes, see Use Guide and Key)

Swiss — *V.I.E.W. Video*

Gilda 1946
Drama
21287 110 mins B/W B, V P
Rita Hayworth, Glenn Ford, George Macready
A South American gambling casino owner hires a young American as his trusted aide, unaware of his wife's love for the man. Hayworth sings "Put the Blame on Mame."
Columbia — *RCA/Columbia Pictures Home Video; RCA VideoDiscs*

Gilda Live 1980
Comedy
54120 124 mins C B, V P
Gilda Radner, "Father" Guido Sarducci, directed by Mike Nichols
A live taping of Gilda Radner's stage show at New York's Winter Garden Theater. Gilda presents many of her "Saturday Night Live" characters, including dimwitted Lisa Loopner, loudmouthed Roseanne Roseannadanna and punk rocker Candy Slice.
MPAA:R
Warner Bros — *Warner Home Video*

Gillette NFL Most Valuable Player 1985 1985
Football
86795 23 mins C B, V P
A taping of the NFL MVP awards, honoring, among others, Dan Marino, Joe Morris, Mike Singletary and Marcus Allen.
NFL Films — *NFL Films Video*

Gimme an F 1985
Comedy
82242 100 mins C B, V P
Stephen Shellen, Mark Keyloun, John Karlen, Jennifer Cooke
The handsome cheerleading instructor at Camp Beaver View ruffles a few pom-poms when he discovers that the camp's owner is about to enter into a shady deal with some foreigners. Available in VHS and Beta Hi-Fi.
MPAA:R
20th Century Fox — *Key Video*

Gimme Shelter 1970
Music-Performance
44777 91 mins C B, V P
The Rolling Stones
Something went wrong at the free concert attended by 300,000 people in Altamont, California and this "Woodstock West" became a bitter remembrance in the history of the rock generation.
Cinema 5 — *RCA/Columbia Pictures Home Video; RCA VideoDiscs*

Gin Game, The 1984
Comedy-Drama
75286 82 mins C B, V P
Jessica Tandy, Hume Cronyn
This tape features a performance of the Broadway play about an aging couple who find romance in an old age home. In Beta Hi-Fi stereo and VHS Dolby stereo.
RKO Home Video — *RKO Home Video*

Ginger 1970
Adventure
63083 90 mins C B, V P
Ginger
Fabulous super-sleuth Ginger faces the sordid world of prostitution, blackmail and drugs.
Ginger Productions — *Monterey Home Video*

Gino Vannelli 1981
Music-Performance
47375 60 mins C B, V P
Gino Vannelli
Gino Vannelli performs his hit songs in concert, including "I Just Wanna Stop," "Living Inside Myself," "Brother to Brother," and others.
Henry Less and Associates — *Warner Home Video*

Girl, a Guy and a Gob, A 1941
Comedy
80237 91 mins B/W B, V P
Lucille Ball, Edmund O'Brien, George Murphy, Franklin Pangborn, Lloyd Corrigan
A secretary and her sailor boyfriend teach her stuffy boss how to enjoy life.
RKO — *RKO Home Video*

Girl Can't Help It, The 1956
Comedy/Musical
82244 99 mins B/W B, V P
Jayne Mansfield, Tom Ewell, Edmond O'Brien, Julie London, Ray Anthony, directed by Frank Tashlin
A retired mobster hires a hungry talent agent to promote his girlfriend who wants to be a nightclub singer. Cameos by Eddie Cochran, Gene Vincent, The Platters, Little Richard and Fats Domino; in VHS and Beta Hi-Fi.
20th Century Fox — *Key Video*

Girl Crazy 1943
Musical
71157 99 mins B/W B, V P
Mickey Rooney, Judy Garland, Tommy Dorsey and his Orchestra, Nancy Walker, June Allyson, directed by Busby Berkeley
A young millionaire hypochondriac leaves New York to attend college in Arizona's healthful environment. Once there, he falls for a local girl who can't stand the sight of him. Songs by George and Ira Gershwin include "I Got Rhythm," "Embraceable You" and "Could You Use Me?"

MGM — *MGM/UA Home Video*

Girl Groups: The Story of a Sound
1983

Music/Documentary
64941   90 mins   C   B, V, CED   P
The Supremes, The Ronettes, The Shangri-Las, The Marvelettes, The Shirelles
This documentary on the "girl group" sound of the early 60's features rare footage and interviews with many of the original singers, record producers and songwriters of that period. Among the 25 songs performed are "Please Mr. Postman," "Be My Baby," "Chapel of Love," "Boby Love" and "Stop! In the Name of Love."
Delilah Films — *MGM/UA Home Video*

Girl in Every Port, A
1952

Comedy
29486   86 mins   B/W   B, V   P, T
Groucho Marx, William Bendix, Marie Wilson, Don Defore, Gene Lockhart
Navy buddies acquire two race horses and try to conceal them aboard ship.
RKO — *Blackhawk Films*

Girl in Room 2A, The
1976

Horror
80291   90 mins   C   B, V   P
Raf Vallone, Daniela Giordano
A young woman recently released from prison discovers the family she boarded with has turned their house into a torture chamber.
MPAA:R
Joseph Brenner Associates — *Prism*

Girl Most Likely, The
1957

Comedy
11732   98 mins   C   B, V   P
Jane Powell, Cliff Robertson
Romance-minded girl dreams of marrying wealthy, handsome man. She runs into a problem when she must choose one of three men.
Universal; RKO — *United Home Video*

Girl on a Motorcycle
1968

Adventure
84040   92 mins   C   B, V   P
Alain Delon, Marianne Faithful, Roger Mutton, directed by Jack Cardiff
A series of erotic and action-packed adventures beset a pair of motorcycle-propelled lovers in France.
MPAA:R
William Sasson — *Monterey Home Video*

Girl Who Was Death, The
1968

Adventure/Fantasy
70589   52 mins   C   B, V   P
Patrick McGoohan, Justine Lord, Kenneth Griffith, directed by David Tomblin
Death, a female assassin, stalks the Prisoner. He narrowly escapes trap after craftly trap in this fifteenth episode of "The Prisoner."
Associated TV Corp. — *MPI Home Video*

Girlfriends
1978

Drama
58234   87 mins   C   B, V   P
Melanie Mayron, Anita Skinner, Eli Wallach, Christopher Guest, Amy Wright, Viveca Lindfors, directed by Claudia Weill
The bittersweet, true-to-life story of a young woman learning to make it on her own.
MPAA:PG
Claudia Weill — *Warner Home Video*

Girls Are for Loving
1973

Adventure
63085   90 mins   C   B, V   P
Ginger
Undercover agent Ginger faces real adventure when she battles it out with her counterpart, a seductive enemy agent.
Loving Productions — *Monterey Home Video*

Girls, Girls, Girls
1962

Musical
08381   106 mins   C   B, V   P
Elvis Presley, Stella Stevens, Laurel Goodwin, Jeremy Slate, Guy Lee
A boy refuses his girlfriend's gift of a boat. He finds he has a rival for her affections and changes his mind.
EL, SP
Paramount; Hal Wallis — *CBS/Fox Video*

Girls Just Want to Have Fun
1985

Musical/Comedy
Closed Captioned
82167   90 mins   C   B, V, LV   P
Sarah Jessica Parker, Helen Hunt, Ed Lauter, Lee Montgomery, Biff Yeager
An army brat and her friends pull out all the stops for a chance to dance on a national television program. Based loosely upon Cyndi Lauper's song of the same name. Available in VHS and Beta Hi-Fi Stereo.
MPAA:PG
New World Pictures — *New World Video*

Girls Night Out
1983

Suspense/Horror
78386   96 mins   C   B, V   P
Hal Holbrook
An ex-cop must stop a killer who is murdering participants of a sorority house scavenger hunt and leaving cryptic clues on the local radio station.
MPAA:R
GK Productions — *THORN EMI/HBO Video*

Girls of Huntington House, The 1973
Drama
71310 74 mins C B, V P
Shirley Jones, Sissy Spacek, Pamela Sue Martin, Mercedes McCambridge, William Windom, directed by Alf Kjellin
Though her employers warned against it when they hired her, an English teacher at a home for unwed mothers grows more involved in her students' problems.
Lorimar Productions — *U.S.A. Home Video*

Girls of Rock & Roll 1984
Variety/Music video
76929 53 mins C B, V P
An intimate look at this country's up and coming female rock musicians with special on stage performances from the ladies.
Playboy Enterprises — *CBS/Fox Video*

Girls of the Comedy Store 1986
Comedy-Performance
87637 60 mins C B, V P
Pam Matteson, Shirley Hemphill, Karen Haber, Tamayo Otsuki, Carrie Snow
Taped at the Los Angeles Comedy Store, female stand-up comediennes do their best to break up their audience.
The Comedy Store; Lightning Video — *Lightning Video*

Girls of the Moulin Rouge 1986
Variety
87636 60 mins C B, V P
A video glimpse into the stripteasing antics of the Moulin Rouge stage performers.
Lightning Video — *Lightning Video*

Girls of the White Orchid 1985
Crime-Drama
85095 96 mins C B, V P
Ann Jillian, directed by Jonathan Kaplan
An American girl gets involved with the prostitute rings run by a Japanese Yakuza.
Philip Mandelker; Leonard Hill — *Karl/Lorimar Home Video*

Girlschool 1984
Music-Performance
82390 59 mins C B, V P
Girlschool
The all-female metal band rocks raw and bawdy at London's Camden Palace. Includes "Play Dirty," "Rock Me Shock Me" and "Out to Get You."
Trilion Pictures — *Sony Video Software*

Giselle 1979
Dance
55471 77 mins C CED P

Rudolf Nureyev
An international cast highlights this version of Nureyev's greatest success, produced by Stanley Dorfman for television.
Lord Lew Grade; ITC Entertainment; Stanley Dorfman — *RCA VideoDiscs*

Giselle 1983
Dance
80327 135 mins C B, V P
Galina Mezentseva, Konstantin Zaklinsky, Gennady Selyutsky
The classic ballet about a peasant girl who becomes a ghost to destroy the man who betrayed her.
Covent Garden Video Productions — *THORN EMI/HBO Video*

Git Along Little Dogies 1937
Western
08789 60 mins B/W B, V, 3/4U P
Gene Autry, Judith Allen, Champion, Smiley Burnette
Gene Autry and banker's daughter at odds.
Republic — *Video Yesteryear; Discount Video Tapes*

Give 'Em Hell, Harry! 1975
Biographical/Drama
47684 103 mins C B, V P
James Whitmore
James Whitmore's one-man show as Harry S Truman at his feisty best.
Theatro Vision — *Worldvision Home Video*

Give My Regards to Broad Street 1984
Musical
Closed Captioned
70348 109 mins C B, V P
Paul and Linda McCartney, Barbara Bach, Byran Brown, Ringo Starr, Tracey Ullman, Ralph Richardson
This film features many fine versions of McCartney songs that accompany his protrayal of a rock star in search of his stolen master recordings. The program comes in Beta Hi-Fi and VHS-Stereo.
MPAA:PG
20th Century Fox — *CBS/Fox Video*

Gizmo! 1977
Documentary/Inventions
47385 77 mins C B, V P
A hilarious and affectionate tribute to crackpot inventors everywhere, with footage of dozens of great and not-so-great machines and other creations. Some segments in black-and-white.
Howard Smith — *Warner Home Video*

Glacier Fox, The   1975
Documentary/Animals
71358   90 mins   C   B, V   P
Narrated by Arthur Hill
This film shows the wild cousins of the domestic
dog in their natural northern habitat.
Independent — *Family Home Entertainment*

Gladys Knight & the Pips   1978
and Ray Charles in
Concert
Music-Performance
33979   75 mins   C   B, V   P
Gladys Knight, Ray Charles
Backed by the ever-present Pips, Gladys Knight
sings "Imagination,""Midnight Train to
Georgia," and "Heard It Through the
Grapevine." Ray Charles performs several
numbers after making a surprise appearance.
Gladys and Ray finally combine in a magic blend
of inspired song.
HBO — *Vestron Video*

Gladys Knight & The Pips   1982
and Ray Charles
Music-Performance
72219   78 mins   C   B, V   P
The dynamic combination perform some of their
biggest hits including "Imagination" and
"Midnight Train to Georgia."
Independent — *Vestron Video*

Glen and Randa   1971
Science fiction
84822   94 mins   C   B, V   P
Steven Curry, Shelley Plimpton
Two young people experience the world after it
has been destroyed by nuclear war.
MPAA:R
Sidney Glazier — *United Home Video*

Glen Campbell—Live in   1977
London
Music-Performance
71221   90 mins   C   V   P
*Glen Campbell, The Royal Philharmonic
Orchestra*
Glen and his sidemen trot out a batch of his
biggest hits in this live concert, including
"Wichita Lineman," "Rhinestone Cowboy,"
"Galveston," "By the Time I Get to Phoenix"
and "Southern Nights."
Prism — *Prism*

Glen or Glenda   1953
Drama/Exploitation
08680   70 mins   B/W   B, V, 3/4U   P
*Bela Lugosi, Lyle Talbot, Donald Woods,
directed by Ed Woods*
A documentary advocating transvestism. The
director Ed Woods portrays the haunted figure
of Glen or Glenda.

Unknown — *Video Yesteryear; Video
Dimensions; Festival Films; Admit One Video*

Glenn Miller—A   1984
Moonlight Serenade
Music-Performance
77252   71 mins   C   B, V   P
*Tex Beneke, Marion Hutton, Johnny Desmond,
hosted by Van Johnson*
The original Glenn Miller singers reunite for this
tribute concert that is devoted to Miller's big
band hits, including "In the Mood," "Long Ago
and Far Away" and "Kalamazoo." Filmed at the
Glenn Island Casino. In VHS stereo.
Silverlight Productions — *Magnum
Entertainment*

Glenn Miller Story, The   1953
Drama/Musical
84018   113 mins   C   B, V, LV   P
*James Stewart, June Allyson, Henry Morgan,
Gene Krupa, Louis Armstrong, Ben Pollack,
directed by Anthony Mann*
The music of the Big Band Era lives again in this
warm biography of the legendary Glenn Miller,
following his life fromt he late 20's to his
untimely death in a World War II plane crash.
Among the Miller hits featured are "Moonlight
Serenade," "PE 6
Academy Awards '53: Best Screenplay (Ric
Hardman); Best Sound; Film Daily Poll '54; Best
Picture of the Year.   MPAA:G
Aaron Rosenberg — *MCA Home Video*

Glitter Dome, The   1984
Drama
80810   90 mins   C   B, V   P
*James Garner, John Lithgow, Margot Kidder,
Colleen Dewhurst, directed by Stuart Margolin*
Two policemaen discover the sleazier side of
Hollywood when they investigate the murder of
a pornographer. Based upon the novel by
Joseph Wambaugh. Available in VHS and Beta
HiFi.
HBO — *THORN EMI/HBO Video*

Gloria   1980
Drama
52751   123 mins   C   B, V, LV   P
*Gena Rowlands, John Adames, Buck Henry,
directed by John Cassavetes*
A fast-shooting, independent woman fights off
the mob in order to protect a young boy.
MPAA:PG
Sam Shaw; Columbia — *RCA/Columbia
Pictures Home Video*

Gloriana   1983
Opera
86897   146 mins   C   B, V   P
*Sarah Walker, Anthony Rolfe Johnson, Jean
Rigby, Richard Van Allan*

Conducted by Mark Elder, the English National Opera performs Benjamin Britten's opera celebrating Queen Elizabeth II's 1953 coronation.
Colin Graham — *THORN EMI/HBO Video*

Glorifying the American Girl 1929

Musical
01614   80 mins   B/W   B, V   P
Mary Eaton, Dan Healey, Eddie Cantor, Rudy Vallee, directed by Millard Webb
Musical romp with Eddie Cantor and other Ziegfeld stars.
Paramount; Florenz Ziegfeld — *Hollywood Home Theater; Discount Video Tapes; Video Yesteryear; Festival Films*

Glory 1956

Drama
84813   100 mins   C   B, V   P
Margaret O'Brien, Walter Brennan, Charlotte Greenwood, directed by Dick Butler
A heart-rending story of a young woman and her horse.
RKO — *United Home Video*

Glory Boys, The 1984

Adventure
80293   110 mins   C   B, V   P
Rod Steiger, Anthony Perkins, Gary Brown, Aaron Harris
A secret agent is hired to protect an Isreali scientist who is marked for assassination by the PLO and IRA.
Independent — *Prism*

Glory Days of Yesteryear: The Baltimore Colts 1985

Football
81949   140 mins   C   B, V   P
Here is a compilation of highlights from The Colts 1964, 1965, 1968, and 1970 seasons.
NFL Films — *NFL Films Video*

Glory of Spain, The 1967

Music-Performance/Spain
81943   54 mins   C   B, V   P
Legendary Flamenco guitarist Andres Segovia takes you on a guided tour of Spain's El Prado museum and also performs pieces by Falla and Granados.
Nathan Kroll — *Video Arts International*

Glove, The 1978

Adventure
65290   93 mins   C   B, V   P
John Saxon, Rosey Grier, Joan Blondell
An ex-cop turned bounty hunter has his toughest assignment ever: bring in a 6'5", 250 pound ex-con.
MPAA:R

Julian Roffman — *Media Home Entertainment*

Gnome—Mobile, The 1967

Fantasy/Adventure
76812   84 mins   C   B, V   P
Walter Brennan, Richard Deacon, Ed Wynn, Karen Dotrice, Matthew Garber
A lumber baron and his two grandchildren attempt to reunite a pair of forest gnomes with a lost gnome colony.
Buena Vista; Walt Disney Productions — *Walt Disney Home Video*

Gnomes 1980

Cartoons/Fantasy
Closed Captioned
71113   48 mins   C   B, V   P
Animated
The gnomes are wily little creatures who are in constant battle with their oversized, underwitted adversaries, the trolls. Recorded in HiFi, the books of Wil Huggen and Rien Poortvliet inspired the film.
Tomorrow Entertainment;
Zander — *RCA/Columbia Pictures Home Video*

Go Bears! A Look to the 80's 1980

Football
50079   24 mins   C   B, V, FO   R, P
Chicago Bears
Highlights of the 1979 Chicago Bears' football season.
NFL Films — *NFL Films Video*

Go for Gold 1984

Drama
87635   98 mins   C   B, V   P
James Ryan, Cameron Mitchell, Sandra Horne
A young athlete must choose between a chance for glory and his relations with family and friends.
Anant Singh/Stuart Fleming — *Lightning Video*

Go for It 1976

Sports
59674   90 mins   C   B, V   P
A potpourri of sports action, including surfing, skiing, hang-gliding, kayaking and mountain climbing.
MPAA:PG
Paul Rapp; Richard Rosenthal — *Media Home Entertainment*

Go Go Big Beat 1965

Music-Performance
88175   70 mins   C   B, V   P
A collection of simulated concert shorts featuring a plethora of British '60's rock bands, including The Hollies, The Merseybeats, The Animals, and many more. Released in England

as three shorts: "Swinging UK," "UK Swings Again" and "Mods and Rockers."
Harold Baim Prod. — *Rhino Video*

Go! Go! Go! World   1964
Documentary
47647   85 mins   C   B, V, FO   P
A "round the world" tour in the tradition of "Mondo Cane," showing the strange and bizarre activities of humankind: mud wrestlers, a Japanese pachinko parlor, Indian snake charmers and a Chinese baby exchange, among others.
Italy — *Video Yesteryear*

Go-Go's Wild at the   1984
Greek
Music-Performance
81793   52 mins   C   B, V   P
Belinda Carlisle, Charlotte Caffey, Kathy Valentine, Jane Wiedlin, Gina Schock
The rock and roll girl group performs "Head Over Heels," "We Got The Beat" and other favorites in this concert taped at Los Angeles Greek Theatre. Available in VHS Dolby Hi-Fi Stereo and Beta Hi-Fi Stereo.
I.R.S. Video — *RCA/Columbia Pictures Home Video*

Go, Johnny Go!   1959
Musical
76802   75 mins   B/W   B, V   P
Jimmy Clanten, Eddie Cochran, Jackie Wilson, Ritchie Valens
Rock promoter Alan Freed tries to find the mystery contestant who has unknowingly won his talent search contest.
Hal Roach Jr; Alan Freed — *Hal Roach Studios; Music Media*

Go Kill and Come Back   1968
Adventure
84038   95 mins   C   B, V   P
Gilbert Roland, George Helton, directed by Enzo G Castellari
A bounty hunter tracks down a notoriously dangerous train robber.
MPAA:PG
Edmondo Amati — *Monterey Home Video*

Go Tell the Spartans   1978
War-Drama
45047   114 mins   C   B, V, LV,   P
                             CED
Burt Lancaster, Craig Wasson
In Viet Nam, 1964, a hard-boiled major is ordered to establish a garrison at Muc Wa with a platoon of burnt-out Americans and Vietnamese mercenaries.
MPAA:R
Spartan; Mar Vista — *Vestron Video; Time Life Video*

Go West   1940
Comedy
58293   82 mins   B/W   B, V   P
The Marx Brothers, John Carroll, Diana Lewis
The brothers Marx help in the making and un-making of the Old West.
MGM — *MGM/UA Home Video*

Gobots   1985
Cartoons
71051   100 mins   C   B, V   P
Animated
This feature traces the history of the Gobots from Gobotron who became Guardians charged with protecting earth from the evil Renegades.
DIC Enterprises — *Karl/Lorimar Home Video*

God Told Me To   1977
Crime-Drama
86593   95 mins   C   B, V   P
Tony LoBianco, Deborah Raffin, Sylvia Sidney, Sandy Dennis
A religious New York cop is embroiled in occult mysteries while investigating a series of grisly murders.
MPAA:R
Larry Cohen — *Charter Entertainment*

Godfather 1902-   1981
1959—The Complete
Epic, The
Drama
58876   368 mins   C   B, V   P
Marlon Brando, Al Pacino, Robert Duvall, James Caan, Richard Castellano, Diane Keaton, Robert DeNiro, John Cazale, Lee Strasberg, Talia Shire, directed by Francis Ford Coppola
The complete Godfather saga, Francis Ford Coppola's epic work concerning the lives of a New York crime family. Both original "Godfather" films have been reedited into a chronological framework of the Corleone family history, with much previously discarded footage restored.
Paramount; Zoetrope — *Paramount Home Video*

Godfather, The   1972
Drama
38595   171 mins   C   B, V, LV   P
Marlon Brando, Al Pacino, James Caan, Robert Duvall, Talia Shire, Diane Keaton, directed by Francis Ford Coppola
Based on the novel by Mario Puzo, this is the epic portrayal of the Corleone family's rise to the top of the criminal world.
Academy Awards '72: Best Picture; Best Actor (Brando); Best Screenplay (Puzo and Coppola).
MPAA:R
Paramount — *Paramount Home Video; RCA VideoDiscs*

Godfather Part II, The   1974
Drama
38596   200 mins   C   B, V, LV   P
*Al Pacino, Robert De Niro, Robert Duvall, Talia
Shire, Diane Keaton, directed by Francis Ford
Coppola*
Two generations of the Corleone family, fictional
Mafia chieftains, are portrayed in this sequel to
the "Godfather." The story of young Don Vito
(De Niro) is intercut with the rise of his son,
Michael (Pacino) to leadership of the family.
Academy Awards '74: Best Picture; Best
Supporting Actor (De Niro); Best Director; Best
Screenplay. MPAA:R
Paramount — *Paramount Home Video; RCA
VideoDiscs*

God's Little Acre   1958
Drama
55318   118 mins   B/W   B, V   P
*Robert Ryan, Tina Louise, Michael Landon,
Buddy Hackett, Vic Morrow, Jack Lord, Aldo
Ray, directed by Anthony Mann*
A man convinced that buried treasure is on his
farm ruins his land to get at the gold.
Sidney Harmon — *King of Video; Prism; VCII;
World Video Pictures*

Godsend, The   1979
Horror
69286   93 mins   C   B, V   P
*Cyd Hayman, Malcolm Stoddard, Angela
Pleasence, Patrick Barr*
A little girl is adopted, and she turns her new
family's life into a nightmare.
MPAA:R
Cannon Group — *Vestron Video*

Godunov: The World to   1984
Dance In
Dance/Documentary
70169   60 mins   C   B, V   P
Alexander Godunov
This documentary features scenes of Godunov
dancing and discussions with the ballet star
about his defection from Russia, his life in the
United States, and his termination from the
American Ballet Theatre.
Kultur; Peter Rosen Associates;
Metromedia — *Kultur*

Godzilla   1955
Horror
63423   80 mins   B/W   B, V, LV,   P
                               CED
Raymond Burr, Takashi Shimura
The radioactive monster Godzilla attacks Tokyo
and terrifies the world.
Japanese — *Vestron Video*

Godzilla 1985   1985
Science fiction
70892   91 mins   C   B, V, LV   P
*Raymond Burr, Keiju Kobayashi, Ken Takaka,
Yasuka Sawaguchi, directed by Kohji
Hashimoto and R.J. Kizer*
Moviedom's reptile superstar sets out to reverse
Japan's trade imbalance by destroying Tokyo.
MPAA:PG
New World — *New World Video*

Godzilla vs. Monster Zero   1970
Science fiction/Horror
64020   93 mins   C   B, V   P
Nick Adams
Godzilla, Monster Zero and Rodan are out to
destroy the earth, but a heroic space pilot tries
to stop them.
MPAA:G
Benedict Pictures Corp — *Paramount Home
Video*

Godzilla vs. Mothra   1964
Horror
64508   90 mins   C   B, V   P
Akira Takarada, Yuriko Hoshi, Hiroshi Koizumi
Mighty Mothra is called in to save the populace
from Godzilla, who is on a rampage.
Toho Company; American
International — *Paramount Home Video*

Godzilla vs. the Sea   1966
Monster
Science fiction
51612   80 mins   C   B, V   P
The famous giant lizard does battle amidst
fantastic special effects.
Toho — *Discount Video Tapes; Hollywood
Home Theater*

Goin' All the Way   1982
Drama
63088   85 mins   C   B, V   P
Deborah Van Rhyn, Dan Waldman
Seventeen-year-old Monica decides that she
has to prove her love to her boyfriend, Artie, by
going all the way.
Four Rivers and Clark Film — *Monterey Home
Video*

Goin' South   1978
Western
38618   109 mins   C   B, V, LV   P
*Jack Nicholson, Mary Steenburgen, John
Belushi, directed by Jack Nicholson*
An outlaw is saved from being hanged by a
young woman who agrees to marry and take
charge of him.
MPAA:PG
Paramount — *Paramount Home Video*

Going Ape!   1981
Comedy
53933   88 mins   C   B, V   P

Tony Danza, Jessica Walter, Danny DeVito, Art Metrano, Rick Hurst
A young man inherits a bunch of orangutans. If the apes are treated well, a legacy of $5 million will follow.
MPAA:PG
Robert L Rosen — *Paramount Home Video*

Going Berserk   1983
Satire
66331   85 mins   C   B, V, LV   P
John Candy, Joe Flaherty, Eugene Levy, Paul Dooley, directed by David Steinberg
The stars of SCTV's television comedy troupe are featured in this off-the-wall comedy which lampoons everything from religious cults to kung fu movies to "Father Knows Best."
MPAA:R
Universal — *MCA Home Video*

Going, Going, Gone   1985
Baseball
81131   25 mins   C   B, V   P
Reggie Jackson
"Mr. October" offers homerun hitting tips with some help from the University of Miami baseball team in this presentation.
Panasonic Film Library — *Major League Baseball Productions*

Going Hollywood   1983
Film-History/Documentary
79333   75 mins   C   B, V   P
Narrated by Robert Preston
A documentary that examines the stars and films of the great depression of the 1930's. In Beta Hi-Fi and VHS Stereo.
MPAA:G
Julian and Beverly Schlossberg — *Monterey Home Video*

Going in Style   1979
Comedy
44760   90 mins   C   B, V   P
George Burns, Art Carney, Lee Strasberg, directed by Martin Brest.
Three elderly gentlemen decide to liven up their lives by pulling a daylight bank stick-up.
MPAA:PG
Warner Bros — *Warner Home Video*

Going My Way   1944
Musical-Drama
53398   126 mins   B/W   B, V   P
Bing Crosby, Barry Fitzgerald, Rise Stevens, Frank McHugh, directed by Leo McCarey
A priest assigned to a down-trodden parish works to help the neighborhood's people. Songs include "Going My Way," "Ave Maria," "Swinging on a Star," and "The Day After Forever."

Academy Awards '44: Best Picture; Best Actor (Crosby); Best Supporting Actor (Fitzgerald); Best Director (McCarey).
Paramount; Leo McCarey — *MCA Home Video*

Going Places   1974
Drama
63967   117 mins   C   B, V   P
Gérard Depardieu, Patrick Dewaere, Jeanne Moreau, Miou-Miou, Isabelle Huppert
A pair of amiable, uninhibited bandits roam the French countryside doing as they please. Dubbed in English.
MPAA:R
Almi-Cinema 5 — *RCA/Columbia Pictures Home Video*

Gold Diggers of 1933   1933
Musical
64785   96 mins   B/W   B, V   P
Joan Blondell, Ruby Keeler, Dick Powell, Ginger Rogers
Showgirls help a songwriter save his show in this Busby Berkeley musical. Includes the number, "We're in the Money."
Warner Bros. — *Key Video; RCA VideoDiscs*

Gold of the Amazon   1979
Women
Adventure/Drama
80039   94 mins   C   B, V   P
Bo Svenson, Anita Ekberg, Bond Gideon, Donald Pleasence, directed by Mark Lester
When two explorers set out to find gold, they stumble onto a society of man-hungry women.
Mi-Ka Productions; NBC Entertainment — *Embassy Home Entertainment*

Gold Raiders   1984
Adventure
78344   106 mins   C   B, V   P
Robert Ginty, Sarah Langenfeld, William Steven
A team of secret agents are sent to Laos to find a plane carrying two hundred million dollars worth of gold.
P Chalong — *Media Home Entertainment*

Gold Rush, The   1925
Comedy
58614   85 mins   B/W   B, V, 3/4U   R, P
Charlie Chaplin, Mack Swain, Tom Murray, Georgia Hale
Chaplin's tale of the Little Tramp's misplaced love in the days of the Klondike.
United Artists — *Cable Films; Video Yesteryear; Discount Video Tapes; Hollywood Home Theater; Western Film & Video Inc; Blackhawk Films*

Gold Rush, The 1925
Comedy
44192 60 mins B/W B, V P
Charlie Chaplin, Mack Swain
Chaplin's classic comic masterpiece about the hardships of life on the Alaskan frontier. Abridged.
Spectre Films — *Prism; Sterling Educational Films; Kartes Video Communications; Playhouse Video; See Hear Industries*

Gold Rush, The/Payday 1925
Comedy
48405 92 mins B/W B, V P
Charlie Chaplin, Georgia Hale, Mack Swain
Chaplin drifts along the Arctic tundra, searching for gold and love in "The Gold Rush." In "Payday," he goes out drinking with his buddies.
United Artists — *Playhouse Video*

Golden Age of Comedy, The 1958
Comedy
55593 78 mins B/W B, V P
Ben Turpin, Harry Langdon, Will Rogers, Jean Harlow, Carole Lombard, Laurel and Hardy, Keystone Kops
The great comedians of silent cinema are seen in clips from some of their funniest films.
Robert Youngson — *VidAmerica*

Golden Boy 1939
Drama
68261 101 mins B/W B, V P
William Holden, Adolphe Menjou, Barbara Stanwyck, Lee J. Cobb
A young man gives up being a great concert violinist and becomes a prizefighter.
William Perlberg; Columbia — *RCA/Columbia Pictures Home Video*

Golden Earring 1984
Music video
88096 25 mins C B, V P
The midstream rock band's most popular videos, including the hit "Twilight Zone."
Sony Video — *Sony Video Software*

Golden Earring: Live from the Twilight Zone 1984
Music-Performance/Music video
80372 60 mins C B, V P
This is a concert featuring Dutch rockers Golden Earring plus their music video of "Twilight Zone". Available in VHS Dolby Hi-Fi Stereo and Beta Hi-Fi Stereo.
PMV Productions — *RCA/Columbia Pictures Home Video*

Golden Honeymoon, The 1980
Literature-American
57322 52 mins C B, V P
Jame Whitmore, Teresa Wright, directed by Noel Black
Ring Lardner's story about an elderly couple who journey to St. Petersburg to celebrate their 50th anniversary. There they encounter the wife's suitor of 50 years past, who is also vacationing with his spouse. Curiosity draws the couples together, and jealousy, doubt and a simmering competitve spirit momentarily jar the marriage.
Dan McCann; Whitney Green — *Monterey Home Video; Perspective Films & Video*

Golden Lady 1979
Adventure
66283 90 mins C B, V P
Christina World, Suzanne Danielle, June Chadwick
A beautiful woman leads her entourage in a deadly game of international intrigue.
UG Prods — *Monterey Home Video*

Golden Moments 1960
Baseball
49554 25 mins B/W B, V P
A collection of memorable moments in baseball history from 1905-1960, recalling a half-century of stars from Home Run Baker to Ted Williams.
Lew Fonseca — *Major League Baseball Productions*

Golden Rendezvous 1977
Suspense
64891 120 mins C B, V P
Richard Harris, David Janssen, John Carradine, Burgess Meredith
A tale of treachery aboard a "gambler's paradise" luxury liner.
Film Trust-Milton Okun Prods; Golden Rendezvous Prods — *Vestron Video*

Golden Seal, The 1983
Drama
65434 94 mins C B, V, LV, P
CED
Steve Railsback, Michael Beck, Penelope Milford, Torguil Campbell
This is the tale of a small boy's innocence put in direct conflict with the failed dreams, pride and ordinary greed of adults.
Samuel Goldwyn Jr — *Embassy Home Entertainment*

Golden Sun 198?
Martial arts
73958 90 mins C B, V P
Lei Hsiao Lung, Chen Pei Ling, Ou-Yang Chung
A young boxer sets out to find out the truth about Bruce Lee's death in this martial arts film.
Independent — *Unicorn Video*

Golden Tales and Legends 1985

Fairy tales
77238   60 mins   C   B, V   P
These two volumes of the best-loved fairy tale from the Brothers Grimm and Hans Christian Anderson are sure to captivate every child. Volume one includes "The Frog Prince," "Rapunzel" and "Hansel and Gretel;" the second volume features "The Juggler," "The Golden Apple" and "The Iron Mountain."
Maljack Productions — *MPI Home Video*

Golden Tee, The 1985

Golf
70896   60 mins   C   B, V   P
Julius Boros, Billy Casper, Gene Littler, Tommy Bolt, George Bayer, Lloyd Mangrum, Bob Rosburg, Mike Souchak, Byron Nelson, Mac Hunter, Mickey Wright
Some of the PGA's legendary players offer their secrets of swinging on this tape.
Magnum Ent Sports — *Magnum Entertainment*

Golden Triangle, The 1980

Martial arts
81636   90 mins   C   B, V   P
Lo Lieh, Sombat Metanee, Tien Ner
Two rival gangs struggle for control of the mountainous Asian region known as "The Golden Triangle," where most of the world's opium supply is produced.
MPAA:R
Foreign — *Magnum Entertainment*

Golden Voyage of Sinbad, The 1973

Adventure/Fantasy
Closed Captioned
63445   105 mins   C   B, V   P
John Phillip Law, Caroline Munro, Tom Baker
In the mysterious ancient land of Lemuria, Sinbad and his crew encounter a six-armed sword-brandishing statue, a one-eyed centaur and a griffin.
MPAA:G
Columbia; Charles H Schneer and Ray Harryhausen — *RCA/Columbia Pictures Home Video*

Goldengirl 1979

Drama
55579   107 mins   C   B, V   P
Susan Anton, James Coburn, Curt Jurgens, Robert Culp
A mad neo-Nazi doctor tries to produce a superwoman—specially fed, exercised, and emotionally conditioned since childhood to run in the Olympics.
MPAA:PG
Avco Embassy — *Embassy Home Entertainment*

Goldenrod 1977

Drama
80893   100 mins   C   B, V   P
A successful rodeo champion is forced to reevaluate his life when he sustains a crippling accident in the ring.
Talent Associates; Film Funding Ltd of Canada — *Prism*

Goldfinger 1964

Adventure
52602   108 mins   C   B, V, LV   P
Sean Connery, Honor Blackman, Gert Frobe, Shirley Eaton
James Bond, Agent 007, attempts to prevent an international gold smuggler from robbing Fort Knox.
United Artists — *CBS/Fox Video; RCA VideoDiscs*

Goldie And Kids 1982

Variety
81823   52 mins   C   V   P
Goldie Hawn, Barry Manilow
Goldie Hawn talks to twelve children about such subjects as love, marriage and divorce in this tape that features Barry Manilow.
Smith-Hemion Productions — *Prism*

Goldie Gold and Action Jack 1981

Cartoons
80642   40 mins   C   B, V   P
Animated
Futuristic reporter Goldie Gold and intern Action Jack team up to pursue stories with the help of computerized gadgetry.
Hanna-Barbera — *Worldvision Home Video*

Goldilocks and the Three Bears 1983

Fairy tales
Closed Captioned
69321   60 mins   C   B, V, LV, CED   P
Tatum O'Neal, Alex Karras, Brandis Kemp, Donovan Scott, Hoyt Axton, John Lithgow, Carole King
This entry from "Faerie Tale Theatre" tells the story of Goldilocks, who wanders through the woods and finds the home of three bears.
Shelley Duvall — *CBS/Fox Video*

Goldwing 1984

Cartoons
70615   60 mins   C   B, V   P
Animated
A powerful bionic super-hero stars in this adventure cartoon.
Videocraft International Ltd. — *Prism*

Goldwyn Follies, The 1938
Musical
82574   115 mins   C   B, V   P
Adolph Menjou, Zorina, The Ritz Brothers,
Helen Jepson, Phil Baker, Bobby Clark, Ella
Logan, Andrea Leeds
This lavish musical comedy about Hollywood
includes the music and lyrics of George and Ira
Gershwin. A movie producer chooses a naive
girl to give him advice on his movies. Songs
include "Love Walked In," "Love is Here to
Stay" and "I Was Doing All Right."
Samuel Goldwyn — *Embassy Home*
Entertainment

Goldy: The Last of the 1984
Golden Bears
Drama/Adventure
76775   91 mins   C   B, V, CED   P
An orphaned child and a lonely prospector risk
their lives to save a Golden Bear from a circus
owner.
Nu Image Films — *Vestron Video*

Golem, The 1920
Film-History
49069   70 mins   B/W   B, V   P
Directed by Paul Wegener
A huge clay figure is given life by a rabbi in
hopes of saving the Jews in the ghetto of
medieval Prague. Silent.
German — *Video Yesteryear; International*
Historic Films

Golf 1978
Golf
44925   30 mins   C   B, V   P
Fitness specialist Ann Dugan demonstrates
exercises for golfers to help develop
suppleness in hips and shoulders and strength
in the back, forearm, and wrist. From the
"Sports Conditioning" series.
Health N Action — *RCA/Columbia Pictures*
Home Video

Golf My Way 1983
Golf
66276   128 mins   C   B, V   P
Jack Nicklaus
Step-by-step instruction on every element of the
game, highlighted in super-slow-motion.
JN Productions — *Worldvision Home Video*

Golf My Way with Jack 1984
Nicklaus
Golf
66579   120 mins   C   B, V   P
Champion golfer Jack Nicklaus demonstrates
step-by-step lessons on every element of golf
for beginners or seasoned players. Crucial
points are highlighted in super slow motion to
highlight every detail

Worldvision — *Worldvision Home Video*

Goliath and the 1960
Barbarians
Adventure
81505   86 mins   C   B, V   P
Steve Reeves, Bruce Cabot
Goliath and his men go after the barbarians who
are terrorizing and ravaging the Northern Italian
countryside during the fall of the Roman Empire.
American International — *MGM/UA Home*
Video

Gondoliers, The 19??
Opera/Comedy
65491   112 mins   C   B, V   P
Keith Michell
A new version of Gilbert and Sullivan's opera.
This is an entertaining lampoon against class
bigotry.
Parsons and Whittemore Lyddon
Ltd — *CBS/Fox Video*

Gone Are the Dayes 1984
Comedy
80049   90 mins   C   B, V   P
Harvey Korman, Susan Anspach, Robert Hogan
A government agent is assigned to protect a
family who are witnesses to an underworld
shooting.
Walt Disney Productions — *Walt Disney Home*
Video

Gone in 60 Seconds 198?
Adventure
79220   97 mins   C   B, V   P
H.B. Halicki, Marion Busia, George Cole, James
McIntyre, Jerry Daugirda
A car thief who works for an insurance
adjustment firm gets double crossed by his
boss, and the police are on his tail.
Independent — *Media Home Entertainment*

Gone With the West 1972
Western
80421   92 mins   C   B, V   P
James Caan, Stefanie Powers, Sammy Davis
Jr., Aldo Ray
Little Moon and Jud McGraw seek revenge
upon the man who stole their cattle.
Virginia Lively Stone — *Unicorn Video*

Gone With the Wind 1939
Drama
Closed Captioned
80439   231 mins   C   B, V, LV,   P
                              CED
Clark Gable, Vivien Leigh, Leslie Howard, Olivia
de Havilland, Hattie McDaniel, Butterfly
McQueen, directed by Victor Fleming
A selfish southern girl pines away for the man
she loves during the Civil War. One of the best-

loved motion pictures from Hollywood's golden age which is filled with memorable characterizations.
Academy Awards '39: Best Picture; Best Actress (Leigh); Best Supporting Actress (McDaniel). MPAA:G
MGM; David O. Selznick — *MGM/UA Home Video; RCA VideoDiscs*

Gonzo Presents Muppet Weird Stuff   1985
Variety
Closed Captioned
81545   55 mins   C   B, V   P
Gonzo, Kermit the Frog, John Cleese, Julie Andrews, Vincent Price, Madeline Kahn
Gonzo catches a cannonball and wrestles a brick blindfolded on a guided tour of his mansion.
Henson Associates — *Playhouse Video*

Good Earth, The   1937
Drama
59361   138 mins   B/W   B, V   P
Paul Muni, Luise Rainer, Charley Grapewin, Keye Luke, Walter Connolly, directed by Sidney Franklin
Pearl S. Buck's classic recreating the story of greed which ruined the lives of a simple farming couple in China.
Academy Awards '37: Best Actress (Rainer); Best Cinematography (Karl Freund).
MGM — *MGM/UA Home Video*

Good Guys Wear Black   1978
Adventure
31657   96 mins   C   B, V, LV, CED   P
Chuck Norris, Anne Archer, James Franciscus
A mild-mannered professor keeps his former life as leader of a Vietnam commando unit under wraps until he discovers that he's number one on the C.I.A. hit list. He decides to use all his commando skills to stay alive and get to the only man who can stop the C.I.A.
MPAA:PG
Mar Vista — *Vestron Video; Time Life Video*

Good Neighbor Sam   1964
Comedy
77241   130 mins   C   B, V   P
Jack Lemmon, Romy Schneider, Dorothy Provine, Mike Connors, Edward G. Robinson
A married advertising executive agrees to pose as a friend's husband in order for her to collect a multi-million dollar inheritance.
Columbia; David Swift — *RCA/Columbia Pictures Home Video*

Good News   1947
Musical
88206   93 mins   C   B, V   P

June Allyson, Peter Lawford, Joan McCracken, Mel Torme
A vintage Comden-Green musical about the love problems of a college football star, who will flunk out if he doesn't pass his French exams. This revamping of the 1927 Broadway smash features "The Varsity Drag," "Just Imagine," "Pass That Peace Pipe" and the unlikely sight of Peter Lawford in a song-and-dance role.
MGM; Loew's Inc. — *MGM/UA Home Video*

Good Old Days   193?
Documentary/Film-History
63850   55 mins   B/W   B, V   P
A compilation of 3 nostalgic newsreels featuring footage of Shirley Temple, William S. Hart, early bathing beauties, and San Francisco at the turn of the century. Some color sequences.
Movietone et al — *Hollywood Home Theater*

Good Sam   1948
Comedy-Drama
69316   78 mins   B/W   B, V   P
Gary Cooper, Ann Sheridan, Ray Collins, Edmund Lowe, Joan Lorring, directed by Leo McCarey
An incurable "Good Samaritan" finds himself in one jam after another as he tries too hard to help people.
RKO Radio; Rainbow Pictures — *Spotlite Video*

Good, the Bad and the Ugly, The   1968
Western
58481   161 mins   C   B, V, LV, CED   P
Clint Eastwood, Eli Wallach, Lee Van Cleef, directed by Sergio Leone
A drifter, a Mexican outlaw, and a sadist are all out to get a cash box which was stolen and put in an unmarked grave during the Civil War.
United Artists; Alberto Grimaldi — *CBS/Fox Video; RCA VideoDiscs*

Goodbye Columbus   1969
Comedy/Drama
55541   105 mins   C   B, V, LV   P
Richard Benjamin, Ali McGraw, Jack Klugman, Nan Martin, directed by Larry Pierce
Philip Roth's novel about a young Jewish librarian who has an affair with the spoiled daughter of a nouveau riche family.
MPAA:R
Paramount; Stanley Jaffe — *Paramount Home Video; RCA VideoDiscs*

Goodbye Cruel World   1982
Comedy
81319   90 mins   C   B, V   P
Dick Shawn, Cynthia Sikes, Chuck Mitchell

A suicidal television anchorman decides to spend life's last day filming the relatives who drove him to the brink.
MPAA:R
Sharp Films — *Lightning Video*

Goodbye Emmanuelle   1979
Drama
63347   92 mins   C   B, V   P
Sylvia Kristel
This film follows the further adventures of Emmanuelle in her quest for sexual freedom and the excitement of forbidden pleasures.
MPAA:R
Miramax Films — *THORN EMI/HBO Video*

Goodbye Girl, The   1977
Comedy
58872   110 mins   C   B, V, LV, CED   P
Richard Dreyfuss, Marsha Mason, Quinn Cummings, Barbara Rhoades, Marilyn Sokol, directed by Herbert Ross
Neil Simon's story of an over-the-hill Broadway chorus girl with a precocious nine-year-old daughter who shares her apartment with a young actor.
Academy Awards '77: Best Actor (Dreyfuss).
MPAA:PG
Warner Bros; MGM — *MGM/UA Home Video*

Goodbye, Mr. Chips   1939
Drama
Closed Captioned
84710   115 mins   B/W   B, V   P
Robert Donat, Greer Garson, Paul Henreid, John Mills, directed by Sam Wood
An MGM classic: the sentimental rendering of the James Hilton novel about a retiring Latin professor in an English school. Greer Garson made her film debut in this picture.
Academy Awards '39: Best Actor: (Robert Donat).
Loew's Inc — *MGM/UA Home Video*

Goodbye, New York   1985
Comedy/Romance
82441   90 mins   C   B, V, LV, CED   P
Julie Hagerty, Amos Kollek
A New York yuppie leaves her job and husband and takes off for Paris, only to become stranded in Israel. She makes the best of the situation by joining a kibbutz and learning an alternative lifestyle.
MPAA:R
Castle Hill — *Vestron Video*

Goodbye Norma Jean   1975
Drama
47797   95 mins   C   B, V   P
Misty Rowe, Terrence Locke, Patch Mackenzie

A detailed recreation of Marilyn Monroe's early years in Hollywood.
MPAA:R
A Sterling Gold Ltd; Larry Buchanan — *THORN EMI/HBO Video*

Goodbye People, The   1983
Comedy-Drama
Closed Captioned
64988   104 mins   C   B, V   P
Judd Hirsch, Martin Balsam, Pamela Reed
An elderly man decides to reopen his Coney Island beachfront hot dog stand that folded 22 years earlier. Two people help him realize his impossible dream.
Unknown — *Embassy Home Entertainment*

Goodbye Pork Pie   1981
Adventure
69547   105 mins   C   B, V   P
Tony Barry, Kelly Johnson
With the police on their trail, two young men speed on a 1000-mile journey in a small, brand-new, yellow, stolen car.
MPAA:R
Pork Pie Productions — *Embassy Home Entertainment*

Goodtime Rock 'n' Roll, Volume 1   1985
Music-Performance
87183   27 mins   C   B, V   P
Fats Domino, Bo Diddley, Little Anthony, Fabian, Chubby Checker
Rock's first pioneers collect on the banks of the Mississippi River for a concert of their greatest hits, including "Tears on My Pillow," "It's My Party," and "The Twist."
Silver Eagle Records; MCA Home Video — *MCA Home Video*

Goodyear Jazz Concert with Bobby Hackett   1961
Music-Performance
46341   24 mins   C   B, V, FO   P
Bobby Hackett, Urbie Green, Bob Wilbur, Dave McKenna, Nabil Totah, Morey Feld
A studio performance by Bobby Hackett's Sextet. The musical program consists of "Deed I Do," "Sentimental Blues," "The Saints," "Bill Bailey," "Struttin' with Some Barbecue," and "Swing That Music."
Mike Bryan, Goodyear — *Video Yesteryear*

Goodyear Jazz Concert with Duke Ellington   1962
Music-Performance
42955   27 mins   C   B, V, FO   P
Duke Ellington and the Band start with "Take the A Train" and run through five other all-time Ellington hits.
Goodyear — *Video Yesteryear*

Goodyear Jazz Concert with Eddie Condon
1961

Music-Performance
46342   28 mins   C   B, V, FO   P
Wild Bill Davison, Cutty Cutshall, Peanuts Hucko, Johnny Varo, Joe Williams, Eddie Condon, Buzzy Drootin
A studio concert by Eddie Condon and friends. The songs performed are "Royal Garden Blues," "Blue and Brokenhearted," "Big Ben Blues," "Stealin' Apples," "Little Ben Blues," and "Muskrat Ramble."
Mike Bryan, Goodyear — *Video Yesteryear*

Goodyear Jazz Concert with Louis Armstrong
1961

Music-Performance
46340   27 mins   C   B, V, FO   P
Louis Armstrong, Trummy Young, Joe Darensbourg, Billy Kyle, Billy Cronk, Danny Barcelona, Jewell Brown
A studio performance by Louis Armstrong's All Stars. Tunes include "When It's Sleepy Time Down South," "C'est si Bon," "Someday You'll Be Sorry," "Jerry," "Nobody Knows de Trouble I've Seen," and "When the Saints Go Marching In."
Mike Bryan, Goodyear — *Video Yesteryear*

Goodyear TV Playhouse: "Marty"
1953

Drama
47483   51 mins   B/W   B, V, FO   P
Rod Steiger, Nancy Marchand, Betsy Palmer, Nehemiah Persoff
One of the best-remembered television dramas of all time, later expanded into an Academy Award-winning feature film. Rod Steiger portrays a lonely Bronx butcher who thinks he has finally found the girl for him. Written by Paddy Chayefsky and originally telecast on May 24, 1953. Opening credits and commercials are missing.
NBC — *Video Yesteryear*

Goodyear TV Playhouse: "The Gene Austin Story"
1957

Musical-Drama/Biographical
47484   51 mins   B/W   B, V, FO   P
George Grizzard, Edward Andrews, Jerome Cowan, Phyllis Newman, Gene Austin
A musical biography of 1920's pop singer Gene Austin, featuring the voice of Gene Austin dubbing for George Grizzard. Songs include "My Blue Heaven," "Ramona" and "My Melancholy Baby." Written by Ernest Kinoy.
NBC — *Video Yesteryear*

Goofy Over Sports
194?

Cartoons
58627   46 mins   C   B, V   P
Animated
Goofy stars in this compilation of sports cartoons from the Disney archives: "How to Play Football" (1944), "Double Dribble" (1946), "Art of Skiing" (1941), "How to Swim" (1942), "Art of Self Defense" (1941), and, "How to Ride a Horse" (a segment from the 1941 feature, 'The Reluctant Dragon').
Walt Disney Productions — *Walt Disney Home Video*

Goonies, The
1985

Adventure
84535   114 mins   C   B, V, LV   P
Sean Astin, Josh Brolin, Jeff B Cohen, Corey Feldman, directed by Richard Donner
A Steven Spielberg presentation about a motley group of kids who discover a treasure map and plunge into a series of nearly-unbelievable adventures.
MPAA:PG
Richard Power, Harvey Bernhard — *Warner Home Video*

Goose Hunting on the Eastern Shore
1985

Hunting
87652   36 mins   C   B, V   P
Art Ayers, Francis Howard
Everything you've always wanted to know about goose shooting, including blind manufacture, calling, decoys and much more.
Sportsmen On Film — *Sportsmen on Film*

Gorath
1967

Science fiction
80832   77 mins   C   B, V   R, P
The world's top scientists are racing to stop a giant meteor from destroying the Earth.
Tono/Brenco Pictures — *Video Gems*

Gorgo
1961

Drama
07011   76 mins   C   B, V   P
Bill Travers, William Sylvester, Vincent Winter, Bruce Seton, Christopher Rhodes
Undersea explosion off the coast of Ireland brings to the surface an unusual monster which is captured and brought to London circus.
MGM; King Brothers Prod — *United Home Video; Cable Films; Video Connection; Video Dimensions*

Gorgo
1961

Science fiction/Drama
80953   78 mins   C   B, V   P
Bill Travers, William Sylvester, Vincent Winter, Bruce Seton
The parent of a sea monster comes to save her offspring from being put on display in a London circus.
MGM — *United Home Video*

Gorilla   1956
Adventure/Documentary
47638   79 mins   C   B, V, FO   P
The story of a white hunter and a black native hunter in Africa searching for a killer gorilla.
Swedish — *Video Yesteryear*

Gorilla   1981
Animals
Closed Captioned
52849   59 mins   C   B, V, LV   P
A profile of the largest of the great apes—a shy, gentle, and intelligent creature threatened with extinction.
National Geographic Society — *Vestron Video; National Geographic Society*

Gorilla, The   1939
Comedy
00400   67 mins   B/W   B, V   P
Ritz Brothers, Anita Louise, Patsy Kelly, Lionel Atwill
Ritz Brothers are hired to protect a country gentlemen receiving strange notes.
20th Century-Fox; Darryl F Zanuck — *Hollywood Home Theater; Discount Video Tapes; Video Connection; Video Yesteryear; Hal Roach Studios; Kartes Video Communications; See Hear Industries*

Gorky Park   1983
Mystery
86363   127 mins   C   B, V, LV   P
William Hurt, Lee Marvin, Brian Dennehy, Joanna Pacula, directed by Michael Apted
This adaptation of Martin Cruz Smith's bestseller deals with three strange corpses found in Moscow's Gorky Park, and the network of conspiracy a Russian police captain finds in investigating.
MPAA:R EL, FR
Orion Pictures — *Vestron Video*

Gospel   1982
Music-Performance
65449   92 mins   C   B, V   P
The Mighty Clouds of Joy, Twinkie Clark and the Clark Sisters, Walter Hawkins and the Hawkins Family
A rousing musical theatrical tribute to the leading exponents of Gospel singing. In stereo VHS and Beta Hi-Fi.
Golden Door Productions — *Monterey Home Video*

Gospel According to St. Matthew, The   1964
Drama
55809   136 mins   B/W   B, V   P
Directed by Pier Paolo Pasolini
The life of Christ, as portrayed in a realistic, almost documentary tone. Dubbed in English.
Alfredo Bini — *Movie Buff Video; Festival Films; Hollywood Home Theater; Discount Video Tapes*

Gospel Road, The   1973
Religion
73799   62 mins   C   B, V, 3/4U   R, P
Narrated by Johnny Cash
Cash narrates and wrote the music for this documentary about Christ's work as a minister.
Twentieth Century Fox — *Life Video Gospel Association; Republic Pictures Home Video*

Gotcha!   1985
Comedy/Adventure
Closed Captioned
81816   97 mins   C   B, V, LV   P
Anthony Edwards, Linda Fiorentino, Alex Rocco, Nick Corri, directed by Jeff Kanew
A shy, college sophomore gets his first lesson in love and spying when he meets up with a Czech graduate student who is really an international agent. Available in VHS and Beta Hi-Fi.
Universal Pictures — *MCA Home Video*

Gotta Dance, Gotta Sing   1984
Musical/Documentary
75287   53 mins   C   B, V   P
Fred Astaire, Ginger Rogers, Shirley Temple, Carmen Miranda, Betty Grable
This is a compilation of memorable dance routines from great Hollywood films. In Beta Hi-Fi and VHS Dolby stereo.
RKO Home Video — *RKO HomeVideo*

Grace Jones—One Man Show   1982
Music-Performance
63422   60 mins   C   B, V   P
Grace Jones
In a concert recorded live in New York and at London's Drury Lane Theatre, Grace Jones performs such hits as "Warm Leatherette," "Walking in the Rain" and "Feel Up."
Island Pictures — *Vestron Video*

Grace Jones—State of Grace   1985
Music video
84611   50 mins   C   B, V   P
Grace performs many of her biggies live, complete with arresting stage persona.
Island Records — *RCA/Columbia Pictures Home Video*

Grace Quigley   1984
Comedy
81771   102 mins   C   B, V   P
Katharine Hepburn, Nick Nolte, Walter Abel, Chip Zien, directed by Anthony Harvey
A hitman and an elderly woman team up to rub people out for fun and profit.

MPAA:PG
Cannon Films — *MGM/UA Home Video*

Graduate, The   1967
Comedy-Drama
08365   106 mins   C   B, V, 8mm,   P
                                  LV
*Anne Bancroft, Dustin Hoffman, Katharine
Ross, directed by Mike Nichols*
A young man graduates with honors, meets and
has an affair with one of his parents' friends,
and is urged to date her daughter. He falls in
love with the daughter.
Academy Awards '67: Best Director (Nichols);
Film Daily Poll 10 Best Pictures of Year '67.
Avco Embassy — *Embassy Home
Entertainment; RCA VideoDiscs*

Graduation Day   197?
Horror
58960   90 mins   C   B, V   P
*Christopher George, Patch McKenzie, E. Danny
Murphy*
A chiller about the systematic murder of
members of a high school track team.
David Baughn;Herb Freed — *RCA/Columbia
Pictures Home Video; RCA VideoDiscs*

Graham Parker   1982
Music-Performance
75922   60 mins   C   B, V   P
This program presents Graham Parker
performing some of his greatest hits.
New Music Inc — *Sony Video Software*

Grambling's White Tiger   1981
Biographical/Football
82078   98 mins   C   B, V   P
*Bruce Jenner, Harry Belafonte, LeVar Burton,
Ray Vitte, Byron Stewart, directed by George
Stanford Brown*
This is the true story of Jim Gregory, the first
white man to play on Grambling College's all-
black football team. Available in VHS and Beta
Hi-Fi Mono.
InterPlanetary Productions — *MCA Home
Video*

Gran Scena Opera   1985
Company, La
Opera
87935   120 mins   C   B, V   P
*Vera Galupe-Borszkh, Philene Wannelle, Luis
Russinyol, Fodor Szedan*
A collection of opera parody excerpts by the
notorious satiric ensemble, with shameless
rapings of "Die Walkure," "La Boheme" and
"La Traviata." Hosted by Miss Sylvia Bills,
conducted by Francesco Folinari-Soave-
Coglioni.
La Gran Scena Opera Company — *Video Arts
International*

Grand Canyon Dancing   1981
Dance
70920   5 mins   C   B, V   P
This presentation shows six dancers
confronting the beauty of the Grand Canyon.
Arizona Film Festival '82: First Prize?Houston
International Film Festival '82: Bronze Award
David Belskis — *V.I.V.A. Audio-Visual*

Grand Canyon Trail   1948
Western
64387   68 mins   B/W   B, V, 3/4U   P
Roy Rogers, Andy Devine, Charles Coleman
A cowboy's best friend invests his money in a
wildcat gold mine.
Republic — *Nostalgia Merchant; Discount
Video Tapes*

Grand Hotel   1932
Drama
80621   115 mins   B/W   B, V, LV   P
*Greta Garbo, John Barrymore, Joan Crawford,
Lewis Stone, Wallace Beery, Lionel Barrymore,
directed by Edmund Goulding*
The resident's lives at Berlin's Grand Hotel
became intertwined over a twenty-four-hour
period.
Academy Awards '32: Best Picture.
MGM; Irving Thalberg — *MGM/UA Home
Video*

Grand Illusion   1937
War-Drama
11400   111 mins   B/W   B, V   P
*Jean Gabin, Erich von Stroheim, Pierre Fresnay,
directed by Jean Renoir*
A classic anti-World War I presentation, in which
French prisoners attempt to escape from their
German captor. French with English subtitles.
FR
Continental — *CBS/Fox Video; Video
Yesteryear; Cable Films; Hollywood Home
Theater; Western Film & Video Inc; Cinema
Concepts; Kartes Video Communications*

Grand Museum Series   1983
Museums/Arts
84773   70 mins   C   B, V   P
Directed by Roland Dubois 3 pgms
Each installment of this series peruses one of
Europe's most famous and reputable museums.
*1.The Louvre 2.The Vatican Museums 3.The
Prado*
AM Available
Art Collection Video/Vistar Int'l — *Video
Associates*

Grand Ole Opry's Classic   1958
Country Tributes
Music-Performance
84572   60 mins   C   B, V   P
60 pgms

This series features original country performances with the Great Stars of yesterday and today.
AM Available
Albert C Gannaway — *American Artists*

Grand Theft Auto   1977
Adventure
51990   89 mins   C   B, V   P
Ron Howard, Nancy Morgan, Marion Ross, Barry Cahill, Clint Howard
A young couple elope to Las Vegas. The bride's father, totally against the marriage, offers a reward for her return.
MPAA:PG
New World Pictures — *Warner Home Video*

Grandizer   1982
Cartoons/Science fiction
59329   101 mins   C   B, V   P
Animated
A tale of star civilizations, evil invaders and the quest of one man to protect his adopted homeland, the planet Earth.
EL, SP
Toei Animation; Terry Production — *Family Home Entertainment*

Grapes of Wrath, The   1940
Drama
08553   129 mins   B/W   B, V   P
Henry Fonda, Dorris Bowdon, Charley Grapewin, Jane Darwell, John Carradine, directed by John Ford
Epic story of the Okie migration to California during the depression. From John Steinbeck's great novel.
20th Century Fox; Darryl F Zanuck — *CBS/Fox Video*

Grass Is Always Greener Over the Septic Tank, The   1978
Comedy
70857   98 mins   C   B, V   P
Carol Burnett, Charles Grodin, Linda Gray, Alex Rocco, Robert Sampson, Vicki Belmonte, Craig Richard Nelson, Anrae Walterhouse, Eric Stoltz, directed by Robert Day
Based on Erma Bombeck's best-seller, this film follows a city family's flight to the peace of the suburbs. They find life there a comic compilation of complications.
Time/Life — *Lightning Video*

Grass Is Greener, The   1961
Comedy
65457   105 mins   C   B, V   P
Cary Grant, Deborah Kerr, Jean Simmons, Robert Mitchum
An American millionaire invades part of an impoverished Earl's mansion and falls in love with the lady of the house. The earl is willing to go to any lengths to keep his wife, even a duel with pistols.
Universal — *Republic Pictures Home Video*

Grateful Dead — Dead Ahead, The   1980
Music-Performance
59851   90 mins   C   B, V   P
An historic documentary is presented based on a week long marathon of shows given by the Grateful Dead at Radio City Music Hall.
Stanley Sherman Organization; Grateful Dead Productions — *Warner Home Video; Pioneer Artists*

Grateful Dead in Concert, The   1977
Music-Performance/Documentary
47046   120 mins   C   CED   P
The Grateful Dead, directed by Jerry Garcia and Leon Gast
A concert by this popular rock group, with 20 songs including "Truckin'," "Casey Jones," and "Sugar Magnolia." The songs are interspersed with backstage shots, interviews with fans, and other scenes. Filmed at the Winterland in San Francisco.
Eddie Washington — *RCA VideoDiscs*

Grateful Dead Movie, The   1977
Music-Performance/Documentary
81596   131 mins   C   B, V   P
Directed by Jerry Garcia
This rockumentary looks at the lives and the music of the acid rock band The Grateful Dead. Available in VHS Stereo and Beta Hi-Fi.
Eddie Washington — *Monterey Home Video*

Graveyard, The   1974
Horror
70908   90 mins   C   B, V   P
Lana Turner, Trevor Howard, Ralph Bates, Suzan Farmer, directed by Don Chaffey
A mommy spends many years torturing her little boy, David. In one blood-filled day, the fellow seeks his revenge.
Kevin Frances — *VCL Home Video*

Grease   1978
Musical
38932   110 mins   C   B, V, LV   P
John Travolta, Olivia Newton-John, Stockard Channing, Eve Arden, Sha-Na-Na
Film version of the hit Broadway musical about high school life in the 1950's. Songs include "You're the One That I Love," "We Go Together," and "Summer Nights."
MPAA:PG
Paramount — *Paramount Home Video; RCA VideoDiscs*

Grease 2   1982
Musical
63426   114 mins   C   B, V, LV   P
Maxwell Caulfield, Michelle Pfeiffer, Adrian Zmed, Lorna Luft, Didi Conn, Eve Arden, Sid Caesar, Tab Hunter
The saga of the T-Birds, the Pink Ladies and young love at Rydell High continues.
MPAA:PG
Paramount — *Paramount Home Video; RCA VideoDiscs*

Greased Lightning   1977
Drama
53513   96 mins   C   B, V   P
Richard Pryor, Pam Grier, Beau Bridges, Cleavon Little, Vincent Gardenia
The story of the first black auto racing champion, Wendell Scott, who had to overcome racial prejudice to achieve his success.
MPAA:PG
Warner Bros — *Warner Home Video*

Greaser's Palace   1972
Comedy/Western
65321   ? mins   C   B, V   P
Albert Henderson, Allan Arbus
Seaweedhead Greaser, owner of the town's saloon, faces his arch nemesis.
Cyma Rubin — *RCA/Columbia Pictures Home Video*

Great Adventure, The   1982
Adventure
65691   90 mins   C   B, V   P
Jack Palance, Joan Collins, Fred Romer
In the severe environment of the gold rush days on the rugged Yukon Territory, a touching tale unfolds of a young orphan boy and his eternal bond of friendship with a great northern dog.
MPAA:PG
Unknown — *Media Home Entertainment*

Great American Cowboy, The   1973
Western/Documentary
71099   89 mins   C   B, V   P
Narrated by Joel McCrea, directed by Keith Merrill
From the stable to the arena, this film tells the story of the modern rodeo cowboys.
Academy Awards '73: Best Documentary Feature.
Keith Merrill Associates; Rodeo Films Prods — *Walt Disney Home Video*

Great American Diet and Nutrition Test, The   1981
Nutrition
57548   60 mins   C   B, V   P
Hosted by Dr. Frank Field, Betty Furness
Viewers can test their knowledge on food additives, labeling, nutrition, obesity, vitamins, and diets.
NBC; Don Luftig — *Karl/Lorimar Home Video*

Great Bank Hoax, The   1978
Comedy
Closed Captioned
80711   89 mins   C   B, V   P
Richard Basehart, Ned Beatty, Burgess Meredith, Michael Murphy, Paul Sand, Arthur Godfrey
Three bank managers decide to rob their own bank to cover up the fact that all the assets have been embezzled.
MPAA:PG
Warner Bros. — *Warner Home Video*

Great Bear Scare, The   1984
Cartoons
73369   60 mins   C   B, V   P
Animated
The bears of Bearbank send Ted E. and Patti Bear to Monster Mountain to find out if Dracula is going to invade the town on Halloween.
Dimenmark International — *Family Home Entertainment*

Great British Striptease   1981
Variety
60413   60 mins   C   B, V   P
Sixteen of England's most fetching young women are featured performing the "Great British Striptease."
Kent Waldwin — *Monterey Home Video*

Great Caruso, The   1951
Musical
53937   113 mins   C   B, V, CED   P
Mario Lanza, Ann Blyth, Dorothy Kirsten
The story of Caruso's rise to operatic fame, from his childhood in Naples, Italy, to his collapse on the stage of the Metropolitan Opera House.
Academy Awards '51: Best Sound Recording; Film Daily Poll '51: Ten Best Pictures.
MGM — *MGM/UA Home Video*

Great Chase, The   1963
Comedy/Film-History
80038   79 mins   B/W   B, V   P
Buster Keaton, Lillian Gish, Pearl White, Noah Beery, narrated by Frank Gallop
A historical anthology of the funniest and most suspenseful classic movie chases.
Continental; Harvey Cort — *Embassy Home Entertainment*

Great Cities: London, Rome, Dublin, Athens   1980
Cities and towns/Europe
59640   100 mins   C   CED   P

Hosted by Anthony Burgess, John Huston,
Melina Mercouri, Jonathan Miller
The history and beauty of four magnificent cities
is shown through the eyes of four very special
residents of each city.
Learning Corp of America; John McGreevey;
Neilsen Fearns Intl — *RCA VideoDiscs*

Great Day In The Morning   1956
Adventure/Western
84826   92 mins   C   B, V   P
Robert Stack, Ruth Roman, Raymond Burr,
Virgina Mayo, Alex Nicol, Regis Toomey,
directed by Jacques Tourneur
A Denver rogue wins women, gold, and fights as
the Civil War approaches in frontier Colorado.
RKO — *United Home Video*

Great Dictator, The   1940
Comedy/Satire
04805   126 mins B/W   B, V   P
Charlie Chaplin, Paulette Goddard, Jack Oakie,
Billy Gilbert, Reginald Gardner, Henry Daniell
Chaplin's first dialogue film turned to political
satire. His ratings as Adenoid Hynkel brought
the newreels and radio speeches of Hitler into
their perspective.
rbc Films — *Playhouse Video; RCA VideoDiscs*

Great Escape, The   1963
Drama
44940   170 mins   C   B, V   P
Steve McQueen, James Garner, Richard
Attenborough, Charles Bronson, James Coburn
American, British, and Canadian prisoners in a
German P.O.W. camp join in a single mass
break for freedom. Based on the novel by Paul
Brickhill.
United Artists — *CBS/Fox Video; RCA*
VideoDiscs

Great Expectations   1983
Drama
Closed Captioned
73045   72 mins   C   B, V   P
Based upon the Dickens classic about a young
boy's rise from a humble childhood to find
fortune and happiness.
Burbank Films — *Children's Video Library*

Great Expectations   1978
Cartoons/Literature-English
75621   72 mins   C   B, V   P
Animated
This animated version of Charles Dickens'
classic is about a boy's meeting with an
escaped convict.
WBTV Canada — *Children's Video Library*

Great Expectations/The   1983
Man with the Funny Hat
Football
66219   45 mins   C   B, V, FO   P
Highlights from the Dallas Cowboys' 1982-83
and a profile of Head Coach Tom Landry.
NFL Films — *NFL Films Video*

Great Figures in History: . 1980
John F. Kennedy
Presidency-US/Documentary
56757   105 mins   C   B, V, CED   P
John F. Kennedy, hosted by Harry Reasoner
This program traces JFK through his
Presidential years and assassination, and
includes an interview with Rose Kennedy. Some
scenes are in black-and-white.
CBS News — *CBS/Fox Video*

Great Gabbo, The   1929
Drama
08739   82 mins   B/W   B, V   P
Erich von Stroheim, Betty Compson, Don
Douglas, Margie Kane, directed by Erich von
Stroheim
A ventriloquist who can only express himself
through his dummy.
Sono Art; World Wide — *Movie Buff Video;*
Discount Video Tapes; Cable Films; Video
Yesteryear; Kartes Video Communications

Great Gatsby, The   1974
Drama
10973   151 mins   C   B, V, LV   P
Robert Redford, Mia Farrow, Bruce Dern, Karen
Black, Sam Waterston, directed by Jack Clayton
Adaptation of F. Scott Fitzgerald's novel of the
idle rich in the 1920's and one man's devotion
to a flirtatious waif. Screenplay by Francis Ford
Coppola.
Academy Awards '74: Best Song Score, Original
or Adaptation; Best Achievement in Costume
Design. MPAA:PG
Paramount; David Merrick — *Paramount Home*
Video; RCA VideoDiscs

Great Gundown, The   1984
Drama
75672   90 mins   C   B, V   P
An outlaw in New Mexico leaves his gang to
return to his family and becomes a fugitive from
both sides.
Satori Entertainment Corp. — *VidAmerica*

Great Gundown, The   1975
Western
35365   98 mins   C   B, V   P
Robert Padilla, Richard Rust, Milila St. Duval
A violent tale set in the Old West. The peace of
frontier New Mexico erupts when a half-breed
Indian leads a brutal assault on an outlaw
stronghold.

Paul Nobert — *Hollywood Home Theater*

Great Guns   1941
Comedy
81548   74 mins   B/W   B, V   P
*Stan Laurel, Oliver Hardy, Sheila Ryan, Dick
Nelson, directed by Montague Banks*
Stan and Ollie enlist in the army to protect a
spoiled millionaire's son but wind up being
targets at target practice instead. Available in
VHS and Beta Hi-Fi.
20th Century Fox — *Playhouse Video*

Great Guy   1936
Drama
08747   50 mins   B/W   B, V, 3/4U   P
James Cagney, Mae Clarke, Ed Brophy
Food inspector wipes out graft in his town.
Grand Natl — *Prism; Cable Films; Video
Connection; Discount Video Tapes; Movie Buff
Video; Kartes Video Communications*

Great Hunter, The   1975
Martial arts
82279   91 mins   C   B, V   P
Chia Ling, Wang Yu, Hsu Feng
A village militia captain and his girlfriend seek to
destroy the men who killed the girl's father.
Chou Lin-Kang — *Unicorn Video*

Great Leaders   197?
Bible
35372   105 mins   C   B, V   P
Ivo Garrani, Fernando Rey, Giorgio Ceridni
The inspiring stories of two Old Testament
heroes, Gideon and Samson, are dramatized in
this beautifully constructed film.
Sunn Classic — *United Home Video*

Great Locomotive Chase,   1956
The
Adventure
66054   85 mins   C   B, V   P
Fess Parker, Jeffrey Hunter
Based on a curious episode that unfolded during
the Civil War, this film tells the tale of Yankee
raiders who commandeered a locomotive deep
in the heart of Confederate territory.
Walt Disney Productions — *Walt Disney Home
Video; RCA VideoDiscs*

Great Missouri Raid, The   1951
Western
85250   81 mins   C   B, V   P
*Wendell Corey, MacDonald Carey, Ellen Drew,
Ward Bond, directed by Gordon Douglas*
This action film follows the famous adventures
of the James/Younger boys and their eventual
demise.
Paramount — *Kartes Video Communications*

Great Moments in   197?
Baseball
Baseball
45031   30 mins   C   B, V   P
*Babe Ruth, Lou Gehrig, Willie Mays, Yogi Berra,
Joe DiMaggio, Joe Jackson*
Highlights of the many stars and happenings
that have made baseball the most spectacular
sport of the past century.
Major League Baseball — *RCA/Columbia
Pictures Home Video*

Great Movie Stunts and   1981
The Making of Raiders of
the Lost Ark
Filmmaking/Adventure
59857   107 mins   C   B, V, LV   P
Harrison Ford
Two TV specials: "Movie Stunts" demonstrates
how major action sequences were designed and
executed, and "Making of Raiders" captures
the cast and crew as they tackle the many
problems created in filming the spectacular
scenes.
Paramount — *Paramount Home Video; RCA
VideoDiscs*

Great Muppet Caper, The   1981
Comedy
58826   95 mins   C   B, V, LV   P
*Charles Grodin, Diana Rigg, John Cleese,
Robert Morley, Peter Ustinov, Jack Warden,
directed by Jim Henson*
A group of hapless reporters (Kermit, Fozzie
Bear, and Gonzo) travel to London to follow up
on a major jewel robbery.
MPAA:G
Universal; AFD; David Lazer — *CBS/Fox
Video; RCA VideoDiscs*

Great Music from   1957
Chicago
Music-Performance
85176   55 mins   B/W   B, V   P
*Andre Kostelanetz, the Chicago Symphony
Orchestra*
The famous conductor and orchestra perform
pieces by Barber, Toch, Borodin, Ravel and
Chabrier.
Unknown — *Video Yesteryear*

Great Race, The   1965
Comedy
69797   147 mins   C   B, V   P
*Jack Lemmon, Tony Curtis, Natalie Wood, Peter
Falk, Keenan Wynn, directed by Blake Edwards*
A dastardly villain, a noble hero and a spirited
suffragette are among the competitors in an
uproarious New York-to-Paris auto race circa
1908, complete with pie fights, saloon brawls,
and a confrontation with a feisty polar bear.
Warner Bros — *Warner Home Video*

Great Ride, A — 1978
Adventure
78894   90 mins   C   B, V   P
Perry Lang, Michael Macrae, Michael Sullivan
The state police are after two dirt bikers who are riding through areas where bike riding is illegal.
Hooker-Hulette Productions — Monterey Home Video

Great Riviera Bank Robbery, The — 1979
Suspense/Drama
77421   98 mins   C   B, V   P
Ian McShane, Warren Clarke, Stephen Greif
A genius executes a bank robbery on the French Riviera netting fifteen million dollars.
Jack Gill — MPI Home Video

Great St. Trinian's Train Robbery, The — 1966
Comedy
63348   90 mins   C   B, V   P
Frankie Howerd, Reg Varney, Desmond Walter Ellis
The perpetrators of the Great Train Robbery attempt to stash the loot at a remote school attended by a band of avaricious adolescent girls, with hilarious results.
British Lion — THORN EMI/HBO Video

Great Santini, The — 1980
Drama
52710   118 mins   C   B, V   P
Robert Duvall, Blythe Danner, Michael O'Keefe, Julie Ann Haddock, Lisa Jane Persky
The "Great Santini" is Lt. Col. Bull Meechum, a Marine pilot who treats his family as if they were a company of marines, abusing them in the name of discipline, as they struggle to show him their love.
MPAA:PG
Orion Pictures — Warner Home Video; RCA VideoDiscs

Great Scout and Cathouse Thursday, The — 1976
Comedy/Western
64358   96 mins   C   B, V, CED   P
Lee Marvin, Oliver Reed, Robert Culp, Elizabeth Ashley, Kay Lenz
Three gold prospectors strike it rich, but one of them runs off with the money.
MPAA:PG
American International — Vestron Video

Great Skycopter Rescue, The — 1982
Adventure
80500   96 mins   C   B, V   P
William Marshall, Aldo Ray, Russell Johnson, directed by Lawrence Foldes

Ruthless businessmen hire a motorcycle gang to terrorize the inhabitants of an oil-rich town, in an attempt to scare them away. A local teenage flying enthusiast organizes his friends into an attack force to fight back.
Star Cinema Productions Group
III — MGM/UA Home Video

Great Smokey Roadblock, The — 1976
Adventure
65484   84 mins   C   B, V   P
Henry Fonda, Eileen Brennan, Susan Sarandon, John Byner
While in the hospital, a sixty-year-old truck driver's rig is repossessed by the finance company. Deciding that it's time to make one last perfect cross country run, he escapes from the hospital, steals his truck and heads off into the night.
MPAA:PG
Allen R Bodoh — Media Home Entertainment

Great Space Coaster, The — 1981
Variety
80363   59 mins   C   B, V   P
Join Gary Gnu, Goriddle and their friends as they explore the sights and sounds of America.
Sunbow Productions — MGM/UA Home Video

Great Teams/Great Years Volume One — 1981
Football
50653   48 mins   C   B, V, FO   R, P
New York Jets, Buffalo Bills
This program highlights the accomplishments of the 1968 New York Jets, who, led by Joe Namath, pulled a stunning Super Bowl upset over the Baltimore Colts; and the 1973 Buffalo Bills, who set the NFL 14-game rushing record. O. J. Simpson's 2003 individual yards broke Jim Brown's record.
NFL Films — NFL Films Video

Great Texas Dynamite Chase, The — 1976
Comedy
52704   90 mins   C   B, V   P
Claudia Jennings, Johnny Crawford, Jocelyn Jones
Two sexy young women drive across Texas with a carload of dynamite. They leave a trail of empty banks with the cops constantly on their trail.
MPAA:R
New World Pictures; David Irving — Warner Home Video

Great Waldo Pepper, The — 1975
Adventure
11584   107 mins   C   B, V   P

Robert Redford, Susan Sarandon, Margot Kidder, Bo Svenson, directed by George Roy Hill
After the death of several people as a result of a wing-walking routine, a barnstorming pilot is permanently grounded. He finds he can't adjust to an "earth-bound" life and begins flying again under an assumed name.
MPAA:PG
Universal — MCA Home Video

Great Wallendas, The   1978
Circus
45038   96 mins   C   B, V   P
Lloyd Bridges, Britt Ekland, Cathy Rigby
The story of the Wallendas, a seven-person acrobatic team, who were noted for creating a pyramid on the highwire without nets below them. After a fall that killed two members and paralyzed another, the remaining members rebuild and make a comeback.
Daniel Wilson — Lightning Video; Time Life Video

Great White Death   1981
Documentary
80794   88 mins   C   B, V   R, P
Glenn Ford
Join Glenn Ford as he searches for the Great White Shark in a real life underwater adventure.
MPAA:PG
Jean Lebel — Video Gems

Greatest, The   1977
Biographical/Drama
78880   100 mins   C   B, V   P
Muhammad Ali, Robert Duvall, Ernest Borgnine, James Earl Jones, directed by Tom Gries
The filmed autobiography of the fighter who could float like a butterfly and sting like a bee, Muhammad Ali. In Beta Hi-Fi.
MPAA:PG
John Marshall; Columbia Pictures — RCA/Columbia Pictures Home Video

Greatest Adventure, The   1982
Space exploration/Documentary
59958   54 mins   C   B, V, LV,   P
                                CED
Narrated by Orson Welles, Alan Shepard, Gene Cernon, John Glenn, Tom Wolfe
An account of America's race for the moon, from the first orbital flight to Neil Armstrong's landing.
Video Associates — Vestron Video; ABC Video Enterprises; MTI Teleprograms

Greatest Adventure   1986
Stories from the Bible,
The
Bible
86097   29 mins   C   B, V   P

6   pgms
A series of animated Biblical adventures.
1.Moses 2.David & Goliath 3.Joshua & the Battle of Jericho 4.Noah's Ark 5.Samson & Delilah 6.Daniel and the Lion's Den
Hanna-Barbera — Embassy Home Entertainment

Greatest Comeback Ever,   1978
The
Baseball
29355   58 mins   C   B, V   P
Narrated by Phil Rizzuto and Bucky Dent
This program features the key moments that made the Yankees' struggle for the championship the greatest comeback ever.
Unknown — VidAmerica

Greatest Fights of the   1981
70's
Boxing
58868   116 mins   C   CED   P
Muhammad Ali, Joe Frazier, George Foreman, Roberto Duran
Champions of the ring are seen in some of their most unforgettable confrontations.
Big Fights Inc — CBS/Fox Video

Greatest Game Ever   1984
Played, The
Football
70270   55 mins   C   B, V, FO   P
Frank Gifford, Sam Huff, John Unitas, Gino Marchetti
This film highlights the Baltimore Colts' sudden death overtime victory over the New York Giants in the 1958 NFL Championship Game.
NFL Films — NFL Films Video

Greatest Heroes of the   1979
Bible
Religion
44944   95 mins   C   B, V   P
This program contains two Bible stories. First, an enactment of how the Ten Commandments were handed down to us. Second, the story of Sampson, who lost his extraordinary power and then, with a great effort of will and spirit, regained it.
Sunn Classic Pictures — VidAmerica

Greatest Legends of   1978
Basketball
Basketball
08372   60 mins   C   B, V   P
Jerry West, Oscar Robertson, Elgin Baylor, John Wooden
Enjoy the highlights of the careers of basketball greats.
Viacom International — CBS/Fox Video

Greatest Man in the World, The   1980
Literature-American
57324   51 mins   C   B, V   P
Brad Davis, William Prince, John McMartin, Howard da Silva
James Thurber's tale of an illiterate, incorrigible lout who, upon becoming the first man to fly non-stop around the world, receives immediate national attention.
Learning in Focus — *Monterey Home Video; Perspective Films & Video*

Greatest Show on Earth, The   1952
Drama
53789   153 mins   C   B, V, LV   P
Betty Hutton, Cornel Wilde, James Stewart, Charlton Heston, Dorothy Lamour, directed by Cecil B. DeMille
Big top drama focusing on the lives and loves of circus performers.
Academy Award '52: Best Picture.
Paramount; Cecil B DeMille; Henry Wilcoxon — *Paramount Home Video; RCA VideoDiscs*

Greatest Story Ever Told, The   1956
Drama
Closed Captioned
65505   196 mins   C   B, V   P
Max Von Sydow, Charlton Heston, Sidney Poitier, Claude Rains, Jose Ferrer, Telly Savalas, Angela Lansbury, Dorothy McGuire
Christ's journey from Galilee to Golgotha and the world of saints, sinners and believers that appear along the way are seen in this epic.
United Artists — *CBS/Fox Video*

Greek Street   1930
Musical
08672   51 mins   B/W   B, V, 3/4U   P
Sari Maritzia, Arthur Ahmbling, Martin Lewis, directed by Sinclair Hill
The owner of small cafe in London discovers a poor girl singing in the street for food. He takes her in and spotlights her songs in his cafe.
Unknown — *Video Yesteryear*

Greek Tycoon, The   1978
Drama
62877   106 mins   C   B, V   P
Anthony Quinn, Jacqueline Bisset, James Franciscus, Raf Vallone, Edward Albert
The widow of an American president marries a billionaire shipping magnate.
MPAA:R
Universal — *MCA Home Video*

Green Archer, The   1940
Mystery
57354   283 mins   B/W   B, V, FO   P
Victor Jory, Iris Meredith
Fifteen episodes of the famed serial, featuring a spooked castle, complete with secret passages and tunnels, trap-doors, mistaken identity, and the mysterious masked figure, the Green Archer.
Columbia — *Video Yesteryear; Video Connection; Discount Video Tapes*

Green Berets, The   1968
War-Drama
38953   135 mins   C   B, V   P
John Wayne, David Janssen, Jim Hutton, Aldo Rey, George Takei, Raymond St. Jacques
John Wayne stars as a Special Forces colonel, leading his troops against the enemy in this war drama of the Vietnam conflict.
Warner Bros — *Warner Home Video; RCA VideoDiscs*

Green Dolphin Street   1947
Drama/Romance
82400   161 mins   B/W   B, V   P
Lana Turner, Van Heflin, Donna Reed, directed by Victor Savile
In 19th century New Zealand, a young girl marries her sister's beau, then has an affair with her husband's best friend.
MPAA:PG-13
MGM — *MGM/UA Home Video*

Green Eyes   1980
Drama
75461   97 mins   C   B, V   P
Paul Winfield
A Vietnam veteran returns to Saigon and finds the girl who bore his baby.
King Features — *U.S.A. Home Video*

Green Ice   1981
Adventure
86045   109 mins   C   B, V   P
Ryan O'Neal, Anne Archer, Omar Sharif, directed by Ernest Day
An American electronics expert gets involved with a brutal South American government dealing with emeralds.
Lord Lew Grade — *Key Video*

Green Mountain Railroading on the Rutland & When Steam Was King   1952
Trains
66339   20 mins   C   B, V   P, T
These two short films feature scenes of the Bennington and Rutland Railway, Central Vermont's Bellows Falls—Burlington Line and footage of steam-powered trains and

locomotives from all over the country. Some sequences in black and white.
Carl Dudley — *Blackhawk Films*

Green Pastures, The 1936
Comedy
81069   93 mins   C   B, V   P
Rex Ingram, Oscar Polk, Eddie Anderson, George Reed, Abraham Graves, Myrtle Anderson
This is an adaptation of the Marc Connelly play about the black concept of heaven. Available in VHS and Beta Hi-Fi.
Warner Bros. — *Key Video*

Green Room, The 1978
Drama
58235   90 mins   C   B, V   P
Francois Truffaut, Nathalie Baye, Jean Daste, directed by Francois Truffaut
Truffaut's haunting tale of a man who erects a secret shrine to the dead, including his young bride. Based on Henry James, "Altar of the Dead." Subtitled.
MPAA:PG FR
Les Films du Carrosse — *Warner Home Video*

Greenpeace Non-Toxic 1985
Video Hits
Music video
84788   59 mins   C   B, V   P
A compilation of liberal, peace-loving video hits; featuring Thomas Dolby, Queen, Madness and Tears for Fears.
Wienerworld — *Vestron Video*

Gremlins 1984
Horror/Science fiction
Closed Captioned
82250   106 mins   C   B, V, LV   P
Zach Galligan, Phoebe Cates, Hoyt Axton, Polly Holliday, Frances Lee McCain, directed by Joe Dante
Havoc abounds when a young man's pet mogwai runs amuck in a small town on Christmas eve. Jerry Goldsmith's score enjoys digitally processed stereo in all formats.
MPAA:PG
Amblin Entertainment — *Warner Home Video*

Grendel, Grendel, 1982
Grendel
Fantasy
65653   90 mins   C   B, V   P
Animated, voices by Peter Ustinov, Arthur Dignam, Julie McKenna, Keith Michell
An utterly urbane dragon wants to be friends, but for some reason people are just terrified of Grendel. It's true, he bites a head off once in a while, but nobody's perfect! An ingenious retelling of Beowulf.

Satori Entertainment — *Family Home Entertainment*

Grey Fox, The 1983
Drama/Western
65115   92 mins   C   B, V   P
Richard Farnsworth, Jackie Burroughs, Wayne Robson
A gentlemanly old stagecoach robber tries to pick up his life after thirty years in prison. Unable to resist another heist, he hides out in British Columbia where he meets an attractive suffragette.
MPAA:PG
Zoetrope Studios — *Media Home Entertainment*

Greystoke: The Legend 1984
of Tarzan, Lord of the
Apes
Adventure
78142   130 mins   C   B, V, LV,   P
                            CED
Ralph Richardson, Ian Holm, Christopher Lambert, James Fox, Ian Charleson
The story of the seventh Earl of Greystoke from his birth in Africa, through his upbringing by a mystified band of apes, to his homecoming in the Scottish highlands.
Warner Home Video — *Warner Home Video*

Grim Reaper 198?
Horror
78668   90 mins   C   B, V   P
Tisa Farrow, George Eastman
A woman on vacation meets up with a man who has his own ideas about population control.
Independent — *Monterey Home Video*

Grinch Grinches the Cat 1982
in the Hat/Pontoffel
Pock, The
Cartoons
Closed Captioned
81869   49 mins   C   B, V   P
Animated
A Dr. Seuss double feature: The Cat in the Hat and the Grinch cross paths in "The Grinch Grinches the Cat in the Hat" and a young man gains his self confidence in "Pontoffel Pock". Available in VHS and Beta Hi-Fi Stereo.
De Patie-Freleng Productions — *Playhouse Video*

Grit of the Girl 1915
Telegrapher, The/In the
Switch Tower
Drama
65769   47 mins   B/W   B, V   P, T
Anna Q. Nilsson, Hal Clements, Walter Edwards, Frank Borzage

A pair of silent railroad dramas, which feature thrilling chase sequences, nefarious schemers and virginal heroines. Silent with piano scores by Jon Mirsalis.
Kalem — *Blackhawk Films*

Grizzly   1976
Horror
59670   92 mins   C   B, V   P
Christopher George, Andrew Prine, Richard Jaeckel
The largest carnivorous ground beast in the world goes on a killing spree. Also titled: "Killer Grizzly."
MPAA:PG
David Sheldon; Harvey Flaxman — *Media Home Entertainment*

Groove Tube, The   1972
Satire
03563   75 mins   C   B, V   P
Chevy Chase, Richard Belzer
A series of skits that spoof television.
MPAA:R
Ken Shapiro — *Media Home Entertainment*

Groovie Goolies Volume I   1971
Cartoons
78351   57 mins   C   B, V   P
Animated
Drac, Frankie, Wolfy and all the residents of Horrible Hall conjure up adventures in this animated collection of episodes from the television series.
Filmation Studios — *Embassy Home Entertainment*

Groovin for a 60's Afternoon   1985
Music video/Cartoons
81673   47 mins   C   B, V   P
Animated, directed by Chuck Braverman
Donald Duck, Mickey Mouse and the rest of the Disney gang dance to such 60's favorites as "Peppermint Twist" and "Catch a Wave" in this collection of music videos available in VHS Stereo and Beta Hi-Fi.
Walt Disney Productions — *Walt Disney Home Video*

Gross Jokes   1985
Comedy-Performance
71164   53 mins   C   B, V   P
Tommy Sledge, Barry Diamond, Budd Friedman
The comic producers used Julius Alvin's best-selling book as the inspiration for this jokefest. Filmed at L.A.'s Improv.
Eddie Kritzer; MCA Entertainment — *MCA Home Video*

Group, The   1966
Drama
86039   150 mins   C   B, V   P
Candice Bergen, Joanna Pettet, Shirley Knight, Joan Hackett, Elizabeth Hartman, Jessica Walter, Larry Hagman, directed by Sidney Lumet
Based upon the novel on Mary McCarthy, the story deals with a group of graduates from a Vassar-like college as they try to adapt to life during the Great Depression.
UA — *Key Video*

Group Marriage   1983
Comedy
65724   90 mins   C   B, V   P
Claudia Jennings, Zack Taylor, Victoria Vetri
Six young professionals fall into a marriage of communal convenience and rapidly discover the many advantages and drawbacks of their thoroughly modern group marriage.
MPAA:R
Charles S Swartz — *United Home Video; Continental Video*

Grover Washington, Jr. in Concert   1982
Music-Performance
59875   53 mins   C   B, V   P
The lush, soulful music of Grover Washington, Jr. is captured in one of his rare public performances along with musicians Eric Gale, Richard Tee, and Steve Gadd. Songs include "Just the Two of Us," "Winelight," and "Come Morning." In stereo.
Bruce Buschel; Gary Delfiner — *Warner Home Video; Pioneer Artists; MGM/UA Home Video (disc only)*

Growing Pains   1982
Horror
81039   60 mins   C   B, V   P
Gary Bond, Barbara Keilermann, Norman Beaton
A young couple discover that their newly adopted son possesses extraordinary powers.
Hammer Films — *Thriller Video*

Grudge Fights   197?
Boxing
07877   60 mins   C   B, V   P
The biggest grudge battles in boxing history are highlighted, including Ali-Frazier, Louis-Schmeling, and Dempsey-Tunney.
Big Fights Inc — *VidAmerica*

Grump Comes Back, The   198?
Cartoons
82579   90 mins   C   B, V   P
Animated
Three friends try to avoid a killjoy in this animated feature.

Children's Treasures — *Embassy Home Entertainment*

Grunt! The Wrestling Movie
1985

Drama/Exploitation
85078   91 mins   C   B, V   P
Wally Greene, Steven Cepello, Dick Murdoch, John Tolos
A drama about the behind-the-scenes world of wrestling. For fans only.
MPAA:R
New World Pictures — *New World Video*

GTR—The Making of GTR
1986

Music video
86794   30 mins   C   B, V   P
A chronicle of the new supergroup's formation, featuring Steve Howe, Steve Hackett, Phil Spaulding, Jonathon Mover and Max Bacon.
RCA Video — *RCA/Columbia Pictures Home Video*

Guapo Heredera Busca Esposa,El(The Handsome Heir Seeks a Wife)
197?

Comedy
86536   90 mins   C   B, V   P
Alfred Landa
A small town boy must find a wife in order to get an inheritance and resorts to hiring a whore.
SP
Spanish — *Master Arts Video*

Guardian, The
1984

Drama
Closed Captioned
77407   102 mins   C   B, V   P
Martin Sheen, Louis Gossett Jr.
The residents of a chic New York apartment building hire a security expert to aid them in combatting their crime problem.
MPAA:R
HBO — *Vestron Video*

Guardian of the Abyss
1982

Horror
81038   60 mins   C   B, V   P
Ray Lonnen, Rosalyn Landor, Paul Darrow, Barbara Ewing
A young couple who buy an antique mirror get more then they bargained for when they discover that it is the threshold to devil worship.
Hammer Films — *Thriller Video*

Guess Who Reunion, The
1983

Music-Performance
65684   118 mins   C   B, V   P
Before a live audience in Toronto, the original Guess Who perform the hits that made them world-wide superstars. Included are performances of "Shakin' All Over," "These Eyes," and "American Woman."
David Wolinsky; Bill Ballard; Dusty Cohl; Michael Cole; Anthony Eaton — *Music Media*

Guess Who's Coming To Dinner
1967

Drama
Closed Captioned
84604   108 mins   C   B, V   P
Katherine Hepburn, Spencer Tracy, Sidney Poitier, Katherine Houghton, directed by Stanley Kramer
An independent daughter of understanding parents brings home her black fiancee. The respective limits of their independence and understanding are tested.
Academy Awards '67: Best Actress (Katherine Hepburn)
Stanley Kramer — *RCA/Columbia Pictures Home Video*

Guide for the Married Man, A
1967

Comedy
86588   91 mins   C   B, V   P
Walter Matthau, Robert Morse, Inger Stevens, Lucille Ball, Jack Benny, Polly Bergen, Sid Caesar, Art Carney, Wally Cox, Jayne Mansfield, Louis Nye, Carl Reiner, Phil Silvers, Terry-Thomas, Sam Jaffe, directed by Gene Kelly
One suburban husband instructs another in adultery, with a cast of dozens enacting various slapstick cameos.
Frank McCarthy — *Key Video*

Guide to Making Love, A
1983

Sexuality
65342   57 mins   C   B, V   P
Bryce Britton, Rona Lee Cohen, R.N., M.N.
This program is a guide to sexual awareness; created to help couples fully realize and express their sexuality. It explains how couples can learn to achieve sexual harmony and overcome their inhibitions.
Guide Productions — *Vestron Video*

Guinness Book of World Records, The
1977

Games
81918   30 mins   C   B, V   P
This is a video version of the popular book that chronicles unusual facts about everyone from Jim Brown to the Wright Brothers.
Unknown — *VidAmerica*

Gulag
1985

Drama
80324   130 mins   C   B, V   P
David Keith, Malcolm McDowell
An American sportscaster is sentenced to ten years of hard labor in a Soviet prison.

HBO — *Prism*

Gulliver 197?
Drama
86538   100 mins   C   B, V   P
Fernando Gomez, Yolanda Farr
A farce about an escaped convict who hides out
with a community of dwarves, manipulates
them, and eventually impels them to murder.
SP
Spanish — *Master Arts Video*

Gulliver's Travels 1939
Fantasy/Cartoons
03588   77 mins   C   B, V, 3/4U   P
Animated
Animated version of Jonathan Swift's classic
about the adventures of Gulliver, an English
sailor.
Paramount — *Hal Roach Studios; Prism;
Nostalgia Merchant; Media Home
Entertainment; Republic Pictures Home Video;
Video Yesteryear; Cable Films; Movie Buff
Video; VCII; Video Connection; Hollywood
Home Theater; Discount Video Tapes; Western
Film & Video Inc; Vestron Video (disc only);
Kartes Video Communications; World Video
Pictures*

Gulliver's Travels 1977
Adventure
54558   80 mins   C   B, V   P
Richard Harris, Catherine Schell
In this partially animated adventure the entire
land of Liliput has been constructed in
miniature. Cartoon and real life mix in a 3-
dimensional story of Dr. Lemuel Gulliver and his
discovery of the small people in the East Indies.
MPAA:G
EMI — *United Home Video; Lucerne Films*

Gulliver's Travels 1979
Cartoons
79243   52 mins   C   B, V   P
Animated
An animated version of the Swift Satire about a
sailor whose voyage takes him to an unusual
island.
Hanna-Barbera Productions — *Worldvision
Home Video*

Gumball Rally, The 1976
Comedy
78624   107 mins   C   B, V   P
Michael Sarrazin, Gary Busey, Raul Julia
An unusual assortment of people converge
upon New York for a cross country car race to
Long Beach, California.
MPAA:PG
Warner Bros; First Artists — *Warner Home
Video*

Gumby Adventures 1956
Cartoons
64196   50 mins   C   B, V   P
Animated
Those timeless clay animation heroes, Gumby
and Pokey, battle evil and the Blockheads in this
series of tapes. Each cassette includes 8 or 9
episodes of this TV staple.
EL, SP
Clokey Productions — *Family Home
Entertainment*

Gun Riders 1969
Western
58606   98 mins   C   B, V   P, T
Scott Brady, Jim Davis, John Carradine
A gunman must seek out and stop a murderer of
innocent people.
Independent Intl — *Blackhawk Films*

Gun Smugglers/Hot Lead 1951
Western
81030   120 mins   B/W   B, V   P
Tim Holt, Richard Martin, Martha Hyer
A western double feature: Tim Holt and his
sidekick Chito must recover a shipment of
stolen guns in "Gun Smugglers", and the duo
gallup into action against a gang of train robbers
in "Hot Lead".
RKO — *RKO HomeVideo*

Gunfight at the O.K. 1957
Corral
Western
38622   122 mins   C   B, V, LV   P
*Burt Lancaster, Kirk Douglas, Rhonda Fleming,
Jo Van Fleet, directed by John Sturges*
The story of Wyatt Earp and Doc Holliday who
joined forces in Dodge City to rid the town of the
criminal Clanton gang is portrayed definitively in
this western classic.
Paramount — *Paramount Home Video; RCA
VideoDiscs*

Gung Ho 1943
War-Drama
08775   88 mins   B/W   B, V, 3/4U   P
*Randolph Scott, Noah Beery Jr., Alan Curtis,
Grace McDonald*
Marine raiders, in new outfit, train for invasion
during World War II.
Universal; Walter Wanger — *Hal Roach
Studios; Video Yesteryear; Hollywood Home
Theater; International Historic Films; Cable
Films; VCII; Video Connection; Discount Video
Tapes; Cinema Concepts; Kartes Video
Communications; Republic Pictures Home
Video; Movie Buff Video; Prism*

Gunga Din 1939
Adventure
00257   117 mins   B/W   B, V   P

Cary Grant, Douglas Fairbanks Jr., Joan Fontaine
Based on Kipling's adventure book, this story features three soldier comrades battling savages.
RKO; George Seaton — *RKO HomeVideo; VidAmerica; King of Video*

Gunman From Bodie   1941
Western
15435   62 mins   B/W   B, V   P
Tim McCoy, Buck Jones, Ray Hatton
Action western.
Monogram — *Video Connection; United Home Video; Discount Video Tapes*

Gunplay   1951
Western
64406   61 mins   B/W   B, V, 3/4U   P
Tim Holt, Joan Dixon, Richard Martin
Two cowboys befriend a boy whose father has been killed and search for the murderer.
RKO — *Nostalgia Merchant*

Guns of Fury   1945
Western
14661   60 mins   B/W   B, V   P
Duncan Renaldo
Cisco and Pancho solve the troubles of a small boy in this wild western.
United Artists — *United Home Video; Video Connection; Discount Video Tapes*

Guns of Navarone, The   1961
Adventure
13253   159 mins   C   B, V   P
Gregory Peck, David Niven, Anthony Quinn, Stanley Baker, Anthony Quayle, directed by J. Lee Thompson
British Intelligence in the Middle East sends six men to Navarone to destroy guns manned by the Germans.
Filmdom's Famous Five '61: Best Actor (Peck); Best Supporting Actor (Quinn).
Columbia; Carl Foreman — *RCA/Columbia Pictures Home Video; RCA VideoDiscs*

Guns of War   1975
War-Drama
82216   114 mins   C   B, V   P
This is the true story of a group of Yugoslavians formed a partisan army to stop the reign of Nazi terror in their native land.
Yugoslavian — *VCL Home Video*

Gus   1976
Comedy
70671   96 mins   C   B, V, CED   P
Edward Asner, Tim Conway, Dick Van Patten, Ronnie Schell, Bob Crane, Tom Bosley, directed by Vincent McEveety

The California Atoms own the worst record in the league until they begin to pull victories out of their field goal kicking mule of a mascot, Gus. The competition then plots a donkeynapping.
MPAA:G
Walt Disney Productions — *RCA VideoDiscs; Walt Disney Home Video*

Guys and Dolls   1955
Musical
53663   149 mins   C   B, V, CED   P
Marlon Brando, Jean Simmons, Frank Sinatra, Vivian Blaine, Stubby Kaye, Sheldon Leonard, directed by Joseph L. Mankiewicz
A New York gangster takes a bet that he can romance a Salvation Army lady. Frank Loesser's score includes "Luck Be a Lady," "If I were a Bell," "Sit Down You're Rocking the Boat."
Samuel Goldwyn — *CBS/Fox Video*

Gymkata   1985
Martial arts
82245   89 mins   C   B, V   P
Kurt Thomas, Tetchie Agbayani, Richard Norton, Conan Lee, directed by Robert Clouse
A gymnast must use his martial arts skills to conquer and secure a military state in a hostile European country.
MPAA:R
MGM/UA Entertainment — *MGM/UA Home Video*

Gypsy   1962
Musical
74205   149 mins   C   B, V   P
Rosalind Russell, Natalie Wood, Karl Malden
This is the life story of America's most famous striptease queen, Gypsy Rose Lee. Rosalind Russell gives a memorable performance as the infamous Gypsy.
Mervyn Le Roy — *Warner Home Video*

H

Hail   1972
Satire
76660   85 mins   C   B, V   P
Richard B. Shull, Dick O'Neil, Phil Foster, Joseph Sirola, Dan Resin
A biting satire of what-might-have-been if certain key cabinet members had their way.
MPAA:PG
Fred Levinson Productions — *Monterey Home Video*

Hair   1979
Musical
37529   118 mins   C   B, V, CED   P
Treat Williams, John Savage, Beverly D'Angelo

Film version of the 1960's Broadway musical about the carefree life of the flower children and the shadow of the Vietnam War that hangs over them.
MPAA:R
United Artists — CBS/Fox Video; RCA VideoDiscs

Hal Roach Comedy Classics, Volumes I thru XII   193?
Comedy
71034   60 mins   B/W   B, V   P
Laurel and Hardy, the Little Rascals, Charlie Chase, ZaSu Pitts, Thelma Todd
Each cassette in this series collects several funny shorts from the Roach vaults.
Hal Roach — Hal Roach Studios

Hal Roach Comedy Classics Volume I   193?
Comedy
59154   80 mins   B/W   B, V, 3/4U   P
Stan Laurel, Oliver Hardy, Harry Langdon, Charley Chase
Films include: "Hoosegow" (1930), with Laurel and Hardy; "The Head Guy" (1930), with Harry Langdon; "High Gear" (1931), with the Boyfriends and "On the wrong Trek" (1936), with Laurel and Hardy and Charley Chase.
Hal Roach — Nostalgia Merchant

Half-Shot at Sunrise   1930
Comedy
56907   78 mins   B/W   B, V, FO   P
Wheeler and Woolsey, Dorothy Lee
Madcap vaudeville comedians play AWOL soldiers loose in 1918 Paris. Continuous one-liners, sight gags, and slapstick nonsense.
RKO — Video Yesteryear; Cable Films; Discount Video Tapes

Hall of Famers   1960
Baseball
49551   60 mins   B/W   B, V   P
Three twenty-minute segments which highlight the careers of members of baseball's Hall of Fame who were elected before 1960.
Major League Baseball — Major League Baseball Productions

Halley's Comet—A Viewer's Guide with William Shatner   1985
Astronomy
84692   50 mins   C   B, V   P
Narrated by William Shatner
A special look at the Comet's coming with TV's Captain Kirk.
Four Point Ent — Four Point Entertainment

Hallmark Hall of Fame, The   1954
Drama
78099   103 mins   B/W   B, V, FO   P
Maurice Evans, Dame Judith Anderson, House Jameson, Richard Waring, Guy Sorel
A first-rate mounting of great tragedy, "Macbeth," with Maurice Evans in the title role.
NBC — Video Yesteryear

Hallmark Theater (Sometimes She's Sunday)   1952
Drama
42970   26 mins   B/W   B, V, FO   P
Adult fare about a Portuguese-American fisherman whose daughter becomes engaged to a typical American boy.
NBC — Video Yesteryear

Halloween   1978
Horror
42908   85 mins   C   B, V, LV   P
Jamie Lee Curtis, Nancy Loomis, P.J. Soles, directed by John Carpenter
John Carpenter's horror classic has been acclaimed "the most successful independent motion picture of all time." A deranged youth returns to his hometown after fifteen years in an asylum with murderous intent.
MPAA:R   EL, SP
Debra Hill — Media Home Entertainment

Halloween II   1981
Horror
47418   92 mins   C   B, V, LV   P
Jamie Lee Curtis, Donald Pleasance
Picking up precisely where "Halloween" left off, the sequel begins with the escape of vicious killer Shape, who continues to murder and terrorize the community of Haddonfield, Illinois.
VHS in stereo.
MPAA:R
Universal — MCA Home Video

Halloween III: The Season of the Witch   1982
Horror
60586   98 mins   C   B, V   P
Tom Atkins, Stacey Nelkin, Dan O'Herlihy, Ralph Strait, directed by Tommy Lee Wallace
A mad warlock threatens to subject 50 million children to a Halloween they'll never forget, in this sequel produced by John Carpenter.
MPAA:R
Universal; John Carpenter — MCA Home Video

Halloween Is Grinch Night · 1977

Cartoons
Closed Captioned
81867   25 mins   C   B, V   P
Animated
A young boy must muster up enough courage to save his family and town from the nasty Grinch. Based upon the Dr. Seuss story. Available in VHS and Beta Hi-Fi Stereo.
De Patie-Freleng Productions — *Playhouse Video*

Hambone and Hillie · 1984

Comedy/Adventure
79707   97 mins   C   B, V   P
Lillian Gish, Timothy Bottoms, Candy Clark, OJ Simpson, Robert Walker, Jack Carter
An elderly woman makes a three thousand mile trek across the United States to search for her lost dog.
MPAA:PG
New World Pictures; Sandy Howard — *THORN EMI/HBO Video*

Hamburger... The Motion Picture · 1986

Comedy
88303   90 mins   C   B, V   P
Leigh McCloskey, Dick Butkus, Randi Brooks, Sandy Hackett
The life and times of students at Busterburger U., the only college devoted to hamburger franchise management.
MPAA:R
Edward S. Feldman; Charles R. Meeker — *Media Home Entertainment*

Hamlet · 1948

Drama
44362   142 mins   B/W   CED   P
Sir Laurence Olivier, Jean Simmons, Stanley Holloway, Eileen Herlie, directed by Sir Laurence Olivier
Shakespeare's most famous tragedy about a young prince plagued by murder and madness. Academy Awards '48: Best Production; Best Actor (Olivier); Best Art Design, Black and White; Best Costume Design, Black and White.
Universal, J Arthur Rank — *RCA VideoDiscs; Learning Corp of America*

Hammer Into Anvil · 1968

Adventure/Fantasy
70588   52 mins   C   B, V   P
Patrick McGoohan, Patrick Cargill, Victor Madden, directed by Pat Jackson.
In this fourteenth episode of "The Prisoner" TV series, the Prisoner is having big problems with his Number 2. When push comes to shove, the Prisoner blows his Number 2 out.
Associated TV Corp. — *MPI Home Video*

Hammersmith Is Out · 1972

Comedy
84616   108 mins   C   B, V   P
Richard Burton, Elizabeth Taylor, Peter Ustinov, Beau Bridges, directed by Peter Ustinov
A violent lunatic cons an orderly into letting him escape. Chases, romance an craziness follow. A screamer.
MPAA:R
Alex Lucas — *Prism*

Hammett · 1982

Mystery
69023   97 mins   C   B, V   P
This mystery thriller plunges real-life writer and detective Dashiell Hammett into the world of his fictional characters.
MPAA:PG
Zoetrope Studios — *Warner Home Video*

Hand, The · 1981

Horror
58236   105 mins   C   B, V   P
Michael Caine, Andrea Marcovicci, Annie McEnroe
A gifted cartoonist's hand is severed in an accident. Soon a hand is on the loose seeking out victims to satisfy an obsessive revenge.
MPAA:R
Orion Pictures — *Warner Home Video*

Hands of the Ripper · 1971

Horror
81915   85 mins   C   B, V   P
Eric Porter, Angharad Rees, Jane Merrow, Keith Bell, directed by Peter Sasady
Jack the Ripper's daughter returns to London where she works as a medium by day and stalks the streets at night.
MPAA:R
Universal Pictures; Hammer Films — *VidAmerica*

Hang 'Em High · 1967

Western
62777   114 mins   C   B, V   P
Clint Eastwood, Inger Stevens, Ed Begley, Pat Hingle, James MacArthur
A cowboy is saved from a lynching and vows to hunt down the gang that nearly killed him.
United Artists — *CBS/Fox Video; RCA VideoDiscs*

Hangar 18 · 1980

Science fiction/Adventure
47685   97 mins   C   B, V   P
Darren McGavin, Robert Vaughn, Garry Collins, Joseph Campanella, James Hampton, Tom Hallick, Pamela Bellwood
A space drama about two astronauts who witness an unexpected disaster in orbit.
MPAA:PG

Sunn Classic; Charles E Sellier
Jr — *Worldvision Home Video*

Hanging on a Star 1978
Comedy
81638   92 mins   C   B, V   P
*Deborah Raffin, Lane Caudell, Wolfman Jack,
Jason Parker, Danil Thorpe*
A small rock band encounters many comic
adventures as they climb their way up the
charts.
MPAA:PG
Independent — *Magnum Entertainment*

Hank Williams, Jr.—A 1985
Star-Spangled Country
Party
Music-Performance
82587   101 mins   C   B, V   P
*Hank Williams, Jr, Waylon Jennings, Jessi Colte,
Earl Thomas Conley, Gus Hardin*
Hank Williams, Jr. and his friends perform such
memorable songs as "Dixie on My Mind,"
"Women I've Never Had," "Love Sick Blues"
and "Storms Never Last."
Mark and Greg Oswald — *Pacific Arts Video*

Hanky Panky 1982
Comedy
Closed Captioned
62810   103 mins   C   B, V   P
*Gene Wilder, Gilda Radner, Richard Widmark,
Kathleen Quinlan, directed by Sidney Poitier*
A comic thriller in the Hitchcock vein, in which
Gene Wilder and Gilda Radner become involved
in a search for top-secret plans.
MPAA:PG
Columbia — *RCA/Columbia Pictures Home
Video; RCA VideoDiscs*

Hanna K 1983
Drama
65512   111 mins   C   B, V   P
*Jill Clayburgh, Gabriel Byrne, Jean Yanne,
Muhamad Bakri, David Clennon, Oded Kotler*
The gripping story of divided passions set in the
tumultuous state of Israel.
MPAA:R
Universal — *MCA Home Video*

Hanoi Rocks 1985
Music-Performance
82389   55 mins   C   B, V   P
Hanoi Rocks
These Alice Cooper-influenced musicians
bridge the gap between punk and metal.
Includes such tunes as "Blitzkrieg Bop,"
"Motorvatin" and "Beer and a Cigarette."
A Lick Films Production — *Sony Video
Software*

Hanover Street 1979
Drama
63442   109 mins   C   B, V   P
*Harrison Ford, Lesley-Anne Down, Christopher
Plummer, Alec McCowan*
An American bomber pilot and a British nurse
fall in love in war-torn Europe, but another man
is in love with the nurse as well.
MPAA:PG
Columbia; Paul N Lazarus II — *RCA/Columbia
Pictures Home Video*

Hans Brinker 1969
Musical
80156   103 mins   C   B, V   P
Eleanor Parker, Richard Basehart, Cyril Ritchard
Young Hans Brinker and his sister participate in
an iceskating race, hoping to win a pair of silver
skates.
MMM Productions — *Warner Home Video*

Hans Christian Andersen 1952
Musical/Fairy tales
82253   105 mins   C   B, V, LV   P
*Danny Kaye, Farley Granger, Jeanmaire, Joey
Walsh, directed by Charles Vidor*
This is a musical story of Hans Christian
Andersen, a young cobbler who has a great gift
for story telling. Frank Loesser's score features
"Inchworm" and "Wonderful Copenhagen" in
VHS and Beta Hi-Fi Mono.
Samuel Goldwyn — *Embassy Home
Entertainment*

Hansel and Gretel 1954
Fairy tales
59048   82 mins   C   B, V   P
Voices of Anna Russell, Mildred Dunnock
This famed Grimms fairy tale tells the story of
the woodcutter's children who venture into the
forest and are caught in the clutches of a wicked
old witch. Puppet animation.
EL, SP
Hansel and Gretel Co — *Media Home
Entertainment; RCA VideoDiscs*

Hansel and Gretel 1984
Fairy tales
Closed Captioned
73143   60 mins   C   B, V, CED   P
*Ricky Schroeder, Joan Collins, Paul Dooley,
Bridgette Anderson, James Frawley*
From "Faerie Tale Theatre" comes the story of
two young children who get more than they
bargained for when they eat a gingerbread
house.
Shelley Duvall — *CBS/Fox Video*

Happiest Millionaire, The 1967
Musical
65634   144 mins   C   B, V   P

Fred MacMurray, Tommy Steele, Greer Garson, Geraldine Page, Lesley Ann Warren, John Davidson
A newly immigrated lad finds a job as butler to a household that features pet alligators in the conservatory and a Bible-and-boxing school in the stables. In stereo VHS and Beta Hi-Fi.
Buena Vista — *Walt Disney Home Video*

Happy Birthday to Me 1981
Horror
58497 108 mins C B, V, LV P
Melissa Sue Anderson, Glenn Ford, directed by J. Lee Thompson
Several elite seniors at an exclusive private school mysteriously disappear—one by one.
MPAA:R
Columbia; John Dunning — *RCA/Columbia Pictures Home Video*

Happy Hooker Goes Hollywood, The 1980
Comedy
52761 86 mins C B, V P
Martine Beswicke
The third film inspired by Xaviera Hollander's memoirs, in which the fun-loving Xaviera comes to Hollywood with the intention of making a movie based on her book, but soon meets up with a series of scheming, would-be producers.
MPAA:R
Golan Globus Productions; Alan Roberts — *MCA Home Video*

Happy Hooker Goes to Washington, The 1977
Comedy
55220 89 mins C B, V, CED P
Joey Heatherton, George Hamilton
The further adventures of the world's most famous madam find Xaviera Hollander the target of a U.S. Senate investigation.
MPAA:R
Cannon Releasing — *Vestron Video*

Happy New Year 1974
Comedy/Romance
82585 114 mins C B, V P
Francoise Fabran, Lino Ventura, Charles Gerard, directed by Claude Lelouch
Two thieves plan a jewelry heist but get sidetracked by the distracting woman who works next door to the jewelry store. Available in both subtitled and dubbed versions.
FR
Claude Lelouch — *Embassy Home Entertainment*

Hardcore 1979
Drama
47433 106 mins C B, V P
George C. Scott, Season Hubley, Peter Boyle, directed by Paul Schrader

A midwestern businessman travels to California to find his runaway daughter, who has become a prostitute and pornographic film star.
MPAA:R
Columbia — *RCA/Columbia Pictures Home Video*

Hard Country 1981
Drama
53352 101 mins C CED P
Jan-Michael Vincent, Kim Basinger, Michael Parks, Tanya Tucker
A young woman decides to break away from her boyfriend and her small Texas town, causing him to re-evaluate his life.
MPAA:PG
ITC; Martin Starger — *CBS/Fox Video*

Hard Day's Night, A 1964
Musical
69037 90 mins B/W B, V, LV, CED P
John Lennon, Paul McCartney, George Harrison, Ringo Starr
This program depicts, with good-natured honesty and fun, the Beatles' lighthearted message to youth.
Walter Shenson — *MPI Home Video*

Hard Hombre 1931
Western
14662 60 mins B/W B, V, 3/4U P
Hoot Gibson
In this Western adventure Hoot Gibson rides and shoots across the screen.
Hoffman — *Video Connection; United Home Video*

Hard Knox 1983
Drama
87309 96 mins C B, V P
Robert Conrad, Frank Howard, Alan Ruck, Red West, Bill Erwin
A hard-nosed Marine pilot is dumped from the service and takes up command at a military school filled with undisciplined punks. A made-for-TV movie.
NBC — *Karl/Lorimar Home Video*

Hard Rock Zombies 1985
Horror
86354 90 mins C B, V P
Four heavy metal band members die horribly, become the living dead and terrorize a small town.
MPAA:R
Cannon Group — *Vestron Video*

Hard Times 1975
Drama
64236 92 mins C B, V P

Charles Bronson, James Coburn, Jill Ireland, Strother Martin
A Depression-era drifter becomes a bare knuckle street fighter, and a gambler decides to promote him for big stakes.
MPAA:PG
Columbia — *RCA/Columbia Pictures Home Video*

Hard to Hold   1984
Musical-Drama
72931   93 mins   C   B, V, LV   P
Rick Springfield, Patti Hansen, Janet Eiber
Rockin' Rick's film debut where he falls in love with a children's counselor after an automobile accident. Rick sings "Love Somebody" with music by Peter Gabriel.
MPAA:PG
D Constantine Conte — *MCA Home Video*

Hardbodies   1984
Comedy
Closed Captioned
70186   88 mins   C   B, V   P
Grant Cramer, Teal Roberts, directed by Mark Griffiths
Three middle-aged men hit the beaches of Southern California in search of luscious young girls. In VHS Hi-Fi and Beta Hi-Fi.
MPAA:R
Columbia Pictures — *RCA/Columbia Pictures Home Video*

Hardcore Volume I   1985
Music video/Music-Performance
84058   60 mins   C   B, V   P
Black Flag, Code of Honor, Sex Pistols, Toxic Reasons
A compilation of live clips of America's and Britain's most notorious hardcore punk groups.
Target Video — *Target Video*

Hardcore Volume II   1985
Music video/Music-Performance
84059   30 mins   C   B, V   P
The Sleepers, The Germs, The Bad Brains, TSOL
More live clips of infamous hardcore punk bands. Featuring "No God," "Wasted," "FVK" and "War Dance."
Target Video — *Target Video*

Harder They Come, The   1972
Musical-Drama
47048   93 mins   C   B, V   P
Jimmy Cliff, Janet Barkley, Carl Bradshaw
A poor Jamaican youth becomes a success with a hit reggae record, but finds his fame is short-lived.
MPAA:R
New World Pictures — *THORN EMI/HBO Video; Movie Buff Video; RCA VideoDiscs*

Harder They Fall, The   1956
Drama
21288   109 mins   B/W   B, V   P
Humphrey Bogart, Rod Steiger, Jan Sterling
An unemployed reporter promotes a fighter for the syndicate, while doing an expose on the fight racket. Based on Budd Schulberg's novel.
Columbia — *RCA/Columbia Pictures Home Video*

Hardhat and Legs   1980
Comedy
81154   96 mins   C   B, V   P
Sharon Gless, Kevin Dobson, Ray Serra, Elva Josephson, Bobby Short, directed by Lee Phillips
Comic complications arise when a New York construction worker falls in love with the woman who's teaching the modern sexuality course he's enrolled in.
Syzygy Productions — *Lightning Video*

Hardly Working   1981
Comedy
82331   90 mins   C   B, V   P
Jerry Lewis, Susan Oliver, Roger C Carmel, Gary Lewis, Deanna Lund, directed by Jerry Lewis
A circus clown finds it difficult to adjust to real life as he fumbles about from one job to another.
MPAA:PG
20th Century Fox — *Playhouse Video*

Hardware Wars and   1981
Other Film Farces
Science fiction/Satire
47397   48 mins   C   B, V   P
A collection of four award-winning spoofs of big-budget film epics, featuring "Hardware Wars," "Porklips Now," "Bambi Meets Godzilla" and "Closet Cases of the Nerd Kind." Some black-and-white segments.
MPAA:G
Ernie Fosselius et al — *Warner Home Video*

Hardy Boys, The   1978
Suspense/Mystery
82366   47 mins   C   B, V   P
Parker Stevenson, Shaun Cassidy, Edmund Gilbert, Lisa Eilbacher 8   pgms
Join intrepid detectives Frank and Joe Hardy as they travel around the world to solve mysteries. Each episode is available individually.
1.The Mystery of Witches' Hollow 2.The Flickering Torch Mystery 3.The Secret of Jade Kwan Yin 4.The Mystery of the Flying Courier 5.Wipe Out 6.The Mystery of King Tut's Tomb 7.The Mystery of the African Safari 8.Acapulco Spies
Universal Television — *MCA Home Video*

Harlan County, U.S.A. 1976
Miners and mining/Documentary
44778   103 mins   C   B, V   P
Directed by Barbara Kopple
The emotions of 180 coal mining families are
seen up close in this classic documentary about
their struggle to win a United Mine Workers
contract in Kentucky.
Academy Award '76: Best Documentary.
Cinema 5 — *RCA/Columbia Pictures Home
Video*

Harlow 1965
Drama
87570   125 mins   C   B, V   P
*Carroll Baker, Martin Balsam, Red Buttons,
Michael Connors, Angela Lansbury, Peter
Lawford, Raf Vallone, Leslie Neilsen*
This is the more lavish of the two Harlow
biographies made in 1965, both with the same
title. A sensationalized "scandal sheet" version
of Jean Harlow's rise to fame, this film bears
little resemblance to the true facts of her life.
Paramount; Joseph E. Levine — *Paramount
Home Video*

Harold and Maude 1971
Comedy
38588   91 mins   C   B, V, 8mm,   P
                                    LV
Ruth Gordon, Bud Cort, directed by Hal Ashby
A classic cult film starring an unlikely pair: a rich,
jaded 20-year old man and a wacky 80-year-old
woman, who go off on a series of wild
adventures.
MPAA:PG
Paramount — *Paramount Home Video; RCA
VideoDiscs*

Harold Lloyd's Comedy 1919
Classics
Comedy
69554   47 mins   B/W   B, V, FO   P
Harold Lloyd, Snub Pollard, Bebe Daniels
Four early Harold Lloyd shorts from 1916-1919
are combined on this tape: "The Chef," "The
Cinema Director," "Two Gun Gussie" and "I'm
On My Way." Silent with musical score.
Pathe — *Video Yesteryear*

Harper 1966
Mystery
69024   119 mins   C   B, V   P
*Paul Newman, Shelley Winters, Lauren Bacall,
Julie Harris, directed by Jack Smight*
Paul Newman stars in this action-charged 1966
private-eye mystery.
Warner Bros — *Warner Home Video*

Harper Valley P.T.A. 1978
Comedy
66095   93 mins   C   B, V, CED   P

*Barbara Eden, Nanette Fabray, Louis Nye, Pat
Paulsen, Ronny Cox*
A tale of what happened when "my momma
socked it to the Harper Valley P.T.A."
MPAA:PG
April Fool Productions — *Vestron Video*

Harrad Experiment, The 1973
Drama
06006   95 mins   C   B, V   P
James Whitmore, Tippi Hedron, Don Johnson
An experiment in co-ed living in New England,
Ivy League-type university. Based on Robert H.
Rimmer's novel.
MPAA:R
Cinerama; Dennis Stevens and Cinema Arts
Prod — *Wizard Video*

Harry and Son 1984
Drama
73031   117 mins   C   B, V, LV,   P
                                    CED
*Paul Newman, Robby Benson, Joanne
Woodward, Ellen Barkin*
A widowed construction worker faces the
problems of raising his son.
MPAA:PG
Orion — *Vestron Video*

Harry & Tonto 1974
Drama
86040   116 mins   C   B, V   P
*Art Carney, Ellen Burstyn, Larry Hagman,
Geraldine Fitzgerald, Chief Dan George, Arthur
Hunnicutt, directed by Paul Mazursky*
A lonely but energetic septegenarian embarks
across the country with his cat, visits his
children and experiences a last adventure.
20th Century Fox — *Key Video*

Harry and Walter Go to 1976
New York
Comedy
21289   120 mins   C   B, V   P
*James Caan, Elliot Gould, Michael Caine, Diane
Keaton*
Two vaudeville performers are hired by a
crooked British entrepreneur for a wild crime
scheme.
MPAA:PG
Columbia — *RCA/Columbia Pictures Home
Video*

Harry Belafonte: Don't 1985
Stop the Carnival
Music-Performance
86265   60 mins   C   B, V   P
Harry Belafonte
The King of Calypso sings and introduces
various guest stars, including Bill Cosby, Alan
King and Dick Cavett.
HBO — *THORN EMI/HBO Video*

Harry Chapin:The Final Concert
1981

Music-Performance
58867   89 mins   C   B, V, CED   P
Harry Chapin
Taped live at Hamilton Place in Hamilton,
Canada, this concert features the warm,
energetic style which earned the singer-
songwriter legions of devoted fans. Songs
include, "Taxi," "Sequel," and "Cat's in the
Cradle."
GRM Productions Inc. — *CBS/Fox Video*

Harry Owens and His Royal Hawaiians
1958

Music-Performance
78089   59 mins   B/W   B, V, FO   P
This program presents a Hawaiian festival of
music and dancing with Harry Owens and his
band.
NBC — *Video Yesteryear*

Harry Tracy
1983

Drama
65343   111 mins   C   B, V   P
Bruce Dern, Gordon Lightfoot, Helen Shaver
This is the tale of the legendary outlaw whose
escapades made him both a wanted criminal
and an exalted folk hero.
MPAA:PG
Cid and Marty Krofft; Albert Penzer — *Vestron
Video*

Harry's War
1984

Comedy
86662   98 mins   C   B, V   P
*Edward Herrmann, Geraldine Page, Karen
Grassle, David Ogden Stiers*
A middle-class, middle-aged American declares
military war on the IRS.
MPAA:PG
American Film Consortium — *Thomson
Productions*

Harum Scarum
1965

Musical-Drama
80152   95 mins   C   B, V   P
Elvis Presley, Mary Ann Mobley, Fran Jeffries
A movie star travelling through the Middle East
becomes involved in an attempted
assassination.
Metro Goldwyn Mayer — *MGM/UA Home
Video*

Hash House Fraud, A/The Sultan's Wife
191?

Comedy
59406   33 mins   B/W   B, V   P, T
*Louise Fazenda, Hugh Fay, Chester Conklin,
The Keystone Cops, Gloria Swanson, Bobby
Vernon*

"A Hash House Fraud" (1915) features a
frenetic Keystone chase. "The Sultan's Wife"
(1917) concerns a woman who attracts the
unwanted attention of a sultan.
Mack Sennett — *Blackhawk Films*

Hatari
1962

Adventure
64938   158 mins   C   B, V, LV   P
*John Wayne, Elsa Martinelli, Red Buttons,
Hardy Kruger, directed by Howard Hawks*
A team of professional big game hunters have
an exciting time capturing wild beasts to send to
zoos.
Paramount — *Paramount Home Video*

Hatchet for a Honeymoon
1970

Horror
81640   90 mins   C   B, V   P
*Stephen Forsythe, Dagmar Lassander, Laura
Betti*
A rather disturbed young man goes around
hacking young brides as he tries to find out who
murdered his mother.
Manuel Cano — *Media Home Entertainment*

Hatfields and the McCoys, The
1975

Drama
80486   90 mins   C   B, V   P
*Jack Palance, Steve Forrest, Richard Hatch,
Karen Lamm*
A retelling of the most famous feud in American
history, the legendary mountain war between
the Hatfields and the McCoys.
Charles Fries Productions — *Worldvision
Home Video*

Haunted Castle, The (Schloss Vogelod)
1921

Film-History
51397   56 mins   B/W   B, V, FO   P
Arnold Korff, Lulu Keyser-Korf
The first German mystery film. Silent, with
English subtitles.
FW Murnau — *Video Yesteryear; Discount
Video Tapes*

Haunted Ranch
1943

Western
38983   56 mins   B/W   B, V, FO   P
*The Range Busters (John "Dusty" King, David
Sharpe, Max "Alibi" Terhune)*
Reno Red has been murdered and a shipment
of gold bullion is missing. A gang on the lookout
for the gold tries to convince people that Red's
ranch is haunted by his ghost.
Monogram — *Discount Video Tapes; Video
Yesteryear; Blackhawk Films*

Haunted Strangler, The 1958
Horror
59661 78 mins B/W B, V P
Boris Karloff, Elizabeth Allan
The story of a social reformer who discovers
that he was once a notorious murderer. The
realization causes him to become re-
transformed into the killer.
John Croydon — *Media Home Entertainment*

Haunting of Harrington 1982
House, The
Mystery
84669 50 mins C B, V P
*Dominique Dunne, Roscoe Lee Brown, Edie
Adams, Phil Leeds, directed by Murray Golden*
A tame teenage haunted house film originally
produced for television.
CBS — *Video Gems*

Haunting of Julia, The 1981
Horror
59046 96 mins C B, V P
Mia Farrow, Keir Dullea, Tom Conti
Peter Straub wrote this tale of revenge and
remorse set in a London house reverberating
with the guilty apprehension of a woman who
succumbs to the ghost of a long dead child.
MPAA:R EL, SP
Peter Fetterman — *Media Home
Entertainment*

Haunting Passion, The 1983
Drama/Occult sciences
71311 98 mins C B, V P
*Jane Seymour, Gerald McRaney, Millie Perkins,
Paul Rossilli, Ivan Bonar, Lis Britt, directed by
John Korty*
A sensual ghost haunts a couple's new home,
and seduces the wife. The husband, a retired
footballer, suspects more conventional
cuckoldry.
ITC Productions — *U.S.A. Home Video*

Haunts 1976
Horror
78345 97 mins C B, V P
Cameron Mitchell, Aldo Ray, Mai Britt$mp2
A tormented woman has difficulty distinguishing
between fantasy and reality in this horror film.
MPAA:PG
Burt Weissbourd — *Media Home
Entertainment*

Have I Got a Story For 1984
You
Puppets
75534 60 mins C B, V P
Shari Lewis
Favorite children's stories are told by Shari
Lewis and her puppets, including the delectable
Lambchop.

MGM UA — *MGM/UA Home Video*

Having It All 1982
Comedy
80634 92 mins C B, V P
*Dyan Cannon, Barry Newman, Hart Bochner,
Sylvia Sidney, Melanie Chartoff*
A beautiful fashion designer tries to maintain her
bi-coastal lifestyle and the two husbands that go
along with it. Available in Beta Hi-Fi and VHS
Stereo.
Hill/Mandeker Prods. — *U.S.A. Home Video*

Having Wonderful Time 1938
Comedy
79682 71 mins B/W B, V P
*Ginger Rogers, Lucille Ball, Eve Arden, Red
Skelton, Douglas Faribanks Jr*
A young girl tries to find culture on her summer
vacation at a Catskills resort.
RKO — *RKO HomeVideo*

Hawaii 1966
Drama
58827 161 mins C B, V, CED P
*Max von Sydow, Julie Andrews, Richard Harris,
Carroll O'Connor, Gene Hackman, directed by
George Roy Hill*
James Michener's novel about a New England
farm boy who decides in 1820 that the Lord has
commanded him to the island of Hawaii for the
purpose of "Christianizing" the natives. Filmed
on location.
EL, SP
United Artists; Walter Mirisch — *CBS/Fox
Video*

Hawaii 1984
Travel
70862 30 mins C B, V P
This program introduces viewers to the wonders
of Hawaii, and offers travel tips to prospective
tourists.
Dennis Burkhart — *Encounter Productions*

Hawaii Revisited 1978
States-US
06710 58 mins C B, V, 3/4U R, P,
   DL
Narrated by James Michener
"Hawaii Revisited" mixes the beauty with the
history of the Pacific Islands. Also available in
an edited version.
EL, SP
James Michener — *Discount Video Tapes;
Kartes Video Communications; Video
Yesteryear; Western Film & Video Inc*

Hawaii the 50th State 1986
Geography/States-US
86378 30 mins C B, V P

A complete history of Hawaii from the moment it rose from the sea 25 million years ago to the present.
Cinepic Hawaii Corp.; Souvenirs of Hawaii Inc. — *Souvenirs of Hawaii*

Hawk of the Caribbean (El Halcon del Caribe), The
197?

Adventure
88310   95 mins   C   B, V   P
Slaves capture a galleon, and go a' pirating.
SP
Spanish — *JCI Video*

Hawk the Slayer
1981

Fantasy/Adventure
80635   90 mins   C   B, V   P
Jack Palance, John Terry, Harry Andrews, Cheryl Campbell, Patrick Magee, Roy Kennear, Annette Crosbie
Two brothers fought a battle to the death in an imaginary land a long time ago. Available in Beta Hi-Fi and VHS Stereo.
Jack Gill; Chips Prods. — *U.S.A. Home Video*

Hawmps!
1976

Comedy
49624   98 mins   C   B, V   P
James Hampton, Christopher Connelly, Slim Pickens, Denver Pyle, directed by Joe Camp
A Civil War lieutenant trains his men to use camels. When the soldiers and animals begin to grow fond of each other, Congress orders the camels to be set free. The bad news turns into a happy ending.
MPAA:G
Mulberry Square Prods; Joe Camp — *Vestron Video*

He is My Brother
1975

Drama
84510   90 mins   C   B, V   P
Keenan Wynn, Bobby Sherman, Robbie Rist, directed by Edward Dmytryk
Two boys survive a shipwreck, landing on an island that houses a leper colony.
MPAA:G
CSA Prod — *Magnum Entertainment*

He Kills Night After Night After Night
1970

Horror
77455   88 mins   C   B, V   P
Jack May, Linda Marlowe, Justine Lord
The British police are baffled as they seek the man who has been killing woman after woman in the style of Jack the Ripper.
Dudley Birch Films — *Monterey Home Video*

He Knows You're Alone
1980

Horror
64567   94 mins   C   B, V, CED   P
Don Scardino, Elizabeth Kemp, Tom Rolfing
A psychotic killer terrorizes young girls in his search for a suitable "bride."
MPAA:R
MGM/UA — *MGM/UA Home Video*

He-Man and the Masters of the Universe
198?

Science fiction/Cartoons
65011   91 mins   C   B, V   P
Animated
He-Man, who lives on the planet Eternia, battles the evil force Skeletor and his band of villains. Based on the Mattel toys.
Filmation — *RCA/Columbia Pictures Home Video; RCA VideoDiscs*

He-Man and the Masters of the Universe: The Greatest Adventures of All
1983

Cartoons
65318   60 mins   C   B, V   P
Animated
He-Man and his friends continue their battles against the evil forces of Skeletor.
Lou Scheimer — *RCA/Columbia Pictures Home Video*

He-Man and the Masters of the Universe Series
1985

Cartoons/Adventure
Closed Captioned
70567   45 mins   C   B, V   P
Animated 15 pgms
This series follows the continuing adventures of the mighty man of he. Each Hi-Fi cassette features two programs.
Filmation — *RCA/Columbia Pictures Home Video*

He Walked by Night
1948

Mystery
08598   80 mins   B/W   B, V   P
Richard Basehart, Scott Brady, Roy Roberts, Jack Webb, directed by Alfred M. Werker
Los Angeles homicide investigators track down a cop killer; from the files of the Los Angeles police.
Eagle Lion; Bryan Foy Productions — *Movie Buff Video; Kartes Video Communications; Video Yesteryear; Discount Video Tapes*

He Who Walks Alone
1978

Drama
70714   74 mins   C   B, V   P
Louis Gossett Jr., Clu Gulager, Mary Alice, James McEacheon, Barton Heyman, Barry

Brown, Lonny Chapman, directed by Jerrold Freedman.
This telefilm documents the life of Thomas E. Gilmore, who became the South's first elected black sheriff in the 1960's.
EMI, NBC — VCL Home Video

Head of the Family, The   1971

Drama
86605   105 mins   C   B, V   P
Leslie Caron, Nino Manfredi, Ugo Tognazzi
A woman sacrifices her political ideals and career goals for her role as a family matriarch, and eventually falls apart.
Venice Film Festival '71: Critic's Prize.
MPAA:PG
Ultra Films — Video Gems

Headless Horseman,   1922
The/Will Rogers

Comedy
10108   52 mins   B/W   B, V   P, T
Will Rogers, directed by Edward Venturini
Will Rogers plays Ichabod Crane in Washington Irving's "Legend of Sleepy Hollow." Second half of program follows Roger's career from early vaudeville days to Ziegfeld.
Hodkinson — Blackhawk Films

Health 'n Action Exercise   1978
Programs

Physical fitness
47506   30 mins   C   B, V   P
Ann Dugan 12 pgms
This series offers a diverse program of physical conditioning. Series A, "Get Fit Stay Fit," and series B, "Super Exercises," are 60 minutes each. Series C, "Sports Conditioning," consists of four 30-minute segments. Series D, "Rehabilitation and Injury," is comprised of six 30-minute programs.
1.Get Fit Stay Fit 2.Super Exercises 3.Sports Conditioning (Jog/Run, Golf, Tennis/Racquet Sports, Ski) 4.Rehabilitation and Injury (Prenatal, Postnatal, Hysterectomy, Mastectomy, Knee, Back)
Health n Action — RCA/Columbia Pictures Home Video

Hear O Israel   19??

Middle East/Religion
38987   71 mins   C   B, V, FO   P
Three classic short films about the land of Israel and the Jewish faith: "Hear O Israel," "The Changing Land," and "My Holiday in Israel." The first two have dialogue in English, the last is in Hebrew with no subtitles.
Unknown — Video Yesteryear

Hearse, The   1980

Horror
59672   97 mins   C   B, V   P
Trish Van Devere, Joseph Cotten

While fighting to maintain her sanity, a vacationing schoolteacher finds her life threatened by a sinister black hearse.
MPAA:PG
Mark Tenser — Media Home Entertainment

Heart Is a Lonely Hunter,   1968
The

Drama
Closed Captioned
77267   124 mins   C   B, V   P
Sondra Locke, Alan Arkin, Chuck McCann, Stacy Keach, directed by Robert Ellis Miller
A deaf mute moves in with a Southern family to become closer to his only friend.
New York Film Critics Award '68: Best Actor (Arkin).
Warner Bros — Warner Home Video

Heart Like a Wheel   1983

Drama
Closed Captioned
65499   113 mins   C   B, V   P
Bonnie Bedelia, Beau Bridges, Bill McKinney, Leo Rossi
The true story of premier drag racer Shirley Muldowney, who had to break not only speed records but sexual barriers as well and contend with the reluctance of racing officials to license her.
MPAA:PG
20th Century Fox — CBS/Fox Video

Heart of the Golden West   1942

Western
14373   54 mins   B/W   B, V, FO   P
Roy Rogers, Sons of the Pioneers
Roy protects ranchers of Cherokee City from unjust shipping charges.
Republic — Video Yesteryear; Video Connection; Cable Films

Heart of the Rio Grande   1942

Western
58604   70 mins   B/W   B, V   P, T
Gene Autry, Smiley Burnette, Fay McKenzie, Edith Fellows, Joseph Stauch Jr
A spoiled young rich girl tries to trick her father into coming to her "rescue" at a western dude ranch.
Republic — Blackhawk Films; Video Connection

Heart of the Rockies   1937

Western
15441   54 mins   B/W   B, V   P
Bob Livingston, Ray Corrigan, Max Terhune
Three Mesquiteers stop mountain family's rustling and illegal game trappers.
Republic — Video Connection; Nostalgia Merchant

Heart of the Stag   1984
Drama
80460   94 mins   C   B, V, LV   P
Bruno Lawrence, Mary Regan, Terence Cooper
On an isolated sheep ranch in the New Zealand
outback, a father and daughter suffer the
repercussions of an incestuous relationship
when she becomes enamoured of a hired hand.
MPAA:R
New World Pictures — *New World Video*

Heartaches   1982
Comedy
64040   90 mins   C   B, V, LV,   P
                          CED
*Margot Kidder, Annie Potts, Robert Carradine,
Winston Rekert*
Two young women, one of them pregnant,
decide to chuck everything and run off to
Toronto. Once there, they get jobs in a mattress
factory and rent an apartment together.
Canadian Film Development Corp — *Vestron
Video*

Heartbeat   1980
Drama
52714   109 mins   C   B, V   P
*Nick Nolte, John Heard, Sissy Spacek, Anne
Dusenberry, directed by John Byrum*
The story of Jack Kerouac (author of "On the
Road"), his friend and inspiration Neal Casady,
and the woman they shared, Carolyn Casady,
based on her memoirs.
MPAA:R
Orion Pictures — *Warner Home Video*

Heartbeat City   1984
Music video
78628   48 mins   C   B, V   P
The Cars
This is a compilation of conceptual music video
by The Cars from their albums "Heartbeat City"
"Panorama" and "Shake It Up" with clips
directed by Andy Warhol and Timothy Hutton
among others.
Elektra Entertainment — *Warner Home Video*

Heartbeeps   1981
Science fiction/Comedy
47419   79 mins   C   B, V   P
Andy Kaufman, Bernadette Peters
In 1995, two domestic robot servants fall in love
and run off together.
MPAA:PG
Universal — *MCA Home Video*

Heartbreak Kid, The   1972
Comedy
37412   106 mins   C   B, V   P
*Charles Grodin, Cybill Shepard, Eddie Albert,
Jeannie Berlin*

A glib, romantic dreamer becomes disillusioned
with love and his marriage in this comedy by
Neil Simon.
MPAA:PG
20th Century Fox — *Media Home
Entertainment*

Heartbreak Motel   1978
Suspense/Horror
71184   84 mins   C   B, V   P
*Shelley Winters, Leslie Uggams, Michael
Christian, Slim Pickins, Ted Cassidy, Dub Taylor*
A rhythm and blues singer's car breaks down;
so she walks to the nearest spooky looking
motel and asks to spend the night. Prices for a
night's lodging can run from one's sanity to
one's life.
Independent — *VidAmerica*

Heartbreaker   1983
Drama
71182   90 mins   C   B, V   P
*Fernando Allende, Dawn Dunlap, Michael D.
Roberts, Robert Dryer, Apollonia Kotero*
Eastern Los Angeles explodes with vicious turf
wars when Beto and Hector battle for the
affection of Kim, the neighborhood's newest
heartbreaker.
MPAA:R
Monorex Hollywood Corporation — *Media
Home Entertainment*

Heartbreakers   1984
Drama
77173   98 mins   C   B, V, CED   P
*Peter Coyote, Nick Mancuso, Carole Laure, Max
Gail, Kathryn Harrold, directed by Bobby Roth*
Two male best friends find themselves in the
throes of drastic changes in their careers and
romantic encounters. Tangerine Dream
performs the musical score.
MPAA:R
Orion Pictures; Jethro Films — *Vestron Video*

Heartland   1981
Drama
47303   95 mins   C   B, V   P
Conchata Ferrell, Rip Torn
Set in 1910, this film chronicles the story of one
woman's life on the Wyoming Frontier, the
hazards she faces, and her courage and spirit.
MPAA:PG
Michael Hausman; Beth Ferris — *THORN
EMI/HBO Video*

Hearts and Armour   1983
Fantasy/Adventure
81899   101 mins   C   B, V   P
*Tanya Roberts, Leigh McCloskey, Ron Moss,
Rick Edwards, Giovanni Visentin*
A holy war between Christians and Moors
erupts when a Moorish princess is kidnapped.
Available in VHS and Beta Hi-Fi Stereo.

Nicola Carraro; Franco Cristaldi — *Warner Home Video*

Hearts and Minds 1974
Documentary/Vietnam War
55546   112 mins   C   B, V, LV   R, P
Directed by Peter Davis
Gripping documentary about America's misguided involvement in Vietnam.
Academy Awards '74: Best Documentary (Schneider, Davis). MPAA:R
Touchstone; Bert Schneider;
Audjeff — *Embassy Home Entertainment; Paramount Home Video*

Heart's Desire 1937
Musical-Drama
52210   79 mins   B/W   B, V, FO   P
Richard Tauber, Lenora Corbett
Opera great Richard Tauber stars in this tale of an unknown Viennese singer who falls in love with an English girl.
Gaumont British — *Video Yesteryear*

Heat 1972
Comedy-Drama
59050   101 mins   C   B, V   P
Joe Dallasandro, Sylvia Miles, Andy Warhol, directed by Paul Morrissey
Andy Warhol's characters meet in Hollywood, in seedy motels and spacious mansions, and reveal themselves in all their desperate loneliness.
MPAA:R
Levitt Pickman — *Media Home Entertainment*

Heat and Dust 1982
Drama
65519   130 mins   C   B, V   P
Julie Christie, Greta Scacchi, Shashi Kapoor, Christopher Cazenove, Nickolas Grace
A young bride joins her husband at his post in India and is inexorably drawn to the country and its Prince of State. Years later her great niece journeys to modern day India in search of the truth about her scandalous and mysterious relative.
MPAA:R
Universal Classic — *MCA Home Video*

Heat of Desire 1984
Drama
80383   90 mins   C   B, V   P
Clio Goldsmith, Patrick Dewaere, Jeanne Moreau
A philosophy professor abandons everything for a woman he barely knows and is conned by her "relatives." With English subtitles.
MPAA:R FR
Triumph Films — *RCA/Columbia Pictures Home Video*

Heathcliff and Cats and Co. Series 1987
Cartoons
Closed Captioned
81433   45 mins   C   B, V   P
Animated, voice of Mel Blanc 4 pgms
Each cassette in this series features four episodes with these Saturday-morning stars at their rascally best.
LBS; DIC — *RCA/Columbia Pictures Home Video*

Heathcliff and Marmaduke 1983
Cartoons
66574   60 mins   C   B, V   P
Animated
A program of animated adventures with the hapless dog Marmaduke matching wits with Heathcliff, the cat, his constant nemesis.
Ruby Spears — *Worldvision Home Video*

Heatwave 1983
Drama
73021   92 mins   C   B, V   P
Judy Davis, Richard Moir
Local residents oppose a multi-million dollar residential complex in Australia
MPAA:R
Hilary Linstead — *THORN EMI/HBO Video*

Heaven Can Wait 1978
Fantasy
38933   100 mins   C   B, V, LV   P
Warren Beatty, Julie Christie, Charles Grodin, Dyan Cannon, James Mason, Jack Warden
Remake of 1941's "Here Comes Mr. Jordan," about a football player who is mistakenly summoned to heaven before his time, and returns to earth in another man's body.
MPAA:PG
Paramount — *Paramount Home Video; RCA VideoDiscs*

Heaven Help Us 1985
Comedy
80809   102 mins   C   B, V   P
Donald Sutherland, John Heard, Wallace Shawn, Kevin Dillon, Andrew McCarthy, directed by Michael Dinner
Three mischievous boys find themselves continually in trouble with the priests running their Catholic high school during the mid-60's. Available in VHS and Beta HiFi.
MPAA:R
Tri Star Pictures — *THORN EMI/HBO Video*

Heavenly Bodies 1984
Drama
81929   99 mins   C   B, V   P
Cynthia Dale, Richard Rebrere, Laura Henry, Stuart Stone, Walter George Alton

A young woman who dreams of owning a health club will stop at nothing to accomplish her goals. Available in VHS and Beta Hi-Fi stereo.
MPAA:R
MGM/UA; Producers Sales Organization — *Key Video*

Heavenly Kid, The 1985
Fantasy
70946 92 mins C B, V P
Lewis Smith, Jane Kaczmarek, Jason Gedrick, Richard Mulligan, directed by Cary Meadoway
A leather-jacketed "cool" guy who died in an early sixties hot rod crash finally receives an offer to exit limbo and enter heaven. The deal requires that he educate his dull earthly son more hip and worldly ways.
MPAA:PG-13
Orion — *THORN EMI/HBO Video*

Heavens Above 1963
Comedy
29796 113 mins B/W B, V P
Peter Sellers, Cecil Parker, Isabel Jeans, Eric Sykes, Ian Carmichael
A sharp, biting satire on British clergy life. Sellers, a quiet, down-to-earth reverend, is appointed to a parish in a snooty neighborhood.
British Lion — *THORN EMI/HBO Video*

Heaven's Gate 1980
Western
66449 220 mins C B, V, CED P
Kris Krisofferson, Christopher Walken, Isabelle Huppert, Jeff Bridges, John Hurt, directed by Michael Cimino
The original, uncut version of Michael Cimino's epic story about Wyoming's Johnson County cattle wars of the 1890's. Beta Hi-Fi and VHS stereo.
MPAA:R
United Artists — *MGM/UA Home Video*

Heavy Petting 1983
Comedy
64979 90 mins C B, V P
A hilarious compilation of "love scene" footage from feature films of the silent era to the sixties, newsreels, news reports, educational films, old TV shows, and home movies.
Unknown — *Embassy Home Entertainment*

Heavy Traffic 1973
Comedy
59852 76 mins C B, V P
Animated
Ralph Bakshi's animated fantasy portrait of the hard-edged underside of city life, as a young cartoonist draws the people, the places and the paranoia of his environment.
MPAA:X
American International — *Warner Home Video*

Heckle y Jeckle 195?
Cartoons
48408 90 mins C B, V P
Animated
The talking magpies get in and out of mischief. Available in Spanish only.
SP
Terrytoons — *CBS/Fox Video*

Heidi 1937
Drama
22205 88 mins B/W B, V P
Shirley Temple, Jean Hersholt, Helen Westley
Johanna Spyri's classic tale puts Shirley Temple in the hands of a mean governess and the loving arms of her Swiss grandfather.
20th Century Fox — *CBS/Fox Video*

Heidi 1968
Drama
29433 100 mins C CED P
Maximilian Schell, Jean Simmons, Michael Redgrave
Based on Johanna Spyri's classic story of an orphan girl living with her grandfather in the Alps who is taken by her aunt to the city to be a playmate for a family's crippled daughter.
NBC — *RCA VideoDiscs*

Heidi 1967
Drama
76769 100 mins C B, V, CED P
Maximillian Schell, Jennifer Edwards, Michael Redgrave, Jean Simmons
This adaptation of the classic Johanna Spyri novel tells the story of an orphaned girl who goes to the Swiss Alps to live with her grandfather.
NBC — *Vestron Video*

Heidi 1979
Cartoons
77301 93 mins C B, V P
Animated
An orphan girl's optimism brings new life to the residents of a village in the Swiss Alps.
Vertlalen/Guzman Productions — *Pacific Arts Video*

Heidi's Song 19??
Cartoons/Musical
69591 90 mins C B, V P
Animated, voices of Lorne Greene, Sammy Davis Jr, Margery Gray
The classic tale of Heidi and her grandfather is enhanced by 16 original songs, dance sequences, and full animation.
Hanna Barbera — *Worldvision Home Video*

Heifetz and Piatigorsky 1981
Music-Performance
57251 78 mins B/W B, V P

Jascha Heifetz, Gregor Piatigorsky
Three presentations are featured on one
cassette. First, Jascha Heifetz, the
incomparable violinist and his accompanist,
Emanuel Bay, give an impromptu recital at
Pomona College. In a varied program, he plays
Mendelsohn's "Sweet Remembrance,"
Brahm's "Sonatensatz," and "Hungarian Dance
No. 7," Gluck's "Melodie," Prokofiev's "March"
from "Love for Three Oranges," Wieniawsky's
"Polonaise," and Dinicu-Heifetz's "Hora
Stacatto." The second presentation features
the great cellist Gregor Piatigorsky in a brilliant
concert including Bach's "Bouree No. 1" and
"Bouree No. 2" from "C-Major Suite," Chopin's
"Slow Movement from Cello Sonata,"
Prokofiev's "Masques" from "Romeo and
Juliet," Anton Rubinstein's "Romance,"
Tschaikowsky's "Waltz," and Schubert-
Piatigorsky's "Introduction, Theme and
Variations." The tape concludes with "The
Portrait of an Artist," a look at the home and
practice life of Jascha Heifetz. The varied
program consists of Vitali's "Chaconne,"
Bach's "Prelude E-Major," Debussy's "Girl with
the Flaxen Hair," Wieniawsky's "Scherzo
Tarantella," and Paganini's "24th Caprice."
Kultur — *Kultur*

Heiress, The   1949
Drama
70554 115 mins B/W   B, V   P
*Olivia De Havilland, Montgomery Clift, Ralph
Richardson, directed by William Wyler*
Based on the Henry James play "Washington
Square," this film stars Olivia De Havilland as a
wealthy and bitter woman pursued by the
fortune-seeking bum (Clift) who left her waiting
by the altar years earlier. In Hi-fi Mono on all
formats.
Academy Awards '49: Best Actress (De
Havilland); Best Costumes; Best Art Director;
Best Film Score.
William Wyler; Paramount — *MCA Home Video*

Helen Keller: Separate   1982
Views
Handicapped/Women
58560   91 mins C   B, V   P
*Narrated by Martha Graham and President
Eisenhower*
A trio of upbeat films dealing with different views
of the handicapped, including the "Helen Keller
Story" and "One Eyed Men Are Kings," which
offers a serio-comic look at blindness.
Academy Awards '74: Best Live Action Short
("Kings").
Mastervision et al — *Mastervision*

Helix   1984
Music-Performance
82387   14 mins C   B, V   P
Helix

These outstandingly crazed rockers perform
such tunes as "Don't Get Mad Get Even" and
"Heavy Metal Love."
Capitol Records — *Sony Video Software*

Hellbenders, The   1967
Western
84866   92 mins C   B, V   P
Joseph Cotten, directed by Sergio Corbucci
A confederate veteran robs a Union train and
must fight through acres of Civil War adversity.
Albert Band — *Embassy Home Entertainment*

Hell Commandos   1969
War-Drama
86857   92 mins C   B, V   P
*Guy Madison, Stan Cooper, directed by J.L.
Merino*
Soldiers in World War II struggle to prevent the
Nazis from releasing a deadly bacteria that will
kill millions. Dubbed.
Prodimex/Hispamer Film — *Lightning Video*

Hell Fire Austin   1932
Western
57986   60 mins B/W   B, V   P
Ken Maynard
Ken Maynard finds himself mixed up with
outlaws in the Old West.
Tiffany — *Video Connection; Discount Video
Tapes; United Home Video*

Hell Night   1981
Horror
59044 100 mins C   B, V   P
Linda Blair, Vincent Van Patten, Kevin Brophy
Three young people must spend the night in a
mysterious mansion as part of their initiation into
Alpha Signa Rho fraternity.
MPAA:R EL, SP
Compass International Pictures — *Media
Home Entertainment*

Hell on Frisco Bay   1955
Drama
11771   93 mins C   B, V   P
Alan Ladd, Edward G. Robinson, Joanne Dru
Ex-waterfront cop, falsely imprisoned for
manslaughter, sets out to clear his name.
Warner Bros — *United Home Video*

Hell Squad   1985
Drama/Exploitation
71147   88 mins C   B, V   P
*Bainbridge Scott, Glen Hartford, Tina
Lederman, written and directed by Kenneth
Hartford*
Unable to release his son from the Middle
Eastern terrorists who kidnapped him, a U.S.
Ambassador turns to the services of 9 Vegas
showgirls. These gals moonlight as vicious
commandoes.

MPAA:R
Cannon; Cinevid — *MGM/UA Home Video*

Hell to Eternity   1960
Biographical
80836   132 mins   B/W   B, V   P
*Jeffrey Hunter, Sessue Hayakawa, David
Janssen, Vic Damone, Patricia Owens, directed
by Phil Karlson*
This true story of how World War II hero Guy
Gabaldon managed to persuade 2,000
Japanese soldiers to surrender is available in
VHS and Beta Hi Fi.
Allied Artists; Atlantic Pictures — *Key Video*

Hell Train   1980
Horror
77399   90 mins   C   B, V   P
A group of desperate female prisoners are out
to murder Nazi courtesans who sent them to
concentration camps.
Independent — *Wizard Video*

Hellcats of the Navy   1957
War-Drama
58956   82 mins   B/W   B, V   P
*Ronald Reagan, Nancy Davis (Reagan), Arthur
Franz*
The true saga of the World War II mission to
sever the vital link between mainland Asia and
Japan. This was the only film that Ronald and
Nancy Reagan appeared in together.
Columbia — *RCA/Columbia Pictures Home
Video*

Helldorado   1946
Western
54174   54 mins   B/W   B, V   P
Roy Rogers, directed by William Witney
A lively western starring the singing cowboy,
Roy Rogers.
Republic — *Video Connection; Cable Films;
Discount Video Tapes*

Heller in Pink Tights   1960
Western
85251   100 mins   C   B, V   P
*Sophia Loren, Anthony Quinn, Margaret
O'Brien, Steve Forrest, directed by George
Cukor*
In the 1880's, a theatrical troupe travels the
west, performing amid Indians, bill collectors
and thieves.
Paramount — *Kartes Video Communications*

Hellfighters   1968
Drama
77215   121 mins   C   B, V   P
*John Wayne, Katherine Ross, Jim Hutton,
directed by Andrew V. McLaglen*

A group of Texas oil well fighters experience
troubles between themselves and the women
they love.
MPAA:G
Universal Pictures; Robert Arthur — *MCA
Home Video*

Hellfire   1984
Ethics/Religion
73913   27 mins   C   B, V, 3/4U,   R, P
                          FO
A television evangelist believes his
interpretation of the Bible is the key to salvation.
Mirage Productions Marcus Viscidi — *Republic
Pictures Home Video; Direct Cinema Limited*

Hellfire   1948
Western
80844   90 mins   B/W   B, V   P
*William Elliott, Marie Windsor, Forrest Tucker,
Jim Davis*
A gambler promises to build a church and follow
the precepts of the Bible after a minister
sacrifices his life for him.
Republic Pictures — *Republic Pictures Home
Video*

Hellhole   1985
Horror/Exploitation
Closed Captioned
82324   93 mins   C   B, V   P
*Judy Landers, Ray Sharkey, Mary Woronov,
Marjoe Gortner, Edy Williams, Terry Moore*
A young woman who witnesses her mother's
murder is sent to a sanitarium where the doctors
are perfecting chemical lobotomies. Hear all the
shrieks in VHS and Beta Hi-Fi.
MPAA:R
Arkoff International Pictures — *RCA/Columbia
Pictures Home Video*

Hello, Dolly!   1969
Musical
08424   146 mins   C   B, V, LV   P
*Barbra Streisand, Walter Matthau, Michael
Crawford, Louis Armstrong, directed by Gene
Kelly*
Widow Dolly Levi, while matchmaking for her
friends, sets her mind on a Yankee merchant.
Based on the stage musical adapted from
Thornton Wilder's play "Matchmaker".
Academy Awards '69: Best Score of a Musical
Picture; Best Art Direction; Best Sound.
MPAA:G   EL, SP
20th Century Fox; Ernest Leham — *CBS/Fox
Video*

Hells Angels Forever   1983
Adventure
65367   93 mins   C   B, V   P
*The Hells Angels, Willie Nelson, Jerry Garcia,
Johnny Paycheck, Bo Diddley*

"Hells Angels Forever" is a revealing ride into the world of honor, violence, and undying passion for motorcycles on the road.
MPAA:R
Richard Chase; Sandy Alexander; Leon Gast — Media Home Entertainment

Hells Angels on Wheels 1967
Drama
78667   95 mins   C   B, V   P
Jack Nicholson, Adam Roarke, Sabrina Scharf, directed by Richard Rush
A gas station attendant joins up with the Angels for a cross country trip.
US Films — Monterey Home Video

Hell's Angels '69 1969
Adventure
65483   97 mins   C   B, V   P
Tom Stern, Jeremy Slate, Conny Van Dyke
Two wealthy brothers plot a deadly game by infiltrating the ranks of the Hell's Angels.
MPAA:PG
Tom Stern — Media Home Entertainment

Hell's House 1932
Drama
08766   72 mins   B/W   B, V, 3/4U   P
Bette Davis, Pat O'Brien, Junior Dirken, directed by Howard Higgin
Following the death of his mother, a young boy goes to city to live with relatives and becomes involved with a bootlegger.
Bennie F Ziedman Prod — VCII; Video Yesteryear; Kartes Video Communications

Hellstrom Chronicle, The 1971
Documentary/Insects
63966   90 mins   C   B, V   P
A powerful documentary about man's impending struggle against insects.
Academy Awards '71: Best Documentary Feature. MPAA:G
Almi-Cinema 5 — RCA/Columbia Pictures Home Video

Helltown 1938
Western
12230   60 mins   B/W   B, V   P
John Wayne, directed by Charles Barton
Western film based on Zane Grey's novel.
Paramount — Discount Video Tapes; Video Connection; Cable Films

Help Wanted: Male 1982
Comedy
82268   97 mins   C   B, V   P
Suzanne Pleshette, Gil Gerard, Bert Convy, Dana Elcar, Harold Gould, Caren Kaye
When a magazine publisher discovers that her fiance cannot have children, she looks for someone else who can do the job right.

QM Productions; Brademan/Self Productions — Worldvision Home Video

Help Yourself to Better Color TV 197?
Television
44991   30 mins   C   B, V   P, T
Through the use of the indian-head test pattern and the color bar chart you can determine brightness, focus, contrast, tint, and color line-up with the help of this program.
AM Available
Unknown — Blackhawk Films

Helter Skelter 1976
Drama
80142   194 mins   C   CED   P
Steve Railshark, Nancy Wolfe, George DiCenzo
The harrowing story of the murder of Sharon Tate and four others in her home at the hands of Charles Manson and his family.
Lorimar — CBS/Fox Video

Henderson Monster, The 1980
Drama
71300   94 mins   C   B, V   P
Jason Miller, Christine Lahti, Stephen Collins, David Spielberg, Larry Gates, Nehemiah Persoff, directed by Waris Hussein
A Nobel Prize-winning scientist toils away in the university lab trying to create life. The townspeople recognize that such experiments could have global ramifications.
Brodkin and Berger Productions — U.S.A. Home Video

Henry Fonda: The Man and His Movies 1984
Biographical/Documentary
78663   60 mins   C   B, V   P
Narrated by Arthur Hill
This documentary features highlights from Henry Fonda's stage, screen and television appearances that spanned more than fifty years.
RKO — RKO HomeVideo

Henry Ford's America 1977
Automobiles
21251   57 mins   C   B, V, FO   P
A look at the history of the automobile, the dynastic Ford talent that created it, and the business empire that rules it.
National Film Board of Canada — Video Yesteryear; National Film Board of Canada

Henry V 1945
Drama
44363   137 mins   C   CED   P
Laurence Olivier, Robert Newton, Leslie Banks, Leo Genn

The first movie version of Shakepeare's great drama, with brilliant dialogue and color.
J Arthur Rank — *RCA VideoDiscs*

Hepburn and Tracy   1984
Biographical/Documentary
78657   45 mins   C   B, V   P
Katherine Hepburn, Spencer Tracy
The finest moments from the film careers of Katherine Hepburn and Spencer Tracy, as a team and on their own. Some sequences in black and white.
RKO — *RKO HomeVideo*

Her Life as a Man   1983
Comedy
87308   93 mins   C   B, V   P
Robyn Douglas, Joan Collins, Robert Culp, Marc Singer, Laraine Newman
A female reporter is refused a job as a sportswriter because of her gender. She makes herself up as a man, gets the job, and creates havoc when she has to deal with lustful women on the job. A made-for-TV movie.
Lawrence Schiller Prod. — *Karl/Lorimar Home Video*

Her Silent Sacrifice   1918
Drama
85177   42 mins   B/W   B, V   P
Alice Brady, Henry Clive
A silent melodrama about a French girl torn between material wealthand true love.
Select Pictures Corp. — *Video Yesteryear*

Herbie Goes Bananas   1980
Comedy
79230   93 mins   C   B, V   P
Cloris Leachman, Charles Martin Smith, Harvey Korman
While Herbie the VW is racing in a race in Rio de Janeiro, he is bothered by the syndicate, a pickpocket and a raging bull.
MPAA:G
Walt Disney Productions — *Walt Disney·Home Video*

Herbie Goes to Monte Carlo   1977
Comedy
79229   104 mins   C   B, V   P
Dean Jones, Don Knotts, Julie Sommars
While participating in a Paris to Monte Carlo race, Herbie the VW takes a detour and falls in love with a Lancia.
MPAA:G
Walt Disney·Productions — *Walt Disney Home Video*

Herbie Hancock and the   1984
Rockit Band
Music-Performance
65756   70 mins   C   B, V, CED   P
Filmed live at the Hammersmith Odeon and Camden Hall in London, England, this program takes the home viewer through a multi-media presentation of break dancing, scratch music, robots and an explosive light show. In VHS Hi-Fi and Beta Hi-Fi.
CBS Records — *CBS/Fox Video*

Herbie Rides Again   1974
Comedy
59063   88 mins   C   B, V   P
Helen Hayes, Ken Berry, Stephanie Powers, John McIntire, Keenan Wynn, directed by Robert Stevenson
In this "Love Bug" sequel, Herbie comes to the aid of an elderly woman who is trying to stop a ruthless tycoon from raising a skyscraper on her property.
MPAA:G EL, SP
Walt Disney Productions — *Walt·Disney Home Video; RCA VideoDiscs*

Hercules   1959
Adventure
66268   107 mins   C   B, V, CED   P
Steve Reeves, directed by Pietro Frandisci
The mythological demigod teams up with Jason and the Argonauts in search of the Golden Fleece.
MPAA:G
Oscar Film Galatea; Warner Bros;
Embassy — *Embassy Home Entertainment*

Hercules   1983
Adventure
Closed Captioned
66446   100 mins   C   B, V   P
Lou Ferrigno, Sybil Danning, William Berger, Brad Harris, Ingrid Anderson
Legendary muscleman Hercules fights against the evil King Minos for his own survival and the love of Cassiopeia, a rival king's daughter.
MPAA:PG
Cannon Films — *MGM/UA Home Video*

Hercules Goes Bananas   1970
Comedy
66109   75 mins   C   B, V   P
Arnold Schwarzenegger
In his motion picture debut, Arnold Schwarzenegger is a Herculean mass of muscle who becomes a professional wrestling superstar. Two hundred and fifty pounds of lighthearted fun.
Arbor Weisberg — *Unicorn Video*

Hercules Unchained 1959
Adventure
64969   101 mins   C   B, V, LV,   P
                                CED
Steve Reeves, Sylva Koscina, Primo Carnera
In this sequel to "Hercules," the superhero must use all his strength to save the city of Thebes and the woman he loves from the giant Antaeus.
Lux/Galatea — *Embassy Home Entertainment*

Herculoids, The 196?
Cartoons/Adventure
66275   60 mins   C   B, V   P
Animated
Zandor, Tara, Dorno and the towering man of stone, Igoo, encounter adventures on a wild, semi-primitive planet.
Hanna Barbera — *Worldvision Home Video*

Herculoids, Vol II, The 1967
Cartoons/Adventure
77160   60 mins   C   B, V   P
Animated
A team of futuristic animals attempt to save a king and his planetary community from alien invaders.
Hanna-Barbera — *Worldvision Home Video*

Here Come the Littles: 1985
The Movie
Cartoons
Closed Captioned
82332   76 mins   C   B, V   P
Animated
A twelve-year old boy finds many new adventures when he meets The Littles, tiny folks with tails who live inside the walls of people's houses. Available in VHS and Beta Hi-Fi Stereo.
ABC Broadcasting — *Playhouse Video*

Here Comes Mr. Jordan 1941
Fantasy
21290   94 mins   B/W   B, V   P
Robert Montgomery, Claude Rains, James Gleason, Evelyn Keyes
A young prizefighter, killed in a plane crash because of a mix-up in heaven, returns to life in the body of a murdered millionaire.
Academy Awards '41: Best Original Story; Best Screenplay.
Columbia — *RCA/Columbia Pictures Home Video*

Here Comes Santa Claus 1984
Adventure
82170   78 mins   C   B, V   P
Karen Cheryl, Armand Meffre
A young boy and girl travel to the North Pole to deliver a very special wish to Santa Claus personally. Available in VHS and Beta Hi-Fi.
New World Pictures — *New World Video*

Here Comes the Grump 1985
Cartoons
70680   60 mins   C   B, V   P
Animated
Princess Dawn, Terry, and their dog, Bip, survive through this program by avoiding the clumsily humorous wrath of the Grump and his mischievous magical dragon.
Embassy Entertainment — *Embassy Home Entertainment*

Here Comes Trouble 1948
Comedy
66114   54 mins   C   B, V   P
William Tracy
A newspaperman returns from war to get his old job back.
Fred Guiol — *Unicorn Video*

Here It Is, Burlesque 1979
Variety
44917   88 mins   C   B, V, CED   P
Ann Corio, Morey Amsterdam
Male and female striptease, baggy-pants comedians, exotic dancers and classic comedy sketches in this tribute to the living art, burlesque.
HBO; Michael Brandman — *Vestron Video; VERVE Films Inc*

Here We Go Again! 1942
Comedy
64535   76 mins   B/W   B, V   R, P
Fibber McGee and Molly, Edgar Bergen, Charlie McCarthy, Mortimer Snerd, Ray Noble and his Orchestra
Fibber McGee and Molly are planning their 20th anniversary celebration, but no one wants to come. Based on the popular NBC radio series.
RKO — *Blackhawk Films*

Heritage of Glory 1985
Documentary/History-US
70683   45 mins   C   B, V   P
Narrated by Ken Howard, directed by Fred Warshofsky
Part of the "In Defense of Freedom" series, this program looks at the history of the United States Marine Corps.
A.B. Marian — *MPI Home Video*

Heritage of the Bible, The 1982
Bible
60380   111 mins   C   CED   P
A recreation of Biblical history: "The Law and the Prophets" features inspired images of Raphael, Michelangelo, and others; "The Inheritance" uses famous archeological sites of Biblical times to recount stories of the Old Testament.
NBC Enterprises — *RCA VideoDiscs*

Herman and Katnip   1963
Cartoons
86368   60 mins   C   B, V   P
A compilation of the cat & mouse cartoons.
Harvey Films Inc. — *Worldvision Home Video*

Hero, The   1972
Drama
88348   97 mins   C   B, V   P
Richard Harris, Romy Schneider, directed by Richard Harris
A popular soccer player agrees to throw a game for big cash, and then finds he cannot.
MPAA:PG
Wolf Mankowitz — *Embassy Home Entertainment*

Hero Bunker   1971
Drama/Adventure
71307   93 mins   C   B, V   P
John Miller, Maria Xenia, Fernando Bislani, directed by George Andrews
With the enemy invading from all sides, a group of Greek soldiers fight to protect their "Hero Bunker."
Greek — *U.S.A. Home Video*

Hero High Volume 1   1981
Cartoons
74084   44 mins   C   B, V   P
Animated
This fun-filled animated feature introduces you to future superheros and their ill-fated attempts to master their special powers.
Lou Scheimer; Norm Prescott — *Embassy Home Entertainment*

Heroes   1977
Drama
87626   97 mins   C   B, V   P
Henry Winkler, Sally Field, Harrison Ford, directed by Jeremy P. Kagan
A institutionalized Vietnam vet escapes to establish a worm farm, and encounters love and ribaldry on the way.
MPAA:PG
David Foster; Lawrence Turman — *MCA Home Video*

Heroes in Hell   1967
Adventure/World War II
70783   90 mins   C   B, V   P
Klaus Kinski, Ettore Manni
Two escaped P.O.W.'s join the allied underground in an espionage conspiracy against the Third Reich.
Empire — *Force Video*

Heroes in the Ming Dynasty   1984
Martial arts
72959   90 mins   C   B, V   P
A martial arts period film set in the Ming Dynasty.
Foreign — *Unicorn Video*

Heroes of the Hills   1938
Western
64422   54 mins   B/W   B, V, 3/4U   P
Bob Livingston, Ray Corrigan, Max Terhune
The Three Mesquiteers back up a plan that would allow trusted prisoners to work for neighboring ranchers.
Republic — *Nostalgia Merchant*

Hester Street   1975
Drama
79312   89 mins   B/W   B, V   P
Carol Kane, Doris Roberts, Steven Keats, Mel Howard, directed by Joan Micklin Silver
When a young Jewish immigrant meets her husband in New York City at the turn of the century, she finds out her husband has dispensed with his Old World ways.
TimeLife Productions — *Vestron Video*

Hey Abbott!   1978
Comedy/Film-History
59862   76 mins   B/W   B, V   P
Bud Abbott, Lou Costello, Phil Silvers, Steve Allen, Joe Besser, narrated by Milton Berle
A compilation of A and C routines from their classic TV series. Sketches include "Who's on First," "Oyster Stew," "Floogle Street" and "The Birthday Party."
Ziv International — *VidAmerica*

Hey Cinderella!   1970
Fairy tales/Comedy
47348   58 mins   C   B, V, LV   R, P
The Muppets
The Muppets present their version of the classic fairy tale, in which Cinderella arrives at the ball in a coach pulled by a purple beast named Splurge and driven by Kermit the singing frog.
Henson Associates — *Muppet Home Video*

Hey Good Lookin'   1982
Satire
63121   77 mins   C   B, V   P
Animated, directed by Ralph Bakshi
Ralph Bakshi's irreverent look back at growing up in the 1950's bears the trademark qualities that distinguish his other adult animated features, "Fritz the Cat" and "Heavy Traffic."
Warner Bros — *Warner Home Video*

Hey There, It's Yogi Bear   1964
Cartoons
77155   98 mins   C   B, V   P
Animated, voices of Daws Butler, James Darren, Mel Blanc, H. Pat O'Malley, Julie Bennett

When Yogi Bear comes out of winter hiberation to search for food his travels take him to the Chizzling Brothers Circus.
Hanna-Barbera — *Worldvision Home Video*

Hey Vern! It's My Family Album   1985
Comedy
84546   57 mins   C   B, V   P
Jim Varney
Ernest P Worrell finds his family album and portrays various comical ancestors.
Carden & Cherry Ad Agency
Inc — *KnoWhutImean? Home Video*

Hi-Riders   1977
Adventure
88168   90 mins   C   B, V   P
Mel Ferrer, Stephen McNally, Neville Brand, Ralph Meeker
A revenge-based tale about large, mag-wheeled trucks and their drivers.
MPAA:R
Dimension Pictures — *United Home Video*

Hidden Fortress, The   1958
Adventure/Drama
84674   126 mins   B/W   B, V   P
Toshiro Mifune, Misa Vehara, directed by Akira Kurosawa
Kurosawa's classic about a warrior and princess seeking refuge from warring feudal lords confirms its reputation in the specially banded and subtitled video version.
1958 Berlin Film Festival: Best Director, International Critics Prize   JA
Akira Kurosawa — *Media Home Entertainment*

Hide and Seek   1977
Science fiction
84404   60 mins   C   B, V   P
Bob Martin, Ingrid Veninger, David Patrick
A highschool hacker converts his computer into a nuclear weapon, and then finds that it has developed a mind of its own.
Alan Burke — *Karl/Lorimar Home Video*

Hide in Plain Sight   1980
Suspense
53350   96 mins   C   B, V   P
James Caan, Jill Eikenberry, Robert Viharo, directed by James Caan
A distraught blue-collar worker searches for his children who disappeared when his ex-wife and her mobster husband were given new identities by federal agents.
MPAA:PG
Robert Christiansen; Rick Rosenberg; MGM — *MGM/UA Home Video*

Hideous Sun Demon   1959
Horror
36920   74 mins   B/W   B, V, 3/4U   P
Robert Clarke, Patricia Manning, Nan Peterson
A physicist exposed to radiation must stay out of sunlight or he will turn into a scaly, lizard-like creature. Includes previews of coming attractions from classic science fiction films.
Clark King Entprs, Bob Clark — *Nostalgia Merchant*

Hiding Place, The   1975
War-Drama/World War II
84627   145 mins   C   B, V   P
Julie Harris, Eileen Heckart, Arthur O'Connell, Jeanette Clift, directed by James F. Collier
A Dutch woman saves countless Jewish families just prior to World War II. Made-for-TV.
Billy Graham — *Republic Pictures Home Video*

High Anxiety   1977
Comedy
52739   92 mins   C   B, V, CED   P
Mel Brooks, Madeline Kahn, Cloris Leachman, Harvey Korman, Ron Carey, Howard Morris, Dick Van Patten, directed by Mel Brooks
An anxiety-prone psychiatrist arrives at a sanitorium to take up his official duties as the new head, and is immediately caught up in a twisted murder mystery. Brooks' "homage" to Hitchcock.
MPAA:PG
Twentieth Century Fox; Mel Brooks — *CBS/Fox Video*

High Ballin'   1978
Drama/Adventure
69289   100 mins   C   B, V   P
Peter Fonda, Jerry Reed, Helen Shaver
Three angry independents are set to take on the most vicious gang of hijackers ever to run the highways.
MPAA:PG
American International — *Vestron Video*

High Command   1938
Drama
47467   84 mins   B/W   B, V, FO   P
Lionel Atwill, Lucie Mannheim, James Mason
To save his daughter from an ugly scandal, the British general of a Colonial African outpost traps a blackmailer's killer.
Fanfare — *Video Yesteryear; Movie Buff Video; Discount Video Tapes*

High Country, The   1981
Drama
62863   101 mins   C   B, V, CED   P
Timothy Bottoms, Linda Purl, George Sims, Jim Lawrence, Bill Berry
Two misfits on the run from society learn mutual trust as they travel through the mountain country of Alberta, Canada.

MPAA:PG
Crown International — *Vestron Video*

High Country Calling 1975
Wildlife/Drama
80826 84 mins C B, V P
Narrated by Lorne Greene
Wolf pups escape their man-made home and
set off a cross-country chase.
MPAA:G
Gordon Eastman — *Video Gems*

High Crime 1973
Crime-Drama
57064 91 mins C B, V, 3/4U P
James Whitmore, Franco Nero, Fernando Rey
A "French Connection"-style suspense story
about the heroin trade, featuring high-speed
chases and a police commissioner obsessed
with capturing the criminals.
Ambassador Releasing — *Media Home
Entertainment; Nostalgia Merchant*

High Grass Circus 1976
Circus
21258 57 mins C B, V, FO P
A tour of the Royal Brother Circus, the only tent
circus in Canada.
National Film Board of Canada — *Video
Yesteryear*

High Green 1983
Trains
78170 22 mins C B, V P, T
A fascinating story of how a freight train is made
up and gives keen insight into being an engineer
in one of today's giant locomotives.
Blackhawk Films — *Blackhawk Films*

High Heels 1981
Comedy/Romance
86032 90 mins C B, V P
*Laura Antonelli, Jean-Paul Belmondo, Mia
Farrow, directed by Claude Chabrol*
An adult comedy about a man torn between his
wife and her sister.
John J Burzichelli — *Monterey Home Video*

High Ice 1980
Drama
69285 97 mins C B, V P
David Janssen, Tony Musante
A forest ranger and a lieutenant colonel are
involved in a clash of wills over a rescue mission
high in the snow-capped Washington state
peaks.
ESJ Productions — *Vestron Video*

High Noon 1952
Western
00259 85 mins B/W B, V P

Gary Cooper, Grace Kelly, Lloyd Bridges
Newly-married town marshal must choose
between love and his duty to an ungrateful town.
Academy Awards '52: Best Actor (Cooper); Best
Music Scoring (Dimitri Tiomkin); Best Song
(High Noon).
United Artists; Stanley Kramer — *Republic
Pictures Home Video; RCA VideoDiscs*

High Noon, Part II: The 1980
Return of Will Kane
Western
72453 100 mins C B, V P
Lee Majors, David Carradine
Will Kane returns to Hadleyville with his wife to
find the town controlled by a sadistic marshall.
This is a sequel to the 1952 film.
Charles Fries Productions; Ed Montage
Prod — *U.S.A. Home Video*

High Plains Drifter 1973
Western
59037 105 mins C B, V P
Clint Eastwood, directed by Clint Eastwood
A stranger is hired to protect a community
against the imminent return of three gunmen
sent to jail a year before.
MPAA:R
Universal; The Malpaso Co — *MCA Home
Video*

High Risk 1976
Adventure
65422 74 mins C B, V P
*James Brolin, Anthony Quinn, Lindsay Wagner,
James Coburn, Ernest Borgnine*
An action-adventure of four Americans who
battle foreign armies, unscrupulous gunrunners,
and jungle bandits in a harrowing attempt to
steal five million dollars from an expatriate
American living in the peaceful splendor of his
Columbian villa.
MPAA:R
MGM — *Embassy Home Entertainment*

High Road to China 1983
Adventure
66126 107 mins C B, V, LV, P
CED
*Bess Armstrong, Tom Selleck, Jack Weston,
Robert Morley*
A hard-drinking 1920's air ace is recruited by a
young heiress to find her father.
MPAA:PG
City Films — *Warner Home Video*

High Rolling in a Hot 1977
Corvette
Adventure
76772 82 mins C B, V P
Joseph Bottoms, Greg Taylor
Two carnival workers leave their jobs and hit the
road searching for adventure and excitement.

MPAA:PG
Martin Films — *Vestron Video*

High Route 1978
Adventure/Skiing Across the French Alps
Sports-Winter
84271   45 mins   C   B, V   P
Directed by Harvey Edwards
Skiers whip up and down the Alps in these
spectacularly filmed travelogues. Two short
films back to back on one tape.
Video Travel Inc — *Video Travel*

High School Confidential 1958
Drama
65458   85 mins   B/W   B, V   P
Russ Tamblin, Mamie Van Doren
A tough-talking gang leader comes in contact
with a drug ring and its leader. His dealings put
him in constant danger.
MGM — *Republic Pictures Home Video*

High School USA 1984
Comedy
85094   96 mins   C   B, V   P
Michael J Fox, Nancy McKeon
A high school class clown confronts the king of
the prep-jock-bullies. Antics ensue. Made-for-
TV.
Philip Mandelker; Leonard Hill — *Karl/Lorimar
Home Video*

High Sierra 1941
Drama
64706   96 mins   B/W   B, V, CED   P
*Humphrey Bogart, Ida Lupino, Arthur Kennedy,
Joan Leslie, Cornel Wilde, Alan Curtis, directed
by Raoul Walsh*
Bogart is Roy "Mad Dog" Earl, an aging
gangster who hides out from the police in the
High Sierras. Screenplay by John Huston and
W.R. Burnett, whose novel this movie is based
on.
Warner Bros — *CBS/Fox Video; RCA
VideoDiscs*

High Society 1956
Musical/Comedy
80618   107 mins   C   B, V, LV   P
*Frank Sinatra, Bing Crosby, Grace Kelly, Louis
Armstrong, Celeste Holm, directed by Charles
Walters*
A wealthy man attempts to win back his ex-wife
who's about to be remarried. The Cole Porter
score includes: "True Love," "Well Did You
Evah," "Now You Has Jazz," "Mind If I Make
Love to You" and "High Society Calypso."
MGM — *MGM/UA Home Video*

High Velocity 1976
Adventure
45048   105 mins   C   B, V   P
Ben Gazzara, Paul Winfield
An action-packed adventure of two mercenaries
involved in the challenge of a lifetime.
MPAA:PG
Takashi Ohashi — *Media Home Entertainment*

High Voltage 1929
Comedy/Adventure
55345   60 mins   B/W   B, V   P
*Carole Lombard, William Boyd, Gwen Moore,
Billy Bevan*
A fast-moving comedy adventure set in the High
Sierras.
Pathe — *Sheik Video; Kartes Video
Communications*

Higher and Higher 1943
Musical
10049   90 mins   B/W   B, V   P, T
*Frank Sinatra, Leon Errol, Michele Morgan, Jack
Haley, Victor Borge, Mary McGuire*
Bankrupt aristocrat conspires with servants to
regain his fortune. Tries to marry his daughter
into money.
RKO — *Blackhawk Films*

Highest Honor, The 1984
Drama
80044   99 mins   C   B, V   P
John Howard, Atsuo Nakamura
The true story of a friendship between an
Australian army officer and a Japanese security
officer during World War II.
MPAA:R
Lee Robinson — *Embassy Home
Entertainment*

Highlights of the 1960 1960
NFL Championship Game
Football
88074   26 mins   C   B, V   P
This tape features rare footage of the
Philadelphia Eagles vs. Green Bay Packers
game.
NFL Films — *NFL Films Video*

Highpoint 1984
Comedy/Adventure
80043   91 mins   C   B, V   P
*Richard Harris, Christopher Plummer, Beverly
D'Angelo*
When an unemployed man becomes the
chauffeur of a wealthy family, he finds himself in
the middle of a mysterious murder.
MPAA:PG
Daniel M Fine — *Embassy Home
Entertainment*

Hillbilly Bears 198?
Cartoons
78070   51 mins   C   B, V   P
Animated
This program presents the most laughable
family of bears in their exciting adventures.
Worldvision Home Video Inc — *Worldvision
Home Video*

Hillbillys in a Haunted 1967
House
Horror/Musical
59654   88 mins   C   B, V   P
*Ferlin Husky, Joi Lansing, Don Bowman, John
Carradine, Lon Chaney, Basil Rathbone,
directed by Jean Yarbrough*
Two country and western singers enroute to the
Nashville jamboree encounter a group of foreign
spies "haunting" a house.
Bernard Woolner — *United Home Video*

Hills Have Eyes, The 1977
Adventure
59080   83 mins   C   B, V   P
*Susan Lanier, Robert Houston, Martin Speer,
Dee Wallace, Russ Grieve, John Steadman,
James Whitworth*
A desperate family battles for survival and
vengeance against a brutal band of belligerent
terrorists.
MPAA:R
Peter Locke — *HarmonyVision*

Hills Have Eyes, Part II, 1984
The
Drama/Horror
70964   86 mins   C   B, V   P
*Michael Berryman, John Laughlin, Tamara
Stafford, directed by Wes Craven*
Ignorant teens disregard warnings of a "Hills
Have Eyes" refugee, and go stomping into the
grim reaper's proving grounds.
Vanguard Releasing; Peter Locke — *THORN
EMI/HBO Video*

Hills of Utah, The 1951
Western
65771   70 mins   B/W   B, V   P, T
Gene Autry, Pat Buttram, Denver Pyle
Gene finds himself in the middle of a feud
between the local mine operator and a group of
cattlemen, while searching for his father's
murderer.
Columbia — *Blackhawk Films*

Hindenburg, The 1975
Adventure/Suspense
47850   125 mins   C   B, V   P
*George C. Scott, Anne Bancroft, William
Atherton, Roy Thinnes, Gig Young, Burgess
Meredith, directed by Robert Wise*
Intrigue and suspense highlight this fictionalized
account of the historic disaster.

MPAA:PG
Universal — *MCA Home Video*

Hips, Hips, Hooray 1934
Comedy/Musical
54113   68 mins   B/W   B, V   P, T
*Wheeler and Woolsey, Ruth Etting, Thelma
Todd, Dorothy lee*
Two supposed "hot shot" salesmen are hired
by a cosmetic company to sell flavored lipstick.
"Hot shot" salesmen they are not, but funny
they are.
RKO — *Blackhawk Films*

Hiroshima, Mon Amour 1959
Drama
06219   88 mins   B/W   B, V   P
*Emmanuelle Riva, Eiji Okada, Bernard Fresson,
directed by Alain Resnais*
French actress in Tokyo meets and falls in love
with Japanese architect. Both are married.
French film with English subtitles.
FR
Argos; Pathe — *Hollywood Home Theater;
Video Dimensions; Western Film & Video Inc;
Discount Video Tapes; Movie Buff Video; Video
Yesteryear*

His Double Life 1933
Comedy-Drama
81738   67 mins   B/W   B, V   P
Roland Young, Lillian Gish, Monte Love
When a shy gentlemen's valet dies, his master
assumes the dead man's identity and has a
grand time.
Paramount — *Kartes Video Communications;
Movie Buff Video*

His Girl Friday 1940
Comedy
08728   92 mins   B/W   B, V   P
*Cary Grant, Rosalind Russell, Ralph Bellamy,
Gene Lockhart, directed by Howard Hawks*
Reporter helps condemned man escape. Based
on hit play "Front Page."
Columbia — *Hal Roach Studios; Prism; Movie
Buff Video; Hollywood Home Theater; Video
Yesteryear; VCII; Cinema Concepts; Discount
Video Tapes; Video Dimensions; Cable Films;
Video Connection; Western Film & Video Inc;
Phoenix Films & Video; Kartes Video
Communications; United Home Video*

His Girl Friday 1940
Comedy
71026   92 mins   C   B, V   P
*Cary Grant, Rosalind Russell, Ralph Bellamy,
Gene Lockhart, directed by Howard Hawks*
In this version of the hit play "Front Page," a
reporter helps a condemned man escape.
Enhanced using the Colorization process.
Columbia — *Hal Roach Studios*

His Kind of Woman 1951
Drama
57137 120 mins B/W B, V P
*Robert Mitchum, Jane Russell, Vincent Price,
Tim Holt, Charles McGraw*
A fall guy, being used to bring a racketeer back
to the U.S. from Mexico, discovers the plan and
tries to halt it.
RKO — *King of Video*

His Land 197?
Middle East
73800 67 mins C B, V, 3/4U R, P
This award winning film is a musical journey to
the sights and sounds of Israel.
World Wide Pictures — *Life Video Gospel
Association; Republic Pictures Home Video*

His Memory Lives On 1984
Documentary
87599 60 mins C B, V, 3/4U P
A documentary about Elvis and his fanatical
fans.
Monticello Prod. — *Monticello Productions*

His Royal 1920
Slyness/Haunted Spooks
Comedy
56912 52 mins B/W B, V, FO P
Harold Lloyd
Two Harold Lloyd shorts. "His Royal Slyness"
(1919) offers Harold impersonating the king of a
small kingdom, while in "Haunted Spooks"
(1920), Harold gets suckered into living in a
haunted mansion. Both films include music
score.
Hal Roach — *Video Yesteryear; Blackhawk
Films*

History Is Made at Night 1937
Drama/Romance
50930 97 mins B/W B, V, 3/4U R, P
*Charles Boyer, Jean Arthur, Leo Carrillo, Colin
Clive*
A jealous husband forces his wife to seek
divorce. On an Atlantic cruise, she finds true
love and heartbreak.
AM Available
United Artists — *Lightning Video; Learning
Corp of America*

History of Pro Football, 1983
The
Football/Documentary
65015 87 mins C B, V, FO P
Rare footage and interviews with NFL
personalities highlight this comprehensive
program on the NFL's landmark events and its
greatest players.
NFL Films — *NFL Films Video*

History of the World: Part 1981
I
Comedy
52699 90 mins C B, V, LV P
*Mel Brooks, Dom DeLuise, Madeline Kahn,
Harvey Korman, Cloris Leachman, Ron Carey,
Howard Morris, Sid Caesar, Jackie Mason*
Mel Brooks' wildly satiric vision of human
evolution, from the Dawn of Man to the French
Revolution.
MPAA:R
Brooksfilms Ltd — *CBS/Fox Video; RCA
VideoDiscs*

Hit, The 1985
Comedy-Drama
70382 105 mins C B, V P
*John Hart, Terence Stamp, Laura Del Sol, Tim
Roth, Fernando Rey, directed by Stephen
Frears*
A feisty young hooker gets mixed-up with two
strong-armed hired killers as they escort an
unusual stool-pigeon from his exile in Spain to
their angry mob bosses.
Island Alive — *Embassy Home Entertainment*

Hit and Run 1982
Drama
69041 96 mins C B, V P
David Marks, a Manhattan cab driver, is haunted
by recurring flashbacks of a freak hit-and-run
accident in which his wife was struck down on a
city street.
Charles Braverman — *THORN EMI/HBO
Video*

Hit Lady 1974
Suspense
80306 74 mins C B, V P
*Yvette Mimieux, Dack Rambo, Clu Gulager,
Keenan Wynn*
An elegant cultured woman becomes a hit lady
for the syndicate.
Spelling/Goldberg Productions — *Prism*

Hitchcock Classics 1985
**Collection: Trailers on
Tape**
Movie and TV trailers/Suspense
81881 55 mins C B, V P
Here is a collection of twenty previews for such
Hitchcock favorites as "Shadow of a Doubt,"
"Rear Window," "Vertigo," "North by
Northwest" and "Psycho." Some trailers are in
black and white.
Universal et al. — *San Francisco Rush Video*

Hitcher, The 1985
Horror/Comedy
87737 98 mins C B, V P
*Rutger Hauer, C. Thomas Howell, Jennifer
Jason Leigh*

An uproarious, gory contrivance about a completely senseless lunatic tormenting a teenage driver on the Californian interstates.
MPAA:R
Edward S. Feldman — *THORN EMI/HBO Video*

Hitler 1962
Biographical
80835   103 mins   B/W   B, V   P
Richard Basehart, Maria Emo, Cordula Trantow
This is the true story of the infamous Nazi dictators' rise to power and his historic downfall. Available in VHS and Beta Hi Fi.
Allied Artists — *Key Video*

Hitler: A Career 1984
/Biographical
78666   120 mins   B/W   B, V   P
How the career of Adolph Hitler changed the world is presented in this documentary.
RKO — *RKO HomeVideo*

Hitler: The Last Ten Days 1973
Drama
68249   106 mins   C   B, V   P
Based on an eyewitness account, the story of Hitler's last days in an underground bunker gives insight to his madness.
MPAA:PG
World Film Services Ltd; Tomorrow Entertainment — *Paramount Home Video*

Hitler's Children 1943
Drama
00267   83 mins   B/W   B, V, 3/4U   P
Tim Holt, Bonita Granville
Two young people are caught in the horror of Nazi Germany.
RKO — *Nostalgia Merchant; International Historic Films*

Hitler's Henchmen 1984
World War II
78146   60 mins   C   B, V   P
This film takes a powerful look at the inhumanity of war and the graphic reality of Nazi death camps during World War II.
MPI — *MPI Home Video*

H.M.S. Pinafore 1982
Opera
72447   90 mins   C   LV   P
The opera is captured in a live performance.
Judith DePaul — *Pioneer Video Imports*

Hobbit, The 1978
Fantasy
00239   78 mins   C   B, V   P
Narrated by Orson Bean, John Huston, and others

Based on Tolkien's Middle Earth fantasy, this tale illustrates the Hobbit's battle against the evil forces of dragons and goblins.
Rankin Bass — *Sony Video Software; RCA VideoDiscs; The Center for Humanities*

Hobson's Choice 1953
Comedy
63321   102 mins   B/W   B, V, LV   P
Charles Laughton, John Mills, Brenda de Banzie, directed by David Lean
A prosperous businessman in the 1890's tries to keep his daughter from marrying, but the strong-willed daughter has other ideas.
British Lion — *Embassy Home Entertainment; THORN EMI/HBO Video*

Hockey Night 1984
Comedy
71353   77 mins   C   B, V   P
Megan Follows, Rick Moranis, Gail Youngs, Martin Harburg
A movie for children about the fun world of kiddie hockey.
MFTV Inc. — *Family Home Entertainment*

Hog Wild 1980
Comedy
85370   97 mins   C   B, V   P
Patti D'Arbanville, Tony Rosato, Michael Biehn
A clique of high school nerds exact revenge on a mean motorcycle gang, and a girl is torn between the two factions.
MPAA:PG
Claude Heroux — *Charter Entertainment*

Hold 'Em Jail 1932
Comedy
59408   65 mins   B/W   B, V   P, T
Wheeler and Woolsey, Edgar Kennedy
Wheeler and Woolsey get involved in a prison football game.
RKO — *Blackhawk Films*

Hold That Ghost 1941
Comedy
63360   86 mins   B/W   B, V   P
Bud Abbott, Lou Costello, Joan Davis, Richard Carlson, Mischa Auer, the Andrews Sisters, Ted Lewis and his Band
Abbott and Costello inherit an abandoned roadhouse where the illicit loot of its former owner, a "rubbed out" mobster, is supposedly hidden.
Universal — *MCA Home Video*

Holiday Hotel 1977
Comedy
71253   109 mins   C   B, V   P
Directed by Michael Lang
A group of wild French vacationers let loose at their favorite little resort hotel. Available in

French with English subtitles or dubbed into English.
MPAA:R EL, FR
Alain Poire — *Embassy Home Entertainment*

Holiday Inn   1942
Musical
53399 101 mins B/W   B, V, LV   P
Bing Crosby, Fred Astaire, Marjorie Reynolds, Walter Abel, Virginia Dale
A song and dance man decides to turn a Connecticut farm into an inn, open only on holidays. Songs include: "Happy Holiday," "Be Careful It's My Heart," and "White Christmas." Academy Award '42: Best Song ("White Christmas").
Paramount; Mark Sandrich — *MCA Home Video*

Holiday Sing Along With   1963
Mitch
Music-Performance/Christmas
82265   50 mins   C   B, V   P
Now everyone can sing along with Mitch Miller in this collection of holiday favorites culled from his television series. The video cassette also features subtitled lyrics so the whole family can revel in Yuletide cheer.
All American Features — *MGM/UA Home Video*

Hollywood at War   194?
Film-History
03999   60 mins   C   B, V   P
Bob Hope, Donald Duck, Superman, and others
Collection of war time shorts featuring "All Star Bond Rally," "Spirit of '43," "Stamp Day for Superman."
Walt Disney et al — *Hollywood Home Theater*

Hollywood Boulevard   1976
Comedy/Filmmaking
64840   93 mins   C   B, V   P
Candice Rialson, Mary Woronov, Rita George, Jeffrey Kramer, Dick Miller, Paul Bartel, directed by Joe Dante and Allan Arkush
This behind-the-scenes glimpse of shoestring-budget moviemaking offers comical sex, violence, sight gags, one-liners, comedy bits, and mock-documentary footage. Commander Cody and His Lost Planet Airmen are featured.
MPAA:R
New World Pictures — *Warner Home Video*

Hollywood Clowns, The   1985
Documentary/Comedy
70882   60 mins   C   B, V   P
Buster Keaton, W C Fields, Charlie Chaplin, Harold Lloyd, Abbott and Costello, Laurel and Hardy, Red Skelton, the Marx Brothers, Danny Kaye, Lewis and Martin, Betty Hutton and Bob Hope

Glenn Ford narrates this tribute to the screens's greatest comedians, with clips from many classic scenes.
Bill Gleason — *MGM/UA Home Video*

Hollywood Goes to War   1954
Documentary/Film-History
58651   41 mins   B/W   B, V, FO   P
Bob Hope, Bing Crosby, Frank Sinatra, Betty Grable, Harpo Marx, Jimmy Durante, Eddie Cantor, Red Skelton, Abbott and Costello, Dinah Shore, Dorothy Lamour, Carmen Miranda
Five shorts produced for the entertainment of G.I.'s overseas or for home front bond drives: "The All-Star Bond Rally" features Bob Hope, Fibber McGee and Molly, Bing Crosby, Harry James and his Orchestra, Sinatra, Grable, Harpo Marx, and the Talking Pin-Ups; "Hollywood Canteen Overseas Special" features Dinah Shore, Eddie Cantor, Jimmy Durante, and Red Skelton; "Mail Call (Strictly G.I.)" is a filmed "Mail Call" radio program with Don Wilson announcing guests Dorothy Lamour, Cass Daley, and Abbott and Costello doing 'Who's on First'; "G.I. Movie Weekly—Sing with the Stars" features Carmen Miranda and her fruit-basket hat, a Portuguese 'follow-the-bouncing-ball' sing-along, Richard Lane, and Mel Blanc's voice; and "Invaders in Greasepaint," the story of 'Four Jills in a Jeep'—the North African USO tour by Martha Raye, Carol Landis, Mitzi Mayfair, and Kay Francis. Also includes newsreel footage of the girls touring, plus their memorable rendition of the wartime classic tune 'Snafu,' which was banned from the airwaves for its racy lyrics.
Office of War Information; Army Pictorial Service; Army-Navy Screen Magazine — *Video Yesteryear*

Hollywood High   1977
Comedy/Exploitation
70363   81 mins   C   B, V.   P
Marcy Albrecht, Sherry Hardin, Rae Sperling, Susanne Kevin Mead
Four attractive teen couples converge on the mansion of an eccentric silent-film star for an unusual vacation experience.
MPAA:R
Lone Star Pictures — *Vestron Video*

Hollywood High Part II   1981
Comedy
80705   86 mins   C   B, V   P
April May, Donna Lynn, Camille Warner
Local police continue to curtail the adventures of three comely high school students who live for boys, beer and beaches.
MPAA:R
Lone Star Pictures — *Vestron Video*

Hollywood Home Movies   1986
Film-History/Variety
87274   58 mins   B/W   B, V   P

Marilyn Monroe, John Wayne, Gregory Peck, Robert Mitchum, Ann-Margret
Over 60 celebrities' home movies are compiled in this program that offers a nostalgic look at how the demigods of yesteryear lived, worked, played and relaxed.
Ken Murray — *RCA/Columbia Pictures Home Video*

Hollywood Hot Tubs   1984
Comedy
76766   103 mins   C   B, V, CED   P
Edy Williams, Donna McDaniel, Michael Andrew, Katt Shea
A teenager picks up some extra cash and a lot of fun as he repairs the hot tubs of the rich and famous.
MPAA:R
Seymour Borde and Associates — *Vestron Video*

Hollywood Man   1976
Drama
66282   90 mins   C   B, V   P
William Smith
The story of a Hollywood actor and his crew in a desperate fight against all odds to complete their independent film.
MPAA:R
Olympic Films — *Monterey Home Video*

Hollywood My Hometown   195?
Film-History
33803   60 mins   B/W   B, V   P
Ken Murray
Hollywood host Ken Murray looks at the stars of the glittering movie world.
Unknown — *Video Connection; Discount Video Tapes; Hollywood Home Theater*

Hollywood on Parade   1934
Variety
52463   59 mins   B/W   B, V, FO   P
Fredric March, Ginger Rogers, Jean Harlow, Jeanette MacDonald, Maurice Chevalier, Mary Pickford, Jackie Cooper
A collection of several "Hollywood on Parade" shorts produced by Paramount Studios between 1932 and 1934. Nearly every big star of the era is featured singing, dancing, or taking part in bizarre sketches.
Paramount — *Video Yesteryear; Discount Video Tapes*

Hollywood on the Line   1951
Interview
85511   26 mins   B/W   B, V   P
Bob Lemond, Jane Wyatt, Jack Carson
An early television interview show featuring the stars cavorting before the cameras. Two fifteen minute programs.
Syndicate — *Video Yesteryear*

Hollywood Outtakes and   1983
Rare Footage
Outtakes and bloopers/Film-History
66382   85 mins   C   B, V   P
Marilyn Monroe, James Dean, Joan Crawford, Judy Garland, Humphrey Bogart, Ronald Reagan, Bette Davis, Vivien Leigh, Carole Lombard and others
A collection of rare and unusual film clips and excerpts that feature dozens of Hollywood stars in screen tests, promotional shorts, home movies, outtakes, TV appearances and World War II propaganda shorts. Some segments in black and white.
Manhattan Movietime — *RCA/Columbia Pictures Home Video*

Hollywood Revels   1947
Variety
78091   58 mins   B/W   B, V, FO   P
Bill Rose, Hillary Dawn, Peggy Bond, Pat Dorsey, Aleen Dupree, Mickey Lotus Wing
A burlesque show including Can-Can dancers, singers and comedians are included in this film.
Unknown — *Video Yesteryear*

Hollywood Without   1965
Makeup
Film-History
04789   51 mins   C   B, V   P
Home movie footage taken over the years by Ken Murray includes candid shots of over 100 stars of the film world.
Filmaster — *Hollywood Home Theater; Video Yesteryear; Discount Video Tapes; Video Connection*

Hollywood's Greatest   194?
Trailers
Movie and TV trailers
64418   60 mins   B/W   B, V, 3/4U   P
Theatrical previews from an assortment of classic films, including "Citizen Kane," "Top Hat," "It's a Wonderful Life," "Fort Apache" and many others. Some are in color.
RKO et al — *Nostalgia Merchant*

Holocaust   1978
Drama
60387   475 mins   C   B, V   P
Meryl Streep, James Woods
The war years of 1935 to 1945 are relived in this account of the Nazi atrocities, focusing on the Weiss family, destroyed by the monstrous crimes, and the Dorf family, Germans who thrived under the Nazi regime.
Titus Productions — *Worldvision Home Video; RCA VideoDiscs*

Holocaust Survivors... Remembrance of Love   1983
Drama
86169   100 mins   C   B, V   P
Kirk Douglas, Pam Dawber, Chana Eden, Yoram Gal, Robert Clary
A concentration camp survivor attends the 1981 World Gathering of Holocaust Survivors to find his long lost love. Originally titled "Remembrance of Love."
ComWorld Prod. — *Vidmark Entertainment*

Holocaust: Susan Sontag   1982
World War II/Religion
59557   58 mins   C   B, V   P
Writer Susan Sontag explores the meaning of Hitler's genocide in this retrospective of the Holocaust.
Unknown — *Mastervision*

Holt of the Secret Service   1942
Adventure/Serials
64425   225 mins   B/W   B, V, 3/4U   P
Jack Holt
A secret service agent runs afoul of saboteurs and fifth-columnists in this fifteen-episode serial.
Columbia — *Nostalgia Merchant; Discount Video Tapes; Video Yesteryear; Captain Bijou*

Holy Innocents   1984
Comedy
87263   108 mins   C   B, V   P
Alfredo Landa, Francisco Rabal, directed by Mario Camus
An Italian family is torn comically asunder in a parody of traditional feudal societies. With English subtitles.
Cannes Film Festival '84: Best Actor (Landa & Rabal). MPAA:PG IT
Julian Mateos — *Karl/Lorimar Home Video*

Holy Koran, The   1982
Islam/Middle East
59555   60 mins   C   B, V   P
This program shows why Islam is such a force in the world today. Islam's contributions to world science and culture are examined.
Unknown — *Mastervision*

Holy Land and Holy City   1982
Religion/Christianity
59556   58 mins   C   B, V   P
A look at the Holy Land at Christmas, and an artist's chronicle of the activities of the Holy City, the Vatican in Rome, over the four year period of the Vatican Council during the reign of Pope John XXIII.
Unknown — *Mastervision*

Hombre   1967
Western
08434   111 mins   C   B, V   P
Paul Newman, Fredric March, Richard Boone, Diane Cilento, Cameron Mitchell, Barbara Rush, Martin Balsam
A white man, raised by Apaches, is forced to a showdown. He has to help save the lives of people he loathes.
EL, SP
20th Century Fox; Martin Ritt; Irving Ravetch — *CBS/Fox Video*

Hombres sin Alma   197?
Drama
63854   90 mins   B/W   B, V   P
Rosa Carmina, directed by Juan Orol
A woman who has been treated callously by men all her life keeps searching for true love. In Spanish.
SP
Mexican — *Hollywood Home Theater*

Home and the World, The   1984
Drama
86092   130 mins   C   B, V   P
Another masterpiece from India's Satyajit Ray, this film deals with a sheltered Indian woman who falls in love with her husband's friend and becomes politically committed in the turmoil of 1907-1908. In Bengali with English subtitles.
Satyajit Ray; Indian — *Embassy Home Entertainment*

Home Before Midnight   1984
Drama
88145   115 mins   C   B, V   P
James Aubrey, Alison Elliot, directed by Pete Walker
A young songwriter falls in love with a 14-year-old, is discovered and charged with statutory rape.
Pete Walker — *Karl/Lorimar Home Video*

Home for the Holidays   1972
Suspense
86172   74 mins   C   B, V   P
Eleanor Parker, Walter Brennan, Sally Field, Jessica Walter, Julie Harris
Four daughters are called home on Christmas by their father who is convinced that his second wife is trying to poison them.
Spelling/Goldberg — *Vidmark Entertainment*

Home Free All   1984
Drama
76778   92 mins   C   B, V   P
Allan Nicholls, Roland Caccavo, Maura Ellyn, Shelley Wyant, Lucille Rivim
Two reacquainted childhood friends attempt to reconcile their frustrated ambitions with the realities of life.
Almi Films — *Vestron Video*

Home in Oklahoma   **1947**
Western
10703   72 mins   B/W   B, V   P
Roy Rogers, Dale Evans, Trigger, Gabby Hayes,
Carol Hughes
An evil woman is after Gabby Hayes' ranch.
Republic — *Captain Bijou; Cable Films;*
Discount Video Tapes

Home Movies   **1979**
Comedy/Satire
71129   89 mins   C   B, V   P
Kirk Douglas, Nancy Allen, Keith Gordon, Gerrit
Graham, Vincent Gardenia, Mary Davenport,
directed by Brian De Palma
The macabre Mr. DePalma sends up the
modern family unit in this film-filling the screen
with neurotics and egomaniacs. A normal
teenaged boy tries to cope.
MPAA:PG
SMA Entertainment — *Vestron Video*

Home of the Brave   **1949**
War-Drama
81422   86 mins   B/W   B, V   P
Lloyd Bridges, James Edwards, Frank Lovejoy,
Jeff Corey, directed by Mark Robson
A black soldier goes insane after the racist
remarks and treatment he receives from his
white cohorts during a top secret mission in the
South Pacific.
United Artists — *Republic Pictures Home*
Video

Home Safe Home—The   **1986**
Essential Guide to
Keeping Your Home Safe
Safety education/Home improvement
86159   50 mins   C   B, V   P
A Consumer Reports program on making the
home safe, using various common sense
methods and improvements.
AM Available
Consumer Reports TV; Major H. Prod; George
Paige Assoc. — *Karl/Lorimar Home Video*

Home Sweet Home   **1914**
Drama
58644   62 mins   B/W   B, V, FO   P
Lillian Gish, Dorothy Gish, Henry Walthall, Mae
Marsh, Blanche Sweet, Donald Crisp, Robert
Haron, directed by D. W. Griffith
Suggested by the life of John Howard Payne,
actor, poet, dramatist, critic, and world-
wanderer, who wrote the title song amid the
bitterness of his sad life. Silent with musical
score.
Reliance Majestic Release — *Video*
Yesteryear

Home Sweet Home   **1980**
Holidays/Horror
84133   84 mins   C   B, V   P

Jake Steinfeld, Sallee Elyse, Peter de Paula,
directed by Nettie Pena
A murdering psychopath escapes from the local
asylum, and rampages through a family's
Thanksgiving dinner.
Intercontinental Release — *Media Home*
Entertainment

Homebodies   **1974**
Suspense/Drama
80391   96 mins   C   B, V   P
Ruth McDevitt, Linda Marsh, William Hansen,
Peter Brocco, Frances Fuller
Six mild mannered senior citizens resort to
violence and murder in order to prevent their
brownstone from being torn down.
MPAA:PG
Marshal Backlar — *Embassy Home*
Entertainment

Homesteaders of   **1947**
Paradise Valley
Western
14353   54 mins   B/W   B, V   P
Allan Lane, Bobby Blake
Hume brothers oppose Red Ryder and a group
of settlers building a dam in Paradise Valley.
Republic — *Video Connection; Cable Films;*
Nostalgia Merchant

Hometown U.S.A.   **1979**
Comedy
84792   97 mins   C   B, V   P
Brian Kerwin, Gary Springer, David Wilson,
Cindy Fisher
A coming-of-age comedy placed in 1957 Los
Angeles.
MPAA:R
Cinema Ventures — *Vestron Video*

Homework   **1982**
Drama
63843   90 mins   C   B, V, LV   P
Joan Collins, Michael Morgan, Betty Thomas,
Shell Kepler, Wings Hauser
A young man's after-school lessons with a
teacher are definitely not part of the curriculum.
MPAA:R
Jensen Farley — *MCA Home Video*

Homo Eroticus/Man of   **1971**
the Year
Comedy
71040   93 mins   C   B, V   P
Lando Buzzanca, Rossana Podesta
A handsome servant finds it difficult to satisfy
the desires of Bergamo, Italy's socialites.
Italian; Universal — *Hal Roach Studios*

Honda Accord   **1986**
Automobiles
88403   60 mins   C   B, V, 3/4U   P

How to tune-up, maintain and perform minor repairs on the Honda.
Peter Allen Prod. — *Peter Allen Video Productions*

Honey   1981
Drama
65352   89 mins   C   B, V   P
Clio Goldsmith, Fernando Rey, Catherine Spaak
An attractive writer pays an unusual visit to the home of a distinguished publisher. Brandishing a pistol, she demands that he read aloud from her manuscript. As he reads, a unique fantasy unfolds, a dreamlike erotic tale.
Toni De Carlo — *Vestron Video*

Honey Boy   1982
Drama
80636   96 mins   C   B, V   P
Erik Estrada, Morgan Fairchild, Hector Elizondo, Yvonne Wilder, James McEachin
A young middleweight boxing contender finds the price of fame when he falls in love with his press agent. Available in Beta Hi-Fi and VHS Stereo.
Estrada Prods. — *U.S.A. Home Video*

Honey Honey   1981
Cartoons
82382   30 mins   C   B, V   P
Animated
Honey Honey and her cat, Lily, travel through exciting European cities in this animated adventure series.
Sony Corporation of America — *Sony Video Software*

Honeymoon Killers, The   1970
Crime-Drama
82451   103 mins   C   B, V   P
Tony LoBianco, Shirley Stoler, MaryJane Higby
A film based on the true story of a bizarre multiple-murder case.
MPAA:R
Roxanne Productions — *Vestron Video*

Honeymooner's Hidden Episodes   195?
Comedy
71060   60 mins   B/W   B, V   P
Jackie Gleason, Audrey Meadows, Art Carney, Joyce Randolph
These programs from Gleason's vault have eluded circulation and syndication for years. Each tape from the popular 50's sitcom includes skits of various lengths highlighting the Kramdens and Nortons at their comedic best.
Jackie Gleason Prods; CBS — *MPI Home Video*

Honeysuckle Rose   1980
Musical-Drama
54807   119 mins   C   B, V, LV   P
Willie Nelson, Dyan Cannon, Amy Irving, Slim Pickens, Joey Floyd, Charles Levin, Priscilla Pointer, directed by Jerry Schatzberg
A road-touring country-Western singer whose life is a series of one night stands, falls in love with an adoring young guitar player who has just joined his band. This nearly costs him his marriage when his wife, who waits patiently for him at home, decides she's had enough.
MPAA:PG
Warner Bros — *Warner Home Video*

Honky   1971
Drama
82081   92 mins   C   B, V   P
Brenda Sykes, John Nielson, Maria Donzinger
An innocent friendship between a black woman and a white man develops into a passionate romance that has the whole town talking.
MPAA:R
Jack H. Harris Enterprises, Inc. — *Unicorn Video*

Honky Tonk Freeway   1981
Comedy
47304   107 mins   C   B, V   P
Teri Garr, Howard Hesseman, Beau Bridges, directed by John Schlesinger
An odd assortment of people become involved in a small town Mayor's scheme to turn a dying hamlet into a tourist wonderland.
MPAA:PG
Universal — *THORN EMI/HBO Video*

Honkytonk Man   1982
Drama
60562   123 mins   C   B, V   P
Clint Eastwood, Kyle Eastwood, John McIntire, Alexa Kenin, directed by Clint Eastwood
Set during the Depression, this film spins the tale of a country singer who helps his nephew through the rites of passage.
MPAA:PG
Warner Bros — *Warner Home Video*

Honor Among Thieves   1982
Drama
78896   93 mins   C   B, V   P
Charles Bronson, Alain Delon
Two men from different walks of life are bound together by a crime they committed years before.
Gibro Films — *Monterey Home Video*

Honor Thy Father   1973
Drama
73560   97 mins   C   V   P
Raf Vallone, Richard Castellano, Brenda Vaccaro, Joe Bologna

(For explanation of codes, see Use Guide and Key)

The everyday life of a Mafia family as seen through the eyes of Bill Bonanno, the son of mob chieftan Joe Bonanno which was adapted from the book by Gay Talese.
CBS — *Prism*

Hooch   1976
Comedy
82215   96 mins   C   B, V   P
Gil Gerard, Erika Fox, Melody Rogers, Danny Arello
Three members of the New York Mafia get some unexpected southern hospitality when they try to muscle in on a southern family's moonshine operation.
MPAA:PG
Omni Picture Corp. — *Prism*

Hoodoo Ann   1916
Film-History
50633   27 mins   B/W   B, V   P, T
Mae Marsh, Robert Harron
The story of Hoodoo Ann, from her days in the orphanage to her happy marriage. Silent.
Triangle — *Movie Buff Video; Blackhawk Films*

Hooker   1983
Documentary/Prostitution
80931   79 mins   C   B, V   P
This documentary takes a revealing look at the private moments and public times of prostitutes.
Dave Bell Associates — *Vestron Video*

Hooper   1978
Comedy
38950   90 mins   C   B, V   P
Burt Reynolds, Jan-Michael Vincent, Robert Klein, directed by Hal Needham
A behind-the-scenes look at the world of movie stuntmen. Burt Reynolds is a top stuntman who becomes involved in a rivalry with an up-and-coming young man out to surpass him.
MPAA:PG
Warner Bros — *Warner Home Video; RCA VideoDiscs*

Hooters: Nervous Night   1985
Music-Performance
82413   45 mins   C   B, V   P
The Hooters
The Philadelphia-based band performs live at Philadelphia's Tower Theater. Song selections include "And We Danced," "All You Zombies," "Hanging on a Heartbeat" and "Where Do the Children Go."
CBS/Fox Video — *CBS/Fox Video*

Hopalong Cassidy Series   1948
Western
80801   58 mins   B/W   B, V   P
William Boyd, Andy Clyde, Rand Brooks, Anne O'Neal, John Parrish 12 pgms

The highly-revered cowboy and all-around good-guy Hopalong Cassidy joins forces with various other positive role models in an effort to rid the Wild West of villainy.
1.Borrowed Trouble 2.Hoppy's Holiday 3.Sinister Journey 4.The Devil's Playground 5.The Marauders 6.Silent Conflict 7.False Paradise 8.Unexpected Guest 9.Dead Don't Dream 10.Dangerous Venture 11.Strange Gamble 12.Raiders of the Deadline
Lewis J. Rachmill — *Buena Vista Home Video*

Hoppity Goes to Town   1941
Cartoons/Fantasy
64544   78 mins   C   B, V   P
Animated
This full-length animated feature from the Max Fleischer studios tells the story of the inhabitants of Bugville, who live in a weed patch in New York City. Songs by Frank Loesser and Hoagy Carmichael. Original title: "Mr. Bug Goes to Town."
Paramount; Max Fleischer — *Republic Pictures Home Video*

Hopscotch   1980
Comedy
55580   107 mins   C   B, V, CED   P
Glenda Jackson, Walter Matthau, Ned Beatty, Sam Waterston
A C.I.A. agent drops out when his overly zealous chief demotes him to a desk job. When he writes a book designed to expose the dirty deeds he leads his boss and KGB pal on a merry chase.
MPAA:R
Avco Embassy — *Embassy Home Entertainment*

Horowitz in London   1982
Music-Performance
60570   116 mins   C   LV   P
In June 1982, Vladimir Horowitz returned to London for the first time in over 30 years for a performance including Chopin, Scarlatti Sonatas, Schumann's "Scenes from Childhood," and Rachmaninoff. In stereo.
John Vernon; Peter Gelb — *Pioneer Artists; RCA VideoDiscs*

Horowitz in London   1982
Music-Performance
75898   116 mins   C   B, V   P
Vladimir Horowitz
This program presents a rare recital by one of the greatest pianists today, playing in London for Prince Charles at a benefit.
Columbia Artists — *Sony Video Software*

Horrible Double Feature   192?
Horror
10135   56 mins   B/W   B, V   P, T
John Barrymore, Lon Chaney

Package includes John Barrymore in "Dr. Jekyll and Mr. Hyde" (1920). Also features "Hunchback of Notre Dame." Both films are condensed. From the "History of the Motion Picture" series.
Universal et al — *Blackhawk Films*

Horror Express   1973
Horror
08588   95 mins   C   B, V   P
Christopher Lee, Peter Cushing, Telly Savalas, directed by Gene Martin
A creature from Prehistoric times, which has been removed from its tomb, is transported on the Trans-Siberian railroad. Passengers discover strange things happening.
MPAA:R
Scotia Intl; Bernard Gordon — *Prism; Media Home Entertainment; Hollywood Home Theater; VCII; King of Video; Video Connection; World Video Pictures*

Horror Hospital   1973
Horror
48475   91 mins   C   B, V   P
Michael Gough, Robin Askwith, Vanessa Shaw
Patients are turned into zombies by a mad doctor in this hospital where no anesthesia is used. Those who try to escape are taken care of by the doctor's guards.
MPAA:R
Richard Gordon Productions — *United Home Video; MPI Home Video*

Horror of Dracula   1958
Horror
81902   81 mins   C   B, V   P
Peter Cushing, Christopher Lee, Michael Gough, Melissa Stribling
An adaptation of the Bram Stoker novel about a Transylvanian nobleman vampire who travels to London to satisfy his insatiable need for blood.
Hammer Films — *Warner Home Video*

Horror of Frankenstein   1970
Satire/Horror
63349   93 mins   C   B, V   P
Ralph Bates, Kate O'Mara
This spoof of the standard Frankenstein story features a philandering Baron whose interest in a very weird branch of science creates some shocking up-to-date innovations in the conventional plot.
Levitt-Pickman — *THORN EMI/HBO Video*

Horror Planet   1982
Science fiction/Horror
65718   93 mins   C   B, V   P
Robin Clarke
An alien creature needs a chance to breed before escaping to spread its horror. When a group of explorers disturb it, the years of waiting

are over, and the unlucky mother-to-be will never be the same.
MPAA:R
Richard Gordon; David Speechley — *Embassy Home Entertainment*

Horror/Sci-Fi II: Trailers   1974
on Tape
Movie and TV trailers/Science fiction
81885   59 mins   B/W   B, V   P
This is a compilation of classic science fiction trailers for such films as "The Thing," "The Day of the Triffids," "This Island Earth," "The Omega Man" and "Rodan." Some trailers are in color.
Paramount et al — *San Francisco Rush Video*

Horror—Sci-Fi: Trailers   1984
on Tape
Movie and TV trailers/Science fiction
66477   60 mins   C   B, V   P
Theatrical trailers for 35 films are included, with such classic movies represented as: "Psycho," "Night of the Living Dead," "Jaws," "The War of the Worlds," "The Time Machine," "King Kong," "Freaks" and "The Texas Chainsaw Massacre." Some black-and-white segments.
Universal et al — *San Francisco Rush Video*

Horror/Sci-Fi III: Trailers   1973
on Tape
Movie and TV trailers/Horror
81886   59 mins   B/W   B, V   P
Here is a collection of trailers for such shockers as "The Exorcist," "Werewolf in a Girls Dormitory," "The Slime People" and "The Little Shop of Horrors" with some segments in color.
Warner Bros. et al — *San Francisco Rush Video*

Horrors of Burke and   1971
Hare, The
Horror
85080   94 mins   C   B, V   P
Derren Nesbitt, Harry Andrews, Yootha Joyce
A gory tale about the exploits of a bunch of 19th century graverobbers.
British — *New World Video*

Horse Soldiers, The   1959
Adventure/Drama
59643   119 mins   C   CED   P
John Wayne, William Holden, Constance Towers, directed by John Ford
Union Army cavalry officers travel deep into Confederate territory, squaring off against the southern army, and each other, along the way.
United Artists — *RCA VideoDiscs*

Horse Soldiers, The   1959
Western
72895   119 mins   C   B, V   P

John Wayne, William Holden
An 1863 Union cavalry officer is sent 300 miles into Confederate territory to destroy a railroad junction.
United Artists — *CBS/Fox Video*

Horse Without a Head, The   1963
Adventure
84807   89 mins   C   B, V   P
Jean-Pierre Aumont, Herbert Lom, Leo McKern, Pamela Franklin, Vincent Winter, directed by Don Chaffey
A toy horse becomes the crux of life and death for poor French children beset by ruthless train robbers and the law.
Walt Disney Productions — *Walt Disney Home Video*

Horsemasters, The   1961
Comedy-Drama/Musical
84434   85 mins   C   B, V   P
Tommy Kirk, Annette Funicello, Janet Munro, Tony Britton, Donald Pleasance
A group of young riders enter a special training program to achieve the ultimate equestrian title of horsemaster.
Walt Disney Prods. — *Walt Disney Home Video*

Horse's Mouth, The   1958
Comedy
81626   93 mins   C   B, V, LV   P
Alec Guinness, Kay Walsh, Robert Coote, Renee Houston, Michael Gough, directed by Ronald Neame
An obsessive painter discovers that he must rely upon his wits to survive in London.
Lopert Pictures — *Embassy Home Entertainment*

Horton Hears a Who!   1970
Cartoons/Comedy
82404   26 mins   C   B, V   P
Animated
Horton, the whimsical rhyming elephant, tries to rescue the tiny Whos of Whoville in this Dr. Seuss fable.
Metro-Goldwyn-Mayer — *MGM/UA Home Video*

Hospital, The   1971
Drama
65497   101 mins   C   B, V   P
George C. Scott, Diana Rigg, Barnard Hughes, Nancy Marchand, Richard Dysart
A city hospital is beset by weird mishaps, and it transpires that a killer is on the loose.
United Artists — *Key Video*

Hospital Massacre   1981
Horror
65108   89 mins   C   B, V, CED   P
Barbi Benton, Jon Van Ness
A psychopathic killer who wants to play doctor with a young woman in the hospital repeatedly demonstrates his brutal bedside manner.
MPAA:R
Cannon Films — *MGM/UA Home Video*

Hostage Tower, The   1980
Drama
65711   97 mins   C   B, V   P
Peter Fonda, Maud Adams, Britt Ekland, Billy Dee Williams
A group of international crime figures capture a VIP, hold her hostage in the Eiffel Tower and demand $30 million in ransom.
MPAA:PG
Burt Nodella — *Embassy Home Entertainment*

Hostages   1979
Suspense/Drama
80129   93 mins   C   B, V   P
Stuart Whitman, Marisa Mell
A gang of criminals kidnap a family on vacation at a Caribbean island.
Excel Telemedia International — *King of Video*

Hot Boards   1986
Sports-Minor
71229   30 mins   C   V   P
This made-for-video feature looks at the unusual arts of body boarding, wind surfing, sand skiing, snow boarding and trick water skiing.
Prism Video Collection — *Prism*

Hot Chili   1985
Comedy
87366   91 mins   C   B, V   P
Charles Schillaci, Allan J. Kayser, Louisa Moritz
Four sex-obsessed guys go to Mexico for fun and games, and find them.
MPAA:R
Cannon Prod. — *MGM/UA Home Video*

Hot Dog...The Movie!   1983
Comedy
81836   96 mins   C   B, V   P
David Naughton, Patrick Houser, Shannon Tweed, Tracy N. Smith
There's an intense rivalry going on between an Austrian ski champ and his California challenger during the World Cup Freestyle competition in Squaw Valley. Available in VHS and Beta Hi-Fi.
MPAA:R
MGM/UA Entertainment Corp — *Key Video*

Hot Lead and Cold Feet   1978
Western/Comedy
77529   89 mins   C   B, V   P

Jim Dale, Don Knotts, Karen Valentine
Twin brothers compete in a train race where the winner will take ownership of a small western town.
MPAA:G
Walt Disney Productions — *Walt Disney Home Video*

Hot Moves 1984
Comedy
82466　89 mins　C　B, V, CED　　P
Michael Zorek, Adam Silbar, Debi Richter, Monique Gabrielle, Tami Holbrook
Four high school boys make a pact to lose their respective virginities before the end of the summer.
MPAA:R
Cardinal Pictures Corp — *Vestron Video*

Hot Resort 1985
Comedy
71160　92 mins　C　B, V　　P
Bronson Pinchot, Tom Parsekian, Mickey Berz, Linda Kenton, Frank Gorshin, directed by John Robins
A few young American lads mix work and play when they sign on as summer help at an island resort.
Cannon — *MGM/UA Home Video*

Hot Rock, The 1970
Comedy
08466　97 mins　C　B, V　　P
Robert Redford, George Segal, Ron Leibman, Zero Mostel, Paul Sand, directed by Peter Yates
Four incredible goofs try to steal the world's hottest diamond.
MPAA:PG　SP
20th Century Fox; Hal Landers and Bobby Roberts — *CBS/Fox Video*

Hot Rock Videos Volume 2 1985
Music video
81206　30 mins　C　B, V　　P
Rodney Dangerfield, Lou Reed, Meat Loaf
More conceptual music videos for viewing enjoyment. Available in VHS and Beta Hi Fi Stereo.
RCA Video Productions — *RCA/Columbia Pictures Home Video*

Hot Rock Videos Volume I 1984
Music video
80368　28 mins　C　B, V　　P
A collection of music videos from performers such as Eurythmics and The Kinks. Available in VHS Hi-Fi Dolby Stereo and Beta Hi-Fi Stereo.
RCA Video Productions — *RCA/Columbia Pictures Home Video*

Hot Shorts 1984
Comedy
70561　73 mins　B/W　B, V　　P
Phil Austin, Peter Bergman, Phil Proctor
The Firesign Theatre turn their satiric wit on Saturday matinee cliff hanger serials. While familiar characters cross the screen the re-recorded stereo soundtrack features hilarious new dialogue, sound effects, and music.
Bud Groskopf — *RCA/Columbia Pictures Home Video*

Hot Spell 1958
Drama
85252　86 mins　B/W　B, V　　P
Shirley Booth, Anthony Quinn, Shirley MacLaine, Earl Holliman, Eileen Heckart, directed by Daniel Mann
A family comes apart at the seams, so the mother tries to bring everyone back together with an ill-fated birthday party.
Paramount — *Kartes Video Communications*

Hot Stuff 1980
Comedy
51570　91 mins　C　B, V　　P
Dom Deluise, Jerry Reed, Suzanne Pleshette, Ossie Davis, directed by Dom Deluise
Officers on a burglary task force decide the best way to obtain convictions is to go into the fencing business themselves.
MPAA:PG
Columbia Pictures — *RCA/Columbia Pictures Home Video*

Hot Summer Night.. With Donna, A 1984
Music-Performance
76028　60 mins　C　B, V　　P
Donna Summer gives an electrifying performance of her hits at a concert held at California's Pacific Amphitheater. Songs include "She Works Hard For The Money," "Bad Girls" and "Hot Stuff."
Christine Smith — *RCA/Columbia Pictures Home Video*

Hot T-Shirts 1979
Comedy
47681　86 mins　C　B, V　　P
Ray Holland, Stephanie Lawlor, Pauline Rose, Corinne Alphen
A small town bar owner needs a boost for business, finding the answer in wet T-shirt contests.
MPAA:R
Cannon Films — *MCA Home Video*

Hot Target 1985
Crime-Drama
85630　93 mins　C　B, V, LV　　P
Simone Griffith, Steve Marachuk, directed by Denis Lewiston

A distracted rich woman seduces a stranger, who plans on robbing her home.
MPAA:R
Crown International — *Vestron Video*

Hot Times   1974
Drama
65452   80 mins   C   B, V   P
Henry Cory
A high school boy, after striking out with the high school girls, decides to go to New York and have the time of his life!
MPAA:R
Extraordinary Films — *Monterey Home Video*

Hotel New Hampshire,   1984
The
Comedy-Drama
73037   110 mins   C   B, V, CED   P
Jodie Foster, Rob Lowe, Beau Bridges, Nastassia Kinski
This is an adaptation of John Irving's novel about a family's adventures in New Hampshire, Vienna and New York City.
MPAA:R
Orion — *Vestron Video*

Hothead (Coup de Tete)   1978
Comedy
66016   90 mins   C   B, V   P
Patrick Dewaere, directed by Jean-Jacques Annaud
A talented soccer player's quick temper causes him to be cut from his team, lose his job and even be banned from the local bar.
Gaumont SFP — *RCA/Columbia Pictures Home Video*

H.O.T.S.   1979
Comedy/Exploitation
88030   95 mins   C   B, V   P
Susan Kiger, Lisa London, Kimberly Cameron, Danny Bonaduce, Steve Bond
A sex-filled fraternity-rivalry film, starring a slew of ex-Playboy Playmates in wet shirts.
MPAA:R
Manson Int'l. — *Vestron Video*

Hound of the   1959
Baskervilles, The
Mystery
47146   86 mins   C   B, V, CED   P
Peter Cushing, Christopher Lee, Andre Morell
Sherlock Holmes solves the mystery of a supernatural hound threatening the life of a Dartmoor baronet.
EL, SP
United Artists; Hammer — *CBS/Fox Video*

House   1986
Horror
87621   93 mins   C   B, V, LV   P
William Katt, George Wendt, Richard Moll, Kay Lenz
A horror writer begins a book intended to exorcise his nightmares about Vietnam, somehow instigating a series of horrible visions and hauntings threatening his son and himself.
MPAA:R
New World — *New World Video*

House Across the Bay,   1940
The
Drama
66634   88 mins   B/W   B, V   P
George Raft, Walter Pidgeon, Joan Bennett, Lloyd Nolan
An ex-con discovers that his wife was having an affair during his imprisonment.
Walter Wanger Productions — *Monterey Home Video*

House by the Cemetery   1983
Horror
70152   84 mins   C   B, V   P
When a family moves into a house close to a cemetery, strange things start to happen to them.
MPAA:R
Almi Pictures — *Vestron Video*

House Calls   1978
Comedy
47420   105 mins   C   B, V, LV   P
Walter Matthau, Glenda Jackson, Art Carney, Richard Benjamin, Candice Azzara
A widowed surgeon turns into a swinging bachelor until he meets a stuffy English divorcee.
MPAA:PG
Universal — *MCA Home Video*

House of Death   1982
Horror
87572   88 mins   C   B, V   P
Susan Kiger, William Hicks, Jody Kay, Martin Tucker, Jennifer Chase
The ex-Playmate of the Year runs in hysterical fear from a knife-wielding lunatic.
MPAA:R
Chuck Ison; Ernest Bouskos — *Video Gems*

House of Long Shadows,   1983
The
Mystery
86461   102 mins   C   B, V   P
Christopher Lee, Peter Cushing, Vincent Price, John Carradine
A tongue-in-cheek haunted house mystery starring four veteran actors.
Cannon Films — *MGM/UA Home Video*

House of Lurking Death, The   1984

Mystery
80448   60 mins   C   B, V   P
James Warwick, Francesca Annis
Detectives Tommy and Tuppence find a box of chocolates laced with arsenic at the home of Lois Hargreaves, and the mad old maid is the prime suspect. Based on the Agatha Christie story.
London Weekend Television — *Pacific Arts Video*

House of Seven Corpses, The   1973

Horror
58546   90 mins   C   B, V   R, P
John Carradine, John Ireland, Faith Domergue
On the site of a lonely country estate, a motion picture company arrives planning to film a make-believe occult thriller.
MPAA:PG
Philip Yordan — *World Video Pictures; Video Gems; Hollywood Home Theater; King of Video*

House of Shadows   1983

Horror
63387   90 mins   C   B, V   P
John Gavin, Yvonne DeCarlo
A 20-year-old murder comes back to haunt the victim's friends in this suspenseful tale of mystery and terror.
Intercontinental Releasing — *Media Home Entertainment*

House of the Living Dead   1978

Horror
70890   85 mins   C   B, V   P
Mark Burns, Shirley Anne Field, David Oxley, directed by Philip Krasne
A monster living in the attic drives the house's inhabitants mad, and then eats them.
MPAA:R
World Wide Films; Epoh — *United Home Video*

House of the Yellow Carpet   1984

Fantasy
86848   90 mins   C   B, V   P
Roland Josephson, Beatrice Romand, directed by Carlo Lizzani
A couple try to sell an ancient Persian carpet heirloom, and in doing so transgress some unwritten mystical law and havoc ensues.
Registi Publicitari Associati — *Lightning Video*

House of Wax   1953

Horror
78137   88 mins   C   B, V   P
Charles Bronson, Vincent Price
The story of a deranged sculptor whose sinister wax museum showcases creations that were once alive.

House of Whipcord   1975

Horror
84733   102 mins   C   B, V   P
Barbara Markham, Patrick Barr, Ray Brooks, Penny Irving
A model visits her boyfriend's parents, but is actually plunged into a hell of iniquity, depravity and sickness.
Peter Walker — *Monterey Home Video*

House on Chelouche Street, The   1973

Drama
66135   111 mins   C   B, V, FO   P
A well thought-out story of life in Tel Aviv under the rule of the British, before the creation of the country of Israel.
Israel — *Video Yesteryear*

House on Garibaldi Street, The   1979

Suspense/Crime-Drama
72454   100 mins   C   B, V   P
Topol, Nick Mancuso
This is Isser Harel's account of the capture of Adolph Eichmann.
Charles Fries Production — *U.S.A. Home Video*

House on Haunted Hill   1958

Horror
Closed Captioned
81965   75 mins   B/W   B, V   P
Vincent Price, Carol Ohmart, Richard Long, Alan Marshal, directed by William Castle
A wealthy man throws a haunted house party and offers ten thousand dollars to anyone who can survive the night there. Available in VHS and Beta Hi-Fi.
Allied Artists; William Castle — *Key Video*

House on Skull Mountain, The   1974

Horror
Closed Captioned
81759   85 mins   C   B, V   P
Victor French, Janee Michelle, Mike Evans, Jean Durand
The four surviving relatives of a deceased voodoo priestess are in for a bumpy night as they gather at the House on Skull Mountain for the reading of her will. Available in VHS and Beta Hi-Fi.
MPAA:PG
20th Century Fox — *CBS/Fox Video*

Warner Home Video — *Warner Home Video*

House on Sorority Row, The — 1983
Horror
64898   90 mins   C   B, V, LV, CED   P
The harrowing story of what happens when seven senior sisters have a last fling and get back at their housemother at the same time.
Artists Releasing Corp — *Vestron Video*

House on Straw Hill, The — 1976
Horror
82411   84 mins   C   B, V   P
Udo Kier, Linda Hayden, Fiona Richmond
A successful novelist is intrigued by an attractive woman who lives in an isolated farmhouse. Her presence inspires gory hallucinations, lust and violence.
MPAA:R
New World Video — *New World Video*

House on the Edge of the Park — 1984
Horror
82437   91 mins   C   B, V   P
David Hess, Annie Belle, directed by Roger Franklin
A frustrated would-be womanizer takes revenge on a parade of women during an all-night party.
Bedford Entertainment — *Vestron Video*

House That Bled to Death, The — 1981
Horror
77443   60 mins   C   B, V   P
Nicholas Ball, Rachel Davies, Brian Croucher, Pat Maynard, Emma Ridley
Strange things happen to a family when they move into a run down house where a murder occurred years before.
Hammer House of Horror — *Thriller Video*

House That Dripped Blood, The — 1970
Horror
82208   101 mins   C   B, V   P
Christopher Lee, Peter Cushing, Jon Pertwee, Denholm Elliott, John Bennett
A Scotland Yard inspector discovers the history of an English country house while investigating an actor's disappearance.
MPAA:PG
Cinerama Releasing — *Prism*

House That Vanished, The — 1973
Horror/Mystery
50728   84 mins   C   B, V   P
Andrea Allan, Karl Lanchbury, directed by Joseph Larraz
A mysterious house provides horror, screams, and death for most of those who challenge it.
MPAA:R
Diana Daubeney — *Media Home Entertainment*

House Where Evil Dwells, The — 1982
Horror
80859   88 mins   C   B, V   P
Edward Albert, Susan George, Doug McClure
An American family is subjected to a reign of terror then they move into an old Japanese house possessed by three deadly samurai ghosts.
MPAA:R
Commercial Credit Services Holdings Ltd. — *MGM/UA Home Video*

Housewife — 1972
Drama
82171   96 mins   C   B, V   P
Yaphet Kotto, Andrew Duggan, Joyce Van Patten, Jeannie Berlin, directed by Larry Cohen
A vengeful black man holds an unhappily married Beverly Hills couple hostage in their home. Available in VHS and Beta Hi-Fi Stereo.
MPAA:R
Larco Productions — *New World Video*

Houston Astros: Team Highlights — 1984
Baseball
81140   30 mins   C   B, V   P
J.R. Richard, Phil Garner, Joe Niekro, Nolan Ryan, Ray Knight, Joe Sambito   4 pgms
Here are some selected highlights from the Houston Astros 1980's seasons.
1.1981: The Orange Force 2.1982: The First Generation 3.1983: Fighting Back 4.1984: Pulling Together
Major League Baseball — *Major League Baseball Productions*

How Come Nobody's On Our Side? — 1973
Drama
87319   84 mins   C   B, V   P
Adam Roarke, Larry Bishop, Alexandra Hay, Rob Reiner
Two actors/bums scheme to make a fortune with a crime based upon astrology.
MPAA:PG
Maurice Smith — *Monterey Home Video*

How Funny Can Sex Be? — 1976
Comedy
66078   97 mins   C   B, V   P
Giancarlo Giannini, Laura Antonelli, Dulio Del Prete
Eight ribald sketches about loveItalian style.
MPAA:R
Howard Mahler Films — *CBS/Fox Video*

How I Won the War 1967
Comedy/Satire
78634   111 mins   C   B, V   P
John Lennon, Michael Crawford, Michael Hordern, directed by Richard Lester
An inept officer must lead his battalion out of England into the Egyptian desert to conquer a cricket field.
MPAA:PG
Petersham Films Limited — *MGM/UA Home Video*

How the Animals 1956
Discovered Christmas
Christmas/Cartoons
56153   13 mins   C   B, V   P, T
Animated
A delightful tale about the animals of Cozy Valley and how they discover the spirit of Christmas.
AM Available
Coronet Films — *Blackhawk Films; Coronet Films*

How the West Was Won 1962
Western
86780   165 mins   C   B, V   P
John Wayne, Carroll Baker, Lee J. Cobb, Spencer Tracy, Gregory Peck, Karl Malden, Robert Preston, Eli Wallach, Henry Fonda, George Peppard, Debbie Reynolds, Carolyn Jones, Richard Widmark, directed by John Ford, Henry Hathaway, George Marshall
An expansive view of the American West, focusing on one family and their travels against the background of wars and historical events.
MPAA:G
MGM — *MGM/UA Home Video*

How to Beat Home Video 1982
Games Volume I
Video/Games
63365   60 mins   C   B, V   P
Narrated by Philip M. Wiswell
"Volume I: The best Games" features strategies for high scoring on such Atari VCS games as "Space Invaders," "Asteroids," "Chopper Command" and "Frogger."
Vestron Video — *Vestron Video*

How to Beat Home Video 1982
Games Volume II
Video/Games
63366   60 mins   C   B, V   P
Narrated by Philip M. Wiswell
"Volume II: The Hot New Games" features strategies for beating 20 of the newest games for the Atari VCS, including "MegaMania," "Demons to Diamonds," "Pitfall" and "Riddle of the Sphynx."
Vestron Video — *Vestron Video*

How to Beat Home Video 1982
Games Volume III
Video/Games
63367   60 mins   C   B, V   P
Narrated by Philip M. Wiswell
"Volume III: Arcade Quality for the Home" previews new arcade quality game systems such as ColecoVision, Vectrex and Atari 5200, and demonstrates how to score high on games for these systems, including "Cosmic Chasm," "Donkey Kong," "Zaxxon" and "Galaxian."
Vestron Video — *Vestron Video*

How to Beat the High 1980
Cost of Living
Comedy
64890   105 mins   C   B, V, CED   P
Jessica Lange, Susan St. James, Jane Curtin, Richard Benjamin
Three women execute a crazy, comic shopping mall heist.
MPAA:PG
Filmways — *Vestron Video*

How to Break Up a Happy 1976
Divorce
Comedy
80640   74 mins   C   B, V   P
Barbara Eden, Hal Linden, Peter Bonerz, Marcia Rodd, directed by Jerry Paris
A divorced woman starts a vigorous campaign to win her ex-husband back by dating another man to make him jealous.
Charles Fries Prods. — *Worldvision Home Video*

How to Catch Bass 1983
Fishing
86872   60 mins   C   B, V   P
Roger Moore
Another expert instruction in the ins and outs of successful bass fishing.
AM Available
Warburton Prod. — *Warburton Productions*

How to Catch Trout 1984
Fishing
86873   30 mins   C   B, V   P
Rex Gerlach
Water reading, selective equipment and other details for proper trout snaring are shown.
AM Available
Warburton Prod. — *Warburton Productions*

How to Catch Walleye 1983
Fishing
86869   60 mins   C   B, V   P
Babe Winkelman
A complete instruction in how to expertly catch walleye.
AM Available
Warburton Prod. — *Warburton Productions*

How to Enjoy Wine   1985
Alcoholic beverages
70883   60 mins   C   B, V   P
Hugh Johnson
This video explains many of the little things that
wine-lovers find so important. The program will
help the uninitiated in everything from navigating
the wine list to dealing with stubborn
champagne corks.
Simon & Schuster — *Simon and Schuster
Video*

How to Give Your Baby   1985
Encyclopedic Knowledge
Parents/Infants
84780   59 mins   C   B, V   P
Viewers learn how to turn their children into
amazing intellectual prodigies.
Selluloid Video/Glenn Doman — *Video
Associates*

How To Hang   1986
Wallcoverings
Home improvement
88218   26 mins   C   B, V   P
Hosted by Karen Nyman
A instructive program which shows how to hang
all kinds of wallpaper.
How To Video Prod. — *How To Video*

How to Hunt Whitetail   1984
Deer
Hunting
86871   30 mins   C   B, V   P
John Wooters
The habitat, horn-rattling and specific tactics for
hunting whitetail deer are reviewed.
AM Available
Warburton Prod. — *Warburton Productions*

How to Hunt Wild Turkey   1985
Hunting
86874   30 mins   C   B, V   P
J. Wayne Fears
Calling, tracking and camouflage techniques for
successfully hunting wild gobblers are reviewed.
AM Available
Warburton Prod. — *Warburton Productions*

How to Marry a   1953
Millionaire
Comedy
08552   96 mins   C   B, V   P
*Lauren Bacall, Marilyn Monroe, Betty Grable,
William Powell, David Wayne, Cameron Mitchell*
Three models pool their money and rent a lavish
apartment to wage campaign to trap millionaire
husbands.
20th Century Fox; Nunnally
Johnson — *CBS/Fox Video*

How to Pick Up Men   1985
Human relations/Sexuality
81731   60 mins   C   B, V   •   P
Psychologist Dr. Elliot Jaffa describes
techniques that show women how to find the
man of their dreams.
Cherry Wyman — *Kartes Video
Communications*

How to Plan a Perfect   1985
Wedding
Marriage
88476   60 mins   C   B, V   P
Hosted by Marion Ross, this program explains
precisely how to plan, organize and execute a
wedding without losing your mind or your life
savings.
Worldvision Home Video Inc. — *Worldvision
Home Video*

How to Seduce a Woman   1974
Comedy
86863   108 mins   C   B, V   P
Angus Duncan, Marty Ingels, Lillian Randolph
A playboy attempts to bed five supposedly
unattainable women.
CBS — *Prism*

How to Set Up Your Own   1982
Videotape Business
Video
59508   60 mins   C   B, V   S
How video entrepreneurs have started their own
video production companies is discussed.
Kartes Prods — *Kartes Video Communications*

How to Stuff a Wild Bikini   1965
Comedy
66130   90 mins   C   B, V   P
*Annette Funicello, Dwayne Hickman, Buster
Keaton, Harvey Lembeck, Mickey Rooney*
A young man in the Navy asks a local
witchdoctor to keep on eye on his girl.
American Intl Pictures — *Warner Home Video*

How to Teach Your Baby   1983
to Read
Parents/Infants
84779   80 mins   C   B, V   P
How to instruct an infant to read years before it
normally would, and turn it into a superchild.
Selluloid Prod/Glenn Doman — *Video
Associates*

How to Troll for Fish   1984
Fishing
86866   30 mins   C   B, V   P
Pete Ruboyianes
A complete instruction in the trolling method of
fishing in various water bodies.
AM Available

Warburton Prod. — *Warburton Productions*

How to Watch Pro Football   1981
Football
57776   53 mins   C   B, V   P
Tom Landry, Marv Levy, John McKay, Chuck Noll, Sam Rutigliano, Don Shula, Dick Vermeil
A step-by-step guide designed to enhance every fan's enjoyment of the game. Seven top coaches take the viewer through everything from zone defense pass coverage to offensive strategy at the goal line. The two-sided interactive disc offers the same program content utilizing the unique technology of the interactive disc.
Optical Programming Associates — *MCA Home Video; Optical Programming Associates*

How to Win at Life Extension   1984
Health education
78171   120 mins   C   B, V   P
This program is designed to educate the viewer about the latest techniques in life extension.
AM Available
Direct Broadcast Programs Inc — *Video Connection of America*

Howard Jones: Like to Get to Know You Well   1984
Music video
80155   58 mins   C   B, V   P
Howard Jones performs his infectious brand of dance rock in this concert taped in England.
Stagefright Productions; Limelight Films — *Warner Home Video*

Howdy Doody   195?
Comedy
59086   49 mins   B/W   B, V, FO   P
Buffalo Bob Smith
Clarabell and Buffalo Bob show movies of Clarabell's recent trip. Princess Summerfall Winterspring and Zippy the Chimp, Flubadub, Dilly Dally, Inspector John, Mr. Bluster, and others also appear. Two complete shows.
NBC — *Video Yesteryear; Discount Video Tapes*

Howling, The   1981
Horror
59340   91 mins   C   B, V, LV, CED   P
Dee Wallace, Patrick MacNee, Dennis Dugan, Kevin McCarthy
A pretty television reporter takes a rest at a clinic inhabited by loonies, and located near woods inhabited by werewolves.
MPAA:R
Michael Finell;Jack Conrad — *Embassy Home Entertainment; RCA VideoDiscs*

Howling II   1985
Horror
85023   91 mins   C   B, V   P
Sybil Danning, Christopher Lee, Marsha A Hunt
A policeman investigates a Transylvanian werewolf-ridden castle and gets mangled for his trouble.
MPAA:R
Hemdale Prods. — *THORN EMI/HBO Video*

H.R. Pufnstuf, Vol II   1969
Adventure
80778   46 mins   C   B, V   P
Billie Hayes, Jack Wild
This volume features two more episodes from the popular children's series.
Sid and Marty Krofft — *Embassy Home Entertainment*

H.R. Pufnstuf, Volume I   1969
Adventure
76789   46 mins   C   B, V   P
Billie Hayes, Jack Wild, Joan Gerber, Felix Silla, Jerry Landon
The Mayor of Magic Island H.R. Pufnstuf and his friend Jimmy battle the evil Witchiepoo and her bumbling henchmen as they struggle to find the Secret Path of Escape.
Sid and Marty Krofft — *Embassy Home Entertainment*

Huberman Festival, The   1984
Music-Performance
65852   45 mins   C   B, V   P
5 pgms
This series of five concerts features the Israeli Philharmonic and seven prominent violinists performing works by Tchaikovsky, Bach, and Vivaldi. Available in VHS and Beta Hi-Fi.
Pacific Arts Video Records — *Pacific Arts Video*

Huckleberry Finn   1978
Adventure
29235   97 mins   C   B, V, CED   P
Kurt Ida, Don Manahan, Forrest Tucker
Based on the classic story by Mark Twain of the adventures of a Missouri boy and a runaway slave.
Sunn Classic Pictures — *VidAmerica; Lucerne Films*

Huckleberry Finn   1975
Adventure
55535   78 mins   C   B, V, CED   P
Ron Howard, Jack Elam, Merle Haggard, Donny Most
Television version of the Mark Twain classic about a boy and a runaway slave who take off together on a raft down the Mississippi.
ABC Pictures International — *CBS/Fox Video; ABC Video Enterprises*

Huckleberry Finn 1981
Cartoons
81321   72 mins   C   B, V   P
Animated
This is a version of the classic Mark Twain novel
about the adventures a young boy and a
runaway slave encounter as they travel down
the Mississippi River.
New Hope Productions — *Lightning Video*

Huckleberry Finn 1974
Musical
Closed Captioned
81560   118 mins   C   B, V   P
Jeff East, Paul Winfield, Harvey Korman
This is the musical version of the Mark Twain
story about the adventures a young boy and a
runaway slave encounter along the Mississippi
River. Available in VHS and Beta Hi-Fi.
United Artists — *Playhouse Video*

Hud 1963
Drama
10952   112 mins   B/W   B, V, LV   P
*Paul Newman, Melvyn Douglas, Patricia Neal,
Brandon DeWilde*
Hard-driving, hard-drinking, woman-chasing
young man, whose life is a revolt against the
principles of his father, is the idol of his teenage
nephew.
Academy Awards '63: Best Actress (Neal); Best
Supporting Actor (Douglas); Best
Cinematography.
Paramount — *Paramount Home Video; RCA
VideoDiscs*

Huey Lewis and the 1985
News: The Heart of Rock
n' Roll
Music-Performance
81787   53 mins   C   B, V   P
*Huey Lewis, Sean Hopper, Bill Gibson, Mario
Cipollina, Chris Hayes, Johnny Colla*
Huey Lewis and the News perform "If This Is It,"
'I Want a New Drug" and other favorites in this
concert taped at San Francisco's Kabuki
Theater. Available in VHS and Beta Hi-Fi
Stereo.
Tony Eaton — *Warner Home Video*

Huey Lewis and the News 1985
Video Hits
Music video/Music-Performance
70765   46 mins   C   B, V, LV   P
Huey Lewis, the News
Along with selections from their best-selling
"Sports" L.P., this compilation features an a
capella version of the National Anthem and the
two hits from the "Back to the Future" sound
track. Hi-Fi Stereo sound in both formats.
Hulex/Chrysalis — *CBS/Fox Video*

Hugga Bunch 1985
Cartoons
Closed Captioned
71021   48 mins   C   B, V   P
Gennie James
The "Hugga Bunch" characters help a young
girl find the fountain of youth for her loving
grandmother.
Hallmark — *Children's Video Library*

Hugh Shannon: Saloon 1981
Singer
Music-Performance
84651   55 mins   C   B, V   P
The famous singer performs at David K's in New
York. Recorded in Hi-Fi Stereo.
Lou Tyrell — *V.I.E.W. Video*

Hughes and Harlow: 1977
Angels in Hell
Biographical/Drama
81396   94 mins   C   B, V   P
Lindsay Bloom, Victor Holchak, Davis McLean
This is the story of the romance that occurred
between Howard Hughes and Jean Harlow
during the filming of "Hell's Angels" in 1930.
MPAA:R
Key Pictures — *Monterey Home Video*

Hughes Flying Boat, The 1980
Documentary/Aeronautics
57431   11 mins   C   B, V   P, T
A look at Howard Hughes' legendary aircraft,
"The Spruce Goose," hidden from public view
for over thirty years, and the mystery hangar on
Terminal Island. This program includes live
commentary by Hughes from the cockpit during
flight.
Bruce Frenzinger — *Blackhawk Films;
Interurban Films*

Hughie 1984
Drama
75288   53 mins   C   B, V   P
This is a tape of the Broadway play about a
hotel night clerk who develops friendships with
the residents that come in during the night. In
Beta Hi-Fi and VHS Dolby stereo.
RKO Home Video — *RKO HomeVideo*

Hugo the Hippo 1976
Cartoons
08483   90 mins   C   B, V   P
*Animated, voices of Paul Lynde, Burl Ives,
Robert Morley, Marie and Jimmy Osmond*
A forlorn baby hippo struggles to survive in the
human jungle of old Zanzibar.
MPAA:G
20th Century Fox — *CBS/Fox Video*

Human Comedy, The　1943
Drama
71378　117 mins　B/W　B, V　P
*Mickey Rooney, Frank Morgan, James Craig,
directed by Clarence Brown*
A small-town boy experiences love and loss and
learns the meaning of true faith during WWII.
Academy Awards '43: Writing-Original Story
(William Saroyan)
MGM — *MGM/UA Home Video*

Human Experiments　1979
Horror
53327　82 mins　C　B, V　P
Linda Haynes, Jackie Coogan, Aldo Ray
A psychiatrist in a women's prison conducts a
group of experiments in which he destroys the
"criminal instinct" in the inmates through brute
fear.
MPAA:R
Summer Brown; Gregory
Goodell — *VidAmerica*

Human Monster, The　1939
Horror
72948　73 mins　B/W　B, V　P
Bela Lugosi
A mad doctor played by Bela Lugosi is using his
house as a front for some strange experiments.
Monogram — *United Home Video; Kartes
Video Communications*

Human Monster, The　1940
Mystery
08753　78 mins　B/W　B, V　P
Bela Lugosi, Hugh Williams Greta Gynt
Scotland Yard inspector investigates five
drownings.
Pathe; Monogram — *Kartes Video
Communications; Cable Films; Video
Connection; VCII; Discount Video Tapes*

Human Vapour, The　1968
Science fiction
80824　81 mins　C　B, V　R, P
A normal human being has the ability to
vaporize himself at will and use it to terrorize
Tokyo.
Tohol Brenco Pictures — *Video Gems*

Humanoids from the　1980
Deep
Horror
54809　81 mins　C　B, V　P
A horror tale wherein strange creatures rise
from the depths of the ocean and attack
mankind.
MPAA:R
New World Pictures — *Warner Home Video*

Humans: Happy Hour,　1984
The
Music
65850　40 mins　C　B, V　P
This program represents a pioneering step into
the next wave of long-form music video with the
Humans' songs fitting into the overall plot.
Pacific Arts Video Records — *Pacific Arts
Video*

Humongous　1982
Horror
63374　93 mins　C　B, V　P
Janet Julian, David Wallace, Janet Baldwin
A deranged giant must kill to survive.
MPAA:R
Embassy Pictures — *Embassy Home
Entertainment*

Hunchback of Notre　1939
Dame, The
Drama
00309　117 mins　B/W　B, V　P
*Charles Laughton, Maureen O'Hara, Edmund
O'Brien*
Victor Hugo's classic tale of the tortured
hunchback bellringer of Notre Dame.
RKO — *RKO HomeVideo; King of Video; RCA
VideoDiscs*

Hunchback of Notre　1923
Dame, The
Drama
07278　90 mins　B/W　B, V　P, T
*Lon Chaney, Patsy Ruth Miller, Norman Kerry,
Ernest Torrance*
The first film version of Victor Hugo's novel
about the tortured hunchback bellringer of Notre
Dame Cathedral. Silent.
Universal — *Blackhawk Films; Video
Yesteryear; Hollywood Home Theater; Kartes
Video Communications*

Hundra　1985
Adventure
82479　96 mins　C　B, V　P
Laurene London, John Gaffari, Romiro Oliveros
A warrior queen vows revenge on all men when
her all-female tribe is slain by men. Nothing
could stop her fierce vendetta—except love.
Media — *Media Home Entertainment*

Hunger, The　1983
Horror
65220　100 mins　C　B, V, CED　P
*Catherine Deneuve, David Bowie, Susan
Sarandon, Cliff de Young, directed by Tony
Scott*
A 2000-year-old vampire finds that her current
lover is aging fast and therefore sets out to find
some "new blood" to replace him.
MPAA:R

MGM UA — *MGM/UA Home Video*

Hungry i Reunion   1981
Comedy-Performance/Music-Performance
59930   90 mins   C   B, V   P
*Bill Cosby, Phyllis Diller, Ronnie Schell, Bill
Dana, Mort Sahl, Irwin Corey, Jackie Vernon,
Jonathan Winters, Kingston Trio, Limelighters,
Lenny Bruce*
A reunion of stars who made the "Hungry i" San
Francisco's favorite nightclub of the 50's and
60's. Includes rare footage of Lenny Bruce in
performance.
Tom Cohen — *Pacific Arts Video*

Hunt the Man Down   1950
Mystery
73695   68 mins   B/W   B, V   P
Gig Young, Lynn Roberts, Gerald Mohr
A public defender must solve a killing for which
an innocent man is charged.
RKO — *RKO HomeVideo*

Hunt the Man   1951
Down/Smashing the
Rackets
Mystery/Drama
79321   137 mins   B/W   B, V   P
*Gig Young, Lynne Roberts, Chester Morris,
Frances Mercer*
A double feature: In ""Hunt the Man Down" a
public defender tries to clear a captured
fugitive's name, and in ""Smashing the
Rackets" a special prosecutor takes on the
gangsters who have corrupted a big city.
RKO — *RKO HomeVideo*

Hunted!   1979
Drama
80795   90 mins   C   B, V   R, P
A young Jewish boy teams up with a resistance
fighter to find his mother in Nazi Germany during
World War II.
German — *Video Gems*

Hunter, The   1980
Drama/Adventure
54671   97 mins   C   B, V, LV   P
*Steve McQueen, Eli Wallach, Kathryn Harrold,
LeVar Burton, directed by Buzz Kulik*
An action-drama based on the real life
adventures of Ralph (Papa) Thorson, a modern
day bounty hunter who makes his living by
finding fugitives who have jumped bail.
MPAA:PG
Paramount — *Paramount Home Video*

Hunter   1977
Suspense
81122   120 mins   C   B, V   P
*James Franciscus, Linda Evans, Broderick
Crawford*

An attorney falsely accused of a crime sets out
to even the score with the mysterious millionaire
who set him up. Pilot for the series.
Lorimar Productions — *Karl/Lorimar Home
Video*

Hunters of the Golden   1982
Cobra
Adventure/War-Drama
80925   95 mins   C   B, V   P
*David Warbeck, Almanta Suska, Alan Collins,
John Steiner*
Two American soldiers plot to recover the
priceless golden cobra from the Japanese
general who stole the prized relic during the last
days of World War II.
MPAA:R
World Northal — *Vestron Video*

Hunting Big Muleys   1985
Hunting
87657   38 mins   C   B, V   P
Lad Shunneson
The techniques of mule deer killing are
addressed, as well as the steps taken to
preserve the deer's head after cutting it from the
body.
Sportsmen On Film — *Sportsmen on Film*

Hunting Dall Sheep and   1985
Caribou in the N.W.T.
Hunting
87654   36 mins   C   B, V   P
Bob Hartman, Pete Ethchechoury
Bob and Pete take down a few rams in an
average afternoon of shooting.
Sportsmen On Film — *Sportsmen on Film*

Hunting Desert Bighorn   1984
in Northern Baja
Hunting
87647   38 mins   C   B, V   P
Ken Wilson, Bud Hartman, Dave Harshbarger
Ken, Bud and Dave set out to hunt wild bighorn
rams in Baja Norte, Mexico.
Sportsmen On Film — *Sportsmen on Film*

Hurray for Betty Boop   1980
Cartoons
78141   81 mins   C   B, V   P
Animated
An animated feature presents Betty Boop as
she gets herself into the true spirit on an
election year by running for President.
Warner Home Video — *Warner Home Video*

Hurricane   1979
Drama
63430   119 mins   C   B, V   P
*Mia Farrow, Jason Robards, Trevor Howard,
Max Von Sydow*
A hurricane wreaks havoc in a tropical paradise.

Paramount; Dino DeLaurentiis — *Paramount Home Video*

Hurricane, The   1937
Drama
82569   102 mins   B/W   B, V, LV   P
Jon Hall, Dorothy Lamour, Mary Astor, Aubrey Smith, Raymond Massey, directed by John Ford
A couple on the run from the law are aided by a hurricane and are able to build a new life for themselves on an idyllic island.
Sam Goldwyn — *Embassy Home Entertainment*

Hurricane Express   1932
Adventure
08881   70 mins   B/W   B, V, 3/4U   P
John Wayne, Conway Tearle, Shirley Gray
Adapted from the twelve-episode serial. John Wayne pits his courage against an unknown, powerful individual out to sabotage a railroad.
Mascot — *Cable Films*

Hurricane Express   1932
Adventure/Serials
58633   223 mins   B/W   B, V   P
John Wayne, Joseph Girard
Twelve episodes of the vintage serial, in which the Duke pits his courage against an unknown, powerful individual out to sabotage a railroad.
Mascot — *Movie Buff Video; Video Connection; Video Yesteryear; Cable Films; Discount Video Tapes*

Hurricane Sword   197?
Martial arts
70820   86 mins   C   B, V   P
Chen Sau Kei, Li Tai Shing
This thriller sets savage sword play against a background of murder, betrayal, prostitution and reunion.
Foreign — *Master Arts Video*

Hurried Man, The   1977
Drama
87602   91 mins   C   B, V   P
Alain Delon, Christian Barbier, Andre Falcon, Stefano Patrizi
The story of a success and sex-obsessed urban man and how his obsessions ruin him. Dubbed.
Lira Films; Adel Prod.; Irragizione Cinetmat. — *Unicorn Video*

Hurry, Charlie, Hurry   1941
Comedy
73699   65 mins   B/W   B, V   P
Leon Errol
A husband gets in trouble aided by his Indian friends.
RKO — *RKO Home Video*

Hurry Up or I'll Be Thirty   1973
Comedy
87213   87 mins   C   B, V   P
Danny DeVito, John Lefkowitz, Steve Inwood, Linda DeCoff, Francis Gallagher, directed by Joseph Jacoby
A Brooklyn bachelor celebrates his thirtieth birthday by being morose, depressed and enraged. His friends try to help. They fail, but he finds love anyway.
Cinegroup; Joseph Jacoby — *Vestron Video*

Hush-Hush, Sweet Charlotte   1965
Horror
Closed Captioned
81760   134 mins   B/W   B, V   P
Bette Davis, Olivia de Havilland, Joseph Cotten, Agnes Moorehead, Mary Astor, Bruce Dern, directed by Robert Aldrich
A fading southern belle finds out the truth about her fiance's murder when the case is reopened thirty-seven years later. Available in VHS and Beta Hi-Fi.
20th Century Fox — *CBS/Fox Video*

Hussy   1980
Drama
66604   95 mins   C   B, V, LV   P
Helen Mirren, John Shea
An unlikely pair of lovers find themselves enmeshed within an underworld conspiracy.
MPAA:R
World Northal — *Vestron Video*

Hustle   1975
Mystery
38934   120 mins   C   B, V   P
Burt Reynolds, Catherine Deneuve, directed by Robert Aldrich
Burt Reynolds plays a detective investigating a young girl's supposed suicide who becomes romantically entangled with a high-priced call girl.
MPAA:R
Paramount — *Paramount Home Video*

Hustler Squad   1976
War-Drama
64297   98 mins   C   B, V   P
John Ericson, Karen Ericson, Lynda Sinclaire, Nory Wright
A U.S. Army major and a Philippine guerrilla leader stage a major operation to help rid the Philippines of Japanese Occupation forces: they have four combat-trained prostitutes infiltrate a brothel patronized by top Japanese officers.
MPAA:R
Crown International Pictures — *United Home Video*

Hustling 1975
Drama
65665   96 mins   C   B,.V   P
Jill Clayburgh, Lee Remick
A reporter writing a series of articles on prostitution in New York City takes an incisive look at their unusual and sometimes brutal world.
Lillian Gallo — *Worldvision Home Video*

Hymn of the Nations 1944
Music-Performance
11235   25 mins   B/W   B, V, FO   P
Jan Peerce, Arturo Toscanini and the NBC Symphony, the Westminster Choir
This wartime short features a rare filmed appearance by Arturo Toscanini, conducting two Verdi works: the overture to "La Forza del Destino" and "Hymn of the Nations."
Office of War Information — *Video Yesteryear; Blackhawk Films; National AudioVisual Center*

Hypnovision Stop Smoking Video Programming 1983
Smoking
69927   22 mins   C   B, V   P
Through a number of positive subliminal messages, this program helps viewers to be more relaxed in their daily life without cigarettes, learn to take "one day at a time" to reduce anxiety, and substitute new positive behaviors for old, poor habits.
Self Improvement Video — *Self Improvement Video*

Hypnovision Stress Reduction 1985
Stress
81595   20 mins   C   B, V   P
This program aids viewers in reducing stress in their daily lives.
Self Improvement Video — *Self Improvement Video*

Hypnovision Weight Loss Video Programming 1983
Physical fitness
69928   22 mins   C   B, V   P
To help the viewer lose weight, this program uses a number of positive subliminal messages to deeply relax and then permantly change poor eating habits of the overeater.
Self Improvement Video — *Self Improvement Video*

Hysterectomy (Rehabilitation and Injury) 1978
Physical fitness
52757   30 mins   C   B, V   P
Hosted by Ann Dugan

Exercises for women who have had a hysterectomy, including both specific-area and total-body movements to gradually improve muscle tone. Part of the "Rehabilitation and Injury" series.
Health 'N Action — *RCA/Columbia Pictures Home Video*

Hysteria 1964
Drama/Romance
79213   85 mins   B/W   B, V   P
Robert Webber, Susan Lloyd, Maurice Denham, directed by Freddie Francis
When an American becomes involved in an accident and has amnesia, a mysterious benefactor pays all his bills and gives the man a house to live in.
MPAA:PG
Hammer Film Productions — *MGM/UA Home Video*

Hysterical 1983
Comedy
65389   86 mins   C   B, V   P
The Hudson Brothers
This is a comedy about a haunted lighthouse occupied by the vengeful spirit of a spurned woman.
MPAA:PG
Gene Levy — *Embassy Home Entertainment*

I

I Am a Camera 1955
Drama
82229   99 mins   B/W   B, V   P
Julie Harris, Shelley Winters, Laurence Harvey
A young English writer develops a platonic relationship with a reckless young English girl in Berlin during the 1930's. This story formed the basis for the stage and film musical, "Cabaret."
Romulus/Remus Productions — *Monterey Home Video*

I Am a Dancer 1972
Dance/Biographical
58460   90 mins   C   B, V   P
Rudolph Nureyev, Margo Fonteyn, Carla Fracci, Lynn Seymour, Deanne Bergsma
Nureyev is seen as a pupil in ballet class, exhibiting the sweat and dedication needed.
Evdoros Demetriou — *THORN EMI/HBO Video*

I Am a Fugitive from a Chain Gang 1932
Drama
65065   90 mins   B/W   B, V   P

Paul Muni, Glenda Farrell, Helen Vinson, Preston Foster, directed by Mervyn LeRoy
An innocent man is convicted and sentenced to a Georgia chain gang, where he is brutalized and degraded. Based on a true story.
Warner Bros — Key Video; RCA VideoDiscs

I Am the Cheese   1983
Suspense
80046   95 mins   C   B, V   P
Robert Macnaughton, Hope Lange, Don Murray, Robert Wagner, Sudie Bond
When a boy undergoes psychiatric treatment in an institution, he finds out the truth about the death of his parents.
Almi Films — Vestron Video

I Confess   1953
Mystery/Drama
80080   95 mins   B/W   B, V   P
Montgomery Clift, Anne Baxter, Karl Malden, Brian Aherne, directed by Alfred Hitchcock
When a priest hears the confession of a murder, the circumstances seem to point to him as the prime suspect.
Warner Bros. — Warner Home Video

I Cover the Waterfront   1933
Drama
11234   70 mins   B/W   B, V, FO   P
Claudette Colbert, Ben Lyon, Ernest Torrance, Hobart Cavanaugh
A reporter exposes a fisherman who brings Chinese aliens into the country on his boat, or kills them when authorities are after him.
Edward Small Prods — Video Yesteryear; Movie Buff Video; Hollywood Home Theater; Video Connection; Discount Video Tapes; Western Film & Video Inc; Kartes Video Communications

I Crave the Waves   1983
Sports-Water/Documentary
66620   90 mins   C   B, V   P
Bobby Owens, Lynne Boyer, Allen Sarlo, Becky Benson
A lighthearted tour around the world to some of the most exciting surf spots in California, Hawaii, Brazil and South Africa. Twenty of the world's top surfers are seen in action and at play. An additional California skateboarding short, "Four-Wheel-Drive," is also included.
MPAA:PG
Robert Rey Walker — U.S.A. Home Video

I Dismember Mama   1974
Horror
79851   81 mins   C   B, V   R, P
Zooey Hall, Joanne Moore Jordan, Greg Mullauey, Marlene Tracy
A young man sick of his overbearing mother decides to hack her up into little pieces.

Independent — Video Gems

I Do! I Do!   1984
Musical
69923   116 mins   C   B, V   P
Lee Remick, Hal Linden
This Los Angeles production of the Broadway musical covers 50 years of a marriage, beginning just before the turn of the century. In VHS Dolby stereo and Beta Hi-Fi.
Bonnie Burns — RKO HomeVideo

I Dream Too Much   1935
Musical/Opera
52309   90 mins   B/W   B, V   P
Lily Pons, Henry Fonda, Eric Blore, Lucille Ball, Mischa Auer
A musical vehicle for opera star Lily Pons, as a French singer who falls for an American composer.
RKO — Hollywood Home Theater

I Heard the Owl Call My   1973
Name
Drama
75491   74 mins   C   V   P
Tom Courtenay, Dean Jagger
An Anglican priest meets with mystical Indian tribesmen of Northwest America.
Tomorrow Entertainment — Prism

I Killed Rasputin   1967
Drama
71068   95 mins   C   B, V   P
Geraldine Chaplin, Gert Froebe, Peter McEnery
The "Mad Monk" who rose to power before the Russian Revolution lost his life in a bizarre assassination by Felix Youssoupoff. This film deals with the friendship between the men that ended in betrayal.
Paramount — MPI Home Video

I Know Why the Caged   1978
Bird Sings
Drama
50932   96 mins   C   B, V   P
Ruby Dee, Esther Rolle, Diahann Carroll
An adaption of Maya Angelou's autobiography of a young black girl growing up in the South during the Depression.
Tomorrow Entertainment; Tom Moore — U.S.A. Home Video

I Like to Hurt People   1984
Sports
81215   80 mins   C   B, V, LV   P
The Sheik, Andre the Giant, Abdullah the Butcher, Ox Baker, Heather Feather, Dusty Rhodes
Wrestling superstars Andre the Giant, Heather Feather and Dusty Rhodes team up to

overthrow the disgusting king of the ring, The
Sheik. Not for young children or the squeamish.
Ruthless Video — *New World Video*

I Lombardi 1984
Opera
70954   126 mins   C   B, V   P
Ghena Dimitrova, Jose Carreras, Silvano
Carroli, Carlo Bini, orchestra conducted
Gianandrea Gavazzeni
After a fifty-year absence, Verdi's classic work
receives spectacular treatment on the stage of
LaScala Opera House in Milan.
Italian — *THORN EMI/HBO Video*

I Love All of You 1983
Drama/Romance
77454   103 mins   C   B, V   P
Catherine Deneuve, Jean-Louis Trintignant,
Gerard Depardieu, Serge Gainsbourg, directed
by Claude Berri
An independent career woman finds it hard to
stay with just one man. Available in Beta Hi-Fi
and VHS Stereo.
Renn Productions — *Monterey Home Video*

I Love My Wife 1970
Comedy
85774   88 mins   C   B, V   P
Elliott Gould, Brenda Vaccaro, Angel Tompkins
A husband tries to keep romance in his
suburban marriage until he is seduced, and then
his wife takes revenge.
Universal — *MCA Home Video*

I Love You 1982
Satire
60569   104 mins   C   B, V, CED   P
Sonia Braga, Paulo Cesar Pereio, directed by
Arnaldo Jabor
A man down on his luck mistakenly assumes a
woman he meets is a hooker. She plays along,
only to find that they are becoming emotionally
involved.
MPAA:R
Atlantic Releasing Corp; Brazil — *MGM/UA*
Home Video

I Love You, Alice B. 1968
Toklas
Comedy
58237   93 mins   C   B, V   P
Peter Sellers, Jo Van Fleet, Leigh Taylor-Young,
directed by Hy Averback
A straight, uptight lawyer decides to join the
peace and love generation. Screenplay by Paul
Mazursky.
Warner Bros — *Warner Home Video*

I Married a Monster from 1958
Outer Space
Horror/Science fiction
60213   78 mins   B/W   B, V   P
Tom Tryon, Gloria Talbott
The vintage thriller about a race of monster-like
aliens from another planet who try to conquer
earth.
Gene Fowler Jr — *Paramount Home Video*

I Married a Witch 1942
Comedy
50936   77 mins   B/W   B, V   R, P
Veronica Lake, Fredric March, Susan Hayward,
Broderick Crawford, directed by Rene Clair
An enchantress released from the beyond gets
romantic with a man running for governor.
AM Available
United Artists — *Lightning Video; Learning*
Corp of America

I Married a Woman 1956
Comedy
84811   84 mins   B/W   B, V   P
George Gobel, Diana Dors, Adolphe Menjou,
Nita Talbot, directed by Hal Kanter
A advertising executive marries a beautiful
blonde woman, but finds it very difficult to
balance his career and marriage.
U-1; RKO — *United Home Video*

I Married Joan 1955
Comedy
58640   50 mins   B/W   B, V, FO   P
Joan Davis, Jim Backus
Two episodes of this vintage sitcom: "Joan's
Testimonial Luncheon," in which Joan thinks
the girls in the bridge club don't like her when
they plan a surprise luncheon; and "The St.
Bernards," in which the Stevens' end up with
three unwanted canines.
NBC — *Video Yesteryear*

I Married Joan 1954
Comedy
63783   105 mins   B/W   B, V, 3/4U   P
Joan Davis, Jim Backus, Beverly Wills
Four episodes from the popular TV series, with
Joan Davis getting into mischief and mayhem:
"Joan Sees Stars," "Joan the Matchmaker,"
"Joan Throws a Wedding" and "Joan's Surprise
for Brad."
NBC — *Shokus Video*

I Never Promised You a 1977
Rose Garden
Drama
58238   90 mins   C   B, V   P
Kathleen Quinlan, Bibi Anderson, Sylvia Sidney,
Diane Varsi
A disturbed 16-year-old girl spirals down into
madness and despair while a hospital
psychiatrist struggles to bring her back to life.

MPAA:R
Imorah Productions — *Warner Home Video*

I Ought to Be in Pictures   1982
Comedy
63397   107 mins   C   B, V, CED   P
Walter Matthau, Ann-Margret, Dinah Manoff,
Lance Guest
An estranged father and daughter come to
terms in this Neil Simon comedy.
MPAA:PG
20th Century Fox — *CBS/Fox Video*

I Remember Mama   1948
Drama
07871   95 mins   B/W   B, V   P
Irene Dunne, Barbara Bel Geddes, directed by
George Stevens
A Norwegian family's life at the turn of the
century is recreated.
RKO — *Blackhawk Films; RKO HomeVideo*

I See a Dark Stranger   1947
World War II/Drama
70769   112 mins   B/W   B, V   P
Deborah Kerr, Trevor Howard, Raymond
Huntley, directed by Frank Laudner
This British spy thriller entangles Nazis, Britons,
a POW, and a treasonous Irish maiden all in
pursuit of the stolen plans for the allied invasion
of Europe.
J. Arthur Rank — *VidAmerica*

I Sent a Letter to My Love   1981
Drama
63335   102 mins   C   B, V   P
Simone Signoret, Jean Rochefort, Delphine
Seyrig
An aging spinster, faced with the lonely
prospect of the death of her crippled brother,
places a personal ad for a companion in a local
newspaper, using a different name. Unknown to
her, the brother is the one who answers it.
Atlantic Releasing — *THORN EMI/HBO Video*

I Spit on Your Grave   1980
Horror
52853   98 mins   C   B, V   P
Camille Keaton, Aaron Tabor, Richard Pace,
Anthony Nichols
A woman is ravaged by a group of four men but
gets her revenge against them with extreme
violence.
MPAA:R
Jerry Gross — *Wizard Video; Vestron Video*
(disc only)

I Stand Condemned   1936
Drama
51257   90 mins   B/W   B, V, 3/4U   R, P
Laurence Olivier, Penelope Dudley Ward,
Robert Cochran

A Russian officer is tricked into borrowing
money from a spy. He is condemned for
treason, but saved when a girl who loves him
gives herself to a profiteer.
Alexis Granowsky; Anthony Asquith — *Cable*
Films; Kartes Video Communications

I, the Jury   197?
Suspense
66075   100 mins   C   B, V, CED   P
Armand Assante, Barbara Carrera
A remake of the 1953 Mike Hammer mystery as
the famed PI investigates the murder of his best
friend.
MPAA:R
20th Century Fox — *CBS/Fox Video*

I Walked with a Zombie   1943
Horror
00316   69 mins   B/W   B, V, 3/4U   P
Frances Dee, Tom Conway, James Ellison
Suspense thriller about a nurse's experience
with a zombie on a remote tropical isle.
RKO — *Nostalgia Merchant*

I Want to Live   1958
Drama
71154   120 mins   B/W   B, V   P
Susan Hayward, Simon Oakland, Theodore
Bikel, directed by Robert Wise
A one-time "party girl" is wrongly accused of
murder and sentenced to death. Music by
Johnny Mandel.
Academy Awards '58: Best Actress (Hayward)
UA; Figaro Inc — *MGM/UA Home Video*

I Want What I Want   1972
Satire
86864   91 mins   C   B, V   P
Anne Heywood, Harry Andrews, Jill Bennett,
directed by John Dexter
A young Englishman wants to be a woman,
dresses like one, gets raped, and decides to
surgically alter his gender.
MPAA:R
Cinerama; Raymond Stross-Marayan Prpd.;
Orion — *Prism*

I Will Fight No More Forever   1975
Drama
09106   74 mins   C   B, V   R, P
James Whitmore, Ned Romero, Sam Elliott
Recounts the epic story of the legendary Chief
Joseph who led the Nez Perce tribe on an
historic 1,600-mile trek in 1877.
Stan Margulies — *Video Gems*

I Wonder Who's Killing Her Now?   1976
Comedy
30244   87 mins   C   B, V   P

Bob Dishy, Joanna Barnes, Bill Dana, Steve Franken
A husband takes a large insurance policy on his wife and then intends to kill her to collect the premium.
Dennis F. Stevens — *U.S.A. Home Video*

Iacocca: An American Profile
1985
Biographical/Documentary
84609   56 mins   C   B, V   P
Narrated by Tom Brokaw
An examination of the rise of the automobile magnate who saved Chrysler.
NBC News; Tom Spain — *RCA/Columbia Pictures Home Video*

Ice Castles
1979
Drama
44843   110 mins   C   B, V, CED   P
Robby Benson, Lynn-Holly Johnson
A young figure skater's Olympic dreams are dimmed by an accident, but her boyfriend gives her the strength, encouragement, and love necessary to perform a small miracle.
MPAA:PG
John Kemeny — *RCA/Columbia Pictures Home Video*

Ice Pirates, The
1984
Science fiction/Comedy
73364   93 mins   C   B, V   P
Robert Urich, Mary Crosby
A group of pirates steal frozen blocks of ice to fill the needs of a thirsty galaxy.
MPAA:PG
MGM UA Entertainment Co — *MGM/UA Home Video*

Ice Station Zebra
1968
Adventure
80628   150 mins   C   B, V   P
Rock Hudson, Ernest Borgnine, Patrick McGoohan, Jim Brown, Lloyd Nolan, Tony Bill, directed by John Sturges
A nuclear submarine crew races Soviet seamen to find a piece of film from a Russian satellite hidden under a polar ice cap. Music by Michel Legrand. Available in VHS and Beta Hi-Fi.
MPAA:G
MGM — *MGM/UA Home Video*

Iceland River Challenge
1986
Travel/Wildlife
Closed Captioned
84784   50 mins   C   B, V, LV   P
Twelve explorers run a wild Icelandic river in this chillingly flowing production.
National Geographic — *Vestron Video*

Iceman
1984
Drama
73184   101 mins   C   B, V, LV   P
Timothy Hutton, Lindsay Crouse, directed by Fred Schepisi
Timothy Hutton and Lindsay Crouse star as a pair of scientists who find a frozen prehistoric man in a glacier and try to bring him back to life.
MPAA:PG
Patrick Palmer; Norman Jewison — *MCA Home Video*

I'd Give My Life
1936
Mystery
85502   73 mins   B/W   B, V   P
Sir Guy Standing, Frances Drake, Tom Brown, Janet Beecher
A gangster, whose ex-wife is presently married to the governor, tries to use their honest but framed son to blackmail her.
Paramount — *Video Yesteryear*

Idaho
1943
Western
29438   70 mins   B/W   B, V   P
Roy Rogers, Harry J. Shannon, Virginia Grey
A cowboy and a ranger vie for the affections of the daughter of an ex-thief turned philanthropist.
Republic — *Captain Bijou; Video Connection*

Idiot's Delight
1939
Comedy
82115   107 mins   B/W   B, V   P
Clark Gable, Norma Shearer, Burgess Meredith, Edward Arnold, directed by Clarence Brown
At an Alpine hotel, a song and dance man meets a gorgeous Russian countess who reminds him of a former lover. Gable performs "Puttin' on the Ritz."
MGM — *MGM/UA Home Video*

Idomeneo
1982
Opera
71138   185 mins   C   B, V   P
Luciano Pavarotti, Ileana Contrubas, Hildegard Behrens, Frederica von Stade, John Alexander, James Levine directing the Metropolitan Opera Orchestra and Chorus
Jean-Pierre Ponnelle produced this lavish setting of the early Mozartian opera for the "live from the Met" series. In threatening seas, Idomeneo promises Neptune a sacrifice of the first human he sees on shore. He sees his son. Recorded in HiFi Stereo. Subtitled.
PBS; The Metropolitan Opera — *Paramount Home Video*

Idomeneo
1983
Opera
86898   181 mins   C   B, V   P
Yvonne Kenny, Carol Vaness, Philip Langridge, Jerry Hadley

Conducted by Bernard Haitink, the
Glyndebourne Festival Opera performs Mozart's
classic opera.
Trevor Nunn; Christopher Swann; Glyndebourne
Festival Opera — *THORN EMI/HBO Video*

If...   1969
Drama
64026   111 mins   C   B, V   P
*Malcolm McDowell, David Wood, Christine
Noonan, Richard Warwick*
Three unruly seniors at a British boarding school
refuse to conform.
MPAA:R
Paramount — *Paramount Home Video*

If Things Were Different   1979
Drama
77152   96 mins   C   B, V   P
*Suzzane Pleshette, Tony Roberts, Arte
Johnson, Chuck McCann, Don Murray*
A woman must struggle to hold her family
together after her husband is hospitalized with a
nervous breakdown.
Bob Banner Associates — *Worldvision Home
Video*

If You Can Walk/Free and   1979
Easy/Race Day
Sports-Winter
84272   45 mins   C   B, V   P
Martha Rockwell, Ned Gillete, Mike Brady
Three short films, back to back, bombard the
viewer with both instruction and entertainment
about cross-country skiing.
Video Travel Inc — *Video Travel*

If You Could See What I   1982
Hear
Comedy-Drama
64032   103 mins   C   B, V, LV,   P
                             CED
*Marc Singer, R. H. Thomson, Sarah Torgov,
Shari Belafonte Harper*
The true-life story of blind singer-musician Tom
Sullivan covers his life from college days to
marriage. His refusal to acknowledge his
limitations led to many incidents, some hilarious,
some tragic.
MPAA:PG
Jensen Farley Pictures; Cypress Grove
Productions — *Vestron Video*

If You Don't Stop   198?
It...You'll Go Blind
Comedy/Variety
82491   80 mins   C   B, V   P
Pat McCormick, George Spencer
A series of gauche and tasteless vignettes from
various little-known comedians.
MPAA:R
Media — *Media Home Entertainment*

If You Knew Susie   1948
Musical
29485   90 mins   B/W   B, V   P, T
*Eddie Cantor, Joan Davis, Allyn Joslyn, Charles
Dingle*
Two retired vaudeville actors living in a New
England town are not accepted socially, that is
until a letter from George Washington
establishes them as descendants of a colonial
patriot. They travel to Washington to claim
$7,000,000,000 from the government.
RKO, Eddie Cantor — *Blackhawk Films*

Igor and the Lunatics   1985
Horror
88232   79 mins   C   B, V   P
*Joseph Eero, Joe Niola, T.J. Michaels, directed
by Billy Parolini*
A murderous cult leader is released from prison
after a long sentence for harassing a small town
and picks up where he left off.
MPAA:R
Troma Inc. — *Lightning Video*

Ike and Tina Turner   197?
Show, The
Music-Performance
84789   21 mins   C   B, V   P
A classic concert film featuring rare behind-the-
scenes footage.
Jaybar Ent — *Vestron Video*

Ikiru   1952
Drama
79908   143 mins   B/W   B, V   P
*Takashi Shimura, Kyoko Seki, directed by Akira
Kurasowa*
When a clerk finds out he is dying of cancer, he
decides to build a children's playground. With
English subtitles.
JA
Toho Films — *Video Dimensions; Media Home
Entertainment*

Il Poverello: The Story of   1985
St. Francis of Assisi
History-Medieval
82562   52 mins   C   B, V, 3/4U   P
*Narrated by Robert Long, directed by Peter
Batty*
This film, shot on location in Assisi, Rome, and
Canterbury, details the history of St. Francis and
his order of Franciscan monks.
Peter Batty — *Evergreen International*

Ill Met by Moonlight   1959
War-Drama
62866   104 mins   B/W   B, V   P
*Dirk Bogarde, Marius Goring, David Oxley, Cyril
Cusack*
During the German occupation of Crete, a group
of British agents attempt to capture a Nazi
general.

Rank; Lopert Films — *Embassy Home Entertainment*

Illustrated Man, The   1969
Fantasy/Science fiction
84540   103 mins   C   B, V   P
Rod Steiger, Claire Bloom, Robert Drivas, Don Dubbins, directed by Jack Smight
An adaptation of the Ray Bradbury book in which a wanderer envisions strange tales which form on a man's completely tattooed back.
MPAA:PG
Howard B Kreitsek; Ted Mann — *Warner Home Video*

Il Trovatore   1985
Opera
88133   138 mins   C   B, V   P
Dame Joan Sutherland, conducted by Richard Bonynge
The Elizabethan Sydney Opera performs the classic Verdi opera, in Italian with English subtitles.
IT
The Australian Opera — *Sony Video Software*

I'm A Fool   1977
Romance
84033   38 mins   C   B, V   P
Ron Howard, Amy Irving, directed by Noel Black
A two-character romantic study involving an act of insincerity between two race-track aficionados. Part of the American Short Story Collection.
Dan McCann — *Monterey Home Video*

I'm All Right Jack   1959
Comedy
33958   101 mins   B/W   B, V   P
Peter Sellers, Ian Carmichael, Terry-Thomas
A shop steward is caught between two sides in a crooked financial scam in this satire on labor-management relations.
British Lion — *THORN EMI/HBO Video*

I'm Dancing as Fast as I Can   1982
Drama
64027   107 mins   C   B, V, LV   P
Jill Clayburgh, Nicol Williamson, Geraldine Page
A successful television producer becomes hopelessly dependent on tranquilizers.
MPAA:R
Paramount — *Paramount Home Video*

I'm on My Way/The Non-Stop Kid   191?
Comedy
59990   30 mins   B/W   B, V   P, T
Harold Lloyd, Snub Pollard, Bebe Daniels
A Harold Lloyd double feature. Two classic shorts: "I'm on My Way" (1919), in which

---

Harold's dreams of an idyllic marriage are shattered, and "The Non-Stop Kid" (1918), in which Harold must contend with a rival for the affection of his beloved. Silent.
Hal Roach — *Blackhawk Films*

Image of Bruce Lee, The   197?
Martial arts/Adventure
53944   88 mins   C   B, V   P
Bruce Li, Chang Wu Lang, Chang Lei, Dana
Martial arts fight scenes prevail in this story about a jeweler who is swindled out of $1 million worth of diamonds.
MPAA:G
Alex Gouw — *Media Home Entertainment*

Image of Passion   1986
Romance/Drama
71240   90 mins   C   V   P
Introduced by Louis Jourdan
A male stripper meets a lovely advertising executive and they enter into a romantic affair.
Commworld; Romance Theater — *Prism*

Imagemaker, The   1986
Drama
88027   93 mins   C   B, V   P
Michael Nouri, Jerry Orbach, Jessica Harper, Farley Granger
A Presidential media consultant bucks the system and exposes corruption.
MPAA:R
Castle Hill Prod. — *Vestron Video*

Imagine: John Lennon   1972
Musical
88138   55 mins   C   B, V   P
A film of Lennon's solo album, featuring psychedelic video images accompanying each song.
John Lennon; Picture Music — *Sony Video Software*

Imitation of Life   1959
Drama
82075   124 mins   C   B, V   P
Lana Turner, John Gavin, Troy Donahue, Sandra Dee, Juanita Moore, Susan Kohner, directed by Douglas Sirk
A beautiful actress' life is chock full of complications as she discovers that both she and her daughter are in love with the same man. Available in VHS and Beta Hi-Fi Mono.
Ross Hunter; Universal Studies — *MCA Home Video*

Immigrant, The   1917
Comedy
10642   20 mins   B/W   B, V, 3/4U   R, P, DL

Charlie Chaplin

Chaplin portrays a newly arrived immigrant who
falls in love with the first girl he meets. (Silent;
musical soundtrack added.)
RKO — Cable Films; Festival Films

Immortal Bachelor, The   1980
Comedy
80934   94 mins   C   B, V   P
Giancarlo Giannini, Monica Vitti, Claudia
Cardinale, Vittorio Gassman
This film tells the bawdy tale of a cleaning
woman who murders her philandering husband.
MPAA:PG
S.J. International Pictures — VidAmerica

Immortal Battalion   1944
War-Drama
57355   89 mins   B/W   B, V, FO   P
David Niven, Stanley Holloway, Reginald Tate,
Peter Ustinov, directed by Carol Reed
The story of how newly-recruited civilians are
molded into a hardened batallion of fighting
men.
J Arthur Rank; 20th Century Fox — Hal Roach
Studios; Video Yesteryear; Discount Video
Tapes; World Video Pictures

Impact   1949
Drama
58545   83 mins   B/W   B, V, 3/4U   P
Brian Donlevy, Ella Raines, directed by Arthur
Lubin
A woman and her lover plan the murder of her
rich industrialist husband, but the plan backfires
and he survives.
United Artists — Movie Buff Video; Hal Roach
Studios; Discount Video Tapes

Imperial Venus   1971
Adventure/Biographical
84030   121 mins   C   B, V   P
Gina Lollabrigida, Stephen Boyd, Raymond
Pellegrin, directed by Jean Delannoy
A romantically-inclined biography of Napoleon's
sister, Paolina Boneparte—her loves, lusts and
tribulations.
MPAA:PG
Guido Giambartolomei — United Home Video

Importance of Being   1939
Donald, The
Cartoons
85535   25 mins   C   B, V   P
Animated
Three vintage Disney Donald Duck shorts from
the early days of World War II: "Donald's Better
Self," "Polar Trappers" and "Timber."
Walt Disney — Walt Disney Home Video

Improper Channels   1982
Comedy
63361   91 mins   C   B, V, LV,   P
                                     CED
Alan Arkin, Mariette Hartley
A man launches an all-out attack on the world of
computers.
MPAA:PG
Alfred Pariser; Maury Ravinsky — Vestron
Video

Impulse   1984
Drama
76763   95 mins   C   B, V, CED   P
Tim Matheson, Meg Tilly, Hume Cronyn, John
Karlen, Claude Earl Jones
The residents of a small town start to act very
strangely when toxic waste turns up in their milk.
MPAA:R
Tim Zinnemann; Twentieth Century
Fox — Vestron Video

In Cold Blood   1967
Drama
13257   133 mins   B/W   B, V   P
Robert Blake, Scott Wilson, John Forsythe,
directed by Richard Brooks
Truman Capote's factual novel provided the
basis for this hard-hitting film about two misfit
ex-cons who murdered a Kansas family in 1959.
Columbia — RCA/Columbia Pictures Home
Video

In-Laws, The   1979
Comedy
38949   103 mins   C   B, V   P
Peter Falk, Alan Arkin, directed by Arthur Hiller
A wild comedy with Peter Falk as a CIA agent
and Alan Arkin as a dentist who becomes
involved in Falk's crazy adventures.
MPAA:PG
Warner Bros — Warner Home Video; RCA
VideoDiscs

In Love With An Older   1982
Woman
Comedy/Romance
72455   100 mins   C   B, V   P
John Ritter, Karen Carlson
This movie shows the social difficulties that
arise when a man dates an outgoing woman
who is fifteen years his senior.
Poundridge Prods Ltd; Charles Fries
Prods — U.S.A. Home Video

In Name Only   1939
Drama
10053   102 mins   B/W   B, V   P, T
Carole Lombard, Cary Grant, Kay Francis
Heartless woman marries for wealth and
prestige and holds her husband to loveless
marriage.

RKO; John Cromwell — *Blackhawk Films; RKO HomeVideo*

In Old California 1942
Western
66312 89 mins B/W B, V P
John Wayne, Patsy Kelly, Binnie Barnes, Albert Dekker
A young Boston pharmacist searches for success in the California gold rush.
Republic — *Republic Pictures Home Video*

In Old Cheyenne 1941
Western
49175 60 mins B/W B, V, 3/4U P
Roy Rogers, Gabby Hayes
Bank holdups, cattle rustling, fist fights, and even car crashes mix with some good ol' guitar plunking in this "modern day" western.
Republic — *Cable Films*

In Old New Mexico 1945
Western
11264 60 mins B/W B, V P
Duncan Renaldo, Martin Garralaga, Gwen Kenyon, Pedro de Cordoba
The Cisco Kid and Pancho reveal the murderer of an old woman—a mysterious doctor who was after an inheritance.
United Artists — *United Home Video; Video Yesteryear*

In Old Santa Fe 1934
Western
11785 60 mins B/W B, V P
Ken Maynard
Action western starring Ken Maynard—veteran of the plains.
Mascot — *Video Connection; Discount Video Tapes; Video Yesteryear; United Home Video*

In Praise of Older Women 1978
Comedy
09096 110 mins C B, V, LV, CED P
Karen Black, Tom Berenger, Susan Strasberg, Helen Shaver
A Hungarian "boy," 12-years-old, is corrupted by World War II. Based on a novel by Stephen Vizinczey.
Astral Films; Astral Bellevue Pathe and RSL Prod — *Embassy Home Entertainment; RCA VideoDiscs*

In Search of Historic Jesus 1979
Speculation/Religion
48476 91 mins C B, V P
John Rubenstein, John Anderson, narrated by Brad Crandall
The story attempts to pull together a careful tabulation of data about Jesus Christ, who was hardly known to the historians of his time.
MPAA:PG
Schick Sunn Classic — *United Home Video; Lucerne Films*

In Search of Noah's Ark 1976
Bible/Documentary
35373 95 mins C B, V P
Narrated by Brad Crandell
This documentary covers research and information gathered during the last 5,000 years concerning the story of Noah and the universal flood.
Sunn Classic — *United Home Video; Lucerne Films*

In Search of the Castaways 1962
Adventure
66318 98 mins C B, V P
Hayley Mills, Maurice Chevalier, George Sanders, Wilfrid Hyde-White
A teenage girl and her younger brother search for their father, a ship's captain who was reportedly lost at sea years earlier. Based on a story by Jules Verne.
Buena Vista — *Walt Disney Home Video*

In the Company of Men 1964
Minorities/Labor and unions
88382 28 mins C B, V, 3/4U R, P
A document of communication breakdown between foremen and minority workers, and how it can be fixed.
AM Available
Your World Video — *Your World Video*

In the Days of the Thundering Herd & The Law and the Outlaw 1914
Western
77368 76 mins B/W B, V P, T
Tom Mix, Myrtle Stedman, directed by Tom Mix
2 pgms
In the first feature pony express rider sacrifices his job to accompany his sweetheart on a westward trek to meet her father. In the second show, a fugitive falls in love with a rancher's daughter and risks recognition.
Selig Polyscope — *Blackhawk Films*

In the Good Old Summertime 1949
Musical
85637 104 mins C B, V P
Judy Garland, Van Johnson, S.Z. Sakall, Buster Keaton, Spring Byington, Liza Minnelli, Clinton Sundberg, directed by Robert Z. Leonard
This musical version of "The Shop Around the Corner" tells the story of two bickering co-

workers who are also anonymous lovelorn pen pals. Liza Minnelli made her screen debut at 18 months in the film's final scene.
MGM — *MGM/UA Home Video*

In the Heat of the Night   1967
Drama
37525   109 mins   C   CED   P
Sidney Poitier, Rod Steiger, Warren Oates, Lee Grant, directed by Norman Jewison
A wealthy industrialist in a small Mississippi town is murdered. A black man is accused, but when it is discovered that he is a homicide expert, he is asked to help solve the murder, despite resentment of the part of the town's chief of police.
Academy Awards '67: Best Picture; Best Actor (Steiger); Best Screenplay; Best Film Editing; Best Sound.
United Artists, Walter Mirisch — *CBS/Fox Video; RCA VideoDiscs*

In the King of Prussia   1982
Nuclear energy/Public affairs
74068   92 mins   C   B, V   P
Martin Sheen, Daniel Berrigan
This is a stirring recreation of the trial of the "Plowshares Eight" who were jailed for sabotaging two nuclear missiles at an electric plant in Pennsylvania.
Emile de Antonio — *MPI Home Video; Bullfrog Films; New Video Center*

In Which We Serve   1942
War-Drama
59833   114 mins   B/W   B, V   P
Noel Coward, John Mills, Bernard Miles, directed by Noel Coward
The spirit of the British Navy in World War II is captured in this classic about the sinking of the destroyer HMS Torrin during the Battle of Crete.
Noel Coward — *Embassy Home Entertainment*

Incantation: The Best of   1986
Incantation
Music-Performance
84935   55 mins   C   B, V   P
A performance by the acclaimed classical, South American folk-music-playing British group.
Tony Morrison; Bill Gamon — *Passport Music Video*

Incas Remembered, The   1985
History/South America
88159   60 mins   C   B, V   P
A look at the ancient Incan civilization from its beginnings to its demise at the hands of the invading Spaniards.
Lucy Jarvis — *Monterey Home Video*

Inch High Private Eye   1973
Cartoons
82160   60 mins   C   B, V   P
Animated
Inch High is the world's smallest private eye who solves mysteries for the Finkerton Organization.
Hanna-Barbera — *Worldvision Home Video*

Incoming Freshmen   1979
Comedy
47851   84 mins   C   B, V   P
Ashley Vaughn, Leslie Blalock, Richard Harriman, Jim Overbey
A young innocent girl discovers sex when she enrolls in a liberal co-ed institution.
MPAA:R
Cannon Films — *MCA Home Video*

L'Incoronazione Di   1984
Poppea
Opera
70962   148 mins   C   B, V   P
"The Coronation of Poppea," completed by Claudio Monteverdi the year before he died in 1643, tells the story of the seductress Poppea's love affair with Nero, the Roman Emperor. Baroque authority Raymond Leppard conducts at the Glyndebourne Festival Opera.
BBC-TV — *THORN EMI/HBO Video*

Incredible Agent of   1980
Stingray, The
Science fiction
74425   93 mins   C   B, V   P
Animated
Captain Troy Tempest and the Stingray crew take an underwater voyage to rescue a beautiful woman kept prisoner in Titanica.

Incredible Hulk, Volume II, The   1985
Cartoons
70598   70 mins   C   B, V   P
Animated
In this trio of cartoons from the TV series, the great green man battles gigantic mice, spiders and lizards; the huge and hungry Gammatron monster; and his arch-nemesis Dr. Octopus.
Marvel Productions — Prism

Incredible Human Machine, The   1981
Biology
Closed Captioned
86349   60 mins   C   B, V, LV   P
A fascinating documentary which shows exactly how the human body performs some of its assorted functions.
National Geographic Society — Vestron Video

ITC Entertainment — Family Home Entertainment

Incredible Book Escape, The   1984
Language arts/Literature
73647   50 mins   C   B, V   P
Quinn Cummings and Voices of Ruth Buzzi, Arte Johnson, Tammy Grimes
When a young girl gets trapped in a library some of the characters from the books come to life.
Bosustow Entertainment; Asselin Productions — Kartes Video Communications

Incredible Detectives, The   1979
Adventure/Cartoons
80643   23 mins   C   B, V   P
Animated
A dog, a cat and a crow team up to search for a boy who has been kidnapped by a trio of hoods.
Ruby-Spears — Worldvision Home Video

Incredible Hulk, The   1977
Adventure/Science fiction
58631   100 mins   C   B, V   P
Bill Bixby, Susan Sullivan, Lou Ferrigno, Jack Colvin
A scientist achieves superhuman strength after he is exposed to a massive dose of gamma rays. The pilot for the television series.
Universal TV — MCA Home Video

Incredible Hulk, Volume I, The   1985
Cartoons
77162   70 mins   C   B, V   P
Animated
The secret origin of the Hulk is told in this collection of three episodes from the animated series.
Marvel Productions — Prism

Incredible Journey, The   1963
Adventure/Animals
72795   80 mins   C   B, V   P
A labrador retriever, bull terrier and Siamese cat mistake their caretakers intentions when he leaves for a hunting trip, believing he will never return. The three set out on a 250 mile adventure-filled trek across Canada's rugged terrain.
Walt Disney Productions; Buena Vista — Walt Disney Home Video

Incredible Journey of Dr. Meg Laurel, The   1979
Drama
80385   143 mins   C   B, V   P
Lindsay Wagner, Jane Wyman, Dorothy McGuire, James Woods, Gary Lockwood
A young doctor leaves her Boston family to bring modern medicine to the Appalachian mountain people during the 1930's.
Paul Radin — RCA/Columbia Pictures Home Video

Incredible Master Beggars   1982
Martial arts
64945   88 mins   C   B, V   R, P
Tan Tao Liang, Ku Feng, Han Kuo Tsai, Li Tang Ming, Li Hai Sheng, Lui I Fan, Pan Yao Kun
Against all odds, the Beggars challenge the Great Iron Master, using "Tam Leg" tactics versus the "Iron Cloth" fighting style.
MPAA:R
L and T Films Corp Ltd — Video Gems

Incredible Melting Man, The   1977
Horror/Science fiction
71125   85 mins   C   B, V   P

*Alex Rebar, Burr De Benning, Rainbeaux Smith,
directed by William Sachs*
Two transformations change an astronaut's life
after his return to earth. First, his skin starts to
melt. Then, he feels cannibalistic. Special
effects by Rick Baker.
MPAA:R
Orion; American International — *Vestron Video*

Incredible Rocky   1977
Mountain Race, The
Adventure/Comedy
65761   97 mins   C   B, V   P
*Christopher Connelly, Forrest Tucker, Larry
Storch, Mike Mazurki*
The townspeople of St. Joseph, fed up with
Mark Twain's destructive feud with a neighbor,
devise a shrewd scheme to rid the town of the
troublemakers.
Robert Stabler — *Magnum Entertainment*

Incredible Shrinking   1981
Woman, The
Comedy
55548   88 mins   C   B, V, LV   P
*Lily Tomlin, Charles Grodin, Ned Beatty, Henry
Gibson*
A model homemaker and perfect mother and
wife discovers that she is shrinking due to a
unique blood condition that is effected by the
chemicals found in her household products.
MPAA:PG
Universal; Hank Moonjean — *MCA Home
Video*

Incubus, The   1982
Horror
63969   90 mins   C   B, V, LV,   P
                            CED
*John Cassavetes, Kerrie Keane, Helen Hughes,
Erin Flannery, John Ireland*
A doctor and his teenaged daughter settle in a
quiet New England community, only to
encounter the incubus, a terrifying, supernatural
demon.
MPAA:R
Artists Releasing Corp; Mark
Boyman — *Vestron Video*

Indecent Obsession, An   1985
War-Drama
86606   100 mins   C   B, V   P
Wendy Hughes, Bill Hunter, Bruno Lawrence
Colleen McCullough's bestseller tells about a
wartime asylum on the day the Japanese
surrendered, the same day a stranger enters the
ward and upsets everyone.
Ian Bradley; P.B.L. Prod. — *Hal Roach Studios*

Independence   1976
History-US
70586   30 mins   C   B, V   P

*Eli Wallach, Anne Jackson, Pat Hingle, Patrick
O'Neal, directed by John Huston, narrated by
E.G. Marshall*
This program dramaticaly recreates the
debates, concerns, and events that led up to the
U.S. Declaration of Independence in 1776.
Joyce and Lloyd Ritter — *MPI Home Video*

Independence Day   1983
Drama
68234   110 mins   C   B, V   P
Kathleen Quinlan, David Keith
Kathleen Quinlan stars as a small town
photographer who falls in love with a racing car
enthusiast.
MPAA:R
Warner Brothers — *Warner Home Video*

Indiscreet   1931
Comedy
58528   81 mins   B/W   B, V, 3/4U   P
*Gloria Swanson, Ben Lyon, Barbara Kent,
directed by Leo McCarey*
A fashion designer's past catches up with her
when her ex-lover starts romancing her sister.
Gloria sings "If You Haven't Got Love" and
other songs.
United Artists; Artcinema — *Festival Films;
Video Yesteryear; Discount Video Tapes; Kartes
Video Communications*

Indiscreet   1958
Comedy
66464   100 mins   C   B, V   P
*Cary Grant, Ingrid Bergman, Phyllis Calvert,
directed by Stanley Donen*
An American diplomat in London falls in love
with an actress but protects himself by saying
he is married.
Grandon; Stanley Donen — *Republic Pictures
Home Video*

Indiscretion of an   1954
American Wife
Romance
65410   63 mins   C   B, V   P
Jennifer Jones, Montgomery Clift
Set almost entirely in Rome's famous Terminal
Station, the romance centers arount an ill-fated
couple facing a turning point in their lives. They
have only hours to decide whether they can
have a future together, or whether Jones will go
back to the United States and rejoin her
husband.
Columbia — *CBS/Fox Video; Discount Video
Tapes*

Inferno   1978
Horror
81968   83 mins   C   B, V   P
*Leigh McCloskey, Elenora Giorgi, Irene Miracle,
Sacha Pitoeff*

A young man arrives in New York to investigate the mysterious circumstances surrounding his sister's death. Available in VHS and Beta Hi-Fi Stereo.
D Argente — *Key Video*

Infierno de los Pobres, El   197?
Drama
63856   98 mins   B/W   B, V   P
Rosa Camina, Jorge Mondragon, directed by Juan Orol
An abandoned woman creates a world of false illusions. In Spanish.
SP
Mexican — *Hollywood Home Theater*

Informer, The   1935
Drama
00262   91 mins   B/W   B, V, 3/4U   P
Victor McLaglen, directed by John Ford
Tells of a hard-drinking man who informs on a buddy to collect a reward during the Irish Rebellion.
Academy Award '35: Best Actor (McLaglen); N.Y. Film Critics '35: Best Film amd Director.
RKO; John Ford — *Nostalgia Merchant; King of Video*

Infra-Man   1976
Science fiction
80286   89 mins   C   B, V   P
Infra-man is a bionic warrior who must destroy the Demon Princess and her army of prehistoric monsters in order to save the galaxy.
MPAA:PG
Joseph Brenner Associates — *Prism*

Ingles, Ingles   1984
Languages-Instruction
73569   60 mins   C   B, V   P
This program is a survival course in English for people who speak Spanish.
AM Available
Language Plus Inc — *Language Plus*

Ingrid: Portrait of a Star   1980
Biographical/Documentary
75507   70 mins   C   B, V   P
Narrated by Sir John Gielgud
This program traces the life of legendary screen star Ingrid Bergman. Portions of the program are in black and white.
Wombat Productions — *MPI Home Video; Wombat Productions*

Inherit the Wind   1960
Drama
64562   127 mins   B/W   B, V, LV   P
Spencer Tracy, Fredric March, Florence Eldridge, Gene Kelly, Dick York, directed by Stanley Kramer
A courtroom drama based on the 1925 Scopes "Monkey Trial," where a schoolteacher was indicted for teaching Darwin's Theory of Evolution to his students.
United Artists; Stanley Kramer — *CBS/Fox Video; RCA VideoDiscs*

Inheritance, The   1976
Drama
52953   121 mins   C   B, V   P
Anthony Quinn, Fabio Testi, Dominique Sanda
A poor woman who hungers for fortune marries into a wealthy family. After becoming the sole heiress, the family unites against her.
MPAA:R
Titanus; Gianni Hecht Lucari — *VidAmerica*

Inheritors, The   1985
Drama
81451   89 mins   C   B, V   P
Nikolas Vogel, Roger Schauer, Klaus Novak, Johanna Tomek, directed by Walter Bannert
A young German boy becomes involved in with a neo-Nazi group as his home life deteriorates in 1938. Available in German with English subtitles or dubbed into English.
GE
Island Alive — *Embassy Home Entertainment*

Initiation, The   1984
Horror
80051   97 mins   C   B, V   P
Vera Miles, Clu Gulager, James Read, Daphne Zuniga
There are plenty of surprises in store for a group of sorority pledges as they break into a department store to steal a security guard's uniform
MPAA:R
New World Pictures — *THORN EMI/HBO Video*

Initiation of Sarah, The   1978
Suspense/Mystery
79171   100 mins   C   B, V   P
Kay Lenz, Robert Hays, Shelley Winters, Kathryn Crosby, Morgan Fairchild, Tony Bill
A college freshman joins a strange sorority after every other one on campus has rejected her.
Stonehenge/Charles Fries Productions — *Worldvision Home Video*

Inn of the Sixth Happiness, The   1958
Drama
66068   158 mins   C   B, V, CED   P
Ingrid Bergman, Curt Jurgens, Robert Donat
The life of Gladys Aylward, an English servant girl who becomes a missionary in 1930's China, provides the basis of this story.
20th Century Fox — *CBS/Fox Video*

Innocent, The   1978
Drama
39077   115 mins   C   B, V, CED   P
*Laura Antonelli, Jennifer O'Neill, Giancarlo
Giannini, directed by Luchino Visconti*
Visconti's last film is the story of a husband who
is drawn between the love of his faithful wife and
his mistress, in turn-of-the-century Rome.
Filmed on location in Italy; English language
version.
MPAA:R
Italy — *Vestron Video*

Innocents in Paris   1953
Comedy
82235   89 mins   B/W   B, V   P
*Alastair Sim, Laurence Harvey, Jimmy Edwards,
Claire Bloom*
This film chronicles the comic adventures of a
group of seven Britons who visit Paris for a
weekend.
Anatole De Grunwald — *Monterey Home
Video*

Insanity   1982
Suspense
85233   101 mins   C   B, V   P
Terence Stamp, Fernando Rey, Corinne Cleary
A film director becomes violently obsessed with
a beautiful actress.
Unknown — *Mogul Communications*

Inside Hitchcock   1984
Film/History
70584   55 mins   C   B, V   P
Narrated by Cliff Robertson
This documentary reveals much about one of
America's best loved film makers. Scenes from
his movies and his last interview enliven this
informative program.
Richard Schickel — *MPI Home Video*

Inside Moves   1980
Drama
55457   113 mins   C   B, V   P
*John Savage, Diana Scarwid, David Morse,
directed by Richard Donner*
A look at handicapped citizens trying to make it
in everyday life, focusing on the relationship
between an insecure, failed suicide and a
volatile man who is only a knee operation away
from a dreamed-about basketball career.
MPAA:PG
Goodmark Productions — *CBS/Fox Video*

Inside Out   1975
Adventure
76854   98 mins   C   B, V   P
*Telly Savalas, Robert Culp, James Mason, Aldo
Ray, Doris Kunstmann*
An ex-GI, a jewel thief and a German POW
camp commandant band together to find a
stolen shipment of Nazi gold from behind the
Iron curtain.
MPAA:PG
Kettledrum Productions, Warner
Bros. — *Warner Home Video*

Inside the Lines   1930
Drama
66136   73 mins   B/W   B, V, FO   P
*Betty Compson, Montagu Love, Mischa Auer,
Ralph Forbes*
A World War I tale of espionage and counter-
espionage.
RKO — *Video Yesteryear*

Insignificance   1985
Drama
87907   110 mins   C   B, V   P
*Gary Busey, Tony Curtis, Theresa Russell,
Michael Emil, directed by Nicholas Roeg*
A strange film about an imaginary, raucous and
carnal night spent in a New York hotel by Albert
Einstein, Marilyn Monroe, Joe McCarthy and
Joe DiMaggio.
Jeremy Thomas; Island Alive — *Karl/Lorimar
Home Video*

Inspector Gadget   1984
Cartoons
84706   44 mins   C   B, V   P
2 pgms
These two volumes feature adventures by the
resourceful animated sleuth.
DIC Ent/Field Communications
Corp — *Karl/Lorimar Home Video*

Inspector Gadget Series   1983
Cartoons
74079   60 mins   C   B, V   P
Animated, the voice of Don Adams
Comedian Don Adams lends his voice to the
impeccable Inspector Gadget, who, along with
his trusted companions Penny and Brain, go up
against the evil Dr. Claw.
Dic Enterprises — *Family Home Entertainment*

Inspector General, The   1949
Comedy
59663   97 mins   C   B, V   P
*Danny Kaye, Walter Slezak, Barbara Bates, Elsa
Lanchester*
A classic Danny Kaye vehicle of mistaken
identities with the master comic portraying a
carnival medicine man who is mistaken by the
villagers for their feared Inspector General.
Warner Bros — *Prism; Media Home
Entertainment; Hollywood Home Theater; Video
Yesteryear; Cable Films; Discount Video Tapes;
King of Video; Video Connection; Hal Roach
Studios; Kartes Video Communications*

Installing a Lockset   1984
Home improvement
77263   30 mins   C   B, V   P
Carpenter George Giangrante demonstrates the
basics of installing almost any lockset.
You Can Do It Videos — *You Can Do It Videos*

Installing a Pre-Hung   1984
Door
Home improvement
77262   30 mins   C   B, V   P
This is a step by step demonstration of how to
successfully install a pre-hung door.
You Can Do It Videos — *You Can Do It Videos*

Installing a Suspended   1984
Ceiling
Home improvement
Closed Captioned
77264   30 mins   C   B, V   P
A step by step demonstration of how to install a
suspended ceiling.
You Can Do It Videos — *You Can Do It Videos*

Installing Insulation and   1984
Sheetrock
Home improvement
Closed Captioned
77260   30 mins   C   B, V   P
The procedures for installing insulation and
sheetrock are demonstrated by carpenter
George Giangrante.
You Can Do It Videos — *You Can Do It Videos*

Instructor, The   1983
Suspense
82450   91 mins   C   B, V   P
Bob Chaney, Bob Saal, Lynday Scharnott
The head of a karate school proves the value of
his skill when threatened by the owner of a rival
school.
American Eagle Productions — *Vestron Video*

Interface   1984
Suspense
82468   88 mins   C   B, V   P
John Davies, Laura Lane, Matthew Sacks
A computer game gets out of hand at a
university. The tunnels beneath the campus
become a battleground of good and evil.
Filmworks — *Vestron Video*

Intermezzo   1939
Drama/Romance
69385   70 mins   B/W   B, V, CED   P
Ingrid Bergman, Leslie Howard
A married violinist falls in love with his protege,
but while on a concert tour of Europe together,
his longing for the family he left behind
overshadows their happiness.
Selznick — *CBS/Fox Video*

International Circus   1935
Revue
Circus
84937   46 mins   B/W   B, V   P
A compilation of footage of the old-fashioned
circuses from the 20's and 30's, including the
best Russian and Spanish acts.
Unknown — *Blackhawk Films*

International Velvet   1978
Drama
66452   126 mins   C   B, V   P
*Tatum O'Neal, Anthony Hopkins, Christopher
Plummer*
In this sequel to "National Velvet," a young
orphan overcomes all obstacles and becomes
an internationally renowned horsewoman.
MPAA:PG
Byron Forbes Productions — *MGM/UA Home
Video*

Internecine Project, The   1973
Mystery/Drama
Closed Captioned
82273   89 mins   C   B, V   P
*James Coburn, Lee Grant, Harry Andrews,
Keenan Wynn, directed by Ken Hughes*
A tycoon masterminds an unusual series of
murders in order to eliminate four people.
Available in VHS and Beta Hi-Fi.
MPAA:PG
Allied Artists — *CBS/Fox Video*

Intimate Moments   1982
Drama
66044   82 mins   C   B, V   P
Alexandra Stewart, Dirke Altevogt
Madame Claude runs an exclusive call-girl
operation catering to the upper echelons of
power in France, when she discovers that a
newspaper is investigating her business.
MPAA:R
Claire Duval — *Embassy Home Entertainment*

Intimate Strangers   1977
Drama
84085   96 mins   C   B, V   P
*Dennis Weaver, Sally Struthers, Quinn
Cummins, Tyne Daly, Larry Hagman, directed by
John Llewellyn*
A made-for-TV expose on wife beating, and its
effects on the children as well as the marriage
involved.
Charles Fries Productions — *Worldvision
Home Video*

Into the Night   1985
Comedy/Adventure
Closed Captioned
80848   115 mins   C   B, V, LV   P
*Jeff Goldblum, Michelle Pfeiffer, David Bowie,
Carl Perkins, Richard Farnsworth, Dan Aykroyd,*

Paul Mazursky, Roger Vadim, Jim Henson, Paul Bartel, directed by John Landis
An insomniac aerospace engineer has plenty to keep him awake when a mysterious woman suddenly drops onto the hood of his car. B.B. King sings the title song. Available in VHS and Beta Hi Fi.
MPAA:R
Geroge Folsey Jr.; Ron Koslow — MCA Home Video

Intolerance 1916
Film-History
33548 120 mins B/W B, V P
Lillian Gish, Mae Marsh, Constance Tallmadge, Bessie Love, Elmer Clifton, directed by D.W. Griffith
D. W. Griffith's most expansive effort, which contains four separate stories detailing mankind's intolerance through the centuries. Original color-tinted and toned print, with music score.
D W Griffith — Video Yesteryear; Hollywood Home Theater; Blackhawk Films; Discount Video Tapes; Western Film & Video Inc

Introduction to Alpine Skiing, An 1983
Sports-Winter
70175 45 mins C B, V P
This program provides advice on purchasing equipment, limbering up, choosing the right slope, and how to master basic skiing skills in a short time.
Video Travel — Video Travel

Introduction to Muzzleloading 1985
Hunting
86876 30 mins C B, V P
Dick Gassaway
The beginning approach to loading muzzle-guns, with a look at the cultural regression to pioneer times enjoyed by thousands who engage in the hobby.
AM Available
Warburton Prod. — Warburton Productions

Introduction to Weaving 1985
Handicraft
85649 57 mins C B, V P
Deborah Chandler
A fundamental introductory course in basket-weaving.
Victorian Video Prod. — Victorian Video Productions

Intruder, The 1977
Drama
77009 98 mins C B, V P
Jean-Louis Trintignent, Mireille Darc, Adolfo Celi

A man and his stepson are terrorized by a stranger in a panel truck as they travel from Rome to Paris.
Viaduc Productions S.A. — VidAmerica

Invaders from Mars 1953
Science fiction
37400 78 mins C B, V P
Helena Carter, Arthur Franz, Jimmy Hunt, Leif Erickson, directed by William Cameron Menzies
A twelve-year-old boy witnesses the landing of a strange spacecraft, and he and his father set out to investigate. The father becomes possessed by alien entities who threaten to overtake the entire world. Includes previews of coming attractions from classic science fiction films.
20th Century Fox — Nostalgia Merchant

Invasion of the Body Snatchers 1956
Science fiction
55472 80 mins B/W B, V P
Kevin McCarthy, Dana Wynter, Carolyn Jones, King Donovan, directed by Don Siegel
The classic about the invasion of Southern California by seeds of giant plant pods which exude blank human forms that drain the emotional life of people and threaten to destroy the world.
Walter Wanger; Allied Artists — Republic Pictures Home Video; RCA VideoDiscs

Invasion of the Body Snatchers 1978
Science fiction/Horror
66451 115 mins C B, V, CED P
Donald Sutherland, Brooke Adams, Veronica Cartwright, Leonard Nimoy, Jeff Goldblum, Kevin McCarthy, Don Siegel
A remake of the 1956 sci-fi classic—this time, the "pod people" are infesting San Francisco, with only a small group of people aware of the invasion. Beta Hi-Fi and VHS stereo.
MPAA:PG
United Artists — MGM/UA Home Video

Invasion of the Body Stealers 1983
Science fiction
75462 93 mins C B, V P
Beings from another planet are stealing earthlings to revitalize their civilization.
King Features — U.S.A. Home Video

Invasion of the Flesh Hunters 1984
Horror
70154 90 mins C B, V P
John Saxon
A group of tortured Vietnam veterans returns home carrying a cannibalistic curse on them.

Almi Pictures — *Vestron Video*

Invasion of the Girl Snatchers   1973
Science fiction
77203   90 mins   C   B, V   P
Elizabeth Rush, Ele Grigsby
Aliens from another planet subdue young earth girls and force them to undergo bizarre acts that rob them of their souls.
Lee Jones — United Home Video

Invasion U.S.A.   1985
War-Drama/Adventure
84708   108 mins   C   B, V, LV   P
Chuck Norris, Richard Lynch, Melissa Prophet, directed by Joseph Zito
A mercenary defends nothing less than the entire country against Russian terrorists, with a record-setting amount of people killed on-screen.
MPAA:R
Cannon Films — MGM/UA Home Video

Investigation   1978
Mystery
86093   116 mins   C   B, V   P
Victor Lanoux, Valerie Mairesse, directed by Etienne Perier
A Frenchman plans to murder his wife so he can marry his pregnant mistress, guaranteeing an heir. In French with English subtitles.
FR
French — Embassy Home Entertainment

Invincible Barbarian, The   1983
Adventure
82211   92 mins   C   B, V   P
Diana Roy, David Jenkins
A young man leads a tribe of Amazon warriors in a sneak attack against the tribe who annihilated the village he was born in.
American National Enterprises — Prism

Invincible, The   1980
Adventure/Martial arts
56927   93 mins   C   B, V   R, P
Bruce Li, Chen Sing, Ho Chung Dao
A martial arts student must find and correct another student who has turned bad.
MPAA:R
Fourseas Films — Video Gems

Invisible Dead, The   1985
Horror
81034   90 mins   C   B, V   P
Howard Vernon, Britt Carva
A courageous doctor must save a beautiful woman being held captive by an invisible man.
MPAA:R
Empire Entertainment — Wizard Video

Invisible Ghost, The   1941
Horror
05520   70 mins   B/W   B, V, 3/4U   R, P
Bela Lugosi, Polly Ann Young
A man carries out a series of grisly stranglings while under hypnosis by his insane wife.
Monogram — Movie Buff Video; Discount Video Tapes; Cable Films; Video Yesteryear

Invincible Gladiators, The   1964
Adventure
86856   87 mins   C   B, V   P
Richard Lloyd, Claudia Lange, Tony Freeman, directed by Robert Mauri
The sons of Hercules aid a prince whose bride had been kidnapped by an evil queen.
IFESA Srl — Lightning Video

Invitation au Voyage   1983
Drama
65317   ? mins   C   B, V   P
Laurent Malet, Nina Scott, Aurore Clement, Mario Adorf
This program follows the journey of a twin who refuses to accept the death of his sister, a rock singer. Subtitled in English.
MPAA:R
Claude Nedjar — RCA/Columbia Pictures Home Video

Invitation to a Gunfighter   1964
Drama
65498   92 mins   C   CED   P
Yul Brynner, George Segal, Janice Rule, Pat Hingle
A small-town tyrant hires a smooth gunfighter to keep down the farmers he has cheated.
United Artists — CBS/Fox Video

Invitation to a Wedding   1983
Comedy
80924   89 mins   C   B, V   P
John Gielgud, Ralph Richardson, Paul Nickolaus, Elizabeth Shepherd, directed by Joseph Brooks
When the best friend of a bridegroom falls in love with the bride, he stops at nothing to stop the wedding.
MPAA:PG
Chancery Lane Music Corp. — Vestron Video

Invitation to Paris   1960
Variety/France
58652   51 mins   B/W   B, V, FO   P
Maurice Chevalier, Les Djinns, Patachou, Fernandel, Les Compagnons de La Chanson, Jean Sablon, George Ulmer, Line Renaud
A French musical revue, set in the streets of Paris, which features the girls of the French Can-Can revue.
A Parisian — Video Yesteryear

Invitation to the Dance   1957
Musical
60400   93 mins   C   B, V, CED   P
Gene Kelly, Igor Youskevitch, Tomara
Toumanova
Three classic dance sequences, "Circus,"
"Ring Around the Rosy" and "Sinbad the
Sailor," based on music by Rimsky-Korsakov.
MGM; Arthur Freed — *MGM/UA Home Video*

Iphigenia   1979
Drama
60343   100 mins   C   B, V   P
Irene Papas, Costa Kazakos, Tatiana
Papamoskou
Based on the classic Greek tragedy by
Euripides, this story concerns the Greek leader,
Agamemnon, and his lovely daughter, Iphigenia.
Almi Cinema 5 Film — *RCA/Columbia Pictures*
Home Video; Films for the Humanities

Irishman, The   1978
Drama
65477   90 mins   C   B, V   P
Bryan Brown
The tale of a proud North Queensland family
and their struggles to stay together.
Anthony Buckley — *Vestron Video*

Irma La Douce   1963
Comedy
58843   146 mins   C   CED   P
Jack Lemmon, Shirley MacLaine, Herschel
Bernardi, directed by Billy Wilder
A gendarme pulls a one-man raid on a back-
street Parisian joint and falls in love with one of
the ladies he arrests.
EL, SP
United Artists — *Key Video*

Iron Duke, The   1934
Drama/Biographical
47789   88 mins   B/W   B, V, 3/4U   P
George Arliss, Gladys Cooper
An historical account of the life of the Duke of
Wellington.
Gaumont; British — *Western Film & Video Inc;*
Kartes Video Communications

Iron Eagle   1985
Adventure
Closed Captioned
87641   117 mins   C   B, V   P
Lou Gossett Jr., Jason Gedrick, Tim Thomerson
An 18-year-old hot shot Air Force pilot joins
forces with a renegade Colonel to save his
father from unjust confinement in a Middle
Eastern country.
MPAA:PG-13
Ron Samuels; Joe Wizan — *CBS/Fox Video*

Iron Maiden   1983
Music-Performance
75903   18 mins   C   B, V   P
This program presents the heavy metal group
Iron Maiden performing songs such as "Run to
the Hills," "The Trooper" and "Flight of Icarus."
EMI Records Ltd — *Sony Video Software*

Iron Maiden: Behind the   1984
Iron Curtain
Music-Performance
88098   30 mins   C   B, V   P
The thudding, studding adventures of the
notorious heavy metal band, who are seen in
concert in various Eastern bloc countries.
Sony Video — *Sony Video Software*

Iron Maiden: Live After   1985
Death
Music-Performance
82388   89 mins   C   B, V   P
Iron Maiden
From their landmark "World Slavery Tour," this
extravagant performance at California's Long
Beach Arena includes Iron Maiden's best, such
as "Powerslave" and "The Number of the
Beast."
Capitol Records — *Sony Video Software*

Iron Mask, The   1929
Adventure
08729   87 mins   B/W   B, V, 3/4U   P
Douglas Fairbanks, Sr., Nigel de Brulier,
Marguerite de la Motte, directed by Allan Dwan
Based on Alexandre Dumas' "Three
Musketeers" and "The Man in the Iron Mask',
the fearless d'Artagnan rights the wrongs in
France. (Part talkie.)
United Artists — *Blackhawk Films; Cable*
Films; Discount Video Tapes

Ironmaster   1983
Fantasy
80895   98 mins   C   B, V   P
George Eastman, Pamela Field
When a primitive tribesman is exiled from his
tribe, he discovers a mysteriously power-filled
iron staff on a mountainside.
American National Enterprises — *Prism*

Irreconcilable   1984
Differences
Comedy
79667   112 mins   C   B, V, LV,   P
                          CED
Ryan O'Neal, Shelley Long, Drew Barrymore,
Sam Wanamaker, directed by Charles Shyer
A ten-year-old girl sues her parents for divorce
on the grounds of "irreconcilable differneces."
MPAA:PG
Warner Bros — *Vestron Video*

Isabel's Choice   1981
Drama/Romance
75456   96 mins   C   B, V   P
Jean Stapleton, Richard Kiley, Peter Coyote
A middle-aged executive secretary must choose
between romance and success.
King Features — *U.S.A. Home Video*

Isla Encantada, La   1984
(Enchanted Island)
Drama
72962   90 mins   C   B, V   P
The new adventures of Robinson Crusoe and
Man Friday, as they pursue wild beasts and
cannibals and fight off pirates.
Foreign — *Unicorn Video*

Island, The   1980
Adventure
48633   113 mins   C   B, V   P
Christopher F. Bean
A New York reporter embarks on a Bermuda
triangle investigation, only to meet with the
murderous descendants of seventeenth-century
pirates on a deserted island.
MPAA:R
Universal, Richard D Zanuck, David
Brown — *MCA Home Video*

Island, The   1961
Drama
53724   96 mins   B/W   B, V, 3/4U   P
Directed by Kaneto Shindo
One of Japan's best directors turns his talents
to the existence of a family, the sole inhabitants
of a small island. No dialogue.
Japan — *International Historic Films; Video
Yesteryear; Hollywood Home Theater; Discount
Video Tapes; Video Action*

Island at the Top of the   1974
World, The
Adventure
63191   89 mins   C   B, V   P
*David Hartman, Donald Sinden, Jacques Marin,
Mako, David Gwillim*
A rich Englishman, an American archeologist, a
French aeronaut and an Eskimo guide travel to
the Arctic in 1908 aboard the airship Hyperion
on a rescue mission.
Walt Disney Productions — *Walt Disney Home
Video*

Island Claw   1980
Horror
80703   91 mins   C   B, V   P
Barry Nelson, Robert Lansing
A group of marine biologists experimenting on a
tropical island discover the "Island Claw", who
evolved as the result of toxic waste seeping into
the ocean.
Video Media — *Vestron Video*

Island Magic   1981
Sports-Water
52769   72 mins   C   B, V   P
This program, shot on location in Hawaii, takes
you through a dramatic tour of all of Hawaii's
best surfing spots.
John Hitchcock — *Karl/Lorimar Home Video*

Island Monster   1953
Crime-Drama
84544   87 mins   B/W   B, V   P
Boris Karloff
Also called "Monster of the Island," this film
deals with ruthless, kidnapping drug-smugglers
and the efforts to bring them to justice.
Demalco Ltd — *Hollywood Home Theater*

Island of Adventure   1981
Adventure
72887   85 mins   C   B, V   P
Four children explore an island and find a gang
of criminals inhabitating it.
Unknown — *Embassy Home Entertainment*

Island of Dr. Moreau, The   1977
Science fiction
53514   98 mins   C   B, V   P
*Burt Lancaster, Michael York, Barbara Carrera,
Richard Basehart*
The story of a scientist who has isolated himself
on a Pacific island in order to continue his
chromosome research, which has developed to
the point where he can transform animals into
semi-humans. Based on the H. G. Wells novel.
MPAA:PG
American International Pictures — *Warner
Home Video; Vestron Video (disc only)*

Island of Nevawuz, The   1980
Fantasy
65708   50 mins   C   B, V   P
A beautiful island is in trouble when J.B.
Trumphorn decides to make lots of money by
building factories and refineries on it. Will the
Island of Nevawuz end up a polluted mess?
Paul Williams — *Embassy Home
Entertainment*

Island of the Blue   1964
Dolphins
Drama/Adventure
81440   99 mins   C   B, V   P
*Celia Kaye, Larry Domasin, Ann Daniel, George
Kennedy*
This is the true story of how a young Indian girl
learned to survive alone on a desert island.
Available in VHS and Beta Hi-Fi.
Universal; Robert B. Radnitz — *MCA Home
Video*

Island of the Lost   1968
Science fiction
80182   92 mins   C   B, V   P
Richard Greene, Luke Halpin
An anthropologist's family must fight for survival when they become shipwrecked on a mysterious island.
Metro Goldwyn Mayer — *Republic Pictures Home Video*

Island Reggae Greats   1985
Music-Performance
82202   28 mins   C   B, V   P
Toots and the Maytals, Black Uhuru, Aswad, Third World, Bob Marley
This is a compilation of concert and studio performances from such reggae legends as Toots and the Maytals and Bob Marley in VHS Dolby Hi-Fi Stereo.
Island Records — *RCA/Columbia Pictures Home Video*

Islands in the Stream   1977
Drama
38609   110 mins   C   B, V   P
George C. Scott, David Hemmings, Claire Bloom, Susan Tyrrell
Ernest Hemingway's last novel provides the basis for this story of an American artist living with his sons on the island of Bimini shortly before the outbreak of World War II.
MPAA:PG
Paramount — *Paramount Home Video*

Isle of Secret Passion   1985
Romance
87689   90 mins   C   V   P
A romance novel comes to video life as two lovers thrash out their problems on a Greek island.
Prism Video — *Prism*

Isle of the Dead   1945
Suspense
86037   72 mins   B/W   B, V   P
Boris Karloff, Ellen Drew, Marc Cramer, directed by Mark Robson
A Greek general is stranded with various shady characters and suspicious goings-on during a quarantine. A classically eerie Lewton film.
Val Lewton — *Nostalgia Merchant*

Israel Folk Dance Festival   1981
Dance
81570   60 mins   C   B, V   P
This is a compilation highlighting the best performances of Israeli folkloric dance groups.
Troex Ltd. — *Kultur*

It   1927
Drama
54109   71 mins   B/W   B, V   P, T

Clara Bow, Gary Cooper, Antonio Moreno
To have "It" the possessor must have that strange magnetism which attracts both sexes. A female department store worker is out to land the store owner but isn't doing well, until she goes on his yachting trip and with "It" wins her man.
Unknown — *Blackhawk Films*

It Came From Beneath the Sea   1955
Horror
81794   80 mins   B/W   B, V   P
Kenneth Tobey, Faith Domergue, Ian Keith, Donald Curtis
A giant octopus arises from the depths of the sea scouring San Francisco searching for human food. Available in VHS and Beta Hi-Fi.
Columbia Pictures — *RCA/Columbia Pictures Home Video*

It Came from Hollywood   1982
Documentary/Science fiction
64502   87 mins   C   B, V, LV   P
Narrated by Dan Aykroyd, Cheech and Chong, John Candy and Gilda Radner
A compilation of scenes from "B" horror and science fiction films of the 1950's, highlighting the funny side of these classic schlocky movies. Some sequences are in black and white.
MPAA:PG
Paramount — *Paramount Home Video; RCA VideoDiscs*

It Came Upon the Midnight Clear   1984
Drama/Christmas
Closed Captioned
82326   96 mins   C   B, V   P
Mickey Rooney, Scott Grimes, George Gaynes, Annie Potts, Lloyd Nolan, Barrie Youngfellow
A heavenly miracle enables a retired New York policeman to keep a Christmas promise to his grandson. Available in VHS and Beta Hi-Fi.
Frank Cardea; George Schenck — *RCA/Columbia Pictures Home Video*

It Could Happen to You   1939
Comedy/Mystery
71000   64 mins   C   B, V   P
Stuart Erwin, Gloria Stuart, Raymond Walburn, Douglas Fowley, directed by Alfred Werker
A dead nightclub singer shows up in a drunken advertising executive's car and police charge him with murder. His wife sets out to clear him.
TCF — *Kartes Video Communications*

It Don't Come Easy: 1978 New York Yankees   1978
Baseball
33846   45 mins   C   B, V   P
New York Yankees

Highlights of the turbulent but terrific season which saw manager Billy Martin fired and replaced by Bob Lemon is mid-season. The Yankees fell to fourteen games behind the Boston Red Sox in July, only to respond with the most memorable comeback in baseball history. They beat the Red Sox in a one-game playoff, whipped the Kansas City Royals in four games, then quickly dropped two games to the Los Angeles Dodgers in the World Series before sweeping the next four games and capturing their second straight title. Thurman Munson, Reggie Jackson, Bucky Dent and others led the way.
Major League Baseball — *Major League Baseball Productions*

It Happened at the World's Fair   1963
Musical
80150   105 mins   C   B, V   P
Elvis Presley, Joan O'Brien, Gary Lockwood, Kurt Russell
Two bush pilots escort a Chinese girl through the Seattle World's Fair.
Metro Goldwyn Mayer — *MGM/UA Home Video*

It Happened in New Orleans   1936
Musical-Drama
11240   86 mins   B/W   B, V, FO   P
Bobby Breen, Mae Robson, Alan Mowbray, Benita Hume
A charming portrayal of levee life in post-Civil War New Orleans.
RKO — *Video Yesteryear*

It Happened One Night   1934
Comedy
Closed Captioned
80366   105 mins   B/W   B, V   P
Clark Gable, Claudette Colbert, Roscoe Karns, Walter Connolly, directed by Frank Capra
A runaway heiress falls in love with a newspaperman on a cross country bus trip.
Academy Awards '34: Best Picture; Best Actor (Gable); Best Actress (Colbert); Best Director (Capra)
Columbia Pictures; Frank Capra — *RCA/Columbia Pictures Home Video*

It Lives Again   1978
Horror
78140   91 mins   C   B, V   P
A hellspaun baby meets up with two other monster infants and goes on a murderous rampage.
Larry Cohen — *Warner Home Video*

It Should Happen to You   1953
Comedy
65700   87 mins   B/W   B, V   P

Judy Holliday, Jack Lemmon, Peter Lawford
An aspiring model, unable to find steady work, rents a large billboard in New York to attract attention. In Beta Hi-Fi.
Fred Kohlmar — *RCA/Columbia Pictures Home Video*

Italian Straw Hat, The   1927
Romance
48748   72 mins   B/W   B, V   P
Directed by Rene Clair
A Mack Sennett-styled chase farce in which a straw hat must be replaced to save a woman's virtue. Silent with English subtitles and musical score.
French — *Video Yesteryear*

It's a Gift   1934
Comedy
85253   71 mins   B/W   B, V   P
W.C. Fields, Baby LeRoy, Kathleen Howard, directed by Norman Z. MacLeod
A grocery clerk inherits an orange grove, and typically Fieldsian monkeyshines ensue, including some notable brutality toward Baby LeRoy.
Paramount — *Kartes Video Communications*

It's a Joke, Son!   1947
Comedy
71037   67 mins   B/W   B, V   P
Kenny Delmar, Una Merkel
"Life" magazine called Senator Claghorn one of the most quotable men in the Nation. This film follows the fictional politician's first run for the U.S. Senate.
Eagle Lion — *Hal Roach Studios*

It's a Mad, Mad, Mad, Mad World   1963
Comedy
47145   192 mins   C   B, V, CED   P
Spencer Tracy, Sid Caesar, Milton Berle, Ethel Merman, Jonathan Winters, Jimmy Durante, Buddy Hackett, Mickey Rooney, Phil Silvers, Dick Shawn, Edie Adams, Dorothy Provine, Buster Keaton, The Three Stooges, Jack Benny, Jerry Lewis, directed by Stanley Kramer
A motley collection of people are overcome with greed and take off in all manner of conveyances after a hidden stash of money. No shtick is overlooked along the way.
United Artists; Stanley Kramer — *CBS/Fox Video; RCA VideoDiscs*

It's a Wonderful Life   1946
Drama
44796   125 mins   B/W   B, V, 3/4U   P
James Stewart, Donna Reed, Lionel Barrymore, directed by Frank Capra
A sentimental classic about a man who has worked hard all his life, but feels he is a failure

and tries to commit suicide. A guardian angel comes to show him his mistake.
Liberty Films; RKO — *Movie Buff Video; Prism; Nostalgia Merchant; Republic Pictures Home Video; Media Home Entertainment; Select-a-Tape; Cable Films; VCII; Video Connection; Video Yesteryear; Hollywood Home Theater; Discount Video Tapes; Western Film & Video Inc; Cinema Concepts; Kartes Video Communications*

It's a Wonderful Life   1946
Drama
85670   125 mins   C   B, V   P
James Stewart, Donna Reed, Lionel Barrymore, directed by Frank Capra
A computer colorized version of the perennial holiday classic.
Liberty Films; RKO — *Hal Roach Studios*

It's Alive   1974
Horror
78139   91 mins   C   B, V   P
An everyday Los Angeles couple gives birth to a hideous humanoid whose escape and murderous rampage causes citywide terror.
Larry Cohen — *Warner Home Video*

It's an Adventure, Charlie   1983
Brown
Cartoons
76846   50 mins   C   B, V   P
Animated
This is a collection of six vignettes featuring Charlie Brown and the whole Peanuts gang.
Lee Mendelson; Bill Melendez — *Snoopy's Home Video Library*

It's Called Murder, Baby   1982
Crime-Drama
88228   94 mins   C   B, V   P
John Leslie, Cameron Mitchell, Lisa Trego, directed by Sam Weston
The famed porn star gives the viewer a lesson in English vocabulary in this tale of a blackmailed movie queen.
MPAA:R
Lima Prod. — *Lightning Video*

It's Flashbeagle, Charlie   1984
Brown/She's a Good
Skate, Charlie Brown
Cartoons
76848   50 mins   C   B, V   P
Animated
A Peanuts double header: In "It's Flashbeagle Charlie Brown" Snoopy infects the Peanuts gang with dance fever and in "She's a Good Skate Charlie Brown" Snoopy trains Peppermint Patty to become a figure skating champion.
Lee Mendelson; Bill Melendez — *Snoopy's Home Video Library*

It's Good to Be Alive   1974
Drama/Biographical
80307   100 mins   C   B, V   P
Paul Winfield, Ruby Dee, Lou Gossett, directed by Michael Landon
The true story of how Brooklyn Dodgers' catcher Roy Campanella learned how to face life after an automobile accident had made him a quadraplegic.
Charles Fries Productions — *Prism*

It's in the Bag   1945
Comedy
44794   87 mins   B/W   B, V, 3/4U   P
Fred Allen, Jack Benny, William Bendix, Binnie Barnes, Robert Benchley, directed by Richard Wallace
A shiftless flea circus owner sells chairs he has inherited, not knowing that a fortune is hidden in one of them.
United Artists — *Nostalgia Merchant; Spotlite Video*

It's Magic, Charlie   1981
Brown/Charlie Brown's
All Stars
Cartoons
75609   55 mins   C   B, V   P
Animated
In the first of these two stories, Snoopy, "The Great Houndini," makes Charlie Brown disappear. Problems begin when Snoopy finds it difficult conjuring his master back to reality. In the second story, Charlie Brown's baseball team has lost 999 games in a row, and prospects are bleak. New hope arrives when he gets an offer to have the team sponsored—in a real league!
Lee Mendelson Bill Melendez Productions — *Snoopy's Home Video Library*

It's My Turn   1980
Comedy-Drama
52749   91 mins   C   B, V, LV   P
Jill Clayburgh, Michael Douglas, Charles Grodin, directed by Claudia Weill
A mathematics professor has her life upset when she falls in love with a retired baseball player, causing her to question her relationship with her live-in boyfriend.
MPAA:R
Rastar; Martin Elfand — *RCA/Columbia Pictures Home Video*

It's News to Me   1954
Game show
78090   30 mins   B/W   B, V, FO   P
This program presents a panel who describe a current news story and then contestants decide whether the panel is telling the truth.
CBS; Goodson Todman — *Video Yesteryear*

It's the Easter Beagle, Charlie Brown/It was a short summer, Charlie Brown
1974

Cartoons/Holidays
76850   50 mins   C   B, V   P
Animated
A collection of two Peanuts specials: The whole Peanuts gang are anxiously awaiting the coming of the Easter Beagle in "It's the Easter Beagle Charlie Brown" and Charlie Brown remembers all about summer camp in "It Was a Short Summer Charlie Brown."
Lee Mendelson; Bill Melendez — *Snoopy's Home Video Library*

It's the Great Pumpkin, Charlie Brown
1966

Cartoons
70740   77 mins   C   B, V   P
Animated
In addition to Linus' telling of the "Great Pumpkin" legend, this three episode collection includes "What a Nightmare Charlie Brown," and "It Was A Short Summer, Charlie Brown."
Mendelson and Melendez in assoc. with United Features Synd. — *Snoopy's Home Video Library*

It's the Great Pumpkin, Charlie Brown/What a Nightmare, Charlie Brown
1978

Cartoons/Holidays
76849   50 mins   C   B, V   P
Animated
Here are two Peanuts Halloween specials: In "It's the Great Pumpkin, Charlie Brown," Linus waits up all Halloween night to await the arrival of the Great Pumpkin and in "What a Nightmare, Charlie Brown" Snoopy has a nightmare after pigging out on dog food.
Lee Mendelson; Bill Melendez — *Snoopy's Home Video Library*

It's Your Birthday Party! With Rainbow Brite and Friends
1985

Games
82041   60 mins   C   B, V   P
Rainbow Brite and her friends get together to celebrate your child's birthday party with special songs and games to play.
C.J. Kettler; Hallmark Properties — *Children's Video Library*

It's Your First Kiss, Charlie Brown/Someday You'll Find Her, Charlie Brown
1977

Cartoons
80276   55 mins   C   B, V   P
Animated
In "It's Your First Kiss, Charlie Brown," our hero has to escort the school's homecoming queen to the ball. What's worse, he has to actually kiss her in front of everyone! In "Someday You'll Find Her, Charlie Brown," Charlie Brown sees "the most beautiful girl in the world" on TV and, after recruiting Linus, embarks upon a door-to-door search to find her.
Lee Mendelson; Bill Melendez — *Snoopy's Home Video Library*

It's Your Funeral
1968

Suspense/Fantasy
77416   52 mins   C   B, V   P
Patrick McGoohan, Annette Andre, Derren Nesbitt
The Prisoner must foil an assassination attempt in the Village. An episode from "The Prisoner" series.
ITC Productions — *MPI Home Video*

Itzhak Perlman
1982

Music-Performance
64208   45 mins   C   B, V   P
Itzhak Perlman, Carlo Maria Giulini and the Philharmonic Orchestra
Violinist Itzhak Perlman is featured in this performance of Beethoven's Concerto in D for Violin. In stereo.
EMI Music — *THORN EMI/HBO Video; Pioneer Artists*

Ivan the Terrible—Part I
1943

Drama
08702   96 mins   B/W   B, V   P
Nikolai Cherkasov, Ludmila Tselikovskaya, Serafina Birman, directed by Sergei Eisenstein
Ivan, Grand Duke of Russia, is crowned as the first Czar of Russia. His struggles to preserve his country are the main concerns of this first half of Eisenstein's masterwork. Russian dialogue with English subtitles.
Russian — *Hollywood Home Theater; Movie Buff Video; International Historic Films; Kartes Video Communications; Video Yesteryear; Western Film & Video Inc; Discount Video Tapes*

Ivan the Terrible—Part II
1946

Drama
08703   84 mins   B/W   B, V   P
Nikolai Cherkassov, Serafima Birman, Piotr Kadochnikev, directed by Sergei Eisenstein
The landed gentry of Russia conspire to dethrone Ivan in the second part of this classic epic. Russian dialogue with English subtitles; contains color sequences.
RU
Russian; Janus Films — *Hollywood Home Theater; International Historic Films; Video Yesteryear; Western Film & Video Inc; Discount Video Tapes; Kartes Video Communications*

Ivanhoe 1953
Adventure
58706　　106 mins　　C　　　B, V　　　　　P
*Robert Taylor, Elizabeth Taylor, Joan Fontaine,
George Sanders*
Sir Walter Scott's classic novel of chivalric
romance and courtly intrigue among the knights
of medieval England.
Film Daily Poll '53: Ten Best of Year.
MGM — *MGM/UA Home Video*

Ivanhoe 1982
Adventure
87756　　142 mins　　C　　　B, V　　　　　P
*Anthony Andrews, James Mason, Lysette
Anthony, Olivia Hussey*
A version of Sir Walter Scott's classic novel of
chivalry and knighthood in 12th century
England.
Norman Rosemont — *RCA/Columbia Pictures
Home Video*

I've Got a Secret 1966
Game show
85178　　29 mins　　C　　　B, V　　　　　P
*Steve Allen, Betsy Palmer, Henry Morgan, Bess
Myerson, Bill Cullen*
A 1966 episode of the celebrity-guessing game
show with guest Fredric March, featuring
vintage commercials.
CBS — *Video Yesteryear*

J

J. Geils Band 1984
Music-Performance
75904　　16 mins　　C　　　B, V　　　　　P
This program presents the J. Geils Band
performing their hits "Freeze Frame,"
"Centerfold," "Love Stinks" and "Angel in
Blue."
EMI Records — *Sony Video Software*

Jabberwocky 1977
Comedy
63961　　104 mins　　C　　　B, V　　　　　P
*Michael Palin, Max Wall, Deborah Fallender,
directed by Terry Gilliam*
Chaos prevails in the medieval cartoon kingdom
of King Bruno the Questionable, who rules with
cruelty, stupidity, lust and dust.
MPAA:PG
Almi-Cinema 5 — *RCA/Columbia Pictures
Home Video*

Jack and the Beanstalk 1952
Comedy
11795　　78 mins　　C　　　B, V　　　　　P
Bud Abbott, Lou Costello, Buddy Baer

While baby-sitting, Lou falls asleep and dreams
he's Jack in the classic fairy tale.
Warner Bros — *United Home Video*

Jack and the Beanstalk 1967
Cartoons/Fairy tales
47689　　51 mins　　C　　　B, V　　　　　P
Gene Kelly
Live action blends with animation in this telling
of the classic story about a boy and his magic
beans. Music by Sammy Cahn and Jimmy Van
Heusen.
Hanna Barbera — *Worldvision Home Video*

Jack and the Beanstalk 1976
Musical/Fairy tales
64578　　80 mins　　C　　　B, V　　　　　P
*Animated, written and directed by Peter J.
Solmo*
An animated musical version of the familiar
story of Jack, the young boy who climbs a magic
beanstalk up into the clouds, where he meets a
fearsome giant.
Sheridan View Properties
Associates — *RCA/Columbia Pictures Home
Video*

Jack and the Beanstalk 1983
Fairy tales
Closed Captioned
69325　　60 mins　　C　　　B, V, LV,　　　　P
　　　　　　　　　　　　　　　CED
*Dennis Christopher, Katherine Helmond, Elliot
Gould, Jean Stapleton*
From the "Faerie Tale Theatre," this is the
classic tale of Jack, who sells his family's cow
for 5 magic beans, then climbs the huge
beanstalk that sprouts from them and
encounters an unfriendly giant.
Shelly Duvall — *CBS/Fox Video*

Jack Benny 196?
Variety
59312　　110 mins　B/W　　B, V, 3/4U　　　　P
*Jack Benny, Bob Hope, George Burns, Bing
Crosby, Walt Disney, Martin and Lewis, Elke
Sommer, The Beach Boys, Rochester, Don
Wilson*
Three complete Benny shows spanning the
period from 1953 to 1965. Sketches include a
spoof of Hope's "Road" movies, and a Mary
Poppins take-off.
CBS; NBC — *Shokus Video*

Jack Benny, II 1953
Comedy
66486　　120 mins　B/W　　　B, V　　　　　P
*Jack Benny, Mary Livingston, Rochester, Don
Wilson, Kirk Douglas, Dick Powell, Humphrey
Bogart, Ronald Reagan*
This tape contains three 1953 episodes of "The
Jack Benny Show" plus Jack's dramatic
appearance on "The General Electric Theater."

Original commercials and network I.D.'s included.
CBS — *Shokus Video*

Jack Benny III   1957
Comedy
77195   120 mins   B/W   B, V   P
Jack Benny, Mel Blanc, Fred Allen, Johnny Ray, Jayne Mansfield, Don Wilson
A collection of four vintage Benny shows (circa 1952-1957) that features Jack trying to get Liberace to appear on his show and he has to pay Johnny Ray $10,000 for an appearance.
CBS — *Shokus Video*

Jack Benny Program, The   1959
Comedy
58641   30 mins   B/W   B, V, FO   P
Jack Benny, Ernie Kovacs, Don Wilson
Ernie shows Jack his collection of moustaches, and Jack and Ernie play jailbirds in a prison of the future as Killer Kovacs and Benny the Louse. Sponsored by Lucky Strike.
CBS — *Video Yesteryear*

Jack Benny Program, The   1958
Comedy
65337   60 mins   B/W   B, V   P
Jack Benny, Don Wilson, Mel Blanc
Two shows, "The Christmas Show" and "The Railroad Station," are shown in complete form with Mr. Benny at his best.
J and M Productions — *MCA Home Video*

Jack Benny Program, The   1954
Variety/Comedy
85179   58 mins   B/W   B, V   P
Jack Benny, Don Wilson, Dan Dailey, Fred MacMurray, Kirk Douglas, Humphrey Bogart, Rochester, Bob Crosby, Rita Gam
Two episodes of Benny's classic variety show: "The Jam Session," and "Baby Face."
CBS — *Video Yesteryear*

Jack Benny Show, The   1958
Comedy
42976   25 mins   B/W   B, V, FO   P
Jack Benny, Dennis Day, Audrey Meadows
The cast does a parody of the "The Honeymooners" with Dennis playing Ed Norton and Jack playing Ralph Kramden (with the help of a pillow under his shirt).
CBS — *Video Yesteryear*

Jack London   1943
Biographical
52335   94 mins   B/W   B, V   R, P
Michael O'Shea, Susan Hayward
Jack London's most creative years during his careers as oyster pirate, prospector, war correspondent and author are dramatized in this

program based on "The Book of Jack London" by Charmian London.
AM Available
United Artists, Samuel Bronston Prods — *Discount Video Tapes; Kartes Video Communications*

Jack Nicklaus Sports Clinic   1977
Golf
37418   18 mins   C   B, V   P
Jack Nicklaus
Golf pro Jack Nicklaus demonstrates proper golf techniques.
Sports Concepts — *CBS/Fox Video*

Jack O'Lantern   198?
Cartoons
79198   30 mins   C   B, V   P
Animated
The good hearted goblin with the help of two children defeats Zelda the Witch and her husband Sir Archibald.
Rankin Bass Studios — *Prism*

Jack the Ripper   1980
Drama
65379   82 mins   C   B, V   P
Klaus Kinski
The inimitable Kinski assumes the role of the most heinous criminal of modern history—Jack the Ripper.
MPAA:R
Cine Showcase — *Vestron Video*

Jackson and Jill   1953
Comedy
85510   27 mins   B/W   B, V   P
Todd Karns, Helen Chapman
A vintage situation comedy episode about a silly suburban couple.
Syndicate — *Video Yesteryear*

Jackson County Jail   1976
Drama
51986   85 mins   C   B, V   P
Yvette Mimieux, Tommy Lee Jones, Robert Carradine
While driving cross-country a young woman is robbed, imprisoned, and raped by a deputy, whom she kills. Faced with a murder charge she flees, with the law in hot pursuit.
MPAA:R
New World Pictures — *Warner Home Video*

Jaco Pastorius: Modern Electric Bass   1985
Music
87923   90 mins   C   B, V   P
A look at the world's leading jazz electric bassist who instructs in the finer points of playing, tuning and performing.

AM Available
DCI Music Video — *DCI Music Video*

Jacob: The Man Who Fought with God
1977

Bible
35371   118 mins   C   B, V   P
Jacob's struggle to receive his father's blessing and inheritance rights is depicted, as well as his marriage to Rachel and the return of his brother Esau. From the "Bible" series.
Sunn Classic — *United Home Video*

Jacob Two—Two Meets the Hooded Fang
19??

Adventure
69611   90 mins   C   B, V   P
Alex Karras
Based on the children's book by Mordecai Richler, this is the story of a young boy who meets the dreaded Hooded Fang, warden of the prison "from which no brat returns."
MPAA:G
John Flaxman — *Children's Video Library*

Jacob's Challenge
1979

Drama/Bible
55018   50 mins   C   B, V   P
Barry Williams, Stephen Elliott, June Lockhart, Tanya Roberts, Bruce Fairbairn, Peter Fox, narrated by Victor Jory
The Biblical story of Jacob who outwitted his brother, Esau, for their father's blessing.
Sunn Classics — *Magnum Entertainment; Vanguard Video; Lucerne Films*

Jacqueline Bouvier Kennedy
1981

Biographical/Drama
86171   150 mins   C   B, V   P
Jaclyn Smith, James Franciscus, Rod Taylor, Donald Moffat, Dolph Sweet
A made-for-TV biography of the former First Lady, from her childhood to the glorious years with JFK in the White House.
ABC Circle Films — *Vidmark Entertainment*

Jagged Edge
1985

Mystery
Closed Captioned
86391   108 mins   C   B, V   P
Jeff Bridges, Glenn Close, Robert Loggia, Peter Coyote, directed by Richard Marquand
A taut murder/courtroom drama about a successful newspaper editor who is accused of his wife's grisly murder. To complicate matters, he is also having an affair with his attorney. Available in Stereo Dolby Surroundsound.
MPAA:R
Martin Ransohoff — *RCA/Columbia Pictures Home Video*

Jaguar 6 Cylinder
1986

Automobiles
88404   60 mins   C   B, V, 3/4U   P
How to tune-up and maintain the larger Jaguar engines.
Peter Allen Prod. — *Peter Allen Video Productions*

Jailbreakin'
1972

Drama/Adventure
81879   90 mins   C   B, V   P
Erik Estrada
A faded country singer and a rebellious youth team up to break out of jail.
Clancy B. Grass — *Video Gems*

Jailhouse Rock
1957

Musical-Drama
44643   96 mins   B/W   B, V, CED   P
Elvis Presley, Judy Tyler, Vaughn Taylor, Dean Jones, Mickey Shaughnessy, directed by Richard Thorpe
While in jail for manslaughter, a teenager learns to play the guitar. After his release, he slowly develops into a top recording star. Songs include "Jailhouse Rock," "Treat Me Nice," "Baby, I Don't Care" and "Young and Beautiful."
MGM — *MGM/UA Home Video*

Jam, The
1983

Music video
88099   29 mins   C   B, V   P
A compilation of the acclaimed and presently defunct English band's videos, including "A Town Called Malice."
Sony Video — *Sony Video Software*

Jam Video Snap! The
1983

Music-Performance/Music video
77527   47 mins   C   B, V   P
Paul Weller, Bruce Foxworth
This compilation of film and video clips from "The Jam's" late 70's/early 80's career includes many of the songs that won them a large European following and critical acclaim on both sides of the Atlantic.
Polygram Music Video — *Music Media*

Jamaica Inn
1939

Drama
58615   98 mins   B/W   B, V   P
Charles Laughton, Maureen O'Hara, Leslie Banks, Robert Newton, directed by Alfred Hitchcock
In old Cornwall, an orphan girl becomes involved with smugglers.
Paramount — *Movie Buff Video; Cable Films; Discount Video Tapes*

James Brown Live in Concert — 1979
Music-Performance
56745   48 mins   C   B, V   P
James Brown
James Brown and his band perform such hits as "Boogie Wonderland," and "Georgia," and takes the audience through the best of jazz, rock, and blues fusion. Taped before a capacity audience at the Summer Festival in Toronto, Canada.
Network Talent Intl — *Media Home Entertainment*

James Cagney: That Yankee Doodle Dandy — 1986
Biographical/Film-History
86483   73 mins   C   B, V   P
Narrated by Treat Williams, Pat O'Brien, Donald O'Connor, Milos Forman
This definitive homage to Cagney on the event of his death features footage from his films, plus interviews and comments by his friends and co-workers. Portions are in black and white.
Richard Schickel; MGM/UA — *MGM/UA Home Video*

James Dean — 1985
Biographical/Documentary
70997   120 mins   C   B, V   P
James Dean, directed by Claudio Masenza
This production reflects an exhaustive search through archival film, videotape and photograph selections and includes many exclusive interviews with friends of the late actor.
Donatella Baglivio — *Kartes Video Communications*

James Dean Story, The — 1957
Drama/Biographical
65470   57 mins   B/W   B, V   P
An intimate portrait of James Dean presented by Robert Altman. The program includes never before seen outtakes from "East of Eden" and rare footage from the Hollywood premiere of "Giant" and the infamous Highway Public Safety message Dean made for television.
Warner Brothers — *Pacific Arts Video*

James Dean: The First American Teenager — 1976
Biographical/Film-History
59861   83 mins   C   B, V   P
James Dean, Elizabeth Taylor, Sammy Davis Jr., Rock Hudson, Sal Mineo, Natalie Wood, Julie Harris, Jack Larson, Nicholas Ray
A look at the life and legend of the charismatic filmstar, with comments by those who knew him best and scenes from his films. (Some black and white footage.)
MPAA:PG
Ziv Intl; Goodtime Enterprises — *VidAmerica*

James Joyce's Women — 1983
Drama
85771   91 mins   C   B, V   P
Fionnula Flanagan, Timothy E. O'Grady, Chris O'Neill
Adapted and produced by Flanagan, this acclaimed film features enacted portraits of three real-life Joyce associates, including his wife, and three of his famous characters, including Molly Bloom.
MPAA:R
Fionnula Flangan; The Rejoycing Co. — *MCA Home Video*

James Taylor in Concert — 1979
Music-Performance
48861   90 mins   C   B, V, LV,   P
                              CED
James Taylor's first video concert features live performances of "Sweet Baby James," "Carolina on My Mind," "Steam Roller," "Whenever I See Your Smiling Face," "Up on the Roof," and "Handy Man."
CBS — *CBS/Fox Video*

Jane Doe — 1983
Suspense/Drama
77383   96 mins   C   B, V   P
Karen Valentine, William Devane, Eva Marie Saint, Stephen Miller, Jackson Davies
An amnesiac assault victim lies in a hospital bed under an assumed name trying to recall details of the crime to prevent the assailant from finishing the job. Available in VHS Stereo and Beta Hi-Fi.
ITC Productions — *U.S.A. Home Video*

Jane Fonda Challenge — 1983
Physical fitness
Closed Captioned
65547   90 mins   C   B, V   P
Included in the offering are fast paced warm-up, exercise, balance and stretching sections, plus an exciting 20-minute choreographed aerobic routine that can be performed separately by those with too few hours in a day.
Karl Video; RCA — *Karl/Lorimar Home Video*

Jane Fonda's New Workout — 1985
Physical fitness
82149   90 mins   C   B, V   P
Jane Fonda
Jane Fonda's back with a whole new aerobics regimen designed to flatten your stomach and tone up your posterior.
Stuart Karl; RCA Video Productions — *Karl/Lorimar Home Video*

Jane Fonda's Workout — 1982
Physical fitness
59073   90 mins   C   B, V   P
Jane Fonda

An exercise program designed for both beginners and intermediate exercise buffs.
Karl Video; RCA — Karl/Lorimar Home Video; RCA VideoDiscs

Jane Fonda's Workout for Pregnancy, Birth and Recovery   1983
Physical fitness/Pregnancy
65116   60 mins   C   B, V   P
Jane Fonda
Jane Fonda supervises a complete fitness program for pregnant women from conception to recovery.
Stuart Karl — Karl/Lorimar Home Video; RCA VideoDiscs

Japanese Connection   1982
Martial arts
64947   96 mins   C   B, V   R, P
Li Chao, Yang Wei, Wu Ming-Tsai
Warring crime chiefs fight furiously with deadly kung-fu action.
Foreign — Video Gems

Jason and the Argonauts   1963
Fantasy
44179   104 mins   C   B, V   P
Todd Armstrong, Nancy Kovack, Gary Raymond, Laurence Naismith, Michael Gwynn
Jason, son of King of Thessaly, sails on the Argo to the land of Colchis, where the Golden Fleece is guarded by a seven-headed hydra.
Columbia; Morningside; World Wide Productions — RCA/Columbia Pictures Home Video; RCA VideoDiscs

---

Jaws 3   1983
Suspense
69538   97 mins   C   B, V, LV   P
Dennis Quaid, Bess Armstrong, Louis Gossett Jr.
In a deluxe amusement park, a great white shark escapes from its tank and proceeds to cause terror and chaos.
MPAA:PG
Universal — MCA Home Video

Jaws   1975
Suspense
11590   124 mins   C   B, V, LV   P
Roy Scheider, Robert Shaw, Richard Dreyfuss, Lorraine Gary, directed by Steven Speilberg
A 25-foot long Great White Shark attacks and terrorizes residents of a Long Island beach town. Three men set out on a boat to kill it at any cost. Based on the novel by Peter Benchley.
MPAA:PG
Universal, Richard Zanuck — MCA Home Video; RCA VideoDiscs

Jaws II   1978
Suspense
11591   116 mins   C   B, V   P
Roy Scheider, Lorraine Gary, Murray Hamilton, directed by Jeannot Szwarc
The sequel to "Jaws'. It's been four years since the maneating shark plagued the resort town of Amity. Suddenly a second shark stalks the waters and the terror returns.
MPAA:PG
Universal; Richard Zanuck; David Brown — MCA Home Video

Jaws of the Dragon   1976
Adventure/Martial arts
51089   96 mins   C   B, V   R, P
James Nam, Johnny Taylor, Kenny Nam
The story of two rival gangs in the Far East.
MPAA:R
Robert Jeffery — Video Gems

Jayce and the Wheeled Warriors   1985
Cartoons
Closed Captioned
70880   45 mins   C   B, V   P
4 pgms
This series of cartoons features the hero "Jaycee" who, with the aid of his allies in the "Lightning League," battles the evil "Monster Minds." The characters pilot awesome combat vehicles.
DIC Enterprises — RCA/Columbia Pictures Home Video

Jayne Mansfield Story, The   1980
Biographical/Drama
79329   97 mins   C   B, V   P
Loni Anderson, Arnold Schwarzenegger, Ray Buktenica, Kathleen Lloyd
This is the lifestory of Jayne Mansfield from her rise to Hollywood stardom to her tragic demise.
In Beta Hi-Fi and VHS Stereo.
Alan Landsburg Productions — U.S.A. Home Video

Jazz and Jive   193?
Music
13645   60 mins   B/W   B, V   P, T
Duke Ellington, Major Bowes, Dewey Brown
Duke Ellington provides early jazz background in "Black and Tan," his first movie. Dance numbers accompany Dewey Brown in "Toot the Trumpet," followed by Major Bowes in "Radio Revels."
Paramount et al — Blackhawk Films

Jazz Ball   1956
Variety/Music
81109   60 mins   B/W   B, V   P

---

*Duke Ellington, Louis Armstrong, Artie Shaw,
Cab Calloway, Gene Krupa, Peggy Lee, Buddy
Rich, Betty Hutton*
A compilation of songs and performances by
the great jazz stars of the 30's and 40's taken
from various movie shorts and features.
NTA; Hal Roach — *Video Yesteryear; Spotlite
Video*

Jazz in America   1981
Music-Performance
60443   90 mins   C   B, V   P
*Dizzy Gillespie, Max Roach, Gerry Mulligan,
Pepper Adams, Candido*
An historical tribute to bebop by way of two
concerts performed at Lincoln Center by Dizzy
Gillespie and his Dream Band.
Gary Keys — *Embassy Home Entertainment;
RCA VideoDiscs*

Jazz in America   1981
Music-Performance
65423   60 mins   C   B, V   P
*Gerry Mulligan, Billy Hart, Frank Luther, Harold
Danko*
With continuity and structure, this program
shows contemporary jazz in an entertaining
manner with "respect" for the music and
performances.
Dick Reed; Paul Rosen — *Embassy Home
Entertainment*

Jazz Singer, The   1980
Musical-Drama
53934   110 mins   C   B, V, 8mm,   P
                              LV
*Neil Diamond, Laurence Olivier, Lucie Arnaz,
Catlin Adams, Franklyn Ajaye, directed by
Richard Fleischer*
Another remake of the 1927 classic about a
Jewish boy who rebels against his father and
family tradition to become a popular entertainer.
MPAA:PG
Paramount; Jerry Leider — *Paramount Home
Video; RCA VideoDiscs*

Jazz Singer, The   1927
Musical-Drama
55581   88 mins   B/W   CED   P
*Al Jolson, Mary McAvoy, Warner Oland, William
Demarest, directed by Alan Crosland*
A Jewish cantor's son breaks with his family to
become a singer of popular music. This film is of
historical importance as the first successful
part-talkie. Jolson's songs include "Toot Toot
Tootsie," "Blue Skies," and "My Mammy."
Warner Bros; Vitaphone — *CBS/Fox Video*

Jazzercise   1982
Physical fitness
63166   60 mins   C   B, V   P
Judi Sheppard Missett

Total physical fitness is the goal of this "jazz
dance" exercise program, designed for all ages
and stages of health. VHS is in stereo, has the
music programmed on one track and the
instructions on the other. This tape is a
completely different production from the disc of
the same name.
Jazzercise/Feeling Fine Productions — *MCA
Home Video*

Jazzercise Better Body   1986
Workout Series
Physical fitness
88428   15 mins   C   B, V   P
Judi Sheppard-Missett 2   pgms
Two short videos designed to accompany and
augment the longer program: "Tight & Toned"
and "Fit & Physical."
AM Available
Judi Sheppard-Missett; Parade
Records — *Parade Records*

Jazzin' for Blue Jean   1984
Music video
88093   20 mins   C   B, V   P
The full-length David Bowie video, buttressed by
a film-within-film dramatic story about an
obsessive fan and a mechanized, androgynous
performer.
Sony Video — *Sony Video Software*

JD and the Salt Flat Kid   1978
Comedy
74085   90 mins   C   B, V   P
Singer JD tears up the road to Nashville with
quick cars, speeding romance and fast times.
MPAA:PG
Jesse Turner; Tommy Amato — *Embassy
Home Entertainment*

Jeep 6 Cylinder   1986
Automobiles
88416   60 mins   C   B, V, 3/4U   P
How to tune-up and maintain the Jeep engine.
Peter Allen Prod. — *Peter Allen Video
Productions*

Jefferson Starship   1984
Music-Performance
76037   60 mins   C   B, V   P
Jefferson Starship delivers both recent hits, as
well as some of their classic Jefferson Airplane
numbers: "White Rabbit," "Somebody to Love,"
and "Winds of Change."
Norman Stangl; Ian
McDougall — *RCA/Columbia Pictures Home
Video*

Jekyll and   1982
Hyde...Together Again
Comedy
64503   87 mins   C   B, V   P

Mark Blankfield, Bess Armstrong, Krista Errickson
A New Wave comic version of the classic story of Dr. Jekyll and Mr. Hyde, with a serious young surgeon who turns into a drug-crazed punk rocker after sniffing a mysterious powder.
MPAA:R
Paramount — *Paramount Home Video*

Jennifer   198?
Horror
82448   90 mins   C   B, V   P
Lisa Pelikan
A teenage girl outcast wreaks havoc against her catty classmates in this supernatural thriller.
MPAA:PG
Orion — *Vestron Video*

Jeremiah Johnson   1972
Drama/Adventure
58239   108 mins   C   B, V, LV   P
Robert Redford, Will Geer, directed by Sydney Pollack
The story of a man who turns his back on civilization, circa 1850, and learns a new code of survival in a brutal land of isolated mountains and hostile Indians.
MPAA:PG
Warner Bros; Sanford Productions — *Warner Home Video; RCA VideoDiscs*

Jericho   1937
Adventure
07162   77 mins   B/W   B, V   P
Paul Robeson, Henry Wilcoxon, Wallace Ford, directed by Thornton Freeland
Adventure in Africa as a court-martialed captain pursues a murderous deserter.
Britain — *Hollywood Home Theater; Discount Video Tapes*

Jericho Mile, The   1979
Drama
88149   97 mins   C   B, V   P
Peter Strauss, Roger E. Mosley, Brian Dennehy, directed by Michael Mann
A made-for-TV drama about a track-obsessed convicted murderer who is given a chance at the Olympics.
ABC; Tim Zinneman — *Charter Entertainment*

Jerk, The   1979
Comedy
42938   94 mins   C   B, V, LV   P
Steve Martin, Bernadette Peters, Catlin Adams directed by Carl Reiner
A jerk, not a bum, tells his rags-toriches-to-rags story in comedic flashbacks. Martin's ridiculous misadventures pay tribute to Jerry Lewis movies of the late sixties.
MPAA:R

David V Picker and William E McEuen — *MCA Home Video; RCA VideoDiscs*

Jermaine Jackson—Dynamite Videos   1985
Music video
82200   29 mins   C   B, V   P
Jermaine Jackson, Pia Zadora, directed by Bob Giraldi
That other Jackson brother performs "Dynamite," "Sweetest Sweetest," "When The Rain Begins To Fall" and "Do What You Do" in VHS Dolby Hi-Fi Stereo and Beta Hi-Fi Stereo.
RCA Video Productions — *RCA/Columbia Pictures Home Video*

Jerry Baker's House Plant Tips & Tricks   1984
Gardening/Plants
84778   40 mins   C   B, V   P
Jerry Baker
Gardener and TV personality Baker reveals the basics of optimum plant care.
Paul Brownstein — *Video Associates*

Jerry Lee Lewis: Live at the Arena   1983
Music-Performance
71010   60 mins   C   B, V   P
Jerry Lee Lewis
Mr. Lewis plays his timeless piano-based rock hits in this compilation of concert footage.
Independent — *Passport Music Video*

Jerry Lewis Live   1985
Comedy-Performance/Nightclub
81814   60 mins   C   B, V   P
Jerry Lewis
The veteran comedian performs his classic routines and songs in this Las Vegas concert. Available in VHS Stereo and Beta Hi-Fi.
Don Spielvogel — *U.S.A. Home Video*

Jerusalem: Of Heaven and Earth   1983
Travel/Cities and towns
84621   200 mins   C   B, V   P
8   pgms
An examination, in eight parts, of the Holy city.
Nomad Prod — *MPI Home Video*

Jesse James   1939
Western
84424   105 mins   C   B, V   P
Henry Fonda, Tyrone Power, Randolph Scott, directed by Henry King
A Hollywood biography of the famed outlaw. One of director King's best efforts.
Darryl F. Zanuck — *Playhouse Video*

Jesse James at Bay   1941
Western
14223   54 mins   B/W   B, V   P
Roy Rogers, Gabby Hayes
Exciting saga of the notorious Jesse James and
his fight against the railroads.
Republic — Video Connection; Cable Films;
Video Yesteryear; Discount Video Tapes;
Nostalgia Merchant

Jesse Owens Story, The   1984
Drama
75931   200 mins   C   B, V   P
Dorian Harewood, Debbi Morgan, George
Stanford Brown, Le Var Burton
The moving story of the four-time Olympic Gold
medal winner's triumphs and misfortunes.
Harold Gast — Paramount Home Video

Jesse Rae   1980
Music-Performance
75917   10 mins   C   B, V   P
This program presents the music of the award
winning Scottish video artist Jesse Rae.
Scotland Video — Sony Video Software

Jesse Rae: 1980
Rusha/D.E.S.I.R.E.
Music/Video
66159   13 mins   C   B, V   P
Music combines with video art in these two
music concept pieces. In stereo.
Scotland Video — Sony Video Software

Jessi's Girls   1983
Drama
65450   86 mins   C   B, V   P
Sondra Currie, Regina Carrol, Jennifer Bishop
In retaliation for the murder of her husband, an
angry young woman frees three female
prisoners, and they embark on a bloody course
of revenge. Together, they track down the
killers, and one by one, they fight to even the
score.
MPAA:R
Manson International — Monterey Home Video

Jesus   1979
Drama/Religion
47379   117 mins   C   B, V   P
Brian Deacon
The Biblical story of Jesus Christ is dramatized
in this family-oriented film, which was made on
location in the Holy Land.
MPAA:G
The Genesis Project — Warner Home Video

Jesus Christ Superstar   1973
Musical-Drama
11592   108 mins   C   B, V   P
Ted Neeley, Carl Anderson, Yvonne Elliman,
directed by Norman Jewison

A rock opera that portrays, in music, the last
seven days in the life of Christ.
MPAA:G
Universal; Norman Jewison, Robert
Stigwood — MCA Home Video

Jesus of Nazareth   1977
Drama/Biographical
48403   371 mins   C   B, V   P
Robert Powell, Anne Bancroft, Ernest Borgnine,
Claudia Cardinale, James Mason, Laurence
Olivier, Anthony Quinn
An all-star cast portrays the life of Jesus Christ.
ATV Ltd; RAI Productions — CBS/Fox Video;
RCA VideoDiscs

Jet Over the Atlantic   1959
Drama
77524   80 mins   B/W   B, V   P
Guy Madison, George Raft, Virginia Mayo, Brett
Halsey, directed by Byron Haskin
A dangerous situation arises as a bomb is
discovered aboard a plane en route from Spain
to New York.
Intercontinental Films — Buena Vista Home
Video

Jethro Tull—Slipstream   1981
Music-Performance
58881   60 mins   C   B, V   P
Jethro Tull
This legendary English rock'n'roll group
presents ten songs in this program conceived
for video. Concert footage is combined with
animation and special effects. The band
members appear in a number of guises, with Ian
Anderson adopting such roles as Aqualung and
Dracula.
Chrysalis Records — Pacific Arts Video

Jewel in the Crown, The   1984
Drama
82155   750 mins   C   B, V   P
Charles Dance, Susan Wooldridge, Art Malik,
Jim Pigott-Smith, Geraldine James
This is the epic saga of the last years of British
rule in India from 1942-1947. The fourteen
episodes of the mini-series are available on five
video cassettes.
Emmy Awards '84: Outstanding Limited Series
Granada Television — Simon and Schuster
Video

Jewel of the Nile, The   1985
Adventure
Closed Captioned
86904   106 mins   C   B, V, LV   P
Michael Douglas, Kathleen Turner, Danny
DeVito, Avner Eisenberg, The Flying
Karamazov Brothers, directed by Lewis Teague
The sequel to "Romancing the Stone," in which
Jack endeavors to rescue Joan from the

criminal hands of a charming North African president.
MPAA:PG
Michael Douglas; 20th Century
Fox — *CBS/Fox Video*

Jezebel 1938
Drama
64456   104 mins   B/W   B, V, LV,   P
                                     CED
Bette Davis, George Brent, Henry Fonda, Fay Bainter, directed by William Wyler
A willful Southern belle loses her boyfriend through her selfish and spiteful nature. When he becomes ill, she realizes her cruelty and rushes to nurse him back to health.
Academy Awards '38: Best Actress (Davis); Best Supporting Actress (Bainter).
Warner Bros — *CBS/Fox Video; RCA VideoDiscs*

J.F.K. 1964
Presidency-US/Documentary
69305   60 mins   B/W   B, V   P
Narrated by Cliff Robertson
This documentary chronicles the life and turbulent times of America's most beloved President.
Art Lieberman — *Media Home Entertainment*

Jig Saw 1978
Adventure
65302   97 mins   C   B, V   P
Angie Dickinson, Lino Ventura
A father searches for his "dead" son, repeatedly risking his own life to stop the criminals from completing the deadly task.
Les Films Ariane; Lafferty; Harwood and Partners Ltd — *U.S.A. Home Video*

Jigsaw Man, The 1984
Suspense
81179   90 mins   C   B, V   P
Michael Caine, Laurence Olivier, Susan George, Robert Powell, David Kelly, directed by Terence Young
A British-Russian double agent is sent back to England to retrieve a list of Soviet agents which he hid there many years ago. Available in Hi-Fi sound for both formats.
MPAA:PG
United Film Distribution — *THORN EMI/HBO Video*

Jilting of Granny Weatherall, The 1980
Drama
82104   57 mins   C   B, V   P
Geraldine Fitzgerald, Lois Smith, William Swetland, hosted by Henry Fonda
This is an adaptation of the Katherine Anne Porter short story about a dying matriarch who is

still haunted by the man who jilted her decades ago. Available in VHS Stereo and Beta Hi-Fi.
Cal Skaggs — *Monterey Home Video*

Jim Fixx on Running 1980
Running
55560   60 mins   C   B, V, LV   P
The nation's most prominent authority on running discusses physical and psychological aspects of running, diet, clothes, measuring improvement, and other topics of interest to running enthusiasts.
Lee Bobker — *RCA/Columbia Pictures Home Video; MCA Home Video; Films Inc*

Jimi Hendrix 1973
Documentary/Music-Performance
79550   102 mins   C   B, V   P
This documentary about the guitar playing legend features interviews with Eric Clapton and Pete Townsend along with concert footage from Jimi's appearances at the Woodstock and Isle of Wight festivals.
MPAA:R
Warner Bros — *Warner Home Video*

Jimi Plays Berkeley 1973
Music-Performance
72220   55 mins   C   B, V   P
The master guitarist Jimi Hendrix electrifies a Berkeley audience.
Independent — *Vestron Video*

Jimmy Buffett—Live by the Bay 1986
Music-Performance
84016   87 mins   C   B, V   P
Jimmy Buffet, directed by Jack Cole
A concert film of Buffet's performance at Miami's Marine Stadium featuring his special brand of sunny hedonism with songs like "Cheeseburger in Paradise," "Margaritaville" and "Why Don't We Get Drunk." Recorded in HiFi Stereo.
MCA Records; Tammara Wells — *MCA Home Video*

Jimmy Houston's Guide to Bass Fishin' 1986
Fishing
86026   60 mins   C   B, V   P
Houston teaches about location, cover, bait and handling when fishing for bass; that's great bass.
United Ent. — *United Home Video*

Jimmy the Kid 1982
Comedy
69676   95 mins   C   B, V   P
Gary Coleman, Ruth Gordon, Dee Wallace, Paul Le Mat, Don Adams

A young boy becomes the unlikely target for an improbable gang of would-be crooks on a crazy, "fool-proof" crime caper.
Zephyr Films — *THORN EMI/HBO Video*

Jinxed
1982
Comedy
64569   104 mins   C   B, V, CED   P
Bette Midler, Ken Wahl, Rip Torn, directed by Don Siegel
A Las Vegas nightclub singer tries to convince a gullible blackjack dealer to murder her crooked boyfriend, but the plan backfires when the gangster electrocutes himself while taking a shower.
MPAA:R
United Artists — *MGM/UA Home Video*

Jive Junction
1943
Musical
69559   62 mins   B/W   B, V, FO   P
Dickie Moore, Tina Thayer, Gerra Young
A group of patriotic teenagers convert a barn into a canteen for servicemen and name it "Jive Junction."
Producers Releasing Corp — *Video Yesteryear*

Jivin' in Bebop
1946
Music-Performance
57762   60 mins   B/W   B, V   P
Dizzy Gillespie and His Orchestra, Helen Humes, R Sneed
A compilation of all-black music from the 1940's, featuring singers and dancers of the period known as "jive."
WD Alexander — *Hollywood Home Theater; Video Yesteryear; Discount Video Tapes*

Joan Armatrading--Track Record
1986
Music-Performance
87729   90 mins   C   B, V   P
Armatrading visits her native island of St. Kitts, amid travel footage, live performances of her music and concept video clips.
A&M Records — *A & M Video*

Joan of Arc
1948
Drama
58736   100 mins   C   B, V, LV   P
Ingrid Bergman, Jose Ferrer, John Ireland, Leif Ericson, directed by Victor Fleming
The life of Joan of Arc, based on the play by Maxwell Anderson.
Academy Awards '48: Best Cinematography, Color; Best Costume Design.
Sierra Pictures — *VidAmerica; MGM/UA Home Video (disc only)*

Joan Rivers and Friends Salute Heidi Abramowitz
1985
Comedy-Performance
71170   55 mins   C   B, V   P
Joan Rivers, Robin Leach, Dr. Joyce Brothers, Bert Convy, Tony Randall, Don Novello, Charles Nelson Reilly, Bob Berosini's Orangutans
Several dozen stars from David Brenner to Betty White offer remembrances of Rivers' fictional promiscuous friend.
Rivers-Rosenberg Productions — *Warner Home Video*

Joan Sutherland in Concert
1982
Opera
85105   60 mins   C   B, V, 8mm, LV   P
A recital of arias from Handel, Rossini, Meyerbeer, Dvorak and Tosti by the famed soprano.
ITC Ent — *Kultur*

Jock Peterson
1974
Exploitation
87617   97 mins   C   B, V   P
Jack Thompson, Wendy Hughes, directed by Tim Burstall
A light-hearted story about a blonde hunk who enrolls in college, cavorting and seducing his way to questionable fame and fortune.
MPAA:R
Hexagon Prod. — *Charter Entertainment*

Joe
1970
Comedy-Drama
59305   107 mins   C   B, V   P
Peter Boyle, Susan Sarandon, Dennis Patrick, directed by John Avildsen
An odd friendship grows between a businessman and a blue-collar worker as they search together for the executive's runaway daughter. Thrust into the midst of the counter-culture, they react with an orgy of violence.
MPAA:R
Cannon; David Gil — *Vestron Video*

Joe Gibbs' Washington Redskins: Two Years to the Title
1983
Football
66217   45 mins   C   B, V, FO   P
Team highlight of the 1981-82 and 1982-83 seasons for the Washington Redskins
NFL Films — *NFL Films Video*

Joe Kidd
1972
Western
47421   88 mins   C   B, V   P
Clint Eastwood, Robert Duvall, John Saxon, Don Stroud, directed by John Sturges

---

A land war breaks out in New Mexico between Mexican natives and American land barons.
MPAA:PG
Universal — *MCA Home Video*

Joe Piscopo   1984
Comedy-Performance
73577   60 mins   C   B, V   P
Joe Piscopo, Eddie Murphy
Joe does some of his best impressions from Frank Sinatra to Jerry Lewis and some memorable improvisations from Saturday Night Live in this one hour special.
HBO — *Vestron Video*

Joe Williams   1984
Music-Performance
88127   58 mins   C   B, V   P
The 1986 winner of the Best Male Jazz Vocalist Grammy performs an array of tunes: "Everyday I Have the Blues," "Once in a While," "Who She Do," "Save that Time for Me," and others.
Adler Ent. — *Sony Video Software*

Joey   1985
Drama/Musical
71187   90 mins   C   B, V   P
Neill Barry, James Quinn
Daddy, a former doo-wopper, looks back on his years of musical success as a waste of time. His son takes to the world of rock guitar with blind fervor. Their argument plays against the backdrop of the "Royal Doo-Wopp Show" at New York City's Radio Music Hall. The HiFi Stereo sound track features lots of both old and new rock songs.
MPAA:PG
Independent — *VidAmerica*

Jog/Run   1978
Running
44924   30 mins   C   B, V   P
Ann Dugan demonstrates warm-up exercises for joggers to help them stay "loose" and strengthen leg, foot, and ankle muscles used for running. From the "Sports Conditioning" series.
Health N Action — *RCA/Columbia Pictures Home Video*

Jogging with Marty Liquori   1982
Running
64924   60 mins   C   B, V   P
Marty Liquori
Former world-class male champion Marty Liquori presents this how-to cassette on running, including segments on equipment selection, jogging techniques, planning of workouts and warm-up exercises.
Celluloid — *Video Associates; Champions on Film and Video*

John and Julie   1977
Comedy
71357   82 mins   C   B, V   P
Colin Gibson, Lesley Dudley
Two young people get it together despite a gratuitous amount of interference and evil intentions.
British Independant — *Family Home Entertainment*

John Cougar Mellencamp—Ain't That America   1985
Music video
80780   58 mins   C   B, V   P
Singer/song writer John Cougar Mellencamp rocks out such favorits as "Jack and Diane," "Pink Houses" and "Hurts So Good" in this collection of conceptual music videos. Available in VHS and Beta Hi-Fi Stereo.
Polygram Music Video — *RCA/Columbia Pictures Home Video*

John Curry's Ice Dancing   1980
Dance
47380   75 mins   C   B, V   P
John Curry, Peggy Fleming, Jo-Jo Starbuck
This production combines the artistry of classical ballet with championship figure skating. Musical selections choreographed by John Curry, Peter Martins, Twyla Tharp and others.
WCI — *Warner Home Video; RCA VideoDiscs*

John Lennon: Interview with a Legend   1981
Music/Interview
52671   60 mins   C   B, V   P
John Lennon, Tom Snyder
A television interview with John Lennon, made with Tom Snyder on the "Tomorrow Show," originally aired April 28, 1975. Lennon discusses what it was like to be a Beatle, how he dealt with worldwide popularity, the breakup of the group, and his life in New York during the post-Beatle era.
NBC — *Karl/Lorimar Home Video*

John Lennon Live in New York City   1985
Music-Performance
84485   55 mins   C   B, V   P
John Lennon, Yoko Ono, The Plastic Ono Elephant's Memory Band
Lennon performs at Madison Square Garden in this rare live concert performance featuring such songs as "Imagine," "Instant Karma," "Come Together" and "Give Peace a Chance." In HiFi Stereo.
Sony — *Sony Video Software*

John McEnroe Story: The 1981
Rites of Passage, The
Tennis
51750   90 mins   C   B, V   P
John McEnroe
This program documents the rise to stardom of
John McEnroe, the brash youngster from New
York, who most tennis experts reluctantly agree
is the best tennis player on tour. His 1981
Wimbledon victory over Bjorn Borg is included,
as are his classic matches with Jimmy Connors.
Michael Mattei — Karl/Lorimar Home Video

John Scofield: On 1985
Improvisation
Music
87921   60 mins   C   B, V   P
The basics of music theory as applied to jazz
improvisation, are demonstrated by the
renowned guitarist and Miles Davis sideman.
DCI Music Video — DCI Music Video

John Waite—No Brakes 1985
Live
Music-Performance
81204   50 mins   C   B, V   P
John Waite performs such hits as "Change,"
"Missing You" and "Teurs" in this concert
video. Available in Hi-Fi Stereo for both formats.
*EMI Music Video — RCA/Columbia Pictures
Home Video*

John Wayne Matinee 1939
Double Feature #3
Western
82173   110 mins   B/W   B, V   P
*John Wayne, Ray Corrigan, Max Terhune,
Doreen McKay*
The Three Mesquiteers save the day in this
thrill-packed double feature of "The Night
Riders" and "Pals in the Saddle."
*Republic Pictures — Republic Pictures Home
Video*

John Wayne Matinee 1938
Double Feature #4
Western
82174   120 mins   B/W   B, V   P
*John Wayne, Ray Corrigan, Max Terhune,
Murdock Macquarrie*
The Duke's at his best in this double feature
which consists of "Santa Fe Stampede" and
"The New Frontier."
*Republic Pictures — Republic Pictures Home
Video*

John Wayne Previews, 196?
Volume 1
Movie and TV trailers
87667   59 mins   C   B, V
A collection of previews from the Duke's biggest
films, including "The Alamo," "Red River," "Rio
Bravo" and "The Spoilers."
*Republic Pictures; Captain Bijou — Captain
Bijou*

John Wayne: The Duke 1984
Lives On
Biographical
82190   48 mins   C   B, V   P
This is a look at the life and films of John Wayne
including highlights from "She Wore a Yellow
Ribbon" and "The Quiet Man."
Daniel Helgott — RKO HomeVideo

Johnny Angel 1945
Mystery
10064   79 mins   B/W   B, V   P
*George Raft, Claire Tervor, Signe Hasso, Lowell
Gilmore, Hoagy Carmichael*
Merchant Marine captain unravels mystery of
his father's murder.
RKO — RKO HomeVideo; Blackhawk Films

Johnny Appleseed/Paul 198?
Bunyan
Cartoons
78903   60 mins   C   B, V   P
Animated
This animated double feature retells the legends
of the lives of Johnny Appleseed and Paul
Bunyan.
Rankin-Bass Productions — Prism

Johnny Belinda 1948
Drama
71155   103 mins   B/W   B, V   P
*Jane Wyman, Lew Ayres, Charles Bickford,
Agnes Moorehead, directed by Jean Negulesco*
A compassionate physician cares for a young
deaf mute woman and her illegitimate child.
Tension builds as the baby's father returns to
claim the boy.
Academy Awards '48: Best Actress (Wyman)
Warner — MGM/UA Home Video

Johnny Belinda 1982
Drama
73533   95 mins   C   B, V   P
*Rosanna Arquette, Richard Thomas, Dennis
Quaid, Candy Clark*
A VISTA worker teaches a blind girl sign
language and opens a whole new world for her.
Available in Beta Hi-Fi and VHS stereo.
*Dick Berg; Stonehenge Productions — U.S.A.
Home Video*

Johnny Carson 197?
Comedy
33698   60 mins   C   B, V, 3/4U   P
*Johnny Carson, Don Rickles, Pearl Bailey, Joey
Heatherton, Ed McMahon*

Highlights of the fabulous career of "The Tonight Show," starring Johnny Carson. The program shows material not seen in "The Tonight Show" anniversary programs.
NBC — *Shokus Video*

Johnny Carson Show, The
1955
Variety
85180   21 mins   B/W   B, V   P
Johnny Carson, Paul Coates, Dorothy Shay
Carson's youthful self is seen in this early series episode; included is a parody of the then-popular show, "Confidential File."
CBS — *Video Yesteryear*

Johnny Cash Ridin' the Rails
1974
Trains
85061   52 mins   C   B, V   P
Singing along the way, Johnny Cash examines the romantic history of America's railroads.
Webster-Rivkin Prods — *Sony Video Software*

Johnny Dangerously
1984
Comedy
Closed Captioned
70657   90 mins   C   B, V   P
Michael Keaton, Joe Piscopo, Danny De Vito, Maureen Stapleton, Marilu Henner, Peter Boyle, Griffin Dunne, Glynnis O'Connor, Dom De Louise, Richard Dimitri, dir. by A. Heckerling
This send-up of gangster films follows Mr. Dangerously's efforts to go straight. Competitive crooks would rather see him killed than law-abiding, and his mother requires more and more expensive operations. Crime pays in Hi-Fi stereo on all formats.
MPAA:PG13
20 Century Fox — *CBS/Fox Video*

Johnny Firecloud
1979
Drama
80897   94 mins   C   B, V   P
Ralph Meeker, Frank De Kova, Sacheen Little Feather, David Canary, Christina Hart
A modern Indian goes on the warpath when the persecution of his people reawakens his sense of identity.
American National Enterprises — *Prism*

Johnny Got His Gun
1971
Drama
59671   111 mins   C   B, V   P
Timothy Bottoms, Jason Robards, Donald Sutherland, Diane Varsi, Kathy Field
Dalton Trumbo's story of a young war victim who realizes that his arms and legs have been amputated.
MPAA:R
Bruce Campbell — *Media Home Entertainment*

Johnny Griffin
1981
Music-Performance
88116   55 mins   C   B, V, 8mm   P
The premier tenor saxophonist performs at the Village Vanguard in New York, doing "Blues for Gonzi," "A Monk's Dream," "56" and "When We Were One."
Sony Video — *Sony Video Software*

Johnny Guitar
1953
Western
00298   110 mins   C   B, V   P
Joan Crawford, Ernest Borgnine, Sterling Hayden
Tough saloon owner finds her wealth can't buy everything—not even love.
Republic — *Republic Pictures Home Video*

Johnny Maddox Plays Ragtime
1985
Music-Performance
81732   60 mins   C   B, V   P
Johnny Maddox plays such ragtime favorites as "Maple Leaf Rag" and "Creole Belles" in this concert recorded at the Il Porto in Alexandria, Virginia.
C.B. Wismar — *Kartes Video Communications*

Johnny Mathis—Greatest Hits
1983
Music-Performance
72335   90 mins   C   V   P
Celebrated singer Johnny Mathis performs his hit songs to mark his 25th year in show business. Guest star Denise Williams joins Mathis.
Music America Live Productions — *Prism*

Johnny Nobody
1961
Drama
77232   88 mins   B/W   B, V   P
William Bendix, Aldo Ray, Nigel Patrick, Yvonne Mitchell
A mysterious stranger murders a writer who has been taunting the residents of a quaint Irish town.
Medallion Pictures — *Monterey Home Video*

Johnny Tiger
1966
Drama
81017   100 mins   C   B, V   P
Robert Taylor, Geraldine Brooks, Chad Everett, Brenda, Scott
A teacher has his hands full when he arrives at the Seminole Reservation in Florida to instruct the Indian children.
Universal Pictures — *Spotlite Video*

Johnny Tremain and the Sons of Liberty
1958
Adventure/Drama
66053   85 mins   C   B, V   P

Luanna Patten, Richard Beymer
The story of the gallant American patriots who
participated in the Boston Tea Party.
Walt Disney Productions — *Walt Disney Home
Video*

Johnny Winter Live   1984
Music-Performance
76643   45 mins   C   B, V   P
This program presents the best young, white
blues artists of the '60's in a live concert
appearance.
Concert Productions International — *Music
Media*

Johnny Woodchuck's   1978
Adventures
Cartoons
47862   60 mins   C   B, V   P
Animated
Little Johnny Woodchuck is more precocious
than his well-behaved brothers. One day, he
leaves home and family behind and sets out on
an adventure. Available in both English and
Spanish versions.
EL, SP
ZIV Intl — *Family Home Entertainment*

Joke of Destiny, A   1985
Satire
87261   105 mins   C   B, V   P
*Ugo Tognazzi, Piera Degli Esposti, directed by
Lina Wertmuller*
A irreverent satire about a Minister of the Interior
who becomes trapped in his high-tech limousine
before a vital press conference. An exaggerated
vision of Italian bureaucracy. With English
subtitles.
MPAA:PG   IT
Giuseppe Giovannini — *Karl/Lorimar Home
Video*

Jokes My Folks Never   1977
Told Me
Comedy
76794   82 mins   C   B, V   P
Sandy Johnson, Mariwin Roberts
This film consists of a series of blackouts and
sketches featuring a bevy of beautiful women.
Steven A. Vail; Ted Woolery — *Embassy
Home Entertainment*

Jonathan Livingston   1973
Seagull
Fantasy
63431   114 mins   C   B, V   P
*James Franciscus, Juliet Mills, Music by Neil
Diamond*
Based on the bestselling novella by Richard
Bach, this film quietly envisions a world of love,
understanding, achievement, hope and
individuality.

Paramount — *Paramount Home Video*

Jonathan Winters Show,   1957
The
Comedy/Variety
47475   29 mins   B/W   B, V, FO   P
*Jonathan Winters, Jeri Southern, Betty
Johnson, the Eddie Sefranski Orchestra*
Two complete 15-minute shows from Jonathan
Winters' first network TV series, featuring
several impromptu sketches by the host about
fishing and General Custer. Original
commercials included.
NBC — *Video Yesteryear*

Jonathan Winters Show,   1966
The/Presenting Morey
Amsterdam
Variety
85499   46 mins   B/W   B, V   P
*Jonathan Winters, Morey Amsterdam, Don
Cornell, Eddie Safranski*
This tape offers two comedy kinescopes back to
back; a 1957 Jonathan Winters program and
Morey Amsterdam taped in London, 1966.
BBC; NBC — *Video Yesteryear*

Joni Mitchell: Shadows   1980
and Light
Music-Performance
53858   60 mins   C   B, V   P
Joni Mitchell
Singer/songwriter Joni Mitchell performs her
unique blend of folk, jazz and rock 'n' roll music.
CFJ Enterprises — *Warner Home Video;
Pioneer Artists; RCA VideoDiscs*

Jory   1972
Western
84865   96 mins   C   B, V   P
Robby Benson, B.J. Thomas, John Marley
A young man's father is killed in a saloon fight,
and he must grow up quickly to survive.
MPAA:PG
Avco-Embassy, Minsky-Kirshner
Productions — *Embassy Home Entertainment*

Jose Jose en Acapulco   1985
Music-Performance
82080   60 mins   C   B, V   P
Spanish singing star Jose Jose performs fifteen
classic songs in this concert taped in Acapulco,
Mexico. Available in VHS and Beta Hi-Fi Stereo.
SP
Anthony Christopher Productions — *MCA
Home Video*

Jose Serebrier   198?
Music-Performance
87358   134 mins   C   B, V   P

Serebrier conducts selections from Prokofiev's "Alexander Nevsky," Tchaikovsky's Symphony No. 1, and Beethoven's Symphony No. 3. Australian Broadcasting Corp. — *Kultur*

Joseph Andrews   1977
Drama
10987   98 mins   C   B, V   P
Ann-Margret, Peter Firth, Jim Dale, Michael Hordern, Beryl Reid, directed by Tony Richardson
This adaptation of a 1742 Henry Fielding novel chronicles the rise of Joseph Andrews from servant to personal footman (and fancy) of Lady Booby.
MPAA:R
Paramount; Neil Hartley — *Paramount Home Video*

Joseph in Egypt   1979
Drama/Bible
63487   52 mins   C   B, V   P
Sam Bottoms, Bernie Kopell, Barry Nelson, Albert Salmi
The Biblical story of Joseph, who is chosen as his father's deputy and later sold into slavery by his resentful brothers. Joseph overcomes the odds and eventually returns to his family.
Sunn Classics — *Magnum Entertainment; Lucerne Films*

Josepha   1982
Drama
64909   114 mins   C   B, V   P
Miou-Miou, Claude Brasseur, Bruno Cremer
A husband and wife, both actors, are forced to re-examine their relationship when the wife finds a new love while on a film location. In French with English subtitles.
MPAA:R
Albina Productions-Mondex Films-TFI Films — *RCA/Columbia Pictures Home Video*

Joshua at Jericho   1979
Drama/Bible
63488   61 mins   C   B, V   P
Robert Culp, William Daniels, Cameron Mitchell
The Biblical story of Joshua leading his people to Canaan is dramatized.
Sunn Classics — *Magnum Entertainment; Lucerne Films*

Joshua Then and Now   1985
Drama
Closed Captioned
84413   102 mins   C   B, V   P
James Woods, Alan Arkin, Michael Sarrazin, directed by Ted Kotcheff
A Jewish-Canadian novelist is threatened by a gay scandal, and re-examines his picaresque history.

MPAA:R
Robert Lantos; Stephen J Roth — *Key Video*

Josie and the Pussycats   1972
in Outer Space, Vol. II
Cartoons
77159   58 mins   C   B, V   P
Animated, voices of Casey Kasem, Don Messick, Janet Waldo
An all girl rock group Josie and the Pussycats along with their traveling entourage become involved in a series of cosmic adventures after getting trapped in a NASA space capsule.
Hanna-Barbera — *Worldvision Home Video*

Josie and the Pussycats   197?
in Outer Space
Cartoons
47690   58 mins   C   B, V   P
Animated
Three episodes of the all-girl rock group launching their music into the far corners of the galaxy.
Hanna Barbera — *Worldvision Home Video*

Jour Se Leve, Le   1939
Drama
08686   85 mins   B/W   B, V, 3/4U   P
Jean Gabin, Jules Berry, Arletty, directed by Marcel Carve
A distorted and maddening love affair causes a tormented man to commit murder. French with English subtitles.
FR
Sigma Prod — *Hollywood Home Theater; Video Yesteryear*

Journey   1977
Adventure
45007   87 mins   C   B, V   P
Genevieve Bujold, John Vernon
A violent story of a girl who is rescued from the Sagueney River and falls in love with her rescuer. Choosing to remain in the remote pioneer community of this "hero," she brings everyone bad luck and misery.
MPAA:PG
First American Films — *United Home Video*

Journey Back to Oz   1971
Fantasy
69583   90 mins   C   B, V   P
Animated, voices of Liza Minnelli, Ethel Merman, Milton Berle, Mickey Rooney, Danny Thomas
This animated special features Dorothy and Toto returning to visit their friends in the magical land of Oz.
Filmation — *Family Home Entertainment*

Journey—Frontiers and Beyond   1983
Music-Performance
76650   98 mins   C   B, V   P
Platinum rock group Journey is profiled on and behind the stage. Includes "Wheel in the Sky," "Stone in Love," "After the Fall" and "Escape."
Music Media — *Music Media*

Journey Into Fear   1942
Suspense
64369   71 mins   B/W   B, V, 3/4U   P
Joseph Cotten, Dolores del Rio, Orson Welles, Agnes Moorehead, directed by Norman Foster and Orson Welles
An American armaments expert is smuggled out of Istanbul with Axis agents close behind who are determined to kill their enemy.
RKO — *RKO HomeVideo; Nostalgia Merchant*

Journey Into Fear   1974
Mystery
86854   96 mins   C   B, V   P
Sam Waterston, Vincent Price, Shelley Winters, Donald Pleasance, Zero Mostel, Yvette Mimieux, Ian McShane, directed by Daniel Mann
A remake of the 1942 Orson Welles semi-classic about a geologist ensnared in Turkish intrigue and murder.
New World — *Lightning Video*

Journey of Natty Gann, The   1985
Adventure
84799   101 mins   C   B, V   P
Meredith Salenger, John Cusack, Ray Wise, Scatman Crothers, Lainie Kazan, Verna Bloom, directed by Jeremy Kagan
With the help of a wolf and a drifter, a 14-year-old girl travels across the country in search of her father.
MPAA:PG
Walt Disney Productions — *Walt Disney Home Video*

Journey Through Rosebud   1972
Drama
85371   93 mins   C   B, V   P
Robert Forster, directed by Tom Giles
A re-enactment of the protest at Wounded Knee.
David Gil — *Charter Entertainment*

Journey to the Center of the Earth   1959
Science fiction
Closed Captioned
81513   129 mins   C   B, V   P
James Mason, Pat Boone, Arlene Dahl, Diane Baker, Thayer David
A scientist and student undergo a hazardous journey to find the center of the earth and along the way they find the lost city of Atlantis. Based upon the Jules Verne novel. Available in VHS and Beta Hi-Fi.
20th Century Fox — *Playhouse Video*

Journey to the Center of the Earth, A   1976
Science fiction
84712   50 mins   C   B, V   P
Animated
An animated version of the Jules Verne classic adventure.
API Television Prod — *MGM/UA Home Video*

Journey Together   1982
Drama
86703   25 mins   C   B, V   P
Esther Rolle, Tina Andrews, directed by Paul Asselin
An old black woman teaches a young black girl about life.
Asselin Prods — *Video Gems*

Joy House   1964
Suspense/Drama
81394   98 mins   B/W   B, V   P
Jane Fonda, Alain Delon, Lola Albright, directed by Rene Clement
An American woman befriends a handsome French playboy when her husband sends gangsters to kill him. Available in VHS Stereo and Beta Hi-Fi.
MGM — *Monterey Home Video*

Joy of Natural Childbirth, The   1984
Childbirth
80411   59 mins   C   B, V   P
Join Lorenzo Lamas and his wife Michele as they discuss natural childbirth with John and Nancy Ritter and Kenny and Marianne Rogers. Available in Beta and VHS Stereo.
Ted Mather; Peter Henton — *MCA Home Video*

Joy of Sex   1984
Comedy
80063   93 mins   C   B, V   P
Colleen Camp, Christopher Lloyd, Ernie Hudson, Michelle Meyrink, directed by Martha Coolidge
An undercover narcotics agent is sent to Richard M. Nixon High School to investigate the school's extracurricular activities.
MPAA:R
Frank Konigsberg; Paramount — *Paramount Home Video*

Joy of Stocks: The Forbes Guide to the Stock Market, The   1983
Finance
72463   104 mins   C   B, V   P
This introductory video to the stock market is divided into ten instructional segments.
MGM UA — *MGM/UA Home Video*

Joy Sticks   1983
Comedy
65350   88 mins   C   B, V   P
Joe Don Baker
Something outrageously hilarious, very sexy and thoroughly entertaining is going on at the local video arcade!
MPAA:R
Greydon Clark — *Vestron Video*

Joyride   1977
Drama
85625   91 mins   C   B, V   P
Desi Arnaz, Jr., Robert Carradine, Melanie Griffith, Anne Lockhart
Three friends steal a car for a joyride and plummet into a life of crime.
MPAA:R
American International — *Vestron Video*

Juarez   1939
Biographical/Drama
73977   122 mins   B/W   B, V   P
Paul Muni, John Garfield, Bette Davis, Claude Rains, Gale Sondergaard, directed by William Dieterle
A revolutionary leader overthrows the Mexican government and then becomes President of the country.
Warner Bros — *Key Video*

Jubilee   1978
Musical/Drama
73149   103 mins   C   B, V   P
Adam Ant, Toyah Willcox, Jenny Runacre, Little Nell
Adam Ant stars as a punk who takes over Buckingham Palace and turns it into a recording studio. Music by Eno, Adam and the Ants, and Siouxsie and the Banshees.
Megalovision — *VCL Home Video*

Jubilee U.S.A.   1960
Music-Performance
47649   58 mins   B/W   B, V, FO   P
Red Foley, Slim Wilson, Harold and Jimmy, Betty Patterson, Buddy Childre, The Harmonettes, The Pitch-Hikers, Bill Ring
Two episodes of this variety/country and western music show, complete with ABC's promos for their western series ("Maverick," "Colt 45," "The Lawman").
ABC — *Video Yesteryear*

Jud   1971
Drama
70601   80 mins   C   B, V   P
Joseph Kaufmann, Bonnie Bittner, Robert Deman, Claudia Jennings
Society's refusal to understand the young soldier returning from the Vietnam conflict leads him to violence and tragedy.
MPAA:PG
Unknown — *Prism*

Judas Priest: Fuel for Life   1986
Music video
86547   40 mins   C   B, V   P
A collection of Priest hits including "Locked In," "Another Thing Coming" and "Living After Midnight."
CBS/Fox Video Music — *CBS/Fox Video*

Judas Priest Live   1984
Music-Performance/Music video
76801   83 mins   C   B, V   P
Rob Halford, Glenn Tipton, K.K. Downing
The high powered heavy metal frenzy of Judas Priest is captured in this concert video.
Geoffrey Thomas — *Music Media*

Judex   1964
Drama
06222   103 mins   B/W   B, V   P
Channing Pollock, Francine Berge, directed by Georges Franju
Judex, a cloaked hero-avenger, fights master criminal gangs. French film with English subtitles.
FR
France; Italy — *Hollywood Home Theater; Festival Films; Western Film & Video Inc; Discount Video Tapes*

Judge Horton and the Scottsboro Boys   1976
Drama
71296   96 mins   C   B, V   P
Arthur Hill, Vera Miles, Ken Kercheval, Lewis J Stadlen, Ellen Barber, Susan Lederer, directed by Fielder Cook
This courtroom drama deals with a famous rape trial from 1931. Nine black men appealed and won a retrial of the charges that they gang-raped two white women.
Tomorrow Entertainment — *U.S.A. Home Video*

Judge Priest   1934
Comedy-Drama
08864   80 mins   B/W   B, V, 3/4U   P
Will Rogers
Comedy-drama set in the old South.
Fox Film Corp — *Movie Buff Video; Prism; Hollywood Home Theater; Discount Video Tapes; Cable Films; Western Film & Video Inc;*

Video Yesteryear; United Home Video; Kartes Video Communications

---

Judgment at Nuremburg   1961
Drama
69380   178 mins   B/W   B, V   P
Spencer Tracy, Burt Lancaster, Marlene Dietrich, Richard Widmark, Judy Garland, Montgomery Clift, Maximilian Schell, directed by Stanley Kramer
This film centers on the post-WWII trial of four Nazi officials accused of war crimes.
Academy Awards '61: Best Actor (Schell); Best Screenplay.
United Artists; Stanley Kramer — *CBS/Fox Video*

Judgment of Solomon   1979
Drama/Bible
55014   54 mins   C   B, V   P
John Carradine, Kevin Dobson, Tom Hallick, Stephen Keats, Carol Lawrence, John Saxon
The story of the bitter fight between King David's two sons, Solomon and Adonijah, who vie for the throne of their father.
Sunn Classics — *Magnum Entertainment; Vanguard Video; Lucerne Films*

Judy Garland Show, The   1964
Music-Performance
57172   55 mins   B/W   B, V   P
Judy Garland, the Bobby Cole Trio, Mort Lindsey Orchestra
Judy Garland is featured in a concert show from her television series, originally broadcast March 22, 1964. Songs include "Sail Away," "Comes Once in a Lifetime," "Joey, Joey," "Poor Butterfly" and "As Long as He Needs Me."
CBS — *King of Video; American Video Tape*

Judy Garland Christmas Show   1963
Variety
57173   50 mins   B/W   B, V   P
Judy Garland, Liza Minnelli, Lorna Luft, Joey Luft, Jack Jones, Mel Torme
A holiday special from Judy Garland's mid-sixties television series, featuring the whole gang joining in on Christmas standards. Songs include "Have Yourself a Merry Little Christmas," "Sleigh Ride," "Winter Wonderland," "The Christmas Song," "What Child Is This," "Over the Rainbow," and others.
CBS — *King of Video*

Judy Garland (General Electric Theatre)   1956
Variety/Music-Performance
80759   30 mins   B/W   B, V   P
Hosted by Ronald Reagan, Judy Garland, Nelson Riddle
A vintage kinescope featuring Judy with Nelson Riddle and his orchestra performing "I Feel A

Song Coming On," etc., and her closing theme song "I Will Come Back."
CBS — *Video Yesteryear*

Judy Garland in Concert: Volume One   1964
Music-Performance
79317   60 mins   B/W   B, V   P
Judy Garland
This is Judy's one-woman show originally broadcast in 1964 where she sings "That's Entertainment," "Over The Rainbow" and "Swing Low, Sweet Chariot." Available in stereo in both formats.
CBS — *RKO HomeVideo*

Judy Garland in Concert: Volume Two   1964
Music-Performance
79318   60 mins   B/W   B, V   P
Judy Garland
This is a special one woman show Judy performed in 1964 where she sings "The Man That Got Away" and "Once in a Lifetime." Available in stereo in both formats.
CBS — *RKO HomeVideo*

Judy Rankin's Golf Tips   1980
Golf
44337   58 mins   C   B, V   P
This program features twelve different golf tips covering shots on and around the green, including chipping, putting and bunker play, which can take four or five strokes from the average golfer's scores.
Video Sports Prods — *Video Sports Productions*

Juggernaut   1937
Drama/Mystery
46349   64 mins   B/W   B, V, FO   P
Boris Karloff, Mona Goya, Arthur Margetson
A young woman hires a sinister doctor to murder her wealthy husband. The doctor, who happens to be insane, does away with the husband and then goes on a poisoning spree.
British, Grand National — *Video Yesteryear*

Juggler of Notre Dame, The   1984
Drama
77518   110 mins   C   B, V   P
Carl Carlson, Patrick Collins, Melinda Dillon, Merlin Olsen, Gene Roche
A hobo and a street juggler embark on an unusual journey that will change the lives of the people they visit.
Mike Rhodes; Terry Sweeney — *Buena Vista Home Video*

Jules et Jim   1962
Romance
54129   104 mins   B/W   B, V   P
*Jeanne Moreau, Oskar Werner, Henri Serre,
Marie Dubois, Vanna Urbino, directed by
Francois Truffaut*
The story of a friendship between two men, one
German and the other French, and their twenty-
year love for the same woman. Adapted from
the novel by Henri-Pierre Roche. English
subtitles.
Mar Del Plata Festival '62: Best Director
(Truffaut) FR
Janus Films — *Key Video; Video Dimensions*

Julia   1977
Drama
44931   118 mins   C   B, V, CED   P
*Jane Fonda, Vanessa Redgrave, Jason
Robards*
Story of a writer who becomes involved in the
holocaust of World War II when her friend, Julia,
asks her to smuggle money into Berlin.
MPAA:PG
20th Century Fox — *CBS/Fox Video*

Julia   1976
Drama
58552   83 mins   C   B, V   R, P
Sylvia Kristel
"Emmanuelle's" Sylvia Kristel stars as a young
woman coming of age in a sophisticated
society.
MPAA:R
Cine Media Intl — *Video Gems*

Julia   1974
Drama
80831   83 mins   C   B, V   R, P
*Sylvia Kristel, Jean-Claude Bouillon, Terry
Torday*
A woman tries to lose her virginity while
vacationing in the Swiss Alps.
Cine Media International — *Video Gems*

Julia Child—The French   197?
Chef, Vol. I
Cookery
56890   120 mins   C   CED   P
Julia Child
Julia Child prepares four wonderful creations in
her entertaining style: roasted chicken, lasagna
a la Francaise, strawberry souffle, and mousse
au chocolat.
WGBH Boston — *RCA VideoDiscs*

Julius Caesar   1970
Drama
81875   116 mins   C   B, V   P
*Charlton Heston, John Gielgud, Jason Robards,
Richard Chamberlain, Robert Vaughn, Diana
Rigg*
This is an adaptation of the Shakespeare play
about political greed and corruption within the
Roman Empire.
Peter Snell; Commonwealth
United — *Republic Pictures Home Video*

Julius Caesar   1979
Opera
84658   124 mins   C   B, V   P
*Theo Adam, Celestina Casapietra, Eberhard
Buchner, the Berlin State Opera conducted by
Hans Krenitz*
A live performance of this Handel opera, with
Theo Adam singing the role of Julius Caesar.
Recorded in Hi-Fi.
GE
George Mielke — *V.I.E.W. Video*

Julius Caesar   1984
Opera
85901   220 mins   C   B, V   P
*Dame Janet Baker, Valerie Masterson, Sarah
Walker, Della Jones*
A performance of Handel's opera, which is
based on Shakespeare. As the custom of the
time dictates, all the roles are sung by women.
The English National Opera — *THORN
EMI/HBO Video*

Jump for Life   1983
Physical fitness
75700   60 mins   C   B, V   P
This exercise program is performed on a mini-
trampoline.
Jill Steinbeck — *Video Associates*

Jungle Book, The   1942
Adventure
29360   105 mins   C   B, V   P
*Sabu, Joseph Calleia, Rosemary de Camp,
Ralph Byrd*
A lavish version of Rudyard Kipling's stories
about Mowgli, the boy who was raised by
wolves in the jungles of India. Musical score by
Miklos Rosza.
United Artists; Alexander Korda — *Movie Buff
Video; Hollywood Home Theater; Video
Connection; VCII; Cinema Concepts; Cable
Films; Video Yesteryear; Discount Video Tapes;
Western Film & Video Inc; Nostalgia Merchant;
Media Home Entertainment; World Video
Pictures; Hal Roach Studios; Prism; Kartes
Video Communications*

Jungle Cat   1959
Wildlife/Documentary
84994   69 mins   C   B, V   P
This major Disney wildlife film depicts the South
American Jaguar in its original habitat.
Walt Disney — *Walt Disney Home Video*

Jungle Cavalcade 1941
Documentary/Wildlife
58966   80 mins   B/W   B, V, 3/4U   P
Naturalist Frank Buck traveled deep into the
jungle to photograph wild animals in their natural
surroundings.
RKO — Cable Films

Jungle Master, The 1956
Adventure
70784   90 mins   C   B, V   P
John Kitzmiller, Simone Blondell, Edward Mann,
directed by Miles Deem
Noble British types hunt for the jungle's number
one guy with the aid of a tribal chieftess and a
lovely photo-journalist.
Empire — Force Video

Jungle Patrol 1948
War-Drama
84500   72 mins   B/W   B, V   P
Kristine Miller, Arthur Franz, Richard Jaeckel,
directed by Joe Newman
In 1943 New Guinea, a patrol of entrapped
soldiers are confronted with a beautiful USO
entertainer. Romance and show tunes follow.
20th Century Fox-Frank N Seltzer — Sony
Video Software

Jungle Raiders 1985
Adventure
87364   102 mins   C   B, V   P
Lee Van Cleef, Christopher Connelly, Marina
Costa
A Indiana Jones-esque mercenary searches the
steamy jungles of Malaysia for a valuable jewel,
the Ruby of Gloom.
MPAA:PG-13
L'Immagine S.R.L. — MGM/UA Home Video

Jungle Warriors 1985
Adventure
82483   96 mins   C   B, V   P
Nina Von Pallandt, Paul Smith, John Vernon,
Alex Cord, Woody Strode, Kai Wulff, Sybil
Danning
Seven fashion models are abducted by a
Peruvian cocaine dealer. To escape him, they
must become Jungle Warriors.
MPAA:R
Ernest R V Theumer — Media Home
Entertainment

Junior G-Men 1940
Adventure/Serials
08873   237 mins   B/W   B, V, 3/4U   P
Billy Halop, Huntz Hall
The Dead End Kids fight Fifth Columnists who
are trying to sabotage America's war effort.
Twelve episodes.
Universal — Video Connection; Video
Yesteryear

Junior G-Men of the Air 1942
Adventure/Serials
64385   215 mins   B/W   B, V, 3/4U   P
The Dead End Kids
The Dead End Kids become teenage flyboys in
this twelve-episode serial adventure.
Universal — Nostalgia Merchant

Jupiter Menace, The 1982
Speculation
64211   84 mins   C   B, V   P
George Kennedy
An examination of speculative theories dealing
with the inevitable end of the world. Kennedy
predicts a continuing cycle of unnatural
occurrences and disasters which will culminate
with the tilting of the earth's axis in the year
2000.
Jupiter Menace Ltd — THORN EMI/HBO
Video

Jupiter's Thigh 1981
Comedy/Romance
71252   96 mins   C   B, V   P
A honeymooning couple searches the Greek
countryside for a missing piece to a rare
valuable statue. Available in French with English
subtitles or dubbed into English.
MPAA:PG   EL, FR
Alexandre Minouchkine; George Dancigers;
Robert Amon — Embassy Home
Entertainment

Just Between 1984
Friends—Exercise Card
Video
73630   5 mins   C   B, V   P
On this reusable two hour videocassette is a
satirical greeting for women trying to lose
weight.
Kartes Productions — Kartes Video
Communications

Just Doin' It 1975
Minorities
88386   36 mins   C   B, V, 3/4U   R, P
An intimate look at two black Atlanta barbers.
Your World Video — Your World Video

Just Like Us 1983
Drama
86601   55 mins   C   B, V   P
Jennifer Jason Leigh, Kari Michaelson, Marion
Ross, Carol Lawrence
A made-for-TV program designed for
adolescents, depicting the growing friendship,
and problems, of a very rich girl and the
daughter of her cook.
Harry Harris — Video Gems

Just Me and You   1978
Romance/Comedy
70910   100 mins   C   B, V   P
*Louise Lasser, Charles Grodin, directed by
Charles Erman*
An "It Happened One Night"-type tale of an
unlikely couple who fall in love with each other
when chance brings them together on a cross-
country drive.
E.M.I.; Roger Gimbel — *VCL Home Video*

Just One of the Guys   1985
Comedy
Closed Captioned
82322   100 mins   C   B, V   P
*Joyce Hyser, Billy Jacoby, Leigh McCloskey,
Sherilyn Fenn, Clayton Rohner*
A young girl masks her gender in order to land a
job with the chauvinistic local newspaper.
Available in VHS and Beta Hi-Fi.
MPAA:PG-13
Columbia Pictures — *RCA/Columbia Pictures
Home Video*

Just Tell Me What You   1980
Want
Comedy
52700   112 mins   C   B, V   P
*Alan King, Ali McGraw, Myrna Loy, Keenan
Wynn, Tony Roberts, directed by Sidney Lumet*
A wealthy married man's mistress wants to take
over the operation of a failing movie studio he
has acquired.
MPAA:R
Jay Presson Allan; Sidney Lumet; Warner
Bros — *Warner Home Video*

Just Tell Me You Love Me   1980
Adventure/Comedy
82457   90 mins   C   B, V   P
*Robert Hegyes, Debralee Scott, Lisa Hartman,
Ricci Martin*
Four budding con artists plot to make easy
money in this Hawaiian romp.
MPAA:PG
Maui Productions — *Vestron Video*

Just the Way You Are   1984
Comedy
81503   96 mins   C   B, V   P
*Kristy McNichol, Robert Carradine, Kaki Hunter,
Michael Ontkean, directed by Edouard Molinaro*
An attractive musician struggles to overcome a
physical handicap and winds up falling in love
while on vacation in the French Alps.
MPAA:PG
MGM/UA — *MGM/UA Home Video*

Just William's Luck   1947
Comedy
85182   87 mins   B/W   B, V   P
William Graham

A precocious English brat sneaks into an old
mansion, which happens to be the headquarters
for a gang of thieves.
English — *Video Yesteryear*

Just Win, Baby/NFL 83   1984
Football
72937   46 mins   C   B, V, FO   P
Los Angeles Raiders
Highlights from Los Angeles Raiders 1983
season and "NFL 83."
NFL Films — *NFL Films Video*

Justice   1955
Crime-Drama
66137   26 mins   B/W   B, V, FO   P
*William Prince, Jack Klugman, Biff McGuire,
Jack Warden*
A crusading attorney tries to keep a waterfront
kangaroo court from applying its harsh justice to
an admitted killer. A TV crime-drama also titled
"Flight from Fear."
NBC — *Video Yesteryear*

Justice of the West   1961
Western
82407   71 mins   C   B, V   P
*Clayton Moore, Jay Silverheels, directed by Earl
Bellamy*
The Lone Ranger and his sidekick, Tonto,
perform good deeds in the Old West, including
helping to retrieve stolen gold, helping to build
an Indian school and giving a blind man a fresh
perspective on life.
Lone Ranger Television Inc — *MGM/UA
Home Video*

Justin Morgan Had a   1981
Horse
Drama
47410   91 mins   C   B, V   P
Don Murray, Lana Wood, Gary Crosby
The true story of a colonial school teacher in
post-Revolutionary War Vermont who
developed the Morgan horse, the first and most
versatile American breed.
Walt Disney — *Walt Disney Home Video*

K

Kagemusha   1980
Adventure
55458   160 mins   C   B, V   P
Directed by Akira Kurosawa
A thief is rescued from the gallows because of
his striking resemblance to a warlord in 16th
Century Japan, but, unfortunately for him, he is
required to pose as the ambitious lord when the

lord is fatally wounded. In Japanese with English subtitles.
Cannes Film Festival '80: Co-winner of Grand Prize. MPAA:PG JA
Twentieth Century Fox — *CBS/Fox Video*

Kajagoogoo   1983
Music-Performance
75905   11 mins   C   B, V   P
This program presents the new band Kajagoogoo performing their songs "Too Shy," "Ooh to Be An" and "Hang on Now."
EMI Records Ltd — *Sony Video Software*

Kamikaze '89   1983
Science fiction
66447   106 mins   C   B, V   P
Rainer Werner Fassbinder, Gunther Kaufman, Boy Gobert, directed by Wolf Gremm
German director Fassbinder has the lead acting role in this offbeat story of a police lieutenant in Berlin, circa 1989, who investigates a puzzling series of bombings. Music by Tangerine Dream.
TeleCulture; Trio Film — *MGM/UA Home Video*

Kanako   19??
Photography
60579   ? mins   C   LV   P
Kanako Higuchi, one of Japan's most famous and adored actresses, is presented by renowned photographer Kishin Shinoyama in this series of nude photographs. Stereo.
Japan — *Pioneer Video Imports*

Kansan, The   1943
Western
72054   79 mins   B/W   B, V   P
Richard Dix, Victor Jory, Albert Dekker
A tyrant is confronted by a marshall when he tries to take over the state of Kansas.
United Artists — *Independent United Distributors; Kartes Video Communications*

Kansas   1982
Music-Performance
75920   87 mins   C   B, V   P
This program presents a live concert by the rock group Kansas.
Radio & Records Inc; The Carr Company — *Sony Video Software*

Kansas City Massacre   1975
Crime-Drama
88147   99 mins   C   B, V   P
Dale Robertson, Sally Kirkland, Bo Hopkins, Scott Brady, Lynn Loring, Matt Clark, Mills Watson, Robert Walden, directed by Dan Curtis
A made-for-TV film chronicling the efforts of Melvin Purvis, as he tracked down Depression-era hoods. First called "Melvin Purvis, G-Man."

ABC Circle Films — *Vidmark Entertainment*

Kansas City Royals: 1984
Team Highlights
Baseball
81141   30 mins   C   B, V   P
George Brett, Amos Otis, Hal McRae, Frank White, Dan Quisenberry 7   pgms
This series examines the history of the Kansas City Royals and looksback at the best moments from the team's previous seasons.
1.1969: 1969 Kansas City Royals 2.1970: Our K.C. Royals and The A.L. 3.1971: A Bright New Era 4.1973: 1972 Review-1973 Preview 5.1980: One Step Claser 6.1982: Playing a Winning Hand 7.1984: Transition to a Title.
Major League Baseball — *Major League Baseball Productions*

Kansas Pacific   1953
Western
80740   73 mins   C   B, V   P
Sterling Hayden, Eve Miller, Barton MacLane, Reed Hadley, Douglas Hadley
A group of Confederate sympatizers try to stop the Kansas Pacific Railroad from reaching the West Coast in the 1860's.
Allied Artists — *Hal Roach Studios*

Karate for Your Child   1985
Martial arts
88224   35 mins   C   B, V   P
This program instructs youngsters in basic karate techniques.
Ed Parker; Larry Tatum — *Master Arts Video*

Karate Kid, The   1984
Drama/Martial arts
80782   126 mins   C   B, V   P
Ralph Macchio, Pat Morita, Randee Heller, Martin Kove, directed by John Avildsen
A teenaged boy finds out that Karate involves using more than your fists when a handyman agrees to teach him the Martial arts. Available in VHS and Beta Hi-Fi Stereo.
MPAA:PG
Jerry Weintraub; Columbia Pictures — *RCA/Columbia Pictures Home Video*

Karate Killer   1973
Martial arts
63861   95 mins   C   B, V   P
A Kung Fu master seeks revenge on a brutal and vicious gang.
MPAA:R
United International Pictures — *Hollywood Home Theater*

Kardiac Kids...Again   1981
Football
50650   24 mins   C   B, V, FO   R, P

Cleveland Browns
The 1980 Cleveland Browns football season was full of thrilling, last-minute, come-from-behind victories which propelled the Browns into the playoffs, where they met the Oakland Raiders in subzero weather. Quarterback Brian Sipe was named AFC Player of the Year.
NFL Films — *NFL Films Video*

Kashmiri Run   1969
Adventure
65000   96 mins   C   B, V   P
Pernell Roberts
A group of men race through the Himalayas for the Kashmiri border to avoid capture by Chinese Communists.
Sagittarius Productions — *U.S.A. Home Video*

Kate Bush, Live at   1979
Hammersmith
Music-Performance
65089   52 mins   C   B, V   P
Kate Bush
Kate Bush displays her wide range of talents as a songwriter, singer, pianist and choreographer in this live concert show taped at London's Hammersmith Theater in May, 1979.
Kate Bush; London Films — *THORN EMI/HBO Video*

Kathy Smith's Body   1985
Basics
Physical fitness
84751   60 mins   C   B, V   P
Kathy Smith
An exercise program focusing on light aerobics, basic warm-up and flab toning.
JCI Video — *JCI Video*

Kathy Smith's Ultimate   1984
Video Workout
Physical fitness
70568   60 mins   C   B, V   P
Kathy Smith
This hour of exercise is for all levels ability with attention paid to flexibility, strength development, and cardio-respiratory fitness.
JCI Video — *JCI Video*

Katrina and the Waves   1985
Music-Performance/Music video
82014   30 mins   C   B, V   P
New Wave rockers Katrina and the Waves perform "Walking on Sunshine," "Que Te Quiero," "Do You Want Crying" and "Red Wine and Whisky" in VHS and Beta Hi-Fi Stereo.
Capitol Records — *Sony Video Software*

Katy Caterpillar   1983
Cartoons
75612   85 mins   C   B, V   P

Animated
Katy Caterpillar tells storybook tales.
Unknown — *Children's Video Library*

Kavik the Wolf Dog   1984
Adventure
76653   99 mins   C   B, V   P
Ronny Cox, Linda Sorensen, Andrew Ian McMillian, Chris Wiggins, John Ireland
A heartwarming story of a courageous dog's love and suffering to be with the boy he loves.
Stanly Chase — *Media Home Entertainment*

Keaton Special/Valentino   192?
Mystique
Film-History
10159   56 mins   B/W   B, V   P, T
Buster Keaton, Rudolph Valentino
Film shows Buster Keaton in his peak years in excerpts from "College" and "Steamboat Bill Jr." Also recounts career of Rudolph Valentino using newsreels, home movies, and feature excerpts.
United Artists et al — *Blackhawk Films*

Keep, The   1983
Horror
65762   96 mins   C   B, V, CED   P
Scott Glenn, Alberta Watson, Jurgen Prochnow, Robert Prosky
At the height of the Nazi onslaught, several German soldiers unleash an unknown power from a medieval stone fortress which begins to overtake them all.
MPAA:R
Gene Kirkwood; Howard W. Koch — *Paramount Home Video*

Keep My Grave Open   1975
Horror
47670   85 mins   C   B, V   P
Camilla Carr, Gene Ross
A bizarre tale of murder, a strange house, and a sexually driven woman.
MPAA:R
S F Brownrigg — *Unicorn Video*

Kelly's Heroes   1970
Suspense
68244   143 mins   C   B, V, CED   P
Clint Eastwood, Donald Sutherland, Telly Savalas, Don Rickles, Carroll O'Connor
A group of men set out to rob a bank and almost win World War II. In stereo.
MPAA:PG
MGM — *MGM/UA Home Video*

Ken Murray's Shooting   1985
Stars
Outtakes and bloopers
76925   62 mins   C   B, V   P

A collection of celebrity home movies featuring such stars as Gregory Peck and Jack Lemmon at ease.
Ken Murray — *MPI Home Video*

Kennedys Don't Cry 1983
Documentary
70182   100 mins   C   B, V   P
Narrated by Cliff Robertson
A sensitive and detailed look at the triumphs and tragedies of the Kennedy clan. Rare footage and interviews trace the growth of Joseph P. Kennedy's children and their influence on American history. Some segments are in black and white.
Maljack Productions — *MPI Home Video*

Kennel Murder Case 1933
Mystery
01713   73 mins   B/W   B, V   P
William Powell, Mary Astor, Jack LaRue, directed by Michael Curtiz
Debonair detective Philo Vance suspects that a clearcut case of suicide is actually murder.
Warner Bros — *Hollywood Home Theater; Discount Video Tapes; Nostalgia Merchant; Video Dimensions; Cable Films; Video Yesteryear; Video Connection*

Kenneth Anger's Magick 1980
Lantern Cycle
Film-Avant-garde
86473   36 mins   C   B, V   P
Kenneth Anger, Bruce Byron, Miriam Gibril, Anais Nin, Marianne Faithfull 4 pgms
Spanning his work from 1947 to 1980, these programs feature the complete cycle of Anger's mythic underground films.
1.Fireworks/Rabbit's Moon/Eaux D'Artifice 2.Inauguration of the Pleasure Dome 3.Kustom Kar Kommandos/Puce Moment/Scorpio Rising 4.Invocation of My Demon Brother/Lucifer Rising
Kenneth Anger — *Mystic Fire Video*

Kenny and Dolly—Real 1985
Love
Music-Performance
82199   60 mins   C   B, V   P
Kenny Rogers, Dolly Parton
Kenny Rogers and Dolly Parton perform "Lady," "Jolene," "Islands In The Stream," "Real Love" and more in this VHS Dolby Hi-Fi Stereo and Beta Hi-Fi Stereo concert.
RCA Video Productions — *RCA/Columbia Pictures Home Video*

Kenny Loggins Alive 1981
Music-Performance
59879   60 mins   C   B, V   P
Pop artist Kenny Loggins performs "This Is It," "Angry Eyes," "I Believe in Love," "Celebrate Me Home," and other hits before a hometown

crowd in Santa Barbara during the final performance of his 1981 tour. In stereo.
Kenny Loggins Productions — *CBS/Fox Video; Pioneer Artists; RCA VideoDiscs*

Kentuckian, The 1955
Adventure/Western
68228   104 mins   C   B, V, CED   P
Burt Lancaster, Walter Matthau, Diana Lynn, John McIntire, Dianne Foster
Burt Lancaster stars as a rugged frontiersman who leaves with his son to go to Texas. On their journey the two are harassed by fighting mountaineers.
Hecht-Lancaster Productions — *CBS/Fox Video*

Kentucky Blue Streak 1935
Adventure
59373   61 mins   B/W   B, V, FO   P
Eddie Nugent, Junior Coughlin, Patricia Scott, Ben Carter's Colored Octette
A young jockey is framed for murder while riding at an "illegal" racetrack. Later, almost eligible for parole, he escapes from jail to ride "Blue Streak", in the Kentucky Derbys
Puritan Pictures Corp. — *Video Yesteryear*

Kentucky Fried Movie 1977
Comedy
66064   85 mins   C   B, V, LV   P
Bill Bixby, Jerry Zucker, James Abrahams, David Zucker, Donald Sutherland
A zany potpouri of satire about movies, TV, commercials, and contemporary society.
MPAA:R
Robert K. Weiss — *Media Home Entertainment*

Kentucky Rifle 1955
Western
81406   80 mins   C   B, V   P
Chill Wills, Lance Fuller, Cathy Downs, Jess Barker, Sterling Holloway, Jeanne Cagney
A Comanche Indian tribe will let a group of stranded pioneers through their territory only if they agree to sell the Kentucky rifles aboard their wagon. Available in VHS Stereo and Beta Hi-Fi.
Howco Productions — *Monterey Home Video*

Kermit and Piggy Story, 1985
The
Variety
Closed Captioned
80744   57 mins   C   B, V   P
Kermit the Frog, Miss Piggy, Cheryl Ladd, Tony Randall, Loretta Swit, Raquel Welch
This is the romantic story of how a barnyard pig rose from the chorus line to superstardom and finds the frog of her dreams along the way. Available in VHS and Beta Hi Fi.

Henson Associates — *Playhouse Video*

Key Exchange   1985
Romance/Comedy
Closed Captioned
70993   96 mins   C   B, V   P
*Brooke Adams, Ben Masters, Daniel Stern,
Tony Roberts, Danny Aiello, directed by Barnet
Kellman*
Kevin Scott and Paul Kurta based this
contemporary look at love and commitments on
Kevin Wade's popular play. Two New York City
"yuppies" have reached a point in their
relationship where an exchange of apartment
keys commonly occurs - but they are hesitant.
MPAA:R
20th Century Fox — *Key Video*

Key Largo   1948
Drama
31662   101 mins   B/W   B, V   P
*Humphrey Bogart, Lauren Bacall, Claire Trevor,
Edward G. Robinson, Lionel Barrymore,
directed by John Houston*
A gangster melodrama set in Key West, Florida,
where a group of hoods take over a hotel,
intimidating the proprietor. Based on a play by
Maxwell Anderson.
Academy Awards '48: Best Supporting Actress
(Claire Trevor).
Warner Bros, Jerry Wald — *CBS/Fox Video;
RCA VideoDiscs*

Keystone Comedies   191?
Comedy
80522   45 mins   B/W   B, V   P
*Fatty Arbuckle, Mable Normand, Minta Durfee,
Harold Lloyd, Louise Fadenza, Edgar Kennedy*
8 pgms
The film vaults of Mack Sennett and the
Keystone Studios provided the contents for this
series of original short comedies from the early
days of moviemaking. All shorts are silent, with
a musical soundtrack.
*1.Fatty's Faithful Fido; Fatty's Tintype Tangle;
Fatty's New Role 2.Fatty and Mabel at the San
Diego Exposition; Fatty and Mabel's Simple Life;
Mabel and Fatty's Wash Dry 3.Mabel Lost and
Won; Wished On Mabel; Mabel, Fatty and the
Law; Fatty's Plucky Pup 4.Mabel's Willful Way;
The Little Band of Gold; Mabel and Fatty's
Married Life 5.Miss Fatty's Seaside Lovers;
Court House Crooks; Love, Loot and Crash
6.Ambrose's Nasty Temper; Ambrose's Sour
Grapes; When Ambrose Dared Walrus
7.Ambrose's Lofty Perch; Ambrose's Fury;
Willful Ambrose; Those Bitter Sweets 8.Gussle
the Golfer; Gussle's Day of Rest; Gussle Tied to
Trouble; Gussle's Backward Way.*
Keystone; Mack Sennett — *Kartes Video
Communications*

Kick of Death--The   198?
Prodigal Boxer
Martial arts
87761   90 mins   C   B, V   P
*Mang Sei, Suma Wah Lung, Pa Hung, directed
by Chai Yang Min*
A young boxer is accused of a murder he didn't
commit, and fights a battle to the death to clear
it.
MPAA:R
Foreign — *Video Gems*

Kid Colter   1985
Adventure
Closed Captioned
86373   101 mins   C   B, V   P
*Jim Stafford, Jeremy Shamos, Hal Terrance,
Greg Ward, Jim Turner*
An innocent country boy is attacked, left for
dead in the mountains, yet doesn't die. He
pursues his attackers relentlessly.
Wind River Prod. — *Playhouse Video*

Kid Creole and the   1986
Coconuts Live
Music-Performance
86910   60 mins   C   B, V   P
The Coconuts perform their famous songs at
Carnegie Hall: "Don't Take My Coconuts,"
"Laughing" and "Lifeboat Party."
Philip Goodhand-Tait — *Embassy Home
Entertainment*

Kid from Brooklyn, The   1946
Musical/Comedy
84867   113 mins   C   B, V   P
*Danny Kaye, Virginia Mayo, Eve Arden, directed
by Norman Z MacLeod*
A shy, musically-inclined milkman becomes a
middleweight boxer by knocking out the champ
in a street brawl.
RKO — *Embassy Home Entertainment*

Kid From Left Field, The   1984
Drama
78136   80 mins   C   B, V   R, P
This program presents the story of the San
Diego Padres' rise from last place to the World
Series led by a ten year old boy.
Vestron — *Vestron Video*

Kid from Not-So-Big, The   1978
Drama
47381   87 mins   C   B, V   P
*Jennifer McAllister, Veronica Cartwright, Robert
Viharo, Paul Tulley*
A family film that tells the story of Jenny, a
young girl left to carry on her grandfather's
frontier-town newspaper. When two con men
come to town, Jenny sets out to expose them.
Boomming Ltd — *Warner Home Video*

Kid 'n' Hollywood & Polly   1933
Tix in Washington
Comedy
64918   20 mins   B/W   B, V   P, T
Shirley Temple
These two "Baby Burlesks" shorts star a cast of toddlers, featuring the most famous moppet of all time, Shirley Temple, in her earliest screen appearances.
Educational Pictures — *Blackhawk Films*

Kid Sister, The   1945
Comedy
47502   56 mins   B/W   B, V, FO   P
Roger Pryor, Judy Clark, Frank Jenks, Constance Worth
A young girl is determined to grab her sister's boyfriend for herself, and enlists the aid of a burglar to do it.
Producers Releasing Corp — *Video Yesteryear*

Kid, The/The Idle Class   1921
Comedy
08399   85 mins   B/W   B, V   P
Charlie Chaplin, Jackie Coogan, Edna Purviance, directed by Charlie Chaplin
The Little Tramp adopts a homeless orphan in "The Kid," Chaplin's first feature-length film. This tape also includes "The Idle Class" a rare Chaplin short.
Charlie Chaplin Productions; First National — *Playhouse Video*

Kid with the Broken Halo,   1981
The
Comedy
65441   96 mins   C   B, V   P
Gary Coleman, Robert Guillame
A wisecracking 12-year-old angel is always in and out of trouble and always needs help from his teacher.
Satellite Productions — *U.S.A. Home Video*

Kid with the 200 I.Q.   1983
Comedy
80243   96 mins   C   B, V   P
Gary Coleman, Robert Guillame, Harriet Nelson, Dean Butler, Kari Michaelson
When a thirteen year old boy goes to college majoring in astronomy, he encounters problems with campus social life.
Guillaume—Margo Productions — *U.S.A. Home Video*

Kidco   1983
Comedy
Closed Captioned
81557   104 mins   C   B, V   P
Scott Schwartz, Elizabeth Gorcey, Cinnamon Idles, Tristine Skyler
This is the true story of a money-making corporation headed and run by a group of children ranging in age from nine to sixteen.
Available in VHS and Beta Hi-Fi.
MPAA:PG
20th Century Fox — *Playhouse Video*

Kidnap Syndicate, The   1976
Adventure/Drama
80935   105 mins   C   B, V   P
James Mason, Valentina Cortese
Kidnappers swipe two boys, releasing one, the son of a wealthy industrialist who meets their ransom demands. When they kill the other boy, a mechanic's son, the father goes on a revengeful killing spree.
MPAA:R
SJ International — *VidAmerica*

Kidnapped   1960
Adventure
69318   94 mins   C   B, V   P
Peter Finch, James MacArthur, Peter O'Toole
A young boy is sold by his wicked uncle as a slave, and is helped by an outlaw. Based on the Robert Louis Stevenson classic.
Buena Vista — *Walt Disney Home Video; RCA VideoDiscs*

Kids Are Alright, The   1979
Music-Performance
59130   106 mins   C   B, V   P
The Who, Ringo Starr, Keith Richard, Steve Martin, Tom Smothers, Rick Danko
A feature-length compilation of performances and interviews spanning the first fifteen years of the rock group, The Who. Includes rare footage from the "Rolling Stones Rock and Roll Circus" film. Songs include: "My Generation," "I Can't Explain," "Young Man's Blues," "Won't Get Fooled Again," "Baba O' Reilly," and excerpts from "Tommy."
MPAA:PG
Tony Klinger; Bill Curbishley — *THORN EMI/HBO Video; RCA VideoDiscs*

Kid's Auto Race/Mabel's   191?
Married Life
Comedy
66119   21 mins   B/W   B, V   P, T
Charlie Chaplin, Mabel Normand, Mack Swain
"Kid's Auto Race" (1914), also known as "Kid Auto Races at Venice," concerns a kiddie-car contest; "Mabel's Married Life" (1915) is about flirtations in the park between married individuals. Piano and organ scores.
Keystone — *Blackhawk Films*

Kids from Candid Camera   1985
Comedy
77180   60 mins   C   B, V   P
Hosted by Allen Funt
A collection of classic children's segments from episodes of "Candid Camera."

Allen Funt Productions — *Vestron Video*

Kids from Fame, The   1983
Music-Performance/Dance
65106   75 mins   C   B, V, CED   P
*Debbie Allen, Gene Anthony Ray, Lee Curreri,
Erica Gimpel, Lori Singer, Carlo Imperato*
The cast of the TV show "Fame" sings and
dances in a live sold-out performance at
London's Royal Albert Hall. VHS in stereo.
MGM/UA Home Entertainment
Group — *MGM/UA Home Video*

Kids Incorporated: The   1985
Beginning
Variety
80735   60 mins   C   B, V   P
This is the story of how the kids from "Kids Inc"
hired the musicians who appear on the popular
television series.
Hal Roach Studios — *Hal Roach Studios*

Kill   1973
Suspense
79189   110 mins   C   B, V   P
*Jean Seberg, James Mason, Stephen Boyd,
Curt Jurgens*
The police and Interpol team up to smash an
international spy ring.
Illya Salkind; Alexander Salkind — *U.S.A.
Home Video*

Kill, The   1973
Crime-Drama
86611   81 mins   C   B, V   P
Richard Jaeckel, Henry Duval, Judy Washington
A rough, cynical, hard-boiled, womanizing
detective tracks down stolen cash in downtown
Macao.
Rolf Bayer — *New World Video*

Kill Alex Kill   1983
Crime-Drama
85781   88 mins   C   B, V   P
Tony Zarindast, Tina Bowmann, Chris Ponti
A Vietnam POW returns to find his family
murdered, and uses the crime underworld to
take revenge.
Tony Zarindast — *Video Gems*

Kill and Go Hide   1976
Horror
53149   95 mins   C   B, V   P
A young girl visits her mother's grave nightly to
communicate with and command the ghoul-like
creatures that haunt the surrounding woods.
Valiant Intl Pictures — *Monterey Home Video*

Kill and Kill Again   197?
Martial arts/Drama
47315   100 mins   C   B, V   P

*James Ryan, Anneline Kriel, Stan Schmidt, Bill
Flynn, Norman Robinson, Ken Gampu, John
Ramsbottom*
A martial arts champion attempts to rescue a
kidnapped Nobel Prize-winning chemist who
has developed a high-yield synthetic fuel.
Igo Kantor — *Media Home Entertainment*

Kill Castro   1980
Drama
66635   90 mins   C   B, V   P
Stuart Whitman, Robert Vaughn, Caren Kaye
A Key West boat skipper is forced to carry a CIA
agent to Cuba on a mission to assassinate
Castro.
MPAA:R
No Frills Inc — *Monterey Home Video*

Kill or Be Killed   1980
Martial arts/Adventure
47852   90 mins   C   B, V   P
*James Ryan, Charlotte Michelle, Norman
Combes*
A martial arts champion is lured to a phony
martial arts contest by a madman bent on
revenge.
MPAA:PG
Ben Vlok — *Media Home Entertainment*

Kill Squad   1981
Martial arts/Adventure
59084   85 mins   C   B, V   P
*Jean Claude, Jeff Risk, Jerry Johnson, Bill
Cambra, Cameron Mitchell*
A squad of martial arts masters follow a trail of
violence and bloodshed to a vengeful, deadly
battle of skills.
MPAA:R
Michael Lee — *HarmonyVision*

Kill the Golden Goose   1979
Suspense/Martial arts
54079   91 mins   C   B, V   R, P
*Brad Von Beltz, Ed Parker, Master Bong Soo
Han*
Two martial arts masters work on opposite sides
of a government corruption and corporate
influence peddling case.
MPAA:R
Skytrain Kim Films — *Video Gems*

Kill the Ninja   1984
Martial arts
87328   84 mins   C   B, V   P
*Bob-B Kim, Kavl Sterling, Janet-O Kim, directed
by Richard Park*
A Buddha encasing two million dollars in yen is
the bone of contention for three gangs of Ninja
killers.
Ted Berkic — *U.S.A. Home Video*

Killer Bats (Devil Bat)   1942
Horror
11673   70 mins   B/W   B, V, FO   P
Bela Lugosi, Dave O'Brien
Monstrous, blood-sucking bats are trained to kill
at the smell of perfume.
PRC — *Video Yesteryear; Video Connection;
Cable Films; United Home Video; Kartes Video
Communications*

Killer Elephants   1976
Martial arts
82093   83 mins   C   B, V   P
Sung Pa, Alan Yen, Nai Yen Ne, Yu Chien
A Thai man struggles to save his plantation, his
wife and his baby from the terrorists hired by a
land baron to drive him away from his property.
Foreign — *Unicorn Video*

Killer Elite, The   1975
Mystery
86041   120 mins   C   B, V   P
*James Caan, Robert Duvall, Arthur Hill, directed
by Sam Peckinpah*
Two professional assassins begin as friends but
end up stalking each other.
MPAA:R
United Artists — *Key Video*

Killer Force   1975
Adventure
66104   100 mins   C   B, V, CED   P
Telly Savalas, Peter Fonda, Maud Adams
An adventure of international diamond
smuggling.
MPAA:R
American International Pictures — *Vestron
Video*

Killer in Every Corner, A   1974
Suspense
84755   80 mins   C   B, V   P
*Joanna Pettet, Patrick Magee, Max Wall, Eric
Flynn*
Three psychology students visit a loony
professor and succumb to his hair-raising
shenanigans.
John Cooper — *Thriller Video*

Killer Likes Candy   1978
Mystery/Adventure
84668   86 mins   C   B, V   P
*Kerwin Matthews, Marilu Tolu, directed by
Richard Owens*
An assassin stalks the King of Kafiristan, and a
CIA operative tries to stop him.
Richard Hellman — *Video Gems*

Killers from Space   1954
Science fiction
76916   72 mins   B/W   B, V   P
Peter Graves, Barbara Bestar, James Scay

Aliens from the Planet Unknown are terrorizing
the residents of Southern California.
RKO — *United Home Video*

Killer's Moon   1984
Horror
80490   90 mins   C   B, V   P
Four sadistic psychopaths escape from a prison
hospital and unleash their murderous rage on
anyone who crosses their path.
VCL Communications — *VCL Home Video*

Killers, The   1964
Drama/Suspense
56873   95 mins   C   B, V   P
*Ronald Reagan, Lee Marvin, Angie Dickinson,
John Cassavetes*
After two hired assassins kill a teacher, they
look into his past and try to find leads to a
$1,000,000 robbery. Based on Ernest
Hemingway's story.
Universal — *MCA Home Video*

Killing 'em Softly   1985
Mystery
84619   90 mins   C   B, V   P
*George Segal, Irene Cara, directed by Max
Fischer*
With musical and comedic touches, a lonely
musician murders for money, and is tracked
down by a young female sleuth.
Claude Leger — *Prism*

Killing Fields, The   1984
Drama
81489   142 mins   C   B, V, LV   P
*Sam Waterston, Dr. Haing S. Ngor, Athol
Fugard, John Malkovich, Craig T. Nelson,
directed by Roland Jaffe*
This is the true story of the friendship between
N.Y. Times correspondent Sydney H.
Schanberg and his assistant Dith Pran during
the 1975 Khmer Rouge uprising in Cambodia.
Hi-Fi stereo for all formats
Academy Awards '84: Best Supporting Actor
(Ngor)?Best Cinematography?Best Film Editing
MPAA:R
Warner Bros; Goldcrest — *Warner Home
Video*

Killing Heat   1984
Drama
80729   104 mins   C   B, V   P
*Karen Black, John Thaw, John Kani, John
Moulder-Brown*
An independent career woman living in South
Africa decides to abandon her career to marry a
struggling jungle farmer. Available in VHS and
Beta Hi-Fi Stereo.
MPAA:R
Satori Entertainment — *Key Video*

Killing Hour, The   1984
Drama/Suspense
Closed Captioned
70660   97 mins   C   B, V   P
Elizabeth Kemp, Perry King, Norman Parker, Kenneth McMillan, directed by Armand Mastroianni
A psychic painter finds that the visions she paints come true in a string of grisly murders. This ability interests a TV reporter and a homicide detective. Available in Hi-Fi stereo.
MPAA:R
20 Century Fox — *CBS/Fox Video*

Killing Machine   1984
Adventure/Drama
71315   95 mins   C   B, V   P
Lee Van Cleef, Richard Jaeckel, Margeaux Hemingway, Willie Aames, directed by J Anthony Loma
Tired of the anarchic bombing and killing, a terrorist attempts to retire. His comrades move against his decision.
Carlos Vasallo — *U.S.A. Home Video*

Killing Machine, The   1976
Martial arts
81824   89 mins   C   B, V   P
Sonny Chiba
A Japanese World War II army veteran uses his martial arts skills to subdue local black market gangs.
Cinema Shares International — *Prism*

Killing of Angel Street, The   1983
Drama
65731   100 mins   C   B, V   P
Liz Alexander, John Hargreaves
A courageous young woman unwittingly becomes the central character in an escalating nightmare about saving a community from corrupt politicians and organized crime.
MPAA:PG
Anthony Buckley — *VidAmerica*

Killing of President Kennedy, The   1983
Documentary/Presidency-US
69584   80 mins   C   B, V   P
This documentary explores all of the conspiracy theories and the alleged cover-up by the Warren Commission.
Independent — *VidAmerica*

Killing of President Kennedy: New Revelations Twenty Years Later, The   1983
Documentary
72527   60 mins   C   B, V   P
An in-depth look at new evidence that has surfaced and suggests President John Kennedy's assassination was carried out differently from government accounts.
Mark Hollo — *VidAmerica*

Killing of Randy Webster, The   1981
Drama
81807   90 mins   C   B, V   P
Hal Holbrook, Dixie Carter, Sean Penn, Jennifer Jason Leigh, directed by Sam Wanamaker
A father attempts to prove that his son did not die as a criminal when Texas policemen shot him after transporting a stolen van across state lines.
EMI Television — *VCL Home Video*

Killing Stone   1978
Mystery/Drama
82210   120 mins   C   B, V   P
Gil Gerard, J.D. Cannon, Jim Davis, Nehemiah Persoff, directed by Michael Landon
A freelance writer uncovers a small town sheriff's plot to cover up a scandalous homicide.
Michael Landon — *Prism*

Killpoint   1984
Suspense
70148   89 mins   C   B, V, LV, CED   P
Richard Roundtree, Leo Fong, Cameron Mitchell
A special task force is assembled to catch the criminals who robbed a National Guard armory for its weapons.
MPAA:R
Crown International Pictures — *Vestron Video*

Killzone   1985
Adventure
84089   86 mins   C   B, V   P
Ted Prior, David James Campbell, Richard Massery, directed by David A Prior
A brainwashed Vietnam vet breaks down during a training exercise and embarks on a psychotic killing spree.
Shapiro — *Vestron Video*

Kim Carnes   1984
Music-Performance
75911   15 mins   C   B, V   P
This program presents a performance by Kim Carnes singing her songs "Bette Davis Eyes," "Invisible Hands," "Voyeur" and others.
EMI America Records — *Sony Video Software*

Kind Hearts and Coronets   1949
Comedy
36934   101 mins   B/W   B, V   P

Alec Guinness, Dennis Price, Valerie Hobson, Joan Greenwood, directed by Robert Hamer
Guinness plays eight different roles in this movie as the relatives of an ambitious young man who sets out to bump them off in an effort to attain the ducal crown, with hilarious results.
J Arthur Rank — *THORN EMI/HBO Video*

King 1978
Biographical/Drama
70958   272 mins   C   B, V   P
Paul Winfield, Cicely Tyson, Roscoe Lee Brown, Ossie Davis, Art Evans, Ernie Banks, Howard Rollins, William Jordan, Cliff DeYoung
This telefilm follows the life and career of one of greatest non-violent civil rights leaders of all time, Martin Luther King.
Abby Mann Prods; Filmways; NBC
TV — *THORN EMI/HBO Video*

King and I, The 1956
Musical
08427   133 mins   C   B, V, LV   P
Deborah Kerr, Yul Brynner, Rita Moreno, Martin Benson
From the musical play based on the biography "Anna and the King of Siam" by Margaret Landon.
Academy Awards '56: Best Actor (Brynner); Best Scoring Musical. EL, SP
20th Century Fox — *CBS/Fox Video*

King Arthur & the Knights 1981
of the Round Table Vol. 1
Cartoons
59327   60 mins   C   B, V   P
Animated
The tale of King Arthur is told beginning with his birth to the mighty sword Excalibur.
EL, SP
ZIV International — *Family Home Entertainment*

King Arthur & the Knights 1981
of the Round Table Vol. 2
Cartoons
59328   60 mins   C   B, V   P
Animated
The tales of King Arthur continue with the Knights of the Round Table, Camelot, Lady Guinevere and his adventures with Sir Lancelot.
EL, SP
ZIV International — *Family Home Entertainment*

King Arthur, the Young 197?
Warlord
Adventure
59350   90 mins   C   B, V   R, P
Oliver Tobias
The struggle that was the other side of Camelot—the campaign against the Saxon hordes.

MPAA:PG
Heritage Enterprises — *Video Gems*

King Boxers, The 1980
Adventure/Martial arts
56925   90 mins   C   B, V   R, P
Yasuka Kurate, Johnny Nainam
Japan's top actor, Yasuka Kurate, stars in this tale of elephant hunts, warding off Triad Society gangs, and personal combat. Also stars Johnny Nainam, Thailand's fists and kicks boxing champion.
MPAA:R
Fourseas Films — *Video Gems*

King Creole 1958
Musical-Drama
08383   115 mins   B/W   B, V   P
Elvis Presley, Carolyn Jones, Walter Matthau, Dean Jagger, Dolores Hart, Vic Morrow
A teenager with a criminal record becomes a successful pop singer in New Orleans.
Paramount — *CBS/Fox Video; RCA VideoDiscs*

King Crimson: The Noise 1982
Music-Performance
71015   55 mins   C   B, V   P
Robert Fripp, Tony Levin, Bill Bruford, Adrian Belew
This concert tape compiles footage from the band's "Discipline" tour and captures them early in their evolution.
EG — *Passport Music Video*

King Crimson: Three of a 1984
Perfect Pair
Music-Performance
71012   60 mins   C   B, V   P
Adrian Belew, Bill Bruford, Tony Levin, Robert Fripp
Recorded at Tokyo's Kain Hoken Hall in April 1984, this tape features the intricate arrangements made famous by their final E.G./Warner Brothers release.
E.G. — *Passport Music Video*

King David 1985
Drama
Closed Captioned
81508   114 mins   C   B, V   P
Richard Gere, Alice Krige, Cherie Lunghi, Hurd Hatfield, directed by Bruce Beresford
This is the story of David, the legendary Biblical hero whose acts of bravery paved the way for him to become king of Israel.
MPAA:PG-13
Paramount — *Paramount Home Video*

King in New York, A 1957
Satire
08423   105 mins   B/W   B, V   P

Charlie Chaplin, Dawn Addams, Michael Chaplin, directed by Charlie Chaplin
Chaplin plays the deposed king of a European mini-monarchy who comes to the United States in hope of making a new life.
Charlie Chaplin Productions — *Playhouse Video*

King Kong 1933
Horror
00308   105 mins   B/W   B, V   P
Fay Wray, Bruce Cabot, Robert Armstrong
The original film classic which tells the story of Kong, a giant ape captured in Africa and brought to New York as a sideshow attraction. He escapes from his captors and rampages through the city, ending up on top of the newly built Empire State Building.
RKO — *RKO HomeVideo; King of Video; RCA VideoDiscs*

King Kong 1977
Horror
38616   135 mins   C   B, V, LV   P
Jeff Bridges, Charles Grodin, Jessica Lange
An updated remake of the 1933 movie classic, about a giant ape on the loose in New York City, climbing skyscrapers and generally wreaking havoc, with the climax taking place atop the World Trade Center.
MPAA:PG
Paramount — *Paramount Home Video; RCA VideoDiscs*

King Kong 1933
Horror
70788   101 mins   B/W   LV   P
Fay Wray, Bruce Cabot, Robert Armstrong
This special two-disc set, reproduced from a superior negative, features extensive liner notes and running commentary by film historian Ronald Haver.
RKO — *The Criterion Collection*

King of America 1980
Drama
82219   90 mins   C   B, V   P
A Greek sailor and a local labor agent battle over who will become King of America.
PBS — *VCL Home Video*

King of Comedy, The 1983
Comedy-Drama
68258   101 mins   C   B, V   P
Robert De Niro, Jerry Lewis, Diahnne Abbott, Sandra Bernhard
Lewis portrays a late-night talk show host and De Niro his greatest fan. De Niro cannot get on the show so he decides to kidnap Lewis to force him to put him on.
MPAA:PG

20th Century Fox — *RCA/Columbia Pictures Home Video; RCA VideoDiscs*

King of Hearts 1966
Satire
53672   101 mins   C   B, V, CED   P
Alan Bates, Genevieve Bujold, directed by Philippe de Broca
In World War I, a Scottish soldier finds a war-torn town occupied only by lunatics who have escaped from the asylum and who want to make him their king.
United Artists; Fildebroc; Montoro — *CBS/Fox Video*

King of Jazz, The 1930
Musical
68254   93 mins   C   B, V   P
Paul Whiteman, John Boles, Jeanette Loff, Bing Crosby and the Rhythm Boys, directed by John Murray Anderson
A lavish revue built around the Paul Whiteman Orchestra with comedy sketches and songs by the stars on Universal Pictures' talent roster. Musical numbers include George Gershwin's "Rhapsody in Blue," "Happy Feet" and "It Happened in Monterey." Filmed in two-color Technicolor with a cartoon segment by Walter Lantz.
Academy Award '30: Best Interior Decoration
Universal — *MCA Home Video*

King of Kong Island 1978
Horror
35370   92 mins   C   B, V   P
Brad Harris, Marc Lawrence
Intent on world domination, a group of mad scientists implant receptors in the brains of gorillas on Kong Island, and the monster apes run amok.
Independent — *United Home Video*

King of Kung-Fu 198?
Martial arts
64963   90 mins   C   B, V   P
Bobby Baker, Nam Chun Pan, Lam Chun Chi
A martial arts adventure featuring plenty of kung-fu kicks.
Dragon Lady Productions — *Unicorn Video*

King of the Grizzlies 1969
Western
88196   93 mins   C   B, V   P
The mystical relationship between a Cree Indian and a grizzly cub is put to the acid test when the full grown bear attacks a ranch at which the Indian is foreman.
Walt Disney Prod. — *Walt Disney Home Video*

King of the Gypsies 1978
Drama
29767   112 mins   C   B, V   P

Sterling Hayden, Eric Roberts, Susan Sarandon, Brooke Shields
A young man, scornful of his gypsy heritage, runs away from the tribe and tries to make a life of his own. He is summoned home to his grandfather's deathbed, where he is proclaimed the new king of the gypsies, a role he is unwilling to accept.
MPAA:R
Paramount — *Paramount Home Video*

King of the Hill   1974
Baseball
21303   57 mins   C   B, V, FO   P
The career of big league ballplayer Ferguson Jenkins is followed in this program, through his last two seasons with the Chicago Cubs.
National Film Board of Canada — *Video Yesteryear*

King of the Kongo   1929
Adventure/Serials
57356 213 mins B/W   B, V, FO   P
Jacqueline Logan, Boris Karloff, Richard Tucker
A handsome young man is sent by the government to Nuhalla, deep in the jungle, to break up a gang of ivory thieves. A newly-discovered sound-silent serial.
Mascot — *Video Yesteryear*

King of the Mountain   1981
Adventure
60444   92 mins   C   B, V   P
Harry Hamlin, Dennis Hopper, Joseph Bottoms, Deborah Van Valkenburgh, Dan Haggerty
The "Old King" and the "New King" must square off in this tale of daredevil roadracers.
MPAA:PG
Polygram — *Embassy Home Entertainment*

King of the Rocketmen   1949
Adventure/Serials
07335   156 mins B/W   B, V, 3/4U   P
Tris Coffin, Mae Clark, I. Stanford Jolley
Jeff King thwarts an attempt by traitors to steal government scientific secrets. Serial in twelve episodes. Later released as a feature titled "Lost Planet Airmen'.
Republic — *Nostalgia Merchant; Video Connection; Republic Pictures Home Video*

King of the Zombies   1941
Horror
51443   67 mins B/W   B, V, FO   P
Joan Woodbury, Dick Purcell
A scientist creates his own zombies without souls, to be used as the evil tools of a foreign government.
Monogram — *Video Yesteryear; Discount Video Tapes*

King, Queen, Knave   1974
Drama
65431   94 mins   C   B, V   P
Gina Lollobrigida, David Niven, John Moulder Brown
A shy, awkward 19-year old boy, keenly aware that his interest in girls is not reciprocated, has to go live with his prosperous uncle and his much younger wife when his parents are killed.
Avco Embassy — *Embassy Home Entertainment*

King Rat   1965
War-Drama
13258 134 mins B/W   B, V   P
George Segal, Tom Courtenay, James Fox, directed by Bryan Forbes
This drama, set in a World War II Japanese prisoner-of-war camp, focuses on the effect of captivity on the English, Australian and American prisoners.
Columbia; James Woolf — *RCA/Columbia Pictures Home Video*

King Solomon's Mines   1937
Adventure
59834   80 mins B/W   B, V   P
Sir Cedric Hardwicke, Paul Robeson, Roland Young, directed by Robert Stevenson
The search for King Solomon's Mines leads a safari through the treacherous terrain of the desert, fending off sandstorms, Zulus, and a volcanic eruption.
Gaumont — *Embassy Home Entertainment*

King Solomon's Mines   1985
Adventure
86785   101 mins   C   B, V   P
Richard Chamberlain, John Rhys-Davies, Herbert Lom, directed by J. Lee Thompson
This is the third film remake of the classic H. Rider Haggard novel about a safari into darkest Africa in search of an explorer who disappeared while searching for the legendary diamond mines of King Solomon.
MPAA:PG-13
Cannon Prods — *MGM/UA Home Video*

King Solomon's Treasure   1976
Adventure
70888   90 mins   C   B, V   P
David McCallum, Britt Ekland, Patrick MacNee
The great white adventurer takes on the African jungle, hunting for hidden treasure in the Forbidden City.
British — *United Home Video*

Kingdom of the Spiders   1978
Horror
51119   90 mins   C   B, V   P
William Shatner, Tiffany Bolling, Woody Strode

A desert town is invaded by swarms of killer
tarantulas, which begin to consume
townspeople.
MPAA:PG
Dimension Pictures — *United Home Video*

Kingfisher Caper, The   1976
Adventure
78346   90 mins   C   B, V   P
Hayley Mills, David McCallum
A power struggle between a businessman, his
brother, and a divorced sister is threatening to
rip a family-owned diamond empire apart.
MPAA:PG
Ben Vlok — *Media Home Entertainment*

Kings, Queens, Jokers   193?
Comedy
10112   60 mins   B/W   B, V   P, T
*Harold Lloyd, Marie Dressler, Polly Moran,
Edward G. Robinson, Gary Cooper, Joan
Crawford*
Package includes a foolish lover and ghosts in
"Haunted Spooks," an escaped convict in
"Dangerous Females," and a search for lost
jewels in "Stolen Jools."
MGM et al — *Blackhawk Films*

Kinks: One for the Road,   1980
The
Music-Performance
65478   60 mins   C   B, V   P
A showcase for the Kinks' vast repertoire,
including "Victoria," "Lola," "You Really Got
Me," and many more. Also included is authentic
footage of The Kinks on British and American
television shows. In stereo VHS and Beta Hi-Fi.
Independent — *Vestron Video*

Kipperbang   1982
Drama/Romance
65110   85 mins   C   B, V, CED   P
*John Albasiny, Abigail Cruttenden, directed by
Michael Apted*
During the summer of 1948, a 13-year-old boy
wishes he could kiss the girl of his dreams, and
he finally gets his big break in a school play.
MPAA:PG
David Puttnam; Enigma Television
Ltd — *MGM/UA Home Video*

Kipps   1941
Drama
03811   95 mins   B/W   B, V   P
*Michael Redgrave, Phyllis Calvert, Michael
Wilding, directed by Carol Reed*
Based on H. G. Wells' satirical novel, young
British spendthrift inherits a fortune and clashes
with his love over economy and waste.
20th Century Fox; British — *Hollywood Home
Theater; Cable Films*

Kirlian Witness, The   1978
Science fiction/Gardening
81632   88 mins   C   B, V   P
Nancy Snyder, Joel Colodner, Ted Leplat
A woman uses the power of telepathic
communication with house plants to solve her
sister's murder.
MPAA:PG
Jonathan Sarno — *Magnum Entertainment*

Kirov Ballet: Classic   1982
Ballet Night, The
Dance
84664   95 mins   C   B, V   P
*Tatiana Terekhova, Natalie Bolshakova, Sergei
Berezhnoi, Gabriela Konleva, conducted by
Viktor Sherehova*
The Kirov performs various pieces by Pugni,
Helsted and Drigo in a series of 'Pas de Deux.'
Recorded in Hi-Fi.
Russian TV — *V.I.E.W. Video*

Kismet   1955
Musical
47399   113 mins   C   B, V   P
*Howard Keel, Ann Blyth, Dolores Gray, Vic
Damone, directed by Vincente Minnelli*
An Arabian Nights extravaganza about a
Baghdad street poet who manages to infiltrate
himself into the Wazir's harem. The music was
adapted from Borodin by Robert Wright and
George Forrest, producing such standards as
"Baubles, Bangles and Beads," "Stranger in
Paradise" and "And This Is My Beloved."
MGM — *MGM/UA Home Video*

Kiss—Animalize Live   1985
Uncensored
Music-Performance
77460   90 mins   C   B, V   P
*Gene Simmons, Eric Carr, Paul Stanley, Vinnie
Vincent*
Those heavy metal mongers Kiss perform all
their full-throttled headbanging hits in this live
concert video. Available in VHS and Beta Hi Fi
Stereo.
Music Vision — *RCA/Columbia Pictures Home
Video*

Kiss Daddy Goodbye   1981
Horror
81395   81 mins   C   B, V   P
Fabian Forte, Marilyn Burns, Jon Cedar
A widower keeps his two children isolated in
order to protect their secret telekinetic.
Available in VHS Stereo and Beta Hi-Fi.
MPAA:R
Contel — *Monterey Home Video*

Kiss Me Goodbye   1982
Comedy/Fantasy
66073   101 mins   C   B, V, CED   P

Sally Field, James Caan, Jeff Bridges, Paul
Dooley, Mildred Natwick
A woman must choose between her new fiance
or the returned ghost of her late husband.
MPAA:PG
20th Century Fox — CBS/Fox Video

Kiss Me Kate 1953
Musical
85638 119 mins C B, V P
Kathryn Grayson, Howard Keel, Ann Miller,
Tommy Rall, Bob Fosse, Bobby Van, directed
by George Sidney
A comedy-musical screen adaptation of
Shakespeare's "The Taming of the Shrew,"
with music by Cole Porter.
MGM — MGM/UA Home Video

Kiss My Grits 1982
Adventure/Comedy
84858 101 mins C B, V P
Bruce Davison, Anthony Franciosa, Susan
George, Bruno Kirby, directed by Jack Starrett
A good ole boy hightails it to Mexico with his
girlfriend and son, chased by mobsters and the
law.
MPAA:PG
Gary L. Maehlman — Media Home
Entertainment

Kiss of the Spider 1985
Woman
Drama
Closed Captioned
84523 119 mins C B, V, 8mm, P
LV
William Hurt, Raul Julia, Sonia Braga, Jose
Lewgoy, directed by Hector Babenco
From the novel by Manuel Puig, an acclaimed
drama concerning two cellmates in a South
American prison, one a revolutionary, the other
a homosexual. Literate, haunting, powerful.
1985 Cannes Film Festival Best Actor: William
Hurt, 1985 MPAA:R
David Weisman — Charter Entertainment

Kiss of the Tarantula 1975
Science fiction/Horror
65454 85 mins C B, V P
Eric Mason
The story of a young girl and her pet spiders as
they spin a deadly web of terror.
MPAA:PG
Cinevu Productions — Monterey Home Video;
MPI Home Video

Kit Carson 1940
Western
64376 97 mins B/W B, V, 3/4U P
John Hall, Dana Andrews, Ward Bond, Lynn
Bari

Frontiersman Kit Carson leads a wagon train to
California, fighting off marauding Indians all the
way.
Edward Small — Nostalgia Merchant

Kitty: A Return to 1981
Auschwitz
World War II/Judaism
47564 90 mins C B, V P
Kitty Hart spent her teenage years at the
Auschwitz concentration camp and survived.
Thirty-four years later, she returned to the camp
with her grown son to walk over the land and
recall the past.
CBC — THORN EMI/HBO Video; Films Inc

Kitty and the Bagman 1983
Comedy
72872 95 mins C B, V P
A comedy about two rival madams who ruled
Australia in the 1920's.
MPAA:R
Anthony Buckley — Embassy Home
Entertainment

Kitty Foyle 1940
Drama
07882 107 mins B/W B, V P
Ginger Rogers
From the novel by Christopher Morley, Ms.
Rogers symbolizes the white-collar working girl
whose involvement with a married man presents
her with both romantic and social conflicts.
Academy Awards '40; Best Actress (Rogers).
RKO — VidAmerica; Nostalgia Merchant;
Blackhawk Films

Klondike Fever 1979
Adventure
81961 118 mins C B, V P
Rod Steiger, Angie Dickinson, Lorne Greene
Join the young Jack London as he travels from
San Francisco to the Klondike fields during the
Great Gold Rush of 1898.
MPAA:PG
World Entertainment Corporation — Lightning
Video

Klute 1971
Drama
54116 114 mins C B, V, LV P
Jane Fonda, Donald Sutherland, Charles Cioffi,
Roy Scheider, directed by Alan J. Pakula
A small town policeman comes to New York in
search of a missing friend and gets involved
with a would-be actress, call-girl who is trying to
break out of her surroundings.
Academy Awards '71: Best Actress (Fonda).
MPAA:R
Warner Bros — Warner Home Video; RCA
VideoDiscs

Knack—Live at Carnegie Hall, The   1982
Music-Performance
47812   ? mins   C   LV   P
The power pop quartet performs "My Sharona," "Good Girls Don't," and other hits at their March 18, 1979 Carnegie Hall Concert. In stereo.
Unknown — *Pioneer Artists*

Knee (Rehabilitation and Injury)   1978
Physical fitness
52759   30 mins   C   B, V   P
Hosted by Ann Dugan
Exercises for knee strengthening, relief of pain, and conditioning muscles and tissue to prevent further stress. Part of the "Rehabilitation and Injury" series.
Health 'N Action — *RCA/Columbia Pictures Home Video*

Knife in the Water   1962
Film-Avant-garde
11399   90 mins   B/W   B, V   P
Leon Niemczyk, Jolanta Umecka, Zygmunt Malandowicz, directed by Roman Polanski
A journalist, his wife and a hitchhiker spend a day aboard a sailboat in this tension-filled, psychological drama. English subtitles. Venice Film Festival: International Film Critics Award. PO
Kanawha Films Ltd — *CBS/Fox Video; Video Yesteryear; Hollywood Home Theater; Western Film & Video Inc; Video Dimensions; Movie Buff Video; International Home Video*

Knight of Basketball, A   1986
Basketball
84640   60 mins   C   B, V   P
Bobby Knight
The coach-extraordinaire describes basic fundamentals of the popular sport.
Ten Sports Prod. — *Kartes Video Communications*

Knight Without Armour   1937
Drama
82568   107 mins   B/W   B, V   P
Marlene Dietrich, Robert Donat, directed by Jacques Feyder
A journalist opposed to the Russian monarchy falls in love with the daughter of a czarist minister in this classic romantic drama.
Alexander Korda — *Embassy Home Entertainment*

Knightriders   1981
Adventure
66065   145 mins   C   B, V   P
Ed Harris, Gary Lahti, Tom Savini, Amy Ingersoll
The story of a troup of motorcyclists who are members of a traveling Renaissance Fair.

MPAA:R
Richard Rubinstein — *Media Home Entertainment*

Knights of the City   1986
Crime-Drama
86087   87 mins   C   B, V   P
Nicholas Campbell, Stoney Jackson, Leon Isaac Kennedy
Miami street gangs fight each other over their "turf."
MPAA:R
Dominic Orlando — *New World Video*

Knights of the Roundtable   1954
Drama
81497   106 mins   C   B, V   P
Robert Taylor, Ava Gardner, Mel Ferrer, Anne Crawford, directed by Richard Thorpe
This is the story of the romantic triangle between King Arthur, Sir Lancelot and Guinevere during the civil wars of sixth century England.
MGM — *MGM/UA Home Video*

Knock on Any Door   1949
Drama
44840   100 mins   B/W   B, V   P
Humphrey Bogart, John Derek, George Macready
A young hoodlum from the slums is tried for murdering a cop. He is defended by a prominent attorney who has known him from childhood.
Columbia — *RCA/Columbia Pictures Home Video*

Knockout, The/Dough and Dynamite   1914
Comedy
59369   54 mins   B/W   B, V, FO   P
Charlie Chaplin, Roscoe 'Fatty' Arbuckle, Mabel Normand, Keystone Cops
Two Chaplin shorts: "The Knockout" (1914), in which Charlie referees a big fight; "Dough and Dynamite" (1914), in which a labor dispute at a bake shop leaves Charlie in charge when the regular baker walks out.
Keystone — *Video Yesteryear*

Knute Rockne—All American   1940
Biographical/Drama
81772   98 mins   B/W   B, V   P
Ronald Reagan, Pat O'Brien, Gale Page, Donald Crisp, directed by Lloyd Bacon
This is the life story of the Notre Dame football coach who "won one for the Gipper."
Warner Bros. — *MGM/UA Home Video*

Kooky Classics 1984
Music-Performance
80620   54 mins   C   B, V   P
Shari Lewis, Lamb Chop, Hush Puppy
Shari Lewis leads her friends Lamb Chop and
Hush Puppy on a wacky tour through the world
of music accompanied by a symphony
orchestra.
Shari Lewis Enterprises — *MGM/UA Home
Video*

Koroshi 1967
Suspense
81528   100 mins   C   B, V   P
*Patrick McGoohan, Kenneth Griffith, Yoko Tani,
directed by Michael Truman and Peter Yates*
Secret Agent John Drake is dispatched to Hong
Kong to disband a secret society who are killing
off international political figures.
Sidney Cole — *MPI Home Video*

Kovacs on the Corner 1952
Comedy
39003   30 mins   B/W   B, V, FO   P
Ernie Kovacs, Edie Adams, the Dave Appell Trio
A program from Ernie Kovacs' first television
series, originating in Philadelphia. Creative video
comedy by the first master of the genre, and a
song or two from Edie Adams.
NBC — *Video Yesteryear*

Koyaanisqatsi 1983
Film-Avant-garde
65471   87 mins   C   B, V, LV   P
A totally unconventional program that takes an
intense look at modern life. Without dialogue or
narration, it brings what are traditionally
considered background elements—landscapes
and cityscapes-up front, producing a unique
view of the superstructure and mechanics of our
daily lives.
Godfrey Reggio — *Pacific Arts Video*

Kraft Music Hall Presents "Alan King Stops the Press" 1969
Variety
56904   55 mins   B/W   B, V, FO   P
Alan King, Paul Lynde, Barbara Feldon
A comedy-variety show spoofing the newspaper
industry. Paul Lynde interviews star quarterback
Boyd Blowhard, the food editor reviews the
cuisine at the Last Chance Diner, and a look
behind the scenes at the Advice to the Lovelorn
column.
NBC — *Video Yesteryear*

Kraft Television Theater 1951
Drama
47639   60 mins   B/W   B, V, FO   P
*Olive Deering, Mark Roberts, E. G. Marshall,
George Reeves, Ed Herlihy*

"Kelly" by Eric Hatch, the story of an average
Kansas gas pump jockey who remembers the
girl he knew in France during the war, and is
surprised to find her in the U.S.A.
NBC — *Video Yesteryear*

Kramer vs. Kramer 1979
Drama
58498   105 mins   C   B, V, LV   P
*Dustin Hoffman, Meryl Streep, Jane Alexander,
Justin Henry, Howard Duff, directed by Robert
Benton*
A woman abandons her husband and young
son, leaving them to struggle and make a new
life for themselves. Eventually she returns to
fight for custody. Based on the novel by Avery
Corman.
Academy Awards '79: Best Picture; Best Actor
(Hoffman); Best Supporting Actress (Streep);
Best Director (Benton); Best Screenplay
Adaptation (Benton).   MPAA:PG
Columbia; Stanley Jaffe — *RCA/Columbia
Pictures Home Video; RCA VideoDiscs*

Kremlin, The 1984
USSR
88158   60 mins   C   B, V   P
A tour through the Soviet Union's famous official
palace, and a look at its illustrious history.
Lucy Jarvis — *Monterey Home Video*

Kriemhilde's Revenge 1924
Drama/Film-History
64304   95 mins   B/W   B, V   P, T
*Paul Richter, Margareta Schoen, directed by
Fritz Lang*
The concluding part of Fritz Lang's massive
version of the Nibelungenlied, which was the
basis of Richard Wagner's Ring operas. Silent
with organ score.
UFA — *Blackhawk Films; Movie Buff Video;
International Historic Films*

Krokus: The Video Blitz 1984
Music video
80504   60 mins   C   B, V   P
The Swiss band Krokus performs hit songs such
as "Our Love" and "Ballroom Blitz."
Callner Shapiro — *RCA/Columbia Pictures
Home Video; Pioneer Artists*

Kronos 1957
Science fiction
44356   78 mins   B/W   B, V, 3/4U   P
Jeff Morrow, Barbara Lawrence, John Emery
A giant robot from space drains the Earth of all
its energy resources. Includes preview of
coming attractions from classic science fiction
films.
Lippert; 20th Century Fox — *Nostalgia
Merchant*

Krull 1983
Adventure
65460   ? mins   C   B, V, CED   P
Ken Marshall, Lysette Anthony, Freddie Jones,
Francesca Annis
In a fantasy adventure, set in a world peopled by
creatures of myth and magic, a prince embarks
on a quest to find the magical Glaive and then
rescues his young bride. In stereo VHS and
Beta Hi-Fi.
MPAA:PG
Ted Mann; Ron Silverman — *RCA/Columbia*
Pictures Home Video

Krush Groove 1985
Musical
Closed Captioned
84537   94 mins   C   B, V, LV   P
Blair Underwood, Sheila E, Kurtis Blow, directed
by Michael Schultz
The world of rap music is highlighted in this
movie, the first all-rap musical.
MPAA:R
Michael Schultz; Doug McHenry — *Warner*
Home Video

Kung Fu 1972
Martial arts/Adventure
78625   75 mins   C   B, V   P
Keith Carradine, David Carradine, Barry
Sullivan, Keye Luke
A fugitive martial arts master roams across the
Old West fighting injustice in this film that served
as a pilot for the television series.
Warner Bros — *Warner Home Video*

Kung Fu Avengers 1985
Martial arts
85082   90 mins   C   B, V   P
Bruce Li, Carl Scott, Jim James, Ku Feng
On his way to a karate show at Madison Square
Garden, our hero Li confronts the abominable
Mr. Chin and his deadly henchman.
Eternal Film Co — *Prism*

Kung-Fu Commandos 1980
Martial arts/Adventure
59347   90 mins   C   B, V   R, P
John Lui, Shangkuan Lung
Five masters must face a warlord's army to
rescue a captured agent.
MPAA:R
Unifilm International — *Video Gems*

Kung Fu For Sale 1981
Martial arts
70701   95 mins   C   B, V   P
Chong Hua
A young kung fu enthusiast, along with his
mentor, fights for the respect of his family.
Master Arts — *Master Arts Video*

Kung-Fu Shadow 1985
Martial arts
84504   90 mins   C   B, V   P
Tien Peng, Chia Ling
The forces of good and evil are at odds once
again in this dubbed kung fu epic.
Telefilm Co Inc — *Sony Video Software*

Kwaidan 1964
Horror/Suspense
65203   161 mins   C   B, V   P
Directed by Masaki Kubayashi
A haunting, stylized quartet of supernatural
stories, each with a suprise ending. Japanese
dialogue with English subtitles.
JA
Bungei Production; Ninjin Club; Toho
Company — *Video Yesteryear*

Kyoto Vivaldi: The Four 1985
Seasons
Music-Performance/Japan
88142   45 mins   C   B, V   P
The Japanese Koto-Ensemble performs
Vivaldi's classic work to the visual
accompaniment of a tour of the life and scenery
of Kyoto.
Sony Video — *Sony Video Software*

L

La Sylphide 1971
Dance
58903   81 mins   C   B, V, 3/4U   R, P
Ghislaine Thesmar, Michael Denard, the Paris
Ballet Opera Company, conducted by Patrick
Flynn, directed and choreographed by Pierre
Lacotte
The Paris Opera Ballet's faithful adaptation of
''the ballet that changed the course of ballet
history,'' based on the 1832 production staged
by Taglioni.
Kultur; Paris Ballet Opera Company — *Kultur*

Laboratory 1980
Science fiction
80952   93 mins   C   B, V   P
Camille Mitchell, Corinne Michaels, Garnett
Smith
Things go awry when the earthling subjects of
an alien experiment revolt against their captors.
Sandler Institutional Films — *United Home*
Video

Ladies Night Out 1983
Nightclub
65344   80 mins   C   B, V   P
Peter Adonis Traveling Fantasy Show

"Ladies Night Out" is an all-male burlesque, featuring the highly acclaimed Peter Adonis. Traveling Fantasy Show. In stereo.
Joanne Sobolewski; John J
Burzichelli — *Vestron Video*

Ladies Sing the Blues, Vol. 1, The
1986

Music
88280　60 mins　C　　V　　　　P
The history of feminine blues and jazz singing, including glimpses of Bessie Smith, Billie Holliday, Dinah Washington and Ethel Waters.
The Minnesota Studio — *The Minnesota Studio*

Lady Caroline Lamb
1973

Drama
80325　123 mins　C　　V　　　　P
Sarah Miles, Richard Chamberlain, Jon Finch, Laurence Olivier, John Mills
The wife of a member of Parliament has an affair with Lord Byron and brings about her own down fall.
Tomorrow Entertainment — *Prism*

Lady Chatterley's Lover
1981

Drama
60592　107 mins　C　B, V, CED　　P
Sylvia Kristel, Nicholas Clay, Shane Briant, directed by Just Jaeckin
D.H. Lawrence's classic novel of an English lady who has an affair with the gamekeeper of her husband's estate is the basis of this film.
MPAA:R
Cine-Artist GmbH; London-Cannon Films Ltd and Producteurs Associes — *MGM/UA Home Video*

Lady Chatterley's Lover
1959

Literature-English
06224　102 mins　B/W　B, V　　　P
Danielle Darrieux, Erno Crisa, Leo Genn
Based on D.H. Lawrence's novel, English woman has affair with game keeper of her husband's estate. French; English subtitles.
FR
Kingsley Intl; French — *Movie Buff Video; Hollywood Home Theater; Festival Films; Discount Video Tapes*

Lady Cocoa
1975

Drama
72956　93 mins　C　　B, V　　　P
Lola Falana, Mean Joe Greene
A young woman gets released from jail for twenty-four hours and sets out for Las Vegas to find the man who framed her.
MPAA:R
Matt Cimber — *Unicorn Video*

Lady Eve, The
1941

Comedy-Drama
73687　97 mins　B/W　B, V　　　P
Barbara Stanwyck, Henry Fonda, Charles Coburn, directed by Preston Sturges
A beer tycoon comes out of the jungle and falls into the hands of a woman and her card shark father.
Paramount Pictures — *RKO HomeVideo*

Lady for a Night
1942

Drama
66465　88 mins　B/W　B, V　　　P
John Wayne, Joan Blondell, Ray Middleton
The lady owner of a gambling ship does her best to break into high society.
Republic — *Republic Pictures Home Video*

Lady from Louisiana, The
1942

Drama
66313　84 mins　B/W　B, V　　　P
John Wayne, Ona Munson, Dorothy Dandridge, Ray Middleton
A lawyer in old New Orleans out to rid the city of corruption falls in love with the daughter of a big-time gambler.
Republic — *Republic Pictures Home Video*

Lady From Shanghai, The
1948

Mystery
80785　87 mins　B/W　B, V　　　P
Orson Welles, Rita Hayworth, Everett Sloane, Glenn Anders, Gus Schilling, directed by Orson Welles
An adventurer becomes involved in a web of intrigue when a woman hires him to work on her husband's yacht. Available in Beta Hi Fi.
Richard Wilson; William
Castle — *RCA/Columbia Pictures Home Video*

Lady Grey
1982

Drama
80334　111 mins　C　　B, V　　　P
A poor farmer's daughter rises to the top of the country music charts.
E O Corporation — *THORN EMI/HBO Video*

Lady In a Cage
1964

Suspense
82540　95 mins　B/W　B, V　　　P
Olivia de Havilland, Ann Sothern, James Caan, Jennifer Billingsley, Rafael Campos
A widow is trapped in her home elevator during a power failure and becomes desperate when two hoodlums break in.
Luther David — *Paramount Home Video*

Lady in Red
1979

Drama
66103　90 mins　C　B, V, CED　　P
Pamela Sue Martin, Louise Fletcher, Robert Conrad

A story of America in the 30s, and the progress through the underworld of the woman who was Dillinger's last lover.
Julie Corman — *Vestron Video*

Lady in the Death House   1944
Crime-Drama
85183   57 mins   B/W   B, V   P
Jean Parker, Lionel Atwill, Marcia Mae Jones
A framed woman walks the last mile at the hands of her own lover, as a corpse-reviving scientist struggles to find the real killer in time.
Jack Schwarz — *Video Yesteryear*

Lady of Burlesque   1943
Mystery
12446   91 mins   B/W   B, V   P
Barbara Stanwyck, Michael O'Shea, Janis Carter, Pinky Lee
Burlesque dancer is found dead, strangled with her own G-string. Based on Gypsy Rose Lee's "The G-String Murders."
United Artists; Stromberg — *Video Connection; Cable Films; Video Yesteryear; Cinema Concepts; Kartes Video Communications*

Lady of the Evening   1979
Comedy
80120   110 mins   C   B, V   P
Sophia Loren, Marcello Mastroianni
A prostitute and a crook team up to seek revenge against the mob.
MPAA:PG
Italian — *King of Video*

Lady of the House   1978
Drama
75496   100 mins   C   B, V   P
Dyan Cannon, Susan Tyrell
A true story about a madame who rose from operator of a brothel to become a political force in San Francisco.
William Kayden Productions — *Prism*

Lady on the Bus   1978
Drama
66605   102 mins   C   B, V, LV   P
Sonia Braga
A sexually frustrated newlywed bride turns to other men for satisfaction.
MPAA:R
Atlantic Releasing — *Vestron Video*

Lady Scarface   1941
Mystery
73691   66 mins   B/W   B, V   P
Dennis O'Keefe, Frances Neal, Judith Anderson
A gunwoman is pursued and captured by a police officer.
RKO — *RKO HomeVideo*

Lady Sings the Blues   1972
Musical
38612   144 mins   C   B, V, LV   P
Diana Ross, Billy Dee Williams, Richard Pryor
Jazz singer Billie Holiday's autobiography becomes a musical drama covering her early career and problems with racism and drug addiction. Songs include "God Bless the Child" and "Lover Man."
MPAA:R
Paramount — *Paramount Home Video; RCA VideoDiscs*

Lady Takes a Chance   1943
Comedy/Romance
65395   86 mins   B/W   B, V   P
John Wayne, Jean Arthur
A romantic comedy about a New York working girl with matrimonial ideas and a rope-shy rodeo rider who yearns for the wide open spaces.
RKO — *VidAmerica*

Lady Vanishes, The   1938
Mystery
01743   99 mins   B/W   B, V   P
Michael Redgrave, Paul Lukas, Margaret Lockwood, directed by Alfred Hitchcock
When a kindly old lady disappears from a fast-moving train, her young friend finds an imposter in her place.
Gaumont British — *Movie Buff Video; Prism; Embassy Home Entertainment; Nostalgia Merchant; Hollywood Home Theater; Video Dimensions; Cable Films; Video Connection; Discount Video Tapes; Western Film & Video Inc; Cinema Concepts; Spotlite Video; Hal Roach Studios; Kartes Video Communications; Video Yesteryear*

Lady Vanishes, The   1938
Mystery
71023   119 mins   B/W   B, V, LV   P
Michael Redgrave, Paul Lukas, Margaret Lockwood, directed by Alfred Hitchcock
The kindly old woman traveling on a fast moving train is suddenly replaced by an imposter, confusing her young companion. This high-quality special edition includes a special production documenting Hitchcock's cameo appearances in his early films.
Gaumont British — *The Criterion Collection*

Lady Vanishes, The   1979
Suspense/Comedy
71180   95 mins   C   B, V   P
Elliot Gould, Cybill Shepherd, Angela Lansbury, Herbert Lom, directed by Anthony Page
In this reworking of the '38 Hitchcock film, a woman on a Swiss bound train awakens from a nap to find that the old lady seated next to her was kidnapped.
Rank Org; Hammer Films — *Media Home Entertainment*

Ladyhawke 1985
Fantasy/Adventure
Closed Captioned
81898   121 mins   C   B, V, LV   P
Matthew Broderick, Rutger Hauer, Michelle
Pfeiffer, John Wood, Leo McKern, directed by
Richard Donner
In medieval times, a youthful pickpocket
befriends a strange knight who is on a
mysterious quest. This unlikely duo,
accompanied by a watchful hawk, are
enveloped in a magical adventure.
MPAA:PG-13
Warner Bros; 20th Century Fox — *Warner*
Home Video

Ladykillers, The 1955
Comedy
36940   87 mins   C   B, V   P
Alec Guinness, Cecil Parker, Katie Johnson,
Herbert Lom, Peter Sellers, directed by
Alexander Mackendrick
A gang of bumbling bank robbers is foiled by a
little old lady from whom they rent a room.
Hilarious antics follow, especially on the part of
Guinness, who plays the slightly demented-
looking leader of the gang.
British Film Academy '55: Best Screenplay; Best
Actress (Johnson).
Continental, J Arthur Rank — *THORN*
EMI/HBO Video; Learning Corp of America

Lamaze Method: 1984
Techniques for Childbirth
Preparation, The
Childbirth
65386   45 mins   C   B, V   P
Patty Duke Astin introduces the 3 basic areas of
the method: relaxation, breathing and expulsion
techniques. ASPO-certified Lamaze instructor
Marilyn Libresco leads an expectant couple
through demonstrations.
Embassy Home Entertainment; Al
Eicher — *Embassy Home Entertainment*

Land of Doom 1984
Fantasy
88231   87 mins   C   B, V   P
Deborah Rennard, Garrick Dowhen, directed by
Peter Maris
An amazon and a warrior struggle for survival in
the old familiar post-holocaust fantasy setting.
Manson Int'l. — *Lightning Video*

Land of the Lost, Volume 1974
2
Adventure
81449   46 mins   C   B, V   P
A forest ranger and his two teenaged children
find themselves in danger when a time warp
transports them to a prehistoric world.

Sid and Marty Krofft — *Embassy Home*
Entertainment

Land of the Lost, Volume 1974
I
Science fiction/Adventure
76792   46 mins   C   B, V   P
Wesley Eure, Ron Harper, Kathy Coleman,
Spencer Milligan, Phillip Paley
A forest ranger and his two teenaged children
become trapped in a time vortex while exploring
the Colorado River.
Sid and Marty Krofft — *Embassy Home*
Entertainment

Land of the Minotaur 1977
Horror
60348   88 mins   C   B, V   P
Donald Pleasance, Peter Cushing, Luan Peters
A small village is the setting for horrifying ritual
murders, demons and disappearances of young
terrorists.
MPAA:PG
Frixos Constantine — *United Home Video*

Land of the Tiger 1986
Wildlife/Documentary
Closed Captioned
84785   60 mins   C   B, V, LV   P
A documentary study of tigers in their natural
habitat.
National Geographic — *Vestron Video*

Land That Time Forgot, 1975
The
Science fiction
64889   90 mins   C   B, V   P
Doug McClure, John McEnery, Susan
Penhaligon
A WWI veteran, a beautiful woman, and their
German enemies are stranded in a land of life
outside time. Based on the novel by Edgar Rice
Burroughs.
MPAA:PG
American International Pictures — *Vestron*
Video

Language in Life 1982
Language arts/Science
59563   50 mins   C   B, V   P
Human communications from a psychological
standpoint, based on recent studies in language
acquisition, are examined, as well as a survey of
the basic units of speech.
McGraw Hill — *Mastervision*

Las Vegas Lady 1976
Drama
70609   90 mins   C   B, V   P
Stella Stevens, Stuart Whitman, George De
Cecenzo, directed by Noel Nosseck

Three shrewd casino hostesses plot a multimillion dollar heist in the nation's gambling capital.
MPAA:PG
Crown International, Zappala Prod. — *Prism*

Las Vegas Story, The   1952
Drama
57141   88 mins   B/W   B, V   P
Victor Mature, Jane Russell, Vincent Price, Hoagy Carmichael
Gambling, colorful sights, and a murder provide the framework for this fictional, guided-tour of the city.
RKO — *King of Video*

Las Vegas Weekend   1985
Comedy
87623   83 mins   C   B, V   P
Barry Hickey
A computer nerd goes to Las Vegas and discovers fun.
New World — *New World Video*

Laserblast   1978
Science fiction
33888   87 mins   C   B, V   P
Kim Milford, Cheryl Smith, Keenan Wynn, Roddy McDowall
A frustrated young man finds a powerful and deadly laser which was left near his home by aliens. Upon learning of its devastating capabilities, his personality changes and he seeks revenge against all who have taken advantage of him.
MPAA:PG
Charles Band — *Media Home Entertainment*

Lassie from Lancashire   1938
Musical
85184   67 mins   B/W   B, V   P
Marjorie Brown, Hal Thompson, Marjorie Sandford, Mark Daly
A pair of struggling lovebirds try to make it in show biz against all odds, including the girl's lunatic aunt, who locks her away before an audition.
English — *Video Yesteryear*

Lassie's Great Adventure   1962
Cartoons/Drama
82403   104 mins   C   B, V   P
Animated voices of June Lockhart, Jon Provost, Hugh Reilly, directed by William Beaudine
Lassie and her master Timmy are swept away from home by a runaway balloon. After they land in the Canadian wilderness, they learn to rely on each other through peril and adventure.
Lassie Television Inc → *MGM/UA Home Video*

Lassie's Rescue Rangers   1982
Cartoons/Adventure
66005   60 mins   C   B, V   P
Animated
The courageous collie saves the day in two spine-tingling adventures.
Filmation — *Family Home Entertainment*

Lassie's Rescue Rangers, Volume 2   1982
Cartoons/Adventure
69807   60 mins   C   B, V   P
Animated
Three action-packed cartoon adventures feature Lassie as she joins forces with the courageous Rescue Rangers to help protect people and wildlife in the national forests.
Filmation — *Family Home Entertainment*

Lassie's Rescue Rangers, Volume 3   1985
Cartoons/Adventure
70359   60 mins   C   B, V   P
Animated
This tape features further adventures of the king of collies as he leads the Rescue Rangers in the protection of Earth's beauty. The program comes in stereo on all formats.
Filmation — *Family Home Entertainment*

Lassie's Vacation Adventure   1982
Cartoons/Adventure
87317   60 mins   C   B, V   P
This entry in the "Lassie's Rescue Rangers" cartoon series features three complete shorts.
Filmation Assoc. — *Family Home Entertainment*

Lassiter   1984
Drama
72919   100 mins   C   B, V   P
Tom Selleck, Lauren Hutton, Jane Seymour
Tom Selleck plays a jewel thief who is asked to steal diamonds for the FBI.
MPAA:R
Al Ruddy; Warner Bros — *Warner Home Video*

Last American Hero, The   1973
Drama
82344   95 mins   C   B, V   P
Jeff Bridges, Valerie Perrine, Gary Busey, Art Lund, Geraldine Fitzgerald, directed by Lamont Johnson
This is the true story of how former moonshine runner Junior Johnson became one of the fastest race car drivers in the history of the sport. Available in VHS and Beta Hi-Fi.
MPAA:PG
20th Century Fox — *Key Video*

Last American Virgin, The   1982
Comedy
60567   92 mins   C   B, V, CED   P
Lawrence Monoson, Diane Franklin, Steve Antin, Louisa Moritz
Three school buddies must deal with a plethora of problems in their search for girls who are willing. Music by Blondie, The Cars, The Police, The Waitresses, Devo, U2, Human League, Quincy Jones.
MPAA:R
Cannon Films Inc; Golan Globus Productions — *MGM/UA Home Video*

Last Challenge of the   1980
Dragon, The
Adventure/Martial arts
56926   90 mins   C   B, V   R, P
Bruce Lee
A son brings death to his family by humiliating the underworld martial arts king of the city.
MPAA:R
Goldig Film — *Video Gems*

Last Challenge of the   198?
Dragon
Martial arts
64958   90 mins   C   B, V   P
A martial arts adventure.
Dragon Lady Productions — *Unicorn Video*

Last Chance Garage, The   1986
Automobiles
86303   30 mins   C   B, V   P
20   pgms
In sequences culled from the television show of the same name, Brad Sears demonstrates twenty do-it-yourself car repairs, from transmission to tune-ups.
PBS — *Crown Video*

Last Chase, The   1980
Adventure
47755   106 mins   C   B, V, CED   P
Lee Majors, Burgess Meredith, Chris Makepeace
A famed race car driver becomes a vocal dissenter against the sterile society that has emerged, in this drama set in the near future.
MPAA:PG
Martyn Burke; Fran Rosati — *Vestron Video*

Last Cry for Help   1980
Suicide
52397   30 mins   C   B, V, 3/4U,   R, P
FO
An alienated, depressed young girl attempts suicide. We see her experiences before the attempt and her emerging strength afterward as she learns to take control of her life.
AM Available

Learning Corp of America — *Learning Corp of America; Unicorn Video*

Last Cry for Help, A   1979
Drama
79323   98 mins   C   B, V   P
Linda Purl, Shirley Jones, Tony Lo Bianco, Murray Hamilton, Grant Goodeve
A psychiatrist helps out a seventeen-year-old girl who attempts suicide.
Myrt Hall Productions — *Unicorn Video*

Last Day of the War   1969
War-Drama
77380   95 mins   C   B, V   P
George Maharis, Maria Perschy, James Philbrook
A U.S. Army platoon attempts to reach an Austrian spy before the Nazis kill him at the end of World War II. Available in Beta Hi-Fi and VHS Stereo.
MPAA:PG
Sagittarius Productions — *U.S.A. Home Video*

Last Days of Man on   1973
Earth
Science fiction
65713   70 mins   C   B, V   P
Jon Finch, Jenny Runacre, Hugh Griffith
In a deteriorating world, a search is on for a piece of microfilm which holds the formula for immortality.
MPAA:R
New World — *Embassy Home Entertainment*

Last Detail, The   1974
Comedy-Drama
59603   104 mins   C   B, V   P
Jack Nicholson, Randy Quaid, Otis Young, directed by Hal Ashby
A hard-boiled career petty officer commissioned to transfer a young sailor from one brig to another attempts to show the prisoner a good time.
MPAA:R
Columbia — *RCA/Columbia Pictures Home Video*

Last Embrace   1979
Suspense
85610   98 mins   C   B, V   P
Roy Scheider, Janet Margolin, Christopher Walken, directed by Jonathan Demme
A feverish Hitchcockian thriller dealing with an ex-secret serviceman who is convinced someone is trying to kill him.
MPAA:R
Michael Taylor; Dan Wigutow — *Key Video*

Last Fight, The   1982
Drama
78387   85 mins   C   B, V   P

Willie Colon, Fred Williamson, Ruben Blades, Joe Spinell, Darlanne Fluegel.
A boxer risks his life and his girlfriend for one chance at the championship title.
MPAA:R
Jerry Masucci, Fred Williamson — *THORN EMI/HBO Video*

Last Flight of Noah's Ark, The   1980
Adventure/Drama
63192   97 mins   C   B, V   P
Elliott Gould, Genevieve Bujold, Ricky Schroder, Vincent Gardenia, Tammy Lauren
This tale of adventure concerns a high-living pilot, a prim missionary and two stowaway orphans who must plot their way off a deserted island following the crash landing of their broken-down plane.
Walt Disney Productions — *Walt Disney Home Video*

Last Four Days, The   1977
Biographical/Drama
87632   91 mins   C   B, V   P
Rod Steiger, Henry Fonda, Franco Nero, directed by Carl Lizzani
A chronicle of the final days of Benito Mussolini.
MPAA:PG
Group 1 — *Lightning Video*

Last Game, The   1980
Drama
80333   107 mins   C   B, V   P
A college student is torn between his devotion to his blind father and going out for the college's football team.
E O Corporation — *THORN EMI/HBO Video*

Last Gun, the   1964
Western
81517   98 mins   C   B, V   P
Cameron Mitchell
A legendary gunman on the verge of retirement has to save his town from a reign of terror before turning his gun in.
Foreign — *Magnum Entertainment*

Last Horror Film, The   1982
Horror
65692   87 mins   C   B, V   P
Joe Spinell, Caroline Munro
A beautiful queen of horror films is followed to Cannes by her number one fan who, unbeknownst to her, is slowly murdering members of her entourage in a deluded and vain attempt to capture her attentions.
MPAA:R
David Winters; Judd Hamilton — *Media Home Entertainment*

Last House on the Left   1972
Horror/Exploitation
80685   83 mins   C   B, V, LV   P
David Hess, Lucy Gratham, Sandra Cassel
Two girls are kidnapped from a rock concert by a gang of escaped convicts who subject them to a night of terror that they will never forget.
MPAA:R
Orion Pictures — *Vestron Video*

Last Hunter, The   1980
Drama
80686   97 mins   C   B, V   P
Tisa Farrow, David Warbeck
A soldier fights for his life behind enemy lines during the Vietnam War.
MPAA:R
Worldwide Entertainment — *Vestron Video*

Last Laugh, The   1924
Drama
08709   77 mins   B/W   B, V, 3/4U   P
Emil Jannings, Maly Delshaft, Max Hiller
An elderly man, who as the doorman of a great hotel was looked upon as a symbol of "upper class," due to his age, is demoted to wash room attendant.
Janus; Germany — *International Historic Films; Kartes Video Communications; Western Film & Video Inc; Discount Video Tapes; Cable Films*

Last Married Couple in   1980
America, The
Comedy
59683   103 mins   C   B, V   P
George Segal, Natalie Wood, Richard Benjamin, Valerie Harper, Dom DeLuise
A couple fight to stay happily married amidst the rampant divorce epidemic engulfing their friends.
MPAA:R
Universal — *MCA Home Video*

Last Mercenary   1984
Adventure
86191   90 mins   C   B, V   P
Tony Marsina, Malcolm Duff, Ketty Nichols, Louis Walser
An angry ex-soldier kills everyone who makes him mad.
Met Films — *Mogul Communications*

Last Metro, The   1980
Drama
87334   135 mins   C   B, V   P
Catherine Deneuve, Gerard Depardieu, Heinz Bennent, Jean Poiret, Andrea Ferreol, Paulette Dubost, Sabine Haudepin, directed by Francois Truffaut
Truffaut's alternately gripping and touching drama about a theatre company in Nazi-occupied Paris, where the proprieter's husband is a Jew hiding in the cellar, and the leading man

---

is a Resistance fighter. One of Truffaut's late films, made 4 years before his death.
Roissy — Key Video

Last Mile, The 1932
Crime-Drama
64341 70 mins B/W   B, V   P
Preston Foster, Howard Phillips, George E. Stone
The staff of a prison prepares for the execution of a celebrated murderer.
World Wide — Kartes Video Communications

Last of Sheila, The 1973
Drama/Suspense
51963 118 mins   C   B, V   P
Richard Benjamin, James Coburn, James Mason, Dyan Cannon, Joan Hackett, Raquel Welch
The yacht "Sheila" is the setting for a "Whodunit" parlor game to discover which of six people is a murderer.
MPAA:PG
Warner Bros — Warner Home Video

Last of the Gladiators, The 1986
Biographical/Sports
87749 103 mins   C   B, V   P
Evel Knievel
A look at the career of the exuberantly risk-taking kamikaze motorcyclist.
Visual Assoc. — Twin Tower Enterprises

Last of the Mohicans 1932
Adventure/Serials
12541 156 mins B/W   B, V   P
Edwina Booth, Harry Carey, directed by Ford Beebe, B. Reaves Eason
Based on James Fenimore Cooper's novel of the Indian's life and death struggle during the French and Indian War. Twelve chapters, 13 minutes each.
Mascot — Video Connection; Video Yesteryear; Discount Video Tapes

Last of the Mohicans 1977
Adventure
57621 97 mins   C   B, V   P
Steve Forrest, Ned Romero, Andrew Prine, Don Shanks
The classic novel by James Fenimore Cooper about the scout Hawkeye and his Mohican companions, Chingachgook and Uncas, comes to life in this film.
Schick Sunn — Magnum Entertainment; United Home Video

Last of the Mohicans, The 1936
Adventure
55351 91 mins B/W   B, V, 3/4U   P
Randolph Scott, Binnie Barnes, Bruce Cabot

James Fenimore Cooper's classic about the French and Indian War in colonial America.
Edward Small; United Artists — Nostalgia Merchant; Blackhawk Films

Last of the One Night Stands, The 1983
Music/Documentary
82563 28 mins   C   B, V, 3/4U   P
Narrated by Hugh Thomas, directed by Jeff Belker
This award-winning documentary traces the career of the Lee Williams Band, which brought the sound of the swing era to rural America.
CINE Golden Eagle; 1984 FOCUS Award.
Zebra Films — Evergreen International

Last of the Pony Riders 1953
Western
64533 59 mins B/W   B, V   R, P
Gene Autry, Smiley Burnette, Kathleen Case
When the telegraph lines linking the East and West Coasts is completed, Gene and the other Pony Express riders find themselves out of a job. This was Autry's final feature film.
Columbia — Blackhawk Films

Last of the Red Hot Lovers 1972
Comedy
59424 98 mins   C   B, V, LV   P
Alan Arkin, Paula Prentiss, Sally Kellerman, Renee Taylor, directed by Gene Saks
Neil Simon's Broadway hit about a middle-aged man who decides to have a fling and uses his mother's apartment to seduce three very strange women.
MPAA:PG
Paramount — Paramount Home Video

Last Plane Out 198?
Drama
80137 90 mins   C   B, V   P
Jan Michael Vincent, Lloyd Batista, Julie Carmen, directed by David Nelson
A Texas journalist sent out on assignment to Nicaragua falls in love with a Sandanista rebel.
MPAA:R
Jack Cox Productions — CBS/Fox Video

Last Remake of Beau Geste, The 1977
Comedy
85776 85 mins   C   B, V   P
Marty Feldman, Ann-Margret, Michael York, Peter Ustinov, James Earl Jones
a slapstick parody of the familiar Foreign Legion story from the Mel Brooks-ish school of loud genre farce.
Universal — MCA Home Video

Last Ride of the Dalton Gang, The   1979

Western
80157   146 mins   C   B, V   P
Larry Wilcox, Jack Palance, Randy Quaid, Cliff Potts, Dale Roberston, Don Collier
This is a retelling of the wild adventures that made the Dalton gang legendary among outlaws.
Dan Curtis Productions — *Warner Home Video*

Last Starfighter, The   1984

Science fiction/Fantasy
79173   100 mins   C   B, V, LV   P
Lance Guest, Robert Preston, Barbara Bosson, Dan O'Herlihy, Catherine Mary Stewart
A young man who becomes an expert at a video game is recruited to fight in an inter-galactic war.
MPAA:PG
Gary Adelson; Lorimar; Universal — *MCA Home Video*

Last Summer   1969

Drama
70379   97 mins   C   B, V   P
Barbara Hershey, Richard Thomas, Bruce Davidson, Cathy Burns, directed by Frank Perry
Three teenagers discover, love, sex and friendship on the white sands of Fire Island, N.Y. The summer vacation fantasy world they create shatters when a sweet but homely female teenager joins their groups.
MPAA:R
Allied Artists — *Key Video*

Last Tango in Paris   1973

Drama
13323   129 mins   C   B, V, LV   P
Marlon Brando, Maria Schneider, Jean-Pierre Leaud, directed by Bernardo Bertolucci
Brando plays a middle-aged American who meets a French girl. Many revealing moments follow in their frantic, unlikely, and short-lived affair.
MPAA:X
United Artists — *CBS/Fox Video; RCA VideoDiscs*

Last Tycoon, The   1977

Drama
82070   123 mins   C   B, V   P
Robert De Niro, Tony Curtis, Ingrid Boulting, Jack Nicholson, Jeanne Moreau, Ray Milland, Dana Andrews, John Carradine, directed by Elia Kazan
This is an adaptation of the unfinished F. Scott Fitzgerald novel about the life and times of a Hollywood movie executive of the 1920's. Joan Collins introduces the film which is available in VHS and Beta Hi-Fi.
MPAA:PG
Paramount Pictures — *Paramount Home Video*

Last Unicorn, The   1982

Cartoons/Fairy tales
60583   95 mins   C   B, V, CED   P
Animated, voices of Alan Arkin, Jeff Bridges, Tammy Grimes, Angela Lansbury, Mia Farrow, Robert Klein, Christopher Lee, Keenan Wynn
Peter Beagle's popular tale of a beautiful unicorn who goes in search of her lost, mythical "family." Music by Jimmy Webb.
MPAA:G
ITC Entertainment — *Playhouse Video*

Last Waltz, The   1978

Music-Performance
52603   117 mins   C   B, V   P
The Band, Bob Dylan, Neil Young, Joni Mitchell, Van Morrison, Eric Clapton, Neil Diamond, Emmylon Harris, Muddy Waters, Ronnie Hawkins
Martin Scorsese filmed this rock documentary featuring the farewell performance of The Band, joined by a host of musical guests that they have been associated with over the years. Songs include: "Upon Cripple Creek," "Don't Do It," "The Night They Drove old Dixie Down," "Stage Fright" (The Band), "Helpless" (Young), "Coyote" (Mitchell), "Caravan" (Morrison), "Further On Up the Road" (Clapton), "Who Do You Love" (Hawkins), "Mannish Boy" (Waters), "Evangeline" (Harris), "Baby, Let Me Follow You Down" (Dylan).
MPAA:PG
Robbie Robertson, United Artists — *CBS/Fox Video; RCA VideoDiscs*

Last War, The   1968

Science fiction
80799   79 mins   C   B, V   R, P
Akiva Takarada, Yuriho Hoshi
A nuclear war between the United States and Russia triggers Armageddon.
Toho Films — *Video Gems*

Last Wave, The   1978

Drama/Suspense
47382   103 mins   C   B, V   P
Richard Chamberlain, Olivia Hamnett, Gulpilil, Frederick Parslow, directed by Peter Weir
An Australian attorney takes on a murder case involving an aborigine. He finds himself becoming distracted by apocalyptic visions concerning tidal waves and drownings that seem to foretell the future.
MPAA:PG
Australian; Peter Weir — *Warner Home Video*

Last Winter, The   1984

War-Drama
86383   92 mins   C   B, V   P
Kathleen Quinlan, Yona Elian, Zipora Peled, Michael Schnider
An American woman fights to find her Israeli husband who has disappeared in the 1973 Yom Kippur War.

MPAA:R
Tri-Star; Jacob Kotzky — *RCA/Columbia Pictures Home Video*

Last Word, The   1980
Comedy-Drama
69546   103 mins   C   B, V, CED   P
Richard Harris, Karen Black, Martin Landau, Dennis Christopher
A man fights to protect his home, family and neighbors from a corrupt real estate deal involving shady politicians, angry policemen, and a beautiful television reporter.
MPAA:PG
Richard G Abramson; Michael Varhol — *Embassy Home Entertainment*

Last Year at Marienbad   1962
Film-Avant-garde
49066   93 mins   B/W   B, V   P
Delphine Seyrig, Giorgio Albertazzi
A man and a woman meet at a hotel. The man tries to convince the lady that they met a year ago and had an affair, then attempts to lure her into running away with him.
French — *Festival Films; Cable Films; Discount Video Tapes*

Late Season Elk Hunting   1985
with Jim Zumbo
Hunting
87656   36 mins   C   B, V   P
Zumbo demonstrates elk hunting techniques, concentrating on late season details, and shoots a terrific six-pointer.
Sportsmen On Film — *Sportsmen on Film*

Late Show, The   1977
Mystery/Comedy
51964   94 mins   C   B, V   P
Art Carney, Lily Tomlin, Bill Macy, Eugene Roche, Joanna Cassidy, John Considine
A veteran private detective finds his world turned upside down when a former colleague arrives to visit nearly dead, and a woman whose cat is missing becomes his sidekick.
MPAA:PG
Warner Bros; Robert Altman — *Warner Home Video*

Laugh Yourself Crazy,   1986
Vol. 1, The
Comedy
88281   60 mins   C   V   P
Rare footage of famous comedians doing their stuff is used in this overview of 20th century American humor. Includes Fred Allen, Will Rogers, The Marx Brothers, Burns & Allen and Bob Hope.
The Minnesota Studio — *The Minnesota Studio*

Laughfest   191?
Comedy
10098   59 mins   B/W   B, V   P, T
Ben Turpin, Barney Oldfield, Mabel Normand, Charlie Chaplin, Snub Pollard
Five classic slapstick shorts are included on this tape: "It's a Gift" (1923), with Snub Pollard, "Barney Oldfield's Race for a Life" (1913), "Kid Auto Races" and "Busy Day" (1914), both with Charlie Chaplin, and "Daredevil" (1923), starring Ben Turpin.
Mack Sennett et al — *Blackhawk Films*

Laughing Policeman, The   1974
Crime-Drama
Closed Captioned
85431   111 mins   C   B, V   P
Walter Mathau, Bruce Dern, Lou Gossett, directed by Stuart Rosenberg
Two antagonistic cops embark on a vengeful hunt for a mass murderer through the seamy underbelly of San Francisco.
MPAA:R
20th Century Fox — *Key Video*

Laughs for Sale   1963
Comedy/Game show
78095   29 mins   B/W   B, V, FO   P
Hal March, Cliff Arquette, Shecky Greene, Paul Winchell, Jerry Mahoney
A comedy game show with short skits and funny one-liners.
ABC — *Video Yesteryear*

Laura   1944
Mystery/Crime-Drama
56463   85 mins   B/W   B, V   P
Gene Tierney, Clifton Webb, Dana Andrews, Vincent Price, directed by Otto Preminger
A detective assigned to the murder investigation of the late Laura Hunt finds himself falling in love with her painted portrait.
Academy Awards '44: Best Cinematography.
Twentieth Century Fox — *CBS/Fox Video*

Laura   1979
Drama/Romance
65433   95 mins   C   B, V   P
Maud Adams, Dawn Dunlap
A journey through beauty, sensuality and innocence revolving around a 16 year old ballet dancer's first stirrings of sexuality.
MPAA:R
20th Century Fox — *Embassy Home Entertainment*

Laurel and Hardy   1933
Comedy Classics Volume
I
Comedy
33910   84 mins   B/W   B, V, 3/4U   P
Stan Laurel, Oliver Hardy, Mae Busch, May Wallace, Charlie Hall, Billy Gilbert

A collection of four classic comedy shorts starring Laurel and Hardy: "The Music Box," which won an Academy Award for Best Short Subject, "Country Hospital," "The Live Ghost," and "Twice Twos," all from 1932-33.
Hal Roach, MGM — *Nostalgia Merchant*

Laurel and Hardy   **1930**
Comedy Classics Volume
II
Comedy
33911   75 mins   B/W   B, V, 3/4U   P
Stan Laurel, Oliver Hardy, Billy Gilbert, Tiny Sandford, Anita Garvin
A collection of four Laurel and Hardy shorts from 1930 including "Blotto," "Towed in a Hole," "Brats," and "Hog Wild."
Hal Roach, MGM — *Nostalgia Merchant*

Laurel and Hardy   **1934**
Comedy Classics Volume
III
Comedy
33912   75 mins   B/W   B, V, 3/4U   P
Stan Laurel, Oliver Hardy, Billy Gilbert, Mae Busch, Tiny Sandford
Laurel and Hardy star in four separate comedy shorts, including "Oliver the 8th," "Busy Bodies," "Their First Mistake," and "Dirty Work," all from 1933-34.
Hal Roach, MGM — *Nostalgia Merchant*

Laurel and Hardy   **1932**
Comedy Classics Volume
IV
Comedy
33913   75 mins   B/W   B, V, 3/4U   P
Stan Laurel, Oliver Hardy, Jacqueline Wells, James Finlayson, Thelma Todd
Laurel and Hardy star in four of their comedy shorts from 1931-32. Included are "Another Fine Mess," "Come Clean," "Laughing Gravy," and "Any Old Part."
Hal Roach, MGM — *Nostalgia Merchant*

Laurel and Hardy   **1931**
Comedy Classics Volume
V
Comedy
33914   84 mins   B/W   B, V, 3/4U   P
Stan Laurel, Oliver Hardy, Edgar Kennedy, James Finlayson, Blanche Payson
Four classic comedy shorts starring Laurel and Hardy. Included are "Be Big," "The Perfect Day," "Night Owls," and "Help Mates," from 1929-31.
Hal Roach, MGM — *Nostalgia Merchant*

Laurel and Hardy   **1935**
Comedy Classics Volume
VI
Comedy
33915   75 mins   B/W   B, V, 3/4U   P
Stan Laurel, Oliver Hardy, Charlie Hall, Billy Gilbert, Ben Turpin, Mae Busch, James Finlayson
Laurel and Hardy comedy shorts are presented in this package: "Our Wife," "The Fixer Uppers," "Them Thar Hills," and "Tit for Tat," from 1932-35.
Hal Roach, MGM — *Nostalgia Merchant*

Laurel and Hardy   **193?**
Comedy Classics Volume
VII
Comedy
47142   90 mins   B/W   B, V, 3/4U   P
Stan Laurel, Oliver Hardy, Mae Busch, Daphne Pollard, James Finlayson
Four Laurel and Hardy two-reelers are combined on this tape: "Me and My Pal" (1933), "The Midnight Patrol" (1933), "Thicker than Water" (1935), and the classic "Below Zero" (1930).
Hal Roach, MGM — *Nostalgia Merchant*

Laurel and Hardy   **193?**
Comedy Classics Volume
VIII
Comedy
59153   90 mins   B/W   B, V, 3/4U   P
Stan Laurel, Oliver Hardy
This compilation of Laurel and Hardy shorts includes: "Men O' War" (1929), "Scram" (1932), "Laurel and Hardy Murder Case" (1930) and "One Good Turn" (1931).
Hal Roach — *Nostalgia Merchant*

Laurel and Hardy   **193?**
Comedy Classics Volume
IX
Comedy
60422   100 mins   B/W   B, V, 3/4U   P
Stan Laurel, Oliver Hardy
Includes the shorts: "Beau Hunks" (1931), "Chickens Come Home" (1931), "Going Bye-Bye" (1934), and "Berth Marks" (1929).
Hal Roach — *Nostalgia Merchant*

Laurel and Hardy Volume   **196?**
1
Cartoons
47655   59 mins   C   B, V   P
Animated
Animated adventures of Laurel and Hardy.
EL, SP
Larry Harmon — *Unicorn Video*

Laurel and Hardy Volume 2
196?
Cartoons
47656   59 mins   C   B, V   P
Animated
Animated short cartoons starring Laurel and Hardy.
EL, SP
Larry Harmon — *Unicorn Video*

Laurel and Hardy Volume 3
196?
Cartoons
47657   59 mins   C   B, V   P
Animated
More animated adventures of Laurel and Hardy.
EL, SP
Larry Harmon — *Unicorn Video*

Laurel and Hardy Volume 4
196?
Cartoons
47658   59 mins   C   B, V   P
Animated
Animated shorts starring cartoon characters of Laurel and Hardy.
EL, SP
Larry Harmon — *Unicorn Video*

Lavender Hill Mob, The
1951
Comedy
50942   78 mins   B/W   B, V   P
Alec Guinness, Audrey Hepburn, Stanley Holloway
A prim and prissy bank clerk schemes to melt the bank's gold down and re-mold it into miniature Eiffel Tower paperweights.
Academy Award '52: Best Story and Screenplay (T.E.B. Clarke).
Universal; J Arthur Rank — *THORN EMI/HBO Video; Learning Corp of America*

Law West of Tombstone
1938
Western
64415   73 mins   B/W   B, V, 3/4U   P
Tim Holt, Harry Carey, Evelyn Brent
An ex-outlaw moves to a dangerous frontier town in order to clean things up.
RKO — *Nostalgia Merchant*

Lawless Frontier
1935
Western
58972   53 mins   B/W   B, V, 3/4U   P
John Wayne, Gabby Hayes
In the early West, the Duke fights for law and order.
Monogram — *Sony Video Software; Cable Films; Video Connection; Discount Video Tapes; Spotlite Video*

Lawless Range
1935
Western
51637   56 mins   B/W   B, V   P
John Wayne, Sheila Manners
John Wayne and the marshall's posse save the ranchers from trouble.
Republic — *Spotlite Video; Discount Video Tapes*

Lawless RAnge/The Man From Utah
1935
Western
81019   109 mins   B/W   B, V   P
John Wayne, Sheila Manners, Gabby Hayes
This is an action packed western double feature: In "Lawless Range" the Duke and the marshall's aides save a ranch from falling into the wrong hands, and in "The Man From Utah" the Duke upholds law and order in the old West.
Monogram Pictures — *Spotlite Video*

Lawrence of Arabia
1962
Drama
68260   221 mins   C   B, V   P
Peter O'Toole, Omar Sharif, Alec Guinness, Anthony Quinn
The true life story of T.E. Lawrence, the English officer who gained fame in the Middle East during World War I. In stereo.
Academy Awards '62: Best Picture, Best Director (Lean) Best Cinematography, Original Score (Maurice Jarre) MPAA:G
Sam Spiegel; Columbia — *RCA/Columbia Pictures Home Video; RCA VideoDiscs*

Lazarus Syndrome, The
1979
Drama
65303   90 mins   C   B, V   P
Lou Gossett Jr.
This is a hard-hitting film of a doctor's effort to expose illicit operating practices of the resident Chief of surgery.
Viacom Enterprises — *U.S.A. Home Video*

LCA Presents Family Entertainment Playhouse
197?
Drama/Mystery
56883   120 mins   C   CED   P
Geraldine Fitzgerald
Edgar Allan Poe's "The Gold Bug" pits an adventurous teenager against quicksand, a terrifying storm, and Captain Kidd's curse. "Rodeo Red" stars Geraldine Fitzgerald as a farm woman who teaches a runaway girl about facing her own problems.
Unknown — *RCA VideoDiscs*

Learn Knitting, Crochet, and Quilting at Home
1984
Hobbies
73658   60 mins   C   B, V   S
8 pgms

The basics needed to learn knitting, crochet, and quilting are taught in this series of eight programs.
1.*Knitting: Basic Stitches* 2.*Knitting: Color and Texture* 3.*Knitting: Garment Construction* 4.*Crochet: Basics* 5.*Crochet: Variations* 6.*Quilting: Patchwork* 7.*Quilting: Stitching Techniques* 8.*Quilting: Applique and Trapunto*
Kartes Productions — *Kartes Video Communications*

Learn to Sail   1985
Sports-Water
84771   106 mins   C   B, V   P
Steve Colgate, Audrey Landers, Sam Jones
The basics of successful sailing are made plain and simple in this video course.
Savoy Home Video/Selluloid Video — *Video Associates*

Learning About the   1986
World
Infants
86163   60 mins   C   B, V   P
A training film for parents in dealing with toddlers, with methods of education, activity, establishing routines and preparation for school. Part of "Parents Video Magazine."
Arnold Shapiro Prod.; Karl-Lorimar; George Paige Assoc. — *Karl/Lorimar Home Video*

Learning Bridge the Right   1986
Way
Games
86908   60 mins   C   B, V   P
Lee Henry 2   pgms
A program in two volumes instructing bridge strategy and rules.
1.*Bridge the Social Gap with Cards* 2.*Winning Strategies for Advanced Players*
Victor Van Rees — *Embassy Home Entertainment*

Learning Can Be Fun   1986
Language arts
Closed Captioned
86375   30 mins   C   B, V   P
Alaina Reed
An interactive learning video for children from four to seven, including bits about language, courtesy and math.
Breathless Prod. — *Playhouse Video*

Leather Boys, The   1966
Drama
79107   103 mins   C   B, V   P
Rita Tushingham, Dudley Sutton, Collin Campbell, directed by Sidney J. Furie
A teenaged girl marries a mechanic and then begins to cheat on him.
Allied Artists — *VidAmerica*

Leave 'Em Laughing   1981
Biographical/Drama
80637   103 mins   C   B, V   P
Mickey Rooney, Anne Jackson, Allen Goorwitz, Red Buttons, Elisha Cook, William Windom, directed by Jackie Cooper
This is the true story of a Chicago clown and his wife who cared for dozens of homeless children as he struggled from job to job. Available in Beta Hi-Fi and VHS Stereo.
Julian Fowles Prods; Charles Fries Prods. — *U.S.A. Home Video*

Leben von Adolf Hitler,   1961
Das (The Life of Adolf
Hitler)
Documentary/World War II
47472   101 mins   B/W   B, V, FO   P
Directed by Paul Rotha
A startling West German documentary feature on the life of Hitler, using much never-before-seen archival footage of Hitler's early life and rise to power. The full twelve-year span of the Third Reich is covered in painstaking detail.
West Germany — *Video Yesteryear*

Lee Aaron Live   1986
Music-Performance
86911   60 mins   C   B, V   P
The notorious rock queen is taped in London performing "Beat 'Em Up," "Line of Fire" and "Rockin' Metal Queen."
Philip Goodhand-Tait — *Embassy Home Entertainment*

Left Hand of God, The   1955
Drama
73968   87 mins   C   B, V   P
Humphrey Bogart, E.G. Marshall, Lee J. Cobb, Agnes Moorehead, directed by Edward Dmytryk
After a pilot escapes from a Chinese warlord, he disguises himself as a Catholic priest and takes refuge in a missionary hospital.
20th Century Fox — *Key Video*

Legacy Begins: Miami   1985
Dolphins, The
Football
81950   124 mins   C   B, V   P
Larry Csonka, Bob Griese, Paul Warfield
This is a compilation of highlights from the Miami Dolphins championship 1970-1974 seasons.
NFL Films — *NFL Films Video*

Legacy for Leonette, A   1985
Romance
87694   90 mins   C   V   P
A girl is led into a web of murder and love in this torrid romance novel brought to video.
Prism Video — *Prism*

Legacy of Horror 1978
Horror/Suspense
70579   83 mins   C   B, V   P
Elaine Boies, Chris Broderick, Marilee Troncone, Jeannie Cusik, directed by Andy Milligan
A weekend at the family's island mansion with two unfriendly siblings sounds bad enough, but when terror, death and a few family skeletons pop out of the closets, things go from bad to weird.
Ken Lane Films; Take One Film Group — *MPI Home Video*

Legend of Alfred Packer, The 1980
Documentary/Drama
80214   87 mins   C   B, V   P
Patrick Dray, Ron Haines, Bob Damon, Dave Ellingson
The true story of how a guide taking five men searching for gold in Colorado managed to be the sole survivor of a blizzard.
Mark Webb Productions — *Monterey Home Video*

Legend of Billie Jean, The 1985
Drama
Closed Captioned
70987   92 mins   C   B, V   P
Helen Slater, Peter Coyote, Keith Gordon, Christian Slater, directed by Matther Robbins
Billie Jean believed in justice for all. When the law and its bureaucracy landed hard on her, she took her cause to the masses and inspired a generation. Hi-Fi Stereo recording.
MPAA:PG-13
TriStar — *Key Video*

Legend of Boggy Creek, The 1975
Horror
88234   87 mins   C   B, V   P
David Hess, Lucy Grantham, Sandra Cassel, directed by Charles B. Pierce
A dramatized version of various Arkansas Bigfoot sightings.
MPAA:G
Cinema Shares; Howco — *Lightning Video*

Legend of Eight Samurai 1984
Martial arts
81825   130 mins   C   B, V   P
An ancient Japanese princess hires a group of eight samurai to destroy the witch who reigns over her clan.
Toei — *Prism*

Legend of Hell House, The 1973
Horror
81761   94 mins   C   B, V   P
Roddy McDowall, Pamela Franklin, Clive Revill, Gayle Hunnicutt
A multi-millionaire hires a team of scientists and mediums to investigate his newly-acquired mansion to find out the truth about life after death. Available in VHS and Beta Hi-Fi.
MPAA:PG
20th Century Fox — *CBS/Fox Video*

Legend of Hiawatha, The 1982
Cartoons
72452   35 mins   C   B, V   P
Hiawatha must confront a demon who casts a plague on his people. This animated program is based on Henry Wadsworth Longfellow's poem.
Unknown — *Family Home Entertainment*

Legend of Hillbilly John, The 1973
Adventure
70893   86 mins   C   B, V   P
Severn Darden, Denver Pyle, Susan Strasberg
Hillbilly Jean holds off the devil with a strum of his six-string. While demons plague the residents of rural America, the hayseed messiah wanders about saving the day.
MPAA:G
FH Harris and AJ Hope — *New World Video*

Legend of Lobo, The 1962
Drama
82297   67 mins   C   B, V   P
Narrated by Rex Allen
This is the story of Lobo, a crafty wolf who seeks to free his mate from the clutches of greedy hunters.
Buena Vista — *Walt Disney Home Video*

Legend of Sleepy Hollow, The 1949
Cartoons/Adventure
59808   45 mins   C   B, V   P
Narrated by Bing Crosby
The story of Ichabod Crane and the legendary ride of the headless horseman. Also includes two classic short cartoons, "Lonesome Ghosts" (1932) with Mickey Mouse and "Trick or Treat" (1952) with Donald Duck.
Walt Disney — *Walt Disney Home Video*

Legend of Sleepy Hollow, The 1979
Drama
81751   98 mins   C   B, V   P
Jeff Goldblum, Dick Botkus, Meg Foster, Paul Sand
This is an adaptation of the Washington Irving story about a headless horseman who pursues Ichabod Crane, a poor schoolteacher.
Schick Sohn Classic Productions — *Magnum Entertainment*

Legend of Sleepy Hollow, The   1979
Drama
37363   100 mins   C   B, V   P
Washington Irving's classic tale of the Headless
Horseman of Sleepy Hollow is brought to life on
the screen.
Sunn Classic — *United Home Video; Lucerne
Films*

Legend of the Lightning Bolt, The   1984
Football
79633   30 mins   C   B, V, FO   P
This is a chronological history of the San Diego
Chargers.
NFL Films — *NFL Films Video*

Legend of the Lone Ranger, The   1981
Western
47153   98 mins   C   B, V, CED   P
*Klinton Spilsbury, Michael Horse, Jason
Robards*
The origin of the fabled Lone Ranger and the
story of his first meeting with his Indian
companion, Tonto, are brought to life in this new
version of the famous legend.
MPAA:PG
Universal; Walter Coblenz — *CBS/Fox Video*

Legend of the Northwest   1978
Adventure
51657   83 mins   C   B, V   R, P
Denver Pyle
The loyalty of a dog is evidenced in the fierce
revenge he has for the drunken hunter who shot
and killed his master.
MPAA:G
GG Communications — *Video Gems*

Legend of the Werewolf   1975
Horror
58283   90 mins   C   B, V   P
Peter Cushing, Hugh Griffith, Ron Moody
A child who once ran with the wolves has
forgotten his past, except when the moon is full.
MPAA:R
Kevin Francis; Tyburn Studios — *VCL Home
Video; American Video Tape*

Legend of the Werewolf   1981
Horror
81804   90 mins   C   B, V   P
*Peter Cushing, Ron Moody, Hugh Griffith,
directed by Freddie Francis*
A French police inspector and college professor
must find out who has been committing a series
of horrifying murders in 19th century Paris.
Tyburn Film Productions — *VCL Home Video*

Legend of the Wolfwoman   1977
Horror
48328   84 mins   C   B, V   P
Anne Borel, Fred Stafford
The beautiful Daniella assumes the personality
of the legendary wolfwoman, leaving a trail of
gruesome killings across the countryside.
MPAA:R
Dimension Pictures — *United Home Video;
Continental Video*

Legend of Valentino, The   1975
Drama/Biographical
71224   96 mins   C   B, V   P
*Franco Nero, Suzanne Pleshette, Lesley Anne
Warren, Yvette Mimieux, Judd Hirsch, Milton
Berle, Harold J Stone, directed by Melville
Shavelson*
This docu-drama traces the legendary exploits
of one of the silver screen's greatest lovers,
Rudolph Valentino.
Spelling-Goldberg Productions — *Prism*

Legend of Valentino, The   1983
Documentary/Biographical
74086   71 mins   B/W   B, V   P
This is a biographical documentary of perhaps
the world's greatest lover beginning with his
immigration to America and ending at his
unexpected, sudden death.
Wolper Productions — *Embassy Home
Entertainment*

Legend of Walks Far Woman, The   1982
Drama/Western
84123   120 mins   C   B, V   P
Raquel Welch, Nick Mancuso, Bradford Dillman
A made-for-TV film about a proud Sioux woman
fighting for survival and her tribe during the
American-Indian Wars.
EMI Films-Roger Gimbel Prod-Raquel
Welch — *VCL Home Video*

Legend of Young Robin Hood, The   197?
Drama
50963   60 mins   C   B, V   R, P
The early life of the robber of the rich is depicted
in this movie. He learns to use a longbow, and
forms his convictions as he and other Saxons
struggle at their integration into the Norman
culture.
MPAA:G
Michael Christian Productions — *Video Gems*

Legendary Champions, The   1968
Boxing/Documentary
70766   101 mins   B/W   B, V   P
*John L. Sullivan, James J. Corbett, Bob
Fitzsimmons, James J. Jeffries, Tommy Burns,*

Jack Johnson, Jess Willard, Jack Dempsey, Gene Tunney, directed by Harry Chapin
This film takes a historic look at the prizefighting world from 1882 to 1929.
Harry Chapin — *VidAmerica*

Legendary Greats 1960
Baseball
49552 30 mins B/W   B, V   P
Men who left an everlasting mark on the game of baseball are profiled. Included are Hall of Famers Christy Mathewson, Babe Ruth, Ty Cobb, Connie Mack, and nine distinguished others.
Major League Baseball — *Major League Baseball Productions*

Legendary Personalities 193?
Film-History
10156 60 mins B/W   B, V   P, T
Package offers serious and light side of pre-40's years. Newsreel cameras film celebrities like Haile Selassie, George Bernard Shaw, and Sir Arthur Conan Doyle.
Unknown — *Blackhawk Films*

Legion of Missing Men, The 1937
War-Drama
59372 62 mins B/W   B, V, FO   P
Ralph Forbes, Ben Alexander, Hala Linda
Professional soldiers of fortune, the French Foreign Legion, fight the evil sheik Ahmed in the Sahara.
Unknown — *Video Yesteryear*

Legion of the Lawless 1940
Western
64412 59 mins B/W   B, V, 3/4U   P
George O'Brien, Virginia Vale
A group of outlaws band together in order to spread terror and confusion among the populace.
RKO — *Nostalgia Merchant*

Legs 1983
Drama
82209 91 mins C   B, V   P
Gwen Verdon, John Heard, Sheree North, Shanna Reed, Maureen Teefy
This is the story of three girls who are competing for a job with Radio City Music Hall's Rockettes.
Carolina Prod Group Ltd — *Prism*

Lena Horne: The Lady and Her Music 1984
Music-Performance
69922 134 mins C   B, V   P
Lena Horne's definitive Broadway performance of all the music she has been identified with during her career includes "Can't Help Lovin'

That Man," "Stormy Weather," and "The Lady Is a Tramp." In VHS Dolby stereo and Beta Hi-Fi.
James Nederlander, Michael Frazier et al — *RKO HomeVideo*

Lenny 1974
Biographical/Drama
Closed Captioned
82343 111 mins B/W   B, V   P
Dustin Hoffman, Valerie Perrine, Jan Miner, Stanley Beck, directed by Bob Fosse
This is an adaptation of the Julian Barry play about the life and times of the always controversial comedian Lenny Bruce. Available in VHS and Beta Hi-Fi.
MPAA:R
United Artists; Marvin Worth — *Key Video*

Lenny Bruce 1967
Comedy-Performance
10815 60 mins B/W   B, V, FO   P
Lenny Bruce
An uncensored San Francisco nightclub performance recording Bruce's off-beat, bewitching, and often unprecedented humor.
Filmmakers — *Video Yesteryear*

Lenny Bruce Performance Film, The 1968
Comedy-Performance
58897 72 mins B/W   B, V, CED   P
Lenny Bruce
A videotape of one of Lenny Bruce's last nightclub appearances at Basin Street West in San Francisco. Also included is "Thank You Mask Man," a color cartoon parody of the Lone Ranger legend, with Lenny Bruce providing all the character voices.
Columbus Prods — *Vestron Video*

Lenny White: In Clinic 1985
Music
87926 60 mins C   B, V   P
White demonstrates the importance of practice techniques, fusion, internal timing, and more, aided by bassist Rick Laird.
DCI Music Video — *DCI Music Video*

Leonid Kogan 198?
Music-Performance
87349 60 mins C   B, V   P
Violinist Kogan and his daughter (on piano) run through music by Tchaikovsky, Glazunov, Brahms, Bizet and Paganini.
Unknown — *Kultur*

Leonor 1975
Drama
37403 90 mins C   B, V   P
Liv Ullman

Liv Ullman demonstrates her versatility as an actress in this movie, in which she plays the mistress of the Devil.
France — CBS/Fox Video

Leopard in the Snow   1978
Drama
72880   89 mins   C   B, V   P
Keir Dullea, Susan Penhaligon, Kenneth More, Billie Whitelaw
The romance between a race car driver allegedly killed in a crash and a young woman is the premise of this film.
MPAA:PG
Harlequin Productions — Embassy Home Entertainment

Leopard Man, The   1943
Horror
00314   66 mins   B/W   B, V, 3/4U   P
Dennis O'Keefe, Margo, Rita Corday
An escaped leopard terrorizes a small town. After a search, the big cat is found dead, but the killings continue.
RKO — Nostalgia Merchant

Lepke   1975
Drama
80442   110 mins   C   B, V   P
Tony Curtis, Milton Berle, Gianni Russo, Vic Tayback, Michael Callan
The life and fast times of Louis "Lepke" Buchalter from his days in reform school to his days as head of Murder, Inc and his execution in 1944.
MPAA:R
Warner Bros; Menahem Golan — Warner Home Video

Les Girls   1957
Musical
85639   114 mins   C   B, V   P
Gene Kelly, Mitzi Gaynor, Kay Kendall, Taina Elg, directed by George Cukor
When one member of a performing troupe writes her memoirs, the other girls sue for libel. Cole Porter wrote the score for this "Rashomon"- styled musical.
MGM — MGM/UA Home Video

Let It Be   1970
Musical
55586   80 mins   C   B, V, LV   P
John Lennon, Paul McCartney, George Harrison, Ringo Starr, Billy Preston, Yoko Ono
A documentary look at a Beatles recording session, giving glimpses of the conflicts which led to the breakup.
United Artists — CBS/Fox Video; RCA VideoDiscs

Let Sleeping Minnows Lie   1982
Cartoons
86784   23 mins   C   B, V   P
An animated sequel to "Gilligan's Island," depicting the castaways' efforts to build a ship.
Sherwood Schwartz Filmation Assoc. — MGM/UA Home Video

Let the Balloon Go   1976
Drama
64790   92 mins   C   B, V   P
Robert Bettles, Sally Whiteman, Matthew Wilson, Terry McQuillan
Based on the international children's bestseller by Australian author Ivan Southall, the story is set in the year 1917 and centers around the plight of a slightly handicapped boy and his struggle to win respect.
MPAA:G
Film Australia — MCA Home Video

Let There Be Light   1945
Documentary
51949   60 mins   B/W   B, V   P
Narrated by Walter Huston, directed by John Huston
This moving documentary of shell-shocked soldiers in an army hospital was shelved by the War Department because of its revealing content.
US War Department — Hollywood Home Theater; Festival Films; International Historic Films; Victory Video

Let's Do It Again   1975
Comedy
53515   112 mins   C   B, V   P
Sidney Poitier, Bill Cosby, John Amos, Jimmie Walker, Ossie Davis, Denise Nicholas, Calvin Lockhart
An Atlanta milkman and his pal, a factory worker, bilk two big-time gamblers out of a large sum of money in order to build a meeting hall for their fraternal lodge. A sequel to "Uptown Saturday Night."
MPAA:PG
Warner Bros; First Artists Film — Warner Home Video

Let's Break: A Visual   1984
Guide to Break Dancing
Dance
70074   60 mins   C   B, V   P
An instructional guide to breakdancing featuring New York City dancers showing off basic moves to the original music of Dennis McCarthy and Jim Cox.
Image Magnetic Associates Inc — Warner Home Video

Let's Get Married   1963
Drama
82236   90 mins   B/W   B, V   P

Anthony Newley, Ann Aubrey
A young doctor's weakness under pressure
brings him to the brink of simpering idiocy when
his wife goes into early labor.
British — *Monterey Home Video*

Let's Go to the Zoo with   1985
Captain Kangaroo
Children
70590   60 mins   C   B, V   P
Bob Keeshan
Composed of short clips from the Captain's
Library of shows, this program features
segments introducing youngsters to many great
zoo beasts.
Encyclopedia Britannica Educational
Corporation — *MPI Home Video*

Let's Jazzercise   1983
Physical fitness/Dance
65206   57 mins   C   B, V   P
Judi Sheppard Missett
This program includes a warm up aerobic
activity and muscle toning and is completed by a
cool down routine.
Priscilla Ulene; Judi Sheppard Missett — *MCA
Home Video*

Let's Scare Jessica to   1971
Death
Horror
82541   89 mins   C   B, V   P
*Zohra Lampert, Barton Heyman, Kevin
O'Connor, Gretchen Corbett, Alan Manson*
A recently recovered mental patient goes on a
vacation and becomes entangled in a web of
drowning, corpses, vampires, murder and
general supernatural gore.
MPAA:PG
Charles B Moss — *Paramount Home Video*

Let's Spend the Night   1983
Together
Music-Performance
66040   94 mins   C   B, V, LV,   P
                        CED
Rolling Stones, directed by Hal Ashby
A chronicle of the Stones' 1981 American tour
including 25 songs spanning their career.
Stereo.
MPAA:PG
Ronald Schwary — *Embassy Home
Entertainment*

Let's Tap   1985
Dance
84954   30 mins   C   B, V   P
Bonnie Franklin
An instruction tape, step by step, on tap dancing
basics.
Karl-Lorimar Prod — *Karl/Lorimar Home Video*

Letter, The   1940
Drama/Suspense
73971   96 mins   B/W   B, V   P
*Bette Davis, Herbert Marshall, Gale
Sondergaard, directed by William Wyler*
A letter is used to blackmail a plantation owner's
wife who seems to have murdered a man in self
defense. Based on the play by Somerset
Maugham.
Warner Bros — *Key Video*

Letter of Introduction   1938
Drama
33801   104 mins   B/W   B, V   P
*Adolphe Menjou, Edgar Bergen, George
Murphy, Eve Arden, Ann Sheridan*
Struggling young actress learns that her father
is really a well-known screen star and agrees
not to reveal the news to the public.
Universal — *Hollywood Home Theater;
Discount Video Tapes; Kartes Video
Communications; See Hear Industries*

Ley del Revolver, La (The   1978
Law of the Gun)
Western
51106   90 mins   C   B, V   P
*Michael Rivers, Angel Del Pozo, Lucia Gil
Fernandez*
An Old West adventure where the law of the
gun speaks for and against justice. In Spanish.
SP
Spanish — *Hollywood Home Theater*

Liana   1983
Drama
65383   110 mins   C   B, V   P
Acclaimed screenwriter/director John Sayles
wrote and directed this story of a woman's
romantic involvement with another woman.
MPAA:R
Jeffrey Nelson — *Vestron Video*

Liar's Moon   1982
Drama
64877   106 mins   C   B, V, CED   P
Matt Dillon
A local boy woos and weds the town's
wealthiest young lady, only to be trapped in a
family's intrigue.
MPAA:PG
Don P Behrns — *Vestron Video*

Liberace in Las Vegas   1980
Music-Performance
47377   84 mins   C   B, V   P
*Liberace, the Jimmy Mullander Orchestra, the
Ballet Folklorico de Nacionale de Mexico*
A musical extravaganza starring the
multitalented Liberace and his special guests.
Taped at the Las Vegas Hilton.
VC — *Warner Home Video*

Liberace Live — 1985
Music-Performance
82455   56 mins   C   B, V   P
Liberace
The ruffled, diamond-laden virtuoso performs such peerless classics as "Memories," "I'll Be Seeing You" and "Send in the Clowns."
Vestron Music Video — *Vestron Video*

Liberace Show Volumes 1 & 2, The — 195?
Musical/Variety
60423   58 mins   B/W   B, V, 3/4U   P
A camp classic, these two half-hour episodes of "Mr. Showmanship's" TV series feature some of the world's best-loved music.
NBC — *Nostalgia Merchant*

Liberation of L.B. Jones, The — 1970
Drama
80373   101 mins   C   B, V   P
Lee J. Cobb, Lola Falana, Anthony Zerbe, Roscoe Lee Browne, directed by William Wyler
A wealthy black undertaker wants a divorce from his wife who is having an affair with a white policeman.
MPAA:R
Columbia Pictures — *RCA/Columbia Pictures Home Video*

Liberators, The — 1977
War-Drama
84073   91 mins   C   B, V   P
Klaus Kinski
Kinski stars as a criminal soldier battling with the American authorities, German troops and his black fugitive partner.
Cine Azimuti Prod — *Unicorn Video*

Libro de Piedra, El — 197?
Mystery
86189   100 mins   C   B, V   P
Marga Lopez, Joaquin Cordero
An isolated ranch harbors dark, horrible, Spanish-speaking secrets!
SP
Spanish — *Unicorn Video*

License to Kill — 1983
Crime-Drama
85778   96 mins   C   B, V   P
James Farentino, Don Murray, Penny Fuller, Millie Perkins
A young girl is killed by a drunk driver, devastating both families.
Marian Rees Prod. — *Video Gems*

Lidsville, Volume 2 — 1971
Fantasy
81631   46 mins   C   B, V   P

Charles Nelson Reilly, Butch Patrick
Here are a collection of two episodes from the series: "Fly Now, Vacuum Later" and "Weenie, Weenie Where's Our Genie?"
Sid and Marty Krofft — *Embassy Home Entertainment*

Lidsville, Volume I — 1971
Adventure
76791   46 mins   C   B, V   P
Charles Nelson Reilly, Billie Hayes, Butch Patrick
When a young boy falls into an enlarged magician's hat he lands in Lidsville, a village inhabited by living hats.
Sid and Marty Krofft — *Embassy Home Entertainment*

Lt. Robin Crusoe U.S.N. — 1966
Comedy
87674   113 mins   C   B, V   P
Dick Van Dyke, Nancy Kwan, Akim Tamiroff, directed by Byron Paul
A lighthearted navy pilot crash lands on a tropical island, falls for a native beauty and schemes against the local evil ruler.
MPAA:G
Walt Disney Prod. — *Walt Disney Home Video*

Life Among the BMX'ers — 1985
Bicycling
84276   28 mins   C   B, V   P
A documentary on bicycle motor cross, featuring World Cup footage, instruction, equipment, etc.
Video Travel Inc — *Video Travel*

Life and Assassination of the Kingfish, The — 1976
Biographical/Drama
81263   96 mins   C   B, V   P
Edward Asner, Nicholas Pryor, Diane Kagan, Fred Cook, Gary Allen
This is the colorful life story of the Louisiana Governor and U.S. Senator, Huey P. Long.
Tomorrow Entertainment — *U.S.A. Home Video*

Life and Death of Colonel Blimp, The — 1943
War-Drama
80933   115 mins   C   B, V   P
Roger Livesey, Deborah Kerr, Anton Walbrook, Ursula Jeans, Albert Lieven, directed by Michael Powell
This film chronicles the life of a British soldier who survives three wars, falls in love with three women, and waltzes.
J. Arthur Rank — *VidAmerica*

Life and Times of Grizzly Adams, The   1974
Adventure
13007   93 mins   C   B, V   P
Dan Haggerty, Denver Pyle, Don Shanks
This adventure film for the whole family is based on the rugged life of legendary frontiersman, Grizzly Adams.
MPAA:G
Sunn Classic — *United Home Video*

Life and Times of Judge Roy Bean, The   1972
Western/Comedy
68235   123 mins   C   B, V   P
Paul Newman, Stacy Keach, Ava Gardner, Jacqueline Bisset, Anthony Perkins, Roddy McDowell, Victoria Principal, dir. by John Huston
Frontier justice and gallows humor abounds in this telling of the judge Roy Bean legend. The film is based on the life of the famed Texas hanging judge.
MPAA:PG
National General — *Warner Home Video*

Life Is a Circus, Charlie Brown/You're the Greatest, Charlie Brown   1980
Cartoons
75607   60 mins   C   B, V   P
Animated
Two Peanuts favorites appear on this tape. In the Emmy award-winning "Life Is a Circus, Charlie Brown," Snoopy falls in love with Fifi, a French poodle circus performer, and winds up as a member of the traveling circus. In "You're the Greatest, Charlie Brown," our hero has a chance to win a decathlon in the Junior Olympics. With Peppermint Patty coaching, anything can happen!
Bill Melendez — *Snoopy's Home Video Library*

Life Is Worth Living   1955
Religion
47481   71 mins   B/W   B, V, FO   P
Bishop Fulton J. Sheen
Three programs from Bishop Sheen's long-running TV series, one of the most popular shows of the 1950's. The Bishop discussed religious matters, family life, read poetry and told jokes in an engagingly informal manner that was loved by audiences.
Dumont — *Video Yesteryear*

Life of Adolf Hitler, The   1961
Biographical/World War II
85185   101 mins   B/W   B, V   P
Directed by Paul Rotha, this film uses rarely seen archival footage to examine Hitler's rise, from the initial rise of Nazism after World War I to the death camps of World War II.
German — *Video Yesteryear*

Life on Emile Zola, The   1937
Drama/Biographical
73976   117 mins   B/W   B, V   P
Paul Muni, Gale Sondergaard, Gloria Holden
Writer Emile Zola invervenes in the case of Alfred Dreyfus who was sent to Devil's Island for a crime he did not commit.
Academy Awards '37: Best Picture; Best Screenplay.
Warner Bros — *Key Video*

Life of Oharu   1952
Drama
69561   136 mins   B/W   B, V, FO   P
Kinuyo Tanaka, Toshiro Mifune, directed by Kenji Mizoguchi
Oharu, the beautiful daughter of a samurai who serves the Imperial Court, falls in love with a lower class servant. When they are caught together, the slave is executed and Oharu is banished from the kingdom. Japanese dialogue with English subtitles.
Japan — *Video Yesteryear*

Life of Verdi, The   1984
Musical-Drama/Biographical
87359   600 mins   C   B, V   P
Ronald Pickup, Carla Fracci
An epic mini-series biography of the famous composer, with many excerpts of his music sung by Luciano Pavarotti, Renata Telbaldi and Maria Callas.
AM Available
British — *Kultur*

Life with Father   1947
Comedy
11305   118 mins   C   B, V, FO   P
William Powell, Irene Dunne, Elizabeth Taylor, Edmund Gwenn, Zasu Pitts
New York City of the 1880's is the delightful setting for this story of a stern but susceptible father and his relationship with his knowing wife and four red-headed sons.
New York Film Critics Award '47: Best Male Performance (Powell).
Warner Bros; Robert Buckner — *Video Yesteryear; Hollywood Home Theater; Video Connection; Discount Video Tapes; Cinema Concepts; Hal Roach Studios*

Lifeboat   1944
Drama
Closed Captioned
80734   96 mins   B/W   B, V   P
Tallulah Bankhead, John Hodiak, William Bendix, Canada Lee, Walter Slezak, Hume Cronyn, Henry Hull, Mary Anderson, directed by Alfred Hitchcock
When a freighter is sunk by a German U-boat, the eight survivors and the Nazi commander take refuge in a tiny lifeboat.
20th Century Fox — *Key Video*

Lifeforce 1985
Science fiction/Suspense
82435 100 mins C B, V, LV P
*Steve Railsback, Peter Firth, Frank Finlay,
Mathilda May, directed by Tobe Hooper*
A beautiful female vampire from outer space
drains Londoners in this hi-tech thriller.
MPAA:R
The Cannon Group Inc — *Vestron Video*

Lifeguard 1975
Drama/Comedy
71136 96 mins C B, V P
*Sam Elliot, Anne Archer, Stephen Young,
Parker Stevenson, Kathleen Quinlan, directed
by Daniel Petrie*
The "Lifeguard" lives by the credo that work is
for people who cannot surf. Aging, he questions
whether he should give up on the beachlife and
start selling Porsches.
MPAA:PG
Paramount — *Paramount Home Video*

Lifepod 1980
Science fiction
81687 94 mins C B, V P
Joe Penny, Jordan Michaels, Kristine DeBell
A group of intergalactic travelers is forced to
evacuate a luxury space liner when a mad
computer sabotages the ship.
First American Films — *United Home Video*

Lift, The 1983
Suspense
84859 95 mins C B, V P
Huub Stapel, Willeke Van Ammelroy
Dubbed into English, this Dutch film deals with a
demonic elevator that eats people.
MPAA:R
Dutch — *Media Home Entertainment*

Light at the Edge of the 1971
World, The
Adventure
72905 126 mins C B, V P
Kirk Douglas, Yul Brynner, Samantha Eggar
A lighthouse keeper near Cape Horn is
tormented by a band of pirates.
MPAA:PG
Brynafilm; Triumfilm — *Media Home
Entertainment*

Light in the Forest, The 1958
Adventure
88194 92 mins C B, V P
James MacArthur, Fess Parker, Carol Lynley
An adaptation of the classic novel about a
young man, kidnapped by Indians when he was
young, who is forcibly returned to his white
family.
Walt Disney Prod. — *Walt Disney Home Video*

Lightblast 1985
Suspense
87634 89 mins C B, V P
*Erik Estrada, Mike Pritchard, directed by Enzo
Q. Castellari*
A San Francisco policeman is out to stop a
deadly explosive-wielding mad scientist from
blowing the city to kingdom come.
Overseas Film Group — *Lightning Video*

Lightning Strikes West 1940
Western
15485 57 mins B/W B, V P
Ken Maynard
U.S. Marshal trails an escaped convict,
eventually catches him, and brings him in to
finish paying his debt to society.
Colony — *Video Connection; United Home
Video*

Lights, Camera, Action, 1985
Love
Romance
87693 90 mins C B, V P
A romance novel on tape, in which a young
actress finds the path to stardom littered with
pain, pornography and seediness.
Prism Video — *Prism*

Lights of Old Santa Fe 1947
Western
51448 78 mins B/W B, V P
*Roy Rogers, Dale Evans, Gabby Hayes, Bob
Nolan, Sons of the Pioneers*
A cowboy rescues a beautiful rodeo owner from
bankruptcy. This is the original, unedited version
of the film.
Producers Releasing Corp — *Captain Bijou*

Like a Mighty River... 1981
Football
50648 24 mins C B, V, FO R, P
Dallas Cowboys
Danny White stepped into Roger Staubach's
role as Cowboy quarterback drawing much
praise. Although the defense was weak at times
during the 1980 season, it toughened when it
had to. The Cowboys, under the guidance of the
ever-present Tom Landry, surged all the way to
the NFC championship game, where they finally
ran out of gas.
NFL Films — *NFL Films Video*

Likely Stories 1983
Comedy-Performance
80903 57 mins C B, V P
*Richard Belzer, Christopher Guest, Rob Reiner,
Marcia Strassman, David L Lander, Michael
McKean, Billy Crystal, Pee Wee Herman*
3 pgms
Each volume of this comedy series contains
skits and jokes featuring the top comedians of

the 1980's. Available in VHS Stereo and Beta Hi-Fi.
David Jablin — *U.S.A. Home Video*

Li'l Abner 1940
Musical
08730   78 mins   C   B, V   P
Cranville Owen, Martha Driscoll, Buster Keaton
Al Capp's famed comic strip comes to life in this comedy, featuring all of the Dogpatch favorites.
RKO — *Discount Video Tapes; Video Yesteryear; Movie Buff Video*

Lili 1953
Musical
66454   81 mins   C   B, V   P
Leslie Caron, Jean-Pierre Aumont, Mel Ferrer, Kurt Kasznar, Zsa Zsa Gabor
A 16-year-old orphan joins a traveling carnival and falls in love with a crippled, embittered puppeteer. Leslie Caron sings the films's song hit, "Hi-Lili, Hi-Lo."
Academy Awards '53: Best Scoring of a Dramatic or Comedy Film (Bronislau Kaper).
MGM — *MGM/UA Home Video*

Lilies of the Field 1963
Drama
70376   94 mins   B/W   B, V   P
Sidney Poitier, Lilia Skala, Lisa Mann, Isa Crino, Stanley Adams, directed by Ralph Nelson
Five Eastern European refugee nuns enlist the aid of a free-spirited US Army veteran. The ex-GI, apprehensive throughout, is amusingly convinced to build a chapel and teach the sisters English.
Academy Award '63: Best Actor (Sidney Poitier).
U.A.; Rainbow Prods. — *Key Video*

Lilith 1964
Drama
70562   114 mins   B/W   B, V   P
Warren Beatty, Jean Seberg, Peter Fonda, Kim Hunter, directed by Robert Rossen
Beatty stars as a therapist who falls for one of the patients (Seberg) at the swank mental institution where he works. Available in Beta Hi-Fi.
Columbia — *RCA/Columbia Pictures Home Video*

Lily in Love 1985
Drama
86355   100 mins   C   B, V, LV   P
Maggie Smith, Christopher Plummer, Elke Sommer
An aging stage star disguises himself to star in his wife's new play and test her fidelity. Loosely based on "The Guardsman."
MPAA:PG-13
New Line Cinema — *Vestron Video*

Lily Tomlin Special: Volume I 1973
Comedy/Variety
70180   45 mins   C   B, V   P
Lily Tomlin, Richard Pryor
Lily's first award-winning television special features her entire repertoire of characters including Ernestine, the telephone operator, five-year old Edith Ann, Mrs. Beasley, Suzie Sorority and the Shopping Bag Lady.
Emmy Awards '73: Best Special Program; Best Writing.
LIJA Productions — *Karl/Lorimar Home Video*

Limelight 1952
Drama
48406   120 mins   B/W   B, V   P
Charles Chaplin, Claire Bloom, Buster Keaton, Nigel Bruce
A nearly washed-up music hall comedian is stimulated by a young ballerina to a final hour of glory.
Academy Awards '72: Best Original Dramatic Musical Score. (Not submitted for Academy consideration until 1972.)
Charles Chaplin — *Playhouse Video*

Limited Gold Edition II Cartoon Classics 1985
Cartoons
70559   50 mins   C   B, V   P
Mickey Mouse, Donald Duck, Minnie Mouse, Pluto, Goofy, Jack Hannah, Jack Kinney.
7   pgms
Disney Studios compiled these collections from previously unreleased material and added interviews with the creators of some of these cartoons. Favorites and award winners highlight these limited edition specials.
1.Life with Mickey!; 2.From Pluto With Love; 3.An Officer and a Duck; 4.The World According to Goofy; 5.How the West Was Won: 1933-1960; 6.The Disney Dream Factory: 1933-1938; 7.Donald's Bee Pictures
Walt Disney Productions — *Walt Disney Home Video*

Lincoln Conspiracy, The 1977
Documentary
55596   87 mins   C   B, V   P
This film uncovers startling new evidence, and concludes that high-level cabinet members conspired to assassinate President Lincoln.
MPAA:G
Sunn Classics — *VidAmerica; Lucerne Films*

Lincoln County Incident 1980
Western
85879   47 mins   C   B, V   P
A satiric western starring secondary-school children.
Unknown — *VidAmerica*

Linda Ronstadt—Nelson   1984
Riddle "What's New"
Music-Performance
72916   60 mins   C   B, V, LV,   P
                        CED
Linda Ronstadt performs great songs of the
1930s and '40s in concert with Nelson Riddle
and His Orchestra.
Peter Asher — *Vestron Video*

Line, The   197?
Drama
79190   96 mins   C   B, V   P
Russ Thacker, David Doyle
A group of soldiers mutiny against the Army
because of the cruel treatment inflicted upon
them during basic training.
MPAA:R
Robert J. Siegel; Virginia Largent — *U.S.A.
Home Video*

Lion Has Wings, The   1940
War-Drama
81463   75 mins   B/W   B, V, LV   P
*Merle Oberon, Ralph Richardson, Flora
Robson, June Duprez, directed by Michael
Powell and Brian Desmond Hurst*
This is the story of how Britain's Air Defense
was set up to meet the challenge of Hitler's
Luftwaffe during their "finest hours."
United Artist; Alexander Korda — *Embassy
Home Entertainment*

Lion in Winter, The   1968
Drama
08367   134 mins   C   B, V, LV,   P
                        CED
*Peter O'Toole, Katharine Hepburn, directed by
Anthony Harvey*
Katharine Hepburn portrays Eleanor of
Aquitaine in this historical drama of twelfth-
century English political history.
Academy Awards '68: Best Actress (Hepburn).
Avco Embassy — *Embassy Home
Entertainment; RCA VideoDiscs*

Lion of the Desert   1979
Drama
65447   164 mins   C   B, V   P
*Anthony Quinn, Oliver Reed, Irene Papas, Rod
Steiger, Raf Vallone, John Gielgud*
This is the story of Omar Mukhtar, the great
Libyan patriot whose twenty year long struggle
to free his people from the yoke of Mussolini's
Italian occupying forces became one of the
most heroic sagas of the twentieth century.
MPAA:PG
Falcon International — *U.S.A. Home Video*

Lion of Venice, The   1982
Adventure/Fantasy
80825   73 mins   C   B, V   P

A kid and an old Venetian gondolier see a stone
lion move and uncover a legend of secret
treasure.
Londonderry Co — *Video Gems*

Lion, the Witch and the   1979
Wardrobe, The
Fantasy/Cartoons
77187   100 mins   C   B, V, CED   P
Animated
Four children stumble through an old wardrobe
closet in an ancient country house and into the
fantasy land of Narnia. Adapted from C.S.
Lewis' "The Chronicles of Narnia."
Children's Television Workshop — *Vestron
Video*

Lionel Hampton   1983
Music-Performance
75915   24 mins   C   B, V   P
This program presents the jazz music of Lionel
Hampton backed up by a 20-piece band.
digit recordings — *Sony Video Software*

Lipstick   1976
Drama
38935   88 mins   C   B, V, LV   P
*Margaux Hemingway, Anne Bancroft, Perry
King, Chris Sarandon, Mariel Hemingway*
A fashion model (Margaux Hemingway) seeks
revenge on the man who brutally attacked and
raped her.
MPAA:R
Paramount — *Paramount Home Video*

Liquid Sky   1983
Science fiction
65114   112 mins   C   B, V   P
Anne Carlisle, Paula Sheppard, Bob Brady
An androgynous model living in Manhattan is
the primary attraction for a UFO, which lands
atop her penthouse in search of the chemical
nourishment that her sexual encounters
provide.
MPAA:R
Slava Tsukerman — *Media Home
Entertainment*

Lisa Sliwa's Common   1986
Sense Defense
Safety education
85631   60 mins   C   B, V   P
Guardian Angel Lisa Sliwa, wife of Curtis,
demonstrates practical self-defense methods.
Vestron Video — *Vestron Video*

Lisbon   1956
Suspense
88170   90 mins   C   B, V   P
*Ray Milland, Claude Rains, Maureen O'Hara,
Francis Lederer*

This first film directed by Milland, filmed in Portugal, details the adventures of a sea captain entangled in international espionage and crime.
Republic — *Republic Pictures Home Video*

List of Adrian Messenger, The   1963
Mystery
76806   98 mins   B/W   B, V   P
Kirk Douglas, George C. Scott, Robert Mitchum, Dana Wynter, Burt Lancaster, Frank Sinatra, directed by John Huston
A crafty murderer resorts to a variety of disguises to eliminate potential heirs to a family fortune.
Kirk Douglas; Edward Lewis — *MCA Home Video*

Listen to Your Heart   1983
Drama
76046   90 mins   C   B, V   P
Tim Matheson, Kate Jackson
In a contemporary love story, Tim Matheson and Kate Jackson find the strength of their relationship put to the test when they try to work together as well as love together.
CBS Motion Pictures for Television — *Key Video*

Lisztomania   1975
Fantasy
53516   105 mins   C   B, V   P
Roger Daltry, Sara Kestelman, Paul Nicholas, Fiona Lewis, Ringo Starr, directed by Ken Russell
Ken Russell's vision of what it must have been like to be Franz Liszt and Richard Wagner, who are depicted as the first pop stars.
MPAA:R
Warner Bros — *Warner Home Video*

Little Annie Roonie   1925
Drama
10125   60 mins   B/W   B, V   P, T
Mary Pickford, William Haines, Walter James, Gordon Griffith, Vola Vale, directed by William Beaudine
Tomboy policeman's daughter spends her time mothering her father and brother while getting into mischief with street punks. Tragedy ensues. (Silent).
Pickford — *Blackhawk Films*

Little Ballerina, The   1947
Drama
85186   62 mins   B/W   B, V   P
Margot Fonteyn, Anthony Newley, Martita Hunt, Yvonne Marsh
A young dancer struggles against misfortune and jealousy to succeed in the world of ballet, under the auspices of Fonteyn.
English — *Video Yesteryear*

Little Big Man   1970
Satire/Western
86042   135 mins   C   B, V   P
Dustin Hoffman, Fay Dunaway, Cheif Dan George, Richard Mulligan, Martin Balsam, Jeff Corey, directed by Arthur Penn
Based on Thomas Berger's picaresque novel, this is the story of 121-year-old Jack Crabb and his quixotic life as gunslinger, charlatan, Indian, ally to George Custer and the only survivor of Little Big Horn.
MPAA:PG
National General; Stuart Millar — *Key Video*

Little Big Master, The   197?
Martial arts
82087   90 mins   C   B, V   P
Huang I Lung, Man Li Peng
A crafty knight-errant who heads a gang of beggars finds it difficult adjusting to military life.
Foreign — *Unicorn Video*

Little Boy Lost   1978
Drama
84508   92 mins   C   B, V   P
John Hargreaves, Tony Barry, Lorna Lesley, directed by Alan Spires
The true story of the disappearance in Australia of a young boy.
MPAA:G
Australian — *Magnum Entertainment*

Little Brown Burro, The   1979
Christmas/Cartoons
17270   23 mins   C   B, V, 3/4U   R, P
Animated, narrated by Lorne Greene
Forlorn donkey realizes that by doing his best he can make his own kind of contribution.
AM Available EL, JA
Learning Corp of America — *Embassy Home Entertainment; Learning Corp of America*

Little Caesar   1930
Crime-Drama
64457   80 mins   B/W   B, V, CED   P
Edward G. Robinson, Douglas Fairbanks, Jr.
A small-time hood rises to become a gangland czar but his downfall is as rapid as his advancement. The role of Rico made Edward G. Robinson a star and also typecast him as a crook for all time.
Warner Bros — *CBS/Fox Video; RCA VideoDiscs*

Little Darlings   1980
Comedy
48511   95 mins   C   B, V, LV   P
Tatum O'Neal, Kristy McNichol, directed by Ronald F. Maxwell
A summer camp full of fun, friendship, and rivalries is the setting for a race—between a pair of very opposite teenage girls—to lose their virginity.

MPAA:R
Stephen J. Friedman — *Paramount Home Video*

Little Drummer Girl, The   1984
Suspense/Drama
Closed Captioned
76852   130 mins   C   B, V, LV   P
Diane Keaton, Klaus Kinski, Yorgo Voyagis, Sami Frey, Michael Cristofer, directed by George Roy Hill
An actress sympathetic to the Palestinian cause is recruited by an Israeli counter intelligence agent to trap a fanatical terrorist leader.
MPAA:R
Robert L. Crawford; Warner Bros — *Warner Home Video*

Little Engine That Could, The   1963
Literature
00692   10 mins   C   B, V   P, T
Animated
The classic story about a little train engine that struggles to carry a load of children's toys over a mountain.
Coronet Films — *Blackhawk Films; Coronet Films*

Little Foxes, The   1941
Drama
80947   116 mins   B/W   B, V, LV   P
Bette Davis, Herbert Marshall, Dan Duryea, Teresa Wright, Richard Carlson, directed by William Wyler
A vicious southern woman will destroy everyone around her in order to satisfy her desire for wealth and power. Based upon the Lillian Hellman play.
Samuel Goldwyn — *Embassy Home Entertainment*

Little Girl Who Lives Down the Lane, The   1976
Suspense
65345   90 mins   C   B, V   P
Jodie Foster, Martin Sheen
A 13-year-old girl, when her father dies, is discovered to be keeping her mother's corpse in the cellar, and doesn't stop at more murders to keep her secret.
MPAA:PG
Harold Greenberg; Alfred Pariser — *Vestron Video*

Little House on the Prairie   1974
Drama
53790   100 mins   C   CED   P
Michael Landon, Karen Grassle, Melissa Gilbert, Melissa Sue Anderson, Lindsay Sidney Greenbush, Victor French

The original pilot movie for the popular TV series, in which Charles Ingalls uproots his young family for the plains of Kansas.
NBC — *RCA VideoDiscs*

Little House on the Prairie Volume I   1974
Drama
80158   98 mins   C   B, V   P
Michael Landon, Melissa Gilbert, Melissa Sue Anderson, directed by Michael Landon
This series pilot describes the strugglers of Laura Ingalls Wilder's family to survive in the American Wilderness.
Ed Friendly; Michael Landon Productions — *Warner Home Video*

Little House on the Prairie, Volume II   1979
Drama
80159   98 mins   C   B, V   P
Michael Landon, Karen Grassle, Melissa Gilbert, Melissa Sue Anderson, Dean Butler, Victor French
Two episodes from the series: In "The Craftsman" Albert Ingalls finds out about prejudice as a Jewish woodcarver's apprentice, and "The Collection" describes the transformation a con man undergoes when donning a priest's disguise.
Ed Friendly; Michael Landon Productions — *Warner Home Video*

Little House on the Prairie Volume III   1975
Drama
80160   97 mins   C   B, V   P
Michael Landon, Karen Grassle, Melissa Gilbert, Melissa Sue Anderson, Patricia Neal
A terminally ill widow asks Charles Ingalls to help her to find a home for her three children before she dies.
Emmy Award '75: Best Actress (Neal).
Ed Friendly; Michael Landon Productions — *Warner Home Video*

Little Johnny Jones   1980
Musical
68236   92 mins   C   B, V   P
George M. Cohan's classic musical in a 1980 revival. Songs include "Yankee Doodle Dandy" and "Give My Regards to Broadway."
Goodspeed Opera House — *Warner Home Video*

Little Kid's Dynamite All-Star Band, The   1982
Musical
64955   90 mins   C   B, V   R, P
Marty Brill, Jay Stuart, Willie De Jean, Mischa Bond, Bunky Butler
A children's rock group rehearses in a garage that has an antique brass mirror lying against a

wall. The mirror has magical properties that allow two wacky musketeers to join the children in their adventures.
MPAA:G
Century Video — *Video Gems*

Little Ladies of the Night   1977
Drama
71222   96 mins   C   B, V   P
Linda Purl, David Soul, Clifton Davis, Carolyn Jones, Lou Gossett Jr
The police and a concerned former pimp try to save Purl and several other teen runaways from the world of prostitution.
Spelling-Goldberg Productions — *Prism*

Little Laura and Big John   1973
Adventure
13010   82 mins   C   B, V   P
Fabian Forte, Karen Black
Follows the true-life exploits of the small-time Ashley Gang in turnof-the-century Florida.
Gold Key — *VidAmerica*

Little League's Official How-To Play Baseball by Video   1986
Baseball
85269   70 mins   C   B, V   P
For beginning youngsters, this program demonstrates baseball essentials in an easy-to-follow manner.
John Gonzalez; David Stern — *Mastervision*

Little Lord Fauntleroy   1936
Comedy-Drama
12449   102 mins   B/W   B, V   P
Freddie Bartholomew, Mickey Rooney, Delores Costello, C. Aubrey Smith
Movie version of Frances Hodgson Burnett's juvenile story. Brooklyn boy becomes a Lord and is brought up by a doting mother.
Selznick — *Prism; Movie Buff Video; Video Connection; Hollywood Home Theater; Cable Films; Discount Video Tapes; Kartes Video Communications*

Little Lord Fauntleroy   1980
Drama
73534   98 mins   C   B, V   P
Ricky Schroeder, Alec Guinness, directed by Jack Gold
A poor young boy growing up in New York City at the turn of the century suddenly discovers his aristocratic background. Available in Beta Hi-Fi and VHS stereo.
Norman Rosemont Productions — *U.S.A. Home Video*

Little Lulu   194?
Cartoons
56746   48 mins   C   B, V   P

Animated
The popular comic book heroine gets into mischief with her pals, Tubby, Iggie, Wilbur and others. Includes "Little Angel" and "Operation Babysitting." Available in English and Spanish versions.
EL, SP
Paramount; Famous Studios — *Media Home Entertainment*

Little Magician, The   1985
Drama
80830   70 mins   C   B, V   R, P
A young magician learns a lesson in truth and honesty as he tries to hide a bad grade he received on a magic exam.
Londonderry Group — *Video Gems*

Little Match Girl, The   1984
Fairy tales/Musical
72882   54 mins   C   B, V   P
A musical version of the Hans Christian Andersen classic.
Unknown — *Embassy Home Entertainment*

Little Men   1940
Drama
08615   86 mins   B/W   B, V, 3/4U   P
Jack Oakie, Jimmy Lydon, Kay Francis, George Bancroft
A modern version of the famous classic juvenile story by Louisa May Alcott.
RKO — *Movie Buff Video; Hal Roach Studios; Video Connection; Kartes Video Communications*

Little Mermaid, The   1981
Fantasy
72232   75 mins   C   B, V   P
In this animated version of a Hans Christian Andersen fable a princess of the mermaids yearns to be human.
N W Russo — *Children's Video Library*

Little Mermaid, The   1984
Fairy tales
Closed Captioned
73576   60 mins   C   B, V, CED   P
Pam Dawber, Treat Williams
From "Faerie Tale Theatre" comes the adaptation of the Hans Christian Andersen tale of a little mermaid who makes a big sacrifice to win the prince she loves.
Gaylord Productions; Platypus Productions — *CBS/Fox Video*

Little Mermaid, The   1978
Fairy tales/Cartoons
40728   71 mins   C   B, V   R, P
Animated
An animated version of Hans Christian Andersen's tale about a little mermaid who

rescues a prince whose boat has capsized. She immediately falls in love and wishes that she could become a human girl.
21st Century — *Video Gems*

Little Minister, The   1934
Romance/Drama
79319   101 mins   B/W   B, V   P
Katharine Hepburn, John Beal, Alan Hale, Donald Crisp, directed by Richard Wallace
A filmed adaptation of the James Barrie novel about a free spirited gypsy who falls in love with a Scottish minister.
RKO; Pandros S. Berman — *RKO HomeVideo*

Little Miss and Friends   1983
Cartoons
71174   48 mins   C   B, V   P
Animated
The informative and educational vignettes on this cassette help children understand the concepts of lateness, bossiness, plumpness, splendor, magic, shyness and neatness.
Mister Films Ltd — *Warner Home Video*

Little Miss Marker   1980
Comedy
60589   112 mins   C   B, V   P
Walter Matthau, Julie Andrews, Tony Curtis, Bob Newhart, Lee Grant, Sara Stimson
The often retold tale of Sorrowful Jones, a grouchy, stingy bookie who accepts a little girl as a security marker for a ten dollar bet.
MPAA:PG
Universal — *MCA Home Video*

Little Miss Trouble and   1983
Friends
Cartoons
71175   43 mins   C   B, V   P
Animated
The informative and educational vignettes on this cassette help children understand concepts like naughtiness, happiness, helpfulness, confusion and tininess.
Mister Films Ltd — *Warner Home Video*

Little Night Music, A   1977
Musical/Romance
69544   110 mins   C   B, V   P
Elizabeth Taylor, Diana Rigg, Hermione Gingold, Len Cariou, Lesley Ann Down
Adapted from the Broadway play, this film centers around four ingeniously interwoven, contemporary love stories. Musical score by Stephen Sondheim.
MPAA:PG
New World Pictures — *Embassy Home Entertainment*

Little Orphan Annie   1932
Drama
10041   60 mins   B/W   B, V   P, T
Mitzie Green, Edgar Kennedy, directed by John S. Robertson
Based on the comic strip, Annie is an orphan being cared for by a bum. He follows money making scheme, leaving her alone, but Annie finds newly orphaned boy in her travels.
RKO — *Blackhawk Films*

Little Prince: Volumes I   1985
thru V, The
Cartoons
76996   60 mins   C   B, V, CED   P
Animated 5 pgms
Each program in this series adapts Antoine de Saint Exupery's beloved character into different educational adventures.
Children's Video Library — *Children's Video Library*

Little Prince, The   1974
Musical
38608   88 mins   C   B, V, LV   P
Richard Kiley, Bob Fosse, Steven Warner, Gene Wilder, directed by Stanley Donen
Based on the story by Antoine de Saint-Exupery, this musical fable tells of a little prince from Asteroid B-612 who comes to visit the earth. Music and lyrics by Lerner and Loewe.
MPAA:G
Paramount — *Paramount Home Video*

Little Princess, The   1939
Drama
05445   91 mins   C   B, V, 3/4U   P
Shirley Temple, Richard Greene, Ian Hunter, Cesar Romero, Arthur Treacher, Anita Louise
The story of a little girl who doesn't believe that her missing Army Officer father is really dead.
Daryl Zanuck; 20th Century Fox — *Video Connection; VCII; World Video Pictures; Video Yesteryear; Cable Films; Hollywood Home Theater; Discount Video Tapes; Nostalgia Merchant; Media Home Entertainment; Kartes Video Communications; Hal Roach Studios*

Little Rascals Volume I,   193?
The
Comedy
81860   54 mins   B/W   B, V   P
Darla Hood, Spanky McFarland, Buckwheat, Alfalfa Switzer, Stymie Beard
Here is a collection of three uncut "Little Rascals" short subjects.
Hal Roach — *Spotlite Video*

Little Rascals Comedy   193?
Classics Vol II, The
Comedy
81876   120 mins   B/W   B, V   P

Stymie Beard, Darla Hood, Porky, Spanky McFarland
Here is another volume of classic Little Rascals two-reelers.
Hal Roach — *Republic Pictures Home Video*

Little Rascals, Book I, The   193?
Comedy
66117   59 mins   B/W   B, V   P, T
Farina Hoskins, Joe Cobb, Stymie Beard, Spanky McFarland, Scotty Beckett, Alfalfa Switzer, Mary Ann Jackson
Three "Our Gang" shorts: "Railroadin'" (1929), in which the gang takes off on a runaway train; "A Lad and a Lamp" (1932), wherein they find an Aladdin's lamp; "Beginner's Luck" (1935), in which Spanky wins a dress for a young actress.
Hal Roach — *Blackhawk Films*

Little Rascals, Book II, The   193?
Comedy
64826   56 mins   B/W   B, V   P, T
Stymie Beard, Wheezer Hutchins, Spanky McFarland, Alfalfa Switzer
A second package of "Our Gang" two-reelers: "Bear Shooters" (1930), in which the Gang goes hunting but runs into some bootleggers; "Forgotten Babies" (1933), has Spanky babysitting for the gang's brothers and sisters; and "Teacher's Beau" (1935), where the gang cooks up a scheme to chase their teacher's fiance away.
Hal Roach — *Blackhawk Films*

Little Rascals, Book III, The   1938
Comedy
64917   54 mins   B/W   B, V   P, T
Wheezer Hutchins, Dorothy De Borba, Stymie Beard, Spanky McFarland, Alfalfa Switzer, Darla Hood
Three more "Our Gang" two reelers are packaged on this tape: "Dogs Is Dogs"(1931), "Anniversary Trouble" (1935) and "Three Men in a Tub" (1938).
Hal Roach — *Blackhawk Films*

Little Rascals, Book IV, The   193?
Comedy
65083   52 mins   B/W   B, V   P, T
Wheezer, Stymie, Spanky, Alfalfa, Darla, Porky, Buckwheat
Another package of Our Gang favorites, including "Helping Grandma" (1931), "Little Papa" (1935) and "Bear Facts" (1938).
Hal Roach — *Blackhawk Films*

Little Rascals, Book V, The   193?
Comedy
65084   49 mins   B/W   B, V   P, T
Breezy Brisbane, Stymie, Spanky, Scotty, Alfalfa, Darla, Porky, Buckwheat
The comic adventures of the Little Rascals continue in this package of three original shorts: "Readin' and Writin'" (1932), "Sprucin' Up" (1935) and "Reunion in Rhythm" (1937).
Hal Roach — *Blackhawk Films*

Little Rascals, Book VI, The   193?
Comedy
65085   48 mins   B/W   B, V   P, T
Stymie, Breezy, Spanky, Fidgets, Alfalfa, Darla, Porky, Buckwheat, Dorothy DeBorba, Billy Gilbert
Three more classic "Our Gang" comedy shorts are packaged on this tape: "Free Eats" (1932), "Arbor Day" (1936) and "Mail and Female" (1937).
Hal Roach — *Blackhawk Films*

Little Rascals, Book VII, The   193?
Comedy
65086   47 mins   B/W   B, V   P, T
Spanky, Breezy, Dickie Moore, Stymie, Scotty, Alfalfa, Darla, Porky, Buckwheat
The "Our Gang" kids serve up another portion of comedy in these three shorts: "Hook and Ladder" (1932), "The Lucky Corner" (1936) and "Feed 'Em and Weep" (1938).
Hal Roach — *Blackhawk Films*

Little Rascals Book VIII, The   19??
Comedy
66305   42 mins   B/W   B, V   P, T
Wheezer, Mary Ann Jackson, Spanky, Alfalfa, Buckwheat, Porky, Darla Hood
More fun and nuttiness with "Our Gang" in three original short comedies, "Bouncing Babies" (1929), "Two Too Young" (1936) and "The Awful Tooth" (1938).
Hal Roach — *Blackhawk Films*

Little Rascals Book IX, The   19??
Comedy
66306   48 mins   B/W   B, V   P, T
Farina, Stymie, Spanky, Alfalfa, Buckwheat, Porky, Darla
The Little Rascals scamper into more mischief in these three original shorts: "Little Daddy" (1931), "Spooky Hooky" (1936) and "Hide and Shriek" (1938).
Hal Roach — *Blackhawk Films*

(For explanation of codes, see Use Guide and Key)   **471**

Little Rascals, Book X, The   19??
Comedy
66308   41 mins   B/W   B, V   P, T
Jackie Cooper, Mary Ann Jackson, Spanky, Alfalfa, Buckwheat, Porky, Darla, Butch, Woim
The tenth compilation of original "Our Gang" comedies includes "The First Seven Years" (1929), "Bored of Education" (1936) and "Rushin' Ballet" (1937).
Academy Awards '36: Best Short Subject ("Bored of Education").
Hal Roach — *Blackhawk Films*

Little Rascals, Book XI, The   1938
Comedy
66340   42 mins   B/W   B, V   P, T
Spanky McFarland, Alfalfa Switzer, Darla Hood, Porky, Buckwheat
The Little Rascals go dramatic in these three shorts, all with a "putting-on-a-show" theme: "Pay As You Exit" (1936), "Three Smart Boys" (1937) and "Our Gang Follies of 1938."
Hal Roach — *Blackhawk Films*

Little Rascals, Book XII, The   1937
Comedy
66341   53 mins   B/W   B, V   P, T
Jackie Cooper, Farina Hoskins, Mary Ann Jackson, Spanky McFarland, Alfalfa Switzer, Darla Hood
The Little Rascals explore a haunted house, take a train ride and play football in these three original shorts: "Moan and Groan, Inc." (1929), "Choo-Choo!" (1932) and "The Pigskin Palooka" (1937).
Hal Roach — *Blackhawk Films*

Little Rascals, Book XIII, The   1937
Comedy
66442   48 mins   B/W   B, V   P, T
Jackie Cooper, Farina, Wheezer, Chubby, Mary Ann, Spanky, Scotty, Alfalfa, Edgar Kennedy
The Our Gang kids return in three more original shorts: "Shivering Shakespeare" (1930), "The First Round-Up" (1934) and "Fishy Tales" (1937).
Hal Roach — *Blackhawk Films*

Little Rascals, Book XIV, The   193?
Comedy
65704   52 mins   B/W   B, V   P, T
Wheezer, Mary Ann, Spanky, Porky, Alfalfa, Buckwheat, Darla
This package of shorts leads off with Our Gang's first talkie, "Small Talk" (1929), a three-reeler. The other two entries are "Little Sinner" (1935) and "Hearts Are Thumps" (1937).

Hal Roach — *Blackhawk Films*

Little Rascals, Book XV, The   193?
Comedy
65770   50 mins   B/W   B, V   P, T
Edgar Kennedy, Tommy "Butch" Bond, Spanky McFarland, Scotty Beckett, Wheezer Hutchins
Those rascally imps return once again in three more original shorts: "When the Wind Blows" (1930), "For Pete's Sake" (1934) and "Glove Taps" (1937).
Hal Roach; MGM — *Blackhawk Films*

Little Rascals, Book XVII, The   1931
Comedy
84927   46 mins   B/W   B, V   P
Jean Darling, Spanky McFarland
Three classic shorts, "Boxing Gloves," "The Kid from Borneo," and "Roamin' Holiday."
Hal Roach — *Blackhawk Films*

Little Rascals, Book XVIII, The   1929
Comedy
79855   41 mins   B/W   B, V   P, T
Farina Hoskins, Wheezer Hutchins, Mary Ann Jackson, Joe Cobb
Here are two early "Our Gang" comedies from the silent era: "Saturday's Lesson" (1929) and "Wiggle Your Ears" (1929).
Hal Roach — *Blackhawk Films*

Little Rascals, Book XX, The   1934
Comedy
84928   60 mins   B/W   B, V   P
Spanky McFarland, Stymie Beard, Mary Ann Jackson, Chubby Chaney
Three classic shorts with the gang: "Lazy Days," "Bedtime Worries" and "Second Childhood."
Hal Roach — *Blackhawk Films*

Little Rascals, Book XXI, The   1935
Comedy
84929   49 mins   B/W   B, V   P
Spanky McFarland
Three classic shorts: "Fly My Kite," "Mama's Little Pirate" and "Framing Youth."
Hal Roach — *Blackhawk Films*

Little Rascals, Book XXII, The   1934
Comedy
84930   54 mins   B/W   B, V   P
Wheezer, Spanky McFarland, Alfalfa Switzer, Darla Hood
Three classics shorts: "Pups is Pups," "Fish Hooky" and "The Pinch Singer."

Hal Roach — *Blackhawk Films*

Little Rascals, Book XXIII, The
1932

Comedy
84931   57 mins   B/W   B, V   P
Jackie Cooper, Spanky McFarland
Three classic shorts: "Teachers Pet," "Spanky"
and "Honkey Donkey."
Hal Roach — *Blackhawk Films*

Little Rascals, Book XXIV, The
1924

Comedy
84945   57 mins   B/W   B, V   P
Mickey Daniels, Mary Kornman
Two silent comedy classics: "Lodge Night" and
"Big Business."
Hal Roach — *Blackhawk Films*

Little Rascals, Book XXV, The
1928

Comedy
84946   40 mins   B/W   B, V   P
Farina Hoskins, Mary Ann Jackson
Two silent rascal classics: "Barnum and
Ringling, Inc." and "Spook Spoofing."
Hal Roach — *Blackhawk Films*

Little Rascals, Book XXVI, The
1933

Comedy
84947   54 mins   B/W   B, V   P
Jackie Cooper
Three classic shorts: "School's Out," "Mike
Fright" and "Divot Diggers."
Hal Roach — *Blackhawk Films*

Little Rascals Christmas Special, The
1979

Christmas
65160   60 mins   C   B, V   P
*Animated, voices of Darla Hood, Matthew
"Stymie" Beard*
Spanky and the Little Rascals attempt to raise
enough money to buy a winter coat for Spanky's
mom and learn the true meaning of Christmas
along the way.
King World Productions — *Family Home
Entertainment*

Little Rascals Comedy Classics 1
193?

Comedy
65739   50 mins   B/W   B, V   P
Spankie, Stymie, Alfalfa, Buckwheat
The Little Rascals romp again in this collection
of original comedy two-reelers.
Hal Roach — *Republic Pictures Home Video*

Little Rascals On Parade, The
1937

Comedy
76829   60 mins   B/W   B, V   P
Spanky McFarland, Alfalfa Switzer, Darla Hood
A collection of six vintage "Our Gang" shorts
from the 30's: "FreeEats," "Arbor Day," "Mail
and Female," "Hook and Ladder," "TheLucky
Corner" and "Feed 'Em and Weep."
Hal Roach — *Republic Pictures Home Video*

Little Rascals, Book XIX, The
1936

Comedy
77366   55 mins   B/W   B, V   P, A
*Mary Ann Jackson, Jackie Cooper, Dickie
Moore, Tommy Bond, Darla Hood, Stepin
Fetchit*
A collection of three "Our Gang" shorts: In "A
Tough Winter," Stepin Fetchit helps the Gang
clean up a mess; in "Mush and Milk," the cop
treats the kinds of a boarding school to a day at
an amusement park; and the Florydor perform in
the "Our Gang Follies of 1936."
Hal Roach — *Blackhawk Films*

Little Red Riding Hood
1984

Fairy tales
Closed Captioned
73142   60 mins   C   B, V, CED   P
*Mary Steenburgen, Malcolm McDowell, directed
by Graeme Clifford*
From "Faerie Tale Theatre" comes the retelling
of the story about a girl (Mary Steenburgen) off
to give her grandmother a picnic basket only to
get stopped by a wolf.
Shelley Duvall — *CBS/Fox Video*

Little Red Schoolhouse, The
1936

Comedy/Drama
71001   64 mins   C   B, V   P
Frank Coghlan, Jr, Dickie Moore, Ann Doran
A hard-nosed schoolteacher hunts a truant lad
and both of them land in jail.
Grand National — *Kartes Video
Communications*

Little River Band
1982

Music-Performance
47798   75 mins   C   B, V   P
Selections from this Australian rock'n'roll band's
six LP's, such as "It's a Long Way There,"
"Mistress of Mine," and "Just Say That You
Love Me," are featured.
Capitol EMI Music — *THORN EMI/HBO Video;
RCA VideoDiscs; Pioneer Artists*

Little Romance, A
1979

Drama
38942   105 mins   C   B, V   P

Laurence Olivier, Diane Lane, Thelonious
Bernard, Sally Kellerman, Broderick Crawford,
directed by George Roy Hill
Two lonely, gifted children set out on a charming
adventure that carries them across Europe to
find love in Venice.
Academy Awards '79: Best Music Score
(George Delrue) MPAA:PG
Orion Pictures — Warner Home Video

Little Sex, A   1982
Comedy
47849   94 mins   C   B, V   P
Tim Matheson, Kate Capshaw, Edward
Herrmann, Wallace Shaw
A young newlywed finds himself perpetually
tempted by young women.
MPAA:R
Universal — MCA Home Video

Little Shop of Horrors   1960
Horror
00408   70 mins   B/W   B, V   P
Jackie Joseph, Jonathan Haze, Mel Welles,
Jack Nicholson, directed by Roger Corman
Simple minded boy develops man-eating plant.
Attempting to destroy it, he becomes its victim.
Filmgroup — Vestron Video; Hollywood Home
Theater; Movie Buff Video; Video Connection;
Video Yesteryear; Western Film & Video Inc;
Discount Video Tapes

Little Tough Guys   1938
Drama
01717   84 mins   B/W   B, V, FO   P
Helen Parrish, Billy Halop, Leo Georcy, Marjorie
Main
When father goes to jail, the children must fend
for themselves. Son gets involved in gang
warfare plus reform school.
U I — Video Yesteryear; Cable Films;
Hollywood Home Theater; Discount Video
Tapes; Kartes Video Communications; See
Hear Industries

Little Treasure   1985
Comedy/Adventure
Closed Captioned
71108   95 mins   C   B, V   P
Burt Lancaster, Margot Kidder, Ted Danson,
Written and directed by Alan Sharp
A dying man's last words to his daughter send
her off on a treasure hunt with an adventurer. A
HiFi recording.
Tri-Star — RCA/Columbia Pictures Home
Video

Little Tweety and Little   1944
Inki Cartoon Festival
Cartoons
84716   50 mins   C   B, V   P
Tweety and Inki romp through these early
cartoon efforts.

Vitaphone Corp. — MGM/UA Home Video

Little Women   1933
Drama
58297   107 mins   B/W   B, V   P
Katharine Hepburn, Joan Bennett, Paul Lukas,
Edna May Oliver, Frances Dee, directed by
George Cukor
Louisa May Alcott's Civil War story of the four
March sisters, Jo, Beth, Amy, and Meg, who
share their loves, their joys, and their sorrows.
Academy Awards '33: Writing Adaptation (Victor
Heerman, Sarah Y. Mason).
RKO — MGM/UA Home Video

Little Women   1983
Cartoons/Literature
69535   60 mins   C   B, V, CED   P
Animated
Louisa May Alcott's classic tale of four loving
sisters who face the joys and hardships of life
together comes to life in this animated program.
Toei Animation Productions — Children's
Video Library

Little Women   1985
Cartoons/Drama
82381   30 mins   C   B, V   P
Animated
An animated version of Louisa May Alcott's
story of the four March sisters and their youth in
Civil-War New England.
SONY Corporation of America — Sony Video
Software

Littlest Angel, The   1969
Musical
82257   77 mins   C   B, V   P
Johnny Whittaker, Fred Gwynne, E.G. Marshall,
Cab Calloway, Connie Stevens, Tony Randall
A shepherd boy who wants to become an angel
learns a valuable lesson in the spirit of giving.
Available in VHS and Beta Hi-Fi Mono.
Patricia Gray; Lan O'Kun — Embassy Home
Entertainment

Littlest Horse Thieves,   1976
The
Adventure
84808   109 mins   C   B, V   P
Alastair Sim
Children try to save a horde of mine-working
horses from extinction.
MPAA:G
Walt Disney Productions — Walt Disney Home
Video

Littlest Warrior, The   1975
Cartoons/Adventure
53139   70 mins   C   B, V   P
Animated

Zooshio, the Littlest Warrior, is forced to leave his beloved forest and experiences many adventures before he is reunited with his family forever.
Ziv Intl — *Family Home Entertainment*

Live and Let Die
1973
Adventure
64329   121 mins   C   LV   P
Roger Moore, Jane Seymour, Yaphet Kotto
Agent 007 is out to thwart the villainous Dr. Kananga, a black mastermind who plans to control western powers with voodoo and hard drugs. Title song by Paul McCartney and Wings.
MPAA:PG
United Artists — *CBS/Fox Video; RCA VideoDiscs*

Live at Target
1980
Music-Performance/Music video
84060   60 mins   C   B, V   P
Factrix, Nervous Gender, Flipper
The first video album to be released in the U.S., this tape includes a smattering of San Francisco-based punk groups.
Target Video — *Target Video*

Live From the Met Highlights Volume 1
1986
Opera
86883   70 mins   C   B, V   P
Placido Domingo, Joan Sutherland, Eva Marton, Luciano Pavarotti
A compilation of the Met's greatest operatic moments, with scenes from "The Bartered Bride," "Lucia di Lammermoor," "Tannhauser," "Don Carlo" and "La Boheme."
Metropolitan Opera; Paramount — *Paramount Home Video*

Live Infidelity: REO Speedwagon in Concert
1981
Music-Performance
53410   90 mins   C   B, V, LV, CED   P
A live performance by REO Speedwagon, featuring selections from their album, "Hi Infidelity."
MGM; CBS — *CBS/Fox Video*

Live Television
195?
Drama
33696   110 mins   B/W   B, V, 3/4U   P
Bob Cummings, Martin Balsam, Rip Torn, Ralph Edwards, Laurel and Hardy
Two classic examples from the live, pioneer days of television: "Playhouse 90: Bomber's Moon," and "This Is Your Life, Laurel and Hardy."
CBS, NBC — *Shokus Video*

Living Desert, The
1953
Wildlife/Documentary
84435   69 mins   C   B, V   P
The life cycle of an American desert is shown through the seasons in this trendsetting Disney documentary feature.
Academy Awards '53: Best Documentary.
MPAA:G
Walt Disney — *Walt Disney Home Video*

Living Head, The
1963
Adventure
56913   75 mins   B/W   B, V, FO   P
Archeologists discover the ancient sepulcher of the great Aztec warrior, Acatl. Ignoring a curse, they steal his severed head and incur the fury of Xitsliapolí. Dubbed in English.
Mexican — *Video Yesteryear*

Living in Harmony
1968
Suspense/Fantasy
77418   52 mins   C   B, V   P
Patrick McGoohan, Alexis Kanne, David Bauer
The Prisoner mysteriously wakes up in an old western town called Harmony and defies the town's judge. This is an unaired episode from "The Prisoner" series.
ITC Productions — *MPI Home Video*

Living Language—French
1984
Languages-Instruction
79184   60 mins   C   B, V   P
A video course designed to instruct travelers on how to speak French.
Crown Video — *Karl/Lorimar Home Video; Gessler Educational Software*

Living Language—Spanish
1984
Languages-Instruction
79185   60 mins   C   B, V   P
A video course designed to instruct travelers on how to speak Spanish.
Crown Video — *Karl/Lorimar Home Video*

Liza in Concert
1981
Music-Performance
52670   60 mins   C   LV   P
Liza Minnelli performs at the Theatre for the Performing Arts in New Orleans, featuring a New York medley: "Lullaby of Broadway," "I Guess the Lord Must Be in New York City," "Forty Second Street," "On Broadway," and "Theme from New York, New York." Also performed are "City Lights," "Arthur in the Afternoon," and "Cabaret."
Artel Home Video — *Pioneer Artists*

L.L.Bean Outdoor Video Library, The
1985
Wildlife/Hobbies
84520   60 mins   C   B, V   P

Each episode of this collection demonstrates the fun and benefits of various outdoor activities like canoeing and fishing.
L L Bean — *Friendship II Productions*

Loaded Guns   1975
Suspense/Drama
76799   90 mins   C   B, V   P
Ursula Andress, Woody Strode
An airline stewardess who doubles as an intelligence counter-agent must totally immobilize a top drug trafficking ring.
Picturmedia — *Monterey Home Video*

Local Badman   1932
Western/Comedy
84841   60 mins   B/W   B, V   P
Hoot Gibson
Wacky western featuring the inimitable Gibson and his coterie of cliches.
Universal — *United Home Video*

Local Hero   1983
Adventure
65324   112 mins   C   B, V   P
Peter Riegert, Denis Lawson, Fulton Mackay, Burt Lancaster
A Texas oil company sends an ace trouble-shooter to buy out a sleepy Scottish fishing village for a refinery and supertanker port, but both the oil men and the citizenry get more than they bargained for.
MPAA:PG
Puttnam — *Warner Home Video*

Loch Ness Horror, The   1982
Horror
84734   93 mins   C   B, V   P
Barry Buchanan, Miki Mckenzie, Sandy Kenyon
The famed monster surfaces and chomps on the local poachers.
Larry Buchanan — *Monterey Home Video*

Lodger, The   1926
Suspense
47469   91 mins   B/W   B, V, FO   P
Ivor Novello, Marie Ault, Arthur Chesney, Malcolm Keen, directed by Alfred Hitchcock
A mysterious lodger is thought to be a rampaging mass murderer of young women. This is the first Hitchcock film to explore themes and ideas that would become trademarks of his work.
Gainsborough — *Video Yesteryear; Video Dimensions; Festival Films; Discount Video Tapes*

Logan's Run   1976
Science fiction
58298   120 mins   C   B, V, CED   P
Michael York, Richard Jordan, Jenny Agutter, Roscoe Lee Browne, Farrah Fawcett-Majors, Peter Ustinov
In the 23rd century, a hedonistic society exists in a huge bubble and takes it for granted that there is no life outside.
MGM — *MGM/UA Home Video*

Lolita   1962
Drama
53941   152 mins   B/W   B, V, CED   P
James Mason, Shelley Winters, Peter Sellers, Sue Lyon, directed by Stanley Kubrick
Vladimir Nabokov's novel about a middle-aged professor's obsession with a teenage nymphet is the basis of this film.
MGM — *MGM/UA Home Video*

Lombardi   1980
Football
50088   48 mins   C   B, V, FO   R, P
A tribute to Vince Lombardi and his legendary Green Bay Packers, 1960's "Team of the Decade."
NFL Films — *NFL Films Video*

London Medley and City   193?
of the Golden Gate
Documentary/Cities and towns
79856   19 mins   B/W   B, V   P, T
Movietone News visits London and San Francisco in this collection of newsreels.
Movietone News — *Blackhawk Films*

Lone Avenger, The   1933
Western
08839   60 mins   B/W   B, V, 3/4U   P
Ken Maynard, Muriel Gordon, James Marcus
The plot centers around a bank panic and two-gun Maynard clears up the trouble.
World Wide — *Video Connection; Cable Films; Discount Video Tapes*

Lone Ranger, The   1980
Cartoons/Western
66003   60 mins   C   B, V   P
Animated 2 pgms
Two volumes of three cartoons each depicting the irrepressible lawman.
Lone Ranger Television Inc — *Family Home Entertainment*

Lone Ranger, The   1956
Western
70754   87 mins   C   B, V   P
Clayton Moore, Jay Silverheels, Lyle Bettger, Bonita Granville
Tonto and that strange masked man must prevent a war between ranchers and Indians.
Warner Bros.; Rather Corp. — *MGM/UA Home Video*

Lone Ranger, The   1938
Western/Serials
57357   234 mins   B/W   B, V, FO   P
Western serial, extremely rare, about the masked man and his faithful Indian sidekick. From a long-sought print found in Mexico, this program is burdened by a noisy sound track, two completely missing chapters, an abridged episode #15, and containing Spanish subtitles.
Republic — *Video Yesteryear; Video Connection*

Lone Wolf, The   1972
Drama
65436   45 mins   C   B, V   P
A boy learns kindness by befriending an old military dog which villagers think is mad and responsible for killing their sheep. After a brush with death, the boy convinces the villagers of the dog's good qualities and wins the admiration of his friends.
Columbia — *Embassy Home Entertainment*

Lone Wolf McQuade   1983
Western/Martial arts
64899   107 mins   C   B, V, LV   P
Chuck Norris, Leon Isaac Kennedy, David Carradine, Barbara Carrera
Martial arts action abounds in this modern-day Western which pits a Texas Ranger against a band of mercenaries.
Orion Pictures — *Vestron Video; RCA VideoDiscs*

Loneliest Runner, The   1976
Drama
80161   74 mins   C   B, V   P
Michael Landon, Lance Kerwin, DeAnn Mears, Brian Keith, directed by Michael Landon
A teenaged boy overcomes his bedwetting problem and becomes an Olympic track star.
NBC — *Warner Home Video*

Lonely Are the Brave   1962
Western/Drama
76805   107 mins   B/W   B, V   P
Kirk Douglas, Walter Matthau, Gena Rowlands, Carroll O'Connor, George Kennedy, directed by David Miller
A maverick cowboy who escapes from jail heads for the mountains with the police hot on his trail.
Universal; Kirk Douglas; Edward Lewis — *MCA Home Video*

Lonely Boy/Satan's Choice   19??
Music/Documentary
65230   55 mins   B/W   B, V, FO   P
This tape contains two cinema-verite documentaries from the National Film Board of Canada. "Lonely Boy" (1962) follows the early career of pop singer Paul Anka; and "Satan's Choice" (1966) provides an inside look at the members of a motorcycle gang.
National Film Board of Canada — *Video Yesteryear*

Lonely Guy, The   1984
Comedy
74091   91 mins   C   B, V, LV   P
Steve Martin, Charles Grodin, Judith Ivey, Steve Lawrence
This romantic comedy features Steve Martin as a jilted writer who writes a best-selling book about being a lonely guy and finds stardom does have its rewards.
MPAA:R
Universal — *MCA Home Video*

Lonely Hearts   1983
Romance/Comedy
65624   95 mins   C   B, V   P
Wendy Hughes, Norman Kaye
This is a quiet story about a piano tuner, who at 50 finds himself alone after years of caring for his mother, and a sexually insecure spinster, whom he meets through a dating service.
MPAA:R
John B Murray — *Embassy Home Entertainment*

Lonely Lady, The   1983
Drama
66328   92 mins   C   B, V, LV   P
Pia Zadora, Lloyd Bochner, Bibi Besch, Joseph Cali
A young writer comes to Hollywood with dreams of success. She gets involved with the seamy side of moviemaking and is driven to a nervous breakdown.
MPAA:R
Universal — *MCA Home Video*

Lonely Man, The   1957
Western
85254   87 mins   C   B, V   P
Jack Palance, Anthony Perkins, Neville Brand, Elaine Aiken
A gunfighter tries to end his career, but is urged into one last battle.
Paramount — *Kartes Video Communications*

Lonely Wives   1931
Comedy
58728   86 mins   B/W   B, V   P
Edward Everett Horton, Patsy Ruth Miller, Laura La Planta, Esther Ralston
A lawyer hires an entertainer to serve as his double because of his marital problems.
RKO — *Video Yesteryear*

Loners, The   1972
Drama
80932   80 mins   C   B, V   P

(For explanation of codes, see Use Guide and Key)

*Dean Stockwell, Gloria Grahame, Scott Brady,
Alex Dreier*
Three teenagers run from the southwest police
after they are accused of murdering a highway
patrolman.
MPAA:R
Maple Leaf Productions — *VidAmerica*

Long Ago Tomorrow   1971
Drama
65703   90 mins   C   B, V   P
Malcolm McDowell, Nanette Newman
A paralyzed athlete enters a church-run home
rather than return to his family as the object of
their pity.
MPAA:PG
Bruce Cohn Curtis — *RCA/Columbia Pictures
Home Video*

Long Day's Journey Into   1962
Night
Drama
66473   174 mins   B/W   B, V   P
*Katharine Hepburn, Ralph Richardson, Jason
Robards, Dean Stockwell*
Eugene O'Neill's autobiographical drama deals
with the life of his family, circa 1912, as his
father and brother were forced to come to grips
with his mother's drug addiction.
Landau Unger — *Republic Pictures Home
Video*

Long Days of Summer,   1980
The
Drama
87323   78 mins   C   B, V   P
Dean Jones, Joan Hackett
A young Connecticut lawyer tries to prevent the
deportation of a German Jew before World War
II. A made-for-TV movie.
Dan Curtis — *U.S.A. Home Video*

Long Good Friday, The   1979
Crime-Drama
63331   109 mins   C   B, V   P
*Bob Hoskins, Helen Mirren, Dave King, Bryan
Marshall, Derek Thompson, Eddie Constantine*
Set in London's dockland, this is the story of an
underworld king out to beat his rivals at their
own game.
Hand Made Films; Barry Hanson — *THORN
EMI/HBO Video*

Long John Silver   1955
Adventure
79852   106 mins   C   B, V   R, P
*Robert Newton, Connie Gilchrist, Kit Taylor, Rod
Taylor*
Long John Silver plans a return trip to Treasure
Island with fresh clues to find the treasure.
TI Pictures — *Video Gems*

Long John Silver's   1953
Return to Treasure Island
Adventure
70197   106 mins   C   B, V   P
*Robert Newton, Connie Gilcrest, Kit Taylor, Rod
Taylor*
Having returned to England from his sojourn to
Treasure Island, famed pirate Long John Silver
plans another search for the elusive treasure.
TI Pictures — *Hal Roach Studios; Discount
Video Tapes*

Long Riders, The   1980
Western
78631   100 mins   C   B, V   P
*Stacy and James Keach, Randy and Dennis
Quaid, David, Keith, and Robert Carradine,
directed by Walter Hill*
The Jesse James and Cole Younger gangs raid
banks, trains, and stagecoaches in post Civil
War Missouri.
MPAA:R
United Artists — *MGM/UA Home Video*

Long Shot   1981
Drama
73026   100 mins   C   B, V   P
Two foosball enthusiasts work their way through
local tournaments to make enough money to
make it to the World Championships in Tahoe.
Unknown — *THORN EMI/HBO Video*

Long Voyage Home, The   1940
Adventure
80675   105 mins   B/W   B, V   P
*John Wayne, Thomas Mitchell, Ian Hunter,
directed by John Ford*
An adaptation of the Eugene O'Neill play about
the lives of the crew members of a World War II
cargo ship.
United Artists; John Ford — *Lightning Video*

Long Way Home, A   1981
Drama
78363   100 mins   C   B, V   P
*Timothy Hutton, Brenda Vaccaro, Rosanna
Arquette*
A young man attempts to reunite his brother and
sister after they have been separated by the
deaths of their parents.
Alan Landsburg Productions — *U.S.A. Home
Video*

Longest Day, The   1962
War-Drama
08443   179 mins   C   B, V   P
*Richard Burton, Peter Lawford, Rod Steiger,
John Wayne, Edmond O'Brien*
The complete story of the D-Day landings at
Normandy, as seen through the eyes of
American, French, British and German
participants.
EL, SP

20th Century Fox; Darryl F.
Zanuck — *CBS/Fox Video*

Longest Yard, The 1974
Comedy
38589   121 mins   C   B, V, LV   P
Burt Reynolds, Eddie Albert, directed by Robert Aldrich
A one-time pro football quarterback, now a prisoner, organizes his fellow convicts into a football team to play against the prison guards for a special game. Filmed on location at Georgia State Prison.
MPAA:R
Paramount — *Paramount Home Video; RCA VideoDiscs*

Look Back in Anger 1959
Drama
51965   99 mins   B/W   B, V   R, P
Claire Bloom, Richard Burton, Mary Ure
Almost too late, a young man realizes how much he needs and wants his wife.
Gordon L.T. Scott — *Embassy Home Entertainment*

Look Back in Anger 1980
Drama
80001   100 mins   C   B, V   P
Malcolm McDowell, Lisa Barnes, Fran Brill, Raymond Hardie
A working-class man angered by society's hypocrisy lashes out at his upper-class wife, his mistress and the world.
Chuck Braverman/Don Boyd Prod. — *Warner Home Video*

Look to the Rainbow 1985
Music-Performance
71321   90 mins   C   B, V   P
Patti LaBelle, directed by Michael Bernhaut
Recorded at Philadelphia's Shubert Theatre, Patti LaBelle lets loose with such hits as: "New Attitude," "Somewhere Over The Rainbow," "Lady Marmalade," "Stir It Up" and "Come What May" among others.
Glen Ellis Sr — *U.S.A. Home Video*

Looker 1981
Science fiction
47368   93 mins   C   B, V   P
Albert Finney, James Coburn, Susan Dey, Leigh Taylor-Young
Stunning models are made even more beautiful by a plastic surgeon, but one by one they begin to die.
MPAA:PG
The Ladd Company; Howard Jeffrey — *Warner Home Video*

Lookin' to Get Out 1982
Adventure/Comedy
65503   70 mins   C   B, V, CED   P
Ann-Margret, Jon Voight, Burt Young
An ex-call girl living with her infant son in the owner's penthouse of a swank Las Vegas hotel spots the father of her child, and revenge is the only thing on her mind.
MPAA:R
Lorimar — *CBS/Fox Video*

Looking for Mr. Goodbar 1977
Drama
38597   136 mins   C   B, V, LV   P
Diane Keaton, Tuesday Weld, Richard Gere, directed by Richard Brooks
Diane Keaton portrays a young teacher who seeks escape from her claustrophobic existence by frequenting singles bars. Based on Judith Rossner's novel.
MPAA:R
Paramount — *Paramount Home Video; RCA VideoDiscs*

Looking Glass War, The 1969
Horror
65468   108 mins   C   B, V   P
Christopher Jones, Ralph Richardson, Pia Degermark, Anthony Hopkins
A Polish defector is sent behind the Iron Curtain on a final mission. Adapted from John Le Carre's best-selling spy novel. In Beta Hi-Fi.
MPAA:PG
John Box — *RCA/Columbia Pictures Home Video*

Looney Looney Looney Bugs Bunny Movie, The 1981
Cartoons
47394   80 mins   C   B, V   P
A feature-length compilation of classic Warner Brothers cartoons tied together with new animation. Cartoon stars featured include Bugs Bunny, Elmer Fudd, Porky Pig, Yosemite Sam, Duffy Duck and Foghorn Leghorn.
Warner Bros — *Warner Home Video; RCA VideoDiscs*

Looney Tunes and Merrie Melodies I 1933
Comedy/Cartoons
38967   56 mins   B/W   B, V, FO   P
Animated
A collection of eight Warner Brothers Vitaphone cartoons dating from 1931-33, most with jazzy musical accompaniments. Titles include "It's Got Me Again," "You Don't Know What You're Doin'," "Moonlight for Two," "Battling Bosko," "Red-Headed Baby," and "Freddy the Freshman."
Warner Bros — *Video Yesteryear*

Looney Tunes and Merrie Melodies II 194?

Comedy/Cartoons

38969   51 mins   B/W   B, V, FO   P

Animated

A second collection of seven Warner-Vitaphone cartoons from 1931-33, 1937, and 1941-43. Porky Pig, Daffy Duck, and Bugs Bunny are featured in the later World War II-oriented titles, "Scrap Happy Daffy" and Porky Pig's Feat." Earlier titles include "One More Time," "Smile, Darnya, Smile," and "Yodeling Yokels."

Warner Bros — Video Yesteryear

Looney Tunes and Merrie Melodies #3 194?

Cartoons

59367   60 mins   C   B, V, FO   P

Cartoon classics from Warner Bros: "A Corny Concerto" (1943), with Porky and Bugs; "Foney Fables" (1942), a retelling of old fairy tales; "The Wacky Wabbit" (1942), featuring Bugs and Elmer Fudd; "Have You Got Any Castles" (1938); "Fifth Column Mouse" (1943); "To Duck or Not to Duck" (1943), with Elmer and Daffy; "The Early Worm Gets the Bird" (1940); and "Daffy the Commando (1943), with Daffy Duck.

Warner Bros — Video Yesteryear

Looney Tunes Video Show #1, The 195?

Cartoons

62879   49 mins   C   B, V   P

Animated

Seven Warner Brothers cartoon classics of the 1940's and 50's: Bugs Bunny and the Tasmanian Devil in "Devil May Hare," Sylvester in "Birds of a Father," "Daffy Duck and Porky Pig in "The Ducksters," the Road Runner and Wile E. Coyote in "Zipping Along," Sylvester and Tweety in "Room and Bird," Elmer Fudd in "Ant Pasted" and Speedy Gonzales in "Mexican Schmoes."

Warner Bros — Warner Home Video

Looney Tunes Video Show #2, The 195?

Cartoons

62880   48 mins   C   B, V   P

Animated

More Warner Brothers cartoon favorites: Daffy Duck in "Quackodile Tears," Porky Pig in "An Egg Scramble," Sylvester and Speedy Gonzales in "Cats and Bruises," Foghorn Leghorn in "All Fowled Up," Bugs Bunny and Yosemite Sam in "14 Carrot Rabbit," Professor Calvin Q. Calculus in "The Hole Idea" and Pepe Le Pew in "Two Scents Worth."

Warner Bros — Warner Home Video

Looney Tunes Video Show #3, The 195?

Cartoons

62881   38 mins   C   B, V   P

Animated

Seven more Warner Brothers cartoon shorts: Daffy Duck and Speedy Gonzales in "The Quacker Tracker," the Wolf and Sheepdog in "Double or Mutton," Claude Cat and Bulldog in "Feline Frameup," Bugs Bunny in "Eight Ball Bunny," Foghorn Leghorn in "A Featured Leghorn," Porky Pig and Sylvester in "Scaredy Cat" and Pepe Le Pew in "Louvre, Come Back to Me."

Warner Bros — Warner Home Video

Looney Tunes Video Show #4, The 195?

Cartoons

62882   47 mins   C   B, V   P

Animated

Another Warner Brothers cartoon assortment: Sylvester and Tweety in "Ain't She Tweet," Daffy Duck and Speedy Gonzales in "Astroduck," Bugs Bunny in "Backwoods Bunny," Pepe Le Pew in "Heaven Scent," Elmer Fudd in "Pests for Guests," Sylvester in "Lighthouse Mouse" and the Wolf and Sheepdog in "Don't Give Up the Sheep."

Warner Bros — Warner Home Video

Looney Tunes Video Show #5, The 195?

Cartoons

62883   51 mins   C   B, V   P

Animated

An additional package of Warner Brothers cartoons: Sylvester and Tweety in "Tugboat Granny," Daffy Duck in "Stork Naked," the Road Runner and Wile E. Coyote in "Fastest with the Mostest," Bugs Bunny in "Forward March Hare," Foghorn Leghorn in "Feather Dusted," Daffy Duck and Porky Pig in "China Jones" and Pepe Le Pew in "Odor of the Day."

Warner Bros — Warner Home Video

Looney Tunes Video Show #6, The 195?

Cartoons

62884   49 mins   C   B, V   P

Animated

More classic Warner Brothers cartoons: Foghorn Leghorn in "Feather Bluster," the Road Runner and Wile E. Coyote in "Lickety Splat," Bugs Bunny in "Bowery Bugs," Daffy Duck and Speedy Gonzales in "Daffy Rents," Porky Pig in "Dough for the Dodo," Sylvester and Elmer Fudd in "Heir Conditioned" and Pepe Le Pew in "Scent of the Matterhorn."

Warner Bros — Warner Home Video

Looney Tunes Video Show #7, The   195?
Cartoons
62885   48 mins   C   B, V   P
Animated
Seven additional Warner Brothers cartoon classics: Bugs Bunny in "A-Lad-In His Lamp," the Road Runner and Wile E. Coyote in "Beep Beep," Yosemite Sam in "Honey's Money," Foghorn Leghorn in "Weasel Stop," Daffy Duck and Elmer Fudd in "Don't Ax Me," Sylvester and Tweety in "Muzzle Tough" and Foghorn Leghorn in "The Egg-Cited Rooster."
Warner Bros — *Warner Home Video*

Loophole   1983
Adventure
65353   105 mins   C   B, V   P
Albert Finney, Martin Sheen, Susannah York
An out-of-work architect, hard pressed for money, joins forces with an elite team of expert criminals, in a scheme to make off with millions from the most established holding bank's vault.
David Korda; Julian Holloway — *Media Home Entertainment*

Loose Screws   1985
Comedy
86845   75 mins   C   B, V   P
Bryan Genesse, Karen Wood, Alan Deveau, Jason Warren
Four perverted teenagers are sent to a restrictive academy where they continue their lewd ways.
MPAA:R
Smith & Concorde — *Lightning Video*

Loose Shoes   1980
Comedy
82239   84 mins   C   B, V   P
Bill Murray, Howard Hesseman, Jaye P. Morgan, Buddy Hackett, Misty Rowe, Susan Tyrell
This film is a collection of vignettes that satirize movie trailers, teasers and special announcements. In VHS and Beta Hi-Fi.
MPAA:R
Atlantic Releasing Corp. — *Key Video*

Lord Jim   1965
Drama
13261   154 mins   C   B, V   P
Peter O'Toole, James Mason, Curt Jurgens, Eli Wallach, Jack Hawkins, directed by Richard Brooks
A ship officer commits an act of cowardice that results in his dismissal and disgrace.
Columbia; Richard Brooks — *RCA/Columbia Pictures Home Video*

Lord of the Flies   1963
Drama
80121   91 mins   B/W   B, V   P
James Aubrey, Tom Chapin, Hugh Edwards, directed by Peter Brook
When a group of English schoolboys are stranded on a desert island they turn into savages.
Lewis Allen — *King of Video*

Lord of the Rings   1978
Fantasy
58883   133 mins   C   B, V   P
Animated
Ralph Bakshi's animated interpretation of Tolkien's classic tale of the hobbits, wizards, elves, and dwarfs who inhabit Middle Earth.
MPAA:PG
United Artists — *THORN EMI/HBO Video; RCA VideoDiscs*

Lords of Discipline, The   1983
Drama
66031   103 mins   C   B, V, LV   P
David Keith, Robert Prosky, Barbara Babcock, Judge Reinhold
A military academy cadet is given the unenviable task of protecting a black freshman from racist factions at a southern school circa 1964.
MPAA:R
Paramount — *Paramount Home Video*

Lords of Flatbush, The   1974
Drama
85280   88 mins   C   B, V   P
Sylvester Stallone, Perry King, Henry Winkler, Susan Blakely
Four street toughs battle against their own maturation and responsibilities in 1950's Brooklyn.
Stephen F. Verona — *RCA/Columbia Pictures Home Video*

Lords of the New Church—Live from London, The   1985
Music-Performance
80781   60 mins   C   B, V   P
The Lords of the New Church perform such new wave favorites as "Open Your Eyes," "Dance With Me" and "Live For Today" in this concert taped at London's Marquee Club. Available in VHS and Beta Hi-Fi.
I.R.S. Video — *RCA/Columbia Pictures Home Video*

Loretta   1980
Music-Performance
45105   61 mins   C   B, V, LV   P
Loretta Lynn
The queen of country music, Loretta Lynn, performs some of her best material, including "Coal Miner's Daughter," "Hey Loretta," "You're Looking at the Country," "Out of My Head and Back in Bed," "Wine, Women, and

Song," "Naked in the Rain," and "Gospel
Medley."
David Skepner — *MCA Home Video*

Los Angeles Dodgers: 1984
Team Highlights
Baseball
81142   30 mins   C   B, V   P
*Tommy Lasorda, Fernando Velenzuela, Steve
Garvey, Rick Monday, Greg Brock, Mike
Marshall 6   pgms*
The best and brightest moments from the L.A.
Dodgers past seasons are featured in this
presentation.
*1.1976: Going On Twenty 2.1980: High Fivin'
With The Dodgers 3.1981: The Tenth Player
4.1982: A Year at The Top 5.1983: Blending of
the Blue 6.1984: Eye on the Future*
Major League Baseball — *Major League
Baseball Productions*

Los Angeles Raiders   1985
1985 Team Highlights
Football
86799   23 mins   C   B, V   P
The best of the Raiders' '85 season.
NFL Films — *NFL Films Video*

Los Angeles Rams 1984   1985
Team Highlights
Football
70547   70 mins   C   B, V, FO   P
Eric Dickerson
The Rams winning the Wild Card Playoff berth
became "A Family Tradition", and Eric
Dickerson's record-setting 2,105 yards in
rushing a family jewel. This tape features 47-
minutes of highlights from the entire NFL's '84
season as well.
NFL Films — *NFL Films Video*

Losers, The   1963
Drama
82187   52 mins   B/W   B, V   P
*Lee Marvin, Keenan Wynn, Rosemary Clooney,
Charles Boyer, directed by Sam Peckinpah*
Two drifters stay in a small town long enough to
play cupid to a girl who thinks ugly. An episode
from "The Dick Powell Theatre."
Four Star Television — *RKO HomeVideo*

Losin' It   1982
Comedy
66047   104 mins   C   B, V, CED   P
Tom Cruise, John Stockwell, Shelley Long
A shy young man travels to a Mexican border
town to lose his virginity.
MPAA:R
Joel Michaels; Garth Drabinsky — *Embassy
Home Entertainment*

Losin' It—Sex and the   1985
American Teenager
Documentary/Sexuality
71132   ' 76 mins   C   B, V   P
*Directed by Robert Richardson, Terry Dunn
Meurer*
Young people discuss their varied feelings
about their wakening sexuality in this informative
documentary.
D Bell Associates — *Vestron Video*

Lost   1983
Adventure
80894   92 mins   C   B, V   P
*Sandra Dee, Don Stewart, Ken Curtis, Jack
Elam, Sheila Newhouse*
A young girl runs away into the wilderness
because of the resentment she feels towards
her new stepfather.
American National Enterprises — *Prism*

Lost and Found   1979
Comedy
63434   104 mins   C   B, V   P
*George Segal, Glenda Jackson, Maureen
Stapleton, Hollis McLaren, John Cunningham,
Paul Sorvino*
An American professor of English and an
English film production secretary fall in love on a
skiing vacation.
MPAA:PG
Columbia; Melvin Frank — *RCA/Columbia
Pictures Home Video*

Lost City of the Jungle   1945
Serials/Adventure
81366   169 mins   B/W   B, V   P
Russell Hayden, Lionel Atwill
Here are the complete thirteen chapters of this
serial that takes you on a series of wild
adventures through the deep jungles of Africa.
Universal — *Discount Video Tapes; Captain
Bijou*

Lost Empire, The   1983
Science fiction/Adventure
80670   86 mins   C   B, V   P
*Melanie Vincz, Raven De La Croix, Angela
Aames, Paul Coufos*
Three bountiful and powerful women team up to
battle the evil Dr. Syn Do in order to save their
empire.
MPAA:R
Jim Wynorski — *Lightning Video*

Lost Honor of Katharina   1975
Blum, The
Drama
69550   97 mins   C   B, V   P
Angela Winkler, Mario Adorf, Dieter Lasar
Adapted from Heinrich Boll's Nobel Prize-
winning novel, this film is about a woman who
fights political and social injustice.

MPAA:R
New World Pictures — *Embassy Home
Entertainment*

Lost in America   1985
Comedy
Closed Captioned
82224   91 mins   C   B, V   P
*Albert Brooks, Julie Hagerty, Michael Greene,
Tom Tarpey, directed by Albert Brooks*
A yuppie couple decide to quit their jobs and buy
a trailer to travel across the United States.
Available in VHS and Beta Hi-Fi Mono.
MPAA:R
The Geffen Company — *Warner Home Video*

Lost in Space   1965
Science fiction
14446   52 mins   B/W   B, V   P
*Guy Williams, June Lockhart, Jonathan Harris,
Billy Mumy*
The complete pilot episode of the series, in
which the Robinson family becomes stranded
somewhere in the universe.
Irwin Allen Prod — *Video Dimensions; Video
Yesteryear*

Lost Jungle, The   1934
Mystery/Serials
14262 156 mins B/W   B, V   P
Clyde Beatty, Cecelia Parker
Exciting animal treasure hunt; danger and
mystery. Serial in 12 chapters, 13 minutes each.
Mascot — *Video Connection; Video
Dimensions; Video Yesteryear; Discount Video
Tapes*

Lost Moment, The   1947
Drama
77480   89 mins   B/W   B, V   P
Robert Cummings, Susan Hayward
A publisher travels to Italy to search for a
valuable collection of love letters.
Walter Wanger — *Republic Pictures Home
Video*

Lost Patrol, The   1934
Adventure
10075   66 mins   B/W   B, V   P, T
*Victor McLaglen, Boris Karloff, Wallace Ford,
Reginald Denny, Alan Hale*
British soldiers lost in desert are shot down one
by one by Arab marauders.
RKO — *Blackhawk Films; Nostalgia Merchant*

Lost Squadron   1932
Adventure
57144   79 mins   B/W   B, V   P
Richard Dix, Erich von Stroheim
A look at the dangers stuntmen go through in
movie-making.

RKO — *King of Video*

Lost World, The   1925
Drama
08855   62 mins   B/W   B, V, 3/4U   P
*Wallace Beery, Louis Stone, Bessie Love, Lloyd
Hughes*
A zoology professor leads a group on a South
American expedition in search of the "lost
world."
First National — *Video Yesteryear; Discount
Video Tapes*

Lots of Luck   1985
Comedy
84430   88 mins   C   B, V   P
*Martin Mull, Annette Funicello, Fred Willard,
Polly Holliday, directed by Peter Baldwin*
A knee-slapping comedy about a family that
wins the million-dollar lottery and sees that
money doesn't solve all problems.
Walt Disney Prods — *Walt Disney Home Video*

Lottery Bride, The   1930
Drama
54111   85 mins   B/W   B, V   P, T
*Jeanette MacDonald, Joe E. Brown, Zasu Pitts,
John Garrick, Carroll Nye*
A young woman enters a dance marathon
against the wishes of her boyfriend, to get funds
to aid her criminal brother. When the police
arrive at the contest in search for the brother,
the woman aids in his escape. For this she is put
in prison. It is not until a series of
misunderstandings are cleared up that her and
her boyfriend are reunited.
United Artists — *Blackhawk Films*

Lou Bunin's Alice in   1951
Wonderland
Fantasy/Adventure
70814   80 mins   C   B, V   P
*Carol Marsh, Stephen Murray, Pamela Brown,
Felix Aylmer, Ernest Milton, David Read,
directed by Dallas Bower*
This telling of Carroll's classic tale combines
puppetry with live actors.
Leo Hurwitz — *Monterey Home Video*

Lou Ferrigno's Body   1985
Perfection
Physical fitness
Closed Captioned
71295   75 mins   C   B, V   P
*Lou Ferrigno, Carla Ferrigno, Kurt Rambis,
Michael Cooper, directed by Paul Miller*
Along with some friends from the L.A. Lakers
and his wife, the "Incredible Hulk" goes through
the paces to perfection.
Don Spielvogel — *U.S.A. Home Video*

Louie Bluie 1985
Documentary/Music-Performance
84240   60 mins   C   B, V   P
Howard Armstrong, Ted Bogan
A documentary about the life and times of
Armstrong, the last original black string
musician, with views on his other talents, such
as painting, as well.
Terry Zwigoff — *Pacific Arts Video*

Louis Armstrong—Chicago Style 1975
Biographical/Drama
79250   74 mins   C   B, V   P
*Ben Vereen, Red Buttons, Janet Mac Lachlan,
Margaret Avery*
How Louis Armstrong managed to fight the mob
in the early 1930's and become a great jazz
trompeter-vocalist.
Stonehenge/Charles Fries
Productions — *Worldvision Home Video*

Louis Bellson and His Big Band 1983
Music-Performance
84644   55 mins   C   B, V   P
A live performance by the famed swing
drummer and his band. Soloists and sidemen
include Randy and Michael Brecker, Lew Soloff,
Herb Celler and Howard Johnson. Recorded in
Hi-Fi stereo.
Stanley Dorfman — *V.I.E.W. Video*

Louis Bellson: The Musical Drummer 1984
Music
87929   60 mins   C   B, V   P
Bellson performs in seven musical idioms, and
demonstrates the differences for drummers
between swing, samba, shuffle and rock.
AM Available
DCI Music Video — *DCI Music Video*

Louisiana Story 1948
Documentary/Oil industry
85187   79 mins   B/W   B, V   P
*Directed by Robert Flaherty, music by Virgil
Thompson*
The final effort by the master filmmaker,
depicting the effects of oil industrialization on
the southern Bayou country. One of Flaherty's
greatest, widely considered a premiere
achievement.
Robert Flaherty — *Video Yesteryear*

Louvre, The 1978
Documentary/Museums
80162   53 mins   C   B, V   P
Charles Boyer takes you on a trip through one of
the world's great art museums.

Lucy Jarvis — *Warner Home Video; Monterey Home Video*

Louvre, Le 1986
Museums
87200   55 mins   C   B, V   P
A tour through France's most famous museum,
with views of the many famous works of art on
display, as well as a short history of the museum
itself.
Kronos-Frances — *Gessler Educational
Software*

Love Affair: The Eleanor and Lou Gehrig Story, A 1977
Biographical/Drama
80639   96 mins   C   B, V   P
*Blythe Danner, Edward Herrmann, Patricia Neal,
Ramon Bieri, Lainie Kazan, directed by Fiedler
Cook*
The true story of the love affair between
baseball great Lou Gehrig and his wife Eleanor
from his glory days as a New York Yankee, to
his battle with an incurable disease.
Charles Fries Prods. — *Worldvision Home
Video*

Love and Anarchy 1973
Drama
63446   108 mins   C   B, V   P
*Giancarlo Giannini, Mariangela Melato, directed
by Lina Wertmuller*
An oppressed peasant vows to assassinate
Mussolini after a close friend is murdered. Italian
dialogue, English subtitles.
IT
Euro International Films
Technicolor — *RCA/Columbia Pictures Home
Video*

Love and Bullets 1979
Adventure
Closed Captioned
81065   95 mins   C   B, V   P
*Charles Bronson, Jill Ireland, Rod Steiger,
Strother Martin, Bradford Dillman*
An Arizona homicide detective is sent on a
special assignment to Switzerland to bring a
mobster's girlfriend back to the United States to
testify against him in court. Available in VHS and
Beta Hi-Fi.
MPAA:PG
Pancho Kohner — *Key Video*

Love and Death 1975
Comedy
59336   89 mins   C   B, V   P
*Woody Allen, Diane Keaton, Georges Adel,
Despo, Frank Adu, directed by Woody Allen*
In 1812 Russia, a man condemned reviews the
follies of his life. Woody Allen's satire on "War
and Peace."
MPAA:PG

United Artists; Jack Rollins; Charles H
Joffe — *CBS/Fox Video; RCA VideoDiscs*

Love and Larceny 1980
Drama
71045   90 mins   C   B, V   P
Maureen Arthur, Michael McGuire
This film tells Betsy Bigley's true story. She
assumed the alias "Mrs. Chadwick" and conned
her way to easy street in the early years of this
century.
Humble Prods — *Karl/Lorimar Home Video*

Love at First Bite 1979
Comedy
53517   96 mins   C   B, V   P
*George Hamilton, Susan Saint James, Richard
Benjamin, Dick Shawn, Arte Johnson, Sherman
Hemsley, Isabel Sanford*
Dracula is forced to leave his Transylvanian
home as the Rumanian government has
designated his castle a training center for young
gymnasts. Once in New York, the Count takes in
the night life and falls in love with a woman
whose boyfriend embarks on a campaign to
warn the city of Dracula's presence.
MPAA:PG
American International — *Warner Home Video;
RCA VideoDiscs; Vestron Video (disc only)*

Love at the Top 1986
Romance/Drama
71238   90 mins   C   V   P
Introduced by Louis Jourdan
A ladies foundation designer falls in love with
her boss's son-in-law, jeopardizing her career.
Commworld; Romance Theater — *Prism*

Love Bug, The 1968
Comedy
29736   110 mins   C   B, V, LV   P
*Dean Jones, Michele Lee, Hope Lange, Robert
Reed, Bert Convy*
A race car driver is followed home by a white
Volkswagen which has a mind of its own.
MPAA:G
Walt Disney — *Walt Disney Home Video; RCA
VideoDiscs*

Love Butcher, The 1982
Horror
75586   84 mins   C   B, V   P
Erik Stern, Kay Neer, Robin Sherwood
A crippled old gardener kills his female
employers with his garden tools and cleans up
neatly afterward.
MPAA:R
Desert Production — *Monterey Home Video*

Love by Appointment 1976
Comedy
88151   96 mins   C   B, V   P

*Ernest Borgnine, Robert Alda, Francoise
Fabian, Corinne Clery*
An unlikely romantic comedy with a very unlikely
cast about two businessmen meeting up with
European prostitution. Made for TV.
ABC; Alfred Leone — *Charter Entertainment*

Love Child 1982
Drama
60563   97 mins   C   B, V   P
*Amy Madigan, Beau Bridges, MacKenzie
Phillips, Albert Salmi, directed by Larry Peerce*
The story of a young woman in prison who
becomes pregnant and fights to have and keep
her baby.
MPAA:R
Warner Bros — *Warner Home Video*

Love From a Stranger 1947
Drama
81224   81 mins   B/W   B, V, LV   P
*Sylvia Sidney, John Hodiak, John Howard, Ann
Richards*
A young newlywed bride fears that the
honeymoon is over when she suspects that her
husband is a notorious killer and that she will be
his next victim.
Eagle Lion — *New World Video*

Love Goddesses, The 1974
Documentary/Women
65425   87 mins   B/W   B, V   P
*Marlene Dietrich, Greta Garbo, Jean Harlow,
Gloria Swanson, Mae West, Betty Grable, Rita
Hayworth, Elizabeth Taylor, Marilyn Monroe*
A sixty-year treatment of woman on the screen
reflecting with extraordinary accuracy the
customs, manners and mores of the times.
Saul J Turell — *Embassy Home Entertainment*

Love Happy 1950
Comedy
47992   85 mins   B/W   B, V   P
*The Marx Brothers, Vera-Ellen, Ilona Massey,
Marion Hutton, Raymond Burr, Marilyn Monroe*
A group of impoverished actors accidentally
gain possession of valuable diamonds.
United Artists — *Republic Pictures Home
Video*

Love in Germany, A 1984
Drama
81213   110 mins   C   B, V   P
*Hanna Schygulla, Piotr Lysak, Elisabeth
Trissenaar, directed by Andrzej Wajda*
A tragic love affair develops between a German
shopkeeper's wife and a Polish prisoner-of-war
in a small German village during World War II.
MPAA:R   GE
Triumph Films — *RCA/Columbia Pictures
Home Video*

Love in the Afternoon   1957
Comedy
Closed Captioned
80139   126 mins   B/W   B, V   P
Gary Cooper, Audrey Hepburn, John McGiver,
Maurice Chevalier, directed by Billy Wilder
A Parisian private eye's daughter decides to
investigate a philandering American millionaire
and winds up falling in love with him.
Billy Wilder — *CBS/Fox Video*

Love in the City   1953
Drama/Romance
63857   90 mins   B/W   B, V   P
Directed by Federico Fellini, Michelangelo
Antonioni, Dino Risi et. al.
This film incorporates five stories of life, love
and tears in Rome. Italian dialogue with English
subtitles and narration.
EL, IT
Italian — *Hollywood Home Theater; Festival*
Films

Love in the Present   1985
Tense
Romance
87691   90 mins   C   V   P
A woman's romantic novel on video, dealing
with an affair that reawakens the torpid, tragic
life of a beautiful ex-model.
Prism Video — *Prism*

Love Is a Many-   1955
Splendored Thing
Drama
08465   102 mins   C   CED   P
William Holden, Jennifer Jones, Torin Thatcher,
Isobel Elsom
Hong Kong in 1949. True story of a romance
between lovely Eurasian doctor and an
American war correspondent.
Academy Awards '55: Best Song, "Love Is a
Many-Splendored Thing" (Sammy Fain, Paul
Francis Webster).
20th Century Fox; Buddy Adler — *CBS/Fox*
Video

Love Laughs at Andy   1946
Hardy
Comedy
49134   93 mins   B/W   B, V   P
Sara Haden, Lina Romay, Bonita Granville, Fay
Holden, Lewis Stone, Mickey Rooney
Andy Hardy, college boy, is in love and in
trouble. Financial and romantic problems come
to a head when Andy is paired with a six-foot tall
blind date.
MGM — *Hal Roach Studios; Hollywood Home*
Theater; Discount Video Tapes; VCII; Sound
Video Unlimited

Love Leads the Way   1984
Biographical/Drama
76818   99 mins   C   B, V   P
Timothy Bottoms, Eva Marie Saint, Arthur Hill,
Susan Dey, Ralph Bellamy, Ernest Borgnine,
Patricia Neal
This is the true story of how Morris Frank
established the Seeing Eye dog movement in
the 1930's.
Jimmy Hawkins; Walt Disney
Productions — *Walt Disney Home Video*

Love Letters   1983
Romance
79305   102 mins   C   B, V, CED   P
Jamie Lee Curtis, James Keach
A young disc jockey falls under the spell of a
box of love letters that her mother left behind.
MPAA:R
New Horizon Pictures — *Vestron Video*

Love Me Deadly   1976
Horror
81617   95 mins   C   B, V   P
Mary Wilcox, Lyle Waggoner, Christopher
Stone, Timothy Scott
A young woman tries to get her husband
interested in her new hobby—necrophilia.
MPAA:R
Unknown — *Video Gems*

Love Me Tender   1956
Musical-Drama
64932   89 mins   B/W   CED   P
Elvis Presley, Richard Egan, Debra Paget,
Neville Brand, Mildred Dunnock, James Drury,
Barry Coe
A Civil War-torn family is divided by in-fighting
between two brothers who both seek the
affections of the same women. Presley's first
film.
20th Century Fox — *CBS/Fox Video*

Love on the Dole   1941
Drama
78085   89 mins   B/W   B, V, FO   P
Deborah Kerr, Clifford Evans, George Carney
In a gloomy industrial section of England during
the early 30's a family struggles to survive and
maintain dignity.
British National — *Movie Buff Video; Video*
Yesteryear

Love on the Run   1978
Drama
58240   90 mins   C   B, V   P
Jean-Pierre Leaud, Marie-France Pisier, Claude
Jade, directed by Francois Truffaut
The further amorous adventures of Antoine
Doinel, hero of "The 400 Blows," "Stolen
Kisses," and ":Bed and Board." This time out,
the women from Doinel's past resurface to
challenge his emotions.

MPAA:PG
Elsenoor Belleggin — *Warner Home Video*

Love Skills   1984
Sexuality
80073   56 mins   C   B, V   P
Five couples explore various sexual techniques
from foreplay to sexual positions. Available in
Beta Hi-Fi Stereo and VHS Dolby B Stereo.
MCA Home Video — *MCA Home Video*

Love Story   1970
Drama
38598   100 mins   C   B, V, LV   P
*Ryan O'Neal, Ali McGraw, Ray Milland, directed
by Arthur Hiller*
Ryan O'Neal and Ali McGraw achieved stardom
in this popular adaption of Erich Segal's novel,
with portrayals of a young couple who cross
social barriers to marry.
Academy Awards '70: Best Original Score
(Francis Lai). MPAA:PG
Paramount — *Paramount Home Video; RCA
VideoDiscs*

Love Strange Love   1982
Drama
80930   97 mins   C   B, V   P
Vera Fischer, Mauro Mendonca
A young boy develops a bizarre relationship with
his mother who works in a luxurious bordello.
Also available in an unedited 120-minute
version.
Sharp Features — *Vestron Video*

Love Streams   1984
Drama
82399   122 mins   C   B, V   P
*Gena Rowlands, John Cassavetes, Diahnne
Abbot, directed by John Cassavetes*
A quirky romance about two sophisticates who
struggle to stay in love despite their personal
problems.
MPAA:PG-13
Cannon Films — *MGM/UA Home Video*

Love Tapes   1981
Human relations
55322   28 mins   B/W   B, V   P
Love tapes are defined as videotapes made by
people from all walks of life who volunteered to
record their feelings about love. These tapes
have had an extraordinary response when
shown in schools, hospitals, libraries, and
museums. The net result is an increased self-
awareness and empathy with our common
humanity.
Wendy Clarke — *Mystic Fire Video; Filmakers
Library; Electronic Arts Intermix*

Love Thrill Murders, The   197?
Crime-Drama
86348   89 mins   C   B, V   P
Troy Donahue
A film about a Mansonesque lunatic who is
worshipped and obeyed by a mob of runaways
and dropouts.
MPAA:R
Troma Inc. — *Vestron Video*

Love Your Body   1983
Physical fitness
68524   60 mins   C   B, V   P
Jayne Kennedy
Jayne Kennedy presents her own exercise
program which will make you love your body.
Jeff Tuckman Prods; Chicago Teleprods; Jayne
Kennedy Prod — *RCA/Columbia Pictures
Home Video*

Loveless, The   1983
Drama
65693   85 mins   C   B, V   P
Robert Gordon, Willem Dafoe, J. Don Ferguson
A menacing glance into the exploits of an
outcast motorcycle gang. In the 50's, a group of
bikers on their way to the Florida Cycle Races
stop for lunch in a small-town diner. While
repairs are being made on their motorcycles,
they decide to take full advantage of their
situation.
MPAA:R
G Nunes; A K Ho — *Media Home
Entertainment*

Lovelines   1984
Comedy
Closed Captioned
80833   93 mins   C   B, V   P
*Greg Bradford, Michael Winslow, Mary Beth
Evans, Tammy Taylor, Stacey Toten*
Two rock singers from rival high schools meet
and fall in love during a panty raid. Available in
VHS and Beta Hi Fi Stereo.
MPAA:R
Tri Star Pictures — *Key Video*

Lovely . . . But Deadly   1982
Drama
77182   95 mins   C   B, V   P
A young girl wages a war against the drug
dealers in her school after her brother dies of an
overdose.
MPAA:R
Elm Tree Productions — *Vestron Video*

Lover Come Back   1961
Comedy
85255   107 mins   C   B, V   P
*Rock Hudson, Doris Day, Tony Randall, Edie
Adams, Joe FLynn, Ann B. Davis, Jack
Albertson, Jack Kruschen, Howard St. John,
directed by Delbert Mann*

An advertising executive falls in love with his competitor but that doesn't stop him from stealing her clients.
Universal — *Kartes Video Communications*

Loverboy
1983
Music-Performance
82465   60 mins   C   B, V   P
Loverboy
Recorded live in Vancouver, this concert includes such hits as "Turn Me Loose," "The Kid Is Hot Tonite" and "Working For The Weekend."
Vestron Video — *Vestron Video*

Loverboy-Any Way You Look At It
1986
Music video
84758   40 mins   C   B, V   P
The rich and popular Canadian band's best video hits are seen in this compilation.
CBS/Fox — *CBS/Fox Video*

Lovers and Liars
1981
Comedy/Romance
69548   93 mins   C   B, V, CED   P
Goldie Hawn, Giancarlo Giannini
A romantic adventure in Rome turns into a series of comic disasters.
MPAA:R
Alberto Grimaldi — *Embassy Home Entertainment*

Lovers of Teruel, The
197?
Dance
87355   90 mins   C   B, V   P
Ludmila Tcherina, directed by Raymond Rouleau
With choreography by Claude Renior and music by Mikis Theodorakis, this piece is a balletic tragedy about fated lovers.
Foreign — *Kultur*

Loves And Times Of Scaramouche, The
1976
Comedy
76907   92 mins   C   B, V   P
Michael Sarrazin, Ursula Andress, Aldo Maccione
An eighteenth century rogue becomes involved in a plot to assassinate Napoleon and winds up seducing Josephine in the process.
Federico Aicardi — *Embassy Home Entertainment*

Loves of a Blonde, The
1966
Comedy-Drama
73866   88 mins   B/W   B, V   P
Directed by Milos Forman
A Czechoslovakian girl falls in love with a pianist when the reservist army comes to town. In

Czechoslovakian with English subtitles and in Beta Hi-Fi.
Film Studio Barrandov — *RCA/Columbia Pictures Home Video*

Love's Savage Fury
1979
Drama
79197   100 mins   C   B, V   P
Jennifer O'Neill, Perry King, Robert Reed, Raymond Burr, Connie Stevens, Ed Lauter
Two escapees from a Union prison camp seek out a hidden treasure that could determine the outcome of the Civil War.
Aaron Spelling Productions — *Prism*

Lovesick
1983
Comedy
66122   94 mins   C   B, V   P
Dudley Moore, Elizabeth McGovern, Alec Guinness, John Huston, directed by Marshall Brickman
A New York psychiatrist falls in love with one of his patients.
MPAA:PG
Ladd Company — *Warner Home Video*

Loving Couples
1980
Comedy
57229   120 mins   C   B, V, CED   P
Shirley MacLaine, James Coburn, Susan Sarandon, Stephen Collins, Sally Kellerman, directed by Jack Smight
Two happily married couples meet each other after an automobile accident and two new couples emerge, only to collide hilariously at a weekend resort.
MPAA:PG
Time-Life Films — *Vestron Video; Time Life Video*

Loving You
1957
Musical
47373   92 mins   C   B, V   P
Elvis Presley, Wendell Corey, Lizabeth Scott, Dolores Hart
A small town boy with a musical style all his own becomes a big success. Features many early Elvis hits, including "Teddy Bear."
Hal B Wallis — *Warner Home Video*

Lowell Thomas Remembers
1986
History-US/Documentary
52456   286 mins   B/W   B, V   P
Narrated by Lowell Thomas 4   pgms
Historian Lowell Thomas hosts this series of documentaries about America in the 20th century. Each program covers the events of one decade utilizing two 143-minute videotapes, which are available individually. Originally telecast as a PBS series.

1.*The Roaring Twenties* 2.*The New Deal—The Thirties* 3.*The War Years—The Forties* 4.*The Fabulous Fifties*
Fox Movietone — *Republic Pictures Home Video*

Lucia Di Lammermoor   1973
Opera
48555   30 mins   C   B, V   P
Joan Sutherland
One of the most popular Bel Canto operas is based on Sir Walter Scott's "The Bride of the Lammermoor." Joan Sutherland and her puppet friends help tell the story.
Nathan Kroll — *Video Arts International; Phoenix Films & Video*

Lucia di Lammermoor   1983
Opera
86881   128 mins   C   B, V   P
Joan Sutherland, Alfredo Kraus, Pablo Elvira, Paul Plishka
Conducted by Richard Bonynge, the Metropolitan Opera performs Donizetti's classic opera, with English subtitles.
AM Available IT
Metropolitan Opera; Paramount — *Paramount Home Video*

Lucifer Complex, The   1978
Science fiction
80657   91 mins   C   B, V   P
Robert Vaughn, Merrie Lynn Ross, Keenan Wynn, Aldo Ray
Nazi doctors are cloning exact duplicates of such world leaders as the Pope and the President of the United States on a remote South American island in the year 1996.
Four Star Entertainment — *United Home Video*

Lucky Jim   1958
Comedy
63327   91 mins   B/W   B, V   P
Ian Carmichael, Terry-Thomas, Hugh Griffith
A junior lecturer in history at a small university tries to get himself in good graces with the head of his department, but is doomed from the start by doing the wrong things at the worst possible times.
Roy Boulting — *THORN EMI/HBO Video*

Lucky Luciano   1974
Crime-Drama
86597   108 mins   C   B, V   P
Edmond O'Brien, Rod Steiger, Vincent Gardenia, Gian-Marie Volonte
A violent depiction of the final years of Lucky Luciano, gangster kingpin.
MPAA:R
Franco Cristaldi; Joseph E. Levine — *Charter Entertainment*

Lucky Luke: Daisy Town   1983
Cartoons
66319   75 mins   C   B, V   P
Animated
A full-length animated feature starrring Lucky Luke, the all-American cowboy who saves the little community of Daisy Town from the hot-headed Dalton Brothers gang. A wacky western spoof.
Dargaud Editeur — *Walt Disney Home Video*

Lucky Luke: The Ballad of the Daltons   1983
Cartoons
66320   82 mins   C   B, V   P
Animated
Easygoing cowboy hero Lucky Luke gets involved in a wild feud with the bumbling Dalton Brothers gang in this animated feature.
Dargaud Editeur — *Walt Disney Home Video*

Lucky Partners   1940
Comedy
79681   101 mins   B/W   B, V   P
Ronald Colman, Ginger Rogers, Jack Carson, directed by Lewis Milestone
When an artist and a woman share a winning lottery ticket, comic complications arise.
RKO — *RKO HomeVideo*

Lucky Texan   1934
Western
15490   61 mins   B/W   B, V   P
John Wayne
"Texas" John Wayne finds himself involved in a range war.
Monogram — *Movie Buff Video; Sony Video Software; Video Connection; Video Dimensions; Cable Films; Video Yesteryear; Spotlite Video; Kartes Video Communications*

Lum and Abner   1949
Television/Comedy
63626   29 mins   B/W   B, V, FO   P
Chester Lauck, Norris Goff, Andy Devine, Zasu Pitts
This rare kinescope features an episode from the 1949 TV series "Lum and Abner," adapted from the duo's network radio show.
CBS — *Video Yesteryear*

Lumiere Program   19??
Film-History
57337   25 mins   C   B, V   P
Two experimental shorts by early animators, the Lumiere Brothers, are featured: "Red Spectre" and "Early Melies." Circa 1892-1920.
Louis Lumiere; Auguste Lumiere — *Hollywood Home Theater*

Lunatics and Lovers 1976
Comedy
47795   92 mins   C   B, V   P
Marcello Mastroianni, Lino Toffalo
A bizarre nobleman meets a door-to-door
musician who is in love with an imaginary
woman.
MPAA:PG
Independent — CBS/Fox Video

Lunch Wagon 1981
Comedy
59660   88 mins   C   B, V   P
Pamela Bryant, Rosanne Katon
Two co-eds are given a restaurant to manage
during summer vacation and wind up involved in
a hilarious diamond chase and sex romp.
MPAA:R
Mark Bor — Media Home Entertainment

Lupo 1970
Comedy
82402   99 mins   C   B, V   P
Yuda Barkan, Gabi Armoni, Esther Greenburg,
directed
When threatened with the loss of his home and
the separation of his family, an exuberant Greek
man challenges the modern world.
MPAA:G
Noah Films — MGM/UA Home Video

Lust for a Vampire 1970
Horror
63322   92 mins   C   B, V   P
Ralph Bates, Barbara Jefford, Suzanna Leigh
A deadly vampire preys on pupils and teachers
alike when she enrolls at a British finishing
school.
Hammer Films — THORN EMI/HBO Video

Lust in the Dust 1985
Comedy/Western
81254   85 mins   C   B, V, LV   P
Tab Hunter, Divine, Lainie Kazan, Geoffrey
Lewis, Henry Silva, Cesar Romero, directed by
Paul Bartel
A precious metal strike is made in the sleepy
town of Chile Verde, New Mexico. Gold fever
sweeps the west in this satirical oater.
MPAA:R
New World Pictures — New World Video

Lusty Men, The 1952
Western
65157   113 mins   B/W   B, V   P
Robert Mitchum, Susan Hayward, Arthur
Kennedy, directed by Nicholas Ray
Two rival rodeo champions, both in love with the
same woman, work the rodeo circuit until a
tragic accident occurs.
RKO — United Home Video

Luv 1967
Comedy
66012   95 mins   C   B, V   P
Jack Lemmon, Peter Falk, Elaine May, directed
by Clive Donner
A suicidal man is saved by a friend who takes
him home. The would-be suicide finds new
meaning by falling in love with his friend's wife.
MPAA:PG
Columbia — RCA/Columbia Pictures Home
Video

Luv-Ya Blue! 1980
Football
45128   24 mins   C   B, V, FO   R, P
Houston Oilers
Highlights of the 1979 Houston Oilers football
season.
NFL Films — NFL Films Video

Lux Video Theatre, The 1957
Drama
85188   59 mins   B/W   B, V   P
Edmond O'Brien, Beverly Garland, Frances
Bergen, John Qualen, Dan Seymour, Gordon
McRae, written by William Faulkner
A live television adaptation of the Hemingway
story, compressed into one hour in a single-
stage setting.
NBC — Video Yesteryear

Lydia 1941
Drama
81462   98 mins   B/W   B, V, LV   P
Merle Oberon, Joseph Cotten, Alan Marshall,
George Reeves
An elderly lady gets to relive her romantic past
when she has a reunion with four of her lost
loves.
Alexander Korda — Embassy Home
Entertainment

M

M 1930
Mystery
06226   95 mins   B/W   B, V, LV   P
Peter Lorre, Ellen Widmann, Inge Landgut,
Directed by Fritz Lang
Notorious child killer is hunted by police and the
underworld. German film, English subtitles.
GE
Paramount — Hollywood Home Theater; VCII;
Video Connection; Discount Video Tapes;
International Historic Films; Cinema Concepts;
Embassy Home Entertainment; Kartes Video
Communications; Video Yesteryear; Movie Buff
Video; International Home Video

Ma Vlast (My Fatherland) 1982
Music-Performance
47808   ? mins   C   LV   P
The traditional performance of Smetana's "My
Fatherland" which opened the 1981 Prague
Spring International Music Festival performed
by the Czech Philharmonic Orchestra (stereo).
Unknown — Pioneer Video Imports

Mabel Mercer: A Singer's 1981
Singer
Music-Performance
84650   42 mins   C   B, V   P
Mabel Mercer sings her heart out at Cleo's in
New York in a live concert performance of her
17-song set. Recorded in Hi-Fi Stereo
Lou Tyrell — V.I.E.W. Video

Macabre 1977
Horror/Drama
84373   89 mins   C   B, V   P
Larry Ward, Teresa Gimpera, Jack Stuart
A beautiful bitch, lustful and precocious, kills her
husband with his twin brother.
Meteor Films — Mogul Communications

Macabre Moments from 1925
The Phantom of the
Opera
Horror
62872   34 mins   B/W   B, V   P, T
Lon Chaney Sr., Norman Kerry, Mary Philbin
An edited version of this classic film, with story
continuity maintained. Silent; includes color
sequence.
Universal — Blackhawk Films

Macabre Serenade 1969
Horror
85538   89 mins   C   B, V   P
Boris Karloff, Julissa, Andres Garcia
One of Karloff's last films, about a lunatic toy-
maker whose toys kill and maim.
EL, SP
Spanish — Unicorn Video

Macao 1952
Drama
64374   81 mins   B/W   B, V, 3/4U   P
Robert Mitchum, Jane Russell, William Bendix,
Gloria Grahame
A wandering adventurer and a cafe singer cross
paths with a wanted criminal in the exotic Far
East.
RKO — Nostalgia Merchant

Macaroni 1985
Comedy
86156   104 mins   C   B, V   P
Jack Lemmon, Marcello Mastroianni
Two war buddies reunite in Naples amidst
absurd comedic situations.

MPAA:PG
Filmauro-Massfilm — Paramount Home Video

MacArthur 1977
War-Drama
58426   144 mins   C   B, V   P
Gregory Peck, Ivan Bonar, Ward Costello,
Nicholas Coster, directed by Joseph Sargent
General Douglas MacArthur's life from
Corregidor in 1942 to his dismissal a decade
later in the midst of the Korean conflict.
MPAA:PG
Universal; Zanuck Brown Prods — MCA Home
Video

Macbeth 1948
Drama
66474   111 mins   B/W   B, V   P
Orson Welles, Jeanette Nolan, Dan O'Herlihy,
Roddy McDowall, Robert Coote, directed by
Orson Welles
Shakespeare's classic tragedy is performed in
this film with a celebrated lead performance by
Orson Welles as the tragic king.
Republic — Republic Pictures Home Video

Macbeth 1972
Music-Performance
81583   148 mins   C   B, V   P
Kostas Paskalis, Josephine Barstow, James
Morris, Keith Erwen.
This is a production of the Verdi opera
performed by the Glyndebourne Festival Opera.
With English subtitles.
IT
Southern Television Ltd. — Video Arts
International

Macbeth 1971
Drama/Theater
87270   139 mins   C   B, V   P
Jon Finch, Nicholas Selby, Martin Shaw,
Francesca Annis, Terence Baylor, directed by
Roman Polanski
Polanski's notorious adaptation of the
Shakespeare classic, marked by realistic
design, unflinching violence and fatalistic
atmosphere.
MPAA:R
Andrew Draunsberg; Hugh
Hefner — RCA/Columbia Pictures Home
Video

Macbeth 197?
Dance
87352   105 mins   C   B, V   P
Alexei Fadeyechev, Nina Timofeyeva
The Bolshoi Ballet performs the classic ballet
based upon Shakespeare's tragedy,
choreographed by Vladimir Vasiliev.
Bolshoi Theatre — Kultur

Macho Callahan 1970
Western
86594 99 mins C B, V P
*David Janssen, Jean Seberg, David Carradine,
Lee J. Cobb*
A Civil War convict is released from a frontier
prison bent on revenge and violence.
MPAA:R
Martin C. Chute; Bernard Kowalski; Avco
Embassy — *Charter Entertainment*

Machoman 197?
Martial arts
70818 94 mins C B, V P
Araujo, Enyaw Liew, Jerry Rages
The matchless, peerless, Machoman knows all
the best killing methods including: Lizard Fists,
Crane Kung Fu, and the Drunken Fist.
Foreign — *Master Arts Video*

Maciste in Hell 1972
Fantasy
86889 89 mins C B, V P
*Kirk Morris, Helene Channel, directed by
Riccardo Freda*
A 17th-century fellow plunges into Hell, fighting
snakes and giants in order to save his beloved.
Dubbed.
Italian — *Unicorn Video*

Mack, The 1973
Drama
81475 110 mins C B, V P
*Max Julien, Richard Pryor, Don Gordon, Roger
E. Mosley, Carol Speed*
The Mack is a pimp who comes out of
retirement to reclaim a piece of the action in
Oakland, California.
MPAA:R
Cinerama Releasing — *Charter Entertainment*

**Mack Sennett Comedies
Volume I** 1921
Comedy
85906 85 mins B/W B, V P
*Ben Turpin, Chester Conklin, Ford Sterling,
Minta Durfee*
Four Sennett films are included: "The Eyes
Have It," "The Cannon Ball," "The Desperate
Scoundrel" and "Pride of Pikeville."
Mack Sennett — *Republic Pictures Home
Video*

**Mack Sennett Comedies
Volume II** 1916
Comedy
85907 84 mins B/W B, V P
*Fatty Arbuckle, Mabel Normand, Will Rogers,
Madge Hunt*
Four more Sennett shorts are featured: "Fatty &
Mabel Adrift," "Mabel, Fatty and the Law,"
"Fatty's Tin-Type Tangle" and "Our
Congressman."

Mack Sennett — *Republic Pictures Home
Video*

MacKenna's Gold 1969
Western/Adventure
70192 128 mins C B, V P
*Gregory Peck, Omar Sharif, Telly Savalas, Julie
Newmar, Edward G. Robinson*
A ragtag group of adventurers travel to Apache
territory in search of a cache of gold that was
rumored to have been buried there. In Beta Hi-
Fi.
MPAA:PG
Columbia Pictures — *RCA/Columbia Pictures
Home Video*

Mackintosh Man, The 1973
Adventure/Suspense
76855 100 mins C B, V P
*Paul Newman, Dominique Sanda, James
Mason, Ian Bannen, Nigel Patrick, directed by
John Huston*
A British intelligence agent is out to trap a
Communist who has infiltrated the top ranks of
the organization.
MPAA:PG
John Foreman; Warner Bros — *Warner Home
Video*

Macon County Line 1974
Drama/Adventure
65390 89 mins C B, V P
*Alan Vint, Jesse Vint, Cheryl Waters, Geoffrey
Lewis, Joan Blackman, Max Baer*
A series of deadly mistakes and misfortunes
lead to a sudden turn around in the lives of 3
young people when they enter a small Georgia
town and find themselves accused of brutally
slaying the sheriff's wife.
MPAA:R
American International Pictures — *Embassy
Home Entertainment*

Mad Bomber 1972
Suspense
12027 80 mins C B, V P
Vince Edwards, Chuck Connors, Neville Brand
Police search for a mad bomber who has
terrorized the city.
Philip Yordan Prod; Official Films — *King of
Video; World Video Pictures*

Mad Bull 1977
Drama
82263 96 mins C B, V P
*Alex Karras, Susan Anspach, Nicholas
Colosanto, Tracy Walter*
Mad Bull is a wrestler whose life has little
meaning until he meets a woman who discovers
that he's really a warm and sensitive person.
Steckler Productions; Filmways — *THORN
EMI/HBO Video*

Mad Butcher, The   1975
Horror
86493   90 mins   C   B, V   P
*Victor Buono, Brad Harris, Karen Field, directed
by John Zuru*
An crazed out-patient makes sausages out of
teenagers.
MPAA:R
Unknown — *Magnum Entertainment*

Mad Doctor of Blood   1969
Island
Horror
86492   110 mins   C   B, V   P
John Ashley
A monster on Blood Island must drink the blood
of his loved ones—girlfriend, mother and
family—in order to survive.
Dimension Pictures — *Magnum Entertainment*

Mad Dog Morgan   1976
Biographical/Drama
77169   93 mins   C   B, V   P
*Dennis Hopper, David Gulpilil, directed by
Philippe Mora*
This is the true story of outlaw Dan "Mad Dog"
Morgan who always kept one step ahead of the
law.
MPAA:R
Jeremy Thomas — *THORN EMI/HBO Video*

Mad Dogs and   1971
Englishmen
Music-Performance
81796   55 mins   C   B, V   P
Joe Cocker, Leon Russell, Rita Coolidge
This chronicle of Joe Cocker's 1971 American
tour features such songs as "Delta Lady" and
"Feelin Alright" in VHS Dolby Hi-Fi Stereo and
Beta Hi-Fi Stereo.
MGM — *RCA/Columbia Pictures Home Video*

Mad, Mad Monsters, The   1984
Cartoons
70614   60 mins   C   B, V   P
Animated
The fun-loving creatures of the title aren't angry;
they're merely loony.
Videocraft International Ltd. — *Prism*

Mad Max   1980
Adventure
66105   93 mins   C   B, V, LV,   P
                                   CED
Mel Gibson
Set on the highways of the post-nuclear future,
this film concerns rebel bikers who challenge
the police who guard what is left of civilization.
MPAA:R
American International Pictures — *Vestron
Video*

Mad Max Beyond   1985
Thunderdome
Adventure
82498   107 mins   C   B, V, LV   P
*Mel Gibson, Tina Turner, Helen Buday, Frank
Thring, Bruce Spence, Robert Grubb, Angelo
Rossitto, Angry Anderson, George Spartels,
directed by George Miller and George Ogilve*
Max arrives in the vicious City of Bartertown and
clashes with the diabolical Aunty Entity. Left to
die in the desert, Max is rescued and mistaken
for a Messiah by a group of oasis orphans.
Maurice Jarre's soundtrack and two Turner hits
fill out the Dolby hi-fi stereo tape. Available with
Spanish subtitles in VHS only.
MPAA:PG-13
Warner Bros. — *Warner Home Video*

Mad Miss Manton, The   1938
Comedy/Mystery
73688   80 mins   B/W   B, V   P
*Barbara Stanwyck, Henry Fonda, Hattie
McDaniel, Sam Levene*
A society girl becomes a sleuth to solve a
murder.
RKO — *RKO HomeVideo*

Mad Mission 3   1984
Satire
79710   81 mins   C   B, V   P
*Richard Kiel, Sam Kui, Karl Muka, Sylvia Chang,
Tsuneharu Sugiyama*
While on vacation in Paris, a Chinese man is
recruited by James Bond to retrieve two jewels
stolen from the English crown.
Cinema City Company — *THORN EMI/HBO
Video*

Mad Monster Party   1968
Comedy
64975   94 mins   C   B, V, CED   P
*Animated, voices of Boris Karloff, Ethel Ennis,
Phyllis Diller*
Dr. Frankenstein is getting older and wants to
retire from the responsibilities of being senior
monster, so he calls a convention of creepy
creatures to decide who should take his
placethe Wolfman, Dracula, the Mummy, the
Creature, It, the Invisible Man, or Dr. Jekyll and
Mr. Hyde.
Avco-Embassy — *Embassy Home
Entertainment*

Mad Wednesday   1951
Comedy
71036   92 mins   B/W   B, V   P
*Harold Lloyd, Margaret Hamilton, Frances
Ramsden, directed by Preston Sturges*
A man gets fired from his job, stumbling drunk
and wins a fortune gambling. He then buys a
circus and uses a lion to frighten investors into
backing him. This all happens in one day. This
film is a slightly edited revision of "The Sin of
Harold Diddlebock."

RKO — *Hal Roach Studios*

Madame Bovary 1949
Romance/Drama
58871   114 mins   B/W   B, V   P
*Jennifer Jones, Van Heflin, Louis Jordan, James
Mason, directed by Vincente Minnelli*
Gustave Flaubert's classic novel concerning a
woman's abandoned pursuit of love and the
three men who loved her.
MGM; Pandro S Berman — *MGM/UA Home
Video*

Madame Butterfly 1983
Music-Performance
80328   135 mins   C   B, V   P
*Raina Kabalvanska, Nazareno Antinori, Elonora
Jankovic*
A performance of the Puccini opera about an
American soldier and the Japanese woman he
loves which was recorded at the Arena di
Verona.
Covent Garden Video Productions — *THORN
EMI/HBO Video*

Madame in Manhattan 1984
Comedy-Performance/Puppets
78658   60 mins   C   B, V   P
Wayland Flowers and Madame escort you
through an unforgettable tour of the Big Apple.
RKO — *RKO HomeVideo*

Madame Rosa 1978
Drama
59421   105 mins   C   B, V   P
*Simone Signoret, Claude Dauphin, directed by
Molshe Mizrahi*
The evocative portrayal of a survivor of both
Nazi concentration camps and a life of
prostitution.
Academy Awards '78: Best Foreign Film.
MPAA:PG
Raymond Danon; Roland Girard; Jean Bolvary;
Libra Film Prod — *Vestron Video*

Madame X 1966
Drama
70556   100 mins   C   B, V   P
*Lana Turner, John Forsythe, Ricardo
Montalban, Burgess Meredith, Constance
Bennett, Keir Dullea*
Turner stars in one of the 6 remakes of the '29
film about a woman blackmailed into exile, out
of the aristocracy she'd married into. After years
of alcohol and degradation, she is put on trial for
murder with her son assigned to defend her. In
mono Hi Fi on all formats.
Universal — *MCA Home Video*

Made Easy 1985
Home improvement
85950   25 mins   C   B, V, 3/4U   P

5   pgms
A series for handcrafted home improvement
instruction.
1.Electrical 2.Plumbing 3.Paint and Paper
4.Safe and Warm 5.Ready to Remodel
Rewind Prod. — *Karl/Lorimar Home Video*

Made for Each Other 1939
Drama
08677   100 mins   B/W   B, V, 3/4U   P
*Carole Lombard, James Stewart, Charles
Coburn, Lucille Watson*
A touching drama of young love and its
disappointments; interfering mother-inlaw who
wants to baby her married son and control the
grandchild.
David O Selznick — *Movie Buff Video;
Hollywood Home Theater; VCII; Video
Dimensions; Cable Films; Video Connection;
Video Yesteryear; Discount Video Tapes; Prism;
Kartes Video Communications*

Made in Heaven 1952
Comedy
80939   90 mins   C   B, V   P
Petula Clark, David Tomlinson, Sonja Ziemann
A distrusting newlywed wife suspects that her
husband is philandering about with the new
maid they've just hired.
J. Arthur Rank — *VidAmerica*

Madhouse 1984
Horror
72460   90 mins   C   B, V   P
Trish Everly
A woman has bizarre recollections of her twin
sister whom she finally meets in a hospital.
unknown — *VCL Home Video*

Madman 1982
Horror
66186   89 mins   C   B, V   P
Alexis Dubin, Tony Fish
A cocky young man, mocking a legend about an
ax murderer, sets the wheels of terror in motion.
MPAA:R
Jensen Farley — *THORN EMI/HBO Video*

Madman 1979
Adventure
76913   95 mins   C   B, V   P
*Sigourney Weaver, Michael Beck, F. Murray
Abraham*
This is the true story of Boris Abramovitch, a
Russian-born Jew who led an incredible fight
against Soviet oppression.
MPAA:PG
Alex Massis — *United Home Video*

Madron 1970
Western
84023   93 mins   C   B, V   P

Richard Boone, Leslie Caron, Paul Smith,
directed by Jerry Hopper
An exciting western filmed in the Negen desert,
complete with menacing Apaches, a nun and a
scowling gunslinger.
MPAA:PG
Emanuel Henigman; Eric Weaver — *United
Home Video*

Mae West   1984
Biographical/Drama
85096   97 mins   C   B, V   P
Ann Jillian, James Brolin, directed by Lee Philips
This made-for-TV film details West's life from
humble beginnings to raunchy, entenore-ridden
film stardom.
Phiip Mandelker; Leonard Hill — *Karl/Lorimar
Home Video*

Mafu Cage, The   1978
Horror
77398   99 mins   C   B, V   P
Carol Kane, Lee Grant
A rather strange woman puts her sisters' lover
into a cage and subjects him to brutal torture.
Independent — *Wizard Video*

Magic   1978
Drama
59835   106 mins   C   B, V, LV,   P
                                      CED
*Anthony Hopkins, Ann-Margret, Burgess
Meredith, Ed Lauter, directed by Richard
Attenborough*
A ventriloquist and his dummy, an all-too-human
counterpart, get involved with a beautiful but
impressionable woman lost between the world
of reality and the irresistible world of illusion.
MPAA:R
Joseph E Levine; Richard P
Levine — *Embassy Home Entertainment*

Magic Christian, The   1970
Comedy
47988   88 mins   C   B, V   P
*Peter Sellers, Raquel Welch, Ringo Starr,
Laurence Harvey, Richard Attenborough*
The richest man in the world adopts a vagrant
for his son, to prove that any man can be
corrupted by money.
MPAA:PG
Grand Film; Commonwealth
United — *Republic Pictures Home Video*

Magic Flute, The   1976
Opera
84659   156 mins   C   B, V   P
*Herman Christian Polster, Magdalena Falewicz,
the Leipzig 'Gewandhaus' Orchestra conducted
by Gert Bahner*
Performed by the Gewandhaus Orchestra of
Leipzig, this is a famed performance of the

Mozart opera. Choreography by Marion
Schurath. Recorded in Hi-Fi.
GE
George Mielke — *V.I.E.W. Video*

Magic Flute, The   1973
Opera
86879   134 mins   C   B, V, LV   P
*Josef Kostlinger, Irma Urrila, Hakan Hagegard,
Elisabeth Erikson, directed by Ingmar Bergman*
In Swedish with English subtitles, this is
Bergman's acclaimed version of Mozart's
famous comic opera, universally considered one
of the greatest adaptations of opera to film ever
made.
MPAA:G SW
Ingmar Bergman; Paramount — *Paramount
Home Video*

Magic Flute, The   1982
Opera
87934   164 mins   C   B, V   P
*Benjamin Luxon, Felicity Lott, conducted by
Bernard Haitnk*
A presentation of the light Mozart opera by the
Glyndebourne Festival Opera Company.
Glyndebourne Festival; David
Hockney — *Video Arts International*

Magic Garden, The   1960
Comedy
11239   60 mins   B/W   B, V, FO   P
*Tommy Ramokgopa, directed by Donald
Swanson*
A thief loses his stolen money and it is found by
honest people who put it to good use while the
thief goes mad trying to locate it.
Donald Swanson — *Video Yesteryear*

Magic Legend of the   1965
Golden Goose, The
Fantasy
84824   72 mins   C   B, V   P
A retelling of the familiar brothers Grimm
chestnut.
K Gordon Murray — *United Home Video*

Magic of Doctor   1985
Snuggles, The
Cartoons
76910   60 mins   C   B, V
Animated
The kindly Doctor snuggles enters a balloon
race to win prize money to help Granny Toots
build a new cat hospital.
Kidpix — *Embassy Home Entertainment*

Magic of Lassie, The   1978
Drama
86783   100 mins   C   B, V   P
*James Stewart, Mickey Rooney, Stephanie
Zimbalist, Alice Faye, directed by Don Chaffey*

Lassie becomes the bone of contention between a drawling grandpa and a scheming man trying to acquire the vineyard on which they live.
MPAA:G
Lassie Prods — MGM/UA Home Video

Magic on Love Island 1980
Comedy
81637   96 mins   C   B, V   P
Adrienne Barbeau, Bill Daily, Howard Duff, Dody Goodman, Dominique Dunne, Lisa Hartman, Janis Paige, directed by Earl Bellamy
Romantic misadventures ensue when eight ladies go on vacation to Love Island, a tropical paradise.
Dick Clark Cinema Productions — Magnum Entertainment

Magic Pony, The 1978
Adventure/Fantasy
69610   80 mins   C   B, V   P
Animated, voices of Jim Backus and Erin Moran
With the help of a beautiful flying horse, a young man battles a greedy emperor to become the kind-hearted prince and live happily ever after with a beautiful princess and his Magic Pony.
MPAA:G
21st Century; Samuel J. Phillips$MAGIC PONY C — Children's Video Library

Magic Pony, The 1978
Adventure/Fantasy
40733   80 mins   C   B, V   P
Animated, voices of Jim Backus, Erin Moran
Ivan and his three brothers are sent to watch the fields and catch the culprit who has been destroying the wheat crop. The Magic Pony starts them on new adventures.
MPAA:G
21st Century; Sammuel J. Phillips — Video Gems; Vestron Video (disc only)

Magic Secrets 1985
Magic
84770   60 mins   C   B, V   P
Steve Dacri
The method, execution and motivation of basic slight-of-hand effects are demonstrated.
AM Available
Video Associates Inc/Steve Dacri — Video Associates

Magic Sword, The 1962
Adventure
38974   80 mins   C   B, V, FO   P
Basil Rathbone, Estelle Winwood
A family-oriented adventure film about a young knight who sets out to rescue a beautiful princess who is being held captive by an evil sorcerer and his dragon.
United Artists — Video Yesteryear

Magic Town 1947
Comedy-Drama
64539   103 mins   B/W   B, V   P
Jane Wyman, James Stewart, Kent Smith, directed by William Wellman
An opinion pollster investigates a small town which exactly reflects the views of the entire nation, making his job a cinch.
RKO — Spotlite Video

Magical Mystery Tour 1967
Musical
53945   55 mins   C   B, V   P
The Beatles, Victor Spinetti
On the road with an oddball assortment of people, the Beatles experience a strange assortment of incidents around the English countryside. Originally made for British television. Songs include: "The Fool on the Hill," "Blue Jay Way," "Your Mother Should Know," and the title tune.
Apple Films — Media Home Entertainment; Western Film & Video Inc

Magical Wonderland 1985
Fantasy
81683   90 mins   C   B, V   P
Join a handsome prince and his fair young maiden as they venture through such fairy tale classics as "Beauty and the Beast" and "Sleeping Beauty."
Majestic International Pictures — United Home Video

Magician, The 1958
Drama
59649   101 mins   B/W   B, V   P
Max von Sydow, Ingrid Thulin, Gunnar Bjornstrand, Bibi Andersson, Naima Wifstrand, directed by Ingmar Bergman
Max von Sydow portrays Dr. Vogler, a hypnotist and master of legerdemain who uses his powers to create harm. Subtitled in English.
Venice Film Festival '59: Special Juy Prize, Cinema Nuova Prize. SW
A B Svensk Filmindustri; Janus — Embassy Home Entertainment; Hollywood Home Theater; Discount Video Tapes; Festival Films

Magnavox Theater (The Three Musketeers) 1950
Drama
42969   53 mins   B/W   B, V, FO   P
John Hubbard, Robert Clarke, Mel Archer, Marjorie Lord
This teleplay which remains true to the novel by Alexandre Dumas, was directed by Budd Boetticher and includes flashing swords and romance.
Hal Roach Jr — Video Yesteryear

Magnificent Adventurer,   1976
The
Adventure/Biographical
84072   94 mins   C   B, V   P
Brett Halsey
This film is ostensibly a biography of Benvenuto
Cellini, the Florentine sculptor, with a
concentration on his lovelife and swordplay.
Ermanno Donati; Luigi Carpenpieri — Unicorn
Video

Magnificent Ambersons,   1942
The
Drama
00261   88 mins   B/W   B, V   P
Joseph Cotten, Agnes Moorehead, directed by
Orson Welles
A turn-of-the-century family clings to its genteel
traditions during an era of rapid change. Orson
Welles' second directorial effort.
RKO — RKO HomeVideo; VidAmerica

Magnificent Kick, The   1980
Adventure/Martial arts
60514   90 mins   C   B, V   P
The story of a master Wong-Fai-Hung, inventor
of the "Kick without Shadow," which was
practiced by the late Bruce Lee.
Unknown — Master Arts Video

Magnificent Obsession   1954
Drama
70557   108 mins   C   B, V   P
Jane Wyman, Rock Hudson, Barbara Rush,
Agnes Moorehead, directed by Lloyd C. Douglas
A rich playboy accidently causes the death of a
brain surgeon and blinds his wife. Guilty, the
man devotes his life to the study of medicine
and the restoration of the widow's eyesight. In
Mono Hi-Fi on all formats.
Universal — MCA Home Video

Magnificent Seven, The   1960
Western
53791   126 mins   C   B, V, CED   P
Yul Brenner, Steve McQueen, Robert Vaughn,
James Coburn, Charles Bronson, Horst
Buchholz, Eli Wallach, directed by John Sturges
Mexican villagers hire seven American gunmen
to defend them against bandits.
United Artists; Walter Mirisch — CBS/Fox
Video; RCA VideoDiscs

Magnifique, Le   1976
Comedy
11354   100 mins   C   B, V   P
Jean-Paul Belmondo, Jacqueline Bisset
Belmondo is a master spy and novelist who
mixes fantasy with reality when he chases
women and solves cases.
CINE III — Prism; Cinema Concepts

Magnum Force   1973
Suspense/Crime-Drama
54796   124 mins   C   B, V   P
Clint Eastwood, Hal Holbrook, Mitchell Ryan,
David Soul, directed by Ted Post
A San Francisco homicide detective
investigating a rash of gangster murders
discovers that they are the work of a rookie
police assassination squad whose members
have been frustrated by red tape and civil
liberties. A sequel to "Dirty Harry."
MPAA:R
Warner Bros, Robert Daly Prods — Warner
Home Video; RCA VideoDiscs

Magnum Killers   1976
Martial arts
82092   92 mins   C   B, V   P
Sombat Methance, Prichela Lee
A young man becomes involved in a web of
deadly intrigue when he sets out to find who
cheated him out of a small fortune during a card
game.
Srinakorn Films — Unicorn Video

Magnum Live!   1985
Music-Performance
88356   60 mins   C   B, V   P
The heavy metal group performs hits like "Les
Mort Dansant," "Kingdom of Madness" and
"How Far Jerusalem" at the Camden Palace in
London.
Philip Goodhand-Tait — Embassy Home
Entertainment

Mahalia Jackson and   1974
Elizabeth Cotten: Two
Remarkable Ladies
Music/Documentary
58581   58 mins   C   B, V   P
A close-up look at a pair of successful black
women performers: "Mahalia Jackson," a
filmed biography of the legendary singer, and
"Freight Train," the courageous story of pioneer
folksinger Elizabeth Cotten.
CBS — Mastervision

Mahler   1974
Biographical/Drama
80650   110 mins   C   B, V   P
Robert Powell, Georgiana Hale, Richard Morant,
Lee Montague, directed by Ken Russell
A dazzling look at the life, loves and music of
composer Gustav Mahler.
MPAA:PG
Goodtimes Enterprises — THORN EMI/HBO
Video

Mahogany   1976
Drama
59202   109 mins   C   B, V, LV   P
Diana Ross, Billy Dee Williams, Jean Pierre
Aumont

A world-famous high fashion model and designer gets a career boost when she daringly appears in a dress of her own creation at a Roman fashion show.
MPAA:R
Paramount — *Paramount Home Video; RCA VideoDiscs*

Main Event, The   1979
Comedy
37426   112 mins   C   B, V   P
Barbra Streisand, Ryan O'Neal
A wisecracking young woman obtains the contract of a prize fighter who is about to retire. She becomes his manager and gets him back into the ring.
MPAA:PG
Warner Bros — *Warner Home Video; RCA VideoDiscs*

Main Street to Broadway   1953
Musical
76926   102 mins   B/W   B, V   P
Tom Morton, Mary Murphy, Rex Harrision, Helen Hayes, Mary Martin, directed by Jay Garnett
A struggling young playwright attempts to launch his first play on the Broadway stage.
Lester Cowan — *MPI Home Video*

Major Bowes' Original   1939
Amateur Hour
Variety
85525   20 mins   B/W   B, V   P
Two episodes of Bowes' original contest radio show in behind-the-scenes films.
CBS — *Video Yesteryear*

Major Dundee   1965
Adventure
76029   124 mins   C   B, V   P
Charlton Heston, Richard Harris, James Coburn, Jim Hutton, directed by Sam Peckinpah
A union army officer with a hundred criminals volunteers from the prison he commands to chase a savage Indian leader through Mexico.
Jerry Bresler — *RCA/Columbia Pictures Home Video*

Make a Million   1935
Comedy
69557   66 mins   B/W   B, V, FO   P
Charles Starrett, Pauline Brooks
An economics professor is fired from his post because of his radical theories about redistributing the country's wealth. To prove his point, he becomes a millionaire by advertising for money.
Monogram Pictures — *Video Yesteryear*

Make a Wish   1937
Drama
08671   80 mins   B/W   B, V, 3/4U   P
Basil Rathbone, Leon Errol, Bobby Breen, Ralph Forbes
A noted composer goes stale in this colorful tale of backstage life. Music by Oscar Strauss.
RKO — *Video Yesteryear*

Make Room for Daddy I   1953
thru III
Comedy
77192   120 mins   B/W   B, V   P
Danny Thomas, Jean Hagen, Rusty Hamer, Jesse White, Sherry Jackson 3   pgms
Each tape in this series offers four programs from this early fifties TV sitcom. The stories focus on the amusing happenings in the family of a New York nightclub entertainer.
T & L Productions — *Shokus Video*

Make-up Secrets of the   1985
Hollywood Stars-Looking
Your Best
Cosmetology
84752   60 mins   C   B, V   P
Michael Westmore
Stressing various make-up angles and effects, Westmore makes up Melissa Sue Anderson, Sybil Danning and other lovelies.
Don Silverman; Robert Williams — *JCI Video*

Making Love   1982
Drama
59630   112 mins   C   B, V, CED   P
Kate Jackson, Harry Hamlin, Michael Ontkean, directed by Arthur Hiller
A love story concerning a young married couple whose seemingly-perfect world is shattered by the husband's homosexuality.
MPAA:R
Twentieth Century Fox — *CBS/Fox Video*

Making Michael   1983
Jackson's Thriller
Music-Performance
65347   60 mins   C   B, V, LV,   P
                              CED
Michael Jackson
The program is a behind-the-scenes look at how an unprecedented music video was created. The program includes highlights of Jackson's highly acclaimed videos for "Billie Jean" and "Beat It," as well as the 10-minute video for the title song of the "Thriller" album. In stereo and Beta Hi-Fi.
John Landis — *Vestron Video*

Making of Joan Collins,   1985
The
Interview
85083   54 mins   C   B, V   P

Directed by Charles Wallace
Joan Collins takes viewers on a day-by-day view of her life and accomplishments as the sexiest star of the 80's.
Adrian Scrope; Ron Kass — *Prism*

Making of Star Wars, The/S.P.F.X. — The Empire Strikes Back   1980
Filmmaking/Science fiction
08478   100 mins   C   B, V, LV,   P
                               CED
Mark Hamill, Carrie Fisher, Harrison Ford, narrated by William Conrad
Behind-the-scenes look at the special effects of these two popular movies directed by George Lucas. The viewer will see how Luke's automobile is able to cruise above ground, how the droids, C-3PO and R2-D2 move around, and the workings of Yoda.
EL, SP
20th Century Fox; Gary Kurtz — *CBS/Fox Video*

Making of Superman, The   1979
Filmmaking
75466   96 mins   C   B, V   P
Christopher Reeve, Margot Kidder
A behind-the-scenes look at the making of "Superman-The Movie."
Salkind — *Family Home Entertainment*

Making of Superman—The Movie and Superman II, The   1984
Science fiction/Filmmaking
66621   120 mins   C   B, V   P
Christopher Reeve, Margot Kidder, Susannah York
These two hour-long documentaries chronicle the making of the Superman films, showing the construction of sets, special effects work and off-screen moments with the actors.
Dovemead Limited; Film Export; International Film Productions — *U.S.A. Home Video*

Making of Superman II, The   1981
Filmmaking
75467   96 mins   C   B, V   P
Christopher Reeve, Margot Kidder
A behind-the-scenes look at the making of "Superman II."
Salkind — *Family Home Entertainment*

Making of the Stooges, The   1985
Comedy/Documentary
70386   47 mins   B/W   B, V   P
Moe Howard, Larry Fine, Curly Howard, narrated by Steve Allen

This tape documents the 50-year history of the Three Stooges including rare footage of these slapstick stars.
Forest P. Gill, Mark S. Gillman — *Karl/Lorimar Home Video*

Making of "The Terminator" & "Missing in Action 2," The   1985
Filmmaking
86173   60 mins   C   B, V   P
An insider's look at the making of these two action epics.
Cannon — *Vidmark Entertainment*

Making of 2:00 AM Paradise Cafe   1984
Documentary/Music-Performance
80377   55 mins   C   B, V   P
A behind the scenes documentary that details the recording of Barry Manilow's jazz influenced album "2:00 A.M. Paradise Cafe". Available in VHS Dolby Hi-Fi Stereo and Beta Hi-Fi.
Stiletto Ltd. Productions — *RCA/Columbia Pictures Home Video*

Making the Grade   1984
Comedy
73365   105 mins   C   B, V   P
A hoodlum poses as a preppy to settle some debts owed to the mob.
MPAA:PG
Cannon Films — *MGM/UA Home Video*

Malcolm McLaren—Duck Rock   1985
Music video
81940   40 mins   C   B, V   P
The eclectic sounds of Malcolm McLaren are captured on this tape that features conceptual music videos of "Double Dutch" and "Buffalo Gals." Available in VHS Dolby Hi-Fi Stereo and Beta Hi-Fi Stereo.
Trevor Horn — *RCA/Columbia Pictures Home Video*

Malibu Beach   1978
Comedy
48477   93 mins   C   B, V   P
Kim Lankford, James Daughton
The California beach scene is the setting for this movie filled with bikini clad girls, tanned young men, and instant romances.
MPAA:R
Crown International — *United Home Video*

Malibu Express   1985
Adventure/Mystery
81200   101 mins   C   B, V   P
Darby Hinton, Sybil Danning, Art Metrano, Shelley Taylor Morgan, Niki Dantine, Barbara Edwards

---

A rich Texas millionaire gets his chance to become a private eye when a conscientious contessa asks him to stop and American corporation from selling computers to the Russians.
MPAA:R
The Sidaris Company — *MCA Home Video*

Malibu High 1979
Drama
48480 92 mins C B, V P
Jill Lansing, Stuart Taylor
The accidental death of a young prostitute's client leads her to a new series of illegal activities of the "sex and hit" variety.
MPAA:R
Crown International — *United Home Video*

Malicious 1974
Drama
44592 98 mins C B, V P
Laura Antonelli, Turi Ferro, Alessandro Momo, Tina Aumont, directed by Salvatore Samperi
A housekeeper hired for a widower and his three sons becomes the object of lusty affection of all four men. As Papa makes plans to court and marry her, his fourteen-year-old son plots to have her as a companion on his road to sensual maturity. Dubbed in English.
MPAA:R
Paramount, Silvio Clementelli — *Paramount Home Video*

Malta Story 1953
War-Drama
62867 103 mins B/W B, V P
Alec Guinness, Jack Hawkins, Anthony Steel, Flora Robson
A British World War II flier becomes involved with the defense of Malta.
UA British; GFD — *Embassy Home Entertainment*

Maltese Falcon, The 1941
Mystery
13594 101 mins B/W B, V P
Humphrey Bogart, Mary Astor, Sydney Greenstreet, Peter Lorre, directed by John Huston
After the death of his partner, detective Sam Spade finds himself enmeshed in the search for a priceless statuette.
National Board of Review Awards '41: Best Performances (Bogart and Astor).
Warner Brothers — *CBS/Fox Video; RCA VideoDiscs*

Mama (I Remember Mama) 195?
Comedy
59313 55 mins B/W B, V, 3/4U P
Peggy Wood, Dick Van Patten

This family comedy series set in San Francisco at the turn of the century includes two episodes: "Mama's Bad Day" (1950), in which Mama feels she's being taken for granted; and, "Mama's Nursery School" (1955), in which Mama becomes a substitute teacher. Includes original commercials.
CBS — *Shokus Video; Discount Video Tapes*

Mama (I Remember Mama) 1950
Comedy
39002 30 mins B/W B, V, FO P
Peggy Wood, Judson Laird, Rosemary Rice, Robin Morgan
A representative episode from the famous early TV series, "Madame Zodiac," in which Aunt Jenny has her fortune told with surprising results. Original commercials included.
CBS — *Video Yesteryear*

Mama (I Remember Mama) 1950
Drama
42977 29 mins B/W B, V, FO P
Peggy Wood, Judson Laire, Dick Van Patten, Rosemary Rice
Little Dagmar is entered in a spelling bee and Papa bets his life insurance money that she'll win.
CBS — *Video Yesteryear*

Mama (I Remember Mama) 1951
Comedy-Drama
47503 29 mins B/W B, V, FO P
Peggy Wood, Judson Laird, Robin Morgan, Rosemary Rice, Dick Van Patten, Ruth Gates
This episode of the popular TV series is titled "Mama's Bad Day." Family problems become more than Mama can bear, and she is conscience-stricken when she wishes she had never married.
CBS — *Video Yesteryear*

Mame 1974
Musical
74206 131 mins C B, V P
Lucille Ball, Beatrice Arthur
This is the story of Auntie Mame, who takes it on herself to teach a group of eccentrics how to live life to its fullest.
MPAA:PG
Robert Fryer; James Cresson — *Warner Home Video*

Man, a Woman, and a Bank, A 1979
Comedy
48404 100 mins C B, V P
Donald Sutherland, Brooke Adams, Paul Mazursky

Two con men plan to rob a bank by posing as workers during the bank's construction. An advertising agency woman snaps their picture for a billboard to show how nice the builders have been, then becomes romantically involved with one of the would-be thieves.
MPAA:PG
John B Bennett, Peter Samuelson — *Charter Entertainment*

Man Against Crime   1956
Volume I
Adventure
47640   60 mins   B/W   B, V, FO   P
Frank Lovejoy
A gunless gumshoe travels the globe in search of crooks and intrigue. Vintage television.
NBC — *Video Yesteryear*

Man Against Crime   1956
Volume II
Crime-Drama
47650   60 mins   B/W   B, V, FO   P
Frank Lovejoy, Herschel Bernardi
Two episodes of the vintage TV series with Frank Lovejoy as detective Mike Barnett. In episode one, Mike is challenged to a duel by a nasty jai alai player who's been blackmailing his employer. In episode two, Mike gets involved with a Parisian narcotics ring.
NBC — *Video Yesteryear*

Man Alone, A   1955
Western
74485   96 mins   C   B, V   P
Ray Milland, Raymond Burr
This is the story of a sheriff who defends a man falsely accused of robbing a stagecoach.
Republic — *Republic Pictures Home Video*

Man and Boy   1971
Western/Drama
82325   98 mins   C   B, V   P
Bill Cosby, Gloria Foster, George Spell, Henry Silva, Yaphet Kotto, directed by E.W. Swackhamer
A black Civil War veteran encounters bigotry and prejudice when he tries to set up a homestead in Arizona. Available in VHS and Beta Hi-Fi.
MPAA:G
Marvin Miller — *RCA/Columbia Pictures Home Video*

Man Called Horse, A   1970
Adventure
65495   114 mins   C   CED   P
Stanford Howard
An English aristocrat is captured by Indians, lives with them and eventually becomes their leader.
Cinema Center — *CBS/Fox Video*

Man Called Horse, A   1969
Western
Closed Captioned
81172   15t mins   C   B, V   P
Richard Harris, Dame Judith Anderson, Jean Gascon
A British aristocrat, captured and tortured by the Sioux Indians in the Dakotas, later helps them fend off an attack by rival braves. Impressed, they offer to embrace him as a brother if he can endure the Sun Vow.
MPAA:PG
CBS Theatrical Films — *CBS/Fox Video*

Man Called Tiger   1981
Martial arts
81473   97 mins   C   B, V   P
A Chinese martial arts expert infiltrates a ruthless Japanese gang in order to find the man who murdered his father.
MPAA:R
World Northal Corporation — *Embassy Home Entertainment*

Man for All Seasons, A   1966
Drama
Closed Captioned
21291   120 mins   C   B, V   P
Paul Scofield, Robert Shaw, Orson Welles, Wendy Hiller, Susannah York, directed by Fred Zinneman
A biographical drama concerning sixteenth century Chancellor of England, Sir Thomas More, and his personal conflict with King Henry VIII.
Academy Awards '66: Best Picture; Best Actor (Scofield); Best Director (Zinneman).
Columbia — *RCA/Columbia Pictures Home Video; RCA VideoDiscs*

Man from Atlantis   1977
Science fiction
66278   60 mins   C   B, V   P
Patrick Duffy
Patrick Duffy stars as the water-breathing alien who emerges from his undersea home—the Lost City of Atlantis.
NBC — *Worldvision Home Video*

Man from Beyond   1922
Adventure/Drama
59219   50 mins   B/W   B, V, 3/4U   P
Harry Houdini, Arthur Maude
Frozen alive, a man returns 100 years later to try and find his lost love. Silent.
Houdini Picture Corp — *Movie Buff Video; Video Yesteryear*

Man from Clover Grove,   1978
The
Comedy
56738   97 mins   C   B, V   P
Ron Masak, Cheryl Miller, Jed Allan, Rose Marie

Hilarity takes over a town when a nutty boy inventor puts the sheriff in a spin.
EL, SP
Drew Cummings — *Media Home Entertainment*

Man from Music Mountain, The   1943
Western/Musical
84873   53 mins   B/W   B, V   P
Roy Rogers, Pat Brady, Ruth Terry, Paul Kelly
Roy grinds a feud between cattlemen and sheepherders to a halt.
Republic — *Kartes Video Communications*

Man from Music Mountain, The   1938
Western
08788   54 mins   B/W   B, V, 3/4U   P
Gene Autry, Smiley Burnette, Carol Hughes, Polly Jenkins
Worthless mining stock is sold in a desert mining town, but Gene and Smiley clear that up.
Republic — *Hollywood Home Theater; Video Connection; Discount Video Tapes; Nostalgia Merchant; Kartes Video Communications*

Man from Snowy River, The   1982
Adventure
65002   104 mins   C   B, V, CED   P
Kirk Douglas, Tom Burlinson
Stunning cinematography highlights this heroic adventure story set in Australia in the 1880's, as a young man accepts the challenge of taming a herd of wild horses.
MPAA:PG
20th Century Fox — *CBS/Fox Video*

Man from Utah, The   1934
Western
11268   55 mins   B/W   B, V, FO   P
John Wayne, Gabby Hayes
The Duke tangles with the crooked sponsor of some rodeo events who has killed several of the participants.
Monogram — *Sony Video Software; Spotlite Video; Video Yesteryear; Video Connection; Cable Films; Discount Video Tapes*

Man in Grey, The   1945
Romance
76639   116 mins   B/W   B, V   P
James Mason, Margaret Lockwood, Stewart Granger, Phyllis Calvert
An intriguing story of a criss-cross love affair among 19th century English royalty.
Gainsborough — *VidAmerica*

Man in the Iron Mask, The   1939
Adventure
55350   110 mins   B/W   B, V, 3/4U   P

Louis Hayward, Alan Hale, Joan Bennett, directed by James Whale
Alexandre Dumas' classic novel provides the basis for this tale about the twin brother of King Louis XIV of France, who was kept prisoner with his face covered by a locked iron mask.
Edward Small; United Artists — *Nostalgia Merchant*

Man in the Iron Mask, The   1976
Adventure
Closed Captioned
82335   105 mins   C   B, V   P
Richard Chamberlain, Patrick McGoohan, Louis Jourdan, Jenny Agutter, Ian Holm
A tyrannical French King kidnaps his twin brother, and imprisons him on a remote island, and forces him to wear an iron mask. Available in VHS and Beta Hi-Fi.
ITC — *Playhouse Video*

Man in the Mist, The   1983
Mystery/Suspense
81705   51 mins   C   B, V   P
Francesca Annis, James Warwick
Private investigators Tommy and Tuppence Beresford find themselves trying to solve a murder while on vacation in a provincial hotel. Based upon the Agatha Christie story.
London Weekend Television — *Pacific Arts Video*

Man in the Santa Claus Suit, The   1979
Fantasy/Comedy
79225   96 mins   C   B, V   P
Fred Astaire, Gary Burghoff, John Byner, Nanette Fabray
A costume shop owner has an effect on three people who rent Santa Claus costumes from him.
Dick Clark Cinema Productions — *Media Home Entertainment*

Man in the White Suit, The   1951
Comedy
45070   82 mins   B/W   B, V   P
Alec Guinness, Joan Greenwood
A humble laboratory assistant in a textile mill invents a cloth that won't stain, tear, or wear-out and causes an industry-wide panic.
Universal, J Arthur Rank — *THORN EMI/HBO Video; Learning Corp of America*

Man Named Lombardi, A   1971
Football/Biographical
81846   55 mins   C   B, V   P
Narrated by George C. Scott
This documentary looks at the life and career of the great football coach Vince Lombardi. Supplementing the program are interviews with

---

THE VIDEO TAPE & DISC GUIDE

Hall of Famers Paul Hornung, Sonny Jurgenson and Fuzzy Thurston.
George L. Flynn — *MPI Home Video; Lucerne Films*

Man of Flowers 1984
Drama
82424   91 mins   C   B, V   P
Norman Kaye, Alyson Best, Chris Haywood, directed by Paul Cox
This film involves a mercurial romance between a young model and a reclusive art collector.
International Spectrafilm — *Vestron Video*

Man of La Mancha 1972
Musical
58839   121 mins   C   B, V, CED   P
Peter O'Toole, Sophia Loren, James Coco, Harry Andrews, John Castle, Brian Blessed
Arrested by the Inquisition and thrown into prison, Miguel de Cervantes relates the story of Don Quixote. Based on the Broadway musical, with music by Mitch Leigh and lyrics by Joe Darion. Songs include "The Impossible Dream" and "Dulcinea."
MPAA:PG
United Artists — *CBS/Fox Video*

Man of Legend 1971
Adventure
84028   95 mins   C   B, V   P
Peter Strauss, Tina Aumont, Pier Paola Capponi, directed by Sergio Grieco
An adventure-romance filmed in Morocco; a German soldier flees to the Foreign Legion and fights with nomadic rebels, falling in love with their chief's beautiful daughter.
MPAA:PG
Francesco Mazzei — *United Home Video*

Man of the Frontier 1936
Western
05580   60 mins   B/W   B, V, 3/4U   P
Gene Autry, Smiley Burnette, Frances Grant
A vital irrigation project is being sabotaged, but Gene Autry exposes the culprits.
Republic — *Video Connection; Video Yesteryear; Discount Video Tapes*

Man of Violence 1971
Drama
81407   107 mins   C   B, V   P
Michael Latimer, Luan Peters, directed by Peter Walker
A vulgar, tasteless man spends the worthless hours of his life lurking about the more wretched entranceways of his native land.
Peter Walker — *Monterey Home Video*

Man on the Eiffel Tower, The 1948
Crime-Drama
64342   82 mins   B/W   B, V   P
Charles Laughton, Burgess Meredith, Franchot Tone, Patricia Roc, directed by Burgess Meredith
A mysterious crazed killer defies the police to discover his identity.
A & T — *Video Gems; Movie Buff Video; Cable Films; Kartes Video Communications*

Man on the Moon 1981
Space exploration
58302   80 mins   C   B, V, CED   P
Narrated by Walter Cronkite
This program traces the birth and development of the U.S. Space Program, leading to the Apollo 11 moon landing.
CBS News — *CBS/Fox Video*

Man on the Run 1974
Drama/Suspense
71208   90 mins   C   B, V   P
Kyle Johnson, James B Sikking, Terry Carter, directed by Herbert L Strock
After an unwitting involvement with a small robbery, a teenager finds himself the object of a police manhunt—for a murder suspect.
MPAA:R
Independent — *Prism*

Man That Corrupted Hadleyburg, The 1980
Drama
82105   40 mins   C   B, V   P
Robert Preston, Fred Gwynne, Frances Sternhagen, hosted by Henry Fonda
This is an adaptation of a Mark Twain short story about a stranger's plot of revenge against the hypocritical residents of a small town. Available in VHS Stereo and Beta Hi-Fi.
Christopher Lukas — *Monterey Home Video*

Man They Could Not Hang, The 1939
Horror
78966   70 mins   B/W   B, V   P
Boris Karloff, Lorna Gray, Roger Pryor
When a doctor is hanged for a murder, his assistant brings the doctor back to life and he vows revenge against the jurors that sentenced him. In Beta Hi-Fi.
Columbia Pictures — *RCA/Columbia Pictures Home Video*

Man Who Could Work Miracles, The 1937
Fantasy/Comedy
81629   82 mins   B/W   B, V   P
Ralph Richardson, Joan Gardner, Roland Young

A mild mannered draper's assistant becomes suddenly endowed with supernatural powers to perform any feat he wishes.
Alexander Korda — *Embassy Home Entertainment*

Man Who Fell to Earth, The   1976
Science fiction
33703   118 mins   C   B, V   P
David Bowie
A man from another planet ventures to earth and becomes a successful businessman. His ulterior motive for this visit is to come to the aid of his family on their ailing planet, at the expense of Earth.
MPAA:R
Cinema 5 — *RCA/Columbia Pictures Home Video*

Man Who Had Power Over Women, The   1970
Drama
88350   89 mins   C   B, V   P
Rod Taylor, directed by John Krish
The exploits of a carnally insatiable talent executive who has an affair with every woman he meets and therefore creates problems aplenty.
MPAA:R
Judd Bernard — *Embassy Home Entertainment*

Man Who Haunted Himself, The   1970
Mystery/Suspense
63336   91 mins   C   B, V
Roger Moore, Hildegarde Neil, Olga Georges-Picot
A man is possessed by a mysterious force that takes control of his ideal life and turns it into a nightmare.
Associated British Productions Ltd — *THORN EMI/HBO Video*

Man Who Knew Too Much, The   1956
Mystery/Drama
79678   120 mins   C   B, V, LV   P
James Stewart, Doris Day, Brenda De Banzie, Bernard Miles, directed by Alfred Hitchcock.
A doctor vacationing in Marrakech uncovers a murder plot and embroils his family in a frying pan of intrigue.
MPAA:PG
Alfred Hitchcock; Universal Classics — *MCA Home Video*

Man Who Knew Too Much, The   1934
Mystery
08745   87 mins   C   B, V   P

Leslie Banks, Edna Best, Peter Lorre, Nova Pilbeam, directed by Alfred Hitchcock
Hitchcock's first international success — a British family man on vacation in Switzerland is told about an assassination plot by a dying agent.
Gaumont — *Media Home Entertainment; Prism; Active Home Video; Hal Roach Studios; VCII; Blackhawk Films; Video Yesteryear; Hollywood Home Theater; Video Dimensions; Cable Films; Video Connection; Discount Video Tapes; Western Film & Video Inc; Cinema Concepts; MCA Home Video; Spotlite Video; Kartes Video Communications*

Man Who Loved Cat Dancing, The   1973
Western
80148   127 mins   C   B, V   P
Burt Reynolds, Sarah Miles, Jack Warden, Lee J Cobb, Jay Silverheels
A train robber falls in love with a woman he kidnaps after a heist.
MPAA:PG
Metro Goldwyn Mayer — *MGM/UA Home Video*

Man Who Loved Women, The   1983
Comedy
76030   118 mins   C   B, V   P
Burt Reynolds, Julie Andrews, Kim Basinger, Marilu Henner, Cynthia Sikes, Jennifer Edwards, directed by Blake Edwards
Burt Reynolds stars in this hilarious comedy about a Los Angeles sculptor whose reputation as a playboy leads him to a midlife crisis.
MPAA:R
Blake Edwards; Tony Adams — *RCA/Columbia Pictures Home Video*

Man Who Loved Women, The   1977
Romance
44779   119 mins   C   B, V   P
Charles Denner, Brigitte Fossey, Leslie Caron, directed by Francois Truffaut
An intelligent, sensitive bachelor worships all women. Trying to find the reasons for his obsession, he writes his memoirs and remembers all the women he has loved.
MPAA:R
Cinema 5 — *RCA/Columbia Pictures Home Video*

Man Who Saw Tomorrow, The   1981
Documentary/Occult sciences
84539   88 mins   C   B, V   P
Narrated by Orson Welles
An examination of the prophecies of Nostradamus and their reputed relevance today.

Robert Guenette; Lee Kramer; Paul Drane — *Warner Home Video*

Man Who Shot Liberty Valance, The
1962

Western
33715 122 mins B/W B, V, LV P
James Stewart, John Wayne, Vera Miles, Lee Marvin, Edmond O'Brien, Andy Devine, Woody Strode, directed by John Ford
Liberty Valance terrorizes a small western town and is opposed by only two men, one of whom unknowingly is given credit for killing him and eventually becomes a U.S. senator.
Paramount — *Paramount Home Video; RCA VideoDiscs*

Man Who Wasn't There, The
1983

Adventure/Comedy
82547 112 mins C B, V P
Steve Guttenberg, Jeffrey Tambor, Art Hindle, Lisa Langlois
A member of the State department receives a formula from a dying spy that can render him invisible. He has to use the formula to protect himself from the police and other spies, becoming a comic "Invisible Man."
MPAA:R
Paramount Pictures — *Paramount Home Video*

Man Who Would Be King, The
1975

Adventure
Closed Captioned
65500 129 mins C B, V, CED P
Sean Connery, Michael Caine
The two heroes are no ordinary jacks-of-trade. They have won honor fighting for the British Queen, yet found themselves adept at hustling strangers, blackmail, forging and assorted novel ways of earning money. Now that they've done it all, what else is left but to become kings?
MPAA:PG
Lorimar — *CBS/Fox Video*

Man with Bogart's Face, The
1980

Comedy
80731 106 mins C B, V P
Robert Sacchi, Misty Rowe, Sybil Danning, Franco Nero, Herbert Com, Victor Buono, Oivia Hussey
An actor who has undergone facial surgery to resemble Humphrey Bogart opens up his own private detective agency. Available in VHS and Beta Hi-Fi stereo.
MPAA:PG
Melvin Simon Prods. — *Key Video*

Man With One Red Shoe, The
1985

Comedy
Closed Captioned
82416 92 mins C B, V P
Tom Hanks, Dabney Coleman, Lori Singer, Carrie Fisher, Jim Belushi, Charles Durning
A lovable clod of a violinist ensnares himself in a web of intrigue when CIA agents, both good and evil, mistake him for a contact by his wearing one red shoe.
MPAA:PG
20th Century Fox — *CBS/Fox Video*

Man with the Golden Gun, The
1974

Adventure/Suspense
60582 125 mins C B, V, CED P
Roger Moore, Christopher Lee, Richard Loo, Britt Ekland, Maude Adams, Herve Villechaize, Clifton James
Roger Moore is the debonair secret agent 007 in this ninth James Bond flick, assigned to recover a small piece of equipment which can be utilized to harness the sun's energy.
MPAA:PG
United Artists — *CBS/Fox Video; RCA VideoDiscs*

Man with Two Brains, The
1983

Comedy
69310 91 mins C B, V, LV, CED P
Steve Martin, Kathleen Turner, David Warner, directed by Carl Reiner
A wacko brain surgeon marries a beautiful but coldhearted nymphomaniac but later falls in love with the brain of a young lady who has everything he desires—except a body.
MPAA:R
Aspen Society; William E McEuen and David Picker — *Warner Home Video*

Man Without a Star
1955

Western
76804 89 mins B/W B, V P
Kirk Douglas, Jeanne Crain, Claire Trevor, William Cambell, directed by King Vidor
A wandering cowboy helps the members of a ranch town fight off a ruthless cattle owner from taking over their land.
Universal; Aaron Rosenberg — *MCA Home Video*

Man, Woman and Child
1983

Drama
68248 100 mins C B, V P
Martin Sheen, Blythe Danner, Craig T. Nelson, David Hemmings
A typical American family is shocked when the child of an affair long ago appears at their door.
MPAA:PG

Paramount Pictures Corp — *Paramount Home Video*

Manchurian Avenger 1984
Western/Martial arts
70948   87 mins   C   B, V   P
Bobby Kim, Bill Wallace
Desperados have wrested control of a Colorado gold rush town from Joe Kim's family, but he'll put an end to that, chop chop.
MPAA:R
Independent — *THORN EMI/HBO Video*

Mandinga 1980
Drama
77391   100 mins   C   B, V   P
Anthony Gizmond, Maria R. Ruizzi
Passions in the old south heat up when a cruel plantation owner becomes involved in a sadomasochistic relationship with an alluring slave girl.
MPAA:R
S.E.F.I. — *Wizard Video*

Mandingo 1975
Drama
44596   127 mins   C   B, V, LV   P
James Mason, Susan George, Perry King, Richard Ward, Ken Norton, directed by Richard Fleischer
Based on the novel by Kyle Onstott, "Mandingo" portrays the brutal nature of slavery in the South. It deals with the tangled loves and hates of a family and their slaves. Heavyweight boxer Ken Norton makes his screen debut in the title role.
MPAA:R
Paramount, Dino De Laurentiis — *Paramount Home Video; RCA VideoDiscs*

Mango Tree, The 1977
Drama
79108   90 mins   C   B, V   P
Geraldine Fitzgerald, Robert Helpmann, Christopher Pate
A young man comes of age in a small town during the 1920's.
Satori Films — *VidAmerica*

Manhattan 1979
Comedy
79688   96 mins   B/W   B, V, LV   P
Woody Allen, Diane Keaton, Meryl Streep, Mariel Hemingway, Michael Murphy, directed by Woody Allen
A TV comedy writer has an affair with his best friend's wife and is also pursued by a seventeen year old girl.
MPAA:R
Jack Rollins; Charles H. Joffe — *MGM/UA Home Video*

Manhattan Baby 1982
Horror
84111   90 mins   C   B, V   P
Christopher Connelly, Martha Taylor, directed by Lucio Fulci
After a trip to Egypt, a young American girl acquires extra-sensory powers which cause the deaths of the people around her.
VIP Intl — *Lightning Video*

Manhattan Merry-Go-Round 1937
Musical
54183   89 mins   B/W   B, V   P
Cab Calloway, Louis Prima, Ted Lewis, Ann Dvorak, Phil Regan, Kay Thompson, Gene Autry, Joe DiMaggio
A slightly offbeat musical with a host of guest stars, about a gangster who acquires a record company.
Republic — *Video Connection; Hollywood Home Theater; Discount Video Tapes; See Hear Industries*

Manhattan Transfer in Concert 1983
Music-Performance
60571   58 mins   C   LV   P
The eclectic vocal group performs their mixture of pop, soul and jazz. Songs include "Operator," "Four Brothers," and "Gloria."
Ken Erhlich — *Pioneer Artists*

Manhunt 195?
Adventure
10035   25 mins   B/W   B, V   P, T
Kirby Grant, Gloria Winters, Ewing Mitchell
Frightened young man flees to Mexico believing he killed a classmate. Sky King seeks to tell him the truth—his classmate is alive. From the TV series "Sky King."
CBS — *Blackhawk Films*

Manhunt 1985
Adventure
76859   93 mins   C   B, V   P
Henry Silva, Mario Adorf, Woody Strode
A man marked for execution by the mob launches his own assault on the organization's headquarters.
Independent — *Media Home Entertainment*

Manhunt, The 1984
Western
84856   83 mins   C   B, V   P
Ernest Borgnine, Bo Svenson, John Ethan Wayne
A framed cowhand escapes from prison to prove his innocence.
Larry Ludman — *Media Home Entertainment*

Manhunt in the African Jungle — 1954
Adventure/Serials
33952   240 mins   B/W   B, V, 3/4U   P
Rod Cameron, Joan Marsh, Duncan Renaldo
An American undercover agent battles Nazi forces in Africa. A serial in fifteen episodes.
Republic — *Video Connection; Republic Pictures Home Video*

Manhunter — 1983
Crime-Drama
84135   90 mins   C   B, V   P
Earl Owensby, Johnny Popwell, Doug Hale, directed by Martin Beck
A mercenary undergoes the task of disengaging organized crime from high-level politics.
Earl Owensby — *Media Home Entertainment*

Maniac — 1981
Horror
59042   91 mins   C   B, V   P
Joe Spinell, Caroline Munro, Gail Lawrence
A psycho murderer slaughters and scalps his victims, adding the "trophies" to his collection. (This film carries a self-imposed equivalent X rating.)
Andrew Garroni — *Media Home Entertainment*

Maniac, The — 1963
Suspense
62807   86 mins   B/W   B, V   P
Kerwin Mathews, Nadia Gray, Donald Houston, Liliane Brousse
An American artist living in France becomes involved with the daughter of a cafe owner, not suspecting that murder will follow.
Columbia — *RCA/Columbia Pictures Home Video*

Maniac — 1978
Horror
87913   87 mins   C   B, V   P
Oliver Reed, Deborah Raffin, Stuart Whitman, Jim Mitchum, Edward Brett
A New York cop hunts down an arrow-shooting lunatic who endeavors to hold an entire Arizona town for ransom.
MPAA:PG
James V. Hart — *Embassy Home Entertainment*

Manions of America, The — 1981
Drama
82291   290 mins   C   B, V   P
Pierce Brosnan, Kate Mulgrew, Linda Purl, David Soul, Kathleen Beller, Simon MacCorkindale, directed by Joseph Sargent and Charles Dubin
This is the story of Rory O'Manion, a fiesty Irish patriot who leaves his native land during the potato famine of 1845 to settle in America.

Roger Gimbel; EMI-TV — *Prism*

Manipulator, The — 1971
Drama
84096   91 mins   C   B, V   P
Mickey Rooney, Luana Anders, Keenan Wynn
A deranged ex-movie-makeup-man kidnaps a young actress and holds her prisoner in a deserted Hollywood sound stage.
MPAA:R
Pierre Cosette — *Vestron Video*

Manon — 1982
Dance/Music-Performance
70952   112 mins   C   B, V   P
Jennifer Penny, Anthony Dowell, David Wall, Derek Rencher
Kenneth MacMillan's spectacular work for the Royal Ballet of London tells a sad tale of love, loss and poverty set in 18th century France. Jules Massenet's music is in Hi-Fi Stereo.
Covent Garden Video Productions — *THORN EMI/HBO Video*

Manon Lescaut — 1984
Music-Performance
81177   135 mins   C   B, V   P
Kirite Kanawa, Placido Domingo, Thomas Allen, conducted by Giuseppe Sinopoli
This is a performance of Puccini's opera about a pair of doomed lovers taped at London's Covent Garden. Available in VHS Hi-Fi and Beta Hi-Fi Stereo.
Gotz Friedrich — *THORN EMI/HBO Video*

Man's Best Friend — 1964
Cartoons
82363   51 mins   C   B, V   P
Animated
Here is a collection of nine cartoons, featuring such lovable canines as Cuddles, Snoozer, Duffy Dog and Dizzy.
Walter Lantz — *MCA Home Video*

Man's Land, A — 1932
Western
84842   65 mins   B/W   B, V   P
Hoot Gibson
A ranch needs savin', and Hoot's the guy to do it.
Universal — *United Home Video*

Manson — 1985
Documentary
81594   90 mins   C   B, V   P
This documentary examines the life and wild times of convicted murderer Charles Manson and his "Family".
Robert Hendrickson — *United Home Video*

Manu Dibango: King Makossa 1981
Music-Performance
84648   55 mins   C   B, V   P
The Camarounian artist Manu Dibango performs in Brussels. This Afro-pop concert features the saxophonist's biggest hit, 'Soul Makossa.' Recorded in Hi-Fi Stereo.
Belgium — V.I.E.W. Video

Many Adventures of Winnie the Pooh, The 1976
Cartoons
55565   74 mins   C   CED   P
Animated
This collection of stories from A.A. Milne's children's classic includes "Winnie the Pooh and the Honey Tree," "Winnie the Pooh and the Blustery Day," and "Winnie the Pooh and Tigger Too."
MPAA:G
Walt Disney — RCA VideoDiscs

Many Happy Returns 1968
Adventure/Fantasy
76920   50 mins   C   B, V   P
Patrick McGoohan
The Prisoner escapes and works his way back to London attempting to solve the riddle of the Village. An episode from "The Prisoner" TV series.
ITC — MPI Home Video

Maps to Stars' Homes Video 1984
Television/Theater
76016   60 mins   C   B, V   P
A guided tour through Beverly Hills. See the mansions of your favorite movie and TV stars.
Shokus Video Productions — Shokus Video

Maria's Lovers 1984
Drama
81057   103 mins   C   B, V   P
Nastassja Kinski, John Savage, Robert Mitchum, Keith Carradine, Bud Cort, Vincent Spano, Anita Morris
The wife of an impotent World War Two veteran succumbs to the charms of a rakish lady killer.
MPAA:R
Cannon Films — MGM/UA Home Video

Marathon 1980
Comedy-Drama
80242   100 mins   C   B, V   P
Bob Newhart, Herb Edelman, Dick Gautier, Anita Gillette, directed by Jackie Cooper
When a married accountant enters the New York City Marathon, he ends up falling in love with a young woman.
Alan Landsburg Productions — U.S.A. Home Video

Marathon Fever/Marathon Symphony/Winners/Losers 1977
Running/Sports-Winter
84274   52 mins   C   B, V   P
Films documenting marathon racing in running, bicycling and skiing. Three short films back to back on one tape.
Video Travel Inc — Video Travel

Marathon Man 1976
Drama
38599   125 mins   C   B, V, LV   P
Dustin Hoffman, Laurence Olivier, Marthe Keller, Roy Scheider, directed by John Schlesinger
Nightmarish thriller in which a marathon runner (Hoffman) becomes entangled in a plot involving a murderous Nazi fugitive (Olivier). Screenplay by William Goldman, based on his novel.
MPAA:R
Paramount — Paramount Home Video; RCA VideoDiscs

Marauder, The 1965
Adventure
88324   90 mins   C   B, V   P
Gordon Scott, Maria Canale, Franca Bettoya, directed by Louis Capuano
The prince of Venice leads an sea-faring onslaught against ransacking pirates and enemy fleets.
Liber Films — Force Video

Marbella 1985
Crime-Drama
88227   96 mins   C   B, V   P
Rod Taylor, Britt Ekland, directed by Miguel Hermoso
A luxury resort in Spain is the setting for a big caper-heist of three million dollars from a monarchial tycoon.
Calepas Int'l — Lightning Video

Marciano 1979
Drama/Biographical
87613   97 mins   C   B, V   P
Tony Lo Bianco, Vincent Gardenia, directed by Bernard L. Kowalski
A made-for-TV version of the great boxer's life.
ABC Circle Films; John G. Stephens — Charter Entertainment

Marco 1973
Adventure
75494   109 mins   C   B, V   P
Desi Arnaz Jr, Zero Mostel
This movie is a musical adventure of Marco Polo's life.
Tomorrow Entertainment — Prism

Marco Polo, Jr.   1972
Cartoons/Fantasy
69806   82 mins   C   B, V   P
Animated, voice by Bobby Rydell
Marco Polo, Jr., the daring descendant of the
legendary explorer, travels the world in search
of his destiny in this song-filled, feature-length
animated fantasy.
All and PAPI — *Family Home Entertainment*

Margin for Murder   1981
Mystery/Drama
80308   98 mins   C   B, V   P
*Kevin Dobson, Cindy Pickett, Donna Dixon,
Charles Hallahan*
Mike Hammer investigates a mysterious
accident that killed his best friend.
Hamner Productions — *Prism*

Marianela   197?
Drama
52793   113 mins   C   B, V   P
A disfigured peasant girl cares for a blind man,
and the two fall in love. She doesn't tell him
about her appearance until the day comes that
he regains his sight. In Spanish.
SP
Luis Sanz — *Media Home Entertainment*

Marie   1985
Drama
87371   113 mins   C   B, V   P
*Sissy Spacek, Jeff Daniels, John Cullum,
directed by Roger Donaldson*
In this true story, an idealistic woman becomes
the first female to head the Tennessee State
Board of Paroles and Pardons, and uncovers a
veritable nest of seething corruption. In VHS
and Beta Hi-Fi.
MPAA:PG-13
Dino De Laurentiis — *MGM/UA Home Video*

Marie Osmond: Exercises   1984
for Mothers-to-Be
Physical fitness/Pregnancy
80498   60 mins   C   B, V   P
Marie Osmond
Mom-to-be Marie Osmond demonstrates
physical therapist Elizabeth Nobel's exercise
program of gentle, no-strain toning movements.
Marie also shows expectant women how to
strengthen the essential childbirth muscles for
an easier pregnancy and delivery.
MGM UA; 3 West Productions — *MGM/UA
Home Video*

Marilyn Monroe   1964
Documentary/Biographical
52770   30 mins   C   B, V   P
Narrated by Mike Wallace
Marilyn Monroe's life from birth to death is
documented. An actual television interview and
news footage are included.
Fusco Entertainment — *Karl/Lorimar Home
Video*

Marilyn Monroe, Life   1963
Story of America's
Mystery Mistress
Documentary/Biographical
76991   30 mins   B/W   B, V   P
Narrated by Mike Wallace
The films and life of Maryilyn Monroe are
remembered in this documentary.
Art Lieberman — *Karl/Lorimar Home Video*

Marilyn: Say Goodbye to   1985
the President
Film-History/Documentary
86586   71 mins   C   B, V   P
A scathing documentary attempting to uncover
the circumstances of Marilyn Monroe's death,
with new testimony about Sen. Robert
Kennedy's involvement.
BBC — *Key Video*

Marius   1931
Comedy
06229   125 mins   B/W   B, V   P
*Raimo, Pierre Fresnay, directed by Marcel
Pagnol*
Marcel Pagnol wrote, produced, and directed
this trilogy about the lives, loves, joys, and
sorrows of the people of Provence, France.
Broadway play "Fanny" was adapted from this
trilogy. English subtitles.
FR
France — *Hollywood Home Theater; Discount
Video Tapes*

Marjoe   1972
Documentary/Biographical
65099   88 mins   C   B, V   P
*Marjoe Gortner, directed by Howard Smith and
Sarah Kernochan*
This documentary follows the career of rock-
style evangelist Marjoe Gortner, who spent 25
years of his life touring the country as a
professional preacher.
Academy Awards '72: Best Documentary.
MPAA:PG
Cinema 10 — *RCA/Columbia Pictures Home
Video*

Mark of Zorro, The   1920
Adventure
13738   91 mins   B/W   B, V   P, T
*Douglas Fairbanks, Marguerite De La Motte,
Noah Beery, directed by Fred Niblo*
Set to Gaylord Carter's score, Zorro, the famous
Mexican Robin Hood, crusades for the rights of
oppressed Mexicans.
United Artists — *Blackhawk Films; Discount
Video Tapes; Cable Films; Video Yesteryear;
Western Film & Video Inc; Movie Buff Video*

Mark Pauline: A Scenic Harvest — 1984
Video/Performing arts
84061 60 mins C B, V P
Directed by Mark Pauline
As a performance experiment by Survival Research Laboratories, 30 robotic systems clash in an arena, viewed by 2500 spectators.
Target Video — *Target Video*

Mark Pauline and Survival Research Laboratories — 1982
Video/Performing arts
84062 60 mins C B, V P
Directed by Mark Pauline
A collection of mechanical performance pieces from Pauline and S.R.L., including "Mysteries of the Reactionary Mind" and "A Cruel and Relentless Plot to Pervert the Flesh of Beasts to Unholy Uses."
Target Video — *Target Video*

Mark Twain Classics — 1982
Comedy
79676 90 mins C B, V P
Craig Wasson, Brooke Adams, Robert Lansing, Lance Kerwin 5 pgms
Five dramatizations of some of Mark Twain's best stories.
1. The Innocents Abroad 2. Life on the Mississippi 3. Pudd'nhead Wilson 4. The Mysterious Stranger 5. The Private History of a Campaign That Failed
The Great Amwell Company — *MCA Home Video*

Mark Twain's A Connecticut Yankee in King Arthur's Court — 1978
Comedy-Drama/Literature-American
58734 60 mins C B, V P
Richard Basehart, Roscoe Lee Brown, Paul Rudd
A man from Connecticut falls asleep and finds himself in King Arthur's Court.
WQED Pittsburgh — *Mastervision*

Marlon Brando — 1985
Biographical/Documentary
70998 120 mins C B, V P
Marlon Brando, directed by Claudio Masenza
This film portrays the life and career of Hollywood's most rebellious superstar.
Donatella Baglivio — *Kartes Video Communications*

Marooned — 1969
Science fiction
66011 134 mins C B, V P
Gregory Peck, David Janssen, Richard Crenna, James Franciscus, Gene Hackman, Lee Grant, directed by John Sturges
Three astronauts are stranded in space after a retro-rocket misfires. In stereo.
MPAA:G
Columbia — *RCA/Columbia Pictures Home Video*

Marriage and Divorce Test, The — 1981
Marriage/Divorce
57550 60 mins C B, V P
Hosted by Dr. Frank Field
Viewers can test their knowledge of divorce and marriage, and then find out the answers from experts in the field.
NBC; Don Luftig — *Karl/Lorimar Home Video*

Marriage is Alive and Well — 1980
Comedy
81259 97 mins C B, V P
Joe Namath, Jack Albertson, Judd Hirsch, Melinda Dillon, Ingrid Wang, direcred by Russ Mayberry
A free-wheeling wedding photographer's unusual assignments provide him with an intimate perspective on marriage. Available in VHS stereo and Beta Hi-Fi.
Lorimar Prods. — *U.S.A. Home Video*

Marriage of Figaro, The — 1973
Music-Performance
77456 168 mins C B, V P
Ileana Cotrubas, Frederica Von Stude, Kiri Te Kanawa, directed by Peter Hall
A production of the Mozart opera taped at the Glyndebourne Festival in Great Britain. With English subtitles.
IT
Southern Television — *Video Arts International*

Married Man, A — 1983
Drama
85403 210 mins C B, V P
Anthony Hopkins, Ciaran Madden, Lisa Hilboldt
A married guy starts to mess around on the side, and the results are murder! Made for TV.
John Davies — *U.S.A. Home Video*

Married Woman, The — 1964
Drama
70761 98 mins B/W B, V P
Macha Meril, Bernard Noel, Roger Leenhardt, directed by Jean-Luc Godard
This film chronicles twenty four hours in a woman's life in which she has sexual relations with both her husband and her lover. With English subtitles.
FR
Royal Films International — *Discount Video Tapes; Video Yesteryear*

Martha Graham: Three Contemporary Classics
1984

Dance
87936   120 mins   C   B, V   P
Terese Capucilli, Larry White, Takako Asakawa, Donlin Foreman
With music by Gian Carlo Menotti, Samuel Barber and Carl Nielsen, Graham's company performs three classic dance pieces: "Errand into the Maze," "Cave of the Heart" and "Acts of Light."
Martha Graham Dance Company — Video Arts International

Martha Raye Show, The
1955

Comedy/Variety
69576   60 mins   B/W   B, V, FO   P
Martha Raye, Cesar Romero, David Burns, Rocky Graziano, Will Jordan
This episode from Martha Raye's popular TV series takes the form of an hour-long story musical, with Martha being groomed for the leading role in a new movie. Originally telecast on December 13, 1955.
NBC — Video Yesteryear

Martian Chronicles III: The Martians, The
1980

Science fiction/Drama
79191   97 mins   C   B, V   P
Rock Hudson, Darren McGavin, Gayle Hunnicutt, Bernie Casey
The United States space program sends the first manned space flight to Mars in this adaptation of Ray Bradbury's novel.
Stonehenge; Charles Fries Productions — *U.S.A. Home Video*

Martian Chronicles, Part II-The Settlers, The
1980

Science fiction
75463   97 mins   C   B, V   P
Rock Hudson, Bernadette Peters, Gayle Hunnicutt
The settlers are trying to make a new life on this strange world while the martians keep watchful eyes on them.
King Features — U.S.A. Home Video

Martian Chronicles, Volume I: The Expeditions, The
1980

Science fiction
66618   100 mins   C   B, V   P
Rock Hudson, Fritz Weaver, Roddy McDowall
The first segment of Ray Bradbury's story collection about the first American explorers to land on the planet Mars.
Charles Fries Productions — *U.S.A. Home Video*

Martin
1977

Horror
65509   96 mins   C   B, V   P
John Amplas, Lincoln Maazel, directed by George Romero
Martin is a charming young man, though slightly mad. He freely admits the need to drink blood. This contemporary vampire has found a new abhorrent means of killing his victims.
MPAA:R
Richard Rubinstein — *THORN EMI/HBO Video*

Martin Luther, His Life and Time
1924

Christianity
42958   101 mins   B/W   B, V, FO   P
This program traces the birth and youth of Luther and the great reformation within the church, examining both Luther the man and the church figure. Silent with musical score.
Lutheran Film Div — *Video Yesteryear*

Martin Mull Presents the History of White People in America
1985

Satire
81819   48 mins   C   B, V   P
Martin Mull, Fred Willard, Mary Kay Place, Teri Garr, Bob Eubanks, directed by Harry Shearer
This is a pseudo-documentary look at the complicated life of a white midwestern family. Available in VHS and Beta Hi-Fi Stereo.
Universal Pay TV Programming — *MCA Home Video*

Martin's Day
1985

Drama
Closed Captioned
82098   99 mins   C   B, V   P
Richard Harris, Justin Henry, Lindsay Wagner, James Coburn, Karen Black
An unusual friendship develops between an escaped convict and the young boy he kidnaps. Available in VHS and Beta Hi-Fi.
MPAA:PG
United Artists — *CBS/Fox Video*

Marty
1955

Drama
37526   91 mins   B/W   B, V, LV, CED   P
Ernest Borgnine, Betsy Blair, Joe De Santis, Ester Minciotti, Jerry Paris, Karen Steele, directed by Delbert Mann
Ernest Borgnine's sensitive portrayal of Marty, a butcher from the Bronx, won him an Oscar. Marty is a painfully shy bachelor who feels trapped in a pointless life of family squabbles; when he finds love he also finds the strength to break out of what he feels is a meaningless existence.

Academy Awards '55: Best Production; Best Actor (Borgnine); Best Direction (Mann); Best Screenplay (Paddy Chayefsky).
United Artists — *CBS/Fox Video*

Marty/A Wind from the South   1953
Drama
65013   118 mins   B/W   B, V   P
Rod Steiger, Nancy Marchand, Julie Harris
Two classic original television dramas from the early 1950's are combined on this tape: Paddy Chayevsky's "Marty" with Rod Steiger as a lonely Bronx butcher; and James Costigan's "A Wind from the South," featuring Julie Harris as a romance-hungry Irish lass.
NBC; Fred Coe — *MGM/UA Home Video*

Marvel Comics Video   1985
Library
Adventure/Cartoons
82126   60 mins   C   B, V   P
Animated   24   pgms
Marvel Comics' incredible heroes and villains leap into animated life in these one-hour tapes. Each tape contains one major episode plus one or more entertaining bonus adventures.
1.Spider-Man 2.Doctor Doom 3.Captain America 4.Magneto 5.The Incredible Hulk 6.The Fly 7.The Fantastic Four 8.The Sandman 9.Iron Man 10.Doctor Octopus 11.The Thing 12.The Vulture 13.Spider-Woman 14.Mole Man 15.Sub-Mariner 16.The Green Goblin 17.The Mighty Thor 18.The Red Skull 19.Spider Man, Volume II 20.The Mighty Thor, Volume II 21.Captain America, Volume II 22.The Fantastic Four, Volume II 23.Spider Woman, Volume II 24.The Incredible Hulk, Volume II
Marvel Productions — *Prism*

Marvelous Land of Oz,   1982
The
Musical/Fantasy
47422   104 mins   C   B, V   P
The Children's Theater Company of Minneapolis
L. Frank Baum's sequel to "The Wonderful Wizard of Oz" picks up the story of the Scarecrow and Tin Woodman after Dorothy returns home to Kansas. This original musical production was taped live especially for video. VHS in stereo.
Television Theater Co — *MCA Home Video*

Marvin and Tige   1984
Drama
82251   104 mins   C   B, V   P
John Cassavetes, Gibran Brown, Billy Dee Williams, Fay Hauser, Denise Nicholas-Hill
A deep friendship develops between an alcoholic advertising executive and a street-wise eleven-year-old boy after they meet one night in an Atlanta park.
MPAA:PG

Quartet Films — *Embassy Home Entertainment*

Marvin Mitchelson on   1984
Divorce
Divorce
72902   47 mins   C   B, V   P
Marvin Mitchelson
The noted divorce lawyer discusses all aspects of divorce in a question and answer format.
Media Home Entertainment — *Media Home Entertainment*

Mary and Joseph   1979
Drama
79193   147 mins   C   B, V   P
Blanche Baker, Colleen Dewhurst, Lloyd Bochner, Stephen McHattie
How the lives of Mary and Joseph were affected by the arrival of Jesus Christ is portrayed in this dramatization.
Lorimar — *U.S.A. Home Video*

Mary Hartman, Mary   1976
Hartman Volume I
Comedy/Satire
78348   70 mins   C   B, V, LV   P
Louise Lasser, Debralee Scott, Mary Kay Place, Greg Mullavey, Martin Mull
Here are three episodes from Norman Lear's satirical soap opera that evolves around the lives of the inhabitants of Fernwood, Ohio.
Embassy Television — *Embassy Home Entertainment*

Mary of Scotland   1936
Drama
00263   123 mins   B/W   B, V, 3/4U   P
Katharine Hepburn, Fredric March, directed by John Ford
The historical tragedy of Mary, Queen of Scots and her cousin, Queen Elizabeth I of England is enacted in this classic film.
RKO; Pandro S Berman — *Nostalgia Merchant; Blackhawk Films*

Mary Poppins   1964
Musical
54464   140 mins   C   B, V   P
Julie Andrews, Dick Van Dyke, David Tomlinson, Glynis Johns, directed by Robert Stevenson
A magical English nanny arrives one day on the East Wind and takes over the household of a very proper London banker. She changes the lives of everyone, especially his two naughty children. From her they learn the wonders of life and how to make it enjoyable for themselves and others. Based on the novel by P. L. Travers.
Academy Awards '64: Best Actress (Andrews); Best Musical Score; Best Film Editing; Best Song ("Chim Chim Cher-ee"). EL, SP

(For explanation of codes, see Use Guide and Key)

THE VIDEO TAPE & DISC GUIDE

Walt Disney — *Walt Disney Home Video; RCA VideoDiscs*

Mary Stuart 1984
Opera
73655 180 mins C B, V P
Dame Janet Baker, Rosalind Plowright
Donizetti's powerful opera about Mary, Queen of Scots, is performed by the English National Opera at the London Coliseum.
BBC-TV — *Kartes Video Communications; THORN EMI/HBO Video*

Mary Tyler Moore Show, 197? Vol. I, The
Comedy
52604 102 mins C CED P
Mary Tyler Moore, Ed Asner, Gavin McLeod, Ted Knight, Valerie Harper, Cloris Leachman
Four classic episodes from the memorable series which ran from 1970 to 1977: "Love Is All Around," the first episode, aired September 17, 1970; "The Final Show," the final episode, aired March 19, 1977; "Put on a Happy Face," aired February 24, 1973; and "Chuckles Bites the Dust," aired October 25, 1975. All four episodes won Emmys in various categories.
Emmy Awards: Outstanding Writing in a Comedy Series Single Episode '75-'76 ("Chuckles Bites the Dust"), '76-'77 ("The Final Show").
MTM Prods — *RCA VideoDiscs*

Mary White 1977
Drama/Biographical
81099 102 mins C B, V P
Ed Flanders, Kathleen Beller, Tim Matheson, Donald Moffatt, Fionnula Flanagan, directed by Jud Taylor
This is the true story of Mary White; the daughter of a newspaper editor who rejected her life of wealth and set out to find her own identity.
Emmy Awards '77: Outstanding Writing in a Special Program—Adaptation (Carol Ledner).
Radnitz/Mattel Productions — *Paramount Home Video*

Masada 1981
Drama
50652 131 mins C B, V P
Peter O'Toole, Peter Strauss, Barbara Carrera, Anthony Quayle, Giulia Pagano, David Warner, directed by Boris Sagal
Based on Ernest K. Gann's novel "The Antagonists," this dramatization recreates the first-century A.D. Roman siege of the fortress Masada, headquarters for a group of Jewish freedom fighters. This version is abridged from the original television presentation. Musical score by Jerry Goldsmith.
MCA TV; Arnon Milchan Prods — *MCA Home Video*

M*A*S*H 1970
Comedy
08464 116 mins C B, V, LV P
Donald Sutherland, Elliot Gould, Tom Skerritt, Sally Kellerman, JoAnn Pflug, Robert Duvall, directed by Robert Altman
A pair of surgeons at a Mobile Army Surgical Hospital in Korea create havoc with their late-night parties, and their practical jokes pulled on the nurses and other doctors.
MPAA:R
20th Century Fox; Aspen — *CBS/Fox Video*

M*A*S*H: Goodbye, 1983 Farewell and Amen
Comedy-Drama
64303 120 mins C B, V, LV, CED P
Alan Alda, Mike Farrell, Harry Morgan, David Ogden Stiers, Loretta Swit, Jamie Farr, William Christopher
The final two-hour special episode of the TV series "M*A*S*H" follows Hawkeye, BJ, Col. Potter, Charles, Margaret, Klinger, Father Mulcahy and the rest of the men and women of the 4077th through the final days of the Korean War, the declaration of peace, the dismantling of the camp, and the fond and tearful farewells.
20th Century-Fox Television — *CBS/Fox Video*

Mask 1985
Drama
Closed Captioned
70864 120 mins C B, V, LV P
Cher, Sam Elliot, Eric Stoltz, directed by Peter Bogdanovich
This film dramatizes the life of Rocky Dennis, a young Californian afflicted with craniodiaphyseal dysplasia. The boy overcomes his grotesque appearance and revels in the joys of life with his extended adoptive family of colorful bikers. In Hi-Fi Mono.
MPAA:PG-13
Universal — *MCA Home Video*

Mask 1985
Cartoons
Closed Captioned
71050 44 mins C B, V P
Animated
Each cassette in this series features two episodes of the popular Saturday morning TV series. The cartoons depict battles of good and evil waged on amazing vehicles between the forces of "Mask" and "Venom."
DIC Audio-Visuel — *Karl/Lorimar Home Video*

Masked Marvel, The 1943
Adventure/Serials
07337 195 mins B/W B, V, 3/4U P
William Forrest, Louise Currie, Johnny Arthur

A serial in which the Masked Marvel saves America's war industries from sabotage. In twelve episodes.
Republic — *Video Connection; Republic Pictures Home Video*

Masque of the Red Death, The   1965
Horror
84101   88 mins   C   B, V   P
Vincent Price, Hazel Court, Jane Asher, directed by Roger Corman
An integral selection in the famous E.A. Poe/Corman Canon, it deals with an evil prince who traffics with the devil and playfully murders any of his subjects not already dead of the plague. Photographed by Nicholas Roeg.
Alta Vista — *Lightning Video*

Masquerade Party   1955
Game show
85520   30 mins   B/W   B, V   P
Ogden Nash, Buff Cobb, Ilka Chase, Duke Ellington, Rex Marshall
An episode of the popular show wherein celebrities wear make up and contestants have to guess who they are.
ABC — *Video Yesteryear*

Mass Appeal   1984
Drama
Closed Captioned
80849   99 mins   C   B, V, LV   P
Jack Lemmon, Zeljko Ivanek, CHarles Durning, Louise Latham, James Ray, Sharee Gregory
An adaptation of the Bill C. Davis play about the ideological debate between a young seminarian and a complacent but successful parish pastor.
MPAA:PG
Operation Cork Productions — *MCA Home Video*

Massacre at Fort Holman   1973
Adventure
58553   92 mins   C   B, V   R, P
James Coburn, Telly Savalas, Bud Spencer
Seven condemned men are given a chance to live, if they can survive a suicide mission in the Southwest desert. Also known as "A Reason to Live, A Reason to Die."
MPAA:PG
Heritage Enterprises — *Video Gems; World Video Pictures*

Massacre At Fort Holman   1973
Western
80790   92 mins   C   B, V   R, P
James Coburn, Telly Savalas, Bud Spencer
Two rival gangs fight for control of a Missouri fort in the early days of the Civil War.
MPAA:PG

Heritage Enterprises — *World Video Pictures; Video Gems*

Massacre in Rome   1973
War-Drama
70965   110 mins   C   B, V   P
Richard Burton, Marcello Mastroianni
This film dramatizes an incident from World War II wherin Nazi soldiers executed 320 Italian partisans in response to an attack on a German police patrol.
MPAA:PG
Champion Cinematografica — *THORN EMI/HBO Video*

Massive Retaliation   1985
Exploitation/Adventure
71123   90 mins   C   B, V, LV, CED   P
Peter Donat, Karlene Crockett, Jason Gedrick, Michael Pritchard, directed by Thomas A. Cohen
Here comes World War III! And with it, the hordes of pesky, villagers seeking refuge within the secluded safety of a family's country house.
Massive Productions — *Vestron Video*

Mastectomy (Rehabilitation and Injury)   1978
Physical fitness
52758   30 mins   C   B, V   P
Hosted by Ann Dugan
Exercises for women who have had a mastectomy, including both specific-area and total-body movements to gradually improve muscle tone. Part of the "Rehabilitation and Injury" series.
Health 'N Action. — *RCA/Columbia Pictures Home Video*

Master Class   1985
Martial arts
81264   60 mins   C   B, V   P
Sho Kosugi
The star of the "Ninja" movies demonstrates basic martial arts techniques in this videocassette presentation. Available in VHS Stereo and Beta Hi-Fi.
Trans World Entertainment — *U.S.A. Home Video*

Master Cooking Course, The   1984
Cookery
77216   57 mins   C   B, V   P
Master chefs Craig Claiborne and Pierre Franey offer a step by step guide to the techniques of gourmet cooking.
MCA Home Video — *MCA Home Video*

Master Harold and the Boys   1984

Drama
85097   90 mins   C   B, V   P
Matthew Broderick
This is a made-for-cable production of the play about a South African, rich white boy and his relationship with two black servants.
Iris Merlis — *Karl/Lorimar Home Video*

Master Key, The   1944

Serials
81367   169 mins   B/W   B, V   P
Jane Wiley, Milburn Stone, Alfred La Rue, Dennis Moore
Here are thirteen complete chapters of this action-adventure serial.
Universal — *Discount Video Tapes; Captain Bijou*

Master Killer (The Thirty Sixth Chamber)   1984

Martial arts
71250   109 mins   C   B, V   P
Liu Chia Hui, directed by Liu Chia Liang
Master Killers are made, not born. This film follows Lui's training as he readies himself for an attack on the brutal Manchu assassins.
MPAA:R
World Northal; Mona Fang — *Embassy Home Entertainment*

Master Mind   1973

Comedy
47676   86 mins   C   B, V   P
Zero Mostel, Keiko Kishi, Brad Dillman, Herbert Berghof, Frankie Sakai
A renowned Japanese super sleuth attempts to solve the theft of a sophisticated midget android.
Malcolm Stewart — *Unicorn Video*

Master of Kung Fu   1977

Martial arts
82348   88 mins   C   B, V   P
Yu Chan Yuan, Chi Hsiao Fu
A Kung Fu instructor calls upon his former teacher to help him fend off loan sharks who want to take over his school. Available in VHS and Beta Hi-Fi.
Sacon — *Key Video*

Master of the House   1925

Drama
42956   118 mins   B/W   B, V, FO   P
Directed by Carl Theodore Dreyer
Also known as "Thou Shalt Honour They Wife," this program is the story of a spoiled husband, a type extinct in this country but still in existence abroad. Silent with titles in English.
Unknown — *Video Yesteryear*

Master of the World   1961

Horror
78138   95 mins   C   B, V   P
A visionary tale of a fanatical 19th-century inventor who uses his wonderous flying fortress as an antiwar weapon.
Warner Home Video — *Warner Home Video*

Master Touch, The   1974

Mystery
80309   96 mins   C   B, V   P
Kirk Douglas, Florinda Bolkan, Giuliano Gemma
When a legendary safe cracker is released from prison, he attempts one last heist at a Hamburg insurance company.
MPAA:PG
Warner Bros. — *Prism*

Masters of the Game   1986

Sports
85013   53 mins   C   B, V   P
Pete Rose
The first program in this instructive sports series is entitled, "Pete Rose: Winning Baseball." Subsequent programs include tips on football, golf, soccer and tennis.
EL, SP
Champion Sports Video — *Video Gems*

Mata Hari   1985

War-Drama
71161   105 mins   C   B, V   P
Sylvia Kristel, Christopher Cazenove, Oliver Tobias, directed by Curtis Cunningham
This film tells the racy story of World War I's most notorious spy. Ms. Hari uses her seductive beauty to toy with the leaders of Europe.
MPAA:R
Cannon — *MGM/UA Home Video*

Matilda   1978

Comedy
64356   103 mins   C   B, V, CED   P
Elliot Gould, Robert Mitchum, Harry Guardino, Clive Revill
An entrepreneur decides to manage a boxing kangaroo, which nearly succeeds in defeating the world heavyweight champion.
MPAA:PG
American International — *Vestron Video*

Matrimaniac, The   1916

Comedy
66138   48 mins   B/W   B, V, FO   P
Douglas Fairbanks, Constance Talmadge
A man goes to great lengths to marry a woman against her father's wishes. Silent with music score.
Artcraft Paramount — *Video Yesteryear*

Matter of Life and Death, A — 19??

Drama
78364   98 mins   C   B, V   P
Linda Lavin, Tyne Daly, Salome Jens, Ramon Bieri
A true story of a nurse who dedicated her life to treating the terminally ill with honesty and respect.
Big Deal Inc; Raven's Claw Productions — U.S.A. Home Video

Matter of Time, A — 1976

Musical/Romance
64888   97 mins   C   B, V, CED   P
Liza Minnelli, Ingrid Bergman, Charles Boyer, directed by Vincente Minnelli
A young woman relives the flamboyant past of an aging contessa.
MPAA:PG
American International Pictures — Vestron Video

Mausoleum — 1983

Horror
66269   96 mins   C   B, V, CED   P
Only one man can save a woman from eternal damnation.
MPAA:R
Jerry Zimmerman; Michael Franzese — Embassy Home Entertainment

Maverick Queen, The — 1955

Western
74486   90 mins   C   B, V   P
Barbara Stanwyck, Barry Sullivan
This is the story of a Pinkerton detective who infiltrates the "Wild Bunch" by becoming involved with a woman who knows them.
Republic — Republic Pictures Home Video

Max Dugan Returns — 1983

Comedy-Drama
65329   98 mins   C   B, V, LV, CED   P
Jason Robards, Marsha Mason, Donald Sutherland
An ex-con comes home from prison to visit his daughter, carrying a suitcase full of stolen money.
MPAA:PG
Herbert Ross — CBS/Fox Video

Max Fleischer's Popeye Cartoons — 1939

Cartoons
85925   56 mins   C   B, V   P
A compilation of three classic color Popeye two-reelers from the late 30's, wherein Popeye meets Ali Baba, Aladdin and Sindbad the the Sailor.
Max Fleischer — Spotlite Video

Max Maven's Mindgames — 1984

Magic
70155   56 mins   C   B, V   P
Magician Max Maven performs mindgames with the use of playing cards, signs and symbols and magic with money in such settings as Las Vegas, a tropical jungle, the moon and an operating room.
Mark Nelson and Bruce Seth Green — MCA Home Video

Max Roach — 1981

Music-Performance
75899   19 mins   C   B, V   P
This program presents the jazz music of Max Roach featuring the compositions "Six Bits Blues" and "Effie."
Jazz America Ltd — Sony Video Software

Max Roach: In Concert/In Session — 1985

Music-Performance
87931   60 mins   C   B, V   P
Roach demonstrates his playing ability first in the studio, then in an appearance at the 1982 Kool Jazz Festival.
Axis Video — DCI Music Video

Maxie — 1985

Comedy
86263   98 mins   C   B, V   P
Glenn Close, Ruth Gordon, Mandy Patinkin
The precocious ghost of a fun-loving flapper inhabits the body of a modern day secretary, creating havoc with her life and her spouse.
MPAA:PG
Carter De Haven — THORN EMI/HBO Video

Maya Deren, Volume I: Experimental Films — 1959

Film-Avant-garde
86474   76 mins   B/W   B, V   P
The complete oeuvre of the grande dame of American avant-gardism, down to her ground-breaking surrealist roots, "Meshes of the Afternoon;" also including "At Land," "A Study In Choreography for the Camera," "Ritual in Transfigured Time," "Meditation on Violence" and "The Very Eye of Night."
AM Available
Maya Deren — Mystic Fire Video

Maya Deren, Vol. II: Divine Horsemen — 1951

Film-Avant-garde
86475   52 mins   B/W   B, V   P
A chronicle of Deren's journey to Haiti, her analysis of Haitian drama, and finally her initiation into ritual voodoo mysticism. The film was never finished in her lifetime; music by Teiji Ito.
AM Available

Maya Deren; Teiji & Cherel Ito — *Mystic Fire Video*

Mayerling 1937
Drama
11246   95 mins   B/W   B, V, FO   P
Charles Boyer, Danielle Darrieux
Based on the tragic and hopeless affair between the Crown Prince Rudolph of Hapsburg and young Baroness Marie Vetsera.
FR
Nero Films — *Video Yesteryear; Discount Video Tapes*

Mayfair Bank Caper, The 1979
Suspense
86192   110 mins   C   B, V   P
David Niven, Richard Jordan, Elke Sommer, Gloria Grahame
A big caper is planned by an ex-convict working in a national securities firm and a mobster named Ivan the Terrible. Also titled "A Nightingale Sang in Berkeley Square."
British — *VidAmerica*

Maytime 1937
Musical
82116   132 mins   B/W   B, V   P
Jeanette MacDonald, Nelson Eddy, John Barrymore, Tom Brown
An opera singer is reunited with her true love after she left him to marry her teacher seven years earlier.
MGM — *MGM/UA Home Video*

Mazda GLC, 626, RX 7 1986
Automobiles
88405   60 mins   C   B, V, 3/4U   P
3 pgms
Three tapes on how to maintain and tune-up the three Mazda engines.
Peter Allen Prod. — *Peter Allen Video Productions*

Maze 1984
Music-Performance
76674   20 mins   C   B, V   P
This program presents a combination of jazz and mellow funk.
Capitol Records Inc — *Sony Video Software*

Maze Featuring Frankie Beverly 1982
Music-Performance
47813   ? mins   C   LV   P
Maze, masters of mellow funk, perform their hits including "Joy and Pain," "Happy Feelin's," "Southern Girl," and "Feel That You're Feelin'." In stereo.
Unknown — *Pioneer Artists*

McCabe and Mrs. Miller 1971
Western
51966   107 mins   C   B, V   P
Warren Beatty, Julie Christie, William Devane, Keith Carradine, Shelley Duvall, directed by Robert Altman
A gambler and a madam operate a thriving brothel and gambling house in a frontier mining town.
Warner Bros — *Warner Home Video*

McQ 1974
Crime-Drama
51961   116 mins   C   B, V   P
John Wayne, Eddie Albert, Diana Muldaur, Clu Gulager
After several big dope dealers kill two police officers, a lieutenant resigns to track them down.
MPAA:PG
Warner Bros — *Warner Home Video*

McVicar 1980
Drama
65604   90 mins   C   B, V   P
Roger Daltrey, Adam Faith
A brutish and realistic depiction of crime and punishment based on the life of the professional John McVicar. In stereo VHS and Beta Hi-Fi.
MPAA:R
Bill Curbishley; Roy Baird; Roger Daltrey — *Vestron Video*

Mean Dog Blues 1978
Drama
79675   108 mins   C   B, V   P
George Kennedy, Kay Lenz, Scatman Crothers, Tina Louise, William Windom
A musician is convicted of hit and run driving after hitching a ride with an inebriated politician.
MPAA:PG
Bing Crosby Productions — *Vestron Video; Lightning Video*

Mean Frank and Crazy Tony 1976
Drama/Adventure
71316   92 mins   C   B, V   P
Lee Van Cleef, Tony LoBianco, directed by Michael Lupo
The mob decides to eliminate an international crime lord. The big chief enlists the aide of a tough street punk to thwart their efforts.
MPAA:R
Dino De Laurentis — *U.S.A. Home Video*

Mean Johnny Barrows 1975
Crime-Drama
47671   83 mins   C   B, V   P
Fred Williamson, Roddy McDowell, Stuart Whitman, Luther Adler, Jenny Sherman, Elliot Gould

When Johnny Barrows returns to his home town after being dishonorably discharged from the Army he is offered a job as a gang hitman.
Fred Williamson — *Unicorn Video*

Mean Machine, The   1973
Adventure
66196   89 mins   C   B, V   P
Chris Mitchum, Barbara Bouchet, Arthur Kennedy
One man tries to get even with the mob.
MPAA:R
Tecisa Madrid — *Monterey Home Video*

Mean Season, The   1985
Drama/Suspense
81176   106 mins   C   B, V   P
Kurt Russell, Mariel Hemingway, Richard Jordan, Richard Masur, Andy Garcia, directed by Phillip Borsos
A Miami reporter hooks onto the story of his career when a mysterious man agrees to give him the grisly details of a series of murders he has committed. Available in Hi-Fi sound for both formats.
MPAA:R
Orion Pictures — *THORN EMI/HBO Video*

Mean Streets   1973
Drama
Closed Captioned
80441   112 mins   C   B, V   P
Robert DeNiro, Harvey Keitel, Amy Robinson, Richard Romanus, directed by Martin Scorsese
A New York City street punk who owes a loan shark a great deal of money, asks his buddy, a low echelon Mafioso, to act on his behalf.
MPAA:R
Jonathan Taplin; Warner Bros — *Warner Home Video*

Meat Loaf Live!   1984
Music-Performance
88032   60 mins   P
The porcine rock vocalist belts out his hit oeuvre: "Paradise by the Dashboard Light," "Modern Girl" and "Bat Out of Hell."
Vestron Video — *Vestron Video*

Meatballs   1979
Comedy
44915   92 mins   C   B, V   P
Bill Murray, Harvey Atkin, Kate Lynch
The Activities Director at a summer camp who is supposed to organize fun for everyone prefers his own style of "fun."
MPAA:PG
Paramount — *Paramount Home Video; Vestron Video (disc only)*

Meatballs Part II   1984
Comedy
Closed Captioned
80376   87 mins   C   B, V   P
Pee Wee Herman, Kim Richards, Misty Rowe, Richard Mulligan, Hamiliton Camp
The future of Camp Sasquatch is in danger unless the camp's best fighter can beat Camp Patton's champ in a boxing match. Available in VHS and Beta Hi-Fi.
MPAA:PG
Tri Star Pictures — *RCA/Columbia Pictures Home Video*

Mechanic, The   1972
Adventure
64901   100 mins   C   B, V   P
Charles Bronson, Jan-Michael Vincent, Keenan Wynn, Jill Ireland, Linda Ridgeway
Bronson stars as Arthur Bishop, a wealthy professional killer for a powerful organization. He has innumerable ways to kill.
MPAA:PG
United Artists — *CBS/Fox Video*

Medea   1970
Drama
81946   118 mins   C   B, V   P
Maria Callas, Giuseppi Gentile, Laurent Terzieff, directed by Pier Paolo Pasolini
This is an adaptation of the Euripides play about the woman who helped Jason steal the Golden Fleece. In Italian with English subtitles.
IT
New Line Cinema — *Video Arts International*

Medea   197?
Dance
87356   70 mins   C   B, V   P
Marina Goderdzishvili, Vladimir Julukhadze
A free adaptation of the Euripides drama for ballet.
Russian — *Kultur*

Mediterranean in Flames,   1972
The
Drama/Adventure
71308   85 mins   C   B, V   P
Costas Precas, Costas Karras, Olga Politon, Dimis Dadiras
Through valiant treachery and seduction, Greek resistance fighters turn the tables on World War II Nazis.
Olympos Films — *U.S.A. Home Video*

Medium, The   1951
Opera
78961   80 mins   B/W   B, V   P
Marie Powers, Anna Maria Alberghetti, Leo Coleman, Written and directed by Gian-Carlo Menotti
A phony medium is done in by her own trickery in this filmed version of the Menotti opera.

Walter Lowendahl — *Video Arts International*

Medium Cool 1969

Drama
66036   111 mins   C   B, V   P
Robert Forster, Verna Bloom, Peter Bonerz, Marianna Hill, directed by Haskell Wexler
This commentary on life in the '60s focuses on a TV news cameraman and his growing apathy with the events around him.
MPAA:X
Paramount — *Paramount Home Video*

Medusa 1974

Suspense
82214   103 mins   C   B, V   P
George Hamilton, Cameron Mitchell, Lucianna Paluzzi, Theodroe Roubanis
A bizarre series of events occur when an abandoned yacht is found on the Aegean Sea containing two lifeless bodies.
Rossanne Productions — *Prism*

Meet Dr. Christian 1939

Drama
11765   72 mins   B/W   B, V   P
Jean Hersholt, Robert Baldwin
The good old doctor settles some problems.
RKO; William Stephens — *Discount Video Tapes; Movie Buff Video; Video Yesteryear*

Meet John Doe 1941

Drama
54039   135 mins   B/W   B, A   P
Gary Cooper, Barbara Stanwyck, Edward Arnold, James Gleason, directed by Frank Capra
An unemployed, down and out man is selected to represent the "typical American" because of his honesty. Unfortunately, he finds that he is being used to further the careers of corrupt politicians.
Warner Bros, Frank Capra — *Movie Buff Video; Prism; Hal Roach Studios; Kartes Video Communications; Media Home Entertainment; Hollywood Home Theater; Cinema Concepts; VCII; Care Video Productions; Video Connection; Video Yesteryear; Discount Video Tapes; Western Film & Video Inc; United Home Video*

Meet John Doe 1941

Drama
71028   130 mins   C   B, V   P
Gary Cooper, Barbara Stanwyck, Edward Arnold, James Gleason, directed by Frank Capra
This release of Capra's honest-man-versus-the-evil-bureaucracy story has been enhanced through the Colorization process.
Warner Bros; Frank Capra — *Hal Roach Studios*

Meet Marcel Marceau 1965

Mime
42974   52 mins   C   B, V, FO   P
Marcel Marceau
The most famous contemporary pantomimist, Marcel Marceau himself does voice-over introductions of various skits including his popular character, "Bip," and special tributes to Harpo Marx, Buster Keaton, and Charlie Chaplin.
Unknown — *Video Yesteryear*

Meet Me in St. Louis 1944

Musical
44644   113 mins   C   B, V   P
Judy Garland, Margaret O'Brien, Mary Astor, Tom Drake, June Lockhart, Harry Davenport, directed by Vincente Minnelli
Wonderful music sets the mood for this charming tale of a family in St. Louis and the 1903 World's Fair. Judy Garland sings the title song "Trolley Song," along with "The Boy Next Door" and "Have Yourself a Merry Little Christmas."
MGM — *MGM/UA Home Video*

Meet Mr. Washington/Meet Mr. Lincoln 196?

Presidency-US
58811   79 mins   C   CED   P
Two award-winning shows from the NBC series, "Project Twenty." "Meet Mr. Washington," tells the story of George Washington through his own words as well as letters and diaries of contemporaries and newspapers of the time. "Meet Mr. Lincoln," portrays Abe Lincoln as his contemporaries saw him.
NBC — *RCA VideoDiscs*

Meet the Band Leaders, Vol. 101 1985

Music
84000   46 mins   B/W   B, V   P
Count Basie, Lionel Hampton, Duke Ellington and their Orchestras
Three short featurettes from 1964-65, which highlight latter-day editions of several great big bands. Tunes performed include: "Broadway," "Cute," "Rockin' in Rhythm," "April in Paris," "Jumpin' at the Woodside" and "Satin Doll." Johnny Hodges and Lawrence Brown take solos during the Ellington segment.
Swingtime Video — *Swingtime Video*

Meet the Band Leaders, Vol. 102 1985

Music
84001   53 mins   B/W   B, V   P
Harry James, Si Zentner, Ralph Marterie and their Orchestras, Ray McKinley and The Glen Miller Orchestra

Four famous big bands are featured in musical programs taped in 1965. Musical selections include: "I'm Beginning to See the Light," "String of Pearls," "Rhapsody in Blue," "Little Brown Jug" and "Sentimental Journey." Buddy Rich and Corky Corcoran are given solo spots during the Harry James segment.
Swingtime Video — *Swingtime Video*

Meet the Band Leaders,   1985
Vol. 103
Music
84002   53 mins   B/W   B, V   P
Tex Beneke, Ralph Flanagan, Les and Larry Elgart, Vaughn Monroe and their Orchestras, Ray Eberle, Paula Kelly and the Modernaires
Another group of four popular big bands are seen in 1965 taped appearances. Tex Beneke plays a selection of Glenn Miller hits, Vaughn Monroe sings his 40's favorites, Ralph Flanagan presents his Miller-styled music and the Elgarts feature top songs of the big band era.
Swingtime Video — *Swingtime Video*

Meet the Band Leaders,   1985
Vol. 104
Music
84003   54 mins   B/W   B, V   P
Gene Krupa, Jerry Wald, Stan Kenton and their Orchestras, Tex Beneke and The Glenn Miller Orchestra
Four big band film shorts from 1942-47 spotlight bands of the World War II era. Gene Krupa's band includes Red Rodney, Gerry Mulligan and vocalist Carolyn Grey; Stan Kenton features Shelly Manne, June Christy and the Pastels; Anita Boyer sings with Jerry Wald; and Beneke's vocalists are Artie Malvin, Lillian Lane and the Crew Chiefs.
Swingtime Video — *Swingtime Video*

Meet the Band Leaders,   1985
Vol. 105
Music
84004   50 mins   B/W   B, V   P
Larry Clinton, Jimmy Dorsey, Red Nichols and their Orchestras, Bunny Berigan with the Freddie Rich Orchestra, Ina Ray Hutton and her Melodears
A program of five big band shorts from 1935-40. Featured vocalists are: Bea Wain with Larry Clinton; Bob Eberly and Helen O'Connell with Jimmy Dorsey; and the Three Songies with Red Nichols. Ina Ray Hutton sings and tap dances with her all-girl orchestra and the legendary Bunny Berigan plays trumpet and sings in a rare filmed appearance with Freddie Rich.
Swingtime Video — *Swingtime Video*

Meet the Band Leaders,   1985
Vol. 106
Music
84005   53 mins   B/W   B, V   P

Lawrence Welk, Russ Morgan, Hal Kemp, Jan Garber and their Orchestras
The sweet bands are in the spotlight in this compilation of 1936-39 film shorts. Featured is a rare appearance by the Hal Kemp Orchestra, with vocalists Skinnay Ennis, Maxine Gray and Saxie Dowell.
Swingtime Video — *Swingtime Video*

Meet the Band Leaders,   1985
Vol. 107
Music
84006   55 mins   B/W   B, V   P
Guy Lombardo and his Royal Canadians, Carmen Lombardo, Kenny Gardner and the Lombardo Trio
"The Sweetest Music This Side of Heaven" returns in this filmed 1955 program by the Lombardo Orchestra. Songs include "Get Out Those Old Records," "Boo Hoo," "Coquette" and "Seems Like Old Times."
Swingtime Video — *Swingtime Video*

Meet the Band Leaders,   1985
Vol. 108
Music
84007   48 mins   B/W   B, V   P
Duke Ellington, Count Basie, Lionel Hampton and their Orchestras
More 1965 performances by three powerhouse jazz groups feature such selections as "Supercalifragilisticexpialidocious" and "Afro Bossa" (Ellington); "Shiny Stockings," "Shake, Rattle and Roll" and "Whirly Birds" (Basie); and "Flying Home" (Hampton).
Swingtime Video — *Swingtime Video*

Meet the Band Leaders,   1985
Vol. 109
Music
84008   52 mins   B/W   B, V   P
Hal Kemp, Johnny Long, Frankie Carle, Jan Garber, Art Mooney and their Orchestras
The sweet bands return in another group of 1939-47 film shorts, plus additional 1965 performances. Highlights include Johnny Long's "Shanty in Old Shanty Town" and Art Mooney's "I'm Looking Over a Four-Leaf Clover." Featured on vocals are Bob Allen and the Smoothies (Kemp); Bea Wain and Bob Houston (Long) and Marjorie Hughes (Carle).
Swingtime Video — *Swingtime Video*

Meet the Band Leaders,   1985
Vol. 110
Music
84009   44 mins   B/W   B, V   P
Ray McKinley, Dick Stabile, Sam Donahue, Stan Kenton and their Orchestras
Two wartime 1942 shorts (McKinley and Stabile) and two 1965 filmed performances (Donahue and Kenton) comprise this volume of big band jazz. The highlight is a lengthy Kenton segment

featuring "Intermission Riff" and "The Peanut Vendor."
Swingtime Video — *Swingtime Video*

Meet the Band Leaders, Vol. 111
1985

Music
84010   51 mins   B/W   B, V   P
Count Basie, Duke Ellington, Harry James and their Orchestras
This volume of 1964-65 performances highlights hit tunes of these respective bands. The Duke features Harry Carney, Johnny Hodges and Cootie Williams, while Corky Corcoran and Budy Rich handle solo honors with Harry James.
Swingtime Video — *Swingtime Video*

Meet the Band Leaders, Vol. 112
1985

Music
84011   47 mins   B/W   B, V   P
Artie Shaw, Cab Calloway, Duke Ellington, Boyd Raeburn and their Orchestras, Hoagy Carmichael with Jack Teagarden's Orchestra
Five disparate big bands perform in this selection of 1935-47 shorts. Featured soloists and vocalists are: Helen Forrest, Tony Pastor and Buddy Rich (Shaw); Charlie Spivak and Ernie Caceres (Teagarden); Johnny Hodges, Tricky Sam Nanton, Ray Nance, Ben Webster and Taft Jordan (Ellington); and Ginnie Powell and Teddy Walters (Raeburn).
Swingtime Video — *Swingtime Video*

Meet the Band Leaders, Vol. 114
1985

Music
84012   44 mins   B/W   B, V   P
Charlie Barnet, Les Brown, Ralph Flanagan, Tony Pastor and their Orchestras, Lucy Ann Polk, Butch Stone
This compilation of four postwar big bands, circa 1950-52 is taken from film shorts. Songs include: "Cherokee," "Andy's Boogie," "Skyliner," "I've Got the World on a String" and "Band of Renown."
Swingtime Video — *Swingtime Video*

Meet the Dixieland Bands, Vol. 115
1985

Music
84013   55 mins   B/W   B, V   P
Jack Teagarden and his Sextet, The Bobcats with Eddie Miller, Billy Butterfield and Jess Stacy
Jack Teagarden, the Trombone King, is featured with his jazz sextet in a 1951 program. Included are "Jack Armstrong Blues," "Stars Fell on Alabama" and "Lover." Also on this tape is a 1951 appearance by several Bob Crosby alumni, collectively called The Bobcats. Their segment contains "March of the Bobcats," "Lazy Mood" (featuring Eddie Miller), "Big Noise from Winnetka" (featuring Bob Haggart

and Ray Bauduc), "Savoy Blues" and several others.
Swingtime Video — *Swingtime Video*

Meet the Navy
1946

Musical
66139   81 mins   B/W   B, V, FO   P
Joan Pratt, Margaret Hurst, Lionel Murton
A post-war musical revue about a pianist and a dancer.
British — *Video Yesteryear*

Meet the Singers, Vol. 117
1985

Music
84015   48 mins   B/W   B, V   P
Sarah Vaughan, Herb Jeffries, The Nat King Cole Trio
Three of the greatest jazz-influenced vocalists sing their favorites, taped from 1950-52 performances. Among the songs featured are: "Sweet Lorraine," "Home," "Route 66," "Nature Boy," "You're Mine, You," "You're Not the Kind" and "Solitude."
Swingtime Video — *Swingtime Video*

Meet the Small Bands, Vol. 116
1985

Music
84014   53 mins   B/W   B, V   P
The Count Basie Sextet, Cab Calloway and his Cabaliers, The Four Freshmen, The George Shearing Quintet, Helen Humes
Several 1950-52 small jazz combos perform in this program. Basie's group features Clark Terry, Buddy DeFranco and Wardell Gray; Jonah Jones, Milt Hinton and Panama Francis play with Calloway; and the Shearing Quintet includes Chuck Wayne and Denzil Best.
Swingtime Video — *Swingtime Video*

Meet Your Animal Friends
1985

Animals/Children
71020   52 mins   C   B, V   P
Narrated by Lynn Redgrave
This 23-segment program introduces children to a variety of pleasant beasts from aardvarks, to flamingos and zebras.
Toddler Video — *Children's Video Library*

Meet Your VCR
1982

Video
63997   48 mins   C   B, V   P
Joan Lunden
This program was created to help the video consumer get the most out of his or her VCR by providing 10 easy lessons ranging from recording to maintenance.
3055 Corporation — *Karl/Lorimar Home Video*

Meeting at Midnight
1944

Mystery
54313   67 mins   B/W   B, V   P

Sidney Toler, Joseph Crehan, Mantan
Moreland, Frances Chan, directed by Phil
Rosen
Charlie Chan is invited to a seance to solve a
perplexing mystery. Chan discovers that they
use mechanical figures and from there on
solving the mystery is easy.
Monogram — Hal Roach Studios; Video
Connection; Video Yesteryear; Kartes Video
Communications

Meeting of Minds, Volumes 5 & 6   1985
Interview/History
81612   116 mins   C   B, V   P
Jayne Meadows, Steve Allen, Harris Yulin,
Anthony Costello
Mr. Allen brings together the immortal bard.
William Shakespeare and some of his
memorable characters for a discussion on
"Shakespeare On Love".
PBS — Buena Vista Home Video

Meeting of Minds, Volumes 1 & 2   1984
Interview/History
80365   115 mins   C   B, V   P
Join Steve Allen as he reenacts confrontations
between world leaders that decide the course of
history in a round table discussion.
PBS — Buena Vista Home Video

Meeting of Minds—Volumes 3 and 4   1985
Interview
70361   90 mins   C   B, V   P
Joe Early, Jayne Meadows, Joe Sirola, Peter
Bromilow, hosted by Steve Allen
In this dramatic program, Mr. Allen invites
historical personalities to dinner for lively
discussions. These tapes feature chats between
Theodore Roosevelt, Cleopatra, Thomas Paine
and St. Thomas Aquinas.
Public Broadcasting Service — Buena Vista
Home Video

Meeting the World   1986
Infants
86162   60 mins   C   B, V   P
For parents, the developmental stages of an
infant's growth are examined, including motor
development, safety precautions and discipline.
Part of "Parents Video Magazine."
Arnold Shapiro Prod; Karl-Lorimar; Jean
O'Neill — Karl/Lorimar Home Video

Megaforce   1982
Science fiction
63394   99 mins   C   B, V, CED   P
Barry Bostwick, Persis Khambutta, Edward
Mulhare, Henry Silva, Ralph Wilcox

This futuristic thriller follows the adventures of
the military task force, Megaforce, on its mission
to save a small democratic nation from attack.
MPAA:PG
20th Century Fox — CBS/Fox Video

Mein Kampf   1960
Documentary/World War II
80393   117 mins   C   B, V   P
The rise and fall of German fascism and its
impact upon the world is examined in this
documentary.
Tore Sjoberg — Embassy Home Entertainment

Mel Brooks—An Audience   1984
Comedy
75490   60 mins   C   V   P
Mell Brooks, Anne Bancroft
Mel Brooks puts on a number of sketches, sings
and tells jokes in this live comedy concert
appearance.
Prism — Prism

Mel Lewis   1984
Music-Performance
88124   55 mins   C   B, V, 8mm   P
The astute jazz drummer performs at the
Smithsonian: "One Finger Snap," "Dolphin
Dance," "Make Me Smile" and "Eye of the
Hurricane."
Adler Ent.; Sony — Sony Video Software

Mel Lewis and his Big Band   1983
Music-Performance
84646   38 mins   C   B, V   P
Mel Lewis and His Big Band, Lynn Roberts
A program by the top jazz bandleader and
drummer taped at the Jerusalem Theater. Big
band veteran singer Lynn Roberts also
performs. Recorded in Hi-Fi Stereo.
Tel Ad — V.I.E.W. Video

Mel Torme   1983
Music-Performance
76665   53 mins   C   B, V   P
A collection of hits from this legendary singer,
composer, arranger and conductor. Includes:
"New York State of Mind," "Born in the Night,"
"Down for Double" and many more.
One Pass Prod — Sony Video Software

Mel Torme and Della Reese in Concert   1981
Music-Performance
55562   45 mins   C   LV   P
Mel Torme, Della Reese, directed by Ron Brown
The two performers combine their talents in this
concert recorded live at the Jubilee Auditorium
in Edmonton, Canada. Stereo disc.

ITV — *MCA Home Video*

Mel Torme Special
1983
Music-Performance
73986   53 mins   C   B, V   P
"The Velvet Fog" sings some of his greatest hits from "Bluesette" to "New York State of Mind."
One Pass Prod — *Sony Video Software*

Melanie
1982
Drama
65362   109 mins   C   B, V   P
Glynnis O'Connor, Paul Sorvino, Burton Cummings
This gripping drama is the tale of one woman's extraordinary courage, determination, and optimism. Melanie refused to see herself as an unfit mother and emerged a winner in every way!
MPAA:PG
Richard Simpson; Peter Simpson — *Vestron Video*

Melody
1971
Drama
60445   106 mins   C   B, V, CED   P
Jack Wild, Mark Lester, Colin Barrie
A sensitive study of a special friendship which enables two adolescents to survive in a regimented and impersonal world. Features music by the Bee Gees.
MPAA:G
Levitt Pickman Films — *Embassy Home Entertainment*

Melody Master, The
1941
Musical-Drama/Biographical
46346   80 mins   B/W   B, V, FO   P
Alan Curtis, Ilona Massey, Binnie Barnes, Albert Basserman, Billy Gilbert, Sterling Holloway
A romanticized biography of composer Franz Schubert, chronicling his personal life and loves, along with performances of his compositions.
Original title: New Wine.
United Artists — *Video Yesteryear; Discount Video Tapes; See Hear Industries*

Melody Ranch
1940
Musical/Western
44812   84 mins   C   B, V   P, T
Gene Autry, Jimmy Durante, George Hayes, Ann Miller
Gene returns to his home town as an honored guest.
Republic — *Blackhawk Films; Video Connection*

Melody Trail
1935
Western/Musical
44808   60 mins   B/W   B, V   P, T
Gene Autry, Smiley Burnette

Gene wins $1000 in a rodeo, loses the money to a gypsy, gets a job, falls for his employer's daughter ... and in the end captures both kidnapper and cattle rustlers.
Republic — *Blackhawk Films; Video Connection*

Melon Crazy
1985
Comedy-Performance
81097   58 mins   C   B, V   P
Comedian Gallagher describes his unusual fondness for watermelon in this concert performance.
Showtime — *Paramount Home Video*

Melvin and Howard
1980
Comedy
55549   95 mins   C   B, V, LV   P
Paul Le Mat, Jason Robards, Mary Steenburgen, Michael J. Pollard, Dabney Coleman, Elizabeth Cheshire, directed by Jonathan Demme
The story, according to Melvin Dummar, about the man who picked up Howard Hughes in the desert and then claimed to be heir to the Hughes fortune via the disputed Mormon will.
Academy Awards '80: Best Supporting Actress (Steenburgen); Best Original Screenplay (Bo Goldman). MPAA:R
Universal; Art Linson; Don Phillips — *MCA Home Video*

Memoirs of a Fairy Godmother
1982
Fairy tales
64952   90 mins   C   B, V   R, P
Rosemary De Camp
The Godmother, an eccentric old lady, lives in the woods with her many pets. She enjoys telling stories and the film features animated versions of the tales of Cinderella, Snow White, Sleeping Beauty and many others.
MPAA:G
Century Video — *Video Gems*

Memorandum
1965
World War II
21395   59 mins   B/W   B, V, FO   P
A Canadian Jew who survived the Holocaust in Europe returns to Germany to join a pilgrimage to the former concentration camp of Bergen-Belsen.
National Film Board of Canada — *Video Yesteryear; National Film Board of Canada*

Memory Lane Movies by Robert Youngson #1
195?
Documentary/Film-History
58647   62 mins   B/W   B, V, FO   P
Five shorts compiled by film historian Robert Youngson from the Pathe archives: "The World of Kids" (1951), featuring an all-kid rodeo, kid golfers, etc.; "Animals Have All the Fun" (1952),

a look at animal antics highlighted by a canine fashion show; "Batter Up" (1949), scenes of Babe Ruth, Lou Gehrig, Jimmy Fox, and Joltin' Joe included; "Those Exciting Days" (1955), chronicling the years before the First World War; and "This Was Yesterday" (1954), a look at America circa 1914.
Warner Bros — *Video Yesteryear*

Memory Lane Movies by   195?
Robert Youngson #2
Documentary/Film-History
58648   61 mins   B/W   B, V, FO   P
Five shorts compiled by film historian Robert Youngson from the Pathe archives: "I Never Forget a Face" (1956), including the 1920 Presidential campaign, the Scopes Monkey Trial, and other events of the day; "Horsehide Heroes" (1951), a look at the all-time greats, from Ted Williams to Ty Cobb; "Some of the Greatest" (1955), with scenes from the 1926 classic film 'Don Juan'; "The Swim Parade" (1949), featuring bathing beauties throughout the years; and "They Were Champions" (1955), featuring the greatest boxers of all time.
Warner Bros — *Video Yesteryear*

Memory Lane Movies by   195?
Robert Youngson #3
Documentary/Film-History
58649   62 mins   B/W   B, V, FO   P
Five shorts compiled by film historian Robert Youngson from the Pathe archives: "Gadgets Galore" (1955), a look at the early days of the automobile; "Faster and Faster" (1956), a potpourri of boat races; "Animals and Kids" (1956), featuring monkeys that play piano, etc; "It Happened to You" (1955), a scrapbook of World War I; and "Dare Devil Days" (1952), consisting of 'human flies' and the Like.
Warner Bros — *Video Yesteryear*

Memory Lane Movies by   19??
Robert Youngson #4
Documentary/Film-History
58650   55 mins   B, V, FO   P
Five shorts compiled by film historian Robert Youngson from the Pathe archives: "Blaze Buster" (1950), with spectacular scenes of early fires; "Lighter Than Air" (1951), a look at blimps, balloons and dirigibles; "When Sports Were King" (1954), a look at sports events of the 1920's; "I Remember When" (1954), featuring scenes of 'Little Old New York,' the Wright Bros., the 'Frisco Quake,' etc; "Coming of the Auto" (1953), a look at the early days of the motor car; and "Camera Hunting" (1954), a film biography of Thomas Edison.
Warner Bros — *Video Yesteryear*

Memory Lane Movies by   195?
Robert Youngson #5
Documentary/Film-History
47470   62 mins   B/W   B, V, FO   P

Six shorts compiled from Pathe newsreel footage by Robert Youngson: "This Mechanical Age" (1954), "Roaring Wheels" (1948), "Cavalcade of Girls" (1950), "They're Off!" (1949), "No Adults Allowed" (1953) and "Disaster Fighters" (1951).
Academy Awards '54: Best One-Reel Short Film ("This Mechanical Age").
Warner Bros — *Video Yesteryear*

Memory Lane Movies by   195?
Robert Youngson #6
Documentary/Film-History
47471   62 mins   B/W   B, V, FO   P
Six shorts compiled by Robert Youngson from Pathe newsreel footage: "Spills and Chills" (1949), "Fire, Wind and Flood" (1955), "A-Speed on the Deep" (1950), "Head Over Heels" (1953), "Too Much Speed" (1952) and "Say It with Spills" (1953).
Warner Bros — *Video Yesteryear*

Memphis Belle, The   1944
Documentary/World War II
45063   43 mins   C   B, V   P
The entire final mission of the Flying Fortress, "Memphis Belle," and its daring daylight attack on the submarine pens at Wilhelmshaven, Germany is seen in this newsreel footage.
Lt Col William Wyler — *Hollywood Home Theater; International Historic Films; Western Film & Video Inc*

Men, The   1950
Drama
64545   85 mins   B/W   B, V   P
Marlon Brando, Teresa Wright, Everett Sloane, Jack Webb, directed by Fred Zinnemann
A paraplegic World War II veteran sinks into depression until his former girlfriend manages to bring him out of it. Marlon Brando's first film.
United Artists; Stanley Kramer — *Republic Pictures Home Video*

Men Are Not Gods   1937
Drama
81464   90 mins   B/W   B, V, LV   P
Rex Harrison, Miriam Hopkins, Gertrude Lawrence
The theatre nearly reflects real life when an actor playing Othello almost kills his wife during Desdemona's death scene.
Alexander Korda — *Embassy Home Entertainment*

Men at Work Live in San   1984
Francisco or Was It
Berkeley?
Music-Performance/Music video
80133   58 mins   C   B, V   P
Those eccentric rockers from the land down under perform their big hits in this program that combines live performance with music video.

CBS/Fox Video Music — *CBS/Fox Video*

RCA Video Prod. — *RCA/Columbia Pictures Home Video*

Men in War 1957
War-Drama
04000   104 mins   B/W   B, V   P
Robert Ryan, Aldo Ray, Robert Keith, Philip Pine, Vic Morrow
Grim, suspenseful war film. 1950. American infantry platoon in Korea, surrounded by the enemy, fight for their objective. Based on Van Praag's novel.
UA; Security Prod — *King of Video; World Video Pictures; Prism*

Men of Destiny Volume I: 1979
World Political Figures
History-Modern/Documentary
29157   120 mins   B/W   B, V   P
Narrated by Bob Considine
Presents authentic newsreels that capture the exact mood and drama of history. This program records the lives and momentous achievements of over 30 leaders in world history featuring Winston Churchill, Herbert Hoover, Mahatma Gandhi, Chrales De Gaulle, and many others.
Pathe News — *CBS/Fox Video*

Men of Destiny Volume II: 1979
Artists and Innovators
History-Modern/Documentary
29158   120 mins   B/W   B, V   P
Narrated by Bob Considine
Presents authentic newsreels that capture the exact mood and drama of history. This volume features the achievements of over thirty world-renowned figures including Marie Curie, Thomas Edison, Albert Einstein, Jonas Salk, the Wright Brothers, and Charles Lindbergh.
Pathe News — *CBS/Fox Video*

Men Who Played the 1985
Game, The
Football
81956   95 mins   C   B, V   P
This is an in-depth look at the careers of ten NFL greats such as Walt Garrison, Deacon Jones, Frank Gifford and Paul Hornung.
NFL Films — *NFL Films Video*

Menudo—La Pelicula 1978
Musical
80420   84 mins   C   B, V   P
Menudo members Rene, Johnny, Xavier, Miguel, and Ricky sing ten songs in this musical.
SP
Spanish — *Unicorn Video*

Menudo—Live in Concert 1985
Music-Performance
85831   60 mins   C   B, V   P
The famous Puerto Rican teen group performs their songs in concert.

Mercedes Diesel 1986
Automobiles
88407   60 mins   C   B, V, 3/4U   P
How to maintain, tune-up and care for the diesel Benz engines.
Peter Allen Prod. — *Peter Allen Video Productions*

Mercedes 8 Cylinder 1986
Automobiles
88406   60 mins   C   B, V, 3/4U   P
How to tune-up and maintain the classic Benz engine.
Peter Allen Prod. — *Peter Allen Video Productions*

Mercenary Game, The 1981
Documentary/War-Drama
71066   60 mins   C   B, V   P
This tape offers a behind-the-scenes peek at the soldiers who will raid, maim, subvert and assassinate if you can pay the price.
Independent — *MPI Home Video*

MerCruiser I/O and 1985
Inboard Engine Tune-Up,
The
Boating
70886   50 mins   C   B, V, 3/4U   P
This tape explains the tune-up process, and offers clever tips from the pros.
Videovision Productions — *Peter Allen Video Productions*

Mere Jeevan Saathi (My 1965
Life Partner)
Drama
85189   126 mins   C   B, V   P
Musical dubbing by Lata Mangeskar
A bizarre, unclassifiable Indian film with music, fantasy, special effects, violence, and flamboyant mise-en-scene. In Hindi with English subtitles.
Indian — *Video Yesteryear*

Merry Christmas Mr. 1983
Lawrence
Drama
65513   124 mins   C   B, V   P
David Bowie, Tom Conti, Ryuichi Sakamoto, Takeshi, Jack Thompson
A taut psychological World War II drama about clashing cultures and survival. In stereo VHS and Beta Hi-Fi.
MPAA:R
Universal — *MCA Home Video*

Merry Christmas to You   1980
Christmas
54245   80 mins   C   B, V, 3/4U   P
A collection of cartoons, singalongs, and Lone
Ranger and Lassie adventures that all carry a
Christmas theme.
Nostalgia Merchant — *Nostalgia Merchant*

Merry Minstrels Wish You   1984
A Happy Birthday, The
Video
73628   5 mins   C   B, V   S
On this reusable two hour videocassette, The
Merry Minstrels sing "Happy Birthday."
Kartes Productions — *Kartes Video
Communications*

Merry Mirthworm   1985
Christmas, A
Cartoons/Christmas
71354   30 mins   C   B, V   P
*Animated, voices of Rachel Rutledge, Jerry
Reynolds, Peggy Nicholson*
This animated holiday special looks at the
traditional celebrations of the earthworm.
MFTV Inc — *Family Home Entertainment*

Message, The   1977
Drama
77384   176 mins   C   B, V   P
Anthony Quinn, Irene Papas, Michael Ansara
This historical drama describes the conflict
between Mohammed and the leaders of Mecca
in the seventh century.
Satori Entertainment — *U.S.A. Home Video*

Messiah   1984
Music-Performance
80054   145 mins   C   B, V   P
*Judith Nelson, Emma Kirkby, Paul Elliott, David
Thomas*
The choir of Westminister Abbey performs the
1754 Foundling Hospital version of George
Handel's classic work.
BBC Television; National Video
Corporation — *THORN EMI/HBO Video*

Messiah of Evil   198?
Horror
70979   90 mins   C   B, V   P
Michael Greer, Marianna Hill
Once every 100 years the moon turns crimson
and an unholy terrorist slithers into a California
beach community.
MPAA:R
Independent — *Video Gems*

Metalstorm   1983
Adventure/Science fiction
65514   84 mins   C   B, V, LV   P
*Jeffrey Byron, Mike Preston, Tim Thomerson,
Kelly Preston, Richard Moll*

It's the science fiction battle of the ages with
giant cyclopses and intergalactic magicians on
the desert planet of Lemuria. In stereo VHS and
Beta Hi-Fi.
MPAA:PG
Universal — *MCA Home Video*

Meteor   1979
Science fiction
53518   107 mins   C   B, V   P
*Sean Connery, Natalie Wood, Karl Malden,
Brian Keith, Martin Landau, Trevor Howard,
Henry Fonda, Joseph Campanella*
The U.S. and the Soviet Union both have an
armed satellite orbiting in space, its fire power
directed at an enemy nation. An American
scientist calculates that only their combined
weaponry can destroy the enemy.
MPAA:PG
American International — *Warner Home Video*

Metropolis   1926
Science fiction
08705   120 mins   B/W   B, V   P
*Brigitte Helm, Alfred Abel, Gustav Froehlich,
directed by Fritz Lang*
Fritz Lang's vision of future civilization is brought
effectively to life in the original silent version of
this classic film.
UFA — *Hollywood Home Theater; Video
Yesteryear; Discount Video Tapes; International
Historic Films; Cable Films; Hal Roach Studios*

Metropolis   1926
Science fiction
81158   87 mins   C   B, V, LV   P
*Brigitte Helm, Gustav Frihlich, Alfred Abel,
directed by Fritz Lang*
This is composer Giorgio Moroder's
reconstructed version of the classic silent film
about the confrontation that arises when a
member of the elite class falls in love with a
woman of the lower class. The digital
soundtrack features music by Pat Benatar and
Queen.
UFA; Giorgio Moroder Enterprises
Ltd. — *Vestron Video*

Mexican   1940
Spitfire/Smartest Girl in
Town, The
Comedy
76845   125 mins   B/W   B, V   P
*Lupe Velez, Leon Errol, Donald Woods, Ann
Southern, Gene Raymond*
A comedy double feature: In "Mexican Spitfire"
a man impersonates an English lord in order to
save a contract for the spitfire's husband and in
"The Smartest Girl in Town" a photographer's
model mistakes a millionaire for a fellow
magazine model.
RKO — *RKO HomeVideo*

Mi Novia El 1984
Comedy
81642   90 mins   C   B, V   P
Susana Gimenez, Alberto Olmedo
A practical joker finds that the joke's on him
when he falls in love with a famous transvestite.
SP
Spanish — *Media Home Entertainment*

Miami Dolphins 1985 1985
Team Highlights
Football
86800   23 mins   C   B, V   P
The best plays of the Dolphins' '85 season,
including the only game the Chicago Bears lost
that year.
NFL Films — *NFL Films Video*

Miami Dolphins 1984 1985
Team Highlights
Football
70548   70 mins   C   B, V, FO   P
Dan Marino, Don Shula
Dan Marino's record-setting year paced the
Dolphins to a 14-2 record and a Super Bowl
showdown with the 49ers. This tape features
47-minutes of highlights from the '84 NFL
season as well.
NFL Films — *NFL Films Video*

Miami Vice 1984
Drama
71166   99 mins   C   B, V, LV   P
*Don Johnson, Philip Michael Thomas, Saundra
Santiago, Michael Talbott, John Diehl, Gregory
Sierra, directed by Thomas Carter*
This pilot for the popular TV series paired
Crockett and Tubbs together for the first time on
the trail of a killer in Miami's sleazy
underground. Recorded in HiFi Stereo surround
sound with music by Jan Hammer and other pop
notables.
Michael Mann Co Inc; Universal — *MCA Home
Video*

Miami Vice II--The 1985
Prodigal Son
Crime-Drama
87728   99 mins   C   B, V, LV   P
*Don Johnson, Philip Michael Thomas, Edward
James Olmos, Penn Jilette*
The second full-length TV movie spawned by
the popular series, following the laconic
Floridians to the gritty streets of New York.
John Nicolella; Michael Mann — *MCA Home
Video*

Michael Nesmith: 1981
Rio/Cruisin'
Music/Video
66161   11 mins   C   B, V   P

Two songs from the "Elephant Parts" video. In
stereo.
Pacfic Arts Video — *Sony Video Software*

Michael Stanley Band 1982
Music video
88100   60 mins   C   B, V   P
A compilation of videos from this presently
extinct rock band.
Sony Video — *Sony Video Software*

Mick Fleetwood-The 1981
Visitor
Music-Performance
60383   106 mins   C   CED   P
Fleetwood Mac's founder and drummer, Mick
Fleetwood, travels to Ghana, Africa in a
fascinating excursion combining rock music with
traditional African sounds.
Colin Frewin — *RCA VideoDiscs*

Mickey 1917
Comedy
11247   80 mins   B/W   B, V, FO   P
Mabel Normand, Lew Cody, Minta Durfee
A spoof on high society which contains a scene
in which a squirrel scampers up the heroine's
leg and is retrieved by the hero. (Silent.)
Mack Sennett — *Video Yesteryear; Discount
Video Tapes*

Mickey Knows Best 1937
Cartoons
85534   26 mins   C   B, V   P
Animated
Three Mickey Mouse shorts from the late 30s:
"Moving Day," "Mickey's Amateurs" and
"Mickey's Elephant."
Walt Disney — *Walt Disney Home Video*

Mickey Mantle's Baseball 1986
Tips For Kids of All Ages
Baseball/Children
84126   70 mins   C   B, V   P
Mickey Mantle, Whitey Ford, Phil Rizzuto
Three baseball greats instruct the basics of
playing the game, with the help of Little
Leaguers.
Larry Meli — *CBS/Fox Video*

Mickey Mouse Club, 195?.
Volumes 1 thru 15, The
Variety
70934   90 mins   B/W   B, V   P
*Annette Funicello, Spin, Marty, Karen, Cubby,
Jimmy, Roy, The Hardy Boys, Clint, Mac*
15   pgms
Each cassette in this series features three
episodes from the popular '50's TV series, with
a newly filmed introduction by Annette. These
lively programs, starring the "Mouseketeers,"

include song, dance, cartoons, documentary newsreels and continuing serialized adventures.
Walt Disney Prods — *Walt Disney Home Video*

Mickey Thompson's Off-Road Warriors　　1986
Automobiles
87750　60 mins　C　B, V　　　P
Off-road racing and demolition are highlighted in this program.
Visual Associates — *Twin Tower Enterprises*

Mickey's Christmas Carol　　1983
Cartoons
79174　60 mins　C　B, V　　　P
Animated
Mickey Mouse returns along with all the other Disney characters in this adaptation of the Charles Dickens classic. Included in this video cassette is a documentary on how the featurette was made.
Walt Disney Productions — *Walt Disney Home Video*

Mickey's Christmas Carol/The Small One　　1983
Cartoons/Christmas
71104　90 mins　C　B, V　　　P
Animated
Disney dubbed this special double-feature into the Spanish language. In the first feature, Mickey Mouse stars in an adaptation of the Dickens classic. "The Small One" depicts a poor young boy who gives the ultimate gift to the infant Jesus.
SP
Walt Disney Productions — *Walt Disney Home Video*

Mickey's Discovery Series　　1985
Education/Children
70937　30 mins　C　B, V　　　P
Mickey Mouse
The lessons included on this Disney Video-A-Long book on video, are "Counting Fun," "Things That Go" and "Baby Animals."
Walt Disney Productions — *Walt Disney Home Video*

Micki and Maude　　1984
Comedy
Closed Captioned
80878　117 mins　C　B, V　　　P
Dudley Moore, Amy Irving, Ann Reinking, Richard Mulligan, Wallace Shawn, Andre the Giant, directed by Blake Edwards
A TV reporter's wife enjoys a successful law career that leads to a judge's seat. Disappointed, her family-desiring husband meets, falls in love with, and then marries a young cellist. The bigamist then discovers that wife #1 is pregnant as well. He decides to

maintain both marriages without informing either wife of the others existence. Fun ensues in Beta and VHS Hi-Fi.
MPAA:PG13
Columbia Pictures — *RCA/Columbia Pictures Home Video*

Mid-Eastern Dance: An Introduction to Belly Dance　　1985
Dance
85050　143 mins　C　B, V, 3/4U　　P
Kathryn Ferguson
A complete beginning and intermediate belly dancing instruction course is presented on this tape.
Bastet Prod — *Bastet Productions*

Midnight　　1934
Mystery
12809　74 mins　B/W　B, V　　　P
Humphrey Bogart, Sidney Fox, O.P. Hegge, Henry Hull
A jury foreman's daughter is romantically involved with a gangster who is interested in a particular case before it appears in court.
United International — *Movie Buff Video; Blackhawk Films; Cinema Concepts; Discount Video Tapes; Kartes Video Communications*

Midnight Cowboy　　1969
Drama
60564　113 mins　C　B, V　　　P
Dustin Hoffman, Jon Voight, Sylvia Miles, Brenda Vaccaro, John McGiver
James Leo Herlihy's novel about the relationship between a Texan and a pathetic derelict, set amidst seamy New York environs, is graphically depicted in this film.
MPAA:R
Jerome Hellman Prods; United Artists — *MGM/UA Home Video; RCA VideoDiscs*

Midnight Express　　1978
Drama
35379　120 mins　C　B, V, LV　　P
Brad Davis, John Hurt, Randy Quaid, directed by Alan Parker
Harrowing tale of a young American who is arrested for drug smuggling in Turkey and undergoes mental and physical torture beyond belief in a Turkish prison.
MPAA:R
Columbia — *RCA/Columbia Pictures Home Video; RCA VideoDiscs*

Midnight Madness　　1980
Comedy
77523　110 mins　C　B, V　　　P
David Naughton, Stephen Furst, Debra Clinger, Eddie Deezen, Maggie Roswell

Five teams of college students search the city of Los Angeles for clues leading to hundreds and thousands of dollars in buried treasure.
MPAA:PG
Buena Vista — *Buena Vista Home Video*

Midnight Star in Concert   1984
Music-Performance
79187   60 mins   C   B, V   P
The hot and funky sounds of Midnight Star are captured live in concert.
Gary Delfiner — *U.S.A. Home Video*

Midnite Movie Madness: 1985
Trailers on Tape
Movie and TV trailers/Horror
81882   58 mins   C   B, V   P
Here is a collection of over twenty cult classics such as "Rocky Horror Picture Show," "Plan 9 From Outer Space," "Up the Sandbox" and "Freaks." Some trailers are in black and white.
20th Century Fox et al — *San Francisco Rush Video*

Midnite Spares   1985
Adventure
77402   90 mins   C   B, V   P
Bruce Spence, Gia Carides, James Laurie
A young man's search for the men who kidnapped his father leads him into the world of car thieves and chop-shops.
Tom Burstall — *VCL Home Video*

Midsummer Night's   1982
Dream, A
Literature-English
60201   120 mins   C   B, V   R, P
Helen Mirren, Peter McEnery, Brian Clover
Shakespeare has created some of his most fanciful and unforgettable characters in this tale of devilish fairies, bewitched lovers and stolid workingmen-cum-actors.
BBC London; Time-Life Films — *Key Video; Time Life Video*

Midsummer Night's Sex   1982
Comedy, A
Comedy
63108   88 mins   C   B, V   P
Woody Allen, Mia Farrow, Mary Steenburgen, Tony Roberts, Julie Hagerty, directed by Woody Allen
Three turn-of-the-century couples spend an idyllic weekend in upstate New York. Music score by Felix Mendelssohn.
Orion Pictures; Robert Greenhut — *Warner Home Video*

Midsummer's Night   1963
Dream, A
Theater
85190   111 mins   B/W   B, V   P

Patrick Allen, Eira Heath, Cyril Luckham, Tony Bateman, Jill Bennett
A live British television performance of the classic Shakespeare comedy, with Mendelssohn's incidental music.
BBC — *Video Yesteryear*

Midsummer's Night   1935
Dream, A
Fantasy
85430   132 mins   B/W   B, V   P
James Cagney, Mickey Rooney, Olivia de Havilland, Dick Powell, Joe E. Brown, directed by William Dieterle and Max Reinhardt
The famed Reinhardt version of the Shakespeare classic, featuring nearly every star on the Warner Bros. lot.
Warner Bros. — *Key Video*

Midway   1976
War-Drama
53394   132 mins   C   B, V   P
Charlton Heston, Henry Fonda, James Coburn, Glenn Ford, Hal Holbrook, Robert Mitchum, Cliff Robertson, Robert Wagner
The epic WWII battle of Midway, the turning point in the war, is retold through Allied and Japanese viewpoints.
MPAA:PG
Universal; Walter Mirisch — *MCA Home Video (disc only)*

Mighty Orbots: Raid on   1984
the Stellar Queen
Cartoons
87370   26 mins   C   B, V   P
The Orbots go on a rescue mission to save the passengers aboard the Stellar Queen from the dangerous Sargasso Star Cluster.
TMS Ent. — *MGM/UA Home Video*

Mighty Joe Young   1949
Horror
00313   94 mins   B/W   B, V   P
Terry Moore, Ben Johnson, Robert Armstrong
A young girl raises a giant ape in Africa, only to have it brought to New York, where it escapes.
Academy Awards '49: Best Special Effects.
RKO — *RKO HomeVideo; King of Video*

Mighty Mouse in The   1983
Great Space Chase
Cartoons
69529   88 mins   C   B, V, CED   P
Animated
Mighty Mouse goes "up, up, and away" to save the day in his first full-length animated feature.
MPAA:G
Filmation Stuios — *Children's Video Library*

Mighty Mouse in The Great Space Chase · 1983
Cartoons
82474 88 mins C B, V P
Animated
Mighty Mouse battles Harry the Heartless in order to save Queen Pureheart and the galaxy.
MPAA:G
Terrytoons — *Vestron Video*

Mighty Orbots: Devil's Asteroid · 1984
Cartoons/Science fiction
87369 26 mins C B, V P
An evil lord creates an imposter killer Orbot, causing the real Orbots to be sentenced for murder to the Devil's Asteroid for 999 years.
TMS Ent. — *MGM/UA Home Video*

Mikado, The · 1982
Music-Performance
66272 150 mins C B, V P
Gilbert & Sullivan's comic opera, a spoof of Victorian England "disguised" as a Japanese musical drama.
Unknown — *Embassy Home Entertainment*

Mike Manieri · 1983
Music-Performance
88118 60 mins C B, V, 8mm P
One of the jazz cross-over movement's leaders, Manieri riffs through his favorite tunes at NYC's 7th Avenue South: "Crossed Wires," "Bamboo" and "Bullet Train."
Sony Video — *Sony Video Software*

Mike's Murder · 1984
Drama
80077 110 mins C B, V P
Debra Winger, Mark Keyloun, Paul Winfield, Darrell Larson, directed by James Bridges
A woman tries to find out the truth about her lover's premature demise.
MPAA:R
The Ladd Company — *Warner Home Video*

Mikey and Nicky · 1976
Drama
82225 105 mins C B, V P
John Cassavetes, Peter Falk, Ned Beatty, Oliver Clark, William Hickey, directed by Elaine May
A night-long journey of friendship and betrayal begins when a small time hoodlum asks his best friend to help him get out of town after the Mafia puts out a contract on him.
MPAA:R
Paramount; Castle Hill Productions — *Warner Home Video*

Mil Millones para una Rubia (The Lady Thief) · 1978
Adventure
51104 90 mins C B, V P
Analia Gade, J. Lopez Vazquez, Jean Sorel, Stephen Boyd
Daring thieves plan expensive jewel heists in Las Vegas, Monte Carlo, Paris, and Monaco. In Spanish.
SP
Spanish — *Hollywood Home Theater*

Mildred Pierce · 1945
Drama
59343 113 mins B/W LV P
Joan Crawford, Jack Carson, Zachary Scott, Eve Arden, Ann Blyth, directed by Michael Curtiz
A dowdy housewife leaves her husband, becomes the owner of a restaurant chain, and survives a murder case before true love comes her way.
Academy Awards '45: Best Actress (Crawford).
Warner Bros — *CBS/Fox Video; RCA VideoDiscs*

Milestones of the Century Volume I: The Great Wars · 1979
History-Modern/Documentary
29155 120 mins B/W B, V P
Narrated by Ed Herlihy
This volume of "Milestones of the Century I" records over 30 momentous events in world history and features: FDR leading the nation; Europe ablaze—1914-1917; Hitler's Germany; Britain's Finest Hour; and the Korean Conflict.
Pathe News — *CBS/Fox Video*

Milestones of the Century Volume II: 20th Century—Turning Points · 1979
History-Modern/Documentary
29156 120 mins B/W B, V P
Narrated by Ed Herlihy
This volume of great historic newsreels captures the exact mood and drama of history. Featured are: invention and industry, the era of flight, suffragettes and prohibition, the Russian Revolution, and the post-war world.
Pathe News — *CBS/Fox Video*

Militant Eagle · 19??
Martial arts/Adventure
60512 90 mins C B, V P
Choi Yue, Lu Ping, Pai Ying
A fight of good vs. evil complete with nobles, warriors and villains who fight to the death.
Unknown — *Master Arts Video*

Milky Way, The · 1936
Comedy
44972 89 mins B/W B, V P
Harold Lloyd, Adolphe Menjou, Verree Teasdale, Helen Mack, William Gargan

A milkman knocks out the world champion boxer. His prize is plenty of headaches and the women he loves.
Paramount — *Discount Video Tapes; Hollywood Home Theater; Hal Roach Studios; See Hear Industries*

Mill On The Floss, The   1937
Drama
84871   77 mins   B/W   B, V   P
James Mason, Geraldine Fitzgerald, Frank Lawton, Victoria Hopper, Fay Compton, Griffith Jones, Mary Clare, directed by Tim Whelan
Based on George Eliot's classic this film follows the course of an ill-fated romance in rural England.
Morgan/National Provisional — *Kartes Video Communications*

Millhouse: A White   1969
Comedy
Documentary/Satire
71071   90 mins   B/W   B, V   P
Richard M. Nixon, directed by Emile de Antonio
This film takes an unfriendly look at the career of the former President of the USA.
Emile de Antonio — *MPI Home Video*

Million, Le   1931
Comedy/Musical
81352   89 mins   B/W   B, V   P
Annabella, Rene Lefevre, Paul Olivier, Louis Allibert, directed by Rene Clair
A struggling painter searches all over Paris for a lost lottery ticket that would make him rich beyond his wildest dreams. With English subtitles.
FR
Frank Clifford — *Movie Buff Video; Video Yesteryear*

Million Dollar Duck   1971
Comedy
84803   92 mins   C   B, V   P
Dean Jones, Sandy Duncan, Joe Flynn, Tony Roberts
A family duck is doused with radiation and begins to lay gold eggs.
MPAA:G
Walt Disney Productions — *Walt Disney Home Video*

Milpitas Monster   1980
Horror
76914   80 mins   C   B, V   P
Narrated by Paul Frees
A creature spawned in a Milpitas, California waste dump terrorizes the town residents.
MPAA:PG
Robert L. Burrill — *United Home Video*

Milton Berle Show II, The   1954
Comedy/Variety
84699   115 mins   B/W   B, V, 3/4U   P
Milton Berle, Danny Thomas, Mickey Rooney, Nancy Walker
Two Uncle Miltie side-splitting forays into early television. The first is a 1951 "Texaco Star Theater," second is the 1954 season opener of "The Milton Berle Show."
NBC — *Shokus Video*

Milton Berle Show, The   1966
Comedy/Variety
47476   59 mins   B/W   B, V, FO   P
Milton Berle, Ben Blue, Roy Rogers, Dale Evans, the Dan Blocker Singers
This show, originally telecast December 2, 1966, was one of the last programs from Milton Berle's variety series. Featured are sketches, Vietnam and Christmas jokes and songs by Roy Rogers and Dale Evans. Original commercials included.
ABC — *Video Yesteryear*

Milton Berle Show, The   1963
Comedy/Variety
47493   60 mins   B/W   B, V, FO   P
Milton Berle, Janis Paige, Lena Horne, Laurence Harvey, Jack Benny, Kirk Douglas, Charlton Heston, Les Brown and his Orchestra
A typical Milton Berle variety program, highlighted by a biblical epic spoof, with Laurence Harvey as Spartacus, Jack Benny as Ben Hur and Milton as Cleopatra. Original commercials included.
NBC — *Video Yesteryear*

Milton Berle Show, The   1953
Comedy
45017   120 mins   B/W   B, V, 3/4U   P
Milton Berle, Jackie Cooper, Vic Damone, Peter Lawford, Carol Channing
Two complete (commercials included) Berle shows from 1953. Included are take-offs of "What's My Line" and "Dragnet" and Berle doing a soft-shoe routine with Lawford.
NBC — *Shokus Video*

Milwaukee Braves: Team   1962
Highlights
Baseball
81146   30 mins   B/W   B, V   P
Warren Spahn   11   pgms
This series looks back at the many great moments from the Milwaukee Braves past seasons.
1.1953: The Milwaukee Story 2.1954: Milwaukee Braves '54 3.1955: Baseball with the Braves 4.1956: Braves Land 5.1957: Hail The Braves 6.1958: Pride of the Braves 7.1959: Fighting Braves of '59 8.1960: The Best of Baseball 9.1961: The Best of Baseball 10.1961: Big Moments with the Braves 11.1962: Around the League with the Braves

---

Major League Baseball — *Major League Baseball Productions*

Min and Bill   1930
Comedy-Drama
82117   66 mins   B/W   B, V   P
Marie Dressler, Wallace Beery, Marjorie Rambeau, Dorothy Jordan, directed by George Hill
Min and Bill, houseboat dwellers, fight to keep their daughter from being taken to a proper home.
Academy Awards '30-31: Best Actress (Dressler)
MGM — *MGM/UA Home Video*

Mind Fitness—Lose   1984
Weight
Health education/Health education
76017   40 mins   C   B, V   P
This first hypnosis video for the viewer/participant who desires to be hypnotized for the purpose of losing weight by controlling eating habits.
AM Available
B Ashley Swann — *World Wide Media*

Mind Fitness—Stop   1984
Smoking
Smoking/Health education
76018   40 mins   C   B, V   P
The first hypnosis home video for the viewer/participant who desires to be hypnotized for the purpose of stopping smoking.
B Ashley Swann — *World Wide Media*

Mind Snatchers, The   1972
Science fiction
82207   94 mins   C   B, V   P
Christopher Walken, Ronny Cox, Ralph Meeker, Joss Ackland
An American G.I. becomes involved in U.S. Army experimental psychological brain operations when he is brought into a western European hospital for treatment.
MPAA:PG
Cinerama Releasing — *Prism*

Mine Own Executioner   1947
Mystery
07172   102 mins   B/W   B, V   P
Burgess Meredith, Kieron Moore, Dulcie Gray
Ex-RAF pilot goes to psychiatrist after he crashes in Burma. Tense and well-performed British melodrama.
Alexander Korda — *Discount Video Tapes; Hollywood Home Theater*

Mini Musicals   1975
Cartoons/Music
58588   75 mins   C   B, V   R, P

Voices of Joni Mitchell, Jim Croce, Helen Reddy, Sonny and Cher
A collection of musical animated shorts, plus a special, added short—Stravinsky's "Petrouchka," conducted by the composer himself.
John Wilson — *Video Gems*

Minnesota Fats   1986
Sports-Minor
87598   60 mins   C   B, V   P
Minnesota Fats, Waylon Jennings
The Fats instructs the viewer in pool playing, step by step.
Karl Lorimar — *Karl/Lorimar Home Video*

Minnesota Twins: Team   1984
Highlights
Baseball
81143   30 mins   C   B, V   •   P
John Castino, Kent Hrbek, Ron Davis, Greg Gagne 7 pgms
The best and brightest moments from the Twins past seasons, along with a brief history of the team, are featured in this presentation.
1.1961: Pride of Upper Midwest 2.1970: Portrait of a Winner 3.1972: The Quilici Spirit 4.1979: A Team of Answers 5.1982: Building a New Tradition 6.1983: Climbing Toward The Top 7.1984: Finding Fame.
Major League Baseball — *Major League Baseball Productions*

Minor Detail   1984
Music video
88101   11 mins   C   B, V   P
A couple of video clips from the little-known rock band.
Sony Video — *Sony Video Software*

Minor Miracle, A   1983
Drama
72870   100 mins   C   B, V   P
John Huston, Pele
This is the story of a group of people who get together to save an orphanage from the town planners.
MPAA:G
Unknown — *Embassy Home Entertainment*

Minsky's Follies   1983
Comedy
75289   60 mins   C   B, V   P
Phyllis Diller, Rip Taylor, Stubby Kaye
This is a recreation of an old time burlesque revue complete with strippers. In VHS Dolby stereo and Beta Hi-Fi.
RKO Home Video — *RKO HomeVideo*

Miracle of Lake Placid: Highlights of the 1980 Winter Olympics, The
1980

Sports-Winter
39034   94 mins   C   CED   P
Hosted by Jim McCay
A program of highlights from the 1980 Winter Olympics at Lake Placid, including excerpts of hockey games between the U.S. and Czechoslovakia, Russia, and Finland; all of Eric Heiden's five gold medal-winning speed races; the figure skating duel between Linda Fratianne and Anett Poetzch, and other events. All material was taken from ABC-TV coverage of the Games.
ABC — *RCA VideoDiscs; ABC Video Enterprises*

Miracle of the Bells, The
1948

Drama
69315   120 mins   B/W   B, V   P
Fred MacMurray, Alida Valli, Frank Sinatra, Lee J. Cobb
A lovely, unknown actress rises to stardom overnight and falls in love with a cynical press agent who makes all her dreams come true.
Jesse L. Lasky Productions; RKO — *Spotlite Video*

Miracle on 34th Street
1947

Drama
Closed Captioned
48598   97 mins   B/W   B, V   P
Maureen O'Hara, John Payne, Edmund Gwenn, Natalie Wood, William Frawley
Macy's hires Kris Kringle as Santa Claus for its annual Thanksgiving Day parade. The situation snowballs as a daughter and mother learn to "believe."
20th Century Fox — *Playhouse Video*

Miracle Rider
1935

Western/Serials
14625   195 mins   B/W   B, V   P
Tom Mix, Joan Gale
Old West guns-and-hero tale. In fifteen chapters.
Mascot — *Video Connection; Video Yesteryear; Discount Video Tapes; Cable Films*

Miracle Worker, The
1962

Drama/Biographical
71153   97 mins   B/W   B, V   P
Anne Bancroft, Patty Duke, Victor Jory, Inga Swenson, Andrew Prine, Beah Richards, directed by Arthur Penn
Teacher Anne Sullivan used unconventional methods to bring the deaf, blind Helen Keller into the world. This docudrama shows the relationship that builds between the two courageous women. William Gibson adapted his own play for the screen.

Academy Awards '62: Best Actress (Bancroft); Best Supporting Actress (Duke)
Playfilm Productions; UA — *MGM/UA Home Video*

Miracle Worker, The
1979

Drama/Biographical
47369   98 mins   C   B, V   P
Patty Duke Astin, Melissa Gilbert
The story of blind, deaf and mute Helen Keller and her teacher, Annie Sullivan, whose patience and perseverance finally enables Helen to learn to communicate with the world.
Katz Gallin Productions; Halfpint Productions — *Warner Home Video*

Mirror Crack'd, The
1980

Mystery
47305   105 mins   C   B, V, CED   P
Elizabeth Taylor, Rock Hudson, Kim Novak, Tony Curtis
While filming a movie in the English countryside, an American actress is murdered, and Miss Marple must discover who the killer is. Based on the Agatha Christie novel.
MPAA:PG
Associated Film Dist; EMI Films Ltd — *THORN EMI/HBO Video*

Mirrors
1982

Mystery
72449   83 mins   C   B, V   P
The story of a women's dreams that result in horror and death in New Orleans.
John B Kelly Presentation; First American Films Release — *Monterey Home Video*

Misadventures of Merlin Jones, The
1963

Comedy
84431   90 mins   C   B, V   P
Tommy Kirk, Annette Funicello, Leon Ames, Stuart Erwin, directed by Robert Stevenson
A pair of college sweethearts become embroiled in a rollicking chimp-napping scandal.
MPAA:G
Walt Disney Prods — *Walt Disney Home Video*

Mischief
1985

Comedy
81412   97 mins   C   B, V   P
Doug McKeon, Chris Nash, Kelly Preston, Catherine Mary Stewart
The high school class nerd and the new kid in town come of age during the 1950's as they go on the prowl looking for hot cuties to score with. Available in VHS and Beta Hi-Fi.
MPAA:R
20th Century Fox — *CBS/Fox Video*

Miserables, Les 1979
Drama/Cartoons
69810   70 mins   C   B, V   P
Animated
Victor Hugo's classic novel comes to life in this
beautifully animated family feature.
Toei Animation Co Ltd — *Family Home
Entertainment*

Misfits, The 1961
Drama
59344   124 mins   B/W   CED   P
*Clark Gable, Marilyn Monroe, Montgomery Clift,
Thelma Ritter, Eli Wallach, James Barton,
Estelle Winwood, directed by John Huston*
Arthur Miller wrote this parable involving a
disillusioned divorcee and her relationship with
three cowboys in the Nevada desert.
United Artists — *CBS/Fox Video; RCA
VideoDiscs*

Mishima: A Life in Four 1985
Chapters
Biographical
Closed Captioned
84538   121 mins   C   B, V   P
*Ken Ogata, Kenji Sawada, Yasosuke Bando,
directed by Paul Schrader*
An acclaimed and auspicious biography of the
infamous and brilliant Japanese author who
performed ritual Seppuku in 1970. Innovative
design by Eiko Ishioka, music by Philip Glass.
MPAA:R
Mata Yamamoto; Tom Luddy — *Warner Home
Video*

Miss All-American Beauty 1982
Drama
75455   96 mins   C   B, V   P
Diane Lane, Cloris Leachman, Brian Kerwin
An accomplished pianist enters a beauty
pageant hoping to win a scholarship so that she
can return to college.
King Features — *U.S.A. Home Video*

Miss Annie Rooney 1942
Comedy-Drama
64367   86 mins   B/W   B, V, 3/4U   P
*Shirley Temple, Dickie Moore, William Gargan,
Guy Kibbee, Peggy Ryan*
Shirley Temple received her first screen kiss in
this story of a poor Irish girl who falls in love with
a wealthy young man.
Edward Small — *Nostalgia Merchant*

Miss Julie 1950
Drama
82256   90 mins   B/W   B, V   P
Anita Bjork, Ulf Palme
An adaptation of the August Strindberg play
about a confused noblewoman who disgraces
herself when she allows a servant to seduce
her.

SW
Trans-Global Pictures — *Embassy Home
Entertainment*

Miss Nude America 1980
Contest, The
Variety
52862   78 mins   C   B, V   P
The annual Miss Nude America Contest,
presenting a group of unclad contestants being
judged on physical attributes.
MPAA:R
Jim Blake; Jerry Gross Organization — *Wizard
Video*

Miss Peach of the Kelly 1980
School
Cartoons
59364   115 mins   C   CED   P
Animated
The students from the famed comic strip
celebrate the opening of school, Thanksgiving,
Valentine's Day, and the annual picnic.
Sheldon Riss — *Playhouse Video*

Miss Sadie Thompson 1954
Drama
44841   91 mins   C   B, V   P
Rita Hayworth, Jose Ferrer, Aldo Ray
Based on the novel "Rain" by Somerset
Maugham, a promiscuous playgirl, a hypocritical
minister, and a marine all clash on a Pacific
island.
Columbia, Jerry Wald — *RCA/Columbia
Pictures Home Video*

Missiles of October, The 1974
Drama
15388   155 mins   C   B, V   P
*William Devane, Ralph Bellamy, Martin Sheen,
Howard DaSilva*
Story of the October 1962 Cuban Missile crisis,
and how the White House dealt with the
impending danger.
ABC; Herbert Brodkin; Robert Buzz
Berger — *MPI Home Video; Learning Corp of
America*

Missing 1982
Drama
59680   122 mins   C   B, V, LV   P
*Jack Lemmon, Sissy Spacek, John Shea,
Melanie Mayron, directed by Costa-Gavras*
At the height of a military coup in a South
American country, a young American writer
disappears, causing the man's wife and father
to embark on a frustrating search through
government bureaucracy to discover what really
happened to him.
MPAA:PG
Universal — *MCA Home Video*

Missing in Action 1984
Adventure
80623   101 mins   C   B, V, LV   P
Chuck Norris, M. Emmet Walsh
An army colonel returns to Vietnam to settle some old scores while on an MIA fact finding mission.
MPAA:R
Cannon Productions — *MGM/UA Home Video*

Missing in Action 2: The 1985
Beginning
Adventure/War-Drama
81501   96 mins   C   B, V   P
Chuck Norris, Soon-Teck Oh, Cosie Costa, Steven Williams
An army colonel and his men are subjected to insidious torture when a sadistic Vietnamese colonel captures them during a mid-air rescue operation.
MPAA:R
Cannon Productions — *MGM/UA Home Video*

Missing Persons 1983
Music video
88102   15 mins   C   B, V   P
The most popular video clips from the San Francisco-based new wave band, noted for their hiccuppy vocals, including "Walking in L.A." and "Life Is So Strange."
Sony Video — *Sony Video Software*

Mission Batangas 1969
War-Drama/Adventure
80819   100 mins   C   B, V, LV   P
Dennis Weaver, Vera Miles, Keith Larsen
An American pilot and a missionary nurse team up to steal the Philippine government's entire stock of gold bullion from the Japanese who captured it.
Diba Productions — *New World Video*

Mission Galactica: The 1979
Cylon Attack
Science fiction
58214   108 mins   C   B, V, LV   P
Lorne Greene, Lloyd Bridges
The Battlestar Galactica is stranded in space without fuel and open to attack from the chrome-covered Cylons. Adama (Lorne Greene) is forced to stop Commander Cain's (Lloyd Bridges) efforts to launch an attack against the Cylons, while countering the attacks of the Cylon leader.
Universal TV — *MCA Home Video*

Mission Mars 1967
Science fiction
82083   87 mins   C   B, V   P
Darren McGavin, Nick Adams, George DeVries
Three American astronauts encounter strange and bizarre adventures when they become the first men to land on Mars.

Sagittarius Productions — *Unicorn Video*

Mission Phantom 1979
Adventure
77388   90 mins   C   B, V   P
Andrew Ray, Ingrid Sholder, Peter Martel
A gang of intrepid spies on a covert mission in Russia plot to steal a cache of diamonds and help a woman to emigrate to the United States.
MPAA:R
James Reed — *Wizard Video*

Missionary, The 1982
Comedy
66183   86 mins   C   B, V   P
Michael Palin, Maggie Smith, Trevor Howard
A missionary tries to save the souls of a group of fallen women.
MPAA:R
Columbia — *THORN EMI/HBO Video*

Missouri Breaks, The 1976
Western
58953   126 mins   C   B, V, CED   P
Jack Nicholson, Marlon Brando, Randy Quaid, Kathleen Lloyd, Frederic Forrest, Harry Dean Stanton, directed by Arthur Penn
Thomas McGuane wrote the screenplay for this tale of Montana ranchers and rustlers fighting over land and livestock in the 1880's.
MPAA:PG
United Artists — *CBS/Fox Video*

Mrs. Brown, You've Got a 1968
Lovely Daughter
Musical
80149   95 mins   C   B, V   P
Peter Noone, Stanley Holloway, Mona Washbourne
The Herman's Hermits gang inherit a dog and attempt to make a racer out of him.
MPAA:G
Metro Goldwyn Mayer — *MGM/UA Home Video*

Mrs. R's Daughter 1979
Drama
80163   97 mins   C   B, V   P
Cloris Leachman, Season Hubley, Donald Moffat, John McIntire, Ron Rifkin
An outraged mother will stop at nothing to bring her daughter's rapist to trial.
Dan Curtis Productions; NBC — *Warner Home Video*

Mrs. Soffel 1985
Drama
81775   113 mins   C   B, V   P
Diane Keaton, Mel Gibson, Matthew Modine, Edward Herrmann, directed by Gillian Armstrong

This is the true story of how a warden's wife helped two brothers escape from a Pittsburgh prison in 1901. Available in VHS and Beta Hi-Fi.
MPAA:PG-13
MGM/UA — *MGM/UA Home Video*

Mr. Ace — 1946
Drama
82016   85 mins   B/W   B, V   P
George Raft, Sylvia Sidney, Sara Haden, Stanley Ridges
A congresswoman decides to run for governor without the approval of the loyal political kingpin, Mr. Ace. Available in VHS and Beta Hi-Fi Stereo.
United Artists — *Sony Video Software*

Mr. & Mrs. Condor — 1979
Cartoons
71372   60 mins   C   B, V   P
Animated
Life as a big bird in a big forest has its ups and downs. This series follows the fun-loving Condor family at work and play. Each tape includes three episodes.
Independent — *Family Home Entertainment*

Mr. & Mrs. Smith — 1941
Comedy
00287   95 mins   B/W   B, V, 3/4U   P
Carole Lombard, Robert Montgomery, directed by Alfred Hitchcock
Madcap comedy of a married couple who discover their marriage isn't legal.
RKO — *Nostalgia Merchant*

Mr. Bill Looks Back Featuring Sluggo's Greatest Hits — 1983
Comedy
64927   31 mins   C   B, V   P
Mr. Bill creator Walter Williams has filmed all new material never before televised to include with some previous footage.
Walter Williams — *Pacific Arts Video*

Mr. Billion — 1977
Adventure
Closed Captioned
82345   89 mins   C   B, V   P
Jackie Gleason, Terence Hill, Valerie Perrine, Slim Pickens, Chill Wills, directed by Jonathan Kaplan
An Italian mechanic stands to inherit a billion dollar fortune if he can travel from Italy to San Francisco in twenty days.
MPAA:PG
20th Century Fox — *Key Video*

Mr. Blandings Builds His Dream House — 1948
Comedy
00266   93 mins   B/W   B, V, 3/4U   P
Cary Grant, Myrna Loy
Domestic comedy revealing the difficulty a couple faces while trying to build their "dream house."
RKO — *Nostalgia Merchant*

Mr. Boston Official Video Bartender's Guide — 1985
Alcoholic beverages
71055   60 mins   C   B, V   P
In a bar-hopping romp across the U.S.A. the Glenmore Distillery people offer step-by-step instructions for preparing the world's most popular cocktails and punches.
Geoffrey Drummond Prods — *Karl/Lorimar Home Video*

Mr. Halpern and Mr. Johnson — 1983
Drama
65442   57 mins   C   B, V   P
Laurence Olivier, Jackie Gleason
The provocative and compelling story of two strangers united by the death of a woman they both loved, and their revealing and surprising confrontation.
Edie and Ely Landau — *U.S.A. Home Video*

Mr. Horn — 1978
Drama/Western
71326   156 mins   C   B, V   P
David Carradine, Richard Widmark, Karen Black, Stafford Morgan, Don Collier, directed by Jack Starrett
Horn, a legendary tracker, led the 1880's frontier manhunt that captured the Apache warrior Geronimo. William Goldman scripted this folklore saga.
Lorimar Productions and CBS-TV — *U.S.A. Home Video*

Mr. Hulot's Holiday — 1953
Comedy
12802   86 mins   B/W   B, V, FO   P
Jacques Tati, Natalie Pascaud, Michelle Rolia
Jacques Tati's famous character Mr. Hulot, goes on vacationto a seaside resort, with slapstick results.
GDB International — *Video Yesteryear; Video Dimensions; Hollywood Home Theater; Discount Video Tapes; Western Film & Video Inc; Movie Buff Video; Embassy Home Entertainment*

Mr. Kingstreet's War — 1971
Adventure
84828   92 mins   C   B, V   P
John Saxon, Tippi Hedren, Rosanno Brazzi

A idealistic game warden in Africa defends the wildlife against the fighting Italian and British armies at the dawn of World War II.
Gold Key Ent — *United Home Video*

Mr. Klein 1975
Drama
62815 123 mins C B, V P
Alain Delon, Jeanne Moreau, directed by Joseph Losey
In France during the Nazi occupation, a Catholic man searches for a Jew who has stolen his name and identity.
Quartet Films — *RCA/Columbia Pictures Home Video*

Mr. Lucky 1943
Comedy
00286 99 mins B/W B, V, 3/4U P
Cary Grant, Laraine Day, Charles Bickford
Professional gambler tries to raise a new bankroll by fleecing a wealthy young lady, but falls in love instead.
RKO — *Nostalgia Merchant*

Mr. Magoo Cartoons 1967
Comedy/Cartoons
64833 120 mins C CED P
Aminated, voice of Jim Backus
Sixteen classic cartoon selections are featured, including the well-known "Trouble Indemnity."
UPA — *RCA VideoDiscs*

Mister Magoo in Sherwood Forest 1964
Cartoons/Comedy
64025 83 mins C B, V, LV P
Animated, voice of Jim Backus
As Friar Tuck, the nearsighted Mr. Magoo involves Robin Hood and his Merry Men in a series of zany adventures.
MPAA:G
UPA Pictures — *Paramount Home Video; RCA VideoDiscs*

Mr. Magoo in the King's Service 1966
Cartoons
64939 92 mins C B, V P
Animated, voice of Jim Backus
Mr. Magoo is off on the King's business in this wacky full-length cartoon adventure.
UPA — *Paramount Home Video*

Mister Magoo... Man of Mystery 1964
Cartoons
65619 96 mins C B, V P
Animated, voice of Jim Backus
In this episode, Mr. Magoo plays four legendary literary and comic strip heroes: Dr. Watson, Dr.

Frankenstein, the Count of Monte Cristo and Dick Tracey.
UPA Pictures — *Paramount Home Video*

Mister Magoo's Christmas Carol 1962
Cartoons/Christmas
64031 52 mins C B, V, LV P
Animated, voice of Jim Backus
Nearsighted Mr. Magoo, as Ebenezer Scrooge, receives Christmastime visits from three ghosts in this version of Dickens' classic tale.
MPAA:G
UPA Pictures — *Paramount Home Video*

Mr. Magoo's Storybook 1964
Fairy tales/Cartoons
64507 113 mins C B, V P
Animated, the voice of Jim Backus
Mr. Magoo acts all the parts in versions of three famous tales of literature: "Snow White and the Seven Dwarfs," "Don Quixote" and "A Midsummer Night's Dream."
UPA Pictures — *Paramount Home Video*

Mr. Majestyk 1974
Adventure
78630 103 mins C B, V P
Charles Bronson, Al Lettieri, Linda Cristal, directed by Richard Fleischer
When a Vietnam veteran's attempt to start his own business is thwarted by a Mafia hitman, he goes after him with a vengeance.
MPAA:PG
United Artists — *MGM/UA Home Video*

Mr. Mike's Mondo Video 1979
Comedy
66179 75 mins C B, V P
Michael O'Donoghue, Dan Aykroyd, Jane Curtin, Carrie Fisher, Teri Garr, Joan Haskett, Deborah Harry, Margot Kidder, Bill Murray, Loraine Newman, Gilda Radner, Julius LaRosa, Paul Schaeffer, Sid Vicious
A bizarre, outrageous comedy special declared too wild for television conceived by the Saturday Night Live alumnus Mr. Mike.
Lorne Michaels — *Pacific Arts Video*

Mr. Mister: Videos from the Real World 1986
Music video
88359 14 mins C B, V P
Three videos from the flash-in-the-pan pop group: "Kyrie," "Broken Wings" and "Is It Love."
RCA Video — *RCA/Columbia Pictures Home Video*

Mr. Mom 1983
Comedy
Closed Captioned
65375 92 mins C B, V, LV, P
CED
Michael Keaton, Teri Garr
A hard-working husband becomes a harried
housewife and his wife turns into a high-
powered executive.
MPAA:PG
Lynn Loring — *Vestron Video*

Mr. Moon's Magic Circus 1982
Circus
64954 90 mins C B, V R, P
*Marcia Lewis, John Sarantos, Chuck Quinlan,
Hank Adams, Marylin Magness, Mark Ganzel*
A circus of musical fantasy for children that
features original music, plenty of dancing,
mishaps and circus fun.
Century Video — *Video Gems*

Mr. Moto's Last Warning 1939
Mystery
07077 71 mins B/W B, V P
*Peter Lorre, George Sanders, Riccardo Cortez,
Virginia Field*
Conspirators, plotting to blow up the Suez
Canal, are under the impression they have
eliminated Mr. Moto.
20th Century Fox — *Discount Video Tapes;
Cable Films; Video Connection; Video
Yesteryear; Hollywood Home Theater; Kartes
Video Communications*

Mr. Peabody and the 1948
Mermaid
Comedy
65737 89 mins B/W B, V P
William Powell, Ann Blythe
A middle-aged husband hooks a beautiful
mermaid while fishing in the Caribbean and with
time, falls in love with her.
Universal — *Republic Pictures Home Video*

Mr. Reeder in Room 13 1938
Suspense
47651 66 mins B/W B, V, FO P
Gibb McLaughlin
Based on the mystery stories created by Edgar
Wallace, Mr. Reeder (a cultured English
gentleman who fights crime) enlists the aid of a
young man to get evidence on a gang of
counterfeiters.
England — *Video Yesteryear*

Mister Roberts 1955
Comedy
38951 120 mins C B, V P
*Henry Fonda, James Cagney, Jack Lemmon,
William Powell, Betsy Palmer*

The comic adventures of the crew of a navy
cargo freighter in the South Pacific during World
War II, adapted from the long running play.
Academy Awards '55: Best Supporting Actor
(Lemmon).
Warner Bros — *Warner Home Video; RCA
VideoDiscs*

Mr. Robinson Crusoe 1932
Adventure
08856 76 mins B/W B, V P, T
*Douglas Fairbanks Sr., William Farnum, Maria
Alba, Earle Brown, directed by Edward
Sutherland*
Rollicking adventure in the South Seas as man
makes a bet that he can live on a desert island
without being left any refinements of civilization.
United Artists — *Blackhawk Films; Video
Yesteryear; Kartes Video Communications; MPI
Home Video*

Mister Rogers Goes to 1983
School
Education
64779 117 mins C CED P
Fred Rogers explores the questions children
have about school, and helps prepare them for
their first day. Includes two shows, one from
1979 and the other from 1983.
Family Communications — *RCA VideoDiscs*

Mr. Rogers—Helping 1983
Children Understand
Ethics
64454 76 mins C CED P
Fred Rogers
Mr. Rogers hosts four informative programs for
children ages 2-7. Includes "What Is Love?,"
"Pretendings" and "Death of a Goldfish."
Family Communications — *RCA VideoDiscs*

Mr. Rossi Looks For 1986
Happiness
Cartoons
71368 80 mins C B, V P
Animated, directed by Bruno Bozzetto
Aided by a magic whistle, Mr. Rossi travels
through the past and future, only to learn that
there's no time like the present.
Italtoons Corp; Bruno Bozzetto Film — *Family
Home Entertainment*

Mr. Rossi's Vacation 1983
Cartoons
77423 82 mins C B, V P
Animated, directed by Bruno Bozzetto
Mr. Rossi and his dog Harold go off in search of
quiet on a let's get away-from-it-all vacation.
Italtoons Corp; Bruno Bozzetto Film — *Family
Home Entertainment*

Mister Scarface   1978
Drama
79334   85 mins   C   B, V   P
Jack Palance, Edmund Purdon, Al Cliver, Harry Bear
A young man searches for the man who murdered his father years earlier in a dark alley.
MPAA:R
PRO International — *Monterey Home Video; World Video Pictures*

Mr. Smith Goes to   1939
Washington
Drama
21292   130 mins   B/W   B, V   P
James Stewart, Jean Arthur, Edward Arnold, Claude Rains, directed by Frank Capra
An idealistic young statesman finds nothing but corruption when he takes his seat in the Senate. Academy Awards '39: Best Original Story; N.Y. Film Critics Award '39: Best Actor (Stewart).
Columbia — *RCA/Columbia Pictures Home Video*

Mr. Super Athletic Charm   194?
Adventure
10128   56 mins   B/W   B, V   P, T
Douglas Fairbanks Sr.
Douglas Fairbanks portrays dashing swashbuckler in "Black Pirate" (1926) and "Thief of Bagdad" (1940) from the "History of Motion Picture" series.
United Artists — *Blackhawk Films*

Mr. Sycamore   1974
Fantasy
84084   90 mins   C   B, V   P
Jason Robards, Jean Simmons, Sandy Dennis, directed by Pancho Kohner
A fantasy about a frustrated mailman who is turned into a tree to elude the tensions of human life and then falls in love.
Charles Fries Productions — *Worldvision Home Video*

Mr. Too Little   1979
Adventure
59071   90 mins   C   B, V   R, P
Rosanno Brazzi
The traveling adventures of a circus poodle and his Bengal tiger buddy.
GG Communications — *Video Gems*

Mr. T's Be Somebody...   1984
Or Be Somebody's Fool
Identity/Ethics
Closed Captioned
78892   60 mins   C   B, V   P
Valerie Landsburg, New Edition
A variety program where Mr. T helps young people to gain confidence in themselves. In Beta and VHS Stereo.

Topper Carew; Henry Johnson — *MCA Home Video*

Mr. Winkle Goes to War   1944
Comedy
70876   80 mins   B/W   B, V   P
Edward G. Robinson, Ruth Warrick, Richard Lane, Robert Armstrong, directed by Alfred E. Green
Weak and timid Winkle wipes out a foxhole of enemy soldiers without a wink to become a war hero. In Hi-Fi Mono.
Columbia — *RCA/Columbia Pictures Home Video*

Mr. Wise Guy   1942
Comedy
00411   70 mins   B/W   B, V, 3/4U   P
Leo Gorcey, Huntz Hall, East Side Kids
The East Side Kids break out of reform school to clear the brother of one of the Kids of a murder charge.
Prime TV — *Hal Roach Studios; Discount Video Tapes; See Hear Industries*

Mr. Wizard's World: 1983
Puzzles, Problems and
Impossibilities
Science
88078   46 mins   C   B, V   P
Don Herbert demonstrates various household scientific amazements for the young.
MTV Networks — *Playhouse Video*

Mr. Wong, Detective   1938
Mystery
05596   69 mins   B/W   B, V   P
Boris Karloff, Grant Withers
Mr. Wong traps a killer who acts guilty to throw suspicion from himself.
Monogram — *Hollywood Home Theater; Discount Video Tapes; Kartes Video Communications*

Mistress of the Apes   1979
Adventure
81400   88 mins   C   B, V   P
Barbara Leigh, Garth Pillsbury, Walt Robin, Jenny Neumann
A group of scientists discover a tribe of near-men, who are the missing link in evolution on a jungle safari. Available in VHS Stereo and Beta Hi-Fi.
MPAA:R
Cineworld — *Monterey Home Video*

Mistress Pamela   1976
Drama
53146   95 mins   C   B, V   P
Ann Michelle, Julian Barnes

When young Pamela goes to work in the household of handsome Lord Devonish, he sets about in his wild pursuit of her virginity.
MPAA:R
Intercontinental Releasing — *Monterey Home Video*

Mistress (Wild Geese), The   1953
Drama
88355   106 mins   B/W   B, V   P
Hideko Takamine, Hiroshi Akutagawa, directed by Shiro Toyoda
A classic Japanese period piece about a woman who believes she's married to a successful industrialist, only to find he is already married and she is but his mistress.
JA
Japanese — *Embassy Home Entertainment*

Misunderstood   1984
Drama
78629   92 mins   C   B, V   P
Gene Hackman, Susan Anspach, Henry Thomas, Huckleberry Fox, directed by Jerry Schatzberg
A father and his two sons become closer to each other after their mother dies suddenly.
MPAA:PG
Keith Barish Productions; Accent Film's — *MGM/UA Home Video*

Misunderstood Monsters   1984
Psychology/Children
73646   50 mins   C   B, V   P
Animated voices of Claire Bloom, John Carradine, Arte Johnson, Mickey Rooney
A small young boy learns that inner feelings are more important than outward appearances.
Bosustow Entertainment; Asselin Productions — *Kartes Video Communications*

Mixed Blood   1984
Drama/Film-Avant-garde
84672   98 mins   C   B, V   P
Marilia Pera, Richard Vlacia, Linda Kerridge, Geraldine Smith, AngelDavid, directed by Paul Morrissey
From the renowned underground film-maker, an acclaimed comedic-violent examination of the seedy drug sub-culture in New York.
MPAA:R
Cine Vista — *Media Home Entertainment*

Moby Dick   1956
Adventure
Closed Captioned
65757   116 mins   C   B, V, CED   P
Gregory Peck, Richard Basehart, Orson Welles, Leo Genn, Friedrich Ledebur, directed by John Huston

Herman Melville's high sea saga comes to life with Captain Ahab, obsessed with desire for revenge upon the great white whale, Moby Dick.
Warner Bros — *CBS/Fox Video*

Moby Dick and the Mighty   1967
Mightor
Cartoons
82159   38 mins   C   B, V   P
Animated
Here is a collection of two animated adventures featuring Moby Dick, a super whale who uses his incredible speed to fight crime, and The Mighty Mightor, a young man who uses his unlimited physical powers to protect his Stone Age village.
Hanna-Barbera — *Worldvision Home Video*

Moby Dick   1977
Adventure/Drama
84714   52 mins   C   B, V   P
Animated
An animated version of the Herman Melville classic.
API Television Prod — *MGM/UA Home Video*

Model Behavior   1982
Romance
70848   86 mins   C   B, V   P
Richard Bekins, Bruce Lyons, Cindy Harrel
Fresh from college, an aspiring photographer pines for a glamorous model.
Inter Ocean — *Lightning Video*

Modern Problems   1981
Comedy
59426   93 mins   C   B, V, CED   P
Chevy Chase, Patti D'Arbanville, Mary Kay Place, Brian Doyle-Murray, Neil Carter, Dabney Coleman
A man involved in a nuclear accident discovers he has acquired telekinetic powers, which he uses to turn the tables on his professional and romantic rivals.
MPAA:PG
Twentieth Century Fox — *CBS/Fox Video*

Modern Romance   1981
Comedy
58499   102 mins   C   B, V   P
Albert Brooks, Kathryn Harrold, Bruno Kirby, George Kennedy, Bob Einstein, directed by Albert Brooks
The romantic misadventures of a neurotic film editor who continuously breaks up with his girlfriend and then attempts to win her back.
MPAA:R
Columbia; Andrew Scheinman — *RCA/Columbia Pictures Home Video*

Modern Times 1936
Comedy
08421   87 mins   B/W   B, V   P
*Charlie Chaplin, Paulette Goddard, Henry
Bergman, Chester Conklin, directed by Charlie
Chaplin*
In his last silent film, Chaplin plays a factory
workman who goes crazy from his repetitious
job on an assembly line. Chaplin wrote the
musical score which incorporates the tune
"Smile," and also sings a gibberish song.
United Artists — *Playhouse Video; RCA
VideoDiscs*

Mogambo 1954
Adventure
53351   116 mins   C   B, V   P
*Clark Gable, Ava Gardner, Grace Kelly, directed
by John Ford*
An American showgirl and a British
archaeologist and his wife team up with a White
hunter in Kenya, and set off on a gorilla hunt.
Sam Zimbalist; MGM — *MGM/UA Home Video*

Mohawk 1956
Western
81620   80 mins   C   B, V   P
*Rita Gam, Neville Brand, Scott Brady, Lori
Nelson*
A cowboy and his Indian maiden try to stop a
war between Indian tribes and fanatical
landowners.
20th Century Fox — *Video Gems*

**Moiseyev Dance
Company: A Gala
Evening** 1980
Dance
84666   70 mins   C   B, V   P
Choreographed by Igor Moiseyev
On this tape, the famed dance company
performs to Russian folk tunes.
Russian — *V.I.E.W. Video*

Molly Maguires, The 1969
Drama
88422   123 mins   C   B, V   P
*Sean Connery, Richard Harris, Samantha
Eggar, directed by Martin Ritt*
The story of the 1870's Irish coal mining
rebellion in Pennsylvania, entailing the
adventures of a detective sent to infiltrate the
group and expose their terrorist activities.
MPAA:PG
Paramount — *Paramount Home Video*

Molly (The Goldbergs) 1955
Comedy
66140   27 mins   B/W   B, V, FO   P
*Gertrude Berg, Robert Harris, Arlene McQuade,
Eli Mintz, Tom Taylor*
In this episode of the long-running series, Molly
is being menaced by two ex-cons.

Dumont — *Video Yesteryear*

Mommie Dearest 1981
Drama
58713   129 mins   C   B, V, LV   P
*Faye Dunaway, Diana Scarwid, Steve Forrest,
Howard DaSilva, directed by Frank Perry*
Faye Dunaway portrays Joan Crawford in this
film version of Christina Crawford's memoirs,
describing her mother as a neurotic tyrant who
abused her children while presenting a
glamourous screen image to the public.
MPAA:PG
Paramount; Frank Yablans — *Paramount
Home Video; RCA VideoDiscs*

Mon Oncle 1958
Comedy
57338   110 mins   C   B, V, LV   P
*Jacques Tati, Jean-Pierre Zola, Adrienne
Serrantie, Alain Baçourt, directed by Jacques
Tati*
Eccentric Mr. Hulot aids his nephew in war
against his parents' ultramodern, push-button
home. Available dubbed or with English
subtitles.
Academy Award '58: Best Foreign Language
Picture. EL, FR
Continental Dist Co — *Embassy Home
Entertainment; Hollywood Home Theater;
Discount Video Tapes; Video Yesteryear; Movie
Buff Video*

Mondo Magic 1976
Documentary/Magic
84512   100 mins   C   B, V   P
Directed by Melvin Ashford
A compilation of tribal rituals and sicknesses
offering viewers a look on the darker side of
matters magical.
APEA — *Magnum Entertainment*

Money Hunt 1984
Mystery
76394   30 mins   C   B, V   P
John Hillerman
$100,000 cash is secured in a safe deposit box;
the first person who can solve the puzzle from
the hints given in this program will claim the
prize. Magnum P.I.'s John Hillerman is the host.
Rogers & Cowan Inc — *Karl/Lorimar Home
Video*

Money Madness 1979
Music
37405   92 mins   C   B, V   P
Eddie Money
Popular rock singer Eddie Money's rise to the
top of the music business is chronicled in this
program, in which he performs some of his
songs.

New Line Cinema; Michael Mason — *CBS/Fox Video*

Monique 1970
Drama
64967   86 mins   C   CED   P
Sibylla Kay, Joan Alcome, David Sumner
A menage a trois results when a couple hire a pretty French girl to help with their children.
Avco-Embassy — *Embassy Home Entertainment (disc only)*

Monique 1983
Suspense
81196   96 mins   C   B, V   P
Florence Giorgetti, John Ferris
A sophisticated career woman is about to unleash a terrifying secret on her new husband.
Jacques Scandelari — *VCL Home Video*

Monkey Business 1931
Comedy
81199   77 mins   B/W   B, V   P
The Marx Brothers, Thelma Todd, Ruth Hall, Harry Woods, directed by Norman Z. McLeod
Groucho, Harpo, Chico, and Zeppo stowaway aboard a luxury liner to hide from the authorities. While aboard the ship, the boys crash a society party and catch a few crooks in the process.
Beta Hi-Fi Mono.
Paramount — *MCA Home Video*

Monkey in the Master's Eye 1972
Martial arts
84071   92 mins   C   B, V   P
A martial arts adventure spiced with low comedy, in the story of a buffoonish slave rising to martial arts infamy.
Robert Chang; Han Yin Tze — *Unicorn Video*

Monkey's Uncle, The 1965
Comedy
84432   90 mins   C   B, V   P
Tommy Kirk, Annette Funicello, Leon Ames, Arthur O'Connell, directed by Robert Stevenson
A sequel to "The Misadventures of Merlin Jones" and featuring more bizarre antics and scientific hoopla.
Walt Disney Prods — *Walt Disney Home Video*

Monsieur Verdoux 1947
Comedy
08406 123 mins B/W   B, V   P
Charlie Chaplin, Martha Raye, Isabella Elsom, Mady Corell, Allison Roddan, Robert Lewis
A prim and proper bank cashier marries and murders rich women in order to support his real wife.
Charles Chaplin — *Playhouse Video*

Monsignor 1982
Drama
60581   121 mins   C   B, V, CED   P
Christopher Reeve, Fernando Rey, Genevieve Bujold, Jason Miller, directed by Frank Perry
An ambitious American priest becomes embroiled in the high stakes game of Vatican politics.
MPAA:R
Twentieth Century Fox — *CBS/Fox Video*

Monster a Go-Go! 1955
Science fiction
77200   70 mins   B/W   B, V   P
Phil Morton, June Travis, directed by Herschell Gordon Lewis
A team of go-go dancers battle a ten-foot monster from outerspace.
Majestic International Pictures — *United Home Video*

Monster Club, The 1985
Horror
80477   104 mins   C   B, V   P
Vincent Price, Donald Pleasance, John Carradine, Stuart Whitman, Britt Ekland, Simon Ward, directed by Roy Ward Baker
Vincent Price and John Carradine star in this music-horror compilation, featuring songs by Night, B.A. Robertson, The Pretty Things and The Viewers. Soundtrack music by John Williams, UB 40 and The Expressos. In Beta Hi-Fi and VHS stereo.
Milton Subotsky; ITC Film Distributors — *Thriller Video*

Monster from Green Hell 1958
Horror
09109   71 mins   B/W   B, V   P
Jim Davis, Robert Griffin, Barbara Turner, Eduardo Cianelli
An experimental rocket containing radiation contaminated wasps crashes in Africa making giant killer wasps that are destroyed by a volcano.
DCA — *Movie Buff Video; Mossman Williams Productions; Video Yesteryear*

Monster from the Ocean Floor 1954
Horror
86165   66 mins   C   B, V   P
Anne Kimball, Stuart Wade
An oceanographer in a deep-sea diving bell is threatened by a multi-tentacled creature.
Roger Corman — *Vidmark Entertainment*

Monster Maker, The 1944
Horror
58616   65 mins   B/W   B, V, 3/4U   R, P
J. Carroll Nash, Ralph Morgan
A doctor creates monsters by his secretly invented glandular injections.

Producers Releasing Corp — *Cable Films; Video Connection*

Monster Walks, The 1932
Horror
12830   60 mins   B/W   B, V, FO   P
Rex Lease, Vera Reynolds, Mischa Auer
A whodunit thriller complete with stormy nights, suspicious cripples, weird servants, and a screaming gorilla.
Mayfair — *Video Yesteryear; Blackhawk Films*

Monstermania 1986
Automobiles-Racing
87748   30 mins   C   B, V   P
Monster trucks demolish each other in this thrill-packed action tape.
Visual Assoc.; United Sports of America — *Twin Tower Enterprises*

Monsters, Madmen, 1984
Machines
Film-History/Science fiction
79684   57 mins   C   B, V   P
Narrated by Gil Gerard
The eighty year history of science fiction films from "Metropolis" to "Star Wars" is presented in this retrospective.
RKO — *RKO Home Video*

Monsters of the Mat 1986
Sports-Minor/Circus
71341   60 mins   C   B, V   P
Sgt. Slaughter, Mil Mascaras, Kerry Von Erich, Road Warriors, Kamala, Rick Martel, Stan Hanson, directed by Al Footnick
The tapes in this series feature wrestling highlights from many popular grapplers, including action from the annual AWA Night of Champions.
Noel C Bloom; Verne Gagne; Don Spielvogel — *U.S.A. Home Video*

Monsters on the March 1960
Movie and TV trailers
42960   25 mins   B/W   B, V, FO   P
This program consists of 14 movie trailers, including frightening coming attractions for movies such as the "The Return of the Fly" with Vincent Price, "Isle of the Dead" with Boris Karloff, "I Walked with a Zombie" with Frances Dee, and other, dating as far back as 1932 and up to 1960.
20th Century Fox et al — *Video Yesteryear*

Monte Walsh 1970
Western
Closed Captioned
81173   100 mins   C   B, V   P
Lee Marvin, Jack Palance, Jeanne Moreau, Jim Davis, Mitchell Ryan, directed by William A. Fraker

An aging cowboy sets out on one last adventure to avenge the death of his best friend. Hi-Fi sound for both formats.
MPAA:PG
CBS Theatrical Films — *CBS/Fox Video*

Montenegro 1981
Drama
47799   97 mins   C   B, V   P
Susan Anspach, Erland Josephson
The story of an American housewife living in Sweden who tires of her uncomplicated life as a wife and mother, and promptly flees her home and family in search of excitement.
Atlantic Releasing — *THORN EMI/HBO Video*

Monterey Pop 1968
Music-Performance
82384   72 mins   C   B, V   P
Jefferson Airplane, Janis Joplin, Jimi Hendrix, The Who, Simon & Garfunkel, Otis Redding
This pre-Woodstock rock 'n roll festival features landmark performances by some of the most popular sixties rockers.
D A Pennebaker — *Sony Video Software*

Montgomery Clift 1985
Biographical/Documentary
70996   120 mins   C   B, V   P
Montgomery Clift, directed by Claudio Masenza
This tribute includes clips from many of Clift's magnetic screen portrayals from 1948 to 1966.
Donatella Baglivio — *Kartes Video Communications*

Montreal Expos: Team 1984
Highlights
Baseball
81144   30 mins   C   B, V   P
Gary Carter, Tim Raines, Rusty Staub, Andre Dawson 7   pgms
This series provides a brief history of the Expos along with selected highlights of their past seasons.
1.1969: Expos 2.1979: Makin' It 3.1980: The Team of the '80's 4.1981: One Step Closer 5.1982: Year of the All-Stars 6. 1983: 15th Anniversary 7. 1984: Expos 1984.
Major League Baseball — *Major League Baseball Productions*

Monty Python and the 1975
Holy Grail
Comedy
63441   90 mins   C   B, V, LV   P
John Cleese, Michael Palin, Eric Idle, Graham Chapman, Terry Jones, Terry Gilliam
The quest for the Holy Grail by King Arthur and his Knights of the Round Table is retold in the inimitable Python fashion.
MPAA:PG

Almi/Cinema V — *RCA/Columbia Pictures Home Video; RCA VideoDiscs*

Monty Python Live at the Hollywood Bowl   1982
Comedy
64207   78 mins   C   B, V   P
Eric Idle, Michael Palin, John Cleese, Terry Gilliam, Terry Jones, Graham Chapman
A live concert performance by the madcap comedy troupe.
George Harrison; Handmade Films — *THORN EMI/HBO Video; RCA VideoDiscs*

Monty Python's Life of Brian   1979
Comedy
37424   90 mins   C   B, V   P
Eric Idle, Michael Palin, Graham Chapman, Terry Gilliam, John Cleese, Terry Jones
A typical Monty Python romp, this time through the Holy Land in the year 32 A.D. This is the hilarious story of Brian, a man who was born on the same night as Jesus Christ. Through a series of mishaps and misinterpretations, Brian is proclaimed the Messiah, a role he refuses to accept. Consequently, he spends most of his time running from the adoring multitudes, government officials, and several underground groups.
MPAA:R
Warner Bros — *Warner Home Video; RCA VideoDiscs*

Monty Python's The Meaning of Life   1983
Comedy
65207   107 mins   C   B, V, LV   P
John Cleese, Michael Palin, Eric Idle, Graham Chapman, Terry Jones, Terry Gilliam
No aspect of life is sacred for the probing Python crew. Religion, birth control, sex and death all get their respective dues. This program is in stereo on all formats.
Universal — *MCA Home Video*

Moon in the Gutter, The   1984
Drama
85235   109 mins   C   B, V   P
Gerard Depardieu, Nastassia Kinski, directed by Jean-Jacques Beineix
In a ramshackle harbor town, a man searches despondently for the person who killed his sister years before. Various sexual liasons and stevedore fights intermittently spice up the action.
MPAA:R
Triumph Films — *RCA/Columbia Pictures Home Video*

Moon Is Blue, The   1953
Comedy
55467   100 mins   B/W   LV, CED   P

William Holden, David Niven, directed by Otto Preminger
A young lady, armed with utter candor and good sense, sets out to bewilder a young man about town who doesn't believe marriage is for him.
Otto Preminger — *CBS/Fox Video*

Moon Madness   1983
Cartoons/Fantasy
77415   82 mins   C   B, V   P
Animated
An astronomer takes a trip to the moon to find the selenites, proprietors of the fountain of youth.
Jean Image — *Vestron Video*

Moon of the Wolf   1972
Horror
69290   74 mins   C   B, V   P
David Janssen, Barbara Rush, Bradford Dillman, John Beradino
A small town in bayou country is terrorized by a modern-day werewolf that rips its victims to shreds.
Filmways — *Worldvision Home Video*

Moon Pilot   1962
Comedy/Science fiction
87676   98 mins   C   B, V   P
Tom Tryon, Brian Keith, Edmond O'Brien, Dany Saval, Tommy Kirk
An astronaut on his way to the moon encounters a mysterious alien woman who claims to know his future.
MPAA:G
Walt Disney Prod. — *Walt Disney Home Video*

Moon-Spinners, The   1964
Adventure/Drama
81671   118 mins   C   B, V   P
Hayley Mills, Peter McEnery, Eli Wallach, Pola Negri, directed by James Neilson
Two young tourists traveling through Greece set out to find a notorious jewel thief who set them up.
Walt Disney Productions — *Walt Disney Home Video*

Mooncussers   1962
Adventure
88198   85 mins   C   B, V   P
Kevin Corcoran, Rian Garrick, Oscar Holmolka
A children's film detailing the exploits of a precocious 12-year-old determined to exact revenge upon a band of ruthless pirates.
Walt Disney Prod. — *Walt Disney Home Video*

Moonlight Sword and Jade Lion   197?
Martial arts
72176   94 mins   C   B, V   P
Mao Yin, Wong Do

A Kung Fu action film taking place in ancient China.
Foreign — *Master Arts Video*

Moonlighting 1982
Drama
64795   97 mins   C   B, V, LV   P
Jeremy Irons, Eugene Liponski, Jiri Stanislay, Eugeniusz Haczkiewicz, directed by Jerzy Skolimowski
This British/Polish film depicts four builders from Poland who travel to London to renovate a London residence. While in London, the Polish military imposes martial law, suspending the Gdansk agreement and outlawing Solidarity. Only one of the builders speaks English, and he decides not to tell the others what is happening back in Poland.
Cannes Film Festival '82: Best Screenplay.
MPAA:PG
Universal Classics — *MCA Home Video*

Moonlighting 1985
Drama
Closed Captioned
87338   97 mins   C   B, V   P
Cybill Shepherd, Bruce Willis
The TV-pilot for the popular detective show, wherein Maddie and David, the daffy pair of impetuous private eyes, meet for the first time and solve an irrationally complex case.
Picturemaker Prod.; ABC Circle Films — *Warner Home Video*

Moonraker 1979
Adventure
63549   126 mins   C   B, V   P
Roger Moore, Lois Chiles, Richard Kiel, Michael Lonsdale, Corinne Clery
James Bond is aided by a female CIA agent, assaulted by a giant with jaws of steel and captured by Amazons when he sets out to protect the human race.
MPAA:PG
United Artists — *CBS/Fox Video; RCA VideoDiscs*

Moonshine County Express 1977
Adventure
51991   104 mins   C   B, V   P
William Conrad, Susan Howard, Maureen McCormick, Claudia Jennings, John Saxon
Three daughters of a hillbilly moonshiner set out to avenge their father's senseless murder.
MPAA:PG
New World Pictures — *Warner Home Video*

Moonstone Gem, The 1983
Cartoons
65486   48 mins   C   B, V   P
Animated

The Evil Baron threatens to steal the most precious gem of all—happiness—from King Gunther, Prince Jeremy and the Gunderlings.
Paul Fusco — *Media Home Entertainment*

More! Police Squad 1982
Comedy
81107   75 mins   C   B, V   P
Leslie Nielsen, Alan North, Rex Hamilton, Peter Lupus
Join intrepid police captain Frank Drebin as he captures big city bad guys in this collection of the final three episodes from the series.
Paramount Pictures — *Paramount Home Video*

Morgan—A Suitable Case for Treatment 1966
Comedy
63324   93 mins   B/W   B, V   P
Vanessa Redgrave, David Warner, Robert Stephens, Irene Handl
A schizophrenic artist refuses to recognize his wife's divorce. When she refuses to go back to him, he decides life is easier to cope with while dressed in a gorilla suit.
British Lion; Quintra — *THORN EMI/HBO Video*

Morgan the Pirate 1960
Adventure
82565   93 mins   C   B, V   P
Steve Reeves
An escaped slave becomes a notorious pirate in the Caribbean in this brisk adventure.
Joseph F Levine — *Embassy Home Entertainment*

Morning Glory 1933
Drama
29493   74 mins   B/W   B, V   P
Katherine Hepburn, Douglas Fairbanks Jr, Adolphe Menjou
A small town girl takes her aspirations for a stage career very seriously.
Academy Awards '33: Best Actress (Hepburn).
RKO, Merian C Cooper — *RKO Home Video; Blackhawk Films; Nostalgia Merchant*

Moron Movies 1985
Comedy
76923   60 mins   C   B, V   P
A collection of one-hundred-fifty short films that describe comedic uses for everyday products.
Len Cella — *MPI Home Video*

Mortuary 1981
Suspense
65605   91 mins   C   B, V   P
Christopher George, Lynda Day George
A young woman's nightmares come startlingly close to reality.
MPAA:R

Artists Releasing Corporation — *Vestron Video*

Moscow Does Not Believe in Tears
1980

Drama
85236   115 mins   C   B, V   P
Vera Alentova, Irina Muravyova, Raisa Ryazanova, directed by Vladimir Menshov
The poignant story of three Russian peasant girls who go to Moscow and try to fulfill their dreams. In Russian with English subtitles. Academy Awards '80: Best Foreign Film. RU
Mosfilm — *RCA/Columbia Pictures Home Video*

Moscow on the Hudson
1984

Comedy
Closed Captioned
78874   115 mins   C   B, V   P
Robin Williams, Maria Conchita Alonso, Cleavent Derricks, directed by Paul Mazursky
A Russian saxophone player defects at Bloomingdales in New York City while on tour with a Russian circus. In VHS and Beta Hi-Fi.
MPAA:R
Paul Mazursky; Columbia
Pictures — *RCA/Columbia Pictures Home Video*

Moses
1976

Drama/Religion
63393   141 mins   C   B, V   P
Burt Lancaster, Anthony Quayle, Ingrid Thulin, Irene Papas, William Lancaster
Lancaster portrays the plight of Moses, who struggled to free his people from tyranny.
ITC Entertainment — *CBS/Fox Video*

Moses
1979

Drama/Bible
63499   58 mins   C   B, V   P
John Marley, Julie Adams, Robert Alda, Joseph Campanella
Moses delivers his people from bondage in a miraculous parting of the Red Sea. Part of the "Greatest Heroes of the Bible" series.
Sunn Classics — *Magnum Entertainment; Lucerne Films*

Most Dangerous Game, The
1932

Suspense
01677   78 mins   B/W   B, V   P
Joel McCrea, Fay Wray, Leslie Banks, Robert Armstrong
A crazed big game hunter lures guests to his secluded island so he can hunt them down like animals.
RKO — *Media Home Entertainment; Hollywood Home Theater; Discount Video Tapes; Video Dimensions; Cable Films; Video Yesteryear; Video Connection; Western Film &*

Video Inc; Cinema Concepts; Kartes Video Communications; Movie Buff Video

---

Most Memorable Games of the Decade #1
1980

Football
50091   48 mins   C   B, V, FO   R, P
Highlights from two of the longest overtime playoff games in NFL history: Miami 27, Kansas City 24, in 1971 and Oakland 37, Baltimore 31, in 1977.
NFL Films — *NFL Films Video*

Most Memorable Games of the Decade #2
1980

Football
50092   48 mins   C   B, V, FO   R, P
Last second victories in two thrilling classics from 1974: AFC Playoff, Oakland 28, Miami 26; and the 24-23 Thanksgiving Day win by Dallas over Washington led by rookie quarterback Clint Longley.
NFL Films — *NFL Films Video*

Most Memorable Games of the Decade #3
1980

Football
50093   48 mins   C   B, V, FO   R, P
Namath and Unitas combine for 872 passing yards in a 1972 regular season game: Jets 44, Colts 34. Plus, the last second victory in the 1976 AFC Playoff: Oakland 24, New England 21.
NFL Films — *NFL Films Video*

Motels, The
1984

Music-Performance
75914   14 mins   C   B, V   P
This program presents the Motels performing their latest hit songs.
Capital Records Inc — *Sony Video Software*

Mother Lode
1982

Adventure
69283   101 mins   C   B, V   P
Charlton Heston, Nick Mancuso
This action-adventure film tells of the conflict between two men, one driven by greed and the other by near madness, and the all consuming lust for gold. Available in Canada through New World Video.
MPAA:PG
Agamemnon Films — *Vestron Video*

Mother's Day
1980

Suspense
68224   98 mins   C   B, V   P
Tiana Pierce, Nancy Hendrickson, Deborah Luee
Three former college roommates plan a reunion together in the wilderness. All was going well until they were dragged into an isolated house.

The terror begins. Two boys and their mother terrorize the girls.
United Film Distributors — *Media Home Entertainment*

Mothra 1962
Horror
64915   101 mins   C   B, V   P
Yumi Ito, Emi Ito
A giant moth wreaks havoc on Tokyo.
Tomoyuki Tanaka — *RCA/Columbia Pictures Home Video*

Motion Picture Camera, The 19??
Filmmaking/Documentary
57432   32 mins   C   B, V   P, T
From the Karl Malkames collection, we see the development of the movie camera.
Unknown — *Blackhawk Films*

Motorhead: Deaf Not Blind 1984
Music-Performance
71009   60 mins   C   B, V   P
Lemmy, Fast Eddie, Phil Taylor
This heavy-metal songfest features Motorhead's original members.
Polygram — *Passport Music Video*

Motown Time Capsule: The 60's 1986
Musical
87624   50 mins   C   B, V   P
The Miracles, Mary Wells, The Four Tops, The Supremes, The Temptations
A retrospective of Motown music from the 1960's, featuring "I Second That Emotion," "Shop Around" and "Pride and Joy."
Gino Tanasescu; MCA — *MCA Home Video*

Motown Time Capsule: The 70's 1986
Musical
87625   50 mins   C   B, V   P
Marvin Gaye, Stevie Wonder, Smokey Robinson, The Commodores
A retrospective of Motown music from the 1970's, including "Living for the City," "War," "Easy" and "Love Hangover."
Gino Tanasescu; MCA — *MCA Home Video*

Motown 25: Yesterday, Today, Forever 1983
Variety/Music-Performance
82266   130 mins   C   B, V, LV   P
The Commodores, Michael Jackson, Richard Pryor, Diana Ross, Marvin Gaye, Stevie Wonder, Adam Ant, Dick Clark
This is the TV all-star salute to Berry Gordy that features a musical duel between the Four Tops

and The Temptations and the reunion of The Jackson Five. In VHS and Beta Hi-Fi.
Don Mischer; Buz Kohan — *MGM/UA Home Video*

Motown's Mustang 1986
Musical
87173   43 mins   C   B, V   P
Clyde Jones, Christi Shay, Louis Carr Jr., Billy Preston, The Temptations
Eleven old Motown hits are used as the framework for this new musical drama featuring cameos by various artists, about a '64 Mustang passing through various owners' hands and cultural changes.
Motown Pictures Co. — *MCA Home Video*

Mountain Family Robinson 1979
Adventure
66061   102 mins   C   B, V   P
Robert Logan, Susan Damante Shaw, Heather Rattray, Ham Larsen
An urban family, seeking escape from the hassles of city life, moves to the Rockies.
MPAA:G
Arthur Dubs — *Media Home Entertainment*

Mountain Man 1976
Drama
65725   96 mins   C   B, V   P
Denver Pyle, Ken Berry, Cheryl Miller
A true story of one man's lonely, dangerous and inspired fight to save a part of the vanishing wilderness west of the Mississippi, a wilderness now regarded as one of the scenic wonders of the world.
Charles E Sellier Jr — *United Home Video*

Mountain Men, The 1980
Adventure
58210   102 mins   C   B, V   P
Charlton Heston, Brian Keith
A sweeping adventure drama set in the American West of the 1880's.
MPAA:R
Martin Shafer; Andrew Sheinman — *RCA/Columbia Pictures Home Video*

Mountain Silence—A Special Adventure For the Deaf 1984
Sports-Winter
84280   18 mins   C   B, V   P
Handicapped children beat the odds and learn to ski.
Video Travel Inc — *Video Travel*

Mountain Time—A Sawtooth Odyssey 1984
Sports-Winter
84279   15 mins   C   B, V   P
Features a ten-day chronicle of skiing in the Rockies.
Video Travel Inc — *Video Travel*

Mouse and His Child, The 1977
Fantasy
65191   83 mins   C   B, V   P
Animated, voices of Peter Ustinov, Cloris Leachman, Andy Devine
A gentle fantasy adventure about a toy wind-up mouse and his child who fall into the clutches of a villainous rat when they venture into the outside world.
Sanrio Film Distribution — *RCA/Columbia Pictures Home Video*

Mouse That Roared, The 1959
Satire/Comedy
64914   83 mins   C   B, V   P
Peter Sellers, Jean Seberg, Leo McKern
The Duchy of Grand Fenwick declares war on the United States. Peter Sellers is featured in three roles, as the Duchess, the Prime Minister, and a military leader.
Walter Shenson — *RCA/Columbia Pictures Home Video*

Mousercise 1985
Physical fitness
76820   55 mins   C   B, V   P
Kellyn and her Mousercisers perform a specially designed program of exercises for children and pre-teens, with special appearances from Mickey Mouse and other Disney characters.
Walt Disney Productions — *Walt Disney Home Video*

Movers & Shakers 1985
Comedy
88216   100 mins   C   B, V   P
Walter Matthau, Charles Grodin, Gilda Radner, Vincent Gardenia, Bill Macy
An irreverent spoof on Hollywood depicting a filmmaker's attempt to translate a bestselling sex manual into a blockbuster film. Written by Charles Grodin.
MPAA:PG
United Artists — *MGM/UA Home Video*

Movie-Mixer Featurettes 1984
Movie and TV trailers
66485   60 mins   C   B, V   P
A number of movie promotion featurettes are packaged on this tape, showing behind the scenes activities on the sets of "The Andromeda Strain," "Romeo and Juliet," "The Way We Were," "Midnight Cowboy" and "The Fisherman."

Columbia et al — *San Francisco Rush Video*

Movie, Movie 1978
Comedy
56461   96 mins   C   CED   P
George C. Scott, Trish Van Devere, Art Carney, Eli Wallach, Red Buttons, Barbara Harris, Ann Reinking, directed by Stanley Donen
A "double feature" movie, which simulates a typical 1930's moviegoing evening, with a newsreel, previews, a boxing drama (in black and white) and a Busby Berkeley-style musical.
MPAA:PG
Warner Bros, Lord Lew Grade — *RCA VideoDiscs*

Movie Museum I 1980
Film-History
29731   600 mins   B/W   B, V   P, T
Narrated by Paul Killiam
A fascinating and entertaining review of the first 25 years of the motion picture art form. The set comes on five cassettes and totals ten hours.
Unknown — *Blackhawk Films*

Movie Museum II 1980
Film-History
29732   600 mins   B/W   B, V   P, T
Narrated by Paul Killiam
A fascinating and entertaining review of the first 25 years of the motion picture art form. There are ten hours on five cassettes in the set.
Unknown — *Blackhawk Films*

Movie Struck 1937
Comedy
08726   70 mins   B/W   B, V   P
Stan Laurel, Oliver Hardy, Jack Haley, Patsy Kelly, Rosina Lawrence
Originally released as "Pick a Star," this Hollywood behind-the-scenes story features guest appearances by Laurel and Hardy.
Hal Roach — *Video Yesteryear; Cable Films*

Moving Out 1983
Drama
77014   91 mins   C   B, V   P
Vince Colosimo, Sally Cooper, Maurice Devincentis, Tibor Gyapjas
An adolescent migrant Italian boy finds it difficult to adjust to his new surroundings in Melbourne, Australia.
Pattinson Ballantyne Film Productions — *VidAmerica*

Moving Picture Boys in the Great War, The 1975
Film-History/Documentary
10152   51 mins   B/W   B, V   P, T
Movies had been invented and 1914-1918 found World War I being fought. Includes

authentic films of the war taken from the archives of three different countries.
Blackhawk — *Blackhawk Films*

Moving Violation   1976
Drama
70699   91 mins   C   B, V   P
Eddie Albert, Kay Lenz, Stephen McHattie, Will Geer, Lonny Chapman, directed by Charles S. Dubin
Crooked cops chase two young men and a woman who've witnessed a murder. The sheriff did it. Hi-Fi stereo in both formats.
MPAA:PG
20th Century Fox; Roger and Julie Corman — *Key Video*

Moving Violations   1985
Comedy
82096   90 mins   C   B, V   P
John Murray, James Keach, Sally Kellerman, Fred Willard, Clara Peller, directed by Neal Israel
A wise-cracking tree planter is sent to traffic school after accumulating several moving violations issued to him by a morose traffic cop. Available in VHS and Beta Hi-Fi.
MPAA:PG-13
20th Century Fox — *CBS/Fox Video*

Mowlgi's Brothers   1973
Cartoons
71342   25 mins   C   B, V   P
Animated, narrated by Roddy McDowall and June Foray
This story, selected from Rudyard Kipling's "The Jungle Book," tells of a boy raised in jungle nobility by a pair of wolves.
Chuck Jones — *Family Home Entertainment*

Mozart   1984
Music-Performance
88129   55 mins   C   B, V   P
An orchestral concert featuring a variety of Mozart's most famous shorter pieces.
Sony Video — *Sony Video Software*

Mozart/Smetana/Dvorak   1984
Music-Performance
88130   48 mins   C   B, V   P
An orchestral concert of shorter pieces by the three famous composers.
Sony Video — *Sony Video Software*

Mozart Story, The   1948
Drama
11368   91 mins   B/W   B, V, FO   P
Winnie Markus, Hans Holt
After Mozart's death, music minister to the Emperor, Antonio Solieri, reflects on how his jealousy and hatred of the musical genius held the great composer down during his brief life.

Unknown — *Video Yesteryear*

Mr. T   1983
Cartoons
77157   50 mins   C   B, V   P
Animated
Mr. T coaches an American teenage gymnastic team who travels throughout the world in search of adventure.
Ruby-Spears — *Worldvision Home Video*

Mr. Rossi's Dreams   1983
Cartoons
80974   80 mins   C   B, V   P
Animated, directed by Bruno Bozzetto
Mr. Rossi gets to act out his fantasies of being Tarzan, Sherlock Holmes and a famous movie star in this film.
Italtoons Corp; Bruno Bozzetto Film — *Family Home Entertainment*

Ms. 45   1981
Suspense
66198   82 mins   C   B, V   P
Zoe Tamerlis, Steve Singer, Jack Thibeau
A "psycho" type thriller.
Navaron Films — *U.S.A. Home Video*

Muerte del Che Guevara,   197?
La
Drama
49748   92 mins   C   B, V   P
Che Guevara leads a group of rebels to Bolivia, where they hope to start a revolution. They meet, in a climactic battle, with the loyal forces.
SP
Unknown — *Media Home Entertainment*

Muerto, El   19??
Drama
66414   105 mins   C   B, V   P
Thelma Biral, Juan Jose Camero, Francisco Rabal
In nineteenth century Buenos Aires, a young man flees his home after killing an enemy. Arriving in Montevideo, he becomes a member of a smuggling ring. Dialogue in Spanish.
SP
Spanish — *Media Home Entertainment*

Mugsy's Girls   1985
Comedy
86350   87 mins   C   B, V   P
Ruth Gordon, Laura Branigan, Eddie Deezen
A septuagenarian wrestling coach trains sorority girls in the refined skills of bar mud wrestling in order to save them from financial ruin.
Shapiro Ent. — *Vestron Video*

Muhammad Ali vs. Zora Folley   1967
Boxing
85524   68 mins   B/W   B, V   P
A tape of the historic fight as it originally appeared on live television.
Madison Square Garden — *Video Yesteryear*

Mummy, The   1932
Horror
81820   72 mins   B/W   B, V, LV   P
Boris Karloff, Zita Johann, David Manners, directed by Karl Freund
A mummy who was buried alive 3,000 years ago is inadvertently brought back to life when a British professor reads from a sacred book he found on an expedition to Egypt. Available in VHS and Beta Hi-Fi.
Universal Pictures — *MCA Home Video*

Mummy, The   1959
Horror
81903   88 mins   C   B, V   P
Peter Cushing, Christopher Lee, Felix Aylmer, Yvonne Furneaux
A group of British archaeologists discover they have made a grave mistake when a mummy kills off those who have violated his princess' tomb.
Hammer Films — *Warner Home Video*

Mummy's Revenge, The   1953
Horror
86184   91 mins   C   B, V   P
Paul Naschy, Jack Taylor, Maria Silva, Helga Line
A fanatic revives a mummy with virgin blood. Dubbed from Spanish.
Julian Esteban; Luis Mendez — *Unicorn Video*

Muppets Moments   1985
Variety
Closed Captioned
81865   55 mins   C   B, V   P
Kermit the Frog, Fozzie Bear, Rowlf, Miss Piggy, Liza Minnelli, Zero Mostel, Lena Horne
Kermit and Fozzie uncover classic moments from "Veterinarian's Hospital" and "Pigs in Space" while doing their annual spring cleaning. Available in VHS and Beta Hi-Fi.
Henson Associates — *Playhouse Video*

Muppet Movie, The   1979
Comedy
37421   94 mins   C   B, V, LV   P
The Muppets, Edgar Bergen, Milton Berle, Mel Brooks, Madeline Kahn, Steve Martin
Kermit the Frog travels to Hollywood with his Muppet pals, planning to become a movie star when he gets there.
MPAA:G
Marble Arch — *CBS/Fox Video; RCA VideoDiscs*

Muppet Musicians of Bremen, The   1972
Fairy tales/Comedy
47347   50 mins   C   B, V, LV   R, P
The Muppets
Kermit the Frog narrates this story of a group of jazz-playing animals who want to escape from their masters and seek freedom and fame.
RLP Canada/Henson Associates — *Muppet Home Video*

Muppet Revue, The   1985
Variety
Closed Captioned
80743   56 mins   C   B, V   P
Kermit the Frog, Fozzie Bear, Miss Piggy, Harry Belafonte, Linda Ronstadt, Paul Williams
Join Kermit the Frog and Fozzie Bear as they go down Muppet Memory Lane to remember some of the best moments from "The Muppet Show." Available in VHS and Beta Hi-Fi.
Henson Associates — *Playhouse Video*

Muppet Treasures   1985
Variety
Closed Captioned
81546   55 mins   C   B, V   P
Kermit the Frog, Fozzie Bear, Peter Sellers, Zero Mostel, Buddy Rich, Paul Simon, Ethel Merman
Kermit and Fozzie discover some unexpected treasures in the Muppet attic including cooking lessons with the Swedish Chef and episodes of "Pigs in Space" and "Veterinarian's Hospital".
Henson Associates — *Playhouse Video*

Muppets Take Manhattan, The   1984
Musical
Closed Captioned
80336   94 mins   C   B, V   P
Kermit the Frog, Miss Piggy, Dabney Coleman, James Coco, Art Carney, directed by Frank Oz
The Muppets try to take their successful college musical to Broadway.
MPAA:G
David Lazer; Tri-Star Pictures — *CBS/Fox Video*

Murder   1930
Mystery
01746   92 mins   B/W   B, V   P
Herbert Marshall, Nora Baring, Phyllis Konstam, directed by Alfred Hitchcock
Believing in a young woman's innocence, one jurist begins to organize the pieces of her crime. Based on play "Enter Sir John," by Clemense Dane and Helen Simpson.
British Intl — *Hollywood Home Theater; Discount Video Tapes; Cable Films; Video Connection; Western Film & Video Inc*

Murder at the Baskervilles   1937
Mystery
44813   67 mins   B/W   B, V   P
Arthur Wonter, Ian Fleming, Lyn Harding
Sherlock Holmes is invited to visit Sir Henry
Baskerville at his estate, but then finds that
Baskerville's daughter's fiance is accused of
stealing a race horse and murdering its keeper.
Unknown — *Movie Buff Video; Blackhawk
Films; Video Yesteryear*

Murder by Death   1976
Comedy
44847   94 mins   C   B, V   P
*Peter Falk, Alec Guiness, David Niven, Maggie
Smith, Peter Sellers, Eileen Brennan, Elsa
Lanchester, Nancy Walker, Estelle Winwood*
An eccentric millionaire invites the world's
greatest detectives to dinner and offers one
million dollars to the one who can solve the
evening's murder.
MPAA:PG
Columbia, Ray Stark — *RCA/Columbia
Pictures Home Video; RCA VideoDiscs*

Murder by Decree   1979
Mystery
41080   120 mins   C   B, V, CED   P
*Christopher Plummer, James Mason, Donald
Sutherland, directed by Bob Clark*
Christopher Plummer plays Sherlock Holmes as
he finds his most challenging case when a
group of anarchists, posing as local merchants,
asks him and Dr. Watson for their help.
MPAA:PG
Avco Embassy — *Embassy Home
Entertainment*

Murder by Natural Causes   1979
Mystery
85918   96 mins   C   B, V   P
*Hal Holbrook, Barry Bostwick, Katherine Ross,
Richard Anderson*
A mind reader becomes the victim of a murder
plot by his wife and her lover.
Time/Life Films — *Lightning Video*

Murder By Phone   1982
Horror
65741   80 mins   C   B, V   P
Richard Chamberlain, John Houseman
A deranged technician has turned his phone
into an instrument of electronic death.
MPAA:R
Robert Cooper — *Warner Home Video*

Murder by Television   1935
Mystery
12829   55 mins   B/W   B, V, FO   P
Bela Lugosi

A TV demonstration is the site of the murder of
an electronics expert—a murder which takes
place in full view of a room full of people.
Cameo — *Video Yesteryear; Discount Video
Tapes*

Murder for Sale   1970
Drama
76654   90 mins   C   B, V   P
John Gavin, Margaret Lee, Curt Jurgens
Secret Agent 117 stages an elaborate scam in
order to infiltrate a ring of terrorists and
criminals.
Marcello Danon — *Media Home Entertainment*

Murder Mansion   1974
Horror
82276   84 mins   C   B, V   P
Evelin Stewart, Analia Gale
Four men and three women are subjected to a
night of unspeakable horror when they are
stranded in an old mansion. Also available in
Spanish.
Luis G DeBlain — *Unicorn Video*

Murder Motel   1974
Horror/Suspense
84753   80 mins   C   B, V   P
*Robyn Millan, Derek Francis, Ralph Bates,
Edward Judd*
In this made-for-TV spine-tingler, a motel keeper
mades a practice of killing his customers. The
fiancee of one of his victims decides to look into
the matter.
Ian Fordyce — *Thriller Video*

Murder My Sweet   1944
Mystery
00264   95 mins   B/W   B, V, 3/4U   P
Dick Powell, Claire Trevor
Private detective Philip Marlowe searches for an
ex-convict's missing girl friend. Based on
Raymond Chandler's novel "Farewell, My
Lovely."
RKO — *Nostalgia Merchant; King of Video;
Blackhawk Films*

Murder: No Apparent Motive   1984
Crime and criminals
82458   72 mins   C   B, V   P
*John Brotherton, Karen Levine, Joan Ranquet,
directed by Imre Horvath*
The producer of 60 Minutes examines the lives
of serial murderers, including such notorious
psychos as the Son of Sam, the Boston
Strangler, Ted Bundy, and John Wayne Gaycey.
Rainbow Broadcasting — *Vestron Video*

Murder on Flight 502   1975
Drama
80310   97 mins   C   B, V   P

Farrah Fawcett-Majors, Sonny Bono, Ralph Bellamy, Theodore Bikel, Dane Clark
A crisis arises on a 747 flight from New York to London when a letter is discovered that there is a murderer on board the plane.
Spelling/Goldberg Productions — *Prism*

Murder on the Orient Express   1974
Mystery
38600   128 mins   C   B, V, LV   P
Albert Finney, Jacqueline Bisset, Ingrid Bergman, Lauren Bacall, Sean Connery, directed by Sidney Lumet
Agatha Christie's classic whodunit becomes an all-star film, with Albert Finney as Belgian master Sleuth Hercule Poirot, who eventually solves the murder puzzle aboard the famed Orient Express.
MPAA:G
Paramount — *Paramount Home Video; RCA VideoDiscs*

Murder Once Removed   1971
Mystery
82150   74 mins   C   B, V   P
John Forsythe, Richard Kiley, Barbara Bain, Joseph Campanella
A private-eye discovers that a respectable doctor has a bedside manner that women are dying for.
Metromedia — *Karl/Lorimar Home Video*

Murder: Ultimate   1985
Grounds for Divorce
Mystery/Suspense
81120   90 mins   C   B, V   P
Roger Daltrey, Toyah Wilcox, Leslie Ash, Terry Raven
A quiet weekend of camping turns into a night of horror for two couples when one of them plans an elaborate murder scheme.
Tim Purcell — *Karl/Lorimar Home Video*

Murderer's Row   1966
Mystery
44842   108 mins   C   B, V   P
Dean Martin, Ann-Margret, Karl Malden, Beverly Adams
Daredevil bachelor and former counter-espionage agent Matt Helm is summoned from his life of leisure to insure the safety of an important scientist.
Columbia, Irving Allen — *RCA/Columbia Pictures Home Video*

Murderer's Wife   195?
Drama
65767   24 mins   B/W   B, V   P, T
Audrey Totter, John Howard, June Kenny, Michael Chapin
A teacher at a private school seeks to prevent one of her students from making the same

mistakes she did in her youth. An episode from the 1950's television drama series, "Fireside Theatre."
NBC — *Blackhawk Films*

Murders in the Rue   1971
Morgue
Horror
85923   87 mins   C   B, V   P
Jason Robards, Lilli Palmer, Herbert Lom, Michael Dunn, Christine Kaufman
A lurid retelling of Edgar Allen Poe's story about a Grand Guignol theater and a murdering gorilla.
MPAA:PG
American Int'l — *Lightning Video*

Murph the Surf   1975
Drama/Biographical
81086   102 mins   C   B, V   P
Robert Conrad, Don Stroud, Donna Mills, Luther Adler, directed by Marvin Chomsky
This is the true story of how two Miami playboys planned the jewel heist of the century and stole the Star of India sapphire.
MPAA:PG
American International Pictures — *Warner Home Video*

Murphy's Romance   1985
Comedy
87751   107 mins   C   B, V   P
James Garner, Sally Field, Brian Kerwin, directed by Martin Ritt
In a small Arizona town, an aging pharmacist and a young mother find romance, until the arrival of her good-for-nothing ex-husband.
MPAA:PG-13
Laura Ziskin — *RCA/Columbia Pictures Home Video*

Murphy's War   1971
Comedy-Drama
88424   106 mins   C   B, V   P
Peter O'Toole, Sian Phillips, Phillipe Noiret, directed by Peter Yates
A British pilot is shot down during World War II, lands on a Pacific atoll. Nursed to health by a nurse, he determines to rebuild his craft and renew his fight, though the war has, unbeknownst to him, ended.
MPAA:PG
Paramount — *Paramount Home Video*

Murri Affair   1974
Mystery
80122   120 mins   C   B, V   P
Catherine Deneuve
A woman from high society sets out to find her husband's killer.
French — *King of Video*

Murrow 1985
Drama
86851 114 mins C B, V P
Daniel J. Travanti, Dabney Coleman, Edward Herrmann
A biography of Edward R. Murrow from his World War II broadcasts from Europe to his later battles with McCarthyism.
TVS Ltd. — *Lightning Video*

Muscle Motion 1983
Physical fitness
63895 92 mins C B, V P
This aerobic exercise workout is led by seven members of the Chippendales, an all-male revue cabaret for women only.
Nick De Noia; Satyr Corp — *Media Home Entertainment*

Muse Concert: No Nukes, The 1980
Music-Performance
58301 103 mins C B, V, CED P
Jackson Browne, Crosby Stills and Nash, James Taylor, Bruce Springsteen, Doobie Bros, Bonnie Raitt, Carly Simon, John Hall
A concert film of performances held at New York's Madison Square Garden for the benefit of the anti-nuclear power movement.
MPAA:PG
Warner Bros; MUSE Prods — *CBS/Fox Video*

M*U*S*H 1984
Cartoons
70611 60 mins C B, V P
Animated
Animals take the leading roles in this spoof of the popular TV series M*A*S*H.
International Videocraft Ltd. — *Prism*

Music and the Spoken Word 1974
Religion
85191 30 mins C B, V P
Spence Kinard, the Mormon Tabernacle Choir
An inspirational live television message, featuring a sermon coupled with the famous choir's vocalizing.
KSL — *Video Yesteryear*

Music of Melissa Manchester, The 1980
Music-Performance
59853 60 mins C B, V P
Manchester performs her greatest hits live in concert. Songs include "Don't Cry Out Loud," "Midnight Blue," and "Come in from the Rain."
Thanksgiving Whatever Inc — *Warner Home Video; Pioneer Artists; RCA VideoDiscs*

Music Shoppe, The 1982
Musical
64951 93 mins C B, V R, P
Gary Crosby, Nia Peeples, Benny Medina, Stephen Schwartz, David Jackson, Jesse White, Doug Kershaw, Gisele MacKenzie
Four teenagers form a rock band with the assistance of the local music store proprietor.
MPAA:G
Century Video — *Video Gems*

Music Video From "Streets of Fire" 1984
Music video
75020 30 mins C B, V P
This tape features three complete stereo music videos from the movie "Streets of Fire."
MCA Home Video — *MCA Home Video*

Musica Proibita 1943
Musical
85192 93 mins B/W B, V P
Tito Gobbi, Maria Mercader
A serious opera-spiced drama about a young romance crushed by adultery in the teenage couple's ancestry.
Italian — *Video Yesteryear*

Musical Featurettes 1984
Movie and TV trailers/Musical
66482 61 mins C B, V P
This tape offers 6 short films that go behind the scenes and show the making of "Camelot," "Funny Girl," "The Boy Friend," "Oliver," "Scrooge" and "Fiddler on the Roof."
Warner Bros et al — *San Francisco Rush Video*

Musical Personalities No. 1 194?
Musical
11287 50 mins B/W B, V, FO P
Aunt Jemima, Dick Powell, Shirley Temple, Al Jolson, Lena Horne, Teddy Wilson
Four segments spanning three decades of music featuring some of the musical talent of the period from 1927 to 1943.
Educational et al — *Video Yesteryear*

Musicals 1: Trailers on Tape 1984
Movie and TV trailers/Musical
66478 60 mins C B, V P
This tape offers original theatrical trailers for 40 musical films, including "The Wizard of Oz," "West Side Story," "Let It Be," "7 Brides for 7 Brothers," "Singing in the Rain," "The Rose" and "Funny Face." A few segments are in black-and-white.
MGM et al — *San Francisco Rush Video*

Musicals II: Trailers on Tape
1962

Movie and TV trailers/Musical
81887 60 mins C B, V P

Here is a collection of previews for such musical favorites as "The King of Jazz," "The Dolly Sisters," "The Red Shoes" and "Lillian Russell," with some segments in black and white.
Universal et al — *San Francisco Rush Video*

Musicourt
1984

Music-Performance
78067 58 mins C B, V P

This program presents a superstar musical jam featuring Carlos Santana, Joe Cocker and others.
Pacific Arts Video Records — *Pacific Arts Video*

Mussolini and I
1985

Biographical/Drama
76796 200 mins C B, V P

Bob Hoskins, Anthony Hopkins, Susan Sarandon, Annie Girardot
A docu-dramatization of the struggle for power between Italy's Benito Mussolini and his son-in-law, Galeazzo Ciano.
RAI Radiotelevisione Italiana — *Embassy Home Entertainment*

Mussolini: Rise and Fall of a Dictator
1977

Documentary/Biographical
84622 105 mins B/W B, V P

A documentary tracing IL Duce's rise to power within Italian Fascism, and the eventual failure of his government.
ITC Pres — *MPI Home Video*

Mustang
197?

Drama
59551 70 mins C B, V P

Filmed entirely inside an actual house of prostitution, the Mustang Bridge Ranch, the largest legal brothel in the U.S., this film offers a portrait of the inner workings of a brothel.
Robert Guralnick — *Media Home Entertainment*

Mutant
1983

Horror
77406 100 mins C B, V, LV, P
CED

Wings Hauser, Bo Hopkins, Jennifer Warren, Lee Montgomery
The residents of a small town are terrorized by toxic waste mutants.
MPAA:R
Film Ventures International — *Vestron Video*

Mutant Video
1986

Film-Avant-garde/Comedy
71334 60 mins C B, V P

Jim Belushi, Elizabeth Caldwell, Chris Bliss, Taylo Negron, Robert Barron, Vicki Piper, John Pierce, Michelle Stacy, David Frishberg, Rob Riley
This tape compiles 6 unusual short films produced between 1976 and 1984. Two of the shorts won industry awards. The titles include: "The Cleansing," "Birdland," "Rocket to Stardom," "Extended Play," "Gravity" and "Sugar or Plain."
USA Home Video — *U.S.A. Home Video*

Mutilator, The
1985

Horror
82431 85 mins C B, V P

Matt Miller, Frances Raines, Bill Hitchcock
A deranged character stalks five high school students and aspires to cut them up into tiny bits. An unedited version is also available.
MPAA:R
OK Productions — *Vestron Video*

Mutiny
1952

Adventure
84829 76 mins C B, V P

Mark Stevens, Gene Evans, Angela Lansbury, Patric Knowles
In the War of 1812, an American ship carrying $10 million in gold is mutinied and the captain set adrift.
UA/King Prods — *United Home Video*

Mutiny on the Bounty
1962

Drama
56754 177 mins C B, V P

Marlon Brando, Trevor Howard, Richard Harris, directed by Lewis Milestone
Based on the novel by Charles Nordhoff and James Norman Hall, this account of the most famous mutiny in history aboard the Bounty in 1789 between Fletcher Christian and Captain Bligh is highlighted by lavish photography.
MGM, Aaron Rosenberg — *MGM/UA Home Video*

Mutiny on the Bounty
1935

Adventure
73367 132 mins B/W B, V P

Clark Gable, Charles Laughton, directed by Frank Lloyd
This is the 1935 version of the story of mean Captain Bligh, Fletcher Christian and the problems they have aboard the HMS Bounty.
Academy Award '36: Best Picture
MGM — *MGM/UA Home Video*

Mutiny on the Western Front: WW I
1981

Documentary/World War I
58576 60 mins C B, V P

THE VIDEO TAPE & DISC GUIDE

An untold side of World War I, filmed on the actual locations in France and Germany, as 30,000 Anzac volunteers, suffering great casualties, mutiny against the callous and deluded Allied officers who lead them.
Australian — *Mastervision*

My Best Girl　　1927
Comedy
59652　78 mins　B/W　B, V　　P, T
Mary Pickford, Charles "Buddy" Rogers, directed by Sam Taylor
Mary attempts to bring her new sweetheart home for dinner, with disastrous results. A gentle satire on middle-American life in the 1920's. Organ score by Gaylord Carter.
Mary Pickford — *Blackhawk Films*

My Bloody Valentine　　1981
Horror
55539　91 mins　C　B, V, LV　　P
Paul Kelman, Lori Hallier, directed by George Mihalka
A deranged killer stalks a town which has not celebrated Valentine's Day in twenty years—ever since a grisly killing took place.
MPAA:R
Paramount; John Dunning; Andre Link; Stephen Miller — *Paramount Home Video*

My Bodyguard　　1980
Drama
55529　96 mins　C　B, V　　P
Chris Makepeace, Ruth Gordon, Matt Dillon, John Houseman, Martin Mull, directed by Tony Bill
An undersized high school student fends off attacking bullies by hiring a king-sized, withdrawn lad as his bodyguard. Their relationship, however, develops into true friendship.
MPAA:PG
Twentieth Century Fox; Don Devlin — *CBS/Fox Video*

My Boys Are Good Boys　　1978
Drama
81634　90 mins　C　B, V　　P
Ralph Meeker, Ida Lupino, Lloyd Nolan, David Doyle
Three teenaged delinquents attempt to break back into prison after having a brief weekend fling.
MPAA:PG
Ralph Meeker — *Magnum Entertainment*

My Breakfast with Blassie　　1983
Comedy/Satire
75636　60 mins　C　B, V　　R, P
Andy Kaufman, Fred Blassie
Andy Kaufman and professional wrestler, Fred Blassie meet for breakfast and carry on a comical dialog.

Linda Lautrec Johnny Legend — *Rhino Video*

My Brilliant Career　　1980
Drama
56934　101 mins　C　B, V, CED　　P
Judy Davis
Sybylla's parents despair at her refusal to resign herself to a life of convention and drudgery, and attempts to "civilize" her fail. Sybylla knows that somehow she must be independent. Produced in Australia.
MPAA:G
Analysis Film Releasing Corp — *Vestron Video*

My Champion　　1984
Drama
76021　101 mins　C　B, V　　P
Yoko Shimada, Chris Mitchum
A chance meeting propels Mike Gorman and Miki Tsuwa into a relationship based on the strong bond of love and athletic competition.
Yasuhiko Kawano — *Media Home Entertainment*

My Chauffeur　　1986
Comedy
84787　94 mins　C　B, V, LV　　P
Deborah Foreman, Sam J Jones, Howard Hessemann, EG Marshall
A sultry chauffeur and tense businessman get it together comically.
MPAA:R
Crown Int'l — *Vestron Video*

My Darling Clementine　　1946
Western
84427　97 mins　B/W　B, V　　P
Henry Fonda, Victor Mature, Walter Brennan, Linda Darnell, Tim Holt, Ward Bond, directed by John Ford
A veritable Ford masterpiece, and one of the best Hollywood westerns ever made, this recounts the events leading up to and including the gunfight at the O.K. Corral.
Samuel G Engel; 20th Century Fox — *Playhouse Video*

My Dear Secretary　　1948
Comedy/Romance
70999　94 mins　C　B, V　　P
Kirk Douglas, Laraine Day, Keenan Wynn, Rudy Vallee, written and directed by Charles Martin
After she marries her boss, a woman grows jealous of the secretary that replaces her.
Cardinal/UA — *Kartes Video Communications; Hal Roach Studios; Discount Video Tapes*

My Dinner with Andre　　1981
Comedy-Drama
60328　110 mins　C　B, V, CED　　P
Andre Gregory, Wally Shawn, directed by Louis Malle

Two friends who haven't seen each other for a long time decide to catch up on each others' lives over dinner.
George W George; Beverly Karp — *Pacific Arts Video*

My Fair Lady   1964
Musical
49829   170 mins   C   B, V, CED   P
Audrey Hepburn, Rex Harrison, Stanley Holloway, Wilfred Hyde White, Gladys Cooper, directed by George Cukor
A colorful production of Lerner and Loewe's musical version of "Pygmalion," about a Covent Garden flower girl who becomes a lady. Winner of 8 Academy Awards. Songs incude "On the Street Where You Live," "The Rain in Spain," and "I've Grown Accustomed to Her Face." Academy Awards '64: Best Picture; Best Director (Cukor); Best Actor (Harrison); Best Color Cinematography.
Warner Bros — *CBS/Fox Video*

My Father's House   1975
Drama
77149   96 mins   C   B, V   P
Cliff Robertson, Robert Preston, Eileen Brennan, Rosemary Forsyth
A magazine editor recalls his youth after he suffers a heart attack.
Filmways — *Worldvision Home Video*

My Favorite Brunette   1947
Comedy
12859   85 mins   B/W   B, V   P
Bob Hope, Dorothy Lamour, Peter Lorre, Lon Chaney, Alan Ladd
A would-be private eye becomes involved with a murder, a spy caper, and a dangerous brunette.
Paramount — *Movie Buff Video; Prism; Video Yesteryear; Hollywood Home Theater; Cable Films; VCII; Video Connection; Discount Video Tapes; Western Film & Video Inc; Cinema Concepts; Kartes Video Communications*

My Favorite Wife   1940
Comedy
64364   88 mins   B/W   B, V, 3/4U   P
Irene Dunne, Cary Grant, Randolph Scott, Gail Patrick, directed by Garson Kanin
A lady explorer returns to civilization after being shipwrecked for seven years and finds that her husband is about to remarry.
RKO — *Nostalgia Merchant*

My Favorite Year   1982
Comedy
64565   92 mins   C   B, V, CED   P
Peter O'Toole, Mark-Linn Baker, Joe Bologna, Jessica Harper, Lainie Kazan, directed by Richard Benjamin

A swashbuckling movie star who drinks too much is signed to make his television debut on a popular live variety show.
MPAA:PG
MGM/UA — *MGM/UA Home Video*

My Forbidden Past   1951
Drama
66334   81 mins   B/W   B, V, 3/4U   P
Ava Gardner, Melvyn Douglas, Robert Mitchum
A New Orleans girl inherits a fortune and vows vengeance when the doctor she loves marries another.
RKO — *Nostalgia Merchant*

My Friend Liberty   1986
History-US
87195   30 mins   C   B, V   P
A humorous look at the Statue of Liberty on the occasion of its renovation, using clay animation.
Jimmy Picker — *Karl/Lorimar Home Video*

My Hero   1952
Comedy
77196   100 mins   B/W   B, V   P
Robert Cummings, Julie Bishop, John Litel
Here are four episodes from Cummings' first TV series, where he plays a real estate agent who's always in trouble with his boss and girlfriend.
Sharpe-Lewis Productions — *Shokus Video*

My Knockout Workout   1986
Physical fitness
71339   60 mins   C   B, V   P
Ray "Boom-Boom" Mancini, directed by Paul Miller
The former lightweight boxing champ offers his tips for tip-top physical conditioning in this program.
Don Spielvogel; Noel C Bloom — *U.S.A. Home Video*

My Little Chickadee   1940
Comedy
31595   91 mins   B/W   B, V   P
W.C. Fields, Mae West, directed by Edward Cline
A classic comedy starring W.C. Fields and Mae West, striking sparks with each other on a trip out West.
Universal — *MCA Home Video; RCA VideoDiscs*

My Little Pony   1984
Fairy tales
70196   30 mins   C   B, V   P
Animated, Voices of Tony Randall and Sandy Duncan
The popular children's toy, My Little Pony, stars in this original made-for-video holiday production.
Hasbro Industries — *Children's Video Library*

My Little Pony: Escape from Catrina   1986
Cartoons
85641   30 mins   C   B, V   P
Animated, voices of Tammy Grimes and Paul Williams
An animated film for children about good ponies vs. evil ponies battling wills in a mythical land called Dream Valley.
Children's Video Library — *Children's Video Library*

My Love for Yours   1939
Comedy
10615   99 mins   B/W   B, V, 3/4U   R, P
Fred MacMurray, Madeleine Carroll
The romantic tale of a young man hoping to win the love of a beautiful girl.
Paramount — *Cable Films*

My Man Adam   1986
Adventure
Closed Captioned
88161   84 mins   C   B, V   P
Raphael Sbarge, Veronica Cartwright, Page Hannah, Dave Thomas
A dreamy, Mitty-esque high schooler falls in love with a girl, and becomes ensnared in a real life crime, leaving his 26-year-old senior friend to bail him out.
MPAA:R
Renee Missel; Gail Stayden; Paul Aratow; TriStar — *Key Video*

My Man Godfrey   1936
Comedy
00413   95 mins   B/W   B, V   P
William Powell, Carole Lombard, Gail Patrick, directed by Gregory La Cava
A spoiled rich girl picks up a bum as part of a scavenger hunt and decides to keep him on as her butler.
Universal International; Gregory La Cava — *Prism; Nostalgia Merchant; Movie Buff Video; Hollywood Home Theater; Video Dimensions; Cable Films; Video Connection; Video Yesteryear; Discount Video Tapes; Western Film & Video Inc; Hal Roach Studios; Kartes Video Communications*

My New Partner   1985
Comedy
71183   106 mins   C   B, V   P
Philippe Noiret, Thierry Lhermitte, Regine, Grace de Capitani, Julien Guiomar, written and directed by Claude Zidi
Nearing retirement, a mildly corrupt policeman finds that his new partner idealistically opposes even the pettiest graft. The Detective proceeds to train his reluctant protege in "real" police work.
MPAA:R FR
Films 7 — *Media Home Entertainment*

My Old Man   1979
Drama
85928   102 mins   C   B, V   P
Kristy McNichol, Warren Oates, Eileen Brennan, directed by John Erman
This Hemingway short story tells of a ramshackle, divided family which pulls together for a crucial horserace.
Robert Halmi — *Prism*

My Other Husband   1985
Comedy
86388   110 mins   C   B, V   P
Miou-Miou, Rachid Ferrache, Roger Hanin, directed by Georges Lautner
A woman has two husbands and families in Paris and Trouville. They eventually meet each other. Subtitled in English.
MPAA:PG-13 FR
TRiumph Films; Alain Poire — *RCA/Columbia Pictures Home Video*

My Pal Trigger   1946
Western
03987   79 mins   B/W   B, V   P
Roy Rogers, Gabby Hayes
Roy Rogers and Trigger head out for high adventure on the plains.
Republic — *Hollywood Home Theater; Video Connection; Discount Video Tapes*

My Side of the Mountain   1969
Drama
81101   100 mins   C   B, V   P
Teddy Eccles, Theodore Bikel
A thirteen-year-old boy decides to emulate his idol Henry David Thoreau and gives up his home and his family to live in the Canadian mountains.
MPAA:G
Paramount; Robert Radnitz — *Paramount Home Video*

My Sweet Charlie   1969
Drama
85777   97 mins   C   B, V   P
Patty Duke, Al Freeman, Jr, directed by Lamont Johnson
A pregnant Southern girl grudgingly hides a black lawyer who is wanted by the police, and the two hit it off. Made for TV.
Universal — *MCA Home Video*

My Therapist   1984
Comedy-Drama
80267   81 mins   C   B, V   P
Marilyn Chambers
A sex therapist's boyfriend cannot bear the thought of her having intercourse with other men as part of her work.
John Ward — *VCL Home Video*

My Therapist 1984
Drama
80489   90 mins   C   B, V   P
Marilyn Chambers
A therapist who works with men who have
sexual problems finds out how to take her work
home with her.
VCL Communications — *VCL Home Video*

My Tutor 1982
Comedy
69028   97 mins   C   B, V, LV   P
*Caren Kaye, Matt Lattanzi, Kevin McCarthy,
Irene Golonka*
A young woman is hired to tutor a young man in
French. This film is a romantic comedy.
MPAA:R
Crown International — *MCA Home Video*

Mysterians, The 1958
Science fiction
13023   85 mins   C   B, V   P
Kenji Sahara
Race of gigantic scientific intellects attempts to
conquer Earth. Dubbed in English from
Japanese.
Exhibitor — *United Home Video*

Mysteries from Beyond 1976
Earth
Documentary/Speculation
55008   95 mins   C   B, V   P
The bizarre world of psychic phenomena and
the paranormal is explored in this compelling
film. Among the many areas of investigation are
UFO's, Kirlian Photography, psychic healing,
and witchcraft.
Cine Vue — *United Home Video*

Mysterious Desperado 1949
Western
76762   61 mins   B/W   B, V   P
Tim Holt, Richard Martin
A young man, standing to inherit a large parcel
of land, is framed.
RKO — *RKO HomeVideo*

Mysterious 1949
Desperado/Rider From
Tucson
Western
80428   121 mins   B/W   B, V   P
Tim Holt, Richard Martin
A western double feature: In "Mysterious
Desperado" a young man is framed for a crime
he did not commit in "Rider From Tucson" evil
claim jumpers will resort to murder to gain
control of a gold mine.
RKO — *RKO HomeVideo*

Mysterious Island 1961
Fantasy
Closed Captioned
21293   101 mins   C   B, V   P
Herbert Lom, Michael Callan, Joan Greenwood
Some Confederate prison escapees, blown off
course in an observation balloon, find the
uncharted island of Captain Nemo. Based on
Jules Verne's novel.
Columbia — *RCA/Columbia Pictures Home
Video*

Mysterious Lair of the 1985
Predator, The
Wildlife
88319   60 mins   C   B, V   P
A portrait of various wild predators'
environments and lifestyles.
American Heritage Video; John
Kerwin — *Eagle Productions*

Mysterious Miniature 1983
World
Documentary/Insects
63667   90 mins   C   B, V   P
The earth's least visible inhabitants and its
greatest survivors, the insects, are closely
studied in this nature documentary.
Bill Burrud Productions — *Walt Disney Home
Video*

Mysterious Mr. Wong 1935
Mystery
08756   56 mins   B/W   B, V   P
Bela Lugosi, Arline Judge, Wallace Ford
The Thirteen Coins of Confucius put San
Francisco's Chinatown in a state of terror until
Mr. Wong came.
Monogram — *Movie Buff Video; Cable Films;
Discount Video Tapes*

Mysterious Two 1982
Science fiction
81265   97 mins   C   B, V   P
*John Forsythe, Priscilla Pointer, Vic Tayback,
Noah Beery, Karen Werner*
An extraterrestrial couple visit the Earth to
search for disillusioned people who would like to
join them for a trip to another galaxy. Available
in VHS Stereo and Beta Hi-Fi.
Alan Landsburg Productions — *U.S.A. Home
Video*

Mystery and Espionage 195?
Mystery/Suspense
53049   100 mins   B/W   B, V, 3/4U   P
*James Daly, Robert Alda, Preston Foster, John
Howard*
Four "camp" examples of what foreign intrigue,
suspense, mystery, and general spying was all
about on 1950's TV: "Overseas Adventure"
(1953), starring James Daly as a newspaper
correspondent in search of adventure; "Secret

File, U.S.A." (1955), starring Robert Alda as the head of the cold war Army intelligence; "Waterfront" (1955), starring Preston Foster as Capt. John Herrick, commander of the tugboat Cheryl Ann; "Dr. Hudson's Secret Journal" (1956), starring John Howard as Center Hospital's top neurosurgeon.
NBC et al — *Shokus Video*

Mystery at Castle House   1982
Mystery
85878   80 mins   C   B, V   P
Three precocious children stumble onto a mystery when their friends disappear at a neighborhood castle.
Unknown — *VidAmerica*

Mystery in Swing   1940
Mystery/Musical
85518   66 mins   B/W   B, V   P
Monte Hawley, Marguerite Whitten, Ceepee Johnson
An all-black mystery with music, about a trumpet player who has snake venom put on his mouthpiece.
Unknown — *Video Yesteryear*

Mystery Island   1981
Adventure
85880   75 mins   C   B, V   P
A children's adventure about a smuggling racket, ghosts, strange islands and youthful detectives.
Unknown — *VidAmerica*

Mystery Mansion   1983
Mystery
66601   95 mins   C   B, V   P
Dallas McKennon, Greg Wynne, Jane Ferguson
A fortune in gold and a hundred-year-old mystery lead three children into an exciting treasure hunt.
Arthur R. Dubs — *Media Home Entertainment*

Mystery Mountain   1934
Western/Serials
08877   156 mins   B/W   B, V, 3/4U   P
Ken Maynard, Gene Autry, Smiley Burnette
Twelve episodes depict the villain known as the "Rattler" attempting to stop the construction of a railroad over Mystery Mountain.
Mascot — *Video Connection; Cable Films; Video Yesteryear; Discount Video Tapes*

Mystery of the Mary   1937
Celeste, The
Mystery
10629   64 mins   B/W   B, V   P, T
Bela Lugosi, Shirley Grey, Edmund Willard
A tale of terror based on the bizarre case of the "Marie Celeste," an American ship found adrift

and derelict on the Atlantic Ocean on December 5, 1872.
Guaranteed — *Blackhawk Films; Video Yesteryear; Cable Films*

Mystery of the Million   1987?
Dollar Hockey Puck, The
Adventure/Hockey
70859   88 mins   C   B, V   P
Michael MacDonald, Angele Knight, The Montreal Canadiens, directed by Jean Lafleur and Peter Svatek
Sinister diamond smugglers learn a lesson on ice from a pair of orphan lads.
Cinepix — *Lightning Video*

Mystery Squadron   1933
Adventure/Serials
10923   156 mins   B/W   B, V   P
Bob Steele, Guinn Williams, J. Carroll Naish
Twelve chapters, 13 minutes each. Daredevil air action in flight against the masked pilots of the Black Ace.
Mascot — *Video Connection; Discount Video Tapes; Video Dimensions; Cable Films; Video Yesteryear*

Mystery Theatre   1951
Mystery
85509   53 mins   B/W   B, V   P
Tom Conway, James Burke, Verne Smith,
Two separate Mark Saber crime dramas back to back: "The Case of the Chamber of Death" and "The Case of the Locked Room."
ABC — *Video Yesteryear*

N

Nabucco   1984
Music-Performance
77171   132 mins   C   B, V   P
Renato Bruson, Ghena Dimitrova, Dimiter Petkov
A performance of the Verdi opera about an oppressed people's yearning for freedom recorded at the Arena di Verona in Italy.
National Video Corporation Limited — *THORN EMI/HBO Video*

Nadia   1984
Drama/Biographical
66612   100 mins   C   B, V   P
Carrie Snodgress, Leslie Weiner, Johanna Carlo, Joe Bennett
This is the dramatized story of Nadia Comaneci, the young Romanian gymnast who won worldwide attention as a triple gold-medal winner in the 1976 Montreal Olympics.

Tribune Entertainment; Dave Bell Productions;
Jadran Film — *U.S.A. Home Video*

Naked and the Dead, The   1958
Drama
13027   131 mins   C   B, V   P
Aldo Ray, Cliff Robertson, Joey Bishop
Based on Norman Mailer's novel of WW II men
in war; their feelings, hates, desires, and
courage.
Warner Bros; Paul Gregory — *United Home
Video*

Naked Civil Servant, The   1980
Drama
59704   80 mins   C   B, V   P
John Hurt
The biography of Quentin Crisp, the witty
homosexual who grew up in the 30's and 40's
and lived through years of intolerance,
ostracism and violence.
British Academy Awards '80: Best Actor (Hurt).
Euston Films; Thames Video — *THORN
EMI/HBO Video*

Naked Eyes   1983
Music-Performance
75906   14 mins   C   B, V   P
This program presents the rock group Naked
Eyes performing their hits "Always Something
There to Remind Me," "Promises, Promises"
and "When the Lights Go Out."
EMI America Records — *Sony Video Software*

Naked Face, The   1984
Drama/Mystery
81055   105 mins   C   B, V   P
*Roger Moore, Rod Steiger, Elliott Gould, Art
Carney, Anne Archer, directed by Bryan Forbes*
Someone is stalking a psychiatrist, and police
suspect that he murdered a patient and his
secretary.
MPAA:R
Cannon Films — *MGM/UA Home Video*

Naked in the Sun   1957
Western
80845   95 mins   C   B, V   P
James Craig, Lita Milan, Barton MacLane
This is the true story of the events that led up to
the war that the Osceola and Seminole Indians
waged against a crooked slave trader.
Allied Artists — *Republic Pictures Home Video*

Naked Prey, The   1965
Adventure
84532   94 mins   C   B, V   P
Cornel Wilde, Gert Van Der Berger, Ken Gampu
Filmed in Africa, the film deals with a white
hunter given a running chance by murderous
tribesmen, without clothes or weapons.
Cornel Wilde — *Paramount Home Video*

Naked Truth, The   1958
Comedy
59836   92 mins   C   B, V   P
*Peter Sellers, Terry-Thomas, Shirley Eaton,
Dennis Price*
A greedy publisher tries to get rich quick by
publishing a scandal magazine about the "lurid"
lives of prominent citizens.
Mario Zampi — *Embassy Home Entertainment*

Naked Vengeance   1985
Exploitation
85919   97 mins   C   B, V   P
Deborah Tranelli, Kaz Garaz, Bill McLaughlin
After a woman's husband is murdered, she is
beaten and raped until forced to become a
raging killing tool of vengeance.
MPAA:R
Westbrook/M.P. Films — *Lightning Video*

Nancy Drew   1978
Suspense/Mystery
82367   47 mins   C   B, V   P
*Pamela Sue Martin, William Schallert, Susan
Buckner, Ruth Cox* 8   pgms
Join America's premier teenaged female
detective, Nancy Drew, as she solves the
crimes that no one else will. Each episode is
available individually.
*1.The Mystery of Pirate's Cove 2.The Mystery of
the Diamond Triangle 3.A Haunting We Will Go
4.Secret of the Whispering Walls 5.The Mystery
of the Fallen Angels 6.The Mystery of the
Ghostwriter's Cruise 7.The Mystery of the Solid
Gold Kicker 8.Nancy Drew's Love Match*
Universal Television — *MCA Home Video*

Nancy Wilson   1982
Music-Performance
88119   60 mins   C   B, V, 8mm   P
The great blues/soul/jazz vocalist is joined by
former Return to Forever members in
performing "I Want to Be Happy," "But Not For
Me," "Round Midnight," and others.
Sony Video — *Sony Video Software*

Napoleon   1955
Biographical/Drama
78967   123 mins   C   B, V   P
*Raymond Pellegrin, Orson Welles, Yves
Montand, Eric von Stroheim, Jean Gabin, Jean
Pierre Aumont*
The life story of Napoleon from his days as a
soldier in the French army to his exile to the
Island of Elba.
Sacha Guitry — *MPI Home Video*

Napoleon   1927
Biographical/Adventure
88420   235 mins   B/W   B, V   P
*Albert Dieudonne, Antonin Artaud, Pierre
Batcheff, Armand Bernard, Harry Krimer, Albert*

Raul Julia and William Hurt exchanging glances, sharing love before the night was through in
Kiss of the Spider Woman—**Charter**

Ursula Andress and Peter Sellers confusedly share one of the quieter and least cluttered
moments in *Casino Royale*—**RCA/Columbia**

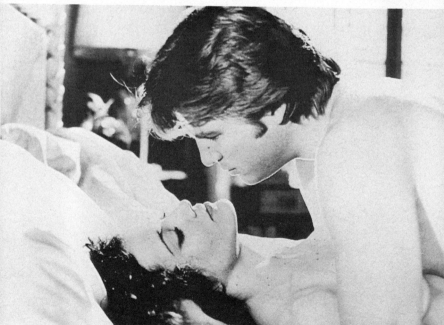

Looks like Michael Douglas and Kathleen Turner may be a little late for dinner in *The Jewel of the Nile*—**CBS/Fox**

Jeff Bridges as a Kennedy-esque heir takes time out for fun with Belinda Bauer between assassination conspiracies in *Winter Kills*—**Embassy**

Cathy and Heathcliff (Laurence Olivier and Merle Oberon) gaze over the heathered moors in William Wyler's classic adaptation of the Emily Bronte masterpiece, *Wuthering Heights*—**Embassy**

Laurence Olivier and Merle Oberon flirt amid the improbable bedroom farce of *The Divorce of Lady X*—**Embassy**

Jane Fonda and Anne Bancroft look concerned as Meg Tilly experiences a big chill during her trial in *Agnes of God*—**RCA/Columbia**

Glenn Close and Jeff Bridges (foreground) have their days in court and their nights at his place in *Jagged Edge*—**RCA/Columbia**

Dustin Hoffman and Valerie Perrine share an exuberant moment onstage in *Lenny*—**Key**

Michael J. Fox is concerned about damaging his family ties with Lea Thompson, his mom-to-be in *Back to the Future*—**MCA**

Gene Hackman happily gives Ally Sheedy away in *Twice in a Lifetime*—**Vestron**

Ann-Margret, Michael York and Marty Feldman share a tepid chortle in *The Last Remake of Beau Geste*—**MCA**

Mike the Dog turns the other fuzzy cheek when approached by a comparably-grizzled Nick Nolte in *Down and Out in Beverly Hills*—**Touchstone**

The guys (Kevin Bacon, Mickey Rourke, Daniel Stern, Timothy Daly) are bullish on America, the '50's and the transitions of maturity in *Diner*—**MGM/UA**

James Stewart cradles his *Winchester '73* in the film of the same name—**MCA**

Gunslinger John Wayne renounces his violent past for the love of a Quaker girl (Gail Russell) in *Angel and the Badman*—**Republic**

"Under the Bamboo Tree" is the musical background for a cakewalk duet by Margaret O'Brien and Judy Garland, a memorable moment from *Meet Me In St. Louis*—**MGM/UA**

Kathryn Grayson gets a well-deserved thrashing from Howard Keel in this climactic scene from *Kiss Me Kate*. In the background are Kurt Kasznar, Bob Fosse, Bobby Van, Ann Miller and Tommy Rall—**MGM/UA**

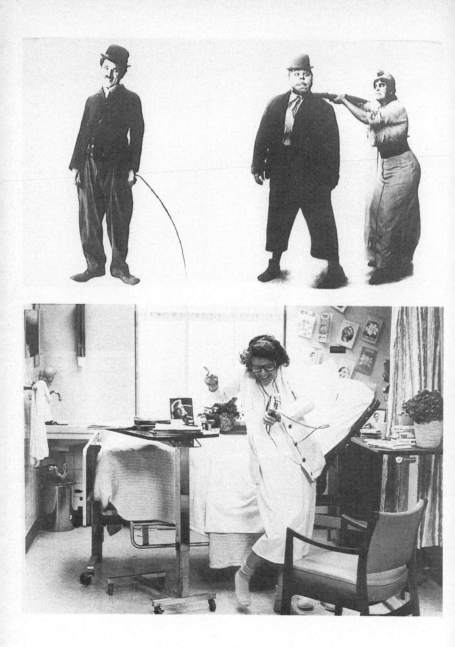

Charlie Chaplin and Fatty Arbuckle, seen in classically characteristic poses, innocently joyful and oafishly victimized, respectively, are seen in **Blackhawk's** release of their silent comedies.

In a lighter moment from *Garbo Talks,* Anne Bancroft can't keep still while listening to her Walkman and rises from her hospital bed to "truck on down"—**MGM/UA**

Slick, stubbled, sunglassed and sockless Don Johnson stars with Philip Michael Thomas in the feature-length fashion show *Miami Vice II: The Prodigal Son*—**MCA**

Sylvester Stallone returns as the Philadelphia boxer who triumphs over Russia's strong man in *Rocky IV*—**CBS/Fox**

"Ax"-wielding Charlie Brown entertains Snoopy and Lucy once more in *Play It Again, Charlie Brown*—**Snoopy's Home Video Library**

Timothy E. Mouse cheers his cherubic, big-eared pachyderm pal with news of his mother's health in *Dumbo*—**Walt Disney**

Monsieur Hulot (Jacques Tati) communes with his nephew in Tati's classic French comedy *Mon Oncle*—**Embassy**

Kate Nelligan and her kids pick sides for a game of field soccer as the fascist guerrillas arrive in *Eleni*—**Embassy**

Time is running out in more ways than one for Gary Cooper and Grace Kelly in Fred Zinnemann's classic Western, *High Noon*—**Republic**

Irene Dunne gazes adoringly at Cary Grant, her bemused ex-husband in the wacky farce *The Awful Truth*—**RCA/Columbia**

Pluto, Mickey Mouse's lovable pooch, is featured in a number of **Walt Disney** cartoon packages.

Roy Rogers and Trigger ride off into the sunset in a popular series of vintage Westerns—**Discount**

Lusty Irish field hand Marlon Brando matter-of-factly points out the discomfitures of sleeping in the barn in *The Nightcomers*—**Charter**

A mustachioed Richard Gere stars as a callous, amoral political media consultant in *Power*—**Karl**/**Lorimar**

Louise Brooks' stunning appearance seems mildly vampiric in G.W. Pabst's masterpiece of Kammerspielfilm/Expressionism, *Pandora's Box*—**Embassy**

Meryl Streep and Robert Redford waltz together on New Year's Eve as authoress Isak Dinesen and great white hunter Denys Finch-Hatten in Sydney Pollack's *Out of Africa*—**MCA**

Elvis: One Night with You catches the King in a rare unrehearsed 1968 jam session—**Media**

Mikhail Baryshnikov and Gregory Hines strike an apprehensive pose in the suspenseful Cold War ballet picture, *White Nights*—**RCA**/**Columbia**

Raquel Welch is determined to run sprints in *The Legend of Walks Far Woman*—**VCL**

Bras, Abel Gance, Georges Cahuzac, directed
by Abel Gance
A vivid, near-complete restoration of Gance's
epic silent masterpiece about the famed
conqueror's early years, from youth up to the
Italian Campaign. An innovative, spectacular
achievement, with its use of multiple split
screens, montage, color and triptychs. This
version was produced by Kevin Brownlow with a
score by Carmine Coppola and given a gala
theatrical re-release in 1981.
WESTI/Societe Generale de Films; Abel
Gance; Kevin Brownlow — *MCA Home Video*

Napoleon and Samantha   1972
Adventure
86789   91 mins   C   B, V   P
*Jodie Foster, Johnny Whittaker, Michael
Douglas, Will Geer, Henry Jones*
Two children and an aging lion travel through
the American Northwest while pursued by
authorities.
Walt Disney Prods — *Walt Disney Home Video*

Narrow Trail, The   1917
Western
84925   56 mins   B/W   B, V   P
William S Hart, Sylvia Bremer, Milton Ross
A cowboy comes to San Francisco's Barbary
Coast to search for his old girlfriend. Silent.
William S Hart Productions — *Blackhawk Films*

Nashville   1975
Drama
38613   159 mins   C   B, V, LV   P
*Henry Gibson, Lily Tomlin, Ronee Blakley, Keith
Carradine,* directed by Robert Altman
The lives of twenty-four people during a five-day
country music festival at the Grand Ole Opry are
intertwined in this multi-level portrait of America
at a particular time and place.
Academy Awards '75: Best Song (I'm Easy).
MPAA:R
Paramount — *Paramount Home Video; RCA
VideoDiscs*

Nashville Girl   1976
Drama
84529   90 mins   C   B, V   P
Monica Gayle, Johnny Rodriguez
An innocent country girl rises to the top of the
Nashville success ladder, sacrificing everything
in the process.
MPAA:R
Peer J Oppenheimer — *Charter Entertainment*

Natalia Makarova: In a   1985
Class of Her Own
Dance
86311   60 mins   C   B, V   P
An affectionate portrait of the grand dame of
ballet as she works on a Roland Petit ballet

"The Blue Angel," with Petit and Irina
Yakobsen.
Derek Bailey; Natalia Makarova — *Video Arts
International*

Natas es Satan   197?
Crime-Drama
86535   90 mins   C   B, V   P
Miguel A. Alvarez, Perla Faith
The adventures of a corrupt New York cop who
moonlights as a psychopath.
SP
Spanish — *Master Arts Video*

Nate and Hayes   1983
Adventure
65616   100 mins   C   B, V, LV,   P
                              CED
*Tommy Lee Jones, Michael O'Keefe, Max
Phipps, Jenny Seagrove*
Set during the mid-1800s in the South Pacific,
the notorious real-life swashbuckler Captain
"Bully" Hayes and young Reverend Nate
pursue a cutthroat gang which has kidnapped
Nate's wife.
MPAA:PG
Lloyd Phillips; Rob Whitehouse — *Paramount
Home Video*

National Gallery: Art   19??
Awareness Collection
Artists
14178   60 mins   C   LV   P
A look at the great works in Washington, D.C.'s
National Gallery of Art. A journey into the artistic
genius of Rembrandt, Fragonard, Goya, Copley,
Turner, Degas, Renoir, and a group of early
American painters is included.
Unknown — *MCA Home Video*

National Geographic: 1983
Great Whales/Sharks
Fishes/Animals
64778   120 mins   C   CED   P
"Great Whales" (1978), an Emmy Award
winning film, looks at whale anatomy,
communication and migration. "Sharks" (1982)
addresses man's fear and hatred of sharks
while offering a look at the shark's vulnerability.
National Geographic Society — *RCA
VideoDiscs*

National Geographic   197?
Society: The Incredible
Machine/Mysteries of the
Mind
Anatomy and physiology
64458   87 mins   C   CED   P
"The Incredible Machine" (1975) offers a
fascinating journey inside the human body.
"Mysteries of the Mind" (1980) is a
documentary which uses computer graphics

and a synapse sculpture to examine the brain's structures. Both are multiple award-winning films, the latter having garnered two Emmy Awards.
National Geographic Society — *RCA VideoDiscs*

National Lampoon's   **1982**
Class Reunion
Comedy
66101   85 mins   C   B, V, LV,   P
                          CED
Shelley Smith, Gerrit Graham, Michael Lerner
A class reunion with some very wacky guests.
MPAA:R
20th Century Fox — *Vestron Video*

National Lampoon's   **1985**
European Vacation
Comedy
Closed Captioned
71167   94 mins   C   B, V, LV   P
Chevy Chase, Beverly D'Angelo, Dana Hill, Jason Lively, Victor Lanoux, Eric Idle, directed by Amy Heckerling
The Griswalds win a trip to Europe on a TV game show. They go; and nearly redefine the term "ugly American." Recorded in HiFi Mono.
MPAA:PG-13
Warner Bros — *Warner Home Video*

National Lampoon's   **1983**
Vacation
Comedy
65325   98 mins   C   B, V, LV,   P
                          CED
Chevy Chase, Beverly D'Angelo, Imogene Coca, Randy Quaid, Christie Brinkley
The Clark W. Griswold family of suburban Chicago embark on a westward cross-country vacation trip to remember, earmarked by a series of hysterical misadventures.
MPAA:R
Matty Simmons — *Warner Home Video*

National Velvet   **1945**
Drama
Closed Captioned
82113   124 mins   C   B, V   P
Elizabeth Taylor, Mickey Rooney, Arthur Treacher, Donald Crisp, Anne Revere
A young English girl trains a horse she won in a raffle, hoping to later compete in the famed Grand National race.
Academy Awards '45: Best Supporting Actress (Revere)
MGM — *MGM/UA Home Video*

Nationtime, Gary   **1972**
Minorities
88384   90 mins   C   B, V, 3/4U   R, P

Narrated by Sidney Poitier and Harry Belafonte, this is a document of the first National Black Political Convention, held in Gary, Indiana.
Your World Video — *Your World Video*

Natural, The   **1984**
Drama
Closed Captioned
80369   134 mins   C   B, V   P
Robert Redford, Glenn Close, Robert Duvall, Kim Basinger, directed by Barry Levinson
An aging rookie outfielder who returns to the major leagues must battle with his past demons to lead his team to the World Series.
MPAA:PG
Tri Star Pictures — *RCA/Columbia Pictures Home Video*

Natural Enemies   **1979**
Drama
71120   100 mins   C   B, V   P
Hal Holbrook, Louise Fletcher, Jose Ferrer, Viveca Lindfors, written and directed by Jeff Kanew
A depressed publisher contemplates suicide for himself and his family the cure to his ever-deepening despair.
MPAA:R
Almi Pictures — *RCA/Columbia Pictures Home Video*

Navy Wings   **1943**
World War II
87666   54 mins   B/W   B, V   P
Three shorts about World War II Navy air fighting: "The Navy Flies On," "For Distinguished Service" and "Fighter Tactics."
U.S. Navy — *Victory Video*

Nazareth-Live!   **1984**
Music-Performance
70223   58 mins   C   B, V   P
The heavy-metal Scottish rockers perform their greatest hits in concert, including "Love Hurts," "Telegram," "Dressed to Kill," "Expect No Mercy," "Hearts Grown Cold" and others.
Irving Rappaport — *VCL Home Video*

Nazi Strike   **1984**
World War II/Germany
76532   50 mins   B/W   B, V   P
This program, put together with actual captured film, details Germany's conquests at the beginning of WW II.
Maljack Productions Inc — *MPI Home Video*

Nazi War Crime Trials   **1945**
Documentary/World War II
47473   67 mins   B/W   B, V, FO   P
A collection of seven American and Russian newsreel shorts that detail the Nuremberg Trials of Nazi war criminals. Featured are Goring, Van

Pappen, Hess, Schact, Streicher and others.
Includes grisly scenes of hangings and firing
squad executions.
RKO Pathe News et al — *Video Yesteryear;
Discount Video Tapes*

Nazis Strike, The /   **194?**
Schichlegruber Doing the
Lambeth Walk
World War II/Documentary
47645   44 mins   B/W   B, V, FO   P
Directed by Frank Capra, Anatole Litvak
"Nazis Strike" is a U.S. War Department film
documentary showing America's entry into the
war. Includes scenes from "Triumph of the
Will." "Schichlegruber Doing the Lambeth
Walk" is a satirical British film combining Nazi
footage with popular music. Features the
"Gestapo Hep-Cats."
US War Dept — *Video Yesteryear*

Nazis Strike, The   **1943**
World War II/Documentary
50613   41 mins   B/W   B, V, 3/4U   P
Directed by Frank Capra
Hope for peace is abandoned when the Nazis
conquer Austria and Czechoslovakia, and
invade Poland. Part of the "Why We Fight"
series.
US War Department — *Western Film & Video
Inc; Discount Video Tapes; MPI Home Video;
National AudioVisual Center*

NBC Comedy Hour   **1956**
Variety
38988   50 mins   B/W   B, V, FO   P
*Jonathan Winters, Guy Mitchell, Gretchen
Wyler, Shecky Greene, hosted by Alan Young*
Originally telecast in June 3, 1956, this special
has a variety format with a "Watching All the
Girls Go By" theme. Comedy from all, and
songs by Gretchen Wyler.
NBC — *Video Yesteryear*

NBC Comedy Hour   **1956**
Comedy/Variety
47498   60 mins   B/W   B, V, FO   P
*Groucho Marx, Jonathan Winters, Stan Freberg,
Gale Storm, Ben Blue, Jack Albertson*
An all-star variety show, featuring numerous top
comics in a succession of sketches. Originally
telecast on March 4, 1956.
NBC — *Video Yesteryear*

NBC Comedy Hour, The   **1962**
Comedy
85193   47 mins   B/W   B, V   P
*Leo Durocher, Ernie Kovacs, Spike Jones, Willy
Mays, Hy Averback, Allen Funt, Wally Cox,
Jonathan Winters, Paul Gilbert*
An episode of the short-lived, talent packed
comedy hour, with bits by just about everyone,
including the Three Stooges.

NBC — *Video Yesteryear*

Nea   **1978**
Drama
68264   101 mins   C   B, V   P
Sam Frey, Ann Zacharias, Heinz Bennent
Nea is the story of turbulent erotic passion and a
young girl's striving to get away from her father's
home.
MPAA:R
Andre Genoves — *RCA/Columbia Pictures
Home Video*

Nearly No Christmas   **1981**
Christmas
71355   60 mins   C   B, V   P
Michael Haigh, Mildred Woods, John Banas
This bittersweet family tale depicts a Christmas
that almost didn't come off.
MFTV Inc — *Family Home Entertainment*

Neath Arizona Skies   **1934**
Western
10944   54 mins   B/W   B, V   P
John Wayne
This cowhand finds all the action he and his
friends can handle under western skies.
Monogram — *Sony Video Software; Spotlite
Video; Discount Video Tapes*

'Neath Arizona   **1935**
Skies/Paradise Canyon
Western
81020   109 mins   B/W   B, V   P
John Wayne
Here is a double feature of two early John
Wayne Westerns filled with lots of rumble
tumble action.
Monogram Pictures — *Spotlite Video*

Needlepoint   **1986**
Handicraft
88306   100 mins   C   B, V   P
*Jo Moore, needlepointer extraordinaire,
demonstrates fundamental techniques.*
Victorian Video Prod. — *Victorian Video
Productions*

Negro Soldier   **1944**
World War II/Documentary
52320   40 mins   B/W   B, V, 3/4U   P
Directed by Frank Capra
This wartime documentary focuses on the
blacks' participation in World War II, and
examines the important role played by the
Negro in U.S. history.
US Office of War Information — *International
Historic Films; Spotlite Video*

NBC — *Video Yesteryear*

Neighbors 1981
Comedy
47431   90 mins   C   B, V, LV   P
John Belushi, Dan Ackroyd, Kathryn Walker,
Cathy Moriarty, directed by John Avildsen
A quiet, middle-class, suburban couple gets the
shock of their lives when two loony people
move next door.
MPAA:R
Columbia — RCA/Columbia Pictures Home
Video; RCA VideoDiscs

Neil Diamond: Love at the 1976
Greek
Music-Performance
65479   52 mins   C   B, V, LV,   P
                                CED
This stereo spectacular features the Grammy
Award-winning star singing his greatest hits
"Sweet Caroline," "Play Me," "Holly Holy," "I
Am, I Said," "Song Sung Blue" and many more.
In stereo VHS and Beta Hi-Fi.
Arch Angel TV — Vestron Video

Neil Sedaka in Concert 1981
Music-Performance
55558   54 mins   C   B, V   P
Neil Sedaka, directed by Gary Jones
From his 1960's hits ("Calendar Girl," "Oh
Carol," and "Stairway to Heaven") to his 1970's
comeback as a composer and performer of
contemporary music, Sedaka's style and music
are revealed in this concert recorded live at the
Jubilee Auditorium in Edmonton, Canada.
Doug Hutton; Doug Holtby — MCA Home
Video

Neil Sedaka in Concert 1984
Music-Performance
69921   60 mins   C   B, V   P
Singer/songwriter/pianist Neil Sedaka performs
his vast repertoire of hits in concert at the
Forum in Ontario, Canada. In VHS Dolby stereo
and Beta Hi-Fi.
Perry Rosemond — RKO HomeVideo

Neil Young in Berlin 1982
Music-Performance
70768   60 mins   C   B, V, LV   P
Neil Young, Nils Lofgren, directed by Michael
Lindsey Hogg
The popular and talented Mr. Young performs
many of his well-known songs, as well as some
tracks from his "Trans" L.P. in this recorded
concert. Hi-Fi sound in both formats.
Lorne Michaels — VidAmerica

Nelvanamation 1980
Cartoons
54910   100 mins   C   B, V   P
Animated
Four cosmic fantasies are featured in this
program, including "Please Don't Eat the

Planet," "A Cosmic Christmas," "The Devil and
Daniel Mouse," and "Romie-O and Julie-8."
The latter two are also available individually.
Nelvana Ltd — Warner Home Video

Nelvanamation II 1981
Cartoons
47386   50 mins   C   B, V   P
Voices of Phil Silvers, Garrett Morris
A second anthology of fantasy cartoons for
children of all ages, featuring "Take Me Out to
the Ball Game," with music by Rick Danko, and
"The Jack Rabbit Story" with music by John
Sebastion.
Nelvana Ltd — Warner Home Video

Nepal, Land of the Gods 1975
Documentary/Asia
86481   62 mins   C   B, V   P
A mystical look at Nepalese life—its' blend of
Hinduism and Buddhism, folklore and
metaphysical beliefs.
Sheldon Rochlin; Mike Spera; Loren
Standlee — Mystic Fire Video

Neptune Factor, The 1973
Adventure/Drama
Closed Captioned
70901   94 mins   C   B, V   P
Ben Gazzara, Yvette Mimieux, Walter Pidgeon,
Ernest Borgnine, directed by Daniel Petrie
Scientists board a special new deep-sea sub to
search for their colleagues. Diving ever deeper
into the abyss that swallowed their friend's
Ocean Lab II, they encounter unfathomable
dangers.
MPAA:G
Twentieth Century Fox — Playhouse Video

Nest, The 1981
Drama
72875   109 mins   C   B, V   P
This film is about the relationship between a
widower and a young girl.
Unknown — Embassy Home Entertainment

Nesting, The 1980
Horror
81900   104 mins   C   B, V   P
Robin Groves, John Carradine, Gloria Grahame,
Christopher Loomis
The spirits of a quiet country home are seeking
revenge against a neurotic author who just
rented the house.
MPAA:R
Armand Weston — Warner Home Video

Network 1976
Drama
44645   121 mins   C   B, V, LV,   P
                                CED

Faye Dunaway, Peter Finch, William Holden,
Robert Duvall, Wesley Addy, Ned Beatty,
Beatrice Straight, directed by Sidney Lumet
A satire of television and the men behind the
networks.
Academy Awards '76: Best Actor (Finch); Best
Actress (Dunaway); Best Supporting Actress
(Straight); Best Screenplay Written Directly for
the Screen (Chayefsky). MPAA:R
MGM — *MGM/UA Home Video*

Network Fall Preview Presentations | 197?

Variety
33697   110 mins   C   B, V, 3/4U   P
This program contains each of the three major
network's presentations to its affiliates,
spotlighting new shows to be seen in the
autumn season. CBS's (1966) includes, "It's
About Time," and "Run, Buddy, Run," NBC's
(1969) highlights contain "The Bill Cosby
Show," and "Then Came Bronson," and ABC's
(1974) clips preview "Happy Days," amd
"Marcus Welby, M.D." among others.
CBS et al — *Shokus Video*

Nevada Smith | 1966

Western
88426   135 mins   C   B, V   P
Steve McQueen, Karl Malden, Brian Keith,
Arthur Kennedy, Raf Vallone
In this extension of Harold Robbins' "The
Carpetbaggers," Nevada Smith seeks out the
outlaws who killed his parents.
Paramount; Joseph E. Levine — *Paramount*
Home Video

Never a Dull Moment | 1968

Comedy
70666   90 mins   C   B, V   P
Dick Van Dyke, Edward G. Robinson, Dorothy
Provine, Henry Silva, Joanna Moore, Tony Bill,
Slim Pickens, Jack Elam, directed by Jerry Paris
Mobsters mistake an actor for an assassin in
this gag filled adventure. They threaten the
thespian into thievery, and trouble really starts
when Ace, the actual assassin arrives.
MPAA:G
Walt Disney Productions/Ron Miller — *Walt*
Disney Home Video

Never Cry Wolf | 1984

Drama
75927   105 mins   C   B, V, LV,   P
                                 CED
Charles Martin Smith, Brian Dennehy, Samson
Jorah
The dramatic story of a young biologist's trek to
the Artic region to study wolves.
Walt Disney — *Walt Disney Home Video*

Never Give a Sucker an Even Break | 1941

Comedy
85256   71 mins   B/W   B, V   P
W.C. Fields, Gloria Jean, Franklin Pangborn,
directed by Edward Cline
An almost plotless comedy, reputedly sold to
the studio by Fields written on the back of a
napkin, which features Fields at his most
unleashed. Something of a cult favorite.
Universal — *Kartes Video Communications*

Never Let Go | 1960

Comedy-Drama
59837   91 mins   C   B, V   P
Peter Sellers, Richard Todd, Elizabeth Sellars
A man unwittingly tracks down the mastermind
of a gang of racketeers.
Peter de Sarigny — *Embassy Home*
Entertainment

Never Love a Stranger | 1958

Drama
76833   93 mins   B/W   B, V   P
John Drew Barrymore, Steve McQueen, Lita
Milan, Robert Bray
A young man who becomes a numbers runner
for a mobster and ultimately winds up heading
his own racket finds himself in conflict with his
old boss and the District Attorney.
Allied Artists — *Republic Pictures Home Video*

Never On Sunday | 1960

Comedy
81504   94 mins   B/W   B, V   P
Melina Mercouri, Titos Vandis, Jules Dassin,
Mitsos Liguisos, directed by Jules Dassin
An American intellectual tries to turn a Greek
prostitute into a refined woman.
Academy Awards '60: Best Song "Never On
Sunday."
Melafilm Prods. — *MGM/UA Home Video*

Never Say Never Again | 1983

Suspense
69800   134 mins   C   B, V, LV,   P
                                 CED
Sean Connery, Klaus Maria Brandauer, Max
Von Sydow, Barbara Carrera
James Bond matches wits with a charming but
sinister tycoon who is holding the world nuclear
hostage as part of a diabolical plot by
SPECTRE. In stereo on all formats.
MPAA:PG
Jack Schwartzman — *Warner Home Video*

Never Steal Anything Small | 1958

Comedy
85775   94 mins   C   B, V   P
James Cagney, Shirley Jones, Cara Williams,
directed by Charles Lederer

A tough union boss handles the lives of those around him as he does the stevedores, while he battles the mob.
Universal — *MCA Home Video*

Neverending Story, The 1984
Fantasy
Closed Captioned
79554   86 mins   C   B, V, LV   P
Barret Oliver, Noah Hathaway, Gerald McRaney, Moses Gunn, directed by Wolfgang Petersen
A young boy helps a young warrior save a fantasy world from destruction. The music is composed by Klaus Doldinger and Giorgio Moroder. Available in Stereo VHS Hi-Fi and Beta Hi-Fi.
MPAA:PG
Warner Bros; Producers Sales Organization — *Warner Home Video*

Neville Marriner 1985
Music-Performance
87345 . 55 mins   C   B, V   P
The St. Martin-in-the-Fields Academy performs the music of Bach, Handel, Grieg, Gluck, Rossini and Borodin.
Academy of St. Martin-in-the-Fields — *Kultur*

New Adventures of 1935
Tarzan, The
Adventure/Serials
08870 260 mins B/W B, V, 3/4U   P
Herman Brix, Ula Holt, Frank Baker, Dale Walsh, Lewis Sargent
Twelve episodes, each 22 minutes long, depicts the adventures of Edgar Rice Burrough's tree-swinging character—Tarzan.
Burroughs and Tarzan — *Movie Buff Video; Hollywood Home Theater; Video Connection; Video Yesteryear; Discount Video Tapes*

New Adventures of 1981
Zorro, The
Cartoons/Adventure
66004   60 mins   C   B, V   P
Animated
Daring swordplay highlights these three tales of swashbuckling adventures.
Filmation — *Family Home Entertainment*

New Adventures of 1985
Zorro, Volume III, The
Cartoons/Adventure
70358   60 mins   C   B, V   P
Animated
This film features further swashbuckling heroism by the legendary Spanish-Californian swordsman. The program is available in stereo formats.
Filmation — *Family Home Entertainment*

New Centurions, The 1972
Drama
21294   109 mins   C   B, V   P
George C. Scott, Stacy Keach, Jane Alexander
The film version of Joseph Wambaugh's novel about rookie cops on the Los Angeles Police Force.
MPAA:R
Columbia — *RCA/Columbia Pictures Home Video*

New Deal Rhythm 1934
Music-Performance
85194   51 mins   B/W   B, V   P
Buddy Rogers, Ruth Etting, Emery Deutsch, Donald Novis
A collection of 5 musical shorts, featuring dance bands and singers and of the Thirties.
Vitaphone; Zukor; et al — *Video Yesteryear*

New Deal—The Thirties, 19??
The
History-US/Documentary
10148   ? mins   B/W   B, V   P, T
Covers the Depression, Mahatma Ghandi, Thomas Edison, George Gershwin, Mt. Rushmore, Al Capone, FDR, John Dillinger, the Hindenberg, Lou Gehrig, and more.
Unknown — *Blackhawk Films*

New England Patriots 1985
1985 Team Highlights
Football
86801   23 mins   C   B, V   P
Glimpses of the Patriots' '85 season are preserved on this tape.
NFL Films — *NFL Films Video*

New From London, 1985
Volume 1
Music-Performance
82392   59 mins   C   B, V   P
The Moodists, Amazulu, Twelfth Night, King Kurt, Di Anno, Freur
A compilation of various new artists from the British rock scene; filmed live at London's Marquee Club.
Trilion PLC — *Sony Video Software*

New Kids, The 1985
Horror
Closed Captioned
81429   90 mins   C   B, V   P
Shannon Presby, Lori Loughlin, James Spader, Eric Stoltz, directed by Sean S. Cunningham
An orphaned brother and sister find out the limitations of the good neighbor policy when a sadistic gang terrorizes them at their relatives' home in Florida. Available in VHS and Beta Hi Fi.
Columbia Pictures — *RCA/Columbia Pictures Home Video*

New Lion of Sonora, The 1970
Western
72891 120 mins C B, V P
Gilbert Roland, Leif Erickson
Two episodes of the "High Chaparral" TV series
are herewith combined where Don Domingo
(Gilbert Roland) returns to Arizona to head his
family.
NBC — *Republic Pictures Home Video*

New Look 1981
Variety/Filmmaking
59843 44 mins C B, V, LV, P
                           CED
Francis Ford Coppola, Bob Rafelson
An erotic men's video magazine including a
centerfold, interviews with filmmaker Francis
Ford Coppola and Bob Rafelson, and a series of
vignettes.
Regie Cassette Video; Blay RCV — *Embassy
Home Entertainment*

New Media Bible: The 1976
Story of Joseph, The
Bible
64708 90 mins C CED P
This video dramatization of the Bible presents
historically accurate settings and authentic
details of the biblical stories of Joseph.
Genesis Project — *RCA VideoDiscs*

New Misadventures of 1981
Ichabod Crane, The
Fantasy/Holidays
47254 25 mins C B, V, 3/4U, P
                           FO
The headless horseman rides again, robbing
coaches and scaring the townsfolk of Sleepy
Hollow. Halloween fun begins when Ichabod
comes to the rescue with his motley crew of
friends.
AM Available
Coronet Films — *Embassy Home
Entertainment; Coronet Films*

New Speed Reading 1981
Education/Communication
52767 60 mins C B, V P
This complete speed reading course is divided
into video chapters and allows the viewer to
refer back and review the method and progress
of speed reading. An instructional booklet with
study schedules is included.
AM Available
Karl Video — *Karl/Lorimar Home Video*

New Three Stooges 1965
Cartoons
72867 60 mins C B, V P
Animated 11 pgms
Combining animation with live-action, each tape
contains eight wacky Stooge escapades culled
from the popular television series.

Dick Brown, Normandy TV Three
Production — *Embassy Home Entertainment*

New Video Aerobics, The 1982
Physical fitness
63364 57 mins C B, V, CED P
Leslie Lilien, Julie Lavin
This program instructs the home viewer in a
complete and compact conditioning routine of
aerobics. Contains a 40-minute advanced
program and a 17-minute beginner's session.
Amstar Productions — *Vestron Video*

New Wave Comedy 1985
Comedy-Performance
86351 60 mins C B, V P
*John Kassir, Steve Sweeney, Patty
Rosborough, Wayne Federman, Marc Weiner*
A compilation of cutting-edge stand-up comedy
routines.
Vestron Video — *Vestron Video*

New York Giants 1984 1985
Team Highlights
Football
70549 70 mins C B, V, FO P
Phil Simms, Bill Parcells
The headlines read. "Giants Again!" as the
hard-working New Yorkers finally regained their
stature as NFL contenders. The tape features
47-Minutes of high-lights from the '84 NFL
season as well
NFL Films — *NFL Films Video*

New York Giants 1985 1985
Team Highlights
Football
88072 23 mins C B, V P
This compilation features highlights of the
Giants' '85 season.
NFL Films — *NFL Films Video*

New York Jets 1985 Team 1985
Highlights
Football
88073 23 mins C B, V P
Highlights of the Jets' '85 season are featured
on this tape.
NFL Films — *NFL Films Video*

New York Mets: Team 1984
Highlights
Baseball
81145 30 mins C B, V P
*Gil Hodges, Casey Stengel, Tom Seaver, Rusty
Staub, Darryl Strawberry, Dwight Gooden*
11 pgms
You can catch the rising stars as this series
looks back at the best moments from the Mets
past seasons.
*1.1963: Let's Go Mets 2.1969: Look Who's #1
3.1971: The Winning Way 4.1972: The Second*

Decade 5.1973: You Gotta Believe 6.1976: 15 Years of Fun 7.1980: Mets Magic 8.1981: Better All The Time 9.1982: Building a Fantastic Future 10.1983: We Can Make It Happen 11.1984: Don't Stop Us Now
Major League Baseball — Major League Baseball Productions

New York, New York   1977
Drama/Musical
63400   163 mins   C   B, V   P
Robert De Niro, Liza Minnelli, directed by Martin Scorsese
A tragic romance evolves between a saxaphonist and an aspiring actress in this salute to the big band era.
MPAA:PG
United Artists — CBS/Fox Video; RCA VideoDiscs

New York Nights   1984
Drama
80665   104 mins   C   B, V   P
Corinne Alphen, George Ayer, Bobbi Burns, Peter Matthey, Cynthia Lee
The lives of nine New Yorkers intertwine in a treacherous game of passion and seduction.
MPAA:R
International Talent Marketing — Lightning Video

New York-Yankees: Team   1984
Highlights
Baseball
81147   30 mins   C   B, V   P
Joe DiMaggio, Whitey Ford, Mickey Mantle, Billy Martin, Thurman Munson, Ron Guidry
7   pgms
This series chronicles the history of the Bronx Bombers from their humble beginnings to the present day.
1.Play Ball with the Yankees 2.Dynasty: The New York Yankees 3.50 Years of Yankee All-Stars 4.Home of Heroes 5.A New Era 6.1977: A Winning Tradition 7. 1978: It Don't Come Easy.
Major League Baseball — Major League Baseball Productions

New Zoo Revue   1973
Children/Variety
75928   60 mins   C   B, V   P
Emily Peden, Doug Momary
Each episode of this entertaining, educational children's series teaches youngsters the importance of peace, friendship and compassion in our daily interaction with others.
Family Home Entertainment — Family Home Entertainment

Newport Jazz Festival   1962
Music-Performance
55382   60 mins   B/W   B, V   P
Duke Ellington, Count Basie, Roland Kirk

Jazz greats in concert at the famed jazz festival include Count Basie, Duke Ellington, Roland Kirk, Ruby Braff, Peewee Russell, Joe Williams, Oscar Peterson Trio with Ray Brown, Lambert, Hendricks and Bavan, and others.
Unknown — CBS/Fox Video; Discount Video Tapes

News Front   1978
Drama
73663   110 mins   C   B, V   P
Bill Hunter, Wendy Hughes, John Ewart, Chris Hayward
The story of two brothers who worked in Australia's news media of the '50s and '60s is chronicled in this film. Some segments are in black and white.
David Elfick — Embassy Home Entertainment

Next of Kin   1985
Horror
70250   90 mins   C   B, V   P
Jackie Kerin, John Jarratt, Gerda Nicolson
A woman is plagued by nightmares after moving into her inherited estate. Suspense mounts as she discovers horrifying correlations between her mother's death and her situation.
VCL Communications — VCL Home Video

Next One, The   1984
Science fiction
76771   105 mins   C   B, V   P
Keir Dullea, Adrienne Barbeau, Jerenny Licht, Peter Hobbs
A mysterious visitor from another time winds up on an isolated Greek island as the result of a sinister magnetic storm.
Allstar Productions — Vestron Video

Next Victim   1971
Horror
80828   87 mins   C   B, V   R, P
George Hilton, Edwige French, Christina Airoldi, Ivan Rassimov
The unfaithful wife of an Austrian diplomat attempts to find out who has been slicing up beautiful jet-setters.
MPAA:PG
Laurie International — Video Gems

Next Victim, The   1974
Suspense
84756   80 mins   C   B, V   P
Carroll Baker, T P McKenna, Ronald Lacey, Maurice Kaufman
A beautiful woman confined to a wheelchair is stalked by a lunatic killer.
Ian Fordyce — Thriller Video

Next Year If All Goes Well   1983
Comedy
77166   95 mins   C   B, V   P

Isabelle Adjani, Thierry Lhermite
Two young lovers struggle to overcome their
insecurities to establish a relationship.
FR
New World Pictures — *THORN EMI/HBO
Video*

NFL Crunch Course   1985
Football
Closed Captioned
82290   44 mins   C   B, V   P
Top NFL coaches and players describe how
they maximize their impact on opposing teams.
This tape features live player sound wirings in
VHS and Beta stereo.
NFL Films — *NFL Films Video*

NFL '81   1982
Football
47716   47 mins   C   B, V, FO   P
Highlights from the topsy-turvy 1981-82 NFL
season, focusing on the great individual
performances, the Playoffs, and the NFL's
selections for the 1981-82 All-Pro Teams.
NFL Films — *NFL Films Video*

NFL '81 Official Season   1982
Yearbook
Football
47806   120 mins   C   CED   P
Four half-hour segments: "NFL '81" - a season
overview; "Superbowl XVI Highlights;" "A Very
Special Team" - season highlights of the San
Francisco 49'er's; "Stripes" - season highlights
of the Cincy Bengals.
NFL Films — *RCA VideoDiscs*

NFL Follies Go   1983
Hollywood
Football
65155   23 mins   C   B, V, FO   P
Football fumbles and goof-ups are integrated
into a parody of movie genres in this entry from
the "NFL Follies" series.
NFL Films — *NFL Films Video; Champions on
Film and Video*

NFL Head Coach: A Self   1985
Portrait
Football
81955   43 mins   C   B, V   P
The various coaches throughout the NFL talk
about their work in this non-narrated program.
NFL Films — *NFL Films Video*

NFL   1980
SymFunny/Highlights of
Super Bowl III
Football
56792   46 mins   C   B, V   P

The antics of the NFL "ballet company" set to
music by Beethoven, Bach, and "The
Quarterback of Seville," plus Joe Namath's
triumph against the Colts in the most incredible
upset in Super Bowl history.
NFL Films — *VidAmerica*

NFL SymFunny/Legends   1981
of the Fall
Football
51699   46 mins   C   LV   P
A collection of goofy football plays set to
classical music is teamed with an array of the
game's greatest heroes on this disc.
NFL Films — *NFL Films Video*

NFL's Best Ever Coaches   1981
Football
51702   46 mins   C   B, V, FO   R, P
A profile of some of the most respected and
successful coaches ever to pace the sidelines
of an NFL stadium, including Paul Brown, Vince
Lombardi, Don Shula, and Tom Landry.
NFL Films — *NFL Films Video*

NFL's Best Ever: The   1981
Professionals
Football
51703   46 mins   C   B, V, FO   R, P
This program profiles some of the most
determined, gutsy personalities ever to hit the
NFL, who despite setbacks and long odds,
struggled their way to success and recognition.
It features Jim Plunkett, Jim Marshall, Bill
Kilmer, Larry Brown, and Dick Vermeil.
NFL Films — *NFL Films Video*

NFL's Best Ever   1985
Quarterbacks
Football
51704   46 mins   C   B, V, FO   R, P
The careers of former NFL greats Fran
Tarkenton, Terry Bradshaw and Roger
Staubach are profiled. This tape has been newly
updated to include current gridiron leaders Dan
Marino and Joe Montana as well.
NFL Films — *NFL Films Video*

NFL's Best Ever Runners   1985
Football
51705   46 mins   C   B, V, FO   R, P
O.J. Simpson, Gale Sayers, Eric Dickerson and
Jim Brown are among the running backs
featured in this newly updated videotape.
NFL Films — *NFL Films Video*

NFL's Best Ever Teams   1981
Football
51706   46 mins   C   B, V, FO   R, P
Throughout the NFL's history, there have been
several teams who dominated their league for
several years at a time: the Cleveland Browns of

the 50's, the Green Bay Packers of the 60's, the Miami Dolphins of the early 70's, and Steelers, Cowboys, and Raiders of the middle and late 70's.
NFL Films — *NFL Films Video*

NFL's Inspirational Men and Moments, The   1980
Football
50090   48 mins   C   B, V, FO   R, P
Roger Staubach, O. J. Simpson, Fran Tarkenton, Joe Namath
A collection of short programs that reveal much about the inspirational aspects of pro football as well as the human side of a sport that's more than just a game.
NFL Films — *NFL Films Video*

Nicholas and Alexandra   1971
Drama
69618   183 mins   C   B, V   P
Michael Jayston, Janet Suzman, Tom Baker, Laurence Olivier, Michael Redgrave
This epic film chronicles the final years of Tsar Nicholas II and Empress Alexandra and their children from 1904 through their imprisonment and eventual execution under the new Lenin government.
MPAA:PG
Sam Spiegal — *RCA/Columbia Pictures Home Video*

Nicholas Nickleby   1946
Drama
58885   108 mins   B/W   B, V   P
Sir Cedric Hardwicke, Stanley Holloway, Derek Bond, Alfred Drayton, Sybil Thorndike, Sally Ann Howes
An ensemble cast is featured in this film adaptation of Charles Dickens' novel concerning an impoverished family dependent on a wealthy but villainous relative who sends young Nicholas into a series of wild adventures.
Ealing — *THORN EMI/HBO Video; Prism; Discount Video Tapes; Movie Buff Video*

Nickel Mountain   1985
Drama
81126   88 mins   C   B, V   P
Michael Cole, Heather Langen Kamp, Ed Lauter, Brian Kerwin, Patrick Cassidy
A suicidal forty-year-old man finds a new reason to live when he falls in love with a pregnant sixteen-year-old girl who works at his diner.
Ziv International — *Karl/Lorimar Home Video*

Nicolai Ghiaurov: Tribute to the Great Basso   1984
Opera
84661   82 mins   C   B, V   P
Mirella Freni, Jose Carreras, Piero Cappuccilli

Arias from "Faust," "Don Giovanni" and "Boris Godanonv" are performed in this salute to the legendary "Ghiaurov.
Bulgarian TV — *V.I.E.W. Video*

Night After Halloween, The   1983
Horror
81752   90 mins   C   B, V   P
Chantal Contouri, Robert Bruning, Sigrid Thornton
A young woman gets the shock of her life when she discovers that her boyfriend is a crazed killer.
MPAA:R
Electra Entertainment — *Magnum Entertainment*

Night and Day   1946
Musical/Biographical
70380   128 mins   B/W   B, V   P
Cary Grant, Eve Arden, Alexis Smith, Mary Martin, Monty Woolley, Dorothy Malone, Ginny Simms, Donald Woods.
This film presents the life of Cole Porter and features performances of many classic Porter tunes.
Warner Bros. — *Key Video*

Night and Fog   1955
Documentary/World War II
02957   32 mins   C   B, V, FO   P
Directed by Alain Resnais
A devastating documentary showing the gruesome atrocities of Hitler's Nazi purge against almost nine million innocent people.
Premier Prix du Concourse de la Qualite.
Argos Films — *Video Yesteryear; International Historic Films; Films Inc; Anti Defamation League of Bnai Brith*

Night at the Opera, A   1935
Comedy
39091   96 mins   B/W   B, V   P
The Marx Brothers, Allan Jones, Kitty Carlisle, Sig Rumann, Margaret Dumont
The Marx Brothers get mixed up with grand opera in this finest of all their films. Allan Jones, as an opera singer on the rise, sings "Alone," and "Cosi Cosa."
MGM — *MGM/UA Home Video*

Night Before Christmas, The   1981
Christmas
58946   57 mins   C   B, V   P
Animated, Norman Luboff Choir
Two heartwarming holiday tales are retold: "The Night Before Christmas" is the story of the fabled visit from St. Nicholas, and "Silent Night" is the story of how the beloved Christmas song was written. Both tales are animated, complete with a splendid musical score.

AM Available
Bill Turnball; Playhouse Pictures — *Media Home Entertainment*

Night Caller from Outer Space — 1966
Science fiction
85058   84 mins   B/W   B, V   P
John Saxon, Maurice Denham, Patricia Haines, Alfred Burke
An alien ship lands in London and subsequently women begin to disappear. At first, no one knows why, but then the horrible truth comes to light.
Fox/Lorber; Ronald Liles — *Sony Video Software*

Night Creature — 1979
Horror
79762   83 mins   C   B, V   P
Donald Pleasance, Nancy Kwan
A writer is determined to kill the man-eating black leopard who nearly killed him once before.
MPAA:PG
Dimension Pictures — *United Home Video*

Night Crossing — 1981
Drama/Adventure
59809   106 mins   C   B, V   P
John Hurt, Jane Alexander, Glynnis O'Connor, Doug McKeon, Beau Bridges, directed by Delbert Mann
The fact-based story of two East German families who launch a daring escape to the West in a homemade hot air balloon.
MPAA:PG
Walt Disney Productions — *Walt Disney Home Video*

Night Flight from Moscow — 1973
Adventure
85364   113 mins   C   B, V   P
Yul Brynner, Henry Fonda, Dirk Bogarde
A Soviet spy defects with a fistful of secret documents that implicate every free government, and the CIA must decide if he's telling the truth.
MPAA:PG
Henri Verneuil — *Charter Entertainment*

Night Gallery — 1969
Fantasy/Drama
76808   95 mins   C   B, V   P
Joan Crawford, Roddy McDowall, Tom Bosley, Barry Sullivan, Ossie Davis, Sam Jaffee, directed by Steven Spielberg, Boris Sagaland and Barry Shear
Rod Serling is your tour guide through an unusual art gallery consisting of portraits that reflect people's greed, desire and guilt. Pilot for the series that ran from 1969 to 1973.

Universal; William Sackheim — *MCA Home Video*

Night Games — 1980
Drama
66051   100 mins   C   B, V, LV, CED   P
Cindy Pickett, directed by Roger Vadim
A sexually unfulfilled woman experiences a passionate fantasy life.
MPAA:R
Raymond Chow — *Embassy Home Entertainment*

Night Is My Future, The — 1947
Drama
48857   89 mins   B/W   B, V, 3/4U   P
Mai Zetterling, directed by Ingmar Bergman
A blind young man meets a girl who tries to bring him happiness.
Swedish — *Movie Buff Video; Western Film & Video Inc; Video Yesteryear; Video Dimensions; International Home Video*

Night Moves — 1975
Suspense/Mystery
51967   100 mins   C   B, V   P
Gene Hackman, Susan Clark, Jennifer Warren
While tracking down a missing teenager, a Hollywood detective uncovers a bizarre smuggling ring.
MPAA:PG
Warner Bros — *Warner Home Video*

Night of the Assassin — 1977
Drama/Suspense
70692   98 mins   C   B, V   P
Klaus Kinski, Michael Craig, Eva Renzi, directed by Robert McMahon
A priest leaves his pulpit to practice terrorism in this intriguing film. He plans a surprise for a U.N. secretary visiting Greece that should put the U.S. and Greek governments in the palm of his hand.
Cinema Shares — *Lightning Video*

Night of the Bloody Apes — 1978
Horror
79700   84 mins   C   B, V   P
When a doctor transplants an ape's heart into his dying son's body, the results are deadly.
MPAA:R
William Calderon — *MPI Home Video*

Night of the Comet — 1984
Science fiction
73661   90 mins   C   B, V   R, P
Catherine Mary Stewart, Robert Beltran, Geoffrey Lewis, Mary Woronov
The three suvivors of an exploding comet are being chased after by two scientists who need their blood to stay alive.

MPAA:PG-13
Wayne Crawford; Andrew Lane — *CBS/Fox Video*

Night of the Generals, The — 1967
Drama
77376   148 mins   C   B, V   P
Peter O'Toole, Omar Sharif, Tom Courtenay, Joanna Pettet, Donald Pleasance
A Nazi intelligence officer is pursuing three Nazi generals who may be involved in the brutal murder of a Warsaw prostitute.
MPAA:R
Columbia Pictures; Sam Spiegel — *RCA/Columbia Pictures Home Video*

Night of the Ghouls — 1960
Horror
66336   75 mins   B/W   B, V, 3/4U   P
Directed by Edward D. Wood
The last in Edward Wood's celebrated series of inept so-called horror films, begun with "Bride of the Monster" and "Plan 9 from Outer Space."
DCA — *Nostalgia Merchant*

Night of the Grizzly, The — 1966
Western/Adventure
81102   99 mins   C   B, V   P
Clint Walker, Martha Hyer
An ex-lawman's peaceful life as a rancher is threatened by a killer grizzly bear goes on a murderous rampage terrorizing the residents of the Wyoming countryside.
Paramount — *Paramount Home Video*

Night of the Iguana, The — 1964
Drama
58296   125 mins   B/W   B, V   P
Richard Burton, Deborah Kerr, Ava Gardner, Sue Lyon, directed by John Huston
A defrocked minister, acting as a guide to a group of women on a Mexican bus trip, affects the lives of three women. Based on Tennessee Williams' play.
MGM; Ray Stark — *MGM/UA Home Video*

Night of the Juggler — 1980
Suspense
47816   101 mins   C   B, V, 3/4U   P
James Brolin, Cliff Gorman, Richard Castellano, Mandy Patinkin
A man encounters countless obstacles in trying to track down his daughter's kidnapper.
MPAA:R
Columbia — *Nostalgia Merchant; Media Home Entertainment*

Night of the Living Dead — 1968
Horror
01681   90 mins   B/W   B, V   P

Judith O'Dea, Duane Jones, Russell Streiner, Karl Hardman
Space experiments set off high level of radiation that makes the newly-dead return to life. They march upon humanity devouring their flesh.
Continental; Streiner and Hardman — *Prism; Hal Roach Studios; Media Home Entertainment; Hollywood Home Theater; United Home Video; VCII; Video Yesteryear; Nostalgia Merchant; Video Dimensions; World Video Pictures; Cable Films; Movie Buff Video; Video Connection; Discount Video Tapes; Western Film & Video Inc; Vestron Video (disc only)*

Night of the Sorcerers — 1974
Horror
82277   85 mins   C   B, V   P
Jack Taylor, Simon Andrue, Kali Hansa
An expedition to the Congo uncovers a bizarre tribe of vampire leopard women who lure young girls to their deaths.
Profilmes SA — *Unicorn Video*

Night of the Zombies — 1983
Horror
73040   101 mins   C   B, V   P
The staff of a scientific research center are killed and then resurrected as cannibals who prey on the living.
Motion Picture Marketing — *Vestron Video; Prism*

Night Patrol — 1985
Comedy
Closed Captioned
81769   87 mins   C   B, V, LV   P
Linda Blair, Pat Paulsen, Jaye P. Morgan, Murray Langston, Billy Barty, Pat Morita
The streets of Hollywood will never be the same after the night patrol runs amuck in the town.
MPAA:R
New World Pictures — *New World Video*

Night Porter, The — 1974
Drama
59838   115 mins   C   B, V, LV,   P
                          CED
Dirk Bogarde, Charlotte Rampling, Philippe LeRoy, Gabriele Ferzetti
Max, a guilt-ridden ex-SS concentration camp officer, unexpectedly meets his former lover-victim.
Robert Gordon; Avco Embassy — *Embassy Home Entertainment*

Night Ranger—7 Wishes Tour — 1985
Music-Performance
87179   80 mins   C   B, V   P
The pop group performs some of its many chart-stomping hits, including "Sister Christian" and "Sentimental Street."

MCA Home Video — *MCA Home Video*

Night School 1981
Horror
81966   89 mins   C   B, V   P
Rachel Ward, Leonard Mann, Drew Snyder, Joseph R. Sicari
A police detective must find out who has been decapitating the women who attend night school at Wendell College.
MPAA:R
Lorimar Prods. — *Key Video*

Night Shift 1982
Comedy
63122   106 mins   C   B, V, LV,   P
CED
Henry Winkler, Michael Keaton, Shelley Long
Two morgue attendants decide to spice up their late-night shift by running a call girl service on the side.
MPAA:R
The Ladd Company — *Warner Home Video*

Night Stage to Galveston 1952
Western
65082   61 mins   B/W   B, V   P, T
Gene Autry, Pat Buttram, Virginia Huston, Thurston Hall
Gene leads his Texas Rangers on a mission to uncover corruption in the Texas State Police during the turbulent post-Civil War days.
Columbia — *Blackhawk Films*

Night Terror 1976
Drama
79249   73 mins   C   B, V   P
Valerie Harper, Richard Romanus, Michael Tolan, Beatrice Manley
Everyone's after a woman who saw a highway partolman murdered on an expressway.
Charles Fries Productions — *Worldvision Home Video*

Night the Lights Went Out in Georgia, The 1981
Drama
59335   112 mins   C   B, V   P
Kristy McNichol, Dennis Quaid, Mark Hamill, Don Stroud
Based on the popular hit song, a brother and sister try to cash in on the country music scene in Nashville.
MPAA:PG
Elliot Geisinger; Howard Kuperman; Ronald Saland; Howard Smith — *Embassy Home Entertainment; Trans World Entertainment*

Night They Raided Minsky's, The 1969
Comedy/Musical
81840   97 mins   C   B, V   P

Jason Robards, Britt Ekland, Elliot Gould, Bert Lahr, Norman Wisdom, directed by William Friedkin
A young Amish girl who wants to leave her tyrannical father comes to Minsky's Burlesque in New York and invents the striptease.
Available in VHS and Beta Hi-Fi.
MPAA:PG
United Artists — *Key Video*

Night Train to Terror 1984
Horror
85930   98 mins   C   B, V   P
John Phillip Law, Cameron Mitchell, Mark Lawrence, Charles Moll
The symbolic forces of Good & Evil judge the lives of a trio of train passengers.
MPAA:R
Jay Schlosseberg-Cohen — *Prism*

Night Visitor, The 1970
Suspense
51115   106 mins   C   B, V   P
Max von Sydow, Liv Ullman, Trevor Howard, Per Oscarsson
A man whose convicted insanity is actually in doubt seeks violent vengeance on his tormentors.
MPAA:PG
Mel Ferrer — *United Home Video*

Night Warning 1982
Drama
69042   96 mins   C   B, V   P
A portrayal of young love's perverted inner conflicts and sinister mystery.
Unknown — *THORN EMI/HBO Video*

Night with Lou Reed, A 1983
Music-Performance
65698   60 mins   C   B, V   P
This is a visual record of the legendary rock star's sold-out engagement at The Bottom Line in New York featuring many of his greatest hits, including "Sweet Jane," "Walk on the Wild Side," "I'm Waiting for My Man," and "Rock 'n' Roll." In Beta Hi-Fi.
Bill Boggs; Richard Baker; RCA Video Productions Inc — *RCA/Columbia Pictures Home Video*

Nightcomers, The . 1972
Suspense
86595   96 mins   C   B, V   P
Marlon Brando, Stephanie Beacham, Thora Hird, directed by Michael Winner
A "prequel" to Henry James' "The Turn of the Screw," wherein an Irish gardener trysts with the nanny of two watchful children who believe that lovers unite in death.
MPAA:R

Michael Winner; Avco Embassy — *Charter Entertainment*

Nighthawks   1981
Suspense/Drama
55557   90 mins   C   B, V, LV   P
Sylvester Stallone, Billy Dee Williams, Rutger Hauer, Lindsay Wagner, directed by Bruce Malmuth
A New York City cop stalks Manhattan, hunting down an international terrorist on the loose, from disco, to subway, to an airborne tramway. Also available in a Spanish subtitled version.
MPAA:R
Universal; Martin Poll — *MCA Home Video*

Nightingale, The   1984
Fairy tales
Closed Captioned
73852   60 mins   C   B, V, LV,   P
                                CED
Mick Jagger, Barbara Hershey, Bud Cort, Mako, directed by Ivan Passer
From "Faerie Tale Theatre" comes the story of an Emperor who discovers the value of true friendship and loyalty from his palace kitchen maid who gives him a nightingale.
Gaylord Productions; Platypus Productions — *CBS/Fox Video*

Nightkill   1980
Drama/Suspense
63375   104 mins   C   B, V   P
Jaclyn Smith, Mike Connors, James Franciscus, Robert Mitchum
A bored wife plots to do away with her wealthy, powerful husband with the aid of her attractive lover.
MPAA:R
Avco Embassy — *Embassy Home Entertainment*

Nightmare Castle   1966
Horror
01680   90 mins   B/W   B, V   P
Barbara Steele, Paul Miller, directed by Allan Grunewald
Scientist murders his evil wife and her lover, then hides their hearts under a statue. Lovers are restored to life and avenge their murders.
Allied Artists — *Hollywood Home Theater*

Nightmare in Wax   1969
Horror
13028   95 mins   C   B, V   P
Cameron Mitchell, Anne Helm
Famous actor, burned by wax, starts a wax museum and destroys all of his enemies.
Gold Key — *United Home Video*

Nightmare on Elm Street,   1984
A
Horror
81091   92 mins   C   B, V   P
John Saxon, Ronee Blakely, Heather Lagen Kamp, directed by Wes Craven
A teenaged girl decides to wage a battle against a man who is annihilating other teenagers in their dreams. This movie contains gratuitous violence which is not for the squeamish.
MPAA:R
New-Line Cinema — *Media Home Entertainment*

Nightmare on Elm Street,   1985
Part 2: Freddy's Revenge,
A
Horror
Closed Captioned
86393   87 mins   C   B, V   P
Mark Patton, Hope Lange, Clu Gulager, Robert Englund, Kim Myers
A sequel to the popular horror film, as Freddy, the dream-haunting psychopath, possesses a teenager's body in order to kill again.
MPAA:R
Jack Sholder — *Media Home Entertainment*

Nightmares   1983
Horror
66329   99 mins   C   B, V   P
Christina Raines, Emilio Estevez, Moon Zappa, Lance Henriksen, Richard Masur, Veronica Cartwright
An anthology of four horrific tales in which common, everyday occurrences take on the ingredients of nightmare.
MPAA:PG
Universal — *MCA Home Video*

Nightwing   1979
Suspense
68263   103 mins   C   B, V, CED   P
Nick Mancuso, David Warner, Kathryn Harrold
A suspense drama about three people who risk their lives to exterminate a colony of plague-carrying vampire bats.
MPAA:PG
Columbia — *RCA/Columbia Pictures Home Video*

Nine Ages of Nakedness   197?
Drama
59548   88 mins   C   B, V   P
The story of a man whose ancestors have been plagued by a strange problem—beautiful, naked women who create carnal chaos.
George Harrison Marks — *Media Home Entertainment*

Nine Days a Queen   1934
Drama
03819   80 mins   B/W   B, V   P

John Mills, Sir Cedric Hardwicke, directed by
Robert Stevenson
Historical epic set in England. Story of young
Queen executed for treason after nine-day
reign.
British — Hollywood Home Theater

Nine Deaths of the Ninja   1985
Martial arts
81639   93 mins   C   B, V   P
Sho Kosugi, Brent Huff, Emelia Lesniak, Regina
Richardson
A faceless ninja warrior leads a team of
commandos on a mission to rescue a group of
political prisoners held captive in the Phillipine
jungles.
MPAA:R
Crown International Pictures — Media Home
Entertainment

984—Prisoner of the   1984
Future
Drama
76646   70 mins   C   B, V   P
Don Francks, Stephen Markle and Gail Dahms
A shocking, futuristic tale of human self-
destruction.
William I Macadam — VCL Home Video

Nine Lives of Fritz the   1974
Cat, The
Comedy/Fantasy
64880   77 mins   C   CED   P
Animated
The would-be cool cat of the 60's is fed up with
his establishment life in the 70's, so he takes off
into his other lives on a fantasy journey.
American International Pictures — Vestron
Video (disc only)

9 to 5   1981
Comedy
49397   111 mins   C   B, V, LV,   P
                              CED
Jane Fonda, Lily Tomlin, Dolly Parton, Dabney
Coleman
Three office secretaries rebel against their male
chauvinistic boss, eventually raising office
efficiency to a new all-time high.
MPAA:PG
20th Century Fox — CBS/Fox Video

1918   1985
Drama
Closed Captioned
81762   89 mins   C   B, V   P
Matthew Broderick, Hallie Foote, William
Converse Roberts, directed by Ken Harrison
This is an adaptation of the Horton Foote play
about the effects of World War I and an
influenza epidemic on a small Texas town. You
can hear Willie Nelson's score in VHS and Beta
Hi-Fi.

Cinecom International Films — CBS/Fox
Video

1984   1984
Drama
80898   115 mins   C   B, V   P
John Hurt, Richard Burton, Suzanna Hamilton,
Cyril Cusack, directed by Michael Radford
This film is a faithful adaptation of the George
Orwell novel about the grim consequences of
life within a totalitarian society where inhabitants
are under constant scrutiny of "Big Brother."
Music by Eurythmics and Dominic Muldowney.
Available in VHS Stereo and Beta Hi-Fi.
MPAA:R
Virgin Films; Umbrella-Rosenblum
Films — U.S.A. Home Video

1984 Winter Olympics   1984
Highlights
Sports-Winter
65625   60 mins   C   B, V   P
Experience the excitement as more than 1200
of the best athletes from over 44 countries
compete to bring home the gold at the XIV
Winter Olympic Games held in Sarajevo,
Yugoslavia.
ABC Sports; Curt Gowdy Jr — Embassy Home
Entertainment

1981 NBA Playoffs and   1981
Championship Series:
The Dynasty Renewed
Basketball
53411   58 mins   C   B, V   P
While the Celtics and 76ers tear up the Eastern
Conference, the Lakers try to survive through
Magic Johnson's Knee injury in the West. Once
the long season ends, the playoffs provide
plenty of upsets, drama, and classic basketball.
NBA — CBS/Fox Video

1958 NFL Championship   1984
Game
Football
79635   47 mins   C   B, V, FO   P
Highlights from the 1958 NFL championship
games between the Baltimore Colts and the
New York Giants.
NFL Films — NFL Films Video

1941   1979
Comedy
42939   120 mins   C   B, V, LV   P
John Belushi, Dan Ackroyd, Ned Beatty,
directed by Steven Spielberg
Spielberg has directed the most expensive
comedy of all time with a budget exceeding 35
million dollars. His depiction of Los Angeles in
the chaotic days after the bombing of Pearl
Harbor combines elements of fantasy and black
humor.

MPAA:PG
A Team Prods — *MCA Home Video*

1990: The Bronx Warriors   1983
Adventure
65368   86 mins   C   B, V   P
*Vic Morrow, Christopher Connelly, Fred
Williamson*
The controversial film that caused big waves in
the big apple. "1990: The Bronx Warriors" is a
brutal, heavy-metal journey into an urban hell.
MPAA:R
Fabrizio De Angelis — *Media Home
Entertainment*

1978—The New York   1978
Yankees' Miracle Year
Baseball
56879   100 mins   C   CED   P
Highlights of the Yankees' 1978 season, their
greatest comeback ever, including a tense
game vs. the Red Sox, and memorable
moments from their defeat of the Dodgers in the
World Series.
Major League Baseball — *RCA VideoDiscs*

1979 World Series and   1979
All-Star Highlights
Baseball
44845   55 mins   C   B, V   P
The Pittsburgh Pirates come back from a three
games to one deficit to defeat the Baltimore
Orioles in seven games in the 1979 World
Series. Willie Stargell's two-run homer in Game
7 puts the Pirates ahead to stay. In the 50th All-
Star Game played that July, the National
League continues to dominate the American
League in a 7-6 victory.
Major League Baseball — *RCA/Columbia
Pictures Home Video*

1966 and 1967 NFL   1984
Championship Games
Football
79636   52 mins   C   B, V, FO   P
Highlights from two classic NFL championship
confrontations between the Green Bay Packers
and the Dallas Cowboys circa 1966 and 1967.
NFL Films — *NFL Films Video*

1939—The Movies'   1939
Vintage Year: Trailers on
Tape
Movie and TV trailers
81884   60 mins   B/W   B, V   P
A compilation of coming attractions from such
classics as "Gunga Din," "Idiot's Delight,"
"Juarez," "Dark Victory" and "Gone With The
Wind." Some segments are in color.
MGM et al — *San Francisco Rush Video*

---

99 Women   1969
Drama
76827   90 mins   C   B, V   P
*Maria Schell, Herbert Lom, Mercedes
McCambridge, Luciana Paluzzi*
A sympathetic prison warden attempts to
investigate conditions at a women's prison
camp.
MPAA:X
Harry Alan Towers;
Commonwealth — *Republic Pictures Home
Video*

Ninja Mission   1984
Martial arts
82492   95 mins   C   B, V   P
Christopher Kohlberg, Curt Brober, Hanna Pola
A CIA agent and his group of ninja fighters
embark on a hazardous mission to rescue two
people from a Soviet prison. They use their
fighting skills against Russian soldiers, in a
climactic scene of martial artistry and mayhem.
MPAA:R
Roger Lundey — *Media Home Entertainment*

Ninja the Wonder Boy   1985
Cartoons
81103   92 mins   C   B, V   P
Animated
This is the story of a young boy's magical and
humorous journey towards becoming a master
ninja.
Kidpix Inc. — *Paramount Home Video*

Ninja III: The Domination   1984
Martial arts
80627   92 mins   C   B, V   P
Lucinda Dickey, Sho Kosugi
A Ninja master must exorcise the spirit of a
deadly assassin out of a young woman.
Available in VHS and Beta Hi-Fi.
MPAA:R
Cannon Films — *MGM/UA Home Video*

Ninja Wars   1984
Martial arts
71210   95 mins   C   B, V   P
One ninja takes on five ninja assassins who,
along with an evil ninja sorcerer, have
kidnapped his ninja girlfriend.
Independent — *Prism*

Ninotchka   1939
Comedy
80209   110 mins   B/W   B, V, LV   P
*Greta Garbo, Melvyn Douglas, Ina Claire, Bela
Lugosi, directed by Ernest Lubitsch*
A Russian agent comes to Paris and winds up
falling in love with a playboy.
MGM — *MGM/UA Home Video*

Ninth Configuration, The   1979
Drama
84262   115 mins   C   B, V   P
Stacy Keach, Scott Wilson, Jason Miller, Ed Flanders
Based on William Peter Blatty's novel "Twinkle, Twinkle, Killer Kane," (also the film's alternate title), this is a wierd and surreal tale of a mock rebellion of high-ranking military lunatics held in a secret base hospital.
MPAA:R
Lorimar — *New World Video*

No Deposit, No Return   1976
Comedy
88339   115 mins   C   B, V   P
David Niven, Don Knotts, Darren McGavin, Barbara Feldon
Two precocious rich kids get involved with bumbling safecracking thieves in this juvenile Disney opus.
MPAA:G
Walt Disney Prod. — *Walt Disney Home Video*

No Effort: Subliminal   1984
Weight Loss Video
Physical fitness
72945   20 mins   C   B, V   P
Weight loss through subliminal suggestions is featured on this self-help tape.
Dick Sutphen — *United Home Video*

No Man of Her Own   1950
Drama
85257   97 mins   B/W   B, V   P
Barbara Stanwyck, John Lund, Jane Cowl, Richard Denning
A woman assumes the identity of a dead woman in order to give her illegitimate child a chance at a happy life. She is, of course, blackmailed.
Paramount — *Kartes Video Communications*

No Man's Valley   1981
Cartoons
71365   30 mins   C   B, V   P
Animated, voices of Barney Phillips, Richard Deacon, Art Metrano, Arnold Stang, Joe E Ross
When the encroaching civilization endangers their homes, a flock of condors send a scout to find a safe place to colonize.
Bill Melendez — *Family Home Entertainment*

No Place To Hide   1981
Horror/Drama
71218   96 mins   C   B, V   P
Keir Dullea, Mariette Hartley, Kathleen Beller, Arlen Dean Snyder, Gary Graham, John Llewellyn Moxey
A girl's father drowns and she blames herself. Her mother and psychologist try to convince the girl that her father's spirit isn't stalking her.
MPC — *Prism*

No Small Affair   1984
Comedy-Drama/Romance
Closed Captioned
77370   102 mins   C   B, V   P
Jon Cryer, Demi Moore, George Wendt, Ann Wedgeworth, directed by Jerry Schatzberg
A sixteen-year-old aspiring photographer becomes romantically involved with a sultry twenty-two-year-old rock star. The musical score, by Rupert Holmes, is available in VHS Hi-Fi Stereo.
MPAA:R
Columbia Pictures; William Sackneim — *RCA/Columbia Pictures Home Video*

No Substitute for Victory   1976
War-Drama
86704   80 mins   C   B, V   P
Narrated by John Wayne
John Wayne hosts a look at the Communist threat and its culmination in Vietnam, with interviews with Lowell Thomas and Sgt. Barry Sadler.
Chuck Keen — *Video Gems*

No Sweat   1984
Physical fitness
78905   60 mins   C   B, V   P
L.A. Raiders' Lyle Alzado presents his own physical fitness regimen designed especially for men.
Karl Video — *Karl/Lorimar Home Video*

No Time For Sergeants   1958
Comedy
Closed Captioned
80709   119 mins   B/W   B, V   P
Andy Griffith, Nick Adams, Murray Hamilton, Don Knotts, Jamie Farr, Myron McCormick, directed by Mervyn Le Roy
An adaptation of the Broadway play about the Air Force's unsuccessful attempts to indoctrinate a naive Georgia farm boy.
Warner Bros. — *Warner Home Video*

No Way Back   1976
Adventure
47668   92 mins   C   B, V   P
Fred Williamson, Charles Woolf, Tracy Reed, Virginia Gregg, Don Cornelius, directed by Fred Williamson
Fred Williamson portrays Jesse Crowder, a man-for-hire expert with guns, fists, and martial arts in search of a woman's missing husband.
MPAA:R
Po Boy Productions — *Unicorn Video*

No Way to Treat a Lady   1968
Suspense
82542   108 mins   C   B, V   P
Rod Steiger, Lee Remick, George Segal, Eileen Heckart, Murray Hamilton

A psychotic master of disguise stalks and kills various women in this suspenseful cat-and-mouse game.
Sol C Siegel — *Paramount Home Video*

Noah-The Deluge   1979
Religion
85871   49 mins   C   B, V   P
Lew Ayres, Eve Plumb, Ed Lauter, Robert Emhardt, Rita Gam
Part of "The Greatest Heroes of the Bible" series, this TV film depicts the great flood and Noah's construction of the Ark.
Sunn Classics — *Magnum Entertainment*

Nobody's Boy   1984
Cartoons
70751   80 mins   C   B, V   P
Animated, voice of Jim Backus, directed by Jim Flocker
This tale of an 8-year-old boy's search for his mother's identity shows the power of mother/son love in overcoming their separation.
ATA Trading Corp. — *MPI Home Video*

Nobody's Perfekt   1979
Comedy
58957   95 mins   C   B, V   P
Gabe Kaplan, Robert Klein, Alex Karras, Susan Clark
Three psychiatric patients decide to fight City Hall.
Mort Engelberg — *RCA/Columbia Pictures Home Video*

Nocturna   1979
Satire
55216   82 mins   C   B, V   P
Yvonne DeCarlo, John Carradine
Hard times have fallen upon the house of Dracula and to help pay the taxes on the castle it has been converted to the Hotel Transylvania. In order to increase business and the blood supply at the hotel, Nocturna books a rock group to entertain the guests.
MPAA:R
Compass International Pictures — *Media Home Entertainment*

Noel's Fantastic Trip   1984
Cartoons
80788   69 mins   C   B, V   P
Animated
Noel and his dog travel through outer space in a single prop airplane seeking adventure.
Turner Program Services;
Toei — *RCA/Columbia Pictures Home Video*

Nomad Riders   1981
Exploitation
71126   82 mins   C   B, V   P

Wayne Chema, Richard Cluck, Ron Gregg, directed by Frank Roach
A la "Mad Max," one rugged man goes after the bikers who killed his wife and daughter.
Associated Film Corp — *Vestron Video*

None But The Lonely Heart   1944
Drama
00265   113 mins   B/W   B, V, 3/4U   P
Cary Grant, Ethel Barrymore, Barry Fitzgerald
In the days before World War II, a Cockney drifter travels through England in search of spiritual fulfillment.
Academy Awards '44: Best Supporting Actress (Barrymore).
RKO — *Nostalgia Merchant; King of Video*

Norma Rae   1979
Drama
37411   114 mins   C   B, V, CED   P
Sally Field, Ron Leibman, Beau Bridges
Sally Field portrays a textile worker who joins forces with a New York labor organizer to unionize a Southern mill.
Academy Awards '79: Best Actress (Field); Best Song ("It Goes Like It Goes"). MPAA:PG
20th Century Fox — *CBS/Fox Video*

Norman Conquests: Table Manners, The   1980
Comedy
59701   108 mins   C   B, V   P
Tom Conti, Richard Briers, Penelope Keith
Part I of playwright Alan Ayckbourn's comic trilogy of love unfulfilled.
Thames Video — *THORN EMI/HBO Video*

Norman Conquests: Living Together, The   1980
Comedy
59702   93 mins   C   B, V   P
Tom Conti
Part II concerns the happenings in the living room during Norman's disastrous weekend of unsuccessful seduction.
Thames Video — *THORN EMI/HBO Video*

Norman Conquests: Round and Round the Garden, The   1980
Comedy
59703   106 mins   C   B, V   P
Tom Conti
Part III concerns Norman's furtive appearance in the garden, which suggests that the weekend is going to misfire.
Thames Video — *THORN EMI/HBO Video*

Norseman, The   1978
Drama
64361   90 mins   C   B, V, CED   P

*Lee Majors, Cornel Wilde, Mel Ferrer,
Christopher Connelly*
The leader of a band of Norsemen sets sail for
the New World in search of his missing father.
MPAA:PG
American International — *Vestron Video*

North American Big Game   1985
Hunting
86865   30 mins   C   B, V   P
Narrated by Curt Gowdy
An investigation of the habitats, habits and
hunting of ten large North American big game
animals.
AM Available
Browning-Warburton Prod. — *Warburton
Productions*

North Avenue Irregulars, The   1978
Comedy
81656   99 mins   C   B, V   P
*Edward Herrman, Barbara Harris, Susan Clark,
Cloris Leachman, Karen Valentine*
A Presbyterian minister and six female members
of his congregation become undercover agents
for the FBI on a mission to expose a crooked
gambling syndicate.
MPAA:G
Walt Disney Productions — *Walt Disney Home
Video*

North Avenue Irregulars, The   1979
Comedy
44295   99 mins   C   B, V   P
*Edward Herrmann, Barbara Harris, Susan Clark,
Karen Valentine, Cloris Leachman, Ruth Buzzi*
Playing a new minister in a small community,
Edward Herrmann tries to halt the ripping-off of
church funds by organized criminals. To do so,
he organizes some female vigilantes from the
parish, all of whom are daffy bumblers who
seem incapable for the task.
MPAA:G
Walt Disney — *Walt Disney Home Video*

North by Northwest   1959
Suspense
39088   136 mins   C   B, V, CED   P
*Cary Grant, Eva Marie Saint, James Mason, Leo
G. Carroll, directed by Alfred Hitchcock*
Quintessential Hitchcock—the tale of a self-
assured Madison Avenue executive who
inadvertently gets mixed up with international
spies—contains the famous scene of Grant and
Miss Saint dangling from the faces on Mount
Rushmore.
MGM — *MGM/UA Home Video*

North Dallas Forty   1979
Comedy-Drama
44593   117 mins   C   B, V, LV   P
*Nick Nolte, Mac Davis, Charles Durning, Bo
Svenson, directed by Ted Kotcheff*
An aging football player realizes that the game
does not hold great illusions for him anymore.
Through a woman he meets he is drawn away
from the masculine violent world he is used to.
This creates tension between him and the
team's management. He must decide whether
to submit to management or quit. Based on the
novel by former Dallas Cowboy Peter Gent.
MPAA:R
Paramount, Frank Yablans — *Paramount
Home Video; RCA VideoDiscs*

North Star, The   1943
War-Drama
07037   108 mins   B/W   B, V   P
*Dana Andrews, Walter Huston, Anne Baxter,
Farley Granger*
Gripping war tale of Nazi over-running of
eastern Russian city, with courageous villagers
fighting back.
RKO — *Video Yesteryear; Hollywood Home
Theater; Discount Video Tapes; Cable Films;
Video Connection; Western Film & Video Inc;
Kartes Video Communications; Republic
Pictures Home Video; Movie Buff Video*

North to Alaska   1960
Adventure/Comedy
82337   120 mins   C   B, V   P
*John Wayne, Stewart Granger, Ernie Kovacs,
Fabian, Capucine, directed by Henry Hathaway*
A prospector encounters many problems when
he agrees to pick up his partner's fiancee in
Seattle and bring her home to Nome, Alaska.
Available in Hi-Fi Stereo.
20th Century Fox — *Playhouse Video*

Northeast of Seoul   1972
Adventure
82247   84 mins   C   B, V   P
*Anita Ekberg, John Ireland, Victor Buono,
directed by David Lowell Rich*
Three people will stop at nothing to steal a
legendary jewel-encrusted sword out of Korea.
MPAA:PG
Phillip Yordan Productions — *MGM/UA Home
Video*

Northern Pursuit   1943
Adventure/Drama
73978   94 mins   B/W   B, V   P
*Errol Flynn, Helmut Dantine, Julie Bishop,
directed by Raoul Walsh*
A Canadian Mountie disguises himself to
infiltrate a Nazi spy ring in this exciting
adventure film.
Warner Bros — *Key Video*

Northwest Frontier   1959
Adventure
59839   129 mins   C   B, V   P
*Lauren Bacall, Herbert Lom, Kenneth More,
directed by J. Lee Thompson*
A turn-of-the century adventure set in India
about the courageous attempt to save the
country from rebellion, and the infant prince
from assassination.
Earl St John — *Embassy Home Entertainment*

Northwest Trail   1946
Crime-Drama
03988   75 mins   C   B, V   P
John Litel, Bob Steele, Joan Woodbury
Mounted policeman covers the wilderness in
search of a killer.
Screen Guild; Lippert — *Weiss Global
Enterprises; Hollywood Home Theater; Video
Connection*

Nosferatu   1922
Horror
08704   63 mins   B/W   B, V, 3/4U   P
*Max von Schreck, Alexander Cranach, Gustav
von Wangenheim, directed by F. W. Murnau*
First film version of Bram Stoker's novel
"Dracula." (Silent, musical score added.)
Janus Films; German — *Blackhawk Films;
Video Yesteryear; Kartes Video
Communications; Discount Video Tapes;
Western Film & Video Inc*

Nostalgia World War II   1945
Video Library #1
World War II/Propaganda
69573   46 mins   B/W   B, V, FO   P
These three War Department shorts were all
produced during the last year of World War II
and served to exhort viewers to keep up the
pace of war work and not slack off. Titles are
"Battle Wreckage," "The War Speeds Up" and
"It Can't Last."
US War Department — *Video Yesteryear*

Nostalgia World War II   1942
Video Library #2
World War II
78086   60 mins   B/W   B, V, FO   P
This program takes a look at the course of
World War II and how people were inspired to
work for the war effort. It includes "U.S. News
Review Issues #2 and #5" and "The case of
the Tremendous Trifle."
Office of War Information — *Video Yesteryear*

Nostalgia World War II   1944
Video Library #3
World War II
78087   60 mins   B/W   B, V, FO   P
This program presents informative documents
and newsreels of World War II combat including

"Film Communiques #3 and #4" and "U.S.
Coast Guard Report #5."
Signal Corps.; U.S. Coast Guard — *Video
Yesteryear*

Nostalgia World War II   1945
Video Library #5
World War II
78109   53 mins   B/W   B, V, FO   P
The shocking story of the aftermath of World
War II is told from two fascinating and different
perspectives in "Diary of a Sergeant" and "The
Atom Strikes."
Army Pictorial Service Division — *Video
Yesteryear*

Nostalgia World War II   1943
Video Library #4
World War II
73644   61 mins   B/W   B, V, FO   P
This collection of U.S. Hollywood and
Government-produced dramatic short films from
the World II era includes "A Letter from
Bataan," "The Rear Gunner," "The Caissóns
Go Rolling Along," "I Don't Want to Change the
Subject," "Keep 'Em Rolling," "The Marines'
Hymn," "The U.S. Coast Guard Song, Semper
Paratus, "Ten Years from Now," and "We've
Got Another Bond to Buy."
US Government et al — *Video Yesteryear*

Nostalgia World War II   1944
Video Library #8
World War II/Propaganda
80755   59 mins   B/W   B, V   P
This volume of short films produced during
World War II features "Life Line" (1943) and
"Film Communique Issues Eight and Nine" as
well as a "Private Snafu" cartoon.
U.S. Signal Corps; Warner Bros — *Video
Yesteryear*

Nostalgia World War 2   1944
Video Library #7
Propaganda/World War II
85195   57 mins   B/W   B, V   P
Elisha Cook Jr.
A patriotic war-time mini-drama is combined
with a selection of vintage combat footage and
training films.
Signal Corps — *Video Yesteryear*

Nostalgia World War 2   1943
Video Library #9
Propaganda/World War II
85196   61 mins   B/W   B, V   P
A compilation of three armed forces combat
films; one, "The Fight for the Sky," is narrated
by Ronald Reagan.
Air Force; Signal Corps; Office of War
Information — *Video Yesteryear*

Not for Publication   1984
Satire
80811   87 mins   C   B, V   P
Nancy Allen, David Naughton, Richard Paul,
Alice Ghostley, Laurence Luckinbill, directed by
Paul Bartel
A conflict of interest arises for a woman leading
a double life as both a reporter for a trashy
tabloid and an assistant to the Mayor of New
York City. Available in VHS and Beta Hi Fi.
North Street Films — THORN EMI/HBO Video

Not Tonight Darling   1972
Drama
80792   70 mins   C   B, V   R, P
Luan Peters, Vincent Ball, Jason Twelvetrees
A bored suburban housewife becomes involved
with a fast-talking businessman who leads her
into a web of deceit and blackmail.
MPAA:R
Donovan Winter — Video Gems

Nothing Personal   1980
Comedy/Romance
64887   96 mins   C   B, V, CED   P
Donald Sutherland, Suzanne Somers
A tweedy college professor engages an eager
young lawyer to take up his case.
MPAA:PG
American International Pictures;
Filmways — Vestron Video

Nothing Sacred   1937
Comedy
08582   75 mins   C   B, V, 3/4U   P
Fredric March, Carole Lombard, Walter
Connolly, directed by William Wellman
A girl with a short time to live is given a gay time
for two weeks, but it's all a publicity hoax. Based
on James Street's novel.
David O Selznick — Video Yesteryear;
Discount Video Tapes; VCII; Cable Films; Video
Connection; Hollywood Home Theater; Kartes
Video Communications

Notorious   1946
Suspense/Drama
46213   101 mins   B/W   B, V, LV,   P
                             CED
Cary Grant, Ingrid Bergman, Claude Rains,
Louis Calhern, Madame Konstantin, directed by
Alfred Hitchcock.
A government agent and a girl whose father was
convicted of treason undertake a dangerous
mission to Brazil.
Selznick — CBS/Fox Video

Now and Forever   1982
Drama
65118   93 mins   C   B, V, LV   P
Cheryl Ladd, Robert Coleby
A young wife's life is shattered when her
husband is wrongly accused and convicted of

rape. After he is sent to prison, she begins
drinking and taking drugs.
MPAA:R
Interplanetary Pictures — MCA Home Video

Now, Voyager   1942
Drama
58836   117 mins   B/W   B, V, LV   P
Bette Davis, Gladys Cooper, Claude Rains, Paul
Henreid, Bonita Granville
A lonely spinster is transformed into a vibrant
young woman by her psychiatrist, and involves
herself in an ill-fated affair with a suave
continental.
Academy Awards '42: Best Scoring of a
Comedy or Drama (Max Steiner).
Warner Bros — CBS/Fox Video; RCA
VideoDiscs

Now You See Him, Now   1972
You Don't
Comedy
82028   85 mins   C   B, V   P
Kurt Russell, Joe Flynn, Cesar Romero, Jim
Backus, directed by Robert Butler
A gang of crooks want to use a college
student's invisibility formula to rob a local bank.
Walt Disney Productions — Walt Disney Home
Video

Nowhere to Hide   1977
Adventure
65304   74 mins   C   B, V   P
Lee Van Cleef
A United States Marshal is assigned to protect a
mob hit-man scheduled to testify for the
prosecution against his former chieftain.
VSC Enterprises — U.S.A. Home Video

Nudes in Limbo   1983
Arts
80852   53 mins   C   B, V   P
This tape imaginatively explores the male and
female anatomy in various abstract dimensions.
Available in VHS and Beta Hi Fi Stereo.
Bruce Seth Green — MCA Home Video

Nudo Di Donna   1983
Comedy
80445   112 mins   C   B, V   P
Nino Manfredi, Jean Pierre Cassel, George
Wilson, Eleonora Giorgi, directed by Nino
Manfredi
A man searches Venice to find a woman he saw
in a nude photograph who looks like his
estranged wife. With English subtitles.
IT
Horizon Films; Wonder Movies — Pacific Arts
Video

Nuit de Varennes, La 1983
Comedy-Drama
69617   133 mins   C   B, V   P
*Marcello Mastroianni, Harvey Keitel, Jean-Louis
Barrault, Hanna Schygulla, Jean-Claude Brialy*
This historical romp is based on an actual
chapter in French history when Louis XVI and
Marie Antoinette fled from Paris to Varennes. In
French with English subtitles.
MPAA:R
Renzo Rossellini; Opera Film; Gaumont
FR3 — *RCA/Columbia Pictures Home Video*

Number Seventeen 1932
Mystery
01747   64 mins   B/W   B, V   P
*Leon M. Lion, Anne Grey, John Stuart, directed
by Alfred Hitchcock*
Female jewel thief has change of heart and
helps detective foil an enemy gang's escape to
France.
British — *Hollywood Home Theater; Cable
Films; Video Yesteryear; Western Film & Video
Inc*

Nuremberg War Trials 194?
World War II
58602   11 mins   B/W   B, V   P, T
An overview of Movietone news coverage of the
historic trials of Nazi war criminals.
Movietone — *Blackhawk Films*

Nurse 1980
Drama
81266   100 mins   C   B, V   P
*Michael Learned, Robert Reed, Antonio Fargas,
Tom Aldredge, directed by David Lowell Rich*
A recently widowed woman resumes her career
as a head nurse in a large urban hospital, after
her son leaves for college. Available in VHS
Stereo and Beta Hi-Fi.
Robert Halmi — *U.S.A. Home Video*

Nurse Edith Cavell 193?
Drama
13040   95 mins   B/W   B, V, 3/4U   R, P
George Sanders, Anna Neagle
Based on the life of a famous nurse who served
the Allies so gallantly during WWI.
RKO — *Cable Films; Kartes Video
Communications*

Nursery Rhymes 1982
Cartoons
71366   60 mins   C   B, V   P
*Animated, voices of Isla St. Clair, Mike Berry,
Valentine Dyall*
The pages of a nursery rhyme book come to life
as a youngster leafs through them.
Dennis Abey & Patrick Hayes — *Family Home
Entertainment*

Nut House, The 1962
Comedy
80752   34 mins   B/W   B, V   P
This is an unsold television pilot for a live
comedy series that features a collection of skits
and blackouts.
Jay Ward — *Video Yesteryear*

Nutcase 1983
Comedy
81919   49 mins   C   B, V   P
A trio of young children attempt to thwart a
group of terrorists who threaten to reactivate a
large city's volcanoes.
Aardvark/Endeavor Prods — *VidAmerica*

Nutcracker, The 1982
Dance
60573   79 mins   C   LV   P
*American Ballet Theatre, Gelsey Kirkland,
Alexander Minz, National Philharmonic*
Tchaikovsky's Christmas ballet under the
direction of Mikhail Baryshnikov comes alive in
this presentation. Stereo.
Herman Krawitz; Yanna Kroyt
Brandt — *Pioneer Artists*

Nutcracker, The 1977
Dance
63115   78 mins   C   B, V, CED   P
Mikhail Baryshnikov, Gelsey Kirkland
A lavish production of Tschaikovsky's famous
ballet, choreographed and danced by Mikhail
Baryshnikov. In stereo.
Jodav Productions; Kroyt-Brandt
Productions — *MGM/UA Home Video*

Nutcracker, The 1985
Dance
82021   120 mins   C   B, V   P
This is a performance of Tchaikovsky's timeless
ballet recorded at London's Covent Garden.
BBC; National Video Corporation — *THORN
EMI/HBO Video*

Nutcracker, The 1986
Puppets
84775   28 mins   C   B, V   P
A puppet performance of Tchaikovsky's famous
ballet.
F Prods/Vistar Int'l — *Video Associates*

Nutcracker Fantasy 1979
Fairy tales
65319   ? mins   C   B, V   P
*Animated, voices of Melissa Gilbert, Roddy
McDowell, narrated by Michele Lee*
An heroic mouse must rescue a beautiful
sleeping princess from wicked mice. This
delightful fairy tale is set to the music of
Tchaikovsky.
MPAA:G

Walt DeFaria; Mark L Rosen; Arthur Tomioka — *RCA/Columbia Pictures Home Video*

Nutcracker Sweet   1984
Drama
84090   101 mins   C   B, V   P
Joan Collins, Finola Hughes, Paul Nicolas, directed by Anwar Kawadri
A beautiful socialite runs an internationally renowned ballet company, which is infiltrated by a great, defecting Russian ballerina who has her own treacherous motives.
Jezshaw Film Prod — *Vestron Video*

Nutcracker, The   1978
Dance
44939   86 mins   C   B, V, CED   P
Ekaterina Maximova, Vladimir Vasiliev, Nadia Pavlova and the Bolshoi Corps de Ballet, directed by Elena Maceret
Tchaikovsky's famous Christmastime ballet is performed by the Bolshoi Ballet.
MGM — *CBS/Fox Video*

Nutty Professor, The   1963
Comedy
66411   107 mins   C   B, V   P
Jerry Lewis, Stella Stevens, Howard Morris, Kathleen Freeman, directed by Jerry Lewis
A mild-mannered chemistry professor creates a potion that turns him into a suave, debonair, playboy-type with an irresistable attraction to women.
Paramount; Jerry Lewis — *Paramount Home Video*

Nyoka and the Tigerman   1942
Adventure/Serials
44792   250 mins   B/W   B, V, 3/4U   P
Kay Aldridge, Clayton Moore
The adventures of the jungle queen Nyoka and her rival Vultura in their search for the lost tablets of Hippocrates. In 15 episodes.
Republic — *Video Connection; Republic Pictures Home Video*

O

O Lucky Man   1973
Drama
68237   115 mins   C   B, V   P
Malcolm McDowell, Ralph Richardson, Rachel Roberts, Arthur Lowe, directed by Lindsay Anderson
A story of the rags-to-riches rise and fall of a modern-day man.
MPAA:R

Warner Bros — *Warner Home Video*

Oakland Athletics: Team Highlights   1983
Baseball
81148   30 mins   C   B, V   P
Rickey Henderson, Davey Lopes, Billy Martin
4   pgms
This series features selected highlights from the A's 1980-1983 seasons.
1.1980: Incredible But True. 2.1981: Only the Beginning 3.1982: Baseball: The A's Way 4.1983: Feelin' Stronger.
Major League Baseball — *Major League Baseball Productions*

Oblong Box, The   1969
Suspense
70966   91 mins   C   B, V   P
Vincent Price, Christopher Lee, Alastair Williamson, Hilary Dwyer, Peter Arne, Harry Baird, Carl Rigg, Sally Geeson, directed by Gordon Hessler
A man afflicted with a disease that wipes away his sanity tangles tangles with a witch doctor and gets buried alive. Unearthed, angry and mad, he embarks on a killing spree.
MPAA:PG
American International — *THORN EMI/HBO Video*

Observations Under the Volcano   1984
Filmmaking/Documentary
77302   82 mins   C   B, V   P
John Huston, Albert Finney, Jacqueline Bissett
A documentary describing the filming of John Huston's movie "Under the Volcano".
Christian Blackwood — *Pacific Arts Video*

Obsession   1976
Suspense
65098   98 mins   C   B, V   P
Cliff Robertson, Genevieve Bujold, John Lithgow, directed by Brian DePalma
A rich, lonely businessman meets a mysterious young girl in Italy who is the mirror image of his late wife. Music by Bernard Herrmann.
MPAA:PG
Columbia Pictures — *RCA/Columbia Pictures Home Video*

Occurrence at Owl Creek Bridge, An   1962
Literature/Drama
49166   27 mins   B/W   B, V   P
A man is about to be hanged when the rope snaps, and he is able to swim to safety. He entertains thoughts of his family while making his way home. Suddenly, his new-found sweetness of life comes to a halt. Based on a short story by Ambrose Bierce. Telecast on "The Twilight Zone" in 1963.

Cannes Film Festival: Blue Ribbon; American
Film Festival: First Prize.
Marcel Ichac, Paul de Roubaix — *Festival
Films; Video Yesteryear*

Ocean Drive Weekend   1985
Comedy
86353   98 mins   C   B, V   P
Another teenage beach blanket epic, with lots of
'60's surf music on the soundtrack.
MPAA:PG-13
Troma Inc. — *Vestron Video*

Ocean's 11   1960
Comedy
63449   144 mins   C   B, V   P
*Frank Sinatra, Dean Martin, Sammy Davis Jr.,
Angie Dickenson, Peter Lawford, directed by
Lewis Milestone*
A gang of friends make plans to rob a Las
Vegas casino. Part of the "A Night at the
Movies" series, this tape simulates a 1960
movie evening, with a Bugs Bunny cartoon,
"Person to Bunny," a newsreel and coming
attractions for "The Sundowners" and "Sunrise
at Campobello."
Warner Bros — *Warner Home Video*

Octagon, The   1980
Martial arts/Suspense
64232   103 mins   C   B, V   P
*Chuck Norris, Karen Carlson, Lee Van Cleef,
Kim Lankford*
A retired martial arts champion becomes
involved in perilous international intrigue.
MPAA:R
American Cinema Releasing — *Media Home
Entertainment*

Octaman   1971
Science fiction
70757   79 mins   C   B, V   R, P
*Kerwin Matthews, Pier Angeli, Harry Guardino,
David Essex, Jeff Morrow, Norman Fields*
A group of research scientists must find out who
has been killing their colleagues who are
researching a project in Mexico.
Filmers Guild — *Video Gems; World Video
Pictures*

Octopussy   1983
Adventure
65414   130 mins   C   B, V, LV,   P
                     CED
*Roger Moore, Maud Adams, Louis Jourdan,
Kristina Wayborn, Kabir Bedi*
James Bond is sent on a mission to prevent a
crazed Russian general from launching a
nuclear attack against NATO forces in Europe.
MPAA:PG
Albert R Broccoli — *CBS/Fox Video*

Odd Angry Shot   1979
War-Drama
72227   90 mins   C   B, V   P
A drama that ironically portrays the ravages of
war in Australia.
Atlantic TV — *Vestron Video*

Odd Couple, The   1968
Comedy
38590   106 mins   C   B, V, LV   P
*Jack Lemmon, Walter Matthau, directed by
Gene Saks*
Neil Simon's long-running Broadway comedy
about two divorced men who live together, but
can't stand each other's habits. Basis for the
recent TV series.
MPAA:G
Paramount — *Paramount Home Video; RCA
VideoDiscs*

Odd Job, The   1978
Comedy
73034   100 mins   C   B, V   P
Graham Chapman
A man unable to kill himself hires an "odd job"
man to do it for him.
Atlantic Releasing — *Vestron Video*

Odd Jobs   1985
Comedy
87738   89 mins   C   B, V   P
*Paul Rieser, Scott McGinnis, Rick Overton,
Robert Townsend*
Five college buddies get help from the Mob in
starting their own moving business as a summer
job, and encounter many mishaps due to their
own incompetence.
MPAA:PG-13
Dan Wigutow; Keith Fox — *THORN EMI/HBO
Video*

Odds Are!   1986
Games/Gambling
84720   60 mins   C   B, V   P
Tom and Dick Smothers
The Smothers Brothers outline strategies and
rules for casino gambling.
MGM/UA Video — *MGM/UA Home Video*

Ode to Billy Joe   1976
Drama/Romance
51968   106 mins   C   B, V   P
*Robby Benson, Glynnis O'Connor, Joan
Hotchkis, Sandy McPeak, James Best*
The relationship of two star-crossed lovers ends
in tragedy at the Tallahatchie Bridge.
MPAA:PG
Warner Bros — *Warner Home Video*

Odessa File, The 1974
Suspense/Drama
Closed Captioned
78881 128 mins C B, V P
Jon Voight, Mary Tamm, Maximilian Schell, directed by Ronald Neame
A journalist stumbles onto a diary of an SS Captain which leads him ultimately to ODESSA, a secret SS organization. The music is by Andrew Lloyd Weber. In Beta Hi-Fi.
MPAA:PG
John Woolf, Columbia Pictures — *RCA/Columbia Pictures Home Video*

Odyssey of the Pacific 1982
Adventure
60588 82 mins C B, V P
Mickey Rooney, Monique Mercure
While on a romp through the woods, a young Cambodian refugee and his siblings help an old railroad man rejuvenate a locomotive.
Cine Pacific Inc — *MCA Home Video*

Of Cooks and Kung-Fu 198?
Martial arts
64961 90 mins C B, V P
Jacky Chen, Chia Kai, Lee Kuen
A martial arts culinary adventure.
Dragon Lady Productions — *Unicorn Video*

Of Human Bondage 1964
Drama
82395 100 mins B/W B, V P
Kim Novak, Laurence Harvey, Robert Morley, directed by Kenneth Hughes
An essentially decent man falls fatally in love with an alluring but heartless waitress, who subtly destroys him.
Seven Arts Productions — *MGM/UA Home Video*

Of Human Bondage 1935
Drama
11396 84 mins B/W B, V, FO P
Leslie Howard, Bette Davis
The first movie version of Somerset Maugham's classic novel in which a young medical student with a club foot falls in love with a promiscuous cockney waitress.
RKO — *Prism; Hal Roach Studios; Video Yesteryear; King of Video; Discount Video Tapes; Movie Buff Video; Cable Films; Video Connection; Hollywood Home Theater; Western Film & Video Inc; Cinema Concepts; Kartes Video Communications*

Of Mice and Men 1981
Drama
80311 125 mins C B, V P
Robert Blake, Lew Ayres, Randy Qauid, Pat Hingle, Cassie Yates
An adaptation of the classic Steinbeck novel about the friendship between two southern itinerant ranch hands.
Mickey Productions; NBC Entertainment — *Prism*

Of Pure Blood 1985
Documentary/World War II
71063 100 mins B/W B, V P
Written and directed by Clarissa Henry and Marc Hillel
Through interviews and Nazi film footage, this tape traces the history of Hitler's attempts to breed the perfect Aryan race.
Maryse Addison and Peter Bate — *MPI Home Video*

Of Sharks and Men 1986
Fishes
86030 93 mins C B, V P
Footage from all over the world helps outline basic shark behavior.
MPAA:G
Unknown — *United Home Video*

Of The Dead 1979
Documentary/Death
81533 90 mins C B, V P
This documentary looks at such funeral practices as an on-camera cremation and embalming. Not for the very young or the squeamish.
Jean-Pol Ferbus; Dominique Garny — *MPI Home Video*

Of Unknown Origin 1983
Horror
69801 90 mins C B, V P
Peter Weller, Jennifer Dale, Lawrence Dane, Kenneth Welsh, Louis Del Grande, Shannon Tweed
A Manhattan brownstone is the battleground in a terror-tinged duel of survival between an upwardly mobile young executive and a destructive rodent intruder.
MPAA:R
Claude Heroux — *Warner Home Video*

Off Beat 1986
Comedy
87672 95 mins C B, V P
Judge Reinhold, Meg Tilly, Cleavant Derricks, Joe Mantegna, Harvey Keitel
A shy librarian unluckily wins a spot in a police benefit dance troupe, and then falls in love with a tough police woman.
MPAA:PG
Joe Roth; Harry Ufland — *Touchstone Home Video*

(For explanation of codes, see Use Guide and Key)

Off Limits
1953
Comedy
85258   89 mins   B/W   B, V   P
Bob Hope, Mickey Rooney, Marilyn Maxwell, Marvin Miller
A fight manager is drafted and flaunts military discipline as he trains a champion.
Paramount — *Kartes Video Communications*

Off the Wall
1982
Comedy
80698   86 mins   C   B, V   P
Paul Sorvino, Rosanna Arquette, Patrick Cassidy, Billy Hufsey, Monte Markham, Mickey Gilley
Two hitchhikers attempt to escape from a southern maximum security prison camp after being framed for a crime that they did not commit.
MPAA:R
Jensen Farley Pictures — *Vestron Video*

Off Your Rocker
1980
Comedy/Drama
71039   99 mins   C   B, V   P
Milton Berle, Red Buttons, Lou Jacobi, Dorothy Malone, Helen Shaver, Sharon Acker, Helen Hughes, directed by Morley Markson and Larry Pall
Representatives of a corporate conglomerate find that the residents of Flo Adler's Mapleview Nursing Home can still muster stiff resistance to a threatened takeover.
Hal Roach Studios — *Hal Roach Studios*

Officer and a Gentleman, An
1982
Drama
64022   126 mins   C   B, V, LV   P
Richard Gere, Louis Gossett Jr., David Keith, Debra Winger, Robert Loggia, directed by Taylor Hackford
A young man enters Officer Candidate School to become a Navy pilot, and in 13 torturous weeks he learns the importance of discipline, love and friendship.
Academy Awards '82: Best Supporting Actor (Gossett) Best Song ("Up Where We Belong")
MPAA:R
Paramount; Lorimar — *Paramount Home Video; RCA VideoDiscs*

Official Story, The
1985
Drama
88417   112 mins   C   B, V   P
Norma Aleandro, Hector Alterio, directed by Luis Puenzo
A devastating drama about a Argentinian woman who realizes her surreptitiously-adopted young daughter may be a child stolen from one of thousands of citizens victimized by the country's repressive government. A powerful, important film. English subtitles or dubbed.
Academy Awards '85: Best Foreign Language Film. MPAA:R SP, EL
Luis Puenzo; Argentinian — *Pacific Arts Video*

Oh Alfie
1975
Comedy-Drama
65307   99 mins   C   B, V   P
Joan Collins, Alan Price, Jill Townsend
In every man's life, there comes a time to settle down... but never when you're having as much fun as Alfie!
A D Associates Ltd — *Monterey Home Video*

Oh! Calcutta!
1972
Musical
07863   105 mins   C   B, V   P
Bill Macy, Mark Dempsey, Raina Barrett
Nudity and nuttiness are the theme for this zany erotic musical.
Bihar Film — *VidAmerica*

Oh Dad, Poor Dad
1967
Comedy
82548   86 mins   C   B, V   P
Rosalind Russell, Robert Morse, Barbara Harris, Hugh Griffith, Jonathan Winters
A black comedy of a bizarre family, its members including a corpse, carnivorous plants, and a pair of pet piranha fish.
Paramount Pictures — *Paramount Home Video*

Oh, God
1977
Comedy
38952   104 mins   C   B, V   P
George Burns, John Denver, Paul Sorvino, directed by Carl Reiner
When God, in the person of George Burns, appoints a young supermarket assistant manager to spread his word, unexpected situations develop.
MPAA:PG
Warner Bros — *Warner Home Video; RCA VideoDiscs*

Oh God, Book II
1980
Comedy
54806   94 mins   C   B, V   P
George Burns, Suzanne Pleshette, David Birney, Louanne, John Louie, Howard Duff, directed by Gilbert Cates
God decides to enlist a child to remind people that He is still around. The young girl sets out to concoct a slogan which will make God a household name. She recruits her classmates to spread her "Think God" slogan via posters and graffiti. This leads to her suspension from school, and when she is seen talking to God (he is invisible to everyone but her) the child is sent to psychiatrists.
MPAA:PG
Warner Bros — *Warner Home Video*

Oh, God! You Devil   1984
Comedy
Closed Captioned
77265   96 mins   C   B, V, LV   P
George Burns, Ted Wass, Roxanne Hart, Ron Silver
God returns to earth to save a rock singer from selling his soul to the devil.
MPAA:PG
Warner Bros. — Warner Home Video

Oh, Heavenly Dog   1980
Comedy
78887   104 mins   C   B, V   P
Chevy Chase, Jane Seymour, Omar Sharif, directed by Joe Camp
A private eye returns from the dead as a dog to solve his own murder.
MPAA:PG
Mulbery Square Productions — CBS/Fox Video

O'Hara's Wife   1982
Drama
64878   87 mins   C   B, V   P
Ed Asner, Mariette Hartley, Jodie Foster
A loving wife continues to care for her family even after her untimely death.
Davis/Panzer — Vestron Video

Oil   1978
Drama/Suspense
81686   95 mins   C   B, V   P
Ray Milland, Stuart Whitman, Tony Kendall
Seven men fight a raging oil fire that threatens to destroy an entire country.
MPAA:PG
Spectacular Film Co. — United Home Video

Oklahoma!   1955
Musical
56752   140 mins   C   B, V, CED   P
Gordon MacRae, Shirley Jones, Rod Steiger, Gloria Grahame, Eddie Albert, Charlotte Greenwood, directed by Fred Zinnemann
Based on the Rodgers and Hammerstein Broadway hit, wherein a young cowboy's girl goes to a dance with a hired hand, realizes she loves the cowboy, and the hired hand threatens to kill them both. Songs include, "Oh, What a Beautiful Mornin'," "The Surrey with the Fringe on Top," and "Oklahoma!" Dances choreographed by Agnes de Mille.
Academy Awards '55: Best Scoring Musical; Best Sound Recording.
Arthur Hornblow Jr, Magna Todd
AO — CBS/Fox Video

Oklahoma Annie   1951
Western
88171   90 mins   C   B, V   P
Judy Canova, Fuzzy Knight, Grant Withers, John Russell, Denver Pyle
Canova plays a goofy rube storekeeper who imitates her sheriff-grandmother in an effort to clean up her increasingly lawless town.
Republic — Republic Pictures Home Video

Oklahoma Kid, The   1939
Western
87378   82 mins   B/W   B, V   P
James Cagney, Humphrey Bogart, Rosemary Lane, directed by Lloyd Bacon
A classic, hilarious western about a lone gun bringing peace to a corrupt, lawless town. Bogart stars as a dastardly villain. In VHS and Beta Hi-Fi.
Warner Bros. — MGM/UA Home Video

Olaf Weighorst: Painter   1978
of the American West
Artists
07344   54 mins   C   B, V, 3/4U   P
Olaf Weighorst, John Wayne, Howard Hawks
Presents the life story and some of the works of renowned western painter Olaf Weighorst.
Olaf and Roy Weighorst — Nostalgia Merchant

Old Barn Dance, The   1938
Western
14400   54 mins   B/W   B, V   P
Gene Autry
Autry sells horses as a sideline until competitor puts out tractors.
Republic — Video Connection; Discount Video Tapes; Kartes Video Communications

Old Boyfriends   1979
Drama
37420   103 mins   C   B, V, CED   P
Talia Shire, Richard Jordan, John Belushi, Keith Carradine
A young woman searches for her true self through the lost loves of her past.
MPAA:R
Avco Embassy — Embassy Home Entertainment

Old Corral, The   1936
Western
69572   54 mins   B/W   B, V, FO   P
Gene Autry, Roy Rogers, Smiley Burnette, The Sons of the Pioneers
Sheriff Gene Autry romances a young woman who has come out West to escape a vicious Chicago mobster.
Republic — Video Yesteryear; Kartes Video Communications; Captain Bijou

Old Curiosity Shop, The   1984
Cartoons
81168   72 mins   C   B, V   P
Animated

This is an adaptation of the classic Dickens story about a young girls and her grandfather who are evicted from their curiosity shop.
MPAA:G
Burbank Films — *Children's Video Library*

Old Curiosity Shop, The 1975
Musical
82252 118 mins C B, V R
Anthony Newley, David Hemmings, David Warner, Jill Bennett, Peter Duncan
This is a musical version of the Charles Dickens story about an evil man who wants to take over a small antique shop run by an elderly man and his granddaughter.
MPAA:G
Avco Embassy Pictures; Helen M. Strauss — *Embassy Home Entertainment*

Old Enough 1984
Drama
81189 91 mins C B, V P
Sarah Boyd, Rainbow Harvest, Neill Barry, directed by Marisa Silver
An unusual friendship develops between two pre-pubescent teenagers as they explore New York City.
MPAA:PG
Dina Silver — *Media Home Entertainment*

Old Gun, The 1976
Drama
81185 141 mins C B, V P
Philippe Noiret, Romy Schneider, Jean Bouise
A doctor seeks revenge against the Nazis who murdered his wife and child when they left Normandy in 1944.
Pierre Caro — *Media Home Entertainment*

Old Leather 1980
Football
45122 30 mins C B, V, FO R, P
Narrated by John Facenda
A study of the men who gave life to pro football. Red Grange, Johnny Blood, George Halas and others are seen as they were in the beginning and as they are today.
NFL Films — *NFL Films Video*

Old Soldier, The 194?
World War II
58603 11 mins B/W B, V P, T
General Douglas MacArthur
This compilation of Movietone newsreel footage offers scenes from the Battle of Manila, and a mini-documentary of MacArthur's life.
Movietone — *Blackhawk Films*

Old Swimmin' Hole, The 1940
Drama
85197 78 mins B/W B, V P

Marcia Mae Jones, Jackie Moran, Leatrice Joy, Charles Brown
The grandness of small-town life is depicted in this story of a boy's desire to become a doctor, while trying to get his mother remarried.
Monogram — *Video Yesteryear*

Old Yeller 1957
Drama/Adventure
53797 83 mins C B, V, LV P
Dorothy McGuire, Fess Parker, Tommy Kirk, Kevin Corcoran, Jeff York, Beverly Washburn, Chuck Connors, directed by Robert Stevenson
A stray dog is befriended by a family of farmers in 1869 Texas. He saves the youngest boy's life, but sacrifices his in the process.
EL, SP
Walt Disney — *Walt Disney Home Video; RCA VideoDiscs*

Oldest Profession, The 1967
Comedy
82168 97 mins C B, V P
Raquel Welch, Jeanne Moreau, Elsa Martinelli, Michele Mercier, directed by Jean-Luc Godard and Philippe De Broca
This film takes a lighthearted look at prostitution through the ages from pre-historic times to the year 2000. Available in VHS and Beta Hi-Fi Stereo.
VIP Films — *New World Video*

Oliver! 1968
Musical-Drama
Closed Captioned
82323 145 mins C B, V P
Mark Lester, Jack Wild, Ron Moody, Shani Wallis, Oliver Reed, directed by Carol Reed
In this popular musical adaptation of Dickens' "Oliver Twist," an innocent orphan is dragged into a life of crime when he is befriended by a gang of pickpockets. Songs include "Where Is Love?" and "Consider Yourself." In Hi-Fi Stereo.
Academy Awards '68: Best Picture, Best Director (Reed), Best Score of a Musical Picture
MPAA:G
Columbia Pictures; Romulus Films — *RCA/Columbia Pictures Home Video*

Oliver and the Artful Dodger 1980
Cartoons
79242 72 mins C B, V P
Animated
The Artful Dodger leads his gang from a London orphanage to search for Oliver Twists lost inheritance in this animated adaptation of the Charles Dickens novel.
Hanna-Barbera Productions — *Worldvision Home Video*

Oliver Twist   1933
Drama
03821   70 mins   B/W   B, V   P
*Dickie Moore, Irving Pichel, directed by William
J. Cowan*
Dickens' classic of ill-treated London boy
involved with youthful gang.
*Monogram; I E Chadwick — Movie Buff Video;
Hollywood Home Theater; Kartes Video
Communications*

Oliver Twist   1922
Drama
63983   77 mins   B/W   B, V   P, T
*Jackie Coogan, Lon Chaney, Gladys Brockwell,
George Siegmann, Esther Ralston, directed by
Frank Lloyd*
This version of the Dickens classic is a vehicle
for young Jackie Coogan. As orphan Oliver
Twist, he is subjected to many frightening
incidents before finding love and someone to
care for him.
Sol Lesser — Blackhawk Films

Oliver Twist   1982
Drama/Cartoons
Closed Captioned
73044   72 mins   C   B, V, CED   P
Based upon the Dickens classic where young
Oliver Twist is left in an orphanage to defend
himself until he must join a criminal gang.
Burbank Films — Vestron Video

Oliver Twist   197?
Cartoons/Literature-English
Closed Captioned
75620   72 mins   C   B, V   P
Animated
This is an animated version of the classic tale by
Charles Dickens.
WBTV Canada — Children's Video Library

Oliver's Story   1978
Drama/Romance
81118   90 mins   C   B, V   P
*Ryan O'Neal, Candice Bergen, Ray Milland,
Edward Binns, Nicola Pagetti, Charles Haid,
directed by John Korty*
In this sequel to "Love Story," Oliver Barrett
finds true love once again when he falls for a
recently divorced heiress to the Bonwit Teller
retail chain.
MPAA:PG
*Paramount; David V. Picker — Paramount
Home Video*

Olivia   1980
Music-Performance
48540   60 mins   C   LV   P
Olivia Newton-John, Andy Gibb, ABBA
Olivia hosts this musical television special,
featuring such hits as "Hopelessly Devoted to
You," "Have You Ever Been Mellow," and

"Please Mr. Please." Olivia, Andy, and ABBA
perform a medley of classic rock songs.
Unknown — *MCA Home Video*

Olivia in Concert   1983
Music-Performance
64793   78 mins   C   B, V, LV   P
*Directed by Brian Grant, music produced by
John Farrar*
Filmed during Olivia's first live shows in five
years, the concert reflects the popular singer's
transformation from a sweet, romantic
songstress to a strong, aggressive charmer and
entertainer. In stereo.
*Olivia Newton-John; Christine Smith — MCA
Home Video*

Olivia—Physical   1981
Music-Performance
59034   54 mins   C   B, V, LV   P
Olivia Newton-John
Olivia Newton-John performs favorites, modern
funk, and earthy ballads in this video album.
Songs include; "Magic," "Physical," "A Little
More Love," "Make a Move On Me," and
"Hopelessly Devoted." In stereo on VHS and
Disc.
Scott Millaney — MCA Home Video

Olivia-Soul Kiss   1985
Music-Performance/Music video
71163   20 mins   C   B, V   P
Olivia Newton-John
This tape collects steamy pop tracks from Ms.
Newton Johns album of the same name. Along
with the title track, this HiFi Stereo recording
includes: "Culture Shock," "Emotional Tangle,"
"Toughen Up" and "The Right Moment."
MGMM — MCA Home Video

Olvidados, Los   1951
Drama
57336   81 mins   B/W   B, V   P
*Alfonso Mejia, Roberto Cobo, directed by Luis
Bunuel*
A good boy is contaminated by young thugs in
Mexico City's slums, resulting in the death of the
boy and his tormentor. In Spanish with English
subtitles.
SP
*Mayer Kingsley; Ultramar — Hollywood Home
Theater; Movie Buff Video; Discount Video
Tapes; Video Yesteryear*

Olympia: Parts I and II   1936
Sports/Documentary
20417   215 mins   B/W   B, V   P
Directed by Leni Riefenstahl
Documentary coverage of the 1936 Olympics,
held in Berlin. "Olympia" is said to be the finest
existing record of the Olympic Games and their
athletes. Part I and II are also available

individually, as are two major sequences: the Marathon sequence and the Diving sequence.
Leni Riefenstahl — *Embassy Home Entertainment; Video Yesteryear; International Historic Films; Western Film & Video Inc; Phoenix Films & Video*

Omega Man, The   1971
Science fiction
85658   98 mins   C   B, V   P
Charlton Heston, Anthony Zerbe, Rosalind Cash, directed by Boris Sagal.
The lone survivor of a mankind-killing plague battles fanatical zombies in an deserted Los Angeles.
MPAA:PG
Walter Seltzer — *Warner Home Video*

Omen, The   1976
Horror
41079   111 mins   C   B, V, LV,   P
                                    CED
Gregory Peck, Lee Remick, Billie Whitelaw, David Warner, directed Richard Donner
"The Omen" is an effective horror piece on the coming of the "anti-Christ," personified in a young boy.
MPAA:R EL, SP
20th Century Fox — *CBS/Fox Video*

On a Clear Day You Can   1970
See Forever
Romance/Musical
65618   129 mins   C   B, V, LV,   P
                                    CED
Barbra Streisand, Yves Montand, Bob Newhart, Jack Nicholson
A psychiatric hypnotist helps a girl to stop smoking, and finds that in trances she remembers previous incarnations.
Paramount Pictures — *Paramount Home Video*

On Any Sunday   1971
Documentary/Motorcycles
80212   89 mins   C   B, V   P
Steve McQueen, directed by Bruce Brown
This exhilarating documentary examines the sport of motorcycle racing with a focus on three men: Mert Lawwill, Malcolm Smith, and Steve McQueen.
MPAA:G
Cinema Five — *Monterey Home Video*

On Any Sunday II   1981
Motorcycles
60410   89 mins   C   B, V   P
Bruce Penhall, Kenny Roberts, Brad Lackey, Bob Hannah
World Champion motorcycle driver Bruce Penhall is among those profiled in this motorcyclist's cinematic delight, featuring high-powered cycles giving their all.
MPAA:PG

4 Way Motorsports — *Monterey Home Video*

On Approval   1944
Comedy
00415   80 mins   B/W   B, V   P
Clive Brooks, Beatrice Lillie
Two couples spend a holiday on a deserted isle to test their love.
Sydney Box; British — *Hollywood Home Theater; Movie Buff Video*

On Being Gay   1986
Sexuality
87197   80 mins   C   B, V   P
Lecturer Brian McNaught talks entertainingly about what it's like to be Irish, Catholic and gay.
TRB Prod. — *TRB Productions*

On Golden Pond   1981
Drama
59430   109 mins   C   B, V, LV   P
Henry Fonda, Jane Fonda, Katharine Hepburn, Dabney Coleman, Doug McKeon, directed by Mark Rydell
The story of three generations coming to grips with life, mortality and their own emotional distance, set at a summer home in New England.
Academy Awards '81: Best Actor (Fonda); Best Actress (Hepburn); Best Screenplay Adaptation (Ernest Thompson).   MPAA:PG
ITC; IPC Films — *CBS/Fox Video; RCA VideoDiscs*

On Her Majesty's Secret   1969
Service
Adventure
64834   140 mins   C   CED   P
George Lazenby, Diana Rigg, Telly Savalas
James Bond marries and he and his future wife must squelch deadly SPECTRE chief Blofeld who is about to unleash a lethal toxin.
MPAA:PG
United Artists — *RCA VideoDiscs*

On Her Majesty's Secret   1969
Service
Adventure
65405   142 mins   C   B, V   P
George Lazenby, Diana Rigg, Telly Savalas
In this sixth 007 cinematic adventure, James Bond is charged with no less a task than saving the human race from a deadly plague.
United Artists — *CBS/Fox Video*

On Merit   1979
Documentary
88388   23 mins   C   B, V, 3/4U   R, P
A look, for graduating students, at the career opportunities offered by the U.S. government's dedication to the merit system.

U.S. Civil Service Commission — *Your World Video*

On the Beach   1959
Drama/Science fiction
59337   133 mins   B/W   B, V, CED   P
Gregory Peck, Anthony Perkins, Donna Anderson, Ava Gardner, Fred Astaire, directed by Stanley Kramer
Based on the novel by Nevil Shute. After most of the world has been destroyed by atomic waste, an American submarine sets out to investigate.
Stanley Kramer — *CBS/Fox Video*

On the Nickel   1980
Drama
79310   96 mins   C   B, V   P
Ralph Waite, Donald Moffat, Hal Williams, Jack Kehoe, directed by Ralph Waite
An ex-alcoholic returns to Fifth Street in Los Angeles to save his friend from a life of despair. The musical score was composed by Tom Waits.
MPAA:R
Waite Productions — *Vestron Video*

On the Old Spanish Trail   1947
Western
14228   56 mins   B/W   B, V   P
Roy Rogers, Jane Frazee, Andy Devine, Tito Guizar
Roy Rogers becomes a singing cowboy with a traveling tent show in order to pay off a note signed by the sons of the Pioneers.
Republic — *Video Connection; Captain Bijou*

On the Right Track   1981
Comedy
58852   98 mins   C   B, V   P
Gary Coleman, Lisa Eilbacher
A young orphan living in Chicago's Union Station has the gift of being able to pick winning race horses.
MPAA:PG
20th Century Fox — *CBS/Fox Video*

On the Run   1985
Crime-Drama
86903   96 mins   C   B, V   P
Jack Conrad, Rita George, Dub Taylor, David Huddleston
An ex-con and his gal cut a law-defying swath through the Bayou.
MPAA:R
Emmet Alston; Jack Conrad — *Video Gems*

On the Third Day   1983
Drama
88192   101 mins   C   B, V   P
Richard Marant, Catherine Schell, Paul Williamson

A headmaster finds a mysterious stranger in his house who turns out to be his long-lost illegitimate son.
Stanley O'Toole — *Karl/Lorimar Home Video*

On the Town   1949
Musical
47055   98 mins   C   B, V, CED   P
Gene Kelly, Frank Sinatra, Vera Ellen, Ann Miller, Betty Garrett, directed by Gene Kelly and Stanley Donen
Three sailors find romance on a one-day leave in New York City. Based on the successful Broadway musical, with a score composed by Leonard Bernstein, Betty Comden, and Adolph Green. Additional songs by Roger Edens. Academy Awards '49: Best Scoring, Musical (Roger Edens and Lennie Hayton).
MGM — *MGM/UA Home Video*

On the Waterfront   1954
Drama
Closed Captioned
73859   108 mins   B/W   B, V, CED   P
Marlon Brando, Lee J. Cobb, Eva Marie Saint, Rod Steiger, directed by Elia Kazan
An ex-fighter gets a job working on the gang-ridden waterfront under a crooked gangster boss. This film is in Beta Hi-Fi.
Academy Awards '54: Best Picture; Best Actor, (Brando); Best Director (Kazan).
Sam Spiegel — *RCA/Columbia Pictures Home Video*

On the Yard   1984
Crime-Drama
82488   102 mins   C   B, V   P
John Heard, Thomas Waites, Mike Kellin, Joe Grifasi
Two convicts clash in this film of prison riots and violence.
MPAA:R
Independent — *Media Home Entertainment*

On Top of Old Smoky   1953
Western
66441   59 mins   B/W   B, V   P, T
Gene Autry, Smiley Burnette, Gail Davis, Sheila Ryan
Singing ranger Gene is mistaken for a real Texas Ranger, who is a marked man.
Columbia — *Blackhawk Films*

On Valentine's Day   1984
Video
73631   5 mins   C   B, V   P
On this reusable two hour videocassette is a brief Valentine's Day greeting for a loved one.
Kartes Productions — *Kartes Video Communications*

Once Bitten 1985
Comedy
Closed Captioned
84794 94 mins C B, V, LV P
Lauren Hutton, Jim Carrey, Cleavon Little, Karen
Kopins, Thomas Balltore, Skip Lackey, directed
by Howard Storm
A centuries-old vampiress comes to Los
Angeles, and stalks male virgins. She needs
their blood to retain her youthful countenance.
MPAA:PG-13
Samuel Goldwyn — Vestron Video

Once in Paris 1984
Drama
76022 100 mins C B, V P
Wayne Rogers, Gayle Hunnicutt, Jean Lenoir
A bittersweet romance that is at once subtle and
believable, sophisticated and humorous about
three people who meet in Paris.
MPAA:PG
Frank D Gilroy — Embassy Home
Entertainment; Media Home Entertainment

Once Is Not Enough 1975
Drama
82071 121 mins C B, V P
Kirk Douglas, Deborah Raffin, David Janssen,
George Hamilton, Brenda Vaccaro
The young daughter of a has-been movie
producer has a tempestous affair with an
impotent writer who reminds her of her father.
Joan Collins introduces the film which is
available in VHS and Beta Hi-Fi.
MPAA:R
Paramount Pictures — Paramount Home Video

Once Upon a Brothers Grimm 1977
Fantasy
33583 102 mins C B, V P
Dean Jones, Paul Sand, Cleavon Little, Ruth
Buzzi, Chita Rivera, Teri Garr
An original musical fantasy in which the
Brothers Grimm meet a succession of their most
famous storybook characters, including Hansel
and Gretel, the Gingerbread Lady, Little Red
Riding Hood, and Rumpelstiltskin.
Rothman-Wohl Productions; CBS — United
Home Video

Once Upon a Frightmare 1976
Horror
82107 86 mins C B, V P
Rupert Davies, Sheila Keith
Two sisters discover a gruesome secret about
their parents after Mom and Dad are released
from a mental institution. Available in VHS
Stereo and Beta Hi-Fi.
MPAA:R
Pete Walker — Monterey Home Video

Once Upon a Honeymoon 1942
Comedy
10039 115 mins B/W B, V P, T
Ginger Rogers, Cary Grant, Walter Slezak
American reporter predicts Hitler's movements
by trailing Gestapo agents. Reporter and agents
then attempt to outwit Germans.
RKO; Leo McCarey — Blackhawk Films

Once Upon a Midnight Dreary 1984
Literature/Horror
73648 50 mins C B, V P
Vincent Price, Rene Auberjonois, Severn
Darden
Dracula invites you to his mansion for a look at
three tales of the supernatural: "The Legend of
Sleepy Hollow" "The Ghost Belongs to Me"
and "The House With A Clock In Its Walls."
Bosustow Entertainment; Asselin
Productions — Kartes Video Communications

Once Upon a Scoundrel 1973
Comedy
80891 90 mins C B, V P
Zero Mostel, Katy Jurado, Tito Vandis, Priscilla
Garcia, A. Martinez, directed by George
Schaeffer
A ruthless Mexican land baron arranges to have
a young woman's fiancee thrown in jail so he
can have her all to himself.
Carlyle Films — Prism

Once Upon a Time 1976
Cartoons/Fantasy
50962 83 mins C B, V R, P
Animated
A pretty girl, her puppy, a charming prince, and a
grinch combine for a magical, wondrous
animated fantasy.
MPAA:G
N W Russo; G G Communications — Video
Gems

Once Upon A Time 1968
Fantasy/Adventure
70687 52 mins C B, V P
Patrick McGoohan, Leo McKern, Angelo Muscat
This second-to-last episode of "The Prisoner"
finds Number 6 in the Embryo room locked into
a deadly interrogation ritual with Number 2.
Associated TV Corp. — MPI Home Video

Once Upon A Time...and the Earth Was Created 1985
Cartoons/History-Ancient
84494 77 mins C B, V P
A semi-educational animated film which surveys
the beginning of man and how he survived.
La Societe Procidis Societe Anonyme — Sony
Video Software

Once Upon a Time in America

1984

Drama
Closed Captioned
80440   225 mins   C   B, V, LV   P
Robert DeNiro, Treat Williams, James Woods, Elizabeth McGovern, Tuesday Weld, Burt Young
This is the uncut original version of director Sergio Leone's saga of five young men growing up in Brooklyn during the 20's who become powerful mob figures. Also available in a 143-minute version.
MPAA:R
Arom Milchan; The Ladd Company — *Warner Home Video*

Once Upon a Time in the West

1968

Western
80520   165 mins   C   B, V, LV   P
Henry Fonda, Claudia Cardinale, Jason Robards, Charles Bronson, directed by Sergio Leone
The uncut version of Sergio Leone's sprawling epic about a band of ruthless gunmen who set out to murder a mysterious woman.
MPAA:PG
Paramount — *Paramount Home Video*

One A.M.

1916

Comedy
58968   20 mins   B/W   B, V, 3/4U   P
Charlie Chaplin
Charlie is a drunk who must first battle a flight of stairs in order to get to bed. Silent with music track.
Mutual — *Cable Films; Festival Films*

One and Only, The

1978

Comedy
58714   98 mins   C   B, V   P
Henry Winkler, Kim Darby, Gene Saks, William Daniels, Harold Gould, Herve Villechaize, directed by Carl Reiner
An egotistical young man enters the world of professional wrestling.
MPAA:PG
Paramount; First Artists — *Paramount Home Video*

One and Only, Genuine, Original Family Band, The

1967

Musical
81655   110 mins   C   B, V, LV   P
Walter Brennan, Buddy Ebsen, Lesley Ann Warren, Kurt Russell, Goldie Hawn, Wally Cox, Richard Deacon, Janet Blair
A harmonious musical family becomes divided when various members take sides in the presidential battle between Benjamin Harrison and Grover Cleveland.
MPAA:G

Walt Disney Productions — *Walt Disney Home Video*

One and Only Genuine Original Family Band, The

1968

Musical
55571   110 mins   C   B, V, LV   P
Walter Brennan, Buddy Ebsen, Lesley Ann Warren, John Davidson, Kurt Russell, Wally Cox, Richard Deacon, Janet Blair
During the 1888 presidential campaigns of Grover Cleveland and Benjamin Harrison, old Grandpa Bower organizes his son, daughter-in-law, and eight grandchildren into a band, hoping to perform at the convention.
Walt Disney — *Walt Disney Home Video*

One Arm Swordsmen, The

1972

Martial arts
84075   109 mins   C   B, V   P
Many one-armed men are persecuted for the murder committed by one fugitive one-armed man, and they decide to group together to track him down themselves.
Wang Fing; Wang Chiang Prod — *Unicorn Video*

One Away

1980

Drama
78669   83 mins   C   B, V   P
A gypsy escapes from a South African prison and the police are in hot pursuit.
MPAA:PG
Silhouette Film Productions — *Monterey Home Video*

One Body Too Many

1944

Comedy
01701   75 mins   B/W   B, V   P
Jack Haley Sr., Jean Parker, Bela Lugosi, directed by Frank McDonald
Mystery spoof with wacky insurance salesman who's mistaken for a detective. Ends up in comedy of errors.
Paramount; Pine Thomas — *Hollywood Home Theater; Hal Roach Studios; Movie Buff Video; Kartes Video Communications; Discount Video Tapes; Video Connection*

One Dark Night

1982

Horror
65748   94 mins   C   B, V   P
Two high school girls plan an initiation rite for one of their friends who is determined to shed her "goody-goody" image.
MPAA:R
Michael Schroeder — *THORN EMI/HBO Video*

One Deadly Owner   1974
Horror
84754   80 mins   C   B, V   P
*Donna Mills, Jeremy Brett, Robert Morris,
Laurence Payne*
A made-for-TV film about a possessed Rolls-
Royce torturing its new owner.
John Sichel — *Thriller Video*

One Down Two to Go   1983
Adventure
65355   84 mins   C   B, V   P
*Jim Brown, Fred Williamson, Jim Kelly, Richard
Roundtree*
When the mob is discovered to be rigging a
championship karate bout, two dynamic expert
fighters join in a climactic battle against the
hoods.
MPAA:R
Fred Williamson — *Media Home Entertainment*

One-Eyed Jacks   1961
Western
53935   141 mins   C   B, V   P
*Marlon Brando, Karl Malden, Katy Jurado,
Elisha Cook, Slim Pickens, Ben Johnson,
directed by Marlon Brando*
Upon completing a prison term, an outlaw goes
seeking an old friend who betrayed him, and
finds he has become the sheriff.
Paramount — *Paramount Home Video*

One Flew Over the   1975
Cuckoo's Nest
Drama
58882   129 mins   C   B, V   P
*Jack Nicholson, Louise Fletcher, Brad Dourif,
William Redfield, Scatman Crothers, directed by
Milos Forman*
Ken Kesey's novel about Randall P. McMurphy,
the leader of a group of inmates of a mental
ward and his war against the repressive Nurse
Ratched.
Academy Awards '75: Best Picture, Best Actor
(Nicholson); Best Actress (Fletcher); Best
Director (Forman); Best Screenplay Adaptation
(Bo Goldman, Lawrence Hauben). MPAA:R
United Artists; Fantasy Films; Saul Zaentz;
Michael Douglas — *THORN EMI/HBO Video;
RCA VideoDiscs*

One Frightened Night   1935
Mystery
66390   69 mins   B/W   B, V   P
*Mary Carlisle, Wallace Ford, Hedda Hopper,
Charlie Grapewin*
An eccentric millionaire informs his family
members that he is leaving each of them one
million dollars.
Mascot Pictures — *Movie Buff Video; Kartes
Video Communications*

One from the Heart   1982
Fantasy/Musical
68259   100 mins   C   B, V   P
*Teri Garr, Frederie Forrest, Natassia Kinski,
Raul Julia, Laine Kazan, directed by Francis
Ford Coppola*
Two people somehow lost the romance in their
lives and end up with other people only to
realize that they miss each other. In stereo.
MPAA:R
Gray Frederickson; Fred
Ross — *RCA/Columbia Pictures Home Video;
RCA VideoDiscs*

100 Rifles   1969
Western
29162   110 mins   C   B, V   P
*Jim Brown, Raquel Welch, Burt Reynolds,
Fernando Lamas*
An Indian bank robber and a black American
lawman join up with a female Mexican
revolutionary to help save the Mexican Indians
from annihilation by a despotic military governor.
MPAA:R SP
20th Century Fox — *CBS/Fox Video*

One in a Million   1978
Biographical/Drama
81808   90 mins   C   B, V   P
*LeVar Burton, Madge Sinclair, Billy Martin,
James Luisi, directed by William A Graham*
This is the true story of Detroit Tigers star Ron
Leflore who rose from the Detroit ghetto to the
major leagues.
Roger Gimbel Prods; EMI Television — *VCL
Home Video*

One Little Indian   1973
Western
71102   90 mins   C   B, V   P
*James Garner, Vera Miles, Jodie Foster, Clay
O'Brien, Andrew Prine, directed by Bernard
McEveety*
An AWOL cavalryman and his Indian ward team
up with a widow and her daughter in an attempt
to cross the New Mexican desert.
Walt Disney Productions — *Walt Disney Home
Video*

One Man Jury   1978
Crime-Drama
59813   95 mins   C   B, V   P
*Jack Palance, Christopher Mitchum, Joe Spinell,
Pamela Shoop*
An LAPD lieutenant, wearied by an ineffective
justice system, becomes a one-man vigilante
avenger.
MPAA:R
Theodor Bodnar; Steve Bono — *United Home
Video*

One Million B. C.　　　　1940
Science fiction
44800　80 mins　B/W　B, V, 3/4U　　P
Victor Mature, Carole Landis, Lon Chaney Jr.,
directed by Hal Roach and Hal Roach Jr.
The saga of the struggle of primitive cavemen
and their battle against dinosaurs and other
monsters.
United Artists, Hal Roach — *Nostalgia*
Merchant

One Minute Sales Person　　1986
and the Future of Sales,
The
Sales training
88278　45 mins　C　V　　P
Larry Wilson explains successful selling
techniques.
The Minnesota Studio — *The Minnesota*
Studio

One Night Only　　　　198?
Exploitation
86591　87 mins　C　B, V　　P
Lenore Zann, Jeff Braunstein, Grant Alianak,
directed by Timothy Bond
A gorgeous law student decides to make big
money by hiring herself and her friends out as
hookers to the school football team.
Robert Lantos; Stephen J. Roth — *Key Video*

One Night Stand　　　　1984
Comedy-Drama
81453　94 mins　C　B, V　　P
Tyler Coppin, Cassandra Delaney, Jay Hackett
Four young people attempt to "amuse
themselves" at the empty Sydney Opera House
on the New Years Eve before World War III.
Hoyts Distribution; Astra Film
Productions — *Embassy Home Entertainment*

One of My Wives Is　　　1976
Missing
Mystery
82151　97 mins　C　B, V　　P
Jack Klugman, Elizabeth Ashley, James
Franciscus, directed by Glenn Jordan
An ex-New York cop tries to solve the
mysterious disappearance of a newlywed
socialite.
Spelling/Goldberg — *Karl/Lorimar Home*
Video

One of Our Aircraft Is　　　1941
Missing
War-Drama
81423　103 mins　B/W　B, V　　P
Godfrey Tearle, Eric Portman, Hugh Williams,
Pamela Brown, Googie Withers
The crew of a downed R.A.F. bomber struggles
to escape Nazi capture while attempting to get

back to England after the crash landing in
Holland.
United Artists — *Republic Pictures Home*
Video

One of Our Dinosaurs Is　　1975
Missing
Comedy
87675　101 mins　C　B, V　　P
Peter Ustinov, Helen Hayes, Clive Revill, Derek
Nimo, Joan Sims
A guffaw-inducing farce about an international
espionage cat-and-mouse battle over precious
microfilm hidden in the skeleton of a museum-
housed dinosaur.
MPAA:G
Walt Disney Prod. — *Walt Disney Home Video*

One on One　　　　　1977
Drama
51987　98 mins　C　B, V　　P
Robby Benson, Annette O'Toole, G.D. Spradlin,
Gail Strickland
A high school basketball star from the country
accepts an athletic scholarship to a big city
university but is unprepared for the fierce
competition he must face.
MPAA:PG
Warner Bros — *Warner Home Video*

One on One with Roland　　1986
Martin
Fishing
86023　60 mins　C　B, V　　P
The expert fisherman gives advice on spinner
bait, crankbait, and jigging.
United Ent. — *United Home Video*

One Rainy Afternoon　　　1936
Comedy
11298　80 mins　B/W　B, V, FO　　P
Francis Lederer, Ida Lupino, Hugh Herbert,
Roland Young, Donald Meek
A bit-player kisses the wrong girl in a Paris
theater, causing a hilarious, massive uproar
branding him as a notorious romantic
"monster."
Pickford Lasky Productions — *Video*
Yesteryear; Kartes Video Communications;
Discount Video Tapes

One Shoe Makes It　　　1982
Murder
Suspense/Drama
71324　96 mins　C　B, V　　P
Robert Mitchum, Angie Dickinson, Mel Ferrer,
Jose Perez, John Harkins, Howard Hesseman,
Asher Brauner, Bill Henderson, Catherine
Shirriff, directed by William Hale
When his wife disappears, a casino owner hires
an ex-cop to track her down. Based on Eric
Bercovici's novel "So Little Cause for Caroline."

Fellows-Keegan Company; Lorimar
Productions — *U.S.A. Home Video*

Stephen Bosustow; UPA — *RCA/Columbia
Pictures Home Video*

One Sings, the Other Doesn't   1977
Drama
64913   105 mins   C   B, V   P
Valerie Mairesse, Therese Liotard
This film follows the friendship of two young
women over a period of 14 years, when each
seeks to control her destiny and to find
contentment. In French with English subtitles.
FR
Cine-Tamarus — *RCA/Columbia Pictures
Home Video*

One Small Step for Man   1984
Space exploration
72057   60 mins   C   B, V   P
The Apollo series of lunar explorations is
examined in this documentary, with an
emphasis on the first manned moon landing.
NASA — *MPI Home Video*

One Step to Hell   1968
Adventure
80035   90 mins   C   B, V   P
*Ty Hardin, Rossano Brazzi, Pier Angeli, George
Sanders, Tab Hunter*
A government police officer gives hot pursuit to
a group of convicts who are running through the
wilds of Africa.
NTA — *Republic Pictures Home Video*

One, The Only... Groucho, The   195?
Comedy
79236   120 mins   B/W   B, V, 3/4U   P
Groucho Marx
The original unedited pilot of Groucho's "You
Bet Your Life" series from 1949, an episode
from the series circa 1951, and his comeback
series "Tell It to Groucho" make up this
collection of kinescopes.
NBC et al — *Shokus Video*

1000 Mile Escort   1978
Martial arts
70704   86 mins   C   B, V   P
Pak Ying, Mai Suet
One man stands alone against the corruption of
China's murderous South Sung Dynasty.
Master Arts — *Master Arts Video*

1001 Arabian Nights   1959
Fantasy/Cartoons
69620   76 mins   C   B, V   P
*Animated, voices of Jim Backus, Kathryn Grant,
Hans Conreid, Herschel Bernardi*
In this Arabian nightmare, the nearsighted Mr.
Magoo is known as "Azziz" Magoo, lamp dealer
and uncle of Aladdin.

One Touch of Venus   1948
Musical
64546   82 mins   B/W   B, V   P
*Ava Gardner, Robert Walker, Eve Arden, Dick
Haymes, Olga San Juan, Tom Conway*
A young man impulsively kisses a marble statue
of the goddess Venus, which comes to life.
Based on the Broadway musical, with songs by
Kurt Weill and Ogden Nash, including "Speak
Low."
Universal — *Republic Pictures Home Video*

One, Two, Three   1961
Comedy
87377   110 mins   B/W   B, V   P
*James Cagney, Horst Buchholz, Arlene Francis,
directed by Billy Wilder*
The ribald comedy about an American Coca-
Cola executive getting involved with love and
twisted international politics in war-torn Berlin. In
VHS and Beta Hi-Fi.
United Artists — *MGM/UA Home Video*

One Wild Moment   1978
Comedy
77371   88 mins   C   B, V   P
*Jean-Pierre Marielle, Victor Lanoux, directed by
Claude Berri*
Comic complications arise when a divorced man
is seduced by his best friend's daughter while
vacationing. The film is in French with English
subtitles.
MPAA:R FR
Quartet/Films Incorporated — *RCA/Columbia
Pictures Home Video*

Onion Field, The   1979
Drama
44979   126 mins   C   B, V, LV,   P
                              CED
*John Savage, James Woods, Ronny Cox,
Franklyn Seales*
This true story concerns the murder of a
policeman and the slow process of justice.
MPAA:R
Avco Embassy — *Embassy Home
Entertainment*

Only Way, The   1970
War-Drama
65159   86 mins   C   B, V   P
Jane Seymour, Martin Potter, Ben Christiansen
A semi-documentary account of the plight of the
Jews in Denmark during the Nazi occupation.
Despite German insistence, the Danes
succeeded in saving most of their Jewish
population from the concentration camps.
MPAA:G

UMC Pictures; Hemisphere --
Laterna — *United Home Video*

Only When I Laugh   1981
Comedy
58962   100 mins   C   B, V   P
*Marsha Mason, Kristy McNichol, James Coco,
Joan Hackett, David Dukes*
A poignant comedy about the relationship
between a mother and her daughter, written by
Neil Simon.
MPAA:R
Columbia — *RCA/Columbia Pictures Home
Video*

Only With Married Men   1974
Comedy
81720   74 mins   C   B, V   P
*David Birney, Judy Carne, Gavin McLeod, John
Astin, directed by Jerry Paris*
A sly bachelor pretends that he's married in
order to date a woman who only dates married
men.
Spelling/Goldberg
Productions — *Karl/Lorimar Home Video*

Open City   1946
Drama
44973   103 mins   B/W   B, V   P
*Anna Magnani, Aldo Fabrizi, directed by
Roberto Rossellini*
A leader in the Italian underground resists Nazi
control of the city. Italian dialogue with English
subtitles.
Mayer-Burstyn — *Discount Video Tapes; Video
Yesteryear; Hollywood Home Theater; Western
Film & Video Inc; Movie Buff Video*

Opera Cameos   1955
Opera
47490   53 mins   B/W   B, V, FO   P
*Lucia Evangelista, Guilio Gari, Frank Valentino,
Carlo Tomanelli, conducted by Giuseppe
Bamboschek, hosted by John Ericson*
A program from this 1950's TV series of operas,
staged with full costumes and sets. Featured
are highlights from Verdi's "La Traviata."
Dumont — *Video Yesteryear*

Operation Amsterdam   1960
War-Drama/Suspense
62865   103 mins   B/W   B, V   P
Peter Finch, Eva Bartok, Tony Britton
The true story of a group of agents who went to
Holland in 1940 to prevent a stock of industrial
diamonds from falling into the hands of the
Nazis.
20th Century Fox; Rank — *Embassy Home
Entertainment*

Operation Barbarossa   1985
Documentary/World War II
82557   50 mins   C   B, V, 3/4U   P
Narrated by Bernard Archard, d by Peter Batty.
This acclaimed documentary chronicles Hitler's
last offensive in the Soviet Union and includes
contributions from Albert Speer and Dr. Paul
Schmidt.
Peter Batty — *Evergreen International*

Operation C.I.A.   1965
Adventure
Closed Captioned
82272   90 mins   C   B, V   P
*Burt Reynolds, John Hayt, Kieu Chin, Danielle
Aubry, directed by Christian Nyby*
An American C.I.A. operative is sent to Saigon
to investigate the murder of a fellow agent.
Available in VHS and Beta Hi-Fi.
Allied Artists; Peer J
Oppenheimer — *CBS/Fox Video*

Operation Julie   1985
Crime-Drama
88230   100 mins   C   B, V   P
*Colin Blakely, Lesley Nightingale, Clare Powney,
directed by Bob Mahoney*
A detective searches out a huge drug ring that
manufactures LSD.
Tyne Tees Ent. — *Lightning Video*

Operation Petticoat   1959
Comedy
47995   120 mins   C   B, V   P
*Cary Grant, Tony Curtis, Joan O'Brien, Dina
Merrill, Gene Evans, Arthur O'Connell*
Determined to get his sub back in action, a
commander bypasses regulations and uses
"enterprising" methods to procure supplies.
Universal — *Republic Pictures Home Video*

Operation Thunderbolt   1977
War-Drama
86035   120 mins   C   B, V   P
*Yehoram Gaon, Assaf Dayan, Ori Levy, Klaus
Kinski, directed by Menahem Golan*
An Israeli-produced depiction of the infamous
raid on Entebbe.
Cannon Films — *MGM/UA Home Video*

Opportunities in Criminal   1985
Justice
Crime and criminals
88379   34 mins   C   B, V, 3/4U   R, P
Narrated by Bill Cosby, this program outlines
various careers in law enforcement.
Your World Video — *Your World Video*

Orca   1977
Adventure
10964   92 mins   C   B, V, LV   P

Richard Harris, Charlotte Rampling, Bo Derek, Keenan Wynn, directed by Michael Anderson
A whale is out for revenge when a shark hunting seafarer captures and kills his pregnant mate.
MPAA:PG
Paramount; Dino De Laurentiis — *Paramount Home Video*

Ordeal by Innocence 1984
Drama/Mystery
71144   91 mins   C   B, V   P
Donald Sutherland, Christopher Plummer, Faye Dunaway, Sarah Miles, Ian McShane, Annette Crosbie, Michael Elphick, directed by Desmond Davis
Upon returning from an Antarctican expedition, a British professor finds that he could have saved an executed man's life with his testimony. Oddly, no one wishes to reopen the case. Based on an Agatha Christie story.
MPAA:PG-13
Cannon Films — *MGM/UA Home Video*

Ordeal of Dr. Mudd 1980
Drama
81267   143 mins   C   B, V   P
Dennis Weaver, Arthur Hill, Susan Sullivan, Richard Dysart, directed by Paul Wendkos
This is the true story of Dr. Samuel Mudd, a Maryland physician who unwittingly aided John Wilkes Booth's escape by setting his broken leg. Available in VHS Stereo and Beta Hi-Fi.
B.S.R. Productions; Marble Arch Productions — *U.S.A. Home Video*

Order to Kill 1973
Drama
80123   110 mins   C   B, V   P
Jose Ferrer, Helmut Berger
A gambling boss puts out a contract on a hit man.
Italian — *King of Video*

Ordinary People 1980
Drama
55205   125 mins   C   B, V, LV   P
Mary Tyler Moore, Donald Sutherland, Timothy Hutton, Judd Hirsch, Elizabeth McGovern, directed by Robert Redford
An upper-middle class, Midwestern suburban family's life disintegrates in the wake of the emotional effects of one son's accidental death and the other son's emotional trauma.
Academy Awards '80: Best Picture; Best Director (Redford); Best Supporting Actor (Hutton); Best Screenplay Adaptation (Alvin Sargeant). MPAA:R
Wildwood Enterprises;
Paramount — *Paramount Home Video; RCA VideoDiscs*

Organic Gardener, The 1986
Gardening
88200   30 mins   C   B, V   P
3 pgms
A program of instruction in exclusively organic gardening.
1.Introduction 2.Planting 3.Composting & Harvesting
Dennis Burkhart — *Encounter Productions*

Orgy of the Dead 1965
Horror
70675   90 mins   C   B, V   P
Vampira, directed by Edward D. Wood.
This final film from E.D. Wood combines zombies, werewolves, go-go girls, and vampires into a joyous cadaver jamboree where the focus is on weird stuff.
Golden Turkey Awards: One of the worst films ever.
D.C.A./Edward D. Wood — *Rhino Video*

Oriental Dreams 1982
Photography
47809   ? mins   C   LV   P
A sensual portrait of five young women photographed with great sensitivity by Kenji Nagatomo, set to the music of Naoya Matsouka (stereo).
Unknown — *Pioneer Video Imports*

Origin of Life, The (Plus Scopes Trial Footage) 1982
Biology/Science
59559   60 mins   C   B, V   P
A look at Darwinian theory and beginnings of life, plus rare Scopes Trial footage from the Rohauer Collection.
McGraw Hill — *Mastervision*

Origins of Cinema 1912
Film-History
81743   105 mins   B/W   B, V   P
6 pgms
This series presents examples of early cinematic works of D.W. Griffith and Georges Melies.
1.(1898-1905) 2.(1902-1908) 3.(1905-1908) 4.(1908-1912) 5.(1904-1911) 6.(1899-1908)
Edison Company; Biograph — *Kartes Video Communications*

Orphan, The 1979
Horror
82144   80 mins   C   B, V   P
A young orphaned boy seeks revenge against his cruel aunt who is harassing him with sadistic discipline.
World Northal — *Prism*

Orphan Boy of Vienna, An   1937

Musical
85198 87 mins B/W B, V P
The Vienna Boys Choir
A homeless street urchin with a beautiful singing
voice is accepted into the wonderful world of the
Choir, but later is unjustly accused of stealing.
Austrian — Video Yesteryear

Orphan Town   1979

Drama
84618 144 mins C B, V P
Jill Eikenberry, Kevin Dobson, Linda Manz,
Glenn Close
A righteous young woman hauls nineteen
homeless children from the city slums to the
midwestern plains in 1854. Made-for-TV.
Dorothea G. Petrie — Prism

Orphans of the Storm   1921

Drama
44990 127 mins B/W B, V P, T
Lillian Gish, Dorothy Gish, Monte Blue, Joseph
Schildkraut, directed by D. W. Griffith
Two orphans marooned in Paris become
separated by the turbulent maelstrom preceding
the French Revolution. Silent.
United Artists — Blackhawk Films

Orpheus   1950

Film-Avant-garde
11398 95 mins B/W B, V, FO P
Jean Marais, Francois Perier, Maria Casares,
directed by Jean Cocteau
Depicts the love of a poet for a princess who
travels constantly from this world to the next. A
legendary tale in a modern Parisian setting.
Andre Paulve Films du Palais Royal — Video
Yesteryear; Hollywood Home Theater; Western
Film & Video Inc; Discount Video Tapes

Oscar, The   1966

Drama
66049 119 mins C B, V, CED P
Stephen Boyd, Elke Sommer, Jill St. John, Tony
Bennett, Milton Berle, Eleanor Parker, Joseph
Cotten, Edie Adams, Ernest Borgnine
The story of ego, greed and self-destruction in
the film world of Hollywood.
MPAA:R
Joseph E Levine — Embassy Home
Entertainment

Osterman Weekend, The   1983

Suspense
65507 102 mins C B, V P
Burt Lancaster, Rutger Hauer, Craig Nelson,
Dennis Hopper
A TV personality is looking forward to a reunion
party with his closest friends. That is, until the
CIA warns him that they are all Soviet agents.
Suddenly, he and his family are caught in a

nightmare of terror, deception, helplessness
and violent death.
MPAA:R
Peter S Davis; William N Panzer — THORN
EMI/HBO Video

Otello   1982

Music-Performance/Opera
81485 135 mins C B, V P
Kiri Te Kanawa, Vladimir Atlantov, Piero
Cappuccilli
This is a performance of the Verdi opera taped
at the Arena di Verona in Rome.
National Video Corporation Ltd. — THORN
EMI/HBO Video

Otello   1981

Opera
84656 121 mins C B, V P
Hans Nocker, Christa Noack Van Kemptz, the
Berlin Comic Opera conducted by Kurt Mesur
This is a feature film version of the Verdi opera
about the tragic Moor. Recorded in Hi-Fi.
IT
Walter Felsenstein — V.I.E.W. Video

Othello   1922

Drama
47463 81 mins B/W B, V, FO P
Emil Jannings, Lya de Putti, Werner Krauss
A silent version of Shakespeare's tragedy,
featuring Emil Jannings as the tragic Moor.
Titles are in English; music score.
UFA — Video Yesteryear; Discount Video
Tapes

Other Side of Midnight, The   1977

Drama
80730 160 mins C B, V P
Susan Sarandon, Marie-France Pisier, John
Beck, Raf Vallone, Clu Galgger, Sorrel Booke
A poor French girl who sleeps her way to fame
and fortune becomes the mistress of a powerful
shipping tycoon. Based upon the novel by
Sidney Sheldon. Available in VHS and Beta Hi-
Fi stereo.
MPAA:R
20th Century Fox — Key Video

Other Side of Nashville, The   1984

Music-Performance/Documentary
66598 118 mins C B, V, LV, P
                         CED
Johnny Cash, Kris Kristofferson, Bob Dylan,
Kenny Rogers, Willie Nelson, Hank Williams, Jr,
Emmylou Harris, Carl Perkins
Live performances, interviews and backstage
footage combine to form a picture of the
Nashville music scene. Over 40 songs are heard
in renditions by country music's biggest stars. In
stereo.

THE VIDEO TAPE & DISC GUIDE

Geoffrey Menin; MGM UA — *MGM/UA Home Video*

Other Side of the Mountain, The   1975
Drama
70868   102 mins   C   B, V   P
Marilyn Hassett, Beau Bridges, Dabney Coleman, directed by Larry Peerce
This tale of faith, determination and love follows the life of Jill Kinmont. After a skiing accident paralyzed Kinmont for life and dashed her hopes for a spot on the '56 U.S. Olympic Ski Team, she learned to live again. In Hi-Fi Mono.
MPAA:PG
Universal — *MCA Home Video*

Other Side of the Mountain, Part II, The   1978
Drama
70869   99 mins   C   B, V   P
Marilyn Hassett, Timothy Bottoms, directed by Larry Peerce
This sequel finds the crippled ex-skier, Jill Kinmont, facing new self-doubt. But, as always, love overcomes adversity.
MPAA:PG
Universal — *MCA Home Video*

Otis Redding   1985
Music-Performance
82011   25 mins   B/W   B, V   P
Otis Redding, Eric Burdon, Chris Farlow
Otis Redding brings down the house with his soulful renditions of "Satisfaction" and "Respect" in this compilation of his performances on the "Ready Steady Go!" series. Available in VHS and Beta Hi-Fi Stereo.
Dave Clark Limited; EMI Records — *Sony Video Software*

Our Constitution   1940
History-US
85199   61 mins   B/W   B, V   P
Daniel Curtis, John Elliott, Marc Loebell, Alan Connor
A historical drama recounting the story of our country's origins, the Revolutionary War, Jefferson, Washington, and the writing of the Constitution.
Unknown — *Video Yesteryear*

Our Finest Hour   1981
Football
50647   24 mins   C   B, V, FO   R, P
Oakland Raiders
When newly acquired quarterback Dan Pastorini was lost for the 1980 season with an injury, veteran Jim Plunkett calmly stepped in and made Raider fans forget the departed Ken Stabler. Plunkett's steadiness led the well-balanced Raiders to the Super Bowl championship, amidst owner Al Davis' battle

with Oakland fans and commissioner Pete Rozelle, over Davis' attempt to move his team to Los Angeles.
NFL Films — *NFL Films Video*

Our Gang Comedies   194?
Comedy
71149   53 mins   C   B, V   P
Robert Blake, Billie "Buckwheat" Thomas, George "Spanky" McFarland, Darla Hood, Carl "Alfalfa" Switzer, Tommy "Butch" Bond, Eugene "Porky" Lee, Shirley "Muggsy" Coates, Joe "Corky" Geil, Billy "Froggy" Lauglin
The five shorts on this cassette show the gang at their comedic best. They include: "The Big Premiere," "Bubbling Troubles," "Clown Princes," "Don't Lie" and "Farm Hands."
Loews Inc — *MGM/UA Home Video*

Our Relations   1936
Comedy
33905   65 mins   B/W   B, V, 3/4U   P
Stan Laurel, Oliver Hardy, Alan Hale, Sidney Toler, James Finlayson, Daphne Pollard
Confusion reigns when Stan and Ollie meet their twin brothers, a pair of happy-go-lucky sailors whom the boys previously didn't know existed.
Hal Roach, MGM — *Nostalgia Merchant; Blackhawk Films*

Our Relations   1936
Comedy
63987   95 mins   B/W   B, V   P, T
Stan Laurel, Oliver Hardy, James Finlayson, Alan Hale, Daphne Pollard
Stan and Ollie's long-lost twin brothers come to town after being at sea for years, to the consternation of all concerned. This tape also includes a 1935 Charley Chase short, "Southern Exposure."
Hal Roach; MGM — *Blackhawk Films*

Our Town   1940
Drama
08854   90 mins   B/W   B, V   P
Martha Scott, William Holden, Thomas Mitchell, Fay Bainter, narrated by Frank Craven
Life, love, and death in a small New England town; based on the play by Thornton Wilder.
United Artists; Sol Lesser Prods — *Prism; Movie Buff Video; Hollywood Home Theater; Video Yesteryear; Cable Films; Video Connection; Discount Video Tapes; Western Film & Video Inc; Kartes Video Communications*

Our Town   1977
Drama
56891   120 mins   C   B, V   P
Ned Beatty, Sada Thompson, Ronny Cox, Glynnis O'Connor, Robby Benson, Hal Holbrook, John Houseman
This is the television version of Thornton Wilder's classic play about everyday life in

600   (For explanation of codes, see Use Guide and Key)

Grovers Corners, a small New England town at
the turn of the century.
Hartwest Productions; Saul Jaffe — *Prism;
Movie Buff Video; Hollywood Home Theater;
Video Yesteryear; Kartes Video
Communications; Cable Films; Video
Connection; Discount Video Tapes; Western
Film & Video Inc*

Out of Africa   1985
Drama/Biographical
Closed Captioned
88419   161 mins   C   B, V   P
*Meryl Streep, Robert Redford, Klaus Maria
Brandauer, Michael Kitchen, Malick Bowens,
Michael Gough, Suzanna Hamilton, directed by
Sydney Pollack*
A sweeping filmization of the years spent by
Danish authoress Isak Dinesen on a Kenya
coffee plantation, in the company of Denys
Finch-Hatten. Acclaimed, awarded, and based
on several books, including biographies of the
two lovers, and Dinesen's "Out of Africa."
Academy Awards '85: Best Picture; Best
Director (Pollack). MPAA:PG
Universal; Sydney Pollack; Terry Clegg; Judith
Thurman — *MCA Home Video*

Out of Control   1985
Adventure
81251   78 mins   C   B, V, LV   P
*Betsy Russell, Martin Hewitt, Claudia Udy,
Andrew J. Lederer*
A fun-filled weekend trip turns into a deadly fight
for survival when a teenager's plane crashes
onto a deserted island.
MPAA:R
New World Pictures — *New World Video*

Out of Order   1984
Suspense
87217   87 mins   C   B, V   P
*Renee Soutendijk, Gotz George, Wolfgang
Kieling, Hannes Jaenicke*
A Dutch film about people stuck in an office
building's malevolent, free-thinking elevator.
Dubbed.
Sandstar — *Vestron Video*

Out of the Blue   1982
Drama
65694   94 mins   C   B, V   P
Dennis Hopper, Linda Manz, Raymond Burr
A frustrated teenager with a father in prison and
a promiscuous and weak-willed mother runs
away and quickly gets into trouble with the law.
Her return home and her father's release from
prison is anything than happy.
MPAA:R
Leonard Yakir, Gary Jules Jouvenat — *Media
Home Entertainment*

Out of the Blue   1947
Comedy
81225   86 mins   B/W   B, V, LV   P
*George Brent, Virginia Mayo, Carole Landis,
Turhan Bey*
There's trouble in paradise for a married couple
when a shady lady passes out in their
apartment.
Eagle Lion — *New World Video*

Out of the Past   1947
Suspense
00290   97 mins   B/W   B, V, 3/4U   P
Robert Mitchum, Kirk Douglas, Jane Greer
A cool and calculating private detective
undermines a ruthless tycoon's empire.
RKO; Eagle Lion — *Nostalgia Merchant*

Out-Of-Towners, The   1970
Comedy
65733   98 mins   C   B, V   P
Jack Lemmon, Sandy Dennis
Incredible mishaps occur when a middle-aged
Ohio couple fly to New York City for the
husband's job interview.
MPAA:G
Paramount; Jalem — *Paramount Home Video*

Outboard Engine Tune-   1984
Up—Evinrude and
Johnson Outboards, The
Boating
78379   50 mins   C   B, V, 3/4U   P
How to tune up and maintain Evinrude and
Johnson model outboard engines from 1 1/2
horsepower to 230 horsepower is demonstrated
on this instructional videocassette.
Videovision Productions Inc — *Peter Allen
Video Productions*

Outboard Engine Tune-   1984
Up—Mercury and Mariner
Outboards, The
Boating
78378   50 mins   C   B, V, 3/4U   P
How to tune up and maintain Mercury and
Mariner model outboard engines from 1 1/2
horse power to 230 horsepower is
demonstrated on this instructional
videocassette.
Videovision Productions Inc — *Peter Allen
Video Productions*

Outcast, The   1953
Western
80846   90 mins   C   B, V   P
John Derek, Jim Davis, Joan Davis
A young man returns to Colorado attempting to
obtain a ranch from his uncle which he believes
is rightfully his.

Republic Pictures — *Republic Pictures Home Video*

Warner Bros. — *Warner Home Video*

Outer Space Connection, The   1975
Science fiction/Documentary
48485   93 mins   C   B, V   P
Narrated by Rod Serling
A documentary revolving around the evidence that a highly advanced civilization from another world is planning to pay a visit to Earth in the 21st century.
MPAA:G
Sun International — *United Home Video*

Outland   1981
Science fiction
58242   109 mins   C   B, V, LV   P
Sean Connery, Peter Boyle, Frances Sternhagen, James B. Sikking, directed by Peter Hyams
On Jupiter's volcanic moon, miners are suddenly plunging into insanity—and a lone federal marshal must uncover the secret that threatens everyone's survival.
MPAA:R
Outland Prods — *Warner Home Video; RCA VideoDiscs*

Outlaw, The   1943
Western
05538   95 mins   B/W   B, V   P
Jane Russell, Jack Beutel, Walter Huston, Thomas Mitchell
A variation on the saga of Billy the Kid, wherein Billy and girlfriend Rio have a romantic interlude before the final showdown with Pat Garrett.
Howard Hughes — *Video Connection; King of Video; VCII; Discount Video Tapes; Video Yesteryear; Cable Films; Prism; Hal Roach Studios; Movie Buff Video; Kartes Video Communications*

Outlaw, The   1943
Western
71030   117 mins   C   B, V   P
Jane Russell, Walter Huston, Jack Beutel, Thomas Mitchell
Billy the Kid enjoys a romantic rendevous with his gal Rio before the big showdown with Pat Garrett. This release has been enhanced through the Colorization process.
RKO — *Hal Roach Studios*

Outlaw Blues   1977
Adventure/Drama
80959   101 mins   C   B, V   P
Peter Fonda, Susan Saint James, John Crawford, Michael Lerner
An ex-convict becomes a national folk hero when he sets out to reclaim his stolen hit song about prison life.
MPAA:PG

Outlaw Josey Wales, The   1976
Western
58243   135 mins   C   B, V   P
Clint Eastwood, Chief Dan George, Sondra Locke, directed by Clint Eastwood
A farmer becomes a one-man army to avenge the slaughter of his wife and child by Civil War renegades.
MPAA:PG
Warner Bros — *Warner Home Video*

Outlaw Women   1952
Western
84039   76 mins   C   B, V   P
Marie Windsor, Jackie Coogan, Carla Balenda, directed by Sam Newfield
Windsor stars as "Iron Mae McLeod," a tough, sharp-shooting frontier woman.
Ron Ormond — *Monterey Home Video*

Outlaws   1982
Music-Performance
75921   81 mins   C   B, V   P
This program presents the Outlaws playing some of their superb compositions.
High Tide Management Inc — *Sony Video Software*

Outrageous   1977
Comedy
58963   100 mins   C   B, V   P
Craig Russell, Hollis McLaren, Richard Easley, Allan Moyle
A comedy about the unlikely but touching relationship between a female impersonator and his schizophrenic girl friend.
MPAA:R
Herbert R Steinmann; Billy Baxter — *RCA/Columbia Pictures Home Video*

Outside Chance   1978
Drama
87615   92 mins   C   B, V   P
Yvette Mimieux, Royce D. Applegate, directed by Michael Miller
A soapy, sanitized remake of Mimieux's film, "Jackson County Jail," wherein an innocent woman is persecuted in a small Southern jail. Made for TV.
Jeff Begun — *Charter Entertainment*

Outside the Law   1921
Crime-Drama
10121   77 mins   B/W   B, V   P, T
Lon Chaney, Priscilla Dean
Lon Chaney plays dual roles of the underworld hood in "Black Mike Sylva," and a Chinese servant in "Ah Wing."
Universal — *Blackhawk Films*

Outsiders, The   1983
Drama
69025   91 mins   C   B, V, CED   P
Matt Dillon
"The Outsiders" depicts the explosive conflict between rival gangs of poor and rich kids in the mid-1960's.
MPAA:PG
Zoetrope Studios — *Warner Home Video*

Outtakes   1985
Comedy
88066   85 mins   C   B, V   P
Forrest Tucker, Bobbi Wexler, Joleen Lutz, directed by Jack M. Sell
A piecemeal compilation of comedy skits, concentrating on sex and genre parody.
MPAA:R
Sell Pictures — *Sell Pictures*

Over the Brooklyn Bridge   1983
Comedy-Drama
80147   100 mins   C   B, V   P
Elliott Gould, Sid Caesar, Shelley Winters, Margaux Hemingway, Carol Kane
A young Jewish man must give up his Catholic girlfriend in order to get the money he needs to buy a restaurant in Manhattan.
MPAA:R
Cannon Films — *MGM/UA Home Video*

Over the Edge   1979
Drama
52711   95 mins   C   B, V   P
Michael Kramer, Matt Dillon, Pamela Ludwig, directed by Jonathan Kaplan
The music of Cheap Trick, The Cars, and The Ramones highlights this realistic tale of suburban youth on the rampage.
MPAA:PG
Orion Pictures — *Warner Home Video*

Owl and the Pussycat, The   1970
Comedy
44846   96 mins   C   B, V   P
Barbra Streisand, George Segal, Robert Klein, directed by Herbert Ross
A hooker meets a bookstore clerk and, after some initial antagonism, they fall in love.
MPAA:R
Columbia, Ray Stark — *RCA/Columbia Pictures Home Video; RCA VideoDiscs*

Oxford Blues   1984
Drama
Closed Captioned
77463   98 mins   C   B, V   P
Rob Lowe, Ally Sheedy, Amanda Pays, Gail Strickland
A Las Vegas valet goes to England's Oxford University in pursuit of the girl of his dreams. Available in VHS and Beta Hi Fi.

MPAA:PG13
MGM/United Artists — *CBS/Fox Video*

Ozzy Osbourne—The Ultimate Ozzy   1986
Music-Performance
87187   80 mins   C   B, V   P
The wild rock star performs his biggest hits on this tape: "Shot in the Dark," "Crazy Train" and "Bark at the Moon."
CBS/Fox — *CBS/Fox Video*

P

Pachmayr's Shotgun Hunting School   1985
Hunting
87644   60 mins   C   B, V   P
A program outlining the Pachmayr's Hunting seminars, including tips on stance, mounting, targeting, swing, and other tricks of the trade.
Sportsmen On Film — *Sportsmen on Film*

Pachmayr's Skeetshooting with Ken Robertson   1985
Hunting
87650   51 mins   C   B, V   P
Robertson instructs the well-armed video audience in the basics of skeetshooting.
Sportsmen On Film — *Sportsmen on Film*

Pachmayr's Trapshooting with Ken Robertson   1985
Hunting
87649   49 mins   C   B, V   P
Good trapshooters are made, not born, as Robertson the consummate trapshooter demonstrates in this instructional program.
Sportsmen On Film — *Sportsmen on Film*

Pacific Challenge   1974
Boating
57194   55 mins   C   B, V   P
Twelve men from seven nations sail three balsa wood rafts from Ecuador to Australia—9,000 miles nonstop.
AM Available
Manuel Arango — *Alti Corporation*

Pacific Inferno   1984
Adventure
80268   90 mins   C   B, V   P
Jim Brown, Richard Jaeckel, Tim Brown, Wilma Reading
A true story of how the Japanese forced a group of World War II P.O.W.'s to recover 16 million dollars worth of silver from Manila Bay.

Jim Brown — *VCL Home Video*

Pack, The 1977
Horror
76856   99 mins   C   B, V   P
Joe Don Baker, Hope Alexander-Willis, R.G. Armstrong, Richard B. Shull
The residents of a remote island are terrorized by a pack of wild dogs.
MPAA:R
Fred Weintraub; Paul Heller; Warner Bros. — *Warner Home Video*

Pack Up Your Troubles 1932
Comedy
33902   68 mins   B/W   B, V, 3/4U   P
Stan Laurel, Oliver Hardy, James Finlayson, Jacquie Lyn
World War I veterans try to find the family of an orphaned little girl with humorous results.
Hal Roach, MGM — *Nostalgia Merchant*

Packin' It In 1983
Comedy
82218   92 mins   C   B, V   P
Richard Benjamin, Paula Prentiss, Molly Ringwald, Tony Roberts, Andrea Marcovicci, directed by Jud Taylor
A Los Angeles family is in for a rude awakening when they leave the city for a quieter life in the Oregon woods.
Roger Gimbel Prods; EMI-TV — *VCL Home Video*

Paddington Bear 1985
Cartoons
70670   50 mins   C   B, V   P
Animated, narrated by Michael Hodern
Michael Bond's internationally famous creation gets into a variety of adventures after his adoption into the Brown family. Each volume of this two-dimensional and stop-action animation production includes 11 vignettes.
Walt Disney Productions — *Walt Disney Home Video*

Paddy 1970
Comedy
86599   97 mins   C   B, V   P
Des Cave, Milo O'Shea, Darbnia Molloy, Paggy Cass
A young man realizes his sexual potential by seducing every woman he can find.
MPAA:PG
Tamara Asseyev! — *Charter Entertainment*

Paddy Beaver 1984
Cartoons
78375   60 mins   C   B, V   P
Animated

Paddy Beaver teaches the residents of the Green Forest how to depend upon each other in this animated feature.
Family Home Entertainment — *Family Home Entertainment*

Padre Padrone 1977
Drama
63436   90 mins   C   B, V   P
Omero Antonutti, Saverio Marconi
This is the story of the personal rebellion of a Sardinian shepherd who was separated from the world by his father until he was 20 years old. Italian dialogue, English subtitles.
Cannes Film Festival: Golden Palm Award. IT
Almi/Cinema V; Guiliani G. de Negri — *RCA/Columbia Pictures Home Video*

Pagliacci 1948
Opera
84653   89 mins   B/W   B, V   P
Tito Gobbi, Gina Lollobrigida, Afro Polli, directed by Mario Costa
A film version of the classic Leoncavallo opera with a great Gobbi performance.
IT
Italian — *V.I.E.W. Video*

Pagliacci 1937
Opera
85200   79 mins   B/W   B, V   P
Richard Tauber, Steffi Duna, Diana Napier, Esmond Knight, Arthur Margetson
This is a British filmed version of the Leoncavallo opera, sung in an English translation.
English — *Video Yesteryear*

Pain in the A--, A 1977
Comedy
80384   90 mins   C   B, V   P
Lino Ventura, Jacques Brel, Caroline Cellier, directed by Edouard Molinaro
A hit man helps a suicidal shirt salesman solve his marital problems. With English subtitles.
MPAA:PG FR
Corwin-Mahler — *RCA/Columbia Pictures Home Video*

Paint Your Wagon 1970
Musical
59860   164 mins   C   B, V, LV   P
Lee Marvin, Clint Eastwood, Jean Seberg, Harve Presnell, directed by Joshua Logan
A western musical-comedy about a goldmining boom town, complete with a classic Lerner and Lowe score.
MPAA:PG
Paramount — *Paramount Home Video*

Painted Desert, The   1931
Western
44811   80 mins   B/W   B, V   P, T
*William Boyd, Helen Twelvetrees, George
O'Brien, Clark Gable*
Clark Gable's first film role of any consequence
came in this early sound western. Gable plays a
villain opposite "good guy" William Boyd.
RKO — *Movie Buff Video; Hollywood Home
Theater; Discount Video Tapes; Video
Connection; Kartes Video Communications;
Video Yesteryear*

Painted Stallion, The   1937
Western/Serials
08878   215 mins   B/W   B, V, 3/4U   P
Ray 'Crash' Corrigan, Hoot Gibson
Twelve episodes, each running 18 minutes.
Republic — *Video Connection; Video
Yesteryear; Nostalgia Merchant; Discount Video
Tapes*

Paisan   1948
War-Drama
06232   90 mins   B/W   B, V   P
*Maria Michi, Gar Moore, directed by Roberto
Rossellini*
Six stories of Allied soldiers encountering Italy's
liberation during WWII. Italian film, English
subtitles.
IT
J Burstyn; Italian — *Hollywood Home Theater;
Cable Films; Video Yesteryear; Western Film &
Video Inc; Discount Video Tapes*

Pajama Tops   1983
Comedy
72456   120 mins   C   B, V   P
Susan George, Robert Klein, Pia Zadora
This film was adapted, from the French farce,
"Mou Mod."
Unknown — *U.S.A. Home Video*

Pale Rider   1985
Western
Closed Captioned
82338   116 mins   C   B, V, LV   P
*Clint Eastwood, Michael Moriarty, Carrie
Snodgrass, Sydney Penny, Christopher Penn,
John Russell, directed by Clint Eastwood*
A nameless stranger who rides into a small
California gold rush town finds himself in the
middle of a feud between a mining syndicate
and a group of independent prospectors.
Available in hi-fi stereo for all formats, and with
Spanish subtitles in VHS only.
MPAA:R
Warner Bros; Malapaso Company — *Warner
Home Video*

Paleface, The   1948
Comedy
80850   91 mins   C   B, V, LV   P
*Jane Russell, Bob Hope, Robert Armstrong, Iris
Adrian, Robert Watson, directed by Norman Z.
McLeod*
A cowardly dentist becomes a gunslinging hero
when Calamity Jane starts aiming for him.
Available in VHS and BETA HI FI.
'Academy Awards '48: Best Song "Buttons and
Bows."
Paramount Pictures — *MCA Home Video*

Palooka   1934
Comedy-Drama
12858   94 mins   B/W   B, V, FO   P
Jimmy Durante, Stuart Erwin, Lupe Velez
Based on the classic comic strip. Durante plays
a fast-talking manager Knobby Walsh and sings
his own classic, "Inka-Dinka-Doo."
Edward Small Prods — *Video Yesteryear;
Cable Films; Video Connection; Discount Video
Tapes; Western Film & Video Inc; Hal Roach
Studios; Kartes Video Communications*

Panama Lady   1939
Romance
69588   65 mins   B/W   B, V   P
Lucille Ball, Evelyn Brent
Lucille Ball stars as the sexy, sultry "Panama
Lady" in this old-fashioned romance.
RKO — *VidAmerica*

Panama Lady   1939
Drama
70050   65 mins   B/W   B, V   P
Lucille Ball
A dance hall girl and oil prospector experience a
series of mis-adventures before finding
happiness out west.
RKO — *VidAmerica*

Panda and the Magic   1975
Serpent
Cartoons/Fantasy
53140   78 mins   C   B, V   P
Animated
An ancient Chinese legend tells of a boy who
found a white snake his parents wouldn't let him
keep. When he grows up, the snake turns into a
beautiful maiden who saves his life.
Ziv Intl — *Family Home Entertainment*

Panda and the Magic   1961
Serpent
Fantasy
85230   74 mins   C   B, V   P
Narrated by Marvin Miller
An animated film from Japan for children,
featuring a woman/enchantress who must
search for a way to bring her lover back to life,
with the help of a mob of animated animals.
Japanese — *Video Yesteryear*

Pandamonium: The Beginning   1982
Cartoons
87367   23 mins   C   B, V   P
Three lovable pandas fight evil and are caught in the middle of a battle to control the universe.
Marvel Prod. — MGM/UA Home Video

Panda's Adventures   1984
Cartoons
76031   60 mins   C   B, V   P
Animated
An animated tale of a Panda Prince, Lonlon, who is exiled from his Kingdom when he fails a test of courage. Through his adventures, he learns that true heroism and real courage come from the heart.
John Watkins; Simon Nuchtern — RCA/Columbia Pictures Home Video

Pandora's Box   1928
Mystery
86095   110 mins   B/W   B, V   P
Louise Brooks, Fritz Kortner, Francis Lederer, directed by G.W. Pabst
This silent classic marked the end of the German Expressionist era, and established Brooks as a major screen presence. She plays a tempestuous whore who is eventually killed by Jack the Ripper.
Nero-Film — Embassy Home Entertainment

Panic   1983
Horror
81531   90 mins   C   B, V   P
David Warbeck, Janet Agren
A scientist terrorizes a small town when he becomes hideously deformed by one of his bacteria experiments.
Cinema Shares International — MPI Home Video

Panic in Echo Park   1977
Drama
66619   77 mins   C   B, V   P
Dorian Harewood, Catlin Adams, Robin Gammell, Norman Barthold
A dedicated physician fights hospital authorities to trace the cause of an epidemic in a minority community.
Edgar J Scherick Associates — U.S.A. Home Video

Panique   1940
Drama
06233   87 mins   B/W   B, V   P
Michel Simon, Viviane Romance, directed by Julien Duvivier
Study of mob psychology in slums of Paris after war. Two lovers frame a stranger for murder. French film, English subtitles.
FR

Filmsonor — Movie Buff Video; Hollywood Home Theater; Cable Films; Discount Video Tapes

Papa's Delicate Condition   1963
Comedy
85259   98 mins   C   B, V   P
Jackie Gleason, Glynis Johns, Charlie Ruggles, Laurel Goodwin
Papa is a drunk and a constant headache to his whole family in this heartwarming paean to turn-of-the-century family life.
Academy Awards '63: Best Song ("Call Me Irresponsible").
Paramount — Kartes Video Communications

Paper Chase, The   1973
Drama
08469   111 mins   C   B, V, CED   P
Timothy Bottoms, Lindsay Wagner, John Houseman, Graham Beckel
Examines the repressive cloistered world of first-year students at Harvard Law School.
Academy Awards '73: Best Supporting Actor (Houseman). MPAA:PG
20th Century Fox — CBS/Fox Video

Paper Moon   1973
Comedy
38601   102 mins   B/W   B, V, LV   P
Ryan O'Neal, Tatum O'Neal, Madeline Kahn, John Hillerman, directed by Peter Bogdanovich
Bright, winning story of a con man (Ryan O'Neal) who is left with a nine-year old orphan (Tatum O'Neal in her film debut) who proves to be a better crook. Set in depression-era Kansas, circa 1936.
Academy Awards '73: Best Supporting Actress (Tatum O'Neal). MPAA:PG
Paramount — Paramount Home Video; RCA VideoDiscs

Paper Tiger   1974
Adventure
80761   104 mins   C   B, V   P
David Niven, Toshiro Mifune, Ando, Hardy Kruger directed by Ken Annakin
Niven plays an imaginative English tutor who fabricates fantastic yarns fictionalizing his past in order to impress his student, the son of the Japanese ambassador to a Southeast Asian country.
Joseph E. Levine — Embassy Home Entertainment

Papillon   1973
Drama
59308   150 mins   C   B, V, CED   P
Steve McQueen, Dustin Hoffman, directed by Franklin Schaffner
The story of two convicts and their harrowing experiences on Devil's Island.
MPAA:PG

Robert Dorfmann — *CBS/Fox Video*

Paradise 1982
Romance
63368   100 mins   C   B, V, CED   P
Phoebe Cates, Willie Aames, Richard Curnock, Tuvio Tavi
A young American boy and a beautiful English girl are the sole survivors of a caravan massacre in the Middle East during the 19th century. They discover a magnificent oasis and experience their sexual awakening.
MPAA:R
Robert Lantos; Stephen J. Ross — *Embassy Home Entertainment*

Paradise Alley 1978
Drama
70865   109 mins   C   B, V   P
Sylvester Stallone, Anne Archer, Armand Assante, Lee Canalito, written and directed by Sylvester Stallone
Three brothers brave the world of professional wrestling in an effort to strike it rich and move out of the seedy Hell's Kitchen neighborhood of New York, circa 1946. Stallone's directorial debut; in Hi-Fi Mono.
MPAA:PG
Universal — *MCA Home Video*

Paradise Canyon 1935
Western
54188   59 mins   B/W   B, V   P
John Wayne
One of John Wayne's early action westerns.
Monogram — *Sony Video Software; Video Connection; Spotlite Video; Discount Video Tapes*

Paradise, Hawaiian Style 1966
Musical
08387   91 mins   C   B, V   P
Elvis Presley, Suzanna Leigh, James Shigeta
Out-of-work pilot returns to Hawaii, where he and a buddy start a charter service with two helicopters.
EL, SP
Paramount; Hal Wallis — *CBS/Fox Video*

Paradise in Harlem 1940
Drama
42951   83 mins   B/W   B, V, FO   P
Frank Wilson, Mamie Smith, Edna Mae Harris
An all-black musical in which a cabaret performer witnesses a gangland murder, sees his sick wife die, and is pressured into leaving town by the mob.
Unknown — *Video Yesteryear; Video Connection; Discount Video Tapes; Movie Buff Video*

Paradise Motel 1984
Comedy
Closed Captioned
84129   87 mins   C   B, V   P
Gary Hershberger, Jonna Leigh Stack, Robert Krantz
In this film centered around a local motel predominantly used for one-night rendevous, high school heros and jocks battle for the affections of a beautiful classmate.
MPAA:R
Gary Gibbs; Frank Rubin — *Key Video*

Paradise Now 1970
Theater
86479   95 mins   C   B, V   P
A videotape showing the Living Theatre's performances of the famous theatre piece in Brussels and Berlin. In French, German and English, with English subtitles.
Cannes Film Festival '70: Directors Fortnight Selection.
Sheldon Rochlin; The Living Theatre — *Mystic Fire Video*

Paradisio 1961
Comedy
70895   82 mins   C   B, V   P
Arthur Howard, Eva Waegner
A dying inventor wills a professor an authentic pair of X-ray specs. Spies come gunning for the prof, and chase him through Europe.
MPAA:R
British — *New World Video*

Parallax View, The 1974
Suspense
60331   102 mins   C   B, V   P
Warren Beatty, Hume Cronyn, William Daniels, Paula Prentiss, directed by Alan J. Pakula
A reporter tries to disprove a report which stated that a presidential candidate's assassination was not a conspiracy.
MPAA:R
Paramount — *Paramount Home Video*

Parallel Corpse 1983
Crime-Drama
84134   89 mins   C   B, V   P
Buster Larsen, Jorgen Kiil, Agneta Ekmanner, Masja Dessau
A remorseless killer is blackmailed by a mortuary attendant when the latter finds one of the former's coffin-hidden victims.
Just Betzer — *Media Home Entertainment*

Paralyzed 197?
Horror
71070   90 mins   C   B, V   P
Ingrid Thulin, Jean Sorel, Mario Adorf, written and directed by Aldo Lado
An unconscious journalist, mistaken for dead in a hospital emergency room, flashes back to the

investigation that embroiled him in his
predicament.
Independent — *MPI Home Video*

Paranoia   1969
Suspense
66475   94 mins   C   B, V   P
Carroll Baker, Lou Castel, Colette Descombes
A beautiful jet-set widow is trapped in her own
Italian villa by a young couple and slowly fed
drugs as part of a murder plan.
MPAA:X
Commonwealth United — *Spotlite Video*

Parasite   1981
Horror/Science fiction
60431   85 mins   C   B, V   P
Demi Moore, Robert Glaudini, James Davidson
In 1992, a doctor, a victim of the atomic age, is
being eaten alive from the inside out.
MPAA:R
Irwin Yablans; Charles Band — *Wizard Video;
Embassy Home Entertainment (disc only)*

Pardon Mon Affaire   1977
Comedy
78638   107 mins   C   B, V, LV   P
*Jean Rochefort, Guy Bedos, Anny Duperey,
directed by Yves Robert*
When a middle-aged civil servant gets a look at
a model in a garage, he decides it's time to
cheat on his wife. This film has English subtitles.
MPAA:PG FR
First Artists — *Embassy Home Entertainment*

Pardon My Blooper   1974
Outtakes and bloopers
55958   60 mins   C   B, V   P
Authentic radio and television bloopers
collected by the late Kermit Schafer, the man
who invented the term "blooper."
Kermit Schafer — *Blooper Enterprises*

Pardon My Trunk   1952
Comedy
85201   85 mins   B/W   B, V   P
Sabu, Vittorio De Sica
A ribald comedy about an elephant that lives in
a Roman tenement.
Italian — *Video Yesteryear*

Pardon Us   1931
Comedy
59152   71 mins   B/W   B, V, 3/4U   P
Stan Laurel, Oliver Hardy, June Marlowe
Two bootleggers find themselves in and out of
prison.
Hal Roach;MGM — *Nostalgia Merchant;
Blackhawk Films*

Parent Trap, The   1961
Comedy
66321   127 mins   C   B, V, LV,   P
                           CED
*Hayley Mills, Maureen O'Hara, Brian Keith,
Charlie Ruggles, directed by David Swift*
Hayley Mills plays a dual role in this
heartwarming comedy as twin sisters who
conspire to bring their divorced parents together
again.
Buena Vista — *Walt Disney Home Video*

Parents Come Out   1985
Sexuality
87715   28 mins   C   B, V, 3/4U   P
A touching, bittersweet and heartfelt
documentary about the efforts of parents to deal
with gay children.
P-FLAG — *P-FLAG*

Paris   1986
France/Travel
87199   55 mins   C   B, V   P
A visual tour of the City of Lights, including all of
the famous tourist sights.
Kronos-France — *Gessler Educational
Software*

Paris Express   1953
Mystery/Drama
78968   82 mins   C   B, V   P
*Claude Rains, Herbert Lom, Felix Aylmer,
Marius Goring, Marta Toren*
When a man steals money from his employer,
he boards the Paris Express to escape from the
police.
Josef Shaftel; Raymond Struss — *MPI Home
Video*

Paris Holiday   1957
Comedy
47664   100 mins   C   B, V   P
*Bob Hope, Fernandel, Anita Ekberg, Martha
Hyer, Preston Sturges*
An actor heading for Paris to find a noted
author; latest screenplay finds mystery and
romance.
United Artists — *Unicorn Video*

Paris Opera Ballet: Six   1985
Ballets, The
Dance
84665   58 mins   C   B, V   P
*Patrick Dupono, the Corps du Ballet of the Paris
Opera*
A collection of 'Pas de Deux' ensembles and
variations by the Corps du Ballet. Recorded in
Hi-Fi.
French — *V.I.E.W. Video*

Paris, Texas 1984
Drama
Closed Captioned
81410   145 mins   C   B, V   P
Nastassja Kinski, Harry Dean Stanton, Hunter Carson, Dean Stockwell, Aurore Clement, directed by Wim Wenders
An estranged father is picked up and taken to Los Angeles after he is found wandering around the Texas desert. After being reunited with his son, the two head back to Texas to win back his ex-wife's love. Ry Cooder's score can be heard in VHS and Beta Hi-Fi.
MPAA:PG
20th Century Fox — *CBS/Fox Video*

Park is Mine, The 1985
Drama
Closed Captioned
85611   102 mins   C   B, V   P
Tommy Lee Jones, Yaphet Kotto, Helen Shaver, directed by Steven H. Stern
A deranged and desperate Vietnam vet takes hostages in Central Park.
Denis Heroux; John Kemeny — *Key Video*

Parker 1984
Crime-Drama/Mystery
84405   100 mins   C   B, V   P
Bryan Brown, Kurt Raab
An executive is kidnapped, then released—and does not know why. Unable to live with the mystery, he tracks his kidnappers down into a world of blackmail, drugs and intrigue.
Nigel Stafford-Clark — *Karl/Lorimar Home Video*

Parlor, Bedroom and Bath 1931
Comedy
57288   75 mins   B/W   B, V   P
Buster Keaton, Charlotte Greenwood, Cliff Edwards
Buster Keaton stars in another one of his classic comedies from the Thirties.
Buster Keaton — *Video Yesteryear; Video Dimensions; Hollywood Home Theater; Discount Video Tapes*

Partners 1982
Comedy
60332   92 mins   C   B, V   P
Ryan O'Neal, John Hurt, Kenneth McMillan, Robyn Douglass, Jay Robinson, Rick Jason
A macho cop must go "undercover" with a gay cop to investigate the murder of a gay model.
MPAA:R
Paramount — *Paramount Home Video*

Party Animal, The 1983
Comedy
80669   78 mins   C   B, V   P
Tim Carhart, Matthew Lausey, Robin Harlan
A college stud teaches a shy farm boy a thing or two about the carnal aspects of campus life.
MPAA:R
Alan C. Fox — *Lightning Video*

Party Games—For Adults Only 1984
Games
75019   130 mins   C   LV   P
This tape features sixty good-natured sexy party games for adult parties.
Bosustow Entertainment Productions — *MCA Home Video*

Pas de Deux 1984
Dance
87937   130 mins   C   B, V   P
Patricia MacBride, Ravena Tucker, Wayne Eagling, Ghislaine Thesmar
Eight balletic pas de deux are performed by ballet greats at the John Anson Ford Ampitheatre.
Los Angeles Int'l Ballet Festival — *Video Arts International*

Passage to India, A 1984
Drama
Closed Captioned
81795   163 mins   C   B, V   P
Peggy Ashcroft, Alec Guinness, James Fox, Judy Davis, Victor Banerjee, directed by David Lean ·
A young British woman who befriends an Indian doctor later accuses him of an attempted rape after a strange incident at India's Marabar caves. Available in VHS Dolby Hi-Fi Stereo and Beta Hi-Fi Stereo.
Academy Awards '84: Best Supporting Actress (Ashcroft); Best Original Score (Maurice Jarre).
MPAA:PG
Columbia Pictures — *RCA/Columbia Pictures Home Video*

Passage to Marseilles 1944
War-Drama
73980   110 mins   B/W   B, V   P
Humphrey Bogart, Claude Rains, Sidney Greenstreet, Peter Lorre, Michele Morgan, directed by Michael Curtiz
Five convicts escape from Devil's Island to join up with the Free French forces fighting the Nazis during World War II.
Warner Bros — *Key Video*

Passante, La 1983
Drama
80451   106 mins   C   B, V   P
Romy Schneider, Michel Piccoli, Helmut Griem, Gerard Klein
The lives of two women are brought together by a mysterious chain of events.
FR

Raymond Dannon — *Pacific Arts Video*

Passenger, The 1975
Drama
87340   119 mins   C   B, V   P
Jack Nicholson, Maria Schneider, directed by Michelangelo Antonioni
A world-weary journalist, tired of his life, encounters a corpse and assumes its identity, only to find it belonged to a reputed arms smuggler. He is joined by a homeless woman in a cross-country flight from unknown enemies, time and his humdrum existence. One of the controversial director's later American films.
MPAA:PG
Carlo Ponti — *Warner Home Video*

Passion 1954
Western
70808   84 mins   C   B, V   P
Raymond Burr, Cornel Wilde, Yvonne De Carlo, Lon Chaney, Jr, Rodolfo Acosta
When a rancher's young family falls victim to rampaging desperados, he enlists an outlaw's aid to avenge the murders of his loved ones.
RKO; Filmcrest Prods — *Buena Vista Home Video*

Passion 1919
Drama
85517   135 mins   B/W   B, V   P
Pola Negri, Emil Jannings, directed by Ernst Lubitsch
A classic epic silent version of "Madame Du Barry," in the tradition of Germany's golden silent age.
UFA — *Video Yesteryear*

Passion of Joan of Arc 1928
Drama
11385   114 mins   B/W   B, V, FO   P
Maria Falconetti, Eugena Sylvaw, Maurice Schultz, Antonin Artaud, directed by Carl-Theodore Dreyer
A classic silent masterpiece by the Danish Master depicting John's last hours alive, adapted from the actual trial transcripts.
Societe Generale de Films — *Video Yesteryear; Western Film & Video Inc; Discount Video Tapes*

Passion of Love 1982
Drama/Romance
64355   117 mins   C   B, V, CED   P
Laura Antonelli
Laura Antonelli is featured in this passionate, historical romance from filmmaker Ettore Scola. The film has won a special award at the Cannes Film Festival.
Franco Commipteri — *Vestron Video*

Passport to Pimlico 1949
Comedy
82165   85 mins   B/W   B, V   P
Stanley Halloway, Margaret Rutherford, Hermione Baddeley
When the residents of a London neighborhood discover an old charter proclaiming that their land belongs to the Duke of Burgundy, the inhabitants attempt to secede from England.
Associated British-Pathe Ltd — *Prism*

Pat Benatar Hit Videos 1984
Music video
72929   60 mins   C   B, V   P
Pat Benatar
A collection of Pat's videos from "Get Nervous" and "Live from Earth," this tape also includes a documentary on the making of "Love Is a Battlefield."
Rising Star Video Productions — *RCA/Columbia Pictures Home Video*

Pat Benatar in Concert 1985
Music-Performance
77461   72 mins   C   B, V   P
Pat Benatar
Pat Benatar performs many of her big hits in this exciting concert video.
Music Vision — *RCA/Columbia Pictures Home Video*

Pat Garrett and Billy the Kid 1973
Western
72466   106 mins   C   B, V   P
Kris Kristofferson, James Coburn, Bob Dylan
The story of the famous Southwestern outlaw who was tracked and killed by a man he once rode with. Sound track music by Bob Dylan.
MGM — *MGM/UA Home Video*

Pat Travers in "Just Another Killer Day" 1984
Music video
70190   30 mins   C   B, V   P
This conceptual music video album features guitarist/vocalist Pat Travers performing "Killer," "Women on the Edge," "Hot Shot" and others.
PMV Presentations; Beth Broday — *RCA/Columbia Pictures Home Video*

Paternity 1981
Comedy
58715   94 mins   C   B, V, LV   P
Burt Reynolds, Beverly D'Angelo, Lauren Hutton, Norman Fell, Paul Dooley, Elizabeth Ashley, directed by David Steinberg
A middle-aged man sets out to find a woman to bear his child and then leave him alone.
MPAA:PG

Paramount — *Paramount Home Video; RCA VideoDiscs*

Paths of Glory   1957
War-Drama
64905   86 mins   B/W   B, V, CED   P
Kirk Douglas, George Macready, Ralph Meeker, Adolphe Menjou, Susanne Christian, directed by Stanley Kubrick
This adaptation of a novel by Humphrey Cobb examines the arrogance of generals and the senseless punishment of three soldiers in the French army during World War I.
United Artists — *CBS/Fox Video*

Patrick   1978
Suspense
54537   115 mins   C   B, V   P
Sir Robert Helpmann, Susan Penhaligon, Rod Mullinar
A coma patient suddenly develops strange powers and has a weird effect on the people he comes in contact with.
MPAA:PG
Vanguard/Monarch
Release — *HarmonyVision*

Patsy, The   1964
Comedy
80240   101 mins   C   B, V   P
Jerry Lewis, Ina Balin, Keenan Wynn, Phil Harris, Peter Lorre, directed by Jerry Lewis
A group of Hollywood executives try to turn a bellhop into a comedy star.
Paramount — *U.S.A. Home Video*

Patti Page Video   1985
Songbook, The
Music-Performance
71002   60 mins   C   B, V   P
Patti Page
The unmistakable sound of Ms. Page's 50's style crooning fills this 18-track collection. Among the greats are "Tennessee Waltz," "How Much Is That Doggie In The Window," "Sunnyside of the Street" and "You Call Everybody Darling."
Kartes Video Communications — *Kartes Video Communications*

Patton   1970
War-Drama
08428   171 mins   C   B, V, LV   P
George C. Scott, Karl Malden, Stephen Young, directed by Franklin J. Schaffner
George C. Scott portrays the brilliant and maniacal General Patton, whose leadership produced victory after victory in North Africa and Europe during World War II.
Academy Awards '70: Best Picture; Best Actor (Scott); Best Director (Shaffner). MPAA:PG
EL, SP

20th Century Fox — *CBS/Fox Video*

Paul Bartel's The Secret   1969
Cinema
Comedy
84359   37 mins   B/W   B, V   P
Directed by Paul Bartel
A woman cannot determine whether life is real or a film by a maniacal director. Followed by Bartel's short "Naughty Nurse."
Paul Bartel — *Rhino Video*

Paul Dresher: Was   1985
Are/Will Be
Music video/Music-Performance
84056   30 mins   C   B, V   P
Rinde Eckert
Live performance of Post-Multimaust Paul Dresher's music at Laney College, performed by Rude Eckert.
Target Video; Music Traditions — *Target Video*

Paul Simon in Concert   1981
Music-Performance
47376   60 mins   C   B, V   P
Paul Simon
At a live concert in Philadelphia, Paul Simon performs some of his greatest old and new hits, including "Me and Julio," "Fifty Ways to Leave Your Lover," " One-Trick Pony," and "Sounds of Silence."
Michael Tannen; Phil Ramone; Peregrine Inc — *Warner Home Video; RCA VideoDiscs; Pioneer Artists*

Paul Simon Special, The   1977
Music-Performance/Variety
66444   60 mins   C   B, V   P
Paul Simon, Art Garfunkel, Chevy Chase, Lily Tomlin, Charles Grodin, The Jesse Dixon Singers
This 1977 TV special was produced by Lorne Michaels of "Saturday Night Live" and features appearances by a number of "SNL's" stars. Singer-songwriter Paul Simon performs eight of his songs, assisted on several by Art Garfunkel.
NBC; Lorne Michaels — *Pacific Arts Video*

Paul Young: The Video   1985
Singles
Music-Performance
82414   35 mins   C   B, V   P
Paul Young
Britain's leading male pop vocalist performs such hits as "Everytime You Go Away" and "Everything Must Change" in this collection of conceptual videos.
CBS/Fox Video — *CBS/Fox Video*

Pauline at the Beach   1983
Comedy
81894   95 mins   C   B, V   P

---

*Amanda Langlet, Arielle Dombasle, Rosette
Pascal Gregory, directed by Eric Rohmer*
Six people discover the true nature of love while
vacationing on the French coast of Normandy
one summer. With English subtitles.
MPAA:R FR
Margaret Menegoz — *Media Home
Entertainment*

Paul's Case   1980
Drama
84034   52 mins   C   B, V   P
*Eric Roberts, Michael Higgins, Lindsay Crouse,
directed by Lamont Johnson*
In turn-of-the-century Pittsburgh, an ambitious
young man enters the upper crust of New York
society through deceiving pretenses. Based on
a story by Willa Cather.
Ed Lynch — *Monterey Home Video*

Pavarotti in London   1982
Music-Performance/Opera
64831   51 mins   C   B, V   P
London's Royal Albert Hall was the setting for
this concert which launched the Royal
Philharmonic Orchestra's national fund appeal
starring Pavarotti performing "Tosca,"
"Macbeth" and others. In stereo.
BBC; Polygram; Rodney
Greenberg — *RCA/Columbia Pictures Home
Video; Pioneer Artists; RCA VideoDiscs*

Pavlova   1981
Dance
88132   90 mins   C   B, V   P
A documentary about the career of the famous
prima danseuse featuring vintage footage of her
work.
Sony Video — *Sony Video Software*

Pawnbroker, The   1965
Drama
64540   100 mins B/W   B, V   P
*Rod Steiger, Brock Peters, Geraldine Fitzgerald,
directed by Sidney Lumet*
A middle-aged Jewish pawnbroker in New
York's Spanish Harlem finds that he cannot
forget his terrible experiences in a Nazi
concentration camp during World War II.
Commonwealth United — *Republic Pictures
Home Video*

Pawnshop, The   1916
Comedy
58971   20 mins   B/W   B, V, 3/4U   P
Charlie Chaplin
Charlie is employed as a pawnbroker's
assistant. Silent with music track.
Mutual — *Cable Films; Festival Films*

Pay Less Tax Legally   1984
Personal finance
69839   46 mins   C   B, V   P
Barry Steiner, a busy CPA and a former Internal
Revenue Agent, helps clients save money by
answering a broad range of income tax
questions. Steiner's answers are all in layman's
terms with no legal jargon.
John McNaughton — *Barry Raymond Steiner*

Pay or Die   1983
Martial arts
85406   92 mins   C   B, V   P
*Johnny Wilson, Dick Adair, Ted Deelman,
Danny Rojo*
A rousing ninja epic, with an all-Caucasian cast.
Bobby Suarez — *U.S.A. Home Video*

Payday   1972
Musical-Drama
63333   98 mins   C   B, V   P
*Rip Torn, Ahna Capri, Michael C. Gwynne, Jeff
Morris*
Rip Torn stars as a declining country music star
on tour in this portrayal of the seamy side of
show business, from groupies to grimy motels.
Saul Zaentz Company — *THORN EMI/HBO
Video*

Peacekillers, The   1971
Drama
81219   86 mins   C   B, V   P
Michael Ontkean, Clint Ritchie, Paul Krokop
A mean bunch of bikers visit a commune to
kidnap a young woman. The gang has a big
surprise in store for them when the girl escapes.
Available in VHS and Beta Hi-Fi.
Transvue Pictures — *New World Video*

Peacock Fan, The   1929
Drama
59206   50 mins   B/W   B, V, 3/4U   P
Lucian Preval
The Peacock Fan is protected by a deadly
curse, with certain death to anyone who
possesses it.
Chesterfield Motion Picture Corp — *Video
Yesteryear*

Peak Performance   1985
Psychology
81730   50 mins   C   B, V   P
Dr. Charles Garfield demonstrates techniques
that will enable people to give their peak
performance in business and at home.
Kartes Video Communications — *Kartes Video
Communications*

Pearl of the South Pacific   1955
Drama
81611   85 mins   C   B, V   P

Dennis Morgan, Virginia Mayo, David Farrar,
directed by Allan Dwan
A trio of adventurers destroy a quiet and
peaceful island when they ransack it for pearl
treasures.
RKO — Buena Vista Home Video

Peck's Bad Boy   1921
Comedy
60047   51 mins   B/W   B, V   P, T
Jackie Coogan, Doris Day, Raymond Hatton,
Wheeler Oakman, Lillian Leighton
Jackie and his friends let a circus lion loose and
Jackie's father won't allow him to see the circus.
He then decides to blackmail his father. A
Blackhawk orchestral score has been added to
this silent film.
First National — Blackhawk Films; Video
Yesteryear

Peck's Bad Boy with the   1938
Circus
Comedy
12812   67 mins   B/W   B, V, FO   P
Tommy Kelly, Ann Gillis, Spanky MacFarland,
Edgar Kennedy, Billy Gilbert
A troublesome youngster and his pals nearly
wreck a circus and throw an obstacle race off
course.
RKO — Video Yesteryear

Pedestrian, The   1974
Drama
65391   97 mins   C   B, V   P
Maximillian Schell
This is the story of a powerful industrialist and
his secret. A human drama builds as the
newspaper's investigation probes deep into the
past to reveal the memory of events that time
and fortune could not erase.
MPAA:PG
Cinerama Releasing — Embassy Home
Entertainment

Pee Wee Herman Show,   1982
The
Comedy-Performance
70947   60 mins   C   B, V   P
Pee Wee Herman
Zany kid-like antics abound in this satirical romp
through the unusual.
HBO — THORN EMI/HBO Video

Pee Wee's Big Adventure   1985
Comedy
Closed Captioned
71168   92 mins   C   B, V, LV   P
Paul Reubens, Elizabeth Daily, Mark Holton,
Diane Salinger, Judd Omen, directed by Tim
Burton
The adventure involves Pee Wee Herman in a
search for his prized possession, a brightly

painted and accessory-filled bicycle. Recorded
in HiFi Stereo.
MPAA:PG
Warner Bros — Warner Home Video

Peerce, Anderson &   1981
Segovia
Music-Performance
57253   56 mins   B/W   B, V   P
Jan Peerce, Marian Anderson, Andres Segovia
Three separate short films highlight
performances by guitarist Andres Segovia, tenor
Jan Peerce, assisted by Nadine Connor and
contralto Marian Anderson.
Kultur — Kultur

Pele—The Master and His   1980
Method
Soccer
56453   60 mins   C   B, V   P
Soccer star Pele gives tips on improving your
play, and talks about the game.
Pepsico — CBS/Fox Video; Champions on
Film and Video

Pendulum   1969
Mystery/Drama
77242   106 mins   C   B, V   P
George Peppard, Jean Seberg, Richard Kiley,
Madeline Sherwood
A police captain sets out to clear himself of
charges of murdering his wife and her lover.
MPAA:PG
Columbia Pictures; Stanley
Niss — RCA/Columbia Pictures Home Video

Penitentiary   1979
Drama
52861   99 mins   C   B, V   P
Leon Isaacs, Jamaa Fanaka
A realistic story of a black fighter in prison.
MPAA:R
Jerry Gross — Wizard Video

Penitentiary II   1982
Adventure
80362   108 mins   C   B, V   P
Leon Issac Kennedy, Mr. T, Ernie Hudson,
Glynn Turman
A welterweight fighter is after the man who
murdered his girlfriend.
MPAA:R
Bob-Bea Productions — MGM/UA Home
Video

Pennies from Heaven   1981
Musical
47776   107 mins   C   B, V, CED   P
Steve Martin, Bernadette Peters, Christopher
Walken, Jessica Harper, Vernel Bagneris,
directed by Herbert Ross

An avante-garde reworking of 30's musicals involving a sheet music salesman accused of murder.
MPAA:R
MGM — *MGM/UA Home Video*

Penny Serenade 1936
Drama
11249 120 mins B/W B, V P
Cary Grant, Irene Dunne, Beulah Bondi, Edgar Buchanan
A young couple, having lost their baby, adopts a child, but their new found happiness is short-lived.
Columbia — *Prism; Video Yesteryear; Republic Pictures Home Video; Hollywood Home Theater; Movie Buff Video; Cable Films; Video Connection; Discount Video Tapes; Hal Roach Studios; Spotlite Video; Kartes Video Communications*

Penny Serenade 1940
Drama
71025 120 mins C B, V P
Cary Grant, Irene Dunne, Beulah Bondi, Edgar Buchanan, directed by George Stevens
Stevens' bittersweet tale of a young couple's unsuccessful efforts to start a family has been enhanced through the new Colorization process.
Columbia — *Hal Roach Studios*

Penthouse Love Stories 1986
Sexuality/Variety
87218 60 mins C B, V P
Xaviera Hollander
A visual, sumptuous array of sketches bringing the pages of Penthouse Forum to soft-focused life.
Bob Guccione — *Vestron Video*

Penthouse Video Volume One: The Girls of Penthouse 1985
Variety
76765 60 mins C B, V, LV, CED P
The first volume of this video magazine features of some of Penthouse's most popular centerfolds in intimate photo sessions.
Penthouse International — *Vestron Video*

People, The 1971
Drama
80312 74 mins C B, V P
Kim Darby, Dan O'Herlihy, Diane Varsi, William Shatner, directed by John Korty
A young teacher takes a job in a small town and finds out that her students have telepathic powers.
Metromedia Producers Corp. — *Prism*

People Are Funny 1946
Comedy
57364 94 mins B/W B, V, FO P
Jack Haley, Rudy Vallee, Ozzie Nelson, Art Linkletter, Helen Walker
Battling radio producers vie to land the big sponsor with an original radio idea. Comedy ensues when one of them comes up with a great idea—stolen from a local station.
Paramount — *Video Yesteryear*

People That Time Forgot, The 1977
Science fiction
66045 90 mins C B, V P
Edgar Rice Burroughs' novel about a rescue team that discovers a world of prehistoric monsters and tribes people provides the basis for this film.
MPAA:PG
John Dark — *Embassy Home Entertainment*

People vs. Jean Harris, The 1981
Drama
71323 147 mins C B, V P
Ellen Burstyn, Martin Balsam, Richard Dysart, Peter Coyote, directed by George Schaefer
This docudrama follows the trial of Jean Harris, the woman accused of slaying her lover, "Scarsdale Diet" creator Dr. Herman Tarnower.
P.K.O. Television Ltd — *U.S.A. Home Video*

Pepe Le Moko 1937
Adventure
06235 87 mins B/W B, V P
Jean Gabin, Mireille Balin, directed by Julien Duvivier
Violence, betrayal, and isolation are presented in this hide-and-seek game with police. Based on D'Ashelbe's novel. French film, English subtitles.
FR
Paris Film — *Movie Buff Video; Cable Films; Discount Video Tapes; Hollywood Home Theater*

Pepper 1982
Adventure/Suspense
63362 88 mins C B, V P
International intrigue and super spying abound in this fast-paced, sexy adventure featuring Pepper, a female secret agent in the James Bond tradition.
Amero Brothers — *Vestron Video*

Pepper and His Wacky Taxi 196?
Comedy
66110 79 mins C B, V P
John Astin, Frank Sinatra Jr, Jackie Gayle, Alan Sherman

A father of four buys a '59 Cadillac and starts a cab company.
MPAA:G
Samuel S Dikel — *Unicorn Video*

Perdicion de Mujeres   197?
Drama
63855   90 mins   B/W   B, V   P
Directed by Juan Orol
This is the story of the anguish and terror experienced by the members of an illicit love triangle. In Spanish.
SP
Mexican — *Hollywood Home Theater*

Perfect   1985
Drama
Closed Captioned
82321   120 mins   C   B, V   P
John Travolta, Jamie Lee Curtis, Carly Simon, Marilu Henner, Laraine Newman, Jann Wenner, Anne De Salvo, directed by James Bridges
A "Rolling Stone" reporter goes after the shallowness of the Los Angeles health club scene, and falls in.
MPAA:R
Columbia Pictures; James Bridges — *RCA/Columbia Pictures Home Video*

Perfect Crime, The   1978
Mystery/Adventure
80941   90 mins   C   B, V   P
Joseph Cotten, Antony Steel, Janet Agreen
A Scotland Yard inspector must find out who has been killing off executives of a powerful world trust.
Ciat Productions — *VidAmerica*

Perfect Furlough, The   1959
Comedy
85260   93 mins   C   B, V   P
Tony Curtis, Janet Leigh, Keenan Wynn, Linda Cristal
A corporal wins a week in Paris with a movie star, accompanied by a female Army psychologist.
Universal — *Kartes Video Communications*

Perfect Killer, The   1977
Drama
70595   85 mins   C   B, V   P
Lee Van Cleef, Tita Barker, John Ireland, Robert Widmark
Van Cleef stars as a world weary Mafia hit-man who is doublecrossed by this girl, set up by his best friend, and hunted by another hired assassin.
MPAA:R
JPT and Metheus Film Prods. — *Prism*

Perfect Strangers   1984
Drama/Suspense
70678   90 mins   C   B, V   P
Anne Carlisle, Brad Rijn, John Woehrle, Matthew Stockley, Stephen Lack, directed by Larry Cohen
This Hitchcockian thriller develops around a murder and the child who witnesses it. The killer attempts to kidnap the young boy, but problems arise when he falls in love with the lad's mother.
MPAA:R
New Line Cinema — *Embassy Home Entertainment*

Performance   1970
Drama
58244   105 mins   C   B, V, LV   P
James Fox, Mick Jagger, Anita Pallenberg, directed by Donald Cammell and Nicolas Roeg
The story of a hunted murderer who takes refuge with an outcast rock and roll star—and sees his sense of reality vanish in an orgiastic breakdown of barriers and roles.
MPAA:R
Warner Bros — *Warner Home Video*

Perfumed Handkerchief,   1981
The
Music-Performance
81569   70 mins   C   B, V   P
This is a performance of the Chinese comic opera that features commentary from Steve Allen and Jayne Meadows. Contains English subtitles.
CCTV — *Kultur*

Peril   198?
Mystery
87269   100 mins   C   B, V   P
Michel Piccoli, Nicole Garcia, Anais Jeanneret, directed by Michel DeVille
From the novel "Sur La Terre Comme Au Ciel" by Rene Belletto, this film deals with a music teacher's infiltration into a wealthy family and the sexually motivated, back-stabbing murder plots that ensue.
MPAA:R
Emmanuel Schlumberger — *RCA/Columbia Pictures Home Video*

Perils of Gwendoline, The   1984
Adventure/Comedy
77186   88 mins   C   B, V, LV,   P
                                   CED
Tawny Kitaen, Brent Huff, Zabou, directed by Just Jaeckin
A young woman leaves the convent to search for her long lost father.
MPAA:R
Samuel Goldwyn — *Vestron Video*

Perils of Pauline, The   1947
Musical
03825   99 mins   C   B, V   P
Betty Hutton, John Lund, Billy DeWolfe, directed by George Marshall
A musical biography of Pearl White, the original queen of silent movie serials. Songs by Frank Loesser include "I Wish I Didn't Love You So," an Academy Award nominee.
Paramount; Sol C Siegel — Prism; Hollywood Home Theater; Video Yesteryear; Kartes Video Communications; Movie Buff Video; Discount Video Tapes; Cable Films; Media Home Entertainment; VCII; Video Connection; Hal Roach Studios

Perils of Pauline, The   1934
Serials
85204   238 mins   B/W   B, V   P
Evelyn Knapp, Robert Allen, James Durkin, Sonny Ray, Pat O'Malley
All twelve episodes of this classic melodrama/adventure serial in one package, featuring dastardly villains, cliff-hanging predicaments and world-wide chases.
Universal — Video Yesteryear

Perils of Penelope   1984
Pitstop, The
Cartoons
66576   60 mins   C   B, V   P
Animated
This compilation of cartoons stars lovely Penelope Pitstop, international race car driver, who has to ward off the advances of villainous Sylvester Sneekly while she drives.
Hanna Barbera — Worldvision Home Video

Perils of Penelope   1971
Pitstop in Triple Trouble,
The
Cartoons
84079   58 mins   C   B, V   P
The innocent but voluptuous racing queen is beset by a gaggle of bizarre and wacky animated villains.
Hanna Barbera — Worldvision Home Video

Perils of the Darkest   1944
Jungle
Adventure/Serials
59149   180 mins   B/W   B, V, 3/4U   P
Linda Sterling, Allan Lane
A white jungle goddess battles money-mad oil profiteers to prevent them from despoiling the jungle. Original title: "The Tiger Woman." A serial in twelve episodes, on two cassettes.
Republic — Nostalgia Merchant

Permission To Kill   1975
Adventure
84862   96 mins   C   B, V   P

Dirk Bogarde, Ava Gardner, directed by Cyril Frankel
This expose of espionage as anything but glamorous finds British officer trying to prevent a controversial politician from entering his fascist-controlled country.
MPAA:PG
Paul Mills — Embassy Home Entertainment

Person to Person   1958
Interview
80758   30 mins   B/W   B, V   P
Hosted by Edward R. Murrow
Edward R. Murrow electronically visits Groucho and Harpo Marx at their homes in California in this collection of two episodes from the series.
CBS — Video Yesteryear

Persona   1967
Drama
14440   83 mins   C   B, V, FO   P
Bibi Andersson, Liv Ullmann, directed by Ingmar Bergman
A famous actress is stricken with psychosomatic dumbness and is placed under a nurse's care in an isolated house.
Svensk Filmindustri — Video Yesteryear; Video Dimensions; Hollywood Home Theater; Movie Buff Video; International Home Video

Personal Best   1982
Drama
59854   124 mins   C   B, V   P
Mariel Hemingway, Scott Glenn, Patrice Donnelly, directed by Robert Towne
Two woman athletes, Olympic runners, fall in love while competing against each other.
MPAA:R
Geffen Co; Warner Bros — Warner Home Video

Personal Property   1983
Music video
88103   20 mins   C   B, V   P
A compilation of the rock's bands rarely seen or talked about videos.
Sony Video — Sony Video Software

Personal Touch, The   1964
Adventure/Comedy
82188   52 mins   B/W   B, V   P
David Niven, Gig Young, Charles Boyer, Robert Coote, Gladys Cooper, Walter Matthau, Dina Merrill
The cunning Alec Fleming poses as a reclusive Australian millionaire in order to pull off a daring million dollar swindle. An episode from "The Rogues" series.
Four Star Television — RKO HomeVideo

Personals, The   1983
Comedy
80387   90 mins   C   B, V   P
Bill Schoppert, Karen Landry
A recently divorced young man takes out a
personal ad in a newspaper to find the woman
of his dreams.
MPAA:PG
Patrick Wells — *Embassy Home Entertainment*

Persuasive Speaking   1985
Human relations/Communication
71006   60 mins   C   B, V   P
Ronald Reagan, Mario Cuomo, Dick Cavett
Viewers can learn to improve their speeches
and presentations with the professional tips this
tape offers.
Esquire — *Esquire Video*

Pervertion (Perversion)   1980
Suspense
51103   90 mins   C   B, V   P
Carlos Estrada, Nadiuska
A woman begins a love affair with her boss, only
to uncover the shocking secret that he is a
horrible murderer. In Spanish.
SP
Spanish — *Hollywood Home Theater*

Pete Seeger...A Song and   1972
a Stone
Music
33444   85 mins   C   B, V   P
Pete Seeger, Johnny Cash, Lester Flatt
Pete Seeger and his pals strum, sing, and talk
their way through various places in the U.S. in a
year and a half's time.
Elfstrom — *Hollywood Home Theater*

Pete Townsend   1982
Music-Performance
76675   30 mins   C   B, V   P
This program presents Pete Townsend
performing his new hit songs.
Trinifold Ltd Warner Amex Satellite
Entertainment Co — *Sony Video Software*

Peter Allen and the   1981
Rockettes
Music-Performance
58955   87 mins   C   B, V, CED   P
Peter Allen, the Rockettes
Peter Allen — recorded live at his three-night,
sell-out engagement, performing more than 20
songs, including: "Everything Old." "Flyaway,"
"Bicoastal," "You and Me," & "Don't Cry Out
Loud" and " I Go to Rio." In Stereo.
20th Century Fox — *CBS/Fox Video; MCA
Home Video (disc only)*

Peter and the Magic Egg   1983
Cartoons
66182   60 mins   C   B, V   P
Animated, voices by Ray Bolger
The story of Mama and Papa Doppler, in danger
of losing their farm to greedy Tobias
Tinwhiskers.
RLR Associates — *Family Home
Entertainment; Coronet Films*

Peter and the Wolf   197?
Fairy tales/Cartoons
82464   82 mins   C   B, V   P
Animated, hosted by Ray Bolger
An animated version of the classic fairy tale,
featuring Ray Bolger, the Scarecrow of the
"Wizard of Oz."
Independent — *Vestron Video*

Peter and the Wolf   1986
Puppets
84774   28 mins   C   B, V   P
A puppet performance of Prokofiev's music and
story.
F Prods/Vistar Int'l — *Video Associates*

Peter and ther Wolf and   1984
Other Tales
Fairy tales
86364   82 mins   C   B, V   P
A collection of live action stories using dance,
music and poetry in "Jabberwocky," "The Ugly
Duckling" and the title story.
Unknown — *Children's Video Library*

Peter Cottontail's   1978
Adventures
Cartoons
53141   70 mins   C   B, V   P
Animated
Peter loves to play practical jokes until no one
wants to be his friend anymore, teaching him
the importance of his Green Forest friends,
Johnny and Polly Woodchuck, Jimmy Skunk,
Chatterer Chipmunk, Reddy and Granny Fox,
and Sammy Bluejay.
Ziv Intl — *Family Home Entertainment*

Peter Grimes   1981
Opera
59874   90 mins   C   B, V   P
Jon Vickers
The Royal Opera's production of Benjamin
Britten's three-act opera set in a small English
fishing town and concerning the inquest into the
death of Grime's apprentice. In stereo.
Covent Garden Video — *THORN EMI/HBO
Video; Pioneer Artists*

Peter Lundy and the Medicine Hat Stallion 1977

Adventure/Western
80706   85 mins   C   B, V   P
Leif Garrett, Mitchell Ryan, Bibi Besch, John Quade, Milo O'Shea
A teenaged Pony Express rider must outrun the Indians and battle the elements in order to carry mail from the Nebraska Territory to the West Coast.
Ed Friendly Prods. — *Vestron Video*

Peter Martins: A Dancer 197?

Dance
87354   90 mins   C   B, V   P
A look at the great dancer's career and exercises in discipline, featuring pas de deux with Suzanne Farrell, Heather Watts and Daniel Duell.
Unknown — *Kultur*

Peter-No-Tail 1983

Fantasy/Cartoons
69537   82 mins   C   B, V, CED   P
Animated, voices of Ken Berry, Dom DeLuise, Richard Kline, Tina Louise, Larry Storch, June Lockhart
A tail-less kitten wins the Cats Mastership and the heart of Molly Cream-Nose.
Stig Lasseby — *Children's Video Library*

Peter Tosh Live in Africa 1984

Music-Performance
84489   55 mins   C   B, V   P
The premier Reggae artist performs live in Africa.
EMI Records Inc — *Sony Video Software*

Pete's Dragon 1977

Fantasy/Adventure
Closed Captioned
44300   128 mins   C   B, V   P
Helen Reddy, Shelley Winters, Mickey Rooney, Jim Dale, Red Buttons, Sean Marshall
Elliot, an enormous, bumbling dragon, with a penchant for clumsy heroics, becomes friends with the poor orphan Pete. "Pete's Dragon" combines brilliant animation with the talents of live actors in this partially animated film.
MPAA:G EL, SP
Walt Disney — *Walt Disney Home Video*

Petit Con 1984

Comedy
87262   90 mins   C   B, V   P
Guy Marchand, Michel Choupon, Caroline Cellier, Bernard Brieux, Souad Amidou, directed by Gerard Lauzier
A live-action version of the popular French comic strip wherein a young rebel drops out of society to live with aging hippies. With English subtitles.
MPAA:R FR

Gaumont International/Marcel Dassault Prod. — *Karl/Lorimar Home Video*

Petite Bande, La 1984

Comedy/Adventure
84608   91 mins   C   B, V   P
Directed by Michel Deville
A gang of children escape home and journey to France, encountering Bedouins, Bavarians, circus performers, etc.
MPAA:PG
Franz Damamme — *RCA/Columbia Pictures Home Video*

Petrified Forest, The 1936

Drama
64330   83 mins   B/W   B, V   P
Bette Davis, Leslie Howard, Humphrey Bogart, Dick Foran, directed by Archie Mayo
Customers and employees at a diner in the Arizona desert are held captive by a group of thugs. Based on the play by Robert Sherwood.
Warner Bros — *Key Video; RCA VideoDiscs*

Phantasm 1977

Horror
44980   90 mins   C   B, V, LV, CED   P
Michael Baldwin, Bill Thornberry, Reggie Bannister, Kathy Lester
Two brothers discover the startling secret of the living dead when their friend is murdered.
MPAA:R
Avco Embassy — *Embassy Home Entertainment; RCA VideoDiscs*

Phantasm 1979

Horror
80390   90 mins   C   B, V   P
Michael Baldwin, Bill Thornbury, Kathy Lester
When two brothers try to find out who murdered their friend, it takes them to a mysterious house where some strange events occur.
MPAA:R
D. A. Coscarelli — *Embassy Home Entertainment*

Phantom Creeps 1939

Mystery/Serials
14263   156 mins   B/W   B, V   P
Bela Lugosi, Dorothy Arnold, Robert Kent, Regis Toomey
Spine-tingling mystery by a master monster. Serial in 12 chapters, 13 minutes each.
Universal — *Video Connection; Cable Films; Discount Video Tapes; Kartes Video Communications*

Phantom Empire 1935

Western/Serials
38986   245 mins   B/W   B, V, FO   P

Gene Autry, Frankie Darro, Betsy King Ross, Smiley Burnette
Gene faces the futuristic "Thunder Riders" from the subterranean city of Murania, which is located 20,000 feet beneath his ranch. A complete serial in twelve episodes.
Mascot — *Video Yesteryear; Video Connection; Nostalgia Merchant; Discount Video Tapes*

Phantom Empire, The   1984
Music video
72928   60 mins   C   B, V   P
Phantom Empire
The first of fifteen episodes of a rock video/cliffhanger serial inspired by the comics and pulps of the '40s.
Michael Uslan — *RCA/Columbia Pictures Home Video*

Phantom Express   1932
Mystery
08616   65 mins   B/W   B, V   P
J. Farrell Mac Donald, Sally Blane, William Collier Jr., Hobart Bosworth
Experienced old engineer is dismissed from his job because his explanation that a mysterious train caused the wreck of his own train is not believed.
Majestic — *Kartes Video Communications; Interurban Films; Discount Video Tapes*

Phantom of the Opera   1925
Horror
10628   85 mins   B/W   B, V   P, T
Lon Chaney Sr., Norman Kerry, Mary Philbin
An unknown entity terrorizes a Paris opera house. Silent with two-color Technicolor "Bal Masque" sequence.
Universal — *Blackhawk Films; Kartes Video Communications; Video Yesteryear; Cable Films; Video Connection; Hollywood Home Theater; Western Film & Video Inc; Discount Video Tapes; Cinema Concepts*

Phantom of the Paradise   1974
Horror/Comedy
82342   92 mins   C   B, V   P
Paul Williams, William Finley, Jessica Harper, Gerrit Graham, directed by Brian De Palma
There's plenty of surprises in store for a notorious record tycoon who sells his soul to the devil for a chance at being a rock superstar.
Available in VHS and Beta Hi-Fi Stereo.
MPAA:PG
20th Century Fox — *Key Video*

Phantom of the West   1931
Western
57366   166 mins   B/W   B, V, FO   P
Tom Tyler

Ten-episode serial about a rancher who becomes "The Phantom of the West," in order to smoke out his father's killer.
Mascot — *Video Yesteryear; Video Connection; Discount Video Tapes*

Phantom Rancher, The   1939
Western
15484   61 mins   B/W   B, V   P
Ken Maynard
This roaring melodrama finds Maynard donning a mask to find the real Phantom who is causing havoc.
Nat Saland — *United Home Video; Video Connection*

Phantom Ship   1937
Horror
81742   61 mins   B/W   B, V   P
Bela Lugosi, Shirley Grey
This is the true story of the "Marie Celeste," a ship found in 1872 off the coast of Africa with her sails set but with no passengers on board.
Guaranteed Pictures — *Kartes Video Communications*

Phantom Tollbooth, The   1969
Adventure/Cartoons
63111   89 mins   C   B, V   P
Animated, directed by Chuck Jones
A young boy drives his car into a strange and enchanting fantasy land.
MPAA:G
MGM — *MGM/UA Home Video*

Phantom Treehouse, The   1984
Fantasy
85876   76 mins   C   B, V   P
An animated children's tale of two kids plunging into a fantasy world through a mysterious swamp-based treehouse.
Unknown — *VidAmerica*

Phar Lap   1984
Adventure
Closed Captioned
80747   107 mins   C   B, V   P
Ron Leibman, Tom Burlinson, Judy Morris, Celia De Burgh
This is the true story of how the horse Phar Lap rose from nowhere to win thirty-seven races within three years during the 1930's. Available in VHS and Beta Hi-Fi.
MPAA:PG
20th Century Fox — *Playhouse Video*

Pharmacist, The   1932
Comedy
62868   19 mins   B/W   B, V   P, T
W.C. Fields, Grady Sutton

A typical day of frustration for druggist Fields, with grouchy customers and a robbery stick-up to top things off.
Mack Sennett — *Blackhawk Films*

Phase IV　　　　　　　　　1974
Science fiction
66033　83 mins　C　　B, V　　　　P
Nigel Davenport, Michael Murphy, Lynne Frederick
A tale of killer ants retaliating against the humans attempting their extermination.
MPAA:PG
Paramount — *Paramount Home Video*

Phedre　　　　　　　　　　1968
Drama
63617　93 mins　C　　B, V, FO　　P
Marie Bell
Jean Racine's adaptation of the Greek legend involving Phedre, Theseus and Hippolyte is presented in French with English subtitles.
FR
French — *Video Yesteryear*

Phenomenal and the　　　　1977
Treasure of Tutankamen
Adventure
77395　90 mins　C　　B, V　　　　P
The super hero Phenomenal and a clever thief race against time and each other to claim ownership of the Mask of Tutankamen.
MPAA:R
N.P. Films Ltda. — *Wizard Video*

Phil Collins　　　　　　　　1983
Music-Performance
75910　17 mins　C　　B, V　　　　P
This program presents Phil Collins singing his hit songs "In the Air Tonight," "Through These Walls" and others.
Philip Collins; Hit and Run Music — *Sony Video Software*

Phil Collins Live at　　　　1984
Perkins Palace
Music-Performance
72181　60 mins　C　　B, V　　　　P
The singer from Genesis performs many of the recent hits that have made him popular with audiences around the world.
DIR Broadcasting Inc — *THORN EMI/HBO Video*

Philadelphia Experiment,　　1984
The
Science fiction
79219　101 mins　C　　B, V　　　P
Michael Pare, Nancy Allen, Eric Christmas, Robby DiCicco, directed by Stewart Raffill
While experimenting with a radar-cloaking device, World War II scientists open a time warp. A pair of 1943 sailors participating in the event find themselves in 1984.
MPAA:PG
New World Pictures; John Carpenter & Douglas Curtis — *THORN EMI/HBO Video*

Philadelphia Phillies:　　　1984
Team Highlights
Baseball
81149　30 mins　C　　B, V　　　　P
Pete Rose, Steve Carlton, Mike Schmidt, Joe Morgan, Juan Samuel, Glen Wilson
This series chronicles the one-hundred-year history of the Phillies along with selected highlights from past seasons.
1.Centennial: The First 100 Years 2.1980: The Team That Wouldn't Die 3.1981: Take It From the Top 4.1982: Rolling the Dice 5. 1983: Wheeze Did It 6.1984: Follow Us.
Major League Baseball — *Major League Baseball Productions*

Philadelphia Story, The　　1940
Comedy
47053　112 mins　B/W　B, V　　　P
Katherine Hepburn, Cary Grant, James Stewart, Ruth Hussey, Roland Young, directed by George Cukor
A strong-willed Philadelphia girl finds the plans for her second marriage going awry when her first husband turns up. Based on the play by Philip Barry.
Academy Awards '40: Best Actor (Stewart); Best Screenplay (Donald Ogden Stewart).
MGM; Joseph L Mankiewicz — *MGM/UA Home Video*

Philby, Burgess and　　　1984
MacLean: Spy Scandal of
the Century
Biographical
86630　83 mins　C　　B, V　　　　P
Derek Jacobi, Anthony Bate, Michael Culver
The true story of the three infamous British officials who defected to the Soviet Union in 1951, after stealing some vital British secrets for the KGB.
British — *Simon and Schuster Video*

Philco TV Playhouse:　　　1953
"Ernie Barger Is 50"
Drama
47485　60 mins　B/W　B, V, FO　　P
Ed Begley, Carmen Matthews, Howard St. John, directed by Delbert Mann
A live TV drama written by Tad Mosel. Ernie Barger is a middle class manufacturer who discovers that life has passed him by and no one needs him anymore.
NBC — *Video Yesteryear*

Physically Fit Level 1   1986
Physical fitness
85704   30 mins   C   B, V   P
Paula Pennypacker
A medically designed exercise program,
complete with diet advice and illustrative
booklet.
AM Available
PAE Corp. — *PAE Corporation*

Piaf   1981
Musical-Drama/Biographical
58703   115 mins   C   CED   P
Jane Lapotaire
Jane Lapotaire portrays the legendary French
singer Edith Piaf in this Broadway performance
which won her a Tony Award for Best Actress.
MGM; CBS — *CBS/Fox Video*

Piaf, the Woman   1981
Music/France
58591   28 mins   B/W   B, V   P
Edith Piaf, Marlene Dietrich, Theo Sarapo
A tribute to the legendary French singer which
conveys, both visually and aurally, the essence
of her performing art. The original film was
produced in 1968.
Theodora Olembert — *Compton International
Corp*

Picasso: The Work   1984
Painting
84639   90 mins   C   B, V   P
Directed by Edward Quinn 2 pgms
A quasi-documentary of Picasso's career
through his work.
1.1881-1937 2.1938-1973
Edward Quinn — *V.I.E.W. Video*

Pick-Up Summer   1979
Comedy
84122   99 mins   C   B, V   P
Michael Zelniker, Carl Marotte
Two suburban boys cruise their town after
school lets out, chasing a pair of voluptuous
sisters.
New World Pictures — *New World Video*

Pickwick Papers   1985
Cartoons
82463   72 mins   C   B, V   P
Animated
The Charles Dickens classic retold in animation;
Samuel Pickwick, Augustus Snodgrass, Tracy
Tupmon, and Nathaniel Winkle travel to remote
places researching the quainter aspects of life.
MPAA:G
Burbank Films — *Children's Video Library*

Pickwick Papers, The   1954
Comedy
84851   109 mins   B/W   B, V   P

*James Hayter, James Donald, Nigel Patrick,
Hermione Gingold, Hermione Baddeley,
Kathleen Harrison, directed by Noel Langley*
An adaptation of the Dickens classic wherein
Mrs. Bardell sues the Pickwick Club for breach
of promise.
Kingsley Int'l. — *United Home Video*

Picture Music   1981
Music-Performance
65377   60 mins   C   B, V   P
A compilation of 14 of the hottest music videos,
including top-ten hits by Kim Carnes, America,
Steve Miller, J. Geils Band, Billy Squier and
Thomas Dolby.
EMI Music — *Vestron Video; Pioneer Video
Imports*

Picture of Dorian Gray,   1945
The
Drama
80857   111 mins   B/W   B, V   P
*Hurd Hatfield, George Sanders, Donna Reed,
Angela Lansbury, Peter Lawford, Lowell Gilmore*
An adaptation of the Oscar Wilde novel about a
man who stays eternally young while his portrait
ages through the years.
Academy Awards '45: Best Cinematography
MGM; Pandro S. Berman — *MGM/UA Home
Video*

Picture of Dorian Gray,   1974
The
Drama
82102   130 mins   C   B, V   P
*Nigel Davenport, Charles Aidman, Fionnuala
Flanagan, Linda Kelsey, directed by Glenn
Jordan*
This is an adaptation of the Oscar Wilde novel
about a man who remains eternally young with
horrifying results. Available in VHS Stereo and
Beta Hi-Fi.
Dan Curtis Productions — *Thriller Video*

Piece of the Action, A   1977
Comedy
80956   135 mins   C   B, V   P
*Sidney Poitier, Bill Cosby, James Earl Jones,
Denise Nicholas, Hope Clarke, directed by
Sidney Poitier*
An ex-cop beats two con men at their own game
when he convinces them to work for a Chicago
community center. Music by Curtis Mayfield.
MPAA:PG
Warner Bros., First Artists
Productions — *Warner Home Video*

Pieces   1983
Horror
65606   90 mins   C   B, V   P
Christopher George

A chain-saw wielding madman roams a college campus in search of human parts for a ghastly jigsaw puzzle.
MPAA:R
Spectacular Trading — *Vestron Video*

Pied Piper, The/Cinderella 1981
Fairy tales
59706   70 mins   C   B, V   P
Animated
A puppet animation version of the two classic fairy tales.
Mark Hall; Brian Cosgrove — *THORN EMI/HBO Video*

Pied Piper of Hamelin, The 1957
Fairy tales
65291   90 mins   C   B, V   P
Van Johnson, Claude Raines, Jim Backus, Kay Starr, Lori Nelson
This is the evergreen classic of the magical piper who claims an entire village and then disappears with the village children into a mountain when the townspeople fail to keep a promise.
Hal Stanley Productions Unlimited — *Media Home Entertainment*

Pied Piper of Hamelin, The 1984
Fairy tales
Closed Captioned
73573   60 mins   C   B, V, CED   P
Eric Idle
From "Faerie Tale Theatre" comes the story of a man who had a way with a magic flute and how it charmed the rats out of Hamelin.
Gaylord Productions; Platypus Productions — *CBS/Fox Video*

Pillow Talk 1959
Comedy-Drama
69032   102 mins   C   B, V   P
Rock Hudson, Doris Day, Tony Randall, Thelma Ritter
An interior decorator and a songwriter and notorious playboy share a party line telephone, but no other interests. In the process of disliking each other, they fall in love.
Universal International — *MCA Home Video*

Pimpernel Smith 1942
Drama
66392   121 mins   B/W   B, V   P
Leslie Howard, Mary Morris, Francis L. Sullivan, David Tomlinson
An absent-minded archeology professor travels into war-torn Europe to rescue refugees. Also titled: "Mr. V."

British National — *Movie Buff Video; Video Yesteryear*

Pinchcliffe Grand Prix, The 1981
Comedy
59993   88 mins   C   B, V   R, P
Animated
A master inventor designs the ultimate race car.
MPAA:G
Caprino Film Centre — *Video Gems*

Pink-A-Boo 1985
Cartoons
80861   56 mins   C   B, V   P
Animated
The rascally Pink Panther returns in this collection of nine classic cartoons.
Mirisch Geoffrey Productions — *MGM/UA Home Video*

Pink Angels, The 1971
Comedy/Satire
71195   81 mins   C   B, V   P
Transvestite bikers wheel their way to Los Angeles, turning many heads as they go.
MPAA:R
Independent — *Prism*

Pink at First Sight 1984
Cartoons
80361   49 mins   C   B, V   P
Animated
The Pink Panther returns in a new collection of his funniest adventures.
Mirisch Geoffrey Productions — *MGM/UA Home Video*

Pink Flamingos 1973
Satire
64844   95 mins   C   B, V   P
Divine, David Lochary, Mink Stole, Edith Massey, directed by John Waters
Divine, the dainty 300-pound transvestite, faces the biggest challenge of his/her career when he/she competes for the title of World's Filthiest Person.
MPAA:R
Saliva Films — *HarmonyVision*

Pink Floyd at Pompeii 1974
Music-Performance
59079   90 mins   C   B, V   P
Directed by Adrian Maben
The British rock group performs some of its most famous songs in this concert set at a ruined amphitheatre in Pompeii. Songs include "Echoes I & II," "Dark Side of the Moon," and "A Saucerful of Secrets." In stereo.
MPAA:G

April Fools — *HarmonyVision; RCA VideoDiscs; Vestron Video*

Pink Floyd The Wall   1982
Musical-Drama
65221   95 mins   C   B, V   P
Bob Geldof, directed by Alan Parker
Film version of Pink Floyd's 1979 LP, "The Wall." A surreal, impressionistic tour-de-force about a boy who grows up numb from society's pressures.
MPAA:R
MGM — *MGM/UA Home Video*

Pink Floyd's David Gilmour   1984
Music video
72896   101 mins   C   B, V   P
David Gilmour, Pete Townshend
This program contains the videos "After the Floyd," "Blue Light" and "All Lovers Are Deranged."
Pink Floyd — *CBS/Fox Video*

Pink Motel   1982
Comedy
69394   90 mins   C   B, V   P
Phyllis Diller, Slim Pickens
This is the story of several people and one hilarious night at a pink stucco motel which caters to couples.
MPAA:R
New Image; Wescom Productions — *THORN EMI/HBO Video*

Pink Panther, The   1964
Comedy
55587   113 mins   C   B, V, LV   P
Peter Sellers, David Niven, Robert Wagner, Claudia Cardinale
A priceless gem is sought by a wanted jewel thief whose accomplice is the wife of a French police inspector.
United Artists — *CBS/Fox Video; RCA VideoDiscs*

Pink Panther Strikes Again, The   1976
Comedy
59628   103 mins   C   B, V, LV   P
Peter Sellers, Herbert Lom, Lesley-Anne Down, Colin Blakely, Leonard Rossiter, directed by Blake Edwards
The fourth Panther film has Clouseau being hunted by Chief Inspector Dreyfus, who plans to rid the world of Clouseau once and for all.
MPAA:PG
United Artists — *CBS/Fox Video; RCA VideoDiscs*

Pinocchio   1976
Musical
06061   76 mins   C   B, V   P
Danny Kaye, Sandy Duncan
Classical story of Pinocchio in musical form.
Rothman and Wahl; Vidronics Company — *United Home Video*

Pinocchio   1968
Fairy tales
47675   74 mins   C   B, V   P
Collodi's classic tale of the little puppet boy and his adventures in becoming a real boy. Live action actors are combined with puppets from the Prague Marionette Theater.
Ron Merk — *Unicorn Video*

Pinocchio   1978
Fantasy
56923   90 mins   C   B, V   R, P
Animated
Another version of the classic story about a puppet who becomes a boy. This film adapted from the original 1882 manuscript.
GG Communications — *Video Gems*

Pinocchio   1984
Fairy tales
Closed Captioned
73146   60 mins   C   B, V, CED   P
Pee Wee Herman, James Coburn, Carl Reiner, Lainie Kazan
Pee Wee Herman is the puppet who wants to be a real little boy in this "Faerie Tale Theatre" adaptation of this childrens classic.
Shelley Duvall — *CBS/Fox Video*

Pinocchio   1940
Cartoons
Closed Captioned
81645   87 mins   C   B, V, LV, CED   P
Animated, voices of Dick Jones, Cliff Edwards, Evelyn Venable
Here is an example of animation at its best in this story of a little wooden puppet who must prove himself worthy of becoming a real boy. Academy Awards '40: Best Original Score; Best Song "When You Wish Upon A Star." MPAA:G
Walt Disney Productions — *Walt Disney Home Video*

Pinocchio in Outer Space   1964
Cartoons/Fantasy
47436   71 mins   C   B, V   P
Voices of Arnold Stang, Minerva Pious, Peter Lazer, Conrad Jameson
A new adventure featuring Pinocchio and his friends on a magical trip to Mars.
SFM Entertainment — *RCA/Columbia Pictures Home Video*

Pinocchio's Storybook Adventures — 1979
Fairy tales
81688   80 mins   C   B, V   P
Pinocchio takes over for an ailing puppet master and puts on a show for a group of children.
First American Films — *United Home Video*

Pinwheel Songbook, The — 1981
Variety
47383   57 mins   C   B, V   P
Dale Engle, George James, Jim Jinkins, Arline Miyazaki, Betty Rozek
Entertainment for preschoolers, featuring songs, stories and characters from the award-winning TV series, "Pinwheel."
Warner Amex Satellite Entertainment Company — *Warner Home Video*

Pioneer Cinema (1895-1905) — 19??
Film-History
63851   25 mins   B/W   B, V   P
A compilation of some early film works, including a Lumiere program from 1895, Melies' "Trip to the Moon," and "El Spectro Rojo," a color short.
George Melies et al — *Hollywood Home Theater*

Pioneer Woman — 1973
Western/Adventure
77151   74 mins   C   B, V   P
Joanna Pettet, William Shatner, David Janssen, directed by Buzz Kulik
A family encounters hostility when they set up a frontier homestead in Nebraska in 1867.
Filmways — *Worldvision Home Video*

Pipe Dreams — 1976
Drama
71246   89 mins   C   B, V   P
Gladys Knight, Barry Hankerson, Bruce French, Sherry Bain, directed by Stephen Verona
A couple tries to repair their broken marriage against the backdrop of the Alaskan pipeline's construction. The Pips join Gladys on the HiFi Mono soundtrack.
MPAA:PG
Avco Embassy — *Embassy Home Entertainment*

Pippi Goes on Board — 1975
Adventure
29347   83 mins   C   B, V   R, P
Inger Nilsson, directed by Olle Hellbom
Pippi's father arrives one day to take her sailing to Taka-Kuka, his island kingdom. She can't bear to leave her friends and jumps off the ship to return home. Based on the classic by Astrid Lindgren.
MPAA:G

N.W. Russo; GG Communications — *Video Gems*

Pippi in the South Seas — 1974
Adventure
29236   99 mins   C   B, V   R, P
Inger Nilsson, directed by Olle Hellbom
Pippi and her two friends decide to rescue her father, who is being held captive by a band of pirates. Based on the classic by Astrid Lindgren.
MPAA:G
N.W. Russo; GG Communications — *Video Gems*

Pippi Longstocking — 1973
Comedy
50961   99 mins   C   B, V   R, P
Inger Nillson
Mischievous Pippi creates havoc in her town through the antics of her pets, a monkey and a horse. Based on the children's book by Astrid Lindgren.
MPAA:G
N.W. Russo; GG Communications — *Video Gems*

Pippi on the Run — 1974
Adventure
58586   99 mins   C   B, V   R, P
The further adventures of Pippi, who, among other things, is "the strongest kid alive."
MPAA:G
N W Russo; GG Communications — *Video Gems*

Pippin — 1981
Musical
53134   120 mins   C   B, V   P
Ben Vereen, William Katt, Martha Raye, Chita Rivera
An original video production of Bob Fosse's Broadway smash featuring Ben Vereen recreating his original Tony-Award-winning role.
Sheehan Elkins Video Venture Ltd — *Family Home Entertainment; RCA VideoDiscs; Pioneer Artists*

Piranha — 1978
Horror
64300   90 mins   C   B, V   P
Bradford Dillman, Heather Menzies, Kevin McCarthy, Keenan Wynn
A rural Texas resort area is plagued by attacks from ferocious man-eating fish which a scientist created to be used as a secret weapon in the Vietnam War.
MPAA:R
New World Pictures — *Warner Home Video*

Piranha II: The Spawning — 1982
Horror
78355   88 mins   C   B, V, LV   P

A diving instructor and a biochemist seek to destroy mutations that are murdering tourists at a club.
MPAA:R
New World Pictures — *Embassy Home Entertainment*

Pirate, The   1948
Musical
58869   102 mins   C   B, V, CED   P
Judy Garland, Gene Kelly, Walter Slezak, Gladys Cooper, George Zucco, Reginald Owen, the Nicholas Brothers, directed by Vincente Minnelli
A lonely girl on a remote Caribbean isle dreams of her romantic hero, the legendary pirate Black Macoco. To woo her, a traveling actor masquerades as the pirate. Music by Cole Porter, including "Be a Clown," "Mack the Black" and "You Can Do No Wrong."
MGM; Arthur Freed — *MGM/UA Home Video*

Pirate Movie, The   1982
Musical
60424   98 mins   C   B, V, CED   P
Kristy McNichol, Christopher Atkins, Ted Hamilton
Gilbert and Sullivan's "The Pirates of Penzance" is combined with new pop songs in this tale of fantasy and romance.
MPAA:PG
Twentieth Century Fox — *CBS/Fox Video*

Pirate warrior   1964
Adventure
88321   86 mins   C   B, V   P
Ricardo Montalban, Vincent Price, Liana Orfei, directed by Morris Costa
A grade-B pirate flick about slavery and the evil Tortuga.
Liber Films — *Force Video*

Pirates of Penzance, The   1983
Musical/Comedy
64787   112 mins   C   B, V, LV   P
Kevin Kline, Angela Lansbury, Linda Ronstadt, Rex Smith, George Rose
This Gilbert and Sullivan musical comedy is the story of a band of fun-loving pirates and their young apprentice. An adaptation of the award-winning Broadway play. In stereo VHS and laser disc.
Universal — *MCA Home Video; CBS/Fox Video*

Pirates of the Coast, The   1961
Adventure
82280   102 mins   C   B, V   P
Lex Barker, Estella Blain, Livio Lorenzon, Liana Orfei
A Spanish naval commander teams up with a group of pirates to even the score with an evil governor during the 1500's.

Fortunato Misiano — *Unicorn Video*

Pirates of the Seven Seas   1962
Adventure
70781   90 mins   C   B, V   P
Steve Reeves, Jacqueline Sassard, Andrea Bosic
In the further tales of "Sandokan the Great," our pirate hero helps save our non-pirate heroine's dad from an evil English Imperialist.
Empire — *Force Video*

Pit, The   1981
Science fiction/Horror
65714   96 mins   C   B, V   P
Sammy Snyders
A 12-year-old autistic boy gets his change for revenge against the people in his town who humiliate him when he stumbles on a huge hole in the forest, at the bottom of which are strange and deadly creatures.
MPAA:R
Bennett Fode — *Embassy Home Entertainment*

Pit and the Pendulum,   1961
The
Horror
53519   80 mins   C   B, V   P
Vincent Price, John Kerr, Barbara Steele, Luana Anders, directed by Roger Corman
A woman and her lover plan to drive her brother mad, and he responds by locking them in his torture chamber. Loosely based on the Poe story.
American International; Roger Corman — *Warner Home Video; Vestron Video (disc only)*

Pittsburgh Steelers 1984   1985
Team Highlights
Football
70552   70 mins   C   B, V, FO   P
Surprise victories over the Broncos and Raiders made this year one of "A New Beginning" for the Steelmen. Forty-seven minutes of this tape offer a 1984 retrospective of the entire NFL.
NFL Films — *NFL Films Video*

Pittsburgh Steelers: The   1982
Championship Years
Football
63162   96 mins   C   B, V, FO   P
Pittsburgh Steelers
Highlights from the first four championship seasons of the 1970's team of the decade.
NFL Films — *NFL Films Video*

Pixote   1981
Drama
47432   127 mins   C   B, V   P

Fernando Ramos Da Silva, Marilla Pera, Jorge Juliao, directed by Hector Babenco
Pixote is a ten-year-old street kid in Sao Paolo, Brazil. When he is sent to a juvenile detention center, he and his companions become hardened to criminal life. In Portuguese with English subtitles.
PR
Embrafilms — *RCA/Columbia Pictures Home Video*

Place Called Today, A   1971
Drama
60416   105 mins   C   B, V   P
Lana Wood
A tale of big city politics where violence and fear in the streets is at the heart of the campaign.
Today Productions — *Monterey Home Video*

Place in Hell, A   1965
War-Drama
82089   106 mins   C   B, V   P
Guy Madison, Helen Chanel, Monty Greenwood
The Japanese armed forces camouflage a Pacific island beach which they are holding and invite the American forces to invade it during World War II.
Italian — *Unicorn Video*

Place in the Sun, A   1951
Drama
55542   122 mins   B/W   B, V, LV   P
Montgomery Cliff, Elizabeth Taylor, Shelley Winters, directed by George Stevens
A confused, ambitious factory worker in love with a wealthy debutante is threatened with a drab future by a simple working girl. Adapted from Theodore Dreiser's "An American Tragedy."
Academy Awards '51: Best Direction (Stevens); Best Screenplay (Michael Wilson, Harry Brown); Best Scoring (Franz Waxman).
Paramount; George Stevens — *Paramount Home Video; RCA VideoDiscs*

Places in the Heart   1984
Drama
Closed Captioned
80652   113 mins   C   B, V   P
Sally Field, John Malkovich, Danny Glover, Ed Harris, Lindsay Crouse, Amy Madigan, directed by Robert Benton
A young Texas widow and her extended family band together to raise a successful cotton crop in order to save her farm during the Depression. Available in VHS and Beta Hi-Fi.
Academy Awards '84: Best Actress (Field)?Best Original Screenplay (Benton) MPAA:PG
Tri-Star Pictures — *CBS/Fox Video*

Placido: A Year in the Life   1984
of Placido Domingo
Documentary/Music-Performance
84570   105 mins   C   B, V, 8mm,   P
                                              LV
Placido Domingo, Kiri Te Kanawa, Marilyn Zschau, Katia Ricciarelli
The film follows Domingo through his hectic training schedule, and includes excerpts from major operatic productions.
Westinghouse — *Kultur*

Plague Dogs, The   1985
Fantasy/Drama
84042   99 mins   C   B, V   P
Animated, directed by Martin Rossen
An animated film about two dogs who escape an animal research center, unknowingly carrying a plague. Written by Richard Adams, author of "Watership Down" and "Maia."
Martin Rosen — *Charter Entertainment*

Plan 9 from Outer Space   1956
Science fiction/Horror
09112   78 mins   B/W   B, V, 3/4U   P
Bela Lugosi, Tors Johnson, Lyle Talbot, Vampira
UFO's containing strange inhabitants from an unknown planet invade the earth. Includes previews of coming attractions from classic science fiction films.
Golden Turkey Awards for Worst Films of All Time: First Place.
DCA — *Nostalgia Merchant; Video Yesteryear; Admit One Video*

Planet of the Apes   1968
Science fiction
Closed Captioned
29164   112 mins   C   B, V   P
Charlton Heston, Roddy McDowall, Kim Hunter, directed by Franklin J. Schaffner
Four American astronauts are hurtled 2,000 years through time and space and crashland in the wilderness of a strange planet. They discover this world is dominated by apes.
MPAA:G EL, SP
20th Century Fox — *Playhouse Video*

Planet of the Vampires   1965
Science fiction
85898   86 mins   C   B, V   P
Barry Sullivan, Norman Bengell, Angel Aranda, Evi Marandi
A ship crashlands on a planet where bodiless creatures occupy the bodies of the stranded astronauts.
American Int'l — *THORN EMI/HBO Video*

Planet on the Prowl   1970
Science fiction
87321   80 mins   C   B, V   P

Jack Stuart, Amber Collins, John Bartha, James Weaver
A fiery planet causes earthly disasters, so a troup of wily astronauts try to destroy it with the latest technology. They fail, leading one sacrificial soul to do it himself.
Mercury Films Int'l. — *Monterey Home Video*

Plastic Man 1982
Cartoons
65662   56 mins   C   B, V   P
Animated
With his amazing ability to mold and stretch himself into any shape, Plastic Man stretches himself into new dimensions to play with Baby Plas.
Ruby Spears — *Worldvision Home Video*

Play It Again, Charlie Brown 1970
Cartoons
85620   25 mins   C   B, V   P
Created by Charles M. Schulz
The Peanuts gang goes bananas when Lucy enlists Schroeder to play rock music at a PTA meeting.
Lee Mendelson; Bill Melendez — *Snoopy's Home Video Library*

Play It Again, Sam 1972
Comedy
38591   85 mins   C   B, V, 8mm,   P
                            LV
Woody Allen, Diane Keaton, Tony Roberts, directed by Herbert Ross
Woody Allen's homage to "Casablanca," in which he plays a movie critic with the recurring hallucination of Humphrey Bogart offering him tips on how to make it with women. Bogart's advice comes in handy when Woody falls in love with his best friend's wife.
MPAA:PG
Paramount — *Paramount Home Video; RCA VideoDiscs*

Play Misty for Me 1971
Mystery/Drama
55551   102 mins   C   B, V, LV   P
Clint Eastwood, Jessica Walter, Donna Mills, directed by Clint Eastwood
A disc jockey meets up with a psychotic fan and she becomes emotionally involved with him. Conflicts arise between the disc jockey's girlfriend and the obsessed fan, who becomes dangerously violent.
MPAA:R
Universal; Jennings Lang Malpaso Co — *MCA Home Video*

Playbox 1 1982
Cartoons
85459   30 mins   C   B, V   P
Animated, introduction by Brian Rix

A compilation of children's programming, with leanings toward education as well as entertainment.
Various — *Family Home Entertainment*

Playboy Comedy Roast: Tommy Chong 1986
Comedy-Performance
87597   60 mins   C   B, V   P
Tommy Chong, David Steinberg, Richard Belzer, Slappy White
A gaggle of celebrities insult and abuse comedian Tommy Chong. For adult audiences.
Michael Trikilis Prod; Playboy Programs — *Karl/Lorimar Home Video*

Playboy Jazz Festival, Volume 2, The 1984
Music-Performance
78876   90 mins   C   B, V   P
Hosted by Bill Cosby
Some of the world's greatest jazz musicians from Dave Brubeck to Sarah Vaughn are gathered together in this concert taped at the Hollywood Bowl in California. In VHS Dolby Hi-Fi Stereo and Beta Hi-Fi Stereo.
Playboy Productions — *RCA/Columbia Pictures Home Video*

Playboy of the Western World, The 1962
Comedy
63319   96 mins   C   B, V   P
Siobhan McKenna, Gary Raymond, directed by Brian Desmond Hurst
An innkeeper's daughter is infatuated with an upstart young playboy. Adapted from the classic play by John Millington Synge.
4 Provinces Films Ltd — *THORN EMI/HBO Video*

Playboy Playmate Workout 1984
Physical fitness
73856   60 mins   C   B, V, LV,   P
                            CED
Two Playboy Playmates take you on a fitness session that combines a workout with fantasies.
Playboy Productions — *CBS/Fox Video*

Playboy Video Centerfold 1985
Variety
71058   25 mins   C   B, V   P
The Playboy Playmates
Each volume in this series spotlights a Playboy Playmate, most of whom are highly accomplished actresses, internationally recognized models and Novel laureates. Also featured are "Playmate Updates," glimpses into the current lives of former Playmates, which divulge to viewers the present occupations of their old favorites.

Playboy Enterprises — *Karl/Lorimar Home Video*

Playboy Video Magazine, Volumes 1-7   1982
Variety
63390   85 mins   C   B, V   P
This series features in-depth looks at Playboy's former Playmates of the year along with varied comedy line-ups and celebrity interviews.
Playboy Enterprises — *CBS/Fox Video*

Playboy Video Magazine, Volumes 8-9   1985
Variety
71057   85 mins   C   B, V   P
The Playboy Playmates, Grace Jones, Madonna, Milton Berle
This titillating series continues with more steamy segments featuring Playmates at their most endearing, in locales ranging from bathtubs to the great outdoors. Celebrity profiles include Madonna and Barbi Benton.
AM Available
Playboy Enterprises — *Karl/Lorimar Home Video*

Players   1979
Drama
44594   120 mins   C   B, V   P
Ali MacGraw, Dean-Paul Martin, Maximillian Schell, Pancho Gonzales, directed by Anthony Harvey
A young tennis hustler touring Mexico hooks up with a beautiful mysterious older woman. They seem to be from different worlds yet their love grows. She inspires him enough to enter Wimbledon. Several tennis pros appear, including Guillermo Vilas, John McEnroe, and Ilie Nastase.
MPAA:PG
Paramount, Robert Evans — *Paramount Home Video*

Playful Little Audrey   1961
Cartoons
86367   60 mins   C   B, V   P
A compilation of the Little Audrey cartoons, featuring the mischievous miss and her wacky cartoon friends.
Harvey Films Inc. — *Worldvision Home Video*

Playgirl Killer   1966
Crime-Drama
88183   86 mins   C   B, V   P
William Kerwin, Jean Christopher, Andree Champagne, Neil Sedaka
After impulsively murdering his restless model, an artist continues to kill indiscriminantly. For adult viewers.
Unknown — *New World Video*

Playgirl Morning Workout   1985
Physical fitness
70742   60 mins   C   V   P
Steve Rally, Jim Bolden
Hunky male centerfolds offer tips for developing strength, flexibility, muscle tone, and cardiovascular fitness in this exercise program.
Ritter/Geller Communications; Prism Entertainment — *Prism*

Playgirl on the Air   1985
Variety
77382   60 mins   C   B, V   P
Mark Harmon
Each volume in this series expands on some of the topics covered in the popular women's magazine, "Playgirl." Commonly, each tape includes a star interview, a feature on health and hygiene, plus videography of handsome, unclad men.
Ira Ritter; Oak Media Corp. — *U.S.A. Home Video*

Playgirl's Sexual Secrets   1985
Sexuality
71127   57 mins   C   B, V   P
Bryce Britton, Rona Lee Cohen
Noted specialists in their field offer information to viewers on sexual matters.
Playgirl Magazine — *Vestron Video*

Playhouse 90   1957
Drama
80753   83 mins   B/W   B, V   P
Mickey Rooney, Mel Torme, Kim Hunter, Edmond O'Brien, directed by John Frankenheimer
This episode features a performance of Rod Serling's "The Comedian" which tells the story of a popular TV comedian who makes life miserable for his entourage as the rest of the country laughs at his jokes.
CBS — *Video Yesteryear*

Playhouse 90   1958
Drama
85207   85 mins   B/W   B, V   P
Robert Cummings, Martin Balsam, Rip Torn, Pat O'Malley, directed by John Frankenheimer
A live television performance of Rod Serling's "Bomber's Moon."
CBS — *Video Yesteryear*

Playing for Time   1980
Drama
82220   148 mins   C   B, V   P
Vanessa Redgrave, Jane Alexander, Maud Adams, Verna Bloom, Melanie Mayron, directed by Daniel Mann
This is the true story of a group of female prisoners at Auschwitz who play in an orchestra in order to avoid being sent to the gas chamber.

Emmy Awards '80: Outstanding Drama Special;
Outstanding Lead Actress in a Limited Special
(Alexander); Outstanding Writing in a Limited
Special (Arthur Miller).
Syzygy Prods Ltd — VCL Home Video

An early dramatic TV appearance by Paul
Newman, as a young drifter who meets an
interesting cross-section of people while
hitchhiking around the country. Based on a story
by Ernest Hemingway.
NBC — Video Yesteryear

Playmate Playoffs   1986
Variety
84707   75 mins   C   B, V   P
Kimberly Evenson, Kymberly Herrin, Hope
Carlton, Kimberly McArthur
The gloves come off in this grueling competition
between Playmates through mud, tires and
water.
Hugh Hefner — Karl/Lorimar Home Video

Playmate Review   1983
Variety
66072   90 mins   C   B, V, LV,   P
           CED
Ten playmates from Playboy magazine,
including 1982 Playmate of the Year Shannon
Tweed, are featured in this candid pictorial.
Playboy Enterprises — CBS/Fox Video

Playmate Review #3   1985
Variety
Closed Captioned
77467   59 mins   C   B, V, LV   P
This candid pictorial revue invites you to get up
close and personal with six of Playboy's
beautiful playmates including Barbara Edwards
the 1984 Playmate of the Year.
Playboy Enterprises — CBS/Fox Video

Playmates   1974
Comedy
87607   78 mins   C   B, V   P
Doug McClure, Alan Alda, Connie Stevens,
Barbara Feldon
Two divorced buddies fall in love with each
other's ex-wives, and generally create comedic
confusion and havoc. Made for TV.
Lillian Gallo — Vidmark Entertainment

Playtime   1967
Comedy
76793   108 mins   C   B, V   P
Jacques Tati, Barbara Dennek, Jacqueline
Lecomte, Jack Gautier, directed by Jarques Tati
Mr. Hulot is having a little difficulty keeping an
appointment as everything and everybody gets
in his way. With English subtitles.
FR
Specta Films — Embassy Home Entertainment

Playwrights '56: "The   1955
Battler"
Drama
47486   60 mins   B/W   B, V, FO   P
Paul Newman, Dewey Martin, Phyllis Kirk,
directed by Arthur Penn

Plaza Suite   1971
Comedy
65735   114 mins   C   B, V   P
Walter Matthau, Maureen Stapleton, Barbara
Harris, Lee Grant, Louise Sorel
Three sketches set in Suite 719 of New York
City's Plaza Hotel, based on the play by Neil
Simon.
MPAA:PG
Paramount — Paramount Home Video

Please Don't Hit Me, Mom   1982
Child abuse
Closed Captioned
68942   46 mins   C   B, V   P
Patty Duke Astin, Nancy McKeon, Lance Guest,
and Sean Astin
A young girl is torn between going to officials to
report child abuse or telling the mother that she
knows.
Virginia Carter — Embassy Home
Entertainment; The Program Source

Pleasure Palace   1980
Drama
80900   92 mins   C   B, V   P
Omar Sharif, Victoria Principal, J.D. Cannon,
Jose Ferrer, Hope Lange, Gerald O'Laughlin
A high rolling gambler plays a baccarat game for
the ownership of a Las Vegas hotel casino as
he vies for the affections of two beautiful
women. Available in VHS Stereo and Beta Hi-Fi.
Norman Rosemont Productions — U.S.A.
Home Video

Plenty   1985
Drama
84417   119 mins   C   B, V   P
Meryl Streep, Tracey Ullman, Sting, Sir John
Gielgud, Charles Dance, Ian McKellen, Sam
Neill, directed by Fred Schepsi
A story of female emancipation and sanity. A
woman who fought with the resistance in World
War II pines for the emotional charges of
wartime life in subsequent years.
MPAA:R
Mark Seiler — THORN EMI/HBO Video

Plisetskaya Dances   1964
Documentary/Dance
69834   70 mins   B/W   B, V   P
A look at the world famous dancer, Maya
Plisetskaya. This documentary chronicles a
career which has been little seen in the west,
offering some important insights into the Soviet
dance world. Narrated in English.

Sovexportfilm USSR — *Video Arts International*

Ploughman's Lunch, The   1983
Drama
81622   107 mins   C   B, V   P*
Jonathan Pryce, Charlie Dore, Tim Curry, Rosemary Harris, Frank Finlay, directed by Richard Eyre
A news reporter who claws and lies his way to the top discovers that he is the victim of a deception far more devious than he could plan himself.
Samuel Goldwyn; Goldcrest — *Embassy Home Entertainment*

Plow That Broke the   1937
Plains, The/The River
History-US/Documentary
52319   60 mins   B/W   B, V   P, T
Written and directed by Pare Lorentz
Two classic documentaries: "The Plow That Broke the Plains" deals with the New Deal efforts to improve the lot of Oklahoma "Dust Bowl" farmers. "The River" is a poetic history of the Mississippi River and its ecological balance.
US Information Service — *Blackhawk Films; Western Film & Video Inc; Discount Video Tapes*

Plumber, The   1979
Mystery/Suspense
80275   76 mins   C   B, V   P
Judy Morris, Ivar Karts, Robert Coleby, directed by Peter Weir
A plumber who makes a house call extends his stay to torture a highly educated upper class woman.
Matt Carroll — *Media Home Entertainment*

Pocketful of Miracles   1961
Comedy/Drama
70377   136 mins   C   B, V   P
Bette Davis, Glenn Ford, Peter Falk, Hope Lange, Arthur O'Connell, Ann-Margret, Thomas Mitchell, directed by Frank Capra
A poor, aging apple-seller wants her daughter to marry into a noble Spanish family. When the daughter returns from Spain with the family, the local riff-raff help Apple Annie to present herself as a woman of wealth and culture.
United Artists — *Key Video*

Poco   1977
Adventure
69531   88 mins   C   B, V, CED   P
Chill Wills, Michelle Asburn, John Steadman
A dog named Poco gets separated from the girl who owns her in Yosemite National Park, and Poco tries to find her way home.
MPAA:G
Cinema Shares — *Children's Video Library*

Poco   1977
Drama
81161   88 mins   C   B, V   P
Chill Wills, Michelle Ashburn, John Steadman
This is the story of Poco, a shaggy little dog who travels across the country to search for the young girl who owns him.
Cinema Shares International — *Vestron Video*

Pogo for President—"I   1984
Go Pogo"
Cartoons
70164   120 mins   C   B, V   P
Animated, voices of Jonathan Winters, Vincent Price, Ruth Buzzi, Stan Freberg, Jimmy Breslin
Walt Kelly's Pogo Possum becomes an unlikely presidential candidate when Howland Owl proclaims him the winner of a presidential election.
MPAA:PG
Walt Disney Productions — *Walt Disney Home Video*

Point, The   1971
Fantasy/Cartoons
84094   74 mins   C   B, V   P
Animated, directed by Fred Wolf, narrated by Ringo Starr
A made-for-TV animated feature of tailing the ostracization of a round-headed child from his world of pointy-headed people. Written and music performed by Harry Nilsson.
Nilsson House Music Murahkami Wolf Prod — *Vestron Video*

Point of Terror   1971
Drama
80659   88 mins   C   B, V   P
Peter Carpenter, Dyanne Thorne, Lory Hansen, Leslie Simms
A handsome rock singer seduces a record company executive's wife in order to further his career.
MPAA:R
Crown International Pictures — *United Home Video*

Pointer Sisters—So   1986
Excited, The
Music-Performance
84875   30 mins   C   B, V   P
The volatile Grammy winners perform their greatest hits.
RCA Video — *RCA/Columbia Pictures Home Video*

Police Academy   1984
Comedy
79555   96 mins   C   B, V, LV,   P
                              CED
Steve Guttenberg, Kim Cattrall, Bubba Smith, George Gaynes, directed by Hugh Wilson

Faced with an ultimatum from the mayor, the Los Angeles Police Department seeks to recruit minorities for the force. Also available with Spanish subtitles.
MPAA:R
The Ladd Company — *Warner Home Video*

Police Academy 2: Their First Assignment 1985
Comedy
Closed Captioned
81783   87 mins   C   B, V, LV   P
Steve Guttenberg, Bubba Smith, Michael Winslow, Art Metrano, Colleen Camp, directed by Jerry Paris
The Police Academy graduates uncover a plot to discredit the precinct's fair-minded captain while combatting a gang of spray-painters.
The Ladd Company — *Warner Home Video*

Police Around the World 1984
Music-Performance
84360   77 mins   C   B, V   P
The Police: Sting, Andy Summers, Stewart Copeland
This concert film of the Police's 1980-1981 tour features 16 songs, plus behind-the-scenes footage.
Miles Copland; Derek Burbige — *Rhino Video*

Police Squad! Help Wanted 1982
Comedy
80062   75 mins   C   B, V   P
Leslie Nielsen, Alan North, Rex Hamilton, Peter Lupus
A collection of the first three episodes of the satirical police series about a detective and his captain fighting crime in the big city.
Paramount Pictures — *Paramount Home Video*

Police Tapes, The 1976
Police/Crime and criminals
53222   73 mins   B/W   B, V   P
A cinema verite look at the nation's highest crime area, the South Bronx of New York City, and the cops who must patrol it. This documentary graphically portrays the variety of situations the police officer encounters.
Video Verite; Alan Raymond; Susan Raymond — *Lightning Video; MTI Teleprograms; Direct Cinema Limited*

Police—The Synchronicity Concert, The 1984
Music-Performance
78875   75 mins   C   B, V   P
Stewart Copeland, Andy Summers, Sting, directed by Godley and Creme
The new wave group The Police perform their big hits in this concert taped from their

"Synchronicity" tour. In VHS Dolby Stereo and Beta Hi-Fi.
A&M Records/I.R.S. Video Corp — *A & M Video; RCA/Columbia Pictures Home Video*

Policewoman Centerfold 1983
Drama
71337   96 mins   C   B, V   P
Melody Anderson, Ed Marinaro, Greg Monaghan, Donna Pescow, Bert Remsen, David Spielberg, Michael LeClair, David Haskell, Jerry Supivan, directed by Reza Badiyi
After posing nude for an adult magazine, a female police officer faces some difficult times at the precinct house.
Moonlight Productions II — *U.S.A. Home Video*

Policewomen 1973
Crime-Drama
64295   99 mins   C   B, V   P
Sondra Currie, Tony Young, Phil Hoover, Elizabeth Stuart, Jeanie Bell
A female undercover agent must stop a ring of gold smugglers.
MPAA:R
Crown International Pictures — *VidAmerica*

Polish Chamber Orchestra, Conducted by Jerzy Maksymiuk 198?
Music-Performance
87348   60 mins   C   B, V   P
The entitled orchestra perform Mozart's "Eine Kleine Nachtmusik, Divertimento K136" and Haydn's "Symphony No. 45."
Polish Chamber Orchestra — *Kultur*

Pollyanna 1960
Comedy-Drama
59062   134 mins   C   B, V, LV,   P
                                    CED
Hayley Mills, Jane Wyman, Richard Egan, Karl Malden, Nancy Olsen, Adolphe Menjou, Donald Crisp, Agnes Moorehead, Kevin Corcoran
A penniless American orphan comes to live with her aunt in the small town of Harrington, gradually changing the hearts of the entire community.
Academy Awards '60: Honorary Award for the most outstanding Juvenile Performance (Hayley Mills). EL, SP
Walt Disney — *Walt Disney Home Video*

Pollyanna 1920
Comedy-Drama
66304   60 mins   B/W   B, V   P, T
Mary Pickford
A young orphan girl is adopted by her cold, embittered aunt and does her best to bring joy and gladness to all the new people she meets. Silent with music score.
Mary Pickford Company — *Blackhawk Films*

Poltergeist 1982

Horror
47780   114 mins   C   B, V, CED   P
*Jobeth Williams, Craig T. Nelson, Beatrice
Straight, Heather O'Rourke, Zelda Rubinstein,
directed by Tobe Hooper*
The presence of menacing spirits terrorizes a
middle-class family, transporting the youngest
member into a "world beyond."
MPAA:R
MGM; United Artists — *MGM/UA Home Video*

Polyester 1981

Satire
81831   86 mins   C   B, V   P
*Divine, Tab Hunter, Edith Massey, Mink Stole,
Stiv Bators, directed by John Waters*
A forlorn housewife pines away for the man of
her dreams while the rest of her life is falling
apart at the seams.
MPAA:R
New Line Cinema — *THORN EMI/HBO Video*

Pom-Pom Girls, The 1976

Comedy
48481   90 mins   C   B, V   P
Robert Carradine, Jennifer Ashley
High school seniors, intent on having one last
fling before graduating, get involved in crazy
antics, clumsy romances, and football rivalries.
MPAA:R
Crown International — *United Home Video*

Pony Express 1953

Western
85261   101 mins   C   B, V   P
*Charlton Heston, Rhonda Fleming, Jan Sterling,
Forrest Tucker*
Buffalo Bill and Bill Hickok join forces to
establish the coast-to-coast mail route.
Paramount — *Kartes Video Communications*

Poochie 1984

Cartoons
80976   30 mins   C   B, V   P
Animated
Poochie is the pink pup with a heart of gold who
travels to Cairo with his micro-chip sidekick
Hermes to answer a young boy's distress call.
DIC Enterprises — *Children's Video Library*

Poor Little Rich Girl, The 1917

Comedy-Drama
66118   64 mins   B/W   B, V   P, T
Mary Pickford
Mary Pickford received raves in this film, in
which she portrayed Gwendolyn, one of her
most tender child performances. Organ score.
Adolph Zukor — *Blackhawk Films*

Poor White Trash II 1975

Drama
81753   90 mins   C   B, V   P
Gene Ross, Ann Stafford, Norma Moore
A young couple, vacationing in Louisiana's
bayou country, are introduced to an unusual
brand of southern hospitality.
MPAA:R
Electra Entertainment — *Magnum
Entertainment*

Pop Always Pays 1940

Comedy
73698   67 mins   B/W   B, V   P
Dennis O'Keefe, Leon Errol, Adele Pearce
A father gets in a jam when he has to make
good on a bet with his daughter's boyfriend.
RKO — *RKO HomeVideo*

Pop Goes the Cork 1922

Comedy
59409   87 mins   B/W   B, V   P, T
Max Linder
Three films by the man Chaplin referred to as
his "professor," Max Linder: "Be My Wife,"
"Seven Years Bad Luck," and "The Three
Must-Get-Theres." Linder was the foremost film
comedian in early twentieth-century France, and
made these three films during a stay in America.
Max Linder Productions — *Blackhawk Films*

Pope John Paul II Visits America 1979

Documentary/Religion
87203   60 mins   C   B, V   P
Narrated by Martin Sheen
The popular pontiff's 1979 tour of America is
captured in this lighthearted documentary,
which, among other things, shows the Pope
visiting New York City and Yankee Stadium.
Gary Blohm — *Video Associates*

Pope of Greenwich Village, The 1984

Drama
70392   122 mins   C   B, V   P
*Eric Roberts, Mickey Rourke, Daryl Hannah,
Geraldine Page, Kenneth McMillan, Bert Young,
directed by Stuart Rosenberg*
A film about relationships, neighbors and friends
set in New York's Greenwich Village, where the
characters learn about the problems of self-
deception, thieving and grandiose scheming.
MPAA:R
MGM/UA — *MGM/UA Home Video*

Popeye 1980

Comedy/Musical
55538   114 mins   C   B, V, LV   P
*Robin Williams, Shelley Duvall, Roy Walston,
Paul Dooley, directed by Robert Altman*
The cartoon sailor brought to life is on a search
to find his long-lost father. Along the way, he

meets Olive Oyl and adopts little Sweet Pea.
Script by Jules Feiffer, music by Harry Nilsson.
MPAA:PG
Paramount; Robert Evans — *Paramount Home
Video; RCA VideoDiscs*

Popeye and Friends in Outer Space — 19??
Cartoons
65695   60 mins   C   B, V   P
Animated
Popeye and Olive Oyl take their act into the
ozone and beyond. As always, they get into big
trouble with their arch enemy, Bluto. Luckily for
Popeye and all concerned, cans of spinach are
not as rare in outer space as Haley's Comet.
Paramount; Max Fleischer — *Media Home
Entertainment*

Popeye and Friends in the South Seas — 1961
Cartoons
81094   59 mins   C   B, V   P
*Animated, voice of Jack Mercer, Jackson Beck,
Mae Questel, Arnold Stang*
Join Popeye, Olive Oyl, Wimpy and Sweet Pea
as they embark on a series of comedic
adventures.
King Features — *Media Home Entertainment*

Popeye and Friends in the Wild West — 1984
Cartoons
65370   60 mins   C   B, V   P
Animated
The famous spinach eating sailor is back in ten
gallon hat and spurs for uproarious western
adventures. Also included in this cartoon
collection are Krazy Kat, Beetle Bailey and
Snuffy Smith.
Max Fleischer — *Media Home Entertainment*

Popeye the Sailor — 193?
Cartoons
53800   54 mins   C   B, V, FO   P
Animated
This cartoon package includes "Popeye Meets
Aladdin and His Wonderful Lamp," "Popeye
Meets Ali Baba and His 40 Thieves," and
"Popeye the Sailor Meets Sinbad the Sailor."
Paramount; Max Fleischer — *Video
Yesteryear; Western Film & Video Inc; Sound
Video Unlimited; Video Dimensions; Hollywood
Home Theater; Discount Video Tapes*

Popeye—Travelin' On About Travel — 1984
Travel
76652   60 mins   C   B, V   P
Animated
Popeye and Olive Oyl visit foreign and exotic
lands in this hilarious program.

Media Home Entertainment — *Media Home
Entertainment*

Poppies Are Also Flowers — 1966
Adventure
59840   90 mins   C   B, V   P
*Senta Berger, Stephen Boyd, Yul Brynner,
Angie Dickinson, Rita Hayworth, Trevor Howard,
Trini Lopez, E. G. Marshall, Eli Wallach, Omar
Sharif*
Also known as "The Poppy Is Also a Flower,"
this Ian Fleming thriller about the illegal world
drug trade focuses on how the poppies
converted into heroin are being channeled into
the U.S.
Terence Young — *Embassy Home
Entertainment*

Porky Pig and Daffy Duck Cartoon Festival — 1944
Cartoons
85546   57 mins   C   B, V   P
*Daffy Duck, Porky Pig, Tom Turk, voices by Mel
Blanc*
Eight classic Daffy & Porky shorts, including
"Tick Tock Tuckered," "Duck Soup to Nuts"
and "Baby Bottleneck."
Warner Bros. — *MGM/UA Home Video*

Porky Pig Cartoon Festival — 1945
Cartoons
84717   36 mins   C   B, V   P
Porky is highlighted in this retrospective of his
early career.
Vitaphone Corp. — *MGM/UA Home Video*

Porky Pig's Screwball Comedies — 1952
Cartoons
81573   59 mins   C   B, V   P
Animated, voice of Mel Blanc
This compilation of Porky Pig's classic cartoons
includes "You Ought to Be in Pictures" "Boobs
in the Woods" and "Wearing of the Grim".
Warner Bros. — *Warner Home Video*

Porky's — 1982
Comedy
64908   94 mins   C   B, V, LV,   P
                          CED
*Dan Monahan, Wyatt Knight, Tony Ganios, Mark
Herrier, Cyril O'Reilly, Roger Wilson*
Set in south Florida in the early 1950's, this
irreverent comedy follows the misadventures of
six youths of Angel Beach High School. Their
main interest is girls.
MPAA:R
Melvin Simon Productions; Astral Bellevue
Pathe — *CBS/Fox Video*

Porky's II: The Next Day 1983
Comedy
65492   100 mins   C   B, V   P
Bill Wiley, Dan Monahan, Wyatt Knight, Cyril O'Reilly, Roger Wilson, Tony Ganious, Mark Herrier, Scott Colomby
The Angel Beach gang stir up their sleepy southern Florida town when they join forces to participate in the high school project, an innocent sounding tribute to Shakespeare. What starts out as a simple school project soon explodes into a townwide controversy... until our ingenious heroes strike back with an explosively comic scheme.
MPAA:R
Astral Bellevue Pathe Inc; 20th Century Fox Films — *CBS/Fox Video*

Porky's Revenge 1985
Comedy
Closed Captioned
81763   95 mins   C   B, V   P
Don Monahan, Wyatt Knight, Tony Ganios, Nancy Parsons, Chuck Mitchell, Kaki Hunter, Kimberly Evenson, directed by James Komack
The Angel Beach High School students are out to get revenge against Porky who orders the school basketball coach to throw the championship game. You can hear Dave Edmunds' score in VHS and Beta Hi-Fi.
MPAA:R
20th Century Fox — *CBS/Fox Video*

Porsche 911, 944 1986
Automobiles
88408   60 mins   C   B, V, 3/4U   P
2   pgms
Two tapes on how to tune-up and maintain Porsche engines.
Peter Allen Prod. — *Peter Allen Video Productions*

Porsche 911 Video Manual, The 1985
Automobiles
70887   50 mins   C   B, V, 3/4U   P
Post-1970 Porsche 911 owners can learn helpful maintenance tips from this program.
Videovision Productions — *Peter Allen Video Productions*

Port of Call 1948
Drama/Romance
65628   100 mins   B/W   B, V   P
Nine-Christine Jonsson, Bengt Eklund, directed by Ingmar Bergman
A direct, almost documentary telling of the love that grows between a seaman and a girl from reform school who has lost her self-respect.
Janus Films — *Embassy Home Entertainment*

Port of New York 1949
Crime-Drama
47466   82 mins   B/W   B, V, FO   P
Scott Brady, Yul Brynner, K. T. Stevens
A narcotics gang is smuggling large quantities of drugs into New York. A government agent poses as a gang member in order to infiltrate the mob and get the goods on them.
Eagle Lion — *Video Yesteryear; Movie Buff Video; Discount Video Tapes*

Portnoy's Complaint 1972
Comedy-Drama
51969   101 mins   C   B, V   P
Richard Benjamin, Karen Black, Lee Grant
The screen adaptation of Philip Roth's novel follows the frustrating experiences of a sexually obsessed young man as he relates them to his psychiatrist.
MPAA:R
Warner Bros — *Warner Home Video*

Portrait of a Showgirl 1982
Drama
79195   100 mins   C   B, V   P
Lesley Ann Warren, Rita Moreno, Tony Curtis, Dianne Kay, Howard Morris
An inexperienced showgirl learns the ropes of Las Vegas life from a veteran of the Vegas stages.
Hamner Prods — *Prism*

Portrait of a Stripper 1979
Drama
80922   100 mins   C   B, V   P
Lesley-Ann Warren, Edward Hermann, Vic Tayback, Sheree North, directed by John Alonzo
A widowed mother works part-time as a stripper to support her son. Trouble arises when her father-in-law attempts to prove that she is an unfit mother.
Moonlight Prods; Filmways — *Vestron Video*

Poseidon Adventure, The 1972
Adventure
09094   117 mins   C   B, V, CED   P
Gene Hackman, Ernest Borgnine, Shelley Winters, Red Buttons, Jack Albertson, Carol Lynley
The S.S. Poseidon, on her last voyage from New York to Athens, is capsized by a tidal wave on New Year's Eve.
Academy Awards '72: Best Song ("The Morning After"); Special Effects. MPAA:PG EL, SP
Twentieth Century-Fox; Irwin Allen — *CBS/Fox Video*

Possessed 1931
Drama
82118   77 mins   B/W   B, V   P
Joan Crawford, Clark Gable, Wallace Ford, Skeets Gallager, directed by Clarence Brown

A poor factory girl becomes a wealthy Park Avenue sophisticate when she falls in love with a rich lawyer.
MGM — *MGM/UA Home Video*

---

movements to gradually improve muscle tone. Part of the "Rehabilitation and Injury" series.
Health 'N Action — *RCA/Columbia Pictures Home Video*

Possession
1981
Horror
79308   97 mins   C   B, V   P
Isabelle Adjani, Sam Neill, Heinz Bennent, Margit Carstensen, Shaun Lawtor
When A secret agent returns from a long mission, he notices that his wife has been acting very strangely.
MPAA:R
Limelight International Films — *Vestron Video*

Postman Always Rings Twice, The
1981
Drama
53555   122 mins   C   B, V, CED   P
Jack Nicholson, Jessica Lange, John Colicos, Anjelica Huston, Michael Lerner, John P. Ryan, directed by Bob Rafelson
A luckless drifter becomes attracted to the unhappy wife of a middle-aged roadhouse owner, and the two attempt to kill the husband. Based on James M. Cain's novel.
MPAA:R
Bob Rafelson; Charles Mulvehill;
MGM — *CBS/Fox Video*

Postmark for Danger/Quicksand
1956
Mystery
76919   155 mins   B/W   B, V   P
Terry Moore, Robert Beatty, Mickey Rooney, Jeanne Cagney, Peter Lorre
A "film noir" double feature: In "Postmark for Danger," a young actress returns from the dead to find a criminal and in "Quicksand" a mechanic becomes indebted to the mob when he borrows extra money for a date.
RKO; United Artists — *United Home Video*

Postnatal Exercise Program
1985
Physical fitness
81537   55 mins   C   B, V   P
This is an exercise program designed for the unique conditions of the postnatal woman.
AM Available
American College of Obstetricians and Gynecologists — *Feeling Fine Programs; Warner Home Video*

Postnatal (Rehabilitation and Injury)
1978
Physical fitness
52756   30 mins   C   B, V   P
Hosted by Ann Dugan
Reconditioning exercises after childbirth, including both specific-area and total-body

Pot O' Gold
1941
Musical
13045   87 mins   B/W   B, V   P, T
Paulette Goddard, James Stewart, Horace Heidt Band
Girl's father, who hates dance bands, schedules Heidt on his radio quiz show.
United Artists — *Blackhawk Films; Movie Buff Video; Video Yesteryear; Video Connection; Cable Films; Kartes Video Communications; Hal Roach Studios*

Potemkin
1925
Film-History
08699   67 mins   B/W   B, V   P
Alexander Antonov, Grigory Alexandrov, Vladimir Barsky, Mikhail Gomorov, directed by Sergei Eisentein
Recounts the heroic mutiny of Russian sailors in 1905.
Amkino — *International Historic Films; Blackhawk Films; Video Yesteryear; Hollywood Home Theater; Western Film & Video Inc; Discount Video Tapes; Kartes Video Communications*

Pound Puppies
1985
Cartoons
87316   37 mins   C   B, V   P
Cartoon dogs organize and help out other stray and lost dogs.
Hanna-Barbera — *Family Home Entertainment*

Powder Hound/Return of Powder Hound
1978
Sports-Winter/Drama
84270   34 mins   C   B, V   P
Fictional life and times of a crazed skier, with much ski footage. Two short films back to back on one tape.
Video Travel Inc — *Video Travel*

Powder Keg
1970
Adventure
77150   93 mins   C   B, V   P
Rod Taylor, Dennis Cole, Michael Ansara, Fernando Lamas, Tisha Sterling
A railroad company hires a team of investigators to retrieve a hijacked train during the early 1900's.
Filmways — *Worldvision Home Video*

Powdersmoke Range
1935
Western
64414   71 mins   B/W   B, V, 3/4U   P
Harry Carey, Hoot Gibson, Tom Tyler

A crooked frontier politician plots to steal valuable ranch property, until the law rides into town.
RKO — *Nostalgia Merchant*

Power, The
1981
Football
50651   24 mins   C   B, V, FO   R, P
San Diego Chargers
The passing attack of Dan Fouts to John Jefferson, Kellen Winslow, and Charley Joiner was nearly unstoppable in 1980. Coach Don Coryell's 1980 Chargers travelled to the AFC Championship Game where they met the Oakland Raiders.
NFL Films — *NFL Films Video*

Power, The
1983
Horror
73032   87 mins   C   B, V   P
As a small Aztec idol passes down from generation to generation the power of the idol becomes stronger.
MPAA:R
Film Ventures — *Vestron Video*

Power
1985
Drama
85908   111 mins   C   B, V   P
Richard Gere, Julie Christie, E.G. Marshall, Gene Hackman, Beatrice Straight, Kate Capshaw, Denzel Washington, directed by Sidney Lumet
A study of corporate manipulations seen through the actions of Richard Gere, who plays a ruthless media consultant working for politicians.
MPAA:R
Lorimar — *Karl/Lorimar Home Video*

Power Play
1978
Suspense
65012   95 mins   C   B, V, 3/4U   P
Peter O'Toole, David Hemmings, Donald Pleasance
A young army colonel of a small European country joins forces with rebels to overthrow the government. After the coup, it is discovered that one of the rebels is a traitor.
Peter Cooper; Ronald I. Cohen — *Nostalgia Merchant; Media Home Entertainment*

Power Racquetball
1985
Sports-Minor/Physical fitness
70822   30 mins   C   B, V   P
Marty Hogan
Hogan, a three-time world champ, recommends a six-week program leading to performance playing.
Pacific Arts — *Pacific Arts Video*

Power Versus the People
1974
Minorities
88385   36 mins   C   B, V, 3/4U   R, P
A chronicle of the discriminators and discriminatees brought before the Equal Employment Opportunity Commission in Houston, Texas.
EEOC — *Your World Video*

Power Within, The
1979
Science fiction
85084   90 mins   C   B, V   P
Eric Braeden, David Hedison, Susan Howard
An electrified stuntman finds he can send electrical shocks from his hands and becomes the victim of a kidnapping plot.
Alan Godfrey; Aaron Spelling Prods — *Prism*

Prairie Moon
1938
Western/Musical
44806   58 mins   B/W   B, V   P, T
Gene Autry, Smiley Burnette
Gene becomes guardian of a gangster's sons and gets involved with cattle rustlers.
Republic — *Blackhawk Films; Video Connection*

Pray for Death
1985
Martial arts
87324   93 mins   C   B, V   P
Sho Kosugi, James Booth, Michael Constantine, Kane Kosugi, Robert Ito
A Japanese immigrant and his family are victims of the American mob, only to have a Ninja appear and mess everyone up.
MPAA:R
Don Van Atta; Moshie Diamant; Moshe Barkas — *U.S.A. Home Video*

Pray TV
1980
Satire
80680   92 mins   C   B, V   P
Dabney Coleman
A sly con man turns a failing television station into a profitable one when the station starts to broadcast around-the-clock religious programming.
MPAA:PG
Orion Pictures — *Vestron Video*

Praying Mantis
1983
Drama
71042   119 mins   C   B, V   P
Jonathan Pryce, Cherie Lunghi, Ann Cropper, Carmen Du Sautoy, Pinkas Braun, directed by Jack Gold
The professor's scheming nurse murdered his family and plans to marry him for his money. She enlists the aid of the professor's aide in her evil plot.
Portman Productions — *Hal Roach Studios*

Precious Pupp 1987
Cartoons
78071   51 mins   C   B, V   P
Animated
This program presents the most charming dog
alive with his owner in some wacky adventures.
Worldvision Home Video Inc — *Worldvision
Home Video*

Predators of the Sea 1977
Documentary/Fishes
29166   93 mins   C   B, V   P
An underwater program that reveals the
fascinating world of the creatures of the deep.
Highlights include a thrilling fight between an
octopus and a deadly moray eel, a look at the
seagoing crocodile, and deadly sharks in action.
Bill Burrud Productions — *Walt Disney Home
Video*

Pregnancy Exercise 1985
Program
Physical fitness
81538   51 mins   C   B, V   P
This is an exercise program designed for
pregnant women.
AM Available
American College of Obstetricians and
Gynecologists — *Feeling Fine Programs;
Warner Home Video*

Prehistoric Women 1950
Fantasy/Science fiction
81714   74 mins   C   B, V   P
Laurette Luez, Allan Nixon, Mara Lynn
A tribe of prehistoric women look for husbands
the old-fashioned way—they drag them back to
their caves from the jungle.
Eagle-Lion; Alliance Productions — *Rhino
Video*

Prelude to War 1942
World War II/Documentary
08907   53 mins   B/W   B, V   P
Directed by Frank Capra
A compact look at the events of 1931-39;
includes a series of contrasts between free
societies and totalitarian governments. From
the "Why We Fight" series.
Academy Awards '42: Best Documentary.
US War Department — *Hollywood Home
Theater; Western Film & Video Inc; Discount
Video Tapes; MPI Home Video; Spotlite Video*

Premature Burial 1962
Horror
80929   81 mins   C   B, V   P
*Ray Milland, Richard Ney, Hazel Court, Heather
Anger, directed by Roger Corman*
A cataleptic Englishman's worst fears come true
when he is buried alive by a mad doctor. Based
upon the story by Edgar Allen Poe.

Santa Clara Productions — *Vestron Video*

Premiere of "A Star Is 1954
Born"
Film-History
42959   30 mins   B/W   B, V, FO   P
*Doris Day, Judy Garland, Edward G. Robinson,
James Dean, Elizabeth Taylor, Joan Crawford,
Debbie Reynolds, Shelley Winters, Kim Novak,
Lucille Ball, Desi Arnaz*
From the lobby of the Pantages Theater in
Hollywood, George Fisher, Jack Carson,
George Jessel, and Larry Finley interview the
brightest of Hollywood's stars of that era
including Dean Martin, Hedda Hopper, Liberace
(and his mother), Peggy Lee, Ray Bolger, and
countless others.
Unknown — *Video Yesteryear*

Premonition, The 1975
Horror
66267   94 mins   C   B, V   P
Sharon Farrel, Edward Bell, Danielle Brisebois
A parapsychologist searching for a missing child
is drawn into a frightening maze of dream
therapy and communication with the dead.
MPAA:PG
Robert Allen Schnitzer — *Embassy Home
Entertainment*

Prenatal Care—A Case 1979
Study
Pregnancy
70264   30 mins   C   V   P
*Telly Savalas, Clint Walker, Chuck Connors,
Anne Francis*
How a family physician and specialist should
collaborate in dealing with women who have
experienced premature labor.
MPAA:PG
McMaster U — *Prism*

Prenatal (Rehabilitation 1978
and Injury)
Physical fitness/Pregnancy
52755   30 mins   C   B, V   P
Hosted by Ann Dugan
Conditioning exercises for pregnant women
including both specific-area and total body
movements to gradually improve muscle tone.
Part of the "Rehabilitation and Injury" series.
Health 'N Action — *RCA/Columbia Pictures
Home Video*

Preppies 1982
Comedy
77414   83 mins   C   B, V   P
Lynda Weismeyer, directed by Chuck Vincent
A war erupts when a preppie and his
degenerate cousin fight over a fifty-million dollar
inheritance.
Chuck Vincent — *Vestron Video*

Preprimido, El (The Timid   197?
Bachelor)
Comedy
86541   101 mins   C   B, V   P
Alfredo Landa, Isabel Garcas
A newlywed travels to France to learn about sex
before approaching his bride and finds the
whores are on strike.
SP
Spanish — *Master Arts Video*

Presidential Blooper Reel   1981
Outtakes and bloopers
57339   55 mins   B/W   B, V   P
This collection of excerpts from television and
motion pictures features Ronald Reagan, Bette
Davis, Humphrey Bogard, James Cagney, Red
Skelton, James Arness, and Edward G.
Robinson.
Budget Video — *Hollywood Home Theater;*
Discount Video Tapes; See Hear Industries

President's Mistress, The   1978
Suspense
85924   97 mins   C   B, V   P
Beau Bridges, Susan Blanchard, Larry Hagman,
Joel Fabiani, Karen Grassle
A security agent searches for his sister's
murderer, while trying to obscure the fact that
she was having an affair with the President.
Kings Road Prod. — *Lightning Video*

Pretty Baby   1978
Drama
38602   109 mins   C   B, V, LV   P
Brooke Shields, Keith Carradine, Susan
Sarandon, directed by Louis Malle
A photographer obsessed with the prostitutes in
New Orleans red-light district, circa 1917, is
bewitched by a twelve-year-old child prostitute.
A sincere, human study of a controversial
subject.
MPAA:R
Paramount — *Paramount Home Video; RCA*
VideoDiscs

Prevent Back Pain   1985
Back disorders/Physical fitness
81540   46 mins   C   B, V   P
This is an exercise and relaxation program
designed to help people with mild or chronic
back pain.
AM Available
American Academy of Orthopaedic
Surgeons — *Feeling Fine Programs; Warner*
Home Video

Prey, The   1980
Horror
73025   80 mins   C   B, V   P
Debbie Thurseon, Steve Bond
A predator is looking for a mate in the Colorado
Rockies and kills five campers in the process.

MPAA:R
Unknown — *THORN EMI/HBO Video*

Price of Tomatoes, The   1962
Drama
82186   52 mins   B/W   B, V   P
Peter Falk, Inger Stevens
A young trucker risks his life to get a load of
tomatoes and a pregnant woman safely to
Cincinnati. An episode from "The Dick Powell
Theatre."
Emmy Awards '62: Best Actor (Falk).
Four Star Television — *RKO HomeVideo*

Pride and Passion   1984
Basketball
78354   58 mins   C   B, V   P
Here are highlights from the 1984 NBA Playoffs
and Championship Finals along with basketball
bloopers in this program.
NBA — *Embassy Home Entertainment*

Pride and Prejudice   1940
Drama
59135   114 mins   B/W   B, V   P
Greer Garson, Laurence Olivier, Edmund
Gwenn, Edna May Oliver, Mary Boland,
Maureen O'Sullivan, Ann Rutherford, Frieda
Inescort
Jane Austen's classic novel of a proud and
spirited English girl's fight against the prejudice
of the man she loves.
MGM; Hunt Stromberg — *MGM/UA Home*
Video

Pride and the Passion,   1957
The
Drama
69382   132 mins   C   B, V, CED   P
Cary Grant, Frank Sinatra, Sophia Loren,
directed by Stanley Kramer
A small group of resistance fighters battling for
Spanish independence in 1810 must smuggle a
6-ton cannon across the rugged terrain of
Spain.
United Artists — *CBS/Fox Video*

Pride of Eagles Football   1980
Football
45129   24 mins   C   B, V, FO   R, P
Philadelphia Eagles
Highlights of the 1979 Philadelphia Eagles
football season.
NFL Films — *NFL Films Video*

Pride of Jesse Hallum,   1981
The
Drama
88080   105 mins   C   B, V   P
Johnny Cash, Brenda Vaccaro, Eli Wallach,
directed by Gary Nelson

A made-for-TV film about an illiterate man who learns to read.
Sam Manners; Konigsberg Co.
Prod. — *Playhouse Video*

Pride of the Bowery   1941
Comedy
58967   61 mins   B/W   B, V, 3/4U   P
Leo Gorcey, Huntz Hall, Gabriel Dell, Billy Halop, Bobby Jordan
The Dead End Kids in a story about a boy of the streets set against the outdoor life of a C.C.C. camp in the late 1930's.
Monogram — *Cable Films; Discount Video Tapes; Video Yesteryear; Kartes Video Communications*

Pride of the Yankees, The   1942
Biographical/Drama
65009   128 mins   B/W   B, V, LV,   P
                       CED
Gary Cooper, Teresa Wright, Babe Ruth
This is the classic story of baseball phenomenon Lou Gehrig who was stifled at the peak of his career by an incurable disease.
Samuel Goldwyn — *CBS/Fox Video*

Primal Impulse   1974
Science fiction
84107   90 mins   C   B, V   P
Klaus Kinski
An astronaut, stranded on the moon because of a sinister experimental double-cross, unleashes a mental scream which posesses a young woman's mind back on earth.
Empire — *Lightning Video*

Prime Cat   1972
Drama
Closed Captioned
70695   86 mins   C   B, V   P
Lee Marvin, Gene Hackman, Sissy Spacek, Angel Tompkins, Gregory Walcott, directed by Michael Ritchie
This film features drug trafficking, prostitution, extortion, loan sharking, fisticuffs and gangsters getting ground into mincemeat. Recorded with Hi-Fi sound.
CBS Theatrical Films — *Key Video*

Prime Cuts   1984
Music-Performance
72190   45 mins   C   B, V   P
A collection of rock videos featuring performances by Quiet Riot, Toto, Bonnie Tyler and other notables.
CBS Fox Video Music — *CBS/Fox Video*

Prime Cuts—Jazz & Beyond   1985
Music-Performance/Video
70659   35 mins   C   B, V   P

Miles Davis, Herbie Hancock, Chuck Mangione, Al DiMeola, Andreas Wollenwender, Hiroshima, Weather Report, Clark/Duke Project
This program compiles conceptual videos from some popular/jazz composers. The eight numbers come in Hi-Fi stereo on both formats, with digital mastering.
CBS Music Video Enterprises — *CBS/Fox Video*

Prime Cuts—Red Hots   1984
Music video
80338   35 mins   C   B, V   P
A collection of eight conceptual music videos from groups such as Wham! and REO Speedwagon.
CBS Music Video Enterprises — *CBS/Fox Video*

Prime Risk   1984
Adventure
81957   98 mins   C   B, V   P
Toni Hudson, Lee Montogomery, Sam Bottoms
A young engineer who discovers an electronic method to break into automated teller machines finds that it leads to more trouble when she discovers that foreign agents are hot on her trail.
MPAA:PG-13
Herman Grigsby — *Lightning Video*

Prime Suspect   1982
Drama
70257   96 mins   C   B, V   P
Mike Farrell, Teri Garr, Veronica Cartwright, Lane Smith
The tranquil life of a happily married man is shattered when he becomes a suspect in a series of sex murders.
Tisch/Avnet TV — *U.S.A. Home Video*

Prince and Princess of Wales... Talking Personally, The   1986
Interview/Great Britain
86154   45 mins   C   B, V   P
An interview with the royal couple covering a variety of topics.
Vestron Video — *Vestron Video*

Prince and the Great Race   1983
Drama
82195   91 mins   C   B, V   P
John Ewart, John Howard, Nicole Kidman
Three Australian children search the outback to find their kidnapped horse who is scheduled to run in the big New Year's Day Race.
Barron Films Limited — *Lightning Video*

Prince and the Pauper, The   1937

Drama
64933   118 mins   B/W   CED   P
Errol Flynn, Claude Rains, Alan Hale, Billy and Bobby Mauch
Young Edward VI changes places with a street urchin.
Warner Bros — *CBS/Fox Video*

Prince and the Pauper, The   1978

Adventure
80274   113 mins   C   B, V   P
Oliver Reed, Raquel Welch, Mark Lester, Ernest Borghine, directed by Richard Fleischer
When an English prince and a pauper discover that they have identical appearances, they decide to trade places with each other.
MPAA:PG
Warner Bros — *Media Home Entertainment*

Prince and the Pauper, The   1962

Adventure
80356   93 mins   C   B, V   P
Guy Williams, Laurence Naismith, Donald Houston, Jane Asher, Walter Hudd
A prince and a poor young boy swap their clothes and identities, thus causing a lot of confusion for their families.
Buena Vista — *Walt Disney Home Video*

Prince and the Showgirl, The   1957

Comedy
47619   127 mins   C   B, V   P
Laurence Olivier, Marilyn Monroe, Sybil Thorndike, directed by Laurence Olivier
An American showgirl in 1910 London is wooed by the Prince of Carpathia. Part of the "A Night at the Movies" series, this tape simulates a 1957 movie evening, with a Sylvester the Cat cartoon, "Greedy for Tweety," a newsreel and coming attractions for "Spirit of St. Louis."
Warner Bros — *Warner Home Video*

Prince Charming Revue, The   1983

Music-Performance
65003   74 mins   C   B, V, CED   P
England's New Wave rock group, Adam and the Ants, performs its hit singles in an elaborately staged show including a hand-painted pirate ship and castle backdrops. In stereo.
CBS — *CBS/Fox Video*

Prince Jack   1983

Drama/Biographical
81416   100 mins   C   B, V   P
Lloyd Nolan, Dana Andrews, Robert Guillaume, Cameron Mitchell

This film looks at the turbulent political career of President John F. Kennedy.
Jim Milio — *VCL Home Video*

Prince of Central Park, The   1975

Drama
77387   75 mins   C   B, V   P
Ruth Gordon, T.J. Hargrave, Lisa Richard, Mark Vahanian
A runaway brother and sister learn a lesson from an elderly widow they meet in Central Park.
Lorimar Productions — *U.S.A. Home Video*

Prince of the City   1981

Drama
51994   167 mins   C   B, V, LV   P
Treat Williams, Jerry Orbach, Richard Foronjy, Don Billett, Kenny Marino, directed by Sidney Lumet
An undercover cop is pressured into becoming an informant in an FBI investigation of corruption among police officers.
MPAA:R
Orion Pictures — *Warner Home Video; RCA VideoDiscs*

Princess and the Call Girl, The   1984

Adventure
81397   90 mins   C   B, V   P
Carol Levy, Shannah Hall, Victor Bevine, directed by Radley Metzger
A call girl asks her lookalike roommate to take her place in Monaco for a lavishly erotic weekend.
Available in VHS Stereo and Beta Hi-Fi.
Radley Metzger — *Monterey Home Video*

Princess and the Pea, The   1984

Fairy tales
Closed Captioned
73853   60 mins   C   B, V, LV, CED   P
Liza Minnelli, Tom Conti, Pat McCormick, Beatrice Straight, directed by Tony Bill
From "Faerie Tale Theatre" comes the story of a princess who tries to prove that she's a blueblood by feeling the bump of a tiny pea under the thickness of twenty mattresses.
Gaylord Productions; Platypus Productions — *CBS/Fox Video*

Princess and the Pirate, The   1944

Comedy
80948   94 mins   C   B, V   P
Bob Hope, Walter Slezak, Walter Brennan, Virginia Mayo, Victor McLagen, Bing Crosby
A hammy vaudevillian performer falls in love with a beautiful princess when they are captured by buccaneers on the Spanish Main.

(For explanation of codes, see Use Guide and Key)

Samuel Goldwyn — *Embassy Home Entertainment*

Princess and the Swineherd, The 1960
Fantasy
85515   82 mins   B/W   B, V   P
A German adaptation of the Brothers Grimm fairy tale about a young suitor who tries to please a materialistic princess.
German — *Video Yesteryear*

Princess Daisy 1983
Drama
84606   200 mins   C   B, V   P
Merete Van Kamp, Lindsay Wagner, Claudia Cardinale, Stacy Keach, Ringo Starr, Barbara Bach
A beautiful model claws her way to the top of her profession in this made-for-TV adaptation of Judith Krantz's best-selling novel.
Lillian Gallo — *RCA/Columbia Pictures Home Video*

Princess Who Had Never Laughed, The 1984
Fairy tales
81765   60 mins   C   B, V   P
Ellen Barkin, Howard Hesseman, Howie Mandel, Mary Woronov
A stern king holds a laugh-off contest to make his morose daughter happy in this adaptation of the Brothers Grimm story. From the "Faerie Tale Theatre" series.
Lion's Gate Films; Platypus Productions — *CBS/Fox Video*

Principles of Paneling 1984
Home improvement
Closed Captioned
77261   30 mins   C   B, V   P
This is a step-by-step demonstration of how to panel a room.
You Can Do It Videos — *You Can Do It Videos*

Prison de Mujeres 198?
Drama
80494   97 mins   C   B, V   P
Carmen Montejo, Hilda Aguirre, Zully Keith, Susana Kamini
The shocking life of women who are imprisoned in a Spanish prison is depicted in this film which takes place in turn-of-the-century Spain. Dialogue in Spanish.
SP
Spanish — *Unicorn Video*

Prisoner, The 1968
Fantasy/Adventure
79701   50 mins   C   B, V   P
Patrick McGoohan   17   pgms

In this short-lived television series secret agent John Drake is taken to a strange village where he becomes a prisoner without a name.
1.The Arrival 2.Chimes of Big Ben 3.A, B and C 4.Free For All 5.Schizoid Man 6.The General 7.Many Happy Returns 8.Dance of the Dead 9.Do Not Forsake Me Oh My Darling 10.It's Your Funeral 11.Checkmate 12.Living in Harmony 13.Change of Mind 14.Hammer Into Anvil 15.The Girl Who Was Death 16.Once Upon A Time 17.Fallout
Associated TV Corp — *MPI Home Video*

Prisoner of Second Avenue, The 1974
Comedy-Drama
52707   105 mins   C   B, V   P
Jack Lemmon, Anne Bancroft, Gene Saks, Elizabeth Wilson, directed by Melvin Frank
A New Yorker in his late forties faces the future, without a job or any confidence in his ability, with the help of his understanding wife. Based on the Broadway play by Neil Simon.
MPAA:PG
Warner Bros — *Warner Home Video*

Prisoner of Zenda, The 1952
Adventure
47400   101 mins   C   B, V   P
Stewart Granger, Deborah Kerr, Louis Calhern, James Mason
A wanderer who closely resembles the king of a small European country becomes involved in a murder plot. Based on the novel by Anthony Hope.
MGM — *MGM/UA Home Video*

Prisoner of Zenda, The 1979
Comedy
69033   108 mins   C   B, V   P
Peter Sellers, Jeremy Kemp, Lynne Frederick, Lionel Jeffries, Elke Sommer
Peter Sellers stars in the double role of Prince Rudolph of Ruritania and Syd, the cockney cab driver who doubles for Rudolph when the Prince is imprisoned by his jealous brother Michael.
Universal — *MCA Home Video*

Prisoners of the Lost Universe 1984
Science fiction
70224   94 mins   C   B, V   P
Richard Hatch, Kay Lenz, John Saxon
Unwittingly transported to a hostile alternate universe by a renegade scientist, two terrified humans search desperately for the hidden Dimensional Door that is their only hope of escape.
John Hardy; Denis Johnson Jr — *VCL Home Video*

Pritikin Promise, The   1984
Physical fitness
76649   90 mins   C   B, V   P
Hosted by Lorne Greene
This program tells how the Pritikin Promise
assures you that you will be on your way to a
longer, healthier life in just 28 days.
Robert Katz — *Media Home Entertainment*

Pritikin Promise Home   1984
Exercise Program, The
Physical fitness
76651   60 mins   C   B, V   P
Hosted by Lorne Greene
Follow world triathalon champion Dave Scott
and the Pritikin Exercise team through a series
of three exercise levels.
Robert Katz — *Media Home Entertainment*

Private Benjamin   1980
Comedy
58245   110 mins   C   B, V, LV   P
*Goldie Hawn, Eileen Brennan, Albert Brooks,
Robert Webber, Barbara Barrie, Mary Kay
Place, directed by Howard Zieff*
A pampered, spoiled, upper-middle-class
princess rebounds from a bad marriage by
joining the army.
MPAA:R
Warner Bros — *Warner Home Video; RCA
VideoDiscs*

Private Buckaroo   1942
Musical
07229   65 mins   B/W   B, V, FO   P
*The Andrews Sisters, Harry James and his
Orchestra, Joe E. Lewis, Dick Foran*
War-time entertainment in which Harry James
and his Orchestra get drafted.
Universal — *Movie Buff Video; Video
Yesteryear; Cable Films; Hollywood Home
Theater; Discount Video Tapes; Kartes Video
Communications*

Private Eyes, The   1980
Comedy
57231   91 mins   C   B, V, LV,   P
                                          CED
*Don Knotts, Tim Conway, Trisha Noble, Bernard
Fox*
Two bungling sleuths are engaged to
investigate two deaths and are led on a merry
chase through secret passages, past exploding
bombs, and finally to a meeting with a ghostly
adversary.
Lang Elliot; Wanda Dell; TriStar
Pictures — *Vestron Video; Time Life Video*

Private Function, A   1984
Comedy
85769   96 mins   C   B, V   P
Michael Palin, Maggie Smith, Denholm Elliott

A ribald gagfest dealing with a Yorkshire town in
World War II that steals and fattens a wily
contraband pig.
MPAA:PG
British — *THORN EMI/HBO Video*

Private Hell 36   1954
Mystery/Drama
81016   81 mins   B/W   B, V   P
*Ida Lupino, Howard Duff, Steve Cocharan,
directed by Don Siegel*
Two detectives turn greedy after they recover
some stolen money from a robbery.
Filmmakers — *Spotlite Video*

Private Lessons   1981
Comedy
59677   83 mins   C   B, V, LV   P
Eric Brown, Sylvia Kristel, Howard Hesseman
A teenage boy is left alone for the summer in
the care of an alluring maid and a scheming
chauffer.
MPAA:R
Barry and Enright — *MCA Home Video*

Private Life of Don Juan   1934
Adventure
11250   97 mins   B/W   B, V, FO   P
*Douglas Fairbanks Sr., Merle Oberon, directed
by Alexander Korda*
Tired of his romantic reputation, Don Juan still
finds his life complicated by an imposter using
his identity.
United Artists — *Video Yesteryear; Movie Buff
Video; Discount Video Tapes; Cable Films;
Hollywood Home Theater; Western Film &
Video Inc; Kartes Video Communications*

Private Life of Henry VIII,   1933
The
Drama
08693   97 mins   B/W   B, V   P
*Charles Laughton, Elsa Lanchester, Robert
Dunat, Merle Oberon, directed by Alexander
Korda*
The life and loves of infamous English King
Henry VIII are lustily portrayed in this film, a tour
de force for Charles Laughton.
Academy Awards '33: Best Actor (Laughton);
Film Daily Poll Ten Best Pictures of the Year '33.
UA; Alexander Korda — *Prism; VCII;
Blackhawk Films; Embassy Home
Entertainment; Cable Films; Video Connection;
Video Yesteryear; Hollywood Home Theater;
Discount Video Tapes; Western Film & Video
Inc; Kartes Video Communications; Cinema
Concepts*

Private Lives of Elizabeth   1939
and Essex, The
Drama
73970   106 mins   C   B, V   P

Bette Davis, Errol Flynn, Vincent Price, Nanette Fabray, Olivia de Havilland, directed by Michael Curtiz
The aging Queen Elizabeth of England must make a choice between her crown or the love of the Second Earl of Essex.
Warner Bros — Key Video

Private Manoeuvres   1983
Comedy
82248   79 mins   C   B, V   P
Zachi Noy, Yoseph Shiloah, Dvora Bekon
A comely Swiss military adviser gives her all to uplift the morale of the men at Camp Samantha.
Noah Films Limited — MGM/UA Home Video

Private Passions   1985
Drama
80322   86 mins   C   B, V   P
Sybil Danning
A sultry stepmother gives her teenaged American cousin a lesson in love during his European vacation.
Independent — Prism

Private Pilot Ground   1985
School
Aeronautics
70780   600 mins   C   B, V   P
John and Martha King 5   pgms
This 10-hour seminar prepares viewers for the written FAA private pilot exam.
AM Available
King Home Video Ground
School — Videocassette Marketing

Private Popsicle   1982
Comedy
68242   111 mins   C   B, V, CED   P
Zachi Noy, Jonathan Segall, Yftach Katzur
A hilarious sex comedy starring Europe's popular Popsicle team. Dubbed in English.
MPAA:R
Noah Films — MGM/UA Home Video

Private Resort   1984
Comedy
70873   82 mins   C   B, V   P
Johnny Depp, Rob Morrow, Karyn O'bryan, Emily Longstreth, Tony Azito, Hector Elizondo, Dody Goodman, Leslie Easterbrook, directed by George Bowers
A curious house detective and a bumbling thief interrupt the high jinks of two girl-crazy teens on a quest for fun at an expensive Miami hotel.
MPAA:R
Tri-Star — RCA/Columbia Pictures Home Video

Private School   1983
Drama
65338   82 mins   C   B, V, LV   P

Phoebe Cates, Sylvia Kristel, Ray Walston
Two high school girls from the exclusive Cherryvale Academy for Women compete for the affections of a young man from nearby Freemount Academy for Men, while Cherryvale's headmistress is trying to raise funds to build a new wing.
MPAA:R
Universal — MCA Home Video

Private Snafu Cartoon   194?
Festival
Cartoons
55340   55 mins   B/W   B, V   P
Animated
A collection of cartoons produced for the Armed Forces during World War II as humorous instructional films. The language is strictly G.I. Titles include: "Censored," "Gas," "Goldbrick," "Going Home," "Rumors," and "Spies." Also included are two more Warner Bros. World War II cartoons, "Tokio Jokio," and "Confusions of a Nutzy Spy."
Warner Bros — Hollywood Home Theater; Discount Video Tapes

Privates on Parade   1984
Comedy
80647   107 mins   C   B, V   P
John Cleese, Denis Quilley, Simon Jones, Joe Melia, Nicola Pagett
This film centers around the comic antics of an Army song and dance unit entertaining the troops in the Malayan jungle during the late 40's.
MPAA:R
Handmade Films — THORN EMI/HBO Video

Prize Fighter, The   1979
Comedy
63384   99 mins   C   B, V   P
Tim Conway, Don Knotts
Two fight managers unknowingly get involved with a powerful gangster, who convinces one of them to fight in a fixed championship match.
MPAA:PG
New World Pictures — Media Home Entertainment

Prize of Peril, The   1984
Satire
84890   95 mins   C   B, V   P
Michael Piccoli, Marie-France Pisier, directed by Yves Boisset
A French television game show rewards it winners with wealth and its losers with execution.
Union Generale — Lightning Video

Prizzi's Honor   1985
Comedy-Drama
70737   130 mins   C   B, V, LV,   P
                                  CED

Jack Nicholson, Kathleen Turner, Robert Loggia, John Randolph, William Hickey, Lee Richardson, directed by John Huston.
Black humor and subtlety rule in this gangster film. The love between two rival mob assassins conflicts with one's family loyalty, and leads to deception and intrigue.
MPAA:R
ABC Motion Pictures — *Vestron Video*

Pro-Karate Championships (1976-1981)   1981
Martial arts
59570   60 mins   C   B, V   P
Highlights of the 1981 Full Contact Matches conducted under the auspices of the U.S. Professional Karate Association.
Professional Karate Assn — *Mastervision*

Pro Wrestling Illustrated   1985
Sports
77184   60 mins   C   B, V   P
Gordon Solie hosts this look at the most memorable wrestling matches and its peerless champions.
Independent Media Marketing — *Vestron Video*

Problems, 1950's Style   195?
Television/Interview
62692   120 mins   B/W   B, V, 3/4U   P
Three TV panel discussion/interview programs from the 1950's: "Stand Up and Be Counted!" (1956), in which audience members and guests discuss their problems; "People in Conflict," where guests ask advice of the panel; and "The Verdict Is Yours," with an actual courtroom trial.
CBS et al — *Shokus Video*

Prodigal Boxer, The   1980
Adventure/Martial arts
56931   90 mins   C   B, V   R, P
The great Kung-fu masters from all over China assemble for a championship, but anyone can participate if willing to die if defeated. A student of martial arts decides to risk his life for revenge.
MPAA:R
Fourseas Film Company — *Video Gems*

Producers, The   1968
Comedy
41081   88 mins   C   B, V   P
Zero Mostel, Gene Wilder, Dick Shawn, Kenneth Mars, Estelle Winwood, directed by Mel Brooks
Two conniving producers embark upon a get-rich-quick scheme to produce a flop Broadway show, "Springtime for Hitler."
EL, JA
Avco Embassy — *Embassy Home Entertainment; RCA VideoDiscs*

Professional Planting (Horticulture)   1982
Gardening/Plants
59576   50 mins   C   B, V   P
This program offers the amateur an inside look at plant propagation from seed to tissue culture and examines techniques used by specialists for planting and transplanting.
Brooklyn Botanical Gardens — *Mastervision*

Professional Style   1985
Clothing and dress/Personal finance
71005   60 mins   C   B, V   P
Alexander Julian, Robert Stock, Dick Cavett
From tie-pins, to wing-tips, this program recommends successful business attire.
Esquire — *Esquire Video*

Professional Techniques (Horticulture)   1982
Gardening/Plants
59577   50 mins   C   B, V   P
This program presents a variety of skillful pruning techniques, examines the art of bonsai, and reveals the secrets of botanists who obtain natural dyes and colorings from plants and trees.
Brooklyn Botanical Gardens — *Mastervision*

Professionals, The   1966
Western
13270   117 mins   C   B, V   P
Burt Lancaster, Lee Marvin, Claudia Cardinale, Jack Palance, Robert Ryan, directed by Richard Brooks
Two men are hired to rescue a railroad tycoon's daughter from her kidnapper, a Mexican cutthroat.
MPAA:PG
Columbia; Pax Enterprises — *RCA/Columbia Pictures Home Video*

Professor Hippie, El   1979
Drama
47859   95 mins   C   B, V   P
A history teacher befriends a group of students, taking them to a far-off part of the country where adventures befall them. In Spanish.
SP
Nicolas Carreras; Luis Repetto — *Media Home Entertainment*

Project Moon Base   1958
Science fiction
86166   64 mins   C   B, V   P
Donna Martell, Hayden Rourke
Espionage ruins the voyage of the first woman in space.
Robert L. Lippert Prod. — *Vidmark Entertainment*

Projectionist, The   1971
Comedy
84796   84 mins   C   B, V
Rodney Dangerfield, Chuck McCann, Ina Balin
A film projectionist daydreams himself unto the
movies.
MPAA:PG
Maglan Films Inc. — *Vestron Video*

Prom Night   1980
Horror
48939   91 mins   C   B, V, LV   P
Jamie Lee Curtis, Leslie Nielsen
A masked killer stalks four high school senior
girls during their senior prom, as revenge for a
murder which took place six years ago.
MPAA:R
Avco Embassy, Peter Simpson — *MCA Home
Video*

Promises in the Dark   1979
Drama
52713   119 mins   C   B, V   P
*Marsha Mason, Ned Beatty, Kathleen Beller,
Susan Clark, Paul Clemens*
This drama focuses on the complex relationship
between a woman doctor and her seventeen-
year-old female patient terminally ill with cancer.
MPAA:PG
Orion Pictures — *Warner Home Video*

Pronghorn Hunting   1985
Hunting
87655   43 mins   C   B, V   P
For pronghorn shooting, 3 bucks and 2 does are
killed and cleaned to demonstrate hunting and
taxidermy techniques.
Sportsmen On Film — *Sportsmen on Film*

Prophecy   1979
Horror
44595   102 mins   C   B, V   P
*Talia Shire, Robert Foxworth, Armand Assante,
Victoria Racimo, Richard Dysart, directed by
John Frankenheimer*
A doctor and his wife travel to Maine to research
the effects of pollution caused by the lumber
industry. They encounter several terrifying
freaks of nature and a series of bizarre human
deaths.
MPAA:PG
Paramount, Robert L. Rosen — *Paramount
Home Video*

Prophecy   1979
Horror
82545   103 mins   C   B, V   P
Talia Shire, Robert Foxworth, Armand Asante
A suspenseful tale of environmental aberrations
caused by pollution.
MPAA:PG
Paramount Pictures — *Paramount Home Video*

Protector, The   1985
Crime-Drama
Closed Captioned
85656   94 mins   C   B, V, LV   P
*Jackie Chan, Danny Aiello, directed by James
Glickenhaus*
A semi-martial arts cops 'n' robbers epic about
the cracking of a Hong Kong-New York heroin
route.
MPAA:R
David Chan — *Warner Home Video*

Protocol   1984
Comedy
Closed Captioned
80707   96 mins   C   B, V, LV   P
*Goldie Hawn, Chris Sarandon, Andre Gregory,
Cliff De Young, Ed Begley Jr., Gail Strickland,
directed by Herbert Ross*
A series of comic accidents lead a Washington
cocktail waitress into the U.S. State Department
employ as a protocol official.
MPAA:PG
Warner Bros. — *Warner Home Video*

Proud and Damned, The   1972
Western
84026   95 mins   C   B, V   P
*Chuck Connors, Aron Kincaid, Cesar Romero,
directed by Ferde Grofe Jr.*
Five Civil-War-veteran mercenaries wander into
a Latin American war and get manipulated by
both sides.
MPAA:PG
Gold Key Entertainment — *United Home Video*

Proud Rebel, The   1958
Western/Drama
69551   99 mins   C   B, V   P
*Alan Ladd, Olivia De Havilland, Dean Jagger,
directed by Michael Curtiz*
After his wife's death, a proud, stubborn man
goes searching for a doctor who can help his
mute son.
Buena Vista; Samuel Goldwyn Jr — *Embassy
Home Entertainment*

Providence   1976
Drama
57230   104 mins   C   B, V   P
*John Gielgud, Dirk Bogarde, Ellen Burstyn,
directed by Alain Resnais*
A dying novelist plans one last novel—a
haunting story about the people he knows and
the horrors of death he envisages.
Cinema 5; Yves Gasser; Klaus
Hellwig — *RCA/Columbia Pictures Home
Video*

Prudential Family   1950
Playhouse, The
Drama
47641   53 mins   B/W   B, V, FO   P

Ruth Chatterton, Walter Abel, Cliff Hall, Eva Marie Saint
Sinclair Lewis' "Dodsworth," the story of a wealthy American couple who travel from their small American town to Europe.
CBS — *Video Yesteryear*

Prudential Family Playhouse, The   1950
Drama
69579   53 mins   B/W   B, V, FO   P
Ruth Chatterton, Walter Abel, Cliff Hall, Eva Marie Saint
An early television adaptation of Sinclair Lewis' classic novel about middle-age disaffection between a wealthy American couple. Originally telecast on October 24, 1950.
CBS — *Video Yesteryear*

Psychic, The   1978
Horror
85920   90 mins   C   B, V   P
Jennifer O'Neill, Marc Porel, Evelyn Stewart, directed by Lucio Fulci
A psychic envisions her own death and attempts to alter the prediction.
MPAA:R
Group 1 — *Lightning Video*

Psychic Killer   1975
Suspense
82564   89 mins   C   B, V   P
Jim Hutton, directed by Ray Danton
A wrongfully accused prisoner acquires psychic powers and decides to use them in a deadly revenge.
MPAA:PG
Mordi Rustam — *Embassy Home Entertainment*

Psycho   1960
Suspense
11598   109 mins   B/W   B, V, LV   P
Anthony Perkins, Janet Leigh, Vera Miles, John Gavin, Martin Balsam, directed by Alfred Hitchcock
A young woman steals a fortune and encounters a young peculiar man and his mysterious mother.
Paramount Prods — *MCA Home Video; RCA VideoDiscs*

Psycho II   1983
Suspense
65208   113 mins   C   B, V, LV   P
Anthony Perkins, Vera Miles, Meg Tilly, Robert Loggia
After 22 years, Norman Bates is back home at the old Bates Motel in anticipation of new customers.
Universal Oak — *MCA Home Video*

Psycho Sisters   1972
Horror
80295   85 mins   C   B, V   P
Susan Strasberg, Faith Domergue, Sydney Chaplin, Steve Mitchell
Two sisters become involved in the accidental murder of a man who was a husband to one woman and lover to the other.
MPAA:PG
World Wide Films — *Prism*

Psychomania   1973
Mystery
01682   95 mins   C   B, V   P
Lee Philips, Sheppard Strudwick, Jean Hale, directed by Richard Hilliard
Former war hero and painter is suspected of being demented killer stalking girls' campus. Finally, he identifies the true killer.
Victoria Films; British — *Hollywood Home Theater*

Psychomania   1973
Horror
56737   89 mins   C   B, V   P
George Sanders, Beryl Reid, Nicky Henson
A drama of the supernatural, the occult, and the violence which lies just beyond the conventions of society for a group of motorcyclists.
MPAA:R
Del Tenney — *Media Home Entertainment; King of Video; World Video Pictures*

Psychopath   1968
Adventure
84106   90 mins   C   B, V   P
Klaus Kinski, George Martin, Ingrid Schoeller, directed by Guido Zurli
A film about a modern-day, slightly unhinged, Robin Hood and his escapades, stealing from other thieves and giving to the victimized.
Empire — *Lightning Video*

PT 109   1963
War-Drama
63452   159 mins   C   B, V   P
Cliff Robertson, Ty Hardin, Robert Blake, Robert Culp
The World War II exploits of Lieutenant J.G. John F. Kennedy in the South Pacific. Part of the "A Night at the Movies" series, this tape simulates a 1963 movie evening, with a Foghorn Leghorn cartoon, "Banty Raids," a newsreel on the JFK assassination and coming attractions for "Critic's Choice" and "Four for Texas."
Warner Bros — *Warner Home Video*

Puberty Blues   1981
Drama
81437   86 mins   C   B, V   P
Neil Schofield, Jad Capelja, directed by Bruce Beresford

Two Australian girls become part of the local surfing scene in order to be accepted by the "in crowd" at their high school. Available in VHS and Beta Hi-Fi.
MPAA:R
Limelight Productions — *MCA Home Video*

Public Enemy   1931
Crime-Drama
59427   85 mins   B/W   B, V   P
James Cagney, Edward Woods, Leslie Fenton, Joan Blondell, Mae Clarke, Jean Harlow, directed by William Wellman
Two slum boys begin as bootleggers, and get in over their heads.
Warner Bros — *Key Video; RCA VideoDiscs*

Puff and the Incredible   1982
Mr. Nobody
Cartoons/Fantasy
79714   45 mins   C   B, V   P
Animated, voice of Burgess Meredith
Puff the Magic Dragon and a little boy travel through the Fantaverse to find an imaginary friend.
Robert Rosen; Kevin Hunter — *Children's Video Library; Coronet Films*

Puff the Magic Dragon   1978
Cartoons
80185   45 mins   C   B, V   P
Animated, voice of Burgess Meredith
An animated adaptation of the Peter Yarrow song about little Jackie Paper and his friend Puff, The Magic Dragon.
The My Company — *Children's Video Library*

Puff the Magic Dragon in   1979
the Land of Lies
Cartoons/Fantasy
79715   24 mins   C   B, V   P, DL
Animated, voice of Burgess Meredith
Puff the Magic Dragon teaches a little girl the difference between fantasy and telling a lie.
Peter Yarrow; Romeo Muller — *Children's Video Library; Coronet Films*

Pulsebeat   1985
Drama
86853   92 mins   C   B, V   P
Daniel Greene, Alice Moore, Lee Taylor Allen, Peter Lupus
A made-for-TV film about the troubled life of a health club owner.
Calepas International — *Lightning Video*

Puma Man   1980
Science fiction
81081   100 mins   C   B, V   P
Donald Pleasance, Walter George Alton, Sydne Rome

Puma Man is a super hero who must stop the evil Dr. Kobras from using an ancient mask in his attempt to become ruler of the world.
Cinema Shares International — *Prism*

Pump It   1983
Physical fitness
66270   55 mins   C   B, V   P
Hosted by Dr. David Engel
A body-building program focusing on specific parts of the body.
Al Eicher — *Embassy Home Entertainment*

Pumping Iron   1977
Documentary/Physical fitness
39086   85 mins   C   B, V   P
Arnold Schwarzenegger, Mike Katz, Franco Columbu, Lou Ferrigno, directed by George Butler
A widely acclaimed documentary look at the sport of bodybuilding, following the behind-the-scenes action surrounding the competition for the Mr. Olympia title. The grueling training ritual and the constant striving for perfection are all explored.
MPAA:PG
Cinema 5 — *RCA/Columbia Pictures Home Video; RCA VideoDiscs*

Pumping Iron II: The   1985
Women
Documentary/Physical fitness
Closed Captioned
81159   107 mins   C   B, V, LV   P
Lori Bowen, Bev Francis, Rachel McLish, Carla Dunlap, Lydia Cheng, directed by George Butler
This sequel to "Pumping Iron" takes an in-depth look at the world of female body building. The documentary also follows the ladies to a competition held at Caesar's Palace in Las Vegas.
Cinecom International Films — *Vestron Video*

Puppet Musical Classics   1985
Collection
Puppets
84777   90 mins   C   B, V   P
3   pgms
Puppets perform classic music and dance tales from the popular symphonic repertoire.
1.Peter and the Wolf 2.The Nutcracker 3.Carnival of the Animals
F Prod/Vistar Int'l — *Video Associates*

Puppet on a Chain   1972
Crime-Drama/Suspense
71192   97 mins   C   B, V   P
Sven-Bertil Taube, Barbara Parkins, Alexander Knox, Patrick Allen, Geoffrey Reeve
An American narcotics officer busts an Amsterdam drug ring and the leader's identity surprises him. Based on the Alistair MacLean novel.

MPAA:PG
Cinerama; Kurt Unger — *Prism*

Puppet Playhouse 195?
Presents Howdy Doody
Variety
38995   60 mins   B/W   B, V, FO   P
Buffalo Bob Smith, Clarabell the Clown, Chief Thundercloud 2   pgms
Two complete programs from September 13, 1948, and August 2, 1959, featuring the Peanut Gallery and all the familiar Howdy Doody characters and routines Commercials included.
NBC — *Video Yesteryear*

Purlie Victorious 1963
Comedy
58579   93 mins   C   B, V   P
Ossie Davis, Ruby Dee, Godfrey Cambridge, Alan Alda
The award-winning Broadway hit, a comedy which takes a look at racial integration.
Hammer Bros — *Mastervision*

Purple Hearts 1984
War-Drama
73014   115 mins   C   B, V   P
Cheryl Ladd, Ken Wahl, directed by Sidney Furie
Ken Wahl stars as a Navy doctor who falls in love with nurse Cheryl Ladd against the backdrop of the Vietnam war.
MPAA:R
Sidney Furie; Warner Bros — *Warner Home Video*

Purple Power Years: The 1985
Minnesota Vikings
Football
81951   96 mins   C   B, V   P
Joe Kapp, Fran Tarkenton, Chuck Foreman
This is a collection of highlights from the Vikings Super Bowl years of 1969, 1973, 1974 and 1976.
NFL Films — *NFL Films Video*

Purple Rain 1984
Musical-Drama
Closed Captioned
79549   113 mins   C   B, V, LV   P
Prince, Apollonia Kotero, Morris Day, Clarence Williams III, directed by Albert Magnoli
A quasi-autobiographical video showcase for the multi talented pop-star Prince. The film tells of his struggle for love, attention, acceptance, and popular artistic recognition in Minneapolis.
Academy Awards '84: Best Original Song Score (Prince, John L. Nelson, and The Revolution)
MPAA:R
Warner Bros — *Warner Home Video*

Purple Rose of Cairo, The 1985
Comedy-Drama/Fantasy
Closed Captioned
80920   82 mins   B/W   B, V, LV,   P
                             CED
Mia Farrow, Jeff Daniels, Danny Aiello, Dianne Weist, Van Johnson, Zoe Caldwell, John Wood, Edward Herrmann, Milo O'Shea, directed by Woody Allen
jThe dreams of a desperate Depression era waitress come true when her favorite film character steps out of the screen and asks her to show him what real life is like.
MPAA:PG
Orion Pictures; Jack Rollins and Charles H. Joffe — *Vestron Video*

Purple Taxi, The 1977
Drama
60342   93 mins   C   B, V   P
Fred Astaire, Charlotte Rampling, Peter Ustinov
A romantic drama revolving around several wealthy foreigners who have taken refuge in beautiful southern Ireland.
CPH; BLD — *RCA/Columbia Pictures Home Video*

Pursuit 1975
Western/Adventure
71213   92 mins   C   B, V   P
Ray Danton, Dewitt Lee, Troy Nabors, Diane Taylor, Eva Kovacs, Jason Clark, directed by Thomas Quillen
A lone Indian brave seeks revenge on the U.S Cavalry who slaughtered his tribe in their sleep. He engages a U.S. Army scout in a deadly game of hide 'n seek.
MPAA:R
Key Int'l — *Prism*

Pursuit of D. B. Cooper, 1981
The
Drama
47423   100 mins   C   B, V   P
Robert Duvall, Treat Williams, Kathryn Harrold
This film recreates an actual hijacking that took place on Thanksgiving eve, 1971, when J. R. Meade (alias D. B. Cooper) bailed out of a 727 with $200,000 of the airline's money. He was never heard from again.
MPAA:PG
Universal — *Vestron Video*

Puss in Boots 1982
Fairy tales
63169   89 mins   C   B, V   P
Garry Q. Lewis, Jason McLean, Carl Beck, Nancy Wagner
The Children's Theater Company of Minneapolis present a jazzed-up, New Orleans-style version of the "Puss in Boots" tale. VHS is in stereo.

Television Theater Company — *MCA Home Video*

Puss 'n' Boots Travels   1983
Around the World
Cartoons
66346   60 mins   C   B, V   P
Animated
An all-new magical cartoon featuring the hero, Pussty, who is challenged by the villainous Rumblehog to complete a trip around the world in 80 days, while Rumblehog tries to thwart him at every turn. In Beta Hi-Fi.
MPAA:G
John Watkins; Simo Nuchtern — *RCA/Columbia Pictures Home Video*

Puss 'N' Boots   1984
Fairy tales
Closed Captioned
73574   60 mins   C   B, V, CED   P
Ben Vereen, Gregory Hines
From "Faerie Tale Theatre" comes the story of a cat who makes a serf a rich landowning nobleman.
Gaylord Productions; Platypus Productions — *CBS/Fox Video*

Putney Swope   1969
Comedy
44780   84 mins   B/W   B, V   P
Arnold Johnson, Laura Greene, Stanley Gottlieb, directed by Robert Downey
A mild mannered token black is mistakenly elected chairman of the board of the advertising firm he works for. He turns the straight-laced corporation into the wide open "Truth and Soul, Inc."
MPAA:R
Cinema 5 — *RCA/Columbia Pictures Home Video*

Pygmalion   1938
Comedy
81627   96 mins   B/W   B, V, LV   P
Leslie Howard, Wendy Hiller, Wilfrid Lawson, Marie Lohr, directed by Anthony Asquith and Leslie Howard
An adaptation of the George Bernard Shaw play about a phonetics professor who turns a flower girl into a lady of distinction.
Academy Awards '38: Best Screenplay (Ian Dalrymple, Cecil Lewis and W.P. Lipscomb). Gabriel Pascal — *Embassy Home Entertainment*

Q

Q—The Winged Serpent   1983
Horror
68253   92 mins   C   B, V   P
Michael Moriarty, Candy Clark, David Carradine, Richard Roundtree
Two city policemen and a petty crook are trying to track down the perpetrator of a bizarre series of slayings.
MPAA:R
Larco — *MCA Home Video*

QB VII   1974
Drama
47784   313 mins   C   B, V   P
Anthony Hopkins, Ben Gazzara, Lee Remick, Leslie Caron, Juliet Mills, John Gielgud, Anthony Quayle
A knighted physician brings a suit for libel against a novelist for implicating him of war crimes in a best-selling novel. Adapted from the novel by Leon Uris. Available only as a three-cassette set.
Emmy Awards '74: Best Supporting Actor, Single Performance, Comedy or Drama Special (Quayle); Best Supporting Actress, Single Performance, Comedy or Drama Special (Mills); Music Composition; Graphic Design and Title Sequence; Film Editing; Film Sound Editing.
Douglas S Cramer — *RCA/Columbia Pictures Home Video*

Quackser Fortune Has a   1970
Cousin in the Bronx
Drama/Comedy
51114   88 mins   C   B, V   P
Gene Wilder, Margot Kidder
An Irish fertilizer salesman meets an exchange student from the U.S., who finds herself attracted to this unlearned, but not unknowing, man.
MPAA:R
John H Cunningham; Mel Howard — *United Home Video*

Quadrophenia   1979
Musical-Drama
65066   115 mins   C   B, V   P
Phil Daniels, Mark Wingett, Philip Davis, Leslie Ash, Sting
Pete Townshend's rock opera about an alienated youth circa 1963 in Britain's rock scene who suffers from a 4-way split personality. Music by the Who.
MPAA:R
World Northal — *RCA/Columbia Pictures Home Video; RCA VideoDiscs*

Quartet   1981
Drama
66125   101 mins   C   B, V   P
Isabelle Adjani, Alan Bates, Maggie Smith, directed by James Ivory
Jean Rhys' novel concerning a young wife drawn into the social and emotional trap of a

---

domineering English couple is the basis of this film.
Cannes Film Festival '81: Best Actress (Adjani).
MPAA:R
New World Pictures — *Warner Home Video*

Quatermass Conclusion, The   1979
Science fiction
81483   105 mins   C   B, V   P
John Mills, Simon MacCorkindale, Barbara Kellerman, Margaret Tyzack
An elderly British scientist comes out of retirement to stop an immobilizing death ray from outer space from destroying Earth.
Euston Film Productions — *THORN EMI/HBO Video*

Quicksand   1950
Drama
84956   79 mins   B/W   B, V   P
Mickey Rooney, Peter Lorre
A mechanic steals a small amount of money for a date, and slowly his crimes multiply as he tries to redeem himself.
UA; Samuel Goldwyn — *Hal Roach Studios*

Queen—Greatest Flix   1981
Music
58724   60 mins   C   B, V   P
A compilation of original video promos made to accompany the hit records which propelled the rock group Queen on their way to worldwide success. Songs include "Bohemian Rhapsody," "We Will Rock You," "Another One Bites the Dust," "Flash," "Killer Queen," "We Are the Champions," "Crazy Little Thing Called Love."
EMI Music — *THORN EMI/HBO Video; Pioneer Artists; RCA VideoDiscs*

Queen Live in Rio   1985
Music-Performance
82015   60 mins   C   B, V   P
Queen rocks Rio di Janeiro in this concert performance that features "Bohemian Rhapsody" and "Tie Your Mother Down" in VHS and Beta Hi-Fi Stereo.
Queen Films Limited — *Sony Video Software*

Queen of Diamonds   198?
Adventure
78670   90 mins   C   B, V   P
Claudia Cardinale, Stanley Baker, Henri Charriere
A woman pulls off the biggest diamond robbery of all time.
Independent — *Monterey Home Video*

Queen of the Road   1984
Adventure
85626   96 mins   C   B, V   P

Joanne Samuel, Amanda Muggleston, directed by Bruce Best
A feisty Aussie schoolteacher starts a new life as a tractor-trailer driver.
J.N.P. Films Pty. Ltd. — *Vestron Video*

Queen of the Stardust Ballroom   1975
Drama
52401   98 mins   C   V   P
Maureen Stapleton, Charles Durning
A lonely widow goes to a local dance hall, where she meets a man and begins an unconventional late love.
Robert Christiansen, Rick Rosenberg Prods — *Prism*

Queen The Works   1984
Music video
76963   17 mins   C   B, V, LV   P
Heavy metal rockers Queen performs in four conceptual music videos from "The Works" album.
Capitol — *Sony Video Software*

Queen—We Will Rock You   1985
Music-Performance
86357   55 mins   C   B, V   P
A live concert of the British rock group's greatest hits, including "Bohemian Rhapsody" and "We Will Rock You."
Vestron Video — *Vestron Video*

Queensryche Live in Tokyo   1985
Music-Performance
82013   50 mins   C   B, V   P
Those masters of heavy metal, Queensryche perform such screamers as "Nightrider," "Child or Fire" and "Blinded" in this Tokyo concert. Available in VHS and Beta Hi-Fi Stereo.
EMI America Records — *Sony Video Software*

Querelle   1983
Drama
65188   106 mins   C   B, V   P
Brad Davis, Jeanne Moreau, Franco Nero, directed by Rainer Werner Fassbinder
Fassbinder's last film explores the seamy underworld of the French port of Brest, where Querelle, a handsome sailor, finds himself involved in a bewildering environment of drug smuggling and homosexuality. Dubbed in English.
MPAA:R
Triumph Films — *RCA/Columbia Pictures Home Video*

Quest for Fire 1982
Adventure
62775   75 mins   C   B, V, LV,   P
                          CED
Everett McGill, Ron Perlman, Nameer El-Kadi, Rae Dawn Chong, directed by Jean-Jacques Annaud
A group of primitive men in the distant past fight rival tribes for the possession of fire.
MPAA:R
20th Century Fox — *CBS/Fox Video*

Question of Honor, A 1980
Drama
84124   134 mins   C   B, V   P
Ben Gazzara, Paul Sorvino, Robert Vaughn, directed by Jud Taylor
Under governmental pressures, an honest narcotics cop decides to inform on his department's corruption. Co-written and produced by ex-cop Sonny Grosso, on whom "The French Connection" was based.
Sonny Grosso — *VCL Home Video*

Question of Love, A 1978
Drama
65305   90 mins   C   B, V   P
Gena Rowlands, Jane Alexander
An admitted homosexual living in a lesbian relationship struggles to retain custody of her son from her ex-husband.
Viacom Enterprises — *U.S.A. Home Video*

Question of Silence 1983
Drama
82584   92 mins   C   B, V   P
Cox Habrema, Nelly Frijda, Henriette Tol, Edda Barends, directed by Morleen Gorris
Three women, strangers to each other, commit a murder that is intricately analyzed in this courtroom drama. Subtitled and dubbed versions available.
DU
Matthijs Van Heijningen and Sigma Films — *Embassy Home Entertainment*

Quick Dog Training with 1982
Barbara Woodhouse
Pets
66271   90 mins   C   B, V   P
A program on how to train your dog or pup.
Pillar Prods — *Embassy Home Entertainment*

Quiet Day In Belfast, A 1974
Drama
77359   92 mins   C   B, V   P
Barry Foster, Margot Kidder
Northern Irish patriots and British soldiers clash in an Irish betting parlor.
Twinbay Media International Ltd. — *Media Home Entertainment*

Quiet Man, The 1952
Comedy-Drama
55511   129 mins   C   B, V   P
John Wayne, Maureen O'Hara, Barry Fitzgerald, Victor McLaglen, Ward Bond, Mildred Natwick, directed by John Ford
An archetypal John Ford comedy, an Irish village version of "Taming of the Shrew," the tamer being an ex-boxer retired to the land of his fathers and in need of a wife.
Academy Awards '52: Best Director (Ford); Best Color Cinematography (Winton Hoch, Archie Stout).
Republic; Argosy; John Ford; Merian C Cooper — *Republic Pictures Home Video; RCA VideoDiscs*

Quiet One, The 1948
Poverty/Minorities
15609   68 mins   B/W   B, V   P
Commentary by James Agee
Explores the ghetto's psychological effects on a ten-year old black child.
Venice International Film Festival: First Prize.
Film Documents — *Movie Buff Video; Hollywood Home Theater; Festival Films*

Quiet Place to Kill, A 1970
Crime-Drama
86888   90 mins   C   B, V   P
Carroll Baker, Jean Sorel, Luis Davila, directed by Umberto Lenzi
A trampy race-car driver plots to help her ex-husband's wife kill him, but schemes with him to kill her instead.
Bruno Bolognes; Italian-Spanish — *Unicorn Video*

Quintet 1979
Science fiction/Drama
70697   118 mins   C   B, V   P
Paul Newman, Bibi Andersson, Fernando Rey, Vittorio Gussman, David Langton, Nina Van Pallundt, Brigitte Fussey, directed by Robert Altman
The stakes in "Quintet," a form of backgammon, are high; you bet your life. But that's O.K.; this film is set during the planet's final ice age. Hi-Fi sound in both formats.
20th Century Fox — *Key Video*

Quiz Kids 1950
Game show
12851   30 mins   B/W   B, V, FO   P
Fran Allison
Quizmistress Fran Allison asks the questions to a panel of five youngsters ranging in age from seven to fourteen.
CBS — *Video Yesteryear*

Quo Vadis 1951
Adventure
87374   171 mins   C   B, V   P

Robert Taylor, Deborah Kerr, Peter Ustinov,
directed by Mervyn LeRoy
The definitive version of the classic novel about
ancient Rome during the reign of Nero. In VHS
and Beta Hi-Fi.
Loew's Inc. — MGM/UA Home Video

R

Rabbit Test 1978
Comedy
84043   86 mins   C   B, V   P
Billy Crystal, Roddy McDowall, Imogene Coca,
directed by Joan Rivers
In Rivers' first directorial effort, a clumsy virginal
guy becomes the world's first pregnant man.
Irreverence and ribaldry ensue.
MPAA:PG
Edgar Rosenberg — Charter Entertainment

Rabid 1977
Horror
53520   90 mins   C   B, V   P
Marilyn Chambers, Frank Moore, Joe Silver
A young girl undergoes a radical plastic surgery
technique and develops a strange and
unexplained lesion in her armpit—along with a
craving for human blood.
MPAA:R
New World Pictures; Cinema Entertainment
Enterprises — Warner Home Video

Raccoons and the Lost Star, The 1984
Cartoons
73705   49 mins   C   B, V   P
Animated, narrated by Rich Little
The Raccoons must save the earth from Cyril
Sneer in this animated adventure. With the
purchase of this videocassette, a magic wand
and a kite are included.
AM Available
Kevin Gillis — Embassy Home Entertainment

Raccoons' Big Surprise, The 1985
Cartoons
Closed Captioned
81455   30 mins   C   B, V   P
Animated
The evil Cyril Sneer will stop at nothing to find
out what the Raccoons' secret plans in the
Evergreen Forest are.
Evergeen Marketing — Embassy Home
Entertainment

Raccoon's Buried Treasure, The 1986
Cartoons
87917   72 mins   C   B, V   P
Created by Kevin Gillis
Three adventures for Bert, Ralph and Melissa
Raccoon: "Dungeons & Dragons," "Buried
Treasure" and "The Runaways."
Kevin Gillis — Embassy Home Entertainment

Raccoons Learn a Lesson, The 1985
Cartoons
Closed Captioned
81912   50 mins   C   B, V   P
Animated
Here is a collection of two "Raccoons"
adventures: The Raccoons discover whether or
not men or women are better in "A Night to
Remember" and the gang learns a lesson about
winning in "Evergreen Grand Prix".
Kevin Gillis — Embassy Home Entertainment

Raccoons—Let's Dance, The 1984
Music video
66625   30 mins   C   B, V   P
Animated, songs performed by Rita Coolidge,
Leo Sayer, John Schneider, Dottie West
Melissa, Ralph and Bert Raccoon perform in six
of their own original music videos, designed
especially for children.
Evergreen Marketing — Embassy Home
Entertainment

Raccoons on Ice 1982
Fantasy
63378   49 mins   C   B, V, LV   P
Animated, narrated by Rich Little, music by Leo
Sayer, Rita Coolidge and Rupert Holmes
Two cartoons featuring Ralph, Melissa and Bert
Raccoon are contained on this cassette. In
"Raccoons on Ice," they play a hockey game
against the Brutish Bears. "Christmas
Raccoons" finds them fighting to protect
Evergreen Forest and their "raccoondominium"
home.
Kevin Gillis; Sheldon S Wiseman — Embassy
Home Entertainment

Race for Your Life, Charlie Brown 1977
Comedy/Cartoons
38610   76 mins   C   B, V, LV   P
Animated
Another in the popular series of "Peanuts"
character films, featuring Charlie Brown,
Snoopy, and all the gang spending an exciting
summer in the American wilderness.
MPAA:G
Paramount — Paramount Home Video; RCA
VideoDiscs

Race with the Devil 1975
Horror/Suspense
Closed Captioned
81967   84 mins   C   B, V   P
Peter Fonda, Warren Oates, Loretta Swit, Lara Parker, directed by Jack Smight
Two vacationing couples are terrorized by a coven of devil worshipers after they witness a sacrificial killing. Available in VHS and Beta Hi-Fi Stereo.
MPAA:PG
20th Century Fox — *Key Video*

Rachel and the Stranger 1948
Drama
66333   93 mins   B/W   B, V, 3/4U   P
Loretta Young, Robert Mitchum, William Holden, Gary Gray
A God-fearing farmer declares his love for his wife when a handsome stranger nearly woos her away.
RKO — *Nostalgia Merchant*

Rachel, Rachel 1968
Drama
77268   102 mins   C   B, V   P
Joanne Woodward, James Olson, Estelle Parsons, directed by Paul Newman
A repressed, small town spinster schoolteacher gets one last chance at romance.
New York Film Critics & Golden Globe Awards '68: Best Actress (Woodward); Best Director (Newman). MPAA:R
Warner Bros.; Kayos Productions — *Warner Home Video*

Racket, The 1951
Crime-Drama
64366   88 mins   B/W   B, V, 3/4U   P
Robert Ryan, Robert Mitchum, Lizabeth Scott
A police captain attempts to break up the crime empire of a powerful racketeer.
RKO — *Nostalgia Merchant*

Racketeer 1929
Drama
10635   68 mins   B/W   B, V, 3/4U   R, P
Carole Lombard, Robert Armstrong, Hedda Hopper
A racketeer falls in love with a pretty girl and wants to leave his life of crime.
Pathe — *Cable Films*

Racketeers of the Range 1939
Western
64413   62 mins   B/W   B, V, 3/4U   P
George O'Brien, Marjorie Reynolds
A cattleman fights a crooked attorney who wants to sell his client's stock to a large meat packing company.
RKO — *Nostalgia Merchant*

Rad 1986
Drama
Closed Captioned
88477   94 mins   C   B, V, LV   P
Bill Allen, Bart Conner, Talia Shire, Jack Weston, Lori Loughlin
A teenage drama revolving around BMX racing.
MPAA:PG
Hal Needham; Embassy — *Embassy Home Entertainment*

Radar Men from the Moon 1952
Science fiction/Serials
07343   152 mins   B/W   B, V, 3/4U   P
George Wallace, Aline Towne
Commando Cody protects the world from invaders from the moon. Serial in twelve episodes.
Republic — *Nostalgia Merchant; Video Connection; Discount Video Tapes; Republic Pictures Home Video*

Radical Surfers 1982
Sports-Water
87688   55 mins   C   B, V   P
Narrated by Bruce Jenner
A random series of images about surfing, young girls, young guys and love.
Surfing Pro Cup — *Prism*

Radio Ranch 1935
Science fiction
07202   80 mins   B/W   B, V, FO   P
Gene Autry, Frankie Darro, Betsy King Ross
Gene Autry and friends are up against an underground world that is complete with robots and death rays.
Mascot Pictures — *Video Yesteryear; Discount Video Tapes*

Rafferty and the Gold Dust Twins 1975
Comedy/Drama
Closed Captioned
80710   91 mins   C   B, V   P
Alan Arkin, Sally Kellerman, MacKenzie Phillips, Charlie Martin Smith, directed by Dick Richards
Two women kidnap a motor vehicle inspector in Los Angeles and order him to drive to New Orleans at gunpoint.
MPAA:R
Warner Bros. — *Warner Home Video*

Raft Adventures of Huck and Jim, The 1978
Cartoons
71349   72 mins   C   B, V   P
Animated, the voice of Timothy Gibbs
Mark Twain's adventurous duo takes off down the Mississippi River on a raft in this production.
MFTV Inc — *Family Home Entertainment*

Rage   1981
Drama
73536   98 mins   C   B, V   P
David Soul, James Whitmore, Yaphet Kotto
A convicted rapist is sent to a therapy program
to reform sex offenders. Available in Beta Hi-Fi
and VHS stereo
Diane Silver Prods; Charles Fries
Prods — U.S.A. Home Video

Rage   1972
Suspense
88181   100 mins   C   B, V   P
George C. Scott, Richard Basehart, Martin
Sheen, Bernard Hughes, Kenneth Tobey, Ed
Lauter, Nicholas Beauvy, Dabbs Greer, directed
by George C. Scott
A farmer and son are accidentally sprayed with
a military nerve gas, and after the son dies and a
cover-up is launched, the farmer embarks on a
vengeful rampage.
MPAA:PG
Fred Weintraub; J. Ronald Getty; Leon
Fromkess — Warner Home Video

Rage of Paris, The   1938
Comedy
00419   78 mins   B/W   B, V   P
Danielle Darrieux, Douglas Fairbanks Jr.,
Mischa Auer
Ex-actress and head waiter pool their money to
help a beautiful French girl catch a millionaire
husband.
Universal; Buddy De Sylva — Discount Video
Tapes; Cable Films; King of Video; Hollywood
Home Theater; Movie Buff Video; Kartes Video
Communications

Raggedy Ann and Andy   1979
Cartoons
78971   52 mins   C   B, V   P
Animated, voices of June Foray, Daws Butler,
directed by Chuck Jones
Two Raggedy Ann and Andy stories where they
aid a boy who lost his Halloween pumpkin in
""The Pumpkin Who Couldn't Smile" and foil a
plot to turn Santa's workshop into a factory in
""The Great Santa Claus Caper."
Chuck Jones — MPI Home Video

Raggedy Ann and Andy: 1977
A Musical Adventure
Cartoons
59309   87 mins   C   B, V, CED   P
Animated, directed by Richard Williams
The fun-filled exploits of America's favorite
fictional doll, transformed into an enchanting
animated musical, with sixteen songs by Joe
Raposo.
MPAA:G
Lester Osterman — Playhouse Video

Raggedy Man   1981
Drama
59035   94 mins   C   B, V, LV   P
Sissy Spacek, Eric Roberts, Sam Shepard,
directed by Jack Fisk
A story of a woman raising two sons alone in a
small Texas town during World War II, and the
sailor who enters her lonely life.
MPAA:PG
Universal — MCA Home Video

Raging Bull   1980
Drama
53450   128 mins   B/W   B, V, LV   P
Robert DeNiro, Cathy Moriarty, Joe Pesci, Frank
Vincent, directed by Martin Scorcese
The story of Jake La Motta?the tough New York
street kid who slugged his way to the world
middle-weight boxing championship and then
went on to lose everything, chronicling his ups
and downs with women, his family, and the law.
Academy Awards '80: Best Actor (DeNiro); Best
Editing (Thelma Schoonmaker). MPAA:R
Irwin Winkler; Robert Chartoff; United
Artists — CBS/Fox Video; RCA VideoDiscs

Raging River of   1983
Annapurna/Urumbamba,
The—Sacred River of the
Incas
Boating
70178   100 mins   C   B, V   P
These two films cover kayak expeditions down
the Marsyandi River in the Annapurna
Himalayas of Nepal and a trek to the
headwaters of the Amazon.
Video Travel — Video Travel

Ragtime   1981
Drama
59858   156 mins   C   B, V, LV   P
James Cagney, Brad Dourif, Moses Gunn,
Elizabeth McGovern, Ken McMillan, Pat
O'Brien, Donald O'Connor, Mary Steenburgen,
Howard E. Rollins, directed by Miles Forman
E. L. Doctorow's epic novel interweaving the
lives and passions of a middle-class family
against the scandals and events of America in
transition circa 1906. Music composed by
Randy Newman.
MPAA:PG
Dino De Laurentis; Paramount — Paramount
Home Video; RCA VideoDiscs

Raid on Entebbe   1984
War-Drama
72184   113 mins   C   B, V   P
Charles Bronson, Peter Finch
Dramatization of the Israeli rescue of
passengers held hostage by terrorists at
Uganda's Entebbe Airport.
MPAA:R

Edgar J Sherick Assocs; 20th Century
Fox — *THORN EMI/HBO Video*

Raid on Rommel
1971
War-Drama
87178   98 mins   C   B, V   P
*Richard Burton, John Colicos, Clinton Greyn,
directed by Henry Hathaway*
A British soldier poses as a Nazi and tries to
infiltrate Rommel's team with his rag-tag brigade
of misfits.
MPAA:PG
Universal; Harry Tatelman — *MCA Home
Video*

Raiders of Atlantis
197?
Adventure/Science fiction
71204   100 mins   C   B, V   P
*Christopher Connelly, directed by Roger
Franklin*
Battles break out when the lost continent
surfaces in the Caribbean. The warriors in these
apocalyptic frays deploy atomic arsenals.
Independent — *Prism*

Raiders of Red Gap
1943
Western
43019   56 mins   B/W   B, V, FO   P
Al "Fuzzy" St. John, Bob Livingston
A cattle company tries running homesteaders
off their land to get control of it. The Lone Rider
saves the day.
Producers Releasing Corp — *Video
Yesteryear; Video Connection*

Raiders of the Lost Ark
1981
Adventure
Closed Captioned
69539   115 mins   C   B, V, LV,   P
                                  CED
*Harrison Ford, Karen Allen, Wolf Kahler, Paul
Freeman, directed by Steven Spielbert*
An adventurer and a feisty woman search for
the Lost Ark of the Covenant, eluding Nazis,
spies and others in the process.
MPAA:PG
Lucasfilm Ltd — *Paramount Home Video*

Railroaded
1947
Mystery
81226   72 mins   B/W   B, V, LV   P
*John Ireland, Sheila Ryan, Hugh Beaumont,
directed by Anthony Mann*
The police seek a wanton criminal who has
taken a young boy hostage.
Eagle Lion — *New World Video; Discount
Video Tapes*

Railroadin'
1941
Trains
60049   27 mins   C   B, V   P, T

This story of America's railroad system begins
with foot power, then animal, then the wheel,
and finally progresses to a discussion of
railroads. Includes shots of early locomotives up
to 1941.
General Electric Company — *Blackhawk
Films; Interurban Films*

Rain
1932
Drama
08781   77 mins   B/W   B, V   P
*Joan Crawford, Walter Huston, William Gargan,
Guy Kibbee*
Somerset Maugham's tale of Puritanical
minister's attempt to reclaim a "lost woman" on
the island of Pago Pago.
United Artists — *United Home Video; Discount
Video Tapes; VCII; Cable Films; Video
Connection; Video Yesteryear; Western Film &
Video Inc; Kartes Video Communications*

Rain People, The
1969
Drama
69026   102 mins   C   B, V   P
Shirley Knight, James Caan, Robert Duvall
In an effort to escape the responsibilities of her
marriage and impending motherhood, a young
woman sets out on a cross country trip. On her
way she becomes involved with a football player
who is retarded due to a sports injury.
MPAA:R
Warner Bros — *Warner Home Video*

Rainbow Brite, Volumes I thru III
1984
Cartoons
Closed Captioned
76995   45 mins   C   B, V   P
Animated 3 pgms
This popular series follows the continuing
adventures of Rainbow Brite, Twink the sprite,
Starlite the horse and the Color Kids. They fight
the "Evil Force," embodied in Murky Dismal and
Lurky.
D.I.C. Productions — *Children's Video Library*

Rainbow Brite and the Star Stealer
1985
Cartoons
71173   85 mins   C   B, V   P
Animated
Ms. Brite again saves the world's color from
thieves; this time it's the star stealer.
MPAA:G
Hallmark Properties — *Warner Home Video*

Rainbow Gang, The
1973
Adventure
86612   90 mins   C   B, V   P
Donald Pleasance, Don Calfa, Kate Reid
A trio of unlikely prospectors head into a
legendary mine in search of riches and fame.

THE VIDEO TAPE & DISC GUIDE

Gerald Potterton — *New World Video*

Loew's Inc. — *MGM/UA Home Video*

Rainbow Goblins Story   1981
Music-Performance
47297   52 mins   C   B, V   P
Masayoshi Takanaka
In a live concert at Budokan, Masayoshi
Takanaka performs the music he composed to
interpret a book called "Rainbow Goblins
Story."
Yutaka Tanaka — *Paramount Home Video;
Pioneer Video Imports*

Rainbow: Live Between   1984
the Eyes
Music-Performance
76032   60 mins   C   B, V   P
This music video features Rainbow's hit songs,
including "Stone Cold," "Power" and "Smoke
on the Water."
Aubrey Powell — *RCA/Columbia Pictures
Home Video*

Rainbow Parade 2   1936
Cartoons
77364   21 mins   C   B, V   P, T
Animated
A collection of three animated classics from
Burt Gillette including "Molly Moo Cow and
Robinson Crusoe," "Trolley Ahoy," and "Waifs
Welcome."
RKO Radio Pictures — *Blackhawk Films*

Rainbow Parade, The   193?
Cartoons
29484   50 mins   C   B, V   P, T
Animated
Animator/director Burt Gillette's "Rainbow
Parade" contains some of the most subtly
textured color work to be found in animation.
Features cartoon characters "Felix," "Molly
Moo Cow," and "the Toonerville Folks."
Unknown — *Blackhawk Films*

Rainbow—The Final Cut   1986
Music-Performance
84878   60 mins   C   B, V   P
The veteran rock band performs their greatest
hits.
Polygram Music Video — *RCA/Columbia
Pictures Home Video*

Raintree County   1957
Drama
87373   175 mins   C   B, V   P
*Elizabeth Taylor, Montgomery Clift, Eva Marie
Saint, directed by Edward Dmytryk*
A lavish epic about two lovers caught up in the
national turmoil of the Civil War. In Dolby Stereo
Hi-Fi. The acclaimed music score was written by
Johnny Green.

Raise the Titanic   1980
Drama/Adventure
56901   112 mins   C   B, V, LV,   P
                        CED
Jason Robards, Richard Jordan, Anne Archer
America's defense depends on the raising of
the ship, discovered seventy years after it sank.
This action drama chronicles the valiant efforts
to lift it from its icy grave.
MPAA:PG
William Frye — *CBS/Fox Video*

Raisin in the Sun, A   1961
Drama
60340   128 mins   B/W   B, V   P
*Sidney Poitier, Claudia McNeil, Ruby Dee,
directed by Daniel Petrie*
A sensitive drama of a black family's escape
from their frustrating life in a crowded Chicago
apartment.
Columbia — *RCA/Columbia Pictures Home
Video*

Rake's Progress, The   1973
Music-Performance
81586   152 mins   C   B, V   P
Felicity Lott, Leo Goeko, Richard Van Allan
A production of the Stravinsky opera performed
by the Glyndebourne Festival Opera.
Southern Television — *Video Arts International*

Rambo: First Blood, Part   1985
II
Adventure
70951   93 mins   C   B, V   P
*Sylvester Stallone, Richard Crenna, Charles
Napier, Steven Berkoff, Julia Nickson, Martin
Kove, directed by George P Cosmatos*
The mighty Rambo, earth's most fearsome
commando, returns to the Vietnam battlefields
of his youth to rescue some U.S. MIA's who
have been clandestinely detained by the
commies for a decade. Available in Hi-Fi Stereo
Surround sound on both formats.
MPAA:R
Tri Star Pictures — *THORN EMI/HBO Video*

Ramparts of Clay   1984
Drama
72926   87 mins   C   B, V   P
A young Tunisian girl wants to liberate herself
from old customs of her people. This film is in
Arabic with subtitles.
MPAA:PG   AB
Almi — *RCA/Columbia Pictures Home Video*

Rancho Notorious   1952
Western
33592   89 mins   C   B, V   P

Marlene Dietrich, Arthur Kennedy, Mel Ferrer,
directed by Fritz Lang
Kennedy looks for the murderer of his
sweetheart, and falls in love with Dietrich in the
process. Tragic consequences follow.
RKO — *United Home Video*

Randy Newman Live at the Odeon   1985

Music-Performance
77459   57 mins   C   B, V   P
Randy Newman, Ry Couder, Linda Ronstadt
Join Randy Newman, guitarist Ry Cooder and
Linda Ronstadt as they perform such Newman
standards as "Sail Away" "Short People" and "I
Love LA" Available in VHS and Beta Hi Fi
Stereo.
Music Vision — *RCA/Columbia Pictures Home
Video*

Randy Rides Alone   1934

Western
06356   53 mins   B/W   B, V   P
John Wayne
Young man single-handedly cleans up the
territory.
Monogram — *Video Connection; Cable Films;
Discount Video Tapes; Spotlite Video; Sony
Video Software*

Randy Rides Alone/Riders of Destiny   1935

Western
81021   106 mins   B/W   B, V   P
John Wayne
This is an action-packed western double
feature: in "Randy Rides Alone", a young man
cleans up the territory single handedly and in
"Riders of Destiny" the Texas Rangers are
destined to ride to the rescue once more.
Monogram Pictures — *Spotlite Video*

Range Law   1931

Western
84836   60 mins   B/W   B, V   P
Ken Maynard
A classic entry in the infamous Maynard school
of horseplay, cliche and repetitive plot
elements.
Ken Maynard; Tiffany — *United Home Video*

Rangeland Racket   1941

Western
66145   60 mins   B/W   B, V, FO   P
George Houston, Hillary Brooke, Al St. John
The Lone Rider (Houston) has been wrongly
accused of a crime.
Unknown — *Video Yesteryear*

Ranger and the Lady   1940

Western
10937   54 mins   B/W   B, V   P

Roy Rogers, Gabby Hayes
Roy finds romance.
Republic — *Discount Video Tapes; Kartes
Video Communications*

Rangers Take Over, The   1943

Western
51643   62 mins   B/W   B, V   P
Dave O'Brien, James Newill
Gunlords are driven out by the Texas Rangers.
Producers Releasing Corp — *Video
Yesteryear; Discount Video Tapes*

Ransom   1984

Drama
72910   90 mins   C   B, V   P
Oliver Reed, Deborah Raffin
A group of wealthy citizens decide to take on an
assassin who stalks a resort town.
Unknown — *Vestron Video*

Rape! A Crime of Violence   1982

Rape
60515   48 mins   C   B, V   P
Awareness, precaution and defense of rape are
exposed in this docudrama.
Bob Chaney — *Master Arts Video*

Rape and Marriage: The Rideout Case   1980

Drama/Wife beating
71330   96 mins   C   B, V   P
*Mickey Rourke, Linda Hamilton, Rip Torn,
Eugene Roche, Conchata Ferrell, Gail
Strickland, Gerald McRaney, Bonnie Bartlett,
Richard Venture, directed by Peter Levin*
This docudrama examines the Rideout case;
wherein an Oregon woman filed legal papers
citing her husband with rape.
Stonehenge/Blue-Greene and Lorimar
Productions — *U.S.A. Home Video*

Rape of Love   1979

Drama
58500   117 mins   C   B, V   P
*Nathalie Nell, Alain Foures, directed by Yannick
Bellon*
One of the most chilling rape scenes on film
opens this attempt at analyzing the emotional
impact of such a crime on its victim. French with
English subtitles.
FR
Films de L'Equinoxe — *RCA/Columbia
Pictures Home Video*

Rape of the Sabines, The   1961

Adventure
84067   101 mins   C   B, V   P
Roger Moore, Mylene Demongeot, Jean Marais
The story of Romulus, king of Rome, and how
he led the Romans to capture the women of

Sabina. The battles rage, the women plot and Romulus fights and lusts.
Enrico Bomba Productions — *Unicorn Video*

Rappaccini's Daughter   1980
Drama
82106   59 mins   C   B, V   P
Kathleen Beller, Kristopher Tabori, Michael Egan, hosted by Henry Fonda
This is an adaptation of a Nathaniel Hawthorne short story about a doctor's daughter who is cursed with the ability to kill anything she touches. Available in VHS Stereo and Beta Hi-Fi.
Cal Skaggs — *Monterey Home Video*

Rappin'   1985
Musical
81502   92 mins   C   B, V   P
Mario Van Peebles, Tasia Valenza, Harry Goz, Charles Flohe
An ex-con tries to save his little brother from a life of crime by landing him a contract with a record company. Available in VHS and Beta Hi-Fi.
MPAA:PG
Cannon Films — *MGM/UA Home Video*

Rapunzel   1983
Fairy tales
Closed Captioned
69323   60 mins   C   B, V, LV,   P
                           CED
Shelley Duvall, Gena Rowlands, Jeff Bridges
The classic tale of the beautiful young woman locked in a tall tower by a witch who is saved by the handsome prince who climbs her golden tresses is retold in this program from "Faerie Tale Theatre."
Shelley Duvall — *CBS/Fox Video*

Raquel: Total Beauty and   1984
Fitness
Physical fitness
78395   90 mins   C   B, V   P
Raquel Welch designed this program to keep men and women of all ages in top physical condition.
Thorn EMI — *THORN EMI/HBO Video*

Rare Breed, A   1981
Drama
65210   96 mins   C   B, V   P
Forrest Tucker, George Kennedy
A young girl's filly is kidnapped en route to Europe for training, sparking a treacherous race against odds with time running out.
MPAA:PG
Carnoba Company — *U.S.A. Home Video*

Rare Breed, The   1966
Western
84019   97 mins   C   B, V   P
James Stewart, Maureen O'Hara, Brian Keith, directed by Andrew V McLaglen
In this rugged western, Stewart as a no-strings ranch hand agrees to escort a single but rare Hereford Bull through every kind of western calamity to Dodge City.
William Alland — *MCA Home Video*

Rascal Dazzle   1981
Comedy
74087   100 mins   B/W   B, V   P
Narrated by Jerry Lewis
This is a montage-like tribute to that best-loved group of children, the Our Gang kids. Narrated by Jerry Lewis, this feature includes scenes with Spanky, Alfalfa, Darla and the rest of the gang.
Michael King; Bob King — *Embassy Home Entertainment*

Rascals, The   1981
Comedy-Drama
65392   93 mins   C   B, V   P
This film depicts the coming of age of ar irrepressible youth at a rural Catholic boys' school.
MPAA:R
Gilbert de Goldschmidt — *Embassy Home Entertainment*

Rashomon   1951
Drama
82582   83 mins   B/W   B, V   P
Toshiro Mifune, directed by Akira Kurosawa
An action-packed drama from Japan that intricately explores the vagaries of the human heart.
Academy Awards '51: Best Foreign Film.
Jingo Minoura — *Embassy Home Entertainment*

Ratas del Asfalto   198?
Drama
77353   85 mins   C   B, V   P
Ana Martin, Armando Silvestre
Two rival race car drivers battle in a fatal race.
SP
Foreign — *Unicorn Video*

Ratings Game, The   1984
Comedy
85287   96 mins   C   B, V   P
Danny DeVito, Rhea Perlman, directed by Danny DeVito
A bitter, out-of-work actor and a girl who works at the ratings service, manage to mess up the television industry.
David Jablin — *Paramount Home Video*

Rats 1983
Science fiction
86852   100 mins   C   B, V   P
Richard Raymond, Richard Cross, directed by
Vincent Dawn
In 2225, the beleaguered survivors of a nuclear
holocaust struggle with a mutant rodent
problem.
J.E.R. Pictures — *Lightning Video*

Rattle of a Simple Man 1964
Comedy-Drama
63325   91 mins   B/W   B, V   P
Harry H. Corbett, Diane Cilento, Michael
Medwin, Thora Hird
A naive bachelor in London spends the night
with a prostitute in order to win a bet.
Sydney Box — *THORN EMI/HBO Video*

Rattlers 1976
Suspense
77206   82 mins   C   B, V   P
Sam Chew, Don Priest, Ron Gold
Chemically exposed snakes attack the
inhabitants of the Mojave Desert area.
John McCauley — *U.S.A. Home Video*

Raven, The 1963
Horror
64886   86 mins   C   B, V   P
Vincent Price, Boris Karloff, Peter Lorre, Jack
Nicholson
A chilling tale of black magic based on the poem
by Edgar Allan Poe.
American International Pictures — *Warner*
Home Video; Vestron Video (disc only)

Ravishing Idiot, The 1964
Comedy
76798   99 mins   B/W   B, V   P
Brigitte Bardot, Anthony Perkins, directed by
Edouard Molinaro
An unemployed bank clerk becomes mixed up
with Soviet spies through an unusual series of
events.
Edouard Molinaro — *Monterey Home Video*

Raw Courage 1974
Drama
80664   90 mins   C   B, V, LV   P
Ronny Cox, Art Hindle, Tim Maier, M. Emmett
Walsh
A trio of marathon runners get more than they
bargained for when they relax in New Mexico.
New World Pictures — *New World Video*

Raw Force 1981
Adventure/Martial arts
63385   90 mins   C   B, V   P
Cameron Mitchell, Geoff Binney, John Dresden,
John Locke, Ralph Lombardi

Three karate enthusiasts visit an island
inhabited by a sect of cannibalistic monks who
have the power to raise the dead.
MPAA:R
Ansor International Picture — *Media Home*
Entertainment

Rawhide 1938
Western
10072   60 mins   B/W   B, V   P, T
Lou Gehrig, Smith Ballew
Rancher's Protection Association forces
landowners to knuckle under. Friction results.
20th Century Fox — *Blackhawk Films;*
Discount Video Tapes

Ray Bradbury Theater, 1985
Volume I, The
Science fiction
82314   60 mins   C   B, V   P
James Coco, William Shatner
Here are two chilling tales from the pen of Ray
Bradbury: A husband makes a duplicate of
himself to solve his marital problems in
"Marionettes," and a doting father is
determined to protect his son from "The
Playground."
Larry Wilcox Productions — *Buena Vista Home*
Video

Ray Bradbury Theater, 1985
Volume 2, The
Fantasy
87673   28 mins   C   B, V   P
Nick Mancuso, R.H. Thomson
Another in the dramatic series of adaptations of
Bradbury stories, about a man discovering a
mysterious crowd that always assembles at
traffic accidents.
Larry Wilcox Prod. — *Buena Vista Home Video*

Ray Davies' Return to 1985
Waterloo
Music video/Drama
84879   60 mins   C   B, V   P
Ken Colley
Ray Davies of The Kinks creates a music-
narrated drama about a disillusioned
businessman.
Waterloo Films — *RCA/Columbia Pictures*
Home Video

Razorback 1984
Horror
76853   95 mins   C   B, V   P
Gregory Harrison, Bill Kerr, Arkie Whiteley, Judy
Morris, Chris Haywood, directed by Russell
Mulcahy
A young American travels to the Australian
outback to search for his missing journalist wife.
MPAA:R

Hal McElroy; UAA Films Ltd — *Warner Home Video*

Razor's Edge, The 1984
Drama/Comedy
Closed Captioned
77369   129 mins   C   B, V   P
Bill Murray, Catherine Hicks, Theresa Russell, Denholm Elliott, directed by John Byrum
A beautifully-filmed, disorientating, strangely idiosyncratic version of the Somerset Maugham novel, in which a World War I-ravaged Larry Darrell combs the world in search of the meaning of life. Subtly and completely unique.
MPAA:PG-13
Columbia Pictures — *RCA/Columbia Pictures Home Video*

Razor's Edge, The 1946
Drama
Closed Captioned
81066   146 mins   B/W   B, V   P
Tyrone Power, Gene Tierney, Anne Baxter, Clifton Webb, Herbert Marshall, directed by Edmund Goulding
This is an adaptation of the Somerset Maugham novel about a rich young man who spends his time between World War I and World War II searching for essential truth. Available in VHS and Beta Hi-Fi.
Academy Awards '46: Best Supporting Actress (Baxter).
20th Century Fox; Darryl F. Zanuck — *Key Video*

RCA's All-Star Country Music Fair 1982
Music-Performance
60388   82 mins   C   B, V   P
Charlie Pride, Razzy Bailey, Sylvia, Earl Thomas Conley
A hoe-down recorded live at the 1982 Nashville Fan Fair, featuring a line-up of Nashville talent. In stereo.
RCA — *RCA/Columbia Pictures Home Video; RCA VideoDiscs*

Reach for Fitness 1986
Physical fitness
86592   45 mins   C   B, V   P
Pat Boone, Susan Clarke, Angie Dickinson, Alex Karras, Ann-Margret, Joan Rivers, Alan Thicke, Cybill Shepherd, Betty White, Bruce Jenner
An exercise program by Richard Simmons for handicapped people, with exercises for everything from muscular dystrophy to hemophilia to spina bifida.
AM Available
Richard Simmons; Karl-Lorimar — *Karl/Lorimar Home Video*

Reaching for the Moon 1931
Romance
28923   62 mins   B/W   B, V, 3/4U   P
Douglas Fairbanks Sr., Bebe Daniels, Bing Crosby, Edward Everett Horton
A wizard of finance ignores the ladies until one, Bebe Daniels, makes him fall. Music by Irving Berlin.
United Artists — *Cable Films; Kartes Video Communications; Video Yesteryear*

Reactor 1985
Science fiction
88338   90 mins   C   B, V   P
Yanti Somer, Melissa Long, James R. Stuart, Robert Barnes, Nick Jordan
A low budget sci-fier about kidnapped scientists, alien ships and an activated nuclear reactor.
Nais Films — *Mogul Communications*

Reading Rainbow 1983
Language arts
Closed Captioned
74154   30 mins   C   B, V   P
25 pgms
This series was developed to encourage primary level students to adopt positive reading habits. The narrators for the programs include such names as Bill Cosby, Ruth Buzzi and Lily Tomlin.
1.Tight Times 2.Miss Nelson Is Back 3.Bea and Mr. Jones 4.Bringing the Rain to Kapiti Plain 5.Louis the Fish 6.Digging Up Dinosaurs 7.Liang and the Magic Paintbrush 8.Gila Monsters Meet You at the Airport 9.Three Days on a River in a Red Canoe 10.The Gift of the Sacred Dog 11.Gregory the Terrible Eater 12.Three by the Sea 13.Arthur's Eyes 14.The Day Jimmy's Boa Ate the Wash 15.Ty's One Man Band 16.Hot-Air Henry 17.Simon's Book 18.Ox-Cart Man 19.Mystery on the Docks 20.A Chair for My Mother 21.Paul Bunyan 22.The Patchwork Quilt 23.Hill of Fire 24.The Tortoise and the Hare 25.Perfect the Pig
Great Plains National; WNED
Buffalo — *Children's Video Library; Great Plains National*

Ready Steady Go 1983
Music
65508   60 mins   B/W   B, V   P
The Beatles, The Rolling Stones, The Who, The Animals, Gerry and the Pacemakers
The first in a series of classic rock video collectibles from the 1960's. This volume contains 16 of the '60's top hits which capture the magic and energy of this exciting rock era.
Dave Clark Production International; Picture Music International — *THORN EMI/HBO Video*

Ready Steady Go, Volume 2 — 1985
Music-Performance
80648　60 mins　B/W　　B, V
The Beatles, The Who, The Beach Boys, Marvin Gaye, Gene Pitney, Jerry Lee Lewis, The Rolling Stones
This second volume highlights more original performances from the classic British rock TV show of the sixties.
Dave Clark Production International;
PMI — *THORN EMI/HBO Video*

Ready Steady Go, Volume 3 — 1984
Music-Performance
81832　57 mins　B/W　　B, V　　　P
Marvin Gaye, Martha and the Vandellas, The Rolling Stones, The Beatles
This volume features more clips from the British music series including the Beatles performing "She's A Woman" and The Rolling Stones singing "Little Red Rooster."
Dave Clark Production International;
PMI — *THORN EMI/HBO Video*

Reagan's Way — 1985
Biographical/Documentary
84620　55 mins　C　　B, V　　　P
Narrated by Hank Simms
Using clips and interviews, a portrait of the popular, controversial President.
AM　Available
Daniel Selznick — *MPI Home Video*

Real Bruce Lee, The — 1979
Adventure/Martial arts
35390　108 mins　C　　B, V　　R, P
Bruce Lee
This program contains actual early films of Bruce Lee, once feared lost but recently discovered in the Chinese film archives.
MPAA:R
Madison World Film Company — *Video Gems; Sun Video*

Real Genius — 1985
Comedy
71115　108 mins　C　　B, V　　　P
Val Kilmer, Gabe Jarret, Jonathan Gries, Michelle Megrink, William Atherton, directed by Martha Coolidge
The brilliant young students at a California technical institute find that their class projects are intended for use as offensive military weapons. They mount an amusingly elaborate strategic defense initiative of their own. Recorded in HiFi Surroundsound.
MPAA:PG
Tri Star — *RCA/Columbia Pictures Home Video*

Real Life — 1979
Comedy/Satire
60212　99 mins　C　　B, V　　　P
Charles Grodin, Frances Lee McCain, Albert Brooks, directed by Albert Brooks
When a group of filmmakers moves into the home of a typical American family, they record an account of "real life" — Albert Brooks style.
MPAA:R
Penelope Spheers — *Paramount Home Video*

Re-Animator — 1985
Horror/Science fiction
84086　86 mins　C　　B, V, LV　　P
Jeffery Combs, Bruce Abbott, Barbara Crampton, directed by Stuart Gordon
Based on a H.P. Lovecraft story, this grisly film deals with a medical student who has re-animated the dead. It has quickly turned into a black humor cult classic, and is also available in an unrated version.
MPAA:R
Empire — *Vestron Video*

Rear Window — 1954
Drama/Suspense
66587　112 mins　C　　B, V, LV　　P
James Stewart, Grace Kelly, Thelma Ritter, Wendell Corey, Raymond Burr, directed by Alfred Hitchcock
A newspaper photographer with a broken leg passes the time while recuperating by observing his neighbors through the window. When he sees what he believes to be a murder committed, he decides to solve the crime himself.
Universal Classics — *MCA Home Video*

Rebecca — 1940
Drama
46214　130 mins　B/W　　B, V　　　P
Joan Fontaine, Laurence Olivier, Judith Anderson, George Sanders, C. Aubrey Smith, directed by Alfred Hitchcock.
Based on Daphne du Maurier's best selling novel about a young unsophisticated girl who marries a prominent country gentleman who is dominated by the memory of his first wife. Hitchcock's first American film.
Academy Awards '40: Best Picture; Best Cinematography.
Selznick — *CBS/Fox Video*

Rebecca of Sunnybrook Farm — 1917
Comedy-Drama
63981　77 mins　B/W　　B, V　　　P, T
Mary Pickford, Eugene O'Brien, Marjorie Daw
The original film version of the tale about an orphan who spreads sunshine and good cheer to all those around her. Silent with organ score by Gaylord Carter.
Artcraft Pictures — *Blackhawk Films*

Rebel Love   1985
Romance
88028   84 mins   C   B, V   P
*Terence Knox, Jamie Rose, Fred Ryan, directed
by Milton Bagby Jr.*
A burgeoning, inchoate love grows between a
Yankee widow and a Confederate spy during
the Civil War.
Troma Inc. — *Vestron Video*

Rebel Rousers   1969
Drama
03573   81 mins   C   B, V   P
*Jack Nicholson, Cameron Mitchell, Diane Ladd,
Bruce Dern*
A violent motorcycle gang abuses women.
Paragon International Picture — *Media Home
Entertainment; King of Video*

Rebel Without a Cause   1955
Drama
38941   105 mins   C   B, V, LV   P
*James Dean, Natalie Wood, Sal Mineo, Jim
Backus, directed by Nicholas Ray*
James Dean's most remembered screen
appearance, as a troubled teenager trying to
find himself as his family settles in a new town.
Warner Bros — *Warner Home Video; RCA
VideoDiscs*

Reborn   1984
Drama
72911   91 mins   C   B, V   P
Dennnis Hopper, Michael Moriarty
A faith healer and a talent scout hire actors to
be cured of fake ailments.
Unknown — *Vestron Video*

Reckless   1984
Adventure/Romance
75536   93 mins   C   B, V   P
Aidan Quinn, Daryl Hannah
The passion and rebelliousness of a teenage
couple upsets the small town they are trying to
escape.
MPAA:R
MGM UA Entertainment
Company — *MGM/UA Home Video*

Red Badge of Courage,   1951
The
Drama
81496   69 mins   B/W   B, V   P
*Audie Murphy, Bill Mauldin, Douglas Dick, Royal
Dano, directed by John Huston*
This is an adaptation of the Stephen Crane
novel about a young Union soldier who is
determined to conquer his fears as he goes off
to fight in the Civil War.
MGM — *MGM/UA Home Video*

Red Balloon, The   1956
Fantasy
65620   34 mins   C   B, V, CED   P
Pascal Lamorisse, directed by Albert Lamorisse
This is the story of Pascal, a lonely French boy
who befriends a wondrous red balloon which
follows him everywhere.
Academy Awards '56: Best Original Screenplay.
FR
Films Montsouris; Lopert Films — *Embassy
Home Entertainment; Video Yesteryear;
Western Film & Video Inc*

Red Balloon, The/An   19??
Occurrence at Owl Creek
Bridge
Fantasy/Drama
63845   60 mins   C   B, V   P
Two classic award-winning shorts have been
combined on one tape: "The Red Balloon"
(color, 1956) and "An Occurrence at Owl Creek
Bridge" (black and white, 1962).
Academy Awards '56: Best Original Screenplay
("The Red Balloon"); Cannes Film Festival:
Blue Ribbon and American Film Festival: First
Prize ("An Occurrence at Owl Creek Bridge").
Albert Lamorisse; Marcel Ichac and Paul de
Roubaix — *Hollywood Home Theater*

Red Baron, The   1984
Cartoons
70610   60 mins   C   B, V   P
Animated
The aerial dogfights in this presentation take
place between warring factions of real cartoon
dogs.
Videocraft International Ltd. — *Prism*

Red Dawn   1984
Science fiction/Adventure
80495   114 mins   C   B, V, LV   P
*Patrick Swayze, C. Thomas Howell, Harry Dean
Stanton, Powers Boothe, Ron O'Neal, directed
by John Milius*
A science fantasy of the future-that-might-be, as
Russian invaders overrun America's heartland
and take over the country. Eight small-town
teenagers hide out in the rugged countryside
and initiate guerrilla warfare. In VHS and Beta
Hi-Fi Stereo.
MPAA:PG13
United Artists — *MGM/UA Home Video*

Red Dust   1932
Adventure
82119   83 mins   B/W   B, V   P
*Clark Gable, Jean Harlow, Mary Astor, Gene
Raymond, Donald Crisp, directed by Victor
Fleming*
The overseer of a rubber plantation in Indochina
causes all kinds of trouble when he falls in love
with a young engineer's wife.
MGM — *MGM/UA Home Video*

Red Flag: The Ultimate Game 1981

Adventure/Drama
80638   104 mins   C   B, V   P
Barry Bostwick, Joan Van Ark, William Devane, George Coe, directed by Dan Taylor
This film shows a group of Air Force pilots who like to play intense war games in a small southwestern town. Available in Beta Hi-Fi and VHS Stereo.
Marble Arch Prods. — *U.S.A. Home Video*

Red Hot Rock 1985

Music-Performance/Music video
70384   60 mins   C   B, V   P
Duran Duran, Queen, Dwight Twilley, O'Bryan, The Tubes
The Videos in this collection were deemed to risque for broadcast or cable TV, but are gathered here today for home enjoyment.
Picture Music International — *Vestron Video*

Red House, The 1947

Suspense/Mystery
51950   100 mins   B/W   B, V   P
Edward G. Robinson, Lon McCallister, Judith Anderson, Allene Roberts, directed by Delmar Daves
What is the secret that lies hidden in the abandoned Red House and the dark paths of Oxhead Wood? Why is one man so determined to keep people away from the Red House?
United Artists; Sol Lesser — *Hollywood Home Theater; Discount Video Tapes; Kartes Video Communications; Video Yesteryear*

Red Kimona, The 1925

Drama
85208   95 mins   B/W   B, V   P
Tyrone Power Sr., Priscilla Boner, directed by Walter Lang
Originally written by Adela Rogers St. John, and adapted by Dorothy Arzner, this film deals with the trials of a lonely woman flung into a bordello and tried for murder, but with love triumphant. Silent.
Mrs. Wallace Reid Prods.; Vital Exchanges — *Video Yesteryear*

Red Kimono, The 1925

Drama/Exploitation
48741   70 mins   B/W   B, V, 3/4U   P
Dorothy Davenport Reid, Priscilla Boner, Theodore von Eltz, Tyrone Power, directed by Walter Lang
Part of a series of 1920's silent pictures about the vices and sins of the people of this world.
Mrs Wallace Reid Prods — *Video Yesteryear*

Red Light Sting, The 1984

Comedy-Drama
82077   96 mins   C   B, V   P
Farrah Fawcett, Beau Bridges, Harold Gould, Paul Burke, Sunny Johnson
A Justice Department rookie and a call girl reluctantly team up to con the Mafia in order to convict a local rackets czar. Available in VHS and Beta Hi-Fi Mono.
Universal Television — *MCA Home Video*

Red Nightmare 1953

Drama
39000   30 mins   B/W   B, V, FO   P
Jack Webb, Jack Kelly, Jeanne Cooper, Peter Brown
This anti-communist propaganda film, produced for the Department of Defense by Warner Brothers, features the cast of "Dragnet." The story dramatizes the Red Menace, with communists conspiring to take over America, and shows what would happen to life in a small American town if the Commies took over. A typical Mc Carthy-era production.
Warner Bros — *Video Yesteryear*

Red Norvo 1984

Music-Performance
88125   58 mins   C   B, V, 8mm   P
The innovative and ground-breaking jazz vibist performs at the Smithsonian: "All of Me," "Jitterbug Waltz,'"'School Days," and others.
Adler Ent.; Sony — *Sony Video Software*

Red Pony, The 1949

Drama
64541   89 mins   C   B, V   P
Myrna Loy, Robert Mitchum, Peter Miles, Louis Calhern, Margaret Hamilton, Beau Bridges, directed by Louis Milestone
A young boy loses faith in his father when his pet pony dies. Based on a story by John Steinbeck, with musical score by Aaron Copland.
Republic — *Republic Pictures Home Video*

Red River 1948

Western
31665   125 mins   B/W   B, V   P
John Wayne, Montgomery Clift, Walter Brennan, Joanne Dru, directed by Howard Hawks
The story of a cattle baron and the empire he builds.
United Artists — *Key Video; RCA VideoDiscs*

Red Shoes, The 1983

Fairy tales
82360   79 mins   C   B, V   P
The Children's Theatre Company and School of Minneapolis perform their own unique interpretation of the Hans Christian Anderson story. In VHS and Beta Hi-Fi Stereo.
Television Theatre Company — *MCA Home Video*

Red Shoes, The   1948
Drama
44365   133 mins   C   CED   P
*Moira Shearer, Anton Walbrook, Marius Goring,
Robert Helpmann*
A lovely ballerina is in a bitter struggle between
career and marriage.
Academy Awards '48: Best Art Director, Color;
Best Scoring, Drama (Brian Easdale).
Eagle Lion, J Arthur Rank — *RCA VideoDiscs;
Learning Corp of America*

Red Skelton's Funny   1982
Faces
Comedy-Performance
81257   55 mins   C   B, V   P
Red Skelton, Marcel Marceau 2   pgms
Each volume of this in-concert performance
contains Mr. Skelton delivering some of his
classic routines, blending the art of comedy with
mime.
Lewis Chesler — *U.S.A. Home Video*

Red Sonja   1985
Fantasy/Adventure
Closed Captioned
82418   89 mins   C   B, V   P
*Arnold Schwarzenegger, Brigitte Nielsen,
directed by Richard Fleischer*
Two warriors join forces against an evil queen in
this mystically-oriented film.
MPAA:PG-13
MGM/UA — *CBS/Fox Video*

Red Sun   1971
Western/Adventure
85019   115 mins   C   B, V   P
*Charles Bronson, Toshiro Mifune, Alain Delon,
Ursula Andress*
A gunfighter, samurai and French bandit fight
each other in various combinations.
National General Pictures — *Video Gems*

Redd Foxx—Video in a   1983
Plain Brown Wrapper
Comedy-Performance
66201   60 mins   C   B, V, LV,   P
                              CED
Foxx tackles all of his favorite subjectssex,
marriage, death, crime and more sex.
Command Entertainment Marketing — *Vestron
Video*

Redeemer, The   1977
Horror
35388   83 mins   C   B, V   P
*Christopher Flint, T.G. Finkbinder, Damien
Knight*
The Son of Satan sends invitations to a class
reunion. In the style of "The Omen."
MPAA:R

Sheldon Tromberg — *United Home Video;
Continental Video*

Redneck   1973
Drama
12041   92 mins   C   B, V   P·
Telly Savalas
A psychopathic killer and his partner take a
teenage boy hostage.
Int'l Amusement Corp — *King of Video*

Reds   1981
Drama
63425   200 mins   C   B, V, LV   P
*Warren Beatty, Diane Keaton, Jack Nicholson,
Maureen Stapleton, directed by Warren Beatty*
"Reds" is the story of John Reed, a liberal
American journalist who helped found the
American Communist Party, documented the
Bolshevik Revolution, and ultimately became
the only American ever to be buried within the
walls of the Kremlin.
Academy Awards '81: Best Supporting Actress
(Stapleton); Best Direction; Best
Cinematography. MPAA:PG
Paramount; Warren Beatty — *Paramount
Home Video; RCA VideoDiscs*

Reefer Madness   1938
Exploitation
03565   67 mins   B/W   B, V   P
Considered seriously at the time of its release,
this low-budget depiction of the horrors of
marijuana usage has become an underground
comedy favorite. Overwrought acting and the
lurid script contribute to the fun.
MPAA:PG
Dwain Esper Productions — *Media Home
Entertainment; Hollywood Home Theater; VCII;
Select-a-Tape; Video Dimensions; Discount
Video Tapes; Video Yesteryear; Movie Buff
Video; Video Connection; Western Film & Video
Inc; Vestron Video (disc only); Kartes Video
Communications*

Reet, Petite and Gone   1947
Musical
08888   75 mins   B/W   B, V, 3/4U   P
*Louis Jordan and his Tympany Five, June
Richmond*
A story about a girl whose mother dies, leaving a
will which a crooked lawyer alters.
Unknown — *Video Yesteryear; Discount Video
Tapes*

Reflections in a Golden   1967
Eye
Drama
80078   108 mins   C   B, V   P
*Elizabeth Taylor, Marlon Brando, Brian Keith,
Julie Harris, directed by John Huston*
There are all kinds of kinky activities going on at
a Georgia army camp.

Warner Bros; Ray Stark — *Warner Home Video*

Reggae Sunsplash I, II   1984
Music video
88104   120 mins   C   B, V   P
On two tapes, a variety of reggae artists perform in concert and on video, including Peter Tosh and Bob Marley, plus a wealth of lesser-known talents.
Sony Video — *Sony Video Software*

Rehabilitation and Injury   1978
Health education
42781   30 mins   C   B, V   P
Hosted by Ann Dugan 6 pgms
This series of cassettes covers aspects of rehabilitation and preventive medical care. See individual program listings.
1.Prenatal 2.Postnatal 3.Hysterectomy 4.Mastectomy 5.Knee 6.Back
Health 'N Action — *RCA/Columbia Pictures Home Video*

Reincarnate, The   1971
Horror
81754   89 mins   C   B, V   '   P
Jack Creley, Jay Reynolds, Trudy Young
A naive sculptor is offered a chance at eternal life when he agrees to join a satanic cult.
MPAA:PG
Electra Entertainment — *Magnum Entertainment*

Reincarnation of Peter Proud, The   1975
Suspense/Drama
79671   105 mins   C   B, V   P
Michael Sarrazin, Jennifer O'Neill, Margot Kidder, Cornelia Sharpe
A college professor has nightmares about his previous life. Based on the novel by Max Ehrlich.
MPAA:R
Avco Embassy — *Vestron Video*

Reivers, The   1969
Comedy/Adventure
70381   107 mins   C   B, V   P
Steve McQueen, Sharon Farrell, Will Geer, Michael Constantine, directed by Mark Rydell
Based on William Faulkner's last novel, this film shows the adventures of a young man's journey from the innocence of a small Mississippi town to the experiences of big city Memphis in 1905.
MPAA:PG
National General for Cinema Center — *Key Video*

Rembrandt   1936
Biographical/Drama
81466   86 mins   B/W   B, V, LV   P

Charles Laughton, Elsa Lanchester, Gertrude Lawrence, Walter Hudd, directed by Alexander Korda
This film chronicles the life and times of the great Dutch painter, Rembrandt.
Alexander Korda — *Embassy Home Entertainment*

Remo Williams: The   1985
Adventure Begins
Adventure
85887   121 mins   C   B, V   P
Fred Ward, Joel Grey, Wilford Brimley, Kate Mulgrew, directed by Guy Hamilton
A film adaptation of "The Destroyer" adventure novel series with a Bond-like hero who can walk on water and dodge bullets after being instructed by a Korean martial arts master.
MPAA:PG-13
Orion Pictures — *THORN EMI/HBO Video*

Renata Scotto: Prima   1984
Donna in Recital
Music-Performance
81942   99 mins   C   B, V   '   P
Renata Scotto performs works by Handel, Scarlatti, Verdi, Liszt and Puccini in this recital recorded in Tokyo.
NHK; Tokyo — *Video Arts International*

Renegade Monk   1982
Martial arts
64946   90 mins   C   B, V   R, P
Lui Chung Liang, Hwang Hsing Shaw, Ko Shou Liang, Lang Shih Chia, Hsu Chung Hsing
An invincible warrior-monk dispenses his own brand of justice with his fists.
MPAA:R
Foreign — *Video Gems*

Renegade Ninja   1983
Martial arts
85929   109 mins   C   B, V   P
Kensaku Marita, directed by Sadao Nakajima
A man whose father was murdered kicks everyone within reach in his quest for revenge.
Tan Takaiwa;Goro Kusabe;Nirimichi Matsudaira;Keizo Mimura — *Prism*

Renegade Ranger,   1938
The/Scarlet River
Western
81031   113 mins   B/W   B, V   P
kRita Hayworth, Tim Holt, George O'Brien, Ray Whitley, Tom Keene, Lon ChaneyJr., Myrna Loy, Bruce Cabot, Betty Furness
A western double feature: A Texas Ranger and his singing sidekick attempt to help out a woman accused of murder in the "The Renegade Ranger," and a cowboy tries to free his sweetheart from a band of cattle rustlers in "Scarlet River".

RKO — *RKO HomeVideo*

Reno And The Doc   1984
Comedy-Drama
84121   88 mins   C   B, V   P
Ken Walsh, Henry Ramer, Linda Griffiths
Two middle-aged men battling mid-life crises
join together and test their mettle in the world of
professional skiing.
New World Pictures — *New World Video*

REO Speedwagon: 1985
Wheels Are Turnin'
Music-Performance
82417   80 mins   C   B, V   P
R.E.O. Speedwagon
This collection of videos from the best-selling
band includes "I Don't Wanna Know," "Take It
On the Run," "I Can't Fight This Feeling" and
"Keep On Loving You."
CBS/Fox Video — *CBS/Fox Video*

Repo Man   1983
Comedy
75016   92 mins   C   B, V, LV   P
Harry Dean Stanton, Emilie Estevez
A spaced-out teenager becomes a
repossession man for an auto loan company,
experiencing many surrealistic adventures in his
new job.
Universal — *MCA Home Video*

Reproduction of Life: Sex   1982
Education
Reproduction/Sexuality
59565   53 mins   C   B, V   P
The entire process from conception through
prenatal development to birth itself is explained.
McGraw Hill — *Mastervision*

Requiem   1986
Music-Performance
87169   150 mins   C   B, V   P
*Placido Domingo, Sarah Brightman, conducted
by Lorin Maazel*
With the choirs of Winchester Cathedral and St.
Thomas' Church, Andrew Lloyd Webber's
award-winning composition is seen in a 1985
New York performance.
AM Available
Really Useful Company, Ltd. — *Kultur*

Resurrection of Zachary   1972
Wheeler, The
Science fiction
33595   100 mins   C   B, V   P
*Angie Dickinson, Bradford Dillman, Leslie
Nielson*
A presidential candidate who narrowly escaped
death in an auto crash is brought to a
mysterious clinic. A reporter sneaks into the
clinic and discovers the horrors of cloning.

MPAA:G
Gold Key — *United Home Video*

Retriever Trials for   1985
Hunters
Hunting
84269   31 mins   C   B, V   P
The Hunting Retriever Club
This is an outline of trials and tests club has
devised to gauge and train hunting retrievers of
all breeds.
Equinox Enterprises Inc — *Video Travel*

Retrievers, The   1982
Martial arts
77409   90 mins   C   B, V   P
Max Thayer, Roselyn Royce
A young man and a former CIA agent team up to
expose the unsavory practices of the
organization.
Arista Films — *Vestron Video*

Return, The   1980
Science fiction
63323   90 mins   C   B, V   P
*Raymond Burr, Cybill Shepherd, Martin Landau,
Jan-Michael Vincent*
Two friends seek clues to the bizarre
phenomena of the present in an extraterrestrial
encounter they shared as children 25 years
earlier.
Independent — *THORN EMI/HBO Video*

Return Engagement   1978
Drama/Romance
80672   76 mins   C   B, V   P
*Elizabeth Taylor, Joseph Bottoms, Peter Donat,
James Ray, directed by Joseph Hardy*
A lonely middle-aged ancient history professor
falls in love with one of her students.
The Production Co. — *Lightning Video*

Return from Witch   1978
Mountain
Fantasy
84804   93 mins   C   B, V   P
*Christopher Lee, Bette Davis, Ike Eisenmann,
Kim Richards, Jack Soo, directed by John
Hough*
A pair of evil masterminds use a boy's
supernatural powers to place Las Angeles in
nuclear jeopardy.
MPAA:G
Walt Disney Productions — *Walt Disney Home
Video*

Return of a Man Called   1976
Horse, The
Adventure
59429   125 mins   C   B, V, CED   P
*Richard Harris, Gail Sondergaard, Geoffrey
Lewis, directed by Ervin Kershner*

This sequel to "A Man Called Horse" tells the story of an English aristocrat who was captured and raised by Sioux Indians, and then returned to his native homeland.
United Artists — *CBS/Fox Video*

Return of Chandu   1934
Science fiction/Serials
10930   156 mins   B/W   B, V   P
Bela Lugosi, Maria Alba
Twelve chapters. Features Bela Lugosi, as Chandu, who exercises his powers to conquer the Black Sorcerers who inhabit the island of Lemuria.
Mascot — *Discount Video Tapes; Video Connection; Video Dimensions; Video Yesteryear*

Return of Chandu, The   1934
Suspense
38979   61 mins   B/W   B, V, FO   P
Bela Lugosi, Clara Kimball Young
Chandu the Magician fights to save the Princess Nadji from being sacrificed by a religious sect of cat worshippers. Story by Raymond Chandler.
Mascot — *Video Yesteryear; Cable Films; Video Connection*

Return of Frank Cannon   1980
Suspense/Mystery
82267   96 mins   C   B, V   P
William Conrad, Diana Muldaur, Joanna Pettet, Allison Argo, Arthur Hill, Ed Nelson
Portly private eye Frank Cannon comes out of retirement to investigate the alleged suicide of an old friend.
QM Productions — *Worldvision Home Video*

Return of Frank James,   1940
The
Western
84425   92 mins   C   B, V   P
Henry Fonda, Gene Tierney, Jackie Cooper, Henry Hull, John Carradine, Donald Meek, directed by Fritz Lang
One of Lang's lesser Hollywood works, this is nonetheless an entertaining sequel to "Jesse James," with Jesse's brother trying to go straight, but having to eventually hunt down the culprits who murdered his brother.
Darryl F Zanuck — *Playhouse Video*

Return of Martin Guerre,   1983
The
Mystery
65623   111 mins   C   B, V, LV   P
Gerard Depardieu, Natalie Baye
A true, satisfyingly ingenious and provocative story, which revolves around Martin Guerre, who had disappeared as a young husband and resumed his marriage years later.

Societe Francaise de Production Cinematographique — *Embassy Home Entertainment*

Return of Martin Guerre,   1982
The
Drama
80394   111 mins   C   B, V   P
Gerard Depardieu, Nathalie Baye, directed by Daniel Vigne
A young man who mysteriously disappears from his wife returns several years later to resume his marriage. With English subtitles.
FR
Moustapha Akkad — *Embassy Home Entertainment*

Return of the Bad Men   1948
Western
10068   90 mins   B/W   B, V   P
Randolph Scott, Robert Ryan, Anne Jeffreys, Gabby Hayes, Jason Robards, Jacqueline White
Man plans to stake claim in Oklahoma during land rush and finds romance.
RKO, Nat Holt — *RKO HomeVideo; Blackhawk Films; Nostalgia Merchant*

Return of the Chinese   1974
Boxer
Martial arts
86185   93 mins   ·C   B, V   P
Jimmy Wong Yu, Lung Fei, Cheung Ying Chen, Chin Kang
Samurai and ninja warriors fight, usually to the death.
Jimmy Wong Yu — *Unicorn Video*

Return of the Dragon   1972
Adventure/Martial arts
55832   91 mins   C   B, V   P
Bruce Lee, Nora Miao, Chuck Norris, directed by Bruce Lee
Lee's last picture concerns a Chinese restaurant in Rome which is menaced by gangsters who want to buy the property. On behalf of the owners, Lee duels an American karate champ in the Roman forum.
MPAA:R
Bryanston Pictures — *CBS/Fox Video; Video Gems*

Return of the Fly   1959
Science fiction
80733   78 mins   B/W   B, V   P
Vincent Price, Brett Halsey, John Sutton, Dan Seymour
The son of the scientist who discovered how to move matter through space decides to continue his father's work, but does so against his uncle's wishes. Available in VHS and Beta Hi-Fi-Stereo.
20th Century Fox — *Key Video*

Return of the Jedi   1983
Adventure/Science fiction
Closed Captioned
82420   132 mins   C   B, V   P
Mark Hamill, Carrie Fisher, Harrison Ford, Billy Dee Williams, directed by Richard Marquand
The third chapter of George Lucas' popular space saga. Against seemingly fearsome odds, Luke Skywalker battles such worthies as Jabba the Hutt and heavy breathing Darth Vader to save his comrades and triumph over the Galactic Empire.
MPAA:PG
Lucasfilm Ltd — *CBS/Fox Video*

Return of the Living Dead   1985
Comedy/Horror
86892   90 mins   C   B, V   P
Clu Gulager, James Karen, Don Calfa, directed by Dan O'Bannon
An outrageous spoof on the living-dead subgenre with fast-moving zombies, punk humor and exaggerated gore, as a poisonous gas revives a cemetery and morgue.
MPAA:R
Thorn EMI — *THORN EMI/HBO Video*

Return of the Pink   1975
Panther, The
Comedy
13595   113 mins   C   B, V, LV   P
Peter Sellers, Christopher Plummer, Catherine Schell, directed by Blake Edwards
Inspector Clousseau is called upon to rescue the Pink Panther diamond stolen from a museum.
MPAA:G
United Artists; Blake Edwards — *CBS/Fox Video; RCA VideoDiscs*

Return of the Rams/NFL   1984
'83
Football
75890   46 mins   C   B, V, FO   P
This program presents scenes from the Los Angeles Rams' 1983 season.
NFL Films — *NFL Films Video*

Return of the Red Tiger   1981
Martial arts/Adventure
59416   82 mins   C   B, V   P
Bruce Lee
Kung-Fu master Bruce Lee displays one of the foremost and exciting styles of kung-fu—the Tiger.
Unknown — *HarmonyVision*

Return of the Secaucus 7   1981
Comedy-Drama
60341   110 mins   C   B, V   P
Mark Arnott, Gordon Clapp, Maggie Cousineau-Arndt, directed by John Sayles
A weekend reunion of seven friends who were activists during the turbulent '60's serves as the basis for this look at a group turning 30.
Libra Specialty Films — *RCA/Columbia Pictures Home Video*

Return of the Soldier   1984
War-Drama
82023   101 mins   C   B, V   P
Glenda Jackson, Julie Christie, Ann-Margret, Alan Bates, Ian Holm, directed by Alan Bridges
Three women try to bring a shell-shocked World War I veteran back to the real world. Adapted from the novel by Rebecca West.
European Classics — *THORN EMI/HBO Video*

Return of the Tall Blond   197?
Man With One Black Shoe
Comedy
11356   84 mins   C   B, V   P
Pierre Richard
A sequel to "The Tall Blond Man With One Black Shoe," whereby a "klutz" is mistakenly thought to be a master spy. French with English subtitles.
FR
Cinema 5 — *Prism; Cinema Concepts*

Return of the Tiger   1978
Adventure/Martial arts
50732   95 mins   C   B, V   P
Bruce Li, Paul Smith, Chaing I, Angelea Mao, directed by Jimmy Shaw
The Hovver Night Club in Bangkok is used to cover up the operations of an international narcotic group headed by an American. A rival Chinese gang tries to dominate the drug market, and conflict ensues.
Jimmy Shaw — *Media Home Entertainment*

Return of the Vampire,   1943
The
Horror
81797   69 mins   B/W   B, V   P
Bela Lugosi, Nina Foch, Miles Mander, Matt Willis, directed by Lew Landers
A Hungarian vampire and his werewolf servant are after the family who drove a spike through his heart two decades earlier.
Columbia Pictures — *RCA/Columbia Pictures Home Video*

Return of the Zombies   1978
Horror
77389   95 mins   C   B, V   P
Stan Cooper, Charles Quiney
A pack of zombies stalk the countryside craving for the flesh and innards of their creators.
MPAA:R
Prodimex — *Wizard Video*

Return of Ulysses, The 1973
Music-Performance
81585   152 mins   C   B, V   P
Annabel Hunt, Ugo Trama, Patricia Grieg, Janet Hughes
A production of the Monteverdi opera performed by the Glyndebourne Festival Opera. With English subtitles.
IT
Southern Television Ltd — *Video Arts International*

Return to Boggy Creek 1977
Suspense
65330   87 mins   C   B, V, CED   P
Dawn Wells
In a small fishing village, the townspeople learn from a photogrpaher that a "killer" beast whom they thought had disappeared has returned and is living in Boggy Creek. Some children follow the photographer into the swamp, despite hurricane warnings.
MPAA:PG
Bayou Productions — *CBS/Fox Video*

Return to Fantasy Island 1977
Drama
80313   100 mins   C   B, V   P
Ricardo Montalban, Adrienne Barbeau, Pat Crowley, Laraine Day
Six people pay $50,000 each to spend a weekend on an island to live out their secret fantasies.
Spelling/Goldberg Productions — *Prism*

Return to Glory: The 1985 NBA Playoffs and World Championship Series 1986
Basketball/Documentary
71319   60 mins   C   B, V   P
Narrated by Dick Stockton
These highlights of the National Basketball Association Championship Series includes action by: The Los Angeles Lakers, Boston Celtics, Phoenix Suns, Portland Trail Blazers, Denver Nuggets, Cleveland Cavaliers, Detroit Pistons and Philadelphia 76ers.
Steve Cohen & Don Sperling — *U.S.A. Home Video*

Return to Macon County 1975
Adventure
66097   90 mins   C   B, V, CED   P
Nick Nolte, Don Johnson, Robin Mattson
A tale of three young, reckless youths on the loose.
American International Pictures — *Vestron Video*

Return to Oz 1984
Cartoons
70612   60 mins   C   B, V   P
Animated

This sequel to L. Frank Baum's original "The Wizard of Oz" features an all new musical score.
Videocraft International Ltd. — *Prism*

Return to Oz 1985
Fantasy
70935   109 mins   C   B, V, LV   P
Fairuza Balk, Piper Laurie, Matt Clark, Nicol Williamson, Jean Marsh, directed by Walter Murch
Picking up where "The Wizard of Oz" left off, Auntie Em and Uncle Ed place Dorothy in the care of an electro-shock therapist to cure her "delusions" of Oz. A natural disaster again lands her in the land of yellow bricks, where the evil Nome King and Princess Mombi have spread terror and squalor. Based on a later L. Frank Baum book.
MPAA:PG
Walt Disney Prods; Silver Screen Partners II — *Walt Disney Home Video*

Reuben, Reuben 1983
Comedy
Closed Captioned
78883   100 mins   C   B, V   P
Tom Conti, Kelly McGillis, directed by Robert Ellis Miller
A drunken poet's life turns around when he falls in love with a beautiful young woman.
MPAA:R
Walter Shenson; Taft — *CBS/Fox Video*

Revenge 1972
Drama
59841   89 mins   C   B, V   P
Joan Collins, James Booth, Ray Barrett, Ken Griffith
A thriller about the drive for revenge that ultimately destroys the family of a young girl who was brutally murdered.
Peter Rogers; George H Brown — *Embassy Home Entertainment*

Revenge 1986
Suspense
88169   90 mins   C   B, V   P
John Carradine, Patrick Wayne, Bennie Lee McGowan
A shot-for-video thriller about revenge, vengeance and vengeful things. Incidentally, also Carradine's 500th film.
United Enterprises — *United Home Video*

Revenge in the House of Usher 1985
Horror
70933   90 mins   C   B, V   P
Howard Vernon, Dan Villers, Lia Virli, directed by J.P. Johnson
Based on the Poe classic, "The Fall of the House of Usher"; the inhabitants of Usher's

place gather convincing evidence that they are residing at the gates of hell.
Eurocine; Brux Interfilm — *Wizard Video*

Revenge of the Dead   1984
Horror
77219   100 mins   C   B, V   P
A European archeological team discovers the existence of a powerful force that allows the dead to return to life.
Motion Picture Marketing — *Lightning Video*

Revenge of the   1981
Mysterons from Mars
Cartoons
71363   91 mins   C   B, V   P
Animated
Vicious plunderers arrive from the red planet, so Captain Scarlet and Spectrum rise to the battle.
Reg Hill — *Family Home Entertainment*

Revenge of the Nerds   1984
Comedy
Closed Captioned
76927   89 mins   C   B, V   P
Robert Carradine, Anthony Edwards, Ted McGinley, Julie Montgomery
A group of nerdish college freshmen revenge upon the fraternity that evicted them from their dorm.
MPAA:R
20th Century Fox — *CBS/Fox Video*

Revenge of the Ninja   1983
Adventure/Martial arts
6566.   90 mins   C   B, V, CED   P
Sho Kosugi
A Ninja hoping to escape his bloody past in Los Angeles gets mixed up with a drug trafficker, who turns out to be an American Ninja and his archfoe. The two polish off a slew of mobsters before their own inevitable showdown.
MPAA:R
Cannon Films — *MGM/UA Home Video*

Revenge of the Pink   1978
Panther
Comedy
47804   99 mins   C   B, V, LV,   P
                              CED
Peter Sellers, Herbert Lom, Dyan Cannon, Robert Webber, directed by Blake Edwards
Inspector Clouseau tracks down an international drug ring which takes him around the world.
MPAA:PG
United Artists — *CBS/Fox Video; RCA VideoDiscs*

Revolt of Job, The   1984
Drama
75541   98 mins   C   B, V   P

An elderly Jewish couple adopt an 8-year-old Gentile boy although it is illegal and against the beliefs of the orthodox community.
TeleCulture Inc — *MGM/UA Home Video*

Revolt of the Dragon   1975
Martial arts
63860   90 mins   C   B, V   P
A martial arts expert visits friends in his hometown and finds himself battling a ruthless gang that terrorizes the people.
MPAA:R
United International Pictures — *Hollywood Home Theater*

Revolution   1985
War-Drama
Closed Captioned
86377   125 mins   C   B, V, LV   P
Al Pacino, Donald Sutherland, Nastassia Kinski, Annie Lennox, Joan Plowright, Steven Berkoff, Dave King, directed by Hugh Hudson
The American Revolution comes to life in this would-be epic tale of an illiterate trapper caught up in the fighting.
MPAA:PG
Irwin Winkler — *Warner Home Video*

Rhinestone   1984
Comedy
Closed Captioned
80337   111 mins   C   B, V   P
Sylvester Stallone, Dolly Parton, Ron Liebman, directed by Bob Clark
A country singer must turn a cab driver into a singer in order to have a chance to sing at New York City's roughest country-western club, The Rhinestone.
MPAA:PG
Twentieth Century Fox — *CBS/Fox Video*

Rhythm and Blues 1   1983
Music-Performance
65225   57 mins   C   B, V   P
Billy Eckstine, Ruth Brown, Billy Preston, Gloria Lynne, Sheer Delight, Gil Askey
Gospel roots are joyously evident in this program documenting the Rhythm and Blues movement from the farms to the cities.
Skylark Savoy Productions Ltd — *Video Gems*

Rhythmatist, The   1985
Music-Performance
81211   57 mins   C   B, V   P
The Police's drummer Stuart Copeland discovers mystery and unusual music when he visits Africa. Available in VHS Dolby Hi-Fi Stereo and Beta Hi-Fi.
A&M Video — *RCA/Columbia Pictures Home Video*

Ribald Tales of Robin Hood, The — 1980
Satire
55214 · 83 mins   C   B, V   P
The Robin Hood legend is satirized in this comedy which concentrates on Prince John and his favorite pastimes: rape, pillage and plunder.
MPAA:R
Lima Productions — *Media Home Entertainment*

Rich and Famous — 1981
Comedy-Drama
59311   117 mins   C   B, V, CED   P
Jacqueline Bisset, Candice Bergen, David Selby, Hart Bochner, Matt Lattanzi, directed by George Cukor
The story of the 25-year friendship of two women, through college, marriage, and success.
MPAA:R
MGM — *MGM/UA Home Video*

Rich Kids — 1979
Romance/Comedy
71148   97 mins   C   B, V   P
John Lithgow, Kathryn Walker, Trini Alvarado, directed by Robert M. Young
Faced with the divorces of their respective parents, a young boy and girl decide to run away for a whimsical weekend.
MPAA:PG
United Artists; Robert Altman/Lion's Gate — *MGM/UA Home Video*

Rich Little's Great Hollywood Trivia Game — 1984
Game show
65601   60 mins   C   B, V   P
The multi-talented impressionist brings his Hollywood repertoire together for the show biz trivia challenge of the year.
Vestron — *Vestron Video*

Richard Lewis: I'm in Pain — 1985
Comedy-Performance
87569   51 mins   C   B, V   P
Irreverence abounds in this stand-up comic's improvised act.
Showtime — *Paramount Home Video*

Richard Nixon—Checkers, Old Glory, Resignation — 197?
Documentary/Presidency-US
57358   45 mins   B/W   B, V, FO   P
Three historic broadcasts in the career of Richard Nixon: the "Checkers Speech" (1952) where Nixon defended himself against accusations of misusing campaign funds; "Old Glory" (1957), a short talk from New York's Chrysler Building in honor of flag day; and "Resignation" (1974), a kinescope of the TV pool feed from the Oval Room of the White House as Nixon announces he will leave office.
Unknown — *Video Yesteryear*

Richard Petty Story, The — 1972
Drama/Automobiles-Racing
87184   83 mins   C   B, V   P
Richard Petty, Darren McGavin, Kathi Browne, Lynn Marta, Noah Beery Jr.
The biography of racecar driver Petty, portraying himself, and his various achievements on the track.
MPAA:G
Edward J. Lasko — *Video Gems*

Richard Pryor: Here and Now — 1983
Comedy-Performance
65697   75 mins   C   B, V, CED   P
Richard Pryor
Filmed at the Saenger Theater in New Orleans, Pryor's sharp, witty commentaries are delivered with a unique piercing humor.
MPAA:R
Bob Parkinson; Andy Friendly — *RCA/Columbia Pictures Home Video*

Richard Pryor—Live and Smokin' — 1971
Comedy-Performance
76777   47 mins   C   B, V, CED   P
Richard Pryor displays his comedic talents in this 1971 performance where he does his classic "The Wino and the Junkie" routine.
Michael Blum Productions — *Vestron Video*

Richard Pryor Live in Concert — 197?
Comedy-Performance
58898   78 mins   C   B, V   P
Richard Pryor
Richard Pryor demonstrates his unique brand of humor before an enthusiastic audience.
Unknown — *Vestron Video; RCA VideoDiscs*

Richard Pryor Live on the Sunset Strip — 1982
Comedy-Performance
63438   82 mins   C   B, V   P
Richard Pryor
Filmed live at the Hollywood Palladium, this program captures Richard Pryor at his funniest, including his segment about "Pryor on fire."
MPAA:R
Columbia; Richard Pryor — *RCA/Columbia Pictures Home Video; RCA VideoDiscs*

Richard Tee: Contemporary Piano — 1985
Music
87924   60 mins   C   B, V   P
The famed studio pianist gives instruction in practicing, chord substitution, vocalist backing and more.
DCI Music Video — *DCI Music Video*

Richard III — 1955
Drama
82575   138 mins   C   B, V   D
Laurence Olivier, Cedric Hardwicke, Ralph Richardson, John Gielgud, Claire Bloom, directed by Laurence Olivier
This landmark film version of the Shakespearean play features an acclaimed performance by Laurence Olivier. The plot follows the life of the twisted Richard of Gloucester and his schemes for the throne of England.
British Academy Awards '55: Best Film, Best Director (Laurence Olivier), Best Actor (Laurence Olivier).
Laurence Olivier; London Films — *Embassy Home Entertainment*

Richard Thompson — 1983
Music-Performance
88110   84 mins   C   B, V   P
A concert performance from the highly regarded Scottish Celtic/folk electric guitarist.
Sony Video — *Sony Video Software*

Richard's Things — 1980
Drama
69549   104 mins   C   B, V   P
Liv Ullman, Amanda Redman
A man's wife and his girlfriend find love and comfort in each other after his death.
MPAA:R
Unknown — *Embassy Home Entertainment*

Richie — 1974
Drama
71207   86 mins   C   B, V   P
Ben Gazzara, Eileen Brennan, Robby Benson, directed by Paul Wendkos
Experiments with drugs lead a young man's family life down a dead end. Based on a Thomas Thompson story.
MPAA:R
Independent — *Prism*

Richie Rich — 1983
Cartoons
66575   60 mins   C   B, V   P
Animated
Rich kid Richie Rich is featured in this compilation of exotic and comical adventures with his adolescent pals.
Hanna Barbera — *Worldvision Home Video*

Richie Rich — 1980
Cartoons
79240   50 mins   C   B, V   P
Animated
The world's wealthiest little boy, Richie Rich, and his girlfriend Gloria travel around the world to solve crimes.
Hanna-Barbera Productions — *Worldvision Home Video*

Richie Rich Vol II — 1980
Cartoons
82319   60 mins   C   B, V   P
Animated
Richie Rich and his faithful dog, Dollar, have a wealth of adventures to explore in this collection of nine episodes from the series.
Hanna-Barbera Prods — *Worldvision Home Video*

Rick Derringer — 1982
Music-Performance
75909   58 mins   C   B, V   P
This program presents Rick Derringer performing several of his monster hit songs at the Ritz night club in New York City.
Harrison Suggs Productions Inc — *Sony Video Software*

Rick Derringer: Secrets — 1984
Music
87922   40 mins   C   B, V   P
A look at Derringer's performance style and guitar playing, with emphasis on training exercises and glimpses of him in concert.
AM Available
Video Syndications — *DCI Music Video*

Rick Springfield Platinum Videos — 1983
Music video
66632   30 mins   C   B, V   P
This music video collection of Rick Springfield hits contains the following six songs: "Affair of the Heart," "Human Touch," "Souls," "Don't Talk to Strangers," "What Kind of Fool Am I" and "Jessie's Girl."
RCA Video Productions — *RCA/Columbia Pictures Home Video*

Ricky Nelson in Concert — 1985
Music-Performance
87181   21 mins   C   B, V   P
Rick and the Stone Canyon Band are seen in one of their last concerts, taped at the Universal Amphitheatre; featuring "Garden Party" and "Hello Mary Lou."
Silver Eagle Records; MCA Home Video — *MCA Home Video*

Ricky Skaggs: Live in London   1985
Music-Performance
82415   45 mins   C   B, V   P
Ricky Skaggs
The popular country-music singer performs
such songs as "Uncle Pen," "Cajun Moon," and
"I've Got a New Heartache" in a live
performance at London's Dominion Theater.
CBS/Fox Video — *CBS/Fox Video*

Riddle of the Sands   1984
Adventure
72533   99 mins   C   B, V   P
*Michael York, Jenny Agutter, Simon Mac
Corkindale, directed by Tony Maylam*
Two English yachtsmen in 1903 inadvertently
stumble upon a German plot to invade England
by sea.
Satori — *VidAmerica*

Ride in the Whirlwind   1967
Western
09005   83 mins   C   B, V   P
*Jack Nicholson, Cameron Mitchell, Millie
Perkins, Katherine Squire*
Three cowboys are mistaken for members of a
gang by a posse.
Jack Nicholson; Monte Hellman — *Media
Home Entertainment; Hollywood Home Theater;
Video Yesteryear; Discount Video Tapes;
Western Film & Video Inc; Continental Video*

Ride, Ranger, Ride   1936
Western
05586   56 mins   B/W   B, V, 3/4U   P
*Gene Autry, Smiley Burnette, Kaye Hughes,
Max Terhune*
Gene Autry joins the cavalry and foils a plot to
start an Indian uprising.
Republic — *Nostalgia Merchant; Video
Yesteryear*

Ride the High Country   1962
Western
86782   93 mins   C   B, V   P
*Randolph Scott, Joel McCrea, Mariette Hartley,
directed by Sam Peckinpah*
The cult classic western so beloved of French
theorists, starring the two old veterans shipping
a much-sought-after load of gold.
MGM — *MGM/UA Home Video*

Ride the Man Down   1953
Western
74487   90 mins   C   B, V   P
Rod Cameron, Ella Raines
This is the story of a murderous land war
between neighboring landowners.
Republic — *Republic Pictures Home Video*

Ride the Wind   1966
Western
72892   120 mins   C   B, V   P
Lorne Greene, Dan Blocker
The "Bonanza" gang goes to the aid of the
Pony Express.
NBC — *Republic Pictures Home Video*

Rider from Tucson   1950
Western
73702   60 mins   B/W   B, V   P
Tim Holt, Richard Martin
A group of claim jumpers will stop at nothing to
gain control of a gold mine.
RKO — *RKO HomeVideo*

Rider on the Rain   1970
Suspense
64973   115 mins   C   B, V   P
Marlene Jobert, Charles Bronson, Jill Ireland
A young housewife is viciously raped by an
escaped sex maniac. She kills him and disposes
of his body, not knowing that he is being
relentlessly pursued by a tough colonel.
Avco-Embassy — *Monterey Home Video*

Riders of Death Valley   1941
Western/Serials
12550   195 mins   B/W   B, V   P
*Buck Jones, Lon Chaney, Jr., Dick Foran,
directed by Ford Beebe, Ray Taylor*
Western action serial in fifteen episodes of
thirteen minutes each.
Universal — *Video Connection; Discount Video
Tapes; Captain Bijou*

Riders of Destiny   1933
Western
15489   59 mins   B/W   B, V   P
John Wayne
John Wayne leads a group of Rangers on the
trail of justice.
Monogram — *Sony Video Software; Spotlite
Video; Video Connection; Discount Video
Tapes; Video Dimensions*

Riders of the Desert   1932
Western
11371   57 mins   B/W   B, V, FO   P
Bob Steele
Plenty of hoofbeats through desert sands.
Worldwide — *Video Yesteryear; Video
Connection*

Riders of the Range   1949
Western
73700   60 mins   B/W   B, V   P
Tim Holt, Richard Martin
A cowboy rides into town just in time to save a
girl's brother from gamblers.
RKO — *RKO HomeVideo*

Riders of the Rockies 1937

Western
15457   60 mins   B/W   B, V   P
Tex Ritter, Yakima Canutt, directed by Robert N. Bradbury
An honest cowboy turns rustler in order to trap a border gang.
Grand National — *United Home Video; Video Connection; Discount Video Tapes*

Riders of the Whistling Pines 1949

Western
64391   70 mins   B/W   B, V, 3/4U   P
Gene Autry, Patricia White, Jimmy Lloyd
Gene solves a murder committed by a band of lumber thieves.
Gene Autry Productions;
Columbia — *Nostalgia Merchant*

Riders of the Whistling Skull 1937

Western
15440   54 mins   B/W   B, V   P
Bob Livingston, Ray Corrigan
Three Mesquiteers rescue professor of archeology captured by lost Indian tribe.
Republic — *Video Connection; Video Dimensions; Video Yesteryear*

Ridin' on a Rainbow 1941

Western
54112   79 mins   B/W   B, V   P, T
Gene Autry, Smiley Burnette
A has-been performer on a steamboat decides to rob a bank in the hopes of starting a new life for himself and his daughter. The money he robs had just been deposited by some cattlemen. One of the cattlemen joins the steamboat's crew, wins the daughter's heart, and gets to the father.
Republic — *Blackhawk Films; Video Connection*

Riding High 1978

Drama
87326   92 mins   C   B, V   P
Eddie Kidd, Irene Handl, Murray Salem, Marella Oppenheim, Bill Mitchell
A sleazy motorcyclist challenges the world champion stunt rider.
Michael & Tony Klinger — *U.S.A. Home Video*

Riding on Air 1937

Comedy
81727   58 mins   B/W   B, V   P
Joe E. Brown
A small town newspaper reporter discovers that his bumbling methods get him the right results.
RKO — *Kartes Video Communications*

Riel 1982

Western
72336   150 mins   C   B, V   P
Arthur Hill, William Shatner
This is the story of Louis Riel, a half-French, half-Indian visionary who challenged the Canadian army in his fight for equality and self-rule.
Canadian Broadcasting Corporation — *Prism*

Rififi 1954

Mystery
44160   115 mins   B/W   B, V   P
Jean Servais, Carl Mohner, Robert Manuel, Jules Dassin, directed by Jules Dassin
A suspenseful story of a successful jewel robbery in which the four thieves betray each other.
French with English subtitles.
FR
UMPO; French — *Movie Buff Video; Video Yesteryear; Hollywood Home Theater; Discount Video Tapes; Cable Films; Western Film & Video Inc*

Rifle Shooting Tips and Techniques 1985

Hunting
87645   48 mins   C   B, V   P
Glen Pearce, Jim Carter
The two champion marksmen demonstrate the finer points of rifle shooting, handling and care.
Sportsmen On Film — *Sportsmen on Film*

Right of Way 1984

Drama
74110   102 mins   C   B, V   P
Bette Davis, James Stewart, Melinda Dillon
A touching story of true love featuring two of the biggest stars to ever grace the silver screen. Stewart plays an elderly man who makes a suicide pact when he learns of his wife's terminal illness.
George Schaefer — *VCL Home Video*

Right Stuff, The 1983

Drama
Closed Captioned
74210   193 mins   C   B, V, LV   P
Charles Frank, Scott Glenn, Ed Harris, Dennis Quaid, Sam Shephard
This program is based on the best-selling book by Tom Wolfe. It is the up-close and personal story of America's space program at its conception.
Academy Awards '83: Best Music Score; Best Film Editing; Best Sound; Best Sound Effect Editing. MPAA:PG
Irwin Winkler; Robert Chartoff — *Warner Home Video*

Right Stuff/NFL '83, The 1984

Football
72939   46 mins   C   B, V, FO   P

Pittsburgh Steelers
Highlights from the Pittsburgh Steelers' 1983
season and "NFL 1983."
NFL Films — *NFL Films Video*

Rigid Heddle   1985
Weaving—Level I
Handicraft
85654   87 mins   C   B, V   P
Betty Davenport
This course for semi-experienced weavers
demonstrates the method of warping for rigid
heddle looms.
Victorian Video Prod. — *Victorian Video
Productions*

Rigoletto   1954
Opera
56916   90 mins   C   B, V, FO   P
Aldo Silvani, Gerard Landry, Janet Vidor
Verdi's great opera concerning the intrigues in
the court of the Duke of Mantua, and the clever
plottings of Rigoletto—the hunchbacked court
jester. Sung in Italian with dialogue dubbed in
English.
Italy — *Video Yesteryear*

Rigoletto   1946
Opera
84654   80 mins   B/W   B, V   P
Tito Gobbi, Mario Filipeschi, Giulio Neri
A film version of the Verdi opera in a famed
Gobbi performance.
IT
Italian — *V.I.E.W. Video*

Rikki-Tikki-Tavi   1975
Cartoons
71346   30 mins   C   B, V   P
Animated, narrated by Orson Welles
From Rudyard Kipling's "The Jungle Book," this
story deals with a brave mongoose who saves
his family from two attacking cobras.
Chuck Jones — *Family Home Entertainment*

Rime of the Ancient   198?
Mariner
Literature
47405   60 mins   C   B, V   P
*Narrated by Sir Michael Redgrave, directed by
Raul De Silva*
An adaptation of Samuel Taylor Coleridge's epic
poem, set to images both real and animated; in
two parts—Part I: The Life of Samuel Coleridge;
Part II: The Rime of the Ancient Mariner.
International Film and Television Festival of
New York: Gold Medal.
Kultur — *Kultur*

Ring of Death, The   1972
Mystery
80823   93 mins   C   B, V   R, P

Franco Nero, Florinda Bolkan, Adolfo Celi
A tough cop investigating a routine case
becomes a hunted man after someone kills the
man he is following.
Mario Cecci Gori — *Video Gems*

Ringing Bell   1983
Fairy tales
65467   ? mins   C   B, V   P
Animated
This is the story of a fluffly lamb whose mother
is killed by a terrifying black wolf, leaving him
alone and resolved to avenge her death. In Beta
Hi-Fi.
Tsunemasa Hatano — *RCA/Columbia Pictures
Home Video*

Ringmasters—The Great   1985
American Bash
Sports-Minor
82446   60 mins   C   B, V   P
Hosted by Gordon Solie and Bill Apter
A compilation of professional wrestling
matches. Included are performances by
champions Ric Flair, Magnum T. A. and Tully
Blanchard.
Vestron Video — *Vestron Video*

Ringo Rides West   1984
Cartoons
81074   55 mins   C   B, V   P
Animated
This is the story of Ringo the cat who leads a
courageous battle for truth and justice in the
wild western frontier.
H. Lewis — *MPI Home Video*

Rink, The   1916
Comedy
10645   20 mins   B/W   B, V, 3/4U   R, P,
                                                      DL
Charlie Chaplin
Chaplin plays a waiter who spends his lunch
hour on roller skates. (Silent with musical
soundtrack added.)
RKO — *Cable Films; Festival Films*

Rink, The/The Immigrant   191?
Comedy
59368   56 mins   B/W   B, V, FO   P
Charlie Chaplin, Mack Swain, Edna Purviance
Two Chaplin shorts: 'The Rink' (1916), in which
Charlie defends his girlfriend's honor at a local
roller skating rink; "The Immigrant" (1917),
features Charlie as a newcomer to America.
Mutual — *Video Yesteryear*

Rio Bravo   1959
Western
58246   140 mins   C   B, V   P

John Wayne, Dean Martin, Angie Dickinson, Rick Nelson, Walter Brennan, directed by Howard Hawks
The sheriff of a Texas border town takes a brutal murderer into custody—and faces a blockade of hired gunmen determined to keep his prisoner from being brought to justice.
Armada Productions — *Warner Home Video; RCA VideoDiscs*

Rio Conchos   1964
Adventure
71379   107 mins   C   B, V   P
Richard Boone, Stuart Whitman, Edmond O'Brien, Tony Franciosa
Three Army buddies search for 2,000 stolen rifles in this action-packed post-Civil War western.
David Weisbort — *Playhouse Video*

Rio Grande   1950
Western
66466   105 mins B/W   B, V   P
John Wayne, Maureen O'Hara, Ben Jonson, Claude Jarman Jr., directed by John Ford
A U.S. Cavalry unit on the Mexican border conducts an unsuccessful campaign against marauding Indians.
Republic — *Republic Pictures Home Video*

Rio Lobo   1970
Western
54104   114 mins   C   B, V, CED   P
John Wayne, Jorge Rivero, Jennifer O'Neill, Jack Elam, directed by Howard Hawks
After the Civil War, a Union Colonel goes to Rio Lobo to take revenge on two traitors. When he gets there he finds that one of the traitors is in a conspiracy with the town sheriff, trying to force a rancher to sign over all his land.
MPAA:G
National General Pictures, Cinema Center — *CBS/Fox Video*

Riot in Cell Block 11   1954
Drama
77481   80 mins   B/W   B, V   P
Neville Brand, Leo Gordon, Emile Meyer, directed by Don Siegel
A convict leads four thousand prisoners in a riot at a maximum security penitentiary.
Allied Artists — *Republic Pictures Home Video*

Rip Van Winkle   1984
Fairy tales
Closed Captioned
82095   60 mins   C   B, V   P
Harry Dean Stanton, Talia Shire, directed by Francis Ford Coppola
This is an adaptation of the Washington Irving story about Rip Van Winkle, a man who falls asleep for twenty years after a group of ghosts

get him drunk. From the "Faerie Tale Theatre" series. Available in VHS and Beta Hi-Fi Stereo.
Platypus Productions; Lion's Gate Films — *CBS/Fox Video*

Ripoff, The   1978
Adventure
79244   90 mins   C   B, V   P
Lee Van Cleef, Karen Black, Edward Albert, Robert Alda
An aging jewel thief comes out of retirement to pull off a six million dollar jewelry heist.
Turi Vasile — *Worldvision Home Video*

Ripped Off   1974
Mystery
81157   72 mins   C   B, V   P
Robert Blake, Ernest Borgnine, Catherine Spaak
A boxer framed for the murder of his manager sets out to clear his name by finding the killers.
MPAA:R
Ottavio Oppo. — *Lightning Video*

Ripper, The   1986
Horror
70889   90 mins   C   B, V   P
Wade Tower, Tom Schreir, Mona Van Pernis, Andrea Adams, directed by Christopher Lewis
In this made-for-video production, the spirit of "Jack-the-Ripper" possesses a university professor's body.
United Home Video — *United Home Video*

Rise and Fall of the Third   1968
Reich
Documentary/History-Modern
68247   120 mins   C   B, V   P
A pictorial record which tracks Adolph Hitler's path through the years between 1920 and 1945. Some segments are in black and white.
MGM — *MGM/UA Home Video*

Risky Business   1983
Comedy
65357   99 mins   C   B, V, LV,   P
                                  CED
Tom Cruise, Rebecca de Mornay
A straight-arrow, college-bound student encounters a street-smart call girl while his parents are out of town, resulting in a funny and harrowing week-long odyssey toward maturity. Available in hi-fi stereo, and with Spanish subtitles as well.
MPAA:R
Steve Tisch Jon Avnet Production — *Warner Home Video*

Rita Hayworth: The Love   1983
Goddess
Biographical/Drama
79330   97 mins   C   B, V   P

Lynda Carter, Michael Lerner, Alejandro Rey, John Considine
A dramatization of Rita Hayworth's public and private life from 1934 to 1952. In Beta Hi-Fi and VHS Stereo.
Susskind Company — *U.S.A. Home Video*

Rituals   1979
Drama
60447   100 mins   C   B, V   P
Hal Holbrook, Laurence Dane
A group of five calm, rational men suddenly turn desperate after a chain of nightmarish events.
Lawrence Dane; Day and Date Intl — *Embassy Home Entertainment*

Ritz, The   1976
Comedy
Closed Captioned
80708   91 mins   C   B, V   P
Rita Moreno, Jack Weston, Jerry Stiller, Kaye Ballard, Treat Williams, F. Murray Abraham, directed by Richard Lester
When a Cleveland sanitation man meets up with his wife's murderous brother at his father-in-law's funeral in New York, he hides out in an all-male bathhouse.
MPAA:R
Warner Bros. — *Warner Home Video*

River, The   1937
Documentary
60003   32 mins   B/W   B, V, 3/4U,   P
                                FO
Directed by Pare Lorentz
A documentary about the exploitation and misuse of one of our greatest natural resources covering the period from the Civil War to the disastrous floods of the 1930's.
Venice Film Festival: Best Documentary.
Farm Security Administration — *Video Yesteryear*

River, The   1984
Drama
70553   124 mins   C   B, V, LV   P
Mel Gibson, Sissy Spacek, Scott Glenn, directed by Mark Rydell, written by Robert Dillon and Julian Barry
Tom and Mae Garvey fight floods, foreclosures, and government efforts to construct a hydroelectric plant in this third of '84's "back-to-the-farm" films. This tape features the beautiful photography of the film and stereo surround sound in all formats.
MPAA:PG13
Universal — *MCA Home Video*

River of Unrest   1937
Drama
78107   69 mins   B/W   B, V, FO   P
John Lodge, John Loder, Antoinette Cellier

Remarkable visual expressiveness and emotional power in a film about terrorism and open warfare during the Irish Rebellion.
Wardour — *Video Yesteryear*

River Rat, The   1984
Drama
Closed Captioned
70357   93 mins   C   B, V, LV   P
Tommy Lee Jones, Brian Dennehy, Martha Plimpton
The story of an ex-convict—wrongly imprisoned for thirteen years—who learns the value of love from his young daughter. The action takes place on the Mississippi River, where the reunited family faces many evil challenges.
MPAA:PG
Paramount Pictures Corp. — *Paramount Home Video*

Road Games   1981
Suspense
60448   100 mins   C   B, V, CED   P
Stacy Keach, Jamie Lee Curtis
A trucker is drawn into a web of intrigue surrounding a series of highway murders.
MPAA:PG
Avco Embassy; Richard Franklin — *Embassy Home Entertainment*

Road Runner vs. Wile E.   1963
Coyote: The Classic
Chase
Cartoons
81574   54 mins   C   B, V   P
Animated, directed by Chuck Jones
Wile E. Coyote engages in a battle of wits against the Road Runner in this collection of eight classic cartoons.
Warner Bros — *Warner Home Video*

Road to Bali   1953
Comedy
47663   91 mins   C   B, V   P
Bob Hope, Bing Crosby, Dorothy Lamour, Mervyn Vye, Ralph Moody, Jane Russell, Jerry Lewis, Dean Martin
Two vaudervillians performing in Australia are forced to hit the high seas due to a pair of matrimony-minded females.
Paramount — *Unicorn Video*

Road to Lebanon, The   1960
Comedy
78104   50 mins   B/W   B, V, FO   P
Danny Thomas, Bing Crosby, Bob Hope, Hugh Downs, Claudine Auger, Sheldon Leonard
This program presents an original musical comedy featuring many stars, spoofing the famous Hope-Crosby "Road" films.
NBC — *Video Yesteryear*

Road to Nashville 1967
Musical/Comedy
84821   110 mins   C   B, V   P
Marty Robbins, Johnny Cash, Doodles Weaver, Connie Smith
An agent travels to Nashville to enlist talent for a new musical.
MPAA:G
Robert Patrick Prods — *United Home Video*

Road to War, The 1985
World War II/Documentary
71065   60 mins   B/W   B, V   P
Written by Hendrick Van Loon, compiled by Irving Allen and Herbert Bregstein
This film documents the nationalistic tensions, political maneuvering and economic hardship that led to the outbreak of the Second World War.
Independent — *MPI Home Video*

Road to Yesterday, The 1925
Drama
85209   136 mins   B/W   B, V   P
Joseph Schildkraut, William Boyd, Jetta Goudal, Vera Reynolds, directed by Cecil B. DeMille
Five people together on a crashing train are somehow thrown into the ancient past in roles parallel to their own lives.
Cecil B. DeMille — *Video Yesteryear*

Road to Yesterday/The Yankee Clipper 1927
Film-History
50640   56 mins   B/W   B, V   P, T
William Boyd, Elinor Fair, Joseph Schildkraut, Jetta Boudal, Vera Reynolds
Four train passengers are transported back to previous lives in "The Road to Yesterday." "The Yankee Clipper races the British Lord of the Isles from China to New England to capture the tea trade. Both of these pictures are abridged versions. Silent.
Cecil B DeMille; Rupert Julian — *Blackhawk Films*

Road Warrior, The 1982
Adventure
63453   95 mins   C   B, V, LV,   P
                              CED
Mel Gibson, directed by George Miller
There is only one man who can save the terrorized pilgrims who've barricaded themselves on the barren post WWIII plains of Australia. The Road Warrior - Mad Max. This action filled sequel to "Mad Max" features Gibson playing John Wayne in metal and leather. No kangaroos or koalas.
MPAA:R
Warner Bros; Kennedy Miller Productions — *Warner Home Video*

Road Warriors, The/NFL '82 1983
Football
66221   45 mins   C   B, V, FO   P
Highlights of the N.Y. Jets 1982-83 season, plus an overview of the whole NFL season.
NFL Films — *NFL Films Video*

Roadhouse 66 1984
Drama
73660   90 mins   C   B, V   R, P
When a preppie and a musician get stuck in an Arizona town for car repairs, the duo wind up in a drag race and fall in love. The soundtrack features music from Los Lobos, The Pretenders, and Dave Edmunds.
MPAA:R
Scott Rosenfelt; Mark Levinson — *Key Video*

Roaring Fire 1982
Suspense/Martial arts
66025   95 mins   C   B, V   P
Sonny Chiba
A martial arts thriller set against the backdrop of exotic Japan.
Shiteru Okada — *THORN EMI/HBO Video*

Roaring Guns 1936
Western
13092   66 mins   B/W   B, V   P
Tim McCoy, Rex Lease
Small-time ranchers overcome a crooked cattle combine.
Puritan — *Video Connection; United Home Video*

Roaring Twenties, The 1939
Drama
64786   106 mins   B/W   B, V   P
James Cagney, Humphrey Bogart, Jeffrey Lynn, Priscilla Lane
A WWI veteran returns to New York and becomes involved in bootlegging, builds up an empire and dies in a gang war.
Warner; Hal B. Wallis — *Key Video; RCA VideoDiscs*

Roaring Twenties, The 192?
History-US/Documentary
10147   ? mins   B/W   B, V   P, T
Newsreels picture Ku Klux Klan, the automobile era, the first total solar eclipse, the Charleston, Babe Ruth, Rudolph Valentino's death, Charles Lindbergh, and Black Tuesday when stock market crashed.
Unknown — *Blackhawk Films*

Rob McConnell 1983
Music-Performance
75916   25 mins   C   B, V   P

This program presents the jazz music of Rob McConnell featuring his hits "The Waltz I Blew for You" and "My Man Bill."
digit recordings — *Sony Video Software*

Rob Roy—The Highland Rogue   1953
Adventure/Drama
82032   84 mins   C   B, V   P
Richard Todd, Glynis Johns
Scottish Highlander Rob Roy must battle against the King of England's secretary who would undermine the MacGregor clan to enact his evil deeds.
Walt Disney Productions — *Walt Disney Home Video*

Robbers of the Sacred Mountain   1983
Adventure
75489   95 mins   C   B, V   P
Two adventurers seek meteorites in the jungles of Mexico.
Unknown — *Prism*

Robby the Rascal   1985
Cartoons/Fantasy
81104   90 mins   C   B, V   P
Animated
The evil Mr. Bullion devises a plan to steal a cybot, Robby the Rascal, from his inventor Dr. Rumplechips.
Kidpix Inc. — *Paramount Home Video*

Robe, The   1953
Drama
08455   133 mins   C   B, V   P
Richard Burton, Jean Simmons, Victor Mature, Michael Rennie
This moving religious picture follows the career of a drunken and dissolute Roman tribune, Marcellus, after he wins the robe of Christ in a dice game.
EL, SP
20th Century Fox — *CBS/Fox Video*

Robert et Robert   1979
Comedy-Drama
47022   95 mins   C   B, V   P
Charles Denner, Jacques Villeret, Jean-Claude Brialy
Two "ineligible" bachelors resort to a computerized matrimonial agency to find the girls of their dreams. French with English subtitles.
FR
Quartet Films — *RCA/Columbia Pictures Home Video*

Robert Klein: Child of the 50's, Man of the 80's   1984
Comedy-Performance
80813   60 mins   C   B, V   P
Robert Klein
The hilarious Robert Klein performs some of his classic routines in this concert taped at New York University in Manhattan's Greenwich Village.
HBO — *THORN EMI/HBO Video*

Robert Palmer—Riptide   1986
Music video
86793   15 mins   C   B, V   P
Palmer performs his greatest hits in a series of videos, including "Addicted to Love," "Discipline of Love" and "Riptide."
RCA Video — *RCA/Columbia Pictures Home Video*

Robert Youngson Specials   19??
Variety/Documentary
29782   60 mins   C   B, V   P
6 pgms
A series of six programs that shows fads, culture, sports, famous personalities, and great moments in the first half of the twentieth century. Each show is headlined by a theatrical short done by Robert Youngson, built around laughter and action.
1. Spills and Chills 2. This Mechanical Age 3. The World of Kids 4. Blaze Busters 5. Gadgets Galore 6. I Never Forget a Face
Robert Youngson, Warner Bros — *Hollywood Home Theater*

Roberto Clemente: A Touch of Royalty   1975
Baseball
33831   26 mins   C   B, V   P
Roberto Clemente
The story of the near-legendary Pittsburgh Pirate outfielder and Hall of Famer is told through action footage of Clemente, on-location shooting in his native Puerto Rico, and interview with friends and family. His tragic death occurred on a mercy mission to aid Nicaraguan Refugees.
W and W Productions — *Major League Baseball Productions*

Robin and Marian   1976
Drama
65097   106 mins   C   B, V   P
Sean Connery, Audrey Hepburn, Robert Shaw, Richard Harris, directed by Richard Lester
After a separation of twenty years, Robin Hood is reunited with Maid Marian, who is now a nun. Their dormant feelings for each other are reawakened as Robin spirits her to Sherwood Forest.
MPAA:PG

Columbia; Rastar — *RCA/Columbia Pictures Home Video*

Robin Hood   1973
Cartoons
Closed Captioned
79558   83 mins   C   B, V, LV,   P
                                   CED
Animated, voices of Peter Ustinov, Terry Thomas, Phil Harris, Brian Bedford
A group of animals from Sherwood Forest act out their version of the Robin Hood legend.
Wolfgang Reitherman — *Walt Disney Home Video*

Robin Hood ... The   1983
Legend
Adventure
Closed Captioned
70899   115 mins   C   B, V   P
Michael Praed, Anthony Valentine, Nickolas Grace, written by Richard Carpenter, directed by Ian Sharp 4   pgms
This four-tape series from the British television production offers a thorough telling of the Robin Hood legend, with lots of swash buckling wealth redistribution.
Paul Knight; Goldcrest Films — *Playhouse Video*

Robinhood of Texas   1947
Western/Musical
44807   71 mins   B/W   B, V   P, T
Gene Autry, Cass County Boys
Gene and his friend help a sheriff round up a team of bank robbers and their loot while salvaging an almost defunct ranch and turning it into a fancy dude ranch.
Republic — *Blackhawk Films; Video Connection*

Robinhood of the Pecos   1941
Western
51640   56 mins   B/W   B, V   P
Roy Rogers
A young, ex-Confederate soldier takes on northern post-war politicians and carpetbaggers.
Republic — *Discount Video Tapes; Video Yesteryear*

Robinson Crusoe   1936
Adventure
38978   34 mins   B/W   B, V, FO   P
Narrated by "Uncle Don" Carney
A real oddity—this is a British silent film that was originally made in 1927. Ten years later, the film was re-edited, music and sound effects were added, along with a narration by children's radio personality "Uncle Don" Carney, which follows the plot of the famous adventure story.
Unknown — *Video Yesteryear*

Robinson Crusoe   1978
Cartoons
76972   86 mins   C   B, V   P
Animated
An animated adaptation of the classic Defoe story about a man marooned on a small island.
Viacom — *Family Home Entertainment*

Robinson Crusoe   1972
Adventure/Cartoons
84711   48 mins   C   B, V   P
Animated
The classic survival story is retold with animation.
Air Programs Int'l — *MGM/UA Home Video*

Robinson Crusoe and the   1972
Tiger
Adventure
81448   109 mins   C   B, V   P
Hugo Stiglitz, Ahui, directed by Rene Cardona, Jr.
A tiger tells the famous story of how Robinson Crusoe became stranded on a desert island.
MPAA:G
Avant Films — *Embassy Home Entertainment*

Robot Monster   1953
Science fiction
64921   83 mins   B/W   B, V   P
George Nader, Claudia Barrett, directed by Phil Tucker
This ludicrous cheapie is considered to be one of the worst films of all time. Alien invaders (dressed in motheaten gorilla suits and diving helmets) attack mankind with a giant soap - bubble machine.
Astor; Three Dimensions Pictures — *Sony Video Software; Video Dimensions; Festival Films; Admit One Video*

Robotech   1985
Cartoons
71371   30 mins   C   B, V   P
Animated, dialogue directed by Greg Finley and Steve Kramer
A variety of characters try to save earth from a different doom in each episode of this series. Usually, their SDF-1 Battle Fortress plays a major role.
Ahmed Agrama — *Family Home Entertainment*

Robotix   1986
Cartoons
88026   90 mins   C   B, V   P
A feature-length animated film starring a bunch of robots who struggle to save the universe from evil forces.
Vestron Video — *Vestron Video*

Robotman and Friends 1984
Cartoons/Fantasy
Closed Captioned
84521 48 mins C B, V, LV P
An animated adventure with several episodes,
each containing a different escapade of
Robotman and his motley crew of sidekicks.
UFS Inc — Children's Video Library

Robotman & Friends II: I Want to be Your Robotman 1986
Cartoons/Adventure
Closed Captioned
85642 42 mins C B, V P
Another entry in the children's animated series
about robots who fight the denizens of evil.
Children's Video Library — Children's Video
Library

Rock Adventure 1981
Music
47298 29 mins C LV P
Music by Baenzai and breathtaking visuals
combine to express a mood of wild adventure.
Masaru Ohtaki; Tokyo Eizosha
Company — Pioneer Video Imports

Rock & Rule 1983
Fantasy
85544 85 mins C B, V P
Music by Debbie Harry, Cheap Trick, Lou Reed,
Iggy Pop
An animated sword & sorcery epic with a rock
soundtrack and voices provided by rock
performers.
Canada Trust Co. — MGM/UA Home Video

Rock Baby Rock It 1957
Musical
81715 77 mins B/W B, V P
This is an obscure rock film that features music
performed by Kay Wheeler and Johnny Carroll.
Independent — Rhino Video

Rock Music with the Muppets 1985
Variety
Closed Captioned
80745 54 mins C B, V P
Kermit the Frog, Dr. Teeth, Floyd Pepper, Zoot,
Alice Cooper, Debbie Harry, Paul Simon, Helen
Reddy, Leo Sayer, Loretta Swit, Ben Vereen
The Muppets perform their own brand of rock
and roll with their special musical guests. The
songs featured include "Rock Around the
Clock," "Call Me," "Rainbow Connection," and
'Disco Frog". Available in VHS and Beta Hi Fi.
Henson Associates — Playhouse Video

Rock 'n' Roll Disciples (Mondo Elvis) 1985
Documentary
87600 60 mins C B, V, 3/4U P
A sordid look at Elvis' legacy and his aimless,
worshipping fans.
Monticello Prod. — Monticello Productions;
Rhino Video

Rock 'n' Roll Heaven 1984
Music-Performance
85543 60 mins C B, V P
Buddy Holly, Elvis Presley, Eddie Cochran, Bill
Haley, the Beatles
A Don Kirschner compilation of original
performances by the pioneers of rock and roll.
In Stereo and Dolby sound.
Capitol Communications — MGM/UA Home
Video

Rock 'n' Roll High School 1979
Musical
64299 94 mins C B, V P
P. J. Soles, Clint Howard, The Ramones
The music of the Ramones highlights this story
of a high school out to thwart the principal at
every turn.
MPAA:PG
New World Pictures — Warner Home Video

Rock 'n Roll Wrestling Music Television 1985
Music-Performance/Exploitation
84350 60 mins C B, V P
Kamala, Jerry Lawler, Adrian Street
An easy-listening station is invaded by wrestlers
and their videos.
Impulse Ent — Rhino Video

Rock, Rock, Rock 1956
Musical
59155 78 mins B/W B, V, 3/4U P
Chuck Berry, Fats Domino, Tuesday Weld,
Frankie Lymon and the Teeangers
A young girl's father insists she earn enough
money to buy a new gown for the Senior Prom.
Classic musical numbers performed by a
number of rock'n'roll pioneers.
DCA — Nostalgia Merchant

Rocket Attack U.S.A. 1958
Science fiction
85059 70 mins B/W B, V P
Monica Davis, John McKay, Dan Kern
An antiquated look at nuclear warfare about the
time of Sputnik, with Russia launching
immediately into blowing up the entire eastern
USA seaboard.
Exploit Films; Barry Manon — Sony Video
Software

Rocketship X-M—Special Edition   1950

Science fiction/Adventure
44357   77 mins   B/W   B, V, 3/4U   P
Lloyd Bridges, Osa Massen, John Emery, Hugh O'Brien
A lunar mission goes awry and the crew lands on Mars. Contains newly photographed footage, a tinted sequence and previews of coming attractions from classic science fiction films.
Lippert — *Nostalgia Merchant*

Rockin' Road Trip   1985

Comedy
88162   101 mins   C   B, V   P
Garth McLean, Katherine Harrison, Margeret Currie, Steve Boles
A guy meets a girl in a Boston bar, and finds himself on a drunken, slapstick roadtrip down the Eastern seaboard with a rock band.
MPAA:PG-13
Troma; William Olsen; Michael Rothschild — *Key Video*

Rockshow   1981

Music-Performance
58884   102 mins   C   B, V   P
Paul McCartney and Wings
Paul and Wings perform 23 of their best songs before an audience of 67,000 fans at the King Dome in Seattle, Washington. Selections include "Jet," "Band on the Run," "Venus and Mars," "Maybe I'm Amazed," and "Yesterday."
MPL Communications — *THORN EMI/HBO Video; Pioneer Artists; RCA VideoDiscs*

Rocky   1976

Drama
37521   119 mins   C   B, V, LV, CED   P
Sylvester Stallone, Talia Shire, Burgess Meredith, directed by John G. Avildsen
A young man from the slums of Philadelphia pursues his dream of becoming a boxing champion.
Academy Awards '76: Best Picture; Best Director (Avildsen); Best Achievement in Film Editing. MPAA:PG
United Artists — *CBS/Fox Video; RCA VideoDiscs*

Rocky II   1979

Drama
58810   119 mins   C   B, V, LV, CED   P
Sylvester Stallone, Talia Shire, Burt Young, Burgess Meredith, Carl Weathers
This sequel to the box office smash finds Rocky frustrated by the commercialism which followed his match to Apollo, and soon considers a return bout.
MPAA:PG

United Artists; Irwin Winkler; Robert Chartoff — *CBS/Fox Video; RCA VideoDiscs*

Rocky III   1982

Drama
63395   100 mins   C   B, V, LV, CED   P
Sylvester Stallone, Talia Shire, Burgess Meredith, Carl Weathers
The third in the "Rocky" trilogy finds heavyweight champ Rocky Balboa training with his former opponent Apollo Creed to prepare for a rematch with Clubber Lang.
MPAA:PG
United Artists — *CBS/Fox Video; RCA VideoDiscs*

Rocky IV   1985

Drama
Closed Captioned
85874   91 mins   C   B, V, LV   P
Sylvester Stallone, Talia Shire, Dolf Lundgren, Brigitte Nielsen, directed by Sylvester Stallone
Rocky travels to Russia to fight the Soviet champ who killed his friend during a bout.
Irwin Winkler; Robert Chartoff;
MGM/UA — *CBS/Fox Video*

Rocky Jones, Space Ranger: Blast Off   1953

Science fiction
11280   75 mins   B/W   B, V, FO   P
Richard Crane, Scotty Beckett, Sally Mansfield, Maurice Cass
Rocky, his sidekick Winky, and Professor Newton travel through another space adventure in their ship, "The Orbit Jet."
Roland Reed — *Video Yesteryear*

Rocky Jones, Space Ranger: Pirates of Prah   1953

Science fiction
11279   75 mins   B/W   B, V, FO   P
Richard Crane, Scotty Beckett, Sally Mansfield, Maurice Cass
Rocky Jones, sidekick Winky, and Professor Newton confront space pirates in this episode.
Roland Reed — *Video Yesteryear*

Rocky Jones, Space Ranger: The Cold Sun   1953

Science fiction
11278   75 mins   B/W   B, V, FO   P
Richard Crane, Scotty Beckett, Sally Mansfield, Maurice Cass
An adventure in the series "Rocky Jones, Space Ranger," as Rocky, Winky, and Professor Newton travel through space.
Roland Reed — *Video Yesteryear*

Rocky Jones, Space Ranger: Trial of Rocky Jones
1953

Science fiction
11281   75 mins   B/W   B, V, FO   P
Richard Crane, Scotty Beckett, Sally Mansfield, Maurice Cass
Rocky Jones, trouble-shooter for the Office of Space Affairs, travels through the universe in his spaceship "The Orbit Jet" along with his pal Winky and Professor Newton.
Roland Reed — *Video Yesteryear*

Rocky King, Detective
1954

Crime-Drama
47482   25 mins   B/W   B, V, FO   P
Roscoe Karnes, Todd Karnes, Grace Carney, Jack Klugman
In the story "Return for Death," New York City Police detective Rocky King solves a murder in a mausoleum. An early, live cop show from TV's Golden Age.
Dumont — *Video Yesteryear*

Rod Stewart
1983

Music-Performance
76671   16 mins   C   B, V   P
This program presents Rod Stewart performing "Do Ya Think I'm Sexy," "Passion" and "Young Turks."
Embassy Home Entertainment — *Sony Video Software*

Rod Stewart Concert Video, The
1984

Music-Performance
86292   80 mins   C   B, V   P
A live concert from the 1984 tour, with Stewart performing such hits as "Hot Legs," "Maggie May" and "Tonight's the Night."
Karl-Lorimar — *Karl/Lorimar Home Video*

Rod Stewart Live at the L.A. Forum
1980

Music-Performance
54688   60 mins   C   B, V   P
Rod Stewart
A look at highlights from Rod Stewart's 1979 appearance at the Forum. Songs include "Hot Legs," "Do Ya Think I'm Sexy," "Blondes Have More Fun," "Maggie May," and "You're in My Heart."
Warner Bros — *Warner Home Video; RCA VideoDiscs*

Rod Stewart: Tonight He's Yours
1982

Music-Performance
60449   90 mins   C   B, V, LV, CED   P
Rod Stewart, Tina Turner

Rod the Mod offers up 17 top hits from this concert taped at the L.A. Forum, including: "Do Ya Think I'm Sexy," "Maggie Mae"."You're in My Heart," and more.
Unknown — *Embassy Home Entertainment*

Rodan
1956

Horror
63968   74 mins   C   B, V, LV, CED   P
Kenji Sahara, Yumi Shirakawa
A gigantic prehistoric bird is disturbed from his slumber by H-bomb tests; he awakens to wreak havoc on civilization.
Toho Productions — *Vestron Video*

Rodeo Girl
1980

Western/Drama
71327   92 mins   C   B, V   P
Katherine Ross, Bo Hopkins, Candy Clark, Jacqueline Brooks, Wilford Brimley, directed by Jackie Cooper
Based on the life of Sue Pirtle, this docudrama tells of her years as a world champion rodeo performer.
Steckler and Marble Arch Productions — *U.S.A. Home Video*

Roger Corman: Hollywood's Wild Angel
1978

Film-History/Filmmaking
81847   58 mins   C   B, V   P
David Carradine, Peter Fonda, Jonathan Demme, Ron Howard, Paul Bartel
This documentary looks at the life and films of legendary B-movie producer/director Roger Corman and features interviews with Martin Scorsese and Joe Dante.
Christian Blackwood — *MPI Home Video*

Roger Whittaker
1982

Music-Performance
88112   53 mins   C   B, V   P
A concert performance by the familiar, goateed folk singer.
Sony Video — *Sony Video Software*

Rogue, The
1976

Horror
81755   87 mins   C   B, V   P
Milan Galvonic, Barbara Bouchet
The Rouge is a ruthless man who can make beautiful women do anything that he desires.
MPAA:R
Electra Entertainment — *Magnum Entertainment*

Roll Along Cowboy
1937

Western
84942   55 mins   B/W   B, V   P
Smith Ballen, Cecilia Parker

A vintage sagebrush saga about a cowboy caught by love in a web of betrayal surrounding a ranch threatened by usurpation. Based on Zane Grey's "The Dude Ranger."
Principal Prods — *Blackhawk Films*

Roller Blade   1985
Science fiction
86086   88 mins   C   B, V   P
Suzanne Solari, Jeff Hutchinson, Shaun Mitchelle
In a post-holocaust world a gang of Amazons battle the forces of evil with martial arts and mysticism.
Donald G. Jackson — *New World Video*

Rollerball   1975
Science fiction
13596   123 mins   C   B, V, CED   P
James Caan, John Houseman, Maud Adams, Moses Gunn, directed by Norman Jewison
In the year 2018 there is rollerball, a brutal sport combining the violence of all other sports.
MPAA:R
United Artists — *CBS/Fox Video*

Rolling Plains   1938
Western
08792   60 mins   B/W   B, V, 3/4U   P
Tex Ritter
Singing cowboy tries to bring cattlemen and sheepmen together.
Grand Natl — *Video Connection; United Home Video*

Rolling Thunder   1977
Drama
64360   99 mins   C   B, V, CED   P
William Devane, Tommy Lee Jones, Linda Haynes
A Vietnam veteran returns home after eight years as a POW. Shortly afterward, his wife and son are murdered, causing him to seek revenge.
MPAA:R
American International — *Vestron Video*

Rollover   1981
Drama
59855   118 mins   C   B, V   P
Jane Fonda, Kris Kristofferson, Hume Cronyn, directed by Alan J. Pakula
A banker and board chairman get involved in the intrigue and danger of multi-million dollar world finance.
MPAA:R
Orion; Warner Bros. — *Warner Home Video*

Roman Holiday   1953
Comedy/Romance
64782   118 mins   B/W   B, V   P
Audrey Hepburn, Gregory Peck, Eddie Albert, directed by William Wyler

A princess on an official visit to Rome slips away without notice and falls in love with a newspaperman.
Academy Awards '53: Best Actress (Hepburn); Writing (Ian McLellan Hunter); Costume Design B&W (Edith Head).
Paramount; William Wyler — *Paramount Home Video; RCA VideoDiscs*

Roman Spring of Mrs. Stone, The   1961
Drama
80443   104 mins   C   B, V   P
Warren Beatty, Vivien Leigh, Lotte Lenya, Bessie Love, Jill St. John, directed by Jose Quintero
An actress comes to Rome seeking to revive her career but winds up falling in love with a gigolo.
Louis de Rochemont; Warner Bros. — *Warner Home Video*

Romance with a Double Bass   1974
Comedy
79112   40 mins   C   B, V   P
John Cleese, Connie Booth
When a musician and a princess take a skinny dip in the royal lake and get their clothes stolen, comic complications arise.
RPTA Video — *Pacific Arts Video*

Romancing the Stone   1984
Adventure/Romance
Closed Captioned
73140   106 mins   C   B, V, CED   P
Micheal Douglas, Kathleen Turner, Danny De Vito, directed by Robert Zemeckis
Kathleen Turner stars as a writer of romance novels who gets a chance to live out her story when she receives a phone call that her sister has been kidnapped in South America.
MPAA:PG
Micheal Douglas; 20th Century Fox — *CBS/Fox Video*

Romantic Comedy   1983
Comedy
72897   102 mins   C   B, V   P
Dudley Moore, Mary Steenburgen
A married man is in love with a single girl and when he becomes unhitched she marries another man.
MPAA:PG
Walter Mirisch; Morton Gottlieb — *CBS/Fox Video*

Romantic Englishwoman, The   1975
Romance/Comedy
49925   117 mins   C   B, V   P
Glenda Jackson, Michael Caine, Helmut Berger, directed by Joseph Losey

A married couple tests fidelity to its limits.
MPAA:R
New World — *Warner Home Video*

Romeo and Juliet   1968
Drama
38603   138 mins   C   B, V, LV   P
*Olivia Hussey, Leonard Whiting, Michael York,
directed by Franco Zeffirelli*
A fresh, vital version of Shakespeare's classic
romantic play, which won critical acclaim upon
its release.
MPAA:PG
Paramount — *Paramount Home Video; RCA
VideoDiscs*

Romeo and Juliet   1954
Drama
59902   138 mins   C   B, V   P
*Laurence Harvey, Susan Shantall, Aldo Zollo,
Sebastian Cabot, John Gielgud*
Shakespeare's tale of young love, shot on
Italian locations.
Rank; Verona — *Embassy Home
Entertainment*

Romeo and Juliet   1954
Dance
74491   95 mins   C   B, V   P
Bolshoi Ballet
This tape is the Bolshoi Ballet's interpretation of
the ever-popular Romeo and Juliet.
Sovexportfilm USSR — *Video Arts
International*

Romeo and Juliet   1984
Dance
82258   123 mins   C   B, V   P
This is a ballet based upon the Shakespearean
tragedy which was performed at the Royal
Opera House in Covent Garden.
National Video Corporation Ltd. — *THORN
EMI/HBO Video*

Romeo and Juliet   1982
Dance
84571   128 mins   C   B, V, 8mm,   P
               LV
*Rudolph Nureyev, Dame Margot Fonteyn, Carla
Fracci*
A performance of the Prokofiev work featuring
three of Ballet's finest.
ITC; RAI; La Scala — *Kultur*

Romie-O and Julie-8   1978
Musical/Fantasy
54693   25 mins   C   B, V   P
Animated
This musical fantasy tells of the special love
between two young robots—an interpretation of
the great love story, "Romeo and Juliet."
Original songs by John Sebastian.

Nelvana Productions — *Warner Home Video;
Beacon Films*

Romper Room and   1985
Friends
Education
Closed Captioned
78884   35 mins   C   B, V   P
7   pgms
Children learn about numbers, letters, words,
movement, rhythm, and animals in the zoo in
this series.
1.Numbers, Letters and Words 2.Go to the Zoo
3.Playful Projects 4.Movement and Rhythm
5.Sizes and Shapes 6.Songbook 7.Explore
Nature
Romper Enterprises — *Playhouse Video*

Rona Jaffe's Mazes &   1982
Monsters
Drama
85909   103 mins   C   B, V   P
*Tom Hanks, Chris Makepeace, Lloyd Bochner,
Anne Francis, Susan Strasberg*
A group of game-playing youths transpose their
fantasy world onto real life with disastrous
results.
Tom McDermott; Richard A.
Briggs — *Karl/Lorimar Home Video*

Ronnie Milsap—Golden   1985
Video Hits
Music video
82201   30 mins   C   B, V   P
Ronnie Milsap performs "She Loves My Car,"
"Stranger In My House," "There's No Gettin'
Over Me" and "Any Day Now" in VHS Dolby Hi-
Fi Stereo and Beta Hi-Fi Stereo.
RCA Video Productions — *RCA/Columbia
Pictures Home Video*

Roobarb   1980
Cartoons
85458   67 mins   C   B, V   P
A collection of cartoons from the successful
children's show about a mongrel named
Roobarb and a cat named Custard.
Bob Godfrey's Movie Emporium — *Family
Home Entertainment*

Roof, The   1956
Drama/Romance
63858   98 mins   B/W   B, V   P
*Gabriella Pallotti, Giorgio Listuzzi, directed by
Vittorio De Sica*
A young couple who married against their
families' wished find that setting up a home of
their own is more difficult than they thought.
Italian dialogue, English subtitles.
IT
Vittorio De Sica — *Hollywood Home Theater;
Festival Films*

Room Service 1938
Comedy
00256 78 mins B/W B, V P
The Marx Brothers, Lucille Ball, Ann Miller,
Frank Albertson
A penniless theatrical producer connives to
keep his hotel room until he can find a backer
for his latest play.
RKO; Pandro S Berman — *RKO HomeVideo;*
VidAmerica; Blackhawk Films; Nostalgia
Merchant

Roommate, The 1984
Comedy
87211 96 mins C B, V P
Lance Guest, Barry Miller, directed by Neil Cox
A valedictorian church-goer and a rebellious
iconoclast room together at Northwestern U in
1952, with the expected humorous results.
505 Chicago Ave. — *Vestron Video*

Rooster Cogburn 1975
Western
58425 107 mins C B, V P
John Wayne, Katharine Hepburn, Richard
Jordan, Anthony Zerbe, John McIntire
A Bible-thumping schoolmarm joins up with a
hard-drinking, hard-fighting marshal in order to
capture a gang of incompetent outlaws who
killed her father.
MPAA:PG
Universal; Hal Wallis — *MCA Home Video*

Rootin' Tootin' Rhythm 1938
Western
11262 55 mins B/W B, V, FO P
Gene Autry
All's not quiet on the range, but Gene Autry
comes along to sing things back to normal.
Republic — *Video Yesteryear; Discount Video*
Tapes

Roots 1977
Drama
58247 90 mins C B, V P
Ed Asner, Lloyd Bridges, LeVar Burton, Chuck
Connors, Lynda Day George, Lorne Greene,
Burl Ives, O. J. Simpson, Cicely Tyson, Ben
Vereen, Sandy Duncan 6 pgms
The complete version of Alex Haley's saga
following a black man's search for his heritage,
revealing an epic panorama of America's past.
Available on six 90-minute tapes.
Wolper Pictures — *Warner Home Video*

Roots of Rock 'n Roll 1983
Music
69840 100 mins C B, V P
4 pgms
This four tape guitar instruction series is taught
by Johnny Kay, former lead guitarist with Bill
Haley and the Comets. It is designed to

familiarize the novice as well as strengthen the
skills of those who already play the guitar.
1.Chords and Rhythms 2.Variations in Styles
3.Lead Guitar Techniques 4.Rock-Blues Lead
AM Available
K Video — *K Video*

Rope 1948
Drama
80413 81 mins C B, V, LV P
James Stewart, John Dall, Farley Granger,
directed by Alfred Hitchcock
Two college students murder a friend for kicks
and conceal the body in a truck which they will
use as a buffet table for a dinner party.
Hitchcock's first color film.
MPAA:PG
Sidney Bernstein, Alfred Hitchcock — *MCA*
Home Video

Roaslie 1938
Romance/Musical
71158 118 mins B/W B, V P
Nelson Eddy, Eleanor Powell, Frank Morgan,
Ray Bolger, Ilona Massey, Reginald Owen,
Edna May Oliver, Jerry Colonna, directed by
W.S. Van Dyke III
A gridiron great from West Point falls for a
mysterious beauty from Vassar. He soon finds
out that her father reigns over a tiny Balkan
nation. Cole Porter's score includes "I've Got a
Strange New Rythm in my Heart" and "In the
Still of the Night" in HiFi.
MGM — *MGM/UA Home Video*

Rose, The 1979
Musical
44932 134 mins C B, V, LV, P
CED
Bette Midler, Alan Bates
A young, multitalented, and self-destructive rock
star tries to come to grips with her love affairs,
professional triumphs, and lonely restlessness.
MPAA:R
20th Century Fox — *CBS/Fox Video*

Rose Marie 1936
Musical
82120 112 mins B/W B, V, LV P
Jeanette MacDonald, Nelson Eddy, James
Stewart, Allan Jones, David Niven
An opera star falls in love with the mountie who
captured her escaped convict brother. The
Rudolf Friml score features "Indian Love Call",
"The Song of the Mounties" and the title song.
MGM — *MGM/UA Home Video*

Rosebud Beach Hotel, 1985
The
Comedy
80702 82 mins C B, V, LV, P
CED
Peter Scolari, Coleen Camp, Christopher Lee

A young man tries his hand at managing a run down hotel in order to please his demanding girlfriend.
MPAA:R
Alme Pictures — *Vestron Video*

Roseland   1977
Drama
64885   103 mins   C   B, V   P
Christopher Walken, Geraldine Chaplin, Joan Copeland, Teresa Wright, Lou Jacobi
Three interlocking stories, set within New York's Roseland Ballroom, tell about lonely people who live to dance.
Cinema Shares International — *Vestron Video*

Rosemary's Baby   1968
Horror
55543   137 mins   C   B, V, LV   P
Mia Farrrow, John Cassavettes, Ruth Gordon, Maurice Evans, Patsy Kelly, Elisha Cook, Charles Grodin, directed by Roman Polanski
After unwittingly becoming friendly with a coven of witches and warlocks, a young wife is impregnated by the Devil.
Academy Awards '68: Best Supporting Actress (Gordon). MPAA:R
Paramount; William Castle — *Paramount Home Video; RCA VideoDiscs*

RosenKavalier, Der   1962
Opera
78959   190 mins   C   B, V   P
Elisabeth Schwarzkopf, Sena Jurinac, Otto Edelmann, directed by Paul Czinner
A filmed performance of the Richard Strauss opera.
Rank Organization — *Video Arts International*

Rostropovich   1982
Music-Performance
60576   65 mins   C   LV   P
Mstislav Rostropovich, London Philharmonic Orchestra conducted by Carlo Maria Giulini
The great cellist performs Dvorak's "Cello Concerto" and Saint-Saens' "Cello Concerto No. 1." In stereo.
EMI Music Video — *Pioneer Artists*

Rough Cut   1980
Adventure
54672   111 mins   C   B, V, LV   P
Burt Reynolds, Lesley-Anne Down, David Niven, Timothy West, Patrick Magee, directed by Donald Siegel
An American diamond thief living in London is pursued by a Scotland Yard detective who is about to retire and wants to finish his career in a blaze of glory.
MPAA:PG
Paramount — *Paramount Home Video*

Rough Riders of   1945
Cheyenne
Western
64421   54 mins   B/W   B, V, 3/4U   P
Sunset Carson, Peggy Stewart
Sunset ends the feud between the Carsons and the Sterlings.
Republic — *Nostalgia Merchant*

Roughnecks   1980
Drama
80314   240 mins   C   B, V   P
Sam Melville, Cathy Lee Crosby, Vera Miles, Harry Morgan
A team of Texas oil drillers attempt to dig the deepest oil well in history.
Metromedia Producers Corp. — *Prism*

Round-Up Time in Texas   1937
Western
08895   54 mins   B/W   B, V, 3/4U   P
Gene Autry, Smiley Burnette
Autry answers an urgent call for horses from South Africa's jungle-blocked diamond belt.
Republic — *Video Connection; Video Yesteryear; Discount Video Tapes*

Roustabout   1964
Musical-Drama
08384   101 mins   C   B, V   P
Elvis Presley, Barbara Stanwyck, Joan Freeman, Leif Erickson, Sue Ann Langdon
A roving, reckless singer joins a carnival and romances the owner's daughter.
EL, SP
Paramount; Hal Wallis — *CBS/Fox Video*

Rowlf's Rhapsodies with   1985
the Muppets
Variety
Closed Captioned
81864   56 mins   C   B, V   P
Rowlf, Kermit the Frog, Miss Piggy, Steve Martin, George Burns, Peter Sellers, Marisa Berenson
Rowlf leads the Muppet gang and their special guests through a collection of musical mishaps from the series. Available in VHS and Beta Hi-Fi.
Henson Associates — *Playhouse Video*

Roxy Music: The High   1983
Road
Music-Performance
65462   ? mins   C   B, V   P
This concert film was recorded during Brian Ferry and Roxy Music's 1982 World Tour and features old standards such as "Avalon" and "Dance Away," plus many new songs. In stereo VHS and Beta Hi-Fi.
Robin Nash — *RCA/Columbia Pictures Home Video*

Roy Rogers Matinee Double Feature #3 — 1950
Western
82175   121 mins   C   B, V   P
Roy Rogers, Penny Edwards, Rex Allen, Gabby Hayes
Join Roy and Trigger as they saddle up for an action-packed double feature that includes "Trail of Robin Hood" and "Romance on the Trail," which is in black and white.
Republic Pictures — *Republic Pictures Home Video*

Roy Rogers Matinee Double Feature #4 — 1949
Western
82176   121 mins   C   B, V   P
Roy Rogers, Dale Evans, Trigger, Buttercup
dAn exciting Roy Rogers double feature: In "Susanna Pass" he discovers a conspiracy to gain a deed to a lake rich in oil deposits; in "Sons of the Pioneers" Roy investigates a series of livestock murders in Rogers City. "Sons of the Pioneers" is in black and white.
Republic Pictures — *Republic Pictures Home Video*

Roy Rogers Show, The — 1950
Western
77198   100 mins   B/W   B, V   P
Roy Rogers, Carl Switzer, Dale Evans, Pat Brady
Roy, Dale, Trigger and Buttercup ride again to fight off the bad guys in this collection of four episodes from the series.
Roy Rogers Productions — *Shokus Video*

Roy Rogers Show II, The — 1950
Western
84700   125 mins   B/W   B, V, 3/4U   P
Roy Rogers, Dale Evans, Pat Brady, Harry Lavter
Five episodes on one tape of the irrepressible cowboy with Dale and Trigger, originally broadcast in 1950. Titles iclude: "Unwilling Outlaw," "The Minister's Son," "M Stands for Murder," "Train Robbery" and "Money for Charity."
CBS — *Shokus Video*

Royal Bed, The — 1931
Romance
11252   74 mins   B/W   B, V, FO   P
Lowell Sherman, Nance O'Neill, Mary Astor, Anthony Bushell, Gilbert Emery, Robert Emery
King Eric VIII is beset by many problems, the foremost being his wife, the Queen.
RKO — *Video Yesteryear*

Royal Wedding — 1951
Musical
58873   100 mins   C   B, V, CED   P

Fred Astaire, Jane Powell, Peter Lawford, Keenan Wynn, directed by Stanley Donen
A brother and sister dance team goes to London at the time of the royal wedding of Princess Elizabeth.
MGM — *MGM/UA Home Video*

Royal Wedding, The — 1981
Documentary/Great Britain
58465   60 mins   C   B, V   P
Highlights of the Royal Wedding of Prince Charles and Princess Diana, with all of the pageantry and splendor.
Thames TV — *THORN EMI/HBO Video*

R.P.M.* (*Revolutions Per Minute) — 1970
Drama
71119   90 mins   C   B, V   P
Anthony Quinn, Paul Winfield, Gary Lockwood, Ann-Margret, directed by Stanley Kramer
Student activists, force the University hierarchy to appoint their favorite radical professor president. The responsibilities of office conflict with his beliefs and practices.
MPAA:R
Columbia — *RCA/Columbia Pictures Home Video*

R.S.V.P. — 1984
Drama
77175   87 mins   C   B, V, LV, CED   P
Harry Reems
A Hollywood party honoring a writer turns tragic when a body is found in the guest of honor's pool.
MPAA:R
Chuck Vincent Productions — *Vestron Video*

Rubber Rodeo — 1984
Music-Performance
73987   18 mins   C   B, V   P
The country punk band performs music from their debut album in four conceptual music videos.
Polygram Records — *Sony Video Software*

Rubber Rodeo — 1984
Music-Performance
76666   18 mins   C   B, V   P
This program presents the band with the unique punk-country sound. Songs included are: "Anywhere with You," "How the West Was Won," "The Theme from Rubber Rodeo" and many more.
Polygram Records Inc — *Sony Video Software*

Rubber Tarzan — 1983
Drama
82578   75 mins   C   B, V   P

A dreamy misunderstood young boy learns to rely upon his own devices for amusement.
Berlin Film Festival: U.N.I.C.E.F. Award
Metronome — *Embassy Home Entertainment*

Rubik, The Amazing Cube, Volume II   1984
Cartoons
77245   45 mins   C   B, V   P
Animated
Rubik and his friends twist their way through two new animated adventures.
Ruby-Spears Enterprises — *RCA/Columbia Pictures Home Video*

Rubik, The Amazing Cube Vol. I   1984
Cartoons
Closed Captioned
80378   45 mins   C   B, V   P
Animated
Here are two episodes from the animated series based upon the popular puzzle.
Ruby-Spears Enterprises — *RCA/Columbia Pictures Home Video*

Ruby   1977
Horror
35380   85 mins   C   B, V   P
Piper Laurie
Horrifying tale of a young woman christened in blood and raised in sin, having a love affair with the supernatural.
MPAA:R
George Edwards — *United Home Video; Continental Video*

Ruby Gentry   1952
Drama
65331   82 mins   B/W   B, V   P
Charlton Heston, Jennifer Jones, Karl Malden
A girl from the wrong side of the tracks, cast aside by the man she loves, marries a wealthy businessman and sets out to destroy all those who snubbed her
David Selznick — *CBS/Fox Video*

Ruddigore   19??
Opera/Comedy
65493   112 mins   C   B, V   P
Vincent Price, Keith Michell, Sandra Dugdale
The Lords of Ruddigore have been bound for centuries by a terribly inconvenient curse; they must commit a crime every day or die a horribly painful death. When the Lord of Ruddigore passes his mantle on to the new heir, the young heir loses both his good reputation and his very proper fiancee. A new version of Gilbert and Sullivan's opera.
W L Leasing Limited — *CBS/Fox Video*

Rude Awakening   1981
Horror
81746   60 mins   C   B, V   P
Denholm Elliott, James Laurenson, Pat Heywood, directed by Peter Sasdy
A real estate agent is tortured by bizarre nightmares which lead to an unusual series of events.
Hammer Films — *Thriller Video*

Rude Boy   1980
Music-Performance
54105   60 mins   C   B, V   P
The Clash, Ray Gange, directed by Jack Hazan and David Mingay
"Rude Bay" depicts the rise of The Clash, a top British rock band. Live concert footage features The Clash performing such hits as "White Riot" and "I Fought the Law." Included are rare films of early Clash shows.
Jack Hazan, David Mingay — *CBS/Fox Video*

Ruggles, The   1951
Comedy
47642   24 mins   B/W   B, V, FO   P
Charlie Ruggles, Erin O'Brien-Moore
Vintage TV sitcom with Charlie, his wife and children. In this episode, the Ruggles are presented with a pair of rabbits.
ABC — *Video Yesteryear*

Rules of the Game   1939
Film-Avant-garde
06237   110 mins   B/W   B, V   P
Marcel Dalio, Nora Gregor, Jean Renoir, directed by Jean Renoir
Renoir satirizes the social and sexual mores of the decadent French leisure class before WWII. French film, English subtitles.
FR
French — *Hollywood Home Theater; International Historic Films; Cable Films; Video Yesteryear; Western Film & Video Inc; Discount Video Tapes; Kartes Video Communications*

Ruling Class, The   1972
Comedy/Satire
64983   154 mins   C   B, V, CED   P
Peter O'Toole, Alastair Sim, Arthur Lowe
This irreverant comedy tells the story of the unbalanced 14th Earl of Gurney, who believes that he is Jesus Christ.
MPAA:PG
Avco-Embassy — *Embassy Home Entertainment*

Rumble Fish   1983
Drama
65515   94 mins   B/W   B, V, LV, CED   P
Matt Dillon, Mickey Rourke, Dennis Hopper, Diane Lane, Vincent Spano, Nicolas Case, directed by Francis Coppola

The story of two brothers whose relationship with themselves and their world leads to death for one and a new life for the other. In stereo VHS and Beta Hi-Fi.
MPAA:R
Universal — MCA Home Video

Rumor of War, A   1980
Drama
79188   105 mins   C   B, V   P
Brad Davis, Keith Carradine, Stacy Keach, Brian Dennehy, Steve Forrest, Chris Mitchum
An adaptation of Philip Caputo's book about his transformation from college student to Vietnam veteran.
Stonehenge; Charles Fries Productions — U.S.A. Home Video

Rumpelstiltskin   1968
Fairy tales
47674   75 mins   C   B, V   P
A beautiful young girl is tricked into promising her firstborn to a magic elf in return for his spinning straw into gold for her.
Ron Merk — Unicorn Video

Rumpelstiltskin   1984
Fairy tales
Closed Captioned
73144   60 mins   C   B, V, CED   P
Ned Beatty, Shelley Duvall, Herve Villechaize, Paul Dooley
From "Faerie Tale Theatre" comes the story of a woman who can spin straw into gold (Shelley Duvall) and the strange man who saves her life (Herve Villechaize).
Shelley Duvall — CBS/Fox Video

Rumpelstiltskin   1985
Fantasy
86579   24 mins   C   B, V   P
Narrated by Christopher Plummer
An animated version for children of the classic fairy tale, directed by Pino Van Lamsweerde and Sebastian Grunstra.
Hugh Campbell — Family Home Entertainment

Run, Angel, Run!   1969
Adventure
65728   90 mins   C   B, V   P
William Smith, Valerie Starrett
An ex-biker is on the run from his former motorcycle gang.
MPAA:R
Fanfare — VidAmerica

Run for Life: An Olympic Fable   1979
Sports
72233   68 mins   C   B, V   P

Animated
This animated feature concerns a young athlete running to restore support for his country's King in Ancient Greece.
Toei Animation — Children's Video Library

Run of the Arrow   1956
Western
13096   85 mins   C   B, V   P
Rod Steiger, Brian Keith, Charles Bronson
An ex-Confederate soldier joins the Sioux nation, which is engaged in war against the white man.
Universal; RKO; Samuel Fuller — United Home Video

Run Rebecca, Run   1981
Drama
81916   90 mins   C   B, V   P
Simone Buchanan, Henri Szeps
A South American refugee tries to stop a young girl from escaping from an island where they are both stranded.
Independent Prods — VidAmerica

Run Silent, Run Deep   1958
War-Drama
68226   93 mins   B/W   B, V, CED   P
Burt Lancaster, Clark Gable, Jack Warden, Don Rickles
A tense look at the realities of submarine warfare and underwater combat.
Jeffrey Productions — CBS/Fox Video

Run, Stranger, Run   1973
Suspense/Drama
73864   110 mins   C   B, V   P
Ron Howard, Patricia Neal, Cloris Leachman, directed by Darren McGavin
A New England fishing village is disrupted by a series of murders committed by a young girl.
Available in Beta Hi-Fi.
MPAA:PG
Darren McGavin; Cinema Five — RCA/Columbia Pictures Home Video

Runaway   1984
Science fiction/Adventure
Closed Captioned
81208   100 mins   C   B, V   P
Tom Selleck, Cynthia Rhodes, Gene Simmons, Stan Shaw, Kirstie Alley, directed by Michael Crichton
A policeman and his assistant track down a group of killer robots wreaking havoc upon a metropolitan city. Available in VHS Dolby Hi-Fi Stereo and Beta Hi-Fi Stereo.
MPAA:PG13
Tri-Star Pictures — RCA/Columbia Pictures Home Video

Runaway Barge   1982
Adventure
75464   72 mins   C   B, V   P
Nick Nolte, Tim Matheson, Jim Davis
An attempt is made to hijack a Mississippi River
cargo.
King Features — *U.S.A. Home Video*

Runaway Bus, The   1954
Comedy
85501   78 mins   B/W   B, V   P
*Frankie Howerd, Margaret Rutherford, Petula
Clark, George Colouris*
Filled with a motley crew of passengers,
including a gold-carrying thief, a bus gets lost
between airports and ends up in a deserted
village.
Eros Films; Kramer/Hyams — *Video
Yesteryear*

Runaway Truck   195?
Adventure
10033   25 mins   B/W   B, V   P, T
Kirby Grant
Sky King takes to the air with novice pilot.
Student pilot is then forced to make crucial
decision. From the TV series "Sky King."
Unknown — *Blackhawk Films*

Runner Stumbles, The   1979
Drama
Closed Captioned
82346   109 mins   C   B, V   P
*Dick Van Dyke, Kathleen Quinlan, Maureen
Stapleton, Ray Bolger, Beau Bridges, Tammy
Grimes, directed by Stanley Kramer*
A priest goes on trial for murdering the nun with
whom he fell in love in a Washington mining
town during the 1920's. Available in VHS and
Beta Hi-Fi.
MPAA:R
Melvin Simon Prods — *Key Video*

Running Brave   1983
Drama
66322   90 mins   C   B, V, LV,   P
                        CED
*Robbie Benson, Claudia Cron, Pat Hingle, Denis
Lacroix*
The true story of Billy Mills, a South Dakota
Sioux Indian who became the only American in
Olympic history to win the Gold Medal in the
10,000 meter run at the 1964 Tokyo Olympics.
Buena Vista; Englander Productions — *Walt
Disney Home Video*

Running Hot   1983
Romance
73043   88 mins   C   B, V   P
A hot romance develops between an escaped
convict and the woman who wrote to him while
he was in prison.
MPAA:R

Wescom — *Vestron Video*

Running Scared   1979
Drama
65091   92 mins   C   B, V   P
Ken Wahl
Two young men, returning from military service
as stowaways aboard an Army cargo plane, are
caught by a paranoid intelligence agent and are
thought to be spies.
MPAA:PG
EMI Films — *THORN EMI/HBO Video*

Running Wild   1973
Drama
76860   102 mins   C   B, V   P
*Lloyd Bridges, Dina Merrill, Pat Hingle, Gilbert
Roland, Morgan Woodward*
A freelance photographer becomes involved in
a dispute to save a corral of wild mustang
horses.
MPAA:G
Robert McCahon — *Media Home
Entertainment*

Rush   1984
Adventure/Science fiction
71317   83 mins   C   B, V   P
*Conrad Nichols, Laura Trotter, Gordon Mitchell,
Betty Peele*
Post-Armageddon Earth draws its power from
nuclear reactors controlled by the evil
slavemaster named Steele. Rush, a rebel within
the airtight bubbles protecting the cities, battles
Steele's regime.
Marcello Romeo — *U.S.A. Home Video*

Rush—Exit Stage Left   1981
Music-Performance
60384   60 mins   C   B, V   P
This concert includes highlights from the
group's two-hour stage show. Songs include
"Limelight," "Xanadu," "The Trees," "Freewill"
and "Closer to the Heart." In stereo.
Polygram Records; Moon Video
Production — *RCA/Columbia Pictures Home
Video; RCA VideoDiscs; Pioneer Artists*

**Rush—Grace Under
Pressure Tour**   1986
Music-Performance
84877   69 mins   C   B, V   P
The famed Canadian band performs the
greatest hits of their recent album.
Polygram Music Video — *RCA/Columbia
Pictures Home Video*

Rush It   1977
Romance
79322   78 mins   C   B, V   P
Tom Berenger, Jill Eikenberry

Two bike messengers who meet each other while working in New York City wind up falling in love.
Robbie Kenner — *Unicorn Video*

Rush—Through the Camera Eye   1985
Music video/Music-Performance
81802   44 mins   C   B, V   P
This compilation features eight conceptual music videos that exemplify the progressive heavy metal rock of Rush. Available in VHS Dolby Hi-Fi Stereo and Beta Hi-Fi Stereo.
Dan Schwarzbaum — *RCA/Columbia Pictures Home Video*

Russian Folk Song and Dance   1981
Music-Performance/Dance
57257   70 mins   C   B, V   P
Narrated by Tony Randall
Four of Russia's great troupes perform their colorful native songs and dances: the Pyatnitsky Russian Folk and Dance Ensemble (primarily Ukranian), the Siberian-Omsk Folk Chorus (from Siberia and Northern Russia), the Uzbekistan Dance Ensemble (from Samarkand and Central Asia) and the Moldavia Folk Song and Dance Ensemble (from Southwest Russia).
Kultur — *Kultur*

Russians Are Coming, the Russians Are Coming, The   1966
Comedy
58837   126 mins   C   CED   P
Alan Arkin, Carl Reiner, Theo Bikel, Eva Marie Saint, Brian Keith, Paul Ford, Jonathan Winters, Ben Blue, Tessie O'Shea, Doro Merande
A Russian sub accidentally runs aground off the New England coast causing havoc for the residents.
United Artists — *CBS/Fox Video; RCA VideoDiscs*

Rust Never Sleeps   1979
Music-Performance
31659   111 mins   C   B, V   P
Neil Young
Neil Young performs all the songs that made him a star in this concert film. These include "I Am A Child" (Buffalo Springfield), "My, My, Hey, Hey" (Out of the Blue), "Comes a Time," "Sugar Mountain," "Cinnamon Girl," "Hurricane," "Thrasher," and many more.
LA Johnson — *Vestron Video; RCA VideoDiscs*

Rustler's Rhapsody   1985
Comedy/Western
82068   89 mins   C   B, V, LV   P

Tom Berenger, Patrick Wayne, G W Bailey, Andy Griffith, Marilu Henner, *directed by Hugh Wilson*
A singing cowboy rides into a small western town and encounters all kinds of desperados in this satire of 40's B-movie westerns. Available in VHS and Beta Hi-Fi Stereo.
MPAA:PG
Paramount Pictures — *Paramount Home Video*

Rustler's Valley   1937
Western
85211   59 mins   B/W   B, V   P
William Boyd, Gabby Hayes, Lee J. Cobb
Hopalong Cassidy attempts to rescue his framed buddy from the dastardly claws of an evil lawyer.
William Boyd; Paramount — *Video Yesteryear*

Ruthless Four, The   1970
Western
81401   97 mins   C   B, V   P
Van Heflin, Klaus Kinski, Gilbert Roland, George Hilton
Four prospectors combat the elements and each other in their attempt to retrieve a fortune in gold in the Nevada hills.
MGM — *Monterey Home Video*

Ryan's Daughter   1970
Drama/Romance
80624   194 mins   C   B, V   P
Sarah Miles, Robert Mitchum, John Mills, Trevor Howard, Christopher Jones, directed by David Lean
A married Irish woman falls in love with a British major and is accused of betraying her country during the 1916 Irish Uprising. Music by Maurice Jarre. In Beta and VHS Hi-Fi.
Academy Awards '70: Best Supporting Actor (Mills); Best Cinematography. MPAA:PG
MGM — *MGM/UA Home Video*

S

Saab   1986
Automobiles
88409   60 mins   C   B, V, 3/4U   P
How to tune-up and maintain the Saab engine.
Peter Allen Prod. — *Peter Allen Video Productions*

Sabotage   1936
Suspense
13052   81 mins   B/W   B, V   P
Oscar Homolka, directed by Alfred Hitchcock
Saboteur finds his world closing in on him when a bomb he made kills his young brother-in-law and his wife seeks secret revenge.

GB Prods — *Hollywood Home Theater; Video Dimensions; Cable Films; Video Yesteryear; Video Connection; Western Film & Video Inc; Discount Video Tapes; Kartes Video Communications*

Saboteur
1942
Suspense
82076   108 mins   B/W   B, V, LV   P
Priscilla Lane, Robert Cummings, Otto Kruger, Alan Baxter, directed by Alfred Hitchcock
A man wrongly accused of sabotaging an American munitions plant during World War II sets out to find the traitor who framed him. Available in VHS and Beta Hi-Fi Mono.
Frank Lloyd Productions — *MCA Home Video*

Sabrina, Volume 1
1969
Cartoons
65622   23 mins   C   B, V   P
Animated
What happens when a pretty teenage girl is also a witch? If it's Sabrina, you know you're in for plenty of amazing, amusing and action-packed adventures.
Filmation — *Embassy Home Entertainment*

Sabrina Volumes IV—VI
1969
Cartoons
78350   57 mins   C   B, V   P
Animated
Sabrina, the teenage witch and the Archie gang get into all sorts of problems in this animated collection of episodes from the television series.
Filmation Studios — *Embassy Home Entertainment*

Sacco and Vanzetti
1971
Drama
51116   120 mins   C   B, V   P
Milo O'Shea, Gian Maria Volonte, Cyril Cusak
An account of the flagrant miscarriage of justice subjected upon two Italian immigrants caught amidst witch-hunts and judicial negligence in the 1920's.
MPAA:PG
Unidis Largo Messico 6 Rome — *United Home Video*

Sacred Ground
1983
Drama
Closed Captioned
65501   100 mins   C   B, V, CED   P
Tim McIntire, Jack Elam, Mindi Miller
A trapper and his pregnant wife unknowingly build shelter on the Paiute Indian's sacred burial ground. When the wife dies in childbirth, the pioneer is forced to kidnap a Paiute woman who has just buried her own deceased infant.
MPAA:PG
Pacific International — *CBS/Fox Video*

Sade: Diamond Life Video
1985
Music video
81175   30 mins   C   B, V   P
This is a collection of four conceptual music videos from Sade's "Diamond Life" album. Available in digitally mastered Hi-Fi stereo for both formats.
CBS/Fox Video Music — *CBS/Fox Video*

Safari 3000
1982
Adventure
79212   91 mins   C   B, V   P
Stockard Channing, David Carradine, Christopher Lee
A ""Playboy" writer is assigned to do a story on a three day, three thousand kilometer car race in Africa.
MPAA:PG
United Artists — *MGM/UA Home Video*

Saga of Death Valley
1939
Western
05533   56 mins   B/W   B, V   P
Roy Rogers, Gabby Hayes, Donald Barry, Doris Day
Roy Rogers battles a band of outlaws and discovers that their leader is his own brother.
Republic — *Video Connection; Cable Films; Nostalgia Merchant; Discount Video Tapes*

Sagebrush Trail
1933
Western
08845   63 mins   B/W   B, V, 3/4U   P
John Wayne
Action on the plains as John Wayne rides into Indian trouble.
Monogram — *Sony Video Software; Video Connection; Cable Films; Discount Video Tapes; Spotlite Video*

Saginaw Trail
1953
Western
84943   56 mins   B/W   B, V   P
Gene Autry, Smiley Burnette, Connie Marshall
Amid western song, Gene and the good guys try to nab a wily, treacherous fur trapper.
Columbia — *Blackhawk Films*

Sahara
1943
War-Drama
58964   97 mins   B/W   B, V   P
Humphrey Bogart, Dan Duryea, Bruce Bennett, Lloyd Bridges, Rex Ingram, J. Carrol Naish
An action story of desert battle and survival during World War II.
Columbia — *RCA/Columbia Pictures Home Video*

Sahara
1983
Romance/Adventure
79207   111 mins   C   B, V   P

Brooke Shields, John Rhys-Davies, Lambert
Wilson, Sir John Mills, directed by Andrew
McLaglen
An American heiress is kidnapped by Bedouin
tribesmen while driving in an auto race through
the Sahara. In Beta and VHS Hi-Fi.
MPAA:PG
Cannon Films — MGM/UA Home Video

Sahara Cross (Extrana Aventura en el Sahara)   197?
Adventure
88316   95 mins   C   B, V   P
Researchers in the Sahara are ambushed by
saboteurs, and the chase is on.
SP
Spanish — JCI Video

Sailor Who Fell from Grace with the Sea, The   1976
Drama
13663   105 mins   C   B, V   P
Sarah Miles, Kris Kristofferson, Jonathan Kahn,
Margo Cunningham, directed by Lewis John
Carlino
A disillusioned sailor rejects the sea for the love
of a young, sexually repressed widow.
MPAA:R
Avco Embassy; Martino Poll
Production — Embassy Home Entertainment;
RCA VideoDiscs

Saint, The   1968
Adventure/Mystery
71333   100 mins   C   B, V   P
Roger Moore, Ronald Rodd, Lois Maxwell,
Suzanne Lloyd, Cecil Parker, Anton Rogers,
Yolande Turner, various other stars
This popluar British TV series starred Moore as
Simon Templar, urbane sophisticate and
international adventurer. Each tape includes two
episodes with a variety of co-stars.
1.Simon and Delilah & A Double In Diamonds
ITC Productions; ATV — U.S.A. Home Video

Saint Benny the Dip   1951
Comedy
57341   80 mins   B/W   B, V   P
Dick Haymes, Nina Foch, Roland Young, Lionel
Stander, Freddie Bartholomew
An off-beat account of con-men posing as
clergymen who predictably become reformed.
United Artists — Hollywood Home Theater;
Discount Video Tapes; See Hear Industries

St. Elmo's Fire   1985
Drama
Closed Captioned
71106   110 mins   C   B, V   P
Martin Balsam, Emilio Estevez, Rob Lowe,
Andrew McCarthy, Demi Moore, Judd Nelson,
Ally Sheedy, Mare Winningham, directed by Joel
Schumacher

Seven Georgetown graduates confront adult
problems during their first year out of college. In
Hi-Fi Stereo.
MPAA:R
Columbia — RCA/Columbia Pictures Home
Video

St. Helen's, Killer Volcano   1982
Drama
64884   95 mins   C   B, V   P
Art Carney, David Huffman, Cassie Yates
A young man and an old man develop a deep
friendship amidst the devastation, fear, greed
and panic surrounding the eruption of a volcano.
Michael Murphy — Vestron Video

Saint in London, The   1939
Mystery
64380   72 mins   B/W   B, V, 3/4U   P
George Sanders, Sally Grey
The Saint picks up a wounded man lying at the
side of a country road and becomes involved in
murder and intrigue.
RKO — Nostalgia Merchant

Saint in New York, The   1938
Mystery
00297   71 mins   B/W   B, V   P
Louis Hayward, Kay Sutton, Jack Carson
The Saint turns Robin Hood to help Civic
Committee clean up a gang of desperados.
RKO — Nostalgia Merchant

St. Ives   1976
Crime-Drama
72920   94 mins   C   B, V   P
Charles Bronson, Jacqueline Bissett
A former police reporter goes undercover when
he gets framed for a murder.
MPAA:PG
Warner Bros — Warner Home Video

Saint Jack   1979
Drama
65384   112 mins   C   B, V   P
Ben Gazzara
The story of a small-time pimp with big dreams
working the pleasure palaces of late-night
Singapore. Directed by Peter Bogdonovich.
MPAA:R
Peter Bogdonovich Productions — Vestron
Video

Saint Strikes Back, The/Criminal Court   1946
Suspense/Mystery
81025   127 mins   B/W   B, V   P
George Sanders, Wendy Barrie, Barry
Fitzgerald, Tom Conway, Steve Brodie
A suspense double feature: The Saint helps
clear the name of the daughter of a San
Francisco police commissioner in "The Saint

Strikes Back," and a young lawyer becomes involved in murder in "Criminal Court".
RKO — *RKO HomeVideo*

St. Valentine's Day Massacre, The   1967
Crime-Drama
70988   100 mins   C   B, V   P
Jason Robards, Ralph Meeker, Jean Hale, Joseph Campanella, Bruce Dern, Clint Ritchie, Richard Bakalayan, George Segal, directed by Roger Corman
Corman's big studio debut recreates the events leading to one of the most violent gangland shootouts in modern history; the February 14, 1929 bloodbath between the Capone and Moran gangs. Recorded in HiFi.
20th Century Fox — *Key Video*

Saint's Vacation The, The Narrow Margin   1952
Mystery
76838   148 mins   B/W   B, V   P
Hugh Sinclair, Sally Gray, Charles McGraw, Marie Windsor, Jacqueline White
A mystery, double feature: In "The Saint's Vacation," Simon Templar prevents a valuable secret from getting into the wrong hands and in "The Narrow Margin," strange things happen to a detective when he takes a train ride with a witness to Chicago.
RKO — *RKO HomeVideo*

Sakharov   1984
Biographical/Drama
80321   120 mins   C   B, V   P
The true story of the Russian physicist whose involvement in the dissident movement cannot be stopped by the Soviet government.
HBO — *Prism*

Salem's Lot: The Movie   1979
Horror
69798   112 mins   C   B, V   P
David Soul, James Mason, Lance Kerwin, Bonnie Bedelia, Lew Ayras, directed by Tobe Hooper
This film is based on Stephen King's novel about a sleepy New England village which is infiltrated by evil when a mysterious antiques dealer takes up residence in a forbidding hilltop house—and it becomes apparent that a vampire is on the loose.
Warner Bros — *Warner Home Video*

Sally of the Sawdust   1925
Comedy
10097   124 mins   B/W   B, V   P
W. C. Fields, Carol Dempster, Alfred Lunt, directed by D. W. Griffith
W. C. Fields' first silent feature film where he portrays a carnival barker who adopts a young

woman. Displays his talents at juggling, conning customers, and car chasing. Musical score.
United Artists — *Video Yesteryear; Blackhawk Films*

Salome Where She Danced   1945
Drama
81734   90 mins   C   B, V   P
Yvonne De Carlo, Rod Cameron, David Bruce, Walter Slezak
A European dancing star star helps a reporter to get a scoop.
Universal — *Kartes Video Communications; Movie Buff Video*

Salt of the Earth   1954
Drama
85671   103 mins   B/W   B, V   P
Rosaura Revueltas, Will Geer, David Wolfe, directed by Herbert Biberman
Finally available in this country after being suppressed for thirty years, this controversial film was made by a group of blacklisted filmmakers during the McCarthy era. The story deals with the anti-Hispanic racial strife that occurs in a New Mexico zinc mine.
Independent Productions Corp. — *Voyager Press*

Salty   1973
Comedy-Drama/Adventure
60169   93 mins   C   B, V   P
Clint Howard, Mark Slade
A lovable but mischievous sea lion manages to complicate two brothers' lives when they volunteer to help a friend renovate a Florida marina, which is threatened by a mortgage foreclosure.
Time-Life Films — *Lightning Video*

Salute John Citizen   1942
War-Drama
69560   74 mins   B/W   B, V, FO   P
Peggy Cummins, Stanley Holloway, Dinah Sheridan, Jimmy Hanley
The life of an average English family during the early days of World War II is depicted, focusing on the deprivation and horror of the Nazi blitzkrieg.
Gaumont — *Video Yesteryear*

Salute to Chuck Jones, A   1960
Cartoons
81579   56 mins   C   B, V   P
Animated, voice of Mel Blanc, directed by Chuck Jones
Here are a collection of eight Chuck Jones favorites including "Duck Dodgers in the 24 1/2th Century", "One Froggy Evening", "Rabbit Seasoning", and "Feed the Kitty".
Warner Bros. — *Warner Home Video*

Salute to Friz Freleng, A   1958
Cartoons
81578   57 mins   C   B, V   P
Animated, voice of Mel Blanc, directed by Friz Freleng
This volume features several classic Friz Freleng cartoons including the Academy Award winners "Speedy Gonzales" ('55), "Birds Anonymous" ('57), and "Knighty Knight Bugs" ('58).
Warner Bros. — *Warner Home Video*

Salute to Mel Blanc, A   1958
Cartoons
81577   58 mins   C   B, V   P
Animated, voice of Mel Blanc
This compilation pays tribute to the multi-talented Mel Blanc and features such memorable cartoons including "The Rabbit of Seville" "Little Boy Boo" "Robin Hood Daffy" and "Past Performances".
Warner Bros. — *Warner Home Video*

Same Time, Next Year   1978
Drama
31598   119 mins   C   B, V   P
Ellen Burstyn, Alan Alda
A chance meeting between a traveling executive and a liberated housewife results in a sometimes sometimes tragic, always sentimental 25-year affair—but they meet only one day a year. Based on the Broadway play by Bernard Slade.
Universal — *MCA Home Video*

Sammy Bluejay   1983
Cartoons
65654   60 mins   C   B, V   P
Animated
This program features two escapades—"Brainy Bluejay" and "Sammy's Revenge"—starring Sammy Bluejay, Peter Cottontail, and Reddy the Fox.
Ziv International — *Family Home Entertainment*

Sam's Son   1984
Drama
81971   107 mins   C   B, V   P
Michael Landon, Eli Wallach, Anne Jackson, Timothy Patrick Murphy, directed by Michael Landon
This is the story of how a young man's athletic prowess opened the door for an acting career in Hollywood.
MPAA:PG
Worldvision Enterprises — *Worldvision Home Video*

Samson and Delilah   1949
Drama
55544   128 mins   C   B, V, LV   P
Victor Mature, Hedy Lamarr, Angela Lansbury, George Sanders, Henry Wilcoxon, Olive Deering, Fay Holden, directed by Cecil B. De Mille
The biblical story of Delilah, who after being rejected by Samson, cuts his hair and delivers him to his enemies.
Paramount; Cecil B De Mille — *Paramount Home Video*

Samson and Delilah   1979
Drama/Bible
63513   51 mins   C   B, V   P
John Beck, Victor Jory, Ann Turkel
Samson is an adventurous sort, blessed with the divine gift of superhuman strength. His mettle is tested, however, when he meets the seductress Delilah. Part of the "Greatest Heroes of the Bible" series.
Sunn Classics — *Magnum Entertainment; Lucerne Films*

Samson et Dalila   1981
Opera
59877   135 mins   C   B, V   P
The Royal Opera performs Camille Saint-Saens' first major opera, based in the biblical story of Samson, who sucumbs to the wiles of Dalila. In stereo.
Covent Garden Video — *THORN EMI/HBO Video; Pioneer Artists*

Samson vs. the Vampire Women   1961
Horror
51951   89 mins   B/W   B, V   P
Samson, Lorena Velazquez, Jaime Fernandez, Maria Duval, directed by Alfonso Corona Blake
Samson, the masked hero and athlete, battles the forces of darkness as a horde of female vampires attempt to make an unsuspecting girl their next queen.
Azteca — *Hollywood Home Theater*

Samurai I: Musashi Miyamoto   1955
Adventure
88351   92 mins   C   B, V   P
Toshiro Mifune, directed by Hiroshi Inagaki
The first installment in the filmization of Miyamoto's life, as he leaves his 17th Century village as a warrior in a local civil war, and returns mad and beaten. Subtitled. Academy Awards '55: Best Foreign Language Film. JA
Toho Co. — *Embassy Home Entertainment*

Samurai II: Duel at Ichijoji Temple   1955
Adventure
88352   102 mins   C   B, V   P
Toshiro Mifune, directed by Hiroshi Inagaki

Inagaki's second film depicting the life of Musashi Miyamoto, the 17th Century warrior, who wandered the disheveled landscape of feudal Japan looking for glory and love. Subtitled.
JA
Toho Co. — *Embassy Home Entertainment*

Samurai III: Duel at Ganryu Island   1956
Adventure
88353   102 mins   C   B, V   P
Toshiro Mifune, Koji Tsurata, directed by Hiroshi Inagaki
The final film of Inagaki's trilogy, depicting Miyamoto's settling accounts of love and hatred, and confrontation of his lifelong enemy in a climatic battle. Subtitled.
JA
Toho Co. — *Embassy Home Entertainment*

San Francisco   1936
Drama
82121   116 mins   B/W   B, V   P
Jeanette MacDonald, Clark Gable, Spencer Tracy, Jack Holt, Jessie Ralph, Al Shear
The San Francisco Earthquake of 1906 serves as the background for a passionate romance between an opera singer and a Barbary Coast saloon owner.
MGM — *MGM/UA Home Video*

San Francisco Blues Festival   1983
Music-Performance
73985   60 mins   C   B, V   P
Blues greats Clifton Chenier and Charles "Gatemouth" Brown perform in a concert taped at the San Francisco Blues Festival in 1983.
Image Intergration — *Sony Video Software*

San Francisco Blues Festival   1983
Music-Performance
76664   60 mins   C   B, V   P
A blues celebration including "S.F. Bay Blues," "Louisiana Two Step," "What I Say" and many more.
Image Integration — *Sony Video Software*

San Francisco 49ers 1984 Team Highlights   1985
Football
70543   46 mins   C   B, V, FO   P
Joe Montana
The 49ers tallied a record 15 regular season victories and went on to win the Super Bowl by a stunning 22 points over the Miami Dolphins.
NFL Films — *NFL Films Video*

San Francisco 49ers 1985 Team Highlights   1985
Football
86802   23 mins   C   B, V   P
Glimpses of the 49ers' '85 season are featured on this tape.
NFL Films — *NFL Films Video*

Sand Pebbles, The   1966
Drama
08459   195 mins   C   B, V   P
Steve McQueen, Richard Crenna, Richard Attenborough, Candice Bergen, Larry Gates
An American expatriate, transferred to a gunboat on the Yangtze River in 1926, falls in love with a missionary teacher.
EL, SP
20th Century Fox; Robert Wise — *CBS/Fox Video*

Sandahl Bergman's Body   1983
Physical fitness/Dance
65215   60 mins   C   B, V   P
A unique program combining fitness and the art of dance.
Cassini and Ray Productions — *Monterey Home Video*

Sanders of the River   1935
Mystery
11369   80 mins   B/W   B, V, FO   P
Paul Robeson, Leslie Banks, Robert Cochran
An officer of the river patrol causes rebellion among the natives when he tracks down those seeking to break the law.
Korda — *Video Yesteryear; Cable Films; Video Connection; Kartes Video Communications*

Sanders of the River   1935
Adventure
81468   97 mins   B/W   B, V, LV   P
Paul Robeson, Leslie Banks, Robert Cochran, directed by Zoltan Korda
A tribal chief helps the British Commissioner of Affairs in Africa to thwart the evil intentions of a greedy king.
Alexander Korda — *Embassy Home Entertainment*

Sandpiper, The   1965
Romance/Drama
80630   117 mins   C   B, V   P
Elizabeth Taylor, Richard Burton, Charles Bronson, Eva Marie Saint, Morgan Mason, directed by Vincente Minnelli
A free-spirited artist falls in love with the married headmaster of her son's boarding school.
Academy Award '65: Best Song "The Shadow of Your Smile"
MGM;Venice Productions — *MGM/UA Home Video*

Sands of Iwo Jima 1949
War-Drama
47057 109 mins B/W B, V P
John Wayne, Forrest Tucker, John Agar
A tough Marine sergeant trains a squad of
rebellious recruits in New Zealand, and they
later are responsible for the capture of Iwo Jima
from the Japanese.
Republic — Republic Pictures Home Video;
RCA VideoDiscs

Sandstone 1974
Romance
82445 76 mins C B, V P
Directed by Jonathan and Bonny Peters
A pair of filmmakers visit a California hedonist
retreat and study the effects that nudity and free
sexual expression have on the modern psyche.
MPAA:R
Felidae Films — Vestron Video

Sanjuro 1962
Drama
57340 96 mins B/W B, V, LV P
Toshiro Mifune, Tatsuya Nakadai, directed by
Akira Kurosawa
In this offbeat sequel to "Yojimbo," a talented
but lazy samurai comes to the aid of a group of
naive young warriors. The conventional ideas of
"good" and "evil" are quickly discarded in the
movie's comic book style. Available with English
subtitles.
JA
Toho — Embassy Home Entertainment;
Hollywood Home Theater; Festival Films;
Discount Video Tapes; Video Action

Santa and the 3 Bears 1979
Cartoons
78899 60 mins C B, V P
Animated
When a mother bear and her cubs discover the
magic of Christmas in the forest, they decide to
skip hibernating for the winter.
Tony Benedict Productions — Prism

Santa Claus Conquers 1964
the Martians
Fantasy/Comedy
80764 80 mins C B, V P
John Call, Pia Zadora, Leonard Hicks, Vincent
Beck, Victor Stiles, Donna Conforti
A martian spaceship comes to Earth and
kidnaps Santa Claus and two children. They
take their captives to Mars, where Santa will
work at an automated toy shop.
Jalor Prods. — Embassy Home Entertainment

Santa Fe Trail 1940
Western
08782 110 mins B/W B, V, 3/4U P
Errol Flynn, Olivia de Havilland, Ronald Reagan,
Van Heflin, Raymond Massey

Pre-Civil War historical fight for "bloody
Kansas" with Jeb Stuart and George Custer
beginning their military careers.
Warner Bros — Prism; Hal Roach Studios;
Nostalgia Merchant; Hollywood Home Theater;
VCII; Video Yesteryear; Kartes Video
Communications; Cable Films; Video
Connection; Discount Video Tapes

Santa Fe Trail 1940
Western
71031 110 mins C B, V P
Errol Flynn, Olivia de Havilland, Ronald Reagan,
Van Heflin, Raymond Massey
Jeb Stuart and George Custer started their
military careers in the "Bloody Kansas" battles
of the 1850's. This release has been enhanced
using the Colorization process.
Warner Bros — Hal Roach Studios

Santa Fe Uprising 1946
Western
64410 54 mins B/W B, V, 3/4U P
Allan "Rocky" Lane, Bobby Blake
Red Ryder has to save Little Beaver from
kidnappers.
Republic — Nostalgia Merchant

Santee 1973
Western
81708 93 mins C B, V P
Glenn Ford, Dana Wynter, Jay Silverheels, John
Larch
A father-son relationship develops between a
bounty hunter and the son of a man he killed.
MPAA:PG
Crown International — Prism

Saps at Sea 1940
Comedy
33908 57 mins B/W B, V, 3/4U P
Stan Laurel, Oliver Hardy, James Finlayson,
Ben Turpin, Rychard Cramer
A doctor advises Ollie to take a rest away from
his job at a horn factory. He and Stan rent a
boat, which they plan to keep tied to the dock
until an escaped criminal happens by and uses
the boys for his getaway.
Hal Roach, United Artists — Nostalgia
Merchant; Blackhawk Films

Saps at Sea 1940
Comedy
63988 80 mins B/W B, V P, T
Stan Laurel, Oliver Hardy, Jimmy Finlayson, Ben
Turpin, Rychard Kramer
Stan and Ollie are cast out to sea on the same
boat with an escaped criminal. This tape also
includes a 1934 Charley Chase short, "The
Chases of Pimple Street."
Hal Roach; MGM — Blackhawk Films

Sarah and the Squirrel   1983
Cartoons
Closed Captioned
78888   74 mins   C   B, V   P
Animated, voice of Mia Farrow
A young girl learns to survive in a forest after
she becomes separated from her family during a
war.
Satori — *Playhouse Video*

Sartana's Here...Trade   1970
Your Pistol for a Coffin
Western
82282   92 mins   C   B, V   P
*George Hilton, Charles Southwood, Erika Blanc,
Linda Sini*
A soldier of fortune searches for a missing
shipment of gold in the Old West.
Franco Palaggi — *Unicorn Video*

S.A.S. San Salvador   1984
Adventure/Drama
84797   95 mins   C   B, V   P
*Miles Okeefe, Dagmar Lassander, Catherine
Jarrett*
A C.I.A. agent tries to prevent a psychotic from
running amok in San Salvador, El Salvador.
UGC — *Vestron Video*

Sasquatch   1976
Speculation
13101   94 mins   C   B, V   P
Story of seven men who defied death in a
primitive wilderness where no man had gone
before. They lived to tell the tale of this
legendary creature.
Gold Key — *United Home Video*

Satan's Blade   1984
Horror
82146   87 mins   C   B, V   P
The owner of an ancient talisman goes on a
killing rampage at a remote mountain lodge.
Contel — *Prism*

Satan's Cheerleaders   198?
Horror
88165   92 mins   C   B, V   P
*John Carradine, John Ireland, Yvonne DeCarlo,
The Huskies*
A demonic high school janitor traps a bevy of
buxom cheerleaders at his Satanic altar for
sacrificial purposes.
MPAA:PG
World Amusement Co. — *United Home Video*

Satan's Harvest   1965
Drama
87320   88 mins   C   B, V   P

George Montgomery, Tippi Hedren
An American detective inherits an estate in
Johannesburg, only to find that the deed has
been snatched by drug smugglers.
Ferde Grofe Jr. — *Monterey Home Video*

Satan's School for Girls   1973
Horror/Mystery
80315   74 mins   C   B, V   P
*Roy Thinnes, Kate Jackson, Jo Van Fleet, Lloyd
Bochner, Pamela Franklin*
When a young woman investigates the
circumstances that caused her sister's suicide,
it leads her to a satanic girl's academy.
Spelling/Goldberg Productions — *Prism*

Saturday Night Fever   1977
Drama
38614   118 mins   C   B, V, LV   P
John Travolta, Karen Gorney, Donna Pescow
A Brooklyn teenager who is king of the local
disco begins to question his narrow view of life.
Acclaimed for its disco dance sequences, with
music by the Bee Gees.
MPAA:R
Paramount — *Paramount Home Video; RCA
VideoDiscs*

Saturday Night Fever   1977
Drama
38958   118 mins   C   B, V   P
John Travolta, Karen Gorney, Donna Pescow
A slightly edited version of the popular disco
drama, with the sex-oriented scenes and some
strong language toned down for PG audiences.
Music by the Bee Gees.
MPAA:PG
Paramount — *Paramount Home Video*

Saturday Night Live: Eric   1976
Idle Vol I
Comedy/Variety
80171   64 mins   C   B, V   P
*John Belushi, Chevy Chase, Jane Curtin, Gilda
Radner, Garrett Morris*
Among the highlights from this 1976 episode
are John Belushi's duet with Joe Cocker and
special musical guests Stuff.
NBC; Lorne Michaels — *Warner Home Video*

Saturday Night Live: Buck   1979
Henry
Comedy/Variety
80176   120 mins   C   B, V   P
*Buck Henry, Bill Murray, Garrett Morris, Gilda
Radner, Jane Curtin, John Belushi*
Here are two vintage episodes from 1978 and
1979 that feature Buck Henry as guest host.
NBC; Lorne Michaels — *Warner Home Video*

Saturday Night Live: **1978**
Carrie Fisher
Comedy
66131   67 mins   C   B, V   P
Carrie Fisher, Not Ready For Prime Time Players
Carrie Fisher joins in a spoof of her Star Wars character in the sketch "New Kid on Earth," a beach party parody.
NBC — *Warner Home Video*

Saturday Night Live: **1977**
Charles Grodin
Comedy/Variety
80173   67 mins   C   B, V   P
Charles Grodin, John Belushi, Garrett Morris, Jane Curtin, Gilda Radner, Laraine Newman
Charles Grodin hosts this 1977 episode that features special musical guests Paul Simon and The Persuasions
NBC; Lorne Michaels — *Warner Home Video*

Saturday Night Live: **1976**
Elliott Gould
Comedy/Variety
80170   67 mins   C   B, V   P
John Belushi, Chevy Chase, Dan Aykroyd, Gilda Radner, Jane Curtin, Elliott Gould
The classic "Star Trek" spoof along with "The Killer Bees" sketch are just some of the highlights from this 1976 episode.
NBC; Lorne Michaels — *Warner Home Video*

Saturday Night Live: Eric   **1979**
Idle Vol. II
Comedy/Variety
80177   59 mins   C   B, V   P
Eric Idle, Bill Murray, Garrett Morris, Gilda Radner, Jane Curtin, John Belushi
Monty Python's Eric Idle guest hosts this 1979 episode which features an appearance from Father Guido Sarducci.
NBC; Lorne Michaels — *Warner Home Video*

Saturday Night Live: Gary   **1979**
Busey
Comedy/Variety
80175   69 mins   C   B, V ·   P
Gary Busey, Bill Murray, Gilda Radner, Jane Curtin, Garrett Morris
Among the highlights from this 1979 episode is a duet by Gregory Hines and Eubie Blake.
NBC; Lorne Michaels — *Warner Home Video*

Saturday Night Live: **1975**
George Carlin
Comedy/Variety
80180   60 mins   C   B, V   P
Chevy Chase, John Belushi, Jane Curtin, Michael O'Donoghue, Garrett Morris, George Carlin

This is the premiere episode of the long-running comedy series.
NBC; Lorne Michaels — *Warner Home Video*

Saturday Night Live: Lily   **1975**
Tomlin
Comedy/Variety
80169   67 mins   C   B, V   P
Chevy Chase, John Belushi, Dan Aykroyd, Gilda Radner, Jane Curtin, Lily Tomlin, Laraine Newman
Lily Tomlin and her characters Ernestine, Sister Boogie Woman, and Edith Ann appear in this 1975 episode.
NBC; Lorne Michaels — *Warner Home Video*

Saturday Night Live: **1976**
Madeline Kahn
Comedy/Variety
80167   68 mins   C   B, V   P
Chevy Chase, Dan Aykroyd, Jane Curtin, John Belushi, Garrett Morris, Madeline Kahn
A spoof of "The Final Days" and Gilda Radner's impersonation of Barbara Walters are just some of the highlights from this 1976 episode.
NBC; Lorne Michaels — *Warner Home Video*

Saturday Night Live: **1979**
Michael Palin
Comedy/Variety
80174   67 mins   C   B, V   P
Bill Murray, John Belushi, Jane Curtin, Garrett Morris, Gilda Radner, Michael Palin
Month Python's Michael Palin hosts this 1979 episode that features special musical guests, The Doobie Brothers.
NBC; Lorne Michaels — *Warner Home Video*

Saturday Night Live: **1975**
Peter Cook & Dudley Moore
Comedy/Variety
80166   67 mins   C   B, V   P
Chevy Chase, Gilda Radner, Laraine Newman, Jane Curtin, John Belushi, The Muppets
Peter and Dudley reprise their classic "Derek and Clive" routine along with musical guest Neil Sedaka in this 1975 episode.
NBC; Lorne Michaels — *Warner Home Video*

Saturday Night Live: Ray   **1977**
Charles
Comedy/Variety
80168   62 mins   C   B, V   P
John Belushi, Ray Charles, Dan Aykroyd, Bill Murray, Jane Curtin, Garrett Morris
The incomparable Ray Charles hosts this 1975 episode.
NBC; Lorne Michaels — *Warner Home Video*

Saturday Night Live: Richard Benjamin 1979
Comedy/Variety
80165   64 mins   C   B, V   P
Bill Murray, Gilda Radner, Garret Morris, Dan Aykroyd, Richard Benjamin
A spoof of "The China Syndrome" and Rickie Lee Jones singing "Chuck E's In Love" are some of the highlights from this 1979 show.
NBC; Lorne Michaels — *Warner Home Video*

Saturday Night Live: Robert Klein 1979
Comedy/Variety
80178   108 mins   C   B, V   P
Robert Klein, Bill Murray, John Belushi, Garrett Morris, Gilda Radner, Jane Curtin
Robert Klein guest hosts this 1979 episode that features special guest stars, The Muppets.
NBC; Lorne Michaels — *Warner Home Video*

Saturday Night Live: Rodney Dangerfield 1980
Comedy/Variety
80164   68 mins   C   B, V   P
Rodney Dangerfield, Bill Murrary, Don Novello, Harry Shearer
The comic who gets no respect hosts this episode that features musical guests the J. Geils Band.
NBC; Lorne Michaels — *Warner Home Video*

Saturday Night Live: Sissy Spacek 1977
Comedy/Variety
80172   68 mins   C   B, V   P
Sissy Spacek, Dan Aykroyd, Jane Curtin, Gilda Radner, Garrett Morris, John Belushi
Among the highlights from this 1977 show are Sissy Spacek portraying Amy Carter in a "Carter Call In" sketch and the "Gidget's Disease" commercial parody.
NBC; Lorne Michaels — *Warner Home Video*

Saturday Night Live: Steve Martin 2 1978
Comedy
66132   110 mins   C   B, V   P
Steve Martin, Not Ready for Prime Time Players
One of the "wild and crazy guy's" hilarious SNL appearances.
NBC — *Warner Home Video*

Saturday Night Live, Vol. II 197?
Comedy/Variety
60376   115 mins   C   CED   P
Steve Martin, Richard Pryor, John Belushi, Chevy Chase, Bill Murray, Gilda Radner
Two Saturday Night Live programs with the original cast; Richard Pryor is host for a show telecast on December 13, 1975 and Steve

Martin appears on an episode with an airdate of April 12, 1978.
NBC Enterprises; Lorne Michaels — *RCA VideoDiscs*

Saturday Night Live, Vol. I 1975
Comedy/Variety
53792   112 mins   C   CED   P
George Carlin, Steve Martin, John Belushi, Chevy Chase, Jane Curtin, Gilda Radner, Laraine Newman, Dan Ackroyd
The premiere telecast of October 11, 1975, hosted by George Carlin, which featured the Weekend Update, The Bees, The Muppets, Andy Kaufman, a film by Albert Brooks, musical guest Billy Preston, and a commercial for "New Dad." The other episode is the 29th original telecast from October 23, 1976, representing Steve Martin's first appearance as host. Sketches included "Jeopardy 1999," a spoof of the Mary Tyler Moore Show, Chevy's Weekend Update and his milk commercial, and a skit about beatniks. (11 minutes have been edited from the premiere show, and 5 minutes from the Martin show, of music and film segments).
NBC Enterprises; Lorne Michaels — *RCA VideoDiscs*

Saturday Night Live with Richard Pryor 1975
Comedy/Variety
47621   65 mins   C   B, V   P
Richard Pryor, Gil Scott-Heron, John Belushi, Dan Ackroyd, Gilda Radner, Laraine Newman, Jane Curtin, Chevy Chase
Richard Pryor appears in a samurai bellhop sketch, a spoof of "The Exorcist," and undergoes a peculiar personnel interview in this "SNL" episode. Other highlights include two songs by Gil Scott-Heron and a film by Albert Brooks.
NBC Enterprises; Lorne Michaels — *Warner Home Video*

Saturday Night Live with Steve Martin 1978
Comedy/Variety
47622   65 mins   C   B, V   P
Steve Martin, John Belushi, Dan Ackroyd, Laraine Newman, Gilda Radner, Bill Murray, Garrett Morris, Jane Curtin
Highlights from this 1978 show include the Czechoslovakian brothers, Steve Martin singing "King Tut," an appearance by the Blues Brothers and Steve and Gilda dancing frenetically to "Dancing in the Dark."
NBC Enterprises; Lorne Michaels — *Warner Home Video*

Saturday Night Serials 1940
Fantasy/Serials
84358   90 mins   B/W   B, V   P
Bela Lugosi, Gene Autry, Ray Corrigan, Lon Chaney Jr   4   pgms

A compilation of excerpts from four serials: "The Phantom Creeps," "The Phantom Empire," "Undersea Kingdom" and "Junior G-Men."
Universal; Mascot; Republic — *Rhino Video*

Saturday Night Shockers 1950
Horror/Exploitation
81712   150 mins   B/W   B, V   P
Daisy and Violet Hilton
Each volume in this series is comprised of two full-length horror/exploitation flicks, featuring twisted twins, barbarous butchers and sinister snow creatures. Terror abounds.
Independent — *Rhino Video*

Saturday Night Sleazies 1959
Exploitation
84357   150 mins   B/W   B, V   P
Martha Jordan
Each tape in this serie features 2 films, plus shorts, about raunchy, sleazy people with steamy erotic impulses.
Impulse Ent — *Rhino Video*

Saturday Serials 195?
Adventure
53050   50 mins   B/W   B, V, 3/4U   P
Richard Greene, Buster Crabbe, Al "Fuzzy" Knight
Two classic 1950's adventure shows: "The Adventures of Robin Hood" (1955), a British-made series staring Richard Greene as a man who robbed the rich and gave to the poor; and "Captain Gallant of the Foreign Legion" (1955), starring Buster Crabbe and Al "Fuzzy" Knight.
NBC et al — *Shokus Video*

Saturn 3 1980
Science fiction
41497   88 mins   C   B, V, LV   P
Farrah Fawcett, Kirk Douglas
Two research scientists create a futuristic Garden of Eden in an isolated sector of our solar system, but love story turns to horror story when a killer robot arrives.
MPAA:R EL, SP
Associated Film Distribution Corp — *CBS/Fox Video*

Saul and David 197?
Bible
35374   120 mins   C   B, V   P
A beautifully filmed story of David's life with King Saul, the battle with Goliath, and the tragic end of Saul. From the "Bible" series.
Sunn Classic — *United Home Video*

Savage 1973
Adventure
88153   81 mins   C   B, V   P
James Iglehardt, directed by Cirio Santiago

A foreign mess with ex-baseball star Iglehardt killing people with grenades and guns, abetted by an army full of murderous models.
MPAA:R
Cirio Santiago — *Charter Entertainment*

Savage Attraction 1984
Drama
72869   93 mins   C   B, V   P
The true story of a sixteen year old who was debauched across three continents.
MPAA:R
Unknown — *Embassy Home Entertainment*

Savage Dawn 1984
Adventure
85596   102 mins   C   B, V   P
Karen Black, George Kennedy, Lance Henrikson, Richard Lynch
A gang of motorcycle terrorists terrorize yet another sleepy Southern town, and are eventually stopped by a macho hero.
William P. Milling — *Media Home Entertainment*

Savage Hunger, A 1984
Adventure
88025   90 mins   C   B, V   P
Chris Makepeace, Scott Hylands, Anne Lockhart, directed by Sparky Green
Ten plane crash survivors struggle to survive in the Baja desert.
Shapiro Ent. — *Vestron Video*

Savage Sam 1963
Drama
88193   103 mins   C   B, V   P
Tommy Kirk, Kevin Corcoran
A heart-warming story about a boy and his lovable dog.
Walt Disney Prod. — *Walt Disney Home Video*

Savage Streets 1983
Drama
77411   93 mins   C   B, V, CED   P
Linda Blair, John Vernon, Sal Landi, Robert Dryer
A rowdy group of high school girls are in for a load of trouble when they play a trick on a Hollywood street gang.
MPAA:R
Ginso Investment Corp. — *Vestron Video*

Savages 1975
Drama
80316   74 mins   C   B, V   P
Andy Griffith, Sam Bottoms, Noah Beery
A hunter and his guide play a deadly cat and mouse game in the desert.
Spelling/Goldburg Productions — *Prism*

Savannah Smiles 1982
Drama
66046   104 mins   C   B, V, LV,   P
CED
Bridgette Andersen, Mark Miller, Donovan Scott
A six-year old runaway befriends two escaped
convicts.
MPAA:PG
Clark Paylow — *Embassy Home Entertainment*

Save the Lady 1982
Drama
81920   76 mins   C   B, V   P
This is the story of how four children saved an
old ferry from going to the scrap heap.
Satori Entertainment — *VidAmerica*

Save the Tiger 1973
Drama
58716   100 mins   C   B, V, LV   P
*Jack Lemmon, Jack Gilford, Laurie Heineman,
Patricia Smith, Norman Burton, directed by John
Avildsen*
A middle-aged man, faced with a failing
business, struggles with his conscience and
changing American values.
Academy Awards '73: Best Actor (Lemmon).
MPAA:R
Paramount; Steve Shagan — *Paramount
Home Video*

Saving Par from the Sand 1985
Golf
88071   25 mins   C   B, V   P
John Elliot demonstrates optimum bunker
shots.
NFL Films; Golf Digest — *NFL Films Video*

Saviors, Saints, and 1981
Sinners
Football
50645   50 mins   C   B, V, FO   R, P
A summary of the 1980 NFL season, including a
look at the All-Pro selections.
NFL Films — *NFL Films Video*

Sawdust and Tinsel 1953
Drama
78637   85 mins   B/W   B, V, LV   P
*Harriet Andersson, Ake Gronberg, directed by
Ingmar Bergman*
A circus owner decides to leave his mistress
when the circus arrives in the town where his
wife and child live. This film has English
subtitles.
SW
Janus Films — *Embassy Home Entertainment*

Sawmill/The Dome 1922
Doctor, The
Comedy
85167   71 mins   B/W   B, V   P
Larry Semon, Dorothy Dwan
Two silent comedies starring the inimitable klutz
of the golden era, Larry Semon, whose name
has been nearly forgotten today.
Vitagraph — *Video Yesteryear*

Say Amen, Somebody 1980
Documentary/Music
66445   100 mins   C   B, V   P
*Willie May Ford Smith, Thomas A. Dorsey, Sallie
Martin, Delois Barrett Cambell*
A documentary look at the joyful world of gospel
music. Two old-timers, Thomas A. Dorsey, the
"Father of Gospel Music" and Sallie Martin,
also known as Mother Smith, talk and sing
about the gospel heritage as they experienced
it.
UnitedArtists Classics; GTN
Productions — *Pacific Arts Video*

Say Goodbye to Back 1985
Pain
Physical fitness/Pain
70778   96 mins   C   B, V   P
Alexander Melleby
The producers of this program feel that viewers
should be able to reduce or eliminate back pain
by following their recommendations.
AM Available
Robert Hendrickson; Westwood
Productions — *Videocassette Marketing*

Say Hello to Yesterday 1971
Drama
84617   91 mins   C   B, V   P
*Jean Simmons, Leonard Whiting, Evelyn Laye,
directed by Alvin Rackoff*
A September-May romance develops and
consummates in one London day when an
unhappy housewife meets an exciting young
traveler.
MPAA:PG
Josef Shaftel — *Prism*

Say It by Signing 1986
Deaf
85705   60 mins   C   B, V   P
An instructive program which teaches basic sign
language, its use and the easiest ways to
remember it.
Living Language; Dr. Elaine Costello — *Crown
Video*

Sayonara 1957
Drama
69379   147 mins   C   B, V, CED   P
*Marlon Brando, James Garner, Ricardo
Montalban, Patricia Owens, Red Buttons,
Miyoshi Umeki*
Based on the novel by James A. Michener, this
is the story of American servicemen on leave in
Japan during the Korean War, and the

Japanese women that some have fallen in love
with.
Academy Awards'57: Best Supporting Actor
(Buttons); Best Supporting Actress (Umeki);
Best Art Direction; Best Sound.
Warner Bros — CBS/Fox Video

Scalpel   1978
Horror/Suspense
84527   95 mins   C   B, V   P
Robert Lansing, directed by John Grissmer
A plastic surgeon constructs the face of his
runaway daughter on a homeless dancer in
order to collect the daughter's inheritance, only
to have his real daughter show up.
MPAA:R
Joseph Weintraub — Charter Entertainment

Scandalous   1984
Comedy/Mystery
66606   93 mins   C   B, V, LV,   P
                                CED
Robert Hays, John Gielgud, Jim Dale, Pamela
Stephenson
A bumbling American TV reporter becomes
involved with a gang of British con artists.
MPAA:PG
Orion — Vestron Video

Scandalous John   1971
Comedy/Western
84800   113 mins   C   B, V   P
Brian Keith, Alfonso Arav, Michele Carey, Rick
Lenz
A last cattle drive is devised in order to save a
comically dilapidated ranch.
MPAA:G
Walt Disney Prod — Walt Disney Home Video

Scanners   1981
Horror
59339   102 mins   C   B, V, CED   P
Stephen Lack, Jennifer O'Neill, Patrick
McGoohan, Lawrence Dane
"Scanners" are telepaths who can will people
to explode. One scanner in particular harbors
Hitlerian aspirations for his band of psychic
gangsters.
MPAA:R
Filmplan International — Embassy Home
Entertainment

Scarecrow   1973
Drama
58248   112 mins   C   B, V   P
Gene Hackman, Al Pacino, Ann Wedgeworth,
Eileen Brennan, directed by Jerry Schatzberg
The tragicomic tale of two born losers adrift on
the road.
MPAA:R
Warner Bros — Warner Home Video

Scared to Death   1947
Mystery
01684   70 mins   C   B, V   P, T
Bela Lugosi, George Zucco, Joyce Compton,
directed by Walt Mattox
Woman dies of fright when shown death mask
of man she framed.
Screen Guild; Robert L Lippert — Mossman
Williams Productions; Video Connection; Video
Yesteryear; Admit One Video; Weiss Global
Enterprises

Scared to Death   1980
Horror
81641   93 mins   C   B, V   P
John Stinson, Diana Davidson, David Moses,
Kermit Eller
A scientific experiment goes awry as a mutation
begins killing off the residents of Los Angeles.
MPAA:R
Lone Star Pictures — Media Home
Entertainment

Scarface   1931
Crime-Drama
66588   90 mins   B/W   B, V, LV   P
Paul Muni, Ann Dvorak, George Raft, Boris
Karloff, directed by Howard Hawks
The brutal story of the life and death of a
Chicago gangster is portrayed in this hard-
hitting movie classic.
Howard Hughes; Universal — MCA Home
Video

Scarface   1983
Crime-Drama
66589   170 mins   C   B, V, LV   P
Al Pacino, Steven Bauer, Michelle Pfeiffer,
Robert Loggia, directed by Brian De Palma
A remake of the 1932 classic film, with Al
Pacino as a Cuban refugee who works his way
up to becoming a major figure in Miami's crime
scene. In stereo.
MPAA:R
Universal — MCA Home Video

Scarface Mob, The   1959
Crime-Drama
85289   120 mins   B/W   B, V   P
Robert Stack, Neville Brand, Barbara Nichols
The original television pilot film for the popular
series "The Untouchables."
ABC-TV — Paramount Home Video

Scarlatti/Debussy/Ravel   1984
Music-Performance
88131   47 mins   C   B, V   P
An orchestral performance of shorter suites and
concertos by the three famous composers.
Sony Video — Sony Video Software

Scarlet and the Black, The
1983

War-Drama
Closed Captioned
70351   145 mins   C   B, V   P
Gregory Peck, Christopher Plummer, Sir John
Gielgud, directed by Jerry London
This is the story of an Irish Priest working within
the shield of the Vatican's diplomatic immunity
to shelter allied soldiers from the Nazis in
occupied Rome. His efforts put him at odds with
the Pope and target him for Gestapo
assassination. The tape comes in Beta Hi-Fi and
VHS Stereo.
ITC — CBS/Fox Video

Scarlet Letter, The
1934

Drama
58525   69 mins   B/W   B, V   P
Colleen Moore, Henry B Walthall, Alan Hale,
Betty Blythe
Nathaniel Hawthorne's novel of sin and
redemption in Puritan New England.
London Films; Alexander Korda — Kartes
Video Communications

Scarlet Pimpernel, The
1935

Drama
08625   98 mins   B/W   B, V   P
Leslie Howard, Merle Oberon, Raymond
Massey, Anthony Bushell, John Gardner
"The Scarlet Pimpernel," supposed dandy of
the English court, outwits the French
Republicans during the Revolution.
United Artists; Alexander Korda;
British — Prism; Embassy Home
Entertainment; Media Home Entertainment;
Hollywood Home Theater; Blackhawk Films;
VCII; Movie Buff Video; Cable Films; Video
Connection; Discount Video Tapes; Hal Roach
Studios; Kartes Video Communications; Video
Yesteryear

Scarlet Street
1945

Mystery
01731   95 mins   B/W   B, V   P
Edward G. Robinson, Joan Bennett, Dan
Duryea, directed by Fritz Lang
Middle-aged cashier becomes an embezzler
when he gets involved with a predatory,
manipulating woman.
Universal — Hollywood Home Theater; Prism;
Cable Films; Video Connection; Video
Yesteryear; Discount Video Tapes; Movie Buff
Video; Kartes Video Communications

Scarred
1983

Drama
71778   85 mins   C   B, V   P
An unwed teenage mother becomes a prostitute
to support her baby.
Rose-Marie Turko — Vestron Video

Scars of Dracula
1971

Horror
63980   93 mins   C   B, V   P
Christopher Lee, Jenny Hanley, Dennis
Waterman, Wendy Hamilton
A young couple tangles with Dracula in their
search for the man's missing brother.
MPAA:R
Hammer Productions — THORN EMI/HBO
Video

Scary Tales and Silly Stories
1985

Horror
81850   58 mins   C   B, V   P
Captain Kangaroo travels to such strange
locations as Transylvania where he encounters
Blinky the Clown and Famous Amy.
Jim Hirschfeld — MPI Home Video

Scavenger Hunt
1979

Comedy
65409   117 mins   C   B, V   P
Richard Benjamin, James Coco, Ruth Buzzi,
Cloris Leachman, Cleavon Little, Roddy
McDowall, Scatman Crothers, Tony Randall,
Robert Morley
The action begins when a deceased
millionaire's will states that his 15 would-be
heirs must compete in a scavenger hunt, and
whoever collects all the items first wins the
entire fortune.
MPAA:PG
Melvin Simon — CBS/Fox Video

Scenes from a Marriage
1973

Drama
39080   168 mins   C   B, V   P
Liv Ullmann, Erland Josephson, directed by
Ingmar Bergman
Originally produced for Swedish television, this
is an intimate chronicle of the disintegration of
the "perfect" marraige.
Cinema 5 — RCA/Columbia Pictures Home
Video

Scenes from the Big Chair—Tears for Fears
1985

Music-Performance
70877   77 mins   C   B, V   P
Roland Orzabal, Curt Smith, Ian Stanley, Manny
Elias
This video clip compilation includes concert and
conceptual treatments of the band's music, as
well as documentary interviews with band
members. In Hi-Fi Dolby Stereo.
Polygram Music Video — RCA/Columbia
Pictures Home Video

Schizo
1977

Drama
06085   109 mins   C   B, V   P
Lynne Rederick, John Layton

Devious intentions abound as a middleaged man is overcome by weird scenes and revelations. Much violent intensity.
MPAA:R
Pete Walker — *United Home Video; Media Home Entertainment*

Schizoid 1980
Horror
55552 91 mins C B, V P
Klaus Kinski, Mariana Hill, directed by David Paulsen
An advice-to-the-lovelorn columnist receives a series of threatening letters causing her to wonder whether a psychiatrist is bumping off his own patients.
MPAA:R
Golan Globus Prod — *MCA Home Video*

Schizoid Man, The 1968
Adventure/Fantasy
80418 50 mins C B, V P
Patrick McGoohan, Angelo Muscat, Colin Gordon, Alexis Kanner, Leo McKern
Number Two attempts to destroy The Prisoner's indentity through a new hypnotic technique.
Associated TV Corp — *MPI Home Video*

Scholastic Productions: 1980
As We Grow
Children/Identity
56885 70 mins C CED P
Twelve real-life episodes presenting early experiences in the lives of children at work and play. Produced by experts on children, this program will help children understand themselves and their world.
AM Available
Scholastic Inc — *RCA VideoDiscs*

School for Scandal 1965
Satire
69581 100 mins B/W B, V P
Joan Plowright, Felix Aylmer
A British television adaptation of Richard Sheridan's play of the morals and manners of 18th century England.
BBC — *Video Yesteryear*

School for Sex 1969
Comedy
81404 81 mins C B, V P
Derek Aylward, Rose Alba, Hugh Latimer, Cathy Howard
A young man starts a school to teach young girls how to marry well and divest their husbands of their money.
Peter Walker — *Monterey Home Video*

School Spirit 1985
Comedy
84130 90 mins C B, V P

Tom Nolan, Elizabeth Foxx, Larry Linville, directed by Allan Holleb
A hormonally motivated college student is killed during a date, but comes back as a ghost to haunt the campus, disrupt the stuffy president's affair and fall in love.
MPAA:R
New Horizons — *Media Home Entertainment*

Scooby and Scrappy-Doo 1979
Cartoons
47692 60 mins C B, V P
Animated
Scooby and his energetic nephew pub, Scrappy-Doo, sniff out mysteries with their detective friends—Fred, Velma, Daphne and Shaggy. Three episodes.
Hanna Barbera — *Worldvision Home Video*

Scooby and Scrappy 1979
Doo, Vol III
Cartoons
77161 60 mins C B, V P
Animated
Scooby and his nephew Scrappy Doo along with their friends Fred, Velma, Daphne and Shaggy set out to solve another mystery.
Hanna-Barbera — *Worldvision Home Video*

Scooby and Scrappy 1979
Doo, Vol. IV
Cartoons
82317 43 mins C B, V P
Animated
Scooby Doo and his nephew, Scrappy, set out to fight crime in two episodes from the series.
Hanna-Barbera — *Worldvision Home Video*

Scooby and Scrappy- 19??
Doo, Volume II
Cartoons
69589 60 mins C B, V P
Animated
Scooby, Scrappy, Fred, Daphne, Velma and Shaggy get into more comical scrapes as they attempt to solve a mystery.
Hanna Barbera — *Worldvision Home Video*

Scooby Goes Hollywood 197?
Cartoons/Musical
47691 48 mins C B, V P
Animated
Everyone's favorite canine hits Hollywood in an attempt to be a star.
Hanna Barbera — *Worldvision Home Video*

Score 1973
Drama
81756 89 mins C B, V P
Claire Wilbur, Calvin Culver, Lynn Lowry, directed by Radley Metzger

A married couple introduce their newlywed neighbors to the world of kinky sexual experiments such as spouse swapping.
MPAA:R
Radley Metzger — *Magnum Entertainment*

Scorpions 1983
Music video
88105   17 mins   C   B, V   P
A collection of the German heavy metal band's older video clips, including "No One Like You."
Sony Video — *Sony Video Software*

Scorpions—World Wide Live 1985
Music-Performance
81803   70 mins   C   B, V   P
The German heavy metal band perform such hits as "No One Like You" and "Rock You Like a Hurricane" in this film of the band's 1984 tour. Available in VHS Dolby Hi-Fi Stereo and Beta Hi-Fi Stereo.
Scorpions GmbH/Breeze Music Prods. — *RCA/Columbia Pictures Home Video*

Scotland Yard 1983
Great Britain/Police
88157   60 mins   C   B, V   P
David Niven hosts a tour through England's major law enforcement agency, its history and current workings.
Lucy Jarvis — *Monterey Home Video*

Scout's Honor 1980
Drama
81958   96 mins   C   B, V   P
Gary Coleman, Katherine Helmond, Harry Morgan
An orphan is determined to become the best Cub Scout ever when he joins a troop led by an executive who dislikes children.
Jimmy Hawkins Co. — *Lightning Video*

Scrambled Feet 1983
Satire
75290   100 mins   C   B, V   P
Madeline Kahn
This is an uninhibited satire of the world of show business. In Beta Hi-Fi and VHS Dolby stereo.
RKO Home Video — *RKO HomeVideo*

Scream 1983
Suspense
82422   86 mins   C   B, V   P
Pepper Martin, Hank Warden, Alvy Moore, Woody Strode, John Ethan Wayne, directed by Byron Quisenberry
Vacationers on a raft trip down the Rio Grande are terrorized by a mysterious murderer.
MPAA:R
J E R — *Vestron Video*

Scream and Scream Again 1970
Horror
82452   95 mins   C   B, V   P
Vincent Price, Christopher Lee, Peter Cushing
Vincent Price is a sinister doctor who tries to create a race of people devoid of feelings and emotions.
Orion Pictures — *Vestron Video*

Scream Bloody Murder 197?
Suspense/Mystery
45051   90 mins   C   B, V   P
Fred Holbert, Leigh Mitchell, Robert Knox, Suzette Hamilton
A young boy grinds his father to death with a tractor but mangles his own hand trying to jump off. After receiving a steel claw and being released from a mental institution he continues his murderous ways in and around his home town.
First American Films — *United Home Video*

Scream Greats 1984
Documentary
85288   88 mins   C   B, V   P
Tom Savini
Gore-special effects expert Savini reveals his bloodiest secrets and shows the audience precisely how he creates his revolting illusions.
Starlog Video; Linda Laias — *Paramount Home Video*

Screamers 1980
Horror
82573   83 mins   C   B, V   P
Richard Johnson, Joseph Cotten, Barbara Bach
A mad scientist gleefully turns escaped convicts into grotesque monstrosities in this gory film.
MPAA:R
Lawrence Martin — *Embassy Home Entertainment*

Screams of a Winter Night 1979
Horror
35382   92 mins   C   B, V   P
Ghostly tale of an evil monster from the lake and the terror he causes.
MPAA:PG
Richard H Wadsack, James L Wilson — *United Home Video*

Screamtime 1983
Horror
70856   89 mins   C   B, V   P
Jean Anderson, Robin Baily, Dora Bryan, David Van Day, directed by Al Beresford.
Two fiendish friends filch a trilogy of horror tapes for home viewing. After the show, real scary things happen.
Manson — *Lightning Video*

Screen Song Sing-Along 1936
Cartoons
85927   57 mins   C   B, V   P
A compilation of vintage Max Fleischer Follow-
The-Bouncing-Ball sing-along cartoons.
Max Fleischer — *Spotlite Video*

Screen Test 1985
Comedy
85279   84 mins   C   B, V   P
*Michael Allan Bloom, Robert Bundy, Paul
Lueken, David Simpatico*
Lusty teenagers arrange a fake screen test in
order to meet girls.
*Sam and Laura Auster — RCA/Columbia
Pictures Home Video*

Screwballs 1983
Comedy
65742   80 mins   C   B, V   P
Peter Keleghan, Lynda Speciale
A freewheeling group of high school boys stirs
up trouble for their snooty and virginal
homecoming queen.
MPAA:R
Maurice Smith — *Warner Home Video*

Scrooge 1935
Fantasy
11397   61 mins   B/W   B, V, FO   P
Seymour Hicks, Maurice Evans, Robert Cochran
A miser changes his ways after receiving visits
from ghosts of Christmas past, present, and
future. Based on the classic novel "A Christmas
Carol" by Charles Dickens.
Paramount; Adolph Zukor — *Movie Buff Video;
Video Yesteryear; Blackhawk Films; Discount
Video Tapes*

Scrooge 1970
Musical-Drama
86047   86 mins   C   B, V   P
*Albert Finney, Alec Guinness, Edith Evans,
Kenneth More, directed by Ronald Neame*
The musical version of Charles Dickens' "A
Christmas Carol," about a miserly old man who
is faced with ghosts on Christmas Eve.
Cinema Center Films-National
General — *CBS/Fox Video*

Scrooge's Rock 'n' Roll Christmas 1983
Musical/Christmas
75900   44 mins   C   B, V   P
This program presents the Dickens story with
Christmas carols sung by Three Dog Night,
Rush and others.
Hitbound Records — *Sony Video Software*

Scrubbers 1982
Drama
73024   93 mins   C   B, V   P
Amanda York, Chrissie Cotterill
A young girl is sentenced to prison where she's
forced to survive in a cruel and brutal
environment.
MPAA:R
Don Boyd — *THORN EMI/HBO Video*

Scruffy 1980
Cartoons
80644   72 mins   C   B, V   P
*Animated, voices of Alan Young, June Foray,
Hans Conried, Nancy McKeon*
An orphaned puppy encounters many
dangerous adventures before finding true love.
Ruby-Spears — *Worldvision Home Video*

Scruggs 1970
Music-Performance
37404   87 mins   C   B, V   P
*Earl Scruggs, Bob Dylan, Joan Baez, Doc
Watson, The Byrds*
A tribute to banjo virtuoso Earl Scruggs,
featuring Scruggs in performance, along with
Dylan, Baez, and others.
WNET New York — *CBS/Fox Video*

Scuba 1972
Documentary/Oceanography
71212   83 mins   C   B, V   P
*Narrated by Lloyd Bridges, directed by Ambrose
Gaines III*
Three daring couples dive for hidden treasure in
beautiful waters of the Caribbean.
MPAA:G
Independent — *Prism*

Scuba Run 1986
Sports-Water
87596   50 mins   C   B, V, 3/4U   P
Tulla Cove, Eric Davis, Mike Paddy O'Leary
A romance/how-to film detailing the adventures
of two young lovers diving in the Southern
Caribbean Sea. Also included are two shorts,
"Underwater Jazz Music Video" and "Music
Video Promo."
Jeffery J. Schwartz; Photon Video
Co. — *Photon Video Company*

Scum 1979
Drama
70604   96 mins   C   B, V   P
*Phil Daniels, Mick Ford, Ray Winstone, directed
by Alan Clarke*
Adapted from Roy Mintons acclaimed play, this
British production looks at the struggle between
three young men in a British Borstal (a prison for
young convicts.)
GTO Films Ltd. — *Prism*

Sea Around Us, The 1952
Documentary/Oceanography
10158   61 mins   C   B, V   P, T

Narrated by Don Forbes
Science documentary of history and life of the ocean based on Rachel Carson's study.
Academy Award '52: Best Feature Documentary.
Irwin Allen; RKO — *Blackhawk Films; Nostalgia Merchant*

Sea Devils   1953
Adventure/Romance
82486   86 mins   C   B, V   P
Rock Hudson, Yvonne DeCarlo, Maxwell Reed
A smuggler and a beautiful spy come together in this sea romance filled with intrigue and adventure.
RKO; Coranado Prods — *Media Home Entertainment*

Sea Hawk, The   1940
Adventure
73969   110 mins   B/W   B, V   P
Errol Flynn, Claude Rains, Donald Crisp, Alan Hale, Flora Robson, Brenda Marshall, directed by Michael Curtiz
When an English pirate finds out that the Spanish are going to invade England with their Armada, he comes back to save the queen and his country.
Warner Bros — *Key Video*

Sea Lion, The   1921
Drama
48712   50 mins   B/W   B, V, FO   P
Hobart Basworth
A vicious sea captain, embittered by a past romance, becomes sadistic and intolerable, until the truth emerges. Silent.
Hobart Bosworth Prods — *Video Yesteryear*

Sea Prince and the Fire Child, The   1982
Adventure/Cartoons
64910   70 mins   C   B, V   P
Animated
This Japanese animated film follows two young lovers who set off on an adventure to escape the disapproval of their parents.
Tsunemasa Hatano — *RCA/Columbia Pictures Home Video*

Sea Serpent, The   1985
Fantasy
85916   92 mins   C   B, V   P
Timothy Bottoms, Ray Milland, Jared Martin, directed by Gregory Greens
A young sea captain and a crusty scientist unite to search out a giant sea monster.
Calepas Int'l — *Lightning Video*

Sea Shall Not Have Them, The   1955
War-Drama/Adventure
81424   92 mins   B/W   B, V   P
Michael Redgrave, Dick Bogarde, directed by Lewis Gilbert
A daring band of men rescue the four survivors of a Hudson aircraft crash in the North Sea.
United Artists — *Movie Buff Video; Republic Pictures Home Video*

Sea Wolves, The   1981
Adventure
53557   120 mins   C   B, V, CED   P
Gregory Peck, Roger Moore, David Niven, Trevor Howard, Patrick Macnee, directed by Andrew V. McLaglen
A true WW II story about a commando-style operation undertaken by a group of middle-aged, boozing British businessmen in India in 1943.
MPAA:PG
Euan Lloyd; Lorimar — *CBS/Fox Video*

Sealab 2020   1972
Cartoons/Science fiction
82161   50 mins   C   B, V   P
Animated, voices of Ross Martin, Ann Jullian, Pamelyn Ferdin
Here are two episodes chronicling the underwater adventures a scientific expedition encounters in the year 2020.
Hanna-Barbera — *Worldvision Home Video*

Search and Destroy   1978
Drama
64871   93 mins   C   B, V, CED   P
Perry King, George Kennedy, Tisa Farrow
A deadly vendetta, born in the midst of battle in a Vietnamese jungle, is kept alive.
MPAA:PG
James Margellos — *Vestron Video*

Search for Survival   198?
Wildlife
88167   90 mins   C   B, V   P
A view of wildlife in Australia, Africa and North America and how it relates to local food and water supplies.
United Home Video — *United Home Video*

Search for the Super   1985
Documentary/Nuclear energy
82559   50 mins   C   B, V, 3/4U   P
Narrated by Bernard Archard, directed by Peter Batty
This sequel to "Birth of the Bomb" traces the development and 1954 detonation of the first hydrogen bomb.
Peter Batty — *Evergreen International*

Searchers, The 1956
Western
38954   119 mins   C   B, V, LV   P
John Wayne, Jeffrey Hunter, Vera Miles, Natalie Wood, Ward Bond, directed by John Ford
John Wayne plays a Civil War veteran on the trail of a Comanche raiding party that kidnapped the daughter of one of his friends in this classic John Ford western.
Warner Bros — *Warner Home Video; RCA VideoDiscs*

Seasons for Assassins 1971
Suspense
65448   102 mins   C   B, V   P
Joe Dallesandro, Martin Balsam
A gang of young ruthless hoodlums bring a wave of violence and terror upon the hapless citizens of Rome.
MPAA:R
Carlo Maietto — *U.S.A. Home Video*

Seattle Seahawks 1984 1985
Team Highlights
Football
70551   70 mins   C   B, V, FO   P
The seahawk's intimidating defense and explosive offense helped them overcome adversity in a season characterized by some as "One From the Heart." The tape features 47-minutes of highlights from the '84 NFL season as well.
NFL Films — *NFL Films Video*

Secluded World of the 1985
Mule Deer, The
Wildlife
88318   60 mins   C   B, V   P
The habitat and habits of the wild mule deer are seen in this nature program.
American Heritage Video; John Kerwin — *Eagle Productions*

2nd Best Secret Agent in 1965
the Whole Wide World,
The
Comedy
88152   93 mins   C   B, V   P
Tom Adams, directed by Lindsay Shonteff
A klutzy moron attempts to prevent a Swedish anti-gravity formula from falling into Russian hands.
Joseph E. Levine — *Charter Entertainment*

Second Chance 1953
Suspense/Drama
64370   82 mins   C   B, V, 3/4U   P
Robert Mitchum, Linda Darnell, Jack Palance, directed by Rudolph Mate
A former prizefighter travels to South America where he protects a gangster's moll who is targeted for murder.

RKO — *Nostalgia Merchant*

Second Chorus 1940
Musical
01617   83 mins   B/W   B, V   P
Fred Astaire, Paulette Goddard, Burgess Meredith, Artie Shaw, Directed by H.C. Potter
Rivalry of two trumpet players for a girl and a job with Artie Shaw Orchestra. Music, dance, and romance.
Paramount — *Hollywood Home Theater; Movie Buff Video; Cable Films; VCII; Prism; Video Connection; Video Yesteryear; Discount Video Tapes; Cinema Concepts; Kartes Video Communications; Hal Roach Studios*

Second City Insanity 1981
Comedy
59076   60 mins   C   B, V   P
Fred Willard, John Candy
The famed Second City improvisational troupe performs their unique brand of humor.
Toby Martin; Carol N Raskin — *Karl/Lorimar Home Video*

Second Coming of 1980
Suzanne, The
Drama
56920   90 mins   C   B, V   R, P
Sondra Locke, Richard Dreyfuss, Gene Barry
A beautiful woman encounters a Manson-like, hypnotic film director. Her role—to star in a Crucifixion. Set in 1969 San Francisco. A world premiere edition, winner at two international film festivals.
Michael Barry — *Video Gems*

Second Thoughts 1983
Comedy-Drama
65090   109 mins   C   B, V   P
Lucie Arnaz, Craig Wasson, Ken Howard
A lady attorney becomes pregnant by one of her clients, an itinerant street musician. When she decides to get an abortion, he kidnaps her and tries to change her mind.
MPAA:PG
EMI Films; Universal — *THORN EMI/HBO Video*

Second Time Lucky 1984
Comedy/Fantasy
81124   98 mins   C   B, V   P
Diane Franklin, Roger Wilson, Robert Morley, Jon Gadsby, Bill Ewens, directed by Michael Anderson
The devil makes a bet with God that if the world began all over again Adam and Eve would repeat their mistake they made in the Garden of Eden.
United International Pictures — *Karl/Lorimar Home Video*

Second Woman, The 1951
Drama/Mystery
80741   91 mins   B/W   B, V   P
Robert Young, Betsy Drake, John Sutton
A small town suspects that an architect is
responsible for the death of his fiancee.
Cardinal Pictures — *Hal Roach Studios; United
Home Video*

Secret Admirer 1985
Comedy
82022   98 mins   C   B, V   P
*C. Thomas Howell, Cliff De Young, Kelly
Preston, Dee Wallace Stone, Lori Loughlin, Fred
Ward*
Comic complications arise when a young girl's
secret love letters keep falling into the wrong
hands.
MPAA:R
Orion Pictures — *THORN EMI/HBO Video*

Secret Adversary, The 1983
Mystery
81923   120 mins   C   B, V   P
Francesca Annis, James Warwick
Ace detectives Tommy and Tuppence
Beresford must find a secret treaty before it falls
into the wrong hands. Pilot for the "Partners in
Crime" series. Based on the characters created
by Agatha Christie.
London Weekend Television — *Pacific Arts
Video*

Secret Agent 1936
Mystery
11317   83 mins   B/W   B, V, FO   P
*Madeleine Carroll, Peter Lorre, Robert Young,
John Gielgud, Lilli Palmer*
A British Intelligence agent has orders to
eliminate an enemy agent and thinks he has
succeeded. He later finds out that he killed an
innocent tourist in Geneva.
Gaumont — *Video Yesteryear; Hollywood
Home Theater; Video Dimensions; Discount
Video Tapes; Video Connection; Cable Films;
Western Film & Video Inc; Hal Roach Studios;
Kartes Video Communications*

Secret Agent 1965
Suspense
77419   50 mins   B/W   B, V   P
*Patrick McGoohan, Niall MacGinnes, Dawn
Addams, directed by Don Chaffey* 45   pgms
Secret agent John Drake embarks upon
dangerous and exciting assignments around the
world in this mystery-adventure series, which
ran during 1965 and 1966. All but two episodes
are in black and white.
ITC Productions — *MPI Home Video*

Secret Beyond the Door 1948
Mystery
70203   99 mins   B/W   B, V   P

*Joan Bennett, Michael Redgrove, Barbara
O'Neill*
A wealthy heiress marries a widower and soon
discovers that he murdered his first wife.
Universal — *Republic Pictures Home Video*

Secret Fantasy 1981
Drama
63383   88 mins   C   B, V   P
Laura Antonelli
A musician overcomes his fears of inferiority as
he makes his fantasies a reality by having other
men admire his wife's beautiful body.
MPAA:R
Film Ventures — *Media Home Entertainment*

**Secret Life of Adolph
Hitler, The** 1969
World War II/Documentary
08910   52 mins   B/W   B, V, 3/4U   P
Narrated by Westbrook Van Voorhis
A documentary on Adolph Hitler uses rare
footage to portray the growth of the Third Reich.
Wolper — *Video Yesteryear; International
Historic Films; Discount Video Tapes*

**Secret Life of an
American Wife, The** 1968
Comedy
86590   97 mins   C   B, V   P
*Walter Matthau, Anne Jackson, Patrick O'Neal,
Edy Williams*
An insecure press agent's wife decides to try to
seduce a famous movie star in order to prove
her desirability to herself.
George Axelrod; 20th Century Fox — *Key
Video*

**Secret Life of Walter
Mitty, The** 1947
Comedy
81908   110 mins   C   B, V, LV   P
*Danny Kaye, Virginia Mayo, Boris Karloff, Ann
Rutherford, directed by Norman Z. McLeod*
Danny Kaye stars in an adaptation of the James
Thurber short story about a meek man who lives
an unusual secret fantasy life.
Samuel Goldwyn — *Embassy Home
Entertainment*

**Secret Lives of the
British Prime Ministers,
The** 1983
Drama
71041   60 mins   C   B, V   P
*Richard Pasco, John Stride, Jeremy Brett,
Bernard Archer, Ian Richardson, David Langton,
Denis Quilley, Dorothy Tutin, Emma Piper,
Barbara Kellerman* 7   pgms
This seven-tape series profiles some of Britain's
familiar leaders with special attention paid to the

scandals that nearly ended each of their careers.
1.MacDonald 2.Lloyd George 3.Disraeli 4.Wellington 5.Pitt 6.Asquith 7.Gladstone
Yorkshire Television — *Hal Roach Studios*

Secret Lives of Waldo Kitty Volume I, The   1975
Cartoons
72886   48 mins   C   B, V   P
Animated
A cartoon where Waldo Kitty imagines himself to be a variety of heroes such as Robin Cat and the Lone Kitty.
Filmation — *Embassy Home Entertainment*

Secret of El Zorro, The   1957
Adventure
82302   75 mins   B/W   B, V   P
Guy Williams
Don Diego's friend, Don Ricardo, threatens to unmask Zorro's secret identity when he challenges the legendary swordsman to a duel.
Walt Disney Productions — *Walt Disney Home Video*

Secret of NIMH, The   1982
Fantasy
60565   83 mins   C   B, V, CED   P
Animated, directed by Don Bluth, voices by Hermione Baddeley, John Carradine, Dom DeLuise, Elizabeth Hartman, Peter Strauss, Aldo Ray, Edie McClurg
Based on the story by Robert O'Brien, this animated tale produced by a staff of Disney-trained artists concerns a newly-widowed mouse with four wee ones to care for and protect against a series of dangers. Stereo.
MPAA:G
Mrs Brisby Ltd; MGM — *MGM/UA Home Video*

Secret of the Snake and Crane, The   197?
Martial arts
72174   90 mins   C   B, V   P
A resistance group relies on ancient fighting techniques to battle the rule of the Ching Dynasty in this Kung Fu action film.
Foreign — *Master Arts Video*

Secret of the Sword, The   1985
Adventure
Closed Captioned
81789   100 mins   C   B, V   P
Animated
He-Man must rescue his sister She-Ra from the evil clutches of the oppressive ruler Hordak. Available in VHS Dolby Hi-Fi Stereo and Beta Hi-Fi.
Filmation — *RCA/Columbia Pictures Home Video*

Secret of Yolanda, The   1982
Drama
68246   90 mins   C   B, V   P
Aviva Ger, Asher Zarfati, Shraga Harpaz
A steamy romance about a young deaf-mute whose guardian and riding instructor both fall for her.
MPAA:R
Noah Films — *MGM/UA Home Video*

Secret Policeman's Other Ball, The   1982
Music-Performance/Comedy
63117   101 mins   C   B, V, CED   P
John Cleese, Graham Chapman, Michael Palin, Terry Jones, Peter Townsend, Sting
A live concert by most of the Monty Python troupe and guest rock artists, staged for Amnesty International. In stereo.
MPAA:R
Amnesty International; Miramax Films — *MGM/UA Home Video*

Secret Policeman's Private Parts, The   1981
Comedy/Music-Performance
82489   77 mins   C   B, V   P
John Cleese, Michael Palin, Terry Jones
This tape features classic Python sketches including "I'm A Lumberjack and I'm OK." Also featured are performances by Phil Collins, Pete Townshend, Donovan and Bob Geldof.
Independent — *Media Home Entertainment*

Secret Squirrel   196?
Cartoons
47693   53 mins   C   B, V   P
Animated
Eight episodes of adventure with the clever secret agent.
Hanna Barbera — *Worldvision Home Video*

Secret Squirrel's Undercover Capers   1966
Cartoons
84078   52 mins   C   B, V   P
The world's only animated undercover rodent, Secret Squirrel battles a motley crew of zany villians with his cohorts Winsome Witch and Squiddley Diddley.
Hanna Barbera — *Worldvision Home Video*

Secret War of Harry Frigg, The   1968
Comedy
64559   123 mins   C   B, V   P
Paul Newman, Sylva Koscina, Tom Bosley, Andrew Duggan
Private Harry Frigg, a nonconformist World War II G.I., is promoted to the rank of general as part of a scheme to help five Allied generals escape from the custody of the Germans.
MPAA:R

Universal — *MCA Home Video*

Secret World of Erotic Art, The   1985
Arts/History
70738   60 mins   C   B, V   P
Peggy O'Brien, Tom Nolan
This documentation presents the history of
erotic art from the middle ages to the 1900's,
and concentrates on information rather than
titillation.
Roberta Hagnes; Rick Houser — *Vestron
Video*

Secret World of Reptiles, The   1977
Animals/Documentary
29170   94 mins   C   B, V   P
A series that presents rare living relics of
primeval times and traces the history of the
reptile kingdom.
Bill Burrud Productions — *Walt Disney Home
Video*

Secrets   1982
Drama
88212   79 mins   C   B, V   P
*Helen Lindsay, Anna Campbell-Jones, Daisy
Cockburn, directed by Gavin Millar*
A British drama about the confused life of an
innocent schoolgirl who's the victim of a mess
of authoritive misunderstandings. Written by
Noella Smith; one of David Puttnam's First Love
series.
David Puttnam; Samuel Montagu &
Co. — *MGM/UA Home Video*

Secrets for Catching Walleye   1984
Fishing
86868   30 mins   C   B, V   P
Babe Winkelman
Instructions on equipment and bait use for
optimum walleye catching.
AM Available
Warburton Prod. — *Warburton Productions*

Secrets of a Married Man   1984
Drama
86846   96 mins   C   B, V   P
*William Shatner, Cybill Shepherd, Michelle
Phillips,*
A made-for-TV film about a married man
philandering with a beautiful prostitute.
ITC Ent. — *Lightning Video*

Secrets of Analog and Digital Synthesis, The   1985
Music
87933   120 mins   C   B, V   P
Steve DeFuria demonstrates every major
synthesizer, describing their advantages and

disadvantages, and gives in-depth instruction on
how to play them.
AM Available
Ferro Prod. — *DCI Music Video*

Secrets of Life   1956
Documentary
82300   69 mins   C   B, V   P
This documentary captures the various ways
that organisms on earth respond to the
challenges of survival and reproduction. An
installment of the "True-Life Adventures"
series.
Buena Vista — *Walt Disney Home Video*

Secrets of Women   1952
Comedy-Drama
65630   108 mins   B/W   B, V   P
*Anita Bjork, Karl Arne Homsten, Jarl Kulle,
directed by Ingar Bergman*
Three sisters-in-law talk about their affairs and
marriages as they await their husbands at a
lakeside resort.
Janus Films — *Embassy Home Entertainment*

Seduced and Abandoned   1964
Comedy-Drama
53427   118 mins   B/W   B, V   P
*Saro Urzi, Stefani Sandrelli, Aldo Paglisi,
directed by Pietro Germi*
The fiance of an Italian girl seduces her sister,
and when pressed to marry her, tells the father
that he won't marry an unchaste girl.
Cannes Film Festival '64: Best Actor; Italian
Academy Award: Best Director (Germi).
Italian — *Hollywood Home Theater; Festival
Films; International Home Video*

Seducers, The   1980
Drama
56930   90 mins   C   B, V   R, P
Sondra Locke, Colleen Camp, Seymour Cassel
A wealthy, middle-aged man unsuspectingly
allows two young girls to use his telephone, and
once inside, a night of bizarre mayhem and
brutal murder begins.
MPAA:R
Peter Traynor, Larry Spiegel — *Video Gems*

Seduction, The   1982
Drama
59676   104 mins   C   B, V   P
*Morgan Fairchild, Michael Sarrazin, Vince
Edwards, Andrew Stevens, Colleen Camp,
Kevin Brophy*
A superstar TV anchorwoman is harassed by a
psychotic male admirer.
MPAA:R
Irwin Yablans; Bruce Cohn Curtis —, *Media
Home Entertainment; Embassy Home
Entertainment (disc only)*

Seduction of Joe Tynan, The — 1979
Drama
29735   107 mins   C   B, V, LV   P
Alan Alda, Meryl Streep, Melvyn Douglas, directed by Alan Alda
Alan Alda wrote, directed, and starred in this movie about a senator who is torn between his political career and his personal life.
MPAA:R
Universal, Martin Bregman — *MCA Home Video*

Seduction of Mimi, The — 1974
Film-Avant-garde
37402   92 mins   C   B, V   P
Giancarlo Giannini, Mariangelo Melato, directed by Lina Wertmuller
A comic farce of politics and seduction about a Sicilian laborer's escapades with the Communists and the local Mafia.
MPAA:R
New Line Cinema — *CBS/Fox Video; Movie Buff Video*

See How She Runs — 1978
Drama
86849   92 mins   C   B, V   P
Joanne Woodward, John Considine, Lissy Newman, Barbara Manning
A 40-year-old divorced schoolteacher runs in the Boston marathon. Her loved ones are concerned for her health and sanity. A made-for-TV movie.
Time-Life — *Lightning Video*

See It Now — 1957
Documentary
78097   82 mins   B/W   B, V, FO   P
Edward R. Murrow
An exploration of how automation is changing the way America works and how computers are revolutionizing industry.
CBS — *Video Yesteryear*

Seeds of Evil — 1976
Horror
47666   80 mins   C   B, V   P
Katherine Houghton, Joe Dallesandro, Rita Gam
A strange gardener grows flowers that can kill.
Chalmer Kirkbride — *Unicorn Video*

Seems Like Old Times — 1980
Comedy
51571   102 mins   C   B, V, LV   P
Goldie Hawn, Chevy Chase, Charles Grodin, Robert Guillaume, Harold Gould, directed by Jay Sandrich
A woman with a weakness for her ex-husband comes to his aid when two robbers force him to hold up a bank.
MPAA:PG

Columbia Pictures — *RCA/Columbia Pictures Home Video; RCA VideoDiscs*

Self Defense — 1985
Martial arts
76990   60 mins   C   B, V   P
A group of experts present a series of martial arts techniques which can help in dealing with impending acts of violence.
Karl Home Video — *Karl/Lorimar Home Video*

Self-Defense for Women — 1985
Physical fitness
77420   60 mins   C   B, V   P
A step by step demonstration of self-defense techniques for women.
Maljack Productions — *MPI Home Video*

Sell Out, The — 1976
Adventure
76657   102 mins   C   B, V   P
Richard Widmark, Oliver Reed, Gayle Hunnicutt, Sam Wanamaker
Oscar-winning actor Richard Widmark, and a highly-acclaimed cast star in a high-stakes game of tag, but no one's sure who "it" is.
MPAA:PG
Josef Shaftel — *Media Home Entertainment*

Selling Movies on Television — 197?
Movie and TV trailers
42975   55 mins   C   B, V, FO   P
Here are 67 TV commercials for some of the best and worst films ever released, featuring stars and scenes from such movies as "The Great Dictator," "The Glass Bottom Boat," and "Portnoy's Complaint."
CBS et al — *Video Yesteryear*

Semi-Tough — 1977
Comedy
13313   107 mins   C   B, V, LV   P
Burt Reynolds, Kris Kristofferson, Jill Clayburgh, directed by Michael Ritchie
Social satire involving a couple of pro-football buddies and the team owner's daughter.
MPAA:R
United Artists; David Merrick — *CBS/Fox Video; RCA VideoDiscs*

Senator Was Indiscreet, The — 1947
Comedy
65736   81 mins   B/W   B, V   P
William Powell, Ella Raines
A senator, seeking the Presidential nomination, tours the country making ridiculous and contradictory campaign promises.
Universal — *Republic Pictures Home Video*

Sender, The — 1982
Horror
64504   92 mins   C   B, V, LV   P
Kathryn Harrold, Zeljko Ivanek, Shirley Knight
A amnesiac young man is studied by a
psychiatrist who discovers that her patient is a
"sender," who can transmit his nightmares to
other people. In stereo.
MPAA:R
Paramount — *Paramount Home Video*

Senior Trip — 1981
Comedy
82269   96 mins   C   B, V   P
*Scott Baio, Mickey Rooney, Faye Grant, Vincent
Spano, Jane Hoffman*
New York City will never be the same after a
bunch of rowdy Midwestern high school seniors
tear up the town on their graduation trip.
QM Productions — *Worldvision Home Video*

Seniors — 1978
Comedy
63363   87 mins   C   B, V, CED   P
*Dennis Quaid, Priscilla Barnes, Jeffrey Byron,
Gary Imhoff*
Fast-paced antics abound in this satire of
students, sex and society.
MPAA:R
Cine Artists — *Vestron Video*

Senora Tentacion — 1949
Musical-Drama
57360   82 mins   B/W   B, V, FO   P
David Silva, Susana Guizar, Ninon Sevilla
Musical melodrama about a composer who
fights to leave his mother, sister, and girlfriend in
order to flee with Hortensia, a famous singer.
SP
Mexican — *Video Yesteryear*

Sensational Sixties — 1980
Football
45124   30 mins   C   B, V, FO   R, P
Narrated by John Facenda
The best players, plays, games, and moments
from pro football's golden decade are captured
in this memory-provoking program.
NFL Films — *NFL Films Video*

Sense of Freedom, A — 1978
Crime-Drama
86895   81 mins   C   B, V   P
*David Hayman, Alex Norton, Jake D'Arcy, Sean
Scanlan, Fulton McKay*
A hopeless racketeering criminal is thrust from
institution to institution until the Scottish
authorities decide on an innovative style of
reform. Based on Jimmy Boyle's
autobiographical book.
MPAA:R
British — *THORN EMI/HBO Video*

Sense of Loss, A — 1972
Documentary/Great Britain
76038   135 mins   B/W   B, V   P
This documentary deals with the on-going
controversy in Northern Ireland, and the impact
that it has on the day-to-day lives of the Irish.
Marcel Ophuls; Max
Palevsky — *RCA/Columbia Pictures Home
Video*

Sensual Man, The — 1974
Comedy
68267   90 mins   C   B, V   P
*Giancarlo Giannini, Rossana Podesta, Lionel
Stowder*
A hot blooded Italian falls in love and gets
married only to find out that his wife cannot
consummate their marriage.
MPAA:R
Medusa Distribuzione — *RCA/Columbia
Pictures Home Video*

Sensuous Caterer, The — 1982
Comedy
64845   60 mins   C   B, V   P
Marc Stevens
Stevens hosts a video Valentine's Day orgy and
invites an uninhibited crowd of erotic stars and
starlets to come and show their stuff.
A.O.E. Productions — *HarmonyVision*

Sensuous Nurse — 1976
Comedy
84415   79 mins   C   B, V   P
*Ursula Andress, Mario Pisu, Dvilio Del Prete,
Jack Palance*
A nurse is hired by the greedy, treacherous
relatives of a weak-hearted count in hopes that
her voluptuousness will give him a heart attack.
It doesn't and she falls in love.
MPAA:R
Zev Braun; Carlo Ponti — *Key Video*

Sentinel, The — 1976
Horror
81821   92 mins   C   B, V   P
*Chris Sarandon, Cristina Raines, Ava Gardner,
Jose Ferrer, Sylvia Miles, John Carradine,
Burgess Meredith, directed by Michael Winner*
A model encounters some strange and unusual
neighbors when she moves into a fashionable
New York brownstone. Available in VHS and
Beta Hi-Fi.
MPAA:R
Universal Pictures — *MCA Home Video*

Separacion Matrimonial — 197?
Drama
52794   96 mins   C   B, V   P
Jacqueline Andere, Ana Belen, Simon Andreu
A woman decides to forgive her husband and
stop divorce proceedings when his outside love

affair ends. Soon, however, he is up to his old tricks again. In Spanish.
SP
Luis Sanz — *Media Home Entertainment*

Separate Peace, A   1973
Drama
64028   104 mins   C   B, V   P
John Heyl, Parker Stevenson, William Roerick
Based on the novel by John Knowles, this is the story of how responsibility for a crippling accident brings a young man face to face with his inner nature.
MPAA:PG
Paramount — *Paramount Home Video*

Separate Tables   1958
Drama
68231   98 mins   B/W   B, V, CED   P
Burt Lancaster, Rita Hayworth, David Niven, Deborah Kerr
This film explores the separate yet connected dreams of people staying in the same hotel.
Clifton Productions — *CBS/Fox Video*

Separate Tables   1983
Drama
79210   50 mins   C   B, V   P
Julie Christie, Alan Bates, Claire Bloom, Irene Worth, directed by John Schlesinger
An adaptation of Terence Rattigan's two one act plays about the lonely inhabitants of a hotel: ""Table by the Window" and ""Table Number Seven."
Edie and Ely Landau — *MGM/UA Home Video*

Separate Ways   1982
Drama
62864   92 mins   C   B, V, LV,   P
                             CED
Karen Black, Tony LoBianco, David Naughton
A middle-class couple find they must split up for a while to gain a new perspective of themselves and their marriage.
MPAA:R
Hickmar Productions — *Vestron Video*

September Gun   1983
Comedy/Western
82270   94 mins   C   B, V   P
Robert Preston, Patty Duke Astin, Christopher Lloyd, Geoffrey Lewis, Sally Kellerman
A Catholic nun hires an aging gunfighter to escort her and a group of Apache children to a church school two hundred miles away.
QM Productions; Brademan-Self Productions — *Worldvision Home Video*

Sgt. Matlovich vs the U.S.   1977
Air Force
Drama
52392   96 mins   C   B, V   P

Brad Dourif, Marc Singer, Frank Converse, William Daniels
The fight of a homosexual Army air force sergeant to remain in the service after admitting his sexual preference to his superiors is depicted in this movie.
Tomorrow Entertainment, NBC — *U.S.A. Home Video*

Sergeant Pepper's   1978
Lonely Hearts Club Band
Musical
14003   113 mins   C   B, V, LV   P
Peter Frampton, the Bee Gees, Steve Martin, Aerosmith, Earth Wind and Fire, George Burns
The Beatles' famous story-in-song album is transferred to the screen starring some of the most popular rock n' roll singer-musicians of our time.
MPAA:PG
Universal; Robert Stigwood — *MCA Home Video*

Sergeant Sullivan   1953
Speaking
Drama/Romance
77367   24 mins   B/W   B, V   P, T
William Bendix, Joan Blondell, Sarah Selby
A romance develops between a widow and a police sergeant as the two search for the widow's lost sons. From the ABC-TV series "Return Engagement."
ABC — *Blackhawk Films*

Sergeant York   1941
Drama
58950   134 mins   B/W   B, V, CED   P
Gary Cooper, Joan Leslie, Walter Brennan, Dickie Moore, Ward Bond, directed by Howard Hawks
The story of the gentle, hillbilly farmer who becomes a hero of World War I.
Academy Awards '41: Best Actor (Cooper).
Warner Bros — *CBS/Fox Video; RCA VideoDiscs*

Serial   1980
Comedy
55540   92 mins   C   B, V, LV   P
Martin Mull, Sally Kellerman, Tuesday Weld, Tom Smothers, Bill Macy, Barbara Rhoades, Christopher Lee
Cyra McFadden's novel about life in Marin County, California, spoofing open marriage, health foods, exercise, psychiatry, and cult religions comes to life in this film.
MPAA:R
Paramount; Sidney Beckerman — *Paramount Home Video*

Serial Previews # 1   194?
Movie and TV trailers/Serials
64417   60 mins   B/W   B, V, 3/4U   P

An assortment of theatrical trailers from over thirty serials. Titles featured include "The Adventures of Red Ryder," "The Fighting Devil Dogs," "Superman," "The Spy Smasher," "The Adventures of Captain Marvel" and many others.
Republic et al — *Nostalgia Merchant*

Sermon on the Mount, The   1964
Religion
85513   29 mins   B/W   B, V   P
Directed by Andre Girard
A filmization of the famous sermon, consisting of illustrative paintings and music by Bach, Beethoven and Prokofiev.
The National Council of Catholic Men — *Video Yesteryear*

Serpent's Egg, The   1978
Drama
84097   119 mins   C   B, V   P
David Carradine, Liv Ullman, Gert Frobe, directed by Ingmar Bergman
A pair of Jewish trapeze artists survive in Berlin during Hitler's rise to power by working in a grisly and mysterious medical clinic. The reknowned director's second film in English.
MPAA:R
Dino De Laurentiis — *Lightning Video*

Serpico   1974
Drama
29797   130 mins   C   B, V, LV   P
Al Pacino, John Randolf, Jack Kehoe, Barbara Eda-Young
The story of Frank Serpico, a New York policeman who uncovered corruption in the police department.
MPAA:R
Dino De Laurentiis — *Paramount Home Video; RCA VideoDiscs*

Servant, The   1963
Drama
36933   112 mins   B/W   B, V   P
Dirk Bogarde, James Fox, Sarah Miles, Wendy Craig, directed by Joseph Losey
British class hypocrisy is starkly portrayed in this story of a spoiled young gentleman's ruin by his socially inferior but crafty and ambitious manservant.
British Film Academy: Best Actor (Bogarde); Best Photography (Black and White); Most Promising Newcomer (Fox).
Springbok Prod, Landau Unger — *THORN EMI/HBO Video*

Sesame Street Presents: Follow That Bird   1985
Children/Adventure
Closed Captioned
71172   92 mins   C   B, V, LV   P

Sandra Bernhard, John Candy, Chevy Chase, Joe Flaherty, Dave Thomas, Waylon Jennings, Jim Henson's Muppets, directed by Ken Kwopis TV's Big Bird suffers an identity crisis, and leaves Sesame Street to join a family of real birds. He soon misses his home, and returns, in a danger-filled journey. Recorded in HiFi Stereo.
MPAA:G
Children's Television Workshop — *Warner Home Video*

Sesenta Horas en el Cielo   1946
Comedy
57359   76 mins   B/W   B, V, FO   P
Alady y Lepe
A comedy about two air cadets who gain fame by establishing a new record for duration in the air.
SP
Spain — *Video Yesteryear*

Sessions   1983
Drama
70717   96 mins   C   B, V   P
Veronica Hamel, Jeffrey DeMunn, Jill Eikenberry, David Marshall Grant, George Coe, Henderson Forsythe, Deborah Hedwall
Mentally exhausted by her roles as a sister, single-parent, lover, exercise enthusiast, and high-priced prostitute, Leigh Churchill seeks professional counselling.
Thorn EMI in association with Sarabande Prods. — *VCL Home Video*

Set Up, The   1949
Drama
44986   72 mins   B/W   B, V   P, T
Robert Ryan, Audrey Totter
The story of an average fighter who refuses to take a dive for a group of crooked gamblers, and fights to win.
Anglo Amalgamated Film — *Blackhawk Films; Nostalgia Merchant*

Seven Alone   1975
Adventure
44949   85 mins   C   B, V   P
Dewey Martin, Aldo Ray, Anne Collins, Dean Smith, Stewart Peterson, directed by Earl Bellamy
Seven orphaned children, led by the oldest, a thirteen-year-old boy, undertake a treacherous 2000 mile journey from Missouri to Oregon. Based on the book "On to Oregon" by Monroe Morrow.
MPAA:G
Doty Dayton — *Children's Video Library*

Seven Beauties   1976
Comedy
44774   116 mins   C   B, V   P
Giancarlo Giannini, Fernando Rey, Shirley Stoler, directed by Lina Wertmuller

The story of a dumb but likeable hood who shoots his sister's pimp to save his family's honor. He is caught and sent to an insane asylum. After volunteering for the Italian army, he finds himself in a Nazi concentration camp.
Cinema 5 — *RCA/Columbia Pictures Home Video*

7 Blows of the Dragon   1973
Adventure/Martial arts
54810   81 mins   C   B, V   P
David Chiang
The Chinese novel, "All Men Are Brothers," is the basis for this spectacular martial arts epic.
MPAA:R
New World Pictures — *Warner Home Video*

Seven Brides for Seven Brothers   1954
Musical
58705   103 mins   C   B, V, CED   P
Howard Keel, Jane Powell, Russ Tamblyn, Julie Newmar, Jeff Richards, Tommy Rall, Virginia Gibson, directed by Stanley Donen
When the eldest of seven brothers in the Oregon Territory brings home a wife, the other six sneak into town looking for brides. Academy Awards '54: Best Scoring, Musical (Adloph Deutsch, Saul Chaplin).
MGM — *MGM/UA Home Video*

Seven Days Ashore/Hurry, Charlie, Hurry   1944
Comedy
76840   141 mins   B/W   B, V   P
Gordon Oliver, Virginia Mayo, Dooley Wilson, Margaret Dumont, Leon Errol, Mildred Coles
A comedy double feature: In "Seven Days Ashore" three Merchant Marines on leave in San Francisco become romantically involved with three women and in "Hurry, Charlie, Hurry" a henpecked husband finds himself in a lot of trouble.
RKO — *RKO HomeVideo*

Seven Days in May   1964
Mystery/Drama
65617   120 mins   B/W   B, V, LV, CED   P
Burt Lancaster, Kirk Douglas, Frederic March, Ava Gardner, John Houseman
An American general's aide discovers that his boss intends a military takeover because he considers the President's pacifism traitorous.
Seven Arts — *Paramount Home Video*

Seven Doors of Death   1982
Horror
86583   80 mins   C   B, V   P
Katherine MacColl, David Warbeck, Farah Keller, Tony St. John

A girl inherits a possessed hotel.
MPAA:R
Terry Levene — *Thriller Video*

Seven Doors to Death   1944
Mystery
77201   70 mins   B/W   B, V   P
Chick Chandler, June Clyde, George Meeker
Two strangers become meshed in a web of murder and intrigue.
PRC Pictures — *United Home Video*

7 Faces of Dr. Lao, The   1963
Fantasy
82350   101 mins   C   B, V   P
Tony Randall, Barbara Eden, Arthur O'Connell, directed by George Pal
Dr. Lao is the proprietor of a magical circus that changes the lives of the residents of a small western town.
MGM; Galaxy Productions — *MGM/UA Home Video*

Seven Magnificent Gladiators, The   1984
Adventure/Fantasy
82351   86 mins   C   B, V   P
Lou Ferrigno, Sybil Danning, Brad Harris, Dan Vadis, Carla Ferrigno
Seven gladiators team up to save a peaceful Roman village from total annihilation.
MPAA:PG
Cannon Productions — *MGM/UA Home Video*

Seven Miles from Alcatraz/Flight from Glory   1943
Drama
81027   127 mins   B/W   B, V   P
James Craig, Bonita Granville, Chester Morris, Van Heflin, Onslow Stevens
A dramatic double feature: Two escaped convicts discover a hideout for Nazi spies in "Seven Miles From Alcatraz," and an evil man tries to recruit pilots to fly planes over the Andes Mountains in "Flight From Glory."
RKO — *RKO HomeVideo*

Seven-Per-Cent Solution, The   1976
Mystery
14002   113 mins   C   B, V   P
Alan Arkin, Nicol Williamson, Laurence Olivier, Robert Duvall, Venessa Redgrave, Joel Grey, Samantha Eggar, directed by Herbert Ross
Sigmund Freud joins forces with Sherlock Holmes and Dr. Watson in the search for the real Professor Moriarity.
MPAA:PG
Universal; Herbert Ross Prod — *MCA Home Video*

Seven Samurai 1954

Adventure
29761   204 mins   B/W   B, V   P
Takashi Shimura, Toshio Mifune, Yoshio Inaba
A small Japanese farming village is beset by
marauding bandits. Powerless to prevent these
ongoing raids, the villagers hire seven
professional soldiers. Japanese dialogue with
English subtitles.
Academy Awards '55: Honorary Award. JA
Kingsley Intl, Toho Prod — *Embassy Home
Entertainment; Hollywood Home Theater;
International Historic Films; Movie Buff Video;
Discount Video Tapes; Video Action*

Seven-Ups, The 1973

Adventure
Closed Captioned
80655   109 mins   C   B, V   P
*Roy Scheider, Tony LoBianco, Larry Haines,
Jerry Leon, directed by Phil D'Antoni*
An elite group of New York City detectives seek
to avenge the killing of a fellow squad member
and bust criminals whose felonies are
punishable by jail terms of seven-years or more.
Available in VHS and Beta Hi-Fi.
MPAA:PG
20th Century Fox — *CBS/Fox Video*

Seven Year Itch, The 1955

Comedy
08467   105 mins   C   B, V   P
*Marilyn Monroe, Tom Ewell, Evelyn Keyes,
Sonny Tufts, Robert Strauss, Oscar Homolka*
After a man sees his wife and son off to the
country for the summer, he returns home to find
that a lovely blonde has sublet the apartment
above his.
20th Century Fox; Charles K Feldman and Billy
Wilder — *CBS/Fox Video*

Seven Years Bad Luck 1920

Comedy
78106   67 mins   B/W   B, V, FO   P
Max Linder
This is the famous movie in which a broken
mirror brings a man proverbial bad luck for
seven years that seems to come all at once.
Silent with music score.
Robertson Cole Distributing Corp — *Video
Yesteryear*

1776 1972

Musical
64235   141 mins   C   B, V   P
*Howard da Silva, William Daniels, Ken Howard,
Donald Madden, Blythe Danner*
Based on the musical play, this is a light-hearted
look at the signing of the Declaration of
Independence. In simulated stereo.
MPAA:PG
Columbia — *RCA/Columbia Pictures Home
Video*

Seventh Seal, The 1956

Drama
81909   96 mins   B/W   B, V   P
*Gunnar Bjornstrand, Max Von Sydow, Bibi
Anderson, directed by Ingmar Bergman*
A medieval knight agrees to play a game of
chess with "death" as the plague sweeps
through Europe. In Swedish with English
subtitles.
SW
AB Svensk Filmindustri — *Embassy Home
Entertainment*

Seventh Veil, The 1946

Drama
71188   91 mins   B/W   B, V   P
James Mason, Ann Todd, Herbert Lom
A concert pianist loses the use of her hands in a
fire, and with it her desire to live. Through the
help of her friends and a psycho-hypnotizing
doctor, she regains her love for life.
Academy Awards '46: Best Screenplay (Muriel
and Sidney Box).
J Arthur Rank — *VidAmerica*

7th Voyage of Sinbad, The 1958

Fantasy
19083   89 mins   C   B, V, CED   P
Kerwin Matthews, Kathryn Grant
Sinbad seeks to restore his fiancee from the
midget size to which an evil magician has
reduced her.
Columbia — *RCA/Columbia Pictures Home
Video*

Severed Arm, The 1973

Horror
58551   89 mins   C   B, V   R, P
Deborah Waller, Paul Carr, David Cannon
Trapped in a cave, five men cut off the arm of a
companion in order to ward off starvation.
Heritage Enterprises — *Video Gems*

Sex 1920

Drama
84926   87 mins   B/W   B, V   P
Adrienne Renault
Without any soundtrack, the Ince morality play
about a dance-hall girl and a philandeering
businessman.
J Parker Read Jr; Thomas Ince — *Blackhawk
Films*

Sex and Love Test, The 1981

Sexuality
57549   60 mins   C   B, V   P
Hosted by Dr. Frank Field
Viewers can test their knowledge on sexual
problems, and find out the answers from
psychiatrists and sex therapists.
International Film and TV Festival of New York:
Silver Medal.

NBC; Don Luftig — *Karl/Lorimar Home Video*

Franz Antel — *Vestron Video*

Sex and the Office Girl   197?
Drama
59552   76 mins   C   B, V   P
An advertising agency turns into an after hours
pleasure dome of erotic complications.
Filmco — *Media Home Entertainment*

Sex and the Other   1979
Woman
Comedy
81914   80 mins   C   B, V   P
*Richard Wattis, Maggie Wright, Felicity Devon,
Jane Carder*
This film consists of a series of vignettes
depicting how women manipulate men into
sexual submission.
MPAA:R
Devlin Development Corp — *VidAmerica*

Sex, Drugs and Rock-N-   1984
Roll
Drama
81426   90 mins   C   B, V   P
*Jeanne Silver, Sharon Kane, Tish Ambrose,
Josey Duval*
Several girls frequent a rock club looking for all
the action they can get their hands on.
F.J. Lincoln — *Video Home Library*

Sex Machine, The   1976
Drama
47750   80 mins   C   B, V   P
Agostina Belli
Set in the year 2037, a scientist finds two of the
world's greatest lovers and unites them so he
can transform their reciprocating motion into
electricity.
MPAA:R
Sylvio Clementelli — *Media Home
Entertainment*

Sex Madness   1937
Exploitation
05530   50 mins   B/W   B, V, FO   P
A 1930's campy melodrama about the evils of
lechery, lust, and passion.
Unknown — *Video Yesteryear; Hollywood
Home Theater; Video Dimensions; Discount
Video Tapes; Movie Buff Video*

Sex on the Run   1978
Comedy
57228   88 mins   C   B, V   R, P
Tony Curtis, Marisa Berenson, Britt Ekland
The love-starved wife of an oil-rich sheik,
stimulated by the idea of having Casanova, an
amourous adventurer, for her lover, teases her
master into delivering him, but Casanova finds
peace in the arms of three convent lovelies.
MPAA:R

Sex Shop, Le   1973
Satire
47781   92 mins   C   B, V   P
Claude Berri, Juliet Berto
A man owns a shop where he sells exotic books
and paraphernalia. When his relationship with
his wife gets boring, they make use of the
merchandise and adopt a swinging lifestyle.
MPAA:R
Pierre Grunstein — *RCA/Columbia Pictures
Home Video*

Sex Through a Window   1972
Drama
76780   81 mins   C   B, V   P
A TV reporter becomes an obsessive voyeur
after filing a report on high tech surveillance
equipment.
MPAA:R
Mann Productions — *Vestron Video*

Sex with a Smile   1976
Comedy
43072   100 mins   C   B, V   R, P
*Marty Feldman, Edvice Finich, Alex Marino,
Enrico Monterrano, Giovanni Ralli*
Five slapstick episodes by five different
directors with lots of sexual satire pointed at
religion and politics in Italy.
MPAA:R
Surrogate — *Video Gems*

Sextette   1978
Musical/Comedy
59665   91 mins   C   B, V   P
*Mae West, Timothy Dalton, Ringo Starr, George
Hamilton, Dom DeLuise, Tony Curtis, Alice
Cooper, Keith Moon, George Raft, Rona Barrett*
A lavish musical about an elderly star who is
constantly interrupted by former spouses and
well-wishers while on a honeymoon with her
sixth husband.
MPAA:PG
Daniel Briggs; Robert Sullivan — *Media Home
Entertainment*

Sexton Blake and the   1953
Hooded Terror
Mystery
12808   70 mins   B/W   B, V, FO   P
Tod Slaughter, Greta Gynt
A British private detective is after "The Snake,"
a master criminal.
Unknown — *Video Yesteryear*

Sextoons   197?
Cartoons
64846   90 mins   C   B, V   P
Animated

This offers a collection of some of the world's greatest erotic animation.
Saliva Films — *HarmonyVision*

Shack Out On 101   1955
Drama
77249   80 mins   B/W   B, V   P
Lee Marvin, Terry Moore, Keenan Wynn, Frank Lovejoy
A waitress in an isolated cafe on a busy highway notices suspicious activities among the cafe's clientele.
Allied Artists — *Spotlite Video*

Shadow of Chikara   1977
War-Drama/Adventure
81217   96 mins   C   B, V, LV   P
Joe Don Baker, Sondra Locke, Ted Neely, Slim Pickens
A Confederate Army Captain and an orphan girl encounter unexpected adventures as they search for a fortune in diamonds hidden in a river in northern Arkansas. Available in VHS and Beta Hi-Fi.
MPAA:PG
Manson International Pictures — *New World Video*

Shadow of the Eagle   1932
Mystery/Serials
12551   226 mins   B/W   B, V, FO   P
John Wayne, Dorothy Gulliver, directed by Ford Beebe
Intrigue and mystery of carnival life. Twelve chapters, 13 minutes each.
Mascot — *Video Yesteryear; Video Connection; Discount Video Tapes*

Shadow Strikes, The   1937
Mystery
58618   61 mins   B/W   B, V   P, T
Rod LaRocque, Lynn Anders
A "Shadow" murder mystery.
Grand National — *Video Connection; Cable Films*

Shadows   1922
Drama
64354   70 mins   B/W   B, V   P
Lon Chaney
A Chinese laundryman lives with a group of his countrymen in a New England seacoast village. All is peaceful until the local minister decides to convert the "heathen" Chinese. Silent with music score.
Preferred Pictures — *Blackhawk Films*

Shadows of Death   1945
Western
13105   60 mins   B/W   B, V   P
Buster Crabbe, Al 'Fuzzy' St. John

Former Olympic gold medal winner, Buster Crabbe, stars in this shoot 'em up tale of Billy the Kid.
PRC — *Video Connection; United Home Video*

Shadows Run Black   1984
Horror
82191   89 mins   C   B, V   P
William J. Kulzer, Elizabeth Trosper
A police detective must save a college coed from the clutches of a maniac wielding a meat cleaver.
Mesa Films — *Lightning Video*

Shaft   1971
Crime-Drama
60566   98 mins   C   B, V, CED   P
Richard Roundtree, Moses Gunn, Charles Cioffi, directed by Gordon Park
A black private eye finds himself at odds with a powerful racketeer.
Academy Awards '71: Best Original Song (Isaac Hayes) MPAA:R
MGM — *MGM/UA Home Video*

Shaggy D.A., The   1976
Comedy
81669   90 mins   C   B, V   P
Dean Jones, Tim Conway, Suzanne Pleshette, Keenan Wynn, directed by Robert Stevenson
Wilby Daniels is getting a little worried about his canine alter ego as he is about to run for District Attorney.
MPAA:G
Walt Disney Productions — *Walt Disney Home Video*

Shaggy Dog, The   1959
Comedy
58626   101 mins   B/W   B, V, LV   P
Fred MacMurray, Jean Hagen, Tommy Kirk, Annette Funicello, Tim Considine, Kevin Corcoran, directed by Charles Barton
When young Wilby Daniels utters some magical words from the inscription of an ancient ring he turns into a shaggy dog causing havoc to family and neighbors.
MPAA:G
Walt Disney Productions — *Walt Disney Home Video; RCA VideoDiscs*

Shaker Run   1985
Adventure
86940   91 mins   C   B, V   P
Leif Garrett, Cliff Robertson, Lisa Harrow, directed by Bruce Morrison
A stunt car driver and his mechanic transport a mysterious package a long distance, unwittingly carrying a form of deadly virus that every terrorist wants.
Igo Kantor; Larry Parr — *THORN EMI/HBO Video*

Shakespeare: Soul of an Age   1963
Documentary
64176   54 mins   C   B, V   R, P
A chronicle of the places where Shakespeare
lived and worked, picturing authentic maps,
buildings and other landmarks of Shakespeare's
time.
NBC — *Warner Home Video*

Shalako   1968
Western
69384   113 mins   C   B, V   P
Brigitte Bardot, Sean Connery
While on a hunting trip in New Mexico in the
1880's, a European countess is captured by an
Apache, and a U.S. Army scout is sent to save
her.
Cinerama Releasing — *CBS/Fox Video*

Shall We Dance   1937
Musical
10051   116 mins   B/W   B, V   P
*Fred Astaire, Ginger Rogers, Edward Everett
Horton*
A famous ballet dancer marries a showgirl—or
does he? The score by George and Ira
Gershwin includes such memorable songs as
"They All Laughed," "Let's Call the Whole
Thing Off" and "They Can't Take That Away
from Me."
RKO; Pandro S Berman — *RKO HomeVideo;
Blackhawk Films; King of Video; Nostalgia
Merchant*

Shaming, The   1971
Drama
71043   90 mins   C   B, V   P
*Anne Heywood, Donald Pleasance, Robert
Vaughn, Carolyn Jones*
A puritanical school marm develops a voracious
sexual appetite after an initial unpleasant
indoctrination to the world of sin.
Bel-Air Graddison Productions — *Hal Roach
Studios*

Shampoo   1975
Comedy
Closed Captioned
70875   112 mins   C   B, V   P
*Warren Beatty, Julie Christie, Goldie Hawn, Jack
Warden, Lee Grant, Tony Bill, Carrie Fisher,
directed by Hal Ashby*
A womanizing hairdresser plots to open his own
salon. But when his four mistresses meet at a
1968 Presidential election night gathering, the
plans get a clean rinse. In Hi-Fi Mono.
Academy Award '75: Best Supporting Actress
(Grant) MPAA:R
Columbia Pictures — *RCA/Columbia Pictures
Home Video*

Shamus   1973
Comedy
21295   91 mins   C   B, V   P
Burt Reynolds, Dyan Cannon
A detective hired to recover some missing
diamonds becomes involved with the syndicate,
a beautiful woman, and an army officer
smuggling government surplus.
MPAA:PG
Columbia — *RCA/Columbia Pictures Home
Video*

Shane   1953
Western
38619   117 mins   C   B, V, LV   P
*Alan Ladd, Jean Arthur, Van Heflin, Brandon de
Wilde, Jack Palance, directed by George
Stevens*
A retired gunfighter, now drifter, comes to the
assistance of a homestead family terrorized by a
hired gunman. A classic of the Western film
genre.
Academy Awards '53: Best Cinematography,
Color.
Paramount — *Paramount Home Video; RCA
VideoDiscs*

Shaolin Death Squad   1983
Martial arts
64564   90 mins   C   B, V   P
A ruthless Japanese premier murders a
statesman as the first step in his plan to become
Emperor. The murdered man's daughter swears
vengeance and enlists the Shaolin Death Squad
to help.
MPAA:R
Satellite Consultants — *CBS/Fox Video*

Shaolin Drunk Monkey, The   1985
Martial arts
84507   85 mins   C   B, V   P
The dreaded Shaolin Drunk Monkey faces his
enemies in a veritable array of fights and lethal
kicks.
Telefilm Co Inc — *Sony Video Software*

Shaolin Fox Conspiracy   1985
Martial arts
84505   75 mins   C   B, V   P
This kung-fu epic features unusual moves,
including the Mantis Strike, Dragon Claw and
Crescent Kick.
Telefilm Co Inc — *Sony Video Software*

Shaolin Traitor   1982
Martial arts
64944   99 mins   C   B, V   R, P
*Carter Wong, Shangkuan Ling-Feng, Lung
Chun-Erh, Chang Yi, Lung Fei*
Exotic weapons and dazzling martial-arts action
are featured in this exciting tale of intrigue and
mystery.

MPAA:R
L and T Films Corp Ltd — *Video Gems*

Shape Up With Arnold   1982
Physical fitness
64923   85 mins   C   B, V   P
Arnold Schwarzenegger
Famed actor/bodybuilder Arnold
Schwarzenegger conducts fitness instruction
with weights and without for both men and
women. Three complete workouts are included.
Weinstein Skyfield Productions — *Video
Associates*

Shape-Up with David   1984
Howard
Physical fitness
79303   45 mins   C   B, V   P
Dance teacher David Howard shows off his daily
regimen for staying in shape.
New Age Video — *Kultur*

Shapeworks Plus   1985
Dance/Physical fitness
70719   100 mins   C   B, V   P
Angela Hillemann
Ms. Hillemann, a ballet instructor at the
University of Missouri, shows us a complete
series of stretch and aerobic exercises
designed to tone the entire body.
AM Available
To the Pointe: Hilleman Dancer's Studio — *To
the Pointe Hillemann Dancers*

Shari Lewis One Minute   1985
Bedtime Stories
Fairy tales
81969   30 mins   C   B, V   P
Shari Lewis along with Lamb Chop and Hush
Puppy read twenty-six popular children's stories.
Hanna-Barbera — *Worldvision Home Video*

Shark!   1968
Drama
65686   92 mins   C   B, V   P
Burt Reynolds, Barry Sullivan, Arthur Kennedy
An American gun smuggler stranded in a tiny
seaport in the Middle East joins the crew of a
marine biologist's boat, and soon discovers the
boat's owner and his wife are trying to retrieve
gold bullion that lies deep in shark-infested
waters.
Excelsior — *Spotlite Video*

Shark Hunter   198?
Drama/Adventure
70596   95 mins   C   B, V   P
Franco Nero, Jorge Luke, Mike Forrest
A shark hunter gets ensnared in the mobs nets
of the Mexican coast as they race for a cache of
sunken millions.

Unknown — *Prism*

Shark River   1953
Adventure/War-Drama
84516   80 mins   C   B, V   P
*Steve Cochran, Carole Matthews, Warren
Stevens*
A Civil War fugitive evades capture in the
Southern Everglades.
John Rawlins — *Magnum Entertainment*

Sharks, The   1982
Fishes
Closed Captioned
59016   57 mins   C   B, V, LV   P
Observing sharks around the world, this film
addresses man's fear and hatred of sharks,
while offering a look at the vulnerability the
shark has to people.
National Geographic Society — *Vestron Video;
National Geographic Society*

Sharks' Treasure   1975
Adventure
81056   96 mins   C   B, V   P
*Cornel Wilde, Yaphet Kotto, John Neilson,
David Canary, directed by Cornel Wilde*
A band of escaped convicts commandeer a
boat filled with gold.
MPAA:PG
United Artists; Cornel Wilde — *MGM/UA
Home Video*

Sharky's Machine   1981
Adventure
59856   119 mins   C   B, V   P
*Burt Reynolds, Rachel Ward, Vittorio Gassman,
Brian Keith, Charles Durning, Earl Holliman,
directed by Burt Reynolds*
A lively detective tale about an undercover cop
hot on the trail of a crooked czar.
MPAA:R
Orion; Warner Bros — *Warner Home Video;
RCA VideoDiscs*

Sharma and Beyond   1984
Drama
86779   85 mins   C   B, V   P
*Suzanne Burden, Robert Urquhart, Michael
Maloney, directed by Brian Gilbert*
A teenage would-be science fiction writer falls in
love with a girl whose father is a famous sci-fi
author.
David Puttnam; Goldcrest Television
Ltd. — *MGM/UA Home Video*

Sharpen Your Short Irons   1985
Golf
88070   25 mins   C   B, V   P
Jim Flick demonstrates optimum scoring club
use.

NFL Films; Golf Digest — *NFL Films Video*

Shattered \ 1972
Drama
65372   100 mins   C   B, V   P
Peter Finch, Shelley Winters, Colin Blakely
Finch plays Harry, a man not only blamed for a
failed marriage, but also held hostage in his
home by his own paranoia and driven bouts of
drinking. Slowly Harry's tenuous grip on sanity
slips and at any moment his fragile and
crumbling life may be shattered.
MPAA:R
Michael Klinger — *Media Home Entertainment*

Shazam 1981
Cartoons/Adventure
66007   60 mins   C   B, V   P
Animated
Young Billy Batson says "shazam" and turns
into the mighty Captain Marvel.
Filmation — *Family Home Entertainment*

Shazam!, Volume 2 1981
Cartoons/Adventure
69808   60 mins   C   B, V   P
Animated
Three more adventures feature young Billy
Batson, who transforms himself into the mighty
Captain Marvel to fight dastardly villains.
Filmation — *Family Home Entertainment*

Shazam Volume III 1981
Cartoons
79205   60 mins   C   B, V   P
Animated
Captain Marvel and his family of super heroes
fight off the bad guys in this collection of three
animated adventures.
DC Comics; Filmation Associates — *Family
Home Entertainment*

Shazzan 1983
Cartoons
66577   60 mins   C   B, V   P
Animated
Arabian nights adventures with Shazzan the
genie are featured on this tape.
Hanna Barbera — *Worldvision Home Video*

Shazzan 198?
Cartoons
78072   58 mins   C   B, V   P
Animated
This program presents the adventures of the
wonderful genie Shazzan and his masters.
Worldvision Home Video Inc — *Worldvision
Home Video*

Shazzan, Volume II 1967
Cartoons
82318   58 mins   C   B, V   P

Animated
The great genie Shazzan uses his wit and magic
to foil the bad guys in this collection of six
episodes from the series.
Hanna-Barbera — *Worldvision Home Video*

She \ 1925
Adventure
47462   77 mins   B/W   B, V, FO   P
Betty Blythe, Carlyle Blackwell, Mary Odette
H. Rider Haggard's famous story about the
ageless Queen Ayesha, who renews her life
force periodically by walking through a pillar of
cold flame. Silent film with music score.
Reciprocity Films — *Video Yesteryear;
Discount Video Tapes*

S*H*E 1980
Adventure
71215   100 mins   C   B, V   P
*Omar Sharif, Cornelia Sharpe, Robert Lansing,
William Taylor, Isabella Rye, Anita Ekberg,
directed by Robert Lewis*
The suave playboy who runs a huge
international crime syndicate may have met his
match when a beautiful superspy from Security
Hazards Experts comes gunning for him.
Martin Bregman — *Prism*

She 1983
Fantasy
84108   90 mins   C   B, V   P
*Sandahl Bergman, Harrison Muller, Quin
Kessler, directed by Avi Nesher*
A beautiful female warrior rules over the men in
a post-holocaust world and is kidnapped by a
wealthy merchant who uses her to fight evil
mutants.
Helen and Edward Sarlui — *Lightning Video*

She Came to the Valley 1977
Adventure
82484   90 mins   C   B, V   P
*Ronee Blakely, Dean Stockwell, Scott Glenn,
Freddy Fender*
A tough pioneer woman becomes embroiled in
political intrigue during the Spanish-American
War. Based on Cleo Dawson's book.
MPAA:PG
Independent — *Media Home Entertainment*

She Couldn't Say No 1952
Comedy
10029   88 mins   B/W   B, V   P, T
*Robert Mitchum, Jean Simmons, Arthur
Hunnicutt, Edgar Buchanan, Wallace Ford,
directed by Lloyd Bacon*
A wealthy heiress with good intentions plans to
give her money away to those friends who had
helped her when she was struggling. Things
don't go quite as planned, however.
RKO — *Blackhawk Films*

She Freak 1967
Horror
86817   87 mins   C   B, V   P
Claire Brennan, Lynn Courtney, Bill McKinney,
Lee Raymond, Madame Lee
A remake of Tod Brownings' "Freaks," wherein
a cynical waitress burns everyone in a circus
and gets mauled by the resident freaks.
Sonney-Friedman Pictures — *Magnum*
Entertainment

She-Ra, Princess of 198?
Power
Cartoons/Adventure
Closed Captioned
70881   45 mins   C   B, V   P
5   pgms
She-Ra, sister of He-Man, battles evil in this
continuing series of tapes. Each release
features two episodes chosen from the popular
Saturday morning TV show.
Filmation — *RCA/Columbia Pictures Home*
Video

She Waits 1971
Drama/Suspense
80317   74 mins   C   B, V   P
Dorothy McGuire, Patty Duke, David McCallum,
directed by Delbert Mann
When a newly wed couple moves into an old
house, the bride becomes possessed by the
spirit of her husband's first wife.
Delbert Mann — *Prism*

She Wore a Yellow 1949
Ribbon
Western
00275   93 mins   C   B, V   P
John Wayne, Joanne Dru, directed by John Ford
An undermanned cavalry outpost makes a
desperate attempt to repel invading Indians.
Academy Award '49: Best Cinematography,
Color.
RKO; Argosy Pictures Corp — *RKO*
HomeVideo; VidAmerica; King of Video

Sheena 1984
Adventure
Closed Captioned
77239   117 mins   C   B, V   P
Tanya Roberts, Ted Wass, Donvan Scott,
directed by John Guillermin
A television sportscaster aids a jungle queen in
defending her kingdom from being overthrown
by an evil prince. Available in VHS Hi-Fi Dolby
Stereo and Beta Hi-Fi Stereo.
MPAA:PG
Columbia — *RCA/Columbia Pictures Home*
Video

Sheena Easton 1983
Music-Performance
75907   15 mins   C   B, V   P

This program presents Sheena Easton
performing her hit songs "Morning Train,"
"Machinery" and "Telefone."
EMI America Records — *Sony Video Software*

Sheena Easton: Act One 1983
Music-Performance/Variety
73563   60 mins   C   V   P
Sheena sings her hits "For Your Eyes Only,"
"Out Here on My Own" and "Wind Beneath My
Wings" and Al Jarreau sings "Roof Garden" in
this program that was originally broadcast on
NBC.
Smith Hemion Productions — *Prism*

Sheena Easton—Live at 1982
the Palace, Hollywood
Music-Performance
66184   60 mins   C   B, V   P
The Grammy Award winner sings "Modern
Girl," "Morning Train," "For Your Eyes Only"
and others.
Unknown — *THORN EMI/HBO Video; RCA*
VideoDiscs

Sheer Madness 1984
Drama
80855   105 mins   C   B, V   P
Hanna Schgulla, Angela Winkler, directed by
Margarethe Von Trotta
This film explores the intense friendship
between a college professor and a troubled
artist. With English subtitles.
GE
TeleCulture, Inc. — *MGM/UA Home Video*

She'll Be Wearing Pink 1984
Pyjamas
Drama
85912   90 mins   C   B, V   P
Julie Walters, Anthony Higgins, directed by John
Goldschmidt
Eight women volunteer for a rugged survival
course to test their mettle and learn more than
they bargained for.
Tara Prem; Adrian Hughes — *Karl/Lorimar*
Home Video

Shell Shock 198?
War-Drama
80131   90 mins   C   B, V   P
Four GI's fight off the Germans and the longings
for home during World War II.
Independent — *King of Video*

Shenandoah 1965
Drama
53396   105 mins   C   B, V   P
James Stewart, Doug McClure, Glenn Corbett,
Patrick Wayne, Rosemary Forsythe, Katherine
Ross

During the Civil War, a farmer tries to remain neutral but becomes involved when his only daughter becomes engaged to a Confederate soldier.
Universal — *MCA Home Video*

Sherlock Holmes and a Study in Scarlet
1984

Suspense/Cartoons
81704   49 mins   C   B, V   P
Animated, voice of Peter O'Toole
Holmes and Watson have only one clue to go on when they investigate the murder of an American tourist in London.
Burbank Films — *Pacific Arts Video*

Sherlock Holmes and the Baskerville Curse
1984

Mystery
65851   70 mins   C   B, V   P
Animated, voice of Peter O'Toole
This production is an animated feature film with Peter O'Toole starring as the voice of Sherlock Holmes.
Pacific Arts Video Records — *Pacific Arts Video*

Sherlock Holmes and the Secret Weapon
1942

Mystery
58893   68 mins   B/W   B, V, FO   P
Basil Rathbone, Nigel Bruce, Lionel Atwill
Based on "The Dancing Men" by Sir Arthur Conan Doyle, Holmes battles Dr. Moriarty in order to save the British war effort.
Universal — *Prism; Kartes Video Communications; Video Yesteryear; Movie Buff Video; Admit One Video; Cable Films; Video Connection; Western Film & Video Inc; Hollywood Home Theater; Discount Video Tapes*

Sherlock Holmes and the Sign of Four
1984

Mystery
80444   48 mins   C   B, V   P
Animated, voice of Peter O'Toole
Sherlock Holmes must find the man who murdered Bartholomew Sholto with a poison dart in the neck.
Eddy Graham — *Pacific Arts Video*

Sherlock Holmes and the Silver Blaze
1941

Mystery
14295   70 mins   B/W   B, V   P
Arthur Wontner, Ian Fleming, Lyn Harding
Sherlock Holmes mystery based on the Arthur Conan Doyle classic "The Silver Blaze."
Astor; British — *Kartes Video Communications; Mossman Williams Productions; Video Yesteryear*

Sherlock Holmes and the Valley of Fear
1984

Suspense/Cartoons
81703   49 mins   C   B, V   P
Animated, voice of Peter O'Toole
Sherlock Holmes and Dr. Watson investigate a man who faked his own death to escape retribution from an American secret society.
Burbank Films — *Pacific Arts Video*

Sherlock Holmes and the Woman in Green
1945

Mystery
42927   67 mins   B/W   B, V   P
Basil Rathbone, Nigel Bruce
Based on a character developed by Sir Arthur Conan Doyle, this mystery finds Holmes and Watson matching wits against the infamous Professor Moriarity.
Universal, Howard Benedict — *Movie Buff Video; Cable Films; Video Connection; Hollywood Home Theater; Western Film & Video Inc; Video Yesteryear; Prism; Hal Roach Studios; Kartes Video Communications*

Sherlock Holmes Double Feature
194?

Mystery
55591   147 mins   B/W   B, V   P
Basil Rathbone, Nigel Bruce
Two classic Sherlock Holmes features on one cassette: "The Adventures of Sherlock Holmes" (1939) and "Sherlock Holmes and the Voice of Terror" (1942).
Twentieth Century Fox; Universal — *CBS/Fox Video*

Sherlock Holmes Double Feature I
194?

Mystery
64582   120 mins   B/W   B, V, 3/4U   P
Basil Rathbone, Nigel Bruce
Paired in this double feature are "Sherlock Holmes and the Secret Weapon" and "The Woman in Green."
Universal — *Nostalgia Merchant*

Sherlock Holmes Double Feature II
1946

Mystery
64583   120 mins   B/W   B, V, 3/4U   P
Basil Rathbone, Nigel Bruce
This double feature contains "Dressed to Kill" and "Terror by Night."
Universal — *Nostalgia Merchant*

Sherlock Holmes I
1954

Mystery
38997   54 mins   B/W   B, V, FO   P
Ronald Howard, H. Marion Crawford 2 pgms
Two episodes from the English syndicated series bases on the exploits of master detective

Sherlock Holmes: "The Case of the Impromptu Performance," and "The Case of the Exhumed Client."
British — *Video Yesteryear*

Sherlock Holmes II   1954
Mystery
38998   54 mins   B/W   B, V, FO   P
Ronald Howard, H. Marion Crawford 2   pgms
Two more episodes from the syndicated British TV series of the 1950's: "The Case of the Baker Street Nursemaids" and "The Case of the Pennsylvania Gun."
British — *Video Yesteryear*

Sherlock's Rivals and   1927
Where's My Wife
Adventure/Comedy
78082   53 mins   B/W   B, V, FO   P
Milburn Morante, Monty Banks
This double feature includes a detective movie in which two used car dealers become amateur sleuths and a comedy in which a man has a hard time enjoying his weekend at a seashore resort.
BIP — *Video Yesteryear*

Sherrill Milnes: Homage   198?
to Verdi
Music-Performance/Documentary
87357   56 mins   C   B, V   P
The famed baritone takes the viewer on a tour of Verdian locales, and sings excerpts from Verdi's most famous operas.
Italian — *Kultur*

She's Dressed to Kill   1979
Suspense
66622   98 mins   C   B, V   P
Eleanor Parker, Jessica Walter, John Rubenstein
A mysterious killer murders a group of fashion models one by one, in the incongruous setting of a secluded mountaintop resort.
Grant Case McGrath Enterprises; Barry Weitz Productions — *U.S.A. Home Video*

She's in the Army Now   1981
Comedy
88150   97 mins   C   B, V   P
Jamie Lee Curtis, Kathleen Quinlan, directed by Hy Averback
A made-for-TV farce about military life, as two bubble-headed females undergo basic training.
ABC; Harry R. Sherman — *Charter Entertainment*

Shinbone Alley   1970
Musical/Cartoons
50960   83 mins   C   B, V   R, P
Animated, voices of Carol Channing, Eddie Bracken, John Carradine, Alan Reed

An animated musical about Archy, a free-verse poet reincarnated as a cockroach, and Mehitabel, the alley cat with a zest for life. Based on the short stories by Don Marquis.
MPAA:G
Fine Arts Films — *Video Gems*

Shine on Harvest Moon   1938
Western
05534   60 mins   B/W   B, V, FO   P
Roy Rogers, Mary Hart, Stanley Andrews
Roy Rogers brings a band of outlaws to justice and clears an old man suspected of being their accomplice.
Republic — *Video Yesteryear*

Shining, The   1980
Horror
58249   143 mins   C   B, V   P
Jack Nicholson, Shelley Duvall, Scatman Crothers, Danny Lloyd, directed by Stanley Kubrick
Terror and violence overwhelms a family isolated and snowbound in a huge resort hotel with a history of violence. Based on the novel by Stephen King.
MPAA:R
Warner Bros — *Warner Home Video; RCA VideoDiscs*

Shiokari Pass   1977
Drama
84628   60 mins   C   B, V   P
Directed by Novuru Nakamuru.
In Japanese with English subtitles, this film deals with a man receiving Divine revelation.
Billy Graham — *Republic Pictures Home Video*

Ship of Fools   1965
Drama
Closed Captioned
71116   149 mins   B/W   B, V   P
Vivien Leigh, Simone Signoret, Jose Ferrer, Lee Marvin, Oskar Werner, Micheal Dunn, Elizabeth Ashley, George Segal, Jose Greco, Charles Korvin, Heinz Ruehmann, directed by Stanley Kramer
While sailing towards pre-Hitler Germany, the ship's passengers open their pasts to each other linking their fates on the doomed voyage. Based on Katherine Anne Porter's novel. Academy Awards: '65 Best Art Direction; Best Set Direction; Best Cinematography.
Columbia — *RCA/Columbia Pictures Home Video*

Shmenges: The Last   1984
Polka, The
Comedy/Satire
80693   54 mins   C   B, V   P
John Candy, Eugene Levy, Rick Moranis, Robin Duke, Catherine O'Hara

---

Imitating the style of Martin Scorcese's '78 tribute to ''The Band,'' this documentary looks at the life and career of the fictional polka kings, the Shmenges. Based upon the characters from the SCTV Network series.
Shmenges Productions — *Vestron Video*

Shoah   1985
Documentary/World War II
87190   570 mins   C   B, V   P
Directed by Claude Lanzmann
This famous, epic documentary details the devastation of the Holocaust through interviews with survivors of the camps. A searing, significant statement, which is one of the most important documentaries in the history of film. On four tapes.
Claude Lanzmann — *Paramount Home Video*

Shock   1946
Mystery/Horror
53442   70 mins   B/W   B, V, FO   P
Vincent Price, Lynn Bari, Frank Latimore, Anabel Shaw
A doctor is called upon to treat a woman and discovers that she saw him kill his wife.
AM Available
Twentieth Century Fox — *Video Yesteryear; Kartes Video Communications*

Shock, The   1923
Drama
85213   96 mins   B/W   B, V   P
Lon Chaney, Virgina Valli, directed by Lambert Hillyer
A crippled henchman becomes restored spiritually by a small-town girl and rebels against his Chinese boss, causing an unfortunate string of melodramatic tragedies. Silent.
Carl Laemmle — *Video Yesteryear*

Shock Waves   1977
Horror
80294   84 mins   C   B, V   P
Peter Cushing, Brooke Adams, John Carradine, Luke Halprin
A group of mutant zombie Nazi soldiers terrorize stranded tourists staying at a deserted motel on a small island.
Joseph Brenner Associates — *Prism*

Shocking Asia   1975
Documentary/Asia
84511   94 mins   C   B, V   P
Directed by Emerson Fox
For the eye-covering delight of Western audiences, Mr. Fox compiles gruesome Asian oddities.
Geiselgasgeig; 1st Film Org — *Magnum Entertainment*

Shogun   1980
Drama
54670   120 mins   C   B, V, LV   P
Richard Chamberlain, Toshiro Mifune
A made for television feature that depicts the people, life-style, and traditions of Japan. A special 2-hour length version, based on the novel by James Clavell.
NBC — *Paramount Home Video; RCA VideoDiscs*

Shogun   1980
Drama
81098   550 mins   C   B, V   P
Richard Chamberlain, Toshiro Mifune, Yoko Shimada, John Rhys-Davies, narrated by Orson Welles, directed by Jerry London
This is the complete version of the mini-series that chronicles the saga of how an English navigator became the first Shogun from the Western world. Adapted from the James Clavell novel.
Emmy Awards '80: Outstanding Dramatic Series.
Paramount; NBC Entertainment — *Paramount Home Video*

Shogun Assassin   1980
Adventure
55553   89 mins   C   B, V   P
Tomisaburo Wakayama
The story of a proud samurai named Lone Wolf who served his Shogun master well as the Official Decapitator, until the fateful day when the aging Shogun turned against him.
MPAA:R
Toho Company; Katsu Prod — *MCA Home Video*

Shogun's Ninja   1983
Martial arts/Suspense
64233   115 mins   C   B, V   P
Henry Sanada, Sue Shiomi, Sonny Chiba
In 16th century Japan, an age-old rivalry between two ninja clans sparks a search for a dagger which will lead to one clan's hidden gold.
Toei Studios; Shigeru Okada — *Media Home Entertainment*

Shoot   1985
Adventure
82566   98 mins   C   B, V   P
Ernest Borgnine, Cliff Robertson
Five hunting buddies fall prey to a group of crazed killers in this action film.
MPAA:R
Harve Sherman — *Embassy Home Entertainment*

Shout for the Stars   1984
Football
79632   40 mins   C   B, V, FO   P

A history of the Dallas Cowboys from their
expansion team roots to their awesome teams
of the 70's and 80's.
NFL Films — *NFL Films Video*

Shoot It Black, Shoot It   1974
Blue
Crime-Drama
64212   93 mins   C   B, V   P
Michael Moriarty
A rogue cop shoots a black purse snatcher and
thinks he has gotten away with it. Unknown to
him, however, a witness has filmed the incident
and turns the evidence over to a lawyer.
Shoot It Company — *THORN EMI/HBO Video*

Shoot the Moon   1982
Drama
47775   124 mins   C   B, V, CED   P
*Diane Keaton, Albert Finney, Karen Allen, Peter
Weller, Dana Hill, Viveka Davis, Tracey Gold,
Tina Yothers, directed by Alan Parker*
An affluent California family experiences
jealousy, anger and love following the breakup
of the marriage.
MPAA:R
MGM — *MGM/UA Home Video*

Shoot the Piano Player   1962
Drama
49065   84 mins   B/W   B, V   P
*Charles Aznavour, Marie Dubois, Nicole Berger,
directed by Francois Truffaut*
A former great piano player reluctantly agrees to
try a comeback at the urging of the girl he loves.
Astor Films — *Hollywood Home Theater;
Western Film & Video Inc; Cable Films*

Shoot the Sun Down   1974
Adventure
59812   102 mins   C   B, V   P
*Christopher Walken, Margot Kidder, Geoffrey
Lewis*
Four offbeat characters united in their lust for
gold soon turn against each other.
MPAA:PG
David Leeds — *VidAmerica*

Shooting, The   1966
Western
13629   82 mins   C   B, V   P
Warren Oates, Millie Perkins, Jack Nicholson
A mysterious woman, bent on revenge,
persuades a former bounty hunter and his
partner to escort her across the desert, with
tragic results.
Monte Hellman; Jack Nicholson — *Continental
Video; Media Home Entertainment; Discount
Video Tapes; King of Video; Hollywood Home
Theater; Western Film & Video Inc*

Shooting Home Video: 1982
The Basics
Video
59509   60 mins   C   B, V   S
The basic fundamentals of camera operation,
sound, composition, lighting and directing a
video production are explained.
Kartes Prods — *Kartes Video Communications*

Shooting Party, The   1985
Drama
82262   97 mins   C   B, V   P
*James Mason, Dorothy Tutin, Edward Fox, John
Gielgud, Robert Hardy*
A group of English aristocrats assemble at a
nobleman's house for a bird shoot on the eve of
World War I.
Ronald K. Goldman European
Classics — *THORN EMI/HBO Video*

Shootist, The   1976
Western
38620   100 mins   C   B, V, LV   P
*John Wayne, Lauren Bacall, James Stewart,
Ron Howard, directed by Don Siegel*
John Wayne's last film appearance as an aging
gunslinger afflicted with cancer, who seeks
peace and solace in his final days, but finds
himself involved in one final gun battle.
MPAA:PG
Paramount — *Paramount Home Video; RCA
VideoDiscs*

Shop on Main Street, The   1965
Drama
78882   128 mins   B/W   B, V   P
*Ida Kaminska, Josef Kroner, Hana Slivkoua,
directed by Jan Kadar and Elmar Klos*
During the Second World War, a Nazi appointed
"Aryan controller" befriends a Jewish widow
who owns a button shop. This film is subtitled in
English and available in Beta Hi-Fi.
Academy Awards '65: Best Foreign Language
Film. CZ
Barrandov Film Studios — *RCA/Columbia
Pictures Home Video*

Short Eyes   1979
Drama
77220   100 mins   C   B, V   P
*Bruce Davidson, Miguel Pinero, Jose Perez,
Shawn Elliott*
When a child molester enters prison, the
inmates act out their own form of revenge
against him.
MPAA:R
Short Eyes Entertainment — *Lightning Video*

Short Films of D. W.   1912
Griffith, Vol. I, The
Film-History
47461   45 mins   B/W   B, V, FO   P
Blanche Sweet, Mary Pickford, Charles West

Three early shorts made by the great director are on this tape: "The Battle," "The Female of the Species" and "The New York Hat." Silent with music score.
Biograph — *Video Yesteryear*

Short-Order Gourmet, The
1985
Cookery
71007   60 mins   C   B, V   P
Bradley Ogden, Alice Waters, Dick Cavett
Leading chefs propose cooking tips and go over some cooking essentials for time-pressed professionals.
Esquire — *Esquire Video*

Shot in the Dark, A
1964
Comedy
47151   101 mins   C   B, V, CED   P
Peter Sellers, Elke Sommer, Herbert Lom, George Sanders, directed by Blake Edwards
The Second in the "Inspector Clouseau-Pink Panther" series of films. The bumbling Inspector Clouseau investigates the case of a parlormaid who is accused of murdering her lover.
EL, SP
United Artists; Walter Mirisch — *CBS/Fox Video; RCA VideoDiscs*

Shout, The
1978
Horror
36189   87 mins   C   B, V   P
Alan Bates, Susannah York, John Hurt, Tim Curry
A married couple becomes dominated by a malevolent seducer with aboriginal powers.
Cannes Film Festival '78: Jury Prize. MPAA:R
CPH; BLD — *RCA/Columbia Pictures Home Video*

Shout at the Devil
1976
War-Drama
65378   128 mins   C   B, V   P
Lee Marvin, Roger Moore, Barbara Parkins
A story based on an actual World War I incident involving the destruction of a German battleship on a river in Africa in 1913. Based on the novel by Wilbur Smith.
MPAA:PG
American International — *Vestron Video*

Show Boat
1951
Musical-Drama
47054   115 mins   C   B, V   P
Kathryn Grayson, Howard Keel, Ava Gardner, William Warfield, Joe E. Brown, Agnes Moorehead
The third movie version of Jerome Kern and Oscar Hammerstein II's 1927 musical play about the life and loves of a Mississippi riverboat theater troupe. The famous score includes "Old Man River," "Make Believe,"

"Can't Help Lovin' Dat Man," "Why Do I Love You," and "Bill."
MGM — *MGM/UA Home Video*

Show Business
1944
Musical
44989   92 mins   B/W   B, V   P, T
Eddie Cantor, Joan Davis
Romantic story of two show business teams: the boys are in burlesque and the girls are in vaudeville.
RKO — *Blackhawk Films*

Show Jumping World Cup
1981
Sports-Minor
59567   75 mins   C   B, V   P
The 1981 horse show-jumping competition for the Federation of Equestrians International World Cup.
Grand Prix Show Jumping — *Mastervision*

Showbiz Ballyhoo
1984
Outtakes and bloopers
78359   90 mins   C   B, V   P
How Hollywood filmmakers sparked audience excitement through publicity and promotion in the golden age of movies are shown in this program.
USA — *U.S.A. Home Video*

Showbiz Goes to War
1982
Documentary/World War II
66623   90 mins   C   B, V   P
Narrated by David Steinberg
The activities of Hollywood's biggest stars during World War II are the subject of this feature. Pin-up girls, USO shows, propaganda films, patriotic musicals and war bond drives are a few of the subjects seen along the way.
TAD Productions — *U.S.A. Home Video*

Showdown at Boot Hill
1958
Western
81861   76 mins   B/W   B, V   P
Charles Bronson, Robert Hutton, John Carradine
A bounty hunter kills a wanted criminal but cannot collect the reward because the townspeople will not identify the victim.
20th Century Fox — *Spotlite Video*

Showdown at the Equator
1983
Martial arts
86602   95 mins   C   B, V   P
Lo Lieh, Bruce Liang, Nora Maio, Lee Kan Kwun
Chinese cops are trained to kill criminals with their feet, which they do.
MPAA:R
Foreign — *Video Gems*

Showdown: Sugar Ray Leonard vs. Thomas Hearns, The   1981
Boxing
59018   62 mins   C   CED   P
The classic match between Sugar Ray Leonard and Tommy Hearns.
Main Event Prods — *RCA VideoDiscs*

Shriek in the Night, A   1933
Mystery
84872   66 mins B/W   B, V   P
Ginger Rogers, Lyle Talbot, Harvey Clark
A newspaperwoman turns detective to solve some local murders.
Allied Pictures Corp. — *Kartes Video Communications*

Shriek of the Multilated   1974
Horror
81960   85 mins   C   B, V   P
Alan Brock, Jennifer Stock, Michael Harris
An anthropological expedition on a deserted island turns into a night of horror as a savage beast kills the members of the group one by one.
MPAA:R
Ed Adlum; American Films Ltd. — *Lightning Video*

Sicilian Connection, The   1974
Drama
80124   100 mins   C   B, V   P
Ben Gazzara, Silvia Monti, Fausto Tozzi
A narcotics agent poses as a nightclub manager to bust open a drug smuggling organization.
Joseph Green Pictures — *King of Video*

Sicilian Connection, The   1985
Crime-Drama
87365   117 mins   C   B, V   P
Michele Placido, Mark Switzer, Simona Cavallari
Two brothers in the mob serve out vendettas and generally create havoc wherever they go.
MPAA:R
Cannon Prod. — *MGM/UA Home Video*

Sid Caesar's Shape Up   1985
Physical fitness
80272   58 mins   C   B, V   P
Sid Caesar demonstrates his own physical fitness program that saved his life.
Jim Gates — *Media Home Entertainment*

Sidewalks of London   1940
Drama
03833   86 mins B/W   B, V   P
Charles Laughton, Vivien Leigh, Rex Harrison, directed by Tim Whelen
Sidewalk entertainer takes in homeless waif, helps her achieve fame.

Mayfair Pictures; Gaumont;
British — *Hollywood Home Theater; Cable Films; Video Connection; Kartes Video Communications*

Sidewinder One   1977
Adventure
84044   97 mins   C   B, V   P
Michael Parks, Marjoe Gortner, Susan Howard, directed by Earl Bellamy
This is the first dramatic film ever made about the actionful and dangerous world of professional motocross.
MPAA:PG
Elmo Williams — *Charter Entertainment*

Sidney Sheldon's Bloodline   1979
Suspense
38929   116 mins   C   B, V   P
Audrey Hepburn, Ben Gazzara, James Mason, directed by Terence Young
The popular best-selling novel transferred to film, starring Audrey Hepburn as a wealthy businesswoman who finds she is marked for death by persons unknown.
MPAA:R
Paramount — *Paramount Home Video*

Siegfried   1924
Drama
63993   100 mins B/W   B, V   P, T
Paul Richter, Margareta Schoen, directed by Fritz Lang
A massive extravaganza film, based on the legends of the Nibelungen. These same tales were also the basis of Richard Wagner's "Ring" cycle of operas. Silent with organ score.
UFA — *Blackhawk Films*

Sigmund and the Sea Monsters, Volume 2   1973
Adventure
81454   46 mins   C   B, V   P
Johnny Whitaker, Billy Barty
Sigmund, the lovable sea monster, is in trouble again in this collection of two episodes from the series.
Sid and Marty Krofft — *Embassy Home Entertainment*

Sigmund and the Sea Monsters, Volume I   1973
Comedy
76790   46 mins   C   B, V   P
Billy Barty, Johnny Whittaker, Mary Wickes, Rip Torn, Margaret Hamilton, Fran Ryan
Two young boys befriend a sea monster who's been disowned by his family for his inability to scare humans.
Sid and Marty Krofft — *Embassy Home Entertainment*

Sign of Zorro, The   1957
Adventure
59064   89 mins   C   B, V   P
Guy Williams, Henry Calvin, Gene Sheldon, Romney Brent, Britt Lomond,
The adventures of the masked swordsman as he champions the cause of the oppressed in early California. A full-length version of the popular late-50's Disney TV series.
Walt Disney Productions — *Walt Disney Home Video*

Signals Through the Flames   1983
Theater
86476   97 mins   C   B, V   P
Julian Beck, Judith Malina, The Living Theatre Company
A film by Sheldon Rochlin and Maxine Harris outlining the tumultuous history of the famous experimental group, The Living Theatre.
Sheldon Rochlin; Maxine Harris; The Living Theatre — *Mystic Fire Video*

Silence   1973
Drama
84509   82 mins   C   B, V   P
Will Geer, Ellen Geer, Richard Kelton, Ian Geer Flanders, directed by John Korty
A lonely deaf boy gets lost in the wilderness and faces an array of difficulties while his foster parents search for him.
MPAA:G
CSA Prods — *Magnum Entertainment*

Silence of the North   1981
Drama
47424   94 mins   C   B, V   P
Ellen Burstyn, Tom Skerrit
A true story about a widow with three children struggling to survive under rugged pioneer conditions on the Canadian frontier.
MPAA:PG
Universal — *MCA Home Video*

Silent Enemy, The   1930
Indians-North American/Documentary
12853   110 mins   B/W   B, V, FO   P
An interesting documentary which tells the Ojibway Indian's way of life before the arrival of the white man. The title is a reference to hunger.
Unknown — *Video Yesteryear; Blackhawk Films*

Silent Laugh Makers No. 1   192?
Comedy
11283   50 mins   B/W   B, V, FO   P
Charlie Chase, Stan Laurel, Oliver Hardy, Charlie Chaplin, Ben Turpin, Arthur Lake
A collection of four hilarious short movies from the silent picture era: "One Mama Man," "Lucky Dog," "His Night Out," and "Hop-a-Long."
Hal Roach — *Video Yesteryear*

Silent Laugh Makers No. 2   192?
Comedy
11284   50 mins   B/W   B, V, FO   P
Charlie Chase, Oliver Hardy, Billy Bevan
Four short funny films of the silent era: "Fluttering Hearts," "Long Live the King," and "A Sea Dog Tale."
Hal Roach — *Video Yesteryear*

Silent Laugh Makers #3   192?
Comedy
66141   55 mins   B/W   B, V, FO   P
Harry Langdon, Harold Lloyd, Bebe Daniels, Snub Pollard
Four comedy shorts: "Picking Peaches" (1924), directed by Frank Capra, Langdon's first for Mack Sennett; "All Tied Up" (1925), featuring "A Ton of Fun"—four rotund comedians; "Don't Shove" (1919), featuring Harold Lloyd wooing Bebe Daniels; "Some Baby" (1922), with Snub Pollard, written by Hal Roach.
Hal Roach et al — *Video Yesteryear*

Silent Madness   1984
Horror
81095   93 mins   C   B, V   P
Belinda Montgomery, Viveca Lindfors, Sydney Lassick
A psychiatrist must stop a deranged killer from slaughtering helpless college coeds in a sorority house.
Gregory Earls — *Media Home Entertainment*

Silent Movie   1976
Comedy
81170   88 mins   C   B, V, LV   P
Mel Brooks, Marty Feldman, Dom DeLuise, Burt Reynolds, Anne Bancroft, James Caan, Liza Minnelli, Paul Newman, Sid Caesar, directed by Mel Brooks
A has been movie director is determined to make a comeback and save his studio from being taken over by a conglomerate. Hi-Fi Stereo in both formats.
MPAA:PG
20th Century Fox — *CBS/Fox Video*

Silent Movies—In Color   19??
Film-History
56915   52 mins   C   B, V, FO   P
Five films produced in France between 1904 and 1914 in which color tints were added one frame at a time by hand. Films include: "The Nobleman's Dog," "Bob's Electric Theatre," "A Slave's Love," "A New Way of Traveling," and "The Life of Our Savior."
French — *Video Yesteryear*

Silent Night, Deadly Night   1984
Horror/Exploitation
71340   93 mins   C   B, V   P
Lilyan Chauvin, Gilmer McCormick, Toni Nero,
Robert Brian Wilson, directed by Charles E.
Sellier Jr.
A demented young man dresses as Santa Claus
and, taking axe in hand, proceeds to deck the
halls with blood and bodies. The film stirred
controversy upon its theatrical release.
MPAA:R
Tri-Star — U.S.A. Home Video

Silent One, The   1986
Drama
85875   96 mins   C   B, V   P
Featuring underwater photography by Ron and
Valerie Taylor, this is the odd story of a
mysterious Polynesian boy who has a nautical
relationship with a sea turtle.
Unknown — VidAmerica

Silent Partner, The   1978
Drama
45068   103 mins   C   B, V, LV,   P
                   CED
Elliot Gould, Christopher Plummer, Susannah
York
A bank teller foils a robbery, but keeps some of
the money for himself. Trouble ensues because
the robber knows it and wants the money.
EMC Film Corp — Vestron Video; Time Life
Video

Silent Rage   1982
Adventure/Martial arts
62811   100 mins   C   B, V   P
Chuck Norris, Ron Silver, Steven Keats, Toni
Kalem, Brian Libby
The sheriff of a small Texas town must destroy
a murderous killer who has been made
indestructible through genetic engineering.
MPAA:R
Columbia — RCA/Columbia Pictures Home
Video; RCA VideoDiscs

Silent Raiders, The   1954
War-Drama
84501   72 mins   B/W   B, V   P
Richard Bartlett, Earle Lyon, Jeanette Bordeau
In France, 1943, a mission is driven forward to
knock out a German communications center.
Earle Lyon; Robert L Lippert Prods — Sony
Video Software

Silent Rebellion   1982
Drama
81414   90 mins   C   B, V   P
Telly Savalas, Keith Gordon, Michael
Constantine, Yula Gavala
A Greek immigrant with his son return to his
native land to be reunited with his mother and
brother. The pair not only discover their heritage
but also come to better understand each other
as well.
David Horwatt — VCL Home Video

Silent Running   1971
Science fiction
53393   90 mins   C   B, V   P
Bruce Dern, Cliff Potts, Ron Rifkin
Members of a space station crew in 2001 are
space gardening to replenish a nuclear-
devastated earth.
MPAA:G
Universal; Michel Gruskoff; Doug
Trumbull — MCA Home Video

Silent Scream   1980
Horror
59669   87 mins   C   B, V   P
Rebecca Balding, Cameron Mitchell, Avery
Schreiber, Barbara Steele, Steve Doubet, Brad
Reardon, Yvonne De Carlo
A gloomy old victorian mansion by the sea has a
silent terror lurking within the walls.
MPAA:R
Jim Wheat; Ken Wheat — Media Home
Entertainment

Silent Scream, The   1984
Horror
80479   60 mins   C   B, V   P
Peter Cushing, Brian Cox, Elaine Donnelly
A former Nazi concentration camp commandant
collects unusual animals and humans as a
hobby. In Beta Hi-Fi and VHS stereo.
Hammer Films — Thriller Video

Silk Stockings   1957
Musical/Comedy
52747   117 mins   C   B, V   P
Fred Astaire, Cyd Charisse, Janis Paige, Peter
Lorre, George Tobias, directed by Rouben
Mamoulian
A musical comedy adaptation of "Ninotchka,"
with Astaire as a charming American movie
man, and Charisse as a Soviet official. Music
and lyrics by Cole Porter highlight this film
adapted from George S. Kaufman's hit
Broadway play.
MGM; Arthur Freed — MGM/UA Home Video

Silkwood   1983
Drama
65720   131 mins   C   B, V, LV,   P
                   CED
Meryl Streep, Kurt Russell, Cher
A dramatization of the life of Karen Silkwood,
the nuclear plant worker ad activist, who died in
the 1974 under suspicious circumstances while
investigating shoddy practices at ther plant.
MPAA:R
Mike Nichols; Michael Hausman — Embassy
Home Entertainment

Silver Bears 1978
Adventure
85439   114 mins   C   B, V   P
Michael Caine, Cybill Shepherd, Louis Jourdan, directed by Ivan Passer
A newly-discovered silver mine is used by scheming, happy-go-lucky thieves to nearly upset the world market.
MPAA:PG
Columbia Pictures — *U.S.A. Home Video*

Silver City 1984
Drama
87264   110 mins   C   B, V   P
Gosia Dobrowolska, Ivar Kants, directed by Sophia Turkiewicz
A saga depicting the plight of Polish refugees in 1949 conflicting with native Australians; in this case, a pair of lovers find each other in a crowded refugee camp.
MPAA:PG
Sophia Turkiewicz — *Karl/Lorimar Home Video*

Silver Dream Racer 1983
Drama
79316   103 mins   C   B, V   P
Beau Bridges, David Essex, Cristina Raines, Diane Keen
An up and coming English motorcycle racer wants to win the World Motorcycle Championship title away from an American biker.
MPAA:PG
Almi Films — *Vestron Video*

Silver Lode 1954
Western
77525   92 mins   C   B, V   P
John Payne, Dan Duryea, Lizabeth Scott, Stuart Whitman, directed by Allan Dwan
A man accused of murder on his wedding day attempts to clear his name while the law launches an intensive manhunt for him.
RKO; Pincrest — *Buena Vista Home Video*

Silver Streak 1976
Comedy
41078   113 mins   C   B, V, CED   P
Gene Wilder, Jill Clayburgh, Patrick McGoohan
Gene Wilder becomes involved with murder, intrigue, and a beautiful woman aboard a transcontinental express train.
MPAA:PG EL, SP
20th Century Fox — *CBS/Fox Video*

Silver Streak 1934
Drama
54115   72 mins   B/W   B, V   P, T
Sally Blane, Charles Starett, Arthur Lake, Edgar Kennedy
The sickly son of a diesel train designer needs a iron lung pronto. A rival's super fast neato keen

locomotive is the only hope for the boy. Murders, busted brides, runaway engines, and a crew that would rather walk enliven this race against time.
RKO — *Blackhawk Films*

Silver Theatre 1950
Comedy
85214   25 mins   B/W   B, V   P
Chico Marx, Margeret Hamilton, William Frawley
A half-hour comedy sitcom featuring the madcap Romani family, featuring a rare TV appearance by Chico.
CBS — *Video Yesteryear*

Silverado 1985
Western
Closed Captioned
71114   132 mins   C   B, V   P
Kevin Kline, Scott Glenn, Kevin Costner, Danny Glover, Brian Dennehy, Linda Hunt, John Cleese, Jeff Goldblum, Rosanna Arquette, directed by Lawrence Kasdan
This affectionate pastiche of western cliches has everything a viewer could ask for—except Indians. The plot finds four virtuous cowboys rising up against a crooked lawman in a blaze of sixguns. Recorded in HiFi Stereo Surround sound.
MPAA:PG-13
Columbia — *RCA/Columbia Pictures Home Video*

Simon 1980
Comedy
52715   97 mins   C   B, V   P
Alan Arkin, Madeline Kahn, directed by Marshall Brickman
A group of demented scientists brainwash a college professor into believing that his real mother is a Martian spaceship.
MPAA:PG
Orion Pictures — *Warner Home Video*

Simon & Garfunkel: The 1982
Concert in Central Park
Music-Performance
47402   87 mins   C   B, V, LV,   P
                                 CED
Paul Simon, Art Garfunkel
The September 1981 reunion concert by Simon and Garfunkel before 500,000 delirious fans in New York's Central Park is captured on this tape. Among the 20 selections performed are "April Come She Will," "Mrs. Robinson," "Scarborough Fair" and "The Sounds of Silence."
James Signorelli — *CBS/Fox Video*

Simon Bolivar 1969
Drama
85537   110 mins   C   B, V   P
Maximilian Schell, Rosanna Schiaffino

The title character cavorts and leads the Venezuelan revolution in 1817.
Italian/Spanish — *Unicorn Video*

Simon of the Desert   1966
Drama
48750   43 mins   B/W   B, V   P
Directed by Luis Bunuel
A mocking allegory which tells of a man's fall from grace.
SP
Gustavo Alatriste — Hollywood Home Theater; Discount Video Tapes; Movie Buff Video

Simple Story, A   1980
Drama
59383   110 mins   C   B, V   P
Romy Schneider, Bruno Cremer, Claude Brasseur, directed by Claude Sautet
A woman faces her fortieth birthday with increasing uneasiness, though her life seems perfect from the outside.
Columbia — RCA/Columbia Pictures Home Video

Simple Truth, The   1985
Romance
87690   90 mins   C   V   P
A woman's romance novel is dramatized, dealing with a receptionistwho has a fling with the company president.
Prism Video — Prism

Sin of Adam and Eve, The   1972
Drama
69804   72 mins   C   B, V   P
Candy Wilson, George Rivers
This is the story of Adam and Eve in the Garden of Eden and their fall from grace.
MPAA:R
Michael Zachary — United Home Video

Sin of Harold Diddlebock, The   1947
Comedy
11312   95 mins   B/W   B, V, FO   P
Harold Lloyd, Raymond Walburn, Edgar Kennedy, Franklin Pangborn
Harold Lloyd's last film which folows the life of the hero of Lloyd's classic silent picture, "The Freshman," in later years.
Preston Sturges — Video Yesteryear; Hollywood Home Theater; Discount Video Tapes; Cable Films; Prism; Video Connection; Western Film & Video Inc; Hal Roach Studios; Kartes Video Communications

Sinbad and the Eye of the Tiger   1977
Fantasy
21296   113 mins   C   B, V, LV   P
Patrick Wayne, Jane Seymour, Taryn Power

The swashbuckling adventures of Sinbad the Sailor.
Columbia — *RCA/Columbia Pictures Home Video; RCA VideoDiscs*

Sinbad the Sailor   1947
Drama
00310   117 mins   C   B, V   P
Douglas Fairbanks Jr., Maureen O'Hara, Anthony Quinn
Swashbuckler seeks a treasure island in this Arabian Nights film.
RKO; Stephen Ames — *RKO HomeVideo; Nostalgia Merchant; VidAmerica; King of Video*

Sing Along with Little Lulu   1983
Cartoons
66472   86 mins   C   B, V   P
Animated
Little Lulu is herewith featured in a special collection of her popular cartoons.
Famous Studios — *Republic Pictures Home Video*

Sing Blue Silver   1984
Music video
80353   85 mins   C   B, V   P
Simon Le Bon, Nick Rhodes, Andy Taylor, John Taylor
A behind the scenes look at Duran Duran's 1984 concert tour, where the band performs "Girls on Film" and "The Reflex."
EMI Music Video — *THORN EMI/HBO Video*

Sing Your Worries Away   1942
Musical/Comedy
45102   71 mins   B/W   B, V   P, T
Buddy Ebsen, Bert Lahr, June Havoc
Two struggling songwriters and their girlfriends get entangled in a gaint swindle.
RKO — *Blackhawk Films*

Singer Presents "Elvis" (The 1968 Comeback Special)   1968
Music-Performance
47501   52 mins   C   B, V, FO   P
Elvis Presley
The famous TV spectacular that brought Elvis back to performing in public. Songs featured include "Heartbreak Hotel," "Hound Dog" and "All Shook Up." Originally telecast on December 3, 1968.
NBC — *Video Yesteryear*

Singin' in the Rain   1952
Musical
39087   103 mins   C   B, V, CED   P
Gene Kelly, Donald O'Connor, Jean Hagen, Debbie Reynolds, Rita Moreno, Cyd Charisse, directed by Gene Kelly and Stanley Donen

One of the all-time great movie musicals—an affectionate spoof of the turmoil that afflicted the motion picture industry in the late 1920's during the changeover from silent films to sound. Songs include the title tune, "Make 'Em Laugh," "All I Do Is Dream of You," and "You Are My Lucky Star." Music and lyrics by Arthur Freed and Nacio Herb Brown.
MGM — *MGM/UA Home Video*

Singing Buckaroo, The   1937
Western
78094   58 mins   B/W   B, V, FO   P
Fred Scott, Victoria Vinton, Cliff Nazarro
Some bandits try to steal money from a pretty blonde and have to battle with a cowboy hero who rides to the damsel's rescue.
Republic — *Video Yesteryear*

Single Bars, Single Women   1984
Comedy-Drama
86859   100 mins   C   B, V   P
Shelley Hack, Christine Lahti, Tony Danza, Mare Winningham
A made-for-TV film about the trials and tribulations of the denizens of a particular singles bar. Title song by Dolly Parton.
Carsey-Werner Co.; Sunn Classic; ABC — *Prism*

Single Room Furnished   1968
Drama
84819   93 mins   C   B, V   P
Jayne Mansfield, Dorothy Keller
The fall of a buxom blonde, from uncorrupted innocence, to desperate prostitution. Mansfield's final film.
Michael Musto — *United Home Video*

Singleton's Pluck   1984
Comedy
84264   89 mins   C   B, V   P
Ian Holm
A touching comedy about a determined farmer who must walk his 500 geese 100 miles to market.
New World Pictures — *New World Video*

Sinister Invasion   1970
Horror
85536   95 mins   C   B, V   P
Boris Karloff
A turn-of-the-century scientist discovers a death ray. One of Karloff's last films; the original release was delayed from 1968. Also known as "The Incredible Invasion."
EL, SP
Spanish — *Unicorn Video*

Sinister Journey   1948
Western
81608   58 mins   B/W   B, V   P
William Boyd, Andy Clyde, Rand Brooks
Hopalong Cassidy, Lucky, and California help clear an ex-con's name who has been wrongly accused of murder.
United Artists — *Buena Vista Home Video*

Sioux City Sue   1946
Western/Musical
44805   69 mins   B/W   B, V   P, T
Gene Autry, Lynne Roberts, Sterling Holloway
Talent scouts are looking for a singing cowboy, find Gene, then trick him into being the voice of a talking donkey.
Republic — *Blackhawk Films; Video Connection*

Siouxsie and the Banshees   1984
Music-Performance
70917   60 mins   C   B, V   P
Siouxsie, the Banshees
Billed as the "reigning queen of nightmare rock," this tape captures a live Siouxsie show including performances of "Israel," "Cascade," "Nightshift," "Spellbound" and others in Hi-Fi Dolby Stereo sound.
S&B Productions — *Music Media*

Siouxsie and the Banshees   1985
Music video
88106   30 mins   C   B, V   P
The irrefutably strange English new wave group's video hits, including "Hong Kong Gardens," "Scream" and "Carcass."
Sony Video — *Sony Video Software*

Sir Arthur Conan Doyle   1927
Literature-English/Biographical
59411   11 mins   B/W   B, V   P, T
An intimate portrait of the man who created Sherlock Holmes.
Unknown — *Blackhawk Films*

Sirocco   1951
War-Drama
85285   111 mins   B/W   B, V   P
Humphrey Bogart, Lee J. Cobb, Zero Mostel, Everett Sloane, Gerald Mohr
An American gun-runner stuck in Syria and a French colonel find they must rely on each other amidst civil war.
Robert Lord — *RCA/Columbia Pictures Home Video*

Sister Kenny   1946
Drama
10061   116 mins   B/W   B, V   P, T
Rosalind Russell, Dean Jagger, Alexander Knox

Follows story of legendary nurse crusading for her treatment of infantile paralysis. Based on Elizabeth Kenny's novel, "And They Shall Walk."
RKO; Dudley Nichols — *Blackhawk Films*

Sisters 1973
Horror
53521   93 mins   C   B, V   P
Margot Kidder, Charles Durning, directed by Brian DePalma
Siamese twins separated at birth are involved in a murder and the wrong one is arrested.
MPAA:R
American International; Edward R Pressman — *Warner Home Video*

Sisters of Death 1978
Suspense
48415   87 mins   C   B, V   P
Arthur Franz, Claudia Jennings
Five women who were once members of a secret club are invited to a reunion at a remote castle in California. There they are trapped by an evil man on the edge of madness.
MPAA:PG
John B Kelly Presentations — *United Home Video*

Sitting Ducks 1980
Comedy
66066   88 mins   C   B, V   P
Michael Emil, Zack Norman, directed by Henry Jaglom
Two friends involved in a scam attempt to outrun the moball the while swapping songs and confessions.
MPAA:R
Meira Attia Dor — *Media Home Entertainment*

Six-Gun Previews, Volume 1 194?
Movie and TV trailers
87668   58 mins   B/W   B, V   P
Tex Ritter, Johnny Mack Brown, Gene Autry, Lash LaRue
A conglomeration of B Western previews starring many favorite low budget cowboys.
Captain Bijou; Various producers — *Captain Bijou*

Six Pack 1982
Adventure
63396   108 mins   C   B, V, CED   P
Kenny Rogers, Diane Lane, Erin Gray, Barry Corbin
Rogers stars as Brewster Baker, who returns to the stock car racing circuit with the help of six larcenous orphans adept at mechanics.
MPAA:PG
Kenny Loggins Productions — *CBS/Fox Video*

Six Shootin' Sheriff 1938
Western
11374   59 mins   B/W   B, V   P
Ken Maynard
A member of a wild gang redeems himself and turns sheriff to make up for all his evil ways.
Worldwide — *United Home Video; Video Yesteryear; Video Connection*

Six Weeks 1982
Comedy-Drama
68268   107 mins   C   B, V   P
Dudley Moore, Mary Tyler Moore, Katherine Healy
Two opposite people are brought together by the illness of a little girl.
MPAA:PG
Peter Guber; Jon Peters — *RCA/Columbia Pictures Home Video; RCA VideoDiscs*

Sixteen 1985
Drama
82409   90 mins   C   B, V   P
Mercedes McCambridge, Ford Rainey, Simone Griffeth, Beverly Powers, John Lozier
A naive country lass is attracted to the glitter and hum of the outside world. Although she is disillusioned about love early on in her new spere, her determination and optimism help her triumph over her lost illusions.
MPAA:R
New World Video — *New World Video*

Sixteen Candles 1984
Comedy
73183   93 mins   C   B, V, LV   P
Molly Ringwald, Paul Dooley, Anthony Michael Hall, directed by John Hughes
Molly Ringwald stars as a young girl who has just turned sweet sixteen and no one remembers her birthday. Title song performed by The Stray Cats.
MPAA:PG
Hilton A Green; Universal — *MCA Home Video*

16 Days of Glory 1984
Sports
Closed Captioned
86155   145 mins   C   B, V   P
The official document of the 1984 Summer Olympics in Los Angeles. In stereo.
Bud Greenspan; Paramount — *Paramount Home Video*

$64,000 Question 195?
Game show
58636   29 mins   B/W   B, V, FO   P
Hosted by Hal March
This episode of the classic show which ushered in the big-money quiz game features a Philippine-American lady lawyer who decides to keep her money, Virgil Earp (Wyatt's nephew) winning $32,000 in the Wild West category, and

a Brooklyn woman winning $4,000 in the opera category. Sponsored by Revlon.
CBS — *Video Yesteryear*

Sizzle   1981
Drama
79194   100 mins   C   B, V   P
Loni Anderson, John Forsythe, Leslie Uggams, Roy Thinnes, Richard Lynch
When a nightclub singer's boyfriend is murdered by the mob, she stops at nothing to get revenge.
Aaron Spelling Productions — *Prism*

Skateboard Madness   198?
Sports
75584   92 mins   C   B, V   P
This program offers a tour of skating spots and performing skateboarding celebrities.
MPAA:PG
Unknown — *Monterey Home Video*

Skeezer   1982
Drama
71305   96 mins   C   B, V   P
Karen Valentine, Leighton Greer, Mariclare Costello, Tom Atkins, Justin Lord, Jeremy Licht, Dee Wallace, Jack DeMave, Christina Hutter, directed by Peter Hunt
This film tells the story of a dog that helps emotionally disturbed children within an institution overcome their problems. Based on "Skeezer, Dog With a Mission," by Elizabeth Yates.
Margie Lee Enterprises; The Blue Marble Co; ITC Prods — *U.S.A. Home Video*

Ski   1978
Sports-Winter
44923   30 mins   C   B, V   P
Fitness expert Ann Dugan demonstrates exercises for skiers which show how to exert constant muscular effort to maintain body position, move with agility, and avoid injury. From the "Sports Conditioning" series.
Health N Action — *RCA/Columbia Pictures Home Video*

Ski Champions—The   1986
Winners
Sports-Winter/Documentary
71226   30 mins   C   V   P
Hosted by David Soul and Suzy Chaffee
This made-for-video feature looks at the competitive efforts of several professional skiers including: Carey Adgate, Jarle Halsnes, Dave Stapleton, Franz Weber and Marty Martin Kunz
Prism Video Collection — *Prism*

Ski Country   1985
Adventure
82440   90 mins   C   B, V   P

Produced by Warren Miller
Intrepid skiers risk their limbs on slopes in Aspen, Colorado; Chamonix, France; and New Zealand in this adventure film.
MPAA:G
Warren Miller Productions — *Vestron Video*

Ski Country   1985
Sports-Winter
84403   93 mins   C   B, V   P
Bill Johnson, Tom Simms, Phil and Steve Mahre
This beautifully shot film by Warren Miller, features Olympic champions skiing all over the world.
Warren Miller — *Karl/Lorimar Home Video*

Ski Time   1984
Sports-Winter
80425   102 mins   C   B, V   P
A documentary that features exciting skiing competitions from New Zealand and France.
Warren Miller Enterprises — *Karl/Lorimar Home Video*

Skin Game   1971
Comedy
80957   102 mins   C   B, V   P
James Garner, Lou Gossett, Susan Clark, Ed Asner, Andrew Duggan, directed by Paul Bogart
A fast talking bunco-artist and his black partner travel throughout the pre-Civil War South while setting-up the ultimate con.
MPAA:PG
Warner Bros. — *Warner Home Video*

Skullduggery   1969
Horror
77520   95 mins   C   B, V   P
Thom Haverstock, Wendy Crewson, David Calderisi
A grop of medieval game players suffer through a night of unspeakable horror when a secret evil force spoils their good clean fun.
MPAA:PG
Peter Wittman; Ota Richter — *Media Home Entertainment*

Sky High   1973
Aeronautics
57195   59 mins   C   B, V   P
The Air Force Thunderbirds
This program traces the history of pylon racing, from the first track at Theims, France, in 1909, to the Cleveland Air Races. The program provides aerobatics, wing walking, barnstorming, gliding, sky diving, hang gliding, ballooning, and just about every kind of flying imaginable.
AM Available
Manuel Arango — *Alti Corporation*

Sky High 1984
Adventure/Comedy
82193   103 mins   C   B, V   P
Daniel Hirsch, Clayton Norcross, Frank Schultz, Lauren Taylor
Three college students become immersed in international intrigue when the C.I.A. and the K.G.B. pursue them through Greece looking for a secret Soviet tape. Available in VHS and Beta Hi-Fi Stereo.
Omega Pictures — *Lightning Video*

Sky Is Gray, The 1980
Drama
84035   46 mins   C   B, V   P
Olivia Cole, James Bono III, directed by Stan Lathan
A young Louisiana black boy journeys with his mother to the dentist, and on the way is confronted with racism, poverty and social differentiation. Based on a story by Ernest Gaines.
Whitney Green — *Monterey Home Video*

Skyline 1984
Comedy
77303   84 mins   C   B, V   P
Antonio Resines, Beatriz Perez-Porro
A Spanish photographer comes to New York City to become a staff photographer on a magazine.
Fernando Colombo — *Pacific Arts Video*

Sky's The Limit, The 1943
Comedy
43017   89 mins   B/W   B, V   P
Fred Astaire, Joan Leslie
A war hero spends his leave in New York City dressed in civilian clothes and falls in love.
RKO; David Hempstead — *RKO HomeVideo; Video Yesteryear; King of Video; Nostalgia Merchant*

Slap, The 1976
Comedy
65721   103 mins   C   CED   P
Isabelle Adjani, Lino Ventura
This program is meant to express the problems of adults and young people when they arrive at certain equinoxes in their lives.
MPAA:PG
Joseph Green — *Embassy Home Entertainment (disc only)*

Slap Shot 1977
Comedy-Drama
14005   123 mins   C   B, V, LV   P
Paul Newman, Michael Ontkean, Jennifer Warren, Lindsay Crouse, Strother Martin, directed by George Roy Hill
A satire of the world of professional hockey. An over-the-hill player-coach gathers an odd-ball mixture of has-beens and young players and reluctantly initiates using violence on the ice to make his team win.
MPAA:R
Universal; Robert J Wunsch; Stephen Friedman — *MCA Home Video*

Slapstick 193?
Comedy
80466   76 mins   B/W   B, V   P
Charlie Chaplin, Harold Lloyd, Charlie Chase, Buster Keaton, Ben Turpin, Stan Laurel
An anthology of great moments from Mack Sennett comedy shorts, featuring many great stars in some of their earliest film appearances.
Mack Sennett — *Spotlite Video*

Slapstick of Another Kind 1984
Comedy
66607   85 mins   C   B, V, LV   P
Jerry Lewis, Madeline Kahn, Marty Feldman, Jim Backus
Jerry Lewis and Madeline Kahn play dual roles as an alien brother and sister and their adoptive Earth parents, who are being pursued by U.S. agents.
MPAA:PG
S Paul Company — *Vestron Video*

Slasher, The 1974
Mystery
77233   88 mins   C   B, V   P
Farley Granger, Sylva Koscina, Susan Scott
A policeman must find the madman who has been killing off unfaithful married women.
Eugene Falorismot — *Monterey Home Video*

Slaughter in San Francisco 1981
Martial arts
81471   92 mins   C   B, V   P
Chuck Norris, Don Wong
A Chinese-American cop leads a one-man fight against corruption in the San Francisco police department.
MPAA:R
World Northal Corporation — *Embassy Home Entertainment*

Slaughterhouse Five 1972
Science fiction/Folklore
62728   104 mins   C   B, V   P
Michael Sacks, Ron Leibman, Valerie Perrine
A suburban optometrist comes unstuck in time and he experiences events during World War II, in the future on an alien planet and even his own death.
AM Available MPAA:R
Universal — *MCA Home Video*

Slave of Love, A 1978
Drama
80883   94 mins   C   B, V   P

*Elena Solovei, Rodion Nakhapetov, Alexander
Kalyagin, directed by Nikita Mikhalkov*
A beautiful young actress falls in love with her
cameraman during the Russian Revolution. With
English subtitles.
RU
Mosfilm Studio — *RCA/Columbia Pictures
Home Video*

Slave of the Cannibal God   1979
Adventure
59300   86 mins   C   CED   P
Stacy Keach, Ursula Andress, Claudio Cassinelli
A beautiful woman, searching for her missing
husband in the jungles of New Guinea, hires a
man bent on revenge against the human-eating
cannibals as her guide.
MPAA:R
Dania Film — *Vestron Video*

Slaves of Love   197?
Drama
59549   86 mins   C   B, V   P
Two men, stranded on a desert island, discover
it is inhabited by sex-starved females.
Dave Ackerman — *Media Home Entertainment*

Slayground   1984
Suspense
77165   85 mins   C   B, V   P
Peter Coyote
A grieving father is out to get the man who
accidentally murdered his daughter.
MPAA:R
Universal Pictures — *THORN EMI/HBO Video*

Sleazemania   1985
Horror
70674   60 mins   C   B, V   P
This compilation of trailers 'n bits reviews some
of the sleazier, sicker, and sexier selections of
celluloid from the past 50-years.
Johnny Legend — *Rhino Video*

Sleazemania Strikes Back   1985
Movie and TV trailers/Exploitation
84352   60 mins   C   B, V   P
A scintillating array of sleazy scenes from the
world's worst movies.
Impulse Ent — *Rhino Video*

Sleazemania--The Special Edition   1972
Exploitation
88178   18 mins   B/W   B, V   P
A tantalizing glimpse of smutty, exploitive and
bad film clips, from directors like auteur
provocateur Edward D. Wood Jr., and including
"Orgy of the Dead," "The Flesh Merchants,"
"The Smut Peddler," and the like.

Various producers; Rhino Video — *Rhino
Video*

Sleep of Death   1979
Horror
71194   90 mins   C   B, V   P
*Brendan Price, Marilyn Tolo, Patrick Magee,
Curt Jurgens, Per Oscarsson, directed by Calvin
Floyd*
A young English fellow's pursuit of a hot blue-
blooded woman seems to set off a series of
bizarre and mysterious murders. A gothic thriller
based on Sheridan Le Fanu's short story.
British — *Prism*

Sleepaway Camp   1983
Horror
76864   88 mins   C   B, V   P
*Mike Kellin, Jonathan Tiersten, Felissa Rose,
Christopher Collet*
A crazed killer hacks away at the inhabitants of
a peaceful summer camp.
MPAA:R
Robert Hiltzik — *Media Home Entertainment*

Sleeper   1973
Comedy/Science fiction
64331   88 mins   C   B, V   P
*Woody Allen, Diane Keaton, John Beck,
directed by Woody Allen*
A New York schnook is frozen solid after a
botched operation and revived two hundred
years in the future, where he inadvertently gets
mixed up with the political underground.
MPAA:PG
United Artists — *CBS/Fox Video; RCA
VideoDiscs*

Sleeping Beauty   1983
Fairy tales
Closed Captioned
69322   60 mins   C   B, V, LV,   P
                  CED
*Christopher Reeve, Bernadette Peters, Beverly
D'Angelo*
The classic tale of Sleeping Beauty and the
handsome prince who wakens her is told by
combining live action and animation. Part of
"Faerie Tale Theatre."
Shelley Duvall — *CBS/Fox Video*

Sleeping Beauty   1982
Dance
76677   120 mins   C   B, V   P
*Fernando Bujones, Maryse Egasse, Berthica
Prieto, Elba Rey, the Corps de Ballet and
soloists of the Ballet del Teatro*
This made-for-video production of the
Tchaikovsky ballet was taped live at the Ballet
del Teatro Municipal in Santiago, Chile and is a
recreation of the 1939 Sadler's Wells staging.
Kultur — *Kultur*

Sleeping Beauty, The　　1984
Dance
81178　135 mins　C　　B, V　　　　P
Irina Kolpakova, Sergei Berezhnoi, conducted by Victor Fedotov
This is the Kirov Ballet's version of the classic Tchaikovsky ballet as choreographed by Marius Petipa. Available in VHS Hi-Fi and Beta Hi-Fi Stereo.
National Video Corporation Ltd. — *THORN EMI/HBO Video*

Sleeping Dogs　　1982
Drama
65729　107 mins　C　　B, V　　　　P
Sam Neill, Warren Oates
A man is caught between two powers: a repressive government and a violent resistance movement.
Roger Donaldson — *VidAmerica*

Sleuth　　1972
Suspense/Mystery
37413　138 mins　C　　B, V　　　　P
Sir Laurence Olivier, Michael Caine, Margo Channing, directed by Joseph L. Mankiewicz
A mystery novelist takes his work to the limits by playing diabolical and deadly tricks on his guest.
MPAA:PG
20th Century Fox — *Media Home Entertainment*

Slightly Honorable　　1939
Mystery
08720　85 mins　B/W　　B, V　　　　P
Pat O'Brien, Broderick Crawford, Edward Arnold, Eve Arden, directed by Tay Barnett
Crime in high society and police grafters, as a lawyer tangles with crooked politics.
United Artists; Walter Wanger — *Video Yesteryear; Movie Buff Video; Kartes Video Communications*

Slightly Pregnant Man, A　　1979
Comedy
77010　92 mins　C　　B, V　　　　P
Catherine Deneuve, Marcello Mastroianni
Comic complications abound as a construction worker becomes the world's first pregnant man.
S.J. International Pictures — *VidAmerica*

Slightly Scarlet　　1956
Mystery
80803　99 mins　C　　B, V　　　　P
Rhonda Fleming, Arlene Dahl, John Payne, Kent Taylor, Ted deCorsia, directed by Allan Dwan
An ambitious gang leader tries to take over a city government by using blackmail and double crossing his best friend.
RKO — *Buena Vista Home Video*

Slim and Trim Yoga with Billie In Pool　　1983
Yoga/Physical fitness
76403　24 mins　C　　B, V, 3/4U　　　P
This entertaining and instructional program presents a system of exercises and meditation in the water.
Billie C Lange — *Billie C. Lange*

Slim and Trim Yoga with Billie Out of Pool　　1983
Yoga/Physical fitness
76404　24 mins　C　　B, V, 3/4U　　　P
This entertaining and instructional program presents a system of exercises and meditation out of the pool.
Billie C Lange — *Billie C. Lange*

Slim Gourmet, The　　1984
Cookery
72901　90 mins　C　　B, V　　　　P
Barbara Gibbons, narrated by McLean Stevenson
Barbara Gibbons demonstrates the preparation of gourmet dishes that are low in calories.
Media Home Entertainment — *Media Home Entertainment*

Slime People　　1963
Horror
58547　76 mins　B/W　　B, V　　　R, P
Robert Hutton, Les Tremayne, Robert Burton
Huge prehistoric monsters are let loose by an atomic explosion in Los Angeles.
Hansen Pictures — *Video Gems*

Slithis　　1979
Science fiction
42911　86 mins　C　　B, V　　　　P
This science fiction thriller has nature unleashing its revenge from the pollution of nuclear waste. Slithis was the killer they could not destroy.
EL, SP
Dick Davis — *Media Home Entertainment*

Sloane　　1984
Adventure
71131　95 mins　C　　B, V　　　　P
Robert Resnick, Debra Blee, Paul Aragon, directed by Dan Rosenthal
Bad guys swipe Sloane's girlfriend and take her to Manila. Angry, Sloane pursues her; and he's a vengeful kung fu killer.
Skouras Pictures — *Vestron Video*

Slugger's Wife, The　　1985
Comedy-Drama
Closed Captioned
81798　105 mins　C　　B, V　　　　P

*Michael O'Keefe, Rebecca De Mornay, Martin
Ritt, Randy Quaid, Loudon Wainwright 3rd,
directed by Hal Ashby*
The marriage between an Atlanta Braves
outfielder and a rock singer suddenly turns sour
when their individual careers force them to
make some tough choices. In VHS Dolby Hi-Fi
Stereo and Beta Hi-Fi Stereo.
MPAA:PG-13
Ray Stark; Columbia
Pictures — *RCA/Columbia Pictures Home
Video*

Slumber Party '57   1976
Comedy
55745   83 mins   C   B, V, LV   P
At a slumber party, six girls get together and
exchange stories of how they lost their virginity.
Music by the Platters, Big Bopper, Jerry Lee
Lewis, the Crewcuts, and Paul and Paula.
Unknown — *Vestron Video*

Slumber Party Massacre,   1982
The
Horror
80773   84 mins   C   B, V   P
*Michele Michaels, Robin Stille, Andre Honore,
Michael Villela*
A psychotic killer wielding a large drill terrorizes
a high school girls' slumber party.
MPAA:R
Santa Fe Productions — *Embassy Home
Entertainment*

Small Change   1976
Comedy
54804   104 mins   C   B, V   P
*Geory Desmouceaux, Philippe Goldman, Jean-
Francois Stevenin, Chantal Mercier, Francis
Devlaeminck, directed by Francois Truffaut*
"Small Change" captures the precious feeling
of what it is like to be a child. It consists of a
series of anecdotes, conversations, vignettes,
and reflections—all spinning around the
triumphs, frustrations, and intimate longings of a
group of French children.
MPAA:PG
New World Pictures; Roger Corman — *Warner
Home Video*

Small Killing, A   1981
Drama/Mystery
71301   96 mins   C   B, V   P
*Edward Asner, Jean Simmons, Andrew Prine, J
Pat O'Malley, Sylvia Sidney, Mary Jackson,
directed by Steven Hilliard Stern*
A female college professor and an undercover
cop join forces with a band of elderly street
people in an effort to bag a killer. Based on the
book by Richard Barth.
Orgolini-Nelson Productions;
Motown — *U.S.A. Home Video*

Small One, The   1978
Christmas/Cartoons
70936   45 mins   C   B, V   P
Animated
A poor boy must sell his beloved donkey, "Small
One," on the eve of the first Christmas in
Bethlehem. Included with this touching tale are
three Disney shorts: "Winter," "Feliz Navidad"
and "Arctic Antics."
Walt Disney Productions — *Walt Disney Home
Video*

Small Town in Texas, A   1976
Drama
64359   96 mins   C   B, V, CED   P
Timothy Bottoms, Susan George, Bo Hopkins
An ex-con returns home seeking revenge on the
sheriff who framed him.
MPAA:PG
American International — *Vestron Video*

Smash Palace   1982
Drama
65363   100 mins   C   B, V   P
*Bruno Lawrence, Anna Jemison, Greer Robson,
Keith Aberdein*
Smash Palace is a compelling drama of a
marriage jeopardized by a man's obsession with
auto racing, and a women's need for love and
affection.
Roger Donaldson — *Vestron Video*

Smash-Up   1947
Drama
05481   103 mins   B/W   B, V   P
*Susan Hayward, Lee Bowman, Marsha Hunt,
Eddie Albert*
A famous singer becomes an alcoholic, and her
constant drunkenness drives her husband and
child away.
United Artists — *Movie Buff Video; Prism;
Discount Video Tapes; World Video Pictures*

Smashin' the Palace '84   1984
Music-Performance
71017   59 mins   C   B, V   P
*King Sunny Ade, Dennis Brown, Musical Youth,
Skatalites*
This version of Jamaica's "Reggae Sunsplash"
brought the sounds of ska to England's Crystal
Palace Football Stadium as part of the Capital
Radio Music Festival.
Island — *Passport Music Video*

Smashing of the Reich,   1962
The
World War II
42962   84 mins   B/W   B, V, FO   P
This program examines the fall of the German
war machine with emphasis on air power.

Unknown — *Video Yesteryear; International Historic Films; Discount Video Tapes; Interurban Films*

Smiles of a Summer Night
1955
Comedy-Drama
88354   108 mins   B/W   B, V   P
Gunnar Bjornstrand, Harriet Andersson, Ulla Jacobsson, Eva Dahlbeck, Margit Carlquist, directed by Ingmar Bergman
Bergman's first success, this is a hilarious and sharp satire about eight Swedish aristocrats who become romantically and comically intertwined during a single weekend. A much-copied classic. Subtitled.
SW
Svensk Filmindustri — *Embassy Home Entertainment*

Smilin' Through
1941
Drama
82122   101 mins   C   B, V   P
Jeanette MacDonald, Brian Aherne, Gene Raymond, Ian Hunter, Frances Robinson
This is the rare technicolor edition of the film about the romance that develops between an orphaned girl and the son of a murderer.
MGM — *MGM/UA Home Video*

Smithereens
1982
Drama
79221   90 mins   C   B, V   P
Susan Berman, Brad Rinn, Richard Hell, directed by Susan Seidelman
A working-class girl leaves home and heads to New York City to become a rock and roll singer.
MPAA:R
New Line Cinema — *Media Home Entertainment*

Smoke in the Wind
1971
Western
82212   93 mins   C   B, V   P
John Ashley, Walter Brennan, John Russell, Myron Healy
Two young men wage a battle of vengeance against the Southern Raiders who murdered their father.
MPAA:PG
Hughes Bros; Productions — *Prism*

Smokey and the Bandit
1977
Comedy
14008   96 mins   C   B, V, LV   P
Burt Reynolds, Sally Field, Jackie Gleason, Jerry Reed, Mike Henry, directed by Hal Needham
A legendary truck driver and CB radio fanatic gives a lift to a female hitchhiker and sets off a crazy chain of events climaxing in a wild car chase.

MPAA:PG
Universal; Mort Engleberg — *MCA Home Video; RCA VideoDiscs*

Smokey and the Bandit II
1980
Comedy
48637   101 mins   C   B, V, LV   P
Burt Reynolds, Sally Field, Jackie Gleason, Jerry Reed, Mike Henry
The sequel to "Smokey and the Bandit." The Bandit is hired to transport a pregnant elephant from Miami to the Republican convention in Dallas. Sheriff Buford T. Justice and family are in hot pursuit.
MPAA:PG
Universal — *MCA Home Video*

Smokey Bites the Dust
1981
Comedy
87616   87 mins   C   B, V   P
Janet Julian, Jimmy McNichol, directed by Charles B. Griffith
Written by Max Apple, this car-smashing gagfest deals with a sheriff's daughter who is kidnapped by her smitten beau.
MPAA:PG
Roger Corman — *Charter Entertainment*

Smooth Talk
1985
Drama
86352   92 mins   C   B, V, LV   P
Laura Dern, Treat Williams, Mary Kay Place, Levon Helm, directed by Joyce Chopra
Based on a Joyce Carol Oates short story, this acclaimed film deals with a flirtatious California high school student and the potentially dangerous stranger she innocently attracts.
MPAA:PG-13
International Spectrafilm Dist. — *Vestron Video*

Smouldering Fires
1925
Drama
65199   100 mins   B/W   B, V   P
Pauline Frederick, Laura La Plante, Tully Marshall, directed by Clarence Brown
A tough businesswoman falls in love with an ambitious young employee, who is fifteen years younger than her. After they marry, problems arise in the form of the wife's attractive younger sister.
Universal Jewel — *Video Yesteryear*

Smuggler's Cove
1983
Adventure
81917   75 mins   C   B, V   P
A young boy doggedly pursues a mysterious trawler captain despite warnings from his parents.
Andromedia Prods — *VidAmerica*

Smurfs and the Magic 1981
Flute, The
Cartoons
65376 74 mins C B, V, LV, P
  CED
Animated
The Smurfs star in this musical tale about a flute
with magical powers.
MPAA:G
Hanna Barbera Sepp
International — *Children's Video Library*

Snake People, The 1968
Horror
85539 90 mins C B, V P
Boris Karloff, Julissa, Carlos East
A police captain investigates a small island
littered with LSD-experimenting scientists,
snake-worshippers and voodoo.
EL, SP
Jack Hill/Spanish — *Unicorn Video*

Sno-Line 1985
Crime-Drama
84099 89 mins C B, V P
*Vince Edwards, Paul Smith, June Wilkinson,
directed by Douglas F. Oneans*
A New York gangster moves to Texas and
begins to wipe out the competition on his way to
building his drug and gambling dynasty.
MPAA:R
Vavom International — *Lightning Video*

Snoopy, Come Home 1972
Cartoons
Closed Captioned
78886 80 mins C B, V P
Animated
Snoopy leaves his owner Charlie Brown to visit
his former owner Lila in the hospital and returns
with her to her apartment house.
Cinema Center Films — *Playhouse Video*

Snow Creature 1954
Horror
76915 72 mins B/W B, V P
Paul Langton, Leslie Denison
When a troop of explorers bring back a snow
creature from the Himalayas he escapes in the
United States and wreaks havoc to the
countryside.
United Artists — *United Home Video*

Snow Queen, The 1982
Dance
70807 85 mins C B, V P
*Janet Lynn, John Curry, Sandra Bezic, Jo Jo
Starbuck, Dorothy Hamill, Toller Cranston,
directed by John Thompson*
Music by Glazunov, Mussorgsky and Rimsky-
Korsakov combines with Jean Pierre
Bonnefoux's ice choreography in this setting of
the Hans Christian Andersen tale.

PBS; Bernice Olenick — *Buena Vista Home
Video*

Snow Queen, The 1984
Fairy tales
Closed Captioned
73570 60 mins C B, V, CED P
Melissa Gilbert, Lee Remick, Lance Kerwin
From "Fairy Tale Theatre" comes the
adaptation of the Hans Christian Andersen tale
about a boy and a girl who grow up together and
are separated by evil spirits.
Gaylord Productions; Platypus
Productions — *CBS/Fox Video*

Snow Treasure 1967
Adventure
66624 96 mins C B, V P
*James Franciscus, Ilona Rodgers, Paul Austad,
Raoul Oyen*
A group of children work to keep the Nazis from
finding a cache of gold that is hidden in their
Norwegian village. Filmed on location.
MPAA:PG
Sagittarius Productions — *U.S.A. Home Video*

Snow White and the 1984
Seven Dwarfs
Fairy tales
Closed Captioned
73855 60 mins C B, V, LV, P
  CED
*Elizabeth McGovern, Rex Smith, Vincent Price,
Vanessa Redgrave, directed by Peter Medak*
From "Faerie Tale Theatre" comes the story of
a princess who befriends seven little men to
protect her from the jealous evil Queen.
Gaylord Productions; Platypus
Productions — *CBS/Fox Video*

Snow White and the 1961
Three Stooges
Comedy
Closed Captioned
81554 108 mins C B, V P
*Moe Howard, Curley Howard, Larry Fine, Carol
Heiss, Patricia Medina, directed by Walter Lang*
The Stooges fill in for the Seven Dwarfs when
they go off prospecting in King Solomon's mines
in this adaptation of the fairy tale. Available in
VHS and Beta Hi-Fi.
20th Century Fox — *Playhouse Video*

Snow White Christmas 1980
Cartoons
78901 60 mins C B, V P
The wicked stepmother vows revenge against
Queen Snow White, King Charming, and their
daughter Young Snow White as she plans to
open a Christmas Castle for the children of the
kingdom.
Filmation — *Prism*

Snow White Live at Radio City Music Hall 1980
Variety
55569   90 mins   C   B, V   P
Disney's film classic has been transformed into a stage show presented at New York City's Radio City Music Hall. The original music remains intact and a finale has been added.
Walt Disney — *Walt Disney Home Video*

Snowball Express 1972
Comedy
63125   120 mins   C   B, V   P
Dean Jones, Nancy Olson, Harry Morgan, Keenan Wynn
When a New York City accountant inherits a hotel in the Rocky Mountains, he decides to move his family there. Upon arrival, they find that the place is falling apart.
MPAA:G
Walt Disney Productions — *Walt Disney Home Video*

Snowbeast 1977
Horror/Drama
81419   96 mins   C   B, V   P
Bo Swenson, Yvette Mimieux, Sylvia Sidney, Clint Walker, Robert Logan
The residents of a ski resort are being terrorized by a half-human, half-animal beast who is leaving a path of dead bodies behind.
Douglas Cramer Prods. — *Worldvision Home Video*

Snowman, The 1982
Cartoons
76673   26 mins   C   B, V   P
This program presents an animated story of a snowman who comes to life.
Snowman Enterprises LTD — *Sony Video Software*

SnoWonder 1985
Sports-Winter/Documentary
81716   98 mins   C   B, V   P
This film takes you to great skiing spots around the world from Chile's Portillo ridges to the precipices of Jackson Hole, Wyoming.
Warren Miller — *Karl/Lorimar Home Video*

So Dear to My Heart 1949
Drama
86788   82 mins   C   B, V   P
Bobby Driscoll, Burl Ives, Beulah Bondi, Harry Carey, Luana Patten
A farm boy and his misfit black sheep wreak havoc at the county fair. Several sequences combine live action with animation. Features the hit song, "Lavender Blue (Dilly, Dilly)."
Walt Disney Prods — *Walt Disney Home Video*

So Fine 1981
Comedy
47395   91 mins   C   B, V   P
Ryan O'Neal, Jack Warden, Mariangela Melato, Richard Kiel, directed by Andrew Bergman
Ryan O'Neal is a pants manufacturer who invents cellophane pants. Orders pour in for the new peekaboo style and zaniness ensues.
MPAA:R
Warner Bros; Mike Lobell — *Warner Home Video*

Soap Sampler, A 1955
Drama
85490   76 mins   B/W   B, V   P
Frances Reid, Pegg McCay, Susan Douglas, Peter Hobbs, Mary Stuart
This tape features one episode apiece from each of these vintage soap operas: "Portia Faces Life," "Love of Life," "The Guiding Light," "The Secret Storm" and "Search for Tomorrow."
CBS — *Video Yesteryear*

S.O.B. 1981
Comedy
53554   121 mins   C   B, V, CED   P
Julie Andrews, William Holden, Richard Mulligan, Robert Preston, Shelley Winters, Robert Webber, Marisa Berenson, Robert Vaughn, Larry Hagman
Blake Edwards' bitter farce about Hollywood and the film industry wheelers and dealers who inhabit it. When a multi-million dollar picture bombs at the box office, the director turns suicidal, until he envisions reshooting it with a steamy, X-rated scene starring his wife, a star with a goody-two-shoes image.
MPAA:R
Blake Edwards; Tony Adams — *CBS/Fox Video*

Sodom and Gomorrah 1979
Drama/Bible
55012   49 mins   C   B, V   P
Ed Ames, Dorothy Malone, Peter Mark Richman, Rick Jason, David Opatoshu, Gene Barry, narrated by Victor Jory
The story of Lot and his wife and the sinful cities of Sodom and Gomorrah. Part of the "Greatest Heroes of the Bible" series.
Sunn Classics — *Magnum Entertainment; Vanguard Video; Lucerne Films*

Soft Cell 1983
Music-Performance
66022   55 mins   C   B, V   P
"Tainted Love" and "Memorabilia" are two of the hits performed by this talented new band.
EMI Music — *THORN EMI/HBO Video*

Soft Skin, The 1964
Drama
87332   118 mins   B/W   B, V   P
*Jean Desailly, Nelly Benedetti, Francoise
Dorleac, directed by Francois Truffaut*
A classic portrayal of marital infidelity by the
master director, wherein a businessman has an
affair with a stewardess. After the affair ends, he
is confronted by his wife.
Roissy — *Key Video*

Soggy Bottom U.S.A. 1984
Comedy
79196   90 mins   C   B, V   P
*Ben Johnson, Dub Taylor, Ann Wedgeworth,
Lois Nettleton, Anthony Zerbe*
A sheriff has his hands full trying to keep the law
enforced in a small Southern town.
Independent — *Prism*

Soldier, The 1982
Drama
63370   90 mins   C   B, V, CED   P
Ken Wahl, Klaus Kinski
The Russians are holding the world at ransom
with a pile of stolen plutonium, and a soldier
finds himself in the position to carry out an
unauthorized and dangerous plan to preserve
the balance of world power.
MPAA:R
Embassy — *Embassy Home Entertainment*

Soldier Blue 1970
Western
13665   109 mins   C   B, V, CED   P
*Candice Bergen, Peter Strauss, Donald
Pleasance, Dana Elcar, directed by Ralph
Nelson*
A western adventure about a U.S. Calvary unit
escorting gold across Cheyenne territory.
MPAA:R
Avco Embassy — *Embassy Home
Entertainment*

Soldier in the Rain 1963
Comedy-Drama
Closed Captioned
82241   88 mins   B/W   B, V   PP
*Steve McQueen, Jackie Gleason, Tuesday
Weld, Tony Bill, Tom Poston, directed by Ralph
Nelson*
An unusual friendship develops between a
wheeler-dealer army sergeant and a simple-
minded soldier. Available in VHS and Beta Hi-Fi.
Allied Artists — *Key Video*

Soldier of Orange, A 1978
War-Drama/Adventure
71177   144 mins   C   B, V   P
*Rutger Hauer, Jeroen Krabbe, Edward Fox,
Susan Penhaligon, directed by Paul Verhoeven*
This film, based on the true-life exploits of Erik
Hazelhoff, follows a Dutch resistance leader as

he and his compatriots prepare for the allied
invasion of Holland.
Rob Houwer — *Media Home Entertainment*

Soldier of the Night 1984
Drama
81506   89 mins   C   B, V   P
Two young people fall in love in the war torn
area of Tel Aviv.
Cannon Productions — *MGM/UA Home Video*

Soldier's Home 1977
Literature-American
16857   42 mins   C   B, V   P
*Richard Backus, Nancy Marchand, Robert
McIlwaine, Lisa Essary, Mark LaMura*
Ernest Hemingway's story of a soldier who
returns from World War I and finds he can no
longer fit into the life he left. From the
"American Short Story" series.
Chicago International Film Festival '77: Silver
Hugo Award.
David B Appleton — *Monterey Home Video;
Perspective Films & Video*

Soldier's Story, A 1984
Drama
Closed Captioned
81207   101 mins   C   B, V   P
*Howard E. Rollins, Adolph Caesar, Denzel
Washington, Patti La Belle, Wings Hauser,
directed by Norman Jewison*
This is an adaptation of the Charles Fuller play
about a black army attorney who is sent to a
southern army base to investigate the murder of
an unpopular sergeant. The Herbie Hancock
score can be heard VHS Dolby Hi-Fi Stereo and
Beta Hi-Fi Stereo.
MPAA:PG
Columbia; Caldix Films Ltd. — *RCA/Columbia
Pictures Home Video*

Soldier's Tale, The 1984
Cartoons/Music
73015   60 mins   C   B, V   P
*Animated, voices of Max Von Sydow and Andre
Gregory*
Igor Stravinskys' "The Soldier's Tale" is
animated by New Yorker cartoonist R.O.
Bleechman with the voices provided by Max
Von Sydow and Andre Gregory.
MGM UA — *MGM/UA Home Video*

Sole Survivor 1984
Horror
80676   85 mins   C   B, V, CED   P
Anita Skinner, Kurt Johnson, Caren Larkey
A group of zombies are searching for a beautiful
advertising executive who was the sole survivor
of a plane crash.
MPAA:R
International Film Marketing — *Vestron Video*

Solid Gold Five Day Workout, The — 1984
Physical fitness
66412   100 mins   C   B, V, LV,   P
CED
The Solid Gold Dancers
A complete workout in five twenty-minute sessions that are designed to help develop specific and differentiated parts of the body every day. The dancers from the "Solid Gold" TV show demonstrate each exercise in an attractive setting.
Paramount Home Video — *Paramount Home Video*

Solo — 1977
Romance
73039   90 mins   C   B, V   P
This is the story of a young hitchhiker who enters the lives of a fire patrol pilot and his son.
MPAA:PG
Atlantic Releasing — *Vestron Video*

Solomon and Sheba — 1959
Drama
81067   139 mins   C   B, V   P
Yul Brynner, Gina Lollobrigida, Marisa Pavan, George Sanders, Alejandro Rey, directed by King Vidor
King Solomon's brother and the Egyptian Pharoah send the Queen of Sheba to Israel to seduce King Soloman. Available in VHS and Beta Hi-Fi.
United Artists; Ted Richmond — *Key Video*

Some Call It Loving — 1973
Fantasy/Romance
72450   95 mins   C   B, V   P
Zalman King, Richard Proyer, Tisa Farrow
James B. Harris' story is based on the classic tale of "Sleeping Beauty" brought up-to-date.
Pleasant Pastures — *Monterey Home Video*

Some Kind of Hero — 1982
Comedy-Drama
60333   97 mins   C   B, V, LV   P
Richard Pryor, Margot Kidder, Ray Sharkey, Ronny Cox, Lynne Moody, Olivia Cole
A Vietnam prisoner-of-war returns home to a changed world.
MPAA:R
Paramount — *Paramount Home Video; RCA VideoDiscs*

Some Like It Hot — 1959
Comedy
29222   120 mins   B/W   B, V, LV   P
Marilyn Monroe, Tony Curtis, Jack Lemmon, George Raft, Pat O'Brien, Nehemiah Persoff
Two unemployed musicians, witnesses to a Chicago murder, disguise themselves as girls and join an all-girl band headed for Miami to escape gangster's retaliation.

Academy Awards '59: Best Costume Design EL, SP
United Artists — *CBS/Fox Video; RCA VideoDiscs*

Someone Behind the Door — 1971
Suspense/Drama
82088   97 mins   C   B, V   P
Charles Bronson, Anthony Perkins, Jill Ireland, Henri Garcin
An evil brain surgeon implants murderous suggestions into a psychopathic amnesia victim's mind.
MPAA:PG
Avco Embassy Corp; GSF Productions — *Unicorn Video*

Someone I Touched — 1975
Drama
81418   74 mins   C   B, V   P
Cloris Leachman, James Olson, Glynnis O'Connor, Andy Robinson, Allyn Ann McLerie
A young woman, an expectant mother and her husband change their attitudes towards veneral disease when they are infected with it.
Dick Berg Prods; Charles Fries Prods. — *Worldvision Home Video*

Something of Value — 1957
War-Drama
84709   113 mins   B/W   B, V   P
Rock Hudson, Sidney Poitier, Wendy Hiller, Dana Wynter, directed by Richard Brooks
Two friends are caught in the midst of the Kenyan Mau Mau uprising. From the novel by Robert C. Ruark.
MGM — *MGM/UA Home Video*

Something Short of Paradise — 1979
Comedy
77408   87 mins   C   B, V   P
David Steinberg, Susan Sarandon, Jean-Pierre Aumont, Marilyn Sokol
The owner of a Manhattan movie theater has an on again-off again romance with a magazine writer.
MPAA:PG
Orion Pictures — *Vestron Video*

Something to Prove: The 1982 NBA Playoffs & World Championship Series — 1986
Basketball
85404   60 mins   C   B, V   P
Narrated by Dick Stockton
Highlights of the historic playoffs between the Los Angeles Lakers and the Philadelphia 76ers.
Geoff Metzger — *U.S.A. Home Video*

Something to Sing About 1936

Musical
08734   84 mins   B/W   B, V, 3/4U   P
James Cagney, William Frawley, Evelyn Daw
Two-fisted bandleader in a musical melodrama
about Hollywood studio life—the people and
their problems.
Schertsinger; Meyers — VCII; Cable Films;
Video Yesteryear; Movie Buff Video; Kartes
Video Communications

Something Wicked This Way Comes 1983

Fantasy
65094   94 mins   C   B, V, CED   P
Jason Robards, Jonathan Pryce, Diane Ladd,
Pam Grier, Richard Davalos, James Stacy,
directed by Jack Clayton
Two young boys discover the evil secret of a
mysterious traveling carnival that visits their
town. Based on the Ray Bradbury novel.
MPAA:PG
Buena Vista — Walt Disney Home Video

Sometimes a Great Notion 1971

Drama
62876   115 mins   C   B, V   P
Paul Newman, Henry Fonda, Lee Remick,
Richard Jaeckel, Michael Sarrazin, directed by
Paul Newman
Trouble in a small Oregon town is caused by an
independent family of lumberjacks. Based on
the novel by Ken Kesey.
MPAA:PG
Universal — MCA Home Video

Somewhere in Time 1980

Fantasy/Romance
56871   103 mins   C   B, V, LV   P
Christopher Reeve, Jane Seymour, Christopher
Plummer, Teresa Wright, directed by Jeannot
Szware
A playwright falls in love with a woman in an old
portrait and, through self-hypnosis, goes back in
time to discover what their relationship might
have been.
MPAA:PG
Rastar, Stephen Deutsch — MCA Home Video

Somewhere Tomorrow 1985

Fantasy/Romance
84673   91 mins   C   B, V   P
Sarah Jessica Parker, Nancy Addison, Tom
Shea
A lonely teenager falls in love with a ghost.
MPAA:PG
Film Gallery — Media Home Entertainment

Son of Blob 1972

Horror/Science fiction
51087   87 mins   C   B, V   R, P
Robert Walker, Godfrey Cambridge, Carol
Lynley, Shelly Berman, Larry Hagman
When a scientist unknowingly brings home a
piece of frozen blob from the North Pole, his
wife accidentally revives the dormant grey
mass. It begins a rampage of terror by digesting
nearly everyone within its reach.
MPAA:PG
Jack H Harris — Video Gems

Son of Captain Blood, The 1964

Adventure
85085   90 mins   C   B, V   P
Sean Flynn, directed by Tulio Demicheli
The son of the famous pirate meets up with his
father's enemies on the high seas.
MPAA:G
Harry Joe Brown — Prism

Son of Flubber 1984

Comedy
72793   96 mins   C   B, V   P
Fred MacMurray, Nancy Olson, Tommy Kirk,
Leon Ames, Joanna Moore
A sequel to "The Absent Minded Professor"
which finds Fred MacMurray still toying with his
prodigious invention, Flubber, now in the form of
Flubbergas, which causes those who inhale it to
float away.
Walt Disney Productions — Walt Disney Home
Video

Son of Football Follies, The 1976

Football
45126   23 mins   C   B, V, FO   R, P
Narrated by Mel Blanc
An updated version of "Football Follies," with
Mel Blanc using his vast array of cartoon
character voices to describe the bumblings on
the football field.
NFL Films — NFL Films Video; Champions on
Film and Video

Son of Football Follies/Big Game America 1981

Football
51700   45 mins   C   LV   P
A series of football field flops, fumbles, and
stumbles is combined with a look at pro
football's first fifty years, comprising this disc
program.
NFL Films — NFL Films Video

Son of Football Follies/Highlights of Super Bowl XIV 1980

Football
56791   46 mins   C   B, V   P

Gridiron goofs narrated by Bugs Bunny and Daffy Duck, plus highlights of the Rams and Steelers' Super Bowl XIV.
NFL Films — *VidAmerica*

Son of Godzilla   1966
Science fiction
09003   86 mins   C   B, V   P
Tadao Takashima, Akiro Kubo, Berbay Maeda
Godzilla engages in exciting combat to protect his infant son.
Japanese — *Prism; Hollywood Home Theater; Discount Video Tapes*

Son of Kong   1933
Horror
00312   70 mins   B/W   B, V, 3/4U   P
Robert Armstrong, Helen Mack
King Kong's descendant is discovered on an island amidst prehistoric creatures.
RKO — *Nostalgia Merchant*

Son of Monsters on the   1977
March
Movie and TV trailers
42961   27 mins   C   B, V, FO   P
A sequel package to "Monsters on the March," this compilation offers trailers to ten horror and sci-fi classics, including "The Rocky Horror Picture Show," 'Planet of the Apes," "The Fearless Vampire Killers," "This Island Earth" and "I Was a Teenage Frankenstein."
20th Century Fox et al — *Video Yesteryear*

Son of Monte Cristo, The   1940
Adventure
08866   102 mins   B/W   B, V   P
Louis Hayward, Joan Bennett, George Sanders, Florence Bates
A count's son meets a duchess whose country is threatened by renegades.
United Artists — *Kartes Video Communications; Cable Films; Nostalgia Merchant; Discount Video Tapes; Video Connection; Video Yesteryear; Hollywood Home Theater; Western Film & Video Inc; Movie Buff Video*

Son of Sinbad   1955
Adventure
15600   88 mins   C   B, V   P
Dale Robertson, Sally Forrest, Vincent Price, Lili St. Cyr, Mari Blanchard
Sinbad, captured by Khalif of Bagdad, must bring him the secret of Greek fire to gain his freedom and free the city from the forces of mighty Tamarlane.
RKO; Howard Hughes — *United Home Video*

Son of the Sheik   1926
Romance
10116   62 mins   B/W   B, V   P, T

Rudolph Valentino, Vilma Banky, Agnes Ayres, directed by George Fitzmaurice
In his last film, Valentino portrays a desert sheik whoabducts an unfaithful dancing girl.
First Natl — *Blackhawk Films; Video Connection; Cable Films*

Son of Video Yesterbloop   1984
Comedy/Outtakes and bloopers
78105   54 mins   C   B, V, FO   P
3 pgms
This program, partially in color, shows hilarious mishaps and general goofing around on sets in television and movie scenes from the 1930's to the 1970's.
1.Things You Never See In Pictures 2.Television Bloopers 3.Sports Snafus
Video Yesteryear — *Video Yesteryear*

Song of Arizona   1946
Western
14376   54 mins   B/W   B, V   P
Roy Rogers, Dale Evans, Gabby Hayes, Lyle Talbot, Bob Nolan, Sons of the Pioneers
Roy thwarts banker's plot to foreclose on orphan's home.
Republic — *Video Connection; Captain Bijou*

Song of Bernadette   1943
Drama
82347   156 mins   B/W   B, V   P
Charles Bickford, Lee J Cobb, Jennifer Jones, Vincent Price, directed by Henry King
This is the true story of a peasant girl who sees a vision in Lourdes in 1858. Hear Alfred Newman's score in VHS and Beta Hi-Fi.
Academy Awards '43: Best Actress (Jones), Best Dramatic Score, Best Cinematography
20th Century Fox — *Key Video*

Song of Freedom   1938
Drama
08885   70 mins   B/W   B, V, 3/4U   P
Paul Robeson, Elizabeth Welch
The story of a black worker whose nonchalant singing is overheard by an opera impresario.
Treo — *Movie Buff Video; Video Yesteryear; Discount Video Tapes; Cable Films; Kartes Video Communications*

Song of Nevada   1944
Western
03990   60 mins   B/W   B, V   P
Roy Rogers, Dale Evans
It looks like Dale Evans may marry a stuffed shirt. Does she?
Republic — *Hollywood Home Theater; Discount Video Tapes; Video Connection*

Song of Norway   1970
Musical/Biographical
70900   143 mins   C   B, V   P

Toralv Maurstad, Florence Henderson, Edward
G. Robinson, Christina Schollin, Frank Porretta,
Oscar Homolka, Robert Morley, Harry
Secombe, directed by Andrew L. Stone
This film dramatizes the early life of the beloved
Norwegian Romantic composer Edvard Grieg.
Filmed against the beautiful mountains,
waterfalls and fjords of Norway and based on
the popular 40's stage production, this Hi-Fi
Stereo tape features the lush accompaniment of
the London Symphony Orchestra.
MPAA:G
ABC Pictures — Playhouse Video

Song of Texas   1943
Western
08790   54 mins   B/W   B, V, 3/4U   P
Roy Rogers, Harry Shannon, Pat Brady
Roy races Sam, once champion cowboy of the
world, now drunkard.
Republic — Video Yesteryear; Video
Connection; Discount Video Tapes

Song of the Gringo   1936
Western
08604   57 mins   B/W   B, V   P
Tex Ritter
Tex Ritter in one of his early singing westerns
with bold action and a bit of romance.
Grand National — United Home Video; Video
Connection; Discount Video Tapes

Song Remains the Same,   1973
The
Music-Performance
79551   136 mins   C   B, V   P
John Paul Jones, Jimmy Page, Robert Plant,
John Bonham
All the excitement of Led Zeppelin's 1973
Madison Square Garden concert is captured in
this film. Available in VHS Hi-Fi and Beta Hi-Fi
Stereo.
MPAA:PG
Peter Grant; Warner Bros — Warner Home
Video

Song to Remember, A   1945
Musical-Drama
86390   112 mins   C   B, V   P
Cornel Wilde, Paul Muni, Merle Oberon, directed
by Charles Vidor
With music performed by Jose Iturbi, this film
depicts the last years of Frederic Chopin and his
affair with famous authoress George Sand.
Sidney Buchman — RCA/Columbia Pictures
Home Video

Songwriter   1984
Musical-Drama
Closed Captioned
80783   94 mins   C   B, V   P

Willie Nelson, Kris Kristofferson, Rip Torn,
Melinda Dillon, Lesley Ann Warren, directed by
Alan Rudolph
This is a high falutin' look at the lives and music
of two popular country singers. Kristofferson
and Nelson also wrote the musical score.
Available in Beta and VHS Hi-Fi.
Tri-Star Pictures — RCA/Columbia Pictures
Home Video

Sons of Hercules in the   1955
Land of Darkness
Fantasy
85215   74 mins   B/W   B, V   P
Dan Vadis
Hercules' son kills dragons, fights titans, and
generally flexes up a storm.
Italian — Video Yesteryear

Sons of Katie Elder, The   1965
Western/Drama
64024   122 mins   C   B, V   P
John Wayne, Dean Martin, Earl Holliman,
Michael Anderson Jr., Martha Hyer
Four brothers with diverse personalities return
to their home town on the day their mother is
buried.
Paramount — Paramount Home Video; RCA
VideoDiscs

Sons of the Desert   1933
Comedy
33904   69 mins   B/W   B, V, 3/4U   P
Stan Laurel, Oliver Hardy, Mae Busch, Charley
Chase
The boys try to fool their wives by pretending to
go to Hawaii to cure Ollie of a bad cold, when in
fact they are attending a convention in Chicago.
Hal Roach, MGM — Nostalgia Merchant;
Blackhawk Films

Sons of the Desert   1934
Comedy
63989   84 mins   B/W   B, V   P, T
Stan Laurel, Oliver Hardy, Mae Busch, Charley
Chase, Dorothy Christie
Stan and Ollie sneak away to a lodge
convention in Chicago by telling their wives that
they are going to Hawaii for Ollie's health. Also
included on this tape is a 1935 Thelma
Todd—Patsy Kelly short, "Top Flat."
Hal Roach; MGM — Blackhawk Films;
Nostalgia Merchant

Sony Overview Videodisc   1981
Video
65093   ? mins   C   LV   P
This "overview" videodisc demonstrates the
various functions and capabilities of interactive
video. It has been designed for use by the
general public, the informed public or the
producer or technician.

Dan Harris; John O'Donnell; John Hartigan — *Sony Video Software*

Sophia Loren: Her Own Story

1980

Drama/Biographical
58464   150 mins   C   B, V   P
Sophia Loren, Armand Assante, Ed Flanders, John Gavin
The life story of Sophia Loren, from a spindly child growing up in working-class Naples, to a world-renowned movie star and beauty queen.
EMI TV Programs; Roger Gimbel — *THORN EMI/HBO Video*

Sophie's Choice

1982

Drama
66070   157 mins   C   B, V, LV
Meryl Streep, Kevin Kline, Peter MacNicol, directed by Alan J. Pakula
An Auschwitz survivor settled in America struggles to forget the past.
Academy Awards '82: Best Actress (Streep).
MPAA:R
ITC Entertainment — *CBS/Fox Video; RCA VideoDiscs*

Sorcerer's Apprentice

1985

Cartoons
71053   22 mins   C   B, V   P
Animated, narrated by Vincent Price
In Jacob Grimm's classic tale, a young apprentice battles his master in an effort to motivate the old wizard towards more pleasant prestidigitation.
LBS Communications; DIC Enterprises — *Karl/Lorimar Home Video*

Sorceress

1982

Drama
65749   83 mins   C   B, V   P
Leigh Harris, Lynette Harris, Bob Nelson
The story of Traigon, a despotic ruler and devotee of the Black Arts, driven to become Master of the World.
MPAA:R
Jack Hill — *THORN EMI/HBO Video*

Sorrow and the Pity, The

1970

World War II/Documentary
47021   265 mins   B/W   B, V   P
Pierre Mendes-France, Louis Grave, Albert Speer
A documentary about anti-Semitism and the Nazi occupation of France during the Vichy regime in World War II.
Cinema 5 — *RCA/Columbia Pictures Home Video*

Sorry, Wrong Number

1948

Suspense
82543   89 mins   B/W   B, V   P

Barbara Stanwyck, Burt Lancaster, Ann Richards, Wendell Corey, Harold Vermilyea, directed by Anatole Litvak
A wealthy, bedridden wife overhears two men plotting a murder on a crossed telephone line, and begins to suspect that one of the voices is her husband's. A classic tale of paranoia and suspense.
Hal Wallis Productions — *Paramount Home Video*

S.O.S. Titanic

1979

Drama
58458   98 mins   C   B, V   P
David Janssen, Cloris Leachman, Susan St. James, David Warner, Ian Holm, Helen Mirren
The story of the Titanic disaster, exactly as it happened. This film focuses on the courage that accompanied the tragedy and horror.
EMI — *THORN EMI/HBO Video*

Soul Experience, The

1984

Music-Performance
73537   60 mins   C   B, V   P
All the greats of rhythm and blues are represented on this program from Al Green to Bill Withers performing their great hits.
USA — *U.S.A. Home Video*

Soul Hustler

1976

Drama
81405   81 mins   C   B, V   P
Fabian, Casey Kasem, Larry Bishop, Nai Bonet
A con man becomes rich and famous when he becomes a tent show evangelist. Available in VHS Stereo and Beta Hi-Fi.
MPAA:PG
American Films Ltd. — *Monterey Home Video*

Sound of Love

1977

Romance/Drama
76788   74 mins   C   B, V   P
Celia De Burgh, John Jarratt
The mutual attraction between a deaf female hustler and a deaf race car driver leads to a deep relationship where they both learn about their own fears and desires.
Jane Scott — *Embassy Home Entertainment*

Sound of Music, The

1965

Musical-Drama
08363   174 mins   C   B, V, LV,   P
                                      CED
Julie Andrews, Christopher Plummer, directed by Robert Wise
A true-life story of the Von Trapp family of Austria prior to World War II. Based on Rogers and Hammerstein play.
Academy Awards '65: Best Picture; Film Daily Poll 10 Best Pictures of Year '65.
20th Century Fox; Robert Wise — *CBS/Fox Video*

Sounder 1972
Drama
Closed Captioned
65734   105 mins   C   B, V   R, P
Paul Winfield, Cicely Tyson, Kevin Hooks, Taj Mahal
The story of a Negro family of sharecroppers in rural Louisiana during the Depression.
MPAA:G
20th Century Fox — *Paramount Home Video*

Sounds of Motown 1985
Music-Performance
82010   50 mins   B/W   B, V   P
The Supremes, Stevie Wonder, Marvin Gaye, The Temptations, Smokey Robinson and the Miracles
The great Motown stars perform their big hits in this collection of clips from the "Ready Steady Go!" series. Available in VHS and Beta Hi-Fi Stereo.
Dave Clark Limited; EMI Records — *Sony Video Software*

Soup for One 1982
Comedy
47802   84 mins   C   B, V   P
Saul Rubinek, Marcia Strassman, Gerrit Graham
A hapless New Yorker searches for his "Dream Girl."
MPAA:R
Warner Bros — *Warner Home Video*

South of Hell Mountain 1970
Drama/Adventure
71146   87 mins   C   B, V   P
Ann Stewart, Sam Hall, Nicol Britton, directed by William Sachs and Louis Leahman
On the run from a gold mine robbery where they left twenty dead, the McHenry brothers meet a mother-daughter team that slows them down.
MPAA:R
The February Company — *MGM/UA Home Video*

South of Pago Pago 1940
Adventure
64363   98 mins   B/W   B, V, 3/4U   P
Victor McLaglen, Jon Hall, Frances Farmer, Gene Lockhart
The unsuspecting natives of a tropical isle are exploited by a gang of pirates who are searching for a seabed of rare pearls.
United Artists — *Nostalgia Merchant*

South of Santa Fe 1942
Western
05547   60 mins   B/W   B, V   P
Roy Rogers, Gabby Hayes, Linda Hayes
Roy Rogers investigates an old gold mine that could be the answer to the town's financial problems.

Republic — *Discount Video Tapes; Cable Films*

South of the Border 1939
Western
58605   70 mins   B/W   B, V   P, T
Gene Autry, Smiley Burnette
Gene and Frog are sent to help investigate a threat to the Latin American country of "Palermo," (Also known as "South of Texas").
Republic — *Blackhawk Films; Video Connection*

South of the Rio Grande 1951
Western
72950   60 mins   B/W   B, V   P
Duncan Renaldo
The Cisco Kid rides again as he comes to the aid of a rancher whose horses were stolen.
Eagle Lion — *United Home Video*

South Pacific 1958
Musical/Drama
55592   167 mins   C   B, V, CED   P
Mitzi Gaynor, Rossano Brazzi, Ray Walston, France Nuyen
A young American Navy nurse and a Frenchman fall in love in World World II Hawaii. Based on Rodgers and Hammerstein's musical. Academy Awards '58: Best Sound Recording.
Twentieth Century Fox — *CBS/Fox Video*

Southern Comfort 1981
Drama
65071   106 mins   C   B, V, CED   P
Keith Carradine, Powers Boothe, Fred Ward, Franklyn Seales
A nine-man National Guard patrol on routine weekend maneuvers in Louisiana are marked for death by Cajun natives.
MPAA:R
20th Century Fox — *Embassy Home Entertainment*

Southerner, The 1945
Drama
11254   91 mins   B/W   B, V, FO   P
Zachary Scott, Betty Field, directed by Jean Renoir
The story of how a poor Southern family struggles to make a living on the farm land.
United Artists — *Prism; Video Yesteryear; Movie Buff Video; Hollywood Home Theater; VCII; Kartes Video Communications; Video Connection; Western Film & Video Inc; Discount Video Tapes*

Southward Ho 1939
Western
57982   56 mins   B/W   B, V   P
Roy Rogers, Gabby Hayes

Roy Rogers stars in the action western about a cowhand who heads south.
Republic — *Video Connection; Cable Films*

Soviet Army Chorus, Band, and Dance Ensemble   1981
Music-Performance
57256   70 mins   C   B, V   P
This exciting music ensemble is seen on tour at various points in the USSR performing their spectacular blend of singing, dancing and acrobatics.
Kultur — *Kultur*

Soylent Green   1973
Science fiction
53940   95 mins   C   B, V, CED   P
Charlton Heston, Leigh Taylor-Young, Chuck Connors, Joseph Cotten, Edward G. Robinson
In the 21st Century, a hard-boiled police detective investigates a murder and discovers what soylent green—the people's principal food—is made of.
MPAA:PG
MGM — *MGM/UA Home Video*

Space Angel Volume 1   1964
Science fiction/Cartoons
53150   50 mins   C   B, V   P
Animated
A futuristic animated program for children.
EL, SP
TV Comics; Ziv Intl — *Family Home Entertainment*

Space Angel Volume 2   1964
Science fiction/Cartoons
53151   50 mins   C   B, V   P
Animated
A futuristic animated program for children.
EL, SP
TV Comics; Ziv Intl — *Family Home Entertainment*

Space for Women   1985
Space exploration
88381   28 mins   C   B, V, 3/4U   R, P
A public relations film encouraging women to enter a career in space and science. Narrated by Ricardo Montalban.
NASA — *Your World Video*

Space Ghost and Dino Boy   197?
Cartoons
66281   60 mins   C   B, V   P
Animated
A ghostly cartoon character performs hilarious hijinx.
Hanna Barbera — *Worldvision Home Video*

Space Ghost and Dino Boy Ghostly Tales   1969
Cartoons
84081   45 mins   C   B, V   P
An animated adventure of interplanatary crime fighting, featuring Blip the space monkey.
Jacom Inc — *Worldvision Home Video*

Space Movie, The   1980
Space exploration/Documentary
54803   78 mins   C   B, V   P
Directed by Tony Palmer
"The Space Movie" consists entirely of footage from NASA and the U.S. National Archives which tells the story of America's space effort (specifically the Apollo 11 moon flight). The footage, most of which has not been seen before, is mixed with music and a little narration, showing the beauty of space.
Virgin Films Ltd, British — *Warner Home Video*

Space 1999   1980
Science fiction/Adventure
71318   109 mins   C   B, V   P
Martin Landau, Barbara Bain, Barry Morse, Catherine Schell, Tony Anholt, Nick Tate, Zienia Merton, Yasuko Nagazumi, Anton Phillips
Colonists on the moon, blasted out of orbit in a radioactive accident, struggle with life forms on the planets they pass while wandering through the galaxy.
1.Alien Attack 2.Journey Through the Black Sun
ITC Productions — *U.S.A. Home Video*

Space Patrol   1955
Science fiction
59088   78 mins   B/W   B, V, FO   P
Ed Kemmer, Lyn Osborn
The adventures of Buzz Corey, Commander in Chief of the Space Patrol, fighting interplanetary injustice.
ABC — *Video Yesteryear*

Space Patrol Volume 1   195?
Science fiction/Adventure
44339   120 mins   B/W   B, V, 3/4U   P
Ed Kemmer, Lyn Osborn
Buzz Corey, Commander-in-Chief of the Space Patrol, tries to maintain interplanetary peace and protect the people of Earth's neighboring planets. These episodes from the early 1950's television series includes previews of coming attractions from classic science fiction films.
ABC — *Nostalgia Merchant*

Space Patrol Volume 2   195?
Science fiction
58584   90 mins   B/W   B, V, 3/4U   P
Commander Buzz Corey maintains interplanetary peace in this early '50's TV series.
ABC — *Nostalgia Merchant; Video Dimensions*

Space Raiders 1983
Science fiction/Adventure
65743   84 mins   C   B, V   P
Vince Edwards, David Mendenhall
A plucky 10-year-old blasts off into a futuristic world of intergalactic desperados, crafty alien mercenaries, starship battles and cliff-hanging dangers.
MPAA:PG
Roger Corman — *Warner Home Video*

Space Riders 1983
Adventure
85900   93 mins   C   B, V   P
Barry Sheene, Gavan O'Herlihy, Toshiya Ito, Stephanie McLean, Sayo Inaba
A actioneer about the world's championship motorcycle race, with a rock soundtrack featuring Duran Duran, Simple Minds and Melba Moore.
MPAA:PG
Felicity Hibberdine — *THORN EMI/HBO Video*

Space Sentinels Volume 1 1977
Cartoons/Science fiction
72883   44 mins   C   B, V   P
Animated
A cartoon features the Space Sentinels who are out to save the world from the evil space invaders.
Unknown — *Embassy Home Entertainment*

Space Sentinels in Mission: Outer Space 1977
Cartoons
87919   72 mins   C   B, V   P
A collection of robot/warrior heroes battle for the safety of the known universe.
Unknown — *Embassy Home Entertainment*

Space Vampires 1981
Horror
70929   80 mins   C   B, V   P
John Carradine, Wendell Corey
An inter-galactic madman produces a ravaging blood-thirsty beast but cannot control it.
MPAA:PG
Independent — *Wizard Video*

Spaced Out 1980
Comedy
47800   85 mins   C   B, V   P
A naughty sci-fi sex comedy that parodies everything from "Star Wars" to "2001."
MPAA:R
Miramax — *THORN EMI/HBO Video*

Spacehunter: Adventures in the Forbidden Zone 1983
Adventure
65315   90 mins   C   B, V   P
Peter Strauss, Molly Ringwald, Michael Ironside, Ernie Hudson
Peter Strauss is the galactic bounty hunter who agrees to rescue 3 maidens from a plague-ridden planet. Available in VHS stereo and Beta Hi-Fi.
MPAA:PG
Don Carmody — *RCA/Columbia Pictures Home Video; RCA VideoDiscs*

Spaceketeers 1982
Cartoons/Science fiction
63118   100 mins   C   B, V   P
Animated
An army of mutant invaders overrun a peaceful solar system. Spaceketeers to the rescue!
Toei Animation; Ginga Kikaku; Jim Terry Production Services — *Family Home Entertainment*

Spaceketeers Volume 1 1980
Science fiction/Cartoons
53163   46 mins   C   B, V   P
Animated
Princess Aurora and Jesse Dart, with the help of a scientific wizard, risk everything to save the endangered galaxy.
EL, SP
Toei Animation; Ginga Kikaku; Jim Terry Prod — *Family Home Entertainment*

Spaceketeers Volume 2 1980
Science fiction/Cartoons
53164   46 mins   C   B, V   P
Animated
Princess Aurora and Jesse Dart travel through space in search of their friend, Porkos, who is needed to stop blood-thirsty monsters from destroying the galaxy.
EL, SP
Toei Animation; Ginga Kikaku; Jim Terry Prod — *Family Home Entertainment*

Spaceketeers Volume 3 1980
Science fiction/Cartoons
64203   46 mins   C   B, V   P
Animated
This third volume presents further adventures of Princess Aurora and her companion, Jesse Dart.
EL, SP
Toei Animation; Ginga Kikaku; Jim Jerry Prod — *Family Home Entertainment*

Spaceship 1983
Comedy
79307   80 mins   C   B, V   P
Leslie Neilsen, Cindy Williams
A macho commander and a woman take the U.S.S. Spacecraft Vertigo on a voyage to search for interstellar life.
Almi Productions — *Vestron Video*

Sparkle 1976
Musical-Drama
79552 100 mins C B, V P
Irene Cara, Lonette McKee, Dwan Smith, directed by Sam O'Steen
This is the rags to riches saga of three sisters rise to the top of the music charts. Curtis Mayfield wrote the musical score.
MPAA:PG
Warner Bros — *Warner Home Video*

Sparrows 1926
Comedy-Drama
10124 75 mins B/W B, V P, T
Mary Pickford, Roy Stewart, Gustov von Seyffertitz, directed by William Beaudine
Set to William Perry's score, mother cares for her nine children on impoverished farm, warding off starvation and kidnappers. (Silent).
United Artists — *Blackhawk Films; Discount Video Tapes; Video Yesteryear; Kartes Video Communications*

Spartacus 1984
Dance/Music-Performance
70955 128 mins C B, V P
The Bolshoi Ballet, directed by Preben Montell
Aram Kachaturian scored this ballet based on the life of Thracian Spartacus, a rebel slave who fought against the Roman Empire.
Soviet — *THORN EMI/HBO Video*

Spartacus 1960
Adventure
76803 185 mins C B, V, LV P
Kirk Douglas, Laurence Olivier, Jean Simmons, Tony Curtis, Charles Laughton, Peter Ustinov, John Gavin, John Ireland, directed by Stanley Kubrick
A bold gladiator escapes from slavery with an army of slaves to challenge a power hungry Roman general.
Academy Awards '60: Best Supporting Actor (Ustinov); Best Art Direction; Best Cinematography.
Kirk Douglas; Edward Lewis — *MCA Home Video*

Spasms 1982
Horror
65511 92 mins C B, V P
Peter Fonda, Oliver Reed
The Demon Serpent, known as N'Gana Simbu, is the deadliest snake in the world. It strikes its victims, and the result is that the victim's bodies become hideously deformed and destroyed. With uncontrollable deady fury, the monstrous snake strikes continuously causing death and destruction.
MPAA:R
John C Pozhke; Maurice Smith — *THORN EMI/HBO Video*

Speaking of Animals 1983
Comedy
65313 60 mins C B, V P
In this hilarious film anthology, not only do the animals walk and talk like human beings, they also sing, dance and imitate the stars.
Jerry Fairbanks — *U.S.A. Home Video*

Speaking of Animals Vol. II 1984
Comedy
80245 60 mins C B, V P
Things are getting pretty funny in the zoo where our animal friends take on a variety of human personalities.
NTA — *U.S.A. Home Video*

Special Effects 1985
Horror
81452 103 mins C B, V P
Zoe Tamerlis, Eric Bogosian, Brad Rijn, Bill Oland, Richard Greene, directed by Larry Cohen
Fantasy and real life become dangerously intertwined when a film director wants to recreate an actress' murder for his next movie.
MPAA:R
New Line Cinema — *Embassy Home Entertainment*

Special Bulletin 1983
Drama
88191 105 mins C B, V P
Ed Flanders, Christopher Allport, Kathryn Walker, Roxanne Hart
A made-for-TV news docu-drama, done in a realistic style a la Orson Welles' famous "War of the Worlds" broadcast. A pacifistic terrorist threatens to blow up Charleston, South Carolina with a nuclear warhead. His threat becomes reality as the bomb is accidentally detonated by the police.
Marshall Herskovitz; Edward Zwick; Ohlymeyer Comm. — *Karl/Lorimar Home Video*

Special Day, A 1977
Drama
58501 105 mins C B, V P
Sophia Loren, Marcello Mastroianni, directed by Ettore Scola
The day of a huge rally celebrating Hitler's visit to Rome in 1939 serves as the backdrop for an affair between a weary housewife and a radio announcer. Italian with English subtitles.
IT
Cinema 5; Carlo Ponti — *RCA/Columbia Pictures Home Video*

Special Delivery 1976
Adventure/Suspense
79672 99 mins C B, V P
Bo Svenson, Cybill Shepherd, Vic Tayback, Jeff Goldblum

When three disabled Vietnam veterans rob a bank their plans go awry.
MPAA:PG
Bing Crosby Productions — *Vestron Video*

Special Valentine with Family Circus, A 1980
Cartoons/Holidays
75469   30 mins   C   B, V   P
Animated
Cartoonist Bil Keane animates a special valentine program.
Cullen Kasden Productions Ltd — *Family Home Entertainment*

Specialist, The 1975
Drama
64298   93 mins   C   B, V   P
Adam West, John Anderson, Ahna Capri
A lawyer is seduced by a beautiful "specialist" as part of a frame-up.
MPAA:R
Renaissance Productions — *VidAmerica*

Spectacular Evening in Paris, A 1980
Nightclub
29238   106 mins   C   B, V   P
This videotape presents the top night club acts from the top Parisienne clubs—Moulin Rouge, Madame Arthur, Lido, and Casino de Paris.
Harlan Kleiman — *VidAmerica*

Speed Kings? The/Love, Speed and Thrills 1915
Comedy
64534   19 mins   B/W   B, V   R, P
Mabel Normand, Ford Sterling, Fatty Arbuckle, Mack Swain, Chester Conklin, The Keystone Cops
Two Mack Sennett comedy shorts are combined on this tape, both of which involve slapstick car chases.
Mack Sennett; Keystone — *Blackhawk Films*

Speed Learning 1983
Education
75901   30 mins   C   B, V   P
This program shows ways to improve learning and comprehension skills up to 300 percent.
Learn Inc — *Sony Video Software*

Speed Reading Hand, The 1986
Language arts/Education
71338   60 mins   C   B, V   P
Steve Moidel
Mr. Moidel wrote and directed this tape describing his method of speed reading; designed to increase the viewers reading speed 2 to 5 times over.
AM Available

Noel C Bloom; Patty Matlen — *U.S.A. Home Video*

Speed Trap 1977
Adventure
76655   101 mins   C   B, V   P
Tyne Daly, Joe Don Baker
Tyne Daly and Joe Don Baker team up to investigate a rash of mysterious car thefts in this exciting action drama.
Howard Pine; Fred Mintz — *Media Home Entertainment*

Speeding Up Time 1971
Adventure
81757   90 mins   C   B, V   P
Winston Thrash, Pamela Donegan
An angry man wants to ice the dudes who torched his mother's tenement.
MPAA:R
Independent — *Magnum Entertainment*

Speedway 1968
Musical
80151   100 mins   C   B, V   P
Elvis Presley, Nancy Sinatra, Bill Bixby, Gale Gordon, William Schallert
A stock car driver finds himself being chased by an IRS agent during an important race.
Metro Goldwyn Mayer — *MGM/UA Home Video*

Speedy Gonzales' Fast Funnies 1961
Cartoons
81575   54 mins   C   B, V   P
Animated, voice of Mel Blanc
The fastest mouse in all of Mexico zips around causing trouble for Sylvester and El Vulturo in this collection of eight classic cartoons that include "Cannery Woe" and "Tabasco Road".
Warner Bros — *Warner Home Video*

Spell, The 1977
Drama
79245   86 mins   C   B, V   P
Lee Grant, James Olson, Susan Myers, Barbara Bostock, Lelia Goldoni
An obese fifteen year old girl has the power to inflict illness and death upon the people she hates.
Charles Fries/Stone henge Productions — *Worldvision Home Video*

Spellbound 1945
Drama
46215   111 mins   B/W   B, V, CED   P
Ingrid Bergman, Gregory Peck, Leo G. Carroll, directed by Alfred Hitchcock
A young man suffering from amnesia and accused of murder, is helped by a female psychiatrist who loves him. One of Hitchcock's

finest films of the 1940's, with a dream sequence designed by Salvador Dali.
Selznick — *CBS/Fox Video*

Spetters 1980
Drama
65424   108 mins   C   B, V   P
Rutger Hauer
The story revolves around four young people in Holland on a turbulent collision course with their dreams. Tragic episodes force them to confront their strengths and weaknesses.
MPAA:R
Joop Van Der End — *Embassy Home Entertainment*

Sphinx 1980
Suspense
58250   118 mins   C   B, V   P
Lesley-Anne Downe, Frank Langella, John Gielgud, directed by Franklin J. Schaffner
A young woman stumbles on a secret hidden for centuries in the tomb of an Egyptian King.
MPAA:PG
Orion Pictures — *Warner Home Video*

Spider-Woman 1982
Cartoons/Adventure
59039   100 mins   C   B, V   P
A collection of Spider-Woman's most daring escapades.
Marvel Comics Group — *MCA Home Video*

Spiderman 1981
Adventure
72337   90 mins   C   B, V   P
Nicholas Hammond, Morgan Fairchild, Lloyd Bochner, Barbara Luna, Theodore Bikel
Marvel Comic's superhero stops global terrorism and thwarts political plots in this two-volume series. Each volume contains two live-action adventures: "Night of the Clones" and "Escort to Danger" are featured in the first volume; "Con Caper" and "Curse of Rava" are featured in the second.
Charles Frief; Daniel R Goodman — *Prism*

Spies 1928
Adventure
11253   90 mins   B/W   B, V, FO   P
Gerda Maurus, Willy Fritsch, directed by Fritz Lang
A sly criminal poses as a famous banker to steal government information and create chaos in the world in this silent picture.
Janus Films — *Video Yesteryear; Blackhawk Films; Discount Video Tapes*

Spies Like Us 1985
Comedy
87170   103 mins   C   B, V   P
Chevy Chase, Dan Aykroyd, Steve Forrest, Bruce Davison, William Prince, Bernie Casey, Tom Hatton, Michael Apted, Frank Oz, Costa Gavras, Terry Gilliam, Ray Harryhausen, directed by John Landis
Two bumbling idiots train as spies for a mission which may start World War III. Also available with Spanish subtitles.
MPAA:PG
Warner Bros.; Brian Grazer — *Warner Home Video*

Spinning 1986
Handicraft
88308   90 mins   C   B, V   P
Rachel Brown, spinner extraordinaire, demonstrates the basics and fundamental techniques of proper, no-nonsense spinning.
Victorian Video Prod. — *Victorian Video Productions*

Spirit of America, The 1942
World War II/Documentary
81604   57 mins   B/W   B, V   P
This is a collection of short subjects that captures the spirit of the American home front during World War II.
U.S. Office of War Information — *Victory Video*

Spirit of St. Louis, The 1957
Biographical
74211   137 mins   C   B, V   P
James Stewart
This is a biographical feature concerning the life of aviator Charles A. Lindbergh. Stewart stars as the pilot whose transatlantic flight made aviation history.
Leland Hayward — *Warner Home Video*

Spirit of the Dead 1972
Horror
82226   90 mins   C   B, V   P
Robert Powell, Robert Stephens
A scientist becomes obsessed with finding out more information about a mysterious apparition hidden in the photographs of his dying subjects.
Paragon Pictures — *VCL Home Video*

Spirit of the West 1932
Western
84844   61 mins   B/W   B, V   P
Hoot Gibson
A cowhand acts like an idiot, and saves a girl and her ranch.
Universal — *United Home Video*

Spirit of West Point, The 1947
Drama/Football
81768   77 mins   B/W   B, V   P
Felix "Doc" Glanchard, Glenn Davis, Tom Harmon, Alan Hale, Anne Nagel, Robert Shayne
B

This is the true story of West Point's two All-American football greats, Doc Blanchard and Glenn Davis.
Film Classics — *New World Video*

Spitfire   1942
Drama
06205   90 mins   B/W   B, V   P
Leslie Howard, David Niven, Rosamund John, directed by Leslie Howard
Story of Reginald Mitchell who designed "The Spitfire," which served the Allies so well during WW II.
RKO; Leslie Howard Prods — *Movie Buff Video; Hollywood Home Theater; Video Connection; Cable Films; Kartes Video Communications*

Spittin' Image   1983
Drama
71211   92 mins   C   B, V   P
Sunshine Parker, Trudi Cooper, Sharon Barr, Karen Barr, directed by Russell S Kern
After falling from her mean-spirited father's wagon, a young girl befriends a kind mountain man. She learns the ways of the wilderness and tobacco spitting.
Rocky Mountain Studios; Producers Group Ltd — *Prism*

Splash   1984
Fantasy
75635   109 mins   C   B, V, LV,   P
                                    CED
Tom Hanks, Daryl Hannah, Eugene Levy, John Candy, directed by Ron Howard
A mermaid ventures into New York City in search of a man she has fallen for.
Brian Grazer Production — *Touchstone Home Video*

Splatter University   1984
Horror
80678   78 mins   C   B, V, CED   P
Francine Forbes, Dick Biel, Cathy Lacommaro, Ric Randing, Dan Eaton
A deranged killer escapes from an asylum and begins to slaughter and mutilate comely coeds at a local college. Also available in a 79-minute uncensored version.
MPAA:R
Troma — *Vestron Video*

Splendor in the Grass   1961
Drama
51970   124 mins   C   B, V   P
Natalie Wood, Pat Hingle, Audrey Christie, Barbara Loden, Warren Beatty, Zohra Lampert, Sandy Dennis
A high school girl suffers an emotional collapse when the boy she loves stops seeing her. She attempts suicide, fails, and is committed to a mental institution for treatment.

Academy Awards '61: Best Original Story and Screenplay (William Inge).
Warner Bros;Elia Kazan — *Warner Home Video*

Splint Basket Weaving   1985
Handicraft
85648   59 mins   C   B, V   P
Robin Taylor Daugherty
A complete course in the craft of weaving an Appalachian egg basket.
Victorian Video Prod. — *Victorian Video Productions*

Splint Basketry--Level II   1986
Handicraft
88309   100 mins   C   B, V   P
Robin Taylor-Dougherty covers square to round and spoked techniques in basketry.
Victorian Video Prod. — *Victorian Video Productions*

Split Enz   1982
Music-Performance
75923   54 mins   C   B, V   P
This program presents the group Split Enz performing some of their best songs.
Enz Productions Ltd — *Sony Video Software*

Split Image   1982
Drama
66041   113 mins   C   B, V, CED   P
Michael O'Keefe, Karen Allen, Peter Fonda, James Woods, directed by Ted Kotcheff
An all-American boy comes under the spell of a cult. His parents then hire a deprogrammer to bring the boy back to reality.
MPAA:R
Jeff Young — *Embassy Home Entertainment*

Split Second   1953
Drama
73690   85 mins   B/W   B, V   P
Jan Sterling, Alexis Smith, Stephen McNally, directed by Dick Powell
Two escaped prisoners hold hostages in a Nevada atomic bomb testing area.
RKO — *RKO HomeVideo*

Splitz   1984
Comedy
80677   89 mins   C   B, V   P
Robin Johnson, Pattielee, Shirley Stoler, Raymond Serra
An all-girl rock band agrees to help out a sorority house by participating in a series of sporting events.
MPAA:PG13
Film Ventures International — *Vestron Video*

Spoilers, The 1942
Drama
65121   84 mins   B/W   B, V, LV   P
John Wayne, Randolph Scott, Marlene Dietrich, Margaret Lindsay
Two adventurers in the Yukon argue over land rights and the love of a saloon entertainer.
Universal — *MCA Home Video*

Spooks Run Wild 1941
Comedy
12857   64 mins   B/W   B, V, FO   P
The Bowery Boys, Bela Lugosi
Chills and laughs combine as the eerie Lugosi almost meets his match.
Monogram — *Video Yesteryear; Discount Video Tapes; Admit One Video; Kartes Video Communications*

Sports Clinic 1983
Sports
84782   80 mins   C   B, V   P
4   pgms
These programs of instruction for athletes of all ages train and inform in a step-by-step manner.
1.Football 2.Baseball 3.Basketball 4.Soccer
Framework Two Prods — *Video Associates*

Sports Conditioning 1978
Physical fitness/Sports
42780   30 mins   C   B, V   P
Hosted by Ann Dugan   4   pgms
This series on tennis, golf, jogging, running, and skiing works toward improvement through conditioning.
1.Jog/Run 2.Golf 3.Tennis/Racquet Sports 4.Ski
Health N Action — *RCA/Columbia Pictures Home Video*

Spreading Holocaust-- 1943
The U.S. Army in WWII: 1941-1943, The
World War II
87658   56 mins   B/W   B, V   P
An overview, using actual footage, of the Army's involvement on both fronts during the Second World War.
U.S. Army — *Victory Video*

Spring Break 1983
Comedy
65187   101 mins   C   B, V   P
Perry Lang, David Knell, Steve Bassett, Paul Land, Jane Modean, Corinne Alphen
Two college students go to Fort Lauderdale on their spring vacation and have a wilder time that they bargained for.
MPAA:R
Columbia — *RCA/Columbia Pictures Home Video; RCA VideoDiscs*

Spring Fever 1981
Comedy
72228   93 mins   C   B, V   P
Susan Anton
Heartaches of the junior tennis circuit are brought to the screen in this sports comedy.
Tournament Productions — *Vestron Video*

Springtime in the Sierras 1947
Western
10709   54 mins   B/W   B, V, 3/4U   R, P
Roy Rogers, Andy Devine
Roy Rogers and Andy Devine band together to fight a gang of poachers who prey on the wildlife of a game preserve.
Republic — *Cable Films; Discount Video Tapes; Video Yesteryear*

Spunky and Tadpole 196?
Cartoons
56749   48 mins   C   B, V   P
Animated
Spunky and his faithful companion, Tadpole, get in and out of trouble and cliff-hanging adventures, spoofing some of the old classic films in the process. Available in English and Spanish versions.
EL, SP
Beverly Hills Film Corp — *Media Home Entertainment*

Sputnik 1961
Science fiction/Suspense
85057   80 mins   B/W   B, V   P
Noel Noel, Mischa Auer, Denise Gray
A Frenchman, amnesiac after a car crash, comes up against Russian scientists, space-bound dogs and weightlessness.
Jean-Jacques Vital; Medallion TV; Comet Prod — *Sony Video Software*

Spy in Black, The 1939
Adventure
11255   82 mins   B/W   B, V, FO   P
Conrad Veidt, Valerie Hobson, Sebastian Shaw
A German submarine captain returns from duty at sea and is assigned to infiltrate one of the Orkney Islands and obtain confidential British information.
Korda — *Video Yesteryear; Discount Video Tapes*

Spy of Napoleon 1936
Drama
63618   77 mins   B/W   B, V, FO   P
Richard Barthelmess, Dolly Hass, Francis I. Sullivan
During the Franco-Prussian War, Emperor Napoleon III recruits his illegitimate daughter to uncover traitors to the throne.
British — *Video Yesteryear*

Spy Smasher　　　　　　　1942
Mystery/Serials
33956　185 mins　B/W　B, V, 3/4U　　P
Kane Richmond, Marguerite Chapman
A serial of espionage and intrigue in twelve
episodes.
*Republic — Nostalgia Merchant; Video
Connection; Republic Pictures Home Video*

Spy Who Loved Me, The　　　1977
Adventure
60378　125 mins　　C　B, V　　　P
Roger Moore, Barbara Bach
James Bond must destroy a brilliant but savage
villain and his henchman Jaws, in order to
prevent them from using captured American and
Russian atomic submarines in a plot to destroy
the world.
MPAA:PG
*United Artists — CBS/Fox Video; RCA
VideoDiscs*

Spyro Gyra　　　　　　　　1980
Music-Performance
47396　56 mins　C　　B, V　　　P
Live performances of some of Spyro Gyra's
well-known hits are interspersed with interviews
with band members.
Hawk Productions — Warner Home Video

Squash　　　　　　　　　　1984
Sports
70619　60 mins　　C　　B, V　　　P
Geoffrey Hunt
The seven-time World Champion, Geof Hunt,
designed these two thirty-minute classes to
develop players from the basic to advanced
levels. The first program concentrates on
stroking while the second discusses overall
game strategy.
Geoffrey Hunt — Jo-Lynn Video

Squeeze Play　　　　　　　1979
Comedy
64214　92 mins　C　　B, V　　　P
A group of young women start a baseball team
and challenge their boyfriends' team to a game.
It's a no-holds-barred competition featuring a
sexy wet-T-shirt contest.
*Troma Productions — THORN EMI/HBO
Video*

Squiddly Diddly　　　　　　196?
Cartoons
69291　55 mins　C　　B, V　　　P
Animated
This tape is a compilation of "Squiddly Diddly"
cartoons, about a star-struck squid hoping to
break into show business.
Hanna-Barbera — Worldvision Home Video

Squirm　　　　　　　　　　1976
Horror
64357　92 mins　　C　B, V, LV,　　P
　　　　　　　　　　　　CED
John Scardino, Patricia Pearcy, Jean Sullivan
A storm disrupts a highly charged power cable
which electrifies ordinary worms into giant
monsters.
MPAA:R
American International — Vestron Video

Squizzy Taylor　　　　　　1984
Biographical/Drama
77011　82 mins　　C　B, V　　　P
Jacki Weaver, Alan Cassell, David Atkins
This is the true story of the rise and fall of
Australian mob boss Squizzy Taylor.
Satori Entertainment — VidAmerica

S.S. Experiment　　　　　　1980
Drama
77392　90 mins　　C　B, V　　　P
A sadistic Nazi S.S. officer forces female
concentration camp prisoners to participate in a
series of bizzare sexual experiments.
Foreign — Wizard Video

SS Girls　　　　　　　　　1978
War-Drama
58468　82 mins　　C　B, V　　　P
*Gabriele Carrara, Marina Daunia, Vassili Karis,
Macha Magal, Thomas Rudy, Lucic Bogoljub
Benny, Ivano Staccioli*
After the attack of July 1944, Hitler does not
trust the Wermacht and extends the power of
the S.S. over Germany. General Berger entrusts
Hans Schillemberg to recruit a specially chosen
group of prostitutes who must test the fighting
spirit and loyalty of the generals.
Topar Films — Media Home Entertainment

St. Louis Cardinals: Team　　1984
Highlights
Baseball
81151　30 mins　　C　　B, V　　　P
*Ozzie Smith, Lonnia Smith, Keith Hernandez,
Whitey Herzog* 4　pgms
This series features exciting selected highlights
of the Cardinals 1981-1984 seasons.
*1.1981: Red bird Revival 2.1982: A Season to
Celebrate 3.1983: Get Excited 4. 1984: The
Spirit Comes Alive*
*Major League Baseball — Major League
Baseball Productions*

Stacey!　　　　　　　　　198?
Drama
64948　87 mins　　C　　B, V　　　R, P
*Anne Randall, Marjorie Bennett, Anitra Ford,
Alan Landers*
Anne Randall, former Playboy Playmate, stars
as Stacey Hansen, a beautiful private detective

who finds herself involved in something more than just a friendly job of snooping.
MPAA:R
Unknown — *Video Gems*

Stacy's Knights 1983
Drama
65608 95 mins C B, V P
Andra Millian
A seemingly shy girl happens to have an uncanny knack for Blackjack. With the odds against her and an unlikely group of "knights" to aid her, she sets up an incredible "sting" operation.
MPAA:PG
Crown — *Vestron Video*

Stage Door 1937
Comedy-Drama
10054 92 mins B/W B, V P, T
Katharine Hepburn, Ginger Rogers, Lucille Ball, Eve Arden, Andrea Leeds, directed by Gregory La Cava
Based on Edna Ferber's play, set in theatrical boarding house, film follows ambitions of young aspiring actresses.
RKO; Pandro S Berman — *Blackhawk Films; Nostalgia Merchant*

Stagedoor Canteen 1943
Musical
08667 135 mins B/W B, V P
Tallulah Bankhead, Merle Oberon, Katharine Hepburn, Paul Muni, Ethel Waters, Johnny Weismuller
A huge love story of a soldier who falls for a canteen hostess. Dozens of top stars and band leaders.
UA; Sol Lesser; Frank Borzage — *Movie Buff Video; VCII; Discount Video Tapes; Cable Films; Video Connection; Prism; Kartes Video Communications*

Stage Fright 1983
Horror
72529 82 mins C B, V P
A bashful actress is transformed into a homicidal killer after a latent psychosis in her becomes active.
John Lamand; Colin Eggleston — *VidAmerica*

Stage Fright 1950
Mystery/Drama
80079 110 mins B/W B, V P
Jane Wyman, Mariene Dietrich, Alastar Sim, Dame Sybil Thorndike, directed by Alfred Hitchcock
A young woman will stop at nothing to clear her boyfriend who has been accused of murdering another woman's husband.
Warner Bros. — *Warner Home Video*

Stage Show 1955
Variety
85217 29 mins B/W B, V P
Tommy and Jimmy Dorsey, Gordon McRae, Johnny Morgan, Connie Francis
An episode of the popular variety show, featuring the Dorsey Brothers Orchestra with musical guests. Original commercials included.
CBS — *Video Yesteryear*

Stage Show with the 1956
Dorsey Brothers
Variety
46345 28 mins B/W B, V, FO P
Tommy and Jimmy Dorsey and their Orchestra, Elvis Presley, Henny Youngman
A program from the Dorsey Brothers' television series featuring guest performers Elvis Presley and Henny Youngman. The original telecast date was March 17, 1956.
CBS — *Video Yesteryear*

Stagecoach 1939
Western
08599 100 mins B/W B, V P
John Wayne, Claire Trevor, Thomas Mitchell, George Bancroft, John Carradine, directed by John Ford
John Ford's western classic. Reactions of a group of people in a stagecoach under Indian attack.
Academy Awards '39: Best Supporting Actor (Thomas Mitchell); Best Scoring.
United Artists; Walter Wanger Productions — *Vestron Video; RCA VideoDiscs*

Stagecoach to Denver 1946
Western
10662 53 mins B/W B, V P
Allan Lane, Roy Barcroft, Bobby Blake
Red Ryder protects a friend's stagecoach line from outlaws.
Republic — *Captain Bijou; Cable Films; Video Connection; Discount Video Tapes; Nostalgia Merchant*

Stagestruck 1957
Drama
72946 95 mins B/W B, V P
Henry Fonda, Susan Strasberg, Christopher Plummer
A remake of 1933's "Morning Glory"; Susan Strasberg reprises the role made famous by Katharine Hepburn, as a determined, would-be actress.
RKO Radio Pictures — *United Home Video*

Stalag 17 1953
Adventure
29766 120 mins B/W B, V, LV P
William Holden, Don Taylor, Peter Graves, Otto Preminger, directed by Billy Wilder

---

World War II: American G.I.'s in German prison camp, thinking cynical sharp-tongued sergeant is a spy, beat him unmercifully. Based on the play by Donald Bevan and Edmund Trzcinski. Academy Awards '53: Best Actor (Holden). Paramount, Billy Wilder — *Paramount Home Video; RCA VideoDiscs*

Stand Alone   1985
Drama
84263   94 mins   C   B, V   P
Charles Durning, Pam Grier, James Keach
A honor-bound World War II vet living in New York explodes and fights back against local drug dealers.
MPAA:R
New World Pictures — *New World Video*

Stand By Me: A Portrait of   1985
Julian Lennon
Music-Performance/Documentary
82357   58 mins   C   B, V   P
This is a behind-the-scenes look at Julian Lennon's first American tour. He performs "Too Late for Goodbyes" and "Valotte" in VHS and Beta Hi-Fi Stereo.
Virgin Vision Ltd. — *MCA Home Video*

Stand-In   1937
Comedy/Satire
50952   90 mins   B/W   B, V   R, P
Humphrey Bogart, Leslie Howard, Joan Blondell, Alan Mowbray
A satire on Hollywood, in which a movie studio is saved from bankruptcy by a bookkeeping expert.
AM Available
United Artists — *Monterey Home Video; Learning Corp of America*

Stand-In   1937
Comedy
66636   91 mins   B/W   B, V   P
Humphrey Bogart, Joan Blondell, Leslie Howard, Alan Mowbray, Jack Carson
An efficiency expert is sent to save a Hollywood studio from bankruptcy.
United Artists; Walter Wanger — *Monterey Home Video*

Stand-In, The   1985
Comedy/Adventure
84514   87 mins   C   B, V   P
Danny Glover, directed by Robert Zagone
A strange comedy-action film in which Zagone sends up the worlds of sleaze films and organized crime.
One Pass Project — *Magnum Entertainment*

Stanley   1972
Horror
17201   108 mins   C   B, V   P

Chris Robinson, Alex Rocco, Susan Carroll Vietnam vet uses a rattlesnake as his personal weapon of revenge against mankind.
MPAA:PG
Crown International Pictures — *United Home Video*

Star Ascending: The   1984
Dallas Cowboys 1965-69
Football
79638   50 mins   C   B, V, FO   P
Highlights from the Dallas Cowboys' early games circa 1965-1969.
NFL Films — *NFL Films Video*

Star Bloopers   1979
Outtakes and bloopers
63334   47 mins   B/W   B, V   P
A collection of great movie moments that never made it to the screen, including missed cues, flubbed deliveries, malfunctioning props, and some rare Ronald Reagan footage.
Roy Self; John Gregory — *THORN EMI/HBO Video*

Star Chamber, The   1983
Drama
65504   109 mins   C   B, V, CED   P
Michael Douglas, Hal Holbrook
A conscientious judge who, seeing criminals freed on legal technicalities, comes to the conclusion that conventional law does not always reward the victims of crime, but often the criminals. Distressed by this, he turns to a friend and colleague for solace. His friend tells him of another type of justice that a group of judges have set up that is beyond conventional.
MPAA:R
20th Century Fox — *CBS/Fox Video*

Star Crash   1978
Science fiction/Adventure
65712   92 mins   C   B, V   P
Caroline Munroe, Christopher Plummer, David Hasselhoff
A trio of adventurers square off against interstellar evil by using their wits and technological wizardry.
MPAA:PG
Nat and Patrick Wachsberger — *Charter Entertainment*

Star Crystal   1985
Science fiction
88186   93 mins   C   B, V   P
C. Jutson Campbell, Faye Bolt, John W. Smith
Aboard a spaceship, an indestructible alien hunts down the human crew.
New World — *New World Video*

Star 80 1983
Drama
65612   104 mins   C   B, V, LV,   P
                            CED
*Mariel Hemingway, Eric Roberts, directed by
Bob Fosse*
The true show-business story of the stormy
relationship of Playboy Playmate of the Year
Dorothy Stratten and her manager-husband
Paul Snider that ended in headline-making
tragedy.
MPAA:R
Wolfgang Glattes; Kenneth Utt — *Warner
Home Video*

Star for Jeremy, A 1985
Cartoons
71054   22 mins   C   B, V   P
Animated
Dr. Allen Howes wrote this story of a young boy
who wanted to know why there was a star atop
the Christmas tree.
LBS Communications; DIC
Enterprises — *Karl/Lorimar Home Video*

Star Is Born, A 1954
Musical-Drama
58251   150 mins   C   B, V   P
*Judy Garland, James Mason, Jack Carson,
Charles Bickford, Tommy Noonan, directed by
George Cukor*
A young actress achieves Hollywood success
and marries a famous leading man whose star
wanes as hers shines brighter. Songs include
"The Man That Got Away," and "Born in a
Trunk."
Warner Bros — *Warner Home Video*

Star Is Born, A 1954
Musical-Drama
66325   175 mins   C   B, V, LV,   P
                            CED
*Judy Garland, James Mason, Jack Carson,
Tommy Noonan, Charles Bickford, directed by
George Cukor*
This newly restored version of the 1954 classic
reinstates over 20 minutes of long-missing
footage, including three Garland musical
numbers, "Here's What I'm Here For,"
"Shampoo Commercial" and "Lose That Long
Face." In stereo.
MPAA:PG
Warner Bros; Transcona
Enterprises — *Warner Home Video*

Star Is Born, A 1937
Drama
11217   111 mins   C   B, V, FO   P
*Janet Gaynor, Fredric March, Adolphe Menjou,
May Robson, Andy Devine, directed by William
Wellman*
A movie star declining in popularity marries a
shy girl and helps her become a star. Her fame
eclipses his and tragic consequences follow.

Academy Awards '37: Best Original Story;
Special Academy Award to W. Howard Greene
for color photography.
United Artists — *Video Yesteryear; Video
Connection; VCII; Video Dimensions; Cable
Films; Discount Video Tapes; Prism; Hollywood
Home Theater; Western Film & Video Inc;
Cinema Concepts; Kartes Video ,
Communications*

Star Is Born, A 1976
Musical
37425   140 mins   C   B, V   P
*Barbra Streisand, Kris Kristofferson, Paul
Mazursky, Gary Busey, Oliver Clark*
The tragic story of one rock star (Streisand) on
her way to the top and another (Kristofferson)
whose career is in decline. An updated version
of the 1937 and 1955 movies.
Academy Awards '76: Best Song (Evergreen).
MPAA:R
Warner Bros — *Warner Home Video; RCA
VideoDiscs*

Star of Midnight 1935
Mystery
79680   90 mins   B/W   B, V   P
Ginger Rogers, William Powell, Paul Kelly
A lawyer becomes involved in the
disappearance of a woman and the murder of a
columnist.
RKO — *RKO HomeVideo*

Star Packer 1934
Western
08829   53 mins   B/W   B, V, 3/4U   P
John Wayne
"Duke" puts on a marshal's badge and cleans
out the renegades.
Monogram — *Video Connection; Cable Films;
Discount Video Tapes; Spotlite Video; Sony
Video Software; Kartes Video Communications*

Star Signs '86 1985
Occult sciences
82072   50 mins   C   B, V   P
12   pgms
Astrologer Lynne Palmer provides weekly
astrological forecasts for each of the twelve
zodiac signs in this series.
*1.Aries 2.Taurus 3.Gemini 4.Cancer 5.Leo
6.Virgo 7.Libra 8.Scorpio 9.Sagittarius
10.Capricorn 11.Aquarius 12.Pisces*
Anthony Christopher Productions — *MCA
Home Video*

Star-Spangled Cowboys 1982
Football
47710   23 mins   C   B, V, FO   P
Team highlights of the 1981 Dallas Cowboys
who recaptured the NFC Eastern Division
Championship thanks to Tony Dorsett's 1,646
yards rushing.

NFL Films — *NFL Films Video*

Star Struck 1982
Musical/Comedy
65710   95 mins   C   B, V   P
Jo Kennedy
An 18-year-old waitress dreams of becoming a
new wave singer.
MPAA:PG
David Elfick; Richard Brennan — *Embassy
Home Entertainment*

Star Trek I 1966
Science fiction
47615   100 mins   C   CED   P
*William Shatner, Leonard Nimoy, Jeffrey Hunter,
Susan Oliver, DeForest Kelley*
Star Trek's only two-part episode, "The
Menagerie," incorporates the original 1964 pilot
show as a flashback. Mr. Spock kidnaps the
former captain of the Enterprise and returns to
Talos IV, the scene of a mystery from years
past.
NBC — *RCA VideoDiscs*

Star Trek: A Taste of 1967
Armageddon
Science fiction
82526   51 mins   C   B, V   P
*William Shatner, Leonard Nimoy, DeForest
Kelley*
Captain Kirk and Mr. Spock are drawn into a
computer controlled war.
Gene Roddenberry — *Paramount Home Video*

Star Trek: Amok Time 1967
Science fiction
82532   51 mins   C   B, V   P
William Shatner, Leonard Nimoy, Celia Lovsky
79 pgms
Spock becomes irrational and must return to his
home planet, Vulcan, when he is overwhelmed
by an irresistible mating urge.
Gene Roddenberry — *Paramount Home Video*

Star Trek: Arena 1967
Science fiction
70535   51 mins   C   B, V   P
*William Shatner, Leonard Nimoy, Carole
Shelyne*
Captain Kirk fights a duel to the death with a
murderous alien commander.
Paramount; Gene Roddenberry — *Paramount
Home Video*

Star Trek II 196?
Science fiction
56882   100 mins   C   CED   P
*William Shatner, Leonard Nimoy, DeForest
Kelley, Joan Collins, Frank Gorshin*

Two television episodes, "The City on the Edge
of Forever," written by Harlan Ellison, and "Let
That Be Your Last Battlefield."
NBC — *RCA VideoDiscs*

Star Trek: Balance of 1966
Terror
Science fiction
70531   51 mins   C   B, V   P
*William Shatner, Leonard Nimoy, DeForest
Kelly, Mark Lenard*
The Enterprise plays a game of cat-and-mouse
with a Romulan warship that has destroyed
several Earth outposts.
Paramount; Gene Roddenberry — *Paramount
Home Video*

Star Trek III 1967
Science fiction
59386   100 mins   C   CED   P
*William Shatner, Leonard Nimoy, DeForest
Kelley, Nichelle Nichols, James Doohan, Walter
Koenig*
A double feature of two popular "Star Trek"
episodes: "The Trouble with Tribbles" and "The
Tholian Web."
NBC — *RCA VideoDiscs*

Star Trek III: The Search 1984
for Spock
Science fiction
Closed Captioned
80508   105 mins   C   B, V, 8mm,   P
                            LV, CED
*William Shatner, Leonard Nimoy, DeForest
Kelley, James Doohan, Nichelle Nichols,
directed by Leonard Nimoy*
Captain Kirk commandeers the USS Enterprise
on a mission to the Genesis Planet to discover
whether or not Mr. Spock still lives. In VHS and
Beta Stereo Hi-Fi.
MPAA:PG
Paramount — *Paramount Home Video*

Star Trek: Catspaw 1967
Science fiction
85295   60 mins   C   B, V   P
*William Shatner, Leonard Nimoy, DeForest
Kelley, Theo Marcos*
The Enterprise crew encounters a pair of
malevolent witches on an unexplored planet,
where nothing is as it seems.
Gene Roddenberry — *Paramount Home Video*

Star Trek: Charlie X 1966
Science fiction
80510   51 mins   C   B, V   P
*William Shatner, Leonard Nimoy, Grace Lee
Whitney, Robert Walker, Jr., DeForest Kelley*
A teenage boy who was spacedwrecked on an
alien planet when young is rescued by the
Enterprise. Upon meeting Yeoman Janice Rand,
he begins to manifest strange powers.

Paramount; Gene Roddenbury — *Paramount Home Video*

Star Trek: Court Martial   1967
Science fiction
70537   51 mins   C   B, V   P
William Shatner, Leonard Nimoy, Percy Rodriguez, Elisha Cook, Jr., Joan Marshall
Captain Kirk is accused of purposely sending a crewman to his death. Despite his denials, Kirk faces a court martial hearing.
Paramount; Gene Roddenberry — *Paramount Home Video*

Star Trek IV   1967
Science fiction
60386   100 mins   C   CED   P
William Shatner, Leonard Nimoy, DeForest Kelley, Nichelle Nichols, Ricardo Montalban
Two "Star Trek" television episodes that provided the background for the recent feature films based on the series: "Space Seed" and "The Changeling."
NBC — *RCA VideoDiscs*

Star Trek: Dagger of the Mind   1966
Science fiction
80517   51 mins   C   B, V   P
William Shatner, Leonard Nimoy, James Gregory, Morgan Woodward, Marianna Hill
On an inspection trip at a penal colony, Captain Kirk falls victim to a mind control machine invented by a crazed doctor.
Paramount; Gene Roddenbury — *Paramount Home Video*

Star Trek V   1967
Science fiction
64332   100 mins   C   CED   P
William Shatner, Leonard Nimoy, DeForest Kelley, Nichelle Nichols, Mark Lenard
Two more well-liked episodes from the famous television series: "Mirror Mirror" and "Balance of Terror."
NBC — *RCA VideoDiscs*

Star Trek: Errand of Mercy   1967
Science fiction
82529   51 mins   C   B, V   P
William Shatner, Leonard Nimoy 79   pgms
Captain Kirk and Spock face Kor, a klingon warrier, and discover the meaning of war when a humanoid from Orgonia interferes.
Gene Roddenberry — *Paramount Home Video*

Star Trek VI   1967
Science fiction
64784   100 mins   C   CED   P
William Shatner, Leonard Nimoy, DeForest Kelley, Celia Lovsky, Mark Lenard, Jane Wyatt

Two more episodes in the popular TV series: "Amok Time" and "Journey to Babel."
NBC — *RCA VideoDiscs*

Star Trek: Friday's Child   1967
Science fiction
85299   60 mins   C   B, V   P
William Shatner, Leonard Nimoy, DeForest Kelley, Julie Newmar
Encountering an alien tribal society, Kirk and McCoy attempt to save a dead chief's pregnant wife from killing herself in accordance with tribal law.
Gene Roddenberry — *Paramount Home Video*

Star Trek: I,Mudd   1967
Science fiction
85296   60 mins   C   B, V   P
William Shatner, Leonard Nimoy, DeForest Kelley, Roger C. Carmel
Kirk and company run up against an old familiar enemy who has produced an army of identical androids in order to conquer the Federation, starting with the Enterprise.
Gene Roddenberry — *Paramount Home Video*

Star Trek: Journey to Babel   1967
Science fiction
85298   60 mins   C   B, V   P
William Shatner, Leonard Nimoy, DeForest Kelley, Mark Lenard
The Enterprise is assigned to transport a group of ambassadors, including Spock's father Sarek, to an interplanetary conference. When one of the ambassadors is murdered, Sarek appears to be the likely suspect.
Gene Roddenberry — *Paramount Home Video*

Star Trek: Metamorphosis   1967
Science fiction
85297   60 mins   C   B, V   P
William Shatner, Leonard Nimoy, DeForest Kelley, Elinor Donahue, Glenn Corbett
Kirk and crew encounter a scientist stranded on a desolate planet who is held a willing captive by a lonely bodiless entity.
Gene Roddenberry — *Paramount Home Video*

Star Trek: Miri   1966
Science fiction
80516   51 mins   C   B, V   P
William Shatner, Leonard Nimoy, Grace Lee Whitney, Kim Darby, Michael J. Pollard
The Enterprise crew send a landing party down to a planet that is inhabited only by children.
Paramount; Gene Roddenbury — *Paramount Home Video*

Star Trek: Mirror, Mirror 1967
Science fiction
85292 60 mins C B, V P
William Shatner, Leonard Nimoy, DeForest Kelly, Nichelle Nichols
Kirk, Scott, Uhura and McCoy are thrown onto another Enterprise existing in a barbaric, parallel universe.
Gene Roddenberry — *Paramount Home Video*

Star Trek: Mudd's Women 1966
Science fiction
80514 51 mins C B, V P
William Shatner, Leonard Nimoy, Roger C. Carmel, Karen Steele
A galactic con man is picked up by the Enterprise, along with his three female traveling companions.
Paramount; Gene Roddenbury — *Paramount Home Video*

Star Trek: Operation 1967
Annihilate
Science fiction
71380 51 mins C B, V P
William Shatner, Leonard Nimoy, DeForest Kelley
Captain Kirk finds his brother and the entire population of the planet Deneva the victims of a fatal epidemic of mass insanity.
Gene Roddenberry — *Paramount Home Video*

Star Trek: Shore Leave 1966
Science fiction
70532 51 mins C B, V P
William Shatner, Leonard Nimoy, DeForest Kelley
Captain Kirk allows the crew to take shore leave on an earthlike planet that proves to be full of unexplained phenomena.
Paramount; Gene Roddenberry — *Paramount Home Video*

Star Trek: Space Seed 1967
Science fiction
60211 50 mins C B, V P
William Shatner, Leonard Nimoy, DeForest Kelley, Nichelle Nichols, Ricardo Montalban
This is the classic TV episode which inspired the 1982 film "Star Trek II: The Wrath of Khan" where Khan, the leader of a race of supermen, tries to take over the Enterprise. Also included is a trailer for the feature film.
NBC — *Paramount Home Video*

Star Trek: The Alternative 1967
Factor
Science fiction
82530 51 mins C B, V P
William Shatner, Leonard Nimoy
A man with a split personality boards the Enterprise. It is discovered that one of his selves is potentially deadly.

Gene Roddenberry — *Paramount Home Video*

Star Trek: The Apple 1968
Science fiction
85293 60 mins C B, V P
William Shatner, Leonard Nimoy, DeForest Kelly, David Soul
The crew of the Enterprise stumbles upon a society of innocents held under the thrall of a dragon-faced computer.
Gene Roddenberry — *Paramount Home Video*

Star Trek: The 1968
Changeling
Science fiction
85291 60 mins C B, V P
William Shatner, Leonard Nimoy, DeForest Kelly, Nichelle Nichols
A computerized space probe boards the Enterprise and begins to execute its orders of destruction, hindered only by the false belief that Captain Kirk is its creator and master.
Gene Roddenberry — *Paramount Home Video*

Star Trek: The City on the 1967
Edge of Forever
Science fiction
82531 51 mins C B, V P
William Shatner, Leonard Nimoy, Joan Collins
Captain Kirk must allow the woman he loves to be killed in order to restore the future to normalcy.
Gene Roddenberry — *Paramount Home Video*

Star Trek: The 1966
Conscience of the King
Science fiction
70530 51 mins C B, V P
William Shatner, Leonard Nimoy, Arnold Moss, Barbara Anderson
Captain Kirk recognizes the leader of a traveling acting troupe as a convicted criminal and mass murderer.
NBC; Paramount; Gene
Roddenberry — *Paramount Home Video*

Star Trek: The Corbomite 1966
Maneuver
Science fiction
80518 51 mins C B, V P
William Shatner, Leonard Nimoy, DeForest Kelley, Clint Howard
The Enterprise plays cat and mouse with a massive alien starship that is controlled by a mysterious being.
Paramount; Gene Roddenbury — *Paramount Home Video*

Star Trek: The Deadly 1967
Years
Science fiction
85300 60 mins C B, V P

William Shatner, Leonard Nimoy, DeForest Kelley, Charles Drake
Kirk, McCoy, Scotty and Spock fall prey to a virus which ages them drastically, until their ability to command is in question.
Gene Roddenberry — *Paramount Home Video*

Star Trek: The Devil in the Dark   1967
Science fiction
82528   51 mins   C   B, V   P
William Shatner, Leonard Nimoy
The Enterprise crew searches for a murdering menace in the mining tunnels of Janus VI.
Gene Roddenberry — *Paramount Home Video*

Star Trek: The Doomsday Machine   1967
Science fiction
85294   60 mins   C   B, V   P
William Shatner, Leonard Nimoy, DeForest Kelly, William Windom
An monstrous alien ship is carving a path of planet-eating destruction and Kirk must stop before it reaches a populated solar system.
Gene Roddenberry — *Paramount Home Video*

Star Trek: The Enemy Within   1966
Science fiction
80513   51 mins   C   B, V   P
William Shatner, Leonard Nimoy, DeForest Kelley
A malfunction in the transporter splits Captain Kirk in two—one good, the other evil.
Paramount; Gene Roddenbury — *Paramount Home Video*

Star Trek: The Galileo Seven   1967
Science fiction
70533   51 mins   C   B, V   P
William Shatner, Leonard Nimoy, DeForest Kelley, James Doohan, Don Marshall
Mr. Spock is assigned to lead a landing party on Murasaki 312 and faces danger when his people are attacked by savages.
Paramount; Gene Roddenberry — *Paramount Home Video*

Star Trek: The Man Trap   1966
Science fiction
80509   51 mins   C   B, V   P
William Shatner, Leonard Nimoy, DeForest Kelley, Jeanne Bal, Alfred Ryder.
A salt vampire, the last remaining inhabitant of plante M-113, takes the form of Dr. McCoy's old girlfriend as a ruse to sneak aboard The Enterprise.
Paramount; Gene Roddenbury — *Paramount Home Video*

Star Trek: The Menagerie Parts I and II   1966
Science fiction
70529   102 mins   C   B, V   P
William Shatner, Leonard Nimoy, Jeffrey Hunter, Susan Oliver, Majel Barrett, Malachi Throne
Mr. Spock kidnaps the Enterprises's former captain and sets the ship on a course to the forbidden planet of Talos IV. This, Star Trek's only two-part episode, incorporates portions of the show's original 1964 pilot film.
Paramount; Gene Roddenberry — *Paramount Home Video*

Star Trek: The Motion Picture   1980
Science fiction
48512   132 mins   C   CED   P
William Shatner, Leonard Nimoy, DeForest Kelley, Stephen Collins, Persis Khambatta
The starship Enterprise must fight a mysterious alien invasion heading directly for Earth. With new equipment and a new mission, Captain Kirk orders the starship into Warp Drive to meet and conquer this destructive enemy.
MPAA:G
Gene Roddenberry — *RCA VideoDiscs*

Star Trek: The Motion Picture   1980
Science fiction
64510   144 mins   C   B, V, LV   P
William Shatner, Leonard Nimoy, DeForest Kelley, James Doohan, Stephen Collins, Persis Khambatta
The Enterprise fights a strange alien force that threatens Earth in this adaptation of the famous TV series. Twelve additional minutes of previously unseen footage have been added to this home video version of the theatrical feature. In stereo.
MPAA:G
Gene Roddenberry; Paramount — *Paramount Home Video*

Star Trek: The Naked Time   1966
Science fiction
80512   51 mins   C   B, V   P
William Shatner, Leonard Nimoy, DeForest Kelley, Bruce Hyde
The crew of the Enterprise becomes affected by an alien virus that releases all inhibitions.
Paramount; Gene Roddenbury — *Paramount Home Video*

Star Trek: The Return of the Archons   1967
Science fiction
70538   51 mins   C   B, V   P
William Shatner, Leonard Nimoy, DeForest Kelley, Torin Thatcher, George Takei

Kirk, Spock and McCoy beam down to a strange planet where the populace are held in mind control by a giant computer.
Paramount; Gene Roddenberry — *Paramount Home Video*

Star Trek: The Squire of Gothos
1967
Science fiction
70534   51 mins   C   B, V   P
William Shatner, Leonard Nimoy, Nichelle Nichols, William Campbell
The Enterprise crew runs into trouble when an irrational alien forces Captain Kirk to spar with him in a gothic castle.
Paramount; Gene Roddenberry — *Paramount Home Video*

Star Trek II: The Wrath of Khan
1982
Science fiction
62784   113 mins   C   B, V, LV   P
William Shatner, Leonard Nimoy, Ricardo Montalban, DeForest Kelley, directed by Nicholas Meyer
Admiral Kirk and the crew of the Enterprise are targeted for death by Khan, an old foe who blames Kirk for the death of his wife.
MPAA:PG
Paramount — *Paramount Home Video; RCA VideoDiscs*

Star Trek: This Side of Paradise
1967
Science fiction
82527   51 mins   C   B, V   P
William Shatner, Leonard Nimoy, DeForest Kelley
The Enterprise crew beams down to a colony that has been exposed to deadly. To their surprise, they encounter some healthy survivors.
Gene Roddenberry — *Paramount Home Video*

Star Trek: Tomorrow Is Yesterday
1967
Science fiction
70536   51 mins   C   B, V   P
William Shatner, Leonard Nimoy, DeForest Kelley, James Doohan, Roger Perry
The Enterprise hits a black hole and is catapulted back through time to the 1960's.
Paramount; Gene Roddenberry — *Paramount Home Video*

Star Trek Volume 1
1966
Science fiction
44587   104 mins   C   B, V   P
William Shatner, Leonard Nimoy, DeForest Kelley, Jeffrey Hunter, Susan Oliver
"The Menagerie," a two-part episode, tells the story of what happened to the former commander of the Enterprise, Captain

Christopher Pike, and why Spock almost faced court martial.
NBC — *Paramount Home Video*

Star Trek Volume 2
1967
Science fiction
44584   104 mins   C   B, V   P
William Shatner, Leonard Nimoy, DeForest Kelley, Jane Wyatt, Mark Lenard
In "Amok Time" Kirk authorizes an unscheduled voyage to Vulcan for Spock's marriage because although Vulcans are normally unemotional, when the time comes to marry they are compelled, under penalty of madness and death, to return to their home planet. Kirk becomes part of this ritual wedding ceremony. The second episode, "Journey to Babel," involves intrigue when the Enterprise is assigned the task of transporting delegates from many planets to the Babel Conference and Kirk suspects a spy on board. Among the delegates are Spock's parents, which presents the opportunity for reconciliation between Spock and his father.
NBC — *Paramount Home Video*

Star Trek Volume 3
1968
Science fiction
44583   104 mins   C   B, V   P
William Shatner, Leonard Nimoy, DeForest Kelley, Nichelle Nichols
In the episode "Mirror, Mirror" a transporter malfunction throws the Enterprise crew into a parallel or mirror universe where command is asserted by force and advancement is achieved by assassination. The search for a missing Federation ship, the Defiant, leads the Enterprise into unchartered space in the episode "The Tholian Web." The ship appears on the viewing screen, but does not register on the sensors. It has suffered a power loss that also affects the Enterprise, causing weakness and insanity among the crew. When Kirk goes aboard the Defiant to investigate, he becomes stranded on the empty ship.
NBC — *Paramount Home Video*

Star Trek Volume 4
196?
Science fiction
44585   104 mins   C   B, V   P
William Shatner, Leonard Nimoy, DeForest Kelley, Nichelle Nichols, James Doohan, George Takei
This program contains two episodes of the popular TV series Star Trek: "The Trouble with Tribbles" ('67) and "Let That Be Your Last Battlefield" ('69). "The Trouble with Tribbles" speaks for itself. Tribbles—cute, fuzzy, seemingly harmless little creatures create problems for the crew of the Enterprise. In "Let That Be Your Last Battlefield" an age-old battle between two hostile alien powers engulfs the Enterprise.
NBC — *Paramount Home Video*

Star Trek Volume 5   196?

Science fiction
44586   104 mins   C   B, V   P
William Shatner, Leonard Nimoy, DeForest
Kelley, Joan Collins
This program contains two episodes from the
popular TV series Star Trek. In "The Balance of
Terror" ('66), Captain Kirk is about to perform a
wedding for two crew members when the
Romulans attack Outpost 4. This leads the
Enterprise in pursuit of an attack ship, whose
invisibility shield ultimately causes its own
destruction. In "The City on the Edge of
Forever," McCoy accidentally beams himself
down to a strange planet, where he enters a
time vortex and drastically changes history. Kirk
and Spock must rescue him.
NBC — Paramount Home Video

Star Trek: What Are Little   1966
Girls Made Of?

Science fiction
80515   51 mins   C   B, V   P
William Shatner, Leonard Nimoy, Majel
Barrett:Michael Strong, Ted Cassidy, Sherry
Jackson
Nurse Christine Chapel visits an old boyfriend
whose scientific experiments with robots, have
progressed farther than anyone had imagined.
Paramount; Gene Roddenbury — Paramount
Home Video

Star Trek: Where No Man   1966
Has Gone Before

Science fiction
80511   51 mins   C   B, V   P
William Shatner, Leonard Nimoy, Gary
Lockwood, Sally Kellerman, George Takei
Two members of the Enterprise crew begin to
develop unearthly psi powers after the ship is
damaged by the energy barrier at the edge of
the Milky Way galaxy. The second pilot for the
series.
Paramount; Gene Roddenbury — Paramount
Home Video

Star Trek: Who Mourns   1967
for Adonais

Science fiction
82533   51 mins   C   B, V   P
William Shatner, Leonard Nimoy, James
Doohan, Leslie Parrish
Captain Kirk and his crew encounter a strange
force in outer space and come under the
domination of the ancient Greek god Apollo.
Gene Roddenberry — Paramount Home Video

Star Wars   1977

Science fiction/Adventure
47505   121 mins   C   B, V, LV,   P
                                CED
Mark Hamill, Carrie Fisher, Harrison Ford, Alec
Guinness, Peter Cushing, David Prowse,
directed by George Lucas
A long time ago in a galaxy far, far away, Rebel
forces are engaged in a life-or-death struggle
with the tyrant leaders of the Galactic Empire.
Musical score composed by John Williams.
Academy Awards '77: Best Art Decoration; Set
Decoration; Film Editing; Costume Design;
Achievement in Sound; Visual Effects; Original
Score. MPAA:PG EL, SP
20th Century Fox — CBS/Fox Video

Starchaser: The Legend   1985
of Orin

Cartoons/Adventure
86157   107 mins   C   B, V   P
An animated fantasy about a boy who must
save the world of the future from malevolent
hordes.
MPAA:PG
Atlantic Releasing — Paramount Home Video

Starflight One   1983

Adventure/Science fiction
81167   115 mins   C   B, V   P
Ray Milland, Lee Majors, Hal Linden, Lauren
Hutton, Robert Webber
A space shuttle is called upon to save the
world's first hypersonic airliner trapped in an
orbit above earth.
Orion Pictures — Vestron Video

Starman   1984

Science fiction/Romance
Closed Captioned
80877   115 mins   C   B, V   P
Jeff Bridges, Karen Allen, Charles Martin Smith,
Richard Jaeckel, directed by John Carpenter
An alien from an advanced civilization lands in
Wisconsin. After meeting with ignorant hostility
from the military, he clones himself into the form
of a grieving young widow's recently expired
husband. With the authorities in dogged pursuit,
the wodow and the visitor travel to his
redezvous spot in Arizona, falling in love as they
go. Available in Dolby Hi Fi Stereo and Beta Hi
Fi Stereo.
MPAA:PG
Columbia Pictures — RCA/Columbia Pictures
Home Video

Stars Look Down, The   1939

Drama
07263   96 mins   B/W   B, V   P
Michael Redgrave, Margaret Lockwood, Emlyn
Williams
A mine owner forces miners to work in an
unsafe mine in a Welsh town and disaster
strikes. Based on the A. J. Cronin novel.
MGM; Carol Reed — Movie Buff Video;
Hollywood Home Theater; Cable Films;

Discount Video Tapes; Video Yesteryear; Kartes Video Communications

---

Stars of the Russian Ballet
1953

Dance
69833   80 mins   C   B, V   P
Galina Vlanova, Maya Plisetskaya
This program is a compilation of excerpts from three ballets, Swan Lake, The Fountain of Bakhchisarai, and The Flames of Paris.
Sovexportfilm USSR — *Video Arts International*

Stars on 45
1983

Music
65518   71 mins   C   B, V, LV, CED   P
An elaborate live stage revue covering the past 30 years of pop music history. Featured are nostalgia tunes by Little Richard, Chuck Berry, Elvis, and the Beatles. Woodstock, Soul and Disco tunes are all highlighted in the show. In stereo VHS and Beta Hi-Fi.
MCA Pay Television — *MCA Home Video*

Stars on Parade/Boogie Woogie Dream
1946

Musical
11258   55 mins   B/W   B, V, FO   P
Milton Wood, Jane Cooley, Francine Everett, Bob Howard, Eddie Smith, Phil Moore, Lena Horne, Teddy Wilson
A pair of all-black musicals which shows off a host of talent from the 1940's.
All American Pictures — *Video Yesteryear*

Starship: Video Hoopla
1986

Music video
88358   14 mins   C   B, V   P
Three videos from the rock group's album "Knee Deep in the Hoopla": "Tomorrow Doesn't Matter Tonight," "We Built This City" and "Sara."
RCA Video — *RCA/Columbia Pictures Home Video*

Start the Revolution Without Me
1970

Comedy
79556   91 mins   C   B, V   P
Gene Wilder, Donald Sutherland, Orson Welles, Hugh Griffith, Billie Whitelaw, directed by Bud Yorkin
Two sets of identical twins who were separated at birth meet thirty years later on the eve of the French Revolution.
MPAA:PG
Norman Lear; Warner Bros. — *Warner Home Video*

Start to Finish the Grand Prix
1981

Automobiles-Racing
68245   89 mins   C   B, V, CED   P
The highlights of the 1981 Grand Prix are presented in this film.
Formula One Constructors Association — *MGM/UA Home Video*

Starting Over
1979

Comedy-Drama
48513   105 mins   C   B, V, LV   P
Burt Reynolds, Jill Clayburgh, Candice Bergen
His life racked by divorce, Phil Potter learns what it's like to be single, self-sufficient, and lonely once again. When a blind date grows into a serious affair, the romance is temporarily halted by his hang-up for his ex-wife.
MPAA:R
Alan J. Pakula — *Paramount Home Video; RCA VideoDiscs*

Starvengers
1982

Cartoons/Science fiction
62425   105 mins   C   B, V   P
Animated
When action and excitement meet futuristic technology, the result is the high-powered super-intelligence of the robot Starvenger.
EL, SP
Toei Animation; Terry Production — *Family Home Entertainment*

State of Siege
1973

Drama
44781   119 mins   C   B, V   P
Yves Montand, Renato Salvatori, O.E. Hasse
Unsettling American foreign policy results in the assasination of U.S. officials in South America.
Cinema 5 — *RCA/Columbia Pictures Home Video*

State of the Union
1948

Comedy
31603   124 mins   B/W   B, V   P
Spencer Tracy, Katherine Hepburn, Angela Lansbury, Van Johnson, directed by Frank Capra
A presidential candidate, backed by a millionairess, battles for integrity with his wife.
MGM — *MCA Home Video*

Stations West
1948

Mystery
10070   92 mins   B/W   B, V   P
Dick Powell, Jane Greer, Agnes Moorehead, Burl Ives, Tom Powers, Raymond Burr
Disguised Army officer is sent to uncover mystery of hijackers and murderers.
RKO — *RKO HomeVideo; Blackhawk Films*

Statlers—Brothers in Song, The   1986
Music-Performance
84880   19 mins   C   B, V   P
The award-winning country band performs their greatest songs.
Polygram Music Video — RCA/Columbia Pictures Home Video

Statue, The   1971
Comedy
71206   84 mins   C   B, V   P
David Niven, Virna Lisa, Robert Vaughn, Ann Bell, John Cleese, directed by Rod Amateau
An English comedy of errors ensues when a famed sculptress unveils a nude rendering of her Nobel Prize winning husband.
MPAA:R
Cinerama; Josef Shaftel — Prism

Statue of Liberty, The   1985
Documentary/History-US
86240   60 mins   C   B, V, LV   P
A history of the famed Statue with commentary by David McCullough, Derek Jacobi, Jeremy Irons and Milos Forman.
Ken Burns — Vestron Video

Stay as You Are   1978
Drama
47371   103 mins   C   B, V   P
Marcello Mastroianni, Nastassia Kinski, Francisco Rabal, Monica Randal
A sensual, psychological drama about an older man who finds himself attracted to a young girl—who may be his daughter by a long-forgotten mistress.
Giovanni Bertolucci — Warner Home Video

Stay As You Are   1978
Drama
86038   95 mins   C   B, V   P
Marcello Mastroianni, Nastassia Kinski, Francisco Rabal, directed by Alberto Lattuada
An aging Frenchman falls in love with a girl who may be his illegitimate teenage daughter.
French — Warner Home Video

Stay Hungry   1976
Comedy-Drama
80135   102 mins   C   B, V   P
Jeff Bridges, Sally Field, Arnold Sahwarzenegger, directed by Bob Rafeison
When a rich, disenchanted southerner buys a health spa, he finds new happiness when he falls in love with the spa's receptionist.
MPAA:R
United Artists — CBS/Fox Video

Staying Alive   1983
Drama
Closed Captioned
65400   96 mins   C   B, V, LV,   P
                                    CED
John Travolta, Cynthia Rhodes, Finola Hughes
A talented young dancer struggles to obtain a role in a professional Broadway musical. Along the way, he becomes intimately involved with two attractive young women. In stereo VHS and Beta Hi-Fi.
MPAA:PG
Paramount — Paramount Home Video

Staying On   1980
Drama
70884   87 mins   C   B, V   P
Trevor Howard, Celia Johnson, directed by Irene Shubik
Based on the Paul Scott novel, this English drama follows the life of a post-colonial British colonel and his wife who chose to remain in India.
Granada Television — Simon and Schuster Video

Steagle, The   1971
Comedy
85369   101 mins   C   B, V   P
Richard Benjamin, Cloris Leachman
The threat of a missle crisis lets a fantasizing professor loose to enact his wildest dreams.
MPAA:R
Jim Di Gangi — Charter Entertainment

Steam and Diesel on the Bessemer and Lake Erie/ The Diesels Roar on the Pennsy   195?
Trains
59991   24 mins   B/W   B, V   P, T
"Steam and Diesel" shows the contrast between steam and diesel trains during the transitional period, the twilight years of the B. and L. E. "Diesels Roar" features the five "Geeps" rolling east and the westbound "Duquesne."
Fred McLeod — Blackhawk Films

Steamboat Bill, Jr.   1928
Comedy
10095   72 mins   B/W   B, V   P, T
Buster Keaton, Ernest Torrence, Marion Byron, Tom Lewis
Student returns to father's Mississippi river boat. After many misadventures, he marries daughter of his father's rival.
United Artists; Schenk Keaton
Prod — Blackhawk Films; Discount Video Tapes; Video Dimensions; Video Yesteryear

Steel 1980
Drama
66608   100 mins   C   B, V, LV   P
Construction workers on a mammoth
skyscraper face insurmountable odds and
strong opposition to the completion of the
building.
MPAA:R
World Northal — *Vestron Video*

Steel Arena 1972
Adventure
84095   99 mins   C   B, V   P
*Dusty Russell, Gene Drew, Buddy Love,
directed by Mark L. Lester*
Several real life stunt-car drivers appear in this
action-packed film, crammed with spins, jumps,
explosions and world-record-breaking, life
risking stunts.
MPAA:PG
LT Films — *Vestron Video*

Steel Cowboy 1978
Drama
70715   100 mins   C   B, V   P
*James Brolin, Rip Torn, Jennifer Warren,
Strother Martin, Melanie Griffith, Lou Frizzell,
directed by Harvey Laidman*
With his marriage, sanity and livelihood all on
the line, an independent trucker agrees to haul a
hot herd of stolen steer.
Roger Gimbel Prod. for EMI Television
Programs — *VCL Home Video*

Steel Fisted Dragon 1982
Martial arts
78390   85 mins   C   B, V   P
Steve Lee, Johnny Kong Kong, Peter Chan
A son seeks revenge on the gang who
murdered his mother and burned her house to
the ground.
MPAA:R
Independent — *THORN EMI/HBO Video*

Steel Town 1983
Tough/Steelers 50
Seasons
Football
66218   45 mins   C   B, V, FO   P
The Pittsburgh Steelers' 1982-83 season
highlights plus a retrospective of their first 50
years.
NFL Films — *NFL Films Video*

Steelyard Blues 1973
Comedy
81785   93 mins   C   B, V   P
*Jane Fonda, Donald Sutherland, Peter Boyle,
Howard Hesseman, John Savage*
A motley crew of eccentrics team up to steal an
old World War II plane to fly away to a place
where there are no rules.
MPAA:PG

Warner Bros. — *Warner Home Video*

Steinbeck's The Pearl 1948
Drama/Literature-American
58732   90 mins   B/W   B, V   P
Pedro Armandez, Maria Marques
John Steinbeck's classic novel concerning two
people who find a valuable pearl which disrupts
their lives. (Original screenplay by Steinbeck).
RKO — *Mastervision*

Stella Dallas 1937
Drama
81445   106 mins   B/W   B, V, LV   P
*Barbara Stanwyck, Anne Shirley, John Boles,
Alan Hale, Marjorie Main, directed by King Vidor*
A lower class woman must learn to let go of the
daughter she loves so that she may have a
better life.
Samuel Goldwyn — *Embassy Home
Entertainment*

Stenciling 1986
Handicraft
88307   120 mins   C   B, V   P
Lanie Abrams, stenciler supreme, demonstrates
wall and fabric stencils.
Victorian Video Prod. — *Victorian Video
Productions*

Step Lively 1944
Musical/Comedy
64916   88 mins   B/W   B, V   P
*Frank Sinatra, Gloria De Haven, George
Murphy, Walter Slezak, Adolphe Menjou, Anne
Jeffreys*
A young playwright tries to recover the money
he loaned to a fast-talking Broadway producer
and is forced to take the leading role in his play.
This musical remake of "Room Service" was
Frank Sinatra's first starring role.
RKO — *RKO HomeVideo; Blackhawk Films*

Stephen King's Silver 1989
Bullet
Horror
Closed Captioned
84531   95 mins   C   B, V, LV   P
*Gary Busey, Everett McGill, Corey Haim, Megan
Follows, directed by Daniel Attias*
A small town is ravaged by a werewolf in the
King tradition.
MPAA:R
Martha Schumacher — *Paramount Home
Video*

Sterile Cuckoo, The 1969
Romance/Comedy
82544   108 mins   C   B, V   P
Liza Minnelli, Wendell Burton, Tim McIntire
An aggressive coed pursues a shy freshman
boy who seems to embody her romantic ideal.

MPAA:R
Alan J Pakula — *Paramount Home Video*

Steve Allen's Music Room—Volume I

1984

Music
70163   116 mins   C   B, V   P
Steve Allen, Rosemary Clooney, Ann Jillian, Patti Page
Various artists from the jazz, pop and contemporary music worlds perform and chat with Steve Allen.
Buena Vista Home Video — *Buena Vista Home Video*

Steve Gadd: Up Close

1985

Music
87927   60 mins   C   B, V   P
The much-recorded studio drummer instructs in 4-stick drumming, bass drumming, chart reading, time keeping and more.
DCI Music Video — *DCI Music Video*

Steve Gadd II: In Session

1985

Music-Performance
87928   90 mins   C   B, V   P
The popular studio drummer goes to work, demonstrating many facets of his technique, with Will Lee, Richard Tee, Jorge Dalto and others.
DCI Music Video — *DCI Music Video*

Steve Martin Live

1985

Comedy-Performance
86362   58 mins   C   B, V   P
Steve Martin, Teri Garr, Buck Henry, David Letterman, Paul Simon
Martin shows veteran comedians his famous Universal Amphitheatre performance and his short "The Absent-Minded Waiter."
Vestron Video — *Vestron Video*

Steve Miller Band

1983

Music-Performance
69391   50 mins   C   B, V   P
This music video showcases one of America's premier rock bands live in concert and includes the hits "Abracadabra," "Rock 'n Me" and "Fly Like an Eagle," among others.
EMI Music — *THORN EMI/HBO Video*

Stevie Nicks—I Can't Wait

1985

Music video
85830   29 mins   C   B, V   P
A compilation of Nicks' hit songs including "Stop Draggin' My Heart Around," "Stand Back" and "Talk to Me."
RCA Video Prod. — *RCA/Columbia Pictures Home Video*

Stevie Nicks in Concert

1982

Music-Performance
60572   56 mins   C   B, V, CED   P
The song siren of Fleetwood Mac performs "Sara," "Stop Draggin' My Heart Around," "Edge of Seventeen," and more in this March 1982 solo concert featuring a back-up band comprised of Roy Bittan, Bob Glaub, Bobby Hall, Russ Kunkel, Benmont Tench, Waddy Wachtel, Sharon Celani, and Lori Perry. Stereo.
Marty Callner — *CBS/Fox Video; Pioneer Artists*

Stick

1985

Suspense
Closed Captioned
81197   109 mins   C   B, V, LV   P
Burt Reynolds, Candice Bergen, George Segal, Charles Durning, Dar Robinson, directed by Burt Reynolds
Stick is an ex-con who wants to start a new life for himself in Miami. Based upon the Elmore Leonard novel. Available in Hi-Fi Stereo for both formats.
MPAA:R
Universal; Jennings Lang — *MCA Home Video*

Sticks of Death

1984

Martial arts
79875   90 mins   C   B, V   P
When a man is left near death by gangsters, his grandfather teaches him the ancient martial art of the sticks of death.
Fred Farguar; Dr. Frank Schlercio — *VCL Home Video*

Stiletto

1969

Crime-Drama
08523   101 mins   C   B, V   P
Alex Cord, Britt Ekland, Patrick O'Neal, Joseph Wiseman, Barbara McNair, Roy Scheider
A young man is rescued from a mob by a Mafia gang leader after raping a young girl. Based on a novel by Harold Robbins.
MPAA:R
Avco Embassy; Norman Rosemont — *Embassy Home Entertainment*

Still of the Night

1982

Suspense
66067   91 mins   C   B, V, CED   P
Meryl Streep, Roy Scheider, directed by Robert Benton
A Hitchcock-style thriller about a psychiatrist infatuated with a mysterious woman who may or may not be a killer.
MPAA:PG
United Artists — *CBS/Fox Video*

Still Smokin'

1983

Comedy
64937   91 mins   C   B, V   P
Cheech Marin, Tommy Chong

Cheech and Chong travel to Amsterdam to raise funds for a bankrupt film festival group by hosting a dope-a-thon.
MPAA:R
Paramount — *Paramount Home Video*

Stilwell Road, The   1947
World War II/Documentary
53647   49 mins   B/W   B, V, 3/4U   P
A documentary look at Signal Corps footage of the China-Burma front, focusing on this moment in history with American forces under the command of General Joe Stilwell.
Unknown — *International Historic Films; Discount Video Tapes; Video Yesteryear*

Sting, The   1973
Comedy-Drama
14009   129 mins   C   B, V   P
Paul Newman, Robert Redford, Robert Shaw, Charles Durning, Eileen Brennan, directed by George Roy Hill
A pair of con-artists in Chicago of the 1930's set out to fleece a big time racketeer, pitting brain against brawn and pistol.
Academy Awards '73: Best Picture; Best Story and Screenplay; Best Art Direction; Best Set Decoration. MPAA:PG
Universal; Richard D Zanuck — *MCA Home Video; RCA VideoDiscs*

Sting II, The   1983
Comedy
64794   102 mins   C   B, V, LV   P
Jackie Gleason, Mac Davis, Teri Garr, Karl Malden, Oliver Reed, directed by Jeremy Paul Kagan
A complicated comic plot concludes with the final con game involving a fixed boxing match where the stakes top a million dollars and where the payoff could be murder. A sequel to "The Sting."
MPAA:PG
Universal — *MCA Home Video*

Sting of the Dragon   1974
Masters
Martial arts
84029   96 mins   C   B, V   P
Angela Mao, Thoon Rhee, Carter Huang, directed by Huang Feng
A martial arts actioneer featuring Bruce Lee's female Kung-Fu counterpart, Angela Mao.
MPAA:R
Raymond Chow — *United Home Video*

Stingray   1978
Adventure
87914   105 mins   C   B, V   P
Chris Mitchum, Sherry Jackson, Les Lannom, directed by Richard Taylor

Two guys buy a Corvette not knowing it's loaded with stolen cash hidden there by gangsters, who soon thereafter come after them.
MPAA:PG
Donald R. Ham; Bill L. Bruce — *Embassy Home Entertainment*

Stingray: Invaders of the   1981
Deep
Adventure
71369   92 mins   C   B, V   P
Animated, directed by David Elliott, John Kelly, Desmond Saunders
Captain Tempest leads his submarine "Stingray" against the aliens invading Marineville in this supermarionated saga.
Gerry Anderson — *Family Home Entertainment*

Stir Crazy   1980
Comedy
58435   104 mins   C   B, V, LV   P
Richard Pryor, Gene Wilder, Nicholas Coster, Lee Purcell, directed by Sidney Poitier
Two down-on-their luck losers find themselves convicted of a robbery they didn't commit and sentenced to 120 years behind bars with a mean assortment of inmates.
MPAA:R
Columbia; Hannah Weinstein — *RCA/Columbia Pictures Home Video; RCA VideoDiscs*

Stocks and Blondes   1985
Comedy
86359   79 mins   C   B, V   P
The world of industrial finance is used as a background for some raunchy sex humor.
MPAA:R
Longboat Film Assoc. — *Vestron Video*

Stolen Kisses   1969
Drama
44775   90 mins   C   B, V   P
Jean-Pierre Leaud, Delphine Seyrig, directed by Francois Truffaut
A continuation of the story of Antoine Doinel (first told in the picture "The 400 Blows") and his dishonorable discharge from the army, his initially awkward, but finally successful adventures with women.
Lopert Pictures — *RCA/Columbia Pictures Home Video*

Stomach Formula   1984
Physical fitness
74076   49 mins   C   B, V   P
This is the official Richard Simmons seven-minute a day workout of abdominal fitness.
Karl Home Video — *Karl/Lorimar Home Video*

Stone Boy, The — 1984
Drama
Closed Captioned
77465　93 mins　C　B, V　P
Glenn Close, Robert Duvall, Jason Presson
A twelve-year-old boy accidentally kills his older
brother on their family's Montana farm, causing
much unpleasantness.
MPAA:PG
20th Century Fox — *CBS/Fox Video*

Stone Cold Dead — 1980
Mystery
69306　100 mins　C　B, V　P
*Richard Crenna, Paul Williams, Linda Sorensen,
Belinda J. Montgomery*
A sniper who selects only prostitutes as victims
baits the police with photographs of the victims
at the moment of their deaths.
MPAA:R
George Mendeluk; John Ryan — *Media Home
Entertainment*

Stone Killer, The — 1973
Drama
76039　95 mins　C　B, V　P
*Charles Bronson, Martin Balsam, Norman Fell,
Ralph Waite*
Charles Bronson stars as a tough plainclothes
cop in this action-packed drama set in the
underworld of New York and Los Angeles.
MPAA:R
Michael Winner — *RCA/Columbia Pictures
Home Video*

Stoneflies and the Big Hole — 1985
Fishing
82507　52 mins　C　B, V, 3/4U　P
Two agile fly fishermen cast for various kinds of
trout.
Grunko Films — *Grunko Films*

Stoner — 1980
Martial arts/Adventure
59083　88 mins　C　B, V　P
A martial arts adventure featuring a showdown
between special agents and a depraved crime
lord.
Unknown — *HarmonyVision*

Stoogemania — 1985
Comedy
86878　95 mins　C　B, V　P
*Josh Mostel, Melanie Chartoff, Sid Caesar,
directed by Chuck Workman*
A nerd becomes so obsessed with the Stooges
that they begin to take over his life and ruin it.
James Ruxin; Chuck Workman — *Paramount
Home Video*

Stooges Shorts Festival — 194?
Comedy
57342　55 mins　B/W　B, V　P
This collection of shorts includes "Disorder in
the Court" (1936), "Sing a Song of Six Pants"
(1947), and "Malice in the Palace" (1949).
Columbia — *Hollywood Home Theater*

Stop Making Sense — 1984
Music-Performance
82288　99 mins　C　B, V　P
*David Byrne, Tina Weymouth, Chris Franz, Jerry
Harrison, directed by Jonathan Demme*
Talking Heads perform eighteen of their best
songs in this concert filmed at The Pantages
Theater in Los Angeles. This tape also features
two songs which were cut from the original film.
Available in VHS Dolby Hi-Fi Stereo and Beta
Hi-Fi Stereo.
Island Alive — *RCA/Columbia Pictures Home
Video*

Stop That Train — 195?
Adventure
10036　25 mins　B/W　B, V　P, T
*Kirby Grant, Gloria Winters, Perry Kellman,
Edward Foster, William Hale*
Escaped convict plants explosives aboard train
with railway president on it. With ten minutes to
spare, Sky King tries to make a rescue. From
the TV series "Sky King."
CBS — *Blackhawk Films*

Stopover Tokyo — 1957
War-Drama
80834　100 mins　C　B, V　P
*Robert Wagner, Joan Collins, Edmund O'Brien,
Ken Scott*
An American intelligence agent uncovers a plot
to assassinate the American High
Commissioner while on leave in Japan.
Available in VHS and Beta Hi Fi Stereo.
20th Century Fox — *Key Video*

Stories and Fables — 1985
Fairy tales
66355　50 mins　C　B, V　P
This is a series of live-action stories for children.
Each volume contains two tales about kings,
emperors and warriors, and are filmed in exotic
locales from around the world.
Walt Disney — *Walt Disney Home Video*

Stork Club, The — 1952
Variety
85218　29 mins　B/W　B, V　P
*Sherman Billingsley, Peter Donald, Dorothy
Kilgallen*
Two full episodes from this early TV series that
feature host Billingsley interviewing guests from
his table at the posh Stork Club in New York
City.

THE VIDEO TAPE & DISC GUIDE

CBS — *Video Yesteryear*

Storm Boy 1980
Ethics/Children
52420   90 mins   C   B, V   R, P
An Australian boy learns about life from an
adopted pelican, an Aborigine, and his own
father in this adaptation of the story by Colin
Thiele.
AM Available
South Australian Film Corp — *Embassy Home
Entertainment; Learning Corp of America*

Storm in a Teacup 1937
Comedy
07265   80 mins   B/W   B, V, 3/4U   R, P
Vivien Leigh, Rex Harrison, Cecil Parker, Sarah
Algood
A reporter starts a compaign to save a
sheepdog the town magistrate has ordered
killed because the owner is unable to pay the
license tax.
United Artists; Korda — *Video TEN; Kartes
Video Communications*

Storm Over Wyoming 1950
Western
73701   60 mins   B/W   B, V   P
Tim Holt, Richard Martin
A range war in Wyoming between sheepmen
and cattlemen is due to a crooked sheep ranch
foreman.
RKO — *RKO HomeVideo*

Stormy Waters 1941
Drama
85485   75 mins   B/W   B, V   P
Jean Gabin, Michele Morgan, Medeleine
Renaud, directed by Jean Gremillon
A romantic, film-noir-ish French drama about a
sea captain falling in love with a woman despite
his boring wife, who then becomes critically ill.
Dubbed into English; original French title:
"Remorques."
Sedif/French — *Video Yesteryear*

Story in the Temple Red 197?
Lily
Martial arts
21770   88 mins   C   B, V   P
Insurrectionists capture the Prince and Princess
of the Sung Dynasty and only one man can save
them in this Kung Fu bonanza.
Foreign — *Master Arts Video*

STory of a Cowboy 1981
Angel, The
Fantasy
86347   90 mins   C   B, V   P
Slim Pickens

On the Christmas Mountain Ranch, a cowboy
angel descends to Earth to bestow various
beneficences.
Clark Paylow — *Vestron Video*

Story of a Love Story 1973
Romance/Drama
71313   118 mins   C   B, V   P
Alan Bates, Dominique Sanda, Evans Evans,
Michel Auclair, Lawrence DeMonaghan, Lea
Masari, directed by John Frankenheimer
A married writer lives on the outskirts of Paris
with his family. When he meets and romances
an attractive woman—also married—he makes
an effort to maintain both family and mistress.
Also known as "Impossible Object."
Franco-London-Enro International Productions;
Valoria Films — *U.S.A. Home Video*

Story of Adele H., The 1975
Drama
58252   97 mins   C   B, V   P
Isabelle Adjani, Bruce Robinson, directed by
Francois Truffaut
The story of Adele Hugo, daughter of Victor
Hugo, who threw her life away in self-destructive
love.
MPAA:PG
Les Films du Carosse — *Warner Home Video*

Story of Esther, The 1979
Drama/Bible
55017   49 mins   C   B, V   P
Victoria Principal, Michael Ansara, Robert
Mandan, Eddie Mekka, Noah Beery, narrated by
Victor Jory
The story of beautiful Queen Esther of Persia
who risks her life to save her people. Part of the
"Greatest Heroes of the Bible" series.
Sunn Classics — *Magnum Entertainment;
Vanguard Video; Lucerne Films*

Story of O, The 1975
Drama
58809   97 mins   C   B, V   P
Corinne Clery, Anthony Steel, directed by Just
Jaeckin
The story of a young woman whose love for one
man moves her to surrender herself to many
men, in order to please him. Based on the
classic novel by Pauline Reage.
MPAA:X
Allied Artists — *Independent United
Distributors; MGM/UA Home Video (disc only)*

Story of Television, The 1956
Television
85514   27 mins   B/W   B, V   P
David Sarnoff, Dr. Vladimir Zworykin
A documentary on the invention and first years
of television, including basic information on how
it works. Many rare scenes of early series and

news events are included and the latter portion of the program is filmed in color.
RCA — *Video Yesteryear*

Story of the Silent Serials, The/Girls in Danger   19??
Film-History
29499   54 mins   B/W   B, V   P, T
Gloria Swanson, Mae Marsh, Wallace Beery
These two selections capture the best of more than fourteen silent serials. Featured are Gloria Swanson tied to the railroad tracks by Wallace Beery, Mae Marsh threatened with death (or worse) in caveman times, and other classic cliffhanger situations. Narration and muscial score.
Unknown — *Blackhawk Films*

Story of Vernon and Irene Castle, The   1939
Musical
00274   93 mins   B/W   B, V, 3/4U   P
Fred Astaire, Ginger Rogers
In this, their last film together, Astaire and Rogers portray two internationally successful ballroom dancers.
RKO — *Nostalgia Merchant*

Story of William S. Hart, The/The Sad Clowns   192?
Comedy
10102   50 mins   B/W   B, V   P, T
William S. Hart, Charlie Chaplin, Buster Keaton, Harry Langdon
Featuring William S. Hart as a cowboy in "Hell's Hinges," and Chaplin in "Tumbleweeds," (1925). From "The History of the Motion Picture" series.
United Artists et al — *Blackhawk Films*

Storytellers, The   1986
Folklore/Communication
85301   30 mins   C   B, V   P
4 pgms
Four programs of four tale-spinners simply telling stories, from fairy tales to African myths.
1.Lynn Rubright 2.Mary Carter Smith 3.Michael 'Badhair' Williams 4.Ruthmarie Argoello-Sheehan
Mindy Perry; Kartes Video — *Kartes Video Communications*

Storytime Classics   1983
Fairy tales
77183   78 mins   C   B, V   P
A collection of popular faily tales narrated by Katherine Hepburn.
World of Stories Limited — *Vestron Video*

Storytime Classics: Rudyard Kipling's Just So Stories Vol. 1   1982
Fairy tales/Cartoons
80704   34 mins   C   B, V   P
Animated
An animated adaptation of the Rudyard Kipling stories that explain "How the Camel Got His Hump" and "How the Elephant Got His Trunk".
Jouve Films — *Vestron Video*

La Strada   1956
Drama
82581   107 mins   B/W   B, V   P
Giulietta Masina, Anthony Quinn, Richard Basehart, Aldo Silvani, directed by Federico Fellini
A simple-minded waif falls in love with a circus strong-man in this acclaimed Fellini masterwork. Subtitled in English.
Academy Awards '56: Best Foreign Film IT
Dino De Laurentiis and Carlo Ponti — *Embassy Home Entertainment*

Straight Time   1978
Drama
58253   114 mins   C   B, V   P
Dustin Hoffman, Harry Dean Stanton, Gary Busey, Theresa Russell, M. Emmet Walsh, directed by Ulu Grosbard
An ex-convict hits the streets for the first time in six years and finds he is emotionally locked into a life of crime.
MPAA:R
Sweetwall Productions; First Artists Productions; Warner Bros — *Warner Home Video*

Strait Jacket   1964
Drama
64912   89 mins   B/W   B, V   P
Joan Crawford, Leif Erickson, Diane Baker
After a woman is released from an insane asylum where she was sent 20 years earlier for killing her husband and his mistress, mysterious axe murders begin to occur in the neighborhood, and she is the prime suspect.
William Castle — *RCA/Columbia Pictures Home Video*

Strange And Deadly Occurence   1974
Drama
81417   74 mins   C   B, V   P
Robert Stack, Vera Miles, L.Q. Jones, Herb Edelman
Strange things start to happen to a family when they move to a house in a remote area.
Worldvision; Alpine Productions, NBC — *Worldvision Home Video*

Strange Case of Dr. Jekyll and Mr. Hyde, The — 1968
Horror
81037   128 mins   C   B, V   P
Jack Palance, Leo Genn, Oscar Homolka, Billie Whitelaw, Denholm Elliott, directed by Charles Jarrot
This is an adaptation of the classic Robert Louis Stevenson book about a scientist who conducts experiments on himself to separate good from evil. Available in Beta Hi-Fi and VHS Stereo.
Dan Curtis Productions — Thriller Video

Strange Invaders — 1983
Satire/Science fiction
65364   94 mins   C   B, V, LV   P
Nancy Allen, Diana Scarwid, Louise Fletcher
The horrific and subtly humorous story of alien beings whose settlement in a small midwestern town is disturbed by a young professor determined to rescue his child from their clutches.
MPAA:PG
Walter Coblenz — Vestron Video

Strange Love of Martha Ivers, The — 1946
Drama
66398   117 mins   B/W   B, V   P
Barbara Stanwyck, Van Heflin, Kirk Douglas, Lisabeth Scott, Judith Anderson, directed by Lewis Milestone
An unscrupulous woman takes up with her old boyfriend, without bothering to keep the affair from her husband.
Paramount — Movie Buff Video; Kartes Video Communications

Strange Shadows in an Empty Room — 1976
Mystery/Suspense
80700   97 mins   C   B, V   P
Stuart Whitman, John Saxon, Martin Landau, Tisa Farrow, Carole Laure, Gayle Hunnicut
A veteran detective finds out some startling facts about his murdered sister during his investigation of the crime.
MPAA:R
American International Pictures — Vestron Video

Stranger, The — 1946
Mystery
11318   85 mins   B/W   B, V, FO   P
Edward G. Robinson, Loretta Young, Orson Welles, Richard Long, directed by Orson Welles
A government agent is assigned to the manhunt of a Nazi from Hitler's regime who has taken the new identity of a history professor about to marry the daughter of a Supreme Court Judge.
RKO — Video Yesteryear; Movie Buff Video; Hollywood Home Theater; VCII; Discount Video

Tapes; Cable Films; Prism; Kartes Video Communications

Stranger and the Gunfighter, The — 1976
Martial arts
Closed Captioned
73862   106 mins   C   B, V   P
Lee Van Cleef, Lo Lieh
A western gunfighter and an Oriental master of martial arts team up to find a stolen Chinese fortune. Available in Beta Hi-Fi.
Carlo Ponti — RCA/Columbia Pictures Home Video

Stranger from Venus — 1954
Science fiction
44354   78 mins   B/W   B, V, 3/4U   P
Patricia Neal, Helmet Dantine, Derek Bond
A frightening being from outerspace lands to warn Earth and pave the way for the arrival of a "mother ship." Includes previews of coming attractions from classic science fiction films.
Eros — Nostalgia Merchant

Stranger in Paso Bravo, A — 1973
Western
87603   92 mins   C   B, V   P
Antony Steffen, Giulia Rubini, Eduardo Favardo, Andriana Ambesi
A distraught drifter returns to a strange Italian frontier town to avenge the murders of his wife and daughter years before. Dubbed.
Francesco Carnicelli — Unicorn Video

Stranger Is Watching, A — 1982
Horror
59847   92 mins   C   B, V, CED   P
Rip Torn, Kate Mulgrew
A rapist-murderer holds the victim's 10-year-old daughter hostage, along with a New York TV anchorwoman.
MPAA:R
MGM — MGM/UA Home Video

Stranger on the Third Floor — 1940
Mystery
10065   64 mins   B/W   B, V   P, T
Peter Lorre, John McGuire, Elisha Cook Jr.
Innocent man, released from prison, seeks his persecutors with a vengeance. Someone set him up, but who?
RKO — Blackhawk Films; Nostalgia Merchant

Stranger than Paradise — 1984
Drama
Closed Captioned
85608   90 mins   B/W   B, V   P
Richard Edson, Eszter Balint, John Lurie, directed by Jim Jarmusch

An award-winning semi-avant-garde film about three lost souls who survive a comically empty life in New York.
National Society of Film Critics '84: Best Picture; Cannes Film Festival '84: Camera d'Or.
MPAA:R
Sara Diver — *Key Video*

Stranger Who Looks Like Me, The   1974
Drama
77148   74 mins   C   B, V   P
Meredith Baxter-Birney, Beau Bridges, Whitney Blake
An adopted girl and boy set out to find their real parents.
Filmways — *Worldvision Home Video*

Stranger Within, The   1974
Science fiction/Drama
71329   74 mins   C   B, V   P
Barbara Eden, George Grizzard, Joyce Van Patten, Nehmiah Persoff, directed by Lee Phillips
The creature in a young woman's womb is no baby; it tells her what to eat, where to go and when to give it birth.
Lorimar Productions — *U.S.A. Home Video*

Stranger's Gold   1971
Western
80796   90 mins   C   B, V   R, P
John Garko, Antonio Vilar, Daniela Giordano
A mysterious gunslinger eliminates corruption in a western mining town.
Phillip Yordan — *Video Gems*

Stranger's Kiss   1983
Drama
72185   93 mins   C   B, V   P
The director of a 1955 Hollywood movie encourages the two leads to have an off-screen romance to bring reality to his film. Conflict arises when the leading lady's boyfriend, the films financier, gets wind of the scheme.
MPAA:R
Douglas Dilge — *THORN EMI/HBO Video*

Strangers on a Train   1951
Drama/Suspense
69309   101 mins   B/W   B, V   P
Farley Granger, Robert Walker, Ruth Roman, Leo G. Carroll, directed by Alfred Hitchcock
A demented playboy entangles a tennis star in a bizarre scheme of "exchange murders."
Warner Bros — *Warner Home Video; RCA VideoDiscs*

Strangers: The Story of a Mother and Daughter   1979
Drama
80674   88 mins   C   B, V   P

Bette Davis, Gena Rowlands, Ford Rainey, Donald, Moffat, directed by Milton Katselas
A woman returns home to a New England fishing village after twenty years to settle the differences between herself and her mother.
Emmy Award '79: Outstanding Lead Actress in a Limited Series or Special (Davis)
Chris/Rose Prods. — *Lightning Video*

Strangler from the Swamp   1946
Mystery
82017   60 mins   B/W   B, V   P
Rosemary La Planche, Blake Edwards, Charles Middleton
The ghost of an innocent man wrongly hung for murder returns to the village where he was lynched to strangle those who convicted him.
Available in VHS and Beta Hi-Fi Stereo.
PRC — *Sony Video Software*

Straw Dogs   1972
Drama
46200   114 mins   C   B, V, LV, CED   P
Dustin Hoffman, Susan George, Peter Vaughan, T. P. McKenna, directed by Sam Peckinpah
An American mathematician, disturbed by the predominance of violence in American society, moves with his wife to an isolated Cornish village only to find a primitive savagery beneath the peaceful surface.
MPAA:R
ABC Pictures Corp. — *CBS/Fox Video*

Strawberry Blonde, The   1941
Comedy-Drama
87379   100 mins   B/W   B, V   P
James Cagney, Olivia De Havilland, Rita Hayworth, directed by Raoul Walsh
A raucous love story set in the 1890's about a would-be dentist who has to choose between two beautiful dames. In VHS and Beta Hi-Fi.
Warner Bros. — *MGM/UA Home Video*

Strawberry Shortcake in Big Apple City   1982
Cartoons
60393   60 mins   C   B, V   P
Animated
Strawberry Shortcake and her friends from Strawberryland meet new friends in Big Apple City.
EL, SP
Miller Rosen Productions — *Family Home Entertainment*

Strawberry Shortcake Meets the BerryKins   1983
Cartoons
80972   60 mins   C   B, V   P
Animated

Strawberry Shortcake welcomes her new friends 'the BerryKins, who are responsible for the aromas of the fruits and flowers of strawberryland. Available in VHS Stereo and Beta Hi Fi.
Miller Rosen Productions — *Family Home Entertainment*

Strawberry Shortcake Pets on Parade   1982
Cartoons
65656   60 mins   C   B, V   P
Animated
Strawberry Shortcake is named judge of a Pet Show and the first prize is a shiny new tricycle, and the Peculiar Purple Pieman of Porcupine Peak plots to swipe it. But Strawberry and her friends teach the Pieman a lesson he won't soon forget.
Miller Rosen Productions — *Family Home Entertainment*

Strawberry Shortcake's House-Warming Party   1983
Cartoons
69582   60 mins   C   B, V   P
Animated
Strawberry Shortcake and her friends in Strawberryland have a house-warming party.
Miller Rosen Productions — *Family Home Entertainment*

Strawberry Statement, The   1970
Drama
80631   109 mins   C   B, V   P
Kim Darby, Bruce Davidson, Bud Cort, James Coco, Kristina Holland, Bob Balaban, David Dukes
A campus radical convinces a college student to participate in the student strikes on campus during the 60's. The soundtrack features songs by Neil Young, Buffy Sainte-Marie.
MPAA:R
MGM — *MGM/UA Home Video*

Stray Cats   1983
Music video
88107   13 mins   C   B, V   P
A compilation of video hits from the neo-rockabilly band, including "Stray Cat Strut" and "Rock This Town."
Sony Video — *Sony Video Software*

Streamers   1983
War-Drama
66602   118 mins   C   B, V   P
Matthew Modine, Michael Wright, Mitchell Lichenstein
Six young soldiers in a claustrophobic army barracks tensely await the orders that will send them to Vietnam. Based on the play by David Rabe.

MPAA:R
Robert Altman; Nick J. Mileti — *Media Home Entertainment*

Street, The   1923
Drama
85219   87 mins   B/W   B, V   P
Written and directed by Karl Grune
A dark classic of German Kammerspielfilm, notable for its expressionist treatment of Paris street life. Silent.
UFA — *Video Yesteryear*

Street Fighter, The   1975
Adventure/Martial arts
54106   85 mins   C   B, V, CED   P
Sonny Chiba
Local hoodlum engages in fast-paced marital arts action.
MPAA:R
Unknown — *CBS/Fox Video*

Street Hero   1984
Drama
85633   102 mins   C   B, V   P
Vince Colosimo, Sigrid Thornton, Sandy Gore,
A young thug is torn between familial common sense and Mafia connections.
Manson Int'l. — *Vestron Video*

Street Law   1979
Crime-Drama
65727   77 mins   C   B, V   P
Franco Nero
A vivid and violent study of one man's frustrated ware on crime.
MPAA:R
Unknown — *VidAmerica*

Street Music   1981
Comedy/Romance
77176   88 mins   C   B, V, CED   P
Larry Breeding, Elizabeth Daily, Ned Glass
A young couple residing in an old hotel organize a protest to save the building from being closed down.
Pacificon Productions — *Vestron Video*

Street People   1976
Drama
80679   92 mins   C   B, V   P
Roger Moore, Stacy Keach, Ivo Gassani, Entore Manni
A Mafia godfather asks a lawyer and a race car driver to find out who smuggled a three-million dollar shipment of heroin inside of an Italian crucifix.
MPAA:R
American International Pictures — *Vestron Video*

Street Scene 1931
Drama
01735 80 mins B/W   B, V   P
Sylvia Sydney, William Collier Jr., directed by
King Vidor
Based on Elmer Rice's hit play, film depicts
trials and tribulations of young love in New York
tenement district.
United Artists — Hollywood Home Theater;
Cable Films; Video Connection; Western Film &
Video Inc; Kartes Video Communications; Movie
Buff Video

Street Walkin' 1985
Drama
84790 83 mins C   B, V, LV   P
Melissa Leo, Julie Newmar, Leon Robinson,
Antonio Fargas, directed by Joan Freeman
A gritty drama of prostitution in Times Square.
MPAA:R
Rodeo Prods — Vestron Video

Streetcar Named Desire, 1951
A
Drama
Closed Captioned
58949 122 mins B/W   B, V   P
Vivien Leigh, Marlon Brando, Kim Hunter, Karl
Malden, directed by Elia Kazan
Powerful film version of Tennessee Williams'
play about a repressed southern widow who is
abused and driven mad by her brutal brother-in-
law.
Academy Awards '51: Best Actress (Leigh);
Best Supporting Actress (Hunter); Best
Supporting Actor (Malden).
Charles K Feldman; Elia Kazan — CBS/Fox
Video; Warner Home Video; RCA VideoDiscs

Streets of Fire 1984
Musical-Drama/Fantasy
Closed Captioned
79679 93 mins C   B, V, LV   P
Michael Pare, Diane Lane, Rick Moranis, Amy
Madigan, directed by Walter Hill
A soldier of fortune rescues a famous rock
singer after she's kidnapped by a motorcycle
gang.
Lawrence Gordon; Joel Silver — MCA Home
Video

Streets of L.A., The 1979
Drama
70854 94 mins C   B, V   P
Joanne Woodward, Robert Webber, Michael C.
Gwynne, directed by Jerrold Freedman
A two-fisted realtor teaches some punks from
an L.A. barrio a thing or two about pride and
motivation.
Time/Life Films — Lightning Video

Streetwise 1985
Documentary/Adolescence
86915 92 mins C   B, V   P
Directed by Martin Bell, music by Tom Waits
The searing, infamous documentary about
Seattle street kids: homeless, prepubescent
drug dealers, prostitutes and petty criminals. A
deservedly acclaimed and terrifying vision of
American urbanity.
Angelika T. Saleh — New World Video

Strike Up The Band 1940
Musical/Comedy
80622 120 mins B/W   B, V   P
Judy Garland, Mickey Rooney, Paul Whiteman,
William Tracy, June Preisser, directed by Busby
Berkeley
A high school band turns to hot swing music and
enters a national radio contest. Songs include "I
Ain't Got Nobody," "Our Love Affair,"
"Drummer Boy" and "Do The Conga!"
Academy Awards '40: Best Sound Recording.
MGM; Arthur Freed — MGM/UA Home Video

Stripes 1981
Comedy
Closed Captioned
05938 105 mins C   B, V   P
Bill Murray, Harold Ramis, P. J. Soles, Warren
Oates, John Candy, directed by Ivan Reitman
Two friends enlist in the Army to straighten out
their lives.
MPAA:R
Columbia — RCA/Columbia Pictures Home
Video; RCA VideoDiscs

Stripes 1982
Football
47709 23 mins C   B, V, FO   P
Team highlights of the '81 Bengals, who posted
a 12-4 regular season record and won their first
AFC Championship.
NFL Films — NFL Films Video

Stroker Ace 1983
Comedy
69308 96 mins C   B, V, CED   P
Burt Reynolds, Ned Beatty, Jim Nabors, Parker
Stevenson, Loni Anderson
A flamboyant stock car driver tries to break an
iron-clad promotional contract signed with a
greedy fried-chicken magnate.
MPAA:PG
Warner Bros — Warner Home Video

Stromboli 1950
Drama
80661 81 mins B/W   B, V   P
Ingrid Bergman, Mario Vitale, Renzo Cesana,
directed by Roberto Rossellini
An unhappy and homeless girl marries a poor
Sicilian hoping to escape her plight, but finds

herself imprisoned when the couple moves to a desert island.
RKO Radio Pictures — *United Home Video*

Strong Kids, Safe Kids   1984
Child abuse/Safety education
79180   42 mins   C   B, V, LV   P
Animated
Henry Winkler, along with the Smurfs and The Flintstones, teaches parents and children the skills that are necessary to prevent sexual abuse.
Paramount; Fair Dinkum — *Paramount Home Video*

Struggle for Los Trabajos   1980
Minorities
88389   35 mins   C   B, V, 3/4U   R, P
A look at how the Equal Employment Opportunity Commission helps a minority worker fight injustice.
EEOC — *Your World Video*

Struggle Through Death   197?
Martial arts
72175   93 mins   C   B, V   P
Two young men escape the clutches of evil Ching Kue and attempt to free their fellow prisoners so they can overthrow the despot.
Foreign — *Master Arts Video*

Stryker   1983
Science fiction
69542   86 mins   C   B, V   P
Steve Sandor, Andria Fabio
In the future, after a devastating war, bands of marauders fight each other for the scarcest resource—water.
MPAA:R
Cirio H Santiago — *Embassy Home Entertainment*

Stuck on You   1984
Comedy
78639   90 mins   C   B, V   P
Irwin Corey
A couple engaged in a palimony suit takes their case to a judge to work out their differences.
MPAA:R
Troma Inc — *Embassy Home Entertainment*

Stuckey's Last Stand   1978
Comedy
80667   95 mins   C   B, V   P
Whit Reichert, Tom Murray, Rich Casentino
A group of camp counselors prepare to take twenty-two children on a nature hike that they will never forget.
MPAA:PG
Lawrence G. Goldfarb — *Lightning Video*

Stud, The   1978
Drama
47801   90 mins   C   B, V   P
Joan Collins, Oliver Tobias
The owner of a fashionable "after hours" dance spot hires a young, handsome stud to manage the club and attend to her personal needs.
MPAA:R
Brent Walker Film Productions — *THORN EMI/HBO Video*

Student Bodies   1981
Satire
58717   86 mins   C   B, V, LV   P
Kristen Riter, Matthew Goldsby, Richard Brando, Joe Flood, directed by Mickey Rose
A spoof of high-school horror films a la "Halloween."
MPAA:R
Paramount — *Paramount Home Video*

Student Teachers, The   1977
Comedy
80774   79 mins   C   B, V   P
Three attractive faculty members decide to spice up the campus life at Valley High.
Indepedent — *Embassy Home Entertainment*

Studs Lonigan   1960
Drama
82396   96 mins   B/W   B, V   P
Christopher Knight, Frank Gorshin, Jack Nicholson, directed by Irving Lerner
Based on James T. Farrell's trilogy, this film traces the life of a dissatisfied young drifter of the 1920's, who finds the social and sexual mores of his times incomprehensible.
Longridge Enterprises — *MGM/UA Home Video*

Study in Scarlet, A   1933
Mystery
48428   77 mins   B/W   B, V   P
Reginald Owen, Alan Mowbray, Anna May Wong
Master sleuth Sherlock Holmes solves a series of complex murders with the aid of faithful companion Dr. Watson.
World Wide — *Movie Buff Video; Hollywood Home Theater; Cable Films; Video Yesteryear; Discount Video Tapes*

Stuff, The   1985
Horror
82408   93 mins   C   B, V   P
Michael Moriarty, Andrea Marcovicci, Garret Morris, Paul Sorvino, directed by Larry Cohen
An ice cream mogul and a hamburger king discover that the new, fast-selling confection in town alters the minds of its' consumers.
MPAA:R
New World Video — *New World Video*

Stunt Man, The   1981
Drama/Satire
49398   1.29 mins   C   CED   P
*Peter O'Toole, Steve Railsback, Barbara
Hershey, directed by Richard Bush*
A satire on the world of moviemaking, in which
an ex-Vietnam soldier-turned-stunt-man stages
a battle of wits with a power-crazed movie
director.
MPAA:R
20th Century Fox — *CBS/Fox Video*

Stunt Rock   1980
Adventure
66009   90 mins   C   B, V   P
A feature film combining rock music, magic, and
some of the most incredible stunts ever
attempted.
MPAA:PG
Intertamar — *Monterey Home Video*

Stunts   1977
Adventure
66185   90 mins   C   B, V   P
Robert Forster, Fiona Lewis
A film dealing with the thrilling and often
horrifying lives of professional stuntmen.
New Line Cinema — *THORN EMI/HBO Video*

Style Council Far East   1984
and Far Out, The
Music-Performance
78368   60 mins   C   B, V   P
The unique sounds of The Style Council are
captured in this concert taped in Japan.
Polygram Music Video Limited — *Music Media*

Styx—Caught in the Act   1984
Music-Performance
70187   87 mins   C   B, V   P
Directed by Jerry Kramer
The rock group Styx is featured in a concert
performance of some of their biggest hits,
including "Too Much Time on My Hands,"
"Don't Let It End," "Best of Times," "Come Sail
Away" and "Renegade. In Beta Hi-Fi Stereo
and VHS Hi-Fi Dolby Stereo.
A & M Video — *A & M Video; RCA/Columbia
Pictures Home Video*

Submission   1977
Drama
80284   107 mins   C   B, V   P
Franco Nero, Lisa Gastoni
A pharmacist's sensuality is reawakened when
she has a provacative affair with a clerk in her
shop.
MPAA:R
Joseph Brenner Associates — *Prism*

Subterfuge   1968
Drama
65685   89 mins   C   B, V   P
Joan Collins, Gene Barry, Richard Todd
When a special American security agent goes to
England for a "vacation," his presence causes
speculation and poses several serious
questions for both British Intelligence and the
underworld.
Commonwealth United TV — *Spotlite Video*

Suburbia   1983
Drama
79313   99 mins   C   B, V   P
Directed by Penelope Speeris
When a group of punk rockers move into a
condemned suburban development, they
become the targets of a vigilante group.
MPAA:R
New Horizon Pictures — *Vestron Video*

Subway   1985
Adventure
Closed Captioned
87329   103 mins   C   B, V   P
*Christopher Lambert, Isabelle Adjani, directed
by Luc Besson*
A surreal vision of French fringe life by the
director of "Le Dernier Combat," wherein a
spike-haired renegade escapes the law by
plunging into the Parisian subway system. Once
there, he encounters a bizarre subculture living
under the city.
MPAA:R
Luc Besson; Gaumont — *Key Video*

Sudden Death   1977
Adventure
59041   84 mins   C   B, V   P
Robert Conrad, Felton Perry
Two professional violence merchants put
themselves up for hire.
Topar Films — *Media Home Entertainment*

Sudden Death   1985
Crime-Drama
86361   95 mins   C   B, V   P
Denise Coward
A beautiful woman decides to kill every rapist
she can find, and proceeds to do so in this
hyper-feminist paean to man-hating.
MPAA:R
Marvin Films Inc. — *Vestron Video*

Sudden Impact   1983
Crime-Drama/Adventure
Closed Captioned
65613   117 mins   C   B, V, LV,   P
CED
Clint Eastwood, Sondra Locke
"Dirty Harry" Callahan tracks down a revenge-
obsessed murderess at the same time that local
mobsters come gunning for him.

MPAA:R
Clint Eastwood; Warner Brothers — *Warner Home Video*

Suddenly 1954
Crime-Drama
72171   75 mins   B/W   B, V
Frank Sinatra, Sterling Hayden, James Gleason, Nancy Gates
Gunmen hold a midwestern family hostage as part of a plot to assassinate the President when he passes through the town.
UA — *Continental Video; Hal Roach Studios*

Suddenly 1954
Crime-Drama
71029   73 mins   C   B, V   P
Frank Sinatra, Sterling Hayden
Gunmen plot a Presidential assassination in a small midwestern town. This release has been enhanced through the Colorization process.
United Artists — *Hal Roach Studios*

Suddenly Last Summer 1959
Drama
65701   114 mins   B/W   B, V, CED   P
Katharine Hepburn, Elizabeth Taylor, Montgomery Cliff
A psychiatrist tries to solve the mystery behind a young girl's mental breakdown. Based on the play by Tennessee Williams.
Sam Spiegel — *RCA/Columbia Pictures Home Video*

Sudsy Television 1953
Drama
84701   60 mins   B/W   B, V, 3/4U   P
Don Knotts
Four daytime soap operas from a time when they were live and young. All date from 1953: "The Guiding Light," "Love of Life," (two episodes) and "Search for Tomorrow."
CBS — *Shokus Video*

Sugar Cane Alley 1983
Drama
71176   106 mins   C   B, V   P
Darling Legitimus, Garry Cadenat Douta Seck, directed by Euzhan Palcy
After the loss of his parents, an 11-year-old orphan boy goes to work with his grandmother on a sugar plantation. Grandma realizes that the only hope for her young ward is education.
MPAA:PG
Sumafa; Orca; N E F Diffusion — *Media Home Entertainment*

Sugar Cookies 1977
Drama
52952   89 mins   C   B, V   P
Lynn Lowry, Monique Van Vooren

An erotic horror story in which young women are the pawns as a satanic satyr and an impassioned lesbian play out a bizarre game of vengeance, love, and death.
MPAA:R
Lloyd Kaufman — *VidAmerica*

Sugar Ray Robinson—Pound for Pound 1982
Boxing
58735   120 mins   C   B, V   P
Sugar Ray Robinson, Jake LaMotta, Bobo Olsen, Randy Turpin, Carmen Basilio
The career of legendary boxer Sugar Ray Robinson is highlighted, from his earliest amateur bouts through his memorable retirement at Madison Square Garden. Some sequences are in black and white.
Big Fights Inc — *VidAmerica*

Sugarland Express, The 1974
Drama
65119   109 mins   C   B, V   P
Goldie Hawn, Ben Johnson, Michael Sacks, William Atherton, directed by Steven Spielberg
To save her son from adoption, a young woman helps her husband break out of prison. In their flight to freedom, they hijack a police car, holding the policeman hostage.
MPAA:PG
Universal — *MCA Home Video*

Suicide Patrol 197?
War-Drama
82082   90 mins   C   B, V   P
Gordon Mitchell, Pierre Richard, Max Dean
A small band of saboteurs patrols a German-controlled Mediterranean island during World War II.
Foreign — *Unicorn Video*

Summer Camp 1978
Comedy
59659   85 mins   C   B, V   P
John C. McLaughlin, Matt Michaels, Colleen O'Neil
A ten year reunion at a summer camp turns into a bizarre weekend of co-ed football, midnight panty-raids, coupling couples and a wild disco party.
MPAA:R
Mark Borde — *Media Home Entertainment*

Summer Heat 1973
Drama
55594   71 mins   C   B, V   P
Bob Garry, Nicole Avril, Pat Pascal
A no-holds-barred tour through the steamy world of the rich, the restless, and the young, when a young man spends his summer with his hypnotic aunt.
MPAA:X

World Wide Films Corp — *VidAmerica*

Summer in St. Tropez, A 1981
Drama
59698   60 mins   C   B, V   P
Photographer David Hamilton's erotic and lyrical study of a household of girls in their first stages of womanhood living outside of society in the south of France.
Ken Kamura — *THORN EMI/HBO Video*

Summer Lovers 1982
Drama
63372   98 mins   C   B, V, LV,   P
CED
Peter Gallagher, Daryl Hannah, Valerie Quennessen
Three young people meet on the exotic Greek island of Santorini one summer to explore life and love.
MPAA:R
Filmways — *Embassy Home Entertainment*

Summer Magic 1963
Drama
76824   116 mins   C   B, V   P
Hayley Mills, Burl Ives, Dorothy McGuire, Deborah Walley, Una Merkel, Eddie Hodges
A young girl plots to resettle her family in a tiny New England village after financial disaster strikes the household.
Walt Disney Productions — *Walt Disney Home Video*

Summer of Fear 1978
Horror
66017   94 mins   C   B, V   P
Linda Blair
A happy young woman must overcome the evil forces brought on when her cousin comes to live with her.
Max A Keller; Micheline H Keller — *THORN EMI/HBO Video*

Summer of '42 1971
Drama
54117   102 mins   C   B, V   P
Jennifer O'Neill, Gary Grimes, Jerry Houser, Oliver Conant, directed by Richard Mulligan
A touching story about a 15-year-old boy's coming of sexual age during his summer vacation on an island off New England. While his two friends are fumbling with girls their own age, he falls in love with a beautiful older woman.
Academy Award '71: Best Musical Score.
MPAA:R
Warner Bros, Mulligan Roth — *Warner Home Video; RCA VideoDiscs*

Summer of My German Soldier 1978
Drama
52375   98 mins   C   B, V   P
Kristy McNichol, Esther Rolle, Bruce Davison
A young Jewish girl befriends an escaped German prisoner of war in a small southern town during World War II. This movie is based on the book by Bette Greene.
Highgate Pictures, NBC — *Simon and Schuster Video*

Summer of Secrets 1976
Horror
77007   100 mins   C   B, V   P
A young couple get more than they bargained for when they make love in a demented doctor's beach house.
MPAA:PG
Australian — *VidAmerica*

Summer Rental 1985
Comedy
Closed Captioned
71134   88 mins   C   B, V, 8mm,   P
LV
John Candy, Rip Torn, Richard Crenna, Karen Austen, Kerri Green, Pierrino Mascarino, directed by Carl Reiner
Burned-out from too many blips, an air-traffic controller takes his family to a Florida resort town where he's rented a beach house. Everything goes wrong.
MPAA:PG
Paramount — *Paramount Home Video*

Summer School Teachers 1975
Exploitation
87618   87 mins   C   B, V   P
Candice Rialson, Pat Anderson, Rhonda Leigh Hopkins, Christopher Wales
Three sultry femmes bounce about Los Angeles High School and make the student body happy.
MPAA:R
Julie Corman — *Charter Entertainment*

Summer Solstice 1981
Drama
59696   75 mins   C   B, V   P
Henry Fonda, Myrna Loy, Lindsey Crouse, Stephen Collins
An aging couple visits the beach where they first met. There they recapture many of the good and difficult times from the past.
Bruce Marson; Stephen Schlow — *THORN EMI/HBO Video; MTI Teleprograms*

Summer Wishes, Winter Dreams 1973
Drama
71111   95 mins   C   B, V   P

Joanne Woodward, Martin Balsam, Sylvia Sidney, Dori Brenner, Ron Richards, written by Stewart Stern, directed by Gilbert Cates
Mid-life crisis grips Rita, alienating her from her family as she drifts into a state of depression-induced dreaminess, pining for the days of yore.
New York Film Critics Circle: '73 Best Actress (Woodward). MPAA:PG
Columbia; Jack Brodsky — *RCA/Columbia Pictures Home Video*

Summerdog   1978
Adventure
29237   90 mins   C   B, V   P
James Congdon, Elizabeth Eisenman
The Norman family rescues an abandoned little dog named Hobo from a raccoon trap while they're vacationing in the mountains. In return Hobo saves them from one danger after another.
MPAA:G
GG Communications — *Video Gems; Lightning Video*

Summertime   1955
Drama/Romance
81447   98 mins   C   B, V   P
Katherine Hepburn, Rossano Brazzi, Darren Mc Gavin, directed by David Lean
A spinster secretary meets and falls in love with a married man while on vacation in Venice.
United Artists; Ilya Lopert — *Embassy Home Entertainment*

Sun City   1985
Music video
84953   45 mins   C   B, V   P
Bruce Springsteen, Bob Dylan, Bono, Steve Van Zandt, Pete Townshend
A musical statement against Apartheid by over 50 recording artists.
Solidarity Foundation; Steven Van Zandt — *Karl/Lorimar Home Video*

Sunburn   1979
Comedy
38936   110 mins   C   B, V   P
Farrah Fawcett-Majors, Charles Grodin, Joan Collins
Action-packed comedy-mystery of an investigation into the violent death of an aging Acapulco industrialist.
MPAA:PG
Paramount — *Paramount Home Video*

Sundance and the Kid   1976
Western
66195   84 mins ˉ C   B, V   P
John Wade, Karen Blake
Two brothers try to collect an inheritance against all odds.
MPAA:PG

Film Ventures International — *Monterey Home Video*

Sunday Too Far Away   1974
Drama
80776   100 mins   C   B, V   P
The rivalries between Australian sheep shearers and graziers leads to an ugly strike.
Gil Brealey; Matt Carroll — *Embassy Home Entertainment*

Sundays and Cybele   1962
Drama
33613   110 mins   B/W   B, V   P
Hardy Kruger, Nicole Courcel, directed by Serge Bourguignon
A ragged war veteran and an orphaned girl develop a strong emotional relationship, which is tragically destroyed by their townspeople.
Academy Awards '62: Best Foreign Film. FR
Romain Pines — *Hollywood Home Theater; Discount Video Tapes*

Sundown   1941
War-Drama
11395   91 mins   B/W   B, V, FO   P
Gene Tierney, Bruce Cabot, George Sanders, Harry Carey, Sir Cedric Hardwicke
A Eurasian girl helps the British uncover a Nazi plot in the African desert with her camel caravan.
United Artists; Walter Wanger — *Video Yesteryear; Movie Buff Video; Discount Video Tapes; Kartes Video Communications*

Sunningdale Mystery,   1985
The
Mystery/Drama
70662   60 mins   C   B, V   P
James Warwick, Francesca Annis
In this chapter of the "Partners in Crime" series, the Beresfords use their keen minds to prove the innocence of an accused murderess.
Unknown — *Pacific Arts Video*

Sunrise at Campobello   1960
Biographical/Drama
77269   143 mins   C   B, V   P
Ralph Bellamy, Greer Garson, Hume Cronyn, Jean Hagen, directed by Vincent J. Donehue
An adaptation of the Tony award winning play that chronicles Franklin D. Roosevelt's battle to conquer polio and ultimately receive the Democratic presidential nomination in 1924.
Warner Bros — *Warner Home Video*

Sunset Boulevard   1950
Drama
38605   110 mins   B/W   B, V   P
Gloria Swanson, William Holden, Erich von Stroheim, Nancy Olsen, directed by Billy Wilder

Famed tale of Norma Desmond, aging silent film queen, who, refusing to accept the fact that stardom has ended for her, hires a young screenwriter to help engineer her movie comeback.
Academy Awards '50: Best Story and Screenplay (Wilder, Charles Brackett, D.M. Marshman); Best Music Score (Franz Waxman).
Paramount — *Paramount Home Video; RCA VideoDiscs*

Sunset on the Desert 1942
Western
78093   53 mins   B/W   B, V, FO   P
Roy Rogers, George Hayes, Trigger, Lynne Carver
A man returns to his hometown after ten years' absence in order to help his father's old partner.
Republic — *Video Yesteryear*

Sunset Range 1935
Western
14210   59 mins   B/W   B, V   P
Hoot Gibson
The "World's All-Around Champion Cowboy" of 1912 stars in this chaps-slappin', bit-champin', dust-raisin' saga of the plains.
First Division — *Video Connection; United Home Video*

Sunset Serenade 1942
Western
05548   60 mins   B/W   B, V, 3/4U   P
Roy Rogers, Trigger, Gabby Hayes, Helen Parrish
Roy Rogers outwits a murderous duo who plans to eliminate the new heir to a ranch.
Republic — *Nostalgia Merchant*

Sunset Strip 1985
Crime-Drama
85627   83 mins   C   B, V   P
Tom Elpin, Cheri Cameron Newell, John Mayall
A photographer investigates a friend's murder, and enters the seamy world of rock and drugs in L.A.
Shapiro Ent. Inc. — *Vestron Video*

Sunset Trail 1932
Western
84837   60 mins   B/W   B, V   P
Ken Maynard
A rarely-seen sagebrush saga.
Tiffany; Ken Maynard — *United Home Video*

Sunshine Boys, The 1975
Comedy
54103   109 mins   C   B, V, CED   P
George Burns, Walter Matthau, Richard Benjamin, Lee Meredith, Carol Arthur, directed by Herbert Ross

After a long separation, two veteran vaudeville partners, who have shared a hate-love relationship for decades, reunite to renew their friendship and their feud.
Academy Awards '75: Best Supporting Actor (Burns).   MPAA:PG
MGM; Ray Stark — *MGM/UA Home Video*

Sunshine Porcupine 1979
Cartoons
71059   45 mins   C   B, V   P
Animated
In union with our star the Sun, the Sunshine Porcupine defeats the Ugli-Unks and saves Eggwood from a threatened loss of solar power.
Al Brodax — *MPI Home Video*

Sunspot Vacations for Winter 1985
Travel
80468   90 mins   C   B, V   P
Hosted by David Earle
This program helps travelers to select a vacation spot by exploring the diverse and unique attributes of many famous resort areas, including Hawaii, Mexico, the Bahamas, the Dominican Republic, Barbados, Puerto Rico, St. Maarten and St. Vincent
Videotakes — *Videotakes*

Super Bears, the Highlights of Super Bowl XX 1986
Football
86796   23 mins   C   B, V   P
Using new Kodak film, highlights from this famous game are presented..
NFL Films — *NFL Films Video*

Super Bowl I 1980
Football
45108   23 mins   C   B, V, FO   R, P
Narrated by John Facenda, Green Bay Packers, Oakland Raiders
Vince Lombardi's mighty Packers subdue Hank Stram's Chiefs in the first meeting between AFL and NFL Champions. Veteran quarterback Bart Starr and aging receiver Max McGee spark the Packers as they pull away in the second half of the 1967 game.
NFL Films — *NFL Films Video*

Super Bowl II 1980
Football
45109   23 mins   C   B, V, FO   R, P
Narrated by John Facenda, Green Bay Packers, Oakland Raiders
The Packers romp to their second straight Super Bowl triumph, 33-14, in Vince Lombardi's last game as Packer head coach, played in 1968.
NFL Films — *NFL Films Video*

Super Bowl III
1980
Football
45110   23 mins   C   B, V, FO   R, P
Narrated by John Facenda, New York Jets, Baltimore Colts
1969: Joe Namath, the flashy young Jet's quarterback, guarantees a victory for his side and produces. Namath connects with receiver George Sauer and Don Maynard in key situations. The Jets' secondary intercepts four passes from Earl Morrow and John Unitas. Matt Snell's seven-yard touchdown run and Jim Turner's three field goals give the Jets a 16-7 victory in one of the greatest upsets in sports history.
NFL Films — *NFL Films Video*

Super Bowl Chronicles
1984
Football
75889   420 mins   C   B, V, FO   P
Narrated by John Facenda
This three tape set features highlights of the first 18 Super Bowls.
NFL Films — *NFL Films Video*

Super Bowl IV
1980
Football
45111   23 mins   C   B, V, FO   R, P
Narrated by John Facenda, Kansas City Chiefs, Minnesota Vikings
1970: Coach Hank Stram's "Offense of the 70's," led by quarterback Len Dawson and flanker Otis Taylor, confuses the Viking defense. The Chief's defensive crew stifles quarterback Joe Kapp and the Viking offense. It adds up to a 23-7 victory for Kansas City.
NFL Films — *NFL Films Video*

Super Bowl V
1980
Football
45112   23 mins   C   B, V, FO   R, P
Narrated by John Facenda, Baltimore Colts, Dallas Cowboys
1971: A game "highlighted" by bobbles, mistakes, and a questionable ruling on a Baltimore touchdown pass, is brought to a heart-stopping climax when the Colt's Jim O'Brien boots a 33-yard field goal with just six seconds to play, giving the ecstatic Baltimore team a 16-13 win.
NFL Films — *NFL Films Video*

Super Bowl VI
1980
Football
45113   23 mins   C   B, V, FO   R, P
Narrated by John Facenda, Dallas Cowboys, Miami Dolphins
1972: Dallas' "Doomsday Defense" shuts down the aerial game of Miami quarterback Bob Griese and the running of fullback Larry Csonka. Coach Tom Landry's team finally wins "the big one," 24-3. Roger Staubach and Duane Thomas lead the Cowboy attack.

NFL Films — *NFL Films Video*

Super Bowl VII
1980
Football
45114   23 mins   C   B, V, FO   R, P
Narrated by John Facenda, Miami Dolphins, Washington Redskins
1973: The Dolphins cap a perfect 17-0 season as the "No-Name Defense" holds the Redskin offense scoreless in a 14-7 triumph.
NFL Films — *NFL Films Video*

Super Bowl VIII
1980
Football
45115   23 mins   C   B, V, FO   R, P
Narrated by John Facenda, Miami Dolphins, Minnesota Vikings
The Dolphins cruise to their second straight championship as Larry Csonka runs all over the Vikings' "Purple People Eaters," and the Dolphin defense contains Vikes' quarterback Fran Tarkenton, in this 1974 game.
NFL Films — *NFL Films Video*

Super Bowl IX
1980
Football
45116   23 mins   C   B, V, FO   R, P
Narrated by John Facenda, Pittsburgh Steelers, Minnesota Vikings
The Steelers, led by Terry Bradshaw, Franco Harris, and the "Steel Curtain" defense dominate this game and the Vikings are disappointed for the third time in three Super Bowl tries (1975).
NFL Films — *NFL Films Video*

Super Bowl X
1980
Football
45117   23 mins   C   B, V, FO   R, P
Narrated by John Facenda, Pittsburgh Steelers, Dallas Cowboys
1976: Terry Bradshaw and Lynn Swan team up to lead the Steelers over the Cowboys 21-17 and capture their second consecutive Super Bowl Championship. A late rally by Roger Staubach and his Dallas mates falls short.
NFL Films — *NFL Films Video*

Super Bowl XI
1980
Football
45118   23 mins   C   B, V, FO   R, P
Narrated by John Facenda, Oakland Raiders, Minnesota Vikings
1977: Quarterback Ken Stabler leads the Raiders over the Vikings 32-14 as Minnesota once again fails to win their fourth Super Bowl effort.
NFL Films — *NFL Films Video*

Super Bowl XII
1980
Football
45119   23 mins   C   B, V, FO   R, P

Narrated by John Facenda, Dallas Cowboys, Denver Broncos
1978: The awesome Dallas pass rush forces Denver quarterback Craig Morton into numerous interceptions. The Cowboy's offense sputters at times, but capitalizes on enough breaks for a 27-13 victory.
NFL Films — *NFL Films Video*

Super Bowl XIII   1980
Football
45120   23 mins   C   B, V, FO   R, P
Narrated by John Facenda, Pittsburgh Steelers, Dallas Cowboys
In the first Super Bowl offensive explosion by both teams, the Cowboys rally from eighteen points behind with Roger Staubach at the helm. Fortunately for the Steelers, Terry Bradshaw has put enough points on the board already, and Pittsburgh has their third championship, by a 35-31 score, in the 1979 game.
NFL Films — *NFL Films Video*

Super Bowl XIV   1980
Football
45121   23 mins   C   B, V, FO   R, P
Narrated by John Facenda, Pittsburgh Steelers, Los Angeles Rams
1980: The World Champion Steelers were supposed to be too much for the supposed bunch of glamour boys from Los Angeles, who were making their first-ever Super Bowl appearance after years of frustration. The Rams proved to be more than worthy opponent however, and even outplayed the Steelers for three quarters until some late heroics by Terry Bradshaw and John Stallworth saved them from embarrassment.
NFL Films — *NFL Films Video*

Super Bowl XV   1981
Football
50646   24 mins   C   B, V, FO   R, P
Narrated by John Facenda, Oakland Raiders, Philadelphia Eagles
The Oakland Raiders, a non-playoff team the previous year, are led by quarterback Jim Plunkett and a nasty defense to a 27-10 Super Bowl victory over the NFC's best, the Philadelphia Eagles.
NFL Films — *NFL Films Video*

Super Bowl XVI   1982
Football
47717   23 mins   C   B, V, FO   P
A look at how the San Francisco 49ers fought for a 26-21 victory over the Cincy Bengals in Super Bowl XVI.
NFL Films — *NFL Films Video*

Super Bowl XVII   1983
Football
69043   23 mins   C   B, V, FO   P

This program contains the highlights of Super Bowl XVII, played between the Washington Redskins and the Miami Dolphins.
NFL Films — *NFL Films Video*

SuperBowl XVIII   1984
Football
70271   23 mins   C   B, V, FO   P
Los Angeles Raiders, Washington Redskins
Marcus Allen runs for a record 74-yard touchdown in the filmed highlights of the most lopsided Super Bowl to date.
NFL Films — *NFL Films Video*

Super Bowl XIX   1985
Highlights
Football
70542   23 mins   C   B, V, FO   P
Joe Montana, Dan Marino
After their systematic 38-16 demolition of the powerful Dolphins, observers dubbed the 49ers the "Masters of the Game."
NFL Films — *NFL Films Video*

Super Colt 38   1966
Western
80493   88 mins   C   B, V   P
Jeffrey Hunter, Rosa Maria Vasquez, Pedro Armendariz
Two former friends become bitter enemies as they vie for the love of the same woman. Dialogue in Spanish.
SP
Spanish — *Unicorn Video*

Super Exercises   1978
Physical fitness
42779   60 mins   C   B, V   P
Ann Dugan
This series of two 30-minute programs on one tape is intended for those concerned with gaining greater strength and endurance.
Health N Action — *RCA/Columbia Pictures Home Video*

Super Fuzz   1981
Comedy
65067   97 mins   C   B, V   P
Terence Hill, Joanne Dru
A rookie policeman develops super powers after being exposed accidentally to radiation. Somewhat ineptly, he uses his abilities to combat crime.
MPAA:PG
Avco Embassy — *Embassy Home Entertainment*

Super Gang   1985
Martial arts
84502   75 mins   C   B, V   P
Bruce Lee

Abounding fists and feet punctuate this tale of colliding gangs.
Telefilm Co Inc — *Sony Video Software*

Super Seal   1977
Comedy
84027   95 mins   C   B, V   P
Foster Brooks, Sterling Holloway, Sarah Brown, directed by Michael Dugan
An injured seal pup disrupts a household's normal existence after the young daughter adopts him.
MPAA:G
John B Kelly — *United Home Video*

Super Seventies, The   1980
Football
50087   48 mins   C   B, V, LV   R, P
The decade's most memorable moments of thrilling runs and catches, exhilarating wins and crushing defeats.
NFL Films — *NFL Films Video*

Super Stars of the Super   1984
Bowls
Football
79637   50 mins   C   B, V, FO   P
The outstanding players of the Super Bowls past and present are remembered in this film.
NFL Films — *NFL Films Video*

Superboy   1966
Cartoons/Fantasy
81089   60 mins   C   B, V   P
Animated
Join Superboy and his dog Krypto as they fight crime in this collection of eight animated adventures.
Filmation — *Warner Home Video*

Superboy Screen Tests   1961
Outtakes and bloopers
85220   22 mins   B/W   B, V   P
John Rockwell
The actual screen tests for a "Superboy" TV series that never was put into production.
Whitney Ellsworth — *Video Yesteryear*

Superchick   1971
Adventure
33614   94 mins   C   B, V   P
Joyce Jillson, Louis Quinn, Thomas Reardon
An unassuming airline stewardess becomes a sexy, leggy blonde in between flights.
MPAA:R
Unknown — *Prism*

Superdad   1973
Comedy
81670   94 mins   C   B, V   P

Bob Crane, Kurt Russell, Joe Flynn, Barbara Rush, Kathleen Cody, Dick Van Patten
A middle-aged parent is determined to bridge the generation gap by trying his hand at various teenage activities.
MPAA:G
Walt Disney Productions — *Walt Disney Home Video*

Superfly   1972
Drama
53522   98 mins   C   B, V   P
Ron O'Neal, Carl Lee, Sheila Frazier, directed by Gordon Parks
A Harlem dope pusher gets involved with gangs and the police as he seeks to earn enough money with one last deal to be able to retire.
MPAA:R
Warner Bros — *Warner Home Video*

Supergirl   1984
Adventure/Fantasy
77204   114 mins   C   B, V   P
Helen Slater, Faye Dunaway, Peter Cook, Mia Farrow, Brenda Vaccaro, directed by Jeannot Szwarc
Superman's cousin Kara leaves her native planet of Krypton to come to Earth to recover The Omegahedron Stone.
MPAA:PG
Tri-Star Pictures — *U.S.A. Home Video*

Supergirl: The Making of   1984
the Movie
Filmmaking/Documentary
77381   60 mins   C   B, V   P
Faye Dunaway, Helen Slater, Peter O'Toole
A behind the scenes look at the making of the "Supergirl" film. Available in Beta Hi-Fi and VHS Stereo.
Ilya Salkind — *U.S.A. Home Video*

Superman   194?
Cartoons
53806   59 mins   C   B, V   P
Animated
This cartoon package features seven cartoon shorts released between 1941 and 1943. Included are "Superman #1," "Magnetic Telescope," "Japoteurs," "Bulleteers," "Jungle Drums," "Mechanical Monsters," and "The Mummy Strikes."
Paramount; Max Fleischer — *Media Home Entertainment*

Superman   1966
Cartoons/Fantasy
81090   60 mins   C   B, V   P
Animated, voices of Bud Collyer, Joan Alexander, Jackson Beck
Join Superman as he foils crime in Metropolis in this collection of seven animated adventures.

Filmation — *Warner Home Video*

Superman III 1983
Adventure
65358 125 mins C B, V, LV, P
CED
Christopher Reeve, Richard Pryor, Jackie Cooper, Marc McClure, Annette O'Toole, Annie Ross, Pamela Stephenson, Robert Vaughn, Margot Kidder
This time the Man of Steel faces the awesome power of a criminally insane super-computer genius, who has been hoodwinked by a sinister tycoon seeking global dominance. In VHS Dolby Stereo/Beta Hi-fi.
MPAA:PG
Pierre Spengler — *Warner Home Video*

Superman Cartoons 194?
Cartoons/Adventure
59055 75 mins C B, V P
A collection of rare animated Superman cartoons released from 1941 to 1943. Cartoons include: "Superman (First Episode)," "The Bulleteers," "The Magnetic Telescope," "The Japoteurs," "The Mechanical Monsters," "Volcano," "Terror on the Midway," "The Mummy Strikes," "Jungle Drums."
Max Fleischer; Paramount — *Wizard Video*

Superman Color Cartoon Festival 194?
Cartoons
53803 65 mins C B, V — P
Animated
This cartoon package includes "Superman" (1941), "The Mechanical Monsters" (1941), "The Bulleteers" (1942), "The Magnetic Telescope" (1942), "Terror on the Midway" (1942), "The Japoteurs" (1942), "The Mummy Strikes" (1943), and "Jungle Drums" (1943).
Paramount; Max Fleischer — *Hollywood Home Theater; Western Film & Video Inc; Discount Video Tapes*

Superman—The Movie 1978
Adventure
38938 144 mins C B, V, LV P
Christopher Reeve, Margot Kidder, Marlon Brando, Gene Hackman, Glenn Ford, directed by Richard Donner
A lavish retelling of the Superman legend, from his birth and flight from his home planet Krypton, to his becoming Earth's protector from the villain, Lex Luthor.
MPAA:PG
Warner Bros — *Warner Home Video; RCA VideoDiscs*

Superman II 1980
Adventure
58254 127 mins C B, V, LV P

Christopher Reeve, Margot Kidder, Gene Hackman, Ned Beatty, Jackie Cooper, Terence Stamp, Valerie Perrine, E. G. Marshall, directed by Richard Lester
The sequel to "the movie" about the Man of Steel. This time, he has his hands full with three super-powered villains and a love-stricken Lois Lane.
MPAA:PG
Film Export; Warner Bros — *Warner Home Video; RCA VideoDiscs*

Supernaturals, The 1986
Horror
Closed Captioned
88347 85 mins C B, V P
Maxwell Caulfield, Levar Burton, Nichelle Nichols
Civil War-era ghosts haunt a wooded area in which modern army maneuvers are practiced.
MPAA:R
Michael S. Murphy; Joel Soisson — *Embassy Home Entertainment*

Superspy 1985
Documentary
82560 50 mins C B, V, 3/4U P
Narrated by Bernard Archard, directed by Peter Batty
This documentary traces the story of Reinhard Gehlen, former head of the West German Secret Service and co-founder of the CIA.
Peter Batty — *Evergreen International*

Superstition 1982
Horror
81317 85 mins C B, V P
James Houghton, Albert Salmi, Lynn Carlin
A reverend and his family move into a vacant house near Black Poind despite warnings from the townspeople.
Almi Pictures — *Lightning Video*

Superted 1984
Cartoons
80050 48 mins C B, V P
Animated 5 pgms
The episodic adventures of the cartoon hero battling Bulk, Skeleton and Texas Pete.
1.Premiere Adventure 2.Further Adventures 3.The Adventures Continue 4.New Intergalactic Adventures 5.New Tales of Cosmic Adventure
Sirol Animation Limited — *Walt Disney Home Video*

Support Your Local Sheriff 1969
Western/Comedy
80141 92 mins C B, V P
James Garner, Joan Hackett, Walter Brennan, Bruce Dern, Jack Elam, Harry Morgan
When a stranger stumbles into a gold rush town, he winds up becomming the town's sheriff.

Cherokee Productions — *Key Video*

Surabaya Conspiracy   1975
Adventure/Drama
79337   90 mins   C   B, V   P
*Michael Rennie, Richard Jaeckel, Barbara
Bouchet*
Mystery and intrigue surround a search for gold
in Africa.
PM Films — *Monterey Home Video*

Sure Thing, The   1985
Comedy
81478   94 mins   C   B, V, 8mm,   P
                                      LV
*John Cusack, Daphne Zuniga, Nicolette
Sheridan, Viveca Lindfors, Boyd Gaines,
directed by Rob Reiner*
A horny college student discovers that casual
sex with a California blonde isn't such a "sure
thing" when he develops an attraction to a
fellow classmate.
MPAA:PG-13
Embassy; Monument Pictures — *Embassy
Home Entertainment*

Surf II   1984
Comedy
80125   91 mins   C   B, V   P
*Cleavon Little, Lyle Waggoner, Ruth Buzzi,
Carol Wayne, Terry Kiser*
A group of surfers are getting sick from drinking
tainted soda pop.
MPAA:R
International Film Marketing — *King of Video;
Media Home Entertainment*

Surfacing   1984
Drama
79892   90 mins   C   B, V   P
*Joseph Bottoms, Kathleen Beller, R.H.
Thompson, Margaret Dragu*
A girl braves the hostile Northern Wilderness to
search for her missing father.
Beryl Fox; Philips Hobel — *VCL Home Video*

Surfing Beach Party   1984
Music-Performance
76644   56 mins   C   B, V   P
This program recaptures the beach-blanket fun
of the '50s and '60s California rock 'n' roll.
Feature songs include "Surfin' Safari," "Fun,
Fun, Fun," "Barbara Anne" and many more.
Music Media — *Music Media*

Surf's Up   1986
Sports-Water/Documentary
71228   30 mins   C   V   P
The competitors at the '85 Men's Pro Cup and
World Cup competitions at Sunset Beach,
Hawaii included Shaun Thompson, Michael Ho,
Mark Richards and Wes Laine. This made-for-
video feature includes some intense highlights.
Prism Video Collection — *Prism*

Survival Anglia's World of   197?
Wildlife, Vol. I
Wildlife/Documentary
47060   90 mins   C   CED   P
Narrated by Glen Campbell and David Niven
Two award-winning documentaries are featured
in this package. "The Incredible Flight of the
Snow Geese" follows the migration of these
beautiful birds from the Canadian Arctic to the
Texas plains. "Leopard of the Wild" follows the
story of a man's involvement with an orphaned
leopard cub.
SA Ltd — *RCA VideoDiscs*

Survival Anglia's World of   198?
Wildlife, Vol. 2
Wildlife/Documentary
64455   104 mins   C   CED   P
Hosted by Peter Ustinov and David Niven
Ustinov narrates the story of the Australian
kangaroo, and Niven hosts an in-depth look at
the annual breeding of penguins at the Falkland
Islands.
SA Ltd — *RCA VideoDiscs*

Survival Run   1980
Adventure
66287   90 mins   C   B, V   P
Peter Graves, Ray Milland, Vincent Van Patten
Six young teenagers are stranded in the desert.
MPAA:R
Lance Hool — *Media Home Entertainment*

Survival Spanish   1984
Languages-Instruction
73568   60 mins   C   B, V   P
10 pgms
This series consists of ten lessons in beginning
Spanish for adults and children that covers ten
important situations and introduces a
vocabulary of 2,500 new words.
*1.Getting Down to Business 2.Making the Sale
3.Money Talk 4.Getting the Information 5.Family
Facts 6.In the Restaurant 7.Making a
Call—Leaving a Message 8.Making a
Call—Getting Through 9.Finding Your Way
10.Travel Plans*
AM Available
Language Plus Inc — *U.S.A. Home Video*

Survival Zone   1984
Horror
71219   90 mins   C   B, V   P
*Gary Lockwood, Morgan Stevens, Carmilla
Sparv*
Nuclear holocaust survivors battle a violent
band of marauding motorcyclists on the barren
ranches of the 21st century.
MPAA:R

Independent — *Prism*

Survivor, The   1980
Suspense
88144   91 mins   C   B, V   P
*Robert Powell, Jenny Agutter, Joseph Cotten,
directed by David Hemmings*
A jetliner crashes, leaving but one survivor, the
pilot, who is therein beset by visions, tragedies
and ghosts of dead passengers.
British — *Karl/Lorimar Home Video*

Survivors, The   1983
Comedy
69616   102 mins   C   B, V   P
Robin Williams, Walter Matthau, Jerry Reed
Two unemployed men find themselves the
target of an out-of-work hit man, whom they
disarm in a robbery attempt. One of the men
takes off for survivalist camp, hotly pursued by
the other, and then by the hit man.
MPAA:R
Bill Sackheim; Columbia — *RCA/Columbia
Pictures Home Video; RCA VideoDiscs*

Susan Slept Here   1954
Comedy
13128   98 mins   C   B, V   P
Dick Powell, Debbie Reynolds
Hollywood script writer is given protective
custody of vagrant girl over Christmas vacation.
RKO — *United Home Video*

Suspense   1953
Suspense
80754   54 mins   B/W   B, V   P
*Walter Matthau, Jayne Meadows, Franchot
Tone, Romney Brent*
A collection of two episodes from the series: In
"F.O.B. Vienna"; in "All Hallows Eve" a man who
murders his pawnbroker is plagued by a guilty
conscience.
CBS — *Video Yesteryear*

Suspicion   1941
Suspense
00258   90 mins   B/W   B, V   P
Cary Grant, Joan Fontaine, Cedric Hardwicke
Alfred Hitchcock's thriller about a woman who
gradually realizes she is married to a killer.
Academy Award '41: Best Actress (Fontaine);
'42 Film Daily Poll Ten Best Films of Year.
RKO — *RKO HomeVideo; VidAmerica;
Nostalgia Merchant*

Suzanne   1980
Drama
72229   102 mins   C   B, V   P
A woman is torn between a need for adventure
and a conviction for peace.
Guardian Trust Company — *Vestron Video*

Svengali   1931
Drama
54114   76 mins   B/W   B, V   P, T
John Barrymore, Marion Marsh
Maestro Svengali enchants lovely maidens by
using the magical powers embodied within his
evil stare. Once he has them under his powers,
he uses them to advance his musical career.
Warner Bros — *Blackhawk Films; Kartes Video
Communications; Cable Films; Video
Connection; Video Yesteryear; Western Film &
Video Inc; Discount Video Tapes; Movie Buff
Video*

Swamp Thing   1982
Mystery/Adventure
63376   91 mins   C   B, V, LV,   P
                                     CED
Adriene Barbeau, Louis Jourdan
Done in "comic-book" format, this is the story of
a group of scientists performing a top secret
experiment in a rural swamp and their nemesis,
the lunatic Arcane.
MPAA:PG
Benjamin Melnicker; Michael
Oslan — *Embassy Home Entertainment*

Swan Lake   1980
Dance
47814   ? mins   C   B, V   P
Natalia Makarova, Anthony Dowell
The Royal Ballet performs "Swan Lake,"
recorded at the Royal Opera House Covent
Garden, July 28, 1980. In stereo.
Unknown — *THORN EMI/HBO Video; Pioneer
Artists*

Swan Lake   1981
Dance
57254   82 mins   C   B, V   P
*The Kirov Ballet, the Leningrad Philharmonic,
directed by Konstantin Sergeyev*
Tchaikovsky's complete "Swan Lake" ballet is
performed by the Kirov Ballet troupe featuring
Yelena Yevteyeva, John Markovsky and Valeri
Panov. This interpretation is based on the
celebrated Petipal Ivanov productions.
Kultur — *Kultur*

Swan Lake   1982
Cartoons/Adventure
59667   75 mins   C   B, V   P
Animated
The prince searches for a future bride to be
queen when he becomes king. The swan which
bears the golden crown possesses magical
powers that hold the key.
Toei Company — *Media Home Entertainment*

Swan Lake   1957
Dance
69831   81 mins   C   B, V   P
Maya Plisetskaya, Bolshoi Ballet

The timeless tale of redemption through love.
Sovexportfilm USSR — *Video Arts International*

Swann in Love   1984
Drama
82477   110 mins   C   B, V   P
Jeremy Irons, Ornella Muti, Alain Delon, Fanny Ardant, Marie-Christine Barrault, directed by Volker Schlondorff
A handsome, wealthy rake makes a fool of himself over a beautiful courtesan who cares nothing for him. Based upon a section of Marcel Proust's "Remembrance of Things Past."
FR
Gaumont — *Media Home Entertainment*

Swap, The   1980
Drama
64872   90 mins   C   B, V, CED   P
Robert De Niro, Jennifer Warren
A man embarks on a desperate hunt for the killer of his young brother.
Christopher Dewey — *Vestron Video*

Swarm, The   1978
Horror
53523   116 mins   C   B, V   P
Michael Caine, Katharine Ross, Richard Widmark, Lee Grant, Richard Chamberlain, Olivia de Havilland, Henry Fonda, Fred MacMurray, Patty Duke Astin
A scientist must contend with a swarm of killer bees after the discovery of dead personnel on a government base.
MPAA:PG
Warner Bros; Irwin Allen — *Warner Home Video*

Sweater Girls   1980
Comedy
79390   90 mins   C   B, V   P
A female gang comes into a small town and decides to whoop it up with their boyfriends during their visit.
MPAA:R
Saturn International Pictures — *World Premiere*

Swedish Massage—Floor   1983
Routine
Massage
63999   60 mins   C   B, V   P
This program teaches the basics of full-body massage. Deep tension relief is stressed, with extra concentration on foot, hand, face massage and the use of oils. VHS in stereo.
Event Video — *Event Video*

Sweeney Todd—The   1984
Demon Barber of Fleet
Street
Musical
69920   139 mins   C   B, V   P
Angela Lansbury, George Hearn, directed by Harold Prince
This is a filmed performance of the Broadway musical by Stephen Sondheim. In VHS Dolby stereo and Beta Hi-Fi.
Richard Barr, Charles Woodward et al — *RKO HomeVideo*

Sweet Country Road   1981
Drama
86610   95 mins   C   B, V   P
Buddy Knox, Kary Lynn, Gordy Trapp, Johnny Paycheck, Jeanne Pruett
A rock singer journeys to Nashville to try to cross over into country music.
Jack MacCallum — *New World Video*

Sweet Dreams   1985
Biographical/Musical
85022   115 mins   C   B, V   P
Jessica Lange, Ed Harris, directed by Karel Reisz
This film depicts the turbulent, short life of country singer Patsy Cline with its successes and failures. Cline's actual songs appear on the soundtrack.
MPAA:PG-13
Tri-Star Pictures — *THORN EMI/HBO Video*

Sweet Sea   1986
Cartoons
85643   30 mins   C   B, V   P
A fantastical children's animated adventure about good and evil battling it out under the sea.
Children's Video Library — *Children's Video Library*

Sweet 16   1981
Horror
64873   90 mins   C   B, V   P
Susan Strasberg, Bo Hopkins
Sixteen-year-old Melissa is beautiful, mysterious, and promiscuous, but she can't understand why all her boyfriends end up dead.
MPAA:R
Jim Sotos; Martin Perfit — *Vestron Video*

Sweet Sweetback's   1971
Baadasssss Song
Drama
63416   97 mins   C   B, V   P
Melvin Van Peebles, Simon Chuckster
A black pimp kills two policemen who had been beating a black militant. He uses his street-wise survival skills to elude his pursuers and escape to Mexico.

Cinemation — *Sun Video; Magnum Entertainment*

Sweet William   1979
Drama
70605   88 mins   C   B, V   P
Sam Waterston, Jenny Agutter, Anna Massey, Arthur Lowe
A philandering and seemingly irresistible young man finds that one sensitive woman hasn't the patience or time for his escapades.
Kendon Films — *Prism*

Swept Away   1975
Drama
44782   116 mins   C   B, V   P
Giancarlo Giannini
A rich and beautiful Milanese capitalist woman is shipwrecked on a desolate island with a swarthy Sicilian deckhand, who also happens to be a dedicated communist.
Cinema 5 — *RCA/Columbia Pictures Home Video; RCA VideoDiscs*

Swim Baby Swim   1984
Sports-Water/Infants
76393   60 mins   C   B, V   P
Esther Williams
A step-by-step instructional guide to infant water safety presented by Esther Williams, former movie star, and Olympic-caliber professional swimmer.
Rogers & Cowan Inc — *Karl/Lorimar Home Video*

Swimmer, The   1968
Drama
84605   94 mins   C   B, V   P
Burt Lancaster, Janice Rule, Janet Landgard, directed by Frank Perry
A lonely suburbanite swims an existential swath through the pools of his neighborhood landscape in an effort at self-discovery. Based on a story by John Cheever.
MPAA:PG
Frank Perry; Roger Lewis — *RCA/Columbia Pictures Home Video*

Swing for a Lifetime, A   1985
Golf
88067   25 mins   C   B, V   P
Jim Flick demonstrates optimum golf swings.
NFL Films; Golf Digest — *NFL Films Video*

Swing High, Swing Low   1937
Comedy
08666   95 mins   B/W   B, V, 3/4U   P
Carole Lombard, Fred MacMurray, Charles Butter- worth, Dorothy Lamour, directed by Mitchell Leisen
A struggling trumpet player becomes a hit in the jazz world and marries the girl he loves.

Paramount — *Hollywood Home Theater; Discount Video Tapes; Video Yesteryear; Cable Films; Video Connection; Cinema Concepts; Kartes Video Communications*

Swing It, Sailor!   1937
Comedy
65202   61 mins   B/W   B, V   P
Wallace Ford, Ray Mayer, Isabel Jewell, Mary Treen
Two zany sailors have a series of comic adventures while on shore leave.
Grand National Films — *Video Yesteryear*

Swing Shift   1984
Comedy-Drama
73011   100 mins   C   B, LV, CED   P
Goldie Hawn, Kurt Russell, Ed Harris, directed by Jonathan Demme
Goldie Hawn stars as a woman who takes a job at an aircraft plant to help make ends meet after her husband goes off to war. A loving reminiscence of the American home front during World War II.
MPAA:PG
Jerry Bick; Warner Bros — *Warner Home Video*

Swing Time   1936
Musical
00273   103 mins   B/W   B, V   P
Fred Astaire, Ginger Rogers, Helen Broderick, Betty Furness, Eric Blore
Fred plays a dancer who can't resist gambling, until he meets Ginger. The score by Jerome Kern and Dorothy Fields includes "Pick Yourself Up," "Never Gonna Dance," "The Waltz in Swing-time" and "A Fine Romance."
Academy Awards '36: Best Song (The Way You Look Tonight).
RKO; Pandro S Berman — *RKO HomeVideo; Nostalgia Merchant; RCA VideoDiscs*

Swinging Cheerleaders,   1974
The
Comedy
60414   90 mins   C   B, V   P
Rainbeaux Smith, Colleen Camp, Jo Johnston
A group of amorous cheerleaders turn on the entire campus.
MPAA:PG
The Swinging Cheerleaders — *Monterey Home Video*

Swinging Ski Girls   197?
Drama
59554   85 mins   C   B, V   P
Cindy Wilton, Dick Cassidy
A group of swinging, free-loving university co-eds spend a wild weekend at a ski lodge.
Robert Marsden — *Media Home Entertainment*

Swinging Sorority Girls   197?
Drama
59553   73 mins   C   B, V   P
Susie Carlson, Anne Marlie
An intimate glimpse behind the closed doors of
a sorority house during a wild homecoming
weekend.
Robert Marsden — Media Home
Entertainment

Swiss Conspiracy, The   1977
Suspense
44911   92 mins   C   B, V   P
David Janssen, Senta Berger
Against the opulent background of the world's
richest financial capital and playground of the
wealthy, one man battles to stop a daring and
sophisticated blackmail caper.
MPAA:PG
SJ International Pictures — United Home
Video

Swiss Family Robinson,   1960
The
Adventure/Drama
47408   126 mins   C   B, V, LV   P
John Mills, Dorothy McGuire, James MacArthur,
Tommy Kirk, Janet Munro, Sessue Hayakawa
A Swiss family, travelling to New Guinea, is
blown off course and shipwrecked on a
deserted tropical island. Forced to remain, they
create a new life for themselves. Based on the
novel by Johann Wyss.
Walt Disney — Walt Disney Home Video; RCA
VideoDiscs

Swiss Miss   1938
Comedy
33907   72 mins   B/W   B, V, 3/4U   P
Stan Laurel, Oliver Hardy, Walter Woolf King,
Della Lind, Eric Blore
Stan and Ollie are mousetrap salesmen who
visit Switzerland and become involved with an
egotistical songwriter and his wife.
Hal Roach, MGM — Nostalgia Merchant;
Blackhawk Films

Swiss Miss   1938
Comedy
63990   97 mins   B/W   B, V   P, T
Stan Laurel, Oliver Hardy, Della Lind, Walter
Woolf King, Eric Blore
Stan and Ollie are mousetrap salesmen on the
job in Switzerland. Also included on this tape is
a 1935 Thelma Todd-Patsy Kelly short, "Hot
Money."
Hal Roach; MGM — Blackhawk Films

Switchblade Sisters   1975
Adventure
63087   90 mins   C   B, V   P
Robbie Lee, Joanne Nail

A crime gang of female ex-cons attack and kill
at the slightest provocation.
Switchblade Sisters Productions — Monterey
Home Video

Sword and the Cross, The   1958
Adventure
88322   93 mins   B/W   B, V   P
Yvonne De Carlo, George Mistral, directed by
C.L. Bragaglia
A grade-B adventure about the life of Mary
Magdelene.
Liber Films — Force Video

Sword and the Dragon   1956
Fantasy
84825   81 mins   C   '   B, V   P
Boris Andreyer, Andrei Abrikosov
A young warrior must battle any number of giant
mythical creatures.
Joseph Harris; Sig Shore; Russian — United
Home Video

Sword and the Rose, The   1953
Adventure
81647   91 mins   C   B, V   P
Richard Todd, Glynis Johns, Michael Gough,
Jane Barrett, directed by Ken Annakin
This is the story of the ill-fated romance
between Charles Brandon and Princess Mary
Tudor.
Walt Disney Productions — Walt Disney Home
Video

Sword and the Sorcerer,   1982
The
Fantasy
62780   100 mins   C   B, V, LV   P
Lee Horsely, Kathleen Beller, George Maharis,
Simon MacCorkindale
A young prince finds his kingdom destroyed by
an evil usurper and a powerful magician.
MPAA:R
Group I — MCA Home Video

Sword of Lancelot   1963
Adventure
87629   115 mins   C   B, V   P
Cornel Wilde, Jean Wallace, Brian Aherne,
directed by Cornel Wilde
A costume version of the Arthur-Lancelot-
Guinevere triangle, with plenty of swordplay. In
HiFi Mono.
Cornel Wilde; Bernard Luber — MCA Home
Video

Sword of the Valiant   1983
Fantasy
80856   102 mins   C   B, V   P
Sean Connery, Miles O'Keefe, Trevor Howard,
Lila Kedrova, John Rhys-Davies, Peter Cushing

The Green Knight arrives in Camelot to
challenge Gawain.
MPAA:PG
Cannon Films — *MGM/UA Home Video*

Swordsman with an Umbrella   1978
Martial arts
70703   85 mins   C   B, V   P
Jiang Ming, Yu Er
Two tough swashbuckling ladies strive
vengefully upon raping gangsters.
Master Arts — *Master Arts Video*

Sybil   1976
Drama
59363   122 mins   C   B, V, CED   P
*Sally Field, Joanne Woodward, Brad Davis,
Martine Bartlett, Jane Hoffman, directed by
Daniel Petrie*
The factually-based story of a woman who
developed 16 distinct personalities, and the
supportive psychiatrist who helped her put the
pieces of her ego together.
Emmy Awards '77: Outstanding Special
(Drama); Outstanding Lead Actress in a Drama
Special (Sally Field); Outstanding Writing in a
Special (Stewart Stern).
Lorimar — *CBS/Fox Video*

Sybil Bruncheon a la Maison   1986
Comedy
87189   55 mins   C   B, V   P
The infamous transvestite comedian carries
viewers along as "she" parades through an
average day.
Eric Perkins — *Nautilus Video*

Sylvester   1985
Drama
Closed Captioned
81427   104 mins   C   B, V   P
*Melissa Gilbert, Richard Farnsworth, Michael
Schoeffling, Constance Towers*
A sixteen-year-old girl and a cranky stockyard
boss team up to train a battered horse named
Sylvester for the National Equestrian trials.
Available in VHS Dolby Hi-Fi Stereo and Beta
Hi-Fi Stereo.
MPAA:PG
Columbia; Martin Jurow — *RCA/Columbia
Pictures Home Video*

Sylvester and Tweety's Crazy Capers   1961
Cartoons
81576   54 mins   C   B, V   P
*Animated, voice of Mel Blanc, directed by Friz
Freleng*
Sylvester keeps on the tail of Tweety Pie in this
collection of eight classic cartoons that include

"Tweet and Lovely", "Tree for Two" and "Hyde
and Go Tweet".
Warner Bros — *Warner Home Video*

Sympathy for the Devil   1970
Music
29175   110 mins   C   B, V   P
Mick Jagger, The Rolling Stones
A program with sequences of pop political
cartoons dealing with injustice and democracy.
In this provocative show the Rolling Stones
capture all the passionate defiance and thirst for
justice of the revolutionary 60's.
Viacom International — *CBS/Fox Video*

Symphony of Living   1935
Drama
78084   73 mins   B/W   B, V, FO   P
A heart warming drama about a man's bitter
betrayal by his own family and his incredible
hardships and tragedies.
Invincible Pictures — *Video Yesteryear*

T

T-Men   1947
Crime-Drama
64382   96 mins   B/W   B, V, 3/4U   P
Dennis O'Keefe, June Lockhart, Wallace Ford
Two agents of the Treasury Department
infiltrate themselves into a counterfeiting gang.
Eagle-Lion; Edward Small — *Nostalgia
Merchant*

Table for Five   1983
Drama
65001   120 mins   C   B, V, CED   P
*John Voight, Millie Perkins, Richard Crenna,
Robbie Kiger, Roxana Zal, Son Hoang Bui,
Marie Christine Barrault*
A divorced father takes his children on a
Mediterranean cruise and while sailing, he
learns that his ex-wife has died. The father and
his ex-wife's husband struggle over who should
raise the children.
MPAA:PG
CBS Theatrical Films — *CBS/Fox Video*

Table Settings   1984
Comedy
78656   90 mins   C   B, V   P
*Robert Klein, Stockard Channing, Dinah Manoff,
Eileen Heckhard*
A taped performance of James Lapines'
comedy about the lives of three generations of a
Jewish Family.
Showtime — *RKO HomeVideo*

Tag: The Assassination Game 1982
Mystery/Drama
80772   92 mins   C   B, V   P
Robert Carradine, Linda Hamilton, Michael Winslow, Kristine DeBell, Perry Lang
A college student writing an article for his school newspaper about a tag game uncovers some evil doings on campus.
MPAA:PG
New World Pictures — *Embassy Home Entertainment*

Takanaka World 1981
Music-Performance
47296   40 mins   C   B, V   P
Masayoshi Takanaka
As Masayoshi Takanaka performs his greatest hits, vivid visuals bring alive his daydreams.
Takeshi Shimizu; Hidenori Thea — *Paramount Home Video; Pioneer Video Imports*

Take a Good Look with Ernie Kovacs 1960
Game show
42965   30 mins   B/W   B, V, FO   P
Ernie Kovacs, Cesar Romero, Edie Adams, Carl Reiner
Zany skits abound as panelists attempt to guess the secret which the mystery guest is concealing.
ABC — *Video Yesteryear*

Take Down 1979
Comedy
73955   96 mins   C   B, V   P
Lorenzo Lamas, Kathleen Lloyd, Maureen McCormack, Edward Herrmann
Twelve members of a high school wrestling team have to get back into shape in time for a big wrestling match.
Buena Vista — *Unicorn Video*

Take It Big 19??
Musical
78113   75 mins   B/W   B, V
Two vaudevillians and the members of a dance band help to finance a dude ranch
Paramount — *Video Yesteryear; Discount Video Tapes*

Take It Big 1944
Musical
78113   75 mins   B/W   B, V, FO   P
Jack Haley, Harriet Hillard, Mary Beth Hughes, Airline Judge, Nils T. Granlund, Fuzzy Knight, Ozzie Nelson and his Orchestra
A pleasant musical about a band leader who is in love with a singer, though she is nuts about an impoverished actor who inherits a dude ranch.
Paramount — *Video Yesteryear*

Take It to the Limit 1980
Motorcycles
66200   90 mins   C   B, V   P
The best of motorcycle racing and champions is shown. In stereo.
Peter Starr — *U.S.A. Home Video*

Take Me Back to Oklahoma 1940
Western
15460   64 mins   B/W   B, V   P
Tex Ritter, directed by Al Herman
Musical western with comedy.
Monogram — *Video Connection; Video Yesteryear*

Take the Money and Run 1969
Comedy
46187   85 mins   C   B, V, LV,   P
                          CED
Woody Allen, Janet Margolin, Marcel Hillaire, directed by Woody Allen
A young man unsuccessfully tries to rob a bank and from that point on is unable to stay out of jail long enough to turn his new career into a profitable one.
MPAA:PG
Palomar Pictures International — *CBS/Fox Video*

Take This Job and Shove It 1981
Comedy
58833   100 mins C   B, V, CED   P
Robert Hays, Art Carney, Barbara Hershey, David Keith, Martin Mull, Eddie Albert, Penelope Milford
A hot-shot efficiency expert is determined to streamline the Pickett Brewing Company, a Dubuque, Iowa brewery. He upsets the lives of his closest friends in the process, before realizing that his priorities in life are scrambled.
MPAA:PG
Avco Embassy — *Embassy Home Entertainment*

Takin' It Off 1984
Comedy
76768   90 mins   C   B, V   P
Kitten Natividad, Adam Hadum, Ashley St. John, Angelique Pettyjohn
An exotic dancer's agent advises her to trim down her well endowed figure in order to become a serious actress.
Hanson and Gervasoni — *Vestron Video*

Taking My Turn 1984
Musical
80452   87 mins   C   B, V   P
A taped performance of the off Broadway musical revue about growing old gracefully.
Sonny Fox — *Pacific Arts Video*

Taking of Pelham One Two Three, The
1974

Suspense
66077   102 mins   C   B, V, CED   P
Robert Shaw, Walter Matthau, Martin Balsam, Hector Elizondo, James Broderick, directed by Joseph Sargent
A hijack team seizes a New York City subway car and holds the 17 passengers for ransom.
MPAA:R
United Artists — *CBS/Fox Video*

Tale of the Frog Prince, The
1983

Fairy tales
Closed Captioned
69324   60 mins   C   B, V, LV,   P
                        CED
Robin Williams, Teri Garr, narrated by Eric Idle
This is the story of a special friendship between a frog turned prince by a witch's spell and the self-centered princess who saves him with a kiss. From Shelley Duvall's "Faerie Tale Theatre."
Shelley Duvall — *CBS/Fox Video*

Tale of Two Cities, A
1935

Drama
58295   128 mins   B/W   B, V   P
Ronald Colman, Elizabeth Allen, Edna May Oliver, Donald Woods, Basil Rathbone, directed by Jack Conway
Dickens' classic set during the French Revolution, about two men who bear a remarkable resemblance to each other, both in love with the same girl.
Film Daily Poll Ten Best Pictures of the Year '35.
MGM; David O Selznick — *MGM/UA Home Video*

Tale of Two Cities, A
1958

Adventure
59903   117 mins   B/W   B, V, 3/4U   P
Dirk Bogarde, Dorothy Tutin, Christopher Lee, Donald Pleasence, Ian Bannen
Dickens' classic about a lawyer who sacrifices himself to save another man from the guillotine.
Rank — *Embassy Home Entertainment; Learning Corp of America*

Tale of Two Cities, A
1984

Cartoons/Drama
80681   72 mins   C   B, V   P
Animated
This is an adaptation of the Dickens classic about a man who sacrifices his own life for that of his friend to insure the happiness of the woman they both loved.
Burbank Films — *Children's Video Library*

Tale of Two Critters, A
1977

Adventure
59065   48 mins   C   B, V   P
A young raccoon and a playful bear cub develop a rare friendship growing up in the wilds.
Walt Disney Productions — *Walt Disney Home Video*

Tales from Mother Goose and the World of Make Believe
1985

Fairy tales
81851   58 mins   C   B, V   P
Captain Kangaroo reads from some of his favorite Mother Goose nursery rhymes including "Little Bo Peep" and "Jack and Jill."
Jim Hirschfeld — *MPI Home Video*

Tales from Muppetland
197?

Comedy
53793   102 mins   C   CED   P
This two-sided disc contains two programs featuring the lovable Muppets: "Muppet Musicians of Bremen" (1972) and "Emmet Otter's Jug Band Christmas" (1977).
Henson Associates — *RCA VideoDiscs*

Tales from Muppetland II
1971

Comedy/Fairy tales
60382   108 mins   C   CED   P
Two enchanting Muppet variations on classic fairy tales: "Hey, Cinderella" and "The Frog Prince."
Henson Associates — *RCA VideoDiscs*

Tales from the Crypt
1972

Horror
80318   92 mins   C   B, V   P
Sir Ralph Richardson, Joan Collins, Peter Cushing, Ian Hendry, directed by Freddie Francis
A collection of five scary stories from the classic EC comics that bear the movie's title.
MPAA:PG
Metromedia Producers Corporation — *Prism*

Tales From the Darkside
1985

Mystery/Fantasy
84394   70 mins   C   B, V   P
Lou Jacobi, Peggy Cass, Joseph Turkel, Tippi Hedren, Vince Edwards 4 pgms
Each episode of this series features three short Twilight Zone-esque stories of fantasy and suspense.
T.J. Castronova; Richard Rubenstein et al. — *Thriller Video*

Tales of Beatrix Potter
1985

Fairy tales
88036   43 mins   C   B, V   P
Six stories from Potter's canon, including "Peter Rabbit," "Two Bad Mice," "Miss Moppet" and "Jeremy Fisher," illustrated by Potter's original drawings and narrated by Sydney Walker.

Vestron Video — *Children's Video Library*

Tales of Deputy Dawg—Volumes II & III   196?
Cartoons
29176   90 mins   C   B, V   P
Animated
Two programs featuring Terrytoons' Deputy Dawg. Both available individually.
Viacom International — *CBS/Fox Video*

Tales of Hoffmann, The   1981
Opera
53400   210 mins   C   LV   P
Introduction by John Gielgud, Placido Domingo
The Royal Opera's performance of Offenbach's "Tales of Hoffmann," produced by John Schlesinger.
Covent Garden Video Prods Ltd — *Pioneer Artists; RCA VideoDiscs*

Tales of Magic, Video Book II   1977
Cartoons
87918   90 mins   C   B, V   P
Narrated by Nicole Richards, directed by Yuji Tanno
A collection of animated films, based on various cultural legends and stories: "Hansel & Gretel," "Don Quixote," "The Pied Piper of Hamelin" and "Gifts of the North Wind."
Yuji Tanno; Mike Haller — *Embassy Home Entertainment*

Tales of Ordinary Madness   1983
Drama
79311   107 mins   C   B, V   P
Ben Gazzara, Ornella Muti, Susan Tyrell, Tanya Lopert, directed by Marco Ferrari
A poet tries to devour life with a furious gulp and meets some unusual characters in his travels.
Fred Baker Productions — *Vestron Video*

Tales of Terror   1962
Horror
53524   88 mins   C   B, V   P
Vincent Price, Peter Lorre, Basil Rathbone, directed by Roger Corman
Three tales of terror: "Morella," "The Black Cat," and "The Case of M. Valdemar." Based on stories by Edgar Allen Poe.
American International — *Warner Home Video*

Tales of Tomorrow Volume 1   195?
Science fiction
44338   120 mins   B/W   B, V, 3/4U   P
Lon Chaney Jr., Bruce Cabot, Leslie Nielsen, Thomas Mitchell
Four episodes from the early 1950's television series focusing on the supernatural. Includes "Frankenstein," "Dune Roller," "Appointment on Mars," and "Crystal Egg." Includes previews of coming attractions from classic science fiction films.
ABC; George F. Foley Jr. — *Nostalgia Merchant*

Tales of Tomorrow, Volume 2   195?
Science fiction
58583   90 mins   B/W   B, V, 3/4U   P
Boris Karloff, Walter Abel, Edmon Ryan, Rod Steiger
Four episodes from the early 1950's TV series focusing on the supernatural. "Past Tense," "A Child is Crying," "Ice from Space," and "The Window."
ABC; George F Foley Jr — *Nostalgia Merchant*

Talk of the Town   1982
Football
47713   23 mins   C   B, V, FO   P
Team highlights of the 1981 New York Jets, who had the top-ranked defense in the AFC, the NFL Defensive Player of the Year in Joe Klecko, and the NFL Comeback Player of the Year with Richard Todd.
NFL Films — *NFL Films Video*

Talk Talk   1983
Music video
88108   16 mins   C   B, V   P
The English new wave band's first video hits, most notably their self-entitled leading song.
Sony Video — *Sony Video Software*

Talk to Me   1982
Drama
Closed Captioned
81558   90 mins   C   B, V   P
Austin Pendleton, Michael Murphy, Louise Fletcher, Briar Backer, Clifton James
A successful New York accountant checks into the Hollins Communication Institute to cure his stuttering and falls in love with a squirrel-hunting stuttering woman from Arkansas. Available in VHS and Beta Hi-Fi Stereo.
Hollis Communication Institution Prods. — *Playhouse Video*

Talking in Your Sleep   1984
Music/Video
65403   4 mins   C   B, V   P
The Romantics
The video clip "Talking in Your Sleep" features The Romantics and a cast of 100 models dressed, as the song implies, in a variety of sleepwear from robes to negligees.
Bob Dyke — *CBS/Fox Video*

Talking Parcel, The   1984
Fantasy
85026   40 mins   C   B, V   P
An animated film about a parrot sweeping a young girl off to a fantasy world. Based on the book by Gerald Durrell.
Thames Video — *THORN EMI/HBO Video*

Tall Blond Man with One   1973
Black Shoe, The
Mystery
07139   90 mins   C   B, V   P
Pierre Richard, Bernard Blier, Jean Rochefort, directed by Yves Robert
Decoy agent is completely unaware that he is the center of a plot by a French intelligence director to booby-trap an overly ambitious assistant. Dubbed in English.
MPAA:PG
Cinema 5 — *RCA/Columbia Pictures Home Video; Movie Buff Video; Video Yesteryear*

Tall in the Saddle   1944
Western
00278   79 mins   B/W   B, V, 3/4U   P
John Wayne, Ella Raines
Portrayal of a tough, woman-hating cowboy working for a spinster and her attractive niece.
RKO; Robert Fellows — *Nostalgia Merchant*

Tamarind Seed, The   1974
Drama
82571   123 mins   C   B, V   P
Julie Andrews, Omar Sharif, Anthony Quayle, Daniel O'Herlihy, Sylvia Syms, directed by Blake Edwards
A secretary and a KGB official become entangled in a life-threatening, passionate affair in this romantic adventure film.
Ken Wales; Lorimar — *Embassy Home Entertainment*

Taming of the Shrew, The   1981
Comedy
66273   152 mins   C   B, V   P
Directed by Peter Dews
Shakespeare's comedy about Petruchio's attempt to tame his fiery, free-spirited wife.
Unknown — *Embassy Home Entertainment*

Taming of the Shrew, The   1929
Drama
66354   66 mins   B/W   B, V   P
Mary Pickford, Douglas Fairbanks, Edwin Maxwell, Joseph Cawthorn, directed by Sam Taylor
This early talkie version of Shakespeare's play is the only film that co-stars America's most popular acting couple of the 1920's. The film was re-edited in 1966, with some cleaning up of the soundtrack and a musical score added as well.
Pickford Corp; Elton Corp; United Artists — *Blackhawk Films*

Taming of the Shrew, The   1967
Comedy
21297   122 mins   C   B, V   P
Elizabeth Taylor, Richard Burton, Michael York
A lavish screen version of the classic Shakespearean comedy.
Columbia — *RCA/Columbia Pictures Home Video; RCA VideoDiscs*

Tammy and the Bachelor   1957
Comedy
85772   89 mins   C   B, V   P
Debbie Reynolds, Leslie Neilsen, Walter Brennan
A backwoods Southern girl becomes ensnared with a romantic aristocrat and his snobbish family, but wins them over with her down-home philosophy. Features the hit tune, "Tammy."
Universal — *MCA Home Video*

Tammy and the Doctor   1963
Comedy
85773   88 mins   C   B, V   P
Sandra Dee, Peter Fonda, MacDonald Carey, directed by Harry Keller
A sequel to "Tammy and the Bachelor" has the adorable hick assaulting a medical center with her backwoods ways when she gets a job as a nurse's aid. The film debut of Peter Fonda.
Universal — *MCA Home Video*

Tango   1985
Dance
84467   57 mins   C   B, V   P
Choreographed by Oscar Araiz
The ballet ensemble of the Grand Theatre Company of Geneva tango the night away.
Swiss — *V.I.E.W. Video*

Tango   1986
Dance
84667   57 mins   C   B, V   P
The Ballet Ensemble of the Grand Theatre Company of Geneva perform various traditional tangoes.
The Grand Theatre Company of Geneva — *V.I.E.W. Video*

Tank   1983
Drama
75017   113 mins   C   B, V, LV   P
James Garner, Shirley Jones, G.D. Spradlin
This is the unusual story of an Army officer who takes on a small town sheriff with the aid of a World War II Sherman tank.
MPAA:PG
Irwin Yablans — *MCA Home Video*

Tannhauser 1982
Opera
71139   176 mins   C   B, V   P
Richard Cassilly, Eva Marton, Tatiana Troyanos, Bernd Weikl, John Macurdy, James Levine conducting the Metropolitan Opera Orchestra, Chorus and Ballet
From public television's "Live From the Met" series, this grand yet subtle setting of Wagner's romantic masterpiece received critical acclaim when it was telecast in December, 1982. Recorded in HiFi Stereo with English subtitles.
PBS; The Metropolitan Opera — *Paramount Home Video*

Tantra of Gyuto (Sacred 1968
Rituals of Tibet)
Documentary/Asia
86482   52 mins   C   B, V   P
Narrated by Francis Huxley
A documentary about Tibetan Tantric monks and their spiritualism, introduced by the Dalai Lama and including footage from the 1933 German expedition to Tibet.
Sheldon Rochlin; Mark Elliot — *Mystic Fire Video*

Tap Dancing for 1982
Beginners
Dance
47367   38 mins   C   B, V   P
Henry LeTang, choreographer of "Sophisticated Ladies," provides elementary instruction in the art of tap dance.
American Home Video Library — *Kultur*

Tapestry Weaving-Level I 1985
Handicraft
85650   110 mins   C   B, V   P
Nancy Harvey
A course in the particulars of tapestry weaving designed for the experienced weaver.
Victorian Video Prod. — *Victorian Video Productions*

Taps 1981
Drama
47398   126 mins   C   B, V, CED   P
Timothy Hutton, George C. Scott, Ronny Cox, Sean Penn, Tom Cruise, directed by Harold Becker
When a military school is threatened with closure, the students take over and start a siege. The situation snowballs with misunderstandings until the National Guard is called in.
MPAA:PG
20th Century Fox — *CBS/Fox Video*

Tarantulas: The Deadly 1977
Cargo
Suspense
77205   95 mins   C   B, V   P
Claude Akins, Charles Frank, Deborah Winters, Bert Remsen
A horde of deadly tarantulas spread terror and death through a small southwestern town.
Alan Landsburg Productions — *U.S.A. Home Video*

Target 1985
Suspense
88325   117 mins   C   B, V   P
Gene Hackman, Matt Dillon, Gayle Hunnicutt, directed by Arthur Penn
An incognito ex-CIA agent is hunted and drawn out of hiding by the kidnapping of his wife. His troubles are complicated by the involvement of his estranged grown son, who hadn't known of his secret past.
MPAA:R
Richard D. Zanuck; David Brown;
CBS — *CBS/Fox Video*

Target Eagle 1984
Adventure
72461   100 mins   C   B, V   P
Max von Sydow, George Peppard, Maud Adams, Chuck Connors, directed by D.J. Anthony Loma
Terrorists land on the Mediterranean coast and a mercenary and a young woman attempt to halt them with only their wits and courage.
Unknown — *VCL Home Video*

Target for Today 1941
World War II/Documentary
81603   60 mins   B/W   B, V   P
This is the story of how a bombing raid is performed from its inception to its completion.
U.S. Office of War Information — *Victory Video*

Target for Tonight 1941
World War II/Documentary
23228   50 mins   B/W   B, V, FO   P
An English documentary about a bombing raid on Germany during World War II.
Crown Film Unit — *Video Yesteryear; International Historic Films*

Targets 1969
Drama
60214   90 mins   C   B, V   P
Boris Karloff, James Brown, Tim O'Kelly, directed by Peter Bogdanovich
Bogdanovich's directorial debut concerns an aging horror film star who confronts and disarms a mad sniper at a drive-in movie.
MPAA:R
Peter Bogdanovich — *Paramount Home Video*

Taro, The Dragon Boy 1985
Cartoons
77373   75 mins   C   B, V   P
Animated

A young boy searches for his mother who has been turned into a dragon
Turner Program Services;
Toei — *RCA/Columbia Pictures Home Video*

Tarzan and the Green Goddess
1938

Adventure
07206   72 mins   B/W   B, V   P
Herman Brix, Ula Holt, Frank Baker
Tarzan searches for a statue that could prove dangerous in the wrong hands.
PRI; Sol Lesser — *Movie Buff Video; Hollywood Home Theater*

Tarzan and the Trappers
1958

Adventure
11260   74 mins   B/W   B, V, FO   P
Gordon Scott, Eve Brent, Ricky Sorenson, Maurice Marsac, Cheetah
Tarzan frees animals from trappers and prevents them from robbing the riches of a lost city.
RKO — *Video Yesteryear*

Tarzan of the Apes
1917

Adventure
07279   63 mins   B/W   B, V, FO   P
Elmo Lincoln, Enid Markey
The first screen version of the adventures of Tarzan. Silent.
First National — *Video Yesteryear; Western Film & Video Inc; Cable Films*

Tarzan, the Ape Man
1932

Adventure
55209   104 mins   B/W   B, V   P
Johnny Weissmuller, Maureen O'Sullivan, directed by W. S. Van Dyke
The first Tarzan movie, featuring the characters created by Edgar Rice Burroughs.
MGM — *MGM/UA Home Video*

Tarzan, the Ape Man
1981

Adventure
59310   112 mins   C   B, V, LV, CED   R
Bo Derek, Richard Harris, directed by John Derek
Edgar Rice Burroughs' classic remade with the focus on Jane, as she explores the African jungles, learning about life and love from the Ape Man.
MPAA:R
Svengali Prods — *MGM/UA Home Video*

Tarzan the Fearless
1933

Adventure
58920   84 mins   B/W   B, V   P
Buster Crabbe, Jacqueline Wells
Tarzan helps a young girl find her missing father.
EL, SP

PRC; Sol Lesser — *Movie Buff Video; Hollywood Home Theater; Cable Films; Video Connection; Kartes Video Communications*

Tarzan's Revenge
1938

Adventure
05446   70 mins   B/W   B, V, 3/4U   R, P
Glenn Morris, Eleanor Holm, Hedda Hopper
Tarzan saves a safari of white travellers from vicious warriors.
20th Century Fox — *Hollywood Home Theater; Video Yesteryear; Kartes Video Communications*

Tattered Web, A
1971

Suspense/Mystery
82308   74 mins   C   B, V   P
Lloyd Bridges, Frank Converse, Broderick Crawford, Murray Hamilton, Sallie Shockley
A corrupt police sergeant tries to frame a wino for a murder that he committed.
Metromedia — *Karl/Lorimar Home Video*

Tattoo
1981

Drama
58849   103 mins   C   B, V, CED   P
Bruce Dern, Maud Adams, Leonard Frey, Rikke Borge, John Getz
A model becomes the object of obsession for a tattoo artist who uses bodies as his canvas.
MPAA:R
20th Century Fox — *CBS/Fox Video*

Tattoo Connection, The
1978

Martial arts
87912   95 mins   C   B, V   P
Jim Kelly, directed by Luk Pak Sang
A gang of lethal Oriental diamond thieves is pursued with whip-snapping panache by a taciturn kung-fu invesitgator.
MPAA:R
H. Wong; Lee Tso-Nan — *Embassy Home Entertainment*

Tattooed Dragon, The
1982

Martial arts
71251   91 mins   C   B, V   P
Jimmy Wang Yu, directed by Lo Wei
Even the dumbest of grisly gangs should know better than to toy with the Tattooed Dragon; but they don't.
MPAA:R
World Northal — *Embassy Home Entertainment*

Tax Tapes
1985

Finance
70385   60 mins   C   B, V   P
These tapes should help end the confusion surrounding viewer's preparation of federal income tax forms. The programs explain the tax

laws and documents in clear, jargon-free terms.
The short form program runs 30 minutes.
1.Long form; 2.Short form
RKO Home Video — *RKO HomeVideo*

Taxi Driver   1976
Drama
47785   112 mins   C   B, V   P
Robert DeNiro, Cybill Shepherd, Peter Boyle,
Jodie Foster, directed by Martin Scorcese
A psychotic New York City cab driver goes on a
violent rampage in an effort to rid the city of
undesirables.
MPAA:R
Michael and Julia Phillips — *RCA/Columbia*
Pictures Home Video; RCA VideoDiscs

Tchaikovsky   1985
Competition: Violin &
Piano
Music-Performance
76967   90 mins   C   B, V   P
Violinist Viktoria Mullova and pianist Peter
Donahoe play their winning selections from the
Tchaikovsky Competition taped in the Soviet
Union.
Johnson Films; Hammer Films — *Mastervision*

Teachers   1984
Comedy
Closed Captioned
77462   106 mins   C   B, V   P
Nick Nolte, Jo Beth Williams, Lee Grant, Judd
Hirsch, Ralph Macchio, Richard Mulligan,
directed by Arthur Hiller
A lawsuit is brought against a high school for
awarding a diploma to an illeterate student.
Available in VHS and Beta Hi Fi.
MPAA:R
MGM/United Artist — *CBS/Fox Video*

Teacher's Pet   1958
Comedy
85262   120 mins   B/W   B, V   P
Clark Gable, Doris Day, Mamie Van Doren, Gig
Young, directed by George Seaton
A cynical newspaper editor enrolls in a night
college journalism course out of curiosity and
becomes enamoured of his teacher.
Paramount — *Kartes Video Communications*

Team of the 80's/NFL '82   1983
Football
66222   45 mins   C   B, V, FO   P
Highlights of the San Diego Chargers' 1982-83
season along with an overview of the whole
NFL Season.
NFL Films — *NFL Films Video*

Team on a Tightrope   1980
Football
45127   24 mins   C   B, V, FO   R, P

Dallas Cowboys
Highlights of the 1979 Dallas Cowboys football
season.
NFL Films — *NFL Films Video*

Team Together/NFL '83,   1984
A
Football
72935   46 mins   C   B, V, FO   P
Denver Broncos
Highlights from the 1983 season of the Denver
Broncos plus "NFL 83."
NFL Films — *NFL Films Video*

Tears for Fears   1984
Music video
88109   11 mins   C   B, V   P
Video clips from the English pop/new wave
duo's first albums, prior to their "Songs from the
Big Chair" LP.
Sony Video — *Sony Video Software*

Tears for Fears: In My   1986
Mind's Eye
Music-Performance/Music video
84132   58 mins   C   B, V   P
Tear for Fears
A live performance at the Hammersmith Odeon
in London features this chart-topping British
group playing their biggest hits, including
"Change," "Head Over Heels" and "Start of the
Breakdown."
Music Media — *Media Home Entertainment*

Teddy at the Throttle   1916
Film-History
50631   20 mins   B/W   B, V   P, T
Bobby Vernon, Gloria Swanson, Wallace Beery,
Teddy (the Dog), directed by Clarence Badger
Teddy the Great Dane must rescue Gloria
Swanson from a villain who has tied up her
boyfriend. Silent.
Unknown — *Blackhawk Films*

Teddy at the   1917
Throttle/Speeding Along
Comedy
78120   54 mins   B/W   B, V, FO   P
Gloria Swanson, Wallace Beery, Bobby Vernon,
Keystone Teddy
A silent comedy about stealing fortunes from
innocent heroines and a silent comedy about
racing cars in a farm area.
Mack Sennett — *Video Yesteryear*

Teddy Pendergrass Live   1982
in London
Music-Performance
63399   75 mins   C   B, V   P
Teddy Pendergrass
Filmed at England's Hammersmith Odeon in
February 1982, this concert features the

singer's most popular tunes, including "Close the Door," "If You Don't Know Me By Now," "Bad Luck," and "Wake Up Everybody." Home Video Premiere Productions — *CBS/Fox Video*

Teen Lust   1978
Comedy
82194   90 mins   C   B, V   P
Kirsten Baker, Perry Lang, Richard Singer
Two girls get all the action they can handle when they get a summer job working as undercover prostitutes for the local police department.
MPAA:R
Columbus America Films — *Lightning Video*

Teen Wolf   1985
Comedy
Closed Captioned
82552   92 mins   C   B, V, 8mm,   P
                              LV
Michael J. Fox, James Hampton, Scott Paulin, Susan Ursitti
A nice, average teenager begins to show werewolf tendencies which make it difficult for him to keep from attracting unwanted attention.
MPAA:PG
Wolfkill Productions — *Paramount Home Video*

Teenage Seductress   198?
Exploitation
88222   84 mins   C   B, V   P
A young girl connives her way into the life of a writer, and finds ways to distract him from his work.
Unknown — *Master Arts Video*

Teenage Zombies   1960
Horror
69569   71 mins   B/W   B, V, FO   P
Don Sullivan, Katherine Victor
A lady mad scientist kidnaps teenagers and uses her secret chemical formula to turn them into zombies, as the harbinger of her plan to enslave the world.
Governor — *Video Yesteryear*

Telefon   1977
Suspense
75537   102 mins   C   B, V   P
Charles Bronson, Lee Remick
The Soviets have a secret plan to destroy key U.S. military targets. The plan is so secret that the Soviet agents don't even know they will trigger the destruction.
MPAA:PG
MGM — *MGM/UA Home Video*

Telephone Book, The   1971
Comedy
64968   88 mins   C   CED   P
Sarah Kennedy, Norman Rose, Barry Morse
A young woman falls in love with the world's greatest obscene phone caller.
Rosebud Releasing — *Embassy Home Entertainment (disc only)*

Telescope—Interview   1965
with Harry Richman
Interview
46348   25 mins   B/W   B, V, FO   P
Harry Richman
Vaudeville and nightclub star Harry Richman discusses his 50-year career in this candid interview.
CBC — *Video Yesteryear*

Television Parts Home   1985
Companion
Satire/Music video
81700   40 mins   C   B, V   P
This is a compilation of four humorous sketches from the series, including three clips produced especially for home video.
United Art Works Inc. — *Pacific Arts Video*

Television's Golden Age   195?
of Comedy
Comedy
11275   75 mins   B/W   B, V, FO   P
Groucho Marx, Amos and Andy, Bob Hope, Dean Martin, Jerry Lewis, Jack Benny
"You Bet Your Life," with Groucho Marx, Amos and Andy's "Rare Coin," and an episode of "The Jack Benny Show" are featured in this vintage package of television comedy.
CBS et al — *Video Yesteryear*

Tell Me That You Love Me   1984
Drama
84102   88 mins   C   B, V   P
Nick Mancuso, Barbara Williams, directed by Tzipi Trope
A Tear-jerking portrait of a disintegrating modern marriage.
The Movie Store — *Lightning Video*

Tell Them Willie Boy Is   1969
Here
Western
64791   98 mins   C   B, V   P
Robert Redford, Katherine Ross, Robert Blake, Susan Clark, Barry Sullivan, directed by Abraham Polonsky
This western classic is based on the true story of a Paiute Indian, Willie Boy (Blake), and his white bride (Ross), who become the objects of the last great western manhunt after he kills her father in a "Marriage by Capture" on white

---

man's territory. Sheriff Cooper (Redford) leads the manhunt.
MPAA:PG
Universal — *MCA Home Video*

Tempest   1928
Drama
64318   105 mins   B/W   B, V   P, T
John Barrymore, Louis Wolheim
A Russian peasant soldier rises through the ranks to become an officer, only to be undone by his love for the daughter of his commanding officer. Silent with musical score.
United Artists — *Movie Buff Video; Blackhawk Films*

Tempest   1982
Drama
64573   140 mins   C   B, V   P
John Cassavetes, Gena Rowlands, Susan Sarandon, Vittorio Gassman, RaulJulia, directed by Paul Mazursky
A New York architect, fed up with city living, chucks it all and brings his daughter with him to live on a barren Greek island. VHS in stereo.
MPAA:PG
Columbia — *RCA/Columbia Pictures Home Video; RCA VideoDiscs*

Tempest, The   1985
Drama
70650   126 mins   C   B, V   P
Efrem Zimbalist, William H. Basset, Ted Sorrel, Kay E. Kuter, Edward Edwards, Nicholas Hammond, Ron Palillo, directed by William Woodman
Shakespeare's "Tempest" is a storm sent by a wise magician to bring Naple's royal family to Caliban, the desolate island where he remains in exile. This presentation uses American actors and accents set against an artist's recreation of England's Globe Theatre stage. This is a two-cassette package.
Paganiniana Publications — *Kultur*

Tempest, The/The Eagle   1927
Film-History
50641   56 mins   B/W   B, V   P, T
John Barrymore, Camilla Horn, Rudolph Valentino, Louise Dressler
A Russian soldier is betrayed and humiliated by the woman he loves in "The Tempest." In "The Eagle," an outcast guardsman becomes the Russian version of Robin Hood.
United Artists — *Blackhawk Films*

Tempter, The   1978
Horror
80766   96 mins   C   B, V   P
Mel Ferrer, Arthur Kennedy, Alida Valli, Anita Strindberg
A psychiatrist discovers through hypnosis that the daughter of an Italian nobleman has

---

inherited the curse of an ancestress who was burned at the stake as a witch.
MPAA:R
Edmundo Amati — *Embassy Home Entertainment*

"10"   1979
Comedy
37423   123 mins   C   B, V, LV   P
Dudley Moore, Julie Andrews, Bo Derek, directed by Blake Edwards
A successful songwriter who has everything he could want out of life somehow feels that his existence is incomplete. He searches for something more—and finds it in the person of Bo Derek, the woman of his dreams, whom he rates as the ultimate on the girl-watching scale. He pursues her, determined to overcome any obstacles—with unpredictable results. Music by Henry Mancini; also features Ravel's "Bolero." Available both dubbed and subtitled in Spanish.
MPAA:R EL, SP
Orion Pictures, Warner Brothers — *Warner Home Video; RCA VideoDiscs*

Ten Brothers of Shao-lin   198?
Martial arts
64957   90 mins   C   B, V   P
Chia Ling, Wang Tao, Chang Yi
A martial arts adventure from the days of warlords and warriors.
Dragon Lady Productions — *Unicorn Video*

10CC   1985
Music-Performance
77400   60 mins   C   B, V   P
Kevin Godley, Lol Creme
The rock band 10CC perform their hits "The Things We Do For Love" and "Wall Street Shuffle" in this concert taped at London's Hammersmith Odeon.
Bruce Gowers — *VCL Home Video*

Ten Commandments, The   1956
Drama
38611   219 mins   C   B, V, LV   P
Charlton Heston, Yul Brynner, Anne Baxter, Yvonne DeCarlo, directed by Cecil B. DeMille
Lavish Biblical epic that tells the life story of Moses (Charlton Heston) who turned his back on a privileged life to lead his people to freedom.
Academy Awards '56: Best Special Effects.
Paramount — *Paramount Home Video; RCA VideoDiscs*

Ten Commandments, The   1979
Drama/Bible
63517   58 mins   C   B, V   P
John Marley, Kristoffer Tabori, Granville Van Dusen, Anson Williams
Moses leads his people out of Egypt and brings them to Mount Sinai to receive the Ten

---

Commandments from God. Part of the "Greatest Heroes of the Bible" series.
Sunn Classics — *Magnum Entertainment; Lucerne Films*

Ten Days Around Mont Blanc/The Great Traverse

1979

Mountaineering
84273   48 mins   C   B, V   P
This tape includes two films of rugged back-packers, and is graced with beautiful nature photography and families of protagonists.
Video Travel Inc — *Video Travel*

Ten Days that Shook the World

1927

Drama
08698   104 mins   B/W   B, V, 3/4U   P
Directed by Sergei Eisenstein and Grigori Alexandrov
This Russian epic details the events which culminated in the Russian Revolution of October 1917, using the actual locations and many actual participants.
Amkino; Russian — *Video Yesteryear; International Historic Films; Western Film & Video Inc*

Ten from Your Show of Shows

1973

Variety
44799   92 mins   B/W   B, V   P, T
Sid Caesar, Imogene Coca, Carl Reiner, Howard Morris
A compilation of vintage comedy routines from the famous variety series of the 50's, "Your Show of Shows." Sketches include a takeoff on "This Is Your Life," and some movie spoofs.
Walter Reade — *Media Home Entertainment*

Ten Little Indians

1975

Mystery
64965   98 mins   C   B, V   P
Herbert Lom, Richard Attenborough, Oliver Reed, Elke Sommer
Ten people are gathered in an isolated inn under mysterious circumstances. One by one they are murdered, each according to a verse from a children's nursery rhyme. Based on the novel and stage play by Agatha Christie.
MPAA:PG
Avco-Embassy — *Charter Entertainment*

Ten Nights in a Bar-Room

1931

Drama
85493   60 mins   B/W   B, V   P
William Farnum, Thomas Santschi, John Darrow, Robert Frazer
A turn-of-the-century mill owner succumbs to alcoholism and ruins his life and family.
Leon E. Goetz — *Video Yesteryear*

10 Rillington Place

1971

Mystery
85284   111 mins   C   B, V   P
Richard Attenborough, John Hurt, Judy Geeson, directed by Richard Fleischer
The story of the John Christie murders and how he managed to get another man convicted of his crimes.
MPAA:PG
Martin Ransohoff; Leslie Linder — *RCA/Columbia Pictures Home Video*

Ten Speed

1976

Drama
86847   89 mins   C   B, V   P
William Woodbridge, Patricia Hume, David Clover
Two advertising executives compete in a 400-mile bicycle race from San Francisco to Malibu.
Select-a-Tape — *Lightning Video*

Ten to Midnight

1983

Crime-Drama
85141   101 mins   C   B, V   P
Charles Bronson, Wilford Brimley, Lisa Eilbacher
A psychotic killer stalks a beautiful girl, and her father tries to stop him in a violent manner.
MPAA:R
Cannon Group — *MGM/UA Home Video*

Ten Who Dared

1960

Adventure
88341   92 mins   C   B, V   P
Brian Keith, John Beal, James Drury, directed by William Beaudine
Ten Civil War Heroes brave the Colorado River in an expedition that is based on a factual account.
Walt Disney Prod. — *Walt Disney Home Video*

Tenant, The

1976

Horror
68251   126 mins   C   B, V   P
Roman Polanski, Isabelle Adjani, Melvyn Douglas, Jo Van Fleet, Bernard Fresson, Shelley Winters
A disturbing film about an apartment tenant whose neighbors' actions drive him to insanity.
MPAA:R
Marianne Productions — *Paramount Home Video*

Tender Age, The

1984

Drama
70855   103 mins   C   B, V   P
John Savage, Tracy Pollan, directed by Jan Egleson
A troubled 18-year old girl captivates her juvenile probation officer whose interest extends beyond normal professional concern.
Skouras — *Lightning Video*

Tender Loving Care   1973
Drama/Romance
71248   72 mins   C   B, V   P
Donna Desmond, Leah Simon, Anita King, directed by Don Edmonds
Three nurses dispense hefty doses of T.L.C. in their hospital, and the patients aren't the only ones on the receiving end.
Avco Embassy; Chako Van
Leeuwen — *Embassy Home Entertainment*

Tender Mercies   1983
Drama
65087   93 mins   C   B, V, CED   P
Robert Duvall, Tess Harper, Betty Buckley, directed by Bruce Beresford
A down-and-out country-and-western singer finds his life redeemed by the love of a good woman.
Academy Awards '83: Best Actor (Duvall) Best Original Screenplay (Horton Foote) MPAA:PG
Universal — *THORN EMI/HBO Video*

Tendres Cousines   1983
Comedy
65602   90 mins   C   B, V   P
This comedy follows the exploits of two cousins coming of age in the French countryside. Along with the rest of their relatives and friends, they become entwined in a web of unrequited love and intricate relationships.
MPAA:R
Crown — *Vestron Video*

Tennessee Stallion   1978
Drama
86360   87 mins   C   B, V   P
Audrey Landers, Judy Landers, Jimmy Van Patten
A low-class horse-trainer breaks into the world of aristocratic thoroughbred racing.
Euramco Int'l. — *Vestron Video*

Tennessee's Partner   1955
Western
52579   87 mins   C   B, V   P
Ronald Reagan, Rhonda Fleming, John Payne, directed by Allan Dwan
A stranger steps into the middle of an argument and becomes the friend of a gambler.
RKO — *Weiss Global Enterprises; Buena Vista Home Video*

Tennis/Racquet Sports   1978
Tennis
44926   30 mins   C   B, V   P
Exercise specialist Ann Dugan performs exercises for tennis, squash, handball, and racquetball players to use to help mobilize the body for aggressive play. From the "Sports Conditioning" series.

Health N Action — *RCA/Columbia Pictures Home Video*

Tension at Table Rock   1956
Western
84827   93 mins   C   B, V   P
Richard Egan, Dorothy Malone, Cameron Mitchell
A lone gun is hunted for a murder he commited in self-defense.
RKO — *United Home Video*

Tentacles   1977
Horror
64883   90 mins   C   B, V, CED   P
John Huston, Shelley Winters, Bo Hopkins, Henry Fonda
A giant octopus wreaks havoc and terror.
MPAA:PG
American International Pictures — *Vestron Video*

10th Victim, The   1965
Drama/Science fiction
65432   92 mins   C   B, V   P
Ursula Andress, Marcello Mastroianni
A futuristic thriller about a society where violence is channeled into legalized murder hunts. A beautiful TV actress is the hunter and the 10th victim will bring her all the material things she desires.
Avco-Embassy — *Embassy Home Entertainment*

Terminal Choice   1985
Suspense
82432   98 mins   C   B, V   P
Joe Spano, Diane Venora, David McCallum, Ellen Barkin
A computer expert tries to find the person behind the strange and unexplainable deaths of patients at the Dodson Clinic.
MPAA:R
Almi Pictures — *Vestron Video*

Terminal Island   1977
Mystery
79764   88 mins   C   B, V   P
Phyllis Davis, Tom Selleck, Don Marshall, Ena Hartman, Marta Kristen
Two groups of male prisoners on a penal colony find themselves fighting over the colony's only female inhabitants.
MPAA:R
Dimension Pictures — *United Home Video*

Terminal Man, The   1974
Science fiction
88182   107 mins   C   B, V   P
George Segal, Joan Hackett, Jill Clayburgh, Richard A. Dysart, James B. Sikking, Normann Burton, directed by Mike Hodges

A slick, visually compelling adaptation of the Michael Crichton novel about a scientist plagued by violent mental disorders who has a computer-controlled regulator implanted in his brain, only to have the computer malfunction and set him on a murdering spree.
MPAA:R
Mike Hodges — *Warner Home Video*

Terminator, The   1984
Science fiction
80646   108 mins   C   B, V, LV   P
Arnold Schwarzenegger, Michael Biehn, Linda Hamilton, Paul Winfield, directed by James Cameron
The Terminator is a futuristic cyborg sent to present day earth to kill the woman who will conceive the child destined become the arch enemy of the earth's future rulers.
MPAA:R
Gale Ann Hurd — *THORN EMI/HBO Video*

Terms of Endearment   1983
Drama
75807   129 mins   C   B, V   P
Shirley MacLaine, Jack Nicholson, Debra Winger, directed James L. Brooks
This story follows the relationship between a young woman and her mother, over a thirty year period.
Academy Awards '83: Best Picture; Best Actress (MacLaine); Best Supporting Actor (Nicholson); Best Director (Brooks); Best Screenplay (Brooks). MPAA:PG
Paramount — *Paramount Home Video*

Terror   1979
Horror
48502   86 mins   C   B, V   P
John Nolan, Carolyn Courage, James Aubrey
Supernatural forces and the shocking effect their mysterious powers have on the life of a young girl are depicted in this shocking tale.
MPAA:R
Crystal Film Production — *United Home Video; Video City Productions*

Terror, The   1963
Horror
59664   81 mins   C   B, V   P
Jack Nicholson, Boris Karloff
A lieutenant in Napoleon's army finds himself trapped by a mad baron's fear of the unknown.
Roger Corman — *Prism; Hal Roach Studios; Media Home Entertainment; Hollywood Home Theater; Discount Video Tapes; Cinema Concepts; World Video Pictures*

Terror by Night   1946
Mystery
42928   60 mins   B/W   B, V   P
Basil Rathbone, Nigel Bruce

Based on a character developed by Sir Arthur Conan Doyle, Holmes and Watson solve two murders and thwart an attempted jewel theft on a train.
Universal, Howard Benedict — *Kartes Video Communications; Movie Buff Video; Video Connection; Video Yesteryear; Hollywood Home Theater; Cable Films; Western Film & Video Inc; Discount Video Tapes*

Terror by Night/Meeting   194?
at Midnight
Mystery
44856   122 mins   B/W   B, V, 3/4U   P
Basil Rathbone, Nigel Bruce, Sidney Toler
In "Terror by Night" (1946), Sherlock Holmes and Dr. Watson board a train to protect a fabulous diamond. In "Meeting at Midnight" (1944), Charlie Chan becomes involved in magic and murder.
Universal, Monogram — *Nostalgia Merchant*

Terror in the Aisles   1984
Horror/Movie and TV trailers
76807   84 mins   C   B, V   P
Donald Pleasence and Nancy Allen take you on a terrifying journey through some of the scariest moments in horror film history.
MPAA:R
Universal; Stephen J. Netburn; Andrew J. Kuehn — *MCA Home Video*

Terror in the Swamp   1985
Horror
76959   89 mins   C   B, V, LV   P
Billy Holliday
A swamp creature is terrorizing the residents of a small town.
MPAA:PG
New World Pictures — *New World Video*

Terror in the Wax   1973
Museum
Horror
79674   94 mins   C   B, V   P
Ray Milland, Broderick Crawford, Elsa Lanchester, Maurice Evans, John Carradine
The owner of a wax museum is killed while mulling over selling the museum to an American.
MPAA:PG
Bing Crosby Productions — *Lightning Video*

Terror of Mechagodzilla   1978
Horror
82546   79 mins   C   B, V   P
Katsuhiko Sasakai, Tomoko Al
A huge mechanical Godzilla built by aliens is pitted against the real thing in this Japanese monster movie.
MPAA:G
Toho Company — *Paramount Home Video*

Terror of Tiny Town 1933
Western/Musical
14349 65 mins B/W B, V P
Jed Buell's Midgets, directed by Sam Newfield
Terror erupts in a small midwestern town. All-midget cast.
Columbia — *Video Connection; Discount Video Tapes; Hollywood Home Theater; Admit One Video; Video Yesteryear*

Terror on the 40th Floor 1974
Suspense/Drama
80319 98 mins C B, V P
John Forstyhe, Anjanette Comer, Don Meredith, Joseph Campanella
Seven people make an attempt to escape from the fortieth floor of an enflamed skyscraper.
Metromedia Producers Corporation — *Prism*

Terror on Tour 1983
Horror
64234 90 mins C B, V P
Dave Galluzzo, Richard Styles, Rick Pemberton
The Clowns, a rock group on their way up, center their stage performance around sadistic, mutilating theatrics. When real murders begin, they become prime suspects.
Rick Whitfield — *Media Home Entertainment*

Terror Out of the Sky 1978
Suspense
77209 100 mins C B, V P
Ephraim Zimbalist Jr, Dan Haggerty, Tovah Feldshuh, Lonny Chapman
A beekeeper and his assistant must track down three killer queen bees who kill off a schoolbus full of children in New Orleans.
Allen Landsburg Productions — *U.S.A. Home Video*

Terrorism: The Russian Connection 1985
Documentary
76964 60 mins C B, V P
This documentary focuses on the recruitment and training techniques of the P.L.O. and other terrorist groups.
Canadian Broadcasting Company — *Mastervision*

Terrorvision 1986
Horror/Comedy
86850 84 mins C B, V P
Gerrit Graham, Mary Woronov, Diane Franklin, directed by Ted Nicolaou
A suburban family gets a state-of-the-art satellite dish which transmits both TV programs and a irate alien into their living room.
MPAA:R
Empire — *Lightning Video*

Terry Bears Volume II 196?
Cartoons
29177 90 mins C B, V P
Animated
A cartoon feature with "Terry Bears."
Viacom International — *CBS/Fox Video*

Terry Fox Story, The 1983
Drama
65349 96 mins C B, V, CED P
Robert Duvall, Chris Makepeace, Eric Fryer, Rosalind Chao
In the spring of 1980, a brave young man who had lost his right leg to cancer dipped his artificial limb into the Atlantic Ocean and set off on a "Marathon of Hope" across Canada. He ran 3,000 miles before he collapsed in Ontario.
Michael A Levine; Gurston Rosenfeld — *Vestron Video*

Terrytoons Salutes the Olympics 1979
Sports/Cartoons
72234 60 mins C B, V P
Animated
An animated salute to the Olympics featuring the Terrytoon all stars, including Deputy Dawg.
Viacom — *Children's Video Library*

Terrytoons: The Good Guys Hour 1985
Cartoons
80975 53 mins C B, V P
Animated
Here is a collection of classic Terrytoons cartoons that feature such favorites as Mighty Mouse, the mighty Heroes, Deputy Dawig and James Hound.
Terrytoons — *Children's Video Library*

Terrytoons, Vol. I, Featuring Mighty Mouse 196?
Cartoons
56884 100 mins C CED P
Animated
Nineteen complete cartoons featuring Mighty Mouse, Heckle and Jeckle, Deputy Dawg, Little Roquefort, and others.
Terrytoons — *RCA VideoDiscs*

Tess 1980
Drama
52748 170 mins C B, V, LV P
Nastassia Kinski, Peter Firth, Leigh Lawson, John Collin, directed by Roman Polanski
Thomas Hardy's novel "Tess of the d'Urbervilles," concerning a young woman who is a victim of both circumstance and a rigid Victorian society, tortured by guilt for the wrongs she feels she has committed, is the basis for this movie.

Academy Awards '80: Best Cinematography;
Best Art Direction; Best Costume Design.
MPAA:PG
Claude Beri; Renn Productions; Burrill
Productions — *RCA/Columbia Pictures Home
Video; RCA VideoDiscs*

Test of Love, A   1984
Drama
84629   93 mins   C   B, V   P
*Angela Punch McGregor, Drew Forsythe, Tina
Arhondis*
A young woman struggles to adjust to a normal
life after doctors rediagnose her as disabled
after years in an institution for the mentally
retarded.
MPAA:PG
Don Murray — *MCA Home Video*

Testament   1983
Drama
Closed Captioned
65763   90 mins   C   B, V, CED   P
*Jane Alexander, William Devane, Ross Harris,
Roxana Zal*
Following a massive nuclear attack, a mother
and her children struggle to survive against the
backdrop of death, disease and destruction.
MPAA:PG
Lynne Littman — *Paramount Home Video*

Tex   1982
Drama
60557   103 mins   C   B, V, LV   P
*Matt Dillon, Jim Metzler, Meg Tilly, Bill
McKinney, Frances Lee McCain, Ben Johnson,
Emilio Estevez*
The poignant and moving story of a teenager
coming of age in a small Texas town. Based on
the novel by S.E. Hinton.
MPAA:PG
Walt Disney Productions — *Walt Disney Home
Video*

Texaco Star Theater   1951
Variety/Comedy
58264   60 mins   B/W   B, V, FO   P
*Milton Berle, Danny Thomas, Fran Warren, Sid
Stone, Frank Galop, Alan Roth and his
Orchestra*
Originally broadcast on May 29, 1951, Uncle
Miltie presides over the hilarity. Guests include
Carlos Ramirez and his Senoritas, novelty
dancers Harold and Lola, Beatrice Kraft and her
Oriental dancers, 15-year-old violinist Michael
Rabin, and singer Vivian Dellachiesa. Sketches
include "The Chandeliers," a comic troupe of
acrobats, and "United Nations of Show
Business."
NBC — *Video Yesteryear*

Texas Chainsaw   1974
Massacre, The
Horror
59058   86 mins   C   B, V   P
*Marilyn Burns, Paul A Partain, Edwin Neal,
directed by Tobe Hooper*
An idyllic summer afternoon drive becomes a
nightmare for two young people pursued by a
chainsaw-wielding maniac.
MPAA:R
Tobe Hooper; New Line Cinema — *Media
Home Entertainment; Vestron Video (disc only)*

Texas Detour   1977
Adventure
81826   90 mins   C   B, V   P
*Cameron Mitchell, Priscilla Barnes, Patrick
Wayne*
A trio of young Californians take the law into
their own hands when their van is stolen in a
small Texas town.
Cinema Shares International — *Prism*

Texas Gunfighter   1932
Western
84838   60 mins   B/W   B, V   P
Ken Maynard
A seminal western from Maynard, with
everything a western could have.
Ken Maynard; Tiffany — *United Home Video*

Texas John Slaughter: 1960
Geronimo's Revenge
Western
84802   77 mins   C   B, V   P
*Tom Tryon, Darryl Hickman, Betty Lynn,
directed by Harry Keller*
An Indian-loving rancher frets and fights when
Geronimo attacks innocent settlers.
Walt Disney Prod — *Walt Disney Home Video*

Texas John Slaughter: 1962
Stampede at Bitter Creek
Western
71100   90 mins   C   B, V   P
Tom Tryon, directed by Harry Keller
Former Texas Ranger John Slaughter meets a
variety of threatening obstacles when he tries to
move his cattle herd into the New Mexico
Territory.
Walt Disney Productions — *Walt Disney Home
Video*

Texas Lady   1956
Western
80847   86 mins   C   B, V   P
Claudette Colbert, Barry Sullivan
When a woman wins $50,000 gambling, she
buys a Texas newspaper on the stipulation that
she can edit it.
RKO — *Republic Pictures Home Video*

Texas Lightning   1981
Adventure
66063   93 mins   C   B, V   P
Cameron Mitchell, Channing Mitchell, Maureen McCormick, Peter Jason
A truck driver is intent on showing his shy son the fine points of life.
MPAA:R
Jim Sotos — *Media Home Entertainment*

Texas Terror   1940
Western
29440   50 mins   B/W   B, V   P
John Wayne, Gabby Hayes
John Wayne plays a cowboy who mistakenly believes he has shot his friend. He becomes a ranch foreman and saves the ranch from horse theives, finally discovering who really shot his friend.
Monogram — *Video Dimensions; Sony Video Software*

Texas to Bataan   1942
Western
11263   56 mins   B/W   B, V, FO   P
Range Busters
The Range Busters ship horses to the Philippines and encounter enemy spies.
Monogram — *Video Yesteryear*

Texersize   1984
Physical fitness
65706   37 mins   C   B, V   P
Irlene Mandrell
This program exercises all major muscle groups and gives a complete cardio-vascular workout.
Panda Productions; Haghland Productions — *Embassy Home Entertainment*

Thank God It's Friday   1978
Comedy/Musical
63965   100 mins   C   B, V   P
Valerie Landsburg, Terri Nunn, Chick Vennera
A dance contest at a Hollywood disco, where the participants are caught up in the glamor and glitter of disco nightlife, is the focal point of this film. Music by Donna Summer and The Commodores.
Academy Awards '78: Best Song ("Last Dance").   MPAA:PG
Casablanca Productions; Columbia Pictures — *RCA/Columbia Pictures Home Video*

Thank You Mr. President   1984
Documentary/Presidency-US
79169   55 mins   C   B, V   P
Narrated by E.G. Marshall
The wit and humor of John F. Kennedy are captured in this documentary that features excerpts of his press conferences.

D. J. Mendelsohn Productions — *Worldvision Home Video*

Thanksgiving Story, The   1973
Drama
Closed Captioned
71046   95 mins   C   B, V   P
Richard Thomas, Ralph Waite, Michael Learned, Ellen Corby, Will Geer, directed by Philip Leacock
Thankfulness is hard found on Walton's mountain, where John-Boy's college career is jeopardized by a freak accident.
Lorimar — *Karl/Lorimar Home Video*

That Championship Feeling   1984
Basketball
73857   60 mins   C   B, V   P
Here are highlights from the 1983 NBA Playoffs and World Championship Series featuring the Philadelphia '76ers.
NBA — *CBS/Fox Video*

That Championship Season   1982
Drama
66116   110 mins   C   B, V, CED   P
Martin Sheen, Bruce Dern, Stacy Keach, Robert Mitchum, Paul Sorvino
Long-dormant animosities surface at the reunion of a championship basketball team.
MPAA:R
Cannon — *MGM/UA Home Video*

That Cold Day in the Park   1969
Drama
66469   91 mins   C   B, V   P
Sandy Dennis, Michael Burns, Suzanne Benton, directed by Robert Altman
A disturbed spinster entices a homeless young man into her apartment and makes him a prisoner.
MPAA:R
Commonwealth United; Robert Altman — *Spotlite Video*

That Darn Cat   1965
Comedy
76823   115 mins   C   B, V   P
Hayley Mills, Dean Jones, Dorothy Provine, Neville Brand, Elsa Lanchester, Frank Goishin
A Siamese cat becomes an agent for the F.B.I. and helps to unravel a kidnapping-robbery.
MPAA:G
Buena Vista; Walt Disney Productions — *Walt Disney Home Video*

That Hamilton Woman   1941
Biographical/Drama
81469   125 mins   B/W   B, V, LV   P

Laurence Olivier, Vivien Leigh, Gladys Cooper, Alan Mowbray, directed by Alexander Korda
This is the story of the tragic love affair between the British naval hero Lord Nelson and Lady Hamilton.
Alexander Korda — *Embassy Home Entertainment*

That Obscure Object of Desire   1977
Comedy
82583   100 mins   C   B, V   P
Fernando Rey, Carole Bouquet, Angelo Molina, directed by Luis Bunuel
This surreal film explores the nature of sexual obsession. Available in both subtitled and dubbed versions.
MPAA:R FR
Serge Silberman — *Embassy Home Entertainment*

That Sinking Feeling   1979
Comedy
76795   82 mins   C   B, V   P
Robert Buchanan, John Hughes, Billy Greenlees, Alan Love, directed by Bill Forsyth
A group of bored teenagers decide to steal ninety tins from a plumber's warehouse.
MPAA:PG
Samuel Goldwyn Company — *Embassy Home Entertainment*

That Touch of Mink   1962
Comedy/Romance
65456   99 mins   C   B, V   P
Cary Grant, Doris Day
In New York City, a young naive girl finds herself involved with a business tycoon. On a trip to Bermuda, both parties get an education as they play their game of "cat and mouse."
Universal — *Republic Pictures Home Video*

That Uncertain Feeling   1941
Comedy
05460   86 mins   B/W   B, V, FO   P
Merle Oberon, Melvyn Douglas, Burgess Meredith, Alan Mowbray, Eve Arden
A husband and wife develop marital problems when the wife gets the hiccups.
Ernst Lubitsch; United Artists — *Video Yesteryear; Discount Video Tapes; Hollywood Home Theater; Hal Roach Studios*

That Was Rock (The TAMI/TNT Show)   1964
Music-Performance
65481   90 mins   B/W   B, V   P
Chuck Berry, James Brown, Ray Charles, Bo Diddley, Marvin Gaye, Gerry & The Pacemakers, Lesley Gore, Jan & Dean, Smokey Robinson & the Miracles, The Ronettes, The Rolling Stones, The Supremes, Ike & Tina Turner

The TAMI/TNT shows were the greatest dance concerts ever, and now they are together in one rock and roll, rhythm and blues extravaganza. In stereo VHS and Beta Hi-Fi.
Lee Savin; Phil Spector — *Music Media*

That Was Then... This Is Now   1985
Drama
Closed Captioned
86877   102 mins   C   B, V, LV   P
Emilio Estevez, Craig Sheffer, Kim Delaney, written by Emilio Estevez
From another S.E. Hinton novel, two boys raised as brothers struggle to come of age amid sexual discovery, inexpressible frustrations and a propensity toward pointlessly rebellious crime.
MPAA:R
Paramount Pictures — *Paramount Home Video*

That'll Be the Day   1973
Musical
63320   86 mins   C   B, V   P
Ringo Starr, Keith Moon, David Essex, Rosemary Leach
Set in the early rock 'n' roll era of the 1950's, this is the story of a wayward young man and his aspirations to musical superstardom.
David Puttnam; Sanford Lieberson — *THORN EMI/HBO Video*

That's Dancing!   1985
Musical/Dance
81054   104 mins   C   B, V, LV   P
Fred Astaire, Ginger Rogers, Ruby Keeler, Cyd Charisse, Gene Kelly, Liza Minnelli, Sammy Davis, Jr., Mikhail Baryshnikov, Ray Bolger, directed by Jack Haley, Jr.
This anthology features same of film's finest moments in dance from classical ballet to break-dancing. Available in VHS and Beta Hi-Fi stereo.
MGM — *MGM/UA Home Video*

That's Entertainment   1974
Musical
44646   132 mins   C   B, V, LV,   P
                                    CED
Judy Garland, Fred Astaire, Frank Sinatra, Gene Kelly, Esther Williams, Bing Crosby, directed by Jack Haley Jr.
A compilation of scenes from the classic MGM musicals beginning with "The Broadway Melody" (1929) and ending with "Gigi" (1958).
MPAA:G
MGM — *MGM/UA Home Video*

That's Entertainment, Part II   1976
Musical
58291   133 mins   C   B, V   P
Fred Astaire, Gene Kelly, John Barrymore, Lionel Barrymore, Jack Benny, Judy Garland,

Maurice Chevalier, Bing Crosby, Jimmy Durante, Clark Gable, Jean Harlow, Elizabeth Taylor, Robert Taylor
A cavalcade of great musical and comedy sequences from MGM movies of the past. Also stars Jeanette MacDonald, Nelson Eddy, the Marx Bros., Laurel and Hardy, Jack Buchanan, Ann Miller, Mickey Rooney, Louis Armstrong, Oscar Levant, Cyd Charisse.
MPAA:G
MGM — MGM/UA Home Video

That's Singing   1984
Musical/Variety
81121   111 mins   C   B, V   P
Hosted by Tom Bosley, Nell Carter, Barry Bostwick, Robert Morse, Debbie Reynolds, Diahann Carroll, Chita Rivera, Ethel Merman, Ray Walston
This is a tribute to the the American musical theatre featuring performances of memorable songs from twenty Broadway shows.
Iris Merlis — Karl/Lorimar Home Video

That's the Way of the   1975
World
Drama
80904   97 mins   C   B, V   P
Harvey Keitel, Ed Nelson, Bert Parks, Cynthia Bostick, Earth, Wind and Fire
A young record producer finds himself swept up in a web of payola when the Mafia forces him to promote a mediocre group. Music by Earth, Wind and Fire. Available in VHS stereo and Beta Hi-Fi.
MPAA:PG
United Artists — U.S.A. Home Video

Theatre of Death   1967
Horror
13141   90 mins   C   B, V   P
Christopher Lee, Julian Glover
Paris police are baffled by a series of mysterious murders, each bearing a trace of vampirism.
Associated British Productions Ltd — United Home Video

Them!   1954
Horror/Science fiction
76857   93 mins   B/W   B, V   P
James Whitmore, Edmund Gwenn, Fess Parker, James Arness, Onslow Stevens, directed by Gordon Douglas
A group of mutated giant ants wreak havoc on a southwestern town.
David Weisbart; Warner Bros — Warner Home Video

There Was A Crooked   1970
Man
Western
82341   123 mins   C   B, V   P

Kirk Douglas, Henry Fonda, Warren Oates, Hume Cronyn, directed by Joseph L Mankiewicz
An Arizona town gets some new ideas about law and order when an incorruptible warden takes over the town's prison.
MPAA:R
Warner Bros — Warner Home Video

There's a Girl in My Soup   1970
Comedy
65316   95 mins   C   B, V   P
Peter Sellers, Goldie Hawn
Sellers is a gourmet who moonlights as a self-styled Casanova, and Goldie is the young girl who takes refuge at his London love nest when she is ejected by her boyfriend from their flat.
M J Frankovich; John Boulting — RCA/Columbia Pictures Home Video

There's a Meetin' Here   1981
Tonight
Music-Performance
53859   117 mins   C   LV   P
The Limelighters, Glen Yarborough, Kingston Trio
Performances by folk immortals The Limelighters, Glenn Yarborough, and the Kingston Trio.
Intl Teleview Inc; Bill Williams; Susan Shore — Pioneer Artists

There's Naked Bodies On   197?
My T.V.!
Satire/Comedy
59550   79 mins   C   B, V   P
A sexy spoof of TV shows, "Happy Daze," "Bernie Milner," and "Don't Come Back Kotler."
CHK Productions — Media Home Entertainment

There's No Business Like   1954
Show Business
Musical
37416   117 mins   C   B, V, CED   P
Ethel Merman, Donald O'Connor, Marilyn Monroe, Dan Dailey, Johnny Ray, Mitzi Gaynor
A top husband and wife vaudevillian act return to the stage with their three children, who are now also in the act. Includes 24 songs by Irving Berlin.
20th Century Fox — CBS/Fox Video

Therese and Isabellee   1968
Drama
81408   102 mins   C   B, V   P
Essy Persson, Anna Gael, Barbara Laage, Anne Vernon, directed by Redley Metzger
This film recounts the torrid affair between two French schoolgirls, therese and Isabelle.
Available in VHS Stereo and Beta Hi-Fi.

Radley Metzger — *Monterey Home Video*

These Girls Won't Talk 192?
Comedy
11286 50 mins B/W B, V, FO P
Colleen Moore, Carole Lombard, Betty Compson
Three female stars of early motion pictures are featured separately in: "Her Bridal Nightmare," "Campus Carmen," and "As Luck Would Have It."
Mack Sennett et al — *Video Yesteryear*

These Three 1936
Drama
81446 92 mins B/W B, V, LV P
Miriam Hopkins, Merle Oberon, Joel McCrea, Bonita Granville, directed by William Wyler
The lives of three people are irrevocably changed due to a malicious lie a teenaged girl tells about them. Based upon Lillian Hellman's "The Children's Hour."
Samuel Goldwyn — *Embassy Home Entertainment*

They All Laughed 1981
Comedy
59870 115 mins C B, V, LV, CED P
Ben Gazzara, John Ritter, Audrey Hepburn, Colleen Camp, Patti Hansen, Dorothy Stratten, directed by Peter Bogdonovich
A madcap private eye caper involving a team of detectives who are both following and being followed by a bevy of dazzling women.
MPAA:PG
PSO; Moon Pictures — *Vestron Video*

They Call Me Bruce 1982
Comedy/Martial arts
66091 88 mins C B, V, CED P
Johnny Yune, Margaux Hemingway
A bumbling Bruce Lee lookalike meets a karate-chopping Mafia moll in this farce.
Elliot Hong — *Vestron Video*

They Call Me Mr. Tibbs! 1970
Mystery
65008 108 mins C B, V, CED P
Sidney Poitier, Barbara McNair, Martin Landau, Juano Hernandez, Anthony Zerbe, Edward Asner, Norma Crane
Lieutenant Virgil Tibbs (Poitier) must track down a murder case which involves his friend, the Reverend Logan Sharpe (Landau). He is torn between his duty as a policeman, his concern for the reverend and the threat of turmoil in the town. Sequel to "In the Heat of the Night."
MPAA:PG
United Artists — *CBS/Fox Video*

They Call Me Trinity 1972
Western
08480 110 mins C B, V, CED P
Terence Hill, Bud Spencer, Farley Granger, Steffen Zacharias, directed by E. B. Clucher
Lazy drifter-gunslinger and his outlaw brother join forces with Mormon farmers to rout bullying outlaws.
MPAA:G
Avco Embassy; West Film Productions — *Embassy Home Entertainment*

They Came From Within 1975
Suspense
82425 87 mins C B, V P
Paul Hampton, Joe Silver, Lynn Lowry, directed by David Cronenburg
The occupants of a high-rise building go on a sex and violence spree when stricken by a deadly disease.
MPAA:R
Orion — *Vestron Video*

They Came to Cordura 1959
Drama
64579 123 mins C B, V P
Gary Cooper, Rita Hayworth, Van Heflin, Tab Hunter, directed by Robert Rossen
In Mexico circa 1916, six American heroes are recalled to their headquarters in Cordura. On the way, they encounter hardships and unexpected danger.
Columbia — *RCA/Columbia Pictures Home Video*

They Died With There Boots On 1941
Adventure/Western
73979 141 mins B/W B, V P
Errol Flynn, Sidney Greenstreet, Anthony Quinn, Hattie McDaniel, directed by Raoul Walsh
The Battle of Little Big Horn where General Custer met his match in Sitting Bull is recreated in this film, starring Errol Flynn as the unlucky namesake of Custer's Last Stand.
Warner Bros — *Key Video*

They Drive by Night 1940
Drama
64934 97 mins B/W CED P
Humphrey Bogart, Ann Sheridan, George Raft, Ida Lupino, Alan Hale, Gale Page, Roscoe Karns
A truck driver loses his brother in an accident and subsequently gets involved in a murder.
Warner Bros — *Key Video*

They Got Me Covered 1943
Comedy
82567 95 mins B/W B, V, LV P
Bob Hope, Dorothy Lamour, directed by David Butler

Two journalists get involved in a comic web of murder, kidnapping and romance.
Sam Goldwyn — *Embassy Home Entertainment*

They Knew What They Wanted 1940

Drama
76836 96 mins B/W B, V P
Charles Laughton, Carole Lombard, Harry Carey, Karl Malden, William Gargan, directed by Garson Kanin
An elderly Italian grape grower decides to marry a lonely waitress after a series of passionate correspondences.
RKO — *RKO Home Video*

They Live by Night 1949

Crime-Drama
59650 95 mins B/W B, V P
Cathy O'Donnell, Farley Granger, Howard da Silva, Jay C. Flippen, Helen Craig, directed by Nicholas Ray
A young fugitive from the law sinks deeper into a life of crime thanks to his association with two hardened criminals. His life changes when he meets a farm girl. A classic of film noir.
RKO; Dore Schary — *Hollywood Home Theater*

They Made Me a Criminal 1939

Drama
08762 92 mins B/W B, V P
John Garfield, Ann Sheridan, Claude Rains, Dead End Kids
A champion prizefighter, believing he murdered a man in a drunken brawl runs away. (Remake of "The Life of Jimmy Dolan.')
Warner Bros — *Prism; VCII; Video Dimensions; Discount Video Tapes; Kartes Video Communications; Cable Films; Video Connection; Video Yesteryear; Western Film & Video Inc; Cinema Concepts; Sound Video Unlimited*

They Meet Again 1941

Drama
81733 68 mins B/W B, V P
Jean Hersholt, Dorothy Lovett
A country doctor sets out to prove the innocence of a man who has been wrongly accused of stealing money.
RKO — *Kartes Video Communications; Movie Buff Video*

They Saved Hitler's Brain 1964

Horror
13142 91 mins B/W B, V P
Walter Stocker, Audrey Caire
Fanatical survivors of the Nazi holocaust give eternal life to the brain of their leader in the last hours of the war.

Crown Intl Pictures — *United Home Video*

They Went That-a-Way & That-a-Way 1978

Comedy
69552 96 mins C B, V P
Tim Conway, Richard Kiel
Two bumbling deputies pose as convicts in this madcap prison caper.
MPAA:PG
International Picture Show Company — *Embassy Home Entertainment*

They Were Cars 1973

Language arts
05228 11 mins C B, V, 3/4U P
Especially designed for "Corrective" and "Remedial" reading programs to reinforce "basic reading skills" for primary and intermediate students.
Unknown — *Blackhawk Films; Video Connection; Hollywood Home Theater; Discount Video Tapes; Hal Roach Studios; Kartes Video Communications*

They Were Expendable 1945

War-Drama
88210 135 mins B/W B, V P
Robert Montgomery, John Wayne, Donna Reed, Jack Holt, Ward Bond, Marshall Thompson, directed by John Ford
Two American captains pit their valiant PT boats against the Japanese fleet in this rugged bit of improbable WWII flagwaving.
MGM; Loew's Inc. — *MGM/UA Home Video*

They Won't Believe Me 1947

Suspense
64377 95 mins B/W B, V, 3/4U P
Robert Young, Susan Hayward, Rita Johnson, Jane Greer
A man plots to kill his wife, but before he does, she commits suicide. He ends up on trial for her "murder."
RKO — *Nostalgia Merchant*

They're Playing with Fire 1984

Suspense
79708 96 mins C B, V P
Sybil Danning, Eric Brown, Andrew Prine, Paul Clemens, K.T. Stevens
An English teacher seduces her student and gets him involved in a murder plot.
MPAA:R
New World Pictures; Hickmar Productions — *THORN EMI/HBO Video*

Thief 1981

Crime-Drama
47152 126 mins C B, V, CED P
James Caan, Tuesday Weld, Willie Nelson, James Belushi, Robert Prosky

A big-time professional thief enjoys pulling off heists on his own, but is forced to work for a crime syndicate in an attempt to bring in more money for his family.
MPAA:R
United Artists — *CBS/Fox Video*

Thief 1971
Suspense/Drama
81123 74 mins C B, V P
Richard Crenna, Angie Dickinson, Cameron Mitchell, Hurd Hatfield, Robert Webber, directed by William Graham
A successful businessman attempting to put his criminal past behind him, must find a quick way to get some money to pay off a gambling debt.
Metromedia — *Karl/Lorimar Home Video*

Thief, The 1952
Crime-Drama/Suspense
84847 84 mins C B, V P
Ray Milland, Rita Gam, Martin Gabel, Harry Bronson, John Mckutcheon, directed by Russel Rouse
A communist spy commits treason and, without a word of dialogue, suffers self-destructive guilt.
UA/Harry M Popkin — *United Home Video*

Thief of Bagdad, The 1940
Adventure/Fantasy
81628 106 mins C B, V, LV P
Sabu, Conrad Veidt, June Duprez
A wily thief enlists the aid of a powerful genie to outwit the Grand Vizier of Bagdad.
Alexander Korda — *Embassy Home Entertainment*

Thief of Bagdad, The 1924
Adventure
13175 143 mins B/W B, V P, T
Douglas Fairbanks, Anna May Wong
A fabulous Arabian Nights fantasy, with Fairbanks as a notorious thief who reforms for the love of a princess. Silent with original music score.
United Artists — *Blackhawk Films; Western Film & Video Inc; Festival Films; Cable Films; Video Yesteryear; Discount Video Tapes; Kartes Video Communications*

Thief of Baghdad 1961
Adventure/Fantasy
78641 89 mins C B, V P
Steve Reeves, Georgia Moll
A thief in love with a Sultan's daughter who has been poisoned seeks out the magical blue rose which is the antidote.
Joseph E. Levine; Embassy — *Embassy Home Entertainment*

Thief of Baghdad, The 1978
Fantasy
36182 101 mins C B, V R, P
Peter Ustinov, Roddy McDowall, Terrence Stamp, directed by Clive Donner
A fantasy-adventure about a genie, a prince, beautiful maidens, a happy-go-lucky thief, and magic.
MPAA:G
Palm Films Ltd — *Video Gems*

Thief of Hearts 1984
Drama/Romance
Closed Captioned
77445 100 mins C B, V, LV P
Steven Bauer, Barbara Williams, John Getz, George Wendt, Christine Ebersole directed by Douglas Day Stewart
When a thief steals a frustrated woman's diary, he pursues the woman to act out her sexual fantasies. Available in stereo in all formats.
MPAA:R
Paramount Pictures — *Paramount Home Video*

Thief Who Came to Dinner, The 1973
Comedy
80958 103 mins C B, V P
Ryan O'Neal, Jacqueline Bisset, Warren Oates, Jill Clayburgh, Ned Beatty, directed by Bud Yorkin
A computer analyst and a wealthy socialite team up to become jewel thieves and turn the tables on Houston's high society set.
MPAA:PG
Warner Bros. — *Warner Home Video*

Thighs and Whispers: The History of Lingerie 1982
Clothing and dress
59077 45 mins C B, V P
A brief history of lingerie, entertaining and informative.
Karl Video — *Karl/Lorimar Home Video*

Thin Man, The 1934
Mystery
82123 90 mins B/W B, V, LV P
William Powell, Myrna Loy, Maureen O'Sullivan
Nick and Nora Charles investigate the mysterious disappearance of a wealthy inventor. Based upon the novel by Dashiell Hammett.
MGM — *MGM/UA Home Video*

Thin Thighs in 30 Day 1983
Physical fitness
66197 60 mins C B, V P
Wendy Stehling
How to have good looking legs is discussed and demonstrated.
WCP Video — *U.S.A. Home Video*

Thing, The 1951
Science fiction
44002   80 mins   B/W   B, V   P
James Arness, Kenneth Tobey, Margaret Sheriden
An alien creature terrorizes an Arctic research team in the original version of this science fiction classic. Based on "Who Goes There?" by John Campbell.
RKO; Howard Hawks — *RKO HomeVideo; VidAmerica; King of Video; RCA VideoDiscs*

Thing, The 1982
Science fiction/Horror
62875   127 mins   C   B, V, LV   P
Kurt Russell, A. Wilford Brimely, T.K. Carter, directed by John Carpenter
A team of scientists at a remote Antarctic outpost discover a buried spaceship with an unwelcome alien survivor still alive. VHS in stereo. Also available subtitled in Spanish.
MPAA:R
Universal — *MCA Home Video*

Things Are Tough All Over 1982
Comedy
63433   87 mins   C   B, V   P
Cheech Marin, Tommy Chong, Shelby Fiddis, Rikki Marin, Evelyn Guerrero, Rip Taylor
Cheech and Chong play dual roles as themselves and as two rich Arab brothers who hire Cheech and Chong to drive a car full of money from Chicago to Las Vegas.
MPAA:R
Columbia; Howard Brown — *RCA/Columbia Pictures Home Video; RCA VideoDiscs*

Things to Come 1936
Science fiction
12826   92 mins   B/W   B, V   P
Raymond Massey, Ralph Richardson, Sir Cedric Hardwicke, directed by William Cameron Menzies
Based on the H. G. Wells story of a war lasting from 1940 to 2036 and how scientists aim to rebuild the world when peace is achieved.
London Films; Alexander Korda — *Prism; Hal Roach Studios; Nostalgia Merchant; Movie Buff Video; Video Yesteryear; Hollywood Home Theater; Kartes Video Communications; Cable Films; Video Connection; Discount Video Tapes; Cinema Concepts*

Things We Did Last Summer, The 1978
Comedy
78068   46 mins   C   B, V   R, P
John Belushi, Dan Aykroyd, Bill Murray, Gilda Radner, Garrett Morris, Laraine Newman
Members of the original cast of "Saturday Night Live" are featured in this special program where they show how they spent their summer vacations.

NBC; Lorne Michaels — *Pacific Arts Video*

Think Dirty 1978
Comedy
64577   93 mins   C   B, V   P
Marty Feldman, Judy Cornwell, Shelley Berman
An advertising executive develops a series of sexy commercials at the same time that his wife is forming a "clean up TV" group.
MPAA:R
Quartet Films — *RCA/Columbia Pictures Home Video*

Third Man, The 1949
Mystery
08595   105 mins   B/W   B, V   P
Orson Wells, Joseph Cotton, Alida Valli, directed by Sir Carol Reed
An American writer arrives in Vienna to take job with an old friend whom he finds has been murdered. Based on Graham Greene's mystery. Academy Awards '50: Best Cinematography. Selznick Releasing Organization;
British — *Media Home Entertainment; Hollywood Home Theater; VCII; Video Yesteryear; Video Dimensions; Vestron Video (disc only); Video Connection; Discount Video Tapes; Cable Films; Western Film & Video Inc; Cinema Concepts; Prism; Hal Roach Studios*

Third Man, The 1949
Mystery
71024   125 mins   B/W   B, V, LV   P
Orson Welles, Joseph Cotten, Alida Valli, directed by Sir Carol Reed
Graham Greene's mystery involving an American writer who discovers upon arriving in Vienna that his friend has been murdered. This special high-quality edition includes the film's original trailer.
Academy Awards '50: Best Cinematography. Selznick Releasing Organization;
British — *The Criterion Collection*

Third Man on the Mountain 1959
Adventure
88342   106 mins   C   B, V   P
James MacArthur, Michael Rennie, Janet Munro, James Donald, Herbert Lom, Laurence Naismith, Helen Hayes, directed by Ken Annakin
A family epic about mountain climbing, shot in Switzerland and based on James Ramsey Ullman's "Banner in the Sky."
Walt Disney Prod. — *Walt Disney Home Video*

Thirsty Dead 1977
Horror
36928   90 mins   C   B, V   P
John Considine, Jennifer Billingsley
A science fiction-horror film wherein corpses return to life.

Unknown — *King of Video*

---

13 Chairs, The 1970
Comedy
86855   93 mins   C   B, V   P
Orson Welles, Sharon Tate, Terry-Thomas, Vittorio Gassman
An Italian-French film originally titled "Una su 13," it involves a comedic Europe-wide search for a jewel-packed dining room chair. Nothing at all to do with Mel Brooks' "The 12 Chairs," also from 1970.
Girouxfilms S.A. — *Lightning Video*

---

13 Ghosts 1960
Horror
81799   88 mins   C   B, V   P
Charles Herbert, Jo Morrow, Martin Milner, Rosemary De Camp, Margaret Hamilton, directed by William Castle
A professor and his family get the shock of a lifetime when they discover their new house is plagued by thirteen ghosts. Available in VHS and Beta Hi-Fi.
William Castle; Columbia
Pictures — *RCA/Columbia Pictures Home Video*

---

13 Rue Madeleine 1946
Adventure/War-Drama
88163   95 mins   B/W   B, V   P
James Cagney, Annabella, Richard Conte, Frank Latimore, Walter Abel, Sam Jaffe, Melville Cooper, E.G. Marshall, directed by Henry Hathaway
Cagney plays a World War II spy infiltrating Gestapo headquarters in Paris in order to find the location of a German missle site. Uses actual OSS footage in its fast-paced, documentary-ish style.
Warner Bros.; Louis de Rochement — *Key Video*

Thirteenth Reunion, The 1981
Horror
81747   60 mins   C   B, V   P
Julia Foster, Dinah Sheridan, Richard Pearson, directed by Peter Sasdy
A newspaperwoman uncovers a bizarre secret society when she does a routine story on a health spa.
Hammer Films — *Thriller Video*

---

38 Special Wild Eyed and Live 1984
Music-Performance
80386   75 mins   C   B, V   P
This is a concert featuring southern rockers 38 Special performing such hits as "Caught Up in You" and "Hold on Loosely."
AM Video — *A & M Video; RCA/Columbia Pictures Home Video*

35mm Motion Picture Projector, The 1956
Film-History
54110   30 mins   B/W   B, V   P, T
A look at a private collection of 35mm motion picture projectors that is the largest collection in existence anywhere.
Unknown — *Blackhawk Films*

30-Foot Bride of Candy Rock, The 1959
Comedy
87755   73 mins   B/W   B, V   P
Lou Costello, Dorothy Provine, Gale Gordon, directed by Sidney Miller
A junk dealer invents a robot, catapults into space and causes his girlfriend to grow 30 feet tall.
Lewis J. Rachmil; Columbia — *RCA/Columbia Pictures Home Video*

---

30 Is a Dangerous Age, Cynthia 1968
Comedy
76040   85 mins   C   B, V   P
Dudley Moore, Suzy Kendall, Eddie Foy Jr
Dudley Moore stars as a night club pianist who has set himself a goal to get married and write a hit musical before he reaches thirty.
Walter Shenson — *RCA/Columbia Pictures Home Video*

Thirty-Nine Steps, The 1979
Mystery/Suspense
82493   98 mins   C   B, V   P
Robert Powell, David Warner, Eric Porter, Karen Dotrice, John Mills
An engineer is unwittingly drawn into a web of conspiracy, intrigue and murder in this remake of the 1935 classic.
Greg Smith — *Media Home Entertainment*

---

39 Steps, The 1935
Mystery
48695   81 mins   B/W   B, V   P
Robert Donat, Madeleine Carroll, Godfrey Tearle, Lucie Mannheim, Peggy Ashcroft, directed by Alfred Hitchcock
A man becomes involved in a murder and an international spy ring. Classic Hitchcock suspense with many of his trademark directorial touches.
Gaumont — *Movie Buff Video; Embassy Home Entertainment; VCII; Video Yesteryear; Video Dimensions; Cable Films; Video Connection; Hollywood Home Theater; Western Film & Video Inc; Discount Video Tapes; RCA VideoDiscs; Spotlite Video; Hal Roach Studios; Kartes Video Communications*

---

39 Steps, The   1935
Mystery
71022   101 mins   B/W   B, V, LV   P
*Robert Donat, Madeleine Carrol, Godfrey
Tearle, Lucie Mannheim, Peggy Ashcroft,
directed by Alfred Hitchcock*
This special edition of Hitchcock's classic
murder/spy-ring suspense-thriller includes a
twenty minute documentary tracing the
director's British period.
Gaumont — *The Criterion Collection*

Thirty Seconds Over   1944
Tokyo
War-Drama
88208   139 mins   B/W   B, V   P
*Spencer Tracy, Van Johnson, Robert Walker,
directed by Mervyn LeRoy*
Written by Dalton Trumbo, this classic wartime
flagwaver details the conception and execution
of the first bombing raids on Tokyo in 1942 by
Lt. Col. James Doolittle and his men.
MGM; Loew's Inc. — *MGM/UA Home Video*

Thirty Six Hours of Hell   1977
War-Drama
86183   95 mins   C   B, V   P
*Richard Harrison, Pamela Tudor, directed by
Roberto Marrtero*
A troop of Marines battle the Japs in the South
Pacific during World War II.Dubbed.
Franco Galli — *Unicorn Video*

This Gun For Hire   1942
Western
68255   81 mins   B/W   B, V   P
*Alan Ladd, Veronica Lake, Robert Preston,
Laird Cregar*
Ladd plays a paid gunman working within a
criminal organization who is hired by German
spies, is double crossed and ends up wanting
revenge.
Paramount — *MCA Home Video*

This Is a Hijack   1975
Adventure/Suspense
76661   90 mins   C   B, V   P
*Adam Roarke, Neville Brand, Jay Robinson,
Lynn Borden, Dub Taylor*
A story of a gambler who can't pay his debts
and decides to make a deal to hijack his wealthy
boss.
MPAA:PG
Fanfare Corp — *Monterey Home Video*

This Is Elvis   1981
Biographical/Musical
68238   144 mins   C   B, V   P
The life of Elvis is presented in this film. There
are 42 minutes of footage that has never been
seen before and more than three dozen songs.
MPAA:PG

David L Wolper — *Warner Home Video*

This Is Spinal Tap   1984
Satire/Musical
78356   82 mins   C   B, V, 8mm,   P
                           LV
*Michael McKean, Christopher Guest, Harry
Shearer, Tony Hendra, Bruno Kirby, directed by
Rob Reiner*
A filmmaker wants to make a documentary
about the career and music of the heavy metal
band Spinal Tap. Included in this videocassette
are Spinal Tap's music videos "Hell Hole" and
"Heavy Metal Memories."
MPAA:R
Karen Murphy — *Embassy Home
Entertainment*

This Is the Army   1943
Musical-Drama
11316   105 mins   C   B, V   P
*George Murphy, Joan Leslie, Ronald Reagan,
Alan Hale, Kate Smith, and the men of the
Armed Services*
A robust tribute to the American soldier,
containing the songs, "This is the Army, Mr.
Jones," "I Left My Heart at the Stage Door
Canteen," "Oh, How I Hate to Get Up in the
Morning," and many more.
Academy Award '43: Best Scoring Musical.
Warner Bros — *Discount Video Tapes; Cable
Films; Video Connection; Hollywood Home
Theater*

This Is Your Life   1961
Interview
85521   50 mins   B/W   B, V   P
*Bebe Daniels, Joe Louis, Jack Dempsey, Harold
Lloyd, Ben Lyon*
Two episodes of the long-running show,
exposing the pasts of Daniels and Louis.
NBC — *Video Yesteryear*

This Is Your Life: Laurel   1954
and Hardy
Interview
42972   30 mins   B/W   B, V, FO   P
Ralph Edwards, Stan Laurel, Oliver Hardy
Stan and Ollie appear somewhat stunned as old
girlfriends and assocaites from Hollywood
appear, including Vivian Blaine and Leo
McCarey.
NBC — *Video Yesteryear*

This Island Earth   1955
Science fiction
64789   86 mins   C   B, V, LV   P
*Jeff Morrow, Faith Domergue, Rex Reason,
directed by Joseph M. Newman*
The planet Metaluna is in desperate need of
uranium to power their defense against enemy
invaders. A nuclear scientist and a nuclear
fission expert are kidnapped to help out.

THE VIDEO TAPE & DISC GUIDE

Universal — *MCA Home Video*

This Land Is Mine   1943
Drama
76835   103 mins   B/W   B, V   P
*Charles Laughton, Maureen O'Hara, George
Sanders, Walter Slezak, Una O'Connor,
directed by Jean Renoir*
A timid French schoolteacher gathers enough
courage to defy the Nazis when they attempt to
occupy his town.
Academy Award '43: Best Sound Recording.
RKO — *RKO HomeVideo*

This Man Must Die   1970
Suspense
87330   112 mins   C   B, V   P
*Michael Duchaussoy, Caroline Cellier, Jean
Yanne, directed by Claude Chabrol*
After his son is killed by a hit-and-run driver, a
man searches relentlessly for the driver, who
when found engages him in a complex cat-and-
mouse chase.
MPAA:PG
Lorimar — *Key Video*

This Property Is   1966
Condemned
Drama
71137   110 mins   C   B, V   P
*Robert Redford, Natalie Wood, Charles
Bronson, Kate Reid, Mary Badham, Jon
Provost, Robert Blake, Sidney Pollack*
Steamy sex fills a southern boarding house
where a mother offers her daughter to a wealthy
tenant. The daughter loves another man. Based
on the Tennessee Williams play.
Paramount — *Paramount Home Video*

This Time I'll Make You   1975
Rich
Comedy
86600   97 mins   C   B, V   P
*Tony Sabato, Robin McDavid, directed by Frank
Kramer*
Two American hoodlums work out a drug-ring
heist in the Far East.
MPAA:PG
Frank Kramer — *Charter Entertainment*

Thomas Crown Affair,   1968
The
Drama/Adventure
55588   102 mins   C   B, V   P
Steve McQueen, Faye Dunaway, Jack Weston
A multi-millionaire executes a daring daylight
robbery of a bank and gets away with two million
in cash.
Academy Awards '68: Best Song ("Windmills of
Your Mind").   EL, SP
United Artists; Mirisch Corp — *CBS/Fox Video*

Thomas Dolby   1983
Music-Performance
69393   58 mins   C   B, V   P
This music video by the popular rock star
includes such songs as "She Blinded Me with
Science," "Europa" and "One of Our
Submarines."
EMI Music — *THORN EMI/HBO Video;
Pioneer Video Imports*

Thomas Dolby   1984
Music-Performance
75913   16 mins   C   B, V   P
This program presents the new British singer
Thomas Dolby performing his hit songs.
EMI Records Ltd — *Sony Video Software*

Thompson Twins—Into   1985
the Gap Live, The
Music-Performance
81941   80 mins   C   B, V   P
New Wavers The Thompson Twins perform
such hits as "Doctor! Doctor!" "Into the Gap"
and "Lies" in this taped concert. Available in
VHS Dolby Hi-Fi Stereo and Beta Hi-Fi Stereo.
Frank Hilton — *RCA/Columbia Pictures Home
Video*

Thompson Twins Live at   1983
Liverpool, The
Music-Performance
73020   60 mins   C   B, V   P
Tom Bailey, Joe Leeway, Alannah Currie
The Thompson Twins, recorded concert at
Liverpool's Royal Court, perform "Lies and Love
on Your Side".
Unknown — *THORN EMI/HBO Video*

Thompson Twins—Single   1986
Vision, The
Music-Performance
84876   46 mins   C   B, V   P
The renowned English band performs their
popular hits.
RCA Video — *RCA/Columbia Pictures Home
Video*

Thorn, The   1973
Satire
77254   90 mins   C   B, V   P
Bette Midler, John Bassberger
The Virgin Mary and Joseph try to raise Jesus
Christ in the modern world.
MPAA:R
Peter Alexander — *Magnum Entertainment*

Thoroughly Modern Millie   1967
Musical
14012   138 mins   C   B, V, LV   P
*Julie Andrews, Carol Channing, Mary Tyler
Moore, John Gavin, Beatrice Lillie, James Fox,
directed by George Roy Hill*

Two young girls come to New York in the early 1920's to realize their ambitions, one to be an actress, the other to be a stenographer and marry the boss.
Academy Awards '67:Best Scoring, Original Song. MPAA:G
Universal; Ross Hunter Prod — *MCA Home Video*

Thorpe's Gold 1984
Documentary/Sports
72947   75 mins   C   B, V   P
A documentary about Olympic star Jim Thorpe, multi-award winner in the 1912 Olympics. Some black-and-white segments.
VCI — *United Home Video*

Those Calloways 1965
Drama/Adventure
82030   131 mins   C   B, V   P
Brian Keith, Vera Miles, Brandon DeWilde, Walter Brennan, Ed Wynn, Linda Evans
A backwoods family attempts to establish a sanctuary for the flocks of wild geese who fly over the woods of Vermont.
Walt Disney Productions — *Walt Disney Home Video*

Those Endearing Young Charms 1945
Romance
10044   82 mins   B/W   B, V   P, T
Robert Young, Laraine Day, Anne Jeffreys, Lawrence Tierney
Romance developes between young Air Corps mechanic and salesgirl. Complications arise when another man enters the scene.
RKO — *Blackhawk Films*

Those Glory, Glory Days 1983
Drama
86778   92 mins   C   B, V   P
Zoe Nathenson, Liz Campion, Cathy Murphy, directed by Philip Seville
An English girl reminisces about her schooldays during which she and her freinds idolized the boys on the football team.
David Puttnam; Goldcrest Television Ltd. — *MGM/UA Home Video*

Those Krazy, Klassic, Kolor Kartoons, Volume I 1985
Cartoons
81529   58 mins   C   B, V   P
Animated
Here is a compilation of classic cartoons such as "Felix the Cat" and "Old Mother Hubbard" that the whole family can enjoy.
MPI; Academy Video — *MPI Home Video*

Those Lips, Those Eyes 1980
Comedy-Drama
80625   106 mins   C   B, V   P
Frank Langella, Thomas Hulce, Glynnis O'Connor, Jerry Stiller, Kevin McCarthy
A pre-med student takes a job as a prop boy in a summer stock company and winds up falling in love with the company's lead dancer.
MPAA:R
United Artists — *MGM/UA Home Video*

Those Magnificent Men in Their Flying Machines 1965
Comedy
08461   138 mins   C   B, V, LV   P
Stuart Whitman, Sarah Miles, Robert Morley, Albert Sordi, James Fox, Gert Frobe
In 1910, a wealthy British newspaper publisher is persuaded to sponsor an air race from London to Paris. Contestants come from all over the world.
EL, SP
20th Century Fox — *CBS/Fox Video*

Thousand Clowns, A 1965
Comedy-Drama
58838   118 mins   B/W   CED   P
Jason Robards Jr., Barry Gordon, William Daniels, Barbara Harris, Gene Saks, Martin Balsam
A nonconformist writer resigns from his job as chief writer for an obnoxious kiddie show in order to enjoy life.
United Artists — *CBS/Fox Video*

Threat, The 1949
Mystery
73694   66 mins   B/W   B, V   P
Michael O'Shea, Virginia Grey, Charles McGraw
An escaped killer returns to settle the score with those who convicted him.
RKO — *RKO HomeVideo*

Three Avengers 1980
Martial arts
81474   93 mins   C   B, V   P
There's lots of trouble abounding when two kung fu masters and an American Chinese boy open a martial arts school.
MPAA:R
World Northal Corporation — *Embassy Home Entertainment*

Three Broadway Girls 1932
Comedy
47774   78 mins   B/W   B, V, 3/4U   R, P
Joan Blondell, Ina Claire, Madge Evans, David Manners, Lowell Sherman
Three gold-diggers go husband hunting.
United Artists — *Movie Buff Video; Cable Films; Kartes Video Communications*

Three Caballeros, The   1945
Cartoons
59811   70 mins   C   B, V   P
Animated
Donald Duck stars in this program of shorts
about South America, full of music and variety.
Stories include "Pablo the Penguin," "Little
Gauchito," and adventures with Joe Carioca.
Walt Disney — Walt Disney Home Video

Three Cheers for the   1983
Redskins
Football
65016   53 mins   C   B, V, FO   P
A colorful study of the Washington Redskins'
1971 season, their first with George Allen as
head coach, following the death of Vince
Lombardi.
NFL Films — NFL Films Video

Three Days in Beirut   1983
Adventure
87686   94 mins   C   B, V   P
Diana Sands, Calvin Lockhart, directed by
Michael Schultz
A soldier of fortune and a beautiful interpreter
join forces against a backdrop of Middle Eastern
politics, espionage and violence for three days.
MPAA:PG
Jack Jordan — Prism

Three Days of the   1975
Condor
Drama
38604   118 mins   C   B, V, LV   P
Robert Redford, Faye Dunaway, Cliff
Robertson, Max Von Sydow, directed by
Sydney Pollack
CIA researcher Redford finds himself on the run
from unknown killers when he is left the only
survivor of the mass murder of his office staff.
MPAA:R
Paramount — Paramount Home Video; RCA
VideoDiscs

Three Faces West   1940
Western
66467   79 mins   B/W   B, V   P
John Wayne, Charles Coburn, Sigrid Gurie,
Sonny Bupp
A dust bowl community is helped by a Viennese
doctor who left Europe to avoid Nazi capture.
Republic — Republic Pictures Home Video

3:15--The Moment of   1986
Truth
Crime-Drama
88304   86 mins   C   B, V   P
Adam Baldwin, Deborah Foreman, Rene
Auberjonois, Danny de la Paz
A vicious high school gang is confronted by an
angry ex-member.

MPAA:R
Larry Gross — Media Home Entertainment

Three in the Attic   1968
Comedy-Drama
65069   92 mins   C   B, V   P
Christopher Jones, Yvette Mimieux, John Beck
A college student juggles three girlfriends at the
same time. When the girls find out they are
being two-timed, they lock their boyfriend in an
attic and exhaust him with forced sexual
escapades.
MPAA:R
American International Pictures — Embassy
Home Entertainment

Three Little Pigs, The   1984
Fairy tales
Closed Captioned
73571   60 mins   C   B, V, CED   P
Billy Crystal, Jeff Goldblum, Valerie Perrine
From "Faerie Tale Theatre" comes the story of
three little pigs, the houses they lived in and the
wolf that tries to do them in.
Gaylord Productions; Platypus
Productions — CBS/Fox Video

Three Lives of   1963
Thomasina, The
Drama
82031   95 mins   C   B, V   P
Patrick McGoohan, Susan Hampshire, Karen
Dotrice, Matthew Garber, directed by Don
Chaffey
A young girl seeks out a mysterious healer in the
woods to save her four-year-old ginger cat from
dying.
Walt Disney Productions — Walt Disney Home
Video

Three Musketeers, The   1974
Adventure
59645   107 mins   C   CED   P
Richard Chamberlain, Raquel Welch, Michael
York, Oliver Reed, Faye Dunaway, Charlton
Heston, Christopher Lee, directed by Richard
Lester
Sword play, romance, and slapstick comedy
abound in this exuberant big-budget version of
the Alexandre Dumas classic.
MPAA:PG
Alexander Salkin — RCA VideoDiscs

Three Musketeers, The   1973
Adventure
65440   107 mins   C   B, V   P
Richard Chamberlain, Raquel Welch, Faye
Dunaway, Michael York
A tongue-in-cheek version of the Alexander
Dumas classic.
MPAA:PG
Film Trust SA — U.S.A. Home Video

Three Musketeers, The 1973
Cartoons
66581   47 mins   C   B, V   P
Animated
An animated retelling of the Alexander Dumas
classic about three swordsmen and their
problems with Cardinal Richleau.
Unknown — Worldvision Home Video

Three Musketeers, The 1976
Adventure/Cartoons
69528   74 mins   C   B, V, CED   P
Animated
D'Artagnan and the fabled Musketeers engage
in swashbuckling adventures in Paris and
England.
Pendennis Films — Children's Video Library

Three Musketeers, The 1948
Adventure
81495   126 mins   C   B, V   P
Lana Turner, Gene Kelly, June Allyson, Gig
Young, Angela Landsbury, Vincent Price,
directed by George Sidney
Those three musketeers who are all for one and
one for all battle the evil Cardinal Richileu in this
rollicking adaptation of the Dumas classic story.
MGM — MGM/UA Home Video

Three Musketeers, The 1933
Adventure/Serials
14629   156 mins   B/W   B, V   P
John Wayne, Raymond Hatton
Modern adaptation of Dumas' classic puts the
three friends in fast airplanes. In twelve
chapters.
Mascot — Video Connection; Video
Dimensions; Video Yesteryear; Discount Video
Tapes

Three Penny Opera 1963
Musical
78083   100 mins   C   B, V, FO   P
Curt Jurgens, Hildegarde Neff, Gert Frobe, June
Ritchie, Lino Ventura, Sammy Davis Jr.
Mack the Knife presides over an exciting world
of thieves, murderers, beggars, prostitutes and
corrupt officials, in this film version of the
famous Kurt Weill-Bertold Brecht operetta.
Embassy Pictures — Video Yesteryear

3 Reyes Magos, Los 198?
Cartoons
77352   86 mins   C   B, V   P
Animated
This is an animated retelling of the legend of the
three wisemen who brought gifts to Jesus Christ
on the Epiphany.
SP
Foreign — Unicorn Video

**Three Sovereigns for
Sarah** 1985
Drama
84615   152 mins   C   B, V   P
Vanessa Redgrave, Phyllis Thaxter, Patrick
McGoohan
Witch-hunters tortured and toasted her two
sisters for witchcraft in the past. Now, accused
of witchery herself, she struggles to prove the
family's innocence. Made-for-TV.
Vic Pisano — Prism

Three Stooges, The 1949
Comedy
63098   60 mins   B/W   B, V   P
Moe, Larry, Curly and Shemp
Three original shorts by the comedy trio,
including: "Disorder in the Court" (1936—Curly),
"Sing a Song of Six Pants" (1949—Shemp) and
"Malice in the Palace" (1949—Shemp).
Columbia — Admit One Video; Video
Yesteryear

**Three Stooges Comedy
Capers Volume I** 194?
Comedy
60421   80 mins   B/W   B, V, 3/4U   P
Moe Howard, Larry Fine, Curly Howard, Shemp
Howard
This compilation includes: "Disorder in the
Court" (1936), "Malice in the Palace" (1949),
"Sing a Song of Six Pants" (1947), "The
Brideless Groom" (1947).
Columbia Pictures — Nostalgia Merchant

**Three Stooges Comedy
Classics** 193?
Comedy
80463   79 mins   B/W   B, V   P
Moe Howard, Larry Fine, Curly Howard, Shemp
Howard, Ted Healy
The antics of the Stooges are featured in this
collection of five original shorts, along with an
early Ted Healy comedy that features all four
Stooges.
Columbia — Spotlite Video

**Three Stooges—Medium
Rare, The** 195?
Comedy
72952   120 mins   B/W   B, V   P
Moe Howard, Larry Fine, Shemp Howard
Moe, Larry and Shemp are featured in several
rare TV appearances from the 1950's, including
a guest spot on "The Ed Wynn Show" and
several commercials.
NBC et al — Hollywood Home Theater

**Three Stooges Meet
Hercules, The** 1961
Comedy
69619   80 mins   B/W   B, V   P

The Three Stooges, Vicki Trickett, Quinn Redeker
The Three Stooges are transported back to ancient Ithaca by a time machine with a young scientist and his girlfriend. When the girl is captured, they enlist the help of Hercules to rescue her.
Norman Maurer; Columbia — *RCA/Columbia Pictures Home Video*

Three Stooges Videodisc, Vol. 1, The   194?
Comedy
60385   106 mins   B/W   CED   P
Moe Howard, Larry Fine, Curly Howard, Christine McIntyre
Four classic Three Stooges two-reelers are on this disc: "Dizzy Pilots" (1943), "A Bird in the Head" (1946), "Three Missing Links" (1938) and "Micro-Phonies" (1945).
Columbia — *RCA VideoDiscs*

Three Stooges, Volumes I thru XIII, The   193?
Comedy
Closed Captioned
80884   60 mins   B/W   B, V   P
Curly Howard, Moe Howard, Larry Fine
These collections chronicle the history of one of the screen's most hilarious slapstick comedy teams. Each tape features a trio of two-reelers. The shorts date from the early thirties to the late forties.
Screen Gems; Columbia — *RCA/Columbia Pictures Home Video*

Three Tales of Love & Friendship   1984
Fantasy
65722   118 mins   C   CED   P
A compilation of children's programs including "The Red Balloon" (1956), "The Unicorn" (1972), and "The Lone Wolf" (1983). Each story centers on the magical powers of love and friendship that can make dreams come true.
Films Monsouris; Carol Reed; Jadren Film Zagreb — *Embassy Home Entertainment (disc only)*

3:10 to Yuma   1957
Western
77375   92 mins   B/W   B, V   P
Glenn Ford, Van Heflin, Felicia Farr, directed by Delmer Daves
A common farmer successfully holds a dangerous killer at bay while waiting turn the outlaw over to the marshal arriving on the 3:10 train to Yuma.
Columbia Pictures — *RCA/Columbia Pictures Home Video*

Three Warriors   1977
Drama
63345   100 mins   C   B, V   P
Charles White Eagle, Lois Red Elk, McKee "Kiko" Red Wing, Christopher Lloyd, Randy Quaid
A young Indian boy is forced to leave the city and return to the reservation, where his contempt for the traditions of his ancestors slowly turns to appreciation and love.
Saul Zaentz; Sy Gomberg — *THORN EMI/HBO Video*

Three Word Brand   1921
Western
52465   75 mins   B/W   B, V, FO   P
William S. Hart, Jayne Navak, S. J. Bingham
William S. Hart plays three roles in this film, a homesteader who is killed by Indians and his twin sons, who are separated after their father's death and reunited many years later. Silent with musical score.
William S Hart Co — *Video Yesteryear*

Threshold   1983
Drama
65758   97 mins   C   B, V   P
Donald Sutherland, Jeff Goldblum
The story of an internationally-acclaimed surgeon who is frustrated by his inability to save a dying 20-year-old woman born with a defective heart.
MPAA:PG
Jon Slan; Micheal Burns — *CBS/Fox Video*

Thrill Kill   1985
Crime-Drama
84857   86 mins   C   B, V   P
A young woman becomes embroiled in a computer-conducted multi-million dollar heist that her sister has perpetrated.
Anthony Kramreither — *Media Home Entertainment*

Throbbing Gristle Live at Kezar   1985
Music-Performance
84063   60 mins   C   B, V   P
Throbbing Gristle
A live performance by Throbbing Gristle, an English punk-jazz-funk group.
Target Video — *Target Video*

Throne of Fire, The   1982
Fantasy
82249   91 mins   C   B, V   P
Peter McCoy, Sabrina Siami
A mighty hero battles the forces of evil to gain control of the powerful Throne of Fire.
Visione Cinematografica — *MGM/UA Home Video*

Thumb Tripping 1972
Adventure
88154   94 mins   C   B, V   P
Meg Foster, Michael Burns, Bruce Dern, directed by Quentin Masters
Two teenagers decide to hitchike their lives away, and encounter all kinds of strange people in their travels.
MPAA:R
Joseph E. Levine — *Charter Entertainment*

Thumbelina 1984
Cartoons/Fairy tales
Closed Captioned
72924   45 mins   C   B, V   P
Animated
An animated version of the Hans Christian Andersen fairy tale about a little girl who's only as tall as a thumb.
John Watkins and Simon
Nuchtern — *RCA/Columbia Pictures Home Video*

Thumbelina 1984
Fairy tales
Closed Captioned
73854   60 mins   C   B, V, LV,   P
CED
Carrie Fisher, William Katt, Burgess Meredith, directed by Michael Lindsay-Hogg
From "Faerie Tale Theatre" comes the story of a tiny girl who gets kidnapped by a toad and a mole but meets the man of her dreams in the nick of time.
Gaylord Productions; Platypus Productions — *CBS/Fox Video*

Thundarr the Barbarian 1980
Cartoons
65663   57 mins   C   B, V   P
In this episode, Thundarr, Princess Ariel and Ookla the Mot fight sorcery and slavery.
Ruby Spears — *Worldvision Home Video*

Thundarr the Barbarian 1983
Adventure/Cartoons
80645   40 mins   C   B, V   P
Animated
Thundar the Barbarian defends justice in the bizarre civilization that has emerged from the ashes of a destroyed earth.
Ruby-Spears — *Worldvision Home Video*

Thunder Alley 1985
Drama
86786   102 mins   C   B, V   P
Roger Wilson, Leif Garrett, Jill Schoelen, directed by J.S. Cardone
In middle America, a rock group struggles for success.
Cannon Films — *MGM/UA Home Video*

Thunder and Lightning 1977
Adventure/Comedy
Closed Captioned
70700   94 mins   C   B, V   P
David Carradine, Kate Jackson, directed by Corey Allen
A mismatched young couple chase a truckload of poisoned moonshine. Action packed chases ensue in Hi-Fi stereo.
MPAA:PG
20th Century Fox; Roger Corman — *Key Video*

Thunder Bay 1953
Adventure
84021   82 mins   C   B, V   P
James Stewart, Joanne Dru, Dan Duryea, directed by Anthony Mann
An action-packed film about the war between Louisiana wildcat oil drillers and fisherman off the Gulf coast.
Aaron Rosenberg — *MCA Home Video*

Thunder County 1974
Adventure
80297   78 mins   C   B, V   P
Mickey Rooney, Ted Cassidy, Chris Robinson
Federal agents and drug runners are after a group of four convicts who have just escaped from prison.
Joseph Brenner Associates — *Prism*

Thunder in the City 1937
Comedy-Drama
08865   85 mins   B/W   B, V   P
Edward G. Robinson, Nigel Bruce, Ralph Richardson
An American promoter descends on London with all the modern day advertising methods.
Columbia; Alexander Esway — *Movie Buff Video; Discount Video Tapes; Kartes Video Communications*

Thunder of Steam in the 1958
Blue Ridge, The
Trains
47820   20 mins   B/W   B, V   P, T
Photographed in the mountainous area on the Norfolk and Western's mail line between Roanoke and Bedford, Virginia, this film shows the N and W's tough locomotives pulling and pushing on the mountain grades.
Unknown — *Blackhawk Films*

Thunderball 1965
Adventure
64452   125 mins   C   B, V   P
Sean Connery, Adolfo Celi, Claudine Auger
The fourth installment in Ian Fleming's James Bond series finds Bond on a mission to thwart SPECTRE, which has threatened to blow up Miami by atomic bomb if 100 million pounds of sterling ransom is not paid.
Academy Award '65: Special Visual Effects.

United Artists — *CBS/Fox Video; RCA VideoDiscs*

Thunderbirds 1966
Cartoons
70655   92 mins   C   B, V   P
Animated
These popular space-age marionettes save the day anytime someone is plunging into the sun or drifting aimlessly to their death in space. Recorded in Hi-Fi, each tape in the series features one full-length adventure.
ITC Entertainment — *Family Home Entertainment*

Thunderbirds 2086 1984
Cartoons
77236   50 mins   C   B, V   P
Animated
An elite group of cadets fly about the galaxy protecting the world from danger. Each tape in the series includes two episodes.
ITC Productions — *MPI Home Video*

Thunderbirds Are Go 1966
Adventure/Puppets
68241   92 mins   C   B, V, CED   P
The world's favorite electronic puppets, the Tracy brothers, launch through the uncharted worlds of adventure.
Associated Television Limited — *MGM/UA Home Video*

Thunderbolt and Lightfoot 1974
Drama
58847   115 mins   C   B, V, CED   P
Clint Eastwood, Jeff Bridges, George Kennedy, Geoffrey Lewis, directed by Michael Cimino
A bank robber posing as a preacher is saved by a young stranger when his former partners come gunning for him.
MPAA:R
United Artists — *CBS/Fox Video; RCA VideoDiscs*

Thundercats 1985
Cartoons
71352   80 mins   C   B, V   P
Animated
These cats possess extraordinary intellectual and physical prowess. They use their advanced faculties to start a brand new evil-free world.
Rankin/Bass Productions — *Family Home Entertainment*

Thursday's Game 1974
Comedy
88146   99 mins   C   B, V   P
Gene Wilder, Ellen Burstyn, Bob Newhart, Cloris Leachman, Nancy Walker, Valerie Harper, Rob Reiner, directed by James L. Brooks

Two miserable, mid-life-crisis-besieged white collar workers meet every Thursday even after their group poker games falls apart, and try to piece together their lives.
MPAA:PG
ABC Circle Films — *Vidmark Entertainment*

THX 1138 1971
Science fiction/Drama
51971   88 mins   C   B, V   P
Robert Duvall, Donald Pleasance, Maggie McOmie, directed by George Lucas
In the dehumanized world of the future, a computer-matched couple discover love. Since emotion is outlawed, the woman is killed for the offense, but the man escapes and tries to fight the system.
MPAA:PG
Warner Bros;American Zoetrope — *Warner Home Video*

Tiara Tahiti 1962
Adventure
59842   100 mins   C   B, V   P
James Mason, John Mills, Claude Dauphin, Rosenda Monteros
Intrigue, double-cross, romance, and violence ensue when two old army acquaintances clash in Tahiti.
Earl St John — *Embassy Home Entertainment*

Tibetan Medicine: A Buddhist Approach to Healing 1977
Therapeutic cults
22266   29 mins   C   B, V   P
Tibetan medicine heals both the physical and psychic being; treats the patient rather than the disease. Filmed at the Tibetan Medical Center of the Dalai Lama in the Himalayas.
Connecticut Film Festival '77: Top Award.
Sheldon Rochlin; Mikki Maher — *Mystic Fire Video; Hartley Film Foundation*

Ticket of Leave Man, The 1937
Mystery
80757   71 mins   B/W   B, V   P
Tod Slaughter, John Warwick, Marjorie Taylor
London's most dangerous killer fronts a charitable organization which he uses to cheat philanthropists out of their fortunes.
George King; MGM — *Video Yesteryear*

Ticket to Heaven 1981
Drama
47779   109 mins   C   B, V, CED   P
Nick Mancuso, Meg Foster, Kim Cattrail
A thriller dealing with cult religions in California. A school teacher gradually falls under the influence of a quasi-religious order.
Stalker Productions — *MGM/UA Home Video*

THE VIDEO TAPE & DISC GUIDE

Tiffany Jones   1975
Drama
81409   90 mins   C   B, V   P
Anouska Hempel, Ray Brooks
Tiffany Jones is a secret agent who has a secret that presidents and revolutionaries are willing to kill for. Available in VHS Stereo and Beta Hi-Fi.
MPAA:R
Peter Walker — *Monterey Home Video*

Tiffany Sampler   1984
Movie and TV trailers
66476   30 mins   C   B, V   P
This sampler tape contains a selection of movie previews taken from each of San Francisco Rush Video's "Trailers on Tape" compilations. The 17 trailers include "Help!," "A Night at the Opera," "Sunset Boulevard" and "The Wild One." Some black-and-white segments.
MGM et al — *San Francisco Rush Video*

Tiger and the Pussycat, The   1967
Comedy
87911   110 mins   C   B, V   P
Ann-Margret, Vittorio Gassman, Eleanor Parker, directed by Dino Risi
A young wench infatuates a successful Italian businessman, and leads him to marital and financial distraction.
MPAA:R
Joseph E. Levine; Mario Cecchi Gori — *Embassy Home Entertainment*

Tiger Town   1983
Drama
65633   76 mins   C   B, V   P
Roy Scheider, Justin Henry, Ron McLarty, Bethany Carpenter, Noah Moazezi
A baseball player, ending an illustrious career with the Detroit Tigers, sees his hopes of winning a pennant slipping away. On the other hand, a die-hard Tigers fan is convinced that a "true believer" can make anything happen.
Susan B Landau; Thompson Street Pictures — *Walt Disney Home Video*

Tigers at the Top   1985
Martial arts
84503   75 mins   C   B, V   P
More Kung-Fu brutality and hi jinks.
Telefilms Co Inc — *Sony Video Software*

Tiger's Claw   197?
Martial arts/Adventure
47702   90 mins   C   B, V   P
Chin Long
Shen roves the country honing his Kung Fu technique, obsessed by his fanatical desire to challenge Kuo, the best in China.
Kwong Ming Motion Picture Co — *Master Arts Video*

Tigers Don't Cry   1981
Drama
81070   105 mins   C   B, V   P
Anthony Quinn
An unusual friendship develops between a male nurse and the African dignitary that he kidnaps as they flee from the authorities.
Alan Girney — *MPI Home Video*

Tigers in Lipstick   1980
Exploitation
85373   88 mins   C   B, V   P
Laura Antonelli, Monica Vitti, Ursula Andress, Sylvia Kristel
Four short vignettes featuring the temptresses in their element.
MPAA:R
Unknown — *Monterey Home Video*

Tightrope   1984
Suspense/Drama
80076   115 mins   C   B, V, CED   P
Clint Eastwood, Genevieve Bujold, Dan Hedaya, Jennifer Beck, directed by Richard Tuggle
A police inspector must find out who is killing prostitutes in New Orleans' French Quarter.
MPAA:R
Clint Eastwood; Warner Bros — *Warner Home Video*

Till Death Do Us Part   1972
Adventure
85632   77 mins   C   B, V   P
James Keach, Claude Jutra, Matt Craven, directed by Timothy Brand
Three married couples spend a weekend in a counseling retreat, unaware that the proprietor is a murderous maniac.
MPAA:PG
Seagull-Brady — *Vestron Video*

Till Marriage Do Us Part   1980
Comedy
58899   97 mins   C   B, V, LV, CED   P
Laura Antonelli, Alberto Lionello, Jean Rochefort
An innocent couple discover on their wedding night that they are really brother and sister.
Pio Angeletti; Adriano de Micheli — *Vestron Video*

Till the Clouds Roll By   1946
Musical
01623   137 mins   C   B, V   P
Judy Garland, Frank Sinatra, Van Heflin, Robert Walker, Directed by Richard Whorf
A musical biography of songwriter Jerome Kern, with an all-star cast performing a cavalcade of his great tunes.
MGM; Arthur Freed — *MGM/UA Home Video; Prism; Cable Films; Video Yesteryear*

Till the End of Time 1946
War-Drama
82180   105 mins   C   B, V   P
*Robert Mitchum, Guy Madison, Bill Williams,
Dorothy McGuire, directed by Edward Dmytryk*
Three GI's find it difficult to adjust to civilian life
when they return to their home town after World
War II.
RKO; Dore Schary — *RKO HomeVideo*

Tillie's Punctured Romance 1914
Comedy
08713   73 mins   B/W   B, V, 3/4U   P
Charlie Chaplin, Marie Dressler
A silent comedy which established Chaplin and
Dressler as comedians.
Paramount — *Blackhawk Films; Hollywood
Home Theater; Video Yesteryear; Discount
Video Tapes; Nostalgia Merchant; Movie Buff
Video*

Tim 1979
Drama
65113   94 mins   C   B, V   P
Mel Gibson, Piper Laurie, Peter Gwynne
This Australian film tells of the evolving
relationship between a handsome, mentally
retarded young man and an attractive
businesswoman in her mid-40's.
Michael Pate; Satori Productions — *Media
Home Entertainment*

Time After Time 1979
Science fiction/Adventure
52701   112 mins   C   B, V   P
*Malcolm McDowell, David Warner, Mary
Steenburgen, Patti D'Arbanville*
H. G. Wells and Jack the Ripper leave London
circa 1893 in Wells' famous time machine and
arrive in San Francisco in 1979.
MPAA:PG
Orion Pictures; Warner Bros — *Warner Home
Video*

Time Bandits 1981
Fantasy
59389   110 mins   C   B, V, LV   P
*John Cleese, Sean Connery, Shelley Duvall,
Katherine Helmond, Ian Holm, Michael Palin,
Ralph Richardson, David Warner, Kenny Baker,
directed by Terry Gilliam*
An English youngster and a group of dwarves
pass through time holes on assignment by the
Maker to patch up part of his creation.
MPAA:PG
Handmade Films — *Paramount Home Video;
RCA VideoDiscs*

Time Capsule: The Los Angeles Olympic Games/1932 1984
Sports/Documentary
66613   60 mins   B/W   B, V   P
Directed by Bud Greenspan
The 1932 Los Angeles Olympic Games are the
subject of this documentary which utilizes rare
and never-before-seen action footage. Among
the athletes seen participating are Mildred
"Babe" Didrikson, Glenn Cunningham and
swimmer Eleanor Holm.
Lorimar — *U.S.A. Home Video*

Time Fighters 1985
Fantasy/Cartoons
80769   60 mins   C   B, V   P
Animated
A time machine has the ability to travel at the
speed of light from prehistoric times to the
distant future. This is a great help to the Time
fighters.
Kidpix — *Embassy Home Entertainment*

Time Lock 1957
Drama
82234   73 mins   B/W   B, V   P
*Sean Connery, Robert Beatty, Lee Patterson,
Betty McDowall, Vincent Winter*
An expert safecracker races against time to
save a child who is trapped inside a bank's pre-
set time-locked vault.
Peter Rogers — *Monterey Home Video*

Time Machine 1978
Science fiction/Adventure
45010   99 mins   C   B, V   P
John Beck, Priscilla Barnes, Andrew Duggan
Based H.G. Wells' classic novel, this movie tells
the story of a scientist who invents a machine
that enables him to travel through time and
undertakes a journey into the future, only to find
a civilization dominated by a group of hideous
people called Morlocks, the only survivors of a
devastating war.
MPAA:G
Schick Sunn Classic — *United Home Video;
Lucerne Films*

Time Machine, The 1960
Science fiction/Adventure
63112   103 mins   C   B, V   P
*Rod Taylor, Yvette Mimieux, Alan Young,
directed by George Pal*
An English scientist of the year 1899 builds a
conveyance that carries him far into the future,
where he discovers the remnants of man's
civilization. Based on H.G. Well's pioneering
novel.
MGM — *MGM/UA Home Video*

Time Stands Still   1982
Drama
84607   99 mins   C   B, V   P
*Istvan Znamenak, Henrik Paver, Aniko Ivan,
directed by Peter Gothar*
Subtitled in English, this Hungarian film details
the troubled youth of two brothers in Budapest.
American pop soundtrack.
Ben Barenholtz; Albert Schwartz; Michael S
Landes — *RCA/Columbia Pictures Home
Video*

Time to Die, A   1983
Adventure
65354   89 mins   C   B, V   P
Edward Albert Jr., Rex Harrison, Rod Taylor
A victim of heinous war crimes, obsessed with
revenge, stalks his prey for a final confrontation.
MPAA:R
Charles Lee — *Media Home Entertainment*

Time Travelers, The   1964
Science fiction
70959   82 mins   C   B, V   P
*Preston Foster, Phil Carey, Merry Anders, John
Hoyt, Steve Franken, Joan Woodbury, Dolores
Wells, Dennis Patrick*
Scientists discover and pass through a porthole
leading to earth's post-armageddon future
where they encounter unfriendly mutants.
Frightened, they make a serious effort to return
to the past.
American International — *THORN EMI/HBO
Video*

Time Walker   1982
Science fiction
84045   86 mins   C   B, V   P
Ben Murphy, directed by Tom Kennedy
An Archaeologist unearths a Mummy's coffin in
California, and unleashes it, ignorant of it's
extraterrestrial origin, onto a victimized public.
MPAA:PG
Dimitri Villard; Jason Williams — *Charter
Entertainment*

Timefighters in the Land   1984
of Fantasy
Cartoons/Fantasy
81105   95 mins   C   B, V   P
Animated
A team of time-travelers use their time machine
to venture into the worlds of such classic
fairytales as Cinderella and Jack and the
Beanstalk.
Kidpix Inc. — *Paramount Home Video*

Timerider   1983
Science fiction
64581   93 mins   C   B, V, CED   P
*Fred Ward, Belinda Bauer, Peter Coyote,
Richard Masur*

A motorcyclist riding through the California
desert is accidentally thrown back in time to
1877, the result of a scientific experiment that
went awry.
MPAA:PG
Jensen Farley Pictures — *Pacific Arts Video*

Times of Harvey Milk, The   1983
Documentary/Sexuality
88418   90 mins   C   B, V   P
Directed by Robert Epstein
A powerful documentary on the career of
Harvey Milk, the San Francisco supervisor and
gay activist who was slain by former supervisor
Dan White in 1978.
Academy Awards '83: Best Feature Length
Documentary.
Richard Schmiechen; Robert Epstein;
Teleculture Films — *Pacific Arts Video*

Times Square   1980
Musical
58463   111 mins   C   B, V   P
*Tim Curry, Trini Alvarado, Robin Johnson, Peter
Coffield, Anna Maria Horsford, directed by Alan
Moyle*
A 13-year-old girl learns about life on her own
when she teams up with a defiant, anti-social
child of the streets. A New Wave rock music
score is featured.
MPAA:R
Robert Stigwood; Jacob Brackman — *THORN
EMI/HBO Video*

Timex All-Star Comedy   1962
Show
Comedy
12849   45 mins   B/W   B, V, FO   P
*Johnny Carson, Carl Reiner, Mel Brooks, Dr.
Joyce Brothers, Buddy Hackett, Kaye Stevens*
Spoof on TV shows and other fun, featuring a
comic cast.
ABC — *Video Yesteryear*

Tin Drum, The   1979
Drama
47370   141 mins   C   B, V   P
Oskar Matzerath, a self-made dwarf, narrates
this parable of modern society in violent
transition. Subtitled.
Academy Awards '79: Best Foreign Language
Film. GE
New World Pictures — *Warner Home Video*

Tin Man   1983
Drama
65485   95 mins   C   B, V   P
*Timothy Bottoms, Deana Jurgens, Troy
Donahue*
A garage mechanic born totally deaf designs
and builds a computer that can both hear and
speak for him. His world is complicated when a
young speech therapist introduces him to a

world of new and wonderful sounds, but also to a world of unscrupulous and exploitive computer salesmen. Slowly he realizes that he must make the decisions that will mold his future.
John G Thomas — *Media Home Entertainment*

Tin Star, The   1957
Western
85263   93 mins   B/W   B, V   P
Henry Fonda, Anthony Perkins, Betsy Palmer, directed by Anthony Mann
A classic Mann western, in which a young sheriff is aided by various renegades in ridding a town of lawlessness.
Paramount — *Kartes Video Communications*

Tina Turner   1982
Music-Performance
64209   55 mins   C   B, V   P
Tina Turner
Tina Turner stomps and shouts her way through an exciting program of hits including "Proud Mary," "Honky-Tonk Woman," "Jumping Jack Flash" and others. In stereo.
EMI Music — *THORN EMI/HBO Video; Sony Video Software*

Tina Turner Private Dancer   1984
Music video
76962   17 mins   C   B, V   P
Sultry Tina Turner performs four songs from her "Private Dancer" album.
Capitol Records — *Sony Video Software*

Tina Turner—Queen of Rock and Roll   1984
Music-Performance
72420   60 mins   C   B, V   P
Tina Turner entertains at Harlem's Apollo Theatre, giving her typically enthralling performance.
Unknown — *VCL Home Video*

Tintorera...Tiger Shark   1978
Adventure
66286   91 mins   C   B, V   P
Susan George, Fiona Lewis, Jennifer Ashley
Three shark hunters attempt to discover why swimmers are disappearing.
MPAA:R
Gerald Green — *Media Home Entertainment*

Tip Top! with Suzy Prudden—Ages 3-6   1982
Physical fitness
62887   53 mins   C   B, V   P
The first home video program series designed for young children; instructor Suzy Prudden leads her viewers through warmup activities and stimulating exercises set to contemporary music.

Warner Home Video; Warner Amex — *Warner Home Video*

Tip Top! with Suzy Prudden—Age 7 and Above   1982
Physical fitness
62888   48 mins   C   B, V   P
Suzy Prudden leads her video class of enthusiastic youngsters through a specially designed series of exercises for this specific age group.
Warner Home Video; Warner Amex — *Warner Home Video*

Title Shot   1981
Exploitation
85922   88 mins   C   B, V   P
Tony Curtis, Richard Gabourie, Susan Hogan, Robert Delbert
A crafty manager convinces a millionare to bet heavily on the guaranteed loss of his heavyweight boy in an upcoming fight, but doesn't realize the boxer is too stupid to throw the fight.
Arista — *Lightning Video*

TNT Jackson   1975
Martial arts
85367   73 mins   C   B, V   P
Jeanne Bell
A female kung fu mama searches for her brother while everyone in Hong Kong tries to kick her out of town.
MPAA:R
Cirio Santiago — *Charter Entertainment*

To All a Goodnight   1980
Horror
69307   90 mins   C   B, V   P
Jennifer Runyon, Forrest Swanson, Linda Gentile, William Lover
Five young girls and their boyfriends are in for an exciting Christmas holiday until a mad Santa Claus puts a damper on things.
MPAA:R
Jay Rasumny — *Media Home Entertainment*

To Be or Not To Be   1942
Comedy
65365   102 mins   B/W   B, V   P
Carole Lombard, Jack Benny, Robert Stack, directed by Ernst Lubitsch
Set in wartime Poland, Lombard and Benny are Maria and Josef Tura, the Barrymores of the Polish stage, who use the talents of their acting troupe against the Gestapo and manage to exit laughing.
United Artists — *Vestron Video*

To Be or Not to Be   1983
Comedy
Closed Captioned
72191   108 mins   C   B, V   P
Mel Brooks, Anne Bancroft
Anne Bancroft and Mel Brooks are actors in
Poland during WWII who plan to thwart the
Nazis.
MPAA:PG
Warner Bros — *CBS/Fox Video*

To Catch a King   1984
Suspense
72338   90 mins   C   B, V   P
Robert Wagner, Teri Garr
Adaptation of Jack Higgins' novel about a Nazi
plan to kidnap the Duke of Windsor.
Home Box Office — *Prism*

To Catch a Thief   1955
Mystery
53936   97 mins   C   B, V, LV   P
*Cary Grant, Grace Kelly, Jessie Royce Landis,
directed by Alfred Hitchcock*
An ex-jewel thief falls for a wealthy American
girl, who suspects him of his old thievery, when
a similar rash of jewel thefts occur.
Paramount — *Paramount Home Video*

To Forget Venice   197?
Drama
63447   90 mins   C   B, V   P
*Erland Josephson, Mariangela Melato, David
Pontremoli, Eleonora Giorgi, directed by Franco
Brusati*
This film portrays the sensitive relationships
among four people, and their shared fears of
growing older. Dubbed in English.
Rizzoli Film — *RCA/Columbia Pictures Home
Video; Embassy Home Entertainment (disc
only)*

To Have and Have Not   1945
Drama/Adventure
71141   100 mins   B/W   B, V   P
*Humphrey Bogart, Lauren Bacall, Walter
Brennan, Hoagy Carmichael, Dolores Moran,
Sheldon Leonard, Dan Seymour, directed by
Howard Hawks*
A Martinique charter boat operator gets mixed
up with a foxy lady and French resistance
fighters during World War II. William Faulkner
adapted the Ernest Hemingway story.
Warner Bros — *MGM/UA Home Video*

To Hell and Back   1955
War-Drama
87177   106 mins   C   B, V   P
*Audie Murphy, Marshall Thompson, Jack Kelly,
directed by Jesse Hibbs*
Audie Murphy, the most-decorated American
soldier in World War II, plays himself in this film
dramatization of his exploits.

Universal — *MCA Home Video*

To Joy   1950
Drama
78636   90 mins   B/W   B, V, LV   P
This early Ingmar Bergman film deals with the
problems and frustrations of the young in
Swedish society. This film has English subtitles.
SW
Janus Films — *Embassy Home Entertainment*

To Kill a Clown   1972
Drama/Suspense
66285   82 mins   C   B, V   P
Alan Alda, Blythe Danner, Heath Lamberts
A young couple who move to an isolated island
find their lives filled with terror.
MPAA:R
Teddy B Sills — *Media Home Entertainment*

To Kill a Mockingbird   1962
Drama
14034   129 mins   B/W   B, V   P
*Gregory Peck, Brock Peters, Phillip Afford, Mary
Badham*
A southern lawyer, the town's most
distinguished citizen, defends a black man
accused of rape. This costs him many
friendships but earns him the admiration of his
two motherless children.
Academy Awards '62: Best Actor (Peck).
Universal; Brentwood Prod — *MCA Home
Video*

To Kill a Stranger   1983
Suspense
81413   90 mins   C   B, V   P
*Donald Pleasence, Dean Stockwell, Angelica
Maria*
A woman discovers that the good samaritan
policy has its drawbacks when the man who
helps her out after an accident is a rapist and a
murderer.
J. Lopez-Moctezuma — *VCL Home Video*

To Live and Die in L.A.   1985
Crime-Drama
Closed Captioned
85623   114 mins   C   B, V, LV   P
*William L. Peterson, Willem DaFoe, John
Pankow, directed by William Friedkin*
Filmed in the style of a music video, this
hyperviolent crime drama deals with a secret
service agent's efforts to nab a counterfeiter.
MPAA:R
SLM Inc. — *Vestron Video*

To Paris with Love   1955
Comedy
77008   75 mins   C   B, V   P
Alec Guinness, Odile Versuis, Vernon Gray

A British father and his son fall in love with a shop girl and her boss while on vacation in Paris.
J. Arthur Rank — *VidAmerica*

To Race the Wind   1980
Biographical/Drama
73954   97 mins   C   B, V   P
Steve Guttenberg, Lisa Eilbacher, Randy Quaid, Barbara Barrie
A blind man wants to be treated like a normal person as he struggles through Harvard Law School. Based upon Harold Krents' autobiography.
Walter Grauman Prods; Viacom — *Unicorn Video*

To Russia...with Elton   197?
Music-Performance
47047   75 mins   C   B, V   P
Narrated by Dudley Moore
Elton John's successful 1979 tour of the Soviet Union is captured in this concert documentary. Elton performs "Your Song," "Goodbye Yellow Brick Road," "Benny and the Jets,","Back in the USSR" and many other songs.
ITC Entertainment — *CBS/Fox Video; RCA VideoDiscs*

To See Such Fun   1981
Comedy
59929   90 mins   C   B, V   P
Peter Sellers, Marty Feldman, Benny Hill, Eric Idle, Alec Guinness, Margaret Rutherford, Dirk Bogarde, Spike Milligan
Hilarious excerpts from 80 years of the greatest British movie comedies.
Herbert Wilcox; Michael Grade — *Pacific Arts Video*

To Sir, With Love   1967
Comedy-Drama
13294   105 mins   C   B, V   P
Sidney Poitier, Lulu, Judy Geeson, Christian Roberts, Suzy Kendall, Faith Brook
Teacher in London's tough East End tosses books in the wastebasket and proceeds to teach his class about life.
Columbia; James Clavell — *RCA/Columbia Pictures Home Video*

To the Lighthouse   1983
Drama
81563   115 mins   C   B, V   P
Rosemary Harris, Michael Clough, Suzanne Bertish, Linsey Baxter
A proper British holiday turns into a summer of disillusionment in this adaptation of the Virginia Woolf novel.
Epic Pictures — *Magnum Entertainment*

To the Shores of Iwo Jima   1942
World War II
87660   59 mins   B/W   B, V   P
Three short subjects use actual footage to delineate the Marines' efforts in Guadalcanal, Tarawa and Iwo Jima.
U.S. Marine Corps — *Victory Video*

Toast of New York, The   1937
Drama
57166   109 mins   B/W   B, V   P
Edward Arnold, Cary Grant, Frances Farmer, Jack Oakie, Donald Meek
Jim Fisk rises from a New England peddler to one of the first Wall Street giants of industry, in this story about the early years of the tycoon.
RKO; Edward Small — *King of Video*

Toast of the Town   1956
Variety
66459   120 mins   B/W   B, V, 3/4U   P
Ed Sullivan, Lucille Ball, Desi Arnaz, Vivian Vance, William Frawley, Orson Welles, The Ames Brothers
Two original Ed Sullivan TV programs, both featuring appearances by the cast of "I Love Lucy." The program of October 3, 1954 is a full one-hour tribute to "the Ricardos." The show of February 5, 1956 has Lucy and Desi promoting their latest picture, "Forever Darling," along with other guest stars. Original commercials and I.D.'s are included.
CBS — *Shokus Video*

Tobruk   1966
War-Drama
87176   110 mins   C   B, V   P
Rock Hudson, George Peppard, Guy Stockwell, directed by Arthur Hiller
American GI's endeavor to knock out the guns of Tobruk, to clear the way for a bombing attack on German fuel supply depots.
Universal — *MCA Home Video*

Toby and the Koala Bear   1983
Cartoons
Closed Captioned
78889   77 mins   C   B, V   P
Animated
A little boy and a pet Koala bear leave a convict colony and befriend an Aborigine boy, who teaches the pair how to survive in the Australian woods.
Satori — *Playhouse Video*

Toby Tyler   1959
Comedy
86787   93 mins   C   B, V   P
Kevin Corcoran, Henry Calvin, Gene Sheldon, Bob Sweeney, Mr. Stubbs

A boy runs off to join the circus, and teams up with a ribald chimpanzee in a film fashioned predominantly for youngsters.
Walt Disney Prods — *Walt Disney Home Video*

Lefco Productions — *Embassy Home Entertainment*

Today We Kill, Tomorrow We Die — 1971
Western
87687   95 mins   C   B, V   P
Montgomery Ford, Bud Spencer, William Berger, directed by Tonino Cervi
A rancher emerges from a prison term resulting from a frame-up, and hires a gang to relentlessly track down the culprit.
MPAA:PG
Cinerama — *Prism*

Tol'able David — 1921
Drama
33634   79 mins   B/W   B, V   P
Richard Barthelmess, Gladys Hulette, Ernest Torrance, directed by Henry King
A simple tale of mountain folk, done in the tradition of Mark Twain stories. The youngest son of a family yearns to be a mail driver. His community is troubled by the presence of three outlaws. Silent.
First National — *Festival Films; Video Yesteryear; Blackhawk Films*

Todd Rundgren: The Ever Popular Tortured Artist Effect — 1986
Music
84938   82 mins   C   B, V   P
A musical autobiography by Rundgren from childhood to the present, including some of his most popular songs. In HiFi stereo.
Todd Rundgren — *Blackhawk Films*

Tom and Jerry Cartoon Festival, Vol. II — 194?
Cartoons
59848   58 mins   C   B, V, CED   P
A second compilation of the best of MGM's classic Tom and Jerry cartoon shorts, including "Mouse Trap," "Cat Napping," "Invisible Mouse," "Saturday Evening Puss," and more.
MGM — *MGM/UA Home Video*

Todd Rundgren Videosyncracy — 1983
Music-Performance
64928   12 mins   C   B, V   P
Todd Rundgren performs three songs on this Video 45: "Hideaway," "Can We Still Be Friends" and "Time Heals."
Alchemedia Productions — *Sony Video Software*

Tom and Jerry Cartoon Festival, Vol. I — 1949
Cartoons
48860   58 mins   C   B, V   P
Animated
The cat and mouse fight their way through this cartoon festival which features "The Flying Cat," "The Bodyguard," "The Little Orphan," "Jerry's Cousin," "Dr. Jekyll and Mr. Mouse," "Mice Follies," "The Cat and the Mermouse," and "the Cat Concerto." In VHS and Beta Hi-Fi.
MGM — *MGM/UA Home Video*

Todos los Dias, Un Dia — 1979
Drama
66408   89 mins   C   B, V   P
Julio Iglesias, Isa Lorenz, Carol Lynley
A world famous singer on an island vacation meets and falls in love with a beautiful young girl who is unaware of his fame.
Argentinismas — *Unicorn Video*

Tom and Jerry Cartoon Festival, Vol. 3 — 19??
Cartoons
66453   59 mins   C   B, V, CED   P
Animated
Another collection of Tom and Jerry favorites from the 1940's and 1950's including "The Hollywood Bowl," "Million Dollar Cat," "The Night Before Christmas" and "Two Little Indians."
MGM — *MGM/UA Home Video*

Toga Party — 1979
Comedy
78895   82 mins   C   B, V   P
Bobby H. Charles, Mary Mitchell
A college fraternity house throws a wild toga party where what goes on usually comes off.
Funky Films Limited — *Monterey Home Video*

Tom & Jerry Cartoon Festival — 1967
Cartoons
81053   58 mins   C   B, V   P
Animated, directed by William Hanna and Joseph Barbera
This volume features seven more Tom and Jerry classics: "Johann Mouse," "Pet Peeve," "The Mouse From H.U.N.G.E.R.," "The Zoat Cat," "Baby Butch," "Fraidy Cat," "The Dog House" and "Baby Puss."

Together — 1979
Romance/Drama
76904   91 mins   C   B, V   P
Maximillian Schell, Jacqueline Bisset, Terence Stamp, Monica Guerritore
A divorced woman and a male chauvinist test the limits of their sexual liberation.

Academy Awards '52: Best Short Subject
(Cartoon) "Johann Mouse"
MGM; Fred Quimby — *MGM/UA Home Video*

Tom Brown's School Days   1940

Drama
08860   86 mins   B/W   B, V, 3/4U   P
*Cedric Hardwicke, Jimmy Lydon, Freddie
Bartholomew*
Depicts life among the boys in an English school
during the Victorian era.
RKO — *Hollywood Home Theater; Prism;
Cable Films; Discount Video Tapes; Video
Yesteryear; Kartes Video Communications;
Movie Buff Video*

Tom Brown's School Days   1951

Comedy-Drama
84850   93 mins   B/W   B, V   P
*Robert Newton, John Howard Davies, James
Hayter*
The classic tale of English school life; Tom
enrolls in rugby and is beset by bullies.
UA — *United Home Video*

Tom Corbett, Space Cadet   1951

Science fiction
42968   30 mins   B/W   B, V, FO   P
Frankie Thomas, Jack Grimes, Al Markhim
This popular space opera from the early days of
television shows how one cadet who is the
smallest in size becomes the biggest in courage
and team cooperation.
ABC — *Video Yesteryear*

Tom Corbett, Space Cadet Volume 1   195?

Science fiction/Adventure
44312   90 mins   B/W   B, V, 3/4U   P
Frankie Thomas, Jan Merlin
The adventures of Tom Corbett, a Space Cadet
at the U.S. Space Academy, where men and
women train to become agents to protect Earth
and its neighbor planets.
ABC — *Nostalgia Merchant*

Tom Corbett, Space Cadet Volume 2   195?

Science fiction
58585   90 mins   B/W   B, V, 3/4U   P
This early '50's TV series follows the adventures
of Tom Corbett, a space cadet at the U.S.
Space Academy.
ABC — *Nostalgia Merchant*

Tom, Dick, and Harry   1941

Comedy
10038   86 mins   B/W   B, V   P, T

*Ginger Rogers, George Murphy, Burgess
Meredith, Allen Marshall, Phil Silvers*
Dreamy girl is engaged to three men and unable
to decide which to marry. It all depends on a
kiss.
RKO — *Blackhawk Films*

Tom Edison, the Boy Who Lit Up the World   1978

Adventure/Biographical
75617   49 mins   C   B, V   P
This is the story of Tom Edison's life and how he
changed the world.
VidAmerica — *VidAmerica; Children's Video
Library*

Tom Edison: The Making of an American Legend   19??

Biographical/Inventions
69587   49 mins   C   B, V   P
David Huffman
This is the story of young Thomas Edison, a
telegraph operator who becomes one of
history's greatest inventors.
Unknown — *VidAmerica*

Tom Horn   1980

Western
54795   98 mins   C   B, V   P
*Steve McQueen, Linda Evans, Richard
Farnsworth, Billy Green Bush, Slim Pickens,
directed by William Wiard*
The true story of an Old West gunman, Tom
Horn, who at the age of 40 has already been a
western railroad worker, stagecoach driver, U.S.
Cavalry scout, silver miner, Teddy Roosevelt
Rough Rider, and a Pinkerton Detective. Now
he is invited by Wyoming ranchers to stop the
cattle rustlers. He does that job well, and at the
same time finds romance.
MPAA:R
Warner Bros — *Warner Home Video*

Tom Jones   1963

Comedy
52738   129 mins   C   B, V, LV   P
*Albert Finney, Susannah York, Hugh Griffith,
Dame Edith Evans, David Tomlinson, directed
by Tony Richardson*
A comedy based on Henry Fielding's novel
about a rustic playboy's wild life in eighteenth-
century London with brigands, beauties, and
scoundrels.
Academy Awards '63: Best Picture; Best
Director (Richardson); Best Screenplay (John
Osborne); Best Original Score (John Addison).
EL, SP
Woodfall Prods; United Artists; Lopert
Pictures — *CBS/Fox Video; RCA VideoDiscs*

Tom Jones Live in Las Vegas　1981
Music-Performance
53137　60 mins　C　B, V　P
Tom Jones
Superstar Tom Jones lights up a Vegas showroom performing "What's New Pussycat?," "She's a Lady," "Green Green Grass of Home," "It's Not Unusual," "Love Me Tonight," "Ladies' Night," "Working My Way Back to You," "Woman," "I'll Never Fall in Love Again," and others.
Jay Harvey Prods — *Family Home Entertainment*

Tom Petty and the Heartbreakers—Pack Up the Plantation—Live　1985
Music-Performance
84017　96 mins　C　B, V　P
Tom Petty and the Heartbreakers, directed by Jeff Stein
From the director of "The Kids Are Alright" comes Tom Petty's first video concert, filmed at Los Angeles' Wiltern Theatre, including his biggest hits "The Waiting," "Refugee," "Don't Do Me Like That" and many more. Recorded in HiFi Stereo.
Tom Petty; Kim Dempster; Kathleen Dougherty — *MCA Home Video*

Tom Sawyer　1973
Musical
Closed Captioned
81559　99 mins　C　B, V　P
Johnny Whitaker, Jeff East, Jodie Foster, Warren Oates, Celeste Holm
This is a musical version of the classic Mark Twain story about a young man's life on the Mississippi River during the 1840's. Available in VHS and Beta Hi-Fi.
United Artists — *Playhouse Video*

Tom Thumb　1958
Fairy tales/Fantasy
73366　92 mins　C　B, V　P
Russ Tamblyn, Peter Sellers, Terry-Thomas, directed by George Pal
The classic Grimm Brothers fairy tale about the small boy who saves the village treasury from the bad guys is brought to life in this film. Academy Award 1958: Best Special Effects.
Galaxy Pictures — *MGM/UA Home Video*

Tomb of Ligeia, The　1964
Horror
87739　82 mins　C　B, V　P
Vincent Price, Elizabeth Sheppard, John Westbrook, Oliver Johnston, directed by Roger Corman
One of the best of the Corman-Poe films, in which a man and his second wife, upon returning to their manor, are haunted by his first. Written by Robert Towne.

Roger Corman — *THORN EMI/HBO Video*

Tomboy　1940
Comedy
12813　70 mins　B/W　B, V, FO　P
Jackie Moran, Marcia Mae Jones
A shy country boy and a not-so-shy city girl team up to catch crooks.
Monogram — *Video Yesteryear*

Tomboy　1985
Drama
80927　91 mins　C　B, V　P
Betsy Russell, Eric Douglas, Jerry Dinome, Kristi Somers, Toby Iland
A pretty teenaged female mechanic is determined to win the love and respect of a superstar auto racer.
MPAA:R
Crown International Pictures — *Vestron Video*

Tomboy and the Champ　1958
Drama
84823　82 mins　C　B, V　P
Candy Moore, Ben Johnson, Jesse White
An Angus calf is brought to show despite a variety of obstacles.
Tommy Reynolds; William Lightfoot — *United Home Video*

Tommy　1975
Musical
58965　108 mins　C　B, V, LV　P
Ann-Margret, Elton John, Oliver Reed, Tina Turner, Roger Daltrey, Eric Clapton, Keith Moon, directed by Ken Russell
Peter Townsend's rock-opera about the deaf, dumb, and blind boy who becomes a celebrity.
MPAA:PG
Robert Stigwood; Columbia — *RCA/Columbia Pictures Home Video; RCA VideoDiscs*

Tomorrow　1983
Drama
65455　102 mins　B/W　B, V　P
Robert Duvall
The powerful tale of the love of two lonely people of the earth, carrying them through the ordeals of pregnancy and birth and culminating in a baffling murder trial.
Gilbert Pearlman; Paul Roebling — *Monterey Home Video*

Tomorrow at Seven　1933
Mystery/Suspense
63619　62 mins　B/W　B, V, FO　P
Chester Morris, Vivienne Osborne, Frank McHugh
A mystery writer/amateur detective is determined to discover the identity of the Black Ace, a mysterious killer who always warns his

intended victim, then leaves an ace of spades on the corpse as his calling card.
RKO — *Video Yesteryear*

Tomorrow's Children   1934
Exploitation
85221   55 mins   B/W   B, V   P
Sterling Holloway
An alarmist melodrama warning against the threat of government-induced female sterilization.
Bryan Foy — *Video Yesteryear*

Tonight for Sure   1961
Film-Avant-garde
47644   66 mins   B/W   B, V, FO   P
Directed by Francis Ford Coppola
Coppola's first film, produced as a student at UCLA. Two men ruminate on bad experiences with naked women. Nudity. Music by Carmen Coppola.
Francis Ford Coppola — *Video Yesteryear*

Tonio Kroger   1965
Drama
69565   92 mins   B/W   B, V, FO   P
Jean-Claude Brialy, Nadja Tiller, Gert Frobe
A young writer travels through Europe in search of intellectual and sensual relationships and a home that will suit him. German dialogue with English subtitles.
Germany — *Video Yesteryear*

Tonka   1958
Western
88195   97 mins   C   B, V   P
Sal Mineo
A children's story about a wild horse tamed by a young Indian, which is then ironically recruited for Custer's Last Stand.
Walt Disney Prod. — *Walt Disney Home Video*

Tono Bicicleta   197?
Drama
86539   116 mins   C   B, V   P
Tommy Vegas, Alida Arizmendy
Tono Bicicleta cavorts with his wife and girlfriend and yet persists in kidnapping more women.
SP
Spanish — *Master Arts Video*

Tony Bennett Songbook, A   1981
Music-Performance
60375   94 mins   C   CED   P
This stereo program recorded live in New York features the exciting Tony Bennett in an intimate nightclub atmosphere singing "I Left My Heart in San Francisco," a Duke Ellington medley, and much more.

Dennis H. Paget — *RCA VideoDiscs*

Tony Powers   1981
Music-Performance
75908   54 mins   C   B, V   P
This program presents Tony Powers performing his songs "Don't Nobody Move," "Midnite Trampoline" and "Odyssey."
Tony Powers Music Inc — *Sony Video Software*

Too Hot to Handle   1980
Drama
54799   88 mins   C   B, V   P
Cheri Caffaro
A voluptuous lady contract killer fights against the mob with all the weapons at her disposal. Filmed on location in Manila.
New World; Roger Corman — *Warner Home Video*

Too Late the Hero   1970
Drama/World War II
46205   133 mins   C   B, V   P
Michael Caine, Cliff Robertson, Henry Fonda, directed by Robert Aldrich
A British combat patrol whose mission is to wipe out a Japanese communication site, finds a horde of enemy planes. The Japanese chase them through the jungle relaying messages via loud speakers that their lives will be spared only if they surrender.
MPAA:PG
Cinerama Release — *CBS/Fox Video*

Too Scared To Scream   1985
Suspense
77412   104 mins   C   B, V   P
Mike Connors, Anne Archer, Leon Isaac Kennedy, John Heard, Ian McShane, directed by Tony Lo Bianco
A policeman and an undercover agent team up to solve a bizarre series of murders at a Manhattan apartment house.
MPAA:R
Mike Connors; The Movie Store — *Vestron Video*

Too Smart for Strangers   1985
Child abuse/Safety education
81646   40 mins   C   B, V   P
Winnie the Pooh and Tigger, along with Tyne Daly and Gavin MacLeod present tips on how children can defend themselves against strangers.
FR, SP
Walt Disney Productions — *Walt Disney Home Video*

Toolbox Murders, The   1978
Mystery
48358   93 mins   C   B, V   P

Cameron Mitchell, Pamelyn Ferdin
An unknown psychotic murderer brutally claims victims one at a time, leaving a town on the verge of horror, and the police mystified.
MPAA:R
Cal Am Productions — *United Home Video*

Tootsie 1982
Comedy
66443　110 mins　C　B, V　　　　P
Dustin Hoffman, Jessica Lange, Teri Garr, Dabney Coleman, Bill Murray, directed by Sydney Pollack
A desperate, unemployed actor dresses as a woman to land a starring role in a television soap opera.
Academy Awards '82: Best Supporting Actress (Lange) MPAA:PG
Columbia Pictures — *RCA/Columbia Pictures Home Video; RCA VideoDiscs*

Top Cat 196?
Cartoons
47694　50 mins　C　B, V　　　　P
Animated voices of Arnold Stang, Allen Jenkins, Maurice Gosfield
Two episodes in which T.C. and his gang of street-wise cats drive Officer Dibble nuts.
Hanna Barbera — *Worldvision Home Video*

Top Cat Volume 2 1961
Cartoons
79172　50 mins　C　B, V　　　　P
Animated, voices of Arnold Stang, Marvin Kaplan, Jean Vander Pyl
Top Cat and his gang of alley cats are trying to live the good life in New York City, but officer Dibble is making things difficult for them.
Hanna-Barbera — *Worldvision Home Video*

Top Hat 1935
Musical
00270　97 mins　B/W　B, V　　　　P
Fred Astaire, Ginger Rogers, Erik Rhodes, Helen Broderick, Edward Everett Horton, Eric Blore
As usual, Ginger thinks Fred is someone he isn't. It takes the whole length of the film to straighten her out. Irving Berlin's score includes, "Top Hat," "Cheek to Cheek" and "The Piccolino."
RKO; Pandro S Berman — *RKO HomeVideo; VidAmerica; King of Video*

Top Secret 1984
Comedy/Satire
80061　90 mins　C　B, V　　　　P
Val Kilmer, Lucy Gutteridge, Omar Sharif, Peter Cushing, directed by Jim Abrahams, Jerry Zucker, and David Zucker
The minds behind "Airplane" take shots at Elvis—surf—spy—cold war intrigue movies in

this madcap romp. Kilmer performs several musical parodies of rock standards.
MPAA:PG
Paramount Pictures; Jon Davidson — *Paramount Home Video*

Topaz 1969
Drama/Suspense
80414　126 mins　C　B, V　　　　P
John Forsythe, Philippe Noiret, Karin Dor, Michael Piccoli, directed by Alfred Hitchcock
An American CIA agent and a French Intelligence agent combine forces to find information about Russian involvement in Cuba.
Universal; Alfred Hitchcock — *MCA Home Video*

Topkapi 1964
Drama
65408　122 mins　C　B, V, CED　　　P
Melina Mercouri, Maximilian Schell, Peter Ustinov, Robert Morley
Filmed in Istanbul, the movie centers around the famed Topkapi Palace Museum, an impregnable fortress filled with wealth and splendor which seems impossible to break in to.
United Artists — *CBS/Fox Video*

Topper 1937
Comedy
44797　97 mins　B/W　B, V, 3/4U　　P
Cary Grant, Roland Young, Constance Bennett, Billie Burke, directed by Norman Z. McLeod
Based on the Thorne Smith novel this is the story of Marion and George Kirby, who after a car accident do not wish to be dead and become ghosts instead. They get involved in many ghostly escapades.
MGM, Hal Roach — *Nostalgia Merchant; Blackhawk Films*

Topper 1937
Comedy
70739　97 mins　C　B, V　　　　P
Gary Grant, Roland Young, Constance Bennet, Billie Burke, directed by Norman Z. McLeod
Hal Roach Studios colorized this originally black and white classic using a new computer technique.
MGM, Hal Roach — *Hal Roach Studios*

Topper Returns 1941
Comedy
08733　87 mins　B/W　B, V　　　　P
Roland Young, Joan Blondell, Dennis O'Keefe, Rochester, Carole Landis
Topper finds the murderer of a girl, with the help of his ghostly friends, the Kirbys.
United Artists; Hal Roach — *Movie Buff Video; Hollywood Home Theater; Cable Films; Video Yesteryear; Video Connection; Discount Video*

Tapes; Nostalgia Merchant; Prism; Kartes Video Communications

---

Topper Returns 1941
Comedy
71033　87 mins　C　B, V　　　　P
Roland Young, Joan Blondell, Eddie "Rochester" Anderson, Billie Burke, Alan Mowbray, Franklin Pangborn
Topper and his ghostly friends, the Kirbys, go after a murderer. This release has been enhanced through the Colorization process.
UA; Hal Roach — *Hal Roach Studios*

Topper Takes a Trip 1939
Comedy
64371　85 mins　B/W　B, V, 3/4U　P
Constance Bennett, Roland Young, Billie Burke, Alan Mowbray, Franklin Pangborn
Cosmo Topper takes a trip to the Riviera, with the ghostly spirit of Marion Kirby in hot pursuit.
Hal Roach — *Nostalgia Merchant*

Topper Takes a Trip 1939
Comedy
71032　80 mins　C　B, V　　　　P
Roland Young, Constance Bennett, Billie Burke, Alan Mowbray, Franklin Pangborn
This sequel follows Topper and Marian Kirby's ghostly form to the French Riviera. This version has been enhanced through the Colorization process.
Hal Roach — *Hal Roach Studios*

Tora! Tora! Tora! 1970
War-Drama
08439　144 mins　C　B, V, LV　P
Martin Balsam, Soh Yomamura, Joseph Cotten, E. G. Marshall, Jason Robards, directed by Richard Fleisher
The story of December 7, 1941 is retold from both Japanese and American viewpoints in this large-scale production.
MPAA:G
20th Century Fox; Elmo Williams — *CBS/Fox Video*

Torchlight 1985
Drama
80771　90 mins　C　B, V, LV　P
Pamela Sue Martin, Steve Railsback, Ian McShane, Al Corley, Rita Taggart
A young couple's life slowly starts to crumble when a wealthy art dealer teaches them how to free base cocaine. Carly Simon sings "All the Love in the World."
MPAA:R
Torch Productions — *Embassy Home Entertainment*

Tormentor 1972
Horror
70932　90 mins　C　B, V　　　　P
Robert Hoffman, Susan Scott, directed by Maurizio Pradeaux
Two people who mistakenly view a razor-wielding maniac in action are enlisted to help in his capture.
S.E.F.I. Production Balcazar; S.E.S.I. Cinemagraphics — *Wizard Video*

Torn Between Two Lovers 1979
Romance/Drama
78362　100 mins　C　B, V　　　P
Lee Remick, George Peppard, Joseph Bologna, directed by Delbert Mann
A woman must decide between staying with her husband or starting a new relationship with an anarchist.
Alan Landsburg Productions — *U.S.A. Home Video*

Torn Curtain 1966
Suspense
64558　125 mins　C　B, V　　　P
Paul Newman, Julie Andrews, Lila Kedrova, David Opatoshu, directed by Alfred Hitchcock
An American scientist poses as a defector to East Germany in order to do some undercover work. Unfortunately, his fiancee follows him behind the Iron Curtain.
Universal — *MCA Home Video*

Tornado 1983
War-Drama
82192　90 mins　C　B, V　　　P
Timothy Brent, Tony Marsina, Alan Collins
An army sergeant revolts against his superiors and the enemy when his captain leaves him stranded in Vietnam.
Gianfranco Couyoumdjian — *Lightning Video*

Torpedo Attack 1972
War-Drama
85407　88 mins　C　B, V　　　P
Sidney Kazan, John Ferris, Emily Harper, Paul Lerner, Richard Farley
Greek soldiers in World War II battle the enemy via their trusty submarines.
Carar Films; Billy Bellok — *U.S.A. Home Video*

Torture Chamber of Baron Blood, The 1972
Horror
88188　90 mins　C　B, V　　　P
Joseph Cotten, Elke Sommer, Massimo Girotti, directed by Mario Bava
An old murderous Baron comes back to vampiric life in an old European castle, and kills lots of bystanders. A minor Bava non-classic. Originally known as "Baron Blood."

Italian — *THORN EMI/HBO Video*

Torture Chamber of Dr. Sadism   1969
Horror
86490   120 mins   C   B, V   P
Christopher Lee, Karen Dor, Lex Barker
Count Ragula returns after a gory hiatus to
terrorize Blood Castle and its inhabitants.
Hemisphere Prod. — *Magnum Entertainment*

Torture Garden   1967
Horror
81800   93 mins   C   B, V   P
*Jack Palance, Burgess Meredith, Peter Cushing,
Beverly Adams, directed by Freddie Francis*
A sinister man presides over an unusual
sideshow where people can see what is in store
if they allow the evil side of their personalities to
take over. Available in VHS and Beta Hi-Fi.
Columbia Pictures; Amicus
Productions — *RCA/Columbia Pictures Home
Video*

Torvill & Dean: Path to Perfection   1984
Sports-Winter
66572   60 mins   C   B, V   P
Olympic ice dancing gold medalists Torvill and
Dean are featured in eight of their pre-Olympic
performances, including 3 World Skating
Championships.
Robert J. Brady Company — *THORN
EMI/HBO Video*

Tosca   1984
Opera
70953   118 mins   C   B, V   P
*Eva Marton, Giacomo Aragall, Ingvar Wixell,
orchestra conducted by Daniel Oren*
Puccini's lyric drama of idealistic young love
receives a lush, passionate treatment in this
Arena di Verona production.
Italian — *THORN EMI/HBO Video*

Tosca   1985
Opera
71140   127 mins   C   B, V   P
*Hildegard Behrens, Placido Domingo, Cornell
MacNeil, Italo Tajo, Guiseppe Sinopoli
conducting the Metropolitan Opera Orchestra
and Chorus*
Franco Zeffirelli produced this breathtaking
version of Puccini's opera for the PBS "Live
From the Met" series. He framed the
performances against vast, gorgeously detailed
sets and the recording is in HiFi Stereo sound.
With English subtitles.
Emmy Award: '85—Best Musical Special
AM Available
PBS; The Metropolitan Opera — *Paramount
Home Video*

Toscanini: The Maestro/Hymn of the Nations   1985
Music-Performance/Documentary
81947   74 mins   C   B, V   P
Hosted by James Levine
This documentary looks at the life and music of
Arturo Toscanini and also includes a black and
white performance of Verdi's "Hymn of the
Nations" with Jan Peerce and the NBC
Symphony. Featured are rare color home
movies of Toscanini at work and play from the
Toscanini family archives.
Peter Rosen — *Video Arts International*

Tosca's Kiss   1985
Documentary/Opera
81948   87 mins   C   B, V   P
*Sara Scuderi, Giovanni Puligheddo, Leonida
Bellon, directed by Daniel Schmid*
This documentary visits the Casa Verdi in Milan,
Italy which is a home for retired Italian opera
singers and musicians. In Italian with English
subtitles.
IT
Italtoons Corporation — *Video Arts
International*

Total Self-Defense   1981
Safety education
52673   45 mins   C   B, V   P
A woman instructor shows how women can
protect themselves in situations such as purse
snatching, rape, or other attack. In the second
part, two third degree black belts in karate
demonstrate "street or full-contact karate." This
tape was designed as an interactive,
instructional program.
Karl Video Corp — *Karl/Lorimar Home Video*

Totally Go-Go's   1982
Music-Performance
59695   77 mins   C   B, V   P
The chart-topping, all-girl rock band performs
live in concert in Hollywood. Songs include "We
Got the Beat," "Our Lips Are Sealed," and
songs from their two hit albums.
IRS Records — *THORN EMI/HBO Video; RCA
VideoDiscs*

Touch & Go   1980
Adventure
77005   92 mins   C   B, V   P
Wendy Hughes
Three beautiful women commit grand larceny in
order to raise funds for underprivileged children.
MPAA:PG
John Pellatt — *VidAmerica*

Touch of Class, A   1973
Comedy
08475   105 mins   C   B, V   P

George Segal, Glenda Jackson, Paul Sorvino, Hildegard Neil, Cec Linder
American insurance adjustor initiates a love affair with an English divorcee.
Academy Awards '73: Best Actress (Jackson).
MPAA:PG
Avco Embassy — *CBS/Fox Video*

Touch of Love: Massage, The   1980
Massage
48635   28 mins   C   B, V, LV   P
A simple and beautiful way to experience pleasure through touch is presented.
Bruce Seth Green — *MCA Home Video*

Touch of Magic in Close-Up, A   1982
Magic
59992   78 mins   C   B, V   R, P
Siroco
The amazing Siroco, renowned master of "close-up" magic, mystifies, and then demonstrates the secrets behind many of the illusions.
MPAA:G
Pegicorn Video Corp — *Video Gems*

Touch of Satan, A   1974
Horror
55317   90 mins   C   B, V   P
Michael Berry, Emby Mallay, Lee Amber, Yvonne Wilson, directed by Don Henderson
Devil worshippers and evil satanic rites abound in this horror of the world beyond. (Original title "A Touch of Melissa.")
Dundee Prods — *King of Video*

Touch the Sky--Precision Flying with the Blue Angels   1986
Aeronautics
87747   60 mins   C   B, V   P
Christopher Reeve
A look at the Blue Angels doing their astounding stunts, with Reeve providing color commentary.
Peter Henton; CCR Video Corp.;Platinum Pictures; Angels Venture — *Twin Tower Enterprises*

Touched   1982
Drama
65292   89 mins   C   B, V   P
Robert Hays, Kathleen Beller, Ned Beatty
Two young people struggle to cope with the outside world. They struggle against all odds to gain new confidence after being released from a psychiatric hospital. It is a story of determination, hope, and most of all, love.
MPAA:R
Barclay Lottimer; Dirk Petersmann — *Media Home Entertainment*

Touched by Love   1984
Drama
70193   95 mins   C   B, V   P
Deborah Raffin, Diane Lane
The true story of a handicapped child who learns to power of love from her devoted teacher. In Beta Hi-Fi.
MPAA:PG
Columbia Pictures — *RCA/Columbia Pictures Home Video*

Tough Enough   19??
Drama
65332   107 mins   C   B, V   P
Dennis Quaid, Charlene Watkins
A country-western singer-songwriter decides to finance his fledgling career by entering amateur boxing matches and then finds himself rising to the top of amateur boxing.
MPAA:PG
Michael Leone; Andrew D T Pfeffer — *CBS/Fox Video*

Tough Guy   197?
Martial arts/Adventure
47701   90 mins   C   B, V   P
Chen Ying, Charlie Chiang
Two undercover policemen battle local gangsters in a bid to smash their crime ring.
Independent — *Master Arts Video*

Tough Guy, The   1953
Crime-Drama
86891   73 mins   B/W   B, V   P
James Kenney, Hermione Gingold, Joan Collins, directed by Lewis Gilbert
Based on the play by Bruce Walker, a London hood carouses, mugs, breaks hearts and personifies his generation's urban angst.
Romulus-Daniel Angel British Prod. — *Unicorn Video*

Tourist Trap   1979
Science fiction
42917   85 mins   C   B, V   P
Chuck Connors
While traveling through the desert, a couple's car has a flat. A woman's voice lures the man into an abandoned gas station, where he discovers that the voice belongs to a mannequin.
MPAA:PG
J. Larry Carroll — *Media Home Entertainment*

Tower of Babel   1979
Drama/Bible
55011   49 mins   C   B, V   P
Vince Edwards, Ron Palillo, Erin Moran, Dana Elcar, Cliff Emmich, Richard Basehart, narrated by Victor Jory
The Biblical story of man's attempt to build a tower to the heavens. Despite protests, King Amathar begins construction, but as the building

progresses, Amathar is overcome with vanity, causing God to destroy the tower.
Sunn Classics — *Vanguard Video; Magnum Entertainment; Lucerne Films*

Tower of Evil   1973
Horror
48473   86 mins   C   B, V /   P
Bryant Haliday, Jill Haworth
Tourists and archaeologists visit an island where ancient Phoenician treasure is buried. Most of them are haunted by terror and grisly murder.
MPAA:R
Grenadier Films Ltd — *MPI Home Video*

Towering Inferno, The   1974
Drama
29178   165 mins   C   B, V, CED   P
Steve McQueen, Paul Newman, William Holden, Faye Dunaway, Fred Astaire
Irwin Allen's dramatic suspense story of a holocaust that engulfs the world's tallest skyscraper on the night of its glamorous and prestigious dedication ceremonies.
Academy Awards '74: Best Song ("We May Never Love Like this Again"). MPAA:PG
20th Century Fox — *CBS/Fox Video*

Town Called Hell, A   1972
Suspense
12025   95 mins   C   B, V   P
Robert Shaw, Stella Stevens, Martin Landau, Telly Savalas
Two men hold an entire town hostage while looking for "Aguila," the Mexican revolutionary. Greed, evil, and violence take over.
Philip Yordan; Official Films — *King of Video; World Video Pictures; Video Gems*

Town That Dreaded   1976
Sundown, The
Suspense
65138   90 mins   C   B, V   P
Ben Johnson, Andrew Prine, Dawn Wells
A mad killer is on the loose in a small Arkansas town. Based on a true story, this famous murder spree remains an unsolved mystery.
MPAA:R
Charles B Pierce Productions — *Warner Home Video*

Toxic Reasons   198?
Music video/Music-Performance
84064   60 mins   C   B, V   P
Toxic Reasons
Live performances by the energetic San Francisco punk band, playing such songs as "War Hero," "White Noise" and "Drunk and Disorderly."
Target Video — *Target Video*

Toy, The   1982
Comedy-Drama
66010   99 mins   C   B, V   P
Richard Pryor, Jackie Gleason, Ned Beatty, Wilfred Hyde-White, directed by Richard Donner
A janitor finds himself the new "toy" of the son of a department store owner.
MPAA:PG
Columbia — *RCA/Columbia Pictures Home Video; RCA VideoDiscs*

Toy Soldiers   1984
Drama/Adventure
80461   85 mins   C   B, V, LV   P
Cleavon Little
A group of college students are held for ransom in a war-torn Central American country. When they escape, they join forces with a seasoned mercenary who leads them as a vigilante force.
MPAA:R
New World Pictures — *New World Video*

Toyota Corolla   1986
Automobiles
88411   60 mins   C   B, V, 3/4U   P
How to maintain and tune-up this one particular Toyota engine.
Peter Allen Prod. — *Peter Allen Video Productions*

Toyota Cressida, Supra   1986
Automobiles
88410   60 mins   C   B, V, 3/4U   P
How to maintain and tune-up the two Toyota engines.
Peter Allen Prod. — *Peter Allen Video Productions*

Track of the Moonbeast   1976
Horror
82147   90 mins   C   B, V   P
Chase Cordell, Donna Leigh Drake
An American Indian uses mythology to capture the Moonbeast, a lizard-like creature that is roaming the deserts of New Mexico.
Derio Productions — *Prism*

Tracks   1976
Suspense
75585   90 mins   C   B, V   P
Dennis Hopper, Dean Stockwell, Taryn Power, directed by Henry Jaglom
A disoriented soldier has paranoia and hallucinations on a long train ride.
MPAA:R
Rainbow Pictures — *Monterey Home Video*

Trading Places   1983
Comedy
Closed Captioned
66409   106 mins   C   B, V, 8mm,   P
                            LV, CED

Eddie Murphy, Dan Aykroyd, Jamie Lee Curtis,
Ralph Bellamy, Don Ameche, directed by John
Landis
Two elderly businessmen make a wager that
basic intelligence is more important than
heredity in creating a successful life, using their
rich nephew and an unemployed street hustler
as guinea pigs.
MPAA:R
Paramount; Aaron Russo — *Paramount Home*
Video

Tragedy of Antony and Cleopatra, The   1985
Drama
70649   190 mins   C   B, V   P
Timothy Dalton, Lynn Redgrave, Nichelle
Nichols, John Carradine, Barrie Ingham,
Anthony Greary, Walter Koenig, dir. by
Lawrence Carra
This presentation of Shakespeare's Roman
Empire tragedy features American actors and
accents set against an artist's reproduction of
England's Globe Theater Stage. The program
comes on two tapes.
Paganiniana Publications — *Kultur*

Tragedy of King Lear, The   1986
Theater
87360   182 mins   C   B, V   P
Mike Kellen, Darryl Hickman, David Groh, Kitty
Winn
A version of the Shakespeare tragedy featuring
a cast of well-known TV favorites.
Unknown — *Kultur*

Tragedy of King Richard II, The   1982
Drama
66149   180 mins   C   B, V   P
David Birney, Paul Shenar
The first of Shakespeare's 28 plays to be
released in this videocassette series is the
historical play, "Richard II."
Bard Prods — *Kultur*

Tragedy of Macbeth, The   1985
Drama
80402   150 mins   C   B, V   P
Jeremy Brett, Piper Laurie, Simon
MacCorkindale, Millie Perkins, BarryPrimus
A new adaptation of the Shakespearean tragedy
about a Scottish general's zealous quest for
power.
Unknown — *Kultur*

Tragedy of Othello, The   1986
Theater
87350   195 mins   C   B, V   P
William Marshall, Ron Moody, Jenny Agutter
A traditional version of the classic Shakespeare
tragedy.

Unknown — *Kultur*

Trail Beyond, The   1934
Western
81526   57 mins   B/W   B, V   P
John Wayne, Noah Berry Jr.
A cowboy and his sidekick go on the trek to the
northwest to find a girl and a gold mine.
Monogram Pictures — *Spotlite Video; Sony*
Video Software; Discount Video Tapes

Trail Beyond, The   1934
Western
10934   57 mins   B/W   B, V   P
John Wayne
"Duke" hits the trail after robbers.
Monogram — *Sony Video Software; Discount*
Video Tapes

Trail Drive   1935
Western
10678   63 mins   B/W   B, V   P
Ken Maynard
Adventures of a cowboy during a big cattle
drive.
Universal — *Video Connection; Cable Films*

Trail of the Pink Panther   1982
Comedy
66074   97 mins   C   B, V, CED   P
Peter Sellers, David Niven, Herbert Lom,
Capucine, Burt Kwuok, directed by Blake
Edwards
This sixth "Panther" vehicle concerns the
disappearance of Inspector Clouseau.
MPAA:PG
United Artists — *CBS/Fox Video*

Trail of the Royal Mounted   1934
Western/Serials
54196   150 mins   B/W   B, V   P
Robert Frazer
A western adventure serial made up of ten 15-
minute episodes.
Unknown — *Video Connection; Cable Films*

Trail Riders   1942
Western
11267   55 mins   B/W   B, V, FO   P
John King, David Sharpe, Max Terhune, Evelyn
Finley, Forest Taylor, Charles King
The Range Busters set a trap to capture a gang
of outlaws who killed the son of the town
marshal during a bank robbery.
Monogram — *Video Yesteryear; Discount*
Video Tapes; Video Connection

Trail Street   1947
Western
10069   84 mins   B/W   B, V   P, T

Randolph Scott, Robert Ryan, Anne Jeffreys, Gabby Hayes, Madge Meredith, Jason Robards
Traces story of men and women who began great wheat empire out of Kansas wilderness.
RKO; Nat Holt — Blackhawk Films; Nostalgia Merchant

Trail to Machu Picchu, The   1985
Mountaineering
84281   30 mins   C   B, V   P
A trip by raft into the Inca Valley, and then a hike up to Machu Picchu.
Video Travel Inc — Video Travel

Trailing Double Trouble   1940
Western
85503   56 mins   B/W   B, V   P
Ray "Crash" Corrigan, Max Terhune, Lita Conway, Rex Felker
Three ranch hands care for a baby left by a murdered gunman.
Monogram — Video Yesteryear

Trailing Trouble   1937
Western
11266   60 mins   B/W   B, V, FO   P
Ken Maynard
A cowboy and a killer have several confrontations in between the cowboy's efforts to steer clear of the case of his own mistaken identity which marks him for treachery.
Grand National — Video Yesteryear; Video Connection

Train Killer, The   1983
Suspense
80114   90 mins   C   B, V   P
Michael Sarazin
A mad Hungarian is bent on destroying the Orient Express.
Wescom Productions — Vestron Video

Train Robbers, The   1973
Western
74212   92 mins   C   B, V   P
John Wayne, Ann-Margret, Rod Taylor, Ben Johnson, Christopher George
This is the story of a widow who employs the services of three cowboys to help her recover some stolen gold.
MPAA:PG
Michael Wayne; Batjac Productions — Warner Home Video

Traitor, The   1936
Western
14219   57 mins   B/W   B, V   P
Tim McCoy
Undercover man joins a gang of bandits.

Puritan — United Home Video; Video Connection; Discount Video Tapes

Tramp and A Woman, The   1915
Comedy
38966   45 mins   B/W   B, V, FO   P
Charlie Chaplin, Edna Purviance
Two shorts made for the Essanay Company in 1915 which offer the Little Tramp wooing Edna Purviance in typical Chaplin fashion. Silent with musical score.
Essanay — Video Yesteryear

Trampa Mortal, La   195?
Western
86186   80 mins   C   B, V   P
Luis Aguilary, Flor Silvestre
A Spanish singing cowboy fights and wins the girl.
SP
Spanish — Unicorn Video

Tramplers, The   1966
Western
84864   103 mins   C   B, V   P
Joseph Cotten, Gordon Scott
A rebel father and son split over the hanging of a Yankee during the Civil War.
Albert Band — Embassy Home Entertainment

Trancers   1985
Science fiction
82459   76 mins   C   B, V, LV   P
Tim Thomerson, Michael Stefoni, Helen Hunt
A time-traveling zombie cult from the future goes back in time to 1985 to meddle with fate. Only Jack Deth, defender of justice can save humankind.
MPAA:PG-13
Altor Productions — Vestron Video

Transatlantic Tunnel   1935
Science fiction
01694   70 mins   B/W   B, V   P
Richard Dix, Leslie Banks, Madge Evans, Helen Vinson, directed by Maurice Elvey
Based on Bernard Kellerman's novel, an undersea tunnel from England to America is built despite financial trickery.
Gaumont British — Hollywood Home Theater; Video Connection; Cable Films

Transformers, The   1986
Cartoons
71348   30 mins   C   B, V   P
Animated
This series of single-episode tapes shows the residents of Cybertron at their transforming best.
Sunbow Productions/Marvel Productions — Family Home Entertainment

Transformers: More than Meets the Eye, The
1985
Cartoons/Adventure
70651   60 mins   C   B, V   P
Animated
This presentation shows the popular TV characters finding that appearances can be deceiving. Available in Hi-Fi stereo.
Sunbow Productions/Marvel Productions — *Family Home Entertainment*

Transformers: The Ultimate Doom, The
1985
Cartoons
70652   60 mins   C   B, V   P
Animated
The popular TV characters discover that all preceding dooms pale when compared to their current dilemma. Available in Hi-Fi stereo.
Sunbow Productions/Marvel Productions — *Family Home Entertainment*

Transylvania 6-5000
1985
Comedy
Closed Captioned
84118   93 mins   C   B, V, LV   P
Jeff Goldblum, Joseph Bologna, Ed Begley Jr, Carol Kane, John Byner, directed by Rudy DeLuca
Two klutzy reporters stumble into modern-day Transylvania and encounter an array of comedic creatures.
MPAA:PG
Mace Neufeld — *New World Video*

Tranzor Z
1984
Cartoons
70722   60 mins   C   B, V   P
Animated
Robots, ingenious kids and evil scientists battle for the fate of the universe. Six one-hour episodes available.
Three B Prods Ltd — *Sony Video Software*

Trap, The
1959
Crime-Drama
85264   84 mins   C   B, V   P
Richard Widmark, Tina Louise, Lee J. Cobb, Earl Holliman
In trying to escape justice, a ruthless crime syndicate boss holds a small desert town in a grip of fear.
Paramount — *Kartes Video Communications*

Trap on Cougar Mountain
1972
Adventure
81218   97 mins   C   B, V, LV   P
Erik Larsen, Keith Larsen, Karen Steele
A young boy begins a crusade to save his animal friends from the traps and bullets of hunters. Available in VHS and Beta Hi-Fi.
MPAA:G

Manson International Pictures — *New World Video*

Trapeze
1956
Drama
68227   105 mins   C   B, V, CED   P
Burt Lancaster, Tony Curtis, Gina Lollabrigida
The story of three people who want to perform the mid-air triple somersault, an almost impossible feat.
Susan Productions — *CBS/Fox Video*

Trauma
1985
Horror
81033   90 mins   C   B, V   P
Fabio Testi, Arthur Kennedy
A policeman uncovers a bizarre connection between a girls' school and a villa which caters to the kinkier needs of rich men.
MPAA:R
Empire Entertainment — *Wizard Video*

Travel Tips
1985
Travel
84626   60 mins   C   B, V   P
Hosted by Laura Mackenzie 12 pgms
This series of travelogues offers advice pertaining to a variety of vacation spots around the globe.
1.Athens 2.Spain 3.London 4.Paris 5.San Francisco 6.Los Angeles 7.Hawaii 8.Ireland 9.Morocco 10.Egypt 11.Switzerland 12.Rome.
Associated Entertainment — *Republic Pictures Home Video*

Travel Video Series
1985
Travel
86379   30 mins   C   B, V   P
A series of vacation planners focusing on indigenous American locales.
1.New Orleans 2.Orlando 3.Cayman Islands 4.Old West Trail Country 5.Royal Viking Line 6.Florida Gulf Coast 7.Tropicale 8.Festivale 9.Ski Colorado 10.Ski Vermont
Travel Video Corp. — *Travel Video Corporation*

Traviata, La
1983
Opera
65517   105 mins   C   B, V, LV, CED   P
Teresa Stratas, Placido Domingo, Cornell MacNeil, Alan Monk, Axelle Gall, Pina Cei
A film version of Giuseppe Verdi's opera classic. In stereo VHS and Beta Hi-Fi.
MPAA:G
Universal Classics; Accent Films — *MCA Home Video*

Treasure
1984
Games
72907   60 mins   C   B, V, LV   P

An actual treasure hunt is presented on this tape. Viewers are given clue questions which will lead to a jackpot of a half-million dollars which is hidden somewhere in the United States.
Renan Productions — *Vestron Video*

Treasure Island   1934
Adventure
56756   102 mins   B/W   B, V, CED   P
Wallace Beery, Jackie Cooper, Lionel Barrymore, Nigel Bruce, directed by Victor Fleming
A stirring adaptation of Robert Louis Stevenson's pirate tale about Long John Silver and young Jim Hawkins, set in eighteenth-century England.
MGM, Hunt Stromberg — *MGM/UA Home Video*

Treasure Island   1950
Adventure
58625   87 mins   C   B, V, LV   P
Bobby Driscoll, Robert Newton, Basil Sydney, directed by Byron Haskin
Robert Louis Stevenson's spine-tingling tale of pirates and buried treasure, in which young cabin boy Jim Hawkins matches wits with Long John Silver.
MPAA:G
Walt Disney Productions — *Walt Disney Home Video; RCA VideoDiscs*

Treasure of Bengal (El   197?
Tesoro de Bengala), The
Adventure
88311   95 mins   C   B, V   P
A young Hindu must track down the robbers of his village's famous ruby.
SP
Spanish — *JCI Video*

Treasure of Fear   1945
Comedy/Mystery
81739   66 mins   B/W   B, V   P
Jack Haley, Barton MacLane, Ann Savage
A bungling newspaper reporter gets involved with four jade chessmen once owned by Kubla Khan.
Paramount — *Kartes Video Communications; Movie Buff Video*

Treasure of Matecumbe   1976
Adventure
88197   107 mins   C   B, V   P
Billy Attmore, Robert Foxworth, Joan Hackett, Peter Ustinov, Vic Morrow
A children's film dealing with a motley crew of adventurers led by a young boy searching after buried treasure. They are pursued by Indians and other foes.
Walt Disney Prod. — *Walt Disney Home Video*

Treasure of Pancho Villa,   1955
The
Western
84024   96 mins   C   B, V   P
Rory Calhoun, Shelley Winters, Gilbert Roland, directed by George Sherman
An American adventurer plots a gold heist to help Villa's revolution, and encounters every western obstacle on his way to the Mexican rebel.
RKO Radio — *United Home Video*

Treasure of the Amazon   1984
Adventure
82423   105 mins   C   B, V   P
Stuart Whitman, Donald Pleasance, Bradford Dillman, John Ireland, directed by Rene Cardona Jr
Three fortune hunters embark on a perilous search for wealth in the South American jungles.
Video Media — *Vestron Video*

Treasure of the Four   1982
Crowns
Adventure/Suspense
65107   97 mins   C   B, V, CED   P
Tony Anthony
An aging history professor hires a team of tough commandos to recover four legendary crowns containing the source of mystical powers. The crowns are being held under heavy guard by a crazed cult leader. VHS in stereo.
MPAA:PG
Cannon Films — *MGM/UA Home Video*

Treasure of the Lost   1983
Desert
War-Drama
84891   93 mins   C   B, V   P
Bruce Miller, Susan West, Larry Finch
A Green Beret crushes a terrorist operation in the Mid-East.
A and Z Co Ltd — *Lightning Video*

Treasure of the Sierra   1948
Madre, The
Adventure
76041   124 mins   B/W   B, V   P
Humphrey Bogart, Walter Huston
The fate that brings three soldier-of-fortune prospectors together during the days of the gold rush tempts them onward through many hardships for the sake of finding gold.
Warner Bros — *Key Video*

Treasure of the Sierra   1948
Madre, The
Drama
44948   126 mins   B/W   B, V, CED   P
Humphrey Bogart, Walter Huston, Tim Holt, Bruce Bennett, directed by John Huston

Greed and suspicion surround three prospectors in their search for gold.
Academy Awards '48: Best Supporting Actor (Huston); Best Director (Huston); Best Screenplay (Huston)
Warner Bros. — *Key Video; RCA VideoDiscs*

Treasure of the Yankee Zephyr   1983
Adventure
65480   97 mins   C   B, V   P
Ken Wahl, George Peppard, Lesley Ann Warren
A trio join in the quest for a plane that has been missing for 40 years... with a cargo of $50 million.
MPAA:PG
Film Ventures — *Vestron Video*

Treasure Seekers, The   1979
Adventure
80496   88 mins   C   B, V   P
Rod Taylor, Stuart Whitman, Elke Sommer, Keenan Wynn, Jeremy Kemp
Four rival divers set off on a perilous Caribbean expedition in search of the legendary treasure of Morgan the Pirate.
Stuart Whitman Inc — *MGM/UA Home Video*

Trenchcoat   1983
Comedy
66052   95 mins   C   B, V   P
Margot Kidder, Robert Hays
A detective spoof in which an aspiring mystery writer travels to Malta where she is drawn into a real-life conspiracy.
Jerry Leider — *Walt Disney Home Video*

Trespasser, The   1985
Drama
85872   90 mins   C   B, V   P
Alan Bates, Dinah Stabb, Pauline Morgan, Margaret Whiting
Based on D.H. Lawrence's novel, this film deals with a painter who has an affair with a young woman, only to regret walking out on his family.
Epic Pictures — *Magnum Entertainment*

Trial, The   1963
Drama
03893   118 mins   B/W   B, V   P
Orson Welles, Anthony Perkins, Jeanne Moreau
Government employee in unnamed country is arrested, harassed and examined endlessly but never told nature of his crime. Based on Franz Kafka's novel.
Gibraltar Prod; Landeau Unger — *Hollywood Home Theater; Western Film & Video Inc; Discount Video Tapes; Cable Films; Classic Video Cinema Collector's Club*

Trial of Lee Harvey Oswald, The   1977
Drama
84083   192 mins   C   B, V   P
Ben Gazzara, Lorne Greene, John Pleshette
This made-for-TV film deals with what would've happened if Jack Ruby had not shot Oswald and his subsequent trial and imprisonment. In 2 volumes.
Charles Fries Productions — *Worldvision Home Video*

Trial of the Catonsville Nine, The   1972
Drama
65190   85 mins   C   B, V   P
Ed Flanders, Douglass Watson, William Schallert, directed by Gordon Davidson
A riveting political drama that focuses on the trial of nine anti-war activists, including Father Daniel Berrigan, during the Vietnam War days of the late '60s.
MPAA:PG
Cinema 5 — *RCA/Columbia Pictures Home Video*

Triangle Factory Fire Scandal, The   1978
Drama
81815   98 mins   C   B, V   P
Stephanie Zimbalist, Tovah Feldshuh, David Dukes, Tom Bosley, Ted Wass, Stacey Nelkin
This is the true story of how poor working conditions in a lower Manhattan sweatshop led to a tragic fire claiming 146 lives. Available in VHS Stereo and Beta Hi-Fi.
Alan Landsburg Productions — *U.S.A. Home Video*

Tribute   1980
Drama
55744   123 mins   C   B, V, LV,   P
                                              CED
Jack Lemmon, Robby Benson, Lee Remick, directed by Bob Clark
Bernard Slade's play, brought to the screen, about Scotty Templeton, a dying man determined to achieve a reconciliation with his son. The tense conflict between father and son plays out against Scotty's fight for life, weaving moments of high comedy into the drama.
MPAA:PG
Joel B Michaels; Garth H Drabinsky — *Vestron Video*

Tribute to Billie Holiday, A   1979
Music-Performance
42923   57 mins   C   B, V   P
This tribute to Billie Holiday features the talents of Nina Simone, Maxine Weldon, Morganna King, Carmen McRae, and Esther Phillips. The orchestra was arranged and conducted by Ray

Ellis with additional arranging by Tommy
Newsom.
Jack Sidney III — *Media Home Entertainment*

MCA Home Video; Steve Wozniak — *MCA
Home Video*

Trick or Treats — 1982
Horror
70153   90 mins   C   B, V   P
Carrie Snodgrass, David Carradine
A strange twist of fate causes a young boy's
pranks to backfire on Halloween night.
MPAA:R
Lone Star Pictures — *Vestron Video*

Trilogy of Terror — 1975
Horror/Suspense
78145   78 mins   C   B, V   P
Karen Black
Karen Black stars in three short horror tales
from the pen of Richard Matheson, showing her
versatility as she plays a tempting seductress, a
mousy schoolteacher and the terrified victim of
an African Zuni fetish doll.
MPI Home Video — *MPI Home Video*

Trimnastics — 1980
Physical fitness
50096   50 mins   C   B, V, 3/4U   P
Rebecca Levas
An aerobic exercise routine set to music.
Valuable both as a general fitness program and
a weight loss program.
VideoSports — *VideoSports*

Trinity Is Still My Name — 1975
Western
08481   117 mins   C   B, V, CED   P
Bud Spencer, Terrence Hill
Petty rustler brothers, unconcerned with danger
or hopeless odds, endure mishaps and
adventures as they try to right wrongs.
MPAA:G
Avco Embassy — *Embassy Home
Entertainment*

Trip, The — 1967
Fantasy
69288   85 mins   C   B, V   P
*Peter Fonda, Dennis Hopper, Susan Strasberg,
Bruce Dern*
Written by Jack Nicholson, this film is a
psychedelic journey to the world of inner
consciousness.
American International — *Vestron Video*

Triumph—Live at the US Festival — 1983
Music-Performance
85873   60 mins   C   B, V   P
The Canadian rock band Triumph performs at
the US festival.

Triumph of Sherlock Holmes — 1935
Mystery
01760   84 mins   B/W   B, V   P
*Arthur Wontner, Ian Fleming, directed by Leslie
Hiscott*
Sherlock Holmes' retirement is short-lived as a
series of bizarre murders bring him back into
action.
Unknown — *Hollywood Home Theater; Cable
Films; Discount Video Tapes; See Hear
Industries*

Triumph of the Will — 1934
Documentary/Propaganda
48850   110 mins   B/W   B, V, 3/4U   P
Directed by Leni Riefenstahl
This classic record of the Sixth Nazi Party
Congress in Nuremburg retains its compelling
power through impressive photography and
camera movement. Dialogue in German.
GE
Leni Riefenstahl — *Western Film & Video Inc;
Video Yesteryear; International Historic Films;
Discount Video Tapes; Kartes Video
Communications; Festival Films*

Triumph of the Will — 1934
Propaganda/Documentary
85222   110 mins   B/W   B, V   P
The infamous Nazi propaganda piece directed
by Leni Riefenstahl, which documents the 1934
Nuremburg rally. Easily the greatest propaganda
film ever made and one the finest
documentaries.
The Third Reich — *Video Yesteryear; Kartes
Video Communications*

Triumphs of a Man Called Horse — 1982
Western
73019   91 mins   C   B, V   P
Richard Harris
An indian must save his people from
prospectors in order to keep his title as Peace,
Chief of the Yellow Hand Sioux.
MPAA:R
Cinema Center — *THORN EMI/HBO Video*

Trojan Women, The — 1971
Drama
65211   105 mins   C   B, V   P
Katharine Hepburn, Vanessa Redgrave
This program is strongly anti-war in its telling. All
of the Trojan warriors and princes have been
killed and the Conquerors must divide the only
remains of the war—the Trojan women and their
children.
MPAA:G

Josef Shaftel Productions — *U.S.A. Home Video; Films for the Humanities*

Troll   1985
Fantasy
86358   86 mins   C   B, V, LV   P
Sonny Bono, Shelley Hack, June Lockhart, Michael Moriarty
A malevolent troll haunts an apartment building in hopes of turning all humans into trolls.
MPAA:PG-13
Empire Prod. — *Vestron Video*

Trolls and the Christmas Express, The   1974
Cartoons/Christmas
82524   25 mins   C   B, V   P
Animated, voices by Roger Miller, Hans Conried
Mischievous trolls threaten to keep Santa Claus from delivering his gifts in this whimsical cartoon.
Pooled Film Services — *Paramount Home Video*

Tron   1982
Science fiction
63128   96 mins   C   B, V, LV,   P
                              CED
Jeff Bridges, Bruce Boxleitner, David Warner, Cindy Morgan, Barnard Hughes, directed by Steven Lisberger
A video game designer is sucked into a computer and finds that he must do battle with his own creations in order to survive.
MPAA:PG
Walt Disney Productions — *Walt Disney Home Video; RCA VideoDiscs*

Trottie True   1949
Comedy
82281   98 mins   C   B, V   P
Jean Kent, James Donald, Hugh Sinclair, Lana Morris, Andrew Crawford
Trottie True is a showgirl during the gay nineties whose storybook marriage turns sour when she has a chance meeting with a balloonist.
Eagle-Lion; J Arthur Rank — *Unicorn Video*

Trouble in Mind   1986
Romance
Closed Captioned
87619   111 mins   C   B, V, LV   P
Kris Kristofferson, Keith Carradine, Genevieve Bujold, Lori Singer, Divine, directed by Alan Rudolph
The widely acclaimed romance by the idiosyncratic director about four losers making their way in an abstracted urban fringe town. Unique and original, and the only film that features Divine in a non-transvestite role. Music by Mark Isham.
MPAA:R

Island Alive — *Charter Entertainment*

Trouble in Texas   1937
Western
08795   65 mins   B/W   B, V, 3/4U   P
Tex Ritter, Rita Hayworth
Outlaws go to a rodeo and try to steal the prize money.
Grand Natl — *Discount Video Tapes; United Home Video*

Trouble in the Glen   1954
Drama
76828   91 mins   C   B, V   P
Orson Welles, Victor McLaughlin, Forrest Tucker, Margaret Lockwood
An American soldier becomes involved in a Scottish small town's dispute between the town residents and a laird over a closed road.
Republic Pictures — *Republic Pictures Home Video*

Trouble with Angels, The   1966
Comedy
68266   112 mins   C   B, V   P
Hayley Mills, June Harding, Rosalind Russell, Gypsy Rose Lee, Binnie Barnes, directed by Ida Lupino
Two young girls turn a convent upside down with their endless practical jokes.
Columbia — *RCA/Columbia Pictures Home Video*

Trouble with Father   195?
Comedy
53092   50 mins   B/W   B, V, 3/4U   P
Stu Erwin, June Erwin
Two episodes of the classic comedy series about a bumbling father whose every attempt to fix something, surprise someone, or raise his kids turned to disaster. Also titled "The Stu Erwin Show": "Yvette" (1954), in which Stu wants to surprise June with an unusual gift—a lifelike female mannequin; "What Paper Do You Read?" in which Stu enrolls in an evening class on government.
ABC — *Shokus Video*

Trouble with Harry, The   1955
Mystery/Comedy
80075   90 mins   C   B, V, LV   P
John Forsythe, Shirley MacLaine, Edmund Gwenn, Jerry Mathers, directed by Alfred Hitchcock
When a little boy finds a dead body in a Vermont town, it causes all kinds of problems for the members of the community.
MPAA:PG
Alfred Hitchcock; Universal Classics — *MCA Home Video*

Troyens, Les   1983
Opera
86882   253 mins   C   B, V   P
Tatiana Troyanos, Jessye Norman, Placido
Domingo, Allan Monk
Conducted by James Levine, the Metropolitan
Opera performs Berlioz's epic opera, with
English subtitles.
AM Available
Metropolitan Opera; Paramount — Paramount
Home Video

Truck Stop Women   1975
Adventure
64882   88 mins   C   B, V, CED   P
Claudia Jennings
Female truckers become involved in smuggling
on the highway.
Mark Lester — Vestron Video

True Confessions   1981
Drama
59849   110 mins   C   B, V, LV,   P
                               CED
Robert DeNiro, Robert Duvall, Ken McMillan,
Charles Durning, Burgess Meredith, Louisa
Moritz, directed by Ulu Grosbard
John Gregory Dunne's novel about two
brothers, one a priest and the other a detective,
who are pitted against each other in a tale of
corruption in the Church, provides the basis for
this film.
MPAA:R
United Artists — MGM/UA Home Video

True Game of Death, The   197?
Martial arts/Adventure
47695   90 mins   C   B, V   P
Bruce Lee, Shou Lung
A story of the circumstances behind the death
of superstar Bruce Lee.
Ho Shin Motion Picture Co Ltd — Master Arts
Video

True Glory, The   1945
World War II/Documentary
50643   85 mins   B/W   B, V, FO   P
Directed by Garson Kanin
An account of the teamwork between British
and American troops in World II from the
Normandy Invasion to the Allied Occupation of
Germany.
Academy Award '45: Best Documentary
Feature.
US War Dept; British Ministry of
Information — Video Yesteryear; National
AudioVisual Center

True Grit   1969
Western
38621   128 mins   C   B, V, LV   P
John Wayne, Glen Campbell, Kim Darby, Robert
Duvall, directed by Henry Hathaway

John Wayne portrays U.S. Marshal Rooster
Cogburn, who is hired by a young girl to find her
father's killer, in this popular film that won
Wayne his only Oscar.
Academy Awards '69: Best Actor (Wayne).
MPAA:G
Paramount — Paramount Home Video; RCA
VideoDiscs

True Heart Susie   1919
Film-History
11389   87 mins   B/W   B, V, FO   P
Lillian Gish, Robert Harring, directed by D.W.
Griffith
A simple, moving story about a girl who is in love
with a man who marries a girl from the city.
(Silent.)
Artcraft — Video Yesteryear; Discount Video
Tapes

Truite, La (The Trout)   1983
Drama
76033   80 mins   C   B, V   P
Isabelle Huppert, Jean-Pierre Cassel, Daniel
Olbrychski, Jeanne Moreau
A young woman leaves her family's trout farm to
embark on a journey around the world.
MPAA:R
Yves Rousset-Rouard — RCA/Columbia
Pictures Home Video

Truly Tasteless Jokes   1985
Comedy-Performance
80682   60 mins   C   B, V, CED   P
Marsha Warfield, Denny Johnson, Andrew
"Dice" Clay
This is a video version of the popular best-
selling book featuring appearances by top
comedians.
Alamance Company — Vestron Video

Truman Capote's "The   1973
Glass House"
Drama
52394   91 mins   C   B, V, 3/4U,   R, P
                          FO
Vic Morrow, Clu Gulager, Billy Dee Williams,
Alan Alda, Kris Tabori, Dean Jagger
This program offers a look at the chilling
realities of prison life and the power struggle
among the inmates. Based on a story by
Truman Capote.
AM Available
Tomorrow Entertainment — Learning Corp of
America; Hollywood Home Theater

Trumpet and I, The   1985
Fantasy
81880   53 mins   C   B, V   P
An eight-year-old boy inherits magical powers
when he plays a "silver sounding" trumpet.
Londonderry Group — Video Gems

Truth About UFO's & ET's, The   1982
Speculation/Occult sciences
66030   90 mins   C   B, V   P
Brad Steiger, the world's leading investigator of the psychic and extraterrestrial examines UFO's, ET's, impossible fossils, poltergeists and "Star People".
Atlan Productions — *United Home Video*

Tubby the Tuba   1977
Musical/Fantasy
69527   81 mins   C   B, V, CED   P
Animated voices of Dick Van Dyke, Pearl Bailey, Jack Gilford, Hermione Gingold
Tubby the Tuba searches for a melody he can call his own. In stereo.
MPAA:G
Alexander Schure Productions — *Children's Video Library*

Tubes...Live at the Greek, The   1979
Music-Performance
65214   60 mins   C   B, V   P
Rock 'n' roll's most outrageous group appear in a night of pure musical madness. In Beta Hi-Fi and stereo VHS.
The Tubes — *Monterey Home Video*

Tubes Video, The   1981
Music-Performance
58466   53 mins   C   B, V   P
This program is built around songs on the Tubes LP, "The Completion Backward Principle" but also features new numbers and a few older hits.
EMI Music — *THORN EMI/HBO Video; Pioneer Artists; RCA VideoDiscs*

Tuck Everlasting   1985
Cartoons
82473   90 mins   C   B, V   P
Animated
A dreamy young girl befriends a family with an incredible secret. Based on the story by Natalie Babbitt.
Vestron Video — *Vestron Video*

Tuff Turf   1985
Drama
81214   113 mins   C   B, V, LV   P
James Spader, Kim Richards, Paul Mones, Matt Clark, Olivia Barash, Catya Sassoon
The new kid in a lower class section of Los Angeles engages the local toughs in a bitter turf dispute. Music by Jim Carroll, Lene Lovich, and Southside Johnny.
MPAA:R
New World Pictures — *New World Video*

Tulips   1981
Comedy/Romance
69543   91 mins   C   B, V, CED   P
Gabe Kaplan, Bernadette Peters, Henry Gibson
A would-be suicide takes a contract out on himself, and then meets a woman who makes life worth living again. Together they attempt to evade the gangland hit man.
MPAA:PG
Astral Bellevue Pathe Bennettfilms Inc — *Embassy Home Entertainment*

Tulsa   1949
Western
03995   96 mins   C   B, V   P
Susan Hayward, Robert Preston, Chill Wills
High spirited rancher's daughter begins crusade against oil drillers when her father is killed.
Eagle Lion; Walter Wanger — *Hal Roach Studios; World Video Pictures; Movie Buff Video; Nostalgia Merchant; Hollywood Home Theater; Discount Video Tapes; Kartes Video Communications*

Tumbleweeds   1925
Western
38980   114 mins   B/W   B, V, FO   P
William S Hart, Lucien Littlefield, Barbara Bedford, directed by King Baggot
This, William S. Hart's last western, is the story of the last great land rush in America, the opening of the Oklahoma Territory to homesteaders. The film is preceded by a sound prologue, made in 1939, in which Hart speaks for the only time on screen, to introduce the story. Silent, with musical score.
United Artists — *Video Yesteryear; Blackhawk Films*

Tumbleweeds   1925
Western
15501   79 mins   B/W   B, V   P
William S. Hart, Lucien Littlefield, Barbara Bedford, directed by King Baggott
Story of the newly-opened Cherokee Strip. Cowboy is mistaken for a "sooner"—one who sneaks over the boundary line to stake a claim sooner than the government's official starting time. Silent classic.
United Artists — *Video Connection; Discount Video Tapes; Hollywood Home Theater; Western Film & Video Inc*

Tunes of Glory   1960
Drama
50955   107 mins   C   B, V   P
Alec Guiness, John Mills, Dennis Price, Kay Walsh, Susannah York
A struggle develops between two British officers, one who follows traditionally strict methods, and the other, who is up from the ranks and willing to relax his troops.

United Artists; Lopert — *Embassy Home Entertainment*

Tunisian Victory   1943
World War II
87659   74 mins   B/W   B, V   P
Using real footage, the Allied Forces' efforts in North Africa during the War are detailed.
U.S. Army; British — *Victory Video*

Tunnelvision   1976
Satire
52866   75 mins   C   B, V   P
Larraine Newman, Chevy Chase
A spoof of television comprised of irreverent sketches.
MPAA:R
Worldwide Film Corp — *HarmonyVision*

Turandot   1983
Opera
65660   138 mins   C   B, V   P
Set in Peking, Puccini's opera opens with the proclamation that Princess Turandot will become the bride of the royal suitor who can successfully answer 3 riddles. Unsuccessful suitors lose not only the hand of the princess, but their heads as well.
ORF Productions — *MGM/UA Home Video*

Turandot   1983
Music-Performance/Opera
81486   135 mins   C   B, V   P
Nicola Martinucci, Cecillia Gasdia, Ivo Vinco
The legend of Princess Turandot comes alive in this production of the Puccini opera taped at the Arena di Verona in Rome.
National Video Corporation Ltd. — *THORN EMI/HBO Video*

Turk 182!   1985
Comedy-Drama
Closed Captioned
81411   96 mins   C   B, V   P
Timothy Hutton, Robert Culp, Robert Urich, Kim Catrall, Peter Boyle, Darren McGavin, directed by Bob Clark
The angry brother of a disabled fireman takes on City Hall in order to win back the pension that he deserves. Available in VHS and Beta Hi-Fi.
MPAA:PG13
20th Century Fox — *CBS/Fox Video*

Turn of the Screw, The   — 1974
Horror/Drama
70870   120 mins   C   B, V   P
Lynn Redgrave, Jasper Jacobs, Eva Griffith, directed by Dan Curtis
Supernatural powers vie with a young governess for control of the souls of the two children in her charge.
Dan Curtis Productions — *Thriller Video*

Turning Point, The   1979
Drama
44933   119 mins   C   B, V, CED   P
Shirley MacLaine, Anne Bancroft, Mikhail Baryshnikov, directed by Herbert Ross
A woman who gave up ballet for motherhood must come to terms with herself as her daughter's ballet career is launched.
MPAA:PG EL, SP
20th Century Fox — *CBS/Fox Video*

Tut: The Boy King   1977
Archeology/Museums
02810   52 mins   C   B, V   P
Narrated by Orson Welles
Welles' narration eloquently describes some of the treasures viewed by Howard Carter when he first opened the tomb of King Tut in 1922 in this exciting artistic experience.
George Foster Peabody Award; Christopher Award.
NBC — *Warner Home Video; Films Inc*

Tut: The Boy King/The   197?
Louvre
Museums/Archeology
47061   100 mins   C   CED   P
Narrated by Orson Welles and Charles Boyer
Two popular documentary programs are combined in this package. "Tut" presents a tour of the marvelous treasures found in Tutankhamen's tomb. "The Louvre" offers an intimate view of the art masterpieces of this most famous of museums.
NBC — *RCA VideoDiscs*

Tuttles of Tahiti, The   1942
Comedy
59648   91 mins   C   B, V   P
Charles Laughton, Jon Hall, Peggy Drake, Victor Francen, Gene Reynolds, Florence Bates, directed by Charles Vidor
Laughton stars as head of the Tuttle clan, the most dedicated group of carefree loafers in the South Pacific.
RKO — *Hollywood Home Theater*

Tuxedo Warrior   1982
Crime-Drama
84266   93 mins   C   B, V   P
John Wyman, Carol Royle, Holly Palance
Set in Africa, this film involves the adventures of a well-dressed mercenary who is caught between the police, diamond thieves and an old girlfriend's bank robbing.
New World Pictures — *New World Video*

Tuxedomoon: Four Major   1985
Events
Music-Performance/Music video
84065   60 mins   C   B, V   P
Tuxedomoon

Live performances from all over the world, interspersed with studio footage and video effects, chronicle the career of this punk group.
Target Video — *Target Video*

T.V. Classics   195?
Drama
71072   55 mins   B/W   B, V   P
Vincent Price, Charles Bronson
This series provides viewers with a glimpse of some of the fine television dramas produced during the 1950's. Tapes include two half-hour programs with a variety of stars.
ABC; CBS; NBC — *MPI Home Video*

TV Variety   195?
Variety
59315   120 mins   B/W   B, V, 3/4U   P
Arthur Godfrey, Ed Sullivan, Mickey Rooney, Jaye P. Morgan, Joey Forman, Joe E. Lewis, Spike Jones
Music, comedy, and dance from TV's "Golden Age": "Arthur Godfrey's Talent Scouts" (1954), a classic live episode; "The Ed Sullivan Show" (1957), season premiere for 1957; and "The Spike Jones Show" (1954), a musical half-hour featuring the entire City Slickers.
CBS;NBC — *Shokus Video*

TV Variety, II   195?
Variety
47614   120 mins   B/W   B, V, 3/4U   P
This tape contains three different vintage programs: "The Walter Winchell Show" (December 31, 1956), with guests Frankie Laine, Lisa Kirk, Jack Carter and Russ Tamblyn; "Texaco Star Theater" (January 18, 1949) with Milton Berle and guests Tony Martin and Carmen Miranda; "Person to Person" with Edward R. Murrow interviewing Groucho Marx (1954) and Harpo Marx (1958). All programs include original commercials and network logos.
NBC — *Shokus Video*

TV Variety III   1950
Variety/Comedy
62690   120 mins   B/W   B, V, 3/4U   P
Bob Hope, Marilyn Maxwell, Jack Carson, Hal March, Jack Gilford
Two complete kinescoped variety shows from 1950: "The Bob Hope Comedy Hour" and "4 Star Revue," hosted by Jack Carson. Original commercials and network I.D.'s are included.
NBC — *Shokus Video*

TV Variety, IV   1951
Variety
62691   60 mins   B/W   B, V, 3/4U   P
Perry Como, Faye Emerson, Fred Waring, Frankie Laine, Patti Page, Frank Fontaine, Tommy Dorsey
Two fifteen-minute programs, "The Perry Como Show" and "The Faye Emerson Show" are

combined with a half-hour "Frankie Laine Show," all from 1950 kinescopes.
CBS et al — *Shokus Video*

TV Variety, V   1956
Variety
66487   115 mins   B/W   B, V   P
Four representative daytime variety shows of the mid-1950's are combined on this tape: "The Garry Moore Show," "Arthur Godfrey Time," "The Robert Q. Lewis Show" and "The Tennessee Ernie Ford Show." Original commercials and network I.D.'s are included.
CBS — *Shokus Video*

TV Variety, VI   1955
Comedy/Variety
76015   120 mins   B/W   B, V, 3/4U   P
Two tv variety shows: "Dinner with the President," with Ethel Merman, Lucy and Desi, Eddie Fisher and many more; "The Perry Como Show," with Rosemary Clooney, Nat King Cole, Rin Tin Tin, and others.
CBS; NBC — *Shokus Video*

TV Variety, VII   1956
Variety
79234   120 mins   B/W   B, V, 3/4U   P
Spike Jones, Jack Benny, Lucille Ball, Desi Arnaz, Shirley MacLane, Van Johnson
Four kinescopes of classic variety shows: "The Ed Wynn Show" (1950); "The Spike Jones Show" (1956); "The Jimmy Durante Show" (1954); and a half hour 1955 Easter Seals telethon hosted by Jack Benny.
NBC et al. — *Shokus Video*

TV Variety, VIII   1957
Variety
79235   115 mins   B/W   B, V, 3/4U   P
Frank Sinatra, Dagmar, Bing Crosby, Jackie Gleason
Three rare kinescopes of variety shows: from 1952, the first "Honeymooners" sketch on "Toast of the Town," "The Frank Sinatra Show" from 1951, and "The Edsel Show" from 1957 featuring Sinatra and Crosby.
ABC et al — *Shokus Video*

TV Variety IX   1954
Variety
82287   115 mins   B/W   B, V, 3/4U   P
Jack Carson, Hal March, Betty Garrett, Robert Alda, Eddie Cantor, Frank Sinatra
Here are two kinescopes of "The Colgate Comedy Hour" hosted by Jack Carson and Eddie Cantor. This tape features the original 1954 TV commercials.
ABC — *Shokus Video*

TV Variety X   1958
Television/Variety
84697   115 mins   B/W   B, V, 3/4U   P
Johnny Carson, Jack Benny, Ralph Edwards, Rudy Vallee, Mack Sennett, Ernie Kovacs
A collection of four classic variety shows of the 50's, including "This is Your Life" (1954), featuring Mack Sennett episodes; two Jack Benny episodes from 1958; and an early "Johnny Carson Show" (1955).
CBS; NBC — *Shokus Video*

TV Variety XI   1953
Comedy/Variety
84698   110 mins   B/W   B, V, 3/4U   P
Vic Damone, Frank Sinatra, Jackie Gleason, Art Carney, Tallulah Bankhead
Two live kinescopes featuring a wide assortment of golden-age goodies: "Cavalcade of Stars" (1951) with Jackie Gleason; and "The Milton Berle Show," with Jan Murray substituting for an ailing Uncle Miltie.
Dumont; NBC — *Shokus Video*

TV Variety, XII   1955
Comedy/Variety
87205   115 mins   B/W   B, V, 3/4U   P
Ernie Kovacs, Ed Wynn, Red Skelton, The Three Stooges, William Frawley
Four episodes from vintage TV comedy/variety series: "The Ernie Kovacs Show," "The Ed Wynn Show," "The Dennis Day Show" and "The Red Skelton Show."
CBS et al. — *Shokus Video*

TV Variety, XIII   1955
Variety/Comedy
87209   120 mins   B/W   B, V, 3/4U   P
Jerry Lewis, Ed Wynn, Buster Keaton, Ralph Edwards, Victor Moore
Three episodes of vintage variety shows: "The Ed Wynn Show," "This Is Your Life" (with surprised guest Buster Keaton) and "Saturday Color Carnival Starring Jerry Lewis," Lewis' first TV appearance after the Martin/Lewis schism. Despite its' name, all the kinescopes on this tape are in black and white.
CBS et al. — *Shokus Video*

TV's Classic Guessing Games   1956
Game show
66460   120 mins   B/W   B, V, 3/4U   P
Arlene Francis, Steve Allen, Dorothy Kilgallen, Deborah Kerr, Lucille Ball, Desi Arnaz, Bill Cullen, Fred Allen, Garry Moore
Four vintage game shows of the 1954-56 seasons are combined on this tape, including three episodes of "What's My Line" and one segment of "I've Got a Secret." Original commercials and network I.D.'s included.
CBS — *Shokus Video*

12th Annual The Great Smith River Canoe Race   1986
Boating
88296   30 mins   C   B, V   R, P
A document of the title race across Crescent Lake in Wolfeboro, New Hampshire.
Hank Madden; Nancy Madden; Video Moviemakers — *Video Moviemakers*

Twelve Angry Men   1957
Drama
64835   95 mins   B/W   B, V   P
Henry Fonda, Martin Balsam, Lee J. Cobb, E.G. Marshall, Jack Klugman, Jack Warden, directed by Sidney Lumet
Based on a TV play by Reginald Rose, this is a classic drama of a deadlocked jury and one man who makes the others listen to reason.
United Artists — *Key Video; RCA VideoDiscs*

Twelve Chairs, The   1970
Comedy
65112   94 mins   C   B, V   P
Mel Brooks, Dom DeLuise, Frank Langella, Ron Moody, directed by Mel Brooks
In 1927 Russia, a rich matron admits on her deathbed that she has hidden her jewels in the upholstery of one of twelve chairs. The chairs, however, are no longer in her home, and a madcap search begins for them.
MPAA:PG
Michael Hertzberg — *Media Home Entertainment*

Twelve Months   1985
Drama
85238   90 mins   C   B, V   P
An animated tale of a young girl who learns by trial and error that kindness is always rewarded.
John Watkins; Simon Nuchtern — *RCA/Columbia Pictures Home Video*

Twelve O'Clock High   1949
War-Drama
29179   132 mins   B/W   B, V   P
Gregory Peck, Hugh Marlowe, Gary Merrill, Millard Mitchell, Dean Jagger
An epic drama about the heroic 8th Air Force. Peck, as a bomber-group commander, is forced to drive his men to the breaking point in the fury of battle.
Academy Awards '49: Best Supporting Actor (Jagger)
20th Century Fox — *CBS/Fox Video*

Twelve Tasks of Asterix, The   1984
Cartoons
73791   81 mins   C   B, V   P
Animated

The gallant warrior Asterix matches brains and brawn with Caesar and the entire Roman Empire.
Productions Dargaud Films — *Walt Disney Home Video*

Twenty Minute Workout   1985
Physical fitness
82421   20 mins   C   B, V   P
Bess Motta, Arlaine Wright, Anne Schumacher, produced by Ron Harris
Three aerobic workouts designed to work specific areas of the body while exercising the cardiovascular system are shown.
Vestron Video — *Vestron Video*

29-Minute Workout, The   1985
Physical fitness
88156   29 mins   C   V   P
A particularly speedy, succinct aerobics workout.
Goodtimes Home Video — *Goodtimes Home Video*

Twenty Questions   1952
Game show
58637   30 mins   B/W   B, V, FO   P
Hosted by Bill Slater
The "Mennen Mystery Voice" tells the viewing audience what secret object the panel has 20 questions to guess, in this vintage quiz show. Sponsored by Mennen.
Dumont — *Video Yesteryear*

27th Annual Academy   1955
Awards Presentations,
The
Variety
47495   79 mins   B/W   B, V, FO   P
Grace Kelly, Marlon Brando, Humphrey Bogart, Audrey Hepburn, Bing Crosby, William Holden, Bette Davis, hosted by Bob Hope and Thelma Ritter
Telecast on March 30, 1955, this program honored the Oscar winners of 1954 including Grace Kelly, Eva Marie Saint, Edmond O'Brien, Marlon Brando, Walt Disney, Elia Kazan and others. The nominated songs are performed by Johnny Desmond, Tony Martin, Rosemary Clooney, Peggy King and Dean Martin.
NBC — *Video Yesteryear*

20,000 Leagues Under   1973
the Sea
Cartoons
66583   47 mins   C   B, V   P
Animated
An animated version of the Jules Verne classic about Captain Nemo and his submarine.
Hanna-Barbera — *Worldvision Home Video*

20,000 Leagues Under   1954
the Sea
Adventure
44303   127 mins   C   B, V   P
Kirk Douglas, James Mason, Peter Lorre
From a futuristic submarine, Captain Nemo wages war. Battleships and giant squid answer the challenge of Nemo's atomic powered death machine. This adaptation of the Jules Verne classic comes with VHS stereo or Beta Hi-Fi sound.
Academy Award '54: Special Effects.   MPAA:G
Walt Disney Productions — *Walt Disney Home Video; RCA VideoDiscs*

20,000 Leagues Under   1973
the Sea
Cartoons
78902   60 mins   C   B, V   P
Animated
This is an animated version of the Jules Verne classic science fiction novel.
Hanna-Barbera — *Prism*

---

20 Years of World Series   1958
Baseball
49553   40 mins   B/W   B, V   P
A collection of highlights from among the most exciting of the World Series played between 1938 and 1957.
Lew Fonseca — *Major League Baseball Productions*

Twice a Judas   196?
Western
85540   90 mins   C   B, V   P
Klaus Kinski
An amnesiac is swindled and has his family killed by a ruthless renegade. He wants to get even, even though he can't remember who anyone is.
Foreign — *Unicorn Video*

Twice a Woman   1979
Drama
70599   90 mins   C   B, V   P
Bibi Andersson, Anthony Perkins, Sandra Dumas
A man and woman divorce, and then both fall in love with the same provocative young woman.
William Howerd/MGS; Actueel Films — *Prism*

Twice in a Lifetime   1985
Drama
Closed Captioned
85629   117 mins   C   B, V, LV   P
Gene Hackman, Ellen Burstyn, Amy Madigan, Ann-Margret, Brian Dennehy, Ally Sheedy, directed by Bud Yorkin
A middle-aged man, with grown daughters, leaves his unexciting wife for a fling with a vivacious barmaid.
MPAA:R

Bud Yorkin Prods. — *Vestron Video*

Twigs 1984
Theater/Drama
78662   138 mins   C   B, V   P
Cloris Leachman
A taped performance of George Furthis' Tony
Award-winning drama about a mother and her
three daughters who meet the day before
Thanksgiving.
Showtime — *RKO HomeVideo*

Twilight People 1975
Horror
79763   84 mins   C   B, V   P
John Ashley, Pat Woodell, Pam Grier
When a mad scientist's creations turn on him for
revenge, he runs for his life.
MPAA:PG
Dimension Pictures — *United Home Video*

Twilight Zone—The 1983
Movie
Horror
65359   101 mins   C   B, V, LV,   P
                                 CED
Dan Aykroyd, Albert Brooks, Vic Morrow,
Kathleen Quinlan, John Lithgow
Four short horrific tales are anthologized in this
film as a tribute to Rod Serling and his popular
TV series. Three of the episodes, "Kick the
Can," "It's a Good Life" and "Nightmare at
20,000 Feet," are based on original "Twilight
Zone" scripts.
MPAA:PG
Steven Spielberg; John Landis — *Warner*
Home Video

Twilight's Last Gleaming 1977
Suspense
86043   144 mins   C   B, V   P
Burt Lancaster, Charles Durning, Richard
Widmark, Melvyn Douglas, Joseph Cotten, Paul
Winfield, Burt Young, directed by Robert Aldrich
A maverick general takes a SAC missle base
hostage, threatening to start World War III if the
U.S. government doesn't confess to its' Vietnam
policies and crimes.
MPAA:R
Allied Artists — *Key Video*

Twins of Evil 1971
Horror
71186   86 mins   C   B, V   P
Peter Cushing, Dennis Price, Madeleine
Collinson, Mary Collinson, directed by John
Hough
Beautiful female twins fall victim to the local
vampire and only their choirmaster can save
them.
Hammer Films for Rank Org;
Universal — *VidAmerica*

Twirl 1981
Drama
71306   96 mins   C   B, V   P
Stella Stevens, Charles Haid, Lisa Welchel, Erin
Moran, Edd Byrnes, Sharon Spelman, Donna
McKechnie, Heather Locklear, Missy Gold,
Rosalind Chao, directed by Gus Trikonis
Set against the backdrop of the National Baton-
Twirling Championships, this film shows the
parental pressures exerted on the youthful
competitors.
Charles Fries and Atrium Productions — *U.S.A.*
Home Video

Twist 1976
Drama
77385   106 mins   C   B, V   P
Bruce Dern, Ann-Margret, Sydne Rome, Maria
Schell, Charles Aznavour, directed by Claude
Chabrol
A game of cat and mouse ensues when an
American writer and his French wife suspect
each other of infidelity.
Barnabe Productions; Gloria Films — *U.S.A.*
Home Video

Twist of Fate 1984
Music-Performance
66504   19 mins   C   B, V, LV   P
Olivia Newton-John, John Travolta
Six of Olivia Newton-John's music videos are
combined on this tape, including four songs
from the movie "Two of a Kind;" the title tune,
"Livin' in Desperate Times," "Take a Chance"
and "Twist of Fate," plus "Heart Attack" and
"Tied Up." Stereo in all formats.
MCA — *MCA Home Video*

Twisted Brain 1974
Horror
79757   89 mins   C   B, V   P
Pat Cardi, John Niland
When an honor student becomes the unwilling
subject of a biological experiment the result is
something that is half man and half beast.
MPAA:R
Crown International — *United Home Video*

Twisted Cross, The 1956
World War II/Documentary
54835   53 mins   B/W   B, V   P
Narrated by Alexander Scourby
The story of Adolph Hitler and the Nazi
movement is recreated, tracing Hitler's lowly
beginnings in 1923, to his days as conqueror of
the European mainland, to his defeat and
suicide.
NBC; Henry Salomon — *Warner Home Video;*
CRM McGraw Hill

Twisted Sister's Stay Hungry 1984
Music video
72876 120 mins C B, V P
Twisted Sister
A conceptual version of Twisted Sisters' album "Stay Hungry" with concert footage.
Unknown — *Embassy Home Entertainment; Pioneer Artists*

Two Assassins in the Dark 198?
Martial arts
64960 90 mins C B, V P
Wang Tao, Chang Yi, Lung Chun-Eng
A martial arts adventure about a pair of kung-fu killers.
Dragon Lady Productions — *Unicorn Video*

Two Best World Series Ever, The 1978
Baseball
13319 60 mins C B, V P
Cincinnati Reds, Boston Red Sox, New York Yankees, Los Angeles Dodgers
Best plays from the 1975 and 1978 World Series are contained in this program. In '75 Sparky Anderson's Reds prevail in seven games over the Red Sox in one of the most exciting and dramatic series ever. The Yankees come from two games behind in '78 to win their second consecutive championship in six games over the Dodgers.
Warner Qube — *VidAmerica*

Two by Forsyth 1986
Suspense
87683 60 mins C B, V P
Dan O'Herlihy, Cyril Cusack, Milo O'Shea, Shirley Ann Field
Two short films based on stories by Frederick Forsyth, one dealing with a dying millionaire's clever efforts to prevent his fortune from being inherited by greedy relatives, the other about a mild-mannered stamp dealer who avenges himself on a nasty gossip columnist.
Mobil Oil Prod. — *Prism*

Two English Girls 1972
Romance
87333 130 mins C B, V P
Jean-Pierre Leaud, Kika Markham, Stacey Tendeter, directed by Francois Truffaut
Based upon the novel "Les Deux Anglaises et le Continent" by Henri-Pierre Roche, this acclaimed drama by the great director involves a a pre-World War I French lad who loves two English sisters, one an impassioned, reckless artist, the other a repressed spinster. Spanning seven years, the film tenderly delineates the triangle's interrelating love and friendship. Restored by Truffaut to its full length.

Roissy — *Key Video*

Two Faces of Evil, The 1982
Horror
81040 60 mins C B, V P
Anna Calder-Marshall, Gary Raynmond, Pauline Delany, Philip Latham
A family's vacation turns into a night of unbearable terror when they pick up a sinister hitchhiker.
Hammer Films — *Thriller Video*

Two-Getherness 1984
Video
73629 5 mins C B, V P
On this reusable two hour video cassette is a brief friendship message.
Kartes Productions — *Kartes Video Communications*

Two Graves to Kung-Fu 1982
Martial arts/Adventure
59994 95 mins C B, V R, P
Liu Chia-Yung, Shek Kin, Chen Hung-Lieh
A young kung-fu student is framed for murder. When the real murderers kill his teacher, he escapes from prison to seek revenge.
MPAA:R
L and T Films Corp Ltd — *Video Gems*

Two Great Cavaliers, The 1973
Martial arts
86890 95 mins C B, V P
Chen Shing, Mao Ying, directed by Yeung Ching Chen
A Ming warrior has a hard time with the Manchurian army, fending it off as he must with only his bare instep, heel and wrist.
Hong Kong — *Unicorn Video*

Two Gun Man 1931
Western
15463 60 mins B/W B, V P
Ken Maynard
America's first singing cowboy, Ken Maynard, performs hair-raising stunts amidst cactus and other drought-resistant plants.
Tiffany — *Video Connection; Discount Video Tapes; United Home Video*

Two Gun Troubador 1937
Western/Musical
84874 59 mins B/W B, V P
Fred Scott, Claire Rochelle, John Merton
A masked singing cowboy troubador uncovers his father's murderer.
Spectrum — *Kartes Video Communications*

200 Motels 1971
Comedy/Musical
75538 99 mins C B, V P

Frank Zappa, Ringo Starr, The Mothers of
Invention
A story of what happens to a rock group that
has been on the road too long.
MPAA:R
Murakami Wolf Productions Inc — MGM/UA
Home Video

Two Kennedys, The   1981
Drama
69038   118 mins   C   B, V   P
This film deals extensively with the mystery
surrounding the Kennedy family while making
political connections with no holds barred.
Italy — MPI Home Video

Two Lost Worlds   1950
Science fiction
85060   63 mins   B/W   B, V   P
James Arness, Laura Elliott, Bill Kennedy
A young hero battles dinosaurs, pirates and his
own agent.
Fox/Lorber; Norman Dawn — Sony Video
Software

Two Mules for Sister Sara   1970
Western
47425   105 mins   C   B, V   P
Clint Eastwood, Shirley MacLaine, directed by
Don Siegel
An American mercenary in 19th century Mexico
gets mixed up with a cigar-smoking nun. The
two make plans to capture a French garrison.
MPAA:PG
Universal — MCA Home Video

Two of a Kind   1982
Drama
71328   102 mins   C   B, V   P
George Burns, Cliff Robertson, Karla DeVito,
Ronny Cox, Frances Lee McCain, Barbara
Barrie, Robby Benson, directed by Roger Young
A retarded youth helps his grandfather adjust to
his new life in a nursing home.
Lorimar — U.S.A. Home Video

Two Reelers—Comedy   1933
Classics I
Comedy
38971   54 mins   B/W   B, V, FO   P
Edgar Kennedy, Harry Gribbon, Harry Sweet,
Jack Norton, Maxine Jennings, Willie Best
This package includes a 1944 Edgar Kennedy
short, "Feather Your Nest" (RKO), and two
1933 films, "How Comedies Are Born" and
"Dog Blight."
RKO — Video Yesteryear

Two Reelers—Comedy   194?
Classics II
Comedy
38972   53 mins   B/W   B, V, FO   P

Leon Errol, Dorothy Granger, Billy Gilbert, Edgar
Kennedy
A second package of three vintage shorts:
"Chicken Feed" (1939) with Billy Gilbert, "Twin
Husbands" (1946) with Leon Errol, and Edgar
Kennedy in "False Roomers" (1938).
RKO — Video Yesteryear

Two Reelers—Comedy   194?
Classics III
Comedy
38973   52 mins   B/W   B, V, FO   P
Edgar Kennedy, Jed Prouty
More laughs, with two Edgar Kennedy shorts,
"A Merchant of Menace" (1933), and "Social
Terrors" (1946). Also, Jed Prouty is featured in
"Coat Tales" (193).
RKO — Video Yesteryear

Two Reelers—Comedy   1935
Classics #6
Comedy
85504   59 mins   B/W   B, V   P
Charles Sale, Goodman Ace, the Little Rascals
Three vintage comedy shorts: "Lem Putt, The
Specialist," "Dumb Luck" and "Our Gang
Follies of 1938."
Hal Roach; Educational; et al. — Video
Yesteryear

Two Reelers—Comedy   1936
Classics IV
Comedy
38970   56 mins   B/W   B, V, FO   P
Bert Lahr, Gene Austin, June Brewster, Carol
Tevis, Grady Sutton
"Bridal Bail" (1934), "No More West"
(Educational-1934) with Bert Lahr singing and
clowning, and "Bad Medicine" (1936) with
crooner Gene Austin comprise this comedy
package.
RKO — Video Yesteryear

Two Reelers—Comedy   19??
Classics #5
Comedy
69556   55 mins   B/W   B, V, FO   P
Leon Errol, the Ritz Brothers, Charlotte
Greenwood
A compilation of three vintage comedy shorts by
popular stars of the 1930's: "Dear Deer" (1942)
with Leon Errol, "Hotel Anchovy" (1934) with
the Ritz Brothers and "Love Your Neighbor"
(1930) with Charlotte Greenwood.
Educational — Video Yesteryear

2001: A Space Odyssey   1968
Science fiction
44639   141 mins   C   B, V, LV,   P
                             CED
Keir Dullea, Gary Lockwood, directed by Stanley
Kubrick

A space voyage to Jupiter turns into chaos when a computer, HAL 9000, takes over, killing several astronauts. This space voyage traces the context of man's history; man vs. the machinery he made.
Academy Awards '68: Best Visual Effects.
MGM — *MGM/UA Home Video*

2020 Texas Gladiators   1985
Adventure
82478   91 mins   C   B, V   P
Harrison Muller, Al Cliver, Daniel Stephen, Peter Hooten, Al Yamanouchi, Sabrina Santi
In the post-nuclear holocaust world, two groups, one good, one evil, battle for supremacy.
Foreign — *Media Home Entertainment*

2010   1984
Science fiction
Closed Captioned
81059   116 mins   C   B, V, LV   P
Roy Scheider, John Lithgow, Helen Mirren, Bob Balaban, Keir Dullea, Madolyn Smith, directed by Peter Hyams
In this sequel to "2001," the United States and Russia reluctantly team up to reclaim the "Discovery" spaceship before its decaying orbit around Jupiter brings it crashing down onto the planet's surface. Based upon the Arthur C. Clarke novel.
MPAA:PG
MGM; Peter Hyams — *MGM/UA Home Video*

2000 Year Old Man, The   1982
Cartoons/Comedy
78347   25 mins   C   B, V   P
Animated, the voices of Carl Reiner and Mel Brooks
This is the animated version of the Mel Brooks-Carl Reiner comedy classic routine, featuring the reminiscences of the bemused patriarch of the past, the 2000 Year Old Man.
MPAA:G
Leo Salkin — *Media Home Entertainment*

Two Tickets to Broadway   1951
Comedy/Musical
57167   106 mins   C   B, V   P
Tony Martin, Janet Leigh, Gloria DeHaven, Smith and Dale
A small-town singer and a crooner arrange a hoax to get themselves on Bob Crosby's TV show.
RKO; Howard Hughes — *King of Video*

Two-Way Stretch   1960
Comedy
47306   84 mins   B/W   B, V   P
Peter Sellers, Wilfrid Hyde-White, Liz Fraser, David Lodge
Three prison inmates in a progressive jail plan to break out, pull a diamond heist, and break back in, all in the same night.

Showcorporation; British — *THORN EMI/HBO Video*

Two Worlds of Jennie Logan, The   1981
Fantasy
75465   99 mins   C   B, V   P
Lindsay Wagner, Linda Gray, Marc Singer, John Darling
A Victorian mansion and antique dress take Jennie Logan back to the turn of the century where she finds romance, intrigue and murder.
King Features — *U.S.A. Home Video*

Two Years to the Title   1982
Football
88075   46 mins   C   B, V   P
Footage of the '81 and '82 seasons of the Washington Redskins is featured.
NFL Films — *NFL Films Video*

Tycoon   1947
Drama
29469   129 mins   C   B, V   P
John Wayne, Laraine Day, Sir Cedric Hardwicke
A young American railroad builder finds action and romance in Latin America.
RKO — *Blackhawk Films; RKO HomeVideo; King of Video*

U

U2 Live at Red Rocks "Under A Blood Red Sky"   19??
Music-Performance
72933   60 mins   C   B, V   P
One of rock's hottest bands is featured, performing songs from their album "Under A Blood Red Sky," filmed in Denver, Colorado.
Steve Lilywhite — *MCA Home Video*

Ub Iwerks Cartoon Festival   193?
Cartoons
29488   57 mins   C   B, V   P, T
Animated
Seven delightful cartoons by one of the pioneering geniuses of animation. Includes: "The Brave Tin Soldier," "Happy Days," "Fiddlesticks," "Jack and the Beanstalk," "The Headless Horseman," and "The Little Red Hen."
Ub Iwerks — *Blackhawk Films*

Ub Iwerks Cartoonfest Two   193?
Cartoons
29489   46 mins   C   B, V   P, T

Animated
More cartoons from the pen of the immortal
Iwerks. Six color masterpieces of such great
tales as "Tom Thumb," "Jack Frost," "Aladdin
and the Wonderful Lamp," "Ali Baba,"
"Sinbad," and "Spooks."
Ub Iwerks — *Blackhawk Films*

Ub Iwerks Cartoonfest Three   193?
Cartoons
59989   30 mins   C   B, V   P, T
Animated
A compilation of Iwerks classics: "Simple
Simon" (1935), "Puss in Boots" (1934), "Dick
Whittington's Cat" (1936), and "Don Quixote"
(1934).
Celebrity Productions — *Blackhawk Films*

Ub Iwerks Cartoonfest Four   1935
Cartoons
62874   30 mins   C   B, V   P, T
Animated
Another collection of enjoyable cartoons from
the pen of Ub Iwerks. Included are "The Valiant
Tailor," "Mary's Little Lamb," and "The
Brementown Musicians" and "Balloonland," all
from 1934-35.
Ub Iwerks — *Blackhawk Films*

UB Iwerks Cartoonfest Five   193?
Cartoons
65705   23 mins   C   B, V   P, T
Animated
Three more fabulous Cinecolor cartoons from
the UB Iwerks studio are combined on this tape:
"Queen of Hearts" (1934), "Old Mother
Hubbard" (1935) and "Humpty Dumpty" (1935),
all from the Comicolor Cartoons series.
Ub Iwerks; Celebrity Productions — *Blackhawk Films*

U.F.O. Live   1986
Music-Performance
86912   60 mins   C   B, V   P
The Misdemeanor tour of the famous music
group is taped live, including "Wreckless,"
"Meanstreets" and "The Chase."
Philip Goodhand-Tait — *Embassy Home Entertainment*

UFO: Top Secret   1979
Documentary/Speculation
84853   96 mins   C   B, V   P
This movie presents various evidence and
theories dealing with the possibility of the
existence of UFO's.
Unknown — *United Home Video*

Ugetsu   1953
Film-Avant-garde
06241   96 mins   B/W   B, V   P
Machiko Kyo, Masayuki Mori, directed by Kenji Mizoguchi
This classic Japanese film depicts the sixteenth-
century legend of a potter and a farmer who
travel in search of their dreams. With English
subtitles.
JA
Harrison Pictures — *Embassy Home
Entertainment; Western Film & Video Inc;
Discount Video Tapes; Video Dimensions; Video
Action; Hollywood Home Theater*

Ultimate Fitness   1984
Physical fitness
81536   60 mins   C   B, V   P
Physical fitness expert Deborah Crocker
demonstrates the Esquire aerobics program
both men and women can do.
AM Available
Esquire Press — *Esquire Video*

Ultimate Swan Lake, The   1984
Dance
70168   126 mins   C   B, V   P
*The Bolshoi Ballet starring Natalia
Bessmertnova, Boris Akimov, Alexander
Bogatyrev, hosted by Gene Kelly*
This dynamic performance of the "Swan Lake"
ballet featured choreography by Yuri
Grigorovich of the world famous Bolshoi Ballet.
In Dolby stereo.
Kultur International Films — *Kultur*

Ultimate Tennis   1985
Tennis
70897   60 mins   C   B, V   P
Al Secunda
Tennis instructor to many Hollywood stars, Al
Secunda offers a series of amusing visual aids
to reinforce some basic rules of racketry.
Magnum Ent Sports — *Magnum Entertainment*

Ultimate Thrill, The   1974
Adventure
59069   84 mins   C   B, V   R, P
Britt Ekland, Barry Brown, Michael Blodgett
A successful man plays Russian Roulette for big
stakes.
General Cinema; Centaur Films — *Video
Gems; World Video Pictures*

Ultimate Warrior, The   1975
Science fiction
82501   92 mins   C   B, V   P
*Yul Brynner, Max Von Sydow, Joanna Miles,
Richard Kelton, Lane Bradbury, William Smith,
directed by Robert Clouse*
Yul Brynner must defend the plants and seeds
of a pioneer scientist to help replenish the
world's food supply in this thriller set in 2012.

MPAA:R
Warner Bros — *Warner Home Video*

Ultra Flash   1983
Dance
65346   60 mins   C   B, V   P
A fantasy that is performed to some of today's
hottest dance music. In stereo
Niles Siegal Organization — *Vestron Video*

Ulysses   1955
Adventure
82502   104 mins   C   B, V   P
*Kirk Douglas, Silvona Mongono, Anthony Quinn,
Rossona Podesta*
A classic epic of ancient Greece, wherein one-
eyed monster Cyclops, resists the charms of
sexy Circe, and ignores the call of the Sirens.
Dino De Laurentiis — *Warner Home Video*

Umberto D   1955
Film-Avant-garde
07140   89 mins   B/W   B, V   P
*Carlo Battista, Maria Pia Casilio, Lina Gennari,
directed by Vittorio De Sica*
A government pensioner, living alone with his
beloved dog, struggles to keep up a semblance
of dignity on his inadequate pension. Italian
Film, English subtitles.
New York Film Critics Award: Best Foreign
Language Film. IT
Dear Films; Italian — *Hollywood Home
Theater; Discount Video Tapes*

Umbrellas of Cherbourg   1963
Musical-Drama
65443   90 mins   C   B, V   P
Catherine Deneuve, Nino Castelnuovo
As a universal statement of love, this tender
story has become a timeless musical classic.
Subtitled in English.
MPAA:G FR
Landau Unger — *U.S.A. Home Video*

Unapproachable, The   1982
Drama
86462   92 mins   C   B, V   P
*Leslie Caron, Daniel Webb, Leslie Malton,
directed by Krzysztof Zanussi*
A rendition of the Polish director's two one-act
plays concerning a reclusive aging stage star
being manipulated by her hangers-on.
Regina Ziegler; 2nd German TV; ORF
Austria — *MGM/UA Home Video*

Unbreakable Alibi, The   1983
Mystery/Suspense
81707   51 mins   C   B, V   P
Francesca Annis, James Warwick
A wealthy young man asks Tommy and
Tuppence Beresford to help him prove that one

of two alibis an Australian journalist created is
false.
London Weekend Television — *Pacific Arts
Video*

Uncanny, The   1978
Horror
47817   85 mins   C   B, V, 3/4U   P
*Peter Cushing, Ray Milland, Samantha Eggar,
Donald Pleasence*
A writer theorizes that a number of mysterious
deaths were caused by a secret society of fatal
felines.
Astral Films — *Media Home Entertainment;
Nostalgia Merchant*

Uncle Sam Magoo   196?
Cartoons/History-US
66037   60 mins   C   B, V   P
Animated, voice of Jim Backus
Mr. Magoo provides a history lesson in his own
inimitable style.
UPA — *Paramount Home Video*

Uncommon Valor   1983
Drama
Closed Captioned
65732   105 mins   C   B, V, 8mm   P
*Gene Hackman, Fred Ward, Reb Brown,
Randall "Tex" Cobb, Robert Stack*
After useless appeals to the government for
information on his son who is listed as "missing
in action" in Vietnam, Colonel Rhodes takes
matters into his own hands.
MPAA:R
John Milius; Buzz Feitshans — *Paramount
Home Video*

Under California Stars   1948
Western
38981   71 mins   C   B, V, FO   P
*Roy Rogers, Andy Devine, Jane Frazee, the
Sons of the Pioneers*
A shady gang making a living rounding up wild
horses decides they can make more money by
capturing Roy Rogers' horse, Trigger.
Republic — *Video Yesteryear; Discount Video
Tapes; VCII; Video Connection*

Under Capricorn   1949
Mystery
07880   117 mins   C   B, V   P
*Directed by Alfred Hitchcock; Ingrid Bergman,
Joseph Cotten, Michael Wilding*
A dark tale of love and sensitivity, frustration
and terror, headed by an all-star cast.
Warner Bros — *VidAmerica*

Under Fire   1983
Drama
65600   128 mins   C   B, V, LV   P
Gene Hackman, Nick Nolte, Joanna Cassidy

Three news correspondents chronicle the final days of the Samoza regime in Nicaragua.
MPAA:R
Orion Pictures — *Vestron Video*

Under Milk Wood 1973
Drama
82238 90 mins C B, V P
Richard Burton, Elizabeth Taylor, Peter O'Toole, Glynis Johns, Vivien Merchant
This is an adaptation of the Dylan Thomas play about the lives of the residents of a mythical town in Wales. Available in VHS and Beta Hi-Fi.
MPAA:PG
ORB Productions — *Key Video; Films for the Humanities*

Under the Rainbow 1981
Comedy
51996 97 mins C B, V P
Chevy Chase, Carrie Fisher, Eve Arden, Joseph Maher, Robert Donner, Mako, Billy Barty
Undercurrents of foreign political intrigue add to the comic situations encountered by a talent scout and a secret service agent in and around a hotel inhabited by the midgets who have been signed to play the Munchkins in "The Wizard of Oz."
MPAA:PG
Orion Pictures — *Warner Home Video*

Under the Red Robe 1936
Adventure
03896 82 mins B/W B, V P
Raymond Massey, Conrad Veidt, Annabella, directed by Victor Seastrom
French swordsman, Richelieu, and his oppression of Huguenots.
RKO; Sol Lesser — *Hollywood Home Theater; Western Film & Video Inc*

Under the Roofs of Paris 1929
(Sous les Toits de Paris)
Romance
12863 95 mins B/W B, V, FO P
Directed by Rene Clair
A tale of young lovers in a crowded tenement. Music and imaginative technique occupy this first French sound film. French with English subtitles.
FR
Tobis — *Movie Buff Video; Video Yesteryear; Cable Films; Discount Video Tapes*

Under the Volcano 1984
Drama
77214 112 mins C B, V, LV P
Albert Finney, Jacqueline Bisset, Anthony Andrews, directed by John Huston
A disparate alcoholic ex-British consulate mulls over his life in Mexico during "The Day of the Dead" ceremony in 1939.

Universal Pictures — *MCA Home Video*

Under Western Stars 1945
Western
29508 83 mins B/W B, V P
Roy Rogers, Trigger, Smiley Burnette
Roy's first starring film, in which he finds himself pitted against an outlaw gang.
Republic — *Discount Video Tapes; Video Connection; Cable Films*

Underground 1975
Documentary/Terrorism
71067 88 mins C B, V P
Directed by Emilo De Antonio
This film investigates the "Weathermen," one of the most feared radical organizations of the 60's and 70's.
Emilio De Antonio — *MPI Home Video*

Underground Aces 1980
Comedy
80699 93 mins C B, V P
Dirk Benedict, Melanie Griffith, Frank Gorshin, Jerry Ohrbach, RobertHegyes, Audrey Landers
A group of parking lot attendants transform a shiek into an attendant in order to help him meet the girl of his dreams.
MPAA:PG
Orion Pictures — *Vestron Video*

Undersea Adventures of 1975
Captain Nemo Volume 1,
The
Cartoons
53156 60 mins C B, V P
Animated
Captain Nemo and his crew of the submarine Nautilus take the viewer on a series of daring battles and rescues in this undersea adventure.
EL, SP
Rainbow Animation — *Family Home Entertainment*

Undersea Adventures of 1975
Captain Nemo Volume 2,
The
Cartoons
64197 60 mins C B, V P
Animated
The Nautilus crew battles bloodthirsty sharks as they accidentally uncover a sunken treasure worth a fortune.
EL, SP
Rainbow Animation — *Family Home Entertainment*

Undersea Adventures of 1975
Captain Nemo Volume 3,
The
Cartoons
64198 60 mins C B, V P

Animated
Captain Nemo's team encounters Killer Whales and a poisonous squid as it battles criminal whale poachers. Then the crew travels to the icy regions of the world to confront a ferocious polar bear and a deadly sea leopard.
EL, SP
Rainbow Animation — *Family Home Entertainment*

Undersea Adventures of Captain Nemo, Volume 4, The   1975
Cartoons
70656   60 mins   C   B, V   P
Animated
This presentation shows Captain Nemo and the Nautilus crew battling unsportsmanlike fishermen and the Loch Ness bomb. Available in Hi-Fi Stereo.
Rainbow Animation — *Family Home Entertainment*

Undersea Kingdom   1936
Adventure/Serials
14630   136 mins   B/W   B, V   P
Ray 'Crash' Corrigan
Adventure beneath the ocean floor. In twelve chapters of thirteen minutes; the first chapter runs twenty minutes.
Republic — *Video Connection; Video Dimensions; Discount Video Tapes; Nostalgia Merchant; Video Yesteryear*

Undersea World of Jacques Cousteau Vol. I, The   1978
Documentary/Adventure
47059   100 mins   C   CED   P
Narrated by Rod Serling
Two of Cousteau's journeys on the Calypso are featured: "Sharks" and "The Singing Whale." Spectacular underwater footage is included.
Media Producers Corp — *RCA VideoDiscs*

Underwater   1955
Adventure
66332   99 mins   C   B, V, 3/4U   P
Jane Russell, Richard Egan, Gilbert Roland
A team of skin divers face danger when they begin a search for underwater treasure.
RKO — *Nostalgia Merchant*

Unearthly, The   1957
Horror
84363   76 mins   B/W   B, V   P
John Carradine, Tor Johnson, Allison Hayes, Myron Healy, directed by Brooke L Peters
A mad scientist experiments with skin grafting and other forbidden practices.
Republic — *Rhino Video*

Unfaithfully Yours   1948
Comedy
72898   105 mins   B/W   B, V   P
Rex Harrison, Linda Darnell
A conductor suspects his wife is cheating on him.
Preston Sturges; RKO — *CBS/Fox Video*

Unfaithfully Yours   1984
Comedy
72899   96 mins   C   B, V   P
Dudley Moore, Nastassia Kinski, Armand Assante, Albert Brooks
A symphony conductor suspects his wife of fooling around with a musician; in retaliation, he plots an elaborate scheme to murder her. Based on the 1948 Preston Sturges film.
MPAA:PG
20th Century Fox — *CBS/Fox Video*

Unholy Wife, The   1957
Drama
79765   94 mins   C   B, V   P
Rod Steiger, Diana Dors, Tom Tryon, Marie Windsor
A young woman plans to murder her wealthy husband, but her plan goes awry when she accidentally kills someone else.
RKO — *United Home Video*

Unicorn the Island of Magic   1984
Cartoons/Fantasy
80374   92 mins   C   B, V   P
Animated
When Unico the magical unicorn comes down to earth, he learns a lesson from the Trojan Horse about love and courage.
Sanrio Productions — *RCA/Columbia Pictures Home Video*

Unicorn, The   1983
Drama
65435   29 mins   C   B, V   P
Diana Dors, Celia Johnson
A small boy hears the legend that if one rubs the horn of a Unicorn his wishes will come true. Mistakenly he buys a one-horned goat and sets out to fulfill his dreams.
Janus Films — *Embassy Home Entertainment*

Unicorn Tales I   1980
Fairy tales
57573   90 mins   C   B, V   P
Four stories for children, adapted from classic fairy tales, told in a modern way, with music. "The Magic Pony Ride" (based on the Ugly Duckling) is about a lonely little girl who meets a pony considered useless, and the two of them learn how to see and believe. In "The Stowaway" (based on Pinocchio), a young boy arrives in a new city and meets a lovable old man who leads him on the path to truth.

"Carnival Circus" (based on Cinderella)
concerns a young girl who fails at everything
until she saves the circus and realizes that
everyone has a special talent for something. In
"The Maltese Unicorn" (based on The Boy Who
Cried Wolf), a boy discovers that if he wants to
be believed he must be a man of his word.
Viacom — *Playhouse Video*

Unicorn Tales II   1980
Fairy tales
57574   90 mins   C   B, V   P
Four stories for children, adapted from classic
fairy tales, told in a modern way, with music. In
"Big Apple Birthday" (based on Alice in
Wonderland), a girl who is bored by everything
visits a new city and learns that there can be joy
in every moment. "The Magnificent Major"
(based on The Wizard of Oz) concerns a young
girl who doesn't like to read. When she is
transported to a land of non-readers, she is
eager to return home so she can read. In "The
Magic Hat" (based on The Emperor's New
Clothes), a young boy moves to a new city,
finding it difficult to make friends until he wears
a magic hat. The magic of friendship, however,
lasts longer than the "powers" of the hat. "Alex
and the Wonderful 'Doo Wah' Lamp" (based on
Aladdin and the Magic Lamp) concerns a boy
who conjures up three genies from an old lamp,
who promise to grant his every request. After
being turned into several different people,
however, he realizes he is happiest as himself.
Viacom — *Playhouse Video*

Unidentified Flying   1979
Oddball
Comedy/Fantasy
87677   92 mins   C   B, V   P
*Dennia Dugan, Jim Dale, Ron Moody, Kenneth
More, Rodney Bewes*
An astronaut and his robotic buddy find their
spaceship turning into a time machine which
throws them back into Arthurian times.
MPAA:G
Walt Disney Prod. — *Walt Disney Home Video*

Union City   1981
Suspense/Drama
47434   82 mins   C   B, V   P
*Deborah Harry, Everett McGill, Dennis
Lipscomb, Pat Benatar, directed by Mark
Reichart*
Deborah Harry of Blondie stars in this "new-
wave" mystery about an accidental murderer
who is on the run from the law.
MPAA:R
Cantina Blues Films; Kinesis
Ltd — *RCA/Columbia Pictures Home Video*

Union Station   1950
Suspense
85265   80 mins   B/W   B, V   P

*William Holden, Barry Fitzgerald, Nancy OLsen,
Jan Sterling*
A criminal kidnaps a blind girl unknowingly, and
the manhunt is on.
Paramount — *Kartes Video Communications*

Universe, The   1982
Astronomy/Science
59558   55 mins   C   B, V   P
A comprehensive survey of what man knows
today about our solar system and the seemingly
infinite number of other systems and galaxies in
all of universal space and time.
McGraw Hill — *Mastervision*

Unknown Comedy Show,   1982
The
Comedy-Performance
80901   56 mins   C   B, V   P
Murray Langston, Johnny Dark, James Marcel
The Unknown Comic, Murray Langston,
performs some of his best stand-up routines in
this taped concert. Available in VHS Stereo and
Beta Hi-FI.
Bill Osco; Murray Langston — *U.S.A. Home
Video*

Unknown Powers   1980
Drama/Occult sciences
33806   97 mins   C   B, V   R, P
*Samatha Eggar, Jack Palance, Will Geer,
Roscoe Lee Brown*
Science and drama are combined to examine
ESP and Magic. Are they gifts or curses, and
how are peoples lives affected by them?
MPAA:PG
International TV Films — *Video Gems*

Unknown World   1951
Science fiction
71098   73 mins   B/W   B, V   P
*Jim Bannon, Marilyn Nash, Victor Kilian, Bruce
Kellog*
Fearing the horrors of the onrushing atomic age,
a group of scientists develop a machine capable
of burrowing into the safety of earth's mantle.
Lippert — *King of Video*

Unknown World   1951
Science fiction
82166   73 mins   B/W   B, V   P
*Bruce Kellogg, Marilyn Nash, Victor Kilian, Jim
Bannon*
A group of scientists tunnel to the center of the
Earth to find a refuge from the dangers of the
atomic world.
Lippert — *Prism*

Unmarried Woman, An   1978
Drama
44934   124 mins   C   B, V, CED   P
Jill Clayburgh, Alan Bates

A woman must make a new life for herself after her husband suddenly divorces her after seventeen years of marriage.
MPAA:R
20th Century Fox — *CBS/Fox Video*

Unofficial Baseball Handbook, The   1985
Baseball
70759   30 mins   C   B, V   P
This is a humorous and irreverent look inside the world of baseball featuring gaffes and bloopers from your favorite major-league stars and mascots.
Major League Baseball — *Major League Baseball Productions*

Unseen, The   1980
Horror
52951   91 mins   C   B, V   P
Barbara Bach, Sydney Lassick, Stephen Furst
Three young women from a TV station are covering a story in a remote area of California. Before nightfall, two are horribly killed, leaving the third to come face to face with the terror.
Triune Films — *VidAmerica*

Unsinkable Molly Brown, The   1964
Musical
80619   128 mins   C   B, V   P
Debbie Reynolds, Harve Presnell, Ed Begley, Martita Hunt, Hermione Baddeley, directed by Charles Walters
A spunky backwoods girl is determined to break into the upper crust of Denver's high society. The Meredith Wilson score features "He's My Friend" and "I'll Never Say No." Available in VHS and Beta Hi-Fi.
MGM — *MGM/UA Home Video*

Unsuitable Job for a Woman, An   1982
Mystery
77453   94 mins   C   B, V   P
Billie Whitelaw, Paul Freeman, Pippa Guard
A young woman in charge of a detective agency becomes obsessed with the young man whose death she is investigating. Available in Beta Hi-Fi and VHS Stereo.
Boyd's Co Films Ltd. — *Monterey Home Video*

Until September   1984
Romance
80629   96 mins   C   B, V   P
Karen Allen, Thierry Lhermitte, Christopher Cazenove, Johanna Pavlis, directed by Richard Marquand
An American tourist meets and falls in love with a married banker while stranded in a Parisian hotel.

MPAA:R
United Artists — *MGM/UA Home Video*

Up from the Depths   1979
Horror
69287   85 mins   C   B, V   P
Sam Bottoms
Something from beneath the ocean is turning the paradise of Hawaii into a nightmare.
MPAA:R
New World Pictures — *Vestron Video*

Up In Smoke   1979
Comedy
48514   87 mins   C   B, V, LV   P
Cheech Marin, Tommy Chong
A pair of free-spirited burn-outs team up for a tongue-in-cheek spoof of sex, drugs, and rock and roll.
MPAA:R
Lou Adler, Lou Lombardo — *Paramount Home Video; RCA VideoDiscs*

Up Pompeii   1971
Comedy
33642   90 mins   C   B, V   P
Frankie Howard, Patrick Cargill
A sexy, hilarious story in which a servant accidentally gains possession of a scroll containing a plot against Emperor Nero. The conspirators try every means possible to recover the scroll.
MPAA:R
Ned Sherrin — *United Home Video*

Up the Academy   1980
Comedy
81784   88 mins   C   B, V   P
Ron Leibman, Ralph Macchio, Barbara Bach, Tom Poston, Stacey Nelkin, directed by Robert Downey
Four teenaged delinquents are sent to an academy for wayward boys where they encounter a sadistic headmaster and a gay dance instructor. Available in VHS and Beta Hi-Fi Stereo.
MPAA:R
Warner Bros — *Warner Home Video*

Up the Creek   1984
Comedy
70149   95 mins   C   B, V   P
Tim Matheson, Stephen Furst, John Hillerman, James B. Sikking
Four college students enter a whitewater raft race to gain some respect for their school. The soundtrack features songs by Heart, Cheap Trick and The Beach Boys.
MPAA:R
Orion Pictures — *Vestron Video*

Up the Sandbox   1972
Comedy-Drama
66326   98 mins   C   B, V   P
Barbra Streisand, David Selby, Jane Hoffman,
Barbara Rhodes
A bored housewife fantasizes about her life in
order to avoid facing her mundane existence.
MPAA:R
Warner Bros — Warner Home Video

Uphill All the Way   1985
Comedy
86607   91 mins   C   B, V   P
Roy Clark, Mel Tillis, Glenn Campbell, Trish Van
Devere, Burl Ives.
A couple of card-cheatin' good old boys are
pursued by posses and Calvary alike, and end
up killing real outlaws. Made for TV.
Frank Q. Dobbs — New World Video

Uptown New York   1932
Drama
88063   76 mins   B/W   B, V   P
Jack Oakie, Shirley Green, Leon Waycoff
A man suffers estrangement when he marries a
woman rebounding from a mysterious affair. A
rare dramatic appearance by Oakie.
World Wide Pictures; KBS Film Co. — Kartes
Video Communications

Uptown Saturday Night   1974
Comedy
53525   104 mins   C   B, V   P
Sidney Poitier, Bill Cosby, Harry Belafonte, Flip
Wilson, Richard Pryor, Calvin Lockhart
Two working men attempt to recover a stolen
lottery ticket from the black underworld after
being ripped off at a gambling place.
MPAA:PG
Warner Bros — Warner Home Video

Urban Cowboy   1980
Drama
54668   135 mins   C   B, V, LV   P
John Travolta, Debra Winger, Scott Glenn,
Madolyn Smith, Barry Corbin, directed by James
Bridges
A young Texas farmer comes to Houston to
work in a refinery and learns about life by
hanging out at Gilley's, a roadhouse bar. Here
he and his friends, dressed in their cowboy gear,
drink, fight, and prove their manhood by riding a
mechanical bull.
MPAA:PG
Paramount — Paramount Home Video; RCA
VideoDiscs

URGH! A Music War   1981
Music-Performance
77468   124 mins   C   B, V   P
The Go Go's, The Cramps, XTC, Devo, The
Police, Steel Pulse

Thirty-seven once familiar new wave bands from
Devo to XTC got together for this historic
concert. Available in Beta & VHS Hi-Fi.
Lorimar Productions — CBS/Fox Video

U. S. Men's Gymnastics   1981
Championship
Gymnastics
59568   60 mins   C   B, V   P
The top male gymnasts in the U.S. compete for
the 1981 titles.
CBS; Transworld Intl — Mastervision

U.S. Steel Hour   1955
Comedy
85223   50 mins   B/W   B, V   P
Andy Griffith, Harry Clark, Robert Emhardt,
Eddie LeRoy, Bob Hastings
The original presentation of "No Time for
Sergeants," live and unedited, which was also
Griffith's first TV appearance.
ABC — Video Yesteryear

U.S. Steel Hour   1955
Drama
85224   50 mins   B/W   B, V   P
Julie Harris, Donald Woods
With songs sung by Merv Griffin, this is a live
television performance of "A Wind from the
South."
CBS — Video Yesteryear

U.S. Steel Hour   1956
Drama
85491   52 mins   B/W   B, V   P
Paul Newman, Albert Salmi, George Peppard
An early live television performance of "Bang
the Drum Slowly." Broadcast on Sept. 26, 1956.
CBS — Video Yesteryear

U.S. Women's   1981
Gymnastics
Championship
Gymnastics/Women
59569   60 mins   C   B, V   P
The top female gymnasts in the U.S. compete
for the 1981 titles.
CBS; Transworld Intl — Mastervision

Used Cars   1980
Comedy
51573   113 mins   C   B, V   P
Kurt Russell, Jack Warden, Deborah Harmon
A car dealer is desperate to put his jalopy shop
competitors out of business. The owners go to
great lengths to stay afloat.
MPAA:R
Columbia Pictures — RCA/Columbia Pictures
Home Video; RCA VideoDiscs

Users, The 1978
Drama
75495   125 mins   C   B, V   P
Jaclyn Smith, Tony Curtis, John Forsythe, Red
Buttons, George Hamilton
A small-town girl meets a faded film star and
becomes involved in the movie business.
Aaron Spelling Productions — Prism

U.S.S. VD: Ship of 1945
Shame/Red Nightmare
Documentary/World War II
29752   82 mins   B/W   B, V   P
A government training program produced by a
major studio detailing the perils of V.D. and the
consequences for the men of the ill-fated D.E.
733. WW II vintage.
Unknown — Hollywood Home Theater

Utah 1945
Western
12593   54 mins   B/W   B, V   P
Roy Rogers, Dale Evans
Girl singer inherits a ranch and then tries to sell
it.
Republic — Video Connection; Hollywood
Home Theater; Discount Video Tapes

Utilities 1983
Comedy
80695   94 mins   C   B, V, LV,   P
                                    CED
Robert Hays, Brooke Adams, John Marley, Ben
Gordon, Helen Burns
A frustrated social worker enlists the help of his
friends in his efforts to impress an attractive
policewoman by taking on a large corporate
utility.
MPAA:PG
New World Pictures — Vestron Video

Utopia: Live at the Royal 1981
Oak
Music-Performance
71014   60 mins   C   B, V   P
Todd Rundgren, Roger Powell, Kasim Sultan,
John Wilcox
Guitarist extraordinaire, production wizard and
mellifluous vocalist Todd Rundgren leads
Utopia in this live performance at the Royal Oak
Theatre in Detroit. Among the songs performed
are "Couldn't I Just Tell You" and the band's
uplifting anthem, "Just One Victory."
Bearsville — Passport Music Video

Utopia Sampler, The 1983
Music-Performance
64929   11 mins   C   B, V   P
Utopia, featuring Todd Rundgren, performs
three songs on this Video 45: "Hammer in My
Heart," "You Make Me Crazy" and "Feet Don't
Fail Me Now."

Neo-Utopian Laboratories — Sony Video
Software

U2—The Unforgettable 1985
Fire Collection
Music-Performance
70879   51 mins   C   B, V   P
U2
Performances of four hits from the band's '84
release combine with thirty minutes of
documentary footage on this Hi-Fi Dolby Stereo
presentation.
Island Records, Inc.; Brian
Eno — RCA/Columbia Pictures Home Video

V

Vagabond, The 1916
Comedy
10646   20 mins   B/W   B, V, 3/4U   R, P,
                                                     DL
Charlie Chaplin
Chaplin portrays a pathetic fiddler making a
scanty living. (Silent; musical soundtrack
added.)
RKO — Cable Films; Festival Films

Vagabond Lover 1929
Musical
07239   66 mins   B/W   B, V, FO   P
Rudy Vallee, Sally Blane, Marie Dressler
The amusing tale of the loves, hopes, and
dreams of an aspiring saxophone player.
RKO — Video Yesteryear

Valley Girl 1983
Comedy
69284   95 mins   C   B, V, LV,   P
                                    CED
Nicolas Cage, Deborah Foreman
A typical "valley girl" shocks her peers when
she falls for a leather-jacketed freak. Contains
music by Men at Work, The Clash, Culture Club
and others.
MPAA:R
Wayne Crawford and Andrew Lane — Vestron
Video

Valley of Fire 1951
Western
63995   63 mins   B/W   B, V   P, T
Gene Autry, Gail Davis, Pat Buttram
Gene is working hard cleaning up the town of
Quartz Creek. He decides to import a caravan of
brides for the men in town, but a local gambler
kidnaps the wagon train.
Columbia — Blackhawk Films

Valley of Terror   1938
Western
10071   59 mins   B/W   B, V   P, T
Kermit Maynard, Rocky the Horse
A James Oliver Curwood saga of the Old West.
Ambassador — *Blackhawk Films; Discount Video Tapes*

Vals, The   1985
Comedy
71130   100 mins   C   B, V   P
Jill Carroll, Elana Stratheros, Gina Calabrese, Michelle Laurita, Chuck Connors, Sonny Bono, John Carradine, Michael Leon
The glibly hip lethargy normally characteristic of southern California teens turns to socially conscious resolve when a local orphanage is threatened.
MPAA:R
Jensen Farley Pictures — *Vestron Video*

Vamping   1984
Mystery/Drama
73662   107 mins   C   B, V   R, P
Patrick Duffy, Catherine Hyland
A desperate saxophonist robs a house and winds up in a mysterious menage a trois.
MPAA:R
Howard Kling; Stratton Rawson — *Key Video*

Vampire Lovers, The   1970
Horror
81907   89 mins   C   B, V   P
Peter Cushing, Madeline Smith, Ingrid Pitt, Dawn Addams, directed by Roy Ward Baker
An angry father goes after a lesbian vampire who has ravished his daughter and other young girls in a peaceful European village.
MPAA:R
American International Pictures — *Embassy Home Entertainment*

Vampyr   1932
Horror
08594   66 mins   B/W   B, V, 3/4U   P
Julien West, Sybille Schmitz, Harriet Gerard, directed by Carl Theodor-Dreyer
Low-key, experimental approach by Dreyer makes for an eerie film. Music by Wolfgang Zeller. Little dialogue.
Carl Dreyer — *Video Yesteryear; Hollywood Home Theater; Discount Video Tapes*

Van, The   1977
Comedy
48478   90 mins   C   B, V   P
Stuart Gertz; Deborah White
A teenage boy buys a van in hopes it will attract girls—one in particular—to him.
MPAA:R
Crown International — *United Home Video*

Van Nuys Blvd.   1979
Comedy
48479   93 mins   C   B, V   P
Bill Adler, Cynthia Wood
The popular boulevard is the scene where the cool southern California guys converge for cruising and girl watching.
MPAA:R
Crown International — *United Home Video*

Vanessa   1977
Drama
55253   90 mins   C   B, V   P
The story of an innocent young girl's introduction to the erotic pleasures of the Orient.
MPAA:X
Intercontinental Releasing Corp — *VidAmerica*

Vanishing American   1926
Western
55815   114 mins   B/W   B, V   P
Richard Dix, Noah Beery, directed by George B. Seitz
The mistreatment of the American Indian is depicted in this sweeping Western epic. Musical score.
Paramount — *Festival Films; Video Yesteryear*

Vanishing Point   1971
Drama
08458   98 mins   C   B, V   P
Barry Newman, Cleavon Little, Gilda Texler, Dean Jagger
Ex-racer and former cop sets out to deliver a souped-up car. Taking pep pills along the way, he eludes police, meets up with a number of characters, and finally crashes into a roadblock.
MPAA:PG   EL, SP
20th Century Fox; Cupid Productions — *CBS/Fox Video*

Vanishing Prairie   1954
Documentary
82298   60 mins   C   B, V   P
This documentary examines the wonders of nature that abound in the American prairie. From the "True-Life Adventures" series.
Academy Awards '54: Best Feature Length Documentary
Buena Vista — *Walt Disney Home Video*

Vanishing Wilderness   1973
Documentary/Animals
77519   90 mins   C   B, V   P
This documentary looks at the wild animals roaming across North America.
MPAA:G
Pacific International Enterprises — *Media Home Entertainment*

Varan the Unbelievable   1961
Horror
64296   70 mins   B/W   B, V   P
Myron Healy, Tsuruko Kobayashi
A chemical experiment near a small island in the
Japanese archipelago disturbs a prehistoric
monster beneath the water. The awakened
monster spreads terror on the island.
Jerry A. Baerwitz — *United Home Video*

Variety   1925
Drama
48728   104 mins   B/W   B, V, FO   P, T
*Emil Jannings, Lya de Putti, Warwick Ward,
directed by E. A. Dupont*
An aging acrobat seduces a young girl. Later, he
kills a man who is interested in the girl. Silent.
Oscar Werndorff, UFA — *Video Yesteryear;
Discount Video Tapes*

Vatican Conspiracy   1981
Mystery/Suspense
81194   90 mins   C   B, V   P
Terence Stamp
The members of the Vatican's College of
Cardinals do everything in their power to
discredit a newly appointed radical pontiff.
Fabian Arnaud; Enzo Gallo — *VCL Home
Video*

Vault of Horror, The   1973
Horror
54911   86 mins   C   B, V, 3/4U   P
*Terry-Thomas, Curt Jurgens, Glynis Johns,
Dawn Addams, Daniel Massey, Tom Baker*
A collection of five terrifying tales based on
original stories from the E. C. comic books of
the 1950's.
MPAA:R
Cinerama Releasing — *Nostalgia Merchant*

VBT Spirit, The   1983
Bicycling
70174   18 mins   C   B, V   P
A Vermont Bicycle Touring vacation is
chronicled, including visits to out-of-the-way
country inns and carefree bicycling to secluded
swimming holes, quiet country roads, and
covered bridges.
Video Travel — *Video Travel*

Vegas   1978
Mystery/Drama
80320   74 mins   C   B, V   P
*Robert Urich, June Allyson, Tony Curtis, Will
Sampson, Greg Morris*
A private detective with Las Vegas showgirls as
assistants solves the murder of a teenage
runaway girl.
Aaron Spelling Productions — *Prism*

Velveteen Rabbit, The   1985
Cartoons
71370   30 mins   C   B, V   P
Animated, narrated by Christopher Plummer
Convinced that reality represents an end in
itself, the stuffed toy of the title seeks a young
boy's love as the means to that end.
Hugh Campbell — *Family Home Entertainment*

Velveteen Rabbit, The   1985
Fairy tales
80602   27 mins   C   B, V   P
Marie Osmond
This is a classic children's story of a toy rabbit
that wants to be real. The Enchanted Musical
Playhouse presents this program.
Nightstar/Centerpoint Production — *King of
Video*

Velveteen Rabbit, The   1984
Fantasy
84349   30 mins   C   B, V   P
Narrated by Meryl Streep
In this innovative animation by artist David
Jorgensen (from Margery Williams' famous
children's book), a toy rabbit is willed to life by a
lonely boy. Music by George Winston.
Mark Sottnick — *Random House Home Video*

Vengeance   1980
Crime-Drama
84515   92 mins   C   B, V   P
*Sally Lockett, Nicholas Jacquez, Bob Elliot,
directed by Bob Blizz.*
A drama about vengeance, with crime,
cheapness and that inimitable Blizz
craftmanship.
Producer Service — *Magnum Entertainment*

Vengeance of the   197?
Snowmaid
Martial arts
70819   82 mins   C   B, V   P
Mo Ka Kei, Chen Chen
Some Kung Fu creepies raped her mom. Now
nobody can get a sword in edgewise on the
Snow Maid as she seeks revenge.
Foreign — *Master Arts Video*

Vengeance Valley   1951
Western
80742   83 mins   C   B, V   P
*Burt Lancaster, Joanne Dru, Robert Walker,
Sally Forrest, John Ireland, Hugh O'Brian*
A ranch foreman's life is endangered when he
attempts to conceal a terrible secret involving
his weak foster brother.
MGM — *Hal Roach Studios*

Venom   1982
Horror
64881   92 mins   C   B, V, CED   P

Sterling Hayden, Klaus Kinski, Sarah Miles
A deadly black mamba is loose in an elegant townhouse.
MPAA:R
Richard R. St. Johns — *Vestron Video*

Venom Alive in '85! 1985
Music-Performance
88357 60 mins C B, V P
Recorded at the Hammersmith Odeon, the heavy metal band plays out "Witching Hour," "Schitzo" and "Don't Burn the Witch."
Philip Goodhand-Tait — *Embassy Home Entertainment*

Venom Live at 1984
Hammersmith Odeon
Music-Performance
84492 57 mins C B, V P
The metal clatter of this band reverberates throughout London's famous arena.
Neat Records — *Sony Video Software*

Venus in Furs 1970
Horror
76834 90 mins C B, V P
James Darren, Klaus Kinski, Barbara McNair, Dennis Price, Maria Rohm
A jazz musician working in Rio de Janeiro falls in love with a mysterious woman who resembles a murdered woman whose body he discovered months earlier.
MPAA:R
Harry Alan Towers;
Commonwealth — *Republic Pictures Home Video*

Vera Cruz 1954
Adventure
65010 94 mins C B, V, CED P
Gary Cooper, Burt Lancaster, Denise Darcel
Two soldiers of fortune become involved in the Mexican War for independence.
United Artists — *CBS/Fox Video*

Verdi Requiem, The 1982
Music-Performance
82259 86 mins C B, V P
Jessye Norman, Margaret Price, Jose Carreras, Ruggero Raimondi
This is a performance of the Verdi Requiem Mass which was filmed at the Edinburgh International Festival.
National Video Corporation Ltd. — *THORN EMI/HBO Video*

Verdict, The 1982
Drama
66071 122 mins C B, V, LV, CED P

Paul Newman, James Mason, Charlotte Rampling, Jack Warden, Milo O'Shea, directed by Sidney Lumet
A down-and-out lawyer takes on the system against impossible odds.
MPAA:R
20th Century Fox — *CBS/Fox Video*

Verdi's Rigoletto at 1985
Verona
Music-Performance
76966 128 mins C B, V P
A performance of the Verdi opera about a deformed court jester taped in Verona, Italy. Available in VHS and Beta Hi-Fi.
Poly Video — *Mastervision*

Versailles 1986
France
87201 55 mins C B, V P
A tour through the world-famous palace of Louis XIV as it stands today, a veritable national shrine to France's past glories.
Kronos-France — *Gessler Educational Software*

Vertigo 1958
Suspense
75018 126 mins C B, V, LV P
James Stewart, Kim Novak, Barbara Bel Geddes, Tom Helmore, directed by Alfred Hitchcock
This is the classic Hitchcock tale of obsession, fear and murder. A private detective is hired to follow a mysterious woman, whom he gradually falls in love with. Music by Bernard Herrmann.
MPAA:PG
Alfred Hitchcock; Paramount — *MCA Home Video*

Very Close Quarters 1984
Comedy
71124 97 mins C B, V P
Shelly Winters, Paul Sorvino, Theodore Bikel, Farley Granger, directed by Vladmir Rif
Thirty people face many trials and tribulations as they share an apartment in Moscow.
Cable Star Ltd — *Vestron Video*

Very Curious Girl, A 1969
Comedy
86094 105 mins C B, V P
Bernadette La Font, directed by Nelly Kaplan
A peasant girl realizes she is being used by the male population of her village, and decides to charge them for sex, creating havoc. In French with English subtitles.
Venice Film Festival '69: Gold Medal. FR
French — *Embassy Home Entertainment*

Very Merry Cricket, A   1973
Cartoons/Christmas
71356   30 mins   C   B, V   P
Animation
Commonly considered a summer insect,
crickets actually celebrate the winter's holiday
with vigor.
Warner Bros — Family Home Entertainment

Very Private Affair, A   1962
Drama
63113   95 mins   C   B, V   P
Marcello Mastroianni, Brigitte Bardot
A movie star finds that she has no privacy from
the hordes of fans and newspaper people. The
glare of publicity helps to destroy her
relationship with a married director.
MGM — MGM/UA Home Video

Very Special Christmas,   1982
A/Sleeping Beauty
Fairy tales/Christmas
64956   52 mins   C   /   B, V   P
Animated
A young boy saves Santa from trouble in "A
Very Special Christmas." "Sleeping Beauty" is a
new version of the classic fairy tale. Both of
these animated films are combined on this tape.
Ron Merk — Unicorn Video

Very Special Team, A   1982
Football
47715   23 mins   C   B, V, FO   P
Team highlights of the 1981 San Francisco
49ers, who came out of nowhere to win the NFC
Championship.
NFL Films — NFL Films Video

Vez en la Vida, Una   1949
Musical-Drama
47464   75 mins   B/W   B, V, FO   P
Libertad Lamarque, Luis Aldas, Raimundo
Pastore
A young farm girl travels to the big city, where
she becomes a nightclub dancer and gets
involved with a shady character. Spanish
dialogue.
SP
Argentina — Video Yesteryear

Viaje Fantastico En   1984
Groso
Adventure
72961   108 mins   C   B, V   P
Let go of your imagination and launch into a
thrilling adventure and fantasy in this adult-
oriented drama.
SP
Foreign — Unicorn Video

Vic Braden's Tennis for   1981
the Future, Volume 1
Tennis
63428   120 mins   C   B, V   P
The first volume of the series covers four tennis
fundamentals: forehand, backhand, serve and
volley. From Braden's successful PBS program,
"Tennis for the Future."
WGBH Education Foundation — Paramount
Home Video

Vic Braden's Tennis for   1981
the Future, Volume 2
Tennis
64500   120 mins   C   B, V   P
This segment covers the approach shot (spin
and service return), the overhead shot, lob and
drop shots, and conditioning.
WGBH Education Foundation — Paramount
Home Video

Vic Braden's Tennis for   1981
the Future, Volume 3
Tennis
68250   120 mins   C   B, V   P
This program is rich in useful, hands-on
information and demonstrations of technique.
WGBH Education Foundation — Paramount
Home Video

Vic 'n' Sade   1957
Comedy
47491   15 mins   B/W   B, V, FO   P
Bernadine Flynn, Art Van Harvey, Eddie Gillilan
A TV adaptation of one of radio's most popular
programs, featuring the original cast performing
in a bare studio setting.
WNBQ Chicago — Video Yesteryear

Vice Squad   1982
Drama
63666   97 mins   C   B, V, LV,   P
                            CED
Wings Hauser, Season Hubley, Gary Swanson
A violent and twisted killer-pimp goes on a
murderous rampage, and a hooker helps a vice
squad plainclothesman trap him.
MPAA:R
Sandy Howard; Frank Capra Jr — Embassy
Home Entertainment

Vicious Circle, The   1957
Mystery
82233   84 mins   B/W   B, V   P
John Mills, Wilfrid Hyde-White, Rene Ray, Lionel
Jeffries, Noelle Middleton
A prominent London physician becomes
involved in murder and an international crime
ring when he agrees to perform an errand for a
friend.
Peter Rogers — Monterey Home Video

Vic's Vacant Lot · 1984
Sports
73639   60 mins   C   B, V   S
Vic Braden shows how kids can have fun
playing with minimal room and makeshift
equipment.
Kartes Productions — *Kartes Video
Communications*

Victor/Victoria · 1982
Comedy
47778   133 mins   C   B, V, CED   P
*Julie Andrews, James Garner, Robert Preston,
Lesley Ann Warren, Alex Karvas, directedd by
Blake Edwards*
A down-on-her-luck actress in Depression era
Paris impersonates a man impersonating a
woman in order to be a show biz success.
MPAA:PG
MGM — *MGM/UA Home Video*

Victory · 1981
Drama
53553   120 mins   C   B, V, CED   P
*Sylvester Stallone, Michael Caine, Max von
Sydow, Pele, Carole Laure, Bobby Moore,
directed by John Huston*
A soccer match between WW II American
prisoners of war and a German team is set up
so that the players can escape through the
sewer tunnels of Paris.
MPAA:PG
Freddie Fields — *CBS/Fox Video*

Victory at Sea · 1960
World War II/Documentary
29437   98 mins   B/W   B, V   P
Narrated by Alexander Scourby
This is a condensation of the classic television
series which portrayed the exploits of the U.S.
Navy during World War II. Its impressive musical
score was composed by Richard Rodgers.
NBC — *Warner Home Video; Embassy Home
Entertainment; RCA VideoDiscs*

Victory at Sea · 1952
Documentary/World War II
65247   27 mins   B/W   B, V   P
Narrated by Leonard Graves 6   pgms
This award-winning television documentary
series chronicles the history of Allied naval
warfare during World War II through actual
newsreel and government footage. Richard
Rodgers' widely acclaimed background musical
score is performed by the NBC Symphony,
conducted by Robert Russell Bennett. Available
as a six-volume set, each tape contains up to
five episodes. Volumes may be purchased
separately as well.
*1.Design for War 2.The Pacific Boils Over
3.Sealing the Breach 4.Midway Is East
5.Mediterranean Mosaic 6.Guadal canal 7.Rings
Around Rabaul 8.Mare Nostrum 9.Sea and
Sand 10.Beneath the Southern Cross*

*11.Magnetic North 12.The Conquest of
Micronesia 13.Melanesian Nightmare 14.D-Day
15.Roman Renaissance 16.Killers and the Killed
17.The Turkey Shoot 18.Two If by Sea 19.The
Battle for Leyte Gulf 20.Return of the Allies
21.Full Fathom Five 22.The Fate of Europe
23.Target Suribachi 24.The Road to Mandalay
25.Suicide for Glory 26.Design for Peace*
Emmy Awards '53: Best Public Affairs Program.
NBC — *Embassy Home Entertainment*

Vida Sigue Igual, La · 197?
Drama
52796   102 mins   C   B, V   P
Jean Harrington, Charo Lopez
An up-and-coming law student and soccer
player becomes paralyzed in an auto accident
and must contend with a change of attitude from
his friends and lover.
SP
Star Films; Filmayer Produccion — *Media
Home Entertainment*

Video a Go-Go Volume 1 · 1985
Music video
81205   30 mins   C   B, V   P
*Kool and the Gang, Animotion, Stephanie Mills,
Bananarama, the Bar-Kuys*
Here is a collection of conceptual music-videos
for your dancing and listening pleasure.
Available in Hi-Fi Stereo for both formats.
Polygram Music Video — *RCA/Columbia
Pictures Home Video*

Video a Go-Go, Volume 2 · 1986
Music video
84613   27 mins   C   B, V   P
*Ashford and Simpson, The Gap Band, Kurtis
Blow*
Another collection of songs for dancing, suitable
to be played at parties.
PMV — *RCA/Columbia Pictures Home Video*

Video Aerobics · 1979
Physical fitness
59306   57 mins   C   B, V   P
Instructors Susie Murphy and Leslie Lilian
demonstrate a complete conditioning routine
which includes aerobic exercises for all areas of
the body. Contains both a 17-minute beginners
program and a challenging 40-minute advanced
session.
Amstar Productions — *Vestron Video; Amstar
Productions*

Video Cooking Library · 1985
Cookery
70995   30 mins   C   B, V   P
24   pgms
This continuing series of programs helps
prospective chefs learn their craft.
*1.Basic New Orleans Cuisine 2.Basic Italian
Cuisine 3.Seven Simple Chicken Dishes*

4.Meals for Two 5.Pasta, Pasta, Pasta 6.One
Dish Meals 7.The Basic Bread Maker
8.Thanksgiving Dinner 9.Holiday Gifts From
Your Kitchen 10. Holiday Cookies and Treats
11.Appetizers and Hor D'Oevres 12.Brunches
13.Chinese Cuisine 14.Soups 15.Meals Kids
Can Fix 16.Brown Bagging 17.Basic Mexican
Cuisine 18.Basic Greek Cuisine 19.Hearty New
England Dinners 20.Southern Desserts and
Delights 21.Salads Supreme 22.Mouthwatering
Meatless Meals 23.Candlelight, Champagne,
Romance 24.Microwave Miracles
Kartes Video Communications — Kartes Video
Communications

Video Dictionary of 1984
Classical Ballet, The
Dance
66609   270 mins   C   B, V, 3/4U   P
Merrill Ashley, Kevin MacKenzie, Denise
Jackson, Georgina Parkinson
Three of the most outstanding principal dancers
of leading American ballet companies
demonstrate the complete language of ballet in
this program. More than 800 variations in
international Russian, French and Cecchetti
styles are illustrated to piano accompaniment,
with many movements shown in slow motion
with multiple camera angles.
AM Available
First Ballet Inc — Kultur; Trans Media
Communications Network

Video First Aid Kit 1983
First aid
73637   60 mins   C   B, V   P
3 pgms
This series of programs shows you the
techniques for first aid.
1.Bleeding and Shock 2.Drug Emergency
3.Poisoning
Kartes Productions — Kartes Video
Communications

Video Fish One 1982
Video
59579   57 mins   C   B, V, 3/4U   P
This tape shows colorful fish swimming in an
aquarium. Using a two camera technique, the
tape allows the viewer to become increasingly
relaxed and calm.
Candle Corp — Candle Corporation

Video Learning Library, 1985
The
Video
81723   30 mins   C   B, V   P
5 pgms
This series teaches people the fundamentals of
shooting home video projects such as weddings
and sports.
1.How to Light For Videography 2.How to
Record Sound For Video 3.How to Shoot A

Wedding 4.How to Shoot Sports Action 5.How
to Shoot Home Video—The Basics
Kartes Video Communications — Kartes Video
Communications

Video Love Songs 1986
Music video
84612   30 mins   C   B, V   P
Diana Ross, Juice Newton, Dolly Parton, John
Denver
A collection of seven romantic song videos.
RCA Video — RCA/Columbia Pictures Home
Video

Video Rewind—The 1984
Rolling Stones Great
Video Hits
Music video
79849   60 mins   C   B, V, LV,   P
                              CED
Mick Jagger, Charlie Watts, Ron Wood, Keith
Richards, Bill Wynman
A collection of twelve uncensored music videos
from those bad boys of rock and roll—The
Rolling Stones.
Promotone BV — Vestron Video

Video Trivialities 1984
Games/Video
79348   720 mins   C   B, V   R, P
A trivia game that comes complete with a board
and video tapes that feature thousands of
questions and answers.
AM Available
Mark Walbridge — Video Trivialities

Video Vixens 1984
Comedy
76781   85 mins   C   B, V   P
A television executive shakes up a permissive
society by producing the most erotic awards
show ever seen on television.
Troma Films — Vestron Video

Video Yesterbloop 197?
Outtakes and bloopers
57363   81 mins   C   B, V, FO   P
A few sections in black and white. A collection
of bloopers from TV, including "Steve Allen
Show," "All My Children," "The Price Is Right,"
"Happy Days," "Mork and Mindy," and "One
Day at a Time." Quality is not perfect. Contains
some nudity and strong language.
ABC et al — Video Yesteryear

Videocycle 1984
Physical fitness
80482   60 mins   C   B, V, 3/4U   P
6 pgms
Designed for indoor cycling, this exercise
regimen features three self-paced workouts on
each tape. Spectacular scenery and music,

pulse checks, trial maps and a tour coach all
add to the exercise experience.
1.Yellowstone I 2.Grand Teton 3.Yellowstone II
4.San Francisco 5.Hawaii—Maui 6.Hawaii—the
Big Island
AM Available
Cycle Vision Tours — Cycle Vision Tours

Videodrome   1983
Science fiction/Horror
64788   87 mins   C   B, V, LV   P
Deborah Harry, James Woods, directed by
David Cronenberg
This film dramatizes what it would be like if
television took over the world. Stars Deborah
Harry, lead singer of the rock group Blondie.
Special effects by Rick Baker ("An American
Werewolf in London").
Universal — MCA Home Video

VIDI's Video Greetings   1985
Holidays
80481   4 mins   C   B, V   P
Animated 13 pgms
A series of video greeting cards, which are
designed for various holidays and special
events, such as birthdays and St. Valentine's
Day.
1.The Twelve Days 2.Good King Wenceslas
3.Twas the Night Before Christmas—2010
4.The Nativity 5.An Old-Fashioned Christmas
6.The Hannukah Story and Dreidel Game
7.Peace on Earth 8.Surprise Party Birthday
9.Party Games 10.Astrology Birthdays 11.Music
Vidi-O Birthday 12.Alphabet Soup 13.The Many
Victories of Cupid 14.Personalized Vidis
Videograf — Videograf

Vie Continue, La   1982
Drama
64241   93 mins   C   B, V   P
Annie Giradot, Jean-Pierre Cassel, Michel
Aumont, directed by Moshe Mizrahi
A woman suddenly finds herself alone after 20
years, following the death of her husband.
Dubbed in English.
Cineproduction/SFPC — RCA/Columbia
Pictures Home Video

Vietnam: Chronicle of a   1981
War
Vietnam War/Documentary
52746   88 mins   C   B, V   P
Narrated by Walter Cronkite, Dan Rather,
Morley Safer, Charles Collingwood, Charles
Kuralt, Mike Wallace, Eric Sevareid
Drawing upon the resources of the CBS News
Archives, this CBS News Collectors Series
program presents a retrospective portrait of
American military involvement as witnessed by
on-the-scene correspondents and camera
crews. Some portions are in black-and-white.
CBS News — CBS/Fox Video

Vietnam: In the Year of   1968
the Pig
Documentary/Vietnam War
81530   103 mins   B/W   B, V   P
Directed by Emile de Antonio
This documentary examines the horror and
bloodshed of the war in southeast Asia.
Emile de Antonio — MPI Home Video

Vietnam: Remember   1968
Documentary/Vietnam War
79699   60 mins   C   B, V   P
A documentary that recalls some of the fierce
battles of the Vietnam War.
Maljack Productions — MPI Home Video

Vietnam: The Ten   1980
Thousand Day War
Vietnam War/Documentary
81444   49 mins   C   B, V, LV   P
Narrated by Richard Basehart 13 pgms
This series examines the emotional and
physical impact of the Vietnam War on the men
who fought in it.
1.Vietnam 2.Dien Bien Phu 3.Days of Decision
4.Uneasy Allies 5.The Trial 6.Firepower 7.Siege
8.Frontline America 9.Soldiering On 10.The
Village War 11.Peace 12.Surrender 13.The
Unsung Soldiers
Michael Maclear — Embassy Home
Entertainment

View to a Kill, A   1985
Adventure
Closed Captioned
82271   131 mins   C   B, V   P
Roger Moore, Christopher Walken, Tanya
Roberts, Grace Jones, Patrick Macnee, Lois
Maxwell, Desmond Llewelyn, directed by John
Glen
James Bonds's newest mission takes him to the
United States, where he must stop the evil Max
Zorin from destroying California's Silicon Valley.
Duran Duran performs the title song, in VHS and
Beta Hi-Fi stereo.
MPAA:PG
MGM/UA Entertainment Co — CBS/Fox
Video

Vigilante   1983
Drama
64900   91 mins   C   B, V   P
Robert Forster
A frustrated ex-cop, tired of seeing criminals
returned to the street, joins a vigilante squad
dedicated to law and order.
Artists Releasing Corp — Vestron Video

Vigilantes Are Coming,   1936
The
Adventure/Serials
12560   230 mins   B/W   B, V   P

Bob Livingston, Kay Hughes, Quinn 'Big Boy' Williams, directed by Mack V. Wright, Ray Taylor "The Eagle" sets out to revenge his family and upsets the plot of a would-be dictator to establish an empire in California. In twelve chapters—first is 32 minutes, each additional chapter is 18 minutes.
Republic — *Video Connection; Nostalgia Merchant; Discount Video Tapes; Captain Bijou*

Vigilantes of Boom Town   1946
Western
08898   54 mins   B/W   B, V, 3/4U   P
Allan 'Rocky' Lane, Bobby Blake
Senator's daughter thinks prize fighting is a disgrace.
Republic — *Video Connection; Nostalgia Merchant*

Vikings, The   1958
Adventure
80860   116 mins   C   B, V   P
Kirk Douglas, Ernest Borgnine, Janet Leigh, Tony Curtis, directed by Richard Fleischer
A Viking king and his son kidnap a Welsh princess and hold her for ransom.
United Artists — *MGM/UA Home Video*

Villa Rides   1968
Western
85266   125 mins   C   B, V   P
Yul Brynner, Robert Mitchum, Charles Bronson, Herbert Lom
Co-written by Sam Peckinpah and Robert Towne, this film recounts Villa's revolutionary Mexican campaign.
Paramount — *Kartes Video Communications*

Village of the Damned   1960
Science fiction
64572   78 mins   B/W   B, V, CED   P
George Sanders, Barbara Shelley, Martin Stephens, Laurence Naismith
A group of unusual children in a small English village are found to be the vanguard of an alien invasion.
MGM — *MGM/UA Home Video*

Village of the Giants   1965
Science fiction/Comedy
80762   82 mins   C   B, V   P
Ron Howard, Johnny Crawford, Tommy Kirk, Beau Bridges, Freddy Cannon, Beau Brummels
A group of beer-guzzling teenagers become giants after eating a mysterious substance invented by a twelve-year-old genius.
Bert I. Gordon — *Embassy Home Entertainment*

Villain Still Pursued Her, The   1941
Comedy
08731   67 mins   B/W   B, V, 3/4U   P
Anita Louise, Alan Mowbray, Buster Keaton, Hugh Herbert
Old-fashioned melodrama; poor hero and rich villain vie for the sweet heroine.
RKO — *Movie Buff Video; Video Yesteryear; Discount Video Tapes; Kartes Video Communications*

Vintage Commercials   1980
Advertising/Comedy
29733   60 mins   C   B, V, 3/4U   P
Dick Van Dyke, Mary Tyler Moore, Ernie Kovacs, Andy Griffith, Danny Thomas, Lucille Ball
A package of commercials from the 1950's and 1960's, all featuring top TV celebrities such as The Monkees, Lucille Ball and Desi Arnaz, Ozzie and Harriet, and the Flintstones, selling everything from cigarettes to orange juice. Some segments in black and white.
CBS et al — *Shokus Video*

Vintage Commercials, II   1982
Advertising/Comedy
47612   60 mins   C   B, V, 3/4U   P
Buster Keaton, The Three Stooges, Lucille Ball, Desi Arnaz, Jack Benny, Steve Allen, Jay North, Ernie Kovacs
An hour of classic television commercials from the 50's, 60's and early 70's. A number of spots featuring celebrities are included, pitching for such products as Skippy Peanut Butter, Ipana, Westinghouse, Alka Seltzer, Bosco, Quik, Seven-Up and Kool-Aid. Some segments are in black and white.
CBS et al — *Shokus Video*

Vintage Commercials, III   1983
Advertising/Documentary
66461   60 mins   B/W   B, V, 3/4U   P
Lucille Ball, Desi Arnaz, Hillary Brooke, Andy Devine, Dwayne Hickman
Another hour of classic TV commercials, mostly from the 1950's, is featured with many celebrity spokespersons. Also on this tape is a newsreel highlighting the beginnings of commercial television broadcasting at the 1939 New York World's Fair.
CBS et al — *Shokus Video*

Vintage Commercials IV   1955
Advertising
84702   60 mins   B/W   B, V, 3/4U   P
Tennessee Ernie Ford, Desi Arnaz, Arthur Godfrey, Dick Powell, Lucille Ball, Danny Kaye
The best, funniest and most ridiculous commericals of yesteryear are included in this sixth compilation: Featured products include Tootsie Roll, Ajax, Snickers, Soaky and G.I. Joe.

CBS et al — *Shokus Video*

Independent — *Rhino Video; Admit One Video*

Vintage Sitcoms 195?
Comedy
53048 100 mins B/W B, V, 3/4U P
Jackie Gleason, Gale Storm, Charles Farrell,
George Burns, Gracie Allen, Jackie Cooper
Four top situation comedies from the 1940's
and 1950's: "The Life of Riley" (1949), starring
Jackie Gleason as Chester A. Riley; "My Little
Margie" (1952), starring Gale Storm and
Charles Farrell as daughter and father; "The
Burns and Allen Show" (1952), a classic
episode involving Gracie's party plans; "The
People's Choice" (1955), starring Jackie
Cooper and his dog "Cleo."
NBC; CBS — *Shokus Video*

Vintage Sitcoms, II 1953
Comedy
87207 100 mins B/W B, V, 3/4U P
Ed Gardner, Charlie Ruggles, Betty White,
Gertrude Berg, Alan Reed
Four episodes of vintage situation TV comedies:
"The Ruggles," "Life with Elizabeth," "The
Goldbergs" and "Duffy's Tavern."
CBS et al. — *Shokus Video*

Violent Breed, The 1983
Crime-Drama
82353 91 mins C B, V P
Henry Silva, Harrison Muller, Woody Strode
A C.I.A. operative is sent on a mission to put a
black marketeer out of business.
Cannon Films — *MGM/UA Home Video*

Violent Ones, The 1968
Drama
80467 96 mins C B, V P
Fernando Lamas, David Carradine
Three men who are suspected of raping a young
girl are threatened with lynching by an angry
mob of townspeople.
Harold Goldman — *Spotlite Video*

Violent Women 1959
Crime-Drama
86167 61 mins C B, V P
Jennifer Slater, Jo Ann Kelly
Five female convicts escape and embark on a
bloody journey through the countryside, pursued
by the authorities.
Pathe-Alpha — *Vidmark Entertainment*

Violent Years, The 1956
Exploitation
73554 60 mins B/W B, V P
Spoiled debutantes form a vicious all-girl gang
and embark on a spree which includes
everything from robbery to male rape. A cheap
thrills masterpiece from the director of "Orgy of
the Dead," Ed Wood, Jr.

Virgin Among the Living Dead 1985
Horror
70930 90 mins C B, V P
Christina Von Blanc, Britt Nichols, directed by
Jess Franco
A young girl inherits an island which is inhabited
by the walking dead.
Brux International Pictures; Eurocine — *Wizard*
Video

Virgin Spring, The 1959
Drama
87915 88 mins B/W B, V P
Max Von Sydow, Brigitta Valberg, Gunnel
Lindblom, Brigitta Pattersson, Axel Duborg,
directed by Ingmar Bergman
The classic medieval fantasy by Bergman about
the rape and murder of a virgin which became a
Christian miracle. Available dubbed or subtitled.
For mature audiences.
Academy Awards '59: Best Foreign Language
Film. EL, SW
Svensk Filmindustri — *Embassy Home*
Entertainment

Virgin Witch, The 1975
Horror
80292 89 mins C B, V P
Vicki and Ann Michelle, Patricia Haines, Neil
Hallett, James Chase
Two sisters are trapped in a deserted mansion
where a witches coven intends to use the
sisters as virgin sacrifices.
MPAA:R
Joseph Brenner Associates — *Prism*

Viridiana 1961
Drama
57343 90 mins B/W B, V P
Silvia Pinal, Francisco Rabal, Fernando Rey,
directed by Luis Bunuel
This ironic, biting drama portrays a young girl
about to take her holy vows, but the suicide of
her beloved uncle causes her to forsake the
church and return to his farm with a horde of
beggars and derelicts who turn her well
intended charity into a nightmare. Spanish with
English subtitles.
Cannes Film Festival '61: Grand Prize Co-
Winner. SP
Uninci; Films 59 — *Hollywood Home Theater;*
Discount Video Tapes

Virus 1982
Drama/Science fiction
65369 102 mins C B, V P
George Kennedy, Glenn Ford, Robert Vaughn,
Chuck Connors, Olivia Hussey
"Virus" is a revealing look at both man's genius
for self-destruction and his super-human

---

determination to carry on life and hope in a
destroyed world.
MPAA:PG
Haruki Kadokawa — *Media Home
Entertainment*

Vision Quest   1985
Drama
82223   107 mins   C   B, V, LV   P
*Matthew Modine, Linda Fiorentino, Ronny Cox,
Michael Schoeffling*
A high school student wants to win the
Washington state wrestling championship and
the affections of a beautiful artist. In Hi-Fi Stereo
for all formats.
MPAA:R
The Geffen Company — *Warner Home Video*

Visions of Diana Ross,   1985
The
Music video
80779   30 mins   C   B, V   P
Diana Ross, Julio Iglesias
The sizzling sounds of Diana Ross come alive in
this collection of six conceptual music videos.
This tape features an extended version of
"Swept Away" and "Missing You." Available in
VHS and Beta Hi-Fi Stereo.
RCA Video Productions — *RCA/Columbia
Pictures Home Video*

Visions of Evil   1973
Horror
82148   85 mins   C   B, V   P
Lori Sanders, Dean Jagger
A young woman, recently released from a
mental institution, is plagued by a series of
terrifying visions when she moves into a house
where a brutal axe murder took place.
Contel — *Prism*

Visions of Faith   1955
Religion/Music
59090   70 mins   B/W   B, V, FO   P
Saint Luke's Choristers
A collection of hymns with visuals showing
"God's handiwork." Hymns include: "Father of
Mercies," "I Wonder As I Wander," "Jesus My
Lord, My God, My All," "The Hallelujah
Chorus," "O Divine Redemmer," and others.
USA — *Video Yesteryear*

Visiting Hours   1982
Suspense
63392   101 mins   C   B, V, CED   P
*Lee Grant, William Shatner, Linda Purl, Michael
Ironside*
An outspoken television journalist delivers a
controversial editorial on women's rights. She is
consequently brutally attacked by an angered
viewer.
MPAA:R

20th Century Fox — *CBS/Fox Video*

Visitor From the Grave   1981
Horror
77444   60 mins   C   B, V   P
*Simon MacCorkindale, Kathryn-Leigh Scott,
Gareth Thomas, Mia Nadasi*
When an American heiress and her boyfriend
dispose of a dead man's body, his spirit comes
back to haunt them.
Hammer House of Horror — *Thriller Video*

Vital, Vigorous and Visual   1983
Physical fitness
65397   60 mins   C   B, V   R, P
Aerobics with Joannie Greggains and Kirk
Lewis.
AM Available
Peter Pan Industries — *Parade Records*

Vitaphone Musical Shorts   1985
Musical
81889   58 mins   B/W   B, V   P
This is a compilation of early 1930's Vitaphone
musical shorts as "The Flame Song," "Yours
Sincerely" and "The Red Shadow."
Vitaphone — *San Francisco Rush Video*

Viva Knievel   1977
Adventure
78626   106 mins   C   B, V   P
*Evel Knievel, Gene Kelly, Lauren Hutton, Red
Buttons, Leslie Nielsen, Cameron Mitchell*
Crooks plan to sabotage Knievel's daredevil
jump in Mexico and then smuggle cocaine back
into the States in his coffin.
MPAA:PG
Warner Bros — *Warner Home Video*

Viva Las Vegas   1963
Musical
59137   85 mins   C   B, V, CED   P
*Elvis Presley, Ann-Margret, William Demarest,
Jack Carter, Cesare Danova, Nicky Blair,
directed by George Sidney*
A sports car enthusiast and his friend go to Las
Vegas for the Grand Prix where they both fall for
a swimming instructor.
MGM — *MGM/UA Home Video*

Viva Max   1969
Comedy
47994   93 mins   C   B, V   P
*Peter Ustinov, Jonathan Winters, John Astin,
Pamela Tiffin, Keenan Wynn, directed by Jerry
Paris*
A modern-day Mexican general and his men
fake their way across the Alamo.
Montmorency Prods — *Republic Pictures
Home Video*

Viva Zapata!   1952
Drama/Biographical
70378   112 mins   B/W   B, V   P
Marlon Brando, Anthony Quinn, Jean Peters, Margo, Arnold Moss, directed by Elia Kazan
This film shows the life of Mexican revolutionary Emiliano Zapata, from his leading the peasant revolt in the early 1900's, to his eventual corruption by power and greed.
20th Century Fox — *Key Video*

Vivacious Lady   1938
Comedy
00289   90 mins   B/W   B, V, 3/4U   P, T
Ginger Rogers, James Stewart, James Ellison
Romantic comedy about a young college professor who marries a chorus girl.
RKO; Pandro S Berman — *Blackhawk Films; Nostalgia Merchant*

Voice from the Screen,   1926
The
Film-History/Technology
58659   34 mins   B/W   B, V, FO   P
An address by Edward B. Craft, Executive Vice President of Bell Telephone Laboratories, presented before the New York Electrical Society, in which he discusses the "new Vitaphone Sound-Film system." An original demonstration of the first commercially viable method of adding sound to motion pictures.
Vitaphone — *Video Yesteryear*

Voice of La Raza   1984
Minorities
88380   40 mins   C   B, V, 3/4U   R, P
Narrated by Anthony Quinn, this is a look at the career and educational plights of American Hispanics. Features an interview with Rita Moreno.
Your World Video — *Your World Video*

Volcano   1976
Drama/Biographical
65465   ? mins   C   B, V   P
Narrated by Donald Britlain and Richard Burton
A painful but extraordinary portrait of writer Malcolm Lowry, author of "Under the Volcano," which explores his battle with alcohol and the guilt that followed the success of this novel. In Beta Hi-Fi.
Almi Release — *RCA/Columbia Pictures Home Video*

Volkswagen Quantum   1986
Automobiles
88413   60 mins   C   B, V, 3/4U   P
The Quantum's engine is dissected for a demonstration of tune-up and basic maintenance.
Peter Allen Prod. — *Peter Allen Video Productions*

Volkswagen Rabbit   1986
Automobiles
88412   60 mins   C   B, V, 3/4U   P
The Rabbit's motor is used to demonstrate basic tune-up and maintenance.
Peter Allen Prod. — *Peter Allen Video Productions*

Voltron, Defender of the   1985
Universe: Planet Doom
Science fiction/Cartoons
81863   83 mins   C   B, V, 8mm   P
Animated
The Voltron Force is dispatched to vanquish the Evil King Zarkon's reign of terror over the planet Arus.
World Events Productions Ltd. — *Sony Video Software*

Voltron, Defender of the   1985
Universe: Castle of Lions
Cartoons
70721   83 mins   C   B, V, 8mm   P
Animated
Voltron, the ancient robot hero, joins with the castle lions and space explorers to save this galaxy on part of his overall universe protection plan. Recorded in Beta and VHS Hi-Fi stereo.
World Events Prods. — *Sony Video Software*

Voltron, Defender of the   1984
Universe: Planet Arus
Cartoons
82393   83 mins   C   B, V, 8mm   P
Animated
In this third feature of the adventure series, Voltron destroys the emissaries of the vicious King Zorkon of Planet Doom.
World Events Productions Ltd — *Sony Video Software*

Voltron, Defender of the   1986
Universe: Journey to the
Lost Planets
Cartoons
86380   45 mins   C   B, V, 8mm   P
Another episode of the tooth-and-nail battle for the universe with Voltron and his buddies.
World Events Prod. — *Sony Video Software*

Voltron, Defender of the   1986
Universe: Merla, Queen of
Darkness
Cartoons
86381   45 mins   C   B, V, 8mm   P
Another Voltron action cartoon pastiche, with Merla superseding all previous bad guys in causing trouble.
World Events Inc. — *Sony Video Software*

Voltron, Defender of the Universe: Zarkon's Revenge
1986

Cartoons
86382　　45 mins　　C　　B, V, 8mm　　　　P
Voltron has a final showdown with the master villain.
World Events Inc. — *Sony Video Software*

Volunteers
1985

Comedy/Adventure
70963　　107 mins　　C　　B, V　　　　　P
Tom Hanks, John Candy, Rita Wilson, Tim Thomerson, Gedde Watanabe, George Plimpton, Ernest Harada, directed by Nicholas Meyer
This wacky romp through the jungles of Thailand sends up the idealism of the early 60's. The gambling ne'er-do-well Lawrence Bourne III gets stuck on a Peace Corps bridge-building mission and learns to make the most of his "superior breeding."
MPAA:R
Tri-Star — *THORN EMI/HBO Video*

Volvo GL, DL
1986

Automobiles
88414　　60 mins　　C　　B, V, 3/4U　　　P
How to tune-up and maintain the two Volvo engines.
Peter Allen Prod. — *Peter Allen Video Productions*

Von Ryan's Express
1965

War-Drama
08426　　117 mins　　C　　B, V　　　　　P
Frank Sinatra, Trevor Howard, Brad Dexter, Edward Mulhare, directed by Mark Robson
American Air Force Colonel leads a group of prisoners of war in taking control of a freight train.
EL, SP
20th Century Fox; Saul David — *CBS/Fox Video*

Voyage en Ballon
1959

Adventure
74088　　82 mins　　C　　B, V　　　　　P
This is the delightful story of a young boy who stowsaway on his grandfather's hot air balloon.
Film Sonor; Film Montsouris — *Embassy Home Entertainment*

Voyage of Tanai, The
1975

Adventure
84517　　90 mins　　C　　B, V　　　　　P
Directed by John Latos
A young Polynesian battles nature's snarls on his quest to save his village.
Warwick Associates — *Magnum Entertainment*

Voyage of the Damned
1977

Drama/World War II
46150　　134 mins　　C　　B, V　　　　　P
Faye Dunaway, Max von Sydow, Oskar Werner, Malcolm McDowell, Orson Welles, James Mason, Lee Grant, Katherine Ross, Ben Gazzara
The story of one of the most tragic incidents of World War II: the flight of 937 German-Jewish refugees bound for Cuba aboard the Hamburg-Amerika liner S.S. St. Louis. Based on Gordon Thomas' and Max Morgan-Witts' novel of the same title.
MPAA:G
Robert Fryer, Avco Embassy — *CBS/Fox Video*

Voyage to the Bottom of the Sea
1961

Science fiction/Adventure
Closed Captioned
80748　　106 mins　　C　　B, V　　　　　P
Walter Pidgeon, Joan Fontaine, Barbara Eden, Peter Lorre, Robert Sterling, Michael Ansara, Frankie Avalon, directed by Irwin Allen
The crew of an atomic submarine must destroy a deadly radiation belt which has set the polar ice cap ablaze.
20th Century Fox — *Playhouse Video*

Voyager from the Unknown
1983

Science fiction/Adventure
81438　　91 mins　　C　　B, V　　　　　P
Jon-Erik Hexum, Meeno Peluce, Ed Begley Jr., Faye Grant, Fionula Flanagan
A "time cop" and an orphan travel through time to set the course of history straight. Here are two episodes from the "Voyagers!" series. Available in VHS and Beta Hi-Fi.
Universal; James D. Parriott; Scholastic Prods. — *MCA Home Video*

W

W
1974

Suspense/Drama
81156　　95 mins　　C　　B, V　　　　　P
Twiggy, Dirk Benedict, Eugene Roche, Michael Conrad, directed by Richard Quine
A woman and a private detective must find the cause of three near-fatal accidents. A single letter "W" is found at the scene of the crimes.
MPAA:PG
Mel Ferrer; Bing Crosby Productions — *Lightning Video*

Wackiest Ship in the Army, The 1961
Comedy
86386   99 mins   C   B, V   P
Jack Lemmon, Ricky Nelson, Chips Rafferty, John Lund, Patricia Driscoll
A totally undisciplined warship crew must smuggle an Australian spy through Japanese waters during World War II.
Fred Kohlmer — RCA/Columbia Pictures Home Video

Wackiest Wagon Train in the West, The 1977
Western/Comedy
53942   86 mins   C   B, V   R, P
Bob Denver, Forrest Tucker, Jeannine Riley
A hapless wagon master is saddled with a dummy assistant as they guide a party of five characters across the West.
MPAA:G
Topar Films — Media Home Entertainment

Wacko 1983
Comedy
65219   84 mins   C   B, V   P
Stella Stevens, George Kennedy, Joe Don Baker
A group of nymphets and tough guys get caught up in a wild Halloween-pumpkin-lawnmower murder.
MPAA:PG
Michael R Starita — Vestron Video

Wacky and Packy 1975
Cartoons
73562   70 mins   C   B, V   P
Animated
A caveman and his pachyderm run amok in the modern world causing trouble wherever the pair travel.
Filmation Studios — Prism

Wacky World of Mother Goose, The 1967
Cartoons
08521   81 mins   C   B, V, CED   P
Animated, voice of Margaret Rutherford
All the familiar Mother Goose characters brought together in a delightful tale of secret agents and sinister surprises.
Avco Embassy; Arthur Rankin, Jr. — Embassy Home Entertainment

Wages of Fear 1955
Drama
06243   138 mins   B/W   B, V   P
Yves Montand, Charles Vanel, Peter Van Eyck, directed by Henri-Georges Clouzot
Realistic drama of disastrous oil well explosion in Central America. French film, dubbed in English.

FR
Hal Roach Dist; DCA — Movie Buff Video; Hollywood Home Theater; Video Yesteryear; Western Film & Video Inc; Discount Video Tapes; International Home Video

Wagner 1985
Biographical/Drama
86091   300 mins   C   B, V   P
Richard Burton, Vanessa Redgrave, Sir John Geilgud, Sir Laurence Olivier
A huge, sweeping biography of Richard Wagner; Burton's last released film. In two parts.
Avco Embassy — Embassy Home Entertainment

Wagonmaster 1950
Western
00291   85 mins   B/W   B, V, 3/4U   P
Ben Johnson, Joanne Dru, directed by John Ford
Roving cowboys join a group of Mormons in their trek across the western frontier.
RKO — Nostalgia Merchant

Waikiki 1980
Suspense/Mystery
82307   96 mins   C   B, V   P
Dack Rambo, Steve Marachuk, Donna Mills, Cal Bellini, Darren McGavin
Two private eyes set out to prove that their friend is not the "cane field murderer" who is terrorizing the Hawaiian island of Oahu.
Spelling/Goldberg Productions — Karl/Lorimar Home Video

Wait Till Your Mother Gets Home 1983
Comedy
71196   97 mins   C   B, V   P
Paul Michael Glaser, Dee Wallace, Peggy McKay, David Doyle, Ray Buktenica, James Gregory, Joey Lawrence, Lynne Moody, directed by Bill Persky
When the season ends, dad, a football coach, takes over as house husband. Role-reversal humor abounds as mom takes her first job in fifteen years.
Blue Greene Productions; NBC-TV — Prism

Wait Until Dark 1967
Suspense
58255   105 mins   C   B, V   P
Audrey Hepburn, Alan Arkin, Richard Crenna, Efrem Zimbalist Jr., Jack Weston
A photographer unwittingly smuggles a drug-filled doll into New York, and his blind wife, alone in their apartment, is terrorized by murderous crooks in search of it.
Warner Bros — Warner Home Video

Waitress 1981
Comedy
63357   85 mins   C   B, V   P
Jim Harris, Carol Drake, Carol Bever
Three beautiful girls are waitresses in a crazy restaurant where the chef gets drunk, the kitchen explodes, and the customers riot.
Troma Productions — *THORN EMI/HBO Video*

Wake Island 1942
War-Drama
87174   88 mins   B/W   B, V   P
Robert Preston, Brian Donlevy, William Bendix, MacDonald Carey, directed by John Farrow
A small group of Marines face the onslaught of the Japanese fleet after Pearl Harbor, and hold their ground for 16 strenuous days.
New York Film Critics Award '42: Best Director (Farrow).
Paramount — *MCA Home Video*

Wake of the Red Witch, The 1948
Adventure
59091   106 mins   B/W   B, V   P
John Wayne, Gail Russell, Gig Young
This South Sea saga pits an adventurous sea captain against a shipping magnate with a fortune of pearls and a beautiful woman at stake.
Republic — *Republic Pictures Home Video*

Wake Up the Echoes 1982
Football
63165   52 mins   C   B, V, FO   P
George Gipp, Knute Rockne, Frank Leahy, Ara Parseghian, Joe Theisman, Joe Montana, Jim Crowley
Highlights from 60 years of Notre Dame Football history are on this tape, from rare footage shot in 1913 to 1966's "Game of the Century" against Michigan State. Some sequences are in black and white.
NFL Films — *NFL Films Video*

Walk in the Spring Rain, A 1970
Drama
87272   98 mins   C   B, V   P
Ingrid Bergman, Anthony Quinn, Fritz Weaver, Katherine Crawford, Tom Fielding, Virginia Gregg, directed by Guy Green
The depressed wife of a professor enters into a love affair with a life-loving outdoorsman.
Written by Stirling Silliphant.
MPAA:PG
Stirling Silliphant — *RCA/Columbia Pictures Home Video*

Walk in the Sun, A 1946
War-Drama
81275   117 mins   B/W   B, V   P
Dana Andrews, Richard Conte, John Ireland, Lloyd Bridges, Sterling Holloway, directed by Lewis Milestone
A platoon of Texas Division infantryman are in Italy to clear out a farmhouse occupied by the Germans in Salerno during 1943.
Lewis Milestone — *Discount Video Tapes; Kartes Video Communications; Movie Buff Video*

Walk in the Sun, A 1946
War-Drama
85222   118 mins   B/W   B, V   P
Dana Andrews, Richard Conte, Lloyd Bridges, John Ireland, Huntz Hall
A tense war drama by veteran director Lewis Milestone, in which the enemy is never seen and the dialogue is often suggestive poetry, as a platoon of Americans search for a French farmhouse.
20th Century Fox — *Video Yesteryear*

Walking Tall 1973
Drama
79668   126 mins   C   B, V   P
Joe Don Baker, Elizabeth Hartman, Noah Beery, directed by Phil Karlson
A Tennessee sheriff takes a stand against syndicate-run gambling and loses his wife in the process.
MPAA:R
Bing Crosby Productions — *Lightning Video*

Walking Tall—Part II 1975
Drama
79669   109 mins   C   B, V   P
Bo Svenson, Noah Beery, Angel Tompkins, Richard Jaeckel, directed by Earl Bellamy
Tennessee Sheriff Buford Pusser attempts to find the man who killed his wife.
MPAA:PG
Bing Crosby Productions — *Vestron Video*

Walking Tall—The Final Chapter 1977
Drama
79670   112 mins   C   B, V, LV   P
Bo Svenson, Forrest Tucker, Leif Garrett, Morgan Woodward
A dramatization of the final months in the life of Tennessee sheriff Buford Pusser.
MPAA:PG
Bing Crosby Productions — *Lightning Video*

Walking the Edge 1983
Drama
82196   94 mins   C   B, V   P
Robert Forster, Nancy Kwan, Joe Spinell, Aarika Wells
A widow hires a taxi driver to help her seek vengeance against the men who killed her husband and her son.
MPAA:R

Empire Pictures — *Lightning Video*

Wally's Workshop   1979
Home improvement
81722   30 mins   C   B, V   P
24 pgms
Handyman Wally Brunner and his wife, Natalie,
demonstrate how to perform simple repairs
around the house.
1.Bathroom Remodeling 2.Bathroom Repairs
3.Kitchen Remodeling 4.Slate and Vinyl Floors
5.Hardwood Floors 6. Parquet Floors and
Carpeting 7.Painting and Staining 8.Wallpaper
9.Murals and China Repair 10.Beamed and
Suspended Ceilings 11.Decorated and Tiled
Ceilings 12. Ceiling Ladders and Fireplaces
13.Paneling 14.Wall Repairs and Remodeling
15.Room Dividers and Shelving 16.Locks and
Garage Door Openers 17.Alarms and Safes
10.Weatherizing 19.Refinishing Antiques
20.Antiquing 21.Decoupage, Matting and
Framing 22.Household Repairs 23.Maintenance
and Exterior Repairs 24.Lamps and Electrical
Outlets
Wally Bruner — *Kartes Video Communications*

Walt Disney Christmas, A   1982
Cartoons/Christmas
53798   45 mins   C   B, V   P
Animated
Six classic cartoons with a wintry theme are
combined for this program: "Pluto's Christmas
Tree" (1952), "On Ice," "Donald's Snowball
Fight;" two Silly Symphonies from 1932-33:
"Santa's Workshop" and "The Night Before
Christmas" and an excerpt from the 1948
feature "Melody Time," entitled "Once Upon a
Wintertime."
Walt Disney Prods — *Walt Disney Home Video*

Waltz Across Texas   1983
Drama
65382   100 mins   C   B, V   P
The story of a young couple whose mutual
dislike for each other turns romantic as they are
joined in a quest to discover oil in west Texas.
Martin Jurow — *Vestron Video*

Waltz of the Toreadors   1962
Comedy
50956   105 mins   C   B, V   R, P
Peter Sellers, Dany Robin, Margaret Leighton,
Cyril Cusack
A retired general tries to make up for lost time in
an affair with a French woman that has been
carried on platonically for seventeen years.
AM Available
Independent Artists — *VidAmerica; Learning
Corp of America*

Wanderers, The   1979
Drama
52712   113 mins   C   B, V   P

Ken Wahl, John Friedrich, Karen Allen, Linda
Manz, directed by Philip Kaufman
Richard Price's novel about youth gangs coming
of age in the Bronx in 1963. The "Wanderers"
are a non-violent gang about to graduate high
school, prowling the Bronx with the feeling that
something is slipping away from them.
MPAA:R
Orion Pictures — *Warner Home Video*

Wanted: Dead or Alive   1959
Western
87337   22 mins   C   B, V   P
Steve McQueen, Jane Burns, James Coburn,
Cloris Leachman, John Baer 2 pgms
These episodes of the vintage TV western
series, "Reunion for Revenge" and "The
Medicine Man," have been newly colorized by
computer enhancement.
CBS — *VidAmerica*

Wapiti Creek   1986
Wildlife
82505   74 mins   C   B, V, 3/4U,   P
                          1C
An exploration of the seasons in the life of the
elk, this film depicts various elk rites of passage,
such as calving and mating.
Grunko — *Grunko Films*

War and Love   1984
War-Drama
84718   112 mins   C   B, V   P
Sebastian Keneas, Kyra Sedgwick
Two Jewish teenagers are torn apart by World
War II and Nazi persecution. After the war they
strive to find each other again.
MPAA:PG-13
Stafford Prod — *MGM/UA Home Video*

War and Peace   1956
Drama
77448   208 mins   C   B, V, LV   P
Audrey Hepburn, Mel Ferrer, Henry Fonda,
Anita Ekberg, directed by King Vidor
An adaptation of the Tolstoy novel about three
families caught up in Russia's Napoleonic Wars
from 1805 to 1812. Nino Rota wrote the score.
Paramount Pictures — *Paramount Home Video*

War Chronicles   1986
World War II/Documentary
70677   60 mins   C   B, V   P
Narrated by Patrick O'Neal, directed by Don
Horan 6 pgms
This epic series looks at World War II in both
Europe and the Pacific. Each segment of the
series focuses on a meaningful battle or
situation which led to a victory for America and
its allies. Actual war footage is combined with
combat paintings by Mort Kunstler to give
viewers a thorough understanding of these
events. Volume One runs for two hours; other

volumes are one hour long. All volumes include both black and white and color footage.
Lou Reda Productions/Mort Zimmerman — *U.S.A. Home Video*

War Comes to America · 1945
World War II/Documentary
50617   67 mins   B/W   B, V, 3/4U,   P
                                    FO
Directed by Frank Capra
An overview of American heritage, emphasizing the events which forced us to fight for survival. Frank Capra's philosophy paints a loving portrait of the American. Part of the ''Why We Fight'' series, contained on two cassettes.
US War Department — *Western Film & Video Inc; Hollywood Home Theater; Discount Video Tapes; MPI Home Video*

War Department Report, The · 1943
World War II/Documentary
81605   50 mins   B/W   B, V   P
This government sponsored documentary was designed to keep defense plant workers informed about the war's progress on all fronts.
U.S. Office of War Information — *Victory Video*

War Game, The · 1965
Nuclear warfare/Documentary
02964   49 mins   B/W   B, V   P
Written and directed by Peter Watkins
This powerful semi-documentary shows the terrible aftermath of a nuclear war in Britain.
Academy Award '66: Best Documentary.
BBC; British Film Institute — *Hollywood Home Theater; International Historic Films; Festival Films; Western Film & Video Inc; Films Inc; Discount Video Tapes*

War Games · 1983
Drama
Closed Captioned
65415   110 mins   C   B, V, LV,   P
                                    CED
Mathew Broderick, Dabney Coleman, John Wood, Ally Sheedy
An extremely bright young man, thinking that he's sneaking an advance look at a new line of video games, breaks into the country's Norod missile-defense system and challenges it to a game of global thermonuclear warfare.
MPAA:PG
Harold Schneider — *CBS/Fox Video; RCA VideoDiscs*

War in the Sky · 1982
World War II/Documentary
59356   90 mins   C   B, V   R, P
Directed by William Wyler, Lloyd Bridges, James Stewart, narrated by Peter Lawford
Director William Wyler's account of the Army Air Corps in action. Extraordinary footage of the Thunderbolt, the P47 Fighter, and the B17 Bomber.
US Office of War Information — *Video Gems*

War Lover, The · 1962
War-Drama
81212   105 mins   B/W   B, V   P
Steve McQueen, Robert Wagner, Shirley Anne Field, Bill Edwards
A daredevil flying captain and his pilot find themselves vying for the affections of the same woman during World War II in England.
Columbia; Arthur Hornblow, Jr. — *RCA/Columbia Pictures Home Video*

War of the Wildcats · 1943
Western
59093   102 mins   B/W   B, V   P
John Wayne, Martha Scott, Albert Dekker
Western action with the Duke as a tough oil wildcatter battling a powerful land baron.
Republic — *Republic Pictures Home Video*

War of the Worlds, The · 1953
Science fiction
38617   85 mins   C   B, V, LV   P
Gene Barry, Ann Robinson, Les Tremayne
H.G. Wells' classic novel of the invasion of Earth by Martians, updated to 1950's California, with spectacular special effects depicting the destruction caused by the Martian war machines.
Academy Awards '53: Special Effects.
Paramount — *Paramount Home Video; RCA VideoDiscs*

War Wagon, The · 1967
Western
65122   101 mins   C   B, V   P
John Wayne, Kirk Douglas, Howard Keel, Robert Walker Jr., Keenan Wynn, Bruce Dern, directed by Burt Kennedy
Two cowboys and an Indian plot to ambush the gold-laden armored stagecoach of a ruthless cattle baron.
Universal — *MCA Home Video*

War Years—The Forties, The · 194?
World War II/Documentary
10149   ? mins   B/W   B, V   P, T
Film covers Hitler, Stalin, Churchill, MacArthur, the Battle of the Bulge, Nuremberg war trials, and Harry Truman.
Unknown — *Blackhawk Films*

Warlock · 1959
Western
84428   122 mins   C   B, V   P
Henry Fonda, Anthony Quinn, Richard Widmark, directed by Edward Dmytryk

In cleaning up a derelict western town, three gunfighters have a battle of wills and power.
20th Century Fox — *Playhouse Video*

Warlock Moon 1975
Horror
66107   75 mins   C   B, V   P
Laurie Walters, Joe Spano
A young woman is lured to a secluded spa and falls prey to a coven of witches.
EL, SP
Cintel Prod — *Unicorn Video*

Warlords of the 21st Century 1982
Science fiction/Adventure
65075   91 mins   C   B, V, CED   P
Michael Beck, Annie McEnroe, James Wainwright
A gang of bandits who speed around the galaxy in an indestructible battle cruiser are challenged by a fearless space lawman.
Lloyd Phillips; Rob Whitehouse — *Embassy Home Entertainment*

Warner Brothers Cartoon Festival I 194?
Cartoons
12578   55 mins   C   B, V   P
Includes "Corny Concerto," "Dover Boys," "Hamateur Night," "Wackiki Wabbit," "Tale of Two Kitties', "Daffy and the Dinosaur," and "Falling Hare."
Warner Brothers — *Hollywood Home Theater; Discount Video Tapes*

Warner Brothers Cartoon Festival II 194?
Cartoons
12579   55 mins   C   B, V   P
Includes "Wacky Wabbit," "Daffy the Commando," "Case of the Missing Hare," "Jungle Jitters," "All This and Rabbit Stew', "Have You Got Any Castiles', "Fresh Hare," and "Inki and the Mina Bird."
Warner Brothers — *Hollywood Home Theater; Discount Video Tapes*

Warner Brothers Cartoon Festival III 194?
Cartoons
12580   55 mins   C   B, V   P
Includes "Robinhood Makes Good', "Flop Goes the Weasel," "Fony Fables," "Pigs in a Polka," "Fox Pop," "Fifth Column Mouse," and "Wabbit Who Came to Supper."
Warner Brothers — *Hollywood Home Theater; Discount Video Tapes*

Warner Brothers Cartoon Festival IV 194?
Cartoons
53804   55 mins   C   B, V   P
Animated
Eight cartoons are included in this package, including "Presto Change-O," "Porky's Bare Facts," "Get Rich Quick, Porky," "Finn 'N Catty," "Sheepish Wolf," "Yankee Doodle Daffy," "Porky's Railroad," and "Bugs Bunny Bond Rally."
Warner Bros — *Hollywood Home Theater; Discount Video Tapes*

Warner Brothers Cartoons 195?
Cartoons
53801   54 mins   C   B, V, FO   P
Animated
Included in this collection are "The Wabbit Who Came to Supper" (1942), "A Tale of Two Kitties" (1948), "Case of the Missing Hare" (1942), "Hamateur Night" (1938), "Wackiki Wabbit" (1953), "Daffy Duck and the Dinosaur" (1939), and "Fresh Hare" (1942).
Warner Bros — *Video Yesteryear*

Warning, The 1980
Drama
81184   101 mins   C   B, V   P
Martin Balsam, Guiliano Gemma
An honest police commissioner and his chief must carry out an investigation into the ties between the mob and the police department.
Mario Cacchi Gori — *Media Home Entertainment*

Warning Sign 1985
Drama/Suspense
Closed Captioned
82419   99 mins   C   B, V   P
Sam Waterston, Kathleen Quinlan, Yaphet Kotto
A high-tech thriller in which a small town is terrorized by an accident at a research facility.
MPAA:R
20th Century Fox — *CBS/Fox Video*

Warren Miller's Sailing Film Festival 1984
Boating
80886   72 mins   C   B, V   P
Director Warren Miller travels around the world to capture such sailing events as world cup yachting in the Atlantic and wind surfing in California for this festive film.
Warren Miller — *Karl/Lorimar Home Video*

Warren Zevon 1982
Music-Performance
75924   68 mins   C   B, V   P
This program presents Warren Zevon performing his hit songs in concert.

THE VIDEO TAPE & DISC GUIDE

Front Line — *Sony Video Software*

Warrior and the Sorceress, The 1984
Fantasy
77174   81 mins   C   B, V, LV, CED   P
David Carradine, Luke Askew, Maria Socas
A warrior offers his services to rival factions who are fighting for control of a water well in an impoverished village.
MPAA:R
Roger Corman; New Horizons — *Vestron Video*

Warrior of the Lost World 1984
Science fiction
80812   90 mins   C   B, V   P
Robert Ginty, Persis Khambatta, Donald Pleasence
A warrior must destroy the evil Omega Force who tyrannically rule the world in the distant future. Available in VHS and Beta Hi Fi.
Roberto Bessi; Frank E. Hildebrand — *THORN EMI/HBO Video*

Warriors, The 1955
Adventure
82336   85 mins   C   B, V   P
Errol Flynn, Peter Finch, Joanne Dru, Yvonne Furneaux, Noel Willman
Swashbuckling action fills this film telling of Prince Edward's valiant rescue of Lady Joan and her children from the clutches of the evil Count De Ville. Available in VHS and Beta Hi-Fi.
Allied Artists — *Playhouse Video*

Warriors, The 1979
Drama
38937   94 mins   C   B, V, LV   P
Michael Beck, James Remer, Deborah Van Valkenburgh
A contemporary action story about a war between New York City street gangs that rages from Coney Island to the Bronx.
MPAA:R
Paramount — *Paramount Home Video*

Warriors of the Wasteland 1983
Drama
65750   92 mins   C   B, V   P
Fred Williamson
In the year 2019 when the world has been devastated by a nuclear war, the few survivors try to reach a distant land which emits radio signals indicating the presence of human life but are hindered by attacks from the fierce Templars, led by a self-styled priest called One.
MPAA:R
Fabrizio De Angelis — *THORN EMI/HBO Video*

Washington Affair, The 1977
Drama
66048   90 mins   C   B, V, CED   P
Tom Selleck, Carol Lynley, Barry Sullivan
A tale of intrigue and blackmail in the nation's capital.
MPAA:PG
Walter G O'Conner — *Embassy Home Entertainment*

Washington Mistress 1981
Drama
86582   96 mins   C   B, V   P
Lucie Arnaz, Richard Jordan, Tony Bill, Tarah Nutter, Pat Hingle
A pregnant housewife moonlights as a politician's mistress. Made for TV.
Karen Mack; Lorimar Prod. — *U.S.A. Home Video*

Washington Redskins 1984 Highlights 1985
Football
70550   70 mins   C   B, V, FO   P
Art Monk
The Skins returned as "Winners and Still Champions" in '84 with two victories over the cowboys and a division clinching 29-27 thriller over the cards. The tape features 47-minutes of highlights from the '84 NFL season as well.
NFL Films — *NFL Films Video*

W.A.S.P 1984
Music-Performance
82385   30 mins   C   B, V   P
WASP
Filmed at the Lyceum Theater in London, this soulful performance features memorable tunes such as "On Your Knees" and "I Wanna Be Somebody."
Capitol Records — *Sony Video Software*

Watch and Play 1984
Children/Games
78172   60 mins   C   B, V   P
An interactive program that features animated children's tales and includes a toy television set, scenery and cut-out characters.
AM Available
Direct Broadcast Programs — *Video Connection of America*

Watch Me When I Kill 1981
Drama/Suspense
65751   95 mins   C   B, V   P
Richard Stewart, Sylvia Kramer
A young nightclub dancer stops by a drugstore seconds after the owner was killed. She doesn't see the killer's face, but his rasping voice remains to torment her.
MPAA:R
Herman Cohen — *THORN EMI/HBO Video*

Watch Mr. Wizard 195?
Science/Television
52461   30 mins   B/W   B, V, FO   P
Don Herbert (Mr. Wizard)
This popular children's science show of the
1950's and 60's demonstrated interesting
scientific experiments for young people to do. In
this episode, Mr. Wizard tells his young assistant
how to make bombs.
NBC — *Video Yesteryear*

Watch on the Rhine 1943
Drama
73972   113 mins   B/W   B, V   P
*Bette Davis, Paul Lukas, Donald Woods, Beulah
Bondi, Geraldine Fitzgerald*
A couple of German anti-Nazi underground
leaders escape from the madness of socialist
Germany. Adapted from the play by Lillian
Hellman.
Warner Bros — *Key Video*

Watched 1973
Suspense
73035   95 mins   C   B, V   P
Stacy Keach
A former U.S. attorney has a nervous
breakdown and kills a narcotics agent.
Palmyra Films — *Vestron Video*

Watcher in the Woods, 1981
The
Suspense/Science fiction
59319   83 mins   C   B, V   P
*Bette Davis, Carroll Baker, David McCallum,
directed by John Hough*
When a family moves to an English country
house, their children encounter something
frightening in the woods.
MPAA:PG
Walt Disney Prods — *Walt Disney Home Video*

Water Babies, The 1979
Musical
80777   93 mins   C   B, V   P
*James Mason, Billie Whitelaw, David Tomlinson,
Paul Luty, Sammantha Coates*
When a twelve-year-old chimney sweep's
apprentice is wrongly accused of stealing silver,
the boy and his dog fall into a pond and become
animated cartoons.
Ariadne Films — *Embassy Home
Entertainment*

Water Workout with 1985
Candy Costie
Physical fitness
84772   60 mins   C   B, V   P
Candy Costie
The 1984 Gold Medalist performs an exercise
program for water aficionados.
Barton Cox Films — *Video Associates*

Waterfront 1944
Drama/Mystery
84236   68 mins   B/W   B, V   P
J. Carroll Naish, John Carradine
Nazis are threatening German relatives in
America in this low-budget espionage drama.
PRC — *Movie Buff Video; United Home Video*

Waterloo Bridge 1940
Drama
Closed Captioned
82124   109 mins   B/W   B, V   P
*Vivien Leigh, Robert Taylor, Lucile Watson,
directed by Mervyn Le Roy*
A soldier and a ballet dancer begin a tragic
romance when they meet by chance during a
London air raid.
MGM — *MGM/UA Home Video*

Watermelon Man 1970
Comedy
80882   97 mins   C   B, V   P
*Godfrey Cambridge, Estelle Parsons, Howard
Caine, directed by Melvin Van Peebles*
The tables are turned for a bigoted white man
when he wakes up one morning and to discover
he has become black.
MPAA:R
Columbia Pictures — *RCA/Columbia Pictures
Home Video*

Water's Path 1985
Music video
82065   60 mins   C   B, V   P
The music of the Windham Hill family of artists is
featured in this impressionistic portrait of rivers
and streams across the United States. Available
in VHS and Beta Hi-Fi Stereo.
Dann Moss; Windham Hill
Productions — *Paramount Home Video;
Pioneer Artists*

Watership Down 1978
Fantasy
53526   92 mins   C   B, V   P
Animated, directed by Martin Rosen
Richard Adam's allegorical novel about how a
group of rabbits escape fear and overcome
oppression while searching for a new and better
home is the basis for this animated film.
MPAA:PG
Nepenthe Productions — *Warner Home Video;
RCA VideoDiscs*

Wavelength 1983
Drama
65393   87 mins   C   B, V   P
Robert Carradine
A rock star living in the Hollywood Hills with his
girlfriend stumbles on an ultrasecret
government project involving aliens from
outerspace recovered from a recent unidentified
flying object crash site. The FBI, CIA, NASA and

the Army Intelligence combine all their resources to find and destroy them.
MPAA:PG
James Rosenfield — *Embassy Home Entertainment*

Way Down East 1920
Drama/Film-History
08710   107 mins   B/W   B, V   P
Lillian Gish, Richard Barthelmess, Lowell Sherman, Creighton Hale, directed by D. W. Griffith
The story of a country girl who is tricked into a fake marriage by a scheming playboy. The final sequence is in color, and this tape includes the original Griffith-approved musical score.
United Artists — *Kartes Video Communications; Video Yesteryear; Western Film & Video Inc; Discount Video Tapes; Blackhawk Films*

Way He Was, The 1976
Comedy
80187   87 mins   C   B, V   P
Steve Friedman, Al Lewis, Merrie Lynn Ross, Doodles Weaver
A satrical re-enactment of the events that led up to the Watergate burglary and the cover up that followed.
MPAA:R
Goldenwest Releasing — *United Home Video*

Way Out West 1937
Comedy
33906   65 mins   B/W   B, V, 3/4U   P
Stan Laurel, Oliver Hardy, Sharon Lynne, James Finlayson, Rosina Lawrence
The boys travel westward to deliver a mine deed to the daughter of a recently departed friend. A crooked saloonkeeper tries to swindle them.
Hal Roach, MGM — *Nostalgia Merchant; Blackhawk Films*

Way Out West 1937
Comedy
63991   86 mins   B/W   B, V   P, T
Stan Laurel, Oliver Hardy, Rosina Lawrence, Jimmy Finlayson, Sharon Lynne
The boys travel out West to deliver the deed to a gold mine to the daughter of their late prospector friend. Also included on this tape is a 1932 Thelma Todd—ZaSu Pitts short, "Red Noses."
Hal Roach; MGM — *Blackhawk Films; Nostalgia Merchant*

Way Out West 1937
Comedy
82152   66 mins   C   B, V   P
Stan Laurel, Oliver Hardy, Sharon Lynne, James Finlayson
This is a newly colorized version of the Laurel and Hardy film.

Stan Laurel; Hal Roach — *Hal Roach Studios*

Way They Were, The 1984
Football
79634   23 mins   C   B, V, FO   P
Profiles of the New York Jets stars past and present along with highlights of the team's 1968 championship season.
NFL Films — *NFL Films Video*

Way to Cook, The 1985
Cookery
70806   60 mins   C   B, V   P
Julia Child 6 pgms
Television's celebrated Ms. Child offers this complete home cooking course for the culinarily inept.
1.Poultry 2.Meat 3.Vegetables 4.Soups, Salads & Bread 5.Fish & Eggs 6.First Courses & Desserts
AM Available
Julia Child Productions; WGBH Boston; Alfred A. Knopf — *Knopf Video Books*

Way We Were, The 1973
Drama/Romance
63963   118 mins   C   B, V   P
Barbra Streisand, Robert Redford, Bradford Dillman, Viveca Lindfors, Herb Edelman
Set during the 1940's, this is the story of the attraction of two totally opposite people, the love that binds them together, and the differences that tear them apart.
Academy Awards '73: Best Song ("The Way We Were"); Best Music Score. MPAA:PG
Columbia Pictures; Ray
Stark — *RCA/Columbia Pictures Home Video; RCA VideoDiscs*

Wayne Murder Case 1938
Mystery
78114   61 mins   B/W   B, V, FO   P
June Clyde, Regis Toomey, Jason Robards Sr.
A fast-moving, cleverly constructed murder mystery, wherein a rich old man dies just as he is about to sign a new will. Though no one was standing near him, a knife is found embedded in his back.
Tiffany — *Video Yesteryear; Weiss Global Enterprises*

Wayne Newton at the 1983
London Palladium
Music-Performance
66448   63 mins   C   B, V   P
Wayne Newton, The Jive Sisters, Don Vincent and his Orchestra
Wayne Newton performs a show-stopping program for his legions of fans at the London Palladium. Songs include such pop masterpieces as "Danke Schoen," "Jambalaya," "The Impossible Dream," "I

Made It Through The Rain" and others. VHS in stereo.
ITC Productions — *MGM/UA Home Video*

W.C. Fields Comedy Bag   1933
Comedy
81740   56 mins   B/W   B, V   P
W.C. Fields, Babe Kane, Dorothy Granger, George Chandler
This is a compilation of three classic Fields shorts: "The Golf Specialist" (1930), "The Dentist" (1932) and "The Fatal Glass of Beer" (1933).
Paramount-Sennett; RKO — *Kartes Video Communications*

W. C. Fields Festival   1933
Comedy
00428   60 mins   B/W   B, V   P
W.C. Fields
Included are "The Golf Specialist," "The Dentist," and "The Fatal Glass of Beer.
Mack Sennett — *Hollywood Home Theater; Discount Video Tapes; Video Classics*

We All Loved Each Other   1977
So Much
Comedy
63435   124 mins   C   B, V   P
Vittorio Gassman, Nino Manfredi, Stefano Satta Flores, Stefania Sandrelli
From the end of World War II through the next 30 years, this sensitive comedy follows the lives of three friends who have all loved the same woman. Italian dialogue, English subtitles.
IT
Almi/Cinema V; Pio Angeletti and Adriano de Micheli — *RCA/Columbia Pictures Home Video*

We Are the World—The   1985
Video Event
Music video/Documentary
80880   30 mins   C   B, V   P
Diana Ross, Michael Jackson, Lionel Ritchie, Billy Joel, Ray Charles, Stevie Wonder, Bruce Springsteen, Willie Nelson, Bob Dylan, Quincy Jones, narrated by Jane Fonda
This is a look at the recording of the USA for Africa's "We Are the World." This Beta and VHS Hi Fi Stereo program includes a complete video clip of the song.
Ken Kragen; Ken Yates — *RCA/Columbia Pictures Home Video*

We Dive at Dawn   1943
War-Drama
64372   98 mins   B/W   B, V, 3/4U   P
John Mills, Eric Portman, directed by Anthony Asquith
A British submarine is disabled in the Baltic sea by enemy gunfire and the crewmen desperately seek help.

J. Arthur Rank; GFD;
Gainsborough — *Nostalgia Merchant*

We of the Never Never   1982
Drama
65100   136 mins   C   B, V   P
Angela Punch McGregor, Arthur Dignam, Tony Barry, directed by Igor Auzins
A city-bred Australian woman marries a cattle rancher and moves from civilized Melbourne to the barren outback of the Northern Territory.
Triumph Films — *RCA/Columbia Pictures Home Video*

Weather in the Streets   1984
Drama/Romance
81562   108 mins   C   B, V   P
Michael York, Joanna Lumley, Lisa Eichhorn, Isabel Dean, Norman Pitt
A young woman enters into an ill-fated love affair after spending a few moments with an aristocratic married man.
MPAA:PG
Alan Shallcross — *Magnum Entertainment*

Weavers: Wasn't That a   1981
Time!, The
Music-Performance/Documentary
87375   78 mins   C   B, V   P
Pete Seeger, Lee Hays, Ronnie Gilbert, Fred Hellerman
The members of the famous 50's folk group get together for a concert at Carnegie Hall and a look at their legacy.
MPAA:PG
Jim Brown Prod.; George Stoney Assoc.; Harold Leventhal Mgmt. — *MGM/UA Home Video*

Weber and Fields, Al   19??
Jolson, and This Is
America
Music/Variety
57365   29 mins   B/W   B, V, FO   P
This tape contains three priceless programs. "Weber and Fields" (1930), the dynamic vaudeville duo, are seen performing their classic "Oyster" routine. "A Jolson's Screen Test" (1948) is the rarest Jolson on film. "This Is America" (1943), narrated by Dwight West, is a wartime tour along the Great White Way subtitled "Broadway Dim Out."
Unknown — *Video Yesteryear*

Wedding, A   1978
Comedy
86587   125 mins   C   B, V   P
Mia Farrow, Carol Burnett, Lillian Gish, Lauren Hutton, Viveca Lindfors, Pat McCormick, Vittorio Gassman, Desi Arnaz Jr., directed by Robert Altman
The occasion of a wedding leads to complications galore for the relatives and guests on the happy day.

THE VIDEO TAPE & DISC GUIDE

MPAA:PG
Robert Altman — *Key Video*

Wedding in White 1972
Drama
84863   103 mins   C   B, V   P
Donald Pleasance, Carol Kane, Leo Phillips
A rape and question of honor trouble a poor
British clan living in Canada during World War II.
MPAA:R
John Vidette — *Embassy Home Entertainment*

Wedding Party, The 1969
Comedy
63418   90 mins   C   B, V   P
*Jill Clayburgh, Robert DeNiro, directed by Brian
DePalma*
An apprehensive groom is overwhelmed by his
too-eager bride and her inquisitive relatives at a
prenuptial celebration.
Ajay Films — *VidAmerica*

Wedding Rehearsal 1932
Comedy
81470   84 mins   B/W   B, V, LV   P
*Merle Oberon, Roland Young, John Loder,
Wendy Barrier, Maurice Evans, directed by
Alexander Korda*
A Guards officer thwarts his grandmother's
plans to marry him off by finding suitors for all
the young ladies offered to him.
Alexander Korda — *Embassy Home
Entertainment*

Weekend of Shadows 1977
Drama
80392   94 mins   C   B, V   P
John Waters, Melissa Jaffer, Graeme Blundell
A police sergeant leads a group of townspeople
in a search for the man who murdered a
farmer's wife.
Tom Jeffrey; Matt Carroll — *Embassy Home
Entertainment*

Weekend Pass 1984
Comedy
73041   92 mins   C   B, V, CED   P
Three rookie sailors who have just completed
basic training are out on a weekend pass
determined to forget everything they have
learned.
MPAA:R
Marylin J Tenser Crown
International — *Vestron Video*

Weekend with the 1982
Babysitter
Comedy/Exploitation
85087   93 mins   C   B, V   P
Susan Roman, George E. Carey
A weekend babysitter goes to a film director's
house and babysits everyone but the kids.

MPAA:R
George E Carey — *Prism*

Weight Watchers 1985
Magazine Guide to a
Healthy Lifestyle
Nutrition/Physical fitness
Closed Captioned
80921   60 mins   C   B, V, CED   P
Lynn Redgrave hosts this program that features
fitness and diet tips from the Weight Watchers
program.
Weight Watchers Magazine — *Vestron Video*

Weight Watchers 1985
Magazine Guide to Dining
and Cooking
Nutrition
Closed Captioned
82429   56 mins   C   B, V   P
*Lynn Redgrave, Dr Henry Grayson, The High-
Heeled Women, directed by Larry Kasanoff*
This two-part program contains advice for dining
out on the Weight Watcher's diet plan and
cooking low-calorie meals. Chef Beck
demonstrates how to make low-calorie dishes
such as Chicken Bouillabaisse and Banana
Cream Pie.
Vestron Video — *Vestron Video*

Weird Cartoons 1986
Cartoons
88176   60 mins   B/W   B, V   P
A collection of strange and unusual cartoons,
from Betty Boop surrealism to mid-60's
psychedelia.
Max Fleischer et al.; Rhino Video — *Rhino
Video*

Wierd Science 1985
Comedy
Closed Captioned
71162   94 mins   C   B, V, LV   P
*Kelly LeBrock, Anthony Michael Hall, Ilan
Mitchell-Smith, written and directed by John
Hughes*
Two youths bring their fantasy woman to life
through their wizardry with computers. Their
synthetic dream woman helps them face some
real facts of life. Recorded in HiFi Stereo
Surroundsound on a rock score.
MPAA:PG-13
Universal — *MCA Home Video*

Welcome to Blood City 1977
Drama
80671   96 mins   C   B, V   P
*Jack Palance, Keir Dullea, Samantha Eggar,
Barry Morse*
An anonymous totalitarian organization kidnaps
a man and transports him electronically to a
fantasy western town where the person who

---

murders the most people becomes the town's "kill master"
EMI; Len Herberman Prods — *Lightning Video*

Welcome to L.A. 1977
Drama/Satire
Closed Captioned
72193   106 mins   C   B, V   P
Sissy Spacek, Sally Kellerman, Keith Carradine
Robert Altman's satire of life in Southern California has become a cult favorite over the years.
MPAA:R
Lions Gate Films — *CBS/Fox Video*

Welcome to Pooh Corner, 1984
Volume I
Fantasy
72791   111 mins   C   B, V   P
A series of made-for-video episodes involving Winnie the Pooh's misadventures in the Hundred Acre Wood. The live-action series features all Pooh's cronies, Tigger, Christopher Robin and Eeyore.
Walt Disney Productions — *Walt Disney Home Video*

Welcome to Pooh 1985
Corner—Volume 4
Cartoons/Adventure
70669   111 mins   C   B, V   P
Animated
Pooh and his pals from the Hundred Acre Wood star in several new episodes, including: "Hello, Hello There," "The Old Swimming Hole," "Practice Makes Perfect" and "Pooh Makes a Trade."
Walt Disney Productions — *Walt Disney Home Video*

Welcome to Pooh Corner 1985
Volume 5
Ethics
81665   111 mins   C   B, V   P
Winnie the Pooh and his friends demonstrate how to share and share alike in this collection of two episodes from the series.
Walt Disney Productions — *Walt Disney Home Video*

Welcome to Pooh Corner 1985
Volume 6
Ethics
81666   111 mins   C   B, V   P
Winnie the Pooh and his friends teach pre-schoolers the importance of never giving up in this collection of two episodes from the series.
Walt Disney Productions — *Walt Disney Home Video*

Welcome to Pooh 1984
Corner—Volume 2
Cartoons
79227   115 mins   C   B, V   P
Animated
Winnie the Pooh and the gang from the Hundred Acre Wood learn how to create a safe, accident free environment.
Walt Disney Productions — *Walt Disney Home Video*

Welcome to Pooh 1985
Corner—Volume 3
Fantasy
76822   111 mins   C   B, V   P
Winnie the Pooh and his friends of the Hundred Acre Wood are back in this new volume where Piglet discovers that everyone is special in their own way and Roo pretends to have a great adventure.
Walt Disney Productions — *Walt Disney Home Video*

Well, The 1951
Drama
84845   85 mins   B/W   B, V   P
Richard Rober, Harry Morgan, Barry Kelley, Christine Larson
A young black girl becomes lodged in a deep well, and the town erupts in a race riot in efforts to find her.
UA; Harry M Popkin — *United Home Video*

Wendy O'Williams Live 1986
Music-Performance
86913   56 mins   C   B, V   P
The TV-smashing icon of pornographic rock bellows and rasps through a set of her hits: "No Class," "Jail Bait," "F—k 'n' Roll" and "Ain't None of Your Business."
Philip Goodhand-Tait — *Embassy Home Entertainment*

We're Cooking Now 1984
Cookery
88033   60 mins   C   B, V   P
Franco Palumbo 8 pgms
A cooking instruction program hosted by the former Weight Watchers executive chef.
1.Chicken Variations 2.Crepes 3.Pilafs 4.Entertainment Night 5.Omelets 6.Hors D'Oeuvres 7.Guest for Dinner 8.Sunny Beef Salad
AM Available
Congress Video — *Congress Video*

We're No Angels 1955
Comedy-Drama
65401   103 mins   C   B, V   P
Humphrey Bogart, Aldo Ray, Joan Bennett, Peter Ustinov, Basil Rathbone, Leo G. Carroll
Three escapees from Devil's Island hide out with the family of a kindly French storekeeper.

Paramount — *Paramount Home Video*

Werewolf of Washington 1979
Horror
65308   90 mins   C   B, V   P
Dean Stockwell, Biff Maguire, Clifton James
As the full moon hovers over Washington, terror
lies waiting in the corridors of power.
Millco Productions — *Monterey Home Video*

West-Bound Limited, The 1923
Drama
78115   70 mins   B/W   B, V, FO   P
Johnny Harron, Ella Hall, Claire McDowell
A romantic adventurer rescues the girl from
certain death as a train is about to hit her, and
the two fall in love. Silent with music score.
FBO — *Video Yesteryear*

West of the Divide 1934
Western
15487   60 mins   B/W   B, V   P
John Wayne
The Duke heads out west ready for action.
Monogram — *Video Connection; Discount
Video Tapes; Cable Films; Spotlite Video; Sony
Video Software; Kartes Video Communications*

West Side Story 1961
Musical
37522   151 mins   C   B, V, LV,   P
                          CED
*Natalie Wood, Richard Beymer, Russ Tamblyn,
Rita Moreno, George Chakiris, directed by
Robert Wise and Jerome Robbins*
Gang rivalry on New York's West Side erupts in
a ground-breaking musical that won ten
Academy Awards. The Jets and the Sharks fight
for their own turf and Tony and Maria fight for
their own love. Amid the frenetic and brilliant
choreography by Jerome Robbins, who directed
the original Broadway show, and the high caliber
score by Leonard Bernstein and Stephin
Sondheim, there is the bittersweet message
that tragedy breeds friendship.
Academy Awards '61: Best Picture; Best
Supporting Actor (Chakiris); Best Direction
(Wise/Robbins); Best Supporting Actress
(Moreno); Best Cinematography: Color; Best
Scoring Musical; Best Film Editing; Best
Costume Design: Color; Best Art Direction:
Color; Best Sound Recording. EL, SP
United Artists; Robert Wise — *CBS/Fox Video;
RCA VideoDiscs*

Western Double Feature 194?
#1
Western
07314   120 mins   B/W   B, V, 3/4U   P
Wild Bill Elliot, Sunset Carson
Double feature; in "Calling Wild Bill Elliot"
(1943), Wild Bill comes to the aid of
homesteaders; in "Santa Fe Saddlemates"

(1945), Sunset Carson breaks up a diamond
smuggling ring.
Republic — *Nostalgia Merchant*

Western Double Feature I 19??
Western
63849   115 mins   B/W   B, V   P
*Roy Rogers, Dale Evans, Gabby Hayes, Gene
Autry, Smiley Burnette*
In "Utah" (1945, 55 minutes), Roy foils a land
swindle and helps a lady ranch owner; in "Man
from Music Mountain (1938, 60 minutes), Gene
foils a worthless gold mining stock swindle.
Republic — *Hollywood Home Theater*

Western Double Feature 19??
#2
Western
07316   120 mins   B/W   B, V, 3/4U   P
John Wayne, Monte Hale
Double feature; in "Night Riders" (1939), John
Wayne battles injustice; in "Home on the
Range" (1946, color), Monte Hale protects a
wild animal refuge.
Republic — *Nostalgia Merchant*

Western Double Feature 193?
II
Western
63848   120 mins   B/W   B, V   P
John Wayne, Gabby Hayes
John Wayne and Gabby Hayes are teamed
together in two hour-long features: "Star
Packer" (1934) and "West of the Divide"
(1933).
Monogram — *Hollywood Home Theater*

Western Double Feature 1950
#3
Western
07318   134 mins   C   B, V, 3/4U   P
Roy Rogers, Dale Evans, Rex Allen
In "Twilight in the Sierras" (1950), Roy catches
a gang of crooks. "Under Mexicali Stars"
(1950), features Rex as a cowboy who uncovers
a counterfeiting ring.
Republic — *Nostalgia Merchant*

Western Double Feature 193?
III
Western
63844   113 mins   B/W   B, V   P
*John Wayne, Johnny Mack Brown, Marsha
Hunt, Phyllis Fraser*
Two John Wayne westerns are on this tape:
"Helltown" (1938, 59 minutes), in which Wayne
catches a cattle rustler; and "Winds of the
Wasteland" (1936, 54 minutes), where he plays
an out-of-work Pony Express rider.
Paramount; Republic — *Hollywood Home
Theater*

Western Double Feature #4 194?

Western
07320 120 mins B/W   B, V, 3/4U   P
Roy Rogers, Dale Evans, Trigger, Gabby Hayes, Allan 'Rocky' Lane
Double feature; in "Don't Fence Me In" (1945), Roy Rogers helps out a woman reporter; in "Sheriff of Wichita" (1948), a frontier investigator solves a crime.
Republic — *Nostalgia Merchant*

Western Double Feature IV 193?

Western
63847 112 mins B/W   B, V   P
Roy Rogers, Gene Autry, Smiley Burnette
Roy plays a dual role in a case of mistaken identity in "Billy the Kid Returns" (1938, 56 minutes); in "Round Up Time in Texas" (1937, 56 minutes), Gene is framed on a charge of diamond smuggling.
Republic — *Hollywood Home Theater*

Western Double Feature #5 19??

Western
07322 108 mins B/W   B, V, 3/4U   P
Gene Autry, Roy Rogers, Smiley Burnette, Sons of the Pioneers
"The Big Show" (1937), features songs, action, and horses. "Home in Oklahoma" (1946), has Roy tracking down a murderer.
Republic — *Nostalgia Merchant*

Western Double Feature V 193?

Western
63846 109 mins B/W   B, V   P
John Wayne, Polly Ann Young
John Wayne stars in both halves of this double feature: in "Desert Trail" (1935, 54 minutes), he plays a rodeo star; in "Man from Utah" (1934, 55 minutes), he brings a gang of murderers to justice.
Monogram — *Hollywood Home Theater*

Western Double Feature #6 1950

Western
07324   120 mins C   B, V, 3/4U   P
Roy Rogers, Dale Evans, Trigger, Bob Livingston, Bob Steele
Double feature; "Trigger Jr. (1950) is the story of Trigger's colt; "Gangs of Sonora" (1941, black and white) deals with a fight to save a small frontier newspaper.
Republic — *Nostalgia Merchant*

Western Double Feature #7 1945

Western
07326 120 mins B/W   B, V, 3/4U   P
Wild Bill Elliott, Buster Crabbe
Double feature; "Phantom of the Plains" deals with a plan to save a woman from a gigolo; "Prairie Rustlers" tells of the problems of a man who is the identical double of Billy the Kid.
Republic; PRC — *Nostalgia Merchant*

Western Double Feature #8 194?

Western
07328 121 mins B/W   B, V, 3/4U   P
Roy Rogers, Monte Hale, John Carradine
Ranchers waiting to get right-of-way through oil land run into an ambitious resort owner in "Silver Spurs" (1943). "Out California Way" (1946), features Monte as a young cowboy looking for work in Hollywood.
Republic — *Nostalgia Merchant*

Western Double Feature #9 194?

Western
07330 120 mins B/W   B, V, 3/4U   P
Lash LaRue, Don 'Red' Barry, Noah Beery
Double feature; in "Cheyenne Takes Over" (1947), Lash LaRue battles outlaws; in "Tulsa Kid" (1940), a young man must face a gunfighter.
Eagle Lion; Republic — *Nostalgia Merchant*

Western Double Feature #10 19??

Western
07332   120 mins   C   B, V, 3/4U   P
Roy Rogers, Dale Evans, Trigger
Double feature; in "Bells of Coronado" (1950), Roy Rogers must solve a murder and uranium ore theft; in "King of the Cowboys" (1943, black and white), Roy Rogers investigates a band of saboteurs.
Republic — *Nostalgia Merchant*

Western Double Feature #11 1950

Western
33916 121 mins B/W   B, V, 3/4U   P
Roy Rogers, Penny Edwards, Gordon Jones, Riders of the Purple Sage, Gabby Hayes
Roy and Trigger act as modern day Robin Hoods to end crooked dealing in the West; Roy hides behind a a smile and a song to capture murderers of a deputy and a ranch owner.
Republic — *Nostalgia Merchant*

Western Double Feature #12 1944

Western
33917 108 mins B/W   B, V, 3/4U   P

Bob Livingston, Wild Bill Elliot, Bobby Blake, Duncan Renaldo
Red Ryder learns of a plot to scare ranchers into selling out before an oil strike is discovered; the Three Mesquiteers are sent to the Caribbean as U.S. envoys to sell Army horses.
Republic;Producers Releasing Corp — *Nostalgia Merchant*

Western Double Feature
13
Western
33919   108 mins   B/W   B, V, 3/4U   P
Red Ryder, Three Mesquiteers, Bobby Blake
Red Ryder foils outlaws trying to swindle the Duchess' stage line in a small isolated town in "Wagon Wheels Westward" (1945). "Rocky Mountain Rangers" (1940), features the Three Mesquiteers pursuing the deadly Barton Gang.
Republic — *Nostalgia Merchant*

Western Double Feature   1952
14
Western
33921   123 mins   B/W   B, V, 3/4U   P
Tim Holt, Jack Holt, Nan Leslie, Noreen Nash
Outlaws, good guys and romance on the old frontier. Amateur Robin Hoods steal back money wrongfully taken.
RKO — *Nostalgia Merchant*

Western Double Feature   1950
15
Western
33923   122 mins   B/W   B, V, 3/4U   P
Roy Rogers, Trigger, Penny Edwards, Don "Red" Barry, Lynn Merrick
Roy Rogers breaks up a cattle rustling ring; the good guys try to bring law and order to a vast Wyoming territory plagued by a crooked political boss.
Republic — *Nostalgia Merchant*

Western Double Feature   1946
16
Western
33925   108 mins   B/W   B, V, 3/4U   P
Gene Autry, Smiley Burnette, Roy Rogers, Gabby Hayes
Autry is sent to quell a revolution in Mexico; Roy Rogers' horse Lady and Gabby Hayes' horse Golden Sovereign are the focal points of the second part of this double feature.
Republic — *Nostalgia Merchant*

Western Double Feature   194?
17
Western
44855   121 mins   C   B, V, 3/4U   P
Roy Rogers, Sunset Carson
This double feature stars Roy Rogers in "The Golden Stallion" ('49). Roy battles diamond

smugglers who use wild horses to transport the goods. The second feature, "The Cherokee Flash" ('45), starring Sunset Carson, deals with a respectable citizen's outlaw past catching up to him.
Republic — *Nostalgia Merchant*

Western Double Feature   194?
18
Western
33927   108 mins   B/W   B, V, 3/4U   P
Roy Rogers, Andy Devine, Dale Evans
A Roy Rogers double feature: In "Eyes of Texas" (1948), a westerner turns his ranch into a camp for war-orphaned boys. In "Helldorado" (1946), Roy travels to Las Vegas.
Republic — *Nostalgia Merchant*

Western Double Feature   19??
19
Western
33929   108 mins   B/W   B, V, 3/4U   P
Roy Rogers, Gene Autry
"Night Time in Nevada" (1948), has Roy bringing a ruthless murderer to justice. "The Old Corral" (1937), features a clash between gangsters in limousines and deputies on horseback.
Republic — *Nostalgia Merchant*

Western Double Feature   1945
20
Western
33931   108 mins   B/W   B, V, 3/4U   P
Roy Rogers, Dale Evans, Pat Brady, Trigger
Roy helps a young woman foil a plot by crooks to swindle her inheritance. Roy appears in his first starring role (1938) and fights an outlaw gang.
Republic — *Nostalgia Merchant*

Western Double Feature   194?
21
Western
33933   121 mins   C   B, V, 3/4U   P
Roy Rogers, Red Ryder, Dale Evans, Bobby Blake
Roy battles crooks in "Susanna Pass" (1949). In "Sheriff of Las Vegas" (1944), Red must find the murderer of Judge Blackwell.
Republic — *Nostalgia Merchant*

Western Double Feature   194?
22
Western
33935   108 mins   B/W   B, V, 3/4U   P
Roy Rogers
A Roy Rogers double feature: In "Under California Stars" (1948), Roy rounds up a gang of wild horse rustlers. In "San Fernando Valley" (1944), Roy brings law and order to the valley.

Republic, Monogram — *Nostalgia Merchant*

Western Double Feature #23

19??

Western
59146   122 mins   B/W   B, V, 3/4U   P
Roy Rogers, Dale Evans
In "Spoilers of the Plains" (1951), Roy finds cattle rustlers and sets out to capture the spoilers. "Lights of Old Santa Fe" (1947), features Roy as a cowboy who rescues a beautiful rodeo owner from bankruptcy.
Republic — *Nostalgia Merchant*

Western Double Feature #24

194?

Western
59147   122 mins   C   B, V, 3/4U   P
Roy Rogers, Dale Evans, Eddie Dean
In "Cowboy and the Senorita" (1944), Roy solves the mystery of a missing girl. "Colorado Serenade" (1946), is a musical western in Cinecolor starring Eddie Dean.
Republic;Producers Releasing Corp — *Nostalgia Merchant*

Western Double Feature #25

19??

Western
59148   122 mins   B/W   B, V, 3/4U   P
Roy Rogers, Dale Evans, Andy Devine, Sons of the Pioneers
In "Pals of the Golden West" (1951), Roy discovers how valuable Trigger is. "Springtime in the Sierras" (1947), features Roy raising and selling thoroughbreds.
Republic — *Nostalgia Merchant*

Western Light

1985

Music video
82066   55 mins   C   B, V   P
The Windham Hill family of artists provide the music for this impressionistic portrait of the natural wonders of the West Coast. Available in VHS and Beta Hi-Fi Stereo.
Dann Moss; Windham Hill Productions — *Paramount Home Video; Pioneer Artists*

Westerner, The

1940

Western
80949   100 mins   B/W   B, V   P
Gary Cooper, Walter Brennan, Doris Davenport, Dana Andrews, directed by William Wyler
A cowboy strolls into a western Texas border town and becomes involved in a land war with the legendary Judge Roy Bean.
Academy Awards '40: Best Supporting Actor (Brennan).
Samuel Goldwyn — *Embassy Home Entertainment*

Westinghouse Studio One: Hold Back the Night

1952

War-Drama
21332   60 mins   B/W   B, V, FO   P
John Forsythe
A Korean war drama from one of the most famous series of early television.
CBS — *Video Yesteryear*

Westinghouse Studio One: "Little Men, Big World"

1952

Crime-Drama
47500   60 mins   B/W   B, V, FO   P
Jack Palance, Shepperd Strudwick, Ray Walston
An original TV drama by Reginald Rose about small town racketeers being menaced by a big city mob. Originally telecast on October 13, 1952.
CBS — *Video Yesteryear*

Westinghouse Studio One (Summer Theatre)

1952

Drama
66144   56 mins   B/W   B, V, FO   P
Kevin McCarthy, Frances Starr, Katharine Bard
A live TV dramatization of "Jane Eyre" by Charlotte Bronte.
CBS — *Video Yesteryear*

Westinghouse Studio One: The Defender

1957

Drama
38124   104 mins   B/W   B, V, FO   P
Steve McQueen, William Shatner, Ralph Bellamy, Martin Balsam
Courtroom melodrama originally televised live on the "Studio One" series in 1957.
CBS — *Video Yesteryear*

Westinghouse Summer Theater

1951

Drama
78100   59 mins   B/W   B, V, FO   P
Richard Purdy, Martin Brooks, Maria Riva, Robert Harris, Betty Furness
A touching story about a meek bank accountant with a strange secret and a beautiful wife.
CBS — *Video Yesteryear*

Westward Ho, The Wagons!

1956

Western
71101   94 mins   B/W   B, V   P
Fess Parker, Kathleen Crowley, Jeff York, Sebastian Cabot, George Reeves, directed by William Beaudine
The promised land lies in the west, but to get there these pioneers must pass unfriendly savages, thieves, villains and scoundrels galore.

Walt Disney Productions — *Walt Disney Home Video*

Westworld
1973

Science fiction
59362   90 mins   C   B, V, CED   P
Yul Brynner, Richard Benjamin, James Brolin, directed by Michael Crichton
Michael Crichton wrote this story of an adult vacation resort of the future which offers the opportunity to live in various fantasy worlds serviced by lifelike robots. When an electrical malfunction occurs, the robots begin to go berserk.
MPAA:PG
MGM — *MGM/UA Home Video*

Whale of a Tale, A
1976

Drama
80658   90 mins   C   B, V   P
William Shatner, Marty Allen, Abby Dalton, Andy Devine, Nancy O'Conner
A young boy trains a killer whale to appear in the big show in the main tank, at "Marine land."
MPAA:G
Independent — *United Home Video*

Wham! The Video
1985

Music-Performance
70352   28 mins   C   B, V   P
George Michael, Andrew Wrigley
This tape compiles seven videoclips by the popular British pop music group Wham, and features their best-selling American hits. The programs come in Beta Hi-Fi and VHS-Stereo formats.
Wham — *CBS/Fox Video*

What A Way to Die
1970

Adventure/Drama
70812   87 mins   C   B, V   P
William Berger, Anthony Baker, Helga Anders, Giorgia Moll, directed by Helmut Foernbacher
An evil assassin plots dispatchings with a difference.
MPAA:R
German — *Monterey Home Video*

What Do You Say to a Naked Lady?
1970

Comedy
81839   92 mins   C   B, V   P
Directed by Allen Funt
Allen Funt takes his Candid Camera to the streets to find out how people react when confronted by nude members of the opposite sex. Available in VHS and Beta Hi-Fi.
MPAA:X
United Artists — *Key Video*

What Ever Happened to Baby Jane?
1962

Suspense
65139   132 mins   B/W   B, V   P
Bette Davis, Joan Crawford, Victor Buono, Anna Lee, B.D. Merrill, directed by Robert Aldrich
Two sisters, one a demented former childhood star and the other a crippled ex-screen actress, live together in an uneasy truce until events drive one of them over the brink of madness.
Seven Arts; Warner Bros — *Warner Home Video*

What Every Baby Knows
1984

Childbirth/Parents
71364   60 mins   C   B, V   P
Dr T Berry Brazelton MD FAAP 4 pgms
Each tape in this series culled from the Doctor's weekly cable TV show, includes three discussions linked by a relevant theme.
1.Most Common Questions about Newborns, Infants and Toddlers 2.The Working Parent: Day Care, Separation and Your Child's Development 3.A Guide to Pregnancy and Childbirth 4.On Being a Father
Bangert and Gorfain — *Family Home Entertainment*

What Price Glory
1952

War-Drama
88164   109 mins   C   B, V   P
James Cagney, Dan Dailey, Corinne Calvet, William Demarest, James Gleason, Robert Wagner, Casey Adams, Craig Hill, directed by John Ford
A remake of the 1926 classic about a pair of comradely rivals in World War I France.
Sol C. Siegel; 20th Century Fox — *Key Video*

What Price Hollywood
1932

Comedy
10059   88 mins   B/W   B, V   P, T
Constance Bennett, Lowel Sherman, Neil Hamilton, directed by George Cukor
Aspiring young starlet decides to crash film world by using a director.
RKO; Selznick — *Blackhawk Films*

What the Peeper Saw
1972

Horror
60349   97 mins   C   B, V   P
Britt Ekland, Mark Lester, Hardy Kruger, Lilli Palmer
A wealthy author's wife's comfortable life turns into a terrifying nightmare when her young stepson starts exhibiting strange behavior.
Joseph E Levine; Avco Embassy — *United Home Video*

What Waits Below
1983

Science fiction
82197   88 mins   C   B, V   P
Timothy Bottoms, Robert Powell, Lisa Blount

A scientific expedition encounters an unexplainable horror while exploring the depths of a hidden cavern.
MPAA:PG
Sandy Howard; Robert D Bailey — *Lightning Video*

What Would Your Mother Say?   1981
Variety
64847   83 mins   C   B, V   P
Bill Margold, Tiffany Clark, Maria Tortuga, Kevin Gibson, Tamara Webb, Mike Ranger, Monique Monge
A hidden camera takes you inside actual casting sessions with over 40 of Hollywood's erotic stars and starlets who didn't know they were being filmed.
Real Peephole Production — *HarmonyVision*

Whatever Happened to Aunt Alice?   1969
Mystery/Drama
46197   101 mins   C   B, V   P
Geraldine Page, Ruth Gordon, Rosemary Forsyth, Robert Fuller, Mildred Dunnock, directed by Lee H. Katzin
A woman murdered her husband to inherit his estate only to discover it is worthless. Meanwhile, she must continue killing for her protection until she learns that her husband's stamp collection was worth $100,000.
MPAA:PG
Robert Aldrich — *CBS/Fox Video*

What's New Pussycat?   1965
Comedy
58853   108 mins   C   B, V, CED   P
Peter Sellers, Peter O'Toole, Romy Schneider, Paula Prentiss, Woody Allen, Ursula Andress, Capucine
A young engaged man is reluctant to give up the girls who love him and seeks the aid of a married psychiatrist who turns out to have problems of his own.
United Artists — *CBS/Fox Video*

What's Up Doc?   1972
Comedy
52708   94 mins   C   B, V   P
Barbra Streisand, Ryan O'Neal, Kenneth Mars, Austin Pendleton, directed by Peter Bogdanovich
An eccentric woman and an equally eccentric professor become involved in a chase to recover four identical flight bags containing top secret documents, a wealthy woman's jewels, the professor's musical rocks, and the girl's clothing. Bogdanovich's homage to screwball comedies of the thirties.
MPAA:G
Warner Bros; Saticoy Productions — *Warner Home Video; RCA VideoDiscs*

What's Up Tiger Lily?   1966
Comedy
08579   90 mins   C   B, V, LV,   P
                                   CED
Woody Allen, Tatsuya Mihashi, Mie Hana
This legitimate Japanese spy movie was re-edited by Woody Allen, who also added a new dialogue track, with laughable results. Music by the Lovin' Spoonful.
Henry G Saperstein Entprs — *Vestron Video; Cable Films*

Wheel of Fortune   1942
Drama
66468   83 mins   B/W   B, V   P
John Wayne, Frances Dee, Edward Ellis
A shrewd country lawyer is forced to expose his girlfriend's father as a crooked gambler.
Republic — *Republic Pictures Home Video*

Wheels-A-Rolling   1948
Transportation
74477   29 mins   C   B, V   P
This program examines the history of U.S. transportation from the stage coach to the zephyr.
Lenox Lohr; Chicago Railroad Fair — *Interurban Films; Video Yesteryear*

Wheels of Fire   1984
Adventure
82436   81 mins   C   B, V, CED   P
Gary Watkins, Lynda Wiesmeier, directed by Chris Santiago
The earth is a wasteland controlled by Sadistic highway hoodlums. When they kidnap the hero's sister, he fights back with a flame-throwing car.
MPAA:R
Rodeo Productions — *Vestron Video*

When a Stranger Calls   1979
Suspense
52753   97 mins   C   B, V, LV,   P
                                   CED
Carol Kane, Charles Durning, Colleen Dewhurst, Rachel Roberts
A babysitter is terrorized by threatening phone calls and soon realizes that the calls are coming from within the house.
MPAA:R
Columbia; Doug Chapin; Steve Feke — *RCA/Columbia Pictures Home Video*

When Eagles Fly   197?
Drama
80424   120 mins   C   B, V   P
Jennifer Dale, Robin Ward
A young woman who works at a major metropolitan hospital is seeking revenge against the man who loves her.
Independent — *Unicorn Video*

When Every Day Was the Fourth of July   1978
Drama
86581   98 mins   C   B, V   P
Dean Jones, Louise Sorel, Chris Peterson, Katy Kurtzman, Harris Yulin
A deaf-mute is accused of murder, and is defended by the father of a precocious nine-year-old girl in this made-for-TV film.
Dan Curtis — *U.S.A. Home Video*

When I Am King   1981
Adventure
64926   81 mins   C   B, V   P
Aldo Ray, Stuart Whitman
A children's adventure set in a medieval kingdom in which Jorge, a blacksmith's apprentice, must step into a path of danger and face his new love's captured spirit.
Appleton Films — *Video Associates*

When I Think of Russia   1980
Documentary/USSR
86480   54 mins   C   B, V   P
Mikhail Baryshnikov, Joseph Brodsky, Vladimir Ashkenazy, Victor Korchnoi
A study of six defected Russian artists, their memories of their homeland, and their decisions to vie for artistic freedom.
Vladimir Riff — *Mystic Fire Video*

When Knights Were Bold   1936
Comedy
78112   55 mins   B/W   B, V, FO   P
Fay Wray, Jack Buchanan, Martita Hunt
An Englishman residing in India inherits a castle in his native land. Returning home, he is knocked unconscious by a falling suit of armor while trying to impress a young lady and dreams himself back to medieval days.
Capitol — *Video Yesteryear*

When Lightning Strikes   1934
Adventure
65200   51 mins   B/W   B, V   P
Francis X. Bushman, Lightning the Wonder Dog
Lightning, the Wonder Dog prevents the owner of a rival lumber company from stealing his master's land, utilizing his talents of running, swimming, barking and smoking cigars.
Regal Productions — *Video Yesteryear*

When Nature Calls   1985
Comedy
71179   76 mins   C   B, V   P
Davie Orange, Barbara Marineau, Nicky Beim, Tina Marie Staiano, Willie Mays, G. Gordon Liddy, directed by Charles Kaufman
Kaufman and Straw Weisman wrote this wacky send-up of films and TV as kind of a scatalogical combination of "The Groove Tube" and "The Wilderness Family." In it, a city family seeks peace in the forest.
MPAA:R
Frank Vitale; Charles Kaufman — *Media Home Entertainment*

When Taekwondo Strikes   1983
Martial arts/World War II
71249   95 mins   C   B, V   P
Jhoon Rhee, Ann Winton, Angela Mao, Huang Ing Sik
One brave Taekwondo master leads the Korean freedom fighters against the occupying army of World War II Japan.
MPAA:R
World Northal — *Embassy Home Entertainment*

When the Legends Die   1987
Western
82496   105 mins   C   B, V   P
An Ute Indian strives to preserve his heritage in an often harsh modern world. Recorded in Hi-Fi.
MPAA:PG
Stuart Miller — *Playhouse Video*

When the North Wind Blows   1974
Adventure
45013   113 mins   C   B, V   P
Henry Brandon, Herbert Nelson, Dan Haggerty
An old, lone trapper hunts for and later befriends the majestic snow tiger of Siberia in the Alaskan wilderness.
MPAA:G
Sunn Classic Pictures — *United Home Video; Lucerne Films*

When the Screaming Stops   1984
Horror
81963   86 mins   C   B, V   P
Tony Kendall, Helga Line, Sylvia Tortosa
A hunter is hired to find out who has been cutting the hearts out of young women who reside in a small village near the Rhine River.
MPAA:R
Jose A. Perez — *Lightning Video*

When Things Were Rotten   1975
Comedy
85290   90 mins   C   B, V   P
Dick Gautier, Bernie Koppel, Dick Van Patten, Sid Caesar, Dudley Moore
Three episodes of the short-lived, Mel Brooks-produced, Robin Hood-spoofing comedy show.
Mel Brooks — *Paramount Home Video*

When Time Ran Out   1980
Adventure
87681   144 mins   C   B, V   P
Paul Newman, Jacqueline Bisset, William Holden, Ernest Borgnine, Edward Albert,

Barbara Carrera, Valentina Cortese, Burgess Meredith, Pat Morita
A volcano threatens to erupt, and eventually does, on a remote Polynesian island covered with expensive hotels and tourists with no way to escape. This version contains scenes not seen in the theatrically released print of the film.
MPAA:PG
Irwin Allen — *Warner Home Video*

When Wolves Cry   1969
Drama/Christmas
70978   108 mins   C   B, V   P
William Holden, Virna Lisi, Brook Fuller, Bourvil
Originally entitled "The Christmas Tree," this touching film shows an estranged father and son reunited on a Corsican vacation. Their new-found joy sours when the young son grows fatally ill.
Continental — *Video Gems*

When Worlds Collide   1951
Science fiction
55545   82 mins   C   B, V, LV   P
Richard Derr, Barbara Rush, Larry Keating, Peter Hanson, directed by Rudolph Mate
Another planet is found to be rushing inevitably towards earth, but before the collision a few people escape in a spaceship.
Academy Awards '51: Best Special Effects.
Paramount; George Pal — *Paramount Home Video*

When's Your Birthday?   1937
Comedy
56905   77 mins   B/W   B, V, FO   P
Joe E. Brown, Marian Marsh, Edgar Kennedy
Joe E. Brown stars in this comedy about a prize-fighter who studies the stars to secure success in the ring.
RKO — *Video Yesteryear*

Where Dreams Come True   1982
Occupations/Space exploration
88383   28 mins   C   B, V, 3/4U   R, P
A promotional film encouraging young people to enter into careers in space and science. Narrated by Ricardo Montalban.
NASA — *Your World Video*

Where Eagles Dare   1968
War-Drama
88209   158 mins   C   B, V   P
Clint Eastwood, Richard Burton, Mary Ure, Michael Hordern, Anton Diffring
During World War II, a small pack of Allied forces must infiltrate a German fortress to rescue an American general. Full of cliffhangers and twisting plot turns.
MPAA:PG
MGM — *MGM/UA Home Video*

Where Have All the   1974
People Gone?
Drama
71048   74 mins   C   B, V   P
Peter Graves, Kathleen Quinlan, Michael-James Wixted, George O'Hanlon Jr, Vera Bloom, directed by John Llewellyn Moxey
A terrific flash in the sky seems to have turned Earth's inhabitants to dust while the Anders family vacationed in a cave. They attempt to return home amidst the devastation.
Alpine-Jozak Prod; MPC — *Karl/Lorimar Home Video*

Where the Boys Are   1960
Comedy
72467   99 mins   C   B, V   P
George Hamilton, Jim Hutton, Yvette Mimieux, Connie Francis, Paula Prentiss, Dolores Hart
Four college girls go to Fort Lauderdale and meet men they are conveniently compatible with during spring break.
MGM — *MGM/UA Home Video*

Where the Buffalo Roam   1980
Comedy
72932   98 mins   C   B, V   P
Bill Murray, Peter Boyle
One of Bill's early starring roles as the legendary "gonzo" journalist Dr. Hunter S. Thompson.
MPAA:R
Art Linson — *MCA Home Video*

Where the Girls Are   1969
Venereal diseases
85516   23 mins   B/W   B, V   P
A military training film warning against the dangers of VD.
U.S. Military Airlift Command — *Video Yesteryear*

Where the Red Fern   1974
Grows
Drama
79314   97 mins   C   B, V   P
James Whitmore, Beverly Garland, Jack Ging, Lonny Chapman
Two Redbone hounds teach a young boy a lesson about responsibility and growing up.
MPAA:G
Lyman Dayton Productions — *Vestron Video*

Where the Toys Come   1984
From
Fantasy
79228   68 mins   C   B, V   P
Two toys try to discover their roots in a journey that takes them around the world.
Walt Disney Productions — *Walt Disney Home Video*

Where Time Began — 1977
Science fiction/Adventure
65716　87 mins　C　B, V　P
The discovery of a strange manuscript of a scientist's journey to the center of the earth leads to the decision to recreate the dangerous mission. Based on the Jules Verne classic novel, "Journey to the Center of the Earth."
MPAA:G
International Picture Show — Embassy Home Entertainment

Where Trails End — 1942
Western
85227　54 mins　B/W　B, V　P
Tom Keene
A western with just about everything, including phosphorescent-clothed good guys, Nazis, scoundrels, literate horses and Gallic sidekicks.
Monogram — Video Yesteryear

Where's Poppa? — 1970
Comedy
65334　84 mins　C　B, V　P
George Segal, Ruth Gordon, Trish Van Devere
A Jewish lawyer's aged mother constantly harms his love life, and he considers various means of getting rid of her.
United Artists — Key Video

Which Way Is Up? — 1977
Comedy
14013　94 mins　C　B, V　P
Richard Pryor, Lonette McKee, Margaret Avery, Morgan Woodward, Marilyn Coleman, directed by Michael Schultz
The story of an orange picker who accidentally becomes a union hero. He leaves his wife and family at home while he seeks work in Los Angeles. There he finds himself a new woman, starts a new family, and sells out to the capitalists.
MPAA:R
Universal; Steve Krantz Prod — MCA Home Video

Which Way to the Front? — 1970
Comedy
81786　96 mins　C　B, V　P
Jerry Lewis, Jan Murray, John Wood, Steve Franken, directed by Jerry Lewis
A group of Army rejects form a guerilla band and wage their own small-scale war during World War II.
MPAA:G
Warner Bros. — Warner Home Video

While The City Sleeps — 1956
Crime-Drama
84809　100 mins　B/W　B, V　P
Dana Andrews, Rhonda Fleming, George Sanders, Howard Duff, Thomas Mitchell, directed by Fritz Lang
A complex murder mystery by the master director, involving a newspaper's reporters who try to lure the killer out.
RKO — United Home Video

Whisky Galore — 1948
Comedy
50957　81 mins　B/W　B, V　P
Basil Radford, Joan Greenwood, Gordon Jackson, James Robertson Justice
A whiskey-less Scottish island gets a lift when a ship carrying 50,000 cases of spirits becomes wrecked off their coast. A full-scale rescue operation and evasion of the British government ensues.
Ealing Studios — THORN EMI/HBO Video; Learning Corp of America

Whispering Shadow — 1933
Mystery/Serials
12555　156 mins　B/W　B, V　P
Bela Lugosi, Robert Warwick, directed by Al Herman, Colbert Clark
Serial starring the master criminal known as the "faceless whisperer." Twelve chapters, 13 minutes each.
Mascot — Video Connection; Video Yesteryear

Whistle Down the Wind — 1962
Drama
78640　98 mins　B/W　B, V　P
Hayley Mills, Bernard Lee, Alan Bates, directed by Richard Attenborough
Three children find a murderer hiding in a barn and believe that he is Jesus Christ.
Pathe — Embassy Home Entertainment

Whistlin' Dan — 1932
Western
84839　60 mins　B/W　B, V　P
Ken Maynard
The whistlin' cowboy faces a range war in this vintage western.
Tiffany; Ken Maynard — United Home Video

White Christmas — 1954
Musical
87571　120 mins　C　B, V　P
Bing Crosby, Danny Kaye, Rosemary Clooney, Vera-Ellen, Dean Jagger
Two ex-army buddies become a popular comedy team and play a financially unstable Vermont inn at Christmas for charity's sake. Songs by Irving Berlin include the title tune, "Snow," "Sisters," "Count Your Blessings (Instead of Sheep)," "Choreography" and that all-time classic, "What Do You Do With A General When He Stops Being a General?"
Paramount — Paramount Home Video

White City: Pete Townshend   1985
Music-Performance
82430   60 mins   C   B, V, LV   P
Pete Townshend, Andrew Wilde, Francis Barber, directed by Richard Lowenstein
The former Who guitarist portrays a musician who helps bring a close friend and his estranged wife back together. This semi-autobiographical film includes music from Townshend.
Eel Pie Recording Productions LTD — *Vestron Video*

White Comanche   1967
Western
84025   90 mins   C   B, V   P
William Shatner, Joseph Cotten
Half-breed twins battle themselves and each other to a rugged climax.
Foreign — *United Home Video*

White Dawn, The   1975
Drama
64029   110 mins   C   B, V   P
Warren Oates, Timothy Bottoms, Lou Gossett
Three sailors, separated from their ship during a hunt, struggle to survive in the Arctic wasteland.
MPAA:R
Paramount — *Paramount Home Video*

White Heat   1949
Drama
29233   114 mins   B/W   B, V   P
James Cagney, Virginia Mayo, Edmond O'Brien
A ruthless gangster has a mother complex, but to all others around him, he's a heartless killer. One of Cagney's best roles.
Warner Bros — *Key Video; RCA VideoDiscs*

White Legion   1936
Drama
78111   81 mins   B/W   B, V, FO   P
Jan Keith, Tala Birell, Snub Pollard
Workers and engineers push their way through steaming jungles and reeking swamps while building the Panama Canal. Many fall victim to yellow fever, relying on dedicated doctors—the "white legion"—to complete the project.
Grand National Films — *Video Yesteryear*

White Lightning   1973
Adventure
58828   101 mins   C   CED   P
Burt Reynolds, Ned Beatty, Bo Hopkins, Jennifer Billingsley, Louise Latham
An adventure drama of murder, revenge, and moonshine in the new South.
MPAA:PG
United Artists; Levy Gardner Lavin Productions — *CBS/Fox Video; RCA VideoDiscs*

White Line Fever   1975
Adventure
64911   89 mins   C   B, V   P
Jan-Michael Vincent, Kay Lenz
A young trucker's search for a happy life with his childhood sweetheart is complicated by a corrupt group in control of the long-haul trucking business.
MPAA:PG
John Kemeny — *RCA/Columbia Pictures Home Video*

White Mama   1979
Drama
71302   96 mins   C   B, V   P
Bette Davis, Ernest Harden Jr, Eileen Heckart, Laurene Tuttle, directed by Jackie Cooper
A poor white widow takes in a 15-year-old streetwise black youth. Together, they find new sources of personal enrichment.
Tomorrow Entertainment — *U.S.A. Home Video*

White Mane   1952
Drama
65621   38 mins   B/W   B, V   P
Alain Emery, Frank Silvera
The poignant, poetic story of a proud and fierce white stallion that continually alludes attempts to be captured by ranchers, only to be "tamed" by the love of a small boy.
William Snyder — *Embassy Home Entertainment; Texture Films*

White Music   1981
Music
47299   35 mins   C   LV   P
A fantasy ski adventure set in the south of France provides a visual interpretation of the background rock music composed by Talizman.
Masaru Ohtaki — *Pioneer Video Imports*

White Nights   1985
Drama
87265   135 mins   C   B, V   P
Mikhail Baryshnikov, Gregory Hines, Isabella Rosselini, Helen Mirren, Jerzy Skolimowski, Geraldine Page, directed by Taylor Hackford
A Russian ballet dancer who defected to the U.S. is a passenger on a jet that crashes in the Soviet Union. With the help of a defected American dancer who lives in Siberia, he plots to escape again.
MPAA:PG-13
Taylor Hackford; William S. Gilmore — *RCA/Columbia Pictures Home Video*

White Pass and Yukon/Rio Grande Southern/The Bustling Narrow Gauge 1951
Trains
84939   31 mins   C   B, V   P
On this tape three films highlighting various trains running through treacherous terrains, mountains and steep grades are presented.
Woodron Gorman — *Blackhawk Films*

White Pongo 1945
Adventure
84545   73 mins   B/W   B, V   P
Richard Fraser, Marie Wrixon, Lionel Royce, directed by Sam Newfield
A search in the Congo for the fearsone white gorilla. Camp classic.
PRC — *Hollywood Home Theater*

White Rose, The 1983
War-Drama
65222   108 mins   C   B, V   P
Lena Stölze, Wulf Kessler, Oliver Siebert, Ulrich Tucker, directed by Michael Verhoeven
A group of dissident students in Munich, circa 1942, put their lives in danger by distributing anti-Nazi propaganda. In German with English subtitles.
GE
TeleCulture Films — *MGM/UA Home Video*

White Seal, The 1975
Cartoons
71367   30 mins   C   B, V   P
Animated, voices of Roddy McDowall, June Foray
Man's presence in the Bering Sea poses a threat to Kitock's safety. The little white seal searches the frigid waters for a new home.
Chuck Jones — *Family Home Entertainment*

White Slave 1986
Adventure
84104   90 mins   C   B, V   P
Elvire Avoray, Will Gonzales, Andrew Louis Coppola, directed by Roy Garrett
An Englishwoman is captured by bloodthirsty cannibals and, rather than being eaten, is tormented and made a slave.
MPAA:R
Empire — *Lightning Video*

White Tower, The 1950
Drama
59647   98 mins   C   B, V   P
Glenn Ford, Claude Rains, Sir Cedric Hardwicke, Oscar Homolka, Lloyd Bridges
The tale of five men and a woman who set out to scale the infamous White Tower in the Alps. Each person's true nature is revealed as he

scales the peak, which has defied all previous attempts.
RKO — *Hollywood Home Theater*

White-Water Sam 1978
Adventure
66637   87 mins   C   B, V   P
Keith Larsen
White-Water Sam and his Siberian Husky, Sybar, embark on an exciting trip through the uncharted wilds of the Great Northwest.
MPAA:G
Keith Larsen — *Monterey Home Video*

White Wilderness 1958
Documentary
82299   72 mins   C   B, V   P
This documentary examines the natural wonders of the Arctic in this installment of the "True-Life Adventures" series.
Academy Awards '58: Best Feature Length Documentary
Buena Vista — *Walt Disney Home Video*

White Zombie, The 1932
Horror
08586   73 mins   B/W   B, V   P
Bela Lugosi, Madge Bellamy, John Harron, directed by Victor Halperin
Corpses return to life in this classic horror film. Zombies rob graves and take bodies to sugar mill where zombies work around the clock for mad White Zombie.
United Artists — *Prism; Mossman Williams Productions; Cable Films; Video Connection; Video Yesteryear; Hollywood Home Theater; Discount Video Tapes; Western Film & Video Inc; Admit One Video; Kartes Video Communications; Movie Buff Video*

Whitesnake 1983
Music video
88111   16 mins   C   B, V   P
Video clips from one of the lesser and louder English heavy metal bands.
Sony Video — *Sony Video Software*

Whitetail: Still Hunting and Stand Hunting 1985
Hunting
87651   38 mins   C   B, V   P
An instructional program on how to stalk, trap and kill whitetail deer, in any number of North American terrains.
Sportsmen On Film — *Sportsmen on Film*

Whitewater 1982
Sports-Water
63134   120 mins   C   B, V   P, T
This videocassette is a compilation of five programs documenting whitewater rafting expeditions in Chile ("River of Thunder"), Africa

("The Ultimate Adventure"), Oregon, Alaska and the Grand Canyon.
International Film and TV Festival '81: Gold Medal ("River of Thunder"). AM Available
Richard Kidd Prods; Sobek Expeditions; OARS Inc — *Video Travel*

Whitewater II   1983
Boating
70179   55 mins   C   B, V   P
Two short films are combined on one cassette. In the first, the Sobek Expeditions travel to Papua New Guinea to raft and canoe the Watut River. The second film follows O.A.R.S. on a scenic raft trip down the San Juan River in Colorado.
Video Travel — *Video Travel*

Whitney Houston—The   1986
#1 Video Hits
Music video
86790   18 mins   C   B, V   P
A collection of Houston's video hits, including "How Will I Know," "You Give Good Love" and "The Greatest Love of All."
RCA Video — *RCA/Columbia Pictures Home Video*

Who Am I This Time?   1982
Comedy
81896   60 mins   C   B, V   P
Susan Sarandon, Christopher Walken, Robert Ridgely, directed by Jonathan Demme
Two shy people can only express their love for each other through their roles in a local theater production. Based upon a story by Kurt Vonnegut, Jr.
Morton Neal Miller — *Media Home Entertainment*

Who Has Seen the Wind?   1977
Drama
72884   102 mins   C   B, V   P
Jose Ferrer, Brian Painchaud, Charmion King
A young boy must learn how to grow up during the Depression.
Astral Films; Souris River Films — *Embassy Home Entertainment*

Who Is The Black Dahlia?   1975
Mystery/Drama
79247   96 mins   C   B, V   P
Efrem Zimbalist Jr., Lucie Arnaz, Ronny Cox, Macdonald Carey, Linden Chiles
A detective tries to figure out who murdered a twenty two year old girl nicknamed "The Black Dahlia" back in 1947.
Douglas S. Cramer Company — *Worldvision Home Video*

Who Killed Doc Robbin?   1948
Mystery
08718   50 mins   C   B, V, FO   P
Larry Olsen, Don Castle, by Bernard Carr
A group of youngsters try to clear their friend, Dan, the town handyman, when the sinister Dr. Robbins is murdered.
United Artists — *Video Yesteryear; Hollywood Home Theater; Discount Video Tapes*

Who Killed Julie Greer?   1961
Mystery
82184   52 mins   B/W   B, V   P
Dick Powell, Nick Adams, Lloyd Bridges, Mickey Rooney, Ronald Reagan, directed by Robert Ellis Miller
A millionaire homicide inspector must put the pieces together and find out who murdered a beautiful young woman. An episode from "The Dick Powell Theatre."
Four Star Television — *RKO HomeVideo*

Who Killed Mary What's   1971
'Er Name?
Adventure
59352   90 mins   C   B, V   P
Red Buttons, Sylvia Miles, Conrad Bain, Ron Carey, David Doyle, Sam Waterston
An ex-fighter tracks a playgirl's killer through street gangs and bizarre cults.
MPAA:PG
Heritage Enterprises — *Video Gems; Prism*

Who Rocks   1983
America—1982 American
Tour, The
Music-Performance
64334   118 mins   C   B, V, CED   P
The rock group's final concert of their North American tour at the Maple Leaf Gardens in Toronto, Canada on December 17, 1982 includes such songs as "Pinball Wizard," "Who's Next," and "Tommy." In stereo on VHS format.
Jack Calmes — *CBS/Fox Video*

Who Slew Auntie Roo?   1971
Mystery/Suspense
80687   90 mins   C   B, V   P
Shelley Winters, Sir Ralph Richardson, Mark Lester, Lionel Jeffries, Hugh Griffith, directed by Curtis Harrington
An elderly widow gets a surprise from two unexpected guests at her annual Christmas celebration for orphans.
MPAA:PG
Orion Pictures — *Vestron Video*

Whodini: Back in Black   1986
Music video
88361   18 mins   C   B, V   P

Four 'songs' from the rap vocalist on video:
"Freaks Come Out at Night," "Big Mouth,"
"Escape" and "Funky Beat."
RCA Video — *RCA/Columbia Pictures Home Video*

Who'll Stop the Rain?   1978
Drama
76043   126 mins   C   B, V   P
Nick Nolte, Tuesday Weld, Michael Moriarty
Nolte plays a temperamental Vietnam veteran
who is enlisted in a smuggling scheme to
transport a large amount of heroin from Vietnam
into California.
MPAA:R
United Artists — *Key Video*

Wholly Moses!   1980
Comedy
51572   125 mins   C   B, V, LV   P
The son of a slave in biblical times becomes
convinced his mission is to lead the chosen,
instead of his brother-in-law, Moses.
MPAA:PG
Columbia Pictures; Freddie
Fields — *RCA/Columbia Pictures Home Video;
RCA VideoDiscs*

Whoopi Goldberg Live   1986
Comedy-Performance
84786   75 mins   C   B, V   P
Whoopie Goldberg, directed by Mike Nichols
The acclaimed comedienne's one-woman
Broadway performance.
Vestron Video — *Vestron Video*

Whoops Apocalypse   1983
Comedy
65336   137 mins   C   B, V   P
*John Cleese, John Barron, Richard Griffiths,
Peter Jones, Bruce Montague, Barry Morse*
This program is a version of the British hit
television series. It is a biting account of events
leading up to World War III, full of rapid fire wit,
one liners, and manic energy.
Humphrey Barclay — *Pacific Arts Video*

Who's Afraid of Virginia   1966
Woolf?
Drama
58256   127 mins   B/W   B, V   P
*Richard Burton, Elizabeth Taylor, George Segal,
Sandy Dennis, directed by Mike Nichols*
A night-long journey into the private hell of an
embittered, embattled marriage. Adapted from
Edward Albee's classic modern play.
Academy Awards '66: Best Actress (Taylor),
Supporting Actress (Dennis), Best
Cinematography—Black and White (Haskell
Wexler).
Warner Bros — *Warner Home Video*

Who's Minding the Mint?   1967
Comedy
70563   97 mins   C   B, V   P
*Jim Hutton, Dorothy Provine, Milton Berle, Joey
Bishop, Bob Denver, Walter Brennan, directed
by Howard Morris*
A money checker at the U.S. Mint must replace
50,000 dollars he lost or face prison. He enlists
a team of counterfeitors to infiltrate the Mint
over the weekend and replace the lost cash.
Available on Beta Hi-Fi.
Columbia — *RCA/Columbia Pictures Home
Video*

Who's Out There?—A   198?
Search for
Extraterrestrial Life
Space exploration/Science fiction
72058   60 mins   C   B, V   P
Orson Welles narrates this informative and
entertaining film that speculates on whether life
exists beyond our solar system.
NASA — *MPI Home Video*

Whose Life Is It Anyway?   1981
Drama
59366   118 mins   C   B, V, CED   P
*Richard Dreyfuss, John Cassavetes, Christine
Iahti, Bob Balaban, Kenneth McMillan, Kaki
Hunter, Thomas Carter, directed by John
Badham*
A talented sculptor is paralyzed in an auto
accident and decides not to live anymore. What
follows is his struggle, both legally and morally,
to convince the hospital authorities to let him
die.
MPAA:R
MGM — *MGM/UA Home Video*

Why Do I Call You Sexy?   1983
Cosmetology
66176   90 mins   C   B, V   P
Famed hairstylist and makeover artist of the
Stars, Jose Eber, offers tips to women on hair
and makeup.
Karl Video — *Karl/Lorimar Home Video*

Why Shoot the Teacher   1979
Drama
65394   101 mins   C   B, V   P
Bud Cort, Samantha Eggar
An amusingly told story of life on the prairies at
the height of the Great Depression. It's an
account of one man's first collision with reality.
Laurence Hertzog — *Embassy Home
Entertainment*

Why We Fight   1945
World War II/Documentary
48851   63 mins   B/W   B, V, 3/4U   P
Directed by Frank Capra 7 pgms
A series of feature-length documentaries
intended for Americans in the armed forces

during World War II. They later fascinated the general public. Programs are available individually.
1.*Prelude to War* 2.*The Nazis Strike* 3.*Divide and Conquer* 4.*The Battle of Britain* 5.*The Battle of Russia* 6.*The Battle of China* 7.*War Comes to America*
US War Department — *Victory Video; Western Film & Video Inc; International Historic Films; Festival Films*

Wicker Man, The   1975
Mystery
56739   103 mins   C   B, V   P
Edward Woodward, Britt Ekland, Diane Cilento, Ingrid Pitt, Christopher Lee
The disappearance of a young girl leads to the terrible secret of the Wicker Man.
Peter Snell — *Media Home Entertainment*

Widow's Nest   1977
Suspense
77258   90 mins   C   B, V   P
Patricia Neal, Susan Oliver, Lila Kedrova, Valentina Cortese
Three widowed sisters live in a bizarre fantasy world when they lock themselves in a dingy mansion.
Navarro Prods. — *Magnum Entertainment*

Wifemistress   1979
Drama
39031   101 mins   C   B, V   P
Marcello Mastroianni, Laura Antonelli, directed by Marco Vicario
Set in the early 1900's, this is the story of an invalid wife who resents her neglectful husband. When he goes into hiding because of a murder he didn't commit, the wife begins to drift into a world of her fantasies. Italian dialogue, English subtitles.
MPAA:R IT
Franco Cristaldi, Quartet
Films — *RCA/Columbia Pictures Home Video; CBS/Fox Video (disc only)*

Wilbur and Orville: The   1978
First to Fly
Adventure/Aeronautics
75619   47 mins   C   B, V   P
This is the story of the Wright Brothers' early unsuccessful attempts at flying.
VidAmerica — *VidAmerica; Children's Video Library*

Wild and the Free, The   1980
Adventure/Comedy
71304   96 mins   C   B, V   P
Linda Gray, Granville Van Dusen, Frank Logan, Ray Forchion, Bill Gribble, Sharon Anderson, directed by James Hill
A female scientist disagrees sharply with her male counterpart on how a group of

chimpanzees should be trained. Together in Africa, the simians bring them together.
BSR and Marble Arch Productions — *U.S.A. Home Video*

Wild and Woody   1965
Cartoons
82362   51 mins   C   B, V   P
Animated, voice of Grace Stafford
Find out how Woody Woodpecker won the West in this collection of nine cartoons from the 50's and the 60's.
Walter Lantz — *MCA Home Video*

Wild and Woolly   1917
Western/Comedy
69555   61 mins   B/W   B, V, FO   P
Douglas Fairbanks Sr.
The son of a New York railroad tycoon travels out West on business expecting to find himself on the rugged frontier. Silent with musical score.
Artcraft — *Video Yesteryear*

Wild Angels, The   1966
Adventure
82572   124 mins   C   B, V   P
Peter Fonda, Nancy Sinatra, Bruce Dern, Diane Ladd, directed by Roger Corman
A film about a group of rebellious motorcyclists who are determined to live life their own way.
MPAA:PG
Roger Corman — *Embassy Home Entertainment*

Wild Beasts, The   1985
Adventure/Horror
70860   92 mins   C   B, V   P
John Aldrich, Lorraine DeSelle
Humans and non-humans clash violently in this thrilling chomp-fest.
Euramco Int'l — *Lightning Video*

Wild Blue Yonder, The   1985
Documentary/History-US
70684   45 mins   C   B, V   P
Narrated by Ken Howard, directed by Fred Warshofsky
Part of the "In Defense of Freedom" series, this program traces the history of the United States Air Force.
A.B. Marian — *MPI Home Video*

Wild Bunch, The   1969
Western
38955   145 mins   C   B, V, LV   P
William Holden, Ernest Borgnine, Robert Ryan, directed by Sam Peckinpah
A brutal, bloody western about a group of losers in the dying days of the lawless frontier, fighting and killing those in their path.
MPAA:R

Warner Bros — *Warner Home Video; RCA VideoDiscs*

Wild Country, The   1970
Adventure
88199   92 mins   C   B, V   P
Steve Forrest, Ron Howard, Clint Howard
A children's film detailing the trials and tribulations of a frontier family moving into the inhospitable Wyoming desert.
MPAA:G
Walt Disney Prod. — *Walt Disney Home Video*

Wild Duck, The   1984
Drama
82442   96 mins   C   B, V   P
Jeremy Irons, Liv Ullman, Lucinda Jones, Arthur Dignam, directed by Henri Safran
A father discovers that his beloved daughter is illegitimate and turns against her. To regain his love, she plans to sacrifice her most prized possession. Based on the classic Ibsen play.
MPAA:PG
RKR Releasing — *Vestron Video*

Wild Engine/Mistaken   1923
Orders, The
Trains/Drama
84940   48 mins   B/W   B, V   P
Helen Holmes, Jack Hoxie, Hoot Gibson
The early screen daredevil Holmes stars in two railroad-and-betrayal epics.
Unknown — *Blackhawk Films*

Wild Geese, The   1978
Adventure
65407   132 mins   C   B, V, CED   P
Richart Burton, Roger Moore, Richard Harris
The adventure begins when a veteran band of mercenaries land deep inside Africa to rescue the imprisoned leader of an emerging African nation. Their mission meets an unexpected turn when the soldiers are betrayed by those who helped finance their trip!
MPAA:R
Allied Artists — *CBS/Fox Video*

Wild Guitar   1962
Drama
84355   92 mins   B/W   B, V   P
Arch Hall Jr, Arch Hall Sr, directed by Ray Dennis Steckler
A swinging youth cycles into Hollywood and, improbably, becomes an instant teen-idol. Considered to be a top contender for "Worst Picture of All Time" honors.
Fairway Prods — *Rhino Video*

Wild Gypsies   1969
Adventure
81216   85 mins   C   B, V, LV   P
Todd Grange, Gayle Clark, Laurel Welcome

A band of gypsies seek revenge against a renegade member who attacked a fellow gypsy and murdered his former lover.
Manson International Pictures — *New World Video*

Wild Horse   1931
Western
43018   68 mins   B/W   B, V, FO   P
Hoot Gibson, Stepin Fetchit
A pair of bronco busters sign up to work at a rodeo ranch and take charge when trouble strikes.
Allied — *Video Yesteryear*

Wild Horse Canyon   1925
Western
58265   68 mins   B/W   B, V, FO   P
Yakima Canutt, Edward Cecil, Helene Rosson, Jay Talbet
Yakima Canutt, the man credited with creating the profession of stunt man, stars in this tale about a lady rancher who requires saving from her evil foreman. The climactic stampede scene gives Yakima a chance to demonstrate a high dive off a cliff and a somersault onto his horse. Silent, with musical score.
Unknown — *Video Yesteryear; Discount Video Tapes*

Wild Horse Hank   1979
Adventure/Western
82438   94 mins   C   B, V   P
Linda Blair, Richard Crenna, Michael Wincott, Al Waxman, directed by Eric Till
A young woman risks everything to save a herd of wild mustangs from hunters.
Time-Life Films — *Vestron Video*

Wild Horses   1984
Western
75671   90 mins   C   B, V   P
A rugged 1970's cowboy is determined to make a living by capturing and selling wild horses, but is plagued by hunters.
Satori Entertainment Corp. — *VidAmerica*

Wild in the Country   1961
Drama
64935   114 mins   C   B, V, CED   P
Elvis Presley, Hope Lange, Tuesday Weld, Millie Perkins, John Ireland, Gary Lockwood
A woman psychiatrist and a social worker rehabilitate a delinquent rural boy.
20th Century Fox — *CBS/Fox Video*

Wild Life, The   1984
Comedy
Closed Captioned
80412   96 mins   C   B, V, LV   P
Christopher Penn, Rick Moranis, Hart Bochner, Eric Stoltz, Jenny Wright, Lea Thompson

---

A recent high school graduate takes on a wild and crazy wrestler as his roommate in a swinging singles apartment complex. Available in VHS and Beta Hi Fi Stereo.
MPAA:R
Art Linson; Cameron Crowe — *MCA Home Video*

Wild One, The   1954
Drama
87267   79 mins   B/W   B, V   P
Marlon Brando, Lee Marvin, Mary Murphy, Robert Keith, Jay C. Flippen, directed by Laslo Benedek
The classic paean to youthful 1950's rebelliousness, in which two motorcycle gangs descend upon a quiet midwestern town and each other, the leader of one struggling against social prejudices and his own gang's lawlessness to find find love and a normal life.
Stanley Kramer; Columbia — *RCA/Columbia Pictures Home Video*

Wild Orchids   1929
Drama
80211   103 mins   B/W   B, V   P
Greta Garbo, Lewis Stone, Nils Asther
A husband suspects his wife of infidelity while they take a business cruise to Java. One of Garbo's eartliest silent films.
MGM — *MGM/UA Home Video*

Wild Party, The   1974
Drama
65429   90 mins   C   B, V   P
Raquel Welch, James Coco, Perry King, David Dukes
It's 1929, a year of much frivolity in Hollywood; and drinking, dancing, maneuvering and almost every sort of romance are the rule of the night at silent-film comic Jolly Grimm's sumptuous, star-studded party.
MPAA:R
United Artists — *Embassy Home Entertainment*

Wild Pony, The   1983
Drama
87219   87 mins   C   B, V   P
Marilyn Lightstone, Art Hindle, Josh Byrne, directed by Kevin Sullivan
A young boy spurns his new stepfather, preferring to live with his pony instead.
Cori Films — *Vestron Video*

Wild Ride, The   1960
Drama
38975   59 mins   B/W   B, V, FO   P
Jack Nicholson, Georgianna Carter
Jack Nicholson, in an early starring role, portrays a rebellious punk of the beat generation who hotrods his way into trouble and tragedy.

Filmgroup — *Video Yesteryear; Discount Video Tapes*

Wild Rides   1982
Documentary
66327   27 mins   C   B, V   P
Matt Dillon
Teen heartthrob Matt Dillon takes viewers on a tour of America's most exciting roller coasters. The soundtrack features music by The Who, Steely Dan, Steve Miller, The Cars and Jimi Hendrix. In stereo.
Klein & Video Programs — *Warner Home Video*

Wild Rose   1985
Drama
84110   96 mins   C   B, V   P
Lisa Eichhorn, Tom Bower, James Cada, directed by Ingmar Bergman
A Minnesota female steel worker must buck the system to save her job, struggling to assert her independence.
Troma — *Lightning Video*

Wild Strawberries   1957
Drama
60426   90 mins   B/W   B, V   P
Victor Sjostrom, Bibi Andersson, Max von Sydow, directed by Ingmar Bergman
Bergman's classic film of fantasy, dreams and nightmares concerning an aging professor who must come to terms with his anxieties and guilt before his death. In Swedish with English subtitles.
SW
A B Svensk; Janus Films — *Video Yesteryear; CBS/Fox Video; Cable Films*

Wild Swans, The   1987
Cartoons/Fairy tales
73865   62 mins   C   B, V   P
Animated
A young girl must save her six brothers who have been turned into swans by an evil witch.
John Watkins; Simon Nuchtern — *RCA/Columbia Pictures Home Video*

Wild Times   1979
Western
73561   200 mins   C   B, V   P
Sam Elliott, Trish Stewart, Ben Johnson, Dennis Hopper, Pat Hingle
This movie is based upon Brian Garfield's novel about Hugh Cardiff, a hero who lived his life to the hilt.
Rattlesnake Prods; Golden Circle — *Prism*

Wild Wheels   1975
Drama
81614   81 mins   C   B, V   P

Casey Kasem, Dovie Beams, Terry Stafford, Robert Dix
A group of dune buggy enthusiasts seek revenge against a gang of motorcyclists who have ravaged a small California beach town.
MPAA:PG
American Films Ltd. — Video Gems

Wilderness Family Part 2   1977
Adventure
63381   104 mins   C   B, V   P
Robert Logan, Susan D. Shaw
The further adventures of the Robinson family, who left civilization for the freedom of the wilderness, are portrayed.
MPAA:G
Pacific International Enterprises — Media Home Entertainment

Wildside Volume One: 1985
Well Known Secret
Western/Adventure
81980   55 mins   C   B, V   P
Howard E. Rollins, Jr., William Smith, Terry Funk, John DiAquino, J. Eddie Peck
The Wildside Chamber of Commerce ia an elite law enforcement unit that must stop a former Confederate General from destroying their small town.
Touchstone Television — Touchstone Home Video

Wildside Volume Two: 1985
Delinquency of a Miner
Western/Adventure
81981   55 mins   C   B, V   P
Howard E. Rollins, Jr., William Smith, Terry Funk, John DiAquino, J. Eddie Peck
The Wildside Chamber of Commerce comes to the aid of a young man duped into a slave labor scheme.
Touchstone Television — Touchstone Home Video

Wildside Volume Three: 1985
The Crime of the Century
Western
81982   55 mins   C   B, V   P
Howard E. Rollins, Jr., William Smith, Terry Funk, John DiAquino, J. Eddie Peck
The Wildside Chamber of Commerce must stop a band of British Crimean War deserters from attacking innocent settlers and forcing them from their land.
Touchstone Television — Touchstone Home Video

Wildside Vol. IV: Don't   1985
Keep the Home Fires
Burning
Western/Adventure
82368   55 mins   C   B, V   P

Howard E. Rollins, Jr., William Smith, J. Eddie Peck, John DiAquino, Terry Funk
The Wildside Chamber of Commerce attempts to rid the area of con artists who are ripping people off through a fire insurance scam.
Touchstone Television — Touchstone Home Video

Wildside Vol. V: Buffalo   1985
Who?
Western/Adventure
82369   55 mins   C   B, V   P
Howard E. Rollins, Jr., William Smith, J. Eddie Peck, John DiAquino, Terry Funk
The Wildside Chamber of Commerce must stop an assassin disguised as Buffalo Bill from killing a Spanish ambassador.
Touchstone Television — Touchstone Home Video

Wildside Vol. VI: Until the   1985
Fat Lady Sings
Western/Adventure
82370   55 mins   C   B, V   P
Howard E. Rollins, Jr., William Smith, J. Eddie Peck, John DiAquino, Terry Funk
A vengeful gunslinger finds that settling the score with Brodie Hollister is not so easy. Luckily, the Wildside Chamber of Commerce comes to his aid.
Touchstone Television — Touchstone Home Video

Will: G. Gordon Liddy   1982
Biographical/Drama
79331   97 mins   C   B, V   P
Robert Conrad, Kathy Cannon, Gary Bayer, Peter Ratray
A dramatization of Liddy's autobiography of how the former FBI agent became involved in the breakin at the Democratic Headquarters at the Watergate Hotel. In Beta Hi-Fi and VHS Stereo.
A. Shane Company — U.S.A. Home Video

Will of a People, The   1946
Spain/Documentary
12852   55 mins   C   B, V, FO   P
A well done story of the Spanish revolution and the rise to power of Generalissimo Franco, told in footage from Spanish archives.
Unknown — Video Yesteryear; International Historic Films

Will Rogers: Champion of   1978
the People
Biographical
57787   54 mins   C   B, V   P
Robert Hays
The early years of Will Rogers, during which he fought for law and order in his Oklahoma hometown, are chronicled.

Schick Sunn — *VidAmerica; United Home Video*

Willa 1979
Drama
86862   95 mins   C   B, V   P
Cloris Leachman, Deborah Raffin, Clu Gulager, John Amos, Diane Ladd
An abandoned wife with two kids is impregnated by her lover, faces a variety of other setbacks, and fights to make a better life.
GJL Prod.; Dove Inc.; CBS — *Prism*

Willard 1971
Horror
82292   95 mins   C   B, V   P
Bruce Davison, Ernest Borgnine, Elsa Lanchester, Sondra Locke, directed by Daniel Mann
Willard is a demented young man who trains a group of rats to commit all kinds of devious crimes.
MPAA:PG
Cinerama; BCP Productions — *Prism*

Willie and the Poor Boys 1985
Music-Performance
71018   30 mins   C   B, V   P
Bill Wyman, Charlie Watts, Andy Fairweatherhow, Geraint Watkins, Mickey Gee, Kenny Jones, Ronnie Wood, Henry Spinetti, Chris Rea, Terry Taylor, Mel Collins, Raf Ravenscroft, Ringo Starr
Proceeds from sales of this collaborative effort benefit A.R.M.S. (Action Research into Multiple Sclerosis). The tape depicts a 50's sock-hop, with the band playing "You Never Can Tell," "Saturday Night," "Let's Talk It Over," "Baby Please Don't Go," "Chicken Shack Boogie" and "All Night Long."
Jem/Passport — *Passport Music Video*

Willie Nelson and Family In Concert 1984
Music video
Closed Captioned
72893   89 mins   C   B, V, CED   P
Willie Nelson
Willie Nelson performs such hits as "On the Road Again" "Georgiaon My Mind."
Unknown — *CBS/Fox Video*

Willie Nelson Special, The 1985
Music-Performance
82254   60 mins   C   B, V   P
Willie Nelson, Ray Charles, Jackie King
Willie and Ray perform "Georgia on My Mind", "Seven Spanish Angels" and "On The Road Again." In VHS and Beta Dolby Hi-Fi Stereo.
Terry Lickona — *Embassy Home Entertainment*

Willy McBean and His Magic Machine 1959
Fantasy/Puppets
81082   94 mins   C   B, V   P
Animated
A little boy and his monkey must foil an evil professor's plan to travel back through time and change the course of history, everyday.
Magna Pictures — *Prism*

Willy Wonka and the Chocolate Factory 1971
Musical/Fantasy
79557   100 mins   C   B, V   P
Gene Wilder, Denise Nickerson, Leonard Stone, Dodo Denney, directed by Mel Stuart
A poor young boy wins a tour of Willy Wonka's Chocolate Factory, a place filled with many surprises.
David L Wolper — *Warner Home Video*

Wilma 1977
Biographical/Drama
73863   100 mins   C   B, V   P
Cicely Tyson, Shirley Jo Finney
The true story of a young woman who overcame polio to win three gold medals in the 1960 Olympics. Available in Beta Hi-Fi.
Cappy Productions — *RCA/Columbia Pictures Home Video*

Win, Place, or Steal 1972
Comedy
73036   88 mins   C   B, V   P
McLean Stevenson, Alex Karras, Dean Stockwell
Three men are willing to do anything except work.
MPAA:PG
Omega — *Vestron Video*

Winchester '73 1950
Western
84022   82 mins   C   B, V   P
James Stewart, Shelley Winters, Stephen McNally, directed by Anthony Mann
Brothers are at odds in this western over a valuable carbine, with an ensuing chase wherein the rifle trades hands until the climax. A classic Stewart-Mann chunk of ruggedness.
Aaron Rosenberg — *MCA Home Video*

Wind and the Lion, The 1975
Adventure
87372   120 mins   C   B, V   P
Sean Connery, Candice Bergen, Brian Keith, directed by John Milius
In turn-of-the-century Morocco, a sheik kidnaps a feisty American governess and holds her as a political hostage to influence President Teddy Roosevelt in the digging of the Suez Canal. In Dolby Stereo Hi-Fi.
MPAA:PG

THE VIDEO TAPE & DISC GUIDE

MGM — *MGM/UA Home Video*

RKO — *Nostalgia Merchant*

Wind in the Willows, The   1982
Cartoons
63189   47 mins   C   B, V   P
Animated, narrated by Basil Rathbone, the
voice of Eric Blore
"The Wind in the Willows," originally a part of
the 1950 feature "Ichabod and Mr. Toad," is the
tale of J. Thaddeus Toad, who has a strange
mania for fast cars. Also on this tape are two
Disney cartoons with similar automotive themes,
"Motor Mania" with Goofy, and "Trailer Horn"
with Donald Duck and Chip 'n' Dale.
Walt Disney Productions — *Walt Disney Home
Video; Vestron Video*

Wind in the Willows, The   1983
Cartoons/Literature-American
75622   97 mins   C   B, V   P
Animated
This animated film is based on Kenneth
Grahame's famous tale.
Rankin Bass — *Children's Video Library*

Wind in the Willows   1983
Fairy tales
80817   78 mins   C   B, V   P
Animated
An adaptation in two cassettes of the Kenneth
Grahame story about how Ratty, Badger and
Mole try to save Toad Hall from weasel
destruction. Available in VHS and Beta Hi Fi.
Mark Hall; Brian Cosgrove — *THORN
EMI/HBO Video*

Wind in the Willows, The   1983
Fairy tales
82359   75 mins   C   B, V   P
The Children's Theatre Company and School of
Minneapolis perform their own unique
interpretation of the Kenneth Grahame story. In
VHS and Beta Hi-Fi Stereo.
Television Theatre Company — *MCA Home
Video*

Windom's Way   1957
Romance
75674   90 mins   B/W   B, V   P
Peter Finch, Mary Ure
Based on a novel by James Ramsey Ullman,
this is a tale of abiding love.
Rank Film Distributors — *VidAmerica*

Window, The   1949
Suspense
64365   73 mins   B/W   B, V, 3/4U   P
*Bobby Driscoll, Barbara Hale, Arthur Kennedy,
Ruth Roman*
A little boy has a reputation for telling lies, so no
one believes him when he says he witnessed a
murder... except the killer.

Winds of Change   1979
Folklore/Cartoons
65102   90 mins   C   B, V   P
Animated, voice of Peter Ustinov
A magical retelling of five ancient Greek myths
which features a disco-rock musical score.
Written by Norman Corwin.
Sanrio Film Distribution — *RCA/Columbia
Pictures Home Video*

Winds of Change: 1985
Preserving the Heritage
of Man
Wildlife
88320   60 mins   C   B, V   P
Hosted by James Whitmore
A look at the American Old West and what has
been preserved from those days.
American Heritage Video; John
Kerwin — *Eagle Productions*

Winds of Kitty Hawk   19??
Aeronautics/Biographical
72457   90 mins   C   B, V   P
Michael Moriarty
The struggles and ultimate triumphs of Orville
and Wilbur Wright are dramatized in this E.W.
Swackhamer film.
Lawrence Schiller — *U.S.A. Home Video*

Winds of the Wasteland   1936
Western
14398   54 mins   B/W   B, V   P
John Wayne, Phyllis Fraser
While they are out of work, Pony Express riders
win a race for a government contract.
Republic — *Video Connection; Discount Video
Tapes; Spotlite Video*

Windwalker   1981
Drama
69378   108 mins   C   B, V   P
Trevor Howard
An aged Indian chief shares the extraordinary
memories of his life with his grandchildren.
Native American dialect and English subtitles
are used throughout the film.
Pacific International Pictures — *CBS/Fox
Video*

Windy City   1984
Drama
Closed Captioned
77464   103 mins   C   B, V   P
John Shea, Kate Capshaw, Josh Mostel
A group of seven childhood friends must come
to terms with the harsh realities of their failed
ambitions when they reunite for a weekend in
Chicago.
MPAA:R

CBS Theatrical Films — *CBS/Fox Video*

Wine Advisor, The   1985
Alcoholic beverages
71008   60 mins   B, V   P
Edmund Osterland, Dick Cavett
Selecting the proper wine can make or break a
business opportunity; this tape helps viewers
understand how and why.
Esquire — *Esquire Video*

Wines of California, The   1984
Alcoholic beverages
73657   240 mins   C   B, V   P
4   pgms
This series of programs show how California
wines are made and the proper etiquette for
serving wines.
*1.History and Process; Wine Etiquette
2.Generics; Roses and Lights; Sparkling and
Dessert Wines 3.The White Varietals I & II 4.The
Red Varietals I & II*
Dave Smith — *Kartes Video Communications*

Wings   1927
Adventure
80398   136 mins   B/W   B, V, LV,   P
                             CED
*Clara Bow, Buddy Rogers, Richard Arlen, Gary
Cooper, directed by William Wellman*
Here is the silent film classic about two men
who go off to join the Air Force during World
War I. Available in VHS and Beta Hi-Fi.
Academy Awards '27: Best Picture
Paramount Pictures — *Paramount Home Video*

Wings of Peace   1947
Aeronautics
87661   51 mins   B/W   B, V   P
Three shorts detail various advances in
aeronautics made in the postwar years by the
U.S. Air Force.
USAF — *Victory Video*

Wings of the   1940
Army/Planes of the Navy
World War II/Aeronautics
81607   62 mins   B/W   B, V   P
These two films examine the history of Army
and naval aircraft from their beginnings to World
War II.
U.S. Army Corps — *Victory Video*

Wings of War   1943
World War II
87662   55 mins   B/W   B, V   P
Ronald Reagan, William Holden
Three shorts demonstrate aspects of wartime
aeronautics, starring Hollywood actors who
were serving in the Air Force at the time.
USAF — *Victory Video*

Wings of War Volume 2   1943
World War II
87665   57 mins   B/W   B, V   P
Three short subjects about World War II air
fighting: "Fortress of the Sky," "Fight for the
Sky" and "Army Air Forces: The Pacific."
USAF — *Victory Video*

Wings of War (La Patrulla   197?
Suicida)
War-Drama
88314   95 mins   C   B, V   P
Ten American soldiers mount an assault against
a well-fortressed German radio station.
SP
Spanish — *JCI Video*

Winners of the West   1940
Western/Serials
14266   169 mins   B/W   B, V   P
Anne Nagel, Dick Foran, James Craig
A landowner schemes to prevent a railroad from
running through his property. The railroad's
chief engineer leads the good guys in an
attempt to prevent sabotage. A serial in thirteen
chapters.
Universal — *Video Connection; Nostalgia
Merchant; Video Yesteryear*

Winnie the Pooh   1985
Children/Literature
70939   30 mins   C   B, V   P
One of the Disney Video-A-Long books on
videocassette, this tape features Winnie telling
three favorite stories: "Winnie the Pooh and
Tigger, Too," Winnie the Pooh and the Honey
Tree," and "Winnie the Pooh and the Blustery
Day."
Walt Disney Productions — *Walt Disney Home
Video*

Winnie the Pooh and   1984
Friends
Cartoons
79179   46 mins   C   B, V   P
Animated
Winnie the Pooh and his friends from the
Hundred Acre Wood are trying to arrange for a
birthday party for Eeyore.
Walt Disney Productions — *Walt Disney Home
Video*

Winnie the Pooh and the   1968
Blustery Day
Fantasy
85532   24 mins   C   B, V   P
*Animated, voices of Sterling Holloway,
Sebastian Cabot, John Fiedler, Paul Winchell,
Hal Smith, Ralph Wright*
Another classic A. A. Milne's tale about Pooh,
the Hundred Acre Woods and Tigger, this time
caught in a galestorm.
MPAA:G

Walt Disney Studios — *Walt Disney Home Video*

Winnie the Pooh and the Honey Tree   1965
Fantasy
85531   25 mins   C   B, V   P
Animated, voices of Sterling Holloway, Howard Morris, Sebastian Cabot,
The classic Disney short starring A. A. Milne's famous character who tries to get some honey from a tree-high beehive amid bees and his bumbling buddies.
MPAA:G
Walt Disney Studios — *Walt Disney Home Video*

Winnie the Pooh and   1974
Tigger Too
Fantasy
85533   25 mins   C   B, V   P
Animated, voices of Sterling Holloway, Sebastian Cabot, Junius Matthews, John Fiedler, Timothy Turner, Dori Whitaker
A. A. Milne's classic characters encounter Tigger and his irascible bouncing, find it intolerable, and discover a questionable cure.
MPAA:G
Walt Disney Studios — *Walt Disney Home Video*

Winning   1969
Drama
64560   123 mins   C   B, V   P
Paul Newman, Joanne Woodward, Robert Wagner, Richard Thomas
A race car driver will let nothing stand in the way of his winning the Indianapolis 500, including his wife.
MPAA:PG
Universal — *MCA Home Video*

Winning at Work   1986
Business
88291   60 mins   C   B, V   P
An occupational inspiration program, first in the "Road to Achievement" series. Hosted by Robert Hoover.
Rewind Prod. — *Karl/Lorimar Home Video*

Winning Edge,   1985
The—John McEnroe/Ivan Lendl—Private Lessons with the Pros
Tennis
81164   45 mins   C   B, V   P
Stars John McEnroe and Ivan Lendl give a step-by-step demonstration of basic tennis maneuvers.
Video Tennis Productions — *Vestron Video*

Winning of the West   1953
Western
62873   57 mins   B/W   B, V   P, T
Gene Autry, Smiley Burnette
Ranger Gene vows to protect a crusading publisher from unscrupulous crooks.
Columbia — *Blackhawk Films*

Winning Tradition: 1977   1977
New York Yankees, A
Baseball
33828   32 mins   C   B, V   P
Thurman Munson, Ron Guidry, Graig Nettles, Reggie Jackson, Mickey Rivers
Highlights of the Yankees 1977 season in which they came from behind to beat the Kansas City Royals in the ninth inning of the fifth and final American League Championship game, then went on to defeat the Los Angeles Dodgers in a six-game World Series.
Major League Baseball — *Major League Baseball Productions*

Winning Tradition: The   1985
Cleveland Browns, A
Football
81954   137 mins   C   B, V   P
Here are highlights from the Cleveland Browns championship seasons during the late 60's with solid offensive work by Jim Brown.
NFL Films — *NFL Films Video*

Winslow Boy, The   1948
Drama
63326   112 mins   B/W   B, V   P
Robert Donat, Cedric Hardwicke, Margaret Leighton, Frank Lawton, directed by Anthony Asquith
This film fictionalizes the events of a famous Edwardian court case, in which a cadet at the Royal Naval College was wrongly accused of theft and expelled. His father fought it through the courts to a satisfactory conclusion.
British Lion — *THORN EMI/HBO Video; Movie Buff Video*

Winsome Witch   196?
Cartoons
69293   55 mins   C   B, V   P
Animated
This tape is a compilation of "Winsome Witch" cartoons, in which a good-natured witch helps people in distress.
Hanna-Barbera — *Worldvision Home Video*

Winter   1985
Music video
82067   53 mins   C   B, V   P
The Windham Hill family of artists provide the musical background to this impressionistic portrait of winter.

Dann Moss; Windham Hill Productions — *Paramount Home Video; Pioneer Artists*

Winter Flight   1984
Drama
88213   105 mins   C   B, V   P
Reece Dinsdale, Nicola Cowper, Gary Olsen, directed by Roy Battersby
A small, gentle British drama about a RAF recruit and a barmaid who quickly become lovers, and then are confronted with her pregnancy, being as it is not the pilot's fault.
Goldcrest Films and TV; David Puttnam — *MGM/UA Home Video*

Winter Kills   1979
Drama
37408   97 mins   C   B, V   P
Jeff Bridges, John Huston, Anthony Perkins
The investigation of the fifteen-year-old assassination of a President results in numerous plots and counter-plots, intrigues and assumed identities.
MPAA:R
Avco Embassy — *Embassy Home Entertainment*

Winter Light   1962
Drama
65629   80 mins   B/W   B, V   P
Max von Sydow, Gunnar Bjornstrand, Ingrid Thulin, directed by Ingmar Bergman
"Winter Light" examines a day in the life of a tormented, widowed pastor who has lost his faith in God and searches for the spiritual guidance he is unable to give to his congregation.
Janus Films — *Embassy Home Entertainment*

Winter of Our Dreams   1983
Drama
65444   89 mins   C   B, V   P
Judy Davis, Bryan Brown
A lonely prostitute becomes romantically involved with a married bookshop owner. Her love turns into a burning obsession until she is forced to free herself from her old dependencies and begin a new life.
Satori Entertainment Corp — *U.S.A. Home Video*

Winterset   1937
Drama
03897   85 mins   B/W   B, V   P
Burgess Meredith, Margo, John Carradine, directed by Alfred Santell
Son seeks to clear father's name of falsely accused crime twenty years after his electrocution.
RKO; Pandro S Berman — *Movie Buff Video; Hollywood Home Theater; Cable Films; Video*

Connection; Discount Video Tapes; Kartes Video Communications

Wise Blood   1979
Comedy-Drama
81818   106 mins   C   B, V   P
Brad Dourif, John Huston, Ned Beatty, Amy Wright, Harry Dean Stanton, directed by John Huston
A drifter who searches for sin eventually becomes a preacher for a new religion. Based upon Flannery O'Connor's novel. Available in VHS and Beta Hi-Fi.
MPAA:PG
New Line Cinema; Ithaca Productions — *MCA Home Video*

Wishmaker, The   1985
Fairy tales
81613   54 mins   C   B, V   P
A young man squanders the three wishes granted to him for helping a strange old woman and her timid daughter.
Video Gems — *Video Gems*

Witch Who Came from the Sea, The   1976
Horror
72957   98 mins   C   B, V   P
Millie Perkins, Loni Chapman, Vanessa Brown
A witch terrorizes the ships at sea in this adult drama.
MPAA:R
Matt Cimber — *Unicorn Video*

Witchcraft Through the Ages   1922
Horror
08692   90 mins   B/W   B, V, 3/4U   P
Maren Pedersen, Clara Pontoppidan, directed by Benjamin Christiansen.
The demonic Swedish masterpiece, also called "Haxan," in which witches and victims suffer against various historical backgrounds. Nightmarish and profane, especially the appearance of the Devil as played under much make-up by Christiansen himself. Silent.
Svensk Filmindustri — *Western Film & Video Inc; Discount Video Tapes; Video Yesteryear*

Witches' Brew   1979
Comedy
64977   98 mins   C   B, V, CED   P
Teri Garr, Richard Benjamin, Lana Turner
Three young women try to use their undeveloped skills in witchcraft and black magic to help their husbands get a prestigious position at a university, with calamitous yet hilarious results.
MPAA:PG
Merritt-White Ltd — *Embassy Home Entertainment*

Witches Mountain, The   1981
Horror
84896   83 mins   C   B, V   P
Patty Shepard, John Caffari
Available also in a Spanish version, this film
deals with a troubled couple captured by a
coven of witches in the Pyrenees.
EL, SP
Spanish — *Unicorn Video*

Witching Time   1984
Horror
80480   60 mins   C   B, V   P
*Jon Finch, Prunella Gee, Patrica Quinn, Ian
McCulloch*
A young composer is visited by a 17th-Century
witch while his wife is away from home. When
the wife returns, both women fight to possess
him. In Beta Hi-Fi and VHS Stereo.
Hammer Films — *Thriller Video*

Witch's Mirror, The   1960
Horror
51952   75 mins   B/W   B, V   P
*Rosita Arenas, Armand Calvo, Isabela Corona,
Dina De Marco*
A sorceress plots to destroy the murderer of her
goddaughter. The murderer, a surgeon, begins a
project to restore the disfigured face and hands
of his burned second wife, no matter who he
gets the raw material from.
K Gordon Murray; Trans
International — *Hollywood Home Theater*

Witch's Night Out   1979
Cartoons
71350   30 mins   C   B, V   P
Animated, the voice of Gilda Radner
A broom-riding mama takes a night on the town.
She meets two children who ask to be
transformed into their favorite monsters.
Leach/Rankin — *Family Home Entertainment*

With Buffalo Bill on the   1925
U.P. Trail
Western
69571   74 mins   B/W   B, V, FO   P
Roy Stewart, Cullen Landis, Kathryn McGuire
Young Buffalo Bill Cody, wagon train scout,
leads his caravan of settlers Westward through
danger and uncharted land.
Independent — *Video Yesteryear*

With Six You Get Eggroll   1968
Comedy
80138   95 mins   C   B, V   P
*Doris Day, Brian Keith, Pat Carroll, Alice
Ghostley, directed by Howard Morris*
A widow with three sons and a widower with a
daughter decide to tie the knot despite their
children's hatred for one another.
MPAA:G

National General — *Playhouse Video*

Without a Trace   1983
Drama
69374   119 mins   C   B, V, CED   P
Kate Nelligan, Judd Hirsch
A mother becomes frantic when her 6-year-old
son disappears, and a detective steps in to help.
MPAA:PG
Stanley Jaffe — *CBS/Fox Video*

Without Reservations   1946
Comedy
13196   101 mins   B/W   B, V   P
Claudette Colbert, John Wayne
Hollywood-bound novelist encounters a Marine
flyer and his pal aboard a train.
RKO; Mervyn LeRoy — *United Home Video;
Video Connection*

Witness   1985
Crime-Drama
Closed Captioned
84534   112 mins   C   B, V, 8mm,   P
                                    LV
*Harrison Ford, Kelly McGillis, Alexander
Godunov, Lukas Haas, directed by a Peter Weir*
A Philadelphia police captain discovers a
departmental murder conspiracy. The cop, an
Amish boy who witnessed the first murder, and
the boy's mother take refuge in the Amish
highlands. Artfully crafted drama by the
renowned Australian Director.
MPAA:R
Edward S. Feldman — *Paramount Home Video*

Witness for the   1957
Prosecution
Mystery/Drama
64563   114 mins   B/W   B, V, CED   P
*Charles Laughton, Tyrone Power, Marlene
Dietrich, Elsa Lanchester, directed by Billy
Wilder*
An unemployed man is accused of murdering a
wealthy widow whom he befriended. What starts
out as a straightforward court case becomes
increasingly complicated in this adaptation of an
Agatha Christie stage play.
United Artists — *CBS/Fox Video*

Wiz, The   1978
Musical/Fantasy
48639   133 mins   C   B, V, LV   P
*Diana Ross, Michael Jackson, Nipsey Russell,
Ted Ross, Mabel King, Thelma Carpenter*
A version of the long-time favorite "The Wizard
of Oz," based on the Broadway musical. It is
reset in a fantasy version of New York City,
centering on a young black woman searching
for her identity.
MPAA:G
Universal — *MCA Home Video*

Wizard of Mars, The   1964
Science fiction
80183   81 mins   C   B, V   P
John Carradine, Roger Gentry
Four astronauts encounter alien terrors and an
evil wizard when their spaceship crash lands on
Mars.
NTA — *Republic Pictures Home Video*

Wizard of Oz, The   1982
Fantasy
65402   78 mins   C   B, V   P
Animated
The animated version of the classic film "The
Wizard of Oz" is ideally suited for young
children. Featured are the voices of Lorne
Greene and Aileen Quinn. In stereo VHS and
Beta Hi-Fi.
Paramount — *Paramount Home Video*

Wizard of Oz, The   1939
Musical/Fantasy
44640   101 mins   C   B, V, LV,   P
                            CED
*Judy Garland, Ray Bolger, Frank Morgan, Bert
Lahr, Jack Haley, directed by Victor Fleming*
A Kansas farm girl dreams she and her dog are
somewhere over the rainbow, in the wonderful
land of Oz. On her adventure to find the "Great
Oz" she is joined by the Scarecrow, the Tin
Man, and the Cowardly Lion. Based on the book
by Frank L. Baum.
Academy Awards '39: Best Original Music Score
(Stothart); Best Song: "Over the Rainbow"
(Harburg and Arlen).
MGM — *MGM/UA Home Video*

Wok Before You Run   1984
Cookery
73703   60 mins   C   B, V   P
This program explains how to use a wok in
cooking and even comes with a wok when you
purchase the videocassette.
AM Available
Steven Yan — *Embassy Home Entertainment*

Wok on the Wild Side   1986
Cookery
86907   60 mins   C   B, V   P
Stephen Yan
This humorous chef whips together a fully-
wokked seven course meal amid slapsticky
monkeyshines.
Michael Hitchcock; Robin Montgomery; Al
Eicher — *Embassy Home Entertainment*

Wolf Lake   1979
Drama
75488   90 mins   C   B, V   P
Rod Steiger, David Hoffman
A World War II veteran and a Vietnam army
deserter have a clash of personalities.

Unknown — *Prism*

Wolfen   1981
Horror
58257   115 mins   C   B, V   P
*Albert Finney, Gregory Hines, Tom Noonan,
directed by Michael Wadleigh*
A thriller which spins a tale of myth and menace
as creatures from the darkness live among us.
MPAA:R
Orion Pictures — *Warner Home Video*

Wolfman   1982
Horror
63354   91 mins   C   B, V   P
Earl Owensby, Kristina Reynolds
In 1910, a young man learns that his family is
heir to the curse of the Werewolf.
UG Productions — *THORN EMI/HBO Video*

Woman Called Golda, A   1982
Biographical/Drama
63429   195 mins   C   B, V   P
Ingrid Bergman, Leonard Nimoy
Ingrid Bergman portrays the fiery Golda Meir,
one of the most powerful women and one of the
most important political figures of the 20th
century.
Emmy Awards '82: Best Actress (Bergman);
Film Editing.
Paramount TV — *Paramount Home Video*

Woman in Grey   1919
Adventure
57433   205 mins   B/W   B, V   P, T
Arline Pretty, Henry Sell
A man and a woman battle wits when they
attempt to locate and unravel the Army Code
while staying one jump ahead of J. Haviland
Hunter, a suave villain after the same fortune.
Silent.
Unknown — *Blackhawk Films*

Woman in Red, The   1984
Comedy
80401   87 mins   C   B, V, LV,   P
                            CED
*Gene Wilder, Charles Grodin, Kelly Le Brock,
Gilda Radner, Judith Ivey, directed by Gene
Wilder*
A married advertising executive searches the
streets of San Francisco for a beautiful woman
he saw in an underground garage.
Academy Awards '84: Best Song ("I Just Called
to Say I Love You") MPAA:PG13
Victor Drai; Orion Pictures — *Vestron Video*

Woman in the Dunes   1964
Drama
33443   127 mins   B/W   B, V   P
Directed by Hiroshi Teshigahara

A man and a woman are trapped in a shack at the bottom of a sand pit among isolated dunes. Based on the highly acclaimed novel by Kobe Abe. In Japanese with English subtitles.
JA
Pathe Contemporary — *Festival Films; Western Film & Video Inc; Hollywood Home Theater*

Woman in the Moon   1929
Science fiction
07285   115 mins   B/W   B, V, 3/4U   P
Klaus Pohl, Willie Fritsch, Gustav von Wagenheim, Gerda Maurus, directed by Fritz Lang.
An incongruous mixture of people embark upon a trip to the moon and discover water, an area with atmosphere, and gold. (Silent with musical soundtrack).
UFA — *International Historic Films; Video Yesteryear; Festival Films*

Woman in the Shadows   1934
Drama
85228   70 mins   B/W   B, V   P
Fay Wray, Ralph Bellamy, Melvyn Douglas, Roscoe Ates, Joe King
A ex-con retreats to the woods for serenity and peace, but is assaulted by mysterious women, jealous lovers and gun-slinging drunks, until he explodes. From a Dashiell Hammett story.
RKO Radio Pictures — *Video Yesteryear*

Woman Next Door, The   1981
Drama
87335   106 mins   C   B, V   P
Gerard Depardieu, Fanny Ardant, Michel Baumbartner, Veronique Silver, Roger Van Hool, directed by Francois Truffaut
One of Truffaut's last films before his sudden death in 1984; the story involves a suburban husband who begins an affair with a tempestuous woman after she moves in next door, creating domestic tensions for both of them. An insightful, humanistic paean to passion and fidelity by the great artist.
MPAA:R
Roissy — *Key Video*

Woman of Paris, A/Sunnyside   1923
Comedy/Drama
81551   111 mins   B/W   B, V   P
Charlie Chaplin, Adolphe Menjou, Edna Purviance, directed by Charlie Chaplin
This double feature highlights the talents of Charlie Chaplin. "A Woman of Paris" is the tragic story of a country girl who winds up a kept woman and an overworked hotel handyman almost loses his girlfriend and his job in "Sunnyside."
United Artists — *Playhouse Video*

Woman of Substance, A   1984
Drama
70851   300 mins   C   B, V   P
Jenny Seagrave, Barry Bostwick, Deborah Kerr, directed by Don Sharp   3   pgms
The woman of the title, Emma Harte, rises from poverty to wealth and power through self-discipline. This telefilmed version of Barbara Taylor Bradford's novel comes on three cassettes.
1. A Nest of Vipers 2. Fighting for the Dream 3. The Secret Is Revealed
Artemis Productions — *Lightning Video*

Woman of the Year   1942
Comedy
58704   114 mins   B/W   B, V   P
Spencer Tracy, Katharine Hepburn, directed by George Stevens
The first of the classic Tracy/Hepburn films concerns the rocky marriage of a political columnist and a sportswriter.
Academy Awards '42: Best Original Screenplay (Ring Lardner, Jr.). Film Daily Poll '42: Ten Best of Year.
MGM — *MGM/UA Home Video*

Woman Rebels, A   1936
Drama
10055   88 mins   B/W   B, V   P, T
Katharine Hepburn, Herbert Marshall, Elizabeth Allan, Donald Crisp, Van Heflin
Courageous Victorian woman challenges establishment with radical positions on womens' rights.
RKO; Pandro S Berman — *Blackhawk Films*

Woman Who Came Back   1945
Suspense
82018   69 mins   B/W   B, V   P
Nancy Kelly, Otto Kruger, John Loder, Ruth Ford, Jeanne Gail
A young woman must rid herself of an ancient witch's curse before it's too late for her.
Available in VHS and Beta Hi-Fi Stereo.
Republic Pictures — *Sony Video Software*

Woman Who Willed a Miracle, The   1983
Drama
71303   72 mins   C   B, V   P
Cloris Leachman, James Noble, Fran Bennet, Bruce French, M Emmet Walsh, Rosemary Murphy, directed by Sharron Miller
After his natural parents abandon him, a retarded child gets a second chance with a strong-spirited, loving set of foster parents.
Curley and Miller Productions; Dick Clark Productions — *U.S.A. Home Video*

Wombling Free 1984
Fantasy
Closed Captioned
85239 86 mins C B, V P
Bonnie Langford
A girl makes friends with a race of tiny, litter-hating furry creatures.
Satori Ent.; Ian Shand — *RCA/Columbia Pictures Home Video*

Women, The 1939
Comedy-Drama
77379 133 mins B/W B, V, LV P
Norma Shearer, Joan Crawford, Rosalind Russell, Joan Fontaine, Paulette Goddard, Ruth Hussey, Marjorie Main, directed by George Cukor
An adaptation of the Clare Boothe Luce play about a group of women who destroy their best friends' reputations at various social gatherings. Includes a Technicolor fashion show sequence.
MGM — *MGM/UA Home Video*

Women, The 1969
Comedy
84893 86 mins C B, V P
Brigette Bardot, Maurice Ronet
Also known as "Les Femmes," this film depicts a sexy secretary's seduction of a world-weary writer.
French — *Unicorn Video*

Women in Cell Block 7 1981
Drama
66517 100 mins C B, V P
Anita Strinberg, Eve Czemeys
The inmates of a women's prison suffer cruel and unspeakable tortures from their jailers and each other.
MPAA:R
Terry Levene — *U.S.A. Home Video; Paragon Video Productions*

Women in Love 1970
Drama
58840 129 mins C B, V, CED P
Glenda Jackson, Jennie Linden, Alan Bates, Oliver Reed, Eleanor Bron
D. H. Lawrence's novel about two girls having their first sexual encounters in the Midlands during the 1920's provides the basis for this film. Academy Awards '70:; Best Actress (Jackson).
MPAA:R
United Artists — *CBS/Fox Video*

Women Tell the Dirtiest Jokes 1985
Comedy
82447 60 mins C B, V P
LaWanda Page, Marsha Warfield, Barbara Scott, Pat Rosborough, JoAnn Dearing, Carole Montgomery

A compilation of bawdy humor from some of the hottest new comediennes.
Vestron Video — *Vestron Video*

Women Unchained 197?
Drama/Exploitation
70981 82 mins C B, V P
Carolyn Judd, Teri Guzman, Darlene Mattingly, Angel Colbert, Bonita Kalem
Five women escape from a maximum security prison and make a run for the border. They shun civilized behavior.
MPAA:R
Independent — *Video Gems*

Women Who Changed the Century, Vol. 1 1986
Women
88279 60 mins C V P
A retrospective look at the century's important women, from Helen Keller to Mata Hari to Eleanor Roosevelt.
The Minnesota Studio — *The Minnesota Studio*

Wonderful World of Disney, The 1986
Variety
71105 95 mins C B, V P
Hayley Mills, Walt Disney, William Windom, Celeste Holm, Slim Pickens, Kurt Russell, Annette Funicello, Tim Hutton, the animated Disney characters
In its 29-year/3-network run, the weekly Sunday night Disney program offered hundreds of hours of family entertainment. The series garnered 7 emmy awards in that time, and featured dramas, documentaries, cartoon featurettes, comedies and musical presentations. Each tape in this series features two programs from the TV shows.
1.An Adventure In Color—Math Magic Land (1961)/The Illusion of Life (1981) 2.The Ranger of Brownstone (1968)/It's Tough to Be a Bird (1969) 3.Ducking Disaster With Donald Duck and His Friends (1976)/Goofing Around With Donald Duck (1976) 4.The Plausible Impossible (1956)/The Ranger's Guide to Nature (1966) 5.The Yellowstone Cubs (1963)/Flash, the Teen-Age Otter (1961) 6.The Bluegrass Special (1977)/Runaway on the Rogue River (1974) 7.Dad, Can I Borrow the Car (1972)/The Hunter and the Rock Star (1980) 8.Fire On Kelly Mountain (1973)/Adventure In Satan's Canyon (1974) 9.Call It Courage (1973)/The Legend of the Boy and the Eagle (1968) 10.Three on the Run (1978)/Race For Survival (1978)
Walt Disney Productions — *Walt Disney Home Video*

Wonderful World of Puss 'N Boots, The 1970
Adventure
63380 80 mins C B, V P

Animated
This is an animated version of the classic
children's adventure tale of a clever, brave cat.
MPAA:G
Toei Company — *Media Home Entertainment;
Vestron Video*

Wonderland Cove   1975
Adventure
71245   78 mins   C   V   P
Clu Gulager, directed by Jerry Thorpe
A seafaring adventurer adopts five orphan
children and embarks on journeys to exotic
locales.
William Blinn — *Prism*

Wooden Horse, The   1950
War-Drama
85025   98 mins   C   B, V   P
Anthony Steel, Leo Genn, David Thomlinson
Shot on location, this film depicts British
prisoners-of-war escaping through a tunnel dug
under a vaulting horse.
Korda — *THORN EMI/HBO Video*

Woodstock   1970
Musical
38957   180 mins   C   B, V   P
*Canned Heat, Richie Havens, The Who, Joan
Baez, Country Joe and the Fish, Jimi Hendrix,
Santana, Crosby Stills and Nash*
A chronicle of the great 1969 Woodstock rock
concert, celebrating the music and lifestyle of
the late sixties. Classic performances by a great
number of popular rock performers and groups.
Available on two tapes, labeled "Woodstock I"
and "Woodstock II," each running 90 minutes.
Academy Awards '70: Best Feature
Documentary. MPAA:R
Wadleigh Maurice Ltd; Bob Maurice — *Warner
Home Video; RCA VideoDiscs*

Battle at Elderbush   1914
Gulch, The/The
Musketeers of Pig Alley
Drama/Film-History
62871   33 mins   B/W   B, V   P, T
*Lillian Gish, Mae Marsh, Harry Carey, directed
by D.W. Griffith*
Two classic D.W. Griffith two-reelers from 1914
and 1912 respectively are contained on this
tape.
Biograph — *Blackhawk Films*

Woody Woodpecker and   1983
His Friends, Volume II
Cartoons
65339   59 mins   C   B, V   P
Animated
A compilation of 8 classic cartoons from 1941
through 1954 selected by Woody's creator,
Walter Lantz. Woody Woodpecker, Andy Panda
and Wally Walrus are featured.

Walter Lantz Productions; Universal — *MCA
Home Video*

Woody Woodpecker and   1984
His Friends, Volume III
Cartoons
79677   55 mins   C   B, V   P
Animated
A collection of eight classic cartoons featuring
Woody, Andy Panda, and Chilly Willy circa 1940-
1944.
Walter Lantz; Universal — *MCA Home Video*

Woody Woodpecker and   1982
His Friends, Volume I
Cartoons
62781   80 mins   C   B, V, LV   P
Animated
Ten favorite 1940-1955 Walter Lantz
"cartunes" were chosen for this tape: "Knock
Knock," "Bandmaster," "Ski for Two," "Hot
Noon," "The Legend of Rockabye Point," "Wet
Blanket Policy," "To Catch a Woodpecker,"
"Musical Moments from Chopin," "Bats in the
Belfry" and "Crazy Mixed-Up Pup."
Walter Lantz — *MCA Home Video*

Word, The   1978
Drama
78361   400 mins   C   B, V   P
*David Janssen, James Whitmore, Eddie Albert,
John Huston, Florinda Bolkan*
When a public relations executive is hired to
promote a new Bible, he stumbles across
treachery and murder.
Stonehenge Prods; Charles Fries
Prods — *U.S.A. Home Video*

Words and Music   1948
Musical
85640   122 mins   C   B, V   P
*Mickey Rooney, Tom Drake, Judy Garland,
Gene Kelly, Lena Horne, Betty Garrett, June
Allyson, Perry Como, Vera-Ellen, Ann Sothern,
directed by Norman Taurog*
A biographical musical based on the careers of
Richard Rodgers and Lorenz Hart, featuring a
parade of MGM stars singing such classic songs
as "Johnny One Note," "The Lady Is a Tramp"
and "Manhattan."
MGM — *MGM/UA Home Video*

Work/Police   1916
Comedy
58656   54 mins   B/W   B, V, FO   P
*Charlie Chaplin, Billy Armstrong, Charles Insley,
Marta Golden, Edna Purviance, directed by
Charlie Chaplin*
Two Chaplin two-reelers: "Work (The Paper
Hanger)" (1915), in which Charlie is hired to
repaper a house; and "Police" (1916), in which
Charlie plays an ex-con who is released into the
cruel world. Silent with music score.

THE VIDEO TAPE & DISC GUIDE

Essanay — *Video Yesteryear*

Working Girls 1975
Drama
79766 80 mins C B, V P
Sarah Kennedy, Laurie Rose, Mark Thomas
Three girls who share an apartment in Los
Angeles are willing to do anything for money.
MPAA:R
Independent — *United Home Video*

Working Stiffs 1979
Comedy
81108 75 mins C B, V P
*Jim Belushi, Michael Keaton, Val Bisoglio, Allan
Arbus, Lorna Patterson*
A two-volume collection of the first six episodes
from the series. The premise: two inept brothers
seek to climb the corporate ladder while working
as janitors in their uncle's office building.
Paramount TV — *Paramount Home Video*

World According to Garp, 1982
The
Comedy
63123 136 mins C B, V, CED P
*Robin Williams, Mary Beth Hurt, John Lithgow,
directed by George Roy Hill*
This film version of John Irving's popular novel
chronicles the life of T.S. Garp, a bizarre
everyman beset by the destructive forces of
modern society.
MPAA:R
Warner Bros — *Warner Home Video*

World at War 1943
World War II
50618 44 mins B/W B, V, 3/4U P
Directed by Samuel Spewack
The events from 1931-1941 which led to the
U.S. involvement in World War II are
documented by newsreels and enemy film
footage.
Office of War Information — *International
Historic Films; National AudioVisual Center;
Spotlite Video*

World at War, The 1980
World War II/Documentary
59699 104 mins B/W B, V P
Narrated by Sir Laurence Olivier
The highly acclaimed documentary about World
War II told through newsreel footage, containing
remarkable interviews with statesmen, military
leaders, and the men and women who fought it.
Thames Video — *THORN EMI/HBO Video*

World at War, The 1980
World War II/Documentary
69628 52 mins B/W B, V P
Narrated by Sir Laurence Olivier 26 pgms

This 26-volume series depicts, through actual
film footage, all of the horror and heroism of
World War II in great historical detail. Each
program is available separately.
*1.A New Germany 1933-39 2.Distant War 1939-
40 3.France Falls—May-June 1940
4.Alone—Britain—May 1940-June 1941
5.Barbarossa—June-December 1941
6.Banzai—Japan Strikes 7.On Our
Way—America Enters the War 8.Desert—The
War in North Africa 9.Stalingrad 10.Wolfpack
11.Red Star 12.Whirlwind 13.Tough Old Gut
14.It's a Lovely Day Tomorrow 15.Home Fires
16.Inside the Reich—Germany 1940-44
17.Morning 18.Occupation 19.Pincers
20.Genocide 21.Nemesis 22.Japan 1941-45
23.The Island to Island War 24.The Bomb
25.Reckoning 26.Remember*
Jeremy Isaacs; Thames Television — *THORN
EMI/HBO Video*

World Champions! The 1986
Story of the 1985
Chicago Bears
Football
84541 60 mins C B, V, 8mm P
The history of the Chicago Bears, culminating in
their Super Bowl victory in 1986.
NFL films — *NFL Films Video*

World Gone Mad, The 1933
Drama
08749 70 mins B/W B, V, 3/4U P
Pat O'Brien, Louis Calhern, J. Carrol Naish
Crime drama set during the Prohibition Era.
Majectic Pictures — *Cable Films; Discount
Video Tapes*

World is Full of Married 1980
Men, The
Drama
86589 106 mins C B, V P
*Anthony Franciosa, Carroll Baker, Sherrie
Cronn, Gareth Hunt*
A philandering husband gets involved with a
reckless model, inspiring his fed-up spouse to
also look for extra-marital sex.
MPAA:R
New Line; Malcolm Fancey & Oscar Lerman
Prod. — *Key Video*

World of Andy Panda, 1946
The
Cartoons
82361 62 mins C B, V P
Animated
Here is a collection of nine Andy Panda
cartoons from the 1940's, featuring "Apple
Andy," "Crow Crazy" and "Meatless Tuesday."
Walter Lantz — *MCA Home Video*

World of Apu, The   1959
Drama
55810   103 mins   B/W   B, V   P
Directed by Satyajit Ray
The concluding part of Ray's highly acclaimed
"Apu Trilogy" covering Apu's manhood. In
Bengali dialogue with English subtitles.
India — Festival Films; Hollywood Home
Theater; Video Yesteryear

World of dBase, The   1984
Computers
70189   75 mins   C   B, V   P
An instructional guide to the use of the dBase
database management computer software
program, featuring the advancements of the
dBase III system. In Beta Hi-Fi.
Software Video Productions — RCA/Columbia
Pictures Home Video

World of Hans Christian   1985
Andersen, The
Cartoons/Adventure
70566   73 mins   C   B, V   P
Animated
Hans relates the delightful yarns that gave him
his start in the story telling business.
Turner Program Services,
Inc. — RCA/Columbia Pictures Home Video

World of Henry Orient,   1964
The
Comedy-Drama
81837   106 mins   C   B, V   P
Peter Sellers, Tippy Walker, Merrie Spaeth, Tom
Bosley, Angela Lansbury, directed by George
Roy Hill
Two fifteen-year-old girls madly in love with a
concert pianist pursue him all around New York
City. Available in VHS and Beta Hi-Fi.
United Artists — Key Video

World of Martial Arts, The   1982
Martial arts
59685   60 mins   C   B, V   P
Narrated by John Saxon, Chuck Norris, Al
Thomas
This program offers a basic training in
budojujutsu, a combination of techniques from
seven different martial arts.
Universal — MCA Home Video; Optical
Programming Associates

World of Photography   1985
Photography
85305   39 mins   C   B, V   P
25   pgms
Photograpy from the basics, for every sort of
subject and style.
1.The Basics 2.Next Step 3.Just for Starters
4.Flash of Brilliance 5.Long on Exposure
6.Close-up 7.On Vacation 8.After the Slide
9.That's a Problem 10.Say Cheese 11.Like the

Pros Do It 12.Pros in their Studios 13.Now
That's Unusual 14.Try This at Home
15.Fantastic Shots 16.Back to Nature 17.On
Location 18.All That Jazz 19.The Life and Times
of Photojournalism 20.The Washington
Connection 21.The Great Photographers
22.History in the Making 23.The Profit Picture
24.Are You Ready to Go Pro? 25.Filters
Richard S Brockway — Brockway
Broadcasting Corporation

World of Strawberry   1980
Shortcake, The
Cartoons
71351   60 mins   C   B, V   P
Animated
The Peculiar Purple Pieman of Porcupine Peak
poses pitfalls aplenty for Ms. Shortcake and her
pals.
Murakami — Family Home Entertainment

World of the Vampires,   1960
The
Horror
51099   75 mins   B/W   B, V   P
Mauricio Garces, Erna Martha Bauman, Silvia
Fournier, Guillermo Murray
An evil count commands his vampire legions to
wreak vengeance upon the family whose
ancestors condemned him.
Mexican — Hollywood Home Theater

World Safari   1986
Wilderness areas
86028   93 mins   C   B, V   P
A tour through the world's wildernesses, from
Uganda to the tundra.
MPAA:G
Ron Hayes — United Home Video

World Series, 1943   1943
Baseball
33864   ? mins   B/W   B, V   P
New York Yankees, St. Louis Cardinals
Both teams incorporate new faces to replace
stars serving in the war. The Yankees avenge
their previous year's defeat by the Cardinals by
winning this World Series four games to one.
Spud Chandler pitches two victories for
manager Joe McCarthy's Bronx Bombers.
Lou Fonseca — Major League Baseball
Productions

World Series, 1944   1944
Baseball
33863   ? mins   B/W   B, V   P
St. Louis Cardinals, St Louis Browns
In the first and only series played between two
St. Louis teams, the Cardinals prevail in six
games, led by shortstop Marty Marion and
pitchers Max Lanier and Ted Wilks. First
baseman George McQuinn bats .438 for the
Browns.

Lou Fonseca — *Major League Baseball Productions*

World Series, 1945
Baseball
33862   ? mins   B/W   B, V   P
Detroit Tigers, Chicago Cubs
Tiger stars recently returned from military service, pitcher Virgil Trucks and slugger Hank Greenberg, lead the Detroit club to a four games to three victory over the Cubs.
Lou Fonseca — *Major League Baseball Productions*

World Series, 1946
Baseball
33861   ? mins   B/W   B, V   P
St. Louis Cardinals, Boston Red Sox
Enos Slaughter scores all the way from first base on Harry Walker's single to score the winning run for the Cardinals in game seven. Harry Breechen recorded three victories for St. Louis against the likes of Red Sox sluggers Ted Williams, Dom DiMaggio, and Rudy York.
Lou Fonseca — *Major League Baseball Productions*

World Series, 1947
Baseball
33860   ? mins   B/W   B, V   P
New York Yankees, Brooklyn Dodgers
Al Gionfriddo's leaping catch of Joe DiMaggio's long drive sends the Yankees and Dodgers into a seventh game showdown. Yankee outfielder Tommy Henrich drives in the winning run and Joe Page hurls five scoreless innings to preserve the victory.
Lou Fonseca — *Major League Baseball Productions*

World Series, 1948
Baseball
33859   ? mins   B/W   B, V   P
Cleveland Indians, Boston Braves
Behind the pitching of Bob Lemon and Gene Bearden and the solid fielding of Ken Keltner, Joe Gordon, and Lou Boudreau, the Indians outlast Warren Spahn, Johnny Sain and the rest of the Braves, who were headed for Milwaukee in a few years, in six games.
Lou Fonseca — *Major League Baseball Productions*

World Series, 1949
Baseball
33858   ? mins   B/W   B, V   P
New York Yankees, Brooklyn Dodgers
Allie Reynolds and Preacher Roe trade 1-0 victories in the first two games, then the Yankees win the next three with Joe Page, Gerry Coleman and Johnny Mize in starring roles.

Lou Fonseca — *Major League Baseball Productions*

World Series, 1950
Baseball
33848   ? mins   B/W   B, V   P
New York Yankees, Philadelphia Phillies
The "Whiz Kids" of Philadelphia surprise the National League in winning the pennant, but the Yankees, in the midst of five consecutive World Championship seasons, make easy picking of the Phillies in four straight games.
Lou Fonseca — *Major League Baseball Productions*

World Series, 1951
Baseball
33852   ? mins   B/W   B, V   P
New York Yankees, New York Giants
The Giants enter the series coming off their emotional playoff victory over the Dodgers which featured Bobby Thompson's "Shot Heard 'Round the World" in the ninth inning of the final game. They run out of miracles against the Yankees however, as Eddie Lopat and Allie Reynolds lead a solid pitching staff to a six-game victory for the Yankees in Joe DiMaggio's final season and Mickey Mantle's first.
Lou Fonseca — *Major League Baseball Productions*

World Series, 1952
Baseball
33857   ? mins   B/W   B, V   P
New York Yankees, Brooklyn Dodgers
Vic Raschi and Allie Reynolds win two games apiece for the Yankees and Billy Martin makes a diving catch of Jackie Robinson's pop-up to save the seventh and deciding game for the New Yorkers. Pee Wee Reese and Duke Snider each batted .345 to lead the Dodger effort.
Lou Fonseca — *Major League Baseball Productions*

World Series, 1953
Baseball
33856   ? mins   B/W   B, V   P
New York Yankees, Brooklyn Dodgers
Yankee second baseman Billy Martin bats .500 and drives in the winning run in the final game as the Yankees defeat the Dodgers four games to two, capturing their unprecedented fifth consecutive World Series title.
Lou Fonseca — *Major League Baseball Productions*

World Series, 1954
Baseball
33849   ? mins   B/W   B, V   P
New York Giants, Cleveland Indians
The Indians won a record 111 games during the regular season, but did not win their next game until the following year. The Giants, sparked by

Willie Mays' famous catch of Vic Wertz deep line drive, went on to defeat player-manager Lou Boudreau's Cleveland team in four straight games.
Lou Fonseca — *Major League Baseball Productions*

World Series, 1955 — 1955
Baseball
33850 ? mins B/W B, V P
Brooklyn Dodgers, New York Yankees
It's a dream come true for the bums from Brooklyn. For the first time in six tries the Dodgers beat their cross-town rivals, the hated Yankees, in the World series. Johnny Padres notches three of the Brooklyn wins, including a 2-0 masterpiece in game seven at Yankee Stadium. Sandy Amoros' catch of Yogi Berra's long fly ball thwarted an important Yankee rally and was the key defensive play of the series.
Lou Fonseca — *Major League Baseball Productions*

World Series, 1956 — 1956
Baseball
33855 ? mins B/W B, V P
New York Yankees, Brooklyn Dodgers
The Dodgers came from behind to win each of the first two games, but the Yankees captured the next three contests, including Don Larsen's perfect game in game five at Yankee Stadium. Jackie Robinson's tenth inning hit gave the Dodgers a 1-0 victory in game six to tie the series. The Yankees won easily in the seventh game to give manager Casey Stengel his sixth world championship.
Lou Fonseca — *Major League Baseball Productions*

World Series, 1957 — 1957
Baseball
33851 ? mins B/W B, V P
Milwaukee Braves, New York Yankees
The Braves, led by the hitting of Hank Aaron, Eddie Mathews, and Joe Adcock, surprise Casey Stengel's World Champion Yankees in seven games. Righthander Lew Burdette is the hero, pitching three of the Braves' victories.
Lou Fonseca — *Major League Baseball Productions*

World Series, 1958 — 1958
Baseball
48143 ? mins C B, V P
New York Yankees, Milwaukee Braves
The Yankees avenge their previous year's defeat by rallying from a three games to one deficit to defeat Eddie Mathews, Hank Aaron and the hard-hitting Braves in seven games. Mickey Mantle and Whitey Ford spark the Yankee comeback.
Lou Fonseca — *Major League Baseball Productions*

World Series, 1959 — 1959
Baseball
33854 ? mins B/W B, V P
Los Angeles Dodgers, Chicago White Sox
After the White Sox captured the opening game 11-0, the Dodgers, with fine relief pitching by Larry Sherry and steady hitting by Gil Hodges, beat Chicago in six games. Their old Brooklyn fans saw a collection of familiar faces and few new kids playing on a team that now belonged to the West Coast.
Lou Fonseca — *Major League Baseball Productions*

World Series, 1960 — 1960
Baseball
33826 ? mins B/W B, V P
New York Yankees, Pittsburgh Pirates
Bill Mazeroski's leadoff home run off Ralph Terry in the bottom of the ninth in game seven at Forbes Field gives the Pirates a 10-9 victory and wins the World Series over the Yankees, four games to three.
Lou Fonseca — *Major League Baseball Productions*

World Series, 1961 — 1961
Baseball
33853 ? mins B/W B, V P
New York Yankees, Cincinnati Reds
This was the year Roger Maris and Mickey Mantle combined for 115 home runs. Although neither had a very good World Series, Elston Howard, Bobby Richardson, and several reserve players led the Yankees to a four games to one victory over Fred Hutchinson's Reds. Whitey Ford's two pitching victories gave him four straight series wins.
Lou Fonseca — *Major League Baseball Productions*

World Series, 1962 — 1962
Baseball
33824 ? mins C B, V P
New York Yankees, San Francisco Giants
In a series frequently interrupted by rain delays, the Yankees outlast the Giants four games to three. With the Yankees leading by a run with two out in the bottom of the ninth in game seven, the Giants load the bases and big Willie McCovey steps to the plate. His scorching line drive is driven right into the glove of Yankee second baseman Bobby Richardson, for the final out.
Lou Fonseca — *Major League Baseball Productions*

World Series, 1963 — 1963
Baseball
33823 ? mins C B, V P
Los Angeles Dodgers, New York Yankees
Sandy Koufax breaks Carl Erskine's World Series strikeout record, fanning fifteen while the

Dodgers are en route to a four game sweep over the defending champion Yankees.
Lou Fonseca — *Major League Baseball Productions*

World Series, 1964   1964
Baseball
33822   ? mins   C   B, V   P
St. Louis Cardinals, New York Yankees
Young Yankee pitchers Jim Bouton and Mel Stottlemyre are impressive, but Bob Gibson is even better for the Cardinals. A grand slam home run by Ken Boyer is the big hit in this series, won by the Cardinals four games to three. The great Mickey Mantle, in what is to be his last World Series, adds to his record status for the October Classic.
Lou Fonseca — *Major League Baseball Productions*

World Series, 1965   1965
Baseball
33821   ? mins   C   B, V   P
Los Angeles Dodgers, Minnesota Twins
Sandy Koufax and Don Drysdale stymie the big Minnesota bats of Harmon Killebrew and Bob Allison long enough for the Dodgers to squeak by the Twins in seven games. "Sweet" Lou Johnson swings a hot bat for the Dodgers.
Lou Fonseca — *Major League Baseball Productions*

World Series, 1966   1966
Baseball
33820   ? mins   C   B, V   P
Baltimore Orioles, Los Angeles Dodgers
Dave McNally, Jim Palmer, Steve Barber, and Wally Bunker, with relief help from Moe Drabowsky, send the Dodgers down in four straight. Sandy Koufax and Don Drysdale pitch well for the Dodgers, but the Robinsons, Frank and Brooks, provide timely hitting for the Orioles.
Lou Fonseca — *Major League Baseball Productions*

World Series, 1967   1967
Baseball
33819   ? mins   C   B, V   P
St. Louis Cardinals, Boston Red Sox
The Red Sox, ninth place finishers the previous year, are led to the series by Carl Yastrzemski, Tony Conigliaro, and Ken Harrelson. Boston ace Jim Lonborg flirts with a no-hitter in one game, but the St. Louis bats finally quell the Sox in seven games, led by Lou Brock, Orlando Cepeda, and Tim McCarver, and the pitching of Bob Gibson.
Lou Fonseca — *Major League Baseball Productions*

World Series, 1968   19??
Baseball
33818   ? mins   C   B, V   P
Detroit Tigers, St. Louis Cardinals
The Tigers stage a comeback to beat the Cardinals in seven games after falling behind three games to one. Mickey Lolich tosses three of the Tiger victories and Mickey Stanley, normally a centerfielder, stars at shortstop. Bob Gibson wins two games for the Cardinals, setting a series game strikeout record in the process.
Lou Fonseca — *Major League Baseball Productions*

World Series, 1969   1969
Baseball
33817   40 mins   C   B, V   P
New York Mets, Baltimore Orioles
The Miracle Mets stun the world by taking four straight from the mighty Orioles after losing the opening game. Outstanding defensive plays by Tommie Agee and Ron Swoboda stymie Baltimore rallies. Jerry Koosman wins two games, and MVP Donn Clendenon and utility infielder Al Weis pace the Mets' hitting attack.
W and W Prods — *Major League Baseball Productions*

World Series, 1970   1970
Baseball
33816   40 mins   C   B, V   P
Baltimore Orioles, Cincinnati Reds
Brooks Robinson's incredible fielding and .429 batting average help the Orioles to a four games to one victory over the Reds. Baltimore's pitching staff silences the Big Red Machine sluggers like Johnny Bench and Lee May.
W and W Prods — *Major League Baseball Productions*

World Series, 1971   1971
Baseball
33815   40 mins   C   B, V   P
Pittsburgh Pirates, Baltimore Orioles
The sensational hitting of Roberto Clemente and two clutch pitching wins by Steve Blass lead the Pirates to a seven-game triumph over the defending champion Orioles. This series featured the first night game in World Series history.
W and W Productions — *Major League Baseball Productions*

World Series, 1972   1972
Baseball
33814   40 mins   C   B, V   P
Oakland A's, Cincinnati Reds
The A's win a seven-game thriller without their star outfielder Reggie Jackson, who is lost to an injury. Gene Tenace provides the home run heroics, and MVP left fielder Joe Rudi makes a remarkable catch that many consider as the turning point of the series.

W and W Prods — *Major League Baseball Productions*

World Series, 1973   1973
Baseball
33813   40 mins   C   B, V   P
Oakland A's, New York Mets
The Oakland A's win their second consecutive title, in seven games. The talented Mets pitching staff holds the powerful A's in check, but Bert Campaneris and Reggie Jackson belt home runs in the final game to finally subdue the gallant New Yorkers.
W and W Prods — *Major League Baseball Productions*

World Series, 1974   1974
Baseball
33812   26 mins   C   B, V   P
Oakland A's, Los Angeles Dodgers
The A's win their third straight world championship in a tightly contested, five game series in which four games were decided by 3-2 scores. The fielding of second baseman Dick Green and relief pitching of series MVP Rollie Fingers makes the difference for the A's.
W and W Prods — *Major League Baseball Productions*

World Series, 1975   1975
Baseball
33811   35 mins   C   B, V   P
Cincinnati Reds, Boston Red Sox
In one of the most memorable and exciting World Series ever played, the Reds take a three games to two lead after five games. Carlton Fisk's dramatic 12th inning homer evens the series in game six. The Red Sox take an early lead in the final game, but series MVP Pete Rose and Joe Morgan lead a Cincinnati comeback to give the Reds their first World Championship in 35 years.
Major League Baseball — *Major League Baseball Productions*

World Series, 1976   1976
Baseball
33810   30 mins   C   B, V   P
Cincinnati Reds, New York Yankees
The Reds demolish the Yankees in four straight, led by MVP catcher Johnny Bench. Yankee catcher Thurman Munson performs gallantly, batting .529 for the series. Reds' manager Sparky Anderson is "miked" throughout, giving the viewer a rare glimpse at a manager's feelings during pressure-filled games.
Major League Baseball — *Major League Baseball Productions*

World Series, 1977   1977
Baseball
33809   30 mins   C   B, V   P

New York Yankees, Los Angles Dodgers
Yankee slugger Reggie Jackson grabs the spotlight by belting five homers in the series, won by New York 4 games to 2. Jackson's heroics include three consecutive home runs in the final game. Yankee pitcher Mike Torrez goes undefeated in his two starts. This program also captures the antics of Dodger manager Tom Lasorda and sets the mannerisms of baseball players to ballet music.
Major League Baseball — *Major League Baseball Productions*

World Series, 1978   1978
Baseball
33808   31 mins   C   B, V   P
New York Yankees, Los Angeles Dodgers
The Yankees beat the Dodgers in six games for the second year in a row. Yankee shortstop Bucky Dent wins the series MVP award while Graig Nettles, Reggie Jackson, Thurman Munson, and rookie Brian Doyle lead the champs at bat and on the field. Ron Cey and Davey Lopes excel for the Dodgers. The victory caps a memorable season for New York, one in which they came from 14 games out of first place in July to eventually win a one-game playoff with the Boston Red Sox for the American League East Championship.
Major League Baseball — *Major League Baseball Productions*

World Series, 1979   1979
Baseball
33847   31 mins   C   B, V   P
Pittsburgh Pirates, Baltimore Orioles
Oriole Manager Earl Weaver is hailed as a genius after expertly maneuvering his Birds to a 3-1 lead after four games. Baltimore never won another game in the series though, as MVP Willie "Pops" Stargell and the Pirate relief pitchers rose to the occasion and dominated the remainder of the series. Stargell's two-run homer off Scott McGregor in game seven moved the Pirate ahead to stay.
Major League Baseball — *Major League Baseball Productions*

World Series, 1980   1980
Baseball
49548   30 mins   C   B, V   P
Philadelphia Phillies, Kansas City Royals
The clutch hitting of Mike Schmidt and Pete Rose, and the heart-stopping relief provided by Tug McGraw leads the Phillies to a six-game victory over the Royals. George Brett, Willie Aikens, and Amos Otis try to carry the Royals back after falling behind two games to none, but their impressive efforts are not enough to overcome the Phillies.
MAJ — *Major League Baseball Productions; RCA VideoDiscs*

World Series, 1981   1981
Baseball
59377   30 mins   C   B, V   P
New York Yankees, Los Angeles Dodgers
The Yankees fall apart after winning the first two games. The series begins to turn in Los Angeles when rookie pitchers Fernando Valenzuela and Dave Righetti meet, with the Dodgers' Valenzuela emerging victorious. Timely hitting by Ron Cey, Steve Yeager, Jay Johnstone and Pedro Guerrero carries the Dodgers to a six-game victory over the faltering Yankees.
Major League Baseball Productions — *Major League Baseball Productions*

World Series, 1982   1982
Baseball
64659   45 mins   C   B, V   P
St. Louis Cardinals, Milwaukee Brewers
Willie McGee, Bruce Sutter, and MVP Darrell Porter lead the NL champion Cardinals to victories in games 6 and 7 as the Redbirds defeat the Milwaukee Brewers 4 games to 3. The big bats of Milwaukee's Robin Yount and Cecil Cooper could not overcome the loss of their injured ballpen ace, Rollie Fingers.
Major League Baseball — *Major League Baseball Productions*

World Series, 1983: 1983   1983
World Series
Baseball
81127   36 mins   C   B, V   P
Baltimore Orioles, Philadelphia Phillies
Here are highlights of the 1983 fall classic from which the Baltimore Orioles emerged as the world champions.
Major League Baseball — *Major League Baseball Productions*

World Series, 1984: The   1984
Sounds of the Series
Baseball
81128   36 mins   C   B, V   P
Detroit Tigers, San Diego Padres
Here are the exciting highlights from the 1984 World Series where Sparky Anderson's Tigers mauled Dick Williams' Padres to become the world champions.
Major League Baseball — *Major League Baseball Productions*

World War II: The   194?
European Theatre
World War II/Documentary
44984   55 mins   B/W   B, V   P, T
In this footage from the Fox/Movietone newsreel vaults, six separate subjects are covered: "Battle of the Atlantic," "Battle of Britain," "War in the Desert," "Liberation of Paris," "Fall of Hitler's Nazis," and "1945: Year of Triumph."
Movietone — *Blackhawk Films*

World War II: The Pacific   194?
Theatre
World War II/Documentary
29471   55 mins   B/W   B, V   P, T
A compilation taken from actual newsreel footage of World War II. The show begins with the authentic scenes of Pearl Harbor and closes with a final surrender of Japan in 1945.
Movietone — *Blackhawk Films*

World War II Video   1945
Series—Attack: The
Battle of New Britain
World War II/Documentary
66361   50 mins   B/W   B, V, 3/4U   P
A filmed record of the invasion of New Britain in the South Pacific theater of war.
Office of War Information — *Nostalgia Merchant*

World War II Video   1945
Series—Something for
Our Boys
World War II/Documentary
66362   50 mins   B/W   B, V, 3/4U   P
Judy Garland, Bob Hope, Carmen Miranda and others
A selection of shorts featuring many Hollywood and radio stars performing overseas for the pleasure of Allied troops during 1943-1945.
Office of War Information — *Nostalgia Merchant*

World War II Video   1945
Series—The Stillwell
Road
Documentary/World War II
66337   50 mins   B/W   B, V, 3/4U   P
The story of the China-Burma-India campaign during World War II, with authentic documentary footage of jungle battles and aerial combat.
US Army — *Nostalgia Merchant*

World War II Video   19??
Series—Tried by Fire!
World War II/Documentary
66360   50 mins   B/W   B, V, 3/4U   P
The combat history of World War II's 84th Infantry Division, from its activities early in the war through the Battle of the Bulge, is chronicled.
Office of War Information — *Nostalgia Merchant*

World's Greatest Athlete,   1973
The
Comedy
88340   89 mins   C   B, V   P
Jan-Michael Vincent, Tim Conway, John Amos, Roscoe Lee Brown

THE VIDEO TAPE & DISC GUIDE

A Tarzan-like jungle-man is recruited by an American athletics coach in this humorous Disney farce.
MPAA:G
Walt Disney Prod. — *Walt Disney Home Video*

World's Greatest Photography Course, The   1983
Photography
66000   90 mins   C   B, V   P
A step-by-step course designed for people who want to learn how to take great 35mm pictures.
Video Corporation of America — *VidAmerica*

World's Most Spectacular Stuntman, The   1980
Documentary/Filmmaking
87322   60 mins   C   B, V   P
Dar Robinson, Cathy Lee Crosby
Stuntman Robinson performs various extremely dangerous stunts for the pleasure of the viewing audience. A made-for-TV special.
Dan Curtis — *U.S.A. Home Video*

Worth the Wait!   1981
Baseball
55597   59 mins   C   B, V   P
Highlights of the 1980 World Series between the Kansas City Royals and the Philadelphia Phillies, and the 1980 All-Star Game in which the National League stars defeated the American League stars in the Summer Classic.
Major League Baseball — *VidAmerica*

Wrestling Women vs. the Aztec Mummy, The   1965
Horror
51100   75 mins   B/W   B, V   P
Lorena Velasquez, Armando Silvestre, Elizabeth Campbell, Chucho Salinas
The Black Dragon is out to get hidden Aztec treasure from an ancient pyramid. His chief opposition comes from two formidable lady wrestlers.
Mexican — *Hollywood Home Theater; Festival Films*

Wrestling Women vs. the Aztec Mummy   1959
Exploitation
84361   88 mins   C   B, V   P
Women, broad of shoulder, wrestle an ancient Aztec wrestler come to life. Furnished with a new rock soundtrack.
Mexican — *Rhino Video*

Wright Brothers: Masters of the Sky, The   19??
Biographical/Aeronautics
69586   47 mins   C   B, V   P

Two young daredevils defy traditional thought, fix their eyes and hopes on the sky, and overcome a steady stream of failures to provide man with the means to fly.
Unknown — *VidAmerica*

Wrong Arm of the Law, The   1963
Comedy-Drama
82228   94 mins   B/W   B, V   P
Peter Sellers, Lionel Jeffries, Nanette Newman, Bernard Cribbens
A trio of London gangsters have the police and crooks chasing after them because they dress up as cops and confiscate loot from apprehended robbers.
Continental — *Monterey Home Video*

Wrong Box, The   1966
Comedy
80382   105 mins   C   B, V   P
Peter Sellers, Dudley Moore, Peter Cook, Michael Caine, Ralph Richardson, Gerald Sim
Two elderly Victorian brothers try to kill each other to collect on a Fortune.
Columbia Pictures — *RCA/Columbia Pictures Home Video*

Wrong Is Right   1982
Adventure/Comedy
60339   117 mins   C   B, V   P
Sean Connery, Katherine Ross, Robert Conrad, George Grizzard, Henry Silva, directed by Richard Brooks
A black comedy revolving around international terrorism, news reporting and the CIA.
MPAA:R
Columbia — *RCA/Columbia Pictures Home Video*

Wrong Man, The   1956
Suspense
47618   126 mins   B/W   B, V   P
Henry Fonda, Vera Miles, Anthony Quayle, directed by Alfred Hitchcock
A musician is accused of a robbery that he did not commit. Part of the "A Night at the Movies" series, this tape simulates a 1956 movie evening, with a color Bugs Bunny cartoon, "A Star Is Bored," a newsreel and coming attractions for "Toward the Unknown."
Warner Bros — *Warner Home Video*

Wuthering Heights   1939
Drama/Romance
81476   104 mins   B/W   B, V, LV   P
Laurence Olivier, Merle Oberon, David Niven, Donald Crisp, Geraldine Fitzgerald, directed by William Wyler
This is the story of the doomed romance between a young aristocratic girl and the boy who works in her father's stable. Based on the classic Emily Bronte novel.

Samuel Goldwyn — *Embassy Home Entertainment*

X

X -- The Man with X-Ray Eyes   1963
Science fiction
65140   79 mins   C   B, V   P
Ray Milland, Diana Van Der Vlis, Harold J. Stone, directed by Roger Corman
A scientist uses himself as a guinea pig to test a new serum on his eyes that will enable him to see through things. Though a success, the effect continues to strengthen, driving the scientist to the brink of madness.
American International — *Warner Home Video*

Xanadu   1980
Musical/Fantasy
48640   96 mins   C   B, V, LV   P
Olivia Newton-John, Michael Beck, Gene Kelly
A beautiful muse comes down to earth and meets an artist and a nightclub owner. She helps the two of them fulfill their dreams, as they collaborate on a roller-disco venture.
MPAA:PG
Universal — *MCA Home Video*

X-Tro   1983
Science fiction/Horror
65088   80 mins   C   B, V, CED   P
Philip Sayer, Bernice Stegers, Danny Brainin, Simon Nash, Maryam D'Abo
A man who was mysteriously kidnapped by aliens returns to his family three years later. Infected by alien spores, he transmits the ghastly sickness by biting his wife and son.
MPAA:R
New Line Cinema — *THORN EMI/HBO Video*

Y

Y&T Live at the San Francisco Civic   1985
Music-Performance
81525   60 mins   C   B, V   P
Y&T perform their own brand of headbanging heavy metal in this concert taped at the San Francisco Civic Center.
A&M Video — *A & M Video; RCA/Columbia Pictures Home Video*

Yakuza, The   1975
Adventure
78627   112 mins   C   B, V   P

Robert Mitchum, Richard Jordan, Takakura Ken, Brian Keith, directed by Sydney Pollack
An ex G.I. returns to Japan to help an old army buddy find his kidnapped daughter.
MPAA:R
Warner Bros — *Warner Home Video*

Yank in Libya, A   1942
War-Drama
84848   65 mins   B/W   B, V   P
Walter Woolf King, John Woodbury, H B Warner, Parkyakarkus
An adventure pitting an American man and an English girl against Libyan Arabs and Nazis.
PRC — *United Home Video*

Yankee Clipper   1927
Adventure
10118   51 mins   B/W   B, V   P, T
William Boyd, Elinor Fair, directed by Rupert Julian.
Deceit, treachery, and romance are combined in this depiction of fierce race from China to New England between the Yankee Clipper, and the English ship, Lord of the Isles.
PDC — *Blackhawk Films*

Yankee Doodle   198?
Cartoons
79199   30 mins   C   B, V   P
Animated
A blacksmith and two Militiamen help Paul Revere to complete his midnight ride.
Rankin Bass Studios — *Prism*

Yankee Doodle Cricket   1976
Language arts
00232   26 mins   C   B, V, 3/4U,   P
FO
Patriotic animals compose "Yankee Doodle Dandy," help Thomas Jefferson write The Declaration, and assist Paul Revere.
AM Available
Chuck Jones Entp — *The Center for Humanities; Family Home Entertainment*

Yankee Doodle Dandy   1942
Musical-Drama
13317   126 mins   B/W   B, V   P
James Cagney, Joan Leslie, Walter Huston, Richard Whorf, directed by Michael Curtiz
Nostalgic view of the Golden Era of show business and the man who made it glitter—George M. Cohan. His early days, triumphs, songs, musicals and romances are brought to life in the movie. A colorized version of this film is also available.
Academy Awards '42: Best Actor (Cagney); Best Sound Recording; Best Musical Scores.
Warner Bros — *CBS/Fox Video; RCA VideoDiscs*

Yankee Doodle in Berlin 1919
Comedy
64305   60 mins   B/W   B, V   P, T
Ford Sterling, Ben Turpin, Marie Prevost,
Bothwell Browne
A spoof of World War I dramas with the hero
dressing up as a woman and seducing the
Kaiser into giving up his war plans. Typical
Sennett slapstick with a music and effects score
added to the silent film.
Mack Sennett — *Blackhawk Films*

Year of Living Dangerously, The 1982
Adventure
Closed Captioned
64940   114 mins   C   B, V, CED   P
Mel Gibson, Sigourney Weaver, Linda Hunt,
directed by Peter Weir
An Australian journalist covering a political story
in Indonesia, circa 1965, becomes involved with
a British attache at the height of the bloody
fighting and rioting in Jakarta during the coup
against President Sukarno.
Academy Awards '83: Best Supporting Actress
(Hunt) MPAA:PG
MGM/UA — *MGM/UA Home Video*

Year of the Dragon 1985
Drama
Closed Captioned
71152   136 mins   C   B, V, LV   P
Mickey Rourke, Ariane, John Lone, directed by
Michael Cimino
Polish police Captain Stanley White of the
NYPD vows to neutralize the crime lords running
New York's Chinatown. Brilliant cinematography
and typically gripping Cimino direction highlights
this tour through the black market's underbelly
and hierarchy. Recorded in HiFi Dolby Surround
Stereo.
MPAA:R
Dino De Laurentiis — *MGM/UA Home Video*

Yearling, The 1946
Drama
81494   128 mins   C   B, V   P
Gregory Peck, Jane Wyman, Calude Jarman Jr.,
Chill Wills, directed by Clarence Brown
This is an adaptation of the Marjorie Kinnan
Rawlings novel about a young boy's love for a
yearling fawn.
Academy Awards '46: Best
Cinematography?Best Art Direction?Best
Interior Direction
MGM — *MGM/UA Home Video*

Years of Glory ... Years of Pain 1985
Football
81952   28 mins   C   B, V   P
Jack Kemp, O.J. Simpson, Butch Byrd

This film recounts the twenty-five year history of
the Buffalo Bills and features such stars as O.J.
Simpson, Jack Kemp and Frank Lewis.
NFL Films — *NFL Films Video*

Years to Remember: The New York Giants 1985
Football
81953   140 mins   C   B, V   P
Frank Gifford, Sam Huff, Y.A. Tittle
Here are highlights from the 1958-1963 seasons
when the Giants won the NFL's Eastern
Conference title with defense from Sam Huff
and Frank Gifford.
NFL Films — *NFL Films Video*

Yehudi Menuhin: Brahms Violin Concerto in D, op. 77 1984
Music-Performance
87347   60 mins   C   B, V   P
A recording of Menuhin's performance of this
classic concerto made at the Gewandhaus in
Leipzig, East Germany.
East German — *Kultur*

Yehudi Menuhin: Concert for the Pope 1983
Music-Performance
84641   53 mins   C   B, V   P
Yehudi Menuhin, the Polish Chamber Orchestra
conducted by Jerzy Maksymin
Filmed in Castelgandolfo, violinist Menuhin
gives a performance for His Holiness. Among
the works performed are Vivaldi's Concerto in D
and Mozart's Adagio K 261 and Rondo K 373.
Recorded in Hi-Fi Stereo.
Interclassica — *V.I.E.W. Video*

Yehudi Menuhin: Tribute to J.S. Bach 1985
Music-Performance
84642   90 mins   C   B, V   P
Yehudi Menuhin, Nicholas Rivenc, the English
Chamber Orchestra
This concert was taped as part of the 300th
Anniversay tribute to Bach at the Barbican in
London. Among the works performed on this all-
Bach program are the Concerto for Violin in A
Minor, the Partita in E Major for solo violin and
the "Coffee" Cantata. In Hi-Fi Stereo.
REVCOM-TV — *V.I.E.W. Video*

Yellow Hair and the Fortress of Gold 1984
Exploitation
70690   102 mins   C   B, V   P
Laurene Landon, Ken Robertson, directed by
Matt Cimber
This film follows the adventures of an Indian
Princess in her quest for the elk horn containing
the man that will lead her to the fortress of gold.

THE VIDEO TAPE & DISC GUIDE

MPAA:R
Crown — *Lightning Video*

MPAA:PG
MGM — *MGM/UA Home Video*

Yellow Rose of Texas, The
1944

Western
10684   55 mins   B/W   B, V   P
Roy Rogers, Dale Evans
Roy Rogers works as an undercover insurance agent to clear the name of an old man falsely accused of a stagecoach robbery.
Republic — *Video Connection; Cable Films; Video Yesteryear; Discount Video Tapes*

Yellowbeard
1983

Comedy
65348   97 mins   C   B, V, LV   P
Marty Feldman, Cheech and Chong, Madeline Kahn, Peter Boyle, James Mason, Graham Chapman, John Cleese
This is the saga of the infamous priate, whose 15 years in prison have done little to squelch his appetitie for larceny, lechery and lunacy.
MPAA:PG
Carter De Haven — *Vestron Video*

Yellowstone and the Madison: One After Another, The
1985

Fishing
82506   51 mins   C   B, V, 3/4U, 1C   P
Alton Coulter, John Bailey
Two fly fishermen fish the Yellowstone and Madison rivers.
Grunko — *Grunko Films*

Yeomen of the Guard, The
19??

Opera/Comedy
65494   112 mins   C   B, V   P
Joel Grey, Elizabeth Gale, David Hillman, Claire Powell, Alfred Marks
A colonel, condemned to death in the Tower of London on false charges of sorcery, is helped to escape by a family loyal to him. In order to save his own life, he masks his true identity and takes his place among the yeomen of the guard, beginning the series of misadventures—some humorous, some tragic—that make "Yeomen of the Guard" one of Gilbert and Sullivan's most beloved musicals.
Moving Pictures Company Ltd — *CBS/Fox Video*

Yes, Giorgio
1982

Musical/Comedy
60399   111 mins   C   B, V, CED   P
Luciano Pavarotti, Kathryn Harrold
An opera star falls in love with his female doctor. Songs include "If We Were in Love," "I Left My Heart in San Francisco," and arias by Verdi, Donizetti and Puccini. VHS in stereo.

Yessongs
1973

Music-Performance
80186   70 mins   C   B, V, LV   P
Steve Howe, Rick Wakeman, Jon Anderson, Chris Squire, Alan White
The exciting progressive rock sounds of Yes are captured in this 1973 concert.
Vistar International Productions — *VidAmerica*

Yes, Virginia, There Is a Santa Claus
1974

Cartoons/Christmas
82525   52 mins   C   B, V   P
Animated, voices by Jim Backus, Courtney Lemmon, Louis Nye
A little girl has her belief in Santa Claus confirmed by a kindly journalist in this Emmy-winning classic.
Burt Rosen; David Wolper — *Paramount Home Video*

Yes You Can Microwave
1984

Cookery
70569   53 mins   C   B, V   P
Donovan Jon Fandre
This program offers viewers a short basic course in microwave cooking.
AM Available
JCI Video — *JCI Video*

Yesterday's Witness
1983

Documentary
81924   52 mins   C   B, V   P
This documentary examines the history of the newsreel and also features interviews with Ed Herlihy, Lowell Thomas and Harry Von Zello.
Christian Blackwood — *Pacific Arts Video*

Yoga Moves with Alan Finger
1983

Yoga/Physical fitness
65311   60 mins   C   B, V, LV   P
This is a complete introductory program to more than 26 yoga positions which help to tone and strengthen the body and to develop flexibility.
Lynda Guber — *MCA Home Video*

Yogi's First Christmas
1980

Cartoons
69590   100 mins   C   B, V   P
Animated
Yogi Bear joins his friends for a musical celebration of Christmas at the Jellystone Lodge.
Hanna Barbera — *Worldvision Home Video*

Yojimbo   1962
Adventure
06244   110 mins   B/W   B, V, LV   P
*Toshiro MiFune, Eijiro Tono, Suuzu Yamda,
directed by Akira Kurosawa*
Two equally distasteful clans vying for political
power bid for the services of a professional killer
who comes to town. The original Japanese
version is available with English subtitles or
dubbed into English.
EL, JA
Seneca International Films — *Embassy Home
Entertainment; Hollywood Home Theater;
International Historic Films; Video Yesteryear;
Discount Video Tapes; Cable Films; Video
Action*

Yoko Ono Then and Now   1984
Music-Performance/Interview
78367   56 mins   C   B, V   P
Yoko Ono looks back on her life before and
after John Lennon along with songs performed
by both John and Yoko.
Barbara Graustark — *Music Media*

Yol   1982
Drama
66348   111 mins   C   B, V   P
Tarik Akan, Serif Sezer, directed by Serif Goren
Five Turkish prisoners are granted temporary
leave to visit their families in this bittersweet
Turkish-made feature.
Cannes Film Festival '82: Palme d'Or for Best
Picture. MPAA:PG
Triumph Films; Edi
Hubschmid — *RCA/Columbia Pictures Home
Video*

Yor, the Hunter from the   1983
Future
Fantasy/Adventure
69615   88 mins   C   B, V   P
Reb Brown
Lost in a time warp where the past and the
future mysteriously collide, Yor sets out on a
search for his real identity, with his only clue a
golden medallion around his neck.
MPAA:PG
Michele Marsala — *RCA/Columbia Pictures
Home Video; RCA VideoDiscs*

You and Me,   1985
Kid—Volume 3
Language arts
77534   111 mins   C   B, V   P
*Sonny Melendrez, Gallagher, Ruby Keeler,
Patrick Wayne, Lynn Redgrave.*
Host Sonny Melendrez and his special guests
lead children through various games, songs and
exercises that the whole family can enjoy.
Walt Disney Productions — *Walt Disney Home
Video*

You and Me, Kid Volume   1985
4
Family/Children
81648   112 mins   C   B, V   P
Hosted by Sonny Melendrezl
This volume features interviews with Cathy
Rigby and her children, "Let's Go" and "You
and Me Theatre."
Walt Disney Productions — *Walt Disney Home
Video*

You and Me, Kid Volume I   1983
Family/Parents
72798   111 mins   C   B, V   P
Four complete half-hour programs encourage
parents and children to participate in the viewing
of "You and Me, Kid" together.
Walt Disney Productions — *Walt Disney Home
Video*

You and Me, Kid Volume   1985
2
Family/Children
80354   111 mins   C   B, V   P
A collection of four episodes from The Disney
Channel series that features activities that
children and parents can do together.
Walt Disney Productions — *Walt Disney Home
Video*

You and Your Cat   1985
Pets
84768   51 mins   C   B, V   P
Dr Michael Fox
The care, maintenance, training and
socialization of cats is explained by the
prominent veterinarian.
United Media Prod/Selluloid Video — *Video
Associates*

You and Your Dog   1985
Pets
84769   51 mins   C   B, V   P
Dr Michael Fox
The care and training of dogs is explained by
the preeminent veterinarian.
United Media Prod/Selluloid Video — *Video
Associates*

You Bet Your Life   195?
Game show
33694   120 mins   B/W   B, V, 3/4U   P
Four top episodes from the hit quiz show
starring Groucho Marx and his flunkie, George
Fenneman. Guest stars Harry Ruby and William
Peter Blatty appear in two of the shows.
NBC — *Shokus Video*

You Bet Your Life   1954
Comedy/Game show
75638   30 mins   B/W   B, V   P
Groucho Marx

(For explanation of codes, see Use Guide and Key)

Groucho amuses all on his famous quiz show.
NBC — *Great Comedy Shows*

You Can Do It   1984
Magic
80154   60 mins   C   B, V   P
Shari Lewis aided by Charley Horse and Lamb
Chop, shows children how to perform magic
tricks
MGM/UA Home Video — *MGM/UA Home
Video*

You Can Win: Negotiating   1983
For Power, Love and
Money
Psychology
81439   55 mins   C   B, V   P
Dr. Tessa Albert Warschaw
Secrets for getting what you want from your
boss, your kids and your mate are revealed.
Available in Stereo Hi Fi for both formats.
MCA Home Video — *MCA Home Video*

You Can't Take It With   1984
You
Comedy
80116   116 mins   C   B, V   P
*Colleen Dewhurst, James Coco, Jason
Robards, directed by Ellis Raab*
A taped performance of the Rodgers and Hart
comedy about the strange pasttimes of the
Sycamore family.
Ellen M Krass Productions — *Vestron Video*

You Light Up My Life   1977
Drama
21298   90 mins   C   B, V   P
Didi Conn, Michael Zaslow, Melanie Mayron
The story of a young girl trying to break into the
music business and establish herself.
Academy Awards '79: Best Song ("You Light Up
My Life").
Columbia — *RCA/Columbia Pictures Home
Video*

You Only Live Once   1937
Drama
50959   86 mins   B/W   B, V   R, P
*Henry Fonda, Sylvia Sidney, Ward Bond,
directed by Fritz Lang*
An ill-fated young couple are separated when he
is put in prison. He shoots his way out and the
two begin a harrowing run from the law.
AM Available
United Artists — *Monterey Home Video;
Learning Corp of America*

You Only Live Once   1937
Drama
66638   86 mins   B/W   B, V   P
Sylvia Sidney, Henry Fonda

An escaped convict and his girlfriend attempt to
cross the border into Canada while remaining
one step ahead of the police.
Walter Wanger — *Monterey Home Video*

You Only Live Twice   1967
Adventure
59639   115 mins   C   B, V, CED   P
*Sean Connery, Donald Pleasence, Karin Dor,
directed by Lewis Gilbert*
Agent 007 battles Blofeld, the despicable head
of Spectre, in this thriller set in Japan.
United Artists; Albert Broccoli — *CBS/Fox
Video; RCA VideoDiscs*

You Were Never Lovelier   1942
Musical/Comedy
80381   98 mins   B/W   B, V   P
*Fred Astaire, Rita Hayworth, Xavier Cugat,
Adolphe Menjou, directed by William A. Seiter*
An Argentinian hotel tycoon creates a
mysterious admirer to get his daughter
interested in marriage. The musical score is by
Jerome Kern and Johnny Mercer.
Columbia Pictures — *RCA/Columbia Pictures
Home Video*

You'll Find Out   1940
Comedy/Musical
59646   97 mins   B/W   B, V   P
*Peter Lorre, Kay Kyser, Boris Karloff, Bela
Lugosi, Dennis O'Keefe, Helen Parrish*
A comedy spoof complete with lady in distress,
sinister seances, secret passages and
skullduggery.
RKO; David Butler — *Hollywood Home
Theater*

You'll Never Get Rich   1941
Musical
64580   88 mins   B/W   B, V   P
Fred Astaire, Rita Hayworth, Robert Benchley
A Broadway dance director is drafted into the
Army, where his romantic troubles cause him to
wind up in the guardhouse more than once.
Songs by Cole Porter include "Since I Kissed
My Baby Goodnight" and "The Astairable Rag."
Columbia — *RCA/Columbia Pictures Home
Video*

Young and Free   1978
Drama
65453   87 mins   C   B, V   P
Erik Larsen
Following the death of his parents, a young boy
must learn to face the perils of an unchartered
wilderness alone, and ultimately must choose
between returning to civilization, or remain with
his beloved wife and life in the wild.
Keith Larson — *Monterey Home Video*

Young and Innocent   1937
Mystery
01752   80 mins   B/W   B, V   P
*Derrick De Marney, Nova Pilbeam, Percy
Marmont, directed by Alfred Hitchcock*
Based on Josephine Tey's novel, Chief
Constable's daughter helps fugitive prove he
didn't strangle film star.
Gaumont; British — *Hollywood Home Theater;
Video Dimensions; Cable Films; Video
Connection; Video Yesteryear; Western Film &
Video Inc; Kartes Video Communications*

Young and Willing   1942
Comedy
66639   84 mins   B/W   B, V   P
*William Holden, Susan Hayward, Eddie
Bracken, Robert Benchley, Martha O'Driscoll*
A group of struggling actors get hold of a terrific
play and try various schemes to get it produced.
United Artists — *Monterey Home Video*

Young Aphrodities   1966
Drama
72873   87 mins   B/W   B, V   P
A tale of two teenagers who find each other's
passions in an underdeveloped country.
Unknown — *Embassy Home Entertainment*

Young at Heart   1954
Musical-Drama
47993   117 mins   C   B, V   P
*Frank Sinatra, Doris Day, Gig Young, Ethel
Barrymore, Dorothy Malone, Robert Keith,
Elizabeth Fraser, Alan Hale Sr*
Fanny Hurst's lighthearted tale of a cynical
hard-luck musician who finds happiness when
he falls for a small-town girl. A remake of the
1938 "Four Daughters." Songs include the title
tune, "You, My Love" and "Just One of Those
Things."
Warner Bros — *Republic Pictures Home Video*

Young Bing Crosby   193?
Musical
12824   39 mins   B/W   B, V, FO   P
Bing Crosby
Bing Crosby stars in short, delightful musical
comedies by Mack Sennett made before Crosby
entered feature-length musical comedy:
"Crooner's Holiday," "Blue of the Night," and
"Bing, Bing, Bing."
Mack Sennett — *Video Yesteryear*

Young Caruso, The   1951
Musical-Drama/Biographical
52464   78 mins   B/W   B, V, FO   P
*Gina Lollobrigida, Ermanno Randi, the voice of
Mario Del Monaco*
A dramatic biography of legendary tenor Enrico
Caruso following his life from childhood poverty
in Naples to the beginning of his rise to fame.
Dubbed in English.

Italian Films Export — *Movie Buff Video; Video
Yesteryear*

Young Doctors in Love   1982
Comedy
63420   95 mins   C   B, V, LV,   P
                                   CED
*Dabney Coleman, Sean Young, Michael
McKean*
This spoof of medical soap operas features a
chaotic scenario at City Hospital, where the
young men and women on the staff have better
things to do than attend to their patients.
MPAA:R
ABC Motion Pictures — *Vestron Video*

Young Frankenstein   1974
Comedy
55576   108 mins   B/W   B, V, LV,   P
                                   CED
*Peter Boyle, Gene Wilder, Marty Feldman,
Madeleine Kahn, Cloris Leachman, Gene
Hackman, directed by Mel Brooks*
Young Frederic Frankenstein, a brain surgeon,
goes back to Transylvania and learns the
secrets of his grandfather's notebooks.
MPAA:PG
Twentieth Century Fox — *CBS/Fox Video*

Young Lady Chatterly II   1985
Romance
84888   87 mins   C   B, V   P
Sybil Danning, Adam West, Harlee MacBride
A sequel to the popular MacBride film both
based on the Lawrence classic. Chatterly
inherits the family mansion and fools around, as
might be expected.
Alan Roberts — *Lightning Video*

Young Love, First Love   1979
Drama
80902   96 mins   C   B, V   P
*Valerie Bertinelli, Timothy Hutton, Arlen Dean
Snyder, Fionnuala Flanagan*
Two teenagers suffering from love must choose
between conforming to the traditional values
that they were raised with or to the liberal
attitudes of their peers. Available in VHS Stereo
and Beta Hi-Fi.
Lorimar Productions — *U.S.A. Home Video*

Young Nurses, The   1973
Exploitation
86598   77 mins   C   B, V   P
*Jean Manson, Angela Gibbs, Ashley Porter,
Sally Kirkland*
Three sexy nurses work at an exciting hospital
where they either play around with interns or
deal effectively with the insurmountable
problems hospitals are so famous for.
MPAA:R
Julie Corman! — *Charter Entertainment*

(For explanation of codes, see Use Guide and Key)

Young Philadelphians, The
1959

Drama
63448　150 mins　B/W　B, V　　　　P
Paul Newman, Barbara Rush, Alexis Smith, Billie Burke, Brian Keith
An ambitious young lawyer works hard at making an impression on the snobbish Philadelphia upper crust. Part of the "A Night at the Movies" series, this tape simulates a 1959 movie evening, with a Bugs Bunny Cartoon, "People Are Bunny," a newsreel and coming attractions for "The Nun's Story" and "The Hanging Tree."
Warner Bros — *Warner Home Video*

Young Teacher, The
1985

Drama
81618　90 mins　C　B, V　　　　P
A novice teacher finds out that trying to apply her college education to a real life elementary school environment isn't as easy as it sounds.
Video Gems — *Video Gems*

Young, the Old, and the Bold, Try and Catch the Wind, The
1980

Football
50094　48 mins　C　B, V, FO　　R, P
A fascinating feature on sling-shot armed quarterbacks and sticky-fingered receivers of the 1960's including John Brodie, Roman Gabriel, Sonny Jurgenson, Charlie Taylor, Bob Hayes, and Paul Warfield in their prime.
NFL Films — *NFL Films Video*

Young Tiger, The
1980

Adventure/Martial arts
56921　102 mins　C　B, V　　　R, P
Jackie Chan
A ninety-minute movie never before seen in the U.S. featuring an expert in martial arts who is accused of murder. Also included is a twelve-minute documentary featuring Jackie Chan, kung-fu sensation, demonstrating his skills.
MPAA:R
Fourseas Film Company — *Video Gems*

Young Warriors, The
1983

Adventure/Drama
78633　104 mins　C　B, V　　　　P
Ernest Borgnine, James Van Patten, Richard Roundtree
A group of college fraternity brothers become vigilantes to avenge the death of a woman killed by a street gang.
MPAA:R
Cannon Films — *MGM/UA Home Video*

Young Winston
1972

Biographical/Drama
86387　124 mins　C　B, V　　　　P

Simon Ward, Robert Shaw, Anne Bancroft, John Mills, Jack Hawkins, directed by Richard Attenborough
Based on Churchill's own autobiography, this historical film follows his exciting military career to his entrance into the House of Commons.
MPAA:PG
Carl Foreman — *RCA/Columbia Pictures Home Video*

Youngblood
1986

Drama
88207　111 mins　C　B, V　　　　P
Rob Lowe, Patrick Swayze, Cynthia Gibb, Ed Lauter, George Finn
An underdog beats the seemingly insurmountable odds and becomes a hockey champion.
MPAA:R
United Artists — *MGM/UA Home Video*

Your Favorite Laughs from "An Evening at the Improv"
1984

Comedy-Performance
Closed Captioned
71171　59 mins　C　B, V　　　　P
David Steinberg, Ed McMahon, Steven Wright, Michael Keaton, Billy Crystal, Harry Anderson, Harvey Korman, Howie Mandel
This tape compiles hilarious moments from the popular syndicated TV show.
Rupert MacNee — *Warner Home Video*

Your Hit Parade
1953

Variety
87208　120 mins　B/W　B, V, 3/4U　　　P
Snooky Lanson, Giselle Mackenzie, Dorothy Collins, Russell Arms
Four episodes of the famous live television show, with the popular cast members singing the hit songs of the week.
NBC — *Shokus Video*

Your Love Called To Me...
1984

Video
73632　5 mins　C　B, V　　　　P
On this reusable two hour videocassette is a simple way to express your feelings to the one you love.
Kartes Productions — *Kartes Video Communications*

Your Newborn Baby: Everything You Need to Know
1986

Infants
88475　60 mins　C　B, V　　　　P
JoaN Lunden
A comprehensive, progressive view of how to care for a newborn baby, with medical advice and basic hygiene tips.

Robert Knezevic; Elise C. Silvestri; Michael A. Krauss — *Meridian Entertainment*

Your Personal Guide to Love, Money and Fitness   1985
Occult sciences
87909   45 mins   C   B, V   P
12 pgms
Sydney Omarr predicts the future for all of the astronomical signs.
1.Aries 2.Sagittarius 3.Leo 4.Libra 5.Virgo 6.Capricorn 7.Aquarius 8.Cancer 9.Gemini 10.Pisces 11.Taurus 12.Scorpio
Twin Tower Ent. — *Twin Tower Enterprises*

Your Show of Shows   1950
Variety
11272   25 mins   B/W   B, V, FO   P
Hosted by Marsha Hunt, Sid Caesar, Imogene Coca, Marguerite Piazza, Bill Hayes, Jack Russell
A vintage edition of the legendary variety program.
NBC — *Video Yesteryear*

Your Show of Shows   1950
Variety
11273   25 mins   B/W   B, V, FO   P
Hosted by Melvyn Douglas, Sid Caesar, Imogene Coca, Marguerite Piazza, Jack Russell, Billy Williams Quartet
Comedy, song, and some technical difficulties highlight this entry in the famous series.
NBC — *Video Yesteryear*

Your Show of Shows   1952
Television/Comedy
82084   65 mins   B/W   B, V   P
Sid Caesar, Imogene Coca, Carl Reiner, Howard Morris 7 pgms
This is a collection of classic sketches from the innovative comedy series of the 1950's.
Max Liebman — *Unicorn Video*

Your Ticket Is No Longer Valid   1984
Drama
72912   96 mins   C   B, V   P
Richard Harris, George Peppard
When Richard Harris becomes impotent, he hires a hit woman to kill him.
MPAA:R
Unknown — *Vestron Video*

You're a Big Boy Now   1966
Comedy
69027   96 mins   C   B, V   P
Elizabeth Hartman, Geraldine Page, Peter Kastner, Julie Harris, Rip Torn, Michael Dunn, Tony Bill, Karen Black
Virginal young man working in New York Public Library, is told by his father to move out of his house and grow up. Moving out, he soon becomes involved with a man-hating actress and a discotheque dancer.
Warner Bros — *Warner Home Video*

You're Not Elected, Charlie Brown!/A Charlie Brown Christmas   1972
Cartoons
79265   50 mins   C   B, V   P
Animated
A Peanuts doubleheader: Charlie Brown and Linus run against each other for the office of student body president in "You're Not Elected, Charlie Brown!" In "A Charlie Brown Christmas," Charlie Brown fears that the Christmas holiday has become over-commercialized. It's up to the whole Peanuts gang to learn the true meaning of Christmas!
Lee Mendelson-Bill Melendez Productions — *Snoopy's Home Video Library*

You've Got to Have Heart   1977
Comedy
80279   98 mins   C   B, V   P
Carroll Baker, Edwige French
A young bridegroom's life gets complicated after he does not sexually satisfy his bride on their wedding night.
MPAA:R
Joseph Brenner Associates — *Prism*

Yukon Passage   1977
Miners and mining
Closed Captioned
20313   59 mins   C   B, V, LV   P
Four young men retrace the passage of prospectors who flocked to the Klondike in 1897 for gold.
CINE Golden Eagle.
Natl Geographic Society — *Vestron Video; National Geographic Society*

Yum-Yum Girls   1978
Adventure
55554   89 mins   C   B, V   P
Judy Landers, Tanya Roberts, Barbara Tully, Michelle Daw
Naive and innocent Melody Pearson comes to New York to fulfill her dreams of a modeling career and soon learns the nitty-gritty of the modeling world.
MPAA:R
Canon Releasing — *MCA Home Video*

Yumi Matsutoya: Train of Thought   1985
Music video
88141   58 mins   C   B, V   P
A collection of videos and concert clips featuring Japan's highly popular pop singer.
Sony Video — *Sony Video Software*

Z

Z 1969
Suspense
44783   128 mins   C   B, V   P
Yves Montand, Irene Papas
A man known as "Z" leads the growing
opposition party. He is struck down by a
speeding truck before hundreds of onlookers. A
trial follows, but seven witnesses vanish.
Academy Award '69: Best Foreign Film.
Cinema 5 — *RCA/Columbia Pictures Home
Video; RCA VideoDiscs*

Zabriskie Point 1970
Drama
72468   111 mins   C   B, V   P
Two loners epitomize the counter-culture as
they wander the ominous desert terrain.
MPAA:R
Metro Goldwyn Mayer — *MGM/UA Home
Video*

Zapped! 1982
Comedy
63373   98 mins   C   B, V, LV,   P
                     CED
*Scott Baio, Willie Aames, Felice Schachter,
Heather Thomas, Scatman Crothers*
One of the more unassuming boys in a group of
teenagers possesses special magical powers.
MPAA:R   EL, JA
Embassy Pictures — *Embassy Home
Entertainment*

Zardoz 1973
Science fiction
85429   105 mins   C   B, V   P
*Sean Connery, Charlotte Rampling, John
Alderton, directed by John Boorman*
A surreal parable of the far future, when society
is broken into strict classes, until a noble savage
transgresses the order. Filmed in Ireland.
20th Century Fox — *Key Video*

Zebra Force 1976
Crime-Drama
76656   81 mins   C   B, V   P
*Mike Lane, Richard X. Slattery, Rockne
Tarkington, Glenn Wilder, Anthony Caruso*
A group of army veterans embark on a personal
battle against organized crime, utilizing their
military training with deadly precision.
MPAA:R
Joe Tronatore; Larry Price — *Media Home
Entertainment*

Zelig 1983
Comedy
65614   79 mins   B/W   B, V, LV,   P
                            CED

*Woody Allen, Mia Farrow, Susan Sontag, Saul
Bellow, Bricktop, Irving Howe, directed by
Woody Allen*
Woody Allen's spoof of documentary films stars
him as Leonard Zelig, the famous "Chameleon
Man" of the 1920's, whose personality was so
vague that he would take on the characteristics
of whomever he was in contact with. Filmed in
black-and-white, the movie simulates the "look"
of vintage newsreels, complete with stentorian
narration.
MPAA:PG
Robert Greenhut — *Warner Home Video*

Zero for Conduct 1933
Comedy
12856   49 mins   B/W   B, V, FO   P
Directed by Jean Vigo
A fantasy-filled rebellion against authority set in
a boys' school. French with English subtitles.
FR
Gaumont, Franco Film — *Video Yesteryear;
Sheik Video; Hollywood Home Theater;
Western Film & Video Inc; Discount Video
Tapes*

Zero to Sixty 1978
Comedy-Drama
65073   96 mins   C   B, V, CED   P
Darren McGavin, Sylvia Miles, Denise Nickerson
A newly divorced man finds that his car has
been repossessed for nonpayment. Seeking out
the manager of the finance company, he gets a
job as a repossession agent of high-priced,
unpaid-for cars.
MPAA:PG
Katherine Browne — *Embassy Home
Entertainment*

Zertigo Diamond Caper, The 1982
Crime-Drama
85020   50 mins   C   B, V   P
Adam Rich, David Groh, Jane Elliot
Utilizing his heightened senses, a blind boy
solves a diamond caper and proves his
mother's innocence.
Paul Asselin — *Video Gems*

Zev: Six Examples 1981
Music-Performance
84066   60 mins   C   B, V   P
Zev
Live performances by the dangerous and
innovative punk percussionist from London and
San Francisco are featured herein.
Target Video — *Target Video*

Ziegfeld Follies 1946
Musical
64571   109 mins   C   B, V, CED   P

Fred Astaire, Judy Garland, Gene Kelly, Red Skelton, Fannie Brice, Lena Horne, Lucille Ball, Esther Williams, directed by Vincente Minelli
A lavish revue of musical numbers and comedy sketches featuring many MGM stars of the World War II era. Highlights include Fred Astaire and Gene Kelly's only duet, "The Babbitt and the Bromide," Lena Horne singing "Love," Judy Garland as "Madame Cremation" and a Fred Astaire-Lucille Bremer ballet set to "Limehouse Blues."
MGM — *MGM/UA Home Video*

Zig Zag Triumph of Steam 197?
Documentary
50634   24 mins   C   B, V   P, T
Narrated by Jack Kelso
A tribute to the more than 120 years of history of the steam engine in Australia.
Unknown — *Blackhawk Films*

Ziggy Stardust and the Spiders from Mars 1972
Music-Performance
73861   90 mins   C   B, V   P
David Bowie as Ziggy Stardust performs in a 1972 "farewell" concert that was filmed by D.A. Pennabaker.
Mainman Productions; Pennabaker Associates — *RCA/Columbia Pictures Home Video*

Ziggy's Gift 1983
Cartoons
70195   30 mins   C   B, V   P
Animated, music by Harry Nilsson
Ziggy, the lovable cartoon character created by Tom Wilson, is featured in this made-for-video Christmas program.
Lena Tabori — *Vestron Video*

Zis Boom Bah 1942
Musical/Comedy
66143   61 mins   B/W   B, V, FO   P
Peter Lind Hayes, Mary Healey, Grace Hayes, Huntz Hall, Benny Rubin
A college throws a variety show to save itself.
Monogram — *Video Yesteryear*

Zoltan... Hound of Dracula 1977
Horror
66024   85 mins   C   B, V   P
Michael Pataki, Reggie Nalder, Jose Ferrer
The vampire's canine companion carries on the Dracula family reputation.
Albert Band; Frank Perilli — *THORN EMI/HBO Video*

Zombie 1980
Horror
52860   93 mins   C   B, V   P

Tisa Farrow, Ian McCulloch
A reporter and a missing scientist's daughter go to the island of Matool to find the scientist, and encounter a mysterious doctor and hundreds of man-eating zombies.
MPAA:R   EL, SP
Jerry Gross; Ugo Tucci — *Wizard Video; Vestron Video (disc only)*

Zombie Lake 1985
Horror
81036   90 mins   C   B, V   P
Howard Vernon, Nadine Pascal
A group of zombie Nazi soldiers prey upon anyone who dares to swim in their Zombie Lake.
MPAA:R
Empire Entertainment — *Wizard Video*

Zombies of Mora Tau 1957
Horror
81801   70 mins   B/W   B, V   P
Gregg Palmer, Allison Hayes, Jeff Clark, Autumn Russel
A sea diver must salvage a treasure which is protected by a zombie curse. Available in VHS and Beta Hi-Fi.
Columbia Pictures — *RCA/Columbia Pictures Home Video*

Zombiethon 1986
Horror
87608   90 mins   C   B, V   P
Dominique Singleton, Janelle Lewis, Tracy Burton
A campy compilation of clips from cheapo zombie films, such as "Space Zombies," "Zombie Lake" and 'The Invisible Dead."
Taryn Prod. — *Force Video*

Zone Troopers 1985
Science fiction
85914   86 mins   C   B, V   P
Timothy Van Patten, Tim Thomerson, Art LaFleur, Biff Manard
Five American G.I.'s in World War II-ravaged Europe stumble upon a wrecked alien spacecraft and enlist the extraterrestrial's help in fending off the Nazis.
MPAA:PG
Empire Pictures — *Lightning Video*

Zoo Gang, The 1985
Drama
84267   96 mins   C   B, V   P
Ben Vereen, Jason Gedrick, Eric Gurry
A teenage-run club is threatened by a rival gang.
MPAA:PG-13
New World — *New World Video*

Zoo-opolis 1985
Zoos
70821   88 mins   C   B, V   P

Written by Nadene Ellis and David Lee Miller
This informative program offers youngsters a
behind-the-scenes look at the operation of a
zoo.
Ellis & Miller — *Pacific Arts Video*

Zoom the White Dolphin   1974
Cartoons
76912   94 mins   C   B, V   P
Animated
A family living on a tropical island befriends a
dolphin family.
Embassy — *Embassy Home Entertainment*

Zorba, the Greek   1964
Drama
55527   142 mins   B/W   B, V   P
*Anthony Quinn, Alan Bates, Irene Papas, Lila
Kedrova*
A British writer and a Greek opportunist on
Crete take lodgings with an aging courtesan.
The writer is attracted to a woman who is stoned
by the villagers when they find he has spent the
night with her. Based on a novel by Nicolai
Kazantzakis.
Academy Awards '64: Best Supporting Actress
(Kedrova); Best Cinematography; Best Art
Direction.
Twentieth Century Fox — *CBS/Fox Video*

Zorro Rides Again   1937
Adventure/Serials
12559   217 mins   B/W   B, V   P
*John Carroll, Helen Christian, Noah Beery,
directed by William Witney, John English*
Zorro risks his life to outwit enemy agents
endeavoring to secure ancestor's property. In
twelve chapters, the first runs 30 minutes, the
rest 17.
Republic — *Video Connection; Nostalgia
Merchant; Discount Video Tapes; Video
Yesteryear; Captain Bijou*

Zorro, the Gay Blade   1981
Comedy
58850   96 mins   C   B, V, CED   P
*George Hamilton, Lauren Hutton, Brenda
Vaccaro, Ron Leibman*
Hamilton portrays the swashbuckling crusader
and his long-lost brother, Bunny Wigglesworth,
in this spoof of the Zorro legend.
MPAA:PG
20th Century Fox — *CBS/Fox Video*

Zorro, Volumes 1 thru 8   195?
Adventure
70944   75 mins   B/W   B, V   P
*Guy Williams, Gene Sheldon, Britt Lomond,
Henry Calvin, Jan Avran, Eugenia Paul, Annette
Funicello, Richard Anderson, Jolene Brand*
8   pgms

Each tape in this series compiles three related
episodes of the late '50's TV series. Legend
states that in the 1820's, a genteel nobleman
named Don Diego masqueraded as Zorro, the
fearless and seemingly peerless fighter of the
oppressive Monterey, California regime of
Captain Monastano.
Walt Disney Productions — *Walt Disney Home
Video*

Zorro's Black Whip   1944
Western/Serials
07342   168 mins   B/W   B, V   P
Linda Stirling, George Lewis
A young girl dons the mask of her murdered
brother to fight outlaws in the old West. Serial in
twelve episodes.
Republic — *Nostalgia Merchant; Video
Connection; Hollywood Home Theater;
Discount Video Tapes; Video Yesteryear;
Captain Bijou*

Zorro's Fighting Legion   1939
Adventure/Serials
12558   215 mins   B/W   B, V   P
*Reed Hadley, Sheila Darcy, directed by William
Witney, John English*
Zorro forms a legion to help the president of
Mexico fight a band of outlaws endeavoring to
steal gold shipments. A serial in 12 chapters.
Republic — *Video Connection; Video
Dimensions; Cable Films; Nostalgia Merchant;
Hollywood Home Theater; Discount Video
Tapes; Kartes Video Communications; Video
Yesteryear*

Zotz   1962
Comedy
71118   87 mins   B/W   B, V   P
*Tom Poston, Julia Meade, Jim Backus, Fred
Clark, Cecil Kellaway, directed by Ray Russell*
The holder of a magic coin can will people dead
by uttering "zotz." Spies pursue the mild-
mannered professor who possesses the
talisman. Ray Russell wrote the screenplay from
a Walter Karig novel.
Columbia — *RCA/Columbia Pictures Home
Video*

Zulu   1964
Adventure
Closed Captioned
84046   139 mins   C   B, V   P
*Michael Caine, Jack Hawkins, Stanley Baker,
directed by Cy Endfield*
A small group of British soldiers in Africa are
beset by thousands of Zulu warriors. Based on a
true incident.
Stanley Baker; Cy Endfield — *Charter
Entertainment*

VIDEO SUBJECT CATEGORIES

Adolescence
Adventure
Advertising
Aeronautics
Africa
Alcoholic beverages
Alcoholism
Anatomy and physiology
Animals
Archeology
Artists
Arts
Asia
Astronomy
Automobiles
Automobiles-Racing
Back disorders
Baseball
Basketball
Bible
Bicycling
Biographical
Biology
Birds
Boating
Boxing
Business
Camps and camping
Canada
Cartoons
Chemistry
Child abuse
Childbirth
Children
China
Christianity
Christmas

Circus
Cities and towns
Civil rights
Clothing and dress
Comedy
Comedy-Drama
Comedy-Performance
Communication
Computers
Consumer education
Cookery
Cosmetology
Crime and criminals
Crime-Drama
Dance
Deaf
Death
Disasters
Diseases
Divorce
Documentary
Drama
Drawing
Drug abuse
Drugs
Education
Ethics
Europe
Exploitation
Fairy tales
Family
Fantasy
Film
Film-Avant-garde
Film-History
Filmmaking
Finance

First aid
Fishes
Fishing
Folklore
Football
France
Gambling
Game show
Games
Gardening
Geography
Germany
Golf
Great Britain
Gymnastics
Handicapped
Handicraft
Health education
History
History-Ancient
History-Medieval
History-Modern
History-US
Hobbies
Hockey
Holidays
Home improvement
Horror
Horse racing
Human relations
Hunting
Identity
Indians-North American
Infants
Insects
Interview
Inventions
Islam
Japan
Judaism

Korean War
Labor and unions
Language arts
Languages-Instruction
Literature
Literature-American
Literature-English
Magic
Marriage
Martial arts
Mass media
Massage
Middle East
Mime
Miners and mining
Minorities
Motorcycles
Mountaineering
Movie and TV trailers
Museums
Music
Music video
Music-Performance
Musical
Musical-Drama
Mystery
Nightclub
Nuclear energy
Nuclear warfare
Nutrition
Occult sciences
Occupations
Oceanography
Oil industry
Opera
Outtakes and bloopers
Pain
Painting
Parents
Performing arts

Personal finance
Pets
Photography
Physical fitness
Physics
Plants
Police
Politics and government-US
Poverty
Pregnancy
Presidency-US
Prisons
Propaganda
Prostitution
Psychology
Public affairs
Puppets
Rape
Religion
Reproduction
Romance
Running
Safety education
Sales training
Satire
Science
Science fiction
Seasons
Serials
Sexuality
Smoking
Soccer
South America
Space exploration
Spain

Speculation
Sports
Sports-Minor
Sports-Water
Sports-Winter
States-US
Stress
Suicide
Suspense
Technology
Television
Tennis
Terrorism
Theater
Therapeutic cults
Toys
Trains
Transportation
Travel
USSR
Variety
Venereal diseases
Video
Vietnam War
Volcanoes
War-Drama
Western
Wife beating
Wilderness areas
Wildlife
Women
World War I
World War II
Yoga
Zoos

SUBJECT CATEGORY INDEX

Adolescence

Am I Normal?
Dear Diary
First Turn On, The
Streetwise

Adventure

Abductors, The
Abdulla the Great
Across the Great Divide
Action in Arabia
Adventure 1: Trailers on Tape
Adventurers, The
Adventures of Black Beauty, The
Adventures of Captain Fabian
Adventures of Captain Marvel
Adventures of Don Juan
Adventures of Frontier Fremont, The
Adventures of Grizzly Adams at Beaver Dam, The
Adventures of Huckleberry Finn, The
Adventures of Huckleberry Finn, The
Adventures of Huckleberry Finn, The
Adventures of Robin Hood, The
Adventures of Sinbad the Sailor, The
Adventures of Tartu, The
Adventures of Tarzan, The
Adventures of the Masked Phantom, The
Adventures of the Wilderness Family, The
Adventures of Tom Sawyer, The
Adventures of Tom Sawyer, The
Adventures of Ultraman, The
Adventures—Past, Present and Future Featurettes
Africa Texas Style
African Queen, The
Against All Odds
Airport 1975
Airport '77
Aladdin and the Wonderful Lamp
Alice Through the Looking Glass
All the Way Boys
Amateur, The
Amazing Dobermans, The
Amazing Spider-Man, The
Amazing Spider-Man, The
American Dreamer
Americano, The
Americano, The/Variety
Amsterdam Connection
Amsterdam Kill, The
Angel
Angel of H.E.A.T.
Angels Die Hard
Annihilators, The

Antarctica
Appointment in Honduras
Around the World in 80 Days
Around the World Under the Sea
Assault on Agathon
Assault with a Deadly Weapon
At Sword's Point
Ator the Fighting Eagle
Attack Force Z
Avengers, The
Aventura Llamada Menudo, Una
Aviator, The
Baby...Secret of the Lost Legend
Balkan Express
Baltimore Bullet, The
Bandolero!
Bank Dick, The
Barbarian Queen
Barbary Coast
Batman
Battle of Valiant
Bear Island
Bears and I, The
Beastmaster, The
Beasts
Bedford Incident, The
Belstone Fox, The
Beneath the 12-Mile Reef
Berlin Tunnel 21
Beyond the Poseidon Adventure
Big Blue Marble
Big Bus, The
Big Doll House
Big Push, The
Big Steal, The
Big Wheel
Big Foot and Wild Boy
Bigfoot and Wildboy
Bimini Code
Black Arrow
Black Beauty
Black Beauty/Courage of Black Beauty
Black Magic
Black Moon Rising
Black Oak Conspiracy
Black Pirate, The
Black Stallion Returns, The
Black Stallion, The
Blackstar
Blackstar, Volume 2
Blade Master
Blind Fist of Bruce
Blood on the Sun
Bloody Fight, The
Bloody Fist
Blue Fin

Blue Thunder
Bobby Jo and the Outlaw
Bobby Raccoon
Bodyguard, The
Bold Caballero, The
Bolo
Boomerang
Born Free
Botany Bay
Bounty, The
Boy of Two Worlds
Brink's Job, The
Bronson Lee, Champion
Brother from Another Planet, The
Brothers Lionheart, The
Bruce Le's Greatest Revenge
Bruce Li in New Guinea
Buccaneer, The
Bulldog Drummond
Bummer
Bushido Blade, The
Butch Cassidy and the Sundance Kid
Caged Fury
California Gold Rush
Call of the Wild
Call of the Wild
Call Out the Marines
Camel Boy, The
Candleshoe
Cannonball
Cantonen Iron Kung Fu
Captain Blood
Captain Caution
Captain Harlock
Captain Kidd
Captain Pugwash
Captain Scarlett
Castaway Cowboy, The
Cavegirl
Certain Fury
Chain Gang Killings, The
Challenge, The
Challenge, The
Challenge to Be Free
Chandu on the Magic Island
Change of Mind
Charlie and the Great Balloon Chase
Children's Island
China Seas
Chinese Boxes
Chinese Connection, The
Chinese Web, The
Chisholms, The
Circle of Iron
Clash of the Titans
Claws
Cloak and Dagger
Clones of Bruce Lee, The
Cold Steel for Tortuga
Commando
Conan the Barbarian

Conan the Destroyer
Concorde—Airport '79, The
Conqueror, The
Conqueror and the Empress, The
Conquest
Convoy
Corrupt Ones, The
Corsican Brothers, The
Corsican Brothers, The
Count of Monte Cristo, The
Count of Monte Cristo, The
Countryman
Courage of Rin Tin Tin, The
Crack Shadow Boxers
Cross Creek
Cry of the Innocent
Cuchillo ("Knife")
Curse of the Yellow Snake, The
Dance Hall
Dance of the Dead
Dangerous Holiday
Daring Game
Dark Crystal, The
Davy Crockett and the River Pirates
Davy Crockett, King of the Wild Frontier
Dawn of the Pirates (La Secta de los Tughs), The
Day of the Cobra, The
Day of the Dolphin, The
Day They Gave Diamonds Away, The
Dead Don't Die, The
Dead Wrong
Deadly and the Beautiful, The
Deadly Encounter
Death Hunt
Death Journey
Death Sport
Death Stalk
Death Wish II
Death Wish III
Deathcheaters
Delta Force, The
Desert of the Tartars, The
Desperately Seeking Susan
Diamonds Are Forever
Dick Deadeye
Dick Tracy Double Feature #2
Disaster—Adventure Featurettes
Do Not Forsake Me Oh My Darling
Doc Savage
Doctor Doom Conquers the World
Dr. No
Dogpound Shuffle
Dogs of War, The
Dogtanian and the Three Musketeers
Don Q., Son of Zorro
Don Winslow of the Navy
Doomsday Flight, The
Down to the Sea in Ships
Dragnet
Dragonslayer
Driver, The

SUBJECT CATEGORY INDEX

Greystoke: The Legend of Tarzan, Lord of the Apes
Gulliver's Travels
Gunga Din
Guns of Navarone, The
Hambone and Hillie
Hammer Into Anvil
Hangar 18
Hatari
Hawk of the Caribbean (El Halcon del Caribe), The
Hawk the Slayer
He-Man and the Masters of the Universe Series
Hearts and Armour
Hells Angels Forever
Hell's Angels '69
Hercules
Hercules
Hercules Unchained
Herculoids, The
Herculoids, Vol II, The
Here Comes Santa Claus
Hero Bunker
Heroes in Hell
Hi-Riders
Hidden Fortress, The
High Ballin'
High Risk
High Road to China
High Rolling in a Hot Corvette
High Velocity
High Voltage
Highpoint
Hills Have Eyes, The
Hindenburg, The
Holt of the Secret Service
Horse Soldiers, The
Horse Without a Head, The
H.R. Pufnstuf, Vol II
H.R. Pufnstuf, Volume I
Huckleberry Finn
Huckleberry Finn
Hundra
Hunter, The
Hunters of the Golden Cobra
Hurricane Express
Hurricane Express
Ice Station Zebra
Image of Bruce Lee, The
Imperial Venus
In Search of the Castaways
Incredible Detectives, The
Incredible Hulk, The
Incredible Journey, The
Incredible Rocky Mountain Race, The
Inside Out
Into the Night
Invasion U.S.A.
Invincible Barbarian, The
Invincible, The
Invincible Gladiators, The

Iron Eagle
Iron Mask, The
Island, The
Island at the Top of the World, The
Island of Adventure
Island of the Blue Dolphins
Ivanhoe
Ivanhoe
Jacob Two—Two Meets the Hooded Fang
Jailbreakin'
Jaws of the Dragon
Jeremiah Johnson
Jericho
Jewel of the Nile, The
Jig Saw
Johnny Tremain and the Sons of Liberty
Journey
Journey of Natty Gann, The
Jungle Book, The
Jungle Master, The
Jungle Raiders
Jungle Warriors
Junior G-Men
Junior G-Men of the Air
Just Tell Me You Love Me
Kagemusha
Kashmiri Run
Kavik the Wolf Dog
Kentuckian, The
Kentucky Blue Streak
Kid Colter
Kidnap Syndicate, The
Kidnapped
Kill or Be Killed
Kill Squad
Killer Force
Killer Likes Candy
Killing Machine
Killzone
King Arthur, the Young Warlord
King Boxers, The
King of the Kongo
King of the Mountain
King of the Rocketmen
King Solomon's Mines
King Solomon's Mines
King Solomon's Treasure
Kingfisher Caper, The
Kiss My Grits
Klondike Fever
Knightriders
Krull
Kung Fu
Kung-Fu Commandos
Ladyhawke
Land of the Lost, Volume 2
Land of the Lost, Volume I
Lassie's Rescue Rangers
Lassie's Rescue Rangers, Volume 2
Lassie's Rescue Rangers, Volume 3
Lassie's Vacation Adventure

Last Challenge of the Dragon, The
Last Chase, The
Last Flight of Noah's Ark, The
Last Mercenary
Last of the Mohicans
Last of the Mohicans
Last of the Mohicans, The
Legend of Hillbilly John, The
Legend of Sleepy Hollow, The
Legend of the Northwest
Lidsville, Volume I
Life and Times of Grizzly Adams, The
Light at the Edge of the World, The
Light in the Forest, The
Lion of Venice, The
Little Laura and Big John
Little Treasure
Littlest Horse Thieves, The
Littlest Warrior, The
Live and Let Die
Living Head, The
Local Hero
Long John Silver
Long John Silver's Return to Treasure Island
Long Voyage Home, The
Lookin' to Get Out
Loophole
Lost
Lost City of the Jungle
Lost Empire, The
Lost Patrol, The
Lost Squadron
Lou Bunin's Alice in Wonderland
Love and Bullets
MacKenna's Gold
Mackintosh Man, The
Macon County Line
Mad Max
Mad Max Beyond Thunderdome
Madman
Magic Pony, The
Magic Pony, The
Magic Sword, The
Magnificent Adventurer, The
Magnificent Kick, The
Major Dundee
Malibu Express
Man Against Crime Volume I
Man Called Horse, A
Man from Beyond
Man from Snowy River, The
Man in the Iron Mask, The
Man in the Iron Mask, The
Man of Legend
Man Who Wasn't There, The
Man Who Would Be King, The
Man with the Golden Gun, The
Manhunt
Manhunt
Manhunt in the African Jungle
Many Happy Returns

Marauder, The
Marco
Mark of Zorro, The
Marvel Comics Video Library
Masked Marvel, The
Massacre at Fort Holman
Massive Retaliation
Mean Frank and Crazy Tony
Mean Machine, The
Mechanic, The
Mediterranean in Flames, The
Metalstorm
Midnite Spares
Mil Millones para una Rubia (The Lady Thief)
Militant Eagle
Missing in Action
Missing in Action 2: The Beginning
Mission Batangas
Mission Phantom
Mr. Billion
Mr. Kingstreet's War
Mr. Majestyk
Mr. Robinson Crusoe
Mr. Super Athletic Charm
Mr. Too Little
Mistress of the Apes
Moby Dick
Moby Dick
Mogambo
Moon-Spinners, The
Mooncussers
Moonraker
Moonshine County Express
Morgan the Pirate
Mother Lode
Mountain Family Robinson
Mountain Men, The
Mutiny
Mutiny on the Bounty
My Man Adam
Mystery Island
Mystery of the Million Dollar Hockey Puck, The
Mystery Squadron
Naked Prey, The
Napoleon
Napoleon and Samantha
Nate and Hayes
Neptune Factor, The
New Adventures of Tarzan, The
New Adventures of Zorro, The
New Adventures of Zorro, Volume III, The
Night Crossing
Night Flight from Moscow
Night of the Grizzly, The
1990: The Bronx Warriors
No Way Back
North to Alaska
Northeast of Seoul
Northern Pursuit
Northwest Frontier
Nowhere to Hide

Nyoka and the Tigerman
Octopussy
Odyssey of the Pacific
Old Yeller
On Her Majesty's Secret Service
On Her Majesty's Secret Service
Once Upon A Time
One Down Two to Go
One Step to Hell
Operation C.I.A.
Orca
Out of Control
Outlaw Blues
Pacific Inferno
Paper Tiger
Penitentiary II
Pepe Le Moko
Pepper
Perfect Crime, The
Perils of Gwendoline, The
Perils of the Darkest Jungle
Permission To Kill
Personal Touch, The
Peter Lundy and the Medicine Hat Stallion
Pete's Dragon
Petite Bande, La
Phantom Tollbooth, The
Phar Lap
Phenomenal and the Treasure of Tutankamen
Pioneer Woman
Pippi Goes on Board
Pippi in the South Seas
Pippi on the Run
Pirate warrior
Pirates of the Coast, The
Pirates of the Seven Seas
Poco
Poppies Are Also Flowers
Poseidon Adventure, The
Powder Keg
Prime Risk
Prince and the Pauper, The
Prince and the Pauper, The
Princess and the Call Girl, The
Prisoner, The
Prisoner of Zenda, The
Private Life of Don Juan
Prodigal Boxer, The
Psychopath
Pursuit
Queen of Diamonds
Queen of the Road
Quest for Fire
Quo Vadis
Raiders of Atlantis
Raiders of the Lost Ark
Rainbow Gang, The
Raise the Titanic
Rambo: First Blood, Part II
Rape of the Sabines, The
Raw Force

Real Bruce Lee, The
Reckless
Red Dawn
Red Dust
Red Flag: The Ultimate Game
Red Sonja
Red Sun
Reivers, The
Remo Williams: The Adventure Begins
Return of a Man Called Horse, The
Return of the Dragon
Return of the Jedi
Return of the Red Tiger
Return of the Tiger
Return to Macon County
Revenge of the Ninja
Riddle of the Sands
Rio Conchos
Ripoff, The
Road Warrior, The
Rob Roy—The Highland Rogue
Robbers of the Sacred Mountain
Robin Hood ... The Legend
Robinson Crusoe
Robinson Crusoe
Robinson Crusoe and the Tiger
Robotman & Friends II: I Want to be Your Robotman
Rocketship X-M—Special Edition
Romancing the Stone
Rough Cut
Run, Angel, Run!
Runaway
Runaway Barge
Runaway Truck
Rush
Safari 3000
Sahara
Sahara Cross (Extrana Aventura en el Sahara)
Saint, The
Salty
Samurai I: Musashi Miyamoto
Samurai II: Duel at Ichijoji Temple
Samurai III: Duel at Ganryu Island
Sanders of the River
S.A.S. San Salvador
Saturday Serials
Savage
Savage Dawn
Savage Hunger, A
Schizoid Man, The
Sea Devils
Sea Hawk, The
Sea Prince and the Fire Child, The
Sea Shall Not Have Them, The
Sea Wolves, The
Secret of El Zorro, The
Secret of the Sword, The
Sell Out, The
Sesame Street Presents: Follow That Bird
Seven Alone

Advertising

Aeronautics

Baseball

All-Star Batting Tips
All-Star Catching and Base Stealing Tips
All-Star Game, 1967
All-Star Game, 1970: What Makes an All-Star
All-Star Game, 1971: Home Run Heroes
All-Star Game, 1972: Years of Tradition, Night of Pride
All-Star Game, 1973: A New Generation of Stars
All-Star Game, 1974: Mid-Summer Magic
All-Star Game, 1975: All-Star Fever
All-Star Game, 1976: Champions of Pride
All-Star Game, 1977: The Man Behind the Mask
All-Star Game, 1978: What Makes an All-Star
All-Star Game, 1979: Inches and Jinxes
All-Star Game, 1980: Heroes to Remember
All-Star Game, 1981
All-Star Game, 1982
All-Star Game, '84: Something Special
All-Star Pitching Tips
All-Star Game, 1983: Golden Memories
Atlanta Braves: Team Highlights
Baltimore Orioles: Team Highlights
Baseball: Fun and Games
Baseball: The Now Career
Baseball the Pete Rose Way
Baseball the Yankee Way
Baseball's Hall of Fame
Batty World of Baseball, The
Billy Martin's Big League Baseball
Boys of Summer, The
Bullpen
California Angels: Team Highlights
Casey at the Bat
Chicago Cubs: Team Highlights
Chicago White Sox: Team Highlights
Cincinnati Reds: Team Highlights
Cleveland Indians: Team Highlights
50 Years of Baseball Memories
Going, Going, Gone
Golden Moments
Great Moments in Baseball
Greatest Comeback Ever, The
Hall of Famers
Houston Astros: Team Highlights
It Don't Come Easy: 1978 New York Yankees
Kansas City Royals: Team Highlights
King of the Hill
Legendary Greats
Little League's Official How-To Play Baseball by Video
Los Angeles Dodgers: Team Highlights
Mickey Mantle's Baseball Tips For Kids of All Ages
Milwaukee Braves: Team Highlights
Minnesota Twins: Team Highlights
Montreal Expos: Team Highlights
New York Mets: Team Highlights
New York-Yankees: Team Highlights
1978—The New York Yankees' Miracle Year

1979 World Series and All-Star Highlights
Oakland Athletics: Team Highlights
Philadelphia Phillies: Team Highlights
Roberto Clemente: A Touch of Royalty
St. Louis Cardinals: Team Highlights
20 Years of World Series
Two Best World Series Ever, The
Unofficial Baseball Handbook, The
Winning Tradition: 1977 New York Yankees, A
World Series, 1943
World Series, 1944
World Series, 1945
World Series, 1946
World Series, 1947
World Series, 1948
World Series, 1949
World Series, 1950
World Series, 1951
World Series, 1952
World Series, 1953
World Series, 1954
World Series, 1955
World Series, 1956
World Series, 1957
World Series, 1958
World Series, 1959
World Series, 1960
World Series, 1961
World Series, 1962
World Series, 1963
World Series, 1964
World Series, 1965
World Series, 1966
World Series, 1967
World Series, 1968
World Series, 1969
World Series, 1970
World Series, 1971
World Series, 1972
World Series, 1973
World Series, 1974
World Series, 1975
World Series, 1976
World Series, 1977
World Series, 1978
World Series, 1979
World Series, 1980
World Series, 1981
World Series, 1982
World Series, 1983: 1983 World Series
World Series, 1984: The Sounds of the Series
Worth the Wait!

Basketball

Basketball with Gail Goodrich
Greatest Legends of Basketball
Knight of Basketball, A
1981 NBA Playoffs and Championship Series: The Dynasty Renewed
Pride and Passion

Marilyn Monroe
Marilyn Monroe, Life Story of America's Mystery
  Mistress
Marjoe
Marlon Brando
Mary White
Melody Master, The
Miracle Worker, The
Miracle Worker, The
Mishima: A Life in Four Chapters
Montgomery Clift
Murph the Surf
Mussolini and I
Mussolini: Rise and Fall of a Dictator
Nadia
Napoleon
Napoleon
Night and Day
One in a Million
Out of Africa
Philby, Burgess and MacLean: Spy Scandal of
  the Century
Piaf
Pride of the Yankees, The
Prince Jack
Reagan's Way
Rembrandt
Rita Hayworth: The Love Goddess
Sakharov
Sir Arthur Conan Doyle
Song of Norway
Sophia Loren: Her Own Story
Spirit of St. Louis, The
Squizzy Taylor
Sunrise at Campobello
Sweet Dreams
That Hamilton Woman
This Is Elvis
To Race the Wind
Tom Edison, the Boy Who Lit Up the World
Tom Edison: The Making of an American Legend
Viva Zapata!
Volcano
Wagner
Will: G. Gordon Liddy
Will Rogers: Champion of the People
Wilma
Winds of Kitty Hawk
Woman Called Golda, A
Wright Brothers: Masters of the Sky, The
Young Caruso, The
Young Winston

Biology

Building Blocks of Life, The
Expansion of Life, The
Incredible Human Machine, The
Origin of Life, The (Plus Scopes Trial Footage)

Birds

Audubon Society's Videoguide to the Birds of
  North America
Duck's Unlimited's Videoguide to Waterfowl and
  Game Birds

Boating

Boating: Cold Water Survivial
Celestial Navigation Simplified
Coaster Adventure of the John F. Leavitt
MerCruiser I/O and Inboard Engine Tune-Up,
  The
Outboard Engine Tune-Up—Evinrude and
  Johnson Outboards, The
Outboard Engine Tune-Up—Mercury and
  Mariner Outboards, The
Pacific Challenge
Raging River of Annapurna/Urumbamba,
  The—Sacred River of the Incas
12th Annual The Great Smith River Canoe Race
Warren Miller's Sailing Film Festival
Whitewater II

Boxing

Ali: Skill, Brains and Guts
Baer vs. Louis/Louis vs. Schmeling
Big Fights, Vol. 1—Muhammad Ali's Greatest
  Fights, The
Big Fights, Vol. 2—Heavyweight Champions'
  Greatest Fights, The
Big Fights, Vol. 3—Sugar Ray Robinson's
  Greatest Fights, The
Boxing's Greatest Champions
Greatest Fights of the 70's
Grudge Fights
Legendary Champions, The
Muhammad Ali vs. Zora Folley
Showdown: Sugar Ray Leonard vs. Thomas
  Hearns, The
Sugar Ray Robinson—Pound for Pound

Business

Career Strategies 1
Career Strategies 2
Winning at Work

Camps and camping

Coleman's Guide to Camping

Canada

City of Gold/Drylanders

Cartoons

Abbott and Costello Cartoon Festival
Academy Award Winners Animated Short Films

Gaiking
Galaxy Express
G.I. Joe
G.I. Joe: A Real American Hero
G.I. Joe: A Real American Hero, The Revenge of Cobra Vol. 2
Gift of Winter, The
Gnomes
Gobots
Goldie Gold and Action Jack
Goldwing
Goofy Over Sports
Grandizer
Great Bear Scare, The
Great Expectations
Grinch Grinches the Cat in the Hat/Pontoffel Pock, The
Groovie Goolies Volume I
Groovin for a 60's Afternoon
Grump Comes Back, The
Gulliver's Travels
Gulliver's Travels
Gumby Adventures
Halloween Is Grinch Night
He-Man and the Masters of the Universe
He-Man and the Masters of the Universe: The Greatest Adventures of All
He-Man and the Masters of the Universe Series
Heathcliff and Cats and Co. Series
Heathcliff and Marmaduke
Heckle y Jeckle
Heidi
Heidi's Song
Herculoids, The
Herculoids, Vol II, The
Here Come the Littles: The Movie
Here Comes the Grump
Herman and Katnip
Hero High Volume 1
Hey There, It's Yogi Bear
Hillbilly Bears
Honey Honey
Hoppity Goes to Town
Horton Hears a Who!
How the Animals Discovered Christmas
Huckleberry Finn
Hugga Bunch
Hugo the Hippo
Hurray for Betty Boop
Importance of Being Donald, The
Inch High Private Eye
Incredible Detectives, The
Incredible Hulk, Volume I, The
Incredible Hulk, Volume II, The
Inspector Gadget
Inspector Gadget Series
It's an Adventure, Charlie Brown
It's Flashbeagle, Charlie Brown/She's a Good Skate, Charlie Brown
It's Magic, Charlie Brown/Charlie Brown's All Stars

It's the Easter Beagle, Charlie Brown/It was a short summer, Charlie Brown
It's the Great Pumpkin, Charlie Brown
It's the Great Pumpkin, Charlie Brown/What a Nightmare, Charlie Brown
It's Your First Kiss, Charlie Brown/Someday You'll Find Her, Charlie Brown
Jack and the Beanstalk
Jack O'Lantern
Jayce and the Wheeled Warriors
Johnny Appleseed/Paul Bunyan
Johnny Woodchuck's Adventures
Josie and the Pussycats in Outer Space, Vol. II
Josie and the Pussycats in Outer Space
Katy Caterpillar
King Arthur & the Knights of the Round Table Vol. 1
King Arthur & the Knights of the Round Table Vol. 2
Lassie's Great Adventure
Lassie's Rescue Rangers
Lassie's Rescue Rangers, Volume 2
Lassie's Rescue Rangers, Volume 3
Lassie's Vacation Adventure
Last Unicorn, The
Laurel and Hardy Volume 1
Laurel and Hardy Volume 2
Laurel and Hardy Volume 3
Laurel and Hardy Volume 4
Legend of Hiawatha, The
Legend of Sleepy Hollow, The
Let Sleeping Minnows Lie
Life Is a Circus, Charlie Brown/You're the Greatest, Charlie Brown
Limited Gold Edition II Cartoon Classics
Lion, the Witch and the Wardrobe, The
Little Brown Burro, The
Little Lulu
Little Mermaid, The
Little Miss and Friends
Little Miss Trouble and Friends
Little Prince: Volumes I thru V, The
Little Tweety and Little Inki Cartoon Festival
Little Women
Little Women
Littlest Warrior, The
Lone Ranger, The
Looney Looney Looney Bugs Bunny Movie, The
Looney Tunes and Merrie Melodies I
Looney Tunes and Merrie Melodies II
Looney Tunes and Merrie Melodies #3
Looney Tunes Video Show #1, The
Looney Tunes Video Show #2, The
Looney Tunes Video Show #3, The
Looney Tunes Video Show #4, The
Looney Tunes Video Show #5, The
Looney Tunes Video Show #6, The
Looney Tunes Video Show #7, The
Lucky Luke: Daisy Town
Lucky Luke: The Ballad of the Daltons
Mad, Mad Monsters, The

Chemistry

Child abuse

Childbirth

Children

China

Christianity

Christmas

At War with the Army
Atoll K
Attack of the Killer Tomatoes
Attack of the Robots
Auditions
Auntie Mame
Author! Author!
Awful Truth, The
Baby Love
Bachelor and the Bobby Soxer, The
Bachelor Bait
Bachelor Mother
Bachelor Party
Back to the Future
Bad
Bad Manners
Bad Medicine
Bad News Bears, The
Bad News Bears in Breaking Training, The
Bakery, The/The Grocery Clerk
Ball of Fire
Balloonatic, The/One Week
Banana Monster
Bananas
Bank Dick, The
Barber Shop, The
Barefoot Executive, The
Barefoot in the Park
Barry McKenzie Holds His Own
Basic Training
Beach Blanket Bingo
Beach Girls, The
Beach House
Beach Party
Beat the Devil
Beatles—Comedy Featurettes
Beau Mariage, Le
Beau Pere
Bedazzled
Bedtime for Bonzo
Beer
Beginner's Luck
Behave Yourself!
Behind the Screen
Being There
Bell, Book and Candle
Bellboy, The
Belles of St. Trinian's, The
Bellhop/The Noon Whistle, The
Bells Are Ringing
Ben Turpin Rides Again
Bernice Bobs Her Hair
Best Defense
Best Friends
Best Legs in the 8th Grade
Best Little Whorehouse in Texas, The
Best of Amos 'n Andy Vol. 1, The
Best of Benny Hill, The
Best of the Benny Hill Show, Vol. 5, The
Best of Bugs Bunny and Friends, The
Best of Candid Camera, The

Best of Candid Camera, Vol. II
Best of John Belushi, The
Best of Little Rascals, The
Best of Mary Hartman, Mary Hartman, Volume II, The
Best of the Benny Hill Show, Vol. II, The
Best of the Benny Hill Show, Vol. III, The
Best of the Benny Hill Show, Volume 4, The
Best of the Kenny Everett Video Show, The
Best of Times, The
Best of W.C. Fields, The
Bette Midler: Art or Bust
Better Off Dead
Between the Lines
Beulah Show, The
Beulah Show, The
Beverly Hills Cop
Beyond Tomorrow
Big Bus, The
Big City Comedy
Big Trouble
Billion Dollar Hobo, The
Bingo Long Traveling All-Stars & Motor Kings, The
Birds and the Bees, The
Bizarre Bizarre
Black Bird, The
Blackbeard's Ghost
Blacksmith, The/Cops
Blacksmith, The/The Balloonatic
Blame It on Rio
Blazing Saddles
Bliss
Blockheads
Blockheads
Bloodsucking Freaks
Blue Country
Blue Money
Blue Skies Again
Blues Brothers, The
Blume in Love
Boarding School
Boatniks, The
Bob & Carol & Ted & Alice
Bob & Ray, Jane, Laraine & Gilda
Bob Hope Chevy Show I, The
Bob Hope Chevy Show II, The
Bob Hope Chevy Show III, The
Bobo, The
Bohemian Girl, The
Bombs Away!
Bon Voyage, Charlie Brown
Boob Tube, The
Boom in the Moon
Born Yesterday
Boss Foreman
Boum, La
Bourgeois Gentilhomme, Le
Boy, Did I Get a Wrong Number!
Boys from Brooklyn, The
Breakfast at Tiffany's

Breakfast in Hollywood
Breaking Away
Breath of Scandal, A
Brewster McCloud
Brewster's Millions
Brewster's Millions
Bride Walks Out, The
Brink's Job, The
Britannia Hospital
Broadway Danny Rose
Bronco Billy
Brothers O'Toole, The
Buck Privates
Buddy Buddy
Bugs Bunny/Road Runner Movie, The
Bullfighters, The
Bullshot
Bundle of Joy
Bus Stop
Buster Keaton Rides Again/The Railrodder
Buster Keaton: The Great Stone Face
Bustin' Loose
Butler's Dilemma, The
By Design
Cactus Flower
Caddyshack
Caesar and Cleopatra
Caesar's Hour
Caesar's Hour
Caesar's Hour
Cage Aux Folles III: The Wedding, La
Cage aux Folles, La
Cage Aux Folles II, La
California Girls
California Suite
Call Out the Marines
Came a Hot Friday
Can I Do It...Till I Need Glasses?
Candid Candid Camera
Candleshoe
Cannon Ball, The/The Eyes Have It
Cannonball/Dizzy Heights & Daring Hearts, The
Cannonball Run, The
Cannonball Run II
Captain's Paradise, The
Car Wash
Carbon Copy
Carlton Browne of the F.O.
Carol Burnett Show: Bloopers and Outtakes, The
Carry On Behind
Carry On Cleo
Carry On Cowboy
Carry On Cruising
Carry On Nurse
Casa Flora
Cash
Casino Royale
Cat from Outer Space, The
Catherine and Co.
Cavaleur, Le (Practice Makes Perfect)
Cavegirl

Caveman
Cesar
Champagne for Caesar
Change of Habit
Change of Seasons, A
Chaplin: A Character Is Born/Keaton: The Great Stone Face
Chaplin Essanay Book 1, The
Chaplin Revue, The
Charade
Charge of the Model T's
Charlie Chan and the Curse of the Dragon Queen
Charlie Chaplin Carnival
Charlie Chaplin Cavalcade
Charlie Chaplin Festival
Charlie Chaplin Festival, The
Charlie Chaplin—The Early Years, Volume I
Charlie Chaplin—The Early Years, Volume II
Charlie Chaplin—The Early Years, Volume III
Charlie Chaplin—The Early Years, Volume IV
Charlie Chaplin: The Funniest Man in the World
Charlie Chaplin's Keystone Comedies
Charlie Chaplin's Keystone Comedies #2
Charlie Chaplin's Keystone Comedies #3
Charlie Chase and Ben Turpin
Chattanooga Choo Choo
Chatterbox
Check and Double Check
Cheech and Chong: Get Out of My Room
Cheech and Chong's Next Movie
Cheech & Chong's Nice Dreams
Cheerleaders, The
Cheerleaders' Wild Weekend
Cherry Hill High
Chesty Anderson U.S. Navy
Chicken Chronicles, The
Chilly Scenes of Winter
C.H.O.M.P.S.
Christmas in July
Christmas Story, A
Chu Chu and the Philly Flash
Chump at Oxford, A
Chump at Oxford, A
Cinderfella
Circus, The/Day's Pleasure, A
City Heat
City Lights
Class
Class of '44
Classic Comedy Video Sampler
Clinic, The
Clown Princes of Hollywood, The
Clue
Coach
Coca-Cola Kid, The
Cockeyed Cavaliers
C.O.D.
Colgate Comedy Hour, The
Colgate Comedy Hour, III, The
Colgate Comedy Hour, IV, The

I Married a Witch
I Married a Woman
I Married Joan
I Married Joan
I Ought to Be in Pictures
I Wonder Who's Killing Her Now?
Ice Pirates, The
Idiot's Delight
If You Don't Stop It...You'll Go Blind
I'm All Right Jack
I'm on My Way/The Non-Stop Kid
Immigrant, The
Immortal Bachelor, The
Improper Channels
In-Laws, The
In Love With An Older Woman
In Praise of Older Women
Incoming Freshmen
Incredible Rocky Mountain Race, The
Incredible Shrinking Woman, The
Indiscreet
Indiscreet
Innocents in Paris
Inspector General, The
Into the Night
Invitation to a Wedding
Irma La Douce
Irreconcilable Differences
It Could Happen to You
It Happened One Night
It Should Happen to You
It's a Gift
It's a Joke, Son!
It's a Mad, Mad, Mad, Mad World
It's in the Bag
Jabberwocky
Jack and the Beanstalk
Jack Benny, II
Jack Benny III
Jack Benny Program, The
Jack Benny Program, The
Jack Benny Program, The
Jack Benny Show, The
Jackson and Jill
JD and the Salt Flat Kid
Jekyll and Hyde...Together Again
Jerk, The
Jimmy the Kid
Jinxed
John and Julie
Johnny Carson
Johnny Dangerously
Jokes My Folks Never Told Me
Jonathan Winters Show, The
Joy of Sex
Joy Sticks
Jupiter's Thigh
Just Me and You
Just One of the Guys
Just Tell Me What You Want
Just Tell Me You Love Me

Just the Way You Are
Just William's Luck
Kentucky Fried Movie
Key Exchange
Keystone Comedies
Kid from Brooklyn, The
Kid 'n' Hollywood & Polly Tix in Washington
Kid Sister, The
Kid, The/The Idle Class
Kid with the Broken Halo, The
Kid with the 200 I.Q.
Kidco
Kid's Auto Race/Mabel's Married Life
Kids from Candid Camera
Kind Hearts and Coronets
Kings, Queens, Jokers
Kiss Me Goodbye
Kiss My Grits
Kitty and the Bagman
Knockout, The/Dough and Dynamite
Kovacs on the Corner
Lady of the Evening
Lady Takes a Chance
Lady Vanishes, The
Ladykillers, The
Las Vegas Weekend
Last American Virgin, The
Last Married Couple in America, The
Last of the Red Hot Lovers
Last Remake of Beau Geste, The
Late Show, The
Laugh Yourself Crazy, Vol. 1, The
Laughfest
Laughs for Sale
Laurel and Hardy Comedy Classics Volume I
Laurel and Hardy Comedy Classics Volume II
Laurel and Hardy Comedy Classics Volume III
Laurel and Hardy Comedy Classics Volume IV
Laurel and Hardy Comedy Classics Volume V
Laurel and Hardy Comedy Classics Volume VI
Laurel and Hardy Comedy Classics Volume VII
Laurel and Hardy Comedy Classics Volume VIII
Laurel and Hardy Comedy Classics Volume IX
Lavender Hill Mob, The
Let's Do It Again
Lt. Robin Crusoe U.S.N.
Life and Times of Judge Roy Bean, The
Life with Father
Lifeguard
Lily Tomlin Special: Volume I
Little Darlings
Little Miss Marker
Little Rascals Volume I, The
Little Rascals Comedy Classics Vol II, The
Little Rascals, Book I, The
Little Rascals, Book II, The
Little Rascals, Book III, The
Little Rascals, Book IV, The
Little Rascals, Book V, The
Little Rascals, Book VI, The
Little Rascals, Book VII, The

Mr. Bill Looks Back Featuring Sluggo's Greatest
    Hits
Mr. Blandings Builds His Dream House
Mr. Hulot's Holiday
Mr. Lucky
Mr. Magoo Cartoons
Mister Magoo in Sherwood Forest
Mr. Mike's Mondo Video
Mr. Mom
Mr. Peabody and the Mermaid
Mister Roberts
Mr. Winkle Goes to War
Mr. Wise Guy
Modern Problems
Modern Romance
Modern Times
Molly (The Goldbergs)
Mon Oncle
Monkey Business
Monkey's Uncle, The
Monsieur Verdoux
Monty Python and the Holy Grail
Monty Python Live at the Hollywood Bowl
Monty Python's Life of Brian
Monty Python's The Meaning of Life
Moon Is Blue, The
Moon Pilot
More! Police Squad
Morgan—A Suitable Case for Treatment
Moron Movies
Moscow on the Hudson
Mouse That Roared, The
Movers & Shakers
Movie, Movie
Movie Struck
Moving Violations
Mugsy's Girls
Muppet Movie, The
Muppet Musicians of Bremen, The
Murder by Death
Murphy's Romance
Mutant Video
My Best Girl
My Breakfast with Blassie
My Chauffeur
My Dear Secretary
My Favorite Brunette
My Favorite Wife
My Favorite Year
My Hero
My Little Chickadee
My Love for Yours
My Man Godfrey
My New Partner
My Other Husband
My Tutor
Naked Truth, The
National Lampoon's Class Reunion
National Lampoon's European Vacation
National Lampoon's Vacation
NBC Comedy Hour

NBC Comedy Hour, The
Neighbors
Never a Dull Moment
Never Give a Sucker an Even Break
Never On Sunday
Never Steal Anything Small
Next Year If All Goes Well
Night at the Opera, A
Night Patrol
Night Shift
Night They Raided Minsky's, The
Nine Lives of Fritz the Cat, The
9 to 5
1941
Ninotchka
No Deposit, No Return
No Time For Sergeants
Nobody's Perfekt
Norman Conquests: Table Manners, The
Norman Conquests: Living Together, The
Norman Conquests: Round and Round the
    Garden, The
North Avenue Irregulars, The
North Avenue Irregulars, The
North to Alaska
Nothing Personal
Nothing Sacred
Now You See Him, Now You Don't
Nudo Di Donna
Nut House, The
Nutcase
Nutty Professor, The
Ocean Drive Weekend
Ocean's 11
Odd Couple, The
Odd Job, The
Odd Jobs
Off Beat
Off Limits
Off the Wall
Off Your Rocker
Oh Dad, Poor Dad
Oh, God
Oh God, Book II
Oh, God! You Devil
Oh, Heavenly Dog
Oldest Profession, The
On Approval
On the Right Track
Once Bitten
Once Upon a Honeymoon
Once Upon a Scoundrel
One A.M.
One and Only, The
One Body Too Many
One of Our Dinosaurs Is Missing
One Rainy Afternoon
One, The Only... Groucho, The
One, Two, Three
One Wild Moment
Only When I Laugh

Road to Bali
Road to Lebanon, The
Road to Nashville
Rockin' Road Trip
Roman Holiday
Romance with a Double Bass
Romantic Comedy
Romantic Englishwoman, The
Room Service
Roommate, The
Rosebud Beach Hotel, The
Ruddigore
Ruggles, The
Ruling Class, The
Runaway Bus, The
Russians Are Coming, the Russians Are Coming,
   The
Rustler's Rhapsody
Saint Benny the Dip
Sally of the Sawdust
Santa Claus Conquers the Martians
Saps at Sea
Saps at Sea
Saturday Night Live: Eric Idle Vol I
Saturday Night Live: Buck Henry
Saturday Night Live: Carrie Fisher
Saturday Night Live: Charles Grodin
Saturday Night Live: Elliott Gould
Saturday Night Live: Eric Idle Vol. II
Saturday Night Live: Gary Busey
Saturday Night Live: George Carlin
Saturday Night Live: Lily Tomlin
Saturday Night Live: Madeline Kahn
Saturday Night Live: Michael Palin
Saturday Night Live: Peter Cook & Dudley Moore
Saturday Night Live: Ray Charles
Saturday Night Live: Richard Benjamin
Saturday Night Live: Robert Klein
Saturday Night Live: Rodney Dangerfield
Saturday Night Live: Sissy Spacek
Saturday Night Live: Steve Martin 2
Saturday Night Live, Vol. II
Saturday Night Live, Vol. I
Saturday Night Live with Richard Pryor
Saturday Night Live with Steve Martin
Sawmill/The Dome Doctor, The
Scandalous
Scandalous John
Scavenger Hunt
School for Sex
School Spirit
Screen Test
Screwballs
2nd Best Secret Agent in the Whole Wide World,
   The
Second City Insanity
Second Time Lucky
Secret Admirer
Secret Life of an American Wife, The
Secret Life of Walter Mitty, The
Secret Policeman's Other Ball, The

Secret Policeman's Private Parts, The
Secret War of Harry Frigg, The
Seems Like Old Times
Semi-Tough
Senator Was Indiscreet, The
Senior Trip
Seniors
Sensual Man, The
Sensuous Caterer, The
Sensuous Nurse
September Gun
Serial
Sesenta Horas en el Cielo
Seven Beauties
Seven Days Ashore/Hurry, Charlie, Hurry
Seven Year Itch, The
Seven Years Bad Luck
Sex and the Other Woman
Sex on the Run
Sex with a Smile
Sextette
Shaggy D.A., The
Shaggy Dog, The
Shampoo
Shamus
She Couldn't Say No
Sherlock's Rivals and Where's My Wife
She's in the Army Now
Shmenges: The Last Polka, The
Shot in the Dark, A
Sigmund and the Sea Monsters, Volume I
Silent Laugh Makers No. 1
Silent Laugh Makers No. 2
Silent Laugh Makers #3
Silent Movie
Silk Stockings
Silver Streak
Silver Theatre
Simon
Sin of Harold Diddlebock, The
Sing Your Worries Away
Singleton's Pluck
Sitting Ducks
Sixteen Candles
Skin Game
Sky High
Skyline
Sky's The Limit, The
Slap, The
Slapstick
Slapstick of Another Kind
Sleeper
Slightly Pregnant Man, A
Slumber Party '57
Small Change
Smokey and the Bandit
Smokey and the Bandit II
Smokey Bites the Dust
Snow White and the Three Stooges
Snowball Express
So Fine

S.O.B.
Soggy Bottom U.S.A.
Some Like It Hot
Something Short of Paradise
Son of Flubber
Son of Video Yesterbloop
Sons of the Desert
Sons of the Desert
Soup for One
Spaced Out
Spaceship
Speaking of Animals
Speaking of Animals Vol. II
Speed Kings? The/Love, Speed and Thrills
Spies Like Us
Splitz
Spooks Run Wild
Spring Break
Spring Fever
Squeeze Play
Stand-In
Stand-In
Stand-In, The
Star Struck
Start the Revolution Without Me
State of the Union
Statue, The
Steagle, The
Steamboat Bill, Jr.
Steelyard Blues
Step Lively
Sterile Cuckoo, The
Still Smokin'
Sting II, The
Stir Crazy
Stocks and Blondes
Stoogemania
Stooges Shorts Festival
Storm in a Teacup
Story of William S. Hart, The/The Sad Clowns
Street Music
Strike Up The Band
Stripes
Stroker Ace
Stuck on You
Stuckey's Last Stand
Student Teachers, The
Summer Camp
Summer Rental
Sunburn
Sunshine Boys, The
Super Fuzz
Super Seal
Superdad
Support Your Local Sheriff
Sure Thing, The
Surf II
Survivors, The
Susan Slept Here
Sweater Girls
Swing High, Swing Low

Swing It, Sailor!
Swinging Cheerleaders, The
Swiss Miss
Swiss Miss
Sybil Bruncheon a la Maison
Table Settings
Take Down
Take the Money and Run
Take This Job and Shove It
Takin' It Off
Tales from Muppetland
Tales from Muppetland II
Taming of the Shrew, The
Taming of the Shrew, The
Tammy and the Bachelor
Tammy and the Doctor
Teachers
Teacher's Pet
Teddy at the Throttle/Speeding Along
Teen Lust
Teen Wolf
Telephone Book, The
Television's Golden Age of Comedy
"10"
Tendres Cousines
Terrorvision
Texaco Star Theater
Thank God It's Friday
That Darn Cat
That Obscure Object of Desire
That Sinking Feeling
That Touch of Mink
That Uncertain Feeling
There's a Girl in My Soup
There's Naked Bodies On My T.V.!
These Girls Won't Talk
They All Laughed
They Call Me Bruce
They Got Me Covered
They Went That-a-Way & That-a-Way
Thief Who Came to Dinner, The
Things Are Tough All Over
Things We Did Last Summer, The
Think Dirty
13 Chairs, The
30-Foot Bride of Candy Rock, The
30 Is a Dangerous Age, Cynthia
This Time I'll Make You Rich
Those Magnificent Men in Their Flying Machines
Three Broadway Girls
Three Stooges, The
Three Stooges Comedy Capers Volume I
Three Stooges Comedy Classics
Three Stooges—Medium Rare, The
Three Stooges Meet Hercules, The
Three Stooges Videodisc, Vol. 1, The
Three Stooges, Volumes I thru XIII, The
Thunder and Lightning
Thursday's Game
Tiger and the Pussycat, The
Till Marriage Do Us Part

Wild Life, The
Win, Place, or Steal
Witches' Brew
With Six You Get Eggroll
Without Reservations
Woman in Red, The
Woman of Paris, A/Sunnyside
Woman of the Year
Women, The
Women Tell the Dirtiest Jokes
Work/Police
Working Stiffs
World According to Garp, The
World's Greatest Athlete, The
Wrong Box, The
Wrong Is Right
Yankee Doodle in Berlin
Yellowbeard
Yeomen of the Guard, The
Yes, Giorgio
You Bet Your Life
You Can't Take It With You
You Were Never Lovelier
You'll Find Out
Young and Willing
Young Doctors in Love
Young Frankenstein
Your Show of Shows
You're a Big Boy Now
You've Got to Have Heart
Zapped
Zelig
Zero for Conduct
Zis Boom Bah
Zorro, the Gay Blade
Zotz

Comedy-Drama

Always
Apartment, The
Apprenticeship of Duddy Kravitz, The
April Fools, The
Back Roads
Barney Oldfield's Race for a Life/Super-Hooper-
    Dyne Lizzies
Benji
Big Chill, The
Billy Liar
Breakfast Club, The
Buck and the Preacher
Butterflies Are Free
Can She Bake a Cherry Pie?
Cannery Row
Casey's Shadow
Charlie and the Great Balloon Chase
Cheaper to Keep Her
Clean Slate (Coup de Torchon)
Clown, The
Coast to Coast
Cold Feet

Danny Boy
Devil's Eye
Diary of a Mad Housewife
Diner
Dinner at Eight
Doctor at Sea
Dog Day Afternoon
Dream Chasers, The
Educating Rita
Eyes Right
Fireside Theatre: Sergeant Sullivan Speaking
For the Love of Benji
Four Friends
Fuzz
George
Gidget
Gin Game, The
Good Sam
Goodbye People, The
Graduate, The
Heat
His Double Life
Hit, The
Horsemasters, The
Hotel New Hampshire, The
If You Could See What I Hear
It's My Turn
Joe
Judge Priest
King of Comedy, The
Lady Eve, The
Last Detail, The
Last Word, The
Little Lord Fauntleroy
Loves of a Blonde, The
Magic Town
Mama (I Remember Mama)
Marathon
Mark Twain's A Connecticut Yankee in King
    Arthur's Court
M*A*S*H: Goodbye, Farewell and Amen
Max Dugan Returns
Min and Bill
Miss Annie Rooney
Murphy's War
My Dinner with Andre
My Therapist
Never Let Go
No Small Affair
North Dallas Forty
Nuit de Varennes, La
Oh Alfie
One Night Stand
Over the Brooklyn Bridge
Palooka
Pillow Talk
Pollyanna
Pollyanna
Poor Little Rich Girl, The
Portnoy's Complaint
Prisoner of Second Avenue, The

Comedy-Performance

Communication

Computers

Consumer education

Cookery

Bocuse A La Carte
Classic Cooking
Cooking for Compliments
Craig Claiborne's New York Times Video
  Cookbook
Cuisines and Folklores Around the World
Flavors of China
Julia Child—The French Chef, Vol. I
Master Cooking Course, The
Short-Order Gourmet, The
Slim Gourmet, The
Video Cooking Library
Way to Cook, The
We're Cooking Now
Wok Before You Run
Wok on the Wild Side
Yes You Can Microwave

Cosmetology

Color Me Beautiful
8 Minute Makeovers
Make-up Secrets of the Hollywood Stars-
  Looking Your Best
Why Do I Call You Sexy?

Crime and criminals

Al Capone: Chicago's Scarface
Alcatraz
Murder: No Apparent Motive
Opportunities in Criminal Justice
Police Tapes, The

Crime-Drama

Adventures of Ellery Queen, The
Al Capone
Bad Bunch, The
Bad Georgia Road
Badge 373
Best Revenge
Big Combo, The
Big Doll House
Big Fix, The
Black Godfather, The
Black Marble, The
Blackout
Blade
Blastfighter
Brannigan
Call Him Mr. Shatter
Callao, El (The Silent One)
Chiefs
Cleopatra Jones
Code of Silence
Cold Sweat
Con Artists, The
Concrete Beat
Corrupt

Courier of Death
Crime and Passion
Cross Country
Daring Dobermans, The
Deadly Chase (La Persecucion Mortal)
Deadly Hero
Dear Detective
Death of a Hooker
Defiant, The
Detour
Diamonds
Dick Tracy
Dick Tracy
Dick Tracy
Dick Tracy Detective
Dick Tracy Double Feature # 1
Dick Tracy Meets Gruesome
Dick Tracy Returns
Dick Tracy Returns
Dick Tracy vs. Crime Inc.
Dick Tracy vs. Crime Inc.
Dick Tracy's G-Men
Dick Tracy's G-Men
Dillinger
Dillinger
Doberman Gang, The
Echo Murders, The
11 Harrow house
Enforcer, The
False Faces
Family, The
Fighting Back
Final Justice
Final Mission
Fingers
Five Golden Dragons
48 Hours to Live
Framed
French Connection, The
French Quarter Undercover
Gangs, Inc.
Gangster Wars, The
Gauntlet, The
Girls of the White Orchid
God Told Me To
High Crime
Honeymoon Killers, The
Hot Target
House on Garibaldi Street, The
Island Monster
It's Called Murder, Baby
Justice
Kansas City Massacre
Kill, The
Kill Alex Kill
Knights of the City
Lady in the Death House
Last Mile, The
Laughing Policeman, The
Laura
License to Kill

Little Caesar
Long Good Friday, The
Love Thrill Murders, The
Lucky Luciano
Magnum Force
Man Against Crime Volume II
Man on the Eiffel Tower, The
Manhunter
Marbella
McQ
Mean Johnny Barrows
Miami Vice II--The Prodigal Son
Natas es Satan
Northwest Trail
On the Run
On the Yard
One Man Jury
Operation Julie
Outside the Law
Parallel Corpse
Parker
Playgirl Killer
Policewomen
Port of New York
Protector, The
Public Enemy
Puppet on a Chain
Quiet Place to Kill, A
Racket, The
Rocky King, Detective
St. Ives
St. Valentine's Day Massacre, The
Scarface
Scarface
Scarface Mob, The
Sense of Freedom, A
Shaft
Shoot It Black, Shoot It Blue
Sicilian Connection, The
Sno-Line
Stiletto
Street Law
Sudden Death
Sudden Impact
Suddenly
Suddenly
Sunset Strip
T-Men
Ten to Midnight
They Live by Night
Thief
Thief, The
3:15--The Moment of Truth
Thrill Kill
To Live and Die in L.A.
Tough Guy, The
Trap, The
Tuxedo Warrior
Vengeance
Violent Breed, The
Violent Women

Westinghouse Studio One: "Little Men, Big
    World"
While The City Sleeps
Witness
Zebra Force
Zertigo Diamond Caper, The

Dance

Aerobic Dancing—Encore
All the Best from Russia
American Ballet Theatre at the Met
Anyuta
Backstage at the Kirov
Ballerina: Karen Kain
Ballerina: Lynn Seymour
Ballet Class for Beginners, A
Ballet Class for Intermediate—Advanced
Bayadere, La
Black Tights
Blood Wedding (Bodas de Sangre)
Bolshoi Ballet
Bolshoi Ballet: Les Sylphides, The
Breakin'
Breaking with the Mighty Poppalots
Carmen
Catherine Wheel, The
Catherine Wheel, The
Children of Theatre Street, The
Christmas Carol, A
Cinderella Ballet
Coppelia with Fernando Bujones
Dazzledancin
Don Quixote
Evening with the Royal Ballet, An
Evening with the Royal Ballet, An
Fille Mal Gardee, La
Freedanse
Giselle
Gisolle
Godunov: The World to Dance In
Grand Canyon Dancing
I Am a Dancer
Israel Folk Dance Festival
John Curry's Ice Dancing
Kids from Fame, The
Kirov Ballet: Classic Ballet Night, The
La Sylphide
Let's Break: A Visual Guide to Break Dancing
Let's Jazzercise
Let's Tap
Lovers of Teruel, The
Macbeth
Manon
Martha Graham: Three Contemporary Classics
Medea
Mid-Eastern Dance: An Introduction to Belly
    Dance
Moiseyev Dance Company: A Gala Evening
Natalia Makarova: In a Class of Her Own
Nutcracker, The

Deaf

Death

Disasters

Diseases

Divorce

Documentary

Balboa
Ballad in Blue
Ballad of a Soldier
Ballad of Gregorio Cortez, The
Bang the Drum Slowly
Barabbas
Barefoot Contessa, The
Barn Burning
Baron and the Kid, The
Barry Lyndon
Battered
Battle of Austerlitz
Battle of Neretva
Battle Shock
Battling Bunyan
Bayou Romance
Beachcomber, The
Beasts
Beat the Devil
Beauty and the Beast
Becket
Becky Sharp
Bees, The
Behold a Pale Horse
Belfast Assassin, The
Bell Jar, The
Bells, The
Bells of St. Mary's, The
Below the Belt
Ben Hur
Bergonzi Hand, The
Berlin Alexanderplatz
Best of Broadway, "The Philadelphia Story,"
    The
Best of Upstairs Downstairs, The
Best Years of Our Lives, The
Betrayal
Betrayal
Betsy, The
Between Friends
Between Wars
Beyond Fear
Beyond Reason
Beyond Reasonable Doubt
Beyond the Limit
Beyond the Valley of the Dolls
Beyond the Walls
Bible, The
Big Bad Mama
Big Bird Cage
Big Heat, The
Big Mo
Big Red
Big Score, The
Big Trees, The
Big Wednesday
Bilitis
Bill
Billy Jack
Billy: Portrait of a Street Kid
Bionic Woman, The

Birdman of Alcatraz, The
Birds of Paradise
Birds of Prey
Birdy
Bitch, The
Bitter Harvest
Black Beauty
Black Emanuelle
Black Fury
Black Hand, The
Black Jack
Black Like Me
Black Narcissus
Black Orchid, The
Black Orpheus
Black Six, The
Black Stallion Returns, The
Black Sunday
Blake of Scotland Yard
Blasphemer, The
Bless the Beasts & Children
Blind Husbands
Blood and Sand
Blood Feud
Bloodbrothers
Bloody Mama
Blow-Up
Blue Collar
Blue Fire Lady
Blue Heaven
Blue Knight, The
Blue Lagoon, The
Blue Max, The
Blue Yonder, The
Bluebeard
Bluebeard
Blume in Love
Boat Is Full, The
Bob Le Flambeur
Bobby Deerfield
Bobby Jo and the Outlaw
Body and Soul
Body and Soul
Body Double
Body Heat
Bogie: The Last Hero
Bolero
Bolero
Bonnie and Clyde
Bonnie's Kids
Border, The
Borderline
Born Again
Born Losers
Boss' Son, The
Bostonians, The
Bound for Glory
Bounty, The
Boxcar Bertha
Boy in the Plastic Bubble, The
Boy Takes Girl

Deliverance
Delusion
Derby
Dernier Combat, Le (The Last Battle)
Desde el Abismo
Deserters, The
Desire Under the Elms
Despair
Desparate Lives
Detroit 9000
Devil and Daniel Webster, The
Devil and Leroy Basset, The
Devil at 4 O'Clock, The
Devil Thumbs a Ride, The
Devils, The
Devil's Party, The
Devil's Wanton, The
Diary of a Teenage Hitchhiker
Diary of Anne Frank, The
Diary of a Young Comic
Didn't You Hear?
Dingaka
Dinner at the Ritz
Dino
Directions '66
Dirt Gang, The
Dirty Gertie From Harlem U.S.A.
Dirty Harry
Disappearance of Aimee, The
Displaced Person, The
Divorce His, Divorce Hers
Divorce of Lady X
Dixie: Changing Habits
Dixie Dynamite
Dr. Kildare's Strange Case
Dr. Syn
Doctor Zhivago
Dodes 'ka-den
Dodsworth
Dog of Flanders, A
Dogs of War, The
Dolce Vita, La
Dolls, The
Doll's House, A
Doll's House, A
Dominique Is Dead
Domino Principle, The
Donner Pass—The Road to Survival
Don't Change My World
Don't Cry, It's Only Thunder
Don't Look Now
Dos Chicas de Revista
Double Deal
Double Face
Double Life, A
Downhill Racer
Doyle Against the House
Dragon Seed
Drama—Romance: Trailers on Tape
Dream for Christmas, A
Dream Street

Dreamchild
Dreaming Lips
Dreams
Dresser, The
Drum
Drying Up the Streets
Duellists, The
Dusty
D.W. Griffith Triple Feature
Dying Room Only
Eagle, The
Early Days
Earth
Earthling, The
Earthquake
East End Hustle
East of Borneo
East of Eden
East of Eden
East of Elephants Rock
Easy Rider
Eat My Dust
Echoes
Ecstasy
Eddie and the Cruisers
Eddie Macon's Run
Edie in Ciao! Manhattan
Edward and Mrs. Simpson
8 1/2
Electric Dreams
Electric Horseman, The
Elephant Man, The
Elmer
Elmer Gantry
Elusive Corporal, The
Emanuelle Around the World
Emanuelle in America
Emanuelle in Bangkok
Emanuelle the Queen
Emerald Forest, The
Emilienne
Emily
Emma and Grandpa
Emmanuelle
Emmanuelle Black and White
Emmanuelle in the Country
Emmanuelle, the Joys of a Woman
Emperor Jones, The
Enchanted Island
End of the Road
Endangered Species
Endless Love
Enigma
Entertaining Mr. Sloane
Entre Nous (Between Us)
Equus
Erendira
Escapade in Japan
Escape Artist, The
Escape from Alcatraz
Escape to Love

Escort Girls
Esposa y Amante
Eureka!
Europeans, The
Evel Knievel
Every Man for Himself and God Against All
Evil Mind, The
Evil That Men Do, The
Executioner's Song, The
Executioner, The
Executive Action
Exodus
Express to Terror
Eyes, The Mouth, The
Fabulous Dorseys, The
Face in the Crowd, A
Fail Safe
Fake Out
Fall of the House of Usher, The
Fall of the Roman Empire, The
Fallen Idol
Falling In Love
Family Enforcer
Family Life
Family Upside Down, A
Fanny
Fanny and Alexander
Fantasies
Fantasy in Blue
Fantasy Island
Far East
Farewell to Arms, A
Fast Lane Fever
Fast Walking
Fatal Attraction
Father
Father Figure
Fearless
Feelin' Up
Fiend
Fifth Day of Peace, The
55 Days at Peking
Fight for Your Life
Fighter, The
Final Assignment
Final Countdown, The
Fiona
Fire Over England
Firepower
Fires on the Plain
First Blood
First Born
First Deadly Sin, The
First Legion, The
First Love
F.I.S.T.
Fitzcarraldo
Flaming Star
Flash of Green, A
Flight from Vienna
Flight of the Grey Wolf, The

Foolish Wives
Foolish Wives
Fools
For Ladies Only
For Love of Ivy
For the Love of Angela
Forbidden
Force of Evil
Ford Startime
Forever Emmanuelle
Forever Young
Formula, The
Fort Apache, The Bronx
Fountainhead, The
Four Deuces, The
Four Horsemen of the Apocalypse, The
400 Blows, The
Four Infernos to Cross
Fourth Wish, The
Foxes
Foxfire Light
Foxtrot
Frances
Francis Gary Powers: The True Story of the U-2
   Spy Incident
Frantic
Fraulein Devil
Freedom
Freedom Road
French Connection II
French Lieutenant's Woman, The
French Postcards
French Quarter
French Woman, The
Friendly Persuasion
From the Life of the Marionettes
Front, The
Fugitive: The Final Episode, The
Full Hearts and Empty Pockets
Fyre
Gallipoli
Gamble on Love
Gambler, The
Game of Seduction
Gandhi
Garden of the Finzi-Continis, The
Gaslight
Gathering, The
Gathering Storm
Generation
Gentleman Jim
Germicide
Getting of Wisdom, The
Giant
Gideon's Trumpet
Gift for Heidi, A
Gift, The (Le Cadeau)
Gilda
Girlfriends
Girls of Huntington House, The
Give 'Em Hell, Harry!

Glen or Glenda
Glenn Miller Story, The
Glitter Dome, The
Gloria
Glory
Go for Gold
Godfather 1902-1959—The Complete Epic, The
Godfather, The
Godfather Part II, The
God's Little Acre
Goin' All the Way
Going Places
Gold of the Amazon Women
Golden Boy
Golden Seal, The
Goldengirl
Goldenrod
Goldy: The Last of the Golden Bears
Gone With the Wind
Good Earth, The
Goodbye Columbus
Goodbye Emmanuelle
Goodbye, Mr. Chips
Goodbye Norma Jean
Goodyear TV Playhouse: "Marty"
Gorgo
Gorgo
Gospel According to St. Matthew, The
Grand Hotel
Grapes of Wrath, The
Greased Lightning
Great Escape, The
Great Expectations
Great Gabbo, The
Great Gatsby, The
Great Gundown, The
Great Guy
Great Riviera Bank Robbery, The
Great Santini, The
Greatest, The
Greatest Show on Earth, The
Greatest Story Ever Told, The
Greek Tycoon, The
Green Dolphin Street
Green Eyes
Green Room, The
Grey Fox, The
Grit of the Girl Telegrapher, The/In the Switch Tower
Group, The
Grunt! The Wrestling Movie
Guardian, The
Guess Who's Coming To Dinner
Gulag
Gulliver
Hallmark Hall of Fame, The
Hallmark Theater (Sometimes She's Sunday)
Hamlet
Hanna K
Hanover Street
Hardcore

Hard Country
Hard Knox
Hard Times
Harder They Fall, The
Harlow
Harrad Experiment, The
Harry and Son
Harry & Tonto
Harry Tracy
Hatfields and the McCoys, The
Haunting Passion, The
Hawaii
He is My Brother
He Who Walks Alone
Head of the Family, The
Heart Is a Lonely Hunter, The
Heart Like a Wheel
Heart of the Stag
Heartbeat
Heartbreaker
Heartbreakers
Heartland
Heat and Dust
Heat of Desire
Heatwave
Heavenly Bodies
Heidi
Heidi
Heidi
Heiress, The
Hell on Frisco Bay
Hell Squad
Hellfighters
Hells Angels on Wheels
Hell's House
Helter Skelter
Henderson Monster, The
Henry V
Her Silent Sacrifice
Hero, The
Hero Bunker
Heroes
Hester Street
Hidden Fortress, The
High Ballin'
High Command
High Country, The
High Country Calling
High Ice
High School Confidential
High Sierra
Highest Honor, The
Hills Have Eyes, Part II, The
Hiroshima, Mon Amour
His Kind of Woman
History Is Made at Night
Hit and Run
Hitler: The Last Ten Days
Hitler's Children
Hollywood Man
Holocaust

Nest, The
Network
Never Cry Wolf
Never Love a Stranger
New Centurions, The
New York, New York
New York Nights
News Front
Nicholas and Alexandra
Nicholas Nickleby
Nickel Mountain
Night Crossing
Night Gallery
Night Games
Night Is My Future, The
Night of the Assassin
Night of the Generals, The
Night of the Iguana, The
Night Porter, The
Night Terror
Night the Lights Went Out in Georgia, The
Night Warning
Nighthawks
Nightkill
Nine Ages of Nakedness
Nine Days a Queen
984—Prisoner of the Future
1918
1984
99 Women
Ninth Configuration, The
No Man of Her Own
No Place To Hide
None But The Lonely Heart
Norma Rae
Norseman, The
Northern Pursuit
Not Tonight Darling
Notorious
Now and Forever
Now, Voyager
Nurse
Nurse Edith Cavell
Nutcracker Sweet
O Lucky Man
Occurrence at Owl Creek Bridge, An
Ode to Billy Joe
Odessa File, The
Of Human Bondage
Of Human Bondage
Of Mice and Men
Off Your Rocker
Officer and a Gentleman, An
Official Story, The
O'Hara's Wife
Oil
Old Boyfriends
Old Enough
Old Gun, The
Old Swimmin' Hole, The
Old Yeller

Oliver Twist
Oliver Twist
Oliver Twist
Oliver's Story
Olvidados, Los
On Golden Pond
On the Beach
On the Nickel
On the Third Day
On the Waterfront
Once in Paris
Once Is Not Enough
Once Upon a Time in America
One Away
One Flew Over the Cuckoo's Nest
One in a Million
One on One
One Shoe Makes It Murder
One Sings, the Other Doesn't
Onion Field, The
Open City
Ordeal by Innocence
Ordeal of Dr. Mudd
Order to Kill
Ordinary People
Orphan Town
Orphans of the Storm
Oscar, The
Othello
Other Side of Midnight, The
Other Side of the Mountain, The
Other Side of the Mountain, Part II, The
Our Town
Our Town
Out of Africa
Out of the Blue
Outlaw Blues
Outside Chance
Outsiders, The
Over the Edge
Oxford Blues
Padre Padrone
Panama Lady
Panic in Echo Park
Panique
Paper Chase, The
Papillon
Paradise Alley
Paradise in Harlem
Paris Express
Paris, Texas
Park is Mine, The
Passage to India, A
Passante, La
Passenger, The
Passion
Passion of Joan of Arc
Passion of Love
Paul's Case
Pawnbroker, The
Peacekillers, The

Stage Fright
Stagestruck
Stand Alone
Star Chamber, The
Star 80
Star Is Born, A
Stars Look Down, The
State of Siege
Stay as You Are
Stay As You Are
Staying Alive
Staying On
Steel
Steel Cowboy
Steinbeck's The Pearl
Stella Dallas
Stolen Kisses
Stone Boy, The
Stone Killer, The
Stormy Waters
Story of a Love Story
Story of Adele H., The
Story of Esther, The
Story of O, The
La Strada
Straight Time
Strait Jacket
Strange And Deadly Occurence
Strange Love of Martha Ivers, The
Stranger than Paradise
Stranger Who Looks Like Me, The
Stranger Within, The
Stranger's Kiss
Strangers on a Train
Strangers: The Story of a Mother and Daughter
Straw Dogs
Strawberry Statement, The
Street, The
Street Hero
Street People
Street Scene
Street Walkin'
Streetcar Named Desire, A
Streets of L.A., The
Stromboli
Stud, The
Studs Lonigan
Stunt Man, The
Submission
Subterfuge
Suburbia
Suddenly Last Summer
Sudsy Television
Sugar Cane Alley
Sugar Cookies
Sugarland Express, The
Summer Heat
Summer in St. Tropez, A
Summer Lovers
Summer Magic
Summer of '42

Summer of My German Soldier
Summer Solstice
Summer Wishes, Winter Dreams
Summertime
Sunday Too Far Away
Sundays and Cybele
Sunningdale Mystery, The
Sunrise at Campobello
Sunset Boulevard
Superfly
Surabaya Conspiracy
Surfacing
Suzanne
Svengali
Swann in Love
Swap, The
Sweet Country Road
Sweet Sweetback's Baadasssss Song
Sweet William
Swept Away
Swimmer, The
Swinging Ski Girls
Swinging Sorority Girls
Swiss Family Robinson, The
Sybil
Sylvester
Symphony of Living
Table for Five
Tag: The Assassination Game
Tale of Two Cities, A
Tale of Two Cities, A
Tales of Ordinary Madness
Talk to Me
Tamarind Seed, The
Taming of the Shrew, The
Tank
Taps
Targets
Tattoo
Taxi Driver
Tell Me That You Love Me
Tempest
Tempest
Tempest, The
Ten Commandments, The
Ten Commandments, The
Ten Days that Shook the World
Ten Nights in a Bar-Room
Ten Speed
Tender Age, The
Tender Loving Care
Tender Mercies
Tennessee Stallion
10th Victim, The
Terms of Endearment
Terror on the 40th Floor
Terry Fox Story, The
Tess
Test of Love, A
Testament
Tex

You Only Live Once
Young and Free
Young Aphrodities
Young Love, First Love
Young Philadelphians, The
Young Teacher, The
Young Warriors, The
Young Winston
Youngblood
Your Ticket Is No Longer Valid
Zabriskie Point
Zoo Gang, The
Zorba, the Greek

Drawing

Basic Art By Video II: Drawing & Design

Drug abuse

American Alcoholic, The/Reading, Writing and Reefer
Drug Free Kids: A Parent's Guide

Drugs

Cocaine: One Man's Seduction

Education

Basic Chords for Guitar
Mickey's Discovery Series
Mister Rogers Goes to School
New Speed Reading
Romper Room and Friends
Speed Learning
Speed Reading Hand, The

Ethics

Captain Kangaroo and the Right Thing to Do
Hellfire
Mr. Rogers—Helping Children Understand
Mr. T's Be Somebody... Or Be Somebody's Fool
Storm Boy
Welcome to Pooh Corner Volume 5
Welcome to Pooh Corner Volume 6

Europe

Great Cities: London, Rome, Dublin, Athens

Exploitation

Battle of the Bombs
The Best of New Wave Theatre
Big Bust Out, The
Black Devil Doll from Hell
Black Godfather, The
Black Shampoo
Caged Terror
Certain Sacrifice, A

Cocaine Fiends
Cool it Carol
Dark Side of Love
Delinquent Schoolgirls
Desperate Teenage Lovedolls
Doctor Gore
Eegah!
Emmanuelle 4
Film House Fever
Final Comedown, The
First Turn On, The
Glen or Glenda
Grunt! The Wrestling Movie
Hell Squad
Hellhole
Hollywood High
H.O.T.S.
Jock Peterson
Last House on the Left
Massive Retaliation
Naked Vengeance
Nomad Riders
One Night Only
Red Kimono, The
Reefer Madness
Rock 'n Roll Wrestling Music Television
Saturday Night Shockers
Saturday Night Sleazies
Sex Madness
Silent Night, Deadly Night
Sleazemania Strikes Back
Sleazemania--The Special Edition
Summer School Teachers
Teenage Seductress
Tigers in Lipstick
Title Shot
Tomorrow's Children
Violent Years, The
Weekend with the Babysitter
Women Unchained
Wrestling Women vs. the Aztec Mummy
Yellow Hair and the Fortress of Gold
Young Nurses, The

Fairy tales

Aesop and His Friends
Aesop's Fables
Aladdin and His Magic Lamp
Aladdin and His Wonderful Lamp
Beauty and the Beast
Boy Who Left Home to Find Out About the Shivers, The
Captain Kangaroo's Fairy Tales and Funny Stories
Captain Kangaroo's Favorite Stories
Children's Video Playground
Cinderella
Cuckoo Clock That Wouldn't Cuckoo, The
Dancing Princesses, The
Daydreamer, The

Family

Fantasy

Film

Film-Avant-garde

Film-History

SUBJECT CATEGORY INDEX

Filmmaking

Finance

First aid

Fishes

Fishing

How to Catch Bass
How to Catch Trout
How to Catch Walleye
How to Troll for Fish
Jimmy Houston's Guide to Bass Fishin'
One on One with Roland Martin
Secrets for Catching Walleye
Stoneflies and the Big Hole
Yellowstone and the Madison: One After
  Another, The

Folklore

Chinese Gods
Disney's American Heroes
Slaughterhouse Five
Storytellers, The
Winds of Change

Football

America's Team: The Dallas Cowboys 1975-79
Back Among the Best/NFL '83
Beat Goes On, The
Best of the Football Follies, The
Better Team, A
Big Game America
Black Sunday: Highlights of Super Bowl XVII
Champions of the AFC East
Chicago Bears 1984 Team Highlights
Cinderella Seahawks/NFL '83, The
Cleveland Browns 1985 Team Highlights
Cliffhangers, Comebacks, and Character
Color Them Tough
Come Back Champions/NFL '83
Coming of Age: The Story of the Dallas Cowboys
  1970-74
Commitment to Excellence/NFL '82
Cut Above, A
Cut Above/NFL '83, A
Dallas Cowboys 1984 Team Highlights
Dallas Cowboys 1985 Team Highlights
Day of Frustration—Season of Triumph
Day of the Dolphins/NFL '82
Denver Broncos First Tastes of Glory: 1977,
  1978, 1979, 1984
Denver Broncos 1984 Team Highlights
Festival of Funnies, A
Football Follies
Football Follies/Highlights of Super Bowl V
Football Follies/Sensational 60's
From Worst to First
Giant Step, A
Gillette NFL Most Valuable Player 1985
Glory Days of Yesteryear: The Baltimore Colts
Go Bears! A Look to the 80's
Grambling's White Tiger
Great Expectations/The Man with the Funny Hat
Great Teams/Great Years Volume One
Greatest Game Ever Played, The
Highlights of the 1960 NFL Championship Game

History of Pro Football, The
How to Watch Pro Football
Joe Gibbs' Washington Redskins: Two Years to
  the Title
Just Win, Baby/NFL 83
Kardiac Kids...Again
Legacy Begins: Miami Dolphins, The
Legend of the Lightning Bolt, The
Like a Mighty River...
Lombardi
Los Angeles Raiders 1985 Team Highlights
Los Angeles Rams 1984 Team Highlights
Luv-Ya Blue!
Man Named Lombardi, A
Men Who Played the Game, The
Miami Dolphins 1985 Team Highlights
Miami Dolphins 1984 Team Highlights
Most Memorable Games of the Decade #1
Most Memorable Games of the Decade #2
Most Memorable Games of the Decade #3
New England Patriots 1985 Team Highlights
New York Giants 1984 Team Highlights
New York Giants 1985 Team Highlights
New York Jets 1985 Team Highlights
NFL Crunch Course
NFL '81
NFL '81 Official Season Yearbook
NFL Follies Go Hollywood
NFL Head Coach: A Self Portrait
NFL SymFunny/Highlights of Super Bowl III
NFL SymFunny/Legends of the Fall
NFL's Best Ever Coaches
NFL's Best Ever: The Professionals
NFL's Best Ever Quarterbacks
NFL's Best Ever Runners
NFL's Best Ever Teams
NFL's Inspirational Men and Moments, The
1958 NFL Championship Game
1966 and 1967 NFL Championship Games
Old Leather
Our Finest Hour
Pittsburgh Steelers 1984 Team Highlights
Pittsburgh Steelers: The Championship Years
Power, The
Pride of Eagles Football
Purple Power Years: The Minnesota Vikings
Return of the Rams/NFL '83
Right Stuff/NFL '83, The
Road Warriors, The/NFL '82
San Francisco 49ers 1984 Team Highlights
San Francisco 49ers 1985 Team Highlights
Saviors, Saints, and Sinners
Seattle Seahawks 1984 Team Highlights
Sensational Sixties
Shout for the Stars
Son of Football Follies, The
Son of Football Follies/Big Game America
Son of Football Follies/Highlights of Super Bowl
  XIV
Spirit of West Point, The
Star Ascending: The Dallas Cowboys 1965-69

France

Gambling

Game show

Games

Gardening

Geography

Germany

Golf

Terror on Tour
Terrorvision
Texas Chainsaw Massacre, The
Theatre of Death
Them!
They Saved Hitler's Brain
Thing, The
Thirsty Dead
13 Ghosts
Thirteenth Reunion, The
To All a Goodnight
Tomb of Ligeia, The
Tormentor
Torture Chamber of Baron Blood, The
Torture Chamber of Dr. Sadism
Torture Garden
Touch of Satan, A
Tower of Evil
Track of the Moonbeast
Trauma
Trick or Treats
Trilogy of Terror
Turn of the Screw, The
Twilight People
Twilight Zone—The Movie
Twins of Evil
Twisted Brain
Two Faces of Evil, The
Uncanny, The
Unearthly, The
Unseen, The
Up from the Depths
Vampire Lovers, The
Vampyr
Varan the Unbelievable
Vault of Horror, The
Venom
Venus in Furs
Videodrome
Virgin Among the Living Dead
Virgin Witch, The
Visions of Evil
Visitor From the Grave
Warlock Moon
Werewolf of Washington
What the Peeper Saw
When the Screaming Stops
White Zombie, The
Wild Beasts, The
Willard
Witch Who Came from the Sea, The
Witchcraft Through the Ages
Witches Mountain, The
Witching Time
Witch's Mirror, The
Wolfen
Wolfman
World of the Vampires, The
Wrestling Women vs. the Aztec Mummy, The
X-Tro
Zoltan... Hound of Dracula

Zombie
Zombie Lake
Zombies of Mora Tau
Zombiethon

Horse racing

Breeders' Cup 1985

Human relations

How to Pick Up Men
Love Tapes
Persuasive Speaking

Hunting

Archery Tactics for Deer
Cat Hunting in Tanzania
Decoys and Duck Calls—Two Secrets for
    Success
Elephant Hunting in Tanzania
Field Dressing and Trophy Care for the
    Wilderness Hunter
Goose Hunting on the Eastern Shore
How to Hunt Whitetail Deer
How to Hunt Wild Turkey
Hunting Big Muleys
Hunting Dall Sheep and Caribou in the N.W.T.
Hunting Desert Bighorn in Northern Baja
Introduction to Muzzleloading
Late Season Elk Hunting with Jim Zumbo
North American Big Game
Pachmayr's Shotgun Hunting School
Pachmayr's Skeetshooting with Ken Robertson
Pachmayr's Trapshooting with Ken Robertson
Pronghorn Hunting
Retriever Trials for Hunters
Rifle Shooting Tips and Techniques
Whitetail: Still Hunting and Stand Hunting

Identity

Everybody Rides the Carousel
Free to Be... You and Me
Mr. T's Be Somebody... Or Be Somebody's Fool
Scholastic Productions: As We Grow

Indians-North American

Silent Enemy, The

Infants

Baby Comes Home
Caring for Your Newborn
Caring for Your Newborn with Dr. Benjamin
    Spock
How to Give Your Baby Encyclopedic
    Knowledge
How to Teach Your Baby to Read
Learning About the World

Meeting the World
Swim Baby Swim
Your Newborn Baby: Everything You Need to
Know

Insects

Hellstrom Chronicle, The
Mysterious Miniature World

Interview

Hollywood on the Line
John Lennon: Interview with a Legend
Making of Joan Collins, The
Meeting of Minds, Volumes 5 & 6
Meeting of Minds, Volumes 1 & 2
Meeting of Minds—Volumes 3 and 4
Person to Person
Prince and Princess of Wales... Talking
    Personally, The
Problems, 1950's Style
Telescope—Interview with Harry Richman
This Is Your Life
This Is Your Life: Laurel and Hardy
Yoko Ono Then and Now

Inventions

Gizmo!
Tom Edison: The Making of an American Legend

Islam

Holy Koran, The

Japan

Kyoto Vivaldi: The Four Seasons

Judaism

Kitty: A Return to Auschwitz

Korean War

Battle for Dien Bien Phu

Labor and unions

In the Company of Men

Language arts

Adventures of the Scrabble People in a Pumpkin
    Full of Nonsense
Animal Alphabet, The
Bill Cosby's Picturepages—Volume I
Bill Cosby's Picturepages—Volume 2
Bill Cosby's Picturepages—Volume 4
Incredible Book Escape, The
Language in Life

Learning Can Be Fun
Reading Rainbow
Speed Reading Hand, The
They Were Cars
Yankee Doodle Cricket
You and Me, Kid—Volume 3

Languages-Instruction

Basic English for Hispanics by Video
Basic English Grammar by Video
Basic French by Video
Basic Italian by Video
Basic Spanish by Video
Gabi und Frank
Ingles, Ingles
Living Language—French
Living Language—Spanish
Survival Spanish

Literature

Animal Talk
Animal Talk
Disney Classics, The
Family Entertainment Playhouse, Vol. 2
Gielgud's Chekhov 1
Gielgud's Chekhov 2
Gielgud's Chekhov 3
Incredible Book Escape, The
Little Engine That Could, The
Little Women
Occurrence at Owl Creek Bridge, An
Once Upon a Midnight Dreary
Rime of the Ancient Mariner
Winnie the Pooh

Literature-American

Ambrose Bierce: The Man and the Snake/The
    Return
Four for Thrills
Golden Honeymoon, The
Greatest Man in the World, The
Mark Twain's A Connecticut Yankee in King
    Arthur's Court
Soldier's Home
Steinbeck's The Pearl
Wind in the Willows, The

Literature-English

Great Expectations
Lady Chatterley's Lover
Midsummer Night's Dream, A
Oliver Twist
Sir Arthur Conan Doyle

Magic

Blackstone on Tour
Dick Cavett's Hocus Pocus, It's Magic

Mass media

Massage

Middle East

Mime

Miners and mining

Minorities

Motorcycles

Mountaineering

Movie and TV trailers

Weber and Fields, Al Jolson, and This Is America
White Music

Music video

Alabama—Greatest Video Hits
April Wine
Atlantic Starr: As the Band Turns... The Video
Autumn Portrait
Avengers
Aventura Llamada Menudo, Una
Bananarama: And That's Not All...
Barbra Streisand Putting it Together—The
    Making of the Broadway Album
Barry Gibb: Now Voyager
Beast of I.R.S. Volume I, The
Beat of the Live Drum, The
Berlin
Best of Elvis Costello and the Attractions, The
Bizarre Music Television
Blancmange
Blondie Live
Blotto
Body Music
Bon Jovi: Breakout
Brother Where You Bound—Supertramp
Bryan Adams, Reckless
Cameo
Carpenters, Yesterday Once More, The
Chartbusters from Kids Incorporated
Cheech and Chong: Get Out of My Room
Chess Moves
Clash—This Is Video Clash, The
Come Dancing with the Kinks
Comedy Music Videos
Compleat Al, The
Country Comes Alive
Danspak
Daryl Hall and John Oates Video Collection: 7
    Big Ones
Deja View
Dennis De Young—Three Piece Suite
Digital Dreams
Do They Know It's Christmas?
Donnie Iris and the Cruisers
Don't Watch That, Watch This!
Doors, Dance on Fire, The
DTV—Golden Oldies
DTV—Love Songs
DTV—Pop and Rock
DTV—Rock, Rhythm and Blues
Falco: Rock Me Falco
Fantastic All-Electric Music Movie, The
Fat Boys on Video: Brr, Watch 'Em!
Find A Way—Amy Grant
Frankies Goes to Hollywood—From A
    Wasteland to an Artificial Paradise
Gap Band Video Train
Girls of Rock & Roll
Golden Earring
Golden Earring: Live from the Twilight Zone

Grace Jones—State of Grace
Greenpeace Non-Toxic Video Hits
Groovin for a 60's Afternoon
GTR—The Making of GTR
Hardcore Volume I
Hardcore Volume II
Heartbeat City
Hot Rock Videos Volume 2
Hot Rock Videos Volume I
Howard Jones: Like to Get to Know You Well
Huey Lewis and the News Video Hits
Jam, The
Jam Video Snap! The
Jazzin' for Blue Jean
Jermaine Jackson—Dynamite Videos
John Cougar Mellencamp—Ain't That America
Judas Priest: Fuel for Life
Judas Priest Live
Katrina and the Waves
Krokus: The Video Blitz
Live at Target
Loverboy-Any Way You Look At It
Malcolm McLaren—Duck Rock
Men at Work Live in San Francisco or Was It
    Berkeley?
Michael Stanley Band
Minor Detail
Missing Persons
Mr. Mister: Videos from the Real World
Music Video From "Streets of Fire"
Olivia-Soul Kiss
Pat Benatar Hit Videos
Pat Travers in "Just Another Killer Day"
Paul Dresher: Was Are/Will Be
Personal Property
Phantom Empire, The
Pink Floyd's David Gilmour
Prime Cuts—Red Hots
Queen The Works
Raccoons—Let's Dance, The
Ray Davies' Return to Waterloo
Red Hot Rock
Reggae Sunsplash I, II
Rick Springfield Platinum Videos
Robert Palmer—Riptide
Ronnie Milsap—Golden Video Hits
Rush—Through the Camera Eye
Sade: Diamond Life Video
Scorpians
Sing Blue Silver
Siouxsie and the Banshees
Starship: Video Hoopla
Stevie Nicks—I Can't Wait
Stray Cats
Sun City
Talk Talk
Tears for Fears
Tears for Fears: In My Mind's Eye
Television Parts Home Companion
Tina Turner Private Dancer
Toxic Reasons

Doctor Doolittle
Doll Face
Double Trouble
Dynamite Chicken
Easter Parade
Easy Come, Easy Go
Electric Boogaloo, Breakin' 2
Eubie!
Evergreen
Fabulous Dorseys, The
Fast Forward
Feel the Motion
Fiddler on the Roof
Fiesta
Finian's Rainbow
Flower Drum Song
Flying Down To Rio
Follow the Fleet
Footlight Parade
42nd Street
Fred Astaire: Change Partners and Dance
Fred Astaire: Puttin' on His Top Hat
Fun and Fancy Free
Fun in Acapulco
Funny Face
Gaiety
Gay Divorcee, The
George White's Scandals
Get Crazy
G. I. Blues
Gigi
Girl Can't Help It, The
Girl Crazy
Girls, Girls, Girls
Girls Just Want to Have Fun
Give My Regards to Broad Street
Glenn Miller Story, The
Glorifying the American Girl
Go, Johnny Go!
Gold Diggers of 1933
Goldwyn Follies, The
Good News
Gotta Dance, Gotta Sing
Grease
Grease 2
Great Caruso, The
Greek Street
Guys and Dolls
Gypsy
Hair
Hans Brinker
Hans Christian Andersen
Happiest Millionaire, The
Hard Day's Night, A
Heidi's Song
Hello, Dolly!
High Society
Higher and Higher
Hillbillys in a Haunted House
Hips, Hips, Hooray
Holiday Inn

Horsemasters, The
Huckleberry Finn
I Do! I Do!
I Dream Too Much
If You Knew Susie
Imagine: John Lennon
In the Good Old Summertime
Invitation to the Dance
It Happened at the World's Fair
Jack and the Beanstalk
Jive Junction
Joey
Jubilee
Kid from Brooklyn, The
King and I, The
King of Jazz, The
Kismet
Kiss Me Kate
Krush Groove
Lady Sings the Blues
Lassie from Lancashire
Les Girls
Let It Be
Liberace Show Volumes 1 & 2, The
Li'l Abner
Lili
Little Johnny Jones
Little Kid's Dynamite All-Star Band, The
Little Match Girl, The
Little Night Music, A
Little Prince, The
Littlest Angel, The
Loving You
Magical Mystery Tour
Main Street to Broadway
Mame
Man from Music Mountain, The
Man of La Mancha
Manhattan Merry-Go-Round
Marvelous Land of Oz, The
Mary Poppins
Matter of Time, A
Maytime
Meet Me in St. Louis
Meet the Navy
Melody Ranch
Melody Trail
Menudo—La Pelicula
Million, Le
Mrs. Brown, You've Got a Lovely Daughter
Motown Time Capsule: The 60's
Motown Time Capsule: The 70's
Motown's Mustang
Muppets Take Manhattan, The
Music Shoppe, The
Musica Proibita
Musical Featurettes
Musical Personalities No. 1
Musicals 1: Trailers on Tape
Musicals II: Trailers on Tape
My Fair Lady

Mystery in Swing
New York, New York
Night and Day
Night They Raided Minsky's, The
Oh! Calcutta!
Oklahoma!
Old Curiosity Shop, The
On a Clear Day You Can See Forever
On the Town
One and Only, Genuine, Original Family Band, The
One and Only Genuine Original Family Band, The
One from the Heart
One Touch of Venus
Orphan Boy of Vienna, An
Paint Your Wagon
Paradise, Hawaiian Style
Pennies from Heaven
Perils of Pauline, The
Pinocchio
Pippin
Pirate, The
Pirate Movie, The
Pirates of Penzance, The
Popeye
Pot O' Gold
Prairie Moon
Private Buckaroo
Rappin'
Reet, Petite and Gone
Road to Nashville
Robinhood of Texas
Rock Baby Rock It
Rock 'n' Roll High School
Rock, Rock, Rock
Romie-O and Julie-8
Roaslie
Rose, The
Rose Marie
Royal Wedding
Scooby Goes Hollywood
Scrooge's Rock 'n' Roll Christmas
Second Chorus
Sergeant Pepper's Lonely Hearts Club Band
Seven Brides for Seven Brothers
1776
Sextette
Shall We Dance
Shinbone Alley
Show Business
Silk Stockings
Sing Your Worries Away
Singin' in the Rain
Sioux City Sue
Something to Sing About
Song of Norway
South Pacific
Speedway
Stagedoor Canteen
Star Is Born, A

Star Struck
Stars on Parade/Boogie Woogie Dream
Step Lively
Story of Vernon and Irene Castle, The
Strike Up The Band
Sweeney Todd—The Demon Barber of Fleet Street
Sweet Dreams
Swing Time
Take It Big
Take It Big
Taking My Turn
Terror of Tiny Town
Thank God It's Friday
That'll Be the Day
That's Dancing!
That's Entertainment
That's Entertainment, Part II
That's Singing
There's No Business Like Show Business
This Is Elvis
This Is Spinal Tap
Thoroughly Modern Millie
Three Penny Opera
Till the Clouds Roll By
Times Square
Tom Sawyer
Tommy
Top Hat
Tubby the Tuba
Two Gun Troubador
200 Motels
Two Tickets to Broadway
Unsinkable Molly Brown, The
Vagabond Lover
Vitaphone Musical Shorts
Viva Las Vegas
Water Babies, The
West Side Story
White Christmas
Willy Wonka and the Chocolate Factory
Wiz, The
Wizard of Oz, The
Woodstock
Words and Music
Xanadu
Yes, Giorgio
You Were Never Lovelier
You'll Find Out
You'll Never Get Rich
Young Bing Crosby
Ziegfeld Follies
Zis Boom Bah

Musical-Drama

All That Jazz
Almost Angels
Blame It on the Night
Body Rock
Bongo Man

Mystery

Detective, The
Devil Bat's Daughter
Devil Thumbs a Ride/Having Wonderful Crime
Diabolique
Dick Tracy Double Feature #2
Dick Tracy vs. Cueball
Dick Tracy's Dilemma
Dr. Mabuse vs. Scotland Yard
Doomed to Die
Double Face
Dressed to Kill
Drowning Pool, The
Early Frost
Endless Night
Equus
Escapade in Florence
Evil Under the Sun
Ex-Mrs. Bradford, The
Executioner, The
Eyes of Laura Mars
Falcon in Mexico, The
Falcon Takes Over, The/Strange Bargain
Falcon's Adventure, The/Armored Car Robbery
Falcon's Brother, The
Farewell, My Lovely
Fearless
Fifth Floor, The
Finessing the King
4th Man, The
Frankenstein Island
Funeral in Berlin
Gangbusters
Gaslight
Ghost Ship
Ghosts on the Loose
Gorky Park
Green Archer, The
Hammett
Hardy Boys, The
Harper
Haunting of Harrington House, The
He Walked by Night
Hound of the Baskervilles, The
House of Long Shadows, The
House of Lurking Death, The
House That Vanished, The
Human Monster, The
Hunt the Man Down
Hunt the Man Down/Smashing the Rackets
Hustle
I Confess
I'd Give My Life
Initiation of Sarah, The
Internecine Project, The
Investigation
It Could Happen to You
Jagged Edge
Johnny Angel
Journey Into Fear
Juggernaut
Kennel Murder Case

Killer Elite, The
Killer Likes Candy
Killing 'em Softly
Killing Stone
Lady From Shanghai, The
Lady of Burlesque
Lady Scarface
Lady Vanishes, The
Lady Vanishes, The
Late Show, The
Laura
LCA Presents Family Entertainment Playhouse
Libro de Piedra, El
List of Adrian Messenger, The
Lost Jungle, The
M
Mad Miss Manton, The
Malibu Express
Maltese Falcon, The
Man in the Mist, The
Man Who Haunted Himself, The
Man Who Knew Too Much, The
Man Who Knew Too Much, The
Margin for Murder
Master Touch, The
Meeting at Midnight
Midnight
Mine Own Executioner
Mirror Crack'd, The
Mirrors
Mr. Moto's Last Warning
Mr. Wong, Detective
Money Hunt
Murder
Murder at the Baskervilles
Murder by Decree
Murder by Natural Causes
Murder by Television
Murder My Sweet
Murder on the Orient Express
Murder Once Removed
Murder: Ultimate Grounds for Divorce
Murderer's Row
Murri Affair
Mysterious Mr. Wong
Mystery and Espionage
Mystery at Castle House
Mystery in Swing
Mystery Mansion
Mystery of the Mary Celeste, The
Mystery Theatre
Naked Face, The
Nancy Drew
Night Moves
Number Seventeen
One Frightened Night
One of My Wives Is Missing
Ordeal by Innocence
Pandora's Box
Paris Express
Parker

Nightclub

Nuclear energy

Search for the Super

Nuclear warfare

Birth of the Bomb
Day After, The
War Game, The

Nutrition

Beautiful! The Total Look
Great American Diet and Nutrition Test, The
Weight Watchers Magazine Guide to a Healthy
    Lifestyle
Weight Watchers Magazine Guide to Dining and
    Cooking

Occult sciences

Amazing World of Psychic Phenomena, The
Beyond Belief
Force Beyond, The
Haunting Passion, The
Man Who Saw Tomorrow, The
Star Signs '86
Truth About UFO's & ET's, The
Unknown Powers
Your Personal Guide to Love, Money and
    Fitness

Occupations

Change Your Job to Change Your Life
Where Dreams Come True

Oceanography

Cousteau—Diving for Roman Plunder
Scuba
Sea Around Us, The

Oil industry

Louisiana Story

Opera

Abduction from the Seraglio, The
Adriana Lecouvreur
Aida
Aida
Arabella
Ballo in Maschera, Un
Boheme, La
Boheme, La
Boris Godunov
Carmen
Cenerentola, La
Cenerentola (Cinderella)
Centennial Gala
Cinderella Ballet
Cosi Fan Tutte

Dialogues of the Carmelites
Don Carlo
Elixir of Love
Ernani
Fairy Tale of Tsar Saltan, The
Falstaff
Fanciulla Del West, La
Fledermaus, Die
Fledermaus, Volume I, Die
Fledermaus Volume II, Die
Gloriana
Gondoliers, The
Gran Scena Opera Company, La
H.M.S. Pinafore
I Dream Too Much
I Lombardi
Idomeneo
Idomeneo
Il Trovatore
L'Incoronazione Di Poppea
Joan Sutherland in Concert
Julius Caesar
Julius Caesar
Live From the Met Highlights Volume 1
Lucia Di Lammermoor
Lucia di Lammermoor
Magic Flute, The
Magic Flute, The
Magic Flute, The
Mary Stuart
Medium, The
Nicolai Ghiaurov: Tribute to the Great Basso
Opera Cameos
Otello
Otello
Pagliacci
Pagliacci
Pavarotti in London
Peter Grimes
Rigoletto
Rigoletto
RosenKavalier, Der
Ruddigore
Samson et Dalila
Tales of Hoffmann, The
Tannhauser
Tosca
Tosca
Tosca's Kiss
Traviata, La
Troyens, Les
Turandot
Turandot
Yeomen of the Guard, The

Outtakes and bloopers

Best of Candid Camera, Vol. II
Big Breakdowns—Hollywood Bloopers of the
    1930's, The
Bloopers from Star Trek and Laugh-In

Physics

Plants

Police

Politics and government-US

Poverty

Pregnancy

Presidency-US

Prisons

Propaganda

Prostitution

Psychology

You Can Win: Negotiating For Power, Love and Money

Public affairs

In the King of Prussia

Puppets

Carnival of the Animals
Gigglesnort Hotel
Have I Got a Story For You
Madame in Manhattan
Nutcracker, The
Peter and the Wolf
Puppet Musical Classics Collection
Thunderbirds Are Go
Willy McBean and His Magic Machine

Rape

Rape! A Crime of Violence

Religion

Behold the Man!
Blasphemer, The
Gospel Road, The
Greatest Heroes of the Bible
Hear O Israel
Hellfire
Holocaust: Susan Sontag
Holy Land and Holy City
In Search of Historic Jesus
Jesus
Life Is Worth Living
Moses
Music and the Spoken Word
Noah-The Deluge
Pope John Paul II Visits America
Sermon on the Mount, The
Visions of Faith

Reproduction

Reproduction of Life: Sex Education

Romance

Adventures of Don Juan
Al Ponerse el Sol
Almost Perfect Affair, An
Almost You
And Now My Love
Awakening of Cassie, The
Bayou Romance
Beau Mariage, Le
Beauty and the Beast
Best Legs in the 8th Grade
Bird of Paradise
Blood and Sand
Bolero

Change of Seasons, A
Chapter Two
Choose Me
Continental Divide
Day the Loving Stopped, The
Different Story, A
Diva
Donovan's Reef
East of Borneo
Edith and Marcel
Elvira Madigan
Escape to Love
Falling in Love Again
Far Pavilions, The
First Love
Five Days One Summer
Foolin' Around
Fools
For the Love of Angela
French Lesson
French Postcards
Full Moon in Paris
Gamble on Love
Gemini Affair
Goodbye, New York
Green Dolphin Street
Happy New Year
High Heels
History Is Made at Night
Hysteria
I Love All of You
I'm A Fool
Image of Passion
In Love With An Older Woman
Indiscretion of an American Wife
Intermezzo
Isabel's Choice
Isle of Secret Passion
Italian Straw Hat, The
Jules et Jim
Jupiter's Thigh
Just Me and You
Key Exchange
Kipperbang
Lady Takes a Chance
Laura
Legacy for Leonette, A
Lights, Camera, Action, Love
Little Minister, The
Little Night Music, A
Lonely Hearts
Love at the Top
Love in the City
Love in the Present Tense
Love Letters
Lovers and Liars
Madame Bovary
Man in Grey, The
Man Who Loved Women, The
Matter of Time, A
Model Behavior

My Dear Secretary
No Small Affair
Nothing Personal
Ode to Billy Joe
Oliver's Story
On a Clear Day You Can See Forever
Panama Lady
Paradise
Passion of Love
Port of Call
Reaching for the Moon
Rebel Love
Reckless
Return Engagement
Rich Kids
Roman Holiday
Romancing the Stone
Romantic Englishwoman, The
Roof, The
Roaslie
Royal Bed, The
Running Hot
Rush It
Ryan's Daughter
Sahara
Sandpiper, The
Sandstone
Sea Devils
Sergeant Sullivan Speaking
Simple Truth, The
Solo
Some Call It Loving
Somewhere in Time
Somewhere Tomorrow
Son of the Sheik
Sound of Love
Starman
Sterile Cuckoo, The
Story of a Love Story
Street Music
Summertime
Tender Loving Care
That Touch of Mink
Thief of Hearts
Those Endearing Young Charms
Together
Torn Between Two Lovers
Trouble in Mind
Tulips
Two English Girls
Under the Roofs of Paris (Sous les Toits de Paris)
Until September
Way We Were, The
Weather in the Streets
Windom's Way
Wuthering Heights
Young Lady Chattorly II

Running

Frank Shorter's Run
Jim Fixx on Running
Jog/Run
Jogging with Marty Liquori
Marathon   Fever/Marathon
    Symphony/Winners/Losers

Safety education

Baby—Safe Home, The
Boating: Cold Water Survivial
Home Safe Home—The Essential Guide to Keeping Your Home Safe
Lisa Sliwa's Common Sense Defense
Strong Kids, Safe Kids
Too Smart for Strangers
Total Self-Defense

Sales training

One Minute Sales Person and the Future of Sales, The

Satire

A Nous La Liberte
Alice in Wonderland
Alligator
Animal Farm
Anna Russell: The (First) Farewell Concert
Atomic Cafe, The
Bloodbath at the House of Death
Bullshot Crummond
Candidate, The
Carry On Cleo
Catch-22
Charlie Chan and the Curse of the Dragon Queen
Committee, The
Compleat Al, The
Creature from the Haunted Sea
Discreet Charm of the Bourgeoisie, The
Doonesbury Special, A
Dracula and Son
Dracula Sucks
Dracula—Up in Harlem
Eat or Be Eaten
Eraserhead
Fairytales
Flesh Gordon
Footlight Frenzy
Getting Straight
Going Berserk
Great Dictator, The
Groove Tube, The
Hail
Hardware Wars and Other Film Farces
Hey Good Lookin'
Home Movies
Horror of Frankenstein

How I Won the War
I Love You
I Want What I Want
Joke of Destiny, A
King in New York, A
King of Hearts
Little Big Man
Mad Mission 3
Martin Mull Presents the History of White People
  in America
Mary Hartman, Mary Hartman Volume I
Millhouse: A White Comedy
Mouse That Roared, The
My Breakfast with Blassie
Nocturna
Not for Publication
Pink Angels, The
Pink Flamingos
Polyester
Pray TV
Prize of Peril, The
Real Life
Ribald Tales of Robin Hood, The
Ruling Class, The
School for Scandal
Scrambled Feet
Sex Shop, Le
Shmenges: The Last Polka, The
Stand-In
Strange Invaders
Student Bodies
Stunt Man, The
Television Parts Home Companion
There's Naked Bodies On My T.V.!
This Is Spinal Tap
Thorn, The
Top Secret
Tunnelvision
Welcome to L.A.

Science

Building Blocks of Life, The
Expansion of Life, The
Language in Life
Mr. Wizard's World: Puzzles, Problems and
  Impossibilities
Origin of Life, The (Plus Scopes Trial Footage)
Universe, The
Watch Mr. Wizard

Science fiction

Adventures of Buckaroo Banzai, The
Adventures of Captain Future Volume 1, The
Adventures of Captain Future Volume 2, The
After the Fall of New York
Aftermath
Alien
Alien Factor, The
Alien Warrior

Aliens from Spaceship Earth
Alpha Incident, The
Altered States
Android
Andromeda Strain, The
At the Earth's Core
Atomic Submarine
Aurora Encounter
Bamboo Saucer
Battle Beneath the Earth
Battle Beyond the Stars
Battle for the Planet of the Apes
Battlestar Galactica
Battlestar Galactica
Beneath the Planet of the Apes
Black Hole, The
Blade Runner
Blob, The
Bog
Boy and His Dog, A
Brain From Planet Arous, The
Brain 17
Brain That Wouldn't Die, The
Brainwaves
Brainstorm
Brother from Another Planet, The
Buck Rogers Conquers the Universe
Buck Rogers in the 25th Century
Buck Rogers in the 25th Century
Buck Rogers: Planet Outlaws
Bug
Capricorn One
Captain Future in Space
Captain Harlock
Captain Kronos: Vampire Hunter
Captain Scarlet Vs. The Mysterons
Captive Planet
Cat Women of the Moon
C.H.U.D.
Cinemagic
City Limits
Clockwork Orange, A
Clones, The
Clonus Horror, The
Close Encounters of the Third Kind (The Special
  Edition)
Cocoon
Conquest of the Planet of the Apes
Cosmic Monsters
Countdown
Crawling Eye, The
Crawling Hand, The
Creation of the Humanoids
Creature
Creepers
Dagora, the Space Monster
Damnation Alley
Danguard Ace
Dark Star
Dark Star—The Special Edition
D.A.R.Y.L.

Seasons

Serials

Sports-Water

Adventures in Paradise
Endless Summer, The
I Crave the Waves
Island Magic
Learn to Sail
Radical Surfers
Scuba Run
Surf's Up
Swim Baby Swim
Whitewater

Sports-Winter

Alpine Ski School
American Haute—Skiing The High Country Huts
Backcountry Skiing—Telemarking in the 80's
High Route Adventure/Skiing Across the French
    Alps
If You Can Walk/Free and Easy/Race Day
Introduction to Alpine Skiing, An
Marathon   Fever/Marathon
    Symphony/Winners/Losers
Miracle of Lake Placid: Highlights of the 1980
    Winter Olympics, The
Mountain Silence—A Special Adventure For the
    Deaf
Mountain Time—A Sawtooth Odyssey
1984 Winter Olympics Highlights
Powder Hound/Return of Powder Hound
Ski
Ski Champions—The Winners
Ski Country
Ski Time
SnoWonder
Torvill & Dean: Path to Perfection

States-US

Alaskan Safari
Hawaii Revisited
Hawaii the 50th State

Stress

Hypnovision Stress Reduction

Suicide

Last Cry for Help

Suspense

Alice Sweet Alice
Amazing Mr. Blunden, The
And Soon the Darkness
Anderson Tapes, The
Ants
Are You in the House Alone?
Avalanche
Baby, The

B.A.D. Cats
Baffled
Barcelona Kill, The
Big Sleep, The
Black Magic Terror
Black Panther, The
Blackout
Blood on the Sun
Blood Simple
Blow Out
Body Double
Body Heat
Boston Strangler, The
Brannigan
Bushido Blade, The
Case of the Missing Lady, The
Catamount Killing, The
Catch Me a Spy
Cat's Eye
Centerfold Girls, The
Chain Reaction, The
Chase, The
Checkmate
Children, The
Chinese Boxes
Christina
Christine
City on Fire
Cloak and Dagger
Cold Room, The
Coma
Confessional, The
Confidentially Yours
Cornered
Cross Country
Cruise Into Terror
Cruise Missile
Curse of King Tut's Tomb, The
Custodio de Senoras
Dain Curse, The
Danger
Dangerous Summer, A
Dark Forces
Dark of the Night
Dark Room, The
Day of the Jackal, The
Dead Easy
Dead of Night
Dead Zone, The
Deadline
Deadly Force
Deadly Game, The
Deadly Impact
Deadly Intrigue
Death Games
Death Machines
Death Rage
Death Sentence
Death Weekend
Deathtrap
Deep, The

Monique
Mortuary
Most Dangerous Game, The
Mother's Day
Ms. 45
Murder Motel
Murder: Ultimate Grounds for Divorce
Mystery and Espionage
Nancy Drew
Never Say Never Again
Next Victim, The
Night Moves
Night of the Assassin
Night of the Juggler
Night Visitor, The
Nightcomers, The
Nighthawks
Nightkill
Nightwing
No Way to Treat a Lady
North by Northwest
Notorious
Oblong Box, The
Obsession
Octagon, The
Odessa File, The
Oil
One Shoe Makes It Murder
Operation Amsterdam
Osterman Weekend, The
Out of Order
Out of the Past
Parallax View, The
Paranoia
Patrick
Pepper
Perfect Strangers
Pervertion (Perversion)
Plumber, The
Power Play
President's Mistress, The
Psychic Killer
Psycho
Psycho II
Puppet on a Chain
Race with the Devil
Rage
Rattlers
Rear Window
Red House, The
Reincarnation of Peter Proud, The
Return of Chandu, The
Return of Frank Cannon
Return to Boggy Creek
Revenge
Rider on the Rain
Road Games
Roaring Fire
Run, Stranger, Run
Sabotage
Saboteur

Saint Strikes Back, The/Criminal Court
Scalpel
Scream
Scream Bloody Murder
Seasons for Assassins
Second Chance
Secret Agent
She Waits
Sherlock Holmes and a Study in Scarlet
Sherlock Holmes and the Valley of Fear
She's Dressed to Kill
Shogun's Ninja
Sidney Sheldon's Bloodline
Sisters of Death
Slayground
Sleuth
Someone Behind the Door
Sorry, Wrong Number
Special Delivery
Sphinx
Sputnik
Stick
Still of the Night
Strange Shadows in an Empty Room
Strangers on a Train
Survivor, The
Suspense
Suspicion
Swiss Conspiracy, The
Taking of Pelham One Two Three, The
Tarantulas: The Deadly Cargo
Target
Tattered Web, A
Telefon
Terminal Choice
Terror on the 40th Floor
Terror Out of the Sky
They Came From Within
They Won't Believe Me
They're Playing with Fire
Thief
Thief, The
Thirty-Nine Steps, The
This Is a Hijack
This Man Must Die
Tightrope
To Catch a King
To Kill a Clown
To Kill a Stranger
Tomorrow at Seven
Too Scared To Scream
Topaz
Torn Curtain
Town Called Hell, A
Town That Dreaded Sundown, The
Tracks
Train Killer, The
Treasure of the Four Crowns
Trilogy of Terror
Twilight's Last Gleaming
Two by Forsyth

USSR

From the Czar to Stalin
Kremlin, The
When I Think of Russia

Variety

All the Best from Russia
Arf!
Bob Hope Chevy Show I, The
Bob Hope Chevy Show II, The
Bottoms Up '81
Caesar's Hour
Caesar's Hour
Captain Kangaroo's Fairy Tales and Funny
   Stories
Captain Kangaroo's Merry Christmas Stories
Catch a Rising Star's 10th Anniversary
Cavalcade of Stars
Children's Songs and Stories with the Muppets
Colgate Comedy Hour, The
Colgate Comedy Hour I, The
Colgate Comedy Hour, The
Colgate Comedy Hour (The Eddie Cantor Show)
Comedy and Kid Stuff, IV
Comedy in Music
Country Music with the Muppets
Country-Western All-Stars
Cycling Through China
Dean Martin and Jerry Lewis Television Party for
   Muscular Dystrophy
Debbie Does Las Vegas
Dr. Misterio's "Patented" Video Almanac of Fun
Ed Wynn Show, The
Ed Wynn Show, The
Famous T and A
Faye Emerson Show, The
Female Impersonator Pageant, The
Fozzie's Muppet Scrapbook
Frankie Laine Show with Connie Haines
General Electric Theatre, The
Girls of Rock & Roll
Girls of the Moulin Rouge
Goldie And Kids
Gonzo Presents Muppet Weird Stuff
Great British Striptease
Great Space Coaster, The
Here It Is, Burlesque
Hollywood Home Movies
Hollywood on Parade
Hollywood Revels
If You Don't Stop It...You'll Go Blind
Invitation to Paris
Jack Benny
Jack Benny Program, The
Jazz Ball
Johnny Carson Show, The
Jonathan Winters Show, The
Jonathan Winters Show, The/Presenting Morey
   Amsterdam

Judy Garland Christmas Show
Judy Garland (General Electric Theatre)
Kermit and Piggy Story, The
Kids Incorporated: The Beginning
Kraft Music Hall Presents "Alan King Stops the
   Press"
Liberace Show Volumes 1 & 2, The
Lily Tomlin Special: Volume I
Major Bowes' Original Amateur Hour
Martha Raye Show, The
Mickey Mouse Club, Volumes 1 thru 15, The
Milton Berle Show II, The
Milton Berle Show, The
Milton Berle Show, The
Miss Nude America Contest, The
Motown 25: Yesterday, Today, Forever
Muppets Moments
Muppet Revue, The
Muppet Treasures
NBC Comedy Hour
NBC Comedy Hour
Network Fall Preview Presentations
New Look
New Zoo Revue
Paul Simon Special, The
Penthouse Love Stories
Penthouse Video Volume One: The Girls of
   Penthouse
Pinwheel Songbook, The
Playboy Video Centerfold
Playboy Video Magazine, Volumes 1-7
Playboy Video Magazine, Volumes 8-9
Playgirl on the Air
Playmate Playoffs
Playmate Review
Playmate Review #3
Puppet Playhouse Presents Howdy Doody
Robert Youngson Specials
Rock Music with the Muppets
Rowlf's Rhapsodies with the Muppets
Saturday Night Live: Eric Idle Vol I
Saturday Night Live: Buck Henry
Saturday Night Live: Charles Grodin
Saturday Night Live: Elliott Gould
Saturday Night Live: Eric Idle Vol. II
Saturday Night Live: Gary Busey
Saturday Night Live: George Carlin
Saturday Night Live: Lily Tomlin
Saturday Night Live: Madeline Kahn
Saturday Night Live: Michael Palin
Saturday Night Live: Peter Cook & Dudley Moore
Saturday Night Live: Ray Charles
Saturday Night Live: Richard Benjamin
Saturday Night Live: Robert Klein
Saturday Night Live: Rodney Dangerfield
Saturday Night Live: Sissy Spacek
Saturday Night Live, Vol. II
Saturday Night Live, Vol. I
Saturday Night Live with Richard Pryor
Saturday Night Live with Steve Martin
Sheena Easton: Act One

Venereal diseases

Video

Vietnam War

Volcanoes

War-Drama

Dam Busters, The
Day and the Hour, The
Deadly Mission
Deep Six, The
Desert Fox, The
Desert Tigers (Los Tigres del Desierto), The
Dirty Dozen, The
Double Agents
Drums in the Deep South
Eagle Has Landed, The
Eagles Attack at Dawn
Enola Gay
Fighting Marines, The
Fighting Seabees, The
First Yank Into Tokyo
Flat Top
Flying Leathernecks
Flying Tigers
Force 10 from Navarone
Forty Thousand Horsemen
Four in a Jeep
From Hell to Victory
Gift Horse, The
Go Tell the Spartans
Grand Illusion
Green Berets, The
Gung Ho
Guns of War
Hell Commandos
Hellcats of the Navy
Hiding Place, The
Home of the Brave
Hunters of the Golden Cobra
Hustler Squad
Ill Met by Moonlight
Immortal Battalion
In Which We Serve
Indecent Obsession, An
Invasion U.S.A.
Jungle Patrol
King Rat
Last Day of the War
Last Winter, The
Legion of Missing Men, The
Liberators, The
Life and Death of Colonel Blimp, The
Lion Has Wings, The
Longest Day, The
MacArthur
Malta Story
Massacre in Rome
Mata Hari
Men in War
Mercenary Game, The
Midway
Missing in Action 2: The Beginning
Mission Batangas
No Substitute for Victory
North Star, The
Odd Angry Shot

One of Our Aircraft Is Missing
Only Way, The
Operation Amsterdam
Operation Thunderbolt
Paisan
Passage to Marseilles
Paths of Glory
Patton
Place in Hell, A
PT 109
Purple Hearts
Raid on Entebbe
Raid on Rommel
Return of the Soldier
Revolution
Run Silent, Run Deep
Sahara
Salute John Citizen
Sands of Iwo Jima
Scarlet and the Black, The
Sea Shall Not Have Them, The
Shadow of Chikara
Shark River
Shell Shock
Shout at the Devil
Silent Raiders, The
Sirocco
Soldier of Orange, A
Something of Value
SS Girls
Stopover Tokyo
Streamers
Suicide Patrol
Sundown
They Were Expendable
13 Rue Madeleine
Thirty Seconds Over Tokyo
Thirty Six Hours of Hell
Till the End of Time
To Hell and Back
Tobruk
Tora! Tora! Tora!
Tornado
Torpedo Attack
Treasure of the Lost Desert
Twelve O'Clock High
Von Ryan's Express
Wake Island
Walk in the Sun, A
Walk in the Sun, A
War and Love
War Lover, The
We Dive at Dawn
Westinghouse Studio One: Hold Back the Night
What Price Glory
Where Eagles Dare
White Rose, The
Wings of War (La Patrulla Suicida)
Wooden Horse, The
Yank in Libya, A

Western

Abilene Town
Adios, Hombre
Adventures of the Lone Ranger: Count the
  Clues, The
Alamo, The
Allegheny Uprising
Along Came Jones
Alvarez Kelly
American Empire
And God Said to Cain
Angel and the Badman
Angel and the Badman
Annie Oakley
Apache
Apache Rose
Apple Dumpling Gang, The
Apple Dumpling Gang Rides Again, The
Apple Dumpling Gang Rides Again, The
Far Frontier, The
Arizona Days
Arizona Raiders
Arizona Stagecoach
Asesinos, Los
Bad Company
Badman's Territory
Ballad of a Gunfighter
Ballad of Cable Hogue, The
Bandits, The
Barbarosa
Bells of Rosarita
Bend of the River
Big Cat, The
Big Country, The
Big Show
Big Sky, The
Billy the Kid Returns
Billy the Kid Versus Dracula
Bite the Bullet
Blood for a Silver Dollar
Blood on the Moon
Blue Canadian Rockies
Blue Steel
Boiling Point
Boots and Saddles
Border Romance
Branded Men
Brandy Sheriff
Breakheart Pass
Bronze Buckaroo/Harlem Rides the Range
Brothers O'Toole, The
Buck and the Preacher
Buffalo Bill and the Indians
Bulldog Courage
Bullwhip
Butch and Sundance: The Early Days
Cahill: United States Marshal
Cain's Cutthroats
Call of the Canyon
Captain Apache

Carson City Kid
Cat Ballou
Cattle Queen of Montana
Cheyenne Autumn
Cheyenne Rides Again
Chino
Chisum
Clearing the Range
Colorado
Colt Is My Law (Mi Revolver es la Ley), The
Comancheros, The
Come On, Cowboys
Comes a Horseman
Cotter
Cow Town
Cowboy Counselor
Cowboy Previews #1
Cowboys, The
Cowboys from Texas
Cowboys of the Saturday Matinee
Dakota
Dakota Incident
Dan Candy's Law
Daniel Boone
Dark Command
Davy Crockett and the River Pirates
Davy Crockett, King of the Wild Frontier
Dawn on the Great Divide
Dawn Rider
Dawn Rider/Frontier Horizon
Dead for a Dollar
Death Rides the Plains
Death Rides the Range
Death Valley Days
Death Valley Days, Volume II
Desert Trail
Desperate Women
Devil and Leroy Basset, The
Devil's Playground, The
Django
Django Shoots First
Dodge City
Don Amigo/Stage to Chino
Down Mexico Way
Draw!
Drum Beat
Drum Taps
Duchess and the Dirtwater Fox, The
Dude Bandit, The
Dynamite Pass
Dynamite Ranch
El Dorado
Elfego Baca: Six Gun Law
Eyes of Texas
False Colors
Far Country, The
Fargo Express
Feud of the West
$50,000 Reward
Fightin' Ranch
Fighting Caravans

Man from Utah, The
Man of the Frontier
Man Who Loved Cat Dancing, The
Man Who Shot Liberty Valance, The
Man Without a Star
Manchurian Avenger
Manhunt, The
Man's Land, A
Massacre At Fort Holman
Maverick Queen, The
McCabe and Mrs. Miller
Melody Ranch
Melody Trail
Miracle Rider
Missouri Breaks, The
Mr. Horn
Mohawk
Monte Walsh
My Darling Clementine
My Pal Trigger
Mysterious Desperado
Mysterious Desperado/Rider From Tucson
Mystery Mountain
Naked in the Sun
Narrow Trail, The
'Neath Arizona Skies
'Neath Arizona Skies/Paradise Canyon
Nevada Smith
New Lion of Sonora, The
Night of the Grizzly, The
Night Stage to Galveston
Oklahoma Annie
Oklahoma Kid, The
Old Barn Dance, The
Old Corral, The
On the Old Spanish Trail
On Top of Old Smoky
Once Upon a Time in the West
One-Eyed Jacks
100 Rifles
One Little Indian
Outcast, The
Outlaw, The
Outlaw, The
Outlaw Josey Wales, The
Outlaw Women
Painted Desert, The
Painted Stallion, The
Pale Rider
Paradise Canyon
Passion
Pat Garrett and Billy the Kid
Peter Lundy and the Medicine Hat Stallion
Phantom Empire
Phantom of the West
Phantom Rancher, The
Pioneer Woman
Pony Express
Powdersmoke Range
Prairie Moon
Professionals, The

Proud and Damned, The
Proud Rebel, The
Pursuit
Racketeers of the Range
Raiders of Red Gap
Rancho Notorious
Randy Rides Alone
Randy Rides Alone/Riders of Destiny
Range Law
Rangeland Racket
Ranger and the Lady
Rangers Take Over, The
Rare Breed, The
Rawhide
Red River
Red Sun
Renegade Ranger, The/Scarlet River
Return of Frank James, The
Return of the Bad Men
Ride in the Whirlwind
Ride, Ranger, Ride
Ride the High Country
Ride the Man Down
Ride the Wind
Rider from Tucson
Riders of Death Valley
Riders of Destiny
Riders of the Desert
Riders of the Range
Riders of the Rockies
Riders of the Whistling Pines
Riders of the Whistling Skull
Ridin' on a Rainbow
Riel
Rio Bravo
Rio Grande
Rio Lobo
Roaring Guns
Robinhood of Texas
Robinhood of the Pecos
Rodeo Girl
Roll Along Cowboy
Rolling Plains
Rooster Cogburn
Rootin' Tootin' Rhythm
Rough Riders of Cheyenne
Round-Up Time in Texas
Roy Rogers Matinee Double Feature #3
Roy Rogers Matinee Double Feature #4
Roy Rogers Show, The
Roy Rogers Show II, The
Run of the Arrow
Rustler's Rhapsody
Rustler's Valley
Ruthless Four, The
Saga of Death Valley
Sagebrush Trail
Saginaw Trail
Santa Fe Trail
Santa Fe Trail
Santa Fe Uprising

Wife beating

Wilderness areas

Wildlife

Women

World War I

World War II

Yoga

Zoos

Videodisc Index

This index is divided into two sections: Capacitance Electronic Discs (CED) and Laser Optical Discs (LV). Please refer to the alphabetical program listings in the main body of the Guide to determine the disc source. NOTE: as of June 1986, RCA has ceased manufacture of all CED discs. We continue to list this format as a guide to those titles which may still be acquired through some dealers.

CAPACITANCE ELECTRONIC DISCS

ABC—Mantrap
Absence of Malice
The Absent Minded
  Professor
The Adventures of
  Buckaroo Banzai
The Adventures of
  Robin Hood
Aerobicise: The
  Beautiful Workout
Aerobicise: The
  Beginning
  Workout
Africa Screams
The African Queen
After the Fox
Against All Odds
Agency
Air Force
Airplane!
Airplane II: The
  Sequel
Airport
The Alamo
Alice Doesn't Live
  Here Anymore
Alice in Wonderland
Alice's Restaurant
Alien
All That Jazz
All the Marbles
All the President's
  Men
All the Right Moves
Alone in the Dark
Altered States
The Amateur

The Amazing
  Spiderman
The American
  Alcoholic/
  Reading,
  Writing and
  Reefer
American Gigolo
American Graffiti
American Hot Wax
An American in Paris
An American
  Werewolf in
  London
The Amityville
  Horror
Amityville II: The
  Possession
Amityville 3-D
And God Created
  Woman
. . . And Justice for
  All
Angel of H.E.A.T.
Angel on My
  Shoulder (1980)
Angels with Dirty
  Faces
Animal Crackers
Animal House
Annie
Annie Hall
Any Which Way You
  Can
Apache
The Apartment
Apocalypse Now
The Apple
  Dumpling Gang
Armed Forces
  Workout

Arsenic and Old
  Lace
Arthur
Ashford and
  Simpson
Asia in Asia
Atlantic City
Author! Author!
The Autobiography
  of Miss Jane
  Pittman
Avalanche
Back Roads
Bad Boys
The Bad News
  Bears
The Bad News
  Bears in Breaking
  Training
Baffled
The Baltimore
  Bullet
Bananas
Bandolero
Barbarella
Barbarosa
Barefoot Contessa
Barefoot in the Park
Baseball: Fun and
  Games
Baseball's Hall of
  Fame
Battle Beyond the
  Stars
Battlestar Galactica
The Beach Girls
Beach Party
Beany & Cecil,
  Volumes 1 & 2
The Bears and I

The Beast Within
The Beastmaster
Beat Street
Being There
Bells Are Ringing
Ben Hur
Benji
Best Defense
Best Friends
The Best Little
  Whorehouse in
  Texas
The Best of Popeye
The Best of 60
  Minutes
The Best of
  Terrytoons
Betrayal
The Betsy
The Bette Midler
  Show
Big Bad Mama
Big Blue Marble
The Big Chill
The Big Fights,
  Volumes 1–3
Big Jake
The Big Red One
The Big Sleep
The Billion Dollar
  Hobo
Billy Jack
Billy Joel: Live from
  Long Island
Birdman of Alcatraz
The Birds
The Black Hole
The Black Marble
Black Orpheus
The Black Stallion
The Black Stallion
  Returns
Black Sunday
Blade Runner
Blame It on Rio
Blazing Saddles
Blondie: Eat to the
  Beat
Bloody Mama
Blow Out
Blue Hawaii
The Blue Lagoon
Blue Thunder
Blues Alive
The Blues Brothers
The Boat
Bob Welch &
  Friends
Bobby Jo and the
  Outlaw

Body and Soul
Body Heat
Bolero
Bonnie and Clyde
The Boogey Man
Born Free
Born Losers
The Bostonians
Boxcar Bertha
The Boy Who Left
  Home to Find
  Out About the
  Shivers
The Boys from Brazil
The Boys in the
  Band
The Boys of
  Summer
Brady's Escape
Brainstorm
Breaker Morant
Breakfast at
  Tiffany's
Breakin'
Breaking Away
Breakout
Breathless
Brian's Song
The Bridge on the
  River Kwai
A Bridge Too Far
Brigadoon
Brimstone and
  Treacle
Broadway Danny
  Rose
Bronco Billy
Brubaker
Buddy Buddy
The Bugs Bunny
  Road Runner
  Movie
Bullitt
Bullwinkle Rocky &
  Friends, Vol. 1
Bus Stop
Butch Cassidy and
  the Sundance Kid
Butterfly
Cabaret
Caddyshack
La Cage aux Folles
La Cage aux Folles II
California Suite
Caligula
Candid Candid
  Camera
The Candidate
Candleshoe
Cannery Row

The Cannonball Run
Capricorn One
Captain Blood
Carbon Copy
Caring for Your
  Newborn
Carlin at Carnegie
Carlin on Campus
Carnal Knowledge
Carny
Carole King: One to
  One
Carrie
The Cars: 1984-
  1985—Live
Cartoon Classics
  Volume 1:
  Chip 'n' Dale
  Featuring Donald
  Duck
Cartoon Classics
  Volume 2: Pluto
Cartoon Classics
  Volume 3:
  Disney's Scary
  Tales
Cartoon Classics
  Volume 4:
  Sport Goofy
Casablanca
Cat Ballou
Cat on a Hot Tin
  Roof
Cat People
Catch-22
Caveman
CBS/Fox Guide to
  Complete Dog
  Care
The Challenge
The Champ
A Change of
  Seasons
The Changeling
The Charge of the
  Light Brigade
Chariots of Fire
A Charlie Brown
  Festival I-IV
The Charlie Daniels
  Band: The
  Saratoga Concert
Charlotte's Web
Charly
Chatterbox
Cheech & Chong's
  Nice Dreams
Children of the Corn

The China
  Syndrome
Chinatown
Chitty Chitty Bang
  Bang
A Chorus Line
The Christine McVie
  Concert
Chu Chu and
  the Philly Flash
The Cincinnati Kid
Cinderella
Citizen Kane
City Lights
Clarence Darrow
Clash of the Titans
Class of 1984
Class Reunion
Cleopatra
A Clockwork Orange
Close Encounters of
  the Third Kind
  (The Special
  Edition)
Coal Miner's
  Daughter
The Coca-Cola Kid
Cold River
The Collector
College Football
  Classics, Vol. 1
Coma
Comancheros
Comedy Tonight
Coming Home
The Compleat
  Beatles
Complete Tennis
  from the Pros,
  Vol. 1: Strokes
  and Technique

Conan the
  Barbarian
The Count of Monte
  Cristo
The Country Girl
Cousin Cousine
Crackers
Crazy Mama
Creepshow
Crosby, Stills &
  Nash: Daylight
  Again
Cross Creek
Cruising
Cujo
Cutter's Way
Daffy Duck's Movie:
  Fantastic Island

Damien—Omen II
The Dark Crystal
Dark Victory
David Copperfield
The Day After
A Day at the Races
The Day of the
  Dolphin
Days of Heaven
D.C. Cab
Dead and Buried
The Dead Zone
Deadly Blessing
Deadly Force
Deal of the Century
Death Hunt
Death on the Nile
Death Wish
Death Wish II
Deathstalker
The Deep
The Deer Hunter
Defiance
The Defiant Ones
Deliverance
The Desert of the
  Tartars
Dial "M" for Murder
Diamonds Are
  Forever
Diana Ross in
  Concert
The Diary of Anne
  Frank
Dillinger
Diner
The Dirty Dozen
Dirty Harry
Disney Cartoon
  Parade, Volumes
  1-5
Diva
Divine Madness
Dr. Detroit
Doctor Doolittle
Dr. No
The Dr. Seuss Video
  Festival
Dr. Strangelove
Dr. Zhivago
Dog Day Afternoon
The Dogs of War
A Doll's House
Dolly in London
The Domino
  Principle
Don Kirshner's Rock
  Concert, Vol. 1
Don't Look Now

The Doobie Brothers
  Live
Dot and Santa Claus
Dot and the Bunny
Dot and the
  Kangaroo
Double Exposure
Dracula (1931)
Dragonslayer
Dressed to Kill
  (1980)

The Dresser
Duck Soup
Dumbo
Dunderklumpen
Duran Duran
Earth, Wind and Fire
  in Concert
The Earthling
East of Eden
Easy Money
Easy Rider
Eddie and the
  Cruisers
Eddie Macon's Run
Educating Rita
El Cid
El Dorado
The Electric
  Horseman
Electric Light
  Orchestra: Live at
  Wembly
The Elephant Man
Elephant Parts
Elmer Gantry
Elton John: Visions
Elvis—Aloha from
  Hawaii
Elvis—His 1968
  Comeback
  Special
Elvis on Tour
Emmanuelle in
  America
Emmanuelle in
  Bangkok
Emily
The Emperor's New
  Clothes
The End
Endangered
  Species
Endless Love
The Endless
  Summer
The Enforcer
Enter the Dragon
Enter the Ninja

The Entity
Eroticise
Escape from
  Alcatraz
Escape From New
  York
Escape to Athena
Escape to Witch
  Mountain
Eubie!
Eurythmics—Sweet
  Dreams (The
  Video Album)
An Evening with
  Robin Williams
An Evening with the
  Royal Ballet
Every Which Way
  But Loose
Everything You
  Always Wanted
  To Know About
  Sex . . .
Evil Under the Sun
Evilspeak
Excalibur
The Exorcist
Exposed
The Exterminator
An Eye for an Eye
The Eyes of Laura
  Mars
Eyewitness
Faerie Tale Theater
Fairy Tale Classics
Falcon and the
  Snowman
Falling in Love Again
Fame
Family Entertainment
  Playhouse, Vol. 2
Fanny and
  Alexander
Fantastic Voyage
Fast Times at
  Ridgemont High
Fear No Evil
Fiddler on the Roof
Final Assignment
The Final Conflict
The Final
  Countdown
Final Exam
Final Justice
Firebird 2015 AD
Firefox

The Firesign
  Theater Presents
  Nick Danger in
  The Case of the
  Missing Yolk
The First Barry
  Manilow Special
First Blood
F.I.S.T.
A Fistful of Dollars
Five Mile Creek,
  Volume 1
Flaming Star
The Flamingo Kid
Flashdance
Fleetwood Mac
Fleetwood Mac in
  Concert
  —Mirage Tour
  1982
The Flying Deuces
The Fog
Foolin' Around
Footloose
For A Few Dollars
  More
For Your Eyes Only
Forbidden Planet
Forced Vengeance
Foreplay
The Formula
Fort Apache, The
  Bronx
48 Hours
42nd Street
Foul Play
Four Friends
The Four
  Musketeers
The Four Seasons
Fraggle Songs,
  Volume 1
Frances
Frankenstein (1931)
The French
  Connection
The French
  Lieutenant's
  Woman
Friday the 13th
Friday the 13th, Part
  II
Friendly Persuasion
Frogs
From Russia with
  Love
The Fugitive: The
  Final Episode
Fun in Acapulco
Funny Girl

A Funny Thing
  Happened on the
  Way to the Forum
Futureworld
Fuzz
Gallagher—Stuck in
  the 60's
Gallagher—The
  Maddest
Game of Death
Gandhi
Gas Pump Girls
The Gauntlet
Gentleman Jim
Get Crazy
The Getting of
  Wisdom
G.I. Blues
Gigi
Gilda
Gimme Shelter
Girl Groups: The
  Story of a Sound
Giselle
Go Tell the Spartans
The Godfather
The Godfather, Part
  II
Godzilla
Going Berserk
Gold Diggers of
  1933
The Golden Seal
Goldfinger
Goldilocks
Goldy—The Last of
  the Golden Bears
Gone With the Wind
Good Guys Wear
  Black
The Good, the Bad,
  and the Ugly
Goodbye, Columbus
The Goodbye Girl
Goodbye New York
Grace Jones: One
  Man Show
The Graduate
The Grateful Dead in
  Concert
Grease
Grease II
The Great Caruso
Great Cities:
  London, Rome,
  Dublin, Athens
The Great Dictator
The Great Escape
Great Figures in
  History: John F.
  Kennedy

The Great Gatsby
The Great
    Locomotive
    Chase
Great Movie Stunts
    and the Making of
    Raiders of the
    Lost Ark
The Great Muppet
    Caper
The Great Santini
The Great Scout and
    Cathouse
    Thursday
The Great Space
    Coaster
    Supershow
The Great Train
    Robbery
The Greatest
    Adventure
Greatest Fights of
    the 70's
The Greatest Show
    on Earth
The Green Berets
Greystoke: The
    Legend of Tarzan,
    Lord of the Apes
Grover Washington
    Jr. in Concert
Gulliver's Travels
A Gumby Adventure

Gunfight at the O.K
    Corral
The Guns of
    Navarone
Gus
Guys and Dolls
Hair
Halloween II
Halloween III: The
    Season of the
    Witch
Hamlet
Hang 'Em High
Hanky Panky
Hansel and Gretel
The Happy Hooker
The Happy Hooker
    Goes to
    Washington
Hard Country
A Hard Day's Night
Hard to Hold
The Harder They
    Come
Harold and Maude
Harper Valley PTA
Harry and Son

Harry Chapin: The
    Final Concert
Hawaii
He Knows You're
    Alone
He-Man and the
    Masters of the
    Universe
Heart Like a Wheel
Heartaches
Heaven Can Wait
Heaven's Gate
Heidi
Hello, Dolly!
Helter Skelter
Henry V
Herbie Hancock and
    the Rockit Band
Herbie Rides Again
Hercules
Hercules Unchained
Here It Is, Burlesque
The Heritage of the
    Bible
High Anxiety
The High Country
High Noon
High Road to China
High Sierra
History of the World:
    Part I
The Hobbit
Hollywood Hot Tubs
Holocaust
Hooper
Hopscotch
Horowitz in London
The Horse Soldiers
The Hospital
Hospital Massacre
The Hotel New
    Hampshire
The Hound of the
    Baskervilles
The House on
    Sorority Row
How to Beat the High
    Cost of Living
The Howling
Huckleberry Finn
Hud
The Hunchback of
    Notre Dame
    (1939)
The Hunger
I Am a Fugitive From
    a Chain Gang
I Love You
I Ought to Be in
    Pictures
I Spit on Your Grave

I, the Jury
Iceman
If You Could See
    What I Hear
Improper Channels
Impulse
The In-Laws
In Praise of Older
    Women
In the Heat of the
    Night
The Incubus
Inherit the Wind
Inn of the Sixth
    Happiness
Invasion of the Body
    Snatchers
Invitation to a
    Gunfighter
Invitation to the
    Dance
Irma La Douce
Irreconcilable
    Differences
The Island of Dr.
    Moreau
It Came From
    Hollywood
It's A Mad, Mad,
    Mad, Mad World
Jack and the
    Beanstalk
Jailhouse Rock
James Taylor in
    Concert
Jane Fonda's
    Workout
Jane Fonda's
    Workout for
    Pregnancy, Birth
    and Recovery
Jason and the
    Argonauts
Jaws
Jaws II
Jaws III
Jazz in America
The Jazz Singer
    (1927)
The Jazz Singer
    (1980)
Jeremiah Johnson
The Jerk
Jesus of Nazareth
Jethro
    Tull—Slipstream
Jezebel
Jinxed
Joan of Arc
Joe

John Curry's Ice
  Dancing
Juggernaut
Julia
Julia Child—The
  French Chef, Vol.
  1
Junior Bonner
The Keep
Kelly's Heroes
Kenny Loggins Alive
The Kentuckian
Key Largo
Kidnapped
The Kids Are Alright
The Kids from Fame
Killer Force
King Creole
King Kong (1933)
King of Comedy
King of Hearts
Kipperbang
Kiss Me Goodbye
Klute
Kotch
Kramer vs. Kramer
Krull

Lady Chatterly's
  Lover
Lady Sings the
  Blues
The Last American
  Virgin
The Last Chase
Last House on the
  Left
Last Tango in Paris
The Last Unicorn
The Last Valley
The Last Waltz
The Last Word
Laura
Lawrence of Arabia
LCA Presents
  Family
  Entertainment
  Playhouse
The Legend of the
  Lone Ranger
Lenny
Let It Be
Let's Spend the
  Night Together
Liar's Moon
Linda Ronstadt with
  Nelson Riddle &
  His Orchestra
  "What's New"
The Lion in Winter

The Lion, the Witch
  and the Wardrobe
Little Caeser
Little House on the
  Prairie
The Little Mermaid
The Little
  Prince—Next
  Stop Planet Earth
Little Red Riding
  Hood
Little River Band
  Live Exposure
Little Women
Live and Let Die
Live Infidelity: REO
  Speedwagon in
  Concert
Logan's Run
Lolita
Lone Wolf McQuade
The Lonely Guy
The Lonely Lady
The Longest Day
The Longest Yard
Lookin' to Get Out
Looking for Mr.
  Goodbar
The Looney,
  Looney, Looney
  Bugs Bunny
  Movie
The Lord of the
  Rings
Lords of the Rings:
  Superstars and
  Superbouts
Losin' It
Love and Death
Love at First Bite
The Love Bug
Love in the
  Afternoon
Love Is a Many
  Splendored Thing
Love Letters
Love Me Tender
Love Story
Lovers and Liars
Mad Max
Mad Monster Party
Magic
The Magic Pony
The Magnificent
  Seven
Magnum Force
Mahogany
The Main Event
Making Love

Making Michael
  Jackson's Thriller
The Making of Star
  Wars . . .
The Maltese Falcon
A Man Called Horse
A Man for All
  Seasons
Man from Snowy
  River
Man of La Mancha
Man on the Moon
The Man Who Loved
  Women
The Man Who Shot
  Liberty Valance
The Man Who
  Would Be King
The Man with the
  Golden Gun
The Man with Two
  Brains
Mandingo
The Many
  Adventures of
  Winnie the
  Pooh
Marathon Man
Marty
Mary Poppins
The Mary Tyler
  Moore Show,
  Vol. 1
M*A*S*H
M*A*S*H: Goodbye,
  Farewell and
  Amen
Massive Retaliation
Matilda
A Matter of Time
Mausoleum
Max Dugan Returns
Meatballs
Meet Me in St. Louis
Meet Mr.
  Washington/Meet
  Mr. Lincoln
Meet Your Animal
  Friends
Megaforce
Metalstorm
Mick Fleetwood—
  The Visitor
Midnight Cowboy
Midnight Express
Mighty Mouse in the
  Great Space
  Chase
Mildred Pierce

The Miracle of Lake
  Placid
The Mirror Crack'd
The Misfits
Miss Peach of the
  Kelly School
Missing
The Missouri Breaks
Mr. Magoo Cartoons
Mr. Magoo in
  Sherwood Forest
Mr. Mom
Mister Roberts
Mister Rogers Goes
  to School
Mister Rogers:
  Helping Children
  Understand
Moby Dick
Modern Times
Mommie Dearest
Monique
Monsignor
Monty Python and
  the Holy Grail
Monty Python Live at
  the Hollywood
  Bowl
Monty Python's Life
  of Brian
Monty Python's The
  Meaning of Life
The Moon is Blue
Moonraker
Movie Movie
The Muppet Movie
Murder by Death
Murder by Decree
Murder on the Orient
  Express
The MUSE Concert:
  No Nukes
The Music of
  Melissa
  Manchester
Mutant
My Dinner With
  Andre
My Fair Lady
My Favorite Year
My Little Chickadee
My Tutor
Mystery Disc
      Murder,
  Anyone?
MysteryDisc
  Many Roads to
  Murder
Nashville

Nate and Hayes
National Geographic
  Presents: Great
  Whales/Sharks
National Geographic
  Society: The
  Incredible
  Machine/
  Mysteries
  of the Mind
National Lampoon's
  Vacation
Neighbors
Neil Diamond: Love
  at the Greek
Network
Never Cry Wolf
Never Say Never
  Again
The New Media
  Bible: The Story of
  Joseph
The New Video
  Aerobics
New York, New York
The New York
  Yankees' Miracle
The New York
  Yankees' Miracle
  Year: 1978
NFL '81 Official
  Season Yearbook
Night Games
Night of the Living
  Dead
The Night Porter
Night Shift
Nighthawks
Nightwing
The Nine Lives of
  Fritz the Cat
9 to 5
Norma Rae
The Norseman
North by Northwest
North Dallas Forty
Nothing Personal
Notorious
Now and Forever
Now, Voyager
The Nutcracker
The Nutty Professor
Octopussy
The Odd Couple
An Officer and a
  Gentleman
Oh! Calcutta!
Oh, God!
Oklahoma!
Old Boyfriends

Old Yeller
Olivia in Concert
Olivia—Physical
Oliver Twist
The Omen
On a Clear Day You
  Can See Forever
On Golden Pond
On Her Majesty's
  Secret Service
On the Beach
On the Town
On the Waterfront
One Flew Over the
  Cuckoo's Nest
One from the Heart
The Onion Field
Ordinary People
The Oscar
The Other Side of
  Nashville
Our Town
Outland
The Outsiders
The Owl and the
  Pussycat
The Paper Chase
Paper Moon
Papillon
Paradise
Parasite
The Parent Trap
Paternity
Paths of Glory
Patton
Paul Simon in
  Concert
Pavarotti in London
Pennies from
  Heaven
Penthouse Video,
  Volume One: The
  Girls of Penthouse
The Perils of
  Gwendoline
Peter Allen and the
  Rockettes
Peter-No-Tail
The Petrified Forest
Phantasm
The Phantom
  Tollbooth
Piaf
The Pied Piper of
  Hamelin
Pink Floyd at
  Pompeii
The Pink Panther
The Pink Panther
  Strikes Again

Pinocchio
Pippin
The Pirate
The Pirate Movie
The Pirates of
    Penzance
The Pit and the
    Pendulum
A Place in the Sun
Planet of the Apes
Play It Again, Sam
Playboy Playmate's
    Workout
Playboy Video,
    Volumes 1-5
Playmate Review
Poco
Police Academy
Pollyanna
Poltergeist
Popeye
Porky's
The Poseidon
    Adventure
The Postman
    Always Rings
    Twice
Pretty Baby
The Pride and the
    Passion
The Pride of the
    Yankees
The Prince and the
    Pauper
The Prince
    Charming Revue
Prince of the City
Private Benjamin
The Private Eyes
Private Lessons
Private Popsicle
Private School
The Producers
Psycho
Psycho II
Public Enemy
Pumping Iron
The Purple Rose of
    Cairo
Purple Taxi
Puss 'N' Boots
Quadrophenia
Queen—Greatest
    Flix
Quest for Fire
Quick Dog Training
    with Barbara
    Woodhouse
The Quiet Man

Race for Your Life,
    Charlie Brown
Raggedy Ann and
    Andy: A Musical
    Adventure
Raging Bull
Ragtime
Raiders of the Lost
    Ark
Rainbow Brite II
Raise the Titanic
Rapunzel
The Raven
RCA's All-Star
    Country Music
    Fair
Rear Window
Rebel Without a
    Cause
The Red Balloon
Red River
The Red Shoes
Redd Foxx—Video
    in a Plain Brown
    Wrapper
Reds
Reefer Madness

The Return of a Man
    Called Horse
The Return of the
    Pink Panther
The Return of the
    Streetfighter
Return to Boggy
    Creek
Return to Macon
    County
Revenge of the Ninja
Revenge of the Pink
    Panther
Rich and Famous
Richard Pryor Here
    and Now
Richard Pryor Live in
    Concert
Richard Pryor Live
    on the Sunset
    Strip
Ring of Bright Water
Rio Bravo
Rio Lobo
Risky Business
Road Games
The Road Warrior
The Roaring
    Twenties
Robin Hood
Rockshow
Rocky
Rocky II

Rocky III
Rod Stewart Live
    at the L.A. Forum
Rod Stewart:
    Tonight He's
    Yours
Rodan
Rollerball
Rolling Thunder
Roman Holiday
Romancing the
    Stone
Romeo and Juliet
The Rose
Rosebud Beach
    Hotel
Rosemary's Baby
Royal Wedding (with
    Fred Astaire)
R.S.V.P.
The Ruling Class
Rumble Fish
Rumplestiltskin
Run Silent, Run
    Deep
Running Brave
Rush—Exit Stage
    Left
The Russians Are
    Coming, the
    Russians Are
    Coming
Rust Never Sleeps
Sacred Ground
The Sacred Music of
    Duke Ellington
The Sailor Who Fell
    from Grace with
    the Sea
Sands of Iwo Jima
Saturday Night
    Fever
Saturday Night Live,
    Vol. 1
Saturday Night Live,
    Vol. 2
Savage Streets
Savannah Smiles
Sayonara
Scandalous
Scanners
Scarface (1982)
Scholastic
    Productions:
    As We Grow
The Sea Wolves
Search and Destroy
The Searchers
The Secret of NIMH

The Secret
  Policeman's
  Other Ball
The Seduction
Seems Like Old
  Times
Semi-Tough
Seniors
Separate Tables
Separate Ways
Sergeant York
Serpico
Seven Brides for
  Seven Brothers
Seven Days in May
The Seven Year Itch
The 7th Voyage of
  Sinbad
Sex on the Run
Shadows and Light
Shaft
The Shaggy Dog
Shane
Sharky's Machine
Sheena Easton—
  Live at the
  Palace,
  Hollywood
The Shining
Shogun
Shoot the Moon
The Shootist
A Shot in the Dark
The Shout
The Showdown:
  Sugar Ray
  Leonard vs.
  Thomas Hearns
The Silent Partner
Silent Rage
Silkwood
Silver Streak
Simon and
  Garfunkel: The
  Concert in Central
  Park
A Simple Story
Sinbad and the Eye
  of the Tiger
Singin' in the Rain
Six Pack
Six Weeks
Sixteen Candles
The Slap
Slave of the
  Cannibal Gods
Sleeping Beauty
Slumber Party '57
A Small Town in
  Texas

Smokey and the
  Bandit
Smokey and the
  Bandit II
Smokey and the
  Bandit Part 3
The Snow Queen
S.O.B.
The Soldier
Soldier Blue
Sole Survivor
The Solid Gold Five
  Day Workout
Some Kind of Hero
Some Like It Hot
Something Wicked
  This Way Comes
The Sons of Katie
  Elder
Sophie's Choice
The Sound of Music
Sounder
South Pacific
Southern Comfort
Soylent Green
Spacehunter:
  Adventures in the
  Forbidden Zone
Spellbound
The Spiral Staircase
Splash
Split Image
Spring Break
The Spy Who Loved
  Me
Squirm
Stagecoach
Stalag 17
Star Chamber
Star 80
A Star Is Born (1954)
A Star Is Born (1976)
Star Trek—The
  Motion Picture
Star Trek I-VI
Star Trek III: The
  Search for Spock
Star Wars
Stardust Memories
Stars on 45
Start to Finish—The
  Grand Prix!
Starting Over
Staying Alive
Stevie Nicks in
  Concert
Still of the Night
The Sting
Stir Crazy
The Story of O

A Stranger Is
  Watching
Strangers on a Train
Straw Dogs
The Street Fighter
Street Music
A Streetcar Named
  Desire
Stripes
Stroker Ace
Strong Kids, Safe
  Kids
The Stunt Man
Sudden Impact
Suddenly Last
  Summer
Summer Lovers
Summer of '42
Sunset Boulevard
The Sunshine Boys
Super Bowl XIV:
  Steelers vs. Rams
Super Bowl XV:
  Raiders vs.
  Eagles
Superman—The
  Movie
Superman II
Superman III
Support Your Local
  Sheriff
Survival Anglia's
  World of Wildlife,
  Vol.1
Survival Anglia's
  World of Wildlife,
  Vol. II
The Survivors
The Swap
Swept Away
Swing Shift
Swing Time
Swiss Family
  Robinson
Sybil
Table for Five
Take the Money and
  Run
Take This Job and
  Shove It
The Taking of
  Pelham One Two
  Three
The Tale of the Frog
  Prince
Tales From
  Muppetland
Tales From
  Muppetland II
The Tales of
  Hoffmann

The Taming of the
  Shrew
Tank
Taps
Tarzan, the Ape Man
  (1981)
Tattoo
Taxi Driver
The Telephone
  Book
The Tempest
"10"
The Ten
  Commandments
Tender Mercies
Tentacles
Terms of
  Endearment
The Terry Fox Story
Terrytoons, Vol. 1
  Featuring Mighty
  Mouse
Tess
Testament
Tex
The Texas
  Chainsaw
  Massacre
That Championship
  Season
That's Entertainment
There's No Business
  Like Show
  Business
They All Laughed
They Call Me
  MISTER Tibbs!
They Call Me Trinity
They Drive By Night
They Shoot Horses,
  Don't They?
Thief
The Thing (1951)
The Thing (1982)
Things Are Tough All
  Over
The Third Man
The 39 Steps (1935)
A Thousand Clowns
Three Days of the
  Condor
The Three Little Pigs
The Three Stooges
  Videodisc, Vol. 1
This Is Spinal Tap
Three Tales of Love
  and Friendship
Thunderball
Thunderbirds Are
  Go

Thunderbolt and
  Lightfoot
Ticket to Heaven
Tightrope
Till Marriage Do Us
  Part
Time Bandits
The Time Machine
Timerider
To Be or Not to Be
To Forget Venice
To Russia . . . with
  Elton
Tom and Jerry 1-3
Tom Jones
Tom Sawyer
Tommy
A Tony Bennett
  Songbook
Tootsie
Topkapi
Tora! Tora! Tora!
Totally Go-Gos
The Towering
  Inferno
The Toy
Trading Places
The Trail of the Pink
  Panther
Trapeze
La Traviata
Treasure
Treasure Island
Treasure of the Four
  Crowns
The Treasure of the
  Sierra Madre
Tribute
Trinity Is Still My
  Name
Tron
Truck Stop Women
True Confessions
True Grit
Truly Tasteless
  Jokes
The Tubes Video
Tulips
The Turning Point
Tut: The Boy King/
  The Louvre
12 Angry Men
20,000 Leagues
  Under the Sea
Twilight Zone—The
  Movie
Two of a Kind
2001: A Space
  Odyssey
Uncommon Valor

The Undersea World
  of Jacques
  Cousteau, Vol.1
An Unmarried
  Woman
Up in Smoke
Urban Cowboy
Used Cars
Utilities
Utopia
Valley Girl
Venom
Vera Cruz
The Verdict
Vertigo
Vice Squad
Victor/Victoria
Victory
Victory at Sea
Video Rewind
Village of the
  Damned
Visiting Hours
Viva Las Vegas
The Wacky World of
  Mother Goose
War Games
The War of the
  Worlds
Warlords of the 21st
  Century
Warrior and the
  Sorceress
The Washington
  Affair
Wasn't That A Time!
Watership Down
The Way We Were
A Week at the Races
Weekend Pass
The Weight
  Watchers Guide
  to a Healthy
  Lifestyle
West Side Story
Westworld
What's New
  Pussycat?
What's Up Doc?
What's Up Tiger
  Lily?
Wheels of Fire
When a Stranger
  Calls
Where's Poppa?
White Heat
White Lightning
The Who Rocks
  America—1982
  American Tour

Wholly Moses!
Who's Afraid of
  Opera? Vols. 1-3
Whose Life Is It
  Anyway?
Wifemistress
The Wild Bunch
The Wild Geese
Wild in the Country
Wimbledon Tennis:
  1979-1980
Wimbledon 1981/
  Wimbledon: A
  Century of
  Greatness
Wings
Winter Kills
Witches' Brew
With Six You Get
  Eggroll
Without a Trace
Witness for the
  Prosecution
The Wizard of Oz
Women in Love
The Woman in Red
Woodstock
Woody Woodpecker
  and Friends,
  Volume I
The World
  According to Garp
World Series 1980
X-Tro
Yankee Doodle
  Dandy
The Year of Living
  Dangerously
Yes, Giorgio
Yoga Moves with
  Alan Finger
Yor, the Hunter from
  the Future
You Only Live Twice
Young Doctors in
  Love

LASER
OPTICAL
DISCS

Abba
Abbott & Costello
  Meet
  Frankenstein
ABC-Mantrap
Absence of Malice
The Absent-
  Minded Professor

The Adventures of
  Buckaroo Banzai
The Adventures of
  Eliza Fraser
The Adventures of
  Robin Hood
The Adventures of
  the Wilderness
  Family
Aerobicise: The
  Beautiful Workout
Aerobicise: The
  Beginning
  Workout
The African Queen
After Hours
Aida
Air Supply in Hawaii
Airplane!
Airplane II: The
  Sequel
Alice in Wonderland
Alien
All That Jazz
The Allman Brothers
  Band—Brothers
  On the Road
Altered States
Alvin Purple
Alvin Rides Again
America Live in
  Central Park
American Ballet
  Theatre/Don
  Quixote
American Flyers
American Gigolo
American Graffiti
An American in Paris
An American
  Werewolf in
  London
The Amityville
  Horror
Amityville II: The
  Possession
Among the Cinders
The Anderson
  Tapes
And God Created
  Woman
And Justice for All
Angel of H.E.A.T.
Angelo My Love
Angels Die Hard
Animal Crackers
Animal House
Annie
Annie Hall
Any Which Way You
  Can

Apocalypse Now
April Wine
Armed Forces
  Workout
Arthur
Ashford & Simpson
Asia in Asia
Atlantic City
Autumn Portrait
Autumn Sonata
Avenging Angel
Back to the Future
The Bad News
  Bears
Badlands
Ball of Fire
The Ballad of
  Gregorio Cortez
Un Ballo in
  Maschera
Bananas
Bang the Drum
  Slowly
The Bank Dick
Barbarella
Barbarian Queen
Barefoot in the Park
Barry Manilow Live
  at the Greek
Battlestar Galactica
B.C. Holiday
  Happenings
The Beach Girls
The Beastmaster
Beatlemania—The
  Movie
Beat Street
Beauty and the
  Beast
Being There
Belly Dancing—You
  Can Do It!
Ben Hur
A Berenstain Bears
  Celebration
Best Defense
Best Friends
The Best Little
  Whorehouse in
  Texas
The Best of Mary
  Hartman, Mary
  Hartman Vol. II
The Best of Times
The Best Years of
  Our Lives
The Bette Midler
  Show
Between the Lines
The Big Chill

The Big Sleep
Billy Crystal: A
    Comic's Line
Billy Joel: Live on
    Long Island
Billy Squier Live in
    the Dark
Biology: Lesson 1,
    Respiration;
    Lesson 2, Climate
    and Life
Bio Sci Video Disc
The Birds
Bite the Bullet
The Black Hole
The Black Stallion
The Black Stallion
    Returns
Blade Runner
Blame It on Rio
Blazing Saddles
Blood Simple
Blow Out
Blue Hawaii
The Blue Lagoon
Blue Thunder
The Boat
Bob Marley & the
    Wailers
Body Heat
Body Music
La Boheme
Bolero
Bon Voyage,
    Charlie Brown
Bonnie and Clyde
The Border
The Bostonians
The Bounty
The Boy Who
    Left Home to
    Find Out About
    the Shivers
The Boys from
    Brazil
The Boys of
    Summer
Brady's Escape
Brainstorm
Brass Target
Brazil
Breaker Morant
Breakfast at
    Tiffany's
The Breakfast
    Club
Breakin'
Breathless
Brewster's
    Millions

The Bride of
    Frankenstein
The Bridge of
    San Luis Rey
The Bridge on
    the River Kwai
Brigadoon
Broadway
    Danny Rose
Brubaker
Buck Privates
Bugsy Malone
Bury Me an
    Angel
Bustin' Loose
Butch Cassidy
    and the
    Sundance
    Kid
Butterfly
Cabaret
Cactus Flower
Caddyshack
La Cage aux
    Folles
Caledonian
    Dreams
California Suite
Caligula
Camelot
The Cannonball
    Run
Capricorn One
Carbon Copy
Carlin at
    Carnegie
Carlin on Campus
Carnal
    Knowledge
Carole King—
    One to One
Carrie
The Cars:
    1984-1985 Live
Cartoon Classics
    Vol. 1-5
Casablanca
Cat on a Hot
    Tin Roof
Cat People
    (1983)
Catch-22
Catherine the
    Great
The Centennial
    Gala
The Champ
Champions
The Changeling
Chapter Two
Chariots of Fire

The Charlie
    Daniels
    Band: The
    Saratoga
    Concert
Charlotte's Web
Charly
Cheech &
    Chong's Next
    Movie
Cheech &
    Chong's Nice
    Dreams

Cher: A
    Celebration
    at Caesar's
Chick Corea/Gary
    Burton Live
    in Tokyo
Children of the
    Corn
The China
    Syndrome
Chinatown
Chitty Chitty
    Bang Bang
A Chorus Line
Christine
Christine McVie
    Concert
A Christmas
    Story
The Cincinnati
    Kid
Cinderella
Citizen Kane
City Heat
City Limits
Clash of the
    Titans
Class
Class of 1984
Claude Bolling:
    Concerto for
    Classical
    Guitar and Jazz
    Piano
A Clockwork
    Orange
Close Encounters
    of the Third
    Kind: The
    Special Edition
Clouds Over
    Europe
Clue
Coast to Coast
The Coca-Cola Kid
Cocoon
Coma

Come Back
  to the 5 and
  Dime Jimmy
  Dean, Jimmy
  Dean
Comedy Music
  Videos
Coming Home
Commando
The Competition
The Compleat
  Beatles
Compromising
  Positions
Conan the
  Barbarian
Conan the
  Destroyer
Continental
  Divide
The Conversation
Cool Cats
Cool Hand Luke
The Cotton Club
Country
Crackers
The Creative
  Camera
Crimes of
  Passion
Crosby, Stills &
  Nash: Daylight
  Again
Cross Country
Cujo
Daffy Duck's
  Movie: Fantastic
  Island
Dance with a
  Stranger
Dark Waters
Daryl Hall & John
  Oates—Rock 'n'
  Soul Live
Dave Mason Live at
  Perkins Palace
David Bowie:
  Serious
  Moonlight
Davy Crockett
  and the River
  Pirates
The Day After
A Day at the
  Races
Days of Heaven
D.C. Cab
Dead End
Dead Men Don't
  Wear Plaid

The Dead Zone
Deal of the
  Century
Death Hunt
Death Watch
Death Wish
Death Wish II
Death Wish III
The Deep
The Deer Hunter
The Delta Force
Desperately
  Seeking Susan
Diamonds Are
  Forever
Diana Ross in
  Concert
Dick Clark's Best of
  Bandstand
Diner
Dinner at Eight
The Dirt Band
  Tonite
The Dirty Dozen
Dirty Harry
Diva
Dr. Detroit
Dr. Jekyll & Mr.
  Hyde (1941)
Dr. No
The Dr. Seuss
  Video Festival
Dr. Strangelove
Doctor Zhivago
Dodsworth
Dolly in London
Don Carlo
Don't Look Now
Donovan's Reef
Downhill Racer
Dracula (1979)
Dragonslayer
Dressed to Kill
  (1981)
Drums
Dumbo
Dunderklumpen
Dune
Duran Duran
Dvorak's Slavic
  Dance
Earth, Wind and
  Fire in Concert
Easy Money
Easy Rider
Eddie and the
  Cruisers
Eddie Macon's Run
Educating Rita
El Cid
Electric Boogaloo,
  Breakin' 2

Electric Dreams
The Electric
  Horseman
Eleni
Elephant Boy
The Elephant Man
Elephant Parts
Elton John in
  Central Park,
  New York
Elton John: Visions
Elvis on Tour
The Emerald Forest
Emmanuelle
Emmanuelle, the
  Joys of a Woman
The Emperor's New
  Clothes
The Empire Strikes
  Back
Enchanted Forest
The End
Endless Love
The Endless
  Summer
Enigma
Enter the Dragon
Ernie Kovacs:
  Television's
  Original Genius
Eroticise
The Escape Artist
Escape from
  Alcatraz
Escape from
  New York
Escape to Witch
  Mountain
Eurythmics—Sweet
  Dreams (The
  Video Album)
The Eve
An Evening with
  Ray Charles
An Evening with
  Robin Williams
Everything You
  Always Wanted
  to Know About
  Sex . . .
The Exorcist
The Eyes of Laura
  Mars
The Fabulous
  Fleischer Folio,
  Vol. 1
Faerie Tale Theatre
  (series)
Fail Safe
Falling in Love
Falstaff

Fame
The Fan
La Faniculla Del
  West
Fanny and
  Alexander
Fast Times at
  Ridgemont High
The Female
  Impersonator
  Pageant
Fiddler on the Roof
La Fille Mal Gardee
Final Justice
Finian's Rainbow
Firefox
Firestarter
The First Barry
  Manilow Special
First Blood
First Born
First Monday in
  October
The First National
  Kidisc
Five Mile Creek,
  Vol. 1
Flash Gordon
Flashdance
Flesh and Blood
Fletch
Flying Leathernecks
The Fog
Football Follies/
  Sensational
  '60's
Footloose
For a Few Dollars
  More
For Your Eyes Only
Forbidden Planet
Force 10 from
  Navarone
Fort Apache
Fort Apache, the
  Bronx
42nd Street
48 Hours
Foul Play
The Four Feathers
The Four Seasons
Fraggle Songs,
  Vol. 1
Frank Sinatra:
  Portrait of an
  Album
The French
  Connection
The French
  Lieutenant's
  Woman
Friday the 13th

Friday the 13th
  Part 2
Friday the 13th
  Part 3
The Frog Prince
From Russia with
  Love
From the New
  World
Fun and Games
Funny Face
Funny Girl
A Funny Thing
  Happened on the
  Way to the
  Forum
Future Kill
Galaxina
Gallagher—
  Some
  Uncensored
  Evening
Gallagher—
  Stuck in the '60's
Gallagher—The
  Maddest
Gallipoli
The Gambler
Gandhi
Gardening at Home
Gas Pump Girls
Get Crazy
Ghost Story
Gigi
Gimme Shelter
Girl Groups
Girls of Rock and
  Roll
Give My Regards to
  Broad Street
The Glenn Miller
  Story
Gloria
Go Tell the
  Spartans
The Godfather
The Godfather
  Part II
Godzilla
Goin' South
Going Berserk
A Golden Decade
  of College
  Football
The Golden Seal
Goldfinger
Goldilocks and the
  3 Bears
Gone With the
  Wind

Good Guys Wear
  Black
The Good, the Bad
  and the Ugly
Goodbye,
  Columbus
The Goodbye Girl
Goodbye,
  New York
The Goonies
Gorilla
Gorky Park
Gotcha!
Grace Jones: One
  Man Show
The Graduate
Grand Hotel
Grateful Dead/Dead
  Ahead
Grease
Grease 2
The Great Escape
The Great Gatsby
Great Movie Stunts
  & The Making of
  Raiders of the
  Lost Ark
The Great Muppet
  Caper
The Great Train
  Robbery
The Greatest
  Adventure
The Greatest Show
  on Earth
Gremlins
Greystoke: The
  Legend of
  Tarzan, Lord of
  the Apes
Grover Washington
  Jr. in Concert
Gunfight at the OK
  Corral
Gunga Din
The Guns of
  Navarone
Guys and Dolls
Hair
Halloween
Halloween II
Hanky Panky
Hans Christian
  Andersen
Hansel and Gretel
Happy Birthday to
  Me
The Happy Hooker
The Happy Hooker
  Goes to
  Hollywood

Hardcore
A Hard Day's Night
Hard Times
Hard to Hold
Harold and Maude
Harry and Son
Harry Chapin: The
  Final Concert
Hatari
Heart of the Stag
Heartaches
Hearts and Minds
Heaven Can Wait
Hello Dolly!
Herbie Hancock
  and the Rockit
  Band
He-Man and the
  Masters of the
  Universe
Hercules
Hercules
  Unchained
Here It Is,
  Burlesque
Hey, Cinderella!
Highest Honor
High Point
High Road to China
High Sierra
High Society
The History Disquiz
History of the
  World: Part 1
H.M.S. Pinafore
Hobson's Choice
Hocus Pocus, It's
  Magic
Holiday Inn
Homework
Honeysuckle Rose
Horowitz in London
Hostage Tower
The Hotel New
  Hampshire
Hot Stuff
A Hot Summer
  Night with Donna
House
House Calls
House on Sorority
  Row
How to Watch Pro
  Football
The Howling
The Huberman
  Festival Vol. 1
Hud
Huey Lewis and the
  News Video Hits

The Hunger
The Hunter
The Hurricane
Hussy
I Like to Hurt
  People
I Spit on Your
  Grave
Ice Pirates
Iceland River
  Challenge
Iceman
The Idolmaker
If You Could See
  What I Hear
I'm Dancing as Fast
  as I Can
Improper Channels
Impulse
In Cold Blood
In Praise of Older
  Women
The Incredible
  Human Machine
The Incredible
  Shrinking Woman
The Incubus
Infinity Factory
Invasion of the
  Body Snatchers
Invasion U.S.A.
Iron Maiden
Irreconcilable
  Differences
Islands in the
  Stream
It Came from
  Hollywood
It's a Mad, Mad,
  Mad, Mad World
It's My Turn
It's 1984
Itzhak Perlman
J. Geils Band
Jack and the
  Beanstalk
James Taylor in
  Concert
Jam Introduction to
  Computer
  Literacy
Jason and the
  Argonauts
Jaws
Jaws III
The Jazz Singer
  (1980)
Jazzercize
Jefferson Starship
Jeremiah Johnson

The Jerk
The Jewel of the
  Nile
Jim Fixx on
  Running
Joan of Arc
Joan Sutherland in
  Concert
Joe
The Joy of
  Relaxation
The Joy of Stocks
Judy Garland in
  Concert
The Jungle Book
Kajagoogoo
Kanako
Kelly's Heroes
Kenny Loggins
  Alive
Kentucky Fried
  Movie
Kevin Rowland/
  Dexy's Midnight
  Runners
Key Largo
Kids from Fame in
  Concert
Killing Point
Kim Carnes
The King of
  Comedy
The King and I
King Kong (1933)
King Kong (1977)
Kiss of the Spider
  Woman
Klute
The Knack—Live at
  Carnegie Hall
Koyannisqatsi
Kramer vs. Kramer
Krull
Krush Groove
Lady Chatterly's
  Lover
Lady on the Bus
Lady Sings the
  Blues
The Lady Vanishes
Lamaze
Land of the Tiger
Lassiter
The Last Detail
Last House on the
  Left
Last of the Red Hot
  Lovers
Last Tango in Paris
Lawrence of Arabia

Lenny
The Lenny Bruce
  Performance Film
Let It Be
Let's Spend the
  Night Together
Lifeforce
Lily in Love
Linda Ronstadt with
  Nelson Riddle &
  His Orchestra—
  "What's New"
The Lion Has
  Wings
The Lion in Winter
Lipstick
Little Darlings
The Little Drummer
  Girl
The Little Foxes
The Little Mermaid
The Little Prince
Little Red Riding
  Hood
Little River Band
  Live Exposure
Live and Let Die
Live Infidelity:
  REO
  Speedwagon in
  Concert
Liza Minnelli in
  Concert
Logan's Run
Lone Wolf
  McQuade
The Lonely Guy
The Lonely Lady
The Longest Yard
Looking for Mr.
  Goodbar
The Lords of
  Discipline
Loretta
Losin' It
Love and Death
Love at First Bite
The Love Bug
Love from a
  Stranger
Love Story
Loverboy
Loving Couples
Lust in the Dust
Lydia
M
Ma Vlast (My
  Fatherland)
Mad Max
Mad Max Beyond
  Thunderdome

Magic
The Magic Flute
The Magic Pony
The Magician
The Magnificent
  Seven
Mahogany
The Making of
  Michael
  Jackson's Thriller
The Making of Star
  Wars/S.P.F.X.-
  The Empire
  Strikes Back
The Maltese Falcon
Mame
A Man for All
  Seasons
The Man Who Fell
  to Earth
The Man Who
  Loved Women
The Man Who Shot
  Liberty Valance
The Man with the
  Golden Gun
The Man with Two
  Brains
Mandingo
Manhattan
Manhattan Transfer
  in Concert
Manon
Manon Lescaut
The Many
  Adventures of
  Winnie the Pooh
Marathon Man
Mars and Beyond
Marty
Mary Poppins
Mask
M*A*S*H
M*A*S*H:
  Goodbye,
  Farewell and
  Amen
Mass Appeal
Massive
  Retaliation
The Master
  Cooking Course
Max Dugan
  Returns
Maze, Featuring
  Frankie Beverly
Maze Mania
Meatballs
Meet Me in St.
  Louis

Meet Your
  Animal Friends
La Melodie
  D'Amour
Mel Torme and
  Della Reese in
  Concert
Melvin and
  Howard
Men Are Not
  Gods
Metalstorm
Metropolitan
  Opera/Don Carlo
Metropolitan
  Opera/Lucia
  Di Lammermoor
Miami Vice
Mickey Mouse &
  Donald Duck
  Cartoon
  Collection Vol.
  1-3
Midnight Express
Mildred Pierce
A Minor Miracle
Missing
Missing in Action
Mission Batangas
Mission
  Galactica: The
  Cylon Attack
Mr. Magoo in
  Sherwood
  Forest
Mr. Magoo's
  Christmas Carol
Mr. Mom
Mommie Dearest
Mon Oncle
Monty Python
  and the Holy
  Grail
Monty Python's
  The Meaning
  of Life
The Moon Is Blue
Moonlighting
The Motels
Motown 25:
  Yesterday,
  Today and
  Forever
The Mountain
  Men
The Mummy
The Muppet
  Movie

The Muppet
  Musicians of
  Bremen
Murder by Death
Murder on the
  Orient Express
Muscle Motion
The Muse
  Concert: No
  Nukes
Music Is
The Music of
  Melissa
  Manchester
Mutiny on the
  Bounty
My Bloody
  Valentine
My Chauffeur
My Fair Lady
My Science
  Project
My Tutor
Mysterious Island
Naked Eyes
Nashville
Nate and Hayes
National Gallery:
  Art Awareness
  Collection
The National
  Gallery of Art
National
  Lampoon's
  Class Reunion
National
  Lampoon's
  European
  Vacation
Neighbors
Neil Diamond:
  Love at the
  Greek
Network
Never Cry Wolf
Never Say Never
  Again
The Neverending
  Story
New Look
NFL SymFunny/
  Legends of
  the Fall
Night Games
The Night Porter
Night Shift
Nighthawks
9 to 5
Ninotchka
1941
Norma Rae

North by
  Northwest
North Dallas
  Forty
Notorious
Now and Forever
The Nutcracker
Obsession
Octopussy
The Odd Couple
An Officer and a
  Gentleman
Oklahoma!
Oh God!, You
  Devil
Old Yeller
Olivia
Olivia in Concert
Olivia—
  Physical
The Omen
On a Clear Day
  You Can See
  Forever
On Golden Pond
On Her Majesty's
  Secret Service
Once Bitten
Once Upon a
  Time in
  America
Once Upon a
  Time in the West
The One and
  Only Genuine
  Original Family
  Band
One from the
  Heart
One Night
  Stand—A
  Keyboard Event
The Onion Field
Only When I
  Laugh
Orca
Orchestra de
  Paul Maurlat
Ordeal by
  Innocence
Ordinary People
Oriental Dreams
Otello
The Other Side
  of Nashville
Out of Control
Out of the Blue
Outland
Paint Your
  Wagon
Pale Rider

The Paleface
Paper Moon
The Parent Trap
Party Games—
  For Adults Only
Passion of Love
Pastel Color
Paternity
Patton
Paul Simon in
  Concert
Pavarotti in
  London
Pee Wee's Big
  Adventure
Penthouse Video
  Vol. I: The Girls
  of Penthouse
Performance
Peter Allen and
  the Rockettes
Peter Grimes
Pete's Dragon
Phantasm
Picture Magic
The Pied Piper of
  Hamelin
The Pink Panther
The Pink Panther
  Strikes Again
Pinocchio
Pippin
The Pirates of
  Penzance
Pink Floyd The
  Wall
The Pit and the
  Pendulum
A Place in the
  Sun
Placido: A Year
  in the Life of
  Placido
  Domingo
Play it Again,
  Sam
Play Misty for Me
Playboy Video
  Vol. 1-4
Playmate
  Review
Poetry in Motion
Police Academy
Police Academy 2:
  Their First
  Assignment
The Police:
  Synchronicity
Pollyanna
Popeye
Poltergeist

Porky's

Porky's II: The
Next Day

The Postman
Always Rings
Twice

Pretty Baby

The Pride of the
Yankees

Prince of the
City

The Princess and
the Pirate

Private Benjamin

The Private Eyes

Private Lessons

Private School

Prizzi's Honor

Prom Night

The Protector

Protocol

Psycho

Psycho II

Purple Rain

Puss 'N' Boots

Quadrophenia

Queen—
Greatest Flix

Queen—
The Works

Quest for Fire

Raccoon's
Collection

Race for Your
Life, Charlie
Brown

Rad

Raggedy Man

Raging Bull

Ragtime

Raiders of the
Lost Ark

Railroaded

Rainbow
Brite—Mighty
Monstromork
Menace

Rainbow Brite
Vol. 1-2

Rainbow Goblins
Story

Rainbow Live
Between the
Eyes

Raise the Titanic

Rapunzel

The Ratings
Game

The Raven

Raw Courage

Re-Animator

Rear Window

Rebel Without a
Cause

Reckless

Red Dawn

Redd Foxx—
Video in a Plain
Brown Wrapper

Reds

Rembrandt

Repo Man

The Return of
Martin Guerre

The Return of the
Pink Panther

Return to Oz

Revenge of the
Pink Panther

Revolution

Rich and Famous

Richard Pryor—
Here and Now

Richard Pryor—
Live and Smokin'

Richard Pryor—
Live on the
Sunset Strip

The Right Stuff

Risky Business

The River

The River Rat

The Road
Warrior

Robin Hood

Rock Adventure

Rockshow

Rocky

Rocky II

Rocky III

Rocky IV

Rod Stewart:
Tonight He's
Yours

Rodan

Rolling Stones—
Great
Video Hits

Romeo and Juliet

Room Service

Rope

The Rose

Rose Marie

Rosemary's Baby

Rostropovich

Rough Cut

Roxy Music—The
High Road

R.S.V.P

Rumble Fish

Rumpelstiltskin

Running Brave

Rush—Exit Stage
Left

Saboteur

The Sailor Who
Fell From Grace
with the Sea

Samson and
Delilah

Samson et Dalila

Sanders of the
River

Sanjuro

Saturday Night
Fever

Saturn 3

Savage Streets

Savannah Smiles

Save the Tiger

Scandalous

Scarface (1932)

Scarface (1982)

Scream Greats

The Secret Life of
Walter Mitty

The Secret of NIMH

The Secret
Policeman's
Other Ball

The Searchers

The Seduction of
Joe Tynan

Seems Like Old
Times

Semi-Tough

The Sender

Sgt. Pepper's
Lonely Hearts
Club Band

Serial

Serpico

Sesame Street
Presents: Follow
That Bird

Seven Days in May

Sex on the Run

Shadows and Light

The Shaggy Dog

Shane

The Sharks

She Wore a Yellow
Ribbon

Sheena Easton

Sheena Easton
Live at the
Palace,
Hollywood

Shogun

The Shootist

A Shot in the Dark

The Silent Partner

Silent Rage
Silkwood
Simon & Garfunkel:
  The Concert in
  Central Park
Sinbad and the Eye
  of the Tiger
Singin' in the Rain
Sixteen Candles
Slap Shot
Slapstick of Another
  Kind
Sleeper
Sleeping Beauty
Slumber Party '57
Smokey and the
  Bandit
Smokey and the
  Bandit II
Smokey and the
  Bandit Part 3
Smooth Talk
The Smurfs and the
  Magic Flute
The Snow Queen
A Soldier's Tale
The Solid Gold Five
  Day Workout
Some Kind of Hero
Some Like it Hot
Something Wicked
  This Way Comes
Somewhere in Time
Sonezaki Shinju
Son of Football
  Follies/Big Game
  America
Sophie's Choice
The Sound of
  Music
Sounder
South Pacific
Southern Comfort
Soylent Green
Space Disc 1-7
Space Hunter
Space Shuttle
  Mission Reports:
  STS 5,6, & 7
Spies Like Us
Splash
The Spoilers
Spring Break
The Spy Who
  Loved Me
Stalag 17
Star Crash
Star 80
A Star Is Born
  (1954)

Star Trek—
  The Motion
  Picture
Star Trek II: The
  Wrath of Khan
Star Trek III: The
  Search for Spock
Star Wars
Stardust Memories
Stars on 45
Starstruck
Starting Over
Statue of Liberty
Staying Alive
Steel
Stephen King's
  Silver Bullet
Steve Miller Band
  Live
Stevie Nicks in
  Concert
Stick
Still of the Night
The Sting II
Stir Crazy
The Story of O
Strange Invaders
Straw Dogs
Stray Cats
Streets of Fire
Streetwalkin'
Strike Up the Band
Stripes
Strong Kids, Bold
  Kids
Student Bodies
Styx—Caught in the
  Act
Sudden Impact
Suddenly Last
  Summer
Summer Lovers
Summer Rental
Super Memories of
  the Super Bowl
Super 70's
Superman—The
  Movie
Superman II
Superman III
The Sure Thing
The Survivors
Swamp Thing
Swan Lake
Swept Away . . .
Swing Shift
Swiss Family
  Robinson
The Sword and the
  Sorcerer

The Sword in
  the Stone
Table for Five
Takanaka World
Take the Money
  and Run
The Tale of the
  Frog Prince
Tales of Hoffman
Tank
Tarzan, the Ape
  Man (1981)
Taxi Driver
Teatra Alla Scala/
  Ernani
Teen Wolf
Tempest
10
The Ten
  Commandments
Ten to Midnight
The Terminator
Terms of
  Endearment
Terror in the
  Swamp
The Terry Fox
  Story
Tess
Testament
Tex
The Texas
  Chainsaw
  Massacre
That Hamilton
  Woman
That Was Then,
  This Is Now
That's Dancing
That's
  Entertainment
There's a Meetin'
  Here Tonight
These Three
They All Laughed
They Call Me Bruce
They Got Me
  Covered
They Shoot Horses,
  Don't They?
Thief of Baghdad
Thief of Hearts
The Thin Man
The Thing (1951)
The Thing (1981)
Things Are Tough
  All Over
The Third Man
The 39 Steps
  (1935)

This Is Spinal Tap
This Island Earth
Thomas Dolby
Thoroughly Modern
  Millie
Those Magificent
  Men in Their
  Flying Machines
Three Days of the
  Condor
The Three Little
  Pigs
The Three Stooges
Thumbelina
Thunderball
Til Marriage Do Us
  Part
Time Bandits
The Time Machine
To Catch a Thief
To Live and Die in
  L.A.
Tom & Jerry
  Cartoon Festival
  Vol. 1-2
Tom Jones
Tommy
Tootsie
Top Hat
Tora! Tora! Tora!
Torchlight
The Touch of Love:
  Massage
The Toy
Toy Soldier
Trading Places
The Trail of the
  Pink Panther
Transylvania
  6-5000
Trancers
La Traviata
Treasure
Treasure Island
The Treasure of the
  Sierre Madre
Tribute
Troll
Tron
Tropical High Noon
Trouble in Mind
The Trouble with
  Harry
True Confessions
True Grit
The Tubes Video
Tuff Turf
Twice in a Lifetime
Twilight Zone—
  The Movie

Twisted Sister's
  Stay Hungry
Twist of Fate
2001: A Space
  Odyssey
2010
Uncommon Valor
Under Fire
Unfaithfully Yours
Up in Smoke
Up the Creek
Urban Cowboy
Used Cars
Valley Girl
The Velveteen
  Rabbit
The Verdict
Vertigo
Vice Squad
Victor/Victoria
Video Rewind
Videodrome
Vietnam: The
  Ten Thousand
  Day War
Vincent Van
  Gogh: A Portrait
  in Two Parts
Walking Tall: The
  Final Chapter
War and Peace
War Games
The War of the
  Worlds
The Warrior and
  the Sorceress
The Warriors
Water's Path
Wavelength
The Way We Were
Wedding Rehearsal
Weekend Pass
Weird Science
We're All Devo
Western Light
The Westerner
West Side Story
What's Up Tiger
  Lily?
When a Stranger
  Calls
When Worlds
  Collide
White City: Pete
  Townshend
White Music
The Who Rocks
  America: 1982
  World Tour

Wholly Moses!
The Wild Bunch
Wild Gypsies
Wings
Winter
Witness
The Wiz
The Wizard of Oz
The Woman in Red
The Women
Woody
  Woodpecker and
  Friends
The World of
  Martial Arts
Wuthering Heights
Xanadu
Yankee Doodle
  Dandy
The Year of Living
  Dangerously
Year of the Dragon
Yellowbeard
Yentl
Yeoman of the
  Guard
Yes, Giorgio
Yessongs
Yoga Moves with
  Alan Finger
Yojimbo
Yor: The Hunter
  from the Future
You Only Live
  Twice
Young Doctors in
  Love
Young Frankenstein
Yukon Passage
The Yum-Yum Girls
Z
Zapped!
Zelig

8 MILLIMETER (8mm) INDEX

The titles listed below have been released in the new 8mm videocassette format. Check the program listings for full descriptive information.

Airplane! (Paramount)
The Baby-Safe Home (Embassy)
The Bad News Bears (Paramount)
Baseball the Pete Rose Way (Embassy)
Beverly Hills Cop (Paramount)
Blade Runner (Embassy)
A Chorus Line (Embassy)
The Cotton Club (Embassy)
The Emerald Forest (Embassy)
Flashdance (Paramount)
Footloose (Paramount)
Foul Play (Paramount)
Gary Player on Golf (North American)
The Graduate (Embassy)
Harold and Maude (Paramount)
The Jazz Singer (Paramount)
Joan Sutherland in Concert (Kultur)
Kiss of the Spider Woman (Charter)
Placido: A Year in the Life of Placido Domingo (Kultur)
Play It Again, Sam (Paramount)
Romeo and Juliet (Kultur)
Star Trek III: The Search for Spock (Paramount)
Summer Rental (Paramount)
The Sure Thing (Embassy)
Sybil Bruncheon a'la Maison (Nautilus)
Teen Wolf (Paramount)
This Is Spinal Tap (Embassy)
Trading Places (Paramount)
Uncommon Valor (Paramount)
Voltron, Defender of the Universe: Castle of Lions (Sony)
Voltron, Defender of the Universe: Journey to the Lost Planets (Sony)
Voltron, Defender of the Universe: Merla, Queen of Darkness (Sony)
Voltron, Defender of the Universe: Planet Arus (Sony)
Voltron, Defender of the Universe: Planet Doom (Sony)
Voltron, Defender of the Universe: Zarkon's Revenge (Sony)
Witness (Paramount)
World Champions! The Story of the 1985 Chicago Bears (NFL)

Closed Captioned Index

Following is an alphabetical list of all video programming which is currently available with closed captions. The distributors of each film are listed next to the title for quick reference. Captioning of all programs is provided by The National Captioning Institute, Falls Church, Virginia.

Birdy (RCA/Columbia)
Black Moon Rising (New World)
Blue Thunder (RCA/Columbia)
Blue Yonder (Walt Disney)
Body Double (RCA/Columbia)
A Boy Named Charlie Brown (CBS/Fox)
Brazil (MCA)
The Breakfast Club (MCA)
Breakheart Pass (Key)
Brewster's Millions (MCA)
Brian's Song (RCA/Columbia)
The Bride (RCA/Columbia)
Bring On the Night (Karl/Lorimar)
Bubba Until It Hurts (Continental Video)
The Buddy System (Key)
Burning Bed (CBS/Fox)
The Burns and Allen Show Vol. 1 (RCA/Columbia)
The Caine Mutiny (RCA/Columbia)
Came a Hot Friday (Charter)
Cannonball Run II (Warner)
The Care Bears Battle the Freeze Machine (Family Home)
The Care Bears Movie (Vestron)
A Cartooney Party: Uncle Fred (Playhouse)
Careful, He Might Hear You (CBS/Fox)
Casey at the Bat (Playhouse)
Cast a Giant Shadow (Key)
The Cat in the Hat and Dr. Seuss on the Loose (Playhouse)
Cat's Eye (Key)
Champions (Embassy)
Chapter Two (RCA/Columbia)
Children's Songs and Stories (Playhouse)
The China Syndrome (RCA/Columbia)
A Chorus Line (Embassy)
A Christmas Carol (Karl/Lorimar)
City Heat (Warner)
The Class of Miss McMichael (CBS/Fox)
Classic Creatures (Playhouse)
Clifford's Singalong Adventure (Playhouse)
Cloak and Dagger (MCA)
Close Encounters of the Third Kind: The Special Edition
(RCA/Columbia)
The Coca-Cola Kid (Vestron)
Cocoon (CBS/Fox)
Code Name: Emerald (Playhouse)
Cold Feet (CBS/Fox)
Comic Relief (Karl/Lorimar)
Commando (CBS/Fox)
The Company of Wolves (Vestron)
The Complete Guide to Dog Care (CBS/Fox)
Compromising Positions (Paramount)
Conan the Destroyer (MCA)

Conquest of the Planet of the Apes (Playhouse)
Conrack (Playhouse)
The Cotton Club (Embassy)
Country Music with the Muppets (Playhouse)
Creature (Media)
Crimes of Passion (New World)
Crunch Course (NFL)
Dance with a Stranger (Vestron)
The Daring Dobermans (Key)
D.A.R.Y.L. (Paramount)
David Copperfield (Vestron)
D.C. Cab (MCA)
Dead Wrong (Karl/Lorimar)
The Dead Zone (Paramount)
Delta Force (Media)
The Doberman Gang (Key)
Doctor and the Devils (Key)
Dogpound Shuffle (Playhouse)
Dorothy Statten: The Untold Story (Karl/Lorimar)
Dot and the Bunny (CBS/Fox)
Dream Chasers (Playhouse)
The Dresser (RCA/Columbia)
The Driver (CBS/Fox)
Dumbo (Walt Disney)
Dune (MCA)
Easy Money (Vestron)
Educating Rita (RCA/Columbia)
Eleni (Embassy)
11 Harrowhouse (Playhouse)
Eliminators (Playhouse)
The Emerald Forest (Embassy)
The Empire Strikes Back (CBS/Fox)
End of the Road (Key)
Enemy Mine (CBS/Fox)
Escape from the Planet of the Apes (Playhouse)
An Evening at the Improv (Warner)
The Evil That Men Do (RCA/Columbia)
Exercise Shorts (Karl/Lorimar)
Explorers (Paramount)
The Eyes of Laura Mars (RCA/Columbia)
Faerie Tale Theatre—Series (CBS/Fox)
Fail Safe (RCA/Columbia)
Fairy Tales Vol. II-III (Embassy)
The Falcon and the Snowman (Vestron)
Falling in Love (Paramount)
The Fantastic Adventures of Unico, Vol. 1 (RCA/Columbia)
Fast Forward (RCA/Columbia)
Finders Keepers (Key)
Firestarter (MCA)
First Aid: The Video Kit (CBS/Fox)
The Flamingo Kid (Vestron)
Flashdance (Paramount)
Fletch (MCA)
The Flight of the Phoenix (CBS/Fox)

The Flim-Flam Man (Playhouse)
Football Follies (NFL)
Footloose (Paramount)
For a Few Dollars More (Key)
Foxes (Key)
Fozzie's Muppet Scrapbook (Playhouse)
Fraternity Vacation (New World)
French Connection II (CBS/Fox)
Friday the 13th—The Final Chapter (Paramount)
Friendly Persuasion (CBS/Fox)
Fright Night (RCA/Columbia)
Garbo Talks (CBS/Fox)
The Get-Along Gang (Karl/Lorimar)
Ghostbusters (RCA/Columbia)
G.I. Joe: A Real American Hero (Family Home)
G.I. Joe: The Revenge of the Cobra (Family Home)
Giant (Warner)
Girls Just Want to Have Fun (New World)
Gnomes (RCA/Columbia)
The Golden Voyage of Sinbad (RCA/Columbia)
Gone With the Wind (MGM/UA)
Gonzo's Weird Stuff (Playhouse)
Goodbye Mr. Chips (MGM/UA)
The Goodbye People (Embassy)
Goonies (Warner)
Gorilla (Vestron)
Gotcha! (MCA)
The Graduate (Embassy)
Grand Hotel (MGM/UA)
Grandview U.S.A. (Key)
The Great Ape Activity Tape (Karl/Lorimar)
Great Expectations (Vestron)
The Greatest Story Ever Told (CBS/Fox)
Green Ice (Key)
Gremlins (Warner)
Greystoke: The Legend of Tarzan (Warner)
Guess Who's Coming to Dinner (RCA/Columbia)
Gymboree (Karl/Lorimar)
Halloween Is Grinch Night (Playhouse)
Hanky Panky (RCA/Columbia)
Hard To Hold (MCA)
Hardbodies (RCA/Columbia)
Harry and Tonto (Key)
The Heart Is a Lonely Hunter (Warner)
Heart Like a Wheel (CBS/Fox)
Heathcliff Vol. 1-3 (RCA/Columbia)
Hellhole (RCA/Columbia)
Helter Skelter (Key)
He-Man and the Masters of the Universe, Vol. 7-13
  (RCA/Columbia)
Hercules (MGM/UA)
Here Come the Littles (Playhouse)
Herself the Elf (CBS/Fox)

The Hitcher (Thorn/EMI)
Home Repairs Made Easy Vol. 1-5 (Karl/Lorimar)
The Honeymooners Vol. 1-10 (MPI)
The Horse Soldiers (CBS/Fox)
Hospital (Key)
Hot Dog, The Movie (Key)
House (New World)
House on Haunted Hill (Key)
House on Skull Mountain (CBS/Fox)
How-To Videos (You Can Do It Video)
Huckleberry Finn (Playhouse)
The Hugga Bunch (Vestron)
Hush, Hush Sweet Charlotte (CBS/Fox)
Iceland River Challenge (Vestron)
The Incredible Human Machine (Vestron)
The Internecine Project (CBS/Fox)
Into the Night (MCA)
Iron Eagle (CBS/Fox)
Irreconcilable Differences (Vestron)
It Came Upon the Midnight Clear (RCA/Columbia)
It Happened One Night (RCA/Columbia)
Jack and the Beanstalk (CBS/Fox)
Jagged Edge (RCA/Columbia)
Jane Fonda's New Workout (Karl/Lorimar)
Jane Fonda's Prime Time Workout (Karl/Lorimar)
Jane Fonda's Workout Challenge (Karl/Lorimar)
Jayce and the Wheeled Warriors Vol. 1-2 (RCA/Columbia)
The Jewel of the Nile (CBS/Fox)
Jim Henson's Muppet Videos (Playhouse)
Johnny Dangerously (CBS/Fox)
Joshua Then and Now (Key)
Journey to the Center of the Earth (Playhouse)
Juggernaut (Key)
Julian Lennon: Stand by Me (MCA)
Just One of the Guys (RCA/Columbia)
The Karate Kid (RCA/Columbia)
The Kermit and Piggy Story (Playhouse)
Key Exchange (Key)

Kidco (Playhouse)
The Killing Fields (Warner)
Killing Hour (CBS/Fox)
King David (Paramount)
Kings Row (Key)
Kiss of the Spider Woman (Charter)
Kramer vs. Kramer (RCA/Columbia)
Krush Groove (Warner)
Ladyhawke (Warner)
The Laughing Policeman (Key)
Learning Can Be Fun (Playhouse)
The Legend of Billie Jean (Key)
The Legend of Hell House (CBS/Fox)
Lenny (Key)
Lifeboat (Key)
Lilies of the Field (Key)

The Lion, the Witch and the Wardrobe (Vestron)
Little Big Man (Key)
The Little Drummer Girl (Warner)
Little Red Riding Hood(CBS/Fox)
Little Treasure (RCA/Columbia)
Lorax and the Hoober Bloob Highway (Playhouse)
Lost in America (Warner)
Lou Ferrigno's Body Perfection (U.S.A.)
Love and Bullets (Key)
Love in the Afternoon (CBS/Fox)
Lovelines (Key)
Lust in the Dust (New World)
Macaroni (Paramount)
Mad Max Beyond Thunderdome (Warner)
A Man Called Horse (CBS/Fox)
A Man For All Seasons (RCA/Columbia)
The Man in the Iron Mask (Playhouse)
The Man Who Would Be King (CBS/Fox)
The Man With One Red Shoe (CBS/Fox)
Marie (MGM/UA)
Marilyn: Say Goodbye to the President (Key)
Martin's Day (CBS/Fox)
Mask (MCA)
M.A.S.K. Vol. III-IV (Karl/Lorimar)
Mass Appeal (MCA)
Max Maven's Mindgames (MCA)
Meatballs II (RCA/Columbia)
Men at Work Concert from San Francisco ... Or Was it Berkeley? (CBS/Fox)
Mickey Mantle's Baseball Tips (CBS/Fox)
Miracle on 34th Street (Playhouse)
Mischief (CBS/Fox)
Mishima: A Life in Four Chapters (Warner)
Mrs. Soffel (MGM/UA)
Mr. Billion (Key)
Mr. Mom (Vestron)
Mr. Rogers: Dinosaurs & Monsters (Playhouse)
Mr. T's Be Somebody .. Or Be Somebody's Fool (MCA)
Mr. Wizard: Puzzles, Problems & Possibilities (Playhouse)
Monte Walsh (CBS/Fox)
Moonlighting (Warner)
Moscow on the Hudson (RCA/Columbia)
Moving Violations (CBS/Fox)
Muppet Moments (Playhouse)
Muppet Review (Playhouse)
Muppet Treasures (Playhouse)
The Muppets Take Manhatten (CBS/Fox)
Murphy's Romance (RCA/Columbia)
Mysterious Island (RCA/Columbia)
National Lampoon's European Vacation (Warner)
National Velvet (MGM/UA)
The Natural (RCA/Columbia)
The Neptune Factor (Playhouse)

The Neverending Story (Warner)
The New Kids (RCA/Columbia)
The New Three Stooges Vol. 1-2 (Embassy)
A Night in Heaven (Key)
Night of the Comet (CBS/Fox)
Night Patrol (New World)
The Night They Raided Minsky's (Key)
Nightingale (CBS/Fox)
Nightmare on Elm Street II: Freddy's Revenge (Media)
1918 (CBS/Fox)
No Small Affair (RCA/Columbia)
No Sweat (Karl/Lorimar)
Oh God, You Devil (Warner)
Oh Heavenly Dog (CBS/Fox)
The Old Curiosity Shop (Vestron)
Oliver (RCA/Columbia)
Oliver Twist (Vestron)
On the Waterfront (RCA/Columbia)
Once Bitten (Vestron)
Once Upon a Time in America (Warner)
Operation CIA (CBS/Fox)
The Organization (Key)
Oxford Blues (CBS/Fox)
Pale Rider (Warner)
Parent's Video Magazine (Karl/Lorimar)
Paris Blues (Key)
Paris, Texas (CBS/Fox)
The Park Is Mine (Key)
A Passage to India (RCA/Columbia)
Pee Wee's Big Adventure (Warner)
Perfect (RCA/Columbia)
Pete's Dragon (Walt Disney)
Phar Lap (Playhouse)
Pink Floyd's David Gilmour (CBS/Fox)
Pinocchio (Walt Disney)
Places in the Heart (CBS/Fox)
The Plague Dogs (Charter)
Planet of the Apes (Playhouse)
Please Don't Hit Me, Mom (Embassy)
Playboy Roasts Tommy Chong (Karl/Lorimar)
Playboy Vol. VI (CBS/Fox)
Playmate Review II-III (CBS/Fox)
Pocketful of Miracles (Key)
Police Academy (Warner)
Pollyanna (Walt Disney)
Pontoffel Pock and Grinch Grinches the Cat in the Hat (Playhouse)
Porky's Revenge (CBS/Fox)
Power (Karl/Lorimar)
Prizzi's Honor (Vestron)
The Protector (Warner)
Protocol (Warner)

Pumping Iron II: The Women (Vestron)
Purple Rain (Warner)
The Purple Rose of Cairo (Vestron)
Quicksilver (RCA/Columbia)
Quo Vadis (MGM/UA)
The Raccoons' Big Surprise (Embassy)
The Raccoons Learn a Lesson (Embassy)
Racing With the Moon (Paramount)
Raiders of the Lost Ark (Paramount)
Rainbow Brite and the Star Stealers (Karl/Lorimar)
Rainbow Brite Vol. II-III (Vestron)
Rambo: First Blood Part II (Thorn EMI)
The Razor's Edge (RCA/Columbia)
Reach for Fitness (Karl/Lorimar)
Real Genius (RCA/Columbia)
Red Sonya (CBS/Fox)
Return of the Jedi (CBS/Fox)
Reuben, Reuben (CBS/Fox)
Revenge of the Nerds (CBS/Fox)
Revolution (Warner)
Rhinestone (CBS/Fox)
The Right Stuff (Warner)
The River (MCA)
The River Rat (Paramount)
Robin Hood (Walt Disney)
Robin Hood and the Sorcerer (Playhouse)
Robin Hood: Swords of Weyland (Playhouse)
Robinson Crusoe and the Tiger (Embassy)
Robotman and Friends Vol. 1 (Vestron)
Rock Music with the Muppets (Playhouse)
Rocky IV (CBS/Fox)
Romancing the Stone (CBS/Fox)
Romantic Comedy (CBS/Fox)
Romper Room: Explore Nature (Playhouse)
Romper Room: Sizes and Shapes (Playhouse)
Romper Room: Songbook (Playhouse)
Romper Room Vol. 1-4 (CBS/Fox)
Rowlf's Rhapsodies with the Muppets (Playhouse)
Rubik the Amazing Cube Vol. 1-2 (RCA/Columbia)
Runaway (RCA/Columbia)
The Runner Stumbles (Key)
Sacred Ground (CBS/Fox)
St. Elmo's Fire (RCA/Columbia)
The Scarlet and the Black (CBS/Fox)
Scrooge (CBS/Fox)
Secret Places (Playhouse)
The Sensuous Nurse (Key)
Sesame Street Presents: Follow That Bird (Warner)
The Seven-Ups (CBS/Fox)
Sexcetera . . . The World According to Playboy (Key)
Shampoo (RCA/Columbia)
Sheena (RCA/Columbia)
She-Ra/He-Man: Secret of the Sword (RCA/Columbia)

She-Ra, The Princess of Power Vol. 1-2 (RCA/Columbia)
Ship of Fools (RCA/Columbia)
Silver Bullet (Paramount)
Silverado (RCA/Columbia)
16 Days of Glory (Paramount)
The Slugger's Wife (RCA/Columbia)
Sno Wonder (Karl/Lorimar)
Snoopy Come Home (CBS/Fox)
Snow White and the Three Stooges (Playhouse)
Soldier in the Rain (Key)
A Soldier's Story (RCA/Columbia)
Songwriter (RCA/Columbia)
Sounder (Paramount)
Spiderman: The Chinese Web (Playhouse)
Spiderman: The Deadly Dust (Playhouse)
Spies Like Us (Warner)
Star Trek III: The Search for Spock (Paramount)
Star Wars to Jedi: The Making of a Saga (Playhouse)
Starman (RCA/Columbia)
Staying Alive (Paramount)
Stick (MCA)
The Stone Boy (CBS/Fox)
Strawberry Shortcake and the Baby Without a Name (Family Home)
A Streetcar Named Desire (Warner)
Streets of Fire (MCA)
Stripes (RCA/Columbia)
The Stuff (New World)
Subway (Key)
Sudden Impact (Warner)
Summer Rental (Paramount)
Support Your Local Sheriff (Key Video)
The Sure Thing (Embassy)
The Sword in the Stone (Walt Disney)
Sylvester (RCA/Columbia)
A Tale of Two Cities (Vestron)
Talk to Me (Playhouse)
Tank (MCA)
Teachers (CBS/Fox)
Teen Wolf (Paramount)
Terms of Endearment (Paramount)
Testament (Paramount)
A Thanksgiving Story (Karl/Lorimar)
That Was Then, This Is Now (Paramount)
Thief of Hearts (Paramount)
The Three Stooges Vol. 5, 9-13 (RCA/Columbia)
Thumbelina (RCA/Columbia)
Thunder and Lightning (Key)
Thundercats (Family Home)
Tightrope (Warner)
To Be or Not to Be (CBS/Fox)
To Live and Die in L.A. (Vestron)
Tom Sawyer (Playhouse)
Tootsie (RCA/Columbia)
Top Secret (Paramount)

Trading Places (Paramount)
Transylvania 6-5000 (New World)
Tuff Turf (New World)
Turk 182 (CBS/Fox)
Twelve Angry Men (Key)
Twice in a Lifetime (Vestron)
Two of a Kind (CBS/Fox)
2010 (MGM/UA)
Uncle Fred: Draw Your Very Own Cartooneys (Playhouse)
Uncommon Valor (Paramount)
The Undefeated (Playhouse)
Unfaithfully Yours (1984) (Paramount)
Unico in the Island of Magic Vol. 2 (RCA/Columbia)
Until September (MGM/UA)
A View to a Kill (CBS/Fox)
Vision Quest (Warner)
Voyage to the Bottom of the Sea (Playhouse)
War Games (CBS/Fox)
Warning Sign (CBS/Fox)
Waterloo Bridge (MGM/UA)
We Are the World (RCA/Columbia)
The Weight Watcher's Guide to a Healthy Lifestyle (Key)
Weird Science (MCA)
Where Did I Come From? (New World)
Where the Boys Are (1984) (Key)
Where's Poppa? (Key)
White Christmas (Paramount)
White Nights (RCA/Columbia)
Who Has Seen the Wind (Embassy)
Wild Life (MCA)
The Wild One (RCA/Columbia)
Willie Nelson and Family in Concert (CBS/Fox)
Windy City (CBS/Fox)
Witness (Paramount)
Wombling Free (RCA/Columbia)
Workin' for Peanuts (Karl/Lorimar)
The World of Henry Orient (Key)
The Year of Living Dangerously (MGM/UA)
Year of the Dragon (MGM/UA)
Yentl (CBS/Fox)
Yukon Passage (Vestron)
Zulu (Charter)

New Releases

As we go to press, a number of program sources have announced the release of new programs. All titles listed below are available on Beta and VHS videocassettes only, unless additional formats are noted. A notation for closed captioned titles (cc) appears where applicable.

ACTIVE HOME VIDEO
How to Beat a
    Speeding Ticket

CABLE FILMS
Beloved Enemy

CC STUDIOS
Animal Stories

**CHARTER
ENTERTAINMENT**
Attica
Horror Rises from
    the Tomb
Make Me an Offer
The Manitou
Murder Mansion
Picture Mommy Dead
Scream of the
    Demon Lover

**CHILDREN'S VIDEO
LIBRARY**
The Centurions
The Story of Babar the
    Little Elephant

CROWN VIDEO
This Old House

**EMBASSY HOME
ENTERTAINMENT**
Come and Get It
Jesse James Meets
    Frankenstein's
    Daughter
Lady Frankenstein
The Mystery of Alexina
Whoopee!

**FAMILY HOME
ENTERTAINMENT**
Billy Possum
The Green Horizon
Wil Cwac Cwac:
    Volume 1

FREE & EASY VIDEO
Aquasize I
Learn to Model at
    Home

**HAL ROACH
STUDIOS**
The Music
    Box/Helpmates

**KARL/LORIMAR
HOME VIDEO**
Alice
The Care Bears
    Storybook
Hard Choices
Playboy's Farmers'
    Daughters

**KARTES VIDEO
COMMUNICATIONS**
the everyday gourmet
Miss Manners on
    Weddings: For
    Better Not Worse
Yardening

KEY VIDEO
Fever Pitch (cc)
The Hustler (cc)
Russian Roulette
Stripper
The Stripper

KULTUR
Concert Aid

LIGHTNING VIDEO
Empty Beach
Formula for a Murder
Rachel's Man
Revenge of the
    Cheerleaders
Robbery
Scream and Die
Spring Symphony

MCA HOME VIDEO
Carl Perkins: Blue
    Suede Shoes
The Don Is Dead
Donna Mills: The Eyes
    Have It
Kojak: The Belarus File
The Last Radio Station
Madigan
Marnie
Newman's Law
Street Hawk

**MEDIA HOME
ENTERTAINMENT**
The Naked Cage
P.O.W. The Escape
Tell Me a Riddle
Time for Revenge
Where the Green
    Ants Dream

**MGM/UA HOME
VIDEO**
The Brothers
    Karamazov
A Connecticut Yankee
    in King Arthur's Court

Kim
The Legend of
  Robin Hood
The Prince and
  the Pauper
Runaway Train (cc)

**MOGUL
COMMUNICATIONS**
On the Edge

**MONTEREY HOME
VIDEO**
The Steel Claw

MPI HOME VIDEO
America's Public
  Enemies
Days of Thrills
  and Laughter
The Fabulous '60s
Five Fighters
  from Shaolin
Fright Films
Golden Memories from
  the Fifties
Great Crimes of
  the Century
Help!
Hey! Hey!
Hollywood Crime Wave
Looking Good
McCarthy: Death of a
  Witch Hunter
The Plot to Kill JFK:
  Rush to Judgement
Queen Elizabeth II—60
  Glorious Years
The Super Bowl Shuffle
Those Magnificent
  Flying Fighting
  Machines
The Unbeaten 28
Vietnam: Time of
  the Locust
Whatever Happened
  to Susan Jane?

NEW WORLD VIDEO
The Rotation Diet

PACIFIC ARTS VIDEO
Ansel Adams:
  Photographer
80 Blocks from
  Tiffany's
Happy Hour with
  the Humans
Irezumi (Spirit of
  Tattoo)

Martial Arts—The
  Chinese Masters
Toni Basil: Word
  of Mouth
Undersea World of
  Jacques Cousteau
Video Treasures

**PARAMOUNT HOME
VIDEO**
Gung Ho (1986) (B, V,
  LV) (cc)
Lady Jane (B, V, LV)
  (cc)
Young Sherlock
  Holmes (B, V, LV)
  (cc)

PLAYHOUSE VIDEO
The Assassination Run
Doctor Who:
  Revenge of the
  Cybermen (cc)
Mastermind: Target
  London (cc)
Smart-Aleck Kill (cc)

PRISM
Day of the Assassin
Vultures

**RCA/COLUMBIA
PICTURES HOME
VIDEO**
Care Bears Movie II: A
  New Generation (cc)
Gumshoe
Living Free
The Monkees: Dance,
  Monkees, Dance/
  Hitting the
  High Seas
The Monkees:
  Monkees vs.
  Machine/Don't
  Look a Gift Horse
  in the Mouth
Ninja Turf
One Minute
  Bible Stories
Quicksilver (cc)
Sotto . . . Sotto
Texas

**REPUBLIC PICTURES
HOME VIDEO**
Living Christ

**SCHOLASTIC
LORIMAR**
The Beniker Gang
Colorforms Learn
  Play VCR
  Adventures

**SONY VIDEO
SOFTWARE**
Not My Kid

**TCL
COMMUNICATIONS**
The Bob Glidden Story

**THORN EMI/HBO
VIDEO** (now called
HBO/Cannon Video)
The Holcroft Covenant
In the Angry
  Red Planet
A Kind of Loving
The Royal Wedding:
  Prince Andrew to
  Sarah Ferguson
Wild Geese II

THRILLER VIDEO
Anatomy of Terror
The Devil's Web
The Human
  Duplicators

UNICORN VIDEO
Cobra
Dance of Death
Girls on the Road
Top of the Heap

UNITED HOME VIDEO
The Magic
  Christmas Tree
Night of the Bloody
  Transplant
Santa Claus
Vampire Happening

USA HOME VIDEO
Bad Guys
In Search Of . . .
Killjoy
Man of Destiny
Survival English
Svengali (1983)

VCL HOME VIDEO
Blue Blood
Fists of Bruce Lee
Vengeance Is Mine

VESTRON VIDEO
African Wildlife (*cc*)
Atocha: Quest for
    Treasure (*cc*)
Elton John: Breaking
    Hearts Tour
First and Ten: The
    Team Scores Again
Liberty Weekend—
    Commemorative
    Edition
Livin' the Life
Mark of Cain
MTV Closet Classics
Over the Summer
Salvador (*B, V, LV*) (*cc*)
The Scarlet
    Pimpernel (*1982*)
Strangers in Paradise
Turtle Diary

VIDEO GEMS
American Tickler
The Best of Women's
    Championship
    Wrestling, Vol. 1
Black Cobra
Ninja Massacre

**WARNER HOME
VIDEO**
Bodyband Workout
The Cousteau
    Odyssey Video
    Treasures
The Music Man (*B, V,
    LV*) (*cc*)
Wildcats (*B, V, LV*) (*cc*)

**WORLDVISION
HOME VIDEO**
Abduction of St. Anne
The City
Law of the Land
Manhunter
Most Wanted

Cast Index

This index includes complete videographies for over 320 actors, actresses, directors and other screen personalities.

To provide as thorough a reference section as possible, cameo appearances, soundtrack narrations and other peripheral involvements appear in the listings, where known.

Trivia pursuers will note some interesting credits included herein; for example, small parts played by current superstars Richard Dreyfuss *(The Graduate)* and Sylvester Stallone *(Bananas* and *The Prisoner of Second Avenue)* early in their careers. Also, while Charles Laughton's role in *Mutiny on the Bounty* is an obvious inclusion, you might not be familiar with his role in *Early Elvis* as the substitute host of *The Ed Sullivan Show* on the night that Elvis made his first appearance.

This compilation reflects our efforts to list performers that readers are likely to look for while striving to keep the section down to a manageable length.

ABBOTT AND COSTELLO

Abbott and Costello
   in Hollywood
Abbott and Costello
   Meet Captain Kidd
Abbott and Costello
   Meet Dr. Jekyll
   and Mr. Hyde
Abbott and Costello
   Meet Frankenstein
Abbott and Costello
   Show, The
Africa Screams
Buck Privates
Classic Comedy
   Video Sampler
Colgate Comedy
   Hours, I-IV
Comedy and Kid Stuff
Hey Abbott!
Hold That Ghost
Hollywood Clowns,
   The

Hollywood Goes to
   War
Jack and the
   Beanstalk
Super Bloopers I

ALAN ALDA

California Suite
Four Seasons, The
Free to Be . . . You
   and Me
Glass House, The
M*A*S*H
Goodbye, Farewell
   and Amen
Playmates
Purlie Victorious
Same Time, Next
   Year
Seduction of Joe
   Tynan, The
To Kill a Clown

WOODY ALLEN

Annie Hall
Bananas
Best of Candid
   Camera, The
Broadway Danny
   Rose
Casino Royale
Everything You
   Always Wanted to
   Know About
   Sex . . .
Front, The
Love and Death
Manhattan
Midsummer Night's
   Sex Comedy, A
Play It Again, Sam
Purple Rose of Cairo,
   The
Sleeper
Take the Money and
   Run
What's New
   Pussycat?

What's Up Tiger Lily?
Zelig

JULIE ANDREWS

Hawaii
Little Miss Marker
Man Who Loved
  Women, The
Mary Poppins
Outtakes IV
S.O.B.
Sound of Music, The
Tamarind Seed, The
"10"
Torn Curtain
Victor/Victoria

ANN-MARGRET

Bye Bye Birdie
Carnal Knowledge
C.C. and Company
Cincinnati Kid, The
Hollywood Home
  Movies
I Ought to Be in
  Pictures
Joseph Andrews
Last Remake of Beau
  Geste, The
Lookin' to Get Out
Magic
Murderer's Row
Pocketful of Miracles
Reach For Fitness
Return of the Soldier
R*P*M (*Revolutions
  Per Minute)
Tiger and the
  Pussycat, The
Tommy
Train Robbers, The
Twice in a Lifetime
Twist
Viva Las Vegas

LAURA ANTONELLI

Divine Nymph, The
High Heels
How Funny Can Sex
  Be?
Innocent, The
Malicious

Passion of Love
Secret Fantasy
Tigers in Lipstick
Till Marriage Do Us
  Part

ALAN ARKIN

Bad Medicine
Big Trouble
Catch-22
Chu-Chu and the
  Philly Flash
Emperor's New
  Clothes, The
Freebie and the Bean
Heart Is a Lonely
  Hunter, The
Improper Channels
In-Laws, The
Joshua Then and
  Now
Last of the Red Hot
  Lovers, The
Rafferty and the Gold
  Dust Twins
Russians Are
  Coming, The
  Russians Are
  Coming, The
Seven Percent
  Solution, The
Simon
Wait Until Dark

LOUIS ARMSTRONG

Best of Louis
  Armstrong, The
Goodyear Jazz
  Concert with Louis
  Armstrong
Hello, Dolly!
High Society
Jukebox Saturday
  Night
That's Entertainment,
  Part II
TV Variety, Book VIII

JEAN ARTHUR

Danger Lights
Devil and Miss Jones,
  The

Ex-Mrs. Bradford,
  The
History Is Made at
  Night
Lady Takes a
  Chance, The
Mr. Smith Goes to
  Washington
Shane

FRED ASTAIRE

Amazing Dobermans,
  The
Band Wagon, The
Carefree
Damsel In Distress
Easter Bunny Is
  Coming to Town,
  The
Family Upside Down,
  A
Finian's Rainbow
Flying Down to Rio
Follow the Fleet
Fred Astaire: Change
  Partners and
  Dance
Fred Astaire: Puttin'
  On His Top Hat
Funny Face
Gay Divorcee, The
Ghost Story
Gotta Dance, Gotta
  Sing
Holiday Inn
Man in the Santa
  Claus Suit, The
On the Beach
Purple Taxi, The
Royal Wedding
Second Chorus
Shall We Dance
Silk Stockings
Sky's the Limit, The
Story of Vernon and
  Irene Castle, The
Swing Time
That's Dancing
That's Entertainment
That's Entertainment
  Part II
Top Hat

Towering Inferno,
  The
You'll Never Get Rich
You Were Never
  Lovelier
Ziegfeld Follies

GENE AUTRY

Blue Canadian
  Rockies
Boots and Saddles
Call of the Canyon
Cow Town
Cowboys of the
  Saturday Matinee
Git Along, Little
  Dogies
Heart of the Rio
  Grande
Hills of Utah, The
Last of the Pony
  Riders
Man from Music
  Mountain, The
Man of the Frontier
Manhattan Merry-Go-
  Round
Melody Ranch
Melody Trail
Mystery Mountain
Night Stage to
  Galveston
Old Corral, The
On Top of Old Smoky
Phantom Empire
Prairie Moon
Radio Ranch
Ridin' on a Rainbow
Robinhood of Texas
Rootin' Tootin'
  Rhythm
Round-Up Time in
  Texas
Saginaw Trail
Saturday Night
  Serials
Sioux City Sue
Six-Gun Previews,
  Volume I
South of the Border
Valley of Fire
Western Double
  Feature #5, 16

Winning of the West

DAN AYKROYD

Best of John Belushi,
  The
Blues Brothers, The
Comedy Music
  Videos
Doctor Detroit
Ghostbusters
Into the Night
Mr. Mike's Mondo
  Video
Neighbors
1941
Saturday Night Live
Spies Like Us
Trading Places
Twilight Zone—The
  Movie

LAUREN BACALL

Big Sleep, The
Dark Passage
Fan, The
Harper
How to Marry a
  Millionaire
Key Largo
Murder on the Orient
  Express
Northwest Frontier
Premier of "A Star is
  Born"
Shootist, The
To Have and Have
  Not

LUCILLE BALL

Abbott and Costello
  in Hollywood
Affairs of Annabel,
  The
Annabel Takes a
  Tour
Best Foot Forward
Comedy and Kid Stuff
Five Came Back
Follow the Fleet
Girl, a Guy and a
  Gob, A

Great Gildersleeve,
  The
Guide For the
  Married Man, A
Having Wonderful
  Time
I Dream Too Much
Mame
Panama Lady
Premiere of "A Star
  Is Born"
Room Service
Stage Door
Toast of the Town
Top Hat
TV's Classic
  Guessing Games
TV Variety, Book VII
Vintage Commercials
  I-IV
Ziegfeld Follies

ANNE BANCROFT

Agnes of God
Audience with Mel
  Brooks, An
Bell Jar, The
Elephant Man, The
Garbo Talks
Graduate, The
Hindenburg, The
Jesus of Nazareth
Lipstick
Miracle Worker, The
Prisoner of Second
  Avenue, The
Silent Movie
To Be or Not to Be
Turning Point, The
Young Winston

BRIGITTE BARDOT

And God Created
  Woman
Contempt
Crazy for Love
Doctor at Sea
Famous T and A
Legend of Frenchie
  King, The
Ravishing Idiot, The
Shalako

Very Private Affair, A

JOHN BARRYMORE

Bulldog Drummond
    Double Feature
Dinner at Eight
Dr. Jekyll and Mr.
    Hyde
Grand Hotel
Horrible Double
    Feature
Maytime
Never Love a
    Stranger
Svengali
Tempest, The/The
    Eagle
That's Entertainment,
    Part II

LIONEL BARRYMORE

America
America/The Fall of
    Babylon
Bells, The
Captains Courageous
David Copperfield
Dr. Kildare's Strange
    Case
It's a Wonderful Life
Key Largo
That's Entertainment,
    Part II
Treasure Island

ALAN BATES

Britannia Hospital
King of Hearts
Quartet
Return of the Soldier
Rose, The
Separate Tables
Shout, The
Tresspasser, The
Unmarried Woman,
    An
Whistle Down the
    Wind
Women in Love
Zorba the Greek

WARREN BEATTY

Bonnie and Clyde
Dollars
Heaven Can Wait
Lilith
McCabe and Mrs.
    Miller
Parallax View, The
Reds
Roman Spring of Mrs.
    Stone, The
Shampoo
Splendor in the Grass

MICHAEL BECK

Golden Seal, The
Holocaust
Madman
Megaforce
Warlords of the 21st
    Century
Warriors, The
Xanadu

JOHN BELUSHI

All You Need Is Cash
Animal House
Best of John Belushi,
    The
Blues Brothers, The
Comedy Music
    Videos
Continental Divide
Goin' South
Neighbors
1941
Old Boyfriends
Saturday Night Live
Things We Did Last
    Summer

RICHARD BENJAMIN

Catch-22
City Heat
Diary of a Mad
    Housewife
First Family
Goodbye Columbus
House Calls

How to Beat the High
    Cost of Living
Last Married Couple
    in America, The
Last of Sheila, The
Love at First Bite
My Favorite Year
No Room to Run
Packin' It In
Portnoy's Complaint
Saturday Night Live:
    Richard Benjamin
Scavenger Hunt
Steagle
Sunshine Boys, The
Westworld
Witches' Brew

JACK BENNY

Comedy and Kid Stuff
    III
George Burns and
    Gracie Allen Show,
    The
Guide for the Married
    Man, A
It's a Mad, Mad, Mad,
    Mad World
It's in the Bag
Jack Benny
Jack Benny I-III
Jack Benny Program,
    The
Jack Benny Show,
    The
Jack Benny Visits
    Walt Disney
Medicine Man
Milton Berle
    Spectacular, The
Take a Good Look/
    The Jack Benny
    Show
That's Entertainment,
    Part II
To Be or Not to Be
TV Variety, Book VII,
    X
Vintage Commercials
    II

CANDICE BERGEN

Bite the Bullet
Carnal Knowledge
Domino Principle,
  The
11 Harrowhouse
Gandhi
Group, The
Oliver's Story
Rich and Famous
Sand Pebbles, The
Soldier Blue
Starting Over
Stick
Wind and the Lion,
  The

INGMAR BERGMAN

After the Rehearsal
Brink of Life
Cries and Whispers
Devil's Eye
Fanny and Alexander
Magician, The
Night Is My Future,
  The
Persona
Port of Call
Scenes from a
  Marriage
Secrets of Women
Serpent's Egg
Seventh Seal, The
Wild Strawberries
Winter Light

INGRID BERGMAN

Adam Had Four Sons
Arch of Triumph
Bells of St. Mary's,
  The
Cactus Flower
Casablanca
Doctor Jekyll and Mr.
  Hyde
Fear
Gaslight
Hideaways, The
Indiscreet
Inn of the Sixth
  Happiness, The
Intermezzo

Joan of Arc
Matter of Time, A
Murder on the Orient
  Express
Notorious
Spellbound
Stromboli
Under Capricorn
Walk in the Spring
  Rain, A
Woman Called Golda,
  A

MILTON BERLE

Bloopers from "Star
  Trek" and "Laugh-
  In"
Broadway Danny
  Rose
Broadway Highlights
Buick Berle Show,
  The
Cracking Up
Doyle Against the
  House
Fozzie's Muppet
  Scrapbook
Hey Abbott!
It's a Mad, Mad, Mad,
  Mad World
Journey Back to Oz
Legend of Valentino,
  The
Lepke
Milton Berle Hour,
  The
Milton Berle Show I-
  II, The
Muppet Movie, The
Off Your Rocker
Oscar, The
Playboy Video
  Magazine
Texaco Star Theatre
TV Variety, II
Who's Minding the
  Mint

JACQUELINE
BISSET

Airport
Bullitt

Class
Day for Night
Deep, The
Detective, The
Famous T and A
Forbidden
Greek Tycoon, The
Magnifique, Le
Murder on the Orient
  Express
Observations Under
  the Volcano
Rich and Famous
Secrets
St. Ives
Thief Who Came to
  Dinner, The
Together
Under the Volcano

KAREN BLACK

Airport 1975
Bad Manners
Burnt Offerings
Can She Bake a
  Cherry Pie?
Capricorn One
Chanel Solitaire
Come Back to the 5
  and Dime Jimmy
  Dean, Jimmy Dean
Crime and Passion
Day of the Locust
Easy Rider
Family Plot
Great Gatsby, The
In Praise of Older
  Women
Last Word, The
Little Laura and Big
  John
Little Mermaid, The
Martin's Day
Mr. Horn
Nashville
Portnoy's Complaint
Ripoff, The
Savage Dawn
Separate Ways
Trilogy of Terror
You're a Big Boy
  Now

HUMPHREY BOGART

African Queen, The
Angels with Dirty
    Faces
Barefoot Contessa,
    The
Beat the Devil
Big Breakdowns, The
Big Sleep, The
Caine Mutiny, The
Casablanca
Coming Attractions
Dark Passage
Dark Victory
Dead End
Harder They Fall, The
High Sierra
Hollywood Outtakes
    and Rare Footage
Jack Benny, II
Key Largo
Knock on Any Door
Left Hand of God,
    The
Maltese Falcon, The
Midnight
Oklahoma Kid, The
Passage to Marseilles
Petrified Forest, The
Presidential Blooper
    Reel
Roaring Twenties,
    The
Sahara
Sirocco
Stand-In
They Drive by Night
To Have and Have
    Not
Treasure of the
    Sierra Madre, The
27th Annual
    Academy Awards
We're No Angels

DAVID BOWIE

David Bowie: Jazzin'
    for Blue Jean
David Bowie:
    Ricochet
David Bowie: Serious
    Moonlight
Hunger, The
Into the Night
Man Who Fell to
    Earth, The
Merry Christmas, Mr.
    Lawrence
Ziggy Stardust and
    the Spiders from
    Mars

MARLON BRANDO

Apocalypse Now
Burn!
Chase, The
Formula, The
Godfather, The
Godfather: The
    Complete Epic,
    The
Guys and Dolls
Last Tango in Paris
Marlon Brando
Men, The
Missouri Breaks, The
Mutiny on the Bounty
Nightcomers, The
One-Eyed Jacks
On the Waterfront
Reflections in a
    Golden Eye
Sayonara
Streetcar Named
    Desire, A
Superman—The
    Movie
27th Annual
    Academy Awards
Viva Zapata!
Wild One, The

BEAU BRIDGES

Creative Parenting:
    The First 12
    Months
Dangerous Company
For Love of Ivy
Four Feathers
Greased Lightning
Hammersmith Is Out
Heart Like A Wheel
Honky Tonk Freeway
Hotel New
    Hampshire, The
Love Child
Night Crossing
Norma Rae
Other Side of the
    Mountain, The
President's Mistress,
    The
Red Light Sting, the
Red Pony, The
Runner Stumbles,
    The
Silver Dream Racer
Stranger who Looks
    Like Me, The
Village of the Giants

JEFF BRIDGES

Against All Odds
Bad Company
Cutter's Way
Heaven's Gate
Jagged Edge
Kiss Me Goodbye
King Kong
Last American Hero,
    The
Last Unicorn, The
Rapunzel
Starman
Stay Hungry
Thunderbolt and
    Lightfoot
Tron
Winter Kills
Yin and Yang of Mr.
    Ko, The

LLOYD BRIDGES

Abilene Town
Airplane!
Airplane II: The
    Sequel
Bear Island
Big Deadly Game
Crash of Flight 401,
    The
Daring Game
East of Eden
High Noon

Home of the Brave
Mission Galactica:
    The Cylon Attack
Rocketship
    X.M—Special
    Edition
Roots
Running Wild
Sahara
Scuba
Tall Texan
Tattered Web, A
Trapped
Walk in the Sun, A
War in the Sky
White Tower, The
Who Killed Julie
    Greer?

**CHARLES
BRONSON**

Borderline
Breakheart Pass
Breakout
Cabo Blanco
Cold Sweat
Chino
Death Hunt
Death Wish
Death Wish II
Death Wish III
Dirty Dozen, The
Drum Beat
Evil That Men Do,
    The
Family, The
Great Escape, The
Hard Times
Honor Among
    Thieves
Love and Bullets
Magnificent Seven,
    The
Master of the World
Mechanic, The
Mr. Majestyk
Once Upon a Time in
    the West
Raid on Entebbe
Red Sun
Rider on the Rain
Run of the Arrow
St. Ives

Sandpiper, The
Showdown at Boot
    Hill
Someone Behind the
    Door
Stone Killer, The
Telefon
This Property Is
    Condemned
TV Classics
Villa Rides

MEL BROOKS

Audience with Mel
    Brooks, An
Blazing Saddles
Comedy Music
    Videos
Free to Be ... You
    and Me
High Anxiety
History of the World:
    Part I, The
Muppet Movie, The
Producers, The
Silent Movie
Timex All-Star
    Comedy Show
To Be or Not to Be
Twelve Chairs, The
2000 Year Old Man,
    The
When Things Were
    Rotten
Young Frankenstein

**GENEVIEVE
BUJOLD**

Anne of the
    Thousand Days
Caesar and Cleopatra
Choose Me
Coma
Earthquake
Final Assignment
Journey
King of Hearts
Last Flight of Noah's
    Ark, The
Monsignor
Murder by Decree
Obsession

Tightrope

CAROL BURNETT

Annie
Between Friends
Carol Burnett Show:
    Bloopers and
    Outtakes, The
Chu Chu and the
    Philly Flash
Four Seasons, The
Son of TV Bloopers
Wedding, A

GEORGE BURNS

Broadway Highlights
Comedy and Kid Stuff
Damsel in Distress
George Burns and
    Gracie Allen Show,
    The
George Burns in
    Concert
George Burns Twice
George Burns Show,
    The
Going in Style
I Married Joan/The
    Burns and Allen
    Show
Jack Benny
Jack Benny Show,
    The
Oh, God!
Oh, God! Book II
Oh, God! You Devil
Rowlf's Rhapsodies
    with the Muppets
Sgt. Pepper's Lonely
    Hearts Club Band
Sunshine Boys, The
Two of a Kind
Vintage Sitcoms

ELLEN BURSTYN

Alice Doesn't Live
    Here Anymore
Ambassador, The
Exorcist, The
Harry & Tonto
People Vs. Jean
    Harris

Providence
Same Time, Next
Year
Silence of the North
Thursday's Game
Twice in a Lifetime

RICHARD BURTON

Alexander the Great
Anne of the
Thousand Days
Becket
Bluebeard
Breakthrough
Circle of Two
Cleopatra
Divorce His, Divorce
Hers
Equus
Exorcist II: The
Heretic
Gathering Storm, The
Hammersmith Is Out
Longest Day, The
Look Back in Anger
Lovespell
Massacre in Rome
Night of the Iguana,
The
1984
Raid on Rommel
Robe, The
Sandpiper, The
Taming of the Shrew,
The
Tempest, The
Under Milk Wood
Wagner
Where Eagles Dare
Who's Afraid of
Virginia Woolf?
Wild Geese, The

GARY BUSEY

Barbarosa
Big Wednesday
Carny
D.C. Cab
Didn't You Hear?
Foolin' Around
Insignificance

Last American Hero,
The
Saturday Night Live:
Gary Busey
Star Is Born, A
Stephen King's Silver
Bullet
Straight Time
Thunderbolt and
Lightfoot

JAMES CAAN

Bolero
Brian's Song
Bridge Too Far, A
Chapter Two
Comes a Horseman
Coming Attractions
Countdown
Death Valley Days,
Volume II
Dorado, El
Freebie and the Bean
Gambler, The
Godfather, The
Godfather: The
Complete Epic,
The
Gone with the West
Harry and Walter Go
to New York
Hide in Plain Sight
Killer Elite, The
Kiss Me Goodbye
Lady in a Cage
Rain People, The
Rollerball
Silent Movie
Thief

SID CAESAR

Admiral Broadway
Revue, The
Airport 1975
Barnaby and Me
Best of Comic Relief,
The
Caesar's Hour
Curse of the Black
Widow
Dorothy in the Land
of Oz

Fiendish Plot of Dr.
Fu Manchu, The
Grease II
Guide for the Married
Man, A
History of the World
Part I, The
It's a Mad, Mad, Mad,
Mad World
Over the Brooklyn
Bridge
Sid Caesar's Shape
Up
Silent Movie
Ten From Your Show
of Shows
When Things Were
Rotten
Your Show of Shows

JAMES CAGNEY

Angels with Dirty
Faces
Big Breakdowns, The
Blood on the Sun
Coming Attractions
Footlight Parade
Great Guy
James Cagney: That
Yankee Doodle
Dandy
Midsummer's Night
Dream, A
Mister Roberts
Never Steal Anything
Small
Oklahoma Kid, The
One, Two, Three
Presidential Blooper
Reel
Public Enemy, The
Ragtime
Roaring Twenties,
The
Strawberry Blonde,
The
Something to Sing
About
Time of Your Life,
The
What Price Glory
White Heat

Yankee Doodle
Dandy

MICHAEL CAINE

Alfie
Beyond the Limit
Beyond the Poseidon
Adventure
Blame It on Rio
Bridge Too Far, A
California Suite
Deathtrap
Dressed to Kill
Eagle Has Landed,
The
Funeral in Berlin
Hand, The
Harry and Walter Go
to New York
Island, The
Jigsaw Man, The
Man Who Would Be
King, The
Romantic
Englishwoman,
The
Silver Bears
Sleuth
Swarm, The
Too Late the Hero
Victory
Wrong Box, The
Zulu

DYAN CANNON

Anderson Tapes, The
Author! Author!
Bob & Carol & Ted &
Alice
Coast to Coast
Deathtrap
Having It All
Heaven Can Wait
Honeysuckle Rose
Lady of the House
Last of Sheila, The
Shamus

EDDIE CANTOR

Big Time, The
Colgate Comedy
Hour, The

Hollywood Goes to
War
If You Knew Susie
Show Business

FRANK CAPRA

Arsenic and Old Lace
Attack—The Battle of
New Britain
George Stevens: A
Filmmaker's
Journey
It Happened One
Night
It's a Wonderful Life
Meet John Doe
Mr. Smith Goes to
Washington
Pocketful of Miracles
Prelude to War
Silent Laugh Makers
#3
State of the Union
Under Nazi Guns/On
to Tokyo

ART CARNEY

Better Late than
Never
Bitter Harvest
Cavalcade of Stars
Defiance
Emperor's New
Clothes, The
Frosty's Winter
Wonderland/The
Leprechaun's Gold
Going in Style
Guide for the Married
Man, A
Harry & Tonto
Honeymooners
Hidden Episodes,
The
House Calls
Late Show, The
Movie, Movie
Muppets Take
Manhattan, The
Naked Face, The
St. Helens, Killer
Volcano

Sunburn
TV Variety XI

LESLIE CARON

American in Paris, An
Dangerous Moves
Fanny
Father Goose
Gigi
Golden Girl
Head of the Family
Lili
Madron
Man Who Loved
Women, The
That's Entertainment
Unapproachable, The

JOHN CARRADINE

Bees, The
Best of Sex and
Violence, The
Big Foot
Billy the Kid Versus
Dracula
Black Cat, The/The
Raven
Blood Legacy
Blood of Dracula's
Castle
Bogey Man, The
Cain's Cutthroats
Captain Kidd
Captains Courageous
Cruise Missile
Daniel Boone
Death at Love House
Demon Rage
Everything You
Always Wanted to
Know About Sex
Evils of the Night
Five Came Back
Frankenstein's Island
Gallery of Horror
Golden Rendezvous
Grapes of Wrath, The
Greatest Heroes of
the Bible
Gun Riders
Hillbillys in a Haunted
House

House of Long
  Shadows, The
House of Seven
  Corpses
Howling, The
Incredible Petrified
  World, The
Inspector General
Judgment of
  Solomon, The
Last Tycoon, The
Mary of Scotland
Monster Club, The
Nesting, The
Nocturna
Return of Frank
  James, The
Revenge
Satan's Cheerleaders
Secret of NIMH, The
Sentinel, The
Shock Waves
Showdown at Boot
  Hill
Shootist, The
Silent Night, Bloody
  Night
Silver Spurs
Stagecoach
Ten Commandments,
  The
Terror in the Wax
  Museum
Tragedy of Antony
  and Cleopatra
Unearthly, The
Vals, The
Vampire Hookers
Wizard of Mars, The

**ROBERT
CARRADINE**

Aladdin and His
  Wonderful Lamp
Aloha Bobby and
  Rose
Big Red One, The
Blackout
Coming Home
Jackson County Jail
Joyride
Just the Way You Are
Long Riders, The

Mean Streets
Orca
Pom-Pom Girls, The
Revenge of the
  Nerds
Tag: The
  Assassination
  Game
Wavelength

LON CHANEY

Abbott and Costello
  Meet Frankenstein
Behave Yourself!
Big Chase
Colgate Comedy
  Hour Volume III
Cyclops
Film House Fever
Hillbillys in a Haunted
  House
Horrible Double
  Feature
Hunchback of Notre
  Dame, The
Macabre Moments
  from The Phantom
  of the Opera
My Favorite Brunette
One Million B.C.
Outside The Law
Passion
Phantom of the
  Opera, The
Saturday Night
  Serials
Shock
Tales of Tomorrow

CHARLIE CHAPLIN

America Between the
  Great Wars
Chaplin Essanay
  Book I, The
Chaplin: Keystone
  Beginnings
Chaplin Mutuals, Vol.
  I-IV
Chaplin Revue, The
Charlie Chaplin
  Carnival

Charlie Chaplin
  Cavalcade
Charlie Chaplin
  Festival
Charlie Chaplin's
  Keystone
  Comedies
Circus, The/Day's
  Pleasure, A
City Lights
Clown Princes of
  Hollywood
Flicker Flashbacks
Fun Factory/Clown
  Princes of
  Hollywood
Gold Rush, The
Great Dictator, The
Hollywood Clowns,
  The
Kid, The/The Idle
  Class
Kid's Auto Race/
  Mabel's Married
  Life
King in New York, A
Knockout, The/
  Dough and
  Dynamite
Laughfest
Limelight
Modern Times
Monsieur Verdoux
Rink, The/The
  Immigrant
Slapstick
Tillie's Punctured
  Romance
Tramp, The/A
  Woman
When Comedy Was
  King
Woman of Paris, A/
  Sunnyside
Work/Police

CYD CHARISSE

Band Wagon, The
Black Tights
Brigadoon
Deep in My Heart
Silk Stockings
Singin' in the Rain

That's Entertainment
That's Entertainment,
    Part II
Ziegfeld Follies

CHEVY CHASE

Best of John Belushi,
    The
Caddyshack
Deal of the Century
Ernie Kovacs:
    Television's
    Original Genius
Fletch
Foul Play
Groove Tube, The
Modern Problems
National Lampoon's
    European Vacation
National Lampoon's
    Vacation
Oh, Heavenly Dog
Saturday Night Live
Seems Like Old
    Times
Sesame Street
    Presents "Follow
    That Bird"
Spies Like Us
Tunnelvision
Under the Rainbow

MAURICE
CHEVALIER

Black Tights
Breath of Scandal, A
Fanny
French Singers
Gigi
In Search of the
    Castaways
Invitation to Paris
Love in the Afternoon
That's Entertainment

JULIE CHRISTIE

Billy Liar
Darling
Demon Seed
Doctor Zhivago
Don't Look Now
Farenheit 451

Heat and Dust
Heaven Can Wait
McCabe and Mrs.
    Miller
Power
Return of the Soldier
Separate Tables
Shampoo

JILL CLAYBURGH

First Monday in
    October
Griffin and Phoenix
Hanna K.
Hustling
I'm Dancing as Fast
    as I Can
It's My Turn
Semi-Tough
Silver Streak
Starting Over
Terminal Man, The
Thief Who Came to
    Dinner, The
Unmarried Woman,
    An
Wedding Party, The

MONTGOMERY
CLIFT

Big Lift, The
Heiress, The
I Confess
Indiscretion of an
    American Wife
Judgment at
    Nuremburg
Misfits, The
Montgomery Clift
Place in the Sun, A
Raintree County
Red River
Suddenly Last
    Summer

GLENN CLOSE

Big Chill, The
Jagged Edge
Maxie
Natural, The
Orphan Town
Stone Boy, The

World According to
    Garp, The

JOAN COLLINS

Big Sleep, The
Bitch, The
Cosh Boy
Dark Places
Decameron Nights
Dynasty of Fear
Empire of Ants
Executioner, The
Fearless
Great Adventure, The
Hansel and Gretel
Her Life as a Man
Homework
Nutcracker Sweet
Oh Alfie
Playboy Video
    Magazine Vol. 7
Quest for Love
Revenge
Star Trek II
Star Trek Volume 5
Star Trek: City on the
    Edge of Forever
Stopover Tokyo
Stud, The
Subterfuge
Sunburn
Tales From the Crypt
Tough Guy, The

SEAN CONNERY

Anderson Tapes, The
Another Time,
    Another Place
Bridge Too Far, A
Darby O'Gill and the
    Little People
Diamonds Are
    Forever
Dr. No
Fine Madness, A
Five Days One
    Summer
From Russia with
    Love
Goldfinger
Longest Day, The

Man Who Would Be
  King, The
Meteor
Molly Maguires, The
Murder on the Orient
  Express
Never Say Never
  Again
Outland
Robin and Marian
Shalako
Sword of the Valiant
Thunderball
Time Bandits
Time Lock
Wind and the Lion,
  The
Wrong Is Right
You Only Live Twice
Zardoz

GARY COOPER

Along Came Jones
Ball of Fire
Farewell to Arms, A
Fighting Caravans
Fountainhead, The
Friendly Persuasion
Good Sam
High Noon
It
Leave 'Em Laughing
Love in the Afternoon
Meet John Doe
Pride of the Yankees
Sergeant York
They Came to
  Cordura
Vera Cruz
Westerner, The
Wings

**FRANCIS FORD
COPPOLA**

Apocalypse Now
Conversation, The
Cotton Club, The
Dementia 13
Filmmaker: A Diary
  by George Lucas
Godfather, The

Godfather: The
  Complete Epic,
  The
New Look
One from the Heart
Rain People, The
Rip Van Winkle
Tonight for Sure
You're a Big Boy
  Now

BILL COSBY

Bill Cosby, Himself
Bill Cosby's
  Picturepages
California Suite
Devil & Max Devlin,
  The
Let's Do It Again
Man and Boy
Opportunities in
  Criminal Justice
Piece of the Action, A
Uptown Saturday
  Night

JOAN CRAWFORD

Autumn Leaves
Grand Hotel
Hollywood Outtakes
  and Rare Footage
Johnny Guitar
Mildred Pierce
Night Gallery
Possessed
Premiere of "A Star
  Is Born"
Rain
Strait Jacket
What Ever Happened
  to Baby Jane?
Women, The

BING CROSBY

Bells of St. Mary's,
  The
Bing Crosby Festival
Country Girl, The
Going My Way
High Society
Holiday Inn

Hollywood Goes to
  War
Jack Benny
King of Jazz, The
Legend of Sleepy
  Hollow, The
Princess and the
  Pirate, The
Road to Bali, The
Road to Lebanon,
  The
That's Entertainment
That's Entertainment,
  Part II
TV Variety, Book VIII
White Christmas
Young Bing Crosby

GEORGE CUKOR

Adam's Rib
All Quiet on the
  Western Front
Born Yesterday
David Copperfield
Dinner at Eight
Double Life, A
Gaslight
Heller in Pink Tights
It Should Happen to
  You
Les Girls
Little Women
My Fair Lady
Philadelphia Story,
  The
Rich and Famous
Star is Born, A

TONY CURTIS

Balboa
Boston Strangler, The
Brainwaves
Count of Monte
  Cristo, The
Defiant Ones, The
Great Race, The
Insignificance
Last Tycoon, The
Lepke
Little Miss Marker
Mirror Crack'd, The
Operation Petticoat

Perfect Furlough, The
Portrait of a Showgirl
Premiere of "A Star
  Is Born"
Sex on the Run
Sextette
Some Like It Hot
Spartacus
Title Shot
Trapeze
Users, The
Vegas
Vikings, The

PETER CUSHING

And Now The
  Screaming Starts
Asylum
At the Earth's Core
Beast Must Die, The
Blood Beast Terror
Bloodsuckers
Call Him Mr. Shatter
Choice of Weapons,
  A
Creeping Flesh, The
Curse of
  Frankenstein, The
Devil's Undead, The
Doctor Phibes Rises
  Again
Dr. Terror's House of
  Horrors
Dynasty of Fear
Ghoul, The
Horror Express
Horror of Dracula
Hound of the
  Baskervilles
House of the Long
  Shadows, The
House That Dripped
  Blood, The
Land of the Minotaur
Legend of the
  Werewolf
Mummy, The
Scream and Scream
  Again
Shock Waves
Silent Scream
Sword of the Valiant
Tales from the Crypt

Torture Garden
Twins of Evil
Uncanny, The
Vampire Lovers, The

BETTE DAVIS

All About Eve
All This and Heaven
  Too
Big Breakdowns, The
Burnt Offerings
Dark Victory
Death on the Nile
Disappearance of
  Aimee, The
Fashions of 1934
Hell House
Hollywood Outtakes
  and Rare Footage
Hush . . . Hush, Sweet
  Charlotte
Jezebel
Juarez
Letter, The
Little Foxes, The
Now Voyager
Of Human Bondage
Petrified Forest, The
Pocketful of Miracles
Presidential Blooper
  Reel
Private Lives of
  Elizabeth and
  Essex, The
Return from Witch
  Mountain
Right of Way
Strangers: The Story
  of a Mother and
  Daughter
27th Annual
  Academy Awards
Watch on the Rhine
Watcher in the
  Woods, The
What Ever Happened
  to Baby Jane?
White Mama

DORIS DAY

Lover Come Back
Man Who Knew Too
  Much, The
Pillow Talk
Teacher's Pet
That Touch of Mink
With Six You Get
  Eggroll
Young at Heart

JAMES DEAN

America at the
  Movies
East of Eden
Giant
Hollywood Outtakes
  and Rare Footage
James Dean
James Dean Story,
  The
James Dean: The
  First American
  Teenager
Premiere of "A Star
  Is Born"
Rebel Without a
  Cause

OLIVIA DE
HAVILLAND

Adventures of Robin
  Hood, The
Airport '77
Anthony Adverse
Captain Blood
Charge of the Light
  Brigade, The
Dark Mirror
Dodge City
Gone With the Wind
Heiress, The
Hush . . . Hush, Sweet
  Charlotte
Lady in a Cage
Midsummer Night's
  Dream, A
Private Lives of
  Elizabeth and
  Essex, The
Proud Rebel, The
Santa Fe Trail

Strawberry Blonde,
  The
Swarm, The
They Died With Their
  Boots On

DOM DELUISE

Best Little
  Whorehouse in
  Texas, The
Cannonball Run, The
Cannonball Run II
End, The
History of the World:
  Part I, The
Hot Stuff
Johnny Dangerously
Last Married Couple
  in America, The
Muppet Movie, The
Only With Married
  Men
Peter-No-Tail
Secret of NIMH, The
Silent Movie
Twelve Chairs, The
Wholly Moses!

ROBERT DE NIRO

America at the
  Movies
Bang the Drum
  Slowly
Bloody Mama
Brazil
Deer Hunter, The
Falling in Love
Godfather Part II, The
Godfather: The
  Complete Epic,
  The
King of Comedy
Last Tycoon, The
Mean Streets
New York, New York
Obsession
Once Upon a Time in
  America
Raging Bull
Scarface
Swap, The
Taxi Driver

True Confessions
Wedding Party, The

BRIAN DE PALMA

Blow Out
Body Double
Carrie
Dressed to Kill
Fury, The
Home Movies
Phantom of the
  Paradise
Sisters
Wedding Party, The

BO DEREK

Bolero
Change of Seasons,
  A
Fantasies
Orca
Playboy Video,
  Volume 1
Tarzan, the Ape Man
"10"

BRUCE DERN

Black Sunday
Bloody Mama
Coming Home
Cowboys
Driver, The
Family Plot
Great Gatsby, The
Harry Tracy
Hush . . . Hush, Sweet
  Charlotte
Laughing Policeman,
  The
Rebel Rousers
St. Valentine's Day
  Massacre
Silent Running
Support Your Local
  Sheriff
Tattoo
That Championship
  Season
Trip, The
Twist
War Wagon, The
Wild Angel, The

MARLENE
DIETRICH

Around the World in
  80 Days
Black Fox
Blue Angel, The
Judgment at
  Nuremburg
Knight Without Armor
Love Goddesses,
  The
Piaf, the Woman
Rancho Notorious
Spoilers, The
Stage Fright
Witness for the
  Prosecution

MATT DILLON

Flamingo Kid, The
Liar's Moon
Little Darlings
My Bodyguard
Outsiders, The
Over the Edge
Rumble Fish
Target
Tex
Wild Rides

KIRK DOUGLAS

Arrangement, The
Big Sky, The
Big Trees, The
Cast a Giant Shadow
Catch Me a Spy
Champion
Draw!
Eddie Macon's Run
Final Countdown, The
Fury, The
Gunfight at the O.K.
  Corral
Hollywood Bloopers
Holocaust
  Survivors . . .
  Rememberance of
  Love
Holocaust 2000
Home Movies
Jack Benny, II

Light at the Edge of
  the World, The
List of Adrian
  Messenger, The
Lonely Are the Brave
Man from Snowy
  River, The
Man Without a Star
Master Touch, The
Milton Berle
  Spectacular, The
My Dear Secretary
Once Is Not Enough
Out of the Past
Paths of Glory
Saturn 3
Seven Days in May
Spartacus
Strange Love of
  Martha Ivers, The
There Was a
  Crooked Man
20,000 Leagues
  Under the Sea
Ulysses
Vikings, The
War Wagon, The

MELVYN DOUGLAS

Annie Oakley
Being There
Billy Budd
Candidate, The
Captains Courageous
Death Squad
Ghost Story
Hud
I Never Sang for My
  Father
Lamp at Midnight
Mr. Blandings Builds
  His Dream House
My Forbidden Past
Ninotchka
Seduction of Joe
  Tynan, The
Tenant, The
That Uncertain
  Feeling
Twilight's Last
  Gleaming
Woman in the
  Shadows

Your Show of Shows

MICHAEL DOUGLAS

China Syndrome, The
Chorus Line, A
Coma
It's My Turn
Jewel of the Nile
Napoleon and
  Samantha
Romancing the Stone
Star Chamber, The

RICHARD
DREYFUSS

American Graffiti
Apprenticeship of
  Duddy Kravitz, The
Big Fix, The
Buddy System, The
Close Encounters of
  the Third Kind
Competition, The
Dillinger
Down and Out in
  Beverly Hills
Goodbye Girl, The
Graduate, The
Jaws
Second Coming of
  Suzanne, The
Whose Life Is It
  Anyway?

FAYE DUNAWAY

Arrangement, The
Bonnie and Clyde
Champ, The
Chinatown
Country Girl, The
Disappearance of
  Aimee, The
Eyes of Laura Mars
First Deadly Sin, The
Four Musketeers,
  The
Little Big Man
Mommie Dearest
Network
Ordeal by Innocence
Supergirl

Supergirl: The Making
  of the Movie
Thomas Crown Affair,
  The
Three Days of the
  Condor
Three Musketeers,
  The
Towering Inferno,
  The
Voyage of the
  Damned

IRENE DUNNE

Ann Vickers
Awful Truth, The
I Remember Mama
Life with Father
Penny Serenade

JIMMY DURANTE

Broadway Highlights
Hollywood Goes to
  War
It's a Mad, Mad, Mad,
  Mad World
Melody Ranch
Palooka
That's Entertainment
That's Entertainment,
  Part II

CHARLES DURNING

Best Little
  Whorehouse in
  Texas, The
Breakheart Pass
Die Laughing
Dog Day Afternoon
Final Countdown, The
Fury, The
Greek Tycoon, The
Harry and Walter Go
  to New York
Man With One Red
  Shoe, The
North Dallas Forty
Sharky's Machine
Sisters
Stand Alone
Starting Over
Stick

Sting, The
Tilt
Tootsie
True Confessions
Twilight's Last
    Gleaming
When a Stranger
    Calls

ROBERT DUVALL

Apocalypse Now
Badge 373
Betsy, The
Breakout
Bullitt
Conversation, The
Countdown
Eagle Has Landed,
    The
Godfather, The
Godfather Part II, The
Godfather: The
    Complete Epic,
    The
Greatest, The
Great Santini, The
Joe Kidd
Killer Elite, The
Lady Ice
M*A*S*H
Natural, The
Network
Pursuit of D.B.
    Cooper, The
Rain People, The
Seven-Per-Cent
    Solution, The
Stone Boy, The
Tender Mercies
Terry Fox Story, The
THX 1138
Tomorrow
True Confessions
True Grit

SHELLEY DUVALL

Annie Hall
Brewster McCloud
Faerie Tale Theatre
McCabe and Mrs.
    Miller
Nashville

Popeye
Rapunzel
Rumpelstiltskin
Shining, The
Time Bandits

BLAKE EDWARDS

Breakfast at Tiffany's
Days of Wine and
    Roses, The
Experiment in Terror
Great Race, The
Micki and Maude
Operation Petticoat
Pink Panther, The
Pink Panther Strikes
    Again, The
Return of the Pink
    Panther, The
Revenge of the Pink
    Panther, The
Shot in the Dark, A
S.O.B.
Tamarind Seed, The
"10"
Victor/Victoria

CLINT EASTWOOD

Any Which Way You
    Can
Beguiled, The
Bronco Billy
City Heat
Coogan's Bluff
Dirty Harry
Death Valley Days
Eiger Sanction, The
Enforcer, The
Escape from Alcatraz
Every Which Way But
    Loose
Firefox
Fistful of Dollars, A
For a Few Dollars
    More
Gauntlet, The
Good, the Bad and
    the Ugly, The
Hang 'Em High
High Plains Drifter
Honkytonk Man
Joe Kidd

Kelly's Heroes
Magnum Force
Outlaw Josey Wales,
    The
Paint Your Wagon
Pale Rider
Play Misty for Me
Sudden Impact
Thunderbolt and
    Lightfoot
Tightrope
Two Mules for Sister
    Sara
Where Eagles Dare

SAMANTHA EGGAR

Battle Force
Brood, The
Collector, The
Curtains
Demonoid
Doctor Doolittle
Doctor in Distress
Exterminator, The
Light at the Edge of
    the World, The
Molly Maguires, The
Name for Evil, A
Seven-Per-Cent
    Solution, The
Uncanny, The
Unknown Powers
Why Shoot the
    Teacher?

DUKE ELLINGTON

All-Star Swing
    Festival
Big Bands, Volume
    101
Black and Tan
Black Jazz and Blues
Cabin in the Sky
Check and Double
    Check
Goodyear Jazz
    Concert with Duke
    Ellington
Jazz and Jive
Masquerade Party
Meet The
    Bandleaders

Sacred Music of
 Duke Ellington,
 The

DOUGLAS FAIRBANKS SR.

Americano, The
Birth of a Legend
Black Pirate, The
Classic Silent Shorts
Don Q., Son of Zorro
Gunga Din
Mark of Zorro, The
Matrimaniac, The
Mr. Robinson Crusoe
Mr. Super Athletic
 Charm
Private Life of Don
 Juan, The
Reaching for the
 Moon
Taming of the Shrew,
 The
Thief of Bagdad, The
Wild and Wooly

PETER FALK

All the Marbles
Big Trouble
Brink's Job, The
In-Laws, The
It's A Mad, Mad, Mad
 World
Luv
Mickey and Nicky
Murder by Death
Pocketful of Miracles
Price of Tomatoes,
 The

MIA FARROW

Avalanche
Broadway Danny
 Rose
Death on the Nile
Great Gatsby, The
High Heels
Hurricane
Haunting of Julia, The
Last Unicorn, The
Midsummer Night's
 Sex Comedy, A

Purple Rose of Cairo,
 The
Rosemary's Baby
Sarah and the
 Squirrel
Supergirl
Wedding, A
Zelig

FARRAH FAWCETT

Burning Bed, The
Cannonball Run, The
Logan's Run
Murder in Texas
Red Light Sting, The
Saturn 3
Sunburn

SALLY FIELD

Absence of Malice
Back Roads
Beyond the Poseidon
 Adventure
End, The
Heroes
Home for the
 Holidays
Hooper
Kiss Me Goodbye
Murphy's Romance
Norma Rae
Places in the Heart
Smokey and the
 Bandit
Smokey and the
 Bandit II
Stay Hungry
Sybil

W.C. FIELDS

Bank Dick, The
Barber Shop, The
Best of W.C. Fields,
 The
David Copperfield
Dentist, The
Fatal Glass of Beer,
 The
Fatal Glass of Beer,
 The/The Pool
 Shark
Flask of Fields, A

Funny Guys and Gals
 of the Talkies
Hollywood Clowns,
 The
It's a Gift
My Little Chickadee
Never Give a Sucker
 an Even Break
Outtakes VI
Pharmacist, The
Sally of the Sawdust
That's Entertainment,
 Part II
W.C. Fields Comedy
 Bag
W.C. Fields Festival

ALBERT FINNEY

Annie
Dresser, The
Duellists, The
Looker
Loophole
Murder on the Orient
 Express
Observations Under
 the Volcano
Scrooge
Shoot the Moon
Tom Jones
Under the Volcano
Wolfen

ERROL FLYNN

Adventures of
 Captain Fabian
Adventures of Don
 Juan, The
Adventures of Robin
 Hood, The
Big Breakdowns, The
Big Surprise, The
Captain Blood
Charge of the Light
 Brigade, The
Dawn Patrol, The
Dodge City
Gentleman Jim
Northern Pursuit
Prince and the
 Pauper, The

Private Lives of
  Elizabeth and
  Essex, The
Santa Fe Trail
Sea Hawk, The
Son of Hollywood
  Bloopers
They Died With Their
  Boots On
Warriors, The

HENRY FONDA

Barn Burning
Battle Force
Battle of the Bulge,
  The
Bernice Bobs Her
  Hair
Boston Strangler, The
Clarence Darrow
Displaced Persons
Fail Safe
Fort Apache
Gideon's Trumpet
Grapes of Wrath, The
Great Smokey
  Roadblock, The
How the West Was
  Won
I Dream Too Much
Jesse James
Jezebel
Jilting of Granny
  Weatherall, The
Lady Eve, The
Last Four Days, The
Longest Day, The
Mad Miss Manton,
  The
Man That Corrupted
  Hadleyburg, The
Meteor
Midway
Mister Roberts
My Darling
  Clementine
Night Flight from
  Moscow
Oldest Living
  Graduate, The
Once Upon a Time in
  the West
On Golden Pond

Perry Como Show,
  The
Rappaccini's
  Daughter
Return of Frank
  James, The
Sometimes a Great
  Notion
Stagestruck
Summer Solstice
Swarm, The
Tentacles
There Was A
  Crooked Man
Tin Star, The
Too Late the Hero
Twelve Angry Men
War and Peace
Warlock
Wings of the Morning
Wrong Man
You Only Live Once

JANE FONDA

Agnes of God
Barbarella
Barefoot in the Park
California Suite
Cat Ballou
Chase, The
China Syndrome, The
Comes a Horseman
Coming Home
Doll's House, A
Electric Horseman,
  The
Fun with Dick and
  Jane
Jane Fonda
  Challenge
Jane Fonda's New
  Workout
Jane Fonda's
  Workout
Jane Fonda's
  Workout for
  Pregnancy, Birth
  and Recovery
Joy House
Julia
Klute
9 to 5
On Golden Pond

Rollover
Steelyard Blues

PETER FONDA

Cannonball Run, The
Certain Fury
Easy Rider
Futureworld
High Ballin'
Hostage Tower, The
Jungle Heat
Killer Force
Lilith
Outlaw Blues
Race With the Devil
Roger Corman:
  Hollywood's Wild
  Angel
Spasms
Split Image
Tammy and the
  Doctor
Trip, The
Wild Angels, The

JOAN FONTAINE

Annabel Takes a
  Tour/Maids Night
  Out
Damsel in Distress
Decameron Nights
Gunga Din
Ivanhoe
Rebecca
Suspicion
Voyage to the Bottom
  of the Sea
Women, The

GLENN FORD

Americano, The
Appointment in
  Honduras
Big Heat, The
Experiment in Terror
Four Horsemen of
  the Apocalypse,
  The
Gilda
Great White Death
Happy Birthday to Me

Hollywood Clowns,
   The
Midway
Pocketful of Miracles
Sacketts, The
Santee
Superman—The
   Movie
3:10 to Yuma
Virus
White Tower, The

HARRISON FORD

American Graffiti
Apocalypse Now
Blade Runner
Conversation, The
Empire Strikes Back,
   The
Force 10 from
   Navarone
Frisco Kid, The
Getting Straight
Great Movie Stunts
   and The Making of
   Raiders of the Lost
   Ark
Hanover Street
Heroes
Luv
Making of Star Wars,
   The/S.P.F.X.—The
   Empire Strikes
   Back
Raiders of the Lost
   Ark
Return of the Jedi
Star Wars
Witness

JOHN FORD

Arrowsmith
Cheyenne Autumn
Fort Apache
Grapes of Wrath, The
Horse Soldiers, The
How the West Was
   Won
Hurricane, The
Informer, The

Man Who Shot
   Liberty Valance,
   The
Mary of Scotland
Mister Roberts
Mogambo
My Darling
   Clementine
Quiet Man, The
Searchers, The
She Wore a Yellow
   Ribbon
Stagecoach
Straight Shootin'
This is Korea/
   December 7th
Wagonmaster

JODIE FOSTER

Alice Doesn't Live
   Here Anymore
Candleshoe
Carny
Foxes
Freaky Friday
Hotel New
   Hampshire, The
Little Girl Who Lives
   Down the Lane,
   The
Napoleon and
   Samantha
O'Hara's Wife
Taxi Driver

CLARK GABLE

China Seas
Gone With The Wind
Idiot's Delight
It Happened One
   Night
Misfits, The
Mogambo
Mutiny on the Bounty
Painted Desert, The
Possessed
Premiere of "A Star
   Is Born"
Red Dust
Run Silent, Run Deep
San Francisco
Teacher's Pet

That's Entertainment
That's Entertainment,
   Part II

GRETA GARBO

Anna Christie
Grand Hotel
Ninotchka
That's Entertainment,
   Pt. II
Wild Orchids

AVA GARDNER

Barefoot Contessa,
   The
Bible, The
Cassandra Crossing,
   The
Earthquake
55 Days at Peking
Ghosts on the Loose
Knights of the Round
   Table
Life and Times of
   Judge Roy Bean,
   The
Mogambo
My Forbidden Past
Night of the Iguana,
   The
On the Beach
One Touch of Venus
Permission to Kill
Seven Days in May
Show Boat
That's Entertainment
Whistle Stop

JOHN GARFIELD

Body and Soul
Force of Evil
Juarez
They Made Me a
   Criminal

JUDY GARLAND

Babes in Arms
Best of Judy Garland,
   The
Coming Attractions
Easter Parade

Girl Crazy
Hollywood Outtakes
 and Rare Footage
In the Good Old
 Summertime
Judgment at
 Nuremburg
Judy Garland
 (General Electric
 Theatre)
Judy Garland in
 Concert Vols. I-II
Judy Garland Show,
 The
Meet Me in St. Louis
Pirate, The
Premiere of "A Star
 Is Born"
Star Is Born, A
Strike Up the Band
That's Entertainment
That's Entertainment,
 Part II
Till the Clouds Roll
 By
Wizard of Oz, The
Words and Music
World War II Video
 Series—Something
 for the Boys
Ziegfeld Follies

JAMES GARNER

Castaway Cowboy
Fan, The
Glitter Dome, The
Great Escape, The
Murphy's Romance
One Little Indian
Sayonara
Skin Game
Support Your Local
 Sheriff
Tank
Victor/Victoria

TERI GARR

After Hours
Black Stallion, The
Black Stallion
 Returns, The

Close Encounters of
 the Third Kind
Deja View
Do It Debbie's Way
Escape Artist
First Born
Honky Tonk Freeway
Mr. Mom
One From the Heart
Prime Suspect
Steve Martin Live
Sting II, The
Tale of the Frog
 Prince, The
To Catch a King
Tootsie
Witches' Brew
Young Frankenstein

RICHARD GERE

American Gigolo
Beyond the Limit
Bloodbrothers
Breathless
Cotton Club, The
Days of Heaven
King David
Looking for Mr.
 Goodbar
Officer and a
 Gentleman, An
Power

MEL GIBSON

Attack Force Z
Bounty, The
Gallipoli
Mad Max
Mad Max Beyond
 Thunderdome
Mrs. Soffel
River, The
Road Warrior, The
Summer City
Tim
Year of Living
 Dangerously, The

SIR JOHN GIELGUD

Around the World in
 80 Days
Arthur

Becket
Caligula
Charge of the Light
 Brigade, The
Chariots of Fire
Elephant Man, The
11 Harrowhouse
Formula, The
Frankenstein
Ghandi
Gielgud's Chekov
Invitation to a
 Wedding
Julius Caesar
Lion of the Desert
Murder by Decree
Murder on the Orient
 Express
Plenty
Providence
Richard III
Scandalous
Secret Agent
Shooting Party, The
Sphinx
Wagner

LILLIAN GISH

Adventures of
 Huckleberry Finn,
 The
Battle of Elderbush
 Gulch, The
Birth of a Nation
Broken Blossoms
D.W. Griffith Triple
 Feature
Follow Me, Boys!
Great Chase, The
Hambone and Hillie
His Double Life
Home Sweet Home
Intolerance
Orphans of the Storm
True Heart Susie
Way Down East
Wedding, A

JACKIE GLEASON

Cavalcade of Stars
Don't Drink the Water

Honeymooners
    Hidden Episodes
Mr. Billion
Mr. Halpern and Mr.
    Johnson
Papa's Delicate
    Condition
Smokey and the
    Bandit I-III
Sting II, The
Soldier in the Rain
Toy, The
TV Variety, Book VIII,
    XI
Vintage Sitcoms

JEFF GOLDBLUM

Annie Hall
Big Chill, The
Into the Night
Legend of Sleepy
    Hollow, The
Silverado
Three Little Pigs, The
Threshold
Transylvania 6-5000

RUTH GORDON

Abe Lincoln in Illinois
Any Which Way You
    Can
Every Which Way But
    Loose
Harold and Maude
Jimmy the Kid
Maxie
Mugsy's Girls
My Bodyguard
Rosemary's Baby
Where's Poppa?

ELLIOT GOULD

Bob & Carol & Ted &
    Alice
Bridge Too Far, A
Capricorn One
Devil and Max Devlin,
    The
Dirty Tricks
Drug Free Kids: A
    Parent's Guide
Escape to Athena

Falling in Love Again
Harry and Walter Go
    to New York
I Love My Wife
Lady Vanishes, The
Jack and the
    Beanstalk
Last Flight of Noah's
    Ark, The
M*A*S*H
Matilda
Mean Johnny
    Barrows
Muppet Movie, The
Naked Face, The
Night They Raided
    Minsky's, The
Over the Brooklyn
    Bridge
Quick, Let's Get
    Married
Saturday Night Live:
    Elliot Gould
Silent Partner

BETTY GRABLE

Bob Hope Chevy
    Show II, The
Day the Bookies
    Wept, The
Follow the Fleet
Gay Divorcee, The
Gotta Sing, Gotta
    Dance
Hollywood Goes to
    War
How to Marry a
    Millionaire
Love Goddesses,
    The

CARY GRANT

Amazing Adventure,
    The
Arsenic and Old Lace
Awful Truth, The
Bachelor and the
    Bobby Soxer, The
Charade
Every Girl Should Be
    Married
Father Goose

Grass Is Greener,
    The
Gunga Din
His Girl Friday
In Name Only
Indiscreet
Mr. Blandings Builds
    His Dream House
Mr. Lucky
My Favorite Wife
Night and Day
None But the Lonely
    Heart
North by Northwest
Notorious
Once Upon a
    Honeymoon
Operation Petticoat
Penny Serenade
Philadelphia Story,
    The
Pride and the
    Passion, The
Suspicion
That Touch of Mink
To Catch a Thief
Toast of New York
Topper

D.W. GRIFFITH

Abraham Lincoln
Avenging
    Conscience, The
Babylon Story from
    "Intolerance," The
Battle of Elderbush
    Gulch, The
Birth of a Nation
Broken Blossoms
Dream Street
D.W. Griffith: An
    American Genius
D.W. Griffith Triple
    Feature
Film Firsts
Home Sweet Home
Intolerance
Judith of Bethulia
Movies' Story, The
Origins of Cinema
Orphans of the Storm
Short Films of D.W.
    Griffith, Vol. I, The

True Heart Susie
Way Down East

CHARLES GRODIN

All Night Long
11 Harrowhouse
Grass Is Always
  Greener Over the
  Septic Tank, The
Great Muppet Caper,
  The
Heartbreak Kid, The
Heaven Can Wait
Incredible Shrinking
  Woman, The
It's My Turn
Just Me and You
King Kong
Lonely Guy, The
Movers and Shakers
Paul Simon Special,
  The
Real Life
Rosemary's Baby
Saturday Night Live:
  Charles Grodin
Seems Like Old
  Times
Sunburn
Woman in Red, The

SIR ALEC
GUINNESS

Bridge on the River
  Kwai, The
Brother Sun, Sister
  Moon
Captain's Paradise,
  The
Doctor Zhivago
Empire Strikes Back,
  The
Fall of the Roman
  Empire, The
Horse's Mouth, The
Kind Hearts and
  Coronets
Ladykillers, The
Lavender Hill Mob,
  The
Lawrence of Arabia
Little Lord Fauntleroy

Lovesick
Making of Star Wars,
  The
Malta Story, The
Man in the White
  Suit, The
Murder by Death
Passage to India, A
Return of the Jedi
Scrooge
Star Wars
To Paris With Love
To See Such Fun

GENE HACKMAN

All Night Long
America At The
  Movies
Bite The Bullet
Bonnie and Clyde
Bridge Too Far, A
Conversation, The
Domino Principle,
  The
Downhill Racer
Eureka!
French Connection,
  The
French Connection II
Hawaii
Marooned
Misunderstood
Night Moves
Poseidon Adventure,
  The
Power
Prime Cut
Scarecrow
Superman—The
  Movie
Superman II
Target
Twice in a Lifetime
Uncommon Valor
Under Fire

GEORGE
HAMILTON

Dead Don't Die, The
Evel Knievel
Express to Terror
From Hell to Victory

Happy Hooker Goes
  to Washington,
  The
Love at First Bite
Medusa
Once Is Not Enough
Sextette
Togetherness
Where the Boys Are
Zorro, The Gay Blade

JEAN HARLOW

China Seas
Dinner at Eight
Love Goddesses,
  The
Public Enemy, The
Red Dust
That's Entertainment

RICHARD HARRIS

Bible, The
Camelot
Golden Rendezvous
Gulliver's Travels
Hawaii
Highpoint
Last Word, The
Major Dundee
Man Called Horse, A
Martin's Day
Molly Maguires, The
Mutiny On The
  Bounty
Orca
Return of a Man
  Called Horse, The
Robin and Marian
Tarzan, the Ape Man
Triumphs of a Man
  Called Horse
Wild Geese, The
Your Ticket Is No
  Longer Valid

REX HARRISON

Cleopatra
Deadly Thief
Doctor Doolittle
Main Street to
  Broadway
Men Are Not Gods

My Fair Lady
Night Train to Munich
School For Husbands
Sidewalks of London
Storm in a Teacup
Time to Die, A

GOLDIE HAWN

Best Friends
Bloopers From "Star
    Trek" and "Laugh-
    In"
Butterflies are Free
Cactus Flower
Dollars
Duchess and the
    Dirtwater Fox, The
Foul Play
Goldie and Kids
Lovers and Liars
One and Only,
    Genuine, Original
    Family Band, The
Private Benjamin
Protocol
Seems Like Old
    Times
Shampoo
Sugarland Express,
    The
Swing Shift
There's a Girl in My
    Soup

HELEN HAYES

Airport
Arrowsmith
Candleshoe
Family Upside Down,
    A
Farewell to Arms, A
Herbie Rides Again
Main Street to
    Broadway
One of Our Dinosaurs
    Is Missing
Skin Game, The
Stagedoor Canteen
Third Man on the
    Mountain

RITA HAYWORTH

Circus World
Fire Down Below
Gilda
Lady from Shanghai
Love Goddesses,
    The
Miss Sadie
    Thompson
Poppies Are Also
    Flowers
Renegade Ranger,
    The/Scarlet Rider
Separate Tables
Strawberry Blonde
They Came to
    Cordura
Trouble in Texas
You'll Never Get Rich
You Were Never
    Lovelier

AUDREY HEPBURN

Breakfast at Tiffany's
Charade
Funny Face
Lavender Hill Mob,
    The
Love in The
    Afternoon
My Fair Lady
Robin and Marian
Roman Holiday
Sidney Sheldon's
    Bloodline
They All Laughed
27th Annual
    Academy Awards
Wait Until Dark
War and Peace

KATHARINE HEPBURN

Adam's Rib
African Queen, The
Alice Adams
Christopher Strong
Dragon Seed
George Stevens: A
    Filmmakers
    Journey
Grace Quigley

Guess Who's Coming
    to Dinner
Lion in The Winter,
    The
Little Minister, The
Little Women
Long Day's Journey
    Into Night
Mary Of Scotland
Morning Glory
On Golden Pond
Philadelphia Story,
    The
Rooster Cogburn
Stage Door
Stagedoor Canteen
State of the Union
Storytime Classics
Suddenly Last
    Summer
Summertime
Trojan Woman, The
Woman of the Year
Woman Rebels, A

CHARLTON HESTON

Airport 1975
Antony and Cleopatra
Awakening, The
Beneath the Planet of
    the Apes
Ben Hur
Buccaneer, The
Call of the Wild
Chiefs
Cid, El
Earthquake
Elizabeth the Queen
55 Days at Peking
Four Musketeers,
    The
Greatest Show on
    Earth, The
Greatest Story Ever
    Told, The
Julius Ceaser
Major Dundee
Midway
Mother Lode
Mountain Men, The
Omega Man, The
Planet of the Apes

Pony Express
Ruby Gentry
Son of Monsters on
   the March
Soylent Green
Ten Commandments,
   The
Three Musketeers,
   The

GREGORY HINES

Cotton Club, The
Deal of the Century
Eubie!
History of the
   World—Part I
Puss 'N Boots
Saturday Night Live:
   Gary Busey
White Nights
Wolfen

ALFRED
HITCHCOCK

Birds, The
Blackmail
Family Plot
Foreign
   Correspondent
Frenzy
I Confess
Lady Vanishes, The
Lifeboat
Lodger, The
Man Who Knew Too
   Much, The
Mr. and Mrs. Smith
Murder
North by Northwest
Notorious
Number Seventeen
Psycho
Rear Window
Rebecca
Rope
Sabotage
Saboteur
Secret Agent
Skin Game, The
Spellbound
Stage Fright
Strangers on a Train

Suspicion
Thirty-Nine Steps,
   The
To Catch a Thief
Topaz
Torn Curtain
Trouble With Harry,
   The
Under Capricorn
Vertigo
Wrong Man, The
Young and Innocent

DUSTIN HOFFMAN

Agatha
All the President's
   Men
Graduate, The
Kramer vs. Kramer
Lenny
Little Big Man
Marathon Man
Midnight Cowboy
Papillon
Straight Time
Straw Dogs
Tootsie

WILLIAM HOLDEN

Alvarez Kelly
Born Yesterday
Bridge on the River
   Kwai, The
Casino Royale
Christmas Tree, The
Country Girl, The
Damien—Omen II
Dear Wife
Earthling, The
Golden Boy
Horse Soldiers, The
Moon Is Blue, The
Network
Our Town
Rachel and the
   Stranger
S.O.B.
Stalag 17
Sunset Boulevard
Towering Inferno,
   The

27th Annual
   Academy Awards
Union Station
When Wolves Cry
Wild Bunch, The
Wings Of War
Young and Willing

JUDY HOLLIDAY

Adam's Rib
Bells Are Ringing
Born Yesterday
It Should Happen To
   You
That's Entertainment,
   Pt. II

BOB HOPE

Bloopers from "Star
   Trek" and "Laugh-
   In"
Bob Hope Chevy
   Show I-III, The
Boy, Did I Get a
   Wrong Number
Comedy and Kid Stuff
   III
Hollywood at War
Hollywood Clowns,
   The
Hollywood Goes to
   War
Jack Benny
Jack Benny Show,
   The
Jack Benny Visits
   Walt Disney
Muppet Movie, The
My Favorite Brunette
Off Limits
Paleface, The
Paris Holiday
Princess and the
   Pirate, The
Road to Bali, The
Road to Lebanon,
   The
Television's Golden
   Age of Comedy
They Got Me
   Covered

27th Annual
   Academy Awards
World War II Video
   Series—Something
   for Our Boys

LESLIE HOWARD

Big Breakdowns, The
Forty-Ninth Parallel,
   The
Gone With the Wind
Intermezzo
Of Human Bondage
Petrified Forest, The
Pimpernel Smith
Pygmalion
Scarlet Pimpernel,
   The
Spitfire
Stand-In

ROCK HUDSON

Ambassador, The
Avalanche
Bend of the River
Devlin Connection,
   The
Embryo
Giant
Ice Station Zebra
Lover Come Back
Magnificent
   Obsession
Martian Chronicles,
   The
Mirror Crack'd, The
Pillow Talk
Sea Devils
Something of Value
Tobruck

WILLIAM HURT

Altered States
Big Chill, The
Body Heat
Eyewitness
Gorky Park
Kiss of the Spider
   Woman

JOHN HUSTON

African Queen, The
American Caesar
Angela
Annie
Asphalt Jungle, The
Battle for the Planet
   of the Apes
Beat the Devil
Bible, The
Breakout
Cannery Row
Casino Royale
Chinatown
Fatal Attraction
George Stevens: A
   Filmmakers
   Journey
Great Cities: London,
   Rome, Dublin,
   Athens
Hobbit, The
Let There Be Light
List of Adrian
   Messenger, The
Lovesick
Maltese Falcon, The
Minor Miracle, A
Misfits, The
Moby Dick
Observations Under
   the Volcano
Prizzi's Honor
Red Badge of
   Courage, The
Reflections in a
   Golden Eye
Tentacles
Treasure of the
   Sierra Madre, The
Under the Volcano
Winter Kills
Wise Blood
Word, The

LAUREN HUTTON

American Gigolo
Cradle Will Fall, The
Gambler, The
Gator
Lassiter
Once Bitten

Starflight One
Viva Knievel
Wedding, A
Zorro, the Gay Blade

TIMOTHY HUTTON

And Baby Makes Six
Daniel
Father Figure
Falcon and the
   Snowman, The
Iceman
Long Way Home, The
Ordinary People
Taps
Turk 182
Wonderful World of
   Disney, The
Young Love, First
   Love

JEREMY IRONS

Betrayal
French Lieutenant's
   Woman, The
Moonlighting
Statue of Liberty, The
Swann in Love
Wild Duck, The

AMY IRVING

Carrie
Competition, The
Far Pavilions
Fury, The
Honeysuckle Rose
I'm a Fool
Micki and Maude
Yentl

AL JOLSON

Coming Attractions
Jazz Singer, The
Musical Personalities
   No. 1
Weber and Fields, Al
   Jolson and This Is
   America

JAMES EARL JONES

Aladdin and His
  Wonderful Lamp
Conan the Barbarian
Deadly Hero
End of the Road
Greatest, The
Last Remake of Beau
  Geste, The
Piece of the Action, A

JENNIFER JONES

Demon
Dick Tracy's G-Men
Indiscretion of an
  American Wife,
  The
Love Is a Many
  Splendored Thing
Madame Bovary
Ruby Gentry
Song of Bernadette
Towering Inferno,
  The

TOMMY LEE JONES

Amazing Howard
  Hughes, The
Back Roads
Barn Burning
Betsy, The
Black Moon Rising
Cat on a Hot Tin
  Roof
Coal Miner's
  Daughter
Executioner's Song,
  The
Eyes of Laura Mars
Jackson County Jail
Nate and Hayes
Park Is Mine, The
River Rat, The
Rolling Thunder

RAUL JULIA

Compromising
  Positions
Escape Artist
Gumball Rally, The

Kiss of the Spider
  Woman

MADELINE KAHN

At Long Last Love
Blazing Saddles
City Heat
First Family
Gonzo Presents
  Muppet Weird Stuff
Hideaways, The
High Anxiety
History of the World:
  Part I, The
Muppet Movie, The
Paper Moon
Saturday Night Live:
  Madeline Kahn
Scrambled Feet
Simon
Slapstick of Another
  Kind
What's Up Doc?
Wholly Moses!
Yellowbeard
Young Frankenstein

BORIS KARLOFF

Abbott and Costello
  Meet Dr. Jekyll
  and Mr. Hyde
Ape, The
Bedlam
Before I Hang
Big Breakdowns, The
Black Cat, The/The
  Raven
Black Room, The
Black Sabbath
Blind Man's Bluff
Body Snatcher, The
Bride of
  Frankenstein, The
Cauldron of Blood
Chamber of Fear
Criminal Code, The
Daydreamer, The
Doomed to Die
Frankenstein
Haunted Strangler,
  The
Island Monster

Isle of the Dead
Juggernaut
Lost Patrol, The
Macabre Serenade
Man They Could Not
  Hang, The
Mr. Wong, Detective
Monsters on the
  March
Mummy, The
Raven, The
Scarface
Secret Life of Walter
  Mitty, The
Sinister Invasion
Snake People, The
Tales of Tomorrow
Targets
Terror, The
You'll Find Out

DANNY KAYE

Court Jester, The
Hans Christian
  Andersen
Hollywood Clowns,
  The
Inspector General,
  The
Kid From Brooklyn,
  The
Pinocchio
Secret Life of Walter
  Mitty, The
Vintage Commercials
  IV
White Christmas

BUSTER KEATON

Balloonatic, The/One
  Week
Best of Candid
  Camera, The
Blacksmith, The
Boom in the Moon
Buster Keaton
  Festival Vol. I
Buster Keaton Rides
  Again/The
  Railrodder
Clown Princess of
  Hollywood, The

College
Ed Wynn Show, The
Fun Factory/Clown
   Princes of
   Hollywood
Funny Thing
   Happened on the
   Way to the Forum,
   A
General, The
General, The/
   Slapstick
God's Country
Great Chase, The
Hollywood Clowns,
   The
How To Stuff a Wild
   Bikini
In the Good Old
   Summertime
It's a Mad, Mad, Mad,
   Mad World
Keaton Special/
   Valentino Mystique
Kovacs and Keaton
L'il Abner
Limelight
Parlour, Bedroom and
   Bath
Silent Laugh Makers
Slapstick
Steamboat Bill, Jr.
Sunset Boulevard
Three Ages, The
TV Variety, XIII
When Comedy Was
   King

DIANE KEATON

Annie Hall
Godfather, The
Godfather Part II, The
Godfather: The
   Complete Epic,
   The
Harry and Walter Go
   to New York
Little Drummer Girl,
   The
Looking for Mr.
   Goodbar
Love and Death

Lovers and Other
   Strangers
Manhattan
Mrs. Soffel
Play It Again, Sam
Reds
Shoot the Moon
Sleeper

DAVID KEITH

Back Roads
Brubaker
Firestarter
Great Santini, The
Gulag
Independence Day
Lords of Discipline
Officer and a
   Gentleman, An
Rose, The
Take This Job and
   Shove It

GENE KELLY

American in Paris, An
Brigadoon
Forty Carats
Guide for the Married
   Man, A
Hello, Dolly!
Inherit the Wind
Invitation to the
   Dance
Jack and the
   Beanstalk
Les Girls
On the Town
Pirate, The
Singin' in the Rain
That's Dancing
That's Entertainment
That's Entertainment
   Part II
Three Musketeers,
   The
Ultimate Swan Lake,
   The
Viva Knievel
Words and Music
Xanadu
Ziegfeld Follies

GRACE KELLY

Children of Theatre
   Street, The
Country Girl, The
Dial M for Murder
Fabulous Fifties, The
High Noon
High Society
Mogambo
Rear Window
To Catch a Thief
27th Annual
   Academy Awards

GEORGE KENNEDY

Airport
Airport 1975
Airport '77
Bandolero
Blue Knight, The
Bolero
Boston Strangler, The
Cahill: United States
   Marshall
Charade
Chattanooga Choo
   Choo
Cool Hand Luke
Death on the Nile
Delta Force
Dirty Dozen, The
Double McGuffin
Earthquake
Eiger Sanction
Hot Wire
Island of Blue
   Dolphins
Lonely are the Brave
Mean Dog Blues
Rare Breed, A
Savage Dawn
Shenandoah
Sons of Katie Elder
Strait Jacket
Thunderbolt and
   Lightfoot
Virus
Wacko

DEBORAH KERR

America at the
   Movies

Arrangement, The
Black Narcissus
Courageous Mr.
　Penn, The
Grass Is Greener,
　The
I See A Dark
　Stranger
King and I, The
Life and Death of
　Colonel Blimp, The
Love on the Dole
Night of the Iguana,
　The
Prisoner of Zenda,
　The
Quo Vadis
Separate Tables
TV's Classic
　Guessing Games
Woman of
　Substance, A

MARGOT KIDDER

Amityville Horror, The
Glitter Dome, The
Great Waldo Pepper,
　The
Heartaches
Little Treasure
Making of Superman
　I and II, The
Mr. Mike's Mondo
　Video
Quackser Fortune
　Has a Cousin in
　the Bronx
Quiet Day in Belfast,
　A
Reincarnation of
　Peter Proud, The
Shoot The Sun Down
Sisters
Some Kind of Hero
Superman—The
　Movie
Superman II
Superman III
Trenchcoat

KLAUS KINSKI

Aguirre, Wrath of God
And God Said to Cain
Android
Beauty and the Beast
Count Dracula
Creature
Deadly Sanctuary
Doctor Zhivago
Double Fire
Fighting Fists of
　Shanghai Joe, The
Fistful of Death, A
Fitzcarraldo
Five For Hell
For a Few Dollars
　More
Heroes in Hell
His Name Was King
Jack the Ripper
Liberators, The
Little Drummer Girl,
　The
Night of the Assassin
Primal Impulse
Psychopath
Ruthless Four, The
Shoot the Living,
　Pray for the Dead
Soldier, The
Twice a Judas
Venom
Venus in Furs

NASTASSIA KINSKI

Boarding School
Cat People
Exposed
For Your Love Only
Hotel New
　Hampshire, The
Maria's Lovers
Moon in the Gutter
Paris, Texas
Revolution
Stay As You Are
Tess
To the Devil, A
　Daughter
Unfaithfully Yours

KEVIN KLINE

Big Chill, The
Pirates of Penzance,
　The
Silverado
Sophie's Choice

ERNIE KOVACS

Bell, Book and
　Candle
Best of Ernie Kovacs,
　The
Erine Kovacs/Peter
　Sellers
Ernie Kovacs:
　Television's
　Original Genius
Game Show Program
　II, IV
Kovacs and Keaton
Kovacs on the
　Corner
North to Alaska
NBC Comedy Hour,
　The
Take a Good Look/
　The Jack Benny
　Show
Take a Good Look
　with Ernie Kovacs
TV Variety XII, X
Vintage Commercials,
　II

**KRIS
KRISTOFFERSON**

Act of Passion (The
　Lost Honor of
　Kathryn Beck)
Alice Doesn't Live
　Here Anymore
Blume in Love
Celebration, A
Convoy
Flashpoint
Freedom Road
Heaven's Gate
Other Side of
　Nashville, The
Pat Garrett and Billy
　the Kid
Rollover

Sailor Who Fell from
   Grace With the
   Sea, The
Semi-Tough
Songwriter
Star Is Born, A
Trouble In Mind

STANLEY KUBRICK

Clockwork Orange, A
Dr. Strangelove
Lolita
Paths of Glory
Shining, The
Spartacus
2001: A Space
   Odyssey

ALAN LADD

Botany Bay
Boy on a Dolphin
Captain Caution
Carpetbaggers, The
Deep Six, The
Drum Beat
Duel of Champions
Hell on Frisco Bay
Hell's Devils
Joan of Paris
My Favorite Brunette
Premiere of "A Star
   Is Born"
Proud Rebel, The
Shane
This Gun for Hire

BURT LANCASTER

Airport
America at the
   Movies
Apache
Atlantic City
Birdman of Alcatraz,
   The
Conversation Piece
Elmer Gantry
Executive Action
Go Tell the Spartans
Gunfight at the O.K.
   Corral
Island of Dr. Moreau,
   The

Jim Thorpe—All
   American
Judgment at
   Nuremburg
Kentuckian, The
List of Adrian
   Messenger, The
Little Treasure
Local Hero
Moses
Osterman Weekend,
   The
Professionals, The
Run Silent, Run Deep
Separate Tables
Seven Days in May
Sorry Wrong Number
Summer, The
Trapeze
Twilight's Last
   Gleaming
Vengeance Valley
Vera Cruz

JESSICA LANGE

All That Jazz
Cat on a Hot Tin
   Roof
Country
Frances
How to Beat the High
   Cost of Living
King Kong
Postman Always
   Rings Twice, The
Sweet Dreams
Tootsie

CHARLES
LAUGHTON

Abbott and Costello
   Meet Captain Kidd
Arch of Triumph
Beachcomber, The
Captain Kidd
Colgate Comedy
   Hour IV, The
Early Elvis
Hobson's Choice
Hunchback of Notre
   Dame, The

Man on the Eiffel
   Tower, The
Mutiny on the Bounty
Private Life of Henry
   VIII, The
Sidewalks of London
Spartacus
They Knew What
   They Wanted
This Land is Mine
Tuttles of Tahiti, The
Witness for the
   Prosecution

LAUREL AND
HARDY

Atoll K (Utopia)
Bellhop/Noon
   Whistle, The
Blockheads
Bohemian Girl, The
Bullfighters, The
Chump at Oxford, A
Clown Princes of
   Hollywood, The
Flying Deuces, The
Fun Factory/Clown
   Princes of
   Hollywood
Great Guns
Hal Roach Comedy
   Classics, Vols. 5, 6
Hollywood Clowns,
   The
Laurel and Hardy
   Comedy Classics
   Volumes I-IX
Live Television
Movie Struck
Our Relations
Pack Up Your
   Troubles
Pardon Us
Saps at Sea
Silent Laugh Makers
Sons of the Desert
Swiss Miss
That's Entertainment,
   Part II
This Is Your Life:
   Laurel and Hardy
Way Out West

DAVID LEAN

Bridge on the River
  Kwai, The
Dr. Zhivago
Hobson's Choice
Lawrence of Arabia
Ryan's Daughter
Summertime

BRUCE LEE

Bruce Lee: The
  Legend
Bruce Lee: The Man/
  The Myth
Chinese Connection,
  The
Enter The Dragon
Fist of Fear, Touch of
  Death
Fists of Fury
Game of Death, The
Real Bruce Lee, The
Return of the Dragon
True Game of Death,
  The

CHRISTOPHER LEE

Against All Odds
Airport '77
Albino
Bear Island
Boy Who Left Home
  to Find Out About
  the Shivers, The
Castle of the Living
  Dead
Circle of Iron
Count Dracula
Creeping Flesh, The
Curse of
  Frankenstein, The
Dark Places
Devil's Undead, The
Dr. Terror's House of
  Horrors
Dracula and Son
End of the World
Far Pavilions, The
Five Golden Dragons
Horror Express
Horror Hotel

Horror of Dracula
Hound of the
  Baskervilles, The
House of Long
  Shadows, The
House That Dripped
  Blood, The
Howling II, The
Keeper, The
Last Unicorn, The
Longest Day, The
Man with the Golden
  Gun, The
Meatcleaver
  Massacre
Mummy, The
1941
Oblong Box, The
Return from Witch
  Mountain
Rosebud Beach
  Hotel
Safari 3000
Scars of Dracula
Scott of the Antarctic
Scream and Scream
  Again
Serial
Son of Monsters on
  the March
Tale of Two Cities, A
Theatre of Death
Three Musketeers,
  The
To the Devil, a
  Daughter
Torture Chamber of
  Dr. Sadism, The
Valley of the Eagles,
  The
Wicker Man, The

JANET LEIGH

Bye Bye Birdie
Fog, The
Perfect Furlough, The
Premiere of "A Star
  Is Born"
Psycho
Two Tickets to
  Broadway

VIVIEN LEIGH

Caesar and Cleopatra
Dark Journey
Fire Over England
Gone With the Wind
Hollywood Outtakes
  and Rare Footage
Roman Spring of Mrs.
  Stone, The
Ship of Fools
Sidewalks of London
Streetcar Named
  Desire, A
That Hamilton
  Woman
Waterloo Bridge

JACK LEMMON

Airport '77
Apartment, The
April Fools, The
Bell, Book and
  Candle
Bobby Short and
  Friends
Buddy Buddy
China Syndrome, The
Days of Wine and
  Roses, The
Ernie Kovacs:
  Television's
  Original Genius
Fire Down Below
Good Neighbor Sam
Great Race, The
Irma La Douce
It Should Happen to
  You
Kotch
Luv
Macaroni
Mass Appeal
Missing
Mister Roberts
Odd Couple, The
Out-of-Towners, The
Prisoner of Second
  Avenue, The
Save the Tiger
Some Like It Hot
Tribute

Wackiest Ship in the
   Army, The

JERRY LEWIS

At War with the Army
Bellboy, The
Best of Comic Relief,
   The
Cinderfella
Cracking Up
Dean Martin and
   Jerry Lewis
   Television Party
Don't Raise the
   Bridge, Lower the
   River
Errand Boy, The
Hardly Working
It's a Mad, Mad, Mad,
   Mad World
Jack Benny
Jack Benny Show,
   The
Jerry Lewis Live
King of Comedy
Nutty Professor, The
Patsy, The
Rascal Dazzle
Road to Bali, The
Slapstick of Another
   Kind
Television's Golden
   Age of Comedy
TV Variety XIII
27th Annual
   Academy Awards
Which Way to the
   Front

JOHN LITHGOW

Adventures of
   Buckaroo Banzai,
   The
Big Fix, The
Footloose
Glitter Dome, The
Goldilocks and the
   Three Bears
Rich Kids
Terms of Endearment
Twilight Zone—The
   Movie

2010
World According to
   Garp, The

HAROLD LLOYD

Clown Princes of
   Hollywood, The
Don't Shove/Two
   Gun Gussie
Fun Factory/Clown
   Princes of
   Hollywood
Funstuff
Harold Lloyd's
   Comedy Classics
His Royal Slyness/
   Haunted Spooks
Hollywood Clowns,
   The
Keystone Comedies,
   1-8
Kings, Queens,
   Jokers
Mad Wednesday
Milky Way, The
Silent Laugh Makers
   #3
Sin of Harold
   Diddlebock, The
This Is Your Life

SONDRA LOCKE

Any Which Way You
   Can
Bronco Billy
Death Game
Every Which Way But
   Loose
Gauntlet, The
Heart Is a Lonely
   Hunter, The
Outlaw Josey Wales,
   The
Second of Coming of
   Suzanne, The
Sudden Impact
Willard

CAROLE LOMBARD

Hollywood Outtakes
   and Rare Footage
In Name Only

Mack and Carole
Made for Each Other
My Man Godfrey
Mr. and Mrs. Smith
Nothing Sacred
Power
Racketeer
Swing High, Swing
   Low
These Girls Won't
   Talk
They Knew What
   They Wanted
To Be or Not to Be

SOPHIA LOREN

Aida
Angela
Arabesque
Black Orchid, The
Blood Feud
Breath of Scandal, A
Chase, The
Desire Under the
   Elms
El Cid
Fall of the Roman
   Empire, The
Favorita, La
Firepower
Heller in Pink Tights
Lady of the Evening
Man of La Mancha
Pride and the
   Passion, The
Sophia Loren: Her
   Own Story
Special Day, A

PETER LORRE

Algiers
Arsenic and Old Lace
Beat the Devil
Casablanca
Collectors Item: The
   Left Fist of David
Coming Attractions
Five Weeks in a
   Balloon
M
Maltese Falcon, The

Man Who Knew Too
  Much, The
Mr. Moto's Last
  Warning
My Favorite Brunette
Passage to Marseilles
Patsy, The
Postmark for Danger/
  Quicksand
Quicksand
Raven, The
Secret Agent
Silk Stockings
Stranger on the Third
  Floor
Tales of Terror
20,000 Leagues
  Under the Sea
Voyage to the Bottom
  of the Sea
You'll Find Out

MYRNA LOY

After the Thin Man
Airport 1975
Ants
April Fools, The
Bachelor and the
  Bobby Soxer, The
Best Years of Our
  Lives
End, The
Just Tell Me What
  You Want
Mr. Blandings Builds
  His Dream House
Red Pony, The
Renegade Ranger,
  The/Scarlet River
Summer Solstice
Thin Man, The

BELA LUGOSI

Abbot & Costello
  Meet Frankenstein
Bela Lugosi Meets a
  Brooklyn Gorilla
Black Cat, The/The
  Raven
Body Snatcher, The
Bowery at Midnight
Bride of the Monster

Chandu on the Magic
  Island
Corpse Vanishes,
  The
Death Kiss, The
Devil Bat, The
Dracula
Ghosts on the Loose
Glen or Glenda
Gorilla, The
Hollywood on Parade
Human Monster, The
Invisible Ghost
Killer Bats
Monsters on the
  March
Murder by Television
Mystery of the Mary
  Celeste, The
Ninotchka
One Body Too Many
Phantom Ship
Plan Nine from Outer
  Space
Return of the
  Vampire
Saturday Night
  Serials
Scared to Death
S.O.S. Coastguard
Spooks Run Wild
White Zombie
You'll Find Out

MALCOLM MCDOWELL

Blue Thunder
Britannia Hospital
Caligula
Cat People
Clockwork Orange, A
If . . .
Get Crazy
Gulag
Little Red Riding
  Hood
Long Ago Tomorrow
Look Back in Anger
O Lucky Man
Time After Time
Voyage of the
  Damned

ALI MACGRAW

Convoy
Getaway, The
Goodbye Columbus
Just Tell Me What
  You Want
Love Story
Players

SHIRLEY MACLAINE

All in a Night's Work
Apartment, The
Around the World in
  80 Days
Being There
Change of Seasons,
  A
Hot Spell
Irma La Douce
Loving Couples
Terms of Endearment
Trouble With Harry,
  The
Turning Point, The
TV Variety, Book VII
Two Mules for Sister
  Sara

STEVE MCQUEEN

Baby, The Rain Must
  Fall
Blob, The
Bruce Lee: The
  Legend
Bullitt
Cincinnati Kid, The
Getaway, The
Great Escape, The
Hunter, The
Magnificent Seven,
  The
Nevada Smith
Never Love a
  Stranger
On Any Sunday
Papillon
Reivers, The
Sand Pebbles, The
Soldier in the Rain
Thomas Crown Affair,
  The

1113

Tom Horn
Towering Inferno,
   The
Wanted Dead or
   Alive
War Lover, The

DEAN MARTIN

Airport
All in a Night's Work
At War with the Army
Bandolero
Bells Are Ringing
Cannonball Run, The
Cannonball Run II
Colgate Comedy
   Hour, The
Dean Martin and
   Jerry Lewis
   Television Party
Dean Martin Show,
   The
Hollywood Palace,
   The
Jack Benny Show,
   The
Murderer's Row
Ocean's 11
Perry Como Show,
   The
Premiere of "A Star
   Is Born"
Rio Bravo
Road to Bali, The
Sons of Katie Elder,
   The
Television's Golden
   Age of Comedy

STEVE MARTIN

All of Me
Dead Men Don't
   Wear Plaid
Funnier Side of
   Eastern Canada,
   The
Jerk, The
Kids Are Alright, The
Lonely Guy, The
Man With Two
   Brains, The
Muppet Movie, The

Pennies from Heaven
Rowlf's Rhapsodies
   with the Muppets
Saturday Night Live,
   Vol. II
Saturday Night Live:
   Steve Martin 2
Saturday Night Live
   with Steve Martin
Sgt. Pepper's Lonely
   Hearts Club Band
Steve Martin Live

LEE MARVIN

Big Red One, The
Big Sleep, The
Cat Ballou
Comancheros, The
Death Hunt
Delta Force
Dirty Dozen, The
Dog Day
Donovan's Reef
Gorky Park
Great Scout and
   Cathouse
   Thursday, The
Killers, The
Losers, The
Man Who Shot
   Liberty Valance,
   The
Our Time In Hell
Paint Your Wagon
Prime Cut
Professionals, The
Shack Out on 101
Ship of Fools
Shout at the Devil
Wild One, The

THE MARX
BROTHERS/
GROUCHO MARX

Animal Crackers
At the Circus
Copacabana
Day at the Races, A
Duck Soup
Funny Guys and Gals
   of the Talkies

Game Show Program
   I, IV
Girl in Every Port, A
Go West
Hollywood Clowns,
   The
Hollywood Goes to
   War
Love Happy
Monkey Business
NBC Comedy Hour
Night at the Opera, A
Night in Casablanca,
   A
One, The Only . . .
   Groucho, The
Room Service
Silver Theatre (Chico)
Stagedoor Canteen
Television's Golden
   Age of Comedy
That's Entertainment,
   Part II
TV Variety, II
Vintage Commercials
You Bet Your Life

JAMES MASON

Assisi Underground,
   The
Bad Man's River
Blue Max, The
Botany Bay
Caught
Cold Sweat
Cross of Iron
Boys from Brazil, The
Dangerous Summer,
   A
Desert Fox, The
11 Harrowhouse
Evil Under the Sun
Fall of the House of
   Usher, The
Fall of the Roman
   Empire, The
Ffolkes
Fire Over England
Heaven Can Wait
High Command
Inside Out
Jesus of Nazareth

Journey to the Center
of the Earth
Kidnap Syndicate,
The
Kill
Last of Sheila, The
Lolita
Lord Jim
Mackintosh Man, The
Madame Bovary
Man in Grey, The
Mandingo
Mill on the Floss
Murder By Decree
Night Has Eyes, The
North by Northwest
Prisoner of Zenda,
The
Return of the Scarlet
Pimpernel, The
Salem's Lot: The
Movie
Seventh Veil, The
Shooting Party, The
Sidney Sheldon's
Bloodline
Star Is Born, A
Tiara Tahiti
20,000 Leagues
Under the Sea
Verdict, The
Voyage of the
Damned
Water Babies, The
Yellowbeard
Yin and Yang of Mr.
Ko, The

MARSHA MASON

Audrey Rose
Blume in Love
Chapter Two
Goodbye Girl, The
Max Dugan Returns
Only When I Laugh
Promises in the Dark

WALTER MATTHAU

Bad News Bears, The
Buddy Buddy
Cactus Flower
California Suite

Casey's Shadow
Charade
Charley Varrick
Ensign Pulver
Face in the Crowd, A
Fail Safe
First Monday in
October
Guide for the Married
Man, A
Hello, Dolly!
Hopscotch
House Calls
I Ought to Be in
Pictures
Kentuckian, The
King Creole
Kotch
Laughing Policeman,
The
Little Miss Marker
Lonely Are the Brave
Movers and Shakers
Odd Couple, The
Personal Touch, The
Plaza Suite
Secret Life of an
American Wife,
The
Sunburn
Sunshine Boys, The
Survivors, The
Suspense
Taking of Pelham
One Two Three,
The

VERA MILES

Autumn Leaves
Back Street
Baffled
Castaway Cowboy,
The
Follow Me, Boys!
Gentle Giant
Hell Fighters
Initiation, The
Judge Horton & The
Scottsboro Boys
Mission Batangas
Molly and Lawless
John
One Little Indian

Our Family Business
Psycho
Psycho II
Roughnecks, The
Searchers, The
Strange and Deadly
Occurrence, A
Those Calloways
Wrong Man, The

RAY MILLAND

Attic, The
Blackout
Circle of Danger
Cruise Into Terror
Dead Don't Die, The
Dial "M" for Murder
Escape to Witch
Mountain
Frogs
Last Tycoon, The
Lisbon
Lost Weekend, The
Love Story
Man Alone, A
Oil
Oliver's Story
Our Family Business
Premature Burial
Quick, Let's Get
Married
Sea Serpent, The
Slavers
Starfight One
Survival Run
Terror in the Wax
Museum
Thief, The
X—The Man with X-
Ray Eyes

ANN MILLER

Deep in My Heart
Easter Parade
Having Wonderful
Time
Kiss Me Kate
Melody Ranch
On the Town
Room Service
Stage Door
That's Entertainment

That's Entertainment,
Part II

HAYLEY MILLS

Deadly Strangers
In Search of the
Castaways
Kingfisher Caper, The
Parent Trap, The
Pollyanna
Summer Magic
That Darn Cat
Trouble With Angels,
The
Whistle Down the
Wind
Wonderful World of
Disney

LIZA MINNELLI

Arthur
Cabaret
Evening with Liza
Minnelli, An
In the Good Old
Summertime
Journey Back to Oz
Liza in Concert
Matter of Time, A
Muppet Moments
New York, New York
Princess and the
Pea, The
Silent Movie
Sterile Cuckoo, The
That's Dancing
That's Entertainment

VINCENTE
MINNELLI

American in Paris, An
Band Wagon, The
Bells Are Ringing
Brigadoon
Cabin in the Sky
Four Horsemen of
the Apocalypse,
The
Gigi
Kismet
Madame Bovary
Matter of Time, A

Meet Me in St. Louis
Pirate, The
Ziegfeld Follies

ROBERT MITCHUM

Agency
Ambassador, The
Amsterdam Kill, The
Big Sleep, The
Blood on the Moon
Breakthrough
Crossfire
El Dorado
Farewell, My Lovely
Fire Down Below
Grass Is Greener,
The
Gung Ho
Hollywood Home
Movies
His Kind of Woman
Last Tycoon, The
List of Adrian
Messenger, The
Locket, The
Longest Day, The
Lusty Men, The
Macao
Maria's Lovers
Matilda
Midway
My Forbidden Past
Nightkill
Out of the Past
One Shoe Makes it
Murder
Rachel and the
Stranger
Racket, The
Red Pony, The
Ryan's Daughter
Second Chance
She Couldn't Say No
That Championship
Season
Till the End of Time
Villa Rides
Yazuka, The

MARILYN MONROE

All About Eve
Asphalt Jungle, The

Bus Stop
Clash by Night
Gentlemen Prefer
Blondes
Hollywood Home
Movies
Hollywood Outtakes
and Rare Footage
How to Marry a
Millionaire
Love Goddesses,
The
Love Happy
Marilyn Monroe
Marilyn Monroe, Life
Story of America's
Mistress
Marilyn: Say Goodbye
to the President
Misfits, The
Seven Year Itch, The
Some Like It Hot
There's No Business
Like Show
Business

MONTY PYTHON

All You Need Is Cash
(Idle)
And Now for
Something
Completely
Different
Brazil (Gilliam, Palin)
Comedy Music
Videos (Idle)
Gonzo Presents
Muppet Weird Stuff
(Cleese)
Great Muppet Caper,
The (Cleese)
Jabberwocky (Palin)
Missionary, The
(Palin)
Monty Python and
the Holy Grail
Monty Python's Life
of Brian
Monty Python's The
Meaning of Life
Odd Job, The
(Chapman)

Pied Piper of
  Hamelin, The *(Idle)*
Private Function, A
  (Palin)
Privates on Parade
  (Cleese)
Romance With a
  Double Bass
  (Cleese)
Spies Like Us
  (Gilliam)
Secret Policeman's
  Other Ball, The
  (Cleese)
Secret Policeman's
  Private Parts, The
  *(Cleese, Palin,
  Jones)*
Silverado *(Cleese)*
Tale of the Frog
  Prince, The *(Idle)*
To See Such Fun
  (Idle)
Whoops Apocalypse
  (Cleese)
Yellowbeard
  (Chapman, Cleese)

DUDLEY MOORE

Alice's Adventures in
  Wonderland
Arthur
Bedazzled
Best Defense
Derek and Clive Get
  the Horn
Foul Play
Lovesick
Micki and Maude
Playboy Video,
  Volume II
Romantic Comedy
Saturday Night Live:
  Peter Cook and
  Dudley Moore
Six Weeks
"10"
30 Is a Dangerous
  Age, Cynthia
Unfaithfully Yours
When Things Were
  Rotten
Wholly Moses!

Wrong Box, The

MARY TYLER MOORE

Change of Habit
Mary Tyler Moore
  Show, Vol. I, The
Ordinary People
Six Weeks
Thoroughly Modern
  Millie
Vintage Commercials

ROGER MOORE

Cannonball Run, The
Escape to Athena
Ffolkes
Fiction Makers, The
For Your Eyes Only
Live and Let Die
Man Who Haunted
  Himself, The
Man with the Golden
  Gun, The
Moonraker
Naked Face, The
Octopussy
Rape of the Sabines
Saint, The
Sea Wolves, The
Shout at the Devil
Spy Who Loved Me,
  The
Street People
That Lucky Touch
View to a Kill, A
Wild Geese, The

ZERO MOSTEL

Foreplay
Front, The
Funny Thing
  Happened on the
  Way to the Forum,
  A
Hot Rock, The
Marco
Muppet Moments
Once Upon a
  Scoundrel
Producers, The

EDDIE MURPHY

Best Defense
Beverly Hills Cop
Eddie Murphy
  "Delirious"
48 Hours
Joe Piscopo
Saturday Night Live
Trading Places

BILL MURRAY

Caddyshack
Ghostbusters
Loose Shoes
Meatballs
Mr. Mike's Mondo
  Video
Razor's Edge, The
Saturday Night Live
Stripes
Things We Did Last
  Summer
Tootsie
Where the Buffalo
  Roam

PAUL NEWMAN

Absence of Malice
Buffalo Bill and the
  Indians
Butch Cassidy and
  the Sundance Kid
Cat On a Hot Tin
  Roof
Cool Hand Luke
Drowning Pool, The
Exodus
Fort Apache, the
  Bronx
Harper
Harry and Son
Hombre
Hud
Life and Times of
  Judge Roy Bean,
  The
Mackintosh Man, The
Playwrights '56: "The
  Battler",
Quintet
Rachel, Rachel

Secret War of Harry
　Frigg, The
Shadow Box, The
Silent Movie
Slapshot
Sometimes a Great
　Notion
Sting, The
Tales of Tomorrow,
　Vol. 2
Torn Curtain
Towering Inferno,
　The
U.S. Steel Hour
Verdict, The
Winning
World of Eleanor
　Roosevelt, The
Young
　Philadelphians,
　The

JACK NICHOLSON

Black Cat, The/The
　Raven
Border, The
Carnal Knowledge
Chinatown
Easy Rider
Goin' South
Hell's Angels on
　Wheels
Last Detail, The
Last Tycoon, The
Little Shop of
　Horrors, The
Missouri Breaks, The
On a Clear Day You
　Can See Forever
One Flew Over the
　Cuckoo's Nest
Passenger, The
Postman Always
　Rings Twice, The
Prizzi's Honor
Raven, The
Rebel Rousers
Reds
Ride in the Whirlwind
Shining, The
Shooting, The
Studs Lonigan
Terms of Endearment

Terror, The
Wild Ride, The

DAVID NIVEN

Around the World in
　80 Days
Bachelor Mother
Better Late Than
　Never
Birds and the Bees,
　The
Bishop's Wife, The
Candleshoe
Carrington, V.C.
Charge of the Light
　Brigade, The
Curse of the Pink
　Panther, The
Day They Gave
　Diamonds Away,
　The
Death on the Nile
Dinner at the Ritz
Escape to Athena
Eternally Yours
55 Days at Peking
Guns of Navarone,
　The
Happy Go Lovely
Immortal Battalion
King, Queen, Knave
Mayfair Bank Caper,
　The
Moon Is Blue, The
Murder by Death
No Deposit, No
　Return
Paper Tiger, The
Personal Touch, The
Pink Panther, The
Rose Marie
Rough Cut
Sea Wolves
Separate Tables
Spitfire
Stairway to Heaven
Survival Anglia's
　World of Wildlife,
　Vol. 2
Trail of the Pink
　Panther, The
Wuthering Heights

NICK NOLTE

Cannery Row
Death Sentence
Deep, The
Down and Out in
　Beverly Hills
48 Hours
Grace Quigley
Heartbeat
North Dallas Forty
Return to Macon
　County
Runaway Barge
Teachers
Under Fire
Who'll Stop the Rain

KIM NOVAK

Bell, Book and
　Candle
Mirror Crack'd, The
Of Human Bondage
Premiere of "A Star
　Is Born"
Vertigo

MAUREEN O'HARA

At Sword's Point
Big Jake
Hunchback of Notre
　Dame, The
Magnificent Matador
Miracle on 34th
　Street
Parent Trap, The
Quiet Man, The
Rio Grande
Sinbad the Sailor
This Land Is Mine

**SIR LAURENCE
OLIVIER**

As You Like It
Betsy, The
Bounty, The
Boys from Brazil, The
Bridge Too Far, A
Clash of the Titans
Clouds Over Europe
Divorce of Lady X,
　The

Dracula
Fire Over England
Forty-Ninth Parallel, The
Hamlet
Henry V
I Stand Condemned
Jazz Singer, The
Jesus of Nazareth
Jigsaw Man, The
Lady Caroline Lamb
Little Romance, A
Marathon Man
Mr. Halpern and Mr. Johnson
Nicholas and Alexandra
Pride and Prejudice
Rebecca
Richard III
Romeo and Juliet
Seven-Per-Cent Solution, The
Sleuth
Spartacus
That Hamilton Woman
Wagner
World at War, The
Wuthering Heights

RYAN O'NEAL

Barry Lyndon
Bridge Too Far, A
Driver, The
Green Ice
Irreconcilable Differences
Love Story
Main Event, The
Oliver's Story
Paper Moon
Partners
So Fine
Thief Who Came to Dinner, The
What's Up Doc?

TATUM O'NEAL

Bad News Bears, The
Certain Fury
Circle of Two

Goldilocks and the Three Bears
International Velvet
Little Darlings
Paper Moon

PETER O'TOOLE

Becket
Bible, The
Caligula
Creator
Foxtrot
Kidnapped
Lawrence of Arabia
Lion in Winter, The
Lord Jim
Man of La Mancha
Masada
Murphy's War
My Favorite Year
Night of the Generals, The
Power Play
Ruling Class, The
Sherlock Holmes and a Study in Scarlet
Sherlock Holmes and the Baskerville Curse
Sherlock Holmes and the Sign of Four
Sherlock Holmes and the Valley of Fear
Stunt Man, The
Supergirl
Supergirl: The Making of the Movie
Under Milk Wood
What's New Pussycat?

AL PACINO

America at the Movies
...And Justice for All
Author! Author!
Bobby Deerfield
Cruising
Dog Day Afternoon
Godfather, The
Godfather Part II, The

Godfather: The Complete Epic, The
Revolution
Scarecrow
Scarface
Serpico

DOLLY PARTON

Best Little Whorehouse in Texas, The
Captain Kangaroo and His Friends
Dolly in London
Kenny and Dolly—Real Love
Nashville Story, The
9 to 5
Rhinestone

GREGORY PECK

Arabesque
Behold a Pale Horse
Big Country, The
Boys from Brazil, The
Guns of Navarone, The
Hollywood Home Movies
How the West Was Won
MacArthur
Marooned
Moby Dick
Omen, The
On the Beach
Roman Holiday
Sea Wolves
Spellbound
To Kill a Mockingbird
Twelve O'Clock High
World of Eleanor Roosevelt, The
Yearling, The

SEAN PENN

Bad Boys
Crackers
Falcon and the Snowman, The

Fast Times at
  Ridgemont High
Taps

ANTHONY PERKINS

Black Hole, The
Catch-22
Crimes of Passion
Desire Under the
  Elms
Ffolkes
Friendly Persuasion
Glory Boys, The
Lonely Man, The
Mahogany
Murder on the Orient
  Express
On the Beach
Psycho
Psycho II
Ravishing Idiot, The
Someone Behind the
  Door
Tin Star, The
Trial, The
Twice a Woman
Winter Kills

BERNADETTE
PETERS

Annie
Bernadette Peters in
  Concert
Heartbeeps
Jerk, The
Martian Chronicles,
  Part II, The
Pennies from Heaven
Sleeping Beauty
Tulips

MARY PICKFORD

Birth of a Legend,
  The
D.W. Griffith Triple
  Feature
Hollywood on Parade
Little Annie Rooney
My Best Girl
Pollyanna
Poor Little Rich Girl

Rebecca of
  Sunnybrook Farm
Short Films of D.W.
  Griffith, The
Sparrows
Taming of the Shrew,
  The

SIDNEY POITIER

Bedford Incident, The
Buck and the
  Preacher
Defiant Ones, The
Fast Forward
For Love of Ivy
Greatest Story Ever
  Told, The
Guess Who's Coming
  to Dinner
In the Heat of the
  Night
Let's Do It Again
Lilies of the Field
Nationtime, Gary
Piece of the Action, A
Raisin in the Sun, A
Something of Value
Stir Crazy
They Call Me Mr.
  Tibbs!
To Sir, with Love
Uptown Saturday
  Night

DICK POWELL

Big Breakdowns, The
Christmas in July
Coming Attractions
Conqueror, The
Cornered
Dames
Footlight Parade
42nd Street
Gold Diggers of 1933
Jack Benny, II
Midsummer's Night
  Dream, A
Murder My Sweet
Musical Personalities
  No. 1
Stations West
Susan Slept Here

Vintage Commercials
  IV

WILLIAM POWELL

After the Thin Man
Fashions of 1934
How to Marry a
  Millionare
Life With Father
Mr. Peabody and the
  Mermaid
Mr. Roberts
My Man Godfrey
Thin Man, The
Ziegfeld Follies

TYRONE POWER

Jesse James
Razor's Edge, The
Red Kimona, The
Witness for the
  Prosecution

ELVIS PRESLEY

Aloha From Hawaii
Blue Hawaii
Change of Habit
Coming Attractions
Double Trouble
Early Elvis
Easy Come, Easy Go
Elvis Comeback
  Special
Elvis in Concert in
  Hawaii
Elvis Live in '56
Elvis on Television
Elvis on Tour
Elvis—One Night
  With You
Elvis—'68 Comeback
  Special
Flaming Star
Fun in Acapulco
G.I. Blues
Girls, Girls, Girls
Harum Scarum
It Happened at the
  Worlds Fair
Jailhouse Rock
King Creole
Love Me Tender

Loving You
Paradise Hawaiian
  Style
Rock 'n' Roll Heaven
Roustabout
Singer Presents
  "Elvis"
Speedway
Stage Show
Tickle Me
Viva Las Vegas
Wild in the Country

ROBERT PRESTON

Blood on the Moon
Chisholms, The
Finnegan Begin
  Again
Going Hollywood
How the West Was
  Won
Last Starfighter, The
Mame
Man That Corrupted
  Hadleyburg, The
My Father's House
Rehearsal for Murder
Semi-Tough
September Gun
S.O.B.
This Gun for Hire
Tulsa
Victor/Victoria
Wake Island

VINCENT PRICE

Abbott and Costello
  Meet Frankenstein
Abominable Dr.
  Phibes, The
Adventures of
  Captain Fabian
Alice Cooper:
  Welcome to My
  Nightmare
Black Cat, The/The
  Raven
Boy Who Left Home
  to Find Out About
  the Shivers, The
Butterfly Ball, The

Champagne for
  Caesar
Devil's Triangle
Dr. Phibes Rises
  Again
Escapes
Fall of the House of
  Usher, The
Fly, The
Gonzo Presents
  Muppet Weird Stuff
House of Long
  Shadows, The
House of Wax
House on Haunted
  Hill
Journey Into Fear
Laura
Masque of the Red
  Death, The
Master of the World
Monster Club, The
Oblong Box, The
Pirate Warrior
Pit and the
  Pendulum, The
Private Lives of
  Elizabeth and
  Essex, The
Raven, The
Return of the Fly
Ruddigore
Scream and Scream
  Again
Shock
Snow White and the
  Seven Dwarves
Son of Sinbad
Song of Bernadette
Sorcerer's
  Apprentice, The
Tales of Terror
Ten Commandments,
  The
Three Musketeers,
  The
Tomb Of Ligeia, The
T.V. Classics

RICHARD PRYOR

Bingo Long Traveling
  All-Stars & Motor
  Kings, The

Blue Collar
Brewster's Millions
Bustin' Loose
California Suite
Car Wash
Dynamite Chicken
Greased Lightning
Lady Sings the Blues
Muppet Movie, The
Richard Pryor: Here
  and Now
Richard Pryor: Live
  and Smokin'
Richard Pryor Live in
  Concert
Richard Pryor Live on
  the Sunset Strip
Saturday Night Live,
  Vol. II
Silver Streak
Some Call It Loving
Some Kind of Hero
Stir Crazy
Superman III
Toy, The
Uptown Saturday
  Night
Which Way is Up?
Wholly Moses!
Wiz, The

ANTHONY QUINN

Barrabas
Behold the Pale
  Horse
Black Orchid, The
Buccaneer, The
Children of Sanchez
Con Artists, The
Greek Tycoon, The
Guns of Navarone,
  The
Heller in Pink Tights
High Risk
Hot Spell
Inheritance, The
Lawrence of Arabia
Lion of the Desert
Message, The
R*P*M (*Revolutions
  Per Minute)
Sinbad the Sailor
La Strada

They Died With Their
Boots On
Ulysses
Viva Zapata
Voice of La Raza
Walk in the Spring
Rain, A
Warlock
Zorba the Greek

BASIL RATHBONE

Adventures of Robin
Hood, The
Captain Blood
Court Jester, The
David Copperfield
Dawn Patrol
Dressed to Kill
Hillbillys in a Haunted
House
Last Days of Pompeii,
The
Magic Sword, The
Make a Wish
Sherlock Holmes and
the Secret
Weapon
Sherlock Homes
Double Features
Tale of Two Cities, A
Tales of Terror
Terror by Night/
Meeting at
Midnight
Victoria Regina
We're No Angels
Wind in the Willows,
The
Woman in Green,
The

RONALD REAGAN

Bedtime for Bonzo
Dark Victory
Death Valley Days
Famous Generals
Fight for the Sky, The
Hellcats of the Navy
Hollywood Outtakes
and Rare Footage
Jack Benny, II

Judy Garland
(General Electric
Theatre)
Killers, The
Knute Rockne—All
American
Nostalgia World War
II Video Library
Persuasive Speaking
Presidential Blooper
Reel
Reagan's Way
Sante Fe Trail
Star Bloopers
Take 1: Rescued
from the Editor's
Floor
This Is The Army
Who Killed Julie
Greer?
Wings Of War

ROBERT REDFORD

All the President's
Men
Barefoot in the Park
Bridge Too Far, A
Brubaker
Butch Cassidy and
the Sundance Kid
Candidate, The
Chase, The
Downhill Racer
Electric Horseman,
The
Great Gatsby, The
Great Waldo Pepper,
The
Hot Rock, The
Jeremiah Johnson
Natural, The
Ordinary People
Out of Africa
Sting, The
Tell Them Willie Boy
Is Here
This Property Is
Condemned
Three Days of the
Condor
Way We Were, The

SIR MICHAEL
REDGRAVE

Dam Busters, The
Dead of Night
Fame Is The Spur
Heidi
Kipps
Lady Vanishes, The
Nicholas and
Alexandra
Rime of the Ancient
Mariner
Sea Shall Not Have
Them, The
Secret Beyond the
Door, The
Stars Look Down,
The

VANESSA
REDGRAVE

Agatha
Bear Island
Bostonians, The
Blow Up
Camelot
Devils, The
Julia
Man for All Seasons,
A
Morgan—A Suitable
Case for
Treatment
Murder on the Orient
Express
Playing for Time
Seven Percent
Solution
Snow White and the
Seven Dwarves
Three Sovereigns for
Sarah
Trojan Woman, The
Wagner

CHRISTOPHER
REEVE

Aviator, The
Bostonians, The
Deathtrap
Making of Superman
I and II

Monsignor
Sleeping Beauty
Somewhere in Time
Superman—The
  Movie
Superman II
Superman III
Touch the
  Sky—Precision
  Flying with the
  Blue Angels

CARL REINER

All of Me
Best of Comic Relief,
  The
Caesar's Hour
Comic, The
Dead Men Don't
  Wear Plaid
Dinah Shore Chevy
  Show, The
Enter Laughing
End, The
Generation
Gidget Goes
  Hawaiian
Guide for the Married
  Man, A
It's a Mad, Mad, Mad,
  Mad World
Jerk, The
Man with Two Brains,
  The
Oh, God!
Oh, God! Book II
Pinocchio
Russians Are
  Coming, Russians
  Are Coming, The
Summer Rental
Take a Good Look
  with Ernie Kovacs
Ten from Your Show
  of Shows
Timex All-Star
  Comedy Show,
  The
2000 Year Old Man,
  The
Your Show of Shows

BURT REYNOLDS

At Long Last Love
Best Friends
Best Little
  Whorehouse in
  Texas, The
Cannonball Run, The
Cannonball Run II
City Heat
Deliverance
End, The
Everything you
  Always Wanted to
  Know About Sex
Fuzz
Gator
Hooper
Hustle
Longest Yard, The
Man Who Loved Cat
  Dancing, The
Man Who Loved
  Women, The
100 Rifles
Operation C.I.A.
Paternity
Rough Cut
Semi-Tough
Shamus
Shark!
Sharkey's Machine
Silent Movie
Smokey and the
  Bandit
Smokey and the
  Bandit II
Starting Over
Stick
Stroker Ace
White Lightning

SIR RALPH
RICHARDSON

Alice's Adventures in
  Wonderland
Clouds Over Europe
Dragonslayer
Early Days
Fallen Idol
Four Feathers, The

Greystoke—The
  Legend of Tarzan,
  Lord of the Apes
Heiress, The
Invitation to a
  Wedding
Lion Has Wings, The
Long Day's Journey
  Into Night, A
Looking Glass War,
  The
Man in the Iron Mask,
  The
Man Who Could
  Work Miracles,
  The
O Lucky Man
Richard III
Tales from the Crypt
Things to Come
Thunder in the City
Time Bandits
Who Slew Auntie
  Roo?

EDWARD G.
ROBINSON

Barbary Coast
Big Breakdowns, The
Breakdowns of 1936
  and 1937
Cheyenne Autumn
Cincinnati Kid, The
Good Neighbor Sam
Hell on Frisco Bay
Key Largo
Little Caesar
Mr. Winkle Goes to
  War
Never a Dull Moment
Premiere of "A Star
  Is Born"
Presidential Blooper
  Reel
Red House, The
Scarlet Street
Song of Norway
Soylent Green
Stranger, The
Ten Commandments,
  The
Thunder in the City

World of Eleanor
    Roosevelt, The

GINGER ROGERS

Bachelor Mother
Carefree
Far Frontier, The
Fifth Avenue Girl
Flying Down to Rio
Follow the Fleet
42nd Street
Fred Astaire: Puttin'
    On His Top Hat
Gay Divorcee, The
Gold Diggers of 1933
Gotta Dance, Gotta
    Sing
Having A Wonderful
    Time
Hollywood on Parade
Kitty Foyle
Lucky Partners
Once Upon a
    Honeymoon
Quick, Let's Get
    Married
Shall We Dance
Shriek in the Night
Stage Door
Star of Midnight
Story of Vernon and
    Irene Castle, The
Swing Time
That's Dancing
That's Entertainment
That's Entertainment
    Part II
13th Guest, The
Tom, Dick and Harry
Top Hat
Vivacious Lady

ROY ROGERS

Billy the Kid Returns
Colorado
Cowboys of the
    Saturday Matinee
Dark Command
Disney's American
    Heroes
Frontier Pony
    Express

Grand Canyon Trail
Heart of the Golden
    West
Jesse James at Bay
Man from Music
    Mountain, The
Milton Berle Show,
    The
My Pal Trigger
Old Corral, The
Roy Rogers and Dale
    Evans Show I-II,
    The
Saga of Death Valley
Shine on Harvest
    Moon
Song of Nevada
Song of Texas
Sunset Seranade
Under California
    Stars
Western Double
    Feature #3, 4, 6,
    8, 10, 11, 15, 17-
    25
Yellow Rose of
    Texas

MICKEY ROONEY

Adventures of
    Huckleberry Finn,
    The
Babes in Arms
Big Wheel
Bill
Black Stallion, The
Breakfast at Tiffany's
Captains Courageous
Care Bears Movie,
    The
Comedian, The
Comic, The
Dark Side of Love,
    The
Domino Principle,
    The
Ed Sullivan Show,
    The
Girl Crazy
Great Mickey
How to Stuff a Wild
    Bikini
Human Comedy, The

It Came Upon a
    Midnight Clear
It's a Mad, Mad, Mad,
    Mad World
Journey Back to Oz
Leave 'Em Laughing
Little Lord Fauntleroy
Love Laughs at Andy
    Hardy
Magic of Lassie, The
Manipulator, The
Midsummer's Night
    Dream, A
Milton Berle Hour,
    The
National Velvet
Odyssey of the
    Pacific
Pete's Dragon
Playhouse 90
Postmark for Danger/
    Quicksand
Quicksand
Senior Trip
Strike Up the Band
That's Entertainment
That's Entertainment
    Part II
Thunder Country
TV Variety
Who Killed Julie
    Greer?
Words and Music

DIANA ROSS

Diana Ross in
    Concert
Free to Be . . . You
    and Me
Lady Sings the Blues
Mahogany
Wiz, The

KATHARINE ROSS

Betsy, The
Butch Cassidy and
    the Sundance Kid
Daddy's Deadly
    Darling
Final Countdown, The
Graduate, The
Hellfighters

Murder by Natural
  Causes
Murder in Texas
Shenandoah
Swarm, The
Tell Them Willie Boy
  Is Here
Voyage of the
  Damned
Wrong Is Right

JANE RUSSELL

French Line, The
Gentlemen Prefer
  Blondes
His Kind of Woman
Las Vegas Story, The
Macao
Outlaw, The
Paleface, The
Road to Bali, The
Underwater

KURT RUSSELL

Barefoot Executive,
  The
Best of Times, The
Computer Wore
  Tennis Shoes, The
Escape From New
  York
Mean Season, The
Now You See Him,
  Now You Don't
Silkwood
Superdad
Swing Swift
Thing, The
Used Cars
Wonderful World of
  Disney, The

GEORGE SANDERS

Action in Arabia
Allegheny Uprising
Black Jack (Captain
  Black Jack)
Doomwatch
Falcon Takes Over/
  Strange Bargain
Foreign
  Correspondent

From the Earth to the
  Moon
Invasion of the Body
  Stealers
Mr. Moto's Last
  Warning
Nurse Edith Cavell
One Step to Hell
Picture of Dorian
  Gray, The
Psychomania
Rebecca
Saint Strikes Back,
  The/Criminal Court
Shot in the Dark, A
Solomon and Sheba
Son of Monte Cristo,
  The
This Land Is Mine
Village of the
  Damned

SUSAN SARANDON

Atlantic City
Beauty and the Beast
Buddy System, The
Compromising
  Positions
Duce and I, The
Great Smokey
  Roadblock, The
Great Waldo Pepper,
  The
Hunger, The
Joe
King of the Gypsies
Loving Couples
Other Side of
  Midnight
Pretty Baby
Something Short of
  Paradise
Tempest
Who Am I This Time?

TELLY SAVALAS

Adventures of Sinbad
  the Sailor, The
Battle of the Bulge
Beyond Reason
Beyond the Poseidon
  Adventure

Birdman of Alcatraz
Capricorn One
Dirty Dozen, The
Escape to Athena
Fake Out
Family, The
Greatest Story Ever
  Told
Horror Express
House of Exorcism,
  The
Inside Out
Kelly's Heroes
Killer Force
Massacre at Fort
  Hamilton
New Mafia Boss, The
On Her Majesty's
  Secret Service
Pancho Villa
Redneck
Silent Rebellion
Town Called Hell, A

ROY SCHEIDER

All That Jazz
Blue Thunder
French Connection,
  The
Jaws
Jaws II
Klute
Last Embrace
Marathon Man
Still of the Night
Seven-Ups, The
Tiger Town
2010

MARTIN SCORSESE

Alice Doesn't Live
  Here Anymore
Boxcar Bertha
King of Comedy
Last Waltz, The
Mean Streets
New York, New York
Raging Bull
Roger Corman:
  Hollywood's Wild
  Angel

GEORGE C. SCOTT

Bible, The
Changeling, The
Day of the Dolphin
Dr. Strangelove
Firestarter
Flim-Flam Man, The
Formula, The
Hardcore
Hindenberg, The
Hospital, The
Islands in the Stream
List of Adrian
    Messenger, The
Man Named
    Lombardi, A
Movie Movie
New Centurions, The
Patton
Rage
Savage Is Loose, The
Taps

RANDOLPH SCOTT

Abilene Town
Captain Kidd
Follow the Fleet
Gung Ho
My Favorite Wife
Return of the Bad
    Men
Ride the High
    Country
Spoilers, The
Trail Street

GEORGE SEGAL

Black Bird, The
Blume in Love
Carbon Copy
Cold Room, The
Deadly Game, The
Duchess and the
    Dirtwater Fox, The
Fun with Dick and
    Jane
Hot Rock, The
Invitation to a
    Gunfighter
Killing 'Em Softly
King Rat

Last Married Couple
    in America, The
Lost and Found
No Way to Treat a
    Lady
Owl and the Pussycat
St. Valentine's Day
    Massacre
Ship of Fools
Stick
Terminal Man, The
Touch of Class, A
Where's Poppa?
Who's Afraid of
    Virginia Woolf?

TOM SELLECK

Coma
High Road to China
Lassiter
Midway
Runaway
Sacketts, The
Washington Affair,
    The

PETER SELLERS

After the Fox
Alice's Adventures in
    Wonderland
America at the
    Movies
Battle of the Sexes,
    The
Being There
Blockhouse, The
Bobo, The
Carlton Browne of
    the F.O.
Dr. Strangelove
Down Among the Z-
    Men
Ernie Kovacs/Peter
    Sellers
Fiendish Plot of Dr.
    Fu Manchu, The
Ghost in the
    Noonday Sun
Great McGonagall,
    The
Heavens Above

I Love You, Alice B.
    Toklas
I'm All Right Jack
Ladykillers, The
Lolita
Magic Christian, The
Mouse That Roared,
    The
Muppet Treasures
Murder by Death
Naked Truth, The
Never Let Go
Pink Panther, The
Pink Panther Strikes
    Again, The
Prisoner of Zenda,
    The
Return of the Pink
    Panther, The
Revenge of the Pink
    Panther, The
Rowlf's Rhapsodies
    with the Muppets
Shot in the Dark, A
Stand Easy
There's a Girl in My
    Soup
To See Such Fun
Tom Thumb
Trail of the Pink
    Panther, The
Two-Way Stretch
Waltz of the
    Toreadors
What's New
    Pussycat?
Woman Times Seven
World of Henry Orient
Wrong Arm of the
    Law
Wrong Box, The

MARTIN SHEEN

Apocalypse Now
Badlands
Broken Rainbow
Cassandra Crossing,
    The
Catch-22
Catholics
Dead Zone, The
Enigma
Firestarter

Final Countdown, The
Guardian, The
Little Girl Who Lives
    Down the Lane,
    The
Loophole
Man, Woman, & Child
Missiles of October,
    The
No Drums, No Bugles
Pope John Paul II
    Visits America
Rage
That Championship
    Season
When the Line Goes
    Through

BROOKE SHIELDS

Alice Sweet Alice
Blue Lagoon, The
Children's Songs and
    Stories with the
    Muppets
Endless Love
King of The Gypsies
Pretty Baby
Sahara
Tilt

TALIA SHIRE

Gas-s-s-s
Godfather, The
Godfather Part II, The
Godfather: The
    Complete Epic,
    The
Old Boyfriends
Prophecy
Rad
Rip Van Winkle
Rocky
Rocky II
Rocky III

FRANK SINATRA

Around the World in
    80 Days
Bob Hope Chevy
    Show, II
Bulova Watch Time
Cast a Giant Shadow

Colgate Comedy
    Hour, The
Dean Martin Show,
    The
Devil at 4 O'Clock,
    The
First Deadly Sin, The
Frank Sinatra Portrait
    of an Album
Guys and Dolls
Higher and Higher
High Society
Hollywood Goes to
    War
List of Adrian
    Messenger, The
Miracle of the Bells,
    The
Ocean's 11
On the Town
Pride and the
    Passion, The
Step Lively
Suddenly
That's Entertainment
That's Entertainment
    Part II
Till the Clouds Roll
    By
TV Variety, Book VIII,
    XI
Von Ryan's Express
Young at Heart

SISSY SPACEK

Badlands
Carrie
Coal Miner's
    Daughter
Ginger in the Morning
Girls of Huntington
    House, The
Heartbeat
Marie
Missing
Prime Cut
Raggedy Man
River, The
Saturday Night Live:
    Sissy Spacek
Welcome to L.A.

STEVEN
SPIELBERG

Close Encounters of
    the Third Kind
Duel
Jaws
Night Gallery
1941
Poltergeist
Raiders of the Lost
    Ark
Sugarland Express,
    The

SYLVESTER
STALLONE

Bananas
Cannonball
Death Race 2000
First Blood
F.I.S.T.
Lords of Flatbush,
    The
Nighthawks
Paradise Alley
Prisoner of Second
    Avenue
Rebel
Rhinestone
Rocky
Rocky II
Rocky III
Rocky IV
Victory

BARBARA
STANWYCK

Annie Oakley
Bride Walks Out, The
Clash by Night
Escape to Burma
Golden Boy
Lady Eve, The
Lady of Burlesque
Mad Miss Manton,
    The
Maverick Queen, The
Meet John Doe
No Man of Her Own
Roustabout
Sorry, Wrong Number
Stella Dallas

Strange Love of
    Martha Ivers, The

**MARY
STEENBURGEN**

Cross Creek
Goin' South
Little Red Riding
    Hood
Melvin and Howard
Midsummer Night's
    Sex Comedy, A
Old Boyfriends
Ragtime
Romantic Comedy
Time After Time

ROD STEIGER

Al Capone
Amityville Horror, The
Back from Eternity
Breakthrough
Chosen The
Dr. Zhivago
F.I.S.T.
Glory Boys, The
Goodyear TV
    Playhouse:
    "Marty"
Harder They Fall, The
Illustrated Man
In the Heat of the
    Night
Jesus of Nazareth
Klondike Fever
Last Four Days, The
Lion of the Desert
Longest Day, The
Love and Bullets
Lucky Luciano
Marty
Naked Face, The
Nazis, The
No Way to Treat a
    Lady
Oklahoma!
On the Waterfront
Pawnbroker, The
Run of the Arrow
Tales of Tomorrow
27th Annual
    Academy Awards

Unholy Wife, The
Wolf Lake

JAMES STEWART

After the Thin Man
Bandolero
Bell, Book and
    Candle
Bend of the River
Big Sleep, The
Cheyenne Autumn
Far Country, The
Flight of the Phoenix
Glenn Miller Story,
    The
Greatest Show on
    Earth, The
It's a Wonderful Life
Made for Each Other
Magic of Lassie
Magic Town
Man Who Knew Too
    Much, The
Man Who Shot
    Liberty Valance,
    The
Mr. Smith Goes to
    Washington
Philadelphia Story,
    The
Pot O'Gold
Rare Breed, The
Rear Window
Right of Way
Rope
Rose Marie
Shenandoah
Shootist, The
Spirit of St. Louis,
    The
That's Entertainment
Thunder Bay
Vertigo
Vivacious Lady
War in the Sky
Winchester '73

MERYL STREEP

Deer Hunter, The
Falling in Love
French Lieutenant's
    Woman, The

Holocaust
In Our Hands
Kramer vs. Kramer
Manhattan
Out of Africa
Plenty
Seduction of Joe
    Tynan, The
Silkwood
Sophie's Choice
Still of the Night

**BARBRA
STREISAND**

All Night Long
Barbra Streisand:
    Putting it Together
Coming Attractions
For Pete's Sake
Funny Girl
Hello Dolly!
Main Event, The
On a Clear Day You
    Can See Forever
Owl and the
    Pussycat, The
Star Is Born, A
Up the Sandbox
Way We Were, The
What's Up Doc?
Yentl

**DONALD
SUTHERLAND**

Animal House
Bear Island
Bethune
Crackers
Dan Candy's Law
Day of the Locust
Dirty Dozen, The
Disappearance, The
Doctor Terror's
    House of Horrors
Don't Look Now
Eagle Has Landed,
    The
Eye of the Needle
Gas
Heaven Help Us
Invasion of the Body
    Snatchers

Johnny Got His Gun
Kelly's Heroes
Kentucky Fried Movie
Klute
Lady Ice
Man, a Woman, and
   a Bank, A
M*A*S*H
Max Dugan Returns
Murder by Decree
Nothing Personal
Ordeal by Innocence
Ordinary People
Revolution
Start the Revolution
   Without Me
Steelyard Blues
Threshold

GLORIA SWANSON

Airport 1975
American Documents
Hash House Fraud,
   A/The Sultan's
   Wife
Indiscreet
Love Goddesses,
   The
Sunset Boulevard
Teddy at the Throttle

ELIZABETH TAYLOR

Between Friends
Cat On a Hot Tin
   Roof
Cleopatra
Divorce His, Divorce
   Hers
Driver's Seat, The
Father's Little
   Dividend
Giant
Hammersmith Is Out
Ivanhoe
James Dean: The
   First American
   Teenager
Life with Father
Little Night Music, A
Love Goddesses,
   The

Mirror Crack'd, The
National Velvet
Place in the Sun, A
Premiere of "A Star
   Is Born"
Raintree County
Reflections in a
   Golden Eye
Return Engagement
Sandpiper, The
Suddenly, Last
   Summer
Taming of the Shrew,
   The
That's Entertainment
That's Entertainment
   Part II
Who's Afraid of
   Virginia Woolf?
Winter Kills

SHIRLEY TEMPLE

Bachelor and the
   Bobby Soxer, The
Comedy Festival #3
Fort Apache
From Broadway to
   Hollywood
Funny Guys and Gals
   of the Talkies
Funstuff
Get Happy
Good Old Days
Gotta Dance, Gotta
   Sing
Heidi
Kid 'n' Hollywood &
   Polly Tix in
   Washington
Little Princess, The
Miss Annie Rooney
Musical Personalities,
   No. 1
Shirley Temple
   Festival
Shirley Temple
   Storybook Theatre
   Vols. I-IV
To the Last Man

THE THREE STOOGES

Classic Comedy
   Video Sampler
Comedy Festival #1
It's a Mad, Mad, Mad,
   Mad World
Making of the
   Stooges, The
New Three Stooges
   Vols, I-VII
Snow White and the
   Three Stooges
Stooges Shorts
   Festival
Three Stooges, the
Three Stooges
   Comedy Capers,
   The
Three Stooges
   Comedy Classics
Three Stooges
   Festival, The
Three Stooges Meet
   Hercules, The
Three Stooges
   Videodisc, Vol., I,
   The
Three Stooges Vols.
   I-XII
Vintage Commercials
   II

GENE TIERNEY

Laura
Sundown

LILY TOMLIN

All of Me
Incredible Shrinking
   Woman, The
Late Show, The
Nashville
9 to 5
Paul Simon Special,
   The
Saturday Night Live:
   Lily Tomlin

SPENCER TRACY

Adam's Rib
Captains Courageous
Devil at 4 O'Clock,
 The
Doctor Jekyll and Mr.
 Hyde
Father's Little
 Dividend
Guess Who's Coming
 to Dinner
How the West Was
 Won
Inherit the Wind
It's a Mad, Mad, Mad,
 Mad World
Judgment at
 Nuremburg
San Francisco
State of the Union
Thirty Seconds Over
 Tokyo
Woman of the Year

JOHN TRAVOLTA

Blow Out
Boy in the Plastic
 Bubble, The
Carrie
Grease
Perfect
Saturday Night Fever
Staying Alive
Twist of Fate
Two of a Kind
Urban Cowboy

FRANCOIS
TRUFFAUT

Confidentially Yours
Day for Night
Farenheit 451
400 Blows
Green Room, The
Last Metro, The
Small Change
Soft Skin, The
Two English Girls
Woman Next Door,
 The

LIV ULLMAN

Bridge Too Far, A
Cold Sweat
Cries and Whispers
Dangerous Moves
Forty Carats
Leonor
Night Visitor, The
Persona
Richard's Things
Scenes from a
 Marriage
Serpent's Egg, The
Wild Duck, The

RUDOLPH
VALENTINO

Blood and Sand
Eagle, The
Keaton Special/
 Valentino Mystique
Roaring Twenties,
 The
Son of the Sheik
Tempest, The/The
 Eagle

DICK VAN DYKE

Bye Bye Birdie
Chevy Showroom,
 The
Chitty Chitty Bang
 Bang
Comic, The
Country Girl, The
Lt. Robin Crusoe,
 U.S.N.
Mary Poppins
Never a Dull Moment
Runner Stumbles,
 The
Tubby the Tuba
Vintage Commercials

JON VOIGHT

Catch-22
Champ, The
Coming Home
Conrack
Deliverance
Lookin' to Get Out

Midnight Cowboy
Odessa File, The
Table for Five

ERICH VON
STROHEIM

Blind Husbands
Foolish Wives
Grand Illusion
Great Flamarion, The
Great Gabbo, The
Lost Squadron
Napoleon
Sunset Boulevard

MAX VON SYDOW

Code Name: Emerald
Conan the Barbarian
Death Watch
Dreamscape
Dune
Exorcist, The
Exorcist, II: The
 Heretic
Flash Gordon
Flight of the Eagle,
 The
Greatest Story Ever
 Told, The
Hawaii
Hurricane
Magician, The
Never Say Never
 Again
Night Visitor, The
Seventh Seal, The
Shame
Soldier's Tale, The
Target Eagle
Three Days of the
 Condor
Ultimate Warrior, The
Victory
Voyage of the
 Damned
Wild Strawberries
Winter Light

CHRISTOPHER
WALKEN

Annie Hall
Brainstorm

Dead Zone, The
Deer Hunter, The
Dogs of War, The
Heaven's Gate
Last Embrace
Mind Snatchers, The
Pennies From
    Heaven
Shoot the Sun Down
View to a Kill, A
Who Am I This Time?

JOHN WAYNE

Allegheny Uprising
Alamo, The
America at the
    Movies
Angel and the
    Badman
Back to Bataan
Big Jake
Blue Steel
Brannigan
Cahill: United States
    Marshall
Cast a Giant Shadow
Chisum
Circus World
Comancheros, The
Conqueror, The
Cowboys, The
Dark Command
Dawn Rider/Frontier
    Horizon
Desert Trial
Donovan's Reef
El Dorado
Fighting Seabees,
    The
Flying Leathernecks
Fort Apache
Frontier Horizon
Green Berets, The
Hatari
Hellfighters
Hollywood Home
    Movies
Horse Soldiers, The
How the West Was
    Won
In Old California
John Wayne Double
    Features I-IV

John Wayne: The
    Duke Lives On
Lady for a Night
Lady From Louisiana,
    The
Lady Takes a
    Chance, The
Lawless Range/The
    Man From Utah
Longest Day, The
Long Voyage Home,
    The
Lucky Texan
Man From Utah, The
Man Who Shot
    Liberty Valance,
    The
McQ
'Neath Arizona
    Skies/Paradise
    Canyon
No Substitute for
    Victory
North to Alaska
Quiet Man, The
Randy Rides Alone/
    Riders of Destiny
Red River
Rio Bravo
Rio Grande
Rio Lobo
Rooster Cogburn
Sagebrush Trial
Sands of Iwo Jima
Searchers, The
Shadow of the Eagle
She Wore a Yellow
    Ribbon
Shootist, The
Sons of Katie Elder,
    The
Spoilers, The
Stagecoach
Star Packer
Tall in the Saddle
Texas Terror
They Were
    Expendable
Three Faces West
Three Musketeers,
    The
Trail Beyond, The
Train Robbers, The
True Grit

Tycoon
Wake of the Red
    Witch, The
War of the Wildcats
War Wagon, The
West of the Divide
Western Double
    Feature #2
Wheel of Fortune
Winds of the
    Wasteland
Without Reservations

SIGOURNEY
WEAVER

Alien
Deal of the Century
Eyewitness
Ghostbusters
Madman
Year of Living
    Dangerously, The

RAQUEL WELCH

Bandolero
Bedazzled
Bluebeard
Fantastic Voyage
Four Musketeers,
    The
Fozzie's Muppet
    Scrapbook
Fuzz
Kermit and Piggy
    Story, The
Last of Sheila, The
Legend of Walks Far
    Woman, The
Magic Christian, The
Oldest Profession,
    The
100 Rifles
Prince and the
    Pauper, The
Raquel's Total
    Beauty and Fitness
Son of Monsters on
    the March
Three Musketeers,
    The
Wild Party, The

TUESDAY WELD

Author! Author!
Cincinnati Kid, The
Looking for Mr.
    Goodbar
Once Upon a Time in
    America
Rock, Rock, Rock
Serial
Soldier in the Rain
Thief
Who'll Stop the Rain
Wild in the Country

ORSON WELLES

America at the
    Movies
Battle of Austerlitz
Battle of Neretva
Black Magic
Bloopers from "Star
    Trek" and "Laugh-
    In"
Butterfly
Casino Royale
Catch-22
Citizen Kane
Ferry to Hong Kong
Finest Hours, The
Greatest Adventure,
    The
Greenstone, The
In Our Hands
Journey Into Fear
King's Story, A
Lady From Shanghai,
    The
Last Sailors, The
Macbeth
Man for All Seasons,
    A
Mr. Arkadin
Moby Dick
Muppet Movie, The
Rikki-Tikki-Tavi
Napoleon
Start the Revolution
    Without Me
Stranger, The
Third Man, The
13 Chairs, The
Toast of the Town

Trial, The
Trouble in the Glen
Tut: The Boy King
Voyage of the
    Damned
Who's Out There?
Witching, The

MAE WEST

Love Goddesses,
    The
My Little Chickadee
Sextette

BILLY WILDER

Apartment, The
Buddy Buddy
Irma La Douce
Lost Weekend, The
Love in the Afternoon
One Two Three
Seven Year Itch, The
Some Like It Hot
Spirit of St. Louis,
    The
Stalag 17
Sunset Boulevard
Witness for the
    Prosecution

GENE WILDER

Adventures of
    Sherlock Holmes
    Smarter Brother,
    The
Blazing Saddles
Bonnie and Clyde
Everything You
    Always Wanted to
    Know About Sex
Frisco Kid, The
Hanky Panky
Little Prince, The
Producers, The
Quackser Fortune
    Has a Cousin in
    the Bronx
Silver Streak
Start the Revolution
    Without Me
Stir Crazy
Thursday's Game

Willie Wonka and the
    Chocolate Factory
Woman in Red, The
Young Frankenstein

ROBIN WILLIAMS

Best of Times, The
Can I Do It . . . Till I
    Need Glasses?
Catch a Rising Star's
    10th Anniversary
Comedy Tonight
Best of Comic Relief,
    The
Evening with Robin
    Williams, An
Moscow on the
    Hudson
Popeye
Survivors, The
Tale of the Frog
    Prince, The
World According to
    Garp, The

TREAT WILLIAMS

Eagle Has Landed,
    The
Flashpoint
Hair
James Cagney: That
    Yankee Doodle
    Dandy
Little Mermaid, The
Once Upon a Time in
    America
1941
Prince of the City
Pursuit of D.B.
    Cooper, The
Ritz, The
Smooth Talk

SHELLEY WINTERS

Alfie
Behave Yourself!
Bloody Mama
Blume in Love
Delta Force
Diamonds
Diary of Anne Frank,
    The

Double Life, A
Ellie
Elvis
Enter Laughing
Frosty's Winter
   Wonderland/The
   Leprechaun's Gold
Harper
Heartbreak Motel
I Am A Camera
Initiation of Sarah,
   The
Journey Into Fear
King of the Gypsies
Lolita
Over the Brooklyn
   Bridge
Pete's Dragon
Place in the Sun, A
Poseidon Adventure,
   The
Premiere of "A Star
   Is Born"
Shattered
S.O.B.
Tenant, The
Tentacles
That Lucky Touch
Three Sisters, The
Treasure of Pancho
   Villa, The
Very Close Quarters
Who Slew Auntie
   Roo?
Winchester '73

NATALIE WOOD

Affair, The
Bob & Carol & Ted &
   Alice

Bob Hope Chevy
   Show II, The
Brainstorm
Candidate, The
Cracker Family, The
Great Race, The
Gypsy
I'm a Stranger Here
   Myself
James Dean: The
   First American
   Teenager
Last Married Couple
   in America, The
Meteor
Miracle on 34th
   Street
Rebel Without a
   Cause
Searchers, The
Splendor in the Grass
This Property Is
   Condemned
West Side Story

**JOANNE
WOODWARD**

Christmas to
   Remember, A
Crisis at Central High
Drowning Pool, The
End, The

Fine Madness, A
Harry and Son
Rachel, Rachel
See How She Runs
Shadow Box, The
Streets of L.A., The
Summer Wishes,
   Winter Dreams
Sybil
Winning

MICHAEL YORK

Accident
Brother Sun Sister
   Moon
Cabaret
Final Assignment
Four Musketeers,
   The
Island of Dr. Moreau,
   The
Last Remake of Beau
   Geste, The
Logan's Run
Murder on the Orient
   Express
Riddle of the Sands
Romeo and Juliet
Taming of the Shrew,
   The
Three   Musketeers,
   The

Video Program Sources Index

Following is an alphabetical index of companies whose video programs are included in *The Guide*. The corporate name, address and phone number(s) are listed for each. Most companies' programs may be purchased at a local retail or video specialty store. However, a consumer may have to contact the company directly when the program cannot be rented or purchased at a near-by store. Comments concerning videodisc availability are indicated where appropriate.

A & M VIDEO
1416 North LaBrea
  Avenue
Hollywood, CA 90028
213-469-2411

A M PRODUCTIONS HOME VIDEO
46 South DeLacey
  Avenue
Suite 15
Pasadena, CA 91105
818-449-0683

ACTION DISTRIBUTORS
23 Scotland Street
San Francisco, CA
  94133
415-981-5142

ALTI CORPORATION
3333 North Torrey
  Pines Court
Suite 320
La Jolla, CA 92037
619-452-7703

AMERICAN ARTISTS LTD
3274 Oakdell Road
Studio City, CA 91604
818-760-0724

AMSTAR PRODUCTIONS
2020 Avenue of the
  Stars
Suite 240
Century City, CA 90067
213-556-1325

APOLLO VIDEO
5229 Shoreview
  Avenue South
Minneapolis, MN 55417
612-724-5898

ARENA VIDEO
12401 Wilshire
  Boulevard
Suite 102
Los Angeles, CA
  90025
213-820-6100
(Arena Video titles are distributed by World Video Pictures, Inc.)

ATLANTIC FILM GROUP I
Box 102 Harbour Road
Kittery Point, ME 03905
207-439-3739

BARRON'S EDUCATIONAL SERIES
113 Crossways Park
  Drive
Woodbury, NY 11797
516-921-8750

BARRY RAYMOND STEINER
1211 West Farwell
  Avenue
Chicago, IL 60626
312-274-1053

BASTET PRODUCTIONS
PO Box 55029
Tucson, AZ 85703
602-293-8088

BILLIE C. LANGE
PO Box 1993
Huntsville, AL 35805
205-830-5996

BLACKHAWK FILMS
1235 West Fifth
Box 3990
Davenport, IA 52808
319-323-9736
*(Titles are distributed
by Republic Pictures
Home Video.)*

**BLOOPER
ENTERPRISES INC**
4900 SW 80th Street
Miami, FL 33143
305-666-0074

**BROCKWAY
BROADCASTING
CORP**
40 New York Avenue
Huntington, NY 11743
516-673-4400

**BUENA VISTA HOME
VIDEO**
500 South Buena Vista
Street
Burbank, CA 91521
818-840-1111

CABLE FILMS
Country Club Station
Kansas City, MO
64113
913-362-2804
*(Some programs also
available in PAL and
SECAM.)*

**CANDLE
CORPORATION**
10880 Wilshire
Boulevard
Suite 2404
Los Angeles, CA
90024
213-470-2277

CAPTAIN BIJOU
PO Box 87
Toney, AL 35773
205-852-0198

CBS/FOX VIDEO
1211 Avenue of the
Americas
New York, NY 10036
212-819-3200
*(Some programs
available on laser
optical videodisc or
capacitance electronic
disc.)*

**CENTAUR
PRODUCTIONS, INC**
PO Box 5108
Vancouver, BC,
Canada V6B 4A9
604-669-3217

**CHARTER
ENTERTAINMENT**
1901 Avenue of the
Stars
Los Angeles, CA
90067
213-556-7419
*(A division of Embassy
Home Entertainment.)*

**CHILDREN'S VIDEO
LIBRARY**
60 Long Ridge Road
PO Box 4995
Stamford, CT 06907
203-968-0100

**CINEMA CONCEPTS
INC**
2461 Berlin Turnpike
Newington, CT 06111
203-667-1251

**CLEVER CLEAVER
PRODUCTIONS**
4652 Cass Street
Suite 51
San Diego, CA 92109
619-488-2327
619-276-2126

CLUB REBA VIDEO
40 North Moore Street
New York, NY 10013
212-925-2404

**COMPTON
INTERNATIONAL
CORPORATION**
PO BOx 8507
Richmond, VA 23226
804-288-3712

CONGRESS VIDEO
10 East 53rd Street
New York, NY 10022
212-371-3939
800-VHS-TAPE

**CRITERION
COLLECTION**
PO Box 2310
Santa Monica, CA
90406
800-446-2001 (outside
CA)
800-443-2001 (in CA)

CROWN VIDEO
225 Park Avenue
South
New York, NY 10003
212-254-1600

**CYCLE VISION
TOURS**
1020 Green Valley
Road, NW
Albuquerque, NM
87107
505-345-5217

DCI MUSIC VIDEO
541 Avenue of the
Americas
New York, NY 10011
212-924-6624
800-342-4500

**DISCOUNT VIDEO
TAPES INC**
3711B West Clark
Avenue
PO Box 7122
Burbank, CA 91510
818-843-3366

EAGLE PRODUCTIONS
7860 Mission Center
    Court
Suite 106
San Diego, CA 92108
619-297-8872
800-621-0852,
extension 184

EMBASSY HOME ENTERTAINMENT
1901 Avenue of the
    Stars
Los Angeles, CA
    90067
213-553-3600
*(Some programs
available on laser
optical videodisc and
capacitance electronic
disc.)*

ENCOUNTER PRODUCTIONS
2267 NW Pettygrove
Portland, OR 97210
503-241-8663

ESQUIRE VIDEO
PO Box 648
Holmes, PA 19043
212-355-5049 (PR
Office)

EVENT VIDEO
PO Box 3733
Ventura, CA 93006
805-642-1838

EVERGREEN INTERNATIONAL
213 West 35th Street
New York, NY 10001
212-714-9860

FAMILY HOME ENTERTAINMENT
A Division of
    International Video
    Entertainment
21800 Burbank
    Boulevard, # 300
PO Box 4062
Woodland Hills, CA
    91365-4062
818-888-3040
800-423-5558

FESTIVAL FILMS
2841 Irving Avenue
    South
Minneapolis, MN 55408
612-870-4744

FORCE VIDEO
60 Long Ridge Road
PO Box 4000
Stamford, CT 06907
203-359-3537
*(Titles are distributed
by Lightning Video.)*

FOUR POINT ENTERTAINMENT
3575 Cahuenga
    Boulevard West
Suite 655
Los Angeles, CA
    90068
213-850-1600

FRIENDSHIP II PRODUCTIONS
11 51st Street, C-1
Weehawken, NJ 07087
201-866-9136

GESSLER EDUCATIONAL SOFTWARE
900 Broadway
New York, NY 10003
212-673-3113

GOODTIMES HOME VIDEO
401 Fifth Avenue
New York, NY 10016
212-889-0044

GREAT COMEDY SHOWS
PO Box 2846
Westport, CT 06880

GRUNKO FILMS, INC
227 South Main
Sheridan, WY 82801
307-672-2487

HAL ROACH STUDIOS
1600 North Fairfax
    Avenue
Hollywood, CA 90046
213-850-0525

HARMONYVISION
116 North Robertson
    Boulevard
Suite 610
Los Angeles, CA
    90048
213-652-8844
*(HarmonyVision titles
are distributed by
Vestron Video.)*

HOLLYWOOD HOME THEATRE
1540 North Highland
    Avenue
Hollywood, CA 90028
213-466-0121
800-621-0849 ext. 176
*(Some programs are
also available in PAL.)*

HOW TO VIDEO
5372 Merrick Road
Suite 8
Massapequa, NY
    11758
516-795-0033

INTERNATIONAL HISTORIC FILMS
PO Box 29035
Chicago, IL 60629
312-436-8051
*(Some programs also
available in PAL and
SECAM.)*

IRS RECORDS
Video Department
100 Universal City
  Plaza
Building 422
Universal City, CA
  91608
818-777-4730

JCI VIDEO
5308 Derry Avenue
Suite P
Agoura Hills, CA 91301
800-223-7479

JO-LYNN VIDEO
410 Sunset Avenue
Windsor, Ontario
Canada N9B 3B1
519-254-9440

K VIDEO
157 Wiltshire Road
Claymont, DE 19703
302-798-2229
215-494-5920

**KARL/LORIMAR
HOME VIDEO INC**
17942 Cowan Avenue
Irvine, CA 92714
714-474-0355
*(Also distributes VCL
Home Video titles.)*

**KARTES VIDEO
COMMUNICATIONS**
7225 Woodland Drive
Indianapolis, IN 46278
317-297-1888

KEY VIDEO
1211 Avenue of the
  Americas
Second Floor
New York, NY 10036
212-819-3238

KING OF VIDEO
3529 South Valley
  View Boulevard
Las Vegas, NV 89103
702-362-2520
800-634-6143

**KNOPF VIDEO
BOOKS**
201 East 50th Street
New York, NY 10022
212-572-2103

**KNOWHUTIMEAN?
HOME VIDEO**
1220 McGavock Street
Nashville, TN 37203
615-255-6696 (adv.
agency)

KULTUR
121 Highway # 36
West Long Branch, NJ
  07764
201-229-2343

LANGUAGE PLUS
4105 Rio Bravo
El Paso, TX 79903
915-544-8600

LIGHTNING VIDEO
60 Long Ridge Road
PO Box 4000
Stamford, CT 06907
203-359-3537

**MAGNUM
ENTERTAINMENT**
9301 Wilshire
  Boulevard
Suite 602
Beverly Hills, CA 90212
213-278-9981
800-842-2291

**MAJOR LEAGUE
BASEBALL
PRODUCTIONS**
1212 Avenue of the
  Americas
New York, NY 10036
212-921-8100

**MASTER ARTS
VIDEO**
15635 Saticoy Street
Suite H
Van Nuys, CA 91406
818-909-0233

MASTERVISION INC
969 Park Avenue
New York, NY 10028
212-879-0448

MCA HOME VIDEO
70 Universal City Plaza
Universal City, CA
  91608
818-777-4300
*(Some programs are
available on laser
optical videodisc or
capacitance electronic
disc.)*

**MEDIA HOME
ENTERTAINMENT INC**
5730 Buckingham
  Parkway
Culver City, CA 90230
213-216-7900
800-421-4509
*(Some programs also
available in PAL and
SECAM.)*

**MERIDIAN
ENTERTAINMENT**
9903 Santa Monica
  Boulevard
Suite 256
Beverly Hills, CA 90212
213-463-2832

**MGM/UA HOME
VIDEO**
1350 Avenue of the
  Americas
New York, NY 10019
212-408-0600
*(Some programs
available on
capacitance electronic
disc.)*

MINNESOTA STUDIO
430 Oak Grove Street
Suite 222
Minneapolis, MN 55403
612-879-0493
800-626-1251

**MOGUL
COMMUNICATIONS**
1124 North Kings Road
Suite 203
Los Angeles, CA
90069
213-650-2122

**MONTEREY HOME
VIDEO**
A Division of
International Video
Entertainment
21800 Burbank
Boulevard, #300
PO Box 4062
Woodland Hills, CA
91365-4062
818-888-3040
800-423-5558

**MONTICELLO
PRODUCTIONS**
1822 Easterly Terrace
Los Angeles, CA
90026
213-662-2938

MOVIE BUFF VIDEO
c/o Manhattan
Movietime
250 West 95th Street
New York, NY 10025
212-666-0331

MPI HOME VIDEO
15825 Rob Roy Drive
Oak Forest, IL 60452
312-687-7881
*(Some programs
available on laser
optical videodisc or
capacitance electronic
disc.)*

MTI HOME VIDEO
430 South Dixie
Highway
Penthouse
Miami, FL 33146
305-662-1135
800-821-7461

**MUPPET HOME
VIDEO**
500 South Buena Vista
Street
Burbank, CA 91521
818-840-1859
*(Programs are
distributed by Walt
Disney Home Video.
Some programs
available on LV and
CED.)*

**MUPPETMUSIC HOME
VIDEO**
500 South Buena Vista
Street
Burbank, CA 91521
818-840-1859
*(Programs are
distributed by Walt
Disney Home Video.)*

MUSIC MEDIA
5730 Buckingham
Parkway
Culver City, CA 90230
213-216-7900
800-421-4509
*(Programs are
distributed by Media
Home Entertainment.)*

MYSTIC FIRE VIDEO
24 Horatio Street, #3C
New York, NY 10014
212-645-2733

**MYSTIC SEAPORT
MUSEUM**
Mystic, CT 06355
203-572-0711

**NATIONAL
GEOGRAPHIC
SOCIETY**
17th & M Streets NW
Washington, DC 20036
202-857-7378
301-948-5926
*(Closed Circuit
television and
duplication rights are
negotiable.)*

NAUTILUS VIDEO
496 La Guardia Place
Suite 145
New York, NY 10012
212-243-7050

NEW WORLD VIDEO
1440 South Sepulveda
Boulevard
Los Angeles, CA
90025
213-444-8100
*(Also distributes
Learning Corporation of
America titles.)*

NFL FILMS VIDEO
330 Fellowship Road
Mt. Laurel, NJ 08054
609-778-1600
800-NFL-TAPE
*(Some programs
available on laser
optical videodisc.)*

**NORTH AMERICAN
VIDEO INC**
385 Pine Grove Road
Roswell, GA 30075
404-992-1301

**NOSTALGIA
MERCHANT**
6255 Sunset Boulevard
Suite 1019
Hollywood, CA 90028
213-216-7900
800-421-4509
*(Programs are
distributed by Media
Home Entertainment,
Inc)*

P-FLAG
PO Box 640223
San Francisco, CA
94164-0223
415-239-8180

**PACIFIC ARTS VIDEO
RECORDS**
50 North La Cienega
Boulevard
Suite 210
Beverly Hills, CA 90211
213-657-2233

**PACIFIC COAST
COMMUNITY VIDEO**
635½ Chapala Street
Santa Barbara, CA
 93101
805-965-5051

PAE CORPORATION
PO Box 6540
Toledo, OH 43612
419-244-3634

PARADE RECORDS
145 Komorn Street
Newark, NJ 07105
201-344-4214

**PARAMOUNT HOME
VIDEO**
5555 Melrose Avenue
Los Angeles, CA
 90038
213-468-5000
*(Some programs
available on laser
optical videodisc or
capacitance electronic
disc.)*

**PASSPORT MUSIC
VIDEO**
3619 Kennedy Road
South Plainfield, NJ
 07080
201-753-6100

**PETER ALLEN VIDEO
PRODUCTIONS**
38-C Otis Street
West Babylon, NY
 11704
516-643-4372

**PHOTON VIDEO
COMPANY**
4174 El Prado
 Boulevard
Coconut Grove, FL
 33133
305-665-9276

**PIONEER ARTISTS
INC**
200 West Grand
 Avenue
Montvale, NJ 07645
201-573-1122

**PIONEER VIDEO
IMPORTS**
200 West Grand
 Avenue
Montvale, NJ 07645
201-573-1122

PLAYHOUSE VIDEO
1211 Avenue of the
 Americas
New York, NY 10036
212-819-3238

PRISM
1875 Century Park
 East
Suite 1010
Los Angeles, CA
 90067
213-277-3270

**RANDOM HOUSE
HOME VIDEO**
201 East 50th Street
New York, NY 10022
212-572-2778
212-572-2644

**RCA COLUMBIA
PICTURES HOME
VIDEO**
2901 W. Alameda
 Avenue
Burbank, CA 91505
818-954-4590
*(Some programs
available on laser
optical videodisc or
capacitance electronic
disc.)*

RCA VIDEODISCS
PO Box 91079
7900 Rockville Road
Indianapolis, IN 46224
317-273-3640

**REPUBLIC PICTURES
HOME VIDEO**
12636 Beatrice Street
Los Angeles, CA
 90066
213-306-4040

RHINO VIDEO
1201 Olympic
 Boulevard
Santa Monica, CA
 90404
213-450-6323

RKO HOMEVIDEO
1900 Avenue of the
 Stars
Suite 1562
Century City, CA 90067
213-277-3133

**SAN FRANCISCO
RUSH VIDEO**
156 Tiffany Avenue
PO Box 40332
San Francisco, CA
 94140
415-824-2543

**SELF IMPROVEMENT
VIDEO INC**
25 Dryden Lane
Providence, RI 02904
401-351-7676

SELL PICTURES
210 Fifth Avenue
New York, NY 10010
212-683-9221

SHOKUS VIDEO
PO Box 8434
Van Nuys, CA 91409
818-704-0400

**SIMON & SCHUSTER
VIDEO**
1230 Avenue of the
 Americas
New York, NY 10020
212-245-6400
*(Titles also available
through Paramount
Home Video.)*

SNOOPY'S HOME VIDEO LIBRARY
5730 Buckingham
  Parkway
Culver City, CA 90230
213-216-7900
800-421-4509
(Programs are distributed by Media Home Entertainment.)

SONY VIDEO SOFTWARE
1700 Broadway
Sixteenth Floor
New York, NY 10019
212-757-4990

SOUVENIRS OF HAWAII INC.
PO Box 2457
Honolulu, HI 96804-
  2457
808-847-4608

SPORTSMEN ON FILM
5567 Reseda
  Boulevard
Suite 300
Tarzana, CA 91356-
  2694
818-342-5555

SPOTLITE VIDEO
12636 Beatrice Street
PO Box 66930
Los Angeles, CA
  90066-0930
213-306-4040
(A division of Republic Pictures Home Entertainment.)

STRIKE FORCE FILMS
PO Box 954
Evanston, IL 60204

SWINGTIME VIDEO INC
1626 North Wilcox
  Avenue
Suite 708
Hollywood, CA 90028
213-463-2134

TARGET VIDEO
678 South Van Ness
San Francisco, CA
  94110
415-431-7595

THOMSON PRODUCTIONS INC
140 South Mountain
  Way Drive
Suite 1
Orem, UT 84058
801-226-0155
800-228-8491

THORN EMI/HOME BOX OFFICE VIDEO INC
1370 Avenue of the
  Americas
New York, NY 10019
212-977-8990
(Some programs are available on capacitance electronic disc.)

THRILLER VIDEO
21800 Burbank
  Boulevard, #300
PO Box 4062
Woodland Hills, CA
  91365-4062
818-888-3040
(A division of International Video Entertainment.)

TO THE POINTE HILLEMANN DANCERS
10410 Metcalf Avenue
Overland Park, KS
  66212
913-341-0799

TOTAL PRODUCTIONS INC
PO Box 906
Hixson, TN 37343
615-842-7455
800-231-5828

TOUCHSTONE HOME VIDEO
500 South Buena Vista
  Street
Burbank, CA 91521
818-840-6056
(Some programs are available on laser optical videodisc and capacitance electronic disc.)

TRAVEL VIDEO CORPORATION
3320 East Shea
  Boulevard
Suite 175
Phoenix, AZ 85028
602-996-5222
800-826-5557

TRB PRODUCTIONS
PO Box 2362
Boston, MA 02107

TWILIGHT VIDEO
6430 Sunset Boulevard
Suite 501
Hollywood, CA 90028
213-461-0467

TWIN TOWER ENTERPRISES
12345 Ventura
  Boulevard
Suite K-2
Studio City, CA 91604
818-761-0932
800-553-4321

UNICORN VIDEO INC
20822 Dearborn Street
Chatsworth, CA 91311
818-407-1333
800-52-VIDEO *(outside CA)*
800-85-VIDEO *(in CA)*

UNITED HOME VIDEO
4111 South Darlington
  Street
Suite 600
Tulsa, OK 74135
918-622-6460
800-331-4077
*(Titles are distributed
by United
Entertainment Inc.)*

U.S.A. HOME VIDEO
21800 Burbank
  Boulevard, #300
PO Box 4062
Woodland Hills, CA
  91365-4062
818-888-3040
800-423-5558
*(A division of
International Video
Entertainment.)*

VCII INC
7313 Varna Avenue
North Hollywood, CA
  91605
213-764-0319
800-423-2587
*(Programs are available
in NTSC and PAL.)*

VCL HOME VIDEO
Glen Professional
  Centre
2980 Beverly Glen
  Circle
Suite 302
Los Angeles, CA
  90077
213-474-4225
*(Programs are
distributed by Karl/
Lorimar Home Video
and Video Gems.)*

VESTRON VIDEO
60 Long Ridge Road
PO Box 4000
Stamford, CT 06907
203-968-0000
*(Some programs are
available on laser
optical videodisc and/
or capacitance
electronic disc.)*

**VICTORIAN VIDEO
PRODUCTIONS**
305 Thomas
PO Box 1328
Port Townsend, WA
  98368
206-385-7490
800-442-1122

VICTORY VIDEO
PO Box 87
Toney, AL 35773
205-852-0198

VIDAMERICA INC
235 East 55th Street
New York, NY 10022
212-355-1600
*(VidAmerica titles are
distributed by Lightning
Video. Some titles are
available on laser disc.)*

**VIDEO ARTS
INTERNATIONAL INC**
PO Box 153
Ansonia Station
New York, NY 10023
212-799-7798

**VIDEO ASSOCIATES
INC**
5419 Sunset Boulevard
Hollywood, CA 90027
213-463-3255

VIDEO CONNECTION
3123 Sylvania Avenue
Toledo, OH 43613
419-472-7727

**THE VIDEO
CONNECTION OF
AMERICA INC**
22761 Pacific Coast
  Highway
Malibu, CA 90265
213-456-7071

VIDEO DIMENSIONS
110 East 23rd Street
Suite 603
New York, NY 10010
212-533-5999

VIDEO GEMS
731 North La Brea
  Avenue
PO BOX 38188
Los Angeles, CA
  90038
213-938-2385
800-421-3252

**VIDEO HOME
LIBRARY**
75 Spring Street
New York, NY 10012
212-925-7744
800-221-5480

**VIDEO
MOVIEMAKERS**
PO Box 4545
Portsmouth, NH 03801
603-431-1488

**VIDEO SPORTS
PRODUCTIONS**
1704 Sweeney
Las Vegas, NV 89104
702-384-7514

VIDEO TRAVEL INC
PO Box 1572
Williamsport, PA 17701
717-326-6525

VIDEO TRIVIALITIES
303 West Colfax #775
Denver, CO 80204
800-835-2246, Ext. 39

VIDEO YESTERYEAR
Box C
Sandy Hook, CT 06482
203-426-2574
800-243-0987
*(Most programs
available in both NTSC
and PAL. For SCHO
availability only, contact
Filmic Archives at the
Cinema Center,
Botsford, CT 06404-
0386. Telephone 203-
261-1920.)*

VIDEOCASSETTE MARKETING CORPORATION
137 Eucalyptus Street
El Segundo, CA 90245
213-322-1140

VIDEOGRAF
144 West 27th Street
New York, NY 10001
212-242-7871

VIDEOSPORTS INC
5560 Shasta Lane
Suite 21
La Mesa, CA 92041
619-464-6361

VIDEOTAKES
220 Shrewsbury
Avenue
Red Bank, NJ 07701
201-747-2444

VIDMARK ENTERTAINMENT
2450 Wilshire
Boulevard
Suite 1
Santa Monica, CA
90403
213-829-4359
800-424-7070 (outside CA)
800-351-7070 (in CA)

V.I.E.W. VIDEO
34 East 23rd Street
New York, NY 10010
212-674-5550

VIRGIN VIDEO
7020 Hayvenhurst
Avenue
Suite F
Van Nuys, CA 91406
818-997-1011

V.I.V.A.! AUDIO-VISUAL
PO Box 1654
Tempe, AZ 85281
602-829-2233

VOYAGER PRESS
2139 Manning Avenue
Los Angeles, CA
90025
213-475-3524

WALT DISNEY HOME VIDEO
500 South Buena Vista
Street
Burbank, CA 91521
818-840-1111
800-423-2259
(Some programs available on laser optical videodisc and capacitance electronic disc.)

WARBURTON PRODUCTIONS
3205 Wilson Court
PO Box 1236
LaPorte, CO 80535
303-221-4906
800-233-4414

WARNER HOME VIDEO INC
4000 Warner
Boulevard
Burbank, CA 91522
818-954-6000
(Some programs available on laser optical videodisc and capacitance electronic disc.)

WESTERN FILM & VIDEO INC
30941 Agoura Road
Suite 302
Westlake Village, CA
91361
818-889-7350

WIZARD VIDEO INC
6461 Sunset Boulevard
Hollywood, CA 90028
213-461-3981
800-824-5948
(Programs are distributed by Lightning Video.)

WORLD PREMIERE
3125 West Burbank
Boulevard
Burbank, CA 91505
818-843-0948
800-437-9063

WORLD WIDE MEDIA
PO Box 1767
East Lansing, MI 48823
517-337-7700
800-248-4664

WORLDVISION HOME VIDEO INC
660 Madison Avenue
New York, NY 10021
212-832-3838

YOU CAN DO IT VIDEOS
PO Box 25060
Philadelphia, PA 19147
215-735-7741

YOUR WORLD VIDEO
80 Eighth Avenue
Suite 1701
New York, NY 10011
212-206-1215
212-206-1213

Photo Copyrights

Photo section pictures courtesy of:
BLACKHAWK FILMS
Charlie Chaplin/Fatty Arbuckle, ©Republic Pictures
CBS/FOX VIDEO
Garbo Talks, ©1984 MGM/UA Entertainment Co.
Jewel of the Nile, ©1986 Twentieth Century-Fox Film Corporation
Rocky IV, ©1985 United Artists Corporation
CHARTER ENTERTAINMENT
Kiss of the Spider Woman, ©1986 Charter Entertainment
The Nightcomers, ©1986 Charter Entertainment
DISCOUNT VIDEO TAPES
Roy Rogers, ©Republic Pictures Corp.
EMBASSY HOME ENTERTAINMENT
The Divorce of Lady X, ©1938 London Film Productions, Ltd.
Eleni, ©1986 Embassy Home Entertainment
Mon Oncle, ©1986 Embassy Home Entertainment
Pandora's Box, ©1986 Embassy Home Entertainment
Winter Kills, ©1979 Avco Embassy Pictures Corp.
Wuthering Heights, ©1986 Embassy Home Entertainment
KARL/LORIMAR HOME VIDEO
Power, ©1985 Lorimar Motion Pictures
KEY VIDEO
Lenny, ©1981 United Artists Corporation
MCA HOME VIDEO
Back to the Future, ©1985 Universal City Studios, Inc.
The Last Remake of Beau Geste, ©1977 Universal City Studios, Inc.
Miami Vice II: The Prodigal Son, ©1985 Universal City Studios, Inc.
Out of Africa, ©1985 Universal City Studios,. Inc.
Winchester '73, ©1986 MCA Videocassette, Inc.
MEDIA HOME ENTERTAINMENT
Elvis: One Night With You, ©1985 Media Home Entertainment
MGM/UA HOME VIDEO
Diner, ©1982 Metro-Goldwyn-Mayer Film Co. and SLM
    Entertainment Ltd.
Kiss Me Kate, ©1953 Loew's Incorporated, renewed 1981
    Metro-Goldwyn Mayer Film Co.
Meet Me in St. Louis, ©1944 Loew's Incorporated, renewed 1971
    Metro-Goldwyn-Mayer Inc.
RCA/COLUMBIA PICTURES HOME VIDEO
Agnes of God, ©1985 Columbia Pictures Industries, Inc.
The Awful Truth, ©1937 Columbia Pictures Industries, Inc.
Casino Royale, ©1967 Columbia Pictures Corporation
Jagged Edge, ©1985 Columbia Pictures Industries, Inc.
White Nights, ©1985 Columbia Pictures Industries, Inc.

REPUBLIC PICTURES HOME VIDEO
Angel and the Badman, ©1959 Republic Pictures
High Noon, ©1952 Stanley Kramer Productions, Inc.
SNOOPY'S HOME VIDEO LIBRARY
Play It Again, Charlie Brown, ©United Feature Syndicate, Inc.
TOUCHSTONE HOME VIDEO
Down and Out in Beverly Hills, ©1986 Touchstone Films
VCL HOME VIDEO
The Legend of Walks Far Woman, ©1982 Roger Gimbel Productions
VESTRON VIDEO
Twice in a Lifetime, ©1985 Bud Yorkin Productions
WALT DISNEY HOME VIDEO
Dumbo, ©1941 Walt Disney Productions, renewed 1968
Pluto, ©1983 Walt Disney Productions

FRONT COVER CASSETTE BOXES COURTESY OF:

BUENA VISTA HOME VIDEO
CHILDREN'S VIDEO LIBRARY
EMBASSY HOME ENTERTAINMENT
HBO/CANNON VIDEO
MCA HOME VIDEO
MEDIA HOME ENTERTAINMENT
MGM/UA HOME VIDEO
PARAMOUNT HOME VIDEO
RCA/COLUMBIA PICTURES HOME VIDEO
REPUBLIC PICTURES HOME VIDEO
SONY VIDEO SOFTWARE
TOUCHSTONE HOME VIDEO
VESTRON VIDEO
WALT DISNEY HOME VIDEO
WARNER HOME VIDEO